National Trade and Professional Associations of the United States

1987
Twenty-second Annual Edition

Craig Colgate, Jr., Publisher
John J. Russell, Editor
Patricia Becker Lee, Editor
Argie M. O'Shea, Editor

COLUMBIA BOOKS INC., Publishers
1350 New York Avenue, N.W., Suite 207
Washington, D.C. 20005
(202) 737-3777

Twenty-second Edition — 1987

ISSN 0734-354X
ISBN 0-910416-63-X

Price U.S. $50.00 paperbound
U.S. $60.00 casebound

TABLE OF CONTENTS

SCOPE OF THE BOOK

This directory, first published in 1966, is completely revised and updated every 12 months.

Its unique value professionally is that it restricts itself to trade and professional associations and labor unions with national memberships. Other groups such as fraternal, sporting, patriotic, hobby and political action organizations are excluded. (Readers may wish to consult our companion directory National Avocational Organizations.

Its chief value to many subscribers has proved to be as a guide to sources of information. The associations it lists are unrivaled repositories of specialized data, either through their headquarters or their memberships. A call or a letter to an organization executive can produce a faster and far more accurate answer to a question than days of routine research.

HOW TO USE IT

The heart of the book is the *Association* Index arranged alphabetically by organization title. Knowing the name, one can turn directly to the group sought and its attendant statistics. Alphabetizing follows the form of the telephone book; all words in a name, "a", "and", "of", "for", "in", etc. (except for initial "The", which follows the pertinent words of the title) are included.

Often, however, the name of a group is known only approximately. Then another method must be followed.

If one knows the product, field or profession with which the organization is concerned, or even a significant word in its title, the *Subject* Index will provide a guide.

If one knows the town or city in which the organization is headquartered, the *Geographic* Index will provide the name.

Both the *Subject* and *Geographic* Indexes have obvious utility in themselves, the first for identifying all organizations concerned with a particular subject, the other for locating all organizations within a specific area.

If one knows the organization's acronym, the *Acronym* Index will provide the full name. Some organizations have adopted an acronym as their formal name, such organizations would also be listed in the *Association* Index under the acronym.

If one is concerned only with organizations of a certain size, consulting the *Budget* Index may prove helpful.

Users of this book are left with a final *caveat*. Informal references to organizations are sometimes imprecise. For example, a person might speak of the International Charolais Association, when he meant the *American* International Charolais Association; or the American Association of Interior Designers, when the correct name is the American *Institute of* Interior Designers. Those who look for an organization without success in the *Association* Index are advised, before giving up, to consult the *Subject* Index for an organization whose name may approximate that of the one sought.

A directory of this type achieves its greatest value when it identifies and offers solutions in so far as practicable to the many individual needs of its users. Suggestions for improving the indexes or categories are always welcome and are given careful consideration.

INTRODUCTION

"Americans of all ages, all conditions, and all dispositions constantly form associations. They have not only commercial and manufacturing companies, in which all take part, but associations of a thousand other kinds, religious, moral, serious, futile, general or restricted, enormous or diminutive. The Americans make associations to give entertainments, to found seminaries, to build inns, to construct churches, to diffuse books, to send missionaries to the antipodes; in this manner they found hospitals, prisons, and schools. If it is proposed to inculcate some truth or to foster some feeling by the encouragement of a great example, they form a society. Wherever at the head of some new undertaking you see the government in France, or a man of rank in England, in the United States you will be sure to find an association."

ALEXIS DE TOCQUEVILLE
Democracy in America, 1835

This directory lists about 6,500 national trade associations, labor unions, professional, scientific or technical societies and other national organizations composed of groups united for a common purpose. Those which do nothing more than accredit have been eliminated.

A trade association was once defined by the late C. Jay Judkins, Chief of the Trade Association Division of the U.S. Department of Commerce from 1930-63 as

> ". . .a nonprofit, cooperative, voluntarily-joined organization of business competitors designed to assist its members and its industry in dealing with mutual business problems in several of the following areas: accounting practice, business ethics, commercial and industrial research, standardization, statistics, trade promotion, and relations with Government, employees and the general public."

A professional society is an organization of individuals with a common background in a subject—medicine, law, engineering, etc., whose chief purpose is to apply their knowledge for professional or monetary gain. For purposes of this book the term "professional" has been construed broadly ("Profession—the occupation, if not commercial, mechanical, agricultural, or the like, to which one devotes oneself," Webster's *New Collegiate Dictionary,* 1958), and as used here includes professional, learned, and scientific societies.

Like a trade association, a professional society is a nonprofit, cooperative, voluntary organization. Academic credentials, an accrediting examination or a state license may be a prerequisite for membership, but not always. Its membership is usually composed of individuals who seek an exchange of ideas and discussion of common problems within their profession. While the ultimate goal of a trade association is increased income from its product or service, the goals of professional societies are commonly considered to point more towards the expansion of knowledge, or the establishment of professional standards. However, the broad range of activities of many professional societies makes them similar to trade associations.

A scientific or learned society, on the other hand, is generally considered to be a group of individuals with a common background in a subject who are primarily concerned with expanding the knowledge of their discipline.

There is no center in the United States for recording national association data. This directory contains more complete and up-to-date information than can be secured anywhere. Although it is sometimes difficult to determine when a new association has been formed or an old one merges or passes away, according to data in the files of Columbia Books there are now more than 3,400 national trade associations in the United States and more than 2,300 professional and learned societies.

Trade Associations—Background

Trade associations are nothing new. Since recorded history men with a common background or objective have united for reinforcement. The Bible contains a reference to a "street of the bakers" and Josephus' *War of the Jews* speaks of the "valley of the cheese-makers," hinting that even 3,000 years ago men with a common trade lived and worked together.

The ancient empires of China, Egypt, Japan and India contained trade groups operating for the benefit of their members, as did Rome, whose groups set wages and prices and fostered apprentice training.

During the Middle Ages European craft and merchant guilds increased in number and power and developed strict regulations and many member services. Merchant guilds were associations of merchants and traders formed originally for protection and increased profit. Craft guilds were made up of artisans and craftsmen producing consumer goods who set quality standards for their work. Both groups set up monopolies with severe entrance requirements and limited the training of apprentices. Cooperation, fellowship and mutual interest were the original foundations underlying these guilds, but as they became better established they developed into instruments for rigid maintenance of the *status quo*.

In the 18th century the rising tide of invention, nationalism and the industrial revolution doomed the efforts of the old guilds to oppose economic and social change and they gradually declined. They had, however, despite their suppression of individual initiative, done some useful things. They encouraged and protected the growth of new industries, improved technical processes and promoted individual skills and training.

Trade Associations in the United States

No regional trade associations existed in colonial America. There is record of a Spermaceti Candlers group in Rhode Island as early as 1762 and the New York Chamber of Commerce, the oldest trade assocation still in existence in North America, was formed by 20 merchants in 1768. The New York Stock Exchange was formed in 1792. The development of national trade associations did not begin in this country, however, until the second half of the 19th century.

Before the Civil War most United States trade associations were local or regional, though the National Association of Cotton Manufacturers was established in 1854, and the American Iron and Steel Association in 1855, groups which today are the Northern Textile Association, and the American Iron and Steel Institute. In the latter part of the 19th century rapid industrial development brought about the establishment of some of the best known national trade associations of today, including thousands of local Chambers of Commerce now organized under the umbrella of the Chamber of Commerce of the United States, the largest and most influential trade association of them all.

The 1880s were characterized by many business agreements, from "informal understandings" to mammoth cartels, some of which were found to be harmful to the national interest. Agreements in restraint of trade were outlawed under the Sherman Anti-Trust Act of 1890. Under the Sherman Act, however, only "undue and unreasonable" business agreements were banned, according to the well-known Standard Oil Company case in 1911, in which the "Rule of Reason" was applied. The Federal Trade Commission Act of 1914 made "unfair methods of competition in commerce" illegal.

Foreign trade is another matter. While cooperation among competing firms to restrict domestic trade has been found harmful to the national interest, cooperation among U.S. exporters can often improve the U.S. balance of payments. This was recognized in the passage of the Webb-Pomerene Export Trade Act of 1918, subtitled "An Act to Promote Trade." This Act enumerates qualified exemptions from the provisions of the Sherman Act, and the Federal Trade Commission and Clayton Acts of 1914. It permits the formation of "Webb-Pomerene" associations to serve as agents for members' goods intended for foreign commerce, undertake joint marketing research, advertising, and shipping, as well as the establishment of uniform contracts, quotas, production standards, and prices. Smaller companies which lacked facilities for ventures abroad could now pool their resources to that end.

In the sixty years since the passage of this Act, export trade associations with memberships from two to several hundred have been formed. Attrition has been high. Associations exporting foodstuffs (grains and flour, milk, dried fruits and vegetable oils), some mineral products, and electrical equipment have been the most successful. The percentage of U.S. exports for which Webb-Pomerene associations are responsible has declined to about 1.5%. The Subject Index of this book lists all active Webb-Pomerene associations now registered with the Federal Trade Commission.

As the advantage of association cooperation in a variety of fields became more apparent, the number of associations grew and their range of activities broadened. The Federal government has always tended to foster association cooperation during national emergencies such as wars or depressions.

There have been three periods of pronounced growth in the number of U.S. national associations. In 1900 there were only about 100. Stimulated by the demands of World War I, by 1920 there were about 1,000.

During the depression of the 1930s their growth was fostered as a way to stimulate the economy. The National Industrial Recovery Act of 1933 encouraged "codes of fair competition." Companies were grouped into trade associations which had the power to set minimum wages and prices and promulgate other regulations. Those who subscribed in writing to the industry code could display the Blue Eagle emblem. About 800 new associations were formed under this law. The whole structure collapsed suddenly in 1935 when the Supreme Court declared the basic Act unconstitutional. Many, but not all, trade associations spawned by the Act disappeared.

World War II necessitated industry-wide streamlining and resulted in a third rapid increase in trade association numbers. By 1943 there were about 1900. After peace in 1945, mergers and consolidations eliminated some, but the total has been gradually increasing ever since.

Membership and Dues

Associations have been formed by participants in almost every form of commercial venture. According to figures released by the United States Commerce Department on national, regional, and local associations, over thirty-five percent represent the retail trade; about twenty percent represent the service trades; and about fifteen percent represent the manufacturing industry. Membership may be based on function (retailers, distributors, or manufacturers), or on product (people concerned with all aspects of the citrus fruit industry). There are also federated trade associations, composed of associations which belong to a "parent" organization, such as the National Forest Products Association. There are associations whose membership includes other associations and individuals such as the American Standards Institute. The total number of U.S. trade associations, their local chapters, and independent local or regional groups is probably around 40,000. One man or company can sometimes be eligible for membership in several. This directory lists only *national* groups.

Trade association membership varies widely. The Motor Vehicle Manufacturers Association, for example, has only ten members, but some are huge. The National Automobile Dealers Association, on the other hand, includes 19,000 companies, but many are small. Professional societies range from the Society of Medical Administrators, which restricts its membership to 50, to the giant American Medical Association with its reported 250,000 physicians.

Staff size may vary from one to several hundred, usually numbering 6-10 people. There are an increasing number of association management companies which run non-profit organizations on a contract basis. The typical "multiple management" firm handles a number of associations, providing a range of skills and services which would be beyond the means of the smaller single association. (A listing of association management companies may be found in a separate section of this directory.)

Top executive officers of associations go by a multiplicity of titles - Secretary, Executive Secretary, Executive Director, Executive Vice President and President. There has been a tendency in recent years to up-grade the title of the chief executive and elevate the salary and prestige of the position. A 1984 survey of 170 not-for-profit groups in the District of Columbia/Maryland/Virginia area revealed an average salary for the top officer of $98,500, the range being $25,500 to $258,000. Both George Washington University (Washington, DC) and DePaul University (Chicago) initiated academic programs leading to graduate degrees in association management in the 1984 fall term. However, in some cases, particularly among the smaller or more specialized societies, the chief operating officer is a Chairman, President or Secretary, usually serving without pay. In such cases the association typically has no permanent headquarters or paid staff.

Association dues are based in most cases upon a flat fee or upon a percentage of annual sales (usually ranging from .01 to .1 percent). Organizations with several classes of membership have different dues for each class. The members of many associations, for example, are the manufacturers. "Associate" members will then be the suppliers of goods and services. Usually only full members have a vote in association affairs. Not infrequently this situation has resulted in tension and ill feeling and the formation by the "associates" of their own trade association. This occurred in 1975 in the motorcycle industry.

What Do Trade Associations Do?

A short and cynical answer was given 200 years ago by Adam Smith who observed in his *Wealth of Nations,* "People of the same trade seldom meet together even for merriment and diversion but the conversation ends in a conspiracy against the public, or in some contrivance to raise prices." An accurate answer is more complicated.

Trade associations are formed by individuals who come together to solve, through concerted action, a problem that they could not solve acting alone. An example is the standardizations of time zones which resulted from concerted action by the nation's railroads. In the 19th century, towns throughout the country chose the "sun-time" of their city hall (noon, when the sun was directly overhead), or that of some prominent landmark such as the city hall of the nearest large city. Railroads ran on the sun-time of their main offices or of an important city on their route. *The Chicago Tribune* once listed twenty-seven local times in Michigan, thirty-eight in Wisconsin, twenty-seven in Illinois, and twenty-three in Indiana. In 1872, a group of railroad superintendents, meeting to agree on the times of summer train schedules, formed an association which eventually became the Association of American Railroads. In 1883, Standard Time was adopted by the railroads and four U.S. time zones were agreed upon. Most of the country accepted "railroad time" immediately.

Another example of concerted association activity is found in air travel. Chaos and inconvenience would prevail if airlines did not cooperate on reservations, ticketing, baggage, cargo handling, confirmations, standbys, and alternate flights. This cooperation results from the work of the Air Transport Association which since 1936 has been coordinating activities of individual airlines with the Civil Aeronautics Board, the Weather Bureau and the Federal Aviation Agency.

Activities of most trade associations tend to follow a pattern which is not always as public-spirited as the above two examples suggest. While not all trade associations do everything, they may promote research on new products, new uses for by-products and improved methods of manufacturing. They may develop market statistics, sponsor quality and certification standards and parts interchangeability. They often sponsor exhibits, contests, awards, and cooperative advertising.

In the field of public relations they may publish pamphlets, yearbooks and articles about their industry. They may draw up news releases furnish photographs, prepare audio-visual materials and sponsor tours, special training courses and demonstrations.

They may compile statistics on all aspects of their industry, sponsor seminars on career guidance and foster discussions of ethical business practice and the prevention of misleading advertising.

Most associations issue some form of periodical in which their membership is kept informed of headquarters activity. Almost all hold annual conventions at which members meet and exchange ideas on common problems.

Lobbying

An excellent overview of the lobby picture in Washington is contained in Columbia Books' companion directory, *Washington Representatives 1987* ($50.00). Contact Columbia Books for further details.

Without question one of the most important functions of the professional staffs of many of the organizations in this book, particularly those headquartered in Washington, is reporting to their membership on governmental developments which might affect their industry, and presenting an industry viewpoint to representatives of the Federal government. In this they have become highly skilled.

Because their membership can be so critically affected by Federal legislation, many associations in recent years have either moved to Washington, established a Washington branch office, or retained a Washington law firm. There is much for these people to do.

Most commonly they direct their efforts at the federal level to three elements of the government; to Congress, and especially its committees where perhaps 90 percent of all laws are formulated; to the executive departments; and to regulatory agencies. They rely, as lobbyists always have, on personal influence arising from familiarity with the law-makers, so entertainment is still a major expense. But more often they supply Congress with detailed information on pending legislation, going so far as to produce drafts of bills that members of Congress may incorporate in whole or in part in measures submitted to the House and Senate. They offer testimony in committee, and they monitor the work of governments on a day-to-day basis. They marshall support from their constituents—the National Rifle Association, for example, has been known to produce five hundred thousand letters from its membership in seventy-two hours—and they get out the vote. In their most controversial role they supply campaign funds and campaign workers on behalf of candidates favorable to their position. They work alone or form shifting and temporary alliances with other lobbies—as in 1946 when the National Association for the Advancement of Colored People, the American Veterans, and the National Farmers Union joined dozens of other disparate groups in support of the employment act of that year.

The result is clear. Virtually no major piece of legislation has been passed through Congress or the state assemblies in this century without some lobby having had a hand in the process.

They do not invariably prevail. In the fall of 1967, for example, the Food and Drug Administration held hearings on proposed rules for prescription medicine advertising intended to insure that doctors not be misled when prescribing for their patients. 96 statements in opposition to these rules (and none in favor) were received from 30 pharmaceutical manufacturers, 46 advertising agencies representing drug manufacturers, 14 magazine publishers, 4 trade associations and 2 individuals. The rules, slightly amended, were issued by FDA in June 1968.

An excellent example of lobbying—almost a textbook case in the art—can be found in MEMBER OF THE HOUSE, Letters of a Congressman, pp. 137-140, by the late Clem Miller, (R), California, edited by John W. Baker, Copyright 1962, Charles Scribner's Sons, and reprinted here in its entirety without change by kind permission of Charles Scribner's Sons. The events Mr. Miller describes probably occurred about 1960.

"In today's world most people are ready to admit that, much as they dislike the word "lobbying," the function carried on under this name is essential to government. (In fact, the right to lobby is protected by the First Amendment.) In recent months there has been a graphic contrast here in effectiveness of lobbying activity between two segments of agriculture important to the economic health of our district: walnut growers and poultrymen. Both groups are in economic trouble because of abundance.

"The walnut growers have a large carry-over from last year which, if placed on top of this year's record production, would break the market. The growers wanted the government to buy walnuts for diversion into the school lunch program, to be financed from existing tariffs on foreign walnut imports.

"In the poultry industry, over production led by huge combines of bankers and feed companies, with million-hen farms, has broken the egg and meat-bird markets wide open. Independent poultrymen are losing six to eight cents per dozen eggs and four to eight cents per pound of meat, and are going bankrupt in droves.

"The walnut industry is well organized. They have been proud that they don't have supports and don't ask the government for "handouts." This is easy to understand. One marketing cooperative controls seventy percent of the state's production. So, when the industry got in trouble and came to Washington, they came well prepared. Each California congressman received a personal, carefully reasoned, five-page letter. It was followed up by another, shorter letter. Then, a telegram called attention to the letters. Finally, there was a telephone call, asking for comments on the letters. By this time, we were fairly wide awake. Quite properly, the group worked through the congressman in whose district the association offices and many growers are located. We received several calls from the congressman's staff, alerting us, keeping us posted, offering help in answering questions.

"After this preliminary barrage, the walnut growers' representative was ready to come to town. He set up headquarters at a nearby hotel. He called on congressmen several times, accompanied by a gentleman from the packing and canning section of the industry. He talked to my legislative assistant. Then we were all invited to a luncheon at the hotel, where the plight of the industry was laid before us and it was announced that a meeting was set up with the Secretary of Agriculture. Meticulous care was taken to be sure that all congressmen and senators who represent walnut growers would be there. In a large Department of Agriculture conference room with numerous department officials present, a skillful "presentation" for the industry was made. Immediately afterward, the walnut congressmen jumped up to demand action. One was self-contained but bitter about department inaction. Another pointed out the illogical Administration position in caustic terms. In turn, each congressman added his bit to the complaint. The Administration was bland and quite self-righteous ('We have more confidence in the walnut grower than he has in himself.'). The exasperation of the Republican congressmen toward the Republican Secretary of Agriculture mounted. 'Would a "shaded" market price have to become a rout before the government moved?" they wanted to know. Administration officials were apparently unshaken.

"However, two weeks later, the Administration did act. The industry was delighted. The work of the lobby had been effective.

"Let's contrast this with the way things are developing in the egg industry. Some time ago I received a long letter from a constituent asking what congressional action was expected in poultry. A check revealed that nothing was contemplated in Congress. Of the seven thousand bills in Congress, there was not one on poultry or eggs. No hearings were scheduled. My interest piqued. I discussed the situation with House Agriculture Committee staff members and with the acting chairman of the subcommittee. The prevailing view was that since there was no leadership in the industry, and no agreement on policy, hearings would serve no purpose. I urged that hearings be scheduled to see if policy might materialize. A day or so later, I heard that a group of distressed poultrymen from New Jersey were asking to meet with their government. The Georgia and Alabama broiler people also asked to be heard.

"All of a sudden, we learned that there was to be a hearing. Citizens were petitioning their government for a redress of grievances. At the hearing a crowd of two hundred poultrymen swarmed into the Agriculture Committee room which had been designed for about seventy-five people. Poultrymen-witnesses testified that the lowest prices in eighteen years for eggs and chickens were bankrupting an industry. As one witness said, in 1957 we were separating the men from the boys; in 1959 it was the men from the giants. One poultryman gave a stark, moving account of his town's plight. He gestured to his friends, sitting somberly at his side. They had been against federal help until a month or so previously, he said. 'We called the people who were down here in 1957 looking for handouts "radicals." Now, we are here ourselves.'

"Throughout two days the same depressing story was recounted as the farmer-witnesses, speaking for themselves and other small producers, took their turn. Technological advances, together with banker-feed company-grower integration, were destroying the independent poultryman. Then the Department of Agriculture spokesman told its story. He confirmed the growers' story but indicated that nothing could be done. It was the inexorable law of supply and demand. Significantly absent were representatives of the larger organized farm groups. At nightfall, the poultrymen had to return to their farms.

"What was the next step? It is up to the interested congressmen they told us. How come, we asked? What are we to do? The leader of the poultrymen said that we had been told the problem. Yes, was the response, but he and his friends should go to see the Secretary of Agriculture. Testimony had indicated that Congress had already given the Secretary all of the authority he needed to act. It would do no good to pass more laws, particularly since they would certainly end with Presidential vetoes.

"All of the men were active poultrymen who had to get back to their flocks. They were leaving that night. Who was to carry the ball for them here in Washington during the next critical weeks? Who was going to do the telephoning? Who was going to coordinate policy between New Jersey, California, Alabama, Wisconsin, Georgia, and Kansas? The answer from them was, 'No one.' We had been given a problem. It was ours now. The result to date: a resolution of the Agriculture Committee urging the Secretary to 'implement such programs of purchase, diversion, and export of poultry products as will lead toward improvement of the present critical situation.' Results for the poultrymen: nothing."

Political Action Committees

A recent development in the association industry has been the growth of political action committees. The modern political action committee grew out of labor's struggle to influence election results, the Non Partisan League of the 1930s and the political action committee of the CIO, its successor. Business, whose political action had been fettered by the Tillman and Federal Corrupt Practices Acts, became restive as it watched increasing political activity by labor unions, although this was considerably reduced by the Smith-Connally Act of 1943.

In 1961 the American Medical Association established a political action committee, the first of them all, whose success sparked the founding by the National Association of Manufacturers in 1963 of the Business and Industry Political Action Committee (BIPAC). Soon many others (realtors, auto dealers, dentists, etc.) formed PACs and the parade was on, especially after the passage of the Federal Election Campaign Act of 1971. Today, (1983) there are more than 350 PACs supported by the business and professional organizations listed in this book. During 1979-80 these groups disbursed about $17 million, a figure which in 1980-81 grew to $20 million. Comparable figures for national labor unions were $14.2 million and $20 million. Association PACs are still forming.

The Concept of Professionalism

The professions, however defined, have always been considered in the United States to constitute an aristocracy of labor. In earlier times in many places the only persons of learning and refinement were considered to be the minister, the doctor and the school teacher—who were accorded general respect. To be "in trade" was often considered slightly reprehensible.

Today many groups are attempting to embrace the word "professional," with its overtones of prestige and financial rewards. The concept of professionalism is constantly evolving. Some professionals are thought not professional enough. Ralph Nader has attacked automotive engineers, for example, for their subservience to the auto industry. To call engineering a profession, he said, perhaps overharshly, is to express a faith rather than describe a reality, and attach a label that "is more an indulgence than a truth." On the other hand, many occupations now seek recognition of a professional status with its concomitants of better pay and faster promotion.

Trade associations are in the forefront of this movement, and accreditation programs, leading to professional status, are multiplying. It is now possible to hire a "Professional Financial Analyst," "Professional Data Processor," "Professional Social Worker," "Certified Assessment Evaluator" and "Certified Professional Secretary," each properly attested to as such by their respective association. The American Society of Association Executives (an association of association and society managers) accredits professional association executives, and awards the title "Certified Association Executive" (CAE).

While defended by most associations and professional societies, this movement towards increasing certification and "professionalism" is not without its critics, who claim that its prime motivation is self-interest. Far from up-grading the services offered the public, they say, the net effect is to drive up prices and restrict the numbers of those who can enter certified and licensed occupations.[1]

This point of view was expressed by Nicholas Von Hoffman in an amusing article in *The Washington Post* for March 14, 1973 on a proposal to license auto mechanics:

"It takes no great imagination to foresee what will happen with licensing of auto mechanics.

"Every state and city which adopts this happy consumer protection measure will have a Board or Commission of Automotive Repair. The members will all be mechanics who will immediately set to work restricting the number of people who can enter the field on the grounds that they're upgrading the profession. Next

[1] For an excellent and easy-to-read discussion of this whole subject see "The Tyranny of the Experts" by Jethro K. Lieberman, Walker and Company, New York, 1970, now, unfortunately, out of print.

they'll promulgate a Code of Automotive Repair Ethics which will have the effect of fixing prices and condemning as illegal and unethical the guy at the gasoline pump who now installs your new set of windshield wipers.

"Lastly, they'll threaten any mechanic with expulsion from their trade who testifies in a malpractice suit against a fellow member of the new fraternity.

"In terms of high prices and low quality, the cost of turning an occupation into a legally licensed profession is invariably prodigious. You can find no better example of this than the organized bar, which is a nice name for an association with the legal sanction to violate the anti-trust laws. If all the people in the retail shoe business were to get together and fix minimum prices for selling shoes they'd be thrown into prison and have to pay triple damages to boot, pun intended.

"State bar associations can fix minimum fee schedules. And the American Bar Association has the gall to inform us that 'habitual charging of fees less than those established by minimum fee schedules may be evidence of unethical conduct.' To make sure that no enterprising lawyer goes around selling $50 divorces or $100 will probates, they have a rule against advertising.

"Any lawyer caught putting an ad in the paper or even hanging up a shingle with letters larger than the prescribed size runs a serious risk of disbarment.

"Armed with the monopoly power to decide who may practice law and how, the professional lawyers' association is in a position to expand the definition of what the practice of law may be. Obviously the more activities that are defined as lawyering, the more money lawyers make. In many places even filling in the blanks of the most routine forms is considered the practice of law.

"This pattern is scarcely confined to law. Doctors go even further by nurturing a whole brigade of sub-professions like nursing and the various kinds of laboratory work. The more professions over which they preside, the greater their status and the more it costs you. The sub-professions are happy to go along for the same reasons.

"Take certified public accountants. They've managed to professionalize themselves to the extent that their services are legally required in the transaction of all kinds of business. The theory is that there are certain universal principles of accounting. By making sure they are followed, C.P.A.s protect the unorganized and unwary public. In fact, C.P.A.s sometimes have certified the most misleading financial statements. Only later, after bankruptcy and scandal blow the mess into the public eye, do they murmur a demur.

"Our present system of protecting the public from organized professions and occupations, be it barbers and beauty culturists, morticians, surgeons or plumbers, simply induces inflation, fraud, manpower shortages and a plethora of low-grade work. As it stands now we're helpless, because most of the practictioners are members in good standing in their professional organizations.

"Instead of contemplating with auto mechanics a repetition of the dismal results from which we suffer, we might consider abandoning licensing altogether. Let anybody follow any occupation he wants, any way he wants. Let there be stringent, but voluntary, public occupational examinations for those people who want to be competent and have a certificate which demonstrates it.

"In this way we'd be swapping ineffectual government regulation for a restoration of the discipline of the free market—but with a mechanism that would enable the buyer to discriminate between the qualified and the unqualified. The legally sanctioned associations we have now have failed."

And still another view of the problem is provided in an editorial from *The Wall Street Journal,* November 7, 1973, entitled "The Right to Make a Living."

"Barber Don Finley decided to offer a new service in his Boca Raton, Florida, shop: shaving women's legs. UPI reports that the service proved popular, and that the presence of women also led to a greater influx of men. Business was booming until the state told Mr. Finley he was violating the barber's code and had to stop.

"Now, any fair-minded person would have to admit that Mr. Finley's innovation was a bit curious. We're curious ourselves why women would pay $5 a leg, which strikes us as a steep price. But we still think Mr. Finley was the victim of arbitrary governmental power. The licensing code says nothing about shaving women's legs, one official explained, but 'If it didn't say you can do it, then you can't do it."

"Which leads to all sorts of philosophical questions. If it isn't barbering, why does Mr. Finley need a license for it at all? Or if it is barbering, why does Mr. Finley need a license for it at all?

"Seventeen years ago Walter Gellhorn noted in his "Individual Freedom and Governmental Restraints," that some states were licensing 'hypertichologists' to remove excessive hair. He also notes that states and municipalities license dealers in scrap, tobacco, threshing machine operators, egg graders, yacht salesmen, well diggers, tile layers and potato growers. Veterinarians in some states were prohibited from ministering to ailing animals unless they first signed a non-Communist oath.

"The licensing mania does not appear to have abated since 1956. Just recently a federal study group on education urged that the government 'adopt a more vigilant antitrust posture toward professional and occupational groups that exert control over who works in their fields of activity.' It noted that the standards employed often bear only a tenuous relationship to the qualifications needed for successful practice. It observed that too often such standards reflect the profession's image of itself and become the means for limiting entry to careers.

"Whatever the motivation behind the recent Florida ruling, requirements for barbers frequently have only slight relationship to the tonsorial trade. Professor Gellhorn noted a Maryland regulation requiring apprentice barbers to receive formal instruction in the 'scientific fundamentals for barbering, hygiene, bacteriology, histology of the hair, skin, nails, muscles and nerves, structure of the head, face and neck, elementary chemistry relating to sterilization and antiseptics, disease of the skin, hair, glands and nails, haircutting, shaving and arranging, dressing, coloring, bleaching, and tinting of the hair.' That law ultimately was declared invalid. But similar requirements remain in other states.

"It is hard to fault the theory of registration requirements for purposes of collecting occupational taxes, or the theory of governmental certification to indicate that one has reached a minimum level of competence. But it is also hard to uphold existing regulations in a host of professions and occupations that seem clearly designed to maintain a closed shop against outsiders."

California has broken away from this concept of self-regulation by the professions, however. Legislation enacted in 1976 has made it mandatory for 38 state licensing boards to draw at least one third, and in some cases the majority, of their members from outside the professions they regulate. Although most lay people view this as a step in the right direction, some California licensing boards, notably in the areas of medicine, law and accountancy, remain unaffected by this new legislation, since their membership is already prescribed by law. California is not the only state to be taking a closer look at its professional licensing boards. Colorado has recently been considering abolishing five such regulatory bodies, and it seems likely that licensing boards will have to work harder at promoting the health, welfare and safety of the public than at protecting the interests of their own professions, if they are to survive in their present form.

The Supreme Court has recently taken action against noncompetitive fee schedules and real estate settlement costs. It ruled that the "learned professions" are not exempt from the provisions of the Sherman Act, and that compulsory minimum fee schedules used by lawyers in real estate settlements are illegal, thus taking a first cautious step towards competitive pricing for professional work.

Then, in 1977, another step was taken when the Supreme Court struck down a seventy-year-old, ABA-inspired ban on advertising by lawyers, deciding that such a ban violated attorneys' rights to free speech, a decision bound to have far-reaching effects on other, notably the medical, professional societies, whose members are not now permitted to advertise.

Ironically, however, some consumer groups are now trying to introduce a kind of reverse price fixing into the medical profession. They are attempting to set "standard" (read "maximum") fees for particular medical services in order to hold down charges passed on to insurance companies or the Government under certain medical programs. The problem they address is the habit of some doctors of raising the fee if the bill is to be paid by someone other than the patient.

A "fair" charge for professional work is often difficult for the rest of us to judge, since one seldom knows how much the service costs the man performing it, how much it is really worth, or, for that matter, the competence of the professional performer. What seems fairly clear, however, is that the law of supply and demand, if allowed to operate freely, should help us to arrive at a just balance.

Scientific, Technical and Learned Societies

Scientific societies, pre-eminent agencies for collecting and diffusing knowledge, originated in Europe during the Renaissance. The first of which we have knowledge seems to have been the Academia Secretorum Naturae, Naples (1560). The next century saw the establishment of the Academia dei Lincei, Rome (1603), the Academia Naturae Curiosum, Leipzig (1651), the Academia del Cimento, Florence (1657), the Royal Society, London (1662) and the Academie des Sciences (1666). The Royal Society was the leading scientific society serving the American colonies before the Revolution. Many Americans contributed to "Philosophical Transactions," the Society's journal which began publication in 1756.

The oldest American scientific society, in continuous existence since its founding in 1743 in Philadelphia by Benjamin Franklin, is the American Philosophical Society. The second oldest is the American Academy of Arts and Sciences, Boston (1780).

Confronted by grave social and economic problems for many years after the Revolution, Americans were slow to establish permanent scientific organizations of national scope, though many local ones were created. Increasing interest in science during the 19th century had led, for example, to the formation of state academies of science in most northern and a few southern states by the outbreak of the Civil War. At the same time many municipal and local academies were established.

By 1840, the need for national bodies had become evident. The following two decades saw the birth of many of our leading professional groups of today: the American Statistical Association (1839), the American Ethnological Society (1842), the American Psychiatric Association (1844), the American Institute of Homeopathy (1845), the American Geographical Society (1852), the American Society of Civil Engineers (1852), the American Pharmaceutical Association (1852), the American Institute of Architects (1857), the National Education Association (1857), and the American Dental Association (1859).

Before the Civil War, most American scientists were generalists whose interests ranged over the whole field of human knowledge. In the latter half of the century science became increasingly specialized. Men devoted more and more time to a particular aspect of a broader subject. This led to a demand for scientific and technical societies of a specialized character.

The development of American scientific societies after the Civil War and up to the beginning of World War I reveals not only an increasing tendency towards specialization, but the formation of purely technological associations in response to the demands of increasing urbanization and industrialization.

During this period scientific and technical societies grew in number and membership and became increasingly significant agencies for the increase and diffusion of knowledge. They held frequent meetings. National scientific and technical gatherings have now become so frequent that it is hard to realize that they developed only within the past century. Such meetings constitute excellent forums for the presentation and discussion of papers and ideas, airing disagreements, and clearing up difficulties before a critical audience of one's peers. In addition to offering recreation and fellowship to those who attend, such gatherings also provide the chance to renew professional contacts and broaden points of view.

Probably even more important as a method of diffusing knowledge and forming thought has been the flood of journals, proceedings and reports of the scientific and technical societies. At the beginning of this century Prof. W. H. Brewer wrote on this subject. "The publications of learned societies, . . . furnish by far the most comprehensive literature of science, philosophy, history, and art, that we have. For a time, this was almost the only way of publishing to the world new discoveries. Today it is as pervasive as it is extensive, and as yet no substitute has been found for this means of publicizing and disseminating the details by which results have been obtained, . . . These publications are an important part of every public library, . . . It is only when we attempt to investigate their number in any branch of science that we can appreciate the great influence such associations must have had in diffusing learning and information among the mass of the people and in making it available for their industries, their comfort and their intellectual pleasure," (W. H. Brewer, "The Debt of the Century to Learned Societies," Connecticut Academy of Arts and Sciences, TRANSACTIONS, XI, 1901).

Cooperation with other research agencies such as the government and the universities has been an important function of American scientific and technical societies. Their relations with universities have been particularly intimate. Not only are many of the officers of the smaller and more specialized societies on the staffs of universities, but, because members find the academic atmosphere congenial, annual meetings are often held at a university.

Many of these societies have also performed a valuable contribution in raising the amateur standards of some disciplines to professional calibre.

Recent years have seen increasing cooperation among such groups in order to avoid overlapping work, the issuance of similar publications, and other forms of unnecessary competition. In an effort to strengthen administrative efficiency and broaden their sphere of influence, scientific societies have formed associations of associations and a wide variety of looser affiliations.

"Horizontal" and "Vertical" Associations

Some professional societies are "horizontal" federations of societies devoted to the same subject. The American Medical Association is now a federation of regional, state and local medical societies, each with its own identity. The American Chemical Society, the National Education Association, and the American Pharmaceutical Association are similar groupings.

A "vertical combination" unites societies devoting their efforts to different subjects. The American Council of Learned Societies (1919), for example, is composed of national scholarly organizations devoted to different fields in the humanities and social sciences, unified only by their common concern for the advancement of fundamental research.

Most of the national learned societies listed in this directory are members of one or more of the "councils," national in scope, which together embrace all aspects of higher learning. Each of these grew out of U.S. efforts during the first World War. They are the American Council on Education, the National Academy of Sciences-National Research Council, the American Council of Learned Societies, and the Social Science Research Council.

In addition, five U.S. so-called "societal institutes" are groupings of learned societies in particular fields, although some admit individuals to membership. These are the American Association for the Advancement of Science, the Federation of American Societies for Experimental Biology, the American Institute of Physics, the American Geological Institute, and the American Institute of Biological Sciences.

Tax Exemption

Many trade and professional associations qualify for tax exemption under Section 501(c)(6) of the U.S. Internal Revenue Service Code. The requirements they must meet to qualify for this exemption have been well set forth by Judge John Kern (Associated Industries of Cleveland, 7T.C.1449, 1465-6 (1946), Acq. 1947-1 C.B. "(1) It must be an association of persons having a common business interest; (2) its purpose must be to promote that common business interest; (3) its activities should be directed to the improvement of business conditions of one or more lines of business; (4) it should not be engaged in a regular business for profit; and (5) its activities should not be confined to the performance of services for individual members." Scientific and learned societies, and some technical societies, also usually qualify for tax exemption under Section 501(c)(3) of the same Code. This section provides that a corporation, fund, or foundation shall be exempt if it is organized for religious, scientific, literary or educational purposes, if no part of its net earnings insure to the benefit of any individual, if no substantial part of its activity consists of propaganda or attempting to influence legislation, and if it plays no part in any political campaign. These tax exemptions and related ones are discussed in depth in *Associations and the Tax Laws* by Robert R. Statham and Richard W. Buek, Washington, DC, U.S. Chamber of Commerce, 1978.

Foundations

An increasing trend has been the establishment of foundations by trade associations under the educational provision of Section 501(c)(3) of the U.S. Internal Revenue Code.

While it is of obvious benefit to an association to have a special-purpose organization not closely connected in the public mind with the self-interest of the parent, most of the benefits flowing from foundations to trade associations seem to be financial. Foundations, for example, can often attract a broader range of financial support, as well as the time and talent of prominent citizens. Then, too, all contributions to a foundation are tax-deductible, and they need not pay income taxes, or several types of excise taxes. Finally, foundations can usually qualify for reduction in postal rates.

Some association-sponsored foundations carry out activities clearly in the public interest under the education provision of Section 501(c)(3). The Highway Users Federation for Safety and Mobility (formerly the Automotive Safety Foundation), for example, works to promote highway safety. The National Foundation for Consumer Credit promotes family credit counseling services. In other cases, however, the word "education" appears broadly defined, and foundation activities seem to contain detectable traces of self-interest. The National Golf Foundation derives considerable support from golf club manufacturers. The Plywood Research Foundation is supported principally by West Coast lumber companies. The Petroleum Marketing Education Foundation is largely the creation of the National Oil Jobbers Council. This list could be extended without difficulty.

Labor Unions

About 220 national labor unions of the United States will be found in this directory. Some organizations classified as labor unions (in the Subject Index) object, claiming that they are professional societies and thus they so regard themselves. However, they represent their members in collective bargaining and many feel that this significant role places them in the labor union category.

The historic merger of the American Federation of Labor and the Congress of Industrial Organizations in December 1955 was expected to set a precedent for affiliated unions with common jurisdictional interests. In the words of the new constitution, it was to encourage "the elimination of conflicting and duplicating organizations and jurisdictions through the process of voluntary merger in consultation with the appropriate officials of the Federation..."

Ten years later, George Meany noted that relatively few unions had responded. The AFL-CIO president declared: "I [do not] suggest that we deviate in any way from the principle that such [merger] action must be entirely voluntary. I do, however, strongly suggest that the responsible officers of many unions, who by all logic and common sense should merge, might well take a broader view of the union as an instrument of progress for the working people rather than an institution devoted to its own perpetuation for the sake of sentiment and tradition."

Although the merging of organizations was slow for

the first decade following the establishment of the AFL-CIO, there has been a noticeable acceleration of mergers since then. There have been 32 mergers since 1965, reducing the number of nationally affiliated unions from 129 to 99 (including new unions formed since 1965).

The merging of organizations, regardless of their function, requires lengthy and delicate negotiations. Labor unions are no exception, and where efforts to merge were successful they frequently required individual sacrifices for the good of the organization. Many merger efforts failed, and some mergers that appeared inevitable have not been seriously attempted. In some instances, intense rivalry over the years ruled out any attempt to reach an accord. Because negotiations of this nature are not conducted in a public forum, it is difficult to identify the roadblocks to success.

It is, however, generally agreed that the strong personality required of a successful union president is often a major deterrent. Aside from the personal attributes of the leadership, differences in union structures, including the degree of local or district autonomy, methods of electing officers, and constitutional procedures often require considerable accommodation. In addition, membership pride and loyalty to the union, as well as fear that craft specialization would not be adequately represented, are thought to thwart some consolidations.

While the roadblocks that were responsible for the relatively low rate of amalgamation after 1955 continued, participants in more recent merger discussions cited factors that work toward amalgamation and are apparently becoming increasingly important. The continued growth of big business and the complexity of the modern market place have forced the labor movement to employ more sophisticated techniques. Unions need increasing resources to negotiate with ever larger multinational corporations, as well as the bloated federal, state and local bureaucracies. Although the staff cost per member has decreased, the other resources necessary in today's economy are expensive and provide incentives for unions to merge.

Some of the labor force is shifting into areas where unions have never been prevalent. There has been a major breakthrough in union development among state and local government employees, especially teachers. The growth of public sector unions, particularly the clerical/white collar workers, has far outrun the growth in the private sector. One partial explanation for this trend is that workers have found it easier to negotiate with the government than with private industry. Another explanation may be that it is just recently that government employees no longer have the job security which used to offset the demand for higher wages. Although public sector unions have not always been successful in achieving their objectives (witness PATCO), the trend to unionize does not appear to be abating in that area.

Outside of the public sector, unions do not appear to be making any dramatic changes in either direction. There is a trend toward internationalizing unions, but this has not always been successful, due to the differing labor situations in foreign economies.

A depressed economy along with inflation gives unions a serious problem. Some workers are simply concerned with job security in a world with increasing unemployment figures. Others are more concerned about receiving adequate pay that keeps up with rampant inflation. Unions have little with which to bargain with managements in industries which are fighting to stay alive. This situation does not attract new membership or swell the union coffers.

Total U.S. membership in unions in 1980 stood at 22.4 million, a mere 20.9% of the total work force. Unions have been winning about the same percentage of representation elections conducted by the National Labor Relations Board, i.e. 48%, for the last five years. This figure is considerably lower than the 62% recorded in 1968. Of the more than 4,000 decertification elections held in this country 1977-1982, labor has lost more than 75%. A recessive economy is bad for unions as well as industry. Fearing layoffs, unorganized workers become less militant and are thankful for any kind of job. When workers are laid off, a union has less dues money to spend on organizing. It is a vicious circle from which unions have yet to break out.

★ ★ ★ ★ ★

National Association Headquarters

Of the 6,200 U.S. organizations listed in this directory, over thirty percent are now located in the Washington area, seventeen percent in the New York area, and eighteen percent in and around Chicago. The rest are scattered, with Philadelphia, Cleveland, Los Angeles and San Francisco having small concentrations.

METROPOLITAN AREA

YEAR	NEW YORK	WASHINGTON	CHICAGO	ELSEWHERE
1971	26%	19%	15%	40%
1972	25	20	15	40
1973	26	24	16	34
1974	25	24	17	34
1975	24	26	16	34
1976	23	27	16	34
1977	22	26	16	36
1978	22	27	16	35
1979	23	28	13	36
1980	21	28	14	37
1981	20	29	15	36
1982	19	30	15	36
1983	19	30	14	37
1984	19	31	18	32
1985	18	30	18	34
1986	17	31	18	34

NATIONAL
TRADE AND PROFESSIONAL ASSOCIATIONS
of the
UNITED STATES

1987

The following listings include about 6,250 active national trade and professional associations, and labor unions. For each organization the latest pertinent information available has been included.

Included among the current listings are the names of organizations, listed in previous directories, that are no longer in existence.

It is not always possible to determine precisely when an organization comes to an end. Some dissolve formally. Others suffer lingering deaths. Associations are sometimes generated by one individual. When he ceases to invigorate his offspring, the association dies. Some associations are set up to solve a problem and fall apart when the problem is solved. Still others are started in competition with older and better established groups, perhaps by dissidents within the original organization. If the going is rough, the struggle may be abandoned after a few years and the dissidents and any who have been attracted to follow them return to the fold. Many are brought to their knees by forces outside their control. The defunct Wool Hat Manufacturers Association, the Brotherhood of Sleeping Car Porters and the Religious Drygoods Association are silent witnesses to changing styles in American life.

The association picture is fluid. People, addresses, budgets, telephone numbers change. Organizations change their names, combine, die. To keep this book in manageable bounds all references to name changes, mergers and deaths more than seven years old have been deleted. Those interested in such history will have to consult previous editions of this directory.

Much effort has been devoted to making this information current and accurate, but errors are undoubtedly present. Any such will be corrected in the next edition of this book if called to the attention of the Editor.

ABCD: The Microcomputer Industry Ass'n (1982)
8725 West Higgins Road, Suite 430, O'Hare Plaza, Chicago IL 60631
Exec. V. President: Bernard F. Whalen
Members: 600 resellers, 60 vendors *Staff:* 4
Annual Budget: $250-500,000 *Tel:* (312) 693-2223
Hist. Note: Formerly (1986) Ass'n of Better Computer Dealers. Members are independent microcomputer resellers who provide technical assistance, training and full maintenance to customers and leading microcomputer software and hardware manufacturers. Membership: $250/yr.
Publications:
Directory. a.
A Better Channel. m.
Annual Meetings:
1987-Florida/Sept./over 400

Abrasive Engineering Soc. (1956)
1700 Painters Run Rd., Pittsburgh PA 15243
Exec. Director: Jack McMillen
Members: 750-800 *Staff:* 2-5
Annual Budget: $100-250,000 *Tel:* (412) 221-0909
Hist. Note: Membership: $35/year.
Publications:
AES Magazine. bi-m. adv.
Proceedings, International Technical Conference. a.
Reference and Buyers Guide. bi-a. adv.
Annual Meetings: Spring/225
1987-Chicago, IL/April or May

Abrasive Grain Ass'n (1933)
712 Lakewood Center North, 14600 Detroit Ave., Cleveland OH 44107
Manager: Allen P. Wherry
Members: 11-15 companies *Staff:* 2-5
Annual Budget: $25-50,000 *Tel:* (216) 226-7700
Hist. Note: Members make natural and artificial grains used in grinding wheels, coated abrasives, etc.
Semi-annual Meetings:

Academy for Implants and Transplants (1972)
Box 223, Springfield VA 22150
Exec. Director: Anthony J. Viscidio, D.D.S.
Members: 250 individuals
Annual Budget: $10-25,000 *Tel:* (703) 451-0001
Hist. Note: Dentists engaged in the field of implants and transplants. Has no paid staff. Membership: $75/yr.
Publication:
Oral Implantologist. semi-a. adv.
Annual Meetings:
1987-New Orleans, LA/March
1988-Las Vegas, NV/April
1989-New Orleans, LA/March
1990-Las Vegas, NV/April

Academy for Sports Dentistry (1983)
The Aerobics Center, 12200 Preston Road, Dallas TX 75230
Secy.-Treas.: Jim Gallman, D.D.S.
Members: 400 *Staff:* 0
Annual Budget: under $10,000 *Tel:* (214) 239-7223
Hist. Note: Dedicated to the promotion of dentistry in sports. Membership: $35/year.
Annual Meetings: June

Academy of Ambulatory Foot Surgery (1972)
910 North 11th St., St. Louis MO 63101
Administrator: Susan Corrington
Members: 1,500 *Staff:* 2-5
Annual Budget: $250-500,000 *Tel:* (314) 231-7500
Hist. Note: Podiatric surgeons who specialize in surgical procedures that do not require hospitalization. Annual membership dues: $285/year. Incorporated in the State of Pennsylvania.
Publications:
Journal of the Academy of Ambulatory Foot Surgery. a. adv.
Newsletter. bi-m. adv.
Annual Meetings:
1987-Orlando, FL/July
1988-Washington, DC/July

Academy of American Poets (1934)
Hist. Note: A non-profit corporation based in New York City administering a permanent trust fund used to award prizes to American poets and foster American poetry.

Academy of Aphasia (1962)
Speech & Hearing Scncs, CUNY Grdt. Cntr.,3 West 42nd Street, New York NY 10036
Board Secretary: Dr. Lorraine Obler
Members: 200
Annual Budget: under $10,000 *Tel:* (212) 790-4366
Hist. Note: Specialists in the study of total or partial loss of speech. Membership: $15/yr.
Annual Meetings: Fall (location determined by availability of volunteer coordinator)
1987-Tucson, AZ/Oct. 25-27/130
1988-Montreal, Quebec, Canada

Academy of Criminal Justice Sciences (1963)
Univ. of Nebraska, 1313 Farnam on the Mall, Omaha NE 68182
Exec. Secretary: Patricia DeLancey
Members: 1,400 *Staff:* 2-5
Annual Budget: $100-250,000 *Tel:* (402) 554-8376
Hist. Note: Professors and institutions who teach courses in criminology, law enforcement and corrections. Membership: $20-30/yr. (individual), $100/yr. (institution).
Publications:
ACJS Today. bi-m. adv.
Justice Quarterly. q. adv.
Membership Directory. a. adv.
Program Book. a. adv.
Annual Meetings: March/900-1,000
1987-St. Louis, MO(Stouffers Riverfront)/March 15-19
1988-San Francisco, CA(Hilton & Tower)/April 5-8

Academy of Dental Materials (1940)
311 East Chicago Ave., Room 10-019, Chicago IL 60611
Exec. Secretary: Sybil Greener
Members: 300 *Staff:* 1
Annual Budget: $10-25,000 *Tel:* (312) 642-9570
Hist. Note: Formerly (1983) American Academy for Plastics Research in Dentistry. Membership: $70/yr. (individual); $500/yr. (organization/company)
Publication:
Dental Materials. bi-m.
Semi-Annual Meetings:
1987-Orlando, FL/Jan. 3-4 and Las Vegas, NV/Oct. 8-9
1988-Chicago, IL/Feb. 12-13

Academy of Dentistry for the Handicapped (1952)
211 E. Chicago, Chicago IL 60611
Exec. Director: Paul Van Ostenberg, DDS, MS
Members: 450 *Staff:* 1
Annual Budget: $10-25,000 *Tel:* (312) 440-2660
Hist. Note: Established as the Academy for Oral Rehabilitation of Handicapped Persons by a group of dentists at a meeting of the American Dental Ass'n in September 1952. Incorporated in Delaware in 1953. In February 1957 the name was changed to the Academy of Dentistry for the Handicapped. Affiliated with the American Dental Ass'n. Membership: $60/year (individual).
Publication:
Special Care in Dentistry. bi-m. adv.
Semi-annual meetings: Spring & Fall.

Academy of Dentistry Internat'l (1974)
7804 Calle Espada, Bakersfield CA 93309-2702
Exec. Director: Dr. Clifford F. Loader
Members: 957 *Staff:* 2
Annual Budget: $100-250,000 *Tel:* (805) 832-3236
Hist. Note: An honorary international dental society established and incorporated in California, ADI promotes and fosters continuing education world-wide for the dental profession. Membership: $60/yr.
Publication:
International Communicator. q.
Semi-annual Meetings: Feb. with Chicago Dental Soc. & Fall with ADA
1987-Las Vegas, NV/Oct. 9-10/380
1988-Washington, DC/Oct. 7-8/320
1989-Honolulu, HI/Nov. 3-4
1990-Boston, MA/Oct 12-13/340

Academy of Denture Prosthetics (1918)
16730 32nd Place N.E., Seattle WA 98155
Secy.-Treas.: Charles Swope, D.D.S.
Members: 90-100 individuals *Staff:* 1
Annual Budget: $10-25,000 *Tel:* (206) 455-5661
Hist. Note: Organized in 1918 as the Nat'l Soc. of Denture Prosthetics. Incorporated in Illinois and name changed to Academy of Denture Prosthetics in 1940.
Publication:
Journal of Prosthetic Dentistry. m. adv.
Annual Meetings: May/150-200

Academy of Dispensing Audiologists (1977)
900 Des Moines St., Suite 200, Des Moines IA 50309
Exec. Director: Karen Loihl
Staff: 2
Annual Budget: $50-100,000 *Tel:* (515) 266-2189
Hist. Note: Professional organization of audiologists dispensing hearing aids in rehabilitative practice. Membership: $70/yr.
Publication:
Newsletter. q. adv.
Annual Meetings: May

Academy of Family Mediators (1981)
Box 4686, Greenwich CT 06830
Exec. Director: Nancy Thode
Members: 750 *Staff:* 1
Annual Budget: $25-50,000 *Tel:* (203) 629-8049
Hist. Note: Members are individuals with backgrounds in the behavioral sciences or law who specialize in helping incompatible married couples achieve an amicable divorce without the necessity of litigation. Membership: $70/year.
Publications:
Mediation News. bi-m.
Mediation Quarterly. q.
Annual Meetings:
1987-New York, NY/July 8-11

Academy of Family Psychology (1958)
Hist. Note: Became a division of the American Psychological Ass'n in 1984.

Academy of General Dentistry (1952)
211 East Chicago Ave., Suite 1200, Chicago IL 60611
Exec. Director: Harold E. Donnell, Jr., CAE
Members: 28,000 *Staff:* 57
Annual Budget: $2-5,000,000 *Tel:* (312) 440-4300
Hist. Note: Membership: $149/yr.
Publications:
AGD Impact. m.
General Dentistry. bi-m. adv.
Annual Meetings: Summer/5-6,000
1987-Seattle, WA(Westin)/July 17-21
1988-Chicago, IL(Hyatt Regency)/July 15-20
1989-New York, NY(Hilton)/July 21-26
1990-San Antonio, TX/July 13-17

Academy of Geriatric Dentistry (1981)
891 Pleasant Ave., Highland Park IL 60035
Exec. Director: S. I. Neiman
Members: 375-400 *Staff:* 2-5
Annual Budget: $100-250,000 *Tel:* (312) 432-2341
Publication:
Member Bulletins.
Annual Meetings: Regionally, four times per year

Academy of Hazard Control Management (1981)
5010A Nicholson Lane, Rockville MD 20852
President: John J. McCambridge
Members: 1,500 *Staff:* 1
Annual Budget: under $10,000 *Tel:* (301) 984-8969
Hist. Note: Sets standards and certifies professionals in government, industry and education who are concerned with occupational and environmental health.
Publication:
Newsletter. 2/yr.

Academy of Health Care Consultants (1958)
Hist. Note: Formerly (1973) Academy of Hospital Counselors and (1975) Academy of Hospital Consultants. Ceased effective operations in 1981.

Academy of Health Professions
Hist. Note: Not a membership organization. Provides administrative services to health organizations.

Academy of Hospital Public Relations (1964)
Hist. Note: Merged with the Public Relations Soc. of America in 1986.

Academy of Internat'l Business (1959)
World Trade Education Center, Cleveland State Univ., Cleveland OH 44115
Exec. Secretary: Ivan R. Vernon
Members: 1,600 *Staff:* 2-5
Annual Budget: $50-100,000 *Tel:* (216) 687-6952
Hist. Note: Formerly (1974) Ass'n for Education in Internat'l Business. Members are teachers, attorneys, executives in the field of international business. Annual membership dues: $25/yr.
Publications:
AIB Newsletter. 4/yr.
Journal of International Business Studies. 3/yr.
Annual Meetings: Fall, generally October
1987-Chicago, IL
1988-San Diego, CA
1989-New Orleans, LA
1990-San Antonio, TX

Academy of Management (1936)
Box KZ, Mississippi State Univ., Mississippi State MS 39762
Secy.-Treas.: Walter B. Newson
Members: 6,900 *Staff:* 2-5
Annual Budget: $500-1,000,000 *Tel:* (601) 325-3928
Hist. Note: Members are teachers of management courses in accredited educational institutions. Budget is $800,000 per year. Membership: $48/yr. (individual).
Publications:
Academy of Management Review. q. adv.
Academy of Management Journal. q. adv.
Academy of Management Executive. q. adv.
Proceedings. a.
Annual Meetings: August/1,600
1987-New Orleans, LA(Sheraton)/Aug. 9-12
1988-Anaheim, CA(Disneyland)/Aug. 4-12
1989-Washington, DC(Hilton)/Aug. 13-16
1990-San Francisco, CA

Academy of Marketing Science (1971)
School of Business Administration, University of Miami, Coral Gables FL 33124
Exec. V. President & Director: Dr. Harold W. Berkman
Members: 900 *Staff:* 2
Annual Budget: $50-100,000 *Tel:* (305) 284-2510
Hist. Note: Professional (academicians and marketing executives) society concerned with fostering education in marketing, advancing the science of marketing and furthering professional standards in the discipline. Sponsors and supports the AMS Foundation which provides grants for both the advancement of the teaching of marketing and research in marketing. Membership: $35/year.
Publications:
Journal of the Academy of Marketing Science. q. adv.
Developments in Marketing Science. a. adv.
Annual Meetings: April/May
1987-Miami Beach, FL(Sheraton Bal Harbor)

Academy of Motion Picture Arts and Sciences (1927)
8949 Wilshire Blvd., Beverly Hills CA 90211
Exec. Director: James M. Roberts
Members: 4,800 *Staff:* 80-85
Annual Budget: over $5,000,000 *Tel:* (213) 278-8990
Hist. Note: Organized on the Pacific coast by motion picture producers as an employee-representation organization to counter the organizing efforts of the Actors' Equity Association. Members today are producers, actors and others connected with the motion picture industry. Presents the annual OSCAR awards. Has an annual budget of $10.3 million. Membership: $150/year (individual).
Publications:
Index to Motion Picture Credits. a.
Players Directory. 3/yr.

Academy of Operative Dentistry (1972)
Box 177, Menomonie WI 54751
Secy.-Treas.: Ralph J. Werner
Members: 1,000-1,100 *Staff:* 1
Annual Budget: $50-100,000 *Tel:* (715) 235-7566
Publication:
Operative Dentistry. q.
Annual Meetings: Winter

Academy of Oral Dynamics (1950)
2363 Philadelphia Ave., Chambersburg PA 17201
Secy.-Treas.: Joseph P. Skellchock, D.D.S.
Members: 75-100 *Staff:* 1
Annual Budget: $10-25,000 *Tel:* (717) 263-2451
Hist. Note: Formerly (1950) Internat'l Academy of Oral Dynamics. Membership composed of dentists interested in the use of engineering principles to diagnose the most favorable force patterns of the human dentition. Membership: $25/yr.
Annual Meetings:
1987-Washington, DC(Hilton)/April 25-26/150
1987-Lancaster, PA(Willow Valley Farms)/June 18-21/45
1987-Baltimore, MD(Convention Center & Sheraton Hotel)/Sept. 12-13/100

Academy of Orthomolecular Medicine (1971)
900 North Federal Highway, Boca Raton FL 33432
Director: Mary Haggarty
Members: 340 *Staff:* 2-5
Annual Budget: $10-25,000 *Tel:* (305) 393-6167
Hist. Note: Founded September 30, 1971 in London in the Dean's Yard of Westminster Abbey as the Academy of Orthomolecular Psychiatry, AOM assumed its present name in 1985. Psychiatrists, physicians, dentists and scientists interested in treatment based on altering molecular levels and concentrations of essential substances necessary to achieve optimum brain function. A division of the Huxley Institute for Bio-social Research. Membership: $95/year (individual MD), $75/year (individual non-MD).
Publication:
Journal of Orthomolecular Medicine. q. adv.
Annual Meetings:
1987-New York, NY(Hilton)/March 21
1987-Atlanta, GA(Marriott)/June 27-28

Academy of Orthomolecular Psychiatry (1971)
Hist. Note: Became the Academy of Orthomolecular Medicine in 1985.

Academy of Osteopathic Directors of Medical Education (1962)
Pontiac Osteopathic Hospital, 50 North Perry, Pontiac MI 48058
Secy.-Treas.: Richard A. Margoles, Ph.D.
Members: 140 *Staff:* 1
Annual Budget: $25-50,000 *Tel:* (313) 338-5392
Hist. Note: Members are medical directors and/or directors of medical education or other qualified individuals charged with this responsibility by the governing body of an osteopathic hospital. Membership: $150/yr. (individual), $300/yr. (institution).
Publications:
AODME Monographs. semi-a.
Newsletter. 3-4/yr.
Semi-annual Meetings: Spring and Fall
1987-Tuscon, AZ/April 28
1987-Orlando, FL/Oct.

Academy of Parish Clergy (1968)
12604 Britton Drive, Cleveland OH 44120
Admin. V. President: Rev. Roger I. Perks
Members: 6-700 *Staff:* 2-5
Annual Budget: $25-50,000 *Tel:* (216) 791-4005
Hist. Note: Formed in Indianapolis as a voluntary self-governing association of clergy who work together in an inter-faith, ecumenical parish setting. Affiliated with the Association of Theological Schools and the Society for the Advancement of Continuing Education for Ministry. Membership: $50/yr. (individual).
Publication:
Sharing the Practice. q.
Annual Meetings: Spring
1987-Atlanta, GA/May 5-7
1988-Dayton, OH/May

Academy of Pharmaceutical Sciences (1965)
2215 Constitution Ave., N.W., Washington DC 20037
Exec. Secretary: Dr. Arthur Horowitz
Members: 3,000 *Staff:* 2-5
Annual Budget: $100-250,000 *Tel:* (202) 628-4410
Hist. Note: The scientific arm of the American Pharmaceutical Association organized to promote the discovery, testing, production and control of drugs. Membership: $110/yr.(through APhA).
Publication:
Academy Reporter. bi-m.
Semi-annual Meetings: Spring (with ApHA) and Fall
1987-Chicago, IL(Hilton)/March 28-April 1/5,000

Academy of Pharmacy Practice (1965)
Hist. Note: A subdivision of the American Pharmaceutical Association. Formerly (1975) Academy of General Practice of Pharmacy.

00002 12 05 86 1233

Academy of Political Science (1880)
2852 Broadway, New York NY 10025-7885
Exec. Director: C. Lowell Harriss
Members: 11,000 individuals, libraries and institutions *Staff:* 6-10
Annual Budget: $250-500,000 *Tel:* (212) 866-6752
Hist. Note: Founded to promote political science and its application to the solution of political, social and economic problems. Membership: $25/year (individual), $35/year (company).
Publications:
Political Science Quarterly. q. adv.
Proceedings. semi-a.
Semi-annual meetings: in New York City

Academy of Product Safety Management (1981)
5010A Nicholson Lane, Rockville MD 20852
Exec. Director: Harold Gordon
Members: 400 *Staff:* 1
Annual Budget: under $10,000 *Tel:* (301) 984-8969
Hist. Note: Sets standards and certifies professionals in government, industry and education who are concerned with protecting the consumer from hazardous products.

Academy of Psychologists in Marital, Sex and Family Therapy (1958)
Hist. Note: Became the Academy of Family Psychology in 1983.

Academy of Psychosomatic Medicine (1953)
70 West Hubbard St., Suite 202, Chicago IL 60610
Exec. Director: Sanford J. Hill
Members: 1,000 *Staff:* 2-5
Annual Budget: $50-100,000 *Tel:* (312) 644-2623
Hist. Note: Founded in New York City in 1953. Incorporated in Massachusetts in 1964. Attempts to advance medicine and allied health professions through interaction of mind, body and environment.
Publication:
Psychosomatics. 9/yr. adv.
Annual Meetings: Fall
1987-Las Vegas, NV/Nov. 12-15

Academy of Screen Printing Technology (1973)
Hist. Note: An honorary non-dues-paying organization affiliated with the Screen Printing Ass'n International, admitting no more than 3 individuals annually.

Academy of Security Educators and Trainers (1980)
P.O. Box 1052, Chesapeake Beach MD 20732
Exec V.P. & Secy.-Treas.: Leonard W. Blankenship
Members: 500 *Staff:* 1
Annual Budget: $25-50,000 *Tel:* (301) 260-4665
Hist. Note: Awards the CST ("Certified Security Trainer") designation. Membership: $55/yr.
Publication:
ASET Newsletter. q.
Annual Meetings: Spring

Academy of Underwater Arts and Sciences (1961)
Hist. Note: A small honorary society of individuals, living and dead, who have made important contributions to an understanding of the underwater world through exploration, scientific and medical research, the arts, and recreation.

Academy of Veterinary Cardiology (1968)
25 Lumber Road, Roslyn NY 11576-2105
Exec. Secretary: Dr. Larry Patrick Tilley
Members: 500 *Staff:* 1
Annual Budget: under $10,000 *Tel:* (516) 484-2700
Hist. Note: Membership includes veterinarians and students interested in veterinary cardiology. Membership: $10/yr.
Publication:
Newsletter. q.
Annual Meetings: With American Animal Hospital Ass'n

Accordion Teachers' Guild (1941)
148 Shorewood Dr., Valparaiso IN 46383
President: Rina Rosa
Members: 225-250
Annual Budget: under $10,000 *Tel:* (219) 465-1236
Publication:
ATG Bulletin. m.
Annual Meetings: Summer

Accountants for the Public Interest (1975)
888 17th St., N.W., Suite 201, Washington DC 20006
Exec. Director: Peter D. Rosenstein
Members: 1,000 *Staff:* 2-5
Annual Budget: $100-250,000 *Tel:* (202) 659-3797
Hist. Note: Through affiliates, members provide pro bono accounting services to non-profit organizations, small businesses and individuals who need such services but are unable to pay for them. Membership: $25/yr. (individual).
Publication:
API Accountant. bi-m.
Annual Meetings: November

Accounting Firms Associated (1978)
2811 N.W. 41st St., Gainesville FL 32606
Exec. Director: Douglas H. Thompson, Jr.
Members: 146 companies; 1,000 individuals *Staff:* 6
Annual Budget: $500-1,000,000 *Tel:* (904) 375-2324
Hist. Note: Accounting Firms Associated, Inc. is an international association of independent public accounting firms founded to pursue and ensure excellence in accounting, financial and business consulting services.
Annual Meetings: August
1987-San Diego, CA
1988-Boston, MA

Accounting Machine Minicomputer Dealers Ass'n of America (1963)
Hist. Note: Also known as the Associated Minicomputer Dealers of America.

Accredited Gemologists Ass'n (1976)
99 Pratt St., Suite 211, Hartford CT 06103
Secretary: Jeffrey Hurwitz
Members: 250 individuals
Annual Budget: under $10,000 *Tel:* (203) 247-1319
Hist. Note: Members must hold a "gemologist" diploma from the Gemological Institute of America or the Gemological Ass'n of Great Britain and pass character, professional, and ethical investigation. Membership: $100/yr.
Annual Meetings: Tucson, AZ(Hotel Park Tucson)/February

ACME, Inc.-The Association of Management Consulting Firms (1929)
230 Park Ave., New York NY 10169
President: Joseph J. Brady
Members: 59 companies *Staff:* 8
Annual Budget: $500-1,000,000 *Tel:* (212) 697-9693
Hist. Note: ACME, founded in 1929 and incorporated in 1933, is a membership organization of major firms engaged in the practice of management consulting for corporate and institutional clients in both the public and private sectors. Formerly (1982) known as the Ass'n of Consulting Management Engineers.
Publications:
Directory of Members. bien.
ACME Newsletter. q.

Acoustical Door Institute (1960)
Hist. Note: Moribund in 1981, attempts were being made in 1982 to reactivate this organization.

Acoustical Soc. of America (1929)
500 Sunnyside Blvd., Woodbury NY 11797
Secretary: Betty H. Goodfriend
Members: 5,900 *Staff:* 2-5
Annual Budget: $250-500,000 *Tel:* (516) 349-7800
Hist. Note: Incorporated in New York City in 1929, where its initial meeting was held May 10-11, 1929 with a charter membership of about 450. A member society of the American Institute of Physics. Membership: $45/year.
Publication:
Journal of the Acoustical Soc. of America. m. adv.
Semi-annual meetings: Spring and Fall/800-1,000
1987-Indianapolis, IN(Hyatt Regency)/May 11-15
1987-Miami, FL(Hyatt)/Nov. 16-20
1988-Seattle, WA(Sheraton)/May 16-20
1988-Honolulu, HI(Sheraton Waikiki)/Nov. 14-18
1989-Syracuse, NY(Syracuse University)/May 22-26
1989-St. Louis, MO(Omni Hotel)/Nov. 6-10
1990-University Park, PA(Pennsylvania State University)/May 21-25
1990-San Diego, CA(Town & Country)/Nov. 26-30

Acoustics, Speech and Signal Processing Soc.
Hist. Note: A subsidiary of the Institute of Electrical and Electronics Engineers. Membership in the Society, open only to IEEE members, includes subscription to a technical periodical in the field published by IEEE. All administrative support provided by IEEE.

Acrylamide Producers Ass'n (1983)
1330 Connecticut Ave., N.W., Suite 300, Washington DC 20036
Secy.-Treas.: Alan W. Rautio
Members: 4 companies *Staff:* 2
Tel: (202) 659-0060
Hist. Note: An affiliate of the Synthetic Organic Chemical Manufacturers Ass'n which provides administrative support.

Acrylonitrile Group (1981)
1330 Connecticut Ave., N.W., Suite 300, Washington DC 20036
Exec. Director: Alan W. Rautio
Members: 10 companies *Staff:* 2-5
Annual Budget: $50-100,000 *Tel:* (202) 659-0060
Hist. Note: An affiliate of the Synthetic Organic Chemical Manufacturers Association, which provides administrative support.

Actors' Equity Ass'n (1913)
165 West 46th St., New York NY 10036
Exec. Secretary: Alan Eisenberg
Members: 35,000 *Staff:* 100
Annual Budget: $2-5,000,000 *Tel:* (212) 869-8530
Hist. Note: Organized in New York City May 26, 1913 by a group of members of the former Actors' Society of America. Chartered in 1919 by the American Federation of Labor it is an autonomous component of Associated Actors and Artistes of America and represents actors on the legitimate stage.
Publication:
Equity News. m. adv.
Semi-annual Meetings:

Acupuncture Internat'l Ass'n (1949)
2330 South Brentwood Blvd., St. Louis MO 63144-2096
Vice President: Dr. William F. White
Members: 3,243 plus local chapters *Staff:* 6-10
Annual Budget: $1-2,000,000 *Tel:* (314) 961-2300
Hist. Note: Doctors of medicine, chiropractic and osteopathy who practice acupuncture. Conducts professional education and public health programs and seminars.
Publication:
Newsletters, bulletins, proceedings and abstracts.
Semi-annual Meetings: April and August
1987-Manila, Philipines/April 1-7
1987-Israel/August 11-17
1988-Las Vegas, NV/April 2-7
1988-Amsterdam, Netherlands/Aug. 6-12
1989-Tel Aviv, Israel
1989-Cruise Ship
1990-San Juan, PR

ADAPSO, the Computer Software and Services Industry Ass'n (1961)
1300 North 17th St., Suite 300, Arlington VA 22209
Interim Exec. Director: Luanne James
Members: 841 companies *Staff:* 30-35
Annual Budget: $2-5,000,000 *Tel:* (703) 522-5055
Hist. Note: Formerly (1985) the Ass'n of Data Processing Service Organizations. Consists of six sections: Software Products, Network Based Information Services, Processing Services, Value-Added Remarketers, Professional Software Services and Microcomputer Software. Absorbed the Ass'n of Independent Software Companies in 1972. Member of the Nat'l Commission on Software Issues in the Eighties. Sponsors and supports the ADAPSO Political Action Committee. Membership fee based on size of company.
Publication:
Directory of Data Processing Service Centers. a.
Semi-annual Meetings: Spring and Fall
1987-Orlando, FL(Hyatt Regency Grand Cypress)/March 29-April 1
1987-Colorado Springs, CO(Broadmoor)/Sept. 27-30

Adhesion Soc. (1977)
Dept. of Chemical Engineering, University of Wisconsin, Madison WI 53706
President: Dr. James Koutsky
Members: 300
Annual Budget: under $10,000 *Tel:* (608) 262-1140
Publication:
Adhesion Society Newsletter.
Annual Meetings: February
1987-Williamsburg, VA(Williamsburg Inn)/Feb. 22-26

Adhesive and Sealant Council (1957)
1500 North Wilson Blvd., Suite 515, Arlington VA 22209
Exec. V. President: Jules Rapp
Members: 176 companies *Staff:* 7-9
Annual Budget: $500-1,000,000 *Tel:* (703) 841-1112
Hist. Note: Formerly (1967) Rubber and Plastic Adhesive and Sealant Manufacturers Council. Members are makers of adhesives and sealants and their suppliers.
Annual Meetings: October
1987-Cincinnati, OH

Adhesives Manufacturers Ass'n (1933)
111 East Wacker Dr., Chicago IL 60601
Exec. Secretary: J. Dollard Carey
Members: 200 individuals; 43 companies *Staff:* 2-5
Annual Budget: $100-250,000 *Tel:* (312) 644-6610
Hist. Note: Members are makers of paper converting and packaging adhesives and hot melts. Known as Adhesives Manufacturers Ass'n of America until 1981.
Publication:
Indicators. bi-m.
Annual Meetings: Spring
1987-Miami, FL(Miami Lakes C.C.)/March 11-14
1988-LaQuinta, CA(La Quinta)/March 9-13
1989-Ft. Lauderdale, FL(Bonaventure)/March 7-11

Adjutants General Ass'n of the United States (1912)
1 Massachusetts Ave., N.W., Washington DC 20001
Exec. Officer: Maj.Gen. John L. France
Members: 50-60 *Staff:* 1
Annual Budget: under $10,000 *Tel:* (202) 789-0031
Hist. Note: Membership composed of the commander of the National Guard in each state, the District of Columbia, the Commonwealth of Puerto Rico, the Virgin Islands and Guam.
Annual Meetings: Spring/300
1987-Salt Lake City, UT/May 10-14
1988-Reno, NV(MGM Grand)/May 15-18
1989-Omaha, NE(Marriott)/May 14-18
1990-Colorado Springs, CO(Broadmoor)/April 22-26
1991-Grand Rapids, MI(Amway Grand Plaza)

Administrative Board of the Dress Industry (1936)
Hist. Note: A group of 6 local New York City trade ass'ns united solely for labor arbitration purposes.

00003 12 05 86 1233

Administrative Management Soc. (1919)
2360 Maryland Rd., Willow Grove PA 19090
Exec. Director: Robert K. Windsor
Members: 10,000 *Staff:* 20
Annual Budget: $1-2,000,000 *Tel:* (215) 659-4300
Hist. Note: Established as the Nat'l Ass'n of Office Managers, it became the Nat'l Office Management Ass'n in 1930 and assumed its present name in 1964. Awards the CAM ("Certified Administrative Manager") designation, recipients of which become members of The Academy of Certified Administrative Managers. Membership: $95/yr. internat'l dues plus chapter and area dues.
Publications:
Managing 87. m.
Management World Magazine. 8/yr. adv.
Manager's Career Letter. bi-m.
Impact: Office Automation. m.
Directory of Office Salaries. a.
Guide to Management Compensation. a.
Data Processing Salaries Report. a.
Annual Meetings: May/June
1987-Chicago, IL(Hyatt Regency)/May 26-29
1988-San Diego, CA(Intercontinental)/May 31-June 3

Adult Education Ass'n of the United States of America (1951)
Hist. Note: Merged with the National Association for Public Continuing and Adult Education in 1982 to become the American Association for Adult and Continuing Education.

Adult Film Ass'n of America (1969)
34 East 30th Street, New York NY 10016
Ms. Lindsay Flora
Members: 275-300 *Staff:* 1
Annual Budget: $50-100,000 *Tel:* (212) 247-1899
Hist. Note: Producers, distributors and exhibitors of sexually explicit films. Has no paid staff or permanent office. Major purpose of association is to combat censorship.
Publication:
The AFAA Bulletin. m. adv.
Annual Meetings: Summer in Los Angeles, CA

Advanced Transit Ass'n (1976)
9019 Hamilton Drive, Fairfax VA 22031
Secy.-Treas.: Jarold A. Kieffer
Members: 200-250 individuals, 5 companies *Staff:* 1
Annual Budget: $10-25,000 *Tel:* (703) 591-8328
Hist. Note: Members are tranportation professionals and others interested in applying advanced technology and planning concepts to urban transportation. Their focus is the current lack of cost and service effective means of urban transit for metro areas. Membership: $35/yr.
Publications:
Journal of Advanced Transportation. 3/yr.
Advanced Transit News. irreg.
Annual Meetings: During the Transportation Research Board Meeting.
1987-Washington, DC(Sheraton Washington)/Jan.

Advertising and Marketing Internat'l Network (1932)
One Bank St., Stamford CT 06901
President: James Marquardt
Members: 31 agencies
Annual Budget: $10-25,000 *Tel:* (203) 327-0890
Hist. Note: A world-wide network of cooperating, non-competitive advertising agencies in 45 cities which provides facilities and branch office services for its members. Formerly called the Continental Advertising Agency Network. Has no permanent office or paid staff. Not a trade association in the strict sense of the word.
Publication:
AMIN News. q.
Annual Meetings:
1987-Vancouver, BC

Advertising Council (1942)
825 Third Avenue, New York NY 10022
President: Robert P. Keim
Staff: 40
Annual Budget: over $5,000,000 *Tel:* (212) 758-0400
Hist. Note: Founded in 1942 as the War Advertising Council. Reorganized after World War II and became the Advertising Council, Inc. Not a trade association in the accepted sense, the Ad Council is a private, non-profit organization of volunteers who conduct advertising campaigns in the public good.
Publications:
Public Service Advertising Bulletin. bi-m.
Annual Report.
Annual Meetings:
1987-Washington, DC(Willard)/April 29

Advertising Media Credit Executives Ass'n, Internat'l (1953)
3803 S. Beverly Hills Drive, Toledo OH 43614
Exec. Secretary: Al W. Kearns
Members: 300 companies, 300-400 individuals *Staff:* 2-5
Annual Budget: $25-50,000 *Tel:* (419) 245-6024
Hist. Note: Members are of the credit executives of newspapers, magazines, radio and television stations. Member: $100/yr.
Publication:
News and Views. q.
Annual Meetings: Fall
1987-Boston, MA(Marriott)/200
1988-St. Louis, MO(Marriott)/200
1989-Albuquerque, NM(Marriott)/200

Advertising Research Foundation (1936)
3 East 54th St., New York NY 10022
President: Michael J. Naples
Members: 350-375 *Staff:* 16-20
Annual Budget: $1-2,000,000 *Tel:* (212) 751-5656
Hist. Note: Founded to improve the scientific practice of advertising and marketing. Supported by the press and the advertising industry. Absorbed the Center for Marketing Communications in 1977.
Publication:
Journal of Advertising Research. bi-m.

Advertising Typographers Ass'n of America (1927)
R.D. 3, Box 643, Stockton NJ 08559
Exec. Secretary: Walter A. Dew, Jr.
Members: 60-70 *Staff:* 2-5
Annual Budget: $100-250,000 *Tel:* (201) 782-4055
Annual Meetings: Fall
1987-Carefree, AZ(The Boulders)/Oct. 11-18/100

Aerobics and Fitness Ass'n of America (1983)
15250 Ventura Blvd., #310, Sherman Oaks CA 91403
President: Linda D. Pfeffer, RN
Members: 12,000 individuals; 350 companies *Staff:* 15
Annual Budget: $100-250,000 *Tel:* (818) 905-0040
Hist. Note: National professional association for the education, training and certification of exercise instructors. Membership: $40/yr.
Publication:
Aerobics & Fitness. 9x/yr. adv.
Annual Meetings: Atlanta, GA(Omni International)/Feb.

Aeronautical Navigator Ass'n (1974)
640 Brumbaugh Drive, New Carlisle OH 45344
Secretary: Major Leland H. Williams
Members: 1,100-1,200 *Staff:* 1
Annual Budget: under $10,000 *Tel:* (513) 849-6082
Hist. Note: Also known as the Navigator Association. Has no paid staff.
Publication:
Navigator Newsletter. m.

Aeronautical Repair Station Ass'n (1984)
1612 K St., N.W., Suite 1400, Washington DC 20006
Acting Exec. Director: Anthony J. Obadal
Members: 75 *Staff:* 4
Annual Budget: $25-50,000 *Tel:* (202) 293-2511
Hist. Note: Established and incorporated in Washington, DC in June, 1984, ARSA represents FAA certified repair stations. Absorbed the Airline Services Ass'n in 1985. Membership: $350/year.
Publication:
The Hotline. bi-m.

Aerospace and Electronic Systems Soc.
Hist. Note: A subsidiary of the Institute of Electrical and Electronics Engineers. Membership in the Society, open only to IEEE members, includes subscription to a technical periodical in the field published by IEEE. All administrative support is provided by IEEE.

Aerospace Department Chairmen's Ass'n (1968)
Dept. of Mechanical Engineering, Howard University, Washington DC 20059
Chairman: Peter M. Bainum
Members: 50-60 individuals
Annual Budget: under $10,000 *Tel:* (202) 636-6612
Hist. Note: Promotes aerospace engineering education and research to stimulate the growth of the aerospace profession. Has no paid staff.
Annual Meetings: Dec.-Jan.
1987-Reno, NV(MGM Grand)/Jan.

Aerospace Education Ass'n
Hist. Note: Reported defunct in 1986.

Aerospace Industries Ass'n of America (1919)
1725 DeSales St., N.W., Washington DC 20036
President: Don Fuqua
Members: 45-50 companies *Staff:* 60-70
Annual Budget: $2-5,000,000 *Tel:* (202) 429-4600
Hist. Note: Established in 1919 as the Aeronautical Chamber of Commerce of America, Inc. Name changed to Aircraft Industries Ass'n of America, Inc. in 1945 and to Aerospace Industries Ass'n of America in 1959.
Publications:
Aerospace. q.
Aerospace Facts and Figures. a.
Directory of Heliports and Helistops. a.
Directory of VTOL Aircraft. a.
Directory of Helicopter Operators. bien.
Semi-annual meetings: Williamsburg (Conf. Center) in May, and Phoenix
(Arizona Biltmore) in November

Aerospace Medical Ass'n (1929)
Washington Nat'l Airport, Washington DC 20001-4977
Exec. V. President: Rufus R. Hessberg, M.D.
Members: 4,200 individuals, 70-80 companies *Staff:* 6-10
Annual Budget: $250-500,000 *Tel:* (703) 892-2240
Hist. Note: Founded October 7, 1929 at the Statler-Hilton Hotel, Detroit as The Aero Medical Society of the United States. Incorporated 1930 in the District of Columbia. Name changed to the Aero Medical Ass'n in 1947 and to The Aerospace Medical Ass'n in 1959. Annual membership dues: $65 (individual); $250 (company).
Publication:
Aviation, Space and Environmental Medicine. m. adv.
Annual Meetings: Spring/2,000
1987-Las Vegas,NV(Hilton)/May 10-14
1988-New Orleans, LA(Marriott)/May 8-12
1989-Washington, DC(Hilton Hotel and Towers)/May 7-11

Aestheticians Internat'l Ass'n (1978)
3606 Prescott, Suite D, Dallas TX 75219
Secretary-Treasurer: H.L. Deason
Members: 1,250 *Staff:* 1
Annual Budget: $250-500,000 *Tel:* (215) 526-0752
Hist. Note: Individuals owning or working in a skin care salon, together with manufacturers and distributors of skin care products. Membership: $50/yr. (individual), $100/yr. (company).
Publications:
Newsletter.q.
News Bulletin. irreg.
Dermascope. bi-m. adv.

Affiliated Advertising Agencies Internat'l (1938)
2280 South Xanadu Way, Suite 300, Aurora CO 80014
President: John L. Del Mar
Members: 80-90 *Staff:* 3
Annual Budget: $250-500,000 *Tel:* (303) 671-8551
Hist. Note: Established as the Affiliated Advertising Agencies Network, it assumed its present name in 1963 after the growth of its foreign membership amounting to about one-third at present. A group of cooperating and non-competing advertising agencies.
Annual Meetings:
1987-New Orleans, LA/Spring

Affiliated Boards of Officials
1900 Association Drive, Reston VA 22091
Exec. Director: Sue G. Mottinger
Members: 5,000 officials; 180 boards *Staff:* 1
Annual Budget: $10-25,000 *Tel:* (703) 476-3451
Hist. Note: A section of the Nat'l Ass'n for Girls and Women in Sport. Rates and trains officials for girls' and women's sports programs. Membership: $15/yr.
Annual Meetings: Not held

Affiliated Warehouse Companies (1953)
Box 295, Hazlet NJ 07730
President: James McBride, III
Members: 85 companies *Staff:* 7
Annual Budget: $100-250,000 *Tel:* (201) 739-2323
Hist. Note: A grouping of public warehouse companies for combined sales promotion, public relations and advertising.
Publications:
Directory. a.
Newsletter. m.
People We'd Like You To Meet. 1-2/yr.
Summary of Sales Work. w.
Public Warehouse Selection Process.
Semi-annual Meetings: Spring and Fall

Afghanistan Studies Ass'n (1971)
Center for Afghanistan Studies, University of Nebraska, Omaha NE 68182
Exec. Director: Thomas E. Gouttierre
Members: 180-200 *Staff:* 1
Annual Budget: under $10,000 *Tel:* (402) 554-2376
Hist. Note: Affiliated with the Ass'n for Asian Studies. Has no paid staff.
Publication:
Newsletter. q. adv.
Annual Meetings: With the Association for Asian Studies

Afram Films
1133 Ave. of the Americas, New York NY 10036
Hist. Note: A Webb-Pomerene Act association. American Motion Picture Export Company (Africa), Inc., at the same address, is also registered as a Webb-Pomerence Act association.

African-American Chamber of Commerce (1964)
Hist. Note: Inactive in 1984.

African American Museums Ass'n (1978)
420 7th St., N.W., Washington DC 20004
Exec. Director: Mrs. Joy Ford Austin
Members: 100 institutions, 227 individuals *Staff:* 5
Annual Budget: $100-250,000 *Tel:* (202) 783-7744
Hist. Note: Membership: $25/yr.(individual), $45/yr.(organization, based on member's budget).
Publications:
SCRIP. q.
Black Museums Calendar. m.
Directory - Blacks in Museums. bi-a.
Annual Meetings: September
1987-Tallahassee, FL/Sept. 25-27
1988-Boston, MA/Sept. 30-Oct. 2

African Heritage Studies Ass'n (1969)
Black Studies Dept., 4-150 NAC Bldg., City College of New York, New York NY 10031
President: Dr. Ofuatey Kodjoies
Members: 600 *Staff:* 1

00004 12 05 86 1233

Annual Budget: under $10,000 *Tel:* (212) 690-8117
Hist. Note: Black researchers and teachers, as well as students, of African history. Membership represents the U.S., the Carribean, and Africa. Has no paid staff; officers change annually.
Annual Meetings: Spring, usually with a like-minded organization

African Studies Ass'n (1957)
255 Kinsey Hall, UCLA, Los Angeles CA 90024
Exec. Secretary: John Distefano
Members: 1,600-1,700 individuals, 5-600 organizations *Staff:* 2-5
Annual Budget: $100-250,000 *Tel:* (213) 206-8011
Hist. Note: Membership: $30-40/yr. (individual); $48/yr. (institution).
Publications:
ASA NEWS. q.
African Studies Review. q. adv.
Issue: Journal of Opinion. irreg.
History in Africa. a.
Annual Meetings: Fall

Aftermarket Body Parts Ass'n (1981)
402 Pierce St., Suite 300, Houston TX 77002
Exec. Director: Stanley A. Rodman
Members: 190 companies *Staff:* 2-5
Annual Budget: $100-250,000 *Tel:* (800) 323-5832
Hist. Note: Founded and incorporated in California in 1980. Formerly (1984) the Aftermarket Body Parts Distributors Ass'n. Members are companies that distribute, supply and/or manufacture automotive bumpers and other auto body crash parts for auto dealers, body shops and garages. Membership: $100/yr. (individual), $300/yr. (company) plus $50/yr. per multiple location.
Publications:
Body Language Newsletter. m.
Collision Parts Journal. q.
Annual Meetings: Fall
1987-Las Vegas, NV(Caesar's Palace)
1988-Dallas, TX(Sheraton Park Central)
1989-San Juan, Puerto Rico(Caribe Hilton)/Nov.

Aftermarket Body Parts Distributors Ass'n (1981)
Hist. Note: Became the Aftermarket Body Parts Ass'n in 1985.

Agricultural and Industrial Manufacturers' Representatives Ass'n (1963)
5845 Horton, Suite 201, Shawnee Mission KS 66202
Exec. Director: Frank A. Bistrom
Members: 125 companies, 35 associates *Staff:* 2-5
Annual Budget: $50-100,000 *Tel:* (913) 262-4511
Hist. Note: Formerly (1972) American Farm and Power Equipment Agents Ass'n.
Publication:
Representative. m.
Annual Meetings: Fall
1987-Reno/Dallas
1988-Atlanta

Agricultural Communicators in Education (1913)
655 15th St., N.W., Suite 300, Washington DC 20005
Coordinator: Donald N. Collins
Members: 685 *Staff:* 1
Annual Budget: $25-50,000 *Tel:* (202) 639-4050
Hist. Note: Formerly (until 1978) the American Ass'n of Agricultural College Editors. Members are writers, editors, broadcasters, graphic designers, teachers and researchers who are involved in the dissemination of agricultural and home economics information. Membership: $45/year.
Publications:
ACE Newsletter. m.
ACE Quarterly. q.
Annual Meetings: Summer/400
1987-Baton Rouge, LA

Agricultural History Soc. (1919)
1301 New York Ave., N.W., Room 1208, Washington DC 20005-4788
Exec. Secretary: Wayne D. Rasmussen
Members: 1,400 *Staff:* 1
Annual Budget: $10-25,000 *Tel:* (202) 786-1896
Hist. Note: Organized to stimulate interest in, promote the study of and facilitate research and publication on the history of agriculture. The Secretariat is based in the Agricultural History Branch of the U.S. Department of Agriculture. Membership: $17.50/yr. (individual); $25/yr. (organization/company)
Publication:
Agricultural History. q. adv.
Annual Meetings: April
1987-Philadelphia, PA(Wyndham Franklin Plaza)/April 2-5
1988-Reno, NV(MGM Grand)/March 30-April 2

Agricultural Publishers Ass'n (1915)
111 East Wacker Drive, Chicago IL 60601
Exec. Director: Walter G. Purcell
Members: 25-30 publishers of farm magazines *Staff:* 1
Annual Budget: $50-100,000 *Tel:* (312) 644-6610
Hist. Note: Membership Fee: Varies according to size of circulation.
Annual Meetings: October

Agricultural Relations Council (1953)
1629 K St., N.W., Suite 1100, Washington DC 20006
Exec. Secretary: Paul Weller
Members: 260 PR executives *Staff:* 4
Annual Budget: $10-25,000 *Tel:* (202) 785-6710
Hist. Note: Association of agricultural public relations professionals. Membership: $100/yr.
Publications:
ARClight. m.
Directory of Members. a.
Annual Meetings: February, with summer seminars in July/August.

Agricultural Research Institute (1951)
9650 Rockville Pike, Bethesda MD 20814
Exec. Director: Wm. Stanwood Cath
Members: 100-125 *Staff:* 2
Annual Budget: $50-100,000 *Tel:* (301) 530-7122
Hist. Note: Originally affiliated with the National Academy of Sciences, the ARI was separately incorporated in 1973, but still maintains close ties with the Board on Agriculture, NAS. Membership: $500/year (organization).
Publications:
ARI Newsletter. q.
Proceedings. a.
Directory. a.
Annual Meetings: October in Washington, DC/100

Agricultural Trade Council (1976)
Hist. Note: Absorbed by the International Trade Council, becoming a subdivision of ITC upon its founding in 1982.

Agriculture Council of America (1973)
1250 Eye St., N.W., Suite 601, Washington DC 20005
President: Orville L. Freeman
Members: 1,200 individuals and companies *Staff:* 7
Annual Budget: $1-2,000,000 *Tel:* (202) 682-9200
Hist. Note: Members include producers, commodity groups/cooperatives, general farm organizations, railroads, port authorities, market development cooperators, private voluntary agencies, retailers and financial institutions. Works to acheive improvement of the U.S. agricultural situation through expansion of export markets.
Publication:
Export Monitor Forum.
Annual Meetings: Fall

Agriculture Pilots Ass'n (1980)

Hist. Note: Address unknown since 1984, reported defunct.

AIDS Internat'l
Hist. Note: Name changed in 1984 to Ass'n of Specialists in Cleaning and Restoration.

Air and Expedited Motor Carriers Conference (1966)
2200 Mill Road, Alexandria VA 22314
Exec. Director: George H. Mundell
Members: 59 companies *Staff:* 3
Annual Budget: $50-100,000 *Tel:* (703) 838-1887
Hist. Note: Formerly (1986) Air Freight Motor Carriers Conference. Affiliated with Film, Air and Package Carriers Conference which provides administrative support. Members are truckers moving freight that has previously been moved by air and handling expedited service.
Annual Meetings:
1987-San Diego, CA(Intercontinental)/Feb. 7-11

Air Brake Ass'n (1893)
Box #1, Wilmerding PA 15148-0001
Secretary-Treasurer: Andrew J. Pommer
Members: 800-1,000 *Staff:* 1
Annual Budget: $10-25,000 *Tel:* (412) 825-1465
Hist. Note: Members are engineers, manufacturers and distributors and suppliers of railway air brakes. Membership: $20/yr.
Publication:
Proceedings. a. adv.
Annual Meetings: September with Railway Supply Ass'n in Chicago, IL
1987-Chicago, IL(Hilton)/Sept. 13-16/3,500

Air Cargo and Mail Ass'n
Hist. Note: Now a part of Nat'l Air Transportation Ass'ns.

Air-Conditioning and Refrigeration Institute (1953)
1501 Wilson Blvd., Suite 600, Arlington VA 22209
President: Arnold W. Braswell
Members: 180 *Staff:* 30
Annual Budget: $2-5,000,000 *Tel:* (703) 524-8800
Hist. Note: Formed in 1953 by a merger of the Refrigeration Equipment Manufacturers Ass'n and the Air Conditioning and Refrigerating Machinery Ass'n. Merged (1965) with the equipment manufacturers of the Nat'l Warm Air Heating and Air-Conditioning Ass'n and (1968) with the Air Filter Institute. Represents manufacturers of air conditioning, refrigeration and heating equipment; membership is divided into sections according to product type. Sponsors and supports the ARI Political Action Committee. Membership fee based upon sales volume.

Publications:
Koldfax. m.
Directories of Performance Rating Standards for Industry Products.
Annual Meetings: November/250
1987-Phoenix, AZ(Wigwam)/Nov. 15-18
1988-Marco Island, FL(Marriott)/Nov. 13-16
1989-Boca Raton, FL(Boca Raton Hotel & Club)/Nov. 12-15
1990-Palm Beach, FL(Breakers)/Nov. 11-14
1991-Palm Springs, CA(Rancho Las Palmas)/Nov. 17-20

Air-conditioning and Refrigeration Wholesalers Ass'n (1935)
1351 S. Federal Highway, Box 640, Deerfield Beach FL 33441
Exec. Director: David L. Kellough
Members: 225-250 (wholesaler) companies, 250-300 associates
Staff: 5
Annual Budget: $500-1,000,000 *Tel:* (305) 421-5500
Hist. Note: Formerly Nat'l Refrigeration Supply Jobbers Ass'n; Refrigeration Equipment Wholesalers Ass'n. Members do not service or install what they sell.
Publications:
Counterline. q.
National Directory. a.
The Wholesaler. m.

Air Conditioning Contractors of America (1969)
1228 17th St., N.W., Washington DC 20036
Exec. V. President: James P. Norris
Members: 2,500-3,000 *Staff:* 11-15
Annual Budget: $1-2,000,000 *Tel:* (202) 296-7610
Hist. Note: Consolidation of Airconditioning and Refrigeration Contractors of America with the contractors of the Nat'l Warm Air Heating and Air Conditioning Ass'n. From 1969 to 1978 known as the Nat'l Environmental Systems Contractors Ass'n. Annual membership dues: $280 to $450 (company). Supports the Air Conditioning Contractors of America Political Action Committee.
Publication:
Newsletter. m.
Annual Meetings: February or March/350
1987-Miami, FL
1988-Tucson, AZ
1989-Charleston, SC

Air Cooled Heat Exchanger Manufacturers Ass'n (1981)
25 North Broadway, Tarrytown NY 10591
Secretary: Richard C. Byrne
Members: 10 companies *Staff:* 2-5
Annual Budget: $10-25,000 *Tel:* (914) 332-0040
Hist. Note: Technical Committee prepares engineering standards for the air cooled heat exchanger industry and cooperates with ASME in developing engineering standards for the gas processing industry.

Air Diffusion Council (1960)
230 North Michigan Ave., Suite 1200, Chicago IL 60601
Exec. Director: George M. Otto
Members: 15-20 companies *Staff:* 2-5
Tel: (312) 372-9800
Hist. Note: Members are makers and suppliers of diffusers, registers, grills, air conditioning terminal units and flexible ducts for air distribution. Membership: $1,000/yr.(company)
Annual Meetings:
1987-Chicago, IL/Jan.

Air Distributing Institute (1947)
4415 W. Harrison Street, Suite 242-C, Hillside IL 60162
Gen. Manager: Patricia H. Keating
Members: 20-25 companies *Staff:* 2-5
Annual Budget: $25-50,000 *Tel:* (312) 449-2933
Hist. Note: Members are manufacturers of prefabricated ducts, pipes and fittings used in residential housing.
Publication:
Bulletin. m.
Semi-annual Meetings: April and October
1987-Phoenix, AZ(Point)/March 29-April 1

Air Force Ass'n (1946)
1501 Lee Hwy., Arlington VA 22209
Exec. Director: David L. Gray
Members: 255,000 *Staff:* 92
Annual Budget: $2-5,000,000 *Tel:* (703) 247-5800
Hist. Note: Absorbed the Air Reserve Ass'n. Military & civilian members supporting development of aerospace power. Membership: $18/year.
Publication:
Air Force Magazine. m. adv.
Annual Meetings: Washington, DC, in September with an attendance of 7-8,000

Air Force Sergeants Ass'n (1961)
Box 50, Temple Hills MD 20748
Exec. Director: James D. Staton
Members: 150,000 *Staff:* 45-50
Annual Budget: $2-5,000,000 *Tel:* (301) 899-3500
Hist. Note: Formed May 3, 1961 by three noncommissioned Air Force officers, and incorporated in the District of Columbia. Members are enlisted personnel in the U.S. Air Force, Air National Guard and U.S. Air Force Reserve. Membership: $15/year.
Publications:
AFSA Federal Digest. m.
AFSA Lobby Ledger. m.

00005 12 05 86 1233

The Sergeants Magazine. m. adv.
Viewpoint. q. adv.
Annual Meetings:
1987-Fort Worth, TX(Worthington)/Aug. 8-13/500

Air Freight Ass'n of America (1947)
1710 Rhode Island Ave., N.W., Washington DC 20036
Exec. V. President and Counsel: Stephen A. Alterman
Members: 20-25 companies *Staff:* 2-5
Annual Budget: $100-250,000 *Tel:* (202) 293-1030
Hist. Note: Formerly (until 1977) the Air Freight Forwarders Ass'n.
Annual Meetings: June, in Washington, DC

Air Freight Motor Carriers Conference
Hist. Note: Became Air and Expedited Motor Carriers Conference in 1986.

Air Line Employees Ass'n, International (1951)
5600 South Central Ave., Chicago IL 60638
President: Victor J. Herbert
Members: 10,000 *Staff:* 25
Annual Budget: $2-5,000,000 *Tel:* (312) 767-3333
Hist. Note: Originally part of the Air Line Pilots Association, ALEA is now an independent chartered affiliate of that group, breaking away about 1963 and representing clerical and passenger service employees.
Publication:
The Air Line Employee. q.
Annual Meetings: Every 5 years (1990)

Air Line Pilots Ass'n, Internat'l (1931)
1625 Massachusetts Ave., N.W., Washington DC 20036
President: Henry A. Duffy
Members: 37,000 pilots *Staff:* 250-275
Annual Budget: over $5,000,000 *Tel:* (703) 689-2270
Hist. Note: Organized in Chicago in 1931 by pilot representatives of various air carriers under the leadership of David Behncke and chartered by the American Federation of Labor the same year. Once included the Air Line Employees Association and the Association of Flight Attendants which became independent chartered affiliates in 1963 and 1973, respectively. Supports the Air Line Pilots Political Action Committee. Has a budget of about $21 million.
Publication:
The Air Line Pilot. m. adv.
Biennial meetings: Even years in Fall.

Air Movement and Control Ass'n (1955)
Exec. V. President: Peter N. Hanly
Members: 186 companies *Staff:* 16-20
Annual Budget: $1-2,000,000
Hist. Note: Manufacturers of centrifugal fans, power roof ventilators, propeller fans, air curtains, ceiling fans, louvers, dampers and shutters. Administers a Certified Ratings Program to insure that products bearing the AMCA seal meet established standards. Formerly (1977) the Air Moving and Conditioning Ass'n, Inc. The Home Ventilating Institute became a division of AMCA in 1984.
Publication:
Directory of Certified Products. a.

Air Movement Institute (1980)
Hist. Note: The research and education arm of the American Fan Ass'n.

Air Pollution Control Ass'n (1907)
Box 2861, Pittsburgh PA 15230
Exec. V. President: G. S. Hart
Members: 8,000-8,500 *Staff:* 22
Annual Budget: $1-2,000,000 *Tel:* (412) 232-3444
Hist. Note: Collects and disseminates information about air pollution and its control.
Publications:
Directory of Government Air Pollution Agencies. a.
Journal. m. adv.
Annual Meetings: June
1987-New York, NY(Hilton)/June 22-26/6,000
1988-Dallas, TX(Hyatt Regency)/June 19-24/5,000
1989-Anaheim, CA(Hilton)/June 26-30/5,000
1990-Pittsburgh, PA(Hilton)/June 25-29/5,000
1991-Denver, CO/June 23-28/5,000

Air Structures Institute (1969)
Hist. Note: Became the Architectural Fabric Structures Institute in 1982.

Air Taxi and Commercial Pilots Ass'n (1974)
7940-2 Airpark Drive, Gaithersburg MD 20879-4127
President: Richard C. Bartel
Members: 250 *Staff:* 1
Annual Budget: under $10,000 *Tel:* (301) 330-6750
Hist. Note: Members are pilots holding a valid Commercial Pilot License or higher issued by the U.S. or a member nation of the I.C.A.O. Has no dues structure or paid staff. Very much the child of its founder and President, ATCPA acts as sort of a mutual benefit society for its members, providing legal and other services.
Publication:
Newsletter. q.
Annual Meetings: January, in Washington, DC

Air Taxi/Charter Ass'n
Hist. Note: Now a part of Nat'l Air Transportation Ass'ns.

Air Traffic Conference of America (1938)
Hist. Note: A division of the Air Transport Ass'n.

Air Traffic Control Ass'n (1956)
2020 North 14th St., Suite 410, Arlington VA 22201
President: Col. Gabriel A. Hartl
Members: 2,000-2,100 *Staff:* 5
Annual Budget: $500-1,000,000 *Tel:* (703) 522-5717
Hist. Note: An independent, non-profit professional organization founded by air traffic controllers seeking professional recognition, it now includes all types of professionals working within the air traffic control system. Membership: $78/yr. (individual); $500-1,000/yr. (company)
Publications:
ATCA Bulletin. m.
Conference Proceedings. a.
Journal of Air Traffic Control. q. adv.
Annual Meetings: October/1,000
1987-Anaheim, CA

Air Transport Ass'n of America (1936)
1709 New York Ave., N. W., Washington DC 20006
President: William F. Bolger
Members: 29 airlines *Staff:* 125-150
Annual Budget: over $5,000,000 *Tel:* (202) 626-4000
Hist. Note: Organized January 5, 1936 at a meeting of airline representatives at the LaSalle-Wacker Building in Chicago. Represents U.S. scheduled airlines in domestic and international passenger and cargo operations. Air Traffic Conference of America is a subsidiary of ATAA.
Annual Meetings: Washington, in December

Airborne Law Enforcement Ass'n (1968)
1450-A North Airport Road, Naples FL 33942
Exec. Director: Carl Meadows
Members: 2,100 *Staff:* 2
Annual Budget: $50-100,000 *Tel:* (813) 643-2200
Hist. Note: Law enforcement officers who use both fixed and rotary wing aircraft, and who are engaged full-time in airborne law enforcement, plus equipment suppliers. Officers elected every 2 years. Membership: $20/yr.
Publications:
Air Bear Magazine. bi-m. adv.
Convention Magazine. a.
Annual Meetings: Summer/800
1987-Sacramento, CA(Red Lion Motor Inn)/July 15-18

Aircraft Electronics Ass'n (1958)
Box 1981, Independence MO 64055
Exec. Director: Monte R. Mitchell
Members: 725 *Staff:* 2-5
Annual Budget: $500-1,000,000 *Tel:* (816) 373-6565
Hist. Note: Companies engaged in the manufacture, installation, and servicing of aviation electronic equipment. Membership fee based on annual sales volume or size of personnel.
Publication:
Avionics News. m. adv.
Annual Meetings: Spring
1987-St. Louis, MO(Adam's Mark)/May 16-20/1,200
1988-Reno, NV(Bally's)/May 5-8/1,300

Aircraft Owners and Pilots Ass'n (1939)
421 Aviation Way, Frederick MD 21701
President: John L. Baker
Members: 260,000 *Staff:* 180-200
Tel: (301) 695-2000
Hist. Note: Represents the interests of general aviation (civil, non-military, non-airline) pilots and aircraft owners. Absorbed the Nat'l Pilots Ass'n in 1979. Sponsors the AOPA Political Action Committee. Membership: $35/yr.
Publications:
Airports U.S.A. a.
AOPA Handbook for Pilots. a.
AOPA Newsletter. m.
AOPA Pilot. m. adv.
Light Plane Maintenance Newsletter. m.
Annual Meetings:
1987-Las Vegas, NV/Oct. 15-17
1988-Nashville, TN/June 15-18
1989-Orlando, FL/Oct. 19-21

AirLifeLine (1979)
1011 St. Andrews Drive, Suite I, El Dorado Hills CA 95630
Admin. Director: Dorothy Simonelli
Members: 730 pilots; 1,600 contributing members *Staff:* 2
Annual Budget: $25-50,000 *Tel:* (916) 933-3060
Hist. Note: A non-profit charitable corporation, AirLifeLine is a network of pilots who donate their fuel and aircraft to fly medical missions. Since 1979, they have flown over 700 missions transporting blood, tissue samples, human organs, mother's milk, and ambulatory patients.
Publication:
AirLifeLine Membership Newsletter. q.
Annual Meetings: June

Airline Industrial Relations Conference (1971)
1709 New York Ave., N.W., Suite 402, Washington DC 20006
Exec. Director: James E. Conway
Members: 26 airlines *Staff:* 5
Annual Budget: $500-1,000,000 *Tel:* (202) 626-4255
Hist. Note: Also known as the AIR Conference. Used by its members as an information exchange for such matters as industrial and personnel relations, equal employment opportunity, and related issues. Although a tenant of the Air Transportation Ass'n of America, the Conference is an independent association; its membership and that of the ATA are not co-extensive.
Annual Meetings: Bi-monthly meetings and annual Board of Directors meeting

Airline Medical Directors Ass'n (1944)
Mayo Clinic, E19A, 200 First St., S.W., Rochester MN 55905
Secretary: C. John Hodgson, M.D.
Members: 150 *Staff:* 2
Annual Budget: under $10,000 *Tel:* (507) 284-2511
Hist. Note: An international organization founded in 1944 to improve the practice and standards of aviation and industrial medicine, particularly as pertaining to domestic and international airline operations, and to encourage research and study of medical problems in these fields. Annual membership dues: $25.
Publication:
Newsletter. 3/yr.
Annual Meetings: With the Aerospace Medical Association in May.
1987-Las Vegas, NV(Hilton)/May
1988-New Orleans, LA(Hilton)May

Airline Operational Control Soc. (1973)
199 Rosemont, Apt. 6, Coroapolis PA 15108
Secy.-Treas.: Robert G. Van Auken
Members: 225-250 individuals and companies *Staff:* 1
Annual Budget: under $10,000 *Tel:* (412) 264-4547
Hist. Note: Membership open to individuals involved with civil aviation operational control. Membership: $15/year (individual), $30/year (organization).
Publication:
AOCS News. q.
Annual Meetings: Fall
1987-Winston-Salem, NC(Hyatt)/Sept. 25-27/60-90

Airline Services Ass'n (1980)
Hist. Note: Absorbed by the Aeronautical Repair Station Ass'n in 1985.

Airport Ground Transportation Ass'n (1946)
901 Scenic Drive, Knoxville TN 37919
Exec. Director: Ray A. Mundy, Ph.D.
Members: 125 companies, 208 individuals *Staff:* 2
Annual Budget: $50-100,000 *Tel:* (615) 525-1108
Hist. Note: Members include airport authorities and operators and industry suppliers of ground transportation. Membership: $300/yr.
Publication:
AGTA News. bi-m.
Semi-annual Meetings:
1987-Ft. Lauderdale, FL(Marriott Cypress Creek)/March 1-4/100
1987-Dallas, TX/Sept.
1988-Los Angeles, CA/Feb.

Airport Operators Council Internat'l (1948)
1220 19th St., N.W., Suite 800, Washington DC 20036
Exec. Director and Sec. General: J. Donald Reilly
Members: 228 *Staff:* 16-20
Annual Budget: $1-2,000,000 *Tel:* (202) 293-8500
Hist. Note: Founded as the Airport Operators Council. Assumed its present name in 1964. Members are boards, commissions, etc. operating public airport facilities. Membership: $900-17,000/yr.
Publications:
Airport Highlights. w.
AOCI Environmental Reporter. m.
AOCI Congressional Reporter. bi-w.
Annual Meetings: October
1987-Miami, FL
1988-Seattle, WA
1989-Houston, TX
1990-Chicago, IL

Airport Security Council (1968)
Box 30705, JFK International Airport, Jamaica NY 11430
Exec. Director: Edward J. McGowan
Members: 35-40 airlines *Staff:* 2-5
Annual Budget: $100-250,000 *Tel:* (516) 328-2990
Hist. Note: Purpose is the development of concerted measures against cargo loss, theft and other airport crimes.

Alcohol and Drug Problems Ass'n of North America (1949)
444 N. Capitol St., N.W., Washington DC 20001
Exec. Director: Karst J. Besteman
Members: 1,500-2,000 *Staff:* 2-5
Annual Budget: $250-500,000 *Tel:* (202) 737-4340
Hist. Note: Established in 1949 as Nat'l States Conference on Alcoholism, it became the North American Ass'n of Alcoholism Programs in 1956 and assumed its present name in 1972. Membership: $45/yr. (individual); $2-600/yr. (organization/company)
Publications:
Newsletter. bi-m.
Special Reports. irreg.
Annual Meetings: Fall
1987-St. Louis, MO

00006 12 05 86 1233

Alexander Graham Bell Ass'n for the Deaf (1890)
3417 Volta Place, N.W., Washington DC 20007
Exec. Director: Donna McCord Dickman, Ph.D.
Members: 6,500-7,000 *Staff:* 20-25
Annual Budget: $500-1,000,000 *Tel:* (202) 337-5220
Hist. Note: Founded by Alexander Graham Bell to promote the teaching of speech, speech-reading, and use of residual hearing. Has three sections: Internat'l Parents Organization of the Hearing Impaired; Internat'l Organization for Education of the Hearing Impaired; Oral Deaf Adults. Membership: $35/yr.
Publications:
Newsounds. m. adv.
Volta Review. 7/yr. adv.
Biennial Meetings: even years
1988-Orlando, FL(Hyatt)

All-America Rose Selections (1938)
Box 218, Shenandoah IA 51601
Exec. Director: George E. Rose
Members: 20 commercial rose growers *Staff:* 2-5
Tel: (712) 246-2884
Hist. Note: A non-profit corporation to test new varieties of roses.
Annual Meetings: Summer, with the American Ass'n of Nurserymen

All-Breeds Rescue Conservancy (1986)
Rainbow Ridge RR Box 100, Ferryville WI 54628
Director: Joan E. Mueller
Members: 20 *Staff:* 1
Annual Budget: under $10,000 *Tel:* (608) 734-3605
Hist. Note: Members are research and practicing veterinarians, sheep and goat breeders, breed association officials, species specialists concerned about containing and eradicating fatal lentiviruses in sheep and goats of all breeds. Disseminates information on these diseases; assists in certifying OPP/CAE-free stock; and maintains a databank of certified flocks to act as a clearinghouse for buyers and sellers of certified stock. Membership: $50 per flock.
Publication:
The ARC Ark. semi-a. adv.
Annual Meetings: Fall

Alliance for Arts Education (1973)
Hist. Note: An arm of the educational program of the Kennedy Center supported by public and private contributions. Not a membership organization.

Alliance for Engineering in Medicine and Biology (1969)
1101 Connecticut Ave., N.W., Suite 700, Washington DC 20036
Exec. Director: Patricia I. Horner
Members: 20 professional societies *Staff:* 3
Annual Budget: $100-250,000 *Tel:* (202) 857-1199
Hist. Note: Established in Chicago, Illinois July 21, 1969 at the 22nd Annual Conference on Engineering in Medicine and Biology by representatives of 14 national engineering, scientific and medical associations. Membership composed of organizations with an active interest in the interaction of engineering and the physical sciences with medicine and the biological sciences in the enhancement of biomedical knowledge and health care.
Publication:
Conference Proceedings. a.
Annual Meetings: Fall/900
1987-Salt Lake City, UT/Sept.
1988-San Antonio, TX/Aug.

Alliance for Responsible CFC Policy (1980)
1901 North Fort Myer Drive, Suite 1204, Arlington VA 22209
Exec. Director: Kevin Fay
Members: 500 companies *Staff:* 1
Annual Budget: $250-500,000 *Tel:* (703) 841-9363
Hist. Note: Members are companies that use or produce chlorofluorocarbons, a family of compounds containing carbon, chlorine, fluorine and sometimes hydrogen. Used primarily as refrigerants, specialty solvents, agents for foamed plastics, etc.
Publication:
Newsletter. m.

Alliance of American Insurers (1922)
1501 Woodfield Road, Suite 400 West, Schaumburg IL 60173
President: Franklin W. Nutter
Members: 175 companies *Staff:* 140
Annual Budget: over $5,000,000 *Tel:* (312) 490-8500
Hist. Note: Founded as the American Mutual Alliance, it became the American Mutual Insurance Alliance in 1956. Broadened membership eligibility to include non-mutual as well as mutual insurers and assumed its present name in 1977. Maintains a Washington office. Supports the Alliance of American Insurers Federal Political Action Committee.
Publication:
Journal of American Insurance. q.
Annual Meetings: May
1987-Quebec City, Quebec(Le Chateau Frontenac Hotel)

Alliance of Independent Colleges of Art (1966)
4th Floor, 633 E St., N.W., Washington DC 20004
Exec. Director: Henry E. Putsch
Members: 8 institutions *Staff:* 3 1/2
Annual Budget: $250-500,000 *Tel:* (202) 393-7060
Hist. Note: Private, independent colleges of art and design. Formerly (until 1982) The Union of Independent Colleges of Art.
Publication:
Newsletter. 3/yr.
Annual Meetings: June

Alliance of Information and Referral Systems (1973)
1100 W. 42nd Street, Suite 310, Indianapolis IN 46208
Director: DebbY Rogers
Members: 277 organizations, 181 individuals *Staff:* 1
Annual Budget: $25-50,000 *Tel:* (317) 923-8727
Hist. Note: Organizations and individuals providing a contact point for those with various social problems so that they can be referred to others who can assist them. Membership: $25/year (individuals); $35-$150/year (agencies).
Publications:
AIRS Newsletter. bi-m. adv.
Journal of Information and Referral. semi-a.
Directory of Information & Referral Services. trien.
Annual Meetings: Spring

Alliance of Metalworking Industries (1974)
1100 17th Street, N.W., Suite 1000, Washington DC 20036
Exec. Director: Ilona M. Hogan
Members: 13 associations *Staff:* 1
Annual Budget: $50-100,000 *Tel:* (202) 223-2431
Hist. Note: Composed of associations representing over 13,000 metalworking firms, among them the American Metal Stamping Ass'n, Forging Industry Ass'n, Nat'l Screw Machine Products Ass'n, Spring Manufacturers Institute, Nat'l Tooling and Machining Ass'n and the Metal Treating Institute. The principal purpose is to carry out legislative and regulatory activities with the federal government.
Annual Meetings: Always Washington, DC(Hyatt Regency)/March/200

Alliance of Motion Picture and Television Producers (1924)
14144 Ventura Blvd., Sherman Oaks CA 91423
President: J. N. Counter, III
Members: 80-85 companies *Staff:* 11-15
Annual Budget: $500-1,000,000 *Tel:* (818) 995-3600
Hist. Note: Merger of Ass'n of Motion Picture Producers (1924) and Alliance of Television Film Producers (1951) and Soc. of Independent Producers. Formerly (1982) Ass'n of Motion Picture and Television Producers.

Alliance of Nonprofit Mailers (1980)
2001 S St., N.W., Suite 510, Washington DC 20009
Exec. Director: Dan Doherty
Members: 75 non-profit organizations *Staff:* 3
Annual Budget: $250-500,000 *Tel:* (202) 462-5132
Hist. Note: A national association of nonprofit organizations and businesses interested in stabilizing nonprofit postal rates. Membership: sliding fee.
Publications:
Alliance Report. w.
Alliance Update.
Annual Meetings: Spring/Early Summer

Allied Artists of America (1914)
145 Lexington Ave., Franklin Square NY 11010
Director: Reta Soloway
Members: 400 regular, 300 associate members
Annual Budget: $10-25,000 *Tel:* (516) 437-4369
Hist. Note: Membership consists of painters and sculptors. Initiated at a meeting at the Grand Union Hotel in New York, January 24, 1914. Purpose is to promote American art and furnish exhibition space for members.
Publications:
Annual Exhibition Catalogue. a. adv.
Newsletter. a.
Annual Meetings: Spring, third Wednesday in April in New York City

Allied Distribution (1933)
16-18 Washington St., Morristown NJ 07960
Exec. V. President: Kenneth Figueiredo
Members: 60 public warehouses and distribution centers *Staff:* 2-5
Annual Budget: $100-250,000 *Tel:* (201) 829-6995
Publication:
Membership Directory. bi-a.

Allied Finance Adjusters Conference (1936)
1263 Bandera Road, San Antonio TX 78228-4088
Division Director: Debbie L. Francis
Members: 200 companies *Staff:* 1
Annual Budget: $25-50,000 *Tel:* (512) 434-1936
Hist. Note: Membership is composed of professional liquidators, repossessors and skip tracers. Membership Fee: Varies with size of population of the city served.
Publications:
Bulletin. q.
Directory. a.
Semi-Annual Meetings: Winter and Summer

Allied Stone Industries (1958)
c/o Biesanz Stone Company, P.O. Box 768, Winona MN 55987
President: Charles Biesanz
Members: 25-30 *Staff:* 1
Annual Budget: $10-25,000 *Tel:* (507) 454-4336
Hist. Note: Members are quarries, fabricators and dealers. Has no paid staff. Membership: $400/yr.
Annual Meetings: February

Allied Trades of the Baking Industry (1920)
Box 398, Memphis TN 38101
Secy.-Treas.: G. E. Maynard
Members: 900-1000 *Staff:* 1
Annual Budget: under $10,000 *Tel:* (800) 238-5765
Hist. Note: Members are salesmen working for companies servicing the baking industry. Membership: $15/yr.
Publication:
The Allied Tradesman. semi-a.
Biennial meetings: odd years

Alpha Alpha Gamma (1922)
7440 University Drive, St. Louis MO 63130
Historian: Miss Betty Lou Custer, FAIA
Members: 1,150 *Staff:* 1
Annual Budget: under $10,000 *Tel:* (314) 621-3484
Hist. Note: Professional sorority, architecture. Affiliated with the Association of Women in Architecture.

Alpha Beta Alpha (1950)
Dept. of Educational Foundations, Winther Hall, University of Wisconsin, Whitewater WI 53190
Exec. Secretary: Dr. W.C. Blankenship
Members: 150 *Staff:* 1
Annual Budget: under $10,000 *Tel:* (414) 472-1380
Hist. Note: A professional fraternity of individuals in library science founded at Northwestern State College of Louisiana on May 3, 1950. In recent years the fraternity has gone into a decline, but newly awakened interest will soon result in a new constitution, providing for a new dues schedule, a newsletter, and regular meetings.
Annual Meetings:
1987-Point Lookout, MO(School of the Ozarks)/March 23-25/120

Alpha Chi Sigma (1902)
2141 North Franklin Road, Indianapolis IN 46219
Nat'l Secretary: Harold J. Wesselman
Members: 43,000 *Staff:* 2-5
Annual Budget: $100-250,000 *Tel:* (317) 357-5944
Hist. Note: A professional fraternity of chemists and chemical engineers founded at the University of Wisconsin December, 1902 and incorporated in Wisconsin.
Publication:
The Hexagon. q.
Biennial Meetings: even years

Alpha Kappa Psi (1904)
3706 Washington Blvd., Indianapolis IN 46205
Exec. Director: Frank J. Brye
Members: 120,000 *Staff:* 2-5
Annual Budget: $250-500,000 *Tel:* (317) 925-1939
Hist. Note: Professional fraternity, business administration. Founded at New York University October 5, 1904 and incorporated in the State of New York the following year.
Publication:
The Diary. q.
Biennial Meetings: uneven years in August
1987-Des Moines, IA/August/500

Alpha Omega (1907)
267 Fifth Ave., New York NY 10016
Admin. Secretary: Robert Young
Members: 10,000-12,000 *Staff:* 4
Annual Budget: $250-500,000 *Tel:* (212) 683-4155
Hist. Note: A professional dental fraternity formed through the merger of the Ramach Fraternity (formed at the Pennsylvania College of Dental Surgery in 1906) and the Alpha Omega Dental Fraternity (formed at the University of Maryland in 1907). Membership: $95/yr.
Publication:
The Alpha Omegan. q. adv.
Annual Meetings: December
1987-Seattle, WA/Dec. 25-Jan. 1/500
1988-Miami Beach, FL/Dec. 25-Jan. 1/600
1989-Jerusalem, Israel/Dec.25-Jan. 1/600

Alpha Psi (1907)
Hist. Note: A professional veterinary fraternity founded at Ohio State University January 18, 1907. Ceased operations January 1, 1983.

Alpha Tau Delta (1921)
14631 North 2nd Drive, Phoenix AZ 85023
National Secretary: Myra Ridder
Members: 10-11,000 *Staff:* 2-5
Annual Budget: $10-25,000 *Tel:* (602) 993-0050
Hist. Note: A professional nursing fraternity founded February 15, 1921 at the Univ. of California at Berkeley. Membership: $10/yr.
Publication:
Caption Magazine. semi-a.
Biennial Meetings: odd years
1987-Decatur, IL(Milikin Univ.)/June 26-29/100

Alpha Zeta Omega (1919)
3416 Swann Ave., Tampa FL 33609
Director of Fraternal Affairs: Bruce Strell
Members: 11,000 *Staff:* 1
Annual Budget: $25-50,000
Hist. Note: Professional pharmacy fraternity founded at the Philadelphia College of Pharmacy in December 1919.

00007 12 05 86 1233

Publication:
Azoan. 3/yr. adv.
Annual Meetings: Second week in July/350
1987-Hartford, CT
1988-Williamsburg, VA
1989-Miami Beach, FL
1990-Baltimore, MD

Alternative Living Managers Ass'n (1983)
1642 N. Winchester, Suite 100, Chicago IL 60622
Exec. Director: Karen K. Kulberg
Members: 350 individuals *Staff:* 2
Annual Budget: $50-100,000 *Tel:* (312) 276-3176
Hist. Note: Members are managers, owners, supervisors, staff members, or administrators of small community-based residences for developmentally disabled persons. Membership: $30/yr.
Publications:
Alma Matters. q. adv.
Directory of Community Based Residences in the U.S. a.

Alternative Wastewater Management Ass'n (1977)
Hist. Note: Reported inactive in 1986.

Aluminum Ass'n (1933)
900 19th St., N.W. Suite 300, Washington DC 20006
President: John C. Bard
Members: 85-90 companies *Staff:* 27
Annual Budget: $2-5,000,000 *Tel:* (202) 862-5100
Hist. Note: Members are manufacturers of aluminum mill products and producers of aluminum. Supports The Aluminum Ass'n Political Action Committee.
Publications:
Aluminum Developments Digest. semi-a.
Aluminum Situation. m.
Aluminum Standards and Data. bien.
Aluminum Statistical Review. a.
World Aluminum Abstracts. m.
Aluminum Report. m.
Semi-annual Meetings: September in White Sulphur Springs, WV and
February in Washington, DC.

Aluminum, Brick and Glass Workers Internat'l Union (1953)
3362 Hollenberg Dr., Bridgeton MO 63044
President: Ernie J. LaBaff
Members: 60,000 *Staff:* 50
Annual Budget: $2-5,000,000 *Tel:* (314) 739-6142
Hist. Note: Chartered by the American Federation of Labor on February 26, 1953 as an outgrowth of the International Council of Aluminum Workers' Union (AFL, founded in 1936) and the Aluminum Workers of America (CIO, founded in 1937). Absorbed the United Brick and Clay Workers of America on September 1, 1981 and assumed its present name. Until 1981 known as the Aluminum Workers International Union. Merged with the United Glass and Ceramic Workers and assumed its prsent name on September 1, 1982.
Publication:
ABG Light. bi-m.
Biennial meetings: Uneven years/450

Aluminum Extruders Council (1951)
4300-L Lincoln Ave., Rolling Meadows IL 60008
President: Donn W. Sanford, CAE
Members: 200 companies *Staff:* 2-5
Annual Budget: $500-1,000,000 *Tel:* (312) 359-8160
Publication:
The Executive Report. m.
Annual Meetings: March

Aluminum Foil Container Manufacturers Ass'n (1955)
Box 271, 736 Main St., Lake Geneva WI 53147
Exec. Secretary: Paul Uetzmann
Members: 11-15 companies *Staff:* 2-5
Annual Budget: $25-50,000 *Tel:* (414) 248-9208
Hist. Note: Manufacturers of aluminum foil containers.
Semi-annual meetings: Late Winter/Spring and Fall/36
1987-Tuscon, AZ(Tuscon National Golf Course)/Feb. 18-22
1987-Wesley Chapel, FL(Saddlebrook Resort)/Oct. 14-18
1988-Pebble Beach, CA(Lodge at Pebble Beach)/May 11-15
1988-Williamsburg, VA(Williamsburg Inn)/Oct. 12-16

Aluminum Recycling Ass'n (1929)
1000 16th St., N.W., Suite 603, Washington DC 20036
Exec. Director: Richard M. Cooperman
Members: 30-35 *Staff:* 2-5
Annual Budget: $100-250,000 *Tel:* (202) 785-0951
Hist. Note: Formerly (1972) Aluminum Smelters Research Institute and (1973) Aluminum Smelters and Recycling Institute. Members recycle aluminum base scrap for reuse in automotive, household, commercial and industrial products.

Aluminum Workers Internat'l Union (1953)
Hist. Note: Became the Aluminum, Brick and Clay Workers International Union on September 1, 1981.

Amalgamated Clothing and Textile Workers Union (1914)
15 Union Square, New York NY 10003
President: Murray H. Finley
Members: 303,000 *Staff:* 500
Annual Budget: over $5,000,000 *Tel:* (212) 242-0700
Hist. Note: Organized by dissidents from the United Garment Workers of America in Webster Hall, New York City on December 26, 1914 with Sidney Hillman as first President. Merged in 1976 with the Textile Workers Union of America (formed in 1939) and assumed its present name. Absorbed the United Shoe Workers of America on March 5, 1979 and the United Hatters, Cap & Millinery Workers in 1982. Affiliated with the Interamerican Textile Leather and Garment Workers Federation, the International Textile, Garment and Leather Workers Federation, the Internat'l Federation of Chemical, Energy and General Workers Union, and the Canadian Labour Congress. Contains about 31,500 Canadian members. Has a budget of about $23 million. Sponsors and supports the Amalgamated Clothing and Textile Workers Union Political Action Committee.
Publication:
Labor Unity. m.
Triennial Meetings:

Amalgamated Lace Operatives of America (1892)
53 Howe Street, Cumberland RI 02864
Secy.-Treas.: Frank Peltier
Members: 110 *Staff:* 1
Annual Budget: under $10,000 *Tel:* (401) 724-2225
Hist. Note: Organized in Philadelphia in 1892 as the Amalgamated Lace Curtain Operatives of America and chartered by the American Federation of Labor in 1894. Became the Charter Society of Amalgamated Lace Operatives of America in 1912 and was expelled from the AFL in 1919. Is now a small independent union.
Annual Meetings: Every 5 years (1988)

Amalgamated Printers' Ass'n (1958)
P.O. Box 2, Leeds MA 01053
Secy.-Treas.: Frank Seamans
Members: 150
Annual Budget: under $10,000
Hist. Note: Active printers, hobbyists and others interested in the preservation of letterpress printing; membership is limited to 150. Has no permanent address or paid staff; officers change biannually.

Amalgamated Transit Union (1892)
5025 Wisconsin Ave., N.W., Washington DC 20016
President: James La Sala
Members: 165,000 *Staff:* 20-25
Annual Budget: over $5,000,000 *Tel:* (202) 537-1645
Hist. Note: Established in Indianapolis on September 15, 1892 as the Amalgamated Association of Street Railway Employees of America and affiliated with the American Federation of Labor in 1893. Became the Amalgamated Association of Street and Electric Railway Employees of America in 1903, the Amalgamated Association of Street, Electric Railway and Motor Coach Employees of America in 1934 and assumed its present name in 1964. The dominant union in the local transit and over the road Bus Industry with membership in the U.S. and Canada. Members are operating, maintenance and administrative employees. Sponsors and supports the Amalgamated Transit Union Political Contributions Committee.
Publication:
In Transit. m.
Annual Meetings: Triennial Meetings

Amatex Export Trade Ass'n (1972)
Textile Hall, Exposition Ave., P.O. Box 6968, Station B, Greenville SC 29606
President: L. Hugh Ballard
Members: 20 companies *Staff:* 2-5
Annual Budget: $100-250,000 *Tel:* (803) 242-9115
Hist. Note: A Webb-Pomerene Act Ass'n; successor to Textile Machinery Export Ass'n

Ambulatory Pediatric Ass'n (1960)
1311-A Dolley Madison Blvd., Suite 3A, McLean VA 22101
Exec. Secretary: Marge Degnon
Members: 1,200 *Staff:* 1
Annual Budget: $50-100,000 *Tel:* (703) 566-9222
Hist. Note: Formerly (1969) Ass'n for Ambulatory Pediatric Services. An organization for those working in child health care programs, who are either involved in teaching and patient care or research in ambulatory pediatrics. Membership: $50/year.
Publication:
Newsletter.
Annual Meetings: Spring
1987-Anaheim, CA(Disneyland)/April 27-May 1
1988-Washington, DC(Sheraton)/May 2-6/4000
1989-Washington, DC(Sheraton)/May 1-5/4000
1990-Anaheim, CA(Hilton)/May 7-11
1991-New Orleans, LA(Riverside Hilton)/April 29-May 3
1992-Baltimore, MD(Convention Ctr.)/May 4-8

America on the Move (1974)
983 West Hawaii Drive, Lakewood CO 80226
President: Ernest A. Witucki, Jr.
Members: 36 individuals, 6 companies *Staff:* 1
Annual Budget: $10-25,000 *Tel:* (303) 987-0158
Hist. Note: Formerly Relocation Assistance Association of America (1986). Relocation and moving consultants, home purchase company agents, realtors and newcomer services. Membership: $100/yr.
Publication:
Aware. m.
Annual Meetings: Summer

American Academy and Board of Neurological and Orthopaedic Surgery (1977)
2320 Rancho Drive, Suite 108, Las Vegas NV 89102
Professor and Chairman: Michael R. Rask, M.D.,Ph.D.
Members: 700 individuals
Tel: (702) 385-6886
Hist. Note: The Academy was formed to fill the need in the realization of the similarity between the mother specialties (i.e., Neurosurgery, Orthopaedic Surgery, Neurology, Physiatry) in dealing with the diseases and injuries of the neuromusculoskeletal system. Membership: $250/yr.
Publications:
The Journal of Neurological & Orthopaedic Medicine & Surgery. q. adv.
The Journal of Bloodless Medicine & Surgery. bi-a. adv.
Annual Meetings: October in Las Vegas, NV(Alexis Park Resort Hotel)
1987-Oct. 20-25
1988-Oct. 24-29
1989-Oct. 24-29
1990-Oct. 23-28

American Academy and Institute of Arts and Letters (1898)
633 West 155th St., New York NY 10032
Exec. Director: Margaret M. Mills
Members: 250 *Staff:* 10
Annual Budget: $1-2,000,000 *Tel:* (212) 368-5900
Hist. Note: An honorary society of native or naturalized U.S. citizens distinguished in the creative arts. An amalgamation of the Nat'l Institute of Arts and Letters (organized in 1898) and the American Academy of Arts and Letters (established in 1904). The Academy's membership of 50 is drawn from the Institute's roster of 250.
Publication:
Proceedings. a
Tri-annual Meetings in New York, NY: Jan., May and Dec.

American Academy for Cerebral Palsy and Developmental Medicine (1948)
2315 Westwood Avenue, Box 11083, Richmond VA 23230
Exec. Director: John A. Hinckley
Members: 1,452 *Staff:* 6-10
Annual Budget: $100-250,000 *Tel:* (804) 355-0147
Publication:
Developmental Medicine & Child Neurology. bi-m.
Annual Meetings: Oct./1,200
1987-Boston, MA(Westin Copley)/Oct. 7-11
1988-Toronto, Canada(Royal York)/Oct. 26-29

American Academy for Plastics Research in Dentistry (1940)
Hist. Note: Became the Academy for Dental Materials in 1983.

American Academy for Professional Law Enforcement
Hist. Note: Reported defunct in 1986.

American Academy of Actuaries (1965)
1729 I St., N.W., 7th Floor, Washington DC 20006
Exec. Director: Stephen G. Kellison
Members: 10,000 *Staff:* 16
Annual Budget: $500-1,000,000 *Tel:* (202) 223-8196
Hist. Note: Founded by the Casualty Actuarial Soc., the Conference of Actuaries in Public Practice, the Fraternal Actuarial Ass'n and the Soc. of Actuaries. Promotes professional standards in actuarial science - the mathematical analysis of pension and insurance plans. Maintains administrative offices in Chicago. Affiliated with the Canadian Institute of Actuaries.
Publications:
Enrolled Actuaries Report. 5/yr.
Journal of The American Academy of Actuaries. a.
Actuarial Update. m.
Year Book. a.
Annual Meetings:
1987-San Antonio, TX(Hyatt Regency)/Nov. 16-17

American Academy of Advertising (1958)
Dept. of Business Administration, The Citadel, Charleston SC 29409
Exec. Secretary: Robert L. King
Members: 500 teachers of advertising *Staff:* 1
Annual Budget: under $10,000 *Tel:* (803) 792-7089
Hist. Note: Membership: $25/year.
Publications:
Contact (newsletter). q.
Journal of Advertising. q.
Proceedings. a.
Membership Directory. a.
Annual Meetings: Spring
1987-Las Vegas, NV

American Academy of Allergy and Immunology (1943)
611 East Wells St., Milwaukee WI 53202
Exec. Director: Donald L. McNeil
Members: 3,800 *Staff:* 6
Annual Budget: $1-2,000,000 *Tel:* (414) 272-6071
Hist. Note: Formed by a merger of the American Association for the Study of Allergy and the Society for the Study of Asthma and Allied Conditions. Membership: $120/year (fellows), $100/year (members).

00008 12 05 86 1233

Publication:
Journal of Allergy and Clinical Immunology. m. adv.
Annual Meetings:
1987-Washington, DC/Feb. 18-25

American Academy of Ambulatory Nursing Administration (1976)
North Woodbury Road, Box 56, Pitman NJ 08071
Exec. Director: Ron Brady
Members: 900 *Staff:* 6-10
Annual Budget: $100-250,000 *Tel:* (609) 582-9617
Hist. Note: Members are registered nurses engaged in the care of ambulatory patients. Membership: $75/year.
Publications:
Ambulatory Nursing Administration Newsletter. bi-m. adv.
Membership Directory. a.
Annual Meetings: Spring
1987-San Francisco, CA(Cathedral Hill)/March 8-11/350
1988-Open
1989-New Orleans, LA

American Academy of Arts and Sciences (1780)
136 Irving St., Cambridge MA 02138
Exec. Officer: Joel Orlen
Members: 2,700-2,800 individuals *Staff:* 25-30
Annual Budget: $1-2,000,000 *Tel:* (617) 492-8800
Hist. Note: Chartered by the Massachusetts legislature in May 1780 at the instigation of John Adams. Promotes and encourages knowledge of the antiquities and natural history of America and encourages "every art and science which may tend to advance the interest, honor, dignity and happiness of a free, independent and virtuous people." A member of the American Council of Learned Societies, it holds monthly meetings.
Publications:
Bulletin of the American Academy of Arts and Sciences. m.
Daedalus. q.
Records. a.
Annual Meetings: Second Wednesday in May in Boston, MA

American Academy of Behavioral Medicine (1979)
12890 Hillcrest Road, Suite 200, Dallas TX 75230
Chancellor: Dr. George R. Mount
Members: 650 *Staff:* 2
Annual Budget: $10-25,000 *Tel:* (214) 458-8333
Hist. Note: Incorporated in the State of Texas as an outgrowth of a regional group of southwestern therapists, the Academy has a membership of psychologists, psychiatrists and others interested in the general field of behavioral medicine and health care. Membership: $20/year.
Publications:
Journal of the AABM. irreg.
Newsletter. q.
Annual Meetings: October

American Academy of Child and Adolescent Psychiatry (1953)
3615 Wisconsin Ave., N.W., Washington DC 20016
Exec. Director: Virginia Q. Anthony
Members: 3,200 physicians and psychiatrists *Staff:* 8
Annual Budget: $250-500,000 *Tel:* (202) 966-7300
Hist. Note: Established in Feb., 1953 as American Academy of Child Psychiatry and incorporated in Delaware in 1959; assumed its present name in 1986. Encourages medical contributions to the knowledge and treatment of psychiatric problems of children and their families.
Publications:
AACP Newsletter. q. adv.
Journal of the American Academy of Child Psychiatry. q.
Annual Meetings: October
1987-Washington, DC/Oct. 21-25

American Academy of Child Psychiatry
Hist. Note: Became the American Academy of Child and Adolescent Psychiatry in 1986.

American Academy of Clinical Psychiatrists (1975)
Box 3212, San Diego CA 92103
Exec. Secretary: Robert P. Budetti
Members: 450 *Staff:* 1
Annual Budget: $10-25,000 *Tel:* (619) 460-2675
Hist. Note: Members are mainly private clinicians and academicians. Has no paid staff or permanent headquarters. Membership: $60/yr.
Publications:
Journal of Clinical Psychiatry. m. adv.
Newsletter. 3/yr.
Annual Meetings: October
1987-Toronto, Canada(Royal York Hotel)/Oct./150

American Academy of Clinical Toxicology (1968)
Comparative Toxicology Lab., Kansas State University, Manhattan KS 66506
Executive Director: F.W. Oehme
Members: 400-450 individuals. 10-15 companies *Staff:* 2
Annual Budget: $25-50,000 *Tel:* (913) 532-5679
Hist. Note: Physicians, research scientists, and analytical chemists, veterinarians and pharmacists active in clinical toxicology. Membership: $75/yr.
Publication:
Veterinary and Human Toxicology. bi-m. adv.
Annual Meetings: Fall
1987-Vancouver, Canada/Oct./350
1988-Baltimore, MD/Oct./375
1989-Atlanta, GA/Oct./375
1990-Tucson, AZ/Oct./400
1991-Toronto, Canada/Oct./400
1992-Open
1993-Houston, TX/Oct./450
1994-Open
1995-Rochester, NY/Oct./450

American Academy of Cosmetic Surgery (1985)
1455 South Potomac, Aurora CO 80012
Secretary: Ron Shippert, M.D.
Members: 950-350
Annual Budget: $1-2,000,000 *Tel:* (303) 751-4224
Hist. Note: Formed by a merger of the American Ass'n of Cosmetic Surgeons (1969) Membership: $350/yr.
Publication:
American Journal of Cosmetic Surgery. q. adv.
Annual Meetings: February

American Academy of Craniomandibular Disorders (1975)
800 Cottage Grove Road, Metacomet Park, Bloomfield CT 06002
Secy.-Treas.: Sheldon Gross
Members: 180-190 *Staff:* 1
Annual Budget: $50-100,000 *Tel:* (203) 232-4344
Hist. Note: Dentists and physicians interested in relieving cranio-facial pain. Until 1979 known as the American Academy of Craniomandibular Orthopedics.
Annual Meetings: Spring
1987-San Francisco, CA(Hyatt on Union Square)/March 26-28/350
1988-New Orleans, LA(Westin Canal Place)/March 17-19/350
1989-New York, NY(The Plaza)/April 13-15/350

American Academy of Crisis Interveners (1977)
215 Breckenridge Lane, Suite 102, Louisville KY 40207
President: Edward S. Rosenbluh, Ph.D.
Members: 200 *Staff:* 1
Annual Budget: under $10,000 *Tel:* (502) 896-0200
Hist. Note: Mental health workers, police and correctional officers, social workers, psychologists, psychiatrists, nurses, clergy, physicians, teachers and others involved in crisis intervention and crisis management. Associated with the Nat'l Conference of Christians and Jews. Has no paid staff.
Publication:
Emotional First Aid-A Journal of Crisis Intervention. a. adv.

American Academy of Crown and Bridge Prosthodontics (1951)
3302 Gaston Ave., Dallas TX 75246
Secretary: Robert S. Staffanou
Members: 405
Annual Budget: $100-250,000 *Tel:* (214) 828-8371
Hist. Note: Organized under the leadership Dr. Stanley D. Tylman, Dr. Claude R. Baker and Dr. George H. Moulton at the Stevens Hotel, Chicago, February 5, 1951. Has no paid staff. Membership: $125/yr.
Publication:
Journal of Prosthetic Dentistry. m.
Annual Meetings: Chicago, IL in February
1987-Chicago Marriott/Feb. 14-15/7-800
1988-Feb. 20-21
1989-Feb. 18-19

American Academy of Dental Electrosurgery (1963)
P.O. Box 374, Planetarium Station, New York NY 10024
Exec. Secretary: Maurice J. Oringer, D.D.S.
Members: 200 *Staff:* 1
Annual Budget: under $10,000 *Tel:* (212) 595-1925
Hist. Note: Supports advancement in research and clinical use of dental electrosurgery. Members required to have five years of dental experience, membership in the American Dental Ass'n or its international equivalents and to have taken electrosurgery courses in continuing education programs. Bestows the Oringer Award for Excellence in Electrosurgery annually to outstanding undergraduate and graduate students.
Publication:
Newsletter. 2-4/yr.
Semi-annual Meetings: Feb. in Chicago, IL and Nov. in New York City

American Academy of Dental Group Practice (1973)
18316 Hermitage Way, Minnetonka MN 55345
Exec. Director: Sue Rains Orlowski
Members: 370 groups *Staff:* 1
Annual Budget: $10-25,000 *Tel:* (612) 474-9285
Publication:
Newsletter. q.
Annual Meetings:
1987-Colorado Springs, CO(Broadmoor)/April 30-May 3/350

American Academy of Dental Practice Administration (1958)
6134 Cheena Drive, Houstony TX 77096
Exec. Director: Linda Doll
Members: 270-280 *Staff:* 1
Annual Budget: $50-100,000 *Tel:* (713) 771-2477
Hist. Note: Membership: $243/year.
Publications:
Journal of Dental Practice Administration. q. adv.
The Communicator (newsletter). q.
Annual Meetings:
1987-Houston, TX(Houstonian)/March 4-8/400

American Academy of Dental Radiology (1949)
Medical College of Georgia, Augusta GA 30912
Secretary: William R. Wege, D.D.S.
Members: 500 *Staff:* 1
Annual Budget: under $10,000 *Tel:* (404) 828-2935
Hist. Note: Formerly (1968) American Academy of Oral Roentgenology.
Publications:
Membership Roster. a.
Oral Surgery, Oral Medicine, Oral Pathology. m.
Annual Meetings: Before meetings of American Dental Ass'n.

American Academy of Dermatology (1938)
1567 Maple Ave., Evanston IL 60201
Exec. Director: Bradford W. Claxton, CAE
Members: 7,000 *Staff:* 32
Annual Budget: $2-5,000,000 *Tel:* (312) 869-3954
Hist. Note: Formerly American Academy of Dermatology & Syphilology. Membership: $200/yr.
Publication:
Journal of the American Academy of Dermatology. m. adv.
Annual Meetings: December/9-10,000
1987-San Antonio, CA(Convention Center)/Dec. 5-10
1988-Washington, DC(Convention Center)/Dec. 2-8
1989-San Francisco, CA(Convention Center)/Dec. 1-6

American Academy of Environmental Engineers (1955)
132 Holiday Court, Suite 206, Annapolis MD 21401
Exec. Director: William C. Anderson
Members: 2,400 *Staff:* 3
Annual Budget: $100-250,000 *Tel:* (301) 266-3311
Hist. Note: Originally (1955) the American Sanitary Engineering Intersociety Board; became the Environmental Engineering Intersociety Board in 1966 and assumed its present name in 1973. Membership: $75/yr.
Publications:
AAEE Roster. a.
The Diplomate. q. adv.
Consultant Directory. a.
Annual Meetings: Late October

American Academy of Environmental Medicine (1965)
Box 16106, Denver CO 80216
Administrative Asst.: J.A. Howard
Members: 450 *Staff:* 3
Annual Budget: $25-50,000 *Tel:* (303) 622-9755
Hist. Note: Originated as the Human Ecology Study Club. Members are interested in studying the effects of the environment on human health. Formerly known as the Soc. for Clinical Ecology.
Publications:
Archives of Clinical Ecology. q. adv.
Newsletter. q.
Annual Meetings: Fall/350
1987-Nashville, TN(Opryland)/Oct. 29-Nov. 1

American Academy of Equine Art (1980)
P.O. Box 1315, Middleburg VA 22117
Exec. Director: Belle T. Cohen
Members: 32 individuals *Staff:* 1
Annual Budget: under $10,000 *Tel:* (703) 687-6701
Hist. Note: Members are professional artists who are willing and qualified to exhibit works of equine art and to teach the subject. Membership: $100/yr (individual), initiation fee $150.
Publications:
Newsletter. irreg.
Prospects of Exhibition. a.

American Academy of Esthetic Dentistry (1975)
211 East Chicago Avenue, Suite 948, Chicago IL 60611
Exec. Director: Peter C. Goulding
Members: 60-70 *Staff:* 2-5
Annual Budget: $50-100,000 *Tel:* (312) 664-2122
Hist. Note: Dentists and other health professionals concerned with 1sthetics in dentistry, medicine and psychology. Affiliated with the Federation of Prosthodontic Organizations. Membership: $425/yr.
Publication:
Newsletter. semi-a.
Annual Meetings: Summer/250
1987-Laguna Beach, CA(Ritz Carleton)/Aug. 5-9

American Academy of Facial Plastic and Reconstructive Surgery (1964)
1101 Vermont Ave., N.W., Suite 404, Washington DC 20005
Exec. V. President: Dr. Lee VanBremen, CAE
Members: 2,750 *Staff:* 10
Annual Budget: $2-5,000,000 *Tel:* (202) 842-4500
Hist. Note: Merger (1964) of American Soc. of Facial Plastic Surgery and American Otorhinologic Soc. for Plastic Surgery Membership: $300/yr.
Publication:
Facial Plastic Time. bi-m.
Semi-annual Meetings: Spring and Fall/500
1987-Denver, CO(Fairmont)/May 1-2
1987-Chicago, IL(Marriott)/Sept. 16-18
1988-Palm Beach, FL(Breakers)/April 29-30
1988-Washington, DC/Sept. 23-24
1989-Toronto, Canada/June 25-29
1989-New Orleans, LA/Sept. 22-23

00009 12 05 86 1233

American Academy of Family Physicians (1947)
1740 West 92nd St., Kansas City MO 64114
Exec. V. President: Dr. Robert Graham
Members: 56,000 family physicians *Staff:* 135
Annual Budget: $2-5,000,000 *Tel:* (816) 333-9700
Hist. Note: Founded in June 1947 in Atlantic City as the American Academy of General Practice. Name changed to the American Academy of Family Physicians in October 1971. Has an annual budget of $10-12 million. Membership: $175/yr. (individual).
Publications:
AAFP Reporter. m.
American Family Physician. m. adv.
Annual Meetings:
1987-San Francisco, CA
1988-New Orleans, LA

American Academy of Forensic Sciences (1948)
225 South Academy Blvd., Suite 201, Colorado Springs CO 80910
Exec. Director: Beth Ann Lipskin
Members: 2,700 *Staff:* 7
Annual Budget: $500-1,000,000 *Tel:* (303) 596-6006
Hist. Note: Formed in St. Louis in 1948 and incorporated in Illinois in 1964. Cooperates with the regional, national and international organizations dedicated to the use of science in the administration of justice. Affiliated with the Forensic Sciences Foundation. The Forensic Sciences Foundation is the Academy's educational, research and testing arm. Membership: $95/yr.
Publications:
Journal of Forensic Sciences. bi-m.
Newsletter. bi-m. adv.
Annual Meetings: February/1,500
1987-San Diego, CA(Town & Country)/Feb. 17-21
1988-Philadelphia, PA(Franklin Plaza)/Feb. 15-20
1989-Las Vegas, NV(Riviera)/Feb. 20-25
1990-Cincinnati, OH(Clarion & Hyatt Regency)/Feb. 19-24

American Academy of Gnathologic Orthopedics (1969)
211 East Chicago Ave., Suite 915, Chicago IL 60611
Exec. Director and Managing Editor: Joanna Carey
Members: 490 *Staff:* 1
Annual Budget: $50-100,000 *Tel:* (312) 642-5834
Hist. Note: Established in Portland, Oregon and incorporated in Wisconsin. Dentists specializing in malformation of the face and jaw. Officers are elected bi-annually. Membership: $90/year.
Publication:
Membership Directory. a.
Annual Meetings: Fall, with the Internat'l Ass'n for Orthodontics
1987-Orlando, FL(Hyatt Orlando)/Sept. 17-20/600
1988-Las Vegas, NV(Caesar's Palace)/Sept. 15-18/600

American Academy of Gold Foil Operators (1952)
2514 Watts Road, Houston TX 77030
Admin. Assistant: Nell Faucett
Members: 400 *Staff:* 1
Annual Budget: $25-50,000 *Tel:* (713) 664-3537
Hist. Note: Members are dentists performing restorative procedures utilizing gold foil and the rubber dam. Membership: $55/yr.
Publication:
Journal of Operative Dentistry. q. adv.
Annual Meetings: Fall/150
1987-Denver, CO(Brown Palace)/Oct. 7-9
1988-Washington, DC(George Washington Univ.)/Oct. 5-7

American Academy of Health Administration (1949)
201 North Figueroa St., 4th Floor, Los Angeles CA 90012
Exec. Director: Marshall P. Gavin
Members: 100-150 *Staff:* 1
Annual Budget: under $10,000 *Tel:* (213) 250-5600
Hist. Note: Founded as the Ass'n of Business Management in Public Health, it became the Ass'n of Management in Public Health and assumed its present name in 1970. Membership: $65/yr.
Annual Meetings: With American Public Health Ass'n

American Academy of Hospital Attorneys (1968)
840 N. Lake Shore Dr., Chicago IL 60611
Director: Shirley Worthy
Members: 2,700 *Staff:* 3
Annual Budget: $500-1,000,000 *Tel:* (312) 280-6601
Hist. Note: Sponsored by the American Hospital Ass'n. Formerly (1971) Soc. of Hospital Attorneys and (1984) American Soc. of Hospital Attorneys.
Publications:
Hospital Law. m.
Membership Roster. a.
Annual Meetings: June
1987-Boston, MA/June 21-24
1988-Maui, HI/June 26-29

American Academy of Implant Dentistry (1952)
Box 2002, Abington MA 02351
Exec. Director: John P. Winiewicz
Members: 1,500 *Staff:* 2-5
Annual Budget: $100-250,000 *Tel:* (617) 878-7990
Hist. Note: Founded in Chicago in February 1952 as the American Academy of Implant Dentures and incorporated in Minnesota in October. Name changed to American Academy of Implant Dentistry in 1966. Membership: $300/yr.
Publication:
Oral Implantology. q. adv.
Annual Meetings: Fall
1987-Las Vegas, NV(Riviera)/Oct. 4-9
1988-Washington, DC(Marriott)/Oct. 10-15
1989-Honolulu, HI/Oct. 29-Nov. 3
1990-Boston, MA/Oct. 7-12

American Academy of Legal and Industrial Medicine (1946)
Box 10, Island Station, Roosevelt Island NY 10044
President: Robert Katz, M.D.
Members: 300-325
Hist. Note: Formerly (1985) American Academy of Compensation Medicine. Members are physicians concerned with the development of medical criteria to determine the relationship between industrial disability and the compensation therefor.
Annual Symposium: March

American Academy of Matrimonial Lawyers (1963)
20 North Michigan, Chicago IL 60602
Exec. Director: Lorraine J. West
Members: 1,150 *Staff:* 2-5
Annual Budget: $100-250,000 *Tel:* (312) 263-6477
Hist. Note: Members are attorneys specializing in the field of marriage and family law. Membership: $100/yr.
Publications:
Proceedings. a.
Newsletter. q.
Semi-annual meetings: Fall in Chicago, IL and Winter
1987-Tucson, AZ(Sheraton El Conquistador)/March 8-15/150

American Academy of Maxillofacial Prosthetics (1953)
3316 Crane Ferry Road, Augusta GA 30907
Exec. Secretary: Dr. Gregory R. Parr
Members: 140 *Staff:* 1
Annual Budget: $10-25,000
Hist. Note: Affiliated with the Federation of Prosthodontic Organizations.
Publication:
Journal of Prosthetic Dentistry. m.
Annual Meetings: Fall/150

American Academy of Medical Administrators (1957)
30555 Southfield, Suite 525, Southfield MI 48076
President: Dr. Thomas R. O'Donovan
Members: 1,600-1,700 *Staff:* 5
Annual Budget: $250-500,000 *Tel:* (313) 540-4310
Hist. Note: Founded in Boston in 1957. Hospital administrators, including department heads in such areas as nursing, food service management, housekeeping, purchasing. Membership: $125/year.
Publications:
AAMA Executive. q.
Executive Newsletter. m.
Annual Meetings: Fall
1987-Las Vegas, NV(Las Vegas Hilton)/Nov. 12-14/250
1988-Orlando, FL(Marriott)/Oct./275
1989-Scottsdale, AZ/Oct./275
1990-New Orleans, LA(Monteleone)/Oct./275
1991-Boston, MA/Oct./275

American Academy of Medical Directors (1974)
4830 West Kennedy Blvd., Suite 648, Tampa FL 33609
Exec. V. President: Roger S. Schenke
Members: 2,200 *Staff:* 12
Annual Budget: $1-2,000,000 *Tel:* (813) 873-2000
Hist. Note: Members hold the title of Medical Director, Chief Medical Officer or have full or part-time responsibilities in medical management and leadership positions. Supports the American College of Physician Executives. Membership: $150/yr.
Publications:
Directory. a.
The Medical Director. bi-m.
Academy Digest. bi-m.
Semi-annual meetings: Spring and Fall
1987-Toronto, Canada(Royal York Hotel)/April 26-29
1987-Scottsdale, AZ(Hyatt)/Nov. 15-19

American Academy of Medical Preventics (1973)
6151 West Century Boulevard, Suite 1114, Los Angeles CA 90045
Exec. Officer: Robert H. Humphreys
Members: 450-575 *Staff:* 2-5
Annual Budget: $500-1,000,000 *Tel:* (213) 645-5350
Hist. Note: Members are physicians interested in chronic diseases of the circulatory system. Membership: $260/yr.
Publications:
Newsletter. m.
Quarterly Magazine. q. adv.
Journal. a. adv.
Monthly Update. m. adv.
Membership Directory. a.
Semi-annual meetings: May and November
1987-Orlando, FL/May/525

American Academy of Microbiology (1955)
Hist. Note: The professional services arm of the American Soc. for Microbiology.

American Academy of Natural Family Planning (1982)
615 South New Ballas Rd., St. John's Hospital, St. Louis MO 63141
Secretary: Maureen Duhn, CNFPP, RN
Members: 12 organizationals; 110 individuals
Annual Budget: $25-50,000 *Tel:* (314) 569-6495
Hist. Note: Formed to foster and promote natural family planning through service, education, leadership and research. Active members must be certified natural family planning teachers. Membership: $100/yr.
Publications:
Academy Activity. q.
Client Connection. q.
Annual Meetings: Summer
1987-Houston, TX(Lincoln Pine Oaks)/June 17-21

American Academy of Neurological Surgery (1938)
Dept. of Neurosurgery, Univ. of Tenn., 956 Court Ave., Memphis TN 38163
Secretary: Dr. Nicholas Zervas
Members: 100 active members; 70 senior members *Staff:* 1
Annual Budget: under $10,000 *Tel:* (901) 528-6374
Hist. Note: Founded in 1938 in Cincinnati. Affiliated with the American Ass'n of Neurological Surgery and the World Federation of Neurological Societies. Membership: $150/yr.
Annual Meetings: Fall
1987-San Antonio, TX(Hyatt Regency)/Oct. 7-10/100

American Academy of Neurology (1948)
2221 University Avenue, S.E., Suite 335, Minneapolis MN 55414
Exec. Director: Jan W. Kolehmainen
Members: 9,200 *Staff:* 16
Annual Budget: $2-5,000,000 *Tel:* (612) 623-8115
Hist. Note: Founded and incorporated in Minnesota in 1948.
Publication:
Neurology. m. adv.
Annual Meetings: April/4,000
1987-New York, NY(Hilton-Sheraton Centre)/April 5-11
1988-Cincinnati, OH(Convention Center)/April 17-23
1989-Chicago, IL(Hyatt Regency)/April 13-19

American Academy of Occupational Medicine (1946)
2340 South Arlington Heights Road, Arlington Heights IL 60005
Exec. Director: Donald L. Hoops
Members: 7-800 *Staff:* 2-5
Annual Budget: $25-50,000 *Tel:* (312) 228-6850
Hist. Note: Concerned with the maintenance and improvement of the health of workers. Members are physicians engaged full time in the field of occupational medicine. Membership: $60/year.
Publication:
Journal of Occupational Medicine. m. adv.
Annual Meetings: Fall

American Academy of Ophthalmology (1896)
655 Beach St., San Francisco CA 94120
Exec. V. President: Dr. Bruce E. Spivey
Members: 13-14,000 *Staff:* 78
Annual Budget: over $5,000,000 *Tel:* (415) 921-4700
Hist. Note: Founded as the Western Ophthalmological, Otolaryngological and Rhinological Ass'n. Name changed to Western Ophthalmologic and Otolaryngologic Ass'n in 1899. Became the American Academy of Ophthalmology and Otolaryngology in 1903. In 1979, the Academy split into the American Academy of Ophthalmology and the American Academy of Otolaryngology. Absorbed the American Association of Ophthalmology, July 1, 1981. Maintains a Washington office. Memberships: $375/yr.
Publications:
Argus. m.
Ophthalmology. m. adv.
Annual Meetings: Fall
1987-Dallas, TX/Nov. 8-12
1988-Las Vegas, NV/Oct. 8-13
1989-New Orleans, LA/Oct. 26-Nov. 2
1990-Atlanta, GA/Oct. 28-Nov. 2

American Academy of Optometry (1929)
5530 Wisconsin Avenue, N.W., Suite 917, Washington DC 20815
Administrator: David Lewis
Members: 3,100 *Staff:* 2-5
Annual Budget: $250-500,000 *Tel:* (301) 652-0905
Hist. Note: Founded to promote optometric education, research, and professional competency. Membership: $65/yr., $25.yr. (student).
Publications:
American Journal of Optometry and Physiological Optics. m. adv.
Newsletter. q.
Annual Meetings: December/1,000
1987-Denver, CO(International Hotel)/Dec. 10-15
1988-Columbus, OH(Hyatt Regency)/Dec. 8-13
1989-New Orleans, LA/Dec. 7-12

American Academy of Oral Medicine (1946)
159 West 53rd Street, Suite 12-B, New York NY 10019
Exec. Coordinator: Dr. Abraham Reiner
Members: 750-800 *Staff:* 1
Annual Budget: $50-100,000 *Tel:* (212) 315-2899
Hist. Note: Founded and incorporated in New York as the American Academy of Dental Medicine, it assumed its present name in 1966. Its purpose is to promote the study and dissemination of knowledge of the cause, prevention and control of diseases of the teeth and oral tissues; and to foster increased scientific understanding and cooperation between the dental and medical professions. Membership: $55/yr.

00010 12 05 86 1233

Publications:
Journal of Oral Medicine. q. adv.
Newsletter of Oral Medicine. 3/yr.
Semi-annual meetings: Spring and Winter/250
1987-Bar Harbour, FL(Sheraton Bal Harbour)/May 4-10
1987-Philadelphia, PA/Dec. 3-6
1988-San Francisco, CA(Sheraton Wharf)/May 8-15
1988-Boston, MA/Dec. 1-4

American Academy of Oral Pathology (1946)
Hist. Note: Still in existence; requested not to list phone and address.

American Academy of Orthodontics for the General Practitioner (1959)
3953 North 76th St., Milwaukee WI 53222
Exec. Secretary: Jane Taylor
Members: 240 individuals *Staff:* 1
Annual Budget: $25-50,000 *Tel:* (414) 464-7870
Hist. Note: Established in order to provide dentists in general practice with an organization in which they can augment their basic knowledge and training in orthodontics. Membership: $45/yr.
Publication:
International Journal of Orthodontics.
Annual Meetings: September
1987-Mishicot, WI(Fox Hills Resort)/Sept. 17-20

American Academy of Orthopaedic Surgeons (1933)
222 South Prospect Ave., Park Ridge IL 60068-4058
Exec. Director: Thomas C. Nelson
Members: 11,500-12,000 *Staff:* 70-75
Annual Budget: over $5,000,000 *Tel:* (312) 823-7186
Hist. Note: Founded October 11, 1933 in Chicago. Incorporated in Illinois in 1948. Provides continuing medical education for practicing orthopaedic surgeons. Maintains a Washington office. Has a budget of $10,000,000. Membership: $300/yr.
Publication:
Bulletin. q.
Annual Meetings: Winter
1987-San Francisco, CA(Convention Center)/Jan. 22-27/15,000
1988-Atlanta, GA(World Congress Center)/Feb. 4-9/16,000
1989-Las Vegas, NV(Convention Center)/Feb. 9-14
1990-New Orleans, LA(Convention Center)/Feb. 8-13

American Academy of Orthotists and Prosthetists (1970)
717 Pendleton St., Alexandria VA 22314
Exec. Director: Brg.Gen. William L. McCulloch
Members: 1,600-1,800 *Staff:* 22
Annual Budget: $500-1,000,000 *Tel:* (703) 836-7118
Hist. Note: Members are individuals who have been certified for practice by the American Board for Certification in Orthotics and Prosthetics. Membership: $150/yr.
Publications:
Clinical Prosthetics & Orthotics-C.P.O. q.
Academician (newsletter). q.
Annual Meetings: Winter
1987-Tampa, FL(Hyatt Regency)
1988-Newport Beach, CA(Marriott Hotel and Tennis Club)
1989-Orlando, FL(Wyndham)
1990-Phoenix, AZ(Hyatt Regency)
1991-Atlanta, GA

American Academy of Osteopathic Surgeons
Hist. Note: Became the American Ass'n of Osteopathic Surgeons in 1984.

American Academy of Osteopathy (1937)
12 West Locust St., P.O. Box 750, Newark OH 43055
Exec. Director: Vicki E. Dyson
Members: 2,000 *Staff:* 2-5
Annual Budget: $100-250,000 *Tel:* (614) 349-8701
Hist. Note: Founded July 6, 1937 in Chicago as The Section of Manipulative Therapeutics of the American Osteopathic Ass'n. Name changed in 1938 to Osteopathic Manipulative Therapeutic and Clinical Research Ass'n. Incorporated in 1944 as the Academy of Applied Osteopathy and became American Academy of Osteopathy in 1970. Affiliated with American Osteopathic Ass'n.
Publications:
Newsletter. q.
Yearbook of Selected Osteopathic Papers. a.
Semi-annual meetings: Spring and Fall, with the American Osteopathic Ass'n
1987-Cincinnati, OH/March 25-28
1988-Charlotte, NC/March 23-26
1989-Colorado Springs, CO/March 22-25

American Academy of Otolaryngic Allergy (1941)
1101 Vermont Ave., N.W., Suite 302, Washington DC 20005
Exec. Director: Sandra L. May
Members: 1,500 *Staff:* 3
Annual Budget: $250-500,000 *Tel:* (202) 682-0456
Hist. Note: Formerly (until 1982) the American Society of Ophthalmologic and Otolaryngologic Allergy. Membership: $225/yr.
Publication:
Newsletter. q.
Annual Meetings:
1987-Chicago, IL/Sept. 17-19/500
1988-New Orleans, LA/Sept./500
1989-Washington, DC/500

American Academy of Otolaryngology-Head and Neck Surgery (1896)
1101 Vermont Avenue, N.W., Suite 302, Washington DC 20005
Exec. V. President: Jerome C. Goldstein, M.D.
Members: 7,900 *Staff:* 28
Annual Budget: $2-5,000,000 *Tel:* (202) 289-4607
Hist. Note: Founded as the Western Ophthalmological, Otolaryngological and Rhinological Ass'n. Name changed to Western Ophthalmologic and Otolaryngologic Ass'n in 1899. Became the American Academy of Ophthalmology and Otolaryngology in 1903 and assumed its present name in 1979 when the ophthalomogists left the Academy and established the American Academy of Ophthalmology. Merged with the American Council of Otolaryngology-Head and Neck Surgery on January 1, 1982. Functions as a national information, liaison and promotional center of otolaryngological endeavors. Affiliated with the International Federation of Oto-Rhino-Laryngological Societies. Coordinates state and federal political action and organizes the Combined Otolaryngological Spring Meetings on behalf of six otolaryngologic societies. Membership: $300/year (individual).
Publications:
The Bulletin. m. adv.
Otolaryngology-Head and Neck Surgery. m.
Annual Meetings: Fall/4,400
1987-Chicago, IL/Sept. 19-23
1988-Washington, DC/Sept. 25-29
1989-New Orleans, LA/Sept. 24-28

American Academy of Pediatric Dentistry (1947)
211 East Chicago Ave., Suite 1036, Chicago IL 60611
Exec. Director: Dr. John A. Bogert
Members: 3,000 *Staff:* 6
Tel: (312) 337-2169
Hist. Note: Formerly (1984) the American Academy of Pedodontics.
Publication:
Pediatric Dentistry. q. adv.
Annual Meetings: Spring/800
1987-New Orleans, LA/May 2-5
1988-Coronado, CA/May 12-15
1989-Orlando, FL/May 27-31

American Academy of Pediatrics (1930)
141 Northwest Point Road, Box 927, Elk Grove Village IL 60009-0927
Exec. Director: James E. Strain, M.D.
Members: 29,000 *Staff:* 140-150
Annual Budget: over $5,000,000 *Tel:* (312) 228-5005
Hist. Note: In 1922 the AMA's Section on Pediatrics dissented from the AMA in support of the Sheppard-Towner Act, a federal proposal to set up a small maternal and child health program. They were censured, causing the nation's pediatricians to realize that they needed a forum of their own. In 1930 35 charter members founded the AACP in Detroit and chartered it in the State of Illinois. Maintains a Washington office. Has an annual budget of $15 million.
Publications:
Pediatrics. m. adv.
Pediatrics-in-Review. m.
AAP News. m. adv.
Annual Meetings: Fall/6,000
1987-New Orleans, LA/Oct. 31-Nov. 5
1988-San Francisco, CA/Oct. 15-20
1989-Chicago, IL/Oct. 21-26
1990-Boston, MA/Oct. 6-11
1991-New Orleans, LA/Oct. 26-31
1992-San Francisco, CA/Oct. 10-15

American Academy of Pedodontics (1947)
Hist. Note: Became the American Academy of Pediatric Dentistry in 1984.

American Academy of Periodontology (1914)
211 East Chicago Ave., Room 1400, Chicago IL 60611
Exec. Director: Alice DeForest
Members: 4,700 *Staff:* 11-15
Annual Budget: $1-2,000,000 *Tel:* (312) 787-5518
Hist. Note: Originated in Cleveland February 21, 1914 as the Academy of Oral Prophylaxis and Periodontology. Became the American Academy of Periodontology in 1919. Incorporated in Michigan in 1934 and merged with the American Soc. of Periodontists in 1967. Membership open to qualified periodontists in the U.S. and Canada. Membership: $250/yr.
Publication:
Journal of Periodontology. m. adv.
Annual Meetings: Fall/3,500
1987-Denver, CO/Oct. 21-24
1988-San Diego, CA/Oct. 26-29

American Academy of Physical Medicine and Rehabilitation (1938)
122 South Michigan Ave., Suite 1300, Chicago IL 60603
Exec. Director: Ike A. Mayeda
Members: 2,400 *Staff:* 7-11
Annual Budget: $500-1,000,000 *Tel:* (312) 922-9366
Hist. Note: Founded in 1938 as the Soc. of Physical Therapy Physicians. Incorporated September 1939 in Chicago. Name changed to American Soc. of Physical Medicine in 1944 and American Academy of Physical Medicine and Rehabilitation in 1956.
Publications:
Archives of Physical Medicine and Rehabilitation. m. adv.
The Physiatrist. q. adv.
Annual Meetings: Fall/1,900-2,000
1987-Orlando, FL(Marriott)/Oct. 18-23
1988-Seattle, WA(Westin/Sheraton)/Oct. 30-Nov. 4

1989-San Antonio, TX(Hilton/Marriott/Hyatt Regency)/Nov. 5-10
1990-Phoenix, AZ(Convention Ctr.)/Oct. 21-26
1991-Washington, DC(Sheraton Washington)/Oct. 27-Nov. 1

American Academy of Physician Assistants (1968)
1117 N. 19th St., Suite 300, Arlington VA 22209
Exec. V. President: F. Lynn May
Members: 10,500 *Staff:* 23
Annual Budget: $2-5,000,000 *Tel:* (703) 525-4200
Hist. Note: 6 Formed by a group of physician assistants at Duke University in April 1968. Sponsors the American Academy of Physician Assistants Political Action Committee. Membership: $145/yr.
Publications:
AAPA News. m.
AAPA Bulletin. bi-w.
Annual Meetings: Spring
1987-Cincinnati, OH
1988-Los Angeles, CA

American Academy of Physiologic Dentistry (1958)
900 East Colfax, South Bend IN 46617
Secretary: Dr. John M. Stenger
Members: 70 individuals *Staff:* 1
Annual Budget: under $10,000 *Tel:* (219) 233-6103
Hist. Note: Membership: $100/yr.
Annual Meetings: 4-6 meetings per year

American Academy of Podiatric Sports Medicine (1970)
1729 Glastonberry Road, Potomac MD 20854
Exec. Director: Larry I. Shane
Members: 850 *Staff:* 1
Annual Budget: $50-100,000 *Tel:* (301) 424-7440
Hist. Note: Affiliated with the American Podiatric Medical Association. Membership: $125/year.
Publication:
Newsletter. q. adv.
Annual Meetings:
1987-Chicago, IL/May 22-24
1988-Boston, MA

American Academy of Psychiatry and the Law (1969)
1211 Cathedral St., Baltimore MD 21201
Admin. Secretary: Kathy L. Smith
Members: 1,200 *Staff:* 2
Annual Budget: $25-50,000 *Tel:* (301) 539-0379
Hist. Note: Members are psychiatrists who have a professional interest in psychiatry and the law and are members of the American Psychiatric Ass'n or an equivalent national organization. Membership: $110/year (individual).
Publications:
Bulletin. q.
Newsletter. 3/year.
Annual Meetings: October
1987-Ottawa, Canada(Westin)/Oct. 21-25
1988-San Francisco, CA/Oct. 20-23
1989-Baltimore, MD

American Academy of Psychoanalysis (1956)
30 East 40th St., Suite 608, New York NY 10016
Exec. Director: Vivian Mendelsohn
Members: 8-900 fellows and associates *Staff:* 2-5
Annual Budget: $100-250,000 *Tel:* (212) 679-4105
Hist. Note: Founded April 29, 1956 in Chicago as the Academy of Psychoanalysis. Incorporated in New York in 1956. Became the American Academy of Psychoanalysis in 1966. The Academy advocates an acceptance of all relevant and responsible psychoanalytic views of human behavior, rather than adherence to one particular doctrine. It holds that divergent views should be made available to psychoanalytic practitioners, candidates in training, and related behavioral scientists. Membership: $265/yr.
Publications:
The Academy Forum. q.
Journal of American Academy of Psychoanalysis. q.
Semi-annual meetings: Spring and Winter
1987-Chicago, IL(Marriott)/May 7-10/300
1987-Scottsdale, AZ(Camelback Inn)/Dec. 10-13/300
1988-Montreal, Canada/May 5-8
1988-New York, NY/Dec. 8-11
1989-San Francisco, CA/May 4-7

American Academy of Religion (1909)
Syracuse University, Syracuse NY 13244-1170
Exec. Director: James B. Wiggins
Members: 4-5,000 *Staff:* 3
Annual Budget: $100-250,000 *Tel:* (315) 423-4019
Hist. Note: Formerly (1964) Nat'l Ass'n of Biblical Instructors. A member of the Council on the Study of Religion and the American Council of Learned Socs. Members include students, persons who study religion outside the field and members of the profession in colleges, universities and seminaries. Membership: $25-$70/yr. (based on salary)
Publications:
Journal of The AAR. q. adv.
Religious Studies News.
Annual Meetings: Winter
1987-Boston, MA(Sheraton & Marriott Copley Square)/Dec. 4-9/3,000

00011 12 05 86 1233

American Academy of Restorative Dentistry (1928)
51 Herkimer St., Hamilton Ontario L8P 2G3
Secy.-Treas.: Emmanuel J. Rajczak
Members: 225-250 *Staff:* 1
Annual Budget: $10-25,000 *Tel:* (416) 523-0133
Hist. Note: Established as the American Soc. of Dental Ceramics at the 1921 meeting of the Nat'l Dental Ass'n (now American Dental Ass'n); it was renamed the American Academy of Restorative Dentistry after the scope of the society was broadened to include more general restorative procedures as well as ceramics.
Publication:
Journal of Prosthetic Dentistry. m. adv.
Annual Meetings: February in Chicago, IL

American Academy of Sports Physicians (1979)
28240 West Agoura Road, Suite 101, Agoura CA 91301
Secretary: Ronald M. Lawrence, M.D.
Members: 120-130 *Staff:* 1
Annual Budget: $10-25,000 *Tel:* (818) 991-6740
Publications:
Annals of Sports Medicine. q. adv.
AASP Newsletter. q.
Annual Meetings: May/June
1987-Nassau, Bahamas/May 13-16

American Academy of Teachers of Singing (1922)
75 Bank St., New York NY 10014
Secretary: William Gephart
Members: 30-40 *Staff:* 1
Annual Budget: under $10,000 *Tel:* (212) 242-1836
Annual Meetings: None held

American Academy of the History of Dentistry (1951)
3804 Hadley Square East, Baltimore MD 21218
Secy.-Treas.: Dr. H. Berton McCauley
Members: 500-600 *Staff:* 1
Annual Budget: $10-25,000 *Tel:* (301) 243-5744
Hist. Note: Seeks to stimulate interest , study and research in the history of dentistry. Membership: $20/yr. (professionals); $7.50/yr. (students)
Publications:
Bulletin of the History of Dentistry. semi-a.
Newsletter. q.
Annual Meetings: Fall, prior to American Dental Ass'n Annual Session/ 50-100
1987-Las Vegas, NV/Oct. 9
1988-Washington, DC/Oct. 7
1989-Honolulu, HI/Nov. 3
1990-Boston, MA/Oct. 12

American Academy of Thermography (1968)
Georgetown Univ. Med. Center, 3800 Reservoir Road, Washington DC 20007
President: Dr. Margaret Abernathy
Members: 500-600 *Staff:* 3
Annual Budget: $100-250,000 *Tel:* (703) 938-6140
Hist. Note: Membership composed of physicians (M.D. and D.O.) involved with the use of infrared and liquid cholesteric imaging in medical diagnosis. Formed as the American Thermographic Society, it assumed its present name in 1983.
Publication:
THERMOLOGY, the Journal of the American Academy of Thermology. q.
Annual Meetings: June
1987-Minneapolis, MN/June 25-27/200

American Academy of Veterinary and Comparative Toxicology (1958)
11 Cardinal Lane, Starkville MS 39759
Secy.-Treas.: H. Dwight Mercer
Members: 250 *Staff:* 1
Annual Budget: $10-25,000 *Tel:* (601) 325-3432
Hist. Note: Organized in 1957, and incorporated Jan. 15, 1958 in Salt Lake City. Formerly (1984) the American College of Veterinary Toxicologists. Concerned with education, research and exchange of proven methods and procedures in the field of veterinary toxicology. Encourages the use of uniform toxicologic nomenclature. Membership: $30/year.
Publication:
Veterinary and Human Toxicology. bi-m. adv.
Annual Meetings: Meets with the American Veterinary Medical Ass'n
1987-Chicago, IL/July 20-23/200
1988-Portland, OR/July 18-21/100
1989-Orlando, FL/July 17-20/250

American Academy of Veterinary Dermatology (1964)
School of Veterinary Medicine, University of Florida, Gainesville FL 32601
Secretary: Gail A. Kunkle, D.V.M.
Members: 90-100
Annual Budget: under $10,000 *Tel:* (904) 392-4751
Hist. Note: Founded in 1964 to foster interest in skin disease of animals. Has no paid staff or permanent headquarters. Officers change annually. Affiliated with the American Animal Hospital Association and The American Veterinary Medical Association.
Publication:
Newsletter. bi-a.
Annual Meetings: With American Animal Hospital Ass'n.

American Academy of Veterinary Nutrition (1956)
452 Old Orchard Circle, Millersvillere MD 21108
Secy.-Treas.: Col. Joseph Milligan
Members: 150 *Staff:* 1
Annual Budget: under $10,000 *Tel:* (301) 981-3342
Hist. Note: Formerly (until 1978) the American Ass'n of Veterinary Nutritionists. Has no permanent address or paid staff; officers change biennially. Membership: $10/yr.
Publication:
Newsletter. irreg.
Annual Meetings: With American Veterinary Medical Ass'n.
1987-Chicago, IL/July/25

American Academy on Mental Retardation (1960)
306 Heavenly Drive, Omahale NB 68154
Secretary: Jack Stark, Ph.D.
Members: 125-150 individuals who hold doctoral degrees
Staff: 1
Annual Budget: under $10,000 *Tel:* (402) 559-7490
Hist. Note: Has no paid staff; officers change annually.
Annual Meetings: With the American Ass'n on Mental Deficiency

American Accordionists Ass'n (1938)
P.O. Box 616, Mineola NY 11501
President: Faithe Deffner
Members: 2,000 *Staff:* 1
Annual Budget: $10-25,000 *Tel:* (516) 746-0145
Hist. Note: Members are teachers, manufacturers, importers and suppliers united to promote the use of the accordion and the development of accordion music. Affiliated with the Nat'l Music Council and the Internat'l Confederation of Accordionists. Membership: $35/yr.
Publications:
AAA Journal. a. adv.
AAA Newsletter. q.
Annual Meetings: Summer

American Accounting Ass'n (1916)
5717 Bessie Drive, Sarasota FL 33583
Exec. Director: Paul L. Gerhardt
Members: 10-12,000 *Staff:* 6-10
Annual Budget: $1-2,000,000 *Tel:* (813) 921-7747
Hist. Note: Founded as the American Association of University Instructors in Accounting, it assumed its present name in 1935. The American Taxation Association is one of its sections. Membership: $45/yr.
Publications:
Accounting Review. q. adv.
Issues in Accounting Education. semi-a.
Accounting Horizons. q.
Annual Meetings: August
1987-Cincinnati, OH
1988-Orlando, FL
1989-Honolulu, HI

American Advertising Federation (1905)
1400 K St., N.W., Suite 1000, Washington DC 20005
President: Howard Hughes Bell
Members: 350 companies, 220 ad clubs, 145 college chapters
Staff: 22
Annual Budget: $1-2,000,000 *Tel:* (202) 898-0089
Hist. Note: Formed by a merger of the Advertising Federation of America and the Advertising Ass'n of the West (formerly Pacific Advertising Ass'n). Supports the Advertising Political Action Committee and the Advertising Hall of Fame.
Publications:
Washington Report. m.
Stateside (state legislative monitor).
American Advertising. q. adv.
Annual Meetings:
1987-Orlando, FL
1988-Los Angeles, CA

American Aerobics Ass'n (1981)
6317 Florida Rd., Durango CO 81301
Director: Jean Rosenbaum, M.D.
Members: 3,000 individuals *Staff:* 2
Annual Budget: $10-25,000 *Tel:* (303) 247-4109
Hist. Note: A non-profit organization whose purposes include research, education, and certification in aerobic exercise. Membership: $75/yr.
Publication:
Newsletter. q.
Annual Meetings: September in Durango, CO(Tammaron Hotel)

American Affiliation of Visiting Nurse Ass'ns and Services
Hist. Note: Superseded by Visiting Nurse Ass'ns of America in 1986.

American Aging Ass'n (1970)
Univ. of Nebraska Medical Center, Omaha NE 68105
Exec. Secretary: Denham Harman, M.D.
Members: 500 *Staff:* 1
Annual Budget: $25-50,000 *Tel:* (402) 559-4416
Hist. Note: Formed to promote biomedical aging research with the long-term goal of increasing the span of healthy, productive life. Membership: $20/year.
Publications:
Age: The Journal of the American Aging Ass'n. q.
Age News. q.
Annual Meetings: Fall

American Agricultural Economics Ass'n (1910)
80 Heady Hall, Iowa State University, Ames IA 50011-1070
Secy.-Treas.: Raymond R. Beneke
Members: 5,000 *Staff:* 2-5
Annual Budget: $250-500,000 *Tel:* (515) 294-8700
Hist. Note: Originated in 1910 as the American Farm Management Ass'n. Became the American Farm Economic Ass'n in 1918 and the American Agricultural Economics Ass'n in 1968. Incorporated in Iowa in 1968. Membership: $150/yr.
Publications:
AAEA Newsletter. bi-m. adv.
American Journal of Agricultural Economics. 5/yr. adv.
Choices. q.
Annual Meetings: Summer
1987-East Lansing, MI/August 2-5
1988-Knoxville, TN/July 31-Aug. 3
1989-Baton Rouge, LA(LSU)/July 30-Aug. 3

American Agricultural Editors Ass'n (1921)
1629 K St., N.W., Suite 1100, Washington DC 20006
Exec. Secretary: Paul S. Weller
Members: 625 *Staff:* 2
Annual Budget: $10-25,000 *Tel:* (202) 785-6710
Hist. Note: Members are editors, writers and photographers associated with agricultural publications. Membership: $50/yr.
Publications:
Byline. m.
Roster. a.
Annual Meetings: Oct./Nov., with summer seminars in July/Aug.

American Agricultural Law Ass'n (1980)
Dept. of Agricultural Economics, U of GA,15 Conner Hall, Athens GA 30602
Secy.-Treas.: Terence Centner
Members: 600 *Staff:* 1
Annual Budget: $10-25,000 *Tel:* (404) 542-0756
Hist. Note: Attorneys, law professors and others interested in agricultural law. Membership: $30/year (individual), $100/year (organization/company).
Publications:
AALA Newsletter. m.
Agricultural Law Update. m.
Membership Directory. bi-a. adv.
Annual Meetings: October
1987-Washington, DC(Omni Shoreham)/Oct. 15-16
1988-Kansas City, MO

American Agricultural Marketing Ass'n (1960)
Hist. Note: Affiliate of the American Farm Bureau Federation.

American Alfalfa Processors Ass'n (1941)
10100 Santa Fe, Suite 305, Overland Park KS 66212
President: Wanda L. Cobb
Members: 125-150 companies *Staff:* 2
Annual Budget: $100-250,000 *Tel:* (913) 648-6800
Hist. Note: Formerly (1984) the American Dehydrators Ass'n. Suppliers to and operators of alfalfa processing firms.
Publication:
Bulletin. w. adv.
Annual Meetings: March/300-400
1987-Albuquerque, NM/March 8-11

American Alliance for Health, Physical Education, Recreation and Dance (1885)
1900 Association Drive, Reston VA 22091
Exec. V. President: Hal Haywood
Members: 42,000 *Staff:* 50-60
Annual Budget: over $5,000,000 *Tel:* (703) 476-3400
Hist. Note: The American Association for Advancement of Physical Education was founded at Adelphi Academy, Brooklyn, NY in 1885. In 1903 the name was changed to the American Physical Education Association and in 1938 to the American Association for Health, Physical Education and Recreation. Incorporated in the District of Columbia in 1969. Became the American Alliance for Health, Physical Education and Recreation in 1974, and assumed its present name in 1979. Composed of the American Association for Leisure and Recreation, Association for the Advancement of Health Education, Association for Research Administration and Professional Councils, National Association for Girls and Women in Sports, National Association for Sport and Physical Education and the National Dance Association. Physical Education and the National Dance Association.
Publications:
Journal of Physical Education and Recreation. 9/yr. adv.
Research Quarterly. q.
School Health Review. bi-m.
Update. 10/yr.
Health Education. 6/yr.
Annual Meetings: Spring
1987-Las Vegas, NV(MGM Grand)/April 13-17/8,000
1988-Kansas City, MO(Bartle Conv. & Expo. Center)/April 6-10/8,000
1989-Boston, MA/April 19-23
1990-New Orleans, LA/March 28-April 1

American Ambulance Ass'n (1977)
3814 Auburn Blvd., Suite 70, Sacramento CA 95821
Exec. V. President: Charles S. Clark
Members: 700 companies *Staff:* 6
Annual Budget: $250-500,000 *Tel:* (916) 483-3827
Hist. Note: A merger of the Ambulance Ass'n of America formed in 1962 and the Nat'l Ambulance and Medical Services Ass'n formed in 1963. Formerly (until 1979) known as the Ambulance and Medical Services Ass'n of America. Members are private ambulance services. Membership: $400/yr.

00012 12 05 86 1233

Publication:
Ambulance Industry Journal. q. adv.
Annual Meetings: Fall
1987-Anaheim, CA(Anaheim Marriott)Nov. 1-4/800
1988-Dallas, TX(Loews Anatole)/Nov. 12-16/800
1989-Las Vegas, NV(Caesar's Palace)/Oct. 22-26/800

American Amusement Machine Ass'n (1980)
205 The Strand, Suite 3, Alexandria VA 22314
Exec. V. President: David A. Weaver
Members: 50-60 makers, distributors and suppliers *Staff:* 2-5
Annual Budget: $250-500,000 *Tel:* (703) 548-8044
Hist. Note: Founded in Des Plaines, Illinois as the Amusement Device Manufacturers Ass'n, it became the Amusement Game Manufacturers Ass'n in 1982 and assumed its present name in 1985. Members are makers of coin-operated games and machines.
Publication:
Coingram. m.
Annual Meetings: Fall

American Analgesia Soc.
30 East 40th St., New York NY 10016
Editor: Randolph Todd, M.D.
Members: 600-650 *Staff:* 1
Annual Budget: $10-25,000 *Tel:* (212) 684-7710
Publication:
Journal of the American Analgesia Society. 3/yr.

American and Delaine-Merino Record Ass'n (1906)
1193 Township Rd. 346, Nova OH 44859
Secy.-Treas.: Elaine A. Clouser
Members: 100-150 *Staff:* 1
Annual Budget: under $10,000 *Tel:* (419) 652-3642
Hist. Note: Owners and breeders of Merino sheep. No membership fee.
Publication:
Consider Merino.
Annual Meetings: Harrisburg, PA(Keystone Internat'l Livestock Expo.)/1st Sat. in Oct.

American Angora Goat Breeder's Ass'n (1900)
Box 195, Rocksprings TX 78880
Secy.-Treas.: Mary Jane Glasscock
Members: 1,900 *Staff:* 1
Annual Budget: under $10,000 *Tel:* (512) 683-4483
Hist. Note: Breeders and fanciers of Angora goats.
Annual Meetings: Rocksprings, 3rd Tuesday in October

American Angus Ass'n (1883)
3201 Frederick Blvd., St. Joseph MO 64501
Exec. V. President: Richard L. Spader
Members: 26,600 *Staff:* 60-65
Annual Budget: $2-5,000,000 *Tel:* (816) 233-3101
Hist. Note: Formerly (1956) American Aberdeen-Angus Breeder's Ass'n. Members are breeders and fanciers of Angus beef cattle. Member of the Nat'l Soc. of Livestock Record Ass'ns.
Publication:
Angus Journal. q. adv.

American Animal Hospital Ass'n (1933)
1746 Cole Blvd. #150, P.O. Box 15899, Denver CO 80215-0899
Exec. Director: John W. Albersl, D.V.M.
Members: 10-11,000 *Staff:* 25-30
Annual Budget: $2-5,000,000 *Tel:* (303) 279-2500
Hist. Note: An association of animal hospitals and small animal practitioners. Founded in 1933 and incorporated in 1935 in Illinois. Membership: $165/yr.
Publications:
Journal of the American Animal Hospital Association. bi-m. adv.
AAHA Trends. bi-m. adv.
Annual Meetings: Late March, Early April
1987-Phoenix, AZ/March 21-27
1988-Washington, DC/April 15-22
1989-St. Louis, MO/April 8-14

American Anthropological Ass'n (1902)
1703 New Hampshire Ave., N.W., Washington DC 20009
Exec. Director: Edward J. Lehman
Members: 10,000 individuals, 3,500 institutions *Staff:* 21-25
Annual Budget: $1-2,000,000 *Tel:* (202) 232-8800
Hist. Note: Established by members of the American Ethnological Soc. of New York, the Anthropological Soc. of Washington and Section H (Anthropology) of the American Ass'n for the Advancement of Science. Incorporated in the District of Columbia in May, 1902. Membership: $35/yr., plus membership in one or more of sixteen constituent sections ($10-40/yr.)
Publications:
American Anthropologist. q. adv.
Guide to Departments of Anthropology. a.
Anthropology Newsletter. m. adv.
American Ethnologist. q. adv.
Ethos. q. adv.
Medical Anthropology Quarterly. q. adv.
Cultural Anthropology. q. adv.
Anthropology and Education Quarterly. q. adv.
Anthropology and Humanism Quarterly. q. adv.
Central Issues in Anthropology. semi-a.
City and Society. semi-a. adv.
Annual Meetings: Fall/3,500
1987-Chicago, IL(Marriott)/Nov. 18-22

American Antiquarian Soc. (1812)
185 Salisbury St., Worcester MA 01609
Director: Marcus A. McCorison
Members: 450-500 *Staff:* 50
Annual Budget: $1-2,000,000 *Tel:* (617) 755-5221
Hist. Note: A learned society founded in 1812 by Isaiah Thomas and others to collect and preserve materials related to American history before 1877, it maintains an outstanding historical research library.
Publications:
Newsletter. semi-a.
Proceedings. semi-a.
Newsletter of the Program in the History of the Book in American Culture.
Annual Meetings:
1987-Worcester, MA(Antiquarian Soc.)/3rd Wed. in Oct.

American Apparel Machinery Trade Ass'n (1933)
c/o SSNC, Inc., 8 Stamford Forum, Stamford CT 06904
Secy.-Treas.: Stephen B. Wiznitzer
Members: 10-15 companies *Staff:* 1
Annual Budget: under $10,000 *Tel:* (203) 356-4200
Hist. Note: Manufacturers of industrial sewing machines and accessories. Formerly (1984) the Sewing Machine Trade Ass'n.
Annual Meetings: New York, NY/October

American Apparel Manufacturers Ass'n (1933)
2500 Wilson Boulevard, Suite 301, Arlington VA 22201
President: G. Stewart Boswell
Members: 900 companies *Staff:* 21-25
Annual Budget: $2-5,000,000 *Tel:* (703) 524-1864
Hist. Note: Formerly the Southern Garment Manufacturers Ass'n, the AAMA absorbed the Nat'l Ass'n of Shirt, Pajama and Sportswear Manufacturers in 1962, the Pacific Coast Garment Manufacturers Ass'n in 1965, the Textile Merchants and Associated Industries of Chicago in 1965, the Corset and Brassiere Ass'n in 1971, the the Lingerie Industry Council in 1971, the New England Rainwear Manufacturers Ass'n in 1974, and the Nat'l Outerwear and Sportswear Ass'n in 1983. It also contains the Boy's and Young Men's Apparel Manufacturers Ass'n as a separate division. Established the American Apparel Manufacturers Political Action Committee.
Publications:
AAMA Apparel Import Digest. m.
AAMA Apparel Management Letter. m.
AAMA Newsletter. m.
Washington Letter. m.
Annual Meetings: Spring and fall/500
1987-San Antonio, TX(Hyatt)/April 22-25
1987-Atlanta, GA(Georgia World Congress Center)/Sept. 15-18

American-Arab Ass'n for Commerce and Industry (1951)
420 Lexington Avenue, Suite 2431, New York NY 10017
President: I. F. Yusif
Members: 175 *Staff:* 2-5
Annual Budget: $250-500,000 *Tel:* (212) 986-7229
Hist. Note: Established as the American-Egyptian Friendship Soc. in New York City. Name changed in 1960 to its present title reflecting growing membership interest in all members of the League of Arab States. Both U.S. and Arab firms are members. Membership: $1,750/yr. (organization).
Publication:
American-Arab Association Bulletin. 10/yr.
Annual Meetings: Spring

American Arbitration Ass'n (1926)
140 West 51st St., New York NY 10020
President: Robert Coulson, CAE
Members: 5,000 *Staff:* 450
Annual Budget: over $5,000,000 *Tel:* (212) 484-4000
Hist. Note: Formed by a merger of the Arbitration Society of America and the Arbitration Foundation. Members are individuals and organizations united to promote the use of arbitration for the settlement of all types of disputes.
Publications:
Arbitration Journal. q. adv.
Arbitration in the Schools. m.
Arbitration Times.
Labor Arbitration in Government. m.
Lawyers' Arbitration Letter and Digest of Court Decisions. q.
Study Time. q.
Summary of Labor Awards. m.
Annual Meetings: New York City in March

American Architectural Manufacturers Ass'n (1936)
2700 River Rd., Suite 118, Des Plaines IL 60018
Exec. Director: William J. Anton, CAE
Members: 200-300 *Staff:* 10-12
Annual Budget: $1-2,000,000 *Tel:* (312) 699-7310
Hist. Note: Merger (1962) of Sliding Glass Door and Window Institute (1954) and Aluminum Window Manufacturers Ass'n (1936) to become the Architectural Aluminum Manufacturers Ass'n. Absorbed (1971) Aluminum Siding Ass'n. Assumed present name in 1984. Manufacturers of storm windows, sliding glass doors, siding, skylights and curtain walls. Membership: $1,000/yr. minimum (company).
Publications:
Pacesetter. q.
Quarterly Review. q.
Semi-annual meetings: Spring and Fall/700
1987-Miami, FL(Doral CC)/March 8-12
1987-Palm Springs, CA(Marriott Desert Springs)/Sept. 27-Oct. 1

1988-Orlando, FL/April 26-30
1988-Seattle, WA
1989-Undecided
1989-Williamsburg, VA(Williamsburg Inn)/Oct. 15-19

American Art Therapy Ass'n (1969)
505 East Hawley St., Mundelein IL 60060-2419
Exec. Director: Edward J. Stygar, Jr.
Members: 2,700 *Staff:* 2-5
Annual Budget: $100-250,000 *Tel:* (312) 949-6064
Hist. Note: Awards the designation ATR to art therapists who reach its standards for certification as registered therapists. Membership: $35-80/yr.
Publications:
Directory. a.
Newsletter. q.
Proceedings. a.
Art Therapy Journal. tri-a.
Annual Meetings: November
1987-Florida
1988-Boston, MA

American Artists Professional League (1928)
c/o Salmagundi Club, 47 Fifth Ave., New York NY 10003
President: Angelo John Grado
Members: 1,000
Annual Budget: under $10,000 *Tel:* (212) 645-1345
Hist. Note: Members are professional painters, sculptors and graphic artists. Membership: $25/yr.
Publications:
Catalog, Grand National Exhibition. a. adv.
News Bulletin. a. adv.
Annual Meetings: Fall, with the Grand National Exhibition
1987-New York, NY(Salmagundi Club)/Sept./1,000

American Arts Alliance (1977)
1319 F St., N.W., Suite 307, Washington DC 20004
Exec. Director: Anne G. Murphy
Members: 350 organizations *Staff:* 6-10
Annual Budget: $250-500,000 *Tel:* (202) 737-1727
Hist. Note: Theater, dance and opera companies, art museums symphony orchestras and choral groups. Incorporated in the State of Delaware in 1977. Gathers and disseminates information about the arts, encourages a national public policy on the arts, and represents the non-profit professional visual and performing arts to legislators and government officials.
Annual Meetings: Not held

American Assembly for Men in Nursing (1971)
600 South Paulina, #474-H, Chicago IL 60612
Chairman: Luther Christman, R.N.
Members: 2-300 *Staff:* 7
Annual Budget: $10-25,000 *Tel:* (312) 942-7117
Hist. Note: Members are primarily registered male nurses as well as male student nurses. Formerly (1982) the National Male Nurse Association. Membership: $25/year for R.N.s ; $15/year for students.
Publication:
Interaction Newsletter. q. adv.
Annual Meetings: June in Chicago, IL/175

American Assembly of Collegiate Schools of Business (1916)
605 Old Ballas Road, #220, St. Louis MO 63141
Exec. V. President: William K. Laidlaw, Jr.
Members: 830 institutions *Staff:* 25-30
Annual Budget: $1-2,000,000 *Tel:* (314) 872-8481
Hist. Note: Formerly (1973) American Ass'n of Collegiate Schools of Business Official accrediting body for business administration/management and accounting education programs at the baccalaureate and master's degree levels.
Publication:
AACSB Newsline. q.
Annual Meetings:
1987-New Orleans, LA/April 12-15/700
1988-Dallas, TX/April 10-13/700

American Ass'n for Adult and Continuing Education (1982)
1201 16th St., N.W., Suite 230, Washington DC 20036
Exec. Director: Judith A. Koloski
Members: 4,000 individuals *Staff:* 6-10
Annual Budget: $250-500,000 *Tel:* (202) 822-7866
Hist. Note: The product of a merger between the Adult Education Ass'n (founded in 1951) and the Nat'l Ass'n for Public and Continuing Adult Education (founded in 1952), AAACE coordinates local, state, regional and national adult education programs, publications and legislation. Membership: $85/year.
Publications:
Adult Education. q. adv.
Lifelong Learning: An Omnibus of Practice and Research. 8/yr. adv.
AAACE Newsletter. 10/yr.
Membership Directory. a.
Annual Meetings: Fall
1987-Washington, DC/Oct. 22-29
1988-Tulsa, OK
1989-Atlantic City, NJ

American Ass'n for Aerosol Research (1981)
Ctr. for Aerosol Technology, Research, Triangle Institute, P.O. Box 12194, Research Triangle Pk NC 27709
Secy.-Treas.: David Ensor
Members: 600

00013 12 05 86 1233

Annual Budget: under $10,000
Hist. Note: Membership: $45/year.
Publication:
Aerosol Science and Technology. q. adv.

American Ass'n for Affirmative Action (1974)
Burnison, Martello & Associates, 11 East Hubbard Street, Chicago IL 60611
Convention Manager: Judith C. Burnison
Members: 800-850 individuals, 225 companies/institutions
Annual Budget: $50-100,000 *Tel:* (312) 329-2512
Hist. Note: Members are affirmative action officers in colleges and universities, private industry and state, federal and local government. Concerned with equal employment and educational opportunities for minorities. Has no paid staff. Membership: $45/yr. (individual); $100-250/yr. (organization/company)
Publication:
Newsletter. 8/yr. adv.
Annual Meetings: Spring
1987-Chicago, IL(Marriott)/April 8-11/400-500
1988-Denver, CO(Fairmont)/April 7-9/400-500

American Ass'n for Applied Linguistics (1977)
1325 18th St., N.W., Suite 211, Washington DC 20036-6501
Secretary-Treasurer: Dr. Albert Valdman
Members: 400 *Staff:* 1
Annual Budget: under $10,000 *Tel:* (202) 835-1714
Hist. Note: Individuals interested in multidisciplinary approaches to language issues and problems.
Publications:
Applied Linguistics. 3/yr.
Newsletter. 3/yr.
Annual Meetings: Winter

American Ass'n for Artificial Intelligence (1979)
445 Burgess Drive, Menlo Park CA 94025
Exec. Director: Claudia C. Mazzetti
Members: 14,000 *Staff:* 11
Annual Budget: $1-2,000,000 *Tel:* (415) 328-3123
Hist. Note: Members are individuals interested in attempting to approximate the human thinking process with computers in such fields as visual data interpretation, export systems, natural language processing, common sense reasoning, automotive problem solving and robotics.
Publications:
AI Magazine. q. adv.
Membership Directory. a.
Conference Proceedings.
Annual Meetings: July/August
1987-Seattle, WA
1988-Minneapolis/St. Paul, MN
1989-Detroit, MI

American Ass'n for Automotive Medicine (1957)
40 Second ave., Arlington Heights IL 60005
Exec. Director: Elaine Petrucelli
Members: 500-600 *Staff:* 2-5
Annual Budget: $10-25,000 *Tel:* (312) 640-8440
Hist. Note: Organized in 1957 and incorporated in Florida. Encourages and promotes the growth and dissemination of new knowledge in the field of traffic and highway safety. Membership is composed of physicians, researchers, educators, engineers, administrators, and other highway and traffic medicine professionals. Membership: $100/yr.
Publications:
AAAM Journal. q.
Proceedings. a.
Annual Meetings: Fall/275
1987-New Orleans, LA(Fairmont)/Sept. 28-30
1988-San Francisco, CA(Fairmont)/Oct. 26-28

American Ass'n for Budget and Program Analysis (1976)
6425 Lakeview Drive, Box 1157, Falls Church VA 22041
Nat'l Exec. Secretary: Marykathryn Kubat
Members: 700-800 *Staff:* 1
Annual Budget: $25-50,000 *Tel:* (703) 941-4300
Hist. Note: The result of a merger between the Budget Officers Conference and the American Public Policy Ass'n, AABPA was chartered as a non-profit educational corp. in Washington, DC in 1976. Members, largely in the DC area, have an interest in program analysis and budgeting. Membership: $30/yr. (individual); $75/yr. (organization/company)
Publications:
Newsletter. m.
Public Budgeting and Finance. q. adv.
Annual Meetings: June
1987-Washington, DC(Nat'l Press Club)/April 9/250

American Ass'n for Cancer Education (1948)
Radiation Oncology, CRTC Building, Room A-1020, UMDNJ, 100 Bergen Street, Newark NJ 07103
Secretary: Stephen M. Stowe, M.D.
Members: 8-900 *Staff:* 2-5
Annual Budget: $25-50,000 *Tel:* (201) 456-5365
Hist. Note: Formerly (1966) Coordinators of Cancer Teaching. Membership includes scientists, surgeons, internists, radiation oncologists, pediatricians, gynecologists, osteopathic physicians, dentists and oncology nursing educators. Concerned with cancer teaching in medical, dental and nursing schools. Membership: $75/yr.
Publications:
American Ass'n for Cancer Education Newsletter q.
Journal of Cancer Education. a. adv.
Annual Meetings: Fall/250
1987-New Orleans, LA
1988-San Diego, CA
1989-Miami, FL

American Ass'n for Cancer Research (1907)
Temple University Medical School, West Bldg., Room 301, Philadelphia PA 19140
Exec. Director: Margaret Foti
Members: 4,200 *Staff:* 2-5
Annual Budget: $1-2,000,000 *Tel:* (215) 221-4565
Hist. Note: Founded 1907 in Washington, DC and incorporated in New York in 1940. An association of research workers for presentation and discussion of new or significant observations and problems in cancer, and to foster research on cancer. Membership: $85/year.
Publication:
Cancer Research. m.
Annual Meetings: Spring/3,000-3,500
1987-Atlanta, Ga(Hilton/Marriott Marquis)/May 20-23
1988-New Orleans, LA(Convention Ctr.)/May 25-28
1989-San Francisco, CA(Moscone Ctr.)/May 24-27
1990-Washington, DC(Convention Ctr.)/May 23-26

American Ass'n for Chinese Studies (1958)
P.O. Box 3158, Ohio State University, Columbus OH 43210
Exec. Secretary: Prof. Wen-Lang Li
Members: 3-400 *Staff:* 2
Annual Budget: under $10,000 *Tel:* (614) 422-1353
Hist. Note: Formerly (1976) the American Ass'n of Teachers of Chinese Language and Culture, Inc.
Publications:
Newsletter. semi-a.
Journal of Chinese Studies. semi-a.
Annual Meetings: Fall
1987-Washington, DC/Nov. 1

American Ass'n for Clinical Chemistry (1948)
1725 K St., N.W., Suite 1010, Washington DC 20006
Exec. V. President: Ronald E. Whorton, M.P.H.
Members: 7,000 *Staff:* 35
Annual Budget: over $5,000,000 *Tel:* (202) 857-0717
Hist. Note: Founded and incorporated in 1948 in New York. Formerly (Jan. 1, 1976) American Ass'n of Clinical Chemists. Members are chemists, physicians and other scientists specializing in clinical chemistry. Provides educational and professional development services to its members in order to improve the level at which chemistry is practiced in chemical laboratories.
Publications:
Clinical Chemistry. m. adv.
Clinical Chemistry News. m. adv.
Endocrinology & Metabolism Continuing Education Program. m.
Therapeutic Drug Monitoring & Emergency Toxicology C.E.P. m.
Annual Meetings: July/August
1987-San Francisco/July 19-24
1988-New Orleans/July 24-29
1989-Atlanta/July 23-28
1990-San Francisco, CA/July 22-27
1991-Washington, DC/July 22-27
1992-Chicago, IL/July 19-24
1993-New York, NY/July 11-16
1994-New Orleans, LA

American Ass'n for Clinical Immunology and Allergy (1964)
Box 912 - DTS, Omaha NE 68101
Exec. Director: Howard Silber
Members: 1,400 *Staff:* 2-5
Annual Budget: $100-250,000 *Tel:* (402) 551-0801
Hist. Note: Sponsors the American Board of Clinical Immunology and Allergy and the Joint Council of Allergy and Immunology.
Publication:
Immunology and Allergy Practice. m. adv.
Annual Meetings:
1987-Palm Desert, CA(Marriott Desert Springs Resort)/Nov. 30-Dec. 3
1988-Orlando, FL(Buena Vista Palace)/Nov. 30-Dec. 3
1989-Las Vegas, NV(Riviera Hotel)/Nov. 29-Dec. 2

American Ass'n for Continuity of Care (1982)
1101 Connecticut Ave., N.W., Suite 700, Washington DC 20036
Exec. Director: Patricia I. Horner
Members: 1,200 *Staff:* 2
Annual Budget: $100-250,000 *Tel:* (202) 857-1100
Hist. Note: Incorporated in Washington, DC, AACC members are multi-disciplinary professionals involved in developing continuity of care, hospital discharge and home health care. Membership: $48/yr. (individual), $175-750/yr. (organization).
Publications:
Access. bi-m. adv.
Directory. a. adv.
Task Force Report a.
Annual Meetings:
1987-Boston, MA(Marriott Copley Place)/Oct. 29-Nov. 1/300-400

American Ass'n for Correctional Psychology (1953)
Arkansas Dept. of Corrections, P.O. Box 8707, Pine Bluff AR 71611
President: Max J. Mobley, Ph.D.
Members: 400
Annual Budget: under $10,000 *Tel:* (501) 247-1800
Hist. Note: Affiliate of the American Correctional Association. Formerly (1983) the American Ass'n of Correctional Psychologists.
Publications:
AACP Newsletter. q.
Criminal Justice and Behavior: An Internat'l Journal of Correctional
Psychology. q. adv.
Annual Meetings: With American Correctional Ass'n

American Ass'n for Counseling and Development (1952)
5999 Stevenson Ave., Alexandria VA 22304
Exec. Director: Dr. Patrick J. McDonough
Members: 52,000 *Staff:* 60
Annual Budget: $2-5,000,000 *Tel:* (703) 823-9800
Hist. Note: AACD, formerly the American Personnel and Guidance Ass'n (1983), is a private, non-profit organization dedicated to the growth and development of the counseling and human development profession. AACD members work in education settings, from pre-school through higher education, in mental health agencies, community organizations, correctional institutions, employment agencies, rehabilitation programs, government, business, industry, research facilities, and private practice. Divisions and organizational affiliates include the following: American College Personnel Ass'n, Ass'n for Counselor Education and Supervision, Nat'l Career Development Ass'n, Ass'n for Humanistic Education and Development, American School Counselor Ass'n, American Rehabilitation Counseling Ass'n, Ass'n for Measurement and Evaluation in Counseling and Development, Nat'l Employment Counselors Ass'n, Ass'n for Multicultural Counseling and Development, Ass'n for Religious and Value Issues in Counseling, Ass'n for Specialists in Group Work, Public Offender Counselors Ass'n, American Mental Health Counselors Ass'n, and Military Educators and Counselors Ass'n. Membership: $52/yr. The present name was assumed in June, 1983.
Publications:
The Guidepost. 18/yr. adv.
Journal of Counseling and Development. m. adv.
Annual Meetings: Spring/8,000
1987-New Orleans, LA/April 22-25
1988-Chicago, IL
1989-Boston. MA

American Ass'n for Crystal Growth (1968)
Solar Energy Research Institute, 1617 Cole Boulevard, Golden CO 80401
Secretary: Dr. Thomas Surek
Members: 600-650 individuals
Annual Budget: $25-50,000 *Tel:* (303) 231-1371
Hist. Note: Formerly (1970) American Committee for Crystal Growth. Members include engineers, scientists, educators, technologists, marketing representatives and students, all with a strong interest in one or more facets of the crystal growth field. Affiliated with the Internat'l Organization for Crystal Growth. Membership: $10/yr.
Publication:
Newsletter. q. adv.
Triennial Meetings:
1987-Monterey, CA(Sheraton)/July 12-17/4-500

American Ass'n for Dental Research (1952)
1111 14th St., N.W., Suite 1000, Washington DC 20005
Exec. Director: Dr. John A. Gray
Members: 4,400 *Staff:* 7
Annual Budget: $500-1,000,000 *Tel:* (202) 898-1050
Hist. Note: Division of Internat'l Ass'n for Dental Research. Membership: $82/yr. (individual); $250-4,000/yr. (company)
Publications:
Journal of Dental Reseach. 16/yr. adv.
Around AADR (newsletter). 6/yr. adv.
Annual Meetings: March
1987-Chicago, IL(Hyatt Regency)/March 11-15/2,900
1988-Montreal/March 9-13/3,500
1989-San Francisco, CA/March 15-19

American Ass'n for Functional Orthodontics (1984)
25 South Kent St., Winchester VA 22601
President: Craig C. Stoner
Members: 2,100 individuals *Staff:* 6
Annual Budget: $250-500,000 *Tel:* (703) 662-2200
Hist. Note: Formerly the American Ass'n of Functional Orthodontists. An independent ass'n of orthodontists, pedodontists, and general dentists from throughout the U.S. and Canada with interests in functional appliance treatment and TMJ therapy. Membership: $125.00/yr.
Publications:
The Functional Orthodontist. bi-m. adv.
AAFO Members' Directory. a.

American Ass'n for Geodetic Surveying (1981)
Hist. Note: A member organization of the American Congress on Surveying and Mapping.

American Ass'n for Geriatric Psychiatry (1978)
1440 Main St., Waltham MA 02254-9132
President: Elliott M. Stein, M.D.
Members: 700
Annual Budget: $10-25,000 *Tel:* (617) 891-3530
Hist. Note: An organization of psychiatrists interested in aging. Purpose is to promote better understanding and care of the mental health of the elderly. Membership: $35/yr.
Publication:
AAGP Newsletter. bi-m.

00014 12 05 86 1233

American Ass'n for Higher Education (1870)
One Dupont Circle, N.W., Suite 600, Washington DC 20036
President: Russell Edgerton
Members: 6-7,000 *Staff:* 11-15
Annual Budget: $500-1,000,000 *Tel:* (202) 293-6440
Hist. Note: Established in 1870 as one of the four original departments of the Nat'l Education Ass'n, it became the Ass'n for Higher Education of NEA in 1952; assumed its present name in 1970 when it became independent from NEA. Membership: $60/yr.
Publications:
AAHE Bulletin. m.
Change Magazine. bi-m. adv.
Annual Meetings: Nat'l Conference on Higher Education
1987-Chicago, IL/March 1-4/2,000
1988-Washington, DC/March 9-12/2,000
1989-Chicago, IL/March 5-8/2,000
1990-Washington, DC(Washington Hilton)/March 25-28/2,000

American Ass'n for Jewish Education (1939)
Hist. Note: Became the Jewish Education Service of North America in 1982.

American Ass'n for Laboratory Accreditation (1978)
656 Quince Orchard Road, Suite 704, Gaithersburg MD 20878
Exec. Director: John W. Locke
Members: 100-125 *Staff:* 2-5
Annual Budget: $100-250,000 *Tel:* (301) 670-1377
Hist. Note: Members are testing laboratories interested in establishing and maintaining quality standards, users of testing services who want to have competent testing services accredited for their use, and general interest people who promote the idea of a comprehensive laboratory accreditation system. Membership does not imply accreditation.
Annual Meetings: February

American Ass'n for Laboratory Animal Science (1948)
70 Timber Creek Drive, Suite 5, Cordova TN 38018
Exec. Director: Donald W. Keene
Members: 3,500 individuals, 550 institutions *Staff:* 6-10
Annual Budget: $500-1,000,000 *Tel:* (901) 754-8620
Hist. Note: Founded in 1948 and incorporated in Illinois in 1953 as the Animal Care Panel. Name changed to American Ass'n for Laboratory Animal Science in 1966. Members are individuals professionally concerned with the production, care and study of laboratory animals.
Publications:
AALAS Newsletter. bi-m.
Laboratory Animal Science. bi-m. adv.
Annual Meetings: Fall
1987-Denver, CO/Nov. 7-12/2,200
1988-Detroit, MI(Westin)/Oct. 9-14/2,400
1989-Little Rock, AR(Excelsior)/Oct. 29-Nov. 3/2,200

American Ass'n for Leisure and Recreation (1938)
1900 Association Dr., Reston VA 22091
Exec. Director: Dr. Barbara M. Sampson
Members: 5,700 professional members, 1,700 students *Staff:* 2-5
Annual Budget: $10-25,000 *Tel:* (703) 476-3400
Hist. Note: Until 1974 the Recreation Division of the American Ass'n for Health, Physical Education and Recreation. Now, an independent member of the Alliance for Health, Physical Education, Recreation and Dance. Members are teachers of leisure studies, recreation, park administration and the like. Membership: $42/yr.
Publications:
AALReporter.
Leisure Today. m. adv.
Annual Meetings: With the American Alliance for Health, Physical Education, Recreation and Dance.
1987-Las Vegas, NV(MGM Grand)/April 13-17

American Ass'n for Marriage and Family Therapy (1942)
1717 K St., N.W., Suite 407, Washington DC 20006
Exec. Director: Mark Ginsberg
Members: 13,000 *Staff:* 21
Annual Budget: $1-2,000,000 *Tel:* (202) 429-1825
Hist. Note: Founded as American Ass'n of Marriage Counselors, it became American Ass'n of Marriage and Family Counselors in 1970 and assumed its present name in 1978. A professional organization of clinical therapists specially trained to work with couples and families. Includes 48 regional divisions in the U.S. and Canada with members around the world. Membership: $75/yr.; must also belong to a state group.
Publications:
Family Therapy News. bi-m. adv.
Journal of Marital and Family Therapy. q. adv.
Annual Meetings:
1987-Chicago, IL(Hilton)/Oct. 29-Nov. 1/3,500
1988-New Orleans, LA(Marriott)/Oct. 27-30/3,500

American Ass'n for Maternal and Child Health
Hist. Note: Ceased operations in 1986.

American Ass'n for Medical Systems and Informatics (1981)
1101 Connecticut Ave., N.W., Suite 700, Washington DC 20036
Exec. Director: Patricia I. Horner
Members: 1,200-1,500 *Staff:* 5
Annual Budget: $100-250,000 *Tel:* (202) 857-1199
Hist. Note: Incorporated in Maryland as the result of a merger between the Soc. for Advanced Medical Systems (founded in 1969) and the Soc. for for Computer Medicine (founded in 1970). Promotes the use of computers and information systems in health care, with emphasis on direct patient care.
Publications:
President's Hotline. q.
Membership Directory. a.
Conference Proceedings. a.
Congress Proceedings. a.
Computer & Biomedical Research. bi-m. adv.
M.D. Computing. bi-m. adv.
Semi-annual Meetings: Spring Congress (West) & Fall Conference (East)
1987-San Francisco, CA(Hilton & Towers)/May 13-16/over 400
1987-Washington, DC(Sheraton)/Oct. 31-Nov. 1/200
1988-San Francisco, CA/May/400
1988-Washington, DC(Sheraton)/Nov. 5-6/over 200

American Ass'n for Medical Transcription (1978)
Box 6187, Modesto CA 95355
Exec. Director: Claudia Tessier
Members: 8,000 *Staff:* 9
Annual Budget: $500-1,000,000 *Tel:* (209) 576-0883
Hist. Note: AAMT is a professional association for medical transcriptionists, supervisors, teachers, students and other interested health personnel. Awards the "CMT" (Certified Medical Transcriptionist) designation by voluntary examination. Membership: $45/yr. (individual); $100-350/yr. (institution/corp.)
Publications:
Journal of the American Ass'n for Medical Transcription. q. adv.
AAMT Newsletter. bi-m. adv.
Annual Meetings: August
1987-New Orleans, LA(Hyatt Regency)
1988-Phoenix, AZ(Cambelback Inn)

American Ass'n for Music Therapy (1971)
Box 359, 66 Morris Ave., Springfield NJ 07081
Exec. Director: Steven Changaris
Members: 500 *Staff:* 1
Annual Budget: $25-50,000 *Tel:* (201) 379-1100
Hist. Note: Formerly(1976) Urban Federation for Music Therapists. Affiliated with the National Association of Schools of Music and the National Music Council. Members are certified music therapists, students of music therapy, schools offering music courses, institutions and interested patrons. Membership: $45/year, $25/year for students.
Publications:
Membership Directory. a.
Music Therapy: AAMT Journal. a.
Newsletter. q.

American Ass'n for Paralegal Education (1981)
Box 40244, Overland Park KS 66204
Exec. Director: Sandra L. Sabanske
Members: 95 institutions *Staff:* 1
Annual Budget: $25-50,000 *Tel:* (913) 381-4458
Hist. Note: Members are educational institutions. Membership: $100/yr.
Publications:
Newsletter. q.
Journal of Paralegal Education. a.
Membership Directory. a.
Annual Meetings: October
1987-Baltimore, MD
1988-Orlando, FL

American Ass'n for Partial Hospitalization (1965)
1221 Massachusetts Ave., N.W., Suite B, Washington DC 20005
Admin. Coordinator: Joan Fridberg
Members: 350 companies; 300 individuals *Staff:* 1
Annual Budget: $50-100,000 *Tel:* (202) 347-1649
Hist. Note: Began in the 1960's as the Partial Hospitalization Study Group; it adopted its present name in 1979 to reflect the fact that the organization had grown into an extensive national network. AAPH is a multidisciplinary organization whose members share a common interest in the development, growth and improvement of partial hospitalization within the continuum of psychiatric treatment. Membership: $40/yr. (individual); $90/yr. (institution)
Publications:
International Journal of Partial Hospitalization. q.
Newsletter. q. adv.
Proceedings. a.
AAPH Bibliography. trien.
Annual Meetings: Aug./Sept.
1987-Boston, MA(Marriott Copley Place)/Aug. 11-17/350
1988-Denver, CO

American Ass'n for Pediatric Ophthalmology and Strabismus (1974)
Canton Eye Center, 800 McKinley Avenue, N.W., Cantongeles OH 44703
Secy.-Treas.: Dr. Elbert H. Magoon, M.D.
Members: 360 *Staff:* 1
Annual Budget: $50-100,000 *Tel:* (216) 452-8884
Hist. Note: Has no paid staff.
Publication:
Journal of Pediatric Ophthalmology and Strabismus. bi-m. adv.
Annual Meetings:
1987-Scottsdale, AZ(Mountain Shadows)/June 15-19/450
1988-Boston, MA/June

American Ass'n for Public Opinion Research (1947)
Box 17, Princeton NJ 08542
Administrator: Diana Druker
Members: 1,100-1,200 *Staff:* 2-5
Annual Budget: $50-100,000 *Tel:* (609) 924-8670
Hist. Note: Members are individuals concerned with public opinion research and the application of its results to advertising, marketing, scholarship and public affairs. Founded at a meeting convoked by Harry H. Field, Director of the National Opinion Research Center, at the Opera House in Central City, Colorado, July 29-31, 1946. Membership: $40-$60/yr.
Publications:
AAPOR News. 3/yr.
Public Opinion Quarterly. q.
Annual Meetings: Late spring at a resort hotel

American Ass'n for Rehabilitation Therapy (1950)
P.O. Box 6412, Gulfport MS 39506
President: Elwood Cavalier
Members: 200 *Staff:* 1
Annual Budget: under $10,000 *Tel:* (601) 865-1078
Hist. Note: A professional society of medical rehabilitation therapists and others interested in the vocational and avocational rehabilitation of the handicapped. Awards the "CRT" (Certified Rehabilitation Therapist) designation. Has no paid staff; officers change annually. Membership: $65/yr.(individual); $100/yr.(organization)
Publications:
American Archives of Rehabilatation Therapy. 3/yr. adv.
Rehabilitation Therapy Bulletin. q. adv.
Annual Meetings: June, usually with Nat'l Ass'n of Rehabilitation Facilities

American Ass'n for Respiratory Care (1947)
1720 Regal Row, Suite 112, Dallas TX 75235
Exec. Director: Sam P. Giordano
Members: 25-26,000 *Staff:* 35-37
Annual Budget: over $5,000,000 *Tel:* (214) 630-3540
Hist. Note: A professional organization of respiratory therapy personnel formed in Chicago and incorporated in the State of Illinois in 1947, it assumed the name, American Ass'n for Inhalation Therapists, in 1954; American Ass'n for Inhalation Therapy in 1967; American Ass'n for Repiratory Therapy in 1973; and its present name in 1986. Sponsored by the American College of Chest Physicians, the American Soc. of Anaesthesiologists and the American Thoracic Soc.
Publications:
AARTimes. m. adv.
Respiratory Care. m. adv.
Annual Meetings: Late Fall
1987-Las Vegas, NV(Conv. Center)/Nov. 14-17/6,000
1988-Orlando, FL(Conv. Center)/Nov. 5-8/6,000
1989-Anaheim, CA(Conv. Center)/Dec. 3-6/6,000
1990-New Orleans, LA(Conv. Center)/Dec. 8-11/6,000

American Ass'n for Respiratory Therapy
Hist. Note: Assumed the name, American Ass'n for Respiratory Care, in 1986.

American Ass'n for Social Psychiatry (1971)
1400 K St., N.W., Suite 411, Washington DC 20005
Secy.-Treas.: Carolyn Robinowitz, M.D.
Members: 600 *Staff:* 1
Annual Budget: $10-25,000 *Tel:* (202) 682-6130
Hist. Note: Members are individuals concerned with the study, prevention and treatment of mental illness and behavioral disorders. Membership: $50/yr.
Publication:
American Journal of Social Psychiatry. q. adv.
Annual Meetings: With The American Psychiatric Association.
1987-Chicago, IL/May 10-14

American Ass'n for State and Local History (1940)
172 2nd Ave. North, Suite 102, Nashville TN 37201
Director: Gerald W. George
Members: 6,100 *Staff:* 24
Annual Budget: $1-2,000,000 *Tel:* (615) 255-2971
Hist. Note: Formerly the Council of Historical Societies. Absorbed the Ass'n of Historic Sites Officials in 1963. An organization of individuals and groups interested in promoting the study of state and local history in the U.S. and Canada.
Publications:
Directory of Historical Societies and Agencies in The United States and Canada. bi-a.
History News. bi-m.
History News Dispatch (newsletter). m.
Annual Meetings: September or October/500
1987-Raleigh, NC
1988-Rochester, NY
1989-Seattle, WA
1990-Jackson Hole, WY
1991-Dearborn, MI
1992-Florida
1993-Hawaii

American Ass'n for Textile Technology (1934)
295 Fifth Ave., Suite 621, New York NY 10016-7201
Exec. Director: Karen Koopman Stone
Members: 1,400-1,500
Annual Budget: $50-100,000 *Tel:* (212) 481-7792
Hist. Note: Organized in 1934 and incorporated in 1945. Encourages the growth and dissemination of knowledge in the field of textile technology and marketing. Membership: $40/yr. (individual); $300/yr. (company).
Annual Meetings:
1987-New York, NY/April 2/200

00015 12 05 86 1233

American Ass'n for the Advancement of Science (1848)
1333 H St., N.W., Washington DC 20005
Exec. Officer: William D. Carey
Members: 132,000 *Staff:* 230
Annual Budget: over $5,000,000 *Tel:* (202) 326-6400
Hist. Note: Founded in September, 1848 in Philadelphia with 461 charter members. Incorporated in Massachusetts in 1874. An umbrella association, the AAAS has nearly 300 affiliates-societies, academies and other organizations which effectively comprise the whole spectrum of U.S. science and engineering. Membership: $65/yr. (individual); $40/yr. (student).
Publications:
AAAS Program.
Science. w. adv.
Science Books and Films- A Quarterly Review. q.
Science Education News. q.
Annual Meetings: February/3,000-4,000
1987-Chicago, IL/Feb. 14-18
1988-Boston, MA/Feb. 11-16
1989-San Francisco, CA/Feb. 16-21

American Ass'n for the Advancement of Slavic Studies (1948)
128 Encina Commons, Stanford University, Stanford CA 94305
Exec. Director: Dr. Dorothy Atkinson
Members: 3,000 *Staff:* 9
Annual Budget: $250-500,000 *Tel:* (415) 723-9668
Hist. Note: Seeks to advance scholarly study, publication and teaching relating to the Soviet Union and Eastern Europe.
Publications:
American Bibliography of Slavic and East European Studies. a.
Newsletter. q.
Slavic Review. q. adv.
Annual Meetings: Fall
1987-Boston, MA(Park Plaza)/Nov. 5-8
1988-Honolulu, HI(Hilton Hawaiian Village)/Nov. 18-21

American Ass'n for the Advancement of Tension Control (1973)
Hist. Note: Became the International Stress and Tension Control Association in 1981.

American Ass'n for the Advancement of the Humanities (1977)
Hist. Note: Defunct, 1983.

American Ass'n for the Comparative Study of Law (1951)
University of Puget Sound Law School, Tacoma WA 98402
Secretary: Prof. Mary Ann Glendon
Members: 60 law schools *Staff:* 2-5
Annual Budget: $25-50,000 *Tel:* (206) 756-3485
Publication:
American Journal of Comparative Law. q. adv.
Annual Meetings: At a law school site

American Ass'n for the History of Medicine (1925)
Univ. of Rochester Medical Center, Rochester NY 14642
Secretary-Treasurer: Edward C. Atwater, M.D.
Members: 1,300 individuals *Staff:* 0
Annual Budget: $50-100,000 *Tel:* (716) 275-2903
Hist. Note: Incorporated in New York in 1958. Membership: $35/yr.
Publications:
Bulletin of the History of Medicine. q. adv.
AAHM Newsletter. 3/yr.
Annual Meetings: Spring
1987-Philadelphia, PA
1988-New Orleans, LA
1989-Birmingham, AL
1990-Baltimore, MD
1991-Cleveland, OH

American Ass'n for the Study of Headache (1959)
Box 25152, Chicago IL 60625
Secretary to the Board: Idell Applebaum
Members: 750 individuals *Staff:* 1
Annual Budget: $100-250,000 *Tel:* (312) 878-8977
Hist. Note: Membership: $85/year.
Publication:
Headache. 10/yr.
Annual Meetings: June

American Ass'n for the Study of Liver Diseases (1949)
6900 Grove Road, Thorofare NJ 08086-9447
Exec. Director: Robert Talley
Members: 1,008 *Staff:* 1
Annual Budget: $100-250,000 *Tel:* (609) 848-1000
Hist. Note: Membership: $85/yr.
Publication:
Hepatology. bi-m. adv.
Annual Meetings: Fall, in Chicago, IL(Marriott)
1987-Oct. 25-28
1988-Nov. 6-9
1989-Nov. 9-12
1990-Nov. 1-4

American Ass'n for the Study of Neoplastic Diseases (1929)
10607 Miles Ave., Cleveland OH 44105
President: Robert H. Jackson, M.D.
Members: 450-500 *Staff:* 1
Annual Budget: $10-25,000 *Tel:* (216) 341-4335
Hist. Note: Physicians interested in the prevention, causation, diagnosis and treatment of neoplastic diseases (tumors), malignant and benign.
Publications:
Bulletin.
Proceedings.
Annual Meetings: June, in conjunction with Internat'l Congress on Neoplastic Diseases

American Ass'n for the Surgery of Trauma (1938)
462 Grider Street, Buffalo, NY 14215
Secy.-Treas.: Dr. Lewis M.. Flint, M.D.
Members: 700-800 *Staff:* 1
Tel: (716) 894-1213
Hist. Note: Organized June 14, 1938 in San Francisco.
Publication:
Journal of Trauma. m. adv.
Annual Meetings: Fall
1987-Montreal, Quebec(Bonaventure Hilton)/Sept. 18-20/500-600
1988-Cosa Mesa(Westin South Coast Plaza)/Oct. 6-8/500-600

American Ass'n for Thoracic Surgery (1917)
13 Elm St., Box 1565, Manchester MA 01944
Exec. Secretary: William T. Maloney, CAE
Members: 900-1,000 *Staff:* 6-10
Annual Budget: $100-250,000 *Tel:* (617) 927-8330
Hist. Note: Organized in New York City in 1917.
Publication:
Journal of Thoracic and Cardiovascular Surgery. m. adv.
Annual Meetings: Spring/2,500
1987-Chicago, IL(Hyatt Regency)/Apr. 8-10
1988-Los Angeles, CA(Century Plaza)/April 18-20
1989-Boston, MA(Sheraton/Hynes Aud.)/May 8-10
1990-Toronto, Ontario(Sheraton Centre)May 7-9
1991-Washington, DC(Hilton)/May 6-8

American Ass'n for Vocational Instructional Materials (1949)
120 Engineering Center, Athens GA 30602
Exec. Director: Richard Hylton
Members: 50 US states, Canadian provinces and territories
Staff: 10-12
Annual Budget: $500-1,000,000 *Tel:* (404) 542-2586
Hist. Note: Purpose is to provide both written and audio-visual instructional materials for job-training programs. Sponsors six programs in vocational, technical and career education for secondary and post secondary education, industry, military and government agencies.
Annual Meetings: October

American Ass'n for Women Podiatrists (1965)
4372 Chamblee Tucker Road, Tucker GA 30084
President: Barbara S. Schlefman
Members: 125
Annual Budget: under $10,000 *Tel:* (404) 491-6762
Hist. Note: Members must be members of the American Podiatry Ass'n. Membership: $40/year.
Publication:
AAWP Newsletter. q.
Annual Meetings: August, in conjunction with the American Podiatry Ass'n
1987-Washington, DC
1988-Anaheim, CA
1989-Las Vegas, NV

American Ass'n of Academic Editors (1980)
813 Branson Park Drive, Muskogee OK 74403
Director: Alex S. Freedman, Ph. D.
Members: 30 *Staff:* 1
Annual Budget: under $10,000 *Tel:* (918) 683-0401
Hist. Note: Editors and publishers of academic books and journals. Membership: $35/yr.
Publication:
Newsletter. irreg.
Annual Meetings: Winter

American Ass'n of Acupuncture and Oriental Medicine (1981)
1424 16th St., N.W., Suite 105, Washington DC 20036
President: Dr. Robert C. Sohn
Members: 1,000 individuals *Staff:* 2
Annual Budget: $10-25,000 *Tel:* (202) 232-1404
Hist. Note: Membership: $25-50/yr. (individual), $150/yr. (organization).
Publication:
The American Acupuncturist. q.
Annual Meetings: Spring
1987-Honolulu, HI

American Ass'n of Advertising Agencies (1917)
666 Third Ave., New York NY 10017
President: Leonard S. Matthews
Members: 722 companies *Staff:* 65-75
Annual Budget: $2-5,000,000 *Tel:* (212) 682-2500
Hist. Note: Maintains a Washington office.
Publication:
Roster and Organization. a.
Annual Meetings: Spring.

American Ass'n of Airport Executives (1928)
4224 King St., Alexandria VA 22302
Exec. V. President: Charles Barclay, AAE
Members: 2,200 *Staff:* 6-10
Annual Budget: $1-2,000,000 *Tel:* (703) 824-0500
Hist. Note: A professional organization of individuals concerned with the management, operation and construction of civil airports. Awards the "A.A.E." (Accredited Airport Executive) designation. Membership: $175/yr. (individual); $350/yr. (company/organization)
Publication:
Airport Report. bi-w.
Annual Meetings: May/June/1,400
1987-San Antonio, TX(Hyatt)
1988-Las Vegas, NV(MGM Grand)
1989-Nashville, TN(Opryland)
1990-St. Louis, MO

American Ass'n of Anatomists (1888)
Box 101, MCV Station, Richmond VA 23298
Secy.-Treas.: William P. Jollie, Ph.D.
Members: 2,850 *Staff:* 1
Annual Budget: $50-100,000 *Tel:* (804) 786-9477
Hist. Note: Established September 17, 1888 at Georgetown University, Washington, DC as the Ass'n of American Anatomists. Name changed in 1908 to American Ass'n of Anatomists. Incorporated in New York in 1947. Regular membership: $40/yr.
Publications:
The American Journal of Anatomy. m.
The Anatomical Record. m.
Annual Meetings: Spring
1987-Washington, DC(Hilton)/May 10-14/1,700
1988-Cincinnati, OH/April 24-28

American Ass'n of Attorney-Certified Public Accountants (1964)
24001 Alicia Parkway, Suite 101, Mission Viejo CA 92691
Exec. Director: Ronald M. DeVore
Members: 1,200 *Staff:* 2
Annual Budget: $100-250,000 *Tel:* (714) 768-0336
Hist. Note: Members are individuals "dually licensed" as both lawyer and CPA. Annual membership dues: $100/yr.
Publications:
The Attorney-CPA Quarterly. bi-m. adv.
Bulletin. a.
Membership List. a. adv.
Semi-annual meetings: Spring and Fall
1987-Jackson Hole, WY(Spring Creek Ranch)/June 27-July 3
1987-San Antonio, TX(Four Seasons)/Nov.
1988-Seattle, WA/June
1988-Albuquerque, NM/Nov.

American Ass'n of Avian Pathologists (1957)
Univ. of Penn., New Bolton Center, Kennett Square PA 19348
Secy.-Treas.: Dr. Robert J. Eckroade
Members: 755 individuals *Staff:* 1
Annual Budget: $100-250,000 *Tel:* (215) 444-5800
Hist. Note: Veterinarians specializing in birds and their diseases. Affiliated with the American Veterinary Medical Ass'n. Membership: $35/yr. (individual).
Publications:
Avian Diseases. q. adv.
Directory. bien.
Annual Meetings: With the American Veterinary Medical Ass'n, in July
1987-Chicago, IL
1988-Portland, OR
1989-Orlando, FL
1990-San Antonio, TX
1991-Seattle, WA

American Ass'n of Bible Colleges (1947)
P.O. Box 1523, Fayetteville AR 72701
Associate Director: Dr. Gary D. Matson
Members: 100-110 colleges *Staff:* 2-5
Annual Budget: $100-250,000 *Tel:* (501) 521-8164
Hist. Note: Colleges, it became the Accrediting Ass'n of Bible Colleges in 1957 Established as the Accrediting Ass'n of Bible Institutes and Bible Bible Colleges, it became the Accrediting Association of Bible and assumed its present name in 1973. Member association of the Council on Postsecondary Education. Incorporated in the State of Illinois. The primary purpose of Bible colleges is to prepare students for church-related vocations.
Publication:
Newsletter. q.
Annual Meetings: Always the last Thursday through Saturday in October/425

American Ass'n of Bioanalysts (1956)
818 Olive, Suite 918, St. Louis MO 63101
Administrator: David Birenbaum
Members: 1,200 *Staff:* 6-10
Annual Budget: $250-500,000 *Tel:* (314) 241-1445
Hist. Note: Merger of Council of American Bioanalysts (founded in 1953) and the National Association of Clinical Laboratories (founded in 1949). Members are directors, managers, and supervisors of medical laboratories concerned with improving laboratory testing and procedures. Membership: $200/yr. (directors), $60/yr. (managers, supervisors).
Publications:
The Bulletin. bi-m. adv.
Test of the Month. m.
Annual Meetings: Spring
1987-Grand Traverse, MI(Grand Traverse Resort)/May 18-22
1988-San Diego, CA(Hotel del Coronado)/May

00016 12 05 86 1233

American Ass'n of Biofeedback Clinicians (1976)
2424 Dempster St., Des Plaines IL 60016
Nat'l Director: Dr. Jeanine Gavin
Members: 1,200 *Staff:* 2-5
Annual Budget: $50-100,000 *Tel:* (312) 827-0440
Hist. Note: Incorporated in the State of Illinois, the AABC takes as its members individuals interested in behavioral medicine and the use of biofeedback techniques for exploring the processes of the human body. Membership: $60/yr.
Publications:
Clinical Biofeedback and Health. semi-a.
The Biofeedback Clinician. q.
Annual Meetings: Fall

American Ass'n of Black Women Entrepreneurs (1982)
814 Thayer Ave., Suite 202, Silver Spring MD 20910
Nat'l President: Brenda Alford
Members: 660 *Staff:* 4
Annual Budget: $50-100,000 *Tel:* (301) 231-3751
Hist. Note: Purpose is to bring black women into the mainstream of the American economic system. Membership: $40-50/yr. (individual); $300/yr. (organization/company)
Publication:
Souvenir Journal. a. adv.
Annual Meetings: Summer
1987-Washington, DC/July 21-25

American Ass'n of Blood Banks (1947)
1117 North 19th St., Suite 600, Arlington VA 22209
Exec. Director: Gilbert M. Clark
Members: 7,000 individuals, 2,400 institutions *Staff:* 40-45
Annual Budget: $2-5,000,000 *Tel:* (703) 528-8200
Hist. Note: Scientists, physicians, nurses, medical technologists and administrators concerned with blood banking and blood transfusion services. Membership $40/yr.
Publications:
News Brief. m.
Transfusion. bi-m. adv.
Blood Bank Week. w.
Annual Meetings: Fall

American Ass'n of Botanical Gardens and Arboreta (1940)
Box 206, Swarthmore PA 19081
Exec. Director: Susan H. Lathrop
Members: 900-1,000 individuals and institutions *Staff:* 2-5
Annual Budget: $100-250,000 *Tel:* (215) 328-9145
Hist. Note: Promotes the botanical, horticultural and educational advancement of botanical gardens and arboreta. Membership: $40/yr.
Publications:
The Public Garden: Journal of the AABGA. q. adv.
Newsletter. m.
Annual Meetings: June/200
1987-Glencoe, IL/June 17-20
1988-Phoenix, AZ

American Ass'n of Bovine Practicioners (1965)
Box 2319, West Lafayette IN 47906
Exec. Secretary: Dr. Harold Amstutz
Members: 5,600 *Staff:* 2-5
Annual Budget: $250-500,000 *Tel:* (317) 494-8560
Hist. Note: Membership is restricted to veterinarians. Membership: $35/yr.
Publication:
Bovine Practitioner. a. adv.
Annual Meetings: Fall/1,500
1987-Phoenix, AZ(Hyatt)/Nov. 10-13/1,600
1988-Calgary, Alberta/Nov. 15-18
1989-Kansas City, MO(Vista International)/1,500

American Ass'n of Business Brokers (1978)
Hist. Note: Reported in 1982 as being defunct.

American Ass'n of Cable TV Owners (1977)
Hist. Note: Inactive since 1983; possible reorganization in 1987.

American Ass'n of Candy Technologists
175 Rock Road, Glen Rock NJ 07452
Secy.-Treas.: Allan R. Allured
Members: 600 individuals *Staff:* 1
Annual Budget: under $10,000 *Tel:* (201) 652-2655
Hist. Note: Has no paid staff. Membership: $25/yr.
Annual Meetings: September

American Ass'n of Ceramic Industries (1925)
1100-H Brandywine Blvd., P.O. Box 2188, Zanesville OH 43702
President: Walter E. Offinger
Members: 60 individuals
Annual Budget: under $10,000 *Tel:* (614) 452-4541
Hist. Note: AACI includes corporations and both corporate and non-corporate individuals in the ceramic industry. Membership: $40/yr. (individual); $100/yr. (corporate)
Publication:
AACI Newsletter. bi-m.
Annual Meetings: October

American Ass'n of Cereal Chemists (1915)
3340 Pilot Knob Rd., St. Paul MN 55121
Exec. V. President: Raymond J. Tarleton
Members: 3,400 *Staff:* 15-20
Annual Budget: $1-2,000,000 *Tel:* (612) 454-7250
Hist. Note: Founded in 1915 at Kansas City, MO, it merged in 1923 with the American Soc. of Milling and Baking Technology; incorporated in Minnesota in 1956. The administrative affiliate of the American Phytopathological Soc., AACC encourages research in cereal grains and related materials, processing and utilization. Membership: $60/yr. (individual), $175/yr. (company).
Publications:
Cereal Chemistry. bi-m.
Cereal Foods World. m. adv.
Annual Meetings: Fall/1,500
1987-Nashville, TN(Opryland)/Nov. 1-5/1,600
1988-San Diego, CA(InterContinental)/Oct. 9-13
1989-Washington, DC(Sheraton Park)/Oct. 29-Nov. 2

American Ass'n of Certified Allergists (1968)
Box 520, Mount Prospect IL 60056
Exec. Director: Joseph J. Lotharius
Members: 500 *Staff:* 2
Annual Budget: $10-25,000 *Tel:* (312) 255-1024
Hist. Note: Membership: $40/yr.
Publication:
President's Newsletter. semi-a.
Annual Meetings: With American Academy of Allergy & American College or Allergists

American Ass'n of Certified Appraisers (1977)
Seven Eswin Drive, Cincinnati OH 45218
Exec. Director: Richard M. Walkenhorst
Members: 2,600-2,700 *Staff:* 3-7
Annual Budget: $100-250,000 *Tel:* (800) 543-2222
Hist. Note: Members are real estate appraisers. Membership: $115/yr. (individual).
Publication:
The Clipboard. bi-m. adv.

American Ass'n of Certified Orthoptists (1940)
NY Eye and Ear Infirmary, 310 East 14th St., New York NY 10003
President: Sara Shippman
Members: 400-450 *Staff:* 1
Annual Budget: $25-50,000
Hist. Note: Founded October 8, 1940 in Cleveland as the American Ass'n of Orthoptic Technicians, it became American Ass'n of Certified Orthoptists in 1966. A charter member of the Internat'l Orthoptic Ass'n and member of the American Orthoptic Council. Membership: $50/yr.
Publications:
AACO Directory. a.
American Orthoptic Journal. a. adv.
Prism. q. adv.
Annual Meetings: With American Academy of Ophthalmology

American Ass'n of Chairmen of Departments of Psychiatry (1967)
Dept. of Psychiatry, OCHSC, 4200 East 9th, Denver CO 80262
Secretary-Treasurer: James H. Shore, M.D.
Members: 120 *Staff:* 1
Annual Budget: $10-25,000 *Tel:* (303) 394-5248
Hist. Note: Chairmen of psychiatry departments in medical schools. Affiliated with the Ass'n of American Medical Colleges and the Council of Academic Societies.
Annual Meetings:
1987-Chicago, IL/May 10

American Ass'n of Children's Residential Centers (1957)
440 First St., N.W., Suite 310, Washington DC 20001
Exec. Secretary: Claudia Waller
Members: 60 institutions, 200 individuals *Staff:* 1
Annual Budget: $50-100,000 *Tel:* (202) 638-1604
Hist. Note: Concerned with maintaining and enhancing sound clinical practice in residential treatment for children with emotional problems. Membership includes psychologists, psychiatrists, social workers, educators and child care specialists, as well as residential treatment agencies. A member of the National Consortium for Child Mental Health Services. Membership: $35/yr.(individual); $750/yr.(agency)
Publications:
Contributions to Residential Treatment. a.
Directory of Organization Members. a.
Newsletter. m.
Annual Meetings: October/150

American Ass'n of Classified School Employees (1958)
2000 Pennsylvania Ave., N.W., Suite 3700, Washington DC 20006
Exec. Director: Craig J. Rancourt
Members: 200,000 *Staff:* 190
Annual Budget: $1-2,000,000 *Tel:* (202) 429-9725
Hist. Note: An independent labor union of public school employees in non-teaching positions. Membership dues: $1.80/year.
Publication:
Classified Times. q. adv.
Annual Meetings: July

American Ass'n of Clinical Urologists (1969)
21510 South Main St., Carson CA 90745
Exec. Director: Frank De Santis
Members: 800 *Staff:* 1
Annual Budget: $50-100,000 *Tel:* (213) 549-3470
Hist. Note: Auxilary of the American Urological Ass'n Membership: $60/yr.
Annual Meetings: With American Urological Ass'n

American Ass'n of College Baseball Coaches (1945)
Hist. Note: Became the American Baseball Coaches Ass'n in 1985.

American Ass'n of Colleges for Teacher Education (1917)
One Dupont Circle, N.W., Suite 610, Washington DC 20036
Exec. Director: David G. Imig
Members: 760 institutions *Staff:* 30
Annual Budget: $500-1,000,000 *Tel:* (202) 293-2450
Hist. Note: Formed by a merger of the American Ass'n of Teachers Colleges, the Nat'l Ass'n of Colleges and Departments of Education and the Nat'l Ass'n of Teacher Education Institutions of Metropolitan Districts. Affiliated with Associated Organizations for Professionals in Education and the ERIC Clearinghouse on Teacher Education.
Publications:
AACTE Briefs. 10/yr. adv.
Journal of Teacher Education. bi-m. adv.
Annual Meetings: February
1987-Arlington, VA(Crystal Gateway Marriott)/Feb. 12-15/1,500
1988-New Orleans, LA(Hyatt Regency)/Feb. 17-20/1,500

American Ass'n of Colleges of Nursing (1969)
One Dupont Circle, N.W., Suite 530, Washington DC 20036
Exec. Director: Dr. Barbara K. Redman
Members: 382 schools of nursing *Staff:* 10
Annual Budget: $500-1,000,000 *Tel:* (202) 463-6930
Hist. Note: Established to answer the need for a national organization exclusively devoted to furthering the goals of baccalaureate and graduate education in nursing. Formerly (1973) American Ass'n of Deans of University and College Schools of Nursing. Member of the Coalition for Health Funding in Washington.
Publication:
Newsletter. m.
Semi-annual meetings: Washington, DC
1987-Washington, DC(Marriott)/March 21-24/250
1987-Washington, DC(Marriott)/Oct. 3-6/250

American Ass'n of Colleges of Osteopathic Medicine (1898)
6110 Executive Blvd., Suite 405, Rockville MD 20852
Exec. Director: Sherry R. Arnstein
Members: 15 institutions *Staff:* 11-15
Annual Budget: $1-2,000,000 *Tel:* (301) 468-0990
Hist. Note: Established a national headquarters and permanent staff in 1972. Operates centralized application processing service.

American Ass'n of Colleges of Pharmacy (1900)
4720 Montgomery Lane, Suite 602, Bethesda MD 20814
Exec. Director: Carl E. Trinca
Members: 70-75 institutions, 1,600 individuals *Staff:* 6-10
Annual Budget: $1-2,000,000 *Tel:* (301) 654-9060
Hist. Note: Founded in May 1900 as the American Conference of Pharmaceutical Faculties. Became the American Ass'n of Colleges of Pharmacy in August 1925. Promotes pharmaceutical education and research. Includes a few foreign institutions. Member of the Coalition for Health Funding in Washington and the Federation of Ass'ns of Schools of the Health Professions.
Publications:
AACP News. m. adv.
American Journal of Pharmaceutical Education. q. adv.
Annual Meetings: Summer
1987-Charleston, SC(Omni)/July 12-15

American Ass'n of Colleges of Podiatric Medicine (1932)
6110 Executive Blvd., Suite 204, Rockville MD 20852
President: Anthony J. McNevin
Members: 7 colleges, 175 hospitals and individuals *Staff:* 6-10
Annual Budget: $500-1,000,000 *Tel:* (301) 984-9350
Hist. Note: Established as the American Association of Colleges of Chiropady, it then became the American Association of Colleges of Podiatry and assumed its present name in 1968. Member of the Coalition for Health Funding in Washington and the Federation of Associations of Schools of the Health Professions. Membership: $20/yr. (individual).
Publications:
Journal of Podiatric Medical Education. semi-a.
AACPM Newsletter. 3/yr.
Annual Meetings: June/80
1987-Washington, DC
1988-Chicago, IL
1989-New York, NY
1990-Philadelphia, PA

American Ass'n of Collegiate Registrars and Admissions Officers (1910)
One Dupont Circle, N.W., Suite 330, Washington DC 20036
Exec. Director: J. Douglas Conner
Members: 7,600 individuals representing 2,100 institutions
Staff: 11-15
Annual Budget: $1-2,000,000 *Tel:* (202) 293-9161
Hist. Note: Founded in 1910 in Detroit as the American Ass'n of College Registrars.
Publication:
College and University. q.
Annual Meetings: Spring/2,500
1987-Las Vegas, NV/April 19-24
1988-Nashville, TN(Opryland)/April 17-22

00017 12 05 86 1233

1989-Chicago, IL(Palmer House)/April 16-21
1990-New Orleans, LA(Hilton Riverside)/April 15-20
1991-Honolulu, HI(Hilton Hawaiian Village)/April 14-19

American Ass'n of Commodity Traders (1965)
Hist. Note: Not a trade association in the accepted sense. This is a privately run outfit, the core of whose so-called membership in 1979 was the body of subscribers to the Commodity Journal, published in New York City.

American Ass'n of Community and Junior Colleges (1920)
One Dupont Circle, N.W., Suite 410, Washington DC 20036
President: Dr. Dale Parnell
Members: 1,000 two-year colleges *Staff:* 30-40
Annual Budget: $2-5,000,000 *Tel:* (202) 293-7050
Hist. Note: Formerly (1972) American Ass'n of Junior Colleges. Membership consists of tax-exempt community, technical and junior colleges which are not private foundations.
Publications:
Community, Technical and Junior College Journal. bi-m. adv.
AACJC Letter. bi-w.
Annual Meetings: April/2,500
1987-Dallas, TX(Loew's Anatole)

American Ass'n of Computer Professionals (1985)
72 Valley Hill Rd., Stockbridge GA 30281
President: Dr. Nancy W. Kelly
Members: 400 individuals *Staff:* 3
Annual Budget: under $10,000 *Tel:* (404) 474-7874
Hist. Note: 4 AACP's primary purpose is to establish and promote high standards for computer professionals and to endorse those who qualify. Membership: $100/yr.
Annual Meetings: Fall

American Ass'n of Correctional Officers (1977)
Hist. Note: Became the Internat'l Ass'n of Correctional Officers in 1986.

American Ass'n of Correctional Training Personnel (1974)
7264 Casablanca Drive, Tucson AZ 85704
Secy.-Treas.: David A. Gaspar
Members: 350 *Staff:* 0
Annual Budget: under $10,000 *Tel:* (602) 297-8276
Hist. Note: Formed in Carbondale, IL to improve the quality of correctional training. An affiliate of the American Correctional Ass'n. Membership: $15/yr. (individual); $25/yr. (institution).
Publication:
Correctional Training Journal. q. adv.
Annual Meetings: With the American Correctional Ass'n

American Ass'n of Cosmetic Surgeons (1969)
Hist. Note: Merged with the American Soc. for Cosmetic Surgery to form the American Academy of Cosmetic Surgery in 1985.

American Ass'n of Cost Engineers (1956)
308 Monongahela Bldg., Morgantown WV 26505
Exec. Director: Kenneth K. Humphreys
Members: 6,100 *Staff:* 6-10
Annual Budget: $500-1,000,000 *Tel:* (304) 296-8444
Hist. Note: A professional society of individuals interested in applying scientific principles to the solution of problems of cost estimating, cost control, planning and scheduling, project management, and profitability. Membership: $60/yr.
Publications:
Cost Engineering. m. adv.
Cost Engineers Notebook. irreg.
Directory. a.
Transactions. a.
Annual Meetings: June or July/1,000
1987-Atlanta, GA(Hilton)/June 28-July 1
1988-New York, NY(July 10-13
1989-San Diego, CA(Town & Country)/June 25-28
1990-Boston, MA(Marriott/Westin)/June 24-27
1991-Seattle, WA(Red Lion Inn/Sea Tac)/June 23-26
1992-Orlando, FL(Marriott World Ctr.)/June 28-July 1
1993-Dearborn, MI(Hyatt Regency)/July 5-9
1994-San Francisco, CA(Marriott)/June 26-29

American Ass'n of Credit Counselors (1955)
Box 372, Grayslake IL 60030
Exec. Secretary: H. Don Morris
Members: 80-90 *Staff:* 1
Annual Budget: under $10,000 *Tel:* (312) 223-0355
Hist. Note: Membership: $50/yr., plus $20/yr./employee to maximum of $200/yr.

American Ass'n of Criminology (1953)
Hist. Note: Founded in 1953 and incorporated in 1955. Members are police and professional criminologists. Address unknown in 1983.

American Ass'n of Critical-Care Nurses (1969)
One Civic Plaza, Newport Beach CA 92660
Exec. Director: Sandra Edson
Members: 55,000 *Staff:* 45-50
Annual Budget: $2-5,000,000 *Tel:* (714) 644-9310
Hist. Note: Founded September 22, 1969 at the Second Cardiac Nursing Symposium, as the American Association of Cardiovascular Nurses. Assumed its present name in 1972. Members are nurses in all areas of critical care, such as hemodialysis, burn care and cardiac intensive care. Membership: $45/yr.
Publications:
Focus on Critical Care.
Heart and Lung, the Journal of Critical Care.
Annual Meetings: Spring/4-5,000
1987-New Orleans(Conv. Center)/May 4-7
1988-Dallas(Conv. Center)/May 8-13

American Ass'n of Crop Insurers (1983)
2501 M St., N.W., #430, Washington DC 20037
Exec. V. President: E. Eugene Gantz
Members: 23 companies *Staff:* 4
Annual Budget: $500-1,000,000 *Tel:* (202) 463-0541
Hist. Note: Members are private sector companies that provide crop insurance protection to farmers. Annual dues vary.
Publication:
Agent Newsletter. q.
Annual Meetings: Feb./March

American Ass'n of Dealers in Ancient, Oriental and Primitive Art (1968)
122 East 93rd St., New York NY 10128
President: Douglas C. Ewing
Members: 60
Annual Budget: under $10,000 *Tel:* (212) 722-1099
Hist. Note: Has no permanent office or staff. Operates from the address of the President.

American Ass'n of Dental Consultants (1977)
5373 Hyland Place, Bloomington MN 55437
Secy.-Treas.: Bruce Keyworth, D.D.S.
Members: 180 *Staff:* 1
Annual Budget: under $10,000 *Tel:* (612) 829-3300
Hist. Note: Members are dental insurance consultants to insurance companies, hospitals, government offices, etc. Membership: $50/year.
Publication:
The Beacon. semi-a.
Annual Meetings: In conjunction with the American Dental Association in October.
1987-Dallas, TX(Westin)/April 24-26
1988-Denver, CO

American Ass'n of Dental Editors (1931)
941 Winona, Chicago IL 60640
Exec. Director: Christine Nolen Taylor
Members: 300 *Staff:* 2
Annual Budget: $10-25,000 *Tel:* (312) 878-0574
Publications:
AADE Editor's Journal. a.
Newsletter. q.
Annual Meetings: With the American Dental Association
1987-Las Vegas, NV(Hilton)/Oct. 9-11/75

American Ass'n of Dental Examiners (1883)
211 E. Chicago Ave., Suite 2134, Chicago IL 60611
Exec. Director: Molly S. Nadler
Members: 700-750 *Staff:* 1
Annual Budget: $50-100,000 *Tel:* (312) 440-7464
Hist. Note: Formerly the National Association of Dental Examiners, members are present and former members of state dental examining boards.
Publications:
The Bulletin. q.
Proceedings. a.
Annual Meetings: Fall/150
1987-Las Vegas, NV(MGM Grand)/Oct. 7-9
1988-Washington, DC/Oct. 5-7
1989-Honolulu, HI/Nov. 1-3

American Ass'n of Dental Schools (1923)
1625 Massachusetts Ave., N. W., Suite 400, Washington DC 20036
Exec. Director: Richard D. Mumma, D.D.S.
Members: 200-500 organization, 3-4,000 individuals *Staff:* 18-20
Annual Budget: $1-2,000,000 *Tel:* (202) 667-9433
Hist. Note: Founded in Omaha January 24, 1923 through the merger of the American Institute of Dental Teachers, Canadian Dental Faculties' Ass'n, Nat'l Ass'n of Dental Faculties and the Dental Faculties' Ass'n of American Universities. Incorporated in Illinois in 1960. Membership includes all U.S. dental schools and many other dental institutions in Canada and the U.S.
Publications:
Bulletin of Dental Education. m.
Journal of Dental Education. m. adv.
Annual Meetings: March/1,500
1987-Chicago, IL(Hyatt Regency)/March 8-11
1988-Montreal(Convention Center)/March 5-9

American Ass'n of Diabetes Educators (1974)
500 N. Michigan Ave., Suite 1400, Chicago IL 60611
Exec. Director: Kate Doyle
Members: 3,000 *Staff:* 2-5
Annual Budget: $500-1,000,000 *Tel:* (312) 661-1700
Hist. Note: Nurses, dietitians, physicians and other allied health professionals involved in teaching self-management to the diabetic Membership: $45/yr.
Publications:
AADE Newsletter. 10/yr.
The Diabetes Educator. q. adv.
Annual Meetings: August-September
1987-Orlando, FL(Marriott)/Sept. 9-13/1,100
1988-Dallas, TX(Convention Center/Hyatt)/Aug. 24-27
1989-Seattle, WA/Aug. 24-27

American Ass'n of Disability Communicators (1983)
2100 Pennsylvania Ave., N.W., Suite 232, Washington DC 20037
President: Robert H. Ruffner
Members: 100 companies; 800 individuals
Annual Budget: under $10,000 *Tel:* (202) 293-5960
Hist. Note: Founded in 1983 by the President's Committee on Employment of the Handicapped and the Nat'l Organization on Disability, AADC is a professional association of writers, editors, journalists, public relations people and broadcasters involved with disability. It holds "media and disability" workshops in the U.S. and Europe two or three times a year; offers professional advice and enrichment. Membership: $25/yr. (individual); $150/yr. (organization)
Publication:
AADC News. q.
Annual Meetings: Spring
1987-Denver, CO(Westin Hotel)/April 22-24
1988-Washington, DC(Washington Hilton)

American Ass'n of Economic Developers (1978)
Hist. Note: Defunct in 1981.

American Ass'n of Electromyography and Electrodiagnosis (1953)
732 Marquette Bank Bldg., Rochester MN 55904
Exec. Director: Ella M. VanLaningham
Members: 2,029 *Staff:* 2-5
Annual Budget: $500-1,000,000 *Tel:* (507) 288-0100
Hist. Note: Founded in 1953 to increase and extend as widely as possible the knowledge of electromyography and electrodiagnosis and to promote the professional association of those physicians and surgeons most interested in electromyography and electrodiagnosis. Membership: $125/yr. (individual); $500/yr. (company).
Publications:
Minimonographs. irreg.
Case Reports. irreg.
Annual Meetings: Fall
1987-San Antonio, TX(Hyatt Regency)/Oct. 15-17/800
1988-San Diego, CA/Oct. 6-9/835
1989-Washington, DC(Shoreham)/Sept. 14-17/870
1990-Chicago, IL(Hyatt Regency)/Sept. 6-9

American Ass'n of Endodontists (1943)
211 E. Chicago Ave., Suite 1501, Chicago IL 60611
Exec. Director: Irma S. Kudo
Members: 3,200 *Staff:* 5
Annual Budget: $500-1,000,000 *Tel:* (312) 266-7255
Hist. Note: Established February 25, 1943 in Chicago. Incorporated in Illinois in 1955. Promotes research on pulp conservation and endodontic treatment. Sponsors the American Board of Endodontics and the AAE Endowment and Memorial Foundation. Membership: $150/yr.
Publication:
Journal of Endodontics. m.
Annual Meetings: April/1,600
1987-San Antonio, TX(Hilton and Hyatt)/April 29-May 3
1988-Anaheim, CA(Marriott)/April 20-24/1,700

American Ass'n of Engineering Societies (1946)
415 2nd St., N.E., Suite 200, Washington DC 20002
Exec. Director: Daniel V. DeSimone
Members: 22 societies *Staff:* 12
Annual Budget: $1-2,000,000 *Tel:* (202) 546-2237
Hist. Note: Formerly the Engineers Joint Council, AAES is a multidisciplinary organization representing over 500,000 engineers in industry, government and education.
Publications:
Directory of Engineering Socs. & Related Orgs. bi-a.
Engineering Manpower Bulletin. 5/yr.
Who's Who in Engineering. bi-&tri-a.
Engineers' Salaries: Special Industry Report. a.
Engineering and Technology Degrees. a.
Engineering & Technology Enrollments. a.
Thesaurus of Engineering and Scientific Terms.
Professional Income of Engineers. a.
Salaries of Engineers in Education. bien.
Annual Meetings: April/100
1987-Williamsburg, VA(Hilton)/April 7-8
1988-Rancho Bernardo, CA/April 6-8

American Ass'n of Equine Practitioners (1955)
Route 5, 22363 Hillcrest Circle, Golden CO 80401
Exec. Director: Brig. Ge Wayne O. Kester, USAF(VC) R
Members: 4,500 *Staff:* 2-5
Annual Budget: $100-250,000 *Tel:* (303) 526-0820
Hist. Note: Members are veterinarians who specialise in horses.
Publications:
Newsletter. 3/yr.
Proceedings Book. a.
Annual Meetings: December
1987-New Orleans, LA
1988-San Diego, CA
1989-Boston, MA
1990-Lexington, KY
1991-San Francisco, CA
1992-Orlando, FL

American Ass'n of Equipment Lessors (1961)
1300 North 17th St., Suite 1010, Arlington VA 22209
President: Michael J. Fleming

00018 12 05 86 1233

Members: 950 companies *Staff:* 6-10
Annual Budget: $2-5,000,000 *Tel:* (703) 527-8655
Hist. Note: Founded as the Ass'n of Equipment Lessors, it assumed its present name in 1974. Members are companies whose principal business is leasing equipment to other users. Sponsors the American Ass'n of Equipment Lessors Capital Investment-Lease Political Action Committee.
Publications:
AAEL News Bulletin. m.
Journal of Equipment Lease Finance. q.
Annual Meetings: Fall
1987-San Francisco, CA(Fairmont Hotel)/Oct. 4-7/1,500
1988-Washington, DC(Washington Sheraton)/Oct. 12-15/1,500
1989-Las Vegas, NV(MGM Grand)/Oct. 20-Nov. 1/1,500

American Ass'n of Esthetics (1956)
113 South Pine St., Hammond LA 70401
President: Mary Tatum Zatariam
Members: 5,000-5,500 *Staff:* 1
Annual Budget: $100-250,000 *Tel:* (504) 542-4320
Hist. Note: Also known as SEDESCO-USA, AAE is the U. S. Branch of SEDESCO, an international association of cosmetologists located in Paris, France. An affiliate of the Nat'l Hairdressers and Cosmetologists Ass'n. Active members are licensed cosmeticians, make-up artists, and skin-care specialists. Membership: $55/yr.
Publication:
Newsletter. irreg.
Annual Meetings:
1987-New York, NY/August/300

American Ass'n of Exporters and Importers (1921)
30th Floor, 11 West 42nd St., New York NY 10036
President: Eugene J. Milosh
Members: 1,000 *Staff:* 11-15
Annual Budget: $500-1,000,000 *Tel:* (212) 944-2230
Hist. Note: Formed in 1921 as the National Council of American Importers with some two dozen member firms in response to protectionism then rampant in America. Until then, no organized national voice represented the interests of a liberal trade policy affecting the consumer and import trade. Became the American Importers Association in 1967 and assumed its present name in 1981. Supports the American Internat'l Trade Political Affairs Committee. Membership fee: depends on volume of business.
Publications:
International Trade Alert. d.
Newsletter. q.

American Ass'n of Feed Microscopists (1953)
1118 Apple Dr., Mechanicsburg PA 17055
Secy.-Treas.: Janet B. Windsor
Members: 300-350 *Staff:* 1
Annual Budget: under $10,000 *Tel:* (717) 766-6039
Hist. Note: A professional society, incorporated in Kentucky, of microscopic analysts for feed manufacturers and state feed control agencies.
Publication:
Proceedings. a.
Annual Meetings: June
1987-St. Louis, MO(Holiday Inn Riverside)/June 21-24/100
1988-Minneapolis, MN

American Ass'n of Feline Practitioners (1970)
5712 Telegraph Road, St. Louis MO 63129
Exec. Secretary: Sharon L. Klingler
Members: 600-700 *Staff:* 1
Annual Budget: under $10,000 *Tel:* (314) 846-6505
Hist. Note: Veterinarians specializing in the treatment of cats. Membership: $25/yr.
Publication:
Journal of the A.A.F.P. semi-a.
Semi-annual Meetings:
1987-Copper Mountain, CO(Copper Mountain Resort)Feb. 7-11/50-75
1987-Hawaii

American Ass'n of Fitness Directors in Business and Industry (1974)
Hist. Note: Became Ass'n for Fitness in Business in 1983.

American Ass'n of Food Stamp Directors (1975)
1125 15th St., N.W., Suite 300, Washington DC 20005
Staff contact: Maura Cullen
Members: 300 *Staff:* 1
Tel: (202) 293-7550
Hist. Note: A constituent unit of the American Public Welfare Association.
Annual Meetings: Fall
1987-Kalispell, MT/Oct. 4-7/250

American Ass'n of Foot Specialists (1958)
1801 Vauxhall Rd., Union NJ 07083
Exec. Secretary: Dr. Jerome J. Erman
Members: 900-1,000 *Staff:* 1
Annual Budget: under $10,000 *Tel:* (201) 688-1616
Hist. Note: Sponsors the American College for Continuing Education for doctors of podiatric medicine; sponsors twelve Educational Conferences each year.
Annual Meetings:
1987-Swan Lake, NY/Aug.

American Ass'n of Foundations for Medical Care (1970)
Hist. Note: Became the American Medical Care and Review Association in 1983.

American Ass'n of Fund-Raising Counsel (1935)
25 West 43 St., New York NY 10036
President: John J. Schwartz
Members: 32 companies *Staff:* 8
Annual Budget: $500-1,000,000 *Tel:* (212) 354-5799
Publications:
Fund Raising Review. semi-m.
Giving-U.S.A. a.
Annual Meetings: November in New York, NY

American Ass'n of Genito-Urinary Surgeons (1886)
Mayo Clinic, Rochester MN 55905
Secy.-Treas.: D.C. Utz, M.D.
Members: 180-190 *Staff:* 1
Annual Budget: under $10,000 *Tel:* (507) 284-3983
Hist. Note: Organized October 16, 1886 in New York City. Has no paid staff.
Annual Meetings: Spring
1987-Southampton, Bermuda(Southampton Princess)/April 9-12
1988-Sea Island, GA(Cloisters)/April 20-23

American Ass'n of Gynecological Laparoscopists (1972)
13021 E. Florence Ave., Santa Fe Springs CA 90670
Chairman: Dr. Jordan M. Phillips
Members: 4,300 *Staff:* 10
Annual Budget: $500-1,000,000 *Tel:* (213) 946-8774
Hist. Note: Obstetricians and gynecologists interested in gynecological endoscopy, the process by which the insides of hollow organs are visualized.
Publication:
Newscope. q. adv.
Annual Meetings: Fall
1987-San Francisco, CA(Sheraton Palace)/Nov. 10-15/250
1988-Dallas, TX(Loew's Anatole)/Nov. 8-12/250
1989-Washington, DC(Sheraton Washington)/Nov. 15-19/250

American Ass'n of Handwriting Analysts (1963)
820 West Maple, Hinsdale IL 60521
V. President, Public Relations: Rose Matousek
Members: 400 *Staff:* 1
Annual Budget: $10-25,000 *Tel:* (312) 325-2266
Hist. Note: Members are proficient in the science of analyzing character through handwriting. Seeks public recognition of the usefulness of handwriting analysis in the authentication of documents and in describing the personality of a writer for counseling, therapy and personnel purposes. Membership: $45/yr.
Publications:
AAHA Newsletter. bi-m.
Annals. a.
Annual Meetings: July

American Ass'n of Healthcare Consultants (1949)
1235 Jefferson Davis Highway, Ste. 602, Arlington VA 22202
President: Vaughan A. Smith
Members: 250 *Staff:* 2-5
Annual Budget: $250-500,000 *Tel:* (703) 979-3180
Hist. Note: Formerly (1984) the American Ass'n of Hospital Consultants. Membership: $480/yr. (plus a firm fee based on professional staff size).
Publications:
Directory of Affiliated Firms. a.
Directory of Individual Members. a.
Semi-annual Meetings:
1987-Sarasota, FL(Old Colony)/March 7-11/100-150
1987-Atlanta, GA
1988-San Diego, CA(Del Coronado)
1988-New Orleans, LA

American Ass'n of Homeopathic Pharmacists (1922)
Box 2273, Falls Church VA 22042
Exec. Director: Helen R. Burton
Members: 17 companies *Staff:* 1
Annual Budget: under $10,000 *Tel:* (703) 532-3237
Hist. Note: Members are manufacturers and distributors of homeopathic remedies and products. Membership: $500/year.

American Ass'n of Homes for the Aging (1961)
1129 20th St., N.W., Suite 400, Washington DC 20036
Exec. V. President: Sheldon L. Goldberg
Members: 2,900 facilities *Staff:* 48
Annual Budget: over $5,000,000 *Tel:* (202) 296-5960
Hist. Note: Primary membership consists of community-based, non-profit nursing homes, independent housing, continuing care communities and homes for the aging. Individuals with an interest in long term care and housing for the aged may join as associate members. Membership: $85/year (individual), $495/year (company).
Publications:
Nonprofit Provider News. bi-w.
Continuing Education Update. semi-a.
Directory of Members. a.
Housing Digest. bi-m.
Legal Memo. bi-m.
Annual Meetings: Fall/2800
1987-Louisville, KY(Conv. Center)/Oct. 12-15
1988-Orland, FL(Marriott World Center)
1989-Baltimore, MD(Conv. Center)/Nov. 6-9
1990-New Orleans, LA(Conv. Center-Hilton)/Nov. 5-8

American Ass'n of Hospital Consultants (1948)
Hist. Note: Became the American Ass'n of Healthcare Consultants in 1984.

American Ass'n of Hospital Dentists (1961)
211 East Chicago Ave., Chicago IL 60611
Exec. Director: Dr. Paul R. Van Ostenberg
Members: 800-900 *Staff:* 2-5
Annual Budget: $100-250,000 *Tel:* (312) 440-2661
Hist. Note: Formerly (1968) American Ass'n of Hospital Dental Chiefs, Inc.
Publications:
Special Care in Dentistry. bi-m. adv.
Interface. q.
Annual Meetings: Fall
1987-Orlando, FL
1988-Boston, MA
1989-London, England

American Ass'n of Hospital Foundations (1980)
Hist. Note: Ceased operations in 1984.

American Ass'n of Housing Educators (1965)
Box 3 AE, New Mexico State University, Las Cruces NM 88003
Secretary: JoAnn Emmel
Members: 400 *Staff:* 1
Annual Budget: $10-25,000 *Tel:* (505) 646-3425
Hist. Note: Teachers, researchers, USDA extension workers, industry representatives and others interested in the field housing and educating the public about it. Formerly (until 1965) known as the Housing Conference to Improve Instruction. Membership: $40/yr.
Publications:
AAHE Newsletter. 3/yr.
Housing and Society. 3/yr.
Proceedings. a.
Annual Meetings: Fall/100
1987-Newport, RI

American Ass'n of Immunologists (1914)
9650 Rockville Pike, Bethesda MD 20814
Exec. Officer: Joseph Saunders, Ph.D.
Members: 4,760 *Staff:* 15
Annual Budget: $250-500,000 *Tel:* (301) 530-7178
Hist. Note: Originally conceived as The Soc. of Vaccine Therapists, the ass'n was founded in June 1913 with 56 charter members, most of whom worked in the laboratories of Sir Amlroth Wright, Mechnikov and Ehrlich. Incorporated in Minnesota in 1913. A member of the Federation of American Societies for Experimental Biology.
Publications:
Journal of Immunology. m. adv.
Newsletter. 3/yr.
Annual Meetings: With The Federation of American Societies for Experimental Biology
1987-Washington, DC/March 29-April 3
1988-Las Vegas, NV/May 1-6
1989-New Orleans, LA/March 19-24

American Ass'n of Independent News Distributors (1971)
Hist. Note: Address unknown in 1985-86.

American Ass'n of Individual Investors (1979)
612 North Michigan Ave., Chicago IL 60611
President: James B. Cloonan
Members: 97,000 *Staff:* 24
Annual Budget: $2-5,000,000 *Tel:* (312) 280-0170
Hist. Note: An independent non-profit corporation formed for the purpose of assisting individuals in becoming effective managers of their own assets through programs of education, information and research. Membership: $48/yr.
Publications:
AAII Journal. 10/year.
Computerized Investing. bi-m.
Annual Meetings:
1987-Boston, MA(Sheraton Boston)/July 12-14/400

American Ass'n of Industrial Management (1899)
Stearns Bldg., 293 Bridge St., Springfield MA 01103
President: Christy Karr
Members: 200-250 companies *Staff:* 11-15
Annual Budget: $100-250,000 *Tel:* (413) 737-8766
Hist. Note: Formerly (1965) Nat'l Metal Trades Ass'n. Concerned with labor and industrial relations, management training. Members are manufacturers, insurance companies and banks, town and city governments, universities and hospitals. A non-profit membership company.
Publications:
The Executive Manager. q.
Signs of the Times. q.
U.S. News Washington Business Report. m.

American Ass'n of Industrial Social Workers (1968)
6501 Wilson Mills Road, Suite K, Cleveland OH 44143
President: Dr. Donald W. Cole, RISW
Staff: 1
Annual Budget: under $10,000 *Tel:* (216) 461-4333

00019 12 05 86 1233

Hist. Note: A non-profit educational association organized to promote an understanding of industrial social work and employee assistance programs. Professional members may use the initials "RISW" after their name (Registered Industrial Social Worker). Membership: $40/yr.
Publications:
The Registry of Industrial Social Workers. a.
Newsletter. q.
Annual Meetings:
1987-Williams Bay, WI(George Williams College)/May 12-15

American Ass'n of Industrial Veterinarians (1954)
MOBAY, Animal Health Division, Box 390, Shawnee KS 66201
Secretary: Terry S. Wollen
Members: 425-475 *Staff:* 1
Annual Budget: under $10,000 *Tel:* (913) 268-3589
Hist. Note: Formerly (1976) Industrial Veterinarian's Ass'n. Has no paid staff.
Publications:
AAIV Highlights. semi-a.
Directory. a.
Annual Meetings: With American Veterinary Medical Ass'n

American Ass'n of Insurance Services (1936)
Hist. Note: Formed by merger of Mutual Marine Conference and Mutual Aircraft Conference. Formerly (1975) Transportation Insurance Rating Bureau. A national rating (advisory) organization and statistical agent for the property and casualty industry based in Bensenville, Illinois and licensed in all states. Also provides technical consulting services. Not a trade association.

American Ass'n of Language Specialists (1957)
1000 Connecticut Ave., N.W., Suite 9, Washington DC 20036
President: Anna Saxon-Forti
Members: 200-210
Annual Budget: under $10,000 *Tel:* (301) 657-2545
Hist. Note: Professional association representing interpreters, translators, and precis writers at the international level, either at conferences or in permanent organizations. Has no paid staff. Membership: $50/year.
Publication:
Yearbook. a.
Annual Meetings: December in New York, NY or Washington, DC

American Ass'n of Law Libraries (1906)
53 West Jackson Blvd., Chicago IL 60604
Exec. Director: William Jepson
Members: 4,100 individuals *Staff:* 6
Annual Budget: $500-1,000,000 *Tel:* (312) 939-4764
Hist. Note: Members are librarians of law libraries in schools, law firms, associations, the government, court systems and other institutions. Membership: $65/yr.
Publications:
Directory of Law Libraries. a.
Law Library Journal. q.
Newsletter. m.
Annual Meetings: Summer/1,500
1987-Chicago, IL(Hyatt)July 5-8/1,400
1988-Atlanta, GA(Marriott)June 26-29
1989-Reno, NV(MGM Grand)/June 18-21
1990-Minneapolis, MN(Hyatt)/June 24-27
1991-New Orleans, LA(Marriott)/June 16-19

American Ass'n of Managing General Agents (1926)
1001 Connecticut Ave., N.W. #800, Washington DC 20036
Exec. V. President: Randy Dyer, CAE
Members: 325 *Staff:* 2-5
Annual Budget: $250-500,000 *Tel:* (202) 223-0388
Hist. Note: Independent insurance managers with contractual authority to perform managerial functions on behalf of insurance companies and syndicates. Annual membership dues: $350-$500/year (company).
Publications:
AAMGA Newsletter. m.
AAMGA Yearbook. a.
Income and Expense Report. a.
Company Contact Report. a.
Annual Meetings: Spring/1,000
1987-Desert Springs, CA(Marriott)/May 3-7
1988-White Sulphur Springs, WV(Greenbriar)
1989-Tuscon, AZ

American Ass'n of Meat Processors (1939)
P.O. Box 269, Elizabethtown PA 17022
Exec. Director: Stephen F. Krut
Members: 1,950 *Staff:* 9
Annual Budget: $250-500,000 *Tel:* (717) 367-1168
Hist. Note: Founded as the Nat'l Frozen Food Locker Institute, it became successively the Nat'l Frozen Food Locker Ass'n, the Frozen Food Locker Institute, the Nat'l Institute of Locker and Freezer Provisioners and finally, in 1973, assumed its present name.
Publications:
AAMPlifier. semi-m.
Capitol Line Ups. semi-m.
Annual Meetings: Summer
1987-Louisville, KY(Galt House)/July 26-29
1988-Albuquerque, NM
1989-Des Moines, IA

American Ass'n of Medical Assistants (1956)
20 North Wacker Drive, #1575, Chicago IL 60606
Exec. Director: Ina L. Yenerich
Members: 17-18,000 *Staff:* 16-20
Annual Budget: $1-2,000,000 *Tel:* (312) 899-1500
Hist. Note: Membership includes medical assistants, medical secretaries, bookkeepers, receptionists, technicians and office nurses. Has program leading to certification as a CMA - Certified Medical Assistant.
Publication:
The Professional Medical Assistant. bi-m. adv.

American Ass'n of Medical Milk Commissions (1907)
1824 North Hillhurst Ave., Los Angeles CA 90027
Secy.-Treas.: Paul Fleiss, M.D.
Members: 30 *Staff:* 1
Annual Budget: $10-25,000 *Tel:* (213) 664-1977
Hist. Note: Professional society of physicians on local Medical Milk Commissions supervising production of Certified Milk from dairies conforming to offical standards. Membership includes physicians, pathologists, pediatricians and veterinarians. Affiliated with the Certified Milk Producers Ass'n of America.
Publication:
Methods and Standards for the Production of Certified Milk. trien.
Semi-annual meetings:
May, with Certified Milk Producers Ass'n of America, and Oct./Nov.

American Ass'n of Medical Soc. Executives (1947)
535 North Dearborn St., Chicago IL 60610
Exec. Director: Robert J. Lindley, CAE
Members: 950 individuals *Staff:* 2-5
Annual Budget: $100-250,000 *Tel:* (312) 645-4975
Hist. Note: Professional organization of executives of medical societies. Formerly Medical Soc. Executives Ass'n. Membership: $110/year (individual), $100-775/year (organization).
Publications:
Medical Executive Magazine. q. adv.
Newsletter. m.
Who's Who in Medical Society Management - Directory. a. adv.
Annual Meetings: Summer/225
1987-New Orleans, LA(Hyatt)/July 29-Aug. 1

American Ass'n of Medico-Legal Consultants (1972)
The Barclay, Rittenhouse Square, Philadelphia PA 19103-6164
Pres. & Exec. Director: Evelyn M. Goldstein
Members: 600 physicians and 150 physician-attorneys *Staff:* 2-5
Annual Budget: $100-250,000 *Tel:* (215) 545-6363
Hist. Note: A national medical malpractice and peer review panel.

American Ass'n of Mental Health Professionals in Corrections (1940)
Box 511, Sacramento CA 95803
Nat'l President: Dr. John S. Zil
Members: 800
Annual Budget: $25-50,000 *Tel:* (916) 322-8595
Hist. Note: Until 1978, the Medical Correctional Association. Membership: $35/year.
Publication:
Corrective and Social Psychiatry Journal. q.
Annual Meetings: With the American College of Forensic Psychiatry.

American Ass'n of Minority Enterprise Small Business Investment Companies (1971)
Hist. Note: Became the Nat'l Ass'n of Investment Companies in 1986.

American Ass'n of Minority Enterprise Small Business Investment Companies
Hist. Note: Became the Nat'l Ass'n of Investment Companies in 1986.

American Ass'n of Motor Vehicle Administrators (1933)
1201 Connecticut Ave., N.W., Suite 910, Washington DC 20036
Exec. Director: Larry E. Lunnen
Members: 66 jurisdictions *Staff:* 35-40
Annual Budget: $2-5,000,000 *Tel:* (202) 296-1955
Hist. Note: Membership composed of state and provincial bodies responsible for the administration and enforcement of motor vehicle and traffic laws in the U.S. and Canada. The Ass'n is comprised, then, of 66 jurisdictions representing 150 agencies and well over 1,000 people.
Publications:
AAMVA Bulletin. m.
The Capital Report.
Personnel Directory of Member Jurisdictions.
Proceedings. a.
Annual Meetings: Fall
1987-Washington, DC(JW Marriott)/Aug. 30-Sept. 3/5-600
1988-Milwaukee, WI(Hyatt Regency)/Sept. 18-22/5-600
1989-New Orleans, LA

American Ass'n of Museums (1906)
1225 Eye St., N.W., Washington DC 20005
Exec. Director: Edward H. Able, Jr.
Members: 10,000 *Staff:* 35
Annual Budget: $2-5,000,000 *Tel:* (202) 289-1818
Hist. Note: Members are curators, registrars, trustees, directors, conservators, volunteers, public relations officers, educators, students, development officers and security managers from art, history and science museums, as well as historic, preservation and art associations, planetariums, zoos, botanical gardens and aquariums. Sponsors an accreditation and assesment program for museums and serves as an information center and job clearinghouse. Affiliated with the Internat'l Council of Museums. Administers 10 standing committees. Membership fee: Individual based on salary; institution based on operating budget.
Publications:
Museum News. bi-m. adv.
Aviso. m.
Official Museum Directory. a.
Annual Meetings: June
1987-San Francisco, CA/June 7-11
1988-Pittsburgh, PA/June 5-9
1989-New Orleans, LA/June 18-22
1990-Denver, CO

American Ass'n of Museums Trustee Committee (1971)
Hist. Note: A Standing Committee of the American Ass'n of Museums, which provides administrative support, established in 1971.

American Ass'n of Nephrology Nurses and Technicians
Hist. Note: Became the American Nephrology Nurses' Association in 1984.

American Ass'n of Neurological Surgeons (1931)
22 South Washington St., Suite 100, Park Ridge IL 60068
Exec. Director: Carl H. Hauber, CAE
Members: 2,850 *Staff:* 15
Annual Budget: 18 *Tel:* (312) 692-9500
Hist. Note: Founded October 10, 1931 as the Harvey Cushing Society. Incorporated in Illinois in 1956 and name changed to American Ass'n of Neurological Surgeons in 1967.
Publication:
Journal of Neurosurgery. m.
Annual Meetings: Spring
1987-Dallas, TX(Loews Anatole)/May 3-5
1988-Toronto, Ontario/April 24-28
1989-Washington, DC/April 2-6
1990-Nashville, TN/April 29-May 3
1991-New Orleans, LA/April 21-25
1992-San Francisco, CA/April 12-16
1993-Boston, MA/April 25-29

American Ass'n of Neuropathologists (1924)
Medical Univ. of South Carolina, Department of Pathology, Charleston SC 29425
Secretary-Treasurer: James M. Powers
Members: 660 *Staff:* 1
Annual Budget: $10-25,000 *Tel:* (803) 792-3581
Hist. Note: Founded as the Club of Neuropatholgists, this professional society of physicians assumed its present name in 1932. Membership: $60-65/year (individual).
Publication:
J Neuropath Exp Neurol. bi-m. adv.
Annual Meetings:
1987-Seattle, WA(Four Seasons)/June 11-14/350
1988-Charleston, SC(Charleston Place)/June 9-12/350

American Ass'n of Neuroscience Nurses (1968)
22 South Washington, Suite 203, Park Ridge IL 60068
Exec. Director: J. Roger Detweiler
Members: 2,200 *Staff:* 2-5
Annual Budget: $250-500,000 *Tel:* (312) 823-9850
Hist. Note: Membership is open to Registered Nurses licensed to practice in the United States or Canada who demonstrate an active or primary interest in neurosurgical or neurological nursing.
Publications:
Journal of Neuroscience Nursing. bi-m. adv.
Synapse. bi-m.
Annual Meetings: Spring
1987-Dallas, TX/May 4-7

American Ass'n of Nurse Anesthetists (1931)
216 Higgins Road, Park Ridge IL 60068-5790
Exec. Director: John F. Garde, CRNA
Members: 20,000 *Staff:* 25-30
Annual Budget: $2-5,000,000 *Tel:* (312) 692-7050
Hist. Note: Established in 1931 as the Nat'l Ass'n of Nurse Anesthetists. Became the American Ass'n of Nurse Anesthetists in 1939. Certifies nurse anesthetists and awards the CRNA (Certified Registered Nurse Anesthetist) designation. Membership: $175/yr.
Publications:
Journal of the AANA. bi-m. adv.
News Bulletin. m.
Annual Meetings: Fall
1987-Cincinnati, OH/Aug. 22-27
1988-Seattle, WA/Aug. 13-18
1989-Boston, MA/Aug. 19-24

00020 12 05 86 1233

American Ass'n of Nurserymen (1876)
1250 Eye St., N.W., Suite 500, Washington DC 20005
Exec. V. President: Robert F. Lederer, CAE
Members: 3,800 *Staff:* 11-15
Annual Budget: $1-2,000,000 *Tel:* (202) 789-2900
Hist. Note: Formed in Chicago on June 14, 1875 as the American Ass'n of Nurserymen, Florists and Seedmen. Became the American Ass'n of Nurserymen in 1887. Contains Garden Centers of America, Horticultural Research Institute, Nat'l Ass'n of Plant Patent Owners, Nat'l Landscape Ass'n, and Wholesale Nursery Growers of America. Supports the Nursery Industry Political Action Committee and the Nursery Marketing Council. Membership Fee: Based on volume of business.
Publications:
ALI. q. adv.
Newsletter. m.
Annual Meetings: July/1,500-2,000
1987-Grand Rapids, MI(Amway Grand Plaza)/July 16-19
1988-Anaheim, CA(Disneyland)/July 16-19
1989-Hartford, CT(Hilton and Sheration)/July 15-18

American Ass'n of Obstetricians and Gynecologists (1888)
Hist. Note: Formerly the American Ass'n of Obstetricians, Gynecologists and Abdominal Surgeons. Merged with the American Gynecological Soc. to form the American Gynecological and Obstetrical Soc. in 1981.

American Ass'n of Occupational Health Nurses (1942)
3500 Piedmont Road, N.E., Atlanta GA 30305
Exec. Director: Matilda A. Babbitz
Members: 11-12,000 *Staff:* 11-15
Annual Budget: $100-250,000 *Tel:* (404) 262-1162
Hist. Note: Founded in Philadelphia in 1942 and incorporated in New York in 1952. The professional association of occupational health nurses. Formerly (1977) the American Ass'n of Industrial Nurses, Inc. Incorporated in the state of Georgia in 1982. Membership: $95/yr.
Publications:
AOHN News. m.
AOHN Journal. m. adv.
Annual Meetings: April
1987-Philadelphia, PA/April 27-May 1
1988-New Orleans, LA/April 21-29

American Ass'n of Ophthalmology (1956)
Hist. Note: Established as the National Medical Foundation for Eye Care, it became the American Association of Ophthalmology in 1965 and merged into the American Academy of Ophthalmology on June 30, 1981.

American Ass'n of Oral and Maxillofacial Surgeons (1918)
211 East Chicago Ave., Ste. 930, Chicago IL 60611
Exec. Director: Bernard J. Degen, II
Members: 4,800 individuals *Staff:* 16-20
Annual Budget: $2-5,000,000 *Tel:* (312) 642-6446
Hist. Note: Formerly (1978) the American Soc. of Oral Surgeons. Supports the Oral and Maxillofacial Surgery Political Action Committee (OMSPAC).
Publications:
AAOMS Forum. 3/yr.
Journal of Oral and Maxillofacial Surgery. m.
Annual Meetings: Fall/3,500
1987-Anaheim, CA(Hilton)/Sept. 16-20
1988-Boston, MA/Sept. 29-Oct. 3
1989-Washington, DC/Sept. 20-24
1990-New York, NY/Sept. 12-16
1991-Chicago, IL(Chicago Hilton)/Sept. 25-29

American Ass'n of Orthodontists (1900)
460 North Lindbergh Blvd., St. Louis MO 63141
Exec. Director: Robert L. Wagner
Members: 9,500 *Staff:* 21-25
Annual Budget: $2-5,000,000 *Tel:* (314) 993-1700
Hist. Note: Formed in 1900 as The American Soc. of Orthodontists. Incorporated in Pennsylvania in 1917 as The American Ass'n of Orthodontists and later, in 1965 after the headquarters was established in St. Louis, incorporated in Missouri. Sponsors the American Ass'n of Orthodontists Foundation.
Publications:
American Ass'n of Orthodontists Bulletin. q.
American Journal of Orthodontics. m. adv.
Annual Meetings: Spring/8-9,000
1987-Montreal, Canada(Convention Center)/May 10-13
1988-New Orleans, LA(Convention Center)/Apr. 29-May 4
1989-Anaheim, CA(Convention Center)/May 14-17
1990-Washington, DC(Convention Center)/May 6-9
1991-Seattle, WA(Convention Center)/May 9-13
1992-St. Louis, MO(Convention Center)/May 5-8

American Ass'n of Orthopaedic Medicine (1982)
926 E. McDowell Road, Suite 202, Phoenix AZ 85006
Secy.-Treas.: Kent L. Pomeroy, M.D.
Members: 250 *Staff:* 2
Annual Budget: $50-100,000 *Tel:* (602) 254-5315
Hist. Note: Professional association of physicians concerned with afflictions of the musculoskeletal system. Absorbed the Prolotherapy Association (founded in 1962). Membership: $75/year.
Publication:
Newsletter. q.
Annual Meetings: February or March
1987-Montreal, Quebec/May 12-16
1988-Dallas, TX/April 20-24
1989-Las Vegas, NV/April 2-6

American Ass'n of Osteopathic Examiners (1935)
Metropolitan Hospital, Springfield Div.,Sproul and Thompson Roads, Springfield PA 19064
President: Dr. A. Archie Feinstein, D.O.
Members: 75-100 *Staff:* 1
Annual Budget: under $10,000 *Tel:* (215) 328-8728
Semi-annual Meetings: July (with American Osteopathic Ass'n) & Nov.

American Ass'n of Osteopathic Specialists (1952)
804 Main Street, Forest Park GA 30050
Exec. Director: Peter P. Tyler, Ph.D.
Members: 250 *Staff:* 2
Annual Budget: $100-250,000 *Tel:* (404) 363-8263
Hist. Note: Membership is open to D.O.'s from all specialty categories. Formerly the American Academy of Osteopathic Surgeons. Assumed its present name in 1984. Membership: $400/yr.
Publications:
AAOS Newsletter. q.
Membership Directory. a.
Annual Meetings: June/350-400
1987-St. Louis, MO(Sheraton)/June 21-25
1988-Philadelphia, PA(Society Hill)/June 19-23
1989-Salt Lake City, UT(Snowbird)/June 18-22
1990-Williamsburg, VA(Lodge)/June 17-21

American Ass'n of Owners and Breeders of Peruvian Paso Horses (1962)
P.O. Box 4851, Chico CA 95927-4851
Exec. Secy./Registrar: MaryLou Johnson
Members: 575 individuals *Staff:* 1
Annual Budget: $50-100,000 *Tel:* (916) 893-9011
Hist. Note: Formed to establish a breed standard for the Peruvian Paso Horse (imported from Peru) and to encourage the breeding, training, and showing of the horse, as well as to inform the general public of the history and attributes of what has been called the "Cadillac of Pleasure Horses." Membership: $35/yr.
Publications:
AAOBPPH Newsletter. q.
Owner/Breeder Membership Directory. a.
Annual Meetings: With Nat'l Championship Show
1987-Reno, NV/Sept.

American Ass'n of Pastoral Counselors (1963)
9508A Lee Highway, Fairfax VA 22031
Exec. Director: James W. Ewing, Ph.D.
Members: 2,550 *Staff:* 5-6
Annual Budget: $250-500,000 *Tel:* (703) 385-6967
Hist. Note: Sponsors a certification program for ordained clergy service centers and training programs in specialized ministries of counseling.
Publications:
Directory. a.
Journal of Pastoral Care. q. adv.
Newsletter. q.
Annual Meetings: Spring/500
1987-New Orleans, LA
1988-Portland, OR

American Ass'n of Pathologists (1976)
9650 Rockville Pike, Bethesda MD 20814
Exec. Officer: Harold Waters
Members: 2,500 *Staff:* 2-5
Annual Budget: $250-500,000 *Tel:* (301) 530-7130
Hist. Note: Formed on July 1, 1976 by a merger of the American Soc. for Experimental Pathology (founded in 1913) and the American Ass'n of Pathologists and Bacteriologists (founded in 1900). Membership: $90/year.
Publication:
American Journal of Pathology. m. adv.
Annual Meetings: Spring, with Federation of American Societies for Experimental Biology
1987-Washington, DC(Marriott)/March 29-April 3
1988-Las Vegas, NV/May 1-6
1989-New Orleans, LA/May 19-24
1990-Washington, DC/April 1-6
1991-Atlanta, GA/April 14-19

American Ass'n of Pathologists' Assistants (1972)
c/o VA Medical Center, West Haven CT 06516
Administrative Chairman: Leo J. Kelly, P.A.
Members: 200 *Staff:* 0
Annual Budget: $10-25,000 *Tel:* (203) 932-5711
Hist. Note: Established and incorporated in Ohio. Membership: $25/year.
Publication:
AAPA Newsletter. q.
Annual Meetings: October/100
1987-Philadelphia, PA

American Ass'n of Petroleum Geologists (1917)
P.O. Box 979, Tulsa OK 74101
Exec. Director: Fred A. Dix, Jr.
Members: 43,000 individuals *Staff:* 73
Annual Budget: over $5,000,000 *Tel:* (918) 584-2555
Hist. Note: Established in Tulsa in 1917 to provide a mechanism for dissemination of scientific and technical ideas and data in the field of geology as it relates to exploration for and production of oil and natural gas. Originally the Southwestern Ass'n of Petroleum Geologists, it became the American Ass'n of Petroleum Geologists in 1918 and was incorporated in Colorado in 1924. A member society of the American Geological Institute. Has a budget of about $8 million. Membership: $40/yr.
Publications:
AAPG Bulletin. m. adv.
AAPG Explorer. m. adv.
Annual Meetings: Spring/6,000
1987-Los Angeles, CA/June 7-10
1988-Houston, TX/March 20-23
1989-San Antonio, TX/April 23-26/5,000
1990-San Francisco, CA/June 3-6/10,000

American Ass'n of Petroleum Landmen (1955)
1470 Continental Plaza, Box 777040, Fort Worth TX 76102
Exec. V. President: Harry L. Sprinkle
Members: 12,400 *Staff:* 11
Annual Budget: $1-2,000,000 *Tel:* (817) 335-2275
Hist. Note: A professional society of petroleum landmen, independent lease brokers, oil operators and company exploration managers. Membership: $50/yr.
Publications:
The Landman. m. adv.
Official Directory of Petroleum Landmen. a. adv.
Annual Meetings: Spring/2,500
1987-Kansas City, MO(Crown Center)/June
1988-Washington, DC(Hilton)/June
1989-Anaheim, CA
1990-San Antonio, TX

American Ass'n of Phonetic Sciences (1973)
Box 14095, Univ. Station, Gainesville FL 32601
Exec. Secretary: William S. Brown
Members: 300 *Staff:* 1
Annual Budget: under $10,000 *Tel:* (904) 392-2046
Hist. Note: Affiliated with Internat'l Soc. of Phonetic Sciences. Membership: $15/year.
Publication:
Newsletter. semi-a. adv.
Annual Meetings: Fall
1987-Maiami, FL(Doral on the Beach)/Nov./100

American Ass'n of Physical Anthropologists (1928)
Dept. of Anthropology, Univ. of Chicago,1126 East 59th St., Chicago IL 60637
President: Dr. Jane E. Buikstra
Members: 1,500 *Staff:* 2-5
Annual Budget: $10-25,000 *Tel:* (312) 962-7701
Hist. Note: Founded in the District of Columbia in 1928. Affiliated with the Internat'l Ass'n of Human Biologists and the Soc. for the Study of Human Biology. Membership: $55/yr.
Publications:
American Journal of Physical Anthropology. q. adv.
Yearbook of Physical Anthropology. a.
Annual Meetings: Spring

American Ass'n of Physicists in Medicine (1958)
335 East 45th St., New York NY 10017
Exec. Director: Elaine-Pevar Osterman
Members: 2,350 *Staff:* 5
Annual Budget: $1-2,000,000 *Tel:* (212) 661-9404
Hist. Note: Founded in Chicago in 1958 and incorporated in Washington in 1965. Promotes the application of physics to medicine and biology. A member society of the American Institute of Physics. Membership: $90/year.
Publications:
Medical Physics. a. adv.
Physics in Medicine and Biology. q.
Annual Meetings: Summer and with the Radiological Society of North America.
1987-Detroit, MI/July 19-23
1988-San Antonio, TX/Aug. 6-13
1989-Memphis, TN/July 23-27
1990-St. Louis, MO/Aug. 5-9

American Ass'n of Physics Teachers (1930)
5112 Berwyn Road, College Park MD 20740
Exec. Officer: Jack M. Wilson
Members: 10-11,000 *Staff:* 16-20
Annual Budget: $500-1,000,000 *Tel:* (301) 345-4200
Hist. Note: Members are university, college, two-year college and high school physicists. Member of the American Institute of Physics. Regular Membership: $40-60/yr.
Publications:
American Journal of Physics. m. adv.
The Physics Teacher. 9/yr. adv.
AAPT Announcer. q. adv.
Semi-Annual Meetings: Jan. (with American Physical Soc.) and June
1987-San Francisco, CA/Jan.
1987-Bozeman, MT(Montana State University)/June
1988-Washington, DC(Crystal City)/Jan.
1988-Ithaca, NY(Cornell University)/June
1989-San Francisco, CA/Jan.

American Ass'n of Plastic Surgeons (1921)
The Johns Hopkins Hospital, 600 North Wolfe St., Baltimore MD 21205
Secretary: John E. Hoopes, M.D.
Members: 300 *Staff:* 1
Annual Budget: $50-100,000 *Tel:* (301) 955-6897
Hist. Note: Formerly (1942) American Ass'n of Oral and Plastic Surgeons. Membership: $250/year (individual).
Publication:
Plastic and Reconstructive Surgery. m. adv.
Annual Meetings: Spring/500
1987-Nashville, TN(Opryland)/May 3-6

00021 12 05 86 1233

1988-Palm Beach, FL(Breakers)/May 1-4
1989-Scottsdale, AZ(Camelback Inn)/May 7-10
1990-Hot Springs, VA(Homestead)/April 29-May 2
1991-San Antonio, TX(Hyatt Regency)/April 12-17
1992-Vancouver, Canada(Hyatt Regency)/May 17-20

American Ass'n of Poison Control Centers (1958)
Arizona Poison and Drug Information Ctr.,oom 3240, 1501 N. Campbell St., Tucson AZ 85725
Secretary: Theodore Tong
Members: 200 individuals, 200 institutions
Annual Budget: $50-100,000 *Tel:* (606) 626-7899
Hist. Note: Members are professional and lay personnel who work in the field of poison control. Has no paid staff. Membership: $50/yr. (individual); $200/yr. (institution).
Publication:
Veterinary and Human Toxicology. bi-m.
Annual Meetings: September/300
1987-Vancouver, BC
1988-Baltimore, MD(Marriott)

American Ass'n of Police Polygraphists (1977)
1918 Sleepy Hollow, Pearland TX 77581
Secy.-Treas.: Holly S. Merrill Canty
Members: 600-650 *Staff:* 1
Annual Budget: $10-25,000 *Tel:* (713) 485-0902
Hist. Note: Polygraphists currently affiliated with a criminal agency or military service. Membership: $30/yr.
Publication:
The Journal. q. adv.
Annual Meetings: Spring/150-200

American Ass'n of Political Consultants (1969)
c/o Cerrell Associates, 320 North Larchmont Blvd., Los Angeles CA 90004
President: Joseph Cerrell
Members: 500 *Staff:* 1
Annual Budget: $50-100,000 *Tel:* (213) 466-3445
Hist. Note: Organized in Jan. 1969 in New York and designed to encompass all facets of political consulting, including public affairs and government relations, in addition to political campaigning. Has no permanent address. The President remains in office 2-4 years. Membership: $150/year (individual), $300/year (corporate).
Publication:
Newsletter. q.
Semi-annual Meetings: February/March and November

American Ass'n of Port Authorities (1912)
1010 Duke St., Alexandria VA 22314
Acting C.E.O.: Erik Stromberg
Members: 123 public port agencies, 300 firms & individuals
Staff: 11
Annual Budget: $500-1,000,000 *Tel:* (703) 684-5700
Hist. Note: Membership: $350/yr.(contributing); for Ports, based on revenues.
Publications:
AAPA Advisory. w.
AAPA Alert. w.
AAPA Handbook. a. adv.
Annual Meetings: Fall
1987-Galveston, TX
1988-San Francisco, CA
1989-Tampa, FL
1990-Nassau, Bahamas

American Ass'n of Preferred Provider Organizations (1983)
101 1/2 South Union St., Alexandria VA 22314
Exec. Director: Sharon Graugnard
Members: 150 companies *Staff:* 4
Annual Budget: $100-250,000 *Tel:* (703) 683-5562
Hist. Note: Membership is open on a corporate basis to entities actively involved in preferred provider operations. Membership: $500/yr.
Publications:
PPO News. m. adv.
Directory of Operational PPOs. bi-a.
Summary of State PPO Enbaling Legislation. bi-a.
Annual Meetings: Nat'l Industry Conference
1987-Irving, TX(Las Colinas Four Seasons)/March/150
1988-Washington, DC
1989-Denver, CO

American Ass'n of Presidents of Independent Colleges and Universities (1968)
Box 300, Grove City College, Grove City PA 16127-2197
Exec. Director: Douglas Dayton
Members: 170-180 *Staff:* 1
Annual Budget: under $10,000 *Tel:* (412) 489-6600
Hist. Note: Formerly (until 1969) known as the American Ass'n of Independent College and University Presidents.
Publications:
Private Higher Education. a.
Report. 3/yr.
Annual Meetings: December

American Ass'n of Professional Bridal Consultants (1955)
Hist. Note: Became the Association of Bridal Consultants in 1981.

American Ass'n of Professional Hypnologists (1969)
Box 1112, Williamsport PA 17701
Exec. Secretary: Rene M Ewing
Members: 200 *Staff:* 2
Annual Budget: under $10,000 *Tel:* (717) 322-8305
Hist. Note: Awards the designation Registered Hypnologist ("R.H."), accredits courses of study, and maintains a nat'l registry for client referral services. Membership: $75(initiation); $50/yr.(dues)
Publication:
American Hypnologist. q.
Annual Meetings:
1987-Philadelphia, PA

American Ass'n of Professional Hypnotherapists (1980)
Box 731, McLean VA 22101
Exec. Director: William S. Brink
Members: 1,525 *Staff:* 3
Annual Budget: $50-100,000 *Tel:* (703) 448-9623
Hist. Note: Members are hypnotherapists, clinical social workers, marriage and family therapists, psychologists, physicians, pastoral counselors, and others trained and experienced in the use of hypnosis in therapy. Membership: $50/yr.
Publications:
Hypnotherapy Today. q.
Nat'l Register of Professional Hypnotherapists. a.

American Ass'n of Professional Standards Review Organizations (1973)
Hist. Note: Became the American Medical Peer Review Association in 1983.

American Ass'n of Professors of Yiddish (1974)
Queens College, NSF 350, Flushing NY 11367
Secretary: Prof. Joseph C. Landis
Members: 150 *Staff:* 1
Annual Budget: under $10,000 *Tel:* (212) 520-7067
Hist. Note: An "allied" organization of the Modern Language Ass'n Has no paid staff.
Publication:
Yiddish and Modern Jewish Studies Annual. 2-3/yr.
Annual Meetings: December, with the Modern Language Ass'n
1987-San Francisco, CA
1988-New Orleans, LA

American Ass'n of Psychiatric Administrators (1961)
1938 Peachtree Street, Atlanta GA 30309
President: Dr. Dave M. Davis
Members: 370 *Staff:* 1
Annual Budget: $10-25,000 *Tel:* (404) 355-2914
Hist. Note: Affiliated with the American Psychiatric Ass'n. Formerly (1975) Ass'n of Medical Superintendents of Mental Hospitals. Has no headquarters or permanent staff. Officers change annually. Membership: $40/yr.
Publication:
Newsletter. q.
Semi-Annual Meetings: Spring and Fall
1987-Chicago, IL/May
1987-Ottawa, Ontario/Oct.

American Ass'n of Psychiatric Services for Children (1948)
1133 15th St., N.W., Washington DC 20005
Exec. Director: John H. Ganoe
Members: 130 organizations, 100 individuals *Staff:* 2-5
Annual Budget: $50-100,000 *Tel:* (202) 429-9440
Hist. Note: Formerly (1970) the American Ass'n of Psychiatric Clinics for Children .
Publications:
Membership Directory. a.
Newsletter of the AAPSC. q. adv.
Annual Meetings: February

American Ass'n of Public Health Dentistry (1937)
10619 Jousting Lane, Richmond VA 23235
President: Joseph Doherty
Members: 5-600
Annual Budget: $25-50,000 *Tel:* (804) 786-3556
Hist. Note: Formerly (1983) the American Ass'n of Public Health Dentists. Membership: $60/yr.
Publications:
Journal of Public Health Dentistry. q.
Communique. q.
Annual Meetings: Two days preceding the American Dental Association's annual meeting and at the same place/200
1987-Las Vegas, NV
1988-Washington, DC

American Ass'n of Public Health Physicians (1954)
Nassau Co. Dept. of Health, 240 Old Country Road, Mineola, L.I. NY 11501
Secy.-Treas.: Norman Schell, M.D.
Members: 200-300
Annual Budget: under $10,000 *Tel:* (516) 535-4922
Hist. Note: Has no paid staff. Membership: $25/yr.
Publication:
The Bulletin. q.
Annual Meetings: With American Public Health Ass'n.
1987-Las Vegas, NV/Fall

American Ass'n of Public Welfare Attorneys (1967)
1125 15th St., N.W., Suite 300, Washington DC 20005
APWA Staff Liaison: Ellen Wells
Members: 300 *Staff:* 1
Annual Budget: under $10,000 *Tel:* (202) 293-7550
Hist. Note: A constituent unit of the American Public Welfare Ass'n. Membership: $35/yr.

American Ass'n of Public Welfare Information Systems Management
1125 15th St., N.W., Suite 300, Washington DC 20005
Exec. Director: Sidney Johnson
Members: 350 *Staff:* 1
Annual Budget: $10-25,000 *Tel:* (202) 293-7550
Hist. Note: A constituent unit of the American Public Welfare Association.
Annual Meetings:
1987-New Orleans, LA(Monte Leone)/Sept. 13-16/350

American Ass'n of Railroad Superintendents (1896)
18154 Harwood Ave., Homewood IL 60430
Secretary: Patricia Weissmann
Members: 1,200 individuals *Staff:* 1
Annual Budget: under $10,000 *Tel:* (312) 799-4650
Hist. Note: Membership: $25/year.
Publication:
Proceedings. a. adv.
Annual Meetings: June/150
1987-Pittsburgh, PA/June 22-25
1988-St. Louis, MO/June 12-15
1989-Toronto, Ontario
1990-Kansas City, MO

American Ass'n of Railway Surgeons (1888)
P.O. Box 503, Daleville VA 24083
Asst. Secy.-Treas.: Lynne B. Harris
Members: 700 *Staff:* 1
Annual Budget: $25-50,000 *Tel:* (703) 981-4978
Hist. Note: Supports medical personnel engaged in the health care of railroad employees. Membership: $30/yr.
Annual Meetings: Always in September at the Drake Hotel in Chicago, IL

American Ass'n of School Administrators (1865)
1801 N. Moore St., Arlington VA 22209
Exec. Director: Dr. Richard D. Miller
Members: 18,000 *Staff:* 60-65
Annual Budget: over $5,000,000 *Tel:* (703) 528-0700
Hist. Note: Founded as the Nat'l Ass'n of School Superintendents, it became the Department of School Superintendence of the Nat'l Education Ass'n 1870, the Department of Superintendence of NEA in 1907 and assumed its present name in 1937. Absorbed the County and Intermediate Unit Superintendents of NEA in 1968. Has an annual budget of $6.5 million. Membership: $145/yr.
Publications:
The School Administrator. m. adv.
Actionline Electronic Newsletter. d.
Annual Meetings: February/17,000
1987-New Orleans, LA/Feb. 20-23
1988-Las Vegas, NV/Feb. 19-22
1989-Orlando, FL/March 3-6
1990-San Francisco, CA/Feb. 23-26
1991-New Orleans, LA/March 1-4

American Ass'n of School Librarians (1951)
50 East Huron St., Chicago IL 60611
Exec. Director: Ann Carlson Weeks
Members: 6,500 *Staff:* 3-50
Annual Budget: $100-250,000 *Tel:* (312) 944-6780
Hist. Note: Membership composed of school media specialists. A division of the American Library Association.
Publication:
School Library Media. q. adv.
Triennial meetings: October

American Ass'n of School Personnel Administrators (1940)
825 Lurline Dr., Foster City CA 94404
Exec. Director: Raymond E. Curry
Members: 1,200 *Staff:* 1
Annual Budget: $50-100,000 *Tel:* (415) 573-1447
Hist. Note: Founded as the American Association of Examiners and Administrators of Educational Personnel, it assumed its present name in 1959.
Publication:
Bulletin. 5/yr.
Annual Meetings: October
1987-San Diego, CA/Oct. 19-23
1988-Valley Forge, PA/Oct. 16-20
1989-Cleveland, OH/Oct. 15-19

American Ass'n of Schools and Departments of Journalism (1921)
Hist. Note: Became the Association of Schools of Journalism and Mass Communication in 1983.

American Ass'n of Scientific Workers (1946)
School of Veterinary Medicine, University of Pennsylvania, Philadelphia PA 19104
Nat'l Secretary: Dr. Robert J. Rutman

00022 12 05 86 1233

Members: 100 *Staff:* 1
Annual Budget: under $10,000 *Tel:* (215) 898-8869
Hist. Note: Established during World War II, this is the U.S. affiliate of the World Federation of Scientific Workers. Membership open to anyone working in science or technology. Has no dues or annual meetings and is preoccupied with the socio-political implications of scientific questions.

American Ass'n of Senior Physicians (1975)
536 North State St., Chicago IL 60610
Exec. Director: Gerald L. Farley
Members: 7,000 *Staff:* 4
Annual Budget: $100-250,000 *Tel:* (312) 645-4970
Hist. Note: Established and incorporated in Chicago with the assistance of the American Medical Ass'n, AASP addresses the needs and interests of the senior physician either in continuing active medical practice or in the pursuit of practice modification or retirement. Membership: $25/yr.
Publication:
AASP Newsletter. bi-m.

American Ass'n of Sex Educators, Counselors and Therapists (1967)
11 Dupont Circle, N.W., Suite 220, Washington DC 20036
Exec. Director: Ruth Hunt
Members: 4,500-5,000 *Staff:* 5
Annual Budget: $250-500,000 *Tel:* (202) 462-1171
Hist. Note: Designates qualified members as AASECT "Certified Sex Educator, Sex Counselor and Sex Therapist." Membership: $100/yr.
Publications:
Journal of Sex Education and Counseling. q. adv.
Newsletter. q.
Annual Meetings:
1987-New York, NY(Marriott Marquis)/April 30-May 3
1988-San Francisco, CA

American Ass'n of Sheep and Goat Practitioners (1969)
248 N.W. Garden Valley Rd., Roseburg OR 97470
Secy.-Treas.: Donald E. Bailey, D.V.M.
Members: 1,100-1,200 *Staff:* 1
Annual Budget: under $10,000 *Tel:* (503) 672-2829
Hist. Note: Formerly (1971) American Ass'n of Sheep Practitioners. Membership: $10/yr.
Publications:
Wool and Wattles. q.
Proceedings. irreg.
Semi-Annual Meetings: February, with Intermountain Veterinary Medical
Health Conference in Las Vegas(Hilton) and Summer, with AVMA
1987-Chicago, IL/July 20-23
1988-Portland, OR/July 18-22
1989-Orlando, FL/July 17-18
1990-San Antonio, TX/July 22-26

American Ass'n of Small Cities (1975)
Route 2, Box 128, DeLeon TX 76444
Exec. Director: Dr. Roy W. Dugger
Members: 2,500-3,000 *Staff:* 2-5
Annual Budget: $50-100,000 *Tel:* (817) 893-5818
Hist. Note: Cities with population of 50,000 or less. Annual membership dues: $25 to $750, depending on population.
Publication:
AASC Newsletter. m.
Annual Meetings: Fall, in Washington, DC

American Ass'n of Small Research Companies (1972)
1200 Lincoln Ave., Suite 5, Prospect Park PA 19076
Exec. Director: Joanne Martin
Members: 500-600 companies *Staff:* 6-10
Annual Budget: $50-100,000 *Tel:* (215) 522-1500
Hist. Note: Members are small research companies, inventors, lawyers; associates are larger research companies.
Publications:
AASRC Newsletter. bi-m.
Members Directory. a.
Annual Meetings: Four Conferences per year.

American Ass'n of Special Educators (1975)
107-20 125th St., Richmond Hill NY 11419
Exec. Director: Louis Marpet
Members: 300 *Staff:* 2-5
Annual Budget: $25-50,000 *Tel:* (718) 641-1224
Hist. Note: Teachers and others who work with handicapped persons.
Publication:
Newsletter.
Annual Meetings:
1987-London, England(Kings College - Chelsea)/July 6-7/250

American Ass'n of Specialized Colleges (1966)
Hist. Note: Defunct in 1985.

American Ass'n of State Climatologists (1976)
Renewable Natural Resources Dept., Univ. of Connecticut, 1376 Storrs Rd., Storrs CT 06268
President: David R. Miller
Members: 100 *Staff:* 1
Annual Budget: under $10,000 *Tel:* (203) 486-2840
Hist. Note: Established in Asheville, NC, by 16 state Climatologists as a method of interaction on climatological matters.
Publication:
State Climatology. q.
Annual Meetings: Summer

American Ass'n of State Colleges and Universities (1961)
One Dupont Circle, N.W., Washington DC 20036-1192
President: Allan W. Ostar
Members: 370 *Staff:* 40-50
Annual Budget: $2-5,000,000 *Tel:* (202) 293-7070
Hist. Note: Formerly the Ass'n of State Colleges and Universities. Absorbed the Ass'n of Upper Level Colleges and Universities and superseded the Ass'n of Teachers of Education Institutions founded in 1951. Membership fee based upon enrollment of institution.
Publications:
AASCU Studies. a.
Memo: to the President. bi-w.
Proceedings of annual meeting. a.
Annual Meetings: November/600
1987-New Orleans, LA(Fairmont)/Nov. 22-24
1988-Baltimore, MD(Hyatt)/Nov. 20-22
1989-San Diego, CA or San Antonio, TX/Nov. 12-4 or Nov. 26-29

American Ass'n of State Highway and Transportation Officials (1914)
444 North Capitol St., N.W., Suite 225, Washington DC 20001
Exec. Director: Francis B. Francois
Members: 53 States & Territories and 5 Canadian provinces
Staff: 19
Annual Budget: $2-5,000,000 *Tel:* (202) 624-5800
Hist. Note: Founded as the American Association of State Highway Officials, it was reorganized in 1973 to represent transportation agencies. The present name was adopted at that time.
Publications:
AASHTO Quarterly. q.
AASHTO Journal Weekly Transportation Report. w.
Annual Meetings:
1987-San Diego(Del Coronado)/Dec. 5-8/800-1,000

American Ass'n of Stratigraphic Palynologists (1967)
Amoco Production Company, Box 3092, Houston TX 77253
Secy.-Treas.: Gordon D. Wood
Members: 850-900 individuals, 120-130 institutions *Staff:* 1
Annual Budget: $25-50,000 *Tel:* (713) 556-3380
Hist. Note: Founded December 8, 1967 in Tulsa, Oklahoma with 32 charter members. Promotes the study of palynology-the study of pollen and spores- especially as it relates to stratigraphic applications and biostratigraphy. Has no paid staff. Membership: $20/yr. (individual); $30/yr. (institutional).
Publications:
Newsletter. q.
Palynology. a.
Contribution Series. irreg.
Membership Directory. a.
Annual Meetings:
1987-Halifax, Canada(Chateau Halifax)/250
1988-Houston, TX(Galleria Oaks)/Oct. 8-12/250

American Ass'n of Suicidology (1968)
2459 S. Ash, Denver CO 80222
Exec. Officer: Julie Perlman, M.S.W.
Members: 1,200 *Staff:* 2
Annual Budget: $50-100,000 *Tel:* (303) 692-0985
Hist. Note: Multi-disciplinary organization of professionals and concerned lay people. Makes available an up-to-date listing of suicide prevention centers established throughout the U.S. Sponsors Nat'l Suicide Prevention Week.
Publications:
Newslink. q.
Proceedings. a.
Suicide and Life Threatening Behavior. q. adv.
Annual Meetings: Spring
1987-San Francisco, CA
1988-Washington, DC

American Ass'n of Sunday and Feature Editors (1948)
Newspaper Center; Box 17407, Dulles Airport, Washington DC 20041
Exec. Secretary: Mary O'Ran
Members: 100-110
Annual Budget: under $10,000 *Tel:* (703) 648-1109
Hist. Note: Concerned with improving the quality of Sunday newspapers. Members include syndicated supplements and news services. Membership: $75/yr.
Publication:
Style. a.
Annual Meetings: Fall
1987-Denver, CO/Sept. 16-18/100

American Ass'n of Surgeon's Assistants (1973)
1980 Isaac Newton Square South, Reston VA 22090
Exec. Director: Richard A. Guggolz
Members: 350 individuals; 4 corporate sponsors *Staff:* 4
Annual Budget: $25-50,000 *Tel:* (703) 435-7311
Hist. Note: Membership: $75/yr.
Publication:
AASA Newsletter. q. adv.

American Ass'n of Swine Practitioners (1969)
5921 Fleur Drive, Des Moines IA 50321
Exec. Secretary: Dr. Tomas A. Neuzil
Members: 1,700 *Staff:* 3
Annual Budget: $100-250,000 *Tel:* (515) 285-7808
Hist. Note: Seeks to improve the quality of swine herd health programs and enhance the scientific knowledge to veterinarians through continued education. Members are graduate veterinarians. Membership: $45/yr.
Annual Meetings: March/600
1987-Indianapolis, IN(Adam's Mark)/March 8-10
1988-St. Louis, MO(Clarion Hotel)/March 6-8

American Ass'n of Teacher Educators in Agriculture (1960)
201 Curtiss Hall, Iowa State University, Ames IA 50010
Exec. Officer: David Williams
Members: 250-300 *Staff:* 1
Annual Budget: under $10,000 *Tel:* (515) 294-5872
Hist. Note: Formerly Teacher Trainers Section of the Agricultural Division of the American Vocational Ass'n; name changed, yet still part of AVA. Officers elected annually; has no permanent headquarters.
Publication:
Journal of the American Ass'n of Teacher Educators in Agriculture.
Annual Meetings: With American Vocational Ass'n.

American Ass'n of Teachers of Arabic (1965)
SAIS, 1740 Massachusetts Ave., N.W., Washington DC 20036
Exec. Director: Gerald Lampe
Members: 150 *Staff:* 5
Annual Budget: under $10,000 *Tel:* (202) 785-6237
Hist. Note: Affiliated in 1964 with the American Council on Teaching of Foreign Languages and in 1970 with the Middle East Studies Association. Membership: $15/yr. (individual), $200/yr. (organization).
Publication:
Al-Arabiyya. a. adv.
Annual Meetings: With Middle East Studies Ass'n of North America in November.

American Ass'n of Teachers of French (1927)
57 E. Armory Ave., Champaign IL 61820
Exec. Director: Fred M. Jenkins
Members: 11,000 *Staff:* 5
Annual Budget: $250-500,000 *Tel:* (217) 333-2842
Hist. Note: Member of the Joint Nat'l Committee on Languages. Sponsors programs for students such as the French honor society at the high school level, a national French contest, traveling realia exhibit; summer scholarships; and placement service. Membership: $27/yr.
Publications:
AATF National Bulletin. m.
French Review. bi-m. adv.
Annual Meetings: July
1987-San Francisco, CA(Meridien)/July 1-5/750
1988-Boston, MA
1989-France

American Ass'n of Teachers of German (1926)
523 Bldg., Suite 201, Route 38, Cherry Hill NJ 08034
Exec. Director: Helene Zimmer-Loew
Members: 7,000 *Staff:* 5
Annual Budget: $500-1,000,000 *Tel:* (609) 663-5264
Hist. Note: AATG sponsors a number of programs for students such as a national high school honor society, summer travel/study programs; competition; and American Ass'n of Students of German. Also provides materials, awards, and placement for teachers. Membership: $20-35/yr. (based on salary)
Publications:
AATG Newsletter. 5/yr.
Die Unterrichtspraxis. semi-a. adv.
German Quarterly. q. adv.
Annual Meetings: Fall
1987-Atlanta, GA(Hyatt)/Nov. 21-25/2,000

American Ass'n of Teachers of Italian (1924)
4 Oakmount Road, Welland Ontario L3C 4X8
Secy.-Treas.: Anthony S. Mollica
Members: 1,600 *Staff:* 1
Annual Budget: $25-50,000 *Tel:* (416) 732-2149
Hist. Note: Formerly allied with the Modern Language Association, but has recently gone its own way. Membership: $25/year (individual), $30/year (institution).
Publications:
Italica. q. adv.
Newsletter. semi-a.
Annual Meetings: December, at the same time and in the same place as the Modern
Language Association.

American Ass'n of Teachers of Slavic and East European Languages (1940)
Foreign Languages Department, Arizona State University, Tempe AZ 85287
Sec.-Treasurery: Prof. Sanford Couch, Jr.
Members: 1,500 *Staff:* 1
Annual Budget: $25-50,000 *Tel:* (602) 965-6394
Publications:
The Slavic and East European Journal. q. adv.
AATSEEL Newsletter. bi-m.

00023 12 05 86 1233

American Ass'n of Teachers of Spanish and Portuguese (1917)
Mississippi State University, P.O. Box 6349, Mississippi State MS 39762-6349
Exec. Director: James R. Chatham
Members: 12,000 *Staff:* 3
Annual Budget: $250-500,000 *Tel:* (601) 325-2041
Hist. Note: Membership: $25/yr.
Publication:
Hispania. q. adv.
Annual Meetings: August/500
1987-Los Angeles, CA/Aug. 12-16

American Ass'n of Textile Chemists and Colorists (1921)
Box 12215, Research Triangle Pk NC 27709
Exec. Director: William R. Martin, Jr.
Members: 7,000 individuals, 250 organizations *Staff:* 20-25
Annual Budget: $500-1,000,000 *Tel:* (919) 549-8141
Hist. Note: Founded in Boston in 1921 with 270 charter members and incorporated in Massachusetts. Promotes the increase of knowledge of the application of dyes and chemicals in the textile industry and the use of textile wet processing machinery. Membership: $50/yr.
Publications:
AATCC Technical Manual. a.
Textile Chemist & Colorist. m. adv.
Membership Directory. a.
Book of Papers from International Conference & Exhibition. a.
Annual Meetings: Oct./3,000
1987-Charlotte, NC(Adams Mark/Marriott/Radisson)/Oct. 13-16
1988-Nashville, TN(Opryland)/Sept. 28-Oct. 1
1990-Boston, MA(Sheraton Boston)/Oct. 3-5

American Ass'n of Tissue Banks (1976)
1117 North 19th St., Suite 402, Arlington VA 22209
Exec. Secretary: Jeanne Mowe
Members: 600 individuals and institutions *Staff:* 2
Annual Budget: $100-250,000 *Tel:* (703) 528-0663
Hist. Note: Incorporated in the State of Maryland. Membership: $60/year (individual), $300/year (institution).
Publications:
AATB Newsletter. q.
AATB Standards for Tissue Banking.
Annual Meetings: Fall
1987-Baltimore, MD

American Ass'n of Trauma Specialists (1974)
Hist. Note: Physicians, emergency room nurses, paramedics, emergency medical technicians and others interested in emergency care. Inactive in 1981.

American Ass'n of University Administrators (1970)
Univ. of Alabama, P.O. Box 6221, Tuscaloosa AL 35487
General Secretary: Dr. John Blackburn
Members: 700 *Staff:* 2-5
Annual Budget: $50-100,000 *Tel:* (205) 348-4767
Hist. Note: A professional association of career educational administrators founded in Buffalo, New York. Membership: $50/yr. (individual); $135/yr. (institution)
Publications:
Communique. bi-m.
Administrator's Update. q.
Annual Meetings: June
1987-Toronto, Ontario(Inn at the Park)/June 28-July 1/200-300

American Ass'n of University Affiliated Programs (1968)
8605 Cameron St., Suite 406, Silver Spring MD 20910
Exec. Director: William Jones
Members: 53 institutions *Staff:* 5-10
Annual Budget: $500-1,000,000 *Tel:* (301) 588-8252
Hist. Note: Members provide clinical settings in universities, teaching hospitals, and clinics operating exemplary services to teach graduate students and others studying developmental disorders such as mental retardation. Founded as the Ass'n of University Affiliated Facilities, it assumed its present name in 1975. Membership: Ranges from $2,500 to $4,500, depending on size of the institution.
Publication:
AAUAP Network News. bi-m. adv.
Annual Meetings: Fall
1987-Kansas City, MO(Crown Palace or Hyatt)/Oct. 17-22/250-275

American Ass'n of University Professors (1915)
1012 14th St., N.W., Suite 500, Washington DC 20005
Gen. Secretary: Ernst Benjamin
Members: 50,000 *Staff:* 35
Annual Budget: $2-5,000,000 *Tel:* (202) 737-5900
Hist. Note: Formed in New York City at the instigation of John Dewey. Promotes academic freedom and profesional standards. Also functions as a labor union, bargaining collectively and representing the economic and legislative interests of full or part-time teachers, scholars, librarians and other academic professionals. Membership: $71/year.
Publication:
Academe: Bulletin of AAUP. bi-m. adv.
Annual Meetings: June, usually in a university environment/300-400
1987-Univeristy of Southern California

American Ass'n of Variable Star Observers (1911)
25 Birch St., Cambridge MA 02138
Director: Dr. Janet Akyuz Mattei
Members: 1,100-1,200 *Staff:* 8-12
Annual Budget: $100-250,000 *Tel:* (617) 354-0484
Hist. Note: Members are amateur and professional astronomers who gather and record data on stars which vary in brightness. Membership: $25/year.
Publications:
AAVSO Circular. m.
Bulletin. a.
Journal of AAVSO. bi-a.
Reports of Variable Star Observations. irreg.
Solar Bulletin. m.
Annual Meetings: Spring

American Ass'n of Veterinary Anatomists (1949)
Veterinary Anatomy, College of, Veterinary Medicine, Texas A&M Univ., College Station TX 77843-4458
Secy.-Treas.: William E. Haensly
Members: 230-250 *Staff:* 1
Annual Budget: under $10,000 *Tel:* (409) 845-3185
Hist. Note: Has no paid staff.
Publications:
AAVA Newsletter. bi-a.
Directory. bien.
Annual Meetings: With American Veterinary Medical Ass'n & American Ass'n of Anatomists

American Ass'n of Veterinary Laboratory Diagnosticians (1958)
3900 E. Timrod, Tucson AZ 85711
Exec. Director: Charlotte Fox
Members: 800 *Staff:* 5
Annual Budget: $50-100,000 *Tel:* (602) 881-1778
Hist. Note: AAVLD, formally the Conference of Veterinary Laboratory Diagnosticians, was organized in 1956 with the express purpose of: dissemination of information relating to the diagnosis of animal disease, coordination of diagnostic activities of regulatory research in service laboratories, establishment of uniform diagnostic techniques and the improvement of existing ones, and the development of a body that could act in a consultant capacity to the United States Animal Health Ass'n on uniform diagnostic criteria involved in regulatory animal disease programs. Membership: $20/yr.
Publications:
Proceedings. a.
Newsletter. tri-a.
Annual Meetings: Fall, with the U.S. Animal Health Ass'n
1987-Salt Lake City, UT(Hotel Utah)/Oct. 25-30

American Ass'n of Veterinary Parasitologists (1956)
The Upjohn Company, Dept. 7923-190-41, Kalamazoo MI 49001
Exec. Secretary-Treasurer: Dr. S.D. 'Bud' Folz
Members: 350 *Staff:* 1
Annual Budget: under $10,000 *Tel:* (616) 385-6523
Hist. Note: Affiliated with the American Veterinary Medical Ass'n.
Annual Meetings: With American Veterinary Medical Ass'n/150
1987-Chicago, IL/July 19-21
1988-Portland, OR/July 17-19
1989-Orlando, FL/July 22-24

American Ass'n of Women Dentists (1921)
211 East Chicago Ave., Suite 948, Chicago IL 60611
Exec. Director: Peter C. Goulding
Members: 1,500 *Staff:* 2-5
Annual Budget: $10-25,000 *Tel:* (312) 337-1563
Hist. Note: Established to encourage women in the pursuit of a dental career. Until 1979 known as the Ass'n of American Women Dentists. Membership: $60/yr.
Publication:
Chronicle. bi-m. adv.
Annual Meetings: Always precedes American Dental Ass'n convention

American Ass'n of Yellow Pages Publishers (1984)
500 Chesterfield Center, Suite 250, Chesterfield MO 63017
Exec. Director: Edward G. Blackman
Members: 40 corporate members
Tel: (314) 532-6515
Hist. Note: Members are publishers of yellow pages and other specialty directories.

American Ass'n of Youth Museums (1962)
c/o Children's Museum of Oak Ridge, Box 3066, Oak Ridge TN 37830
President: Selma Shapiro
Members: 35-40
Annual Budget: under $10,000 *Tel:* (615) 482-1074
Hist. Note: Membership composed of museums with formal experience-oriented programs of which at least 70% of the participants are children. Formerly (1967) Ass'n of Youth Museum Directors. Affiliated with American Ass'n of Museums. Has no paid staff or permanent office. Membership: $25-100/yr. based on a percentage of member museum's annual budget.
Annual Meetings: June, with the American Ass'n of Museums

American Ass'n of Zoo Keepers (1967)
Topeka Zoo, 635 Gage Blvd., Topeka KS 66606
Administrative Secretary: Barbara Manspeaker
Members: 1,915 *Staff:* 2
Annual Budget: $25-50,000 *Tel:* (913) 272-5821
Hist. Note: Membership: $25/year.
Publications:
Animal Keepers' Forum. m.
Membership Directory. a.
Conference Proceedings. a.
Annual Meetings:
1987-Milwaukee, WI/Oct. 4-8

American Ass'n of Zoo Veterinarians (1945)
Box 49325, Atlanta GA 30359
Exec. Secretary: Morton S. Silberman, D.V.M.
Members: 600 *Staff:* 2-5
Annual Budget: $25-50,000 *Tel:* (404) 321-0948
Hist. Note: Organized to advance programs of preventive medicine for captive wild animals and to disseminate information about veterinary medicine in that field. Membership: $100/yr.
Publications:
The Journal of Zoo Animal Medicine. q. adv.
Proceedings. a. adv.
Newsletter. q.
Annual Meetings: Fall
1987-Kahuku, HI(Turtle Bay Hilton)/Sept. 2-6/450
1988-Toronto, Ontario(Sheraton Center)/Oct.

American Ass'n of Zoological Parks and Aquariums (1924)
Oglebay Park, Wheeling WV 26003
Exec. Director: Robert O. Wagner
Members: 4,500 *Staff:* 6-10
Annual Budget: $250-500,000 *Tel:* (304) 242-2160
Hist. Note: Formerly a branch of the American Institute of Park Executives and the National Recreation and Park Ass'n, it became an independent organization in 1971.
Publication:
AAZPA Newsletter. m.
Annual Meetings: Fall/1,200
1987-Portland, OR/Sept.
1988-Milwaukee, WI/Sept.

American Ass'n on Mental Deficiency (1876)
1719 Kalorama Road, N.W., Washington DC 20009
Exec. Director: Dr. Albert J. Berkowitz
Members: 10,000 individuals *Staff:* 21-25
Annual Budget: $1-2,000,000 *Tel:* (202) 387-1968
Hist. Note: Organized June 6, 1876 in Elwyn, Pennsylvania as the Ass'n of Medical Officers of American Institutions for Idiotic and Feeble-Minded Persons. Name changed to American Ass'n for the Study of the Feeble-Minded in 1906 and became American Ass'n on Mental Deficiency in 1933. Incorporated in Pennsylvania in 1938. Affiliated with the American Academy on Mental Retardation and the Internat'l Ass'n for the Scientific Study of Mental Retardation.
Publications:
American Journal of Mental Deficiency. bi-m. adv.
Mental Retardation. bi-m. adv.
Monograph Series. irreg.
Annual Meetings:
1987-Los Angeles, CA(Hilton)/May 24-28/2,000
1988-Washington, DC(Washington Hilton)/May 29-June 2/2,400
1989-Chicago, IL(Palmer House Hotel)/May 28-June 1/2,400
1990-Atlanta, GA(Atlanta Hilton)/May 27-31/2,400

American Astronautical Soc. (1953)
6212-B Old Keene Mill Court, Springfield VA 22152
Exec. Director: Carolyn F. Brown
Members: 1,500 *Staff:* 4-6
Annual Budget: $250-500,000 *Tel:* (703) 866-0020
Hist. Note: Founded at the American Museum of Natural History in New York in November 1953 by a small group of engineers, scientists and others who wished to initiate an American activity similar to the British Interplanetary Society as spokesman for a substantive space program. Incorporated in the State of New York in 1954. Dedicated to the advancement of the astronautical sciences and spaceflight engineering and the encouragement of the astronautic arts. Regular memberships are for professionals involved in the field of astronautics with six years of related training and/or work experience. Membership: $50/yr.
Publications:
AAS Newsletter. bi-m.
Journal of the Astronautical Sciences. q.
Advances in the Astronautical Sciences.
Science and Technology Series.
AAS History Series.
AAS Microfiche Series.
Annual Meetings: Fall/300-500

American Astronomical Soc. (1899)
2000 Florida Ave., N.W., Suite 300, Washington DC 20009
Exec. Officer: Dr. Peter B. Boyce
Members: 4,300 *Staff:* 2-5
Annual Budget: $2-5,000,000 *Tel:* (202) 328-2010
Hist. Note: Organized September 6, 1899 at the Yerkes Observatory, Green Bay, Wisconsin as the Astronomical and Astrophysical Soc. of America. Name changed to American Astronomical Soc. in 1914. Incorporated in Illinois in 1928. A member of the American Institute of Physics. Membership: $65/yr.
Publications:
Astronomical Journal. m.
Astrophysical Journal. semi-m.
Bulletin of the American Astronomical Society. 4/yr.
Semi-annual meetings: Summer and Winter
1987-Pasadena, CA(Mt. Wilson Observatory/Caltech)/Jan. 4-8/1,000

00024 12 05 86 1233

1987-Vancouver, BC/June 14-18/800
1988-Austin, TX/Jan. 10-14/800

American Athletic Trainers Ass'n and Certification Board (1978)
660 West Duarte Road, Arcadia CA 91006
Board Chairman: Joseph Borland, RPT
Members: 1,500-1,600 *Staff:* 1
Annual Budget: $10-25,000 *Tel:* (818) 445-1978
Hist. Note: Athletic trainers are skilled in the prevention and care of injuries as well as physical therapy under a physician's direction. Membership: Ranges from $40/yr.(qualified certified trainers) to $7/yr.(student trainers).
Publication:
Newsletter. q.
Annual Meetings: June

American Auto Racing Writers and Broadcasters Ass'n (1955)
922 North Pass Ave., Burbank CA 91505
Exec. Director: Norma 'Dusty' Brandel
Members: 500-550 *Staff:* 1
Annual Budget: under $10,000 *Tel:* (818) 842-7005
Hist. Note: Established in Indianapolis in 1955 with 17 charter members.
Publication:
Newsletter. m. adv.
Annual Meetings: May, in Indianapolis, IN

American Automatic Control Council (1957)
1051 Camino Velasquez, Green Valley AZ 85614
Secretary: William E. Miller
Members: 7 societies *Staff:* 1
Annual Budget: $100-250,000 *Tel:* (602) 625-0401
Hist. Note: Founded in Chicago, IL in March, 1957 as North American Control Council, it assumed its present name in October of that year. AACC is a federation of sponsoring societies, including: American Institute of Aeronautics and Astronautics, American Institute of Chemical Engineers, American Soc. of Mechanical Engineers, Ass'n of Iron and Steel Engineers, Institute of Electrical and Electronic Engineers, Instrument Soc. of America and Soc. for Computer Simulation. Serves as the U.S. representative in Internat'l Federation of Automatic Control. Membership: $800/yr. (organization)
Publications:
AACC Newsletter. q.
Prodeedings of the American Contol Conference. a.
Annual Meetings: American Control Conference in June/700
1987-Minneapolis, MN(Hyatt Regency)/June 10-12
1988-Atlanta, GA(Hilton & Towers)/June 15-17
1989-Pittsburgh, PA

American Automotive Leasing Ass'n (1955)
1001 Connecticut Ave., N.W., Suite 1201, Washington DC 20036
Exec. Director: John H. Fitch, Jr.
Members: 180 companies *Staff:* 2-5
Annual Budget: $250-500,000 *Tel:* (202) 223-2600
Hist. Note: Formed in late 1955 by 19 charter auto leasing companies in response to an effort by the IRS to deny leasing companies capital gains treatment on the sale of their used vehicles.
Publications:
Newsletter. m.
Washington Report. m.
Issue Alert. irreg.
Tax Advisory. irreg.
Legal Advisory.
Annual Meetings: Every September at a mid-west location
1987-Rancho Mirage, CA(Las Palmas)/Feb. 27-March 6
1988-Palm Beach, FL (PGA Sheraton)/March 6-9
1989-La Costa, CA(La Costa Hotel)/March 5-9
1990-Miami, FL(Doral)/March 4-7

American Bakers Ass'n (1897)
1111 14th St., N.W., Washington DC 20005
President: Robert J. Wager
Members: 325 companies *Staff:* 11-15
Annual Budget: $500-1,000,000 *Tel:* (202) 296-5800
Hist. Note: Supports the BREAD Political Action Committee. Formed at a meeting in Walter Baker & Co.'s room in the Mechanics' Building, Boston, October 20, 1897 at which eleven states and two Canadian provinces were represented. Known originally as the National Association of Master Bakers and then the American Association of the Baking Industry, it has operated under its present name since 1921. Incorporated in Illinois in 1917, it is affiliated with the American Institute of Baking. Supports the BREAD Political Action Committee.
Semi-annual Meetings: Spring and Fall

American Bandmasters Ass'n (1929)
2019 Bradford Dr., Arlington TX 76010
Secy.-Treas.: Jack H. Mahan
Members: 300-350 *Staff:* 1
Annual Budget: under $10,000 *Tel:* (817) 261-8629
Hist. Note: Formed at a meeting on July 5, 1929 at the Hotel Pennsylvania in New York City. Incorporated March 13, 1930 in the State of New York.
Publications:
Journal of Band Research. semi-a.
Directory. a.
Annual Meetings:
1987-Knoxville, TN/March 25-28
1988-Ashland, OR/March 2-5
1989-Tallahassee, FL/March 1-4
1990-Champaign-Urbana, IL/March 7-10
1991-Tempe, AZ/March 6-9

American Bankers Ass'n (1875)
1120 Connecticut Ave., N.W., Washington DC 20036
Exec. V. President: Donald G. Ogilvie
Members: 12-13,000 *Staff:* 400
Annual Budget: over $5,000,000 *Tel:* (202) 663-5000
Hist. Note: Organized in Saratoga, NY, July 20-22, 1875. Absorbed the Charge Account Bankers Ass'n and the Foundation for Full Service Banks in 1972. The association now has a budget of more than sixty million dollars and represents over 95% of the nation's banks. The American Institute of Banking is a section of the ABA; BankPac, its political action committee, and the Bank Marketing Ass'n are affiliates of ABA.
Publications:
ABA Bank Card Letter. m.
ABA Bank Installment Lender Report. m.
ABA Banking Journal. m. adv.
Agricultural Banker. m.
Bank Insurance & Protection Bulletin. m.
Bank Marketing Newsletter. m.
Bank Personnel News. m.
ABA Bankers Weekly. w.
Leaders Letter. m.
Thruput. m.
Trust Letter. m.
Trust Management Update. m.
Annual Meetings: Fall
1987-Dallas, TX(Convention Ctr.)/Oct. 17-21/9,000
1988-Honolulu, HI(Hilton Village and Sheraton)/Oct. 8-12/11,000
1989-Washington, DC(Convention Ctr.)/Oct. 14-18/10,000

American Bankruptcy Institute (1982)
122 Maryland Ave, N.E., P.O. Box 2187, Washington DC 20013
Exec. Director: G. Timothy Leighton
Members: 2,000 individuals *Staff:* 2
Annual Budget: $100-250,000 *Tel:* (202) 543-1234
Hist. Note: Incorporated in Nebraska. The ABI is a professional ass'n providing a multi-disciplinary forum for the exchange of ideas and information on bankruptcy issues. Membership: $90/yr.
Publications:
ABI Newsletter. bm. adv.
Bulletins. irreg.
Semi-Annual Meetings: Summer and Winter
1987-Washington, DC/Feb. 2-3 and July 19-21

American Bar Ass'n (1878)
750 N. Lake Shore Drive, Chicago IL 60611
Exec. Director and C.O.O.: Thomas H. Gonser
Members: 313,564 *Staff:* 575
Annual Budget: over $5,000,000 *Tel:* (312) 988-5000
Hist. Note: the bar). Represents more than 50% of practising lawyers in the U.S. Federally approved accrediting agency for law schools. The American Law Student Ass'n is a division of the ABA. Maintains the nationally-honored Code of Professional Responsibility. Operates the Center for Professional Responsibility, and an information center for the bar admission and bar disciplinary agencies. Has an annual budget of $50,000,000. Membership: $15-$140/year (depending upon number of years admitted to the bar).
Publications:
American Bar Association Journal. m.
Barrister. q. adv.
Student Lawyer. 9/yr. adv.
Annual Meetings: August
1987-San Francisco, CA/Aug. 6-13
1988-Toronto, Ontario/Aug. 4-11
1989-Honolulu, HI/Aug. 3-10

American Barter Trade Export Ass'n
Hist. Note: A Webb-Pomerene Act association. Address unknown in 1984. Probably defunct.

American Baseball Coaches Ass'n (1945)
1614 N. Lincoln Ave., Urbana IL 61801
Exec. Director: Lee Eilbracht
Members: 5,000 *Staff:* 3
Annual Budget: $100-250,000 *Tel:* (217) 328-7780
Hist. Note: Formerly (1985) the American Ass'n of College Baseball Coaches. Membership: $15/year (individual).
Publication:
Digest. q. adv.
Annual Meetings: January
1987-San Diego, CA/Jan. 8-12/1,500
1988-Atlanta, GA/Jan. 7-11

American Bashkir Curly Registry (1971)
Box 453, Ely NV 89301
Secretary: Sunny Martin
Members: 390 individuals *Staff:* 2
Annual Budget: under $10,000 *Tel:* (702) 289-4228
Hist. Note: Members are owners and breeders of rare horses with curly coats. Membership: $10/yr.
Publication:
Curly Cues. semi-a.
Annual Meetings: June in Ely, NV(Bristlecone Convention Ctr.)/150

American Beauty Ass'n (1985)
Box 1608, Boynton Beach FL 33425
Exec. Director: S.D. Frohlich
Staff: 1
Annual Budget: $25-50,000 *Tel:* (305) 736-7897
Hist. Note: Result of a merger of the Nat'l Beauty and Barber Manufacturers Ass'n and the UBA in 1985. Membership: $300/yr.
Publication:
ABA Newsletter. 10/yr.

American Bed & Breakfast Ass'n (1981)
Box 23294, Washington DC 20026
Director: Sarah Sonke
Members: 11,000 B&B's *Staff:* 3
Annual Budget: $10-25,000 *Tel:* (703) 237-9777
Hist. Note: Acts as a clearinghouse of information on B&B's. Membership: $50-75/yr.
Publications:
A Treasury of B&B. a. adv.
Shoptalk. m.
Annual Meetings: Spring

American Beefalo Ass'n (1975)
Hist. Note: Merged with the Internat'l Beefalo Breeders' Registry and the World Beefalo Ass'n to form the American Beefal World Registry in 1983.

American Beefalo World Registry (1975)
116 Executive Park, Louisville KY 40207
Admin. Assistant: Bonnie Priddy
Members: 900-1,000 breeders *Staff:* 2-5
Annual Budget: $50-100,000 *Tel:* (502) 897-1650
Hist. Note: Formed in November, 1983 by a merger of the American Beefalo Ass'n (1975), the World Beefalo Ass'n and Internat'l Beefalo Breeders' Registry (1980). Absorbed the Bison Hybrid Internat'l Ass'n. Maintains a registry of full-blood and percentage Beefalo stock (full-blood is an exact 3/8 bison & 5/8 bovine cross); also maintains a registry for bison cross animals not qualifying as Beefalo, and a Beefalo Meat Regisrtry. Membership: $60/yr.
Publication:
Beefalo Nickel. bi-m. adv.

American Beekeeping Federation (1943)
13637 N.W. 39th Ave., Gainesville FL 32606
Secy.-Treas.: Frank A. Robinson
Members: 1,800-1,900 *Staff:* 2-5
Annual Budget: $50-100,000 *Tel:* (904) 332-0012
Hist. Note: Formerly Nat'l Federation of Beekeepers Ass'ns. Members are honey producers, packers, shippers and suppliers. Membership: $15/yr. (commercial), $75/yr. (manufacturers/retailers)
Publication:
Federation Newsletter. bi-m. adv.
Annual Meetings: January, and odd years with the Apiary Inspectors of America.
1987-New Orleans, LA(Hyatt Regency)/Jan.
1988-Houston, TX
1989-Indianapolis, IN/Jan. 20-25

American Berkshire Ass'n (1875)
P.O. Box 2436, 1769 US 52 North, W. Lafayette IN 47906
Exec. Secretary: Jack W. Wall
Members: 400 *Staff:* 2-5
Annual Budget: $100-250,000 *Tel:* (317) 497-3618
Hist. Note: Breeders and fanciers of Berkshire swine. Member of the National Society of Livestock Record Associations. Membership: $20/year.
Publication:
The Purebred Picture. 10/yr. adv.
Annual Meetings: Summer

American Beverage Alcohol Ass'n (1938)
10 East 40th St., Room 2000, New York NY 10016
Gen. Counsel: Abraham M. Buchman
Members: 50-55 *Staff:* 1
Annual Budget: $10-25,000 *Tel:* (212) 953-0440
Hist. Note: Successor to the Whiskey Brokers of America, Inc. Until 1982 known as the Independent American Whiskey Ass'n. The above address is the law firm of Buchman, Buchman, & O'Brien.
Annual Meetings: with Wine and Spirits Wholesalers of America

American Bleached Shellac Manufacturers Ass'n (1924)
c/o William Zinsser Co., 39 Belmont Dr., Somerset NJ 08873
President: Gardner R. Cunningham
Members: 5-10 companies *Staff:* 1
Annual Budget: under $10,000 *Tel:* (201) 469-8100

American Blind Lawyers Ass'n (1971)
1010 Vermont Ave., N.W., Suite 1100, Washington DC 20005
Contact: Roberta Douglas
Members: 200 individuals *Staff:* 0
Annual Budget: under $10,000 *Tel:* (800) 424-8666
Hist. Note: No paid staff. Officers change annually. Administrative services provided by the American Council of the Blind, located at the above address. Membership: $10-15/yr.
Publication:
Newsletter. bi-m.
Annual Meetings: July
1987-Los Angeles, CA(Airport Hilton)/July 11-18/100

American Blonde D'Aquitaine Ass'n (1973)
79 East Center St., Gunnison UT 84634
Office Manager: Joan Newman
Members: 325-350 *Staff:* 1
Annual Budget: under $10,000 *Tel:* (801) 528-3123
Hist. Note: Breeders and fanciers of Blonde D'Aquitaine cattle. Merged with the Nat'l Blonde D'Aquitaine Foundation in 1985. Membership: $25/yr.

00025 12 05 86 1233

Publication:
The Bulletin. q.
Annual Meetings: February
1987-Houston, TX

American Blood Commission (1975)
1117 North 19th St., Suite 501, Arlington VA 22209
Exec. Director & Asst. Secy.: Nancy R. Holland
Members: 34 organizations *Staff:* 2
Annual Budget: $100-250,000 *Tel:* (703) 522-8414
Hist. Note: The Commission is a non-governmental organization established in 1975 to implement the National Blood Policy (issued by the federal government in 1973) which calls for a safe, adequate supply of voluntarily donated blood at a reasonable cost. The active membership of the ABC includes representation of the donor, the patient, the hospital, the private physician, the third party payer, as well as the three major organizations representing blood service facilities. It serves as a public policy forum for dialogue on blood service issues.
Annual Meetings: March
1987-Arlington, VA(Hyatt Regency)/100

American Blood Resources Ass'n (1972)
Box 3346, Annapolis MD 21403
President: Robert W. Reilly
Members: 90-100 companies *Staff:* 2-5
Annual Budget: $250-500,000 *Tel:* (301) 263-8296
Hist. Note: Members are commerical blood processors, blood component collectors, distributors and manufacturers. Membership: $600/year (company) each operating location.
Publications:
ABRA Newsletter. m.
Plasma Quarterly Magazine. q. adv.
Annual Proceedings Plasma Forum. a.
Annual Meetings: June in Arlington, VA/300

American Blue Cheese Ass'n (1954)
Hist. Note: A division of the Nat'l Cheese Institute.

American Board of Medical Specialties (1933)
One American Plaza, #805, Evanston IL 60201
Exec. V. President: Dr. Donald G. Langsley
Members: 25-30 organizations *Staff:* 20
Annual Budget: $500-1,000,000 *Tel:* (312) 491-9091
Hist. Note: Established as the Advisory Board for Medical Specialties, ABMS assumed its present name in 1970. As the "parent" organization for the 23 medical specialty Boards in the USA, it works closely with the American Hospital Ass'n, the Ass'n of American Medical Colleges, the American Medical Ass'n and the Council of Medical Specialty Societies as parent and sponsor of accrediting agencies for graduate and continuing medical education. Membership: $2,000/yr. (organization)
Publications:
ABMS Compendium of Certified Medical Specialists. bien.
Directories for each medical specialty. bien.
Semi-annual Meetings: Spring and Fall in Chicago at Hyatt O'Hare,
O'Hare Westin or O'Hare Marriott/175
1987-March 19 & Sept. 17
1988-March 17 & Sept. 22
1989-March 16 & Sept. 21
1990-March 22 & Sept. 13

American Boarding Kennels Ass'n (1977)
4575 Galley Road, Suite 400A, Colorado Springs CO 80915
Exec. Director: James J. Krack, CAE
Members: 1,000 *Staff:* 4
Annual Budget: $250-500,000 *Tel:* (303) 591-1113
Hist. Note: Persons or firms that board pets; kennel suppliers and others interested in the kennel industry. Membership: $120/year.
Publication:
Boarderline. bi-m. adv.
Annual Meetings: Fall
1987-St. Louis, MO(Clarion)/Nov. 1-4
1988-Atlanta, GA(Omni)/Oct. 23-27
1989-Nashville, TN(Opryland)/Nov. 12-15

American Boat and Yacht Council (1954)
Box 806, Amityville NY 11701
Exec. Director: G. James Lippmann
Members: 1,200 individuals, 200 companies *Staff:* 6-10
Annual Budget: $100-250,000 *Tel:* (516) 598-0550
Hist. Note: Members are individuals concerned with the design, construction, and maintenance of recreational boats and related equipment. Develops standards and recommended practices . Membership: $50/yr. (individual); $75/yr. (company)
Publication:
American Boat and Yacht Council News. irreg.
Annual Meetings: January, in New York, NY
1987-New York, NY(Jacob Javits Convention Ctr.)/Jan. 2/100

American Boat Builders and Repairers Ass'n (1943)
715 Boylston St., Boston MA 02116
Exec. V. President: Richard S. Guild, CAE
Members: 500 *Staff:* 1
Annual Budget: $100-250,000 *Tel:* (617) 266-6800
Hist. Note: Established as the Atlantic Coast Boat Builders and Repairers Association, it assumed its present name in 1955.
Publication:
Newsletter. m.
Annual Meetings:
1987-Hamilton, Bermuda(Hamilton Princess)

American Boiler Manufacturers Ass'n (1888)
950 North Glebe Road, Suite 160, Arlington VA 22203
Exec. Director: William H. Axtman
Members: 100-125 companies *Staff:* 6-10
Annual Budget: $250-500,000 *Tel:* (703) 522-7350
Hist. Note: Formerly (1960) American Boiler Manufacturers Ass'n and Affiliated Industries.
Semi-annual meetings: Winter and early Summer/260
1987-Charleston, SC(Kiawah Resort)/June 21-23

American Book Producers Ass'n (1980)
319 East 52nd St., New York NY 10022
President: Paul Fargis
Members: 50 companies *Staff:* 1
Annual Budget: $10-25,000 *Tel:* (212) 982-8934
Hist. Note: Members are book producing houses that develop the concepts for books and, based on a contractual agreement with a publisher, a business or other source, may produce finished books or production-ready film, camera-ready mechanicals, finished manuscripts, art and layouts. Membership: $300/year (company).
Publications:
Directory. a.
Newsletter. m.
Monthly Meetings:

American Booksellers Ass'n (1900)
122 East 42nd St., New York NY 10168
Exec. Director: Bernard Rath
Members: 5,600 *Staff:* 30-35
Annual Budget: $2-5,000,000 *Tel:* (212) 867-9060
Hist. Note: The trade association of U.S. retail bookstores. Started at the call of six booksellers in November, 1900, three from New York, and one from Grand Rapids, Cleveland and St. Paul and formally organized the following year with an initial membership of 748. Membership: $35/year (individual), $125 and up/yr. (company).
Publications:
ABA Newswire. w. adv.
ABA Sideline Directory. a. adv.
American Bookseller. m. adv.
Basic Book List. a.
Book Buyer's Handbook. a.
Annual Meetings: Spring/15,000
1987-Washington, DC(Convention Center)/May
1988-Anaheim, CA
1989-Washington, DC

American Bottled Water Ass'n (1958)
Hist. Note: Became the International Bottled Water Association in 1982.

American Brahman Breeders Ass'n (1924)
1313 La Concha Lane, Houston TX 77054
Exec. V. President: Wendell E. Schronk
Members: 3,650 *Staff:* 16-20
Annual Budget: $500-1,000,000 *Tel:* (713) 795-4444
Hist. Note: Breeders and fanciers of Brahman beef cattle. Member of the Nat'l Soc. of Livestock Record Ass'ns. Membership: $200/yr.
Publication:
The Brahman Journal. m. adv.
Annual Meetings: February, in Houston

American Breed Ass'n (1976)
306 South Avenue A, Portales NM 88130
Exec. Secretary: Jewell W. Jones
Members: 195 *Staff:* 2
Annual Budget: $10-25,000 *Tel:* (505) 356-8019
Hist. Note: Breeders and fanciers of a breed of cattle consisting of 1/2 Brahman, 1/4 Charolais, 1/8 Bison, 1/16 Hereford and 1/16 Shorthorn. Member of the Nat'l Pedigree Livestock Council. Membership: $50/yr.
Publication:
American Breed Newsletter. bi-m. adv.
Annual Meetings: Third Saturday in July/150

American Bridge Teachers' Ass'n (1957)
1905 East 58th St., Tulsa OK 74105
Business Secretary: Mary C. Hills
Members: 650 *Staff:* 1
Annual Budget: $10-25,000 *Tel:* (918) 747-8562
Hist. Note: Membership: $25/year.
Publication:
ABTA Quarterly Magazine. q. adv.
Annual Meetings: Precedes Summer Nationals of the American Contract Bridge League
1987-Baltimore, MD(Hyatt Regency & Omni)/July 15-17/100
1988-Salt Lake City, UT(Hotel Utah & Marriott)/July 27-29/100
1989-Chicago, IL(Hilton)July 26-28/100

American Broncho-Esophagological Ass'n (1917)
155 North Michigan Ave., Suite 325, Chicago IL 60601
Secretary: Lauren D. Holinger, M.D.
Members: 300 individuals *Staff:* 1
Annual Budget: under $10,000 *Tel:* (312) 938-1990
Hist. Note: Established as the American Bronchoscopic Society, it assumed its present name in 1928. Affiliated with the American Academy of Otolaryngology - Head and Neck Surgery.
Annual Meetings: Spring
1987-Denver, CO/April 27-28
1988-Palm Beach. FL/April 23-23
1989-San Francisco, CA/April 1-2
1990-Palm Beach, FL/April 29-30

American Brush Manufacturers Ass'n (1918)
1900 Arch St., Philadelphia PA 19103
Exec. Secretary: G.A. Taylor Fernley
Members: 225 companies *Staff:* 2-5
Annual Budget: $100-250,000 *Tel:* (215) 564-3484
Hist. Note: Absorbed the National Broom and Mop Council in 1982.
Annual Meetings: March/300
1987-Rancho Mirage, CA(Rancho Las Palmas)/March 19-22
1988-Orlando, FL(Hyatt Regency)/March 10-13
1989-Marco Island, FL(Marriott's Marco Beach Resort)/March 22-25
1990-Phoenix, AZ(Point Tapatio Cliffs)/March 22-25

American Bryological and Lichenological Soc. (1898)
Dept. of Biology, Texas A&M University, College Station TX 77843
Secy.-Treas.: Dale M.J. Mueller
Members: 525-550 *Staff:* 1
Annual Budget: $25-50,000 *Tel:* (409) 845-7772
Hist. Note: Originated in 1898 in Plymouth, New Hampshire as the Sullivant Moss Chapter of the Agassiz Ass'n. Became independent in 1900 under the name of Sullivant Moss Soc. Name changed to American Bryological Soc. in 1949 and to the American Bryological and Lichenological Soc. in 1969. Incorporated in Missouri in 1965. Affiliated with American Institute of Biological Sciences. Devoted to th study of all aspects of bryophytes and lichens. Membership: $30/yr.
Publications:
The Bryologist. q.
Evansia. irreg.
Annual Meetings: Summer
1987-Columbus, OH(Ohio State Univ.)/Aug. 9-13/100

American Buckskin Registry Ass'n (1962)
Box 3850, Redding CA 96049-3850
Office Secretary: Lori Williams
Members: 5-6,000 *Staff:* 2
Annual Budget: under $10,000 *Tel:* (916) 223-1420
Hist. Note: Established as the Buckskin Registry Ass'n, it assumed its present name in 1965. Members are owners, breeders, and dealers of the Buckskin horse. Membership: $15/yr.
Publication:
Buckskin News. m. adv.
Quarterly Meetings:

American Buffalo Ass'n (1975)
Stockyard Station Box 16660, Denver CO 80216
Exec. Secretary: Laurie Dineen
Members: 450-500 *Staff:* 1
Annual Budget: $100-250,000 *Tel:* (303) 292-2833
Hist. Note: Members are producers and marketers of buffalo products; their purpose is to preserve the American Bison and by-products. Membership: $55/yr.
Publications:
ABA Buffalo Journal. a. adv.
Buffalo World (newsletter). bi-m. adv.
Office Newsletter. bi-m.
Semi-annual Meetings: Jan. at Nat'l Western Stock Show and Summer
1987-Denver, CO(Denver Plaza)/Jan. 22-24/150-200
1987-Custer, SD(Custer State Park)/Aug. 19-23/200-250
1988-Denver, CO/Jan./150-200

American Bureau of Metal Statistics (1920)
Box 1405, Plaza Station, Secaucus NJ 07094
President: William J. Lambert
Members: 14 companies *Staff:* 12
Annual Budget: $250-500,000 *Tel:* (201) 863-6900
Hist. Note: Merged on January 1, 1975 with the Copper Institute (organized in 1927) and the United States Copper Association (established in 1934). Collects and disseminates statistical industry data on copper, lead, zinc and other non-ferrous metals. Membership open to non-ferrous metal producers in the Western Hemisphere.
Publications:
Industry Reports. m.
Yearbook of the ABMS. a.

American Bureau of Shipping (1862)
45 Eisenhower Drive, Paramus NJ 07652
Chairman: William N. Johnston
Members: 480 *Staff:* 1,500
Annual Budget: over $5,000,000 *Tel:* (201) 368-9100
Hist. Note: Certifies the soundness of merchant ships, mobil and fixed offshore drilling units, and other marine structures. Publishes over 30 Rules and Guides related to the construction and certification of ships, mobile offshore drilling units, containers, machinery and other equipment.
Publications:
Record of The American Bureau of Shipping. a.
ABS Activity Report. q.
Semi-annual Meetings: April and September

American Burn Ass'n (1967)
Good Samaritan Medical Center, 1130 East McDowell Road, Suite B-2, Phoenix AZ 85006
Secretary: Thomas L. Wachtel, M.D.
Members: 3,000 *Staff:* 3
Annual Budget: $25-50,000 *Tel:* (602) 239-2391
Hist. Note: Members are individuals concerned with the care, treatment and prevention of burns. Membership: $40/yr.
Publications:
Journal of Burn Care and Rehabilitation. q. adv.
Roster of the ABA. a.

00026 12 05 86 1233

Burn Care Services in North America. a.
Annual Meeting Abstract. a.
Annual Meetings: Spring
1987-Washington, DC(Sheraton)/April 29-May 2
1988-Seattle, WA/March 30-April 3
1989-New Orleans, LA(Hyatt)/March 15-18
1990-Las Vegas, NV/April 1-6

American Bus Ass'n (1926)
1025 Connecticut Ave., N.W., Suite 308, Washington DC 20036
President: Norman R. Sherlock
Members: 3,500 companies *Staff:* 20-25
Annual Budget: $2-5,000,000 *Tel:* (202) 293-5890
Hist. Note: Formerly the Motor Bus Division and later the Nat'l Motor Bus Division of the American Automobile Ass'n. Name changed to the Nat'l Ass'n of Motor Bus Operators until 1960 when it became the Nat'l Ass'n of Motor Bus Owners until it assumed its present name on Sept. 19, 1977. Privately owned bus companies, bus manufacturers, accessory manufacturers, travel-tourism business and organizations and others concerned with bus service. Connected with the Bus Industry Public Affairs Committee. Sponsors and supports the BusPac-Political Action Committee.
Publications:
Destinations. m.
Travel Scan. m.
Bus Operator. bi-m.
Annual Meetings:
1987-Orlando, FL(Peabody)/February 3-6/1,000

American Business Conference (1980)
1730 K St., N.W., Suite 703, Washington DC 20006
President: William Lilley, III
Members: 100 companies *Staff:* 6-10
Annual Budget: $1-2,000,000 *Tel:* (202) 822-9300
Hist. Note: An association of 100 medium size growth companies, represented by their chief executive officers, founded in Washington June 24, 1980 under the sponsorship of Arthur Levitt, Jr. Chairman of the American Stock Exchange. Is concerned with tax and regulatory reform and preservation of the free enterprise system. Membership: $12,500/year.

American Business Law Ass'n (1923)
Dept. of Insurance, Legal Studies and, Real Estate, Univ. of Georgia, Athens GA 30602
Exec. Secretary: Dr. Jan W. Henkel
Members: 1,200 *Staff:* 1
Annual Budget: $25-50,000 *Tel:* (404) 542-2126
Hist. Note: Members are teachers of business law, legal environment and other law-related courses in colleges and universities other than professional law schools. Membership: $25/yr.
Publications:
American Business Law Journal. q. adv.
Journal of Legal Studies Education. semi-a.
ABLA Newsletter. semi-a.
Annual Meetings: August
1987-Philadelphia, PA/Aug. 19-22
1988-New Orleans, LA

American Business Press (1965)
Hist. Note: Became the Ass'n of Business Publishers in 1985.

American Business Women's Ass'n (1949)
9100 Ward Parkway, Box 8728, Kansas City MO 64114
Exec. Director: Carolyn B. Elman
Members: 112,000 individuals *Staff:* 40
Annual Budget: $2-5,000,000 *Tel:* (816) 361-6621
Hist. Note: Dedicated to the professional, educational, cultural and social advancement of business women. Provides networking support. Membership: $25/yr.
Publications:
Women In Business. bi-m. adv.
Chapter Newsletters. bi-m.
National Member Newsletter. a.
Annual Meetings:
1987-Los Angeles, CA/Oct. 21-25
1988-Orlando, FL/Oct. 12-16
1989-Nashville, TN/Nov. 1-5
1990-Dallas, TX/Oct. 30-Nov. 4

American Butter Institute (1908)
699 Prince Street, Box 20047, Alexandria VA 22320
Exec. Director: Robert F. Anderson
Members: 100 *Staff:* 2-5
Annual Budget: $10-25,000 *Tel:* (703) 549-2230
Hist. Note: Organized as the Nat'l Ass'n of Creamery Butter Manufacturers in 1908, ABI is the nation's oldest dairy product association.

American Camping Ass'n (1910)
Bradford Woods, Martinsville IN 46151
Exec. V. President: Armand B. Ball, Jr. CAE
Members: 2,400 camps; 5,600 individuals *Staff:* 25-30
Annual Budget: $2-5,000,000 *Tel:* (317) 342-8456
Hist. Note: Established in 1910 as the Camp Directors Ass'n. Became the Camp Directors' Ass'n of America in 1924 and the American Camping Ass'n in 1935. Sponsors accreditation programs for camps and certification/educational programs for camp director/owners.
Publications:
Camping Magazine. 7/yr. adv.
Camping Update.
Parents' Guide to Accredited Camps. a. adv.
Annual Meetings:
1987-Washington, DC(Shoreham)/March 2-7/1,000
1988-Nashville, TN(Opryland)/Feb. 17-20/1,000
1989-Seattle, WA(Westin)/Feb. 28-March 3/1,000
1990-Boston, MA(Sheraton)/1,200
1991-Dearborn, MI(Hyatt)/1,100

American Cancer Soc. (1913)
90 Park Ave., New York NY 10016
Exec. V. President: G. Robert Gadberry
Members: 2,500,000 individuals *Staff:* 275-300
Annual Budget: over $5,000,000 *Tel:* (212) 736-3030
Hist. Note: Formerly (1913) the American Society for the Control of Cancer; Incorporated (1922). Name changed (1944) to American Cancer Society, Inc. Has an annual budget of $260,000,000.
Publications:
CA- a Cancer Journal for Clinicians. bi-m.
Cancer. m. adv.
Cancer Facts and Figures. a.
Cancer News. semi-a.
Annual Meetings: New York City in November

American Canoe Manufacturers Union (1982)
439 East 51st St., New York NY 10022
Exec. Director: Dwight Rockwell
Members: 6 companies *Staff:* 2
Annual Budget: under $10,000 *Tel:* (212) 421-5220
Hist. Note: Formed to promote canoeing as a lifetime sport and activity to America's youth and young adults. Membership: $3,000/yr.
Publications:
Canoe Book List. a.
Learn Canoeing! a.
Semi-Annual Meetings: Summer and Fall

American Car Rental Ass'n (1978)
2011 Eye St., N.W., Fifth Floor, Washington DC 20006
Exec. Director: M. Jane Moss
Members: 600 companies *Staff:* 6-10
Annual Budget: $250-500,000 *Tel:* (202) 223-2118
Hist. Note: Became separate organization in 1978 on the dissolution of the Car and Truck Renting and Leasing Ass'n.
Publications:
ACRA Report. bi-m.
ACRA Alert. m.
Annual Meetings: Spring
1987-Tampa, FL(Saddlebrook Resort/March 25-29/325
1988-Los Angeles, CA(Century Plaza)/mid-March

American Carbon Soc. (1957)
The Stackpole Corp., St. Mary's PA 15857
Secy.-Treas.: Dr. William A. Nystrom
Members: 500 *Staff:* 1
Annual Budget: $10-25,000 *Tel:* (814) 781-8410
Hist. Note: Individuals interested in the scientific aspects of a class of materials ranging from organic crystals and polymers through chars and carbons to graphite. Has an international membership. Formerly (1973) the American Carbon Committee.
Publication:
Carbon. bi-m.
Biennial Meetings: Uneven years
1987-Worcester, MA(Worcester Polytechnic Institute)

American Cardiology Technologists Ass'n (1957)
1980 Isaac Newton Square South, Reston VA 22090
Exec. Director: George M. Cate
Members: 3,000 *Staff:* 2-5
Annual Budget: $100-250,000 *Tel:* (703) 435-9466
Hist. Note: Originated in Miami in February, 1957 as the Southern Cardiology Technologists Ass'n. Chartered as the American Technologists Ass'n in Dade County, Florida, on April 10, 1958. Affiliated with the American Society of Allied Health Professions and the National Health Council. Membership: $50/yr.
Publication:
ACTA Newsletter. m.

American Cargo War Risk Reinsurance Exchange (1939)
14 Wall St., Rm. 2120, New York NY 10005
Secretary: Carroll W. Dawson
Members: 100-125 ocean marine insurance companies *Staff:* 2-5
Tel: (212) 233-3180
Hist. Note: During W.W.I, American insurance companies were dependent upon foreign insurers for reinsurance of war risks on cargo. In order to provide an independent domestic market for such risks, the Exchange was organized in June 1939, just prior to W.W.II. It has provided a stable and economical reinsurance market for war risks on ocean cargoes since that time.
Annual Meetings: New York City in Spring

American Carnation Soc. (1852)
Hist. Note: Became inactive in 1981.

American Cartographic Ass'n (1981)
Hist. Note: A member organization of the American Congress on Surveying and Mapping.

American Catfish Marketing Ass'n (1971)
Box 34, Jackson MS 39205
Exec. Director: George Williams
Members: 8 companies *Staff:* 1-2
Annual Budget: $10-25,000 *Tel:* (601) 353-7916
Hist. Note: Major processors of domestic catfish.
Annual Meetings: September in Jackson, MS

American Catholic Correctional Chaplains Ass'n (1952)
2900 King Drive, Cleveland OH 44104
Secretary: Fr. Dismas Boeff
Members: 200 *Staff:* 2-5
Annual Budget: under $10,000 *Tel:* (216) 721-5300
Hist. Note: Affiliated with The American Correctional Ass'n. Formerly the American Catholic Prison Chaplains Ass'n. Membership: $15/year.
Publication:
Chaplett. q.
Annual Meetings: Summer, with the American Correctional Ass'n.

American Catholic Historical Ass'n (1919)
Catholic Univ. of America, Washington DC 20064
Secretary: Rev. Robert Trisco
Members: 1,000-1,100 *Staff:* 1
Annual Budget: $10-25,000 *Tel:* (202) 635-5079
Hist. Note: A professional society of those interested in the history of the Catholic church and the promotion of historical scholarship among Catholics. Founded in Cleveland, Ohio in December, 1919 by a small group of historians under the leadership of Peter Guilday and incorporated in the District of Columbia. Membership: $25/yr.
Publication:
Catholic Historical Review. q. adv.
Annual Meetings: December, with the American Historical Ass'n/150-200
1987-Washington, DC(Sheraton Washington & Omni Shoreham)/Dec. 28-30

American Catholic Philosophical Ass'n (1926)
Catholic University, Washington DC 20064
Nat'l Secretary: Dr. Daniel O. Dahlstrom
Members: 2,000 members and subscribers *Staff:* 4
Annual Budget: $50-100,000 *Tel:* (202) 635-5518
Hist. Note: Members are scholars and individuals interested in Catholic philosophy. Membership: $31-40/yr. (individual); $40-50yr. (institution)
Publications:
Newsletter. q. adv.
The New Scholasticism. q. adv.
Proceedings. a. adv.
Annual Meetings: Spring
1987-Buffalo, NY(Hyatt Regency)/March 27-29/2-300
1988-Louisville, KY/April 8-10/2-300
1989-New Orleans, LA(Marriott)/April 7-9/2-300

American Cement Trade Alliance (1985)
1331 Pennsylvania Ave., N.W., Suite 910, Washington DC 20004
President: Richard C. Creighton
Members: 19 companies *Staff:* 4
Annual Budget: $250-500,000 *Tel:* (202) 662-7416
Hist. Note: Established and incorporated in the District of Columbia to address issues relating to the portland cement industry. Supported by companies representing more than 70% of U.S. cement production. Membership: assessed per ton of clinker capacity
Annual Meetings: January

American Cemetery Ass'n (1887)
5201 Leesburg Pike, Suite 1111, Falls Church VA 22041
Exec. V. President: Stephen L. Morgan
Members: 2,300 *Staff:* 14
Annual Budget: $1-2,000,000 *Tel:* (703) 379-5838
Hist. Note: Founded as the Ass'n of American Cemetery Superintendents, it became the Ass'n of American Cemeteries in 1944 and became the American Cemetery Ass'n in 1945. Merged with the Nat'l Ass'n of Cemeteries in Oct., 1980. Members are cemetery owners and managers and their suppliers.
Publication:
Cemetery Management. m. adv.
Annual Meetings: Fall
1987-Cincinnati, OH(Convention Ctr.)/Nov. 3-7

American Ceramic Soc. (1899)
757 Brooksedge Plaza Drive, Westerville OH 43081-2821
Exec. Director: W. Paul Holbrook
Members: 330 companies, 10,500 individuals *Staff:* 44
Annual Budget: $2-5,000,000 *Tel:* (614) 890-4700
Hist. Note: Founded February 6, 1899 by Edward Orton, Jr. with 15 charter members. Incorporated in Ohio in 1905. A member of the Internat'l Commission on Glass and the Inter-Society Color Council. The Nat'l Institute of Ceramic Engineers and the Ceramic Education Council are affiliated classes of the ACerS. Membership: $60/yr.
Publications:
Ceramic Bulletin. m. adv.
Journal of the American Ceramic Society/Communications. m.
Ceramic Abstracts. bi.-m.
Ceramic Engineering and Science Proceedings. bi-m.
Advance Ceramic Materials. q. adv.
Ceramic Source. a. adv.
Annual Meetings: Spring
1987-Pittsburgh, PA/April 26-30/6,500-7,000
1988-Cincinnati, OH(Convention Ctr.)/May 1-5/4,500

00027 12 05 86 1233

American Ceramic Tableware Council (1979)
Hist. Note: Defunct in 1982.

American Chain Ass'n (1971)
152 Rollins Ave., Suite 208, Rockville MD 20852
Exec. Secretary: Raymond J. Lloyd
Members: 9 companies *Staff:* 3
Annual Budget: $100-250,000 *Tel:* (301) 984-9080
Hist. Note: Formerly (1971) American Sprocket Chain Mfrs. Ass'n, successor to: Ass'n of Roller & Silent Chain Mfrs. and Malleable Chain Mfrs. Inst. Member, Machinery and Allied Products Institute.
Annual Meetings: February

American Chain of Warehouses (1911)
55 West Quackenbush Ave., Dumont NJ 07628
Exec. V. President: Charles E. Kessler
Members: 50 commercial warehouses *Staff:* 6
Tel: (201) 387-2600
Hist. Note: Membership: Dues are set according to formula.
Publication:
Report for Members. m.
Annual Meetings: With American Warehousemen's Ass'n alternately in Chicago & New York
1987-Chicago, IL/Fall

American Chamber of Commerce Executives (1914)
1454 Duke St., Alexandria VA 22314
President: Paul J. Greeley, Jr.
Members: 4,000 *Staff:* 31
Annual Budget: $2-5,000,000 *Tel:* (703) 836-7904
Hist. Note: Merger of American Ass'n of Commercial Executives and Central Ass'n of Commercial Secretaries. Formerly (1949) Nat'l Ass'n of Commercial Organization Secretaries. Grants the professional CCE (Certified Chamber Executive) designation.
Publication:
Chamber Executive. m. adv.
Annual Meetings: October/500
1987-Montreal, Quebec(Bonaventure)
1988-Denver, CO(Fairmont)
1989-Minneapolis, MN(Marriott City Center)
1990-Atlanta, GA(Marriott Marquis)
1991-Phoenix, AZ(Pointe Tappatio)

American Chamber of Commerce Researchers Ass'n (1962)
c/o ACCE, 1454 Duke St., Alexandria VA 22314
Manager, Ass'n Services: Rosemary Harper
Members: 200 companies; 250 individuals
Annual Budget: $10-25,000 *Tel:* (703) 836-7904
Hist. Note: Officers are elected annually. Administrative support provided by the American Chamber of Commerce Executives.
Publication:
Cost of Living Index. q.
Annual Meetings: Spring
1987-Columbus, OH/June/100

American Chemical Soc. (1876)
1155 16th St., N.W., Washington DC 20036
Exec. Director: Dr. John Crum
Members: 136,000 *Staff:* 1,550
Annual Budget: over $5,000,000 *Tel:* (202) 872-4600
Hist. Note: Founded in New York City on April 6, 1876. Incorporated in 1877. Granted a national charter by the Congress in 1937. Encourages the advancement of all branches of chemistry in the broadest and most liberal manner. Membership: $76/yr.
Publications:
Accounts of Chemical Research. m.
Analytical Chemistry. m. adv.
Biochemistry. bi-w. adv.
Chemical Abstracts. w.
Chemical and Engineering News. w. adv.
Chemical Reviews. 6/yr.
Chemical Titles. bi-w.
CHEMTECH m. adv.
Environmental Science and Technology. m. adv.
I&EC Research. m.
Inorganic Chemistry. bi-w. adv.
Journal of Agricultural and Food Chemistry. bi-m. adv.
Journal of the American Chemical Society. bi-m. adv.
Journal of Chemical and Engineering Data. q.
Journal of Chemical Information and Computer Sciences. q. adv.
Journal of Medicinal Chemistry. m. adv.
Journal of Organic Chemistry. bi-w. adv.
Journal of Physical & Chemical Reference Data. q.
Journal of Physical Chemistry. bi-w. adv.
Macromolecules. m. adv.
Organometallies. m.
Energy & Fuels. bi-m.
Langmuir. bi-m.
Semi-annual meetings: Spring and Fall
1987-Denver, CO/April 5-10
1987-New Orleans, LA/Aug. 30-Sept. 4

American Cheviot Sheep Soc. (1924)
R.R. 1, Box 100, Clarks Hill IN 47930
Secretary: Ruth Bowles
Members: 6-700 *Staff:* 1
Annual Budget: under $10,000 *Tel:* (317) 523-2193
Hist. Note: Breeders and fanciers of Cheviot sheep. Member of the National Society of Livestock Record Associations. Membership: $10/life.
Publications:
Sheep Breeder-Sheepman. m. adv.
Breeders Directory. a.
Cheviot Journal. a.
Annual Meetings: November, in Louisville, KY

American Chianina Ass'n (1972)
Box 890, Platte City MO 64079
C.E.O.: Robert H. Vantrease
Members: 4,000 *Staff:* 11
Annual Budget: $250-500,000 *Tel:* (816) 431-2808
Hist. Note: Breeders and fanciers of Chianina beef cattle. Member of the Nat'l Soc. of Livestock Record Ass'ns.
Publication:
ACA Journal. m. adv.
Annual Meetings: Fall

American Chiropractic Ass'n (1930)
1701 Clarendon Blvd., Arlington VA 22209
Exec. V. President: Dr. Gerald M. Brassard
Members: 20,000 *Staff:* 25-30
Annual Budget: $2-5,000,000 *Tel:* (703) 276-8800
Hist. Note: Founded in 1930 as the Nat'l Chiropractic Ass'n, it assumed its present name in 1963; chartered in Delaware. Sponsors the following specialty councils: Diagnosis and Internal Disorders, Nutrition, Orthopedics, Neurology, Physiological Therapeutics, Sports Injuries and Physical Fitness, Diagnositc Imaging, Mental Health and Technic. Promotes the philosophy, science and art of chiropractic, and the professional welfare of its members; promotes legislation defining chiropractic health care and public education of chiropractic. Conducts chiropractic survey and statistical study. Oversees the work of the ACA-PAC, its political action arm. Membership: $400/yr.
Publications:
ACA Journal of Chiropractic. m. adv.
ACA Membership Directory. a.
Annual Meetings: June
1987-Las Vegas, NV
1988-Philadelphia, PA
1989-San Antonio, TX

American Choral Directors Ass'n (1959)
Box 6310, Lawton OK 73506
Exec. Director: Dr. Gene Brooks
Members: 13,000 *Staff:* 6-10
Annual Budget: $250-500,000 *Tel:* (405) 355-8161
Hist. Note: A non-profit professional organization whose active membership is composed of choral musicians from schools, colleges and universities, community and industrial organizations, churches and professional groups. Active Membership: $25/yr.
Publication:
The Choral Journal. 10/yr. adv.
Biennial meetings: uneven years
1987-San Antonio, TX(Convention Center)/March 11-14/5,000

American Choral Foundation (1954)
251 South 18th St., Philadelphia PA 19103
Exec. Director: Janice F. Kestler
Members: 1,100-1,200 *Staff:* 5
Annual Budget: $50-100,000 *Tel:* (215) 545-4444
Hist. Note: Members are choral conductors, school music administrators, music libraries and others concerned with choral music. Formerly (1959) the American Concert Choir and Choral Foundation. Absorbed the Ass'n of Choral Conductors in 1985. Administrative support provided by the Ass'n of Professional Vocal Ensembles. Membership: $27.50/yr.
Publications:
American Choral Review. q. adv.
Research Memoranda. q.

American Cinema Editors (1950)
4416-1/2 Finley Ave., Los Angeles CA 90027
President: James Blakely
Members: 250-300 *Staff:* 2-4
Annual Budget: $10-25,000 *Tel:* (213) 660-4425
Hist. Note: An honorary professional society. Presents the annual "Eddie" award for film editing. Has no permanent officers or staff. Membership, though international, is concentrated in the Los Angeles area.
Publication:
American Cinemeditor. q. adv.
Annual Meetings: 4th Tuesday in May

American Classical League (1919)
Miami Univ., Oxford OH 45056
Manager: Geri Dutra
Members: 3,500 *Staff:* 2-5
Annual Budget: $25-50,000 *Tel:* (513) 529-4116
Hist. Note: High school and college teachers of Latin and Greek. Supports the Junior Classical League - high school Latin and Greek students.
Publication:
Classical Outlook. q. adv.
Annual Meetings:
1987-Washington, DC(Georgetown University)/June 17-20

American Cleft Palate Ass'n (1943)
331 Salk Hall, Univ. of Pittsburgh, Pittsburgh PA 15261
Exec. Director: Jane Angelone Graminski
Members: 1,800 individuals *Staff:* 2-5
Annual Budget: $100-250,000 *Tel:* (412) 681-9620
Hist. Note: Founded in Harrisburg, PA, April 4, 1943 as the American Academy of Cleft Prosthesis. Became the American Ass'n for Cleft Palate Rehabilitation in 1949 and later assumed its present name. Members consist of doctors, dentists and others concerned with deformities of the mouth and face. Membership: $60/yr.
Publication:
Cleft Palate Journal. q.
Annual Meetings: Spring/400
1987-San Antonio, TX/April
1988-Williamsburg, VA/April
1989-San Francisco, CA/April
1990-St. Louis, MO
1991-Hilton Head, SC
1992-Portland

American Clinical and Climatological Ass'n (1884)
Dept. of Medicine, Med. Univ. of S.C., 171 Ashley Ave., Charleston SC 29425
Secy.-Treas.: James C. Allen, M.D.
Members: 300-325 *Staff:* 1
Annual Budget: $25-50,000 *Tel:* (803) 792-2911
Hist. Note: Members are engaged in the clinical study of disease. Membership: (invitation only) $100/yr.
Publication:
Transactions of the American Clinical and Climatological Ass'n. q.
Annual Meetings: October/300-350
1987-Ponte Vedra Beach, FL(Ponte Vedra Inn)/Oct. 18-21
1988-Sea Island, GA(The Cloisters)/Oct. 23-26
1989-Bermuda(Southampton Princess)/Oct. 22-25
1990-Hot Springs, VA(The Homestead)/Oct. 21-24

American Clinical Laboratory Ass'n (1971)
1919 Pennsylvania Ave., N.W., Suite 800, Washington DC 20006
General Counsel: H. Robert Halper
Members: 25 *Staff:* 2-5
Annual Budget: $100-250,000 *Tel:* (202) 887-1400
Hist. Note: Members are clinical laboratories licensed and regulated under Medicare and the Interstate Laboratory Program. The above address is the law firm of O'Connor and Hannan. Membership: Dues vary by organization size.
Annual Meetings:
1987-Washington, DC/Oct.

American Cloak and Suit Manufacturers Ass'n (1919)
450 Seventh Ave., New York NY 10123
Exec. Director: Peter Conticelli
Members: 185 *Staff:* 3-4
Tel: (212) 244-7300
Hist. Note: Membership concentrated in the New York metropolitan area. Major function is to represent its members in bargaining with labor.

American Coal Ash Ass'n (1968)
1819 H St., N.W., Suite 510, Washington DC 20006
President: Tobias Anthony
Members: 100 companies *Staff:* 2-5
Annual Budget: $250-500,000 *Tel:* (202) 659-2303
Hist. Note: Formerly (1985) the Nat'l Ash Ass'n. Formed and incorporated in the State of New York with 28 charter members, the National Coal Association, 23 electric utilities and 4 coal companies. Members are companies producing fly ash from the combustion of coal and are interested in promoting its use.
Publication:
Ash at Work. bi-m.
Annual Meetings: Washington, DC, 1st Wednesday in April

American Cocoa Research Institute (1948)
7900 Westpark Dr., Suite 514, McLean VA 22102
President: Richard T. O'Connell, CAE
Members: 15-20 companies *Staff:* 2-5
Annual Budget: $250-500,000 *Tel:* (703) 790-5011
Hist. Note: Affiliate of Chocolate Manufacturers Ass'n of the U.S.A., which provides administrative support.
Annual Meetings: With the Chocolate Manufacturers Ass'n

American Coke and Coal Chemicals Institute (1944)
1255 Twenty-Third St., N.W., Washington DC 20037
Exec. V. President: Mark T. Engle
Members: 50-60 companies *Staff:* 2-5
Annual Budget: $100-250,000 *Tel:* (202) 452-1140
Hist. Note: Members are national and international firms representing companies which produce oven coke and metallurgical coal; producers and processors of chemicals derived from petroleum, coal or tar; and builders of major components to the industry.
Annual Meetings: In White Sulphur Springs, WV(Greenbrier)/Sept.-Oct./250

American Collectors Ass'n (1939)
4040 West 70th St., Minneapolis MN 55435
Exec. V. President: John W. Johnson, CAE
Members: 3,200 credit collection companies *Staff:* 75
Annual Budget: $1-2,000,000 *Tel:* (612) 926-6547
Hist. Note: Organized in 1939 by a group of Western states collectors, ACA's purpose is to promote the general welfare of the collection profession. Activities include education, publishing, research, public affairs, group buying, public relations, conventions, trade show and data processing service. Membership: $145/yr. (minimum)
Publications:
Collector. m. adv.
Roster. a.

00028 12 05 86 1233

Annual Meetings: Summer
1987-Orlando, FL/June 30-July 3
1988-Maui, HI(Marriott)/July 5-8
1989-Minneapolis, MN(Hyatt Regency)/July 4-7
1990-Reno, NV(Bally's)/July 3-6
1991-New York, NY
1992-Banff, Canada
1993-San Antonio, TX
1994-Colorado Springs, CO
1995-Palm Desert, CA
1996-Salt Lake City, UT

American College for Continuing Education (1968)
Hist. Note: Sponsored by the American Ass'n of Foot Specialists.

American College Health Ass'n (1920)
15879 Crabbs Branch Way, Rockville MD 20855
Exec. Director: Stephen D. Blom
Members: 475 institutions, 900 individuals *Staff:* 8
Annual Budget: $500-1,000,000 *Tel:* (301) 963-1100
Hist. Note: Founded as the American Student Health Ass'n. Membership: $10-$195/yr. (individual); $200-3,000/yr. (institution)
Publications:
Action. 10/yr.
Journal of the ACHA. bi-m. adv.
Annual Meetings: Spring/1,250
1987-Chicago, IL(Marriott)/May 27-30
1988-Denver, CO(Hilton)/May 25-28
1989-Washington, DC

American College of Allergists (1942)
800 East Northwest Hwy., Suite 101, Mount Prospect IL 60056
Exec. Director: James R. Slawny
Members: 2,600 *Staff:* 2-5
Annual Budget: $1-2,000,000 *Tel:* (312) 255-0380
Hist. Note: An organization of qualified allergists, physicians and scientists who have a special interest in allergy and/or immunology. Membership: $120/yr.
Publication:
Annals of Allergy. m. adv.
Annual Meetings:
1987-Las Vegas, NV/Jan. 17-21 and Boston, MA/Nov. 14-18

American College of Anesthesiologists (1936)
Hist. Note: A section of the American Soc. of Anesthesiologists.

American College of Angiology (1955)
1044 Northern Blvd., Suite 103, Roslyn NY 11576
Director, CME: Denise M. Kapeluck
Members: 1,900-2,000 individuals *Staff:* 5-7
Annual Budget: $250-500,000 *Tel:* (516) 484-6880
Hist. Note: Members are individuals interested in the study of blood circulation, lymph glands and the heart. Membership: $150/yr.
Publications:
Journal of Angiology. m. adv.
Vascular Surgery. bi-m. adv.
Semi-annual meetings: Summer and Fall
1987-Montreux, Switzerland(Hyatt Continental Montreux)/July 26-Aug. 1
1987-Paradise Island, Bahamas(Resorts Internat'l)/Oct. 18-23

American College of Apothecaries (1940)
874 Union Ave., Memphis TN 38163
Exec. V. President: Dr. D. C. Huffman
Members: 1,000 *Staff:* 5
Annual Budget: $100-250,000 *Tel:* (901) 528-6037
Hist. Note: Members are pharmacists owning ethical prescription pharmacies. Membership: $150/year.
Publications:
A.C.A. Newsletter. m.
Patron's Newsletter. m.
Physician's Newletter. m.
Professional Practice Newsletter. m.
Voice of The Pharmacist. q.
Annual Meetings:
1987-San Diego, CA

American College of Cardiology (1949)
9111 Old Georgetown Rd., Bethesda MD 20814
Exec. V. President: William D. Nelligan, CAE
Members: 15,000 *Staff:* 75-80
Annual Budget: over $5,000,000 *Tel:* (301) 897-5400
Hist. Note: Formed in 1949 and incorporated in the District of Columbia. Has an annual budget of $10 million.
Publications:
Journal of the American College of Cardiology. m. adv.
Newsletter. m.
Affiliates Newsletter. q.
Annual Meetings: Spring
1987-New Orleans, LA/March 8-12
1988-Atlanta, GA/March 27-31
1989-Anaheim, CA/March 19-23
1990-New Orleans, LA/March 18-22
1991-Atlanta, GA/April 28-May 2

American College of Chemosurgery (1967)
c/o American Academy of Dermatology, 1567 Maple Ave., Evanston IL 60201
Secy.-Treas.: Martin Braun, III
Members: 200 *Staff:* 1
Annual Budget: $25-50,000 *Tel:* (312) 869-3954
Hist. Note: Members are physicians utilizing chemosurgery for the microscopically controlled excision of skin cancers.
Publication:
Bulletin of the American College of Chemosurgery. q.
Annual Meetings:
1987-Castle Harbour, Bermuda(Marriott's Castle Harbour)/April 27-29

American College of Chest Physicians (1935)
911 Busse Highway, Park Ridge IL 60068
Exec. Director: Dr. Alfred Soffer
Members: 13,000 *Staff:* 38-40
Annual Budget: $2-5,000,000 *Tel:* (312) 698-2200
Hist. Note: Founded in 1935 and incorporated in Illinois in 1942. Associated member of the Council of Internat'l Organizations. Membership: $175/yr.
Publication:
CHEST. m. adv.
Annual Meetings: Fall
1987-Atlanta, GA(Hilton)/Oct. 26-30/4,000
1988-Anaheim, CA(Hilton)/Oct. 3-7/4,000

American College of Clinical Pharmacology (1969)
19 South 22nd St., Philadelphia PA 19103
Exec. Director: William F. Chaveas
Members: 575-600 *Staff:* 2-5
Annual Budget: $100-250,000 *Tel:* (215) 563-9560
Hist. Note: Individuals who have earned a doctorate in the biomedical sciences or who have had at least three years of training in basic science, internal medicine or an allied field.
Publications:
Journal of Clinical Pharmacology. 8/yr. adv.
Directory. bien.
Annual Meetings: Fall
1987-Philadelphia, PA(College of Physicians)/Oct. 15-16

American College of Clinical Pharmacy (1979)
3101 Broadway, Suite 350, Kansas City MO 64111
Exec. Secretary: Robert M. Elenbaas
Members: 725 *Staff:* 1
Annual Budget: $100-250,000 *Tel:* (816) 531-2177
Hist. Note: Internat'l society founded in October 1979 in Kansas City. Promotes the rational use of medications in health care, the advancement of knowledge regarding drug therapy and the development of clinical pharmacy. Membership: $75/yr. (individual).
Publications:
ACCP Reprot. q.
Membership Directory. a.
Residency & Fellowship Directory. a.
Annual Meetings: Summer
1987-Austin, TX(Four Seasons)/July 19-23/500
1988-Philadelphia, PA/July 24-27/550
1989-Kansas City, MO/July 23-26/600
1990-San Francisco, CA/July 22-25/650

American College of Cryosurgery (1977)
150 East Kennedy Blvd., Lakewood NJ 08701
Corresp. Secretary: Emanuel G. Kuflik, M.D.
Members: 500-525 *Staff:* 1
Annual Budget: $10-25,000 *Tel:* (201) 364-0515
Hist. Note: Cryosurgery is a method of destroying tissue by coolants such as nitrous oxide, liquid nitrogen, freon, etc. Members are physicians, general surgeons, scientists and veterinarians involved in the clinical application of cryosurgery. Membership: $20/yr.
Publication:
Newsletter. q.

American College of Dentists (1920)
7315 Wisconsin Ave., Suite 352N, Bethesda MD 20814
Exec. Director: Dr. Gordon H. Rovelstad
Members: 4,500-5,000 *Staff:* 2-5
Annual Budget: $250-500,000 *Tel:* (301) 986-0555
Hist. Note: Founded in Cedar Rapids in 1920 and incorporated in Maryland in 1970. Membership: $115/yr.
Publications:
Journal of the American College of Dentists. q.
News and Views. q.
Annual Meetings: Fall
1987-Las Vegas/Oct. 9-10/1,100
1988-Washington, DC(Sheraton)/Oct. 8/1,200
1989-Honolulu, HI/Nov. 4/800
1990-Boston, MA/Oct. 13/1,200

American College of Emergency Physicians (1968)
Box 619911, Dallas TX 75261-9911
Exec. Director: Colin C. Rorrie, Jr. PhD.
Members: 11,000 *Staff:* 68
Annual Budget: over $5,000,000 *Tel:* (214) 550-0911
Hist. Note: Maintains a Washington office. Has an annual budget of $6 million. Membership: $310/year.
Publications:
Annals of Emergency Medicine. m. adv.
ACEP News. m. adv.
Annual Meetings:
1987-San Francisco, CA(Moscone Center)/Nov. 2-5
1988-New Orleans, LA(Convention Center)/Sept. 26-29

American College of Foot Orthopedists (1949)
Box 202, 1377 K St., N.W., Washington DC 20005
Exec. Secretary: Dr. Richard Baerg
Members: 400 *Staff:* 1
Annual Budget: $25-50,000 *Tel:* (301) 652-6888
Hist. Note: A professional society of podiatrists specializing in diseases and deformities of the foot. Affiliated with the American Podiatric Medical Ass'n. Membership: $65/yr.
Publication:
ACFO Newsletter. q.
Annual Meetings: August, with American Podiatric Medical Ass'n
1987-Washington, DC
1988-Anaheim, CA

American College of Foot Specialists
Hist. Note: Became the American College for Continuing Education in 1983.

American College of Foot Surgeons (1940)
1601 Dolores St., San Francisco CA 94110-4906
Exec. Director: John L. Bennett
Members: 1,800 *Staff:* 6
Annual Budget: $250-500,000 *Tel:* (415) 826-3200
Hist. Note: A voluntary scientific and fraternal surgical organization which sponsors scientific seminars on surgical procedures. Membership in the American Podiatric Medical Ass'n and its component state society required. Membership: $150/yr.
Publication:
Journal of Foot Surgery. bi-m. adv.
Annual Meetings: February
1987-Los Angeles, CA
1988-Las Vegas, NV
1989-Hollywood, FL
1990-New Orleans, LA
1991-San Francisco, CA
1992-Las Vegas, NV
1993-Sarasota, FL
1994-Houston, TX
1995-Scottsdale, AZ
1996-Las Vegas, NV

American College of Gastroenterology (1932)
13 Elm St., Box 1565, Manchester MA 01944
Exec. Director: Gardner V. McCormick
Members: 1,800 *Staff:* 2-5
Annual Budget: $250-500,000 *Tel:* (617) 927-8330
Publication:
American Journal of Gastroenterology. m. adv.
Annual Meetings:
1987-Dallas, TX(Fairmont)/Oct. 24-28/900
1988-New York, NY(Hilton)/Oct. 14-19/1,000

American College of General Practitioners in Osteopathic Medicine and Surgery (1950)
2045 S. Arlington Heights Road, #104, Arlington Heights IL 60005
Exec. Director: Bette Vaught
Members: 7,500 *Staff:* 6
Annual Budget: $1-2,000,000 *Tel:* (800) 323-0794
Hist. Note: Founded in California in 1950 and chartered in Illinois. An affiliate of the American Osteopathic Ass'n.
Publications:
Newsletter. m.
Osteopathic Medical News. q.
Annual Meetings: Spring
1987-Scottsdale, AZ(Sheraton)/March 10-15
1988-Jamaica/March

American College of Health Care Administrators (1962)
8120 Woodmont Ave., Suite 200, Bethesda MD 20814
Exec. V. President: Kathleen M. Griffin, Ph.D., CAE
Members: 6,000-6,500 individuals *Staff:* 20-25
Annual Budget: $1-2,000,000 *Tel:* (301) 652-8384
Hist. Note: Administrators of non-profit, voluntary, municipal, profit, and religious long-term care institutions. Founded as the American College of Nursing Home Administrators, it assumed its present name in 1983. Sponsors and supports the Foundation of American College of Health Care Administrators. Membership: $185/year.
Publications:
The Journal of Long-Term Care Administration. q.
Long-Term Care Administrator. bi-m.
Annual Meetings: Spring
1987-Washington, DC/April 5-9

American College of Healthcare Executives (1933)
840 North Lake Shore Drive, Chicago IL 60611
President: Stuart A. Wesbury, Jr.
Members: 20,000 *Staff:* 100
Annual Budget: over $5,000,000 *Tel:* (312) 943-0544
Hist. Note: A professional society of hospital and health service administrators. Incorporated in the State of Illinois in 1933. Formerly (1985) the American College of Hospital Administrators. Full Membership: $160/yr.
Publications:
Directory. bi-a
Hospital & Health Services Administration. bi-m.
Healthcare Executive. bi-m.
Annual Meetings: With American Hospital Association
1987-Atlanta, GA(Marriott Marquis)/July 24-28
1988-New Orleans, LA/Aug. 5-9

American College of Healthcare Marketing (1984)
5530 Wisconsin Ave., N.W., Suite 917, Washington DC 20815
Exec. Director: David Lewis
Members: 100-150 *Staff:* 4
Annual Budget: $50-100,000 *Tel:* (202) 331-1223

00029 12 05 86 1233

Hist. Note: Founded to encourage interchange of ideas among practitioners and decision-makers involved in healthcare marketing; to provide education; to promote professional standards; and to further the development of marketing within the healthcare industry as a means of controlling costs by strengthening the free market system. Membership: $150/yr.
Publications:
Healthcare Marketeer. bi-m.
ACHM Membership Directory. a.
Annual Meetings: Symposium
1987-Orlando, FL/March

American College of Hospital Administrators (1933)
Hist. Note: Became the American College of Healthcare Executives in 1985.

American College of Internat'l Physicians (1975)
11704 Wilshire Boulevard, Suite 208, Los Angeles CA 90025
Board Chairman: Dr. Robert N. Braun
Members: 1,000 fellows *Staff:* 2-5
Annual Budget: $50-100,000 *Tel:* (213) 478-9555
Hist. Note: Physicians educated in foreign countries and the U.S. who are licensed and practicing in the U.S. Main interests of the College are medical education, research, ethics and international activities. Absorbed the National Association of Foreign Medical Graduates in 1976. Membership: $75/year.
Publications:
ACIP Bulletin. q. adv.
Annual Program & Report.
Annual Meetings: 986-Dallas/July 4-7/400
1987-Atlantic City, NJ(Bally's)/June 18-21/2-300

American College of Laboratory Animal Medicine (1957)
Dept. of Comparative Medicine, Hershey Medical Center, Hershey PA 17033
Secy.-Treas.: C. Max Lang, D.V.M.
Members: 322 individuals *Staff:* 2-5
Annual Budget: $50-100,000 *Tel:* (717) 531-8460
Hist. Note: Founded in 1957 as the American Board of Laboratory Animal Medicine. Incorporated in Illinois in 1957. Affiliated with the American Veterinary Medical Ass'n and the American Ass'n for Laboratory Animal Science. Established to encourage education, training and research in laboratory animal medicine and to provide standards for veterinarians professionally concerned with the health of laboratory animals.
Publication:
ACLAM Newsletter. q.
Annual Meetings: with American Veterinary Medical Ass'n.

American College of Legal Medicine (1955)
Box 190, Maple Glen PA 12002
Exec. Secretary: Thomas Teal
Members: 750 *Staff:* 2-5
Annual Budget: $100-250,000 *Tel:* (215) 646-6800
Hist. Note: Founded in April 1955 and incorporated in Delaware September 1960. Members are doctors, lawyers, hospital administrators, insurance personnel and others interested in the relationship between law and medicine. Fellows of the College must have both a medical and law degree. Full Membership: $190/yr.
Publications:
ACLM Newsletter. q.
Journal of Legal Medicine. q. adv.
Legal Aspects of Medical Practice. m. adv.
Annual Meetings: Spring
1987-Long Beach, CA(Queen Mary)/May 6-9/300

American College of Medical Group Administrators (1956)
1355 S. Colorado Blvd., Suite 900, Denver CO 80222
Admin. Director: Fred E. Graham, Ph.D.
Members: 1,000 *Staff:* 2-5
Annual Budget: $50-100,000 *Tel:* (303) 753-1111
Hist. Note: A voluntary certification organization drawing its membership from the Medical Group Management Association. Founded as the American College of Clinic Managers, it became the American College of Medical Group Administrators in 1976. Membership: $85/yr. (individual).
Publication:
The College Review.
Annual Meetings: With Medical Group Management Ass'n
1987-Washington, DC/Oct. 25-29
1988-Kansas City, MO/Oct. 9-13
1989-Las Vegas, NV/Oct. 29-Nov. 2
1990-Toronto, Canada(Convention Center)/Oct. 28-Nov. 1/2,950
1991-San Antonio, TX(Convention Center)/Oct. 27-31

American College of Musicians (1929)
808 Rio Grande St., Box 1807, Austin TX 78767
President: Walter Merchant
Members: 11,000
Annual Budget: $500-1,000,000 *Tel:* (512) 478-5775
Hist. Note: A standardizing agency granting degrees and diplomas to worthy musicians, ACM consists of two divisions: the Nat'l Guild of Piano Teachers and the Nat'l Fraternity of Student Musicians. Members are individuals whose qualifications make them eligible to judge.
Publication:
Piano Guild Notes. bi-m.
Annual Meetings: Not held

American College of Neuropsychiatrists (1939)
30400 Telegraph Road, Suite 133, Birmingham MI 48010
Exec. Director: Dr. Louis E. Rentz, DO, FACN
Members: 250-300 individuals *Staff:* 2-5
Annual Budget: $10-25,000 *Tel:* (313) 647-3400
Hist. Note: Affiliated with the American Osteopathic Association.
Publication:
Journal. q. adv.
Annual Meetings: With the American Osteopathic Association
1987-Orlando, FL/Oct. 4-8/150
1988-Las Vegas, NV(Hilton)November/150

American College of Neuropsychopharmacology (1961)
Vanderbilt University, Box 1823, Station B, Nashville TN 37235
Secretary: Dr. Oakley Ray
Members: 430 individuals
Annual Budget: $100-250,000 *Tel:* (615) 327-5326
Annual Meetings: December

American College of Nuclear Medicine (1972)
Box 5887, Columbus GA 31906
Exec. Director: Dr. John D. Watson, MD
Members: 600 *Staff:* 1
Annual Budget: $25-50,000 *Tel:* (404) 322-8049
Hist. Note: Members are scientists and physicians working in the field of nuclear medicine. Membership: $100/yr.
Publications:
Newsletter. m.
Directory. biennial.
Annual Meetings: With Soc. of Nuclear Medicine & American College of Nuclear Physicians
1987-Washington, DC/mid-Sept.

American College of Nuclear Physicians (1974)
1101 Connecticut Ave., N.W., Suite 700, Washington DC 20036
Exec. Director: Carol A. Lively
Members: 1,160 individuals *Staff:* 2-5
Annual Budget: $100-250,000 *Tel:* (202) 857-1135
Hist. Note: Physicians doing diagnostic work with radio-active pharmaceuticals. Members must pass a Specialty Board in nuclear medicine.
Publication:
ACNP Newsletter. bi-m.
Semi-annual Meetings: summer and winter

American College of Nurse-Midwives (1955)
1522 K St., N.W., Suite 1120, Washington DC 20005
Exec. Director: Mary Rita Prah
Members: 2,500 *Staff:* 11
Annual Budget: $500-1,000,000 *Tel:* (202) 347-5445
Hist. Note: Formerly (1969) American College of Nurse-Midwifery. Certifies nurse-midwives and awards the CNM (Certified Nurse-Midwife) designation. Membership: $200/yr.
Publications:
Journal of Nurse-Midwifery. bi-m. adv.
Quickening. bi-m. (for members only)
Registry of Services. adv.
Annual Meetings: Spring/8-900
1987-Orlando, FL(Peabody)/May 3-8
1988-Detroit, MI(Westin)

American College of Nursing Home Administrators (1962)
Hist. Note: Became the American College of Health Care Administrators in 1983.

American College of Nutrition (1959)
Box 831, White Plains NY 10602
Exec. Director: Mildred S. Seelig, M.D.
Members: 850, mostly physicians *Staff:* 2-5
Annual Budget: $100-250,000 *Tel:* (914) 948-4848
Hist. Note: Members are holders of doctoral degrees appropriate for the application of clinical nutrition to patient care, the teaching of nutrition and/or research in nutrition. Officers change biennially. Membership: $100/yr.
Publication:
ACN Journal. bi-m. adv.
Annual Meetings: Fall
1987-Chicago, IL(Pheasant Run)/Sept. 20-23/300-350
1988-New Orleans, LA

American College of Obstetricians and Gynecologists (1951)
600 Maryland Ave., S.W., Suite 300, Washington DC 20024
Exec. Director: Warren H. Pearse, M.D.
Members: 25,000 *Staff:* 140
Annual Budget: over $5,000,000 *Tel:* (202) 638-5577
Hist. Note: Doctors specializing in childbirth and female disorders. Formerly (1956) American Academy of Obstetrics and Gynecology. Promotes further education and standards of practice. Has an annual budget of $11 million. Membership: $265/yr.
Publication:
Obstetrics and Gynecology. m. adv.
Annual Meetings: Spring/7,000
1987-Las Vegas, NV(Hilton)/April 27-30
1988-Boston, MA/May 1-5
1989-Atlanta(Hilton)/May 22-25

American College of Oral and Maxillofacial Surgeons (1975)
1100 N.W. Loop 410, Suite 500, San Antonio TX 78213
Secy.-Treas.: Dr. James E. Bauerle
Members: 700-750 surgeons *Staff:* 3
Annual Budget: $25-50,000 *Tel:* (512) 344-4477
Hist. Note: First called the Association of Diplomates of the American Board of Oral Surgery. Membership limited to Diplomates of the American Board of Oral and Maxillofacial Surgery, who actively practice in that specialty. Membership: $80/year (individual).
Publication:
ACOMS Review. q. adv.
Annual Meetings: Spring
1987-San Francisco, CA(Meridian)/Feb. 26-28/250

American College of Osteopathic Emergency Physicians (1975)
5200 South Ellis Ave., Chicago IL 60615
President: Dr. James F. Grate
Members: 225-250 *Staff:* 1
Annual Budget: $10-25,000 *Tel:* (312) 947-2704
Publication:
Newsletter. 3-4/yr.
Annual Meetings: Spring
1987-Chicago, IL

American College of Osteopathic Internists (1943)
14750 N.W. 77th Ct. 130, Miami Lakes FL 33016-1507
Secy.-Treas.: Dr. Ralph J. Tomei
Members: 450-475 *Staff:* 2-5
Annual Budget: under $10,000 *Tel:* (305) 556-0600
Publication:
Newsletter. q.
Annual Meetings: Fall

American College of Osteopathic Obstetricians and Gynecologists (1934)
900 Auburn Rd., Pontiac MI 48057
Exec. Director: Jerry Polsinelli, D.O.
Members: 346 *Staff:* 2
Annual Budget: $100-250,000 *Tel:* (313) 332-6360
Hist. Note: Formed in Wichita, Kansas during the annual meeting of the American Osteopathic Association by ten charter practicing obstetricians in the profession of osteopathy. Originally the American College of Osteopathic Obstetricians, the present name was assumed in 1949. Chartered in the State of Missouri. Membership: $200/year.
Publications:
Newsletter. q.
Membership Directory. a.
Annual Meetings: March
1987-Maui, HI(Maui Marriott)/March 7-14/175
1988-Miami Beach, FL(Fontainbleau Hilton)/March 19-24/160

American College of Osteopathic Pediatricians (1940)
210 Carnegie Center, Suite 207, Princeton NJ 08540
Exec. Director: Theresa E. Goeke
Members: 266 *Staff:* 2
Annual Budget: $50-100,000 *Tel:* (609) 987-0077
Hist. Note: Organized in 1940 in California and incorporated in 1967 in Illinois. Membership: $200/yr.
Publications:
Newsletter. q.
Directory. a.
Annual Meetings: Spring
1987-Hilton Head, SC/April 23-27
1988-San Francisco, CA/April 14-18
1989-Boston, MA
1990-Virgin Islands

American College of Osteopathic Surgeons (1927)
122 C St., N.W., Suite 875, Washington DC 20001
Exec. Director: Guy D. Beaumont, Jr.
Members: 1,200 *Staff:* 5
Annual Budget: $500-1,000,000 *Tel:* (202) 639-8115
Hist. Note: Organized June 1926 and incorporated in Missouri in 1927. Affiliated with the American Osteopathic Ass'n. Membership: $350/yr.
Publications:
ACOS News. m. adv.
Directory and By-Laws. a.
Annual Meetings: Fall/1,000
1987-Honolulu, HI(Sheraton Waikiki)/Oct. 18-21
1988-New York, NY(Hilton)/Oct. 16-20

American College of Physician Executives (1978)
4830 W. Kennedy Blvd., Suite 648, Tampa FL 33609
Exec. V. President: Roger S. Schenke
Members: 350 *Staff:* 10
Annual Budget: $50-100,000 *Tel:* (813) 873-2000
Hist. Note: An honorary society of physicians whose primary professional responsibility is the management of health care organizations. Affiliated with the American Academy of Medical Directors, to which its members must belong. Membership: $190/yr.
Semi-annual meetings: Spring and Fall
1987-Conference/Toronto, Canada(Royal York Hotel)/April 26-29
1987-Institute/Scottsdale, AZ(Hyatt)/Nov. 15-19

00030 12 05 86 1233

American College of Physicians (1915)
4200 Pine St., Philadelphia PA 19104
Exec. V. President: Dr. John R. Ball, M.D.
Members: 50,000-plus *Staff:* 200-250
Annual Budget: over $5,000,000 *Tel:* (800) 523-1546
Hist. Note: Merged with the Congress of Internal Medicine in 1925. Patterned after Great Britain's Royal College of Physicians, ACP was founded as a communications link among medical scientists, clinical researchers and practicing physicians. Members are certified, practicing internists. "Fellows" are certified internists recognized by their colleagues for their scholarship and professional excellence. Has an annual budget of $20 million.
Publications:
Annals of Internal Medicine. m. adv.
ACP Observer. m. adv.
Annual Meetings: Spring/7,000
1987-New Orleans, LA(Hilton)/April 2-5
1988-New York, NY/March 28-31

American College of Podiatric Radiologists (1942)
1 Lincoln Road Bldg., Suite 308, Miami Beach FL 33139
Secretary: Dr. Irving H. Block, D.P.M.
Members: 65-70 *Staff:* 1
Annual Budget: under $10,000 *Tel:* (305) 531-9866
Hist. Note: Established as the American College of Chiropodial Roentgenologists, it became the American College of Foot Roentgenologists in 1962 and assumed its present name in 1974. Affiliated with the American Podiatric Medical Ass'n.
Publication:
Newsletter. q.

American College of Podopediatrics (1977)
10515 Carnegie Ave., Cleveland OH 44106
Vice President: Irving Lewis, D.P.M.
Members: 175-200 *Staff:* 1
Annual Budget: under $10,000 *Tel:* (216) 231-3300
Hist. Note: Established in Cleveland by a group of podiatrists and others interested in promoting children's foot health. Affiliated with the American Podiatric Medical Ass'n. Has no paid staff or permanent officers. Membership: $35/yr.
Publication:
Newsletter. irreg.
Annual Meetings: August
1987-Washington, DC

American College of Preventive Medicine (1954)
1015 15th St. N.W., Washington DC 20005
Exec. Director: William M. Kane, Ph.D.
Members: 2,000 *Staff:* 6-10
Annual Budget: $250-500,000 *Tel:* (202) 789-0003
Hist. Note: Physicians specializing in preventive medicine, occupational medicine, public health and aerospace medicine. Membership: $155/yr.
Publication:
American Journal of Preventive Medicine. bi-m. adv.
Annual Meetings: Spring in Atlanta, GA(Westin Peachtree)/500
1987-April 9-12

American College of Probate Counsel (1949)
2716 Ocean Park Blvd., #1080, Santa Monica CA 90405-5207
Exec. Director: Gerry Vogt
Members: 2,400 *Staff:* 4
Annual Budget: $500-1,000,000 *Tel:* (213) 450-2033
Hist. Note: Membership, by invitation only, consists of lawyers specializing in probate law. Membership: $200/yr.
Publications:
Membership Roster. a.
Newsletter. q.
Annual Meetings: February/900
1987-Maui, HI(Hyatt Regency)/Feb. 10-15/900
1988-Marco Island, FL(Marriott)/Feb. 23-28/900

American College of Prosthodontists (1970)
84 N.E. Loop 410, Suite 273 W., San Antonio TX 78216
Office Director: Linda Wallenborn
Members: 1,700 *Staff:* 1
Annual Budget: $50-100,000 *Tel:* (512) 340-3664
Hist. Note: Members are dentists who are diplomates of the American Board of Prosthodontics; board eligible prosthodontists; and students in prosthodontic training.
Publication:
Newsletter. 3/yr.
Annual Meetings: October
1987-San Diego, CA
1988-Baltimore, MD
1989-Tucson, AZ

American College of Psychiatrists (1963)
Box 365, Greenbelt MD 20770
Exec. Director: Alice C. Martinez
Members: 500 active, 300 emeritus *Staff:* 2-5
Annual Budget: $500-1,000,000 *Tel:* (301) 345-3534
Hist. Note: An honorary society limited to 500 active members and 500 emeritus members. Publications and meetings limited to members only. Membership: $200/yr.(active); $25/yr.(emeritus).
Publications:
Newsletter. q.
Proceedings. a.
Annual Meetings: February/500
1987-Maui, HI(Maui Marriott)/Feb. 11-15/500
1988-Tucson, AZ(Loew's Ventana Canyon Resort)/Feb. 11-15/500
1989-Monterey, CA(Hyatt Regency)/1st week in Feb.

American College of Radiology (1924)
1891 Preston White Drive, Reston VA 22091
Exec. Director: John J. Curry
Members: 20,000 *Staff:* 150
Annual Budget: over $5,000,000 *Tel:* (703) 648-8900
Hist. Note: Founded in June 1923 in San Francisco and incorporated in California in 1924. Purpose of the ACR is to improve the art and science of radiological practice through coordination of national radiological societies, promotion of research, standardization of procedures, safeguarding of patients and operators and continuing medical education. Has an annual budget over $10 million. Membership: $325/year.
Publication:
American College of Radiology Bulletin. m. adv.
Annual Meetings: Fall/700

American College of Real Estate Consultants (1972)
Hist. Note: Became the International College of Real Estate Consulting Professionals in 1981.

American College of Sports Medicine (1955)
ACSM National Center, Box 1440, Indianapolis IN 46206
Exec. Director: John A. Miller
Members: 10-11,000 *Staff:* 15-20
Annual Budget: $2-5,000,000 *Tel:* (317) 637-9200
Hist. Note: The College is concerned with the effect of sports, exercise and other motor activities on general health. Membership includes team physicians, orthopedic surgeons, athletic trainers and others. Affiliated with the Federation Internationale de Medicine Sportive. Membership: $90/yr.
Publications:
ACSM Newsletter. q.
Medicine & Science in Sports & Exercise. q. adv.
Annual Meetings: May/2-2,500
1987-Las Vegas(MGM Grand)
1988-Dallas, TX

American College of Surgeons (1913)
55 East Erie St., Chicago IL 60611
Director: Paul A. Ebert
Members: 49,000 fellows *Staff:* 170
Annual Budget: over $5,000,000 *Tel:* (312) 664-4050
Hist. Note: Founded in 1913 and incorporated in Illinois. U.S. member of the Internat'l Federation of Surgical Colleges. An association of surgeons devoted to advancing the science of surgery and its competent practice. Has an annual budget of $14.7 million. Membership: $270/year (individual).
Publications:
Bulletin. m.
Surgery, Gynecology and Obstetrics. m. adv.
Yearbook. trien.
Annual Meetings: Fall/18,000
1987-San Francisco, CA(Fairmont & Moscone Center)/Oct. 11-16
1988-Chicago, IL(Hilton & Towers)/Oct. 23-28
1989-Atlanta, GA/Oct 15-20
1990-San Francisco, CA/Oct. 7-12

American College of Toxicology (1977)
9650 Rockville Pike, Bethesda MD 20814
Exec. Director: Alexandra Ventura
Members: 850 *Staff:* 1
Annual Budget: $50-100,000 *Tel:* (301) 530-0033
Hist. Note: Incorporated in The State of Illinois. A multidisciplinary society composed of professionals having a common interest in toxicology. Membership: $58/yr.
Publications:
Journal of The American College of Toxicology. q. adv.
Newsletter. q.
Annual Meetings: November-December/400-500
1987-Baltimore, MD(Sheraton Inner Harbor)/Dec. 7-9
1988-Baltimore, MD(Sheraton Inner Harbor)/Oct. 31-Nov. 2

American College of Trial Lawyers (1950)
10889 Wilshire Blvd., Los Angeles CA 90024
Exec. Director: Robert A. Young
Members: 3,700-4,000 *Staff:* 2-5
Annual Budget: $500-1,000,000 *Tel:* (213) 879-0143
Hist. Note: An honorary society of lawyers, former lawyers and judges.
Annual Meetings: March

American College of Utilization Review Physicians (1973)
30 North 36th St., Camp Hill PA 17011
Exec. Director: Betty J. Hamman, BA
Members: 1,200 *Staff:* 6-10
Annual Budget: $250-500,000 *Tel:* (717) 737-5660
Hist. Note: Organized and incorporated in the State of Pennsylvania, October 13, 1973 to set standards, provide continuing medical education and measure competence in the fields of quality assurance and utilization review. Members are doctors, related health personnel and hospitals. Membership: $140/yr. (individual), $350/yr. (company).
Publications:
Newsletter. m. adv.
Study Guide in Quality Assurance and Utilization Review.
Quality Assurance and Utilization Review. q. adv.
Cost Containment Syllabus.
Annual Meetings: October
1987-San Juan(El Caribe Hilton & La Condado Plaza)Oct. 25-27/400-500

American College of Veterinary Internal Medicine (1972)
805 Horseshoe Lane, Blacksburg VA 24060
Secy.-Treas.: R. Lee Pyle
Members: 371 *Staff:* 1
Annual Budget: $250-500,000 *Tel:* (703) 951-8543
Hist. Note: Governing organization for veterinary specialists who deal with the diagnosis and non-surgical treatment of diseases of the internal organs. Encompasses internal medicine, cardiology, gastroenterology, endocrinology, oncology, nephrology, hematology and neurology. Membership: $75/yr.
Publications:
Directory. a.
Proceeding Book. a.
Annual Meetings: May
1987-San Diego, CA(Sheraton Harbor Island)/May/1,100
1988-Washington, DC(Sheraton Washington)/May/1,200

American College of Veterinary Microbiologists (1962)
Pitman-Moore, Inc., Box 344, Washington Crossing NJ 08560
Secy.-Treas.: Dr. D. E. Kahn
Members: 190-200 *Staff:* 1
Annual Budget: under $10,000 *Tel:* (609) 737-7244
Hist. Note: Formerly (1966) the American Ass'n of Veterinary Bacteriologists. Incorporated (1968) following approval by the American Veterinary Medical Ass'n. Sponsors a board examination leading to the certification "Diplomate." Membership: $20/year (individual).
Publication:
Newsletter. 3-4/yr. adv.
Annual Meetings: With American Veterinary Medical Ass'n

American College of Veterinary Ophthalmologists (1969)
10661 Ellis Ave., Suite A, Fountain Valley CA 92708
Secy.-Treas.: Dr. John D. Lavach
Members: 75 *Staff:* 1
Annual Budget: under $10,000 *Tel:* (714) 964-4644
Hist. Note: Affiliated with The American Veterinary Medical Ass'n. Membership: $110/yr.
Annual Meetings: With American Academy of Ophthalmology

American College of Veterinary Pathologists (1949)
382 West Street Road, Kennett Square PA 19348
Secy.-Treas.: Dr. Helen Acland
Members: 801 *Staff:* 2
Annual Budget: $50-100,000 *Tel:* (215) 444-3432
Hist. Note: Membership: $85/yr.
Publication:
Veterinary Pathology. 6/yr. adv.
Annual Meetings: Fall
1988-Kansas City, KS(Hyatt Regency)/Nov. 1-4
1989-Baltimore, MD(Hyatt Regency)/Oct. 29-Nov. 3
1990-Phoenix, AZ
1991-Orlando, FL

American College of Veterinary Radiology (1961)
School of Veterinary Medicine, University of California at Davis, Davis CA 95616
Secretary: Dr. Joseph Morgan
Members: 106 *Staff:* 1
Annual Budget: under $10,000 *Tel:* (916) 752-0814
Hist. Note: Originally established as a specialty board in veterinary radiology under the jurisdiction of the American Veterinary Medical Association, it had become the American Board of Veterinary Radiology with 11 charter members in 1966 and was incorporated in the State of Illinois. The present name was assumed in 1969. Membership: $50/yr.
Publication:
Veterinary Radiology. bi-m. adv.
Annual Meetings: With the Radiological Soc. of North America
1987-Chicago, IL/Nov. 29-Dec. 4

American College of Veterinary Surgeons (1965)
405 Park Lane Drive, Champaign IL 61820
Exec. Secretary: Dr. A.G. Schiller
Members: 300 *Staff:* 1
Tel: (217) 333-5337
Hist. Note: Maintains rigid membership requirements including certification by examination.
Publication:
Journal of Veterinary Surgery. q. (published by Lippincott).
Semi-Annual Meetings: Fall in Chicago, IL and rotating sites in Feb.

American College of Veterinary Toxicologists (1958)
Hist. Note: Became the American Academy of Veterinary and Comparative Toxicology in 1984.

American College Personnel Ass'n (1924)
5999 Stevenson Ave., Alexandria VA 22304
Exec. V. President: Patrick J. McDonough
Members: 7-8,000 *Staff:* 2-5
Annual Budget: $10-25,000 *Tel:* (703) 823-9800
Hist. Note: Established in 1924 to serve as the collective voice of the college student profession, including teachers, counselors, deans, department heads and researchers. A division of the American Ass'n for Counseling and Development. Membership: $15/yr.
Publications:
The Journal of College Student Personnel. bi-m. adv.
ACPA Developments Newsletter. q.

00031 12 05 86 1233

Annual Meetings: With the American Ass'n for Counseling and Development
1987-New Orleans, LA/April 22-25

American Collegiate Retailing Ass'n (1948)
Department of Marketing, Shippensburg University, Shippensburg PA 17257
President: Dr. Myron Gable
Members: 300 individuals *Staff:* 1
Annual Budget: under $10,000 *Tel:* (717) 532-1610
Hist. Note: Organization of faculty from colleges with specialized curricula in retailing. Conducts annual Retail Management Seminar for retail store executives. Affiliated with the Council for Professional Education for Business. Has no paid staff.
Publication:
Newsletter. q.
Semi-annual Meetings: January in New York, NY with Nat'l Retail Merchants Ass'n and April

American Commercial Collectors Ass'n (1969)
4040 West 70th St., Minneapolis MN 55435
Exec. Director: David J. Peterson
Members: 225-250 companies *Staff:* 2
Annual Budget: $50-100,000 *Tel:* (612) 925-0760
Hist. Note: Specialists in the collection of commercial accounts receivable.
Publications:
Blue Book of Commercial Collectors. a.
Scope. m. adv.
Annual Meetings: October/80
1987-Hilton Head, SC

American Committee for Irish Studies (1959)
English Dept., Indiana Univ./Purdue Univ., Fort Wayne IN 46805
Secretary: Mary Helen Thuente
Members: 1,500
Annual Budget: $10-25,000 *Tel:* (219) 481-6765
Hist. Note: Scholars interested in Irish history, language and culture. Affiliated with the American Historical Ass'n and the Modern Language Ass'n of America. Membership: $18/year.
Publications:
ACIS Newsletter.
Irish Literary Supplement.
Annual Meetings: Spring/200
1987-Dublin, Ireland(University College)

American Community Theatre Ass'n
Hist. Note: A division of the American Theatre Association.

American Community TV Ass'n (1978)
Hist. Note: Became the American Low Power TV Association in 1982.

American Comparative Literature Ass'n (1960)
Univ. of Michigan, Ann Arbor MI 48109
Secy.-Treas.: Stuart Y. McDougal
Members: 800 *Staff:* 1
Annual Budget: under $10,000 *Tel:* (313) 763-9157
Hist. Note: An "allied" organization of the Modern Language Association.
Publication:
ACLA Newsletter. m.
Annual Meetings: Annual Meeting except on those years when the Internat'l Comparative Literature Ass'n holds its triennial meeting (1988, 1991, etc.)

American Compensation Ass'n (1954)
6619 N. Scottsdale Road, Scottsdale AZ 85253
Exec. Director: F.W. Miller
Members: 10,000 *Staff:* 22
Annual Budget: $2-5,000,000 *Tel:* (602) 951-9191
Hist. Note: Established as the Ohio Wage and Salary Association, it assumed its present name in 1957 and superseded the Midwest Compensation Association in 1963. Members are individuals responsible for the administration and management of all forms of employee compensation in their organization - wages, salaries, benefits, executive compensations and other forms of remuneration. Membership: $75/yr.
Publications:
Conference Proceedings. a.
Membership Directory. a.
Newsletter. bi-m.
Annual Meetings: October/800-900
1987-Toronto, Canada(Hilton)
1988-San Francisco, CA(Hyatt)
1989-San Antonio, TX(Hyatt)
1990-Chicago, IL(Marriott)

American Composers Alliance (1938)
170 West 74th St., New York NY 10023
Exec. Director: Rosalie Calabrese
Members: 301 *Staff:* 6-10
Annual Budget: $100-250,000 *Tel:* (212) 362-8900
Hist. Note: Established in late 1937 by 48 musicians under the leadership of Aaron Copland, its first president, to protect the rights of its members and the use and understanding of their music. Since 1972, Broadcast Music, Inc. has performed this function, and all ACA members now belong to Broadcast Music. Distributes members' music through its subsidiary, American Publishers Edition. Membership: $45/yr.
Publication:
Catalogues of New Music.
Annual Meetings: December in New York City

American Concrete Institute (1905)
Box 19150, Redford Sta., Detroit MI 48219
Exec. V. President: George F. Leyh
Members: 18-19,000 individuals, 5-600 organizations *Staff:* 54
Annual Budget: over $5,000,000 *Tel:* (313) 532-2600
Hist. Note: Founded in 1905 as the Nat'l Ass'n of Cement Users; became the American Concrete Institute in 1913 and was incorporated in Michigan in 1964. ACI gathers and disseminates information for the improvement of the design, construction, manufacture and maintenance of concrete products and structures. Its members include designers, architects, civil engineers, educators, contractors, concrete craftsmen and technicians, materials suppliers, testing laboratories and manufacturers. Has an annual budget of $5.5 million. Membership: $94/yr.
Publications:
Concrete Abstracts. bi-m.
Concrete International: Design and Construction. m. adv.
ACI Structural Journal. bi-m.
ACI Materials Journal. bi-m.
Semi-annual Meetings: Spring and Fall
1987-Mexico City/March 22-27 and Seattle, WA/Nov. 8-13
1988-Orlando, FL/March 20-25 and Houston, TX/Oct. 30-Nov. 4
1989-Atlanta, GA/Feb. 19-24 and San Diego, CA/Oct. 29-Nov. 3
1990-Toronto, Ontario/March 25-30 and Philadelphia, PA/Nov. 11-16
1991-Los Angeles, CA/March 17-22 and Dallas, TX/Oct. 27-Nov. 1
1992-Washington, DC/March 8-13 and Salt Lake City, UT/Oct. 25-30

American Concrete Pavement Ass'n (1964)
2625 Clearbrook Dr., Arlington Heights IL 60005
President: Marlin J. Knutson
Members: 200-225 *Staff:* 6-10
Annual Budget: $250-500,000 *Tel:* (312) 640-1020
Hist. Note: Until 1981 known as the American Concrete Paving Association. Membership: Dues depend on the type of member company.
Publications:
Bulletin. irreg.
Newsletter. m.
Annual Meetings: November/250-300
1987-Palm Springs, CA(Canyon Hotel)/Nov. 29-Dec. 2
1988-San Antonio, TX

American Concrete Pipe Ass'n (1907)
8320 Old Courthouse Rd., Vienna VA 22180
President: Richard E. Barnes, CAE
Members: 250-300 *Staff:* 15-20
Annual Budget: $1-2,000,000 *Tel:* (703) 821-1990
Hist. Note: Conceived by a small group of concrete farm drain tile manufacturers who needed some means of exchanging ideas and establishing quality standards. Membership rapidly expanded to include culvert and sanitary sewer pipe makers throughout the world and today more than 40 countries are represented.
Publication:
Concrete Pipe News. bi-m.
Annual Meetings: Usually March
1987-Colorado Springs, CO(Broadmoor)/Mar. 29-Apr. 4
1988-Tuscon, AZ(Ventana Canyon)/March 20-25

American Concrete Pressure Pipe Ass'n (1950)
8320 Old Courthouse Road, Vienna VA 22180
President: Richard E. Barnes, CAE
Members: 5-10 *Staff:* 2-5
Annual Budget: $500-1,000,000 *Tel:* (703) 821-1990
Publication:
Concrete Pressure Pipe Digest. bi-m.

American Concrete Pumping Ass'n (1974)
1034 Tennessee St., Vallejo CA 94590
Exec. V. President: James R. Hubbard
Members: 260 companies *Staff:* 2
Annual Budget: $100-250,000 *Tel:* (707) 553-1732
Hist. Note: Membership Fee: Varies by company size and activity from $125-575/yr.
Publications:
Update (newsletter). bi-m.
Concrete Pumping & Placing. bi-m.
Annual Meetings: Winter
1987-Houston, TX(Warwick)/Jan. 25-29/20,000

American Conference of Academic Deans (1944)
1818 R St., N.W., Washington DC 20009
Staff Assistant: Shelagh Casey
Members: 675-700 *Staff:* 1
Annual Budget: $10-25,000 *Tel:* (202) 387-3760
Hist. Note: Chief academic officers of four-year colleges of arts and sciences.
Publication:
Proceedings. a. 5/yr.
Annual Meetings: With Ass'n of American Colleges

American Conference of Governmental Industrial Hygienists (1938)
6500 Glenway Ave., Bldg. D-7, Cincinnati OH 45211
Exec. Secretary: William D. Kelley
Members: 3,000 *Staff:* 15
Annual Budget: $1-2,000,000 *Tel:* (513) 661-7881
Hist. Note: Formerly (1945) Nat'l Conference of Governmental Industrial Hygienists. A professional society of government and university employees engaged in full-time programs of industrial hygiene. Membership: $25/year.
Publications:
Threshold Limit Values. a.
Transactions. a.
Bulletin Board. bi-a.
Applied Industrial Hygiene. q. adv.
Membership Directory. a.
Annual Meetings: May, with American Industrial Hygiene Ass'n, and Fall
1987-Montreal, Canada(Conv. Center)/May 30-June 5
1988-Salt Lake City, UT(Conv. Center)/May 15-20
1989-St. Louis, MO(Conv. Center)/May 21-26

American Congress of Rehabilitation Medicine (1921)
130 South Michigan Ave., Suite 1310, Chicago IL 60603
Exec. Director: Ike A. Mayeda
Members: 2,900 *Staff:* 7-11
Annual Budget: $500-1,000,000 *Tel:* (312) 922-9368
Hist. Note: Founded September 18, 1923 as the American College of Radiology and Physiotherapy. Name changed in 1926 to the American College of Physical Therapy and in 1930 to the American Congress of Physical Therapy. In 1945 it again changed its name to the American Congress of Physical Medicine and in 1953 it further became the American Congress of Physical Medicine and Rehabilitation. In 1967 it adopted its present name. It was incorporated in Illinois in 1930. Membership: $120/yr. (individual).
Publication:
Archives of Physical Medicine and Rehabilitation. m. adv.
Annual Meetings:
1987-Orlando, FL(Marriott)/Oct. 18-23/1,900-2,100
1988-Seattle, WA(Westin/Seattle Sheraton)/Oct. 30-Nov. 4/1,900-2,100
1989-San Antonio, TX(Hilton,Marriott,Hyatt Regency)/Nov. 5-10/1,900
1990-Phoenix, AZ(Convention Center)/Oct. 21-26/1,900
1991-Washington, DC(Sheraton Washington)/Oct. 27-Nov. 1/2,000

American Congress on Surveying and Mapping (1941)
210 Little Falls St., Falls Church VA 22046
Exec. Director: Richard F. Dorman, CAE
Members: 11,000 individuals, 100-110 companies *Staff:* 10-15
Annual Budget: $1-2,000,000 *Tel:* (703) 241-2446
Hist. Note: Founded in the District of Columbia in 1941 and incorporated there in 1951. Composed of three member organizations: the Nat'l Soc. of Professional Surveyors, the American Ass'n for Geodetic Surveying and the American Cartographic Ass'n. Affiliated with state land surveyor societies, also the Accreditation Board for Engineering and Technology, and the National Council of Engineering Examiners. Member of the Internat'l Federation of Surveyors, the Internat'l Cartographic Ass'n and the Internat'l Soc. of Mine Surveyors. Promotes the profession of surveying and mapping science. Sponsors and supports the ACSM/NSPS Political Action Committee. Membership: $70/yr.
Publications:
ACSM Bulletin. bi-m. adv.
The American Cartographer. q. adv.
Surveying and Mapping. q. adv.
Semi-annual meetings: Spring and Fall
1987-Baltimore, MD(Conv. Center)/March 29-April 3/5,000
1987-Reno, NV(MGM Grand)/Oct. 4-9/2,000
1988-St. Louis, MO(Conv. Center)/March 13-18/5,000
1988-Virginia Beach, VA(Conv. Center)/September 12-16/2,000
1989-Baltimore, MD(Conv. Center)/March 12-17
1989-Cleveland, OH(Stouffers)/Sept. 7-12/2,000
1990-Denver, CO/March 18-24
1990-Atlantic City, NJ(Harrah's Boardwalk)/Sept. 23-28
1991-Washington, DC/March
1991-Portland, OR/Sept. 16-20
1992-Detroit, MI/Sept.-Oct.
1993-New Orleans, LA/Sept.-Oct.

American Connemara Pony Soc. (1956)
Hoshiekon Farm, Box 513, Goshen CT 06756
Secretary: Elizabeth A. O'Brien
Members: 350 *Staff:* 1
Annual Budget: under $10,000 *Tel:* (203) 491-3521
Hist. Note: Breeders and exhibitors of the Connemara pony developed in Ireland in the 18th and 19th centuries.
Publication:
The American Connemara. q. adv.
Annual Meetings: Fall
1987-West Coast

American Consultants League (1984)
2030 Clarendon Blvd., Suite 206, Arlington VA 22201
Exec. Director: Audrey S. Wyatt
Members: 1,050 individuals *Staff:* 2-5
Annual Budget: $100-250,000 *Tel:* (703) 528-4493
Hist. Note: An association of part-time and full-time consultants in every field of expertise from all over the United States, Canada, and several foreign countries. Assists consultants in the setting up and managing of the business end of their consultancies by providing educational materials and continuing education through the Consultants Institute, a home study course which is the education arm of the League. Membership: $78/yr.
Publications:
Consulting Intelligence (newsletter). bi-m. adv.
The ACL Directory.

00032 12 05 86 1233

American Consulting Engineers Council (1973)
1015 15th St., N.W., Suite 802, Washington DC 20005
President and Acting Exec. V. President: Lester Poggemeyer
Members: 4,600 firms *Staff:* 45
Annual Budget: $2-5,000,000 *Tel:* (202) 347-7474
Hist. Note: Independent, private practice engineering companies. Provides information on federal legislation, insurance business practices, international markets and public relations to member firms. Merger of the American Institute of Consulting Engineers (1910) and the Consulting Engineers Council of the U.S.A. (1956).
Publications:
Last Word. w.
Member Directory. a.
Special Reports. m.
Guidelines to Practice.
Semi-Annual meetings: Spring and Fall
1987-Minneapolis, MN(Hyatt Regency)/May 17-21/600

American Copper Council (1974)
10 West 33rd St., Suite PH-A, New York NY 10001
Exec. Director: Mary C. Boland
Members: 130 *Staff:* 2-5
Annual Budget: $100-250,000 *Tel:* (212) 714-2249
Hist. Note: Organized in 1974 as as successor to the committee for the Release of Stockpile Copper, the Council represents all segments of the industry, dividing it into 18 sectors.
Publications:
Coppertalk Newsletter. q.
Directory of Member Companies. a.
Biennial Meetings:
1988-El Paso, TX/Feb.-March/250

American Corn Millers Federation (1918)
6707 Old Dominion Dr., #240, McLean VA 22101
President: Betsy Faga
Members: 50-75 companies *Staff:* 2-5
Annual Budget: $50-100,000 *Tel:* (703) 821-3025
Hist. Note: ACMF is comprised of companies engaged in corn dry milling.
Publication:
ACMF Newsletter. m.
Semi-annual Meetings: Spring and Fall/40
1987-San Antonio, TX(Four Seasons)/March 25-27
1987-Key Largo, FL(Ocean Reef Club)/Fall

American Corporate Counsel Ass'n (1982)
1225 Connecticut Ave., N.W., Suite 202, Washington DC 20036
Exec. Director: Nancy A. Nord
Members: 7-8,000 *Staff:* 9
Annual Budget: $500-1,000,000 *Tel:* (202) 296-4523
Hist. Note: Members are lawyers who practice law in a corporation and who do not hold themselves out to the public for the practice of law. Membership: $75/year. Organized in Dallas, Texas March 11, 1982 by 52 corporate attorneys from 45 companies.
Publications:
The Docket-quarterly newsletter
The Docket. q.

American Correctional Ass'n (1870)
4321 Hartwick Rd., Suite L-208, College Park MD 20740
Exec. Director: Anthony P. Travisono
Members: 20,200 *Staff:* 60
Annual Budget: $2-5,000,000 *Tel:* (301) 699-7600
Hist. Note: Founded as the Nat'l Prison Ass'n. Became the American Prison Ass'n and assumed its present name in 1954. Membership consists of individuals of all types involved in the correctional field-wardens, psychologists, sociologists, probation officers, etc. Membership: $25-65/yr.
Publications:
Corrections Today. 8/yr. adv.
Directory of Correctional Institutions and Agencies. a.
On the Line. bi-m.
Proceedings. a.
Probation & Parole Directory. bien.
National Jail & Adult Detention Directory. bien.
Semi-annual meetings: January and August
1987-Atlanta, GA/Jan. 15-18
1987-New Orleans, LA/Aug. 2-6

American Correctional Chaplains Ass'n (1885)
Maryland Correctional Training Center, 1837 Virginia Ave., Hagerstown MD 21740
President: Rev.Fr. Kloman F. Riggi
Members: 450-500
Annual Budget: under $10,000 *Tel:* (301) 791-7200
Hist. Note: An affiliate of the American Correctional Ass'n.
Annual Meetings: With American Correctional Ass'n.

American Correctional Food Service Ass'n (1969)
277 E. 6100 South, Salt Lake City UT 84107
Nat'l Coordinator: Marvin C. Zitting
Members: 550-600 *Staff:* 2-5
Annual Budget: $10-25,000 *Tel:* (801) 268-3000
Hist. Note: An affiliate of the American Correctional Association. Members are food service employees in government correctional institutions.
Publications:
Newsletter. bi-m.
Directory. a.
Annual Meetings: Summer
1987-Ft. Worth, TX/August

American Correctional Health Services Ass'n (1975)
5530 Wisconsin Ave., Suite 917, Washington DC 20815
Administrator: David Lewis
Members: 1,400 *Staff:* 3
Annual Budget: $50-100,000 *Tel:* (301) 652-1172
Hist. Note: Multidisciplinary society of health care professionals and representatives from diverse areas of the corrections field. An affiliate of the American Correctional Association. Membership: $25/yr. (individual), $125/yr. (non-profit organization), $250/yr. (for-profit organization).
Publication:
CORHEALTH. bi-m.
Semi-annual conferences: Spring and Winter
1987-Philadelphia, PA/April

American Corrective Therapy Ass'n (1946)
259-08 148th Road, Rosedale NY 11422
Exec. Director: David Ser
Members: 800 *Staff:* 2-5
Annual Budget: $10-25,000 *Tel:* (718) 276-0721
Hist. Note: Professional society of corrective and exercise therapists. Corrective Therapy is the applied science of medically prescribed therapeutic exercise, education and adapted physical activities to improve the quality of life and health of adults and children, by developing physical fitness, increasing functional mobility and independence, and improving psychosocial behavior. Affiliated with American Alliance for Health, Physical Education and Recreation. Formerly (1967) Ass'n for Physical and Mental Rehabilitation.
Publication:
American Corrective Therapy Journal. bi-m. adv.
Annual Meetings:
1987-Portland, OR
1988-Nashville, TN

American Corriedale Ass'n (1916)
Hist. Note: Breeders and fanciers of Corriedale Sheep. Address unknown in 1985.

American Cotton Exporter's Ass'n (1975)
Cotton Exchange Bldg., Suite 1, Mezz., P.O. Box 3366, Memphis TN 38173
Secretary: Earle N. Billings
Members: 60 *Staff:* 1
Annual Budget: under $10,000 *Tel:* (901) 525-2272
Hist. Note: A Webb-Pomerene Act Ass'n. Incorporated in New York on Feb. 4, 1975.

American Cotton Shippers Ass'n (1924)
Cotton Exchange Building, P.O. Box 3366, Memphis TN 38173
Exec. V. President & Secy.: Earle N. Billings
Members: 500-550 *Staff:* 6-10
Tel: (901) 525-2272
Hist. Note: Members are cotton merchants, cotton shippers, and exporters of raw cotton and firms allied with the industry. Its membership is composed of five Federated Associations: Arkansas-Missouri Cotton Trade Ass'n; Atlantic Cotton Ass'n; Southern Cotton Ass'n; Texas Cotton Ass'n; and the Western Cotton Shippers Ass'n. Maintains the Cotton States Arbitration Board in conjunction with the American Textile Manufacturers Institute. Maintains a Washington office. Membership: $300/yr.
Annual Meetings: Spring
1987-Washington, DC(Mayflower)
1988-Dallas, TX(Fairmont)
1989-New Orleans, LA(Fairmont)

American Council for Competitive Telecommunications (1976)
Hist. Note: Merged with the Ass'n of Long Distance Telephone Companies to form the Competitive Telecommunications Ass'n in 1984.

American Council for Construction Education (1976)
Hist. Note: Address unknown in 1984.

American Council for Elementary School Industrial Arts
Hist. Note: Became the Technology Education for Children Council in 1986.

American Council for the Arts (1960)
1285 Avenue of the Americas, New York NY 10019
President: Milton Rhodes
Members: 4,000 organizations and individuals *Staff:* 10
Annual Budget: $500-1,000,000 *Tel:* (212) 245-4510
Hist. Note: Municipal, community and state art councils, community leaders, local and national arts organizations, art centers, universities, libraries, corporations, foundations and individuals. Absorbed Advocates for the Arts of the American Council for the Arts. Established as Community Arts Councils Inc., it became Arts Councils of America in 1965, Associated Councils of the Arts in 1966 and assumed its present name in 1977. Membership: $25-250/year.
Publication:
Update. m.
Annual Meetings: Spring

American Council of Highway Advertisers (1936)
304 Pennsylvania Ave., S.E., Suite 300, Washington DC 20003
President: Richard R. Roberts
Members: 50 companies *Staff:* 2-5
Annual Budget: $100-250,000 *Tel:* (202) 546-0555
Hist. Note: Formerly (1949) American Highway Sign Ass'n and (1985) Roadside Business Ass'n. ACHA represents sign and billboard companies, hotels, motels, restaurants, tourist attractions, service stations and other businesses that depend on attracting highway travelers and customers. Supports the Highway Advertisers Political Action Committee (HAPAC).
Publication:
Bulletin. bi-m.
Annual Meetings: Fall
1987-Point Clear, AL(Marriott's Grand Hotel)/Oct. 13-15/100
1988-Maui, HI(Intercontinental Wailea)/Nov. 15-18/125

American Council of Independent Laboratories (1937)
1725 K St., N.W., Suite 301, Washington DC 20006
Exec. Director: Joseph F. O'Neil
Members: over 300 *Staff:* 4-6
Annual Budget: $250-500,000 *Tel:* (202) 887-5872
Hist. Note: Founded as the American Council of Commercial Laboratories, it assumed its present name in 1953. Members are independent laboratories doing testing, scientific analyses and applied research for others on a contract basis.
Publication:
ACIL Directory. bien.
Annual Meetings: Fall/250
1987-New York, NY/Oct. 8-13
1988-Austin, TX/Oct 15-20
1989-Hawaii/Oct. 21-26

American Council of Industrial Arts State Ass'n Officers (1955)
Dept. of Industrial Studies, Univ. of Wisconsin - Platteville, Platteville WI 53818
President: Dr. Jack Kirby
Annual Budget: under $10,000 *Tel:* (608) 342-1246
Hist. Note: A division of the Internat'l Technology Education Ass'n, it has no permanent headquarters or paid staff; officers change annually. Members are teachers of industrial arts who belong to state industrial arts associations.
Publication:
President's Newsletter. semi-a.
Annual Meetings: With Internat'l Technology Education Ass'n

American Council of Industrial Arts Supervisors (1951)
Utah State Board of Education, 250 East 500 South, Salt Lake City UT 84111
President: Jerry P. Balistreri
Members: 300
Annual Budget: under $10,000 *Tel:* (801) 533-5371
Hist. Note: Members work for the U.S. Office of Education, state departments of education and local school districts. Affiliated with the American Industrial Arts Ass'n. Has no paid staff or permanent address. Officers change annually.
Publication:
Newsletter. q.
Annual Meetings: With the American Industrial Arts Ass'n

American Council of Learned Societies (1919)
228 E. 45th St., New York NY 10017
President: Stanley M. Katz
Members: 45 societies *Staff:* 15-20
Annual Budget: $1-2,000,000 *Tel:* (212) 697-1505
Hist. Note: Organized in Washington DC September 19, 1919 by twelve scholarly organizations in the humanities and social sciences. Its immediate purpose was to provide U.S. representation in the International Academic Union. Its member organizations today are all national in scope and concerned with the advancement of fundamental research in humanistic studies.
Publications:
ACLS Newsletter. q.
Annual Report. a.
Annual Meetings: Spring

American Council of Life Insurance (1976)
1850 K St., N.W., Washington DC 20006
President: Richard S. Schweiker
Members: 630 legal reserve life insurance companies *Staff:* 275
Annual Budget: over $5,000,000 *Tel:* (202) 862-4000
Hist. Note: A merger on January 1, 1976 of the American Life Insurance Ass'n (1973) and the Institute of Life Insurance (1939), both of which operate as semi-autonomous divisions of the Council. Has an annual budget of approximately $20 million. Sponsors and supports the American Council of Life Insurance Political Action Committee.
Publication:
Council Review. m.
Annual Meetings: Fall/1,200
1987-Washington, DC(Sheraton)/Nov. 15-18
1988-New York, NY(Waldorf Astoria)/Nov. 13-16
1989-Washington, DC(JW Marriott)/Nov. 12-15
1990-Houston, TX(Westin Galleria)/Nov. 11-14

American Council of Nanny Schools (1983)
Director, Home & Family Living Programs, University Center MI 48710
Director: Joy Shelton
Members: 15 schools *Staff:* 0
Annual Budget: under $10,000 *Tel:* (517) 686-9417
Hist. Note: A non-profit coalition of accredited nanny schools seeking to educate, standardize, and promote the professional status of nannies in this country through accrediting new

00033 12 05 86 1233

schools, providing professional support, and developing and administering a national competency test for nannies. Membership: $100-200/yr.
Semi-Annual Meetings: June and November

American Council of Otolaryngology-Head and Neck Surgery, Inc. (1968)
Hist. Note: Founded August 28, 1968 in the District of Columbia and incorporated there the same year. Formerly (until 1980) known as the American Council of Otolaryngology, Inc. Merged with the American Academy of Otolaryngology-Head and Neck Surgery on December 31, 1981.

American Council of Railroad Women (1944)
201 Mission St., 30th Floor, San Francisco CA 94105
President: Susan P. Saltzer
Members: 100
Annual Budget: under $10,000 *Tel:* (415) 974-4677
Hist. Note: Membership restricted to corporate officers and professional or high level supervisors/managers in the railroad industry. Established as the National Association of Railroad Women, it assumed its present name in 1952. Membership: $30/yr.
Publication:
ACRW Bulletin. irreg.
Annual Meetings: Fall

American Council of Teachers of Russian (1974)
815 New Gulph Road, Bryn Mawr PA 19010
Director of USSR Programs: Dr. Dan E. Davidson
Members: 30 institutions, 1,100 individuals *Staff:* 7-8
Annual Budget: $500-1,000,000 *Tel:* (215) 525-6559
Hist. Note: Professional organization of teachers of Russian language as well as literature and culture. Operates an extensive academic exchange program under a direct cooperative agreement with the Pushkin Institute of the Russian Language in Moscow. Membership: $15/yr.
Publications:
ACTR Newsletter. 5/year. adv.
Russian Language Journal q. adv.
Annual Meetings: December 27 or 28
1987-Washington, DC
1988-New York, NY
1989-Chicago, IL

American Council on Consumer Interests (1953)
240 Stanley Hall, University of Missouri, Columbia MO 65211
Exec. Director: Dr. Barbara J. Slusher
Members: 2,000 *Staff:* 2-5
Annual Budget: $100-250,000 *Tel:* (314) 882-3817
Hist. Note: Founded at the University of Minnesota as the Council on Consumer Information with 21 charter members for the purpose of stimulating the exchange of ideas among persons interested in the welfare of the consumer. The present name was adopted in 1969. ACCI is an affiliate member of Joint Council on Economic Education, the Internat'l Organization of Consumers UNions and the Consumer Federation of America. Membership: $30/yr. (individual), $55/yr. (organization).
Publications:
ACCI Happenings. q.
ACCI Newsletter. 9/yr.
Journal of Consumer Affairs. semi-a.
Conference Proceedings. a.
Annual Meetings: April or March/250
1987-Denver, CO(Marriott)/April 1-4
1988-Chicago, IL
1989-Baltimore, MD

American Council on Education (1918)
One Dupont Circle, N.W., Suite 800, Washington DC 20036
President: Robert H. Atwell
Members: 1,600 institutions and associations *Staff:* 175
Annual Budget: over $5,000,000 *Tel:* (202) 939-9300
Hist. Note: Organized by eleven national educational associations to coordinate the work of educational institutions during World War I. It has always placed particular emphasis on higher education and today plays a leading role in the resolution of questions regarding higher education and the Federal Government. Has an annual budget exceeding $10 million.
Publications:
Educational Record. q.
Higher Education and National Affairs. semi-m.
Educational Record. q. adv.
Annual Meetings: January/1,000
1988-Washington, DC

American Council on Education for Journalism (1945)
Hist. Note: Became the Accrediting Council on Education in Journalism and Mass Communication in 1981.

American Council on Industrial Arts Teacher Education
Hist. Note: Became Council on Technology Teacher Education in 1986.

American Council on Internat'l Personnel (1971)
510 Madison Ave., Suite 500, New York NY 10022
Exec. Director: Lucia A. Trovato
Members: 1,000 companies
Annual Budget: $100-250,000 *Tel:* (212) 688-2437
Hist. Note: Membership is open to all companies and organizations that employ at least 1,000 persons worldwide, including overseas and U.S. affiliates and subsidiaries. ACIP's purpose is to serve the business community on immigration matters.
Publications:
Newsletter. m.
Employment of Foreign Nationals in the U.S.
Annual Meetings: May
1987-Washington, DC

American Council on Schools and Colleges (1924)
Hist. Note: Address unknown in 1987.

American Council on Science and Health (1978)
18th Floor, 1995 Broadway, New York NY 10023
Exec. Director: Elizabeth M. Whelan
Members: 3,000 individuals; 400 corporations *Staff:* 16-20
Annual Budget: $500-1,000,000 *Tel:* (212) 362-7044
Hist. Note: A consumer education association providing the public with scientifically balanced evaluations of food, chemicals, the environment and health. Membership: $35/year (individual), $1,000/year (organization).
Publications:
ACSH News and Views. bi-m.
Inside ACSH. q.
The ACSH Media Update. q.

American Council on the Teaching of Foreign Languages (1967)
579 Broadway, Hastings-on-Hudson NY 10706
Exec. Director: C. Edward Scebold
Members: 7-8,000 *Staff:* 10-15
Annual Budget: $500-1,000,000 *Tel:* (914) 478-2011
Hist. Note: Founded in 1967 as part of the Modern Language Ass'n of America and incorporated in 1974. Became a separate organization in 1977. Membership: $35/yr.
Publications:
Foreign Language Annals. bi-m. adv.
PAN Newsletter. bi-m.
Annual Meetings: November
1987-Atlanta, GA(Westin Peachtree Plaza)/Nov. 20-22/1,500
1988-Undecided
1989-Boston, MA(Marriott Copley Place)/Nov. 17-19/1,500

American Court and Commercial Newspapers (1930)
4333 Glenwood Ave., Minneapolis MN 55422
Secy.-Treas.: W. Dexter Moss, Jr.
Members: 56 *Staff:* 1
Tel: (612) 377-6627
Hist. Note: Newspapers dealing primarily with court news, financial matters, real estate and business matters. Established as Associated Court and Commercial Newspapers, it assumed its present name in 1979.
Semi-annual meetings:

American Craft Council (1943)
40 W. 53rd St., New York NY 10019
Exec. Director: Norton Berman
Members: 33,000 *Staff:* 40
Annual Budget: $2-5,000,000 *Tel:* (212) 956-3535
Hist. Note: Formerly the American Craftsmen's Council, ACC exists to stimulate appreciation of the products of Americans working in ceramics, wood, glass, metal, textiles, etc. Membership fee ranges from $39.50-500/yr.
Publication:
American Craft. bi-m. adv.
Annual Meetings: Summer

American Creditors Ass'n (1975)
Hist. Note: A wholly-owned subsidiary of the National Revenue Corporation in Columbus, Ohio. The approximately 85,000 members are the clients of the Corporation.

American Criminal Justice Ass'n (1937)
Box 61047, Sacramento CA 95860
Exec. Secretary: Karen K. Campbell
Members: 5,000 *Staff:* 1
Annual Budget: $25-50,000 *Tel:* (916) 484-6553
Hist. Note: Also known as Lambda Alpha Epsilon, its official title until 1970. Members are criminal justice specialists working in law enforcement, prosecution-defense, courts and corrections as well as college students of the field. Membership: $27/year.
Publication:
LAE Journal of the American Criminal Justice Ass'n. q.
Annual Meetings: Spring
1987-San Jose, CA(San Jose Hyatt)/April 16-21/400
1988-Chicago, IL

American Crossbred Pony Register (1957)
R.D. 1, Box 151, Branchville NJ 07826
Registrar: Lois A. Pellow
Staff: 1
Annual Budget: under $10,000 *Tel:* (201) 875-6399
Publication:
Pony Prints. bi-m.

American Crystallographic Ass'n (1949)
335 East 45th St., New York NY 10017
Admin. Secretary: Ethel E. Snider
Members: 1,800-1,900 *Staff:* 1
Annual Budget: $10-25,000 *Tel:* (212) 661-9404
Hist. Note: Created in 1949 through a merger of the Crystallographic Soc. of America and the American Soc. of X-ray and Electron Diffraction. Incorporated in New York in 1971. Member of the American Institute of Physics.
Publications:
Newsletter. bi-m.
Transactions of The A.C.A. a.
Semi-annual meetings: Summer and Winter

American Culinary Federation (1929)
Box 3466, St. Augustine FL 32084
Exec. Director: L. Edwin Brown
Members: 15,000 *Staff:* 7
Annual Budget: $250-500,000 *Tel:* (904) 824-4468
Hist. Note: Professional chefs and others serving the food service industry. Awards the CEC ("Certified Executive Chef") designation, as well as the "Master Chef Program". Sponsors the American Academy of Chefs (Honorary). Absorbed the American Institute of Chefs as well as the Professional Chefs Association of America. Affiliated with the Canadian Federation of Chefs and the World Ass'n of Cooks Societies. Membership: $35/yr.
Publication:
Culinary Review. m. adv.
Annual Meetings: July
1987-Phoenix, AZ(Arizona Biltmore)
1988-Charlotte, NC(Charlotte Convention Center)

American Cultured Dairy Products Institute (1958)
888 16th St., N.W., Washington DC 20006
President: Glenn P. Witte
Members: 125-150 companies *Staff:* 2-5
Annual Budget: $50-100,000 *Tel:* (202) 223-1931
Hist. Note: Founded as the American Cottage Cheese Institute, it assumed its present name in 1966. Affiliated with the Milk Industry Foundation and the Internat'l Ass'n of Ice Cream Manufacturers.
Publication:
Cultured Dairy Products Journal. q. adv.
Annual Meetings: March

American Cutlery Manufacturers Ass'n (1947)
1133 15th St., N.W., Suite 620, Washington DC 20005
Exec. Director: David W. Barrack
Members: 35-40 companies *Staff:* 2-5
Annual Budget: $50-100,000 *Tel:* (202) 293-5910
Publications:
Bulletin. m.
Directory. a.
Annual Meetings: May

American Dairy Ass'n (1940)
6300 North River Rd., Rosemont IL 60018
President: Joseph B. Kelsch
Members: 200-210,000 dairy farmers *Staff:* 15
Annual Budget: over $5,000,000 *Tel:* (312) 696-1880
Hist. Note: A division of the United Dairy Industry Ass'n, ADA is a federation of 20 regional and state dairy farmers' associations. It is the largest commodity promotion organization in the U.S., representing 95% of the nation's dairy farmers and 85% of the milk produced; it conducts $50 million annual advertising and sales promotion program for domestic milk and non-milk products on a non-brand basis. Affiliated with Nat'l Dairy Promotion and Research Board.
Publication:
Dairy Promotion Quarterly. q.
Annual Meetings: With United Dairy Industry Ass'n

American Dairy Goat Ass'n (1904)
Box 865, Spindale NC 28160
Secy.-Treas.: Don Wilson
Members: 18,400 *Staff:* 16-20
Annual Budget: $500-1,000,000 *Tel:* (704) 286-3801
Hist. Note: Breeders and fanciers of dairy goats. Formerly American Milch Goat Record Association and American Milk Goat Record Association. Member of the National Society of Livestock Record Associations. Membership: $15/yr.
Publications:
ADGA Handbook. a. adv.
ADGA Newsletter. m.
Dairy Goats, Breeding/Feeding/Management. m. adv.
Annual Meetings: Fall
1987-San Antonio, TX

American Dairy Products Institute (1986)
130 North Franklin St., Chicago IL 60606
Exec. Director: Warren S. Clark, Jr.
Members: 159 companies *Staff:* 11-15
Annual Budget: $500-1,000,000 *Tel:* (312) 782-5455
Hist. Note: Product of a merger between the American Dry Milk Institute and the Whey Products Institute in 1986. Seeks to promote the acceptance and utilization of processed dairy products, to maintain liaison and represent the industry in dealings with governmental agencies and legislative bodies, to support technical and marketing research and to assemble and disseminate statistics and other information about processed dairy products.
Annual Meetings: Chicago/April/550
1987-(Hyatt Regency O'Hare)/April 8-9
1988-(O'Hare Marriott)/April 18-22/550
1989-April 12-13/550

00034 12 05 86 1233

American Dairy Science Ass'n (1906)
309 West Clark St., Champaign IL 61820
Exec. Secretary: Carl D. Johnson
Members: 2,400 individuals, 2,000 companies *Staff:* 16-20
Annual Budget: $250-500,000 *Tel:* (217) 356-3182
Hist. Note: Incorporated in the District of Columbia in 1906. Members are equipment manufacturers and suppliers, farmers, educators, researchers and breeders interested in strengthening all aspects of the dairy industry.
Publication:
Journal of Dairy Science. m. adv.
Annual Meetings:
1987-Columbia, MO(University of Missouri)/June 21-24
1988-Raleigh, NC(North Carolina State University)/June 26-29
1989-Lexington, KY/Aug. 1-4

American Dance Guild (1956)
33 West 21st St., 3rd Floor, New York NY 10010
Exec. Director: Richard Allan Ploch
Members: 400
Annual Budget: $25-50,000 *Tel:* (212) 627-3790
Hist. Note: Performers, teachers, critics, choreographers and students of all forms of dance. Formerly (until 1956) known as the Dance Teachers Guild, until 1966 the Nat'l Dance Teachers Guild, and until 1968 the Nat'l Dance Guild. Maintains a speakers bureau and job registry. Membership: $40/year.
Publications:
Newsletter. bi-m. adv.
American Dance. semi-a.
Annual Meetings: June
1987-Washington, DC(Geo. Washington Univ.)/June 4-7/200

American Dance Therapy Ass'n (1966)
2000 Century Plaza, Suite 108, Columbia MD 21044
Exec. Director: James D. Mitchell
Members: 1,100 *Staff:* 2-5
Annual Budget: $100-250,000 *Tel:* (301) 997-4040
Hist. Note: Individuals and institutions concerned with the dance as a therapeutic agent. Awards the DTR and the ADTR designations to those meeting prescribed professional standards. Membership: $60/year.
Publications:
American Journal of Dance Therapy. a.
Newsletter. q.
Annual Meetings: Fall
1987-Long Beach, CA(Queen Mary)/Oct. 27-Nov. 1
1988-Baltimore, MD

American Deafness and Rehabilitation Ass'n (1966)
814 Thayer Ave., Silver Spring MD 20910
President: Steve Slager
Members: 1,000-1,200 *Staff:* 2-5
Annual Budget: $50-100,000 *Tel:* (301) 589-0880
Hist. Note: Founded in St. Louis, Missouri in 1966 as Professional Rehabilitation Workers with the Adult Deaf and incorporated the following year. The present name was assumed in 1976. Membership: $36/yr.
Publications:
Journal of Rehabilitation of the Deaf. q. adv.
Newsletter. semi-m.
Semi-annual Meetings:
1987-Minneapolis, MN/May-June

American Defense Preparedness Ass'n (1919)
Rosslyn Center, Suite 900, 1700 North Moore St., Arlington VA 22209
President: Gen. Henry A. Miley, Jr. (Ret.)
Members: 916 companies; 38,000 individuals *Staff:* 30
Annual Budget: $2-5,000,000 *Tel:* (703) 522-1820
Hist. Note: Merged (1965) with Armed Forces Chemical Ass'n and (1974) Armed Forces Management Ass'n. Formerly (1948) Army Ordnance Ass'n and (1973) American Ordnance Ass'n. Membership: $20-90 (based on length of desired membership).
Publications:
Common Defense. m.
Directory. a.
National Defense. 10/yr. adv.
Technical Bulletin. q.
Annual Meetings: Spring/1,200
1987-Washington, DC(Shoreham)/May 20-21

American Dehydrators Ass'n (1941)
Hist. Note: Became the American Alfalfa Processors Ass'n in 1984.

American Dental Assistants Ass'n (1924)
666 North Lake Shore Dr., Suite 1130, Chicago IL 60611
Exec. Director: John C. Thiel
Members: 25,000 *Staff:* 11-16
Annual Budget: $500-1,000,000 *Tel:* (312) 664-3327
Hist. Note: Requires tripartite membership (local, state, and national).
Publication:
The Dental Assistant. bi-m. adv.
Annual Meetings: Fall
1987-Houston, TX

American Dental Ass'n (1859)
211 East Chicago Ave., Chicago IL 60611
Exec. Director: Thomas J. Ginley, Ph.D.
Members: 140,000 *Staff:* 350-400
Annual Budget: over $5,000,000 *Tel:* (312) 440-2500
Hist. Note: Founded August 3, 1859 in Niagara Falls. United with the Southern Dental Ass'n in 1897 and changed its name to the Nat'l Dental Ass'n. In 1922 the name was changed to the American Dental Ass'n. Incorporated in Illinois. Supports the American Dental Political Action Committee. Maintains a Washington office.
Publications:
ADA Directory. a.
ADA News. w. adv.
Dental Abstracts. m. adv.
Index to Dental Literature. q.
Journal of the ADA. m. adv.
Annual Meetings: Fall
1987-Las Vegas, NV/Oct. 10-15
1988-Washington, DC/Oct. 8-11
1989-Honolulu, HI/Nov. 5-9
1990-Boston, MA/Oct. 14-18

American Dental Hygienists' Ass'n (1923)
444 North Michigan Ave., Suite 3400, Chicago IL 60611
Exec. Director: Albert J. Sunseri, CAE
Members: 32,000 *Staff:* 30-40
Annual Budget: $2-5,000,000 *Tel:* (312) 440-8900
Hist. Note: Supports ADHA-HY-PAC, a political action committee. Membership: $99/yr. (individual(, $500/yr. (organization/company).
Publications:
Dental Hygiene. m. adv.
Educational Directions. q. adv.
Horizons. bi-m. 35,000 circ.
Annual Meetings: June
1987-St. Louis, MO(Omni Union Station)/June 17-24/800-1,000
1988-Seattle, WA

American Dental Interfraternity Council (1923)
884 Brighton Road, Tonawanda NY 14150
Exec. Secretary: Dr. Edward J. Dweck
Members: 4
Annual Budget: under $10,000 *Tel:* (716) 836-4590
Hist. Note: A federation of professional Greek letter societies united to promote better public relations for the dental profession.
Annual Meetings: Fall

American Dental Soc. of Anesthesiology (1953)
211 East Chicago Ave., Suite 948, Chicago IL 60611
Exec. Director: Peter C. Goulding
Members: 3,500 *Staff:* 2-5
Annual Budget: $100-250,000 *Tel:* (312) 664-8270
Hist. Note: Members are dentists with a special interest in pain control. Membership: $75/yr.
Publications:
Anesthesia Progress. bi-m. adv.
Newsletter. bi-m.
Annual Meetings: Spring/250
1987-Anaheim, CA(Marriott)/April 24-26

American Dental Trade Ass'n (1882)
4222 King St., Alexandria VA 22302
President & C.E.O.: Nikolaj M. Petrovic, CAE
Members: 150 companies *Staff:* 5
Annual Budget: $500-1,000,000 *Tel:* (703) 379-7755
Hist. Note: Membership: $500-40,000/yr.
Publication:
Update. bi-m.
Annual Meetings: Fall
1987-Orlando, FL(Hyatt Grand Cypress)/Nov. 10-15/350
1988-Palm Desert, CA(Marriott Desert Springs)/Oct. 26-30/350
1989-Maui, HI(Hyatt Regency)/Oct. 30-Nov. 3/600
1990-Hilton Head, SC/Sept. 27-30/350-400
1991-Scottsdale, AZ(Hyatt Gainey Ranch)/Nov. 6-9/350-400

American Dermatologic Soc. for Allergy and Immunology (1975)
Dept. of Dermatology, Mayo Clinic, Rochester MN 55905
Secy.-Treas.: Suzanne M. Connolly
Members: 250 *Staff:* 1
Annual Budget: $10-25,000 *Tel:* (507) 284-2555
Hist. Note: Membership: $25/yr.
Annual Meetings: Fall/200
1987-Washington, DC

American Dermatological Ass'n (1876)
Department of Dermatology, University Hospitals BT 2045-1, Iowa City IA 52242
Secretary: John S. Strauss, MD
Members: 350 *Staff:* 1
Annual Budget: $25-50,000 *Tel:* (319) 356-2274
Hist. Note: Organized September 6, 1876 and incorporated in 1930 to advance dermatologic knowledge, teaching and research. Membership: $150/yr.
Annual Meetings: Spring

American Dexter Cattle Ass'n (1912)
Box 56, Decorah IA 52101
Exec. Secy.-Treas.: Kay Moore Baker
Members: 125-150 *Staff:* 1
Annual Budget: under $10,000 *Tel:* (507) 735-5772
Hist. Note: Established as the American Kerry and Dexter Club, it assumed its present name in 1957.
Publications:
Bulletin. q.
Herd Book. a.

American Diabetes Ass'n (1940)
Nat'l Service Center, P.O. Box 25757, Alexandria VA 22313
Exec. V. President: Robert S. Bolan
Members: 215,000 *Staff:* 80
Annual Budget: over $5,000,000 *Tel:* (703) 549-1500
Hist. Note: Founded in 1940 in Cincinnati as a professional society of medical doctors; converted in 1965 to a voluntary health agency. Operates as a federation of affiliated associations, each of which is responsible for fund raising and program activities within its geographic region. Has an annual budget of $15 million. Membership: $20/yr.
Publications:
ADA Forecast. m. adv.
Clinical Diabetes. bi-m. adv.
Diabetes. m. adv.
Diabetes Care. bi-m. adv.
Diabetes '86. q. adv.
Annual Meetings: June/5,000
1987-Indianapolis, IN(Hyatt)/June 4-9
1988-New Orleans, LA(Convention Center)/June 9-14
1989-Detroit, MI(Westin)/June 1-6
1990-Atlanta, GA(Marriott, Congress Center)/June 14-19
1991-Washington, DC(Convention Center)/June 20-28

American Dialect Soc. (1889)
Dept. of English, MacMurray College, Jacksonville IL 62650
Exec. Secretary: Allan Metcalf
Members: 560 individuals, 300 institutions *Staff:* 1
Annual Budget: $10-25,000 *Tel:* (217) 245-6151
Hist. Note: Members are educators and others interested in the English language in North America. Sponsors the Dictionary of American Regional English. Membership: $20/yr.
Publications:
American Speech. q.
Newsletter of the American Dialect Society. 3/yr. adv.
Publication of the American Dialect Society (PADS). irreg.
Annual Meetings: With the Modern Language Association, December 27-30 each year.

American Die Casting Institute (1928)
2340 Des Plaines Ave., Des Plaines IL 60018
President: Peter A.R. Findlay
Members: 250-300 companies *Staff:* 6-10
Annual Budget: $500-1,000,000 *Tel:* (312) 298-1220
Hist. Note: Supports the Die Casting Research Foundation.
Publication:
Die Casting Management. bi-m.
Annual Meetings: Fall, in the Chicago area/225

American Dietetic Ass'n (1917)
430 North Michigan Ave., Chicago IL 60611
Exec. Director: Julian Haynes, Ph.D.
Members: 54,000 *Staff:* 110
Annual Budget: over $5,000,000 *Tel:* (312) 280-5000
Hist. Note: The nation's largest professional society of dietitians established in Cleveland, MO in 1917 and incorporated in Illinois in 1923. Members are employed in hospitals, schools, colleges, universities as well as in business institutions and industry. The American Dietetic Ass'n Foundation, established 1967, is its education and research arm. Sponsors and supports the American Dietetic Ass'n Political Action Committee. Has an annual budget of approximately $8.7 million. Membership: $90/yr.
Publication:
Journal of the American Dietetic Ass'n. m. adv.
Annual Meetings: Fall/10-12,000
1987-Atlanta, GA(Convention Ctr.)/Oct. 19-23
1988-San Francisco, CA(Convention Ctr.)/Oct. 3-7
1989-Kansas City, MO(Convention Ctr.)/Oct. 23-27

American Digestive Disease Soc. (1973)
7720 Wisconsin Ave., Bethesda MD 20814
Exec. Director: Martin I. Hassner
Members: 10,000 *Staff:* 7
Annual Budget: $500-1,000,000 *Tel:* (301) 652-9293
Hist. Note: Lay/community leadership working with physicians specializing in the diagnosis and treatment of digestive diseases. ADDS is the only national, voluntary, educational organization in its field. Sponsors a national physicians referral service, provides educational materials, and works to stimulate federal research in digestive diseases. Membership: $30/yr. (individual), $100/yr. (company).
Publications:
Dialogue. irreg.
Living Healthy. m. adv.
Person to Person. irreg.
Annual Meetings: Spring

American Dinner Theatre Institute (1972)
Box 2537, Sarasota FL 33578
Exec. Secretary: Marvin H. Poons
Members: 30-40 *Staff:* 1
Annual Budget: $25-50,000 *Tel:* (813) 365-1754
Hist. Note: Founded at a conference of dinner theatre operators held in Dallas, TX in October 1972. Acts as a clearinghouse for information on all phases of dinner theatre operation.
Publication:
Newsletter. m.

American Diopter and Decibel Soc. (1960)
3518 5th Ave., Pittsburgh PA 15213
Meetings Coordinator: Jeannine Nee
Members: 175-200 *Staff:* 2-5
Annual Budget: $10-25,000 *Tel:* (412) 963-6304
Hist. Note: Physicians specializing in diseases of the eye, ear, nose and throat. Membership: $50/year.

00035 12 05 86 1233

Publication:
Proceedings. a.
Biennial Meetings:
1987-Acapulco, Mexico(Acapulco Princess)/Jan. 24-31/100

American Donkey and Mule Soc. (1967)
2901 N. Elm St., Denton TX 76201
Secretary: Betsy Hutchins
Members: 3,000 *Staff:* 1
Annual Budget: $25-50,000 *Tel:* (817) 382-6845
Hist. Note: Breeders, owners, and organizations interested in donkeys and mules. Maintains the American Donkey Register, a stud book, sets show standards, prepares and disseminates educational books and literature. Membership: $12/yr.
Publication:
The Brayer. q. adv.
Annual Meetings: Nat'l Mule Show

American Down Ass'n (1983)
3830 Watt Ave., Suite 10, Sacramento CA 95821
Exec. Director: Howard Winslow
Members: 48 companies *Staff:* 4-5
Annual Budget: $100-250,000 *Tel:* (916) 971-1135
Annual Meetings: Semi-Annual Meetings

American Driver and Traffic Safety Education Ass'n (1956)
123 North Pitt St., Suite 509, Alexandria VA 22314
Exec. Director: Dr. William D. Cushman
Members: 1,500
Annual Budget: $100-250,000 *Tel:* (703) 836-4748
Hist. Note: A professional society of driving and safety educators, it was established as the American Driver and Safety Education Ass'n, it became the American Driver Education Ass'n in 1957 and assumed its present name in 1963. Membership: $15-100/yr. (individual); $400/yr. (organization/company)
Publications:
Journal of Traffic Safety Education. q. adv.
Washington Wire. 4-7/yr.
Annual Meetings: August/3-400
1987-Spokane, WA/Aug. 9-13

American Dry Milk Institute (1925)
Hist. Note: Merged with the Whey Products Institute in 1986, to become the American Dairy Products Institute.

American Dye Manufacturers Institute
Hist. Note: Ceased operations in early 1987.

American Economic Ass'n (1885)
1313 21st Ave. South, Nashville TN 37212
Secretary: Dr. C. Elton Hinshaw
Members: 19-20,000 individuals, 6,000 companies *Staff:* 25-30
Annual Budget: $1-2,000,000 *Tel:* (615) 322-2595
Hist. Note: Founded in Saratoga, NY in 1885. A member of the American Council of Learned Societies and affiliated with the Social Science Research Council, the American Ass'n for the Advancement of Science and the Internat'l Economic Ass'n. Encourages economic research, particularly historical and statistical studies of industrial life. The umbrella organization for U.S. economists. Membership: $38.50/yr. (individual); $110/yr. (organization/company).
Publications:
American Economic Review. 5/yr. adv.
Journal of Economic Literature. q. adv.
Annual Meetings: Late December
1987-Chicago, IL(Hyatt)/Dec. 28-30/6,000
1988-New York, NY(Marriott/Sheraton)/Dec. 28-30/7,500
1989-Atlanta, GA(Hilton/Marriott)/Dec. 28-30/6,000

American Economic Development Council (1926)
4849 North Scott St., Suite 22, Schiller Park IL 60176
President: Edward J. Collins, Jr. CAE
Members: 1,250 individuals *Staff:* 6
Annual Budget: $500-1,000,000 *Tel:* (312) 671-5646
Hist. Note: Originally a part of the Chamber of Commerce of the United States, AEDC is a tax-exempt incorporated organization of professionals active in the field of industrial and economic development. Splitting from the Chamber in 1926 as the American Industrial Development Council, it assumed its present name in 1980. Membership: $250/yr.
Publications:
AEDC Newsletter. m.
Legislative Affairs Report. m.
Economic Development Review Journal. semi-a.
Membership Directory. a.
Annual Meetings: Spring/400
1987-Fort Worth, TX/May 30-June 3
1988-Tucson, AZ

American Educational Research Ass'n (1915)
1230 17th St, N.W., Washington DC 20036
Exec. Officer: William J. Russell
Members: 14,000 *Staff:* 16-20
Annual Budget: $1-2,000,000 *Tel:* (202) 223-9485
Hist. Note: Founded in 1915 in Cincinnati as the Nat'l Ass'n of Directors of Educational Research, an affiliate of the Nat'l Education Ass'n. In 1930 the name was changed to the American Educational Research Ass'n. In 1968 the affiliation with NEA was dropped and the organization was incorporated in the District of Columbia. AERA is an international professional organization of educators, directors of research, testing, or evaluation in federal, state, and local agencies; counselors; evaluators, graduate students; and behavioral scientists concerned with educational research and its application to practice. Membership: $45/yr.
Publications:
American Educational Research Journal. q. adv.
Educational Evaluation and Policy Analysis. q. adv.
Educational Researcher. 10/yr. adv.
Journal of Educational Statistics. q.
Review of Educational Research. q.
Review of Research in Education. a.
Annual Meetings: Spring
1987-Washington, DC(Sheraton)/April 20-24/6,200
1988-New Orleans, LA(Marriott/Sheraton)/April 5-9/6,000
1989-San Francisco, CA/March
1990-Boston, MA/April
1991-Chicago, IL/April

American Educational Studies Ass'n (1968)
Dept. of EDPA, College of Education, University of Maryland, College Park MD 20742
Secretary: Nancy King
Members: 600
Annual Budget: $10-25,000 *Tel:* (301) 454-4032
Hist. Note: Concerned with the comprehensive view of education including the underlying philosophy, history, sociology and psychology of education and dedicated to research and the improvement of teaching in these areas. Membership: $20/year.
Publications:
AESA Newsletter. q.
Educational Studies. q. adv.
Educational Foundations. 3/a.
Semi-annual Meetings: March with American Ass'n of Colleges for
Teacher Education and November
1987-Chicago, Il(Americana)/Nov. 3-8
1988-Toronto, Canada

American Egg Board (1939)
1460 Renaissance Dr., Suite 301, Park Ridge IL 60068
President: Louis B. Raffel
Members: 18 individuals representing 5,000 producers *Staff:* 25
Annual Budget: over $5,000,000 *Tel:* (312) 296-7044
Hist. Note: Established as the Poultry and Egg National Board, a federation of egg producers. The name was changed in 1973 to the American Egg Board. An act of Congress in 1976 gave this official status, permitted dues check offs from egg producers, and the appointment by the Secretary of Agriculture of the members of the Board. Concerned with advertising, promotion and research activities for eggs and egg products. Has an annual budget of $6,500,000.

American Electroencephalographic Soc. (1946)
2579 Melinda Drive, N.E., Atlanta GA 30345
Exec. Director: Fay Tyner
Members: 1,350 *Staff:* 2-5
Tel: (404) 320-1746
Hist. Note: A professional society of electroencephalographers and neurophysiologists.
Publications:
Newsletter. semi-a.
Journal of Clinical Neurophysiology. q.
Annual Meetings: Fall
1987-St. Louis, MO/Sept.
1988-San Diego, CA

American Electrology Ass'n (1958)
710 Tennent Road, Englishtown NJ 07726
Exec. Director: Jerome Enis
Members: 1,800 individuals *Staff:* 2
Annual Budget: $100-250,000 *Tel:* (201) 536-6477
Hist. Note: Founded in Boston in Feb., 1958 as American Electrolysis Ass'n, it assumed its present name in 1986. Membership composed of electrologists (hair removers). Sponsors national certification program, national accreditation program and continuing education. Membership: $100/yr.
Publications:
Electrolysis World. bi-m. adv.
Membership Directory. a. adv.
Journal of Electrology. semi-a. adv.
Biennial conventions: even years; Annual Meetings in Fall

American Electrolysis Ass'n
Hist. Note: Became the American Electrology Ass'n in 1986.

American Electronics Ass'n (1943)
2670 Hanover, P.O. Box 10045, Palo Alto CA 94303
President: J. Richard Iverson
Members: 2,900 companies *Staff:* 125
Annual Budget: over $5,000,000 *Tel:* (415) 857-9300
Hist. Note: Founded in California in 1943 by 25 electronics manufacturers, it is now the largest trade ass'n serving the electronics and information technology industries. Maintains a Washington office, which is one of its eight offices in the U.S., and has a budget of over $12.5 million. Formerly (1971) the Western Electronic Manufacturers Ass'n and, until 1978, WEMA. Supports the American Electronics Ass'n ElectroPAC. A member of the Nat'l Commission on Software Issues in the Eighties. Membership fee varies with size of company.
Publications:
Update. m.
Directory. a.

American Electroplaters and Surface Finishers Soc. (1909)
Central Florida Research Park, 12644 Research Parkway, Orlando FL 32826
Exec. Director: J. Howard Schumacher, Jr.
Members: 9-10,000 *Staff:* 20-25
Annual Budget: $1-2,000,000 *Tel:* (305) 281-6441
Hist. Note: Founded in New York City in 1909 as the Nat'l Electro-Platers Ass'n. Became American Electroplaters' Soc. in 1913 and assumed its present name in 1985. Incorporated in New Jersey in 1946. Promotes all aspects of electroplating and surface finishing.
Publications:
Plating and Surface Finishing. m. adv.
Sur/Fin Proceedings. a.
Sur/Fin Shopguide a. adv.
Annual Meetings: Summer
1987-Chicago, IL(Hilton/McCormick Ctr.)/July 13-16
1988-Los Angeles, CA/June 27-30
1989-Cleveland, OH
1990-Boston, MA(Hynes Aud.)/July 7-15/5,000
1991-Toronto, Ontario

American Electroplaters' Soc. (1909)
Hist. Note: Became the American Electroplaters and Surface Finishers Soc. in 1985.

American Embryo Transfer Ass'n (1981)
Association Bldg., 9th and Minnesota, Hastings NE 68901
Exec. V. President: Don Ellerbee
Members: 100 individuals and companies *Staff:* 2-5
Annual Budget: $25-50,000 *Tel:* (402) 462-9032
Hist. Note: Seeks to promote the use of embryo transfer as a means to improve livestock and encourages cooperative relationships among companies and individuals engaged in embryo transfer. Has developed a Certification Program for embryo transfer companies in order to identify those who meet certain criteria in their commercial activities.
Publication:
Convention Proceedings. a.
Annual Meetings: October

American Endodontic Soc. (1969)
1440 N. Harbor Blvd. Suite 719, Fullerton CA 92635
Exec. Director: Dr. Ramon Werts
Members: 7000 individuals *Staff:* 2-5
Annual Budget: $100-250,000 *Tel:* (714) 870-5590
Hist. Note: Members are dentists specializing in root canal work.
Publications:
AES Newsletter. q.
Hotline. q.
Annual Meetings: Fall

American Engineering Model Soc. (1968)
Box 2066, Aiken SC 29802
Exec. Director: Raymond J. Hale
Members: 500 *Staff:* 2
Annual Budget: $50-100,000 *Tel:* (803) 649-6710
Hist. Note: Members are individuals and institutions building, designing and applying engineering models (physical, scale and computer) in all fields of industrial activity. Membership includes designers, engineers, management personnel and skilled model makers. Membership: $35/yr.
Publications:
Newsletter. m. adv.
Seminar Proceedings. a.
Annual Meetings: May/300

American Entomological Soc. (1859)
1900 Race St., Philadelphia PA 19103
Office Secretary: Mildred G. Morgan
Members: 300-350 individuals *Staff:* 1
Annual Budget: under $10,000 *Tel:* (215) 561-3978
Hist. Note: Founded in Philadelphia in 1859 as the Entomological Soc. of Philadelphia. In 1867 the name was changed to American Entomological Soc. The Society's library has been merged into that of the Academy of Natural Sciences of Philadelphia. Membership: $7/yr.
Publications:
Entomological News. 5/yr.
Memoirs. irreg.
Transactions. q.
Five Meetings Each Year: February, March, April, October & November
in either Philadelphia, Pennsylvania or Newark, Delaware.

American Epidemiological Soc. (1927)
Emory Univ. Sch. of Medicine, MPH Prog.,735 Gatewood Road, N.E., Atlanta GA 30322
Secy.-Treas.: Philip S. Brachman
Members: 300 *Staff:* 1
Annual Budget: under $10,000 *Tel:* (404) 329-7806
Hist. Note: Members are individuals interested in the study of disease occurrence.
Annual Meetings: March

American Epilepsy Soc. (1946)
179 Allyn St., #304, Hartford CT 06103
Exec. Director: Priscilla Bourgeois
Members: 1,300 *Staff:* 2-5
Annual Budget: $100-250,000 *Tel:* (203) 246-6566
Hist. Note: Founded as the American League Against Epilepsy, it assumed its present name in 1959. Members are physicians and scientists engaged in research and practice in epilepsy or closely related fields. Membership: $89/yr.

00036 12 05 86 1233

Publication:
Epilepsia. bi-m. adv.
Annual Meetings: Fall
1987-Baltimore, MD/Dec. 6-10/600

American Equilibration Soc. (1955)
8726 N. Ferris Avenue, Morton Grove IL 60053
Office Director: Shel Marcus
Members: 1,500 *Staff:* 2-5
Tel: (312) 965-2888
Hist. Note: Membership consists of dentists and physicians interested in the structure and functions of the temporomandibular region and related parts of the mouth.
Publication:
Compendium. a.
Annual Meetings:
1988-Australia

American Ethnological Soc. (1842)
Dept. of Anthropology, University of South Florida, Tampa FL 33620
Secretary: Dr. Alvin W. Wolfe
Members: 1,100-1,200 *Staff:* 1
Annual Budget: $50-100,000 *Tel:* (813) 974-2150
Hist. Note: Organized in 1842, "to make inquiries into the origin, progress and characteristics of the various races of man." Became inactive in the 1860s but was re-organized in 1871 as the Anthropological Institute, and shortly thereafter it assumed its present name. Affiliated with American Anthropoligical Ass'n. Has elected officers and no permanent address. Membership: $40/yr.
Publication:
American Ethnologist. q. adv.
Semi-annual Meetings: Spring and Fall

American Family Therapy Ass'n (1977)
1255 Twenty-Third St., N.W., #850, Washington DC 20037
Exec. Director: Susan C. Watson
Members: 900 *Staff:* 2-5
Annual Budget: $100-250,000 *Tel:* (202) 659-7666
Hist. Note: Members are teachers, researchers, and clinical therapists specially trained to work with couples and families. Its purpose is to advance therapies and theories that regard the family as a unit within a broader context; to promote research in family therapy; and to make information available to the public and practitioners in other fields. Membership: $110/yr.
Publications:
AFTA Newsletter. q. adv.
Membership Directory. a.
Annual Meetings: June
1987-Chicago, IL(Drake)
1988-Montreal, Canada

American Fan Ass'n (1980)
Box 1481, East Lansing MI 48823
President: D. Gravatt Huber
Members: 32 *Staff:* 3-5
Annual Budget: $100-250,000 *Tel:* (517) 349-5566
Hist. Note: Membership includes both manufacturers and distributors of electric fans. Supports the Air Movement Institute, a non-profit research and educational subsidiary of AFA.
Publication:
AFA Blade. m. adv.
Semi-annual Meetings:

American Farm Bureau Federation (1920)
225 Touhy Ave., Park Ridge IL 60068
President: Dean R. Kleckner
Members: 49 states and Puerto Rico *Staff:* 100-110
Annual Budget: over $5,000,000 *Tel:* (312) 399-5700
Hist. Note: Members are the state Farm Bureaus in 49 states and Puerto Rico. These, in turn, represent nearly 3,000 county Farm Bureaus and over 3,200,000 families. The American Agricultural Marketing Ass'n, American Agricultural Insurance Company, American Farm Bureau Service Company, and American Agricultural Communications System are affilated companies. Maintains a Washington office.
Publication:
Farm Bureau News. w.
Annual Meetings: January
1987-Anaheim, CA/Jan. 11-15
1988-New Orleans, LA/Jan. 10-14
1989-San Antonio, TX/Jan. 8-12

American Farriers Ass'n (1971)
Box 695, Albuquerque NM 87103
President: Bruce B. Daniels
Members: 2,000 farriers, 20 manufacturers/suppliers *Staff:* 1
Annual Budget: $50-100,000 *Tel:* (505) 345-2784
Hist. Note: An association of professional horseshoers. Membership: $50/yr.
Publication:
American Farriers Journal. bi-m. adv.
Annual Meetings:
1987-Albuquerque, NM(Hilton)/Feb. 24-28/1,000
1988-Lexington, KY
1989-Reno, NV
1990-Lubbock, TX

American Fastener and Closure Ass'n (1986)
3008 Millwood Ave., Columbia SC 29205
President: J. Edgar Eubanks
Members: 30 companies *Staff:* 3
Annual Budget: $100-250,000 *Tel:* (803) 252-5646
Hist. Note: Formerly (1986) Slide Fastener Ass'n. Incorporated in South Carolina. Membership: based on sales.

American Fastener Enclosure Ass'n (1950)
3008 Millwood Ave., Columbia SC 29205
President: J. Edgar Eubanks
Members: 18 companies *Staff:* 8
Tel: (803) 252-5646
Hist. Note: Formerly Slide Fastener Manufacturers Ass'n of America and (1986) Slide Fastener Ass'n. Members are zipper makers in the U.S., 85% of which are represented in the association. Membership: Based on company sales.

American Federation for Clinical Research (1940)
6900 Grove Rd., Thorofare NJ 08086
Exec. Secretary: Peter Slack
Members: 12,500 *Staff:* 6-10
Annual Budget: $250-500,000 *Tel:* (609) 848-1000
Hist. Note: Promotes research in clinical and laboratory medicine. Membership: $40/yr.
Publication:
Clinical Research. q. adv.
Annual Meetings: Spring
1987-San Diego, CA/May 1-4
1988-Washington, DC/Apr. 30-May 3

American Federation of Government Employees (1932)
80 F St., N.W., Washington DC 20001
President: Kenneth T. Blaylock
Members: 200,000 *Staff:* 275-300
Annual Budget: over $5,000,000 *Tel:* (202) 737-8700
Hist. Note: Established by dissidents from the National Federation of Federal Employees in 1932 who wished to extend the civil service classification system to skilled crafts in government. Chartered by the American Federation of Labor the same year. Merged in 1971 with the Association of Engineers and Scientists. Sponsors and supports the American Federation of Government Employees Political Action Commitee.
Publications:
The Government Standard/Agenda. m.
Political Action. m.
AFGE Bulletin. bi-w.
Biennial meetings: Even years in Summer

American Federation of Grain Millers Internat'l Union (1936)
4949 Olson Memorial Hwy., Minneapolis MN 55422
President: Robert W. Willis
Members: 30,000 *Staff:* 26-30
Annual Budget: $2-5,000,000 *Tel:* (612) 545-0211
Hist. Note: Organized in Toledo, Ohio July, 1936 as the Grain Processors Council. Became the National Council of Grain Processors in 1939. Chartered by the American Federation of Labor July 26, 1948 under its present title.
Publication:
Grain Miller News. q.
Biennial meetings: Uneven years

American Federation of Home Health Agencies (1981)
1320 Fenwick Lane, Suite 500, Silver Spring MD 20910
Exec. Director: Ann Howard
Members: 300 *Staff:* 2-5
Annual Budget: $100-250,000 *Tel:* (301) 588-1454
Hist. Note: Has a political action committee. Works with government agencies to develop policies and implement the provisions of Medicare legislation.
Publication:
Insider. semi-m.
Annual Meetings: May
1987-Washington, DC

American Federation of Information Processing Societies (1961)
1899 Preston White Drive, Reston VA 22091
President: Dr. Jack Moshman
Members: 150,000 in 11 constituent societies *Staff:* 25
Annual Budget: over $5,000,000 *Tel:* (703) 620-8900
Hist. Note: Formed in 1961 as successor to Nat'l Joint Computer Committee. Incorporated in Delaware in 1970. Consists of The American Soc. for Information Science, American Statistical Ass'n, Ass'n for Computational Linguistics, The Ass'n for Computing Machinery, Inc., Ass'n for Educational Data Systems, Data Processing Management Ass'n Inc., The Computer Soc. of the Institute of Electrical and Electronics Engineers, Instrument Soc. of America, Soc. for Computer Simulation, Soc. for Industrial and Applied Mathematics, Soc. for Information Display. The umbrella organization of the professional societies serving the U.S. computer industry. U.S. Representative to The International Federation for Information Processing. Has an annual budget of $12 million.
Publications:
AFIPS Washington Activities Report.
Annals of the History of Computing. q. adv.
Proceedings of the National Computer Conference. a.
Proceedings of Office Automation Conference. a.

American Federation of Labor and Congress of Industrial Organizations (1955)
815 16th St., N. W., Washington DC 20006
President: Lane Kirkland
Members: 13,100,000 *Staff:* 200-250
Annual Budget: over $5,000,000 *Tel:* (202) 637-5000
Hist. Note: The American Federation of Labor was founded in 1886 by 13 national unions on the principle of autonomy for its members. Samuel Gompers was the first president and served 38 years. In 1935 nine of its unions broke away under the leadership of John L. Lewis to form the Congress of Industrial Organizations to push industrial (as opposed to craft) unionism. After 20 years of independence, the AFL and CIO were merged in 1955. The AFL-CIO consists of 96 separate unions, 51 state organizations and about 740 local units broken into 96 separate unions. Has a budget of about $40 million.
Publication:
AFL-CIO News. w.
Biennial meetings: Odd years
1987-Chicago, IL/Sept. 14-17

American Federation of Musicians of the United States and Canada (1896)
1501 Broadway, Suite 600, New York NY 10036
President: Victor W. Fuentealba
Members: 230,000 *Staff:* 100
Annual Budget: over $5,000,000 *Tel:* (212) 869-1330
Hist. Note: Organized October 19, 1896 in Indianapolis as the American Federation of Musicians and chartered by the American Federation of Labor the same year. Assumed its present name in 1965. Supports the A.F.M.-Tempo Political Contributions Committee.
Publication:
International Musician. m. adv.
Biennial meetings: odd years
1987-Las Vegas, NV/June

American Federation of Physicians and Dentists
Hist. Note: No paid staff; address unknown in 1986.

American Federation of Police (1966)
1100 N.E. 125th St., Suite 100, North Miami FL 33161
Exec. Director: Gerald S. Arenberg
Members: 30-35,000 *Staff:* 11-15
Annual Budget: $1-2,000,000 *Tel:* (305) 891-1700
Hist. Note: Established as the United States Federation of Police, this is largely an educational organization, offering insurance benefits, a placement service and various types of awards to its members. Merged with the American Law Enforcement Officers Association in 1977. Maintains an office in Washington, DC.
Publications:
Police Times Magazine. bi-m.
International Criminal Investigator. q.
Biennial Meetings: even years

American Federation of School Administrators (1971)
853 Broadway, Suite 2109, New York NY 10003
President: Martin Kalish
Members: 10,000 *Staff:* 6-10
Annual Budget: $250-500,000 *Tel:* (212) 477-2580
Hist. Note: Established in 1971 as the School Administrators and Supervisors Organizing Committee. Assumed its present name on July 7, 1976. Affiliated with the AFL-CIO in 1976.
Publication:
AFSA News. 8/yr.
Annual Meetings: Every 3 years in Summer (1988)

American Federation of Small Business (1953)
407 South Dearborn St., Chicago IL 60605
Exec. V. President: Thomas H. Latimer
Members: 25,000 *Staff:* 11-15
Tel: (312) 427-0206
Hist. Note: AFSB grew out of the Illinois Small Businessmen's Ass'n and the Conference of American Small Business Organizations (both founded in 1938); AFSB absorbed the CASBO in 1982. Dedicated to conservative economics, AFSB promotes free enterprise and opposes big government and labor monopoly. Membership: $50-500/yr.
Publication:
Member Letters. bi-m.
Annual Meetings: January
1987-Chicago, IL
1988-Philadelphia, PA
1989-Boston, MA
1990-Hawaii

American Federation of State, County and Municipal Employees (1936)
1625 L Street., N.W., Washington DC 20036
President: Gerald W. McEntee
Members: 1,100,000 *Staff:* 225-250
Annual Budget: over $5,000,000 *Tel:* (202) 452-4800
Hist. Note: Organized in Chicago December 9, 1933 and chartered by the American Federation of Labor the following year. Merged (April 1978) with the Civil Service Employees Ass'n of New York. Has a budget of about $40 million. Sponsors and supports the American Federation of State, County and Municipal Employees Political Action Committee.
Publication:
The Public Employee. m.
Biennial Meetings: Even years in late Spring

American Federation of Teachers (1916)
555 New Jersey Ave., N.W., Washington DC 20001
President: Albert Shanker
Members: 610,000 *Staff:* 100
Annual Budget: over $5,000,000 *Tel:* (202) 879-4400
Hist. Note: Organized in Chicago April 15, 1916 and affiliated with the American Federation of Labor. Has a budget of about $25 million. Sponsors and supports the AFT Cope Political

00037 12 05 86 1233

Action Committee.
Publications:
American Educator. q.
American Teacher. m. adv.
Biennial Meetings: Summer

American Federation of Television and Radio Artists (1937)
1350 Avenue of the Americas, 2nd Floor, New York NY 10019
Nat'l Exec. Secretary: John Hall, Jr.
Members: 66,000 *Staff:* 21-25
Annual Budget: $2-5,000,000 *Tel:* (212) 265-7700
Hist. Note: Chartered August 16, 1937 by Associated Actors and Artistes of America as an autonomous branch union representing radio performers. It has since come to represent performers on live or videotaped TV programs as well. Merged with the Television Authority in 1950.
Publication:
AFTRA Magazine. q. adv.
Annual Meetings: Summer

American Feed Industry Ass'n (1909)
1701 N. Fort Myer Drive, Arlington VA 22209
President: Oakley M. Ray
Members: 550 *Staff:* 16
Annual Budget: $1-2,000,000 *Tel:* (703) 524-0810
Hist. Note: Formerly (1985) the American Feed Manufacturers Ass'n. Membership includes firms which manufacture formula feed to sell, firms which manufacture formula feed only for their own poultry or livestock, and firms which provide ingredients, services, equipment, and supplies to feed manufacturers. Absorbed the Midwest Feed Manufacturers Association in 1975.
Publications:
Membership Directory. a. adv.
Newsletters.
Software Directory.
Buyers Guide.
Annual Meetings: Spring
1987-Indianapolis, IN/April 26-29/4,000

American Feed Manufacturers Ass'n (1909)
Hist. Note: Became the American Feed Industry Ass'n in 1985.

American Fern Soc. (1893)
Department of Botany, University of Tennessee, Knoxville TN 37996
Treasurer: Dr. James D. Caponetti
Members: 700-800 *Staff:* 1
Annual Budget: $10-25,000 *Tel:* (615) 974-6219
Hist. Note: Founded in 1893 as the Linnaean Fern Chapter of the Aggasiz Ass'n with 24 charter members. Became The American Fern Soc. in 1905 and was incorporated in the District of Columbia in 1936. Affiliated with the American Institute of Biological Sciences. Has an internat'l membership of pteridologists, botanists and others interested in growing or studying ferns. Has no paid staff. Membership: $6-10/yr. (individual), $12/yr. (organization).
Publications:
American Fern Journal. q. adv.
Fiddlehead Forum Newsletter. bi-m.
Annual Meetings: With the American Institute of Biological Sciences.
1987-Columbus, OH(Ohio State Univ.)/Aug. 9-13
1988-Davis, CA(University of California)/Aug. 14-18

American Fertility Soc. (1944)
2131 Magnolia Ave., Suite 201, Birmingham AL 35256
Medical Director: Herbert H. Thomas, M.D.
Members: 9,500 *Staff:* 12
Annual Budget: $500-1,000,000 *Tel:* (205) 251-9764
Hist. Note: Founded and incorporated in 1944 in California as the American Society for the Study of Sterility, it assumed its present name in 1966. Promotes knowledge of all aspects of reproductive medicine including fertility. Membership: $85/year.
Publications:
Fertility & Sterility. m. adv.
Fertility News. q.
Annual Meetings: Fall
1987-Reno, NV(MGM Grand)/Sept. 27-Oct. 1/1,500
1988-Atlanta, GA(Hilton)/Oct. 7-14/1,500
1989-San Francisco, CA(Hilton)
1990-Washington, DC(Hilton)

American Film Marketing Ass'n (1980)
1000 Washington Blvd., Culver City CA 90232
President: Jonas Rosenfield
Members: 74 companies *Staff:* 8
Annual Budget: $1-2,000,000 *Tel:* (213) 275-3400
Hist. Note: Member companies are engaged in the distribution, marketing, and in some cases the production of independent English language feature motion pictures. The association fosters the interests of its members in areas of copyright protection and trade barrier problems; operates the American Film Market in February of each year in Los Angeles, CA. Membership: $3,000/yr.
Publication:
AFMA News. bi-m.
Semi-annual meetings: Film Market in Los Angeles in Feb. and meeting in June
1987-(Beverly Hilton)/Feb. 26-March 6
1988-(Beverly Hilton/Feb. 25-March 4

American Finance Ass'n (1940)
Grad. School of Business Admin., New York Univ., 100 Trinity Place, New York NY 10006
Exec. Secy. & Treas.: Prof. Michael Keenan
Members: 7,000 *Staff:* 2-5
Annual Budget: $100-250,000 *Tel:* (212) 285-6140
Hist. Note: Established in 1940 and incorporated in Illinois in 1952. Membership consists of both individuals and institutions interested in finance. Affiliated with Allied Social Sciences Ass'n, which manages the annual convention. Membership: $35/yr. (individual); $50/yr. (organization)
Publication:
Journal of Finance. 5/yr. adv.
Annual Meetings: Late December
1987-Chicago, IL/Dec. 28-30

American Financial Services Ass'n (1916)
4th Floor, 1101 14th St., N.W., Washington DC 20005
President: Robert B. Evans
Members: 550 companies *Staff:* 25-30
Annual Budget: $2-5,000,000 *Tel:* (202) 289-0400
Hist. Note: The national trade association for finance and industrial banking companies in the United States. Its member companies are the financial institutions which specialize in consumer installment financing and counseling. Merged (1971) with the American Industrial Bankers Ass'n which had, in 1965, absorbed the American Finance Conference. Established as the National Consumer Finance Ass'n, it assumed its present name in 1983. Maintains the Consumer Credit Institute and the Consumer Finance Political Action Committee.
Publications:
Consumer Finance Law Bulletin. q.
Credit. bi-m. adv.
Finance Facts Newsletter. m.
Finance Facts Yearbook. a.
The Financial Forum. semi-a.
Annual Meetings: Spring
1987-Honolulu, HI(Sheraton Waikiki)/May 18-22/1,300
1988-Toronto, Ontario(Hilton Harbour Castle)/May 22-26/1,300
1989-San Francisco, CA(Fairmont Hotel)/May 14-18/1,300
1990-Dallas, TX(Loew's Anatole Hotel)/May 13-17/1,300

American Fine China Guild (1955)
Box 7386, Trenton NJ 08628
Secretary: Mark Z. Segal
Members: 3 dinnerware manufacturers *Staff:* 1
Annual Budget: under $10,000 *Tel:* (609) 883-6600
Annual Meetings: January, New York City

American Fire Chiefs Ass'n (1978)
Hist. Note: Defunct in 1983.

American Fire Sprinkler Ass'n (1981)
11325 Pegasus, Suite E-109, Dallas TX 75238
Exec. Director: J. Frank Riseden
Members: 325 companies *Staff:* 7
Annual Budget: $500-1,000,000 *Tel:* (214) 349-5965
Hist. Note: Members are manufacturers, contractors, and suppliers of fire sprinkler systems, as well as fire protection consultant firms. Membership fee based on sales volume.
Publication:
Sprinkler Age. m. adv.
Annual Meetings: Fall
1987-Honolulu, HI/Sept. 20-23/700
1988-Marco Island, FL/Oct./700

American Fish Farmers Federation (1965)
Hist. Note: Ceased effective operations about 1969. Reactivated in about 1976, it had no paid staff and spent the small dues it was able to collect primarily on publication of a newsletter detailing environmental regulations passed by the government that affected fish farmers. Defunct again about 1981.

American Fisheries Soc. (1870)
5410 Grosvenor Lane, Bethesda MD 20814
Exec. Director: Carl R. Sullivan
Members: 8,300 *Staff:* 16
Annual Budget: $1-2,000,000 *Tel:* (301) 897-8616
Hist. Note: Founded Dec. 20, 1870 in New York, NY as the American Culturists' Ass'n, it became the American Fish Cultural Ass'n in 1878 and the American Fisheries Soc. in 1884; incorporated in the District of Columbia in 1911. Promotes the conservation and development of commercial and recreational fisheries.
Publications:
Fisheries. bi-m. adv.
North American Journal of Fisheries Management bi-m.
Transactions. bi-m.
Progressive Fish-Culturist. q.
Annual Meetings: August or September
1987-Winston-Salem, NC
1988-Toronto, Ontario
1989-Anchorage, AK

American Fishing Tackle Manufacturers Ass'n (1933)
2625 Clearbrook Dr., Arlington Heights IL 60005
Exec. V. President: Thomas P. Conley
Members: 500 companies *Staff:* 11-15
Annual Budget: $1-2,000,000 *Tel:* (312) 364-4666
Hist. Note: Formerly Associated Fishing Tackle Manufacturers. Promotes Nat'l Fishing Week each June.
Publication:
Tackle Times. m.
Annual Meetings: Trade Show/8,500
1987-Atlanta, GA/Aug. 6-9
1988-Las Vegas, NV/July 28-31
1989-Las Vegas, NV/July 27-30

American Flint Glass Workers Union (1878)
1440 South Byrne Rd., Toledo OH 43614
President: George M. Parker
Members: 21,700 *Staff:* 20-25
Annual Budget: $2-5,000,000 *Tel:* (419) 385-6687
Hist. Note: Organized in Pittsburgh July 1, 1878 as the United Flint Glass Workers. Became the American Flint Glass Workers' Union of North America in 1912 when it affiliated with the American Federation of Labor. Adopted its present name in 1975.
Publications:
American Flint Magazine. m.
Trade Circular. m. adv.
Biennial meetings: Uneven years in June

American Folklore Soc. (1888)
c/o American Anthropological Ass'n, 1703 New Hampshire Ave., N.W., Washington DC 20009
Secy.-Treas.: Charles Camp
Members: 1600 individuals, 1400 organizations
Tel: (202) 232-8800
Hist. Note: Organized in Cambridge, MA, January 4, 1888 to collect, publish and preserve original folklore material. An affiliate of the American Anthropological Association, which provides business and administrative support. Membership: $25/yr.
Publications:
American Folklore Newsletter. bi-m.
Journal of American Folklore. q. adv.

American Football Coaches Ass'n (1921)
7758 Wallace Road, Suite 1, Orlando FL 32819
Exec. Director: Charlie McClendon
Members: 5,000 *Staff:* 3
Tel: (305) 351-6113
Hist. Note: Originally organized to promote college football and to discuss mutual problems. Later interests include a voice in the rule making process, the promotion of safe techniques and the formulation/enforcement of a code of ethics. Membership: $15/year (college coaches), $10/year (other coaches).
Publications:
Proceedings Manual. a.
Summer Mannual. a.
Directory. a.
The Extra Point. 5/yr.
Annual Meetings: January
1987-San Diego, CA(Sheraton Harbor Island)/Jan. 5-7/2,500
1988-Atlanta, GA(Hilton Towers)/Jan. 4-6/2,800
1989-Nashville, TN(Opryland)/2,800
1990-Orlando, FL(Marriott World Center)/3,000

American Footwear Industries Ass'n (1869)
Hist. Note: Merged with the American Shoe Center in 1982 to become the Footwear Industries of America.

American Forage and Grassland Council (1944)
2021 Rebel Road, Lexington KY 40503
Exec. Director: J. Kenneth Evans
Members: 5-6,000 *Staff:* 2-5
Annual Budget: $25-50,000 *Tel:* (606) 278-0177
Hist. Note: Membership: $15/year (individual), $50-600/year (organization/company) Established July 17, 1944 at Rutgers University as the Joint Committee on Grassland Farming. Reorganized on December 19, 1957 as the American Grassland Council. The name was changed July 15, 1968 to the American Forage and Grassland Council. Membership: $15/year (individual), $50-600/year (organization/company) depending on type and size.
Publication:
Proceedings. a.
Annual Meetings:
1987-Springfield, IL/March/300-500
1988-Baton Rouge, LA/April/300-500

American Foreign Law Ass'n (1925)
Marsh & McLennan, Inc., 1221 Avenue of the Americas, New York NY 10020
Secretary: Damira Buzdovacic
Members: 5-600 *Staff:* 2-5
Annual Budget: $10-25,000 *Tel:* (212) 997-5922
Publications:
AFLA Newsletter. 3-4/yr.
Ross Report. a.
Annual Meetings: April/May in New York, NY

American Foreign Service Ass'n (1918)
2101 E St., N.W., Washington DC 20037
Director for Administration: Sue Schumacher
Members: 8,800 *Staff:* 20
Annual Budget: $500-1,000,000 *Tel:* (202) 338-4045
Hist. Note: Acts as the elected representative of all Foreign Service personnel in the AID and State Department bargaining units. Membership fee: Varies by grade.
Publication:
Foreign Service Journal. m. adv.
Annual Meetings: Summer

00038 12 05 86 1233

American Forensic Ass'n (1948)
Univ. of Wisconsin, River Falls WI 54022
Secretary: James Pratt
Members: 1,200 *Staff:* 2-5
Annual Budget: $25-50,000 *Tel:* (715) 425-3198
Hist. Note: Established in 1948 to promote effective and responsible oral communication. Membership composed primarily of college and high school directors of debate and speech programs. Affiliated with the Speech Communication Ass'n. Membership: $20/yr. (individual); $25/yr. (organization/company).
Publications:
Journal. q. adv.
Newsletter. 3/yr. adv.
Annual Meetings: With Speech Communication Ass'n

American Forest Council (1932)
1250 Connecticut Ave., N.W., Suite 320, Washington DC 20036
President: Laurence D. Wiseman
Members: 70-80 *Staff:* 20-30
Annual Budget: $2-5,000,000 *Tel:* (202) 463-2455
Hist. Note: Formerly (19680 American Forest Products Industries, Inc. and (1986) American Forest Institute. A nonprofit, nonpolitical organization, it provides information and education on the importance of forestry and forest products. Encourages the development and productive management of the nation's commercial forest lands by government, industry and private landowners. Administers the 58,000-member American Tree Farm System.
Publications:
American Tree Farmer Magazine.
Greenamerica.

American Forestry Ass'n (1875)
1319 18th St., N.W., Washington DC 20036
Exec. V. President: R. Neil Sampson
Members: 40,000 *Staff:* 20-25
Annual Budget: $1-2,000,000 *Tel:* (202) 467-5810
Hist. Note: Founded September 10, 1875 in the Grand Pacific Hotel in Chicago for "the protection of the existing forests of the country from unnecessary waste, and the promotion of the propagation and planting of useful trees". Merged in 1882 with the American Forestry Congress. Membership: $24/yr.
Publications:
American Forests. m. adv.
Resource Hotline. bi-w.
Annual Meetings: Fall

American Formalwear Ass'n (1973)
111 East Wacker Drive, Suite 600, Chicago IL 60601
Exec. Director: Jack Springer
Members: 300-325 companies *Staff:* 2-5
Annual Budget: $100-250,000 *Tel:* (312) 644-6610
Hist. Note: Formerly a division of the Menswear Retailers of America, AFA became autonomous on July 1, 1981. Administrative support provided by the Men's Fashion Ass'n of America.
Publications:
American Formalwear Newsletter. bi-m. adv.
Formalwear News Bureau. bi-m.
Semi-annual meetings: Spring and Fall
1987-Tucson, AZ(El Conquistador)/Feb. 28-March 2
1987-St. Louis, MO(Adam's Mark)/Sept. 10-13

American Foundrymen's Soc. (1896)
Golf & Wolf Roads, Des Plaines IL 60016-2277
Exec. V. President: Charles H. Jones
Members: 14,000 *Staff:* 45
Annual Budget: $2-5,000,000 *Tel:* (312) 824-0181
Hist. Note: Founded as the American Foundrymen's Ass'n, it assumed its present name in 1948. AFS is a technical society of individuals concerned with the castings industry. The Cast Metals Institute is the educational arm of the AFS.
Publications:
Modern Casting. m. adv.
Transactions. a.
Annual Meetings: April-May
1987-St. Louis, MO/April 6-10
1988-Hartford, CT/April 24-29/2,000
1989-San Antonio, TX/May 7-12/2,000
1990-Detroit, MI(Cobo Hall)/April 23-27/15,000

American Fox Trotting Horse Breed Ass'n (1971)
Box 666, Marshfield MO 65706000
Secretary:
Members: 1,500 *Staff:* 1
Annual Budget: $25-50,000
Hist. Note: Members breed, own or train American Fox Trotting horses, a medium sized, three gaited breed. Membership: $10/yr.
Publications:
American Fox Trotting Horse. a. adv.
Breed Journal. a.

American Fracture Ass'n (1938)
Box 668, Bloomington IL 61701
Exec. Secretary: Barbara J. Dehority
Members: 500 *Staff:* 2-5
Annual Budget: $10-25,000 *Tel:* (309) 663-6272
Hist. Note: Founded in 1938 in Macomb, Illinois and was known as the Ambulatory Fracture Ass'n until 1952 when the name was changed to the American Fracture Ass'n. Membership limited to 500.
Publication:
Orthopedic Abstracts. a.
Annual Meetings: Spring
1987-Chicago, IL(Hyatt)/May 23-27

American Franchise Ass'n (1982)
2730 Wilshire Blvd., Suite 400, Santa Monica CA 90403
Exec. Director: Russell L. Berney
Members: 30,000
Tel: (213) 829-0841
Hist. Note: Members are francise owners, attorneys, accountants, brokers and other interested individuals.
Publication:
Franchise Reporter. q. adv.

American Frozen Food Export Ass'n (1981)
Hist. Note: A Webb-Pomerene Act Association. Inactive in 1983.

American Frozen Food Institute (1942)
1764 Old Meadow Rd., Suite 350, McLean VA 22102
President: Thomas B. House, CAE
Members: 400-500 *Staff:* 16-20
Annual Budget: $2-5,000,000 *Tel:* (703) 821-0770
Hist. Note: Formerly (1970) Nat'l Ass'n of Frozen Food Packers. Absorbed the California Freezers Ass'n in 1967. Supports the Freezers Political Action Committee. Affiliated with the Internat'l Frozen Food Ass'n; Frozen Potato Products Institute; Nat'l Frozen Pizza Institute; and Frozen Vegetable Council.
Publications:
AFFI Letter. bi-m.
Frozen Food Report. m.
Membership Directory & Buyers Guide. a. adv.
Annual Meetings: Fall
1987-Dallas, TX(Loew's Anatole)/Oct. 11-14

American Fur Industry (1958)
101 West 30th St., New York NY 10001
Exec. Director: Sandy Blye
Members: 120 ass'ns *Staff:* 2-5
Annual Budget: $500-1,000,000 *Tel:* (212) 564-5133
Hist. Note: Includes (1962) the Fur Industry Marketing Institute, (1971) the Fur Conservation Institute of America, and (1972) the American Fur Industry. Formerly (until 1980) known as the Fur Information and Fashion Council, Inc. Supports FURPAC, a political action committee.
Publications:
Fashion Reports. m.
Furs Naturally Booklet.
Newsletter.
Annual Meetings: New York City, in January

American Fur Merchant's Ass'n (1898)
101 West 30th St., New York NY 10001
Exec. Director: Dorothy L. Banculli
Members: 80 *Staff:* 1
Annual Budget: $50-100,000 *Tel:* (212) 736-9200
Hist. Note: Members, most of which are concentrated in the New York area, include: dealers, brokers, silk and supply houses, manufacturers, credit bureaus, retailers, importers, and auction houses.
Publication:
News Bulletin. m.
Annual Meetings: New York City in Spring.

American Furniture Manufacturers Ass'n (1905)
Box HP-7, High Point NC 27261
Exec. V. President: Douglas L. Brackett
Members: 275-300 companies *Staff:* 11-15
Annual Budget: $500-1,000,000 *Tel:* (919) 884-5000
Hist. Note: Manufacturers of household and institutional furniture. Founded as the Southern Furniture Manufacturers Ass'n. Assumed its current name in 1984 when it merged with the Nat'l Ass'n of Furniture Manufacturers. Maintains a government affairs office in Washington, DC.
Publication:
Who's Who in the Southern Furniture Industry. a.
Annual Meetings: Fall

American Galloway Breeders Ass'n (1888)
Route 1, Box 106A, Athol ID 83801
Secretary: Jim Carney
Members: 120-150 *Staff:* 1
Annual Budget: $10-25,000 *Tel:* (208) 772-5585
Hist. Note: Formed in Chicago, November 23, 1882 by U.S. and Canadian breeders of Galloway cattle. Incorporated in the State of Montana. Absorbed the Galloway Performance International in 1973. Membership: $50/yr.
Publication:
American Galloway Breeders Newsletter. semi-a.
Annual Meetings: October
1987-Billings, MT

American Gas Ass'n (1919)
1515 Wilson Blvd., Arlington VA 22209
President: George H. Lawrence
Members: 300 companies, 3,200 individuals *Staff:* 400
Annual Budget: over $5,000,000 *Tel:* (703) 841-8400
Hist. Note: Formed by a merger of the Gas Institute and the Commercial Gas Ass'n in 1918. Connected with the Gas Employees Political Action Committee (GASPAC).
Publications:
A.G.A. Monthly. m.
Operating Section Proceedings. a.
Pipeline Research Summary. a.
Research & Development Report. a.
Washington Letter. w.
Annual Meetings: Fall

American Gastroenterological Ass'n (1897)
6900 Grove Road, Thorofare NJ 08086
Exec. Secretary: Charles B. Slack
Members: 5,200 *Staff:* 2-5
Annual Budget: $100-250,000 *Tel:* (609) 848-1000
Hist. Note: Membership: $135/yr.
Publication:
Gastroenterology. m. adv.
Annual Meetings: Spring/5,000
1987-Chicago, IL(Hyatt Regency)/May 9-15
1988-New Orleans, LA(Convention Center)/May 14-20
1989-Washington, DC(Sheraton Washington Hotel)/May 13-19
1990-San Antonio, TX(Convention Center)/May 12-18

American Gear Manufacturers Ass'n (1916)
1500 King St., Suite 201, Alexandria VA 22314
Exec. Director: Richard Norment
Members: 350 companies *Staff:* 6-10
Annual Budget: $500-1,000,000 *Tel:* (703) 684-0211
Hist. Note: Members are gear manufacturers, makers of gear cutting and checking equipment, gearing teachers, suppliers to the industry and purchasers of gear products.
Publication:
News Digest. m.
Annual Meetings: First weekend in June.

American Gelbvieh Ass'n (1971)
5001 Nat'l Western Drive, Denver CO 80216
Exec. Director: James A. Spawn
Members: 1,100 *Staff:* 7
Annual Budget: $250-500,000 *Tel:* (303) 296-9257
Hist. Note: Breeders and promoters of Gelbvieh cattle. Membership: $25/yr.
Publication:
Gelbvieh World. m. adv.
Annual Meetings: Denver, in January, with an attendance of 300.

American Gem and Mineral Suppliers Ass'n (1950)
Box 2166, Upland CA 91786
Exec. Secretary: Irene Elliott
Members: 150-175 *Staff:* 1
Annual Budget: under $10,000 *Tel:* (714) 981-8588
Hist. Note: Provides an opportunity for members to become professional in their business activities through an exchange of ideas with each other. The purpose is to promote a high standard of ethics and business methods in the industry. Membership: $48/yr.
Publication:
Min-A-Gram. bi-m.
Semi-annual Meetings: Feb. and August
1987-Tucson, AZ/Feb. and Pasadena, CA/Aug.

American Gem Soc. (1934)
5901 West Third Street, Los Angeles CA 90036
Executive Director: George Kramer
Members: 1,600 retail jewelry firms, 3,600 individuals *Staff:* 16
Annual Budget: $1-2,000,000 *Tel:* (213) 936-4367
Hist. Note: A professional association of U.S. and Canadian jewelers. Certifies members as Registered Jewelers, Certified Gemologists or Certified Gemologist Appraisers.
Publications:
Spectra. m.
Gems and Jewelry Fact Sheets. q.
Gem Trends. q.
Annual Meetings: Spring/800-1,000
1987-San Francisco, CA/April 24-28
1988-Toronto, Canada/April 22-26

American Gem Trade Ass'n (1981)
#181 World Trade Center, 2050 Stemmons Expy., Box 581043, Dallas TX 75258
Exec. Director: Shelly Kuehn
Members: 450 firms *Staff:* 2
Annual Budget: $250-500,000 *Tel:* (214) 742-4367
Hist. Note: Established in Tucson, AZ and incorporated in New York, AGTA is a trade association for the colored gemstone industry. Membership: $125/yr. (affiliate), $225/yr. (firm).
Publications:
Newsletter. q.
Directory. a.
Annual Meetings: February, in Tucson, Arizona
1987-(Doubletree Hotel)/Feb. 7-12

American Genetic Ass'n (1903)
818 18th St., N.W., Washington DC 20006
Mng. Editor: Barbara C. Kuhn
Members: 1,600-1,800 *Staff:* 2-5
Annual Budget: $250-500,000 *Tel:* (202) 659-2096
Hist. Note: Established as the American Breeders Ass'n in December 1903 in St. Louis by a committee from the Ass'n of Land Grant Colleges. Name changed in 1913 to the American Genetic Ass'n when it was incorporated in the District of Columbia. Affiliated with the American Ass'n for the Advancement of Science. A member society of the Internat'l Genetics Federation. Promotes the study of genetics and its application to plant and animal improvement and human welfare. Membership: $25/yr.
Publication:
Journal of Heredity. bi-m. adv.
Annual Meetings: January

American Geographical Soc. (1851)
156 5th Ave., New York NY 10010
Director: Mary Lynne Bird

00039 12 05 86 1233

Members: 7000 fellows and subscribers *Staff:* 2-5
Annual Budget: $250-500,000 *Tel:* (212) 242-0214
Hist. Note: Initiated in 1851 and incorporated on May 22, 1852 in New York as The American Geographical and Statistical Soc. Name changed to its present form in 1871. Over the years, sponsored research projects, symposia and lectures and published books, periodicals and maps. Membership: $20/yr. (individual); $1,000/yr. (organization).
Publications:
Focus. q. adv.
Geographical Review. q. adv.
AGS Newsletter. irreg.

American Geological Institute (1948)
4220 King St., Alexandria VA 22302
Exec. Director: Marvin E. Kauffman
Members: 17 societies, 80,000 individuals *Staff:* 55
Annual Budget: $2-5,000,000 *Tel:* (703) 379-2480
Hist. Note: Founded in Washington in 1948 and operated as part of the Nat'l Academy of Sciences, 1948-1963. Incorporated as separate entity in 1963 in the District of Columbia. A federation of societies, the Institute is a member of the American Ass'n for the Advancement of Science, Scientific Manpower Commission, Board on Earth Sciences (NRC) .
Publications:
Geotimes. m. adv.
Earth Science. q.
Directory of Geoscience Departments, US & Canada. a. adv.
Minerals Exploration Alert.
Bibliography and Index of Geology. m.
Semi-annual Meetings: Spring and Fall

American Geophysical Union (1919)
2000 Florida Ave., N.W., Washington DC 20009
Exec. Director: Dr. Athelstan F. Spilhaus, Jr.
Members: 20,000 *Staff:* 65
Annual Budget: over $5,000,000 *Tel:* (202) 462-6903
Hist. Note: Established in 1919 by the Nat'l Research Council to act as the U.S. Nat'l Committee for the Internat'l Union of Geodesy and Geophysics. Promotes the study of problems connected with the physics and chemistry of the earth. Member society of the Renewable Natural Resources Foundation.
Publications:
EOS, Transactions. w. adv.
Journal of Geophysical Research. w.
Water Resources Research. semi-m.
Geophysical Research Letters. m.
Radio Science. m.
Tectonics. bi-m.
Reviews of Geophysics. q.
Paleoceanography. q.
Semi-annual Meetings: Spring-East Coast, Fall-West Coast

American Geriatrics Soc. (1942)
770 Lexington Ave., #400, New York NY 10021
Exec. V. President: Linda Hiddemen Barondess
Members: 5,000 *Staff:* 9
Annual Budget: $250-500,000 *Tel:* (212) 308-1414
Hist. Note: Founded in Atlantic City in 1942. Incorporated in Rhode Island in 1952 and later in New York in 1963. Members are licensed physicians and allied health care professionals whose practice emphasis is in geriatric medicine and whose interests lie in geriatric medicine and gerontology. Affiliated with the American Federation for Aging Research, the Gerontological Soc. of America and the Internat'l Ass'n of Gerontology. Membership: $115/yr.
Publications:
Journal of the American Geriatrics Society. m. adv.
Newsletter. bi-m. adv.
Annual Meetings: Second or third week in May
1987-New Orleans, LA(Hyatt Regency)/May 14-17
1988-Anaheim, CA(Disneyland Hotel)/May 19-22

American Goat Soc. (1935)
Rt. 2, Box 112, De Leon TX 76444
Secretary: H. Wayne Hamrick
Members: 1,500 *Staff:* 2-5
Annual Budget: under $10,000 *Tel:* (817) 893-6431
Hist. Note: Breeders and fanciers of dairy goats. Membership: $10/yr.
Publication:
The Voice of AGS. a.
Annual Meetings:
1987-San Antonio, TX

American Greenhouse Vegetable Growers Ass'n (1984)
P.O. Box 20228, Columbus OH 43220
Exec. Secretary: Carol Laymon
Members: 125 *Staff:* 1
Annual Budget: $10-25,000 *Tel:* (614) 459-1498
Hist. Note: Merger of the Nat'l Ass'n of Greenhouse Vegetable Growers (1937) and the Western Greenhouse Vegetable Growers Ass'n. Members are persons or organizations with production area 2,500 square feet or greater and actively engaged in the business of greenhouse vegetables for the primary purpose of making a profit. Membership: $50/yr.
Publications:
Greenhouse Grower (newsletter). q. adv.
Proceedings. a.
Annual Meetings: Fall
1987-Reno, NV/August/150
1988-Washington, DC/Sept./300

American Greyhound Track Operators Ass'n (1946)
1065 N.E. 125th Street, Suite 219, North Miami FL 33161
Exec. Director: George D. Johnson, Jr.
Members: 48 tracks *Staff:* 4
Annual Budget: $250-500,000 *Tel:* (305) 893-2101
Hist. Note: Represents U.S. pari-mutual greyhound tracks.
Semi-annual meetings: Spring and Fall
1987-Rancho Mirage, CA(Marriott's Rancho Las Palmas)/March 8-13/300

American Group of CPA Firms (1963)
246 Janata Blvd., Suite 241, Lombard IL 60148
Exec. Director: Nancy R. Saulinski
Members: 20 *Staff:* 3
Annual Budget: $100-250,000 *Tel:* (312) 495-8488
Hist. Note: Seeks to maintain and enhance the ability of member firms to serve clients on a national and international basis and to increase public awareness of those objectives. Members are certified public accounting firms.
Publications:
Directory. a.
Newsletter. semi-a.
Annual Meetings: Committee Meetings throughout country

American Group Practice Ass'n (1949)
1422 Duke St., Alexandria VA 22314
Exec. V. President: Donald W. Fisher, Ph.D.
Members: 300 clinics *Staff:* 12
Annual Budget: $1-2,000,000 *Tel:* (703) 838-0033
Hist. Note: Formerly (1974) American Ass'n of Medical Clinics. Members are group practice medical clinics. Accredits medical clinics and maintains a physician placement service. Supports the American Group Practice Political Action Committee.
Publications:
Directory. a.
Group Practice Journal. m. adv.
Executive News Service.
Annual Meetings: Fall/750
1987-New Orleans, LA/Sept. 16-20
1988-San Diego, CA/Sept. 14-17
1989-Minneapolis, MN/Sept. 12-15

American Group Psychotherapy Ass'n (1943)
25 East 21st St., 6th Floor, New York NY 10010
Chief Exec. Officer: Marsha Block
Members: 3,300 individuals *Staff:* 8-10
Annual Budget: $250-500,000 *Tel:* (212) 477-2677
Hist. Note: Includes psychiatrists, psychologists, social workers, psychiatric nurses and others in the mental health field interested in the theory, practice and research of group psychotherapy. Established June 16, 1943 in New York City at the Jewish Board of Guidance as the American Group Therapy Association.
Publications:
AGPA Newsletter q. adv.
International Journal of Group Psychotherapy. q. adv.
Annual Meetings: February/1,200
1987-New Orleans, LA
1988-New York, NY

American Guernsey Cattle Club (1877)
2105-J South Hamilton Road, Box 27410, Columbus OH 43227
Secy.-Treas.: James F. Cavanaugh
Members: 1,800 *Staff:* 10-15
Annual Budget: $500-1,000,000 *Tel:* (614) 864-2409
Hist. Note: Breeders of Guernsey dairy cattle. Maintains herd registry. Member of the Nat'l Pedigreed Livestock Council. Membership: $50/life.
Publication:
Guernsey Breeder's Journal. 10/yr. adv.
Annual Meetings:
1987-Pittsburgh, PA/April 9-13/450

American Guides Ass'n (1981)
8909 Dorrington Ave., West Hollywood, Los Angelos CA 90048
President: Anne C. Faerovik
Members: 20 companies, 300 individuals *Staff:* 3
Annual Budget: under $10,000 *Tel:* (213) 550-7660
Hist. Note: AGA promotes professionalism, sets guidelines, and improves standards within the guiding profession; encourages the travelling public to purchase escorted and guided tours; acts as a liaison between the Tour Managing/Guiding professions and other industry-related organizations. Membership: $50/yr. (individual); $250/yr. (company). Affiliated with the American Tour Managers Ass'n.
Publication:
Newsletter. m.
Annual Meetings: January

American Guild of Authors and Composers (1931)
Hist. Note: Became the Songwriters Guild in 1984.

American Guild of Music (1901)
Box 3, Downers Grove IL 60515
Registered Agent: Elmer Herrick
Members: 1,400-1,500 *Staff:* 1
Annual Budget: $10-25,000 *Tel:* (312) 968-0173
Hist. Note: Professional string musicians, formerly (1953) the American Guild of Banjoists, Mandolinists and Guitarists. Membership: $15/yr.
Publication:
American Guild Associate News. q. adv.
Annual Meetings: Summer
1987-Nashville, TN

American Guild of Musical Artists (1936)
1841 Broadway, New York NY 10023
Nat'l Exec. Secretary: Gene Boucher
Members: 5,500-6,000 *Staff:* 15-16
Annual Budget: $500-1,000,000 *Tel:* (212) 265-3687
Hist. Note: Founded March 11, 1936 in New York City by Lawrence Tibbett and Jascha Heifetz. Became an autonomous branch union of Associated Actors and Artistes of America August 30, 1937 and merged at the same time with the Grand Opera Artists Ass'n. Absorbed the Grand Opera Choral Alliance in 1938. Now is the exclusive bargaining agent for all concert musical artists, opera singers, ballet dancers and stage personnel in those fields.
Publication:
Agmazine. q.
Semi-annual meetings: Regional

American Guild of Organists (1896)
815 2nd Ave., Suite 318, New York NY 10017
Exec. Director: Daniel N. Colburn, II
Members: 23,000 individuals *Staff:* 10
Annual Budget: $500-1,000,000 *Tel:* (212) 687-9188
Hist. Note: Chartered by the Board of Regents of the University of the State of New York to conduct examinations of organists and choir-masters. Its purpose is to advance the cause of organ and choral music. Membership: $40/yr.
Publication:
The American Organist. m. adv.
Biennial meetings: Even years
1988-Houston, TX/2,000
1990-Worcester, MA/1,700

American Guild of Variety Artists (1939)
184 Fifth Ave., New York NY 10010
President: Rod McKuen
Members: 5,000 *Staff:* 20-25
Annual Budget: $250-500,000 *Tel:* (212) 675-1003
Hist. Note: An autonomous component of Associated Actors and Artistes of America (AFL-CIO).
Annual Meetings: Every 4 years (1988)

American Gynecological and Obstetrical Soc. (1981)
Univ. of Rochester, 601 Elmwood Ave., Rochester NY 14642
Secretary: Henry Thiede
Members: 300
Annual Budget: $50-100,000 *Tel:* (716) 275-5201
Hist. Note: Formed by a merger of the American Gynecological Soc. and the American Ass'n of Obstetricans and Gynecologists in 1981. Membership: $250/year.
Publication:
Transactions of the American Gynecological and Obstetrical Soc. a.
Annual Meetings: September
1987-Phoenix, AZ(Biltmore)/Sept. 10-12/400
1988-Napa Valley, CA(Silverado)/Sept. 8-10/400
1989-Hot Springs, VA(The Homestead)/Sept. 7-9/400
1990-Hot Springs, VA(The Homestead)/Sept. 6-8/400

American Gynecological Soc. (1876)
Hist. Note: Merged with the American Ass'n of Obstetricians and Gynecologists to form the American Gynecological and Obstetrical Society in 1981.

American Hackney Horse Soc. (1891)
Box 174, Pittsfield IL 62363
Exec. Secretary: Luciel M. Hanks
Members: 675 *Staff:* 2
Annual Budget: $50-100,000 *Tel:* (217) 285-2472
Hist. Note: Promotes the breeding, registering and showing of registered Hackney horses and Hackney ponies. Regular Membership: $25/yr.
Publication:
AHHS Stud Book. bien.
Annual Meetings: January
1987-Nashville, TN(Opryland Hotel)/Jan. 9-10/100

American Hair Replacement Ass'n (1972)
Hist. Note: Ceased operations in 1984.

American Hampshire Sheep Ass'n (1889)
P.O. Box 345, Ashland MO 65010
Secy.-Treas.: Jim Cretcher
Members: 2,300-2,400 *Staff:* 2-5
Annual Budget: $100-250,000 *Tel:* (314) 657-9012
Hist. Note: Breeders and fanciers of Hampshire sheep. Members of the Nat'l Soc. of Livestock Record Ass'ns.
Annual Meetings: Fall
1987-San Francisco, CA/Oct. or Nov./80

American Hanoverian Soc. (1971)
831 Bay Ave., Office 2E, Capitola CA 95010
Exec. Secretary: Kathy Schoeneman
Members: 3-4,000 *Staff:* 1
Annual Budget: $50-100,000 *Tel:* (408) 476-4461
Hist. Note: Members own and breed Hanoverian horses. Membership: $60/yr.
Publications:
Members Forum. bi-m. adv.
Yearbook. a. adv.

00040 12 05 86 1233

American Hardboard Ass'n (1976)
520 N. Hicks Road, Palatine IL 60067
Exec V. President: James E. Nolan, CAE
Members: 11 companies *Staff:* 2-5
Annual Budget: $250-500,000 *Tel:* (312) 934-8800
Hist. Note: A merger of the Acoustical and Insulating materials Ass'n, founded in 1968, and the American Hardboard Ass'n founded in 1952. Became the American Board Products Ass'n in 1976. Changed to its present name in 1978. Represents most of the major U.S. producers of hardboard.
Publication:
Membership Directory.

American Hardware Manufacturers Ass'n (1901)
931 North Plum Grove Rd., Schaumburg IL 60195
Exec. Director: William P. Farrell
Members: 1,200 companies *Staff:* 11-15
Annual Budget: $2-5,000,000 *Tel:* (312) 885-1025
Publication:
Newsletter. bi-m.
Trade Shows: National Hardware Show (70,000 attendance) in August;
Conventions: National in October (1,800 attendance); Southern in
April (1,400 attendance).

American Health and Beauty Aids Institute (1981)
111 East Wacker Drive, Suite 600, Chicago IL 60601
Exec. Director: Lafayette Jones
Members: 21 companies *Staff:* 8
Annual Budget: $250-500,000 *Tel:* (312) 644-6610
Hist. Note: Members are makers of beauty products for ethnic minorities.
Publications:
AHBAI News. q. adv.
ACCESS. bi-m.
Annual Meetings: Spring
1987-Palm Springs, CA(Marquis)/April 8-12

American Health Care Ass'n (1956)
1200 15th St., N.W., 8th Floor, Washington DC 20005
Exec. V. President: Paul R. Willging, Ph.D.
Members: 8,600 state licensed facilities *Staff:* 35-40
Annual Budget: over $5,000,000 *Tel:* (202) 833-2050
Hist. Note: A federation of state associations of health care facilities formed by a merger of the American Ass'n of Nursing Homes and the Nat'l Ass'n of Registered Nursing Homes (founded in 1949). Formerly (1974) the American Nursing Home Ass'n. Absorbed the Nat'l Council of Health Centers in 1984 merger. Supports the American Nursing Home Education and Political Action Committee.
Publications:
AHCA Notes. bi-m.
AHCA Journal. m. adv.
Annual Meetings: Alternately East, West, Mid-west
1987-New York, NY(Sheraton Ctr.)/Sept. 27 - Oct. 2

American Health Planning Ass'n (1972)
1110 Vermont Ave., N.W., Suite 950, Washington DC 20005
Exec. Director: Shirley H. Wester
Members: 1,500-1,600 *Staff:* 8
Annual Budget: $500-1,000,000 *Tel:* (202) 861-1200
Hist. Note: State, regional and national health planning and other organizations. Formerly the Association of Areawide Health Planning Agencies and (1978) the American Association for Comprehensive Health Planning. Provides national voice for health care consumers, purchasers, providers and business and labor representatives who are interested in health planning to improve health care system. Membership: $60/yr. (individual), $750-6,000/yr. (organization).
Publication:
Today in Health Planning. w. adv.
Annual Meetings: June/800

American Healthcare Radiology Administrators (1973)
Box 334, Sudbury MA 01776
Communications Director: Teresa V. Cryan
Members: 2,600 *Staff:* 2-5
Annual Budget: $250-500,000 *Tel:* (617) 443-7591
Hist. Note: Formerly (1986) American Hospital Radiology Administrators. Membership: $80/yr.
Publications:
Announcement. m. adv.
Directory. a.
Radiology Management. q. adv.
Annual Meetings: August/1,300
1987-Miami Beach, FL(Fontainebleau)/August 9-14
1988-Las Vegas, NV(Caesar's Palace)/July 31-Aug. 5

American Heart Ass'n (1924)
7320 Greenville Ave., Dallas TX 75231
Exec. V. President: Dudley Hafner
Staff: 2,500
Annual Budget: over $5,000,000 *Tel:* (214) 750-5300
Hist. Note: Incorporated in New York in 1924. Reorganized in 1948 as a national voluntary health agency. Has an annual budget of $150 million.
Publications:
Cardiovascular Nursing. q.
Circulation. m. adv.
Circulation Research. m. adv.
Hypertension. bi-m. adv.
Modern Concepts of Cardiovascular Disease. m.
Stroke-Current Concepts of Cerebrovascular Disease. q.
Arterial Sclerosis. bi-m.
Annual Meetings: Fall
1987-Anaheim, CA/Nov. 16-19

American Heartworm Soc. (1974)
1511 K St., N.W., #716, Washington DC 20005
Administrative Director: Ralph Johnson
Members: 1,000 individuals *Staff:* 2
Annual Budget: $50-100,000 *Tel:* (202) 638-6077
Hist. Note: Members are practitioners and research scientists dedicated to research and dissemination of knowledge about canine heartworm disease. Membership: $20/yr. (member), $25/yr. (subscriber).
Publications:
American Heartworm Society Bulletin. q.
Proceedings of Heartworm Symposium. a.
Heartworm Disease in Dogs.
Triennial: 1989

American Helicopter Soc. Internat'l (1943)
217 N. Washington St., Alexandria VA 22314
Exec. Director: John F. Zugschwert
Members: 8,000 individuals, 145 companies *Staff:* 5-7
Annual Budget: $500-1,000,000 *Tel:* (703) 684-6777
Hist. Note: Founded and incorporated in 1943 in Connecticut. Membership: $30/year.
Publications:
Journal of the American Helicopter Society. q.
Proceedings of The National Forum. a.
Vertiflite. bi-m. adv.
Annual Meetings: Spring
1987-St. Louis, MO(Convention Ctr. & Sheraton)/May 18-20/3,000
1988-Washington, DC(Sheraton)

American Herbal Products Ass'n (1981)
5925 63rd St., Maspeth NY 11378
Exec. Director: Lynda Sadler
Members: 45 companies *Staff:* 1
Annual Budget: $10-25,000 *Tel:* (718) 894-8200
Hist. Note: Membership: $400/yr.
Publications:
Herbalgram. q.
Herb Leaf. q. adv.
Annual Meetings:
1987-Anaheim, CA(Jolly Roger Hotel)/March

American Hereford Ass'n (1881)
P.O. Box 4059, Kansas City MO 64101
Exec. V. President: H.H. Dickenson
Members: 20,000 *Staff:* 50-75
Annual Budget: $1-2,000,000 *Tel:* (816) 842-3757
Hist. Note: Breeders and fanciers of Hereford beef cattle. Member of the National Society of Livestock Record Associations. Membership: $100/life.
Publication:
American Hereford Journal. m. adv.
Annual Meetings: November in Kansas City, MO

American Historical Ass'n (1884)
400 A St., S.E., Washington DC 20003
Exec. Director: Amb. Samuel Gammon
Members: 15,000 *Staff:* 15-20
Annual Budget: $500-1,000,000 *Tel:* (202) 544-2422
Hist. Note: An off-shoot of the American Social Science Ass'n which came into being at the annual meeting of the Ass'n in Saratoga, NY in 1884. Its founders were a group of historians who felt that the ASSA had over-specialized in such matters as prison reform, charity, etc. Incorporated by Congress in 1889 to promote historical studies, collect and preserve historical manuscripts and disseminate the fruits of historical research. A member of the American Council of Learned Societies. Membership: $20-60/yr. (individual); varies with income.
Publications:
American Historical Review. 5/yr. adv.
Annual Report. a.
Perspectives (Newsletter). 9/yr. adv.
Recently Published Articles. 3/yr.
Grants and Fellowships of Interest to Historians. a.
Doctoral Dissertations in History. semi-a.
Annual Meetings: Always December 28-30.
1987-Washington, DC(Sheraton Washington)

American Hockey Coaches Ass'n (1947)
22 Tryon Ave., Rumford RI 02916
Secretary-Treasurer: Herb Hammond
Members: 250 *Staff:* 1
Annual Budget: $10-25,000 *Tel:* (410) 863-2236
Hist. Note: Resolves local and intersectional differences on rules, officiating and recruiting. Conducts placement service. Membership: $25/yr. (individual).
Publications:
Newsletter. 5/yr.
American Hockey Coaches Directory. a.
Annual Meetings: 4
May
1987-Naples, FL(Naples Beach Hotel & Golf Club)/April 24-28/350

American Hockey League (1936)
218 Memorial Avenue, West Springfield MA 01089
V. Pres. & Secy.: Gordon C. Anziano
Members: 13 clubs *Staff:* 2-5
Annual Budget: $500-1,000,000 *Tel:* (413) 781-2030
Publications:
AHL Guide. a. adv.
AHL Official Rule Book. a. adv.
AHL Playoff Guide. a. adv.
AHL Schedule. a. adv.
Annual Meetings:
1987-Bermuda(Castle Harbour)
1988-Hilton Head, SC(Palmetto Dunes)

American Holistic Medical Ass'n (1978)
2727 Fairview Ave., Seattle WA 98102
Admin. Director: Craig Salins
Members: 670 *Staff:* 2-5
Annual Budget: $100-250,000 *Tel:* (206) 322-6842
Hist. Note: Holistic medicine is a system of health care which emphasizes the necessity of looking at the whole person, when diagnosing and treating an illness, with emphasis on patient responsibility for self-health. Members are licensed physicians and medical and osteopathic students. Related to the American Holistic Medical Foundation, an educational and research foundation. Membership: $250/yr.
Publications:
Journal of Holistic Medicine. semi-a.
Holistic Medicine. bi-m. adv.
Annual Meetings: Regional

American Holistic Nurses' Ass'n (1981)
205 St. Louis Street, Suite 506, Springfield MO 65806
Exec. Director: Cynthia L. Wheeler
Members: 1,100 *Staff:* 3
Annual Budget: $50-100,000 *Tel:* (417) 864-5160
Hist. Note: AHNA is a non-profit, educational association for nurses and allied health care professionals embracing the concept of holistic health, a harmony between mind, body and spirit. Provides a support system, communications network, recognition and educational opportunities. Membership: $65/yr.
Publications:
Beginnings (newsletter). m.
Journal of Holistic Nursing. semi-a.
Annual Meetings: Summer
1987-Rhinebeck, NY(Omega Institute)/June 16-20/250
1988-Hawaii

American Home Economics Ass'n (1909)
2010 Massachusetts Ave., N. W., Washington DC 20036
Exec. Director: Joan R. McFadden
Members: 25,000 individuals *Staff:* 30
Annual Budget: $2-5,000,000 *Tel:* (202) 862-8300
Hist. Note: Founded at Lake Placid, NY December 31, 1908 and incorporated in New York in 1909. Reincorporated in the District of Columbia in 1951. A professional organization of individuals working to help individuals and families develop living skills, adjust to limited resources and a changing environment. Membership: $60/year (individual), $1,000/year (organization/company).
Publications:
AHEA Action. 5/yr. adv.
Home Economics Research Journal. q. adv.
Journal of Home Economics. q. adv.
Annual Meetings: End of June/5,000
1987-Indianapolis, IN(Hyatt)/June 29-July 2
1988-Baltimore,MD/June 20-23
1989-Denver, CO/June 26-29
1990-Baltimore, MD/June 24-27

American Home Lighting Institute (1945)
435 North Michigan Ave., Suite 1717, Chicago IL 60611
Managing Director: James S. Nicol
Members: 500-550 *Staff:* 2-5
Annual Budget: $500-1,000,000 *Tel:* (312) 644-0828
Hist. Note: Members are manufacturers, showrooms and manufacturers' representatives of portable lamps, fixtures, bulbs, and their components and accessories.
Publication:
Lightrays. bi-m.
Annual Meetings: Fall/700
1987-Monterey, CA

American Home Sewing Ass'n (1928)
1375 Broadway, 4th Fl., New York NY 10018
Exec. V. President: Leonard Ennis
Members: 500 companies *Staff:* 7
Annual Budget: $1-2,000,000 *Tel:* (212) 302-2150
Hist. Note: Formerly (1976) the Nat'l Notion Ass'n; a new Nat'l Notion Ass'n was incorporated at this time with different objectives. AHSA was known as the Nat'l Home Sewing Ass'n from 1976 until 1978 when it merged with the American Home Sewing Council to create the present group. Members are manufacturers of all types of home sewing items, as well as fabric stores and chains. Affiliate members include wholesalers and manufacturers' representatives.
Publications:
Sewing Seeds. q.
Trade and Show Journal a. adv.
Annual Meetings: March/4,000
1987-Las Vegas, NV(Bally's)/March 15-18
1988-San Francisco, CA(Moscone Ctr.)/March 6-9
1989-Long Beach, CA(Convention Ctr.)/March 19-22
1990-Las Vegas, NV(Bally's)/March 18-21
1991-San Francisco, CA(Moscone Ctr.)/March 3-6

American Honey Producers Ass'n (1969)
Box 368, Minco OK 73059
President: Glenn Gibson
Members: 550-600 *Staff:* 2-5
Annual Budget: $25-50,000 *Tel:* (405) 352-4126
Hist. Note: Formed by members of The American Beekeeping Federation who wished for an organization representing the interests of beekeepers. Voting members of AHPA must derive 50% of their income from bees. Membership: $10-80/yr.

00041 12 05 86 1233

Publication:
Newsletter. bi-m.
Annual Meetings: Winter
1987-Corpus Christi, TX(Sheraton)/Jan. 13-17/350

American Horse Council (1969)
1700 K St., N.W., Suite 300, Washington DC 20006
President: R. Richards Rolapp
Members: 145-155 organizations; 2,204 individuals *Staff:* 6-10
Annual Budget: $500-1,000,000 *Tel:* (202) 296-4031
Hist. Note: Supports the American Horse Council Committee on Legislation and Taxation (COLT). The trade association of the equine industry. Members are organizations and individuals who need to be kept informed of tax and regulatory developments affecting such matters as gambling, funding of livestock research, import-export restrictions and similar matters affecting those who live by horses. Membership: $100/yr. (individual), $1,000/yr. (organization).
Publications:
AHC Newsletter. m.
Horse Industry Directory. a.
Tax Bulletin. m.
AHC Business. q.
Annual Meetings: Spring
1987-Washington, DC(Hyatt Regency Capital Hill)/June 7-10/400

American Horse Publications (1970)
515 Emerald Park Drive, McHenry IL 60050
Exec. Director: Gail Blanchard
Members: 100 publications *Staff:* 1
Annual Budget: $10-25,000 *Tel:* (815) 385-9445
Hist. Note: An association of horse-oriented publications in the U.S. and Canada. Membership: $50-$150/year.
Publication:
Newsletter.
Semi-annual Meetings: Jan. and June

American Horticultural Soc. (1922)
Box 0105, Mount Vernon VA 22121
Exec. Director: Dr. Charles A. Huckins
Members: 40,000 *Staff:* 20-25
Annual Budget: $1-2,000,000 *Tel:* (703) 768-5700
Hist. Note: Founded in Washington, D.C. in 1922. Merged in 1926 with the National Horticultural Society. Incorporated in 1932 in the District of Columbia and consolidated in 1959 with the American Horticultural Council. Membership includes the widest range of horticultural concerns, with individuals, scientific organizations, institutions and commercial enterprises spanning interests from technical research to amateur gardening. Membership: $25/yr. (individual), $100-5,000/yr. (organization).
Publications:
American Horticulturist. bi-m. adv.
American Horticulturist Magazine. bi-m. adv.
Annual Meetings: Fall/350
1987-New York/May 13-17
1988-Atlanta, GA/April
1989-Minneapolis, MN
1990-Seattle, WA

American Hospital Ass'n (1898)
840 North Lake Shore Drive, Chicago IL 60611
President: Carol M. McCarthy, Ph.D.
Members: 6,100 institutions, 40,000 individuals *Staff:* 900
Annual Budget: over $5,000,000 *Tel:* (312) 280-6000
Hist. Note: Formerly (1906) Ass'n of Hospital Superintendents of the United States and Canada. Affiliated with the Hospital Research and Educational Trust. Maintains a Washington Office. Sponsors the AHA Political Action Committee, established in 1978.
Publications:
Hospital Literature Index. q.
Hospital Week. w.
Hospitals. semi-m. adv.
The Hospital Medical Staff. m.
The Volunteer Leader. m. adv.
Trustee. m. adv.
Annual Meetings: Late Summer
1987-Atlanta, GA/July 27-29
1988-New Orleans, LA/Aug. 8-10

American Hospital Radiology Administrators
Hist. Note: Became the American Healthcare Radiology Administrators in 1986.

American Hot Dip Galvanizers Ass'n (1935)
1101 Connecticut Avuenue, N.W., Suite 700, Washington DC 20036-4303
Exec. V. President: Timothy J. Gorman
Members: 100-125 companies *Staff:* 10-15
Annual Budget: $500-1,000,000 *Tel:* (202) 857-1119
Hist. Note: Organized in 1933 and incorporated in 1935 in the Commonwealth of Pennsylvania Represents the after-fabrication hot dip galvinizing industry whose members provide anti-corrosion coatings to steel products.
Publications:
Directory. a.
Newsletter. bi-m. (for members)
Newsletter. q. (for industry)
Annual Meetings: Spring/200
1987-Carlsbad, CA(LaCosta)/April 5-9
1988-Orlando, FL(Hyatt Grand Cypress)/April 24-28
1989-Irving, TX(Las Colinas Inn & Conference Ctr.)/March 31-April 7

American Hotel and Motel Ass'n (1910)
888 Seventh Ave., New York NY 10106
Exec. V. President: Kenneth F. Hine
Members: 8,800 properties; 1,300,000 rooms *Staff:* 50-60
Annual Budget: over $5,000,000 *Tel:* (212) 265-4506
Hist. Note: A federation of state hotel ass'ns. Formerly (1917) American Hotel Protective Ass'n and (1962) American Hotel Ass'n. Supports the American Hotel-Motel Political Action Committee. Maintains a Washington office. Has an annual budget of $10 million.
Publications:
Directory of Hotel & Motel Systems. a. adv.
Hotel & Motel Red Book. a. adv.
Lodging Magazine. 10/yr. adv.
Washington Report. m.
AHMA Reports. m.
AHMAgram. m.
State Capital Happenings. bi-a.
Annual Meetings:
1987-San Francisco, CA(Fairmont and Westin St. Francis)/June 21-24
1988-Dallas, TX(Loew's Anatole)/April 15-18
1989-Boston, MA

American Hotel and Motel Brokers (1959)
Hist. Note: Became the Hotel and Motel Brokers of America in 1985.

American Humor Studies Ass'n (1974)
Department of English, S.W. Texas State University, San Marcos TX 78666
Secy.-Treas.: Michael Hennessy
Members: 200 *Staff:* 1
Annual Budget: $10-25,000 *Tel:* (512) 245-3654
Hist. Note: An "allied" organization of the Modern Language Ass'n, AHSA has no paid staff or permanent headquarters.
Publications:
Studies in American Humor. q. adv.
American Humor. a.
Annual Meetings: December, with Modern Language Ass'n

American Hungarian Educators Ass'n (1974)
707 Snider Lane, Silver Spring MD 20904
Exec. Director: Eniko Molnar Basa
Members: 250 *Staff:* 1
Annual Budget: under $10,000 *Tel:* (301) 384-4657
Hist. Note: Chartered in the State of Maryland in 1976. Educators concerned with the teaching and dissemination of Hungarian history, language, literature, art and music. Attempts to further Hungarian studies in American and Canadian universities. Has no permanent office. Officers are elected biennially. Membership: $12/yr.
Publication:
American Hungarian Educator. 3/yr.
Annual Meetings: Spring/300
1987-Montclair, NJ(Montclair State College)

American Hypnotists' Ass'n (1959)
1159 Green St., Ste 6, San Francisco CA 94109
President: Rafael M. Bertuccelli, M.D.
Members: 400-450 *Staff:* 2
Annual Budget: under $10,000 *Tel:* (415) 775-6130
Annual Meetings: Spring
1987-Los Angeles, CA/June/200
1988-Las Vegas, NV/May/250
1989-Mexico City/May/150

American Immigration Lawyers Ass'n (1946)
1000 16th St., N.W., Washington DC 20036
Exec. Director: Warren Leiden
Members: 2,000 *Staff:* 6-7
Annual Budget: $500-1,000,000 *Tel:* (202) 331-0046
Hist. Note: Formerly (1981) the Ass'n of Immigration and Nationality Lawyers. Attorneys practicing in the field of immigration and naturalization law. Membership: $200/yr.
Publications:
Immigration Journal. q. adv.
AILA Monthly Mailing. m. adv.
Directory. a. adv.
Annual Meetings: June/600
1987-Philadelphia, PA
1988-San Diego, CA
1989-Washington, DC
1990-Seattle, WA

American Importers Ass'n (1921)
Hist. Note: Became the American Association of Exporters and Importers in 1981.

American Independent Refiners Ass'n (1983)
50 F St., N.W., Suite 1040, Washington DC 20001
Exec. Director: Raymond F. Bragg, Jr.
Members: 25 companies *Staff:* 2-5
Annual Budget: $250-500,000 *Tel:* (202) 543-8811
Hist. Note: Members are independent refiners. The product of a merger April 1, 1983 of the American Petroleum Refiners Association (formed in 1961) and the Independent Refiners Association of America (formed in 1949).
Annual Meetings: August

American Indian Health Care Ass'n (1975)
245 East 6th St., Suite 815, St. Paul MN 55101
Director: William LaRoque
Members: 37 programs *Staff:* 5
Annual Budget: $100-250,000 *Tel:* (612) 293-0233
Hist. Note: Nat'l organization of urban Indian health programs which promotes the health and social well-being of those Indian people residing off reservation in urban areas. Membership: $20/yr. (individual), $50/yr. (company).
Publication:
Urban Indian Health Program Summary Booklet. a.
Annual Meetings:
1987-San Diego, CA/January 27-30

American Industrial Arts Ass'n (1939)
Hist. Note: Became the Industrial Technology Education Ass'n in 1985.

American Industrial Arts Student Ass'n (1978)
1908 Association Drive, Reston VA 22091
Exec. Director: Kay Schaeffer
Members: 45,000 *Staff:* 2-5
Annual Budget: $100-250,000 *Tel:* (703) 860-9000
Hist. Note: A vocational high school student association composed of students enrolled in industrial arts courses. Membership: $4/yr. (students), $5/yr. (professional/adult), $10/yr. (alumni).
Publications:
The School Scene. q.
The Advisor Update. m.
Annual Meetings: June/1,500
1987-Baton Rouge, LA
1988-Valley Forge, PA
1989-North Carolina
1990-Ohio

American Industrial Health Council (1977)
1330 Connecticut Ave., N.W., Washington DC 20036
Exec. Director: Ronald A. Lang
Members: 100 *Staff:* 6-10
Annual Budget: $1-2,000,000 *Tel:* (202) 659-0060
Hist. Note: An organization representing the chemical and other industries formed to address the scientific issues related to proposed standards of federal agencies for identifying and regulating products suspected of causing cancer, and other chronic health hazards. Affiliated with the Synthetic Organic Chemical Manufacturers Ass'n, which provides administrative support.
Publications:
Status Report. m.
Newsletter. bi-m.
Annual Meetings: November/December

American Industrial Hygiene Ass'n (1939)
475 Wolf Ledges Parkway, Akron OH 44311
Exec. Director: Frederick Motts
Members: 7,000 individuals, 400 companies and organizations
Staff: 30
Annual Budget: $1-2,000,000 *Tel:* (216) 762-7294
Hist. Note: To promote the study and control of environmental stresses arising in or from the work place or its products, in relation to the health or well-being of workers and the public. Membership: $40/yr.(individual); $150/yr.(organization)
Publication:
American Industrial Hygiene Association Journal. m. adv.
Annual Meetings: Summer
1987-Montreal, Quebec(Convention Ctr.)/May 30-June 5/6,700
1988-San Francisco, CA(Moscone Ctr.)/May 15-20
1989-St. Louis, MO/May 21-26

American Innerspring Manufacturers (1966)
1918 North Parkway, Memphis TN 38112
Exec. Director: Arthur Grehan
Members: 22 companies *Staff:* 2
Annual Budget: $50-100,000 *Tel:* (901) 274-9030
Hist. Note: Formerly the Association of Innerspring Manufacturers. Members make and sell innerspring units and box springs to mattress manufacturers.
Annual Meetings: Spring

American Institute for Archaeological Research (1982)
Box 6068, Newburyport MA 01950
Exec. Director: Dorothy L. Hayden
Members: 150 *Staff:* 5
Annual Budget: under $10,000 *Tel:* (617) 465-9247
Hist. Note: Founded in New Hampshire in February, 1982 to carry out research in the fields of archaeology and anthropology with particular emphasis on stonework and inscriptions of North America from pre-colonial times. Membership: $25/yr.
Publications:
Institute News. m.
On Site. a.
Semi-annual Meetings: Spring and Fall

American Institute for Conservation of Historic and Artistic Works (1973)
3545 Williamsburg Lane, N.W., Washington DC 20008
Exec. Director: A. Gilson Brown
Members: 2,400 individuals, 150 institutions *Staff:* 3-6
Annual Budget: $250-500,000 *Tel:* (202) 364-1036
Hist. Note: Formerly (until 1973) an affiliate of the Internat'l Institute for Conservation of Historic and Artistic Works. The AIC is a professional organization of conservators, curators, educators, librarians and scientists. Purpose is to disseminate information on conservation, encourage high standards of practice, and provide continuing education opportunities for conservators. Membership: $70/year (Fellow), $55/year (Professional), $80/year (institution).

00042 12 05 86 1233

Publications:
Directory. a. adv.
Journal. semi-a. adv.
Newsletter. bi-m. adv.
Annual Meetings: May, Memorial Day weekend/1,000
1987-Vancouver, BC
1988-New Orleans, LA

American Institute for Decision Sciences (1969)
Hist. Note: Became the Decision Sciences Institute in 1985.

American Institute for Design and Drafting (1948)
966 Hungerford Drive, Suite 10-B, Rockville MD 20850
Exec. Director: Philip Nowers, CAE
Members: 2,600 *Staff:* 5
Annual Budget: $100-250,000 *Tel:* (301) 294-8712
Hist. Note: Founded as the Ass'n of Professional Draftsmen and assumed its present name in 1960. Membership includes individuals, corporations and educational institutions. Seeks to promote improved quality and efficiency in the drafting/designing profession and industry. Membership: $50/yr.
Publication:
Design and Drafting News. m. adv.
Annual Meetings: Spring
1987-St. Louis, MO(Sheraton)/March 31-April 2
1988-New Orleans(Conv. Center)/March 16-18

American Institute for Exploration (1954)
Hist. Note: Formerly (1961) the Institute of Regional Exploration. Has no paid staff. Inactive in 1982.

American Institute for Homeopathy (1844)
1500 Massachusetts Ave., N.W., Suite 41, Washington DC 20005
Exec. Director: Suzanne B. Roethel
Members: 115 *Staff:* 2-5
Annual Budget: $25-50,000 *Tel:* (202) 223-6182
Hist. Note: Members are doctors of medicine, dentistry and osteopathy practicing according to laws propounded by Samuel C.F. Hahnemann (1755-1843). Membership: $150/yr.
Publications:
Journal. q. adv.
Newsletter. m.

American Institute for Imported Steel (1950)
11 West 42nd St., New York NY 10036
Exec. Director: Carol P. Quinn
Members: 70 companies *Staff:* 2-5
Annual Budget: $100-250,000 *Tel:* (212) 921-1765
Hist. Note: An information-gathering organization keeping its members informed concerning trade and tariff legislation and importing concerns. Founded during the Korean War at government urging to help alleviate the then-current steel shortage. Members are U.S. companies, or U.S. affiliates of foreign producers incorporated in the U.S, importing steel. Bulk of the membership concentrated on the East and Gulf coasts.

American Institute for Patristic and Byzantine Studies (1967)
R.R. 1, Box 353A, Kingston NY 12401
President: Dr. Constantine N. Tsirpanlis
Members: 375 *Staff:* 3
Annual Budget: under $10,000 *Tel:* (914) 336-8797
Hist. Note: Promotes research in eastern Patristic, literature, history, theology, and culture. Founded as the American Society for Neo-Hellenic Studies, it assumed its present name in 1981. Membership: $35/yr. (individual), $40/yr. (organization).
Publication:
Patristic and Byzantine Review. trien.
Annual Meetings: 2nd week in October

American Institute for Property and Liability Underwriters (1942)
720 Providence Road, Malvern PA 19355
Manager of Communications: Karen Vaughn
Members: 1,000 companies *Staff:* 110
Annual Budget: over $5,000,000 *Tel:* (215) 644-2100
Hist. Note: Affiliated with the Insurance Institute of America. Determines qualifications for professional certification of insurance personnel and awards the designation Chartered Property Casualty Underwriter (CPCU).
Publications:
CPCU/IIA Catalog. a.
CPCU/IIA Key Information. a.
Institute Insights Newsletter. bi-a.

American Institute for Shippers Ass'ns (1961)
Box 33457, Washington DC 20033
Executive Assistant: Carole Elipsitz
Members: 150 companies *Staff:* 2-5
Annual Budget: $100-250,000 *Tel:* (202) 628-0933
Hist. Note: Shippers associations are cooperatives formed for the purpose of consolidating freight to obtain volume transportation rates. Membership: $125-2,500/year, based on gross revenues.
Publications:
AISA Guide to Shipping Cooperatives. a. adv.
AISA News. m.
Annual Meetings: Spring-Early Summer/250
1987-Phoenix, AZ(Pointe)/May 3-7
1988-Ft. Lauderdale, FL(Marriott)/April 24-28

American Institute of Aeronautics and Astronautics (1963)
1633 Broadway, New York NY 10019
Exec. Director: James J. Harford
Members: 36,000 *Staff:* 180
Annual Budget: over $5,000,000 *Tel:* (212) 581-4300
Hist. Note: Formed in 1963 by a merger of the American Rocket Soc. (1931) and the Institute of the Aeronautical Sciences (1932). Maintains a Washington office and is planning to move headquarters to Washington in summer, 1987. Has an annual budget of over $8 million.
Publications:
AIAA Journal. m.
AIAA Student Journal. q. adv.
Aerospace America.
International Aerospace Abstracts. semi-m.
Journal of Aircraft. m.
Journal of Energy. bi-m.
Journal of Guidance, Control and Dynamics. bi-m.
Journal of Spacecraft and Rockets. bi-m.

American Institute of Architects (1857)
1735 New York Ave., N.W., Washington DC 20006
Exec. V. President: Louis L. Marines
Members: 50,000 licensed architects *Staff:* 200
Annual Budget: over $5,000,000 *Tel:* (202) 626-7300
Hist. Note: Incorporated in New York April 15, 1857; incorporated The Western Ass'n of Architects in 1889. As the umbrella organization of the U.S. architectural profession, AIA promotes the standards of architecture and interests of architects. Supports the American Institute of Architects Foundation (educational arm) and the American Institute of Architects Political Action Committee. Has an annual budget of $25 million. Membership: $90/yr.
Publications:
ARCHITECTURE, The AIA Journal. m. adv.
Memo. m.
Annual Meetings: Late Spring/ 6-8,000
1987-Orlando, FL/June 19-22
1988-New York, NY/May 8-11
1989-St. Louis, MO/May 7-10
1990-Houston, TX(George Brown Convention Ctr.)/May 20-23

American Institute of Baking (1919)
Hist. Note: Research and educational center for the baking industry. Affiliated with the American Bakers Association.

American Institute of Banking (1900)
Hist. Note: A section of The American Bankers Ass'n.

American Institute of Biological Sciences (1947)
730 11th St., N.W., Washington DC 20001-4584
Exec. Director: Charles M. Chambers
Members: 7,200 individuals; 4,500 institutions *Staff:* 25-30
Annual Budget: $2-5,000,000 *Tel:* (202) 628-1500
Hist. Note: Established within the National Research Council at a meeting of the Organizing Board in April, 1946. Incorporated as an independent, non-profit entity in the District of Columbia on Jan. 12, 1985. Charter membership closed Dec. 31, 1987. A federation of professional societies with an interest in the life sciences, AIBS also has individual members and promotes all aspects of the biological sciences, including agriculture, environment, and medicine. Absorbed the American Soc. of Professional Biologists in 1969. Membership: $37.50/yr.; $19.50/yr. (student).
Publications:
BioScience. m. adv.
Forum. bi-m.
Membership Directory. a.
Departmental Directory.
Annual Meetings: August/3,000
1987-Columbus, OH(Ohio State Univ.)/Aug. 9-13
1988-Davis, CA(Univ. of CA)/Aug. 6-12
1989-Toronto, Ontario(Univ. of Toronto)/Aug. 6-10
1990-Raleigh, NC(NC State Univ.)/Aug.
1991-San Antonio, TX(Trinity Univ.)/Aug.
1992-Honolulu, HI(Univ. of HI)/Aug.
1993-Ames, IA(Iowa State Univ.)

American Institute of Building Design (1950)
1412 19th St., Sacramento CA 95814
Exec. Director: Diana Darling-Lewis
Members: 750 *Staff:* 2-5
Annual Budget: $50-100,000 *Tel:* (916) 447-2422
Hist. Note: Formerly (1958) United Designers Ass'n Established in California as the United Designers Association, it assumed its present name in 1958. Seeks to unify the building design field, develop better design education standards, encourage inter-professional relations among designers and promote research into the aesthetic and technical aspects of the field. Membership: $90/yr. (individual), $225/yr. (company).
Publications:
Newsletter. q. adv.
Professional Designer. adv.
Annual Meetings: Summer/250
1987-Portland, OR/July
1989-Houston, TX

American Institute of Certified Planners (1978)
1776 Massachusetts Ave., N.W., Washington DC 20036
Exec. Director: Israel Stollman
Members: 5,500 *Staff:* 7
Annual Budget: $500-1,000,000 *Tel:* (202) 872-0611
Hist. Note: The professional institute of the American Planning Ass'n. Members are those members of APA who have met the required qualifications of education, experience and examination in the field of planning. Awards the designation "AICP". Membership: $60/yr. (required membership in APA)
Publications:
Roster of Members.
AICP Notes.
Annual Meetings: With American Planning Ass'n.

American Institute of Certified Public Accountants (1887)
1211 Ave. of the Americas, New York NY 10036-8775
President: Philip B. Chenok
Members: 250,000 *Staff:* 550
Annual Budget: over $5,000,000 *Tel:* (212) 575-6200
Hist. Note: Founded as the American Ass'n of Public Accountants. Became the Institute of Accountants in the U.S.A. in 1916 and the American Institute of Accountants in 1917. Merged in 1937 with the American Soc. of Certified Public Accountants. Became the American Institute of Certified Public Accountants in 1957. Administers the national uniform CPA exam. Supports the AICPA Effective Legislation Committee. Has an annual budget of over $50,000,000. Maintains a Washington office.
Publications:
CPA Letter. m.
Journal of Accountancy. m. adv.
Tax Adviser. m. adv.
Annual Meetings: Fall
1987-New York, NY/Sept. 19-23

American Institute of Chemical Engineers (1908)
345 East 47th St., New York NY 10017
Exec. Director: Dr. J. Charles Forman
Members: 60,000 *Staff:* 90
Annual Budget: over $5,000,000 *Tel:* (212) 705-7338
Hist. Note: Organized June 22, 1908 in Philadelphia and incorporated in New York in 1910. A member of the Accreditation Board for Engineering and Technology, the American Nat'l Standards Institute, the American Ass'n of Engineering Societies and other related organizations. Has an annual budget of over $10,000,000. Membership: $80/yr.
Publications:
AIChE Journal. m. adv.
Chemical Engineering Progress. m. adv.
Energy Progress. q. adv.
Environmental Progress. q. adv.
International Chemical Engineering. q. adv.
Plant/Operations Progress. q. adv.
Symposium Series. 10/yr.
Biotechnology Progess. q. adv.
Chemical Engineering Faculties. a.
Directory of Chemical Engineering Consultants. a.
Annual Meetings: November/4,000
1987-New York, NY(Hilton)/Nov. 15-20
1988-Washington, DC(Hilton)/Nov. 27-Dec. 2
1989-San Francisco, CA(Hilton)/Nov. 5-10
1990-Chicago, IL(Palmer House)/Nov. 11-16

American Institute of Chemists (1923)
7315 Wisconsin Ave., Bethesda MD 20814
Exec. Director: David A. H. Roethel
Members: 6,000 *Staff:* 2-5
Annual Budget: $250-500,000 *Tel:* (301) 652-2447
Hist. Note: Founded in New York City in 1923 and incorporated in New York in 1926 and in Maryland in 1974. A member of the Commission on Professionals in Science and Technology, Engineers and Scientists Joint Committee on Pensions and sponsor of the American Board of Clinical Chemistry, the Nat'l Registry in Clinical Chemistry, the Nat'l Certification Commission in Chemistry and Chemical Engineering and the AIC Student Research and Recognition Foundation.
Publications:
The Chemist. 11/yr. adv.
Membership Directory. a. adv.
Annual Meetings: Spring
1987-Philadelphia, PA/April 23-26
1988-Los Angeles, CA/Sept. 22-25

American Institute of Commemorative Art (1951)
2446 Sutter Court, N.E., Grand Rapids MI 49505
Exec. Director: Donald J. Patten
Members: 50 *Staff:* 1
Annual Budget: $25-50,000 *Tel:* (616) 361-7827
Hist. Note: Members are devoted to high standards of design and ethics in the monument field. Limited to 50 members by its constitution. Membership: $350/yr.
Publication:
Milestone. m.
Annual Meetings:
1987-Charleston, SC(Omni)/Sept. 27-30/90-100
1988 Clearwater Beach, FL(Adam's Mark)/Dec. 4-7/90-100
1989-Louisville, KY

American Institute of Constructors

American Institute of Cooperation (1925)
50 F St., N.W., Suite 900, Washington DC 20001
President & CEO: David C. Thomas
Members: 900 *Staff:* 9
Annual Budget: $500-1,000,000 *Tel:* (202) 347-1080
Hist. Note: A national educational organization of farmer cooperatives chartered as a university.
Publications:
AIC Newsletter. m.
American Cooperation. a.
Annual Meetings: Summer/1,800-2,000
1987-St. Louis, MO(Clarion Hotel)/Aug. 10-13

00043 12 05 86 1233

American Institute of Criminology (1953)
Hist. Note: Educational and Social Services division of The American Association of Criminology.

American Institute of Financial Brokers (1959)
Box 802063, Dallas TX 75380
President: Allan Clark
Members: 4-500 *Staff:* 1
Tel: (214) 931-9494
Hist. Note: Members are individuals engaged in negotiating loans, letters of credit, prime bank notes and other forms of commercial financing and loan counseling.

American Institute of Fishery Research Biologists (1956)
Box 271, La Jolla CA 92038
President: Hugh R. MacCrimmon
Members: 1,300 *Staff:* 1
Annual Budget: under $10,000

American Institute of Food Distribution (1928)
28-12 Broadway, Fair Lawn NJ 07410
President: Roy Harrison
Members: 2,783 *Staff:* 11-15
Annual Budget: $500-1,000,000 *Tel:* (201) 791-5570
Hist. Note: An international information and research organization serving, and maintained by, companies concerned with distribution of food products. Maintains a Washington, DC area office.
Publications:
Food Institute Report w.
Food Retailing Review. a.
Food Business Mergers & Aquisitions. a.

American Institute of Graphic Arts (1914)
1059 Third Ave., New York NY 10021
Director: Caroline Hightower
Members: 5,000 *Staff:* 6-10
Annual Budget: $500-1,000,000 *Tel:* (212) 752-0813
Hist. Note: Promotes good design in graphic communication, and architectural and environmental graphics. Conducts interrelated programs of competitions, exhibitions, publications and educational activities to promote excellence in graphic design. Membership: $100/yr.
Publications:
Journal. q.
Graphic Design USA. a.
Biennial meetings: uneven years
1987-San Francisco, CA(St. Francis/Masonic Auditorium)/Sept. 3-5/1,800

American Institute of Hydrology (1981)
3416 University Ave., S.E., Suite 200, Minneapolis MN 55414
Exec. Manager: Helen Klose
Members: 500-600 *Staff:* 1
Annual Budget: $50-100,000 *Tel:* (612) 379-0901
Hist. Note: Incorporated March 1981 in the State of Minnesota. Registers and certifies hydrologists and hydrogeologists. Membership: $47.50/yr. (individual); $125/yr. (organization/company)
Publications:
Hydrological Science and Technology. q. adv.
AIH Bulletin. q. adv.
Semi-Annual Meetings: Spring and Fall
1987-San Francisco, CA/March 26-27
1988-Atlanta, GA/Oct. 1-2

American Institute of Hypnosis (1955)
Hist. Note: Address unknown, 1981. Possibly defunct.

American Institute of Indian Studies (1961)
Foster Hall, Room 212, Univ. of Chicago, Chicago IL 60637
President: Joseph Elder
Members: 41 institutions *Staff:* 1
Annual Budget: under $10,000 *Tel:* (312) 962-8638
Hist. Note: Colleges and universities which support study and research in the art, archeology and languages of India.

American Institute of Industrial Engineers (1948)
Hist. Note: Became the Institute of Industrial Engineers in 1981.

American Institute of Kitchen Dealers (1963)
Hist. Note: Became the National Kitchen and Bath Association in 1982.

American Institute of Landscape Architects (1957)
Hist. Note: Merged with the American Society of Landscape Architects on January 1, 1982.

American Institute of Maintenance (1958)
Hist. Note: Absorbed by the Cleaning Management Institute in 1985.

American Institute of Marine Underwriters (1898)
14 Wall St., New York NY 10005
President: Ward L. Mauck
Members: 120 companies *Staff:* 6-10
Annual Budget: $500-1,000,000 *Tel:* (212) 233-0550
Hist. Note: Tracing its origins to 1820, its member companies write ocean marine insurance in the United States.
Annual Meetings: New York, NY in November

American Institute of Medical Climatology (1958)
1023 Welsh Rd., Philadelphia PA 19115
Exec. V. President: George W. K. King
Members: 75-100 *Staff:* 2
Annual Budget: under $10,000 *Tel:* (215) 673-8368
Hist. Note: Promotes the sciences of bioclimatology and biometerology, which address the relationship between climate, weather and the entire spectrum of life.
Publication:
Bulletins. q.
Annual Meetings: Philadelphia, end of October

American Institute of Merchant Shipping (1969)
1000 16th St., N.W., Suite 511, Washington DC 20036
Vice President: Ernest J. Corrado
Members: 24 companies *Staff:* 5-7
Annual Budget: $500-1,000,000 *Tel:* (202) 775-4399
Hist. Note: Merger (1969) of Committee of American Steamship Lines (1952), Pacific American Steamship Ass'n (1919) and The American Merchant Marine Institute (1938). Members are owners and operators of U.S. flag vessels, primarily tankers, bulk-carriers and container ships. Represents members' interests in dealings with internat'l and domestic agencies concerned with merchant shipping.
Publication:
Newsline. irreg.
Annual Meetings: Washington, DC/January-February

American Institute of Mining, Metallurgical, and Petroleum Engineers (1871)
345 East 47th St., New York NY 10017
Exec. Director: Robert H. Marcrum
Members: 99,000 *Staff:* 130-140
Annual Budget: over $5,000,000 *Tel:* (212) 705-7695
Hist. Note: Founded in Wilkes-Barre, Pennsylvania in 1871 as the American Institute of Mining Engineers to "further the arts and sciences employed to recover the earth's minerals and convert them to useful products." Incorporated in 1905, the name was changed in 1919 to American Institute of Mining and Metallurgical Engineers after absorbing the American Institute of Metals. In 1957 the name American Institute of Mining, Metallurgical and Petroleum Engineers, Inc. was adopted and the Institute was reorganized into constituent societies which now consist of The Metallurgical Soc. of AIME, the Soc. of Mining Engineers of AIME, the Soc. of Petroleum Engineers of AIME and the Iron and Steel Soc. of AIME. Publications of these societies (listed below) should be obtained directly from the society in question. A member of American Association of Engineering Societies. Has a budget of over $10 million.
Publications:
The Iron and Steelmaker. m. adv.
Journal of Metals. m. adv.
Journal of Petroleum Technology. m. adv.
Mining Engineering. m. adv.
Annual Meetings: February/March
1987-Denver, CO(Radisson Hotel)/Feb. 23-27

American Institute of Nail and Tack Manufacturers (1947)
25 North Broadway, Tarrytown NY 10591
Secretary: Richard C. Byrne
Members: 8-10 companies *Staff:* 2-5
Annual Budget: $10-25,000 *Tel:* (914) 332-0040
Hist. Note: Develops safety programs and engineering standards for products of industry.
Annual Meetings: Spring

American Institute of Nutrition (1928)
9650 Rockville Pike, Bethesda MD 20814
Exec. Officer: Richard G. Allison
Members: 2,400 *Staff:* 5
Annual Budget: $1-2,000,000 *Tel:* (301) 530-7050
Hist. Note: An outgrowth of the increasing interest in nutrition research by certain members of the American Society of Biological Chemists who in 1928 incorporated the AIN for the purpose of publishing The Journal of Nutrition. In 1934 AIN turned to the Wistar Institute to publish the Journal and AIN was reorganized as a membership society, with 178 charter members. AIN is a professional society of nutrition research scientists and member of the Federation of American Societies for Experimental Biology. Membership: $70/yr.
Publications:
Journal of Nutrition. m. adv.
AIN Nutrition Notes. q.
Annual Meetings: Spring, with Federation of American Socs. for Experimental Biology
1987-Washington, DC(Washington Hilton)/March 29-April 3
1988-Las Vegas, NV/May 1-6
1989-New Orleans, LA/March 17-24
1990-Washington, DC/April 1-6
1991-Atlanta, GA/April 14-19

American Institute of Oral Biology (1931)
Box 481, South Laguna CA 92677
Exec. Secretary: Barbara P. Ward
Members: 650 *Staff:* 2-5
Annual Budget: $25-50,000 *Tel:* (714) 499-1286
Publication:
Proceedings Manual. a.
Annual Meetings: Fall/100-150

American Institute of Parliamentarians (1958)
124 W. Washington Blvd., Suite 144, Fort Wayne IN 46802
Exec. Director: Bob Leiman
Members: 1,300-1,400 *Staff:* 4
Annual Budget: $50-100,000 *Tel:* (219) 422-3680
Hist. Note: Promotes the use of the democratic process and effective parliamentary procedures. Awards the designations CP(Certified Parliamentarian) and CPP (Certified Professional Parliamentarian). Membership: $25/yr.
Publications:
The Communicator. q.
Parliamentary Journal. q.
Annual Meetings:
1987-Arlington, VA(Stouffer's - Crystal City)/Aug. 13-16/150-200
1988-Los Angeles, CA

American Institute of Physics (1931)
335 East 45th St., New York NY 10017
Exec. Director: H. William Koch
Members: 10 socs., 18 affiliated socs., 107 associates *Staff:* 515
Annual Budget: over $5,000,000 *Tel:* (212) 661-9404
Hist. Note: Organized in New York under the leadership of Karl Compton and George Pegram as a means of preserving communication within the community of physicists whose energies were being dispersed into an increasing number of special fields. A federation of ten societies in physics: Acoustical Soc. of America, American Crystallographic Ass'n, American Physical Soc., Optical Soc. of America, Soc. of Rheology, American Ass'n of Physicists in Medicine, American Vacuum Soc., and American Geophysical Union. Incorporated in New York in 1932. Has a budget of approximately $46 million.
Publications:
Applied Physics Letters. w.
Current Physics Index. q.
Journal of Applied Physics. m.
Journal of Mathematical Physics. m.
Journal of Physical and Chemical Reference Data. q.
Physics Today. m. adv.
The Journal of Chemical Physics. semi-m.
The Physics of Fluids. m.
The Review of Scientific Instruments. m. adv.
Annual Meetings: Not Held

American Institute of Plant Engineers (1954)
3975 Erie Ave., Cincinnati OH 45208
Exec. Director: Michael J. Tillar
Members: 8,000 individuals, 50 companies *Staff:* 11-15
Annual Budget: $500-1,000,000 *Tel:* (513) 561-6000
Hist. Note: Individuals involved in the full spectrum of facilities management required to create a product or provide a service. Membership: $60/yr.
Publications:
Facilities forum. bi-m.
AIPE Facilities Management, Operations & Engineering. bi-m.
AIPE Newsline.

American Institute of Professional Geologists (1963)
7828 Vance Drive, Suite 103, Arvada CO 80003
Exec. Director: Victor C. Tannehill
Members: 4,700 *Staff:* 2-5
Annual Budget: $250-500,000 *Tel:* (303) 431-0831
Hist. Note: Founded November 15, 1963 and incorporated in Colorado in 1964. A member of the American Geological Institute.
Publications:
The Professional Geologist. m. adv.
Membership Directory. a.
Annual Meetings: Fall

American Institute of Real Estate Appraisers (1932)
430 North Michigan Ave., Chicago IL 60611
Exec. V. President: Richard B. Gaskins
Members: 6,400 *Staff:* 45-50
Annual Budget: $2-5,000,000 *Tel:* (312) 329-8559
Hist. Note: The only professional appraisal organization affiliated with the National Ass'n of Realtors. Awards the designations MAI (Member of the Appraisal Institute) and RM (Residential Member).
Publications:
Appraisal Journal. q.
The Appraiser. 10/yr.
Semi-annual meetings:
1987-Chicago, IL/May
1987-Hawaii/November

American Institute of Reciprocators (1938)
15601 Chilcoat Road, Sparks MD 21152
Exec. Secretary: John M. Julian
Members: 7-800 individuals *Staff:* 2-5
Annual Budget: $50-100,000
Hist. Note: Membership: $125/year.
Publication:
AIR Journal. q.
Annual Meetings: Spring/500

American Institute of Steel Construction (1921)
400 North Michigan Ave., Chicago IL 60611-4185
President: Neil W. Zundel
Members: 400-440 companies *Staff:* 55-60
Annual Budget: $2-5,000,000 *Tel:* (312) 670-2400
Hist. Note: Fabricators and erectors of structural steel. Maintains an office in Washington, DC. Membership: $50/yr. (individual), $1.40/ton/yr. (company).

00044 12 05 86 1233

Publications:
Modern Steel Construction. q.
The Engineering Journal. q.
Annual Meetings: Fall/400
1987-Boca Raton, FL(Boca Raton Hotel & Club)/Nov. 1-4
1988-White Sulphur Springs, WV(Greenbrier)/Sept. 11-14
1989-Colorado Springs, CO(Broadmoor)/Sept. 10-13
1990-White Sulphur Springs, WV(Greenbrier)/Sept. 9-12

American Institute of Technical Illustrators Ass'n (1974)
2424 Sylvan Lane, Alton IL 62002-5502
President: Dr. John F. White
Members: 648 individuals, 334 companies *Staff:* 2-5
Annual Budget: $500-1,000,000 *Tel:* (314) 458-2248
Hist. Note: Provides information on requirements and needs of technical illustrators. Membership: $75/year.
Publication:
Newsletter. m.
Annual Meetings: Fall
1987-Anaheim, CA
1988-Chicago, IL

American Institute of the History of Pharmacy (1941)
Pharmacy Bldg., Madison WI 53706-1508
Business Manager: Joann A. Esser
Members: 1,200 *Staff:* 2-5
Annual Budget: $50-100,000 *Tel:* (608) 262-5378
Hist. Note: Founded in Madison, Wisconsin as a non-profit historical agency specializing in pharmacy and drugs, with emphasis on the USA. Individual memberships are nation-wide, governed by a nationally representative Council. The historical and publishing office has been at the University of Wisconsin School of Pharmacy since the founding. Fosters investigations, publications, teaching, and interest in the history of pharmacy; collects historical records and makes them available; sponsors awards and site markers. Activities remain dependent upon volunteer officers and committees with the aid of part-time support personnel. Membership: $25/yr. (individual); $200/yr. (organization/company)
Publications:
AIHP Notes. q.
Pharmacy in History. q.
Annual Meetings: With American Pharmaceutical Ass'n
1987-Chicago, IL/March 29-April 1
1988-Atlanta, GA/March 12-16

American Institute of Timber Construction (1952)
333 W. Hampden Ave., Englewood CO 80110
Exec. V. President: Ewell H. Davenport
Members: 200 *Staff:* 12
Annual Budget: $500-1,000,000 *Tel:* (303) 761-3212
Hist. Note: Members are manufacturers and erectors of laminated structural timber, engineers, architects, etc.
Annual Meetings: Spring
1987-Destin, FL/April 19-22
1988-Bermuda
1989-Palm Springs, CA
1990-Key West, FL

American Institute of Ultrasound in Medicine (1951)
4405 East-West Hwy., Suite 504, Bethesda MD 20814
Director of Conventions: Barbara Hairfield
Members: 7,000 *Staff:* 11
Annual Budget: $1-2,000,000 *Tel:* (301) 656-6117
Hist. Note: Began at a meeting in a Denver hotel room of 24 physiatrists attending the annual meeting of the American Congress of Physical Medicine and Rehabilitation who wished to expand the scope of physical medicine as a new specialty. Members ar physicians, scientists, engineers and sonographers concerned with the use of diagnostic medical ultrasound. Membership: $85/year.
Publications:
Journal of Ultrasound in Medicine. m. adv.
Sonic Exchange. a. adv.
Scientific Meeting Abstracts. a.
Annual Meetings: Fall/5,000
1987-New Orleans, LA/Oct. 7-10
1988-Washington, D.C.(Convention Center)/Oct. 16-22

American Institutions Food Service Ass'n (1981)
277 East 6100 South, Salt Lake City UT 84107
Exec. Director: Marvin C. Zitting
Members: 90-100 *Staff:* 2-5
Annual Budget: $10-25,000 *Tel:* (801) 268-3000

American Insurance Ass'n (1964)
1025 Connecticut Ave., N.W., Suite 415, Washington DC 20036
President: Robert E. Vagley
Members: 171 companies *Staff:* 325-350
Annual Budget: over $5,000,000 *Tel:* (202) 293-3010
Hist. Note: Formed by a merger of the National Board of Fire Underwriters (founded in 1866), the Association of Casualty and Surety Companies (founded in 1927) and the old American Insurance Association (founded in 1953). Maintains a Washington office. Supports the American Insurance Association Political Action Committee. Membership fee based on market share.
Publications:
Newsletter. bi-w.
Directory.
Annual Meetings: November

American Insurers Highway Safety Alliance (1920)
1501 Woodfield Road, Suite 400 West, Schaumburg IL 60173
President: Franklin W. Nutter
Members: 16 companies *Staff:* 2-5
Annual Budget: $500-1,000,000 *Tel:* (312) 490-8500
Hist. Note: Formerly (1977) Nat'l Ass'n of Automotive Mutual Insurance Companies. Members are automobile insurance companies.
Annual Meetings: With Alliance of American Insurers

American Intellectual Property Law Ass'n (1897)
2001 Jefferson Davis Hwy., Suite 203, Arlington VA 22202
Exec. Director: Michael W. Blommer
Members: 5,500 *Staff:* 6-10
Annual Budget: $500-1,000,000 *Tel:* (703) 521-1680
Hist. Note: Formerly (1914) Patent Law Ass'n of Washington and (1984) the American Patent Law Ass'n. Membership in this voluntary bar ass'n consists of lawyers whose specialty is trademark, copyright and patent law. Field of concern is U.S. trademark, copyright and patent laws, and the federal rules and regulations that administer them. Member of Nat'l Council of Patent Law Ass'ns and the National Commission on Software Issues in the Eighties. Membership: $100/yr. (individual).
Publications:
Bulletin of AIPLA. bi-m. adv.
Journal of AIPLA. q.
Membership Directory. bien.
Economic Survey. bien.
Series of monographs.
Semi-annual Meetings: Spring and Mid-Winter
1987-Washington, DC/May
1988-Washington, DC/May
1989-Arlington, VA/May
1990-Washington, DC/May

American Internat'l Automobile Dealers Ass'n (1970)
1128 16th St., N.W., Washington DC 20036
President: Robert M. McElwaine
Members: 7,000-8,000 *Staff:* 15
Annual Budget: $1-2,000,000 *Tel:* (202) 659-2561
Hist. Note: Connected with the AIADA Political Action Committee. Founded as the Volkswagen American Dealers Association, it became the American Imported Automobile Dealers Association in 1972. Assumed its present name in 1980.
Publications:
AIADA Confidential Newsletter. m.
Internat'l Automobile Dealer. q.
Annual Meetings: May

American Internat'l Charolais Ass'n (1957)
11700 N.W. Plaza Circle, Box 20247, Kansas City MO 64195
Exec. V. President: Dr. Joe Garrett
Members: 3,500 *Staff:* 20-25
Annual Budget: $1-2,000,000 *Tel:* (816) 464-5977
Hist. Note: Formed (1957) by merger of American Charolais Breeders Ass'n and Internat'l Charolais Ass'n. Absorbed (1967) American Charbray Breeders Ass'n. Members are breeders and fanciers of Charolais beef cattle. Member of the National Society of the Livestock Record Associations and the United States Beef Breeds Council. Membership: $50/yr.
Publication:
Charolais Journal. m. adv.
Annual Meetings: Winter/350
1987-Denver, CO(Airport Hilton)/Jan. 12-15
1988-Denver, CO/Jan.
1989-Kansas City, MO

American Internat'l Marchigiana Soc. (1973)
Marky Cattle Ass'n, Box 198, Walton KS 67151-0198
Exec. Secretary: Martie Knudsen
Members: 250-280 cattle breeders *Staff:* 1
Annual Budget: under $10,000 *Tel:* (316) 837-3303
Hist. Note: An association founded in 1973 to foster raising of the marchigiana breed of cattle in the United States. Also known as the Marky Cattle Association. Membership: $35/yr., $100/lifetime.
Publication:
The Marky Newsletter. m. adv.
Annual Meetings: Kansas or Nebraska/March
1987-Wichita, KA(Kansas Coliseum & Red Coach Inn)/March 12-14

American Intraocular Implant Soc.
Hist. Note: Became American Soc. of Cataract and Refractive Surgery in 1986.

American Iron and Steel Institute (1855)
1000 16th St., N.W., Washington DC 20036
President: Robert B. Peabody
Members: 1,700 individuals, 60 companies *Staff:* 45
Annual Budget: over $5,000,000 *Tel:* (202) 452-7100
Hist. Note: The American Iron Ass'n was founded in 1855 and absorbed by the American Iron and Steel Ass'n in 1864. This, in turn, was absorbed in 1912 by the American Iron and Steel Institute which had been incorporated March 31, 1908 in New York. Promotes the interests of the iron and steel industry.
Publication:
Annual Statistical Report. a.
Annual Meetings: May in Washington, DC at the Capitol Hilton
1987-May 20-21
1988-May 18-19
1989-May 17-18

American Iron Ore Ass'n (1882)
915 Rockefeller Bldg., 614 Superior Ave., N.W., Cleveland OH 44113-1306
President: Lawrence C. Turnock, CAE
Members: 15-20 companies *Staff:* 2-5
Annual Budget: $250-500,000 *Tel:* (216) 241-8261
Hist. Note: Established as the Western Iron Ore Ass'n, it became the Lake Superior Iron Ore Ass'n in 1895 And assumed its present name in 1957. Members are iron mining companies.
Publications:
Statistical Reports - Ore Consumed & Inventory. m.
Iron Ore - Statistical. a.
Membership Directory. a.
Industry Directory. triennial.
Annual Meetings: June

American-Israel Chamber of Commerce and Industry (1953)
500 Fifth Ave., New York NY 10110-0380
Administrator: D. Ferrante
Members: 425-450 *Staff:* 3
Annual Budget: $100-250,000 *Tel:* (212) 354-6510
Publications:
Economic Horizons. a.
I.Q.: Israel Quality. q.
Made in Israel Directory. bi-a.
Annual Dinner Dance: Winter in New York, NY

American Jail Ass'n (1981)
Box 2158, Hagerstown MD 21742
Secretary: Richard Fordan
Members: 1,675 individuals *Staff:* 2
Annual Budget: $50-100,000 *Tel:* (301) 790-3030
Hist. Note: Members are jail personnel and persons whose work is closely associated with jails. The result of a merger between the National Jail Association (formed in 1939) and the National Jail Managers Association (formed in 1973). Membership: $20/yr.
Publications:
AJA Newsletter. q. adv.
Nprth American Jail Gazette. q. adv.
Annual Meetings: May
1987-Clearwater Beach, FL(Sheraton-Sand Key)/May 2-8/750
1988-Los Angeles, CA
1989-San Antonio, TX

American Jersey Cattle Club (1868)
Box 27310, Columbus OH 43227-0310
Exec. Secretary: Maurice E. Core
Members: 2,500 *Staff:* 40
Annual Budget: $2-5,000,000 *Tel:* (614) 861-3636
Hist. Note: Breeders of Jersey dairy cattle. Member of the Nat'l Soc. of Livestock Record Ass'ns. Membership: $50/lifetime.
Publication:
Jersey Journal. m. adv.
Annual Meetings: June
1987-Eau Claire, WI(Holiday)/June/400

American Jewelry Distributors Ass'n (1908)
Hist. Note: Became the American Jewelry Marketing Ass'n in 1986.

American Jewelry Marketing Ass'n (1908)
1900 Arch St., Philadelphia PA 19103
Exec. Director: William L. Robinson
Members: 200 *Staff:* 2-5
Annual Budget: $25-50,000 *Tel:* (215) 564-3484
Hist. Note: Formerly (until 1978) the Nat'l Wholesale Jewelers Ass'n and the American Jewelry Distributors Ass'n (until 1986).
Publications:
Newsletter. irreg.
Membership Directory. a.
Annual Meetings: March

American Jewish Correctional Chaplains Ass'n (1937)
10 East 73rd St., New York NY 10021
Exec. Director: Rabbi Paul L. Hait
Members: 90 *Staff:* 2
Annual Budget: under $10,000 *Tel:* (212) 879-8415
Hist. Note: Affiliated with the American Correctional Ass'n and the American Correctional Chaplains Ass'n. Formerly Nat'l Council of Jewish Correctional Chaplains and Nat'l Council of Jewish Prison Chaplains. Membership: $10/yr.
Semi-annual Meetings:
1987-Catskill Mts., NY(Homowock Hotel)/May

American Jewish Historical Soc. (1892)
2 Thornton Road, Waltham MA 02154
Director: Bernard Wax
Members: 3,500-3,600 *Staff:* 6-10
Annual Budget: $250-500,000 *Tel:* (617) 891-8110
Hist. Note: The Society is a museum, library and film archives and educational institution interested in public service. It is the repository for the archives of such organizations as the Council of Jewish Federations and the American Jewish Congress, and the Synagogue Council of America. Its collections provide information on Jewish communal and institutional life, social welfare services, immigration, synagogue records, prominent Jewish individuals, the Colonial Period and the early 19th century, and the ties between American Jewry and events overseas. Membership: $50/year.
Publications:
American Jewish History. q. adv.
Heritage (newsletter). bi-a.

00045 12 05 86 1233

Annual Meetings:
1987-Boston, MA

American Jewish Press Ass'n (1943)
12 Millstone Campus Drive, St. Louis MO 63146
President: Robert A. Cohn
Members: 150 newspapers, 50 individuals *Staff:* 1
Annual Budget: $10-25,000 *Tel:* (314) 432-3353
Hist. Note: Members are Jewish community newspapers. Formerly the American Association of English Jewish Newspapers. Membership: $100/yr. (individual); $280/yr. (full newspaper)
Publication:
Membership Bulletin. bi-w.
Semi-annual meetings: spring and fall
1987-Philadelphia, PA(Society Hill Sheraton)/May 19-22/60
1987-Miami, FL/November/85
1988-Kansas City, MO/May/60
1989-San Francisco, CA/May/60

American Judges Ass'n (1960)
300 Newport Ave., Williamsburg VA 23187-8798
Secretariat Representative: Keith A. Goehring
Members: 1,600
Annual Budget: $50-100,000 *Tel:* (804) 253-2000
Hist. Note: An independent organization of judges of all jurisdictions in the United States and Canada. Affiliated with the American Judges Foundation and the American Academy of Judicial Education. Formerly (1965) the Nat'l Ass'n of Municipal Judges and (1972) the North American Judges Ass'n. Membership: $50/year.
Publications:
Court Review. q.
AJA Benchmark Newsletter. q.
Annual Meetings: Fall/250
1987-Catskill Mountains, NY
1988-Nashville, TN

American Judicature Soc. (1913)
25 East Washington St., Suite 1600, Chicago IL 60602
Exec. V. President: George H. Williams
Members: 25,000 *Staff:* 22
Annual Budget: $1-2,000,000 *Tel:* (312) 558-6900
Hist. Note: Lawyers, judges, educators and others interested in the effective administration of justice.
Publications:
Court Improvement Bulletin. semi-a.
Judicature. semi-m.
Judicial Conduct Reporter. q.
Citizens Forum on the Courts. q.
Semi-annual Meetings: Winter & Summer

American Karakul Fur Sheep Registry (1965)
Hist. Note: Became the American Karakul Sheep Registry in 1985.

American Karakul Sheep Registry (1965)
Route 1, Box 179, Rice WA 99167
Secretary: Julie O'Neill
Annual Budget: under $10,000 *Tel:* (509) 738-6310
Hist. Note: Formerly Karakul Fur Sheep Registry, (1979) Empire Karakul Registry and (1985) American Karakul Fur Sheep Registry. The breed was imported from Russia as pelt animals--the young being killed at birth to produce Russian lamb pelts.
Annual Meetings: Not held

American Ladder Institute (1935)
111 East Wacker Dr., Chicago IL 60601
Exec. Director: James M. Dickinson
Members: 60 *Staff:* 3
Annual Budget: $100-250,000 *Tel:* (312) 644-6610
Hist. Note: Manufacturers of wood, metal and fiberglass ladders. Suppliers to the industry are eligible for membership as associates.
Annual Meetings: 987-Detroit, MI/Oct. 11-13
Semi-annual Meetings: Spring and Fall
1987-Hawaii/March 15-18
1987-Detroit, MI/Oct. 11-13

American Lamb Council
Hist. Note: Became an operating division of the American Sheep Producers Council.

American Laminators Ass'n (1984)
419 Norton Building, Seattle WA 98104-1584
Exec. Director: Arthur S. Langlie
Members: 22 companies *Staff:* 1
Annual Budget: $50-100,000 *Tel:* (206) 622-0666
Hist. Note: Trade Association for the thermoset decorative panel products industry. Concenered with promotion, marketing, certification, standards and other common industry interests. Firm Membership: $850/year.
Publication:
Bulletins. irreg.
Semi-annual meetings: Spring and Fall.

American Land Development Ass'n (1969)
Hist. Note: Became the American Resort and Residential Development Ass'n in 1985.

American Land Title Ass'n (1907)
1828 L St., N.W., Washington DC 20036
Exec. V. President: Michael B. Goodin
Members: 2,600 corporations *Staff:* 11-15
Annual Budget: $2-5,000,000 *Tel:* (202) 296-3671
Hist. Note: Membership is composed of title insurers, agents, title abstracters, lawyers and other specialists in real estate law. Formerly (1963) American Title Ass'n. Supports the Title Industry Political Action Committee.
Publications:
ALTA Capital Comment. m.
Title News. n. adv.
Management Newsletter-ALTA-Update.
Abstracter-Agent Newsletter.
Annual Meetings: Fall/950
1987-Seattle, WA(Westin)/Oct. 18-21
1988-Toronto, Canada(Hilton Harbour Castle)/Oct. 16-19/1,300
1990-Colorado Springs, CO(Broadmoor)/Oct. 7-11

American Landrace Ass'n (1950)
Box 2340, West Lafayette IN 47906
Exec. Secretary: Don Verhoff
Members: 350 *Staff:* 2-5
Annual Budget: $100-250,000 *Tel:* (317) 497-3718
Hist. Note: Members are breeders and fanciers of landrace swine. Member of the Nat'l Pedigree Livestock Council. Membership: $20/yr.
Publication:
Purebred Picture. m. adv.
Annual Meetings: January
1987-Murfreesboro, TN(Best Western)/Jan. 8-10/200

American Laryngological Ass'n (1878)
230 Lothrop St., Pittsburgh PA 15213
Secretary: Eugene N. Myers, M.D.
Members: 150 *Staff:* 1
Annual Budget: under $10,000 *Tel:* (412) 647-2110
Hist. Note: Members are individuals concentrating on the advancement of medicine and surgery of the upper aerodigestive tract. Membership: $150/year.
Publication:
Transactions. a.
Annual Meetings: Spring
1987-Denver, CO(The Fairmont)/April 25-26
1988-Palm Beach, FL(The Breakers)
1989-San Francisco

American Laryngological, Rhinological and Otological Soc. (1895)
P.O. Box 155, East Greenville PA 18041
Exec. Secretary: Frank N. Ritter
Members: 700-750 *Staff:* 1
Annual Budget: $10-25,000 *Tel:* (215) 356-8348
Hist. Note: Organized June 19, 1895 and incorporated December 5, 1917. Also known as the Triological Society.
Publications:
Triologistics. 3/yr.
Transactions. a.
Annual Meetings: Spring
1987-Denver, CO(Fairmont)/April 28-30
1988-Palm Beach, FL(Breakers)/April 26-28
1989-San Francisco, CA(Fairmont)/April 4-6
1990-Palm Beach, FL(Breakers)/May 1-3

American Law Institute (1923)
4025 Chestnut St., Philadelphia PA 19104
Director: Geoffrey C. Hazard, Jr.
Members: 2,751 *Staff:* 85
Annual Budget: $2-5,000,000 *Tel:* (215) 243-1600
Hist. Note: Membership, by invitation only, consists of lawyers, judges, educators and government officials interested in simplifying, clarifying and codifying the law. Its program of legal education is conducted in close association with the American Bar Ass'n. Membership: $150/year (practicing lawyers), $75/year (teachers and judges).
Publications:
Proceedings. a.
ALI Reporter. q.
Annual Meetings:
1987-Washington, DC(Mayflower)/May 19-22
1988-Chicago, IL(Hyatt-Regency)May 17-20
1989-Washington, DC(Mayflower)/May 16-19

American Law Student Ass'n (1949)
Hist. Note: Division of The American Bar Ass'n

American League of Financial Institutions (1949)
1511 K St., N.W., Suite 516, Washington DC 20005
President: Theresa L. Watson
Members: 76 institutions *Staff:* 6-10
Annual Budget: $250-500,000 *Tel:* (202) 628-5624
Hist. Note: Founded April 22, 1949 as the American Savings and Loan League. Assumed present name in 1984. Members are minority savings and loan institutions.
Publication:
The Ledger. m.
Annual Meetings: November

American League of Lobbyists (1978)
404 Fairchild Bldg., 499 S. Capitol St., Washington DC 20003
Exec. Director: L.W. "Bill" Bonsib
Members: 250 *Staff:* 1
Annual Budget: $50-100,000 *Tel:* (202) 546-7000
Hist. Note: Established in December 1978 in Washington to improve the image of lobbyists and to monitor efforts to reform laws concerning lobbying and related activities. Members are government relations specialists. Membership: $125/year.

American League of Professional Baseball Clubs (1900)
350 Park Ave., New York NY 10022
President: Robert W. Brown, M.D.
Members: 14 clubs *Staff:* 9
Annual Budget: $1-2,000,000 *Tel:* (212) 371-7600
Publication:
American League Redbook. a.
Annual Meetings: December

American Leather Chemists Ass'n (1903)
Tanners Building, University of Cincinnati, Cincinnati OH 45221
Exec. Secretary: Velma Becker
Members: 710 *Staff:* 2-5
Annual Budget: $50-100,000 *Tel:* (513) 475-2707
Hist. Note: Founded in 1903 and incorporated in New Jersey in 1937. Member of the Internat'l Union of Leather Chemists Societies. Membership: $50/yr.
Publication:
Journal of the American Leather Chemists Association. m. adv.
Annual Meetings: June/350-400
1987-Hershey, PA(Hershey Hotel)/June 14-18
1988-Mackinac Island, MI(Grand Hotel)/June 25-28

American Legal Clinic Ass'n (1977)
Hist. Note: Became the Association of Advertising Lawyers in September 1981.

American Legend Cooperative (1985)
400 Strander Blvd., P.O. Box 58308, Seattle WA 98188
Chief Exec. Officer: Tom Haass
Members: 1,500 *Staff:* 2-5
Annual Budget: $250-500,000 *Tel:* (206) 244-1303
Hist. Note: Formed in 1985 by a merger of the Great Lakes Mink Ass'n and the Emba Mink Breeders Ass'n (1942).
Publication:
Newsletter. 3-4/yr.

American Library Ass'n (1876)
50 East Huron St., Chicago IL 60611
Exec. Director: Thomas J. Galvin
Members: 43,500 *Staff:* 200-225
Annual Budget: over $5,000,000 *Tel:* (312) 944-6780
Hist. Note: An educational association of U.S. libraries and librarians, the ALA represents all types of libraries - state, public, school, academic and special libraries serving persons in government, commerce, armed services, hospitals, prisons and other institutions. ALA has 11 membership units (divisions) focusing on specific types of libraries or library services: American Ass'n of School Librarians, American Library Trustee Ass'n, Ass'n for Library Service to Children, Ass'n of College and Research Libraries, Ass'n of Specialized and Cooperative Library Agencies, Library Administration and Management Ass'n, Library Information and Technology Ass'n, Public Library Ass'n, Reference and Adult Services Division, Resources and Technical Services Division, and Young Adult Services Division. ALA also counts 56 independent library associations in states, regions and territories of the U.S. as chapters. 22 independent national and international organizations with purposes similar to the ALA are affiliates. Maintains a Washington, DC office.
Publications:
American Libraries. 11/yr. adv.
Booklist. semi-m. adv.
Choice. 11/yr. adv.
College and Research Libraries. q. adv.
Information Technology and Libraries. q. adv.
Library Resources and Technical Services. q. adv.
Library Technology Reports. bi-m.
Newsletter on Intellectual Freedom. bi-m.
R Q. q. adv.
School Library Media Quarterly. q. adv.
Top of the News. q. adv.
ALA Washington Newsletter. 12/yr.
College and Research Libraries News. 11/yr. adv.
Documents to the People. bi-m. adv.
Semi-Annual Meetings: Winter and Summer
1987-Chicago, IL/Jan. 17-22
1987-San Francisco, CA/June 27-July 2
1988-San Antonio, TX/Jan. 9-14
1988-New Orleans, LA/July 9-14
1989-Washington, DC/Jan. 7-12
1989-Dallas, TX/June 24-29
1990-Chicago, IL/Jan. 13-18
1990-Chicago, IL/June 23-28

American Library Trustee Ass'n (1961)
50 East Huron St., Chicago IL 60611
Exec. Director: Sharon L. Jordan
Members: 1,700-1,800 *Staff:* 2
Annual Budget: $25-50,000 *Tel:* (312) 944-6780
Hist. Note: Originally founded in 1890 as a section of the American Library Ass'n, became a division of the ALA in 1961. Membership: $30/yr. (individual), $50/yr. (company). Restricted to ALA members.
Publication:
ALTA Newsletter. bi-m.
Annual Meetings: Summer/250
1987-San Francisco, CA/June 27-July 2
1988-New Orleans, LA/July 9-14
1989-Dallas, TX/June 24-29
1990-Chicago, IL/June 23-28
1991-Atlanta, GA/June 29-July 4

00046 .12 05 86 1233

American Licensed Practical Nurses Ass'n (1984)
1110 Vermont Ave., N.W., Suite 840, Washington DC 20005
Exec. Director and General Counsel: Paul M. Tendler
Members: 3,000 *Staff:* 5
Annual Budget: $250-500,000 *Tel:* (202) 785-6300
Hist. Note: A professional association of licensed practical/vocational nurses. Membership: $25/year.
Publication:
ALPNA Newsletter. q.
Annual Meetings:
1988-San Francisco, CA
1989-New Orleans, LA

American Literary Translators Ass'n (1978)
Univ. of Texas-Dallas, Box 830688, Richardson TX 75083-0688
Exec. Secretary: Stephanie Stearns
Members: 800 *Staff:* 2
Annual Budget: $50-100,000 *Tel:* (214) 690-2093
Hist. Note: Translators into English of books in literature and the humanities. Maintains the Translation Clearinghouse and Translation Library. Currently funded by the University of Texas and a grant from the Nat'l Endowment for the Arts. Membership: $20/yr. (individual); $100/yr. (organization/company)
Publications:
ALTA Newsletter. q.
Translation Review. 3/yr. adv.
Annual Meetings: Fall/200
1987-Montreal, Quebec/Oct. 16-19

American Littoral Soc. (1961)
Sandy Hook, Highlands NJ 07732
Exec. Director: Derrickson W. Bennett
Members: 4,000-5,000 *Staff:* 2-5
Annual Budget: $100-250,000 *Tel:* (201) 291-0055
Hist. Note: Founded in 1961 at the Sandy Hook Marine Laboratory and incorporated in 1962 in New Jersey. Promotes the study and conservation of the coastal zone habitat. Membership: $20/yr.(regular)
Publications:
Coastal Reporter. q.
Underwater Naturalist. q. adv.
Annual Meetings: Fall
1987-New England/Oct. 9-12/200

American Logistics Ass'n (1920)
1133 15th St., N.W., Suite 500, Washington DC 20005
Exec. V. President: A. Kolbet Schrichte
Members: 450 companies, 2,500 individuals *Staff:* 14
Annual Budget: $1-2,000,000 *Tel:* (202) 466-2520
Hist. Note: A trade association of companies and individuals involved in marketing to the military - commissaries, exchanges, clubs, snack bars, ship's stores, mess halls, service stations, etc. Formerly the Quartermaster Ass'n and (1972) Defense Supply Ass'n. Membership: $50/yr.(individual); $1,100/yr.(company)
Publications:
Interservice Magazine. q. adv.
Worldwide Directory. a. adv.
Executive Briefing Newsletter. q.
Interchange Newsletter. q.
Annual Meetings: Fall
1987-Illinois
1988-Washington, DC
1989-New Orleans, LA

American Longevity Ass'n (1980)
330 South Spalding Drive, Suite 304, Beverly Hills CA 90212
President: Robert J. Morin, M.D.
Members: 1,200 *Staff:* 6-10
Annual Budget: $100-250,000 *Tel:* (213) 553-8554
Hist. Note: Professionals and laypeople interested in research in aging, arteriosclerosis and other degenerative diseases. Membership: $47/yr.
Publication:
Longevity Letter. m.

American Loudspeaker Manufacturers Ass'n (1965)
3413 North Kennicott Ave., Arlington Heights IL 60004
Exec. Director: C. Andrew Larsen, CAE
Members: 26 *Staff:* 2-5
Annual Budget: $10-25,000 *Tel:* (312) 577-7200
Hist. Note: Membership: $360/yr.
Publications:
Newsletter. q.
Manuals and Reports.
Semi-annual Meetings: Fall and Spring

American Low Power TV Ass'n (1978)
Hist. Note: Inactive in 1983.

American Luggage Dealers Ass'n (1975)
111 E. Wacker Drive, Suite 600, Chicago IL 60601
Exec. Director: Bonnie Sweetman
Members: 65 companies *Staff:* 6
Annual Budget: $100-250,000 *Tel:* (312) 644-6610
Hist. Note: Formed to develop, through mutual group action and cooperative effort, a progressive merchandise program such as publication of catalogs, specific merchandise opportunities, etc.
Publication:
"Giftables" Catalog. a.
Annual Meetings: February

American Lung Ass'n (1904)
1740 Broadway, New York NY 10019
Managing Director: James A. Swomley
Members: 5-6,000 *Staff:* 125-150
Annual Budget: over $5,000,000 *Tel:* (212) 315-8700
Hist. Note: Established as the National Association for the Study and Prevention of Tuberculosis, it became the National Tuberculosis Association in 1918, the National Tuberculosis and Respiratory Disease Association in 1968 and assumed its present name in 1973. A federation of state and local associations, the American Thoracic Society acts as its medical arm. Member of the Coalition for Health Funding in Washington. Has an annual budget of $9 million.
Publication:
American Review of Respiratory Disease. m. adv.
Annual Meetings: May
1987-New Orleans, LA(Sheraton/Marriott)/May 10-13
1988-Las Vegas, NV(Hilton)/May 8-11
1989-Cincinnati, OH(Clarion/Hyatt)/May 14-17
1990-Boston, MA(Sheraton)/May 20-23

American Machine Tool Distributors Ass'n (1925)
4720 Montgomery Lane, Bethesda MD 20814
Exec. V. President: Robert A. Gale
Members: 4-500 companies *Staff:* 15-20
Annual Budget: $1-2,000,000 *Tel:* (301) 654-1200
Hist. Note: Founded in Cincinnati by 22 charter distributors of machine tools. Sponsors the American Machine Tool Distributors' Association Political Action Committee.
Publications:
AMTDA Membership Directory. a.
Tool Talk.
Annual Meetings: Spring/500
1987-Orlando, FL(Disneyworld)/April 5-9
1988-San Diego, CA(Del Coronado)/March 6-9
1989-Boca Raton, FL(Boca Raton Hotel & Club)/April 30-May 3

American Maine-Anjou Ass'n (1969)
567 Livestock Exchange Bldg., Kansas City MO 64102
Exec. V. President: Steven P. Bernhard
Members: 950 *Staff:* 2-5
Annual Budget: $100-250,000 *Tel:* (816) 474-9555
Hist. Note: Formerly (1971) the Maine-Anjou Soc. and (1975) the Internat'l Maine-Anjou Ass'n. Members are breeders and fanciers of Maine-Anjou Beef Cattle. Member of the Nat'l Cattlemen's Ass'n. Membership: $35/yr.
Publications:
Maine-Anjou International.
Maine-Anjou Review.
Annual Meetings: Winter
1987-Ft. Worth, TX(Stockyards Hotel)/Feb. 1-3

American Malacological Union (1931)
3706 Rice Blvd., Houston TX 77005
Recording Secretary: Constance E. Boone
Members: 750-800 *Staff:* 1
Annual Budget: $10-25,000 *Tel:* (713) 668-8252
Hist. Note: An international society of individuals and organizations who are interested in the study of mollusks and shells.
Publications:
Bulletin. semi-a.
Newsletter. semi-a.
Annual Meetings: Summer
1987-Key West, FL(Casa Marina Marriott)/July 19-25
1988-Charleston, SC(University of Charleston)/July

American Malting Barley Ass'n (1945)
735 North Water St., Milwaukee WI 53202
President: Larry K. Neuman
Members: 12 companies *Staff:* 2-5
Annual Budget: $500-1,000,000 *Tel:* (414) 272-4640
Hist. Note: Founded as the Midwest Barley Improvement Ass'n, it became the Malting Barley Improvement Ass'n in 1954 and assumed its present name in 1982. Absorbed Malt Research Institute. Members are maltsters and brewers.
Publication:
Proceedings of Barley Improvement Conference. bien.
Annual Meetings: Usually November in Milwaukee, WI

American Management Ass'n (1923)
135 West 50th St., New York NY 10020
President & C.E.O.: Thomas R. Horton
Members: 75,000 *Staff:* 700
Annual Budget: over $5,000,000 *Tel:* (212) 586-8100
Hist. Note: Merger (1973) of the American Management Ass'n (1923), the American Foundation for Management Research (1960), the Internat'l Management Ass'n (1956), the Presidents Ass'n (1961) and the Soc. for Advancement of Management (1912), the oldest society in the U.S. devoted to all types of management education. Maintains offices in New York City, Atlanta, Chicago, and Washington, DC. Has an annual budget of approximately $100 million.
Publications:
Comp Flash. m.
Compensation & Benefits Review. bi-m.
Management Review. m.
Organizational Dynamics. q.
Personnel. m.
The President. m.
Management Solutions. m.
Supervisory Sense. m.
Entreprenurial Excellence. m.
Trainer's Workshop. m.
Annual Meetings: New York City, in September.

American Maritime Ass'n (1961)
485 Madison Avenue, New York NY 10022
Admin. Assistant: Marlena Schroeder
Members: 30 companies *Staff:* 1
Annual Budget: $100-250,000 *Tel:* (212) 319-9217
Hist. Note: Membership: participation fee of $800/yr. per vessel.
Annual Meetings: June, in New York City

American Marketing Ass'n (1915)
250 South Wacker Dr., Suite 200, Chicago IL 60606
Exec. V. President: Wayne A. Lemburg, CAE
Members: 46,000 *Staff:* 63
Annual Budget: over $5,000,000 *Tel:* (312) 648-0536
Hist. Note: Formerly (1915) Nat'l Ass'n of Teachers of Advertising; (1926) Nat'l Ass'n of Teachers of Marketing & Advertising; (1932) Nat'l Ass'n of Teachers of Marketing; (1937) merged with American Marketing Soc. to form the American Marketing Ass'n. Membership: $45/yr.
Publications:
Journal of Marketing. q. adv.
Journal of Marketing Research. q. adv.
Journal of Health Care Marketing. q. adv.
Marketing News. bi-w. adv.

American Massage and Therapy Ass'n (1943)
Hist. Note: Became the American Massage Therapy Ass'n in 1984.

American Massage Therapy Ass'n (1943)
Box 1270, Kingsport TN 37662
Exec. Secretary: James C. Bowling
Members: 4,200 *Staff:* 1
Annual Budget: $50-100,000 *Tel:* (615) 245-8071
Hist. Note: Members are professional massage therapists or technicians. Formerly (1984) the American Massage and Therapy Ass'n. Membership: $200/yr.
Publications:
Massage Therapy Journal. q. adv.
Newsletter. q.
Registry. a.
Annual Meetings: 2nd week in August/400
1987-Chicago, IL(McCormick)
1988-Washington, DC
1989-Colorado
1990-Texas
1991-Pennsylvania

American Mathematical Soc. (1888)
Box 6248, Providence RI 02940
Exec. Director: Dr. William J. Leveque
Members: 19,700 individuals, 500 institutions *Staff:* 200
Annual Budget: over $5,000,000 *Tel:* (401) 272-9500
Hist. Note: Organized in New York City on November 24, 1888 by six members of the mathematics department of Columbia University as the New York Mathematical Soc. Became the American Mathematical Soc. in 1894. Incorporated in the District of Columbia in 1923. Membership: $64/yr. Has a budget of about $13 million.
Publications:
Bulletin of the AMS. q.
Current Mathematical Publications. tri-w.
Employment Information in the Mathematical Sciences. 6/yr.
Mathematical Reviews. m. adv.
Mathematics of Computation. q. adv.
Mathematics of the USSR-Izvestiya. 6/yr.
Mathematics of the USSR-Sbornik. 8/yr.
Memoirs of the American Mathematical Society. bi-m.
Notices of the AMS. 8/yr. adv.
Proceedings. m.
Proceedings of the Steklov Institute of Mathematics. q.
Soviet Mathematics-Dokl. 3/yr.
Theory of Probability and Mathematical Statistics. 2/yr.
Transactions of the AMS. m.
Transactions of the Moscow Mathematical Society. a.
Vestinik of the Leningrad University (Mathematics).
Abstracts of the AMS. 6/yr.
Annual Meetings: With The Mathematical Association of America/2,800
1987-San Antonio, TX(Convention Center)/Jan. 21-24
1988-Atlanta, GA(Hyatt Regency)/Jan. 6-9
1989-Phoenix, AZ(Convention Center)/Jan. 11-14

American Meat Institute (1906)
1700 North Moore Street, Suite 1600, Arlington VA 22209
President: C. Manly Molpus
Members: 950-1,000 companies *Staff:* 30-35
Annual Budget: $2-5,000,000 *Tel:* (703) 841-2400
Hist. Note: The national trade organization of the meat packing and processing industry. Founded in 1906 as the Ass'n of American Meat Packers, it became the American Meat Packers Ass'n in 1919 and the American Meat Institute in 1940. Absorbed the American Meat Institute Foundation as its research arm. Absorbed the Nat'l Meat Ass'n in 1984. Connected with the American Meat Institute Political Action Committee.
Annual Meetings:
1987-Chicago, IL(McCormick Place)/Oct. 15-18/10,000-12,000
1988-Las Vegas, NV(Hilton)/Oct. 1-4/1,500-1,800

American Meat Science Ass'n (1948)
Nat'l Live Stock & Meat Board, 444 North Michigan Ave., Chicago IL 60611
Secy.-Treas.: H. Kenneth Johnson
Members: 900 *Staff:* 1
Annual Budget: $10-25,000 *Tel:* (312) 467-5520

00047 12 05 86 1233

Hist. Note: Established as the Reciprocal Meat Conference in 1948 and became the American Meat Science Ass'n in 1964. Promotes education and research in meat and related subjects.
Publications:
Directory of Members. a.
Proceedings of the Reciprocal Meat Conference. a.
Annual Meetings: June, at a university environment.
1987-St. Paul, MN(Univ. of MN)

American Medallic Sculpture Ass'n (1982)
American Numismatic Soc., Broadway & 155th St., New York NY 10032
President: Alan Stahl
Members: 175 *Staff:* 1
Annual Budget: under $10,000 *Tel:* (212) 234-3031
Hist. Note: Organized in February, 1982 in New York City by a group of medallic artists to promote improvement in medallic art. U.S. Member of The Federation Internationale de la Medaille. Membership: $25/yr.
Publication:
Medallic Sculpture. semi-a.
Annual Meetings: May

American Medical Ass'n (1847)
535 North Dearborn St., Chicago IL 60610-4377
Exec. V. President: James H. Sammons, M.D.
Members: 255,000 *Staff:* 1,000
Annual Budget: over $5,000,000 *Tel:* (312) 645-5000
Hist. Note: Established in Philadelphia in 1847 and incorporated in Illinois in 1897. Principal spokesman for the U.S. medical profession with about 2000 local and regional medical societies. Maintains a Washington office. It and its affiliates support numerous political action committees throughout the country. Has an annual budget of over $125 million. Membership: $360/year.
Publications:
American Medical News. w. adv.
Journal of the American Medical Ass'n. w. adv.
American Journal of Diseases of Children. m. adv.
Archives of Dermatology. m. adv.
Archives of General Psychiatry. m. adv.
Archives of Internal Medicine. m. adv.
Archives of Neurology. m. adv.
Archives of Ophthalmology. m. adv.
Archives of Otolaryngology. m. adv.
Archives of Pathology and Laboratory Medicine. m. adv.
Archives of Surgery. m. adv.
The Citation. bi-w.
Legislative Roundup. w. (during congressional sessions).
Semi-annual meetings: Summer and Winter

American Medical Care and Review Ass'n (1970)
5410 Grosvenor Lane, Suite 210, Bethesda MD 20814
Exec. V. President: Ronald A. Hurst
Members: 400 plans *Staff:* 11-15
Annual Budget: $1-2,000,000 *Tel:* (301) 493-9552
Hist. Note: Founded as American Ass'n of Foundations for Medical Care, it assumed its present name in 1983. AMCRA represents Individual Practice Associations (IPAs), IPA-type Health Maintenance Organizations (IPA/HMOs), Preferred Provider Organizations (PPOs), Foundations for Medical Care (FMCs), Peer Review Organizations (PROs) and other competitive medical plans. The Institute for Internat'l Health Initiatives (IIHI) is the non-profit foundation affiliate of the AMCRA. Supports the AMCRA Political Action Committee.
Publications:
AMCRA Newsletter. 10/yr.
PPO Newsletter. 10/yr.
PPO Directory. semi-a.
HMO Directory. a.
Annual Meetings: Fall
1987-Monterey, CA
1988-Boston, MA
1989-Dallas, TX
1990-San Diego, CA

American Medical Electroencephalographic Ass'n (1964)
850 Elm Grove Rd., Elm Grove WI 53122
Exec. Secretary: Robert H. Herzog
Members: 800 *Staff:* 1
Annual Budget: $100-250,000 *Tel:* (414) 784-3646
Hist. Note: Membership: $125/yr.
Publication:
Clinical EEG Journal. q.
Annual Meetings: Fall
1987-Savannah, GA(Savannah Sheraton)/Oct. 15-18/150

American Medical Peer Review Ass'n (1973)
440 First St., N.W., Suite 510, Washington DC 20001
Exec. V. President: Andrew Webber
Members: 123 institutions; 372 individuals *Staff:* 8-12
Annual Budget: $500-1,000,000 *Tel:* (202) 628-1853
Hist. Note: Established as the American Ass'n of Professional Standards Review Organizations to present the point of view of medical peer review groups to the Federal government Assumed its present name in 1983. Membership: $50/yr.(individual); variable fee for institutions.
Publications:
AMPRA Bulletin. 20/year.
AMPRA Review. bi-m. adv.
Annual Meetings:
1987-Washington, DC/May (Legislative Policy Conference)

American Medical Publishers' Ass'n (1961)
Administrative Secretariat, P.O. Box 944, Crystal Lake IL 60014
President: John F. Dill
Members: 48 companies *Staff:* 1
Annual Budget: under $10,000 *Tel:* (815) 459-3712
Hist. Note: Formerly (1974) Ass'n of American Medical Book Publishers. Has no paid staff.
Publication:
AMPA Newsletter. q.
Semi-annual Business Meetings and Biennial Workshop (Odd Years):
1987-Princeton, NJ(Hyatt Regency)/March 1-3/200

American Medical Record Ass'n (1928)
875 North Michigan Ave., Chicago IL 60611
Exec. Director: Rita Finnegan, RRA
Members: 27,000 *Staff:* 60
Annual Budget: $2-5,000,000 *Tel:* (312) 787-2672
Hist. Note: Founded in Boston in 1928 as the Ass'n of Record Librarians of North America. Became the American Ass'n of Medical Record Librarians in 1935. Incorporated in Illinois in 1953 and became the American Medical Record Ass'n in 1969. Membership: $80-$100/year.
Publication:
Journal of AMRA. m. adv.
Annual Meetings: October/3,000
1987-Baltimore, MD(Convention Ctr.)/Oct. 18-22
1988-Dallas, TX(Fairmont Hotel)/Oct. 9-14
1989-Orlando, FL(Marriott)/Oct. 22-27
1990-Seattle, WA(Convention Ctr.)

American Medical Student Ass'n (1950)
1890 Preston White Drive, Reston VA 22091
Exec. Director: Paul R. Wright
Members: 32,000 *Staff:* 25-30
Annual Budget: $1-2,000,000 *Tel:* (703) 620-6600
Hist. Note: Founded as the Student American Medical Ass'n, it assumed its present name in 1975. Membership: $35/4 years.
Publications:
Inside AMSA. m. adv.
New Physician. m. adv.
AMSA Task Force Newsletters. q. (each of 16 TF's)
AMSA Focus.
Annual Meetings: March
1987-New Orleans, LA
1988-Washington, DC

American Medical Technologists (1939)
710 Higgins Road, Park Ridge IL 60068
Exec. Director: Chester B. Dziekonski
Members: 16,500 *Staff:* 17
Annual Budget: $1-2,000,000 *Tel:* (312) 823-5169
Hist. Note: Founded in 1939 and incorporated in New Jersey. Grants the MT (Medical Technologist), MLT (Medical Laboratory Technician), and RMA (Registered Medical Assistant) designations. Membership: $75/yr.
Publications:
AMT Events. bi-m.
Published with the American Society for Medical Technology: Journal
of Medical Technology. bi-m. adv.
Annual Meetings: Summer
1987-New Orleans, LA(Sheraton)/July 26/700

American Medical Women's Ass'n (1915)
465 Grand St., New York NY 10002
Exec. Director: Carol Davis-Grossman
Members: 9,000 individuals *Staff:* 6-10
Annual Budget: $500-1,000,000 *Tel:* (212) 477-3788
Hist. Note: Founded November 1915 in Chicago and incorporated in Illinois in 1916 as the Medical Women's Nat'l Ass'n. Reincorporated in New York in 1924 and name changed to American Medical Women's Ass'n, Inc. in 1937. Membership restricted to women physicians, interns, residents and medical and osteopathic students. U.S. affiliate of the Medical Women's International Association. Membership: $10-$100/yr. (individual).
Publications:
Journal of the American Medical Women's Association. bi-m.
What's Happening in AMWA. q.
Annual Meetings: November
1987-Orlando, FL
1988-Chicago, IL
1989-San Diego, CA
1990-Boston, MA

American Medical Writers Ass'n (1940)
5272 River Rd., Suite 410, Bethesda MD 20816
Exec. Director: Lillian Sablack
Members: 2,600 *Staff:* 2-5
Annual Budget: $250-500,000 *Tel:* (301) 986-9119
Hist. Note: Originated September 25, 1940 at Rock Island, IL as the Mississippi Valley Medical Editors' Ass'n. Became American Medical Writers' Ass'n in 1948. Incorporated in Illinois in 1951. Concerned with the advancement and improvement of medical communications.
Publications:
AMWA Freelance Directory. every 1 1/2 yrs.
AMWA Membership Directory. a.
AMWA Newsletter. bi-m.
Annual Meetings: Fall
1987-Chicago, IL(Drake Hotel)/Nov. 4-7
1988-Philadelphia, PA(Hershey Hotel)/Oct. 26-29
1989-Boston, MA(The Lafayette Hotel)/Nov. 15-18

American Mental Health Counselors Ass'n (1977)
5999 Stevenson Ave., Alexandria VA 22304
Exec. Director: Dr. Patrick J. McDonough
Members: 10,000-11,000 *Staff:* 1
Annual Budget: under $10,000 *Tel:* (703) 823-9800
Hist. Note: A division of the American Ass'n for Counseling and Development. Membership: $30/yr.
Publications:
AMHCA Journal. q. adv.
AMHCA News. 7/yr.
Annual Meetings: With the American Ass'n for Counseling and Development
1987-New Orleans, LA/April 22-25

American Metal Detector Manufacturers Ass'n (1978)
2814 National Drive, Garland TX 75041
President: Charles Garrett
Members: 6 companies *Staff:* 1
Annual Budget: under $10,000 *Tel:* (214) 278-6151
Hist. Note: Has no paid staff. Officers change periodically but the above will remain the address of the association.

American Metal Importers Ass'n (1955)
Box 117, Demerest NJ 07627
President: Mr. Julie Lipper
Members: 25 *Staff:* 1
Annual Budget: under $10,000 *Tel:* (201) 487-1188
Hist. Note: Established as the American Importers of Brass and Copper Mill Products, it merged in 1964 with the American Association of Aluminum Importers and Warehouse Distributors and changed its name to the American Metal Importers Association in 1966. Presently operating at a reduced level of activity. Membership: $150/yr.

American Metal Stamping Ass'n (1942)
27027 Chardon Rd., Richmond Heights OH 44143
President: Jon E. Jenson
Members: 1,000 companies *Staff:* 16-20
Annual Budget: $2-5,000,000 *Tel:* (216) 585-8800
Hist. Note: Manufacturers of metal stampings, precision sheet metal fabrications and metal spinnings in the U.S. and Canada. Formerly (1961) Pressed Metal Institute, established in 1942. Sponsors the American Metal Stamping Ass'n Political Action Committee. Charter member of the Alliance of Metal working Industries with whom it works closely to make the metal stamping industry's position known on federal and state legislation and issues. Membership: $500/yr.
Publications:
Metal Stamping. m. adv.
Sources for Stampings. a. adv.
Annual Meetings: Fall

American Meteorological Soc. (1919)
45 Beacon St., Boston MA 02108
Exec. Director: Dr. Kenneth C. Spengler
Members: 9,700 individuals, 120-130 corporations *Staff:* 21-25
Annual Budget: $2-5,000,000 *Tel:* (617) 227-2425
Hist. Note: Founded December 29, 1919 in St. Louis and incorporated in the District of Columbia in 1920. Permanent headquarters were established in Boston in 1946 and the Society was reincorporated in Massachusetts in 1958. Certifies consulting meteorologists, and grants Seal of Approval to television and radio meteorologists.
Publications:
Bulletin of The AMS. m. adv.
Journal of Climate and Applied Meteorology. m.
Journal of the Atmospheric Sciences. m.
Journal of Physical Oceanography. m.
Monthly Weather Review. m.
Journal of Atmospheric and Ocean Technology. q.
Weather and Forecasting. q.
Meterological and Geoastrophysical Abstracts. a.
Annual Meetings: January

American Microchemical Soc. (1935)
Chemistry Dept., Rutgers University, 73 Warren St., Newark NJ 07102
Chairman: Dr. Roger Lalancette
Members: 150 individuals
Annual Budget: under $10,000
Hist. Note: Established as the New York-New Jersey section of the Microchemical Soc., it became the Metropolitan Microchemical Soc. in 1938 and assumed its present name in 1963. Has no paid staff; officers change annually. Most of the members are from the New York area; those who are not have joined mainly because of the discount they obtain on subscriptions to the Microchemical Journal.
Publication:
Microchemical Journal. q.

American Microscopical Soc. (1878)
Box 368, Lawrence KS 66044
Treasurer: Melvin W. Denner
Members: 6-700 *Staff:* 1
Annual Budget: $10-25,000 *Tel:* (913) 843-1234
Hist. Note: A professional society of microscopical biologists and microscopists established in 1878 to promote the use of the microscope in research and teaching. Membership: $24/yr. (individual), $35/yr. (company).
Publication:
Transactions of the American Microscopical Soc. q.
Annual Meetings: December
1987-New Orleans, LA/Dec. 27-31
1988-San Francisco, CA/Dec. 27-31

00048 12 05 86 1233

American Milking Shorthorn Soc. (1912)
Box 449, Beloit WI 53511
Office Manager and Treasurer: Leslie Ann Stuff
Members: 550 *Staff:* 4
Annual Budget: $100-250,000 *Tel:* (608) 365-3332
Hist. Note: Breeders and fanciers of Milking Shorthorn dairy cattle. Formed in 1912 as the Milking Shorthorn Club within the framework of the American Shorthorn Breeders Ass'n. Adopted its present name and became incorporated as a separate association in 1948. Member of the National Society of Livestock Record Associations and the Purebred Dairy Cattle Association.
Publication:
Journal of the Milking Shorthorn and Illawarra Breeds. m. adv.
Annual Meetings: April/300
1987-Jamesville, WI
1988-Portland, OR
1989-Springfield, MO

American Millinery Manufacturers Ass'n (1931)
Hist. Note: Established as the Eastern Women's Headwear Association it assumed its present name in 1965. Reported as defunct in 1982.

American Mining Congress (1897)
1920 N St., N.W., Suite 300, Washington DC 20036
President: John A. Knebel
Members: 500-550 companies *Staff:* 60
Annual Budget: over $5,000,000 *Tel:* (202) 861-2800
Hist. Note: AMC is an industry association that encompasses producers of most of America's metals, coal, industrial and agricultural minerals; manufacturers of mining and mineral processing machinery, equipment and supplies; and engineering and consulting firms and financial institutions that serve the mining industry. The AMC is both a clearinghouse for information and coordinator for action on behalf of the mining industry. Membership fee is based upon a rolling three-year average of sales or production of mineral commodities. (Minimum fee: $500/yr.)
Publication:
American Mining Congress Journal. m. adv.
Semi-annual meetings: Spring (Coal) and Fall (Mining)
1987-Cincinnati, OH/May 3-6/2,500
1987-San Francisco, CA/Sept. 13-16/3,500
1988-Chicago, IL/April 24-28/15,000
1988-Denver, CO/Sept. 25-28/2,500

American Montessori Soc. (1960)
150 Fifth Ave., New York NY 10011
Nat'l Director: Bretta Weiss
Members: 8,000 individuals; over 700 schools *Staff:* 6-10
Annual Budget: $500-1,000,000 *Tel:* (212) 924-3209
Hist. Note: Members are teachers, schools and others interested in the approach to early learning through self-motivation developed by Dr. Maria Montessori in 1907. Membership: $27.50/yr. (individual), $7.50/yr./child (school).
Publication:
AMS Constructive Triangle. q. adv.
Annual Meetings: Spring/over 500
1987-Miami Beach, FL(Konover Hotel)/April 24-26
1988-Cincinnati, OH(Clarion Hotel)/April 14-17

American Monument Ass'n (1904)
6902 North High St., Worthington OH 43085
Exec. V. President: Pennie L. Sabel
Members: 98 companies *Staff:* 2-5
Annual Budget: $250-500,000 *Tel:* (614) 885-2713
Hist. Note: Founded as the National Association of American Granite Producers, it became the American Granite Association in 1914 and assumed its present name in 1946. Members are quarries, fabricators and dealers of memorial and monument stone.
Publication:
Stone in America Magazine. m. adv.
Annual Meetings:
1987-Atlanta, GA

American Morgan Horse Ass'n (1909)
Box 1, Westmoreland NY 13490
Exec. Director: Georgine Winslett
Members: 12,000 *Staff:* 30
Annual Budget: $1-2,000,000 *Tel:* (315) 735-7522
Hist. Note: Established as the Morgan Horse Club, Inc., it assumed its present name in 1971. Members are breeders of the Morgan horse, a type of light horse which originated in Vermont around 1800. Membership: $20/yr. (individual); $30/yr. (family)
Publications:
The Morgan Horse Magazine. m. adv.
AMHA Newsletter. q.
The Morganizer (youth newsletter). q.
American Morgan Horse Register. a.
Annual Meetings: Fall
1987-Albuquerque, NM(Regent)/Feb. 19-23/500
1988-California
1989-Florida

American Mosquito Control Ass'n (1935)
P.O. Box 5416, Lake Charles LA 70606
Office Manager: Sharon A. Colvin
Members: 2,000 *Staff:* 2-5
Annual Budget: $100-250,000 *Tel:* (318) 474-2723
Hist. Note: Established in 1935 as the Eastern Ass'n of Mosquito Control Workers and assumed its present name in 1944. Incorporated in New Jersey (1948), California (1974) and Louisiana (1986). Members are involved in the control of mosquitoes and other vectors. Has members throughout the world, though the bulk come from Canada and the United States. Membership: $25/year.
Publications:
Journal of the AMCA. q. adv.
Mosquito Systematics. q.
Annual Meetings: Spring/800
1987-Seattle, WA/March 29-April 2
1988-Denver, CO/Feb. 21-25
1989-Boston, MA/April 2-6

American Movers Conference (1943)
2200 Mill Road, Alexandria VA 22314
President: Maj.Gen Charles C. Irions, USAF(Ret.)
Members: 1,350 *Staff:* 11-15
Annual Budget: $500-1,000,000 *Tel:* (703) 838-1930
Hist. Note: Formed by a merger of the Movers Conference of America (founded in 1943 as the Household Goods Carriers' Conference) and the American Movers Institute (founded in 1960). Affiliated with American Trucking Associations.
Publications:
American Mover. m. adv.
Moving Scene.
Military News.
Annual Meetings: Fall/3-400
1987-San Diego, CA(Intercontinental)/Oct. 11-14
1988-Ft. Lauderdale, FL(Marriott Harbor Beach)/Oct. 5-9

American Murray Grey Ass'n (1970)
1222 North 27th St., Suite 208, Box 30085, Billings MT 59107
Exec. Director: Joan L. Turnquist
Members: 400 *Staff:* 1-2
Annual Budget: $25-50,000 *Tel:* (406) 248-1266
Hist. Note: Established as a national breed registry for Murray Grey Cattle. Members are breeders and fanciers of Murray Grey Beef Cattle. Member of the National Society of Livestock Record Associations. Membership: $40/yr.
Publications:
Murray Grey News. bi-m. adv.
AMGA Herd Book. a. adv.
Annual Meetings: Fall
1987-Billings, MT/Oct.

American Mushroom Institute (1955)
907 East Baltimore Pike, Kennett Square PA 19348
Exec. Director: Charles R. Harris
Members: 300-350 *Staff:* 2-5
Annual Budget: $100-250,000 *Tel:* (215) 388-7806
Hist. Note: AMI represents growers and marketers of cultivated and exotic mushrooms in the United States. Its major purposes are research and information dissemination, the development of better methods of growth and marketing of mushrooms, representation of the industry to governmental bodies and increasing the consumption of mushrooms.
Publications:
Mushroom News. m. adv.
Membership Directory. a.
Annual Meetings:
1988-New Orleans, LA(Fairmont)/Oct. 6-10/500

American Music Conference (1947)
303 E. Wacker Dr., 12th Floor, Chicago IL 60601
Director/Administrative Services: Paul Bjoneberg
Members: 150 *Staff:* 2
Annual Budget: $100-250,000 *Tel:* (312) 856-8888
Hist. Note: A public relations and promotional arm of the music industry with members including retailers, firms, educators and music industry organizations interested in the promotion of music.
Publication:
Music USA-Industry Statistics a.
Annual Meetings: June

American Musicians Union (1948)
8 Tobin Court, Dumont NJ 07628
President: Ben Intorre
Members: 1,000
Annual Budget: under $10,000 *Tel:* (201) 384-5378
Hist. Note: Formed by a small group of musicians who chose to remain independent of the AFL-CIO merger of labor unions; joined the Nat'l Federation of Independent Unions in 1961. Membership is open to all musicians and vocalists; they are provided a contract book, but are not required to use the official contract form. Also has no binding wage scale. Membership: $20/yr. plus $10 initiation fee.
Publication:
Quarternote. q. adv.

American Musicological Soc. (1934)
201 South 34th St., Philadelphia PA 19104
Exec. Director: Alvin H. Johnson
Members: 3,200-3,300 *Staff:* 2-5
Annual Budget: $100-250,000 *Tel:* (215) 898-8698
Hist. Note: In 1929 the American Council of Learned Societies, feeling that "the history and science of music forms an important branch of learning," formed a standing committee on musicology. Out of this was formed the independent American Musicological Society in 1934, a learned society of professional musicologists and educators. Membership: $30/yr.
Publications:
Journal of The AMS. 3/yr. adv.
Newsletter. semi-a.
Directory. a.
Annual Meetings:
1987-New Orleans, LA(Sheraton)/Oct. 15-18/1,200
1988-Baltimore, MD(Omni Int'l)/Nov. 3-6/1,200
1989-Austin, TX(Hyatt Regency)/Oct. 26-29/1,000
1990-Oakland, CA(Hyatt Regency)/Nov. 7-10/1,200

American Mustang Ass'n (1962)
Box 338, Yucaipa CA 92399
President: George Snyder
Members: 100-150 *Staff:* 1
Annual Budget: under $10,000 *Tel:* (714) 685-5250
Hist. Note: Members are owners and breeders of the Mustang horse of the Western plains. Membership: $10/yr.
Publication:
AMA Newsletter. bi-m. adv.

American Name Soc. (1951)
7 East 14th St., Apt. 17-U, New York NY 10003
Exec. Secretary: Wayne H. Finke
Members: 900-1,000 *Staff:* 1
Annual Budget: $10-25,000 *Tel:* (212) 929-8434
Hist. Note: A professional society of onomatologists and others interested in the study of the origin and meaning of names, geographic, personal, scientific, etc. Membership: $25/yr. (individual); $30/yr. (company/organization).
Publications:
ANS Newsletter. q.
Names. q.
Annual Meetings: With Modern Language Ass'n in late December
1987-San Francisco, CA/Dec. 27-30/300

American Naprapathic Ass'n (1909)
5913 West Montrose Ave., Chicago IL 60634
Corresp. Secretary: Roy P. Krueger
Members: 125-150 manipulative therapists *Staff:* 1
Annual Budget: $50-100,000 *Tel:* (312) 685-6020
Hist. Note: Members are practitioners of naprapathy, the science and system of manipulation (administered by the hands) designed to cure physical ailments. Membership: $142/yr.
Publication:
The Voice of Naprapathy. q.
Semi-annual Meetings: 2nd Sunday in Jan. and last weekend in June

American Nat'l Metric Council (1973)
1010 Vermont Ave., N.W., Suite 320-321, Washington DC 20005
President: Albert M. Navas
Members: 600 *Staff:* 6
Annual Budget: $250-500,000 *Tel:* (202) 628-5757
Hist. Note: Coordinates metric activities of commerce and industry.
Publication:
Metric Reporter. m.
Annual Meetings: Spring
1987-Washington, DC/250

American Nat'l Standards Institute (1918)
1430 Broadway, New York NY 10018
President: Donald L. Peyton
Members: 240 ass'ns, 1,000 companies *Staff:* 110
Annual Budget: over $5,000,000 *Tel:* (212) 354-3300
Hist. Note: Originated in 1918 as the American Engineering Standards Committee. Became the American Standards Ass'n in 1928 and the United States of America Standards Institute in 1966. Incorporated in New York in 1948. Became the American Nat'l Standards Institute, Inc. in 1969. A member of the Internat'l Organization for Standardization, the Pacific Area Standards Congress, and the International Electrotechnical Commission. Promotes the knowledge and voluntary use of approved standards for industry, engineering, and safety design. Has an annual budget over $7 million.
Publications:
Catalog. a.
Standards Action. bi-w.
ANSI Reporter. bi-w.
Annual Meetings: Spring
1987-Arlington, VA(Marriott Crystal Gateway)/March 25-26/400

American Natural Soda Ash Corporation (1984)
8 Wright St., Westport CT 06880
Director, Planning & Development: Jim Skelly
Members: 6 companies
Annual Budget: over $5,000,000 *Tel:* (203) 226-9056
Hist. Note: A Webb-Pomerene Act association.

American Nature Study Soc. (1908)
5881 Cold Brook Road, Homer NY 13077
Treasurer: John A. Gustafson
Members: 750-1,000 *Staff:* 1
Annual Budget: under $10,000 *Tel:* (607) 749-3655
Hist. Note: Main concern is nature and conservation education. Membership: $13/year.
Publications:
Nature Study. q. adv.
ANSS Newsletter. q.
Annual Meetings: With American Ass'n for the Advancement of Science

American Nephrology Nurses' Ass'n (1969)
Box 56, North Woodbury Road, Pitman NJ 08071
Exec. Director: Ronald P. Brady
Members: 3,200 individuals *Staff:* 6-10
Annual Budget: $500-1,000,000 *Tel:* (609) 589-2187
Hist. Note: Nurses specializing in the structure, function and diseases of the kidneys, as well as dieticians, physicians, social workers and technicians. Formerly the American Ass'n of Nephrology Nurses and Technicians, assumed its present name in 1984. Membership: $50/yr.

00049 12 05 86 1233

Publications:
ANNA Journal. bi-m.
Update. bi-m.
Publications List Available.
Annual Meetings: Spring
1987-New York, NY(Marriott Marquis)/May 16-18
1988-Reno, NV(MGM Grand)/May 1-4

American Neurological Ass'n (1875)
Box 14730, Minneapolis MN 55414
Exec. Director: Jan W. Kolehmainen
Members: 750-800 *Staff:* 2
Annual Budget: $100-250,000 *Tel:* (612) 378-3290
Hist. Note: Founded in 1875 and incorporated in New York in 1947.
Publication:
Annals of Neurology. m. adv.
Annual Meetings: Sept.-Oct.
1987-San Francisco, CA(Hilton & Towers)/Oct. 18-20/7-800
1988-Philadelphia, PA(Wyndham)/Oct. 8-12/7-800
1989-New Orleans, LA(Sheraton)/Sept. 24-27/7-800

American Newspaper Publishers Ass'n (1887)
The Newspaper Center, 11600 Sunrise Valley Dr., Reston VA 22091
Exec. V. President and General Manager: Jerry W. Friedheim
Members: 1,400 *Staff:* 180
Annual Budget: over $5,000,000 *Tel:* (703) 648-1000
Hist. Note: Founded in Rochester, New York and established an office in New York City until 1972 when it moved to its present location. Represents over 90% of total U.S. daily and Sunday circulation, and includes newspapers from Canada and elsewhere in the Western Hemisphere. Sponsors the ANPA Foundation and ANPA Credit Bureau, Inc., a wholly-owned subsidiary. Has an annual budget of $12 million.
Publication:
Presstime. m.
Annual Meetings: Spring/2,400
1987-New York, NY(Waldorf)/April 27-28
1988-Honolulu, HI(Sheraton Waikiki)/April 25-27
1989-Chicago, IL(Hyatt Regency)/April 24-26
1990-Los Angeles, CA/April 23-25
1991-New York, NY/April 22-24
1992-Vancouver, BC/April 20-22

American Normande Ass'n (1974)
Hist. Note: Merged with the North American Normande Ass'n in 1985.

American Nuclear Energy Council (1975)
410 First St., S.E., Washington DC 20003
President: Edward M. Davis
Members: 100 companies *Staff:* 11-15
Annual Budget: $1-2,000,000 *Tel:* (202) 484-2670
Hist. Note: Members consists of companies engaged in some aspect of the nuclear fuel cycle, from mining, to engineering and fabrication, to waste disposal. Represents the industry point of view to Congress and Federal agencies.

American Nuclear Insurers (1957)
The Exchange, 270 Farmington Ave., Suite 245, Farmington CT 06032
President and C.E.O.: Burt C. Proom, CPCU
Members: 140-150 companies *Staff:* 115-120
Tel: (203) 677-7305
Hist. Note: A merger in 1974 of the Nuclear Energy Property Insurance Ass'n and the Nuclear Energy Liability Insurance Ass'n both established in 1957. Formerly (until 1978) the Nuclear Energy Liability Property Insurance Ass'n.

American Nuclear Soc. (1954)
555 North Kensington Ave., La Grange Park IL 60525
Exec. Director: Octave J. Du Temple
Members: 15,000 *Staff:* 90
Annual Budget: over $5,000,000 *Tel:* (312) 352-6611
Hist. Note: Established December 11, 1954 in the Nat'l Academy of Sciences in Washington, DC to advance science and engineering relating to the atomic nucleus and allied sciences and arts. Has an annual budget of $8 million.
Publications:
ANS News. m.
Nuclear Technology. m.
Nuclear News. m. adv.
Nuclear Science and Engineering. m.
RSTD Proceedings. a.
Transactions. semi-a.
Fusion Technology. bi-m.
Nuclear Standards News. m.
Semi-Annual Meetings: Spring and Fall
1987-Dallas, TX(Loews Anatole)/June 6-12
1987-San Francisco, CA(Hilton)/Nov. 8-13
1988-San Diego, CA(Town & Country)/June 12-17
1988-Washington, DC(Sheraton)/Nov. 13-18
1989-Atlanta, GA(Hilton)/June 4-8
1989-San Francisco, CA(Hilton)/Nov. 26-Dec. 1

American Numismatic Soc. (1858)
Broadway and 155th St., New York NY 10032
Director: Leslie A. Elam
Members: 2,219 *Staff:* 25-30
Annual Budget: $500-1,000,000 *Tel:* (212) 234-3130
Hist. Note: Organized April 16, 1858 in New York City under the present name. Incorporated in 1865 as the American Numismatic and Archeological Society but reverted to the present name in 1907. Its purpose is "the collection and preservation of coins and medals, with an investigation into the history, and other subjects connected therewith." Maintains a significant numismatic library and museum. Membership: $20/yr.
Publications:
ANS Museum Notes. a.
Newsletter. q.
Numismatic Literature. semi-a.
Numismatic Notes and Monographs. irreg.
Numismatic Studies. irreg.
Sylloge Nummorum Graecorum. irreg.
Annual Meetings: January

American Nurses' Ass'n (1896)
2420 Pershing Rd., Kansas City MO 64108
Exec. Director: Judith A. Ryan
Members: 188,000 *Staff:* 185
Annual Budget: over $5,000,000 *Tel:* (816) 474-5720
Hist. Note: Founded in New York City in 1896. Incorporated 1901 as the Nurses Associated Alumnae of the United States and Canada. Became the American Nurses' Ass'n in 1911 and was incorporated in the District of Columbia in 1917. The national professional organization of registered nurses, ANA is composed of 53 constituent state and territorial associations and over 900 district associations of nurses. Maintains a Washington office and sponsors N-CAP, a political action committee.
Publication:
The American Nurse. m. adv.
Biennial meetings: Even years in June.
1988-Louisville, KY/June 10-16

American Occupational Medical Ass'n (1915)
2340 South Arlington Heights Road, Arlington Heights IL 60005
Exec. Director: Dr. Donald L. Hoops
Members: 4,300 physicians *Staff:* 11-15
Annual Budget: $1-2,000,000 *Tel:* (312) 228-6850
Hist. Note: Established in Illinois in 1915 as the American Ass'n of Industrial Physicians and Surgeons and chartered in Illinois in 1916. Became the Industrial Medical Ass'n in 1951 and the American Occupational Medical Ass'n in 1974. Membership: $125/year (individual).
Publication:
Journal of Occupational Medicine. m. adv.
Annual Meetings: Spring/4,000
1987-Philadelphia, PA/April 26-May 1
1988-New Orleans, LA/April 24-29
1989-Boston, MA/April 30-May 5
1990-Houston, TX

American Occupational Therapy Ass'n (1917)
1383 Piccard Drive, Suite 300, Rockville MD 20850
Exec. Director: James J. Garibaldi
Members: 43,000 *Staff:* 85
Annual Budget: over $5,000,000 *Tel:* (301) 948-9626
Hist. Note: Formed in 1917 in Clifton Springs, NY with 5 members as the Soc. for the Promotion of Occupational Therapy, it became the American Occupational Therapy Ass'n and was incorporated in the District of Columbia in 1917. AOTA's purpose is to act as an advocate for occupational therapy in order to enhance the health of the public in its medical community and educational environments through research, education, action, service and establishment and endorsement of standards. Sponsored the formation of the American Occupational Therapy Foundation in 1965. Supports the American Occupational Therapy PAC. Has an annual budget of $6.3 million. Membership: $100/yr.
Publications:
American Journal of Occupational Therapy. m. adv.
Newsletter. m. adv.
Annual Meetings: Spring
1987-Indianapolis, IN(Hyatt & Convention Ctr.)/April 6-10/3,000
1988-Phoenix, AZ(Convention Ctr.)/April 17-20/3,500
1989-Baltimore, MD(Convention Ctr.)/April 16-19/3,500
1990-New Orleans, LA(Hyatt & Dome)/April 22-25/3,000

American Oceanic Organization (1967)
Box 2249, Springfield VA 22152
President: John Carey
Members: 600
Tel: (703) 451-1730
Hist. Note: Purpose is to stimulate discussion of current issues related to the developmental, economic and strategic importance of national oceanic, coastal and inland marine resources. Members are drawn from government agencies, U.S. Congress, industry and academia. Formerly (1968) the American Oceanology Ass'n. Membership: $30/yr. (individual); $300/yr. (organization/company).
Monthly Meetings: Washington, DC

American Oil Chemists' Soc. (1909)
508 S. Sixth St., Champaign IL 61820
Exec. Director: James Lyon
Members: 4,000 *Staff:* 16-20
Annual Budget: $1-2,000,000 *Tel:* (217) 359-2344
Hist. Note: Founded in 1909 in Memphis, TN as the Soc. of Cotton Products Analysts. Incorporated in Louisiana in 1922 as the American Oil Chemists' Soc. Encourages the advancement of technology and research in oils, other lipids and associated substances. Membership: $50/year (individual).
Publications:
Journal of the American Oil Chemists' Society. m. adv.
Lipids. m.
Annual Meetings: Spring
1987-New Orleans, LA(Fairmont)/May 6-10/1,600
1988-Phoenix, AZ(Convention Center)/May 8-12/1,700
1989-Cincinnati, OH(Conv. Center)/April 30-May 4/1,800

American Ontoanalytic Ass'n (1959)
Hist. Note: Reported as inactive in 1981.

American Ophthalmological Soc. (1864)
200 First St. S.W., Rochester MN 55905
Secy.-Treas.: Thomas P. Kearns, M.D.
Members: 250 individuals *Staff:* 1
Annual Budget: $25-50,000 *Tel:* (507) 284-3726
Hist. Note: The oldest specialty society in American medicine and the second oldest ophthalmology society in the world. Membership restricted to 225 active members. Awards the Howe Medal for distinguished service to ophthalmology.
Publication:
Transactions. q.
Annual Meetings: May, usually at The Homestead at Hot Springs, Va.

American Optometric Ass'n (1898)
243 North Lindbergh Blvd., St. Louis MO 63141
Exec. Director: O. Gordon Banks, CAE
Members: 24,000 individuals, 550-600 local societies *Staff:* 100-105
Annual Budget: over $5,000,000 *Tel:* (314) 991-4100
Hist. Note: Founded as the American Optical Ass'n in 1898. Became the American Optometric Ass'n in 1919. A federation of state optometric associations. Seeks to improve the quality, availability, and accessibility of eye/vision care, to represent the optometric profession to government, third parties and the public , and to assist members in conducting practices successfully in accordance with the highest standards of of patient care and efficiency. Affiliated with the International Optometric and Optical League. Connected with the American Optometric Ass'n Political Action Committee. Maintains Washington Office.
Publications:
AOA News. semi-m. adv.
Journal of The American Optometric Association. m. adv.
Annual Meetings: Summer
1987-Orlando, FL
1988-Chicago, IL
1989-New York, NY
1990-Hawaii

American Organization of Nurse Executives (1967)
840 North Lake Shore Dr., Chicago IL 60611
Exec. Director: Connie Curran, Ed.D. RN
Members: 3,700 *Staff:* 2-5
Annual Budget: $500-1,000,000 *Tel:* (312) 280-6409
Hist. Note: An affiliate of the American Hospital Association. Formerly (1978) American Soc. for Hospital Nursing Service Administrators and (1985) the American Soc. for Nursing Service Administrators. Membership: $100/year.
Publication:
Nurse Executive. q.
Annual Meetings: Fall

American Oriental Soc. (1842)
329 Sterling Library, Yale Station, New Haven CT 06520
Secretary: Jonathan Rodgers
Members: 1,350 *Staff:* 1
Annual Budget: $50-100,000 *Tel:* (203) 432-1842
Hist. Note: Established in 1842 to encourage research in the languages and literatures of Asia and North Africa. Member of the American Council of Learned Societies. Membership: $25/yr.
Publications:
Journal of The American Oriental Society. q.
American Oriental Series. irreg.
Annual Meetings: Spring
1987-Los Angeles, CA

American Ornithologists' Union (1883)
Nat'l Museum of Natural History, Smithsonian Institution, Washington DC 20560
Secretary: Stephen Russell
Members: 5,000
Annual Budget: $100-250,000 *Tel:* (202) 357-1970
Hist. Note: Founded September 29, 1883 at the American Museum of Natural History in New York City with 21 charter members. Incorporated 1888 in the District of Columbia. Affiliated with the American Ass'n for the Advancement of Science. Officers change annually, but mailing address remains as above. Membership: $26/yr.
Publications:
The Auk. q. adv.
Ornithological Newsletter. bi-m.
Ornithological Monographs. irreg.
Membership List. trien.
Checklist of North American Birds. irreg.
Annual Meetings: August
1987-San Francisco, CA/Aug. 9-14
1988-Fayetteville, AR(University of Arkansas)/Aug. 15-18/500
1989-Pittsburgh, PA/Aug. 7-11

American Orthodontic Soc. (1975)
9550 Forest Lane, Suite 215, Dallas TX 75243
Exec. Administrator: Murray Forsvall
Members: 2,000 *Staff:* 2-5
Annual Budget: $500-1,000,000 *Tel:* (214) 343-0805
Annual Meetings: With the Internat'l Ass'n for Orthodontics
1987-Orlando, FL(Hyatt)
1988-Las Vegas, NV(Caesar's Palace)

00050 12 05 86 1233

American Orthopaedic Ass'n (1887)
222 S. Prospect Ave., Park Ridge IL 60068
Exec. Secretary: Lois Stratemeier
Members: 300-325
Annual Budget: $2-5,000,000 *Tel:* (312) 823-7186
Hist. Note: Membership: $250/year.
Publication:
Journal of Bone and Joint Surgery. 8/yr. adv.
Annual Meetings: Summer/6-700
1987-Washington, DC(Convention Ctr.)/May 3-8/6,000

American Orthopaedic Soc. for Sports Medicine (1972)
70 West Hubbard St., Suite 202, Chicago IL 60610
Exec. Director: Sanford J. Hill
Members: 1,000 *Staff:* 2-5
Annual Budget: $50-100,000 *Tel:* (312) 644-2623
Hist. Note: Promotes the prevention, recognition and orthopedic treatment of sports injuries.
Publication:
American Journal of Sports Medicine. bi-m. adv.
Annual Meetings:
1987-Orlando, FL(Peabody Hotel)/June 29-July 2

American Orthopsychiatric Ass'n (1924)
19 West 44th St., New York NY 10036
Exec. Director: Marion F. Langer, Ph.D.
Members: 10-11,000 *Staff:* 11-15
Annual Budget: $500-1,000,000 *Tel:* (212) 354-5770
Hist. Note: Founded in New York City in 1924 and incorporated in New York in 1937. Interdisciplinary association of mental health professionals concerned with the study of human behavior and development, and the promotion of mental health.
Publications:
American Journal of Orthopsychiatry. q. adv.
Readings: A Journal of Reviews & Commentary in Mental Health. q. adv.
Annual Meetings: Spring/6,000
1987-Washington, DC(Hilton)/March 25-29
1988-San Francisco, CA(Hilton)/March 27-31
1989-New York, NY(Hilton)/March 31-April 4
1990-Miami Beach, FL(Fontainebleau Hilton)/April 25-29

American Orthotic and Prosthetic Ass'n (1917)
717 Pendleton St., Alexandria VA 22314
Exec. Director: William L. McCulloch
Members: 940 companies *Staff:* 15-20
Annual Budget: $500-1,000,000 *Tel:* (703) 836-7116
Hist. Note: Manufacturers and fitters of braces and artificial limbs. Formerly (1937) Ass'n of Limb Manufacturers of America and (1959) Orthopedic Applicance and Limb Manufacturers Ass'n. Sponsors and supports the American Orthotic and Prosthetic Association Political Action Committee.
Publications:
AOPA Almanac. m. adv.
Orthotics and Prosthetics. q. adv.
The AOPA Yearbook. a. adv.
Annual Meetings: October
1987-San Francisco, CA(Hyatt Regency Hotel)/Sept. 22-27

American Osteopathic Academy of Orthopedics (1941)
1217 Salem Ave., Dayton OH 45406
Secy.-Treas.: Donald Siehl, D. O.
Members: 250-275 *Staff:* 1
Annual Budget: $10-25,000 *Tel:* (513) 274-7151
Hist. Note: Affiliated with the American Osteopathic Ass'n. Membership: $250/yr.
Publications:
The Orthopod. m.
The AOAO Journal.
Annual Meetings: Spring
1987-Philadelphia, PA(Sheraton Society Hill)/June 5-6/150
1988-Dearborn, MI(Hyatt Regency)/May 6-7/200
1989-Phoenix, AZ(Camelback)/May 5-6/150-175
1990-Dearborn, MI(Hyatt Regency)/May 4-5/200-225

American Osteopathic Academy of Sclerotherapy (1938)
2222 Lindsay Michelle Drive, Alpine CA 92001
Exec. Secretary: Rayma Kulik
Members: 125-130 individuals *Staff:* 1
Annual Budget: under $10,000 *Tel:* (619) 445-6386
Hist. Note: Founded in 1938 as the American Osteopathic Soc. of Herniologists. Members are physicians who treat by injecting certain medications (sclerosants) to stimulate the production of fibrous connective tissue to strengthen weakened areas. Affiliated with American Osteopathic Ass'n.
Annual Meetings: With American Osteopathic Ass'n
1987-White Sulphur Springs, WV(Greenbrier)/May 22-24/100

American Osteopathic Academy of Sports Medicine (1975)
7034 West North Ave., Chicago IL 60635
Administrator: Thomas Miller
Members: 1,000 *Staff:* 1
Annual Budget: $100-250,000 *Tel:* (312) 622-9131
Hist. Note: Affiliated with the American Osteopathic Ass'n.
Publications:
Journal. q.
Membership Directory. a.
Annual Meetings: Fall, with the American Osteopathic Ass'n

American Osteopathic Ass'n (1897)
212 East Ohio St., Chicago IL 60611
Exec. Director: John P. Perrin
Members: 25,500 individuals *Staff:* 70-80
Annual Budget: $2-5,000,000 *Tel:* (312) 280-5800
Hist. Note: Organized in April 1897 as the American Osteopathic Ass'n for the Advancement of Osteopathy. Became the American Osteopathic Ass'n in 1901 and was incorporated in Illinois in 1923. A federation of divisional societies organized within state, provincial and foreign country boundaries, the present association has numerous affiliations with other osteopathic organizations. It institutes the official structure of the osteopathic profession. Maintains a Washington office. Sponsors and supports the Osteopathic Political Action Committee. Membership: $275/year (individual).
Publications:
The D.O. m. adv.
The Journal of the A.O.A. m. adv.
The Yearbook & Directory of Osteopathic Physicians. a. adv.
Annual Meetings: Fall
1987-Orlando, FL(Conv. Center)/Oct. 4-8
1988-Las Vegas, NV
1989-Anaheim, CA(Conv. Center)/Nov. 12-15

American Osteopathic College of Allergy and Immunology (1975)
Box 74, Lathrup Village MI 48076
Secretary: Laurie P. Ruderman
Members: 100 *Staff:* 1
Annual Budget: under $10,000 *Tel:* (313) 559-8808
Hist. Note: Provides an examining board to certify physicians in the areas of allergy and immunology. Affiliated with the American Osteopathic Ass'n. Membership: $75/year.
Publication:
Newsletter. 2-3/yr.
Annual Meetings: 2nd week in November

American Osteopathic College of Anesthesiologists (1952)
3511 Blue Jacket Dr., Lee's Summit MO 64063
Secy.-Treas.: A.A. Mannarelli, D.O.
Members: 325 physicians
Tel: (816) 373-4700
Publication:
Newsletter. 3/yr.
Annual Meetings: Fall/1,000
1987-Hawaii, HI(Sheraton Waikiki)/Oct. 11-16
1988-New York, NY(Hilton)/Oct. 16-19

American Osteopathic College of Dermatology (1955)
1847-A Peeler Road, Atlanta GA 30338
Exec. Director: Cathy M. Garris
Members: 200 individuals *Staff:* 2
Annual Budget: under $10,000 *Tel:* (404) 399-6865
Annual Meetings: With American Osteopathic Ass'n

American Osteopathic College of Nuclear Medicine (1979)
Hist. Note: Affiliated with the American Osteopathic Association. Address unknown in 1985-86.

American Osteopathic College of Pathologists (1954)
Hist. Note: Founded in Toronto, Canada in 1954 and incorporated in Illinois. Affiliated with the American Osteopathic Ass'n. Address unknown in 1985-86.

American Osteopathic College of Proctology (1927)
3210 Westminster, Pearland TX 77541-8933
Secy.-Treas.: Lester Tavel, DO
Members: 155
Annual Budget: under $10,000 *Tel:* (713) 997-1473
Hist. Note: Formed for the study of ano-rectal diseases. Membership: $75/yr.
Publication:
Procto-Review.
Annual Meetings: Fall
1987-Honolulu, HI(Sheraton Waikiki)/Oct. 18-21/50
1988-New York, NY

American Osteopathic College of Radiology (1941)
Route 2, Box 75, Milan MO 63556
Exec. Director: Pamela A. Smith
Members: 550 individuals *Staff:* 2
Annual Budget: $100-250,000 *Tel:* (816) 265-4991
Hist. Note: Membership: $325/yr.
Publication:
View Box. q.
Annual Meetings: Fall/125
1987-Tucson, AZ/Oct. 18-21

American Osteopathic College of Rehabilitation Medicine (1954)
Hist. Note: Affiliated with American Osteopathic Ass'n Formerly (1955) American Osteopathic Academy of Physical Medicine and Rehabilitation and (1970) American Osteopathic College of Physical Medicine and Rehabilitation. Address unknown since 1984.
Publications:
Directory. a.
Newsletter. irreg.
Annual Meetings: With American Osteopathic Ass'n

American Osteopathic Hospital Ass'n (1934)
55 West Seegers Road, Arlington Heights IL 60005
President: Richard A. Strano
Members: 300-320 *Staff:* 20-25
Annual Budget: $1-2,000,000 *Tel:* (312) 952-8900
Hist. Note: Maintains a Washington office. Sponsors the Osteopathic Hospital Political Action Committee.
Publications:
Directory of Osteopathic Hospitals. a. adv.
Directory of Postdoctoral Education. a. adv.
Health Highlights. bi-m.
Osteopathic Hospitals/Leadership. 8/yr. adv.
Capitol Insights.
Marketing Profiles.
Annual Meetings: Fall
1987-Kansas City(Hyatt)/Oct. 11-14
1988-Florida

American Otological Soc. (1868)
4500 San Pablo Road, Jacksonville FL 32224
Secy.-Treas.: Dr. D. Thane R. Cody
Members: 200
Annual Budget: $10-25,000 *Tel:* (904) 223-2000
Hist. Note: Organized July 22, 1868 in Newport, RI and incorporated in New York in 1926. Promotes research and education on diseases of the ear.
Publication:
Transactions of The American Otological Society. a.
Annual Meetings: Spring
1987-Denver, CO
1988-Palm Beach, FL

American Oxford Sheep Ass'n (1882)
Route 4, Ottawa IL 61350
Exec. Secretary: Wallace W. Watts
Members: 280 *Staff:* 2
Annual Budget: under $10,000 *Tel:* (815) 433-2946
Hist. Note: Founded in Xenia, Ohio as the American Oxford Down Record Ass'n and assumed its present name in 1981. Membership: $10/yr.
Publication:
Oxford Newsletter. semi-a.
Annual Meetings: Ottawa, IL/2nd Saturday in June

American Package Express Carriers Ass'n (1969)
2200 Mill Road, Alexandria VA 22314
Exec. Director: George H. Mundell
Members: 86 companies *Staff:* 3
Annual Budget: $50-100,000 *Tel:* (703) 838-1887
Hist. Note: Affiliated with Film, Air and Package Carriers Conference, which provides administrative support. Members are messenger courier companies and carriers of small packages.
Publications:
Service Directory. a.
Air Courier Rate and Routing Guide.
Annual Meetings:
1987-San Diego, CA(Intercontinental)/Feb. 6-11

American Pain Soc. (1978)
70 West Hubbard, Suite 202, Chicago IL 60610
Exec. Director: Marilyn Notkin
Members: 1,300 *Staff:* 2
Annual Budget: $50-100,000 *Tel:* (312) 644-2623
Hist. Note: Physicians, dentists, psychologists, nurses, physical and occupational therapists and scientists interested in the control of pain. American chapter of the Internat'l Ass'n for the Study of Pain. Incorporated in the District of Columbia in August, 1978.
Publication:
Abstracts. a.
Meet two years out of every three:

American Paint Horse Ass'n (1962)
Box 18519, Fort Worth TX 76118
Exec. Secretary: Ed Roberts
Members: 16-18,000 owners and breeders *Staff:* 45-50
Annual Budget: $2-5,000,000 *Tel:* (817) 439-3400
Hist. Note: Merger of American Paint Stock Horse and American Paint Quarter Horse Ass'ns. Collects, records, and preserves the pedigrees of Paint horses. Member of the Nat'l Soc. of Livestock Record Ass'ns. Membership: $20/yr.
Publications:
The Paint Horse Journal. m. adv.
Stud Book and Registry. bien.
Member Newsletter. q.
Annual Meetings: Fall
1987-St. Paul, MN/Sept. 24-26
1988-Calgary, Alberta

American Paper Institute (1964)
260 Madison Ave., 10th Floor, New York NY 10016
President: Red Cavaney
Members: 175 companies *Staff:* 140-145
Annual Budget: over $5,000,000 *Tel:* (212) 340-0600
Hist. Note: Formerly (1965) Pulp, Paper and Paperboard Institute U.S.A. Successor to American Paper and Pulp Ass'n (1878) and the Nat'l Paperboard Ass'n (1925). Absorbed the Bleached Converting and Packaging Paper Manufacturers Ass'n (1932); Glassine and Greaseproof Manufacturers Ass'n (1930); The Kraft Paper Ass'n (1933); Newsprint Service Bureau (1918); Printing Paper Manufacturers Ass'n (1933); Specialty Paper and Board Affiliates (1933); U.S. Pulp Producers Ass'n (1933); Vegetable Parchment Manufacturers Ass'n (1935); Writing Paper Manufacturers Ass'n (1861); Fourdrinier Kraft Board Institute (1977). Member of the Forest Industries Council. Has an annual budget of $10,000,000.

00051 12 05 86 1233

Publications:
API Report. m.
Monthly Statistical Summary. m.
Capacity Report. a.
Statistics of Paper. a.
Annual Meetings: March, in New York, NY(Waldorf Astoria)/2,000

American Park Rangers Ass'n (1981)
1100 N.E. 125th St., Miami FL 33161
Exec. Director: Gerald Arenberg
Members: 100-125 *Staff:* 1
Annual Budget: under $10,000 *Tel:* (305) 891-1700
Hist. Note: Formerly Nat'l Ass'n of Park Rangers (1982). Membership: $12/yr.
Publication:
Police Times.

American Parquet Ass'n (1963)
1660 Union National Plaza, Little Rock AR 72201
Exec. Director: Al Pollard
Members: 5 companies *Staff:* 2-5
Annual Budget: $25-50,000 *Tel:* (501) 375-5377
Hist. Note: Makers of hardwood parquet flooring.

American Patent Law Ass'n (1897)
Hist. Note: Became the American Intellectual Property Law Ass'n in 1984.

American Pavement Marking Ass'n (1981)
Hist. Note: Dissolved in 1984.

American Peanut Export Corporation
P.O. Box 458, Dothan GA 36302
Hist. Note: A Webb-Pomerene Act association.

American Peanut Research and Education Soc. (1969)
376 Ag Hall, Oklahoma State University, Stillwater OK 74078
Exec. Officer: Dr. J. Ronald Sholar
Members: 700 *Staff:* 1
Annual Budget: $100-250,000 *Tel:* (405) 624-6423
Hist. Note: Organized in Norfolk, Virginia July 1968 as the American Peanut Research and Education Association as an outgrowth of the Peanut Improvement Working Group dating back to 1957. The present name was adopted in 1979. Membership, which is drawn from government, academia and private industry, now includes individuals from over 20 countries. Membership: $15/yr. (individual), $$25/yr. (company).
Publications:
APRES Proceedings. a.
Peanut Research. q.
Peanut Science. semi-a.
Annual Meetings: July
1987-Orlando, FL(Orlando Marriott)/July 13-17/350
1988-Tulsa, OK(Sheraton Kensington)/250
1989-North Carolina

American Pediatric Soc. (1888)
450 Clarkson Ave., Box 49, Brooklyn NY 11203
Secy.-Treas.: Dr. Audrey K. Brown
Members: 1,000 *Staff:* 2-5
Tel: (718) 270-1692
Hist. Note: Organized September 18, 1888 and incorporated in New York in 1962.
Publication:
Pediatric Research. m.
Annual Meetings: Spring/3,000
1987-Anaheim, CA(Disneyland)/April 27-May 1
1988-Washington, DC(Sheraton Washington)
1989-Washington, DC(Sheraton Washington)
1990-Anaheim, CA(Hilton)
1991-New Orleans, LA(Hilton)

American Personnel and Guidance Ass'n (1952)
Hist. Note: Became the American Association for Counseling and Development in June 1983.

American Pet Products Manufacturers Ass'n (1958)
60 East 42nd St., New York NY 10165
Exec. Secretary: Jules Schwimmer
Members: 200-225 *Staff:* 2-5
Annual Budget: $500-1,000,000 *Tel:* (212) 867-2290
Hist. Note: Sponsors the Pet Information Bureau, established in 1978, with the purpose of teaching the public responsible pet ownership.
Publication:
Newsbriefs. bi-m.
Annual Meetings: June
1987-Washington, DC(Sheraton)/June 18-20
1988-Boston, MA(Boston Sheraton)

American Petroleum Institute (1919)
1220 L St., N.W., Washington DC 20005
President: Charles J. DiBona
Members: 6,000 individual members; 230 companies *Staff:* 480
Annual Budget: over $5,000,000 *Tel:* (202) 682-8000
Hist. Note: Incorporated March 20, 1919 in the District of Columbia. The petroleum industry's major trade ass'n, API is an umbrella organization for the major oil companies, independent oil producers and fuel distributors, service-station owners and other related concerns. Sets standards and performance requirements for the industry and publishes petroleum statistics. Membership: $250/year (individual).
Publications:
Petroleum Today. q.
Washington Report. w.
Other numerous pamphlets and manuals.
Annual Meetings: Rotates between Chicago (every third year), New York, San Francisco and Houston in November
1987-Chicago, IL(Conrad Hilton & Towers)/Nov. 8-10/2,500
1988-New York, NY(Hilton)/Nov. 13-15

American Petroleum Refiners Ass'n (1961)
Hist. Note: Merged April 1, 1983 with the Independent Refiners Association of America to form the American Independent Refiners Association.

American Pewter Guild, Ltd. (1958)
P.O. Box 1113, c/o Fischer Pewter, Midlothian VA 23113
Exec. Director: Nellie M. Fischer
Members: 45-50 manufacturers of pewter *Staff:* 1
Annual Budget: $25-50,000 *Tel:* (804) 379-3282
Hist. Note: The association perpetuates the traditions of European craft guilds in order to maintain high standards of quality for pewter, network with other international pewter guilds and trade organizations, and develop consumer awareness of the attributes of pewter products. Members represent both foreign and domestic concerns, large manufacturers and individual hobbyist.
Publication:
Pewter Review. q.
Semi-annual Meetings: Spring and Fall

American Pharmaceutical Ass'n (1852)
2215 Constitution Ave., N.W., Washington DC 20037
President: Dr. John F. Schlegel
Members: 50,000 *Staff:* 75
Annual Budget: over $5,000,000 *Tel:* (202) 628-4410
Hist. Note: Founded in Philadelphia in 1852 and incorporated in the District of Columbia in 1888, AphA is a national professional association of pharmacists. Its constituent sections include: Academy of Pharmacy Practice, Academy of Pharmaceutical Sciences, Academy of Pharmaceutical Management and Student AphA. Has an annual budget of $5 to $6 million. Administer a political action committee, AphA-PAC. Membership: $90/yr.
Publications:
Pharmacy Weekly. w.
American Pharmacy. m. adv.
Journal of Pharmaceutical Sciences. m. adv.
Annual Meetings: Spring/5,000
1987-Chicago, IL/March 28-April 1

American Philological Ass'n (1869)
617 Hamilton Hall, Columbia Univ., New York NY 10027
Secy.-Treas.: Harry B. Evans
Members: 2,500-3,000 *Staff:* 2-5
Annual Budget: $100-250,000 *Tel:* (212) 280-4051
Hist. Note: Organized in Poughkeepsie, New York in July, 1869 by classical scholars from the Classical Section of the American Oriental Society and the Greek Club of New York City. A member of the American Council of Learned Societies.
Publications:
Newsletter. q.
Positions for Classicals and Archaeologists. m.
Transaction and Proceedings. a.
American Classical Studies. irreg.
Philological Monographs. irreg.
Annual Meetings: Always Dec. 28-30

American Philosophical Ass'n (1900)
Univ. of Delaware, Newark DE 19716
Exec. Secretary: David A. Hoekema
Members: 6,800 individuals *Staff:* 3
Annual Budget: $100-250,000 *Tel:* (302) 451-1112
Hist. Note: Formed in New York City in November, 1901 with 98 charter members. Merged in 1927 with the Western Philosophical Ass'n and later with the Soc. of Philosophy, the latter a Pacific Coast organization. Members are professors of philosophy at the college level, graduate students and others with a special interest in the field. A member of the American Council of Learned Societies and the Federation Internationale des Societes de Philosophie. Membership: $15-60/year (individual) by income, $50/year (company).
Publications:
Proceedings and Addresses. 5/yr. adv.
Jobs for Philosophers. 5/yr.
Shopping List. 3/yr. adv.
Newsletters on Phil. & Law, Phil. & Medicine and Teaching Phil. adv.
Tri-annual Meetings: March, April and December
1987-San Francisco, CA(Golden Gateway Holiday Inn)/March 26-28
1987-Chicago, IL(Palmer House)/April 30-May 2
1987-New York, NY(Sheraton)/Dec. 27-30

American Philosophical Soc. (1743)
104 South Fifth St., Philadelphia PA 19106-3387
Exec. Officer: Dr. Herman H. Goldstine
Members: 600-625 *Staff:* 20-25
Annual Budget: $2-5,000,000 *Tel:* (215) 627-0706
Hist. Note: Founded in 1743 in Philadelphia by Benjamin Franklin, APS evolved in 1769 through a merger of the American Philosophical Soc. and the American Soc. for Promoting Useful Knowledge; chartered in 1780 in Pennsylvania. The full name is the American Philosophical Soc. Held at Philadelphia for Promoting Useful Knowledge. A member of the American Council of Learned Societies. Promotes and advances all useful branches of knowledge; provides financial assistance to scholars; publishes scholarly books, monographs and articles; and maintains a library.
Publications:
Memoirs. 5-7/yr.
Proceedings. q.
Transactions. 6-8/yr.
Yearbook. a.
Semi-Annual Meetings: Philadelphia, PA(Philsophical Hall)/April & Nov.

American Photographic Artisans Guild (1970)
1921 Mizpah Church Road, Rural Hall NC 27045
President: Linda Weaver
Members: 1,000
Annual Budget: under $10,000 *Tel:* (919) 725-5812
Hist. Note: Formerly Nat'l Professional Colorists of America and American Photographic Artists Guild. Affiliated with Professional Photographers of America. Membership: $20/yr.
Publication:
Palette Page. q.
Annual Meetings: In conjunction with Professional Photographers of America
1987-Rosemont, IL(Convention Headquarters)

American Physical Soc. (1899)
335 East 45th St., New York NY 10017
Exec. Secretary: W. W. Havens, Jr.
Members: 36,000 *Staff:* 50-60
Annual Budget: over $5,000,000 *Tel:* (212) 682-7341
Hist. Note: Organized May 20, 1899 at Columbia University under the leadership of Professors Ernest Merritt and Edward L. Nichols of Cornell and Arthur Gordon Webester of Clark University, a man who became known as the "Father of the American Physical Society." A constituent member of the American Institute of Physics. Has an annual budget of $8 million. Membership: $30/yr.
Publications:
Bulletin. m.
Physical Review Letters. w.
Reviews of Modern Physics. q.
The Physical Review. m.
Annual Meetings: March/4,000
1987-New York, NY(Hilton)/March 16-20
1988-New Orleans, LA(Marriott)/March 21-25
1989-St. Louis, MO(Cervantes Convention Center)/March 20-24
1990-Anaheim, CA(Anaheim Hilton)/March 26-30

American Physical Therapy Ass'n (1921)
1111 North Fairfax St., Alexandria VA 22314
Interim Exec. Director: Eugene Michels
Members: 41,000 *Staff:* 84
Annual Budget: over $5,000,000 *Tel:* (703) 684-2782
Hist. Note: Founded as the American Women's Therapeutic Ass'n, it became the American Physiotherapy Ass'n in 1922 and assumed its present name in 1948; APTA is a professional society of physical therapists. Affiliated with the National Health Council. Has an annual budget of $7 million. Membership: $115/yr.
Publications:
Clinical Management in Physical Therapy. q. adv.
Physical Therapy. m. adv.
Progress Report. 11/yr.
PT Bulletins. w.
Publication List Available.
Annual Meetings: June/4-5,000
1987-San Antonio, TX(Conv. Center)/June 28-July 2

American Physiological Soc. (1887)
9650 Rockville Pike, Bethesda MD 20814
Exec. Secy.-Treas.: Dr. Martin Frank
Members: 6,800 *Staff:* 50-55
Annual Budget: $2-5,000,000 *Tel:* (301) 530-7164
Hist. Note: Founded December 30, 1887 at a meeting held in the physiology laboratory of the College of Physicians and Surgeons, New York City. Incorporated in Missouri in 1923. A member of the Federation of American Societies for Experimental Biology (FASEB). Membership: $80/yr.
Publications:
American Journal of Physiology. m. adv.
Journal of Applied Physiology. m. adv.
Journal of Neurophysiology. bi-m. adv.
Physiological Reviews. q. adv.
The Physiologist. q. adv.
Semi-annual Meetings: Spring (with FASEB) and Fall
1987-Washington, DC(Conv. Center)/March 29-April 3
1987-San Diego, CA/Oct 11-16
1988-Las Vegas, NV(Conv. Center)/May 1-6
1988-Montreal, Canada(Conv. Center)/Oct. 9-14
1989-New Orleans, LA/Mar 19-24
1990-Washington, DC/April 1-6

American Phytopathological Soc. (1908)
3340 Pilot Knob Rd., St. Paul MN 55121
Exec. V. President: Raymond J. Tarleton
Members: 4,400 *Staff:* 25-30
Annual Budget: $1-2,000,000 *Tel:* (612) 454-7250
Hist. Note: Founded December 30, 1908 in Baltimore with 130 charter members and Incorporated in the District of Columbia in 1915. Promotes all aspects of knowledge of plant diseases and control. Affiliated with the American Ass'n for the Advancement of Science, the American Institute of Biological Sciences, and the Council for Agricultural Science & Technology. Membership: $61/yr. (individual), $250/yr. (organization).
Publications:
Phytopathology. m.
Plant Disease. adv.

00052 12 05 86 1233

Annual Meetings: Summer
1987-Cincinnati, OH(Clarion & Conv. Center)/Aug. 2-6/1,900
1988-San Diego, CA(Town & Country)/Nov. 13-17/2,000
1989-Richmond, VA(Marriott)/Aug. 20-24/1,800

American Pilots' Ass'n (1884)
1055 Thomas Jefferson St., N.W, Suite 404, Washington DC 20007
President: Capt. Pat J. Neely
Members: 59 state associations of pilots *Staff:* 2-5
Annual Budget: $100-250,000 *Tel:* (202) 333-9377
Hist. Note: Established the American Pilots' Ass'n Political Action Committee.
Biennial Meetings: Even years

American Pinzgauer Ass'n (1973)
RR 1, Box 104E, Kelley IA 50134
Secretary: Peg Meents
Members: 500 *Staff:* 2
Annual Budget: $50-100,000 *Tel:* (515) 597-3010
Hist. Note: Owners and breeders of the Pinzgaur breed of cattle, which originated in the Pinzgau Valley, Austria.
Publications:
North American Pinzgauer. q. adv.
Pinzgauer Newsline (newsletter). bi-m.
Annual Meetings: October
1987-Chehalis, WA/Oct.
1988-Tampa, FL/Feb.

American Pipe Fittings Ass'n (1938)
8136 Old Keene Mill Road, Suite B311, Springfield VA 22152
Exec. Director: Paul H. Engle, Jr.
Members: 30-35 companies *Staff:* 2-5
Annual Budget: $100-250,000 *Tel:* (703) 644-0001
Hist. Note: Formerly Pipe Fittings Mfrs. Ass'n Seeks to promote use of American pipe fittings, contribute to development of standards, collect statistics, and cooperate with government agencies on matters affecting the industry. Membership: $960/yr.
Annual Meetings:
1987-Houston, TX(Westin Oaks Hotel)/Jan. 26-28
1988-Williamsburg, VA(Kings Mill on the James)/May 18-20
1989-Rancho Mirage, CA(Marriott's Rancho Las Palmas)/Sept. 20-23

American Planning Ass'n (1917)
1776 Massachusetts Ave., N.W., Washington DC 20036
Exec. Director: Israel Stollman
Members: 22,000 *Staff:* 55-60
Annual Budget: $2-5,000,000 *Tel:* (202) 872-0611
Hist. Note: Membership is open not only to practicing planners (city, local, state, regional, rural, privately or publicly employed), but to elected officials, students and teachers, citizens and public administrators. Includes the American Institute of Certified Planners, a professional institute which provides national certification of planners. Membership fee depends upon salary range.
Publications:
JobMart. semi-m.
Journal of the American Planning Association. q. adv.
Land Use Law and Zoning Digest. m.
Planning Advisory Service Reports. 10/yr.
Planning. m. adv.
Zoning News. m.
Annual Meetings: Spring
1987-New York, NY/April 26-30
1988-San Antonio, TX/April 30-May 4
1989-Atlanta, GA/April 29-May 3

American Plywood Ass'n (1936)
P.O. Box 11700, Tacoma WA 98411
President: William T. Robison
Members: 140-150 mills *Staff:* 180
Annual Budget: over $5,000,000 *Tel:* (206) 565-6600
Hist. Note: Formerly (1964) Douglas Fir Plywood Ass'n. Trade association of producers of plywood and other structural panels. Members must meet the association's quality standards in order to use the APA Trademark on their products. Member of the Forest Industries Council. Has an annual budget of $11.5 million.
Publication:
Management Report. m.
Annual Meetings: Fall
1987-Portland, OR(Red Lion/Columbia River)/Oct.

American Podiatric Medical Ass'n (1912)
20 Chevy Chase Circle, N.W., Washington DC 20015
Exec. Director: Norman Klombers, D.P.M.
Members: 9,000 *Staff:* 35-40
Annual Budget: $2-5,000,000 *Tel:* (202) 537-4900
Hist. Note: Organized July 1, 1912 as the Nat'l Ass'n of Chiropodists. Incorporated in New York in 1912; became the American Podiatry Ass'n in 1958 and the American Podiatric Medical Ass'n in 1984. Over 50 component podiatry societies and numerous affiliates. Supports the Podiatry Political Action Committee. Membership: $500/yr. (individual).
Publications:
APMA News. m. adv.
Journal of the American Podiatry Association. m. adv.
Annual Meetings: August/2,000
1987-Washington, DC/Aug. 5-9
1988-Anaheim, CA/Aug. 17-21

American Podiatry Ass'n (1912)
Hist. Note: Became the American Podiatric Medical Ass'n in 1984.

American Police Academy
Hist. Note: Educational arm of the National Association of Chiefs of Police.

American Political Science Ass'n (1903)
1527 New Hampshire Ave., N.W., Washington DC 20036
Exec. Director: Dr. Thomas E. Mann
Members: 13,000 individuals and institutions *Staff:* 20-25
Annual Budget: $1-2,000,000 *Tel:* (202) 483-2512
Hist. Note: Founded in New Orleans in 1903 at a joint meeting of the American Historical and American Economic Associations. Incorporated in 1951 in the District of Columbia. Member of the American Council of Learned Societies. Membership: $40-$75/year.
Publications:
American Political Science Review. q. adv.
PS. q. adv.
NEWS for Teachers of Political Science. q. adv.
Annual Meetings: August-September/3,400
1987-Chicago, IL(Palmer House)/Sept. 3-6
1988-Washington, DC(Hilton)/Sept. 1-4
1989-Atlanta, GA(Hilton)/Aug. 31-Sept. 3
1990-San Francisco, CA(Hilton)/Aug. 30-Sept. 2

American Polled Hereford Ass'n (1901)
4700 East 63rd St., Kansas City MO 64130
President: Dr. T.D. Rich
Members: 16,000 *Staff:* 49
Annual Budget: $2-5,000,000 *Tel:* (816) 333-7731
Hist. Note: Established as the American Polled Hereford Cattle Club, it assumed its present name in 1907. Members are breeders and fanciers of Polled Hereford beef cattle. Membership: $15/yr.
Publication:
Polled Hereford World. m. adv.
Annual Meetings: Winter
1987-Jackson, MS/Feb. 12

American Polled Shorthorn Soc.
Box 156, Virginia IL 62691
Secretary: Darryl Rahn
Members: 1,400-1,500 *Staff:* 1
Annual Budget: under $10,000 *Tel:* (217) 452-3051
Hist. Note: Breeders and fanciers of polled shorthorn cattle.
Publication:
Shorthorn Country. m. adv.

American Polygraph Ass'n (1966)
Box 8037, Chattanooga TN 37411
Manager: Robbie S. Bennett
Members: 2,800 *Staff:* 2-5
Annual Budget: $50-100,000 *Tel:* (615) 892-3992
Hist. Note: A merger of Academy of Scientific Interrogation, American Academy of Polygraph Examiners, and Nat'l Board of Polygraph Examiners. Membership: $100/yr.
Publications:
APA Membership Directory. a. adv.
APA Newsletter. bi-m.
Polygraph. q. adv.
Polygraph Law Reporter. q.
Annual Meetings: August/400
1987-Fort Worth, TX(Worthington)/Aug. 2-7
1988-Miami, FL(Doral Hotel On-the-Beach)
1989-Virginia Beach, VA

American Polypay Sheep Ass'n (1979)
Hist. Note: Address unknown in 1985.

American Pomological Soc. (1848)
103 Tyson Bldg., University Park PA 16802
Business Manager: Dr. Loren D. Tukey
Members: 900-1,000 individuals *Staff:* 1
Annual Budget: under $10,000 *Tel:* (814) 863-2198
Hist. Note: Formed in Buffalo September 1, 1848 at a conference called by the New York Agricultural Soc. First called the North American Pomological Convention, the group became the American Pomological Congress in 1849 and the American Pomological Soc. in 1852. The first U.S. national association to promote fruit variety improvement. Affiliated with The Internat'l Soc. of Horticultural Science.
Publication:
Fruit Varieties Journal. a. adv.
Annual Meetings: With the American Society for Horticultural Science
1987-Orlando, FL(Hyatt Orlando)/Nov. 6-14
1988-East Lansing, MI(MI State Univ.)/Aug. 7-12
1989-Tulsa, OK/July 30-Aug. 4
1990-Arizona/Nov. 4-9

American Portrait Soc.
Hist. Note: Address unknown in 1986.
Publication:
Directory of American Portrait Artists. bien.

American Postal Workers Union (1971)
1300 L St., N.W., Washington DC 20005
President: Moe Biller
Members: 245,000-250,000 *Staff:* 70-80
Annual Budget: over $5,000,000 *Tel:* (202) 842-4200
Hist. Note: Merger (1971) of Nat'l Ass'n of Post Office and General Services Maintenance Employees (1937); Nat'l Ass'n of Special Delivery Messengers (1932); Nat'l Federation of Post Office Motor Vehicle Employees (1925); Nat'l Postal Union; United Federation of Postal Clerks (1966). Affiliated with AFL-CIO. Has a budget of about $18,000,000. Sponsors and supports the Political Fund Committee of the American Postal Workers Union. Membership: $77.40/yr.
Publication:
The American Postal Worker. m. adv.
Biennial Meetings: Even years in Summer

American Poultry Ass'n (1873)
26363 South Tucker Road, Estacada OR 97023
Secretary-Treasurer: Nona N. Shearer
Members: 3,500 *Staff:* 1
Annual Budget: $10-25,000 *Tel:* (503) 630-6759
Hist. Note: The oldest livestock organization in North America, established in Buffalo, New York by a group of poultrymen interested in fostering purebred poultry. Membership: $6/year (individual), $8/year (organization/company).
Publications:
APA News and Views. q.
APA Yearbook. a. adv.
Semi-annual Meetings:
1987-Houston, TX/Feb. 28-Mar. 1
1987-Claremore, OK/Nov. 27-31

American Poultry Historical Soc. (1952)
Poultry Science Dept., Univ. of WI, 1675 Observatory Drive, Madison WI 53706
Secy.-Treas.: Lou Arrington
Members: 250-300 *Staff:* 1
Annual Budget: under $10,000 *Tel:* (608) 296-2525
Hist. Note: Membership: $10/yr.
Annual Meetings: Usually with Southeastern Poultry and Egg Ass'n

American Powder Metallurgy Institute (1958)
105 College Rd. East, Princeton NJ 08540
Exec. Director: Kempton H. Roll
Members: 2,200 *Staff:* 12
Annual Budget: $100-250,000 *Tel:* (609) 452-7700
Hist. Note: Membership: $55/yr.
Publications:
P/M Technology Newsletter. m.
Internat'l Journal of Powder Metallurgy. q. adv.
Annual Meetings: Spring
1987-Dallas, TX/May-June/1,000

American Prepaid Legal Services Institute (1974)
750 N. Lake Shore Drive, Chicago IL 60611
Exec. Director: Alec M. Schwartz
Members: 275 companies *Staff:* 4
Annual Budget: $250-500,000 *Tel:* (312) 988-5751
Hist. Note: Founded by the American Bar Ass'n to serve as a national umbrella organization dedicated to the growth and development of prepaid legal services. Membership: $250/yr.
Publications:
API Newsbriefs. m.
Publications List Available.
Annual Meetings: Fall

American Printed Fabrics Council (1966)
Hist. Note: Formed by members of the Textile Distributors Association to promote printed fabrics; administrative support provided by TDA.

American Producers of Italian Type Cheese Ass'n (1941)
c/o Twin Town Cheese Factory Inc., Route 1, Almena WI 54805
President: John Ludy
Members: 80-85 *Staff:* 1
Annual Budget: under $10,000 *Tel:* (715) 357-3775
Hist. Note: Has no paid staff or established office. Major concern is coordinated response to Federal regulations.
Annual Meetings: Fall/50-75

American Production and Inventory Control Soc. (1957)
500 West Annandale Road, Falls Church VA 22046
Exec. Director: Michael J. Stack
Members: 62,000 individuals, 1,100 companies *Staff:* 59
Annual Budget: over $5,000,000 *Tel:* (703) 237-8344
Hist. Note: An organization of professionals in the field of production and inventory management. Sponsors Special Interest Groups (SIGs) for members intersted in collecting, validating and disseminating information in areas not included in the existing body of knowledge. Conducts a voluntary certification program leading to the "CPIM" (Certified in Production and Inventory Management) designation. Supports an Educational and Research Foundation. Has an annual budget of $9.5 million. National Membership: $40/yr.
Publications:
APICS News. m.
Production and Inventory Management. q.
Journal of Operations Management. q.
APICS Conference Proceedings. a.
Annual Meetings: Fall/6-8,000
1987-St. Louis, MO(Cervantes Conv. Center)
1988-Las Vegas, NV
1989-Orlando, FL
1990-New Orleans, LA
1991-Seattle, WA

00053 12 05 86 1233

American Productivity Management Ass'n (1975)
4711 Golf Road, Suite 412, Skokie IL 60076
Exec. Director: Leon N. Skan
Members: 300 companies *Staff:* 4
Annual Budget: $250-500,000 *Tel:* (312) 677-9141
Hist. Note: A not-for-profit membership organization of companies with corporate wide productivity improvement efforts. Membership: $850/yr.
Publications:
APMA Update. m.
Tapping the Network. m.
Annual Meetings: Tri-annual meetings

American Professional Racquetball Organization (1977)
5089 N. Granite Reef Road, Scottsdale AZ 85253
Exec. Director: Mort Leve
Members: 400-450 *Staff:* 1
Annual Budget: $10-25,000 *Tel:* (602) 945-0143
Hist. Note: Members are racquetball instructors and others who derive income from racquetball. Has twelve regional groups which sponsor clinics and workshops.
Publications:
Teacher's Court. q.
Teacher's Manual.
Annual Meetings: Summer or Fall

American Prosthodontic Soc. (1928)
919 North Michigan Ave., Ste. 2108, Chicago IL 60611
Exec. Director: Dr. Howard J. Harvey, DDS
Members: 1,200-1,300 *Staff:* 6-10
Annual Budget: $100-250,000 *Tel:* (312) 944-7618
Hist. Note: Membership: $150/year (individual).
Annual Meetings: Prior to the Chicago Dental Society
1987-Chicago, IL(Drake Hotel)/Feb. 12-13

American Protestant Correctional Chaplains' Ass'n (1953)
5235 Greenpoint Drive, Stone Mountain GA 30088
Director: Ralph Graham
Members: 375-400 *Staff:* 1
Annual Budget: $10-25,000 *Tel:* (404) 469-8294
Hist. Note: Works to improve the ministry of Protestant clergy in correctional institutions. Certifying agency for correctional chaplains. Membership: $25-$40/year.
Publications:
Journal of Pastoral Care.
Newsletter. q.
Annual Meetings: With American Correctional Ass'n and American Correctional Chaplains Ass'n.

American Protestant Health Ass'n (1920)
1701 E. Woodfield Road, Suite 311, Schaumburg IL 60195
President: Charles D. Phillips
Members: 1,600-1,700 *Staff:* 6-10
Annual Budget: $250-500,000 *Tel:* (312) 843-2701
Hist. Note: Formerly the American Protestant Hospital Ass'n, it assumed its present name in 1984.
Publication:
Bulletin. q. adv.
Annual Meetings: March/1,600
1987-New Orleans, LA(Regency Hyatt)/March 14-19

American Protestant Hospital Ass'n
Hist. Note: Became the American Protestant Health Ass'n in 1984.

American Psychiatric Ass'n (1844)
1400 K St., N.W., Washington DC 20005
Medical Director: Dr. Melvin Sabshin
Members: 32,000 *Staff:* 200
Annual Budget: over $5,000,000 *Tel:* (202) 682-6000
Hist. Note: A professional society consisting solely of psychiatrists. The oldest national medical society in the U.S., founded in Philadelphia in 1844 as the Ass'n of Medical Superintendents of American Institutions for the Insane. In 1892 it became the American Medico-Psychological Ass'n and in 1921 the American Psychiatric Ass'n. Incorporated in the District of Columbia in 1927. Has an annual budget of $18 million. Membership: $300/yr.
Publications:
American Journal of Psychiatry. m. adv.
Hospital and Community Psychiatry. m. adv.
Psychiatric News. m. adv.
Annual Meetings: Spring
1987-Chicago, IL/May 9-15
1988-Montreal, Canada/May 7-13
1989-San Francisco, CA/May 6-12

American Psychoanalytic Ass'n (1911)
309 E. 49th St., New York NY 10017
Admin. Director: Helen Fischer
Members: 2,800-2,900 *Staff:* 10-12
Annual Budget: $500-1,000,000 *Tel:* (212) 752-0450
Hist. Note: Formed to study and advance psychoanalysis; to advocate and maintain standards for the training and practice of psychoanalysis; and to foster the integration of psychoanalysis with other branches of medicine.
Publications:
A.Psa.A Newsletter. q.
Journal of the A.Psa.A. q.
Roster of the A.Psa.A.
Semi-Annual meetings: Spring and Fall
1987-Chicago, IL(Hyatt Regency)/May 6-10/1,500
1987-New York, NY(Waldorf-Astoria)/Dec. 16-20/2,000
1988-Montreal, Quebec(Queen Elizabeth)/May 4-8/1,500
1988-New York, NY(Waldorf)/Dec. 14-18/2,000

American Psychological Ass'n (1892)
1200 17th St., N.W., Washington DC 20036
Exec. Officer: Leonard D. Goodstein
Members: 90,000 individuals *Staff:* 390
Annual Budget: over $5,000,000 *Tel:* (202) 955-7600
Hist. Note: Founded at a meeting convoked by G. Stanley Hall at Clark University, July 8, 1892 and incorporated in the District of Columbia in 1925. Has a number of autonomous divisions which collectively advance psychology as a science, profession and means of promoting human welfare. Absorbed the American Psychology-Law Soc. in 1985. Membership $110/year. Has an annual budget of $40 million.
Publications:
APA Monitor. m. adv.
American Psychologist. m. adv.
Behavioral Neuroscience. bi-m. adv.
Contemporary Psychology. m. adv.
Developmental Psychology. bi-m. adv.
Journal of Abnormal Psychology. q. adv.
Journal of Applied Psychology. q. adv.
Journal of Comparative Psychology. q. adv.
Journal of Consulting and Clinical Psychology. bi-m. adv.
Journal of Counseling Psychology. q. adv.
Journal of Educational Psychology. q. adv.
Journal of Experimental Psychology: Animal Behavior Processes. q. adv.
Journal of Experimental Psychology: General. q. adv.
Journal of Experimental Psychology: Learning, Memory, and Cognition.
q. adv.
Journal of Experimental Psychology: Human Perception and Performance.
bi-m. adv.
Journal of Personality and Social Psychology. m. adv.
Professional Psychology. bi-m. adv.
Psychological Abstracts. m.
Psychological Bulletin. bi-m. adv.
Psychological Review. q. adv.
Psychology Today. m. adv.
Psychology and Aging.
PsycSCAN: Clinical Psychology. q.
PsycSCAN: Developmental Psychology. q.
PsycSCAN: LD/MR. q.
PsycSCAN: Applied Psychology. q.
Annual Meetings: August, with an attendance of 15,000
1987-New York, NY
1988-Atlanta, GA
1989-New Orleans, LA

American Psychology-Law Soc. (1968)
Hist. Note: Merged into the American Psychological Ass'n in 1985.

American Psychopathological Ass'n (1910)
Univ. of Iowa Medical School, Iowa City IA 52242
Secretary: Dr. Nancy Andreasen
Members: 500 individuals *Staff:* 1
Annual Budget: under $10,000 *Tel:* (319) 353-3932
Hist. Note: Founded in New York City in 1910. Promotes research on problems of psychopathology. Membership limited to 500.
Publications:
Comprehensive Psychiatry. bi-m. adv. (Editor: Dr. Ralph O'Connell,
St. Vincent's Hospital, New York, NY)
Annual Meetings: Always in New York City

American Psychosomatic Soc. (1943)
1311 A Dolley Madison Blvd., McLean VA 22101
Exec. Director: George K. Degnon
Members: 900 individuals *Staff:* 3
Tel: (703) 556-9222
Hist. Note: Organized in 1943 as the American Soc. for Research in Psychosomatic Problems and incorporated in 1944. Became The American Psychosomatic Soc., Inc. in 1948. Membership: $75/year.
Publication:
Psychosomatic Medicine. bi-m. adv.
Annual Meetings: March
1987-Philadelphia, PA(Sheraton Society Hill)/March 26-29

American Public Gas Ass'n (1961)
Box 1426, Vienna VA 22180
Exec. Director: Arie M. Verrips
Members: 200-225 *Staff:* 2-5
Annual Budget: $250-500,000 *Tel:* (703) 281-2910
Hist. Note: Members are municipal natural gas systems and their suppliers.
Publications:
Directory of Municipal Natural Gas Systems. a. adv.
Newsletter. semi-m.
Legislative Report. bi-w.
Meetings: Three times per year.

American Public Health Ass'n (1872)
1015 15th St., N.W., Washington DC 20005
Exec. Director: William H. McBeath, M.D.
Members: 32,000 individuals *Staff:* 65
Annual Budget: over $5,000,000 *Tel:* (202) 789-5600
Hist. Note: Established September 12, 1872 at Long Branch, NJ and incorporated in Massachusetts in 1918, APHA represents health professionals in over 40 disciplines in the development of health standards and policies. Member of the Coalition for Health Funding in Washington. Has an annual budget of $6.2 million. Membership: $60/yr. (individual); $750/yr. (organization/company)
Publications:
American Journal of Public Health. m. adv.
The Nation's Health. m. adv.
Annual Meetings: Fall
1987-New Orleans, LA
1988-Boston, MA
1989-Chicago, IL
1990-New York, NY
1991-Atlanta, GA
1992-Washington, DC

American Public Power Ass'n (1940)
2301 M St., N.W., Washington DC 20037
Exec. Director: Lawrence S. Hobart
Members: 1,700-1,800 *Staff:* 60
Annual Budget: $2-5,000,000 *Tel:* (202) 775-8300
Hist. Note: Members are publicly-owned electric utility systems. Membership: based on kWh sales and revenues.
Publications:
Public Power Weekly. w.
Public Power. bi-m. adv.
Public Power Innovations. a.
Legal Reporting Service. m.
APPA Washington Report.
Public Power Quarterly Communicator. q.
Human Resources Report. q.
DEED Digest. q.
Annual Meetings: Spring/2,000
1987-San Antonio, TX(Convention Center)/May 18-20
1988-Seattle, WA(Westin-Sheraton)/June 26-29

American Public Transit Ass'n (1882)
1225 Connecticut Ave., N.W., Suite 200, Washington DC 20036
Exec. V. President: Jack Gilstrap
Members: 800 *Staff:* 60
Annual Budget: over $5,000,000 *Tel:* (202) 828-2800
Hist. Note: Founded in 1882 as the American Street Railway Ass'n, it became the American Street and Inter-Urban Railway Ass'n in 1905 and later the American Electric Railway Ass'n. The name was changed in 1910 to American Transit Ass'n which merged in 1974 with the Institute of Rapid Transit (1961) to form the present organization.
Publications:
Passenger Transport. w. adv.
Transit Fact Book. a.
Annual Meetings: Fall
1987-San Francisco, CA(Hilton)/Sept. 27-Oct. 1/12,000
1988-Montreal, Quebec(Queen Elizabeth)/Oct. 2-6/2,500
1989-Atlanta, GA(Hilton)/Sept. 24-28/2,500
1990-Houston, TX/Sept. 30-Oct. 4/12,000

American Public Welfare Ass'n (1930)
1125 15th St., N.W., Suite 300, Washington DC 20005
Exec. Director: A. Sidney Johnson, III
Members: 6,000 individuals; 945 agencies *Staff:* 35-40
Annual Budget: $1-2,000,000 *Tel:* (202) 293-7550
Hist. Note: Members are individuals and institutions working in the social welfare field. Two Councils and six affiliate groups are a part of the association: the Nat'l Council of State Human Service Administrators, the Nat'l Council of Local Public Welfare Administrators, the American Ass'n of Public Welfare Attorneys, the American Ass'n of Public Welfare Information Systems Management, the Ass'n of Administrators of the Interstate Compact on the Placement of Children, the American Ass'n of Food Stamp Directors, the State Medicaid Directors' Ass'n and the Nat'l Ass'n of Public Child Welfare Administrators. Membership: $35/yr. (individual); agency dues vary.
Publications:
Public Welfare. q. adv.
Public Welfare Directory. a.
This Week in Washington. w.
W-Memo. 30/yr.

American Public Works Ass'n (1894)
1313 East 60th St., Chicago IL 60637
Exec. Director: Robert D. Bugher
Members: 24,000 *Staff:* 35-40
Annual Budget: $1-2,000,000 *Tel:* (312) 667-2200
Hist. Note: Government officials, engineers, administrators and others engaged in some aspect of public works. Merger (1937) of American Soc. of Municipal Engineers and Internat'l Ass'n of Public Works Officials. Maintains a Washington office.
Publications:
The APWA Reporter. m. adv.
The APWA Directory. a.
Annual Meetings: Fall

American Publicists Guild (1981)
Hist. Note: Ceased operations in 1985.

American Pulpwood Ass'n (1934)
1025 Vermont Ave., N.W., Suite 1020, Washington DC 20005
President: Kenneth S. Rolston, Jr. CAE
Members: 350-400 companies *Staff:* 16-20
Annual Budget: $500-1,000,000 *Tel:* (202) 347-2900
Hist. Note: Member of the Forest Industries Council. Consumers, producers and distributors of pulpwood.
Publications:
Technical Papers. m.
Technical Releases. m.
Annual Meetings: Spring/500
1987-Washington, DC(Mayflower)/March
1988-Boston, MA(Park Plaza)/March
1989-Memphis, TN(Peabody)/March
1990-Charlotte, NC(Adam's Mark)/March 31-April 4

00054 12 05 86 1233

American Purchasing Soc. (1969)
Box 543, Lisle IL 60532
Exec. Director: Harry E. Hough
Members: 925-950 individuals *Staff:* 2-5
Annual Budget: $10-25,000 *Tel:* (312) 852-1991
Hist. Note: Members include purchasing agents, buyers, procurement specialists, purchasing managers, purchasing executives and others who buy goods and services.
Publications:
Executips. m.
Journal of The American Purchasing Society. Semi-a.
Today's Executive. m.
Annual Meetings: September

American Pyrotechnics Ass'n (1948)
Box 213, Chestertown MD 21620
Exec. Director: Dr. John A. Conkling
Members: 170 companies *Staff:* 2-5
Annual Budget: $100-250,000 *Tel:* (301) 778-6825
Hist. Note: Fireworks importers, distributors, suppliers and manufacturers. Incorporated in Delaware. Absorbed the Nat'l Pyrotechnic Distributors Ass'n in 1979.
Publication:
Bulletin. m.
Annual Meetings: September
1987-New Orleans, LA/300

American Quarter Horse Ass'n (1940)
2701 I-40 East, Box 18519, Amarillo TX 79168
Exec. V. President: Ronald Blackwell
Members: 150,000 owners and breeders *Staff:* 225-250
Annual Budget: over $5,000,000 *Tel:* (806) 376-4811
Hist. Note: Organized in 1940 to collect, register, and preserve the pedigree of Quarter horses. Has an annual budget of $13 million. Member of the Nat'l Soc. of Livestock Record Ass'ns and the American Horse Council. Membership: $10/yr.
Publication:
Quarter Horse Journal. m. adv.
Annual Meetings: Spring

American Quaternary Ass'n (1969)
Dept. of Geological Sciences, Univ. of Michigan, Ann Arbor MI 48109
Secretary: Dr. William R. Farrand
Members: 1,000 individuals *Staff:* 1
Annual Budget: under $10,000 *Tel:* (313) 764-1473
Hist. Note: Established in 1969 and held its first meeting at Montana State University in Bozeman in 1970. Members are natural scientists studying the history of the environment during the last two million years. Affiliated with The Internat'l Quaternary Ass'n. Membership: $8/year.
Publications:
Qauternary Times (newsletter). q.
Program with Abstracts. bien.
Biennial meetings: even years
1988-Amherst, MA(Univ. of MA)/June/300-400

American Quick Printing Ass'n
Hist. Note: Reported as defunct in 1986.
Publication:
Newsletter. m.

American Rabbit Breeders Ass'n (1910)
1925 South Main St., Box 426, Bloomington IL 61701
Secretary: Glen C. Carr
Members: 35,000 *Staff:* 6-10
Annual Budget: $500-1,000,000 *Tel:* (309) 827-6623
Hist. Note: Members are Commercial or Fancy breeders of rabbits and guinea pigs--Commercial breeders being those who breed for profit and Fancy, those who breed for pleasure (about 90% of the membership). Founded as the Nat'l Breeders and Fanciers Ass'n, it became the American Pet Stock Ass'n in 1923, the American Rabbit and Cavy Ass'n in 1928 and assumed its present name in 1954. Has chartered about three dozen Specialty Clubs, all of which are listed in NTPA's companion directory, National Avocational Organizations, for fanciers of various types of rabbits. Membership: $10/yr.
Publications:
ARBA Yearbook. a. adv.
Domestic Rabbits. bi-m. adv.
Annual Meetings: Fall
1987-Portland, OR/Oct. 12-15/4,000

American Radio Ass'n (1948)
Hist. Note: Labor union affiliated with AFL-CIO. Merged into the International Organization of Masters, Mates and Pilots, Marine Division of the International Longshoremen's Association January 3, 1981.

American Radium Soc. (1916)
925 Chestnut St., Philadelphia PA 19107
Exec. Secretary: Suzanne Bohn
Members: 850 *Staff:* 1
Annual Budget: $50-100,000 *Tel:* (215) 574-3179
Hist. Note: Founded in 1916 by physicians interested in radiation therapy. Promotes the study of cancer in all its aspects.
Publication:
American Journal of Clinical Oncology. m. adv.
Annual Meetings: Spring/300
1987-London, England(The Portman)/April 6-10
1988-Seattle, WA/April 16-20
1989-St. Thomas, Virgin Islands

American Railway Bridge and Building Ass'n (1891)
18154 Harwood Ave., Homewood IL 60430
Secretary: Patricia Weissmann
Members: 700 individuals *Staff:* 1
Annual Budget: under $10,000 *Tel:* (312) 799-4650
Hist. Note: Established as Ass'n of Railway Superintendents of Bridges and Buildings, it assumed its present name in 1908. Members are rail officials and others concerned with the construction and maintenance of railway structures. Membership: $20/yr.
Publication:
Proceedings of Annual Convention. a. adv.
Annual Meetings: Fall
1987-Kansas City, MO
1988-Chicago, IL
1989-Toronto, Ontario

American Railway Car Institute (1915)
20280 Governors Hwy., Office Park 1, Suite 101, Olympia Fields IL 60461
President: E.T. Ahnquist
Members: 30 companies *Staff:* 2
Annual Budget: $50-100,000 *Tel:* (312) 747-0511

American Railway Development Ass'n (1906)
Consolidated Rail Corporation, 1812 Six Penn Center Plaza, Philadelphia PA 19103
President: Robert E. Mortensen
Members: 100-125 individuals
Annual Budget: under $10,000 *Tel:* (215) 977-4208
Hist. Note: Members are marketing, real estate and industrial development officers of railroads. Has no permanent staff; officers change annually.
Publications:
Newsletter. 3-4/yr.
Proceedings. a.
Annual Meetings: May
1987-Philadelphia, PA(Sheraton Society Hill)/May 20-22

American Railway Engineering Ass'n (1899)
50 F St., N.W., Suite 7702, Washington DC 20001
Exec. Director: Louis T. Cerny
Members: 4,400 *Staff:* 6
Annual Budget: $250-500,000 *Tel:* (202) 639-2190
Hist. Note: Members are railway officials responsible for the construction and maintenance of railroad fixed structures and rights of way. Membership: $35/yr.
Publication:
Area Bulletin. q. adv.
Annual Meetings: Chicago, IL(Palmer House)/March/1,000
1987-March 16-18
1988-March 21-23

American Rambouillet Sheep Breeders Ass'n (1891)
2709 Sherwood Way, San Angelo TX 76901
Secy.-Treas.: JoAnn Custer
Members: 1,088 breeders *Staff:* 2-5
Annual Budget: $100-250,000 *Tel:* (915) 949-4414
Hist. Note: Breeders and fanciers of Rambouillet sheep. Membership: $10/yr.
Publication:
Newsletter. q.
Annual Meetings: Summer
1987-Sedalia, MO/June 23-26

American Real Estate and Urban Economics Ass'n (1965)
School of Business, Dept. of Real Estate,ndiana University, 10th and Fee Lane, Bloomington IN 47405
Secy.-Treas.: Jeffrey D. Fisher
Members: 750-800 *Staff:* 1
Annual Budget: $10-25,000 *Tel:* (812) 335-3297
Hist. Note: Established and incorporated in 1965 as American Real Estate Ass'n. Name changed in 1966 to American Real Estate and Urban Economics Ass'n. Individuals both academically and commercially involved in real estate and urban economics.
Publication:
AREUEA Journal. q.
Annual Meetings: Participant in the Allied Social Science Ass'ns Conference

American Reciprocal Insurance Ass'n
Hist. Note: Dissolved December 31, 1982.

American Recovery Ass'n (1965)
4450 General DeGaulle Drive, Suite 1122,P.O. Box 6788, New Orleans LA 70174
Exec. Director: Huey Mayronne
Members: 420 repossession companies *Staff:* 3-5
Annual Budget: $500-1,000,000 *Tel:* (504) 367-0711
Hist. Note: The world's largest organization of professional finance adjusters and repossession specialists. ARA members represent banks, credit unions, finance companies, leasing companies, savings and loan associations and other financial institutions in the recovery of collateral on defaulted installment contracts. Formerly (1972) American Repossessors Ass'n, Inc.
Publications:
Directory. a. adv.
News and Views. m.
Annual Meetings: Fall/250
1987-Washington, DC(Willard Hotel)
1988-Hawaii

American Recreation Coalition (1979)
1331 Pennsylvania Ave., N.W., Suite 1001, Washington DC 20004
President: Derrick A. Crandall
Members: 100 ass'ns and companies *Staff:* 4
Annual Budget: $250-500,000 *Tel:* (202) 879-2560
Hist. Note: Formed by the recreation industry and related organizations to present a united approach to such topics of legislative interest as land use and energy, and to educate the government and the public about the value of recreation.

American Recreational Equipment Ass'n (1926)
Box 557, Delaware OH 43015
Exec. Director: Richard J. Coulter
Members: 60 companies *Staff:* 2-5
Annual Budget: $50-100,000 *Tel:* (614) 363-9715
Hist. Note: Formerly (1934) Manufacturers Division, Nat'l Ass'n of Amusement Parks. Members are makers of rides, walk-throughs and other equipment and devices purchased by carnivals, circuses and amusement parks. Membership: $150-1,200/yr.(Based on annual business).
Annual Meetings: November, with Internat'l Ass'n of Amusement Parks

American Red Brangus Ass'n (1956)
Box 1326, Austin TX 78767
Exec. Director: Penny Kammeier
Members: 1,300 *Staff:* 2-5
Annual Budget: $250-500,000 *Tel:* (512) 451-0469
Hist. Note: Founded in Austin, Texas. Breeders and fanciers of Red Brangus cattle, a crossbreed of Brahman and Angus cattle. Membership: $25/year.
Publications:
Bull Pen. 8/yr.
American Red Brangus Journal. q.
Membership Directory. a.
Annual Meetings: November in rotating locations

American Red Poll Ass'n (1883)
Box 35519, Louisville KY 40232
Secy.-Treas.: Carrie H. Schueler
Members: 500 *Staff:* 1
Annual Budget: $100-250,000 *Tel:* (502) 635-6540
Hist. Note: Breeders and fanciers of Red Poll beef cattle. Formerly (1976) Red Poll Cattle Club of America. Member of the National Society of Livestock Record Associations. Absorbed The Red Poll Beef Breeders Internt'l in 1979.
Publication:
Red Poll News. 3/yr. adv.
Annual Meetings: October

American Registry of Certified Professionals in Agronomy, Crops and Soils (1976)
677 South Segoe Rd., Madison WI 53711-1068
Director/Coordinator: Jean M. MacCubbin
Members: 2,000-2,500 *Staff:* 2-5
Annual Budget: $50-100,000 *Tel:* (608) 273-8080
Hist. Note: A membership activity of the American Soc. of Agronomy. Certifies professionals as agronomists, crop scientists/specialists, soil scientists/specialists and soil classifiers. Membership: $25-45/yr.
Annual Meetings: Winter, with the American Soc. of Agronomy
1987-Atlanta, GA/Nov. 29-Dec. 4/4,000

American Registry of Clinical Radiography Technologists (1955)
1616 South Blvd., Edmond OK 73013
Exec. Director: William A. McNeil
Members: 5-6,000 *Staff:* 2
Annual Budget: $100-250,000 *Tel:* (405) 348-5071
Hist. Note: Formed to maintain high standards of education and training in the field of radiography technology. Membership: $65/yr.
Publications:
X-Rayport. q. adv.
Newsletter. m.
Annual Meetings:
1987-Atlanta, GA/July 23-25/100

American Registry of Professional Entomologists (1970)
P.O. Box AJ, College Park MD 20740
Exec. Manager: William H. Wymer, CAE
Members: 1,900 *Staff:* 2-5
Annual Budget: $50-100,000 *Tel:* (301) 864-1336
Hist. Note: Professionals engaged in the study of insects and such related activities as pest management. Affiliated with the Entomological Soc. of America. Formerly (1973) American Registry of Certified Entomologists. Membership: $40/year.
Publications:
ARPE News. q.
Registry Notes. q.
Register of Registered Professional Entomologists. bien.
Annual Meetings: December/150-200
1987-Boston, MA(Sheraton)/Dec. 6-10
1988-Louisville, KY(Galt House)/Dec. 5-9
1989-Houston, TX

American Rehabilitation Counseling Ass'n (1957)
5999 Stevenson Ave., Alexandria VA 22304
Exec. Director: Dr. Patrick J. McDonough
Members: 3,500
Annual Budget: $25-50,000 *Tel:* (703) 823-9800

00055 12 05 86 1233

Hist. Note: Members are rehabilitation counselors working with people with physical, mental or emotional handicaps. Division of the American Ass'n for Counseling and Development. Membership: $15/yr.
Publications:
Rehabilitation Counseling Bulletin. q. adv.
ARCA News.
Annual Meetings: With American Ass'n for Counseling and Development
1987-New Orleans, LA/April 22-25

American Rental Ass'n (1955)
1900 19th St., Moline IL 61265
Exec. Director: C.A. Siegfried, Jr. CAE
Members: 3,100 *Staff:* 19
Annual Budget: $2-5,000,000 *Tel:* (309) 764-2475
Hist. Note: Formerly (1961) American Associated Rental Operators. Supports ARAPAC, its political action committee. In 1986, the Nat'l Rental Service Ass'n merged with ARA.
Publications:
Action News Newsletter. m.
Rental Age. m. adv.
Annual Meetings: Late Winter/7,000
1987-New Orleans, LA(Convention Ctr.)/Feb. 8-12

American Resort and Residential Development Ass'n (1969)
1220 L St., N.W., Suite 510, Washington DC 20005
President: Gary A. Terry
Members: 700 *Staff:* 17
Annual Budget: $1-2,000,000 *Tel:* (202) 371-6700
Hist. Note: Formerly (1985) the American Land Development Ass'n. Represents the recreational, resort and residential real estate development industry, including timesharing and R.V. camp resorts. Sponsors and supports the American Land Development Association Political Action Committee.
Publication:
Developments. m. adv.
Annual Meetings: Spring
1987-San Diego, CA/May 10-13
1988-Las Vegas, NV(Bally's)/April 17-20

American Restaurant China Council (1937)
Hist. Note: Address unknown in 1987.

American Retail Ass'n Executives (1918)
100 West 31st St., New York NY 10001
Exec. Director: Beatrice L. Cohen
Members: 100 *Staff:* 1
Annual Budget: under $10,000 *Tel:* (212) 244-8780
Hist. Note: Formerly the Nat'l Ass'n of Retail Secretaries, members are executives of retail merchants associations and similar organizations. Membership: $50/yr.
Annual Meetings: With Nat'l Retail Merchants Ass'n in New York, NY/January
1987-(Hilton)/Jan. 11-14

American Retail Federation (1935)
1616 H St., N.W., Washington DC 20006
President: Joseph P. O'Neill
Members: 185 companies and associations *Staff:* 11-15
Annual Budget: $1-2,000,000 *Tel:* (202) 783-7971
Hist. Note: A federation of national and state retail ass'ns. Concerns itself principally with national issues and problems affecting legislation and federal regulation. Divisions: Central Council of Nat'l Retail Ass'ns and Nat'l Conference of State Retail Ass'ns. Connected with the Retail Political Action Committee.
Annual Meetings: Washington, in May/175

American Retreaders' Ass'n (1957)
Box 17203, Louisville KY 40217
Mng. Director: Edward J. Wagner
Members: 1,600 companies *Staff:* 6-10
Annual Budget: $250-500,000 *Tel:* (502) 367-9133
Hist. Note: Founded as the Central States Retreaders' Association, it assumed its present name in 1964.
Annual Meetings: Louisville(Kentucky Fair and Exposition Center) in Apr./7-8,000
1987-April 10-12
1988-April 15-17

American Rheumatism Ass'n (1934)
17 Executive Park Drive, N.E., #480, Atlanta GA 30329
Exec. Vice President: Dallas Whaley
Members: 4,800 *Staff:* 16
Annual Budget: $1-2,000,000 *Tel:* (404) 633-3777
Hist. Note: The professional society for Rheumatologists. Members are physicians, teachers and individuals with an interest in disease of joints and connective tissues. Membership: $169/yr.
Publication:
Arthritis and Rheumatism. m. adv.
Annual Meetings:
1987-Washington, DC(Sheraton)/June 8-13/4,000
1988-Houston, TX/May 23-28
1989-Cincinnati, OH/June 13-17
1990-Seattle, WA/Oct. 28-Nov. 3

American Rhinologic Soc. (1954)
2929 Baltimore, Suite 105, Kansas City MO 64108
Secretary: Dr. Pat A. Barelli
Members: 300 *Staff:* 2
Annual Budget: under $10,000 *Tel:* (816) 561-4423
Hist. Note: Formed in Chicago in 1954 by Dr. M.H. Cottle. Members are physicians who are diplomates of the American Board of Otolaryngology; promotes research and education on disorders and surgery of the nose.
Publications:
Journal of International Rhinology. q. adv.
Newsletter. q.
Annual Meetings: Fall, with the American Academy of Otolaryngology

American Risk and Insurance Ass'n (1932)
Dept. of Finance, College of Business, Admin., Univ. of Central Florida, Orlando FL 32816
Exec. Director: Dr. David R. Klock
Members: 1,800 *Staff:* 1
Annual Budget: $50-100,000 *Tel:* (305) 275-2525
Hist. Note: A learned society devoted exclusively to furthering the science of risk and insurance through education, research, literature and communications. Formerly (1961) American Ass'n of University Teachers of Insurance. Membership: $40/yr.(individual); $500/yr.(sponsoring institution)
Publication:
Journal of Risk and Insurance. q. adv.
Annual Meetings: August
1987-Montreal, Quebec/Aug. 16-19
1988-Reno, NV/Aug. 14-17
1989-Denver, CO(Fairmont Hotel)
1990-Orlando, FL(World Marriott Hotel)

American Road and Transportation Builders Ass'n (1902)
525 School St., S.W., ARTBA Building, Washington DC 20024
President: Daniel J. Hanson, Sr.
Members: 4,000 *Staff:* 20-25
Annual Budget: $1-2,000,000 *Tel:* (202) 488-2722
Hist. Note: Founded as American Road Makers, it became the American Road Builders Association in 1910, absorbed the Better Highway Information Foundation in 1969 and assumed its present name in 1977. Sponsors the ARTBA-525-PAC, a political action committee.
Publications:
American Transportation Builder. q. adv.
ARTBA Newsletter. w.
Annual Meetings:
1987-Lake Buena Vista, FL/Nov. 18-22/1,200

American Roentgen Ray Soc. (1900)
880 Woodward Ave., Suite 105, Pontiac MI 48053
Secretary: Dr. Raymond A. Gagliardi, M.D.
Members: 1,600 physicians *Staff:* 2-5
Annual Budget: $50-100,000 *Tel:* (313) 858-3040
Hist. Note: Organized in 1900 in St. Louis as the Roentgen Soc. of the United States. Became the American Roentgen Ray Soc. in 1906. Incorporated in the District of Columbia in 1922. Membership: $100/yr. (individual).
Publication:
American Journal of Roentgenology. m. adv.
Annual Meetings: Spring/3,000
1987-MiamiBeach, FL(Fontainebleau)/April 22-May 1
1988-Los Angeles, CA(Bonaventure)/May 1-6
1989-New Orleans, LA(Hilton)/May 7-12
1990-Washington, DC(Sheraton)/May 10-18

American Romney Breeders Ass'n (1909)
29515 N.E. Weslinn Drive, Corvallis OR 97333
Secy.-Treas.: Dr. John H. Landers, Jr.
Members: 350 *Staff:* 1
Annual Budget: under $10,000 *Tel:* (503) 753-7603
Hist. Note: Breeders and fanciers of Romney sheep. Maintains a registry of pedigrees. Membership: $10/yr.
Annual Meetings: Nov./Dec.

American Rose Council (1982)
1625 Eye St., N.W., Suite 1015, Washington DC 20006
Exec. Officer: Andrew P. Murphy, Jr.
Members: 2-5 *Staff:* 1
Annual Budget: $10-25,000 *Tel:* (202) 728-1070
Hist. Note: Members are U.S. growers of roses in Central America united to oppose a suggested tariff on imported roses. The above address is the law office of Coan, Couture, Lyons, and Moorhead.

American Rural Health Ass'n (1977)
Hist. Note: Merged with Nat'l Rural Health Care Ass'n in 1986.

American Saddlebred Horse Ass'n (1891)
4093 Iron Works Pike, Lexington KY 40511
Director of Adminstration: Patricia G. Nichols
Members: 6,000 *Staff:* 15
Annual Budget: $500-1,000,000 *Tel:* (606) 259-2742
Hist. Note: Members are owners and breeders of Saddle horses united to record and preserve a five-generation pedigree of each horse of this breed in the world. Known as the American Saddle Horse Breeders Ass'n before 1980. Member of the Nat'l Soc. of Livestock Record Ass'ns. Membership: $35/yr.
Publications:
American Saddlebred Magazine. bi-m. adv.
American Saddle Horse Register. a.
Membership Directory. a. adv.
Annual Meetings:
1987-Lexington, KY(Marriott)/Feb. 27-March 2/350-400

American Safe Deposit Ass'n, The (1924)
330 West Main St., Greenwood IN 46142
Exec. Manager: Joyce A. McLin
Members: 2,800-2,900 banks *Staff:* 2-5
Annual Budget: $50-100,000 *Tel:* (317) 888-1118
Hist. Note: A federation of regional and local associations of banks, trust companies and others engaged in the safe deposit business. Formerly (1947) Nat'l Safe Deposit Advisory Council.
Publications:
"ACCESS" Magazine. q. adv.
Educational Bulletin. q.
Annual Meetings: Spring
1987-Providence, RI
1988-Durango, CO
1989-Orlando, FL

American Salmon Growers Ass'n
Hist. Note: Reported as inactive in 1984.

American Savings and Loan League (1964)
Hist. Note: Became the American League of Financial Institutions in 1984.

American Schizophrenia Ass'n (1964)
Huxley Institute, 900 North Federal Hwy., Suite 330, Boca Raton FL 33432
Exec. Director: Mary Roddy Haggerty
Members: 3,000 physicians and lay people *Staff:* 2-5
Annual Budget: $100-250,000 *Tel:* (305) 393-6167
Hist. Note: A division of the Huxley Institute for Biosocial Research promoting biochemical research and orthomolecular medicine for the prevention and amelioration of schizophrenia, alcoholism, learning disability, drug addiction, memory loss, diseases of the aging and related conditions affecting brain functions.
Publications:
Newsletter. q.
Orthomolecular Psychiatry. q. adv.

American School and Community Safety Ass'n (1959)
Hist. Note: Became The Safety Society in 1985.

American School Band Directors' Ass'n (1953)
Box 146, Otsego MI 49078
Office Manager: James J. Hewitt
Members: 1,000-1,100 individuals and companies *Staff:* 1
Annual Budget: $10-25,000 *Tel:* (616) 694-2092
Hist. Note: Organized in Cedar Rapids, Iowa, November 21-22, 1953. Members are professionally trained instrumental music teachers with at least seven years of experience. Officers change annually on January 1st. Membership: $45/year (individual), $35/year (institution).
Publication:
School Musician. m. (Sept-June). adv.
Annual Meetings: June/500
1987-Interlochen, MI/June 24-27

American School Counselor Ass'n (1953)
5999 Stevenson Ave., Alexandria VA 22304
Exec. Director: Dr. Patrick J. McDonough
Members: 10,000-11,000 *Staff:* 2-5
Annual Budget: $100-250,000 *Tel:* (703) 823-9800
Hist. Note: Division of the American Ass'n for Counseling and Development. Membership: $23/yr.
Publications:
Elementary School Guidance Counseling. 4/yr. adv.
The School Counselor. 5/yr. adv.
ASCA Counselor. irreg.
Annual Meetings: With American Ass'n for Counseling and Development
1987-New Orleans, LA/April 22-25

American School Food Service Ass'n (1946)
5600 S. Quebec Ave., Englewood CO 80111
Exec. Director: Ann G. Smith
Members: 55,000 *Staff:* 20-25
Annual Budget: $2-5,000,000 *Tel:* (800) 525-8575
Hist. Note: Members are individuals working in food services in educational institutions. Membership: $15/yr.
Publications:
School Foodservice Journal. 11/yr. adv.
ASFSA Business Report. bi-m.
Research Review. bi-a.
Annual Meetings: July/5-6,000
1987-Salt Lake City, UT(Hilton)/July 26-30
1988-San Antonio, TX(Hilton)/July 21-28
1989-Orlando, FL/July 23-27
1990-New Orleans, LA
1991-Seattle, WA

American School Health Ass'n (1927)
ASHA Building, 1521 South Water St., Box 708, Kent OH 44240
Exec. Director: Dana A. Davis
Members: 8,000 *Staff:* 6-10
Annual Budget: $250-500,000 *Tel:* (216) 678-1601
Hist. Note: Established in Albany, NY in 1927 as the American Ass'n of School Physicians. Became the American School Health Ass'n in 1938. Incorporated in Ohio in 1971. Membership: $55/yr.
Publication:
Journal of School Health. m. adv.
Annual Meetings: Fall/500

00056 12 05 86 1233

1987-Indianapolis, IN/Oct. 7-10
1988-Orlando, FL/Sept. 28-Oct. 1
1989-Illinois

American Schools Ass'n (1914)
201 South, 180 Allen Road, Atlanta GA 30328
President: Carl M. Dye
Tel: (404) 255-8308
Hist. Note: Main purpose is to coordinate educational counseling and consulting.
Publication:
Directory of College Transfer Information. bien.

American Schools of Oriental Research (1900)
4243 Spruce St., Philadelphia PA 19104
Office Administrator: Susan M. Wing
Members: 170 institutions *Staff:* 6-10
Annual Budget: $500-1,000,000 *Tel:* (215) 222-4643
Hist. Note: Universities and individuals involved in Middle Eastern research, especially Biblical archaeology, ancient history. Membership: $15-66/yr.
Publications:
Biblical Archaeologist. q.
Bulletin. q.
Journal of Cuneiform Studies. 2/yr.
Newsletter. 8/yr.

American Science Film Ass'n (1962)
Hist. Note: Dissolved in 1982.

American Scientific Glassblowers Soc. (1954)
1507 Hagley Rd., Toledo OH 43612
Exec. Secretary: Theodore Bolan
Members: 900 *Staff:* 1
Annual Budget: $50-100,000 *Tel:* (419) 476-5478
Hist. Note: Founded in Wilmington, DE in 1952 and incorporated in Delaware in 1954. Membership: $45/yr.
Publications:
Fusion. q. adv.
Symposium Proceedings. a.
Annual Meetings: Summer
1987-Boston, MA/July 27-Aug. 2
1988-Atlantic City, NJ/June 26-July 1
1989-Milwaukee, WI
1990-Atlanta, GA

American Scotch Highland Breeder's Ass'n (1948)
Box 81, Remer MN 56672
Secretary: Francine A. Hogate
Members: 550-600 *Staff:* 1
Annual Budget: under $10,000 *Tel:* (218) 566-1321
Hist. Note: Formed at Belvidere, South Dakota by a group of ranchers meeting at the ranch of Baxter and Lyndall Berry. Member of the Nat'l Soc. of Livestock Records Ass'ns. Membership: $25/year.
Publication:
The Bagpipe. q.
Annual Meetings: Summer

American Seafood Retailers Ass'n (1981)
67 River Road, Cos Cob CT 06807
President: R. Woodman Harris
Members: 175-185 *Staff:* 2-5
Annual Budget: $100-250,000 *Tel:* (203) 661-2959
Annual Meetings: Not held

American Seat Belt Council (1961)
4010 South 57th Ave., Suite 202, Lake Worth FL 33463
Exec. Director: Michael R. Cloney
Members: 20-25 companies *Staff:* 2-5
Annual Budget: $50-100,000 *Tel:* (201) 521-4441
Hist. Note: Formerly (1969 to 1977) the American Safety Belt Council, Inc. Supercedes the Automobile Safety Belt Council founded in 1955.
Annual Meetings:
1987-Boca Raton,FL(Boca Raton Hotel and Club)/March

American Seed Trade Ass'n (1883)
1030 15th St., N.W., Suite 964, Washington DC 20005-1593
Exec. V. President: William T. Schapaugh
Members: 700 companies *Staff:* 10
Annual Budget: $500-1,000,000 *Tel:* (202) 223-4080
Hist. Note: Active members are producers of seeds for planting purposes. Affiliates are state seed associations, and the like, while associates are suppliers to the industry and corresponding members are overseas seed companies. Sponsors the American Seed Trade Ass'n Political Action Committee and the American Seed Research Foundation.
Publications:
Corn and Sorghum Seed Conference Proceedings. a.
Soybean Seed Conference Proceedings. a.
Farm Seed Conference Proceedings. a.
Annual Meetings: June/1,000
1987-Boston, MA(Weston)/June 28-July 2
1988-Seattle, WA/June 19-23

American Sheep Producers Council (1955)
200 Clayton St., Denver CO 80206
Exec. Director: Roger L. Wasson
Members: 25 *Staff:* 30-35
Annual Budget: $2-5,000,000 *Tel:* (303) 399-8130
Hist. Note: Organized to promote consumption of lamb and wool and is divided into the American Lamb Council and the American Wool council. Promotional activities are funded by deductions from Department of Agrilture incentive payments to individual sheep raisers.
Publication:
American Sheep Producer. m. adv.
Annual Meetings: Denver,CO/third Thursday in October.

American Shetland Pony Club (1888)
Box 3415, Peoria IL 61614
Secretary: T.R. Huston
Members: 800 *Staff:* 2-5
Annual Budget: $50-100,000 *Tel:* (309) 691-9661
Hist. Note: Members are owners and breeders of Shetland ponies and miniature horses. Member of the Nat'l Soc. of Livestock Record Ass'ns. Membership: $17.50/yr.
Publication:
The Pony Journal. bi-m. adv.

American Shire Horse Ass'n (1885)
1687 N.E. 56th St., Altoona IA 50009
Secy.-Treas.: Lowell Wagoner
Members: 250 *Staff:* 1
Annual Budget: under $10,000 *Tel:* (515) 265-7676
Hist. Note: Members are owners and breeders of Shire horses. Records pedigrees of Shire draft horses and promotes their breeding. Membership: $15/yr.
Publications:
Directory of Shire Owners and Breeders. a.
Shire Newsletter. q.
Annual Meetings: Nat'l Shire Show

American Short Line Railroad Ass'n (1913)
2000 Massachusetts Ave., N.W., Washington DC 20036
President: Paul Howard Croft
Members: 300 railroads, 150 associate companies *Staff:* 6-10
Annual Budget: $500-1,000,000 *Tel:* (202) 785-2250
Hist. Note: The American Short Line Railroad Association is a non-profit, unincorporated association principally comprised of Class III line-haul, switching and terminal companies located in 45 states with a Board of Directors elected regionally. The action of the Association is advisory only and not binding on any of its members. A Short Line Railroad Association was founded in New York City in 1910 to have Congress amend the Railway Mail Pay Law such that short lines might obtain an increase in pay for transporting the mail. This group was short lived as were other groups in Southern and Pacific Coast territories. In 1913, representatives of twenty-two short-line railroads organized the Short Line Railroad Association of the Southeast. Accumulated experience led to the general belief that this Association should become national in scope. Subsequently the name was changed to The American Short Line Railroad Association; and in March, 1917, the general office of the Association was established in Washington, D.C. Membership grew to 177 members by 1918, and in 1920 the railroads in the Western Association of Short Line Railroads affiliated with this Association.
Annual Meetings: Fall/500
1987-Albuquerque, NM(Marriott)/Oct. 4-7
1988-Nashville, TN(Opryland)/Oct. 2-5

American Shorthorn Ass'n (1846)
8288 Hascall St., Omaha NE 68124
Exec. Secretary: Dr. Roger E. Hunsley
Members: 2,500 *Staff:* 16-20
Annual Budget: $250-500,000 *Tel:* (402) 393-7200
Hist. Note: Breeders and promoters of Shorthorn Beef Cattle. Member of the Nat'l Pedigreed Livestock Council; the U.S. Beef Breeds Council; and the Nat'l Cattlemen's Ass'n. Membership: $35/yr.
Publication:
Shorthorn Country. m. adv.
Annual Meetings: November/January
1987-Denver, CO(Stouffers Concourse)/Jan./500
1988-Louisville, KY(Executive Inn)/Nov./500
1989-Denver, CO(Stouffers Concourse)/Jan./500

American Shrimp Canners and Processors Ass'n
Hist. Note: Became the American Shrimp Processors Ass'n in 1984.

American Shrimp Processors Ass'n (1962)
Box 50774, New Orleans LA 70150
Exec. Director: William D. Chauvin
Members: 20-30 companies *Staff:* 1
Annual Budget: $50-100,000 *Tel:* (504) 368-1571
Hist. Note: Formerly (1977) the American Shrimp Canners Association and the American Shrimp Canners and Processors Ass'n. Assumed its present name in 1984. Membership: $1,000/year.

American Shrimpboat Ass'n (1971)
Hist. Note: Defunct in 1982.

American Shropshire Registry Ass'n (1884)
Box 1970, Monticello IL 61856
Secy.-Treas.: Elizabeth R. Glasgow
Members: 1,000 sheep breeders *Staff:* 1
Annual Budget: $10-25,000 *Tel:* (217) 762-7321
Hist. Note: Breeders and fanciers of Shropshire sheep, which were introduced into the U.S. in 1855 from England and are bred both for their meat and wool production.
Publication:
Shropshire Voice. 3/yr.
Annual Meetings: Fall/150

American Sightseeing Internat'l (1947)
309 Fifth Ave., New York NY 10016
President and C.E.O.: Richard J. Valerio
Members: 100 companies *Staff:* 5
Annual Budget: $250-500,000 *Tel:* (212) 689-7744
Hist. Note: Established as the American Sightseeing Ass'n, it assumed its present name in 1971. Members are independent sightseeing companies worldwide, usually one per city.
Publications:
American Sightseeing-International Tariff. a.
ASI Worldwide Tour Planning Manual. a. adv.
Annual Meetings: Fall, usually just before that of the American Soc. of Travel Agents.

American Simmental Ass'n (1969)
One Simmental Way, Bozeman MT 59715
Exec. V. President: Earl B. Peterson
Members: 12,500 *Staff:* 30
Annual Budget: $2-5,000,000 *Tel:* (406) 587-4531
Hist. Note: Breeders and fanciers of Simmental and Simbrah cattle.
Publication:
Simmental Shield.
Annual Meetings: Winter

American Ski Federation (1979)
207 Constitution Ave., N.E., Washington DC 20002
President: Joseph Prendergast
Members: 1,000 corporations; 6 ass'ns *Staff:* 2-5
Annual Budget: $250-500,000 *Tel:* (202) 543-1595
Hist. Note: Represents the interests of the American skiing industry. Membership includes the National Ski Areas Association, National Ski Patrol System, Professional Ski Instructors of America, Ski Retailers Council, the National Ski Touring Operators Association and Ski Industries America. Sponsors and supports the American Ski Federation Political Action Committee.
Publication:
ASF Washington Letter. m.

American Ski Teachers Ass'n of Natur Teknik (1960)
Box 34, Marshall Creek PA 18335
Secretary: Diane Hannan
Members: 400-450 *Staff:* 2-5
Annual Budget: under $10,000 *Tel:* (717) 223-0730
Hist. Note: Formerly (1970) American Ski Teachers Ass'n. Members are certified ski instructors united to promote high standards of ski instruction. Sponsors competitions; certifies ski instructors. Membership: $10/yr.
Publications:
Directory of Certified Instructors. a.
Newsletter. 3/yr.

American Small and Rural Hospital Ass'n
Hist. Note: Absorbed by the Nat'l Rural Health Care Ass'n in 1986.

American SMR Network Ass'n (1985)
1700 North Moore St., Suite 910, Rosslyn VA 22209
Administrative Asst.: Barbara J. Wake
Members: 120 companies, 10 individuals
Annual Budget: $25-50,000 *Tel:* (703) 528-5115
Hist. Note: Established and incorporated in Washington, DC, ASNA members are Specialized Mobile Radio (SMR) system licensees. ASNA represents the interests of its members in federal regulatory and legislative activities; maintains data concerning the assignment and use of frequency assignments; and provides research services at a separate Gettysburg, PA office. Membership: $150/yr. for 5 or fewer channels; $1 for each additional channel.
Publications:
ASNA Newsletter. m. adv.
Membership News Bulletins. irreg.
FCC Rules and Regulations (Abridged), Part 90. a.
Annual Meetings: June
1987-Boston, MA(Westin Copley Place)/June 25-26

American Soc. for Adolescent Psychiatry (1967)
24 Green Valley Rd., Wallingford PA 19086
Exec. Secretary: Mary D. Staples
Members: 1,700 individuals; 27 groups *Staff:* 1
Annual Budget: $25-50,000 *Tel:* (215) 566-1054
Hist. Note: In 1958 a group of New York psychiatrists formed the Soc. for Adolescent Psychiatry. Shortly thereafter similar groups were set up in Philadelphia, Los Angeles and Chicago. In 1967 these groups confederated into the present ASAP, which is now a confederation of psychiatric societies throughout the United States and Canada. Encourages and supports research on the psychopathology and treatment of adolescents and provides a forum for the exchange of psychiatric knowledge about them. Membership: $55/yr.
Publications:
Annals of Adolescent Psychiatry. a.
Membership Directory. a.
Newsletter. q. adv.
Annual Meetings: May, before the convention of the American Psychiatric Ass'n/300
1987-Chicago, IL/May 8-10
1988-Montreal, Canada/May 6-8
1989-San Francisco, CA/May 5-7

American Soc. for Aerospace Education (1976)
Hist. Note: Superceded by the Aerospace Education Ass'n in 1983.

00057 12 05 86 1233

American Soc. for Aesthetic Plastic Surgery (1967)
3912 Atlantic Ave., Long Beach CA 90807
Exec. Director: Robert G. Stanton
Members: 757 *Staff:* 6
Annual Budget: $500-1,000,000 *Tel:* (213) 595-4275
Hist. Note: Members are specialists in the area of aesthetic plastic surgery certified by the American Board of Plastic Surgery. Membership: $375/yr.
Publication:
Aesthetic Society News. 3/yr.
Annual Meetings: Spring
1987-Los Angeles, CA(Century Plaza)/March 22-27/1,200-1,500
1988-San Francisco, CA(Hyatt Regency)/March 19-26/1,200-1,600
1989-Orlando, FL(Hyatt Regency-Grand Cypress)/April 9-14/1,300-1,700
1990-Chicago, IL(Hilton & Towers)/April 1-5/1,500-1,600

American Soc. for Aesthetics (1942)
C.W. Post Center of Long Island Univ., Greenvale NY 11548
Secy.-Treas.: Dr. Arnold Berleant
Members: 750 *Staff:* 2-5
Annual Budget: $25-50,000 *Tel:* (516) 299-3054
Hist. Note: Organzied as an interdisciplinary society on April 25, 1942 at Catholic University to encourage scholarly study, research, discussion and publication in aesthetics and the arts. Member, American Council of Learned Societies. Membership: $20/yr.
Publications:
Journal of Aesthetics and Arts Criticism. q. adv.
Newsletter.
Annual Meetings:
1987-Kansas City, MO/Oct. 28-31

American Soc. for Artificial Internal Organs (1955)
Box C, Boca Raton FL 33429
Exec. Director: Karen K. Burke
Members: 1,421 *Staff:* 4
Annual Budget: $250-500,000 *Tel:* (305) 391-8589
Hist. Note: Established June 1955 in Atlantic City. Members are physicians, scientists and engineers from academia, industry, research institutions and government agencies who have made a significant contribution to the development and/or understanding of of artificial organs. Membership: $80/yr.
Publications:
ASAIO Abstracts. a.
Transactions of the ASAIO. q.
Annual Meetings: Spring
1987-New York, NY(Marriott Marquis)/May 18-21

American Soc. for Cell Biology (1960)
9650 Rockville Pike, Bethesda MD 20814
Exec. Officer: Dorothea C. Wilson
Members: 5,000 *Staff:* 6
Annual Budget: $500-1,000,000 *Tel:* (301) 530-7153
Hist. Note: Formed in 1960 and incorporated in New York in 1961. Affiliated with The Federation of American Societies for Experimental Biology. Membership: $65/yr.
Publications:
ASCB Directory. a.
Journal of Cell Biology. m.
Newsletter. q.
Annual Meetings: Fall
1987-St. Louis, MO(Cervantes Conv. Center)/Nov. 16-20/5,000
1989-San Francisco, CA(Moscone Conv. Center)/Jan. 29-Feb. 2/8,000
1989-Houston, TX(Brown Conv. Center)/Nov. 6-10/5,000
1990-San Diego, CA(Conv. Center)/Nov. 5-9/5,000
1991-Boston, MA(Conv. Center)/Nov. 10-14/5,000
1992-New Orleans, LA(Conv. Center)/Nov. 1-5/5,000

American Soc. for Clinical Investigation (1909)
c/o Slack Inc., 6900 Grove Road, Thorofare NJ 08086
Central Office Mgr.: Jean Marie Dolloff
Members: 2,061 *Staff:* 1
Annual Budget: $10-25,000 *Tel:* (609) 848-1000
Hist. Note: Founded in Atlantic City in 1909 as the American Soc. for the Advancement of Clinical Investigation. Name changed to American Soc. for Clinical Investigation in 1916. Encourages scientific investigation by the medical practitioner. Membership: $150/yr.
Publication:
Journal of Clinical Investigation. m. adv.
Annual Meetings: Spring
1987-San Diego, CA(Town & Country)/May 1-4
1988-Washington, DC/April 29-May 2
1989-Washington, DC/April 28-May 1
1990-Washington, DC/May 4-7

American Soc. for Clinical Nutrition (1959)
9650 Rockville Pike, Bethesda MD 20814
Exec. Officer: Gilda M. Knight
Members: 650 *Staff:* 4-6
Annual Budget: $250-500,000 *Tel:* (301) 530-7110
Hist. Note: A division of the American Institute of Nutrition
Publication:
American Journal of Clinical Nutrition. m. adv.
Annual Meetings: With the American Federation for Clinical Research

American Soc. for Clinical Pharmacology and Therapeutics (1900)
1718 Gallagher Rd., Norristown PA 19401-2810
Exec. Secretary: Elaine Galasso
Members: 1,700-1,800 *Staff:* 2-5
Annual Budget: $250-500,000 *Tel:* (215) 825-3838
Hist. Note: Organized May 1, 1900 as the American Therapeutic Society. Merged in 1969 with the American College of Clinical Pharmacology and Chemotherapy (founded in 1963) and incorporated in the District of Columbia under its present name. Membership: $90/year.
Publication:
Clinical Pharmacology and Therapeutics. m.
Annual Meetings: Spring/950-1100
1987-Orlando, FL(Marriott)/March 25-28
1988-San Diego, CA(Town & Country)/March 9-11
1989-Nashville, TN(Opryland)/March 8-10
1990-San Francisco, CA(Marriott-Moscone Center)/March 21-23
1991-San Antonio, TX/March

American Soc. for Colposcopy and Cervical Pathology (1964)
6900 Grove Road, Thorofare NJ 08086
Exec. Director: Robert Talley
Members: 1,515 *Staff:* 2
Annual Budget: $25-50,000 *Tel:* (609) 848-1000
Hist. Note: Obstetricians, gynecologists and others interested in promoting the accurate and ethical application of colposcopy. Formerly The American Society for Colposcopy and Colpomicroscopy.
Publication:
The Colposcopist. q. adv.
Biennial Meetings: Even years

American Soc. for Concrete Construction (1957)
3330 Dundee Road, Suite N4-B, Northbrook IL 60062-0270
Exec. Director: Burr Bennett
Members: 800 companies *Staff:* 2-5
Annual Budget: $100-250,000 *Tel:* (312) 291-1340
Hist. Note: Formerly (1964) the Nat'l Concrete Contractors Ass'n.
Publications:
Hotline Summary. bi-m.
Literature Roundup. bi-m.
Management Report. bi-m.
Membership Bulletin. bi-m.
Annual Meetings: Winter
1987-Houston, TX/Jan. 25-29
1988-Las Vegas, NV/Jan. 17-21
1989-Atlanta, GA/Feb. 19-23
1990-Houston, TX/Jan. 21-25

American Soc. for Conservation Archaeology (1974)
1584 Thursnton Ave., #302, Honolulu HI 96822
Secretary: Peter Miller
Members: 375-400 individuals and institutions *Staff:* 1
Annual Budget: under $10,000
Hist. Note: Promotes and coordinates the preservation and protection of historic and prehistoric sites.
Publication:
ASCA Report. q.
Annual Meetings: Spring with the Soc. for American Archaeology

American Soc. for Cybernetics (1964)
Dept. of Decision Sciences, George Mason University, Fairfax VA 22030
V. President: Prof. Stephen S. Ruth
Members: 800 *Staff:* 7
Annual Budget: $10-25,000 *Tel:* (703) 323-2738
Hist. Note: Cybernetics--the science of communication and control or the science of system regulation, whether the system is a machine, a biological organism or a social organization. Absorbed the American Cybernetics Ass'n in 1979. Membership: $25/yr.
Publications:
ASC Newsletter. 10/yr.
Cybernetic. q.
Annual Meetings:
1987-Switzerland/March

American Soc. for Cytotechnology (1979)
10480 Gregory Circle, Cypress CA 90630
Secy.-Treas.: Elsie V. Carruthers
Members: 1,200-1,300 *Staff:* 1
Annual Budget: $25-50,000 *Tel:* (714) 828-0621
Hist. Note: Members are individuals concerned with the evaluation of cells for early signs of malignancy. Full members must have passed a qualifying cytotechnology exam and have either graduated from a school of cytology or worked in the field for three years. Membership: $25/yr.
Publication:
ASCT News. m. adv.
Annual Meetings: Spring

American Soc. for Dental Aesthetics (1978)
635 Madison Ave., New York NY 10022
President: Dr. Irwin Smigel
Members: 100 *Staff:* 1
Annual Budget: $10-25,000 *Tel:* (212) 371-4575
Hist. Note: Members are dentists who have demonsrated excellence in an area of aesthetic dentistry. Applicants must be dentists for 5 years, then submit photos of five (before and after) cases which are scrupulously reviewed before their acceptance. Fellowships to the Society are granted to members who have been active for three years and have advanced the society's standards.
Publication:
Newsletter. semi-a.
Semi-annual Meetings: Spring and Fall

American Soc. for Dermatologic Surgery (1970)
1567 Maple Ave., Evanston IL 60201
Secretary: Neil Swanson
Members: 1,650 *Staff:* 1
Annual Budget: $100-250,000 *Tel:* (312) 869-3959
Hist. Note: Membership: $150/yr.
Publication:
Journal of Dermatologic Surgery and Oncology. m.
Annual Meetings:
1987-Castle Harbour, Bermuda(Marriott's Castle Harbour)/April 29-May 3

American Soc. for Engineering Education (1893)
11 Dupont Circle, N.W., Suite 200, Washington DC 20036
Exec. Director: F. Karl Willenbrock
Members: 10,000 individuals; 550 institutions *Staff:* 26
Annual Budget: over $5,000,000 *Tel:* (202) 293-7080
Hist. Note: Originated in 1893 as the Soc. for the Promotion of Engineering Education. Merged in 1946 with the Engineering College Research Ass'n to form the American Soc. for Engineering Education. Incorporated in Pennsylvania in 1943. A member of the American Ass'n of Engineering Societies, Accreditation Board for Engineering and Technology, the American Ass'n for the Advancement of Science and the American Council on Education. A participating society of the World Federation of Engineering Organizations. Membership: $40/yr.(individual); $110-600/yr.(organization).
Publications:
Chemical Engineering Education. q. adv.
Civil Engineering Education. bi-a.
COED (Computers in Education Division) Journal. q.
Engineering Design Graphics. 3/yr. adv.
Engineering College Research and Graduate Directory. a. adv.
Mechanical Engineering News. q. adv.
The Engineering Economist. q.
Engineering Education News. 8/yr. adv.
Journal of Engineering Technology. semi-a.
Annual Meetings: June/2,500
1987-Reno, NV(Univ. of Nevada)/June 21-25
1988-Portland, OR(Univ. of Portland)/June 19-23
1989-Nashville, TN(Vanderbilt Univ.)/June 18-22

American Soc. for Engineering Management (1979)
301 Harris Hall, Univ. of Missouri-Rolla, Rolla MO 65401-0249
Exec. Director: Daniel L. Babcock
Members: 750 individuals *Staff:* 1
Annual Budget: $25-50,000 *Tel:* (314) 341-4560
Hist. Note: Founded in 1979 by a group of engineering management professionals from academic, industrial, and governmental organizations to promote the development of engineering management as a professional discipline and academic specialty and to maintain a high professional standard among its members. Membership: $40/yr.
Publications:
Newsletter. q.
Proceedings of Annual Meeting. a.
Engineering Management International. a.
Annual Meetings: Fall
1987-St. Louis, MO/Oct.

American Soc. for Enology and Viticulture (1950)
Box 1855, Davis CA 95617
Exec. Director: Lyndie McHenry Boulton
Members: 3,000 *Staff:* 6
Annual Budget: $250-500,000 *Tel:* (916) 753-3142
Hist. Note: Formerly (1984) the American Soc. of Enologists. The American Soc. for Enology and Viticulture is an international, professional society dedicated to the interests of enologists, viticulturists and others in the fields of wine and grape production. It is a non-profit association formed by 98 charter members on January 27, 1950 which received formal recognition of tax-exempt status on May 25, 1951. Originally composed of researchers of the University of California and winemaker members of the California industry, the Society has enjoyed a steady enlargement. It includes members from other parts of the U.S. and 35 foreign nations. The Society has an Eastern chapter at Cornell University, a Pacific Northwest chapter in Pullman,WA, and a chapter in Japan. Membership: $45/yr., individual; $150/yr, company.
Publication:
American Journal of Enology and Viticulture. q. adv.
Annual Meetings: June
1987-Anaheim, CA(Marriott)/June 25-27
1988-Reno, NV(MGM Grand)/June 22-24
1989-Anaheim, CA(Disneyland)/June 29-July 1

American Soc. for Environmental Education (1971)
Box 800, Wheeler Professional Park, Hanover NH 03755
President: Dr. William L. Mayo
Members: 800 *Staff:* 7
Annual Budget: $250-500,000 *Tel:* (603) 643-3536
Hist. Note: ASEE is a professional organization for environmental educators at all educational levels from primary school to graduate university studies. Incorporated in Michigan, ASEE was formerly (1976) known as American Soc. for Ecological Education. Membership: $25/year (individuals/non-profit institutions), $500/year (companies).
Publication:
Environmental Education Report and Newsletter. q.
Annual Meetings: Summer

00058 12 05 86 1233

American Soc. for Ethnohistory (1953)
c/o Duke University Press, Box 6697, College Station, Durham NC 27708
Jounrals Manager: Stephen Cohn
Members: 1,200 *Staff:* 2-5
Annual Budget: $25-50,000 *Tel:* (919) 684-2173
Hist. Note: Anthropologists, historians, art historians, geographers and other professionals interested in research in the cultural history of non-industrial peoples. Formerly (until 1966) known as the American Indian Ethnohistoric Conference.
Publication:
Ethnohistory. q.
Annual Meetings: Fall

American Soc. for Gastrointestinal Endoscopy (1941)
13 Elm St., Box 1565, Manchester MA 01944
Exec. Director: William T. Maloney, CAE
Members: 3,050 *Staff:* 6-10
Annual Budget: $100-250,000 *Tel:* (617) 927-8330
Hist. Note: Formerly American Gastropic Club. Seeks to advance the use of endoscopy as a diagnostic technique.
Publication:
Gastrointestinal Endoscopy. q. adv.
Annual Meetings: January
1987-Washington, DC(Hilton)/Jan. 30-Feb. 1/400
1988-Dallas, TX/Jan. 25-29/400

American Soc. for Geriatric Dentistry (1964)
211 East Chicago Ave., Chicago IL 60611
Exec. Director: Paul Van Ostenberg
Members: 450 *Staff:* 1
Annual Budget: $10-25,000 *Tel:* (312) 440-2660
Hist. Note: Established and incorporated in Chicago, IL. Membership: $50/year.
Publications:
Special Care in Dentistry. bi-m. adv.
ASGO Newsletter. q.
Annual Meetings: Fall, with the American Dental Ass'n.

American Soc. for Head and Neck Surgery (1959)
Stanford Univ. Medical Center, Stanford CA 94305-5328
Secretary: Dr. Willard E. Fee
Members: 600 *Staff:* 1
Annual Budget: $50-100,000 *Tel:* (415) 725-6500
Hist. Note: Members are fellows of the American College of Surgeons whose primary interest is head and neck surgery. Membership: $100/year.
Publication:
Archives of Otolaryngology. a.
Annual Meetings: Spring/600
1987-Denver, CO(Fairmont)/April 25-May 2
1988-Palm Beach, FL(Breakers)
1989-San Francisco, CA
1990-Palm Beach, FL(Breakers)
1991-Maui, HI

American Soc. for Healthcare Education and Training (1970)
840 North Lake Shore Dr., Chicago IL 60611
Director: James B. Gantenberg
Members: 1,800-2,000 *Staff:* 2
Annual Budget: $250-500,000 *Tel:* (312) 280-6113
Hist. Note: Membership composed of persons engaged in the educating and training of health care, wellness and health promotion personnel. Affiliated with the American Hospital Ass'n. Formerly (1983) American Soc. for Health Manpower Education and Training. Membership: $60/yr.
Publications:
Hospitals. semi-m. adv.
Healthcare Education Dateline. q.
Journal of Healthcare Education and Training. q.
Annual Meetings: June/450-500
1987-San Francisco, CA/June 7-10
1988-St. Louis, MO(Adam's Mark)/June 17-22
1989-Chicago, IL(Marriott)/June 8-13
1990-Orlando, FL(Marriott Orlando)/June 9-12

American Soc. for Healthcare Human Resources Administration (1964)
840 North Lake Shore Drive, Chicago IL 60611
Director: V. Brandon Melton
Members: 2,300-2,400 *Staff:* 3
Annual Budget: $25-50,000 *Tel:* (312) 280-6111
Hist. Note: An affiliate of the American Hospital Ass'n. Formerly (1975) American Soc. for Hospital Personnel Directors. Dedicated exclusively to the education and professional development of hospital personnel administrators. Membership: $70/year.
Publication:
Newsletter. bi-m.
Annual Meetings: July/500
1987-Nashville, TN/July 19-23
1988-Kansas City, MO(Westin Crown Ctr.)/July 17-21
1989-Waikiki, HI(Sheraton)/July 16-20

American Soc. for Histocompatability and Immunogenetics (1970)
211 East 43rd St., Suite 301, New York NY 10017
Exec. Director: Margaret Glos, CAE
Members: 900-1,000 *Staff:* 6-10
Annual Budget: $250-500,000 *Tel:* (212) 867-4193
Hist. Note: Physicians, blood banks and others involved in the testing of blood to determine its compatability with organs to be used in transplants. Formerly (1984) the American Ass'n for Clinical Histocompatibility Testing. Membership: $50/yr. (individual), $750/yr. (institutional).
Publications:
ASHI Quarterly. q. adv.
Human Immunology. m.
Annual Meetings: Fall
1987-New York, NY(Waldorf)/Nov. 21-23/700
1988-San Francisco, CA(Hyatt Embarcadero)/Oct.
1989-Toronto, Canada/Oct.

American Soc. for Horticultural Science (1903)
701 North Saint Asaph St., Alexandria VA 22314
Exec. Director: Cecil Blackwell
Members: 5,000 *Staff:* 6-10
Annual Budget: $1-2,000,000 *Tel:* (703) 836-4606
Hist. Note: Founded in 1903 in Boston and incorporated in 1961 in the District of Columbia. Promotes and encourages national and international interest in scientific research and education in all branches of horticulture (the production, marketing, processing, and utilization of fruits, nuts, vegetables, flowers, ornamental and landscape plants).
Publications:
HortScience. bi-m. adv.
Journal of the ASHS. bi-m.
ASHS Newsletter. m. adv.
Annual Meetings:
1987-Orlando, FL(Hyatt Orlando)/Nov. 6-12/1,800
1988-East Lansing, MI(MI State Univ.)/Aug. 7-12/1,600
1989-Tulsa, OK/July 30-Aug. 4/1,500
1990-Arizona/Nov. 4-9/1,500
1991-University Park, PA(Penn State Univ.)/Aug./1,500
1992-Hawaii/Aug./1,500

American Soc. for Hospital Central Service Personnel (1967)
840 North Lake Shore Drive, Chicago IL 60611
Director: Clarence W. Daly
Members: 1,600-1,700 *Staff:* 2-5
Annual Budget: $250-500,000 *Tel:* (312) 280-6160
Hist. Note: An affiliate of the American Hospital Ass'n. Membership: $50/yr.
Publication:
Hospital Central Service. bi-m.
Annual Meetings: Fall/500
1987-Dallas, TX(Hyatt Regency)/Sept. 22-25
1988-Anaheim, CA/Oct.

American Soc. for Hospital Engineering (1962)
840 North Lake Shore Drive, Chicago IL 60611
Director: V. James McLarney
Members: 3,800 *Staff:* 7
Annual Budget: $1-2,000,000 *Tel:* (312) 280-6144
Hist. Note: An Affiliate of the American Hospital Ass'n. Membership: $75/yr. (individual); $250/yr. (institution).
Publications:
Directory. a.
Hospital Engineering Bulletin. m.
Newsletter of ASHE. q.
Annual Meetings: June
1987-San Diego, CA/(Town&Country)/600
1988-Grand Rapids, MI
1989-New Orleans, LA
1990-Las Vegas, NV
1991-Orlando, FL

American Soc. for Hospital Food Service Administrators (1967)
840 North Lake Shore Drive, Chicago IL 60611
Director: Kathleen Pontius
Members: 2,200 individual *Staff:* 2-5
Annual Budget: $250-500,000 *Tel:* (312) 280-6416
Hist. Note: Affiliate of the American Hospital Ass'n. Formerly (1976) the American Soc. for Hospital Food Service.
Publication:
Newsletter. q.
Annual Meetings: July/500-600
1987-Chicago, IL(Palmer House)/July 8-12
1988-Dallas, TX(Hyatt Regency)/July 18-21
1989-Boston, MA(Marriott Copley Place)/July 10-13

American Soc. for Hospital Marketing and Public Relations (1964)
840 North Lake Shore Drive, Chicago IL 60611
Director: Lauren A. Barnett
Members: 2,800 *Staff:* 2-5
Annual Budget: $250-500,000 *Tel:* (312) 280-6359
Hist. Note: Established under the aegis of the Board of Trustees of the American Hospital Ass'n as the American Soc. for Hospital Public Relations Directors in May, 1964; became the American Soc. for Hospital Public Relations and assumed its present name in 1984. Affiliated with the American Hospital Ass'n. Membership: $75-$120/year.
Publication:
Hospital Marketing and Public Relations. bi-m.
Annual Meetings:
1987-San Antonio, TX
1988-Washington, DC

American Soc. for Hospital Materials Management (1962)
840 North Lake Shore Dr., Chicago IL 60611
Director: Marcie Anthony
Members: 2,000 individuals *Staff:* 2-5
Annual Budget: $100-250,000 *Tel:* (312) 280-6137
Hist. Note: Affiliated with the American Hospital Ass'n. Formerly (1975) the American Soc. for Hospital Purchasing Agents and (1983) the American Soc. for Hospital Purchasing and Materials Management. Membership: $50/yr.
Publications:
Hospital Materials Management News. bi-m.
Perspectives. q.
Conference Proceedings. a.
Fellowship Readings. a.
Technical Articles. bi-m.
Job Descriptions for Materials Management.
Annual Meetings: Summer
1987-Atlanta, GA/July 27-29/300

American Soc. for Hospital Personnel Administration
Hist. Note: Became the American Soc. for Healthcare Human Resources Administration in 1986.

American Soc. for Hospital Public Relations
Hist. Note: Became the American Soc. for Hospital Marketing and Public Relations in 1984.

American Soc. for Hospital Purchasing and Materials Management (1962)
Hist. Note: Became the American Society for Hospital Materials Management in 1983.

American Soc. for Hospital Risk Management (1980)
840 North Lake Shore Drive, Chicago IL 60611
Director: David R. Meyers
Members: 1,200 *Staff:* 2-5
Annual Budget: $250-500,000 *Tel:* (312) 280-6425
Hist. Note: An affiliate of the American Hospital Ass'n. Members are hospital employees involved in risk management as well as insurance personnel, hospital administrators, attorneys, physicians and healthcare management consultants.
Publication:
Perspectives in Hospital Risk Management. q.

American Soc. for Industrial Security (1955)
1655 N. Fort Myer Drive, Suite 1200, Arlington VA 22209
Exec. V. President: Ernest J. Criscuoli, Jr.
Members: 24,000 *Staff:* 38
Annual Budget: $2-5,000,000 *Tel:* (703) 522-5800
Hist. Note: Members include security professionals and company representatives for security products, and services. Operates The ASIS Foundation. Membership: $55/year.
Publications:
Directory. a.
Security Management. m. adv.
ASIS Dynamics. bi-m.
Annual Meetings:
1987-Las Vegas, NV(Hilton)/Sept. 28-Oct. 1
1988-Boston, MA(Sheraton)/Sept. 26-29
1989-Nashville, TN/Sept. 11-14
1990-San Francisco, CA/Sept. 10-13

American Soc. for Information Science (1937)
1424 16th St., N.W., Suite 404, Washington DC 20036
Exec. Director: Linda Resnik
Members: 4,200 *Staff:* 9
Annual Budget: $500-1,000,000 *Tel:* (202) 462-1000
Hist. Note: Founded in Washington, DC in 1937 as the American Documentation Institute and incorporated in Delaware the same year. Became the American Soc. for Information Science in 1968. Promotes the creation and application of knowledge concerning information and its transfer. A member of the American Federation of Information Processing Societies. Membership: $75/yr. (individual); $350 & $550/yr. (company)
Publications:
Annual Review of Information Science and Technology. a.
Bulletin of the American Society for Information Science. bi-m. adv.
Journal of the American Society for Information Science. bi-m. adv.
Proceedings. a.
ASIS Handbook and Directory. a.
Semi-annual: Fall and Spring
1987-Cincinnati, OH(King Island Inn & Conference Ctr.)/May 17-20
1987-Boston, MA/Oct. 4-8
1988-Atlanta, GA/Oct. 23-27
1989-San Diego, CA/Oct. 29-Nov. 2

American Soc. for Laser Medicine and Surgery (1980)
813 2nd St., Suite 200, Wausau WI 54401
Secretary: Dr. Ellet H. Drake, FACC
Members: 900 *Staff:* 2
Annual Budget: $100-250,000 *Tel:* (715) 845-9283
Hist. Note: Founded through an initial grant from the A. Ward Ford Memorial Institute in Wausau, and incorporated in the State of Wisconsin by 150 charter members. Membership: $110/yr. (physician), $75/yr. (scientist).
Publications:
Laser Medicine and Surgery News. bi-m.
Lasers in Surgery and Medicine. bi-m.
Annual Meetings:
1987-San Francisco, CA(Hyatt Regency Embarcadero)/April 11-13
1988-Dallas, TX(Fairmont Hotel)/April 24-27

00059 12 05 86 1233

American Soc. for Legal History (1956)
College of Law, Georgia State Univ., Atlanta GA 30303-3092
Secretary: L. Lynn Hogue
Members: 1,200 *Staff:* 1
Annual Budget: under $10,000 *Tel:* (404) 658-2048
Hist. Note: A member of the American Council of Learned Societies. Membership: $18/yr. (individual), $30/yr. (institution).
Publications:
Law & History Review. semi-a.
Newsletter. semi-a.
Annual Meetings: Third week in October.
1987-Philadelphia, PA/Oct. 23-24
1988-Charleston, SC/Oct. 21-21
1989-San Francisco, CA/Oct. 20-21

American Soc. for Mass Spectrometry (1969)
Box 1508, East Lansing MI 48823
Admin. Secretary: Judith Watson
Members: 1,900-2,000 *Staff:* 1
Annual Budget: $50-100,000 *Tel:* (517) 337-2548
Hist. Note: Academic and industrial chemists and scientists who use the mass spectrograph as an analytical and physical tool.
Publication:
Proceedings. a.
Annual Meetings: Spring
1987-Denver, CO

American Soc. for Medical Technology (1932)
3 Metro Center, Suite 750, Bethesda MD 20814
Exec. Director: Lynn Podell
Members: 25,000 *Staff:* 25-30
Annual Budget: $2-5,000,000 *Tel:* (301) 961-1931
Hist. Note: Formerly (1936) the American Soc. of Clinical Laboratory Technicians and (1972) the American Soc. of Medical Technologists. Members have an associate, a B.S. degree, and/or clinical training or experience in a branch of medical technology, or the medical laboratory sciences. Supports the Medical Laboratory Technology Political Action Committee. Membership: $80/yr.
Publications:
Journal of Medical Technology. m. adv.
ASMT News. m. adv.
Annual Meetings: June/3-4,000
1987-Las Vegas, NV(Hilton, Conv. Center)/June 14-19
1988-San Antonio, TX/June 19-24
1989-Atlanta, GA/June 11-16
1990-New Orleans, LA/June 24-29

American Soc. for Metals (1913)
Metals Park OH 44073
Mng. Director: Edward L. Langer
Members: 52-53,000 *Staff:* 105
Annual Budget: over $5,000,000 *Tel:* (216) 338-5151
Hist. Note: Originated in Detroit as the Steel Treaters Club in 1913. Name changed to the American Soc. for Steel Treating in 1920 and the American Soc. for Metals in 1933. Incorporated in Ohio in 1920. Membership: $36/year. Has a budget of about $12 million.
Publications:
ASM News. m. adv.
Bulletin of Alloy Phase Diagrams. q.
Internat'l Metals Review. bi-m.
Journal of Applied Metalworking q.
Journal of Heat Treating q.
Journal of Materials for Energy Systems. q.
Metal Progress. m. adv.
Metallurgical Transactions A. m.
Metallurgical Transactions B. q.
Metals Abstracts. m.
Metals Abstracts Index. m.
Annual Meetings: Fall

American Soc. for Microbiology (1899)
1913 Eye St., N.W., Washington DC 20006
Exec. Director: Dr. Michael I. Goldberg
Members: 34,000 *Staff:* 65-70
Annual Budget: over $5,000,000 *Tel:* (202) 833-9680
Hist. Note: Founded in New Haven, CT in 1899 as the Soc. of American Bacteriologists. Became the American Soc. for Microbiology in 1960, and merged with the American Academy of Microbiology in 1969. Incorporated in the District of Columbia in 1947. A member of the Internat'l Union of Microbiological Societies. Promotes scientific knowledge of microbiology and related subjects through discussions, reports and publications. The American Academy of Microbiology is the professional services arm of the ASM. The ASM has an annual budget of $12,000,000.
Publications:
Abstracts of the Annual Meeting. a. adv.
Antimicrobial Agents and Chemotherapy. m. adv.
Applied and Environmental Microbiology. m. adv.
ASM News. m. adv.
Microbiological Reviews. q. adv.
Directory. adv. a.
Infection and Immunity. m. adv.
International Journal of Systematic Bacteriology. q. adv.
Journal of Bacteriology. m. adv.
Journal of Clinical Microbiology. m. adv.
Journal of Virology. m. adv.
Molecular and Cellular Biology. m. adv.
Annual Meetings: March
1987-Atlanta, GA(World Congress Ctr.)/March 1-6/10,000
1988-Miami Beach, FL(Convention Ctr.)/May 8-13/10,000
1989-New Orleans, LA(Convention Ctr.)/May 14-19/10,000

American Soc. for Neo-Hellenic Studies (1967)
Hist. Note: Became the American Institute for Patristic and Byzantine Studies in 1983.

American Soc. for Neurochemistry (1969)
1340 Old Chain Bridge Road, Suite 300, McLean VA 22101
Secretary: Richard J. Burk, Jr.
Members: 800-900 *Staff:* 1
Annual Budget: $25-50,000 *Tel:* (703) 790-1745
Hist. Note: Organized in 1968-1969 by U. S., Canadian and Mexican members of the Internat'l Soc. for Neurochemistry and incorporated in the District of Columbia, August 6, 1969. Membership: $30/yr.
Publication:
Transactions of the ASN. a.
Annual Meetings: Late Winter
1987-Caracas, Venezuela

American Soc. for Nondestructive Testing (1941)
4153 Arlingate Plaza, Columbus OH 43228
Mng. Director: Desmond D. Dewey
Members: 8,900 *Staff:* 24
Annual Budget: $2-5,000,000 *Tel:* (614) 274-6003
Hist. Note: Founded in August 1941 with nine charter members as the American Industrial Radium and X-Ray Soc. In 1947 became officially known as the Soc. for Nondestructive Testing, Inc. and in 1967 the name was changed to the American Soc. for Nondestructive Testing, Inc. Incorporated in Illinois in 1967. Engineers, metallurgists and managers in the field of nondestructive testing using radiation, magnetics, electricity and sound and heat for the transportation, chemical, petroleum and nuclear industries. Membership: $50/yr.
Publication:
Materials Evaluation. m. adv.
Semi-annual Meetings: Spring and Fall
1987-Phoenix, AZ(Hilton)/April 6-9
1987-Atlanta, GA(Hilton)/Oct. 5-9

American Soc. for Nursing Service Administrators (1967)
Hist. Note: Became the American Organization of Nurse Executives in 1985.

American Soc. for Parenteral and Enteral Nutrition (1975)
8605 Cameron St., Suite 500, Silver Spring MD 20910
Exec. Director: Barney Sellers
Members: 4,000 individuals *Staff:* 6-10
Annual Budget: $500-1,000,000 *Tel:* (301) 587-6315
Hist. Note: Physicians, dieticians, nurses, pharmacists, nutritionists, hospital administrators and others who work on hospital nutrition care teams. Concerned with the care of patients who cannot digest food normally, and therefore have to be fed parenterally (intravenously) or enterally (by tube). Membership: $65-$125/year.
Publications:
Journal of Parenteral and Enteral Nutrition. bi-m. adv.
Nutrition in Clinical Practice. bi-m.
Annual Meetings: Winter
1987-New Orleans, LA(Hilton)

American Soc. for Pediatric Neurosurgery (1978)
New York University Medical Ctr., 550 First Ave., New York NY 10016
President: Dr. Fred Epstein
Members: 25 *Staff:* 1
Annual Budget: under $10,000 *Tel:* (212) -

American Soc. for Performance Improvement (1966)
c/o Metro Waste Control Commission, 350 Metro Square Bldg., 7th & Robert St., St. Paul MN 55101
Nat'l President: Jean M. Erickson
Members: 800-900 *Staff:* 1
Annual Budget: $100-250,000 *Tel:* (612) 222-8423
Hist. Note: Formerly (1972) American Soc. for Zero Defects. Administrators of quality, productivity and performance improvement programs. Membership: $40/yr.
Publication:
Focus. q. adv.

American Soc. for Personnel Administration (1948)
606 N. Washington St., Alexandria VA 22314
President: Ronald C. Pilenzo
Members: 35,000 *Staff:* 55
Annual Budget: over $5,000,000 *Tel:* (703) 548-3440
Hist. Note: A professional society of personnel and industrial relations executives, and others involved in human resources management. Has an annual budget of $7 million. Membership: $135/yr.
Publications:
Personnel Administrator. m. adv.
Resource. m. adv.
Washington Insider. bi-w.
Annual Meetings: Spring/4,000-6,000
1987-Kansas City, MO(Vista Internat'l)/June 28-July 1
1988-San Francisco, CA(Hilton and Meridien)/June 26-30
1989-Boston, MA(Sheraton)
1990-Atlanta, GA

American Soc. for Pharmacology and Experimental Therapeutics (1908)
9650 Rockville Pike, Bethesda MD 20814
Exec. Officer: Kay A. Croker
Members: 3,800 *Staff:* 6-10
Annual Budget: $1-2,000,000 *Tel:* (301) 530-7060
Hist. Note: Organized at Johns Hopkins University on December 28, 1908 with 18 charter members. Incorporated in Maryland in 1933. A member of the Federation of American Societies for Experimental Biology, Internat'l Union of Pharmacology, and American Ass'n for the Advancement of Science, the U.S. Pharmacopeial Convention and the Nat'l Research Council, Assembly of Life Sciences. Membership: $65/yr.
Publications:
Clinical Pharmacology and Therapeutics. m. adv.
Drug Metabolism and Disposition. bi-m. adv.
Journal of Pharmacology and Experimental Therapeutics. m. adv.
Molecular Pharmacology. m. adv.
Pharmacological Reviews. q. adv.
The Pharmacologist. q. adv.
Rational Drug Therapy. m. adv.
Drug Metabolism Newsletter. q. adv.
Semi-annual Meetings: April and August
1987-Washington, DC/April 6-10
1987-Honolulu, HI/Aug. 15-19

American Soc. for Photobiology (1972)
1340 Old Chain Bridge Road, Suite 300, McLean VA 22101
Exec. Secretary: Richard J. Burk, Jr.
Members: 1,500 *Staff:* 6-10
Annual Budget: $50-100,000 *Tel:* (703) 790-1745
Hist. Note: Founded in 1972 to further the scientific study of the effects of light on all living organisms. Membership: $30/yr.
Publications:
ASP Newsletter. m.
Photochemistry and Photobiology. m. adv.

American Soc. for Photogrammetry and Remote Sensing (1934)
210 Little Falls St., Falls Church VA 22046-4398
Exec. Director: William D. French
Members: 7,600 *Staff:* 13
Annual Budget: $100-250,000 *Tel:* (703) 534-6617
Hist. Note: Founded as the American Soc. of Photogrammetry in Washington, DC in 1934 with 12 charter members and incorporated the same year in DC. Promotes the use of aerial photography and remote sensing. Membership: $45/yr.
Publication:
Photogrammetric Engineering and Remote Sensing. m. adv.
Semi-annual Meetings: Spring and Fall with the American Congress on
Surveying and Mapping
1987-Baltimore, MD(Convention Ctr.)/March 29-April 3/6,000
1987-Reno, NV(MGM Grand)/Oct. 4-9
1988-St. Louis, MO(Convention Ctr.)/March 13-18/6,000
1988-Virginia Beach, VA(Convention Center)/Sept. 12-16
1989-Baltimore, MD(Convention Center)/April 2-7
1989-Cleveland, OH/Sept. 7-12
1990-Denver, CO/March 18-24/8,000
1990-Atlantic City, NJ/Sept. 23-28
1991-Portland, OR/Sept. 16-20
1992-Detroit, MI/Sept.-Oct.
1993-New Orleans, LA/Sept.-Oct.

American Soc. for Psychoprophylaxis in Obstetrics (1960)
1840 Wilson Blvd., #204, Arlington VA 22201
Exec. Director: Robert H. Moran
Members: 5,000 *Staff:* 11-15
Annual Budget: $500-1,000,000 *Tel:* (703) 524-7802
Hist. Note: Founded and incorporated in New York in 1960. Begun as a medical society, the membership now includes childbirth educators, parents and physicians. Promotes prepared childbirth by the Lamaze method.
Publications:
GENESIS. bi.-m.
Lamaze Parents' Magazine. a.
Annual Meetings: Fall
1987-Chicago, IL

American Soc. for Public Administration (1939)
1120 G St., N.W., Suite 500, Washington DC 20005
Exec. Director: Keith F. Mulrooney
Members: 16,600 *Staff:* 19
Annual Budget: $1-2,000,000 *Tel:* (202) 393-7878
Hist. Note: A professional society of public service employees and others interested in the career of public administration. Affiliated with the Nat'l Ass'n of Schools of Public Affairs and Administration. The Nat'l Academy of Public Administration is a division of the ASPA. Membership: $20-70/yr.
Publications:
Public Administration Review. bi-m. adv.
Public Administration Times. bi-w. adv.
Annual Meetings: Spring
1987-Boston, MA(Sheraton)/March 28-April 1
1988-Portland, OR(Marriott-Hilton)/April 16-20
1989-Miami, FL(Hyatt-Conv. Center)/April 8-12
1990-Los Angeles(Hilton)/March 29-April 4

American Soc. for Quality Control (1946)
310 West Wisconsin Ave., Milwaukee WI 53203
Acting Exec. Director: Michael Thiel
Members: 49,000 *Staff:* 50
Annual Budget: $2-5,000,000 *Tel:* (414) 272-8575

00060 12 05 86 1233

Hist. Note: Founded and incorporated in New York State in 1946. Promotes the art of quality control and its application to industrial products and processes. Designates proficiency in specific areas of the field. Membership: $50/yr.
Publications:
Journal of Quality Technology. q.
Quality Progress. m. adv.
Technometrics. q. (with Am. Stat. Ass'n)
Annual Meetings: Spring
1987-Minneapolis, MN
1988-Dallas/Fort Worth, TX

American Soc. for Reformation Research (1947)
Hist. Note: Became the Society for Reformation Research in 1985.

American Soc. for Stereotactic and Functional Neurosurgery (1968)
6560 Fannin St., Suite 1530, Houston TX 77030
Secy.-Treas.: Dr. P.L. Gildenberg
Members: 175-200 *Staff:* 1
Annual Budget: under $10,000 *Tel:* (713) 790-0795
Hist. Note: Formerly (1972) the American Branch of the World Soc. for Research in Stereoencephalotomy. Members are surgeons using techniques for inserting delicate instruments into precise areas of the nervous system.
Publication:
Applied Neurophysiology. bi-m.
Biennial Meetings: Odd years

American Soc. for Surgery of the Hand (1946)
3025 South Parker Road, Suite 65, Aurora CO 80014
Admin. Director: Gail M. Gorman
Members: 811 *Staff:* 8
Annual Budget: $1-2,000,000 *Tel:* (303) 755-4588
Hist. Note: Established in 1946. Incorporated in Ohio in 1947. Membership: $175/yr.
Publications:
Bibliography for Surgery of the Hand. a.
Journal of Hand Surgery. q.
Annual Meetings:
1987-San Antonio, TX(Convention Center)/Sept. 9-12/1,500

American Soc. for Testing and Materials (1898)
Hist. Note: Became ASTM in 1983.

American Soc. for the Advancement of Anesthesia in Dentistry (1929)
475 White Plains Rd., Eastchester NY 10707
Exec. Secretary: Antonio Reyes-Guerra
Members: 6-700 *Staff:* 2-5
Annual Budget: under $10,000 *Tel:* (914) 961-8136
Hist. Note: Founded in 1929 by Dr. M. Hillel Feldman for the training of dentists in the use of nitrous oxide and oxygen. Incorporated in New Jersey in 1929. As new drugs and techniques developed, the Society studied them and expanded its role to include all aspects of pain control. Formerly (1965) the American Soc. for the Advancement of General Anesthesia in Dentistry. Membership: $40/year.
Publication:
Modern Pain Control. bi-a. adv.
Semi-Annual Meetings: Spring and Fall

American Soc. for the Study of Orthodontics (1945)
50-12 204th St., Bayside NY 11364
Exec. Secretary: Daisy N. Buchalter
Members: 250 *Staff:* 1
Annual Budget: $10-25,000 *Tel:* (212) 224-8898
Hist. Note: Formerly (1962) New York Soc. for the Study of Orthodontics. Affiliated with the Federation of Orthodontic Ass'ns.
Publication:
International Journal of Orthodontics. q. adv.
Annual Meetings: November, in conjunction with the greater New York Dental Meeting.

American Soc. for the Study of Religion (1959)
Dept. of Religious Studies, Rice University, Houston TX 77001
Secretary: Niels C. Nielsen, Jr.
Members: 105 (by election) *Staff:* 1
Annual Budget: under $10,000 *Tel:* (713) 527-4995
Hist. Note: Founded in Chicago by a group of scholars in the comparative study of religion under the leadership of Mircea Eliade and Joseph Kitagawa. Membership: $5/yr.
Publication:
Newsletter. irreg.
Annual Meetings: April or May

American Soc. for Theatre Research (1956)
Theatre Arts Program/DI, University of Pennsylvania, Philadelphia PA 19104
Secretary: Cary M. Mazer
Members: 6-700 *Staff:* 1
Annual Budget: $10-25,000 *Tel:* (215) 898-7382
Hist. Note: Members are scholars of the theatre. Affiliated with the Internat'l Federation for Theatre Research. Membership: $20/year.
Publications:
ASTR Newsletter. semi-a.
Theatre Survey. semi-a.
Internat'l Bibliography of Theatre. a.
Annual Meetings: November
1987-New York, NY/Oct.
1988-Undecided/Nov. 17-20
1989-New York, NY/Nov. 16-19

American Soc. for Therapeutic Radiology and Oncology (1955)
1891 Preston White Drive, Reston VA 22091-4326
Exec. Director: Sheila A. Aubin
Members: 2,200 *Staff:* 2-5
Annual Budget: $50-100,000 *Tel:* (703) 648-8900
Hist. Note: Physicians who limit their practice to radiation therapy. Formerly (1984) the American Soc. for Therapeutic Radiology and Oncology.
Publications:
Cancer. m.
Internat'l Journal of Radiation, Oncology, Biology and Physics.
Annual Meetings: September
1987-Seattle, WA
1988-Cincinnati, OH
1989-Minneapolis, MN

American Soc. for Training and Development (1944)
1630 Duke St., Box 1443, Alexandria VA 22313
Exec. V. President: Curtis E. Plott
Members: 25,000 *Staff:* 75
Annual Budget: over $5,000,000 *Tel:* (703) 683-8100
Hist. Note: Formerly (1964) American Soc. of Training Directors. ASTD is an educational society of trainers and human resource development professionals. Has an annual budget of approximately $7 million. Membership: $100/year.
Publications:
ASTD Nat'l Report. semi-m.
Training and Development Journal. m. adv.
Annual Meetings: Spring
1987-Atlanta, GA/June 21-26
1988-Dallas, TX/May 22-27

American Soc. of Abdominal Surgeons (1959)
675 Main St., Melrose MA 02176
Exec. Secretary: Blaise F. Alfano, M.D.
Members: 9,000-10,000 *Staff:* 11-15
Annual Budget: $250-500,000 *Tel:* (617) 665-6102
Hist. Note: Founded and incorporated in Delaware in 1959.
Publication:
Journal of Abdominal Surgery. m. adv.
Annual Meetings:
1987-Tampa, FL(National Study Center)
1988-Williamsburg, VA
1989-Tampa, FL(National Study Center)

American Soc. of Access Professionals (1980)
P.O. Box 76865, Washington DC 20013
President: Catherine McMillan
Members: 350
Annual Budget: $10-25,000 *Tel:* (202) 653-6460
Hist. Note: A group of individuals - government employees, lawyers, journalists, etc. - who are concerned with access to government data under current personal privacy and public information statutes. Has no paid staff; officers are elected annually. Membership: $20/yr.
Publication:
ASAP Newsletter. m.
Annual Meetings: Fall

American Soc. of Aerospace Pilots
Hist. Note: Reported defunct in 1986.

American Soc. of Agricultural Consultants (1963)
Enterprise Center, 8301 Greensboro Dr., Suite 260, McLean VA 22102
Exec. V. President: Frank Frazier
Members: 380 *Staff:* 2-5
Annual Budget: $100-250,000 *Tel:* (703) 356-2455
Hist. Note: Membership: $260/yr.
Publication:
Newsletter. irreg.
Annual Meetings: Fall

American Soc. of Agricultural Engineers (1907)
2950 Niles Road, St. Joseph MI 49085
Exec. V. President: Roger R. Castenson
Members: 12,000 *Staff:* 30-35
Annual Budget: $2-5,000,000 *Tel:* (616) 429-0300
Hist. Note: Founded in Madison, WI in 1907 and incorporated in Michigan in 1935.
Publications:
Agricultural Engineering. 7/yr. adv.
Transactions of the ASAE. bi-m.
ASAE Standards. a.
Semi-annual meetings: Summer and Winter
1987-Baltimore, MD/June 28-July 1
1987-Chicago, IL(Hyatt Regency)/Dec. 15-18
1988-Rapid City, SD(Conv. Center)/June 26-29
1988-Chicago, IL(Hyatt Regency)/Dec. 13-16
1989-Quebec City, Canada(Conv. Center)/June 25-28

American Soc. of Agronomy (1907)
677 South Segoe Rd., Madison WI 53711
Exec. V. President: Robert F. Barnes
Members: 13,000 *Staff:* 25-30
Annual Budget: $1-2,000,000 *Tel:* (608) 273-8080
Hist. Note: Founded December 13, 1907 and incorporated in 1948. Promotes the acquisition and diffusion of knowledge concerning the nature and interrelationship of plants, soils and the environment. Shares headquarters facilities with the Crop Science Soc. of America and the Soil Science Soc. of America. Membership: $32/year.
Publications:
Agronomy Journal. bi-m. adv.
Crops and Soils. 9/yr. adv.
Journal of Environmental Quality. q.
Journal of Agronomic Education. a.
Agronomy News. m.
Annual Meetings: Fall
1987-Atlanta, GA(Hyatt Regency/Hilton/Westin)/Nov. 29-Dec. 4/4,000

American Soc. of Allied Health Professions (1967)
1101 Connecticut Ave., N.W., Washington DC 20036
Exec. Director: Carolyn M. Del Polito
Members: 1,000-1,500 *Staff:* 6
Annual Budget: $500-1,000,000 *Tel:* (202) 857-1100
Hist. Note: Formerly (1974) Ass'n of Schools of Allied Health Professions. Membership includes allied health schools and programs, associations, and individual educators.
Publications:
Allied Health Trends. m.
Journal of Allied Health. q. adv.
Annual Meetings: Winter

American Soc. of Anesthesiologists (1905)
515 Busse Highway, Park Ridge IL 60068
Exec. Secretary: John W. Andes
Members: 23,000 *Staff:* 25-30
Annual Budget: over $5,000,000 *Tel:* (312) 825-5586
Hist. Note: Organized in 1905 in Brooklyn, NY as the Long Island Soc. of Anesthetists. Became the New York Soc. of Anesthetists in 1912 and incorporated in 1936 as the American Soc. of Anesthetists, Inc. Became the American Soc. of Anesthesiologists in 1945. Absorbed the Wood Library-Museum of Anesthesiology (founded in 1936) in 1974. The American College of Anesthesiologists is a section of the ASA. Membership: $175/yr.
Publications:
Anesthesiology. m. adv.
Newsletter. m.
Annual Meetings: Fall
1987-Atlanta, GA(World Congress Ctr.)/Oct. 10-14/9,000
1988-San Francisco, CA(Moscone Ctr.)/Oct. 8-12/12,000
1989-New Orleans, LA/Oct. 14-18/12,000
1990-Las Vegas, NV(Convention Ctr.)/Oct. 19-23/12,000

American Soc. of Animal Science (1908)
309 West Clark St., Champaign IL 61820
Exec. Secretary: Carl D. Johnson
Members: 4,000 *Staff:* 1
Annual Budget: $250-500,000 *Tel:* (217) 356-3182
Hist. Note: Founded in 1908 in Chicago as the American Soc. of Animal Nutrition. Became the American Soc. of Animal Production in 1912 and the American Soc. of Animal Science in 1941. Affiliated with the Nat'l Block and Bridle Club.
Publication:
Journal of Animal Science. m. adv.
Annual Meetings: Summer
1987-Logan, UT(Utah State Univ.)/July 28-31
1988-New Brunswick, NJ(Rutgers Univ.)/July 26-29
1989-Lexington, KY(Univ. of KY)/Aug. 1-4
1990-Ames, IA(Iowa State Univ.)/Aug. 1-4

American Soc. of Appraisers (1952)
11800 Sunrise Valley Drive, Suite 400, Reston VA 22091
Exec. Director: A.W. Carson
Members: 5,200 *Staff:* 10
Annual Budget: $1-2,000,000 *Tel:* (703) 620-3838
Hist. Note: Formed by a merger of the Soc. of Technical Appraisers (founded in 1939) and the American Soc. of Technical Appraisers (founded in In 1985 the Ass'n of Governmental Appraisers merged with ASA. Awards the ASA designation to appraisers with five years of experience who pass a written examination and awards the FASA designation to Fellows among this group selected by the Board of Governors.
Publications:
Appraisal and Valuation Manual. a.
Newsline. bi-m.
Valuation. a.
Annual Meetings: June
1987-Minneapolis, MN/June 29-July 1
1988-Washington, DC/June 27-29
1989-St. Louis, MO/June 26-28

American Soc. of Artists (1972)
Box 1326, Palatine IL 60078
President: Nancy J. Fregin
Members: 800-900 *Staff:* 14
Annual Budget: $50-100,000 *Tel:* (312) 751-2500
Hist. Note: An organization of professional artists, which sponsors art and crafts festivals and a lecture service and other services for members.
Publications:
Art Lovers' Art and Craft Fair Bulletin. q. adv.
A.S.A. Artisan. q. adv.
Annual Exhibits: 25-30

American Soc. of Ass'n Executives (1920)
1575 Eye St., N.W., Washington DC 20005
President: R. William Taylor, CAE
Members: 13,500 *Staff:* 100-105
Annual Budget: over $5,000,000 *Tel:* (202) 626-2723
Hist. Note: Founded in Lenox, Massachusetts in 1920 as American Trade Ass'n Executives, a successor organization to the Nat'l Trade Organization Secretaries. Name changed in 1956 to American Soc. of Ass'n Executives. A professional society of paid employees of associations and societies. Certifies association executives and awards the CAE (Certified

00061 12 05 86 1233

Association Executive) designation. Sponsors the ASAE Foundation. Connected with A-PAC. Membership: $140/yr. Has an annual budget of $12 million.
Publications:
Association Management. m. adv.
Inside ASAE. bi-w.
Who's Who in Association Management. a. adv.
Leadership Magazine. a.
Semi-annual Meetings: March and August/4,000
1987-Anaheim, CA(Convention Ctr.)/March 21-25
1987-New York, NY(Jacob K. Javits Convention Ctr.)/Aug. 22-26
1988-Dallas, TX(Convention Ctr.)/March 26-30
1988-Toronto, Ontario(Convention Ctr.)/Aug. 13-17

American Soc. of Aviation Writers (1980)
6 West Park Place, Great Neck NY 11023
Director: Ron Bernthal
Members: 57 *Staff:* 1
Annual Budget: $10-25,000 *Tel:* (516) 466-5353
Hist. Note: A small group of newspaper and magazine journalists in the United States involved in covering commercial aviation, space technology and airport facilities.
Annual Meetings: January/100

American Soc. of Bakery Engineers (1924)
2 North Riverside Plaza, Chicago IL 60606-2747
President: Robert A. Fischer
Members: 2,700 *Staff:* 2-5
Annual Budget: $250-500,000 *Tel:* (312) 332-2246
Hist. Note: Membership: $75/yr.
Publications:
E.I.S. Reports. irreg.
Proceedings. a.
Technical Bulletins. irreg.
Annual Meetings: Chicago(Chicago Marriott/March/1,200

American Soc. of Bariatric Physicians (1950)
7430 East Caley Ave., Bldg. 1, Suite 210, Englewood CO 80111
Exec. Director: James F. Merker, CAE
Members: 600-650 *Staff:* 2-5
Annual Budget: $250-500,000 *Tel:* (303) 779-4833
Hist. Note: Formerly (1972) American Soc. of Bariatrics. Members are physicians specializing in the treatment of obesity.
Publication:
The Bariatrician. q.
Annual Meetings: Fall/200-250
1987-Las Vegas, NV(MGM Grand)/Sept. 24-27
1988-Orlando, FL

American Soc. of Biological Chemists (1906)
9650 Rockville Pike, Bethesda MD 20814
Exec. Officer: Charles C. Hancock
Members: 6,500 *Staff:* 11-15
Annual Budget: $2-5,000,000 *Tel:* (301) 530-7145
Hist. Note: Founded December 26, 1906 in New York City under the leadership of Doctors John C. Abel and C. A. Herter and incorporated in New York in 1919. A founder and constituent member of the Federation of American Societies for Experimental Biology as well as the Pan American Ass'n of Biochemical Societies. A member of the American Ass'n for the Advancement of Science and the Council of Academic Societies of the American Ass'n of Medical Colleges. Membership: $40/yr.
Publication:
Journal of Biological Chemistry. 3x/m. adv.
Annual Meetings: Spring
1987-Philadelphia, PA
1988-Las Vegas, NV
1989-San Francisco, CA(Moscone Conv. Center)/Jan. 29-Feb. 2
1990-New Orleans, LA
1991-Atlanta, GA
1992-Houston, TX
1993-St. Louis, MO

American Soc. of Body Engineers (1945)
24634 Five Mile Road, Redford MI 48239
Business Manager & Director: Hyatt Eby, Jr.
Members: 1,620 *Staff:* 2
Annual Budget: $25-50,000 *Tel:* (313) 533-2600
Hist. Note: Automotive engineers and auto body designers. Membership: $25/yr.
Publications:
ASBE Newsletter. bi-m.
Body Engineering Technical Journal. semi-a. adv.
Semi-annual Meetings: April and Detroit area, in October.

American Soc. of Brewing Chemists (1934)
3340 Pilot Knob Rd., St. Paul MN 55121
Exec. Officer: Raymond J. Tarleton
Members: 750-800 *Staff:* 2-5
Annual Budget: $100-250,000 *Tel:* (612) 454-7250
Hist. Note: A professional society of brewing chemists. Formerly the Malt Analysis Standards Committee. Membership: $70/yr. (individual), $150/yr. (corporate).
Publications:
Journal. q.
Newsletter. q.
Annual Meetings: Spring
1987-Cincinnati, OH(Hyatt Regency)/May 22-26
1988-Denver, CO(Marriott)/April 23-27

American Soc. of Business Press Editors (1949)
4445 Gilmer, Cleveland OH 44143
Exec. V. President: Jeanne Ribinskas
Members: 350 *Staff:* 1
Annual Budget: $10-25,000 *Tel:* (216) 531-8306
Hist. Note: Formerly (1964) Soc. of Business Magazine Editors. Membership: $50/yr.
Publications:
The Editor's Notebook. bi-m.
ASBPE Newsletter. bi-m.
Annual Meetings: Summer
1987-Washington, DC(Marriott)/June 14-17

American Soc. of Cartographers (1965)
Hist. Note: Address unknown in 1985-86.

American Soc. of Cataract and Refractive Surgery (1974)
3700 Pender Drive, Suite 108, Fairfax VA 22030
Exec. Director: David A. Karcher
Members: 4,500 *Staff:* 6
Tel: (703) 591-2220
Hist. Note: Formerly (1986) American Intraocular Implant Soc. Disseminates and facilitates the flow of information concerning lens implantation within the ophthalmic community. Added a division in 1986: American Soc. of Ophthalmic Administrators (ASOA) comprised of 500 members. Membership: $175/yr.
Publication:
Journal of Cataract and Refractive Surgery. bi-m. adv.
Annual Meetings: Spring/2,500
1987-Orlando, FL(Marriott's World Ctr.)/April 6-10
1988-Los Angeles, CA(Century Plaza)/March 27-30
1989-Washington, DC(Hilton)/April 25-28
1990-Los Angeles, CA(Centuray Plaza)/March 25-28
1991-Boston, MA/April 6-11

American Soc. of Certified Business Counselors (1979)
11500 Olive Street Road, Suite 182, Creve Coeur MO 63141
Contact Person: Judith Ellman
Members: 35-40 *Staff:* 1
Annual Budget: under $10,000 *Tel:* (314) 567-9277
Hist. Note: Founded as the American Society of Certified Financing Counselors, it assumed its present name in 1981.

American Soc. of Certified Engineering Technicians (1964)
P.O. Box 7789, Shawnee Mission KS 66207
Exec. Director: Jim Wilhoit, CET
Members: 5,000-5,500 *Staff:* 2-5
Annual Budget: $100-250,000 *Tel:* (816) 941-9760
Hist. Note: Members are individuals who have been certified by the Nat'l Institute for Certification in Engineering Technologies as either an Associate Engineering Technician (AET), Engineering Technician (ET), Senior Engineering Technician (SET), or Engineering Technologists. Affiliated with the Nat'l Soc. of Professional Engineers. Membership: $40/yr. (individual), $250-500/yr. (organization/company).
Publication:
Certified Engineering Technician. bi-m. adv.
Annual Meetings: June
1987-El Paso, TX

American Soc. of Chartered Life Underwriters
Hist. Note: Became the American Soc. of CLU & ChFC in 1986.

American Soc. of Church History (1888)
305 E. Country Club Lane, Wallingford PA 19086
Secy.-Treas.: William B. Miller
Members: 1400-1500 *Staff:* 2-5
Annual Budget: $50-100,000 *Tel:* (215) 566-7126
Hist. Note: Affiliated with the American Historical Ass'n. A member of the Council on the Study of Religion.
Publication:
Church History. q.
Annual Meetings: With American Historical Ass'n in late December

American Soc. of Cinematographers (1919)
1782 North Orange Drive, Hollywood CA 90078
Secretary: Alfred Keller
Members: 275-300 *Staff:* 9
Annual Budget: $250-500,000 *Tel:* (213) 876-5080
Hist. Note: Membership is by invitation $200/yr. (individual), $300/yr. (organization/company).
Publications:
American Cinematographer. m. adv.
American Cinematographer Manual. quadrennial.
Monthly Meetings: except July, August and September.

American Soc. of Civil Engineers (1852)
345 East 47th St., New York NY 10017
Exec. Director: Dr. Edward O. Pfrang
Members: 104,000 *Staff:* 150
Annual Budget: over $5,000,000 *Tel:* (202) 705-7496
Hist. Note: Founded November 5, 1852 in New York City as the American Soc. of Civil Engineers and Architects. Dormant 1855-1867. Revived in 1868 as the American Soc. of Civil Engineers and incorporated in New York in 1877. Annual budget is $16 million. Membership: $75/yr.
Publications:
ASCE Publications Abstracts. bi-m.
Civil Engineering. m. adv.
Journals of 18 Technical Divisions. m. bi-m. q.
Transactions. a.
ASCE News. m.
Semi-annual meetings: Spring and Fall/1,750
1987-Atlantic City, NJ(Resorts International)/April 26-30
1987-Anaheim, CA(Disneyland)/Oct. 26-30
1988-Nashville, TN(Opryland(/May 9-13
1988-St. Louis, MO(Sheraton St. Louis & Convention Center)/Oct. 24-28

American Soc. of Clinical Hypnosis (1957)
2250 East Devon Ave., Suite 336, Des Plaines IL 60018
Exec. V. President: William F. Hoffman, Jr.
Members: 4,000 *Staff:* 5
Annual Budget: $500-1,000,000 *Tel:* (312) 297-3317
Hist. Note: Established the American Soc. of Clinical Hypnosis-Education and Research Foundation in 1962. Affiliated with the American Ass'n for the Advancement of Science. Membership: $95/yr.
Publication:
American Journal of Clinical Hypnosis. q.
Annual Meetings:
1987-Las Vegas, NV(Riviera)/April 6-11/400
1988-Chicago, IL(Hyatt Regency)/March 14-19
1989-Nashville, TN(Vanderbilt Plaza)/March 13-18

American Soc. of Clinical Oncology (1964)
435 N. Michigan Ave., Chicago IL 60611
Exec. Director: Alfred Van Horn, III
Members: 6,157 *Staff:* 2-5
Annual Budget: $500-1,000,000 *Tel:* (312) 644-0828
Hist. Note: Founded November 5, 1964 and incorporated in 1965 to promote the study of neoplastic diseases, clinical research and patient care. Members are academicians in universities, medical centers, teaching and research facilities affiliated with cancer centers, major hospitals or in community practice.
Publications:
Proceedings. a.
Journal of Clinical Onclogy.
Annual Meetings: With American Ass'n for Cancer Research.
1987-Atlanta, GA(World Congress)/May 17-19/5,000
1988-New Orleans, LA/May 22-24/5,000
1989-San Francisco, CA(Moscone Center)/May 21-23/5,500

American Soc. of Clinical Pathologists (1922)
2100 West Harrison St., Chicago IL 60612
Secretary and Chief of Staff: Robert A. Dietrich, M.D., J.D.
Members: 48,000 *Staff:* 175
Annual Budget: over $5,000,000 *Tel:* (312) 738-1336
Hist. Note: Founded in St. Louis, ASCP is a professional society of clinical pathologists, clinical scientists, chemists, microbiologists and medical technologists. Its purpose is to promote a wider application of pathology and laboratory medicine to the diagnosis and treatment of disease, to conduct educational programs and published educational materials in the field of clinical and anatomic pathology and to conduct a program for the examination and certification of medical laboratory personnel. It presents awards and has numerous scientific councils and committees. Maintains a Washington office. Has an annual budget over $13 million. Membership: $230/yr.
Publications:
American Journal of Clinical Pathology. m. adv.
Laboratory Medicine m. adv.
ASCP Newsletter. m.
Semi-annual Meetings: with the College of American Pathologists
1987-San Francisco, CA(Hilton)/March 28-April 2
1987-New Orleans, LA(Conv. Center-Sheraton)/Oct. 24-30
1988-Kansas City, MO(Westin-Hyatt)/April 16-21
1988-Las Vegas, NV(Conv. Center-Hilton)/Oct. 22-28
1989-Chicago, IL(Hyatt Regency)/March 11-16
1989-Washington, DC(Conv. Center)/Oct. 28-Nov. 3

American Soc. of CLU & ChFC (1928)
270 Bryn Mawr Avenue, Bryn Mawr PA 19010
Exec. V. President & Mng. Director: John R. Driskill, CLU, ChFC
Members: 32,000 *Staff:* 50-55
Annual Budget: over $5,000,000 *Tel:* (215) 526-2500
Hist. Note: Formerly (1986) American Soc. of Chartered Life Underwriters. The Society is a national organization of insurance and financial service professionals who have earned the designations "CLU" (Chartered Life Underwriter) or "ChFC" (Chartered Financial Consultant) through the American College, Bryn Mawr, PA. Has an annual budget of $5.5 million. Membership: $100/yr.
Publications:
Journal of the American Society of CLU and ChFC. bi-m. adv.
Query. m.
Assets. bi-m.
Financial Monitor. bi-m.
Annual Meetings: October
1987-Washington, DC(Sheraton Washington)/Oct. 4-7/2,000

American Soc. of Colon and Rectal Surgeons (1899)
#1717, 615 Griswold, Detroit MI 48226
Exec. Director: Harriette Gibson
Members: 1,350 *Staff:* 2-5
Annual Budget: $100-250,000 *Tel:* (313) 961-7880
Hist. Note: Founded in Columbus, Ohio in 1899 as the American Proctologic Soc. with 12 charter members. Incorporated in Delaware in 1947. Name changed in 1973 to the American Soc. of Colon and Rectal Surgeons. Sponsored the formation of the American Board of Colon and Rectal Surgery and in 1957 founded the American Society of Colon and Rectal Surgeons Research Foundation. Membership: $200/year (individual).

00062 12 05 86 1233

Publication:
Diseases of the Colon and Rectum. m. adv.
Annual Meetings: Spring/800
1987-Washington, DC(Sheraton)/April 5-10/900-1,000
1988-Anaheim, CA(Disneyland)/June 12-17/900-1,000

American Soc. of Composers, Authors and Publishers (1914)
One Lincoln Plaza, New York NY 10023
President: Morton Gould
Members: 35,000 *Staff:* 800
Annual Budget: over $5,000,000 *Tel:* (212) 595-3050
Hist. Note: America's first performing rights Society was organized in 1914 by the composer Victor Herbert and eight of his colleagues. The goal of the Society was to license all commercial users of copyrighted music so that the musical creative talent of this country and their publishers might receive just financial returns. Budget over $200 million. Membership: $10/yr. (writers); $50/yr. (publishers).
Publication:
ASCAP in Action. irreg.

American Soc. of Computer Dealers (1981)
3131 McKinney Ave., Suite 700, Dallas TX 75204
Gen. Counsel: Bryan Kent Ford
Members: 60 *Staff:* 1
Annual Budget: $25-50,000 *Tel:* (214) 871-0700
Hist. Note: Members are dealers, leasing companies, brokerage firms and refurbishment maintenance companies. Moving in early 1987; mail will be forwarded.
Publication:
Newsletter. semi-a.

American Soc. of Consultant Pharmacists (1969)
2300 9th St., South, Arlington VA 22204
Exec. Director: R. Tim Webster
Members: 2,500 *Staff:* 8-10
Annual Budget: $500-1,000,000 *Tel:* (703) 920-8492
Hist. Note: Pharmacists specializing in service to long-term care facilities and geriatric institutions. Membership: $125/yr. (individual), $500/yr. (company).
Publications:
Update Newsletter. m.
Clinical Consult. q.
Consultant Pharmacist Journal. bi-m. adv.
Annual Meetings: November/1,200
1987-New York, NY(Marriott Marquis)/Nov. 4-8
1988-Las Vegas, NV(Caesar's Palace)/Nov. 9-13
1989-Chicago, IL(Hyatt Regency)/Nov. 8-12

American Soc. of Consulting Arborists (1967)
700 Canterbury Road, Clearwater FL 33546
Exec. Director: Jack Siebenthaler
Members: 190-210 *Staff:* 1
Annual Budget: $25-50,000 *Tel:* (813) 446-3356
Hist. Note: A professional society of individuals skilled in growing and caring for shade and ornamental trees. Membership: $125/yr.
Publication:
Arboricultural Consultant. bi-m.
Annual Meetings:
1987-Santa Barbara, CA(Red Lion Inn)/Oct. 14-17/125-150

American Soc. of Consulting Planners (1966)
210 Seventh St., S.E., Suite 647, Washington DC 20003
Exec. Administrator: Pamela H. Wev
Members: 120-130 firms *Staff:* 1
Annual Budget: $25-50,000 *Tel:* (202) 544-0035
Hist. Note: Formed as a spin-off from the American Institute of Planners to represent the interests of private, as opposed to public, planners. Incorporated in the District of Columbia. Members are planning firms engaged in the private practice of planning. Membership: $150-300/yr. (company)
Publications:
Bulletin. m.
Newsletter. q.
Membership Directory. a.
Annual Meetings: Spring, in conjunction with the American Planning Ass'n

American Soc. of Contemporary Medicine, Surgery and Ophthalmology (1970)
233 East Erie, #710, Chicago IL 60611
Director: Dr. John G. Bellows
Members: 15,000-16,000 *Staff:* 6-10
Annual Budget: $250-500,000 *Tel:* (312) 951-1400
Hist. Note: Formed by a merger of the American Soc. for Contemporary Ophthalmology (formed in 1966) and the American Soc. of Contemporary Medicine and Surgery (formerly the Soc. of Cryosurgery, formed in 1968).
Publications:
Annals of Ophthalmology. m. adv.
Comprehensive Therapy. m.
Glaucoma. bi-m. adv.
Journal of Ocular Therapy and Surgery. bi-m. adv.
Annual Meetings:
1987-Las Vegas, NV(Caesar's Palace)/March 14-20/1,000

American Soc. of Corporate Secretaries (1946)
1270 Avenue of the Americas, New York NY 10020
President: Donald D. Geary
Members: 2,900 *Staff:* 11-15
Annual Budget: $1-2,000,000 *Tel:* (212) 765-2620
Hist. Note: Members are officers of corporations who deal with the board of directors, shareholders and senior management. Membership: $335/yr.
Publication:
The Corporate Secretary. 10/yr.
Annual Meetings: 7
Summer/1,200
1987-White Sulphur Springs, WV(Greenbrier)/June 28-July 1
1988-Colorado Springs, CO(Broadmoor)/June 26-29
1989-Boca Raton, FL(Boca Raton Hotel & Club/May 31-June 3
1990-San Francisco, CA(St. Francis)/June 13-16
1991-Quebec, Canada(Hilton)/June 26-29
1992-White Sulphur Springs,WV(Greenbrier)/July 5-8
1993-San Antonio, TX(Hyatt Regency)/May 26-29

American Soc. of Criminology (1941)
1314 Kinnear Rd., Columbus OH 43212
Exec. Secretary: Dr. Charles Wellford
Members: 2,000 *Staff:* 1
Annual Budget: $50-100,000 *Tel:* (614) 422-9207
Hist. Note: Established in Berkeley, California as the Soc. for the Advancement of Criminology, it absorbed the Ass'n of College Police Training Officials in 1947 and assumed its present name in 1956. Affiliated with the American Ass'n for the Advancement of Science, members are criminologists, psychologists, sociologists and students in institutions of higher learning. Possibly moving in early 1987; mail to the above address will be forwarded.
Publications:
The Criminologist. bi-m. adv.
Criminology: An Interdisciplinary Journal. q. adv.
Annual Meetings: November
1987-Montreal, Quebec/Nov. 11-14
1988-Chicago, IL/Nov. 8-12

American Soc. of Cytology (1951)
1015 Chestnut St., Suite 1518, Philadelphia PA 19107
President: Dr. Thomas A. Bonfiglio, M.D.
Members: 4,100-4,200 *Staff:* 2-5
Tel: (215) 922-3880
Hist. Note: Founded in 1951 as the Inter-Society Cytology Council. Incorporated in Massachusetts in 1959. Became American Soc. of Cytology in 1961.
Publication:
The Cytotechnologist's Bulletin. bi-m. adv.
Annual Meetings: November

American Soc. of Dentistry for Children (1927)
211 East Chicago Ave., Ste. 920, Chicago IL 60611
Exec. Officer: Dr. George W. Teuscher
Members: 7,000 *Staff:* 9
Annual Budget: $500-1,000,000 *Tel:* (312) 943-1244
Hist. Note: Membership: $70/yr.
Publications:
ASDC Newsletter. bi-m.
Journal of Dentistry for Children. bi-m. adv.
Annual Meetings: Fall/350
1987-Tucson, AZ(El Conquistador)/Oct. 14-18
1988-Orlando, FL(Hyatt Cypress Gardens)/Oct. 12-16

American Soc. of Dermatopathology (1962)
Denver General Hospital, 777 Bannock Street, Denver CO 80204
Secy.-Treas.: Dr. Loren E. Golitz, M.D.
Members: 650 individuals *Staff:* 1
Annual Budget: $100-250,000 *Tel:* (303) 983-6063
Publication:
Journal of Cutaneous Pathology. (published in Denmark)
Annual Meetings:
1987-San Antonio, TX(Hyatt Regency)/Dec. 3-4
1988-Washington, DC/Dec. 1-2
1989-San Francisco, CA/Nov. 30-Dec. 1

American Soc. of Directors of Volunteer Services (1968)
840 North Lake Shore Dr., Chicago IL 60611
Director: Elizabeth Dudley
Members: 1,700 *Staff:* 4
Annual Budget: $250-500,000 *Tel:* (312) 280-6436
Hist. Note: Affiliated with the American Hospital Ass'n. Membership: $60-90/yr.
Publication:
Newsletter for Society Members. q.

American Soc. of Echocardiography (1975)
1100 Raleigh Bldg., Box 2598, Raleigh NC 27602
Exec. Director: Sharon Perry
Members: 3,000 individuals *Staff:* 2-5
Annual Budget: $50-100,000 *Tel:* (919) 821-1435
Hist. Note: Physicians, nurses and technicians concerned with ultrasound diagnosis of heart disease. Incorporated in the state of Indiana. Membership: $20-30/year.
Publication:
Echocardiography. q.
Annual Meetings: With the American Heart Association

American Soc. of Educators
1511 Walnut St., Philadelphia PA 19102
Exec. Director: Laurie Wagman
Members: 26,000 *Staff:* 6-10
Annual Budget: $250-500,000 *Tel:* (215) 563-3501
Hist. Note: Members are individuals interested in the development and use of electronic and audio-visual technologies as teaching aids. Membership: $27/yr.
Publication:
Media and Methods. 5/yr. adv.

American Soc. of EEG Technologists (1959)
Hist. Note: Became the American Soc. of Electro-eurodiagnostic Technologists in 1985.

American Soc. of Electro-Neurodiagnostic Technologists (1959)
Sixth at Quint, Carroll IA 51401
Exec. Secretary: M. Fran Pedelty
Members: 2,200 *Staff:* 2-5
Annual Budget: $100-250,000 *Tel:* (712) 792-2978
Hist. Note: Formerly (1985) the American Soc. of EEG Technologists. Membership: $40/year.
Publications:
American Journal of EEG Technology. q. adv.
ASET Newsletter. q.
Annual Meetings: With American Electroencephalographic Soc.
1987-St. Louis, MO/Sept. 14-18

American Soc. of Electroplated Plastics (1966)
1133 15th St., N.W., Suite 620, Washington DC 20005
Exec. Director: David W. Barrack
Members: 85-90 companies *Staff:* 2-5
Annual Budget: $50-100,000 *Tel:* (202) 293-5910
Hist. Note: Organized in 1966 and incorporated in 1967 in Pennsylvania.
Publications:
Bulletin. q.
Directory. a.
Annual Meetings: Fall
1987-Phoenix,AZ/Oct. 19-23
1988-Orlando,FL/Oct. 18-21

American Soc. of Enologists (1950)
Hist. Note: Became the American Soc. for Enology and Viticulture in 1984.

American Soc. of Extra-corporeal Technology (1964)
1980 Isaac Newton Square South, Reston VA 22090
Exec. Director: George M. Cate
Members: 1,600 *Staff:* 2-5
Annual Budget: $250-500,000 *Tel:* (703) 435-8556
Hist. Note: Doctors, nurses and technicians concerned with the function of heart-lung machines, artificial kidneys, and other life-sustaining machines. Formerly (until 1968) the American Soc. of Extracorporeal Circulation Technicians. Membership: $50/yr.
Publications:
Journal of Extracorporeal Technology. q.
Perfusion Life. 10/yr. adv.
Annual Meetings: Spring
1987-Louisville, KY/March 20-22

American Soc. of Farm Managers and Rural Appraisers (1929)
950 S. Cherry St., Suite 106, Denver CO 80222
Exec. V. President: John Olson
Members: 4,000 *Staff:* 8
Annual Budget: $500-1,000,000 *Tel:* (303) 758-3513
Hist. Note: Awards the AFM (Accredited Farm Manager) and ARA (Accredited Rural Appraiser) designations. Membership: $50-$110/yr.
Publications:
Journal of the ASFMRA. semi-a.
Newsletter. bi-m.
Annual Meetings: Fall/500-675
1987-San Antonio, TX(Marriott)/Nov. 15-18
1988-Indianapolis, IN(Hyatt Regency)/Nov. 13-16
1989-Savannah, GA

American Soc. of Forensic Odontology (1969)
2101 East 41st St., Ashtabula OH 44004
President: Curtis Mertz
Members: 150 individuals *Staff:* 1
Annual Budget: under $10,000 *Tel:* (216) 992-3143
Hist. Note: Dentists and others interested in the study of teeth for identification purposes, particularly in relation to malpractice, child abuse, and bite mark identification.
Publications:
Internat'l Journal of Forensic Odontology. 3/yr. adv.
Newsletter. 3/yr.
Annual Meetings:
1987-San Diego, CA(Town & Country)/Feb./150

American Soc. of Furniture Designers (1981)
Box 2688, High Point NC 27261
Exec. Secretary: Judith Reagan
Members: 200-250 individuals; 30 corporations *Staff:* 2-5
Annual Budget: $25-50,000 *Tel:* (919) 884-4074
Hist. Note: The only nationwide, non-profit membership organization for furniture designers. Founded in High Point, North Carolina in October 1981. Membership: $150/yr. (individual); $375/yr. (organization/company)
Publications:
The Designer Forum. q. adv.
Concerning Us (newsletter). m.
Semi-Annual Meetings: Spring and Fall
1987-Chicago, IL/June

American Soc. of Gas Engineers (1954)
P.O. Box 936, Tinley Park IL 60477
Exec. Director: Ray Kendall
Members: 600 *Staff:* 1

00063 12 05 86 1233

Annual Budget: $10-25,000 *Tel:* (312) 532-5707
Hist. Note: Formerly (1973) Gas Appliance Engineers Soc. Membership: $5-40/yr.
Publication:
Tech Digest. 3-4/yr.
Annual Meetings:
1987-Itasca, IL(Carson Inn-Nordic Hills)/May 14-15/50-75

American Soc. of Genealogists (1940)
Box 4970, Washington DC 20008
Secretary: Neil D. Thompson
Members: 50
Annual Budget: $10-25,000
Hist. Note: An honorary society, limited to 50, of genealogists chosen on the basis of their published work. Has no paid staff, dues or permanent address.
Annual Meetings: October
1987-Washington, DC

American Soc. of Golf Course Architects (1946)
221 North LaSalle St., Chicago IL 60601
Exec. Secretary: Paul Fullmer
Members: 80-90 individuals *Staff:* 1
Annual Budget: $25-50,000 *Tel:* (312) 372-7090
Hist. Note: Membership: $200/yr.
Publication:
Suppliers Directory. a. adv.
Annual Meetings: Spring
1987-Maui, HI(Royal Lahaina)/Feb. 15-19

American Soc. of Group Psychotherapy and Psychodrama (1942)
116 East 27th St., New York NY 10003
Exec. Director: Stephen Wilson
Members: 800 *Staff:* 2-5
Annual Budget: $10-25,000 *Tel:* (212) 725-0033
Hist. Note: Membership includes psychiatrists, psychologists, sociologists and nurses.
Annual Meetings: Usually Spring, in New York City.

American Soc. of Hand Therapists (1977)
1027 Highway 70 West, Garner NC 27529
Exec. Director: Charlene B. Barbour
Members: 340
Annual Budget: $50-100,000 *Tel:* (919) 779-2748
Hist. Note: Members are physical or occupational therapists specializing in working with patients with hand problems. Membership: $100/yr.
Publications:
ASHT Newsletter. q. adv.
Hand Journal. q.
Annual Meetings:
1987-San Antonio, TX/Sept. 11-14

American Soc. of Heating, Refrigerating and Air-Conditioning Engineers (1894)
1791 Tullie Circle, N.E., Atlanta GA 30329
Exec. Directory/Secretary: Frank M. Coda
Members: 50,000 *Staff:* 75-80
Annual Budget: over $5,000,000 *Tel:* (404) 636-8400
Hist. Note: Organized in 1894 and incorporated in 1895 as the American Soc. of Heating and Ventilating Engineers. Became the American Soc. of Heating and Air-Conditioning Engineers in 1954. Merged in 1959 with the American Soc. of Refrigerating Engineers (established 1904) to form the American Soc. of Heating, Refrigerating and Air-Conditioning Engineers. Maintains a Washington office. Has an annual budget of $9.41 million. Membership: $75/year.
Publications:
ASHRAE Journal. m. adv.
ASHRAE Transactions. semi-a.
ASHRAE Handbook. a.
Insights. m. a.
Annual Meetings: Summer
1987-Nashville(Opryland)/Jun. 28-July 1
1988-Ottawa, Canada(Chateau Laurier)/Jun 26-29
1989-Vancouver, Canada(Hyatt-Four Seasons)/June 25-28

American Soc. of Hematology (1957)
6900 Grove Road, Thorofare NJ 08086-9447
Exec. Director: Ira Weiss
Members: 3,400 *Staff:* 2
Annual Budget: $500-1,000,000 *Tel:* (609) 848-1000
Hist. Note: Affiliated with Internat'l Soc. of Hematology. Membership: $85 initial fee; $80/yr. to renew.
Publications:
Blood. m. adv.
Membership Directory. bien.
Meeting Program. a.
Annual Meetings: December
1987-Washington, DC(Sheraton)/Dec. 4-8/3,400
1988-San Antonio, TX(Convention Ctr.)/Dec. 3-6/3,500
1989-Atlanta, GA(Hilton and Marriott)/Dec. 2-5/3,600
1990-Boston, MA(Convention Ctr.)/Nov. 28-Dec. 4/3,600
1991-St. Louis, MO(Convention Ctr.)/Dec. 6-13/3,600

American Soc. of Home Inspectors (1975)
1010 Wisconsin Ave., N.W., Suite 630, Washington DC 20007
Exec. Director: Anita S. Bollt
Members: 400 individuals *Staff:* 2-5
Annual Budget: $100-250,000 *Tel:* (202) 965-7510
Hist. Note: Members are professional home inspectors. Membership: $150/year.
Publications:
ASHI Reporter. m.
Annual Conference Proceedings. a.
Annual Meetings: February
1987-San Francisco, CA
1988-Orlando, FL

American Soc. of Hospital Attorneys (1968)
Hist. Note: Became the American Academy of Hospital Attorneys in 1984.

American Soc. of Hospital-Based Emergency Air Medical Services
Hist. Note: Uses its acronym, ASHBEAMS, as its official title.

American Soc. of Hospital Pharmacists (1942)
4630 Montgomery Ave., Bethesda MD 20814
Exec. V. President: Dr. Joseph A. Oddis
Members: 20-21,000 *Staff:* 110
Annual Budget: over $5,000,000 *Tel:* (301) 657-3000
Hist. Note: Founded in 1942 as the American Soc. of Hospital Pharmacists, an outgrowth of the Sub-Section of Hospital Pharmacy of the American Pharmaceutical Ass'n. Incorporated in the District of Columbia in 1955. Reincorporated in Maryland in 1984. Sponsors and supports the American Soc. of Hosptial Pharmacists Research and Education Foundation. Has an annual budget of $14,000,000. Membership: $85/yr.
Publications:
American Hospital Formulary Service. a.
American Journal of Hospital Pharmacy. m. adv.
ASHP Newsletter. m.
Clinical Pharmacy. bi-m. adv.
International Pharmaceutical Abstracts. bi-w.
Semi-annual Meetings: June and December
1987-Washington, DC(Convention Ctr.)/May 31-June 4/4,000
1987-Atlanta, GA(George World Congress Ctr.)/Dec. 6-10/10,000
1988-San Francisco, CA/June 5-9/4,000
1988-Dallas, TX(Convention Ctr.)/Dec. 4-8/10,000

American Soc. of Human Genetics (1948)
15501-B Monona Drive, Derwood MD 20855
Administrative Director: Gerry Gurvitch
Members: 2,900 *Staff:* 6
Annual Budget: $500-1,000,000 *Tel:* (301) 424-4120
Hist. Note: Incorporated in North Carolina in 1952 and reincorporated in Maryland in 1985. Affiliated with the American Ass'n for the Advancement of Science. Membership: $55/yr.
Publications:
American Journal of Human Genetics. m. adv.
Membership Directory. biennial.
Annual Meetings: Fall
1987-San Diego(Town & Country)/Oct. 7-10
1988-New Orleans(Hyatt)/Oct. 12-16
1989-Baltimore, MD(Convention Center)/Nov. 11-15/1,800

American Soc. of Ichthyologists and Herpetologists (1913)
Florida State Museum, University of Florida, Gainesville FL 32611
Secretary: Dr. Carter R. Gilbert
Members: 3,200 individuals and institutions *Staff:* 1
Annual Budget: $100-250,000 *Tel:* (904) 392-6572
Hist. Note: Incorporated in the District of Columbia. Purpose is to advance the study of fishes, amphibians and reptiles. Has no permanent address; the Secretary stays in office 3-5 years.
Publication:
Copeia. q.
Annual Meetings: Summer
1987-Albany, NY(N.Y. State Museum)/June 21-26
1988-Ann Arbor, MI(Univ. of Michigan)/June
1989-San Francisco, CA(S.F. State University & CA Academy of Sciences)

American Soc. of Indexers (1968)
1700 18th St., N.W., Washington DC 20009
President: Ben-Ami Lipetz
Members: 500
Annual Budget: $10-25,000 *Tel:* (215) 837-9615
Hist. Note: Members include freelance and salaried indexers, abstracters, librarians, editors, publishers annd organization employing indexers. Membership: $30/yr.
Publications:
ASI Register of Indexers. a.
The Indexer. semi-a.
ASI Newsletter. bi-m.
Annual Meetings: April-May
1987-New York, NY/May 1/200

American Soc. of Interior Designers (1975)
1430 Broadway, New York NY 10018
Exec. Director: Robert H. Angle
Members: 22,000 *Staff:* 30-35
Annual Budget: $2-5,000,000 *Tel:* (212) 944-9220
Hist. Note: A consolidation of the American Institute of Interior Designers (1931) and the Nat'l Soc. of Interior Designers (1957).
Annual Meetings: Summer/2,000
1987-Toronto, Canada

American Soc. of Internal Medicine (1956)
1101 Vermont Ave., N.W., Suite 500, Washington DC 20005
Exec. V. President: Joseph F. Boyle, M.D.
Members: 20,000 *Staff:* 39
Annual Budget: $2-5,000,000 *Tel:* (202) 289-1700
Hist. Note: Formed in 1956 as a national federation of state societies representing over 20,000 internists, subspecialists of internal medicine, and neurologists. The society focuses on all aspects of medicine, including quality, availability, and cost of medical services. Membership: $165/yr.
Publications:
The Internist. m. adv.
The Internist's Intercom. m.
Annual Meetings: Fall
1987-Washington, DC(Marriott)/Oct. 15-17/500-700

American Soc. of Internat'l Executives (1964)
1777 Walton, Suite 419, Blue Bell PA 19422
President: Anthony Swartz
Members: 400 *Staff:* 2
Annual Budget: $10-25,000 *Tel:* (215) 643-3040
Hist. Note: Founded in April 1964 under the sponsorship of the Foreign Traders Ass'n of Philadelphia and incorporated in 1975, ASIE is a professional society which sets standards, gives examinations and bestows appropriate recognition through certification on career personnel engaged in international trade. Awards the titles "CDS" (Certified Documentary Specialist), "CIE" (Certified International Executive), both through examination, and "EIE" (Experienced International Executive). Membership: $20-50/yr. (individual); $75/yr. (corporate)
Publications:
ASIE Bulletin. m.
Roster. a.
Annual Meetings: Spring in Philadelphia, PA

American Soc. of Internat'l Law (1906)
2223 Massachusetts Ave., N.W., Washington DC 20008
Exec. Director: John Lawrence Hargrove
Members: 5,000 *Staff:* 18-20
Annual Budget: $500-1,000,000 *Tel:* (202) 265-4313
Hist. Note: Organized in 1906 and incorporated in 1950 by a special act of Congress. Promotes international relations on the basis of law and justice.
Publications:
American Journal of International Law. q. adv.
International Legal Materials. bi-m.
Newsletter. bi-m.
Proceedings of The ASIL. a.
Studies in Transnational Legal Policy. irreg.
Annual Meetings: Spring, in Washington DC/700

American Soc. of Interpreters (1965)
P.O. Box 5558, Washington DC 20016-1158
Secretary: Eva F. Desrosiers
Members: 75-80
Annual Budget: under $10,000 *Tel:* (301) 657-3337
Hist. Note: Members are accredited professional interpreters. Has no paid staff. Membership: $35/yr. (individual); $100/yr. (company)
Annual Meetings: Washington or New York/Spring

American Soc. of Journalism School Administrators (1944)
Hist. Note: Absorbed by the Ass'n of Schools of Journalism and Mass Communication in 1985.

American Soc. of Journalists and Authors (1948)
1501 Broadway, Suite 1907, New York NY 10036
Exec. Secretary: Alexandra Cantor
Members: 700-750 *Staff:* 2
Annual Budget: $100-250,000 *Tel:* (212) 997-0947
Hist. Note: Established in 1948 as the Soc. of Magazine Writers, Inc. Became the American Soc. of Journalists and Authors, Inc. in 1975. Freelance nonfiction writers whose bylines appear on books and in leading periodicals. Membership: $120/yr.
Publications:
Newsletter. m.
ASJA Directory of Professional Writers. a.
Annual Meetings: Nonfiction Writers' Conference/First Saturday in May/700

American Soc. of Knitting Technologists (1960)
386 Park Ave. South, New York NY 10016
Secretary: David Gross
Members: 125-130 *Staff:* 1
Annual Budget: under $10,000 *Tel:* (212) 683-7520
Hist. Note: Members are technologists employed in the knitting industry in various capacities. Sponsored by the National Knitwear and Sportswear Ass'n, the U.S. section of the Internat'l Federation of Knitting Technologists which is headquartered in Switzerland. Membership: $25/yr.
Semi-annual Conferences: Spring and Fall

American Soc. of Laboratory Animal Practitioners (1967)
Washington State University, Pullman WA 99164
Secy.-Treas.: Farol Tomson, DVM
Members: 275-325 *Staff:* 1
Annual Budget: under $10,000 *Tel:* (509) 335-6246
Hist. Note: Veterinarians engaged in laboratory animal practice. Affiliated with the American Veterinary Medical Ass'n and the American Ass'n for Laboratory Animal Science.
Publications:
Synapse. q.
Membership Roster. a.
Annual Meetings: Summer/300
1987-Chicago, IL/July 20-23
1988-Portland, OR/July 18-21
1989-Orlando, FL/July 17-21
1990-San Antonio, TX/July 23-26
1991-Seattle, WA/July 28-Aug. 1

00064 12 05 86 1233

American Soc. of Landscape Architects (1899)
1733 Connecticut Ave., N.W., Washington DC 20009
Exec. V. President: David R. Bohardt
Members: 8,000 *Staff:* 32
Annual Budget: $2-5,000,000 *Tel:* (202) 466-7730
Hist. Note: Founded in New York City by eleven charter members and incorporated in Massachusetts in 1916. Works closely with the Landscape Architecture Foundation. Membership: $135/yr.
Publications:
Landscape Architectural News Digest. m.
Landscape Architecture. bi-m. adv.
Garden Design. bi-m. adv.
Annual Meetings: Fall
1987-Baltimore, MD(Conv. Center)/Oct. 31-Nov. 3/2,500
1988-Northwest
1989-Southeast

American Soc. of Law and Medicine (1972)
765 Commonwealth Ave., 16th Floor, Boston MA 02215
Exec. Director: Larry Gostin
Members: 4,500 *Staff:* 6
Annual Budget: $500-1,000,000 *Tel:* (617) 262-4990
Hist. Note: An outgrowth of two founding organizations--the Massachusetts Soc of Examining Physicians (1911) and the Massachusetts Soc. of Law and Medicine (1971). Multi-disciplinary membership of professionals concerned with the interrelation of law, medicine, and health care. Membership: $85/yr.
Publications:
American Journal of Law and Medicine. q.
Law, Medicine & Health Care. bi-m.
Bi-monthly Meetings:

American Soc. of Limnology and Oceanography (1936)
Virginia Institute of Marine Science, College of William & Mary, Gloucester Point VA 23062
Secretary: Polly A. Penhale
Members: 3,500 *Staff:* 3
Annual Budget: $250-500,000 *Tel:* (804) 642-7000
Hist. Note: Founded January 1, 1936 in St. Louis as the Limnological Soc. of America. Assumed its present name in 1949 and was incorporated in Wisconsin in 1956.
Publication:
Limnology and Oceanography. bi-m.
Semi-annual Meetings: Winter and Summer at a University site
1987-Madison, WI(Univ. of WI)/June 14-18

American Soc. of Local Officials
Hist. Note: Disbanded in 1986.

American Soc. of Lubrication Engineers (1944)
838 Busse Highway, Park Ridge IL 60068
Exec. Director: Maxine E. Hensley
Members: 3,700 individuals, 198-200 companies *Staff:* 6-10
Annual Budget: $500-1,000,000 *Tel:* (312) 825-5536
Hist. Note: Founded to advance the science of lubrication (tribology). Membership: $45/yr.
Publications:
Lubrication Engineering. m. adv.
Transactions. q.
Annual Meetings: Spring
1987-Anaheim, CA(Disneyland)/May 10-14/1,200-1,500
1988-Cleveland, OH(Stouffer's)/May 8-12/1,200-1,500
1989-Atlanta, GA(Westin)/April 30-May 5
1990-Denver, CO(Denver Hilton)/April 30-May 3
1991-Montreal, Canada(Queen Elizabeth Hyatt)/April 29-May 2
1992-Philadelphia, PA/April 26-30
1993-Calgary, CN(Skyline-Palliser-Delta Bow Valley-Westin)/May 17-20
1994-Pittsburgh, PA

American Soc. of Magazine Editors (1963)
575 Lexington Ave., New York NY 10022
Exec. Director: Robert E. Kenyon, Jr.
Members: 600 *Staff:* 2
Annual Budget: $250-500,000 *Tel:* (212) 752-0055
Hist. Note: A professional society of senior magazine editors. Affiliated with the Magazine Publishers Association. Membership: $100/yr.
Annual Meetings: With the Magazine Publishers Ass'n

American Soc. of Magazine Photographers (1944)
205 Lexington Ave., New York NY 10016
Exec. Director: Patrice Garrison
Members: 4,500 *Staff:* 6-10
Annual Budget: $500-1,000,000 *Tel:* (212) 889-9144
Hist. Note: Known as the Soc. of Photographers in Communications from 1971 to 1979. Membership: $225/yr. (individual); $500/yr. (organization/company)
Publications:
ASMP Bulletin. m. adv.
Membership Directory. a. adv.
Professional Business Practices in Protogtaphy. Every 4 yrs.
Stock Photography Handbook. Every 4 yrs.

American Soc. of Mammalogists (1919)
Dept. of Zoology, Brigham Young University, Provo UT 84602
Secy.-Treas.: H. Duane Smith
Members: 3,600 *Staff:* 2-5
Annual Budget: $100-250,000 *Tel:* (801) 378-2482
Hist. Note: Founded and incorporated in the District of Columbia in April 1919. Affiliated with the Internat'l Union for the Conservation of Nature. Membership: $20/yr.
Publications:
Journal of Mammalogy. q. adv.
Mammalian Species. a.
Annual Meetings: June/800

American Soc. of Marine Artists (1977)
212 Second Ave., Milford CT 06460
President: Peter E. Egeli
Members: 300 *Staff:* 1
Annual Budget: under $10,000 *Tel:* (203) 877-7305
Hist. Note: Members are artists, collectors and historians. Has no paid staff. Membership: $25/yr.
Publication:
ASMA News. q.
Annual Meetings: Fall

American Soc. of Master Dental Technologists (1976)
Box 248, Oakland Gardens NY 11364
Exec. Secretary: Susan Heppenheimer
Members: 100 *Staff:* 1
Annual Budget: under $10,000 *Tel:* (718) 428-0075
Hist. Note: A professional society formed to raise the educational standards of dental technicians. Awards the designation "MDT"-Master Dental Technologist. Membership: $60/year.
Annual Meetings: Fall
1987-New York, NY

American Soc. of Maxillofacial Surgeons (1947)
233 North Michigan Ave., Chicago IL 60601
Acct. Executive: Lousanne Lofgren
Members: 280 *Staff:* 1
Annual Budget: $25-50,000 *Tel:* (312) 856-1818
Publication:
Maxillofacial Surgeons. q.
Annual Meetings: Fall
1987-Atlanta, GA/Nov. 8-13

American Soc. of Mechanical Engineers (1880)
345 East 47th St., New York NY 10017
Exec. Director: Paul F. Allmendinger
Members: 114,000 *Staff:* 300
Annual Budget: over $5,000,000 *Tel:* (212) 705-7722
Hist. Note: Founded in 1880 and incorporated in New York in 1881, ASME is a technical society with 34 technical divisions and extensive programs in the development of safety codes and equipment standards, educational guidance for student members, professional development, and government relations. Conducts one of the largest technical publishing operations in the world. Has an annual budget of $28.8 million. Membership: $60/year.
Publications:
Applied Mechanics Reviews. m.
Journal of Applied Mechanics. q.
Journal of Biomechanical Engineering. q.
Journal of Dynamic Systems, Measurements and Control. q.
Journal of Energy Resources Technology. q.
Journal of Engineering for Industry. q.
Journal of Engineering for Gas Turbines and Power. q.
Journal of Engineering Materials and Technology. q.
Journal of Fluids Engineering. q.
Journal of Heat Transfer. q.
Journal of Tribology. q.
Journal of Mechanisms, Transmission and Automation in Design. q.
Journal of Pressure Vessels Technology. q.
Mechanical Engineering. m. adv.
Solar Energy Engineering. q.
Vibration, Acoustics, Stress and Reliability in Design. q.
Transactions. a. adv.
Semi-annual meetings: Summer and Winter
1987-Toronto, Canada/June 7-12/600
1987-New York, NY(Marriott Marquis)/Nov. 15-20/3,000

American Soc. of Military Comptrollers (1949)
Box 91, Mount Vernon VA 22121
Exec. Director: Col. Edmund W. Edmonds, Jr. USAF
Members: 15,000 *Staff:* 1
Annual Budget: $100-250,000 *Tel:* (703) 780-6164
Hist. Note: Successor (1955) to Soc. of Military Accountants and Statisticians. Membership: $15/yr. (individual), $125/yr. (company).
Publication:
Armed Forces Comptroller. q.
Annual Meetings: May
1987-San Antonio, TX
1988-Denver, CO
1989-Jacksonville, FL
1990-Oakland, CA
1991-Indianapolis, IN

American Soc. of Missiology (1972)
Box 1092, Elkhart IN 46515
Secy.-Treas.: Wilbert R. Shenk
Members: 550 *Staff:* 1
Annual Budget: $25-50,000 *Tel:* (219) 294-7523
Hist. Note: Members are individuals interested in the scholarly study of theological, historical and social questions regarding the missionary dimension of the Christian church. Member of the Council on the Study of Religion. Membership: $20/yr.
Publication:
Missiology: an International Review. q. adv.

American Soc. of Naturalists (1883)
Division of Biological Sciences, Univ. of Kansas, Lawrence KS 66045
Secretary: Philip Hedrick
Members: 700 individuals *Staff:* 1
Annual Budget: $25-50,000 *Tel:* (913) 864-3763
Hist. Note: Affiliated with the American Ass'n for the Advancement of Science. One of the older scientific learned societies, the American Society of Naturalists has been called "the old grandmother of scientific societies" since more than 20 groups have splintered from it to form their own societies.
Publication:
The American Naturalist. m. adv.

American Soc. of Naval Engineers (1888)
1452 Duke St., Alexandria VA 22314
Exec. Director: Capt. James L. McVoy, USN(Ret.)
Members: 7,800 *Staff:* 12
Annual Budget: $500-1,000,000 *Tel:* (703) 836-6727
Hist. Note: Founded in the District of Columbia in 1888 and incorporated there in 1946. Membership: $36/yr.
Publications:
Membership Directory. bi-a. adv.
Naval Engineers Journal. bi-m. adv.
Annual Meetings: Spring, in Washington, DC at the Shoreham/3,300
1987-April 30-May 1
1988-May 4-6
1989-May 4-5
1990-May 3-4
1991-May 2-3

American Soc. of Nephrology (1967)
6900 Grove Road, Thorofare NJ 08086
Meeting Manager: Jan Sharkey
Members: 3,000 *Staff:* 2-5
Annual Budget: $50-100,000 *Tel:* (609) 848-1000
Hist. Note: Members are nephrologists.
Publication:
Abstract Book of the ASN. a.
Annual Meetings: December/3,000
1987-Washington, DC(Sheraton Washington)/Dec. 13-16
1988-San Antonio, TX(Conv. Center)/Dec. 11-14
1989-Washington, DC(Sheraton Washington)/Dec. 3-6
1990-Washington, DC(Sheraton Washington)/Dec. 2-5

American Soc. of Neuroimaging (1977)
Three Gates Circle, Buffalo NY 14209
President: Lawrence Jacobs, M.D.
Members: 550-600
Annual Budget: $25-50,000 *Tel:* (716) 887-4071
Hist. Note: Established as the Society for Computerized Tomography and Neuroimaging and affiliated with the American Academy of Neurology, it assumed its present name in 1980. Members are specialists in CT scanning and other neurodiagnostic techniques. Membership: $100/yr.
Publication:
ASN Newsletter. 2-3/year.
Annual Meetings: Winter
1987-Tampa, FL(Hyatt Regency)/Feb. 28-March 3

American Soc. of Neuroradiology (1962)
1415 West 22nd St., Tower B, Oak Brook IL 60521
Secretary: Peter E. Weinberg, M.D.
Members: 950-1,000 *Staff:* 2-5
Annual Budget: $500-1,000,000 *Tel:* (312) 574-8082
Hist. Note: Senior Membership: $175/yr.
Publication:
American Journal of Neuroradiology. bi-m. adv.
Annual Meetings: May
1987-New York, NY(NY Hilton)/May 10-15/1,000
1988-Chicago, IL(Hilton & Towers)/May 14-19/1,000

American Soc. of Newspaper Editors (1922)
Box 17004, Washington DC 20041
Exec. Director: Lee Stinnett
Members: 900-1,000 *Staff:* 2-5
Annual Budget: $500-1,000,000 *Tel:* (703) 620-6087
Hist. Note: Offices are located in the Newspaper Center, 11600 Sunrise Valley Drive, Reston, VA.
Publication:
Bulletin. 9/yr.
Annual Meetings: Spring

American Soc. of Notaries (1965)
918 16th St., N.W., Washington DC 20006
Exec. Director: Eugene E. Hines
Members: 24,500 *Staff:* 2-5
Annual Budget: $250-500,000 *Tel:* (202) 955-6162
Hist. Note: ASN was organized to improve notarial practices and to uphold high standards for notaries public. Membership: $15/yr.
Publication:
The American Notary. bi-m.

American Soc. of Ophthalmic Administrators (1974)
Hist. Note: A division of the American Soc. of Cataract and Refractive Surgery.

American Soc. of Ophthalmic Registered Nurses (1976)
655 Beach Street, San Francisco CA 94109
Administrator: Sue Brown

00065 12 05 86 1233

Members: 1,500 individuals; 11 companies *Staff:* 2-5
Annual Budget: $50-100,000 *Tel:* (415) 921-4700
Hist. Note: Membership: $35/year.
Publication:
Insight. bi-m. adv.
Annual Meetings: With the American Academy of Ophthalmology

American Soc. of Opthalmologic and Otolaryngologic Allergy (1941)
Hist. Note: Became the American Academy of Otolaryngologic Allergy in 1982.

American Soc. of Outpatient Surgeons (1978)
3960 Park Blvd., Suite E, San Diego CA 92103
Exec. Director: Karen M. Delaney
Members: 35 companies; 400 individuals *Staff:* 2
Annual Budget: $100-250,000 *Tel:* (619) 692-9918
Hist. Note: Formerly (1986) Soc. for Office Based Surgery. A national non-profit professional organization dedicated to improved surgical care at lower cost. Surgical specialists/board certified surgeons admitted to membership. Membership: $175/yr.
Publication:
Newsletter. bi-m.
Annual Meetings: Spring
1987-Tempe, AZ(Wescourt in the Buttes)/Feb. 27-March 1

American Soc. of Papyrologists (1961)
Dept. of Greek and Latin, Wayne State University, Detroit MI 48202
Secy.-Treas.: Kathleen McNamara
Members: 175 *Staff:* 1
Annual Budget: $25-50,000 *Tel:* (313) 577-3032
Hist. Note: The ASP is an association of scholars and students concerned with classical and Egyptian antiquity, in particular with the editing and study of texts preserved on papyrus. Affiliated with the Association Internationale de Papyrologues, Brussels, Belgium.
Publications:
American Studies in Papyrology. irreg.
Bulletin of the ASP. q. adv.
Annual Meetings: In conjunction with the American Philological Ass'n and the Archaeological Institute of America.

American Soc. of Paramedics (1975)
Hist. Note: Defunct in 1983.

American Soc. of Parasitologists (1924)
Department of Biological Sciences, University of N. Colorado, Greeley CO 80639
Secy.-Treas.: Dr. Gerald D. Schmidt
Members: 1,300-1,400 *Staff:* 1
Annual Budget: $50-100,000 *Tel:* (303) 351-2467
Hist. Note: Formed in Washington under the leadership of a group of parasitologists from the Baltimore-Washington area, December 30, 1924 at a meeting of the American Ass'n for the Advancement of Science. Incorporated in the District of Columbia in 1932. Membership: $45/yr.
Publication:
Journal of Parasitology. bi-m. adv.
Annual Meetings: Summer
1987-Lincoln, NE(Univ. of NE)/Aug. 1-7
1988-Winston-Salem, NC(Wake Forest Univ.)/Aug.
1989-Vancouver, BC(Univ. of British Columbia)/Aug.
1990-East Lansing, MI(MI State Univ.)/Aug.

American Soc. of Pension Actuaries (1966)
2029 K St., N.W., Fourth Floor, Washington DC 20006
Exec. Administrator: Becky Panneton
Members: 2,200 *Staff:* 8
Annual Budget: $250-500,000 *Tel:* (202) 659-3620
Hist. Note: Awards the designations MSPA and FSPA (Member and Fellow of the Society of Pension Actuaries) and CPC (Certified Pension Consultant).
Publication:
The Pension Actuary. m.
Annual Meetings: Fall, in Washington, DC at the Hyatt.

American Soc. of Petroleum Operations Engineers (1976)
Box 24009, Richmond VA 23224
Secretary: Edward Crumpler
Members: 125-150 *Staff:* 1
Annual Budget: under $10,000 *Tel:* (804) 232-8956
Hist. Note: Individuals concerned with the design, production and use of petroleum marketing equipment from the refinery to the ultimate consumer-trucks, gas stations, etc. Membership: (by exam only) $50/yr.

American Soc. of Pharmacognosy (1959)
School of Pharmacy, Northeast Louisiana University, Monroe LA 71209
Secretary: Dr. William J. Keller
Members: 700-800 *Staff:* 4
Annual Budget: $100-250,000 *Tel:* (318) 342-3080
Hist. Note: Founded in 1959 and incorporated in the District of Columbia in 1965. Promotes the study of the composition, production, use and history of drugs of natural origin. Absorbed the Plant Science Seminar. Membership: $45/yr.
Publications:
Journal of Natural Products Lloydia. bi-m.
Newsletter. 4/yr.
Annual Meetings: July/August/300-400
1987-Kingston, RI(Univ. of Rhode Island)/July
1988-Salt Lake City, UT/July
1989-San Juan, PR/July

American Soc. of Photogrammetry
Hist. Note: Changed to American Soc. for Photogrammery and Remote Sensing in March, 1985.

American Soc. of Photographers (1937)
Box 52900, Tulsa OK 74152
President: Jerry L. Cornelius
Members: 500
Annual Budget: $25-50,000 *Tel:* (918) 743-2122
Hist. Note: Membership in Professional Photographers of America is a pre-requisite for membership in ASP: members must be either a Master of Photography, a Photographic Craftsmen, or a Photographic Specialist.
Publication:
ASP Newsletter. q.
Annual Meetings: Summer

American Soc. of Physician Analysts (1950)
Hist. Note: Merged with the American Ass'n of Psychoanalytic Physicians to form the American Soc. of Psychoanalytic Physicians in 1985.

American Soc. of Picture Professionals (1966)
Box 5283, Grand Central Station, New York NY 10163
Nat'l Secretary: John Schultz
Members: 600 *Staff:* 2-5
Annual Budget: $10-25,000 *Tel:* (212) 685-3870
Hist. Note: Founded in 1966, and incorporated in 1970 in New York. Members include photographers, graphic designers, picture librarians, archivists, editors and researchers. Membership: $50/yr.
Publication:
The Picture Professional. q. adv.
Annual Meetings: Fall in New York City

American Soc. of Plant Physiologists (1924)
15501-A Monona Drive, Rockville MD 20855
Exec. Director: Melvin J. Josephs
Members: 4,200 *Staff:* 7
Annual Budget: $1-2,000,000 *Tel:* (301) 251-0560
Hist. Note: Founded at the University of Chicago in 1924 and incorporated in the District of Columbia the same year. Affiliated with the American Ass'n for the Advancement of Science, adherent society of the American Institute of Biological Sciences and member of the Internat'l Ass'n for Plant Physiology. Membership: $35/yr.
Publications:
ASPP Newsletter. bi-m.
Journal of Plant Physiology. m.
Annual Meetings: July/Aug.
1987-St. Louis, MO(Chase Park Plaza)/July 19-23/1,400
1989-Toronto, Ontario

American Soc. of Plant Taxonomists (1937)
Dept. of EPO Biology, University of Colorado, Boulder CO 80309
Secretary: Dr. Meredith A. Lane
Members: 1,000
Annual Budget: $25-50,000 *Tel:* (303) 492-5530
Hist. Note: Founded in 1935 and incorporated in 1964. Affiliated with the American Ass'n for the Advancement of Science, the American Institute of Biological Sciences, the National Research Council and the Botanical Society of America.
Publication:
Systematic Botany. q. adv.
Annual Meetings: With American Institute of Biological Sciences

American Soc. of Plastic and Reconstructive Surgeons (1931)
233 North Michigan Ave., Suite 1900, Chicago IL 60601
Exec. Director: Thomas R. Schedler, CAE
Members: 2,500-2,600 *Staff:* 25-35
Annual Budget: $2-5,000,000 *Tel:* (312) 856-1818
Hist. Note: Founded in New York City in 1931 and incorporated in New York in 1945. Reincorporated in Illinois in 1975.
Publications:
Plastic and Reconstructive Surgery. m. adv.
Plastic Surgery Newsletter. semi-m.
Plastic Surgeon. m.
Annual Meetings: Fall/4,500
1987-Atlanta, GA(Conv. Center)/Nov. 8-13
1988-Toronto, Canada/Oct. 2-7
1989-San Francisco, CA(Moscone Center)/Oct. 29-Nov. 3

American Soc. of Plastic and Reconstructive Surgical Nurses (1975)
North Woodbury Road, Box 56, Pitman NJ 08071
Exec. Director: Ron Brady
Members: 920 *Staff:* 2-5
Annual Budget: $25-50,000 *Tel:* (609) 589-6247
Hist. Note: Membership: $50/yr.
Publications:
Journal of Plastic and Reconstructive Surgical Nursing. q. adv.
ASPRSNews. bi-m.
Annual Meetings: Fall
1987-Atlanta, GA/Nov. 8-12

American Soc. of Plumbing Engineers (1964)
3617 Thousand Oaks Blvd., Suite 210, Westlake CA 91362
Exec. Director: John S. Shaw, CAE
Members: 5,000 *Staff:* 6
Annual Budget: $500-1,000,000 *Tel:* (805) 495-7120
Publications:
ASPE Data Book. bien. adv.
ASPE Journal. q.
Plumbing Engineer. bi-m. adv.
Biennial meetings: Even years/4,000
1988-Long Beach, CA(Convention Center)/Nov. 13-16
1990-Cincinnati, OH(Convention Center)/Nov. 4-7

American Soc. of Podiatric Assistants (1964)
Hist. Note: Became the American Soc. of Podiatric Medical Assistants in 1985.

American Soc. of Podiatric Dermatology (1967)
3900 16th St., N.W., Washington DC 20011
Secy.-Treas.: Dr. Samuel Moskow
Members: 300 *Staff:* 1
Annual Budget: $10-25,000 *Tel:* (202) 234-5420
Hist. Note: An affiliate of the American Podiatric Medical Ass'n
Annual Meetings: With the American Podiatric Medical Ass'n

American Soc. of Podiatric Medical Assistants (1964)
2204 Washington Ave., Waco TX 76701
Exec. Director: Zelda Walling Vicha, P.A.C.
Members: 900 *Staff:* 1
Annual Budget: $10-25,000 *Tel:* (817) 754-1811
Hist. Note: Members must have at least one year on-the-job training. Formerly (1985) American Soc. of Podiatric Assistants. An affiliate of the American Podiatric Medical Ass'n. Membership: $50 initial fee; $35/yr. (renewal)
Publication:
The Podiatric Assistant. q.
Annual Meetings: With the American Podiatric Medical Ass'n

American Soc. of Podiatric Medicine (1944)
Hist. Note: An affiliate of the American Podiatry Ass'n. Formerly (1972) American College of Podiatric Medicine, Inc. Address unknown since 1984.
Publications:
ASPM Seminar Journal. a. adv.
Newsletter. 3/yr.
Annual Meetings: Spring

American Soc. of Post-Anesthesia Nurses (1980)
2315 Westwood Ave., Box 11083, Richmond VA 23230
Exec. Secretary: John A. Hinckley
Members: 3,500-4,000 *Staff:* 6-10
Annual Budget: $250-500,000 *Tel:* (804) 359-3557
Hist. Note: An organization of post-anesthesia care nurses. Membership: $50/yr.
Publications:
Breathline. q. adv.
Journal of Post-Anesthesia Nursing. q. adv.
Annual Meetings: April/1,000
1987-Los Angeles(Century Plaza)/April 20-24
1988-Fort Worth(Hyatt)/April 10-14
1989-Orlando(Hyatt)/April 2-6

American Soc. of Primatologists (1976)
Endocrine Research Ctr., Michigan State Univ., East Lansing MI 48824
President: Richard Dukelow
Members: 550 *Staff:* 1
Annual Budget: $10-25,000 *Tel:* (517) 355-7475
Hist. Note: Members are individuals specializing in the study of monkeys, apes, and other primates. Membership: $12/yr.
Publications:
The Bulletin of The ASP. bi-m.
American Journal of Primatology. q.
Annual Meetings: Usually at an academic center in the summer/350

American Soc. of Professional and Executive Women (1979)
1511 Walnut St., Philadelphia PA 19102
Exec. Director: Laurie Wagman
Members: 18,000 *Staff:* 6-10
Annual Budget: $100-250,000 *Tel:* (215) 563-4415
Hist. Note: Promotes a positive additudinal environment for career women via practical information and benefits. Membership: $42/yr.
Publication:
Successful Woman. bi-m.
Annual Meetings: Not held

American Soc. of Professional Consultants (1980)
Hist. Note: Dissolved in September, 1982.

American Soc. of Professional Draftsmen and Artists (1966)
Hist. Note: Members are professionals in the fields of drafting, commercial and technical art. Address Unknown, 1981. Possibly defunct.

00066 12 05 86 1233

American Soc. of Professional Estimators (1956)
6911 Richmond Hwy., Suite 230, Alexandria VA 22306
Exec. Director: L. Douglas Cox
Members: 3,000 *Staff:* 2-5
Annual Budget: $100-250,000 *Tel:* (703) 765-2700
Hist. Note: Construction trade estimators. Membership: $85/yr.
Publication:
The Estimator. m. adv.
Annual Meetings:
1987-Albuquerque, NM(Marriott)
1988-Hartford, CT(Sheraton)
1989-Cleveland, OH or St. Paul, MN
1990-West Coast

American Soc. of Professional Surveyors (1981)
Hist. Note: Became the National Society of Professional Surveyors in 1983.

American Soc. of Psychoanalytic Physicians (1985)
904 Dryden St., Silver Spring MD 20901
Exec. Secretary: Deborah C. Skolnik
Members: 360 *Staff:* 1
Annual Budget: under $10,000 *Tel:* (301) 681-7385
Hist. Note: Formed as a merger of the American Soc. of Physician Analysts and the American Ass'n of Psychoanalytic Physicians.
Publication:
Bulletin. q. adv.
Annual Meetings: May, in conjunction with the American Psychiatric Ass'n

American Soc. of Psychopathology of Expression (1964)
WPIC, 3811 O'Hara St., Pittsburgh PA 15213
President: Irene Jakab, M.D.
Members: 100 *Staff:* 1
Annual Budget: under $10,000 *Tel:* (412) 624-4947
Hist. Note: Members are psychiatrists, psychologists, art therapists, artists, and others interested in the problems of verbal and non-verbal expression. Membership: $25/year.
Publication:
Proceedings.

American Soc. of Psychosomatic Dentistry and Medicine (1948)
Hist. Note: Absorbed by the Internat'l Psychosomatics Institute in 1986.

American Soc. of Questioned Document Examiners (1942)
139 Fulton St., New York NY 10038
Secy.-Treas.: Paul A. Osborn
Members: 100-110 *Staff:* 1
Annual Budget: $10-25,000 *Tel:* (212) 406-8912
Hist. Note: Purpose is to foster education; sponsor scientific research; establish standards; and provide training in the field of questioned document examination and promote justice in matters that involve questions about documents. Membership: $50/yr.
Publications:
ASQDE Newsletter. q.
Membership Directory. a. (for members only)
Annual Meetings: Summer/100-130
1987-Vancouver, BC(Hyatt Regency)/Aug. 2-7
1988-Denver, CO

American Soc. of Radiologic Technologists (1920)
15000 Central Ave., S.E., Albuquerque NM 87123
Exec. Director: Ward M. Keller
Members: 15,000 *Staff:* 17
Annual Budget: $1-2,000,000 *Tel:* (505) 298-4500
Hist. Note: Founded in Chicago in October 1920 as the American Ass'n of Radiologic Technicians, it became the American Soc. of Radiographers in 1930. Incorporated in Minnesota in 1932. Became the American Soc. of X-Ray Technicians in 1934 and the American Soc. of Radiologic Technologists, Inc. in 1936. Affiliated with the American Registry of Radiologic Technologists. Membership: $60/yr. (individual)
Publications:
ASRT Scanner. bi-m. adv.
Radiologic Technology. bi-m. adv.
Annual Meetings: Summer
1987-Washington, DC/June 27-July 2
1988-Albuquerque, NM/June 12-17/800

American Soc. of Real Estate Counselors (1953)
430 N. Michigan Ave., Chicago IL 60611
Exec. V. President: Lois Hofstetter
Members: 660 *Staff:* 7
Annual Budget: $500-1,000,000 *Tel:* (312) 329-8427
Hist. Note: Established in November 1953 to meet the public need for advice and guidance rendered by qualified real estate experts on a fee basis. Awards the CRE (Counselor of Real Estate) designation. Affiliated with the Nat'l Ass'n of Realtors (formerly the Nat'l Ass'n of Real Estate Boards) since 1954. Membership: $525/yr.
Publications:
The Counselor. q.
Directory. a.
Real Estate Issues. semi-a.
Technical Monographs and Bulletins. irreg.
Annual Meetings: With Nat'l Ass'n of Realtors

American Soc. of Regional Anesthesia (1976)
Box 11083, 2315 Westwood Ave., Richmond VA 23230
Exec. Secretary: John A. Hinckley
Members: 4,000 *Staff:* 2-5
Annual Budget: $100-250,000 *Tel:* (804) 358-0305
Hist. Note: Physicians and anesthetists interested in the induction of insensibility over a certain area by nerve blocking or field blocking.
Publications:
Newsletter.
Regional Anesthesia. a. adv.
Annual Meetings: March
1987-Orlando, FL(Disneyworld)/March 24-29
1988-Las Vegas, NV(MGM)/March 19-20
1989-Hilton Head, SC(Inter-Continental)/March 7-11

American Soc. of Safety Engineers (1911)
1800 East Oakton, Des Plaines IL 60018-2187
Exec. Director: Judy T. Neel, CAE
Members: 20,000 *Staff:* 30
Annual Budget: $2-5,000,000 *Tel:* (312) 692-4121
Hist. Note: Founded in 1911 as the United Ass'n of Casualty Inspectors and merged with the Nat'l Safety Council in 1924, becoming its Engineering Section. It again became independent in 1947 as the American Soc. of Safety Engineers and incorporated in Illinois in 1962. Membership is open to individuals whose employment, education, and experience are safety-related. Membership: $55/yr.
Publications:
Professional Safety. m. adv.
Society Update. q.
Annual Meetings: Spring/1,200
1987-Baltimore, MD(Convention Center)/June 14-17

American Soc. of Sanitary Engineering (1906)
Box 40362, Bay Village OH 44140
Exec. Secretary: Gael H. Dunn
Members: 2,500-3,000
Annual Budget: $50-100,000 *Tel:* (216) 835-3040
Hist. Note: Originated in January 1906 in the District of Columbia as the American Soc. of Inspectors of Plumbing and Sanitary Engineers. Became the American Soc. of Sanitary Engineering in 1914 and incorporated in the District of Columbia in 1937. Membership: $54/year (inidivudal), $125/year (organization/company).
Publications:
ASSE Yearbook. a. adv.
Newsletter. m.
Refresher Course Proceedings. a. adv.
Annual Meetings: Fall/250-300
1987-New York, NY
1989-New Orleans, LA

American Soc. of Sugar Beet Technologists (1935)
1311 South College Ave. (P.O. Box 1546), Fort Collins CO 80522
Secretary: James H. Fischer
Members: 6-700 *Staff:* 2-5
Annual Budget: $10-25,000 *Tel:* (303) 482-8250
Hist. Note: Membership: $20/2 years.
Publication:
Journal of the ASSBT. semi-a.
Biennial Meetings: odd years in Feb./March
1987-Phoenix, AZ(Hilton)/March 1-5/600-700

American Soc. of Test Engineers (1981)
114 N. Hale St., Wheaton IL 60187
Exec. Secretary: William D. Ashman
Members: 450-500 *Staff:* 1
Annual Budget: $10-25,000 *Tel:* (312) 260-1055
Hist. Note: Members are companies and individuals involved in electronic testing.
Publication:
Bulletin. q.
Annual Meetings: Winter

American Soc. of Therapeutic Radiologists (1955)
Hist. Note: Became the American Soc. for Therapeutic Radiology and Oncology in 1984.

American Soc. of Traffic and Transportation (1946)
Hist. Note: Became the American Soc. of Transportation and Logistics in 1984.

American Soc. of Transportation and Logistics (1946)
Box 33095, Louisville KY 40232
Exec. Director: Carter M. Harrison
Members: 2,500-3,000 *Staff:* 2-5
Annual Budget: $100-250,000 *Tel:* (502) 451-8150
Hist. Note: Organized in Cincinnati, Ohio March 1, 1946 and incorporated later the same year in the State of Indiana as the American Soc. of Traffic and Transportation, AST&L assumed its present name in 1984. A professional society of individuals involved in or concerned with the various management functions of transportation, physical distribution and logistics. Awards the "CTL" (Certified in Transportation and Logistics) designation. Membership: $65/yr.
Publications:
ASTRALOG Newsletter. bi-m.
Pro-Development Letter. bi-m.
Transportation Journal. q.
Annual Meetings: Late Summer/Fall
1987-San Jose, CA(Red Lion Inn)/Oct. 14-17

American Soc. of Travel Agents (1931)
4400 MacArthur Blvd., N.W., Washington DC 20007
President: W. Ray Shockley
Members: 21,000 *Staff:* 80-85
Annual Budget: over $5,000,000 *Tel:* (202) 965-7520
Hist. Note: Established in 1931 in New York as the American Steamship and Tourist Agents' Ass'n. The name was changed in 1944 to American Soc. of Travel Agents, Inc. Maintains Washington and West Coast offices. Sponsors the American Society of Travel Agents Political Action Committee. Has an international membership of about 20%.
Publications:
A.S.T.A. Travel News. m. adv.
A.S.T.A. Notes. w.
Annual Meetings: Fall
1987-Houston, TX/Oct./6,500

American Soc. of Trial Consultants (1982)
Speech and Mass Commmunications, Towson State University, Towson MD 21204
Exec. Secretary: Ronald J. Matlon, Ph.D.
Members: 150 individuals *Staff:* 1
Annual Budget: $10-25,000
Hist. Note: Organized in Phoenix, October, 1982. Formerly (1986) the Ass'n of Trial Behavior Consultants, ASTC assumed its present name in January, 1987. Members are trial consultants from a variety of academic backgrounds who work within court systems on jury selection, behavioral counseling, etc. Membership: $60/yr. (individual), $36/yr./person (company).
Publications:
Annual Directory of Members. a.
Court Call Newsletter. q.
Annual Meetings: October

American Soc. of Tropical Medicine and Hygiene (1952)
Box 29837, San Antonio TX 78229
Secy.-Treas.: Dr. John E. Scanlon
Members: 2,000 *Staff:* 1
Annual Budget: $250-500,000 *Tel:* (512) 691-6845
Hist. Note: Organized November 17, 1951 in Chicago as an amalgamation of the American Soc. of Tropical Medicine, formed in 1903, and the Nat'l Malaria Soc., founded in 1916. Incorporated in Delaware in 1952. Membership: $40/year (individual).
Publications:
American Journal of Tropical Medicine and Hygiene. bi-m.
Tropical Medicine and Hygiene News. bi-m.
Annual Meetings: December/600
1987-Los Angeles, CA
1988-Washington, DC
1989-Honolulu, HI
1990-New Orleans, LA
1991-Boston, MA

American Soc. of TV Cameramen (1974)
Hist. Note: Address unknown in 1985-86. Also known as American Society of Videographers.

American Soc. of Ultrasound Technical Specialists (1969)
Hist. Note: Became the Society of Diagnostic Medical Sonographers in 1981.

American Soc. of University Composers (1965)
250 West 54th St., Room 300, New York NY 10019
Exec. Secretary: Martin Gonzalez
Members: 850 *Staff:* 2-5
Annual Budget: $25-50,000 *Tel:* (212) 247-3121
Hist. Note: Composers and musicians interested in contemporary American music.
Publications:
ASUC Journal of Music Scores. bi-a.
News-Bulletin. bi-m.
Annual Meetings:
1987-Evanston, IL(Northwestern University)

American Soc. of Veterinary Ophthalmology (1957)
1528 Shalamar, Stillwater OK 74074
Secy.-Treas.: Dr. A. J. Quinn, D.V.M.
Members: 200-210 *Staff:* 1
Annual Budget: under $10,000 *Tel:* (405) 377-2134
Hist. Note: Founded in 1957 in Miami Beach during a meeting of the American Animal Hospital Association. Affiliated with American Veterinary Medical Ass'n Membership: $25/yr.
Publications:
Directory. a.
Newsletter. q.
Semi-annual Meetings: Spring, with American Animal Hospital Ass'n and summer with American Veterinary Medical Ass'n
1987-Phoenix, AZ/March 21-27
1987-Chicago, IL/July 20-23
1988-Washington, DC/April 15-22
1988-Portland, OR/July 17-20
1989-St. Louis, MO/April 8-14
1989-Orlando, FL/July 17-20

American Soc. of Veterinary Physiologists and Pharmacologists (1946)
School of Veterinary Medicine, UW, 2015 Lindon Drive, West, Madison WI 53706
Secy.-Treas.: Andy Kiorpes

00067 12 05 86 1233

Members: 200-225 *Staff:* 1
Annual Budget: under $10,000 *Tel:* (608) 263-9804
Hist. Note: Affiliated with Nat'l Soc. for Medical Research. Membership: $15/year.
Publication:
ASVPP Newsletter. 3/yr.
Annual Meetings: With the American Veterinary Medical Ass'n

American Soc. of Videographers
Hist. Note: Alternative name for the American Soc. of TV Cameramen. Address unknown for 1985-86.

American Soc. of Women Accountants (1938)
35 East Wacker Drive, Suite 1036, Chicago IL 60601
Exec. Director: Miriam Green
Members: 7,500 *Staff:* 2-5
Annual Budget: $50-100,000 *Tel:* (312) 726-9030
Hist. Note: Membership: $40/yr.
Publications:
The Coordinator. m.
The Women C.P.A. q. adv.

American Soc. of Zoologists (1890)
Box 2739, California Lutheran University, Thousand Oaks CA 91360
Exec. Officer: Mary Adams-Wiley
Members: 4,100 *Staff:* 6
Annual Budget: $2-5,000,000 *Tel:* (805) 492-3585
Hist. Note: The Eastern Branch of the American Soc. of Zoologists was founded in 1890 as the American Morphological Ass'n; the Central Branch developed from the Central Naturalists, founded in 1899; the two merged in 1901-3 and the present unified organization emerged from a joint meeting in Philadelphia in 1913. Incorporated in Illinois in 1964. Membership is open to individuals who have had scientific training equivalent to the doctorate, who are actively engaged in the field of zoology and who have been nominated by a member of the society. Membership: $48/year (individual).
Publication:
American Zoologist. q. adv.
Annual Meetings: December/1,500
1987-New Orleans, LA(Hyatt)/Dec. 27-30
1988-San Francisco, CA(Marriott-Moscone Center)Dec. 27-30
1989-Boston, MA(Marriott & Westin-Copley Plaza)/Dec. 27-30

American Soc. on Aging (1954)
833 Market St., Suite 516, San Francisco CA 94103
Exec. Director: Gloria H. Cavanaugh
Members: 300 companies; 5,500 individuals *Staff:* 15
Annual Budget: $1-2,000,000 *Tel:* (415) 543-2617
Hist. Note: Founded as the Western Gerontological Soc. ASA's goal is the well-being of older Americans and those who work with them and for them. Membership includes educators, service providers, researchers, administrators, policy makers, business people, advocates, and elders. Membership: $60/yr. (individual); $135/yr. (non-profit organization); and $250/yr. (profit organization)
Publications:
Generations. q. adv.
The ASA Connection. bi-m. adv.
Annual Meetings: March
1987-Salt Lake City, UT
1988-San Diego, CA

American Sociological Ass'n (1905)
1722 N St., N. W., Washington DC 20036
Exec. Officer: William V. D'Antonio
Members: 13,000 *Staff:* 15-20
Annual Budget: $1-2,000,000 *Tel:* (202) 833-3410
Hist. Note: Formed as the American Sociological Society in December 1905 in Baltimore at a joint meeting of the American Historical, Economic and Political Science Associations to promote sociological research and intercourse between persons engaged in the scientific study of society. Incorporated in the District of Columbia in 1943 and became the American Sociological Ass'n in 1960. A member of the American Council of Learned Societies.
Publications:
American Sociological Review. bi-m. adv.
ASA Footnotes. 9/yr. adv.
Contemporary Sociology. bi-m. adv.
Employment Bulletin. m.
Journal of Health and Social Behavior. q. adv.
Social Psychology Quarterly.
Sociology of Education. q. adv.
Teaching Sociology. q. adv.
Sociological Theory. semi-a. adv.
Annual Meetings: Late Summer/4,000
1987-Chicago, IL(Palmer House)/Aug. 17-21
1988-Atlanta, GA(Marriott)/Aug. 24-28

American Sod Producers Ass'n (1967)
4415 W. Harrison Street, Suite 309-C, Hillside IL 60162
Exec. Director: Douglas H. Fender
Members: 525 companies *Staff:* 2
Annual Budget: $250-500,000 *Tel:* (312) 449-2890
Publications:
ASPA Turf News. bi-m. adv.
ASPA Business Management Newslette. bi-m.
Semi-annual meetings: Summer and Winter

American Solar Energy Ass'n (1977)
Hist. Note: Absorbed by the National Association of Solar Contractors in 1981.

American Solar Energy Soc. (1970)
2030 17th Street, Boulder CO 80302
Conference Director: Susie Burley
Members: 3,000 *Staff:* 3
Annual Budget: $500-1,000,000 *Tel:* (303) 443-3130
Hist. Note: Established in 1970 and incorporated in Florida. Formerly (1982) the Internat'l Solar Energy Soc., American Section. Affiliated with the Internat'l Solar Energy Soc. Membership: $50/yr.
Publications:
Annual Proceedings. a.
ASES News.
Solar Energy. m. adv.
Sun World. q.
Passive Proceedings. a.
Annual Meetings:
1987-Portland, OR

American Southdown Breeders Ass'n (1882)
R.D. 4, Box 14B, Bellefonte PA 16823
Secretary: Florence W. Strouse
Members: 700 *Staff:* 1
Annual Budget: $10-25,000 *Tel:* (814) 355-9841
Hist. Note: Breeders and fanciers of Southdown sheep. Membership: $10/life.
Annual Meetings: Fall

American Soybean Ass'n (1920)
Box 27300, 777 Craig Rd., St. Louis MO 63141-1700
Chief Executive Officer: Kenneth L. Bader
Members: 29,000 *Staff:* 175
Annual Budget: over $5,000,000 *Tel:* (314) 432-1600
Hist. Note: Aims to keep soybean farming profitable by export/market expansion, education, research and legislative action.
Publications:
The Soybean Digest. m. adv.
The Soya Blue Book. a. adv.
Annual Meetings: Summer
1987-St. Louis, MO(Cervantes Convention Hall)/Aug. 1-4/2,500
1988-New Orleans, LA(Rivergate)/July 29-Aug. 2/2,500

American Specialty Surety Council (1980)
Hist. Note: Became the American Surety Ass'n in 1984.

American Speech-Language-Hearing Ass'n (1925)
10801 Rockville Pike, Rockville MD 20852
Exec. Director: Frederick T. Spahr, CAE
Members: 45,000 individuals *Staff:* 125
Annual Budget: over $5,000,000 *Tel:* (301) 897-5700
Hist. Note: ASHA is the professional, scientific and accrediting association of speech-language pathologists and audiologists. Founded in 1925 as the American Academy of Speech Correction. Became the American Soc. for the Study of Disorders of Speech in 1927 and the American Speech Correction Ass'n in 1934. In 1947 the name was again changed to the American Speech and Hearing Ass'n and the organization was incorporated in Kansas. Changed to its present name in 1979. Member of the Council of Communication Societies and the Internat'l Ass'n of Logopedics and Phoniatrics. Has an annual budget of $9.5 million. Membership: $120/yr.
Publications:
Asha. m. adv.
Journal of Speech and Hearing Disorders. q.
Journal of Speech and Hearing Research. q.
Language, Speech and Hearing Services in Schools. q.
Annual Meetings: Fall/9-10,000
1987-New Orleans, LA/Nov. 13-16
1988-Boston, MA/Nov. 18-21
1989-St. Louis, MO/Nov. 17-20
1990-Seattle, WA/Nov. 16-19

American Spice Trade Ass'n (1907)
Box 1267, Englewood Cliffs NJ 07632
Exec. V. President: Thomas F. Burns
Members: 300-310 spice companies *Staff:* 2-5
Annual Budget: $250-500,000 *Tel:* (201) 568-2163
Annual Meetings: Spring
1987-Laguna Niguel, CA(Ritz-Carlton)/May 3-7

American Spinal Injury Ass'n (1972)
250 E. Superior Street, Rm. 619, Chicago IL 60611
President: J. Darrell Shea
Members: 330 *Staff:* 2
Annual Budget: $50-100,000 *Tel:* (312) 908-3425
Hist. Note: Membership: $125/yr.
Publication:
ASIA Bulletin.
Annual Meetings:
1987-Boston, MA(Westin-Copley Plaza)/March 20-22/450

American Sportcasters Ass'n (1979)
150 Nassau St., New York NY 10038
Exec. Director: Louis O. Schwartz
Members: 500-600 *Staff:* 3
Annual Budget: $50-100,000 *Tel:* (212) 227-8080
Hist. Note: Members are radio and TV sportscasters; the ASA is the forerunner of the American Sportscasters Charitable Trust. Membership: $40/yr.
Publication:
Insiders Sportsletter. m.
Annual Meetings: Fall
1987-New York, NY(Marriott Marquis)/Nov. 18/600

American Stamp Dealers' Ass'n (1914)
5 Dakota Drive, #102, Lake Success NY 11042
Exec. Officer: Joseph B. Savarese
Members: 1,000 *Staff:* 2-5
Annual Budget: $250-500,000 *Tel:* (516) 775-3600
Hist. Note: Membership: $175/yr.
Publications:
A.S.D.A. Newsletter. m.
A.S.D.A. Directory. a.
Annual Meetings: November in New York City

American Statistical Ass'n (1839)
806 15th St., N.W., Suite 640, Washington DC 20005
Exec. Director: Fred C. Leone
Members: 15,000 *Staff:* 25-30
Annual Budget: $1-2,000,000 *Tel:* (202) 393-3253
Hist. Note: Founded in Boston November 27, 1839 and incorporated in Massachusetts in 1841. ASA, a non-profit professional organization, fosters statistics and their application in the broadest manner, promotes unity and effective effort among all concerned with statistical problems and works to increase the contribution of statistics to human welfare.
Publications:
American Statistician. q. adv.
AMSTAT News. m. adv.
Current Index to Statistics. a.
Journal of Business and Economic Statistics. q.
Journal of the American Statistical Ass'n. q. adv.
Journal of Educational Statistics. q.
Proceedings. a.
Technometrics. q.
Annual Meetings: Summer
1987-San Francisco, CA/Aug./3,500
1988-New Orleans, LA/Aug./2,500
1989-Washington, DC/Aug./5,000

American Stock Exchange (1911)
86 Trinity Place, New York NY 10006
Chairman: Arthur Levitt, Jr.
Members: 518 member firms, 864 individuals *Staff:* 799
Annual Budget: over $5,000,000 *Tel:* (212) 306-1000
Hist. Note: Founded as an outdoor market in New York before 1800, it became successively the New York Curb Agency in 1908, the New York Curb Market Ass'n in 1911, the New York Curb Market in 1921 with its move indoors, the New York Curb Exchange in 1929 and the American Stock Exchange in 1953. Individual members are distinguished as regular members (661) and options principals members (203).
Publications:
Quarterly Reports.
Annual Report.
Annual Meetings: New York City, 2nd Monday in April.

American Stock Yards Ass'n (1932)
205 Livestock Exchange Bldg., Sioux City IA 51107
President: L.V. Kuhl
Members: 22 companies *Staff:* 1
Annual Budget: $25-50,000 *Tel:* (712) 258-5531
Annual Meetings: Summer
1987-Santa Barbara, CA(Biltmore)/June 23-26
1988-Colorado Springs, CO(Broadmoor)/June 21-24

American Stone Importers Ass'n (1930)
Hist. Note: Merged with the American Gem Trade Ass'n in 1985, and became the New York Guild of the AGTA. Formerly Precious Stone Dealers Ass'n.

American String Teachers Ass'n (1946)
Box 2066, University Station, Athens GA 30612
Exec. Director: J. Kimball Harriman
Members: 5-6,000 *Staff:* 2-5
Annual Budget: $100-250,000 *Tel:* (404) 542-5254
Hist. Note: Founded in 1946 and incorporated in Iowa in 1955. An associate organization of the Music Educators Nat'l Conference and member of the Nat'l Music Council and Associated Councils of the Arts. Membership is open to teachers and performers of stringed instruments including Guitar and Harp; students; schools or libraries; and commercial institutions interested in supporting its programs. Membership: $25/yr. (individual); $29/yr. (school or library); and $75/yr. (business).
Publication:
American String Teacher. q. adv.
Annual Meetings: With Music Educators Nat'l Conference
1987-Baltimore, MD/March 5-9/5-600

American Student Dental Ass'n (1971)
211 East Chicago Ave., Suite 840, Chicago IL 60611
Exec. Director: Julia Hensley
Members: 18,000 *Staff:* 6-10
Annual Budget: $250-500,000 *Tel:* (312) 440-2795
Hist. Note: Founded in Chicago, Illinois in February 1971 at a conference of dental students as the Student American Dental Association. The present name was assumed in 1971. Seeks to involve its members in the interprofessional activities of the dental profession. Membership: $25/yr.
Publications:
ASDA News. m. adv.
Dentistry '86. q.
ASDA Handbook. a.

00068 12 05 86 1233

ASDA Guide to General Practice Residencies. a.
Annual Meetings:
1987-Baltimore, MD(Omni)/Sept. 23-27/200

American Studies Ass'n (1951)
309 College Hall, Univ. of Pennsylvania, Philadelphia PA 19104-6403
Exec. Director: Dr. John F. Stephens
Members: 2,600 individuals and institutions *Staff:* 2-5
Annual Budget: $100-250,000 *Tel:* (215) 898-5408
Hist. Note: Founded in 1951 and incorporated in 1951 to foster the study of American culture and civilization as an entity rather than from the viewpoint of a single discipline. Admitted to membership in the American Council of Learned Societies in 1958.
Publications:
American Quarterly. q. adv.
ASA Newsletter. q. 3,000 circ.
Annual Meetings:
1987-New York, NY(NY Hilton)/Nov. 20-24/1,200
1988-Miami Beach, FL(Fontainebleau)/Oct. 27-30
1989-Toronto, Canada(Sheraton Centre)/Nov. 2-5/1,000

American Subcontractors Ass'n (1966)
1004 Duke St., Alexandria VA 22314
Exec. V. President: Christopher S. Stinebert
Members: 6,000 companies *Staff:* 16
Annual Budget: $1-2,000,000 *Tel:* (703) 684-3450
Hist. Note: ASA is a trade association representing subcontractors and specialty trade contractors in the construction industry. Sponsors and supports the American Subcontractors Association Political Action Committee. Membership: $105/yr.
Publications:
ASA Journal. a. adv.
The Subcontractor Magazine. m. adv.
The Leadergram. bi-w.
Annual Meetings: March
1987-Orlando, FL(Peabody)/March 24-29/500
1988-Hawaii(Undecided)

American Suffolk Sheep Soc. (1929)
P.O. Box 256, 17 West Main St., Newton UT 84327
Secretary: VeNeal J. Jenkins
Members: 3,500 *Staff:* 2-5
Annual Budget: $10-25,000 *Tel:* (801) 563-6105
Hist. Note: Breeders and fanciers of Suffolk sheep. Member of the National Society of Livestock Records Associations. Membership: $10/yr.
Publication:
The Modern Suffolk.
Annual Meetings: Every year in Salt Lake City, UT/August

American Sugar Cane League of the U.S.A. (1922)
416 Whitney Building, New Orleans LA 70130-2692
V. President & Gen. Manager: R. Charles Hodson, Jr.
Members: 3,500 *Staff:* 6-10
Annual Budget: $250-500,000 *Tel:* (504) 525-6848
Hist. Note: Formed by a merger of the Louisiana Sugar Planters Ass'n (founded in 1887), the American Cane Growers Ass'n (founded in 1919) and the Producers and Manufacturers Ass'n (founded in 1921). Sponsors the American Sugar Cane League Political Action Committee.
Publication:
Sugar Bulletin. semi-m. adv.
Annual Meetings: Last Friday of September in New Iberia, LA.

American Sugarbeet Growers Ass'n (1977)
1156 15th St., N.W., Suite 1020, Washington DC 20005
Exec. V. President: Luther A. Markwart
Members: 10-15 regional ass'ns *Staff:* 2-5
Annual Budget: $100-250,000 *Tel:* (202) 833-2398
Hist. Note: A federation of state and regional associations of sugarbeet growers. Formerly (until 1977) Nat'l Sugarbeet Growers Ass'n.
Publication:
Capitol Sugargram. q.
Annual Meetings: February
1987-San Francisco, CA

American Sulphur Export Corporation (1982)
Box 2967, Pennzoil Place, Houston TX 77252-2967
Managing Director: J. Colin Anderson
Members: 2 companies *Staff:* 1
Annual Budget: under $10,000 *Tel:* (713) 546-4400
Hist. Note: A Webb-Pomerene Act Ass'n, it is also known as AMSULEX. Member companies are Pennzoil Sulphur Co.(Houston) and Freeport McMoran Inc.(New Orleans).

American Supply and Machinery Manufacturers Ass'n (1905)
1230 Keith Bldg., Cleveland OH 44115-2180
Business Manager: Charles M. Stockinger
Members: 600-650 companies *Staff:* 2-5
Annual Budget: $500-1,000,000 *Tel:* (216) 241-7333
Hist. Note: Manufacturers of industrial supplies and machinery sold through industrial distributors.
Annual Meetings: Spring
1987-Los Angeles, CA/May 10-13
1988-Orlando, FL/May 8-11
1989-Chicago, IL/May 14-17
1990-Atlanta, GA/May 13-16
1991-San Francisco, CA/May 12-15

American Supply Ass'n (1894)
20 North Wacker Drive, Suite 2260, Chicago IL 60606
Exec. V. President: Peter Schwartz
Members: 1,200 companies *Staff:* 15
Annual Budget: $1-2,000,000 *Tel:* (312) 236-4082
Hist. Note: Merger (1970) of Central Supply Ass'n of Chicago and the American Institute of Supply Associations. Members are plumbing and heating wholesalers and distributors.
Publications:
Newsletter. m.
ASA News.
Washington Alert.
Membership Directory.
Annual Meetings: Fall/4,000
1987-New York City, NY(Hilton)/Oct. 14-18
1988-New Orleans, LA(Hilton, Marriott and Sheraton)

American Surety Ass'n (1980)
2045 North 15th St., Suite 1000, Arlington VA 22201
Exec. V. President: Dr. John F. Magnotti
Members: 120-130 companies *Staff:* 2-5
Annual Budget: $50-100,000 *Tel:* (703) 528-0072
Hist. Note: Small and minority contractors interested in the surety bond guarantee of the Federal government. Formerly (1984) the American Specialty Surety Council.
Annual Meetings: Fall

American Surgical Ass'n (1880)
Department of Surgery, University of Louisville, Louisville KY 40292
Secretary: Dr. H. Polk
Members: 500-600
Tel: (502) 588-5442
Hist. Note: Founded in 1880 in Philadelphia as the American Surgical Soc., the name was subsequently changed to the American Surgical Ass'n.
Publications:
Annals of Surgery. semi-a. adv.
Transactions. a.
Annual Meetings: Spring
1987-Palm Beach, FL/April 21-23
1988-San Francisco, CA/May 2-4
1989-Colorado Springs, CO/April 10-12
1990-Washington, DC/April 5-7
1991-Boca Raton, FL/April 10-12
1992-Palm Desert, CA/April 6-8
1993-Baltimore, MD
1994-Chicago, IL

American Surgical Trade Ass'n (1903)
Hist. Note: Became the Health Industry Distributors Association in 1983.

American Swimming Coaches Ass'n (1958)
1 Hall of Fame Drive, Fort Lauderdale FL 33316
Exec. Director: John Leonard
Members: 2,600 *Staff:* 2-5
Annual Budget: $250-500,000 *Tel:* (305) 462-6267
Hist. Note: Membership: $35/yr.
Publications:
ASCA Newsletter. 6/yr.
Clinic Book. a.
Journal of Swimming Research. q.

American Symphony Orchestra League (1942)
633 E St., N.W., Washington DC 20004
Chief Exec. Officer: Catherine French
Members: 900 orchestras; 4,500 individuals; 425 orgs. *Staff:* 37
Annual Budget: $2-5,000,000 *Tel:* (202) 628-0099
Hist. Note: Founded in 1942 and chartered by Congress in 1962, the purpose of the League is to ensure the artistic, organizational and financial success of American orchestras. Services include: training programs, publications, research and analysis, technical assistance, and government relations for professional, avocational and youth orchestras, and for trustees, management staff, conductors, artistic staff and volunteers.
Publication:
Symphony Magazine. bi-m. adv.
Annual Meetings: June
1987-New York, NY(Waldorf-Astoria)/June 10-14
1988-Chicago, IL
1989-Washington, DC

American Tarentaise Ass'n (1973)
P.O. Box 206, North Platte NE 69103
Exec. Secretary: Bette Sexson
Members: 700 cattle breeders *Staff:* 2-5
Annual Budget: $50-100,000 *Tel:* (308) 532-7911
Hist. Note: Tarentaise cattle originated in Southeastern France, and were recognized as a breed in 1866. The association if the official breed registry for Tarentaise cattle. Membership: $50/yr.
Publication:
Tarentaise Recorder. 10/yr. adv.
Annual Meetings: January
1987-Denver, CO(Dillon Inn)/Jan. 15-18/125

American Tarpan Studbook Ass'n
Hist. Note: No paid staff; address unknown in 1986.

American Taxation Ass'n (1975)
Hist. Note: A section of the American Accounting Association, which provides administrative support. Members are university professors teaching courses dealing with federal tax matters. Membership: $12.50/year.
Publication:
ATA Journal. semi-a.
Annual Meetings: With the American Accounting Association.

American Technical Education Ass'n (1928)
North Dakota State School of Science, Wahpeton ND 58075
Exec. Director: Betty Krump
Members: 2,000-2,500 *Staff:* 2-5
Annual Budget: $25-50,000 *Tel:* (701) 671-2240
Hist. Note: Established in 1928 as the American Ass'n of Technical High Schools and Institutes, it assumed its present name in 1950 and was incorporated in New York in 1960. From 1944 to 1969, the association was associated with the American Vocational Ass'n. Composed of post-secondary institutions, businesses and industrial concerns, ATEA is involved in expanding and improving the quality of technical education. Membership: $25/yr. (individual); $50/yr. (industry/business); and $75/yr. (institution/agency)
Publication:
ATEA Journal. bi-m.
Annual Meetings: Spring
1987-Cleveland, OH/March 28-30
1988-Nashville, TN/March 24-27

American Telemarketing Ass'n (1983)
104 Wilmot Road, Suite 201, Deerfield IL 60015-5195
Managing Director: Carl A. Wangman, CAE
Members: 700 *Staff:* 2-5
Annual Budget: $500-1,000,000 *Tel:* (312) 940-8800
Hist. Note: Membership open to all companies and individuals who use the telephone to give or receive information from customers and/or prospective customers. Membership: $125/yr. (individual); $375/yr. (company)
Publication:
Newsletter. m. adv.
Annual Meetings: November
1987-Monterey, CA(Sheraton Doubletree)/Nov. 1-4
1988-Boston, MA/Nov. 9-13
1989-San Antonio, TX/Oct. 11-14

American Textile Machinery Ass'n (1907)
7297 Lee Highway, Suite N, Falls Church VA 22042
Exec. V. President: Harry W. Buzzerd, Jr. CAE
Members: 125-130 *Staff:* 6-10
Annual Budget: $250-500,000 *Tel:* (703) 533-9251
Hist. Note: Formerly (1933) Nat'l Ass'n of Textile Machinery Manufacturers. Member, Machinery and Allied Products Institute. Sponsors and supports the Textile Machinery Good Government Political Action Committee.
Publications:
Product Directory Guide. bien.
ATMA Executive Report. 6-8/yr.
Annual Meetings:
1987-Nashville, TN(Sheraton)

American Textile Manufacturers Institute (1949)
1101 Connecticut Ave., N.W., Suite 300, Washington DC 20036
Exec. V. President: Carlos Moore
Staff: 38
Annual Budget: $2-5,000,000 *Tel:* (202) 862-0500
Hist. Note: Merger in 1949 of the American Cotton Manufacturers Ass'n and the Cotton Textile Institute to form the American Cotton Manufacturers Institute. Absorbed the Nat'l Federation of Textiles in 1958. Name changed to present title in 1962. Merged in 1964 with the Ass'n of Cotton Textile Merchants of NY. Absorbed the Nat'l Ass'n of Finishers of Textile Fabrics in 1965, and the Nat'l Ass'n of Wool Manufacturers in 1971. Supports the American Textile Industry Committee for Good Government. Membership: $1,000/yr. (individual); corporate based upon percent of value added.
Publications:
Textile Hi-Lights. q.
Textile Hi-Lights Supplement. m.
Annual Meetings: Spring/775-850
1987-New Orleans, LA(Fairmont)/April 9-11
1988-San Francisco, CA(Fairmont)/April 6-9

American Theatre Ass'n
Hist. Note: Reported as defunct in 1986.

American Theatre Critics Ass'n (1974)
c/o The Tennessean, 1100 Broad St., Nashville TN 37202
Exec. Secretary: Clara Hieronymus
Members: 345 *Staff:* 1
Annual Budget: under $10,000
Hist. Note: Organized at the O'Neill Theater Center in Waterford, CT in 1974 to make possible greater communication among theatre critics, to encourage freedom of expression in theater and theater criticism, to advance standards of criticism and to increase public awareness of the theater as a national resource. Membership: $25/yr.
Publication:
ATCA Newsletter. q.
Semi-annual Meetings: January in New York, NY and June
1987-Canada(Shakespeare Festival)/June
1988-Houston, TX/June

American Theological Library Ass'n (1947)
St. Meinrad School of Theology, Archabbey Library, St. Meinrad IN 47577
Exec. Secretary: Fr. Simeon Daly
Members: 160 libraries, 450 individuals *Staff:* 2-5
Annual Budget: $250-500,000 *Tel:* (812) 357-6718
Hist. Note: An outgrowth of the Religious Books Round Table of the American Library Ass'n; incorporated in 1973. International membership includes persons from Christian, Jewish and non-Judeo-Christian traditions interested in the

00069 12 05 86 1233

practice, support or promotion of theological librarianship, information systems or bibliography. All inquiries regarding the Religion Index should be directed to: 5600 Woodlawn Ave., Chicago, IL, 60637.
Publications:
Newsletter. q.
Proceedings. a.
Religion Index I: Periodical Literature. semi-a.
Religion Index II: Multi-Author Works. a.
Annual Meetings: June
1987-San Francisco, CA(Univ. of Southern CA)/June 21-26
1988-Wilmore, KY(Asbury School of Theology)/June 20-24
1989-Columbus, OH(Trinity Lutheran Seminary)/June 18-23

American Thermographic Soc. (1969)
Hist. Note: Became the American Academy of Thermography in 1983.

American Thoracic Soc. (1905)
1740 Broadway, 15th Floor, New York NY 10019
Exec. Director: S.R. Iannotta
Members: 8,700 *Staff:* 6-10
Annual Budget: $1-2,000,000 *Tel:* (212) 315-8700
Hist. Note: Founded in 1905 as the American Sanatorium Ass'n. Became the American Trudeau Soc. in 1939. In 1960 the name was changed to the American Thoracic Soc. Acts as the medical section of the American Lung Ass'n.
Publications:
American Review of Respiratory Disease. m. adv.
ATS News. q.
Annual Meetings: Spring, with the American Lung Ass'n
1987-New Orleans, LA(Marriott)/May 10-13
1988-Las Vegas, NV/May 8-11
1989-Cincinnati, OH/May 14-17
1990-Boston, MA/May 20-23

American Thyroid Ass'n (1923)
Mayo Clinic, Rochester MN 55905
Secretary: Colum A. Gorman, M.D.
Members: 650 *Staff:* 1
Tel: (507) 284-4738
Hist. Note: Founded as the American Ass'n for the Study of Goiter, it became the American Goiter Ass'n in 1948 and assumed its present name in 1960.
Publication:
Newsletter. q.
Annual Meetings: Fall
1987-Washington, DC/Sept. 15-19
1988-Montreal, Quebec/Sept. 27-Oct. 1

American Tin Trade Ass'n (1928)
Box 1347, New York NY 10150
Secretary: Terry Ford
Members: 30-40 tin traders *Staff:* 1
Annual Budget: under $10,000 *Tel:* (212) 599-8300
Hist. Note: Membership: $250/year.
Annual Meetings: New York City, always second Thursday in May/40-50

American Tinnitus Ass'n (1971)
Box 5, Portland OR 97207
Exec. Director: Gloria E. Reich
Members: 50,000 *Staff:* 2-5
Annual Budget: $100-250,000 *Tel:* (503) 248-9985
Hist. Note: Physicians, audiologists, hearing aid dispensers and individuals who suffer from noises in the head and ears. Membership: $15/year.
Publication:
Newsletter. q.
Annual Meetings:
1987-Chicago, IL/Sept. 20
1988-San Francisco, CA/Sept. 26
1989-New Orleans, LA/Sept. 25
1990-Washington, DC/Sept. 10

American Tour Managers Ass'n (1981)
8909 Dorrington Ave., West Hollywood, Los Angelos CA 90048
President: Anne C. Faerovik
Members: 20 companies, 300 individuals *Staff:* 3
Annual Budget: under $10,000 *Tel:* (213) 550-7660
Hist. Note: ATMA promotes professionalism, sets guidelines, and improves standards within the tour managing (directing) field; encourages the travelling public to purchase escorted and guided group tours; acts as a liaison between the Tour Managing/Guiding professions and other industry-related organizations. Membership: $50/yr. (individual); $250/yr. (company) Affiliated with the American Guides Ass'n.
Publication:
Newsletter. m.
Annual Meetings: January

American Traffic Safety Services Ass'n (1966)
408 Westwood Office Park, Fredericksburg VA 22401
Exec. Director: Robert M. Garrett
Members: 300 companies *Staff:* 6
Annual Budget: $500-1,000,000 *Tel:* (703) 371-8800
Hist. Note: Started as the American Traffic Safety Control Devices Association. Became the American Traffic Services Ass'n in 1971 and assumed its present name in 1984.
Publications:
ATSSA Flash. m.
ATSSA Signal. q.
ATSSA Bulletin. irreg.
ATSSA Membership Directory. a.
Annual Meetings: March/600
1987-Las Vegas, NV(Riviera)
1988-Orlando, FL

American Traffic Services Ass'n (1966)
Hist. Note: Became the American Traffic Safety Services Ass'n in 1984.

American Train Dispatchers Ass'n (1917)
1401 S. Harlem Ave., Berwyn IL 60402
President: Robert J. Irvin
Members: 2,600 *Staff:* 2-5
Annual Budget: $100-250,000 *Tel:* (312) 242-1691
Hist. Note: First organized as a local union in Spokane, Washington on November 1, 1917, this shortly developed into the Western Train Dispatchers' Association and, before the end of 1918, The American Train Dispatchers Association was formed. Chartered by AFL-CIO in 1957.
Publication:
The Train Dispatcher. 8/yr. adv.
Annual Meetings: Every 4 years in Fall (1987)
1987-Las Vegas, NV/3rd week in October

American Trainers Ass'n (1934)
Hist. Note: Address unknown in 1985-86.

American Trakehner Ass'n (1974)
5008 Pine Creek Drive, Suite B, Westerville OH 43081
Exec. Director: Marlisa K. Bannister
Members: 1,400 *Staff:* 8
Annual Budget: $100-250,000 *Tel:* (614) 895-1466
Hist. Note: Members are owners and breeders of Trakehner horses, a breed originating in Trakehnen, East Prussia in 1732. Membership: $55/yr.
Publications:
American Trakehner. q. adv.
Handbook. a.
Newsletter.
Annual Meetings: Fall

American Translators Ass'n (1959)
109 Croton Ave., Ossining NY 10562
Staff Administrator: Rosemary Malia
Members: 2,200-2,300 *Staff:* 1
Annual Budget: $25-50,000 *Tel:* (914) 941-1500
Hist. Note: Members are translators and interpreters. Has a testing and accreditation program. Membership: %40/yr. (individual), $60/yr. (institution), $125/yr. (company).
Publications:
ATA Chronicle. m. adv.
Translation Services Directory. bien.
Proceedings. a.
Annual Meetings: Fall
1987-Albuquerque, NM
1988-Seattle, WA
1989-Boston, MA
1990-New Orleans, LA
1991-Salt Lake City, UT

American Trauma Soc. (1968)
Box 13526, Baltimore MD 21203
Exec. Director: Sandra Bond-Lillicropp
Members: 5,000 *Staff:* 6
Annual Budget: $100-250,000 *Tel:* (301) 528-6304
Hist. Note: Dedicated to reducing needless death and disability by improving trauma care through traum system development, professional and para-professional training, public education and prevention. Membership includes both lay and professional individuals, institutions, and corporations. Membership: $20/yr. (individual); $500/yr. (corporate); $1,000/yr.(institution).
Publications:
Traumagram. q.
EMS Newsletter. q.
Trauma Center Newsletter. q.
Annual Meetings: May, in Washington, DC
1987-May 13-16

American Truck Dealers Ass'n
Hist. Note: A division of the National Automobile Dealers Association.

American Truck Stop Operators Ass'n (1981)
P.O. Box 14126, North Palm Beach FL 33408
President: Lloyd L. Golding
Members: 800 companies *Staff:* 4
Annual Budget: $250-500,000 *Tel:* (305) 848-9999
Hist. Note: Trade association of full facility truck stop operators. Membership: $500/year.
Publication:
Bulletin. m.

American Trucking Ass'ns (1933)
2200 Mill Road, Alexandria VA 22314
President: Thomas J. Donohoe
Members: 3,400 *Staff:* 290
Annual Budget: over $5,000,000 *Tel:* (703) 838-1700
Hist. Note: A federation of state trucking associations, national truck conferences and individual motor carriers and suppliers. Formed by a merger of the American Highway Freight Ass'n and the Federated Truck Ass'ns of America. Has a budget of approximately $30 million.
Publications:
Transport Topics. w. adv.
Interstate Information Report. m.
Motor Carrier Advisory Service. m.
Financial & Operating Statistics: Annual Report. a.
Financial & Operating Statistics: Quarterly Report. q.
Monthly Truck Tonnage Report. m.
Weekly Truck Tonnage Report. w.
Trucksource: SOurce of Trucking Industry Information. a.
Official Directory of Motor Carrier Consultants. a. adv.
National Motor Carrier Directory. a. adv.
Annual Meetings: Fall/4,000
1987-New York, NY(Hilton)/Oct. 25-29
1988-Los Angeles, CA(Westin Bonaventure)/Oct. 16-20
1989-Las Vegas, NV(Hilton)/Oct. 22-26
1990-Anaheim, CA(Anaheim Hilton & Towers)/Oct. 7-11
1991-Washington, DC(Washington Hilton)/Oct. 20-24

American Tube Ass'n (1979)
7297 Lee Highway, Suite N, Falls Church VA 22042
Exec. Director & Secretary: David S. O'Bryon
Members: 200 individuals *Staff:* 2
Annual Budget: $25-50,000 *Tel:* (703) 533-0250
Hist. Note: Membership: $75/yr.
Publication:
Newsletter. q.
Annual Meetings: Winter

American Tunaboat Ass'n (1923)
1 Tuna Lane, San Diego CA 92101
President: August Felando
Members: 40-500 *Staff:* 4-50
Annual Budget: $250-500,000 *Tel:* (619) 233-6405
Hist. Note: Established as the American Fisherman's Protective Ass'n, ATA has also been known as American Fisherman's Tunaboat Ass'n (1929) and American Tunaboat Ass'n (1947). Sponsors the American Tunaboat Association Political Action Committee. Membership: $100/yr.
Publication:
Newsletter. irreg.
Annual Meetings: December
1987-San Diego, CA

American Turpentine Farmers Ass'n Co-op (1936)
1204 North Patterson St., Valdosta GA 31601
President: Jim L. Gillis, Jr.
Members: 400 *Staff:* 2-5
Annual Budget: $50-100,000 *Tel:* (912) 242-6785
Hist. Note: Formed as a cooperative marketing association for producers of turpentine, rosin, and their by-products.
Regional Meetings:

American Underground-Space Ass'n (1976)
511 11th Ave. South, Box 320, Minneapolis MN 55415
Exec. Director: Susan R. Nelson
Members: 500 *Staff:* 2
Annual Budget: $50-100,000 *Tel:* (612) 339-5403
Hist. Note: Membership consists of engineers, architects, planners, developers, and others interested in the development of underground commercial, industrial, residential, and transport structures. Membership: $40/year (individual), $200/year (company/institution).
Publications:
Newsletter.
Underground Space. q.
Annual Meetings: Not regularly scheduled

American Urological Ass'n (1902)
1120 North Charles St., Baltimore MD 21201
Exec. Secretary: Richard J. Hannigan
Members: 5,700 *Staff:* 11-15
Annual Budget: over $5,000,000 *Tel:* (301) 727-1100
Hist. Note: Founded in 1902 and incorporated in Maryland. Has an annual budget of $5.4 million. Membership: $240/year.
Publication:
Journal of Urology. m. adv.
Annual Meetings: Spring/4,500-5,000
1987-Anaheim, CA(Convention Ctr./Hilton)/May 17-21
1988-Boston, MA(Hynes Convention Ctr./Marriott Copley Place)/June 3-7
1989-Dallas, TX(Infomart/Loew's Anatole)/May 7-11
1990-New Orleans, LA(Convention Ctr./Hilton)/May 13-17
1991-Las Vegas, NV(Convention Ctr./Hilton)/April 28-May 2
1992-Washington, DC(Convention Ctr./Grand Hyatt)/May 10-14
1993-Houston, TX(Brown Convention Ctr.)/May 16-20

American Urological Ass'n Allied (1972)
6845 Lake Shore Dr., Raytown MO 64133
Exec. Director: Bruce R. Hagen
Members: 1,500 individuals *Staff:* 2
Annual Budget: $100-250,000 *Tel:* (816) 358-3317
Hist. Note: Established in Baltimore, MD, in 1972, AUAA is recognized by the American Urological Ass'n as the sole provider of education for all health professionals in urology: RN's, LPN/LVN's, physicians and physician's assistants, technicians, industry sales personnel and office staff. Membership: $50/yr.
Publications:
AUAA Journal. q. adv.
Uro-Gram (newsletter). q.
Annual Meetings: Spring
1987-Anaheim, CA(Sheraton Anaheim)/May 17-21
1988-Boston, MA(Lafayette Hotel)/June 3-7
1989-Dallas, TX(Sheraton Dallas Hotel)/May 7-11
1990-New Orleans, LA/May 13-17
1991-Las Vegas, NV/April 28-May 2
1992-Washington, DC/May 10-14
1993-Houston, TX/May 16-20

00070 12 05 86 1233

American Vacuum Soc. (1953)
335 East 45th Street, New York NY 10017
Exec. Secretary: Nancy L. Hammond
Members: 5,200 *Staff:* 2-5
Annual Budget: $2-5,000,000 *Tel:* (212) 661-9404
Hist. Note: Established in 1953 as the Committee on Vacuum Techniques. Incorporated in Massachusetts in the same year. Became the American Vacuum Soc. In 1958. Affiliated with the American Institute of Physics, and the Internat'l Union for Vacuum Science, Techniques and Applications. Membership: $50/year
Publications:
Journal of Vacuum Science & Technology A. bi-m. adv.
Journal of Vacuum Science & Technology B. bi-m. adv.
Annual Meetings: Fall
1987-Anaheim, CA(Hilton & Conv. Center)/Nov. 3-6
1988-Atlanta, GA(Hilton)/Oct. 4-7
1989-Boston, MA(Sheraton Boston)

American Venereal Disease Ass'n (1934)
P.O. Box 22349, San Diego CA 92122
Secy.-Treas.: William Harrison, M.D.
Members: 1,650-1,700 *Staff:* 1
Annual Budget: $25-50,000 *Tel:* (619) 453-3238
Hist. Note: Member of the Internat'l Union against the Venereal Diseases and the Treponematoses. Founded as the American Neisserian Medical Association. Assumed its present name in 1967. Has no paid staff.
Publication:
Sexually Transmitted Diseases. q. adv.
Annual Meetings: Fall

American Veterinary Exhibitors Ass'n (1936)
Box 19006, Birmingham AL 35219
Exec. Director: Bob Willis, Ed.D.
Members: 100 companies *Staff:* 1
Annual Budget: $10-25,000 *Tel:* (205) 979-0830
Hist. Note: Members are firms which exhibit at veterinary meetings.
Publications:
Newsletter. q.
Schedule of Veterinary Conventions. a.
Annual Meetings: With the American Veterinary Medical Ass'n

American Veterinary Medical Ass'n (1863)
930 North Meacham Rd., Schaumburg IL 60196
Exec. V. President: Dr. Arthur Freeman
Members: 43,000 *Staff:* 50-60
Annual Budget: over $5,000,000 *Tel:* (312) 885-8070
Hist. Note: Founded in 1863 as the United States Veterinary Medical Ass'n, the name became American Veterinary Medical Ass'n in 1898. Incorporated in Illinois in 1917. Sponsors the American Veterinary Medical Association Political Action Committee. Membership: $115/year.
Publications:
American Journal of Veterinary Research. m. adv.
Journal of AVMA. semi-m. adv.
Annual Meetings: July
1987-Chicago, IL/July 20-23
1988-Portland, OR/July 18-21
1989-Orlando, FL/July 17-20
1990-San Antonio, TX/July 23-26

American Veterinary Soc. of Animal Behavior (1975)
10010 N.W. 11th Manor, Coral Springs FL 33065
Secy.-Treas.: Walter F. Burghardt, Jr.,DVM
Members: 120
Annual Budget: under $10,000 *Tel:* (305) 753-8759
Hist. Note: Formerly the American Soc. of Veterinary Ethology. Membership restricted to veterinarians, veterinary students, and animal behavior consultants. Has no paid staff. Membership: $12/yr.
Publication:
Newsletter. q.
Annual Meetings: July
1987-Chicago, IL/July 20-23
1988-Portland, OR/July 18-21
1989-Orlando, FL/July 17-20

American Vocational Ass'n (1926)
1410 King St., Alexandria VA 22314
Exec. Director: Charles H. Buzzell
Members: 45-46,000 *Staff:* 40-45
Annual Budget: $2-5,000,000 *Tel:* (703) 683-3111
Hist. Note: Founded in 1906 as the Nat'l Soc. for the Promotion of Industrial Education. Name changed in 1918 to the Nat'l Soc. for Vocational Education. Merged in 1925 with the Vocational Ass'n of the Middle West to form the American Vocational Ass'n and incorporated in Indiana in 1929. A federation of state vocational ass'ns.
Publications:
Update. 6/yr. adv.
Voced Journal. 8/yr. adv.
Annual Meetings: December

American Vocational Education Research Ass'n (1966)
Illinois State University, Department of Home Economics, Normal IL 61761
President: Connie Ley
Members: 275-300
Annual Budget: under $10,000 *Tel:* (309) 438-2517
Hist. Note: Affiliated with the American Vocational Ass'n.
Publications:
The Beacon. q.
The Journal of Vocational Educational Researching. q.
Annual Meetings: With the American Vocational Ass'n

American Warehousemen's Ass'n (1891)
1165 North Clark St., Chicago IL 60610
President: Jerry Leatham
Members: 500-550 *Staff:* 6-10
Annual Budget: $500-1,000,000 *Tel:* (312) 787-3377
Publications:
AWA Newsgram. q.
Warehousing Review. q.
Annual Meetings: Spring/550
1987-Boca Raton, FL(Racquet Club)/Feb. 22-27
1988-Colorado Springs, CO(Broadmoor)/March 15-20

American Warmblood Registry (1981)
Box 395, Hastings NY 10706
Exec. Director: Sonja K. Lowenfish
Staff: 2
Annual Budget: $10-25,000 *Tel:* (914) 693-4829
Hist. Note: Members are owners and breeders of American Warmblood horses. Membership: $45/yr.
Publications:
Directory of Stallions at Stud. a.
American Warmblood Bulletin. m.
Annual Meetings: Fall

American Watch Ass'n (1933)
1201 Pennsylvania Ave., N.W., Box 464, Washington DC 20044
Exec. Director: Emilio G. Collado, III
Members: 40-50 companies *Staff:* 2-5
Annual Budget: $100-250,000 *Tel:* (703) 759-3377
Hist. Note: Founded as the American Watch Assemblers Ass'n, it assumed its present name in 1951. Members are importers of watch and clock movements and cases; domestic manufacturers and assemblers.
Annual Meetings: New York, NY/March

American Watch Workers Union
Hist. Note: Independent labor union. Affiliated with the National Federation of Independent Unions. Address unknown since 1984, probably defunct.
Publication:
American Watch Worker. m.
Biennial meetings: Uneven years

American Watchmakers Institute (1960)
3700 Harrison Ave., Box 11011, Cincinnati OH 45211
Exec. Secretary: Milton C. Stevens
Members: 7,500-8,000 individuals and institutions *Staff:* 6-10
Annual Budget: $500-1,000,000 *Tel:* (513) 661-3838
Hist. Note: Merger of Horological Institute of America and United Horological Ass'n of America. Offers correspondence courses in clockmaking and micro-electronics for watches, and an examination and certification program for master watchmakers.
Publication:
Horological Times. m.

American Water Resources Ass'n (1964)
5410 Grosvenor Lane, Suite 220, Bethesda MD 20814
Exec. Director: Kenneth D. Reid, CAE
Members: 2,700 *Staff:* 2-5
Annual Budget: $250-500,000 *Tel:* (301) 493-8600
Hist. Note: Incorporated in Illinois in March 1964, AWRA is a multidisciplinary non-profit scientific, educational association dedicated to the advancement of research, planning, management, development and education in water resources. Member Society of the Renewable Natural Resources Foundation. Membership includes engineers, hydrologists, biologists, attorneys, chemists and social scientists. Membership: $45/yr.
Publications:
Hydata News and Views. bi-m.
Proceedings. a.
Water Resources Bulletin. bi-m.
Semi-annual meetings:
American Water Resourses Symposium in the spring.
Annual American Water Resources Conference in the fall.
1987-(Conference & Symposium)Syracuse, NY/May 17-20
1987-(Conference & Symposium)Salt Lake City,UT/Oct. 31-Nov. 6
1988-(Conference & Symposium)Milwaukee,WI/Nov. 6-11
1989-(Conference & SYmposium)Tampa, FL/Sept. 17-22

American Water Works Ass'n (1881)
6666 W. Quincy Ave., Denver CO 80235
Exec. Director: Paul A. Schulte
Members: 36,000 individuals, 4,000 organizations *Staff:* 82
Annual Budget: over $5,000,000 *Tel:* (303) 794-7711
Hist. Note: Organized at Washington University, St. Louis, on March 29, 1881 and incorporated in Illinois in 1912. Membership: $53/yr.(individual); organizational fee varies by size. Has an annual budget over $9 million.
Publications:
Community Relations Newsletter. m.
Journal. m. adv.
Mainstream. m.
OpFlow. m.
Washington Report. 9/yr.
Water World News. bi-m.
Annual Meetings: June/7,500
1987-Kansas City, MO(Convention Ctr.)/June 14-18
1988-Orlando, FL(Convention Ctr.)June 19-22
1989-San Diego, CA(Convention Ctr.)/June 18-22
1990-Cincinnati, OH/June 17-21
1991- Philadelphia, PA/June 23-27

American Waterways Operators (1944)
1600 Wilson Blvd., Suite 1000, Arlington VA 22209
President: Joseph A. Farrell, III
Members: 250-275 *Staff:* 15-20
Annual Budget: $1-2,000,000 *Tel:* (703) 841-9300
Hist. Note: Members include carriers transporting commodities by water, shipyards, terminals, and affiliated businesses. Works to preserve the waterways system and develop the nation's infrastructure. Supports the American Waterways Operators PAC.
Publications:
AWO Letter. bi-w.
Annual Report. a.
Membership Directory. a.
Affiliate Directory. a.
Tri-annual Board Meetings:

American Waterways Shipyard Conference (1976)
1600 Wilson Blvd., Arlington VA 22209
Manager, Shipyard Operations: Marcia Y. Kinter
Members: 40-50 shipyards *Staff:* 1
Annual Budget: $50-100,000 *Tel:* (703) 841-9300
Hist. Note: Supported by the American Waterways Operators which provides administrative support.
Publication:
Shipyard Survey. a.
Quarterly Meetings:

American Welding Soc. (1919)
550 N.W. LeJeune Road, Box 351040, Miami FL 33135
Exec. Director: Paul Ramsey
Members: 32,000 *Staff:* 69
Annual Budget: over $5,000,000 *Tel:* (305) 443-9353
Hist. Note: Organized in March 1919 as an outgrowth of the Welding Committee of the Emergency Fleet Corporation, U.S. Shipping Board. Incorporated in New York in 1932. Has an annual budget of $6.5 million.
Publication:
Welding Journal. m. adv.
Annual Meetings: Spring/14,000
1987-Chicago, IL/March 22-27
1988-New Orleans, LA/April 17-22

American Wholesale Booksellers Ass'n (1984)
702 S. Michigan, South Bend IN 46518
Exec. Secretary: Michael J. Raymond
Members: 30 *Staff:* 0
Annual Budget: under $10,000 *Tel:* (219) 232-8500
Hist. Note: Members are companies engaged in the wholesale distribution of books whose sales of books account for at least 75% of total sales. Membership: $200/yr.
Publications:
Newsletter. q.
Directory of Members. a.
Annual Meetings: May/June

American Wind Energy Ass'n (1974)
1017A King St., Alexandria VA 22314
Exec. Director: Thomas O. Gray
Members: 200 companies, 400 individuals *Staff:* 2-5
Annual Budget: $250-500,000 *Tel:* (703) 684-5196
Hist. Note: The trade association for the wind energy industry, AWEA is composed of manufacturers of wind systems and components, siting equipment, wind farm developers, investors, and others with an interest in wind energy. Membership: $35/year (individual), $250-5,000/year (industry).
Publications:
AWEA Wind Energy Weekly. w.
Windletter. 8/yr.
Annual Meetings: Fall
1987-San Francisco, CA/October/400

American Window Coverings Manufacturers Ass'n (1985)
355 Lexington Ave., 15th Fl., New York NY 10017
Exec. Secretary: Peter S. Rush
Members: 20 companies *Staff:* 2-5
Annual Budget: $50-100,000 *Tel:* (212) 661-5300
Hist. Note: Originally the Venetian Blind Institute (1942); the Venetian Blind Ass'n (1977); and most recently (1985) the United States Venetian Blind Ass'n. Represents manufacturers of hard window coverings.
Annual Meetings: Fall

American Wine Ass'n
10 East 40th Street, New York NY 10016
General Counsel: Abraham M. Buchman
Members: 15-20 companies *Staff:* 1
Annual Budget: $10-25,000 *Tel:* (212) 953-0440
Hist. Note: Membership consists principally of East Coast wineries.

American Wire Cloth Institute (1933)
2000 Maple Hill St., Yorktown Heights NY 10598
Secretary: Peter M. Miranda
Members: 20-25 companies *Staff:* 2-5
Tel: (914) 962-9052
Hist. Note: Formerly (1978) the Industrial Wire Cloth Institute.

American Wire Producers Ass'n (1964)
1101 Connecticut Ave., N.W., Suite 700, Washington DC 20036
Mng. Director: Robert T. Chancler
Members: 80-90 companies *Staff:* 2-5
Annual Budget: $50-100,000 *Tel:* (202) 857-1155

00071 12 05 86 1233

Hist. Note: Founded as the Independent Wire Drawers Ass'n, it became the Independent Wire Produers Ass'n in 1975 and assumed its present name in 1981 when it merged with the Specialty Wire Ass'n. Members are companies producing wire by drawing metal through a disk.
Publication:
Wireline. m.
Annual Meetings: Winter
1987-Palm Springs, CA(La Quinta)/Feb. 14-16
1988-Naples, FL(Registry Hotel)/Feb.

American Woman's Soc. of Certified Public Accountants (1933)
500 North Michigan Ave., Suite 1400, Chicago IL 60611
Exec. Director: Lydia Lewis
Members: 4-5,000 *Staff:* 2-5
Annual Budget: $100-250,000 *Tel:* (312) 661-1700
Hist. Note: Membership: $45/yr.
Publication:
The Woman C.P.A. q.
Annual Meetings: With the American Soc. of Women Accountants

American Women Composers (1976)
c/o Levine Music Center, 1690 36th St., N.W., Suite 410, Washington DC 20007
President: Tommie Ewert Carl
Members: 250 *Staff:* 3
Annual Budget: $10-25,000 *Tel:* (202) 342-8179
Hist. Note: Members are women composers, performers, and musicologists. Maintains a music library and holds various symposia and concerts throughout the year. Produces records under the Capriccio label.
Publication:
AWC News/Forum. semi-a.

American Women in Radio and Television (1951)
1101 Connecticut Ave., N.W., Suite 700, Washington DC 20036
Exec. V. President: Carolyn Del Polito
Members: 2,700-3,000 *Staff:* 3
Annual Budget: $250-500,000 *Tel:* (202) 429-5102
Hist. Note: Prior to 1951 a group known as the Ass'n of Women Broadcasters was an adjunct to the Nat'l Ass'n of Radio and Television Broadcasters, the predecessor to the Nat'l Ass'n of Broadcasters. AWB was discontinued in October, 1950. The present organization was established at the Hotel Astor in New York, April 6-8, 1951 and consists of individuals in numerous job categories in the radio-TV industry and its affiliated or supporting organizations. Membership: $95/yr.
Publications:
News & Views. bi-m.
Membership Directory. a. adv.
Convention Program. a. adv.
Annual Meetings: Spring
1987-Los Angeles, CA(Beverly Hilton)/June 10-13
1988-Pittsburgh, PA/June

American Wood Chip Export Ass'n (1974)
900 S.W. Fifth Avenue, 23rd Floor, c/o Stoel, Rives, Boley, Fraser and Wyse, Portland OR 97204
Secretary: David P. Miller
Members: 7 companies *Staff:* 1
Annual Budget: under $10,000 *Tel:* (503) 224-3380
Hist. Note: A Webb-Pomerene Act association.

American Wood Council (1968)
1250 Connecticut Ave., N.W., Suite 230, Washington DC 20036
President: Carl E. Darrow
Members: 7 ass'ns *Staff:* 6-10
Annual Budget: $500-1,000,000 *Tel:* (202) 833-1595
Hist. Note: Merger (1969) of Wood Marketing, Inc. and Forest Products Promotion Council Member of the Forest Industries Council. Major purpose is promotion of wood products.

American Wood-Preservers' Ass'n (1904)
P.O. Box 849, Stevensville MD 21666
Secy.-Treas.: John D. Ferry
Members: 1,800-1,900 *Staff:* 2-5
Annual Budget: $50-100,000 *Tel:* (301) 643-4163
Hist. Note: Membership: $55/yr.
Publications:
AWPA Book of Standards. a.
AWPA Proceedings. a. adv.
Annual Meetings:
1987-Toronto, Canada(Toronto Hilton)/May 10-13

American Wood Preservers Bureau (1971)
Box 5283, Springfield VA 22150
President: Charles E. Thomas, Jr.
Members: 300 companies *Staff:* 6-10
Annual Budget: $500-1,000,000 *Tel:* (703) 339-6660
Hist. Note: Spun off from The American Wood Preservers Institute, AWPB operates a quality control laboratory and testing program, certifies wood preservation inspection agencies, and provides a quality mark certification program for pressure treated wood.
Annual Meetings: December

American Wood Preservers Institute (1921)
1945 Old Gallows Road, Suite 405, Vienna VA 22180
President: John F. Hall
Members: 86 *Staff:* 6-10
Annual Budget: $500-1,000,000 *Tel:* (703) 893-4005
Hist. Note: The government affairs arm of the industry.
Annual Meetings: Fall

American Word Processing Ass'n (1972)
Hist. Note: Became the Information Management and Processing Ass'n in 1984 and ceased operations in 1986.

American Yarn Spinners Ass'n (1967)
Box 99, Gastonia NC 28053
Exec. V. President: Jim H. Conner
Members: 125-150 companies *Staff:* 5
Annual Budget: $100-250,000 *Tel:* (704) 824-3522
Hist. Note: Merger of Carded Yarn Ass'n (1936) and Combed Yarn Spinners (1908). Affiliated with the Ass'n of Synthetic Yarn Manufacturers and the Craft Yarn Council of America. Absorbed the Long Staple Yarn Ass'n in 1974, the Yarn Dyers Ass'n in 1976 and the Carpet Yarn Ass'n in 1981.
Annual Meetings: September in Sea Island, GA at the Cloisters

American Yorkshire Club (1935)
R.R. 2, Box 49, Roanoke IL 61561
President: Bruce Leman
Members: 4-5,000 *Staff:* 10
Annual Budget: $500-1,000,000 *Tel:* (317) 463-3593
Hist. Note: Breeders and fanciers of Yorkshire swine.
Publication:
Yorkshire Journal. 10/yr. adv.
Semi-annual Meetings: January and July

Amerifax Cattle Ass'n (1977)
Box 149, Hastings NE 68901
Secretary: John Quirk
Members: 140 *Staff:* 1
Annual Budget: $25-50,000 *Tel:* (402) 463-5289
Hist. Note: Promotes the Amerifax breed of cattle. Maintains a herd book. Membership: $20/year, $50 initiation fee.
Publication:
Amerifax News. q. adv.
Annual Meetings: January

Amusement and Music Operators Ass'n (1948)
111 East Wacker Drive, Chicago IL 60601
Exec. V. President: William W. Carpenter
Members: 1,500 *Staff:* 2-5
Annual Budget: $500-1,000,000 *Tel:* (312) 644-6610
Hist. Note: Formerly (1977) Music Operators of America, Inc. Established as the Music Operators of America, it assumed its present name in 1977. Members are companies making, servicing or selling coin operated record players or amusement devices.
Publication:
Location Newsletter. m.
Annual Meetings: Fall
1987-Chicago, IL(Hyatt Regency)/Nov.5-7/7,000

Amusement Game Manufacturers Ass'n (1980)
Hist. Note: Became the American Amusement Machine Ass'n in 1985.

Analytical Laboratory Managers Ass'n (1980)
P.O. Box 258, Montchanin DE 19710
Exec. Secretary: Dr. Bob Stalzer
Members: 300
Annual Budget: under $10,000 *Tel:* (302) 571-8216
Hist. Note: Created to promote the exchange of information about management and operation of analytical laboratories. Members include university, industrial and government laboratories. Founded as the University Laboratory Managers Association, ALMA assumed its present name in 1981.
Publication:
ALMA Newsletter. 3/yr.
Annual Meetings: Fall

Aniline Ass'n (1982)
1330 Connecticut Ave., N.W., Suite 300, Washington DC 20036
Exec. Director: Alan W. Rautio
Members: 6 companies *Staff:* 2
Annual Budget: $25-50,000 *Tel:* (202) 659-0060
Hist. Note: An affiliate of the Synthetic Organic Chemicals Manufacturers Ass'n which provides administrative support.

Animal Behavior Soc. (1964)
Dept. of Psychology, Tulane University, New Orleans LA 70118
Secretary: Dr. Terry Christenson
Members: 2,500 *Staff:* 1
Annual Budget: $50-100,000 *Tel:* (504) 865-5331
Hist. Note: Membership: $32/year (individual). Professionals and students involved in animal behavior research. Affiliated with the American Soc. of Zoologists. Membership: $32/year (individual).
Publications:
Animal Behaviour. q.
Newsletter. q.
Annual Meetings: June
1987-Williamstown, MA(Williams College)/June 21-26/500

Animal Health Institute (1941)
119 Oronoco St., Box 1417-D50, Alexandria VA 22313
President: Fred H. Holt
Members: 50-75 *Staff:* 11-16
Annual Budget: $1-2,000,000 *Tel:* (703) 684-0011
Hist. Note: AHI is the U.S. industry trade association representing the manufacturers of the veterinary pharmaceuticals, biologicals, feed additives and animal pesticides used in agriculture and veterinary medicine.
Publications:
Animal Drug News. bi-m.
Annual Report. a.
Membership Directory. a.
Annual Meetings: May/250
1987-Tucson, AZ(El Conquistador)

Animal Nutrition Research Council (1939)
c/o Diversified Laboratories, Inc., 3251 Old Lee Highway, Fairfax VA 22030
Secy.-Treas.: Dr. Roger L. Garrett
Members: 425-450 *Staff:* 1
Annual Budget: under $10,000 *Tel:* (703) 273-2011
Hist. Note: Founded as the Animal Vitamin Research Council, it assumed its present name in 1946. Membership: $10/yr. (individual).
Publication:
Proceedings of Annual Symposium. a.
October, in Washington, DC: Every third year, with a 3 year rotation
with Poultry Science Ass'n and Animal Science Ass'n.

Animation Producers' Ass'n
Hist. Note: Reported defunct in 1982.

Ankina Breeders (1975)
5803 Oakes Rd., Clayton OH 45315
President: James K. Davis, Ph.D.
Members: 250 *Staff:* 1
Annual Budget: under $10,000 *Tel:* (513) 837-4128
Hist. Note: Breeders and fanciers of Ankina beef cattle. Membership: $25/yr.

Antennas and Propagation Soc.
Hist. Note: A subsidiary of the Institute of Electrical and Electronics Engineers. Membership in the society, open only to IEEE members, includes subscription to a technical periodical in the field published by IEEE. All administrative support is provided by IEEE.

Anthracite Industry Ass'n (1981)
208 N. 3rd St., Suite 310, Harrisburg PA 17101
Exec. Director: Mazie Mohney
Members: 60 companies *Staff:* 2-5
Annual Budget: $25-50,000 *Tel:* (717) 233-1808
Hist. Note: Successor organization to the Anthracite Institute (1931-1973). Incorporated in the State of Pennsylvania. Members are producers of anthracite coal, which happens to occur only in Pennsylvania. Has a Washington office.

Anti-Friction Bearing Manufacturers Ass'n (1933)
1101 Connecticut Ave., N.W., Suite 700, Washington DC 20036
President: Michael L. Payne
Members: 40-50 *Staff:* 2-5
Annual Budget: $250-500,000 *Tel:* (202) 857-1100

Antiquarian Booksellers Ass'n of America (1949)
50 Rockefeller Plaza, New York NY 10020
Admin. Assistant: Janice Farina
Members: 425-450 companies *Staff:* 1
Tel: (212) 757-9395
Hist. Note: Members are rare book dealers. Affiliated with the Internat'l League of Antiquarian Booksellers.
Annual Meetings: April in New York, NY

Antique Appraisal Ass'n of America (1972)
11361 Garden Grove Blvd., Garden Grove CA 92643
Secretary: Andrew Nolan
Members: 250 individuals *Staff:* 1
Annual Budget: under $10,000 *Tel:* (714) 530-7090
Hist. Note: Certifies members to professionally appraise antiques.
Publication:
Newsletter. bi-m.
Annual Meetings: Not held

ANV Export Corporation (1980)
c/o Valley Marketing Cooperative, Inc., 100 S. Ottawa, St. Johns MI 48879
Hist. Note: A Webb-Pomerene Act association.

Apartment Owners and Managers Ass'n of America (1966)
65 Cherry Plaza, Box 238, Watertown CT 06795-0238
President: Robert J. McGough
Members: 4,100 *Staff:* 2-5
Annual Budget: $100-250,000 *Tel:* (203) 274-2589
Hist. Note: Membership open to anyone engaged in the planning, construction, financing, ownership and management of multi-family housing. Membership: $125/yr. (individual), $200/yr. (company).
Publications:
Apartment Management Report. m. adv.
AOMA Newsletter. m. adv.

APEC (1985)
Miami Valley Tower, 40 West 4th St., Suite 2100, Dayton OH 45402
Exec. Director: Doris J. Wallace
Members: 220 companies *Staff:* 3
Annual Budget: $250-500,000 *Tel:* (513) 228-2602
Hist. Note: Formerly (1985) Automated Procedures for Engineering Consultants. Membership consists of professional design firms who pool their resources to develop computer software for use in building systems design. Membership:

00072 12 05 86 1233

$500-1,500/yr. (based on firm size).
Publication:
APEC Journal. 3/yr.
Annual Meetings: November

Apiary Inspectors of America (1932)
Maryland Dept. of Agriculture, 50 Harry S. Truman Pkwy., Annapolis MD 21401
Secretary: I. Barton Smith, Jr.
Members: 40-50 *Staff:* 1
Annual Budget: under $10,000 *Tel:* (301) 841-5920
Hist. Note: Members are state apiarists of the U.S. and Canada. Formerly Nat'l Apiary Inspectors. Membership: $35/yr. (individual); $50/yr. (state).
Publication:
Proceedings of the Annual Conference. a.
Annual Meetings: January
1987-Biloxi, MS/Jan. 26-30/50
1988-Beltsville, MD

Appalachian Hardwood Manufacturers (1928)
Box 427, High Point NC 27261
Exec. V. President: James L. Gundy
Members: 150 companies *Staff:* 2-5
Annual Budget: $100-250,000 *Tel:* (919) 885-8315
Publication:
Appalachian Hardwood Year Book. biennial.
Semi-annual Meetings: Winter and Summer
1987-Charleston, SC(Omni Charleston Place)/Feb. 19-20
1987-White Sulphur Springs, WV(Greenbrier)/July 27-28
1988-New Orleans(Royal Sonesta)/Feb. 18-19
1988-Asheville, SC(Grove Park Inn)/July 25-26
1989-Miami, FL(Doral Hotel & Country Club)/Feb. 23-24
1989-White Sulphur Springs, WV(Greenbrier)/July 24-25
1990-Washington, DC(J.W. Marriott)/Feb. 22-23
1991-Sea Island, GA(The Cloister)/Feb. 21-22
1991-White Sulphur Springs, WV(Greenbrier)/July 28-30
1992-Hilton Head, SC(Intercontinental)/Feb.

Appaloosa Horse Club (1938)
Box 8403, Moscow ID 83843
Exec. Secy.: Ronald A. Robison
Members: 22,000 *Staff:* 100
Annual Budget: $2-5,000,000 *Tel:* (208) 882-5578
Hist. Note: Owners and breeders of the Appaloosa horse. Member of the Nat'l Soc. of Livestock Records Ass'ns. Membership: $25/yr. (individual).
Publications:
Appaloosa News. m. adv.
ApHC Racing Chart Book. q.
Racing Newsletter. m.
Annual Meetings: Summer
1987-Albuquerque, NM(New Mexico State Fairgrounds)/June 30-July 12

Apparel Guild (1978)
147 West 33rd St., New York NY 10001
President Emeritus: Mac Hoyt
Members: 200-225 *Staff:* 1
Annual Budget: under $10,000 *Tel:* (212) 279-4580
Hist. Note: Membership: $100/yr. the Garment Salesmen's Guild New York (founded in 1938). A fraternal, benevolent and charitable association of wholesale apparel salesmen. Affiliated with the Bureau of Wholesale Sales Representatives (formerly NAWCAS/NAMBAC) Membership: $75/year.
Publication:
Trade Wind. m. adv.
Annual Meetings: May

Apparel Manufacturers Ass'n (1977)
Hist. Note: Formed by a merger of the Nat'l Dress Manufacturers Ass'n and the Popular Priced Dress Manufacturers Group, Inc. Affiliated with the Federation of Apparel Manufacturers. Sole purpose is labor arbitration with ILGWU.

Appliance Parts Distributors Ass'n (1937)
c/o Servall Company, 228 East Baltimore Street, Detroit MI 48202
Exec. V. President: Kenneth Adler
Members: 70-80 companies *Staff:* 2-5
Annual Budget: $100-250,000 *Tel:* (313) 872-3658
Hist. Note: Formerly Appliance Parts Jobbers Association. Membership: based on the number of company branches.
Semi-annual Meetings: Spring and Fall
1987-Bermuda(Castle Bermuda)/May 10-15/300
1987-Orlando, FL(Hyatt Grand Cypress)/Sept. 14-18/200

Appraisers Ass'n of America (1949)
60 East 42nd St., Suite 2505, New York NY 10165
Exec. Director: Victor Wiener
Members: 1,200-1,300 *Staff:* 2-5
Annual Budget: $100-250,000 *Tel:* (212) 867-9775
Hist. Note: A professional society primarily of personal property appraisers.
Publication:
The Appraiser. 10/yr.
Annual Meetings: Spring, in New York City.

Aquatic Plant Management Soc. (1961)
Box 16, Vicksburg MS 39180
Secy.-Treas.: William N. Rushing
Members: 600 *Staff:* 1
Annual Budget: $10-25,000 *Tel:* (601) 634-3542
Hist. Note: Individuals and companies interested in the control of water plants hindering recreation or navigation. Membership: $25/yr. (individual), $200/yr. (company).
Publications:
Journal of Aquatic Plant Management. semi-a.
Newsletter of the APMS. 3-4/yr.
Annual Meetings: July
1987-Savannah, GA(Hyatt)/July 12-15/200
1988-New Orleans, LA(Fairmont)/July 10-13/200
1989-Phoenix, AZ/mid-July/150

Arabian Horse Registry of America (1908)
12000 Zuni St., Westminster CO 80234
Secretary: Ralph F. Clark
Members: 23,000 *Staff:* 60
Annual Budget: $500-1,000,000 *Tel:* (303) 450-4748
Hist. Note: Owners and breeders of Arabian horses. Members of the Nat'l Pedigree Livestock Council.
Publication:
Registry News. m.
Three Meetings/Year: March, July and November in Westminster, CO.

Archaeological Institute of America (1879)
Box 1901-Kenmore Station, Boston MA 02215
Director, Nat'l Headquarters: Joan Bowen
Members: 9-10,000 *Staff:* 25
Annual Budget: $1-2,000,000 *Tel:* (617) 353-9361
Hist. Note: Founded in 1879 in Boston under the aegis of Charles Eliot Norton and incorporated in 1906. Member of the American Council of Learned Societies and affiliate of the American Ass'n for the Advancement of Science and numerous other societies and institutes. Membership: $25-$200/yr.
Publications:
American Journal of Archaeology. q.
Archaeology. bi-m. adv.
Archaeological Fieldwork Opportunities Bulletin. a.
Annual Meetings: Winter/1,200
1987-New York, NY(Marriott Marquis)/Dec. 27-30
1988-Baltimore, MD/Jan. 5-9

Archery Manufacturers Organization (1946)
200 Castlewood Drive, North Palm Beach FL 33408
Exec. Director: Anthony L. Kucera
Members: 58 companies *Staff:* 2-4
Annual Budget: $50-100,000 *Tel:* (305) 842-4100
Hist. Note: Founded as the Archery Manufacturers and Dealers Ass'n, it became the Archery Manufacturers Ass'n in 1952 and assumed its present name in 1965. Supports the American Archery Council as its promotional arm.
Semi-Annual Meetings:

Archery Range and Retailers Organization (1981)
4609 Femrite Drive, Madison WI 53716
President: Gordon Bentley
Members: 73 companies
Tel: (608) 221-2697
Hist. Note: Formerly (until 1980) known as the Archery Lane Operators Association, ARRO is primarily a cooperative buying assocation. Membership: $300/yr. (company).
Annual Meetings: Winter
1987-New Orleans, LA/Jan. 8-11

Architectural Acoustics Soc. (1977)
Hist. Note: Reported as defunct in 1983.

Architectural Aluminum Manufacturers Ass'n (1936)
Hist. Note: Became the American Architectural Manufacturers Ass'n in 1984.

Architectural Fabric Structures Institute (1969)
104 Wilmot Road, Suite 201, Deerfield IL 60015-5195
Exec. V. President: David L. Stumph
Members: 26 *Staff:* 2
Annual Budget: $25-50,000 *Tel:* (312) 940-8800
Hist. Note: Formerly a division of Industrial Fabrics Association International, AFSI became an independent organization in 1985. Membership composed of architectural fabric structure manufacturers, material and equipment suppliers, contractors, architects, engineers, code agency representatives, insurance or testing associations. Formerly (until 1982) The Air Structures Institute. Membership: $1,190/yr.

Architectural Precast Ass'n (1966)
825 East 64th St., Indianapolis IN 46220
Exec. Director: Robert W. Walton
Members: 65-70 companies *Staff:* 6-10
Annual Budget: $25-50,000 *Tel:* (317) 251-1214
Hist. Note: Makers of precast concrete elements.
Publication:
The Architectural Precaster. bi-m.
Annual Meetings: Spring
1987-Bermuda/April 5-10

Architectural Secretaries Ass'n (1965)
Hist. Note: Became the Soc. of Architectural Administrators in 1983.

Architectural Woodwork Institute (1953)
2310 South Walter Reed Dr., Arlington VA 22206
Exec. V. President: William H. Winter
Members: 750-850 *Staff:* 6-10
Annual Budget: $1-2,000,000 *Tel:* (703) 671-9100
Hist. Note: Absorbed the Millwork Cost Bureau. Members are manufacturers and suppliers of paneling, fixtures, cases, laminates and doors.
Publications:
1985 Quality Standards. a.
Design Solutions Journal. q. adv.
National Membership Directory. a. adv.
Buyers Guide to Associate Member Services. a. adv.
Annual Meetings: Fall/over 900
1987-Los Angeles, CA(LA Hilton)/Oct. 21-23
1988-Orlando, FL/Oct. 12-14

Argentina-American Chamber of Commerce (1919)
50 West 34th Street, 6th Floor, C-2, New York NY 10001
Exec. Director: Julian M. Magdaleno
Members: 4-500 companies *Staff:* 6-10
Annual Budget: $100-250,000 *Tel:* (212) 564-3855
Publications:
Argentine-American Business Review Directory. a. adv.
Argentine News-Letter. w.
Annual Meetings: Spring in New York, NY/4-500

Armed Forces Broadcasters Ass'n (1982)
Box 12013, Arlington VA 22209
Exec. V. President: Robert P. Bubniak
Members: 600 *Staff:* 1
Annual Budget: under $10,000 *Tel:* (609) 924-3600
Hist. Note: Enhances camaraderie among former, present, and future members of the military broadcasting community; provides employment search assistance. Membership: $20/yr.
Publication:
Transmitter. q.
Annual Meetings: April

Armed Forces Communications and Electronics Ass'n (1946)
AFCEA Internat'l Headquarters, 4400 Fair Lakes Court, Fairfax VA 22033-3899
President: Dr. Jon L. Boyes, V.Adm, USN
Members: 33,000 individuals; 750 corporations *Staff:* 60
Annual Budget: over $5,000,000 *Tel:* (703) 631-6100
Hist. Note: Originated May 1946 as the Army Signal Ass'n. Name changed to Armed Forces Communications Ass'n in 1948 and to the Armed Forces Communications and Electronics Ass'n in 1955. Fosters cooperation between free world industries, governments and C3I professionals. Has an annual budget of over $8 million. Membership: $16/yr. (individual); corporation fee varies by size.
Publication:
Signal. m. adv.
Bi-monthly Meetings:

Armed Forces Marketing Council (1969)
1750 New York Ave., N.W., Suite 340, Washington DC 20006
Exec. V. President: Rip Rowan
Members: 10-15 companies *Staff:* 2-5
Annual Budget: $100-250,000 *Tel:* (202) 783-8228
Hist. Note: Members are companies supplying military exchanges, commissaries, clubs and veterans' canteens.

Army Theatre Arts Ass'n
Hist. Note: A division of the American Theatre Association.

Aromatic Red Cedar Closet Lining Manufacturers Ass'n (1950)
221 North LaSalle St., Chicago IL 60601
Director: Leo Floros
Members: 2 companies *Staff:* 1
Annual Budget: $10-25,000 *Tel:* (312) 372-7090
Hist. Note: Sustains a small publicity campaign for red cedar but is comparatively inactive. Members consist of one manufacturer is North Carolina and one in Missouri. The above address is that of a public relations firm.

Art and Antique Dealers League of America (1926)
353 East 78th St., Suite 19A, New York NY 10021
Secretary: Joseph H. Kilian
Members: 90-100 *Staff:* 1
Annual Budget: $10-25,000 *Tel:* (212) 879-7558
Hist. Note: Oldest and principal antiques and fine arts organization in America. An outgrowth of the Antique Dealers Luncheon Club which on January 7, 1926 met at the Madison Hotel, New York City and formed the Antique and Decorative Arts League, which became the Art and Antique Dealers League of America, Inc., in 1942. Member of the Internat'l Art Dealers Confederation (CINOA - Confederation Internationale des Negociantes en Oeuvres d'Art), a worldwide organization encompassing 14 countries.
Publication:
The Clarion. semi-a.
Annual Meetings: not held

Art and Craft Materials Institute (1934)
715 Boylston St., Boston MA 02116
Exec. V. President: Deborah Fanning, CAE
Members: 80 companies *Staff:* 2-5
Annual Budget: $100-250,000 *Tel:* (617) 266-6800
Hist. Note: Members are makers of art and craft products, many of which are used by children. The Institute conducts a certification program to assure that these products are non-toxic, or properly labelled.

00073 12 05 86 1233

Art Dealers Ass'n of America (1962)
575 Madison Ave., New York NY 10022
Admin. V. President: Gilbert S. Edelson
Members: 110-120 *Staff:* 2-5
Annual Budget: $100-250,000 *Tel:* (212) 940-8590
Hist. Note: Dealers in paintings, drawings, sculpture, prints and photographs. Incorporated in the State of New York in March, 1962.
Annual Meetings: Always held at a gallery in New York City.

Art Libraries Soc./North America (1972)
3900 E. Timrod St., Tucson AZ 85711
Exec. Director: Pamela Parry
Members: 1,250 *Staff:* 1
Annual Budget: $100-250,000 *Tel:* (602) 881-8479
Hist. Note: A professional organization of art information specialists, the society includes individual (librarians, historians, curators, and students) and institutional (colleges and universities, museums and galleries, historical societies and libraries) members. Membership: $45/yr. (individual); $75/yr. (insititutional)
Publications:
Art Documentation. q. adv.
ARLIS/NA Update. q. adv.
Handbook and List of Members. a. adv.
Conference Abstracts. a.
Occasional Papers. irreg.
Annual Meetings: February
1987-Washington, DC(Capital Hilton)/Feb. 13-19/450
1988-Dallas, TX(Sheraton Hotel & Towers)/Feb. 4-11/400
1989-Phoenix, AZ

Art Material Board of Trade
Hist. Note: Ceased operations in 1984.

Arthroscopy Ass'n of North America (1974)
70 West Hubbard St., Suite 202, Chicago IL 60610
Exec. Director: Sanford J. Hill
Members: 500 *Staff:* 2-5
Annual Budget: $250-500,000 *Tel:* (312) 644-2623
Hist. Note: The North American chapter of the International Arthroscopy Association. Incorporated in the State of Illinois in 1982. Membership: by invitation only, $300/yr.
Publication:
Journal of Arthroscopic Surgery. q. adv.
Annual Meetings:
1987-Houston, TX(Westin Galleria)/March 11-14
1988-Washington, DC/March 24-27
1989-Seattle, WA/April 13-16

Artificial Flower Manufacturers Board of Trade (1938)
225 West 34th St., New York NY 10022
Exec. Director: Sheldon Edelman
Members: 10 companies *Staff:* 2-5
Annual Budget: $25-50,000 *Tel:* (212) 564-2500

Artists Equity Ass'n (1947)
Hist. Note: Became the Nat'l Artists Equity Ass'n in 1984.

Asbestos Information Ass'n/North America (1970)
1745 Jefferson Davis Hwy., Suite 509, Arlington VA 22202
President: B.J. Pigg
Members: 40 companies *Staff:* 6-10
Annual Budget: $250-500,000 *Tel:* (703) 979-1150
Hist. Note: Incorporated in 1971. The public relations arm of U.S. and Canadian asbestos producers and asbestos products manufacturers. Provides information on asbestos and health.
Publication:
Newsletter. m.
Annual Meetings: Washington, DC area in September
1987-Arlington, VA(Stouffer's Concourse)

ASHBEAMS (1980)
612 Pennsylvania Ave., San Diego CA 92103
Exec. Director: Nina Merrill
Members: 180 Aero medical service providers *Staff:* 2
Annual Budget: $100-250,000 *Tel:* (619) 542-0388
Hist. Note: The acronym, ASHBEAMS, represents: American Soc. of Hospital-Based Emergency Air Medical Services. Established in Houston, Texas and incorporated in Iowa, ASHBEAMS is an association of hospitals operating emergency helicopter/fixed wing transport services. Membership: $50/yr.(individual); $225-450/yr. (organization/company)
Publication:
Aeromedical Journal. bi-m. adv.
Annual Meetings: Late Fall
1987-Milwaukee, WI(Hyatt Regency)/Oct. 14-16
1988-Boston, MA
1989-Phoenix, AZ

Asian/Pacific American Librarians Ass'n (1980)
c/o Baker & Taylor, 652 East Main St., Box 6920, Bridgewater NJ 08807
President: Asha Capoor
Members: 200 individuals
Annual Budget: under $10,000 *Tel:* (201) 218-3976
Hist. Note: Open to all librarians/information specialists of Asian/Pacific descent working in U.S. libraries/information centers and other such related organizations. Affiliated with the American Library Ass'n. Membership: $10/yr. (individual); $25/yr. (institution).
Publication:
APALA Newsletter. 3/yr.
Annual Meetings: With the American Library Ass'n
1987-San Francisco, CA/June 27-July 2
1988-New Orleans, LA/July 9-14
1989-Dallas, TX/June 27-29

Asphalt Emulsion Manufacturers Ass'n (1973)
1133 15th St., N.W., Suite 620, Washington DC 20005
Exec. Director: John H. Ganoe
Members: 120 companies *Staff:* 2-5
Annual Budget: $100-250,000 *Tel:* (202) 293-5910
Hist. Note: Members are manufacturers of asphalt emulsion (Active) and suppliers to the industry (Associate). A member of the Materials and Services Division of the American Road and Transportation Builders Ass'n.
Publications:
AEMA Directory. a. adv.
AEMA Newsletter. bi-m. adv.
Annual Meetings: Spring/400
1987-Montreal, Canada(Sheraton Center)/April
1988-Maui, HI(Royal Lahaina)/March

Asphalt Institute (1919)
Asphalt Institute Building, College Park MD 20740
President: Gerald Triplett
Members: 55-60 *Staff:* 40-45
Annual Budget: $1-2,000,000 *Tel:* (301) 277-4258
Hist. Note: Founded as the Asphalt Ass'n, it assumed its present name in 1929. Members are companies making asphalt products from crude petroleum.
Publications:
ASPHALTNEWS. q.
Catalog of Publications and Audio-Visual Programs. a.
Annual Meetings: December (By invitation only)
1987-Ft. Lauderdale, FL(Bonaventure Hotel & Spa)/Nov. 29-Dec. 2
1988-San Diego, CA(Rancho Bernardo Inn)/Dec. 4-7

Asphalt Recycling and Reclaiming Ass'n (1976)
#3 Church Circle, Suite 250, Annapolis MD 21401
Exec. Director: Michael R. Krissoff
Members: 160-170 *Staff:* 2-5
Annual Budget: $100-250,000 *Tel:* (301) 267-0023
Hist. Note: Promotes the collective interests of those individuals, firms or corporations engaged in the asphalt recycling industry as contractors, owners or manufacturers of equipment, engineers suppliers, and public highway officials. Membership: $750/yr. (organization/company).
Publications:
ARRA Newsletter. q. adv.
Membership Directory. a. adv.
Semi-annual Meetings: Winter/200 and Fall
1987-Scottsdale, AZ(Doubletree)/March 4-7
1987-Kansas City, MO(Marriott)/Sept. 15-16
1988-Tampa, FL(Hyatt Westshore)/Feb. 24-27
1988-Kansas City, MO(Marriott)/Sept. 13-14
1989-San Diego, CA(Del Coronado)/Feb. 15-16
1989-Kansas City, MO(Marriott)/Sept. 19-20
1990-Kansas City, MO(Marriott)/Sept. 18-19
1990-Kansas City, MO(Marriott)/Sept. 17-18

Asphalt Roofing Manufacturers Ass'n (1919)
6288 Montrose Road, Rockville MD 20852
Exec. V. President: Richard D. Snyder, CAE
Members: 25-30 companies *Staff:* 2-5
Annual Budget: $500-1,000,000 *Tel:* (301) 231-9052
Hist. Note: Formerly (1969) Asphalt Roofing Industry Bureau.
Publication:
ARMA Newsletter. m.
Annual Meetings: October
1987-Miami, FL(Doral Country Club)/Oct. 21-23

Asphalt Rubber Producers Group (1985)
5235 South Kyrene Road, Suite 210, Tempe AZ 85283
Exec. Director: Donna J. Carlson
Members: 15 companies *Staff:* 3
Annual Budget: $100-250,000 *Tel:* (602) 267-8806
Hist. Note: Incorporated in Arizona in 1985, ARPG members are companies involved in the manufacture or application of asphalt-rubber membranes or in the rubber recycling business. Membership: $250/year (individual).
Publication:
Rebounder. q. adv.

Aspirin Foundation of America (1981)
1330 Connecticut Ave., N.W., Washington DC 20036
Exec. Director: Gary W. Goodwin
Members: 11 companies *Staff:* 2-5
Annual Budget: $1-2,000,000 *Tel:* (202) 659-0060
Hist. Note: An affiliate of the Synthetic Organic Chemical Manufacturers Association, which provides administrative support.

Assembly of Episcopal Hospitals and Chaplains
Hist. Note: No paid staff; address unknown in 1986.

Assembly of Governmental Employees
Hist. Note: Defunct in 1986.

Associated Accounting Firms Internat'l (1966)
1612 K St., N.W., Suite 1102, Washington DC 20006
President: Robert G. Taylor
Members: 35 Firms *Staff:* 2-5
Annual Budget: $250-500,000 *Tel:* (202) 463-7900
Hist. Note: Established in New York as the Ass'n of Regional CPA Firms, it assumed its present name in 1967. AAFI is an association of independent CPA firms with offices in most major cities in the U.S. and UK; its purpose is to share expertise and information to make each firm more efficient and better able to serve its clients.
Publication:
AAFI Newsletter. semi-a.
Semi-Annual Meetings: Spring and Fall

Associated Actors and Artistes of America (1919)
165 West 46th St., New York NY 10036
President: Frederick O'Neal
Members: 9 nat'l unions with a total membership of 90,000
Staff: 2-5
Annual Budget: $50-100,000 *Tel:* (212) 869-0358
Hist. Note: Affiliated with AFL-CIO. Chartered by the American Federation of Labor on August 28, 1919, AAAA is the successor organization to the White Rats Actors Union of America established in 1910. An umbrella coordinating organization comprising nine autonomous branches: Actors' Equity Association, American Federation of Television and Radio Artists, American Guild of Musical Artists, American Guild of Variety Artists, Asociacion Puertorriquena de Artistas y Technicos del Espectaculo, Hebrew Actors Union, Italian Actors Union, Screen Actors Guild and Screen Extras Guild.
Biennial meetings: Uneven years in New York City on the second
Thursday in June.

Associated Air Balance Council (1965)
1518 K St., N.W., Washington DC 20005
Exec. Director: Kenneth M. Sufka
Members: 90 individuals, 72 companies *Staff:* 2
Annual Budget: $100-250,000 *Tel:* (202) 737-0202
Hist. Note: Members are independent testers of air handling systems.
Publications:
Newsletter. m.
Publications List Available.
Annual Meetings: October

Associated Antique Dealers of America (1978)
Box 88454, Indianapolis IN 46208
President:
Members: 200 *Staff:* 1
Annual Budget: under $10,000
Hist. Note: Members are antique dealers who have been in business for at least 3 years. Membership: $50/yr.
Publications:
AADA News. 8/yr.
Directory. a.
Annual Meetings:
1987-Toronto, Ontario/June

Associated Builders and Contractors (1950)
729 15th St., N.W., Washington DC 20005
Exec. V. President: Daniel J. Bennet
Members: 18,500 companies *Staff:* 75
Annual Budget: over $5,000,000 *Tel:* (202) 637-8800
Hist. Note: Incorporated in Baltimore, MD in 1950. Members are merit shop construction companies. Sponsors and supports the Associated Builders and Contractors Political Action Committee. Has an annual budget of $5-6 million. Membership fee varies by volume.
Publications:
Builder and Contractor. m. adv.
Merit Shop Newsline. m.
National Membership Directory. a. adv.
Annual Meetings: March
1987-Orlando, FL(Marriott's World Center)/March 5-9
1988-San Francisco, CA(St. Francis)/March 6-10
1989-Washington, DC(J.W. Marriott)/March 19-23
1990-New Orleans, LA(Marriott)/March 4-8
1991-San Diego, CA(Intercontinental)/March 10-14

Associated Business Writers of America (1945)
1450 South Havana St., Aurora CO 80012
Director: Donald E. Bower
Members: 100-125 freelance writers *Staff:* 1
Annual Budget: under $10,000 *Tel:* (303) 751-7844
Hist. Note: An affiliate of the National Writers Club. Comparatively inactive. Membership: $50/yr.
Publications:
Authorship. bi-m.
Membership Directory. a. adv.
Annual Meetings: With National Writers Club
1987-Ft. Collins, CO

Associated Church Press (1916)
Box 306, Geneva IL 60134-0306
Exec. Secretary: Donald F. Hetzler
Members: 170 *Staff:* 1
Annual Budget: $50-100,000 *Tel:* (312) 232-1055
Hist. Note: Formerly (1937) Editorial Council of the Religious Press. Protestant, Anglican, Catholic and Orthodox church-affiliated periodicals.
Publications:
Newslog. bi-m.
Associated Church Press Directory. a. adv.
Annual Meetings: April-May

00074 12 05 86 1233

1987-Ssn Antonio, TX(Hyatt Regency)/May 19-22
1988-Nashville, TN(Opryland)/April 16-20

Associated Collegiate Press, Nat'l Scholastic Press Ass'n (1921)
620 Rarig Center, 330 21st Ave. South, Minneapolis MN 55455
Exec. Director: Tom E. Rolnicki
Members: 2,500 publications *Staff:* 6-10
Annual Budget: $100-250,000 *Tel:* (612) 625-8335
Hist. Note: Founded to promote the growth and quality of high school and college student publications.
Publication:
Scholastic Editor's Trends in Publications. 7/yr. adv.
Semi-annual Meetings: ACP last weekend in October, NSPA in November/1,000
1987-St. Louis, MO(Sheraton)/(ACP)
1987-Kansas City, MO/(NSPA)
1988-Atlanta, GA/(ACP)
1989-New Orleans, LA/(ACP)

Associated Construction Publications (1938)
16231 West Ryerson, New Berlin WI 53151
Exec. V. President: John D. Weatherhead
Members: 14 regional publications *Staff:* 2-5
Annual Budget: $2-5,000,000 *Tel:* (414) 782-0960
Semi-annual meetings: January and June

Associated Cooperage Industries of America (1915)
2100 Gardiner Lane, Suite 100-E, Louisville KY 40205
Secy.-Treas.: Janice Bishop
Members: 48 companies *Staff:* 1
Annual Budget: $25-50,000 *Tel:* (502) 459-6113
Semi-annual meetings: May in the midwest and November in the Southeast

Associated Corset and Brassiere Manufacturers Ass'n (1933)
475 Fifth Ave., Suite 1908, New York NY 10017
Exec. Director and Counsel: Jack Glauberman
Members: 30 *Staff:* 2
Annual Budget: $50-100,000 *Tel:* (212) 532-6960
Hist. Note: Membership is concentrated in the Eastern United States - New York, New Jersey and Pennsylvania.
Annual Meetings: Nov./Dec.

Associated Credit Bureaus (1906)
16211 Park Ten Place, Houston TX 77084
Senior V. President: Barry Connelly
Members: 1,400 credit bureaus; 1,100 collection agencies *Staff:* 45-50
Annual Budget: $2-5,000,000 *Tel:* (713) 492-8155
Hist. Note: Founded as Nat'l Ass'n of Retail Credit Agencies, it became the Nat'l Ass'n of Mercantile Agencies in 1908 and the Associated Credit Bureaus of America in 1937; assumed its present name in 1968. Membership is divided into two classes: Credit Reporting Offices and Collection Service Offices. Supports the Associated Credit Bureaus Political Action Committee.
Publication:
Communicator. m.
Annual Meetings: June
1987-Seattle, WA/June 10

Associated Equipment Distributors (1919)
615 West 22nd St., Oak Brook IL 60521
Exec. V. President: P. D. Hermann, CAE
Members: 1,300-1,400 *Staff:* 30-35
Annual Budget: $2-5,000,000 *Tel:* (312) 574-0650
Hist. Note: Distributors and manufacturers of construction, mining, logging, and road maintenance equipment. Formerly Nat'l Distributors Ass'n of Construction Equipment. Affiliated with the Canadian Ass'n of Equipment Distributors. Connected with the Associated Equipment Distributors Political Action Committee and the AED Research and Services Corp. Maintains a Washington office.
Publications:
Construction Equipment Distribution. m. adv.
Distributor Executive "Contact". semi-m.
Annual Meetings: Winter/4,000
1987-Chicago, IL/Jan. 17-20
1988-New Orleans, LA/Jan. 30-Feb. 2
1989-Anaheim, CA/Jan. 28-31
1990-Chicago, IL/Jan. 20-23
1991-Atlanta, GA/Feb. 2-5

Associated Footwear Manufacturers (1933)
Hist. Note: Ceased operations in 1985.

Associated Funeral Directors Service (1939)
810 Stratford Avenue, Box 7476, Tampa FL 33603
Exec. Director: Frank P. Pryor
Members: 2,500 funeral homes *Staff:* 6-10
Annual Budget: $50-100,000 *Tel:* (813) 228-9105
Hist. Note: Membership fee based on population of member's service area.
Publications:
AFDS Bulletin & Roster. semi-a. adv.
Newsletter. semi-a.
Annual Meetings: October
1987-Salt Lake City, UT/750
1988-New Orleans, LA/750
1989-Baltimore, MD
1990-Louisville, KY
1991-Las Vegas, NV

Associated Gas Distributors (1963)
1001 Pennsylvania Ave., N.W., Washington DC 20004
General Counsel: Frederick Moring
Members: 50 companies *Staff:* 2-5
Tel: (202) 624-2500
Hist. Note: East Coast gas distributors, no pipelines or producers. Mailing address is the law firm of Crowell and Moring.

Associated General Contractors of America (1918)
1957 E St., N.W., Washington DC 20006
Exec. V. President: Hubert Beatty
Members: 27,000 *Staff:* 90-100
Annual Budget: over $5,000,000 *Tel:* (202) 393-2040
Hist. Note: Membership consists of heavy (as opposed to light) construction contractors organized in state and local groups. Supports various state and regional political action committees, and also the Associated General Contractors Political Action Committee.
Publications:
Constructor. m. adv.
National Newsletter. w.
Directory. a.
Annual Meetings: March/8,000
1987-Washington, DC/March 5-10
1988-New Orleans, LA/March 10-15
1989-Atlanta, GA/March 2-7

Associated Glass and Pottery Manufacturers (1874)
2800 East Military Rd., Zanesville OH 43701
Secretary: Harold L. Hayes
Members: 16-20 companies *Staff:* 1
Annual Budget: under $10,000 *Tel:* (614) 452-8329
Hist. Note: Manufacturers of semi-vitrified and vitrified ceramic and glass dinnerware.

Associated Independent Dairies of America
Hist. Note: Address unknown in 1986; probably defunct.

Associated Independent Distributors (1959)
13507 Branch View, Dallas TX 75234
Exec. Secretary: Karen Crum
Members: 4-500 companies *Staff:* 2-5
Annual Budget: $100-250,000 *Tel:* (214) 241-1124
Hist. Note: Manufacturers and distributors of replacement parts for construction equipment.
Annual Meetings: Fall/450

Associated Independent Electrical Contractors of America (1956)
Hist. Note: Became Independent Electrical Contractors in 1981.

Associated Information Managers (1978)
1776 E. Jefferson St., 4th Floor, Rockville MD 20852
Exec. Director: Sheila Brayman
Members: 1,000 individuals & corporations *Staff:* 2-5
Annual Budget: $50-100,000 *Tel:* (301) 231-7447
Hist. Note: Professional information managers who work for private corporations, government agencies and non-profit institutions. Membership also includes directors of libraries and information centers, records and research managers, and office automation experts. Membership: $85/year (individual), $500-3,000/year (corporate).
Publications:
AIM Network. bi-w.
Career Exchange Clearinghouse. bi-w.
Who's Who in Information Management. a.
Conference Proceedings. a.
Annual Meetings: Spring
1987-Washington, DC(Omni Shoreham)/May 18-20

Associated Laboratories (1958)
641 S. Vermont St., Palantine IL 60067
President: Robert F. Hutchison
Members: 16-20 *Staff:* 1
Annual Budget: under $10,000 *Tel:* (312) 358-7400
Hist. Note: Regional water treatment companies.
Publication:
Water Treatment Newsletter. m.
Annual Meetings: Semi-annual meetings

Associated Landscape Contractors of America (1961)
405 North Washington St., Suite 104, Falls Church VA 22046
Exec. Director: Terry Peters
Members: 1,200 *Staff:* 6
Annual Budget: $500-1,000,000 *Tel:* (703) 241-4004
Publications:
Action Letter. m. adv.
Who's Who in Landscape Contracting. a. adv.
Annual Meetings:
1987-San Antonio, TX(Hyatt Regency)
1988-San Diego, CA

Associated Locksmiths of America (1956)
3003 Live Oak St., Dallas TX 75204
Exec. Director: Webster W. Sharp
Members: 7,100 *Staff:* 10
Annual Budget: $1-2,000,000 *Tel:* (214) 827-1701
Hist. Note: Membership: $75/yr. (individual); $300/yr. (company).
Publication:
Keynotes. m. adv.
Annual Meetings: Summer/6,000
1987-Dallas, TX(Hyatt Regency & Convention Ctr.)June 28-July 5

Associated Master Barbers and Beauticians of America/Hair Internat'l (1924)
Box 220782, Charlotte NC 28222
Executive Director: Joy Nettles
Members: 2,000-3,000 *Staff:* 4
Annual Budget: $250-500,000 *Tel:* (704) 366-5177
Hist. Note: A professional organization of barbers and cosmetologists. Membership: $80/yr. (individual); $150/yr. (organization).
Publication:
Hair International News. m. adv.
Triennial Meetings: 1988

Associated Minicomputer Dealers of America (1963)
4323 E. Lancaster, Fort Worth TX 76101-0627
Exec. Secretary: William T. Ewell
Members: 110 companies *Staff:* 2
Annual Budget: $25-50,000 *Tel:* (817) 531-1371
Hist. Note: Organized in 1963 as the Accounting Machine Dealers Ass'n of America. In 1977 it became the Accounting-machine Minicomputer Dealers of America. Assumed its present name in 1983. Annual company membership: $350/year.
Publication:
AMDA Newsletter. m. adv.
Meetings every nine months:
1987-Seattle, WA(Four Seasons Olympic Seattle Hotel)/July 8-12
1988-New Orleans, LA/April-May

Associated Minority Contractors of America (1978)
Hist. Note: Ceased effective operations in 1982.

Associated Pimiento Canners (1941)
Hist. Note: Defunct in 1985.

Associated Pipe Organ Builders of America (1941)
c/o Dobson Organ Co., 200 North Illinois St., Lake City IA 51449
President: Lynn Dobson
Members: 25 companies
Annual Budget: under $10,000 *Tel:* (712) 464-8065
Hist. Note: Formerly Associated Organ Builders of America. Formed originally to get metal priorities during World War II. Has no permanent address or staff; officers rotate annually.
Annual Meetings: Spring
1987-Louisville, KY

Associated Press Broadcasters (1941)
1825 K St., N.W., Washington DC 20006
Exec. Director: John Bennitt
Members: 6,000
Tel: (202) 955-7212
Hist. Note: Formerly (1970) Associated Press Radio-Television Ass'n and (1974) Associated Press Broadcasters Ass'n. Radio and TV stations that are members of the Associated Press.
Publication:
Air Play. m.
Semi-annual Meetings:
1987-Washington, DC and Southern California

Associated Public-Safety Communications Officers (1935)
Sandpiper Plaza, 930 3rd Ave., New Smyrna Beach FL 32069
Exec. Director: Robert E. Tall
Members: 6,000 *Staff:* 13
Annual Budget: $500-1,000,000 *Tel:* (904) 427-3461
Hist. Note: The oldest and largest public safety communications group, APCO is recognized by the Federal Communications Commission as the frequency coordination body for police, local government and 800 MHZ public safety radio services. Members of the Public Safety Communications Council and the Land Mobile Communications Council. Offers a certification and testing program for electronics technicians, and a dispatcher training course.
Publications:
The APCO Bulletin. m. adv.
APCO Reports. m.
Annual Meetings: Summer
1987-Baltimore, MD(Hyatt)/August 27-29
1988-Little Rock, AR(Excelsior)
1989-Reno, NV(Sparks Nugget)

Associated Reinforcing Bar Producers-CRSI (1974)
Hist. Note: Merged with the Concrete Reinforcing Steel Institute in 1982.

Associated Schools of Construction (1965)
Hist. Note: Address unknown in 1986.

00075 12 05 86 1233

Associated Specialty Contractors (1950)
7315 Wisconsin Ave., Bethesda MD 20814
President: Daniel Walter
Members: 8 associations *Staff:* 1
Annual Budget: $50-100,000 *Tel:* (301) 657-3110
Hist. Note: A federation of eight construction specialty contractors associations: Mechanical Contractors Ass'n of America, Inc.: Nat'l Ass'n of Plumbing-Heating-Cooling Contractors; Nat'l Electrical Contractors Ass'n, Inc.; Sheet Metal and Air Conditioning Contractors' Nat'l Ass'n, Inc.; Mason Contractors Ass'n of America; National Insulation Contractors Ass'n; National Roofing Contractors Association and Painting and Decorating Contractors of America. Formerly (1973) Council of Mechanical Specialty Contracting Industries, Inc.
Semi-annual Meetings: May and December

Associated Surplus Dealers (1950)
1666 Corinth Ave., Los Angeles CA 90025
Administrator: Walter J. Fletcher
Members: 450-500 *Staff:* 11-15
Annual Budget: $2-5,000,000 *Tel:* (213) 477-2556
Hist. Note: Membership: $50/yr. (individual or company).
Publications:
ASD Buyers Guide. a. adv.
ASD/AMD Trade News. m.
Annual Meetings: Holds five trade shows per year, usually in Las Vegas, Reno, and
Atlantic City
1987-Las Vegas, NV(Hilton, Riviera and Sahara Hotels)/March 8-12
1987-Atlantic City, NJ(Convention Center)/May 31-June 3
1987-Las Vegas, NV(Hilton and Riviera Hotels)/Aug. 16-20
1987-Atlantic City/NJ(Convention Center)/Oct. 18-21
1987-Reno, NV(Bally's)/Nov. 8-11

Associated Telephone Answering Exchanges (1946)
320 King St., Suite 500, Alexandria VA 22314
Exec. V. President: Joseph N. Laseau
Members: 1,100-1,200 companies *Staff:* 6-10
Annual Budget: $500-1,000,000 *Tel:* (703) 684-0016
Hist. Note: Formed in 1946 to represent the telephone answering service industry, ATAE has expanded with the industry and now represents the full range of messaging and communications service bureaus, including TAS, voice mail, voice store and forward.
Publication:
The Answer. bi-m. adv.
Annual Meetings: May/June
1987-San Francisco, CA(Hilton)/700
1988-Orlando, FL(Disneyland)

Associated Third Class Mail Users (1947)
Hist. Note: Became the Third Class Mail Association on October 25, 1981.

Associated Two-Year Schools in Construction (1970)
Clemson University, Lee Hall, Clemson SC 29631
Exec. Director: Roger Liska
Members: 25 schools, 30 individuals *Staff:* 1
Annual Budget: under $10,000 *Tel:* (803) 656-3081
Hist. Note: Members are colleges, technical schools and post-secondary units offering couses leading to two-year degrees or certificates in Contstruction technology or related fields and faculty/staff of such facilities. Membership: $15/year (individual).
Annual Meetings: April
1987-Indianapolis, IN

Associated Wire Rope Fabricators (1976)
Box 42464, Houston TX 77242
Exec. V. President: Robert P. Moffett
Members: 180-185 companies *Staff:* 2-5
Annual Budget: $100-250,000 *Tel:* (713) 266-1027
Hist. Note: Members make or sell components or devices for lifting or towing.
Publication:
Slingmakers. q.
Semi-annual meetings: March and October

Associated Writing Programs (1967)
Old Dominion University, Norfolk VA 23508
Acting Exec. Director: Gale C. Arnoux
Members: 7,500 individuals, 110 universities *Staff:* 5
Annual Budget: $100-250,000 *Tel:* (804) 440-3839
Hist. Note: An organization of writers, teachers, students and educational institutions concerned with creative and professional writing. Founded at Brown University. Membership: $40/yr. (individual); $320-475/yr. (institution)
Publications:
AWP Newsletter. bi-m. adv.
Intro: An Anthology of Student Fiction and Poetry. a.
AWP Catalogue of Writing Programs. irreg.
Annual Meetings: Spring
1987-Austin, TX(The Driskill)/April 2-5/250-300

Ass'n for Academic Surgery (1966)
Dept. of Surgery, Univ. of Cin. Med. Ctr,31 Bethesda Ave. (ML558), Cincinnati OH 45267
Secy.-Treas.: Dr. Richard N. Bell
Members: 1,990 *Staff:* 2-5
Annual Budget: $50-100,000 *Tel:* (513) 872-7207
Hist. Note: Founded in 1966 as an organization serving needs of academic surgeons, particularly those under 40 years of age. Dedicated to interchange of scientific, educational, social and political information relative to the surgical profession.
Publication:
Journal of Surgical Research. m.
Annual Meetings: November
1987-Orlando,

Ass'n for Advanced Life Underwriting (1957)
1922 F St., N.W., Washington DC 20006
Exec. Director: Madelyn Guilian
Members: 1,300 individuals *Staff:* 2-5
Annual Budget: $500-1,000,000 *Tel:* (202) 331-6081
Hist. Note: A Conference of the Nat'l Ass'n of Life Underwriters. Members are individuals specializing in estate analysis, pension planning, employee benefit plans and similar fields involving the placement of a large volume of life insurance. Membership: $500/yr.
Publications:
Washington Report. irreg.
AALU Roster. a.
Annual Meeting Proceedings. a.
Annual Meetings: Spring in Washington, DC/700
1987-(JW Marriott)/March 1-4
1988-March 6-9
1989-March 5-8
1990-March 4-7

Ass'n for Advancement of Behavior Therapy (1966)
15 West 36th St., New York NY 10018
Exec. Director: Mary Jane Eimer
Members: 3,600 *Staff:* 8
Annual Budget: $250-500,000 *Tel:* (212) 279-7970
Hist. Note: Founded and incorporated in New York in 1966 as the Ass'n for Advancement of the Behavioral Therapies. Became Ass'n for Advancement of Behavior Therapy in 1968. Membership: $50/yr.
Publications:
Advances in Behavior Therapy. a.
The Behavior Therapist. bi-m. adv.
Behavior Therapy. 5/yr.
Behavioral Assessment. q. adv.
Graduate Study Directory. a.
Annual Meetings: November/December/2,500
1987-Boston, MA(Sheraton)/Nov. 12-15/2,100

Ass'n for Applied Psychoanalysis (1952)
116 Village Walk Drive, Royal Palm Beach FL 33411
Exec. Director: Dr. William D. Katz
Members: 300 *Staff:* 2-5
Annual Budget: $10-25,000 *Tel:* (305) 793-0686
Hist. Note: Members are practicing psychoanalysts who must have had at least 300 hours of personal psychoanalysis. Membership: $35/year.
Publications:
American Imago. q. adv.
Directory. a.
Newsletter. q. adv.

Ass'n for Asian Studies (1941)
1 Lane Hall, Univ. of Michigan, Ann Arbor MI 48109
Sec'y-Treas.: L.A. Peter Gosling
Members: 5,000 individuals, 2,200 institutions *Staff:* 6-10
Annual Budget: $250-500,000 *Tel:* (313) 665-2490
Hist. Note: Organized as the Far Eastern Association on June 9, 1941, the Ass'n for Asian Studies assumed its present name in 1957 to reflect a growing interest in Asia East of the Middle East. A member of the American Council of Learned Societies.
Publications:
Asian Studies Newsletter. 5/yr.
Bibliography of Asian Studies. a.
Journal of Asian Studies. q. adv.
Meeting Program. a. adv.
Doctoral Dissertations on Asia. a.
Annual Meetings: Spring
1987-Boston, MA(Sheraton Boston)April 10-12

Ass'n for Behavior Analysis (1974)
Dept. of Psychology, Western Michigan University, Kalamazoo MI 49008
Business & Convention Manager: Sharon Myers
Members: 1,840 *Staff:* 2-5
Annual Budget: $100-250,000 *Tel:* (616) 383-1629
Hist. Note: Until 1979 the Midwestern Association for Behavior Analysis. ABA's membership consists of individuals interested in the applied experimental and theoretical analysis of behavior and the enhancement of behavior analysis as a profession. Full members of ABA have at least a Master's degree in psychology or a related discipline and have demonstrated competence in either applied or experimental behavior analysis.
Publication:
ABA Newsletter. q.
Annual Meetings:
1987-Nashville(Opryland Hotel)/May 25-28/1,400
1988-Philadelphia, PA(Franklin Plaza)/May 26-29/1,400
1989-Milwaukee, WI(Hyatt Regency)/May 25-28/1,400
1990-Nashville, TN(Opryland)/May 27-21/1,400

Ass'n for Biology Laboratory Education (1979)
Biochemistry Dept., Purdue University, West Lafayette IN 47907
Secretary: Anna M. Wilson
Members: 300 individuals
Annual Budget: under $10,000 *Tel:* (317) 494-1644
Hist. Note: ABLE's purpose is primarily to facilitate communication between teachers actively involved with laboratory instruction in the various areas of biology and to provide reliable lab exercises, organisms and materials. Membership: $20/yr.
Publications:
LABSTRACTS (newsletter). 3/yr.
Proceedings. a.
Annual Meetings: June
1987-St. Paul, MN(Univ. of MN)/June 15-19

Ass'n for Biomedical Research (1979)
Hist. Note: Became the Nat'l Ass'n for Biomedical Research in 1985.

Ass'n for Birth Psychology (1978)
444 East 82nd St., New York NY 10028
Exec. Director: Leslie Feher
Members: 360 *Staff:* 1
Annual Budget: under $10,000 *Tel:* (212) 988-6617
Hist. Note: Members are professionals interested in the study of the correlation between the perinatal experience and later personality development. Membership: $30/year.
Publication:
Birth Psychology Bulletin. semi-a.
Annual Meetings:
1987-Florida

Ass'n for Bridge Construction and Design (1976)
c/o Wilbur Smith and Associates, 2100 Smallman St., Pittsburgh PA 15222
President: George Tomich
Members: 400 individuals; 30 companies *Staff:* 1
Annual Budget: under $10,000 *Tel:* (412) 261-0101
Hist. Note: Has no paid staff. Membership: $15/yr. (individual); $125/yr. (company).
Publication:
Newsletter. bi-m.
Annual Meetings: June, in Pittsburgh in conjunction with the Nat'l Bridge Conference.

Ass'n for Broadcast Engineering Standards (1963)
2000 M St., N.W., Suite 600, Washington DC 20036
Secretary: William Potts
Members: 80-90 stations *Staff:* 2-5
Annual Budget: $50-100,000 *Tel:* (202) 331-0606
Hist. Note: Formerly (1970) Ass'n on Broadcasting Standards. Broadcast licensees united to support maintenance of optimum aural broadcast engineering standards.
Annual Meetings: With Nat'l Ass'n of Broadcasters.

Ass'n for Business Communication (1935)
English Building, 608 S. Wright St., Urbana IL 61801
Exec. Director: Robert D. Gieselman
Members: 1,700 individuals, 700 institutions *Staff:* 2-5
Annual Budget: $100-250,000 *Tel:* (217) 333-1007
Hist. Note: Formerly (1968) American Business Writing Ass'n. Membership consists of teachers, training directors, business executives and consultants; 75% of ABC members are university professors. Membership: $35/yr.
Publications:
Bulletin of the ABC. q. adv.
Journal of Business Communication. q. adv.
Annual Meetings: October/2-300
1987-Atlanta, GA(Peachtree Plaza)
1988-Indianapolis, IN
1990-San Antonio, TX

Ass'n for Business Simulation and Experiential Learning (1974)
Crummer Graduate School of Business, Rollins College, Winter Park FL 32789
Exec. Director: Frank Dasse
Members: 200-250 *Staff:* 1
Annual Budget: $10-25,000 *Tel:* (305) 646-2404
Hist. Note: ABSEL was created to encourage the association of business simulators and those interested in developing and using experiential learning techniques in the fields of business and administration. Membership: $35/yr. (individual).
Publications:
Newsletter. semi-a. adv.
Proceedings. a. adv.
Annual Meetings: March
1987-Hilton Head, SC/March 25-27
1988-New Orleans, LA

Ass'n for Canadian Studies in the United States (1971)
One Dupont Circle, N.W., Suite 620, Washington DC 20036
Exec. Director: Dr. Ellen Reisman Babby
Members: 1,200 *Staff:* 2-5
Annual Budget: $100-250,000 *Tel:* (202) 887-6375
Hist. Note: Promotes the study of Canada on all educational levels. The core of its membership is comprised of university professors involved in teaching about Canada. Membership: $25/yr.(individual); $40/yr.(institution)
Publications:
American Review of Canadian Studies. q. adv.
Canadian Studies Update. bi-a.
Directory. a.
Biennial meetings: odd years
1987-Montreal(Bonaventure)/Oct. 8-10

Ass'n for Child Psychoanalysis (1965)
4524 Forest Park, St. Louis MO 63108
Secretary: Moisy Shopper, M.D.
Members: 375-400 *Staff:* 2-5
Annual Budget: $10-25,000 *Tel:* (314) 361-4646
Hist. Note: Formerly (1971) American Ass'n for Child Psychoanalysis.
Publication:

00076 12 05 86 1233

Ass'n for Childhood Education Internat'l (1892)
11141 Georgia Ave., Suite 200, Wheaton MD 20902
Exec. Director: James S. Packer
Members: 12,000 *Staff:* 11-15
Annual Budget: $500-1,000,000 *Tel:* (301) 942-2443
Hist. Note: Established in 1892 as the Internat'l Kindergarten Union. In 1931 merged with the Nat'l Council of Primary Education and became Ass'n for Childhood Education Internat'l. Members are teachers, teacher educators, school administrators, students of education, librarians and parents. Membership: $32/year (individual), $40/year (organization).
Publications:
Childhood Education. 5/yr. adv.
Journal of Research in Childhood Education. semi-a. adv.
ACEI Exchange Newsletter. 10/yr.
Annual Meetings: Spring
1987-Omaha, NE(Red Lion Inn)
1988-Salt Lake City, UT

Ass'n for Clinical Pastoral Education (1939)
1549 Clairmont Road, Suite 103, Decatur GA 30033
Exec. Director: Rev. Duane Parker, Ph.D.
Members: 4,000 *Staff:* 2-5
Annual Budget: $250-500,000 *Tel:* (404) 320-1472
Hist. Note: A combination of the CPE functions of the Lutheran Council of the U. S. A., the Association of Clinical Pastoral Educators, the Council for Clinical Pastoral Education and the Institute of Pastoral Care. Originally the Council for the Clinical Training of Theological Students, it became the Council for Clinical Training in 1967 and assumed its present name in 1968. Membership: $35/yr. (individual); $50/yr. (institution)
Publication:
Journal of Pastoral Care. q. adv.
Annual Meetings: Fall
1987-Philadelphia, PA(Sheraton Society Hill)/Nov.

Ass'n for Communication Administration (1971)
5105 Backlick Road, #E, Annandale VA 22003
Exec. Secretary: Robert N. Hall
Members: 700 *Staff:* 2
Annual Budget: $25-50,000 *Tel:* (703) 750-0534
Hist. Note: Founded in San Francisco as the Ass'n for Departments and Administrators in Speech Communication; it assumed its present name in 1975 and incorporated in the State of Virginia in 1982. Membership generally comprises administrators teaching Communication, Humanities, Theatre, Radio-TV, or English at the college level. Membership: $40/yr.
Publications:
Bulletin of ACA. q.
Directory of Theatre Programs. bien. adv.
Careers in Communication Arts and Sciences. bien.
Directory of Radio-Television-Film Programs. bien.
Annual Meetings: Fall/125
1987-Boston, MA/Nov. 5-6/125
1988-New Orleans, LA/Nov. 3-4/125
1989-San Francisco, CA/Nov. 18-19/100

Ass'n for Commuter Transportation (1976)
1776 Massachusetts Ave., N.W., #521, Washington DC 20036
Exec. Director: Sandra Spence
Members: 5-600 *Staff:* 2-5
Annual Budget: $100-250,000 *Tel:* (202) 659-0602
Hist. Note: Formed in Savannah, Georgia in August 1976 by 31 charter van pool pioneers as the Nat'l Ass'n of Van Pool Operators; assumed its present name in 1984. Absorbed the Ass'n of Ridesharing Professionals in 1986. Members are corporations, public agencies, transit authorities, vanpool management companies, real estate developers and individuals involved in promoting alternatives to drive-alone commuting. Membership: $49/yr. (individual); $200/yr. (organization/company)
Publications:
ACT NOW. bi-m. adv.
Membership Directory. a. adv.
Annual Meetings: September
1987-Seattle, WA

Ass'n for Comparative Economic Studies (1972)
Dept. of Economics, Univ. of Notre Dame, Notre Dame IN 46556
Exec. Secretary: Dr. Roger Skurski
Members: 400 *Staff:* 1
Annual Budget: $10-25,000 *Tel:* (219) 239-7016
Hist. Note: A member of the Allied Social Science Ass'ns. Merger of the Ass'n for the Study of Soviet-Type Economics (1959) and Ass'n for Comparative Economics (1963). Membership: $10/yr. (individual); $25/yr. (organization/company)
Publications:
Journal of Comparative Economics. q.
Comparative Economic Studies. q.
Annual Meetings: With the Allied Social Science Ass'n
1987-Chicago, IL/Dec. 28-30
1988-New York, NY/Dec. 28-30

Ass'n for Computational Linguistics (1962)
Bell Communications Research, 445 South St., MRE 2A379, Morristown NJ 07960-1961
Secy.-Treas.: Dr. Donald E. Walker
Members: 2,000 individuals *Staff:* 1
Annual Budget: $50-100,000 *Tel:* (201) 829-4312
Hist. Note: Formerly (1968) Ass'n for Machine Translation and Computational Linguistics. Affiliated with the Internat'l Committee on Computational Linguistics and the American Federation of Information Processing Societies. Computational linguistics deals with algorithms, models, and computer systems or components of systems for research on language and scholarly investigation.
Publications:
Computational Linguistics. q.
Proceedings of Annual Meetings. a.
Proceedings of European Chapter Meetings. bien.
Annual Meetings: Summer
1987-Stanford, CA(Stanford Univ.)/July 6-9/500

Ass'n for Computer Art and Design Education
(1984)
88 Garfield Ave., Madison NJ 07940
Exec. Secretary: Verdenal H. Johnson
Staff: 1
Annual Budget: under $10,000 *Tel:* (201) 377-9333
Hist. Note: Founded in 1984 in response to the need for recognition of the unique requirments of computer-assisted fine art and graphic design programs. Purpose is to help individuals and institutions interested in integrating the computer into fine art and graphic design curricula. Membership: $35/yr.
Publication:
Newsletter.
Annual Meetings: June/July

Ass'n for Computers and the Humanities (1978)
English Dept, University of Minnesota, Minneapolis MN 55455
Exec. Secretary: Donald Ross
Members: 380 individuals *Staff:* 0
Annual Budget: under $10,000 *Tel:* (612) 625-2888
Hist. Note: Formed to foster computer-aided scholarship and teaching in the humanities and arts fields. Membership: $35/yr.
Publications:
ACH Newsletter. q. adv.
Computers and the Humanities. q. adv.
Biennial: (1988)

Ass'n for Computing Machinery (1947)
11 West 42nd St., New York NY 10036
Exec. Director: Dr. Richard Hespos
Members: 72-73,000 *Staff:* 80
Annual Budget: over $5,000,000 *Tel:* (212) 869-7440
Hist. Note: Founded September 15, 1947 at Columbia University as the Eastern Association for Computing Machinery. Constitution and by-laws adopted in 1949. Incorporated in Delaware in 1954. Affiliated with the American Association for the Advancement of Science, the American Federation of Information Processing Societies, Conference Board of the Mathematical Sciences, National Academy of Sciences-National Research Council and the American National Standards Institute.
Publications:
ACM Transactions on Database Systems. q.
ACM Transactions on Mathematical Software. q.
Collected Algorithms from ACM. q.
Communications of the ACM. m. adv.
Computing Reviews. m.
ACM Computing Surveys. q.
Journal of the ACM. q.
Transactions on Programming Languages and Systems. q.
Transactions on Office Information Systems. q.
Transactions on Graphics. q.
Transactions on Computer Systems. q.
Annual Meetings: Fall Joint Computer Convention with the IEEE
1987-Dallas, TX/Oct. 25-29

Ass'n for Conservation Information, The (1938)
Dept. of Natural Resources, Wallace Bldg., Des Moines IA 50319
President: Ross Harrison
Members: 60-70
Annual Budget: under $10,000 *Tel:* (515) 281-5973
Hist. Note: Organized originally as the American Association for Conservation Information, ACI works to upgrade the quality of all forms of communication in and among agencies devoted to the protection and management of natural resources and wildlife. Members are officials of state fish and game departments, parks, recreation, soil and forestry organizations, as well as affiliates of federal and regional natural resource agencies. Has no paid staff or permanent address. Officers change annually.
Publications:
The Balance Wheel. q.
Membership Directory. a.
Semi-annual Meetings: Winter Workshop and Summer Conference
1987-Nevada/Winter
1987-Baton Rouge, LA/July 12-18

Ass'n for Consumer Research (1969)
Graduate School of Management, Brigham Young Univ., Provo UT 84602
Exec. Secretary: Keith Hunt
Members: 1,200 *Staff:* 1
Annual Budget: under $10,000 *Tel:* (801) 378-2080
Hist. Note: Business people, educators and government officials interested in consumer research. Membership: $20/yr.
Publication:
Advances in Consumer Research. a.
Annual Meetings: Fall
1987-Cambridge, MA(Hyatt)/Oct. 8-11/400

Ass'n for Continuing Higher Education (1939)
College of Graduate & Continuing Studies,niv. of Evansville, 1800 Lincoln Ave., Evansville IN 47722
Exec. V. President: Dr. Roger H. Sublett
Members: 1,300 individuals *Staff:* 2-5
Annual Budget: $50-100,000 *Tel:* (812) 479-2472
Hist. Note: Established as Ass'n of University Evening Colleges by a group of evening college administrators attending the 1939 annual meeting of Ass'n of Urban Universities; assumed its present name in 1973. Membership consists of individuals whose prime commitment is continuing education and regionally accredited institutions of higher learning which have programming or administrative units responsible for continuing education. Membership: $35/yr. (individual); $200/yr. (institution)
Publications:
Journal of Continuing Higher Education. q.
Five Minutes with ACHE. 9/yr.
Proceedings. a.
Membership Directory. a.
Annual Meetings: Fall/400
1987-Indianapolis, IN(Hyatt Regency)/Nov. 8-11
1988-Salt Lake City, UT(Hotel Utah)/Oct. 30-Nov. 2

Ass'n for Continuing Professional Education
(1922)
Dept. of Curriculum and Instruction, Northern Illinois University, DeKalb IL 60115
Exec. V. President: Dr. John J. Dlabal, Jr.
Members: 45-50 institutions *Staff:* 1
Annual Budget: under $10,000 *Tel:* (815) 753-0381
Hist. Note: Established as Ass'n for Field Services in Teacher Education, it assumed its present name in 1975.
Publications:
Newsletter. q.
New Campus. a.
Annual Meetings: Fall with the Ass'n for Continuing Higher Education

Ass'n for Corporate Growth (1954)
104 Wilmot Road, Suite 201, Deerfield IL 60015-5195
Exec. Director: John C. Mommsen, Jr.
Members: 2,700 acquisition and merger specialists *Staff:* 3-5
Annual Budget: $250-500,000 *Tel:* (312) 724-2622
Hist. Note: Founded as the Ass'n for Corporate Growth and Diversification by Peter Hilton and a group of businessmen as a professional society and forum for ideas related to both external and internal growth - joint ventures, acquisitions and divestitures, and new or expanded products and services. Membership: $60/yr. (individual only)
Publications:
Journal for Corporate Growth. bi-a.
Proceedings. a.
Directory. a.
Annual Meetings: Spring
1987-Naples, FL(Ritz Carlton)/April 5-8/375
1988-Tucson, AZ(Westin LaPaloma)/March 27-30/360
1989-Palm Beach, FL(Breakers)/April 5-8/400
1990-Phoenix, AZ(Biltmore)/April 18-21/400
1991-Boca Raton, FL(Hotel & Club)/April 10-13/425

Ass'n for Correctional Research and Information Management (1971)
Div. of Criminal Justice,, Cal. State Univ., 6000 J St., Sacramento CA 95819
President: Dr. Thomas Johnson
Members: 100
Annual Budget: under $10,000 *Tel:* (916) 278-6487
Hist. Note: An affiliate of the American Correctional Ass'n. Formerly (1981) the Association for Correctional Research and Information Statistics.
Annual Meetings: With American Correctional Ass'n.

Ass'n for Counselor Education and Supervision
(1940)
5999 Stevenson Ave., Alexandria VA 22304
Exec. Director: Dr. Patrick J. McDonough
Members: 2,500-3,500
Annual Budget: $50-100,000 *Tel:* (703) 823-9800
Hist. Note: Division of the American Ass'n for Counseling and Development. Membership: $25/yr.
Publications:
Counselor Education and Supervision. q. adv.
ACcESs. q.
Annual Meetings: With the American Ass'n for Counseling and Development
1987-New Orleans, LA/April 22-25

Ass'n for Creative Change within Religious and other Social Systems (1968)
P.O. Box 219, Frederick MD 21701
Exec. Director: Lydia Walker
Members: 500-600 *Staff:* 2-5
Annual Budget: $25-50,000 *Tel:* (301) 635-6464
Hist. Note: Established as the Ass'n of Religion and Applied Behavorial Science, changed to its present name in 1973. A professional membership organization of individuals committed to effecting corporate and individual change through insights derived from applied behavioral science and theology. Membership: $90/yr.
Publications:
Directory of Membership. a.
Journal of Religion and the Applied Behavioral Sciences. 3/yr. adv.
Annual Meetings: June
1987-Atlanta, GA(Ogelthorpe College)/June 8-11
1988-Toronto, Ontario

Ass'n for Documentary Editing (1979)
History Dept., The Johns Hopkins University, Baltimore MD 21218
Secy.-Treas.: Elizabeth S. Hughes
Members: 25 companies; 400 individuals *Staff:* 0
Annual Budget: $10-25,000 *Tel:* (301) 338-8363
Hist. Note: Members of the ADE are working on editions in history, literature, philosophy, the arts, and the sciences. Many members are teachers or archivists as well as editors; others are full-time editors. All share the goal of promoting documentary

00077 12 05 86 1233

editing through cooperation and exchange of ideas. Membership: $15/yr.
Publications:
Documentary Editing. q.
Membership Directory. a.
Annual Meetings: October
1987-Boston, MA(Colonnade Hotel)/Nov. 4-7
1988-New Orleans, LA(Monteleone)

Ass'n for Dressings and Sauces (1933)
5775 Peachtree-Dunwoody Rd., Suite 500D, Atlanta GA 30342
President: Robert H. Kellen
Members: 180 companies *Staff:* 8
Tel: (404) 252-3663
Hist. Note: Formerly Mayonnaise and Salad Dressing Manufacturers Ass'n and (1973) Mayonnaise and Salad Dressings Institute.
Semi-annual meetings: Spring and Fall
1987-Tampa, FL/April 5-7
1987-New Orleans, LA/Oct. 18-20

Ass'n for Education and Rehabilitation of the Blind andVisually Impaired (1984)
206 North Washington St., Alexandria VA 22314
Exec. Director: Kathleen Megivern
Members: 6,100 *Staff:* 5
Annual Budget: $250-500,000 *Tel:* (703) 548-1884
Hist. Note: The result of a consolidation of the American Ass'n of Workers for the Blind (1895) and the Ass'n for Education of the Visually Handicapped (1905) in 1984.
Publications:
Yearbook of AER. a.
AER Report. bi-m.
Job Exchange. m.
Biennial Meetings: Even years (international) & Odd years (regional)

Ass'n for Education in Journalism and Mass Communication (1912)
1621 College Street, University of South Carolina, Columbia SC 29208-0251
Exec. Director: Jennifer McGill
Members: 2,000 *Staff:* 5
Annual Budget: $250-500,000 *Tel:* (803) 777-2005
Hist. Note: Formerly (1951) American Ass'n for Teachers of Journalism. Membership: $60/yr. (individual), $100/yr. (organization).
Publications:
AEJMC News. 7/yr.
Journalism Educator. q. adv.
Journalism Monographs. q.
Journalism Quarterly. q. adv.
Journalism Directory. a. adv.
Journalism Abstracts. a.
Annual Meetings: Summer/over 700
1987-San Antonio, TX(Trinity University)/Aug. 1-4
1988-Portland, OR(Portland Hilton)/July 2-6
1989-Washington, DC

Ass'n for Education of the Visually Handicapped (1853)
Hist. Note: Consolidated with the American Ass'n of Workers for the Blind to become the Ass'n for Education and Rehabilitation of the Blind and Visually Impaired in 1984.

Ass'n for Educational Communications and Technology (1923)
1126 16th St., N.W., Washington DC 20036
Manager: Stan Zenor
Members: 5,500 *Staff:* 12
Annual Budget: $1-2,000,000 *Tel:* (202) 466-4780
Hist. Note: Founded in 1923 as the Department of Visual Instruction of the Nat'l Education Ass'n. Incorporated in the District of Columbia in 1969. Reorganized in 1970 as a national affiliate of the Nat'l Education Ass'n and became independent as the Ass'n for Educational Communications and Technology in July 1970. Membership: $50/yr.
Publications:
Educational Communication & Technology Journal. q.
TechTrends. 8/yr. adv.
Journal of Instructional Development. q.
Annual Meetings: January
1987-Atlanta, GA/Jan. 7-12
1988-New Orleans, LA/Jan. 13-18

Ass'n for Educational Data Systems (1962)
Hist. Note: Address unknown in 1987. Probably defunct.

Ass'n for Employee Health and Fitness (1974)
965 Hope St., Stamford CT 06907
Exec. Director: Harv Ebel, Ph.D.
Members: 3,500 individuals *Staff:* 4
Annual Budget: $500-1,000,000 *Tel:* (203) 359-2188
Hist. Note: Founded as the American Ass'n of Fitness Directors in Business and Industry in 1974; became the Ass'n for Fitness in Business in 1983; and assumed its present name in 1986. Members include fitness directors, physicians, health promotion specialists, physiologists, benefit managers, product manufacturers, nutritionists, psychologists, personnel directors, exercise instructors, and health policy experts. Membership: $75/yr.
Publications:
AFB Action Newsletter. bi-m.
Fitprints Research Bulletin. bi-m.
Fitness in Business Journal. bi-m.
Annual Meetings: Fall
1987-St. Louis, MO/Oct. 14-19
1988-Buffalo, NY

Ass'n for Evolutionary Economics (1965)
Dept. of Economics, Univ. of Nebraska, Lincoln NE 68588
Secy.-Treas.: Dr. F. Gregory Hayden
Members: 850 economists, 1,200 libraries and organizations
Staff: 2-5
Annual Budget: $25-50,000 *Tel:* (402) 472-3867
Hist. Note: Seeks to foster the development of economic study and of economics as a social science based on the complex interrelationships of man and society. A member of the Allied Social Science Ass'ns. Membership: $22/yr.
Publication:
Journal of Economic Issues. q. adv.
Annual Meetings: With the Allied Social Science Ass'ns
1987-Chicago, IL

Ass'n for Experiential Education (1977)
Box 249-CU, Boulder CO 80309
Exec. Director: Dr. Mitchell Sakofs
Members: 1,000 *Staff:* 2-5
Annual Budget: $100-250,000 *Tel:* (303) 492-1547
Hist. Note: An international network of diverse individuals, schools, and other educational organizations which share a common interest in and commitment to experience-based teaching and learning. Membership: $35/yr. (individual); $100/yr. (organization).
Publications:
Journal of Experiential Education. 3/yr.
Jobs Clearinghouse. m.
Adventure Alternatives in Corrections, Mental Health & Special Pops. a
Annual Meetings: Fall
1987-Port Townsend, WA/Oct. 1-4

Ass'n for Federal Information Resources Management (1979)
P.O. Box 28506, Washington DC 20038
Chairperson: Carol Becker
Members: 20-30 companies; 250 individuals *Staff:* 0
Annual Budget: $10-25,000 *Tel:* (202) 663-1139
Hist. Note: AFFIRM's primary goal is to improve the management of information systems and resources of the Federal Government. Members are professionals from the various component disciplines of information resources management. Membership: $20/yr.
Publications:
The Affirmation. m.
Membership Directory. a.
Annual Meetings: Annual Seminar held in the Fall in Washington, DC

Ass'n for Field Archaeology (1970)
Boston University, 232 Bay State Road, Boston MA 02215
Managing Editor: Al Wesolowsky
Members: 1,600 *Staff:* 1
Annual Budget: under $10,000 *Tel:* (617) 353-2357
Hist. Note: Members are individuals involved with the primary analysis of excavated archaeological materials; concerned with the timely publication of archaeological reports; the illicit international trade in antiquities; and in "public archaeology"/ cultural resource management. Membership: $40/ yr.(individual); $50/yr.(company-subscription only).
Publication:
Journal of Field Archaeology. q. adv.
Annual Meetings: With Archaeological Inst. of America & Soc. for American Archaeology

Ass'n for Finishing Processes (1975)
One SME Dr., Box 930, Dearborn MI 48121
Exec. Director: Michael G. Bell
Members: 3,000 *Staff:* 2
Annual Budget: $100-250,000 *Tel:* (313) 271-1500
Hist. Note: Sponsored by the Soc. of Manufacturing Engineers. Technicians, engineers and scientists who use industrial finishes such as powder coating, radiation curing, waterborne high solids and other custom coatings. Membership: $55/yr.
Publication:
Newsletter. q.
Biennial Meetings: Uneven years in Fall.
1987-Cincinnati, OH/Sept. 21-24/5,000-7,000

Ass'n for Fitness in Business
Hist. Note: Became Ass'n for Employee Health and Fitness in 1986.

Ass'n for Genealogical Education
Hist. Note: Merged with the National Genealogical Society in 1981.

Ass'n for Gerontology in Higher Education (1974)
600 Maryland Ave., SW, West Wing 204, Washington DC 20024
Exec. Director: Elizabeth B. Douglass
Members: 270 institutions *Staff:* 2-5
Annual Budget: $100-250,000 *Tel:* (202) 484-7505
Hist. Note: The association grew out of an ad hoc committee of educators interested in the development and improvement of gerontological programs and resources. Its membership comprises colleges and universities in the U.S. and Canada concerned with gerontological education, training and research. Membership: $175-275/yr. (institution).
Publications:
AGHE Exchange. q. adv.
National Directory of Educational Programs in Gerontology. bi-a.
Annual Meetings: Feb./March
1987-Boston, MA(Park Plaza)/March 5-8/500
1988-Chicago, IL(Bismarck)/March 3-6
1989-Tampa/St. Petersburg, FL/Feb.-March

Ass'n for Gnotobiotics (1961)
Roswell Park Memorial Institute, 666 Elm Street, Buffalo NY 14263
Exec. Secretary: Dr. Patricia M. Bealmear
Members: 400 *Staff:* 1
Annual Budget: under $10,000 *Tel:* (716) 845-3105
Hist. Note: Individuals interested in germ-free research and applications. Formerly (1968) Ass'n for Applied Gnotobiotics. Membership: $10/yr.(individual); $250/yr.(organization)
Publications:
Newsletter. m.
Membership Directory. a.
Annual Meetings: Annual Meeting alternates between June and October
1987-Raleigh, NC/Oct.
1988-New Orleans, LA/June
1989-Columbus, OH/June
1990-Buffalo, NY/Oct.

Ass'n for Healthcare Quality (1969)
Hist. Note: Dissolved in 1985.

Ass'n for Hospital Medical Education (1956)
1101 Connecticut Ave., N.W., Suite 700, Washington DC 20036
Exec. Director: Donna Cantor
Members: 600 individuals, 400 hospitals *Staff:* 2-5
Annual Budget: $100-250,000 *Tel:* (202) 857-1196
Hist. Note: Formerly (1968) Ass'n of Hospital Directors of Medical Education. Members are concerned with medical education, primarily in community hospitals.
Publication:
AHME News. m.
Annual Meetings: Spring
1987-Tucson, AZ(Loew's Venetian Canyon)/April 22-25

Ass'n for Humanist Sociology (1976)
Hist. Note: Arose out of discussions in 1975 of the need for a more humanized emphasis in sociological research and teaching. Has no paid staff. Address unknown since 1984.

Ass'n for Humanistic Education and Development (1931)
5999 Stevenson Ave., Alexandria VA 22304
Exec. Director: Dr. Patrick J. McDonough
Members: 2,500 *Staff:* 2-5
Annual Budget: $25-50,000 *Tel:* (703) 823-9800
Hist. Note: Division of the American Ass'n for Counseling and Development. Formerly (1975) Student Personnel Ass'n for Teacher Education. Membership: $11/yr.
Publications:
Journal of Humanist Education and Development. q. adv.
Infochange. q.
Annual Meetings: With the American Ass'n for Counseling and Development
1987-New Orleans, LA/April 22-25

Ass'n for Humanistic Psychology (1962)
325 Ninth St., San Francisco CA 94103
Exec. Director: Paul DuBois
Members: 4,000 *Staff:* 4
Annual Budget: $250-500,000 *Tel:* (415) 626-2375
Hist. Note: Founded in Palo Alto in December 1962 as the American Ass'n for Humanistic Psychology. Incorporated in California in 1965. Name changed to Ass'n for Humanistic Psychology in 1969.
Publications:
AHP Perspective. m.
Journal of Humanistic Psychology. q. adv.
Annual Meetings: August
1987-Oakland, CA(Mills College)/Aug. 5-9

Ass'n for Information and Image Management (1943)
1100 Wayne Ave., Silver Spring MD 20910
Exec. Director: Bettie A. Steiger
Members: 8,000 *Staff:* 19
Annual Budget: $2-5,000,000 *Tel:* (301) 587-8202
Hist. Note: Established and incorporated in Michigan as the Nat'l Microfilm Ass'n, it became the Nat'l Micrographics Ass'n in 1975 and assumed its present name in 1983. Merged in 1974 with Users of Automatic Information Display Equipment. Members are users and manufacturers of equipment, supplies and services for the information and image management industry. Membership: $75/yr. (individual); $350/yr. (organization/company).
Publications:
Journal of Information and Image Management. m. adv.
FYI/IM Newsletter. m.
Annual Meetings: Spring/10,000
1987-New York, NY(Conv. Center)/April 27-30
1988-Chicago, IL(McCormick Place)/April 11-14
1989-Philadelphia, PA(Civic Center)/May 1-4
1990-Boston, MA(Hynes Auditorium)/April 9-12
1991-Washington, DC(Conv. Center)/April 29-May 2

00078 12 05 86 1233

Ass'n for Institutional Research (1965)
314 Stone Building, Florida State University, Tallahassee FL 32306-3038
Admin. Director: Jean C. Chulak
Members: 2,000 individuals *Staff:* 2-5
Annual Budget: $100-250,000 *Tel:* (904) 644-4470
Hist. Note: Members are involved in research to improve institutions of postsecondary education. Membership: $55/yr.
Publications:
A.I.R. Newsletter. q.
New Directions for Institutional Research. q.
Professional File. q.
Research in Higher Education. 8/yr.
Yearbook. a.
Annual Meetings: Spring/800
1987-Kansas City, MO/May 3-6
1988-Phoenix, AZ/May 15-18

Ass'n for Integrated Manufacturing Technology (1962)
P.O. Box 1234, Beloit WI 53511
Exec. Director: Monte Jenkins
Members: 3,800-4,000 individuals *Staff:* 2-5
Annual Budget: $250-500,000 *Tel:* (608) 364-7949
Hist. Note: Founded June 15, 1962 and incorporated in 1963. Individuals and companies involved with the field of computer-integrated design and manufacturing, particularly in metal working. Membership: $60/yr.
Publications:
Directory. a. adv.
Integrated Manufacturing Report. m. adv.
Annual Meetings: Spring
1987-Boston, MA

Ass'n for Integrative Studies (1979)
School of Interdisciplinary Studies, 185 Peabody Hall, Miami University, Oxford OH 45056
Secy.-Treas.: Prof. William H. Newell
Members: 310
Annual Budget: under $10,000 *Tel:* (513) 529-2213
Hist. Note: Established and incorporated in Ohio, AIS members are primarily faculty and administrators engaged in interdisciplinary teaching and research or who are interested in exploring interdisplinary topics and methodology. Membership: $20/year (individual), $30/year (institution).
Publications:
AIS Newsletter. q.
Issues in Integrative Studies. a.
Annual Meetings: October/November/100
1987-University Park, PA(Pennsylanvia State University)/Oct. 8-11

Ass'n for Internat'l Marathons (AIMS) (1981)
9 E. 89th St., New York NY 10128
Director: Fred Lebow
Members: 50 *Staff:* 1
Annual Budget: $25-50,000 *Tel:* (212) 860-4455
Hist. Note: Members are directors of marathons around the world.

Ass'n for Jewish Studies (1969)
Widener Library, Harvard University, Cambridge MA 02138
Exec. Secretary: Charles Berlin
Members: 1,000 *Staff:* 1
Annual Budget: under $10,000
Hist. Note: Promotes the teaching of Jewish studies at the college level.
Publication:
Journal. semi-a.

Ass'n for Library and Information Science Education (1915)
471 Park Lane, State College PA 16803
Exec. Secretary: Janet C. Phillips
Members: 90 schools, 600 individuals *Staff:* 1
Annual Budget: $50-100,000 *Tel:* (814) 238-0254
Hist. Note: Member of the American Library Ass'n and the Internat'l Federation of Library Ass'ns. Formerly (until 1983) known as the Association of American Library Schools.
Publication:
Journal of Education for Library & Information Science. 5/yr.
Annual Meetings: Semi-annual meetings prior to those of American Library Ass'n/3-400

Ass'n for Library Service to Children (1901)
American Library Ass'n, 50 East Huron St., Chicago IL 60611
Exec. Director: Susan Roman
Members: 3,000 individuals; 1,000 libraries *Staff:* 2-5
Annual Budget: $100-250,000 *Tel:* (312) 944-6780
Hist. Note: The association is interested in the improvement and extension of library service to children in all types of libraries; it is responsible for the evaluation and selection of book and non-book library materials and for the improvement of techniques of library service to children from pre-school to 8th grade when such materials and techniques are intended for use in more than one type of library. A division of the American Library Ass'n. Formerly (until 1956) the Children's Library Ass'n and (until 1977) the Children's Services Division. Membership: $25/year (Membership in ALA required).
Publications:
ALSC Newsletter. semi-a.
Top of the News. q. adv.
Annual Meetings: Summer with the American Library Ass'n
1987-San Francisco, CA/June 27-July 2
1988-New Orleans, LA/July 9-14
1989-Dallas, TX/June 24-29
1990-Chicago, IL/June 23-28
1991-Atlanta, GA/June 29-July 4

Ass'n for Living Historical Farms and Agricultural Museums (1970)
Museum of American History, Room 5035, Washington DC 20560
Editor: Dr. George Terry Sharrer
Members: 350 institutions *Staff:* 1
Annual Budget: under $10,000 *Tel:* (202) 357-2813
Hist. Note: Members include those involved in living historical farms, agricultural museums and outdoor museums of history and folklife. Membership: $8/yr.
Publications:
Living Historical Farms Bulletin. bi-m.
Proceedings. a.
Annual Meetings: June/250
1987-Ann Arbor, MI(University of Michigan)
1988-Bethpage, NY(Old Bethpage Village)
1989-Nobelsville, IN(Conner Prairie Museum)
1990-Sturbridge, MA(Old Sturbridge Village)

Ass'n for Major Symphony Orchestras (1937)
Hist. Note: Became the Ass'n of Major Symphony Orchestra Volunteers in 1985.

Ass'n for Management Excellence (1903)
Hist. Note: Reported as defunct in 1984.

Ass'n for Manufacturing Excellence (1985)
380 West Palatine Road, Wheeling IL 60090
Managing Director: Charles G. Whitchurch
Members: 900 *Staff:* 2-5
Annual Budget: $250-500,000 *Tel:* (312) 520-3282
Hist. Note: A non-profit organization founded to cultivate the understanding, analysis and exchange of world class productivity methods and their successful application in the pursuit of excellence.
Annual Meetings:
1987-Lake Buena Vista, FL(Buena Vista Palace)/Oct. 7-9

Ass'n for Maternal and Child Health and Crippled Children's Programs (1955)
Dept. of Health Services, Div. of, Maternal & Child Health, 275 E. Main St., Frankfort KY 40621
Secy.-Treas.: Dr. Patricia K. Nicol, M.P.H.
Members: 120-130
Annual Budget: $10-25,000 *Tel:* (502) 564-4830
Hist. Note: Established as the Association of State Maternal and Child Health and Crippled Children Directors, it assumed its present name in 1982.
Publication:
Newsletter. q.
Annual Meetings: Winter

Ass'n for Measurement and Evaluation in Counseling and Development (1965)
5999 Stevenson Ave., Alexandria VA 22304
Exec. Director: Dr. Patrick J. McDonough
Members: 17-1800
Annual Budget: $25-50,000 *Tel:* (703) 823-9800
Hist. Note: Division of the American Ass'n for Counseling and Development. Formerly (1984) the Ass'n for Measurement and Evaluation in Guidance. Membership: $12/yr.
Publications:
Measurement & Evaluation in Counseling & Development Journal. q. adv.
AMECD Newsnotes.
Annual Meetings: With American Ass'n for Counseling and Development
1987-New Orleans, LA/April 22-25

Ass'n for Measurement and Evaluation in Guidance (1965)
Hist. Note: Became the Ass'n for Measurement and Evaluation in Counseling and Development in 1984.

Ass'n for Multi-Image International (1974)
8019 N. Himes Ave., Suite 401, Tampa FL 33614
Exec. Director: Marilyn J. Kulp
Members: 3,300 individuals, 50-75 companies *Staff:* 6-10
Annual Budget: $500-1,000,000 *Tel:* (813) 932-1692
Hist. Note: AMI members are actively engaged in the field of multi-image production utilization. AMI promotes the use of multi-image as a medium for education, communication and entertainment. Incorporated in Pennsylvania. Membership: $80/yr.
Publication:
Multi-Images Journal. bi-m. adv.

Ass'n for Multicultural Counseling and Development (1971)
5999 Stevenson Ave., Alexandria VA 22304
Exec. Director: Dr. Patrick J. McDonough
Members: 1,900-2,000
Tel: (703) 823-9800
Hist. Note: Formerly (1985) Ass'n for Non-White Concerns in Personnel and Guidance. A division of the American Ass'n for Counseling and Development. Membership: $15/yr.
Publications:
Journal of Multicultural Counseling and Development. 3/yr. adv.
AMCD Newsletter.
Annual Meetings: With American Ass'n for Counseling and Development
1987-New Orleans, LA/April 22-25

Ass'n for Non-White Concerns in Personnel and Guidance (1971)
Hist. Note: Became the Ass'n for Multicultural Counseling and Development (1985).

Ass'n for Payroll Management (1981)
Hist. Note: Address unknown in 1984.

Ass'n for Persons with Severe Handicaps (1974)
7010 Roosevelt Way, N.E., Seattle WA 98115
Exec. Director: Elizabeth Lindley
Members: 6,000 *Staff:* 6-10
Annual Budget: $100-250,000 *Tel:* (206) 523-8446
Hist. Note: Founded as the American Ass'n for the Education of the Severely-Profoundly Handicapped. It became the Ass'n for the Severely Handicapped in 1979 and assumed its present name in 1984. Members are teachers, social workers, psychologists, physical therapists, legal administrators, special education administrators, parents and students. Membership: $55/yr.
Publications:
TASH Journal. q. adv.
TASH Newsletter. m. adv.
Annual Meetings:
1987-Chicago, IL(McCormick Center Hotel)/Oct. 29-31/2,500
1988-Washington, DC(Washington Hilton & Tower)/Dec. 8-10/2,500

Ass'n for Politics and the Life Sciences (1980)
Hist. Note: Defunct in 1985.

Ass'n for Population/Family Planning Libraries and Information Centers, Internat'l (1968)
Population Information Program, 624 N. Broadway, Baltimore MD 21205
President: Judy Mahachek
Members: 150-200
Annual Budget: under $10,000 *Tel:* (301) 955-8200
Hist. Note: Members are librarians, information researchers, resource coordinators and the population and family-planning related agencies that they serve. Incorporated in the District of Columbia in May 1972.
Publications:
APLICommunicator. q. adv.
Proceedings. a.
Annual Meetings: Spring/50
1987-Chicago, IL/April 30-May 2

Ass'n for Practitioners in Infection Control (1972)
505 East Hawley St., Mundelein IL 60060
Exec. Director: Edward J. Stygar, Jr.
Members: 7,000 *Staff:* 2-5
Annual Budget: $250-500,000 *Tel:* (312) 949-6052
Hist. Note: Physicians, nurses, medical technologists, sanatarians and others professionally concerned with infection control. Membership: $60/yr. (domestic); $80/yr. (foreign)
Publications:
American Journal of Infection Control. q. adv.
APIC News.
Update.
Annual Meetings: Spring/1,200
1987-Miami Beach, FL(Fountainbleau)/May 3-8
1988-Dallas, TX(Loews Anatole)/May 1-5
1989-Reno, NV(MGM Grand)/May 21-26

Ass'n for Professional Education for Ministry (1950)
Hist. Note: Ceased operations in 1984.

Ass'n for Psychoanalytic Medicine (1945)
4560 Delafield Ave., New York NY 10471
Admin. Secretary: Mrs. Terry Montgomery
Members: 225-250 *Staff:* 1
Annual Budget: $25-50,000 *Tel:* (212) 548-6088
Hist. Note: Formerly Ass'n for Psychoanalytic and Psychosomatic Medicine. Affiliated with American Psychoanalytic Ass'n.
Publication:
Bulletin. 3-4/yr. adv.
Annual meetings: June, always in New York City

Ass'n for Recorded Sound Collections (1966)
Box 75082, Washington DC 20013
Exec. Director: Phillip Rochlin
Members: 1,000 *Staff:* 1
Annual Budget: $10-25,000 *Tel:* (703) 591-6746
Hist. Note: ARSC serves the interests of the private collector, discographer, librarian, archivist, and specialty dealer in all fields of record collecting and development of historical discographic information for classical, jazz, pop, rock, country, folk-ethnic and spoken word sound recordings. Membership: $15/yr.
Publications:
Bulletin. a.
Journal. 3/yr.
Newsletter. q.
Membership Directory. bi-a.
Annual Meetings: Spring

00079 12 05 86 1233

1987-Washington, DC/May 28-30/100
1988-Toronto, Ontario

Ass'n for Regulatory Reform (1985)
1331 Pennsylvania Ave., N.W., Suite 508, Washington DC 20004
President: Danny Ghorbani
Members: 20 companies *Staff:* 3-4
Annual Budget: $250-500,000 *Tel:* (202) 783-4087
Hist. Note: Represents the interests and views of manufacturers and producers of manufactured housing. Dedicated to the reform of unnecessary regulation of American enterprise.
Publications:
ARR Washington Update. bi-m.
ARR News. irreg.
Deregualtor Position Papers. irreg.
Annual Meetings: May
1987-Washington, DC

Ass'n for Religious and Value Issues in Counseling (1955)
5999 Stevenson Avenue, Alexandria VA 22304
Exec. Director: Dr. Patrick J. McDonough
Members: 2,500-3,500 *Staff:* 6-10
Annual Budget: $10-25,000 *Tel:* (703) 823-9800
Hist. Note: A division of the American Ass'n for Counseling and Development. Formerly (1958) Catholic Counselors in APGA; (1960) Nat'l Conference of Diocesan Guidance Councils; (1962) Nat'l Conference of Catholic Guidance Councils; and (1978) Nat'l Catholic Guidance Conference. Membership: $12/yr.
Publications:
Counseling and Values Journal. semi-a.
ARVIC Newsletter.
Annual Meetings: With the American Ass'n for Counseling and Development
1987-New Orleans, LA/April 22-25

Ass'n for Research, Administration, Professional Councils and Societies (1949)
1900 Association Dr., Reston VA 22091
Exec. Director: Dr. Raymond A. Ciszek
Members: 8-9,000 *Staff:* 2-5
Annual Budget: $10-25,000 *Tel:* (703) 476-3430
Hist. Note: Established originally as a division of the American Ass'n for Health, Physical Education and Recreation. In 1974 became an independent member of the American Alliance for Health, Physical Education, Recreation and Dance. Coordinates the work of special interest councils in health, physical education and recreation. Membership: $42/year.
Annual Meetings: Spring, with AAHPERD/6,000
1987-Las Vegas, NV/April 13-17
1988-Kansas City, MO/April 6-10
1989-Boston, MA/April 19-23
1990-New Orleans, LA/March 28-April 1

Ass'n for Research in Growth Relationships (1956)
32 Linden Drive, Kingston RI 02881
Exec. Secretary: Thomas P. Nally
Members: 75 *Staff:* 1
Annual Budget: under $10,000 *Tel:* (401) 783-7172
Hist. Note: A professional society of workers in child psychology, development, growth and education.

Ass'n for Research in Nervous and Mental Disease (1920)
Mt. Sinai School of Medicine, New York NY 10029
Secy.-Treas.: Bernard Cohen, M.D.
Members: 900-1,000 *Staff:* 1
Annual Budget: $10-25,000 *Tel:* (212) 348-8133
Hist. Note: Established as the Neuropsychiatric Research Society, it assumed its present name in 1922. Membership: $50/yr.
Publication:
Proceedings. a.
Annual Meetings: First Friday & Saturday in December in New York City

Ass'n for Research in Vision and Ophthalmology (1928)
9650 Rockville Pike, Bethesda MD 20814
Exec. Director: Kathleen C. McCasland
Members: 4,100 *Staff:* 3
Annual Budget: $500-1,000,000 *Tel:* (301) 530-7000
Hist. Note: Founded as the Ass'n for Research in Ophthalmology and incorporated in New York in 1936; assumed its present name in 1971. Memberhip: $75/yr. (individual); $125/yr. (organization/company)
Publication:
Investigative Ophthalmology and Visual Science. m. adv.
Annual Meetings: Sarasota, FL(Hyatt)/Spring/3,200
1987-May 4-8
1988-May 2-6
1989-May 1-5

Ass'n for School, College and University Staffing (1934)
DAVEA Center, 301 S. Swift Road, Addison IL 60101
Exec. Director: Charles A. Marshall
Members: 1,000 *Staff:* 2-5
Annual Budget: $100-250,000
Hist. Note: Personnel in educational placement in colleges, universities and school districts. Formerly (1962) Nat'l Institutional Teacher Placement Ass'n.
Publications:
ASCUS Staffer. q.
ASCUS Annual. a. adv.
Directory of Membership and Subject Field Index. a.
Directory of Public School Systems in the U.S. a.
Teacher Supply and Demand Report. a.
Annual Meetings: October/200
1987-San Diego, CA(Town & Country)/Oct. 20-23

Ass'n for Social Anthropology in Oceania (1967)
Royal Roads Military College, F.M.O. Victoria, Victoria British Columbia VOS 1B0
Secretary: James A. Boutilier
Members: 320-330 individuals; 40-50 institutions *Staff:* 1
Annual Budget: under $10,000 *Tel:* (604) 380-4545
Hist. Note: Formerly known as the Ass'n for Social Anthropology in Eastern Oceania.
Publication:
ASAO Newsletter. q.
Always the last week of February or early March. Three year cycle:
meetings on the East coast, Mid-West, and West coast.

Ass'n for Social Economics (1941)
College of Administration & Business, Louisiana Tech. Univ., Box 10318, Ruston LA 71272
Secretary: Edward J. O'Boyle
Members: 500
Annual Budget: $10-25,000 *Tel:* (318) 257-3701
Hist. Note: Formerly (1970) Catholic Economic Ass'n Membership: $25/year. The Association has no paid staff.
Publications:
Forum and Newsletter. semi-a.
Review of Social Economy. 3/yr.
Annual Meetings: With the Allied Social Science Ass'n in late December.
1987-Chicago, IL

Ass'n for Software Protection (1981)
Hist. Note: Members are developers of computer software who seek to protect their copyrighted product from unauthorized use. Address unknown since 1984.

Ass'n for Specialists in Group Work (1973)
5999 Stevenson Ave., Alexandria VA 22304
Exec. Director: Dr. Patrick J. McDonough
Members: 3,000-3,100 *Staff:* 2-5
Annual Budget: $25-50,000 *Tel:* (703) 823-9800
Hist. Note: A division of the American Ass'n for Counseling and Development. Membership: $12/yr.
Publications:
Journal of Specialists in Group Work. q.
ASGW Newsletter.
Annual Meetings: With the American Ass'n for Counseling and Development
1987-New Orleans, LA/April 22-25

Ass'n for Supervision and Curriculum Development (1943)
125 North West St., Alexandria VA 22314
Exec. Director: Dr. Gordon Cawelti
Members: 72,000 *Staff:* 60
Annual Budget: over $5,000,000 *Tel:* (703) 549-9110
Hist. Note: Merger in 1943 of the Soc. for Curriculum Study (1929) and the Department of Supervisors and Directors of Instruction of the Nat'l Education Ass'n to form the Department of Supervision and Curriculum Development of NEA. Changed to its present title in 1946. Became independent of NEA in 1975. Members are curriculum coordinators and consultants, professors of education and educational administrators. Has an annual budget of $8 million. Membership: $48/yr.
Publication:
Educational Leadership. m. adv.
Annual Meetings: March
1987-New Orleans, LA/March 1-5,000

Ass'n for Symbolic Logic (1936)
Dept. of Mathematics, Univ. of Illinois,1409 West Green St., Urbana IL 61801
Secretary-Treasurer: C. Ward Henson
Members: 1,400-1,500 *Staff:* 2-5
Annual Budget: $100-250,000 *Tel:* (217) 333-3350
Hist. Note: Founded and incorporated in Rhode Island in 1936. Affiliated with the American Mathematical Soc., the Conference Board of the Mathematical Sciences and the Internat'l Union for the History and Philosophy of Science. Promotes research and studies in mathematical logic and related fields. Membership: $32/yr. (individual); $200/yr. (institution); and $500/yr. (corporate).
Publication:
Journal of Symbolic Logic. q.
Annual Meetings: December or January
1987-San Antonio, TX/Jan. 21-25

Ass'n for Systems Management (1947)
24587 Bagley Rd., Cleveland OH 44138
Exec. Director: Richard L. Irwin, CAE
Members: 9-10,000 *Staff:* 15-20
Annual Budget: $2-5,000,000 *Tel:* (216) 243-6900
Hist. Note: Formerly (1969) Systems and Procedures Ass'n. Members are analysts and executives of information systems. Member of the Nat'l Commission on Software Issues in the Eighties. Membership: $80/yr.
Publication:
Journal of Systems Management. m. adv.
Annual Meetings: Spring/1,500
1987-Louisville, KY/April 26-29
1988-San Diego, CA/April 17-20
1989-Dallas, TX

Ass'n for the Advancement of Health Education (1937)
1900 Association Drive, Reston VA 22091
Exec. Director: Becky J. Smith, Ph.D.
Members: 7,500 *Staff:* 2-5
Annual Budget: $10-25,000 *Tel:* (703) 476-3440
Hist. Note: Until 1974 a division of the American Ass'n for Health, Physical Education and Recreation. Now an independent member of the American Alliance for Health, Physical Education, Recreation and Dance. Membership: $42/year.
Publications:
Health Education. bi-m.
HE-XTRA. 3/yr.
Annual Meetings: With AAHPERD.

Ass'n for the Advancement of International Education (1964)
University of Florida, Norman Hall, Room 200, Gainesville FL 32611
Exec. Director: Dr. Gordon E. Parsons
Members: 601 companies, 450 individuals *Staff:* 2
Annual Budget: $100-250,000 *Tel:* (904) 392-1542
Hist. Note: Established in Washington, DC. Members include head adminstrators of American schools, colleges and universities located in major cities worldwide. Membership: $300/yr.
Publication:
Inter-Ed. 3/yr. a.
Annual Meetings:
1987-New Orleans, LA(Inter Continental)/Feb. 17-19/600
1988-San Diego, CA/Feb. 15-18/650
1989-Orlando, FL/early March/650

Ass'n for the Advancement of Medical Instrumentation (1967)
1901 North Ft. Myer Drive, Ste. 602, Arlington VA 22209-1699
Exec. Director: Michael J. Miller, CAE
Members: 5,000 *Staff:* 15-20
Annual Budget: $1-2,000,000 *Tel:* (703) 525-4890
Hist. Note: A non-profit professional association of health care providers who develop, use or manage medical technology. Founded and incorporated in Massachusetts in 1967. Individual membership: $100/yr.; institutional membership fee varies.
Publications:
AAMI News. bi-m.
Medical Instrumentation. bi-m. adv.
Biomedical Technology Today. bi-m.
Annual Meetings: Spring
1987-Los Angeles, CA(Westin Bonaventure)/May 16-20/2,000
1988-Washington, DC(Sheraton Washington)/May 14-18/2,000

Ass'n for the Advancement of Psychoanalysis (1941)
329 East 62nd St., New York NY 10021
Secretary: Susan Rudnick, C.S.W.
Members: 80-90 *Staff:* 1
Annual Budget: $10-25,000 *Tel:* (212) 751-2724
Hist. Note: Membership: $175/year (individual).
Publications:
American Journal of Psychoanalysis. q. adv.
Newsletter. q.
Annual Meetings: New York City.

Ass'n for the Advancement of Psychology (1974)
1200 17th St., N.W., Washington DC 20036
Exec. Director: Clarence Martin
Members: 6,000 *Staff:* 6-10
Annual Budget: $250-500,000 *Tel:* (202) 466-5757
Hist. Note: Merged in 1975 with the Council for the Advancement of the Psychological Professions and Sciences (1971). Members are psychologists and educators. Works in close alliance with the American Psychological Ass'n. Primarily a government liaison operation. Supports Psychologists for Legislative Action Now (PLAN).
Publication:
Newsletter.
Annual Meetings: Labor Day weekend, with the American Psychological Ass'n.

Ass'n for the Advancement of Psychotherapy (1939)
114 East 78th St., New York NY 10021
President: Stanley Lesse, M.D.
Members: 400-500 *Staff:* 2-5
Annual Budget: $100-250,000 *Tel:* (212) 288-4466
Publication:
American Journal of Psychotherapy. q. adv.
Annual Meetings: Fall

Ass'n for the Anthropological Study of Play (1974)
Leisure Beh. Research Lab., Children's, Research Center, 51 East Gerty Drive, Champaign IL 61820
Secy.-Treas.: Dr. Garry Chick
Members: 240 individuals; 28 organizations
Annual Budget: under $10,000 *Tel:* (217) 333-6434
Hist. Note: TAASP's broad focus includes many disciplines and scholarly interests involved with the study of play. Membership: $15/yr.

00080 12 05 86 1233

Publications:
TAASP Newsletter. q.
TAASP Proceedings. a.
Annual Meetings: Spring/100-150
1987-Montreal, Quebec/March 25-28
1988-Berkeley, CA

Ass'n for the Bibliography of History (1978)
Department of History, Georgia State University, Atlanta GA 30303
Secy.-Treas.: Gerald H. Davis
Members: 180-200 *Staff:* 1
Annual Budget: under $10,000 *Tel:* (404) 658-3255
Hist. Note: Established in San Francisco at the 1978 annual meeting of the American Historical Association. Members are historians and librarians interested in developing better bibliographic tools and skills for historical research. Membership: $7/yr.
Publication:
ABH Newsletter. 3/yr. adv.
Annual Meetings: With the American Historical Association

Ass'n for the Care of Children's Health (1965)
3615 Wisconsin Ave., N.W., Washington DC 20016
Exec. Director: Beverley Johnson
Members: 3,900 *Staff:* 15
Annual Budget: $250-500,000 *Tel:* (202) 244-1801
Hist. Note: Pediatricians, child psychologists, child life activity specialists, nurses and others concerned with the health and well-being of children and families in health care settings. Membership: $48/yr.
Publications:
Journal of the Association for the Care of Children's Health. q. adv.
Newsletter.
Annual Meetings: Spring/1,600
1987-Halifax, Canada

Ass'n for the Coordination of University Religious Affairs (1959)
Ball State Univ., Muncie IN 47306
Secy.-Treas.: George W. Jones
Members: 70 *Staff:* 1
Annual Budget: under $10,000 *Tel:* (317) 285-1092
Hist. Note: An association of personnel involved in religious affairs at instutions of higher education. Affiliated with the Coordinating Council of Professional Religious Associations in Higher Education. Membership: $25/yr. (individual), $60/yr. (institution).
Publication:
Dialogue on Campus. q.
Annual Meetings:
1987-Nashville, TN(Vanderbilt University)/Feb. 23-25

Ass'n for the Development of Computer-Based Instructional Systems (1968)
Western Washington University, Miller Hall, Room 409, Bellingham WA 98225
Exec. Director: Gordon P. Hayes
Members: 2,400 *Staff:* 2-5
Annual Budget: $100-250,000 *Tel:* (206) 676-2860
Hist. Note: Formerly (1973) Ass'n for Development of Instructional Systems. Membership: $45/year.
Publications:
Journal of Computer-Based Instruction. q.
Newsletter. bi-m.
Conference Proceedings. a.
Annual Meetings: Fall
1987-Oakland, CA/Nov. 9-12

Ass'n for the Education of Teachers in Science (1953)
University of Tennessee, 315 Claxton Addition, Knoxville TN 37996-3400
Exec. Secretary: Jill D. Wright
Members: 600 *Staff:* 1
Annual Budget: under $10,000 *Tel:* (615) 974-0998
Hist. Note: Affiliated with the Nat'l Science Teachers Ass'n. Has no paid staff.
Publications:
AETS Newsletter. q.
Science Education. q. adv.
Annual Meetings:
1987-Washington, DC/March 26-29

Ass'n for the Gifted
Hist. Note: TAG is a division of the Council for Exceptional Children.

Ass'n for the Improvement of Teaching
Hist. Note: Address unknown in 1986.

Ass'n for the Psychophysiological Study of Sleep (1961)
Hist. Note: Became the Sleep Research Society in 1983.

Ass'n for the Sociology of Religion (1938)
Washington and Jefferson College, Washington PA 15301
Exec. Officer: Dr. Theodore E. Long
Members: 5-600 *Staff:* 3
Annual Budget: $25-50,000 *Tel:* (412) 223-6162
Hist. Note: Formerly (1971) American Catholic Sociological Soc. Has no paid staff. Membership: $20/yr. (individual), $40/yr. (company).
Publications:
Directory. bien.
News and Announcements. q.
Sociological Analysis. q.
Annual Meetings: August/over 125, prior to the American Sociological Ass'n.
1987-Chicago, IL/Aug. 14-16
1988-Atlanta, GA/Aug. 21-23
1989-San Francisco, CA/Aug. 6-8

Ass'n for the Study of Afro-American Life and History (1915)
1407 14th St., N.W., Washington DC 20005
Exec. Director: Dr. Bonnie J. Gillespie
Members: 2,200 *Staff:* 3-5
Annual Budget: $100-250,000 *Tel:* (202) 667-2822
Hist. Note: Organized by Dr. Carter G. Woodson in Chicago September 9, 1915 as the Ass'n for the Study of Negro Life and History and incorporated in the District of Columbia the same year. Assumed its present name in 1973. Promotes an appreciation of the life and history of the Afro-American, creates an understanding of his present status and works to improve his promise for the future. Membership $40/year.
Publications:
Journal of Negro History. q. adv.
The Negro History Bulletin q. adv.
Annual Meetings: October
1987-Raleigh, NC(Sheraton University Ctr.)/Oct. 9-11
1988-Chicago, IL

Ass'n for the Study of Man-Environment Relations (1969)
Box 57, Orangeburg NY 10962
President: Aristide H. Esser
Members: 200 *Staff:* 1
Annual Budget: $10-25,000 *Tel:* (914) 634-8221
Hist. Note: Founded in 1969 as an ass'n of social and behavioral scientists and design professionals. An affiliate of the American Ass'n for the Advancement of Science.
Publication:
Man-Environment Systems. bi-m. adv.
Annual Meetings: With American Ass'n for the Advancement of Science

Ass'n for Tropical Biology (1961)
Missouri Botanical Garden, P.O. Box 299, St. Louis MO 63166
Secy.-Treas.: Dr. Elsa Zardini
Members: 1,400 individuals; 600 libraries *Staff:* 3
Annual Budget: $50-100,000 *Tel:* (314) 577-5171
Hist. Note: Membership: $18-24/yr. (individual), $40/yr. (institution).
Publication:
Biotropica. q.
Annual Meetings: August with AIBS.

Ass'n for University Business and Economic Research (1947)
College of Commerce and Business Admin.,Univ. of Alabama, Box AK, Tuscaloosa AL 35487
1st. V. President: Carl E. Ferguson, Jr.
Members: 164
Annual Budget: $10-25,000 *Tel:* (205) 348-6191
Hist. Note: Members are business and economic research centers in universities and colleges. Organized in January 1947 in Atlantic City as the Associated University Bureaus of Business and Economic Research at a meeting of the American Statistical Association, the American Economic Association and other related groups. Name changed to its present form in 1970.
Publications:
AUBER Bibliography. a. adv.
Directory. a.
Semi-annual Meetings: Spring in Washington, DC and Fall
1987-San Francisco, CA/Fall

Ass'n for Unmanned Vehicle Systems (1972)
1133 15th St., N.W., suite 620, Washington DC 20005
Exec. Director: John H. Ganoe
Members: 1,400-1,450 *Staff:* 1
Annual Budget: $50-100,000 *Tel:* (202) 293-5910
Hist. Note: Established in Dayton, Ohio as the National Association for Remotely Piloted Vehicles, it assumed its present name in 1977. Members are companies and individuals concerned with the development and manufacture of space vehicles, weapons systems, guidance controls, etc. Membership: $15/year (individual), $200-500/year (business), $100/year (educational institution).
Publications:
News Bulletin. q.
Unmanned Systems. bi-m. adv.
Annual Meetings: Early summer.
1987-Washington, DC/July

Ass'n for Vital Records and Health Statistics (1933)
Box 95007, Lincoln NE 68509
Secretary: Mary Lou Eastman
Members: 200-250 *Staff:* 1
Annual Budget: under $10,000 *Tel:* (402) 471-2241
Hist. Note: Organized in 1933 as the American Ass'n of Registration Executives. Became American Ass'n for Vital Records and Public Health Statistics in 1958; assumed its present name in 1980.
Publication:
AVRHS Journal. bi-m.
Annual Meetings: Summer

Ass'n for Volunteer Administration (1960)
Box 4584, Boulder CO 80306
Director: Jacqueline Callahan
Members: 1,400 *Staff:* 2
Annual Budget: $25-50,000 *Tel:* (303) 497-0238
Hist. Note: Formerly (1981) American Association of Volunteer Services Coordinators. Regular Membership: $75/yr.
Publications:
Newsletter. bi-m.
The Journal of Volunteer Administration. q.
Annual Meetings: October
1987-Chicago, IL/Oct. 8-11

Ass'n for Women Geoscientists (1977)
Box 1005, Menlo Park CA 94026
President: Carol Dickerson
Members: 1,000 *Staff:* 1
Annual Budget: $50-100,000 *Tel:* (415) 231-1248
Hist. Note: Established in 1977 in San Francisco as the Ass'n of Women Geoscientists, AWG assumed its present name in 1982 and was incorporated in California in 1983. A member society of the American Geological Institute. Has no paid staff or permanent address beyond the above. Officers change annually. Membership: $25/yr.
Publication:
Gaea Newsletter. bi-m. adv.
Annual Meetings:
1987-San Franciso, CA/Spring/200

Ass'n for Women in Computing (1978)
1133 15th St., N.W., Suite 620, Washington DC 20005
Association Administrator: Phyllis Call
Members: 1,000 individuals, 17 chapters *Staff:* 1
Annual Budget: $25-50,000 *Tel:* (202) 293-5910
Hist. Note: Has no paid staff, permanent headquarters or phone. Membership: $30/year (individual).
Publications:
AWC Source. bi-m. adv.
Conference Proceedings. a.

Ass'n for Women in Mathematics (1971)
Box 178, Wellesley College, Wellesley MA 02181
Admin. Assistant: Margaret T. Munroe
Members: 1,600 *Staff:* 1
Annual Budget: under $10,000 *Tel:* (617) 235-0320
Hist. Note: Formerly (1973) Ass'n of Women Mathematicians. Membership: $15/year.
Publication:
AWM Newsletter. bi-m. adv.
Semi-annual meetings: With the American Mathematical Soc. and the
Mathematical Association of America

Ass'n for Women in Psychology (1969)
666 Pelham Road, #2G, New Rochelle NY 10805
Spokesperson: Joan C. Chrisler, Ph.D.
Members: 2,000
Hist. Note: Formerly (1970) Ass'n for Women Psychologists. Major objectives are to promote unbiased scientific research on gender in order to establish fact and eliminate myths and assumptions about the "natures" of women and men, and to gain equality of opportunity with men in the profession. Membership: $7.50-50/year (individual).
Publication:
AWP Newsletter. q. adv.
Annual Meetings: March
1987-Denver, CO/March 5-8

Ass'n for Women in Science (1971)
2401 Virginia Ave., N.W., Suite 303, Washington DC 20037
Exec. Director: Diana M. Tycer
Members: 3,200 individuals *Staff:* 3
Annual Budget: $50-100,000 *Tel:* (202) 833-1998
Hist. Note: Founded in April, 1971 in Chicago. Affiliated with the Federation of Organizations for Professional Women, the American Ass'n for the Advancement of Science, and the Nat'l Coalition for Women and Girls in Education. Membership: $10-50/year (varies with income).
Publications:
Newsletter. bi-m. adv.
AWIS Job Bulletin. m.
AWIS Legislative Update. bi-m.
Annual Meetings: With the American Ass'n for the Advancement of Science

Ass'n for Women Veterinarians (1947)
P.O. Box 1051, Littleton CO 80523
Secretary: Dr. Lynn C. Anderson
Members: 600
Annual Budget: under $10,000
Hist. Note: Founded as the Women's Veterinary Ass'n, it became the Women's Veterinary Medical Ass'n in 1950 and assumed its present name in 1980. Membership: $25/yr.
Publication:
AWV Bulletin. q. adv.
Annual Meetings: With the American Veterinary Medical Ass'n

Ass'n of Academic Health Centers (1971)
11 Dupont Circle, N.W., Suite 210, Washington DC 20036
President: John R. Hogness, M.D.
Members: 100 centers *Staff:* 5
Annual Budget: $500-1,000,000 *Tel:* (202) 265-9600
Hist. Note: Founded in 1968 and incorporated in Indiana as the Organization of University Health Center Administrators and assumed its present name in 1971.
Semi-annual Meetings: Spring and Fall.

00081 12 05 86 1233

Ass'n of Academic Health Sciences Library Directors (1978)
Basic Med. Sci. Lib., NE Ohio University,ollege of Medicine, State Route 44, Rootstown OH 44272
Secy.-Treas.: Karen L. Brewer
Members: 120-130 institutions
Annual Budget: $25-50,000 *Tel:* (216) 325-2511
Hist. Note: Formed to provide a medium for communication among academic health sciences library directors for addressing common concerns on planning, program and policy developments; to extend contacts nationally to provide a forum for joint action. Compiles statistics on medical school libraries in the U.S. and Canada annually. Membership: $300/yr.
Publications:
AAHSLD News. q.
Annual Report. a.
Annual Meetings: Fall
1987-Washington, DC/Nov. 10-17
1988-Chicago, IL/Nov. 12-17

Ass'n of Academic Physiatrists (1967)
8000 Five Mile Road, Suite 340, Cincinnati OH 45230
Exec. Director: Carolyn L. Braddom, M.A.
Members: 500 *Staff:* 2
Annual Budget: $50-100,000 *Tel:* (513) 232-8833
Hist. Note: Members are academic physicians specializing in physical medicine and rehabilitation. Affiliated with the Association of American Medical Colleges. Membership: $78/yr.
Publications:
Directory. a.
Newsletter. a.
Semi-annual meetings: Spring and Fall/50-100
1987-San Diego, CA(Sheraton Harbor Island)/Feb. 19-22/100
1987-Toronto, Canada(Sheraton)/April 15-18

Ass'n of Accounting Administrators (1983)
Box 11000, Washington DC 20008
Exec. Director: Clifford M. Brownstein
Members: 350 individuals *Staff:* 3
Annual Budget: $100-250,000 *Tel:* (202) 537-1220
Hist. Note: Members are accounting administrators, office managers and administrative partners in accounting firms and corporate accounting departments. Membership: $150/year (individual), $300-800/year (organization).
Publications:
AAA Report. q. adv.
Membership Directory. a.
Annual Meetings: Spring
1987-Denver, CO/June 18-19

Ass'n of Administrative Law Judges (1960)
Room 2646, Kluczynski Bldg., 230 South Dearborn St., Chicago IL 60604
Registered Agent: Judge Francis O'Byrne
Members: 475-500 *Staff:* 1
Annual Budget: $25-50,000 *Tel:* (312) 886-5538
Hist. Note: Incorporated in the State of Illinois in 1980, members are employees of the Health and Human Services Department of the U.S. Government. Officers are elected annually. Membership: $104/yr.
Publication:
AALJ Newsletter. bi-m.

Ass'n of Administrators of the Interstate Compact on the Placement of Children (1969)
1125 15th St., N.W., Suite 300, Washington DC 20005
Project Manager: Betsey Rosenbaum
Members: 49 state and the Virgin Islands
Tel: (202) 293-7550
Hist. Note: A constituent unit of the American Public Welfare Ass'n. Members are state administrators of the uniform law for the placement of children across state lines.

Ass'n of Advanced Rabbinical and Talmudic Schools (1971)
175 Fifth Ave., New York NY 10010
Exec. Director: Bernard Fryshman, Ph.D.
Members: 57 institutions *Staff:* 3
Annual Budget: $100-250,000 *Tel:* (212) 477-0950
Hist. Note: Formerly (1971) the Council of Roshei Yeshivas.

Ass'n of Advertising Lawyers (1977)
Hist. Note: Ceased operations in 1985.

Ass'n of Agricultural Computer Companies (1984)
120 North Harrison, Alexandria IN 46001
Secy.-Treas.: Kurt Harter
Members: 140 companies; 160 individuals
Annual Budget: $10-25,000 *Tel:* (317) 843-2441
Hist. Note: Active membership is open to representatives of any company engaged in the manufacture, marketing and/or distribution of computer hardware, software, peripheral equipment and support services in agriculture.. Membership: $120/yr.
Publication:
AACC Newsletter. q.
Annual Meetings: December

Ass'n of Allergists for Mycological Investigations (1938)
Hist. Note: No paid staff; address unknown in 1986.

Ass'n of American Air Travel Clubs (1970)
700 Diplomat Pkwy., Hallandale FL 33009
Exec. Director: John F. Monahan
Members: 6-10 *Staff:* 2-5
Annual Budget: under $10,000 *Tel:* (305) 944-3100
Hist. Note: Air travel clubs and industry suppliers recommending federal guidelines for regulation of air travel.
Annual Meetings: Winter

Ass'n of American CIRP Industrial Sponsors (1975)
Hist. Note: Reported defunct in 1983.

Ass'n of American Colleges (1915)
1818 R St., N.W., Washington DC 20009
President: John W. Chandler
Members: 590 institutions *Staff:* 30-35
Annual Budget: $1-2,000,000 *Tel:* (202) 387-3760
Hist. Note: AAC, through grants and publications, promotes liberal education and its inclusion in preprofessional programs in colleges and universities. Members are public and private, two- and four-year colleges and universities. The Council for Liberal Learning (founded 1985) is an individual membership organization within AAC which conducts public relations and lobbying efforts. Membership fee based on sliding scale.
Publication:
Liberal Education. 5/yr.
Annual Meetings: Winter/900
1987-Washington, DC(JW Marriott)/Jan. 15-17
1988-Washington, DC/Jan. 14-16

Ass'n of American Dentists (1962)
Hist. Note: Not a professional society or affiliated with the American Dental Association. Based in Dallas, Texas, the members constitute a study group meeting annually to consider the tax aspects of their work and to perform "research in money" and "the philosophy and economics of the private practice of dentistry." Membership is not divulged but in 1982 was probably less than 100.

Ass'n of American Editorial Cartoonists (1957)
c/o Rocky Mountain News, 400 West Colfax, Denver CO 80204
Secy.-Treas.: Ed Stein
Members: 300 *Staff:* 1
Annual Budget: under $10,000 *Tel:* (501) 741-8747
Publications:
AAEC Notebook. q.
Membership Directory. bien.
Annual Meetings: May or June/150

Ass'n of American Feed Control Officials (1909)
Box 3160, College Station TX 77841
Secretary: Barbara J. Sims
Members: 300-350
Annual Budget: $10-25,000 *Tel:* (409) 845-1121
Hist. Note: Officials of government agencies at the State, Provincial, Dominion and Federal levels engaged in the regulation of production, analysis, labeling, distribution and sale of animal feeds and livestock remedies.
Publication:
Official Publication. a.
Annual Meetings:
1987-Oklahoma City, OK
1988-Portland, ME
1989-San Antonio, TX

Ass'n of American Geographers (1904)
1710 16th St., N. W., Washington DC 20009
Exec. Director: Dr. Robert T. Aangeenbrug
Members: 5,500 *Staff:* 6-10
Annual Budget: $500-1,000,000 *Tel:* (202) 234-1450
Hist. Note: Founded in Philadelphia in 1904 at a meeting of the American Ass'n for the Advancement of Science and incorporated in the District of Columbia in 1937. Merged in 1948 with the American Soc. of Professional Geographers. A member of the American Council of Learned Societies. Membership: $65/yr.
Publications:
Annals. q. adv.
The Professional Geographer. q. adv.
Annual Meetings: Spring/2,300
1987-Portland, OR(Hilton & Marriott)/April 22-26
1988-Phoenix, AZ(Hilton & Hyatt)/April 7-10

Ass'n of American Law Schools (1900)
One Dupont Circle, N.W., Suite 370, Washington DC 20036
Exec. Director: Millard H. Ruud
Members: 151 institutions *Staff:* 10
Annual Budget: $500-1,000,000 *Tel:* (202) 296-8851
Hist. Note: Organized in Saratoga Springs, New York on August 29, 1900 with thirty-two schools as charter members. Incorporated in the District of Columbia in 1971.
Publications:
AALS Newsletter. q.
Directory of Law Teachers. a.
Journal of Legal Education. q.
Placement Bulletin. bi-m.
Proceedings. a.
Annual Meetings: January/2,000
1987-Los Angeles, CA

Ass'n of American Library Schools (1915)
Hist. Note: Became the Association for Library and Information Science Education in 1983.

Ass'n of American Medical Colleges (1876)
One Dupont Circle, N.W., Washington DC 20036
President: Dr. Robert G. Petersdorf
Members: 127 schools, 76 societies, 432 hospitals *Staff:* 165
Annual Budget: over $5,000,000 *Tel:* (202) 828-0400
Hist. Note: Seeks the advancement of medical education, biomedical research and the nation's health.
Publication:
Journal of Medical Education. m. adv.
Annual Meetings: Fall
1987-Washington, DC(Washington Hilton)/Nov. 7-12

Ass'n of American Pesticide Control Officials (1947)
2004 Le Suer Road, Richmond VA 23229
Secretary: Harry Rust
Members: 50-60 *Staff:* 1
Annual Budget: $10-25,000 *Tel:* (804) 288-8181
Hist. Note: An association comprised of state, municipal and federal officials dedicated to a uniform approach throughout North America to the enforcement of laws relating to proper and safe use of pesticide chemicals. Formerly Ass'n of Economic Poisons Control Officials.
Annual Meetings: August.
1987-Oklahoma, OK
1988-Maui, HI

Ass'n of American Physicians (1886)
Washington University Medical School, St. Louis MO 63110
Secretary: Dr. Stuart Kornfeld
Members: 900-1000 *Staff:* 1
Annual Budget: $10-25,000 *Tel:* (314) 362-8803
Hist. Note: Members are medical school professors. Membership: $75/yr.
Publication:
Transactions of the Association of American Physicians. a.
Annual Meetings: Spring/4,500
1987-San Diego, CA(Town & Country)/May 1-4
1988-Washington, DC(Sheraton)/April 29-May 2

Ass'n of American Physicians and Surgeons (1943)
5201 Lyngate Court, Burke VA 22015
Exec. Secretary: E. Sue Ackley
Members: 5,000 *Staff:* 2-5
Annual Budget: $100-250,000 *Tel:* (703) 425-6300
Hist. Note: Represents physicians in the socio-economic aspects of medical practice. Supports the Ass'n of American Physicians and Surgeons Political Action Committee.
Publication:
Newsletter. m.
Annual Meetings: Fall
1987-New Orleans, LA/Oct. 8-10

Ass'n of American Plant Food Control Officials (1946)
Div. of Reg. Services, Univ. of Kentucky, Lexington KY 40546
Secretary: D. L. Terry
Members: 175-200 *Staff:* 1
Annual Budget: under $10,000 *Tel:* (606) 257-2668
Hist. Note: Formerly (1970) Ass'n of American Fertilizer Control Officials.
Publication:
Official Publication of AAPFCO. a.
Annual Meetings: August
1987-Oklahoma
1988-Maine
1989-San Antonio, TX
1990-Greensboro, NC

Ass'n of American Publishers (1970)
220 East 23rd St., New York NY 10010
President: Nicholas Veliotes
Members: 340 companies *Staff:* 35
Annual Budget: $2-5,000,000 *Tel:* (212) 689-8920
Hist. Note: Formed by a merger of the American Educational Publishers Institute (founded in 1942 and formerly known as the American Textbook Publishers Institute) and the American Book Publishers Council (founded in 1946 and which included the former Technical, Scientific and Medical Book Publishers). The voice of the American publishing industry. Connected with the American Book Publishers Political Action Committee. Maintains a Washington office.
Publication:
AAP Newsletter. adv.
Annual Meetings: Spring

Ass'n of American Railroads (1872)
50 F St., N.W., Washington DC 20001
President: William H. Dempsey
Members: 243 railroads *Staff:* 825
Annual Budget: over $5,000,000 *Tel:* (202) 635-2100
Hist. Note: Formed to arrange summer passenger train schedules; the Time-Table Convention then formed became sucessively the General Time Convention, the American Railway Ass'n and, finally, in 1934 the Ass'n of American Railroads. This was the result of a merger with the Ass'n of Railway Executives, the Railway Accounting Officers Ass'n, the Railway Treasury Officers Ass'n and the Bureau of Railway Economics. Maintains a Hazardous Materials division, formerly the Bureau of Explosives. Also maintains a 36-mile test track in Pueblo, CO. Membership: $1,350/yr. (organization/company)

00082 12 05 86 1233

Ass'n of American Seed Control Officials (1956)
Utah Department of Agriculture, 350 North Redwwod Road, Salt Lake City UT 84116
Secy.-Treas.: Richard Wilson
Members: 52 individuals *Staff:* 1
Annual Budget: under $10,000 *Tel:* (801) 533-4129
Hist. Note: U.S. and Canadian officials who administer state/provincial seed regulations. One member from each state, one from Canada and one from the U.S. Dept. of Agriculture. Has no paid staff.
Annual Meetings:
1987-Virginia
1988-California
1989-New York
1990-Nebraska

Ass'n of American State Geologists (1906)
c/o American Geological Institute, 4220 King St., Alexandria VA 22302
Secy.-Treas.: R. Thomas Segall
Members: 49
Annual Budget: under $10,000 *Tel:* (703) 379-2480
Hist. Note: Founded in 1906 as the Ass'n of State Geologists of the Mississippi Valley; assumed its present name May 12, 1908 in the District of Columbia. A member of the American Geological Institute, which provides administrative support. Members of the association are chief executives of State Geological Surveys.
Publication:
The State Geologists Journal. a.
Annual Meetings: June

Ass'n of American Universities (1900)
One Dupont Circle, N.W., Suite 730, Washington DC 20036
President: Robert M. Rosenzweig
Members: 56 *Staff:* 16-20
Annual Budget: $500-1,000,000 *Tel:* (202) 466-5030
Hist. Note: Members are chief executives of major research universities. Affiliated with the Association of Graduate Schools.
Semi-annual meetings: Spring and Fall

Ass'n of American University Presses (1937)
One Park Ave., Room 1103, New York NY 10016
Exec. Director: Frances Gendlin
Members: 98 presses *Staff:* 20
Annual Budget: $100-250,000 *Tel:* (212) 889-6040
Hist. Note: Operates marketing and management subsidiary, American University Press Services, Inc., with which it shares headquarters.
Publication:
Directory. a.
Annual Meetings: June

Ass'n of American Veterinary Medical Colleges (1948)
1522 K St., N.W., Suite 834, Washington DC 20005
Exec. Director: B.E. Hooper, D.V.M.
Members: 40 institutions *Staff:* 2
Annual Budget: $100-250,000 *Tel:* (202) 371-9195
Hist. Note: In 1984 the association bylaws were amended to provide for only institutional membership. Membership: $5,000/yr.
Publication:
Journal of Veterinary Medical Education. 2/yr.
Annual Meetings: July/500
1987-Chicago,IL/July 20-23
1988-Portland,OR/July 18-21
1989-Orlando,FL/July 17-20
1990-San Antonio,TX/July 22-26
1991-Seattle, WA/July 28-Aug. 1

Ass'n of American Vintners (1978)
Box 84, Watkins Glen NY 14891
Admin. Director: J. William Moffett
Members: 90-100 *Staff:* 1
Annual Budget: $25-50,000 *Tel:* (607) 535-4144
Hist. Note: Members are wine producers.
Annual Meetings: First week in February

Ass'n of American Woodpulp Importers (1911)
100 Park Ave., New York NY 10017
Secretary: William L. Weidenfeller
Members: 28 companies *Staff:* 1
Annual Budget: under $10,000 *Tel:* (212) 532-7300
Hist. Note: Representatives, mainly in the New York area, of U.S., Canadian and Scandinavian companies bringing woodpulp into the United States. Has no paid staff or permanent address; officers change biannually.

Ass'n of Appliance and Home Entertainment Distrbutors (1980)
Hist. Note: Ceased operations in 1983.

Ass'n of Applied Insect Ecologists (1966)
Box 254, Bakersfield CA 93302-0254
Exec. Director: John F. Plain
Members: 250-275 *Staff:* 1
Annual Budget: $10-25,000 *Tel:* (805) 324-0932
Hist. Note: Members are specialists in agricultural pest control.
Publications:
AAIE Bulletin. q. adv.
AAIE Conference Abstracts. a. adv.
Annual Meetings: Winter/300-400
1987-Indian Wells, CA(Erawan Garden Hotel)/Feb. 2-4
1988-Napa Valley, CA/Feb.

Ass'n of Architectural Librarians (1974)
1735 New York Ave., N.W., Washington DC 20006
Secretary: Stephanie C. Byrnes
Members: 300 *Staff:* 1
Annual Budget: under $10,000 *Tel:* (202) 626-7494
Hist. Note: An informal organization without officers, dues, or paid staff, which has been loosely administered since its birth by the library of the American Institute of Architects.
Publication:
Newsletter. q.

Ass'n of Area Business Publications (1979)
202 Legion Ave., Annapolis MD 21401
Exec. Director: Lewis M. Conn
Members: 93 *Staff:* 2
Annual Budget: $100-250,000 *Tel:* (301) 263-0015
Hist. Note: Members are local and regional business papers. AABP provides a forum for local business papers to cooperate and exchange information and promotes these papers in the national business community. Membership: $500-2,100/yr.
Publications:
Newsletter. q. adv.
Membership Directory. a.
Semi-annual Meetings: Winter and Summer
1987-Puerto Vallarta, Mexico/Jan. and San Francisco, CA/June

Ass'n of Art Museum Directors (1916)
615 Belmont St., Room 101, Montreal Quebec H3B 2L8
Administrator: Millicent Hall Gaudieri
Members: 150-175 *Staff:* 1
Annual Budget: $50-100,000 *Tel:* (514) 875-4598
Hist. Note: Membership: $500/yr.
Semi-annual Meetings: January and June
1987-Houston, TX(Jan.) and Boston, MA(June)

Ass'n of Artist-Run Galleries (1974)
164 Mercer St., New York NY 10012
Program Director: Dennis Corbett
Members: 20-30 galleries *Staff:* 1
Annual Budget: $10-25,000 *Tel:* (212) 226-3107
Hist. Note: Essentially a service organization for alternative cooperative non-profit galleries, membership in the AARG is available to individual members of artist-run galleries. Membership: $15/yr.
Annual Meetings: Exhibitions throughout the year

Ass'n of Asbestos Cement Pipe Producers (1972)
1600 Wilson Blvd., Suite 1008, Arlington VA 22209
President: Joseph C. Jackson
Members: 29 companies *Staff:* 1
Annual Budget: $250-500,000 *Tel:* (703) 841-1556
Hist. Note: An international association incorporated in Pennsylvania in 1972. Also known as the A/C Pipe Producers Ass'n. Represents international manufacturers of asbestos-cement pipes for use in water, sewage and irrigation systems.
Publications:
A/C Advisory. m.
Special Reports. q.
Annual Meetings: April

Ass'n of Asian-American Chambers of Commerce (1965)
Hist. Note: Became inactive in 1983.

Ass'n of Asphalt Paving Technologists (1926)
Univ. of Minnesota, 134 CME Building, 500 Pillsbury Drive, S.E. Minneapolis MN 55455-0220
Secy.-Treas.: Eugene L. Skok, Jr.
Members: 800 *Staff:* 1
Annual Budget: $50-100,000 *Tel:* (612) 635-8062
Hist. Note: Formed in Chicago in 1926 with 19 charter members and incorporated in Minnesota in 1969. Membership: $60/yr.
Publication:
Asphalt Paving Technology. a.
Annual Meetings: February
1987-Reno, NV/Feb. 16-18
1988-Williamsburg, VA/Feb. 29-March 2
1989-Nashville, TN/Feb. 20-22

Ass'n of Audio-Visual Technicians (1975)
Box 9716, Denver CO 80209
Exec. Director: Elsa C. Kaiser
Members: 1,200 *Staff:* 2-5
Annual Budget: $25-50,000 *Tel:* (303) 698-1820
Hist. Note: Members are U.S. and foreign audio-visual technicians in schools, industry and service shops. Membership: $35/yr. (individual); $65/yr. (company).
Publication:
Fast Foreward. m. adv.
Annual Meetings: In conjunction with COMMTEX

Ass'n of Average Adjusters of the U.S. (1879)
101 Murray St., New York NY 10007
Secretary: Frank Hourigan
Members: 900 *Staff:* 2-5
Annual Budget: $10-25,000 *Tel:* (212) 962-4111
Hist. Note: Marine insurance adjusters and ship and cargo appraisers. Membership principally in New York area.
Annual Meetings: October, in New York, NY

Ass'n of Aviation and Space Museums (1980)
Hist. Note: Reported inactive in 1985.

Ass'n of Bank Holding Companies (1958)
730 15th St., N.W., Washington DC 20005
President: Donald L. Rogers
Members: 145 *Staff:* 9
Annual Budget: $1-2,000,000 *Tel:* (202) 393-1158
Hist. Note: Membership consists of companies registered with the Federal Reserve Board under the Bank Holding Company Act of 1956. Formerly (1975) Ass'n of Registered Bank Holding Companies.
Publication:
Bank Holding Company Facts. a.
Annual Meetings: Spring/300
1987-Boston, MA(Copley Hyatt)/May 20-22
1988-Colorado Springs, CO(Broadmoor)/May 25-27

Ass'n of Baptist Professors of Religion
Hist. Note: Became the Nat'l Ass'n of Baptist Professors of Religion in 1983.

Ass'n of Bedding and Furniture Law Officials
Texas Dept. of Health, Product Safety, Division, 1100 West 49th St., Austin TX 78756
Secy.-Treas.: Mackie Lawrence
Members: 35-40
Annual Budget: under $10,000 *Tel:* (512) 458-7519
Hist. Note: Organized to secure the adoption of uniform bedding and upholstery laws; members supervise the inspection of bedding materials and upholstered furniture at the state and local levels. Has no permanent staff or address. Membership: $45/yr.
Annual Meetings: Spring
1987-New Orleans, LA(International Hotel)/March 18-22/25

Ass'n of Better Computer Dealers (1982)
Hist. Note: Name changed to ABCD: The Microcomputer Industry Ass'n in 1986.

Ass'n of Biomedical Communications Directors (1973)
Louisiana State Univ. Medical Center, Shreveport LA 71130
Secretary: Dennis Pernotto
Members: 80-90 *Staff:* 1
Annual Budget: $10-25,000 *Tel:* (318) 674-5260
Hist. Note: Members are directors of bio-medical communications units in teaching instutitions. Membership: $50/year.
Publications:
ABCD Exchange. q. adv.
The Journal of Biocommunication. q. adv.
Joint Membership Directory. a. adv.
Annual Meetings: Summer
1987-Seattle, WA(Rosario Resort)/June 14-17/60

Ass'n of Biotechnology Companies (1983)
1220 L St., N.W., Suite 615, Washington DC 20005
Managing Director: Warren C. Hyer, Jr.
Members: 165 *Staff:* 5
Annual Budget: $100-250,000 *Tel:* (202) 842-2229
Hist. Note: ABC is an international trade association composed of firms involved in the use of recombinant DNA, hybridoma and immunological technologies in a wide range of applications including human health care, animal husbandry, agriculture and specialty chemical production. Membership is presently concentrated in North America. Membership: $875/yr.
Publication:
ABC Dialogue. m.
Annual Meetings:
1987-Washington, DC

Ass'n of Bituminous Contractors (1968)
2020 K Street, N.W., Suite 800, Washington DC 20006
Secretary and General Counsel: William H. Howe
Members: 350 *Staff:* 1
Annual Budget: $100-250,000 *Tel:* (202) 785-4440
Hist. Note: General and independent contractors constructing coal mines and coal mine facilities. Bargains with the United Mine Workers. The above address is the law firm of Loomis, Owen, Fellman and Howe.
Publication:
Update Newsletter. q.
Annual Meetings: March

Ass'n of Black CPA Firms
Hist. Note: Address unknown in 1986; probably defunct.

Ass'n of Black Psychologists (1968)
P.O. Box 55999, Washington DC 20040-5999
National Office Manager: Dr. Ruth G. King
Members: 600-700 individuals *Staff:* 2-5
Annual Budget: $50-100,000 *Tel:* (202) 722-0808
Hist. Note: An organization of black psychologists, organized at the 1968 San Francisco meeting of the American Psychological Association. Membership: $90/yr. (individual); $200/yr. (company).
Publications:
Journal of Black Psychology. semi-a.
Newsletter. bi-m. adv.
Annual Meetings: August
1987-Atlanta, GA(Downtown Hilton)/Aug. 12-16/500-700
1988-Washington, DC/Aug. 10-14/500-800

00083 12 05 86 1233

Ass'n of Black Sociologists (1970)
c/o Dept. of Sociology, University of Michigan, Ann Arbor MI 48109
President: Prof. Aldon Morris
Members: 200-225
Annual Budget: under $10,000 *Tel:* (313) 764-5561
Hist. Note: Affiliated with the American Sociological Ass'n. Formerly (1977) Caucus of Black Sociologists.
Publication:
The Black Sociologist. semi-a.
Annual Meetings: Last week in August

Ass'n of Bone and Joint Surgeons (1947)
222 South Prospect, Suite 127, Park Ridge IL 60068
Exec. Director: Carole Murphy
Members: 210 *Staff:* 1
Annual Budget: $25-50,000 *Tel:* (312) 823-7186
Hist. Note: Founded in Oklahoma City in April 1949 and incorporated the same year in Oklahoma.
Publication:
Clinical Orthopaedics and Related Research. m.
Annual Meetings: Summer

Ass'n of Brass and Bronze Ingot Manufacturers (1950)
Bay State Refining Co., Box 269, Chicopee MA 01021
President: Paul Rothery
Members: 13 companies *Staff:* 1
Annual Budget: under $10,000 *Tel:* (413) 594-4736
Hist. Note: Has no paid staff or permanent office; officers change annually.

Ass'n of Bridal Consultants (1981)
200 Chestnutland Road, New Milford CT 06776-2521
President: Gerard J. Monaghan
Members: 190 companies and individuals *Staff:* 2
Annual Budget: $10-25,000 *Tel:* (203) 355-0464
Hist. Note: Composed of independent consultants as well as owners of wedding- related businesses. Formed from the defunct American Ass'n of Professional Bridal Consultants which was established in 1955. Membership: $100/yr.
Publication:
Newsletter. bi-m. adv.
Annual Meetings:
1987-San Francisco, CA

Ass'n of Business and Professional Women in Construction
Hist. Note: Became Professional Women in Construction in 1982.

Ass'n of Business Officers of Preparatory Schools (1924)
Kent School, Kent CT 06757
President: Richard Lindsey
Members: 36
Annual Budget: under $10,000 *Tel:* (203) 927-3501
Hist. Note: Membership is limited to non-military, independent secondary boarding schools whose enrollment of students is more than one-half boarding; and whose business management is of sufficient importance to demand the services at the school of an officer whose time is largely devoted to this purpose. Has no permanent office or paid staff.

Ass'n of Business Publishers (1906)
205 East 42nd St., New York NY 10017
Exec. Director: William G. O'Donnell
Members: 118 companies, 618 publications *Staff:* 14-16
Annual Budget: $2-5,000,000 *Tel:* (212) 661-6360
Hist. Note: Formed by a merger of Associated Business Publications (founded in 1906) and National Business Publications (founded in 1948). Formerly American Business Press, the Association assumed its present name in 1985. Supports the Specialized Periodical Action Committee. Members are specialized business magazines with audited circulation.
Annual Meetings: Spring/350
1987-Wesley Chapel, FL(Saddlebrook Resort)/May 3-6
1988-Boca Raton, FL(Boca Raton Hotel & Club)/April 17-20

Ass'n of Buying Offices (1933)
Hist. Note: Dissolved in 1984.

Ass'n of Catholic Colleges and Universities (1899)
One Dupont Circle, N.W., Suite 650, Washington DC 20036
Exec. Director: Sr. Alice Gallin
Members: 215 *Staff:* 4
Annual Budget: $250-500,000 *Tel:* (202) 457-0650
Hist. Note: Founded in 1899, ACCU in 1904 became the College and University Department of the Nat'l Catholic Education Ass'n. Although still a department of that latter organization, it reassumed its former name in 1978.
Publications:
Current Issues in Catholic Higher Education. semi-a.
Update. bi-m.
Annual Meetings: January-February in Washington, DC at the Hyatt Regency/250

Ass'n of Catholic TV and Radio Syndicators (1975)
12 East 48th St., New York NY 10017
V. President/Treasurer: Mary Jane Hopkins
Members: 40 companies
Annual Budget: under $10,000 *Tel:* (212) 759-4050
Hist. Note: Affiliated with UNDA-USA, the U.S. arm of the international association of Catholic broadcasters. Members are producers and syndicators of Catholic radio and television programs. Has no paid staff.

Ass'n of Chairmen of Departments of Mechanics (1970)
Th. & Appl. Mechanics, Thurston Hall, Cornell University, Ithaca NY 14853
President: F. Moon
Members: 100-125 institutions *Staff:* 1
Annual Budget: under $10,000 *Tel:* (607) 256-5062
Hist. Note: Has no paid staff or permanent headquarters.
Semi-Annual Meetings:

Ass'n of Choral Conductors (1959)
Hist. Note: Absorbed by the American Choral Foundation in 1985.

Ass'n of Christian Librarians (1957)
Box 4, Cedarville OH 45314
Treasurer: Steve Brown
Members: 300
Annual Budget: under $10,000 *Tel:* (513) 766-2211
Hist. Note: Membership composed of evangelical Christian librarians representing primarily evangelical institutions of higher education and other interested individuals who subscribe to the purposes and position of the association. ACL seeks to bring together Christian librarians from evangelical institutions of higher education for fellowship and professional advancement; to define standards and improve practices. Formerly (1981) Christian Librarians Fellowship.
Publications:
Christian Librarian. q.
Christian Periodical Index. 3/yr.
Annual Meetings: June
1987-Upland, IN(Taylor University)

Ass'n of Christian Schools Internat'l (1978)
731 Beech Blvd., La Habra CA 90631
Exec. Director: Dr. Paul A. Kienel
Members: 2,500 *Staff:* 55
Annual Budget: $2-5,000,000 *Tel:* (213) 694-4791
Hist. Note: Privately funded schools with a religious orientation emphasizing a "back to basics" curriculum. The result of a merger on July 1, 1978 of the Western Ass'n of Christian Schools, the Ohio Ass'n of Christian Schools and the Nat'l Christian School Education Ass'n.
Publications:
Christian School Comment. m.
Christian School Journal. q.
Annual Meetings: Late fall

Ass'n of Cinema and Video Laboratories (1953)
P.O. Box 1758, Memphis TN 38101-1758
Contact: Martha Barnett
Members: 100 *Staff:* 1
Annual Budget: $25-50,000 *Tel:* (901) 774-4944
Hist. Note: The ACVL provides an opportunity for the discussion and exchange of ideas in connection with the technical, administrative and managerial problems of the motion-picture and video laboratory industry. The Association is concerned with government relations, public and industry relations, product specifications, improvements of technical practices and procedures and other interest areas for film and video laboratories. Formerly Association of Cinema Laboratories.
Publication:
Handbook.

Ass'n of Civilian Technicians (1960)
932 Hungerford Drive, Suite 34A, Rockville MD 20850
President: John T. Hunter
Members: 8,500 *Staff:* 6-10
Annual Budget: $250-500,000 *Tel:* (301) 762-5656
Hist. Note: Union of civilian employees of the Army and Air National Guard and Army and Air Reserve civilian employees. Sponsors and supports the Ass'n of Civilian Technicians Political Action Committee.
Publication:
The Technician. bi-m.
Semi-annual meetings: Spring and Fall

Ass'n of Clinical Scientists (1949)
University of Connecticut Medical School,63 Farmington Ave., Farmington CT 06032
Secy.-Treas.: F. William Sunderman, Jr. M.D.
Members: 760 individuals *Staff:* 1
Annual Budget: $25-50,000 *Tel:* (203) 674-2328
Hist. Note: Organized as the Clinical Science Club in 1949. Became Ass'n of Clinical Scientists in 1956. Chartered by the State of Pennsylvania as a nonprofit scientific organization in 1957. Affiliated with the American Ass'n for the Advancement of Science.
Publications:
Annals of Clinical and Laboratory Science. bi-m. adv.
Proceedings. a.
Annual Meetings: Fall
1987-Charleston, SC(Charleston Place Hotel)/May 14-17
1988-Tampa, FL(Lincoln Hotel)/Nov. 12-15

Ass'n of Co-operative Educators (1965)
510-119 Fourth Ave. South, Saskatoon Saskatchewan S7N 5X2
Exec. Secretary: Myrna Barclay
Members: 400 *Staff:* 1
Annual Budget: under $10,000 *Tel:* (306) 244-3600
Hist. Note: Founded in Banff as the Ass'n for Cooperative Education, the name was changed in 1970 to its present form. Membership consists of individuals professionally engaged in educational, training or personnel programs of cooperative organizations. Membership: $30/yr.
Publications:
ACE News. q.
Membership List. a.
Annual Meetings: Annual institutes in June or July at educational institutions.
1987-Saskatoon, Saskatchewan
1988-Kingston, Jamaica

Ass'n of College and Research Libraries (1938)
50 East Huron St., Chicago IL 60611
Exec. Director: JoAn Segal
Members: 1,100 libraries; 8,700 individuals *Staff:* 40-45
Annual Budget: $1-2,000,000 *Tel:* (312) 944-6780
Hist. Note: Represents academic and research librarians and libraries. This includes all types of academic libraries - community and junior college, college, and university - as well as comprehensive and specialized research libraries and their professional staffs. Formerly Ass'n of College and Reference Libraries. A division of the American Library Ass'n. Membership: $25/yr.
Publications:
Rare Books & Manuscripts Librarianship. q. adv.
C & RL News. 11/yr. adv.
College and Research Libraries. bi-m. adv.
Choice. m. adv.
Annual Meetings: With American Library Ass'n, midwinter and summer annual conference
1989-Cincinnati, OH(Conv. Center)/April 5-8

Ass'n of College and University Auditors (1958)
Colorado State University, 309 Administration Bldg., Ft. Collins CO 80523
President: Thomas M. Grip
Members: 500 institutions *Staff:* 1
Annual Budget: $100-250,000 *Tel:* (303) 491-7100
Hist. Note: Members are educational institutions with their own auditing staffs. Administrative support provided by the National Association of College and University Business Officers.
Publication:
Newsletter. q.
Annual Meetings: Fall
1987-Hawaii
1988-Birmingham, AL

Ass'n of College and University Housing Officers-Internat'l (1952)
101 Curl Drive, Suite 140, Columbus OH 43210-1195
Manager: Rhea Dawn Smith
Members: 729 colleges & universities *Staff:* 2-3
Annual Budget: $100-250,000 *Tel:* (614) 292-0099
Hist. Note: Organized in 1952 at the Univ. of California, Berkeley, as a direct outgrowth of the first Nat'l Campus Housing Conference held in 1949 at the Univ. of Illinois. Added International to its name in 1981. Members are college and university staff members with responsibility for student residence, food service, developmental programming, administration and related operations. Membership: $50/yr. (individual), $120-140/yr. (institution).
Publications:
Talking Stick. m. adv.
International Directory. a. adv.
Journal of College and University Student Housing. semi-a. adv.
Annual Meetings: Summer/1,200
1987-Los Angeles, CA(Univ. of Southern California)/July 12-16
1988-College Park, MD(Univ. of Maryland)/July 10-14

Ass'n of College and University Printers (1964)
University of Maryland Printing Dept., Bldg. 005, College Park MD 20742
Program Chairman: Charles H. Fisher
Members: 125-150
Annual Budget: under $10,000 *Tel:* (301) 454-3128
Hist. Note: An informal group of managers of printing services in colleges and universities, membership in which is achieved principally by attending the annual conference.
Annual Meetings: Usually at a University Environment
1987-College Park, MD(Center for Adult Education)/April 27-May 1

Ass'n of College and University Telecommunications Administrators (1971)
101 South Webster St., Madison WI 53702
President: Michael A. Toner
Members: 600 *Staff:* 1
Annual Budget: $25-50,000 *Tel:* (608) 267-7355
Hist. Note: Membership: $75/yr.
Publication:
Newsletter. m.
Annual Meetings: Summer/400
1987-Minneapolis, MN
1988-San Diego, CA

00084 12 05 86 1233

Ass'n of College Honor Societies (1925)
1257 Haslett Road, Box 547, Haslett MI 48840
Secy.-Treas.: Dorothy I. Mitstifer
Members: 60 societies *Staff:* 1
Annual Budget: $10-25,000 *Tel:* (517) 339-3324
Hist. Note: Acts as the coordinating agency for college and university honor societies.
Annual Meetings: February
1987-Scottsdale, AZ/Feb. 19-22
1988-Jacksonville, FL

Ass'n of College Unions-Internat'l (1914)
400 East Seventh St., Bloomington IN 47405
Exec. Director: Richard D. Blackburn
Members: 900-1,000 *Staff:* 6-10
Annual Budget: $500-1,000,000 *Tel:* (812) 332-8017
Hist. Note: Founded as the Association of College Unions, it assumed its present name in 1961.
Publications:
Bulletin. bi-m.
Directory of Members. a. adv.
Newsletter. 10/yr.
Proceedings. a.
Annual Meetings: Early Spring/1,000
1987-Boston, MA(Marriott)/March 22-25
1988-New Orleans, LA(Marriott)/March 16-19
1989-Columbus, OH(Hyatt)/March 19-22
1990-Portland, OR(Red Lion)/April 1-4
1991-St. Louis, MO(Adams Mark)/March 24-27

Ass'n of College, University and Community Arts Administrators (1957)
6225 University Ave., Madison WI 53705
Exec. Director: Susan Hardy
Members: 1,400 *Staff:* 6-10
Annual Budget: $500-1,000,000 *Tel:* (608) 233-7400
Hist. Note: Formerly (1974) Ass'n of College and University Concert Managers, Inc. Members are colleges, universities and nonprofit arts organizations.
Publication:
Bulletin. 11/yr.
Annual Meetings: Third Week in December in New York, NY

Ass'n of Collegiate Schools of Architecture (1912)
1735 New York Ave., N.W., Washington DC 20006
Exec. Director: Richard McCommons
Members: 110 full members plus candidate members *Staff:* 6
Annual Budget: $500-1,000,000 *Tel:* (202) 785-2324
Hist. Note: U.S. and Canadian faculties of professional architectural degree programs.
Publications:
ACSA News. every six weeks. adv.
Architecture Schools of North America. a.
Journal of Architectural Education. q.
Annual Meetings: Spring
1987-Los Angeles, CA/March 14-17

Ass'n of Collegiate Schools of Planning (1959)
Georgia Institute of Technology, City Planning Program, Atlanta GA 30332-0155
President: David Sawlcki
Members: 102 schools *Staff:* 1
Annual Budget: $50-100,000 *Tel:* (404) 894-2351
Publication:
Journal of Planning Education and Research. q.
Annual Meetings: Semi-annual meetings

Ass'n of Commercial Mail Receiving Agencies (1982)
10131 Coors Road, N.W., Albuquerque NM 87114
Exec. Director: James W. Baer
Members: 450 *Staff:* 2
Annual Budget: $100-250,000 *Tel:* (505) 892-3331
Hist. Note: Businesses providing services such as mail boxes, mail forwarding, parcel shipping as well as telephone answering and secretarial service. Membership: $100/yr.
Publications:
Mail Center News. m. adv.
Member Directory. a. adv.
Annual Meetings: May/200
1987-Scottsdale, AZ
1987-Los Angeles, CA

Ass'n of Commercial Records Centers (1980)
9715 James Ave. South, Minneapolis MN 55431
Exec. Director: David Mattes
Members: 160 *Staff:* 1
Annual Budget: $50-100,000 *Tel:* (612) 888-4090
Hist. Note: Members are companies and individuals providing professional full service off-site records storage including vault service for magnetic or micrographic media and/or business paper storage. Membership: $100/yr. (individual), $350/yr. (company).
Publication:
For the Record. q.
Annual Meetings: November
1987-New Orleans, LA(Royal Sonesta)/Nov. 4-7
1988-San Diego, CA(Del Coronoado)/Nov. 9-12

Ass'n of Community Cancer Centers (1974)
11600 Nebel St., Suite 201, Rockville MD 20852
Exec. Director: Lee E. Mortenson
Members: 500 *Staff:* 2-5
Annual Budget: $100-250,000 *Tel:* (301) 984-9496
Hist. Note: Voting members are primarily community hospitals with cancer-care programs.
Publications:
Journal of Cancer Program Management.
Community Cancer Programs in the U.S. a.
Annual Meetings: March

Ass'n of Community College Trustees (1972)
6928 Little River Turnpike, Suite A, Annandale VA 22003
Exec. Director: William H. Meardy
Members: 500-600 districts *Staff:* 11-15
Annual Budget: $1-2,000,000 *Tel:* (703) 941-0770
Hist. Note: Formerly (1972) the Council of Community College Boards, National School Boards Ass'n. Membership: $400-1,600/yr. (institution, based on enrollment).
Publications:
ACCT-O-LINE. w.
Advisor. m. adv.
Trustee Quarterly. q.
Annual Meetings: Fall/1,500-2,000
1987-Orlando, FL(Marriott)/Oct. 7-11
1988-Louisville, KY(Galt House-Hyatt)/Oct. 5-9
1989-Vancouver, BC(Hyatt Regency-Hotel Vancouver)/Sept. 20-24
1990-Baltimore, MD(Bayshore-Pan Pacific)/Oct. 10-14

Ass'n of Community Travel Clubs (1966)
2330 South Brentwood Blvd., Suite 666, St. Louis MO 63144-2096
President: Leroy Blitz
Members: 487 organizations or clubs *Staff:* 13
Annual Budget: $1-2,000,000 *Tel:* (314) 961-2300
Hist. Note: Formerly (1969) Ass'n of Transport Flying Clubs.
Publications:
Bulletin. m.
Country Club Travel Group News.
Semi-annual Meetings:
1987-Rome and Tokyo
1988-Belfast, Ireland and Valetta, Malta
1989-Cruise and Israel
1990-Amsterdam and Hong Kong
1991-Sidney, Australia

Ass'n of Computer Programmers and Analysts (1970)
Hist. Note: Absorbed the Society of Professional Data Processors in 1974 and the Chicago Area PL/I Users Group in 1976. Inactive and probably moribund in 1983.

Ass'n of Computer Retailers (1983)
107 South Main St., Suite 202, Chelsea MI 48118
President: Patrice Johnson
Members: 200 *Staff:* 5
Annual Budget: $250-500,000 *Tel:* (517) 475-1378
Hist. Note: Members are independent resellers of computers and software. Membership: $250/yr.
Publication:
Newsletter. m.
Annual Meetings: Fall

Ass'n of Concert Bands (1977)
19 Benton Circle, Utica NY 13501
Exec. Secretary: J. Edward Hacker
Members: 400-450 bands, companies and individuals *Staff:* 1
Annual Budget: under $10,000 *Tel:* (315) 732-2737
Hist. Note: Formerly (1983) Ass'n of Concert Bands of America. Devoted to the development and growth of community and concert bands in America and abroad. Membership: $25/yr. (individual); $35/yr. (organization)
Publications:
The Instrumentalist. m.
Newsletter. 10/yr. adv.
Annual Meetings: Spring
1987-Rochester, MN(Holiday Inn)/April 23-26/100
1988-Sarasota, FL/100

Ass'n of Conservation Engineers (1961)
Alabama Dept. of Conservation, 64 North Union St., Montgomery AL 36130
Secy.-Treas.: William P. Allinder
Members: 200
Annual Budget: under $10,000 *Tel:* (205) 261-3476
Hist. Note: Members are engineers and allied personnel employed by state, federal and provincial conservation and recreation departments, who have a specialized interest in the areas of fish, wildlife, parks, forests and related conservation-recreation fields. Membership: $15/yr. (individual).
Publications:
ACE Newsletter.
Membership Directory. a.
Annual Meetings: Fall
1987-Madison, WI

Ass'n of Consulting Chemists and Chemical Engineers (1928)
50 East 41st St., Suite 92, New York NY 10017
Exec. Secretary: Roland D. Glenn
Members: 100-125 *Staff:* 1
Annual Budget: $25-50,000 *Tel:* (212) 684-6255
Hist. Note: Members are independent consulting chemists and chemical engineers. Chartered in 1928 in the State of New York. Membership: $200/year.
Publications:
Consulting Services Directory. bien.
Your Consultant. q.
Annual Meetings: Fourth Tuesday in October in New York, NY

Ass'n of Consulting Foresters (1948)
5410 Grosvenor Lane, Suite 205, Bethesda MD 20814
Exec. Director: Arthur F. Ennis
Members: 375-400 *Staff:* 2-5
Annual Budget: $25-50,000 *Tel:* (301) 530-6795
Hist. Note: Technically trained foresters who have demonstrated their professional competency and whose services are available to the general public on a fee or contract basis. Membership: $100/yr.
Publications:
ACF Membership Specialization Directory. a.
The Consultant. q. adv.
Annual Meetings: Last week in June.
1987-Washington (State)
1988-Charleston, SC/June 20-24

Ass'n of Consulting Management Engineers
Hist. Note: Became ACME, Inc. - The Association of Management Consulting Firms in 1982.

Ass'n of Cosmetologists and Hairdressers (1985)
1811 Monroe, Dearborn MI 48124
President: Mary Ann Neuman
Members: 40 companies; 1,800 individuals *Staff:* 3
Annual Budget: $50-100,000 *Tel:* (313) 563-0360
Hist. Note: Membership includes hairdressers and cosmetologists, as well as wholesalers, manufacturers, buyers, distributors, and retailers.
Publication:
Newsletter. q.

Ass'n of Country Entertainers (1976)
Hist. Note: Address unknown in 1983. Reported defunct in 1984.

Ass'n of Crafts and Creative Industries (1975)
1100-H Brandywine Blvd., P.O. Box 2188, Zanesville OH 43702
President: Walter E. Offinger
Members: 1,860 *Staff:* 10
Annual Budget: $50-100,000 *Tel:* (614) 452-4541
Hist. Note: Formerly (1984) the Mid-America Craft Hobby Ass'n. National membership is comprised of professionals in the craft supply industry. Object of ACCI is to offer a means of exchange to all those engaged in the buying, selling or manufacturing of craft, art, miniature, needlework and floral supplies merchandise. Membership: $10-50/yr.
Publication:
Ass'n of Crafts & Creative Industries Newsletter. bi-m.
Semi-Annual: Trade Market/Trade Show & Convention
1987-Orlando, FL(Orange Cty. Convention/Civic Ctr.)/April 14-16
1987-Chicago, IL(Rosemont/O'Hare Exposition Ctr.)/July 18-20

Ass'n of Credit Union League Executives
Box 431, Madison WI 53701
Exec. Director: William Sterner
Members: 250-300 *Staff:* 2-5
Annual Budget: $100-250,000 *Tel:* (608) 231-4000
Hist. Note: Founded as the Internat'l Ass'n of Managing Directors, it assumed its present name in 1979. Members are chief executives of credit union leagues, all of whom are affiliated with the Credit Union Nat'l Ass'n.
Publication:
League Letter. m.
Annual Meetings: July
1987-Honolulu, HI

Ass'n of Dark Leaf Tobacco Dealers and Exporters (1947)
Box 335, Mayfield KY 42066
President: James Marvin
Members: 20-25 *Staff:* 1
Annual Budget: under $10,000 *Tel:* (502) 247-2682
Hist. Note: An affiliate of Burley and Dark Leaf Tobacco Export Ass'n, ADLTDE was organized to promote the use of dark-fired and dark air-cured tobaccos both domestically and abroad.
Semi-annual Meetings:

Ass'n of Data Processing Service Organizations (1961)
Hist. Note: Became ADAPSO, the Computer Software and Services Industry Ass'n in 1985.

Ass'n of Diesel Specialists (1956)
9140 Ward Parkway, Kansas City MO 64114
Exec. V. President: Martin Fromm
Members: 800-850 *Staff:* 6-10
Annual Budget: $100-250,000 *Tel:* (816) 444-3500
Hist. Note: Members are companies and individuals whose primary interest is the technology and service of diesel fuel injection, governor and turbocharger systems.
Publication:
Nozzle Chatter. q.
Annual Meetings: August/September
1987-Nashville, TN/Aug. 23-27
1988-Las Vegas, NV/Sept. 25-29
1989-Atlanta, GA/Sept. 24-28

00085 12 05 86 1233

Ass'n of Direct Marketing Agencies (1971)
c/o Clark Direct Marketing, 801 2nd Ave., New York NY 10017
President: Junnes Clark, III
Members: 50 *Staff:* 2-5
Annual Budget: $25-50,000 *Tel:* (212) 661-9230
Hist. Note: Established as the Association of Direct Marketing Agencies and Consultants, it assumed its present name in 1971. Membership predominantly in the Eastern U.S. Members are direct response advertising agencies.
Annual Meetings: June

Ass'n of Diving Contractors (1968)
405 Gretna Blvd., #212, Gretna LA 70053
Exec. Secretary: Dianna Calmes
Members: 150 companies *Staff:* 2-5
Annual Budget: $100-250,000 *Tel:* (504) 362-0074
Hist. Note: Commercial diving contractors, manufacturers and suppliers of diving equipment, and diving schools.
Publication:
Commercial Diving Journal. q. adv.
Annual Meetings: Internat'l Diving Symposium
1987-New Orleans, LA/Feb. 9-11

Ass'n of Drilled Shaft Contractors (1971)
Box 280379, Dallas TX 75228
Exec. Director: Scot Litke
Members: 443 companies *Staff:* 2-5
Annual Budget: $100-250,000 *Tel:* (214) 681-5994
Hist. Note: Founded as a Texas-based organization in the 1960's; now has chapters throughout the United States. ADSC is comprised of foundation drilling contractors, manufacturers and suppliers to the foundation drilling industry and engineering and design professionals.
Publications:
Foundation Drilling. 8/yr.
Membership Directory. a.
Technical Library Catalog. a.
Annual Meetings: Semi-Annual Meetings
1987-Dallas, TX
1987-Ft. Collins, CO(Univ. Park Holiday Inn)/July 12-18/80
1987-Monterey, CA(Monterey Plaza Hotel)/July 22-26/150
1988-Orlando, FL(Hilton Hotel, Walt Disney World)/Jan. 20-24/200
1988-Boston, MA/July/200

Ass'n of Earth Science Editors (1967)
American Geological Institute, 4220 King Street, Alexandria VA 22302
Secy.-Treas.: Kathleen Krafft
Members: 325-350
Annual Budget: under $10,000 *Tel:* (703) 379-2480
Hist. Note: Founded to strengthen the profession of earth science editing, AESE promotes the exchange of ideas of problems of selection, editing and publication of research manuscripts, journals, serials, periodicals and maps pertaining to earth sciences. Affiliated with the American Geological Institute and the American Ass'n for the Advancement of Science. Membership: $20/yr.
Publications:
Blueline (newsletter). q.
Membership Directory. a.
Annual Meetings: October/100
1987-Alexandria, VA
1988-Albuquerque, NM
1989-Ottawa, Ontario
1990-Tulsa, OK

Ass'n of Edison Illuminating Companies (1885)
51 East 42nd St., New York NY 10017
Secy.-Treas.: Arthur N. Anderson
Members: 90-100 privately-owned utilities *Staff:* 2-5
Annual Budget: $100-250,000 *Tel:* (212) 697-1336
Hist. Note: Organized in 1885 by licensees of Thomas A. Edison for the advancement of electric service to the public for light, heat and power.

Ass'n of Editorial Businesses (1980)
116 4th St., S.E., Washington DC 20003
Secy.-Treas.: Shirley Rosenberg
Members: 25-30 companies *Staff:* 1
Annual Budget: under $10,000 *Tel:* (202) 293-0077
Hist. Note: Members are providers of editorial services, such as research, writing, editing, proofreading and indexing. Established October 14, 1980 and incorporated in the District of Columbia. Most of the members at present are concentrated in the Washington area. Membership: $40/yr. (individual).
Publication:
AEB Newsletter. m.
Annual Meetings: Bimonthly meetings in Washington, DC

Ass'n of Energy Engineers (1977)
4025 Pleasantdale Rd., Suite 420, Atlanta GA 30340
Exec. Director: Albert Thumann, P.E.
Members: 6,200 *Staff:* 9
Annual Budget: $500-1,000,000 *Tel:* (404) 447-5083
Hist. Note: Licensed professional engineers, architects, utility managers and consultants with experience in energy management and cogeneration. Absorbed the Energy Management and Controls Soc. in Jan., 1986.
Publications:
Strategic Planning and Energy Management. q.
Energy Engineering. bi-m. adv.
Cogeneration Journal. 3/yr.
Annual Meetings: Fall

Ass'n of Engineering Geologists (1957)
3479 Rambow Drive, Palo Alto CA 94306
Exec. Director: Patricia S. Osiecki
Members: 3,000 *Staff:* 1
Annual Budget: $100-250,000 *Tel:* (415) 494-6785
Hist. Note: Founded by 12 charter members in Sacramento, CA as the California Ass'n of Engineering Geologists; assumed its present name and became an international organization in 1962. A member society of the American Geological Institute. Membership is open to anyone possessing a college degree in geology or engineering geology, or having a serious interest in the subject. Full Membership: $70/yr.
Publications:
AEG Bulletin. q. adv.
AEG Directory. a. adv.
AEG Newsletter. q. adv.
Annual Meetings: Fall
1987-Atlanta, GA/Oct. 4-10
1988-Kansas City, MO/Oct. 17-22
1989-Vail, CO
1990-Pittsburgh, PA

Ass'n of Environmental Engineering Professors (1963)
Dept. of Civil Engineering, University of Texas, EJC 8.6, Austin TX 78712
Secretary: Desmond Lawler
Members: 380
Annual Budget: $10-25,000 *Tel:* (512) 471-4595
Hist. Note: Formerly (1972) American Ass'n of Professors in Sanitary Engineering. Individuals working or teaching in the fields of health, the environment, air and water resources and related areas. Has no permanent staff or address; officers change annually.
Publication:
AEEP Newsletter. q. adv.
Semi-annual Meetings: With the Water Pollution Control Federation and with the American Water Works Ass'n

Ass'n of Environmental Scientists and Administrators (1985)
Hist. Note: Address unknown in 1986.

Ass'n of Environmental Scientists and Engineers (1983)
Hist. Note: Became the Ass'n of Environmental Scientists and Administrators (1985).

Ass'n of Episcopal Colleges (1962)
815 Second Avenue, New York NY 10017
President: Linda Armstrong Chisholm, Ph.D.
Members: 6-10 *Staff:* 2-5
Annual Budget: $100-250,000 *Tel:* (212) 986-0989
Hist. Note: Formerly (1965) Foundation for Episcopal Colleges, and (1966) Fund for Episcopal Colleges.
Publication:
News & Views. q.
Annual Meetings: 2nd Sunday after Easter. (Directors)
1987-Monrovia, Liberia(Ducor Hotel)/June 13/20
1988-San Francisco, CA/20

Ass'n of Executive Search Consultants (1959)
151 Railroad Ave., Greenwich CT 06830
Exec. Director: Janet Jones-Parker
Members: 70-80 executive search firms *Staff:* 2-5
Annual Budget: $250-500,000 *Tel:* (203) 661-6606
Hist. Note: Established as the Association of Executive Recruiting Consultants, it assumed its present name in 1982.
Publication:
AESC Report. q.

Ass'n of Existential Psychology and Psychiatry (1960)
40 East 89th St., New York NY 10028
Secretary: Dr. Louis E. DeRosis
Members: 1,600-1,700 individuals *Staff:* 2-5
Annual Budget: under $10,000 *Tel:* (212) 348-3500
Hist. Note: Individuals interested in a "a multi-dimensional dialogue between all the disciplines which further the non-technological aspects of human existence."
Publication:
Human Inquiries. 3/yr.
Semi-annual Meetings: New York City and Washington, D.C.

Ass'n of Family and Conciliation Courts (1963)
AFCC-Oregon Health Sciences University, Dept. of Psychiatry, Gaines Hall #149, Portland OR 97201
Exec. Director: Stanley Cohen, Ph.D.
Members: 1,000-1,200 *Staff:* 1
Annual Budget: $50-100,000 *Tel:* (503) 220-5651
Hist. Note: AFCC was established to: develop and improve the practice and procedures of family counseling as a complement to the judicial process; to promote ethical standards in court related marriage and divorce counseling; and to provide a forum for the exchange of ideas and assistance in establishing programs in this field. Members include lawyers, judges and marriage counselors. Membership: $60/yr. (individual); $120/yr. (institution)
Publications:
Newsletter. 4/yr.
Conciliation Courts Review. bi-a.
Publications List Available.
Semi-annual Meetings: May and December
1987-Honolulu, HI/May and Las Vegas, NV/Dec.
1988-Los Angeles, CA/May

Ass'n of Federal Communications Consulting Engineers (1948)
P.O. Box 19333, 20th St. Station, Washington DC 20036-0333
President: Charles Gallagher
Members: 180-190 individuals
Annual Budget: $25-50,000 *Tel:* (202) 223-6700
Hist. Note: Organization of Professional Engineering Consultants serving the broadcasting and telecommunications industry. Associate membership composed of engineering executives of broadcast group owners and equipment manufacturers. AFCCE maintains close relationship with the Federal Communications Commission. Has no paid staff. Officers change annually.
Annual Meetings: Spring

Ass'n of Federal Investigators (1957)
1612 K St., N.W., Suite 202, Washington DC 20006
Exec. Director: June Stafford
Members: 2,000 *Staff:* 3
Annual Budget: $250-500,000 *Tel:* (202) 466-7288
Hist. Note: Formerly (1963) Ass'n of Former Civil Service Investigators. Membership: $45/yr.
Publications:
AFI Report. m.
Investigators' Journal.
Job Board.
Annual Meetings: November, in Washington, DC/500.

Ass'n of Federal Photographers (1957)
Hist. Note: Address unknown in 1985.

Ass'n of Federal Safety and Health Professionals (1971)
7549 Wilhelm Drive, Lanham MD 20706
Secy.-Treas.: Abraham M. Kooiman, CSP
Members: 470
Annual Budget: under $10,000 *Tel:* (301) 552-2104
Hist. Note: Founded as the Ass'n of Federal Safety Employees in Chicago, assumed its present name in 1979. Merged with the Guild of Government Safety Professionals in 1978 and accepted the Air Force Safety Technicians Ass'n as a division in 1981. Membership: $20/yr.
Publications:
AFS&HP Newsletter. q.
Directory.
Annual Meetings: Held in conjunction with the Nat'l Safety Congress

Ass'n of Field Service Managers, Internat'l (1976)
3475 Prudential Court, Suite B, Fort Myers FL 33907
Exec. Director: George B. Keller
Members: 4,500 *Staff:* 4
Annual Budget: $1-2,000,000 *Tel:* (800) 237-5044
Hist. Note: Members are managers of personnel who service computers and high technology equipment. Added "Internat'l" to its title in 1986. Membership: $85/yr. (individual) plus $15 initiation fee.
Publication:
The Field Service Manager. bi-m. adv.
Annual Meetings: Fall
1987-Toronto, Canada/mid-Oct.

Ass'n of Film Commissioners (1979)
Box 6299, San Jose CA 95150
President: Joseph J. O'Kane
Members: 150-200 *Staff:* 1
Annual Budget: $100-250,000 *Tel:* (408) 295-9600
Hist. Note: Members are officials serving as film commissioners. The purpose of the AFC is to act as liaison between the visual communications industry and local governments or organizations in order to facilitate on-location production. Membership: $100/yr.
Publications:
AFC News. q.
Trade Show Book. a.
Semi-Annual Meetings:
1987-Beverly Hills, CA(Beverly Hills Hilton)/Feb.-March
1987-Jackson Hole, WY

Ass'n of Firearm and Toolmark Examiners (1969)
7857 Esterel Dr., La Jolla CA 92037
Secretary: Eugenia A. Bell
Members: 500 individuals *Staff:* 1
Annual Budget: under $10,000 *Tel:* (619) 453-0847
Hist. Note: Organized February 26, 1969 at the Chicago Police Department and formally constituted there a year later.
Publication:
AFTE Journal. q.
Annual Meetings: Spring
1987-Seattle, WA/June 15-19

Ass'n of Flight Attendants (1945)
1625 Massachusetts Ave., N.W., Washington DC 20036
President: Susan Bianchi Sand
Members: 27,000 *Staff:* 54
Annual Budget: over $5,000,000 *Tel:* (202) 328-5400
Hist. Note: Formerly (1973) the Stewards and Stewardesses Division of the Air Line Pilots Ass'n, International. Now, independently affiliated with the AFL-CIO. Sponsors and supports the Flight PAC Political Action Committee. Membership: $26/yr.
Publication:
Flight Log. q. adv.
Annual Meetings: November/100
1987-St. Louis, MO

00086 12 05 86 1233

Ass'n of Flock Processors (1968)
Hist. Note: A professional society of printers using paper or textiles with raised impressions. Defunct, 1983.

Ass'n of Food and Drug Officials (1896)
Box 3425, York PA 17402
Exec. Assistant: Whitney W. Almquist
Members: 500 *Staff:* 1
Annual Budget: $50-100,000 *Tel:* (717) 757-2888
Hist. Note: Founded in 1896 to promote the passage of federal regulations to prevent the misbranding and adulteration of foods, drugs, cosmetics and devices, and to promote uniformity among the states in regulating the above. Members are individuals concerned with the development and enforcement of uniform food, drug and other consumer protection laws. Membership: $35/yr. (individual); $200/yr. (association).
Publications:
Bulletin. q.
News and Views. q.
Membership Directory. a.
Annual Meetings: June. Hosted in rotation by the seven regional chapters of the ass'n
1987-Tulsa, OK/June 20-24

Ass'n of Food Industries (1906)
Box 776, Matawan NJ 07747
Exec. V. President: Richard J. Sullivan
Members: 370 companies *Staff:* 5
Annual Budget: $250-500,000 *Tel:* (201) 583-8188
Hist. Note: Formed by a merger of the Bean Ass'n, the Dried Fruit Ass'n of New York and the Food Brokers Ass'n. Membership now composed of the Olive Oil Ass'n of America, the Maraschino Cherry and Glace Fruit Processors, the Metropolitan Food Brokers Ass'n, Processed Foods and Nut and Agricultural Products. Formerly (1982) Association of Food Distributors. Membership: $500-1,300/yr.
Publications:
AFI Annual. a. adv.
AFI Newsletter. m.
Annual Meetings:
1987-Sarasota, FL(Longboat Key Club)/April 23-26

Ass'n of Footwear Distributors (1956)
284 Harbor Way, San Francisco CA 94080
Secretary: David Goldfine
Members: 11-15 companies *Staff:* 1
Annual Budget: under $10,000 *Tel:* (415) 873-1434
Hist. Note: Loose-knit group of footwear wholesale distributors; has no permanent staff or address.
Semi-annual Meetings: Winter and Spring with New York Shoe Show

Ass'n of Former Agents of the U.S. Secret Service (1970)
Box 31073, Temple Hills MD 20748
Exec. Secretary: Floyd M. Boring
Members: 500 *Staff:* 1
Annual Budget: under $10,000 *Tel:* (301) 894-2115
Hist. Note: Dedicated to welfare of former special agents of the U.S., of their families when in need; to the continuing improvement and effectiveness of law enforcement; and to awarding scholarships and honoring those law enforcement officers whose performance merits special recognition. Membership: $10/yr.
Publications:
Directory. a.
Pipeline. q.
Annual Meetings: Fall

Ass'n of Former Intelligence Officers (1975)
6723 Whittier Ave., Suite 303A, McLean VA 22101
Exec. Director: John K. Greaney
Members: 3,500 *Staff:* 2-5
Annual Budget: $50-100,000 *Tel:* (703) 790-0320
Hist. Note: Founded in May 1975 by a group of intelligence professionals, who served with or retired from one of the U.S. intelligence organizations, concerned about the future of the U.S. intelligence system in consequence of the prevalent media reporting. Chartered originally as the Ass'n of Retired Intelligence Officers, the present name was adopted in Dec. 1976. Incorporated as a non-profit organization in the State of Virginia. Membership: $25/yr.
Publication:
Periscope. q.
Annual Meetings: September/400

Ass'n of Fundraising List Professionals (1983)
499 South Capitol St., S.W., Suite 501, Washington DC 20003
Secretary: Mary Richardson
Members: 42 companies; 60 individuals *Staff:* 0
Annual Budget: under $10,000 *Tel:* (202) 484-5000
Hist. Note: Professionals who deal in political or charitable/humanitarian fund- raising. Membership: $100/yr.
Annual Meetings: April

Ass'n of General Merchandise Chains (1933)
1625 Eye St., N. W., Washington DC 20006
President: Edward T. Borda
Members: 500 companies *Staff:* 6-10
Annual Budget: $1-2,000,000 *Tel:* (202) 785-2060
Hist. Note: Formerly (1969) Variety Stores Ass'n, Inc. Members are variety and discount general merchandise retailers and their vendor companies. Sponsors the AGMC Political Action Committee.
Publications:
AGMC Newsletter. m.
AGMC Membership Directory. a.
Annual Meetings:
1987-Williamsburg, VA(Colonial Williamsburg Foundation)/Oct. 11-15

Ass'n of Governing Boards of Universities and Colleges (1921)
One Dupont Circle, N.W., Ste. 400, Washington DC 20036
President: Robert L. Gale
Members: 1,500-1,550 tax-exempt institutions *Staff:* 20-25
Annual Budget: $1-2,000,000 *Tel:* (202) 296-8400
Hist. Note: Founded originally as an informal organization of public university trustees, AGB established an office in Washington with its first full-time staff in 1964. It became a national organization the same year when membership was opened to both public and private college and university governing boards.
Publications:
AGB News Notes. bi-m.
AGB Reports. bi-m.
Annual Meetings: Spring
1987-New Orleans, LA/March 22-24

Ass'n of Government Accountants (1950)
727 South 23rd St., Ste. 100, Arlington VA 22202
Exec. Director: W. Fletcher Lutz
Members: 12,500 *Staff:* 12
Annual Budget: $500-1,000,000 *Tel:* (703) 684-6931
Hist. Note: Established in 1950 as the Federal Government Accountants Ass'n. The name was changed to Ass'n of Government Accountants in 1975. Members are engaged in financial management at the federal, state and local levels of government. Membership: $35.00/yr.
Publications:
Financial Management Topics. m.
The Government Accountants Journal. q. adv.
Annual Meetings: June
1987-New Orleans, LA
1988-Washington, DC
1989-Los Angeles, CA

Ass'n of Governmental Appraisers (1961)
Hist. Note: Formerly (until 1980) known as the Ass'n of Federal Appraisers. Merged January 1, 1980 with the Soc. of Government Appraisers and the Ass'n of Government Appraisers to form the Ass'n of Governmental Appraisers. Merged with the American Soc. of Appraisers in 1985.

Ass'n of Graduate Liberal Studies Programs (1975)
School for Summer & Continuing Education,Georgetown University, Washington DC 20057
President: Dr. Phyllis O'Callaghan
Members: 75 institutions *Staff:* 1
Annual Budget: under $10,000 *Tel:* (202) 625-3014
Hist. Note: Members are interested in maintaining the quality of interdisciplinary, graduate-level degree programs in liberal studies.
Publication:
Newsletter. semi-a.
Annual Meetings: Fall

Ass'n of Graduate Schools in Ass'n of American Universities (1948)
One Dupont Circle, N.W., Suite 730, Washington DC 20036
Senior Federal Relations Officer: John Vaughn
Members: 56 *Staff:* 1
Annual Budget: under $10,000 *Tel:* (202) 466-5032
Hist. Note: Members are Deans of graduate studies of the fifty-six research universities belonging to the Ass'n of American Universities. Purpose is to consider matters of common interest relating to graduate study and research.
Annual Meetings: Fall
1987-Charlottesville, VA/Oct.

Ass'n of Graphic Arts Consultants (1976)
1730 North Lynn St., Arlington VA 22209
Exec. Director: Nancy M. Yancey
Members: 48 individuals *Staff:* 1
Annual Budget: $10-25,000 *Tel:* (703) 841-8136
Hist. Note: A special industry group of the Printing Industries of America.

Ass'n of Ground Water Scientists and Engineers (1985)
Hist. Note: A division of the Nat'l Water Well Ass'n.

Ass'n of Group Travel Executives (1965)
424 Madison Ave., Suite 707, New York NY 10017
President: Arnold H. Light
Members: 650-700 individuals *Staff:* 2-5
Annual Budget: $25-50,000
Hist. Note: Affiliated with the Travel Industry Association of America.
Publication:
Topics. bi-m.
Annual Meetings: Not held.

Ass'n of Hispanic Arts (1975)
200 E. 87th St., 2nd Floor, New York NY 10028
Exec. Director: Jane Delgado
Members: 150 companies; 3,000 individuals *Staff:* 5
Annual Budget: $250-500,000 *Tel:* (212) 369-7054
Hist. Note: Founded in 1975 by a network of Hispanic Art Organization representatives for the purpose of addressing issues relevant to the growth and stability of the Hispanic Arts community; membership is open to all Hispanic arts organizations and invididual artists. Membership: $25-125/yr.(according to budget)
Publications:
AHA Hispanic Arts News. 10/yr. adv.
Directory of Private Funding Sources. bi-a.
Directory of Hispanic Arts Organizations. tri-a.

Ass'n of Home Appliance Manufacturers (1967)
20 North Wacker Drive, Chicago IL 60606
President: Robert L. Holding
Members: 136 companies *Staff:* 30-35
Annual Budget: $1-2,000,000 *Tel:* (312) 984-5800
Hist. Note: Formed in 1967 by a merger of the Consumer Products Division of the Nat'l Electrical Manufacturers Ass'n and the American Home Laundry Manufacturers' Ass'n. Composed of manufacturers and suppliers to the major appliance and portable appliance industry. Maintains a Washington office.
Annual Meetings: Spring
1987-Amelia Island, FL(Amelia Island Plantation)/April 22-25/350

Ass'n of Hospital Television Networks (1979)
401 Fallowfield Road, Camp Hill PA 17011
Director:
Members: 40 networks *Staff:* 2
Tel: (717) 761-2272
Hist. Note: National consortium of hospital television networks either receiving teleconferences produced by AHTN or producing their own local medical programs. Membership: $250/yr.
Publications:
Health Programming Monthly. m.
Producer of Medical Teleconferences. irreg.

Ass'n of Human Resource Systems Professionals (1980)
P.O. Box 8040-A202, Walnut Creek CA 94596
Nat'l Administrator: Susan Giese Goldenberg
Members: 2,100 *Staff:* 2-5
Annual Budget: $250-500,000 *Tel:* (415) 945-8428
Hist. Note: Beginning in 1978 as an informal San Francisco Bay Area group, HRSP became a national organization, incorporating in 1980. Members are personnel, data processing and other professionals concerned with the development, maintenance and operation of human resource systems. Membership: $80/year (individual).
Publication:
HRSP Newsletter. q.
Annual Meetings: Spring
1987-Minneapolis, MN(Marriott City Ctr.)/May 31-June 3
1988-San Francisco, CA
1989-Houston, TX(Westin Galleria)/April 16-19
1990-Atlanta, GA(Westin Peachtree)/April 29-May 2
1991-Pittsburgh, PA(Westin William Penn)/April 26-29

Ass'n of Immigration and Nationality Lawyers (1946)
Hist. Note: Became the American Immigration Lawyers Association in 1982.

Ass'n of Importers-Manufacturers for Muzzleloading (1973)
Hist. Note: Inactive in 1986.

Ass'n of Independent Camps (1939)
60 Madison Ave., #1012, New York NY 10010
Exec. Director: Mathilde D. Sheinbaum
Members: 150-175 *Staff:* 1
Annual Budget: $50-100,000 *Tel:* (212) 679-3230
Hist. Note: Formerly (until 1978) the Ass'n of Private Camps, Inc.
Publications:
AIC Camp Directory. a. adv.
Guide for Selecting a Private Camp. a. adv.
Annual Meetings:
1987-Old Greenwich, CT(Hyatt Regency)/March 20-21/200

Ass'n of Independent Colleges and Schools (1912)
One Dupont Circle, N.W., Suite 350, Washington DC 20036
President: Dr. Jerry W. Miller
Members: 800 institutions *Staff:* 23-25
Annual Budget: $2-5,000,000 *Tel:* (202) 659-2460
Hist. Note: In 1950 the Nat'l Ass'n and Council of Accredited Commercial Schools and the Nat'l Council of Business Schools merged to form the Nat'l Ass'n and Council of Business Schools. This, in turn, merged with the American Ass'n of Business Schools (formerly the American Ass'n of Commercial Colleges) to form the United Business Schools Ass'n in 1962. Assumed its present name in 1973.
Publications:
The Compass. m. adv.
Directory of Accredited Schools. a.
Annual Meetings: Fall
1987-Washington, DC(J.W. Marriott)/Oct. 28-Nov. 1
1988-London, England/Nov. 2-6
1989-New Orleans, LA(Fairmont)/Oct. 18-22
1990-San Francisco, CA(Fairmont)/Oct. 24-28
1991-Dallas, TX(Fairmont)/Oct. 23-27

00087 12 05 86 1233

Ass'n of Independent Commercial Producers
(1973)
100 East 42nd St., New York NY 10017
General Counsel: Stephen Steinbrecher
Members: 300-350 *Staff:* 1
Annual Budget: $50-100,000 *Tel:* (212) 867-5720
Hist. Note: Independent producers of television commercials and their suppliers.

Ass'n of Independent Conservatories of Music
(1969)
11021 East Blvd., Cleveland OH 44106
President: Milton Salkind
Members: 8 *Staff:* 2-5
Annual Budget: under $10,000 *Tel:* (216) 791-9191
Hist. Note: Independent music schools, such as The Juilliard School and the Peabody Conservatory of Music. Formerly known as the Ass'n of Independent Colleges of Music and the Council of Independent Professional Schools of Music.

Ass'n of Independent Corrugated Converters
(1974)
801 North Fairfax St., Suite 211, Alexandria VA 22314
Exec. V. President: J. Richard Troll
Members: 400-600 *Staff:* 2-5
Annual Budget: $250-500,000 *Tel:* (703) 836-2422
Hist. Note: Represents non-mill owning and non-mill owned segment of corrugated container industry.
Publications:
AICC Newsletter. q.
AICC Membership Directory. a.
Semi-annual Meetings: Spring and Fall
1987-Boca Raton, FL(Boca Raton)/Mar. 11-15
1987-Toronto, Canada(Westin)/Oct. 14-17
1988-Maui, HI(Hyatt Regency)/April 13-16
1988-Boston, MA(Westin)/Oct. 12-15
1989-Scottsdale, AZ(Registry)/April 12-15

Ass'n of Independent Mailing Equipment Dealers
(1975)
600 Shoemaker Ave., Unit 5, Columbus OH 43201
Exec. Director: Neil McBride
Members: 175-200 companies *Staff:* 1
Annual Budget: $50-100,000 *Tel:* (614) 299-7759
Hist. Note: Association of dealers in all things concerned with mail and paper handling equipment. Membership: $200/yr.
Publication:
Newsletter. 10/yr.
Annual Meetings: Even years in Washington, DC, rotating in odd years
1987-Las Vegas, NV

Ass'n of Independent Microdealers (1984)
3010 North Sterling Ave., Peoria IL 61604
President: Ronald A. Wallace
Members: 140 companies *Staff:* 1
Annual Budget: $50-100,000 *Tel:* (309) 685-4843
Hist. Note: Membership: $125/yr.
Publication:
Apple Computer Users Guide. q. adv.

Ass'n of Independent Music Publishers (1977)
Box 930, 1626 North Wilcox, Hollywood CA 90028
Secretary: Joan Schulman
Members: 80 companies
Annual Budget: under $10,000 *Tel:* (213) 469-8371
Hist. Note: The Ass'n was formed to further and enhance the interests and image of music publishers in all fields of the industry: public performance, recording, print, copyright matters, etc.
Monthly Meetings:

Ass'n of Independent Television Stations (1972)
1200 18th St., N.W., Suite 502, Washington DC 20036
President: Preston R. Padden
Members: 321 *Staff:* 15
Tel: (202) 887-1970
Hist. Note: Members include commercial independent television broadcasting stations not primarily affiliated with a national network (154) and national sales representatives, program distributors, and other related broadcasting companies and organizations (112). Primary purpose is to act and speak for independent stations in an industry oriented towards national networks and their affiliated stations. Towards this end, it conducts a continuing market research development program among national advertising agencies, informs the FCC and Congress of members' concerns, speaks for the stations in industry councils, serves as a common ground for suppliers and the independent stations and a clearinghouse for sales and promotions, and compiles statistics. Sponsors and supports the Ass'n of Independent Television Stations Political Action Committee.
Publications:
Newsletter. bi-w.
INTV Quarterly Journal. q.
Annual Meetings: Always in January/February
1987-Los Angeles, CA/Jan. 7-11

Ass'n of Independent Video and Filmmakers
(1974)
625 Broadway, 9th Floor, New York NY 10012
Exec. Director: Lawrence Sapadin
Members: 4,000 *Staff:* 8-12
Annual Budget: $100-250,000 *Tel:* (212) 473-3400
Hist. Note: Membership is open to anyone involved in independent video and film creation. Educational arm of the Foundation for Independent Video and Film (FIVF). Sponsors cultural programs with grants from the Nat'l Endowment for the Arts and the New York State Council on the Arts. Membership: $35/yr.
Publication:
The Independent. m. adv.
Annual Meetings: New York/March-April

Ass'n of Industrial Manufacturers' Representatives (1972)
5845 Horton, Suite 201, Mission KS 66202
Exec. Director: Frank Bistrom
Members: 225-250 *Staff:* 2-5
Annual Budget: $50-100,000 *Tel:* (913) 262-0163
Hist. Note: AIM/R began as an auxiliary of the now defunct Association of Industry Manufacturers, first becoming independent in June, 1976 in Minneapolis. Incorporated September 14, 1977. Members are independent manufacturer's representatives throughout the United States; membership draws heavily in the plumbing, heating and air conditioning fields.
Annual Meetings:
1987-Boston, MA(Marriott Copley Place)/June 12-14

Ass'n of Industrial Metallizers, Coaters and Laminators (1956)
61 Blue Ridge Rd., Wilton CT 06897
Exec. Director: William H. Troph
Members: 95 companies *Staff:* 2-5
Annual Budget: $100-250,000 *Tel:* (203) 762-5611
Hist. Note: Formerly (1973) Vacuum Metallizers Ass'n. Producers of metallized film, vacuum metallizing equipment, laminated and coated flexible packaging and industrial materials. Membership: $875/yr.
Publication:
Newsletter. q.
Tri-annual Meetings: Winter, Spring and Fall

Ass'n of Information and Dissemination Centers
(1968)
Box 8105, Athens GA 30603
President: Marjorie Hlava
Members: 100-150 organizations *Staff:* 1
Annual Budget: $10-25,000 *Tel:* (404) 542-6820
Hist. Note: Formerly (1976) the Ass'n of Scientific Information Dissemination Centers. Members are industrial, educational and government information centers which build, maintain, search and/or distribute online databases; online or computer database vendors, producers and high volume searchers.
Publication:
ASIDIC Newsletters. semi-a.
Semi-annual meetings: Spring and Fall
1987-New Orleans, LA(Royal Sonesta)/April 4-6
1987-Newport, RI(Viking)/Sept. 17-19
1988-San Antonio, TX/March
1988-Canada/Sept.

Ass'n of Information Managers Financial Institutions (1966)
111 East Wacker Drive, Suite 2221, Chicago IL 60601
Exec. Director: Richard A. Yingst
Members: 650 *Staff:* 2
Annual Budget: $100-250,000 *Tel:* (312) 938-2576
Hist. Note: Until 1980, the Systems Automation Division of the Financial Managers Society for Savings Institutions. Membership: $195/yr. (individual)
Publications:
Directory of the Financial Management Society. a.
AIM Newsletter.
AIM Automation Survey.
AIM Software Directory.
Annual Meetings: Fall
1987-Boston, MA(Boston Center/Oct. 4-7/300

Ass'n of Information Systems Professionals
(1972)
1015 North York Road, Willow Grove PA 19090
Managing Director: Mark S. Hertzog
Members: 10,000 *Staff:* 15
Annual Budget: $1-2,000,000 *Tel:* (215) 657-6300
Hist. Note: Originally an affiliate of the Administrative Management Soc., AISP became completely independent in 1977. Concerned with office information systems and applications of automation in information processing. Conducts specialized education and research, maintains library and speakers bureau. Until 1981 known as the Internat'l Word Processing Ass'n and until 1983, as the Internat'l Information/Word Processing Ass'n. Membership: $75/yr. (U.S.); $90/yr. (Canada)
Publications:
Words. bi-m. adv.
Education & Training Exchange. q.
Format. bi-m.
Papers and Proceedings. a.
Salary Survey Results. a.
Prompts. m.
Annual Meetings: SYNTOPICAN
1987-Dallas, TX(Loew's Anatole)/June 29-July 2

Ass'n of Insurance Attorneys (1937)
600 Jefferson Bank Bldg., Peoria IL 61602
Secretary: Gary M. Peplow
Members: 675 lawyers *Staff:* 1
Annual Budget: $25-50,000 *Tel:* (309) 676-0400
Hist. Note: Attorneys with at least 5 years trial experience with insurance cases and insurance matters. Membership: $115/year.
Annual Meetings: Spring/250
1987-Palm Beach, FL(Breakers)/April 1-4
1988-Phoenix, AZ/April 6-10

Ass'n of Interior Decor Specialists (1971)
Hist. Note: Name changed in 1984 to Ass'n of Specialists in Cleaning and Restoration.

Ass'n of Internal Management Consultants (1971)
Box 304, East Bloomfield NY 14443
Exec. Secretary: Margaret Custer
Members: 245 *Staff:* 1
Annual Budget: $50-100,000 *Tel:* (716) 657-7878
Hist. Note: Established in Baltimore February 19, 1971 by forty-two charter members under the leadership of Walter J. Sistek of the Maryland National Bank. Incorporated in the State of New York in 1975. Individuals engaged in the practice of internal management consulting, with five or more years experience and operating at a senior or project leader level. Membership: $100/yr.
Publications:
AIMC Newsletter. 3-4/yr.
AIMC Forum. semi-a.
Membership Directory. a.
Annual Meetings: Spring
1987-Captiva Island, FL(South Seas Plantation)/May 10-13

Ass'n of Internat'l Health Researchers (1982)
2665 Pleasant Valley, Mobile AL 36606
Exec. Director: Dr. Roy E. Kadel
Members: 83 individuals
Annual Budget: under $10,000 *Tel:* (205) 473-3946
Publication:
AIHR Journal. bi-m.
Annual Meetings: June

Ass'n of Internat'l Photography Art Dealers (1979)
93 Standish Road, Hillsdale NJ 07642-1110
Exec. Secretary: Bernard J. Ellis
Members: 63 *Staff:* 2-5
Annual Budget: $100-250,000 *Tel:* (201) 664-4600
Hist. Note: Galleries and private dealers in fine art photography who have been in business for at least three years. Membership: $250/yr.
Annual Meetings:
1987-Los Angeles, CA(Ambassador Hotel)/March 12-14
1988-Houston, TX(Warwick Hotel)/March 4-6

Ass'n of Interpretive Naturalists (1961)
6700 Needwood Road, Derwood MD 20855
Exec. Manager: Jan Hockenberry
Members: 1,300-1,400 *Staff:* 2-5
Annual Budget: $50-100,000 *Tel:* (301) 948-8844
Hist. Note: Members are specialists in the preparation of interpretive exhibits and educational programs in museums, parks, historic sites, etc. Membership: $25-75/yr. (individual), $50-100/yr. (company).
Publications:
Journal of Interpretation. semi-a. adv.
National Newsletter. m.
Workshop Porceedings. a. adv.
Annual Meetings: Fall
1987-St. Louis, MO/Nov. 8-12
1988-St. Paul, MN/Oct. 6-10

Ass'n of Investment Brokers (1939)
49 Chambers St., Suite 820, New York NY 10007
President: Merrill J. Chapman
Members: 1,000 *Staff:* 2-5
Annual Budget: $25-50,000 *Tel:* (212) 608-5656
Hist. Note: Formerly the Association of Customers' Brokers.
Publication:
Tickertape. 10/yr.
Annual Meetings: May in New York City

Ass'n of Iron and Steel Engineers (1907)
Three Gateway Center, Suite 2350, Pittsburgh PA 15222
Mng. Director: Herschel B. Poole
Members: 11,000 *Staff:* 16-20
Annual Budget: $2-5,000,000 *Tel:* (412) 281-6323
Hist. Note: Originated in 1907 as the Ass'n of Iron and Steel Electrical Engineers; became the Ass'n of Iron and Steel Engineers in 1936. Promotes the technical and engineering phases of the production and processing of iron and steel. Membership: $45/yr.(domestic); $55/yr.(foreign)
Publications:
Directory of Iron and Steel Plants. a. adv.
Iron and Steel Engineer. m. adv.
Making Shaping and Treating Steel.
Semi-Annual Meetings: Spring and Fall
1987-St. Louis, MO/April 13-15/1,200
1987-Pittsburgh, PA(Expo. & Convention)/Sept. 21-24/20,000
1988-Baltimore, MD/May 2-4/1,200
1988-Cleveland, OH/Sept. 19-21/1,200

Ass'n of Jesuit Colleges and Universities (1970)
1424 16th Street, N.W., Suite 300, Washington DC 20036
President: Rev. William McInnes
Members: 28 *Staff:* 2-5
Annual Budget: $100-250,000 *Tel:* (202) 667-3889
Hist. Note: Formed in 1970 when the Jesuit Educational Ass'n split to form the Ass'n of Jesuit Colleges and Universities and the Jesuit Secondary Education Ass'n. Absorbed the Jesuit Research Council of America.
Publications:
ACJU Higher Education Report. m.
Directory. a.

00088 12 05 86 1233

Jesuit Degree Programs.
International Resource Book.
Semi-annual meetings: Small and closed to public

Ass'n of Jewish Book Publishers (1962)
838 Fifth Ave., New York NY 10021
President: Bernard Levinson
Members: 35 publishers
Annual Budget: $10-25,000 *Tel:* (212) 249-0100
Hist. Note: Membership concentrated in the New York area.
Annual Meetings: Not held

Ass'n of Jewish Center Workers (1918)
15 East 26th Street, New York NY 10010
Administrative Director: Lois Carol Schlar
Members: 1,000 *Staff:* 2
Annual Budget: $50-100,000 *Tel:* (212) 532-4949
Publications:
Conference Papers. a.
Related Research Reporter. bi-a.
Viewpoints. bi-a.
Kesher.

Ass'n of Jewish Chaplains of the Armed Forces (1946)
15 East 26th St., New York NY 10010
Director: Rabbi David Lapp
Members: 850-900
Annual Budget: under $10,000 *Tel:* (212) 532-4949
Hist. Note: Administration are members of the Association. Jewish Chaplains in the Army, Air Force, Navy, and Veterans Administration are members of the Association. Membership $10/year.
Publication:
CHAPLINES Newsletter. q.
Annual Meetings: January-February
1987-Monticello, NY/Feb. 1-4/100

Ass'n of Jewish Family and Children's Agencies (1972)
40 Worth St., Suite 800, New York NY 10013-2908
Exec. Director: Bert J. Goldberg
Members: 125 agencies *Staff:* 4
Annual Budget: $100-250,000 *Tel:* (212) 608-6660
Hist. Note: Members are local Jewish family and children service agencies in the U.S. and Canada.
Publications:
Newsletter. q.
Directory. a.
Annual Meetings: April
1987-San Francisco, CA
1988-Baltimore, MD

Ass'n of Jewish Libraries (1965)
122 East 42nd Street, Room 1512, New York NY 10168
Corres. Secretary: Esther Nussbaum
Members: 600-650 individuals *Staff:* 1
Annual Budget: $10-25,000 *Tel:* (212) 490-2280
Hist. Note: Merger of the Jewish Library Ass'n (founded in 1946) and the Jewish Librarians Ass'n (founded in 1962). Membership: $25/yr.
Publications:
AJL Newsletter. q. adv.
Judaica Librarianship. semi-a. adv.
Annual Meetings: June
1987-Livingston, NJ/June 21-24
1988-Kansas City, MO

Ass'n of Junior Leagues (1921)
825 Third Ave., New York NY 10022
Exec. Director: Deborah L. Seidel
Members: 163,000 members in 266 leagues *Staff:* 55-60
Annual Budget: $1-2,000,000 *Tel:* (212) 355-4380
Hist. Note: The first Junior League was established in New York City in 1901 by Mary Harriman and a group of 85 young women to promote volunteer service in the settlement houses of the city. They founded the Junior League for the Promotion of Settlement Movements, later shortened to the Junior League. Following New York's lead, women in Boston, Brooklyn, Portland, Baltimore, Chicago and Cleveland began to organize Junior Leagues. From work in the settlement houses, early Junior Leagues rapidly expanded their programs to found well baby clinics, conduct classes in home nursing, establish orphanages and organize garment factories to employ needy women. The New York Junior League started the first residence for young working women. As Leagues multiplied, the need for an overall organization was recognized and, in 1921 the Association of the Junior Leagues of America was incorporated with 24 Leagues as charter members. The present name was adopted in 1971.
Publications:
AJL Newsline. bi-m.
Junior League Review. 2-3/yr.
Annual Meetings: Spring/850
1987-Nashville, TN(Opryland)/May 2-6
1988-Chicago, IL(Hyatt Regency)/April 28-May 1
1989-Anaheim, CA(Anaheim Hilton)/May

Ass'n of Knitted Fabrics Manufacturers (1935)
100 East 42nd Street, New York NY 10017
Exec. Director: Jacob P. Rosenbaum
Members: 15 *Staff:* 1
Annual Budget: under $10,000 *Tel:* (212) 867-5720

Ass'n of Labor-Management Administrators and Consultants on Alcoholism (1971)
1800 North Kent St., Suite 907, Arlington VA 22209
Exec. Director: Thomas J. Delaney
Members: 4,200 *Staff:* 11
Annual Budget: $500-1,000,000 *Tel:* (703) 522-6272
Hist. Note: Members are individuals involved in occupational alcoholism programs. Membership: $85/year (individual), $150/year (organization/company).
Publications:
ALMACAN. m. adv.
Directory. a.
Annual Meetings: Fall
1987-Chicago, IL(Hilton)/Oct. 4-7/1,600
1988-Los Angeles, CA(Westin Bonaventure)/Nov. 12-16/1,600
1989-Florida

Ass'n of Labor Relations Agencies (1952)
Hist. Note: Ceased operations in 1985.

Ass'n of Legal Administrators (1971)
104 Wilmot Road, Suite 205, Deerfield IL 60015-5195
Exec. Director: Richard M. Tempero
Members: 5,100 *Staff:* 10
Annual Budget: $2-5,000,000 *Tel:* (312) 940-9240
Hist. Note: Members are individuals responsible for the administration of private law firms, corporate legal departments and government agencies.
Publications:
ALA News. 8/yr. adv.
Legal Administrator. q. adv.
Compensation Survey. a.
Directory. semi-a. adv.
Management & Administration Newsletter. bi-m.
Systems & Technology Newsletter. q.
Financial Management Newsletter. q.
People-to-People Newsletter. bi-m.
Annual Meetings: Spring/1,500
1987-Orlando, FL/May 17-22
1988-Chicago, IL/April 30-May 6
1989-Toronto, Canada/April 30-May 6
1990-Seattle, WA

Ass'n of Life Insurance Counsel (1913)
1740 Broadway, New York NY 10010
Secy.-Treas.: Marianne Dowling
Members: 1,000 *Staff:* 1
Annual Budget: $25-50,000 *Tel:* (212) 679-1110
Hist. Note: Legal counsels of life insurance companies. Membership: $100/yr. (individual).
Publication:
Proceedings of the ALIC. trien.
Annual Meetings: May, in White Sulphur Springs, WV(Greenbrier)
1987-May 3-5
1988-May 22-24
1989-May 20-22
1990-May 20-22

Ass'n of Life Insurance Medical Directors of America (1889)
One Tower Square, Hartford CT 06183-1030
Secretary: Joseph R. Jurkoic, M.D.
Members: 800
Annual Budget: $25-50,000 *Tel:* (203) 277-4193
Hist. Note: Membership: $100/year (individual).
Publications:
Journal of Insurance Medicine. q.
Transactions. a.
Annual Meetings: Fall/300
1987-Minneapolis, MN(Hyatt Regency)/Oct. 11-14

Ass'n of Local Air Pollution Control Officials (1971)
444 North Capitol St., N.W., Suite 306, Washington DC 20001
Exec. Director: S. William Becker
Members: 220 individuals *Staff:* 3
Annual Budget: $100-250,000 *Tel:* (202) 624-7864
Hist. Note: Shares headquarters and staff with the State and Territorial Air Pollution Program Administrators. In addition to its semi-annual meetings for members, the association sponsors an annual Conference, Air Toxics Control Conference.
Publication:
Washington Update. m. (for members only)
Semi-annual Meetings: June and Dec. (for members only)

Ass'n of Local Housing Finance Agencies (1982)
1101 Connecticut Ave., N.W., Suite 700, Washington DC 20036
Exec. Director: John Murphy
Members: 196 *Staff:* 3
Tel: (202) 857-1197
Hist. Note: Regular members of ALHFA are county and city agencies issuing or supportive of issuing tax-exempt bonds to provide single and multifamily affordable housing; affiliate members are organizations providing technical assistance to issuers. Serves as an advocate before Congress and the Executive branch on affordable housing issues.
Publication:
Newsletter. bi-m.
Semi-Annual Meetings: Spring and Fall
1987-Philadelphia, PA(Four Seasons)/March 31-April 3

Ass'n of Local Transport Airlines (1957)
Hist. Note: Disbanded in 1985.

Ass'n of Long Distance Telephone Companies (1981)
Hist. Note: Merged with the American Council for Competitive Telecommunications in 1984 to form the Competitive Telecommmunications Ass'n.

Ass'n of Lutheran College Faculties (1935)
Luther College, Decorah IA 52101
President: Dr. Wilfred F. Bunge
Members: 50 *Staff:* 1
Annual Budget: under $10,000 *Tel:* (319) 387-1054
Hist. Note: Interested faculty who teach in Lutheran church-related colleges and universities.
Annual Meetings:
1st weekend in October
1987-River Forest, IL/Oct. 2-4

Ass'n of Machinery and Equipment Appraisers (1983)
1110 Spring St., Silver Spring MD 20910
President: Roland Grenier
Members: 250 *Staff:* 1
Annual Budget: $25-50,000 *Tel:* (301) 587-9335
Hist. Note: Members are appraisers of metal working machinery and equipment. Establishes standards and acredits appraisers. Membership: $100/yr.
Publications:
Auction Summaries. bi-a.
Membership Directory. a.
Annual Meetings: May
1987-Hollywood, FL

Ass'n of Major City Building Officials (1974)
481 Carlisle Drive, Herndon VA 22070
Secretariat: Robert Wible
Members: 31
Annual Budget: under $10,000 *Tel:* (703) 437-0100
Hist. Note: Provides a forum for building officials of 31 major cities in the U.S. to discuss mutual interests and seek solutions to common problems to building code and public safety issues.
Annual Meetings: Fall

Ass'n of Major Symphony Orchestra Volunteers (1937)
c/o AMSOV Archives, 1420 Locust St., #320, Philadelphia PA 19102
President: Mrs. Carl Koch
Members: 35 groups *Staff:* 0
Annual Budget: under $10,000 *Tel:* (215) 893-1956
Hist. Note: Membership extended to women's committees and guilds of major symphony orchestras in the U.S. and Canada that have annual budgets exceeding $3,500,000. Formerly (1957) Ass'n of Women's Committees for Symphony Orchestras and (1981) Women's Ass'n for Symphony Orchestras and (1985) Ass'n for Major Symphony Orchestras. Officers change every two years.
Publication:
Highlights. a.
Annual Meetings: Biennial meetings
1987-Boston, MA

Ass'n of Management Analysts in State and Local Government (1975)
c/o Fels Center of Government, University of Pennsylvania, Philadelphia PA 19104
Secretary-Treasurer: Tom Mills
Members: 200 *Staff:* 1
Annual Budget: $10-25,000 *Tel:* (215) 898-4758
Hist. Note: Has no paid staff. Officers are elected annually.
Publication:
Newsletter. q.
Annual Meetings: Spring
1987-Philadelphia, PA(Univ. of PA)

Ass'n of Management Consultants (1959)
500 N. Michigan Ave., Suite 1400, Chicago IL 60611
Members: 100-125
Annual Budget: $25-50,000 *Tel:* (312) 266-1261
Hist. Note: Members are professional management consulting firms.
Publication:
Update. m.

Ass'n of Management Consulting Firms (1929)
Hist. Note: See ACME, Inc.-The Ass'n of Management Consulting Firms.

Ass'n of Marine Engine Manufacturers (1945)
2550 M Street, N.W., Suite 425, Washington DC 20037
Exec. Secretary: Ron Stone
Members: 25-30 companies *Staff:* 2-5
Tel: (202) 296-4588
Hist. Note: Established as the Outboard Motor Manufacturers Association, AMEM became the Marine Engine Manufacturers Ass'n in 1978 and assumed its present name in 1985. It is a "partner-affiliate" of the Nat'l Marine Manufacturers Ass'n which provides AMEM with administrative support and with which it shares offices.

00089 12 05 86 1233

Ass'n of Master of Business Administration Executives (1970)
AMBA Center, 227 Commerce St., East Haven CT 06512
President: Albert P. Hegyi
Members: 25,000 individuals *Staff:* 11-15
Tel: (203) 467-8870
Hist. Note: A membership organization providing career information and professional services.
Publications:
MBA Employment Guide. a. adv.
MBA Executive. q. adv.
AMBA Network News. q.

Ass'n of Maximum Service Telecasters (1956)
1730 M St., N.W., Suite 713, Washington DC 20036
President: Tom E. Paro
Members: 250 TV stations *Staff:* 5
Tel: (202) 457-0980
Hist. Note: Individuals, partnerships, firms and corporations who own and operate TV stations, UHF or VHF.
Annual Meetings: Early spring/350
1987-Dallas, TX/March 27-April 1
1988-Las Vegas, NV/April 8-13
1989-Las Vegas, NV/April 28-May 3
1990-Dallas, TX/March 22-28
1991-Dallas, TX/April 11-17

Ass'n of Media Producers (1976)
Hist. Note: Absorbed by the National Audio-Visual Association in 1982.

Ass'n of Medical Illustrators (1945)
2692 Huguenot Springs Road, Midlothian VA 23113
Exec. Director: Margaret H. Henry
Members: 704 *Staff:* 3
Annual Budget: $250-500,000 *Tel:* (804) 794-2908
Hist. Note: Incorporated in the State of Illinois. Has an international membership Membership: $135/yr.
Publications:
The Journal of Biocommunication. q.
Newsletter. bi-m. adv.
Medical Illustration Sourcebook. a.
Directory. a.
Annual Meetings: Late Summer/Fall
1987-Bloomington, MN(Radisson South)/Aug. 15-19
1988-San Diego, CA
1989-Dallas, TX(Fairmont)/Aug. 12-17

Ass'n of Medical Rehabilitation Directors and Coordinators (1953)
87 Elm St., Framingham MA 01701
Exec. Director: Frank S. Deyoe
Members: 400 *Staff:* 1
Annual Budget: $10-25,000 *Tel:* (617) 877-0517
Hist. Note: Members are the chief administrative officers of rehabilitation facilities and agencies of all types. Sponsors the American Board for Certification of Medical Rehabilitation Directors and Coordinators, an independent body to certify AMRDC members. Membership: $45/yr.
Publications:
Bulletin. q. adv.
Membership Directory. a.

Ass'n of Medical School Pediatric Department Chairmen (1961)
Department of Pediatrics, UCI Medical Center, 101 City Dr. S, Orange CA 92668
Secy.-Treas.: Dr. Beverly C. Morgan
Members: 140-150 *Staff:* 1
Annual Budget: $10-25,000 *Tel:* (714) 634-6483
Hist. Note: Chairman of pediatrics of U.S. and Canadian accredited medical schools. Has no paid staff.

Ass'n of Men's Belt Manufacturers
Hist. Note: Merged with the Belt Ass'n in 1986.

Ass'n of Mental Health Administrators (1959)
840 North Lake Shore Dr., Suite 1103W, Chicago IL 60611
Exec. Director: Laurie Poul
Members: 1,575 *Staff:* 2
Annual Budget: $100-250,000 *Tel:* (312) 943-2751
Hist. Note: Established as American Soc. of Mental Hospital Business Administrators, it assumed its present name in 1969. AMHA is the professional association for administrators of services for the emotionally disturbed, mentally ill or retarded, developmentally disabled and those with problems of alcohol and substance abuse. Membership: $100/yr.
Publications:
Newsletter. m.
Journal of Mental Health Administration. semi-a.
Annual Meetings: September
1987-Hollywood, FL(Diplomat)/Sept. 27-30

Ass'n of Mental Health Clergy (1948)
12320 River Oaks Pt., Knoxville TN 37922
Exec. Director: Chaplain George Doebler
Members: 540 *Staff:* 2-5
Annual Budget: $25-50,000 *Tel:* (615) 544-9717
Hist. Note: Formerly (1975) Ass'n of Mental Hospital Chaplains. An interfaith organization for ministers, priests and rabbis professionally concerned with mental health. The first meeting was held in Washington, DC with the American Psychiatric Ass'n, and the AMHC retains close affiliative ties with that organization. Certifies competence in mental health ministry among clinically trained clergy serving in psychiatric facilities, community mental health centers, facilities for the developmentally handicapped, and religious congregations. Membership: $45/yr.
Publications:
Cura Animarum. 3/yr.
Journal of Pastoral Care. q.
Annual Meetings: With the American Psychiatric Association.

Ass'n of Mental Health Librarians (1964)
1400 K Street, N.W., Washington DC 20005
Correspondent: Zing Jung
Members: 100 individuals
Annual Budget: under $10,000 *Tel:* (202) 682-6080
Hist. Note: Formed (1964) as the Soc. of Mental Health Librarians, it assumed its present name in 1980. The Ass'n provides an opportunity for the exchange of information and the continuing education of its members. Membership: $15/year.
Annual Meetings: Fall
1987-Boston, MA

Ass'n of Metropolitan Sewerage Agencies (1970)
477 H St., N.W., Washington DC 20001
Exec. Director: Ron M. Linton
Members: 100 agencies *Staff:* 6-10
Annual Budget: $250-500,000 *Tel:* (202) 682-5886
Hist. Note: Incorporated in the District of Columbia in 1970. Members consist of sewerage agencies of areas with more than 250,000 people. Formed to exchange technical data of mutual benefit and deal with the Federal Government on environmental and regulatory matters.
Publications:
AMSA Monthly Report. m.
Law Digest. bi-m.
Annual Meetings: Spring

Ass'n of Microbiological Diagnostic Manufacturers (1973)
1575 Eye St., N.W., Suite 800, Washington DC 20005
Administrator: Catherine B. Maimon
Members: 75 companies *Staff:* 3
Annual Budget: $25-50,000 *Tel:* (202) 789-7539
Hist. Note: Membership open to any manufacturer, processor, repackager or distributor of microbiological diagnostic devices or device components. Membership fee based upon number of employees.
Annual Meetings: October
1987-Las Vegas, NV(Flamingo Hilton)/Oct. 19-22/100

Ass'n of Military Colleges and Schools of the U.S. (1914)
7009 Arbor Lane, McLean VA 22101
Exec. Director: Maj. Gen. Willis D. Crittenberger, Jr. USA
Members: 42 *Staff:* 1
Annual Budget: $10-25,000 *Tel:* (703) 827-0155
Hist. Note: Members are educational institutions with regionally accredited academic programs and Defense Department-approved military or naval programs. Absorbed the Nat'l Ass'n of Military Schools in 1972. Membership fee varies from $200-550/yr., depending upon the size of the student body.
Annual Meetings: March
1987-Alexandria, VA(Holiday Inn)/March 11-13/50-70
1988-Atlanta, GA

Ass'n of Military Surgeons of the U.S. (1891)
10605 Concord St., Suite 306, Kensington MD 20895
Exec. Director: Lt.Gen. Max B. Bralliar, USAF(Ret.)
Members: 15,000 *Staff:* 12
Annual Budget: $500-1,000,000 *Tel:* (301) 933-2801
Hist. Note: Established in 1891 and incorporated by an act of Congress in 1903. Membership consists of commissioned officers or civilians employed by the armed services, the Public Health Service or the Veterans Administration, or medical consultants. Membership: $25/yr. (individual), $400/yr. (institution).
Publication:
Military Medicine. m. adv.
Annual Meetings: Fall-Winter/7,000
1987-Las Vegas, NV/Nov. 6-13
1988-San Antonio, TX(Convention Center)/Oct. 30-Nov. 4
1989-San Diego/Nov. 12-17

Ass'n of Mill and Elevator Mutual Insurance Companies (1897)
1 Pierce Place, Itasca IL 60143-1269
President and C.E.O.: Robert W. Hill
Members: 7 companies *Staff:* 200
Annual Budget: over $5,000,000 *Tel:* (312) 250-8600

Ass'n of Minicomputer Users (1978)
Hist. Note: Ceased operations in 1983.

Ass'n of Motion Picture and Television Producers (1924)
Hist. Note: Became the Alliance of Motion Picture and Television Procers in 1982.

Ass'n of Muslim Scientists and Engineers (1969)
Box 38, Plainfield IN 46168
President: Talat Sultan
Members: 590 *Staff:* 2
Annual Budget: $50-100,000 *Tel:* (317) 839-8157
Hist. Note: Established and incorporated in Indiana. Membership: $15/yr.
Publication:
Muslim Scientist. q. adv.

Ass'n of Nat'l Advertisers (1910)
155 East 44th St., New York NY 10017
President: DeWitt F. Helm, Jr.
Members: 400-500 *Staff:* 25-30
Annual Budget: $2-5,000,000 *Tel:* (212) 697-5950
Hist. Note: Founded in 1910 as Ass'n of Nat'l Advertising Managers, it assumed its present name four years later. A.N.A. is exclusively committed to serving the interest of companies which advertise either regionally or nationally. Maintains a Washington office. Membership fee based on advertiser's expenditures.
Publications:
Washington Newsletter. irreg.
Annual Report.
Catalog of A.N.A. Publications.
Annual Meetings: Fall

Ass'n of Naval R.O.T.C. Colleges and Universities (1946)
3528 Indianbrook Drive, Lafayette IN 47905
Exec. Assistant to President: Dorothy A. Bolder
Members: 60 *Staff:* 1
Annual Budget: $10-25,000 *Tel:* (317) 474-0574
Hist. Note: Membership: $200/yr. (institution).
Annual Meetings: Fall/75-100
1987-Orlando, FL
1988-San Diego, CA

Ass'n of Newspaper Classified Advertising Managers (1920)
Box 267, Danville IL 61834
Gen. Manager: Frank B. Harris
Members: 700-800 *Staff:* 2-5
Annual Budget: $100-250,000 *Tel:* (217) 442-2057
Publications:
Ancam Exchanges. 11/yr. adv.
Conference Digest. a. adv.
Membership Directory. a. adv.
Best of the Best Ad Ideas. a.
Annual Meetings: June
1987-San Diego, CA(del Coronado)/June 21-24
1988-Ft. Lauderdale, FL(Marriott Harbor Beach)/June 26-30
1989-Ft. Worth, TX(Americana)/June 18-22
1990-Calgary, Alberta

Ass'n of North American Directory Publishers (1898)
351 Longley Road, Groton MA 01450-1028
Admin. Director: Carol C. Hill
Members: 85 *Staff:* 2-5
Annual Budget: $100-250,000 *Tel:* (617) 448-3573
Hist. Note: Members are publishers of city and telephone directories. Purpose is to foster and maintain high standards of directory service. Membership: $750 to $14,000, depending on gross advertising dollar.
Publication:
The Directory Journal. bi-m.
Annual Meetings: Spring
1987-Tucson, AZ(Westin La Paloma)/March 16/150
1987-Rancho Mirage, CA(Marriott's Rancho Las Palmas)/Oct. 26/150
1988-Naples, FL(Ritz)/March 2/170

Ass'n of North American Missions (1941)
Box 9710, Madison WI 53715
Assoc. Director: Jack M. Rood
Members: 33 *Staff:* 2-5
Annual Budget: $50-100,000 *Tel:* (608) 835-5489
Hist. Note: Founded as the Nat'l Home Missions Fellowship, it assumed its present name in 1980. Members are North American missions with more than five missionaries.
Publications:
Prayer Letter. m.
Roundtable. 3/yr.
Update. bi-m.
Notes and Quotes. bi-m.
Annual Meetings: Spring
1987-Clearwater, FL
1988-Olcott, NY

Ass'n of Official Analytical Chemists (1884)
1111 North 19th St., Suite 210, Arlington VA 22209
Exec. Director: Dr. David B. MacLean
Members: 2,500 *Staff:* 21
Annual Budget: $2-5,000,000 *Tel:* (703) 522-3032
Hist. Note: Founded in Washington, DC in 1884 as the Ass'n of Official Agricultural Chemists and became the Ass'n of Official Analytical Chemists in 1965. Originally this group had quasi-official status and received governmental support and office space, among other benefits. In 1978 it became fully independent and fully self-supporting. The purpose of AOAC is to approve analytical methods for products or substances affecting public health and safety, consumer protection or the quality of the environment and to encourage analytical chemical research related to agriculture, public health and regulatory control of commodities in these fields. Membership: $45/yr. (individual)
Publication:
Journal of the A.O.A.C. bi-m. adv.
Annual Meetings: Aug.-Sept.
1987-San Francisco, CA(Cathedral Hill)/Sept. 14-17

00090 12 05 86 1233

1988-Palm Beach, FL(Breakers)/Aug. 29-Sept. 1
1989-St. Louis, MO(Clarion)/Sept. 25-28
1990-New Orleans, LA/Sept. 9-13

Ass'n of Official Racing Chemists (1947)
Box 19232, Portland OR 97219
Secretary: Margaret A. Sullivan
Members: 100-125 *Staff:* 1
Annual Budget: $10-25,000 *Tel:* (503) 644-9224
Hist. Note: Formed in Chicago by a group of chemists from the United States and several other countries. The international membership consists of individuals concerned with detection of drugs in racing samples. Affiliated with the Nat'l Ass'n of State Racing Commissioners.
Publication:
Proceedings. a.
Annual Meetings: Spring
1987-Los Angeles, CA(Airport Hilton)/March 22-26

Ass'n of Official Seed Analysts (1908)
801 Sangamon Ave., Springfield IL 62706-1001
Secretary-Treasurer: James N. Lair
Members: 325-350 individuals *Staff:* 1
Annual Budget: $25-50,000 *Tel:* (217) 785-8487
Hist. Note: Established in 1908 by 16 states, the U.S. Department of Agriculture and Canada. Cooperates with the Internat'l Seed Testing Ass'n, the Soc. of Commercial Seed Technologists and the Commercial Seed Analysts Ass'n of Canada. Membership: $35/yr. (individual), $150/yr. (organization).
Publications:
Journal of Seed Technology. semi-a.
Newsletter. 3/yr.
Annual Meetings: Summer/250-300
1987-Sacramento, CA
1988-Grand Isle, NY

Ass'n of Official Seed Certifying Agencies (1919)
3709 Hillsborough St., Raleigh NC 27607
Exec. V. President: Foil McLaughlin
Members: 45-50 agencies, 4-500 individuals *Staff:* 1
Annual Budget: $25-50,000 *Tel:* (919) 737-2851
Hist. Note: Formerly (1968) The Internat'l Crop Improvement Ass'n. Members are state seed certifying agencies and their employees.
Annual Meetings:
1987-Nashville, TN/July 12-16/250
1988-Seattle, WA/June 26-July 2

Ass'n of Oil Pipe Lines (1947)
1725 K St., N.W., Suite 1205, Washington DC 20006
Exec. Director: Patrick H. Corcoran
Members: 90-100 *Staff:* 2-5
Annual Budget: $500-1,000,000 *Tel:* (202) 331-8228
Hist. Note: Founded as the Committee for Pipe Line Companies, a voluntary, unincorporated association of common carrier pipeline companies, the name was later changed to the Committee for Oil Pipe Lines, and in 1960 to Ass'n of Oil Pipe Lines.
Publications:
Shifts in Petroleum Transportation. a.
Oil Pipelines of the U.S. - Progress and Outlook. irreg.
Bibliography of Source Material. irreg.
Semi-annual Meetings: Winter in Washington, DC and June
1987-Banff, Alberta, Canada/June 21-23/235
1988-Laguna, CA(Ritz-Carlton)/June 27-28/220

Ass'n of Oilwell Servicing Contractors (1956)
6060 No. Central Expressway, Suite 428, Dallas TX 75206
Exec. V. President: John T. Haggin
Members: 700 companies *Staff:* 6-10
Annual Budget: $500-1,000,000 *Tel:* (214) 692-0771
Hist. Note: Supports the Workover and Well Servicing Action Committee (WOWSAC).
Publications:
Newsletter. m.
Well Servicing. bi-m. adv.
Directory. a.
Semi-annual meetings: Late Winter and July
1987-Dallas, TX/Feb. and Snowmass, CO/July

Ass'n of Old Crows (1964)
2300 9th St. South, Suite 300, Arlington VA 22204
Exec. Director: A.G. Slayton
Members: 24,000 individuals *Staff:* 5-9
Annual Budget: over $5,000,000 *Tel:* (703) 920-1600
Hist. Note: Members are electronic warfare specialists or individuals working in electronic companies. Grew from a similar World War II organization whose symbol was the raven. Membership: $15/yr.
Publication:
Journal of Electronic Defense. m. adv.
Annual Meetings: Fall/4,000

Ass'n of Operating Room Nurses (1954)
10170 E. Mississippi Ave., Denver CO 80231
Exec. Director: Clifford H. Jordan
Members: 35,500 *Staff:* 75
Annual Budget: over $5,000,000 *Tel:* (303) 755-6300
Hist. Note: Has an annual budget of $6 million. Membership: $35/year (individual).
Publications:
AORN Journal. m. adv.
Chapter Newsletter. m.
Annual Meetings: Late Winter
1987-Atlanta, GA/March 8-13

Ass'n of Operative Millers (1896)
4901 Main, #414, P.O. Box 30299, Kansas City MO 64112
Exec. V. President: G. Robert Coughenour
Members: 1,500 *Staff:* 2-5
Annual Budget: $100-250,000 *Tel:* (816) 561-4171
Hist. Note: Millers, superintendents, engineers, plant managers, and others in the cereal milling industry. Membership: $65/yr.
Publication:
Technical Bulletin. m.
Annual Meetings: Spring/1,000
1987-Toronto, Canada(Sheraton Centre)/May 17-21
1988-Denver, CO(Marriott)/May 21-26
1989-Seattle, WA(Sheraton)/May 20-24
1990-Orlando, FL(Hyatt Orlando)/April 21-25

Ass'n of Osteopathic State Executive Directors (1918)
226 Bailey Avenue, Fort Worth TX 76107
Exec. V. President: Tex Roberts, CAE
Members: 58 *Staff:* 2-5
Annual Budget: $10-25,000 *Tel:* (817) 336-0549
Hist. Note: Regular members are Osteopathic State executive directors; affiliate members include related medical associations.
Publication:
AOSED News. q. adv.
Annual Meetings: In conjunction with the American Osteopathic Ass'n
1987-Chicago, IL(Warwick)/July/50

Ass'n of Otolaryngology Administrators (1982)
Dept. of Otolaryngology, Univ. of Iowa, P.O. Box 3150, Iowa City IA 52244-1078
Exec. Secretary: Patrick R. Connolly
Members: 200
Annual Budget: $10-25,000 *Tel:* (319) 356-2371
Hist. Note: Active members are individuals responsible for the business aspects of an otolaryngology practice. Membership: $60/yr.
Publication:
Otoscope. q. adv.
Annual Meetings: Fall
1987-Chicago, IL/Sept. 18-20
1988-Washington, DC/Sept. 23-25
1989-New Orleans, LA/Sept. 22-24
1990-San Diego, CA/Sept. 7-9
1991-Kansas City, MO/Sept. 20-22

Ass'n of Outplacement Consulting Firms (1982)
364 Parsippany Road, Parsippany NJ 07054
Exec. Director: Jeanne O'Donnell
Members: 33 companies *Staff:* 2-5
Annual Budget: $50-100,000 *Tel:* (201) 887-6667
Hist. Note: Established at a dinner meeting at the Yale Club, New York City, on March 16, 1982 to promote standards of professional practice in the outplacement business. Membership: $1,500/yr.
Annual Meetings: February
1987-Boca Raton, FL(Hotel & Club)/Feb. 13-15

Ass'n of Overseas Educators (1955)
Indiana University of Pennsylvania, Indiana PA 15705
Director: Dr. Robert L. Morris
Members: 200 active members *Staff:* 1
Annual Budget: under $10,000 *Tel:* (412) 357-2295
Hist. Note: Formerly (1959) American Overseas Educators Organization.
Publication:
Newsletter. semi-a.
Annual Meetings: August

Ass'n of Paid Circulation Publications (1964)
1627 K St., N.W., Suite 400, Washington DC 20006
Exec. Director: Jackie Jackson
Members: 35-40 *Staff:* 2-5
Annual Budget: $10-25,000 *Tel:* (202) 296-8487
Hist. Note: Established in 1964 as the Paid Circulation Committee, it changed its name in 1965 to the Paid Circulation Council. In 1974 it became the Association of Second Class Mail Publications, in 1979 the Association of Second Class Mail Publishers and in 1982 assumed its present name.

Ass'n of Paroling Authorities (1961)
Board of Pardons and Paroles, 2503 Lake Road, Suite 2, Huntsville TX 77340
President: Ronald Jackson
Members: 150-175 *Staff:* 1
Annual Budget: under $10,000 *Tel:* (409) 291-2161
Hist. Note: Affiliate of the American Correctional Ass'n. Members are State Parole Board members. Membership: $25/yr.
Publication:
Newsletter. semi-a.
Annual Meetings: Immediately before the American Correctional Ass'n.
1987-San Francisco, CA(Holiday Inn Union Square)/April 7-11/125

Ass'n of Part-Time Professionals (1978)
Flow General Bldg., 7655 Old Springhouse Road, McLean VA 22102
President: Dr. Diane Rothberg
Members: 1,500 individuals *Staff:* 5
Annual Budget: $50-100,000 *Tel:* (703) 734-7975
Hist. Note: Members are individuals and organizations concerned with part-time employment. Encourages employers to hire professionals on a permanent part-time basis and to pay pro-rated benefits. Incorporated in the District of Columbia in 1981. Membership: $15/yr.
Publication:
National Newsletter. q.

Ass'n of Pathology Chairmen (1967)
Department of Pathology, West Virginia University, Morgantown WV 26506
Secy.-Treas.: Nathaniel F. Rodman
Members: 140 *Staff:* 1
Annual Budget: $50-100,000 *Tel:* (304) 293-3213
Hist. Note: Formerly (1976) American Ass'n of Chairmen of Medical School Departments of Pathology, Inc.
Publication:
Newsletter. q.
Annual Meetings:
1987-Orlando, FL/Sept.
1988-Washington, DC/March

Ass'n of Pediatric Oncology Nurses (1973)
2081 Business Center Dr., Suite 290, Irvine CA 92715
President: Mary Waskerwitz
Members: 600 *Staff:* 1
Annual Budget: $10-25,000 *Tel:* (714) 852-1250
Hist. Note: Nurses caring for children with cancer. Membership: $45/yr. (individual), $150/yr. (company).
Publication:
Journal of the Ass'n of Pediatric Oncology Nurses. q.
Annual Meetings: October

Ass'n of Petroleum Re-refiners (1950)
1915 I St., N.W., Suite 500, Washington DC 20006
Exec. Director: George T. Booth, III
Members: 50 *Staff:* 2-5
Annual Budget: $50-100,000 *Tel:* (202) 639-4490
Hist. Note: Membership consists of companies re-refining or reclaiming used oil and petroleum products and suppliers to the industry.
Publication:
APR Review. bi-m.
Annual Meetings: October

Ass'n of Petroleum Writers (1947)
Hist. Note: A loosely-structured organization whose principal activity has been described as its annual banquet, the association exists solely for the support of its members.

Ass'n of Philosophy Journals Editors (1971)
University of Cincinnati, Cincinnati OH 45221-0206
Secretary: Arnold Wilson
Members: 90-100 *Staff:* 1
Annual Budget: under $10,000 *Tel:* (513) 475-2073
Hist. Note: Membership: $10/yr.
Annual Meetings: With the American Philosophical Ass'n

Ass'n of Physical Fitness Centers (1975)
600 Jefferson St., Suite 202, Rockville MD 20852
President: Dr. Jimmy D. Johnson
Members: 100 operators, 575 facilities *Staff:* 4
Annual Budget: $250-500,000 *Tel:* (301) 424-7744
Hist. Note: Members are owners of health spas.
Publication:
APFC Newsletter. m.
Annual Meetings: April/May
1987-Dallas, TX(Registry Hotel)/April 28-30/800
1988-Las Vegas, NV(Caesars Palace)/April 19-21/800

Ass'n of Physical Plant Administrators of Universities and Colleges (1914)
1446 Duke Street, Alexandria VA 22314-3492
Exec. Director: Walter A. Schaw, CAE
Members: 2,900 *Staff:* 11-15
Annual Budget: $1-2,000,000 *Tel:* (703) 684-1446
Hist. Note: Members are accredited non-profit institutions of higher education with an independent physical plant, and university or college system offices which supervise the physical plants of two or more campuses. Membership: $135-465/year (based on enrollment).
Publications:
APPA Newsletter. m. adv.
Facilities Management Magazine. m. adv.
Proceedings. a.
Annual Meetings: Summer/1,200
1987-New Orleans, LA/June 21-24
1988-Washington, DC/July 24-27
1989-Reno, NV/July

Ass'n of Physician Assistant Programs (1972)
1117 North 19th St., Suite 300, Arlington VA 22209
Director APAP Affairs: Nancy Tilson
Members: 52 programs *Staff:* 1-3
Annual Budget: $50-100,000 *Tel:* (703) 525-4200
Hist. Note: Formed to further the concept of the physician assistant.
Publications:
Nat'l Directory of Physician Assistant Programs. bien.
Selected and Annotated Physican Assistant Profession Bibliography.
Annual Meetings: May
1987-Cincinnati, OH
1988-Los Angeles, CA

00091 12 05 86 1233

Ass'n of Planned Parenthood Professionals (1963)
645 N. Michigan Ave., Suite 1058, Chicago IL 60611
Vice President: Dan Hill
Members: 700-750 *Staff:* 1
Annual Budget: $25-50,000 *Tel:* (312) 787-8456
Hist. Note: Physicians with an active interest in family planning. Formerly (1973) American Ass'n of Planned Parenthood Physicians. Affiliated with Planned Parenthood World Population.
Semi-annual Meetings: Spring and Fall

Ass'n of Plastic Raw Materials Distributors
Hist. Note: Dissolved in 1986.

Ass'n of Political Risk Analysts (1980)
1133 15th St., N.W., Suite 1000, Washington DC 20005
Exec. Director: Joan Walsh Cassedy
Members: 500 individuals and companies *Staff:* 2
Annual Budget: $50-100,000 *Tel:* (202) 293-5913
Publications:
Political Risk Review. bi-m.
Membership Directory. a.
Proceedings. a.
Annual Meetings:
1987-Washington, DC(Washington Plaza)/May 13-14/150

Ass'n of Primary Dealers in U. S. Government Securities (1969)
Hist. Note: Absorbed by the Public Securities Ass'n in 1983.

Ass'n of Private Pension and Welfare Plans (1967)
1331 Pennsylvania Ave., N.W., Suite 719, Washington DC 20004
Exec. Director: Stuart J. Brahs
Members: 475-500 *Staff:* 6-10
Annual Budget: $500-1,000,000 *Tel:* (202) 737-6666
Hist. Note: Focus is on government regulations and legislation concerning private, voluntary retirement savings and welfare benefit arrangements. Members are investment firms, attorneys, benefits administrators, banks, actuaries, associations, accounting firms and employer/plan sponsors. Sponsors and supports the Association of Private Pension and Welfare Plans Political Action Committee.
Publications:
APPWP Newsletter. m.
APPWP Legislative & Regulatory Report.
Legislative Report. a.
Annual Meetings: Spring
1987-Washington, DC(Loew's L'Enfant Plaza)/May 6-9/250-30

Ass'n of Private Postal Systems (1975)
Box 324, Millburn NJ 07041
Exec. Director: Joy Rudy
Members: 60-70 companies *Staff:* 1
Annual Budget: $10-25,000 *Tel:* (201) 376-4996
Hist. Note: Members are companies delivering advertising mail, mostly door to door. Membership: $240/yr. base
Publication:
Update. m.
Annual Meetings: February
1987-Miami, FL/Feb. 5-8

Ass'n of Productivity Specialists (1977)
200 Park Ave., Suite 303E, New York NY 10166
Administrator: Raymond Blydenburgh
Members: 8 companies; 110 individuals *Staff:* 2-5
Annual Budget: $10-25,000 *Tel:* (212) 286-0943
Hist. Note: Membership: $25/yr. (individual); $800/yr. (organization/company)
Publication:
APS Spokesman. irreg.
Annual Meetings: Spring

Ass'n of Professional Bridge Players (1982)
P.O. Box 7104, Berkeley CA 94707
Chief Exec. Officer: Ron Feldman
Members: 150 individuals
Annual Budget: $25-50,000 *Tel:* (415) 548-0862
Hist. Note: Established and incorporated in California. Membership: $50/yr.
Annual Meetings:
1987-Anaheim, CA
1988-Salt Lake City, UT
1989-Chicago, IL(Americana Congress)/July 27-Aug. 7

Ass'n of Professional Color Laboratories (1968)
3000 Picture Place, Jackson MI 49201
Exec. Secretary: Roy S. Pung
Members: 700 companies *Staff:* 2-5
Annual Budget: $100-250,000 *Tel:* (517) 788-8146
Hist. Note: Laboratories doing processing for professional photographers. Managed by The Photo Marketing Association International. Membership: $150/yr.
Publications:
Colorgram. m.
Down to Business. m.
Membership Roster. a.
Glossary of Terms. a.
Annual Meetings: Late Winter
1987-Orlando, FL(Buena Vista Place)/Feb. 5-8
1988-San Francisco, CA(Hyatt Regency Emarcadero)/Jan. 28-31

Ass'n of Professional Design Firms (1985)
117 N. Jefferson St., Suite 305, Chicago IL 60606
President: W. Daniel Wefler
Members: 60 companies *Staff:* 2
Annual Budget: $100-250,000 *Tel:* (312) 559-0320
Hist. Note: Membership is open to firms engaged in graphic, industrial, and commercial interior design. Membership: $750/yr. minimum, based on number of employees.
Publication:
APDF Bulletin. m.
Annual Meetings: June

Ass'n of Professional Directors of YMCAs in the United States (1871)
40 W. Long St., Columbus OH 43215
Exec. Director: James G. Stooke
Members: 3,500-4,000 *Staff:* 2-5
Annual Budget: $100-250,000 *Tel:* (614) 224-2514
Hist. Note: Formerly (1969) Ass'n of Secretaries, Young Men's Christian Ass'ns of North America.
Publications:
Perspective. m. adv.
Journal of Physical Education. 8/yr.
Annual Meetings: Fall

Ass'n of Professional Genealogists (1979)
Box 11601, Salt Lake City UT 84147
President: Glade I. Nelson
Members: 300-400 *Staff:* 2-5
Annual Budget: under $10,000
Hist. Note: Mail to the above address will be forwarded. Membership: $35/year.
Publications:
APG Quarterly. q.
APG List of Professional Genealogists and Related Services. a.
Semi-annual Meetings: Spring and Fall
1987-Raleigh, NC

Ass'n of Professional Material Handling Consultants (1960)
1548 Tower Rd., Winnetka IL 60093
Secretary: Robert B. Footlik
Members: 40 individuals, 30 companies *Staff:* 1
Annual Budget: under $10,000 *Tel:* (312) 441-5920
Hist. Note: Independent material handling consultants, and those who coordinate material handling within multi-plant operations.
Publication:
Newsletter. semi-a.
Semi-annual Meetings:

Ass'n of Professional Orchestra Leaders (1979)
Hist. Note: Address Unknown in 1986.

Ass'n of Professional Vocal Ensembles (1977)
251 South 18th St., Philadelphia PA 19103
Exec. Director: Janice F. Kestler
Members: 220 organizations, 80 individuals *Staff:* 1
Annual Budget: $100-250,000 *Tel:* (215) 545-4444
Hist. Note: Voting members are choral organizations which employ a minimum of 25% of the total ensemble membership or twelve professional singers, whichever is less, and can verify a perfomance scedule of at least four programs for each of two consecutive seasons. Administers the American Choral Foundation. Membership: $30-50/year (individual), .01% of operating budget $50/year minimum (organization).
Publication:
VOICE. bi-m. adv.
Annual Meetings:
1987-San Francisco, CA
1988-Washington, DC
1989-Great Falls, MT

Ass'n of Professional Writing Consultants (1982)
3924 South Troost, Tulsa OK 74105
Secretary: Suzanne S. Webb
Members: 100 individuals
Annual Budget: under $10,000 *Tel:* (918) 743-4793
Hist. Note: Members are full-time independent writing consultants, part-time consultants who primarily teach in colleges and universities, in-company writing consultants, and training professionals. Its purpose is to provide a network and group services for writing consultants, to ensure the quality of writing seminars and other consulting practices, and to inform business and industry about writing consultants. Membership: $20/yr.
Publications:
The Professional Writing Consultant. semi-a.
Membership Directory. a.
Bibliography. a.
Annual Meetings: March
1987-Atlanta, GA(Westin Peachtree Plaza)/March 19-21/50

Ass'n of Professors and Researchers in Religious Education (1970)
1100 East 55th St., Chicago IL 60615
Exec. Secretary: Dr. Donald F. Williams
Members: 325 *Staff:* 1
Annual Budget: under $10,000 *Tel:* (312) 538-3456
Hist. Note: Professors and researchers in religious education in institutions of higher learning, denominational and ecumenical organizations, and other agencies. Originated as the Professors and Research Section of the Division of Christian Education of the Nat'l Council of Churches; Ecumenical, Interfaith, and International since 1970. Became an independent organization in 1970. Member of the Council of Socs. for the Study of Religion. Membership: $25/year.
Publications:
Newsletter. semi-a.
Religious Education. q.
Membership Directory. a.
Annual Meetings: Fall/150

Ass'n of Professors of Gynecology and Obstetrics (1962)
600 Maryland Ave., S.W., Suite 300 East, Washington DC 20024-2591
Administrator: Leona Zanetti
Members: 1,000 *Staff:* 1
Annual Budget: $100-250,000 *Tel:* (202) 393-4417
Hist. Note. Members are drawn from faculties of medical school departments of obstetrics and gynecology.
Publications:
Academic Positions Report. q.
APGO Newsletter. q.
Annual Meetings: February-March in New Orleans at the Fairmont/500

Ass'n of Professors of Medicine (1954)
655 15th St., N.W., Suite 425, Washington DC 20005
Special Asst. for Policy Activities: Lynn Morrison
Members: 125 *Staff:* 2-5
Annual Budget: $50-100,000 *Tel:* (202) 393-1655
Hist. Note: Chairpersons of medical school departments of medicine.
Publication:
APM Monthly News. m.
Semi-annual meetings: Spring and Fall

Ass'n of Professors of Missions (1952)
Boston Univ., School of Theology, 755 Commonwealth Ave., Boston MA 02215
Secretary-Treasurer: Dr. Dana Robert
Members: 100-150 *Staff:* 1
Annual Budget: under $10,000 *Tel:* (617) 353-3064
Hist. Note: Professors teaching in the field of missions in colleges and seminaries. Member of the Council on the Study of Religion.
Annual Meetings: June

Ass'n of Program Directors in Internal Medicine (1978)
969 Madison Avenue, Suite 1103, Memphis TN 38104
Exec. Director: Constance N. Adcock
Members: 400 institutions, 740 individuals *Staff:* 2-5
Annual Budget: $100-250,000 *Tel:* (901) 521-0602
Hist. Note: Seeks to advance medical education through assisting accredited hospital internal medicine education programs. Membership: $400/yr. (institution)
Publication:
Careers in Internal Medicine. q.
Semi-annual Meetings: Spring with American College of Physicians and Fall with Ass'n of American Medical Colleges
1987-New Orleans, LA(Intercontinental)/April 1-2
1987-New Orleans, LA(Fairmont)/Oct. 24-26

Ass'n of Progressive Rental Organizations (1980)
1866 InterFirst Tower, Austin TX 78701
Exec. Director: Elizabeth T. Johnston
Members: 489 companies *Staff:* 10-12
Annual Budget: $500-1,000,000 *Tel:* (512) 478-6521
Hist. Note: Members are television, appliance and furniture dealers who rent merchandise with an option to purchase. Membership: $300-3,000/yr.(dealers); $300/yr.(suppliers).
Publications:
Progressive Rentals. bi-m. adv.
APRO Show Guide. a. adv.
Who's Who in Rent to Own Directory. a. adv.
Annual Meetings: July
1987-New Orleans, LA(Fairmont)/1,600
1988-Las Vegas, NV(Caesar's Palace)/1,700
1989-Undecided
1990-Las Vegas, NV(Caesar's Palace)/1,700

Ass'n of Public Data Users (1975)
Princeton Univ. Computing Center, 87 Prospect Ave., Princeton NJ 08544
Secretariat: Susan Anderson
Members: 150 organizations *Staff:* 1
Annual Budget: $25-50,000 *Tel:* (609) 452-6052
Hist. Note: Facilitates the utilization of public data through the sharing of knowledge about files and applicable software, exchange of documentation, and joint purchasing of data. APDU is committed to increasing the knowledge base of its members about new sources of information and increasing the awareness of Federal agencies about the requirements of data users. Membership: $100/year (individual), $200/year (organization).
Publications:
APDU Newsletter. m.
APDU Membership Directory. a.
Annual Meetings: Fall, in the Washington, DC area

Ass'n of Publicly Traded Investment Funds (1962)
c/o Niagara Share Corporation, 70 Niagara St., Buffalo NY 14202
Chairman: Robert J.A. Irwin
Members: 17 funds *Staff:* 1
Annual Budget: $25-50,000 *Tel:* (716) 856-2600
Hist. Note: Formerly (1977) the Ass'n of Closed-End Investment Companies.

00092 12 05 86 1233

Ass'n of Publishers' Representatives (1950)
Hist. Note: Became the National Association of Publishers' Representatives in 1982.

Ass'n of Racquetsports Manufacturers and Suppliers (1982)
9292 East 131st St., Noblesville IN 46060
Exec. Director: Phil Trotter, Jr.
Members: 25-30 companies *Staff:* 2-5
Annual Budget: $50-100,000 *Tel:* (317) 849-6181
Hist. Note: Members are companies producing goods or services needed in the construction and operation of various types of racquet facilities.
Annual Meetings: With the International Racquet Sports Association.

Ass'n of Radio Reading Services (1978)
1133 20th St., N.W., Washington DC 20036
Nat'l Director: Bernard Posner
Members: 115 reading services *Staff:* 2-5
Annual Budget: $10-25,000 *Tel:* (800) 255-2777
Hist. Note: In the late 1970's, the 15 reading services on the air formed the Ass'n of Radio Reading Services; numbers grew rapidly afterwards, and today 157 transmittal sites exist in all states. Membership open to radio reading services for the blind and other print-handicapped persons. Membership: $100/yr. (individual); $150/yr. (organization/company)
Publication:
Hearsay. q.
Annual Meetings: Spring
1987-Washington, DC(Mayflower Hotel)/May 27-29/150

Ass'n of Railroad Advertising and Marketing (1924)
3706 Palmerston Rd., Shaker Heights OH 44122
Exec. Secretary: Joe D. Singer
Members: 125-150 *Staff:* 1
Annual Budget: under $10,000 *Tel:* (216) 751-9673
Hist. Note: Members are employees of railroad companies and railroad supply companies responsible for advertising, marketing or communications. Established as the Ass'n of Railroad Advertising Managers, it assumed its present name in 1983. Membership: $50/yr.
Annual Meetings: Spring
1987-San Diego, CA(del Coronado)/May 16-20/125

Ass'n of Railroad Editors (1922)
Hist. Note: Became the Ass'n of Railway Communicators in 1985.

Ass'n of Railway Communicators (1922)
c/o Ass'n of American Railroads, American Railroads Bldg., 50 F St., N.W., Washington DC 20001
Secy.-Treas.: J. Ronald Shumate
Members: 130 *Staff:* 1
Annual Budget: under $10,000 *Tel:* (202) 639-2562
Hist. Note: Established as Railway Employees' Magazine Ass'n, it became the Conference of Railway Editors in 1924, the American Railway Magazine Editors Ass'n in 1925, the Ass'n of Railroad Editors in 1964 and assumed its present name in 1985. Membership: $35/year.
Publication:
Proof. m.
Annual Meetings: Fall
1987-Asheville, NC(Grove Park Inn)/Sept. 29-Oct. 2
1988-Hilton Head, SC(Mariner's Inn)/Oct. 4-9

Ass'n of Railway Museums (1961)
P.O. Box 3311, City of Industry CA 91744-0311
Secretary: Brian L. Norden
Members: 48 museums
Annual Budget: under $10,000 *Tel:* (818) 814-1438
Hist. Note: Members are museums of electric and steam railways. Has no paid staff or permanent address. Professional Affiliate Member of American Ass'n of Museums. Membership: $45/yr.
Publication:
ARM Report. q.
Annual Meetings: Fall/200
1987-Riverside, CA/Oct. 16-19
1988-Galveston, TX
1989-Edmonton, Alberta
1990-New Haven, CT

Ass'n of Records Managers and Administrators (1956)
Box 8540, Prairie Village KS 66208
Exec. Director: Louis G. Snyder
Members: 9,000 *Staff:* 6-10
Annual Budget: $1-2,000,000 *Tel:* (913) 341-3808
Hist. Note: Formerly (1975) American Records Management Ass'n. Absorbed (1975) Ass'n of Records Executives and Administrators. Affiliated with the Institute of Certified Records Managers. Membership: $55/yr.
Publication:
ARMA Records Management Quarterly. q. adv.
Annual Meetings: Fall
1987-Anaheim, CA/Sept. 14-17/2,000
1988-Baltimore, MD/Oct. 3-6
1989-New Orleans, LA/Oct. 2-5
1990-San Francisco, LA/Nov. 5-8
1991-Orlando, FL/Sept. 23-26
1992-Detroit, MI/Oct. 19-22

Ass'n of Regional Religious Communicators (1960)
500 Wall St., Suite 415, Seattle WA 98121
President: J. Grayley Taylor
Members: 65-75 *Staff:* 1
Annual Budget: under $10,000 *Tel:* (206) 682-0608
Hist. Note: Members are interfaith broadcasters.
Publication:
Newsletter. bi-m.

Ass'n of Rehabilitation Nurses (1974)
2506 Gross Point Rd., Evanston IL 60201
Exec. Director: Dagny N. Engle, R.N.
Members: 4,500 *Staff:* 2-5
Annual Budget: $250-500,000 *Tel:* (312) 475-1000
Hist. Note: Formed and supports the Rehabilitation Nursing Foundation as its educational and research arm.
Publications:
Rehabilitation Nursing. bi-m. adv.
Newsletter. bi-m.
Annual Meetings: Fall
1987-Anaheim, CA(Disneyland)/Oct. 14-18

Ass'n of Rehabilitation Programs in Data Processing (1978)
18100 Frederick Pike, Bldg. 975/4E22, Gaithersburg MD 20879
Contact: Irv Kaplan
Members: 620 *Staff:* 1
Annual Budget: under $10,000 *Tel:* (301) 670-5444
Hist. Note: Membership includes rehabilitation programs as well as individuals interested in promoting data processing as a career for the handicapped. Has no permanent office or staff; officers change biannually. Membership: $100/year/project, $15/year (individual, associate).
Publication:
Viewpoint. q.
Semi-annual Meetings: May and October

Ass'n of Representatives of Professional Athletes (1978)
10000 Santa Monica Blvd., Suite 312, Century City CA 90067
Exec. Director: Richard S. Brinkman
Members: 175-200 *Staff:* 2-5
Annual Budget: $25-50,000 *Tel:* (213) 553-5607
Hist. Note: Members are lawyers, CPAs and others interested in the efficient representation of professional sports figures. Membership: $300/yr.
Publications:
ARPA newsletter. 10/yr.
Directory a. adv.
Annual Meetings: Spring

Ass'n of Reproduction Materials Manufacturers (1954)
901 N. Washington St., Alexandria VA 22314
Exec. Director: Philip P. Nowers
Members: 40-50 companies *Staff:* 2-5
Annual Budget: $100-250,000 *Tel:* (703) 548-7500
Hist. Note: Formerly (1969) Nat'l Ass'n of Blueprint & Diazotype Coaters.
Annual Meetings: October

Ass'n of Research Directors (1945)
Lever Research, 45 River Rd., Edgewater NJ 07020
Secretary-Treasurer: Dr. A.H. Gilbert
Members: 180 *Staff:* 0
Annual Budget: under $10,000 *Tel:* (201) 943-7100
Hist. Note: A loosely structured group which draws its membership principally from the New York area. Officers change annually, though the Secretary remains two years.

Ass'n of Research Libraries (1932)
1527 New Hampshire Ave., N.W., Washington DC 20036
Exec. Director: Shirley Echelman
Members: 118 libraries *Staff:* 16-20
Annual Budget: $500-1,000,000 *Tel:* (202) 232-2466
Hist. Note: The Association's primary function is to identify and solve problems fundamental to large research libraries. Membership: $5,500/yr.
Publications:
Minutes. semi-a.
Newsletter. bi-m.
Salary Survey. a.
Statistics. a.
Semi-annual Meetings: Spring & Fall/150
1987-Pittsburgh, PA(William Penn)/May 6-8
1987-Washington, DC(Georgetown)/Oct. 22-23
1988-Berkeley, CA(Claremont)/May 4-6
1988-York, England/Sept.
1989-Providence, RI/May
1989-Washington, DC/Oct.
1990-New Orleans, LA/May
1990-Washington, DC/Oct.

Ass'n of Reserve City Bankers (1911)
1710 Rhode Island Ave., N.W., Suite 500, Washington DC 20036
Exec. Director: Dr. Anthony T. Cluff
Members: 400 *Staff:* 2-5
Annual Budget: $250-500,000 *Tel:* (202) 296-5709
Hist. Note: Executive officers of U.S. banks holding deposits from other banking institutions and conducting national banking business.

Ass'n of Reserve Officers of the U.S. Public Health Service (1945)
4349 Klingle St., N.W., Washington DC 20016
Exec. Secretary: James Q. Gant, Jr. M.D.
Members: 400-500 *Staff:* 1
Annual Budget: under $10,000 *Tel:* (202) 363-0744
Hist. Note: Founded in 1945 at the National Institutes of Health.
Biennial meetings: Even years

Ass'n of Retail Marketing Services (1957)
3 Caro Ct., Red Bank NJ 07701
Exec. Director: George Meredith
Members: 140 individuals, 125 companies *Staff:* 6-10
Annual Budget: $100-250,000 *Tel:* (201) 842-5070
Hist. Note: Formerly (1982) Trading Stamp Institute of America and TSIA, Inc., The Ass'n of Retail Marketing Services. Assumed its present name in 1983. Membership: $300/yr.
Publications:
Creative Marketing Newsletter. q.
The Register Newsletter. m.
Directory of Members. a.
Annual Meetings: Fall
1987-Chicago, IL

Ass'n of Retail Travel Agents (1962)
25 South Riverside, Croton on Hudson NY 10520
President: Ronald A. Santana
Members: 3,000-3,400 *Staff:* 6-10
Annual Budget: $100-250,000 *Tel:* (914) 271-9000
Publication:
ARTA FACTS. m.
Semi-annual meetings: Spring and Fall

Ass'n of Rotational Molders (1976)
435 N. Michigan Ave., Suite 1717, Chicago IL 60611
Exec. Director: Joan W. Shelton
Members: 200 companies *Staff:* 2-3
Annual Budget: $250-500,000 *Tel:* (312) 644-0828
Hist. Note: Plastic fabricators employing rotating molds.
Publication:
Roto-Molders Review. semi-m.
Annual Meetings: Semi-annual Meetings

Ass'n of Sales Administration Managers (1981)
P.O. Box 737, Harrison NJ 07029
Contact: Bill Martin
Members: 85-90 individuals
Annual Budget: under $10,000 *Tel:* (201) 481-4800
Hist. Note: Although membership is comprised mainly of companies in the health and beauty field, ASAM seeks to expand its membership to all consumer goods manufacturers. Relatively inactive 1985-86.

Ass'n of School Business Officials Int'l (1910)
1760 Reston Ave., Suite 411, Reston VA 22090
Exec. Director: Ronald A. Allen, CAE
Members: 6,800 *Staff:* 12-15
Annual Budget: $1-2,000,000 *Tel:* (703) 478-0405
Hist. Note: Management-level school business administrators, professors of business and education, students, and businessmen of school-related firms. Membership: $80/yr.
Publications:
ASBO Accents Newspaper. m. adv.
Directory. a. adv.
School Business Affairs. m. adv.
Annual Meetings: Fall
1987-San Antonio, TX(Convention Ctr.)/Oct. 18-22/5,000
1988-Detroit, MI(Cobo Hall)/Oct. 2-6/5,000
1989-Orlando, FL/Oct. 15-19
1990-Toronto, Ontario/Oct. 14-18
1991-New Orleans, LA/Oct. 27-31
1992-Anaheim, CA/Oct. 4-8
1993-Boston, MA/Oct. 31-Nov. 4
1994-Seattle, WA/Oct. 2-6
1995-Nashville, TN/Sept. 30-Oct. 4

Ass'n of Schools and Colleges of Optometry (1941)
6100 Executive Blvd., Suite 514, Rockville MD 20852
Exec. Director: Lee W. Smith
Members: 18 institutions *Staff:* 2-5
Annual Budget: $100-250,000 *Tel:* (301) 231-5944
Hist. Note: Represents professional programs of optometric education in the U.S. and Canada. Membership: $10,500/yr. (organization)
Publications:
Journal of Optometric Education. q. adv.
Optometric Faculty Directory. a.
Survey of Optometric Education. a.
Residency and Graduate Program Directory. a.
Annual Meetings: With the American Optometric Ass'n
1987-Orlando, FL(Marriott Center)/July 2-5/65
1988-Chicago, IL/June
1989-New York, NY/June

Ass'n of Schools of Journalism and Mass Communication (1921)
College of Journalism, Univ. of SC, 1621 College St., Columbia SC 29208-0251
Exec. Director: Jennifer McGill
Members: 170 institutions *Staff:* 5
Annual Budget: $50-100,000 *Tel:* (803) 777-2005
Hist. Note: Founded as the Ass'n of Accredited Schools and Departments of Journalism, it became the American Ass'n of Schools and Departments of Journalism in 1954 and assumed its present name in 1983. Absorbed the American Soc. of

00093 12 05 86 1233

Journalism School Administrators in 1985. Affiliated with the Ass'n for Education in Journalism and Mass Communication. Membership: $200-400/yr. (insititution).
Annual Meetings:
1987-San Antonio, TX(Trinity Univ.)/Aug. 1-4
1988-Portland, OR(Portland Hilton)/July 2-5
1989-Washington, DC

Ass'n of Schools of Public Health (1941)
1015 15th St., N.W., Suite 404, Washington DC 20005
Exec. Director: Michael Gemmell
Members: 23 schools *Staff:* 5
Annual Budget: $500-1,000,000 *Tel:* (202) 842-4668
Hist. Note: The only national organization representing the deans, faculty and students of the twenty-three schools of public health. Established in 1941 to facilitate communication among leadership of the schools.

Ass'n of Science Museum Directors (1960)
Natural History Museum, P.O. Box 1390, San Diego CA 92112
Contact: Charles A. McLaughlin
Members: 90-100 *Staff:* 1
Annual Budget: under $10,000 *Tel:* (619) 232-3821
Publication:
Science Museum News. bi-a.
Annual Meetings: With American Ass'n of Museums

Ass'n of Science-Technology Centers (1973)
1413 K St., N.W., 10th Floor, Washington DC 20005
Exec. Director: Bonnie Van Dorn
Members: 215 museums *Staff:* 11-12
Annual Budget: $500-1,000,000 *Tel:* (202) 371-1171
Hist. Note: Members are science museums and related institutions.
Publication:
ASTC Newsletter. bi-m. adv.
Annual Meetings: Fall/250
1987-Seattle,WA
1988-Boston, MA

Ass'n of Scientists and Engineers of the Naval Sea Systems Command (1975)
Naval Sea Systems Command, PMS415-2, P.O. Box 15684, Arlington VA 22215
Secretary: Dolly Hoffman
Members: 750 *Staff:* 1
Annual Budget: $10-25,000 *Tel:* (202) 692-1227
Hist. Note: Formed in 1975 by the merger of the Ass'n of Naval Weapons Engineers and Scientists (1952) and the Ass'n of Senior Engineers of the Naval Ship Systems Command (1946). Formerly (1978) known as Ass'n of Scientists and Engineers in the Naval Air and Sea Systems Commands. Members are all civilian technical employees of the Navy. Has no paid staff or permanent officers. Membership: $10/yr.
Publication:
The Scientist and Engineer. 10/yr.
Annual Meetings: Spring in Washington

Ass'n of Second Class Mail Publishers (1964)
Hist. Note: Became the Association of Paid Circulation Publications in 1982.

Ass'n of Seventh-day Adventist Educators (1970)
6840 Eastern Avenue, N. W., Washington DC 20012
Exec. Secretary: Gordon Madgwick
Members: 800 *Staff:* 2-5
Annual Budget: under $10,000 *Tel:* (202) 722-6424
Hist. Note: Formerly Ass'n of Seventh-day Adventist Institutions of Higher Learning and Secondary Schools.
Publications:
Journal of Adventist Education. 5/yr.
Seventh-Day Adventist Yearbook. a.

Ass'n of Ship Brokers and Agents (U.S.A.) (1934)
305 Broadway, Room 804, New York NY 10007
Secretary: Virginia M. Dougherty
Members: 105 *Staff:* 2
Annual Budget: $100-250,000 *Tel:* (212) 608-6888
Hist. Note: Founded as the Association of Ship Brokers and Agents on January 9, 1934 in the Arbitration Room of the New York Produce Exchange at Two Broadway. The Association incorporated in 1954 and assumed its present name in 1970. Members are ship brokers and ship agents.
Publications:
American Tanker Rate Schedule. a.
ASBA Newsletter. q.
Yearbook. a. adv.
Annual Meetings: Second Tuesday in January

Ass'n of Sleep Disorders Centers (1975)
604 Second St., S.W., Rochester MN 55902
Administrator: Carol C. Westbrook
Members: 150 centers *Staff:* 2-5
Annual Budget: $100-250,000 *Tel:* (507) 287-6006
Hist. Note: Formerly (1976) American Ass'n of Sleep Disorder Centers.
Publications:
ASDC Newsletter. q.
SLEEP. q. adv.
Annual Meetings: Fall

Ass'n of Small Business Development Centers (1980)
1050 17th St., N.W., Washington DC 20036
Washington Counsel: Allen Neece, Jr.
Members: 50 *Staff:* 1
Annual Budget: $100-250,000 *Tel:* (202) 887-5599
Hist. Note: SBDCs are small business development centers which provide management and technical assistance to small business concerns and are jointly funded by federal and state governments. Previously the Small Business Development Center Directors Ass'n.

Ass'n of Social and Behavioral Scientists (1935)
Box 4371, Fort Valley State College, Fort Valley GA 31030
Exec. Secretary: Dr. Yvonne Buford
Members: 300
Annual Budget: $10-25,000 *Tel:* (912) 825-6446
Hist. Note: Founded in Charlotte, NC in October 1935 as the Ass'n of Social Science Teachers in Negro Schools. Became the Ass'n of Social and Behavioral Scientists in 1968.
Publication:
Journal of Social and Behavioral Sciences. q. adv.
Annual Meetings: Spring

Ass'n of Soil and Foundation Engineers (1969)
8811 Colesville Rd., Suite G106, Silver Spring MD 20910
Exec. Director: John P. Bachner
Members: 300 companies, 2,500 individuals *Staff:* 7
Annual Budget: $100-250,000 *Tel:* (301) 565-2733
Hist. Note: Seeks the enhancement of professionalism and the reduction of liability loss exposure. Formerly (1975) Associated Soil and Foundation Engineers.
Publication:
Newslog. 8/yr.
Semi-Annual Meetings: April and October

Ass'n of Southern Baptist Colleges and Schools (1915)
901 Commerce, Suite 600, Nashville TN 37203-3260
Exec. Secretary: Arthur L. Walker, Jr.
Members: 69 institutions *Staff:* 6-10
Tel: (615) 244-2362
Hist. Note: Consists of the presidents and chief academic officials of Southern Baptist colleges, universities, seminaries, Bible schools and academies. Formerly known as the Southern Ass'n of Baptist Colleges and Schools.
Publication:
Southern Baptist Educator. m.
Annual Meetings: June/125
1987-Kansas City, MO(Marriott-Plaza)/June 29-July 1
1988-Greenville, SC/June 27-29

Ass'n of Specialists in Cleaning and Restoration (1945)
5205 Leesburg Pike, Suite 1408, Falls Church VA 22041-3802
Acting Managing Director: Helen Bradley
Members: 5-600 companies *Staff:* 6-10
Annual Budget: $500-1,000,000 *Tel:* (703) 845-1400
Hist. Note: Formerly (1984) the Ass'n of Interior Decor Specialists. Divisions: Carpet & Upholstery Cleaning Institute (1971); Drapery Specialists Institute (1971); Nat'l Institute of Fire Restoration (1968); and Nat'l Institute of Rug Cleaning (1945). Membership: $3-700/yr.
Publication:
Cleaning and Restoration. m. adv.
Annual Meetings: Spring
1987-St. Louis, MO(Omni Internat'l)/March 10-15/400
1988-Orlando, FL(Wyndham)/April 5-10/400

Ass'n of Specialized and Cooperative Library Agencies (1944)
50 East Huron St., Chicago IL 60611
Exec. Director: Sandra M. Cooper
Members: 1,450 *Staff:* 2-5
Annual Budget: $50-100,000 *Tel:* (312) 944-6780
Hist. Note: Division of the American Library Ass'n. Formerly known as the Ass'n of State Library Agencies, the Ass'n of Hospital and Institution Libraries (until 1974), and Health and Rehabilitative Library Services (until 1978).
Publication:
Interface. q.
Annual Meetings: With the American Library Ass'n

Ass'n of Sports Museums and Halls of Fame (1971)
4 West Dale Road, Wilmington DE 19810
Exec. Director: Al Cartwright
Members: 65 organizations *Staff:* 1
Annual Budget: under $10,000 *Tel:* (302) 475-7068
Hist. Note: Established as the Ass'n of Sports Hall of Fame Directors, it assumed its present name in 1972. Membership: $50/yr.
Publications:
Newsletter. q. adv.
Organizing a Sports Museum/Hall of Fame.
Annual Meetings: Fall, usually at a Hall of Fame.

Ass'n of State and Interstate Water Pollution Control Administrators (1962)
444 North Capitol St., N.W., Suite 330, Washington DC 20001
Exec. Director: Robbi J. Savage
Members: 63 *Staff:* 2-5
Annual Budget: $100-250,000 *Tel:* (202) 624-7782
Hist. Note: The chief water pollution control administrators from 50 states, Guam, Virgin Islands, Puerto Rico, the District of Columbia, and 5 interstate agencies. Establishes objectives, policies, and standards for state water pollution control activities.
Annual Meetings:
1987-Hartford, CT(Sheraton Hartford)/Aug. 9-12

Ass'n of State and Territorial Dental Directors (1942)
State Dept. of Health & Environ Sciences,ogswell Bldg., Helena MT 59620
Secy.-Treas.: Dr. William Haggberg
Members: 50-55 *Staff:* 1
Annual Budget: under $10,000 *Tel:* (406) 444-4740
Hist. Note: Established in 1942. Affiliate of the Ass'n of State and Territorial Health Officials. Has no paid staff or permanent office. Membership: $25/yr.
Publication:
Newsletter. q. adv.
Annual Meetings: Spring
1987-Mobile, AL

Ass'n of State and Territorial Directors of Nursing (1935)
South Carolina Dept. of Health, 2600 Bull St., Columbia SC 29201
President: Lillian McCreight
Members: 54
Annual Budget: under $10,000 *Tel:* (803) 734-4890
Hist. Note: Established in 1935 as a council of the American Public Health Ass'n, it later became Ass'n of State and Territorial Directors of Public Health Nursing. In 1966 the name was changed to Ass'n of State and Terrritorial Directors of Nursing. Affiliated with Ass'n of State and Territorial Health Officials. Has no paid staff or permanent address. The President is elected for a 2-year term.
Annual Meetings: May, with the Ass'n of State and Territorial Health Officials.

Ass'n of State and Territorial Health Officials (1942)
1311 Dolley Madison Blvd., #3A, McLean VA 22101
Exec. Director: George K. Degnon, CAE
Members: 55 *Staff:* 2
Annual Budget: $50-100,000 *Tel:* (703) 556-9222
Hist. Note: Formerly (1975) Ass'n of State and Territorial Health Officers. Members are state and territorial health authorities.
Publications:
State Health Agency Directory. bi-a.
Prevention Notes (newsletter). bi-m.
Annual Meetings: Spring
1987-Tempe, AZ/May 3-6
1988-Charleston, SC/May

Ass'n of State and Territorial MCH-CC Directors (1955)
Hist. Note: Became the Association of Maternal and Child Health and Crippled Children's Programs in 1982.

Ass'n of State and Territorial Solid Waste Management Officials (1974)
444 North Capitol St., N.W., Suite 345, Washington DC 20001
Exec. Director: Sue Moreland
Members: 110-120 individuals *Staff:* 2-5
Annual Budget: $250-500,000 *Tel:* (202) 624-5828
Hist. Note: Members are directors of state solid and hazardous waste programs, and associate members are program staff. Membership: $20/yr.
Annual Meetings: Fall

Ass'n of State Correctional Administrators (1960)
National Institute of Correction, Spring Hill West, South Salem NY 10590
Exec. Officer: George M. Camp
Members: 58 *Staff:* 4
Annual Budget: $100-250,000 *Tel:* (914) 533-2562
Hist. Note: Formerly (1967) Correctional Administrators Association of America. ASCA's membership consists of the directors of all fifty state correctional agencies, the Federal Bureau of Prisons, and several large urban prison systems. It's purpose is to provide leadership and direction on national correctional policy and practice.
Annual Meetings: Semi-annual meetings

Ass'n of State Drinking Water Administrators (1985)
1911 North Fort Myer Drive, Suite 803, Arlington VA 22209
Exec. Director: G. Wade Miller
Members: 57 states & territories *Staff:* 3
Annual Budget: $100-250,000 *Tel:* (703) 524-2428
Hist. Note: Members include all 57 states and territories; individuals who work for state or local water utilities are also eligible for membership.
Publication:
Newsletter. q.
Annual Meetings: February
1987-San Diego, CA/Feb. 23-26

Ass'n of State Juvenile Justice Administrators (1968)
Hist. Note: Merged with the Nat'l Ass'n of Juvenile Correctional Agencies in 1984.

00094 12 05 86 1233

Ass'n of Steel Distributors (1943)
111 E. Wacker Drive, Chicago IL 60601
Exec. Director: Edward Craft
Members: 155 companies *Staff:* 3
Annual Budget: $250-500,000 *Tel:* (312) 644-6610
Hist. Note: Members are service centers, warehouses, processors, traders, depots and manufacturers. Membership: $1200/yr.
Publication:
News & Views.
Annual Meetings: Spring
1987-Miami, FL(Doral Country Club)/March/125-150

Ass'n of Surgical Technologists (1969)
8307 Shaffer Parkway, Littleton CO 80127
Exec. Director: Sandra L. Wilkins
Members: 10-11,000 *Staff:* 11-15
Annual Budget: $500-1,000,000 *Tel:* (303) 978-9010
Hist. Note: Incorporated as a non-profit educational association under the name Ass'n of Operating Room Technicians; the present name was assumed in 1978. Awards the CST ("Certified Surgical Technologist") designation. Membership $55/yr.
Publication:
Surgical Technologist. bi-m. adv.
Annual Meetings: Spring
1987-Las Vegas, NV(Riviera)/May 12-15

Ass'n of Synthetic Yarn Manufacturers (1970)
Box 66, Gastonia NC 28053
Exec. Director: Jim H. Conner
Members: 25-30 companies *Staff:* 2-5
Annual Budget: $25-50,000 *Tel:* (704) 824-3522
Hist. Note: Formerly Synthetic Yarn Manufacturers Ass'n. Affiliated with American Yarn Spinners Ass'n.
Annual Meetings: February

Ass'n of Systematics Collections (1972)
730 11 St., N.W. Third Floor, Washington DC 20001
Assistant Director: Lincoln Fairchild
Members: 78 institutions, 20 societies *Staff:* 3
Annual Budget: $100-250,000 *Tel:* (202) 347-2850
Hist. Note: Members are museums, colleges and universities using their natural history collections for systematics (the study and classification of organisms according to their natural relationships). Professional societies of individuals interested in the systematics of organisms are also included in the membership. Membership: $550, 1,700 or 4,500/yr. (based on size of organization).
Publication:
Newsletter. bi-m. adv.
Annual Meetings: Spring, near a member institution in a museum environment

Ass'n of Teacher Educators (1920)
1900 Association Dr., Suite ATE, Reston VA 22091
Exec. Director: Dr. Robert J. Stevenson
Members: 3,000-3,100 *Staff:* 2-5
Annual Budget: $100-250,000 *Tel:* (703) 620-3110
Hist. Note: Founded as the National Association of Supervisors of Student Teaching, it became the Association for Student Teaching in 1946 and assumed its present name in 1970. Originally a division of the National Education Association, it became independent in 1975. Membership: $45/year.
Publications:
ATE Newsletter. bi-m.
Action in Teacher Education. q. adv.
Annual Meetings: February/1,000
1987-Houston, TX/Feb. 15-18
1988-San Diego, CA/Feb. 13-17

Ass'n of Teachers of English as a Second Language (1951)
Hist. Note: Section of the Nat'l Ass'n for Foreign Student Affairs

Ass'n of Teachers of Japanese (1963)
East Asian Languages & Literature, Univ. of Wisconsin, 1206 Linden Dr., Madison WI 53706
President: James O'Brien
Members: 600 *Staff:* 1
Annual Budget: under $10,000 *Tel:* (608) 262-2291
Publications:
ATJ Newsletter. 3/yr.
Journal of The Association of Teachers of Japanese. semi-a. adv.
Annual Meetings: With Ass'n for Asian Studies

Ass'n of Teachers of Latin American Studies (1970)
252-58 63rd Ave., Flushing NY 11362
President: Daniel J. Mugan
Members: 815 *Staff:* 2-5
Annual Budget: $50-100,000 *Tel:* (718) 428-1237
Hist. Note: An organization of educators and other persons interested in the promotion of study about Latin America in our education institutions. Membership: $10/yr.
Publications:
Perspective (newsletter). q. adv.
Curriculum Guides on Ecuador, Brazil and Argentina.
Annual Meetings: Semi-annual Meetings

Ass'n of Teachers of Preventive Medicine (1942)
1030 15th St., N.W., Suite 1020, Washington DC 20005
Exec. Director: Dennis Barbour, J.D.
Members: 650 individuals, 40 institutions *Staff:* 5
Annual Budget: $250-500,000 *Tel:* (202) 682-1698
Hist. Note: Teachers of preventive medicine and community health in medical schools. Sponsors the ATPM Foundation. Affiliated with the Ass'n of American Medical Colleges and the Council on Education for Public Health. Membership: $65/yr. (individual); $300/yr. (institution)
Publications:
American Journal of Preventive Medicine. q.
ATPM Newsletter. q.
Perspectives on Prevention. q.
ATPM Roster. a.
Annual Meetings: Spring, with American College of Preventive Medicine

Ass'n of Teachers of Technical Writing (1973)
Dept. of English, Texas Tech Univ., Lubbock TX 79409-4530
Secy.-Treas.: Carolyn Rude
Members: 1,200
Annual Budget: $10-25,000
Hist. Note: An "allied" organization of the Modern Language Ass'n and the Conference on College Composition and Communication, ATTW's purpose is to provide communication among teachers of technical writing. Begun in 1973 with a dozen or so members, ATTW is now an international organization. Membership includes teachers from all levels and all types of educational institutions, and technical writers from government and industry. Has no paid staff.
Publication:
The Technical Writing Teacher. 3/yr.
Semi-annual Meetings: March with CCCC and Dec. with MLA

Ass'n of Tennis Professionals (1972)
611 Ryan Plaza Drive, 6th Fl., Arlington TX 76011-9990
Exec. Director: Ron Bookman
Members: 300-350 *Staff:* 20-25
Tel: (817) 860-1166
Hist. Note: Founded in 1972 at Forest Hills, New York. Membership restricted to leading touring professional players. Operates the official computerized player ranking system.
Publication:
International Tennis Weekly. w. adv.

Ass'n of Tequila Producers (1979)
P.O. Box 58083, Dallas TX 75258
Director: Herbert H. Lee
Members: 15 companies *Staff:* 2
Annual Budget: $100-250,000 *Tel:* (214) 239-9578
Hist. Note: Seeks to educate the members of the trade and consumers about facts concerning the history, production and uses of tequila.
Publication:
Tequila Book.

Ass'n of the Customs Bar (1917)
Hist. Note: Became the Customs and International Trade Bar Association in 1982.

Ass'n of the Institute for Certification of Computer Professionals (1971)
2200 East Devon Ave., Suite 268, Des Plaines IL 60018
President: William W. Fly
Members: 2,200 *Staff:* 2
Annual Budget: $25-50,000 *Tel:* (312) 299-4227
Hist. Note: AICCP has been designated by the Institute for Certification of Computer Professionals as the membership organization for holders of the Certificate in Data Processing (CDP), the Certificate in Computer Programming (CCP), the Certificate for Systems Professionals (CSP), and the Associate Computer Professional (ACP). Its purpose is to promote professionalism and certification in the computer professions. Membership: $35/yr.
Publication:
AICCP Newsletter. m. adv.
Annual Meetings: Not held

Ass'n of the Nat'l Panhellenic Conference Central Office (1943)
Hist. Note: Became the Central Office Executives Ass'n of the Nat'l Panhellenic Conference (1985).

Ass'n of the Nonwoven Fabrics Industry
Hist. Note: See INDA, Ass'n of the Nonwoven Fabrics Industry.

Ass'n of the United States Army (1950)
2425 Wilson Blvd., Arlington VA 22201
Exec. V. President: Maj.Gen. Robert F. Cocklin, AUS(Ret.)
Members: 165,000 *Staff:* 65-70
Annual Budget: over $5,000,000 *Tel:* (703) 841-4300
Hist. Note: Formed by a merger of the U.S. Infantry Ass'n and the U.S. Field Artillery Ass'n. Absorbed (1955) the U.S. Antiaircraft Ass'n. Active, retired and reserve military personnel. Has budget of $9 million. Membership: $16/yr.
Publications:
Army Magazine. m. adv.
AUSA News. m.
Annual Meetings: October, in Washington, DC at the Sheraton with an attendance of 25,000.
1987-Oct. 12-14
1988-Oct. 17-19
1989-Oct. 16-18

Ass'n of the Wall and Ceiling Industries-Internat'l (1918)
25 K St., N.E., Suite 300, Washington DC 20002
Exec. V. President: Joe M. Baker, Jr., CAE
Members: 1,300 *Staff:* 10-15
Annual Budget: $2-5,000,000 *Tel:* (202) 783-2924
Hist. Note: Formerly (until July 1, 1979) known as the IAWCC/GDCI. A consolidation in July, 1976 of the Gypsum Drywall Contractors Internat'l and the Internat'l Ass'n of Wall and Ceiling Contractors. The Gypsum Drywall Contractors Internat'l was founded in 1957 as the Internat'l Drywall Contractors Ass'n, and became the GDCI in 1959. The Internat'l Ass'n of Wall and Ceiling Contractors was founded in 1918 as the Contracting Plasterers' Internat'l Ass'n, became the Contracting Plasterers' and Lathers' Internat'l Ass'n in 1956, and changed to the IAWCC in 1970. Supports the Wall and Ceiling Political Action Committee, the Foundation of the Wall & Ceiling Industry, and the Asbestos Abatement Council. Membership: $400/yr.
Publications:
First Tuesday. m.
Construction Dimensions. m. adv.
Asbestos Abatement. m. adv.
Annual Meetings: Feb./March/April
1987-New Orleans, LA(Hyatt Regency)/March 4-8
1988-Nashville, TN(Opryland)/March 16-20

Ass'n of Theological Schools in the United States and Canada (1918)
P.O. Box 130, 42 E. National Rd., Vandalia OH 45377
Exec. Director: Dr. Leon Pacala
Members: 200-205 *Staff:* 11-15
Annual Budget: $1-2,000,000 *Tel:* (513) 898-4654
Hist. Note: Founded as the Conference of Theological Seminaries of the United States and Canada, it became the American Association of Theological Schools in 1936, absorbed the American Association of Schools of Religious Education in 1965 and assumed its present name in 1975. Incorporated in 1955. The association is the recognized accrediting agency for graduate schools of theology.
Publications:
Bulletin. bi-a.
Directory. a.
Theological Education. semi-a.
Biennial Meeings: even years
1988-San Francisco, CA/June 13-15

Ass'n of Tile, Terrazzo, Marble Contractors and Affiliates (1947)
626 Lakeland East Drive, Jackson MS 39208
Exec. Director: Joe A. Tarver
Members: 550 companies *Staff:* 3
Annual Budget: $250-500,000 *Tel:* (601) 939-2071
Hist. Note: Formerly Southern Tile, Terrazzo, Marble Contractors Ass'n. Membership limited to individuals, firms, and corporations engaged in the installation, manufacture, or sale of ceramic tile, terrazzo, marble and allied products. Membership: $150/yr.
Publications:
Tileletter. m. adv.
Buyers Guide. a. adv.
Annual Meetings: Spring
1987-Orlando, FL(Peabody)/April 22-25/1,000-1,200

Ass'n of Tongue Depressors (1978)
Hist. Note: Address unknown in 1985-86; probably defunct.

Ass'n of Transportation Practioners (1929)
1211 Connecticut Ave., N.W., Suite 310, Washington DC 20036
Exec. Director: Norma L. Iser
Members: 2,200 *Staff:* 4
Annual Budget: $250-500,000 *Tel:* (202) 466-2080
Hist. Note: Formerly (1939) Ass'n of Practitioners before the Interstate Commerce Commission and (1983) Ass'n of Interstate Commerce Commission Practitioners. Attorneys and transportation specialists admitted to practice before the I.C.C. and other transportation regulatory agencies. Membership: $85/yr. (individual).
Publications:
Transportation Practitioners Journal. q.
Eastern Transportation Law Seminar Papers & Proceedings. bi-a.
Western Transportation Law Seminar Papers & Proceedings. bi-a.
Annual Meetings:
1987-Fontane, WI(Abbey on Lake Geneva)/June 28-July 1
1988-San Diego, CA(Islandia Hyatt)/June 26-30

Ass'n of Travel Marketing Executives (1980)
804 D St., N.E., Washington DC 20002
Exec. Director: Cynthia K. Hawkins
Members: 250-300 *Staff:* 2-5
Annual Budget: $10-25,000 *Tel:* (202) 546-9409
Hist. Note: Members work in an executive or managerial capacity that is primarily but not exclusively related to marketing a travel product or service. Membership: $95/yr.
Publications:
Travel and Tourism. m. adv.
Executuve Newsletter.

00095 12 05 86 1233

Ass'n of Trial Behavior Consultants (1982)
Hist. Note: Became the American Soc. of Trial Consultants in January, 1987.

Ass'n of Trial Lawyers of America (1946)
1050 31st St., N.W., Washington DC 20007
Exec. Director: Marianna S. Smith
Members: 70,000 *Staff:* 100
Annual Budget: over $5,000,000 *Tel:* (202) 965-3500
Hist. Note: Founded as the NACCA Bar Ass'n (Nat'l Ass'n of Claimant's Compensation Attorneys); became the American Trial Lawyers Ass'n in 1964 and the Ass'n of Trial Lawyers of America in 1972. Affiliated with the Nat'l Conference of Law Reviews. Sponsors the Attorneys Congressional Campaign Trust, a political action committee interested principally in electing members of Congress who will oppose no-fault insurance and strengthen the adversary system of tort litigation. Sponsors the Nat'l College of Advocacy. Has an annual budget of 8,000,000.
Publications:
ATLA Law Journal. biennial.
ATLA Law Reporter. 10/yr.
ATLA Advocate. 10/yr.
Products Liability Law Reporter. 10/yr.
Trial. m. adv.
Professional Negligence Reporter.
Annual Meetings: Summer/2,500
1987-San Diego/July

Ass'n of Umbrella Manufacturers and Suppliers
Reported as defunct in 1982.

Ass'n of United States Night Vision Manufacturers (1980)
918 16th St., N.W., Suite 702, Washington DC 20006
Exec. V. President: John F. Cove
Members: 9 companies *Staff:* 2-5
Annual Budget: $100-250,000 *Tel:* (202) 638-3707
Hist. Note: Members are makers of night vision devices, systems, or components.
Publication:
Nightlines. m.
Annual Meetings: January

Ass'n of United States University Directors of Interant'l Agricultural Programs (1964)
Univ. of Illinois, Urbana IL 61801
Secy.-Treas.: Dr. Thomas A. McCowen
Members: 240 *Staff:* 1
Annual Budget: under $10,000 *Tel:* (217) 333-6422
Hist. Note: Members are international development professionals representing educational, research and extension interests in international agriculture. Affiliated with the Nat'l Ass'n of State Universities and Land Grant Colleges. Membership: $10/year.
Annual Meetings:
1987-Kingston, RI(University of Rhode Island)/June 2-4

Ass'n of Universities for Research in Astronomy (1957)
2100 Pennsylvania Ave., N.W., Suite 820, Washington DC 20037
President: Dr. Goetz Oertel
Members: 20 institutions *Staff:* 4
Annual Budget: $500-1,000,000 *Tel:* (202) 955-9000
Hist. Note: A consortium of universities managing government-financed observatories in the U.S. and abroad.
Annual Meetings: Spring
1987-Tucson, AZ/March

Ass'n of University Anesthetists (1953)
Dept. of Anesthesia, Box 238, University of Virgina Medical Center, Charlottesville VA 22908
Secretary: Dr. Edward D. Miller, Jr.
Members: 300 *Staff:* 1
Annual Budget: under $10,000 *Tel:* (804) 924-2283

Ass'n of University Architects (1955)
Kansas Bd. of Regents, Suite 609 Capitol, Tower, 400 S.W. Eighth St., Topeka KS 66603
President: Warren Corman
Members: 90-100
Annual Budget: under $10,000 *Tel:* (913) 296-3421
Hist. Note: Licensed architects whose full-time job is the development of the university or college employing them.
Publications:
Annual Report. a.
Newsletter. q.
Annual Meetings: At various University locations

Ass'n of University Programs in Health Administration (1948)
1911 North Fort Myer Drive, Suite 503, Arlington VA 22209
President: Gary L. Filerman
Members: 1,000 *Staff:* 20-25
Annual Budget: $1-2,000,000 *Tel:* (703) 524-5500
Publications:
Health Administration Education. bien.
Journal of Health Administration Education. q.
Staff Report. m.
Annual Meetings: Spring
1987-Montreal, Quebec(Queen Elizabeth Hotel)/April 30-May 3/300-400
1988-Washington, DC(Grand Hyatt)/April 14-17/300-400

Ass'n of University Programs in Occupational Health and Safety (1981)
Hist. Note: This organization has no dues or paid staff beyond a lobbyist in Washington. Members are twelve universities having graduate, OSHA-funded, medical programs in such areas as accident prevention, toxicology, etc.

Ass'n of University Radiologists (1953)
1891 Preston White Drive, Reston VA 22091
Exec. Secretary: Sheila A. Aubin
Members: 1,300 *Staff:* 2-5
Annual Budget: $25-50,000 *Tel:* (703) 648-8900
Hist. Note: Members are full-time academic radiologists, involved in teaching and laboratory and clinical investigation. Associate member of the Coalition for Health Funding in Washington.
Publication:
Newsletter. m.
Annual Meetings: Spring/450
1987-Charleston, SC/March 22-27

Ass'n of University Summer Sessions (1917)
Summer Sessions Of., Maxwell Hall 254, Indiana University, Bloomington IN 47405
Recorder: Dr. Leslie J. Coyne
Members: 50 institutions
Annual Budget: under $10,000 *Tel:* (812) 335-5048
Hist. Note: Formerly (1964) Ass'n of Summer Sessions Deans and Directors.
Annual Meetings: October
1987-Palo Alto,CA
1988-Chicago, IL(Northwestern Univ.)

Ass'n of Urban Universities (1914)
1225 Connecticut Ave., N.W., Room 306, Washington DC 20036
President: Jim Harrison
Members: 30 *Staff:* 3
Tel: (202) 387-2130
Hist. Note: Established by about 20 universities to work for reauthorization and funding of the Urban Grant Act (now Title XI, Higher Education Act) and to represent the legislative and regulatory interests of the nation's urban universities.

Ass'n of Vacuum Equipment Manufacturers (1969)
230 North Michigan Ave., Room 1200, Chicago IL 60601
Exec. Secretary: Kenneth B. Andersen, CAE
Members: 35 companies *Staff:* 1
Annual Budget: $10-25,000 *Tel:* (312) 853-0432
Hist. Note: Membership: $315-862.50/yr.
Annual Meetings: Fall, with the American Vacuum Soc.

Ass'n of Visual Communicators (1957)
900 Palm Ave., Suite B, South Pasadena CA 91030
Exec. Director: Michael Adrio
Members: 800 *Staff:* 2-5
Annual Budget: $250-500,000 *Tel:* (818) 441-2274
Hist. Note: Originally (1957) Industry Film Producer Ass'n; most recently (1985) Information Film Producers of America. Members are audio-visual professionals using the media of film, video, slides, filmstrips, multi-image and video disks to communicate information. Membership: $60/yr.
Publications:
AVC Communicator. bi-m. adv.
AVC Directory. a. adv.

Ass'n of Visual Science Librarians (1968)
Pacific University, The Library, Forest Grove OR 97116
President: Laurel Gregory
Members: 50 *Staff:* 1
Annual Budget: under $10,000 *Tel:* (503) 359-2204
Hist. Note: Established in Beverly Hills, California at the 1968 meeting of the American Academy of Optometry. Members are librarians whose collections or services include the literature of vision. Has no paid officers or staff. Officers serve for two years.
Annual Meetings: With the American Academy of Optometry in December and with the Medical Library Ass'n in June

Ass'n of Vitamin Chemists (1943)
Hist. Note: An organization of individuals dedicated to the advancement of vitamin methodology. Has no permanent staff; officers change annually. Address unknown in 1987.

Ass'n of Voluntary Action Scholars (1971)
Lincoln Filene Ctr., Tufts University, Medford MA 02155
Secretary: Louise Choate
Members: 460 individuals
Annual Budget: $25-50,000 *Tel:* (617) 381-3450
Hist. Note: A professional and scholarly association for all those who are concerned with better understanding of citizen involvement and volunteer participation. Membership: $35/yr. (individual); $60/yr. (organization/company)
Publications:
Citizen Participation and Voluntary Action Abstracts. q.
Journal of Voluntary Action Research. m.
Newsletter. m.
Annual Meetings: Fall
1987-Kansas City, MO

Ass'n of Volunteer Bureaus (1951)
Hist. Note: Reported as defunct in 1984.

Ass'n of Water Transportation Accounting Officers (1912)
Box 53, Bowling Green Sta., New York NY 10004
Secy.-Treas.: Vincent Fiorenza
Members: 325-350 *Staff:* 1
Annual Budget: $25-50,000 *Tel:* (212) 264-1384
Hist. Note: Formerly (until 1943) the Ass'n of Water Line Accounting Officers. Members are officers in the accounting departments of water transportation companies. Membership: $40/yr. (individual); $125/yr. (organization/company)
Publications:
Annual Report. a.
Bulletin. bi-m.
Annual Meetings: Fall, in the East
1987-Whitehaven, PA(Pocono Hershey)/Sept. 18-19

Ass'n of Women Government Contractors (1980)
Hist. Note: Merged in March 1983 with the National Association of Women Federal Contractors to form the National Association of Women Government Contractors.

Ass'n of Women in Architecture (1922)
7440 University Dr., St. Louis MO 63130
Historian: Betty Lou Custer, FAIA
Members: 1,100-1,200 *Staff:* 1
Annual Budget: under $10,000 *Tel:* (314) 621-3484

Ass'n of World Trade Chamber Executives (1951)
Hist. Note: Address unknown since 1984, probably inactive.

Ass'n of Yarn Distributors
Hist. Note: No paid staff; address unknown in 1986.

Ass'n on Handicapped Student Service Programs in Postsecondary Education (1978)
P.O. Box 21192, Columbus OH 43221
Exec. Director: Jane E. Jarrow
Members: 742 *Staff:* 3
Annual Budget: $100-250,000 *Tel:* (614) 488-4972
Hist. Note: Members are committed to improving post-secondary educational opportunities for handicapped students. Membership: $50/yr. (professional); $125/yr. (institution)
Publications:
ALERT Newsletter. bi-m.
AHSSPPE Bulletin. q.
Membership Directory. a.
Annual Meetings: July
1987-Washington, DC(Mayflower Hotel)/July 22-25
1988-New Orleans, LA(Sheraton)/July 20-23

Ass'n on Programs for Female Offenders (1960)
Georgia Dept. of Correction, 2 Martin Luther King Dr., S.E., Atlanta GA 30334
President: Elaine DeCostanzo
Members: 90 *Staff:* 1
Annual Budget: under $10,000 *Tel:* (404) 656-4543
Hist. Note: Formerly (1975) Women's Correctional Ass'n, APFO is an affiliate of the American Correctional Ass'n. Organized by corrections professionals, APFO is open to all persons in related fields who are dedicated to the improvement of services to female offenders as well as in the total corrections field. Membership: $15/yr.
Publication:
Newsletter. q.
Annual Meetings: With American Correctional Ass'n

Ass'n to Advance Ethical Hypnosis (1956)
2500 East Hallandale Beach Blvd., Hallandale FL 33009
Exec. Director: Martin Segall
Members: 1,500-2,000 *Staff:* 1
Annual Budget: under $10,000 *Tel:* (305) 458-3039
Publications:
Journal of the Ass'n to Advance Eyhical Hypnosis.
Suggestion. bi-m.
Annual Meetings: October

ASTM (1898)
1916 Race St., Philadelphia PA 19103
President: Joseph G. O'Grady
Members: 30,000 *Staff:* 200
Annual Budget: over $5,000,000 *Tel:* (215) 299-5400
Hist. Note: Originated in 1898 as the American Section of the Internat'l Ass'n for Testing Materials. Became the American Soc. for Testing Materials in 1902 and incorporated in 1904. The world's largest source of voluntary consensus standards for materials, products, systems and services, ASTM also promotes related technical knowledge. Maintains a Washington office. Has a budget of $16,000,000. Membership: $50/year.
Publications:
ASTM Standardization News. m. adv.
Book of Standards. a.
Cement and Concrete Aggregates Journal. semi-a.
Composites Technology & Research. q.
Geotechnical Testing Journal. q.
Journal of Forensic Science. q. adv.
Journal of Testing and Evaluation. bi-m.
Annual Meetings: Not held

Astrologers Guild of America (1927)
Hist. Note: Address unkown in 1987. Presumed defunct.

Athletic Equipment Managers Ass'n (1974)
723 Kiel Court, Bowling Green OH 43402
President: Bill Kelly
Members: 475-500 *Staff:* 1
Annual Budget: under $10,000 *Tel:* (419) 352-1207
Hist. Note: Membership: $15/yr.
Publication:
Newsletter. q.
Annual Meetings: June
1987-Dayton, OH/June 10-12

Athletic Goods Team Distributors (1970)
Hist. Note: A division of the National Sporting Goods Association. Its 2,700 members are dealers to high school, community and institutional athletic teams.

Atlantic and Gulf American Flag Berth Operators (1956)
Hist. Note: Became the Trans-Atlantic American Flag Liner Operators in 1985.

Atomic Industrial Forum (1953)
7101 Wisconsin Ave., Bethesda MD 20814
President: Dr. Carl Walske
Members: 500 organizations *Staff:* 80
Annual Budget: over $5,000,000 *Tel:* (301) 654-9260
Hist. Note: First suggested by Dr. T. Keith Glennan, AIF was founded in New York in April, 1953 and incorporated in that state to serve as the voice of the nuclear energy industry. Members consist of utilities, manufacturers of electrical generating equipment, researchers, architects, engineers, labor unions, milling and mining companies, constructors, laboratories, educational institutions and government agencies.
Publications:
INFO Newsletter. m.
Nuclear Industry. m.
NESP Report. bi-m.
Annual Meetings: November
1987-Los Angeles, CA

Audio Engineering Soc. (1948)
60 East 42nd St., Rm. 2520, New York NY 10065
Exec. Director: Donald J. Plunkett
Members: 9,700 individuals, 130 companies *Staff:* 11-18
Annual Budget: $2-5,000,000 *Tel:* (212) 661-8528
Hist. Note: Members are professionals throughout the world active in audio engineering or acoustics. Membership: $50/yr.
Publication:
Journal of the Audio Engineering Society. 10/yr. adv.
Tri-annual Meetings:
1987-London, England(Queen Elizabeth II Conf. Ctr.)/March 10-13
1987-Tokyo, Japan/June 17-19
1987-New York, NY/Oct. 16-19

Audio Visual Management Ass'n (1946)
6311 North O'Connor Road, Suite 110, Irving TX 75039
Exec. Director: F.M. Wehrli
Members: 115-150 *Staff:* 1
Annual Budget: $50-100,000 *Tel:* (214) 869-4325
Hist. Note: A professional society of individuals managing audio-visual communications departments in business and industry. Formerly (until 1980) known as the Industrial Audio-Visual Association.
Semi-annual meetings: Spring and Fall

Audit Bureau of Circulations (1914)
900 N. Meacham Road, Schaumburg IL 60173-4968
President: M. David Keil
Members: 5,100 *Staff:* 205
Annual Budget: over $5,000,000 *Tel:* (312) 885-0910
Hist. Note: Members are newspapers and periodicals, advertisers and advertising agencies. Purpose is to audit claimed circulation figures and publish the results. Has a budget of over $11 million.
Publications:
FAS-FAX. semi-a.
News Bulletin. q.
Publisher's Statements. semi-a.
Audit Reports. a.
Magazine Trends Report. a.
Canadian Newspaper Factbook. a.
Canadian Circulation of U.S. Magazines. a.
Magazine Coverage Reports. a.
ABC Casebook. q.
Rate Book. a.
County Penetration Report. semi-a.
Annual Meetings: November/500

Auger and Elevator Manufacturers Council
Hist. Note: A division of the Farm and Industrial Equipment Institute.

Authors Guild (1921)
234 West 44th St., New York NY 10036
Exec. Secretary: Helen A. Stephenson
Members: 6,000 *Staff:* 6-10
Annual Budget: $250-500,000 *Tel:* (212) 398-0838
Hist. Note: Affiliated with the Authors League of America and the Dramatists Guild. Membership: $60/year.
Publication:
Bulletin. q.
Annual Meetings: February in New York, NY

Authors League of America (1912)
234 West 44th St., New York NY 10036
Administrator: Nancy Weidner
Members: 13,500 *Staff:* 2-5
Tel: (212) 391-9198
Hist. Note: Promotes the professional interests of authors and dramatists in such areas as taxation, copyright and freedom of expression. Affiliated with the Authors Guild and the Dramatists Guild.
Publications:
Authors Guild Bulletin. q.
Dramatists Guild Quarterly. q.

Auto Internacional Ass'n (1983)
11540 East Slauson Ave., Whittier CA 90606
Nat'l Director: Dick Wells
Members: 350 companies *Staff:* 18
Annual Budget: $100-250,000 *Tel:* (213) 692-9402
Hist. Note: Members are manufacturers, importers, exporters and distributors of parts and accessories for imported vehicles. Shares administrative staff with the Specialty Equipment Market Ass'n. Membership: $750/yr.
Publication:
AIA Update. bi-m.
Annual Meetings: October or November in Las Vegas

Autobody Filler Manufacturers Ass'n (1978)
Hist. Note: In 1985, AFMA disbanded and the member companies became part of the Autobody Supply and Equipment Manufacturers Council, a division of the Motor and Equipment Manufacturers Ass'n.

Autoleather Guild (1917)
776 Waddington Rd., Birmingham MI 48009
Director: Lorraine H. Schultz
Members: 2-5 companies *Staff:* 2-5
Annual Budget: $100-250,000 *Tel:* (313) 646-5250
Hist. Note: Public relations, marketing, and merchandising affiliate of the Leather Industries of America for genuine leather used in covering seats of major automobile manufacturers, trucks, and airlines. Formerly (1977) The Upholstery Leather Group.
Annual Meetings: With the Tanners' Council of America.

Automated Procedures for Engineering Consultants (1966)
Hist. Note: Shortened name to the acronym, APEC, Inc., in 1985.

Automated Storage/Retrieval Systems (1967)
8720 Red Oak Blvd., Suite 201, Charlotte NC 28210-3957
Management Exec.: John Nofsinger
Members: 15-20 companies *Staff:* 2-5
Annual Budget: $25-50,000 *Tel:* (704) 522-8644
Hist. Note: A product section of the Material Handling Institute, Inc. Until 1975 known as Controlled Mechanical Storage Systems. Membersip: $2,400/yr.
Annual Meetings: Fall, with The Material Handling Institute.
1987-Boca Raton, FL(Hotel & Club)/Nov. 7-11
1988-Phoenix, AZ(Biltmore)/Oct. 8-12

Automated Vision Ass'n (1984)
900 Victors Way, Box 3724, Ann Arbor MI 48106
Managing Director: Jeffrey A. Burnstein
Members: 40 companies *Staff:* 12
Annual Budget: $100-250,000 *Tel:* (313) 994-6088
Hist. Note: Established and managed by the Robotic Industries Ass'n. Members are machine vision manufacturers, users or suppliers of related equipment and services for the machine vision industry. Membership: $500-1,000/yr.
Publication:
AVA Buyer's Guide. a. adv.
Annual Meetings:
1987-Detroit, MI(Cobo Hall)/June 9-11/7,500

Automatic Damper Manufacturers Ass'n (1977)
Box 6212, Harrisburg PA 17122
Chairman: Joe Windish
Members: 10 companies *Staff:* 1
Annual Budget: $10-25,000 *Tel:* (717) 652-0761
Hist. Note: Members are makers of automatic vent dampers for oil and gas heating equipment.
Annual Meetings: Summer

Automatic Fire Alarm Ass'n
Hist. Note: No paid staff; address unknown in 1986.

Automatic Guided Vehicle Systems (1982)
8720 Red Oak Blvd., Suite 201, Charlotte NC 28210-3957
Management Exec.: Richard E. Ward
Members: 13 *Staff:* 2-5
Annual Budget: $10-25,000 *Tel:* (704) 522-8644
Hist. Note: A product section of the Material Handling Institute.
Annual Meetings:
1987-Boca Raton, FL(Boca Raton Hotel & Club)

Automatic Identification Manufacturers (1972)
1326 Freeport Road, Pittsburgh PA 15238
Exec. Director: W. P. Hakanson
Members: 86 *Staff:* 8
Tel: (412) 963-8588
Hist. Note: Affiliated with The Material Handling Institute, Inc.
Annual Meetings: 3/year and an annual trade show

Automatic Transmission Rebuilders Ass'n (1954)
2472 Eastman Ave., Suite 23, Ventura CA 93003
Exec. Director: Gene M. Lewis
Members: 1,800 *Staff:* 16
Annual Budget: $500-1,000,000 *Tel:* (805) 654-1700
Hist. Note: Members are rebuilders and suppliers.
Publication:
The Good Guys. m. adv.
Annual Meetings: Fall
1987-Las Vegas, NV

Automobile Importers of America (1964)
1725 Jefferson Davis Hwy., Suite 1002, Arlington VA 22202
President: George C. Nield
Members: 30-40 *Staff:* 13
Annual Budget: $2-5,000,000 *Tel:* (703) 979-5550
Hist. Note: Founded as the Imported Car Group, it assumed its present name in 1965. Members are manufacturers of imported automobiles. Disseminates information concerning federal and state regulations affecting the auto industry.
Annual Meetings: Fall, usually in New York City

Automotive Advertisers Council (1941)
444 North Michigan Ave., Suite 2000, Chicago IL 60611
Admin. Asst.: Joan Watkiss
Members: 60-65 *Staff:* 1
Annual Budget: $10-25,000 *Tel:* (312) 836-1300
Hist. Note: Administrative services provided by the Automotive Service Industry Ass'n. Chief executive is the President, who is elected annually.
Semi-Annual Meetings: May and October

Automotive Affiliated Representatives (1934)
111 East Wacker Drive, #600, Chicago IL 60601
Exec. Director: James M. Dickinson
Members: 350-400 companies *Staff:* 4
Annual Budget: $100-250,000 *Tel:* (312) 644-6610
Hist. Note: Members are professional sales representatives in the automotive aftermarket. Manufacturers may apply for associate membership. Membership: $300/year.
Publications:
AAR News. m.
AAR Membership Directory. a.
Auto Know Newsletter. m.
Annual Meetings: Fall/Winter

Automotive Battery Charger Manufacturers Council (1980)
300 Sylvan Ave., Englewood Cliffs NJ 07632
Exec. Secretary: Stephen A. Bomer
Members: 8 companies *Staff:* 2-5
Annual Budget: $10-25,000 *Tel:* (201) 836-9500
Hist. Note: Affiliated with the Motor and Equipment Manufacturers Ass'n.
Annual Meetings: Fall

Automotive Booster Clubs Internat'l (1921)
501 West Algonquin Road, Arlington Heights IL 60005-4411
Exec. V. President: James E. Bates, CAE
Members: 2,750 individuals *Staff:* 2-5
Annual Budget: $50-100,000 *Tel:* (312) 593-8350
Hist. Note: Founded in Boston on February 21, 1921. Members are salespersons of auto replacement parts, supplies and accessories for the automotive aftermarket. Membership: $25/yr.
Publication:
Booster Cable Topics and Trends. q.
Annual Meetings: Second week in November

Automotive Cooling System Institute (1976)
222 Cedar Lane, Teaneck NJ 07666
Secretary: John D. Trott
Members: 15-20 companies *Staff:* 1
Annual Budget: $10-25,000 *Tel:* (201) 836-9500
Hist. Note: A service activity of the Motor and Equipment Manufacturers Ass'n. Formed by a group of makers of cooling system maintenance products to expand the market for their products.

Automotive Dismantlers and Recyclers Ass'n (1943)
1133 15th St., N.W., Suite 620, Washington DC 20005
Exec. V. President: Russell F. McKinnon
Members: 5,000 auto wrecking yards *Staff:* 6-10
Annual Budget: $500-1,000,000 *Tel:* (202) 293-5910
Hist. Note: Incorporated in the State of New York. Formerly (1973) Nat'l Auto and Truck Wreckers Ass'n (NATWA), and (1975) Ass'n of Auto and Truck Recyclers, Inc. Members are dismantlers and recyclers of domestic and foreign auto truck and motorcycle parts for construction and farm equipment.
Publications:
The ADRA Newsletter. m.
Dismantlers Digest. bi-m. adv.
Membership Directory. a. adv.
Annual Meetings: Fall
1987-Orlando, FL(Marriott)/Oct.
1988-Palm Springs, CA(Marriott)/Sept.

00097 12 05 86 1233

Automotive Engine Rebuilders Ass'n (1922)
234 Waukegan Road, Glenview IL 60025
President: Barry E. Soltz
Members: 3,900 *Staff:* 6-10
Annual Budget: $100-250,000 *Tel:* (312) 729-6400
Hist. Note: Active members include: automotive jobber machine shops, custom automotive machine shops, heavy-duty, deisel and industrial shops, production engine rebuilders, and high performance and marine shops. Associate membership is available for suppliers of automotive parts, tools, equipment, and chemicals and services.
Publications:
Technical, Service, and News Bulletins. m.
Specifications Manuals. irreg.
Annual Meetings: June
1987-Dallas,TX(Market Hall)/June 18-20/4,000
1988-Atlanta,GA(Hilton)/June 17-19/1,000
1989-Reno,NV(MGM Grand)/June 15-17/1,000

Automotive Exhaust Systems Manufacturers Council (1970)
222 Cedar Lane, Teaneck NJ 07666
Exec. Director: Ralph W. Van Demark
Members: 5 companies *Staff:* 2
Tel: (201) 836-9500
Hist. Note: Formed by a group of companies making exhaust systems parts to expand the market for their products and monitor noise and emission control legislation.

Automotive Filter Manufacturers Council (1971)
300 Sylvan Ave., Englewood Cliffs NJ 07632
Exec. Secretary: Stephen A. Bomer
Members: 26 companies *Staff:* 2-5
Annual Budget: $25-50,000 *Tel:* (201) 836-9500
Semi-annual Meetings: Spring and Fall/70-75
1987-Jacksonville, FL(Ponte Verda Club)/April 2-4

Automotive Fleet and Leasing Ass'n (1969)
2512 Artesia Blvd., Redondo Beach CA 90278
Exec. Director: Edward J. Bobit
Members: 310 *Staff:* 2-5
Annual Budget: $50-100,000 *Tel:* (213) 376-8788
Hist. Note: AFLA is designed to improve communications among buyers, sellers, fleet administrators, lending institutions, lessors, used vehicle marketers and allied automotive service companies. Membership: $125/yr.
Publication:
AFLA Forum. q.
Semi-annual meetings: April and September
1987-Montreal, Quebec(Hilton Bonaventure)/April 23-25/400
1987-Phoenix, AZ(Pointe Resort)/Sept. 24-26/250
1988-San Francisco, CA(St. Francis)/April 28-30/400
1988-Fort Lauderdale, FL(Marriott Harbor Beach)/Sept. 22-24/250

Automotive Industry Action Group (1982)
17117 W. Nine Mile Rd., Suite 830, Southfield MI 48075
Office Manager: Barbara Youngert
Members: 450 companies, 800 individuals *Staff:* 10
Annual Budget: $500-1,000,000 *Tel:* (313) 569-6262
Hist. Note: A non-profit association composed of the major North American vehicle manufacturers and their suppliers. Membership fee depends on annual sales.
Publications:
Actionline. m. adv.
Standards Publications. irreg.
Annual Meetings:
1987-Detroit, MI

Automotive Information Council (1972)
29200 Southfield Road, Southfield MI 48076
President: Charles Charpie
Members: 700 companies & associations *Staff:* 2-5
Annual Budget: $100-250,000 *Tel:* (313) 559-5922
Hist. Note: The public relations arm of the industry.

Automotive Lift Institute (1945)
3008 Millwood Ave., Columbia SC 29205
President: J. Edgar Eubanks
Members: 10-15 companies *Staff:* 8-10
Tel: (803) 252-5646
Hist. Note: Makers of hyraulic automotive lifts.

Automotive Market Research Council (1966)
300 Sylvan Ave., Englewood Cliffs NJ 07632
President: Terrance Winslow
Members: 85-100 companies, 250-300 individuals *Staff:* 1
Annual Budget: $10-25,000 *Tel:* (201) 836-9500
Hist. Note: AMRC is a loosely organized association of companies whose business is the manufacture of vehicles and vehicular parts, components, subassemblies, or accessories for sale as original or replacement equipment. Marketing research is one of the primary responsibilities of the professional marketing personnel who represent their company in the Council through active participation on organization committees. Has no paid staff; administrative support is provided by the Motor and Equipment Manufacturers Ass'n. All officers change annually.
Publications:
Newsletter. 4-6/yr.
Press release. semi-a.
Semi-annual meetings: Spring and Fall

Automotive Occupant Protection Ass'n (1978)
110 South Kenyon Ave., Margate City NJ 08402
Secy.-Treas.: Thomas C. McGrath, Jr.
Members: 10-15 companies *Staff:* 1
Annual Budget: $10-25,000 *Tel:* (609) 823-1511
Hist. Note: Members are manufacturers interested in promoting auto safety equipment.

Automotive Parts and Accessories Ass'n (1967)
5100 Forbes Blvd., Lanham MD 20706
President: Julian C. Morris
Members: 1,400 companies *Staff:* 30-35
Annual Budget: $2-5,000,000 *Tel:* (301) 459-9110
Publications:
APAA Report. m.
Government Affairs Reporter. m.
Monitor. m.
Annual Meetings: Trade Show in the Fall

Automotive Parts Rebuilders Ass'n (1947)
6849 Old Dominion Drive, Suite 352, McLean VA 22101
Exec. V. President: Lawrence P. Mutter, CAE
Members: 1,300 *Staff:* 6-10
Annual Budget: $1-2,000,000 *Tel:* (703) 790-1050
Hist. Note: Membership: $265-$920/year (based on number of employees).
Publications:
Update. m.
APRA Membership Roster & Trade Directory. a.
Annual Meetings: Fall
1987-Salt Lake City, UT(Hotel Utah)/Sept. 27-30/2,500
1988-Orlando, FL(Sheraton World)/Nov. 11-14
1989-Toronto, Ontario(Royal York)/Oct. 15-18
1990-Albuquerque, NM(Regency)/Oct. 8-11

Automotive Products Export Council (1979)
5100 Forbes Blvd., Lanham MD 20706
Executive Manager: Robert W. McMinn
Members: 6 associations *Staff:* 0
Annual Budget: $50-100,000 *Tel:* (301) 459-5927
Hist. Note: An organization of 6 automotive trade associations which are engaged in promotion of export sales of U.S. automotive products. APEC has organized U.S. Pavilions at several foreign trade shows, including the U.S. Pavilion at the 1986 Automechanika Show in Frankfurt, FDR. Membership: $1,100/yr.
Tri-Annual Meetings: January, May and August in Washington, DC

Automotive Refrigeration Products Institute (1983)
5100 Forbes Blvd., Lanham MD 20706
Exec. Director: Timothy B. Tierney
Members: 15 companies *Staff:* 4
Annual Budget: $10-25,000 *Tel:* (301) 731-5195
Hist. Note: Trade association of companies engaged in the manufacture, distribution and/or packaging of automotive refrigeration products. Membership: $1,200/yr.
Publication:
Frostlines. q.
Annual Meetings: Fall

Automotive Service Ass'n (1986)
1901 Airport Freeway, Suite 100, Bedford TX 76021-0929
Exec. V. President: George W. Merwin
Members: 12,000 *Staff:* 25
Annual Budget: $2-5,000,000 *Tel:* (817) 283-6205
Hist. Note: Consolidation of Automotive Service Councils, Inc. (formed in 1955) and Independent Automotive Service Ass'n (formed in 1949). Members are businesses providing automotive service in mechanical, auto body and transmission, along with other fields. Membership: $150/yr.
Publications:
AutoInc. m. adv.
Bulletin. q.
Annual Meetings:
1987-Congress of Automotive Repair & Service/Fall/1,500
1987-Nat'l Autobody Congress & Expo/Las Vegas, NV(Bally's)/Fall/6,000

Automotive Service Councils (1955)
Hist. Note: Merged with Independent Automotive Service Ass'n in 1986 to form the Automotive Service Ass'n.

Automotive Service Industry Ass'n (1924)
444 North Michigan Ave., Chicago IL 60611
President: John W. Nerlinger, CAE
Members: 8,500 *Staff:* 40
Annual Budget: $2-5,000,000 *Tel:* (312) 836-1300
Hist. Note: Merger (1959) of Nat'l Standard Parts Ass'n and Motor Equipment Wholesalers Ass'n. Absorbed (1974) Automotive Electric Ass'n. Members are independent automotive wholesalers, including auto trim wholesalers, auto paint, body supply and equipment wholesalers, distributors, manufacturers, remanufacturers and manufacturers' representatives. Membership fee based on sales volume.
Publications:
Voice of the Industry. m.
Buyers Guide. bi-a.
Membership Directory. bi-a.
Annual Meetings: Late Winter or Early Spring/3,000
1987-Atlanta, GA/March 7-9
1988-Las Vegas, NV(MGM Grand)/Feb. 27-March 1
1989-Chicago, IL(Hyatt Regency)/Feb. 25-27
1990-Las Vegas, NV(MGM Grand)/Feb. 25-27
1991-Chicago, IL(Hyatt Regency)/Feb. 23-25

Automotive Trade Ass'n Executives (1917)
8400 Westpark Drive, McLean VA 22102
Exec. Director: C. Alan Marlette
Members: 105 associations *Staff:* 2-5
Annual Budget: $50-100,000 *Tel:* (703) 821-7072
Hist. Note: Members are executives of state and local automobile dealer associations. Formerly (1984) Automotive Trade Ass'n Managers.
Semi-annual meetings: Feb. and July

Automotive Trade Ass'n Managers (1917)
Hist. Note: Became Automotive Trade Ass'n Executives in 1984.

Automotive Warehouse Distributors Ass'n (1947)
9140 Ward Parkway, Kansas City MO 64114
President: Martin Fromm
Members: 550-600
Annual Budget: $2-5,000,000 *Tel:* (816) 444-3500
Hist. Note: Distributors of automotive parts and supplies. Sponsors and supports the Automotive Warehouse Distributors Association Political Action Committee.
Publications:
AWDA Leadership Directory. a.
AWDA News. bi-m.
AWDA Annual Progress Report. a.
AWDA University Catalog. a.
Annual Meetings: Always in Las Vegas, NV(Caesar's Palace)/Fall
1987-Oct. 26-30
1988-Oct. 31-Nov. 4
1989-Oct. 30-Nov. 3
1990-Oct. 29-Nov. 2
1991-Oct. 28-Nov. 1

Aviation Crime Prevention Institute (1986)
P.O. Box 3443, Frederick MD 21701
President: Robert J. Collins
Staff: 1
Annual Budget: $50-100,000 *Tel:* (301) 694-5444
Hist. Note: Established in 1986 as a non-profit foundation, the ACPI is comprised of individuals working to prevent thefts of aircraft and equipment.
Publications:
Newsletter. m.
Alert. q.

Aviation Distributors and Manufacturers Ass'n Internat'l (1943)
1900 Arch St., Philadelphia PA 19103
Exec. V. President: John W. Kane
Members: 100-110 *Staff:* 2-5
Annual Budget: $50-100,000 *Tel:* (215) 564-3484
Hist. Note: Promotes friendly business relations and mutual confidence among its members and others in the industry; represents the distributors and manufacturers of aviation parts, supplies and equipment in all matters of national importance; and cooperates with various government agencies, including the Federal Aviation Administration.
Publication:
Aviation Education News Bulletin. m.
Semi-Annual Meetings: Spring and Fall

Aviation Facilities Energy Ass'n (1983)
Box 45171, Atlanta GA 30320
Membership Secretary: Linda Wood
Members: 9 companies, 145 individuals *Staff:* 1
Annual Budget: $25-50,000 *Tel:* (404) 530-2105
Hist. Note: Organized under the sponsorship of the American Ass'n of Airport Executives, the Airport Operators Council Internat'l and the Air Transport Ass'n of America and incorporated in Texas in 1984. Members are individuals responsible for, or active in, aviation facilities energy management/conservation.
Publication:
AFEA Ballast. q.
Annual Meetings:
1987-New York, NY/mid-May

Aviation Maintenance Foundation (1972)
Box 2826, Redmond WA 98073
President and Exec. Director: Richard S. Kost
Members: 6,000 individuals; 150 companies *Staff:* 8
Annual Budget: $250-500,000 *Tel:* (206) 823-0633
Hist. Note: Incorporated in March, 1972. Members are aircraft maintenance personnel. Membership: $30/yr.
Publications:
AMFI Technical Bulletin. q.
Industry News. bi-m.
Industry Statistical Surveys.
Annual Meetings:
1987-Reno, NV(MGM Grand)/Oct. 20-22/1,200
1988-Atlanta, GA/Oct. 18-20/1,200

Aviation Safety Institute (1973)
P.O. Box 304, Worthington OH 43085
President: John B. Galipault
Members: 35 companies; 382 individuals *Staff:* 9
Annual Budget: $250-500,000 *Tel:* (614) 885-4242
Hist. Note: A not-for-profit research organization that depends primarily upon tax-deductible contributions and consequently serves as a wholly independent "third party" in the promotion of aviation safety. Membership: $50/yr.
Publication:
Monitor. bi-w.

00098 12 05 86 1233

Aviation Security Ass'n of America Internat'l (1981)
Hist. Note: Reported defunct in 1985.

Aviation/Space Writers Ass'n (1938)
17 S. High St., Suite 1200, Columbus OH 43215
Exec. Director: David W. Field, CAE
Members: 1,400-1,500 *Staff:* 2-5
Annual Budget: $100-250,000 *Tel:* (614) 221-1900
Hist. Note: Member of the Council of Communication Societies. Membership: $75/yr.
Publications:
AWA News. q.
Yearbook & Directory. a. adv.
Annual Meetings:
1987-San Diego, CA

Avocado Export (1984)
17620 Fitch, P.O. Box 17925, Irvine CA 92713
Members: 5 companies
Tel: (714) 852-0311
Hist. Note: A Webb-Pomerene Act association.

Avocado Growers Bargaining Council (1968)
P.O. Box 151, Fallbrook CA 92028
Secretary: Margaret Jerram
Tel: (714) 728-6014
Hist. Note: Formerly (1972) Avocado Growers Council. Members are grove owners and growers.
Publication:
Avocado Growers Bargaining Council Newsletter. irreg.

Ayrshire Breeders Ass'n (1875)
2 Union Street, Brandon VT 05733
Operations Officer: Judith M. Disorda
Members: 1,100 *Staff:* 10
Annual Budget: $100-250,000 *Tel:* (802) 247-5774
Hist. Note: Breeders and fanciers of Ayrshire dairy cattle. Member of the Nat'l Soc. of Livestock Record Ass'ns. Membership: $45/three years; $100/ten years.
Publication:
Ayrshire Digest. 11/yr. adv.
Annual Meetings: Spring
1987-New Hampshire
1988-Minnesota
1989-Maryland-Delaware

Bakery, Confectionery and Tobacco Workers' Internat'l Union (1886)
10401 Connecticut Ave., Kensington MD 20895
President: John DeConcini
Members: 145,000 *Staff:* 60
Annual Budget: $2-5,000,000 *Tel:* (301) 933-8600
Hist. Note: Organized on January 13, 1886 in Pittsburgh and chartered by the American Federation of Labor on February 23, 1887. Merged (1969) with American Bakery and Confectionery Workers' Internat'l Union. Affiliated with AFL-CIO, CLC. Formerly (until 1978) known as the Bakery and Confectionery Workers Internat'l Union of America. Merged with the Tobacco Workers Internat'l Union in August, 1978, and assumed its present name at that time. Has a budget of about $8 million. Sponsors and Supports the Bakery, Confectionery and Tobacco Workers International Union Political Action Committee.
Publications:
BC&T News. 10/yr.
BC&T Report .m.
Annual Meetings: Every 4 years (1990)

Bakery Equipment Manufacturers Ass'n (1918)
111 East Wacker Drive, Suite 600, Chicago IL 60601
Chairman of the Board: William W. Carpenter
Members: 100 companies *Staff:* 2-5
Annual Budget: $50-100,000 *Tel:* (312) 644-6610
Publication:
BEMA Newsletter. bi-m.
Annual Meetings: Summer

Baking Industry Sanitation Standards Committee (1949)
111 E. Wacker Drive, Suite 600, Chicago IL 60601
Exec. Director: Bonnie Sweetman
Members: 5 Associations *Staff:* 2-5
Annual Budget: $10-25,000 *Tel:* (312) 644-6610
Publication:
Sanitation Standards.
Semi-annual meetings: Fall and Winter

Balloon Manufacturers Ass'n
Hist. Note: A division of the Industrial Fabrics Association International.

Bank Administration Institute (1924)
60 Gould Center, Rolling Meadows IL 60008
President: Ronald G. Burke
Members: 9,000 banks *Staff:* 150
Annual Budget: over $5,000,000 *Tel:* (312) 228-6200
Hist. Note: Established as the National Association for Bank Auditors and Controllers, it became NABAC, the Association for Bank Audit, Control and Operation in 1959 and assumed its present name in 1967. Provides operational assistance and educational programs for bankers. Has an annual budget of $23 million.
Publications:
Bank Administration. m. adv.
Issues in Bank Regulation. q.
World of Banking. q.
Annual Meetings: Fall

Bank Marketing Ass'n (1915)
309 West Washington St., Chicago IL 60606
Exec. V. President: Raymond M. Cheseldine
Members: 4,500 *Staff:* 65
Annual Budget: $2-5,000,000 *Tel:* (312) 782-1442
Hist. Note: Formerly (1947) the Financial Advertisers Ass'n, (1965) the Financial Public Relations Ass'n and (1970) the Bank Public Relations and Marketing Ass'n.
Publications:
Bank Marketing. m. adv.
Community Bank Marketing Newsletter. 9/yr.
IC Newsletter. q.
Resource. bi-m.
Marketing Update. m.
ActionGrams. irreg.
Annual Meetings: Fall
1987-Phoenix, AZ(Hilton)/Sept. 27-30
1988-San Francisco, CA(Hilton)/Oct. 30-Nov. 2

Bank Stationers Ass'n (1964)
Hist. Note: Became the Financial Stationers Ass'n in 1984.

Bankers' Ass'n for Foreign Trade (1921)
1600 M St., N.W., 7th Floor, Washington DC 20036
Exec. Director: Mary Condeelis
Members: 200-225 banks *Staff:* 5
Annual Budget: $250-500,000 *Tel:* (202) 452-0952
Hist. Note: BAFT serves as a trade association of professional international commercial bankers dedicated to promoting international trade and finance. Members include virtually all the U.S. commercial banks with significant international banking activities and foreign banks having operations in the U.S. Through its Center for International Banking Studies (CIBS), BAFT offers educational programs updating professional banking practices.
Publications:
"BAFT Update". m. adv.
Annual Report.
Annual Meetings: April/May
1987-Boca Raton, FL(Boca Raton Hotel & Club)/April 26-30
1988-Boca Raton, FL(same)/April 24-28
1989-Open
1990-Boca Raton, FL(Boca Raton Hotel & Club)/April 29-May 3

Baptist Public Relations Ass'n (1954)
Box 728, Brentwood TN 37027
Admin. Coordinator: Barbara J. Fly
Members: 400
Annual Budget: $10-25,000 *Tel:* (615) 373-2255
Hist. Note: Main purpose is educational. Membership: $30/yr.
Publications:
BPRA Newsletter. bi-m.
BPRA Directory. a.
Annual Meetings: Spring
1987-Atlanta, GA
1988-Louisville, KY
1989-Dallas-Ft. Worth, TX
1990-Nashville, TN

Barbecue Industry Ass'n (1958)
710 E. Ogden Ave., Suite 113, Naperville IL 60540
President: Arthur W. Seeds, CAE
Members: 60 *Staff:* 2-5
Annual Budget: $250-500,000 *Tel:* (312) 369-2404
Hist. Note: Formerly (1966) Wood Charcoal Briquet Producers Ass'n, (1969) Barbecue Briquet Institute, (1977) Charcoal Briquet Institute, and (1978) Charcoal Barbecue Industry Ass'n. Member companies manufacture and sell barbecue products. BIA's primary purpose is increasing the amout of consumer barbecuing.
Annual Meetings: Fall
1987-Ft. Lauderdale, FL(Bonaventure Resort & Spa)/Oct. 17-19

Barley and Malt Institute (1946)
Hist. Note: Address unknown in 1985-86; probably defunct.

Barre Granite Ass'n (1889)
51 Church St., Barre VT 05641
Exec. V. President: Norman James
Members: 25 *Staff:* 12
Annual Budget: $100-250,000 *Tel:* (802) 476-4131
Publication:
Barre Life. q.
Annual Meetings: Barre, Vermont

Barzona Breeders Ass'n of America (1968)
Box 631, Prescott AZ 86302
President: Pete Jameson
Members: 80 *Staff:* 2-5
Annual Budget: $25-50,000 *Tel:* (602) 445-5150
Hist. Note: Breeders and fanciers of Barzona cattle. Membership: $75/yr.
Publication:
The Barzonian. q. adv.
Annual Meetings: Winter
1987-Buellton, CA/Feb. 26-27

Baseball - Office of Commissioner (1921)
350 Park Avenue, 17th Floor, New York NY 10022
Commissioner: Peter V. Ueberroth
Members: 160-170 professional clubs *Staff:* 30-35
Annual Budget: $2-5,000,000 *Tel:* (212) 371-7800

Baseball Writers Ass'n of America (1908)
36 Brookfield Road, Fort Salonga NY 11768
Secy.-Treas.: Jack Lang
Members: 800 *Staff:* 1
Annual Budget: under $10,000 *Tel:* (516) 757-0562
Hist. Note: Members are sports writers on direct assignment to major league teams.
Annual Meetings: In October at the site of the World Series

Basic and Traditional Food Ass'n (1978)
Hist. Note: Became inactive in 1983.

Battery Council Internat'l (1924)
111 East Wacker Dr., Chicago IL 60601
Exec. Secretary: William W. Carpenter
Members: 225-250 companies *Staff:* 2-5
Annual Budget: $100-250,000 *Tel:* (312) 644-6610
Hist. Note: Established as the Nat'l Battery Manufacturers Ass'n. Became the Ass'n of American Battery Manufacturers in 1940, and the Battery Council Internat'l in 1969. Distributors, manufacturers and suppliers to the electrical storage battery industry. Maintains a Washington Office.
Publications:
Data Book Statistic. a.
Convention Proceedings. a.
Annual Meetings:
1987-New Orleans, LA(Hilton)/800-900
1988-Osaka, Japan(Royal Osaka)/600-700
1989-Fort Lauderdale, FL(Wyndham)/600-700

BCA-Credit Information (1972)
Hist. Note: Became the Broadcast Credit Ass'n, Inc. in 1985.

Bearing Specialist Ass'n (1966)
800 Roosevelt Rd., Bldg. C., Suite 20, Glen Ellyn IL 60137
Exec. Director: Richard W. Church
Members: 100-125 companies *Staff:* 3
Annual Budget: $100-250,000 *Tel:* (312) 858-7337
Hist. Note: Merger of Anti-Friction Bearing Distributors Ass'n and Ass'n of Bearing Specialists. Members are anti-friction bearing distributors.
Publication:
News and Views. bi-m.
Annual Meetings: Spring
1987-Maui, HI(Hyatt Regency)/April 26-30
1988-Bermuda(Southampton Princess)/April 10-14
1989-Tuscon, AZ(Loew's Ventana Canyon)/April 9-12

Beauty and Barber Supply Institute (1904)
155 North Dean St., Englewood NJ 07631
Exec. Director: Frank Vella
Members: 1,400-1,500 *Staff:* 6-10
Annual Budget: $250-500,000 *Tel:* (201) 871-1810
Hist. Note: Formerly the Barber Supply Dealers of America.
Publication:
The Communicator. m.
Annual Meetings:
1987-Las Vegas, NV
1988-Chicago, IL
1989-Las Vegas, NV
1990-Las Vegas, NV

Beef Improvement Federation (1968)
Box 7621, North Carolina State University, Raleigh NC 27695-7621
Exec. Director: Roger McCraw
Members: 80 organizations *Staff:* 1
Annual Budget: $10-25,000 *Tel:* (919) 737-2761
Hist. Note: Membership, by organization, consists of groups of beef cattle breeders and state improvement associations. Membership: $50-$600/year.
Annual Meetings: Spring/300
1987-Wichita, KS/April 29-May 1

Beefmaster Breeders Universal (1961)
6800 Park Ten Blvd., Suite 290 West, San Antonio TX 78213
Exec. V. President: Gene Kuykendall
Members: 3,500 *Staff:* 13
Annual Budget: $1-2,000,000 *Tel:* (512) 732-3132
Hist. Note: Owners and breeders of Beefmaster cattle. Member of the National Society of Livestock Record Associations. Membership: $30/yr.
Publication:
The Beefmaster Cowman. m.
Annual Meetings: Fall
1987-San Antonio, TX(Marriott Riverwalk)/Oct. 25-28
1988-Atlanta, GA

Beer Institute (1986)
1750 K St., N.W., Washington DC 20006
President: James C. Sanders
Members: 40 brewers; 75 suppliers *Staff:* 10
Tel: (202) 466-2400
Hist. Note: Successor organization to the United State Brewers Ass'n, formerly (1944) United Brewers Industrial Foundation and (1961) United States Brewers Foundation. Absorbed Brewers Hop Research Institute. Members are the major national breweries and suppliers to the brewing industry.
Publication:

00099 12 05 86 1233

Beet Sugar Development Foundation (1945)
1311 So. College Ave., Box 1546, Fort Collins CO 80522
Secy.-Manager: James H. Fischer
Members: 10-15 *Staff:* 25-30
Annual Budget: $250-500,000 *Tel:* (303) 482-8250
Hist. Note: Members are U.S. and Canadian sugar beet companies and primary suppliers of sugar beet seed.
Annual Meetings: February

Behavior Genetics Ass'n (1972)
Institute for Behavioral Genetics, Univ. of Colorado, Box 447, Boulder CO 80309
Secretary: James R. Wilson
Members: 400 *Staff:* 1
Annual Budget: $10-25,000 *Tel:* (303) 492-7362
Hist. Note: Organized May 9, 1972 in Illinois to promote scientific study of the interrelationships of genetic mechanisms and behavior, to aid and encourage education to that end and to disseminate and interpret knowledge in that regard to the public. Affiliated with the International Genetics Association. Has no paid staff. Membership: $40/yr.
Publication:
Behavior Genetics. 6/yr. adv.
Annual Meetings: June/130
1987-Minneapolis, MN
1988-The Netherlands
1989-Virginia
1990-France

Behavior Therapy and Research Soc. (1970)
Temple University Medical School and, Medical College of Pennsylvania, Philadelphia PA 19129
Admin. Secretary: Pearl Epstein
Members: 200-250 individuals *Staff:* 1
Annual Budget: under $10,000 *Tel:* (215) 849-0607
Hist. Note: Promotes research on the theory and practice of behavior therapy.
Publications:
Journal of Behavior Therapy and Experimental Psychiatry. q. adv.
Roster of Clinical Fellows. a.
Annual Meetings: With Ass'n for Advancment of Behavior Therapy.

Belgian American Chamber of Commerce in the United States (1925)
350 Fifth Ave., Suite 703, New York NY 10118
Exec. Director: Claire F. Raick
Members: 600 *Staff:* 2-5
Annual Budget: $250-500,000 *Tel:* (212) 967-9898
Publications:
Belgian American Trade Review. 6/yr. adv.
Directory of Belgian-U.S. Trade. Irreg.
Listing of Belgian Companies in the United States. irreg.
Listing of Belgian Exporters/Importers. irreg.

Belgian Draft Horse Corp. of America (1887)
125 Southwood Drive, Box 335, Wabash IN 46992
Secy.-Treas.: Rollin F. Christner
Members: 3,300 *Staff:* 6-10
Annual Budget: $100-250,000 *Tel:* (219) 563-3205
Hist. Note: Originated as the American Ass'n of Importers and Breeders of Belgian Draft Horses and assumed its present name in 1937. The pedigree ass'n for owners and breeders of Belgian Draft Horses. Membership: $50 for lifetime membership.
Publication:
Belgian Review. a. adv.
Annual Meetings: December

Below/Hook Lifters Ass'n
8720 Red Oak Blvd., Suite 201, Charlotte NC 28210-3957
Management Exec.: Tom Meinert
Members: 12 *Staff:* 2
Annual Budget: under $10,000 *Tel:* (704) 522-8644
Hist. Note: A product Section of the Material Handling Institute. Membership: $1,350/yr.
Annual Meetings:
1987-Boca Raton, FL(Boca Raton)/Nov. 6-12

Belt Ass'n (1934)
225 West 34th St., New York NY 10122
Exec. Director: Sheldon M. Edelman
Members: 75-100 companies *Staff:* 6-10
Annual Budget: $50-100,000 *Tel:* (212) 564-2500
Hist. Note: Members are manufacturers of ladies' belts. Absorbed the Ass'n of Men's Belt Manufacturers in 1986.

Beta Alpha Psi (1919)
5717 Bessie Drive, Sarasota FL 33583
Dir. of Administration: Nancy Harke
Members: 8-10,000 *Staff:* 1
Annual Budget: $250-500,000 *Tel:* (813) 924-7818
Hist. Note: An honorary, professional accounting fraternity. Organized February 12, 1919 at the University of Illinois.
Publication:
Newsletter. 3/yr.
Annual Meetings: Summer, before the convention of the American Accounting Ass'n

Better Lawn and Turf Institute (1957)
County Line Road, Box 108, Pleasant Hill TN 38578
Director: Eliot C. Roberts
Members: 125-150 *Staff:* 2-5
Annual Budget: $50-100,000 *Tel:* (615) 277-3722
Hist. Note: Organized orginally by midwestern bluegrass harvesters but soon spread to include growers of all improved turfgrasses in the Northwest and included marketing groups, associations and suppliers such as fertilizer, chemical and equipment companies. Known also as The Lawn Institute. Membership: $75/year.
Publications:
Harvests. q.
Press Kits. semi-a.
Lawn-O-Gram. q.
Annual Meetings: With the American Seed Trade Ass'n

Better Vision Institute (1929)
230 Park Ave., New York NY 10169
Exec. Secretary: Lawrence O. Aasen, CAE
Members: 3,400-4,000 *Staff:* 6-10
Annual Budget: $100-250,000 *Tel:* (212) 682-1731
Hist. Note: The public relations arm of the ophthalmic community. Membership includes all groups in the eye care field: manufacturers, wholesalers, opticians, optometrists, ophthalmologists, educational institutions and other general members. Membership: $30/yr. (individual), $300/yr. (company).
Publication:
BVI Newsletter. irreg.
Annual Meetings: Spring

Beverage Alcohol Information Council (1979)
Hist. Note: Became the Licensed Beverage Information Council in 1982.

Beverage Machinery Manufacturers Ass'n (1941)
1511 K St., N.W., Suite 508, Washington DC 20005
Exec. V. President: R. Mickey Gorman, CAE
Members: 55 companies *Staff:* 1
Annual Budget: $25-50,000 *Tel:* (202) 347-3250
Hist. Note: Dormant in 1978, this organization was revived in December 1982.
Publications:
Newsletter. m.
Membership Directory. a.
Annual Meetings: March
1987-St. Louis, MO/50

Beverage Manufacturers' Agents Ass'n (1980)
Hist. Note: Defunct in 1983.

Bibliographical Soc. of America (1904)
Box 397, Grand Central Station, New York NY 10163
Exec. Secretary: Irene Tichenor
Members: 1,400 *Staff:* 2
Annual Budget: $100-250,000 *Tel:* (718) 638-7957
Hist. Note: Organized in Washington, D.C. as an outgrowth of the Bibliographical Society of Chicago. Incorporated in 1927. A member of the American Council of Learned Societies. Membership is open to all interested in bibliograhical problems and projects. Membership: $20/yr.
Publication:
Papers. q. adv.
Annual Meetings: January in New York, NY/300

Bicycle Manufacturers Ass'n of America (1965)
1055 Thomas Jefferson St. N.W., Suite 308, Washington DC 20007
Exec. Director: Thomas Shannon
Members: 3 companies, 16 associate members *Staff:* 3
Annual Budget: $500-1,000,000 *Tel:* (202) 333-4052

Bicycle Wholesale Distributors Ass'n (1940)
1900 Arch St., Philadelphia PA 19103
Exec. Director: Don White
Members: 200 *Staff:* 4-6
Annual Budget: $50-100,000 *Tel:* (215) 564-3484
Hist. Note: Formerly (1960) Cycle Jobbers Ass'n.
Publication:
Newsletter. q.
Annual Meetings: October/300
1987-Coronado, CA(Hotel del Coronado)/Oct. 10-15
1988-Naples, FL(Ritz-Carlton)/Oct. 22-26

Billiard and Bowling Institute of America (1934)
200 Castlewood Drive, North Palm Beach FL 33408
Administrator: Sebastian DiCasoli
Members: 100-125 manufacturers & distributors *Staff:* 2-5
Annual Budget: $50-100,000 *Tel:* (305) 842-4100
Hist. Note: A component of the Sporting Goods Manufacturers Ass'n.
Publications:
BBIA Flashes. m.
Directory of Membership and Products Made. a.
Annual Meetings: Spring
1987-San Diego, CA(Hilton)/April 26-29

Billiard Congress of America (1948)
9 South Linn St., Iowa City IA 52240
Mng. Director: Robert E. Froeschle
Members: 2,000 *Staff:* 2-5
Annual Budget: $100-250,000 *Tel:* (319) 351-2112
Publications:
BCA Break. q.
Official Rule and Record Book. a.
Annual Meetings: Semi-annual meetings

Binding Industries of America (1955)
70 East Lake St., Chicago IL 60601
Exec. Director: James R. Niesen
Members: 275-300 *Staff:* 2-5
Annual Budget: $250-500,000 *Tel:* (312) 751-0440
Hist. Note: A special industry group of Printing Industries of America. Formerly (1971) Trade Binders and Loose Leaf Division of P.I.A. Membership: $200-600/yr.
Publication:
Binders Bulletin. 6/yr.
Annual Meetings: March
1987-Scottsdale,AZ/March 15-19/500
1988-Naples,FL(Ritz-Carlton)/March/500

Bioelectromagnetics Soc. (1978)
120 W. Church St., #4, Frederick MD 21701
Exec. Director: William Wisecup
Members: 400-425 *Staff:* 2-5
Annual Budget: $10-25,000 *Tel:* (301) 663-4252
Hist. Note: A scientific society promoting research concerned with the interaction of electromagnetic energy with biological systems.
Publications:
Bioelectromagnetics. q.
Abstracts. a.

Biofeedback Soc. of America (1969)
10200 West 44th Ave., Suite 304, Wheatridge CO 80033
Exec. Director: Dr. Francine Butler, CAE
Members: 2,000 *Staff:* 2-5
Annual Budget: $100-250,000 *Tel:* (303) 422-8436
Hist. Note: Psychologists, psychiatrists and health care professionals reducing tension by the use of techniques to measure biologic responses not normally felt or measured.
Publication:
Biofeedback and Self-Regulation. q. adv.
Annual Meetings: Spring
1987-Boston, MA/March
1988-San Antonio, TX/March

Biological Photographic Ass'n (1931)
115 Stoneridge Drive, Chapel Hill NC 27514
Exec. Director: Thomas Hurtgen
Members: 1,300-1,400 *Staff:* 2
Annual Budget: $100-250,000 *Tel:* (919) 967-8247
Hist. Note: Membership: $65/yr.(individual); $500/yr.(organization).
Publications:
Journal of Biological Photography. q.
BPA News. 7/yr.
Annual Meetings: Summer
1987-Ann Arbor, MI(University of Michigan)/Aug. 7-10
1988-Rochester, NY(Rochester Plaza)/Aug. 5-8

Biological Stain Commission (1922)
Univ. of Rochester Medical Center, Box 626, Rochester NY 14642-3197
Secretary: Eric A. Schenk, M.D.
Members: 90-100 individuals, 15-20 societies *Staff:* 3
Annual Budget: $50-100,000 *Tel:* (716) 275-3197
Hist. Note: To standardize biological stains and promote their perfection and use. Originated as a special committee of the Nat'l Research Council and later became the Commission on Biological Stains. Incorporated in New York in 1943 as the Biological Stain Commission, Inc. Tests samples submitted by manufacturers and those approved are awarded the Certified Biological Stain distinction.
Publication:
Stain Technology. bi-m. adv.
Annual Meetings: June/30
1987-Rochester, NY
1988-Washington, DC

Biomedical Engineering Soc. (1968)
Box 2399, Culver City CA 90231
Secy.-Treas.: Fred J. Weibell
Members: 850-900 *Staff:* 1
Annual Budget: $25-50,000 *Tel:* (213) 206-6443
Hist. Note: Incorporated February 1, 1968 in order to give equal weight to those interested in biomedical and engineering questions. Membership: $35/year.
Publications:
Annals of Biomedical Engineering. bi-m. adv.
Bulletins. q.
Annual Meetings: April
1987-Washington, DC(Hilton)/March 29-April 3/13,000
1988-Las Vegas, NV/May 1-6/20,000

Biomedical Marketing Ass'n
505 East Hawley St., Mundelein IL 60060
Exec. Director: Robert B. Willis
Members: 550 individuals *Staff:* 5-10
Tel: (312) 949-6054
Hist. Note: Membership consists of diagnostic marketers in biomedical field. Membership: $95/yr.
Publications:
Directory. a.
The Messenger. bi-m.
Annual Meetings:
1987-Rye Brook, NY(Rye Town Hilton)/Feb. 11-13/125

Biometric Soc. (ENAR) (1947)
Box 269, Washington DC 20044
Secy.-Treas.: Barbara Tilley
Members: 2,700 *Staff:* 1

00100 12 05 86 1233

Annual Budget: $50-100,000 *Tel:* (215) 661-6734
Hist. Note: The internat'l organization, The Biometric Soc., was founded at Woods Hole, September 1947 as a result of a report at the First Internat'l Biometric Conference. The North American components are divided between an Eastern and a Western Region, lying on either side of 104 degrees of longitude in the U.S. and Canada. Promotes the application of mathematical and statistical techniques to biology. Membership: $26/yr.
Publication:
Biometrics. q. adv.
Annual Meetings: March
1987-Dallas, TX(Hyatt Regency)/March 22-25
1988-Boston, MA(Park Plaza)/March 27-30

Biophysical Soc. (1957)
9650 Rockville Pike, Room L110, Bethesda MD 20814
Secretary: Dr. Winona C. Barker
Members: 4,000 *Staff:* 2
Annual Budget: $250-500,000 *Tel:* (301) 493-6114
Hist. Note: Founded in Columbus, Ohio in 1957. Members are individuals interested in applying physical laws and techniques to the investigation of biological phenomena.
Publication:
Biophysical Journal. m.
Annual Meetings: Winter/2,800
1987-New Orleans, LA/Feb. 22-26
1988-Baltimore, MD/Feb. 29-March 3

Bioprocess Engineering Soc. Internat'l (1985)
Hist. Note: Address unknown in 1986.

Biscuit and Cracker Distributors Ass'n (1944)
111 East Wacker Drive, Chicago IL 60601
Exec. Director: Barbara Chalik
Members: 200 *Staff:* 2-5
Annual Budget: $50-100,000 *Tel:* (312) 644-6610
Annual Meetings: Fall

Biscuit and Cracker Manufacturers Ass'n (1901)
888 16th St., N.W., Washington DC 20006
President: Francis P. Rooney
Members: 225-250 companies *Staff:* 2-5
Annual Budget: $250-500,000 *Tel:* (202) 223-3127
Hist. Note: Absorbed the Biscuit Bakers Institute in 1965.
Annual Meetings: April
1987-Scottsdale, AZ(Hyatt Regency)/April 5-7
1988-Naples, FL(Ritz Carlton)/April 10-13

Bituminous and Aggregate Equipment Bureau (1960)
111 East Wisconsin Ave., Suite 1700, Milwaukee WI 53202
Exec. V. President: Fred J. Broad
Members: 25-30 *Staff:* 2-5
Annual Budget: under $10,000 *Tel:* (414) 272-0943
Hist. Note: A Bureau of the Construction Industry Manufacturers Ass'n. Formerly (1976) the Bituminous Equipment Manufacturers Bureau. Members are manufacturers of equipment used in asphalt paving.

Bituminous Coal Operators Ass'n (1950)
918 16th St., N.W., Suite 303, Washington DC 20006
President: Joseph P. Brennan
Members: 35 member companies or company groups *Staff:* 12
Annual Budget: $1-2,000,000 *Tel:* (202) 783-3195
Hist. Note: BCOA was formed in 1950 to represent mine operators in negotiation of the National Bituminous Coal Wage Agreement, in order to avoid the chaotic situation resulting from separate company negotiations with the United Mine Workers of America. Dues are established by the Board of Directors, using tonnage produced as the basis.
Annual Meetings: Second Tuesday in May

Black Music Ass'n (1978)
1500 Locust St., Suite 1905, Philadelphia PA 19102
Finance Director: Virginia Glover
Members: 1,000-2,000 *Staff:* 2-5
Annual Budget: $50-100,000 *Tel:* (215) 545-8600
Hist. Note: Established to further black music and bring blacks into music, not only as performers but also as businessmen.
Publication:
Innervisions. bi-m.
Annual Meetings: Fall

Black Psychiatrists of America (1969)
Box 370659, Decatur GA 30037
President: Dr. Richard A. Fields, M.D.
Members: 500
Annual Budget: $10-25,000 *Tel:* (404) 243-2110
Hist. Note: Organized in Miami, Florida and incorporated in New York, BPA membership includes black psychiatrists in the United States, Canada, and the Carribean. BPA is a non-profit, professional organization promoting excellence within the field with particular emphasis on the concerns of ethnic minority groups and the economically depressed. Membership: $200/yr. (individual).
Publication:
BPA Quarterly. q. adv.
Semi-annual Meetings: May and November

Black Top and Nat'l Delaine-Merino Sheep Breeders Ass'n (1885)
R.D. 4, Box 228F, McDonald PA 15057
Secy.-Treas.: Irwin Y. Hamilton
Members: 6-10 *Staff:* 1
Annual Budget: under $10,000 *Tel:* (412) 745-1075
Hist. Note: The product of a merger between the National Delaine Merino Sheep Ass'n and the Black Top Sheep Breeders Ass'n.

Blue Cross and Blue Shield Ass'n (1946)
676 N. St. Clair St., Chicago IL 60611
President: Bernard R. Tresnowski
Members: 79 *Staff:* 700
Annual Budget: over $5,000,000 *Tel:* (312) 440-6000
Hist. Note: Formerly Blue Cross Ass'n and Nat'l Ass'n of Blue Shield Plans; merged in 1978 to become the Blue Cross and Blue Shield Ass'n. Members must be medical and/or hospital plans and operate according to established standards. Offers information, consulting, representation and operation services to members.
Publication:
Inquiry. q.
Annual Meetings: November

Board of Trade of the Wholesale Seafood Merchants (1933)
7 Dey St., Suite 805, New York NY 10007
Exec. Secretary: Dennis F. Ryan
Members: 400 *Staff:* 2-5
Annual Budget: $25-50,000 *Tel:* (212) 732-4340
Hist. Note: The commodity exchange for U. S. and Canadian wholesale seafood merchants.
Annual Meetings: New York City

Boarding Schools (1976)
18 Tremont St., Boston MA 02108
Director: Richard Cowan
Members: 235 schools *Staff:* 2-5
Annual Budget: $100-250,000 *Tel:* (617) 723-3629
Hist. Note: Sponsored by the Nat'l Ass'n of Independent Schools and the Secondary School Admissions Test Board, Boarding Schools (otherwise known as the Committee on Boarding Schools) rents space from NAIS but has its own dues structure and staff. Its members, essentially, are the members of NAIS who have boarding departments. Serves 235 member schools by improving public awareness of boarding schools and expanding the markets of students. Membership: $700-1,000/yr.
Publications:
Boarding Schools Directory. a.
Special Programs. a.
Boarding School Life. semi-a.
Annual Meetings: March, in conjunction with NAIS
1987-Boston, MA(Sheraton)/Feb. 26-28

Boating Writers Internat'l (1970)
56 Hickory Hill Road, Wilton CT 06897
Exec. Secretary: Robert G. Black
Members: 250 *Staff:* 1
Annual Budget: $10-25,000 *Tel:* (203) 762-2711
Hist. Note: Individuals who write about boating and outdoor sports for magazines, newspapers, television and radio. Reports on legislation affecting boating and seeks to encourage boating as a recreational and competitive sport.
Publication:
BWI Bulletin. m.
Annual Meetings: Held in conjunction with the Chicago Boat Show.

Book Industry Study Group (1976)
160 Fifth Ave., Suite 604, New York NY 10010
Manager: Sandra K. Paul
Members: 190 individuals, companies and ass'ns *Staff:* 2-5
Annual Budget: $100-250,000 *Tel:* (212) 929-1393
Hist. Note: Publishers, manufacturers, suppliers, wholesalers, retailers, librarians and others engaged professionally in the development, production and dissemination of books. Purpose is to sponsor and encourage research within and about the book industry, to increase readership, improve distribution of books of all kinds, and expand the market for books.
Publications:
Research Reports. irreg.
Book Industry Trends. a.
Trends Update. q.

Book Manufacturers Institute (1920)
111 Prospect St., Stamford CT 06901
Exec. V. President: Douglas E. Horner
Members: 100 companies *Staff:* 2-5
Annual Budget: $100-250,000 *Tel:* (203) 324-9670
Hist. Note: Established as the Employing Bookbinders of America, it assumed its present name in 1933.
Semi-annual Meetings: Spring and Fall

Botanical Soc. of America (1906)
Biology Dept., Indiana University, Bloomington IN 47405
Secretary: Dr. David L. Dilcher
Members: 3,000-3,500 *Staff:* 2-5
Annual Budget: $100-250,000 *Tel:* (812) 335-9455
Hist. Note: The American Botanical Club was organized in 1883 as a segment of the American Ass'n for the Advancement of Science. In 1894 25 members of this group constituted themselves the Botanical Soc. of America. This merged in 1906 with the Soc. for Plant Morphology and Physiology (formed in 1896) and the American Mycological Soc. (formed in 1903) and at a meeting in New York City the present Society was formed and later incorporated in Connecticut in 1939. An affiliate of the American Ass'n for the Advancement of Science and an adherent society of the American Institute of Biological Sciences. Goals are to promote research and teaching, cooperation among scientists and to disseminate knowledge of plants for application to practical problems. Membership: $35/yr.
Publications:
American Journal of Botany. m. adv.
Plant Science Bulletin. q.
Directory. bien.
Abstracts. a.
Annual Meetings: Summer
1987-Columbus, OH(Ohio State Univ.)/Aug. 9-13
1988-Davis, CA(Univ. of California)/Aug. 6-12
1989-Toronto, Ontario(Univ. of Toronto)/Aug. 6-10

Bow Tie Manufacturers Ass'n (1952)
75 Livingston St., Brooklyn NY 11201
Counsel: Leonard Brodsky
Members: 6-10 companies *Staff:* 1
Annual Budget: under $10,000 *Tel:* (718) 875-2300
Hist. Note: Major purpose of the association is to represent its members in labor negotiations. Closely associated with the National Neckwear Ass'n. Membership: $600/yr.

Bowling Proprietors Ass'n of America (1932)
Box 5802, Arlington TX 76005
Exec. Director: V.A. Wapensky
Members: 4,000-4,200 *Staff:* 30
Annual Budget: $2-5,000,000 *Tel:* (817) 649-5105
Hist. Note: Supports the Bowling Proprietors' Ass'n of America Political Action Committee.
Publication:
The Bowling Proprietor. 11/yr. adv.
Annual Meetings: Summer
1987-Hawaii(Hawaiian Hilton)
1988-New York, NY(Hilton)/Jan. 20-24/500
1989-Orlando, FL(Marriott's World Center)/June 18-23
1990-Washington, DC(Sheraton Washington)/June 25-29
1991-Louisville, KY/June 25-29

Bowling Writers Ass'n of America (1934)
6357 Siena St., Dayton OH 45459
Secy.-Treas: Mike Hennessy
Members: 350 *Staff:* 1
Annual Budget: $10-25,000 *Tel:* (513) 433-8363
Hist. Note: Formerly (1931) Nat'l Bowling Writers' Ass'n. Membership: $15/year.
Annual Meetings: With American Bowling Congress tournament.
1987-Niagara Falls, NY
1988-Jacksonville, FL
1989-Reno, NV

Box Office Management Internat'l (1980)
1572 Second Ave., Suite 2N, New York NY 10028
President: Patricia Spira
Members: 600 *Staff:* 2-3
Annual Budget: $250-500,000 *Tel:* (212) 570-1099
Hist. Note: Membership is comprised of box office managers, treasurers, marketing and systems directors and other administrators from the performing arts and sports fields. Performing arts centers and entertainment facilities are also represented as are industry vendors and suppliers. Membership: $135/yr.
Publications:
Newsletter. bi-m.
Membership Directory.
Annual Meetings: January
1987-San Antonio, TX(Marriott)/Jan. 27-30/over 600
1988-Las Vegas, NV(Caesar's Palace)
1989-Tampa, FL(Hyatt)

Boxboard Research and Development Ass'n (1953)
350 South Kalamazoo Mall, Suite 207, Kalamazoo MI 49007
Exec. Director: Jon D. Hamelink
Members: 30-40 companies *Staff:* 3
Annual Budget: $100-250,000 *Tel:* (616) 344-0394
Hist. Note: An association of U.S., Canadian and other foreign companies interested in cooperative research and development in technical and operational aspects of the recycled combination boxboard industry.
Annual Meetings: Chicago, first week in May.

Boys' and Young Men's Apparel Manufacturers Ass'n (1947)
Hist. Note: Formerly Boy's Apparel & Accessories Mfrs. Ass'n A division of the American Apparel Manufacturers Ass'n.

Boys Clubs of America (1906)
771 First Ave., New York NY 10017
Nat'l Director: William R. Bricker
Members: 1,300,000 youth *Staff:* 150
Annual Budget: over $5,000,000 *Tel:* (212) 557-7755
Hist. Note: A congressionally chartered national federation established as the Boys Club Federation of America; assumed its present name in 1931. Has an annual budget over $11 million. Membership: $1-2/year (individual).
Publications:
Boys Club Bulletin. semi-a.
Connections. q.
Executive Newsletter. bi-m.
Commentary. bi-m.

00101 12 05 86 1233

Annual Meetings: Spring/1,000
1987-Orlando, FL

Boys Clubs Professional Ass'n (1953)
808 Inca St., P.O. Box 4306, Denver CO 80204
President: William Cope
Members: 500
Annual Budget: $25-50,000 *Tel:* (303) 893-2600
Hist. Note: Members are workers in boys clubs. Membership: $50/year.
Publication:
Profiles. q. adv.
Annual Meetings: With Boys Clubs of America

BPI . . .A Growers' Organization (1969)
Box 286, Okemos MI 48864
Exec. Director: Terry Humfeld
Members: 3,800 *Staff:* 6-10
Annual Budget: $500-1,000,000 *Tel:* (517) 349-3924
Hist. Note: Formerly known as Bedding Plants, Inc. Members are growers, wholesalers, retailers, educators, and allied tradesmen of the bedding plant industry.
Publication:
BPI News. m.
Annual Meetings: Fall/1,500
1987-Rochester, NY/Oct. 4-8
1988-San Antonio, TX(Hyatt)/Oct. 4-8
1989-Cincinnati, OH/Oct. 1-5

Brake System Parts Manufacturers Council (1973)
222 Cedar Lane, Teaneck NJ 07666
Exec. Director: Ralph W. Van Demark
Members: 21 companies *Staff:* 2
Tel: (201) 836-9500
Hist. Note: Formed by a group of companies making brake systems parts to expand the market for their products.

Branch Warehouse Ass'n (1958)
Hist. Note: Defunct in 1983.

Brass and Bronze Ingot Institute (1928)
33 North La Salle St., Room 3500, Chicago IL 60602
Ass't. Secretary: Julie A. Butler
Members: 5 companies *Staff:* 1
Annual Budget: $10-25,000 *Tel:* (312) 236-2715
Hist. Note: Formerly Non-Ferrous Metal Ingot Institute. Has no office, as such. The above address is the law firm of Gorham, Metge, Bowman and Hourigan.

Brazilian American Chamber of Commerce (1968)
22 West 48th St., Suite 404, New York NY 10036-1886
Exec. Director: Frank J. Devine
Members: 325-350 *Staff:* 2-5
Annual Budget: $100-250,000 *Tel:* (212) 575-9030
Hist. Note: Founded as the Brazilian-American Association, it incorporated and assumed its present name in 1968. Membership is made up of Brazilian and U.S. businessmen concerned with forging closer ties between the business communities of both nations. Membership: $175/yr.(individual); $550/yr.(corporate).
Publications:
Brazilian American Business Review/Directory. a. adv.
News Bulletin. m.
Brazil-U.S. Listing. irreg. adv.
Annual Meetings: March in New York, NY

Brewers Ass'n of America (1942)
541 West Randolph St., Chicago IL 60606
Exec. Secretary: William M. O'Shea
Members: 400 *Staff:* 2-5
Annual Budget: $100-250,000 *Tel:* (312) 782-2306
Hist. Note: Founded as the Small Brewers Association, it assumed its present name on September 11, 1952. Members are breweries and suppliers to the industry.
Publication:
Newsletter. m.
Annual Meetings: Ft. Lauderdale, FL(Pier 66)/Fall

Brick Institute of America (1934)
11490 Commerce Park Drive, Suite 300, Reston VA 22091
President: Nelson J. Cooney
Members: 100-125 *Staff:* 20-25
Annual Budget: $1-2,000,000 *Tel:* (703) 620-0010
Hist. Note: Founded as the Structural Clay Products Institute, it assumed its present name in 1972. Sponsors the Brick Political Action Committee.
Annual Meetings: Fall
1987-White Sulfur Springs, WV(Greenbrier)/Oct. 18-21/650
1988-Boca Raton, FL(Hotel & Club)/Oct. 23-26/650
1989-White Sulphur Springs, WV(Greenbrier)/Oct. 15-18/650

Bridal and Bridesmaids Apparel Ass'n (1957)
c/o Bridal Expo, 510 Montauk Hwy, West Islip NY 11795
Secretary: William Heaton
Members: 35-40 companies *Staff:* 1
Annual Budget: under $10,000 *Tel:* (516) 669-1272

Bright Belt Warehouse Ass'n (1945)
P.O. Box 12004, Raleigh NC 27605
Managing Director: Mac Dunkley
Members: 250-300 *Staff:* 2-5
Annual Budget: $50-100,000 *Tel:* (919) 828-8988
Hist. Note: Represents the flue-cured tobacco warehouse industry.
Annual Meetings: June

British-American Chamber of Commerce (1920)
275 Madison Ave., Room 1714, New York NY 10016
Exec. Director: Fabienne M. Edmeades
Members: 6-700 *Staff:* 2-5
Annual Budget: $100-250,000 *Tel:* (212) 889-0680
Hist. Note: Encourages commerce, cultivates reciprocal interest in, and comity between the United States and the United Kingdom.
Publications:
British-American Trade News. m. adv.
Year Book and Classified Membership Directory. a. adv.
BACC Trade Bulletin.
Directory of U.S. Subsidiaries of British Firms. a. adv.

Broadcast, Cable and Consumer Electronics Soc.
Hist. Note: Subsidiary of the Institute of Electrical and Electronics Engineers. Membership in the Society, open only to IEEE members, includes subscription to a technical periodical in the field published by IEEE. All administrative support is provided by IEEE.

Broadcast Credit Ass'n (1972)
1259 Route 46 East, Box 5356, Parsippany NJ 07054-0332
Exec. V. President: Robert E. McAuliffe
Members: 500 *Staff:* 5
Annual Budget: $250-500,000 *Tel:* (201) 299-1965
Hist. Note: A subsidiary of the Broadcast Financial Management Ass'n, Inc. Known as BCA-Credit Information from 1976 to 1985.
Publications:
Aging Summary of Accounts Receivable. m.
Creditopics. m.
Membership Directory. a.
Credit and Collection Survey. a.
Annual Meetings: With Broadcast Financial Management Ass'n
1987-Boston, MA(Marriott Copley Place)/April 26-29
1988-New Orleans, LA/April 17-20

Broadcast Education Ass'n (1955)
1771 N St., N.W., Washington DC 20036
President: Dr. Harold Niven
Members: 300-325 institutions, 400-450 individuals
Annual Budget: $50-100,000 *Tel:* (202) 429-5355
Hist. Note: Formerly (1973) Ass'n for Professional Broadcasting Education. Member of the Council of Communication Societies. Institutional members are colleges and universities with training programs in radio and television.
Publications:
Feedback. q.
Journal of Broadcasting and Electronic Media. q.
Annual Meetings: Spring, with Nat'l Ass'n of Broadcasters

Broadcast Financial Management Ass'n (1961)
701 Lee Street, Suite 1010, Des Plaines IL 60016
Exec. Director: Robert E. McAuliffe, CAE
Members: 1,200 *Staff:* 2-5
Annual Budget: $500-1,000,000 *Tel:* (312) 296-0200
Hist. Note: Formerly (1977) Institute of Broadcasting Financial Management.
Publication:
Broadcast Financial Journal. bi-m. adv.
Annual Meetings: Spring
1987-Boston, MA(Marriott Copley)/April 26-29/1,100

Broadcast Promotion and Marketing Executives (1956)
402 East Orange St., Lancaster PA 17602
Admin. Director: Patricia A. Evans
Members: 1,750 companies *Staff:* 2-5
Annual Budget: $1-2,000,000 *Tel:* (717) 397-5727
Hist. Note: Directors of public relations and advertising for radio and television stations. Formerly (1984) the Broadcaster' Promotion Ass'n.
Publications:
Image Magazine. m. adv.
Membership Roster. a.
Annual Meetings: June
1987-Atlanta, GA(Westin Peachtree)/June 10-14/1,700
1988-Los Angeles, CA(Westin Bonaventure)/June 8-12/1,700
1989-Detroit, MI(Renaissance Center)/June 22-25/2,000

Broadcast Rating Council (1964)
Hist. Note: Became the Electronic Media Rating Council in 1983.

Broadcasters' Promotion Ass'n (1956)
Hist. Note: Became the Broadcast Promotion and Marketing Executives in 1984.

Broker Management Council (1980)
117 Miramar Ave., Biloxi MS 39530
Exec. Director: William R. Bess
Members: 30-40 individuals; 20-30 companies *Staff:* 2-5
Annual Budget: $25-50,000 *Tel:* (601) 374-6537
Hist. Note: Independent food brokers who specialize in hotel and restaurant food service products.
Publication:
Management Letter. m.
Semi-annual Meetings: spring and fall/35
1987-New Orleans, LA(Royal Sonesta)/May 1-4

Brotherhood of Book Travelers (1883)
Hist. Note: Became the Ass'n of Book Travelers in 1980.

Brotherhood of Locomotive Engineers (1863)
1365 Ontario Street, Room 1112 Engineers Building, Cleveland OH 44114
President: R.E. Delaney
Members: 32,000 *Staff:* 55-60
Annual Budget: $2-5,000,000 *Tel:* (216) 241-2630
Hist. Note: Established in Detroit March 17, 1863 as Division Number One, Brotherhood of the Footboard. After 1864 became the Grand Internat'l Division of the Brotherhood of Locomotive Engineers. Sponsors and supports the Brotherhood of Locomotive Engineers Legislative League Political Action Committee.
Publication:
Locomotive Engineer. w.
Annual Meetings: Every 5 years (1991)

Brotherhood of Maintenance of Way Employes (1887)
12050 Woodward Ave., Detroit MI 48203-3596
President: Geoffrey N. Zeh
Members: 80,000 *Staff:* 50-60
Annual Budget: $2-5,000,000 *Tel:* (313) 868-0490
Hist. Note: Established in July 1887 in Alabama as the order of Railroad Trackmen. On October 13, 1891 the Brotherhood of Railway Section Foremen of North America, founded in La Porte City, Iowa, merged with the Order of Railroad Trackmen to become the International Brotherhood of Railway Track Foremen of America. Became the Brotherhood of Railway Trackmen in 1896 and absorbed the United Brotherhood of Railroad Trackmen (Canadian) in 1900, affiliating with the American Federation of Labor the same year. Became the United Brotherhood of Maintenance of Way Employes and Railway Shop Laborers in 1918 and assumed its present name in 1925. Has a budget of about $8 million.
Publications:
BMWE Railway Journal. m.
Along The Way m.
Every 4 years: next meeting in July, 1990

Brotherhood of Railroad Signalmen (1901)
601 West Golf Road, Box U, Mount Prospect IL 60056
President: R.T. Bates
Members: 12,000-13,000 *Staff:* 11-15
Annual Budget: $1-2,000,000 *Tel:* (312) 439-3732
Hist. Note: Organized in the signal tower of the Altoona, Pennsylvania railroad yard in 1901 and chartered by the American Federation of Labor in 1914. Sponsors and supports the Brotherhood of Railroad Signalmen Political Action Committee.
Publication:
The Signalmen's Journal. adv.
Annual Meetings: Every 3 years in Summer (1988)

Brotherhood of Railway, Airline and Steamship Clerks, Freight Handlers, Express and Station Employees (1899)
3 Research Place, Rockville MD 20850
President: Richard I. Kilroy
Members: 200,000 *Staff:* 100-125
Annual Budget: over $5,000,000 *Tel:* (301) 948-4910
Hist. Note: Established in Sedalia, Missouri December 31, 1899 as the Order of Railroad Clerks of America and chartered by the American Federation of Labor the following year. Became the Brotherhood of Railway and Steamship Clerks, Freight Handlers, Express and Station Employees in 1919 and assumed its present name in 1967. In 1969 it absorbed the Transportation-Communication Employees Union, the Railway Patrolmen's International Union and the Federation of Business Machine Technicians and Engineers. In 1975 it merged with the United Transport Service Employees of America (founded in 1937), and in 1978 merged with the Brotherhood of Sleeping Car Porters (founded in 1925). Absorbed the American Railway and Airway Supervisors Association in 1980; in 1986, BRAC merged with Brotherhood Railway Carmen of the United States. Has a budget of about $15 million. Sponsors and supports the Responsible Citizens Political League.
Publications:
Interchange. 9/yr.
International President's Bulletin. q.
Leadership Action Lines. m.
Quadrennial Meetings: Next 1987.

Brotherhood of Shoe and Allied Craftsmen (1933)
Box 390, East Bridgewater MA 02333
President: Edward M. Smith, -
Members: 700 *Staff:* 2-5
Annual Budget: $50-100,000 *Tel:* (617) 587-2606
Hist. Note: Independent labor union.

Brotherhood Railway Carmen of the United States and Canada (1888)
4929 Main St., Kansas City MO 64112
President: C.E. Wheeler
Members: 70-76,000 *Staff:* 20-25
Annual Budget: $2-5,000,000 *Tel:* (816) 561-1112
Hist. Note: The result of a merger on September 9, 1890 of the Brotherhood of Car Repairers of North America (founded in Cedar Rapids October 27, 1888) and the Carmen's Mutual Aid

00102 12 05 86 1233

Ass'n (founded in Minneapolis on November 23, 1888). Merged with the Car Inspectors, Repairers and Oilers Mutual Benefit Association in 1891 and with the Brotherhood of Railway Carmen of Canada the next year. Affiliated with the American Federation of Labor in 1910. Has a budget of about $6 million. Sponsors and supports the Railway Carmen Political League Political Action Committee. Membership: $318/yr. (individual).
Publication:
Railway Carmen's Journal. m.
Annual Meetings: Every 5 years in Summer
1988-Kansas City, MO(Radisson)/Aug. 14/500

Brown Swiss Cattle Breeders Ass'n of the U.S.A. (1880)
800 Pleasant St., Box 1038, Beloit WI 53511-1038
Secy.-Treas.: George W. Opperman
Members: 1,100 *Staff:* 20-25
Annual Budget: $500-1,000,000 *Tel:* (608) 365-4474
Hist. Note: Breeders and fanciers of Brown Swiss dairy cattle. Member of the Nat'l Soc. of Livestock Record Ass'ns. Membership: $50/lifetime (individual); $50/10 yrs. (company)
Publication:
Brown Swiss Bulletin. m. adv.
Annual Meetings: July
1987-Dayton, OH(Marriott)/July 14-16/300-350
1988-Rockford, IL(Clock Tower Inn)

Builders Hardware Manufacturers Ass'n (1925)
60 East 42nd St., Suite 511, New York NY 10165
Exec. Director: J. Dudley Waldner, CAE
Members: 70-80 *Staff:* 2-5
Annual Budget: $250-500,000 *Tel:* (212) 682-8142
Hist. Note: Formerly (1961) Hardware Manufacturers Statistical Ass'n.
Publication:
ANSI/BHMA Standards.
Semi-Annual Meetings: Spring and Fall

Building Officials and Code Administrators Internat'l (1915)
4051 W. Flossmoor Road, Country Club Hills IL 60477
Exec. Director: Clarence R. Bechtel
Members: 8,000 *Staff:* 40-45
Annual Budget: $2-5,000,000 *Tel:* (312) 799-2300
Hist. Note: Formerly (1970) Building Officials Conference of America, Inc., BOCAI is the oldest organization of building officials and code administrators in the country. Promulgates and maintains model building codes, promotes the use of safe, suitable and modern construction techiques and materials. Membership: $75/yr. (minimum)
Publications:
Boca Bulletin. bi-m.
The Building Official. m. adv.
Annual Meetings: Summer/5-600
1987-Alexandria, VA/June 21-26
1988-Columbus, OH/June 19-24
1989-Schaumburg, IL/June 18-23

Building Owners and Managers Ass'n Internat'l (1908)
1250 Eye St., N.W., Washington DC 20005
Exec. V. President: Noel R. Leary
Members: 6,000 *Staff:* 34
Annual Budget: $2-5,000,000 *Tel:* (202) 289-7000
Hist. Note: Formerly (1968) Nat'l Ass'n of Building Owners and Managers. International membership consists of building owners, developers, managers, service companies, investors and brokers. Its 90 federated associations are in North America and around the world. Sponsors the Building Owners and Managers Institute International, an educational arm which provides educational programming leading to two professional designations: "RPA" (Real Property Administrator) and "SMA" (Systems Maintenance Administrator). Also sponsors the Building Owners and Managers Ass'n Political Action Action Committee. Membership: $150/yr.
Publications:
Convention Directory. a. adv.
Experience Exchange Report. a.
Membership/Committee Directory. a. adv.
Skylines. m.
Annual Meetings: June
1987-Toronto, Ontario(Metro Toronto Conv. Ctr.)/June 28-July 1/3,200
1988-Cincinnati, OH(Convention Center)/June 19-22/3,300
1989-Atlanta, GA(Merchandise Mart)/June 18-21/3,400

Building Service Contractors Ass'n Internat'l (1965)
8315 Lee Highway, Suite 301, Fairfax VA 22031
Exec. V. President: Carol A. Dean
Members: 1,300 *Staff:* 15-20
Annual Budget: $1-2,000,000 *Tel:* (703) 698-8810
Hist. Note: Formerly (1974) Nat'l Ass'n of Building Service Contractors. Members are companies offering cleaning, maintenance, security and janitorial services, and their suppliers. Membership: $300-1,400/yr. (based on annual gross service sales of prior business year.
Publications:
SERVICES magazine. m. adv.
Who's Who in Building Service Contracting. a. adv.
Annual Report. a.
Annual Meetings: Spring
1987-Washington, DC(Sheraton Washington)/April 1-5/1,000

Building Service Managers Institute (1957)
Hist. Note: A component of the Environmental Management Association.

Building Stone Institute (1919)
420 Lexington Ave., New York NY 10017
Exec. V. President: Dorothy Kender
Members: 400 companies *Staff:* 6-10
Annual Budget: $250-500,000 *Tel:* (212) 490-2530
Hist. Note: Formerly (1955) Internat'l Cut Stone Quarrymen's Ass'n. Stone dealers, contractors and quarry owners.
Publication:
Building Stone Magazine. bi-m. adv.
Annual Meetings: February

Building Systems Institute
1230 Keith Building, Cleveland OH 44115
General Manager: Charles M. Stockinger
Members: 3 ass'ns *Staff:* 2-5
Annual Budget: $10-25,000 *Tel:* (216) 241-7333
Hist. Note: Membership consists of national trade associations operating within the building systems industry.
Publication:
Building Systems Architecure, Design, and Planning Guidelines.

Built-in Cleaning Systems Institute (1967)
c/o H.P. Products, 512 W. Gorgas St., Louisville OH 44641-1332
President: Paul Bishop
Members: 6-10 companies *Staff:* 1
Annual Budget: under $10,000 *Tel:* (216) 875-5556
Hist. Note: Manufacturers trade association.

Bumper Recycling Ass'n of North America (1969)
1133 15th St., N.W., Suite 620, Washington DC 20005
Exec. Director: David W. Barrack
Members: 135-40 companies *Staff:* 10
Annual Budget: $50-100,000 *Tel:* (202) 293-5910
Hist. Note: Incorporated in the State of California in 1969 as the Bumper Reconditioning Association of North America. Assumed its present name August 5, 1972. Members are companies which recycle the bumpers of motor vehicles.
Publication:
BRANA Newsletter. bi-m. adv.
Semi-annual meetings: March and August

Bureau of Explosives (1907)
Hist. Note: Became Ass'n of American Railroads - Hazardous Materials in 1985.

Bureau of Salesmen's Nat'l Ass'ns (1948)
1718 Peachtree Rd., N.W., Suite 600, Atlanta GA 30309
Mng. Director: Sherwyn E. Syna
Members: 19-20,000 apparel salesmen *Staff:* 6-10
Tel: (404) 881-0933
Hist. Note: A federation of national, state and local groups; consists of the Bureau of Wholesale Sales Representatives, the Nat'l Shoe Travelers Ass'n and the Southeastern Toy Travelers Ass'n.

Bureau of Wholesale Sales Representatives (1943)
1718 Peachtree Street, N.W., Suite 600, Atlanta GA 30309
Exec. Director: Sherwyn E. Syna
Members: 16,000 salesmen *Staff:* 21-25
Annual Budget: $250-500,000 *Tel:* (404) 881-0933
Hist. Note: Members are wholesale men's and boy's clothing salespersons. Formerly (1959) Nat'l Ass'n of Men's Apparel Clubs and (1980) Nat'l Ass'n of Men's and Boy's Apparel Clubs. A member of The Bureau of Salesmen's National Associations. Sponsors and supports the Bureau of Wholesale Sales Representatives Political Action Committee. Membership: $75/yr.
Publication:
Bureau News. m. adv.
Annual Meetings: December

Burlap and Jute Ass'n (1923)
P.O. Box 1649, Darien CT 06820
Secy.-Treas.: Linda Miller
Members: 12 companies; 12 associates *Staff:* 1
Annual Budget: under $10,000 *Tel:* (203) 655-8221
Hist. Note: Members are importers of burlap and jute.
Annual Meetings: New York City, in December/20

Burley and Dark Leaf Tobacco Export Ass'n (1947)
1100 17th St., N.W., Suite 902, Washington DC 20036
V. President & Mng. Director: Benjamin F. Reeves
Members: 10-15 ass'ns *Staff:* 2
Annual Budget: $100-250,000 *Tel:* (202) 296-6820
Hist. Note: A federation of ass'ns. Directors of these constitute the membership.
Annual Meetings:
1987-Owensboro, KY(Executive Inn)/Sept. 24-26/200

Burley Auction Warehouse Ass'n (1946)
Box 670, Mount Sterling KY 40353
Mng. Director & Gen. Counsel: Thomas M. Edwards, Jr.
Members: 200-225 *Staff:* 2-5
Annual Budget: $25-50,000 *Tel:* (606) 498-2002
Hist. Note: Members are warehouse companies selling burley tobacco at auction in the eight burley-producing states.
Annual Meetings: June
1987-Nashville, TN(Opryland)/June 10-12/300-350

Burley Leaf Tobacco Dealers Ass'n (1942)
Austin Co., P.O. Box 1360, Greenville TN 37744-1360
Secy.-Treas.: Frank Jennings
Members: 20-25 companies
Annual Budget: $10-25,000 *Tel:* (615) 638-4124
Hist. Note: A member of Burley and Dark Leaf Tobacco Export Ass'n.

Burley Tobacco Growers Cooperative Ass'n (1922)
620 South Broadway, Lexington KY 40508
Exec. Secretary: A. R. Beckley
Members: 500,000 *Staff:* 15-20
Annual Budget: $250-500,000 *Tel:* (606) 252-3561

Buses Internat'l Ass'n (1981)
Box 1472, Spokane WA 99210
Exec. Director: William A. Luke
Members: 100 *Staff:* 1
Annual Budget: under $10,000 *Tel:* (509) 328-9181
Hist. Note: Members are management-level personnel in the bus industry or its suppliers. Membership: $25/yr.
Publication:
Buses International. q.

Business and Institutional Furniture Manufacturers Ass'n (1973)
2335 Burton St., S.E., Grand Rapids MI 49506
Exec. Director: Stephen D. Channer
Members: 230 companies *Staff:* 2-5
Annual Budget: $250-500,000 *Tel:* (616) 243-1681
Hist. Note: A member of the Coalition for Common Sense in Government Procurement.

Business Council (1933)
888 17th St., N.W., Washington DC 20006
Exec. Secretary: Jean H. Carter
Members: 225 Individuals *Staff:* 2-5
Annual Budget: $250-500,000 *Tel:* (202) 298-7650
Hist. Note: A forum for the exchange of ideas between top corporate executives and government officials. Established originally as the Business Advisory Council to the Department of Commerce, it assumed its present name in 1961 and broke away from the Department of Commerce.
Annual Meetings: Three each year, one in Washington and two in Hot Springs

Business Education Research Associates (1901)
Hist. Note: Became Business Education Research of America in 1984.

Business Education Research of America
Hist. Note: No paid staff; address unknown in 1986.

Business Forms Management Ass'n (1958)
P.O. Box 40468, Portland OR 97240
Administrator: Katy Smith
Members: 2,000-2,100 individuals *Staff:* 2-5
Annual Budget: $2-5,000,000 *Tel:* (503) 232-0232
Hist. Note: An international, non-profit association of individuals interested in the effective management of forms and related information sources. Membership Fee: Depends upon area.
Publications:
News and Views. m.
Journal of Forms Management. q. adv.
BFMA Directory. a.
Annual Meetings: May/500
1987-Phoenix, AZ/May 17-21
1988-Toronto, Ontario
1989-Kansas City, MO
1990-Atlanta, GA

Business History Conference (1955)
Box 18, 1407 W. Gregory, Urbana IL 61801
Exec. Secretary: Jeremy Atack
Members: 210 *Staff:* 1
Annual Budget: under $10,000 *Tel:* (217) 333-7300
Hist. Note: Membership: $15/year.
Publication:
Papers of the Business History Conference. a.
Annual Meetings: In a university environment.
1987-Wilmington, DE/March
1988-Atlanta, GA/March

Business Planning Board (1985)
10 Paragon Drive, Box 433, Montvale NJ 07645
Consulting Director: Jonathan B. Schiff
Members: 1,500 *Staff:* 2
Annual Budget: $100-250,000 *Tel:* (201) 573-6225
Hist. Note: 5 Established in New Jersey in January, 1985, BPA members are Chief Executive Officers, Chief Financialo Officers and others directly involved in corporate planning. Affiliated with the Nat'l Ass'n of Accountants. Membership: $75/yr. (individual).
Publications:
Business Planning Update. m.
Business Planning. q.
Who's Who in Business Planning Today. a.

00103 12 05 86 1233

Business/Professional Advertising Ass'n (1922)
205 East 42nd St., #1518, New York NY 10017
Mng. Director: Ronald L. Coleman
Members: 4,500 individuals *Staff:* 6-10
Annual Budget: $500-1,000,000 *Tel:* (212) 661-0222
Hist. Note: Formerly (1959) Nat'l Industrial Advertisers Ass'n and (1974) Ass'n of Industrial Advertisers. Membership: $125/yr.
Publications:
Marketing/Advertising/Research Newsletter.
The B/PAA Communicator.
Marketing Communications Newsletter.
Marketing/High Tech Trends.
Annual Meetings: June/5-600
1987-Boca Raton, FL(Hotel & Club)/June 14-17
1988-San Francisco, CA(Fairmont)/June 19-22
1989-Montreal, Quebec(Sheraton Centre)/June 11-14
1990-Hilton Head, SC(Hyatt)/June 10-13
1991-New York, NY
1992-Atlanta, GA(Marriott Marquis)/June 7-10

Business Publications Audit of Circulation (1931)
360 Park Ave. South, New York NY 10010
President: Joseph Foley
Members: 2,000 *Staff:* 75
Annual Budget: $2-5,000,000 *Tel:* (212) 532-6880
Hist. Note: Members are advertising agencies, advertisers and publishers of business, professional or technical publications. Purpose is to audit their claimed paid or controlled circulation. Formerly Controlled Circulations Audit.
Publication:
BPA News. q.
Annual Meetings:
1987-New York, NY/May

Business Records Manufacturers Ass'n (1951)
1726 M St., N.W., Washington DC 20036
Exec. Director: John C. Vickerman
Members: 16-20 companies *Staff:* 2-5
Annual Budget: $25-50,000 *Tel:* (202) 457-0909
Hist. Note: Formerly (until 1972) the Loose Leaf and Blank Book Manufacturers Ass'n.
Annual Meetings: Semi-annual

Cab Manufacturers Council
Hist. Note: A division of the Farm and Industrial Equipment Institute.

Cable Televison Administration and Marketing Soc. (1976)
1220 L St., N.W., Suite 625, Washington DC 20005
Exec. Director: Victor S. Parra
Members: 1,600 *Staff:* 5
Annual Budget: $1-2,000,000 *Tel:* (202) 371-0800
Hist. Note: CTAM members are general managers, regional managaers and systems level executives of cable television companies. Incorporated in Washington, DC. Membership: $125/yr.
Publication:
CTAM Newsletter. q.

Cadmium Council (1980)
292 Madison Ave., New York NY 10017
President: Werner T. Meyer
Members: 11 companies *Staff:* 2-5
Annual Budget: $100-250,000 *Tel:* (212) 578-4750
Hist. Note: Formerly a council of the Zinc Institute, the Council is the marketing, research and promotional arm of the cadmium industry. Members are producers and consumers of cadmium. Shares an administrative staff with the Zinc Institute and the Lead Industries Association.
Publications:
CadmiumLines. 3/yr.
Annual Report.

Cajal Club (1947)
4200 Ninth Ave., Box B-111, Denver CO 80262
Secy.-Treas.: David G. Whitlock, M.D.
Members: 450-475 *Staff:* 1
Annual Budget: under $10,000 *Tel:* (303) 394-8201
Hist. Note: Members are neuroanatomists. Named after Sr. Don Santiago Ramon y Cajal, a pioneer in the field of neuroanatomy. Has no headquarters or paid staff. Membership: $10/yr.
Publication:
Proceedings. irreg.
Annual Meetings: With the American Ass'n of Anatomists.

California Dried Fruit Export Ass'n (1925)
P.O. Box 270A, 303 Brokaw Rd., Santa Clara CA 95052
Secy.-Treas.: Frank A. Mosebar
Members: 30-35
Annual Budget: $25-50,000 *Tel:* (408) 727-9302
Hist. Note: A Webb-Pomerene Act Ass'n of dried fruit and tree nut exporters.

California Export Ass'n (1984)
1095 Hillsdale Ave., Box 5699, San Jose CA 95150
Members: 10 packing companies
Hist. Note: A Webb-Pomerene Act association.

California Redwood Ass'n (1916)
591 Redwood Highway, Suite 3100, Mill Valley CA 94941
Exec. V. President: L. Keith Lanning
Members: 4 companies *Staff:* 11-15
Annual Budget: $1-2,000,000 *Tel:* (415) 381-1304
Publication:
Redwood News. q.

California Valley Exports (1982)
Hist. Note: A Webb-Pomerene Act association. Ceased operations in 1985.

Callerlab-Internat'l Ass'n of Square Dance Callers (1971)
Box 679, Pocono Pines PA 18350
Exec. Secretary: John Kaltenthaler
Members: 1,850 *Staff:* 2-5
Annual Budget: $100-250,000 *Tel:* (717) 646-8411
Hist. Note: An organization of currently active square dance callers. Incorporated in the State of California. Has an international membership. Membership: $50/yr.
Publications:
Direction. bi-m.
Guidelines. q.
Annual Meetings: Mon.-Wed. before Easter
1987-New Orleans, LA(Hyatt)April 13-15/1,000
1988-Reno, NV(MGM Grand)/March 28-20/1,200
1989-Nashville, TN(Opryland)/March 20-22
1990-Orlando, FL(Hyatt)/April 9-11
1991-Las Vegas, NV(Bally's)/March 25-27

Calorie Control Council (1966)
5775 Peachtree-Dunwoody Rd., Suite 500D, Atlanta GA 30342
President: Robert H. Kellen
Members: 65 *Staff:* 11-15
Tel: (404) 252-3663
Hist. Note: An international association of manufacturers and suppliers of dietary foods and beverages. Objectives include maintaining and enhancing communication between the calorie food control industry and government and reulatory bodies, scientific and medical professionals and consumers.
Annual Meetings: Fall

Calorimetry Conference (1947)
Chemistry Dept., Eyring Science Center, Brigham Young University, Provo UT 84602
Secy.-Treas.: Juliana Boerio-Goates
Members: 250
Annual Budget: $10-25,000 *Tel:* (801) 378-2302
Hist. Note: Scientists interested in the measurement of heat. Formerly (1950) the Low Temperature Calorimetry Conference. Membership: $10/yr.
Annual Meetings: Summer
1987-Boulder,CO(Univ. of Colorado)/July
1988-Bartlesville, OK

CAMEO (1978)
17 Clara Road, Framingham MA 01701
President: Larry Blakely
Members: 25 companies; 30 individuals
Annual Budget: $10-25,000 *Tel:* (617) 877-4651
Hist. Note: A non-profit organization made up of professional audio and music electronics manufacturers and distributors. Provides educational information for dealers and end-users; promotes and expands professional audio and music electronics industries. Membership: $500/yr. (charter); $200/yr. (standard)
Publication:
CAMEO Dictionary of Creative Audio Terms.
Annual Meetings: Winter
1987-Anaheim, CA/Jan. 18
1988-Anaheim, CA/Jan. 17
1989-Anaheim, CA/Jan. 22

Camp Horsemanship Ass'n (1967)
Box 188, Lawrence MI 49064
Exec. Secretary: Sally Edwards-Butler
Members: 200 organizations, 900 instructors *Staff:* 1
Annual Budget: $25-50,000 *Tel:* (616) 674-8074
Hist. Note: Founded in Texas in 1967 and incorporated in Michigan in 1980. Members are camp owners, camp directors, colleges, stables, riding instructors and others interested in riding instruction and safety. Sets standards and provides certification for instructors. Membership: $45/yr. (organization), $5/yr. (individual/non-voting).
Publication:
CHA Newsletter. semi-a.
Annual Meetings: October
1987-Michigan

Campground Owners Ass'n (1969)
Hist. Note: Officially known as Kampground Owners Association.

Can Manufacturers Institute (1939)
1625 Massachusetts Ave., N.W., Washington DC 20036
President: John M. Dunn
Members: 100-110 companies *Staff:* 16-20
Annual Budget: $500-1,000,000 *Tel:* (202) 232-4677
Hist. Note: Absorbed the Carbonated Beverage Container Manufacturers Ass'n in 1974.
Publications:
Executive Focus. m.
Legislative Review. w.
Metal Can Shipments Report. m.
Annual Meetings: Spring, in Washington, DC

Canadian-American Motor Carriers Ass'n (1978)
1850 M St., N.W., Suite 280, Washington DC 20036
General Counsel: William H. Shawn
Members: 25 *Staff:* 1
Annual Budget: $10-25,000 *Tel:* (202) 887-1400
Hist. Note: Members are U. S. and Canadian trucking firms operating across the border who wish to induce their respective governments to arrive at consistent regulations.
Publication:
CAMCA Bulletin. m.
Annual Meetings: March

Candy Brokers Ass'n of America (1960)
Hist. Note: Became the National Candy Brokers and Sales Association in 1981.

Candy, Chocolate and Confectionery Institute (1958)
Hist. Note: Inactive in 1984.

Canned and Cooked Meat Importers Ass'n (1971)
1700 North Moore St., Suite 1600, Arlington VA 22209
Exec. Secretary: Dr. A. Dewey Bond
Members: 25 *Staff:* 1
Annual Budget: under $10,000 *Tel:* (703) 841-2400
Hist. Note: Incorporated in the District of Columbia in 1971. Primarily a legislative interest group whose members import meat from South American countries. The above address is that of the American Meat Institute.

Canned Salmon Institute (1957)
Hist. Note: Became the Salmon Institute in 1981.

Canon Law Soc. of America (1939)
Caldwell Hall, Room 431, Catholic Univ., Washington DC 20064
Exec. Coordinator: Edward G. Pfnausch
Members: 2,000 *Staff:* 2-5
Annual Budget: $50-100,000 *Tel:* (202) 269-3491
Hist. Note: Individuals interested in the study of church law and ecclesiastical jurisprudence. Membership: $50/yr.
Publications:
Proceedings. a.
Newsletter. 3/yr.
Annual Meetings: Fall/400
1987-Nashville, TN(Hyatt)/Oct. 12-15
1988-Baltimore, MD(Hilton)/Oct. 10-15
1989-Seattle, WA(Westin)/Oct. 9-12
1990-Cleveland, OH(Bond Court)/Oct. 15-18

Cantors Assembly (1947)
150 Fifth Ave., New York NY 10011
Exec. V. President: Samuel Rosenbaum
Members: 325-400 individuals *Staff:* 2-5
Annual Budget: $50-100,000 *Tel:* (212) 691-8020
Hist. Note: Promotes and advances the traditions of Conservative Judaism.
Publications:
Journal of Synagogue Music. q.
Proceedings. a.

Cap Screw and Special Threaded Products Bureau (1929)
Hist. Note: Formerly (1973) United States Cap Screw and Special Thread Products Service. Dissolved in 1983

Captive Insurance Companies Ass'n (1973)
205 East 42nd St., New York NY 10017
Administrator: Lisa Mueller
Members: 177 companies *Staff:* 1
Annual Budget: $50-100,000 *Tel:* (212) 687-4501
Hist. Note: Single insurance companies completely owned by a parent organization or industry. Membership: $300/yr. (company) plus $100 initiation fee.
Publication:
CICA Newsletter. q.
Annual Meetings: Fall/100
1987-Dallas, TX(Sheraton Park Central)
1988-Boston, MA

Car Audio Specialists Ass'n (1978)
2101 L St., N.W., Suite 903, Washington DC 20037
Exec. Director: Cheryl J. Hollins
Members: 250 companies & individuals *Staff:* 2-5
Annual Budget: $100-250,000 *Tel:* (202) 828-2270
Hist. Note: Manufacturers, importers, distributors, retailers and installers involved in the production, sale and installation of radios, tape and cassette decks and other sound equipment for motor vehicles. Association members are concerned that such devices do not become standard equipment in new vehicles. Formerly (1983) the Custom Automotive Sound Ass'n. Membership fee: Based on annual car audio sales volume or flat rate.
Publications:
CASA Newsletter. m.
OEM Car Audio Policy. a.
Tri-annual Membership Meetings:
January and June with Consumer Electronics Trade Show
August in Toronto, Ontario

00104 12 05 86 1233

Car Care Council (1969)
600 Renaissance Center, Detroit MI 48243
President: Arthur H. Nellen
Members: 145
Annual Budget: $100-250,000 *Tel:* (313) 259-4612
Hist. Note: Originally comprised of aftermarket manufacturers, CCC now includes distributors and dealers. Provides public service material on car maintenance for the media.
Annual Meetings: March, with the Internat'l Automotive Aftermarket Show
1987-Atlanta, GA/March 11
1988-Las Vegas, NV/March 2
1989-Chicago, IL/March 1

Car Department Officers Ass'n (1901)
101 North Wacker Drive, 9th Floor, Chicago IL 60606
Secy.-Treas.: E.T. Zasadil
Members: 800 *Staff:* 1
Annual Budget: under $10,000 *Tel:* (312) 853-3223
Hist. Note: Companies and individuals involved in the construction, maintenance and repair of freight and passenger railway cars. Founded as Interchange Car Inspectors, it became the Railway Car Department Officers Ass'n the same year, the Master Car Builders Ass'n in 1926 and assumed its present name in 1928.
Publication:
Proceedings. a.
Annual Meetings: September

Carbonated Beverage Institute (1945)
1101 16th St., N.W., Washington DC 20036
Administrative Consultant: Donald Prescott
Members: 25-30 independent bottlers *Staff:* 0
Tel: (202) 463-6745
Annual Meetings: January

Card Clothing Manufacturers Ass'n (1934)
Hist. Note: Reported inactive from 1982-85.

Carded Packaging Institute (1972)
71 East Ave., Norwalk CT 06851
Exec. Director: Penny Dalziel
Members: 30-35 companies *Staff:* 2-5
Annual Budget: $10-25,000 *Tel:* (203) 852-7168
Hist. Note: Membership open to reputable firms engaged in the production of carded packages and industry suppliers of materials and equipment. Membership: $875/yr.
Publication:
CPI Newsletter. bi-m.
Semi-annual meetings: Spring and Fall

Cardio Pulmonary Contractors Ass'n (1975)
Hist. Note: Service contractors offering to set up and maintain respiratory therapy departments in hospitals. Address unknown in 1983.

Career Apparel Institute (1970)
1156 Ave. of the Americas, Suite 700, New York NY 10036
Exec. Director: Bernard J. Lepper
Members: 400 companies *Staff:* 2-5
Annual Budget: $100-250,000 *Tel:* (212) 869-0670
Hist. Note: Members are manufacturers of uniforms, mills, fibre producers, and dealers. CAI is a division of the Nat'l Ass'n of Uniform Manufacturers and Distributors.
Annual Meetings: With Nat'l Ass'n of Uniform Manufacturers and Distributors

Caricaturist Soc. of America (1947)
255 West 43rd St., New York NY 10036
President: Joseph Kaliff
Members: 90-100
Annual Budget: under $10,000 *Tel:* (212) 221-2627
Hist. Note: Professional caricaturists. Membership concentrated in the New York area.

Carpet and Rug Institute (1969)
310 S. Holiday Ave., P.O. Box 2048, Dalton GA 30722-2048
President: Ronald E. VanGelderen
Members: 200 companies *Staff:* 11
Annual Budget: $500-1,000,000 *Tel:* (404) 278-3176
Hist. Note: Formed by a merger of the American Carpet Institute (1928) and the Tufted Textile Manufacturers Ass'n (1945). Maintains a Washington office.
Publications:
CRI Directory and Report. a.
CRI News. m.
Annual Meetings. Fall

Carpet and Upholstery Cleaning Ass'n (1971)
Hist. Note: A division of the Ass'n of Specialists in Cleaning and Restoration.

Carpet Cushion Council (1976)
P.O. 465, Southfield MI 48037
Exec. Director: David T. Lipton
Members: 32 companies *Staff:* 1
Annual Budget: $100-250,000 *Tel:* (313) 356-6656
Hist. Note: Involved in public relations to encourage distribution and use of separate carpet cushions. Works with regulatory agencies at the national, state, and local levels. Formerly a division of the Carpet and Rug Institute, the Council is now independent and incorporated in the District of Columbia. Membership: based on sales volume

Carpet Manufacturers Marketing Ass'n (1979)
300 Emory Square, Suite 203, Dalton GA 30720
Exec. Director: Jane Osborne
Members: 170-180 companies *Staff:* 2-5
Annual Budget: $50-100,000 *Tel:* (404) 278-4101
Hist. Note: Established as a non-profit organization in August 1979 by 34 charter members. Membership: $600/year.
Publications:
Newsletter. q.
Directory. semi-a.
Semi-annual Meetings: May and December (temporarily)
1987-Chattanooga, TN(Convention and Trade Center)/Dec. 4-6

Carpet Yarn Ass'n (1971)
Hist. Note: Became a division of the American Yarn Spinners Association in 1981.

Cartoonists Guild (1967)
30 East 20th St., New York NY 10003
Exec. Director: Susan Dooha
Members: 150 *Staff:* 3
Annual Budget: $10-25,000 *Tel:* (212) 777-7353
Hist. Note: Founded as the Magazine Cartoonists Guild, it assumed its present name in 1973. The Guild is a national organization of professional cartoonists. Formally affiliated with the Graphic Artists Guild in 1984. Membership: $110/yr.

Carwash Operators Ass'n (1968)
Hist. Note: Address unknown since 1984. Probably inactive or defunct.

Casket Manufacturers Ass'n of America (1913)
708 Church St., Evanston IL 60201
Exec. Director: George W. Lemke
Members: 200 *Staff:* 3
Annual Budget: $100-250,000 *Tel:* (312) 866-8383
Hist. Note: Membership Fee: Based on sales volume.
Publication:
CMA Newsletter. m.
Annual Meetings: Fall/225
1987-Orlando, FL(Hyatt Grand Cypress)/Sept. 13-16
1988-San Diego, CA(del Coronado)/Sept. 13-16
1989-San Antonio, TX(Four Seasons)/Sept. 26-29
1990-Montreal, Canada(Hilton Bonaventure)

Cast Bronze Institute
Hist. Note: Reported inactive in 1986.

Cast Iron Pipe Research Ass'n (1915)
Hist. Note: Became the Ductile Iron Pipe Research Association in 1981.

Cast Iron Soil Pipe Institute (1949)
1499 Chain Bridge Rd., Suite 203, McLean VA 22101
Exec. V. President: Edward M. Bailey
Members: 11 foundries *Staff:* 6-10
Annual Budget: $500-1,000,000 *Tel:* (703) 827-9177
Hist. Note: Manufacturers of cast iron soil pipe and fittings.
Annual Meetings: November

Cast Metals Ass'n (1986)
455 State St., Suite 201, Des Plaines IL 60016
President: Charles T. Sheehan
Staff: 2-5
Annual Budget: $100-250,000 *Tel:* (312) 297-2430
Hist. Note: CMA was formed in April, 1986 as a merger of the Nat'l Foundry Ass'n (founded in 1898) and Cast Metals Ass'n (founded in 1972). It was organized to promote the welfare of the metal casting industry through: industry interaction with federal and governmental agencies and representatives; promotion of public interest in the industry; collection and dissemination of statistical data; encouragement of safe working conditions; management development; and the development of equitable relationships between employers and employees. In addition to the annual meeting, CMA holds several other meetings and conferences throughout the year. Maintains a Washington, DC office.
Publications:
Labor Letter. semi-m.
Labor Case Comments. semi-m.
Labor Agreement Settlement Data. 9-12/yr.
Management Safety and Health Newsletter. 9/yr.
Nat'l Survey of Wages and Benefits in the Foundry Industry. a.
CMA Salary Survey. bien.
Annual Meetings: March in Washington, DC

Cast Metals Federation
Hist. Note: Merged with Nat'l Foundry Ass'n in April, 1986 to form the Cast Metals Ass'n.

Cast Metals Institute
Hist. Note: Not a trade assocation. The educational branch of the American Foundrymen's Society.

Caster and Floor Truck Manufacturers Ass'n (1933)
800 Custer St., Evanston IL 60202
Exec. Secretary: Thomas D. Dolan
Members: 30-40 companies *Staff:* 2-5
Annual Budget: $10-25,000 *Tel:* (312) 864-8444

Casting Industry Suppliers Ass'n (1919)
111 East Wacker Drive, Suite 600, Chicago IL 60601
Exec. Secy.-Treas.: Jim Dickinson
Members: 65-70 companies *Staff:* 2-5
Annual Budget: $50-100,000 *Tel:* (312) 644-6610
Hist. Note: Formerly (1984) Foundry Equipment Manufacturers Ass'n and (1986) Foundry Equipment and Materials Ass'n. Founded as the result of common industry problems during and after World War I. Members are makers of foundry equipment and supplies. Merged in 1963 with the Foundry Supply Manufacturers Group.
Publications:
Bulletin. m.
Directory. a.
Annual Meetings: March

Casualty Actuarial Soc. (1914)
One Penn Plaza, 51st Floor, New York NY 10119
V. President of Admin.: Richard H. Snader
Members: 1,280 *Staff:* 2-5
Annual Budget: $50-100,000 *Tel:* (212) 560-1018
Hist. Note: Formerly (1921) Casualty Actuarial and Statistical Soc. of America. Membership contigent upon examination. Actuaries dealing in casualty and fire insurance, to the exclusion of life insurance. Affiliated with the American Academy of Actuaries.
Publications:
Proceedings. a.
Yearbook. a.
Semi-annual Meetings: May and Nov.
1987-Orlando, FL/May and San Antonio, TX/Nov.

Catalysis Soc. of North America (1966)
c/o DuPont Experimental Station, Building 402, Wilmington DE 19898
Editor: William J. Linn
Members: 2,500 *Staff:* 1
Annual Budget: $10-25,000 *Tel:* (302) 772-4655
Hist. Note: Members are chemists and chemical engineers engaged in the study and use of reactions involving catalysts, substances used to accelerate reactions and which may be recovered virtually unchanged. Has no paid staff.
Publication:
The Catalysis Society Newsletter. q.
Biennial meetings: uneven years
1987-San Diego, CA

Catfish Farmers of America (1968)
Box 34, Jackson MS 39205
Exec. V. President: George Williams
Members: 600 *Staff:* 4
Annual Budget: $250-500,000 *Tel:* (601) 353-7916
Publications:
The Catfish Journal. m. adv.
Newsletter. m.

Cathodic Protection Industry Ass'n (1980)
Box 227, Hawthorne NJ 07507
President: Edgar W. Dreyman
Members: 20 companies *Staff:* 1
Annual Budget: $10-25,000 *Tel:* (201) 427-8540
Hist. Note: Members manufacture, sell, install and maintain electronic anti-corrosion systems, which are affixed to such areas as docks and pipelines.
Publication:
CPIA News. bi-a.
Annual Meetings: With the National Association of Corrosion Engineers.

Catholic Actors Guild of America (1914)
1501 Broadway, Suite 2400, New York NY 10036
Exec. Secretary: Suzanne Richardson
Members: 550 *Staff:* 1
Annual Budget: $50-100,000 *Tel:* (212) 398-1868
Hist. Note: Strives to promote the best interests of theatre by bringing members of the profession together on spiritual and professional lines. Membership: $20/yr.
Publication:
Call Board. 5/yr. adv.

Catholic Audio-Visual Educators (1985)
Box 9257, Pittsburgh PA 15224
Nat'l Exec. Director: John Manear
Members: 2,000 *Staff:* 2
Annual Budget: under $10,000 *Tel:* (412) 561 3583
Hist. Note: Formerly the Catholic Audio-Visual Educators Ass'n.(1985) Membership: $10.
Publication:
Newsletter. q.
Annual Meetings: Easter Week with National Catholic Educational Association.
1987-New Orleans

Catholic Audio-Visual Educators Ass'n (1948)
Hist. Note: Changed name to Catholic Audio-Visual Educators in 1985.

Catholic Biblical Ass'n of America (1936)
Catholic University, 620 Michigan Ave., N.E., Washington DC 20064
Exec. Secretary: Joseph Jensen, O.S.B.

00105 12 05 86 1233

Members: 1,106 *Staff:* 2-5
Annual Budget: $100-250,000 *Tel:* (202) 635-5519
Hist. Note: Members are Catholic Biblical scholars. Member of the Council on the Study of Religion.
Publications:
Catholic Biblical Quarterly. q. adv.
Old Testament Abstracts. 3/yr. adv.
Annual Meetings: August

Catholic Campus Ministry Ass'n (1969)
300 College Park Ave., Dayton OH 45469
Exec. Director: Donald R. McCrabb
Members: 1,000 *Staff:* 2-5
Annual Budget: $100-250,000 *Tel:* (513) 229-4648
Hist. Note: Formerly (1968) Nat'l Newman Chaplains Ass'n. CCMA is a national voluntary organization of individuals and groups of campus ministers who associate to foster their theological and professional growth and the promote the ministry of the Catholic Church in higher education. Membership: $50/yr.
Publications:
CCMA Newsletter. m.
Journal of The Catholic Campus Ministry Association. 3/yr.
CCMA Directory. a.
Semi-annual Study Weeks: Eastern in Jan. and Western in April
1987-Miami, FL(Barry University)/Jan. 2-6/2-300
1987-Malibu, CA(Sewa Retreat)/April 20-24/100

Catholic Charities USA (1910)
1319 F St., N.W., Washington DC 20004
Exec. Director: Rev. Thomas J. Harvey
Members: 3,500-4,000 *Staff:* 16-20
Annual Budget: $1-2,000,000 *Tel:* (202) 639-8400
Hist. Note: Formerly (1986) Nat'l Conference of Catholic Charities.
Publications:
Charities USA. 10/yr.
Social Thought. q.
Annual Meetings: Fall
1987-San Antonio, TX/Sept.

Catholic Fine Arts Soc. (1955)
St. John's University, Staten Island NY 10301
President: Dr. Michael F. Capobianco
Members: 75-100 *Staff:* 5
Annual Budget: under $10,000 *Tel:* (718) 447-4343
Hist. Note: College, high and elementary school art teachers and artists. Founded at Catholic University, Washington DC in 1955. Has no paid staff or permanent address; its affairs are directed by a biennially-elected President. Membership: $15/yr.
Publication:
CFAS Newsletter. q.
Annual Meetings: Columbus Day Weekend
1987-Philadelphia, PA

Catholic Health Ass'n of the United States (1915)
4455 Woodson Road, St. Louis MO 63134
President: John E. Curley, Jr.
Members: 600-700 hospitals; 200-300 nursing homes *Staff:* 80-90
Annual Budget: over $5,000,000 *Tel:* (314) 427-2500
Hist. Note: Formerly (until 1979) known as The Catholic Hospital Ass'n.
Publications:
Catholic Health World. bi-w. adv.
Health Progress. 10/yr. adv.
Law Reports. 10/yr.
Annual Meetings: June/1,100-1,200
1987-Pittsburgh, PA(Hilton)/June 7-10
1988-Nashville, TN(Opryland)/June 19-22
1989-Seattle, WA(Westin)/June 11-14
1990-Washington, DC(Hilton)/June 10-13
1991-Montreal, Quebec

Catholic Library Ass'n (1921)
461 West Lancaster Ave., Haverford PA 19041
Exec. Director: Matthew R. Wilt
Members: 3,100-3,200 *Staff:* 6-10
Annual Budget: $100-250,000 *Tel:* (215) 649-5250
Hist. Note: Membership: $35/yr. (individual); $40-85/yr. (institution).
Publications:
Catholic Library World. bi-m. adv.
Catholic Periodical and Literature Index. 6/yr.
Annual Meetings: With Nat'l Catholic Educational Ass'n
1987-New Orleans, LA/April 20-23/600

Catholic Press Ass'n (1912)
119 North Park Ave., Rockville Center NY 11570
Exec. Director: James A. Doyle
Members: 291 publications, 264 individuals *Staff:* 6
Annual Budget: $100-250,000 *Tel:* (516) 766-3400
Hist. Note: Founded in Columbus, Ohio, August 24-25, 1911 by forty-seven charter member publications. Incorporated the following year in New York. Membership: based on size and frequency of publications.
Publications:
Catholic Journalist. m. adv.
Catholic Press Directory. a. adv.
Annual Meetings: Spring
1987-San Antonio, TX/May 20-22
1988-Boston, MA/April 13-15
1989-Baltimore, MD
1990-Nashville, TN/April 16-22

Catholic Theological Soc. of America (1946)
Loyola University, Chicago IL 60626
Secretary: Rev. Edward H. Konerman
Members: 1,300 *Staff:* 1
Annual Budget: under $10,000 *Tel:* (312) 274-3000
Hist. Note: Members are individuals engaged in scholarly research, writing, and teaching of theology in seminaries and universities. Membership: $25/yr.
Publication:
CTSA Proceedings. a.
Annual Meetings: June
1987-Philadelphia, PA/June 10-13

Caucus for Women in Statistics (1970)
Box 3000, NCAR, Boulder CO 80307
Secretary: Ginger A. Caldwell
Members: 325-350
Annual Budget: under $10,000 *Tel:* (303) 497-1229
Hist. Note: Formed to focus on specific problems associated with the participation of women in statistically oriented professions, the Caucus strives to foster opportunities for the education, employment and advancement of women in statistics. The Caucus is an independent organization; it is informally associated with the American Statisical Ass'n for purposes of its annual meeting and cooperation on various ASA committees. Membership: $10/yr.
Publications:
Newsletter. q.
Membership Directory. a.
Annual Meetings: August
1987-San Francisco, CA/Aug. 17-20/75
1988-Fort Collins, CO/Aug. 8-11/80
1989-Washington, DC

CAUSE (1962)
737 29th St., Boulder CO 80303
Exec. Director: Jane N. Ryland
Members: 700 institutions *Staff:* 8
Annual Budget: $500-1,000,000 *Tel:* (303) 449-4430
Hist. Note: Formerly College and University Systems Exchange, it began as an informal group of 20 college and university data processing directors who met for the purpose of exchanging information on changes in a rapidly developing field. Incorporated in the State of Illinois in 1971 and opened a national office in Boulder the same year. CAUSE serves as the professional association for computing and information technology in higher education. Membership: $126-1,900/yr.
Publications:
CAUSE/Effect. 6/yr.
CAUSE/Information. 6/year.
CAUSE Monograph Series.
Proceedings. a.
Annual Meetings: December
1987-Tarpon Springs, FL(Innisbrook)/Dec. 1-4/700

Ceilings and Interior Systems Construction Ass'n (1950)
104 Wilmot Road, Suite 201, Deerfield IL 60015-5195
Exec. V. President: Carl A. Wangman
Members: 500-550 *Staff:* 6-10
Annual Budget: $500-1,000,000 *Tel:* (312) 940-8800
Hist. Note: Formerly (1970) Nat'l Acoustical Contractors Ass'n
Publication:
Interior Construction. m. adv.
Annual Meetings: Spring/6-700
1987-New Orleans, LA(Sheraton)/April 4-9/700
1988-Coronado, CA(del Coronado)/April 10-14/500
1989-Orlando, FL(Marriott's World Ctr.)/April 2-6/600
1990-Vancouver, BC(Hyatt Regency Vancouver)/April 21-26/700
1991-Colorado Springs, CO(Broadmoor)/April 13-18/750

Cell Kinetics Soc. (1977)
NYU School of Medicine, Goldwater Hospital, Roosevelt Island NY 10044
Secretary: Robert J. Sklarew
Members: 350 *Staff:* 1
Annual Budget: $10-25,000 *Tel:* (212) 750-6766
Hist. Note: A multidisciplinary professional society of individuals with an interest in cell kinetics. Membership: $45/yr. (individual), $500/yr. (sustaining company).
Publications:
Cell and Tissue Kinetics.
Membership Directory. a.
Annual Meetings:
1987-Vancouver, BC(Pan Pacific)/March 26-28/150

Cellular Communications Industry Ass'n (1984)
Hist. Note: Became the Cellular Telecommunications Industry Ass'n in 1985.

Cellular Radio Communications Ass'n (1983)
Hist. Note: Absorbed by the Cellular Communications Industry Ass'n in 1985.

Cellular Telecommunications Industry Ass'n (1984)
1150 17th St., N.W., Suite 607, Washington DC 20036
President: Robert W. Maher
Members: 85 companies *Staff:* 5
Annual Budget: $500-1,000,000 *Tel:* (202) 785-0081
Hist. Note: Formerly (1984) the Cellular Communications Industry Ass'n. Members are companies holding licenses, permits or having a reasonable expectation of receiving a cellular authorization from the FCC. Absorbed the Cellular Radio Communications Ass'n in 1985. Membership: $2,500-70,000/yr. (based on size of market).

Publication:
Director's Report. m.
Semi-annual: winter, late Spring
1987-Phoenix, AZ(The Pointe/Tapitio Cliffs)/Jan. 19-21
1988-Arlington, VA(Hyatt Regency)/June 17-19

Cellulose Manufacturers Ass'n (1979)
Hist. Note: Address unknown in 1982, reported defunct.

Cement Employers Ass'n (1946)
2 Village Drive, Saugerties NY 12477
Exec. V. President: Kenneth M. Flicker
Members: 40 companies *Staff:* 2-5
Annual Budget: $100-250,000 *Tel:* (914) 246-4935
Hist. Note: A grouping of cement companies united to promote personnel and industrial relations.
Annual Meetings: Fall/50-60

Cemented Carbide Producers Ass'n (1955)
712 Lakewood Center North, 14600 Detroit Avenue, Cleveland OH 44107
Commissioner: Allen P. Wherry
Members: 24-27 companies *Staff:* 2-5
Annual Budget: $50-100,000 *Tel:* (216) 226-7700
Hist. Note: Members are makers of sintered carbide containing tungsten.

Central Conference of American Rabbis (1889)
21 East 40th Street, New York NY 10016
Exec. V. President: Rabbi Joseph B. Glaser
Members: 1,475 *Staff:* 6-10
Annual Budget: $1-2,000,000 *Tel:* (212) 684-4990
Hist. Note: Professional rabbinic organization of Reform Judaism.
Publications:
CCAR Yearbook. a.
Journal of Reform Judaism. q. adv.
Annual Meetings: Spring
1987-Tarpon Springs, FL(Innisbrook)/May
1988-Israel(Laromme)/March
1989-Cincinnati, OH(Hyatt)/June
1990-Seattle, WA(Sheraton)/June
1991-Nashville, TN(Opryland)/June
1992-San Antonio, TX(Hyatt)/April
1993-Montreal, Quebec(Queen Elizabeth)/June

Central Council of Nat'l Retail Ass'ns (1921)
Hist. Note: A division of the American Retail Federation. Until 1943, The Retailers Nat'l Council.

Central Office Executives Ass'n of the Nat'l Panhellenic Conference (1943)
7730 Carondelet #333, St. Louis MO 63105
President: Virginia Fry
Members: 26
Annual Budget: under $10,000
Hist. Note: Formerly (1985) the Ass'n of Nat'l Panhellenic Conference Central Office. Members are the executive directors of the member organizations of the Nat'l Panhellenic Conference. Has no paid staff or permanent address and modest dues.
Biennial Meetings: With Nat'l Panhellenic Conference

Central Shippers (1984)
c/o LoBue Bros., Inc., 201 South Sweet Brier Ave., Lindsay CA 93247
G.A. Wollenman
Members: 5 companies
Hist. Note: A Webb-Pomerene Act association.

Central Station Electrical Protection Ass'n (1950)
1120 19th St., N.W., Suite LL-20, Washington DC 20036
Exec. Director: Richard J. Lucas
Members: 100 companies *Staff:* 4
Annual Budget: $50-100,000 *Tel:* (202) 296-9595
Hist. Note: Underwriters Laboratories listed central stations and suppliers to the industry.
Publications:
CS Newsletter. m.
Directory. a.
Semi-annual Meetings: Spring and Fall

Ceramic Arts Federation Internat'l (1983)
2031 East Via Burton, Suite A, Anaheim CA 92806
Exec. Director: Frank Pynn
Members: 236 companies; 166 individuals *Staff:* 1
Annual Budget: $25-50,000 *Tel:* (714) 533-3820
Hist. Note: Formed by a merger of the Nat'l Ceramics Manufacturers Ass'n, the Ceramic Distributors of America, the Nat'l Ceramic Dealers Ass'n, and the Nat'l Ceramic Teachers Ass'n in 1983.
Annual Meetings: Summer
1987-Cincinnati, OH
1988-New Orleans, LA
1989-Niagara Falls, NY

Ceramic Distributors of America (1969)
Hist. Note: Absorbed by the Ceramic Arts Federation Internat'l in 1983.

00106 12 05 86 1233

Ceramic Educational Council (1926)
Hist. Note: Formerly (1938) the Ass'n of Ceramic Educators. Education arm of the American Ceramic Soc. Membership open only to ACerS members.

Ceramic Tile Distributors Ass'n (1978)
15 Salt Creek Lane, Suite 422, Hinsdale IL 60521
Exec. Director: Eleanor Schulte
Members: 400 companies *Staff:* 2
Annual Budget: $1-2,000,000 *Tel:* (312) 665-3270
Hist. Note: A national trade association of wholesale distributors or ceramic tile incorporated in Arizona and Illinois. Its goals are to increase members' professionalism through information, education and product knowledge and to promote use of ceramic tile in the U.S. Membership: $300/yr.
Publication:
News & Views. bi-m.
Annual Meetings:
1987-Orlando, FL(Peabody & Orlando Conv. Ctr.)/Nov. 1-3/3,500
1988-San Francisco, CA(Hilton & Masconi Ctr.)/July 17-20/4,000
1989-Dallas, TX(Loews Anatole & Conv. Ctr.)/April/4,500

Ceramic Tile Institute of America (1954)
700 North Virgil Ave., Los Angeles CA 90029
Administrative Coordinator: Timothy C. Hengst
Members: 300 companies *Staff:* 6-10
Annual Budget: $250-500,000 *Tel:* (213) 660-1911
Hist. Note: Members are installers and makers of ceramic tiles.
Annual Meetings: February, in the Los Angeles area.

Ceramic Tile Marketing Federation (1983)
1615 L St., N.W., Suite 925, Washington DC 20036
Exec. Director: Sanford J. Hill
Members: 150 companies *Staff:* 1
Annual Budget: $100-250,000 *Tel:* (202) 296-9200
Hist. Note: Organization of manufacturers of ceramic tiles and allied products, distributors, contractors and importers which carries on promotion programs to stimulate increased uses of professionally installed ceramic tiles in the building industry.
Publication:
Newsletter. q.

Certified Ballast Manufacturers Ass'n (1939)
772 Hanna Building, Cleveland OH 44115
Secy.-Treas.: M. R. Davies
Members: 6-10 fluorescent lamp ballast makers *Staff:* 2-5
Annual Budget: $50-100,000 *Tel:* (216) 241-0711
Publication:
CBM News. q.

Certified Color Manufacturers Ass'n (1972)
900 17th St., N.W., Suite 650, Washington DC 20006
General Counsel: Daniel R. Thompson
Members: 5 companies *Staff:* 1
Annual Budget: $25-50,000 *Tel:* (202) 293-5800
Hist. Note: Makers of certified colors for food, drugs, and cosmetics. The above address is the law office of Mr. Thompson.

Certified Milk Producers Ass'n of America (1908)
Alta Dena Dairy, P.O. Box 388, 17637 E. Valley Blvd., City of Industry CA 91747
Treasurer: R.M. L'Heureux
Members: 4 farms *Staff:* 1
Annual Budget: under $10,000 *Tel:* (818) 964-6401
Hist. Note: Members are farms producing raw "certified" (pure, but unpasteurized) milk. Membership fee based on production.
Annual Meetings: May, with American Ass'n of Medical Milk Commissions.

Chain Link Fence Manufacturers Institute (1960)
1101 Connecticut Ave., N.W., Suite 700, Washington DC 20036
Exec. V. President: Mark Levin, CAE
Members: 42 companies *Staff:* 2-5
Annual Budget: $100-250,000 *Tel:* (202) 857-1140
Annual Meetings: Summer

Chamber Music America (1977)
545 8th Ave., New York NY 10018
Exec. Director: Dean K. Stein
Members: 450 ensembles; 200 presenters & schools *Staff:* 2-5
Annual Budget: $250-500,000 *Tel:* (212) 244-2772
Hist. Note: Incorporated in New York in September, 1977. Members are conductorless ensembles, one musician to a part (instrumental or vocal), performing concerts for professional fees, presenters of chamber music concerts, training institutions and individuals and businesses interested in the development and growth of the chamber music field. Membership: $25/yr.(individual);$55/yr.(organization).
Publications:
Chamber Music Magazine. q. adv.
Membership Directory. a.
Directory of Summer Festivals, Workshops and Schools. bien.
New Music Repertoire Directory. a.
Management Monographs.
Annual Meetings: December

Chamber of Commerce of Latin America (1940)
One World Trade Center, Suite 2342, New York NY 10048
Exec. Secretary: Ronald W. Ramirez
Members: 500 *Staff:* 2-5
Annual Budget: $25-50,000 *Tel:* (212) 432-9313
Hist. Note: Membership: $150/yr. (individual); $250/yr. (organization/company)
Publications:
Inter-American Trade News. q. adv.
Inter American Foreign Trade. semi-a.
Annual Meetings: December

Chamber of Commerce of the United States of America (1912)
1615 H St., N.W., Washington DC 20062
President: Dr. Richard L. Lesher
Members: 180,000 *Staff:* 1,300
Annual Budget: over $5,000,000 *Tel:* (202) 659-6000
Hist. Note: Organized at a conference called by President Taft on April 22, 1912 in Washington, DC. The Chamber was formed on the recommendation of President Taft, who saw the need for a "central organization" to give Congress the benefit of the thinking of the business community on national problems and issues affecting the economy. Now, it is generally regarded as the spokesgroup for U.S. business. It is the world's largest business federation composed of more than 180,000 companies plus several thousand other organizations such as local and state chambers of commerce and trade and professional associations. Supports the Nat'l Chamber Alliance for Politics. Has an annual budget of $65 million.
Publications:
Nation's Business. m. adv.
The Business Advocate. w. adv.
Annual Meetings: Held in Washington, Sunday, Monday, and Tuesday of the week in which May 1st falls 2-3,000

Char-Swiss Breeders Ass'n (1961)
407 Chambers St., Marlin TX 76661
Secy.-Treas.: G. T. Fairbairn
Members: 230-240 *Staff:* 1
Annual Budget: under $10,000 *Tel:* (817) 883-2592
Hist. Note: Breeders and fanciers of Char-Swiss beef cattle, a crossbreed of Charolais and Brown Swiss cattle.

Cheese Importers Ass'n of America (1943)
460 Park Ave., New York NY 10022
Secretary: Virginia Sheahan
Members: 160 *Staff:* 2-5
Tel: (212) 753-7500
Publications:
Bulletin. semi-m.
Year Book. a. adv.

Chefs de Cuisine Ass'n of America (1916)
c/o Hotel Paramount, 235 W. 46th St., Suite 325, New York NY 10036
Manager: Salvatore Petrolino
Members: 400-425 *Staff:* 1
Annual Budget: $50-100,000 *Tel:* (212) 719-2949
Hist. Note: Formerly (1964) Executive Chefs de Cuisine Ass'n of America. Membership concentrated largely in the New York area. Membership: $40/yr. Ass'n may move its office in January or February 1987.
Publication:
Newsletter. m.
Annual Meetings: September, in New York, NY

Cheiron: The Internat'l Soc. of the History of Behavioral and Social Sciences (1968)
Dept. of Psychology, Texas A&M University, College Station TX 77843
Exec. Secretary: Rand B. Evans
Members: 220 *Staff:* 1
Annual Budget: under $10,000
Hist. Note: Formerly Internat'l Soc. for the History of Behavioral and Social Sciences. Scholars in the United States and other countries interested in the history of the behavioral and social sciences. Membership: $10/yr.
Publication:
Cheiron Newsletter. semi-a.
Annual Meetings: June/80
1987-Newport, RI(College of Newport)
1988-Princeton, NJ(Princeton Univ.)
1989-Kingston, Ontario(Queens Univ.)

Chemical Coaters Ass'n (1970)
Box 241, Wheaton IL 60189
Exec. Director: Matt Heuertz
Members: 750-800 individuals and companies *Staff:* 2
Annual Budget: $100-250,000 *Tel:* (312) 668-0949
Hist. Note: Users and suppliers of industrial cleaners, paints, coatings and equipment. Membership: $40/yr.(individual); $400/yr.(company).
Publication:
Newsletter. q.
Annual Meetings: Spring
1987-Milwaukee, WI(Convention Ctr./Hyatt Regency)/May 19-21

Chemical Communications Ass'n (1964)
c/o Monsanto, 1460 Broadway, New York NY 10036
Corres. Secy.: Phillip P. Fried
Members: 125 individuals *Staff:* 1
Annual Budget: under $10,000 *Tel:* (212) 382-9601
Hist. Note: An organization of editors, writers, corporate public relations and agency people who work in and around the chemical industry, mostly in the New York area. Has no paid staff. Membership: $25/yr.

Chemical Fabrics and Film Ass'n (1927)
1230 Keith Bldg., Cleveland OH 44115-2180
Exec. Secretary: Charles M. Stockinger
Members: 15 companies *Staff:* 2-5
Annual Budget: $50-100,000 *Tel:* (216) 241-7333
Hist. Note: Established as the Plastic Coatings and Film Ass'n, CFFA became the Vinyl Fabrics Institute and assumed its present name in 1971. Members are manufacturers of vinyl and urethane products, and of pyroxylin - a substance used in making plastics, lacquers and films.
Annual Meetings: December

Chemical Industry Institute of Toxicology (1974)
Hist. Note: Studies toxicological issues associated with the manufacture, distribution and disposal of industrial chemicals. Address unknown since 1984.

Chemical Manufacturers Ass'n (1872)
2501 M St., N.W., Washington DC 20037
President: Robert A. Roland
Members: 200 companies *Staff:* 160
Annual Budget: over $5,000,000 *Tel:* (202) 887-1100
Hist. Note: Established in May, 1872 by 17 makers of sulfuric acid for "... protection against unwise legislation and unjust freight discrimination . . . and . . . joint action . . . for the purchase of goods at reasonable prices. . ." The name was changed to the Manufacturing Chemists' Ass'n in 1950 when it absorbed the Plastics Materials Manufacturers Ass'n; assumed its present name in 1979. Canadian companies were admitted to membership in 1953. Today the membership consists of companies whose primary business is the manufacture of chemicals in the United States or Canada, and who sell a substantial portion of chemicals produced by them to others in the open market.
Publication:
Chemecology. m.
Semi-annual Meetings: June in White Sulphur Springs, WV and Fall

Chemical Marketing Research Ass'n (1940)
139 Chestnut Ave., Staten Island NY 10305
Exec. Secretary: Mary J. Carrick
Members: 900 *Staff:* 1
Tel: (212) 727-0550
Hist. Note: Formerly (1945) Chemical Market Research Group. Assumed its present name in 1965. Members are professionals within the chemical and allied products industries. Membership: $95/yr.
Publication:
Chemical Marketing & Management Journal. q. adv.
Triannual Meetings:
1987-Houston, TX(Westin Galleria)/Feb. 2-4
1987-Philadelphia, PA(Hershey Philadelphia Hotel)/May 4-6
1987-Miami, FL(Doral Country Club)/Sept. 20-23

Chemical Specialties Manufacturers Ass'n (1914)
1001 Connecticut Ave., N.W., Washington DC 20036
President: Ralph Engel
Members: 380-420 *Staff:* 25-28
Annual Budget: $1-2,000,000 *Tel:* (202) 872-8110
Hist. Note: Established as the Nat'l Ass'n of Insecticide and Disinfectant Manufacturers, it assumed its present name in 1948. Sponsors the Chemical Specialties Manufacturers Association Political Action Committee.
Publications:
Chemical Times and Trends. q. adv.
Executive Newswatch, Legislative Report. w.
Semi-annual Meetings: April/May and December
1987-Chicago, IL(Marriott)/April 26-29/1,000
1987-Washington, DC(JW Marriott)/Dec. 6-9/1,000

Chemical Waste Transportation Council (1982)
1730 Rhode Island Ave., N.W., Suite 1000, Washington DC 20036
Exec. Director: Suellen Pirages
Members: 75 companies *Staff:* 2-5
Annual Budget: $50-100,000 *Tel:* (202) 659-4613
Hist. Note: Affiliated with Nat'l Solid Wastes Management Ass'n; companies must join NSWMA before they can become eligible to join CWTC. Formerly (1985) Liquid Waste and Sludge Transporter Council.
Publication:
Information Packets. m.
Annual Meetings: With Nat'l Solid Wastes Management Ass'n

Cherry Exporters Ass'n (1982)
Hist. Note: A Webb-Pomerene Act association. Address unknown in 1984. Probably defunct.

Chester White Swine Record Ass'n (1930)
1803 West Detweiller, Peoria IL 61615
Secretary: Daniel Parrish
Members: 872 *Staff:* 4
Annual Budget: $250-500,000 *Tel:* (309) 691-0151
Hist. Note: Breeders of Chester White swine. The Chester White Breed originated in Chester County, PA, in the early 19th century. Member of the National Society of Livestock Record Associations.
Publication:
Chester White Journal. m. adv.
Annual Meetings: July
1987-Elkhorn, WI/July 16

00107 12 05 86 1233

Chief Executives Organization (1958)
2000 Palm Beach Lakes Blvd., Suite 900, West Palm Beach FL 33409
Exec. Director: Terry J. Mooney
Members: 860 *Staff:* 6-10
Annual Budget: $500-1,000,000 *Tel:* (305) 689-1352
Hist. Note: Members are individuals formerly in the Young Presidents' Organization who have become 49, the mandatory retirement age. Formerly (1983) Chief Executives Forum.
Publications:
CEO News. q.
Membership Directory. a.
Semi-annual Meetings: Spring and Fall

Chief Officers of State Library Agencies (1973)
California State Library, Box 2037, Sacramento CA 95809
Chairman: Gary Strong
Members: 51 individuals *Staff:* 1
Annual Budget: $25-50,000 *Tel:* (916) 445-4027
Hist. Note: An independent organization of the men and women who head State and Territorial agencies responsible for library development. Provides a mechanism for dealing with state and territorial library problems.

Chief Petty Officers Ass'n (1969)
5520-G Hempstead Way, Springfield VA 22151
Exec. Secretary: C. R. Castor
Members: 8,000 *Staff:* 2
Annual Budget: $100-250,000 *Tel:* (703) 941-0395
Hist. Note: Chief Petty Officers of the U.S. Coast Guard, active, retired and reserve. Constituent member of the Combined Organization of Military Ass'ns. Membership: $18/yr.
Publication:
The Chief. q. adv.
Annual Meetings: August
1987-Cleveland, OH

Children's Book Council (1945)
67 Irving Place, New York NY 10003
President: John Donovan
Members: 75 publishers *Staff:* 6-10
Annual Budget: $500-1,000,000 *Tel:* (212) 254-2666
Hist. Note: Publishers of children's books interested in promoting literature for children. Sponsors Children's Book Week each November.
Publication:
CBC Features. semi-a.

Children's Eye Care Foundation (1970)
Hist. Note: Became (1982) National Children's Eye Care Foundation.

Children's Literature Ass'n (1972)
210 Education, Purdue University, W. Lafayette IN 47907
Publications Mgr.: Jill B. May
Members: 1,000 individuals *Staff:* 1
Annual Budget: $25-50,000 *Tel:* (317) 494-2355
Hist. Note: Membership consists of teachers, librarians, authors and publishers. Encourages research and scholarship in the field of children's literature. Membership: $40/yr. (individual); $50/yr. (institution)
Publications:
Children's Literature: An International Journal. a.
ChLA Quarterly. q.
Proceedings. a.
Annual Meetings: May
1987-Ottawa, Canada(Carleton Univ.)/May 14-17

Children's Theatre Ass'n of America (1944)
Hist. Note: A division of the American Theatre Association. Formerly the Children's Theatre Conference.

Childrenswear Manufacturers Ass'n (1976)
66 E. Main St., Moorestown NJ 08057
Exec. Director: William L. MacMillan, III
Members: 125 companies *Staff:* 2-5
Annual Budget: $50-100,000 *Tel:* (609) 234-9155
Publication:
Newsletter. irreg.

China Clay Producers Group (1978)
1666 K St., N.W., Suite 800, Washington DC 20006
General Counsel: Gordon O. Pehrson, Jr.
Members: 6 companies *Staff:* 1
Annual Budget: $250-500,000 *Tel:* (202) 872-7800
Hist. Note: A trade group of kaolin producers. Supports the China Clay Producers Group Political Action Committee. The above address is the law firm of Sutherland, Asbill and Brennan.
Semi-annual meetings: Spring and Fall
1987-Washington, DC/Spring and Savannah, GA/Fall

China, Glass and Giftware Ass'n (1948)
1115 Clifton Ave., Clifton NJ 07013
Exec. Secretary: Donald Doctorow
Members: 300 *Staff:* 1
Annual Budget: $10-25,000 *Tel:* (201) 779-1600
Hist. Note: Established in 1948. Formerly (1975) China, Glass and Pottery Ass'n of America, Inc.
Semi-Annual Meetings: January in Atlantic City, May in New York City

Chinese-American Librarians Ass'n (1973)
Hist. Note: Formerly the Mid-West Chinese American Librarians Association. Affiliated with the American Library Association. Has no paid staff. Address unknown since 1984.

Chinese Language Computer Soc. (1976)
Knowledge Systems Institute, Box 41, Glencoe IL 60022
President: Shi-Kuo Chang
Members: 300-400 *Staff:* 1
Annual Budget: under $10,000 *Tel:* (312) 567-3401
Hist. Note: Professionals interested in Chinese language data processing. Membership: $10/year.
Publication:
Newsletter. 3/yr.

Chinese Language Teachers Ass'n (1962)
Institute of Far Eastern Studies, 162 S. Orange Ave., Seton Hall Univ., South Orange NJ 07079
Secy.-Treas.: John Young
Members: 700 *Staff:* 2
Annual Budget: $10-25,000 *Tel:* (201) 762-4973
Hist. Note: Affiliated with the Association for Asian Studies and the American Council for the Teaching of Foreign Languages. Membership: $20/year.
Publications:
Journal of The Chinese Language Teachers Association. 3/yr.
Newsletter. 3/yr.
Annual Meetings: November, with the American Council for the Teaching of Foreign Languages.

Chlorinated Parafin Industry Ass'n
Hist. Note: An affiliate of the Synthetic Organic Chemical Manufacturers Ass'n which provides administrative support.

Chlorine Institute, The (1924)
2001 L St., N.W., Suite 506, Washington DC 20036
President: Robert G. Smerko
Members: 140-150 companies *Staff:* 10
Annual Budget: $1-2,000,000 *Tel:* (202) 775-2790
Hist. Note: Members are producers of gaseous and liquid chlorine and others associated in some way with manufacture, processing, packaging, transporting, and use. Membership: $1,400/yr.
Publication:
CI General Publications List. m.
Annual Meetings: Feb./March
1987-Washington, DC(Mayflower)/March 15-19
1988-New Orleans, LA(Fairmont)/March 6-10

Chlorobenzene Producers Ass'n (1978)
1330 Connecticut Ave., N.W., Suite 300, Washington DC 20036
Exec. Director: Alan W. Rautio
Members: 3 companies *Staff:* 2-5
Annual Budget: $100-250,000 *Tel:* (202) 659-0060
Hist. Note: An affiliate of the Synthetic Organic Chemical Manufacturers Ass'n, which provides administrative support.

Chocolate Manufacturers Ass'n of the U.S.A. (1923)
7900 Westpark Drive, Suite 514, McLean VA 22102
President: Richard T. O'Connell, CAE
Members: 15-20 *Staff:* 6-10
Annual Budget: $100-250,000 *Tel:* (703) 790-5011
Hist. Note: Founded as the Association of Cocoa and Chocolate Manufacturers of the United States, it assumed its present name in 1958.
Publication:
Newsletter. m.
Annual Meetings: New York, NY in Spring

Choristers Guild (1949)
2834 W. Kingsley Drive, Garland TX 75041
Exec. Director: John T. Burke
Members: 9,500-10,000 *Staff:* 6-10
Annual Budget: $250-500,000 *Tel:* (214) 271-1521
Hist. Note: Members are directors of children's choirs in churches and schools seeking to enhance the religious and musical training of their students. Incorporated in the states of Tennessee and Texas. Membership: $30/yr.
Publication:
The Choristers Guild Letter. 10/yr.
Annual Meetings: First week of February in Dallas

Christian Booksellers Ass'n (1950)
2620 Venetucci Ave., Box 200, Colorado Springs CO 80901
President: William R. Anderson
Members: 3,520 companies *Staff:* 60
Annual Budget: $2-5,000,000 *Tel:* (303) 576-7880
Hist. Note: A trade association serving book stores, publishers and suppliers for all major Christian denominations.
Publications:
Bookstore Journal. m. adv.
CBA Suppliers Directory. a. adv.
Current Christian Books. a.
Annual Meetings: July/8,000
1987-Anaheim, CA(Convention Center)/July 11-16
1988-Dallas, TX(Convention Center)/July 16-21
1989-Atlanta, GA(World Congress Center)/July 8-13

Christian College Coalition (1976)
6th Floor, 1776 Massachusetts Ave., N.W., Washington DC 20036
President: John R. Dellenback
Members: 75 institutions *Staff:* 6-10
Annual Budget: $500-1,000,000 *Tel:* (202) 293-6177
Hist. Note: Seeks to encourage national development of, and cooperation among, regionally-accredited, evangelical Christian liberal arts colleges and universities. Originally a sub-group of the 13-member Christian College Consortium, the Coalition became fully independent and incorporated in the District of Columbia in 1982.
Publications:
Christian College News. m.
A Guide to Christian Colleges. bien.

Christian College Consortium (1971)
6 Pine Tree Drive, Suite 180, St. Paul MN 55112
President: Dr. Carl Lundquist
Members: 13 colleges *Staff:* 2-5
Annual Budget: $100-250,000 *Tel:* (612) 638-6155
Hist. Note: Organized in 1971, the Consortium consists of thirteen colleges united by regional accreditation, concentration upon liberal arts studies, educational strengths that can be shared, nationwide distribution and a common affirmation of faith. Membership: $2,000/yr.
Publication:
Synthesis. irreg.
Annual Meetings: Spring

Christian Labor Ass'n of the United States of America (1931)
Box 65, 9820 Gordon St., Zeeland MI 49464
President: Donald E. Leep
Members: 4,000-5,000 *Staff:* 9-10
Annual Budget: $250-500,000 *Tel:* (616) 772-9153
Hist. Note: Independent labor union
Annual Meetings: Holland, MI in May

Christian Legal Soc. (1961)
P.O. Box 1492, Merrifield VA 22116
Exec. Director: Samuel E. Ericsson
Members: 5,000 *Staff:* 25-30
Annual Budget: $1-2,000,000 *Tel:* (703) 560-7314
Hist. Note: An evangelical Christian organization of lawyers, judges, law professors and law students.
Publications:
Focus. m.
Religious Freedom Reporter. m.
Reconciler. a.
CLS Quarterly. q.
Briefly. q.
Lawyers' Quest. q.
Jurist. q.
Semi-annual Meetings: April and October

Christian Medical Soc. (1931)
Box 830689, Richardson TX 75083-0689
General Director: Edwin A. Blum
Members: 6,100 *Staff:* 30-35
Annual Budget: $2-5,000,000 *Tel:* (214) 783-8384
Hist. Note: Members are religiously-oriented medical and dental personnel, some of whom serve as medical missionaries. Membership: $275/yr. (inidividual).
Publications:
CMS Journal. q.
News and Reports. bi-m. adv.
Annual Meetings: May
1987-New Orleans, LA
1988-Seattle, WA

Christian Ministries Management Ass'n (1976)
P.O. Box 4638, Diamond Bar CA 91765
Exec. Director & CEO: Sylvia Flaten
Members: 1,000 organizations; 2,300 individuals
Annual Budget: $500-1,000,000 *Tel:* (714) 861-8861
Hist. Note: Non-profit organization designed to assist those involved in the management of Christian organizations. Membership: $70/yr.
Publications:
Christian Management Report. bi-m. adv.
Membership Directory. a. adv.
Christian Management Institute Handbook. a. adv.
Publications List Available.
Annual Meetings: February
1987-Los Angeles, CA(Hilton)/Feb. 23-26
1988-Orlando, FL/Feb. 22-25
1989-Feb. 20-23
1990-Feb. 19-22

Christian Schools Internat'l (1920)
3350 E. Paris Ave., Grand Rapids MI 49508
Director: Dr. Michael T. Ruiter
Members: 440 protestant private schools *Staff:* 21-25
Annual Budget: $250-500,000 *Tel:* (616) 957-1070
Hist. Note: Established as the National Union of Christian Schools, it assumed its present name in 1978.
Publications:
Christian Home and School. 10/yr. adv.
Christian School Directory. a.
Annual Meetings: July/August
1987-Mequon, WI

00108 12 05 86 1233

Church and Synagogue Library Ass'n (1967)
Box 1130, Bryn Mawr PA 19010
Exec. Secretary: Dorothy J. Rodda
Members: 1,900 *Staff:* 2-5
Annual Budget: $50-100,000 *Tel:* (215) 853-2870
Hist. Note: An outgrowth of library workshops held for several years by the library school of Drexel University in Philadelphia. A member of the Council of National Library Associations. Membership: $12/year.
Publication:
Church & Synagogue Libraries. bi-m. adv.
Annual Meetings: June
1987-Philadelphia, PA(Haverford College)/June 28-30
1988-Oberlin, OH(Oberlin College)/June 19-21

Church Furniture Manufacturers Ass'n (1961)
Hist. Note: Formerly a division of the Nat'l Ass'n of Furniture Mfrs. In 1984 merged into the American Furniture Manufacturers Ass'n, no longer exists as a separate entity.

Church Music Publishers Ass'n (1926)
c/o Holt Publishing Co., 380 South Main Place, Carol Stream IL 60187
President: George Shorney
Members: 25-30 companies
Annual Budget: under $10,000 *Tel:* (800) 323-1049
Hist. Note: Formerly Church and Sunday School Music Publishers Ass'n. Members publish music for Christian churches and schools. Has no paid staff of permanent address.
Annual Meetings: Spring

Cigar Ass'n of America (1937)
1100 17th St., N.W., Suite 504, Washington DC 20036
President: Norman F. Sharp
Members: 75 *Staff:* 2-5
Annual Budget: $500-1,000,000 *Tel:* (202) 466-3070
Hist. Note: Established in 1937 as the Cigar Manufacturers Ass'n of America, Inc. Became the Cigar Ass'n of America, Inc. in 1974 through a merger of the Cigar Research Council, the Cigar Manufacturers Ass'n of America, the Cigar Institute of America and the State and Local Tax Council. Represents the producers of about 95% of the cigars sold in the U.S. Sponsors the Cigar Political Action Committee.
Publications:
Statistical Bulletin. m.
Imports of Cigars and Leaf Tobacco. m.
Trademark Bulletin. irreg.
Annual Meetings: December
1987-Boca Raton, FL(Hotel & CLub)/Dec. 3-6

Circuits and Systems Soc.
Hist. Note: A subsidiary of the Institute of Electrical and Electronic Engineers. Membership in the Society, open only to IEEE members, includes subscription to a technical periodical in the field published by IEEE. All administrative support is provided by IEEE.

City and Regional Magazine Ass'n (1978)
801 2nd Ave. #1400, New York NY 10017
Exec. Director: C. Whitford McDowell
Members: 40-50 companies *Staff:* 2-5
Annual Budget: $100-250,000 *Tel:* (212) 697-3580
Publication:
Newsletter.
Annual Meetings: Spring
1987-New Orleans, LA(Fairmont)/May 11-13/150-200

Civil Aviation Medical Ass'n (1948)
775 Bank Lane, Lake Forest IL 60045
Business Counsel: Albert Carriere
Members: 800 *Staff:* 2
Annual Budget: $25-50,000 *Tel:* (312) 234-6330
Hist. Note: Established in 1948 as the Airline Medical Examiners Ass'n, it assumed its present name in 1955. Became a constituent organization of Aeromedical Ass'n, now known as Aerospace Medical Ass'n. CAMA is comprised of physicians concerned with the welfare and growth of civil aviation, including aviation medical examiners and physicans who are pilots, aviation medical educators, flight instructors and fixed base operators. Membership: $60/yr. (individual); $200/yr. (organization/company)
Publication:
CAMA Bulletin. q.
Annual Meetings:
1987-Chicago, IL
1988-London, England

Classification Soc. of North America (1964)
Room 2C-551, c/o AT&T Bell Laboratories,600 Mountain Ave., Murray Hill NJ 07974
Secretary: James Corter
Members: 450 *Staff:* 1
Annual Budget: under $10,000 *Tel:* (201) 582-6665
Hist. Note: Information scientists and others interested in classification and pattern recognition. Has no paid staff. Membership: $30/yr. (individual); $52/yr. (library).
Publications:
Journal of Classification.
Classification Literature Automated Search Service. a.
Annual Meetings: June

Classroom Publishers Ass'n (1948)
2020 K St., N.W., Suite 800, Washington DC 20006
General Counsel: Stephen F. Owen, Jr.
Members: 6-10 companies *Staff:* 1
Annual Budget: $25-50,000 *Tel:* (202) 296-5680
Hist. Note: Founded as the Classroom Periodical Publishers Ass'n, it assumed its present name in 1978. Has no permanent office; the above address is the law firm of Loomis, Owen, Fellman and Howe.

Clay Minerals Soc. (1962)
Box 2295, Bloomington IN 47402
Office Manager: Susan Wintsch
Members: 750-800 *Staff:* 1
Annual Budget: $100-250,000 *Tel:* (812) 332-9600
Hist. Note: Incorporated in the District of Columbia July 18, 1962. Supersedes the Committee on Clay Minerals of the National Academy of Sciences/National Research Council. Members are individuals concerned with the scientific study and applications of clays and related silicate minerals.
Publication:
Clays and Clay Minerals. bi-m.
Annual Meetings: Summer or Fall
1987-Socorro, NM/Oct./400

Cleaning Equipment Manufacturers Ass'n (1980)
111 East Wacker Drive, Suite 600, Chicago IL 60601
Exec. V. Pres./Secy.: William W. Carpenter
Members: 110 companies *Staff:* 3
Annual Budget: $50-100,000 *Tel:* (312) 644-6610
Hist. Note: Members are manufacturers of pressure washer systems and their components.
Publication:
Newsletter. m. adv.
Semi-annual Meetings: Spring and Fall

Cleaning Management Institute (1985)
15550-D Rockfield Blvd., Irvine CA 92718
Exec. Director: Beryl Caron
Members: 1,000 *Staff:* 2-5
Annual Budget: $250-500,000 *Tel:* (714) 770-5008
Hist. Note: Successor organization to the American Institute of Maintenance (1958) in 1985. Members are individuals and companies involved in building cleaning maintenance operations. Membership: $65/yr.
Publication:
Cleaning Management Magazine. m. adv.
Annual Meetings:
1987-Anaheim, CA/Jan.27-30/3,000
1987-Atlanta, GA/May 5-8/3,000

Clear Channel Broadcasting Service (1934)
1776 K St., N.W., Suite 1100, Washington DC 20006
Legal Counsel: R. Russell Eagan
Members: 10-20 stations
Tel: (202) 429-7020
Hist. Note: Membership composed of Class I-A and I-B Clear Channel standard broadcast (AM) stations. Has no permanent headquarters or staff. The above address is the law firm of Wiley & Rein.

Clinical Laboratory Management Ass'n (1971)
193-195 West Lancaster Ave., Paoli PA 19301
Exec. Director: L. Joan Logue
Members: 5,000 *Staff:* 2-5
Annual Budget: $500-1,000,000 *Tel:* (215) 353-9116
Hist. Note: Established as the American Association of Clinical Laboratory Supervisors and Administrators, it assumed its present name in 1976. Members are laboratory executives and their suppliers. Membership: $75/yr.
Publications:
CLMA Newsletter. m.
Journal.
Annual Meetings: Fall
1987-Dallas, TX(Loews Anatole)/Sept. 15-18/1,400

Clinical Ligand Assay Soc. (1977)
Box 67, Wayne MI 48184
Secretary: Deborah A. Rakoczy
Members: 1,250 *Staff:* 2-5
Annual Budget: $250-500,000 *Tel:* (313) 722-6290
Hist. Note: Founded in 1977 as the Clinical Radioassay Society, it assumed its present name in 1981. A ligand assay is a subspecialty of clinical laboratory medicine by which substances (drugs, hormones, etc.) are measured in small quantities. Membership: $38/yr.
Publication:
Journal of Clinical Immunoassay. q. adv.
Annual Meetings: Spring
1987-St. Louis, MO/April 22-25
1988-Washington, DC/Baltimore,MD
1989-Los Angeles, CA
1990-Philadelphia, PA

Clinical Orthopaedic Soc. (1912)
8424 Naab Road, Indianapolis IN 46260
Secy.-Treas.: Dr. Frank Throop
Members: 600-650 *Staff:* 1
Annual Budget: $50-100,000 *Tel:* (317) 924-3486
Hist. Note: Membership consists mainly of mid-western orthopaedic surgeons.
Publication:
Directory. a.
Annual Meetings: Fall
1987-Chicago, IL/Oct. 6-9
1988-Cincinnati, OH/Oct. 5-7

Clinical Soc. of Genito-Urinary Surgeons (1921)
Dept. of Urology, University Hospital, Box 422, Charlottesville VA 22908
Business Manager: Sally Field
Members: 40-50 *Staff:* 1
Annual Budget: under $10,000 *Tel:* (804) 924-2224

Closure Manufacturers Ass'n (1963)
1133 20th St., N.W., #321, Washington DC 20036
Exec. V. President: Charles H. Emely
Members: 14 companies *Staff:* 2
Annual Budget: $250-500,000 *Tel:* (202) 223-9050
Hist. Note: Founded as the Closure Committee of the Glass Packaging Institute, CMA in 1981 became an independent affiliate of the Institute. Members are companies which make metal and plastic closures for all types of containers.
Publication:
The Closure Industry Report (newsletter). semi-a.
Semi-annual Meetings: Spring and Fall (Members Only)
1987-Scottsdale, AZ(Registry)/May 13-14
1987-White Sulphur Springs, WV(Greenbrier)/Sept. 13-15

Clothing Manufacturers Ass'n of the U.S.A. (1907)
1290 Avenue of the Americas, New York NY 10104
Exec. Director: Robert A. Kaplan
Members: 350-400 *Staff:* 2-5
Annual Budget: $100-250,000 *Tel:* (212) 757-6664
Hist. Note: Has absorbed many of the members of the inactive Association of Boys and Students Clothing Manufacturers. Principal activity is labor and government relations. Membership Fee: Based on sales volume.
Publications:
Statistical Report on Sales, Production, and Profit in Men's and Boy's
Tailored Clothing Industry. a.
Publications List Available.

Clowns of America, Internat'l (1968)
1315 Boulevard, New Haven CT 06511
President: Arnold S. Firine
Members: 5,800-6,000 *Staff:* 2-5
Annual Budget: $50-100,000 *Tel:* (203) 624-0438
Hist. Note: Formerly (1968) Clown Club of America and Circus Clown Club. Members are amateur and professional entertainers.
Publication:
New Calliope. m. adv.
Annual Meetings: April
1987-San Diego, CA

Club Managers Ass'n of America (1927)
7615 Winterberry Place, Bethesda MD 20817
Exec. V. President: James A. Schuping
Members: 3,500 *Staff:* 20-25
Annual Budget: $1-2,000,000 *Tel:* (301) 229-3600
Hist. Note: Established and incorporated in Michigan in 1927. Membership: $280/yr.
Publications:
Club Management Magazine. m. adv.
Outlook. m.
Annual Meetings: Winter
1987-Las Vegas, NV(Bally's)/Jan. 18-24

Clydesdale Breeders of the United States (1879)
17378 Kelly Road, Pecatonica IL 61063
Secretary: Betty J. Groves
Members: 500 *Staff:* 1
Annual Budget: under $10,000 *Tel:* (815) 247-8780
Hist. Note: Members own and breed Clydescale horses. Formerly the American Clydesdale Ass'n and Clydesdale Breeders Ass'n of the U.S.
Publication:
Clydesdale. a. adv.

Coal Exporters Ass'n of the United States (1945)
1130 17th St., N.W., Washington DC 20036
Exec. Director: Constance D. Holmes
Members: 40 companies *Staff:* 1
Annual Budget: $25-50,000 *Tel:* (202) 463-2639
Hist. Note: Affiliated with Nat'l Coal Ass'n.
Publication:
Bulletin. m.
Annual Meetings: With Nat'l Coal Ass'n

Coal Fuel Mixtures Ass'n (1982)
Hist. Note: Dissolved in 1983.

Coalition for Common Sense in Government Procurement (1979)
1990 M St., N.W., Suite 400, Washington DC 20036
Exec. Director: Yvonne M. Kidd
Members: 100 companies, 10 associations *Staff:* 2-5
Annual Budget: $100-250,000 *Tel:* (202) 331-0975
Hist. Note: Members are firms who provide commercial goods to the federal government, and related associations.
Publication:
Off the Shelf. m.
Semi-annual Meetings: Spring and Fall

Coalition for Health and the Environment (1979)
Hist. Note: An umbrella organization of health, environmental, labor, consumer, business and insurance groups formed to promote public recognition of the interrelated nature of a healthy environment and disease prevention. Formerly (1981) National Coalition for Disease Prevention and Environmental

00109 12 05 86 1233

Health. Reported as defunct in 1982.

Coalition of American Public Employees (1972)
Hist. Note: Inactive in 1982, reported defunct.

Coalition of Automotive Ass'ns
Hist. Note: Non-profit organization formed to provide administrative support for the Specialty Equipment Market Ass'n and Auto Internat'l Ass'n.

Coalition of Labor Union Women (1974)
15 Union Square, New York NY 10003
Exec. Director: Lee Levin
Members: 18,000 *Staff:* 2-5
Annual Budget: $50-100,000 *Tel:* (212) 242-0700
Hist. Note: Founded in 1974 to work towards full equality of opportunities and rights for employed women. Members are women in the labor movement, and others interested in advancing the participation of women within unions. Concerned with such issues as labor law reform, passage of ERA, child care, safety in the workplace and pay equity. Membership: $20/yr.
Publication:
CLUW News. bi-m.
Annual Meetings: Four Conferences/Board Meetings per year

Coated Abrasives Fabricators Ass'n (1980)
Hist. Note: Ceased operations in 1984.

Coated Abrasives Manufacturers' Institute (1933)
1230 Keith Bldg., Cleveland OH 44115-2180
Mng. Director: Charles M. Stockinger
Members: 6-10 companies *Staff:* 2-5
Annual Budget: $25-50,000 *Tel:* (216) 241-7333

Coblentz Soc. (1954)
Perkin-Elmer Corp., 761 Main Ave., Norwalk CT 06859-0903
Secretary: Dr. Robert W. Hannah
Members: 600 *Staff:* 1
Annual Budget: under $10,000 *Tel:* (203) 431-7797
Hist. Note: Founded in 1954 and incorporated in Connecticut the same year. Named for the infrared spectroscopist, Dr. W. W. Coblentz, active 1900-1908. Members are molecular spectroscopists.
Publication:
Coblentz Society Mailings. q.
Annual Meetings: Spring

Cocoa Merchants' Ass'n of America (1924)
Box 5476, Grand Central Station, New York NY 10163
President: Johann J. Scheu
Members: 100-125
Annual Budget: $250-500,000 *Tel:* (212) 883-9523
Hist. Note: Has no paid staff. Membership: $1,500/yr.
Publication:
Annual Report.
Annual Meetings: February

Coffee, Sugar and Cocoa Exchange (1882)
4 World Trade Center, New York NY 10048
President: Bennett J. Corn
Members: 527 *Staff:* 95
Annual Budget: over $5,000,000 *Tel:* (212) 938-2800
Hist. Note: The Coffee, Sugar & Cocoa Exchange, Inc. was founded in 1882 as the Coffee Exchange of the City of New York. Originally created to trade coffee futures, the Exchange added the trading of sugar futures in 1914 to replace European raw sugar markets closed by the World War. In 1916, the Exchange changed its name to the New York Coffee and Sugar Exchange, Inc. On September 28, 1979, the Exchange merged with the New York Cocoa Exchange, Inc. and officially became the Coffee, Sugar & Cocoa Exchange, Inc. The New York Cocoa Exchange opened for business on October 1, 1925, establishing the world's first exchange for trading in cocoa beans. The Coffee, Sugar & Cocoa Exchange is the world's leading marketplace for futures trading in these three important commodities. In addition to coffee, sugar, and cocoa futures, options on sugar, coffee, and cocoa futures and CPI (Consumer Price Index) futures are also traded the CSCE. The Exchange's 527 membership seats are held by representatives from every segment of the coffee, sugar and cocoa industries as well as by floor brokers and futures commission merchants. The Exchange is regulated by the federal Commodity Futures Trading Commission (CFTC) which was created after Congress significantly amended the Commodity Exchange Act in 1974. With the creation of the CFTC, internationally traded commodities were brought under federal regulation for the first time. Has a budget of approximately $5-$6 million.
Publications:
Coffee, Sugar & Cocoa Exchange Daily Market Report. d.
Coffee, Sugar & Cocoa Exchange Weekly Review of Market. w.
Statistical Annual. a.
Newsletter.
Economic Index Market.
Annual Meetings: 3rd Wednesday in March (at Exchange)

Cognitive Science Soc. (1980)
Psychology Dept., Carnegie-Mellon Univ., Pittsburgh PA 15213
Secy.-Treas.: Kurt VanLehn
Members: 600-650 *Staff:* 1
Annual Budget: $25-50,000 *Tel:* (412) 268-3790
Hist. Note: Members are university and industrial researchers with doctorates.
Publication:
Cognitive Science. q. adv.

Coin Laundry Ass'n (1960)
1314 Butterfield Road, Suite 212, Downers Grove IL 60515
President: Frank J. Vitek
Members: 2,600 *Staff:* 6-10
Annual Budget: $500-1,000,000 *Tel:* (312) 963-5547
Hist. Note: Established as the National Automatic Laundry and Cleaning Council, it assumed its present name in 1983. Members are self-service laundry and dry cleaning establishments together with manufacturers and distributors of the equipment, services and supplies they use. Membership: $120-5,000/yr.
Publications:
CLA Management Guidelines. m.
CLA News. m.
Washington Dateline. m.
Annual Meetings: Spring/17-19,000
1987-Atlanta, GA/Apr. 27-30
1989-Dallas, TX/March 6-9

Cold Finished Steel Bar Institute (1971)
1120 Vermont Ave., N.W., Suite 1000, Washington DC 20005
Members: 27 companies *Staff:* 1
Annual Budget: $100-250,000 *Tel:* (202) 857-0059
Publication:
Barometer.
Semi-annual Meetings: Washington, DC(Watergate)/June and December/50

Collector Car Appraisers Internat'l (1980)
24 Myrtle Avenue, Buffalo NY 14204
President: James T. Sandoro
Members: 25 individuals *Staff:* 3
Annual Budget: $25-50,000 *Tel:* (716) 855-1931
Hist. Note: Members are licensed and bonded individuals with at least ten years experience handling antique, classic, special interest collector cars, trucks, motorcycles, etc. Certifies members to act as expert witnesses in law suits and arbitration. Maintains a 3,740 volume library. Membership: $1,000/yr.
Publication:
Actual Cash Value, Car Guide. a.
Annual Meetings:
1987-New York, NY
1988-Scottsdale, AZ
1989-Los Angeles, CA

Collector Platemakers Guild (1977)
Box 1474, Northbrook IL 60062
Exec. Officer: Hunter Haines
Members: 40 companies *Staff:* 1
Annual Budget: $25-50,000 *Tel:* (312) 272-0028
Hist. Note: Makers or importers of commemorative or limited edition plates who wish to encourage plate collecting as a hobby.
Publication:
Newsletter. m.
Annual Meetings: Summer

College and Universities Systems Exchange (1971)
Hist. Note: See CAUSE.

College and University Personnel Ass'n (1947)
11 Dupont Circle, Suite 120, Washington DC 20036
Exec. Director: Richard C. Creal
Members: 1,300 colleges and universities *Staff:* 10
Annual Budget: $500-1,000,000 *Tel:* (202) 462-1038
Hist. Note: Members are colleges and universities united to improve the effectiveness of their personnel administration. Sliding scale membership fee.
Publications:
Administrative Compensation Survey. a.
The Journal of the College and University Personnel Ass'n. q. adv.
Personnelite. w.
Faculty Salary Survey. a.
Annual Meetings: Late Summer or early Fall/500
1987-Boston, MA(Marriott)/Aug. 9-12
1988-St. Louis, MO(Marriott)/Oct. 23-26
1989-Salt Lake City, UT/August 6-9/500
1990-New Orleans, LA/Oct. 21-24

College Art Ass'n of America (1911)
149 Madison Ave., New York NY 10016
Exec. Director: Susan L. Ball
Members: 8,500-9,000 *Staff:* 6-10
Annual Budget: $500-1,000,000 *Tel:* (212) 889-2113
Hist. Note: Founded at the Cincinnati Art Museum in May, 1911 at a meeting of the Western Drawing and Manual Training Ass'n. A professional organization of art historians, studio artists and museum personnel united to improve the standards of art scholarship, art teaching and art history. Member of the American council of Learned Socs. Membership: $35-100/yr. (individual); $75/yr. (institution)
Publications:
The Art Bulletin. q.
Art Journal. q. adv.
CAA Newsletter. q.
Annual Meetings: Winter
1987-Boston, MA(Copley Marriott & Westin)/Feb. 12-14/4,500
1988-Houston, TX(Hyatt Regency)/Feb. 11-13/4,000
1989-San Francisco, CA(Hilton)/Feb. 10-12/3,600

College Athletic Business Managers Ass'n (1951)
U.S. Military Academy, Box 27, West Point NY 10996
Secy.-Treas.: Janet La Casse
Members: 350-400 *Staff:* 1
Annual Budget: under $10,000 *Tel:* (914) 446-5982
Hist. Note: Affiliated with Nat'l Collegiate Athletic Ass'n. Members are business and ticket managers of athletic programs. Has no paid staff.
Annual Meetings: With NCAA

College Band Directors Nat'l Ass'n (1941)
Box 8028, University of Texas, Austin TX 78713
Secy.-Treas.: Richard L. Floyd
Members: 900 *Staff:* 1
Annual Budget: $25-50,000 *Tel:* (512) 471-5883
Hist. Note: Membership: $40/year.
Publications:
Newsletter. q.
Journal. semi-a.
Biennial Meetings: Odd years
1987-Evanston, IL(Northwestern University)/Feb. 25-28/500
1989-Austin, TX(University of Texas)/Feb. 22-25/500

College English Ass'n (1939)
Nazareth College of Rochester, Rochester NY 14610
Exec. Director: Dr. John J. Joyce
Members: 2,000-2,200 individuals, 350-375 libraries *Staff:* 3
Annual Budget: $25-50,000 *Tel:* (716) 586-2525
Hist. Note: Concerned with practical applications of scholarship to teaching English literature and language at the college level. Membership: $20/yr. (individual), $24/yr. (institution).
Publications:
The CEA Critic. q. adv.
The CEA Forum. q. adv.
Annual Meetings: April
1987-Charleston, SC
1988-New Orleans, LA

College Football Ass'n (1977)
6688 Gunpark Dr., Suite 201, Boulder CO 80301-3339
Exec. Director: Charles M. Neinas
Members: 66 *Staff:* 4
Annual Budget: $500-1,000,000 *Tel:* (303) 530-5566
Hist. Note: Organized to provide major football playing universities a forum to discuss matters of mutual interest and concern. Membership: $1,500/yr.
Publication:
Sidelines. m.
Annual Meetings: June

College Fraternity Editors Ass'n (1923)
3920 Lytham Court, Columbus OH 43320
President: Mrs. Charles Hyatt
Members: 110 fraternities and sororities *Staff:* 1
Annual Budget: $10-25,000 *Tel:* (614) 451-6633
Hist. Note: Organized December 1, 1923 at the Hotel Pennsylvania in New York City. Membership consists of full-time editors of fraternity magazines. Officers change annually in June.
Publication:
The Fraternity Editor. irreg.
Annual Meetings: June
1987-Vail, CO

College Language Ass'n (1937)
Atlanta University, Atlanta GA 30314
Secretary: Lucy Grigsby
Members: 350
Annual Budget: $10-25,000 *Tel:* (404) 681-0251
Hist. Note: Established as the Ass'n of Language Teachers in Negro Colleges, it assumed its present name in 1949. An "allied" organization of the Modern Language Ass'n, the Nat'l Council of Teachers of English and the Conference on College Composition and Communications. Has no paid staff. Membership: $30/yr.
Publication:
Journal. q.
Annual Meetings: April
1987-Washington, DC

College Media Advisers (1954)
Dept. of Journalism, Memphis State Univ., Memphis TN 38152
Director: Ronald E. Spielberger
Members: 5-600 *Staff:* 2-5
Annual Budget: $50-100,000 *Tel:* (901) 454-2403
Hist. Note: Established as the Nat'l Council of College Publication Advisors, it assumed its present name in 1983 to reflect the growing importance of electronic media. Members are advisers to college student newspapers, yearbooks, magazines, radio and TV stations. Membership: $45/yr.
Publications:
College Media Review. q. adv.
CMA Newsletter. m.
Semi-annual Meetings: Mid-March in New York City and Fall
1987-New York, NY/March
1987-St. Louis, MO(Sheraton)/Oct./1,300
1988-New York, NY/March
1988-Atlanta, GA(Hyatt)/Nov. 2-5/1,300
1989-New York, NY/March
1989-New Orleans, LA(Montleone)/Nov. 16-19/1,300

College Music Soc. (1958)
1444 15th St., Boulder CO 80302
Exec. Director: Robby D. Gunstream
Members: 5,750 *Staff:* 2-5

00110 12 05 86 1233

Annual Budget: $100-250,000 *Tel:* (303) 449-1611
Hist. Note: Formed by a merger of the Soc. of Music in the Liberal Arts Colleges and the College Music Ass'n. Members are college teachers of music. Considers and disseminates ideas of the philosophy and practice of music in higher education.
Publications:
College Music Symposium. a.
Directory of Music Faculties. bien.
Newsletter. 10/yr.
Annual Meetings: Fall
1987-New Orleans, LA

College of American Pathologists (1947)
5202 Old Orchard Road, Skokie IL 60077-1034
Chief Exec. Officer: Howard E. Cartwright
Members: 10,000 *Staff:* 180
Annual Budget: over $5,000,000 *Tel:* (312) 677-3500
Hist. Note: Founded and incorporated May 14, 1947. Fellowship is restricted to physicians certified by the American Board of Pathology. Has an annual budget of $18,000,000. Membership: $150/yr.
Publications:
Pathologist. The Journal of the College of American Pathologists. m. adv.

Semi-Annual Meetings: With American Soc. of Clinical Pathologists
1987-San Francisco, CA/March 28-April 2
1987-New Orleans, LA/Oct. 24-30
1988-Kansas City, MO/April 16-21
1988-Las Vegas, NV/Oct. 22-28
1989-Chicago, IL/March
1989-Washington, DC/Oct.-Nov.

College of Diplomates of the American Board of Orthodontics (1979)
6402 Odana Road, Madison WI 53719
Secy.-Treas.: Dr. R.C. Thurow
Members: 1,000 *Staff:* 1
Annual Budget: $25-50,000 *Tel:* (608) 274-5223
Hist. Note: Limited to diplomates of the American Board of Orthodontics. Membership: $15/year.
Publication:
Newsletter. semi-a.
Annual Meetings: July
1987-Hot Springs, VA(Homestead)/July 12-16/250
1989-Newport, RI(Sheraton)

College of Optometrists in Vision Development (1970)
Box 285, Chula Vista CA 92012
Secretary: Robert M. Wold, O.D.
Members: 850-900 *Staff:* 1
Annual Budget: $100-250,000 *Tel:* (619) 425-6191
Hist. Note: Optometrists concerned with vision therapy, particularly in the area of learning disabilities. Affiliated with the American Optometric Ass'n. Formed by a merger of the Nat'l Optometric Soc. for Developmental Vision Care, the Nat'l Soc. for Vision and Perception Training and the Southwest Developmental Vision Soc.
Publication:
Journal of Optometric Vision Development. q. adv.
Annual Meetings: Fall

College of Osteopathic Healthcare Executives (1954)
55 West Seegers Road, Arlington Heights IL 60005
President: Richard A. Strano
Members: 150-200 *Staff:* 2-5
Annual Budget: $100-250,000 *Tel:* (312) 952-8900
Hist. Note: COHE provides continuing education to excutives of osteopathic health care facilities to ensure their professional excellence. It also certifies their levels of educational achievement.
Publications:
Directory. a.
News Briefs. q.
In Perspective. q.
Annual Meetings: Spring/350
1987-San Diego, CA(Hilton Tennis and Beach Resort)

College Placement Council (1956)
62 Highland Ave., Bethlehem PA 18017
Acting Exec. Director: Warren E. Kauffman
Members: 2,600 colleges and employers *Staff:* 30-33
Annual Budget: $2-5,000,000 *Tel:* (215) 868-1421
Hist. Note: Formerly (1953) Ass'n of School and College Placement. Serves as the interface between higher education and employers of college graduates. Membership: $250/yr.
Publications:
Spotlight. 21/yr.
Journal of College Placement. q. adv.
Salary Survey. q.
College Placement Annual. a.
CPC Nat'l Directory: Who's Who... a.
Triennial Meetings: 1989

College Sports Information Directors of America (1957)
Texas A&I Univ., Campus Box 114, Kingsville TX 78363
Secretary: Fred Nuesch
Members: 1,400 *Staff:* 2-5
Annual Budget: $25-50,000 *Tel:* (512) 592-0389
Hist. Note: Originally a section of the American College Public Relations Ass'n. Became independent in 1957. Sponsors Academic All-American teams in football, basketball, baseball, volleyball, and softball and a post-graduate scholarship.
Publications:
CoSIDA Digest. m. adv.
CoSIDA Directory. a. adv.
Annual Meetings: June
1987-Portland, OR/June 28-July 2

College Swimming Coaches Ass'n of America (1922)
Pomona-Pitzer Colleges, 210 E 2nd St., Claremont CA 91711-6347
President: Penny Lee Dean
Members: 7-800 *Staff:* 3
Annual Budget: $25-50,000 *Tel:* (714) 621-8176
Hist. Note: Chartered in the State of Florida, September 14, 1967. Has no paid staff; officers rotate annually.
Publication:
CSCAA Newsletter. bi-m.
Annual Meetings: Fall

College Theology Soc. (1954)
Theology Department, Loyola Marymount University, Los Angeles CA 90045
Secretary: Marie Anne Mayeski
Members: 800 *Staff:* 1
Annual Budget: $10-25,000 *Tel:* (213) 642-2700
Hist. Note: Formerly (1967) Soc. of Catholic College Teachers of Sacred Doctrine. Member of the Council on the Study of Religion. Membership: $25/yr.
Publication:
Horizons: The Journal of the College Theology Society. semi-a. adv.

Collegiate Commissioners Ass'n (1939)
1111 Plaza Drive, Schaumburg IL 60195
Secy.-Treas.: John D. Dewey
Members: 13 *Staff:* 0
Annual Budget: $50-100,000 *Tel:* (312) 885-3933
Hist. Note: Members are commissioners and staffs of the major collegiate athletic conferences of the U.S. Founded as the National Association of Football Commissioners, it became the National Association of Collegiate Commissioners in 1948 and assumed its present name in 1965. Publishes a number of annual handbooks for officials. Has no paid staff or permanent headquarters.
Annual Meetings: June

Colombian American Ass'n (1927)
111 Broadway, Suite 1408, New York NY 10006
Secy.-Treas.: Paul E. Calvet
Members: 66 companies, 41 individuals *Staff:* 3
Annual Budget: $25-50,000 *Tel:* (212) 233-7776
Hist. Note: Seeks to facilitate commerce and trade between the Republic of Colombia and the United States, to foster and advance cultural relations and good will between the two nations, and to encourage safe and sound investments. Membership: $150/yr.(individuals); $350/yr.(corporate).
Publication:
Colombian Newsletter. m.

Colonial Waterbird Society (1976)
Dept. of Biological Sciences, East Texas State University, Commerce TX 75428
Editor: James A. Kushlan
Members: 20 companies, 400 individuals
Annual Budget: under $10,000 *Tel:* (214) 886-5377
Hist. Note: Established in Charleston, S.C., the group consists of members concerned with the study, conservation and management of aquatic birds. Membership: $20/yr. (individual).
Publication:
Colonial Waterbirds. semi-a. adv.
Annual Meetings: Fall
1987-Halifax, NS
1988-Washington, DC

Color Ass'n of the United States (1915)
343 Lexington Ave., New York NY 10016
Exec. Director: Marielle Bancou
Members: 1,500 *Staff:* 10
Tel: (212) 683-9531
Hist. Note: Formerly (1954) The Textile Color Card Ass'n of the U.S., Inc. Membership: $150/yr. (individual), $420/yr. (company).
Publications:
CAUS Color Design//Newsletter.
Seasonal Color Forecasts. bi-a.
Standard Color Reference of America. Every 10 yrs.
Trend Reports
Annual Meetings: New York,NY

Color Marketing Group (1962)
1133 15th St., N.W., Suite 1000, Washington DC 20005
Managing Director: Everett R. Call
Members: 900 *Staff:* 2-5
Annual Budget: $250-500,000 *Tel:* (202) 429-9440
Hist. Note: Membership: $235/yr.
Semi-annual Meetings: Spring and Fall
1987-Miami, FL(Hyatt)/May 3-6/500

Colorado Ranger Horse Ass'n (1938)
1162 Chestnut, Muskogee OK 74403
Exec. Secretary: Nancy Van Orden
Members: 1,300 *Staff:* 1
Annual Budget: $10-25,000 *Tel:* (918) 683-2252
Hist. Note: Members are owners and breeders of Colorado Ranger horses. Records and registers horses that can trace unbroken and direct descent from one of two foundation sires, Patches 1 and Max 2. Membership: $10/yr.
Publication:
Rangerbred News. bi-m. adv.
Annual Meetings: September

Columbia Sheep Breeders Ass'n of America (1942)
Box 272, Upper Sandusky OH 43351
Exec. Secretary: Richard L. Gerber
Members: 1,500 *Staff:* 2-5
Annual Budget: $50-100,000 *Tel:* (614) 482-2608
Hist. Note: Breeders and fanciers of Columbia sheep. Member of the National Society of Livestock Record Associations.
Publication:
Speaking of Columbias. m. adv.

Combustion Institute (1954)
5001 Baum Blvd., Pittsburgh PA 15213
Exec. Secretary: Mrs. Marge Salamony
Members: 3,500-4,000 *Staff:* 2-5
Tel: (412) 687-1366
Hist. Note: An international organization with sections in several foreign countries, including Canada. Absorbed the Standing Committee on Combustion Symposia in 1954.
Publications:
Combustion and Flame. m.
Proceedings. bien.
Biennial meetings: even years

Comedy Writers Ass'n (1977)
GPO Box 3341, Brooklyn NY 11202
Director: Robert Makinson
Members: 110 individuals
Annual Budget: under $10,000 *Tel:* (718) 855-5057
Hist. Note: Membership open to anyone who can create comedy and market it. Membership: $12/yr.
Publications:
Latest Jokes. bi-m. adv.
Comedy Writer's Bulletin. a.
Comedy Buyer's Bulletin. a.

Comics Magazine Ass'n of America (1954)
60 East 42nd St., Suite 511, New York NY 10165
Exec. Secretary: J. Dudley Waldner, CAE
Members: 11 companies *Staff:* 2-5
Annual Budget: $50-100,000 *Tel:* (212) 682-8144
Hist. Note: Sponsors the Comics Code Authority, an agency for pre-publication evaluation of all editorial and advertising matter appearing in comic books.
Publication:
CMAA Newsletter. q.
Annual Meetings: Winter in New York, NY

Commercial Development Ass'n (1943)
1133 15th St., N.W., Suite 620, Washington DC 20005
Administrator: John H. Ganoe
Members: 900 *Staff:* 1
Annual Budget: $100-250,000 *Tel:* (202) 293-5910
Hist. Note: Formerly (1970) Commercial Chemical Development Ass'n. An association of individuals, primarily chemists, with primary responsibility for managing commercial development of industrial products in their companies. Founded in 1943 as the Technical Service Ass'n.
Publications:
CDA Reporter. bi-m.
Business Development Review. q.
Semi-annual Meetings: March and October

Commercial Food Equipment Service Ass'n (1963)
60 Revere Drive, Northbrook IL 60062
Exec. Director: Carla M. Helm
Members: 200 companies *Staff:* 2-5
Annual Budget: $50-100,000 *Tel:* (312) 480-9080
Hist. Note: Members are companies with a minimum of three years experience servicing or repairing food preparation equipment for hotels, restaurants or institutions.
Publication:
Newsletter. bi-m.
Semi-annual Meetings: May and November

Commercial Law League of America (1895)
222 West Adams St., Chicago IL 60606
Acting Exec. Director: Max Moses
Members: 5,500-6,000 *Staff:* 6-10
Annual Budget: $500-1,000,000 *Tel:* (312) 236-4942
Hist. Note: Membership: $120/yr.
Publications:
Commercial Law Journal. m. adv.
Commercial Law Bulletin. m. adv.
Annual Meetings: July/600-800
1987-Asheville, NC(Grove Park)
1988-Palm Beach, FL(Breakers)
1989-Maui, HI(Hyatt)
1990-Bermuda(Southampton Princess)

Commercial Refrigerator Manufacturers Ass'n (1933)
1101 Connecticut Ave., Suite 700, Washington DC 20036
Exec. Director: Robert T. Chancler
Members: 29 companies *Staff:* 2
Annual Budget: $25-50,000 *Tel:* (202) 857-1145

00111 12 05 86 1233

Hist. Note: Members include individuals and corporations who manufacture commercial refrigerators for sale in the U.S. and industry suppliers. Membership fee is determined by company's sales volume.
Publication:
Newsletter. q.
Semi-annual Meetings: January and June
1987-Palm Springs, CA(Jan.) and Washington, DC(June)

Commercial Travelers Insurance Federation (1900)
Hist. Note: Formerly Internat'l Federation of Commercial Travelers Insurance Organizations. Address unknown in 1984. Probably defunct.

Commission on Professionals in Science and Technology (1953)
1500 Massachusetts Ave., N.W., Suite 831, Washington DC 20005
Exec. Director: Betty M. Vetter
Members: 320 *Staff:* 2-5
Annual Budget: $100-250,000 *Tel:* (202) 223-6995
Hist. Note: Formerly (1986) Scientific Manpower Commission. A private non-profit corporation formed by fourteen scientific societies to focus attention on common manpower problems. Is concerned with the recruitment, training and utilization of scientific personnel. Membership: $45/yr. (individual); $65/yr. (institution); and $600/yr. (corporate and society).
Publications:
Scientific, Engineering, Technical Manpower Comments. 10/yr.
Professional Women & Minorities: A Manpower Data Resource Service. a.
Salaries of Scientists, Engineers & Technicians.
The Technological Marketplace.
Opportunities in Science and Engineering.
The International Flow of Scientific Talent.
The Science and Engineering Talent Pool.
Annual Meetings: Sept. in Washington, DC - Limited to Commissioners

Commission on Software Issues in the Eighties (1980)
Hist. Note: Ceased operations in 1985.

Commissioned Officers Ass'n of the United States Public Health Service (1947)
1400 Eye Street, N.W., Suite 725, Washington DC 20005
Exec. Director: William J. Lucca, Jr., CAE
Members: 7,000 *Staff:* 6-10
Annual Budget: $250-500,000 *Tel:* (202) 289-6400
Publications:
C.O.A. Bulletin. m.
COA Directory. a. adv.
Proceeding Program. a. adv.
Annual Meetings:
1987-Las Vegas, NV/Nov. 8-12
1988-Scottsdale, AZ(Camelback Inn)

Committee of Small Magazine Editors and Publishers
Hist. Note: Began using the acronym, COSMEP, with Internat'l Ass'n of Independent Publishers in 1986.

Committee on Federal Contracting Practices (1979)
Hist. Note: Absorbed by the Professional Services Council in 1983.

Commodity Exchange (1933)
Hist. Note: See New York Mercantile Exchange.

Common Carrier Conference-Irregular Route (1941)
Hist. Note: Merged July 1, 1983 with the Contract Carrier Conference to form the Interstate Carriers Conference.

Communications Marketing Ass'n (1974)
501 W. Algonquin Road, Arlington Heights IL 60005-4411
Exec. Secretary: Francis C. Rebedeau
Members: 175-200 companies *Staff:* 2-5
Annual Budget: $25-50,000 *Tel:* (312) 593-8360
Hist. Note: Independent manufacturers and independent sales rep companies of two-way mobile radio equipment.
Publication:
CMC Update. bi-m.
Annual Meetings: Always the weekend before Thanksgiving.

Communications Security Ass'n (1984)
655 15th St., N.W., Suite 320, Washington DC 20005
President: James A. Ross
Members: 250 individuals
Annual Budget: $10-25,000 *Tel:* (202) 639-4620
Hist. Note: Membership is open to all persons and businesses interested in the security of communications and information. Membership: $50/yr.
Publication:
COMSEC Letter. m.
Annual Meetings: December

Communications Soc.
Hist. Note: A subsidiary of the Institute of Electrical and Electronics Engineers. Membership in the Society, open only to IEEE members, includes a subscription to a technical periodical in the field published by IEEE. All administrative support is provided by IEEE.

Communications Workers of America (1938)
1925 K St. N. W., Washington DC 20006
President: Morton Bahr
Members: 650,000 *Staff:* 225-250
Annual Budget: over $5,000,000 *Tel:* (202) 728-2300
Hist. Note: Established in Chicago June 5, 1938 as the Nat'l Federation of Telephone Workers, it was named the Communications Workers of America in 1947; joined the Congress of Industrial Organizations in 1949 and merged with Telephone Workers Organizing Committee. It has a budget of about $10 million. Sponsors and supports the CWA-COPE Political Action Committee.
Publications:
CWA News. m.
CWA Newsletter. w.
Annual Meetings: Spring

Community Antenna Television Ass'n (1973)
Box 1005, Fairfax VA 22030-1005
President: Stephen R. Effros
Members: 2,000 systems *Staff:* 3
Annual Budget: $250-500,000 *Tel:* (703) 691-8875
Hist. Note: An association of over 2,000 systems serving 12,000,000 subscribers.
Publications:
CATAcable. m.
CATAssociate. q.

Community Ass'ns Institute (1973)
1423 Powhatan St., Alexandria VA 22314
Exec. V. President: C. James Dowden
Members: 7,000 firms and condominium associations *Staff:* 22
Annual Budget: $2-5,000,000 *Tel:* (703) 548-8600
Hist. Note: Sponsored by the Nat'l Ass'n of Home Builders and the Urban Land Institute. Composed of community and condominium owners, builders and managers. Absorbed (1975) Nat'l Federation of Condominium Ass'ns and the Condominium Research and Education Soc.
Publications:
CAI News. m. adv.
Community Association Law Reporter. m.
GAP Report. q.
Common Ground Magazine. bi-m. adv.
Annual Meetings: Spring
1987-San Diego, CA(Sheraton Harbor Island East)/April 8-12/4-500

Community Broadcasters Ass'n (1954)
Hist. Note: Dissolved in 1985.

Community College Journalism Ass'n (1968)
County College of Morris, Randolph NJ 07869
Exec. Secy-Treas.: Mary E. Hires
Members: 200 individuals *Staff:* 1
Annual Budget: under $10,000 *Tel:* (201) 361-5000
Hist. Note: Formerly the Junior College Journalism Association, membership is comprised of journalism instructors in community and junior colleges. Affiliated with the Association for Education in Journalism. Membership: $25/yr. (individual), $35/yr. (company).
Publications:
Community College Journalist. q. adv.
Newsletter. 3/yr.
Annual Meetings: With the Ass'n for Education in Journalism.
1987-San Antonio, TX(Trinity University)/Aug. 1-4

Community College Social Science Ass'n (1970)
Hist. Note: Became the Association for the Improvement of Teaching in 1983.

Community Design Center Directors Ass'n (1977)
c/o American Institute of Architects, 1735 New York Ave., N.W., Washington DC 20006
AIA Staff Coordinator: Bruce M. Kriviskey
Members: 55-60 *Staff:* 1
Annual Budget: under $10,000 *Tel:* (202) 626-7452
Hist. Note: Formed to strengthen goals and address common problems of Community Design Centers which are non-profit, community-based organizations that provide architectural design, planning and related technical assistance to community groups and individuals who could not afford such services. Affiliated with the American Institute of Architects.
Publications:
Newsletter.
Directory.
Annual Meetings: Washington, DC/AIA Headquarters/May

Community/Urban Symphony Orchestras
Hist. Note: A sub-group of the American Symphony Orchestra League without dues structure or separate headquarters.

Compact Disc Group (1984)
Hist. Note: Address unknown in 1987.

Comparative and Internat'l Education Soc. (1956)
College of Education, University of Akron, Akron OH 44325
General Secretary: Dr. Abdul A. Al-Rubaiy
Members: 2,500 *Staff:* 2-5
Annual Budget: $25-50,000 *Tel:* (216) 375-6953
Hist. Note: Formerly (1974) Comparative Education Soc. Membership: $28/yr.(individual); $53/yr.(organization).
Publications:
C.I.E.S. Newsletter. q.
Comparative Education Review. q. adv.

Competitive Telecommunications Ass'n (1981)
120 Maryland Ave., N.E., Washington DC 20002
Exec. Director: Jerry McAndrews
Members: 150 companies *Staff:* 8
Annual Budget: $250-500,000 *Tel:* (202) 546-9022
Hist. Note: Members are retailers and manufacturers of long distance telephone equipment. Formed by a merger of Ass'n of Long Distance Telephone Companies and the American Council for Competitive Telecommunications in 1984. Membership: $1,000-36,000/yr. (carriers, based on revenues); $2,500- 10,000/yr. (suppliers, based on revenues).

Components, Hybrids and Manufacturing Technology Soc.
Hist. Note: A subsidiary of the Institute of Electrical and Electronics Engineers. Membership in the Society, open only to IEEE members, includes subscription to a technical periodical in the field published by IEEE. All administrative support provided by IEEE.

Composite Can and Tube Institute (1933)
1742 N St., N.W., Washington DC 20036
Exec. V. President: Robert W. Foster
Members: 65-70 companies *Staff:* 2-5
Annual Budget: $100-250,000 *Tel:* (202) 223-4840
Hist. Note: Formed in New York City as the National Fibre Can and Tube Institute, it assumed its present name in 1970. Manufacturers of composite cans, tubes, spools, cores, ribbon blocks, mailing packages, cones, and bobbins. Membership Fee: Based on sales volume.
Publications:
Cantube Bulletin. m. adv.
Safety Bulletin. q.
Industry Directory. a.
Annual Meetings: Spring/100
1987-Charleston, SC(Kiawah Island)/May 17-19
1988-Phoenix, AZ(Biltmore)/May 22-24
1989-Key Largo, FL(Ocean Reef Club)/May 21-23

Composites Group of SME
Hist. Note: A special interest group within the Soc. of Manufacturing Engineers CoG/SME is concerned with the intergration of fiber reinforced plastics/composites into the manufacturing sector.

Composites Institute (1946)
355 Lexington Ave., New York NY 10017
Manager: Catherine A. Randazzo
Members: 500 individuals, 400 companies *Staff:* 6
Annual Budget: $500-1,000,000 *Tel:* (212) 503-0600
Hist. Note: Formerly (1986) Reinforced Plastics/Composites Institute. Division of the Soc. of the Plastics Industry. Members are molders and fabricators of glass and other fibre-reinforced plastics as well as materials suppliers.
Publication:
Proceedings. a.
Annual Meetings: Winter/3,000
1987-Cincinnati, OH(Convention Ctr.)/Feb. 2-6
1988-Cincinnati, OH/Feb. 1-5

Compressed Air and Gas Institute (1915)
1230 Keith Bldg., Cleveland OH 44115-2180
Secy.-Treas.: John H. Addington
Members: 60 companies *Staff:* 2-5
Annual Budget: $250-500,000 *Tel:* (216) 241-7333
Hist. Note: The Compressed Air and Gas Institute is a non-profit organization of companies which manufacture air and gas compressors or pneumatic tools and machinery; products which have many applications world-wide in construction, manufacturing, mining and the process and natural gas industries. The forerunner of the present Institute, the Compressed Air Society, was formed in 1915 to provide an instrument for solving the problems common to all member companies and to promote the industry. In 1933 the group became the Compressed Air Institute. The name Compressed Air and Gas Institute was adopted in 1945.

Compressed Gas Ass'n (1913)
1235 Jeff Davis Highway, Arlington VA 22202
President: Bernhard K. Kuehn
Members: 300 companies *Staff:* 11-15
Annual Budget: $500-1,000,000 *Tel:* (703) 979-0900
Hist. Note: Established as the Compressed Gas Manufacturers Ass'n, it assumed its present name in 1949; absorbed the Internat'l Acetylene Ass'n. CGA member companies include manufacturers, distributors and transporters of compressed, liquefied and cryogenic gases, as well as manufacturers of valves, cylinders, transportation equipment and other products related to the compressed gas industry. CGA's main concern is the promotion of safety in the compressed gas industry.
Publications:
Compressions. m.
List of Publications. a.
Annual Meetings: January

00112 12 05 86 1233

1987-Chicago, IL(Hyatt Regency)/Jan. 25-27
1988-Boca Raton, FL(Hotel & Club)/Jan. 17-19
1989-New Orleans, LA(Fairmont)/Jan. 22-24
1990-Washington, DC(JW Marriott)/Jan. 21-23
1991-San Diego, CA(Sheraton Harbour Island)/Jan. 20-22
1992-Orlando, FL(Buena Vista Palace)/Jan. 26-28

Computer Aided Manufacturing-Internat'l (1972)
611 Ryan Plaza Drive, Suite 1107, Arlington TX 76011
President: William A. Carter
Members: 200 companies and organizations *Staff:* 25
Annual Budget: $1-2,000,000 *Tel:* (817) 265-5328
Hist. Note: Members are companies throughout the world interested in computer-assisted manufacturing and the general field of robotics. About two-thirds of the membership is from the United States. Membership: $8,500/yr.
Publication:
CAM-I News Alert. bi-m.

Computer and Automated Systems Ass'n of SME (1975)
Box 930, One SME Dr., Dearborn MI 48121
Asst. Manager: Sally Davis
Members: 12,000 individuals, 124 companies *Staff:* 6
Tel: (313) 271-1500
Hist. Note: The CASA/SME was founded in 1975 to provide comprehensive coverage of computers and automation in the overall advancement of manufacturing. Since that time, CASA/SME has become an organizational home for engineers, managers, and other professionals involved with computers and automated systems. CASA/SME is applicaion-oriented and addresses all phases of research, design, installation, operation, and maintenance of the total manufacturing enterprise. With a goal of continuing education for manufacturing engineers and managers, CASA/ SME actitities include major conference and expositions, short courses local chapter participation, and publications. Membership: $48/yr. (individual), $163/yr. (company).
Publications:
CASA/SME Newsletter. m.
Bibliography of CASA/SME Related Technical Papers.
CIM Series Booklets. irreg.
Annual Meetings: Fall-AUTOFACT Conference and Exposition in Detroit, MI at Cobb Hall

Computer and Business Equipment Manufacturers Ass'n (1916)
311 First St., N.W., Suite 500, Washington DC 20001
President: Vico E. Henriques
Members: 35-40 companies *Staff:* 25-30
Annual Budget: $2-5,000,000 *Tel:* (202) 737-8888
Hist. Note: Formerly (1962) Office Equipment Manufacturers Institute and (1973) Business Equipment Manufacturers Ass'n. Serves as Secretariat for the American National Standards Institute Committee on Information Processing Systems (X3). Acts on domestic and international issues that affect the high-technology industry.
Semi-annual Meetings: Spring and Fall
1987-Washington, DC(Sheraton Grand)/April 7-8
1987-Napa, CA(Silverado)/Oct. 18-21

Computer and Communications Industry Ass'n (1972)
666 11th St., N.W., Washington DC 20001
President: A.G.W. Biddle
Members: 70 companies *Staff:* 11-15
Annual Budget: $500-1,000,000
Hist. Note: Formerly (1976) Computer Industry Ass'n. CCIA is comprised of manufacturers and providers of computer information processing and telecommunications-related products and services; companies are represented by senior executives. It represents the interests of its members in domestic and foreign trade, capital formation and tax policy, Federal procurement policy and industry standards.
Publications:
CEO Report. semi-m.
International Trade Report. m.
Federal Procurement Policy Update. m.
Telecommunications Update. m.
Triannual Membership Meetings:

Computer Dealers and Lessors Ass'n (1981)
1212 Potomac St., N.W., Washington DC 20007
President: James F. Benton
Members: 312 *Staff:* 2-5
Annual Budget: $250-500,000 *Tel:* (202) 333-0102
Hist. Note: Buyers, lessors and sellers of computers. Formed by a merger of the Computer Dealers Association (established 1972) and the Computer Lessors Association (established 1968).
Publications:
CDLA Newsletter. q.
News Digest. m.
Semi-annual Meetings: Spring and Fall

Computer Law Ass'n (1971)
9520 Lee Highway, Suite A, Fairfax VA 22031
Exec. Director: Barbara Fieser
Members: 1,200 individuals *Staff:* 1
Annual Budget: $25-50,000 *Tel:* (703) 591-7014
Hist. Note: Formerly (1973) Computer Lawyers Group and (1975) Computer Lawyers Ass'n. Incorporated in Jan., 1973. Members are concerned with legal problems arising from the invention, evolution, production, marketing, acquisition and use of computer-communications technology. Member of the Nat'l Commission on Software Issues in the Eighties. Membership: $50/year.
Publications:
Computer Law Ass'n Newsletter. q.
International Update Newsletter. q.
Membership Directory. a.
Semi-Annual Meetings: March and October
1987-Chicago, IL/March 5-6

Computer Measurement Group (1969)
6397 Little River Turnpike, Alexandria VA 22312
Admin. Asst.: Vicki Garrett
Members: 5-6,000 *Staff:* 2
Tel: (703) 354-3306
Hist. Note: Membership: $55/year.
Publications:
CMG Proceedings.a.
CMG Transactions.q.
Annual Meetings: First week in December.

Computer Micrographics Technology
1800 Pickwick Ave., Glenview IL 60025
Exec. Director: John C. Mommsen, Jr.
Members: 20 companies; 800 individuals *Staff:* 2-5
Annual Budget: $25-50,000 *Tel:* (312) 724-7700
Publication:
Comtec Newsletter. 3/yr. adv.
Annual Meetings: February

Computer Security Institute (1974)
360 Church St., Northboro MA 01532
Exec. Director: John C. O'Mara
Members: 3,000 *Staff:* 6-10
Annual Budget: $1-2,000,000 *Tel:* (617) 393-2600
Hist. Note: Membership services designed for data processing managers, security officers, auditors and others with an interest in computer security. Membership: $95/yr.
Publications:
Computer Security Handbook.
Computer Security Journal. semi-a.
Computer Security Newsletter. bi-m.
Computer Security Buyers Guide.
Semi-Annual Meetings: July and November
1987-Chicago, IL/July 12-15
1987-Anaheim, CA/Nov. 8-12

Computer Soc. of the Institute of Electrical and Electronics Engineers (1952)
1730 Massachusetts Ave., N.W., Washington DC 20036-1903
Exec. Director: Dr. T. Michael Elliott
Members: 90,000 individuals *Staff:* 35-40
Annual Budget: over $5,000,000 *Tel:* (202) 371-0101
Hist. Note: The largest technical society within the Institute of Electrical and Electronics Engineers and the world's largest association of computer professionals. Promotes the development of information processing. A founding member and cooperating partner of the American Federation of Information Processing Socs. and the Institute for Certification of Computer Professionals. Has an annual budget of over $14 million. Membership: $39/yr. (Soc. membership only); $82/yr. (IEEE and Soc. membership).
Publications:
Computer Magazine. m. adv.
IEEE Computer Graphics & Applications. m. adv.
MICRO. bi-m. adv.
Transactions on Computers. m.
Transactions of Pattern Analysis and Machine Intelligence. bi-m.
Transactions on Software Engineering. m.
Design and Test. bi-m. adv.
SOFTWARE. bi-m. adv.
EXPERT. q. adv.
Lightwave Technology. m.
Robotics and Automation. q.
Journal of Solid State Circuits. q.
Holds three major conferences a year: Compcon Spring in San Francisco,
CA, Compcon Fall in Washington, DC, and Compsac in Chicago, IL.

Computer Use in Social Services Network (1981)
P.O. Box 19129, Arlington TX 76019-0129
Coordinator: Dick Schoech
Members: 200 companies; 800 individuals
Annual Budget: under $10,000 *Tel:* (817) 273-3964
Hist. Note: Members share expertise and resources in the application of computers in human service settings. Provides automated skill bank and software clearinghouse, special interest groups in education and hospital services, and an electronic network. Membership: $10/yr.(individual); $15/yr.(institution).
Publication:
CUSS Network Newsletter. q. adv.

Computerized Radiology Soc. (1977)
Georgetown Univ. Medical Center, 3900 Resevoir Road., N.W., Washington DC 20007
Exec. Director: Dr. Robert S. Ledley
Members: 300 *Staff:* 1
Annual Budget: under $10,000 *Tel:* (202) 625-2121
Hist. Note: Members are radiologists interested in using the computer to scan X-rays of selected planes of the body.
Publication:
Computerized Radiology. bi-m.
Annual Meetings: With American Ass'n for the Advancement of Science

Computerized Tomography Soc.
Hist. Note: Became the Computerized Radiology Society in 1984.

Concert Music Broadcasters Ass'n (1969)
c/o WCLV, 26501 Emery Industrial Pkwy., Cleveland OH 44128
Editor: C.K. Patrick
Members: 100-125 individuals *Staff:* 1
Annual Budget: $10-25,000 *Tel:* (216) 464-0900
Hist. Note: Organization of radio stations playing classical music on a commercial basis more than twenty hours per week. Has no permanent headquarters or paid staff. Mail to the above address will be forwarded.
Publication:
CMBN Directory. a.
Annual Meetings: First Week in May

Concord Grape Ass'n (1966)
5775 Peachtree-Dunwoody Rd., Suite 500D, Atlanta GA 30342
President: Robert H. Kellen
Members: 13 *Staff:* 3
Tel: (404) 252-3663
Hist. Note: Founded as the Concord Grape Council, it became the American Concord Grape Association in 1974 and assumed its present name in 1980.
Annual Meetings:
1987-Palm Beach, FL/March 22

Concrete Pipe Ass'n (1907)
8320 Old Courthouse Rd., Suite 201, Vienna VA 22180
President: Richard E. Barnes, CAE
Members: 2 Associations *Staff:* 1
Annual Budget: $1-2,000,000 *Tel:* (703) 821-1990
Hist. Note: Formed to handle matters of common concern to American Concrete Pipe and American Concrete Pressure Pipe Ass'ns.
Publication:
Newsletter. m.
Annual Meetings: Spring
1987-Colorado Springs, CO(Broadmoor)/March 28-April 2

Concrete Plant Manufacturers Bureau (1963)
900 Spring St., Silver Spring MD 20910
Exec. Secretary: Terrence J. Keenan
Members: 7 companies *Staff:* 2-5
Annual Budget: $25-50,000 *Tel:* (301) 587-1400
Hist. Note: An affiliate of the Nat'l Ready Mix Concrete Ass'n. Primary purpose is developing engineering standards,
Annual Meetings: Spring

Concrete Reinforcing Steel Institute (1924)
933 North Plum Grove Road, Schaumburg IL 60195
Exec. V. President: Victor A. Walther, Jr.
Members: 245 *Staff:* 15
Annual Budget: $1-2,000,000 *Tel:* (312) 490-1700
Hist. Note: Firms engaged in the production and fabrication of reinforcing bars and accessories. Absorbed the Associated Reinforcing Bar Producers in 1982 and the Fusion Bonded Coaters Ass'n in 1985.
Publication:
Shop Talk. q.
Annual Meetings:
1987-Napa, CA(Silverado Country Club)/May 10-14
1988-Hot Springs, VA(The Homestead)/May 2-6
1989-Palm Springs, CA(America's Canyon Hotel)/April 23-28

Concrete Sawing and Drilling Ass'n (1972)
6077 Roswell Road, N.E., Suite 205, Atlanta GA 30328
Exec. Director: Ed Thorn
Members: 200 companies *Staff:* 2-5
Annual Budget: $50-100,000 *Tel:* (404) 257-1177
Hist. Note: Contractors of concrete sawing and drilling and producers of diamond sawblades and drills.
Publication:
Concrete Openings Newsletter. q.
Annual Meetings: Winter
1987-Palm Springs, CA/Feb. 26-March 1

Conductors Guild
Hist. Note: A sub-group of the American Symphony Orchestra League without dues structure or separate headquarters.

Conference Board of Major Printers (1976)
1730 North Lynn St., Arlington VA 22209
Exec. Director: Laura M. Yoder
Members: 50 companies *Staff:* 1
Annual Budget: $100-250,000 *Tel:* (703) 841-4803
Hist. Note: A section of Printing Industries of America composed of representatives of large printers. Collects market statistics, prepares special studies, etc.
Publications:
Index of Sales Activity. m.
Newsline. m.
Update. m.

Conference Board of the Mathematical Sciences (1960)
1529 18th St., N.W., Washington DC 20036
Admin. Officer: Peter L. Renz
Members: 14 professional societies *Staff:* 2
Annual Budget: $25-50,000 *Tel:* (202) 293-1170
Hist. Note: A group of professional societies formed to present their point of view to the Government, CBMS consists of: American Mathematical Soc., Ass'n for Symbolic Logic, Institute of Mathematical Statistics, Mathematical Ass'n of

00113 12 05 86 1233

America, Nat'l Council of Teachers of Mathematics, Soc. for Industrial and Applied Mathematics, American Mathematical Ass'n of Two-Year Colleges, American Statistical Ass'n, Ass'n for Women in Mathematics, Nat'l Council of Supervisors of Mathematics, Operations Research Soc. of America, Soc. of Actuaries, Institute of Management Sciences and Ass'n of State Supervisors of Mathematics.
Semi-annual Meetings: May and December/35
1987-Washington, DC

Conference for Secondary School English Department Chairpersons (1970)
1111 Kenyon Road, Urbana IL 61801
Secy.-Treas.: John C. Maxwell
Members: 1,300 *Staff:* 1
Annual Budget: under $10,000 *Tel:* (217) 328-3870
Hist. Note: A subsidiary of the National Council of Teachers of English, to which all members of the Conference must first belong, and which provides administrative support. Membership: $45/year.
Publication:
CSSEDC Quarterly. q.
Annual Meetings: Fall, with the Nat'l Council of Teachers of English.

Conference Group on German Politics (1968)
1321 N.W. 49th Terrace, Gainesville FL 32605
Contact: David Conradt
Members: 300-350
Annual Budget: under $10,000
Hist. Note: Founded in 1968 by a group of American social scientists as an association of scholars dealing with German politics, both foreign and domestic.
Publication:
CCGP Newsletter. q.
Annual Meetings: Fall

Conference of Actuaries in Public Practice (1950)
500 Park Blvd., Itasca IL 60143
Director of Administration: Claudia Krueger
Members: 900 *Staff:* 2
Annual Budget: $100-250,000 *Tel:* (312) 773-8140
Hist. Note: Members include consulting and government actuaries. Affiliated with the American Academy of Actuaries. Awards the designations "FCA," "MCA" and "ACA" (Fellow, Member and Associate of the Conference of Actuaries). Membership: $135/yr.(fellow); $110/yr.(member); $85/yr.(associate).
Publication:
The Proceedings. a.
Annual Meetings: Fall/300
1987-Tarpon Springs, FL(Innisbrook)/Oct. 5-7
1988-San Francisco, CA(Embarcadero)/Nov. 1-3
1989-Hot Springs, VA(Homestead)/Sept. 25-27
1990-Palm Desert, CA(Marriott's Rancho Las Palmas)/Oct. 22-24
1991-Colorado Springs, CO(Broadmoor)/Sept. 30-Oct. 2

Conference of American Renting and Leasing Assn's (1978)
2011 Eye St., N.W., 5th Floor, Washington DC 20006
Exec. Director: Roger A. Murch
Members: 35-40 *Staff:* 2-4
Annual Budget: under $10,000 *Tel:* (202) 223-3217
Hist. Note: Sole Responsibility: Publishes the annual Directory, The Vehicle.
Publication:
The Vehicle. a.

Conference of American Small Business Organizations (1942)
Hist. Note: A group of companies and individuals interested in defending the free enterprise system. Merged with the National Small Business Association in 1982.

Conference of Casualty Insurance Companies (1930)
Box 68695, 3707 Woodview Trace, Indianapolis IN 46268
Exec. V. President: Larry Kahl
Members: 122 companies *Staff:* 2-5
Annual Budget: $100-250,000 *Tel:* (317) 872-4061
Hist. Note: Formerly (1977) Conference of Mutual Casualty Companies. Members are insurance companies active in writing casualty coverages. CCIC is an education organization only: sponsors eight departmental and one management seminar each year and a "Claim Arbitration Program." Management and offices provided by the Nat'l Ass'n of Mutual Insurance Companies. Membership Fee: Based on premiums written.
Publications:
CCIC Newsletter.
Directory and Yearbook. a.
Annual Meetings: June
1987-Asheville, NC(Grove Park Inn)/June 21-25

Conference of Chief Justices (1949)
Nat'l Center for State Courts, 300 Newport Ave., Williamsburg VA 23187-8798
Secretariat: Brenda A. Williams
Members: 57 *Staff:* 1
Annual Budget: under $10,000 *Tel:* (804) 253-2000
Hist. Note: Administration provided by the Nat'l Center for State Courts.
Annual Meetings: Summer Membership Meeting
1987-Rapid City, SD/Aug. 2-6
1988-Portland, ME/July 31-Aug. 4
1989-Lake Tahoe, NV/Aug.

Conference of Educational Administrators Serving the Deaf (1868)
Box 2016 Columbia MD 21045

Members: 800 *Staff:* 8
Annual Budget: $50-100,000 *Tel:* (301) 461-9988
Hist. Note: CEASD's purpose is to promote effective management of educational programs for the deaf. Orginially known as the Ass'n of Superintendents and Principals, a splinter group from the Convention of American Instructors of the Deaf (established 1850). Formerly (until 1980) known as the Conference of Executives of American Schools for the Deaf, Inc.
Publications:
American Annals of the Deaf. 5/yr. adv.

Annual Meetings: In odd years with Convention of American Instructors of the Deaf
1987-Santa Fe, NM
1989-San Diego, CA

Conference of Local Environmental Health Administrators (1938)
Hist. Note: Became the Nat'l Conference of Local Environmental Health Administrators in 1983.

Conference of Major Superiors of Men, U.S.A. (1956)
8808 Cameron St., Silver Spring MD 20910
Exec. Director: Roland Faley, T.O.R.
Members: 250-275 *Staff:* 2-5
Annual Budget: $100-250,000 *Tel:* (301) 588-4030
Hist. Note: Formerly the Conference of Major Superiors of Men's Institutes. Members are supervisors of the various Roman Catholic religious orders.

Conference of Nat'l Park Concessioners (1919)
Box 29041, Phoenix AZ 85038
Chairman: Rex G. Maughan
Members: 125 *Staff:* 1
Annual Budget: $50-100,000 *Tel:* (602) 967-6006
Hist. Note: Individuals and companies holding contracts with the Department of the Interior to provide goods and services to visitors to U.S. national parks. Established in 1919. Incorporated in 1975. Supports the Concessioners Political Action Committee.
Semi-annual Meetings: Washington, DC/March & National Park/Oct.

Conference of Public Health Laboratorians (1985)
Box 9083, Austin TX 78766
Secy.-Treas.: Charles E. Sweet
Members: 286 *Staff:* 1
Annual Budget: under $10,000 *Tel:* (512) 458-7318
Hist. Note: Originally Conference of State and Provincial Public Health Laboratory Directors. Most recently (1985) Conference of Public Health Laboratory Directors. Membership includes state health department laboratory directors and directors of military, hospital, and other laboratories. Has no paid staff. Membership: $10/yr.
Publication:
Newsletter (for members only).
Annual Meetings: With the American Public Health Ass'n

Conference of Public Health Laboratory Directors (1920)
Hist. Note: Changed its name to Conference of Public Health Laboratorians (1985).

Conference of Public Health Veterinarians (1946)
Dept. of Health, Room 701, 109 Governor St., Richmond VA 23219
Secretary: Suzanne R. Jenkins
Members: 150-170
Annual Budget: under $10,000 *Tel:* (804) 786-6261
Hist. Note: Seeks to amalgamate into one organization all persons who are professionally engaged or actively interested in the application of veterinary medicine to the prevention of disease, protection of life, and the promotion of the well-being and efficiency of man.
Publication:
Newsletter. q.
Annual Meetings: With the American Veterinary Medical Ass'n

Conference of Radiation Control Program Directors (1968)
71 Fountain Place, Frankfort KY 40601
Exec. Secretary: Charles M. Hardin
Members: 380 individuals *Staff:* 6
Annual Budget: $500-1,000,000 *Tel:* (502) 227-4543
Hist. Note: Members are or have been employed by state, local or foreign radiation control programs. The conference provides a forum for the exchange of information between radiation control programs of states, and between the states and federal government. Membership: $10-25/yr.
Publication:
Newsletter. q.
Annual Meetings: Spring
1987-Boise, ID(Red Lion Inn)/May 18-21
1988-Nashville, TN/May 23-26

Conference of Research Workers in Animal Diseases (1920)
Ohio Ag. Res. & Develop. Center, Wooster OH 44691
Secy.-Treas.: Dr. Erwin M. Kohler
Members: 600 *Staff:* 1
Annual Budget: under $10,000 *Tel:* (216) 264-1021
Hist. Note: Approximately 300 presentations of unpublished research results of studies in animal heath and disease are presented annually. Membership: $5/yr.
Annual Meetings: Fall-Chicago(Americana Congress)/500
1987-November 15-16
1988-November 8-9
1989-November 14-15

Conference of State and Territorial Directors of PublicHealth Education (1946)
Office of Health Education, VA Dept. of Health, Rm. 100 Governor St., Richmond VA 23219
President: Linda Redman, MPH
Members: 52 *Staff:* 1
Annual Budget: 1
Hist. Note: Members are director of state public health education programs. Affiliated with the Ass'n of State and Territorial Health Officials.
Publications:
Conference Call. q.
Proceeding. a.
Roster of Members. a.

Conference of State and Territorial Epidemiologists
Hist. Note: Became the Council of State and Territorial Epidemiologists in 1986.

Conference of State Bank Supervisors (1902)
1015 18th St., N.W., Suite 606, Washington DC 20036
Exec. V. President: Dr. Lawrence E. Kreider
Members: 54 *Staff:* 18
Annual Budget: $2-5,000,000 *Tel:* (202) 296-2840
Hist. Note: Founded in 1902 as the Nat'l Ass'n of Supervisors of State Banks. Current name assumed in 1970. The professional organization of the state bank regulators of the 50 States, Guam, Puerto Rico, the Virgin Islands, and Washington, DC. Associate membership offered, to state-chartered commercial and mutual savings banks.
Publications:
A Profile of State Chartered Banking. bi-a.
Capitol Comments. m.
The Supervisor. m.
Annual Meetings: Spring
1987-San Diego, CA(Del Coronado)/April 5-7
1988-Orlando, FL(Contemporary)/April 10-12
1989-Colorado Springs, CO(Broadmoor)/May 7-10

Conference of State Court Adminstrators (1955)
Nat'l Center for State Courts, 300 Newport Ave., Williamsburg VA 23187-8798
Director of Secretariat Services: Marilyn M. Roberts
Members: 55 *Staff:* 2-5
Annual Budget: $50-100,000 *Tel:* (804) 253-2000
Hist. Note: Established as Nat'l Conference of Court Administrative Officers, it became Nat'l Conference of State Court Administrators in 1972 and assumed its present name in 1975. Administration provided by Nat'l Center for State Courts.
Annual Meetings: Late Summer
1987-Rapid City, SD/Aug. 2-6
1988-Portland, ME/July 31-Aug. 4
1989-Lake Tahoe, NV/Aug.

Conference of State Manufacturers' Ass'ns
Hist. Note: Has no dues structure, paid staff or permanent address. Officers rotate annually. Mail sent to the National Association of Manufacturers will be forwarded as necessary.

Conference of State Sanitary Engineers (1920)
P.O. Box 2071, Westminster MD 21157-9071
Exec. Director: Betty L. Maugans
Members: 150-175 *Staff:* 2
Annual Budget: $25-50,000 *Tel:* (301) 876-2584
Hist. Note: Established May 20, 1920 to coordinate the public health engineering activities of the official state and territorial health oganizations. Members are officials of state agencies concerned with environmental matters. Membership: $40/yr.
Publication:
CSSE News. q.

Conference on College Composition and Communication (1949)
1111 Kenyon Rd., Urbana IL 61801
Exec. Secy.-Treas.: John C. Maxwell
Members: 6,900 individuals, 1,500 institutions *Staff:* 1
Annual Budget: $100-250,000 *Tel:* (217) 328-3870
Hist. Note: A subsidiary of the National Council of Teachers of English, to which members of the Conference must first belong and which provides administrative support. Members are teachers of freshman English at the college level. Membership: $43/year.
Publication:
College Composition and Communication. a. adv.
Annual Meetings: Spring/3,000, and Fall with the Nat'l Council of Teachers of English.
1987-Atlanta, GA(Peachtree Plaza)/March 19-21
1988-St. Louis, MO(Clarion Hotel)/March 17-19

00114 12 05 86 1233

1989-Seattle, WA(Sheraton)/March 15-18
1990-Chicago, IL(Palmer House)/March 14-17

Conference on Consumer Finance Law (1927)
200 Beneficial Center, Peapack NJ 07977
Editor: Bernice B. Stein
Members: 1,100-1,200 lawyers
Annual Budget: $25-50,000 *Tel:* (201) 781-3729
Hist. Note: Formerly (1984) Conference on Personal Finance Law. The objects of the Conference are to encourage research in the small loan and consumer finance field, to promote by discussion and publication the improvement of legal procedures affecting small loans and installment finance, and to afford a forum at which interested lawyers may meet and exchange opinions.
Publication:
Consumer Finance Law. q.
Annual Meetings: With the American Bar Ass'n in August
1987-San Francisco, CA
1988-Toronto, Ontario
1989-Honolulu, HI

Conference on Data Systems Languages (1959)
29 Hartwell Ave., Lexington MA 02173
Chairman: Jan Prokop
Members: 150-200 individuals *Staff:* 1
Annual Budget: under $10,000 *Tel:* (617) 860-6350
Hist. Note: Established May 21, 1959, with the support of the Pentagon, to develop COBOL. CODASYL is an entirely voluntary organization whose purpose is to develop specifications for languages used in computer applications with the intention that these languages will be "common across the machines of different vendors." These specifications are published as "Journals of Development" and submitted as candidates for national and international standardization. Member of the Commission on Software Issues in the Eighties.
Publications:
Journal of Development for:
COBOL. irreg.
Common Operating System Control Language. irreg.
Data Description Language. irreg.
Fortran Data Manipulation Language. irreg.

Conference on English Education (1963)
1111 Kenyon Rd., Urbana IL 61801
Secy.-Treas.: John C. Maxwell
Members: 1,500 *Staff:* 1
Annual Budget: under $10,000 *Tel:* (217) 328-3870
Hist. Note: A subsidiary of the National Council of Teachers of English, to which all members of the Conference must first belong and which provides administrative support. Members are state and local supervisors of English instruction and college English education teachers. Membership: $47/year.
Publication:
English Education. a. adv.
Semi-Annual Meetings: In the Fall with the Nat'l Council of Teachers of English and in the Spring

1987-Louisville, KY(Galt House)/March 26-28
1988-Boston, MA(Marriott Copley Plaza)/March 23-26
1989-Charleston, SC(Omni Charleston Plaza)/April 5-8

Conference on Personal Finance Law (1927)
Hist. Note: Became the Conference on Consumer Finance Law in 1984.

Congress of County Medical Societies (1965)
P.O. Box 12489, Oklahoma City OK 73157
President: Dr. Francis A. Davis
Members: 155 county medical societies
Tel: (405) 943-2318
Publication:
Private Practice Magazine. m. adv.

Congress of Independent Unions (1958)
303 Ridge St., Alton IL 62002
President: R. Richard Davis
Members: 10 independent labor unions *Staff:* 6-10
Annual Budget: $250-500,000 *Tel:* (618) 462-2447
Annual Meetings: October/November

Congress of Lung Ass'n Staff (1912)
1740 Broadway, New York NY 10019
Exec. Director: Bethmarie Fahey
Members: 600-700 *Staff:* 2-5
Annual Budget: $100-250,000 *Tel:* (212) 315-8700
Hist. Note: Formerly Nat'l Conference of Tuberculosis Workers, and (1973) Nat'l Respiratory Disease Conference. Members are executives and professional staff of voluntary lung associations.
Publication:
CLAS Communicator. m.
Annual Meetings: May
1987-New Orleans, LA(Marriott)
1988-Las Vegas, NV(Hilton)
1989-Cincinnati, OH
1990-Boston, MA

Congress of Neurological Surgeons (1951)
Univ. of Southern California Med Sch., 1200 N. State St., Suite 5046, Los Angeles CA 90033
Secretary: Steven Giannotta, M.D.
Members: 3,000 *Staff:* 1
Annual Budget: $500-1,000,000 *Tel:* (213) 226-7421
Hist. Note: A professional society with members both from the United States and a number of foreign countries. Membership: $75/yr.
Publication:
Neurosurgery. m.
Annual Meetings: Fall
1987-Baltimore, MD/Oct. 9-14
1988-Seattle, WA/Oct. 9-14

Congress on Research in Dance (1965)
Dept. of Dance Education, NYU, 35 West 4th St., Room 675, New York NY 10003
Admin. Secretary: Jennifer Corrie
Members: 500 individuals; 500 institutions *Staff:* 1
Annual Budget: $25-50,000 *Tel:* (212) 598-3459
Hist. Note: Formerly (until 1979) known as the Committee on Research in Dance. Dance scholars who conduct research in various areas of dance and dance-related fields. Membership: $30/yr. (individual); $54/yr. (organization/company)
Publications:
Dance Research Annual. a.
Dance Research Journal. semi-a. adv.
Newsletter. semi-a.
Annual Meetings:
1987-New York, NY/700

Conservation Education Ass'n (1947)
University of Wisconsin, Green Bay WI 54301
Exec. Secretary: Dennis Bryan
Members: 400 *Staff:* 2
Annual Budget: $10-25,000 *Tel:* (414) 465-2397
Hist. Note: Formerly (1953) Nat'l Committee on Policies in Conservation Education. Promotes environmental conservation education for people of all ages. Has no paid staff. Membership: $20/yr.(individual); $35/yr.(organization).
Publication:
CEA Newsletter. q.
Annual Meetings: August/250
1987-Golden Pond, KY(TVA/Land Between the Lakes)/Aug. 2-6
1988-Dingsmon Ferry, PA(Pocono Environ. Ed. Center)/July 31-Aug. 4

Conservative Orthopedics Internat'l Ass'n (1982)
1811 Monroe, Dearborn MI 48124
President: Dr. Stephen R. Castor
Members: 2,000 individuals *Staff:* 3
Annual Budget: $500-1,000,000 *Tel:* (313) 563-0360
Hist. Note: Doctors of medicine, chiropractic, osteopathy, and other individuals interested in non-surgical treatment for the prevention and rehabilitation of musculoskeletal related disorders. Membership: $100/yr.
Publications:
Bulletin. bi-m.
Newsletter. m.
Annual Meetings: Semi-annual Meetings

Consolidated Tape Ass'n (1974)
c/o New York Stock Exchange, 11 Wall St., New York NY 10005
Administrator: J.F. Cipriano
Members: 16 individuals, 8 companies *Staff:* 1
Annual Budget: under $10,000 *Tel:* (212) 656-2052
Hist. Note: Members are interested in melding the reporting from the various stock exchanges.

Consortium of University Film Centers (1971)
330 University Library, Kent State Univ., Kent OH 44242
Exec. Director: John P. Kerstetter
Members: 200 *Staff:* 1
Annual Budget: $10-25,000 *Tel:* (216) 672-3456
Hist. Note: Members are college and university film/video rental librarians, film/video producers, distributors and individuals.
Publication:
CUFC Leader Newsletter. bi-a.
Semi-annual meetings: Winter and Fall
1987-Atlanta, GA/Feb. 25-28

Construction Equipment Advertisers and Public Relations Council (1939)
111 East Wisconsin Ave., Milwaukee WI 53202
Chairman: Greg Sitek
Members: 200 *Staff:* 2
Annual Budget: under $10,000 *Tel:* (414) 272-0943
Hist. Note: Became a branch of the Construction Industry Manufacturers Ass'n in 1976. Membership consists of individuals concerned with marketing, promotion or advertising of construction equipment.
Semi-annual: Spring and Fall

Construction Equipment Council
Hist. Note: A division of the Farm and Industrial Equipment Institute.

Construction Financial Management Ass'n (1981)
40 Brunswick Ave., Suite 202, Edison NJ 08818
Admin. Director: Maryanne Graham
Members: 1,600 *Staff:* 2
Annual Budget: $50-100,000 *Tel:* (201) 287-2777
Hist. Note: Members are CPAs, accountants, comptrollers and other individuals in the construction industry concerned with financial controls. Officers are elected annually.
Publication:
CFMA Newsletter. m.
Semi-annual meetings: Spring and Fall

Construction Industry Management Board (1974)
1101 15th St., N.W., Suite 1040, Washington DC 20005
Chairman: Frank R. Kruse
Members: 25-30 groups *Staff:* 1
Annual Budget: under $10,000 *Tel:* (202) 223-1510
Hist. Note: At first affiliated with the Contractors Mutual Association but now administered by the National Construction Employers Council, CIMB is composed of regional groups of employers united to bargain collectively.

Construction Industry Manufacturers Ass'n (1909)
Marine Plaza-1700, 111 East Wisconsin Avenue, Milwaukee WI 53202
Exec. V. President: Fred J. Broad
Members: 200-250 companies *Staff:* 16-20
Annual Budget: $500-1,000,000 *Tel:* (414) 272-0943
Hist. Note: Members are manufacturers of construction equipment and related components used in the general construction, housing, roadbuilding, mining, energy and forestry fields. Subsidiaries include: Power Crane and Shovel Ass'n; Construction Equipment Advertisers and Public Relations Council; and Bituminous and Aggregate Equipment Bureau. Maintains a Washington office.
Publications:
Catalog of Safety, Technical, and Information Materials on Construction Machines.
Annual Meetings: Hosts Internat'l Construction Equipment Exposition every 6 years
1987-Las Vegas, NV(Las Vegas Convention Center)/Feb. 21-26

Construction Management Ass'n of America (1981)
1025 Thomas Jefferson St., N.W., Suite 400 E, Washington DC 20007
Exec. Director: Karl F. Borgstrom
Members: 535 firms and individuals *Staff:* 2-5
Annual Budget: $100-250,000 *Tel:* (202) 944-3651
Hist. Note: The Association is comprised of firms that provide total management of a construction project from conception through completion as a professional service. CMAA will be moving in February, 1987 to 12355 Sunrise Valley Drive, Reston, VA.
Publications:
CM Adviser. bi-m.
CMA Manual: Standards
Annual Meetings: Fall
1987-Boca Raton, FL/Sept. 27-30

Construction Products Manufacturers Council (1921)
1600 Wilson Blvd., Suite 1005, Arlington VA 22209
Exec. V. President: W. Brit Dewey
Members: 80 companies *Staff:* 4-6
Annual Budget: $250-500,000 *Tel:* (703) 522-0613
Hist. Note: Manufacturers of building products. Formerly (until 1980) known as the Producers' Council, Inc.
Publications:
CPMC Bulletin. m.
Chapter Profile. q. adv.
Annual Directory. a.
Annual Meetings:
1987-Tampa, FL(Saddlebrook)/March 25-27

Construction Specifications Institute (1948)
601 Madison St., Alexandria VA 22314-1791
Exec. Director: Joseph A. Gascoigne
Members: 18,000 *Staff:* 45
Annual Budget: over $5,000,000 *Tel:* (703) 684-0300
Hist. Note: Founded in the District of Columbia in 1948 and incorporated in Maryland, CSI provides a forum for architects, engineers, specifiers, contractors, construction product representatives, and others interested in the construction industry. Membership: $110/yr.
Publications:
Construction Specifier. m. adv.
CSI Newsdigest. m.
Annual Meetings: Spring
1987-Detroit, MI/June 26-28
1988-Washington, DC/June 24-26
1989-New Orleans, LA/June 23-25

Construction Writers Ass'n (1957)
Box 259, Poolesville MD 20837
Secretary-Treasurer: E. E. Halmos, Jr.
Members: 120 *Staff:* 1
Annual Budget: under $10,000 *Tel:* (301) 972-7440
Hist. Note: Has no paid staff. Membership: $30(individual);$100(company).
Publication:
Newsletter. irreg.
Annual Meetings:
1987-Las Vegas, NV/Feb.

Consular Law Soc. (1940)
450 Park Ave., New York NY 10022
President-Elect: M. Curt Meltzer
Members: 100 official members, 300 ex-officio members *Staff:* 1
Annual Budget: under $10,000 *Tel:* (212) 371-4900
Hist. Note: Members of the Bar and other professionals concerned with legal developments in the field of consular, diplomatic and international law. Membership: $75/yr.
Annual Meetings:
1987-New York, NY(Harvard Club)/June

00115 12 05 86 1233

Consumer Bankers Ass'n (1919)
1300 North 17th St., Suite 1200, Arlington VA 22209
President: Thomas E. Honey
Members: 700-750 *Staff:* 11-15
Annual Budget: $1-2,000,000 *Tel:* (703) 276-1750
Hist. Note: Members are commercial banks, savings & loan associations, credit unions and mutual savings banks with a prime interest in retail banking. Formerly (1947) Morris Plan Bankers Ass'n. Supports the Consumer Bankers Ass'n Political Action Committee.
Publication:
CBA Reports. bi-w.
Annual Meetings: Fall/425
1987-Tucson, AZ(Westin La Paloma)/Oct. 3-6
1988-San Diego, CA(Hotel del Coronado)/Sept. 24-27

Consumer Credit Insurance Ass'n (1951)
307 North Michigan Ave., Chicago IL 60601
Exec. V. President: William F. Burfeind
Members: 200 *Staff:* 6-10
Annual Budget: $500-1,000,000 *Tel:* (312) 726-9895
Hist. Note: Members are insurance companies that provide insurance in connection with credit transactions.
Annual Meetings: Spring
1987-Napa, CA(Silverado)/June 18-21/300
1988-Tarpon Springs, FL(Innisbrook)/March 25-30/300
1989-Scottsdale, AZ(Registry Hotel)/April 30-May 3
1990-Hilton Head, SC(Hyatt Regency)/April 22-25

Consumer Federation of America (1967)
1424 16th St., N.W., Suite 604, Washington DC 20036
Exec. Director: Stephen Brobeck
Members: 225 organizations *Staff:* 12
Annual Budget: $500-1,000,000 *Tel:* (202) 387-6121
Hist. Note: Absorbed Electric Consumers Information Committee. Affiliated with Internat'l Organization of Consumers Unions. Membership consists of consumer organizations, labor unions, rural-electric cooperatives and state & local consumer protection officials. Supports the C.F.A. Political Action Fund.
Publications:
CFA News. m.
Voting Record of U.S. Congress. a.
Indoor Air News.
CPS Newsletter.
Annual Meetings: Consumer Assembly, Washington, DC in January or February.
1987-Washington, DC(Washington Plaza)/Feb. 12-13

Contact Lens Ass'n of Opthalmologists (1963)
2620 Jena St., New Orleans LA 70115
Exec. V. President: Dr. Oliver H. Dabezis, Jr.
Members: 2,000 *Staff:* 2
Tel: (504) 891-5442
Hist. Note: Established at the Essex House, New York City, in October 1963 by a group of members of the American Academy of Ophthalmology.
Publication:
CLAO Journal. q. adv.
Annual Meetings: January
1987-Las Vegas, NV(Riviera)/Jan. 14-18

Contact Lens Manufacturers Ass'n (1962)
P.O. Box 5252, Fletcher NC 28732-5252
Exec. Director: Mary J. Quick
Members: 181 companies *Staff:* 2
Annual Budget: $100-250,000 *Tel:* (800) 343-5367
Hist. Note: Membership fee based upon annual sales.
Publication:
The Contact Report. m. adv.
Annual Meetings: Fall
1987-New Orleans, LA(Clarion)/Oct. 14-17/400
1988-Orlando, FL(Wyndham)/Oct. 17-20/400

Contact Lens Soc. of America (1955)
10339 Democrary Lane, P.O. Box 10115, Fairfax VA 22030
Exec. Secretary: Tina M. Schott
Members: 1,200 *Staff:* 2-5
Annual Budget: $100-250,000 *Tel:* (703) 385-5898
Hist. Note: Members are fitters, as well as manufacturers, of contact lenses.
Publication:
CLSA Eyewitness Newsletter. m. adv.
Annual Meetings: Spring
1987-Charleston, SC(Omni Hotel)/March 27-30
1988-Las Vegas, NV

Containerization and Intermodal Institute (1960)
P.O Box 1593, North Caldwell NJ 07007
Exec. Director: Barbara Spector Yeninas
Members: 300 *Staff:* 2-5
Annual Budget: $50-100,000 *Tel:* (201) 226-0160
Hist. Note: Formerly (1960) Bulk Packaging and Containerization Institute, and (1967) The Containerization Institute. Membership includes transportation carriers, domestic and import-export lessors of containers and unit-load devices, terminal and port managers.
Publication:
Membership Bulletin. m.
Annual Meetings: June

Continental Ass'n of Funeral and Memorial Socs. (1963)
2001 S St., N.W., Suite 530, Washington DC 20009
Exec. Director: Carol Coile
Members: 160 societies *Staff:* 2-5
Annual Budget: $50-100,000 *Tel:* (202) 745-0634
Hist. Note: Burial and funeral consumer groups formed to reduce funeral expense and anxiety.
Publication:
Newsbulletin. m.
Biennial meetings: Even years

Continental Basketball Ass'n (1946)
425 S. Cherry St., Suite 230, Denver CO 80222
Commissioner: Carl Scheek
Members: 12 teams *Staff:* 30
Annual Budget: $1-2,000,000 *Tel:* (303) 331-0404
Hist. Note: Established April 23, 1946 as the Eastern Basketball League, it later became the Eastern Basketball Ass'n and assumed its present name on Jan. 1, 1978. Supported as a feeder league by the Nat'l Basketball Ass'n.
Publications:
CBA Newsweekly. w. adv.
CBA Official Guide. a.
CBA Official Team Yearbook. a.
Semi-annual Meetings: May and October

Continental Dorset Club (1898)
Box 506, Hudson IA 50643
Secy.-Treas.: Marion A. Meno
Members: 1,700 *Staff:* 2-5
Annual Budget: $25-50,000 *Tel:* (319) 988-4122
Hist. Note: Breeders and fanciers of Dorset sheep. Member of the National Pedigree Livestock Council.
Publication:
Dorset Journal. q.

Contract Carrier Conference (1938)
Hist. Note: Merged July 1, 1983 with the Common Carrier Conference-Irregular Route to form the Interstate Carriers Conference.

Contract Furnishings Council (1973)
1190 Merchandise Mart, Chicago IL 60654
Exec. V. President: Mariann B. Gregory
Members: 90-100 dealers *Staff:* 2-5
Annual Budget: $25-50,000 *Tel:* (312) 321-0563
Hist. Note: Members are full service dealers who supply furnishings to businesses and institutions. Membership: $500/yr.
Publications:
Bulletin. m.
Newsletter. q.

Contract Services Ass'n of America (1965)
605 14th St., N.W., Suite 500, Washington DC 20005
Exec. Director: W. Jackson Coleman
Members: 40 companies *Staff:* 6
Annual Budget: $500-1,000,000 *Tel:* (202) 347-0600
Hist. Note: Formerly (1986) Nat'l Council of Technical Services Industries. Members are larger companies performing contract services for the government. Supports the Committee on Contracting-Out. Membership: $2,800-16,000/yr.
Annual Meetings: Winter
1987-Coral Gables, FL(Biltmore)/Jan. 28-30/120

Contractors Pump Bureau (1928)
P.O. Box 5858, Rockville MD 20855
Exec. Director: Walter D. Anderson
Members: 20 companies *Staff:* 1
Annual Budget: $25-50,000 *Tel:* (301) 977-3919
Hist. Note: Members are makers of pumping machinery and engines for pumps for the construction industry. Membership: $1,100-6,600/yr.
Publication:
Pumpline (newsletter). m.
Annual Meetings: September
1987-Amelia Island, FL(Plantation)/Sept. 11-13/50-60

Control Systems Soc.
Hist. Note: A subsidiary of the Institute of Electrical and Electronics Engineers. Membership in the Society, open only to IEEE members, includes subscription to a technical periodical in the field published by IEEE. All administrative support is provided by IEEE.

Controlled Release Soc. (1978)
16 Nottingham Drive, Lincolnshire IL 60015
Administrative Assistant: M. Judith Roseman
Members: 950 *Staff:* 1
Tel: (312) 940-4277
Hist. Note: Members are firms concerned with basic and applied research on controlled release delivery systems. Membership: $20/yr. (indvidual); $100/yr. (company).
Publication:
Proceedings. a.
Annual Meetings:
1987-Toronto, Ontario(Sheraton Centre)/Aug. 2-7/600
1988-Basel, Switzerland/Aug. 15-19

Controllers Council (1985)
10 Paragon Drive, Box 433, Montvale NJ 07645
Consulting Directory: Jonathan B. Schiff
Members: 3,000 *Staff:* 2
Annual Budget: $100-250,000 *Tel:* (201) 573-6225
Hist. Note: Established in New Jersey in January, 1985, the Council is affiliated with the Nat'l Ass'n of Accountants. Membership: $75/yr. (individual).
Publications:
Controllers Update. m.
Controllers Quarterly. q.
Who's Who Among Controllers Today. a.

Convenient Automotive Services Institute (1983)
1600 Wilson Blvd., Suite 1008, Arlington VA 22209
Exec. Director: Joseph C. Jackson
Members: 329 companies *Staff:* 3
Annual Budget: $50-100,000 *Tel:* (703) 841-1556
Hist. Note: Founded by owners and operators of quick oil change and lubrication service stores to promote the growth of the industry through education, marketing, and management support services. Membership: $250/yr.(minimum)
Annual Meetings: September

Convention Liaison Council (1949)
1575 Eye St., N.W., Washington DC 20005
Exec. Director: LaRue Frye
Members: 20 associations *Staff:* 1
Annual Budget: $100-250,000 *Tel:* (202) 626-2764
Hist. Note: Members are associations which are directly involved in the convention, exposition, trade show, and meeting industry, and travel and tourism generally. Provides a focal point for the industry to exchange information, recommend solutions to industry problems, develop programs to serve the industry and to create a public awareness of the size of the industry. Membership: $600/yr.
Publications:
Convention Liaison Manual. 5/yr.
Legal Review Newsletter. q.
Convention Industry Glossary. 5/yr.
Annual Meetings: Fall
1987-Indianapolis, IN(Holiday Inn)/May 17-18/100-120

Convention of American Instructors of the Deaf (1850)
Box 2163Columbia MD 21045
Members: 1,600
Annual Budget: $50-100,000 *Tel:* (301) 461-9988
Hist. Note: Incorporated in 1897 by act of Congress. Membership: $40/yr.
Publications:
American Annals of the Deaf. 5/yr.. adv.
Biennial Meetings: Uneven years
1987-Santa Fe, NM
1989-San Diego, CA

Converting Equipment Manufacturers Ass'n (1984)
Box 359, 66 Morris Ave., Springfield NJ 07081
Exec. Director: William T. Thiel
Members: 35 companies *Staff:* 1
Annual Budget: $25-50,000 *Tel:* (201) 379-1100
Hist. Note: Membership open to any company or corporation engaged on a commercial scale in the manufacture of coaters, laminators, slitters/rewinders, printing press, metalizers, sheeters, extruders, calenders, forming, bag or envelope machinery used to perform a complete web converting function. Membership: $1,000/yr. (full); $500/yr. (associate).
Annual Meetings: May or June

Conveyor Equipment Manufacturers Ass'n (1933)
152 Rollins Avenue, Suite 208, Rockville MD 20852
Exec. V. President: Raymond J. Lloyd
Members: 55-60 companies *Staff:* 4
Annual Budget: $100-250,000 *Tel:* (301) 984-9080
Hist. Note: Founded as the Ass'n of Conveyor and Material Preparation Equipment Manufacturers, it became the Conveyor Ass'n in 1935 and assumed its present name in 1945. A member of the Machinery and Allied Products Institute.
Publications:
Bulletin. q.
Directory. a.
Annual Meetings: Spring
1987-Tampa, FL(Saddlebrook)/March 14-18
1988-Scottsdale, AZ(McCormick Ranch)/March 12-16

Cookware Manufacturers Ass'n (1922)
P.O. Box 271, Lake Geneva WI 53147
Exec. V. President: Paul Uetzmann
Members: 20-25 companies *Staff:* 2-5
Annual Budget: $50-100,000 *Tel:* (414) 248-9208
Hist. Note: Formerly (until 1963) the Aluminum Wares Association and (until 1981) the Metal Cookware Manufacturers Association.
Annual Meetings: Spring/90
1987-Boca Raton, FL(Boca Raton)/March 25-29
1988-Colorado Springs, C0(Broadmoor)/April 13-20

Cooling Tower Institute (1950)
Box 73383, Houston TX 77273
Admin. Manager: Dorothy Garrison
Members: 250-300 *Staff:* 2-5
Annual Budget: $250-500,000 *Tel:* (713) 350-1995
Hist. Note: Promotes improvement in technology, design, performance and maintenance of cooling towers. Also concerned with water and air pollution and conservation of water as a natural resource.
Publications:
CTI Journal. semi-a. adv.
CTI News. q.
Annual Meetings: Winter/300
1987-New Orleans, LA(Sheraton)/Feb. 25-27
1988-Houston, TX(Intercontinental)/Feb. 8-10

00116 12 05 86 1233

Cooperative Education Ass'n (1963)
655 15th St., N.W.,, Washington DC 20005
Exec. Director: Rita Reyerson
Members: 1,250 *Staff:* 2
Annual Budget: $50-100,000 *Tel:* (202) 637-4770
Hist. Note: Represents all aspects of cooperative education, the integration of classroom work and practical experience in an organized college program.
Publications:
CEA Membership Directory. a.
Journal of Cooperative Education. 3/yr.
Newsletter. 6/yr.
Annual Meetings:
1987-Los Angeles, CA/500

Cooperative Food Distributors of America (1937)
Hist. Note: Merged in 1982 with the National Association of Retail Grocers of the United States to become the National Grocers Association.

Cooperative League of the USA (1916)
Hist. Note: Became the Nat'l Cooperative Business Ass'n in 1985.

Coopers' Internat'l Union of North America (1890)
400 Sherburn Lane, Suite 207, Louisville KY 40207
President: Ernest D. Higdon
Members: 1,100 *Staff:* 2-5
Annual Budget: under $10,000 *Tel:* (502) 897-3151
Hist. Note: Organized in Titusville, Pennsylvania November 10, 1890 and chartered by the American Federation of Labor the following year.
Publication:
Coopers' Journal. 3/yr.
Quadrennial Meetings: 1988

Coordinating Council for Computers in Construction (1983)
1221 Avenue of the Americas, New York NY 10020
Chairman: Harry Mileaf
Members: 6,000 individuals *Staff:* 4
Annual Budget: $10-25,000 *Tel:* (212) 512-3268
Hist. Note: Open to architects, engineers, contractors, and building product manufacturers. Purpose is to facilitate use of computers in the construction process. Membership: Free.
Publication:
Techpointers. q.
Annual Meetings: Ad Hoc

Coordinating Council of Literary Magazines (1967)
666 Broadway, New York NY 10012
Exec. Director: Kay Ann Cassell
Members: 375 *Staff:* 4
Annual Budget: $250-500,000 *Tel:* (212) 614-6551
Hist. Note: Membership open to any noncommercial literary magazine that has been in operation for at least one year and published at least two issues. Sponsors a grants program, regional meetings, publications, library and subscription services, technical assistance and an advertising program. Membership: $10/yr. (circ. under 1,500); $30/yr. (circ. over 1,500)
Publications:
CCLM News. q.
Directory of Literary Magazines. a.
Catalog of Undergraduate Magazines.

Coordinating Research Council (1942)
219 Perimeter Center Parkway, Atlanta GA 30346
Gen. Manager: Alan E. Zengel
Members: 800-900 *Staff:* 11-15
Annual Budget: $1-2,000,000 *Tel:* (404) 396-3400
Hist. Note: Coordinates research between the petroleum, automotive equipment and transportation industries.
Publication:
Annual Report.

Copier Dealers Ass'n (1977)
P.O. Box 610, Enfield CT 06082
Secy.-Treas.: Elliot M.L. Bloom
Members: 60 companies *Staff:* 2
Annual Budget: $25-50,000 *Tel:* (203) 745-0364
Hist. Note: Members are photocopy machine dealers.
Tri-annual Meetings:

Copper and Brass Fabricators Council (1964)
1050 17th St., N.W., Suite 440, Washington DC 20036
President: Robert J. Wardell
Members: 20-25 companies *Staff:* 2-5
Annual Budget: $50-100,000 *Tel:* (202) 833-8575
Hist. Note: Formerly (1966) Copper & Brass Fabricators Foreign Trade Ass'n, Inc.

Copper and Brass Servicenter Ass'n (1951)
251 West DeKalb Pike, Adams Bldg., Suite 109, King of Prussia PA 19406
Exec. V. President: R. Franklin Brown, Jr.
Members: 90-100 companies *Staff:* 2-5
Annual Budget: $100-250,000 *Tel:* (215) 265-6658
Hist. Note: Formerly (1976) Copper and Brass Warehouse Ass'n. CBSA is composed of wholesale distributors (Servicenters) of fabricated copper and brass mill products; the Association's Associate Members are the brass mills (fabricators) who manufacture these products.
Publications:
Membership Directory. a.
FLASH Report - Statistical Survey. m.
Annual Meetings: Spring
1987-Rancho Mirage, CA(Marriott's Rancho Las Palmas)/ March 25-28/300

Copper Development Ass'n (1963)
2 Greenwich Office Park, Box 1840, Greenwich CT 06836-1840
President: George M. Hartley
Members: 100 companies *Staff:* 30-40
Annual Budget: $2-5,000,000 *Tel:* (203) 625-8210
Hist. Note: Supersedes the Copper and Brass Research Ass'n as the market and technical development arm of the copper and brass industry. Membership is composed of both U.S. and Canadian companies.
Publication:
Copper Topics. 3/yr.
Semi-annual meetings: Winter & Spring

Copyright Soc. of the U.S.A. (1953)
New York Univ. Law School, New York NY 10012
Ass't Exec. Director: Kate McKay
Members: 1,000
Tel: (212) 598-2280
Hist. Note: Established to foster interest in and advance the study of copyright law and of rights in literature, music, art, the theatre, motion pictures and other forms of intellectual property.
Publication:
Journal. q. adv.
Annual Meetings:
1987-Los Angeles, CA/Feb.

Cordage Institute (1920)
314 Lincoln St., Suite 568, Hingham MA 02043
Exec. Director: G.P. Foster
Members: 25 *Staff:* 2-5
Annual Budget: $50-100,000 *Tel:* (617) 749-1016
Hist. Note: Membership consists of manufacturers and suppliers of natural and fiber and synthetic rope and twine.
Publication:
Newsletter. bi-m.
Semi-annual meetings: February and October

Corn Refiners Ass'n (1913)
1001 Connecticut Ave., N.W., Washington DC 20036
President: Robert C. Liebenow
Members: 8 companies *Staff:* 6-10
Annual Budget: $500-1,000,000 *Tel:* (202) 331-1634
Hist. Note: Formerly (1923) American Manufacturers' Ass'n of Products from Corn; (1932) Associated Corn Products Manufacturers; (1966) Corn Industries Research Foundation. Represents the corn wet milling industry in the U.S. Members operate plants which produce corn syrup, corn starch, dextrose, corn oil and various animal feed ingredients.
Publication:
Corn Annual. a.

Corporate Aviation Management Ass'n (1982)
Hist. Note: Address unknown in 1987. Probably defunct.

Correctional Education Ass'n (1945)
4321 Hartwick Road, Suite L-208, College Park MD 20740
Exec. Director: Stephen J. Steurer
Members: 2,100 *Staff:* 2-5
Annual Budget: $50-100,000 *Tel:* (301) 277-9088
Hist. Note: The largest affiliate of the American Correctional Ass'n and the only one with a national headquarters and paid staff, CEA is a non-profit professional association serving educators and administrators who provide services to students in correctional settings. Its members include adult and juvenile educational administrators, academic and vocational educators, correctional officers, childcare counselors, clinicians, researchers and librarians. Membership: $35/yr. (individual); $50/yr. (library); and $75/yr. (institution).
Publications:
Journal of Correctional Education. q. adv.
CEA Newsletter. q. adv.
Annual Meetings:
1987-San Francisco, CA/July 26-29
1988-Detroit, MI
1989-Colorado Springs, CO

Correctional Industries Ass'n (1942)
706 Middlebrook Circle, Tallahassee FL 32312
Exec. Secretary: Paul A. Skelton, Jr.
Members: 1,500 *Staff:* 1
Annual Budget: $10-25,000 *Tel:* (904) 385-4878
Hist. Note: Members are supervisory personnel in prison industries. Affiliated with the American Correctional Association. Membership: $15/yr.(individual); $40/ yr.(organization).
Publications:
CIA Newsletter. q. adv.
CIA Directory. a. adv.
Annual Meetings: With The American Correctional Ass'n, August.

Correctional Service Federation-U.S.A. (1962)
Wisconsin Correctional Service, 436 West Wisconsin Ave., Milwaukee WI 53203
Pres./Treas.: Erwin J. Heinzelmann
Members: 20 private correctional agencies *Staff:* 1
Annual Budget: under $10,000 *Tel:* (414) 271-2512
Hist. Note: Affiliate of the American Correctional Ass'n and International Prisoners Aid Ass'n. Membership: $50/year.
Publication:
Newsletter. q.
Annual Meetings: With American Correctional Ass'n.

Corrugated Plastic Tubing Ass'n (1973)
66 Kempemfelt Drive, Barrie Ontario L4M 1C1
Exec. Secretary: Edwin T. Brent
Members: 60-70 *Staff:* 1
Annual Budget: $25-50,000 *Tel:* (705) 722-4538
Hist. Note: Membership: $500-2,000/yr.
Publication:
CPTA News. q.
Annual Meetings: March

COSMEP, Internat'l Ass'n of Independent Publishers (1968)
Box 703, San Francisco CA 94101
Exec. Director: Richard Morris
Members: 1,000 *Staff:* 2-5
Annual Budget: $50-100,000 *Tel:* (415) 922-9490
Hist. Note: Formerly the Cooperative of Small Magazine Editors and Publishers, it became the Committee of Small Magazine Editors and Publishers; it know uses the acronym COSMEP as its title since 80% of it members are book publishers, not magazines. Members are "small" publishers who are concerned with improving the promotion and distribution of their magazines and book titles. Membership: $45/yr.
Publication:
COSMEP Newsletter. m.
Annual Meetings: June
1987-Chicago, IL

Cosmetic Executive Women (1954)
217 East 85th St., Suite 214, New York NY 10028
President: M. Susan Hays
Members: 600 *Staff:* 1
Annual Budget: $100-250,000 *Tel:* (212) 535-6177
Hist. Note: Organized in 1954 and incorporated in the State of New York in 1959. Membership is limited to women who have served at least 3 years in an executive capacity in the cosmetic industry. Formerly (1981) Cosmetic Career Women.
Publication:
CEW Dateline. q.
Annual Meetings: New York, NY

Cosmetic Industry Buyers and Suppliers (1948)
c/o Avon Products, 9 W. 57th St., New York NY 10019
President: Gordon Wilkins
Members: 325-350
Annual Budget: $25-50,000 *Tel:* (212) 546-7143
Hist. Note: Members are individuals providing and obtaining essential oils, chemicals, packaging and other goods for the cosmetic industry. Memberhip concentrated in the New York area. Has no paid staff or permanent address.

Cosmetic, Toiletry and Fragrance Ass'n (1894)
1110 Vermont Ave., N.W., Washington DC 20005
President: E. Edward Kavanaugh
Members: 500-525 companies *Staff:* 50-60
Annual Budget: over $5,000,000 *Tel:* (202) 331-1770
Hist. Note: Founded as the Manufacturing Perfumers Association of the United States, it became the American Manufacturers of Toilet Articles in 1921, the Associated Manufacturers of Toilet Articles in 1932, the Toilet Goods Association in 1935 and assumed its present name in 1971. Sponsors the Cosmetic, Toiletry and Fragrance Association Political Action Committee. Has an annual budget of approximately $5.5-6 million.
Publications:
Executive Newsletter. bi-w.
Inside News From CTFA. semi-m.
Legislative Bulletin. w.
Trademark Bulletin. semi-m.

Costume Jewelry Salesmen's Ass'n (1951)
303 5th Ave., New York NY 10016
Treasurer: Jack Wishnew
Members: 100
Annual Budget: under $10,000 *Tel:* (212) 683-3896
Hist. Note: Became a component of the Marketing and Distributive Association in 1982. Has no paid staff or permanent address and operates principally with volunteers.
Annual Meetings: April

Cotton Council Internat'l (1956)
1030 15th Street, N.W., Suite 700, Washington DC 20005
Exec. Director: K. Adrian Hunnings
Members: 21 companies *Staff:* 6-10
Annual Budget: $1-2,000,000 *Tel:* (202) 833-2943
Hist. Note: The overseas operations arm of the Nat'l Cotton Council of America.
Publication:
U.S. Cotton Handbook. a.

Cotton Warehouse Ass'n of America (1969)
1150 Connecticut Ave., N.W., Suite 507, Washington DC 20036
Exec. V. President: Donald L. Wallace, Jr.
Members: 250-300 *Staff:* 2-5
Annual Budget: $100-250,000 *Tel:* (202) 331-4331
Hist. Note: Merger (1969) of the American and the National Cotton Compress and Cotton Warehouse Ass'ns. Supports the Cotton Warehouse Government Relations Committee.

00117 12 05 86 1233

Publication:
Cotton Comments. m.
Annual Meetings: Spring
1987-New Orleans, LA(Fairmont)/March 31-April 4/250

Council for Adult and Experiential Learning (1976)
10840 Little Patuxent Parkway, Columbia MD 21044
President: Morris T. Keeton
Members: 500 *Staff:* 21-25
Annual Budget: $1-2,000,000 *Tel:* (301) 997-3535
Hist. Note: Established in 1976 as Council for the Advancement of Experiential Learning (AEL), it assumed its present name in 1985 to reflect changing program priorities. A non-profit, higher education association whose basic mission is the advancement of experiential learning and the improvement of services to adult learners. Membership: $84.50/yr.(individual); $495/yr.(organization).
Publication:
CAEL News. bi-m. adv.
Annual Meetings: Fall

Council for Advancement and Support of Education (1974)
11 Dupont Circle, Suite 400, Washington DC 20036
President: Gary L. Quehl
Members: 2,800 institutions, 12,000 individuals *Staff:* 40-50
Annual Budget: $2-5,000,000 *Tel:* (202) 328-5900
Hist. Note: Merger (1974) of American College Public Relations Ass'n and American Alumni Council. Formerly (1975) AAC/ACPRA.
Publication:
Case Currents. m.
Annual Meetings: July
1987-Boston, MA

Council for Agricultural Science and Technology (1972)
137 Lynn Ave., Ames IA 50010-7120
Exec. V. President: William W. Marion
Members: 4,500 individuals, 26 scientific societies *Staff:* 2-5
Annual Budget: $250-500,000 *Tel:* (515) 292-2125
Hist. Note: Chartered in the State of Iowa as a non-profit corporation to provide accurate information, based on agricultural science and technology, to the government, the news media and the public about national or regional agricultural subjects of broad concern. Membership: $20/year.
Publications:
COMMENTS from CAST. bi-m.
NewsCAST. q.
Science of Food and Agriculture. q.

Council for American Private Education (1971)
1625 Eye St., N.W., Room 822, Washington DC 20006
Exec. Director: Robert L. Smith
Members: 15 nat'l private school organizations *Staff:* 2-5
Annual Budget: $100-250,000 *Tel:* (202) 659-0016
Publication:
CAPE Outlook. m. adv.
Annual Meetings: October and March in Washington,DC

Council for Basic Education (1956)
725 15th St., N.W., Washington DC 20005
Exec. Director: A. Graham Down
Members: 5,000 *Staff:* 10-12
Annual Budget: $1-2,000,000 *Tel:* (202) 347-4171
Hist. Note: National advocate of the liberal arts for all elementary and secondary school students. Primarily concerned with strengthening the position of the basic curriculum - English, Math, Science, Foreign Languages, History and the Arts. Membership: $40/yr.
Publication:
Basic Education. m.
Annual Meetings: Fall

Council for Children with Behavioral Disorders
Hist. Note: CCBD is a division of the Council for Exceptional Children.

Council for Educational Development and Research (1971)
1201 16th St., N.W., Suite 305, Washington DC 20036
Exec. Director: E. Joseph Schneider
Members: 16 companies *Staff:* 6-10
Annual Budget: $250-500,000 *Tel:* (202) 223-1593
Publication:
R & D Preview. bi-m.
Annual Meetings: Fall

Council for Educational Diagnostic Services
Hist. Note: CEDS is a division of the Council for Exceptional Children.

Council for European Studies (1970)
1509 International Affairs Bldg., Columbia University, New York NY 10027
Exec. Director: Dr. Ioannis Sinanoglou
Members: 65 institutions, 900 individuals *Staff:* 2-5
Annual Budget: $100-250,000 *Tel:* (212) 280-4172
Hist. Note: Members are social scientists interested in Western Europe and colleges and universities that have programs dealing with the history, culture and economics of Western Europe. Membership: $20/yr. (individual); $250/yr. (institution).
Publication:
European Studies Newsletter. bi-m. adv.
Biennial Meetings:
1987-Washington, DC(Georgetown Hotel)/Oct. 30-Nov. 1/300-400

Council for Exceptional Children (1922)
1920 Association Drive, Reston VA 22091
Exec. Director: Jeptha V. Greer
Members: 50,000 *Staff:* 55
Annual Budget: $2-5,000,000 *Tel:* (703) 620-3660
Hist. Note: Formerly (1958) International Council for Exceptional Children. CEC is a professional organization whose members include teachers, administrators, teacher educators, students, support services, professionals and parents. Its goals include the promotion of professional standards of practice for persons involved in the education of exceptional persons; the extension of special education services to exceptional children not presently being served; and the support of the development and advancement of new knowledge, technology, methodology, curriculum and materials. Special divisions within CEC (which publish their own periodicals, see below) include: Council for Children with Behavioral Disorders; Career Development; Council for Educational Diagnostic Services; Mental Retardation; Children with Communication Disorders; Early Childhood; Teacher Education; Ass'n for the Gifted; and Technology and Media. Hosts symposia, the ERIC Clearinghouse on Handicapped and Gifted Children, the Center for Special Education Technology and the Special Education Software Center.
Publications:
Exceptional Children. bi-m. adv.
Teaching Exceptional Children. q. adv.
Exceptional Child Education Resources. q.
Behavioral Disorders. q.
Career Development for Exceptional Individuals. semi-a.
Diagnostique. q.
Education and Training of the Mentally Retarded. q.
Journal of Childhood Communication Disorders. semi-a.
Journal of the Division for Early Childhood. semi-a.
Learning Disability Focus. semi-a.
Learning Disabilities Research. semi-a.
Teacher Education and Special Education. q.
Journal for the Education of the Gifted. q.
Journal of Special Education Technology. q.
Annual Meetings: Spring
1987-Chicago, IL(Convention Ctr.)/April 20-24
1988-Washington, DC(Convention Ctr.)
1989-San Francisco, CA(Convention Ctr.)/April 24-28

Council for Export Trading Companies (1982)
1225 Connecticut Ave., N.W., Suite 415, Washington DC 20036
Exec. Director: Ronald C. Wakeford
Members: 92 companies *Staff:* 2
Annual Budget: $25-50,000 *Tel:* (202) 861-4705
Hist. Note: Promotes exports by small and medium-sized companies through the development and use of Export Trading Companies. ETC's are special entities exempt by law from anti-trust statutes for the purpose of selling American goods and services abroad.
Publications:
CEC Newsletter. m.
Handbook for Export Trading Companies. a.
Annual Meetings: Spring in Washington, DC

Council for Intercultural Studies and Programs (1967)
Ramapo College of New Jersey, 505 Ramapo Valley Road, Mahwah NJ 07430
President: Walter T. Brown
Members: 250 colleges and universities, 10 associations *Staff:* 2-5
Annual Budget: $10-25,000 *Tel:* (201) 529-7405
Hist. Note: Member institutions have undergraduate programs in intercultural studies. Formerly (1972) Nat'l Council of Ass'ns for Internat'l Studies.
Publication:
Intercultural Studies Information Service. 6/academic yr.

Council for Interinstitutional Leadership (1967)
One Dupont Circle, N.W., Suite 20, Washington DC 20036
Coordinator: Holly Hexter
Members: 40 consortia of institutions *Staff:* 2
Annual Budget: $25-50,000 *Tel:* (202) 939-9354
Hist. Note: Encourages voluntary cooperation between colleges and universities. Formerly known as the Cooperative Program of the American Ass'n for Higher Education. Membership: $100/yr.(individual); $450/yr.(organization).
Publications:
Consortium Directory. a.
CIL Newsletter.
Annual Meetings: Fall

Council for Jewish Education (1926)
426 West 58th St., New York NY 10019
Exec. Director: Philip Gorodetzer
Members: 400
Tel: (212) 713-0290
Hist. Note: Formerly (until 1981) the Nat'l Council for Jewish Education. Members are college and university teachers of Hebrew and faculty of Jewish teacher training schools.

Council for Noncollegiate Continuing Education (1974)
530 East Main St., Suite 501, Richmond VA 23219
Exec. Director: Larry K. Dodds, Ed.D.
Members: Over 260 institutions and their 600 branches *Staff:* 6
Annual Budget: $250-500,000 *Tel:* (804) 648-6742
Hist. Note: Members are associations, private educational institutions, unions, and companies who conduct continuing education programs. The Council's purpose is to accredit and help improve such programs.
Publication:
The Growing Edge. q.
Annual Meetings: November

Council for Periodical Distributors Ass'ns (1955)
60 East 42nd St., Suite 2134, New York NY 10165
Exec. V. President: John Harrington
Members: 450 *Staff:* 2-5
Annual Budget: $500-1,000,000 *Tel:* (212) 818-0234
Hist. Note: Wholesale distributors to U.S. and Canadian retailers and newsstands of books, newspapers, magazines, etc. Formerly Council for Independent Distribution. Affiliated ass'ns are the Atlantic Coast Independent Distributors Ass'n, Mid-America Periodical Distributors Ass'n, Pacific Coast Independent Magazine Wholesalers Ass'n, and the Periodical Distributors of Canada.
Publications:
CPDA News. m. adv.
Single Copy. bi-m.

Council for Religion in Independent Schools (1898)
Box 780, Nyack NY 10960
Director: Dr. Barbara Jones
Members: 420 schools *Staff:* 2-5
Annual Budget: $100-250,000 *Tel:* (914) 358-4900
Hist. Note: A non-profit educational organization incorporated in the State of New York helping schools to initiate, evaluate and improve the teaching of religion and ethics.
Publication:
Newsletter. m.
Annual Meetings: Fall

Council for Responsible Nutrition (1973)
2100 M St., N.W., Suite 602, Washington DC 20037
President: J. B. Cordaro
Members: 50 companies *Staff:* 4-7
Annual Budget: $500-1,000,000 *Tel:* (202) 872-1488
Hist. Note: Manufacturers and distributors of dietary supplements.
Publication:
CRN Newsletter. q.
Annual Meetings: Fall
1987-Scottsdale, AZ(Camelback Inn)/Sept. 13-17/150

Council for the Advancement of Experiential Learning (1974)
Hist. Note: Became the Council for Adult and Experiential Learning in 1985.

Council for Therapeutic Recreation Certification (1981)
P.O. Box 16126, Alexandria VA 22302
Admin. Officer: Peg Connolly
Members: 6,000 *Staff:* 2
Annual Budget: $250-500,000 *Tel:* (703) 820-3993
Hist. Note: An independently administered body of the Nat'l Recreation and Park Ass'n, its primary purposes are: to establish national evaluation standards for the certification of individuals who possess the competencies of the therapeutic recreation profession; grant recognition to individuals who voluntarily apply and meet those standards; and moniter adherence to the standards by certified therapeutic recreation personnel.
Publications:
NCTRC Newsletter.
Registry.
Annual Meetings: April

Council for Tobacco Research-U.S.A. (1954)
900 3rd Ave., New York NY 10022
President: Robert F. Gertenbach
Members: 10-15 companies *Staff:* 15-20
Annual Budget: over $5,000,000 *Tel:* (212) 421-8885
Hist. Note: Organized by tobacco companies as the sponsoring agency for a program of research into questions of the effects of tobacco on human health. Originally the Tobacco Industry Research Committee, it assumed its present name in 1965. Has an annual budget of approximately $12 million.
Publication:
Annual Report.

Council of Active Independent Oil and Gas Producers (1977)
Hist. Note: Ceased operations in 1985.

Council of Administrators of Special Education
Hist. Note: A division of the Council for Exceptional Children.

Council of American Building Officials (1972)
5203 Leesburg Pike, Suite 708, Falls Church VA 22041
President: Richard P. Kuchnicki
Members: 3 ass'ns *Staff:* 4
Annual Budget: $250-500,000 *Tel:* (703) 931-4533
Hist. Note: Members are the Southern Building Code Congress International, Building Officials and Code Administrators International, and the International Conference of Building Officials. The Council represents the interests of these organizations in Washington.

00118 12 05 86 1233

Council of American-Flag Ship Operators (1977)
1627 K St., N.W., Suite 1200, Washington DC 20006
Exec. V. President and Gen. Counsel: Albert E. May
Members: 5-10 companies *Staff:* 6-10
Annual Budget: $500-1,000,000 *Tel:* (202) 466-5388
Hist. Note: Established January 1, 1978, by eight major cargoliner companies, who were previously members of the Liner Council of the American Institute of Merchant Shipping. Primarily concerned with the promotion and maintenance of a United States merchant marine, owned, operated, built and manned by U.S. citizens. Membership is open to all owners and operators of U.S.-flag vessels in the foreign and domestic trades.

Council of American Maritime Museums (1974)
Chesapeake Bay Maritime Museum, St. Michaels MD 21663
Secretary: Richard J. Dodds
Members: 35 *Staff:* 1
Annual Budget: under $10,000 *Tel:* (301) 745-2916
Hist. Note: Affiliated with the International Congress of Maritime Museums and the American Association of Museums.
Annual Meetings: Late Spring

Council of American Master Mariners (1936)
17 Battery Place, New York NY 10004
Nat'l Secy.-Treas.: Capt. Raymond E. Salman
Members: 1,200 *Staff:* 1
Annual Budget: $25-50,000 *Tel:* (212) 248-5047
Hist. Note: Membership: $35/yr.
Publication:
Sidelights. q.

Council of American Overseas Research Centers (1980)
Smithsonian Institution, NHB Room 354, Washington DC 20560
Exec. Director: Mary Ellen Lane
Members: 11 centers *Staff:* 2
Annual Budget: $50-100,000 *Tel:* (202) 842-8636
Hist. Note: Established to "advance higher learning and scholarly research by providing a forum for communication and cooperation among American overseas advanced research centers."
Annual Meetings: Board Meetings in September

Council of American Survey Research Organizations (1975)
3 Upper Devon Belle Terre, Port Jefferson NY 11777
Exec. Director: Diane K. Bowers
Members: 130 private survey research companies *Staff:* 2-5
Annual Budget: $100-250,000 *Tel:* (516) 928-6954
Hist. Note: Membership: $450-1,750/yr.
Annual Meetings: Fall
1987-Princeton, NJ(Scanticon)/Sept. 16-18/140

Council of Ass'n Attorneys (1966)
Hist. Note: Formerly (1971) Council of Trade Ass'n Attorneys Address unknown since 1984.

Council of Better Business Bureaus (1971)
1515 Wilson Blvd., Arlington VA 22209
President: William H. Tankersley
Members: 900-1,000 *Staff:* 100
Annual Budget: over $5,000,000 *Tel:* (703) 276-0100
Hist. Note: Merger (1970) of the Ass'n of Better Business Bureaus (1921) and the Nat'l Better Business Bureau (1912). Membership consists of national companies and local Better Business Bureaus. Has an annual budget of $15 million.
Annual Meetings: Fall

Council of Biology Editors (1957)
9650 Rockville Pike, Bethesda MD 20814
Exec. Director: Philip L. Altman
Members: 800 *Staff:* 2-5
Annual Budget: $100-250,000 *Tel:* (301) 530-7036
Hist. Note: Founded in 1957 and incorporated in 1965 in the District of Columbia. Membership consists of individuals concerned with communications in biology and related fields. Membership: $40/yr.(individual); $200/yr.(organization).
Publication:
CBE Views. q.
Annual Meetings: Spring
1987-Vancouver, BC(UBC Conference Ctr.)/May 9-12/200
1988-Baltimore, MD(Marriott Inner Harbor)/May 14-17/250
1989-Rochester, MN(Kahler Hotel)/May 20-23/250

Council of Chief State School Officers (1927)
400 North Capitol St., N.W., Suite 379, Washington DC 20001
Exec. Director: William F. Pierce
Members: 57 *Staff:* 30-35
Annual Budget: $2-5,000,000 *Tel:* (202) 393-8161
Hist. Note: Established as the National Council of Chief State School Officers, it assumed its present name in 1954.
Publication:
Chiefline. w.
Annual Meetings: November
1987-North Carolina

Council of Colleges of Arts and Sciences (1965)
Eisenhower Hall, Kansas State Univ., Manhattan KS 66506
Exec. Director: Dr. Linda P. Frank
Members: 275 *Staff:* 1
Annual Budget: $10-25,000 *Tel:* (913) 532-6900
Hist. Note: Eligibility for membership in CCAS is conferred by membership in the Nat'l Ass'n of State Universities and Land-Grant Colleges (NASULGC) or the American Ass'n of State Colleges and Universities (AASCU). CCAS members are deans of arts and sciences of state-supported universities. Membership: $100-300/yr.(based on the number of BA/BS degree awarded).
Publication:
Newsletter. bi-m.
Annual Meetings: November
1987-San Francisco, CA(Hotel Meridien)/Nov. 18-21
1988-Atlanta, GA(Colony Square)/Nov. 2-5
1989-Boston, MA(Westin Copley Place)/Nov. 15-18
1990-New Orleans, LA(Sheraton New Orleans)/Nov. 14-17

Council of Communication Management (1955)
Box 3970, Grand Central Station, New York NY 10163
Secretary: Art York
Members: 150-200 individuals
Annual Budget: $25-50,000 *Tel:* (212) 254-3985
Hist. Note: Individuals in member companies responsible for communication with the public, government and employees. Has no paid staff; officers change annually.
Publication:
CCM Communicator. m.
Annual Meetings: October

Council of Communication Societies
Hist. Note: Disbanded in 1985.

Council of Community Blood Centers (1962)
Old Brick House Square, 113 Rowell Court, Falls Church VA 22046
Exec. Director: James MacPherson
Members: 31 *Staff:* 2-5
Annual Budget: $250-500,000 *Tel:* (703) 237-0833
Hist. Note: Formerly (1971) Community Blood Bank Council. A national association of independent regional and community blood centers dedicated to serving the public interest by promoting excellence in blood services. Membership fee based on annual blood collection.
Publication:
Newsletter. w.

Council of Defense and Space Industry Ass'ns (1964)
1620 Eye St., N.W., Suite 1000, Washington DC 20006
Admin. Officer: Ruth W. Franklin
Members: 8 associations *Staff:* 2-5
Annual Budget: $25-50,000 *Tel:* (202) 659-5013
Hist. Note: Established June 30, 1964 by industry ass'ns having common interests in the defense and space fields, CODSIA functions as a voluntary, coordinating, non-profit, consultative body. It addresses policies, regulations, directives and procedures relating to the supplier-purchaser relationship between government and industry. Members are Aerospace Industries Ass'n of America, Electronic Industries Ass'n, Motor Vehicle Manufacturers A'ssn, Nat'l Security Industrial Ass'n, Shipbuilders Council of America, American Electronics Ass'n, Computer and Business Equipment Manufacturers Ass'n and the Professional Services Council.

Council of Distributive Teacher Educators (1960)
Hist. Note: An affiliate of the American Vocational Association. Became a component of the Marketing and Distributive Education Association in 1982.

Council of Educational Facility Planners, Internat'l (1921)
1060 Carmack Rd., Suite 160, Columbus OH 43210
Acting Exec. Director: Robert Hedley
Members: 1,100 *Staff:* 4-6
Annual Budget: $100-250,000 *Tel:* (614) 422-1521
Hist. Note: Formerly (1967) Nat'l Council on Schoolhouse Construction. Members are companies and persons who plan, design, build, equip and maintain educational facilities. Membership: $95/yr. (individual), $245/yr. (company).
Publication:
CEFP Journal & Guide For Planning Educational Facilities. bi-m. adv.
Annual Meetings: Fall
1987-Edmonton, Canada(Fantasyland Hotel)/Oct. 3-6/400
1988-Milwaukee, WI(Hyatt Regency)/Oct. 9-12/350
1989-Cincinnati, OH/350

Council of Engineering and Scientific Soc. Executives (1949)
c/o Electrochemical Soc., 10 South Main St., Pennington NJ 08534-2896
President: V.H. Branneky
Members: 500 *Staff:* 1
Annual Budget: $25-50,000 *Tel:* (609) 737-1902
Hist. Note: Formerly (1972) Council of Engineering and Scientific Soc. Secretaries. Has no paid staff or permanent officers.
Publication:
CESSE Quill. 3/yr.
Annual Meetings: Summer/350
1987-Cleveland, OH
1988-New York, NY
1989-Houston, TX

Council of Fashion Designers of America (1963)
575 Seventh Avenue, New York NY 10018
President: Zachary Solomon
Members: 90-100 *Staff:* 1
Annual Budget: under $10,000 *Tel:* (212) 921-8500
Hist. Note: Members are persons engaged in creative fashion design, ie wearing apparel, fabrics, jewelry, accessories, etc.

Council of Fleet Specialists (1967)
8245 Nieman Road, Suite 111, Shawnee Mission KS 66214
Exec. V. President: U. J. Reese
Members: 200-225 *Staff:* 2-5
Annual Budget: $250-500,000 *Tel:* (913) 492-1620
Hist. Note: Members are distributors of parts and servicers for heavy-duty trucks. Membership: $700/yr.
Publication:
Parts/Equipment Buyers' Guide and Services Directory. a. adv.
Annual Meetings: Spring/1,100
1987-New Orleans, LA(Hyatt)/May 2-6
1988-Dallas, TX(Hyatt)/April 16-20

Council of Food Processors Ass'n Executives (1937)
1401 New York Ave., N.W., Suite 400, Washington DC 20005
Secretary: Sharon Hughes
Members: 25-30 *Staff:* 1
Annual Budget: under $10,000 *Tel:* (202) 639-5929
Hist. Note: Formerly (1962) Ass'n of Canners' State and Regional Secretaries, and (1979) Council of Canning Ass'n Executives.
Annual Meetings: With Nat'l Food Processors Ass'n and Food Processing Machinery and Supplies Ass'n.

Council of Graduate Schools in the U.S. (1961)
One Dupont Circle, N.W., Suite 430, Washington DC 20036
President: Jules LaPidus
Members: 390-395 *Staff:* 6-10
Annual Budget: $250-500,000 *Tel:* (202) 223-3791
Publications:
Newsletter. m.
Proceedings. a.
Annual Meetings: Winter
1987-Washington, DC(Capital Hilton)/Dec. 2-5
1988-Colorado Springs, CO(Broadmoor)/Nov. 29-Dec. 2
1989-Washington, DC

Council of Independent Colleges (1956)
One Dupont Circle, N.W., Ste. 320, Washington DC 20036
President: Dr. Allen P. Splete
Members: 280 colleges *Staff:* 11-15
Annual Budget: $500-1,000,000 *Tel:* (202) 466-7230
Hist. Note: Members are independent four-year colleges of liberal arts and sciences with full-time enrollments under 3,000. Formerly (1981) the Council for the Advancement of Small Colleges.
Publication:
Newsletter. q.
Semi-annual Meetings: President's (Jan.) & Dean's (Nov.) Institutes
1987-Miami Lakes, FL/Jan. 2-7

Council of Industrial Boiler Owners (1979)
5817 Burke Center Pkwy., Burke VA 22015
President: William B. Marx
Members: 50 companies *Staff:* 2-5
Annual Budget: $250-500,000 *Tel:* (703) 250-9042
Hist. Note: Owners and operators of industrial steam boilers.
Annual Meetings: October/85-100
1987-Charlottesville, VA(Boar's Head Inn)/Oct. 21-23
1988-Woodstock, VT(Woodstock Inn)/Oct. 19-21

Council of Intergovernment Coordinators
Hist. Note: See the National Association of Counties' Council of Intergovernment Coordinators.

Council of Landscape Architectural Registration Boards (1961)
309 S. Franklin St., Syracuse NY 13202
Exec. Secretary: Johanna G. Luce
Members: 39 state boards *Staff:* 1
Annual Budget: $100-250,000 *Tel:* (315) 472-1717
Hist. Note: An independent service organization whose only members are the legally constituted state regulatory agencies, the Council's main objectives are to: promote high standards for landscape architecture; foster the enactment of uniform laws for landscape architecture; compile, maintain and transmit certified records of qualified practitioners for registration; and equalize and improve the examination of applicants through a uniform national licensing examination. Membership: $600/yr. (state board)
Annual Meetings: September
1987-Baltimore, MD(Marriott)/Sept. 25-26
1988-Lexington, KY/Sept. 23-24

Council of Library Ass'n Executives (1975)
Box 1534, Trenton NJ 08607
President: Abigail Studdiford
Members: 25-30 *Staff:* 1
Annual Budget: under $10,000 *Tel:* (609) 394-8032
Hist. Note: Members are executive directors, or equivalent, of state, provincial and regional library associations. Membership: $25/yr.

00119 12 05 86 1233

Publication:
CLAE Newsletter. semi-a.
Semi-annual Meetings: in conjunction with the American Library Ass'n
1987-Chicago, IL/Jan.
1987-San Francisco, CA/June
1988-San Antonio, TX/Jan.
1988-New Orleans, LA/June
1989-Washington, DC/Jan.
1989-Dallas, TX/June
1990-Chicago, IL/Jan.
1990-Chicago, IL/June

Council of Logistics Management (1963)
2803 Butterfield Road, Suite 380, Oak Brook IL 60521
Exec. V. President: George A. Gecowets
Members: 6,000 *Staff:* 12
Annual Budget: $2-5,000,000 *Tel:* (312) 574-0985
Hist. Note: Formerly (1985) the Nat'l Council of Physical Distribution Management. A professional organization of individuals concerned with transportation, warehousing, inventory, materials, logistics and/or physical distribution management. Membership: $150/year.
Publications:
Conference Proceedings. a.
Journal of Business Logistics. semi-a.
Logistics Comment. bi-m.
Physical Distribution Bibliography. a.
Annual Meetings: Fall
1987-Atlanta, GA(Marriott/Hyatt/Hilton)/Sept. 27-30/2,700
1988-St. Louis, MO(Cervantes Center)/2,800
1989-Boston, MA(Marriott/Westin Copley)/2,800

Council of Medical Specialty Societies (1965)
Box 70, Lake Forest IL 60045
Exec. V. President: Richard S. Wilbur, M.D.
Members: 24 medical societies *Staff:* 6-10
Annual Budget: $500-1,000,000 *Tel:* (312) 295-3456
Hist. Note: Founded as the Tri-College Council by the American College of Obstetricians and Gynecologists, the American College of Physicians and the American College of Surgeons. As other specialty societies joined, the present name was adopted in 1967. Each member society represents one of the 24 specialties with a certifying board sanctioned by the American Board of Medical Specialties. Provides a forum for discussion, action and policy formulation on national issues affecting medical practice. Incorporated in Illinois in 1976 when a permanent office was set up with a paid staff.
Publication:
Newsletter. m.
Annual Meetings: Chicago in November at Westin O'Hare Hotel.

Council of Mutual Savings Institutions (1962)
521 Fifth Ave., New York NY 10017
Exec. Director: Kenneth Virch
Members: 250-275 *Staff:* 6-10
Annual Budget: $250-500,000 *Tel:* (212) 867-2776
Hist. Note: Formerly the Ass'n of Mutual Savings Institutions. Members are depositor-owned savings institutions dedicated to research, legislation and public education on behalf of mutual savings institutions and the people they serve. Annual membership fee: $10 per one million of assets.
Publication:
Mutual Savings Reporter. m.
Annual Meetings:
1987-New York, NY or Chicago, IL/May

Council of Nat'l Library and Information Ass'ns (1942)
461 West Lancaster Ave., Haverford PA 19041
Chairman: Norma Yueh
Members: 20 associations *Staff:* 1
Annual Budget: under $10,000 *Tel:* (215) 649-5251
Hist. Note: Formerly (until 1979) known as the Council of Nat'l Library Ass'ns, CNLIA was established as a forum for the discussion of library and information problems. Membership is open to any national library/information association of North America.
Semi-annual Meetings: May and November in New York City

Council of Nat'l Organizations for Adult Education (1952)
Hist. Note: Defunct in 1982.

Council of Natural Waters (1979)
Hist. Note: Defunct in 1982.

Council of Planning Librarians (1957)
1313 East 60th St., Chicago IL 60637-2897
President: Mary Ravenhall
Members: 160 *Staff:* 1
Annual Budget: $100-250,000 *Tel:* (312) 947-2007
Hist. Note: Originally an ad-hoc committee of librarians interested in planning materials convened in 1957; became an official organization in 1960. Members are librarians, academics, professional planners, and public and private planning agencies. Cooperates with several other professional associations, including the Council of Nat'l Library Ass'ns, the Internat'l City Management Ass'n, and the American Planning Ass'n. Membership: $25/yr. (individual); $45/yr. (institution)
Publications:
CPL Bibliographies.
CPL Newsletter. q. (Members only)
Annual Meetings: Spring/50
1987-New York, NY
1988-Houston, TX/April 13-16

Council of Pollution Control Financing Agencies (1978)
477 H St., N.W., Washington DC 20001
Exec. Director: Ron M. Linton
Members: 50 *Staff:* 2-5
Annual Budget: $100-250,000 *Tel:* (202) 682-3996
Hist. Note: State and local government agencies and other organizations interested financing and establishing economic incentives for pollution control facilities.
Publication:
Report. m.
Annual Meetings: Summer

Council of Professional Ass'ns on Federal Statistics (1980)
806 15th St., N.W., Suite 440, Washington DC 20005
Exec. Director: Katherine K. Wallman
Members: 16 organizations *Staff:* 2-5
Annual Budget: $50-100,000 *Tel:* (202) 783-5808
Hist. Note: Established to monitor the priorities, scope and compatibility of the Federal statistical effort. Has a multidisciplinary membership of ass'ns. Also has 35 affiliates. Membership: $1,100-13,500/yr.
Publication:
News From COPAFS. m.

Council of Sales Promotion Agencies (1969)
176 Madison Ave., New York NY 10016
President: Joseph Flanagan
Members: 40 agencies *Staff:* 3
Annual Budget: $100-250,000 *Tel:* (212) 532-0096
Hist. Note: A trade association of sales promotion agencies with at least two years experience, 25% of whose membership is foreign.
Publications:
CSPA Report. q.
Opportunity: Promotion Advantage. a.
Agency Selection Guide. a.
Membership Roster. a.

Council of Scientific Soc. Presidents (1973)
1155 16th St., N.W., Washington DC 20036
Exec. Officer: R. Eric Leber
Members: 37 individuals *Staff:* 2
Annual Budget: $25-50,000 *Tel:* (202) 872-4452
Hist. Note: Members are chief elected officers of scientific societies. Formerly (1977) the Committee of Scientific Soc. Presidents.
Semi-annual Meetings: Washington, DC/May and December

Council of Socs. in Dental Hypnosis (1960)
Hist. Note: Inactive in 1984-85. Address unknown in 1985.

Council of State Administrators of Vocational Rehabilitation (1940)
1055 Thomas Jefferson St., N.W., Suite 401, Washington DC 20007
Exec. Director: Joseph H. Owens, Jr.
Members: 75-100 *Staff:* 2-5
Annual Budget: $250-500,000 *Tel:* (202) 638-4634
Hist. Note: Composed of the chief administrators of the public vocational rehabilitation agencies for physically and mentally handicapped persons in the states, District of Columbia, and the territories.
Semi-annual: May and Fall in Washington.

Council of State and Territorial Epidemiologists (1951)
New Jersey Dept. of Health CN 360, Trenton NJ 08625
Secy.-Treas.: William E. Parkin
Members: 65
Annual Budget: under $10,000 *Tel:* (609) 292-4046
Hist. Note: Formerly (1986) Conference of State and Territorial Epidemiologists. Affiliated with Ass'n of State and Territorial Health Officials.
Annual Meetings: Spring
1987-Santa Fe, NM(Hilton)/May 17-20

Council of State Chambers of Commerce (1932)
122 C St., N.W., Suite 200, Washington DC 20001
President: William R. Brown
Members: 40 chambers *Staff:* 6
Annual Budget: $250-500,000 *Tel:* (202) 484-8103
Hist. Note: A federation of state and regional chambers of commerce founded as the National Association of State Chambers of Commerce which assumed its present name in 1948.
Annual Meetings: Fall
1987-Williamsburg,VA(Colonial)
1988-New Orleans,LA(Royal Sheraton)

Council of State Community Affairs Agencies (1974)
444 North Capitol St., N.W., Suite 251, Washington DC 20001
Exec. Director: John Sidor
Members: 50 *Staff:* 4-6
Annual Budget: $250-500,000 *Tel:* (202) 393-6435
Hist. Note: Members are employees of state community affairs agencies representing all 50 states.
Publications:
State CDBG Update. 11/yr.
Housing Update. 10/yr.
Public Facilities Clearinghouse Notes. 10/yr.
Annual Meetings: September
1987-Key West, FL/100

Council of State Governments (1933)
Iron Works Pike, Box 11910, Lexington KY 40578
Exec. Director: Carl W. Stenberg
Members: 50 states *Staff:* 75
Annual Budget: $2-5,000,000 *Tel:* (606) 252-2291
Hist. Note: Founded as the American Legislators Ass'n, it assumed its present name in 1933. The Council seeks to preserve and strengthen the role of the state in the federal system; it serves as a research and service agency for 50 state governments and associations of state officials.
Publications:
Legislative Research Checklist. bi-m.
The Book of the States. bien.
Journal of State Government. q.
State Government News. m.
Annual Meetings: Late Fall

Council of State Housing Agencies (1971)
444 North Capitol St., N.W., Hall of the States, Suite 118, Washington DC 20001
Exec. V. President: Carl W. Riedy, Jr.
Members: 55 *Staff:* 11
Annual Budget: $1-2,000,000 *Tel:* (202) 624-7710
Hist. Note: Members are the state housing agencies, also District of Columbia, Virgin Islands and Puerto Rico.
Publications:
HFA Update. m.
Survey of State Housing Finance Agencies. a.
Directory of State Housing Finance Agencies. a.
Washington Update. w.
Annual Meetings:
1987-Boston, MA

Council of State Planning Agencies
Hist. Note: Became the Council of State Policy and Planning Agencies in 1986.

Council of State Policy and Planning Agencies (1966)
400 North Capitol St., N.W., Suite 291, Washington DC 20001
Exec. Director: James M. Souby
Members: 155 *Staff:* 6-10
Annual Budget: $1-2,000,000 *Tel:* (202) 624-5386
Hist. Note: Formerly (1986) Council of State Planning Agencies, it is affiliated with the Nat'l Governors Ass'n, with whom it shares offices. A membership organization comprised of policy and planning executives of the nation's Governors, it provides assistance to states on a wide spectrum of policy and technical matters through publications, seminars, and direct assistance to individual states.
Publications:
State Planning Information Report. q.
State Planning Issues. bi-a. adv.
Stateside. q.
Report to the Governors. bi-m.
Annual Meetings: September

Council of the Americas (1958)
680 Park Ave., New York NY 10021
President: George W. Landau
Members: 185-200 *Staff:* 11-15
Annual Budget: $1-2,000,000 *Tel:* (212) 628-3200
Hist. Note: Founded in New York City in 1958 as the United States Inter-American Council, Inc. The name was changed in 1965 to Council for Latin America, Inc. and in 1970 to Council of the Americas, Inc. Maintains a Washington office. Membership: $5,000/yr.
Publications:
CoA Agenda. m.
President's Letter. m.
Washington Report. m.

Council of the Great City Schools (1961)
1413 K St., N.W., Washington DC 20005
Exec. Director: Samuel B. Husk
Members: 25-36 *Staff:* 8-11
Annual Budget: $250-500,000 *Tel:* (202) 371-0163
Hist. Note: Members are large city school districts. Formerly known as the Research Council of the Great Cities Program for School Improvement. Membership: $10,000.

Council of Writers Organizations (1979)
Plaza Hotel Suite 1723, New York NY 10019
Secretary: Robert Scott Milne
Members: 25 associations
Annual Budget: under $10,000 *Tel:* (212) 759-6744
Hist. Note: Formed in December, 1978 in New York City. An umbrella agency for organizations representing professional writers. Membership: $200/year (organization).
Publication:
Word Wrap. m.
Annual Meetings: Late Winter
1987-New York, NY(Algonquin Hotel)/March

Council of 1890 College Presidents (1913)
Langston University, President's Office, Langston OK 73050
Secy.-Treas.: Ernest Holloway

00120 12 05 86 1233

Members: 15-20 *Staff:* 1
Annual Budget: under $10,000 *Tel:* (405) 466-2231
Hist. Note: Presidents of land grant colleges with predominantly black enrollment. Formerly (until 1955) known as the Conference of Presidents of Negro Land Grant Colleges and (until 1979) the Council on Cooperative College Projects. Membership: $100/yr.
Annual Meetings: November

Council on Alternate Fuels (1980)
1301 Pennsylvania Ave., N.W., Suite 325, Washington DC 20004
President: Michael Koleda
Members: 25-30 companies *Staff:* 3-5
Annual Budget: $500-1,000,000 *Tel:* (202) 347-7069
Hist. Note: Established as the Nat'l Council on Synthetic Fuels Production in 1980. Formerly (1985) Council on Synthetic Fuels; assumed its present name in 1986. Regular members are producers of synthetic fuels; associate members are research and development and engineering companies.
Annual Meetings: Semi-Annual Meetings

Council on Diagnostic Imaging to the A.C.A. (1936)
Box 1655, Ashtabula OH 44004
Secy.-Treas.: Dr. Clark L. McClain
Members: 4,500 *Staff:* 1
Annual Budget: $100-250,000 *Tel:* (216) 993-7213
Hist. Note: A part of the American Chiropractic Ass'n. Founded as the Nat'l Council of Chiropractic Roentgenologists, it later became the Council on Roentgenography, (1964) the American Council on Chiropractic Roentgenology, (1968) the Council on Roentgenology to the A.C.A. and assumed its present name in 1986.
Publication:
Roentgenological Briefs. m.
Annual Meetings: With American Chiropractic Ass'n
1987-Orlando, FL(Buena Vista)
1988-Nashville, TN

Council on Electrolysis Education (1972)
911 S. Brentwood Blvd., #236, St. Louis MO 63105
Chairman: Dorothy Graves
Members: 11 ass'ns
Annual Budget: under $10,000 *Tel:* (314) 862-2111
Hist. Note: Members are organizations of professional electrologists (hair removers). Has no paid staff.
Semi-annual meetings: Spring and Summer

Council on Employee Benefits (1946)
1144 East Market St., Akron OH 44316
Secy.-Treas.: Carl S. Lazaroff
Members: 190 companies *Staff:* 2-5
Annual Budget: $250-500,000 *Tel:* (216) 796-4008
Hist. Note: An employer organization for the exchange of information on all aspects of employee benefit plans. Founded as the Federation of Employee Benefit Associations, it became the Council on Employee Benefit Plans in 1950 and assumed its present name in 1961.
Publication:
Reporter. a.
Semi-annual meetings: Spring (members only) and October

Council on Foundations (1949)
1828 L St., N.W., Washington DC 20036
President & C.E.O.: James A. Joseph
Members: 800 foundations, 155 corporation grant makers
Staff: 40-45
Annual Budget: $2-5,000,000 *Tel:* (202) 466-6512
Hist. Note: Established in 1949 as an information clearinghouse and representative for foundations and other philanthropic organizations. Provides advisory services to its members and to the grantmaking field.
Publications:
Council on Foundations Newsletter. bi-w.
Foundation News. bi-m.
Annual Report. a.
Community Foundation News. irreg.
Washington Update. irreg.
Communications Update. irreg.
International Dateline. irreg.
Annual Meetings: Spring
1987-Atlanta, GA/March 30-April 1
1988-Los Angeles, CA/April 25-27
1989-Toronto, Ontario/April 10-12
1990-Boston, MA/April 2-4
1991-Chicago, IL

Council on Governmental Ethics Laws (1978)
Iron Works Pike, Box 11910, Lexington KY 40578
Staff Director: Edward D. Feigenbaum
Members: 56 agencies *Staff:* 2
Annual Budget: $10-25,000 *Tel:* (606) 252-2291
Hist. Note: Established in Minneapolis, the Council is the only organization existing solely as an international professional association for agencies and individuals with responsibilities in governmental ethics, elections, campaign finance and lobby law regulation. Membership: $175/yr. (governmental agency)
Publications:
Campaign Finance, Ethics & Lobby Law Blue Book. bien.
COGEL Newsletter. bi-m.
Annual Meetings:
1987-Quebec City, Quebec/Sept. 27-30

Council on Hotel, Restaurant and Institutional Education (1946)
311 First St., N.W., Washington DC 20001
Exec. V. President: Douglas E. Adair
Members: 800-1,000 *Staff:* 3
Annual Budget: $100-250,000 *Tel:* (202) 628-0038
Hist. Note: A non-profit professional association representing the schools and educators, firms, professional executives and students of the hospitality industry concerned with the education of cooks, bakers, hotel, restaurant and institutional administrators. Founded as the Nat'l Council on Hotel and Restaurant Education, it assumed its present name in 1959. Membership: $95/yr.(individual); $300/yr.(organization).
Publications:
Hospitality Educator. m. adv.
Hospitality Education and Research Journal. semi-a. adv.
Conference Proceedings. a. adv.
Directory of HRI Schools. a. adv.
CHRIE Communique.
Annual Meetings: Summer/250
1987-Atlanta, GA(Marriott Marquis)/Aug. 5-9
1988-Toronto, Ontario/August

Council on Library-Media Technical-Assistants (1967)
Cuyahoga Community College, SC-126, 2900 Community College Avenue, Cleveland OH 44115
Exec. Secretary: Margaret R. Barron
Members: 500 individuals and institutions
Annual Budget: under $10,000 *Tel:* (216) 348-4000
Hist. Note: Formerly (1973) Council on Library Technology and (1977) Council on Library Technical-Assistants. Affiliated with the American Library Ass'n. Members are individuals employed as library-media technical-assistants with an associate's or bachelor's degree in that speciality. Currently operating a certification task force exploring certifcation for library-media technicians on a national level.
Publications:
Newsletter. m.
Membership Directory and Data Book. a.
Conference Proceedings. a.
Annual Meetings: Holds both regional and annual meetings

Council on Oceanic Engineering Soc.
Hist. Note: A subsidiary of the Institute of Electrical and Electronics Engineers. Membership in the Society, open only to IEEE members, includes subscription to a technical periodical in the field published by IEEE. All administrative support is provided by IEEE.

Council on Postsecondary Accreditation (1975)
One Dupont Circle, N.W., Suite 305, Washington DC 20036
President: Richard M. Millard
Members: 50 accrediting bodies *Staff:* 7
Annual Budget: $250-500,000 *Tel:* (202) 452-1433
Hist. Note: Formed in 1975 through the merger of the Federation of Regional Accrediting Commissions of Higher Education and the Nat'l Commission on Accrediting, COPA works to foster and facilitate the role of accrediting bodies in promoting and insuring the quality and diversity of American postsecondary education. Constituent groups within COPA include: Assembly of Institutional Accrediting Bodies; Assembly of Specialized Accrediting Bodies; and Assembly of Nat'l Postsecondary Educational Organizations.
Publications:
President's Bulletin. m.
Accreditation. q.
Accredited Institutions of Postsecondary Education. a.
Factbook. bien.
Semi-annual Board Meetings: April and October
1987-Baltimore, MD/April and San Francisco, CA/Oct.

Council on Roentgenology to the A.C.A.
Hist. Note: Became the Council on Diagnostic Imaging to the A.C.A. in 1986.

Council on Social Work Education (1952)
1744 R St., N.W., Washington DC 20009
Exec. Director: Eunice O. Shatz
Members: 5,000 *Staff:* 25
Annual Budget: $1-2,000,000 *Tel:* (202) 667-2300
Hist. Note: Accredits Baccalaureate and Masters degree programs of social work at colleges and universities. Formed by a merger of the Nat'l Council on Social Work Education, the Nat'l Ass'n of Schools of Social Administration and the American Ass'n of Schools of Social Work.
Publications:
Journal of Education for Social Work. 3/yr. adv.
Summary Information on Master of Social Work Programs. a.
Statistics on Social Work Education . a.
Annual Meetings: Feb./March
1987-St. Louis, MO(Clarion Hotel)/March 8-11/2,000

Council on Soil Testing and Plant Analysis (1970)
Georgia University Station, P.O. Box 2007, Athens GA 30612-0007
Secy.-Treas.: J. Benton Jones, Jr.
Members: 300-350 *Staff:* 1
Annual Budget: $10-25,000 *Tel:* (404) 542-2471
Hist. Note: Promotes uniform soil test and plant analysis methods, use, interpretation and terminology.
Publication:
Soil-Plant Analyst. q.
Annual Meetings: Fall, with the American Soc. of Agronomy.

Council on Synthetic Fuels
Hist. Note: Became Council on Alternate Fuels in 1986.

Council on Technology Teacher Education (1950)
Industrial Technology Dept., Eastern Michigan University, Ypsilanti MI 48197
Membership Secretary: Everett N. Israel
Members: 1,000 *Staff:* 1
Annual Budget: $10-25,000 *Tel:* (313) 487-2040
Hist. Note: Formerly (1986) American Council on Industrial Arts Teacher Education. Affiliated with the Internat'l Technology Education Ass'n (ITEA). Membership: $10/yr.
Publications:
Newsletter. a.
Yearbook. a.
Annual Meetings: March with Internat'l Technology Education Ass'n
1987-Tulsa, OK/March 23-27/1,500-2,000
1988-Norfolk, VA/March 21-25
1989-Dallas, TX/March 20-24

Country Day School Headmasters Ass'n of the U.S. (1912)
Norfolk Academy, 1585 Weslayan Drive, Norfolk VA 23502
Secretary: John H. Tucker, Jr.
Members: 80-100 *Staff:* 1
Annual Budget: under $10,000 *Tel:* (804) 461-6236
Private Meeting: Usually at a college site

Country Music Ass'n (1958)
P.O. Box 22299, Nashville TN 37202
Exec. Director: Jo Walker-Meador
Members: 7,250 individuals; 450 organizations *Staff:* 11-15
Annual Budget: $500-1,000,000 *Tel:* (615) 244-2840
Hist. Note: Membership is open to any individual or organization deriving income from country music. Membership: $50/yr.(individual); $125-1,250/yr.(organization).
Publication:
Close-Up. m.
Annual Meetings: Oct., in Nashville, TN

CPA Associates (1957)
230 Park Ave., New York NY 10169
President: Christopher W. Seidel
Members: 40 companies *Staff:* 2-5
Annual Budget: $500-1,000,000 *Tel:* (212) 818-9700
Hist. Note: Members, predominantly American, are accounting firms.
Publication:
Outlook. q.

Cranberry Institute (1951)
Hist. Note: Ceased operations in 1984.

Crane and Rigging Ass'n
Hist. Note: A section of the Specialized Carriers and Rigging Ass'n.

Crane Manufacturers Ass'n of America (1927)
8720 Red Oak Blvd., Suite 201, Charlotte NC 28210
Managing Director: Albert L. Leffler
Members: 19 companies *Staff:* 2-5
Annual Budget: $25-50,000 *Tel:* (704) 522-8644
Hist. Note: Formerly (1968) Electric Overhead Crane Institute, Inc. Member of the Machinery & Allied Products Institute.
Annual Meetings: With the Material Handling Institute, Inc.

Cranial Academy (1947)
1140 West Eighth St., Meridian ID 83642
Exec. Director: Madeline Rathjen
Members: 500 *Staff:* 1
Annual Budget: under $10,000 *Tel:* (208) 888-1201
Hist. Note: Affiliated with the American Academy of Osteopathy. Formerly (1960) Osteopathic Cranial Ass'n.
Publication:
News Letter. q.
Annual Meetings: Summer

Crayon Water Color and Craft Institute (1934)
Hist. Note: Became the Art and Craft Materials Institute in 1983.

Credit Union Executives Soc. (1962)
Box 14167, Madison WI 53714-0167
President: Mike Welch
Members: 3,000-3,200 *Staff:* 15-20
Annual Budget: $2-5,000,000 *Tel:* (608) 271-2664
Hist. Note: Membership: $220/yr.
Publications:
Credit Union Management Magazine. m. adv.
CU Marketing Magazine. q. adv.
FYI Management Memo. semi-m.
CU Directory.
Annual Meetings: June
1987-Las Vegas, NV(Hilton)/June 17-July 2
1988-Orlando, FL

00121 12 05 86 1233

Credit Union Nat'l Ass'n (1934)
5710 Mineral Point Rd., Box 431, Madison WI 53701
President: Jim R. Williams
Members: 52 State credit union leagues *Staff:* 200-225
Annual Budget: over $5,000,000 *Tel:* (608) 231-4000
Hist. Note: Formerly (1970) CUNA Internat'l Inc. Certifies qualified credit union employees and awards the CCUE (Certified Credit Union Executive) designation. Maintains a Washington Office. Supports the Credit Union Legislative Action Council, 1730 Rhode Island Ave., N.W., Washington, DC 20036. Has a budget of approximately $19 million.
Publications:
Credit Union News Watch. w.
Credit Union Executive. q. adv.
Credit Union Manager. bi-m.
Everybody's Money. q.
Directors Newsletter. m.
The Credit Union Magazine. m. adv.
Lending Letter. m.
Annual Meetings: Fall
1987-New Orleans, LA/Oct. 18-23/2,000

Credit Women-Internat'l (1930)
6500 Chippewa, Suite 225, St. Louis MO 63109
Exec. V. President: Esther Worthington
Members: 12-13,000 *Staff:* 2-5
Annual Budget: $100-250,000 *Tel:* (314) 752-9535
Hist. Note: Members are persons employed in credit or collections departments of business firms, professional offices or companies. Membership: $15/yr.
Publication:
Internat'l. semi-a.
Annual Meetings: June/600
1987-Seattle, WA(Westin)
1989-San Antonio, TX

Cremation Ass'n of North America (1913)
111 East Wacker Drive, Suite 600, Chicago IL 60601
Exec. Director: Jack M. Springer
Members: 700-800 *Staff:* 2-5
Annual Budget: $100-250,000 *Tel:* (312) 644-6610
Hist. Note: Formerly (1976) Cremation Ass'n of America. Members are crematories, cemeteries, funeral directors and suppliers. Membership: $150/yr. (plus $50 initiation fee)
Publications:
Cremationist. q. adv.
CANA Update. bi-m.
Annual Meetings: August
1987-Orlando, FL(Wyndham Hotel - Seaworld)/Aug. 26-29/325
1988-Chicago, IL(Fairmont Hotel)/Aug. 9-12
1989-Vancouver, Canada

Criminal Justice Statistics Ass'n (1972)
444 North Capitol St., N.W., Suite 606, Washington DC 20001
Exec. Director: Hildy Saizon
Members: 125 *Staff:* 4
Annual Budget: $250-500,000 *Tel:* (202) 347-4608
Hist. Note: Funding and administrative support is provided by the Federal Bureau of Justice Statistics. Members are directors of state criminal statistics analysis centers and individuals engaged in applied statistical analysis in criminal justice agencies at the state and local level. Purpose is to foster standardization of criminal justice statistics in the states & facilitate exchange of statistics among states. Membership: $40/yr.
Publications:
FORUM. q.
Directory of Criminal Justice Issues in the States. a.

Crop Dryer Manufacturers Council
Hist. Note: Affiliate of Farm & Industrial Equipment Institute

Crop-Hail Insurance Actuarial Ass'n (1948)
209 West Jackson Blvd., Room 700, Chicago IL 60606
Exec. V.P. & Manager: Lloyd W. Lindstrom
Members: 125-150 companies *Staff:* 53
Annual Budget: $2-5,000,000 *Tel:* (312) 922-7722
Hist. Note: Statistical and rating office for insurance on growing crops against the perils of weather, fire and transit.
Annual Meetings: February/March
1987-Granada Royale(Embassy Suites)/March 1-3/300

Crop Insurance Research Bureau (1964)
3707 Woodview Trace, P.O. Box 68700, Indianapolis IN 46268
Exec. V. President: Henry A. Butler
Members: 43 companies *Staff:* 2-5
Annual Budget: $100-250,000 *Tel:* (317) 875-5250
Hist. Note: Members are crop insurance and other related companies. Sponsors CIRB-PAC and crop insurance industry research. Provides industry liaison to the U.S. Department of Agriculture.
Publication:
Member News Bulletin.
Annual Meetings: February
1987-San Diego, CA

Crop Quality Council (1922)
Hist. Note: Dissolved August 31, 1983.

Crop Science Soc. of America (1955)
677 South Segoe Rd., Madison WI 53711
Exec. V. President: Robert F. Barnes
Members: 5,800 *Staff:* 25
Annual Budget: $250-500,000 *Tel:* (608) 273-8080
Hist. Note: Founded in 1955 and incorporated in Wisconsin in 1963. Shares headquarters with the American Soc. of Agronomy and the Soil Science Soc. of America.
Publications:
Crop Science. bi-m.
Journal of Environmental Quality. q.
Agronomy News. m.
Annual Meetings: With American Soc. of Agronomy and Soil Science Soc. of America
1987-Atlanta, GA(Hilton/Hyatt Regency/Westin)/Nov. 29-Dec. 4/4,000

Cross Country Ski Areas of America (1976)
RD 2 Bolton Road, Winchester NH 03451
Exec. Director: Chris Frado
Members: 180 *Staff:* 1
Annual Budget: $50-100,000 *Tel:* (603) 239-6387
Hist. Note: CCSAA is the industry representative of cross country ski area operators. It was formed to promote cross country skiing in North America, protect the interests of operators and establish standards of protection for the skier and operator. Membership: $250/yr.
Publication:
Newsletter. bi-m.
Annual Meetings: May

Crucible Institute (1919)
Hist. Note: Dissolved in 1984.

Cruise Lines Internat'l Ass'n (1975)
17 Battery Place, New York NY 10004
President: James G. Gordon
Members: 20 companies *Staff:* 12
Annual Budget: $1-2,000,000 *Tel:* (212) 425-7400

Crusher and Portable Plant Ass'n (1969)
30 Oak St., Stamford CT 06905
Secretary & Counsel: Herbert S. Blake, III
Members: 7 companies *Staff:* 2-5
Annual Budget: $10-25,000 *Tel:* (203) 324-0700
Hist. Note: Manufacturers of cone, jaw, gyratory, roll crushers, impactors, hammermills, and portable crushing plants.
Annual Meetings: With the Vibrating Screen Manufacturers Association.

Cryogenic Soc. of America (1964)
c/o Huget Advertising, 1033 South Blvd., Oak Park IL 60302
Recording Secretary: Werner K. Huget
Members: 250-300 *Staff:* 1
Annual Budget: under $10,000 *Tel:* (312) 383-7053
Hist. Note: Founded in Los Angeles in September, 1964 and incorporated in California the same year. Reincorporated in Illinois in 1984. Absorbed the Helium Soc. in 1971. Promotes the engineering and science of low temperatures. Membership: $30/yr.(individual); $200/yr.(corporate).
Publication:
Cold Facts. q.

Cultured Marble Institute (1974)
435 North Michigan Ave., Suite 1717, Chicago IL 60611
Exec. Director: Roy A. Brewer
Members: 185 companies *Staff:* 2-5
Tel: (312) 644-0828
Hist. Note: Manufacturers and suppliers of polester resin-based synthetic marble products.
Publications:
Cultured Marble News. q. adv.
Membership Directory-Supplier's Guide. a.
Annual Meetings: Spring
1987-Houston, TX
1988-Jacksonville, FL
1989-San Diego, CA

Cultured Pearl Ass'n of America (1954)
411 5th Ave., Room 801, New York NY 10016
Exec. Secretary: Barbara Perrin
Members: 60 *Staff:* 2-5
Annual Budget: $50-100,000 *Tel:* (212) 686-2720
Hist. Note: A group of cultured pearl importers in the New York area united for promotion and public relations.
Quarterly Meetings:

CUNA Internat'l (1934)
Hist. Note: Abbreviation for the Credit Union National Association.

Custom Clothing Guild of America (1982)
c/o Sew-It-Seams Magazine, Box 2698, Kirkland WA 98083
Publisher: Sharon Lewis
Members: 275 individuals *Staff:* 1
Annual Budget: under $10,000 *Tel:* (206) 244-4417
Hist. Note: Organization of professionals involved in the design and manufacture of clothing, accessories, textiles, and related services. Membership: $40/yr. Reported as relatively inactive in 1986, but inquiries are handled at the above number and address.
Publications:
Pacific Northwest Newsletter. m.
National Newsletter. q.

Custom Roll Forming Institute (1972)
522 Westgate Tower, Cleveland OH 44116
President: Robert Boeddener
Members: 25-30 companies *Staff:* 2-5
Annual Budget: $25-50,000 *Tel:* (216) 333-8848
Hist. Note: Members are makers of metal mouldings (such as curtain tracks) cold-rolled to customer specifications.
Annual Meetings: Fall

Custom Tailors and Designers Ass'n of America (1881)
565 5th Ave., New York NY 10017
Exec. Director: Irma B. Lipkin
Members: 350 *Staff:* 2-5
Annual Budget: $50-100,000 *Tel:* (212) 661-1960
Hist. Note: Trade association for men's custom tailoring industry. Formerly the Merchant Tailors and Designers Association of America. Membership: $175/yr. (minimum).
Publication:
The Custom Tailor. 3/yr. adv.
Annual Meetings: Late Winter
1987-Scottsdale, AZ(La Posada)/March 1-4/150

Customs and Internat'l Trade Bar Ass'n (1917)
c/o Siegel, Mandall and Davidson, 1 Whitehall Street, New York NY 10004
Secretary: Brian Goldstein
Members: 190-200
Annual Budget: under $10,000 *Tel:* (212) 425-0060
Hist. Note: Attorneys admitted to practice before the United States Court of International Trade (previously the United States Customs Court) and specializing in Customs and International Trade law in the United States. Formerly (until 1982) The Association of the Customs Bar.
Publication:
Newsletter. a.

Cutting Die Institute (1946)
420 Madonna, Venice FL 33596
Exec. Manager: Charles P. Arn
Members: 20 companies *Staff:* 2-5
Annual Budget: $50-100,000 *Tel:* (813) 426-1910
Hist. Note: Manufacturers of steel dies used to cut softer materials-plastics, leather, rubber, etc.
Annual Meetings: Spring
1987-Miami Beach, FL/March

Cutting Tool Manufacturers Ass'n (1943)
Hist. Note: Became the Cutting Tool Manufacturers of America in 1984.

Cutting Tool Manufacturers of America (1943)
1230 Keith Building, Cleveland OH 44115-2180
Exec. Director: C.M. Stockinger
Members: 175-200 companies *Staff:* 2-5
Annual Budget: $50-100,000 *Tel:* (216) 241-7333
Hist. Note: Trade association of manufacturers of tools and toolholders designed for cutting materials through use of a power driven machine tool. Formerly (1984) the Cutting Tool Manufacturers Ass'n. Membership: $365-1250/year (varies by number of employees).
Publication:
Cutting Tool Directory. bi-a.
Annual Meetings: Late winter

Cycle Parts and Accessories Ass'n (1942)
181 Salem Road, East Hills NY 11577
Exec. Director: John Auerbach
Members: 23 companies *Staff:* 2
Annual Budget: $100-250,000 *Tel:* (516) 484-7194
Annual Meetings: February/March in New York, NY

Cylinder Manufacturers Ass'n (1977)
1055 Thomas Jefferson St., N.W., Washington DC 20007
General Counsel: William W. Scott
Members: 16-20 companies
Annual Budget: $10-25,000 *Tel:* (202) 342-8400
Hist. Note: Established as the American Cylinder Manufacturers Committee, it assumed its present name in 1980. Members are makers of metal cylinders for industrial gases or fire extinguishing materials. The above address is the law firm of Collier, Shannon, Rill and Scott.

Cystic Fibrosis Foundation (1955)
6931 Arlington Road, Bethesda MD 20814
President and C.E.O.: Robert K. Dresing
Members: 25,000 *Staff:* 100-115
Annual Budget: over $5,000,000 *Tel:* (301) 951-4422
Hist. Note: Founded as Nat'l Cystic Fibrosis Research Foundation, it assumed its present name in 1975. Member of the Coalition for Health Funding in Washington. Has an annual budget of $20 million.
Publication:
Commitment. q.
Annual Meetings: Winter
1987-Washington, DC/Jan. 30-31

Dairy and Food Industries Supply Ass'n (1919)
6245 Executive Blvd., Rockville MD 20852
Exec. V. President: John M. Martin
Members: 600-645 *Staff:* 14
Annual Budget: $1-2,000,000 *Tel:* (301) 984-1444
Hist. Note: Founded as the Dairy and Ice Cream Machinery and Supplies Ass'n, it became the Dairy Industries Supply Ass'n and assumed its present name in 1963. Absorbed the

00122 12 05 86 1233

Nat'l Ass'n of Food and Dairy Equipment Manufacturers in 1976. Members are manufacturers and distributors of dairy and food industry machinery, equipment and supplies.
Publications:
DFISA Reporter. bi-m.
DFISA Marketing News. bi-m.
Annual Meetings: Spring/400
1987-Orlando, FL(Buena Vista Palace)/March 29-April 1
1988-Palm Springs, CA(Americana Canyon Hotel)/March 13-16

Dairy Research (1969)
6300 North River Road, Rosemont IL 60018
President: Anthony J. Luksas
Members: 350,000 *Staff:* 3
Tel: (312) 696-1860
Hist. Note: The commercial research and development arm of the United Dairy Industry Association. Formally known as Dairy Research, Inc.
Publication:
Dairy Research Digest. m.

Dairy Soc. Internat'l (1946)
7185 Ruritan Drive, Chambersburg PA 17201
Mng. Director: George W. Weigold
Members: 200 companies and associations *Staff:* 2-5
Annual Budget: $25-50,000 *Tel:* (717) 375-4392
Hist. Note: Founded as the Dairy Industry Societies, International, it assumed its present name in 1956. Members are associations and companies interested in expanding world consumption of milk and milk products. Has an international membership.
Publications:
Dairy Situation Review. 5/yr.
DSI Bulletin. 3/yr.
Market Frontier News. 6/yr.
Annual Meetings: Fall, usually with another dairy organization.

Dance Critics Ass'n
Box 47, Planetarium Station, 127 West 83rd St., New York NY 10024
Administrator: Karen Onoda
Members: 350 *Staff:* 1
Annual Budget: $10-25,000
Hist. Note: Professionals who review dance either on a regular basis or freelance; teachers, historians, publicists and others interested in dance writing. Conducts workshops on subjects of practical interest to dance critics.
Publication:
Newsletter. q.

Dance Educators of America (1932)
Box 509, Oceanside NY 11572-0509
Exec. Director: Grace Wakefield
Members: 2,000 *Staff:* 2-5
Annual Budget: $250-500,000 *Tel:* (516) 766-6615
Publication:
Official Bulletin. 5/yr. adv.
Annual Meetings: Summer.
1987-Las Vegas, NV

Dance Masters of America (1884)
Box 1117, Wauchula FL 33873
Exec. Secretary: Sharon Sockalosky
Members: 2,500 *Staff:* 2-5
Annual Budget: $250-500,000 *Tel:* (813) 773-2417
Hist. Note: An organization of dance teachers. Formerly (until 1926) known as the American Nat'l Ass'n, Masters of Dancing.
Publications:
DMA Bulletin. 5/yr. adv.
DMA Magazine. bi-m. adv.
Annual Meetings: August/500
1987-New York, NY/Aug. 1-8
1988-Miami Beach, FL
1989-New York, NY
1990-St. Louis, MO
1991-New York, NY
1992-San Francisco, CA
1993-New York, NY
1994-Lexington, KY

Danish-American Chamber of Commerce (USA) (1931)
825 3rd Ave., New York NY 10022
Exec. Secretary: Marianne Bork
Members: 150 companies, 150 individuals *Staff:* 1
Annual Budget: $50-100,000 *Tel:* (212) 980-6240
Hist. Note: Formed through a merger of the Danish-American Trade Council (1964) and the Danish Luncheon Club (1931). Members are concentrated in the New York City area. Membership: $60/yr. (individual); $175/yr. (corporate)
Publication:
Newsletter. bi-m. adv.
Monthly Meetings: in New York City

Data Entry Management Ass'n (1976)
750 Summer St., Stamford CT 06901
Exec. Director: Marilyn S. Bodek
Members: 2,000 *Staff:* 2-5
Tel: (203) 967-3500
Hist. Note: Membership: $66/year.
Publication:
Newsletter. m.
Annual Meetings: Fall/500

Data Processing Management Ass'n (1951)
505 Busse Hgwy., Park Ridge IL 60068
Exec. Director: John A. Venator
Members: 32,000 individuals *Staff:* 32
Annual Budget: $2-5,000,000 *Tel:* (312) 693-5070
Hist. Note: Formerly (1962) Nat'l Machine Accountants Ass'n. Members are managers of data processing installations; supervising systems and methods analysts; and programmers. Includes 18 Canadian chapters. A member of the National Commission on Softwares Issues in the Eighties, the American Federation of Information Processing Societies and the Institute for the Certification of Computer Professionals.
Publications:
Data Management. m. adv.
Your Computer Career. q.
Annual Meetings: Fall/10-12,000
1987-San Francisco, CA(Hilton and Tower)/Nov. 1-4
1988-Dallas, TX(Convention Ctr./Oct. 16-19

Daytime Broadcasters Ass'n (1953)
Hist. Note: Became inactive around 1972 but resumed operations about 1976. Merged with the Nat'l Ass'n of Broadcasters in 1985.

Dealer Bank Ass'n (1972)
529 14th St., Suite 200, Washington DC 20045
Exec. Director: Richard DeCair
Members: 175-185 banks *Staff:* 6-10
Annual Budget: $1-2,000,000 *Tel:* (202) 662-8766
Hist. Note: The trade association for commercial banks engaged in underwriting of and dealing in public securities. Sponsors the Dealer Bank Association Political Action Committee.
Publication:
The Dealer. m.
Annual Meetings: Spring
1987-San Diego, CA(del Coronado)/March 12-14

Decision Sciences Institute (1969)
University Plaza, Atlanta GA 30303
Exec. Director: Carol J. Latta
Members: 3,200 individuals, 700 libraries and companies *Staff:* 2-5
Annual Budget: $250-500,000 *Tel:* (404) 658-4005
Hist. Note: Formerly (1985) American Institute for Decision Sciences. Membership consists mainly of business school faculties and management specialists who use quantitative and behavioral techniques to apply theories of administrative decision-making.
Publications:
Decision Line. bi-m. adv.
Decision Sciences Journal. q. adv.
Annual Meetings: Fall/1,200
1987-Boston(Marriott-Copley Place/Nov. 23-25
1988-Las Vegas(Riviera Hotel)/Nov. 21-23
1989-New Orleans(Sheraton)/Nov. 20-22

Decorative Laminate Products Ass'n (1956)
600 South Federal St., Suite 400, Chicago IL 60605
Exec. Director: Charles Stolberg
Members: 220-230 companies *Staff:* 2-5
Annual Budget: $100-250,000 *Tel:* (312) 346-1600
Hist. Note: Members are manufacturers of decorative laminate-surface products such as countertops, cabinets, institutional casegoods, store fixtures, commercial millwork and furniture, interior doors and toilet compartments. Known as the Nat'l Ass'n of Plastic Fabricators until 1984.
Publications:
Membership Directory. a. adv.
DLPA NEWS. a. adv.
Annual Meetings: May
1987-Orlando, FL(Hotel Royal Plaza/May 12-17
1988-Tuscon, AZ(Sheraton El Conquistador)/May 17-22

Deep Foundations Institute (1975)
P.O. Box 281, Sparta NJ 07871-0281
Exec. Director: Robert Compton
Members: 625-650 *Staff:* 2-5
Tel: (201) 729-9679
Hist. Note: Incorporated in New Jersey in January, 1976. Concerned with the design, installation and stability of deep foundations of all types of structures.
Publication:
Deep Foundation News.

Defense Research Institute (1960)
750 North Lake Shore Drive, Suite 500, Chicago IL 60611
Exec. Director: Louis B. Potter
Members: 12,500 *Staff:* 20-25
Annual Budget: $2-5,000,000 *Tel:* (312) 944-0575
Hist. Note: Members are defense lawyers, insurance and manufacturing executives, and defendants. The Institute's primary purpose is to increase the professional skill and enlarge the knowledge of defense lawyers. Products and professional liability, insurance, environmental and equal opportunity law are some of the subjects with which members are concerned. Operates an arbitration service and provides a Brief Bank Index and Expert Witness Index.
Publication:
For the Defense. m.
Annual Meetings: With Internat'l Ass'n of Insurance Counsel.

Dehydrated and Convenience Foods Council (1964)
Hist. Note: Established in 1964 as Dehydrated Foods Industry Council. Became Dehydrated and Convenience Foods Council in 1975. Reported defunct in 1982.

Delta Dental Plans Ass'n (1965)
211 East Chicago Ave., Suite 1010, Chicago IL 60611
Exec. V. President: James Bonk
Members: 40-50 plans & dental societies *Staff:* 6-10
Annual Budget: $1-2,000,000 *Tel:* (312) 337-4707
Hist. Note: Formerly the Nat'l Ass'n of Dental Service Plans. A group of dental service corporations seeking to expand the provision of dental care on a pre-paid basis.
Publications:
Newsletter. m.
Membership Directory. a.
Annual Meetings: June
1987-Minneapolis, MN(Marriott)/June 25-29/200-300
1988-Boston, MA
1989-San Francisco, CA

Delta Omicron (1909)
1352 Redwood Court, Columbus OH 43229
Exec. Secretary: Jane Wiley Kuckuk
Members: 20-30,000
Annual Budget: $25-50,000 *Tel:* (614) 888-2640
Hist. Note: An international music fraternity founded September 6, 1909 at the Cincinnati Conservatory of Music and incorporated in the State of Ohio the same year.
Publications:
The Wheel of Delta Omicron. q.
The Whistle. a.
Triennial Meetings:
1987-Jefferson City, TN(Carson-Newman College)

Delta Pi Epsilon (1936)
Gustavus Adolphus College, St. Peter MN 56082
Exec. Director: Dr. Ellis J. Jones
Members: 10-11,000 *Staff:* 2-5
Annual Budget: $100-250,000 *Tel:* (507) 931-4184
Hist. Note: Professional Society in graduate business education. Founded at New York University in 1936 and incorporated in the State of New York, December 3, 1937. Reincorporated in Minnesota in 1983. Members are teachers of business subjects. National Membership: $25/yr.
Publications:
Business Education Index. a.
DPE Journal. q.
Annual Meetings: November
1987-Indianapolis, IN(Sheraton Meridian)/Nov. 11-14/125
1988-Fort Worth, TX(Hyatt Regency)/Nov. 9-12/250
1989-Pittsburgh, PA/Nov. 8-11/125
1990-Columbus, OH/Nov. 7-10/250
1991-Little Rock, AR/Nov. 13-16/125

Delta Sigma Delta (1882)
10885 Ventura Circle, Boynton Beach FL 33436
Supreme Scribe: Dr. Harry L. Hodges
Members: 26,000 *Staff:* 2-5
Annual Budget: $100-250,000 *Tel:* (305) 736-4979
Hist. Note: A professional dental fraternity founded at the University of Michigan November 15, 1882. Membership: $12/yr.
Publication:
Desmos of Delta Sigma Delta. q. adv.
Annual Meetings: Fall/150-200
1987-Las Vegas, NV/Oct. 7-10
1988-Washington, DC/Oct. 5-8
1989-Honolulu, HI/Nov. 1-4
1990-Boston, MA/Oct. 10-13

Delta Sigma Pi (1907)
330 South Campus Ave., Box 230, Oxford OH 45056-0230
Exec. Director: Michael J. Mazur
Members: 127,000 *Staff:* 11-15
Annual Budget: $500-1,000,000 *Tel:* (513) 523-4189
Hist. Note: Professional fraternity, commerce and business administration, founded at New York University November 7, 1907.
Publication:
The Deltasig. q.
Biennial Meetings: uneven years/650
1987-New Orleans(Fairmont)/Aug.
1989-St. Louis

Delta Soc. (1976)
321 Burnett Ave. S., Suite 303, Renton WA 98055
Exec. Director: Linda M. Hines
Members: 100 companies; 1,300 individuals *Staff:* 4
Annual Budget: $250-500,000 *Tel:* (206) 226-7357
Hist. Note: The Society is an international, educational, research and service resource on the relationships between people, animals and the environment. Members include veterinarians, psychiatrists, health workers, volunteers, administrators and teachers. Membership: $35/yr. (individual); $50/yr. (non-profit organization); $125/yr. (corporation)
Publications:
People-Animals-Environment. semi-a. adv.
Interactions. semi-a.
Anthrozos: Journal of the Delta Society. q.
Annual Meetings: October
1987-Vancouver, BC
1988-Orlando, FL

Delta Theta Phi (1913)
666 High St., Worthington OH 43085-4106
Assistant: Eileen Kobee
Members: 90,000 *Staff:* 2-5
Annual Budget: $250-500,000 *Tel:* (614) 888-2600
Hist. Note: Professional legal fraternity formed at the Cleveland Law School of Baldwin University, September 27, 1913 by merger of Alpha Kappa Phi, Delta Phi Delta and Theta Lambda Phi. Membership: $25/year.

00123 12 05 86 1233

Publication:
The Paper Book. q.
Biennial Meetings: uneven years, Summer.
1987-Minneapolis, MN/Aug. 12-15

Dental Dealers of America (1944)
1118 Land Title Bldg., Philadelphia PA 19110
Exec. Secretary: Dr. Edward B. Shils
Members: 90 wholesale distributors *Staff:* 2
Annual Budget: $25-50,000 *Tel:* (215) 563-2588
Annual Meetings: February, in Chicago with the Dental Manufacturers of America and Fall with the American Dental Association.

Dental Gold Institute (1981)
140 The Fenway, Boston MA 02115
Exec. Director: Louis J. P. Calisti, MPH
Members: 11-15 companies *Staff:* 1
Annual Budget: $100-250,000 *Tel:* (617) 423-1645
Hist. Note: Members are dental gold manufacturers united to promote the use of gold in dentistry following the dramatic rise in the price of gold in 1980.

Dental Group Management Ass'n (1971)
Hist. Note: Address unknown in 1987.

Dental Laboratory Conference (1941)
Warwick Hotel, Suites 411-412, 17th & Locust Sts., Philadelphia PA 19103
Exec. Director: Robert Gitman
Members: 200 *Staff:* 6-10
Annual Budget: $100-250,000 *Tel:* (215) 546-2313
Hist. Note: Membership: $800/yr.
Publication:
DLC New and Views. q. adv.
Semi-annual Meetings: Jan. and June
1987-Marco Island, FL/Jan. and San Francisco, CA/June
1988-Virgin Islands/Jan. and Cape Cod, MA/June

Dental Manufacturers of America (1932)
1118 Land Title Bldg., Philadelphia PA 19110
Exec. Director: Dr. Edward B. Shils
Members: 150 companies *Staff:* 3
Annual Budget: $100-250,000 *Tel:* (215) 563-2588
Three times a year: February, with the Dental Dealers of America;
fall, with the American Dental Association; and summer, membership meeting.

Dermatology Nurses Ass'n (1982)
Box 56, North Woodbury Road, Pitman NJ 08071
Exec. Secretary: Sherry K. Schussler
Members: 650 *Staff:* 2-5
Annual Budget: $10-25,000 *Tel:* (609) 582-1915
Hist. Note: Founded in New Orleans in December, 1982 and incorporated in the State of New Jersey. Membership: $50/yr.
Publication:
DNA Focus. bi-m. adv.
Annual Meetings: December
1987-San Antonio, TX(Wyndham)/Dec. 3-6

Detachable Container Ass'n (1955)
1730 Rhode Island Avenue, N.W., 10th Fl., Washington DC 20036
Exec. Director: Eugene Wingerter
Members: 70-80 companies
Annual Budget: under $10,000 *Tel:* (202) 659-4613
Hist. Note: An affiliate of the Nat'l Solid Wastes Management Ass'n, originally termed the Dempster Contract Haulers Ass'n. Members are makers and operators of trash collecting equipment that can be separated from its locomotive force. Administrative supports is provided by NSWMA.
Annual Meetings: Spring, with Nat'l Solid Wastes Management Ass'n

Devon Cattle Ass'n (1918)
Hist. Note: Address unknown in 1986. Probably defunct.

Diamond and Gemstone Remarketing Ass'n (1981)
Box 674, Frederick MD 21701
President: Will Hurwitz
Members: 25-30 brokers *Staff:* 1
Annual Budget: under $10,000 *Tel:* (301) 663-3501
Hist. Note: Members are brokers who remarket non-professional's diamonds and gems. Publishes a listing of available stones.
Annual Meetings: Summer in New York City

Diamond Core Drill Manufacturers Ass'n (1929)
3008 Millwood Ave., Columbia SC 29205
Secy.-Treas.: J. Edgar Eubanks
Members: 30 companies *Staff:* 8-10
Annual Budget: $10-25,000 *Tel:* (803) 252-5646
Hist. Note: Manufacturers of rotary exploration and masonry drills and equipment, and suppliers.
Annual Meetings: March, with the National Drilling Federation.

Diamond Council of America (1944)
9140 Ward Pkwy., Kansas City MO 64114
Exec. Director: Jerry Fogel
Members: 900-1,000 *Staff:* 6-10
Annual Budget: $50-100,000 *Tel:* (816) 444-3500
Hist. Note: Conducts correspondence course in gemology. Certifies employees as "Guild Gemologist" and "Certified Diamontologist". Supplies members with merchandising tools, advertising copy, displays, etc. to feature diamonds and other gems as a professional specialty.
Publication:
The Diamontologist. bi-m.
Semi-annual: February and July in New York City.

Diamond Manufacturers and Importers Ass'n of America (1932)
147 Willis Ave., Mineola NY 11501
Ass'n Attorney: Ben Kinzler
Members: 150-200 *Staff:* 2-5
Tel: (212) 944-2066
Hist. Note: Formerly the Diamond Manufacturers Association. Members are importers, cutters and polishers of rough diamonds.

Diamond Trade Ass'n of America (1940)
15 West 47th St., New York NY 10036
Secretary: Manny Cohen
Members: 700-800 *Staff:* 2-5
Annual Budget: $100-250,000 *Tel:* (212) 869-5200
Annual Meetings: 2nd Tuesday of January in New York, NY

Diamond Wheel Manufacturers Institute (1963)
712 Lakewood Center North, 14600 Detroit Ave., Cleveland OH 44107
Manager: Allen P. Wherry
Members: 32 companies *Staff:* 2-5
Tel: (216) 226-7700
Hist. Note: Members are makers of diamond-coated grinding wheels.

Die Casting Federation
Hist. Note: Reported inactive in 1986.

Die Casting Research Foundation (1951)
2340 Des Plaines Ave., Des Plaines IL 60018
President: Peter A. R. Findlay
Members: 200-250 companies *Staff:* 6-10
Annual Budget: $100-250,000 *Tel:* (312) 298-1220
Hist. Note: A subsidiary of the American Die Casting Institute.
Annual Meetings: With the American Die Casting Institute, Fall, in the Chicago area.

Die Set Manufacturers Service Bureau (1951)
25 North Broadway, Tarrytown NY 10591
Secretary: Richard C. Byrne
Members: 5-7 companies *Staff:* 2-5
Annual Budget: $10-25,000 *Tel:* (914) 332-0040
Hist. Note: Establishes inch and metric standards. Technical Committee serves both nationally and internationally in the setting of engineering standards. Membership open to all manufacturers of standard and special die sets.
Annual Meetings: Fall

Diesel Engine Manufacturers Ass'n (1944)
712 Lakewood Center North, 14600 Detroit Ave., Cleveland OH 44107
Secy.-Treas.: Allen P. Wherry
Members: 6-10 companies *Staff:* 2-5
Annual Budget: $25-50,000 *Tel:* (216) 226-7700
Hist. Note: Trade association of U.S. manufacturers of diesel and/or internal combustion engines whose product line includes units of 1,000 or more horsepower.
Semi-annual Meetings: June and November

Dietary Managers Ass'n (1960)
4410 W. Roosevelt Road, Hillside IL 60162
Exec. Director: William St. John
Members: 12,000 individuals *Staff:* 6-10
Annual Budget: $500-1,000,000 *Tel:* (312) 449-2770
Hist. Note: Formerly (1984) the Hospital, Institution and Educational Food Service Soc. Members are people with managerial responsiblities in kitchens.
Publication:
Issues. bi-m.
Annual Meetings: July/August
1987-Pittsburgh,PA/Aug. 2-6
1988-Kansas City,MO/July 31-Aug. 4

Diplomatic and Consular Officers, Retired (1952)
1801 F St., N.W., Washington DC 20006
Exec. Director: Allen B. Moreland
Members: 2,200-2,300 *Staff:* 2-5
Annual Budget: $100-250,000 *Tel:* (202) 682-0500
Hist. Note: Established as the Retired Foreign Service Officers Association, it assumed its present name in 1952. Members are principally active and retired Foreign Service officers. Now accepts members with overseas experience from other government agencies and operates Dacor House in Washington.
Publication:
Dacor Bulletin. m.
Annual Meetings: Washington, DC in Spring.

Direct Mail Fundraisers Ass'n (1972)
1501 Broadway, Suite 610, New York NY 10036
President: Mary E. Cooke
Members: 200-225 *Staff:* 1
Annual Budget: under $10,000 *Tel:* (212) 581-7400
Hist. Note: Members are primarily direct mail managers for charity organizations. Has no paid staff; officers change annually. Membership: $50/yr.
Publication:
Newsletter. semi-a.
Monthly Luncheon Meetings:

Direct Marketing Ass'n (1917)
6 East 43rd St., New York NY 10017
President and C.E.O.: Jonah Gitlitz
Members: 2,770 companies; 5,500 individuals *Staff:* 100
Annual Budget: over $5,000,000 *Tel:* (212) 689-4977
Hist. Note: Formerly Direct Mail/Marketing Ass'n and Direct Mail Advertising Ass'n. Absorbed the Business Mail Foundation. Maintains a Washington office. Supports the Direct Marketing Ass'n Political Action Committee. Has an annual budget of approximately $12 million.
Publications:
Fact Book. a.
International Fact Book. a.
Washington Report (Members Only). m.
Direct Line (Members Only). m.
Directions (Members Only). bi-m.
DMA Matters (Members Only). q.
Dateline: DMA (Members Only). q.
Semi-annual Meetings: Spring and Fall/6,000

Direct Marketing Computer Ass'n (1982)
315 W. 58th St., 25th Floor, New York NY 10019
Exec. Secretary: Sheila Nero
Members: 150 companies *Staff:* 2
Annual Budget: $250-500,000 *Tel:* (212) 245-0167
Hist. Note: Members are companies and individuals using computers for direct mail marketing. Membership: $750/yr.
Publication:
Input/Output Newsletter. bi-m.
Annual Meetings: February

Direct Marketing Creative Guild (1972)
516 Fifth Ave., New York NY 10036
Member-at-Large: Andi Emerson
Members: 900 individuals
Annual Budget: $10-25,000 *Tel:* (212) 213-0320
Hist. Note: Founded as the Nat'l Ass'n of Direct Mail Writers. Incorporated as the Direct Marketing Writers' Club in 1972. Became the Direct Marketing Writers' Guild, Inc., in 1975. Assumed its present name in 1980. Has no paid staff. Membership: $50/yr.
Publication:
Creative Forum. m. adv.

Direct Marketing Credit Ass'n (1965)
The History Book Club, Inc., 40 Guernsey St., Box 790, Stamford CT 06904
President: William Duhigg
Members: 40-50 *Staff:* 1
Annual Budget: under $10,000 *Tel:* (203) 359-4250
Hist. Note: Individuals in the mail order industry concerned with credit and collections. Affiliated with Direct Mail/Marketing Association. Until 1979 known as the Direct Mail Credit Association. Membership: $125/yr.
Annual Meetings: Monthly meetings in New York City

Direct Selling Ass'n (1910)
1776 K St., N.W., Suite 600, Washington DC 20006
President: Neil H. Offen
Members: 100-200 *Staff:* 25-30
Annual Budget: $2-5,000,000 *Tel:* (202) 293-5760
Hist. Note: Formerly (1969) Nat'l Ass'n of Direct Selling Companies. Sponsors Direct Selling Education Foundation. Manufacturers and distributors retailing products via door-to-door, party plan and other direct-to-consumer methods. Supports the Direct Selling Association Political Action Committee and the Direct Selling Education Foundation.
Publications:
Action Needed Bulletin. irreg.
Advisory Memorandum. irreg.
At Home wih Consumers. q.
Briefing for Members. m.
International Bulletin. q.
State and Federal Tax Notes. Irreg.
Annual Meetings: Spring/450
1987-White Sulphur Springs, WV(Greenbrier)/May 31-June 3

Directors Guild of America (1936)
7950 Sunset Blvd., Hollywood CA 90046
Nat'l Exec. Director: Michael H. Franklin
Members: 8,000 *Staff:* 85
Annual Budget: over $5,000,000 *Tel:* (213) 656-1220
Hist. Note: Independent labor union. Merger of Screen Directors Guild of America, the Radio and Television Directors Guild, Screen Directors Int'l Guild, and IATSE Asst. Dirs.
Publication:
DGA Directory of Members. a.
Biennial meetings: Uneven years

Display Distributors Ass'n (1968)
Art R. Cohen Co., 949 Pennsylvania Ave., Pittsburgh PA 15222
Exec. Director: Paul Cohen

00124 12 05 86 1233

Members: 19 companies *Staff:* 1
Annual Budget: $25-50,000 *Tel:* (412) 281-4052
Hist. Note: Members are companies distributing display products. Incorporated in the State of Illinois.
Semi-annual Meetings: June & Dec. in New York, NY(Warwick Hotel)

Distilled Spirits Council of the United States (1973)
1250 Eye St., N.W., Suite 900, Washington DC 20005
President/C.E.O.: F. A. Meister
Members: 35 companies *Staff:* 60
Annual Budget: over $5,000,000 *Tel:* (202) 628-3544
Hist. Note: A trade association of domestic distillers; also known as DISCUS. Merger of the Distilled Spirits Institute (1933), the Bourbon Institute (1958), and Licensed Beverage Industries (1946). Absorbed the Tax Council-Alcoholic Beverage Industries. Connected with the Distilled Spirits Council Political Action Committee. Has an annual budget of $7-10,000,000.
Publications:
Facts Book. a.
Public Revenues. a.
Statistical Review. a.
Annual Meetings: Winter/300

Distillers Feed Research Council (1947)
P.O. Box 23097, Des Moines IA 50322
Exec. Director: Robert H. Hatch
Members: 15-20 *Staff:* 2-5
Annual Budget: $100-250,000 *Tel:* (515) 224-6802
Hist. Note: Members are beverage distillers who process grain and recover therefrom other products such as animal feed and pharmaceutical products.
Publication:
Distillers Feed Conference Proceedings. a.
Annual Meetings: Spring/300

Distillery, Wine and Allied Workers' Internat'l Union (1940)
66 Grand Ave., Englewood NJ 07631
President: George J. Orlando
Members: 20,000 *Staff:* 6-10
Annual Budget: $1-2,000,000 *Tel:* (201) 569-9212
Hist. Note: Chartered December 20, 1940 by the American Federation of Labor as the Distillery, Rectifying and Wine Workers International Union. Became the Distillery, Rectifying, Wine and Allied Workers International Union of America in 1962 and adopted its present name in 1978.
Publication:
DWU Newsletter (internal). q.
Quadrennial Meetings (for members only): 1988

Distribution Codes Institute
1900 Arch St., Philadelphia PA 19103
President: Robert G. Clifton
Members: 12 wholesale associations *Staff:* 1
Annual Budget: $10-25,000 *Tel:* (215) 564-3484
Hist. Note: Maintains and develops information on DC code for industrial and commercial products. Note: DC code has merged with UPC code for retail and industrial goods. Formerly Distribution Number Bank.

Distribution Contractors Ass'n (1961)
531 Harvard Tower, Tulsa OK 74135
Mng. Director: James R. Upton
Members: 125 companies *Staff:* 2-5
Annual Budget: $100-250,000 *Tel:* (918) 743-1513
Hist. Note: Membership consists of firms engaged in underground pipeline construction and manufacturers and suppliers of construction equipment.
Publication:
Newsletter. bi-w.
Annual Meetings: Winter
1987-Palm Springs, CA/Feb. 1-4

Distributive Education Clubs of America (1947)
1908 Association Drive, Reston VA 22091
Exec. Director: Frederick L. Williford
Members: 190-200,000 individuals *Staff:* 20-25
Annual Budget: $1-2,000,000 *Tel:* (703) 860-5000
Hist. Note: Members are individuals, for the most part students, concerned with distribution, marketing, merchandising and management.
Publications:
New Dimensions. q. adv.
DECA Advisor.
Annual Meetings: Spring
1987-New Orleans, LA/April 29-May 3 and May 6-10
1988-Salt Lake City, UT/April 28-May 1 and May 4-8
1989-Orlando, FL/April 27-30 and May 3-7

Div. of Applied Experimental and Engineering Psychology (1953)
Institute of Aviation, Univ. of Illinois, Willard Airport, One Airport Road, Savoy IL 61874
Secretary: Henry L. Taylor
Members: 680 *Staff:* 1
Annual Budget: under $10,000 *Tel:* (217) 333-2411
Hist. Note: A division of the American Psychological Ass'n. Formerly (1984) the Soc. of Engineering Psychologists and (1985) the Soc. of Applied Experimental and Engineering Psychology. Membership: $105/yr.
Publication:
Newsletter. q.
Annual Meetings: With American Psychological Ass'n
1987-Dallas, TX

Diving Equipment Manufacturers Ass'n (1972)
Box 217, Tustin CA 92681
Exec. Director: Robert L. Gray
Members: 220-240 companies *Staff:* 2-5
Annual Budget: $500-1,000,000 *Tel:* (714) 730-0650
Hist. Note: Membership: $300-$500/year.
Annual Meetings: January/4,000
1987-Las Vegas, NV(Convention Center)/Jan. 22-25
1988-New Orleans, LA(Convention Center)/Jan. 28-31
1989-Las Vegas, NV(Convention Center)/Jan. 26-29
1990-Orlando, FL(Convention Center)/Jan. 18-21

Do-It-Yourself Research Institute (1981)
770 North High School Road, Indianapolis IN 46224
Liaison: Rhonda McKittrick
Members: 37 companies *Staff:* 5
Annual Budget: $250-500,000 *Tel:* (317) 241-1070
Hist. Note: Members are manufacturers, wholesalers and retailers involved in the "do-it-yourself" market (i.e. self home improvement, auto repair, landscaping/gardening, etc.). Membership: $1,000-10,000/year.
Publications:
Newsletter. q.
DIY Consumer Outlook: A Reference Guide. a.
The DIY Industry Looking Ahead: A Delphi Study. a.

Domestic Petroleum Council (1975)
Hist. Note: Address unknown in 1986. Probably defunct.

Domestic Wildcatters Ass'n (1975)
Hist. Note: Comparatively inactive in 1985-86.

Door and Hardware Institute (1934)
7711 Old Springhouse Road, McLean VA 22102-3474
Exec. V. President: Richard M. Hornaday, CAE
Members: 4,000 individuals *Staff:* 14-17
Annual Budget: $2-5,000,000 *Tel:* (703) 556-3990
Hist. Note: Founded as the Nat'l Contract Hardware Ass'n, it became the Nat'l Builders Hardware Ass'n in 1954. The Door and Hardware Institute is the result of a merger in 1975 with the American Soc. of Architectural Hardware Consultants. Distributors and manufacturers of doors and builders' hardware, and architectural hardware and certified door consultants.
Publications:
Doors and Hardware. m. adv.
DHI Blueprint. bi-m.
DHI Distributor. q.
DHI Membership Directory. a.
Canadian Viewpoint. q.
DHI Buyer's Guide. bi-a.
Annual Meetings: Fall/3,000
1987-Anaheim, CA(Disneyland)
1988-Toronto, Canada
1989-Houston, TX
1990-Philadelphia, PA
1991-Denver, CO
1992-Nashville, TN
1993-Vancouver, BC

Door and Operator Dealers (1973)
Box 117, 28 Lowry Drive, West Milton OH 45383
Exec. V. President: Christopher S. Long
Members: 6-700 companies *Staff:* 2-5
Annual Budget: $100-250,000 *Tel:* (513) 698-4186
Hist. Note: Formerly Door and Operator Dealers of America. Members are makers and installers of overhead garage door systems.
Publication:
DODA News. bi-m. adv.
Annual Meetings: Summer
1987-Nashville, TN

Door and Operator Dealers of America (1973)
Hist. Note: Name changed to Door and Operator Dealers in 1986.

Door Operator and Remote Controls Manufacturers Ass'n (1959)
655 West Irving Park, Suite 201 Park Place, Chicago IL 60613-3198
Exec. Secretary: Frank S. Fitzgerald, CAE
Members: 15-20 companies *Staff:* 2-5
Annual Budget: $50-100,000 *Tel:* (312) 525-2644
Triannual Meetings: Chicago, IL(Skybird Mutiny Ctr.)/Jan.,April,Sept.

Dramatists Guild (1921)
234 West 44th St., New York NY 10036
Exec. Director: David E. LeVine
Members: 8,000 *Staff:* 16-20
Annual Budget: $500-1,000,000 *Tel:* (212) 398-9366
Hist. Note: Affiliated with Authors League of America and the Authors Guild, Inc. The professional association of American playwrights, composers and lyricists. Members are entitled to use the Guild's "Approved Production Contract". Membership: $35/yr. (individual), $50/yr. (company).
Publications:
Dramatists Guild Quarterly. q.
Newsletter. m.
Annual Meetings: New York City

Drapery Specialists Institute (1971)
Hist. Note: A division of the Ass'n of Specialists in Cleaning and Restoration.

Driving School Ass'n of America (1973)
111 West Pomona Blvd., Monterey Park CA 91754
Co-Founder and Editor: George R. Hensel
Members: 600
Annual Budget: $25-50,000 *Tel:* (213) 728-2100
Hist. Note: Trade association of professional and state licensed driving schools in the U.S. and Canada, as well as spokesmen of state associations. Membership: $60-300/year.
Publication:
Dual News. adv.
Annual Meetings: November

Drug, Chemical and Allied Trades Ass'n (1890)
42-40 Bell Blvd., Suite 604, Bayside NY 11361
Exec. V. President: Joseph D. Madden, CAE
Members: 500 companies *Staff:* 2-4
Annual Budget: $250-500,000 *Tel:* (718) 229-8891
Hist. Note: Until 1961, the Drug, Chemical and Allied Trades Section of the New York Board of Trade. Represents all segments of the drug, chemical and cosmetics industries, such as manufacturers, advertising agencies, agents and brokers. Membership dues based on number of employees in the firm.
Publication:
Digest of Current Activities and Trends. m.
Annual Meetings: Fall/500
1987-Boca Raton, FL(Hotel & Club)/Oct. 14-18
1988-Palm Beach, FL(Breakers)/Oct. 19-23
1989-Palm Desert, CA(Marriott's Desert Springs)/Nov. 15-19
1990-Boca Raton, FL(Hotel & Club)/Oct. 24-28
1991-Hilton Head, SC(Intercontinental)/Oct. 23-27

Drug Information Ass'n (1965)
P.O. Box 113, Maple Glen PA 19002
Admin. Director: Thomas W. Teal
Members: 4,000 *Staff:* 2-5
Annual Budget: $1-2,000,000 *Tel:* (215) 628-2288
Hist. Note: Members are individuals from the pharmaceutical industry, government, and academia responsible for processing and disseminating information on medicine and drugs in medicine, biology, pharmacy, and allied human/animal fields. Membership: $40/yr.
Publications:
Drug Information Journal. q. adv.
Newsletter.
Annual Meetings: June/600-700
1987-San Francisco, CA(Hyatt)
1988-Toronto, Ontario(Sheraton Centre)

Drug Wholesalers Ass'n (1974)
Hist. Note: The Pharmaceutical Distributors International (formed in 1956) and the Federal Wholesale Druggists Association of the the U.S.A. and Canada (formed in 1916) merged in 1974 to form the International Pharmaceutical Distributors Association. This, in turn, became the Drug Wholesalers Association on April 23, 1976. Merged into the Nat'l Wholesale Druggists' Ass'n in 1984.

Dry Color Manufacturers Ass'n (1922)
P.O. Box 20839, Alexandria VA 22320-1839
Exec. V. President: J. Lawrence Robinson, CAE
Members: 50 companies *Staff:* 2-5
Annual Budget: $250-500,000 *Tel:* (703) 684-4044
Hist. Note: Manufacturers of organic and inorganic color pigments.
Annual Meetings: White Sulphur Springs, WV/June

Dry Process Ceramic and Steatite Manufacturers Ass'n (1978)
25 North Broadway, Tarrytown NY 10591
Secretary: Richard C. Byrne
Members: 12 companies *Staff:* 2-5
Annual Budget: $25-50,000 *Tel:* (914) 332-0040
Hist. Note: Established through a merger of the Steatite Manufacturers Ass'n (founded in 1956) and the Dry Process Ceramic Manufacturers Ass'n. Members are makers of ceramics and steatite used in the manufacturer of various electronic products.

Ductile Iron Pipe Research Ass'n (1915)
245 Riverchase Pkwy. East, Suite 0, Birmingham AL 35244
President: Troy F. Stroud
Members: 6 companies *Staff:* 20-25
Annual Budget: $1-2,000,000 *Tel:* (205) 988-9870
Hist. Note: Established as the Cast Iron Pipe Publicity Bureau, it later became the Cast Iron Pipe Institute, and the Cast Iron Pipe Research Association in 1928. Assumed its present name in 1981.
Publications:
Ductile Iron Pipe News. semi-a.
Ductile Iron Pipe Handbook. a.
Quarterly Meetings: March, June, Sept., Nov.

Ductile Iron Soc. (1958)
615 Sherwood Pkwy., Mountainside NJ 07092
Exec. Director: Keith D. Millis
Members: 80-90 foundries *Staff:* 2-5
Annual Budget: $100-250,000 *Tel:* (201) 232-3080

00125 12 05 86 1233

Hist. Note: Ductile Iron is a casting material having properties similar to cast steel and processing characteristics similar to cast iron. Membership: $1,400-6,000/yr. (based on sales).
Publications:
Ductile Iron News. 3/yr.
Ductile Technical Notes and Items. q.
Annual Meetings: Three annually
1987-Akron, OH(Quaker Square Hilton)/June 3-5/150

Dude Ranchers' Ass'n (1926)
Box 471, LaPorte CO 80535
Exec. Secretary: Amey Grubbs
Members: 60-65 guest ranches *Staff:* 2-5
Annual Budget: $25-50,000 *Tel:* (303) 493-7623
Hist. Note: Organized in Billings, Montana in November 1926 to protect the image of the dude ranch industry, promote ranch properties and preserve the western ranch way of life. Membership: $15/yr.(individual); $25/yr.(commercial).
Publications:
The Dude Rancher. semi-a.
Dude Ranch Vacations Directory. a.
Annual Meetings: December or January, by vote of the previous convention.
1987-Anaheim, CA(Conestoga Hotel)/Jan. 5-8

Dump Transport Industries Ass'n
Hist. Note: Reported defunct in 1986.

Durene Ass'n of America
Hist. Note: Dissolved in 1986.

Durum Wheat Institute (1944)
Hist. Note: Members are millers of durum wheat. Durum wheat is grown principally in Northeastern North Dakota, and is ground into semolina, or flour for making spaghetti, macaroni, noodles and similar products. Absorbed by the Millers' Nat'l Federation in 1982.

Dutch Belted Cattle Ass'n of America (1909)
Hist. Note: Address unknown in 1987.

Dyes Environmental and Toxicology Organization (1977)
Hist. Note: Dissolved in 1982 and replaced by the U.S. Operating Committee of the Ecological and Toxicological Association of the Dyestuffs Manufacturing Industry (ETAD), an international organization.

Early Sites Research Soc. (1973)
Long Hill, Rowley MA 01969
Director: James Whittall
Members: 200-250 *Staff:* 1
Annual Budget: under $10,000 *Tel:* (617) 948-2410
Hist. Note: Membership, concentrated in the Northeast, is composed of archeologists involved in exploring unidentified antiquities.
Publication:
Early Sites Bulletin. semi-a.
Semi-annual Meetings: Spring and Fall

Ecological and Toxilogical Ass'n of the Dyestuffs Manufacturing Industry (1982)
Hist. Note: An international trade association; the United States Operating Committee of ETAD is the U.S. affiliate.

Ecological Soc. of America (1915)
Dept. of Botany, Univ. of Tennessee-Knoxville, Knoxville TN 37996
Secretary: Hazel R. Delcourt
Members: 6,100 *Staff:* 4
Annual Budget: $250-500,000 *Tel:* (615) 974-3094
Hist. Note: Organized December 1915 in Columbus, Ohio at the annual meeting of the American Association for the Advancement of Science. A professional society of individuals interested in the study of living things in relation to their environment. Member society of the American Institute of Biological Sciences. Represented on the Council of the American Ass'n for the Advancement of Science and the Nat'l Research Council. Membership: $45/year.
Publications:
Bulletin of the Ecological Soc. of America. q.
Ecology. bi-m.
Ecological Monographs. q.
Annual Meetings: Summer
1987-Columbus, OH(Ohio State University)/Aug. 9-16/2,000

Econometric Soc. (1930)
Dept. of Economics, Northwestern Univ., Evanston IL 60201
Exec. Director: Julie Gordon
Members: 6,000 *Staff:* 2-5
Annual Budget: $100-250,000 *Tel:* (312) 492-3615
Hist. Note: An international society for the advancement of economic theory in its relation to mathematics and statistics. Organized in Cleveland, Ohio, December 29, 1930 with Professor Irving Fisher of Yale University as first president.
Publications:
Econometrica. bi-m. adv.
Programs and Abstracts of Papers. a.
Tri-annual Meetings:
1987-Berkeley, CA(Univ. of CA)/June 24-27
1987-New Zealand(Univ. of Canterbury)/Aug. 26-28
1987-New Orleans, LA/Dec. 28-30

Economic History Ass'n (1940)
c/o Hagley Museum and Library, Box 3630, Greenville DE 19807
Secy.-Treas.: Richmond D. Williams
Members: 3,300 *Staff:* 1-3
Annual Budget: $50-100,000 *Tel:* (302) 658-2400
Hist. Note: Member American Council of Learned Societies.
Publication:
Journal of Economic History. q. adv.
Annual Meetings: September

Economics News Broadcasters Ass'n (1977)
Hist. Note: Incorporated in 1977 in the District of Columbia. Members are broadcasters of business news on radio and television, interested in stimulating public demand for more economic information on the air. Address unknown since 1984.

ECRI (1955)
5200 Butler Pike, Plymouth Meeting PA 19462
President: Dr. Joel J. Nobel
Members: 2,400 hospitals *Staff:* 110
Annual Budget: over $5,000,000 *Tel:* (215) 825-6000
Hist. Note: Consultation services related to health care technology and clinical engineering. Founded as the Graduate Pain Research Foundation, it became the Emergency Care Research Institute in 1968 and assumed its present name in 1980. Membership: $975/yr.
Publications:
Health Devices. m.
Health Devices Alerts. w.
Technology in Health Care Newsletter. m.
Health Devices Sourcebook. q.
Hospital Risk Control.
Issues in Health Care Technology.
Journal of Health Care Technology.
Product Comparison Journals in: Hospital Products, Clinical Laboratory
Products, Imaging and Radiology Products, and Operating Rm. Products.

Ecuadorean American Ass'n (1932)
111 Broadway, Suite 1408, New York NY 10006
Secretary: Linda Calvet
Members: 70 companies, 50 individuals *Staff:* 3
Annual Budget: $25-50,000 *Tel:* (212) 233-7776
Hist. Note: Promotes greater knowledge and understanding of modern Ecuador; seeks seeks to disseminate information on current events and on economic and financial matters of concern to investors in Ecuador; and promotes commercial and cultural relations and good will among the people of the two countries. Membership: $150/yr.(individual); $350/yr.(corporate).
Publications:
News Digest. m.
Special Reports. irreg.

Edison Electric Institute (1933)
1111 19th St., N.W., Washington DC 20036-3691
President: William McCollam, Jr.
Members: 200 *Staff:* 280-300
Annual Budget: over $5,000,000 *Tel:* (202) 828-7400
Hist. Note: Investor-owned electric utility companies. Absorbed (Feb. 1, 1975) the Electric Energy Ass'n (1972), which now serves as the Conservation and Energy Management Division. Merged, August 1, 1978, with the Nat'l Ass'n of Electric Companies, which now serves as the Institute's Governmental Affairs Division. Sponsors the Constructive Congress Committee of the Edison Electric Institute, a political action committee.
Publication:
Electric Perspectives. q.
Annual Meetings: Spring/2,500
1987-Cincinnati, OH/June 8-10
1988-Washington, DC/June 13-15
1989-Portland, OR/June 5-7
1990-Kansas City, MO/June 4-6
1991-San Diego, CA/June 3-5

Editorial Freelancers Ass'n (1975)
Box 2050, Madison Square Station, New York NY 10159
Co-Executive: Trumbull Rogers
Members: 500-600 *Staff:* 1
Annual Budget: $25-50,000 *Tel:* (212) 677-3357
Hist. Note: Members provide freelance editorial services to the publishing and communications industries.
Publications:
Newsletter. bi-m.
Directory. a.
Annual Meetings: New York, NY/June

EDP Auditors Ass'n, The (1969)
455 Kehoe Blvd., Suite 106, Carol Stream IL 60188
Exec. Director: Gerard Fee
Members: 9,000 individuals *Staff:* 6-10
Annual Budget: $1-2,000,000 *Tel:* (312) 682-1200
Hist. Note: Formed to help auditors, managers and systems specialists address electronic data processing system control problems and develop methods and techniques to eliminate them. Maintains a research and education subsidiary, The EDP Auditors Foundation; belongs to the Nat'l Commission on Software Issues in the Eighties. Membership: $70/yr.
Publications:
Control Objectives. a.
EDP Auditor Journal. q. adv.
EDP Auditor Update. bi-m. adv.
Annual Meetings: June

1987-Seattle, WA
1988-New Orleans, LA
1989-Toronto, Ontario
1990-New York, NY
1991-San Francisco, CA

Education Soc.
Hist. Note: A subsidiary of the Institute of Electrical and Electronics Engineers. Membership in the Society, open only to IEEE members, includes subscription to a technical periodical in the field published by IEEE. All administrative support is provided by IEEE.

Education Writers Ass'n (1947)
1001 Connecticut Ave., N.W., Washington DC 20036
Exec. Director: Lisa J. Walker
Members: 400-500 individuals *Staff:* 2-5
Annual Budget: $50-100,000
Hist. Note: Members work for newspapers, magazines and broadcasting stations and freelance. Absorbed the Nat'l Council for the Advancement of Education Writing in 1975. Membership: $50/year.
Publications:
The Education Reporter. bi-m.
EWA Membership Directory. a.
Annual Meetings: Spring
1987-San Francisco, CA(Sir Francis Drake)/April 2-5/110-150
1988-Washington, DC

Educational Dealers and Suppliers Ass'n Internat'l (1984)
P.O. Box 3551, Covina CA 91722
Exec. Director: Dawn M. Mancuso
Staff: 2
Tel: (818) 331-7633
Hist. Note: EDSA Internat'l was formed and incorporated in California with the goal of providing member services in a cost-effective manner to all sectors of the education market. Membership: $25/yr. (company only)
Publication:
EDSA International News. bi-m. adv.
Annual Meetings: Spring
1987-Orlando, FL(Omni/Expo Centre)/April 3-5

Educational Film Library Ass'n (1943)
45 John St., Suite 301, New York NY 10038
Exec. Director: Marilyn J. Levin
Members: 1,500 *Staff:* 6-10
Annual Budget: $250-500,000 *Tel:* (212) 227-5599
Hist. Note: Internationally known as the sponsor of the American Film Festival, the most important nontheatrical film/video competition in the U.S. Membership: $45/yr.(individual); $175-265/yr.(company).
Publications:
EFLA Bulletin. q.
EFLA Evaluations. q.
Sightlines. q. adv.
American Film Festival: May-June
1987-New York, NY(International Vista Hotel)/June 18-23

Educational Paperback Ass'n (1975)
Hist. Note: Address unknown in 1985-86.

Educational Press Ass'n of America (1895)
Glassboro State College, Glassboro NJ 08028
Exec. Director: Don Stoll
Members: 550-600 *Staff:* 2-5
Annual Budget: $25-50,000 *Tel:* (609) 863-7349
Hist. Note: Members are writers and editors of educational publications. Membership: $35/yr.(individual); $75/yr.(organization).
Publications:
Edpress News. 10/yr.
Edpress Membership Roster and Free-Lance Directory. a.
Annual Meetings: Summer

EDUCOM (1964)
Rosedale Road, Box 364, Princeton NJ 08540
V. President: Daniel A. Updegrove
Members: 450 institutions *Staff:* 35
Annual Budget: $2-5,000,000 *Tel:* (609) 734-1915
Hist. Note: A non-profit consortium of colleges, universities and other nonprofit institutions to facilitate the introduction, use and management of information technology. Formerly (1984) the Interuniversity Communications Council. Membership: $450-2,100/yr. (institution, varies with enrollment).
Publications:
EDUCOM Bulletin. q.
EDUCOM Networking. q.
Annual Meetings: October
1987-Los Angeles, CA/2,000

Egyptian-American Chamber of Commerce (1980)
One World Trade Center, Suite 8741, New York NY 10048
Exec. Director: Farouk A. Zaki
Members: 200 companies *Staff:* 2-5
Annual Budget: $100-250,000 *Tel:* (212) 466-1866
Hist. Note: Promotes trade and investment between the U.S. and Egypt; members are senior executives representing organizations, from the full spectrum of the business community, having an involvement in Egyptian American business relations. Membership: $300/yr.
Publications:
Egyptian-American Business Review. q.
Business Opportunities Bulletin.

00126 12 05 86 1233

Membership Directory. a.
Annual Meetings: New York City/March/400

Eight Sheet Outdoor Advertising Ass'n (1950)
Box 457, Independence MO 64051
Exec. Director: Ronald Waggener
Members: 120-130 companies *Staff:* 2-5
Annual Budget: $100-250,000 *Tel:* (816) 373-6305
Hist. Note: Members are lessors of eight-sheet outdoor poster panels (Jr 8 Poster Panels) which are small, 6' x 12', panels used in outdoor advertising. Formerly (until 1979) known as the Junior Panel Outdoor Advertising Ass'n.
Publications:
Rate and Allotments Book. a.
Eight-Sheet Outdoor. m.
Sources. a.
Annual Meetings:
1987-Scottsdale, AZ(Sheraton)/Oct. 18-21/200

Electric Housewares Distributors Ass'n (1975)
1018 Circle Dr., P.O. Box 11297, Green Bay WI 54304
President: Jack Tuttle
Members: 15 companies
Annual Budget: under $10,000 *Tel:* (414) 499-9918
Hist. Note: Dedicated to the support and improvement of the distribution of electric housewares. Only full functioning distributors with no wholly-owned retail stores may belong. Membership: $500/year.

Electric Motor Distributors Ass'n (1981)
Hist. Note: Defunct in 1983.

Electric Power Research Institute (1972)
Box 10412, Palo Alto CA 94303
President: Floyd L. Culler, Jr.
Members: 500 *Staff:* 700
Annual Budget: over $5,000,000 *Tel:* (415) 855-2000
Hist. Note: Research relating to the production, transmission, distribution and utilization of electric power. Members are electric utility companies. Maintains a Washington office. Has an annual budget of about $300 million.
Publications:
EPRI Guide. q.
EPRI Journal. m.

Electric Vehicle Council (1967)
Hist. Note: Reported as dissolved in 1984.

Electrical Apparatus Service Ass'n (1933)
1331 Baur Blvd., St. Louis MO 63132
Exec. V. President: August A. Baechle
Members: 2,800-2,900 *Staff:* 11-15
Annual Budget: $1-2,000,000 *Tel:* (314) 993-2220
Hist. Note: Established as the Nat'l Industrial Service Ass'n, it assumed its present name in 1961. Members are firms selling, servicing and rebuilding electric motors, generators, transformers and related equipment.
Annual Meetings: Summer/2,300-2,500
1987-Washington, DC(Washington Hilton)/June 28-July 1
1988-Orlando, FL(Marriott)/June 26-29

Electrical-Electronics Materials Distributors Ass'n (1970)
Box 214, Sea Girt NJ 08750
Vice President: Paul E. Saunders
Members: 45-50 companies *Staff:* 2
Annual Budget: $10-25,000 *Tel:* (201) 974-1900
Hist. Note: Distributors of electrical and electronic insulating materials and industry suppliers. Affiliated with the Nat'l Ass'n of Wholesaler-Distributors.
Publications:
EEMDA Circuits. m.
Annual Business Survey.
Annual Meetings: May/150
1987-Hilton Head, SC

Electrical Equipment Representatives Ass'n (1948)
1308 Pennsylvania, Kansas City MO 64105
Exec. Director: John S. McDermott, CAE
Members: 90-100 companies *Staff:* 1
Annual Budget: $50-100,000 *Tel:* (816) 221-0918
Hist. Note: Membership: $475/yr.
Publication:
EERA Directory. a.
Annual Meetings: Spring/235
1987-Orlando,FL(Buena Vista Estates)/May 3-7
1988-Tuscon, AZ(Ventana Canyon Resort)/May 15-19

Electrical Generating Systems Ass'n (1963)
Box 9257, Coral Springs FL 33065
Exec. Director: Anthony Raucci
Members: 382 companies in the U.S. *Staff:* 2-5
Annual Budget: $250-500,000 *Tel:* (305) 755-2677
Hist. Note: Founded as the Engine Generator Set Manufacturers Association, it became the Electrical Generating Systems Marketing Association in 1973 and assumed its present name in 1983. Formed in 1963 by 14 companies manufacturing engine generator sets, who were interested in standardizing specifications for products to be purchased by the U.S. government, primarily the military. In 1972, dealers and distributors of electrical generating equipment were invited to become full members, and the focus of the ass'n was changed to developing programs which would be of benefit to them.

Publications:
Powerline. bi-m.
Membership/Product Directory. a.
Semi-annual Meetings: Winter and Fall/400
1987-San Diego, CA(Intercontinental)/Feb. 18-21
1987-Boston, MA(Sheraton)/Sept. 16-18
1988-Ft. Lauderdale, FL(Bonaventure)/Feb. 17-20
1988-St. Louis, MO(Sheraton)/Sept. 14-16
1989-Tucson, AZ(Sheraton El Conquistador)/March 1-3

Electrical Industry Study Board (1975)
Hist. Note: A technical and market research arm of the electrical contracting industry. Defunct, 1983.

Electrical Insulation Soc.
Hist. Note: A subsidiary of the Institute of Electrical and Electronics Engineers. Membership in the Society, open only to IEEE members, includes subscription to a technical periodical in the field published by IEEE. All administrative support is provided by IEEE.

Electrical Women's Round Table (1925)
5008 Pine Creek Drive, Suite B, Westerville OH 43081
Exec. Director: Marlisa K. Bannister
Members: 500-600 *Staff:* 2
Annual Budget: $10-25,000 *Tel:* (614) 895-1355
Hist. Note: Members are women in electric utilities or firms connected with the electrical industry who hold consumer-related positions in public relations, advertising, editing, education and the like. Formed in New York City October 5, 1925 with about 50 charter members and incorporated in the State of New York in 1927. Membership: $35/yr.
Publication:
Newsletter. q.
Annual Meetings: Fall/300
1987-Morristown, NJ(Headquarters Plaza)/Oct. 14-16
1988-Atlanta, GA(Colony Square)/Sept. 28-30

Electricity Consumers Resource Council (1976)
1707 H St., N.W., Suite 1050, Washington DC 20006
Exec. Director: Dr. John A. Anderson
Members: 20 companies *Staff:* 6
Tel: (202) 466-4686
Hist. Note: Members are industrial consumers of electricity who support regulatory practices that assure adequate supplies of electricity at prices based on cost of service.
Publication:
Elcon Report. q.
Annual Meetings: Washington, DC in February/55

Electrochemical Soc. (1902)
10 South Main St., Pennington NJ 08534-2896
Exec. Secretary: V.H. Branneky
Members: 6,000 *Staff:* 11-15
Annual Budget: $1-2,000,000 *Tel:* (609) 737-1902
Hist. Note: Formed in Philadelphia April 3, 1902 as the American Electrochemical Soc., it became the Electrochemical Soc., Inc. in 1930 and incorporated in New York. Membership: $50/year.
Publication:
Journal of The Electrochemical Society. m. adv.
Semi-annual Meetings: May and Oct./1,500
1987-Philadelphia, PA(Adam's Mark)/May 10-15
1987-Honolulu, HI(Hilton Hawaiian Village)/Oct. 18-23
1988-Atlanta, GA(Hilton)/May 15-20
1988-Chicago, IL(Palmer House)/Oct. 15-20
1989-Los Angeles, CA(Bonaventure)/May 7-12
1989-Hollywood, FL(Diplomat)/Oct. 15-20
1990-Montreal, Quebec(Queen Elizabeth)/May 6-11

Electrolysis Soc. of America (1935)
Hist. Note: Reported to have merged with the Nat'l Electrolysis Organization to form the Soc. of Clinical and Medical Electrologists.

Electromagnetic Compatibility Soc.
Hist. Note: A subsidiary of the Institute of Electrical and Electronics Engineers. Membership in the Society, open only to IEEE members, includes subscription to a technical periodical in the field published by IEEE. All administrative support is provided by IEEE.

Electromagnetic Energy Policy Alliance (1984)
1255 Twenty-Third St., N.W., Washington DC 20037
Exec. Director: Richard H. Ekfelt
Members: 50 *Staff:* 5
Annual Budget: $100-250,000 *Tel:* (202) 452-1070
Hist. Note: The Alliance is an association of manufacturers and users of electronic and electrical systems that utilize non-ionizing electromagnetic energy in telecommunications, broadcasting, manufacturing and consumer services. Its primary objective is to work for a responsible and rational public policy regarding electromagnetic energy. Membership: $395/yr. (individual); $1,200-4,800 (corporate)
Publication:
EEPA News Bulletin. bi-m.
Annual Meetings: Spring
1987-Washington, DC/April

Electron Devices Soc. (1951)
Hist. Note: Formerly (1976) Group on Electron Devices. A Council of the Institute of Electrical and Electronics Engineers. Scientists, students and engineers concerned with the study and practice of electrical and electronic device engineering. Membership in the Society, open only to IEEE members, includes a subscription to a technical periodical in the field published by IEEE. All administrative support is provided by IEEE.

Electron Microscopy Soc. of America (1942)
Box EMSA, Woods Hole MA 02543
Business Office Manager: Morton Maser
Members: 3,700 *Staff:* 2-5
Annual Budget: $100-250,000 *Tel:* (617) 540-7639
Hist. Note: Established November 27, 1942 as the Electron Microscope Society of America at the Second National Chemical Exposition in Chicago and incorporated in Delaware. An affiliate of the American Institute of Physics and the American Ass'n for the advancement of Science. Has no paid staff. Membership: $20/yr.(individual); $100/yr.(organization).
Publications:
Bulletin. semi-a. adv.
Proceedings. a.
Annual Meetings: August/2,000
1987-Baltimore, MD(Convention Center)
1988-Milwaukee, WI(Mecca)

Electronic Funds Transfer Ass'n (1981)
1726 M St., N.W., Suite 1000, Washington DC 20036
President: Dale L. Reistad
Members: 150 companies; 100 individuals *Staff:* 12
Annual Budget: $1-2,000,000 *Tel:* (202) 659-2100
Hist. Note: Encourages use of EFT (Electronic Funds Transfer), such as automatic teller machines, retail point-of-sale systems, home financial services and corporate payment systems. Chartered in the District of Columbia. Membership: $480/yr. (individual), $2,000/yr. (council), $6,000/yr. (corporation).
Publications:
Executive Report. m.
Washington Report. m.
Sources of EFT Information. a.
Primer of EFT Standards. a.
Annual Meetings: Spring
1987-Las Vegas, NV(Caesar's Palace)/March 29-April 1/2,000
1988-Washington, DC(Sheraton)/April 10-13

Electronic Industries Ass'n (1924)
2001 Eye St., N.W., Washington DC 20006
President: Peter F. McCloskey
Members: 1,100 companies *Staff:* 150
Annual Budget: over $5,000,000 *Tel:* (202) 457-4900
Hist. Note: Formerly Radio Manufacturers Ass'n (1924-50); Radio-Televesion Manufacturers Ass'n (1950-53); Radio-Electronics-Television Manufactureres Ass'n (1953-57). Became Electronic Industries Ass'n on August 5, 1957. Includes former Magnetic Recording Industry Ass'n. Absorbed Ass'n of Electronic Manufacturers in 1975, and the Institute of High Fidelity in 1980. Sponsors the Joint Electron Device Engineering Council, the Electronics Political Action Committee, the Electronic Industries Foundation, and Consumer Electronics Shows. Members are companies involved in the manufacture of electronic components, parts, systems and equipment for communications, industrial, government and consumer-end uses.
Publications:
Executive Report. a.
Market Trends. m.
Semi-annual meetings: Spring in Washington, DC and Fall in California

Electronic Industry Show Corporation (1935)
222 South Riverside Plaza, Suite 2710, Chicago IL 60606
Exec. V. President: David L. Fisher
Members: 300 companies *Staff:* 5
Annual Budget: $250-500,000 *Tel:* (312) 648-1140
Hist. Note: Members are manufacturers who sell their products through electronics distributors. EISC's main purpose is to conduct an annual trade show for these manufacturers. Affiliated with Electronic Industries Ass'n, Electronic Representatives Ass'n, and Nat'l Electronic Distributors Ass'n.
Publication:
Bulletin. m.
Annual Meetings: April/7,500-8,000
1987-Las Vegas, NV(MGM Grand)/April 26- May 3

Electronic Media Rating Council (1964)
420 Lexington Ave., New York NY 10017
Exec. Director: Melvin Goldberg
Members: 22 *Staff:* 2-5
Annual Budget: $250-500,000 *Tel:* (212) 687-7733
Hist. Note: Established by broadcast industry, trade groups and major networks to maintain industry confidence in the integrity of broadcast rating services. Conducts an accreditation system involving regular audits by professional CPA firms of all aspects of the operation of the independent companies which produce radio and TV ratings. Founded as the Broadcast Rating Council, it assumed its present name in 1983.
Annual Meetings: New York City

Electronic Motion Control Ass'n (1981)
230 North Michigan Ave., Suite 1200, Chicago IL 60601
Exec. Director: George M. Otto
Members: 230 individuals and companies *Staff:* 2-5
Annual Budget: $50-100,000 *Tel:* (312) 372-9800
Hist. Note: Members are users, suppliers and manufacturers of motion control devices such as brakes, clutches, analog tachometers, adjustable-speed drives, position-sensing components, digital postitioning systems and torque-sensing devices. Membership: $35/yr.(individual); $750/yr.(company).
Publication:
Motion Magazine. bi-m. adv.
Annual Meetings: October

00127 12 05 86 1233

Electronic Music Consortium (1977)
School of Music, Ohio State Univ., 1866 College Road, Columbus OH 43210
Chairman: Dr. Thomas Wells
Members: 55-65 *Staff:* 1
Annual Budget: under $10,000 *Tel:* (614) 292-7837
Hist. Note: Affiliated with the American Soc. of University Composers. Members are composers and studio directors.
Publication:
ASUC Newsletter. q.
Annual Meetings: With the American Soc. of University Composers
1987-Evanston, IL

Electronic Pest Control Ass'n (1980)
710 East Ogden, Suite 113, Naperville IL 60540
Exec. V. President: Arthur W. Seeds, CAE
Members: 5 companies *Staff:* 1
Annual Budget: $25-50,000 *Tel:* (312) 369-2406
Hist. Note: Makers of electronic insect killing devices.
Publications:
Industry Updates. 2/3 per yr.
News About Electronic Pest Control (To Trade Press). q.
Semi-annual Meetings:

Electronic Representatives Ass'n (1935)
20 East Huron St., Chicago IL 60611
Exec. V. Pres.: Raymond J. Hall
Members: 9,000 individuals; 2,200 companies *Staff:* 16
Annual Budget: $500-1,000,000 *Tel:* (312) 649-1333
Hist. Note: Founded as the Representatives of Radio Parts Manufacturers, it became the Representatives of Electronic Parts Manufacturers in 1942 and assumed its present name in 1959.
Publications:
Directory of Electronic Reps. a. adv.
The Representor. q. adv.
Annual Meetings: Spring

Electronics Manufacturing Group of SME
Hist. Note: A special interst group within the Soc. of Manufacturing Engineers which addresses the concerns of electronics manufacturing professionals.

Electronics Technicians Ass'n Internat'l (1978)
604 N. Jackson St., Greencastle IN 46135
President: Dick Glass
Members: 1,545 *Staff:* 3-6
Annual Budget: $50-100,000 *Tel:* (317) 653-3849
Hist. Note: Incorporated November 14, 1978 in the State of Indiana. Members are involved in such fields as medical, industrial, computer, satellite communications, and military electronics, as well as sound equipment and other electronic service. Operates a "Certified Electronics Technician" Program through Iowa State University. Membership: $15-25/yr. (individual), $125/yr. (company).
Publications:
Technician Ass'n News. m.
EEA Training Program. m.
Management Update. m.
Membership Directory. a.
Telecom Monograph. m.
Annual Meetings:
1987-Greencastle, IN(Waldon Inn & DePauw University)/June 4-5/150

Emba Mink Breeders Ass'n (1942)
Hist. Note: Merged with the Great Lakes Mink Ass'n in 1985 to form the American Legend Cooperative.

Embroidery Council of America (1973)
512 23rd St., Union City NJ 07087
Exec. V. President: I. Leonard Seiler
Members: 225-250 companies *Staff:* 2-5
Tel: (201) 863-2069
Hist. Note: Members are manufacturers of machine-made embroidery and laces under union contract. Formerly Schiffli Lace and Embroidery Institute.
Publication:
Fashion Perspective. a.

Emergency Lighting Manufacturers Ass'n (1976)
Hist. Note: Defunct, 1981.

Emergency Medicine Management Ass'n (1978)
600 Courtland St., Suite 420, Orlando FL 32804
Exec. Director: Barbara Zee
Members: 200-225 *Staff:* 2
Annual Budget: $25-50,000 *Tel:* (305) 629-0933
Hist. Note: Members are administrators, managers of and suppliers to emergency medicine practices. Incorporated in the State of Michigan. Membership: $110/yr.
Publication:
The Lifeline. bi-m.
Annual Meetings: Fall
1987-San Francisco, CA/Nov.
1988-New Orleans, LA/Sept.
1989-Washington, DC/Sept.

Emergency Medicine Residents' Ass'n (1974)
Box 619911, Dallas TX 75261
Staff Liaison: Sandra L. Riggins
Members: 1,100 *Staff:* 2
Annual Budget: $25-50,000 *Tel:* (214) 550-0920
Hist. Note: Physicians training in the specialty of emergency medicine. Membership: $35/yr.
Publication:
EM Resident. bi-m.
Semi-Annual Meetings: Spring & Fall
1987-Philadelphia, PA/May

Emergency Nurses Ass'n (1970)
666 North Lakeshore Dr., Chicago IL 60611
Exec. Director: Torry Mark Sansone
Members: 15,000 *Staff:* 15
Annual Budget: $1-2,000,000 *Tel:* (312) 649-0297
Hist. Note: Formerly (1974) Nat'l Emergency Department Nurses Ass'n and the Emergency Department Nurses Ass'n. Assumed its present name in 1984. Members are registered nurses committed to emergency nursing. Membership: $50/year.
Publication:
Journal of Emergency Nursing. bi-m. adv.
Annual Meetings: Fall/1,200
1987-Boston, MA/Sept. 23-27

Employee Benefit Research Institute (1978)
2121 K St., N.W., Suite 860, Washington DC 20037
President: Dallas L. Salisbury
Members: 250 companies *Staff:* 20-25
Annual Budget: $2-5,000,000 *Tel:* (202) 659-0670
Hist. Note: Plan sponsors, consultants and others interested in employee benefit plans. The Institute's main purpose is to conduct public policy research, particularly in the area of retirement, health, and welfare plans. Established September 1978 in Washington DC.
Publications:
Employee Benefit Notes. bi-m.
Issue Briefs. m.
Annual Meetings: In Washington, DC/April

Employee Relocation Council (1964)
1720 N St., N.W., Washington DC 20036
Exec. V. President: H. Cris Collie
Members: 10,000 *Staff:* 20-25
Annual Budget: $2-5,000,000 *Tel:* (202) 857-0857
Hist. Note: Organized by a handful of large companies who wished to lessen the impact of relocation on their employees productivity, efficiency and morale. Formerly (1973) Employee Relocation Real Estate Advisory Council.
Publications:
E-R-C Directory. a.
Mobility. bi-m.

Employers Council on Flexible Compensation (1981)
1660 L St., N.W., Suite 715, Washington DC 20036
Director: Kenneth E. Feltman
Members: 200 companies *Staff:* 4
Annual Budget: $500-1,000,000 *Tel:* (202) 659-4300
Hist. Note: A national, non-profit business league committed to the promotion and improvement of flexible compensation plans. Membership open to employers that have adopted or are considering adopting any program of flexible compensation, including benefit departments of state and local governments. Associate membership is to insurance companies, accounting firms, consulting actuaries, and others that design or administer employee benefit plans. Membership fee based upon size and type of organization.
Publications:
ECFC Newsletter. m.
ECFC Bulletin. bi-w.
Flexible Compensation. a.
Flexible Compensation Sourcebook. a.
Annual Meetings: February in Washington, DC at the Mayflower Hotel

Employment Management Ass'n (1969)
1100 Raleigh Building, Raleigh NC 27601
Exec. Director: Hollis Smith
Members: 1,500 *Staff:* 4-6
Annual Budget: $500-1,000,000 *Tel:* (919) 821-1435
Hist. Note: Employment and personnel executives. "Third party" professionals (providers of support services to the employment process) are eligible as affiliate, non-voting members. Membership: $95/year.
Publications:
EMA Employment Resources Guide. a. adv.
EMA Reporter. m.
Semi-Annual Meetings: Spring and Fall

Endocrine Soc. (1918)
9650 Rockville Pike, Bethesda MD 20814
Exec. Director: Mrs. Nettie C. Karpin
Members: 5,300 *Staff:* 5
Annual Budget: $500-1,000,000 *Tel:* (301) 530-9660
Hist. Note: A professional society of physicians and research scientists founded as the Association for Study of Internal Secretions. Membership: $75/yr.
Publications:
Endocrine Review. m. adv.
Endocrinology. m. adv.
Journal of Clinical Endocrinology and Metabolism. m. adv.
Annual Meetings: June/4,000
1987-Indianapolis,IN(Convention Center)
1988-New Orleans,LA(Convention Center)
1989-Seattle,WA(Convention Center)
1990-Atlanta,GA(Convention Center)

Energy Consumers and Producers Ass'n (1977)
Box 1726, Petroleum Plaza, Seminole OK 74868
President: E. L. Stewart, Jr.
Members: 700 *Staff:* 3
Annual Budget: $100-250,000 *Tel:* (405) 382-5363
Hist. Note: Members are small independent oil and gas producers as well as recipients of oil and gas royalties. Main purpose is to combat government regulations. Sponsors the Energy Consumers and Producers Association Political Action Committee. Membership: $150/yr.
Publication:
ECPA Newsline. m.

Energy Management and Controls Soc.
Hist. Note: Merged with the Ass'n of Energy Engineers in Jan., 1986.

Energy Telecommunications and Electrical Ass'n (1928)
Box 795038, Dallas TX 75379-5038
V. President: Martha G. Fike
Members: 125-130 companies *Staff:* 2
Annual Budget: $250-500,000 *Tel:* (214) 578-1900
Hist. Note: Affiliated with Petroleum Electric Supply Ass'n and Petroleum Electric Power Ass'n. Formerly (until 1978) the Petroleum Industry Electrical Ass'n. Membership is composed of companies and corporations in the energy industries employing personnel having managerial, engineering or technical responsibility in the electrical, electronics, communications and allied fields. Membership: $200/yr.
Publications:
ENTELEC Newsletter. q.
ENTELEC Bound Technical Papers. a.
Annual Meetings: March
1987-Houston, TX(Hyatt/Albert Thomas Convention Ctr.)/March 15-18
1988-Dallas, TX(Hyatt/Convention Ctr.)/March 13-16
1989-Houston, TX(Brown Convention Ctr.)/March 12-15
1990-San Antonio, TX(Convention Ctr.)/March 22-25
1991-New Orleans, LA(Hyatt/Dome)/March 19-22

Engine Manufacturers Ass'n (1933)
111 East Wacker Drive, Chicago IL 60601
Exec. Director: Thomas C. Young, CAE
Members: 20-25 companies *Staff:* 2-5
Annual Budget: $250-500,000 *Tel:* (312) 644-6610
Hist. Note: Formerly (1968) Internal Combustion Engine Institute. Members are makers of internal combustion engines used for any purpose except exclusive aircraft or passenger car use.
Annual Meetings: Three board meetings per year

Engine Service Ass'n (1970)
710 North Plankinton Ave., Milwaukee WI 53203
Exec. Secretary: Delores Liebherr-Morris
Members: 60 companies *Staff:* 2-5
Annual Budget: $50-100,000 *Tel:* (414) 271-2263
Hist. Note: Members are central warehouse distributors of internal combustion engines.

Engineering College Magazines Associated (1920)
12935 Castlebar Drive, Sun City West AZ 85375
Exec. Secretary: Howard J. Schwebke
Members: 40 *Staff:* 1
Annual Budget: under $10,000 *Tel:* (602) 584-2524
Hist. Note: Members are engineering colleges that publish engineering journals for students.
Annual Meetings: Spring

Engineering Foundation (1914)
Hist. Note: Founded in New York City in 1914 as an operating department of United Engineering Trustees, Inc. by the five major engineering societies American Soc. of Civil Engineers, American Institute of Mining, Metallurigical and Petroleum Engineers, American Soc. of Mechanical Engineers, Institute of Electrical and Electronics Engineers and the American Institute of Chemical Engineers. Supports research in science and engineering and the advancement in any other manner of the arts and sciences of engineering and the good of mankind. The Foundation funds interdisciplinary grants and holds like conferences on regular annual cycles. It publishes the final reports from the research projects and the conferences that it sponsors. Not a membership organization.

Engineering in Medicine and Biology Soc.
Hist. Note: A subsidiary of the Institute of Electrical and Electronics Engineers. Membership in the Society, open only to IEEE members, includes a subscription to a technical periodical in the field published by IEEE. All administrative support is provided by IEEE. Not to be confused with the Alliance for Engineering in Medicine and Biology.

Engineering Management Soc.
Hist. Note: A subsidiary of the Institute of Electrical and Electronics Engineers. Membership in the Society, open only to IEEE members, includes a subscription to a technical periodical in the field published by IEEE. All administrative support is provided by IEEE.

Engineering Reprographic Soc. (1974)
1400 E. 78th St., Suite 306, Minneapolis MN 55423
Membership V. President: Pattie Murphy Bukowski
Members: 500-600 *Staff:* 2-5

00128 12 05 86 1233

Annual Budget: $10-25,000 *Tel:* (612) 887-8049
Hist. Note: Formerly (1977) the Engineering Reprographics Management Ass'n. Supervisors of in-house engineering reprographics departments.
Publication:
Newsletter. bi-m.
Annual Meetings: October

Engraved Stationery Manufacturers Ass'n (1911)
Box 120539, 1000 17th Ave. South, Nashville TN 37212
Manager: David F. Bacon
Members: 150 companies *Staff:* 2-5
Annual Budget: $50-100,000 *Tel:* (615) 327-4444
Hist. Note: Founded in 1911 as the Nat'l Ass'n of Steel and Copper Plate Engravers. Assumed its present name in 1938.
Publication:
ESMA Newsletter. m.
Semi-annual Meetings: Winter and Summer

Enteral Nutrition Council (1983)
5775 Peachtree-Dunwoody Rd., Suite 500D, Atlanta GA 30342
President: Robert H. Kellen
Members: 7 companies *Staff:* 5
Tel: (404) 252-3663
Hist. Note: Members are manufacturers and marketers of enternal formulas - foods for special dietary use.
Annual Meetings:
1987-Atlanta, GA/June

Entomological Soc. of America (1889)
4603 Calvert Rd., College Park MD 20740
Exec. Director: W. Darryl Hansen
Members: 9,200 *Staff:* 16
Annual Budget: $2-5,000,000 *Tel:* (301) 864-1334
Hist. Note: Formed in 1953 by the consolidation of the American Ass'n of Economic Entomologists (1889) and the Entomological Soc. of America (1906). Incorporated in the District of Columbia in 1954. Membership: $60/yr.
Publications:
Annals of ESA. bi-m.
Bulletin. q. adv.
Environmental Entomology. bi-m.
ESA Newsletter. m.
Insecticide and Acaricide Tests. a.
Journal of Economic Entomology. bi-m.
Annual Meetings: Week after Thanksgiving/2,500
1987-Boston, MA(Sheraton)
1988-Louisville, KY(Galt House)

Envelope Manufacturers Ass'n of America (1933)
1600 Duke St., Suite 440, Alexandria VA 22314-3421
Exec. V. President: T. Randolph Shingler
Members: 200-250 *Staff:* 2-5
Annual Budget: $500-1,000,000 *Tel:* (703) 739-2200
Hist. Note: A merger of the American Envelope Manufacturers Association (founded in 1909) and the Bureau of Envelope Manufacturers Association of America (founded in 1916).
Publication:
Newsletter. m.
Semi-annual meetings: spring and fall/3-400
1987-Phoenix, AZ(Biltmore)/April 4-8
1987-Colorado Springs, CO(Broadmoor)/Oct. 25-28

Environmental Industry Council (1976)
1825 K St., N.W., Suite 210, Washington DC 20006
Exec. Director: John Adams
Members: 25 companies *Staff:* 2-5
Annual Budget: $50-100,000 *Tel:* (202) 331-7706
Hist. Note: Membership includes corporations which manufacture environmental protection equipment and materials. Organized as a result of the first environmental industry conference in December 1975. Incorporated in the District of Columbia.

Environmental Management Ass'n (1957)
1019 Highland Ave., Largo FL 33540
President and C.E.O.: Harold C. Rowe
Members: 45-50,000 individuals *Staff:* 11-15
Annual Budget: $250-500,000 *Tel:* (813) 586-5710
Hist. Note: Formed by a merger of the Ass'n of Food Industry Sanitarians, the Industrial Sanitation Management Ass'n and the Nat'l Ass'n of Bakery Sanitarians. Formerly the Institute of Sanitation Management. Maintains the following institutes: Buildings-Grounds Subsidiary, Food Sanitation Institute, Health Care, and Sanitation Suppliers and Contractors.
Publication:
Professional Sanitation Management. bi-m. adv.
Annual Meetings: October
1987-St. Louis, MO/Oct. 10-15
1988-Norfolk, VA/Oct. 15-20

Environmental Mutagen Soc. (1969)
NCI-FCRF, Box B, Bldg. 538, Frederick MD 21701
Secretary: Rosalie Elespuru
Members: 1,100
Annual Budget: $50-100,000 *Tel:* (301) 698-1223
Hist. Note: Focus is to encourage the study of mutagens in the human environment, particularly as they affect public health. Membership: $55/yr. (individual), $500/yr. (company).
Publications:
Environmental Mutagenesis. bi-m.
EMS Newsletter. q.
Annual Meetings: Spring
1987-San Francisco, CA/April 8-11
1988-Charleston, SC/March 26-31
1989-Cleveland, OH(Case Western Reserve)

Epigraphic Soc. (1974)
6625 Bamburgh Drive, San Diego CA 92117
President: Dr. Barry Fell
Members: 1,100 *Staff:* 1
Annual Budget: $10-25,000 *Tel:* (619) 571-1344
Hist. Note: Members are archeologists and other scholars interested in the comparative study of ancient inscriptions. Major interest is in North and South America, Western Europe and Arab countries. Membership: $22.50/year
Annual Meetings:
1987-San Francisco, CA/Spring/200

Episcopal Conference of the Deaf (1881)
1210 Locust St., St. Louis MO 63103
Exec. Secretary: Rev. Robert Grindrod
Members: 900 *Staff:* 1
Annual Budget: $50-100,000 *Tel:* (314) 966-2808
Hist. Note: Organized as the Conference of Church Workers among the Deaf, ECD assumed its present name in 1970. Membership: $3/yr.
Publication:
Deaf Episcopalian. q.
Annual Meetings: Summer
1987-St. Louis
1988-Boston

Epsilon Sigma Phi (1927)
3641 46th Ave. South, Minneapolis MN 55406
Secy.-Treas.: William A. Milbrath
Members: 11,200 *Staff:* 2-5
Annual Budget: $50-100,000 *Tel:* (612) 721-3742
Hist. Note: A fraternity of professional workers in U. S. land grant universities and U. S. Department of Agriculture Extension programs. Established in Montana January 10, 1927.
Publications:
Journal of Extension.
The People and the Profession. q.
Newsletter.

Equipment and Tool Institute (1947)
1545 Waukegan Rd., Glenview IL 60025
Exec. Manager: Donn R. Proven
Members: 75-80 companies *Staff:* 2-5
Annual Budget: $100-250,000 *Tel:* (312) 729-8550
Hist. Note: Members are makers of automotive service equipment and tools.
Publication:
ETI's News Break. q.
Annual Meetings: Fall

Equipment Interchange Ass'n (1958)
6410 Kenilworth Ave., Suite 108, Riverdale MD 20737
Managing Director: Albert J. Mascaro
Members: 150 companies *Staff:* 5
Annual Budget: $25-50,000 *Tel:* (301) 277-8830
Hist. Note: Formerly 1961 Nat'l Motor Equipment Interchange Committee. Promotes uniform equipment interchange practices among common carriers of general commodities engaged in interstate and foreign commerce, operating under a certificate of public convenience and necessity granted by the Interstate Commerce Commission. Membership: $100/yr.
Publication:
Interchange Bulletin. m.
Semi-annual meetings: Spring and Summer

Equipment Maintenance Council (1981)
Hist. Note: Address unknown in 1987.

Equipment Service Ass'n (1960)
Box 452, Plymouth IN 46563
Exec. Director: Georgia S. Palmitessa
Members: 150-175 companies *Staff:* 1
Annual Budget: $50-100,000 *Tel:* (219) 935-5188
Hist. Note: Organized as the International Hydraulic Equipment Rebuilders Association at a meeting of hydraulic jack rebuilders convoked by the Hydraulic Jack Manufacturers Association. Members are companies repairing, rebuilding and servicing industrial and automotive service equipment. Membership: $175/yr.
Publications:
Bulletin. m.
Membership Directory. a.
Annual Meetings: Spring
1987-St. Petersburg Beach, FL
1988-Milwaukee, WI(Marc Plaza)/225

ESOP Ass'n (1979)
1725 De Sales St., N.W., Suite 400, Washington DC 20036
Exec. Director: David Binns
Members: 900 companies and professionals *Staff:* 7
Annual Budget: $500-1,000,000 *Tel:* (202) 293-2971
Hist. Note: Formed in May 1979 as the ESOP Ass'n of America through a merger of the Nat'l Ass'n of ESOP Companies and the Employee Stock Ownership Council of America, both formed in 1977; assumed its present name in July, 1982. Incorporated in the District of Columbia. Members are companies with employee stock ownership plans as well as professionals who specialize in these plans. Maintains a Washington office. Membership: $300-2,000/yr.
Publications:
ESOP Report. m.
Profiles. m.
Annual Meetings: May-June/6-700
1987-Washington, DC(Marriott)/May 13-15
1988-Washington, DC(Grand Hyatt)/May 18-20

Estuarine Research Federation (1969)
Marine Sciences Research Center, SUNY, Stony Brook NY 11794-5000
President: Dr. J.R. Schubel
Members: 2,000 individuals
Annual Budget: $50-100,000 *Tel:* (516) 246-6543
Hist. Note: Promotes research in estuarine and coastal waters, and is available as a source of advice in matters concerning estuaries and the coastal zone.
Publication:
Estuaries. q.
Biennial Meetings: Odd years

Ethylene Oxide Industry Council (1981)
2501 M St., N.W., Washington DC 20037
Program Manager: Dr. Bob Romano
Members: 35-40 companies *Staff:* 2-5
Annual Budget: $500-1,000,000 *Tel:* (202) 887-1196
Hist. Note: A Special Programs Division of the Chemical Manufacturers Ass'n. Ethylene Oxide is a gas used in the conversion of other chemical products. It is a major component of anti-freeze and is used as a sterilant of medical devices.

Evangelical Christian Publishers Ass'n (1974)
Box 2439, Vista CA 92083-0770
Exec. Director: C. E. Andrew
Members: 50-60 companies *Staff:* 2-5
Annual Budget: $100-250,000 *Tel:* (619) 941-1636
Hist. Note: Organized on October 10, 1974, at a meeting of publishers of Christian literature. Membership: $720-4,200/yr.
Publication:
Mondayletter. w.
Annual Meetings: Sept./Oct.

Evangelical Church Library Ass'n (1970)
Box 353, Glen Ellyn IL 60138
Exec. Secretary: Nancy Dick
Members: 700 *Staff:* 1
Annual Budget: $10-25,000 *Tel:* (312) 668-0519
Hist. Note: Established to assist churches in setting up and maintaining library resource centers. Membership: $10/yr.
Publication:
Librarian's World. q. adv.
Annual Meetings: Fall in Wheaton, IL/200

Evangelical Press Ass'n (1948)
Box 4550, Overland Park KS 66204
Exec. Director: Gary Warner
Members: 320-350 *Staff:* 2-5
Annual Budget: $50-100,000 *Tel:* (913) 381-2017
Publications:
EP News Service. w.
Liaison. bi-m.
Membership Directory. a.
Annual Meetings: Spring
1987-Asheville, NC/May 11-13

Evangelical Teacher Training Ass'n (1930)
110 Bridge St., Box 327, Wheaton IL 60189
President: Paul E. Loth
Members: 210 colleges and seminaries *Staff:* 11-15
Annual Budget: $250-500,000 *Tel:* (312) 668-6400
Hist. Note: Active member seminaries and colleges present courses using ETTA materials to prepare students for professional church leadership and to train church volunteers. These courses lead to the Christian Education Diploma or the Standard Teachers Diploma of the association.
Publication:
Teacher Training Profile. q.
Biennial meetings: Odd years.

Evaporated Milk Ass'n (1923)
Box 4188, Rockville MD 20850
Exec. V. President: Dr. J. C. Flake
Members: 8 companies *Staff:* 1
Annual Budget: $25-50,000 *Tel:* (301) 424-2150

Evidence Photographers Internat'l Council (1968)
600 Main St., Honesdale PA 18431
President: Robert Jennings
Members: 500 *Staff:* 3
Annual Budget: under $10,000 *Tel:* (717) 253-1520
Hist. Note: EPIC is a non-profit educational and scientific organization dedicated to the advancement of forensic photography in civil evidence and law enforcement. Membership: $60/year.
Publication:
Journal of Evidence Photography. semi-a. adv.
Annual Meetings: Fall

Excess and Casualty Reinsurance Ass'n (1958)
Hist. Note: Merger of Excess Reinsurance Ass'n (1934) and Casualty Reinsurance Ass'n of America (1949) Dissolved December 31, 1982.

Exchange Carriers Standards Ass'n (1983)
4 Century Drive, 3rd Fl., Parsippany NJ 07054
Exec. Director: O.J. "Gus" Gusella, Jr.
Members: 300 telephone companies *Staff:* 6
Annual Budget: $1-2,000,000 *Tel:* (201) 538-6111
Hist. Note: Open to all telephone companies. Provides technical standards for exchange, interexchange, manufacturers and users of telephone services. Membership: Scaled by size of company.

00129 12 05 86 1233

Publication:
Tielines. q.
Annual Meetings: October
1987-Orlando, FL/Oct. 15
1988-New York, NY/Oct. 15

Executive Assistant Ass'n (1981)
Hist. Note: Orginated in the Chicago area as a forum of expression for assistants to senior executives but never grew significantly, probably because of the great turnover in such positions and lack of any real area of common concern.

Executive Women Internat'l (1938)
965 East 4800 South, Suite 1, Salt Lake City UT 84117
Exec. Director: Mary L. Johnson
Members: 5,000 *Staff:* 2-5
Annual Budget: $10-25,000 *Tel:* (801) 263-3296
Hist. Note: Women employed as executive secretaries or administrators. Membership is by invitation only and through company representation. Formerly (until 1978) Executives' Secretaries, Inc.
Publication:
The Times. q.
Annual Meetings: September
1987-Houston, TX
1988-San Francisco, CA
1989-Pittsburgh, PA
1990-Minneapolis, MN
1991-Nashville, TN

Exhaust Systems Professional Ass'n (1973)
Hist. Note: Independent muffler shops. Defunct, 1981.

Exhibit Designers and Producers Ass'n (1937)
1411 K St., N.W., Suite 801, Washington DC 20005
Exec. Director: Robert C. Lohse
Members: 340 companies *Staff:* 2-5
Annual Budget: $2-5,000,000 *Tel:* (202) 393-2001
Hist. Note: Designers and builders of displays for exhibits and trade shows. Sets standards for creators of exhibits and promotes education in the use of three-dimensional media.
Publications:
Dimensions Magazine. m. adv.
Membership Directory. a. adv.
Annual Meetings: December
1987-Orlando, FL(Hyatt Grand Cypress)/Nov. 29-Dec. 4/3-400
1988-Tucson, AZ(El Conquistador)/Dec. 1-7/3-400

Exhibition Validation Council (1981)
Hist. Note: Established by the Trade Show Bureau to develop a standardized form for reporting attendance and other data from trade shows, and to act as a clearinghouse where information on trade shows can be registered. A subsidiary of the Trade Show Bureau.

Expanded Metal Manufacturers' Ass'n
Hist. Note: Dissolved in 1986.

Expanded Shale, Clay and Slate Institute (1952)
6218 Montrose Road, Rockville MD 20852
Mng. Director: Harry C. Robinson
Members: 40-50 *Staff:* 2-5
Annual Budget: $100-250,000 *Tel:* (301) 231-9497
Hist. Note: Founded as the Expanded Shale Institute, it assumed its present name in 1955. Members are producers of shale, clay and slate aggregates used in lightweight structural concrete and concrete masonry. Membership fee based on aggregate that is sold.
Annual Meetings: Oct.
1987-Boston,MA(Marriott Long Wharf)/Oct. 4-7
1988-Salt Lake City,UT(Hotel Utah)/Oct. 2-5
1989-Montreal

Expansion Anchor Manufacturers Institute (1972)
Hist. Note: Inactive in 1983.

Expansion Joint Manufacturers Ass'n (1954)
25 North Broadway, Tarrytown NY 10591
Secretary: Richard C. Byrne
Members: 11 companies *Staff:* 2-5
Annual Budget: $10-25,000 *Tel:* (914) 332-0040
Hist. Note: The Association's Technical Committee prepares industry standards. Cooperates with ASME in the development of engineering standares for metallic expansion joints for use in piping systems.

Experimental Ballistics Associates (1960)
110 Kensington Ave., Trenton NJ 08618
Coordinator: Edward M. Yard
Members: 30 *Staff:* 1
Annual Budget: under $10,000 *Tel:* (609) 393-5804
Hist. Note: A small group of individuals, many from the arms industry, informally organized to exchange information on the technical aspects of ballistics and explosive propulsion. Has no dues structure, paid staff or elected officers.

Exposition Service Contractors Ass'n (1970)
1516 South Pontius Ave., Los Angeles CA 90025
Exec. Director: Randy Bauler, CAE
Members: 110 firms *Staff:* 2
Annual Budget: $50-100,000 *Tel:* (213) 478-0215
Hist. Note: Members are full-service general exposition contractors, as well as support firms to the exposition service industry such as security, audio-visual, electrical and floral companies. Membership: $400-600/yr.
Publications:
ESCA Voice. m.
Annual Guide to Exposition Service. a. adv.
Annual Meetings: Fall with the Nat'l Ass'n of Exposition Managers

Exterior Insulation Manufacturers Ass'n (1981)
P.O. Box 75037, Washington DC 20013
Exec. Director: Susan H. Dove
Members: 85 companies *Staff:* 2-5
Annual Budget: $100-250,000 *Tel:* (202) 783-6582
Hist. Note: An outgrowth of the Association of the Wall and Ceiling Industries International, EIMA became an independent association in 1981.
Publications:
Newsletter. q.
Directory. a.

Eye Bank Ass'n of America (1961)
1511 K St., N.W., Suite 830, Washington DC 20005-1401
President: Thomas J. Moore
Members: 85-90 eye banks *Staff:* 2-5
Annual Budget: $100-250,000 *Tel:* (202) 628-4280
Hist. Note: Established in 1961 under the auspices of the American Academy of Ophthalmology.
Publication:
Foresight. q.
Annual Meetings: With the American Academy of Ophthalmology

Fabric Salesmen's Ass'n (1982)
450 7th Ave., Suite 1900, New York NY 10001
President: Mel Block
Members: 375 *Staff:* 2-5
Tel: (212) 594-4283
Hist. Note: Membership concentrated in New York City area. Formerly (1982) the Piece Goods Salesmen's Ass'n and the Fabric Salesmen's Guild.

Fabricating Manufacturers Ass'n (1975)
Hist. Note: Became the Fabricators and Manufacturers Ass'n, Internat'l in 1985.

Fabricators and Manufacturers Ass'n, Internat'l (1970)
7811 North Alpine Rd., Rockford IL 61111
President and C.E.O.: John P. Nandzik
Members: 500 companies *Staff:* 22
Annual Budget: $1-2,000,000 *Tel:* (815) 654-1902
Hist. Note: Manufacturers of metal fabricating equipment and manufacturers using metal fabricating processes. Formerly (1975) Fabricating Machinery Ass'n, Inc. Also, Formerly (1985) Fabricating Manufacturers Ass'n. Membership: $65/yr.(individual); $250/yr.(company).
Publications:
The Fabricator. 8/yr. adv.
FMA Newsletter. m.
FMA Membership Directory. a.
Literature Resource Directory. a.
Annual Meetings: April

Facing Tile Institute (1934)
Hist. Note: Ceased operations in 1985.

Factory Mutual System (1835)
1151 Boston-Providence Turnpike, Norwood MA 02062
Vice President, Training Resource Center: Bruce P. Mattoon
Members: 3 companies *Staff:* 70
Annual Budget: $2-5,000,000 *Tel:* (617) 762-4300
Hist. Note: Formerly Associated Factory Mutual Insurance Companies. Members are mutual insurance companies insuring industrial and commercial properties.
Publication:
Factory Mutual Record. bi-m.

Family Service America (1911)
11700 W. Lake Park Drive, Milwaukee WI 53224
President & C.E.O.: Geneva B. Johnson
Members: 300 agencies *Staff:* 65
Annual Budget: $2-5,000,000 *Tel:* (414) 359-2111
Hist. Note: Formerly known as the Family Welfare Ass'n of America and the Family Service Ass'n of America, it assumed its present name in 1984. Members are local agencies which provide counseling and other social services to families.
Publications:
Directory of Member Agencies. a.
Highlights. bi-m.
Social Casework. 10/yr. adv.
Biennial meetings: Odd years
1987-Cincinnati, OH/1,100
1989-Tampa, FL
1991-Seattle, WA

Far East-America Council of Commerce and Industry (1943)
Hist. Note: Dissolved in 1984.

Far East Merchants Ass'n (1932)
Hist. Note: Defunct in 1982.

Farm and Industrial Equipment Institute (1893)
410 North Michigan Ave., Chicago IL 60611
President: Emmett Barker
Members: 350-400 *Staff:* 15
Annual Budget: $1-2,000,000 *Tel:* (312) 321-1470
Hist. Note: Established in 1893. Formerly Nat'l Ass'n of Agricultural Implement and Vehicle Manufacturers, (1933) Nat'l Ass'n of Farm Equipment Manufacturers and (1965) Farm Equipment Institute. Merged (1969) with Industrial Equipment Manufacturers. Maintains the following councils: Auger and Elevator Manufacturers, Cab Manufacturers, Construction Equipment, Crop Dryer Manufacturers, Fertilizer and Farm Chemical Equipment, Forestry Equipment, Grain Bin Manufacturers, Manufacturers of Aerial Devices and Digger-Derricks, Manufacturers of Telescoping and Articulating Cranes, Marketing and Management, Materials Handling, Milking Machine Manufacturers, Power Sprayer and Duster, Tillage Equipment, Underground Equipment, and Wheel Tractor and Attachments.
Publications:
Membership Roster. a.
Newsletter. m.
Retail Sales Reports. m.
State of the Industry. semi-a.
Annual Meetings: September-October.

Farm and Land Institute
Hist. Note: Changed its name to REALTORS Land Institute in Feb., 1986.

Farm Credit Council (1983)
50 F St., N.W., Suite 900, Washington DC 20001
President: John A. Waits
Members: 13 organizations *Staff:* 7
Annual Budget: $500-1,000,000 *Tel:* (202) 393-3744
Hist. Note: Members are the 12 Farm Credit Councils together with the Central Bank for Cooperatives. Affiliated with the National Council of Farmer Cooperatives.
Publication:
FCC Newsletter. m.
Annual Meetings: January
1987-Anaheim, CA(Disneyland Hotel)/Jan. 27

Farm Equipment Manufacturers Ass'n (1950)
243 North Lindbergh Blvd., St. Louis MO 63141
Exec. V. President: Robert K. Schnell
Members: 700 companies *Staff:* 2-5
Annual Budget: $500-1,000,000 *Tel:* (314) 991-0702
Hist. Note: Founded as the Allied Farm Equipment Manufacturers Association, it assumed its present name in 1956. Membership: $210-700/yr.
Publication:
Shortliner. semi-m.
Semi-annual Meetings: Spring and Fall
1987-Corpus Christi,TX(Hershey)/March 21-25
1987-Atlanta, GA(Hyatt Regency)/Nov. 15-18
1988-San Diego,CA(Hyatt)/April 9-13
1988-Reno,NV(Bally's)/Oct. 23-27
1989-Nashville, TN(Opryland Hotel)/Oct. 29-Nov. 2
1990-St. Louis, MO(Adam's Mark)/Nov. 4-8

Farm Equipment Wholesalers Ass'n (1945)
1927 Keokuk St., Iowa City IA 52240
Exec. V. President: Thomas L. Irwin, Jr.
Members: 125-150 *Staff:* 2-5
Annual Budget: $100-250,000 *Tel:* (319) 354-5156
Hist. Note: Originally organized as an association of farm equipment and supplies wholesalers. Membership now includes wholesalers of farm, light industrial, irrigation, lawn and garden, turf care, park, golf course and institutional maintenance and sports and recreation equipment. Wholesalers of such items as boats, motors, snowmobiles and golf carts are also eligible for membership.
Publication:
TIPS. m.
Annual Meetings: November

Farmers Educational and Co-operative Union of America (1902)
Nat'l Farmers Union, Denver CO 80251
President: Cy Carpenter
Members: 300,000 families *Staff:* 30-35
Annual Budget: $1-2,000,000 *Tel:* (303) 337-5500
Hist. Note: Also known as Nat'l Farmers Union, Farmers Union. Maintains a Washington Office. Members are farm families throughout the nation united for legislative, insurance, cooperative and educational purposes.
Publication:
Washington Newsletter. m.
Annual Meetings: March/1,200-1,500
1987-Fort Worth, TX(Hyatt Regency)/March 1-4
1988-Albuquerque, NM(Hilton)/March 6-9
1989-Little Rock, AR(Excelsior)/March 5-8
1990-Omaha,NE (Holiday Inn Central)/March 4-7

Farmstead Equipment Ass'n (1945)
410 North Michigan Ave., Chicago IL 60611
Exec. Director: J.H. Ebbinghaus
Annual Budget: under $10,000 *Tel:* (312) 321-1470
Hist. Note: Merger (1967) of Barn Cleaner, Cattle Feeder, Silo Unloader Ass'n and Barn Equipment Ass'n. An auxiliary of the Farm and Industrial Equipment Institute. Membership fee based on sales volume.

00130 12 05 86 1233

Fashion Group (1931)
9 Rockefeller Plaza, 17th Floor, New York NY 10020
Exec. Director: Lenore Benson
Members: 6,000 women fashion executives *Staff:* 6-10
Annual Budget: $500-1,000,000 *Tel:* (212) 247-3940
Publications:
The Fashion Group Bulletin. 6/yr.
FG Newsflash. m.
Annual Meetings: New York City

Fashion Jewelry Ass'n of America (1985)
Box S-8, Regency East, One Jackson Walkway, Providence RI 02903
Office Secretary: Mildred Schuster
Members: 175-200 individuals *Staff:* 1
Annual Budget: $10-25,000 *Tel:* (401) 273-1515
Hist. Note: Founded as the Manufacturing Jewelers Sales Ass'n in 1952; assumed its present name in 1985. Membership: $150/yr.
Annual Meetings: Co-sponsors the United Jewelry Show with Manufacturing Jewelers and
Silversmiths of America in Providence, RI in March and September.

Fatty Acids Producers Council (1951)
Hist. Note: Division of the Soap and Detergent Ass'n. Merged with the Glycerine Producers Ass'n to form the the Glycerine and Fatty Acid Producers Ass'n in 1983.

FCIB-NACM Corp. (1919)
520 Eighth Ave., New York NY 10018-6571
Exec. V. President: Gerd-Peter Lota
Members: 1,100 banks, exporters, and manufacturers *Staff:* 16-20
Annual Budget: $500-1,000,000 *Tel:* (212) 947-5070
Hist. Note: Sponsored by Nat'l Ass'n of Credit Management. Formerly (1967) the Foreign Credit Interchange Bureau.
Publications:
FCIB Bulletin. bi-w.
FCIB Minutes of Round Table Conference. m.
Newsletter. m.
Credit and Collection Survey. semi-a.
Country Credit Reports. m.
European Meeting: 3/yr. in various cities
Asian Meeting: 1/yr. in various cities
North American Meeting: 5/yr. in various cities; 10/yr. in New York

Feather and Down Ass'n (1964)
Hist. Note: Became the American Down Association in 1983.

Federal Administrative Law Judges Conference (1947)
1815 H St., N.W., Room 424, Washington DC 20006
Secretary: Norman Zenkel
Members: 700 *Staff:* 1
Annual Budget: $25-50,000 *Tel:* (202) 633-0525
Hist. Note: Formerly (1973) Federal Trial Examiners Conference. Individuals who preside at administrative hearings within federal agencies. Has no permanent staff. Officers are elected annually. Mail is received at the National Lawyers Club. Membership: $40/yr.
Publications:
Newsletter. m. adv.
Proceedings of Annual Trial Examiners' Seminar.
Annual Meetings: September in the Washington, DC area

Federal Bar Ass'n (1920)
1815 H St., N.W., Suite 408, Washington DC 20006
Exec. Director: John G. Blanche, III
Members: 15,000 *Staff:* 13
Annual Budget: $1-2,000,000 *Tel:* (202) 638-0252
Hist. Note: Professional society of attorneys currently and formerly employed by the Federal Government; also associate members who have no employment connection but have a substantial interest in federal law. Membership: $40/year.
Publications:
Federal Bar News/Journal. m. adv.
Lawyers Job Bulletin Board. m.
Annual Meetings:
1987-Memphis, TN(Holiday Inn Crowne Plaza)/Sept. 16-19/500

Federal Communications Bar Ass'n (1936)
Box 35546, Washington DC 20033
Secretary: Thomas Schattenfield
Members: 1,500
Annual Budget: $50-100,000 *Tel:* (202) 857-6020
Hist. Note: Members are lawyers who practice before the Federal Communications Commission and FCC staff attorneys; the majority of members practice in Washington, DC. Has no permanent address beyond the above post box; officers change annually. Incorporated in the District of Columbia in 1943. Membership: $55/yr.
Publication:
Federal Communications Law Journal. q.
Annual Meetings: June in Washington, DC

Federal Construction Council (1952)
c/o Nat'l Academy of Sciences, 2101 Constitution Ave., N.W., Washington DC 20418
Exec. Secretary: Henry A. Borger
Members: 13 agencies, 180 individuals *Staff:* 6-10
Annual Budget: $500-1,000,000 *Tel:* (202) 334-3378
Hist. Note: Members are professional employees of federal agencies and members of the Building Research Board of the Nat'l Academy of Sciences. Encourages cooperation among the several federal construction agencies. Sponsors 12 consulting committees composed of federal agency employees plus ad hoc advisory committees composed of nationally recognized experts in building technology.

Federal Court Clerks Ass'n (1922)
U.S. District Court, 500 Camp St., Room C151, New Orleans LA 70130
Historian: Nelson Jones
Members: 2,400-2,500
Annual Budget: $10-25,000
Hist. Note: Clerks and deputy clerks of the U.S. District Courts, U.S. Courts of Appeal, and six independent courts of the U.S.
Annual Meetings:
1987-Honolulu, HI/August 2-6
1988-Boston, MA

Federal Design Council (1951)
Hist. Note: Founded as the Society of Federal Artists and Designers, it assumed its present name in 1971. Members are individuals engaged in visual communications programs in the Federal Government. Reported inactive in 1985.

Federal Energy Bar Ass'n (1946)
1800 M St., N.W., Suite 700 N, Washington DC 20036
Administrator: Thomas A. Mars
Members: 1,600 *Staff:* 1
Annual Budget: $100-250,000 *Tel:* (202) 872-4815
Hist. Note: Lawyers engaged in promoting proper administration of federal laws relating to the production, development, conservation, transmission, and economic regulation of energy. Formerly (1977) the Federal Power Bar Ass'n. Membership: $40/year.
Publications:
Energy Law Journal. semi-a. adv.
Directory.
Annual Meetings: May
1987-Washington, DC(Capitol Hilton)/May 14/600

Federal Executive and Professional Ass'n (1981)
210 N. Adams St., Rockville MD 20850-1829
Manager: Mary Moneymaker
Members: 1,000-1,100 *Staff:* 1
Annual Budget: $25-50,000 *Tel:* (301) 294-2625
Hist. Note: The result of a merger between the Federal Professional Association (founded 1962) and the Federal Executive League (founded 1973). Members, 2/3rds of whom are in the Washington area, are professionals employed by or retired from the federal government.
Annual Meetings: Spring in Washington, DC area

Federal Law Enforcement Officers Ass'n (1978)
106 Cedarhurst Ave., Selden NY 11784
Exec. V. President: Thomas Doyle
Members: 4,500 *Staff:* 2-5
Annual Budget: $100-250,000 *Tel:* (516) 698-0179
Hist. Note: Members are criminal investigators in the 1811 series employed by the U.S. Government. Membership: $50/year.
Publication:
FLEOA Newlettter. m.
Annual Meetings: Fall

Federal Librarians Round Table (1972)
110 Maryland Ave., N.E., Washington DC 20002
Staff Liaison: Anne Heanue
Members: 500-550 *Staff:* 1
Annual Budget: under $10,000 *Tel:* (202) 547-4440
Hist. Note: An affiliate of the American Library Association. A Round Table is a membership unit established to promote a field of librarianship not within the scope of any single division of the ALA. Individuals in the Federal library system may join the FLRT after first joining the ALA and paying an additional $8 annual dues. Membership: $8/yr. (individual); $10/yr. (organization/company)
Publication:
The Federal Librarian. q.
Annual Meetings: With the American Library Ass'n
1987-San Francisco, CA/June 27-July 3
1988-New Orleans, LA/July 9-14
1989-Dallas, TX/June 24-29
1990-Chicago, IL/June 23-28
1991-Atlanta, GA/June 29-July 4

Federal Managers Ass'n (1913)
1000 16th St., N.W., Washington DC 20006
Exec. Director: David W. Sanasack
Members: 20,000 *Staff:* 7
Annual Budget: $500-1,000,000 *Tel:* (202) 778-1500
Hist. Note: Organized in 1913 in Washington, DC as the Nat'l Ass'n of Supervisors, with members solely from the U.S. Navy. Disbanded in 1922, but was reactiviated in 1933. In 1950, the ass'n became the Nat'l Ass'n of Supervisors, Department of Defense; in 1968 became the Nat'l Ass'n of Supervisors, Federal Government; and in 1979 assumed its present name. Membership includes managers and supervisors in all federal agencies. Membership: $34/yr. (individual), $40/yr. (company).
Publications:
Federal Managers Quarterly. q. adv.
Federal Managers Newletter. m. adv.
Annual Meetings: In Washington, DC
1987-(Crystal City Marriott)/March 13-17/300

Federal Plant Quarantine Inspectors Nat'l Ass'n (1954)
Hist. Note: Became the Nat'l Ass'n of Agriculture Employees in 1982.

Federal Probation Officers Ass'n (1955)
U.S. District Court, 3rd & Constitution, N.W., 2nd Floor, Washington DC 20001
President: Ralph Ardito
Members: 1,200
Annual Budget: $10-25,000 *Tel:* (202) 633-0446
Hist. Note: An affiliate of the American Correctional Ass'n.
Publication:
FPOA Newsletter. q.
Annual Meetings: Spring

Federal Statistics Users' Conference (1956)
Hist. Note: Members were organizations dependent on Federal statistics and concerned with improving their quality. Ceased operations in 1984.

Federal Timber Purchasers Ass'n (1969)
Hist. Note: Members are companies who purchase timber from Government forests and who wish to continue to do so on favorable terms. Reported in 1983 as defunct.

Federal Water Quality Ass'n (1941)
c/o WH 547, U.S. EPA, 401 M St., S.W., Washington DC 20460
President: Jim Groff
Members: 375-400 *Staff:* 1
Annual Budget: under $10,000 *Tel:* (202) 833-8383
Hist. Note: Formerly the Federal Sewage Research Ass'n; now affiliated with the Water Pollution Control Federation. Membership consists of federal employees, consultants, industry and association representatives concerned with sewage and industrial waste treatment and disposal. 80% of members are in the Washington area. Membership: $8/yr.
Publication:
FWQA Newsletter. 8/yr.
Annual Meetings: Spring

Federally Employed Women (1968)
1010 Vermont Ave., N.W., Suite 821, Washington DC 20005
Exec. Officer: Karen Scott
Members: 220-230 local groups *Staff:* 5-8
Annual Budget: $100-250,000 *Tel:* (202) 638-4404
Hist. Note: Most members are employees of the Federal government. The association's goal:to end sex discrimination and increase job opportunities for women in government service.
Publication:
FEW News and Views. bi-m. adv.
Annual Meetings: July
1987-St. Louis, MO
1988-Baltimore, MD
1989-Memphis, TN
1990-San Antonio, TX

Federated Ambulatory Surgery Ass'n (1974)
700 N. Fairfax, Suite 520, Alexandria VA 22314
Exec. Director: Gail D. Durant
Members: 500 individuals, 30 companies, 150 facilities
Annual Budget: $250-500,000 *Tel:* (703) 836-8808
Hist. Note: First incorporated in Arizona in 1974 as the Society for the Advancement of Freestanding Ambulatory Surgical Care, became the Freestanding Ambulatory Surgery Ass'n in 1984 and assumed its present name in 1986. Facility Membership: $500-2,000/yr. Individual: $250/yr. Auxiliary: $500/yr.
Publication:
FASA Update. bi-m.
Annual Meetings: Spring/600
1987-Phoenix, AZ(Hyatt Regency)/May 6-9
1988-Washington, DC(Shoreham)
1989-New Orleans, LA(Hyatt Regency)
1990-Anaheim, CA(Marriott Anaheim)

Federated Pecan Growers' Ass'ns of the U.S. (1946)
Knapp Hall, L.S.U., Room 268E, Baton Rouge LA 70803
Secy.-Treas.: Dr. E. Earl Puls
Members: 9 state and regional associations *Staff:* 1
Annual Budget: under $10,000 *Tel:* (504) 388-2222
Hist. Note: Formerly Federated Pecan Growers of the United States.

Federation of American Controlled Shipping (1958)
50 Broadway, Suite 3400, New York NY 10004
Chairman: Philip J. Loree
Members: 20 companies *Staff:* 6-10
Annual Budget: $500-1,000,000 *Tel:* (212) 344-1483
Hist. Note: Represents the interests of U.S. companies operating under the Liberian, Panamanian and Bahamian flags. Formerly (1972) American Committee for Flags of Necessity. Maintains a Washington office.
Publication:
FACS Forum. m.
Annual Meetings: New York City in December.

00131 12 05 86 1233

Federation of American Health Systems (1966)
1111 19th St., N.W., Suite 402, Washington DC 20036
Exec. Director: Michael D. Bromberg
Members: 1,300 hospitals *Staff:* 25-35
Annual Budget: $500-1,000,000 *Tel:* (202) 833-3090
Hist. Note: Formerly (1986) the Federation of American Hospitals. Originally an association of investor-owned hospitals, FAHS members now include a broad range of health-care delivery systems. Sponsors the Federation of American Hospitals Political Action Committee.
Publications:
Annual Report. a.
Directory. a.
Hotline. semi-m.
Review. bi-m. adv.
Annual Meetings: Spring
1987-Orlando, FL(Marriott)/March 11-13

Federation of American Hospitals (1966)
Hist. Note: Became the Federation of American Health Systems in 1986.

Federation of American Scientists (1945)
307 Massachusetts Ave., N.E., Washington DC 20002
Director: Jeremy J. Stone
Members: 5,100 *Staff:* 10-12
Annual Budget: $250-500,000 *Tel:* (202) 546-3300
Hist. Note: Organized in 1945 for the purpose of lobbying to help insure civilian control of atomic energy. Membership: $25/yr.
Publication:
FAS Public Interest Report. 10/yr.

Federation of American Societies for Experimental Biology (1912)
9650 Rockville Pike, Bethesda MD 20814
Exec. Director: Robert W. Krauss, Ph.D.
Members: 28,440 *Staff:* 100
Annual Budget: over $5,000,000 *Tel:* (301) 530-7090
Hist. Note: In 1912 the American Physiological Soc., the American Soc. of Biological Chemists and the American Soc. of Pharmacology and Expermental Therapeutics formed the Federation of American Societies for Experimental Biology (FASEB). The Federation was joined by the American Soc. of Experimental Pathology (now named the American Ass'n of Pathologists) in 1913, the American Institute of Nutrition in 1940 and the American Ass'n of Immunologists in 1942. Incorporated in the District of Columbia in 1954. Has a budget of approximately $10 million.
Publication:
Federation Proceedings. m. adv.
Annual Meetings: Spring
1987-Washington, DC/March 29-April 3
1988-Las Vegas, NV/May 1-6
1989-New Orleans, LA/March 19-24
1990-Washington, DC/April 1-6
1991-Atlanta, GA/April 14-19
1992-Anaheim, CA/April 5-10
1993-New Orleans, LA/March 28-April 2

Federation of Analytical Chemistry and Spectroscopy Societies (1972)
Wayne State University, 175 Chemistry, Detroit MI 48207
General Chairman: Dr. Ronald Schroeder
Members: 5 organizations *Staff:* 1
Annual Budget: $100-250,000 *Tel:* (313) 226-7658
Hist. Note: Members are the analytical division of the American Chemical Soc., the Chromatography Forum of the Delaware Valley, the Coblentz Soc., the Instrument Soc. of America and the Soc. for Applied Spectroscopy. Purpose is to provide a national forum for analytical chemistry through an exhibition and technical papers.
Annual Meetings: Fall
1987-Detroit, MI/Oct. 5-9

Federation of Apparel Manufacturers (1977)
450 Seventh Ave., New York NY 10123
Asst. Exec. Director: Cory R. Greenspan
Members: 8 associations *Staff:* 20
Annual Budget: over $5,000,000 *Tel:* (212) 594-0810
Hist. Note: The eight member associations represent manufacturers of women's and children's apparel and are primarily concentrated in the New York metropolitan area.

Federation of Ass'ns of Regulatory Boards (1973)
Drawer 609, Wallace NC 28466
Secretary: Dr. John D. Robinson
Members: 10-15 boards *Staff:* 1
Annual Budget: under $10,000 *Tel:* (919) 285-3167
Hist. Note: Formerly (1985) Federation of Ass'ns of Health Regulatory Boards, the ass'n is now open to any regulated profession.
Publication:
The Wire. q.
Annual Meetings:
1987-San Francisco, CA/Feb. 6-9

Federation of Biocommunicators
Hist. Note: An informal organization without headquarters or staff consisting of the Association of Medical Illustrators, the Association of Biomedical Communicators and the Health Sciences Communications Association.

Federation of Computer Users in the Medical Sciences (1983)
Pacific Technology Center, Box 15579, San Francisco CA 94115
President: Dr. Daniel Moody
Members: 1,250 practices *Staff:* 5
Annual Budget: $500-1,000,000 *Tel:* (415) 626-4600
Hist. Note: Members are physicians and dentists concerned with the employment of computers in practice management. Membership: $95/year (individual).
Publications:
FOCUS on Computers. q.
Medimarketing. q. adv.

Federation of Dental Diagnostic Sciences (1976)
San Antonio Dental School, 7703 Floyd Curl Drive, San Antonio TX 78284
Secy.-Treas.: Olaf E. Langland
Members: 8 *Staff:* 1
Annual Budget: under $10,000 *Tel:* (512) 691-6961
Hist. Note: Consists of delegates from the American Academy of Dental Radiology, the American Academy of Oral Pathology, the American Academy of Oral Medicine and the Organization of Teachers of Oral Diagnosis. Purpose is to promote diagnostic science in dentistry.
Annual Meetings: Spring

Federation of Digestive Disease Societies (1981)
Hist. Note: Dissolved in 1984.

Federation of Insurance and Corporate Counsel (1985)
15 Ridge Road, Marblehead MA 01945
Admin. Secretary: Harrison G. Ball
Members: 1,300 *Staff:* 1
Annual Budget: $500-1,000,000 *Tel:* (617) 639-0698
Hist. Note: Founded in 1936 as the Federation of Insurance Counsel; assumed its present name in 1985. Members are lawyers who are actively engaged in the legal aspects of the insurance business, officials and executives of insurance companies, and corporate counsel engaged in defense of claims. Membership: $185/yr.
Publication:
FICC Quarterly. q.
Semi-Annual Meetings: Winter and Summer
1987-Palm Springs, CA(Marriott's Rancho Las Palmas)/Feb. 25-28
1987-Colorado Springs, CO(Broadmoor)/Aug. 4-8
1988-Maui. HI(Hyatt Regency)/Feb. 17-21
1988-Bermuda(Southampton Princess)/Aug. 3-7

Federation of Insurance Counsel (1936)
Hist. Note: Became the Federation of Insurance and Corporate Counsel in 1985.

Federation of Internat'l Country Air Personalities (1976)
Hist. Note: Ceased operations in 1984.

Federation of Materials Societies (1972)
1707 L St., N.W., Washington DC 20036
Exec. Director: Betsy Houston
Members: 15-20 *Staff:* 2-5
Annual Budget: $50-100,000 *Tel:* (202) 296-9282
Hist. Note: Promotes cooperation among societies concerned with the understanding, development and application of materials and processes.
Publication:
FMS Newsletter. bi-m.
Annual Meetings: Biennial
1988-Fredericksburg, VA(Sheraton Fredericksburg)/June 20-23/200

Federation of Mental Health Centers (1960)
Hist. Note: Defunct, 1983.

Federation of Modern Painters and Sculptors (1940)
340 West 72nd St., New York NY 10023
Corres. Secretary: Elisabeth Model
Members: 60 *Staff:* 1
Annual Budget: under $10,000 *Tel:* (212) 568-2981
Hist. Note: Professional painters and sculptors. Purpose is to improve the economic and working conditions of professional artists and facilitate the exhibition of their work. Has no permanent headquarters or paid staff. Membership concentrated in the New York area. Membership: $10/yr.

Federation of Nat'l Ass'ns (1974)
Hist. Note: Dissolved in 1983.

Federation of Nurses and Health Professionals (1978)
555 New Jersey Ave., N.W., Washington DC 20001
President: Albert Shanker
Members: 30,000 *Staff:* 6-10
Annual Budget: $1-2,000,000 *Tel:* (202) 879-4400
Hist. Note: A division of the American Federation of Teachers.
Publication:
Health Wire. 8/yr.
Annual Meetings: With the American Federation of Teachers in July/August.

Federation of Organizations for Professional Women (1972)
2437 15th St., N.W., Suite 309, Washington DC 20009
Exec. Director:
Members: 50 organizations *Staff:* 2-5
Annual Budget: $50-100,000 *Tel:* (202) 328-1415
Hist. Note: A federation of affiliated women's organizations to promote equal status for women in all education levels and career fields. The above building address will be taken over by D.C. Government; plans are under discussion for a new location. Membership: $30/yr. (individual); $100-200/yr. (organization).
Publications:
Alert. q.
Woman's Yellow Book. a.
Washington Woman's Directory. a.

Federation of Orthodontic Ass'ns (1969)
3953 North 76th St., Milwaukee WI 53222
Exec. Director: Dr. David H. Watson
Members: 2 ass'ns *Staff:* 2-5
Annual Budget: $25-50,000 *Tel:* (414) 461-8884
Hist. Note: Membership: $2,000/yr.
Publication:
Internat'l Journal of Orthodontics. semi-a.
Annual Meetings: Fall

Federation of Postal Police Officers (1975)
Hist. Note: Address unknown in 1987.

Federation of Professional Athletes (1978)
1300 Connecticut Ave., N.W., Suite 407, Washington DC 20036
President: Gene Upshaw
Members: 4,500 *Staff:* 2
Annual Budget: under $10,000 *Tel:* (202) 463-2200
Hist. Note: Labor federation affiliated with the AFL-CIO. FPA represents the players' associations of the Nat'l Football League, the Major Indoor Soccor League, and the United States Football League. Formerly (1980) Professional Athletes International.
Publications:
Directory a.
Football Law Newsletter. w.
Football Newspaper. m.
Football Newsletter. m.

Federation of Professional Writers of America (1981)
Hist. Note: Inactive in 1984.

Federation of Prosthodontic Organizations (1965)
211 East Chicago Ave., Suite 948, Chicago IL 60611
Exec. Director: Peter C. Goulding
Members: 16 organizations *Staff:* 2-5
Annual Budget: $100-250,000 *Tel:* (312) 642-7538
Hist. Note: Federation of national and regional dental organizations interested in prosthetic dentistry.
Publications:
Journal of Prosthetic Dentistry. m. adv.
Federation of Prosthodontic Organizations Newsletter. q.
Annual Meetings: Always in Chicago at the American Dental Ass'n Building, usually the second week of September.

Federation of Societies for Coatings Technology (1922)
1315 Walnut St., Philadelphia PA 19107
Exec. V. President: Frank J. Borrelle
Members: 6,500-7,000 *Staff:* 11-15
Annual Budget: $1-2,000,000 *Tel:* (215) 545-1506
Hist. Note: Established June 15, 1922 as the Federation of Paint and Varnish Production Clubs. Became the Federation of Societies for Paint Technology in 1959. The name was later changed to Federation of Societies for Coatings Technology. Membership: $20/yr.
Publications:
Journal of Coatings Technology. m. adv.
Membership Directory. a. adv.
Convention Program Book. a. adv.
Annual Meetings: Fall/6,000
1987-Dallas, TX(Convention Ctr.)/Oct. 5-7
1988-Chicago, IL/Oct. 19-21
1989-New Orleans, LA(Rivergate)/Nov. 8-10
1990-Washington, DC(Convention Ctr.)/Oct. 29-31
1991-Toronto, Ontario(Convention Ctr.)/Nov. 4-6

Federation of State Medical Boards of the U. S. (1912)
2630 West Freeway, Suite 138, Fort Worth TX 76102
Exec. V. President: Bryant L. Galusha, M.D.
Members: 64 boards *Staff:* 12
Annual Budget: $2-5,000,000 *Tel:* (817) 335-1141
Hist. Note: Parent organization of all state medical boards, the Federation was organized in Chicago at the Congress Hotel on February 29, 1912 with a charter membership of ten boards and eighteen fellows. It was incorporated in 1966. Maintains derogatory information submitted by state boards on physicians. Offers Federation Licensing Examination (FLEX) given by all states. Keeps statistics regarding requirements for licensure for ready reference to inquiries. Membership: $1,000/year (state board).
Publications:
The Federation Bulletin. m.
FSMB Newsletter. q.
Legislative EXCHANGE. a.

00132 12 05 86 1233

Directory. a.
Annual Meetings: Spring
1987-St. Louis, MO(Adams Mark)/April 23-25/350

Federation of Tax Administrators (1937)
444 North Capitol St., N.W., Washington DC 20001
Exec. Director: Leon Rothenberg
Members: 51 *Staff:* 6-10
Annual Budget: $250-500,000 *Tel:* (202) 624-5890
Hist. Note: Established by the Nat'l Ass'n of Tax Administrators, the North American Gasoline Tax Conference and the Nat'l Tobacco Tax Ass'n. Members are the tax agencies of the 50 state governments and the District of Columbia.
Publication:
Tax Administrators News. m.

Federation of Trainers and Training Programs in Psychodrama (1976)
5435 Balboa Blvd., Suite 200, Encino CA 91316
Membership Chairman:
Members: 50 *Staff:* 1
Annual Budget: under $10,000 *Tel:* (818) 789-6151
Hist. Note: Trainers, educators and practitioners of psychodrama.
Publication:
Newsletter. a.

Fellowship of Religious Humanists (1963)
P.O. Box 278, Yellow Springs OH 45387
President: Paul Beattie
Members: 500 *Staff:* 2-5
Annual Budget: $25-50,000 *Tel:* (412) 621-8008
Hist. Note: An organization with an educational purpose, most of whose members are connected with the organizations with which it is affiliated: the American Ethical Union, the American Humanist Ass'n, the Internat'l Ass'n for Religious Freedom, the Internat'l Humanist and Ethical Union, and the Unitarian Universalist Ass'n. Membership: $12/yr.
Publications:
The Communicator. q.
Religious Humanism. q. adv.
Annual Meetings: October, in an academic or religous setting.

Fellowship of United Methodists in Worship, Music and Other Arts (1956)
Box 6867, North Augusta SC 29841
Exec. Secretary: Jerry W. Henry
Members: 2,500 *Staff:* 1
Annual Budget: $25-50,000 *Tel:* (803) 279-4961
Hist. Note: Formerly (1974) Nat'l Fellowship of United Methodist Musicians, and (1979) Fellowship of United Methodist Musicians. Membership: $20/yr.
Publication:
News Notes. m.
Biennial meetings: Uneven years

Ferroalloys Ass'n (1971)
1511 K St., N.W., Suite 833, Washington DC 20005
President: George A. Watson
Members: 12 companies *Staff:* 2-5
Annual Budget: $100-250,000 *Tel:* (202) 393-0555
Quarterly Meetings:

Ferrous Scrap Consumers Coalition (1979)
1055 Thomas Jefferson St., N.W., Washington DC 20007
Counsel: Paul C. Rosenthal
Members: 900-950 *Staff:* 1
Annual Budget: $50-100,000 *Tel:* (202) 342-8485
Hist. Note: Members are foundries, steel companies and individuals working in the steel and foundry industry. The above address is that of the law firm, Collier, Shannon, Rill, and Scott. Membership Fee: Based on size of the company.
Annual Meetings: None held

Fertilizer and Farm Chemical Equipment Council
Hist. Note: A division of the Farm and Industrial Equipment Institute.

Fertilizer Institute (1970)
1015 18th St., N.W., 11th Floor, Washington DC 20036
President: Gary D. Myers
Members: 300-325 companies *Staff:* 30-35
Annual Budget: $2-5,000,000 *Tel:* (202) 861-4900
Hist. Note: Merger of the Nat'l Plant Food Institute (1955) and Agricultural Nitrogen Institute (1951). Formerly (1970) Nat'l Plant Food Institute. Members are brokers, producers, importers, dealers and manufacturers of fertilizer and fertilizer-related equipment. Supports the FERT Political Action Committee.
Publication:
Fertilizer Progress. bi-m. adv.
Semi-annual Meetings: June in White Sulphur Springs, WV(Greenbrier) and February

Fiber Soc. (1941)
Box 625, Princeton NJ 08542
Secy.-Treas.: George Lamb
Members: 300-400 *Staff:* 1
Annual Budget: $10-25,000 *Tel:* (609) 924-3150
Hist. Note: A professional group of researchers on fibers, fiber products and fibrous compounds. Membership: $15/yr.
Semi-Annual Meetings: Spring in the South and Fall in the North
1987-Greensboro, NC(Sheraton)/May 4-6

Fiberglass Fabrication Ass'n (1979)
1010 Wisconsin Ave., N.W., Suite 630, Washington DC 20007
Executive: Sandra K. Heydt
Members: 400 companies *Staff:* 2-5
Annual Budget: $250-500,000 *Tel:* (202) 544-0262
Hist. Note: Membership is open to any person, firm or corporation performing the hand layup or sprayup method of fiberglass fabrication in open molds or engaged in filament winding or resin transfer molding. Incorporated in 1979 in Washington, DC. Membership Fee: Based on sales volume of fiberglass products.
Publications:
FFA News. m.
Membership Directory/Buyers Guide. a.
Annual Meetings: Fall
1987-New Orleans, LA/Oct. 28-Nov. 1

Fibre Box Ass'n (1940)
8725 West Higgins Road, Chicago IL 60631
Exec. V. President: Bruce Benson
Members: 110 *Staff:* 6
Annual Budget: $500-1,000,000 *Tel:* (312) 693-9600
Hist. Note: Members are makers of corrugated boxes.
Annual Meetings: Spring
1987-San Francisco, CA(Fairmont)/April 1-3/200
1988-Williamsburg, VA(Conference Ctr.)/April 24-26/250

Fibre Drum Technical Council (1974)
1228 31st St., N.W., Box 25576, Washington DC 20007
General Counsel: Lawrence W. Bierlein
Members: 9 companies *Staff:* 1
Annual Budget: under $10,000 *Tel:* (202) 333-9199
Hist. Note: An outgrowth of the old Fibre Drum Manufacturers Association, the council was formed to represent the industry in technical matters concerning shipping containers with a 2-gallon minimum capacity.

Film, Air and Package Carriers Conference (1936)
2200 Mill Road, Alexandria VA 22314
Exec. Director: George H. Mundell
Members: 160 companies *Staff:* 3
Annual Budget: $100-250,000 *Tel:* (703) 838-1887
Hist. Note: Formerly (1969) Film Carriers Conference. Umbrella organization of the Air and Expedited Motor Carriers Conference, which deals in air freight and expedited service, the American Package Express Carriers Ass'n, which delivers shipments of 100 pounds or less, and the Nat'l Film Carriers, Inc., which transports movie film to and from theatres. An affiliate of the American Trucking Ass'ns, Inc.

Film Library Information Council (1967)
Hist. Note: Ceased operations in 1985.

Financial Analysts Federation (1947)
1633 Broadway, New York NY 10019
President: Alfred C. Morley
Members: 15,000 *Staff:* 16-20
Annual Budget: $2-5,000,000 *Tel:* (212) 957-2860
Hist. Note: Formerly Nat'l Federation of Financial Analysts Societies. Established the Institute of Chartered Financial Analysts in 1959.
Publications:
Financial Analysts Journal. bi-m. adv.
Membership Directory. a.
Annual Meetings: Spring/1,500
1987-Philadelphia,PA
1988-San Francisco,CA
1989-Montreal, Canada

Financial Executives Institute (1931)
10 Madison Avenue, P.O. Box 1938, Morristown NJ 07960
President: Robert W. Moore
Members: 13,000 *Staff:* 35-40
Annual Budget: $2-5,000,000 *Tel:* (201) 898-4600
Hist. Note: Formed by eight corporate controllers in New York City as the Controllers Institute of America, December 29, 1931 and incorporated December 31 in the District of Columbia. Assumed its present name in 1962. A professional organization of individuals performing the duties of Controller, Treasurer or Vice President of Finance. Maintains a Washington government liaison office.
Publication:
FE. m. adv.
Annual Meetings: October/1,000
1987-Boston, MA(Marriott)/Oct. 4-7
1988-San Francisco, CA

Financial Institutions Marketing Ass'n (1985)
111 E. Wacker Drive, Chicago IL 60601
President: Tom J. Hefter
Members: 1,800-2,000 *Staff:* 6-10
Annual Budget: $500-1,000,000 *Tel:* (312) 938-2570
Hist. Note: Originally founded as the Savings Institutions Marketing Soc. of America in 1965; most recently Financial Institutions Marketing Soc. of America (1985). Members include banks, investment companies, and credit unions.
Publication:
Financial Marketing. m.
Annual Meetings: Feb./March
1987-Orlando, FL/Feb. 22-25
1988-San Diego, CA/Feb. 14-18
1989-San Antonio, TX/March 19-22
1990-Orlando, FL/Feb. 18-21

Financial Institutions Marketing Soc. of America (1965)
Hist. Note: Became the Financial Institutions Marketing Ass'n in 1985.

Financial Management Ass'n (1970)
College of Business Administration, University of South Florida, Tampa FL 33620
Administrator: Jack S. Rader
Members: 8,000 individuals and institutions *Staff:* 6-10
Annual Budget: $250-500,000 *Tel:* (813) 974-2084
Hist. Note: Members are college teachers of financial management and corporate and organizational financial officers. Membership: $30/yr.
Publications:
Financial Management. q. adv.
Financial Management Collection. 3/yr. adv.
Annual Meetings: October/1,200
1987-Las Vegas, NV(Hilton)
1988-New Orleans, LA(Marriott)
1989-Boston, MA
1990-Lake Buena Vista, FL
1991-Chicago, IL
1992-San Francisco, CA

Financial Managers Soc. (1949)
111 East Wacker Drive, Suite 2221, Chicago IL 60601
President: B. Clyde Hampton
Members: 4,800 individuals *Staff:* 11-15
Annual Budget: $1-2,000,000 *Tel:* (312) 938-2576
Hist. Note: Formerly (1967) The Soc. of Savings and Loan Controllers, (1974) The Nat'l Soc. of Controllers and Financial Officers of Savings Institutions and (1982) The Financial Managers Soc. for Savings Institutions.
Publication:
Printout. m.
Annual Meetings: May
1987-Reno, NV(Bally's)/May 10-13/2,600
1988-Boston, MA(Marriott/Westin Copley Place)/May 15-18
1989-Nashville, TN(Opryland Hotel)/May 7-10
1990-Honolulu, HI(Hilton Hawaiian Village)/May 20-23
1991-Orlando, FL(Marriott's World Ctr.)/May 19-22
1992-Chicago, IL(Palmer House)/May 10-13

Financial Printers Ass'n (1983)
1730 North Lynn St., Arlington VA 22209
Exec. Director: Betty B. Horn
Members: 50 companies *Staff:* 2
Annual Budget: $25-50,000 *Tel:* (703) 841-8122
Hist. Note: A special interest section of the Printing Industries of America.
Publication:
FPA Bulletin. m.

Financial Stationers Ass'n (1964)
1101 Connecticut Ave., N.W., Suite 700, Washington DC 20036
Exec. Director: Michael L. Payne
Members: 70-80 companies *Staff:* 2-5
Annual Budget: $50-100,000 *Tel:* (202) 857-1144
Hist. Note: Formerly Bank Stationers Section of Lithographers and Printers Nat'l Ass'n and the Bank Stationers Ass'n. Assumed present name in 1984.
Publication:
Newsletter. q.
Annual Meetings:
1987-Palm Beach, FL(Breakers)/March 22-25/120
1988-Kamuela, HI(Mauna Kea Beach)/April 30-May 5/120
1989-Montebello, Quebec, Canada(Chateau Montebello)/June 24-28/120

Fine Hardwoods-American Walnut Ass'n (1971)
5603 West Raymond St., Suite "0", Indianapolis IN 46241
President: Larry R. Frye
Members: 40-45 companies *Staff:* 2-5
Annual Budget: $100-250,000 *Tel:* (317) 244-3311
Hist. Note: Merger of The American Walnut Ass'n (1914) and The Fine Hardwoods Ass'n (1933). Members are hardwood lumber and veneer manufacturers.
Publications:
Wood Unlimited Newsletter. q.
Fine Hardwoods Selectorama. a.

Finnish American Chamber of Commerce (1948)
Finland House, 540 Madison Ave., New York NY 10022
Exec. Secretary: Juhani Vehkaoja
Members: 150-175 companies *Staff:* 1
Annual Budget: $25-50,000 *Tel:* (212) 832-2588
Hist. Note: Membership: $40/yr.(individual); $200/yr.(company).
Publication:
FACC Newsletter. 8/yr. adv.
Annual Meetings: June

Fir and Hemlock Door Ass'n
Hist. Note: Ceased operations in 1986.

00133 12 05 86 1233

Fire Equipment Manufacturers' Ass'n (1925)
1230 Keith Bldg., Cleveland OH 44115-2180
Exec. Director: John H. Addington
Members: 20-25 companies *Staff:* 2-5
Annual Budget: $100-250,000 *Tel:* (216) 241-7333
Hist. Note: Established as the Fire Extinguisher Manufacturers' Ass'n, Inc., it assumed its present name in 1936. Members are companies making all types of devices that control or extinguish fires in residential or commercial buildings.
Annual Meetings: Fall

Fire Marshals Ass'n of North America (1906)
1110 Vermont Ave., N.W., Suite 1210, Washington DC 20005
Exec. Secretary: Robert B. Smith
Members: 1,100 *Staff:* 2-5
Annual Budget: $25-50,000 *Tel:* (202) 667-7441
Hist. Note: Organized in 1906, it became a Section of the Nat'l Fire Protection Ass'n in 1927. Members are fire marshals, fire prevention officers or similar government officials charged with investigating or preventing fires.
Publications:
Fire Journal. bi-m.
Fire News.
Fire Marshals Bulletin.
Fire Marshals Directory. a.
Semi-annual Meetings: With the Nat'l Fire Protection Ass'n
1987-Cincinnati, OH/May 18-21 and Portland, OR/Nov. 16-19
1988-Los Angeles, CA/May 16-20 and Nashville, TN/Nov. 14-17
1989-Washington, DC/May 14-18 and Seattle, WA/Nov. 13-16
1990-San Antonio, TX/May 14-17 and Miami, FL/Nov. 12-15

Fire Retardant Chemicals Ass'n (1971)
851 New Holland Ave., Box 3535, Lancaster PA 17604
Exec. V. President: Russell Kidder
Members: 30-40 companies *Staff:* 2-5
Annual Budget: $50-100,000 *Tel:* (717) 291-5616
Hist. Note: Promotes fire safety while creating and maintaining the best possible industry climate for our member companies to individually market their products and services. Membership Fee based on sales volume.
Publications:
Newsletter. q.
Proceedings. bi-a.
Semi-annual meetings: Spring and Fall/100
1987-New Orleans, LA/March 23-25
1987-Monterey, CA/Oct.

Fire Suppression Systems Ass'n (1982)
1740 E. Joppa Road, P.O. Box 28279, Baltimore MD 21234
Exec. Director: Calvin K. Clemmons
Members: 80-90 companies *Staff:* 2-5
Annual Budget: $100-250,000 *Tel:* (301) 661-6400
Hist. Note: Founded in Chicago and incorporated in the State of Illinois, members are makers, designers, suppliers and installers of fire control equipment.
Publication:
Systems Scene. bi-m.
Annual Meetings: Winter
1987-Naples, FL(Registry)/Jan. 17-21/250

First Amendment Lawyers Ass'n (1970)
1737 Chestnut St., Suite 1200, Philadelphia PA 19103
Admin. Director: Albert B. Gerber
Members: 125 *Staff:* 1
Annual Budget: $10-25,000 *Tel:* (215) 665-1600
Hist. Note: Lawyers concentrating on defending clients under the 1st Amendment to the Constitution - free speech, assemblage, petition, etc. Membership: $125/year.
Semi-annual Meetings: Winter and Summer

Flat Glass Marketing Ass'n (1949)
3310 Harrison St., Topeka KS 66611
Exec. V. President: William J. Birch
Members: 125 companies *Staff:* 2-5
Annual Budget: $100-250,000 *Tel:* (913) 266-7013
Hist. Note: Formerly (1969) Flat Glass Jobbers Ass'n.
Publication:
Glass Reflections. m.

Flavor and Extract Manufacturers Ass'n of the United States (1909)
900 17th St., N.W., Suite 650, Washington DC 20006
Attorney and Exec. Secretary: Daniel R. Thompson
Members: 115-120 companies *Staff:* 2-5
Annual Budget: $500-1,000,000 *Tel:* (202) 293-5800
Hist. Note: Formerly the Flavoring Extract Manufacturers Association of the U.S. Merged with the National Manufacturers of Beverage Flavors in 1965. Has no headquarters of its own. The above address is the law firm of Daniel R. Thompson, P.C.
Publications:
Newsletter. m.
Proceedings. a.
Semi-annual meetings: Spring and Fall

Fleischner Soc. (1969)
Dept. of Radiology, Box 615, MCV Station,edical College of Virginia, Richmond VA 23298
Secretary: Anthony V. Proto, M.D.
Members: 62 *Staff:* 1
Annual Budget: $50-100,000 *Tel:* (804) 786-5864
Hist. Note: Named for Dr. Felix Fleischner, an eminent chest radiologist, the society is dedicated to advancing the knowledge of chest diagnosis, with an emphasis on radiology. Membership is international and interdisciplinary, although most members are Americans and radiologists.
Publication:
Syllabus of Course Material. a.
Annual Meetings: Symposium on Chest Disease/May
1987-San Francisco, CA(St. Francis)/May 21-23
1988-Montreal, Quebec/May 16-18
1989-London, England/June 5-7

Flexible Packaging Ass'n (1950)
1090 Vermont Ave., N.W., Suite 500, Washington DC 20005
President: Glenn E. Braswell
Members: 180-200 *Staff:* 11-15
Annual Budget: $1-2,000,000 *Tel:* (202) 842-3880
Hist. Note: Includes former Industrial Bag and Cover Ass'n and Waxed Paper Institute. Formerly (until 1979) known as Nat'l Flexible Packaging Ass'n.
Annual Meetings: March, in Boca Raton, FL

Flexicore Manufacturers Ass'n (1952)
Box 1807, Dayton OH 45401
Exec. Director: John B. Henry
Members: 16-20 *Staff:* 2-5
Annual Budget: $100-250,000 *Tel:* (513) 226-8849
Hist. Note: Members are makers of pre-stressed, pre-cast concrete.
Semi-annual Meetings: Winter and Spring

Flexographic Technical Ass'n (1958)
95 West 19 St., Huntington Station NY 11746
Exec. Director: George J. Parisi
Members: 1,100 printers, suppliers, and end-users *Staff:* 17
Annual Budget: $1-2,000,000 *Tel:* (516) 271-4224
Hist. Note: Members are printers using the flexographic process, a method of rotary printing using flexible rubber plates and fast-drying inks.
Publication:
FLEXO Journal.
Annual Meetings: Spring/650
1987-Orlando, FL/May 3-6
1988-Nashville, TN/May 1-4

Flight Engineers' Internat'l Ass'n (1948)
905 16th St., N. W., Washington DC 20006
President: Alan Widdicombe
Members: 2,000 *Staff:* 2
Annual Budget: $100-250,000 *Tel:* (202) 347-4511
Hist. Note: Affiliated with AFL-CIO; Int'l Transport Workers' Federation; Flight Safety Foundation; Society of Accident Investigators.
Annual Meetings: Fall

Flight Safety Foundation (1945)
5510 Columbia Pike, Suite 303, Arlington VA 22204
President: John Enders
Members: 445 *Staff:* 10
Annual Budget: $500-1,000,000 *Tel:* (703) 820-2777
Hist. Note: An international membership organization of airlines, aerospace manufacturers, aviation professionals, and others interested in flight safety. Membership: $1,000/yr.
Publications:
Accident Prevention Bulletin. m.
Air Taxi/Commuter Safety Bulletin. bi-m.
Airport Operations Safety Bulletin. bi-m.
Aviation Mechanics Bulletin. bi-m.
Cabin Crew Safety Bulletin. bi-m.
FSF Flight Safety Digest. m.
Helicopter Safety Bulletin. bi-m.
Human Factors Bulletin. bi-m.
Newsletter. m.
Pilot Safety Exchange Bulletin. bi-m.
Semi-annual meetings: Spring and Fall
1987-Tokyo, Japan and San Francisco, CA
1988-Sydney, Australia and Williamsburg, VA
1989-Athens, Greece
1990-Rome, Italy

Floor Covering Installation Contractors Ass'n (1982)
Box 2048, Dalton GA 30722-2048
Contact Person: Ron VanGelderen
Members: 101 companies
Annual Budget: $10-25,000 *Tel:* (404) 226-5488
Hist. Note: Established July 1982 and incorporated in Georgia. Officers are elected annually.
Publication:
FCICA Newsletter. q.
Annual Meetings: Spring

Florists' Transworld Delivery Ass'n (1910)
29200 Northwestern Hwy., Southfield MI 48037
Exec. V. President: William A. Maas
Members: 23,000 *Staff:* 457
Annual Budget: over $5,000,000 *Tel:* (313) 355-9300
Hist. Note: Formerly Florists Telegraph Delivery Ass'n. A partner of InterFlora, Inc., the international florists' delivery organization. Has an operating budget of $100 million. Membership: $154/yr.
Publications:
Florist. m. adv.
FTD News. m. adv.
Annual Meetings: August
1987-Dallas,TX
1988-Boston,MA
1989-Honolulu,HI
1990-Chicago, IL

Flue-Cured Tobacco Cooperative Stabilization Corporation (1946)
Box 12300, Raleigh NC 27605
General Manager: Fred G. Bond
Members: 600,000-700,000 *Staff:* 55-65
Annual Budget: $500-1,000,000 *Tel:* (919) 821-4560
Hist. Note: Flue-cured tobacco producers' marketing cooperative for six southern states.
Publication:
Newsletter. m.
Annual Meetings: In corporation office.

Fluid Controls Institute (1921)
Box 9036, 31 South St., Morristown NJ 07960
Exec. Secretary: Edward C. Rutter
Members: 95-100 companies *Staff:* 2-5
Annual Budget: $25-50,000 *Tel:* (201) 829-0990
Hist. Note: Manufacturers of devices for fluid control, such as temperature and pressure regulators, strainers, gauges, control valves, solenoid valves, steam traps, etc. Established as the National Association of Steam and Fluid Specialty Manufacturers, it became the National Steam Specialty Club in 1941 and assumed its present name in 1955.
Publication:
News and Views. q.
Annual Meetings: Spring/225
1987-Sea Island(Cloister)/May 24-27/175
1988-Boca Raton, FL(Boca Raton Hotel)/May 15-18/175

Fluid Power Distributors Ass'n (1974)
1900 Arch St., Philadelphia PA 19103
Exec. Director: Kenneth R. Dickson
Members: 275-300 companies *Staff:* 2-5
Annual Budget: $100-250,000 *Tel:* (215) 564-3484
Hist. Note: Membership is composed of wholesalers who supply hydraulic and pneumatic equipment.
Publications:
Power Planner. m.
Directory. a.
Annual Meetings: April
1987-Naples, FL(Ritz Carlton)/March 28-April 1
1988-Scottsdale, AZ(Camelback Inn)
1989-Marco Island,FL(Marriott)/March

Fluid Power Soc. (1957)
2900 North 117th St., Milwaukee WI 53222
President: Raymond F. Hanley
Members: 2,440 individuals and companies *Staff:* 1
Annual Budget: $100-250,000 *Tel:* (414) 257-0910
Hist. Note: An outgrowth of a local Detroit organization called the Industrial Hydraulics Training Ass'n. This came to the attention of the Nat'l Fluid Power Ass'n. and the concept of the Fluid Power Soc. developed. Incorporated in Illinois in 1957. Membership: $30/yr.
Publications:
Membership Directory. a.
Pressure. bi-m. adv.
FPS Newsletter. q.
Annual Meetings: Spring

Fluid Sealing Ass'n (1933)
2017 Walnut St., Philadelphia PA 19103
Secy.-Treas.: Brent H. Farber, Jr.
Members: 200 companies *Staff:* 9
Annual Budget: $50-100,000 *Tel:* (215) 569-3650
Hist. Note: Formerly (1970) Mechanical Packing Ass'n. Members are makers of asbestos, rubber and leather packing used in mechanical seals.
Publication:
Newsletter. 3/yr.
Tri-annual Meetings: Mid-winter, Spring and the Annual Meeting

Food and Drug Law Institute (1949)
1701 K St., N.W., Suite 904, Washington DC 20006
President: Frank A. Ducksworth
Members: 150 companies *Staff:* 5-7
Annual Budget: $250-500,000 *Tel:* (202) 833-1601
Hist. Note: Formerly (1965) Food Law Institute.
Publication:
Food Drug Cosmetic Law Journal. m.
Annual Meetings: December in Washington, DC/1,200

Food and Energy Council (1957)
Hist. Note: Became the Nat'l Food and Energy Council in 1982.

Food Equipment Manufacturers Ass'n
111 East Wacker Drive, Chicago IL 60601
Exec. Secretary: Maxine Lee Couture
Members: 35-40 companies *Staff:* 2-5
Annual Budget: $10-25,000 *Tel:* (312) 644-6610
Hist. Note: Members are fabricators of commercial kitchen equipment.
Semi-annual Meetings:
1987-Maui, HI(Hyatt)
1988-Miami, FL(Doral C.C.)

Food Industries Suppliers' Ass'n (1968)
Box 603, Milford MI 48042
Exec. V. President: Thomas M. Watkins
Members: 125 *Staff:* 2-5
Annual Budget: $10-25,000 *Tel:* (313) 685-9380
Hist. Note: Affiliated with Nat'l Ass'n of Wholesaler-Distributors. Members are distributors who sell equipment and supplies to the food processing industry. Membership: $300/yr.

00134 12 05 86 1233

Publication:
FISA Distributor News. m.
Semi-Annual meetings: Spring and Fall

Food Industry Ass'n Executives (1927)
1001 Connecticut Ave., N.W. #800, Washington DC 20036
Exec. V. President: William S. Bergman, CAE
Members: 160 individuals *Staff:* 1
Annual Budget: $50-100,000 *Tel:* (202) 452-1520
Hist. Note: Formerly (1959) the National Grocery Secretaries Association. Members are executives of retail grocer associations on the national, state and local levels.
Publication:
Insight. m.
Annual Meetings: November
1987-Hawaii/Nov. 12-19

Food Industry Ladies of America (1962)
Hist. Note: Division of Nat'l American Wholesale Grocers Ass'n

Food Machinery Service Institute (1932)
Hist. Note: Established as the United Saw Service Association, it assumed its present name in 1983. Merged with the Meat Industry Supplier Ass'n in 1984.

Food Marketing Institute (1977)
1750 K St., N.W., Suite 700, Washington DC 20006
President: Robert O. Aders
Members: 1,500 companies *Staff:* 90
Annual Budget: over $5,000,000 *Tel:* (202) 452-8444
Hist. Note: Formed Jan. 3, 1977 by a merger of the Super Market Institute, Inc. and the Nat'l Ass'n of Food Chains. Members are food retailers and wholesalers. Supports the Food Marketing Institute Political Action Committee.
Publications:
FMI Issues Bulletin. m.
Reference Point. m.
Common Ground. q.
Annual Meetings: Always in Chicago, IL(McCormick Place)/ May
1987-May 3-6
1988-May 8-11
1989-May 7-10

Food Merchandisers of America (1955)
Hist. Note: Dissolved in 1985.

Food Processing Machinery and Supplies Ass'n (1885)
1828 L St., N.W., Suite 700, Washington DC 20036
Director, Administration: Ford Oxaal
Members: 484 companies *Staff:* 6-10
Annual Budget: $1-2,000,000 *Tel:* (202) 833-1790
Hist. Note: Formerly (1968) Canning Machinery and Supplies Ass'n.
Publications:
FOCUS. m.
Trade Opportunities. m.
Membership Directory and Locator Guide. bien.
U.S. Guide to Manufacturers of Food Equipment. bien.
Biennial Meetings: Odd years
1987-Chicago, IL(McCormick Place)/Jan. 24-28/18,000
1989-Anaheim, CA(Convention Center)/Jan. 28-Feb. 1/18,000

Food Processors Institute (1973)
Hist. Note: A division of Nat'l Food Processors Ass'n, the FPI meets the educational and training needs of the food processing industry. Also known as the Nat'l Food Processors Institute

Food Protein Council (1971)
Hist. Note: Became the Soy Protein Council in 1982.

Food Sanitation Institute (1957)
Hist. Note: A component of the Environmental Management Association.

Food Service Brokers of America, Inc. (1984)
2779 Clairmont Rd., Suite F-9, Atlanta GA 30329
President: David M. Guinee
Members: 301 companies *Staff:* 2
Annual Budget: $50-100,000 *Tel:* (404) 633-9404
Hist. Note: Membership available to any food brokerage company who has at least one person who works exclusively in sales to the food service industry and/or deli-bakery industry. Membership: $300/yr.
Publications:
FSBA Association Update. q.
Membership Directory. a.
Newsletter. q.

Foodservice and Lodging Institute (1965)
1919 Pennsylvania Ave., N.W., Washington DC 20006
Exec. Secretary: William G. Giery
Members: 40-50 companies *Staff:* 2-5
Annual Budget: $100-250,000 *Tel:* (202) 659-9060
Hist. Note: Formerly (1973) American Restaurant Institute. Membership limited to major multi-unit, multi-state food and lodging operators.

Foodservice Consultants Soc. Internat'l (1979)
12345 30th Ave., N.E., Suite H, Seattle WA 98125-5405
Exec. V. President: C. Russell Nickel
Members: 620 *Staff:* 2-5
Annual Budget: $250-500,000 *Tel:* (206) 367-3274
Hist. Note: The result of a merger in 1979 between the Food Facilities Consultants Soc. (founded in 1955) and the Internat'l Soc. of Food Service Consultants (founded in 1958). A professional society for consultants in design, equipment, engineering and management to the foodservice industry and furthers reseach, development and education in the foodservice field. Membership: $295/yr.
Publications:
The Consultant.
Spec Sheet (for members only).
Semi-Annual Meetings: Spring in Chicago, IL and Fall

Foodservice Equipment Distributors Ass'n (1933)
332 South Michigan Ave., Suite 1242, Chicago IL 60604
Exec. Director: Raymond Herrick
Members: 300-350 companies *Staff:* 2-5
Annual Budget: $100-250,000 *Tel:* (312) 427-9605
Hist. Note: Formerly (1972) Food Service Equipment Industry, Inc. Dealers in and distributors of foodservice equipment and supplies.
Publication:
FEDA News & Views. bi-m. adv.
Annual Meetings: March

Football Writers Ass'n of America (1941)
Box 1022, Edmond OK 73083
Exec. Director: Volney Meece
Members: 750 *Staff:* 1
Annual Budget: under $10,000 *Tel:* (405) 341-4731
Hist. Note: Established to improve working conditions in college press boxes. Now picks All-America Football team, National championship Football Team, College Coach of the year and winner of Outland Award, which goes to outstanding collegiate guard, tackle or center. Membership: $10/year.
Publication:
The 5th Down. 6/yr.
Annual Meetings: Early June during the American Football League Coaches Ass'n golf tournament in Dallas.

Footwear Council
Hist. Note: Dissolved in January 1986.

Footwear Industries of America (1869)
3700 Market St., Suite 303, Philadelphia PA 19104
President: Carl Bontemps
Members: 185 companies *Staff:* 25-30
Annual Budget: $2-5,000,000 *Tel:* (215) 222-2282
Hist. Note: Formerly (1905) the Nat'l Boot and Shoe Manufacturers Ass'n; (1965) the Nat'l Shoe Manufacturers Ass'n; (1969) Nat'l Footwear Manufacturers Ass'n. Merged in 1972 with the New England Footwear Ass'n (1869) to form the American Footwear Industries Ass'n Inc. and assumed its present name in 1982 after merging with the American Shoe Center. Incorporated in Massachusetts. Supports the Footwear Industry Political Action Committee (FOOTPAC). Maintains a Washington office. Membership: $750/yr.
Publication:
Footwear Manual. a.
Annual Meetings: Spring

Footwear Retailers of America (1944)
1319 F St., N.W., Suite 700, Washington DC 20004
President: Peter T. Mangione
Members: 30 companies *Staff:* 5
Annual Budget: $500-1,000,000 *Tel:* (202) 737-5660
Hist. Note: Founded as the Popular Price Shoe Retailers Ass'n, it became the Nat'l Ass'n of Shoe Chain Stores in 1965, the Volume Footwear Retailers Ass'n in 1969, the Volume Footwear Retailers of America in 1972, and assumed its present name in 1985.

Footwear Traffic and Distribution Council (1964)
Hist. Note: Sponsored by the Footwear Industries of America and the Volume Footwear Retailers of America. Formerly (1969) the Footwear Industry Traffic Council, and (1979) the Footwear Industry Traffic and Distribution Council. Concentrates on tariffs, taxes and physical distribution problems of the shoe industry. Has no dues structure, staff or permanent headquarters.

Foragers of America (1897)
515 Madison Ave., Suite 1313, New York NY 10022
President: Ed Ott
Members: 200
Tel: (212) 838-8600
Hist. Note: Organization of cosmetic buyers and sales executives with membership concentrated in New York City.
Annual Meetings: New York, NY

Foreign Credit Insurance Ass'n (1962)
40 Rector St., 11th Floor, New York NY 10006
President: John A. Hanson
Members: 4 companies *Staff:* 175
Annual Budget: over $5,000,000 *Tel:* (212) 306-5000
Hist. Note: The association, in cooperation with the Export-Import Bank of the United States provides foreign credit insurance to United States exporters and their financing institutions covering the risks incurred under commercial and political credit exposures. The insurance provides for payment in the event of nonpayment by buyers of United States products and services exported to creditworthy nationals and foreign governments.
Publication:
FCIA News. m.
Annual Meetings: Mid-March

Forest Farmers Ass'n (1941)
4 Executive Park East, Box 95385, Atlanta GA 30329
Exec. V. President: B. Jack Warren
Members: 3-4,000 timber growers *Staff:* 3
Annual Budget: $250-500,000 *Tel:* (404) 325-2954
Hist. Note: Covers 15 southeastern states. Seeks to give private timberland owners and related interests a greater voice in matters affecting their business. Membership: $30/yr.
Publications:
Forest Farmer. m. adv.
Forest Farmer Manual. a. adv.
Annual Meetings: Spring/350-400
1987-Savannah, GA(DeSoto Hilton)/May 13-15

Forest History Soc. (1946)
701 Vickers Ave., Durham NC 27701
Exec. Director: Harold K. Steen
Members: 1850-2,000 *Staff:* 6-10
Annual Budget: $250-500,000 *Tel:* (919) 682-9319
Hist. Note: Preceded by two unincorporated organizations, the Forest Products History Foundation (1946-52) and the American Forest History Foundation (1951-55), the Forest History Soc. was incorporated in Minnesota in 1955. It moved to New Haven in 1964 where it was associated with the Yale School of Forestry, and moved to Santa Cruz in 1969, where it was associated with the University of California. In 1984 it affiliated with Duke University and moved to Durham, NC. A non-profit educational institution advancing the historical understanding of mankind's interaction with his physical environment. Membership: $20/yr.
Publications:
Forest History Cruiser. q.
Journal of Forest History. q.
Annual Meetings: Fall
1987-Durham, NC/Oct.

Forest Industries Council
Hist. Note: Reported inactive in 1986.

Forest Industries Telecommunications (1947)
Box 5446, Eugene OR 97405
Exec. V. President: James H. Baker
Members: 1,800 *Staff:* 6-10
Annual Budget: $250-500,000 *Tel:* (503) 485-8441
Hist. Note: Organized in 1947 to assist the forest industry in radio matters before the FCC. Recognized by the FCC as the official representative of the Forest Products Radio Service.
Publication:
Two Way Transmissions. m.
Annual Meetings: Fall
1987-Williamsburg, SC

Forest Products Research Soc. (1947)
2801 Marshall Court, Madison WI 53705
Exec. V. President: Arthur B. Brauner
Members: 5,500-6,000 *Staff:* 13
Annual Budget: $500-1,000,000 *Tel:* (608) 231-1361
Hist. Note: Focus is on wood industry development, research, production, distribution and use, including all phases from logging to finished product and use of by-products.
Publication:
Forest Products Journal. m. adv.
Annual Meetings: Summer/500-600
1987-Louisville, KY(Hyatt)/June 21-25
1988-Quebec, Canada(Hilton)/June 19-23
1989-Reno, NV(MGM)/June 18-22

Forest Products Safety Conference (1934)
Weldwood of Canada, Ltd., 1055 West Hastings St., Box 2179, Vancouver British Columbia V6B 3V1
Secretary: Gordon Gray
Members: 100-120 companies *Staff:* 1
Annual Budget: $25-50,000 *Tel:* (604) 662-2848
Hist. Note: A group of U.S. and Canadian lumber companies united to promote safer working conditions. Established as the Western States Safety Conference, it became the Western Safety Conference in 1938, the Western Forest Products Safety Conference in 1945 and assumed its present name in 1951.
Publication:
Conference Proceedings. a.
Annual Meetings: April
1987-Eugene, OR(Hilton)/April 23-24

Forest Timber Purchasers Ass'n (1969)
Hist. Note: Dissolved in 1983.

Forestry Conservation Communications Ass'n (1944)
Hall of the States, 444 North Capitol, N.W., Washington DC 20001
Secy.-Treas.: James A. Caponey
Members: 125-150 organizations
Annual Budget: under $10,000
Hist. Note: An automomous part of the Internat'l Ass'n of Game, Fish and Conservation Commissions; affiliated with Nat'l Ass'n of State Foresters.
Publication:
FCAA Newsletter. m.

00135 12 05 86 1233

Forestry Equipment Council
Hist. Note: A division of the Farm and Industrial Equipment Institute.

Forged Eye Bolt Manufacturers Ass'n (1976)
25 North Broadway, Tarrytown NY 10591
Secretary: Richard C. Byrne
Members: 6-8 companies *Staff:* 2-5
Annual Budget: under $10,000 *Tel:* (914) 332-0040
Hist. Note: Cooperates with the American Nat'l Standards Institute in the preparation of design and safety standards for forged eye bolts.
Annual Meetings: Fall

Forging Industry Ass'n (1913)
1121 Illuminating Bldg, 55 Public Square, Cleveland OH 44113
Exec. V. President: Robert W. Atkinson, CAE
Members: 250 *Staff:* 11-15
Annual Budget: $500-1,000,000 *Tel:* (216) 781-6260
Hist. Note: Formerly Drop Forging Ass'n. Producers of forgings and raw materials, major equipment and supplies used in the forging industry. Sponsors the Forging Industry Political Action Committee.
Annual Meetings: May
1987-San Francisco, CA/May 6-10
1988-San Diego, CA/May 8-12

Formaldehyde Institute (1979)
1330 Connecticut Ave., N.W., Washington DC 20036
President: John F. Murray
Members: 40-50 companies *Staff:* 2-5
Annual Budget: $1-2,000,000 *Tel:* (202) 659-0060
Hist. Note: Users and producers of formaldehyde concerned with health and environmental problems arising therefrom. An affiliate of the Synthetic Organic Chemical Manufacturers Ass'n, which provides administrative support.
Annual Meetings: Fall/125

Forum for Health Care Planning (1950)
1101 Connecticut Ave., N.W., Suite 700, Washington DC 20036
Exec. Director: Carol A. Lively
Members: 600 individuals *Staff:* 2-5
Annual Budget: $50-100,000 *Tel:* (202) 857-1162
Hist. Note: Formerly (1986) American Ass'n for Hospital Planning. The Forum is a national membership organization committed to strengthening the planning for hospitals and health care delivery systems to meet community needs. Its members include health care practitioners, executives, consultants, architects, managers, voluntary community leaders, planners, teachers and researchers in the health care field. Membership: $95/yr.
Publications:
Newsletter. q.
Membership Directory. a.
Annual Meetings: Health Planning Forum
1987-Atlanta, GA/July 25/200

Foundation for Internat'l Meetings (1983)
1726 M St., N.W., Suite 1002, Washington DC 20036
President: John C. Vickerman
Members: 200 *Staff:* 3
Annual Budget: $50-100,000 *Tel:* (202) 457-0909
Hist. Note: Founded in Washington, DC in early 1983. Members are C.E.O.'s of associations and corporations which meet internationally and have an ongoing international program. Associate members are respresentatives of foreign convention sites. Membership: $225/yr. (by invitation).
Publication:
Newsletter. m.
Annual Meetings: Winter

Foundation for Savings Institutions (1952)
1522 K St., N.W., Suite 910, Washington DC 20005
President: Stephen R. Seiter
Members: 1,000 savings and loan organizations *Staff:* 6-10
Annual Budget: $2-5,000,000 *Tel:* (202) 842-4300
Hist. Note: Founded as the Savings and Loan Foundation (1952) and assumed its present name in 1983. Members are associations insured by the Federal Savings and Loan Insurance Corporation. Serves as the advertising arm of the U.S. Savings and Loan industry.
Publication:
Bulletin. m.

Foundation of the American Soc. of Ass'n Executives (1963)
Hist. Note: Established in 1963 by the American Society of Association Executives and incorporated in the District of Columbia in 1967. Receives its support from business organizations and associations whose executives are members of ASAE. Supports research on the future of association operations and provides information to increase the effectiveness of voluntary associations.

Foundry Equipment and Materials Ass'n
Hist. Note: Became Casting Industry Suppliers Ass'n in 1986.

Fourdrinier Kraft Board Group of the American Paper Institute (1977)
260 Madison Ave., New York NY 10016
V. President: William V. Driscoll
Members: 30 *Staff:* 7
Annual Budget: $500-1,000,000 *Tel:* (212) 340-0760
Hist. Note: Absorbed (1977) by the American Paper Institute, Inc. Members are involved in the containerboard industry.
Annual Meetings: Biennial.

Fourdrinier Wire Council (1924)
Box 849, Stevensville MD 21666
Secy-Treas: John D. Ferry
Members: under 50 *Staff:* 2-5
Tel: (301) 643-4161
Hist. Note: Formerly (1965) Paper Mill Fourdrinier Wire Cloth Manufacturers Ass'n. Founrdrinier machines manufacture paper through a process requiring wire cloth, which is manufactured by members of this ass'n.

Fragrance Foundation (1949)
142 East 30th St., New York NY 10016
Director: Annette Green
Members: 150-200 *Staff:* 4-6
Annual Budget: $100-250,000 *Tel:* (212) 725-2755
Hist. Note: The educational arm of the perfume industry. Membership Fee: Based on annual sales volume.
Publications:
Fragrance Forum. q.
Publications List Available.
Annual Meetings: November in New York, NY at the Plaza

Fragrance Materials Ass'n of the United States (1979)
900 17th St., N.W., Suite 650, Washington DC 20006
Exec. Secretary: Daniel R. Thompson
Members: 86 companies
Annual Budget: $250-500,000 *Tel:* (202) 293-5800
Hist. Note: Successor to the Essential Oils Ass'n, which was dissolved in 1980. Has no directly employed staff or headquarters; the above address is the law firm of Daniel R. Thompson, P.C.
Publication:
FMA Bulletin. m.
Annual Meetings: January

Fraternal Ass'n of Steel Haulers (1967)
Hist. Note: Dissolved in 1985.

Fraternal Field Managers Ass'n (1935)
100 W. Lawrence St., Appleton WI 54911
Exec. Secretary: Howard Pleuss
Members: 70-75 individuals *Staff:* 1
Annual Budget: under $10,000 *Tel:* (414) 734-7172
Hist. Note: Members are sales managers of fraternal life insurance societies. Awards the designation "FIC" (Fraternal Insurance Counselor). A section of the National Fraternal Congress of America, it sponsors the National Association of Fraternal Insurance Counselors. Has no paid staff. Membership: $10/yr.
Semi-annual meetings:
1987-Milwaukee, WI(Hyattt)/April 29-May 1/50

Fraternal Order of Police (1915)
2100 Gardiner Lane, Louisville KY 40205
Nat'l Secreatry: Ralph Orms
Members: 173,400 *Staff:* 8
Annual Budget: $500-1,000,000 *Tel:* (502) 451-2700
Hist. Note: Full time law enforcement officers seeking economic benefits and professional advancement. Membership: $3/yr.
Publications:
National FOP Journal. q.
Fair Labor Standards Handbook. a.
Biennial meetings: Uneven years in Summer
1987-Mobile, AL(Riverview Plaza)/August/8-10,000

Fraternity Executives Ass'n (1930)
c/o Alpha Gamma Rho Fraternity, Box 20246, Kansas City MO 64195
President: Philip Josephson
Members: 58 fraternities *Staff:* 1
Annual Budget: $50-100,000 *Tel:* (816) 891-9200
Hist. Note: Formerly (1970) College Fraternity Secretaries Ass'n. Serves chief executive officers of male fraternities.
Publication:
News and Notes. m.
Annual Meetings: Normally with College Fraternity Editors Ass'n, usually in June.

Freight Forwarders Institute (1941)
1055 Thomas Jefferson St., N.W., Suite 403, Washington DC 20007
Exec. Secretary: Faye Adams
Members: 25-30 *Staff:* 2-5
Annual Budget: $100-250,000 *Tel:* (202) 333-4580
Hist. Note: Formerly (1942) Freight Consolidators and Forwarders Institute. Connected with the Part IV Freight Forwarders Political Action Committee.

French-American Chamber of Commerce in the United States (1896)
509 Madison Ave., New York NY 10022
General Manager: Mrs. Chantal Soichet
Members: 2,000 United States, 800 France *Staff:* 10
Annual Budget: $500-1,000,000 *Tel:* (212) 371-4466
Hist. Note: Formerly (1977) French Chamber of Commerce in the United States. Furthers trade and fosters economic, commercial and financial relations between France and the U.S. Also provides a forum for French and American business and professional people with international interests. Operates eleven chapters in the U.S. and an office in Paris. Membership: $550/yr.
Publications:
Directory. a. adv.
French American Commerce. q. adv.
News. bi-m. adv.

Fresh Garlic Ass'n (1978)
Box 2151, Gilroy CA 95020
Secy.-Treas.: David Martin
Members: 15-20
Annual Budget: $10-25,000 *Tel:* (408) 847-1100
Hist. Note: Membership consists of garlic growers, shippers and handlers. FGA's main purpose is promotion of garlic. Has no paid staff; officers are elected annually.
Annual Meetings: October, in Santa Clara County, CA

Friction Materials Standards Institute (1948)
E-210, Route 4, Paramus NJ 07652
Exec. Director: Edward W. Drislane
Members: 30-40 companies *Staff:* 2-5
Annual Budget: $100-250,000 *Tel:* (201) 845-0440
Hist. Note: Formerly Brake Lining Manufacturers Ass'n. Manufacturers of brake linings and clutch facings.
Publications:
Automotive Data Book. a.
Brake Block Identification Catalog. a.
Annual Meetings: June/35

Frozen Onion Ring Packers Council (1973)
Hist. Note: Dissolved in 1982.

Frozen Potato Products Institute (1958)
1764 Old Meadow Lane, Suite 350, McLean VA 22102
Exec. Director: Steven C. Anderson
Members: 12 companies *Staff:* 2-5
Annual Budget: $25-50,000 *Tel:* (703) 821-0770

Fulfillment Management Ass'n (1945)
21 Stony Brook Rd., Branchburg NJ 08876
President: Stuart Boysen
Members: 575-600
Annual Budget: $10-25,000 *Tel:* (201) 526-3577
Hist. Note: Established as the Subscription Fulfillment Managers Association, it assumed its present name in 1972. Members are direct mail fulfillment, marketing and circulation executives, concentrated in the New York area. Has no paid staff. Membership: $75/yr.
Publication:
FMA Bulletin. 10/yr. adv.
Annual Meetings: Third Week in June

Fur Conservation Institute of America (1970)
Hist. Note: A subsidiary of the American Fur Industry, Inc.

Fur Industry Marketing Institute (1962)
Hist. Note: A subsidiary of the American Fur Industry, Inc.

Furniture Rental Ass'n of America (1964)
5008 Pine Creek Drive, Suite B, Westerville OH 43081
Exec. Director: James R. Bannister
Members: 100 companies *Staff:* 2
Annual Budget: $100-250,000 *Tel:* (614) 895-1273
Hist. Note: Incorporated 1972 in Massachusetts, FRAA is the only trade association serving the furniture renting and leasing industry exclusively. Membership: $400-1,000/yr.
Publication:
FRAA Newsletter. bi-m.
Annual Meetings: Feb.-March
1987-Hollywood, FL(Diplomat Resort)Feb. 24-27
1988-New Orleans, LA(Fairmont Hotel)/March 9-12

Fusion Bonded Coaters Ass'n (1975)
Hist. Note: Became a division of the Concrete Reinforcing Steel Institute (1985).

Fusion Power Associates (1979)
2 Professional Drive, Suite 249, Gaithersburg MD 20879
President: Dr. Stephen O. Dean
Members: 50 companies, 500 individuals *Staff:* 2
Annual Budget: $250-500,000 *Tel:* (301) 258-0545
Hist. Note: Incorporated in California in 1979, the association is concerned with the development of practical applications of fusion science and technology. Membership: $35/year (individual), $3,000/yr. (corporate).
Publications:
Executive Newsletter. m.
What's New in Fusion. q.
Fusion Facilities Directory. a.
Annual Meetings: Semi-annual meetings in Winter and Spring.

Future Business Leaders of America-Phi Beta Lambda (1942)
Box 17417, Dulles, Washington DC 20041
President: Edward D. Miller
Members: 200,000 individuals *Staff:* 11-15
Annual Budget: $500-1,000,000 *Tel:* (703) 860-3334
Hist. Note: A vocational student organization whose members are high school and college students preparing for business and office careers. Membership: $4/yr.

00136 12 05 86 1233

Publication:
Tomorrow's Business Leader. q. adv.
Annual Meetings: July

Future Farmers of America (1928)
National FFA Center, Box 15160, Alexandria VA 22309
Nat'l Advisor: Dr. Larry D. Case
Members: 434,643 *Staff:* 100
Annual Budget: $2-5,000,000 *Tel:* (703) 360-3600
Hist. Note: A vocational student organization organized under the National Vocational Education Act to foster character, leadership and good citizenship. Absorbed the New Farmers of America in 1965. Membership: $2.50/year.
Publications:
Between Issues. bi-m.
National Future Farmer Magazine. bi-m. adv.
Update. m.
Annual Meetings: November in Kansas City, MO

Future Homemakers of America (1945)
1910 Association Drive, Reston VA 22091
Exec. Director: Louisa Liddell
Members: 315,000 *Staff:* 20-25
Annual Budget: $1-2,000,000 *Tel:* (703) 476-4900
Hist. Note: A vocational high school student organization, composed of home economics students, sponsored by the Department of Education and the American Home Economics Association. Members focus on personal growth, leadership development, family life education and vocation preparation. Absorbed the New Homemakers of America in 1965. Membership: $4/year.
Publication:
Teen Times. q.
Annual Meetings: July
1987-Washington, DC(Washington Hilton)/July 19-24
1988-Cincinnati, OH(Clarion Hotel)/July 11-14

Futures Industry Ass'n (1955)
1825 Eye St., N.W., Suite 1040, Washington DC 20006
President: John M. Damgard
Members: 105 companies, 159 associates *Staff:* 6-10
Annual Budget: $1-2,000,000 *Tel:* (202) 466-5460
Hist. Note: National trade organization of commodity futures brokerage houses. Formerly (1975) Association of Commodity Exchange Firms, Inc. Sponsors the Futures Industry Political Action Committee.
Publications:
Bulletin. w.
FIA Review. bi-m.
Futures Trading Volume Report. m.
Congressional Report.
CFTC Report.
Futures Trading Course.
Annual Meetings: Spring

Galiceno Horse Breeders Ass'n (1959)
Box 219, Godley TX 76044
Secretary: Chris Giles
Members: 100
Annual Budget: under $10,000 *Tel:* (817) 389-3547
Hist. Note: Members are owners and breeders of Galiceno horses. Membership: $10/yr.
Publication:
Newsletter. m.
Annual Meetings: January

Galvanized Ware Manufacturers Council (1932)
Hist. Note: Makers of pails, cans, tubs, etc. Ceased effective operations in 1980.

GAMA
Hist. Note: See Game Manufacturers Ass'n.

Game Manufacturers Ass'n (1975)
3304 Crater Lane, Plano YX 75023
Exec. Director: Howard Baraschaik
Members: 109 companies
Annual Budget: $10-25,000 *Tel:* (214) 242-1516
Hist. Note: Formerly (1986) GAMA. Members are companies that manufacture historical, fantasy, science fiction, and abstract games which are played on tables, computers, boards, or plain paper for the adventure game and hobby markets. Membership: $25/yr.(individual); $250/yr.(company).
Publication:
Newsletter. q.
Annual Meetings: June/July
1987-Baltimore, MD(Hyatt)/July 3-5/5,000

Gamma Iota Sigma (1965)
1775 College Rd., Columbus OH 43210
Exec. V. President: Dr. Alan C. Williams
Members: 1,600 *Staff:* 1
Annual Budget: under $10,000 *Tel:* (614) 422-2061
Hist. Note: Student professional insurance society. Founded at The Ohio State University in 1965. The Griffith Foundation for Insurance Education is the parent organization.
Publication:
The Sextant. semi-a.
Annual Meetings: First Tuesday in March

Garage Door Council (1982)
655 Irving Park at Lake Shore Drive, Chicago IL 60613-3198
President: Frank S. Fitzgerald, CAE
Staff: 2-5
Annual Budget: under $10,000 *Tel:* (312) 525-2644
Hist. Note: A federation available to trade groups of companies making and distributing garage doors and components; main task is conducting public information campaigns.
Annual Meetings: May at Corporate Headquarters

Garden Centers of America (1972)
1250 I St., N.W., Washington DC 20008
Administrator: Patrick Redding
Members: 600 companies *Staff:* 2
Annual Budget: $50-100,000 *Tel:* (202) 789-2900
Hist. Note: Established and incorporated in Washington, DC. Trade association of retail nurseries, members must be members of the American Ass'n of Nurserymen. Membership: $100/year.
Publication:
Garden Centers of America Newsletter. 10/year.
Annual Meetings: February

Garden Writers Ass'n of America (1948)
1218 Overlook Road, Eustis FL 32726
Exec. Director: W.J. Jung
Members: 1,160 *Staff:* 1
Annual Budget: $25-50,000 *Tel:* (904) 589-8888
Hist. Note: Membership: $40/yr.
Publication:
Garden Writers Bulletin. bi-m.
Annual Meetings: October
1987-Akron, OH/Oct.
1988-Portland, OR/Oct.

Gas Appliance Manufacturers Ass'n (1935)
Box 9245, Arlington VA 22209
President: Harry A. Paynter
Members: 235 companies *Staff:* 25-30
Annual Budget: $1-2,000,000 *Tel:* (703) 525-9565
Hist. Note: Founded as the Association of Gas Appliance and Equipment Manufacturers, it assumed its present name in 1946 and absorbed the Institute of Appliance Manufacturers (founded in 1872) in 1967. Manufacturers of residential, commercial and industrial gas appliances and equipment; gas, electric and oil-fired water heaters; oil-fired central furnaces and equipment used in the production, transmission and distribution of natural gas.
Publications:
Patent Digest. m.
Statistical Highlights. m.
Annual Meetings: Spring/500
1987-Palm Beach, FL(Breakers)/March 29-April 1
1988-Boca Raton, FL(Hotel & Club)/May 1-4
1989-White Sulphur Springs, WV(Greenbrier)/May 7-10
1990-Laguna Niguel, CA(Ritz-Carlton)/April 8-11

Gas Processors Ass'n (1921)
6526 E. 60th St., Tulsa OK 74145
Exec. Director: Ronald E. Cannon
Members: 225 companies *Staff:* 6-10
Annual Budget: $500-1,000,000 *Tel:* (918) 493-3872
Hist. Note: Established in 1921 as Ass'n of Natural Gasoline Manufacturers and became Natural Gasoline Ass'n of America in 1922. The name was changed to Natural Gas Processors Ass'n in 1961 and Gas Processors Ass'n in 1974. Membership consists of firms handling natural gasoline and other hydrocarbon products at gas-processing plants.
Publication:
Proceedings. a.
Annual Meetings: March/3,500
1987-Denver, CO(Marriott)/March 16-18
1988-Dallas, TX(Anatole)/March 14-16
1989-San Antonio, TX(Convention Center)/March 13-15
1990-Phoenix, AZ(Convention Center)/March 11-15

Gas Processors Suppliers Ass'n (1927)
6526 E. 60th St., Tulsa OK 74145-9202
Secretary: Ronald E. Cannon
Members: 475 companies *Staff:* 6-10
Annual Budget: $100-250,000 *Tel:* (918) 493-3872
Hist. Note: Formerly (1974) Natural Gas Processors Suppliers Ass'n. Membership: $150/yr.
Annual Meetings: With Gas Processors Ass'n
1987-Denver, CO(Marriott)/March 16-18/3,000
1988-Dallas, TX(Anatole)/March 14-16/3,000
1989-San Antonio, TX(Convention Center)/3,000
1990-Phoenix, AZ(Convention Center)/March 11-15/3,000

Gasket Fabricators Ass'n (1979)
2017 Walnut St., Philadelphia PA 19103
Exec. Director: Brent H. Farber, Jr.
Members: 125 companies *Staff:* 10
Annual Budget: $25-50,000 *Tel:* (215) 569-3650
Hist. Note: National trade association of fabricators whose products include metallic and non-metallic sealing devices and allied products. Membership: $700/yr.
Publication:
Newsletter.
Semi-Annual Meetings: Spring and Fall

Gasoline and Automotive Service Dealers Ass'n (1929)
6338 Avenue N, Brooklyn NY 11234
Exec. Director: Stanley M. Schuer
Members: 700 companies; 300 individuals *Staff:* 7
Annual Budget: $250-500,000 *Tel:* (718) 241-1111
Hist. Note: Formerly (1977) Gasoline Merchants. Members are owners and/or operators of service stations or auto repair facilities. GASDA seeks to education and strengthen professionalism in the industry. Membership: $240/yr.
Publications:
Newsletter. irreg.
Directory and Buyers Guide. a.

Gasoline Pump Manufacturers Ass'n (1934)
c/o Morgan, Lewis and Bockius, 1800 M St., N.W., Suite 700 North, Washington DC 20036
General Counsel: Mark Joelson
Members: 5-10 companies *Staff:* 1
Tel: (202) 872-5000

Gastroenterology Research Group (1955)
c/o Mayo Clinic, Rochester MN 55905
Secretary: Dr. Sidney Phillips
Members: 650-700 *Staff:* 1
Annual Budget: under $10,000 *Tel:* (507) 285-5711
Hist. Note: Affiliated with American Gastroenterological Ass'n and American Ass'n for the Study of Liver Disease.
Annual Meetings: Spring
1987-Chicago, IL/May 9-15

Gay and Lesbian Press Ass'n (1981)
P.O. Box 8185, Universal City CA 91608-0185
Admin. Director: R.J. Curry
Members: 300 publications & individuals
Annual Budget: $10-25,000 *Tel:* (213) 877-1045
Publication:
Newsletter. q.
Annual Meetings: May
1987-San Diego, CA/May 22-25

Gelatin Manufacturers Institute of America (1956)
516 Fifth Ave., Room 507, New York NY 10036
Secy.-Treas.: James Foley
Members: 5 companies *Staff:* 1
Annual Budget: $10-25,000 *Tel:* (212) 575-1234
Hist. Note: The above address is a telephone answering service that advises callers to put their concerns in writing.

General Agents and Managers Conference of NALU (1951)
1922 F St., N.W., Washington DC 20006
Exec. V. President: Dennis G. Stork
Members: 7,000
Annual Budget: $1-2,000,000 *Tel:* (202) 331-6088
Hist. Note: Founded to provide educational and training opportunities for those engaged in field management within the life insurance industry. Membership: $75/yr.
Publications:
GAMC News. bi-m. adv.
Leaders Letter. bi-m.
Conference Call. q.
Agency Management Today. 8/yr.
Annual Meetings: March/1,500
1987-New Orleans, LA(Hyatt Regency)/March 22-25
1988-San Diego, CA(Sheraton)/March 27-30
1989-Nashville, TN(Opryland)/March 19-22
1990-Dallas, TX(Loews Anatole)/March 18-21

General Aviation Manufacturers Ass'n (1970)
1400 K St., N.W., Suite 801, Washington DC 20005
President: Edward W. Stimpson
Members: 38 companies *Staff:* 11-15
Annual Budget: $1-2,000,000 *Tel:* (202) 393-1500
Hist. Note: An outgrowth of the former Utility Aircraft Council of the Aerospace Industries Association, members of GAMA are manufacturers of small airplanes, their accessories and components. Works on airport/airway technical matters and safety issues to develop a better climate for growth of general aviation. Supports the General Aviation Political Action Committee.

General Federation of Women's Clubs (1890)
1734 N St., N.W., Washington DC 20036
Exec. Director: Quincalee Brown
Members: 11,000 clubs; 500,000 individuals *Staff:* 16-20
Annual Budget: $1-2,000,000 *Tel:* (202) 347-3168
Hist. Note: GFWC is a non-denominational, non-partisan, international service organization of volunteer women.
Publication:
Clubwoman Magazine. m. adv.
Annual Meetings: June/1,400
1987-San Diego, CA(Sheridan Harbor)
1988-Grand Rapids, MI(Amway Grand Plaza)
1989-undecided
1990-New York, NY(Marriott Marquis)

General Merchandise Distributors Council (1970)
1275 Lake Plaza Drive, Colorado Springs CO 80906
President and CEO: Richard W. Tilton
Members: 650-700 *Staff:* 6-10
Annual Budget: $1-2,000,000 *Tel:* (303) 576-4260
Hist. Note: Founded in 1970 as a national trade association for the general merchandise units of wholesale grocers and their suppliers of non-food products.
Publication:
The Exchange. bi-m.
Tri-annual Meetings:

00137 12 05 86 1233

1987-Scottsdale, AZ(Cambelback Inn)/Jan. 7-9 (Candy/Tobacco/Conf.)
1987-Palm Desert, CA(Desert Springs Resort)/May 16-22 (Health/Beauty)
1987-Marco Island, FL(Marco Beach Resort)/Sept. 11-17 (Gen. Merch.)
1988-Candy/Tobacco/Conf. - undetermined
1988-Orlando, FL(Marriott World Ctr.)/June 3-9 (Health/Beauty Aids)
1988-Phoenix, AZ(Pointe, South Mountain)/Sept. 23-29 (Gen. Merch.)
1989-Candy/Tobacco/Conf. - undetermined
1989-Marco Island, FL(Marco Beach Resort)/May (Health/Beauty Aids)
1989-Monterey, CA(Doubletree & Sheraton)/Sept. 16-22 (Gen. Merch.)
1990-Candy/Tobacco/Conf. - undetermined
1990-Palm Desert, CA(Desert Springs Resort)/May 11-18 (Health/Beauty)
1990-Orlando, FL(Marriott World Ctr.)/Sept. 7-13 (Gen. Merch.)

Generic Pharmaceutical Industry Ass'n (1981)
200 Madison Ave., Suite 2404, New York NY 10016
President: Dee Fensterer
Members: 19 companies *Staff:* 4
Tel: (212) 683-1881
Hist. Note: Promotes the recognition, acceptance, and use of generic prescription drug products and seeks to increase the availability of equivalent generic pharmaceuticals on the market. Facilitates the identification, development, and marketing of drug treatments for rare diseases through its Institute for Orphan Drugs.
Publication:
Generics. q. adv.

Genetic Toxicology Ass'n (1977)
c/o Toxicology Professionals Inc., Box 369, Oakton VA 22124
Secretary: Dr. Michael Farrow
Members: 375
Annual Budget: under $10,000 *Tel:* (703) 938-1952
Hist. Note: Promotes the study of mutagenicity- the capacity to induce mutations in living organisms. Incorporated in the State of Delaware. Has no paid staff. Officers are elected annually. Membership: $5/year.
Publication:
GTA Newsletter. q.
Semi-annual Meetings: Spring and Fall/100-125

Genetics Soc. of America (1931)
15501-B Monona Drive, Derwood MD 20855
Administrative Director: Gerry Gurvitch
Members: 2,800 individuals *Staff:* 6
Annual Budget: $500-1,000,000 *Tel:* (301) 762-1424
Hist. Note: Organized in 1931 in New Orleans as an outgrowth of the Genetics Section of the American Soc. of Zoologists and the Botanical Soc. of America. Incorporated in Maryland in 1984. Membership: $45/yr.
Publications:
Genetics. m.
Membership Directory. bien.
Annual Meetings: Summer
1987-San Francisco, CA(Hilton)/June 14-16

Geochemical Soc. (1955)
Dept. of Geological Sciences, Wright State University, Dayton OH 45435
Secretary: Bryan Gregor
Members: 1,600 *Staff:* 3
Annual Budget: $10-25,000 *Tel:* (513) 873-3442
Hist. Note: Founded November 7, 1955 and incorporated in the District of Columbia in 1956. Encourages the application of chemistry to the solution of geological and cosmological problems. Membership: $40/yr. (individual), $340/yr. (company).
Publications:
Geochimica et Cosmochimica Acta. m. adv.
Geochemical News. bi-a.
Annual Meetings: With Geological Soc. of America.

Geological Soc. of America (1888)
3300 Penrose Place, Box 9140, Boulder CO 80301
Exec. Director: F. Michael Wahl
Members: 16,200 *Staff:* 39
Annual Budget: $2-5,000,000 *Tel:* (303) 447-2020
Hist. Note: Founded in 1888 and incorporated in New York in 1929. Soc. includes ten topical divisions; Archaeological Geology, Coal Geology, Engineering Geology, Geophysics, History of Geology, Hydrogeology, Planetary Geology, Quaternary Geology and Geomorphology, Sedimentary Geology and Structural Geology and Tectonics. Also has six regional sections, each of which holds its own annual meeting in the spring. A member society of the American Geological Institute. Membership: $70/yr. (Members/Fellows)
Publications:
GSA News and Information. m.
Geological Society of America Bulletin. m.
Geology. m.
Membership Directory. a.
Annual Meetings: Fall
1987-Phoenix, AZ/Oct. 26-29
1988-Denver, CO/Oct. 31-Nov. 3
1989-St. Louis, MO/Nov. 6-9
1990-Dallas, TX/Oct. 29-Nov. 1
1991-San Diego, CA/Oct. 21-24
1992-Cincinnati, OH/Oct. 26-29
1993-Boston, MA/Oct. 25-28

Geoscience and Remote Sensing Soc.
Hist. Note: A subsidiary of the Institute of Electrical and Electronics Engineers. Membership in the Society, open only to IEEE members, includes subscription to a technical periodical in the field published by IEEE. All administrative support is provided by IEEE.

Geoscience Information Soc. (1965)
c/o American Geological Institute, 4220 King St., Alexandria VA 22302
Secretary: Miriam Sheaves
Members: 290
Annual Budget: under $10,000 *Tel:* (703) 379-2480
Hist. Note: Founded in Kansas City, GIS was incorporated in the District of Columbia in 1966. Affiliated with the Geological Soc. of America and the American Geological Institute. Membership: $30/yr.(individual); $50/yr.(institution)
Publications:
GIS Newsletter. bi-m.
Proceedings. a.
Membership Directory. a.
Annual Meetings: Fall with the Geological Soc. of America
1987-Phoenix, AZ/Oct. 26-29
1988-Denver, CO/Oct. 31-Nov. 3

Geothermal Resources Council (1972)
Box 1350, Davis CA 95617
Exec. Director: David N. Anderson
Members: 1,350-1,400 *Staff:* 6-10
Annual Budget: $500-1,000,000 *Tel:* (916) 758-2360
Hist. Note: Members are individuals interested in the development of geothermal energy. Membership: $45/year.(individual); $250/yr.(institution/company).
Publication:
List available upon request.
Annual Meetings: Fall

German American Chamber of Commerce (1947)
666 5th Avenue, New York NY 10103
Exec. Director: Werner Walbrol
Members: 3,000
Tel: (212) 974-8830
Hist. Note: Membership: $400/yr.
Publications:
American Subsidiaries of German Firms. a. adv.
German Business Weekly. w.
United States-German Economic Survey. a. adv.
Membership Directory. a.
Annual Meetings: New York, NY

Gerontological Soc. of America (1945)
1411 K St., N.W., Suite 300, Washington DC 20005
Exec. Director: John M. Cornman
Members: 6,200 *Staff:* 16-15
Annual Budget: $1-2,000,000 *Tel:* (202) 393-1411
Hist. Note: An outgrowth of the Club for Research in Ageing organized in 1939. Incorporated in New York in 1945. A member of the American Ass'n for the Advancement of Science, and the Internat'l Ass'n of Gerontology. Members are researchers, educators and professionals in the field of aging. Membership: $70/yr.
Publications:
Journal of Gerontology. bi-m. adv.
The Gerontologist. bi-m. adv.
Gerontology News. 10/yr.
Annual Meetings: Fall
1987-Washington, DC(Washington Hilton)/Nov. 18-22/2,700
1988-San Francisco, CA(Hilton)/Nov. 18-22/2,700
1989-Minneapolis, MN(Hyatt & Holiday Inn)/Oct. 15-19/2,700
1990-Boston, MA(Marriott Copley Place)/Oct. 16-20/2,900
1991-West Coast

Gift Ass'n of America (1952)
1511 K St., N.W., Suite 716, Washington DC 20005
Managing Director: Jerome A. Miller
Members: 1,100 *Staff:* 1
Annual Budget: $10-25,000 *Tel:* (202) 638-6080
Hist. Note: The association conducts seminars on subjects of interest to the gift industry at various gift marts throughout the United States. Fomerly (1982) Gift and Decorative Accessories Ass'n of America. Membership: $50/yr, retail; $100/yr., wholesale.

Gift Retailers, Manufacturers and Representatives Ass'n (1986)
1100-H Brandywine Blvd., P.O. Box 2188, Zanesville OH 43702
President: Walter E. Offinger
Members: 100 individuals
Annual Budget: under $10,000 *Tel:* (614) 452-4541
Hist. Note: Membership: $20/yr.
Publication:
GRMRA News. bi-m. adv.
Annual Meetings: August
1987-Columbus, OH(Veterans Memorial)/Aug. 9-11
1988-Columbus, OH(Veterans Memorial)/Aug. 21-25

Gift Wrappings and Tyings Ass'n (1961)
Hist. Note: Dissolved 1984.

Girls Clubs of America (1945)
205 Lexington Ave., New York NY 10016
Nat'l Exec. Director: Margaret Gates
Members: 240 clubs *Staff:* 25-30
Annual Budget: $2-5,000,000 *Tel:* (212) 689-3700
Hist. Note: Established in 1945 by nineteen charter clubs serving young women. GCA serves 240 girls club centers serving 250,000 girls aged 6-18. Maintains a National Resource Center in Indianapolis, IN.
Publication:
Voice for Girls. 3/yr.
Annual Meetings: Spring
1987-Dallas, TX(Westin)/April 23-26
1988-Washington, DC
1989-Denver, CO

Glass Art Soc. (1971)
20300 North Greenway St., Southfield MI 48076
Treasurer: Sylvia Vigiletti
Members: 6-700 *Staff:* 1
Annual Budget: $25-50,000 *Tel:* (313) 357-0783
Hist. Note: A professional society of artists working in glass. Membership: $25/yr.
Publication:
Glass Art Society Journal. a.
Annual Meetings: Spring

Glass Bottle Blowers of the United States and Canada (1890)
Hist. Note: Merged in August 1982 with the International Brotherhood of Pottery and Allied Workers to form the Glass, Pottery, Plastics and Allied Workers International Union.

Glass Packaging Institute (1945)
1133 20th St., N.W., Suite 321, Washington DC 20036
President: Lewis D. Andrews, Jr.
Members: 38 companies *Staff:* 5
Annual Budget: $2-5,000,000 *Tel:* (202) 887-4850
Hist. Note: Formerly (1976) Glass Container Manufacturers Institute, Inc.
Annual Meetings: Always in White Sulphur Springs, WV/Sept./130

Glass, Pottery, Plastics and Allied Workers Internat'l Union (1982)
608 East Baltimore Pike, Box 607, Media PA 19063
Internat'l President: James E. Hatfield
Members: 75,000 *Staff:* 45
Tel: (215) 565-5051
Hist. Note: Product of merger between the Internat'l Brotherhood of Pottery and Allied Workers and the Glass Bottle Blowers Ass'n of the United States and Canada, both of which were formed in 1890. Supports the Glass, Pottery, Plastics and Allied Workers Political Education League.
Publication:
GPPAW Horizons. m.
Quadrennial Meetings: 1989

Glass Tempering Ass'n (1958)
3310 Harrison St., Topeka KS 66611
Exec. V. President: William J. Birch
Members: 30-35 companies *Staff:* 2-5
Annual Budget: $50-100,000 *Tel:* (913) 266-7064
Publication:
Engineering Standards Manual. a.
Semi-Annual Meetings:

Glutamate Ass'n, The (United States) (1977)
5775 Peachtree-Dunwoody Rd., Suite 500D, Atlanta GA 30342
President: Robert H. Kellen
Members: 14 companies *Staff:* 5
Tel: (404) 252-3663
Hist. Note: Provides information on glutamic acid and its salts, including monosodium glutamate (MSG). Serves as a regulatory and scientific liaison for industry concerning glutamates.
Annual Meetings:
1987-Teaneck, NJ/March 30-31

Glycerine and Fatty Acid Producers Ass'n
Hist. Note: A division of the Soap and Detergent Ass'n.

Gold Filled Ass'n (1985)
49 Pearl St., Attleboro MA 02703
Secretary: Chris Sheridan
Members: 6 companies *Staff:* 2-5
Annual Budget: $100-250,000 *Tel:* (617) 222-3666
Hist. Note: Formerly (1985) Gold Filled Manufacturers Ass'n. Manufacturers of sheet, wire, and tubing of solid mechanically bonded bimetals and trimetals using gold, silver, and other precious metals.
Annual Meetings: February, in Providence, RI

Gold Filled Manufacturers Ass'n (1954)
Hist. Note: Changed its name to Gold Filled Ass'n.(1985)

Gold Institute (1976)
1026 16th St., N.W., Suite 101, Washington DC 20036
Mng. Director: John H. Lutley
Members: 80 companies *Staff:* 6-10
Annual Budget: $250-500,000 *Tel:* (202) 783-0500
Hist. Note: The Gold Institute, incorporated in Canada with an international membership, is the developmental, technical and industrial information arm of leading producers of gold and products using gold. Maintains a financial office in Toronto.

00138 12 05 86 1233

Publications:
The Gold News/Nouvelles de l'Or. bi-m.
Modern Gold Coinage. a.
Gold Mine Production. a.
Your Introduction to Investing in Gold.

Golf Ball Manufacturers Ass'n (1924)
Hist. Note: See Nat'l Golf Foundation.

Golf Ball Manufacturers Ass'n
Hist. Note: Reported as inactive in 1986.

Golf Coaches Ass'n of America
Wooster College, Wooster OH 44619
President: Robert Nye
Members: 225-250 *Staff:* 1
Annual Budget: under $10,000 *Tel:* (216) 263-2000
Hist. Note: Formerly (1969) NCAA Golf Coaches Ass'n. Coaches at 4-year colleges and universities which are members of the Nat'l Collegiate Athletic Ass'n. Membership: $25/yr.
Annual Meetings:
1987-Columbus, OH(Ohio State University)/June 7-9/50-70

Golf Components Ass'n
Hist. Note: Merged with the Golf Products and Distributors Association in 1982 to become the Golf Products and Components Association.

Golf Course Ass'n (1976)
8030 Cedar Ave. South, Suite 228, Minneapolis MN 55420
Exec. Director: Curt Walker
Members: 250 clubs *Staff:* 2-5
Annual Budget: $100-250,000 *Tel:* (612) 854-8482
Hist. Note: Established as the National Association of Public Golf Courses under the aegis of the National Golf Foundation, it became fully independent under its present name on May 1, 1982.
Publications:
Golf Course Association News. m.
Management Letter. m.
Annual Meetings: Winter
1987-Orlando, FL(Hilton Walt Disney World)/Jan. 19-23/250
1988-Scottsdale, AZ(Camelback Inn)/Jan. 19-24/300

Golf Course Builders of America (1970)
4361 Northlake Blvd., Palm Beach Gardens FL 33410
Exec. Director: Don A. Rossi
Members: 30 companies *Staff:* 1
Annual Budget: $10-25,000 *Tel:* (305) 694-2977
Publication:
Directory. a. adv.

Golf Course Superintendents Ass'n of America (1926)
1617 St. Andrews Dr., Lawrence KS 66046-9990
Exec. Director: John M. Schilling
Members: 6,800 *Staff:* 25
Annual Budget: $2-5,000,000 *Tel:* (913) 841-2240
Hist. Note: Formerly Nat'l Greenkeeping Superintendents Ass'n. Sponsors program leading to certification of Superintendents. Has a U.S. and Canadian membership.
Publication:
Golf Course Management. m. adv.
Annual Meetings: Winter
1987-Phoenix, AZ(Civic Center)/Jan. 26-Feb. 2/10,000
1988-Houston, TX

Golf Products and Components Ass'n (1982)
Hist. Note: See Nat'l Golf Foundation.

Golf Products and Distributors Ass'n
Hist. Note: Merged with the Golf Components Association in 1982 to become the Golf Products and Components Association.

Golf Writers Ass'n of America (1947)
P.O. Box 37324, Cincinnati OH 45222
Secretary: Robert D. Rickey
Members: 575 *Staff:* 1
Annual Budget: $10-25,000 *Tel:* (513) 631-4400
Annual Meetings: Augusta with the Masters Tournament.

Government and Industrial Surplus Equipment and Material Dealers Ass'n
Hist. Note: Reported as inactive in 1982.

Government Finance Officers Ass'n of the United States and Canada (1906)
180 North Michigan Ave., Suite 800, Chicago IL 60601
Exec. Director: Jeffrey L. Esser
Members: 10,000 *Staff:* 50
Annual Budget: $2-5,000,000 *Tel:* (312) 977-9700
Hist. Note: Formerly (1927) Nat'l Ass'n of Comptrollers and Accounting Officers and (1984) Municipal Finance Officers Ass'n of the United States and Canada. Members are finance officers from city, county, state, provincial, and federal governments, school, and other special districts; retirement systems, colleges, universities, public accounting firms, financial institutions and others in the United States and Canada interested in government finance. Maintains six centers: Career Development; Federal Liaison; Government Finance Research; Publications; Technical Services; and Member Services.
Publications:
Newsletter. semi-m.
GAAFR Review. m.
Public Investor. m.
Government Finance Review. bi-m. adv.
Annual Meetings: Spring
1987-Washington, DC/May 31-June 3
1988-Atlanta, Ga
1989-Seattle, WA

Government Management Information Sciences (1969)
City & County of Denver, 3840 L York St., Denver CO 80205
Exec. Director: Joseph M. Lewis
Members: 330 government agencies *Staff:* 1
Annual Budget: $25-50,000 *Tel:* (303) 575-2838
Hist. Note: GMIS is an organization of state and local governments involved in data processing and of educational institutions dealing in the affairs of state, county or local governments which are involved in data processing. Membership: $25-$100/year (based on agencies EDP budget).
Publication:
GEM. bi-m.
Annual Meetings: Summer/150
1987-Minneapolis, MN(Plaza)/June 14-18
1988-Reno, NV(MGM Grand)/June 19-24
1989-Virginia Beach, VA
1990-Gulf Shores, AL

Governmental Refuse Collection and Disposal Ass'n (1961)
Box 7219, Silver Spring MD 20910
Exec. Director: H. Lanier Hickman, P.E.
Members: 2,200 individuals, 550 companies *Staff:* 7
Annual Budget: $500-1,000,000 *Tel:* (301) 585-2898
Hist. Note: Government solid waste agency managers and their suppliers, vendors and consultants.
Publications:
GRCDA Newsletter. m.
Proceedings of Equipment, Services and Systems Show. a.
Annual Meetings: Summer
1987-St. Paul, MN(Radisson/Civic Ctr.)/Aug. 10-14/1,200
1988-Baltimore, MD(Hyatt/Sheraton/Convention Ctr.)/Aug. 22-26/1,200
1989-Tulsa, OK(Excelsior/Williams/Convention Ctr.)/Aug. 14-18/1,400
1990-Vancouver, BC(Convention Ctr.)/Aug. 20-24/1,500

Governmental Research Ass'n (1914)
24 Province St., 8th Floor, Boston MA 02108
President: Donald Goodrich
Members: 400 *Staff:* 1
Annual Budget: $10-25,000 *Tel:* (617) 720-1000
Hist. Note: Members work in government research organizations sponsored by universities, chambers of commerce, etc. Membership: $50/yr.
Publication:
GRA Reporter. q.

Grain Bin Maufacturers Council
Hist. Note: A division of the Farm and Industrial Equipment Institute.

Grain Elevator and Processing Soc. (1930)
Box 15026, Commerce Station, Minneapolis MN 55415-0026
Exec. V. President: John J. Healy, CAE
Members: 3,000 individuals *Staff:* 6
Annual Budget: $500-1,000,000 *Tel:* (612) 339-4625
Hist. Note: Formerly Soc. of Grain Elevator Superintendents. Membership: $65/yr.
Publications:
In-Grain (newsletter). m.
Membership Directory and Yearbook. a. adv.
Annual Meetings: Late Winter
1987-Columbus, OH(Ohio Ctr.)/March 8-11
1988-Wichita, KS(Century II Conv. & Cultural Ctr.)/Feb. 28-March 3
1989-Vancouver, BC(Canada Place)/Feb. 26-March 1
1990-San Antonio, TX(Convention Ctr.)/March 18-21

Grain Equipment Manufacturers' Ass'n
Hist. Note: Disbanded in 1986.

Grain Processing Machinery Manufacturers' Ass'n (1951)
Hist. Note: Became the Grain Equipment Manufacturers' Ass'n in 1984.

Grain Sorghum Producers Ass'n (1955)
Hist. Note: Became the Nat'l Grain Sorghum Producers Ass'n in 1985.

Graphic Artists Guild Nat'l (1969)
4th Floor, 30 East 20th St., New York NY 10003
Exec. Director: Susan Dooha
Members: 5,000 *Staff:* 6-10
Annual Budget: $250-500,000 *Tel:* (212) 777-7353
Hist. Note: A labor organization whose membership includes any person engaged or employed in the creation or production of original creative works of art intended for graphic presentation either as originals or reproductions. Includes the Illustrators' Guild, a division for free-lance illustrators, and the Textile Designers Guild for textile and surface designers, graphic designers, cartoonists guild and computer artists. Membership: $110/yr.
Publication:
National Newsletter. m. adv.
Semi-annual Meetings:

Graphic Arts Advertisers and Exhibitors Council (1960)
Baldwin Technology Corp., 417 Shippan Ave., Stamford CT 06902-0979
Exec. Officer: Garrett W. Walker
Members: 50-55 companies *Staff:* 1
Annual Budget: $10-25,000 *Tel:* (203) 348-4400
Hist. Note: Members are graphics arts manufacturers and are represented usually by their marketing or advertising manager.

Graphic Arts Ass'n Executives (1913)
Hist. Note: Inactive since 1983.

Graphic Arts Employers of America (1887)
1730 North Lynn St., Arlington VA 22209
President: William D. Solomon
Members: 4,000-5,000 companies *Staff:* 5
Annual Budget: $250-500,000 *Tel:* (703) 841-8150
Hist. Note: A division of Printing Industries of America, of which it was the originating organization. Represents graphic arts firms whose production departments are partially or wholly organized. Formerly (1981) the Graphic Arts Union Employers of America (UEA).
Publications:
Industrial Relations Bits & Pieces. bi-w.
Around the Bargainning Loop. m.
Industrial Relations Reporter. bi-m.
Annual Meetings: Spring

Graphic Arts Equipment and Supply Dealers Ass'n (1960)
1730 North Lynn St., Arlington VA 22209
Exec. Director: William C. Strackbein
Members: 250 companies *Staff:* 2-5
Annual Budget: $100-250,000 *Tel:* (703) 841-8169
Hist. Note: A section of Printing Industries of America. Members are companies that sell, make, service or distribute graphic arts equipment and supplies.
Publications:
Newsletter. m.
Member Directory. a.
Annual Meetings: Spring
1987-Kona, HI(Kona Surf)/March 25-29/275

Graphic Arts Internat'l Union (1972)
Hist. Note: Merged on July 1, 1983 with the International Printing and Graphic Communications Union to form the Graphic Communications International Union.

Graphic Arts Marketing Information Service (1966)
1730 North Lynn St., Arlington VA 22209
Exec. Director: Mark Favus
Members: 60-65 companies *Staff:* 2-5
Annual Budget: $500-1,000,000 *Tel:* (703) 841-8179
Hist. Note: GAMIS is a section of Printing Industries of America. Membership: $5,500/yr.
Publications:
Graphcomm: The Future of Print as We Know It.
Index of Print Sales Activity.
Geographic Market Potentials.
Material Handling Study.
Business Forms Study.
Annual Meetings:
1987-Charleston, SC(Kiawah)

Graphic Arts Technical Foundation (1924)
4615 Forbes Ave., Pittsburgh PA 15213
Exec. Director: Gilbert W. Bassett
Members: 6,400 *Staff:* 98
Annual Budget: over $5,000,000 *Tel:* (412) 621-6941
Hist. Note: Formerly (1963) Lithographic Technical Foundation. Absorbed the Education Council of the Graphic Arts Industry (1955) and the Nat'l Scholarship Trust Fund for the Printing and Publishing Industry in 1966. GAFT is a non-profit, member supported and directed educational, research, and technical organization. It serves the graphic communications industries worldwide. Membership: $15-25/yr.(individual); Corporate - based on sales volume.
Publications:
Annual Report. a.
Annual Research Department Report. a.
ECB Newsletter. 10/yr.
Environmental Control Report. q.
GASC/GATF Teachers Report. 3/yr.
GATF '86 Newsletter. 10/yr.
Graphic Arts Abstracts. m.
NSTF National Scholarship Porgram Booklet. a.
Productivity and Training Report. q.
Products & Services Catalogue. a.
Programs & Events Calendar. semi-a.
Seminar Catalogue. a.
Workshop Catalogue. 10/yr.
Learning Modules. irreg.
Market Research Newsletter. irreg.
Research Project Report. irreg.
Technical Services Report. irreg.
Techno-Economic Forecasts. irreg.
Techno-Economic Market Profiles. irreg.
Techno-Economic Niche Reports. irreg.
Annual Meetings: Fall

00139 12 05 86 1233

1987-Point Clear, AL(Grand)/ Oct. 8-11
1988-Castle Harbour, Bermuda/Oct. 20-23
1989-Laguna Niguel, CA(Ritz Carlton)/Oct. 19-22
1990-Naples, FL(Ritz Carlton)/Oct. 25-28

Graphic Communications Ass'n (1966)
1730 North Lynn St., Suite 604, Arlington VA 22209
President: Norman W. Scharpf
Members: 325 companies and organizations *Staff:* 10-12
Annual Budget: $1-2,000,000 *Tel:* (703) 841-8160
Hist. Note: Organized as Graphic Communications Computer Ass'n, GCA assumed its present name in 1981. Has a broad-based membership of printing, publishing, newspaper, supplier and government organizations and advertising agencies. Seeks productivity, technical and market improvements in the creation, production and distribution of publications and printed materials. Affiliated with Printing Industries of America.
Publications:
Newsletter. bi-m.
Membership Directory. a.

Graphic Communications Internat'l Union (1983)
1900 L St., N. W., Washington DC 20036
President: James J. Norton
Members: 200,000 *Staff:* 100-125
Annual Budget: $2-5,000,000 *Tel:* (202) 462-1400
Hist. Note: The Amalgamated Lithographers of America and the International Photoengravers Union of North America merged on September 7, 1964 to form the Lithographers and Photoengravers International Union. This, in turn, merged September 4, 1972 with the International Brotherhood of Bookbinders (founded 1892) to form the Graphic Arts International Union which merged July 1, 1983 with the International Printing and Graphic Communications Union to form the present organization. Affiliated with AFL-CIO, Canadian Labor Congress and International Graphical Federation. Sponsors and supports the Graphic Communications Internat'l Union Political Contributions Committee.
Publication:
Graphic Communicator. 10/yr.
Convention every four years: 1988, 1992, etc.

Graphic Preparatory Ass'n (1960)
415 E. Hitt St., Mount Morris IL 61054
Exec. Officer: Ronald S. Ballard
Members: 125 companies *Staff:* 2-5
Annual Budget: $50-100,000 *Tel:* (815) 734-4178
Hist. Note: The result of a merger between the Lithographic Preparatory Services Ass'n (founded in 1960) and the Printing Platemakers Ass'n (founded in 1897). A section of Printing Industries of America, members are companies making negatives, positives, plates, supplies or equipment used for the graphic arts industry.
Annual Meetings: Fall

Gravure Research Institute (1947)
22 Manhasset Ave., Port Washington NY 11050
Exec. V. President: Harvey F. George
Members: 125 *Staff:* 11-15
Annual Budget: $500-1,000,000 *Tel:* (516) 883-6670
Publications:
Gravure Environmental Reporter. m.
GRI Membership Directory. a.
GRI Newsletter. q.
Annual Meetings: Fall

Gravure Technical Ass'n (1949)
60 East 42nd St., New York NY 10165
Exec. V. President: McKinley M. Luther
Members: 300 companies *Staff:* 9-12
Annual Budget: $500-1,000,000 *Tel:* (212) 661-8936
Hist. Note: Members are gravure printers and converters. The Gravure Advertising Council and Gravure Packaging Council are subsidiaries. Supports the Gravure Education Foundation, established in 1979.
Publication:
Gravure Bulletin. q. adv.
Annual Meetings: Spring
1987-Chicago,IL
1988-New York

Great Lakes Shipowners Ass'n (1945)
Hist. Note: Members are ICC certificated common carriers operating on the Great Lakes. Reported as inactive in 1983.

Greater Blouse, Skirt and Undergarment Ass'n (1933)
225 West 34th St., New York NY 10122
Exec. Director: Harold Siegel
Members: 700 *Staff:* 11-15
Tel: (212) 563-5052
Hist. Note: Formerly (1967) Greater Blouse and Skirt Contractors Ass'n. Membership concentrated in the New York area.
Annual Meetings: Early Fall

Greater Clothing Contractors Ass'n (1932)
31 West 15th St., New York NY 10011
Manager: Richard Indelicato
Members: 100-125 clothing manufacturers *Staff:* 6-10
Annual Budget: $100-250,000 *Tel:* (212) 255-6900
Hist. Note: Major purpose is to represent its members in union negotiations.

Green Olive Trade Ass'n
325 14th St., Carlstadt NJ 07072
President: Edward Culleton
Members: 10 companies *Staff:* 1
Annual Budget: under $10,000 *Tel:* (201) 935-0233
Hist. Note: Formerly Ass'n of American Importers of Green Olives and (1969) Ass'n of American and Canadian Importers of Green Olives.
Annual Meetings: May

Greeting Card Ass'n (1941)
1350 New York Ave., N.W., Suite 615, Washington DC 20005
Exec. V. President: Marianne McDermott
Members: 110-120 companies *Staff:* 2-5
Annual Budget: $250-500,000 *Tel:* (202) 393-1778
Hist. Note: Founded as the Greeting Card Ass'n, it became the Nat'l Ass'n of Greeting Card Publishers from 1967-83 and resumed its original name in 1983. Membership fee based on annual sales volume.
Publications:
Card News. m.
Industry Directory. a.
Artist's and Writer's Market List. irreg.
Annual Meetings: September

Grinding Wheel Institute (1914)
712 Lakewood Center North, 14600 Detroit Ave., Cleveland OH 44107
Manager: Allen P. Wherry
Members: 35-40 *Staff:* 2-5
Annual Budget: $100-250,000 *Tel:* (216) 226-7700
Hist. Note: Formerly (1948) Grinding Wheel Manufacturers Ass'n.

Grocery Manufacturers of America (1908)
1010 Wisconsin Ave., N.W., Suite 800, Washington DC 20007
President/C.E.O.: George W. Koch
Members: 135-140 companies *Staff:* 40-45
Annual Budget: $2-5,000,000 *Tel:* (202) 337-9400
Hist. Note: Members are manufacturers of branded products sold in grocery stores.
Publication:
State Legislative Reporting and Analysis Service. w.
Annual Meetings: White Sulphur Springs, WV in June

Groundwater Management Districts Ass'n (1975)
1125 Maize Road, Colby KS 67701
Secretary: Wayne A. Bossert
Members: 140 *Staff:* 1
Annual Budget: under $10,000 *Tel:* (913) 462-3915
Hist. Note: Membership includes districts, consulting organizations and individuals concerned with the management and conservation of water resources. Seeks effective information transfer between member districts, associations, and organizations responsible for water resource management. Affiliated with the Nat'l Water Resources Ass'n. Membership: $15/yr. (individual), $100/yr. (organization).
Annual Meetings:
1987-Reno, NV(MGM Grand)
1988-Spokane, WA

Group Health Ass'n of America (1959)
1129 20th St., N.W., Washington DC 20036
President: James F. Doherty
Members: 1,000-1,100 *Staff:* 47
Annual Budget: $2-5,000,000 *Tel:* (202) 778-3200
Hist. Note: Formed by a merger of the Group Health Federation of America and the American Labor Health Association. Members are group practice pre-payment health plans, related organizations and individuals supporting the Health Maintenance Organization movement. Sponsors the Group Health Association of America Political Action Committee. Membership: $60/yr. (individual).
Publications:
Group Health Journal. Semi-a.
Group Health News. bi-m.
HMO Managers Letter. semi-m.
Medical Directors. m.
Proceedings. a.
HMO Manager's Letter. semi-m.
HMO Directory. bi-a.
Annual Meetings: June
1987-Seattle, WA(Westin/Sheraton Hotels)/June 21-24
1988-Chicago, IL(Palmer House)/June 26-29/2,000
1989-Atlanta, GA(Hilton)/June 25-28/2,100
1990-Los Angeles, CA(Westin Bonaventure)/June 10-13/2,100
1991-New York, NY(Hilton)/June 23-26

Guild of Book Workers (1906)
521 Fifth Ave., 17th Floor, New York NY 10175
President: Frank Mowery
Members: 500-600 *Staff:* 1
Annual Budget: under $10,000
Hist. Note: Established to continue and foster the growth of the hand book crafts, including binding, calligraphy, illumination, and papermaking. An affiliate of the American Institute of Graphic Arts from 1948 to 1978. Has no paid staff; all contact handled through mail.
Publications:
Guild of Book Workers Journal. semi-a.
Newsletter. bi-m.
Annual Meetings: June in New York, NY

Guild of Natural Science Illustrators (1968)
Box 652, Ben Franklin Station, Washington DC 20044
Liaison: Elaine Hodges
Members: 900 *Staff:* 1
Annual Budget: $25-50,000 *Tel:* (202) 357-2128
Hist. Note: Professional illustrators in the field of the natural sciences. Has no paid staff. Membership: $25/yr.
Publication:
Newsletter. m.
Annual Meetings: Summer
1987-Athens, GA/June

Guild of Temple Musicians (1974)
1329 Lincoln Avenue South, Highland Park IL 60035
President: Bernhard Ebstein
Members: 300 *Staff:* 1
Annual Budget: under $10,000 *Tel:* (312) 433-0368
Hist. Note: Affiliated with the American Conference of Cantors.
Annual Meetings: Summer

Guitar and Accessories Music Marketing Ass'n (1924)
135 West 29th Street, New York NY 10001
Exec. V. President: Jerome Hershman
Members: 25 companies *Staff:* 1
Annual Budget: $10-25,000 *Tel:* (212) 564-0251
Hist. Note: Established as the National Association of Musical Merchandise Manufacturers, it became the Guitar and Accessory Manufacturers of America in 1963 and assumed its present name in 1982. Members are distributors of domestic or fretted instruments and allied accessories.
Annual Meetings: June with Nat'l Ass'n of Music Merchants.

Guitar and Accessory Manufacturers Ass'n of America (1924)
Hist. Note: Became the Guitar and Accessories Music Marketing Association in 1982.

Gummed Industries Ass'n (1920)
P.O. Box 92, Greenlawn NY 11740
Managing Director: Robert W. McKellar
Members: 30-35 companies *Staff:* 2-5
Annual Budget: $100-250,000 *Tel:* (516) 261-0114
Hist. Note: Membership consists of converters of water-activated gummed paper products and suppliers of basic raw materials.
Annual Meetings: Fall
1987-Sarasota, FL(Longboat Key Club)/Oct. 4-7

Gypsum Ass'n (1930)
1603 Orrington Ave., Evanston IL 60201
President: A. Victor Abnee, Jr.
Members: 16 companies *Staff:* 11-15
Annual Budget: $500-1,000,000 *Tel:* (312) 491-1744
Hist. Note: Members are gypsum miners and manufacturers of gypsum products. Membership fee based on tonnage of gypsum mined.
Annual Meetings: Fall
1987-Point Clear, AL/Oct.
1988-Phoenix, AZ(Wigwam)/Oct.
1989-Hot Springs, VA(Homestead)/Oct.

Gyro Internat'l (1912)
1096 Mentor Ave., Box 489, Painesville OH 44077
Secy.-Treas.: John H. Harding
Members: 5,500 *Staff:* 2-5
Annual Budget: $100-250,000 *Tel:* (216) 352-2501
Hist. Note: A federation of business and professional men's civic service clubs. Formerly (1924) Association of Gyro Clubs.
Publication:
Gyroscope. q.
Annual Meetings: July
1987-Victoria,BC(Empress Hotel)/June 25-28
1988-Long Beach,CA/June 23-26
1989-Kelowna, BC
1990-Ft. Lauderdale, FL
1991-St. Catherines, Ontario
1992-Denver, CO

Hack and Band Saw Manufacturers Ass'n of America (1959)
1230 Keith Bldg., Cleveland OH 44115-2180
Secy.-Treas.: Charles M. Stockinger
Members: 9 companies *Staff:* 2-5
Annual Budget: $25-50,000 *Tel:* (216) 241-7333
Hist. Note: Formed by a merger of the Hack Saw Ass'n (1928) and the Metal Cutting Band Saw Ass'n.

Halogenated Solvents Industry Alliance (1980)
2315 M St., N.W., Washington DC 20037
Exec. Director: Paul Cammer, Ph.D.
Members: 150 companies *Staff:* 3-5
Annual Budget: $500-1,000,000 *Tel:* (202) 223-5890
Hist. Note: Members are producers, users, distributors, and equipment manufacturers for the industry. Established to develop constructive programs on problems involving halogenated solvents. Seeks fair legislation and regulations; provides industry comments and information to government agencies; represents the industry at regulatory and legislative hearings. Membership: $50-500/yr.
Publications:
HSIA Newsletter. bi-m.
HSIA Solvents Update. m.
Annual Meetings: Quarterly regional seminars

00140 12 05 86 1233

Hampshire Swine Registry (1893)
1111 Main St., Peoria IL 61606
Exec. Secretary: Rick Maloney
Members: 2,000 *Staff:* 8
Annual Budget: $250-500,000 *Tel:* (309) 674-9134
Hist. Note: Breeders and fanciers of Hampshire swine. Member of the National Society of Livestock Record Associations. Membership: $20/yr.
Publication:
American Hampshire Herdsman. m. adv.
Annual Meetings:
1987-Murpheesboro, TN(Best Western Wayside Inn)/Jan. 9-11/250

Hand Tools Institute (1939)
25 North Broadway, Tarrytown NY 10591
Exec. Director: Richard C. Byrne
Members: 70 companies *Staff:* 8-10
Annual Budget: $100-250,000 *Tel:* (914) 332-0040
Hist. Note: Absorbed the Vise Manufacturers Ass'n in 1969. Formerly (1973) Service Tools Institute.
Semi-annual meetings: April and October

Handweavers Guild of America (1969)
65 LaSalle Rd., West Hartford CT 06107
Coordinator: Natalie Sarrazin
Members: 13,000 *Staff:* 10
Annual Budget: $500-1,000,000 *Tel:* (203) 233-5124
Hist. Note: Individuals, companies and organizations promoting interest in and creation of handcrafted textiles. Membership: $25/yr.
Publication:
Shuttle Spindle & Dyepot. q. adv.
Biennial meetings: Even years
1988-Chicago, IL/June

Hardware Affiliated Representatives (1972)
Hist. Note: Reported as permanently disbanded in 1984.

Hardwood Dimension Manufacturers Ass'n (1929)
Hist. Note: Became Nat'l Dimension Manufacturers Ass'n in 1985.

Hardwood Manufacturers Ass'n (1935)
805 Sterick Bldg., Memphis TN 38103
President: James H. Lee
Members: 90-100 *Staff:* 5
Annual Budget: $250-500,000 *Tel:* (901) 525-8221
Hist. Note: Formerly Southern Hardwood Producers Inc. and the Southern Hardwood Lumber Manufacturers Ass'n. Assumed present name in 1984.
Annual Meetings: March

Hardwood Plywood Manufacturers Ass'n (1921)
Box 2789, Reston VA 22090-2789
President: Clark E. McDonald, CAE
Members: 61 members; 52 supplier members; veneer div.-59
Staff: 12
Annual Budget: $1-2,000,000 *Tel:* (703) 435-2900
Hist. Note: Established in Chicago in 1921 as the Plywood Manufacturers Ass'n. Formerly Plywood Manufacturing Institute and Hardwood Plywood Institute. Absorbed the Southern Plywood Manufacturers Ass'n in 1953 and became the Hardwood Plywood Manufacturers Ass'n in 1964. Affiliated with Nat'l Forest Products Ass'n, Internat'l Conference of Building Officials, Southern Building Code Congress, Building Officials and Code Administrators Internat'l, and the U.S. Dept. of Commerce Nat'l Voluntary Laboratory Accreditation Program. Membership: $1,400/yr. minimum.
Publications:
Members Bulletin. m.
Where to Buy Hardwood Plywood and Veneer. a.
Semi-Annual Meetings: Spring and Fall
1987-Louisville, KY(Hyatt Hotel)/April 22-24
1987-Anaheim, CA(Hilton)/Oct. 13-16
1988-San ANtonio, TX(Hilton Palacio del Rio)/April 19-22
1988-Quebec City, Canada(Chateau Frontenas)/Oct. 4-7

Hardwood Research Council (1953)
Box 34518, Memphis TN 38184
Exec. Director: John A. Pitcher
Members: 90 individuals, 1,200 companies *Staff:* 2
Annual Budget: $50-100,000 *Tel:* (901) 377-1824
Hist. Note: Promotes research and technology transfer in hardwood forest management, utilization and marketing.
Publication:
Hardwood Forestry Bulletin. m.
Annual Meetings:
1987-Memphis, TN(Peabody Hotel)/May 10-13/150

Harness Horsemen Internat'l (1964)
1800 Silas Deane Hwy., Suite 220, Rocky Hill CT 06067
Exec. Director: Michael L. Kalil
Members: 40,000 individuals, 25 member ass'ns *Staff:* 9
Annual Budget: $250-500,000 *Tel:* (203) 563-1910
Hist. Note: HHI represents 40,000 owners, trainers, drivers and breeders of standardbred racehorses.
Publications:
News from HHI (newsletter). every 3 weeks.
Directory of Associations. a.
Careers in Harness Racing.
Semi-annual Meetings: Winter and Summer
1987-Ft. Lauderdale, FL(Marriott Cypress Creek)/Jan. 28-Feb. 1

Harness Tracks of America (1954)
35 Airport Rd., Morristown NJ 07960
Exec. V. President: Stanley F. Bergstein
Members: 48 pari-mutuel harness tracks *Staff:* 6-10
Annual Budget: $250-500,000 *Tel:* (201) 285-9090
Hist. Note: A trade association for North American harness race tracks. Issues monthly economic studies, reports, position papers, a weekly newsletter and special surveys on legal and legislative matters affecting the sport and industry.
Publications:
Directory. a.
Track Topics. w.
Annual Meetings: Winter

Harness Tracks Security
Hist. Note: Ceased operations in 1986.

Harvey Soc. (1905)
Mt. Sinai School of Medicine, 5th Ave & 100th Streets, Rm. 17-76, New York NY 10029
Secretary: Robert J. Desnick, Ph.D.,M.D.
Members: 1,650-1,700 *Staff:* 1
Annual Budget: $25-50,000 *Tel:* (212) 570-6944
Hist. Note: Named after William Harvey, British physician who discovered the circulation of the blood in the 17th century, the Society consists of individuals interested in or capable of making a contribution to the literature of medicine. Membership: $30/yr.
Publication:
The Harvey Lectures. a.
Annual Meetings: New York City

Hatters Machinery and Equipment Ass'n
Hist. Note: Recorded in 1978 as being inactive or defunct.

Hazardous Waste Services Ass'n
Hist. Note: Dissolved in 1986.

Hazardous Waste Treatment Council (1982)
1919 Pennsylvania Ave., N.W., Suite 300, Washington DC 20006
Exec. Director: Richard C. Fortuna
Members: 45 companies *Staff:* 5
Annual Budget: $250-500,000 *Tel:* (202) 296-0778
Hist. Note: Established and incorporated in Washington, DC. Trade association of waste disposal firms employing high technology treatment techniques rather than land disposal. Membership: $5,000-20,000/yr. (company, based on size).

Headmasters Ass'n (1893)
Westminster School, Simsbury CT 06070
Secretary: Donald Werner
Members: 100 *Staff:* 1
Annual Budget: under $10,000 *Tel:* (203) 658-4444
Hist. Note: Heads of secondary schools of all types who have completed at least one year. Limited to one hundred members, twenty-five from public schools and seventy-five from non-public schools. Membership: $75/yr.
Annual Meetings: Princeton, NJ(Chauncey Conference Center)/Feb./150

Headwear Institute of America (1974)
Hist. Note: Reported as inactive in 1984.

Health Associated Representatives
Hist. Note: Became the Health Industry Representatives Ass'n (1985).

Health Care Exhibitors Ass'n (1930)
5775 Peachtree-Dunwoody Road, Suite 500-D, Atlanta GA 30342
Exec. Director: Robert C. Gelardi
Members: 340 companies *Staff:* 6
Tel: (404) 252-3663
Hist. Note: Formerly (1973) Medical Exhibitors Ass'n, Inc. Members are manufacturers and distributors of products exhibited at surgical, medical, dental and hospital meetings.
Publication:
Handbook and Schedule of Conventions.
Annual Meetings: June
1987-Nashville, TN/June 21-24

Health Care Institute
Hist. Note: A component of the Environmental Management Association.

Health Education Media Ass'n
Hist. Note: Address unknown in 1986; probably defunct.

Health Industries Institute (1963)
Hist. Note: Ceased operations 1982-1983.

Health Industry Distributors Ass'n (1903)
1701 Pennsylvania Ave., N.W., Suite 470, Washington DC 20006
President: Paul B. Simmons
Members: 800 companies *Staff:* 6-10
Annual Budget: $1-2,000,000 *Tel:* (202) 659-0050
Hist. Note: Founded as the American Surgical Trade Ass'n, it assumed its present name in 1983. Trade association for all sectors of the medical products distribution industry. Sponsors the Health Industry Educational Foundation and the Health Industry Distributors Ass'n Political Action Committee. Membership: $380-420/yr.
Publications:
Medical Products Sales. m. adv.
HIDA Headlines. bi-w.
Annual Meetings: Fall/5,000
1987-New Orleans, LA(Rivergate)/Sept. 19-23
1988-Kansas City, MO(Conv. Center)/Sept 24-28
1989-Chicago, IL(Hyatt Regency)/Sept. 23-27

Health Industry Manufacturers Ass'n (1903)
1030 15th St., N.W., Suite 1100, Washington DC 20005
President: Frank E. Samuel, Jr.
Members: 300 companies *Staff:* 50
Annual Budget: $2-5,000,000 *Tel:* (202) 452-8240
Hist. Note: Established as the Wholesale Surgical Trade Ass'n. Became Manufacturers Surgical Trade Ass'n in 1944 and the Medical-Surgical Manufacturers Ass'n in 1967. Merged in 1974 with the Health Industries Ass'n to form the Health Industry Manufacturers Ass'n. Represents domestic manufacturers of medical devices and diagnostic products. Sponsors the Health Industry Manufacturers Association Political Action Committee. Membership fee based on sales volume.
Annual Meetings: January-March

Health Industry Representatives Ass'n (1978)
5845 Horton, Suite 201, Mission KS 66202
Exec. Director: Frank A. Bistrom
Members: 200 *Staff:* 2-5
Annual Budget: $100-250,000 *Tel:* (913) 262-4513
Hist. Note: Manufacturers representatives who sell medical equipment and other products in the health care field. Formerly (1985) Health Associated Representatives.
Publication:
HIRA News. m.
Annual Meetings:
1987-Scottsdale, AZ/April

Health Insurance Ass'n of America (1956)
1025 Connecticut Ave., N.W., Suite 1200, Washington DC 20036
President: James L. Moorefield
Members: 300-350 *Staff:* 89
Annual Budget: over $5,000,000 *Tel:* (202) 223-7780
Hist. Note: Formed by a merger of the Bureau of Accident and Health Underwriters and the Health and Accident Underwriters Conference. Members are accident and health insurance companies. Sponsors the Health Insurance Political Action Committee. Has annual budget in excess of $10 million.
Semi-annual Meetings: Spring and Fall

Health Physics Soc. (1956)
1340 Old Chain Bridge Road, Suite 300, McLean VA 22101
Exec. Secretary: Richard J. Burk, Jr.
Members: 7,104 *Staff:* 6-10
Annual Budget: $100-250,000 *Tel:* (703) 790-1745
Hist. Note: Founded and incorporated in the District of Columbia in 1956. Reincorporated in Tennessee in 1969. Fosters the protection of man and the environment from radiation. Affiliated with the Internat'l Radiation Protection Ass'n.
Publications:
Health Physics Journal. m. adv.
Newsletter. m.
Membership Handbook. a.
Semi-annual Meetings: Summer and Winter
1987-Reno, NV/Feb. 8-12
1987-Salt Lake City, UT/July 5-9
1988-Boston/July 4-8
1988-San Antonio, TX/Dec. 4-8
1989-Albuquerque, NM/June 18-22

Health Sciences Communications Ass'n (1959)
6105 Lindell Blvd., St. Louis MO 63112
Exec. Director: Lionelle H. Elsesser
Members: 800 individuals; 80 institutions *Staff:* 1
Annual Budget: $100-250,000 *Tel:* (314) 725-4722
Hist. Note: Organized in 1959 as the Council on Medical Television as part of the Institute for Advancement of Medical Communication. Incorporated in North Carolina in 1964 under its own charter. Became the Health Sciences Communications Ass'n in 1972. A professional association of individuals interested in application of educational technology to the health sciences field. Membership: $85/yr.
Publications:
HeSCA Feedback. bi-m.
Journal of Biocommunication. q.
Annual Meetings: Spring
1987-Norfolk, VA(Omni)/May 22-27
1988-San Diego, CA(Town & Country)/May 12-19
1989-St. Louis, MO(Clarion)/April 30-May 4

Healthcare Financial Management Ass'n (1946)
1900 Spring Rd., Suite 500, Oak Brook IL 60521
President: Richard L. Clarke, FHFMA
Members: 25,000 individuals *Staff:* 61
Annual Budget: over $5,000,000 *Tel:* (800) 252-4362
Hist. Note: Formerly (1968) the American Ass'n of Hospital Accountants and (1982) the Hospital Financial Management Ass'n. Awards the rating of Fellow or Certified Manager of Patients Accounts. Members are directly or indirectly associated with financial management in healthcare organizations in the U.S., Canada, and several other countries, and belong to one of 75 local chapters. Membership: $130/yr.
Publications:
Healthcare Financial Management. m. adv.
Patient Accounts. m.
Chiefly Financial. m.

00141 12 05 86 1233

Annual Meetings:
June
1987-Anaheim, CA(Disneyland)/June 21-26/1,500

Healthcare Information Systems Sharing Group (1967)
1980 Isaac Newton Square South, Reston VA 22090
Exec. Director: Rick Guggolz
Members: 130 *Staff:* 2-5
Annual Budget: $50-100,000 *Tel:* (703) 437-5440
Hist. Note: Formerly (1986) Hospital Information Systems Sharing Group. Members are hospitals, health care facilities, health care computer hardware and software vendors, consultants and others interested in hospital information systems. HISSG's mission is to serve as a primary resource for advancing the understanding of the use and management of automated information systems that support quality. Membership: $125/yr.(individual); $305/yr.(institution)
Publications:
Newsletter. q.
Computers and Healthcare. bi-m.
Semi-annual Meetings: January and July
1987-San Diego, CA(Hilton)/Jan. 27-30/125
1987-Nashville, TN(Opyrland)/June 30-July 1/125

Healthcare Internal Audit Group (1981)
2506 Gross Point Road, Evanston IL 60201
Exec. Director: Dagny N. Engle, RN, CAE
Members: 600 *Staff:* 2-5
Annual Budget: $100-250,000 *Tel:* (312) 475-1000
Hist. Note: HIAG was established to promote cost containment and increased productivity in healthcare institutions through internal auditing. Membership: $60/yr.
Publications:
Highlights. q.
New Perspectives. q.
Semi-annual Meetings: Spring and Fall

Hearing Industries Ass'n (1955)
1255 Twenty-Third St., N.W., Washington DC 20037
Exec. Director: Sheldon J. Hauck
Members: 40 companies *Staff:* 2-5
Annual Budget: $250-500,000 *Tel:* (202) 833-1411
Hist. Note: Formerly (1977) the Hearing Aid Industry Conference.
Publications:
HIA Newsletter. q.
The Marketing Edge. q.
Annual Meetings:
1987-Scottsdale, AZ(Loew's Paradise Valley)/March 10-14/100
1988-Palm Springs, CA(The Royce Resort)/Feb. 100

Heat Exchange Institute (1933)
1230 Keith Bldg., Cleveland OH 44115
Secy.-Treas.: John H. Addington
Members: 18 companies *Staff:* 2-5
Annual Budget: $50-100,000 *Tel:* (216) 241-7333
Hist. Note: Members are manufacturers of heat exchange and/or vacuum apparatus.
Tri-annual Meetings:

Heavy Duty Business Forum (1977)
300 Sylvan Ave., Englewood Cliffs NJ 07632
Administrator: Stephen A. Bomer
Members: 50 *Staff:* 2
Tel: (201) 836-9500
Hist. Note: A discussion group affiliated with the Motor and Equipment Manufacturers Association concerned with issues affecting makers of products for heavy duty vehicles. Members are management and marketing executives.
Semi-annual: Spring and Fall

Heavy Duty Manfacturers Ass'n
222 Cedar Lane, Teaneck NJ 07666
Exec. Director: John D. Trott
Tel: (201) 836-9500

Heavy Duty Representatives Ass'n (1974)
4015 Marks Rd., Suite 2B, Medina OH 44256
Exec. Dir.: Cara R. Giebner
Members: 55 companies *Staff:* 1
Annual Budget: $25-50,000 *Tel:* (216) 725-7160
Hist. Note: Independent sales agents, representing manufacturers of parts, equipment and accessories for the heavy-duty vehicle and equipment market. Associate membership opened to manufacturers in the heavy- duty trucking industry.
Annual Meetings:
1987-Louisville, KY(Executive West Hotel)/March 19

Heavy-Duty Truck Manufacturers Ass'n (1970)
Hist. Note: Ceased effective operations in 1983.

Hebrew Actors Union (1887)
31 East 7th St., New York NY 10003
Secy.-Treas.: Bernard Sauer
Members: 200-225 *Staff:* 1
Annual Budget: $10-25,000 *Tel:* (212) 674-1923
Hist. Note: An autonomous branch union of Associated Actors and Artistes of America. Membership: $20/year.
Annual Meetings: New York, NY in October

Helicopter Airline Ass'n (1982)
1619 Duke St., Alexandria VA 22314
President: Frank Jensen
Members: 200 companies *Staff:* 1
Annual Budget: under $10,000 *Tel:* (703) 683-4646
Hist. Note: Members are airlines using helicopters to carry passengers on a fixed schedule. Incorporated in the District of Columbia, HAA is just getting started and anticipates more members and a greater budget in the near future.
Publications:
Rotornews. q.
Rotorgrams. irreg.
Helicopter Annual.

Helicopter Ass'n Internat'l (1948)
1619 Duke St., Alexandria VA 22314-3406
President: Frank L. Jensen, Jr.
Members: 1,150 *Staff:* 20-25
Annual Budget: $1-2,000,000 *Tel:* (703) 683-4646
Hist. Note: Began as the California Helicopter Ass'n with seven charter members. Became the Helicopter Ass'n of America in 1951 and assumed its present name in 1981. Now has an international membership from 35-40 countries. Membership consists of companies that own and operate helicopters for hire, use helicopters for private and corporate transport and helicopters in public service. Sponsors and supports the Helicopter Ass'n Internat'l Political Action Committee.
Publications:
Helicopter Annual a. adv.
Rotorgram. irreg.
Rotor News. q.
Annual Meetings: Winter/11,000
1987-Dallas, TX/Feb. 26-28
1988-Anaheim, CA/Feb. 7-9
1989-New Orleans, LA/Jan. 15-17
1990-Dallas, TX/Feb. 4-6
1991-Anaheim, CA/Jan. 27-29
1992-Las Vegas, NV/March 1-3

Herb Trade Ass'n (1976)
Hist. Note: Individuals and companies associated with all aspects of the herb industry. Defunct in 1982.

Herpetologists' League (1936)
Department of Biology, Elmhurst College, Elmhurst IL 60126
Treasurer: Dr. James Berry
Members: 1,800 individuals and institutions *Staff:* 1
Annual Budget: $50-100,000 *Tel:* (312) 279-4100
Hist. Note: An organization with international membership founded in 1936. Fosters the study of the biology of amphibians and reptiles. Regular Membership: $25/yr. Use extension 200 with phone number above.
Publications:
Herpetologica. q.
Herpetological Monographs. irreg.
Annual Meetings: In conjunction with the Soc. for the Study of Amphibians and Reptiles.

Hickory Handle Ass'n (1900)
2923 22rd Ave. South, Nashville TN 37215
Secretary: F. Donald Cowan
Members: 9 companies *Staff:* 1
Annual Budget: under $10,000 *Tel:* (615) 269-6436
Annual Meetings: Early September in Nashville.

High Speed Rail Ass'n (1983)
1225 Connecticut Avenue, N.W., 7th Floor, Washington DC 20036
Exec. Director: Robert J. Casey
Members: 180 companies, organizations, and unions
Annual Budget: $100-250,000 *Tel:* (717) 787-8748
Hist. Note: The HSRA was organized to further the development of high speed rail passenger transportation systems. Membership: $300-1,500/yr.
Publications:
SPEEDLINES. 10 per year. adv.
Yearbook of High Speed Rail Ass'n. a. adv.
News. 25/yr.
Semi-Annual: May & November.
1987-Las Vegas, NV(Bally Grand)/May 26-29
1987-Washington, DC(Hyatt)/Nov. 12
1988-Houston, TX/May
1988-Washington, DC/Nov.
1989-Washington, DC/May
1989-Paris, France/November

Highway Users Federation for Safety and Mobility (1970)
1776 Massachusetts Ave., N.W., Washington DC 20036
President: Lester P. Lamm
Members: 550-600 *Staff:* 45-50
Annual Budget: $2-5,000,000 *Tel:* (202) 857-1200
Hist. Note: A consolidation of the Automotive Safety Foundation (1937), Auto Industries Highway Safety Committee (1946) and Nat'l Highway Users Conference (1932). Absorbed the Auto Dealers Traffic Safety Council in 1975. Members are users of highways who profit from the movement of goods and people. Also includes manufacturers of vehicles, tire, and related accessories.
Publications:
At Issue. q.
State Legislative Report. q.
Buckle-Up Clearinghouse. q.
For Members Only. q.
Annual Meetings: Fall

Hispanic Nat'l Bar Ass'n (1972)
P.O. Box 20663, Cathedral Finance Station, New York NY 10025
President: William Mendez, Jr.
Members: 3,000
Annual Budget: $50-100,000 *Tel:* (212) 878-0000
Hist. Note: Founded in California as LaRaza Nat'l Bar Ass'n; assumed present name in 1980; and was re-incorporated in Washington, DC in 1983. Membership: $35/yr.
Publication:
Noticias. q. adv.
Annual Meetings: Fall
1987-Miami, FL(Hyatt)/Oct. 8-11
1988-Phoenix, AZ/Oct.

Histochemical Soc. (1950)
NIH-NIDR, Bldg. 10, Room 1A23, Bethesda MD 20892
Secretary: Dr. Constance Oliver
Members: 300 *Staff:* 1
Annual Budget: $25-50,000 *Tel:* (301) 496-2922
Hist. Note: Founded in 1950 and incorporated in 1963 in New York. Studies the chemical, biochemical and physical characteristics of living material as these apply to both normal and abnormal conditions. Has no paid staff. Membership: $78/year.
Publication:
The Journal of Histochemistry and Cytochemistry. m. adv.
Annual Meetings: Spring
1987-New Orleans, LA
1988-Washington, DC

Historic House Ass'n of America (1978)
Hist. Note: Became the Center for Historic Houses of the Nat'l Trust for Historic Preservation.

History of Earth Sciences Soc. (1982)
c/o Museum of Natural History, E-501, Washington DC 20560
Secretary: Ellis L. Yochelson
Members: 450 individuals *Staff:* 1
Annual Budget: under $10,000 *Tel:* (202) 343-3232
Hist. Note: Seeks to foster the study of all phases of history of the earth sciences. Membership: $15/yr. (individual), $25/yr. (institution).
Publication:
Earth Sciences History. semi-a.
Annual Meetings: None held

History of Economics Soc. (1972)
Dept. of Economics, University of Tennessee, Knoxville TN 37996
Secy.-Treas.: Prof. Hans Jensen
Members: 700 *Staff:* 2
Annual Budget: under $10,000 *Tel:* (615) 974-1688
Publication:
The History of Economics Society Bulletin. semi-a.

History of Education Soc. (1960)
School of Education, Indiana University, Bloomington IN 47405
Managing Editor: Amy Schutt
Members: 425 *Staff:* 2
Annual Budget: $50-100,000 *Tel:* (812) 335-9334
Hist. Note: For the advancement of interest, study and research in the history of education Membership: $20/year (individual), $47/year (institutional).
Publications:
History of Education Quarterly. q. adv.
The Network. m.
Annual Meetings: Fall

History of Science Soc. (1924)
School of Humanities & Social Sciences, North Carolina State Univ., Box 8101, Raleigh NC 27695-8101
Secretary: Edith D. Sylla
Members: 4,000 *Staff:* 1
Annual Budget: $250-500,000
Hist. Note: Founded in 1924 to foster interest in the history of science and its social and cultural relations. Member American Council of Learned Societies. Membership: $29/yr.
Publications:
Isis. q. adv.
Newsletter. q.
Osiris. a.
Annual Meetings:
1987-Raleigh, NC

Hobby Industry Ass'n of America (1940)
319 East 54th St., Elmwood Park NJ 07407
Exec. Director: Frederic P. Polk, CAE
Members: 2,300 *Staff:* 6-10
Annual Budget: $1-2,000,000 *Tel:* (201) 794-1133
Hist. Note: Founded in Chicago as the Model Industry Association with 87 charter members, it assumed its present name in 1956. The Hobby Industry Association is a grouping of manufacturers, wholesalers, retailers, publishers and others affiliated with the hobby industry.
Publication:
Hobby Horizons. m.
Annual Meetings: Meeting and trade show in January

Hoist Manufacturers Institute (1968)
8720 Red Oak Blvd., Suite 201, Charlotte NC 28210
Managing Director: A.L. Leffler
Members: 17 companies *Staff:* 3
Tel: (704) 522-8644

00142 12 05 86 1233

Hist. Note: Formerly Hoist Manufacturers Ass'n. Affiliated with the Material Handling Institute, Inc.
Annual Meetings: With the Material Handling Institute, Inc.
1987-Boca Raton, FL(Hotel & Club)/Nov. 6-11
1988-Phoenix, AZ(Biltmore)/Oct. 7-12

Holstein-Friesian Ass'n of America (1885)
One Holstein Place, Box 808, Brattleboro VT 05301
Chief Executive Officer: Zane V. Akins
Members: 45,000 *Staff:* 275-300
Annual Budget: over $5,000,000 *Tel:* (802) 254-4551
Hist. Note: Breeders of Holstein-Friesian dairy cattle. Member of the National Society of Livestock Records Association. Has an annual budget of $10,000,000. Membership: $4/yr.
Publications:
Holstein Association News. m.
Holstein World. bi-m. adv.
Annual Meetings: June/2,000-2,500
1987-Indianapolis, IN(Hyatt)/June 19-25
1988-San Diego, CA/June 24-30
1989-Minneapolis, MN

Home Economics Education Ass'n (1927)
1201 16th St., N.W., Washington DC 20036
Exec. Director: Catherine A. Leisher
Members: 2,700-2,800 *Staff:* 2-5
Annual Budget: $50-100,000 *Tel:* (202) 822-7844
Hist. Note: Established as Dept. of Supervisors and Teachers of Home Economics of the Nat'l Education Ass'n, it became the Dept. of Home Economics in 1938 and assumed its present name in 1969. It is a nongovernance affiliate of the NEA. Membership: $15/year.
Publications:
Bulletin. semi-a.
Newsletter. q.
Semi-annual Meetings:
June with American Home Economics Ass'n
December with American Voctional Ass'n

Home Economists in Business (1922)
5008 Pine Creek Drive, Suite B, Westerville OH 43081
Exec. Director: Marlisa K. Bannister
Members: 3,000 individuals *Staff:* 16
Annual Budget: $100-250,000 *Tel:* (614) 890-4342
Hist. Note: Individuals employed as professional home economists in companies. A section of the American Home Economics Ass'n. Membership: $20/yr.
Publications:
HEIB Directory. a.
News Notes (newsletter).
Stepping Stones (professional development newsletter).
Annual Meetings: June, before the American Home Economics Ass'n meeting

Home Fashion Products Ass'n (1968)
P.O. Box 5126, Old Bridge NJ 08857
Manager: Bette Katz
Members: 100-120 *Staff:* 2-5
Annual Budget: $50-100,000
Hist. Note: Formerly (until 1981) the National Curtain, Drapery and Allied Products Ass'n. Membership: $350/yr.
Semi-annual Meetings: Spring and Fall in New York, NY

Home Health Services and Staffing Ass'n
Hist. Note: Merged with Nat'l Ass'n for Home Care in 1986.

Home Office Life Underwriters Ass'n (1930)
General American Life Insurance Co., 13045 Tesson Ferry Road, St. Louis MO 63128
Secretary: Roland Ricketts
Members: 525-550 individuals *Staff:* 1
Annual Budget: $10-25,000 *Tel:* (314) 525-5656
Hist. Note: Membership: $40/yr.
Publication:
Proceedings. a.
Annual Meetings: Spring
1987-New Orleans(Fairmont)/April 26-29
1988-Hot Springs, VA(Homestead)/May 15-18

Home Ventilating Institute (1956)
Hist. Note: Became a division of the Air Movement and Control Ass'n in 1984. HVI will continue its certification and consumer education programs under AMCA auspices.

Honey Industry Council of America (1950)
13637 N.W. 39th Ave., Gainesville FL 32606
Exec. Secretary: Frank A. Robinson
Members: 9 *Staff:* 2
Tel: (904) 332-0012
Hist. Note: Members represent all segments of the honey industry. Absorbed the American Honey Institute in 1979. Membership: $250/yr.
Annual Meetings: with the American Beekeeping Federation

Hong Kong Trade Development Council (1966)
548 Fifth Ave., New York NY 10036
Manager: Steven Wong
Staff: 11-15
Annual Budget: over $5,000,000 *Tel:* (212) 730-0777
Hist. Note: Additional offices in North America: Chicago, Dallas, Los Angeles and Toronto.
Publications:
Apparel Magazine. semi-a.
Enterprise-HK. m.
Hong Kong Trader. m.
Toys Magazine. a.

Hoo-Hoo Internat'l
Hist. Note: See Internat'l Concatenated Order of Hoo-Hoo.

Hop Growers of America (1956)
504 North Naches Ave., Suite 5, Yakima WA 98901
Manager: Bill Harris
Members: 4 state associations, 200-225 growers *Staff:* 2-5
Annual Budget: $25-50,000 *Tel:* (509) 453-4749
Hist. Note: Membership is concentrated in four western states which host in turn the annual meeting.
Publication:
Newsletter. m.
Annual Meetings: January
1987-San Diego, CA

Horsemen's Benevolent and Protective Ass'n (1940)
2800 Grand Route, St. John, New Orleans LA 70119
Nat'l Secy.-Treas.: Kim Callihan
Members: 35-40,000 *Staff:* 15-20
Annual Budget: $500-1,000,000 *Tel:* (504) 945-4500
Hist. Note: Members are owners and trainers of thoroughbred horses.
Publication:
Horsemen's Journal. m. adv.
Semi-annual meetings: Summer and Winter

Horticultural Dealers Ass'n (1945)
Hist. Note: Formerly the American Wholesale Bulb Dealers Association and the American Wholesale Horticultural Dealers Association. Merged in 1984 with the North American Flowerbulb Wholesalers Association.

Horticultural Research Institute (1962)
1250 Eye St., N.W., Suite 500, Washington DC 20005
Administrator: Duane F. Jelinek
Members: 230 companies, 40-50 trade assn's *Staff:* 2-5
Annual Budget: $50-100,000 *Tel:* (202) 789-2990
Hist. Note: A non-profit affiliate of American Ass'n of Nurseymen. Supports and conducts horticulture research with the aid of outside institutions. Membership: $150/yr.
Publication:
Journal of Environmental Horticulture. q.
Annual Meetings: With American Association of Nurserymen

Hospital Financial Management Ass'n (1946)
Hist. Note: Became the Healthcare Financial Management Association in 1982.

Hospital Information Systems Sharing Group (1967)
Hist. Note: Became Healthcare Information Systems Sharing Group in 1986.

Hospital, Institution and Educational Food Service Soc. (1960)
Hist. Note: Became the Dietary Managers Ass'n in 1984.

Hospital Management Systems Soc. (1961)
840 North Lake Shore Dr., Chicago IL 60611
Director: Richard P. Covert
Members: 1,700-1,800 *Staff:* 2-5
Annual Budget: $250-500,000 *Tel:* (312) 280-6023
Hist. Note: A division of the American Hospital Ass'n. Membership: $65/yr.
Publication:
Health Care Systems. q.
Annual Meetings: Feb/March in conjunction with the Health Services Division of the American Institute of Industrial Engineers
1987-Las Vegas, NV(Riviera)/Feb. 11-13/550
1988-Houston, TX(Galleria Oaks)/March 9-11/450
1989-Hollywood, FL(Diplomat)/March 8-10/500
1990-New Orleans, LA(Marriott)/Feb. 21-23/550
1991-San Diego, CA(Sheraton Harbor)/Feb. 25-March 1/550

Hospital Presidents Ass'n (1983)
801 Main St., Concord MA 01742
Chairman: Robert R. Lovejoy
Members: 71 individuals *Staff:* 2
Annual Budget: $25-50,000 *Tel:* (617) 369-1290
Hist. Note: HPA is an educational association dedicated to the design and presentation of programs for the most advanced practitioners of health care management among the Chief Executive Officers of hospitals in the U.S. and abroad. Membership: $500/yr.
Semi-annual Meetings:

Hot Melt Equipment Manufacturers Ass'n (1977)
Hist. Note: Disbanded in 1984.

Hotel and Motel Brokers of America (1985)
10920 Ambassador Drive, Kansas City MO 64153
Exec. V. President: Robert H. Kralicek
Members: 35-40 brokers *Staff:* 2-5
Annual Budget: $250-500,000 *Tel:* (816) 891-7070
Hist. Note: Founded as the Motel Brokers of America in 1959; became the American Hotel and Motel Brokers in 1984 and assumed its present name in 1985. Members are real estate agents specializing in the sale of motel and hotel properties. Membership: $3,700/yr.
Publication:
Inside Issues. bi-m.
Annual Meetings: Winter
1987-Lake Buena Vista, FL(Hilton)/Jan. 6-11/100

Hotel Employees and Restaurant Employees Internat'l Union (1891)
1219 28th St., N.W., Washington DC 20007
Gen'l President: Edward T. Hanley
Members: 400,000 *Staff:* 100-125
Annual Budget: over $5,000,000 *Tel:* (202) 393-4373
Hist. Note: Founded in April 1891 as the Waiters and Bartenders Nat'l Union. Became the Hotel and Restaurant Employees Nat'l Alliance in 1892 and the Hotel and Restaurant Employees' Internat'l Alliance and Bartenders' Internat'l League of America in 1898. Merged in 1935 with the Food Workers Industrial Union to become the Hotel and Restaurant Employees and Bartenders Internat'l Union and assumed its present name in 1982. Has a budget of about $14 million. Sponsors and supports the HEREIU "TIP" (To Insure Progress) a Political Action Committee.
Publication:
Catering Industry Employee. m.
Quadrennial Meetings: 1991

Hotel Sales and Marketing Ass'n Internat'l (1927)
1400 K St., N.W., Suite 810, Washington DC 20005
Exec. V. President: Leonard H. Hoyle, Jr. CAE
Members: 7,000 *Staff:* 6-10
Annual Budget: $500-1,000,000 *Tel:* (202) 789-0089
Hist. Note: Formerly (1983) Hotel Sales Management Ass'n Internat'l. Awards the CHSE (Certified Hotel Sales Executive) designation. Membership: $115-385/yr. (individual)
Publications:
Update. m.
HSMA Marketing Review. q.
Annual Meetings: Fall
1987-Atlanta, GA(Hyatt Regency)/Nov. 21-24/650-700
1988-Kansas City, MO(Westin Crown Plaza)/Nov. 19-22/700-750

Hotel Sales Management Ass'n Internat'l (1927)
Hist. Note: Became the Hotel Sales and Marketing Association International in 1983.

Household Goods Carriers' Bureau (1936)
1611 Duke St., Alexandria VA 22314
President: Joseph M. Harrison
Members: 1,500-2,000 *Staff:* 20-25
Annual Budget: $1-2,000,000 *Tel:* (703) 683-7410
Hist. Note: Members are movers licensed by the Interstate Commerce Commission to transport household goods.
Publications:
Tariff Question Box. q.
Member Advisory Bulletin.
Mileage Guide.
Transportation Fact Book.
Moving Industry Financial Statistics.
Digest of Household Goods Carriers' ICC Annual Report Data.
National Zip Code Mileage Guide.
Fuel Report. m.
Operating Statistics. q.
Annual Meetings: February or March

Household Goods Forwarders Ass'n of America (1962)
1500 Massachusetts Ave., N.W., Suite 525, Washington DC 20005
President: Calvin W. Stein
Members: 650 *Staff:* 2-5
Annual Budget: $250-500,000 *Tel:* (202) 293-1800
Hist. Note: Active members (76) are companies transporting household goods by the door-to-door container method for the Department of Defense, national accounts and individuals. Associate members are suppliers and related organization, here and abroad.
Publication:
The Portal. m.
Annual Meetings: Fall/650
1987-Orlando, FL(Wyndham Hotel)/Oct. 5-10

HSIA Water Work Group (1981)
Hist. Note: A division of the Halogenated Solvent Industrial Alliance which in turn is an affiliate of the Synthetic Organic Chemical Manufacturers Ass'n.

Human Factors Soc. (1957)
P.O. Box 1369, Santa Monica CA 90406
Exec. Administrator: Marian G. Knowles
Members: 4,500 *Staff:* 5
Annual Budget: $250-500,000 *Tel:* (213) 394-1811
Hist. Note: A multidisciplinary society of those engaged in research on problems of the safety, comfort and convenience of people in the environment. Established in 1957 in Tulsa. Formerly known as the Human Factors Society of America.
Publications:
Bulletin. m. adv.
Directory. a. adv.
Human Factors. bi-m. adv.
Proceedings of Annual Meeting.

00143 12 05 86 1233

Cumulative Index. Every 5 yr.
Human Factors Review. a.
Annual Meetings: October
1987-New York, NY/Oct. 19-23

Human Resource Planning Soc. (1977)
Box 2553, Grand Central Station, New York NY 10163
Exec. Director: Joy Ann Buss
Members: 1,500 *Staff:* 4
Annual Budget: $500-1,000,000 *Tel:* (212) 490-6387
Hist. Note: Manpower planning and development specialists, staffing analysts, business planners and others concerned with planning for employee recruitment, development and utilization. Membership: $125/year (individual), $500/year (organization).
Publications:
Human Resource Planning. q.
Newsletter. bi-m.
Annual Meetings: March
1987-San Francisco, CA(Fairmont)/March 1-4/550
1988-Washington, DC(JW Marriott)/March 20-23

Hybrids and Manufacturing Technology Components Soc.
Hist. Note: A subsidiary of the Institute of Electrical and Electronics Engineers. Membership in the Society, open only to IEEE members, includes subscription to a technical periodical in the field published by IEEE. All administrative support is provided by IEEE.

Hydraulic Institute (1917)
712 Lakewood Center North, 14600 Detroit Ave., Cleveland OH 44107
Secy.-Treas.: Allen P. Wherry
Members: 65-70 industrial pump manufacturers *Staff:* 5-10
Annual Budget: $100-250,000 *Tel:* (216) 226-7700
Annual Meetings: Triannual meetings
1987-Chicago, IL/May 8-11
1987-New Orleans, LA(Royal Orlean)/Sept. 20-23
1988-Chicago, IL/May 14-17
1988-Sea Island, GA(The Cloister)/Sept. 18-21

Hydraulic Tool Manufacturers Ass'n (1974)
Box 1337, Milwaukee WI 53201
Exec. Secretary: John W. Petersen
Members: 10 companies *Staff:* 1
Annual Budget: under $10,000 *Tel:* (414) 639-6770
Hist. Note: Members are firms engaged in the primary marketing of a line of portable hydraulic-powered tools which carry a brand name particularly ascribed to the firm doing the marketing. Has no paid staff. Membership: $300/yr.
Annual Meetings: November

Hydronics Institute (1915)
35 Russo Place, Berkeley Heights NJ 07922
General Manager: John C. Kaussner
Members: 70-80 heating equipment companies *Staff:* 11-15
Annual Budget: $1-2,000,000 *Tel:* (201) 464-8200
Hist. Note: Merger (1970) of The Better Heating-Cooling Council (1950) and The Institute of Boiler and Radiator Manufacturers (1915).
Semi-Annual meetings: Absecon, NJ(Seaview Country Club)/ June-Oct.

Hydroponics Soc. of America (1978)
P.O. Box 6067, Concord CA 94524
Corresponding Secy.: Gene Brisbon
Members: 300 companies and individuals
Annual Budget: $10-25,000 *Tel:* (415) 682-4193
Hist. Note: Organized to promote the development of hydroponics - the growing of plants in nutrient solutions, without soil. Membership: $25/yr.
Publications:
Newsletter. bi-m. adv.
Conference Proceedings. a.
Directory. bi-m.
Annual Meetings:
1987-San Francisco, CA(Airport Marriott)/April 3-4/200

ICAAAA Coaches Ass'n (1919)
402A Yale Station, New Haven CT 06520
Secy.-Treas.: Stephen Bartold
Members: 110-115 schools *Staff:* 1
Annual Budget: under $10,000 *Tel:* (203) 432-1406
Hist. Note: Track and field coaches from eastern colleges and universities affiliated with the Intercollegiate Ass'n of Amateur Athletes of America (ICAAAA). Has no paid staff.
Annual Meetings: Fall

Ice Skating Institute of America (1959)
1000 Skokie Blvd., Wilmette IL 60091
Exec. Director: Justine Townsend Smith
Members: 20,000 *Staff:* 6-10
Annual Budget: $250-500,000 *Tel:* (312) 256-5060
Hist. Note: Membership comprised of ice rink owners, operators, instructors, builders/suppliers, and skaters. Sponsors the annual National Team Championships in August.
Publications:
Journal. q.
Newsletter. m.
Annual Meetings: May
1987-Las Vegas, NV(Hilton)/May 25-28

IFPA- Film and Video Communicators (1957)
Hist. Note: Acronym for Information Film Producers of America, Inc.

Illuminating and Allied Glassware Manufacturers Ass'n
Hist. Note: Dissolved in 1986.

Illuminating Engineering Soc. of North America (1906)
345 East 47th St., New York NY 10017
Exec. V. President: Rogers B. Finch
Members: 9,000-10,000 *Staff:* 20-25
Annual Budget: $1-2,000,000 *Tel:* (212) 705-7926
Hist. Note: Organized February 13, 1906 with 178 charter members and incoporated in New York in 1907. Sponsors the Lighting Research Institute.
Publications:
Journal of the Illuminating Engineering Society. q.
Lighting Design and Application. m. adv.
IES Times. bi-m.
Annual Meetings: Summer/700
1987-Scottsdale, AZ(Camelback)/Aug. 2-6
1988-Minneapolis, MN(Amfac)/Aug. 7-11
1989-Orlando, FL/Aug. 6-10
1990-Baltimore, MD
1991-Montreal, Canada

Illustrators' Guild
Hist. Note: A division of the Graphic Artists Guild for free-lance illustrators.

Immigration History Soc. (1965)
Minnesota Historical Soc., 690 Cedar St., St. Paul MN 55101
Editor: Prof. Carlton C. Qualey
Members: 870 *Staff:* 1
Annual Budget: under $10,000 *Tel:* (612) 296-5662
Hist. Note: Historians, sociologists, economists and others interested in immigration to the U.S. Affiliated with the American Historical Ass'n and the Organization of American Historians.
Publications:
Journal of American Ethnic History. semi-a.
Immigration History Newsletter. semi-a.
Annual Meetings: April, with the Organization of American Historians

Imported Hardwood Products Ass'n (1956)
Hist. Note: Became the International Hardwood Products Association in 1982.

In-Flight Food Service Ass'n
304 West Liberty St., Suite 301, Louisville KY 40202
Exec. V. President: Phillip S. Cooke
Members: 200 *Staff:* 2-5
Tel: (502) 583-3783
Hist. Note: Association for those involved with providing foodservice and products to airlines.

In-Plant Management Ass'n (1964)
2475 Canal St., Suite 300, New Orleans LA 70119
Exec. Director: Larry E. Aaron
Members: 3,000 *Staff:* 5
Annual Budget: $250-500,000 *Tel:* (504) 822-2877
Hist. Note: Founded as the In-Plant Printing Management Ass'n, it became IPMA-A Graphic Communications Management Ass'n in 1982 and assumed its present name in 1986. Members are managers or supervisors of company-owned or in-plant graphic communications departments. Awards the CGCM ("Certified Graphic Communications Manager") designation. Membership: $100/yr.
Publications:
Perspectives. m.
Inside IPMA. m.
Annual Meetings: June
1987-San Antonio, TX(Hyatt)/June 10-12/300
1988-San Diego, CA(Holiday Inn at the Embarcadero)/April 20-23/400

In-Plant Powder Metallurgy Ass'n (1958)
Hist. Note: A constituent part of the Metal Powder Industries Federation. Merged with the P/M Industries Ass'n to form the Metal Powder Technology Ass'n in 1985.

In-Plant Printing Management Ass'n (1964)
Hist. Note: Became IPMA-A Graphic Communications Management Association in 1982.

Incentive Manufacturers Representatives Ass'n (1963)
710 East Ogden Ave., Suite 113, Naperville IL 60540
Exec. Director: Arthur W. Seeds, CAE
Members: 200-225 companies *Staff:* 2-5
Annual Budget: $100-250,000 *Tel:* (312) 369-2425
Hist. Note: Formerly (1977) Nat'l Premium Manufacturers Representatives, Inc. Members are incentive marketing specialists. Membership: $450/yr.
Publication:
News and Views. q.
Annual Meetings: Spring
1987-Tampa Bay, FL(Saddlebrook Hotel)/March 8-12/300
1988-Scottsdale, AZ(Sheraton Scottsdale Resort)/March 20-24/300

INDA, Ass'n of the Nonwoven Fabrics Industry (1968)
1700 Broadway, New York NY 10019
President: John J. Mead, CAE APR
Members: 100-125 companies *Staff:* 10-12
Annual Budget: $1-2,000,000 *Tel:* (212) 582-8401
Hist. Note: Formerly (1972) the Disposables Ass'n and (1977) the Internat'l Nonwovens and Disposables Ass'n. Suppliers of fibers, adhesives, chemicals, fluff pulp, plastic film and related materials; roll goods producers; machinery and equipment suppliers; finishers and converters; and marketers of finished products.
Publications:
INDA Newsletter. m.
INDA Washington Report. semi-m.
International Directory of the Nonwoven Fabrics Industry. bien. adv.
Annual Meetings: February
1987-Marco Island, FL(Marriott's Marco Beach Resort)/Feb. 22-24

Independent Aluminum Residential Fabricators Ass'n (1977)
Hist. Note: Companies fabricating building components from aluminum. Inactive in 1982.

Independent American Whiskey Ass'n (1938)
Hist. Note: Became the American Beverage Alcohol Association in 1982.

Independent Armored Car Operators Ass'n (1973)
Security Armored Car Service, 1022 South 9th St., St. Louis MO 63104
Secy.-Treas.: Ronald Bray
Members: 35-40 companies *Staff:* 2-5
Annual Budget: $10-25,000 *Tel:* (314) 231-4030
Publication:
The Money Mover. q.
Semi-annual Meetings: April and October

Independent Automotive Damage Appraisers Ass'n (1964)
2200 South 108th St., Milwaukee WI 53227
Exec. Director: Paul Cinquemani
Members: 100-125 *Staff:* 2-5
Annual Budget: $100-250,000 *Tel:* (414) 541-6050
Hist. Note: Founded by a group of independent appraisers sponsored and screened in selected areas after World War II by the Association of Casualty and Surety Companies and the Association of Mutual Companies.
Publications:
IADA News. q.
IADA Service Directory. a.
Annual Meetings: June/200
1987-Milwaukee, WI(Prister Hotel)/June 25-27

Independent Automotive Service Ass'n (1949)
Hist. Note: Merged with Automotive Service Councils, Inc. in 1986 to form the Automotive Service Ass'n.

Independent Bakers Ass'n (1967)
Box 3731, Washington DC 20007
President: Robert N. Pyle
Members: 300 companies *Staff:* 2-5
Annual Budget: $100-250,000 *Tel:* (202) 223-2325
Hist. Note: Members are baking companies not part of any national chain. Sponsors BAKE PAC, a political action committee.
Annual Meetings: June/250

Independent Bankers Ass'n of America (1930)
One Thomas Circle, N.W., Suite 950, Washington DC 20005
Exec. V. Pres.: Kenneth Guenther
Members: 7,000-7,500 *Staff:* 20-25
Annual Budget: $2-5,000,000 *Tel:* (202) 659-8111
Hist. Note: Membership consists generally of small, independent, community-owned banks. Supports the Independent Bankers Political Action Committee.
Publications:
The Independent Banker. m. adv.
Washington Weekly Report. w.
Annual Meetings: Spring
1987-Orlando, FL/April 1-4
1988-Honolulu/March 13-17

00144 12 05 86 1233

Independent Battery Manufacturers Ass'n (1955)
100 Larchwood Drive, Largo FL 33540
Exec. Secretary: Celwyn Hopkins
Members: 306 battery companies and suppliers *Staff:* 6-10
Annual Budget: $250-500,000 *Tel:* (813) 586-1408
Hist. Note: Established in 1955 by ten charter members as the Independent Battery Manufacturers of America and incorporated in the State of Ohio. The present name was assumed in 1966 to reflect increased foreign membership.
Publications:
The Battery Man. m. adv.
SLIG Buyers' Guide. bi-a. adv.
Annual Meetings: Chicago in October/400

Independent Cash Register Dealers Ass'n (1945)
711 East Morehead St., Charlotte NC 28202
Secy.-Treas.: Curtis Kennington
Members: 420 companies *Staff:* 2-5
Annual Budget: $100-250,000 *Tel:* (704) 376-8516
Hist. Note: Membership: $200/yr. (individual), $500/yr. (company).
Publications:
Data Link Newsletter. m. adv.
Membership Directory. a. adv.
Semi-annual meetings: January and July
1987-Honolulu, HI(Sheraton Waikiki)/Feb. 1-4/800
1987-Montreal, Canada(Sheraton Le Centre)/July 26-29/1,000

Independent Cold Extruders Institute (1966)
Hist. Note: Ceased operations in 1984.

Independent College Funds of America (1958)
420 Lexington Ave., Suite 2725, New York NY 10170
Vice President: Robert L. Graze
Members: 39 state ass'ns, 601 colleges and universities *Staff:* 2-5
Annual Budget: $250-500,000 *Tel:* (212) 682-8355
Hist. Note: Members are state associations of private colleges united for a coordinated fund raising approach to business and industry.
Publication:
Directory of State Associations. a.
Annual Meetings: April
1987-San Francisco, CA/April 9-12

Independent Computer Consultants Ass'n (1976)
Box 27412, St. Louis MO 63141
Exec. Director: John Christensen
Members: 5,000 individuals; 1,900 companies *Staff:* 2-5
Annual Budget: $100-250,000 *Tel:* (314) 997-4633
Hist. Note: Represents individuals, partnerships and companies providing computer-related products and services. A member of the National Commission on Software Issues in the Eighties.
Publication:
The Independent. bi-m.
Annual Meetings: Spring
1987-San Francisco, CA

Independent Cosmetic Manufacturers and Distributors (1974)
400 Country Club Drive, P.O. Box 727, Bensenville IL 60106-0727
Exec. Director: Jerome N. Michell
Members: 300 companies
Tel: (800) 334-2623
Hist. Note: Membership fee based upon annual sales volume.
Publication:
Digest. 10/yr.
Annual Meetings: June

Independent Data Communications Manufacturers Ass'n (1971)
5th Floor, 1201 Pennsylvania Ave., N.W., Washington DC 20004
General Counsel: Herbert E. Marks
Members: 6 companies *Staff:* 5
Tel: (202) 626-6600
Hist. Note: Manufacturers of data communications equipment not affiliated with a common carrier. Participates in government policy proceedings to fosters competition in telecommunications. The above address is the law firm of Squire, Sanders and Dempsey.

Independent Educational Counselors Ass'n (1976)
Box 125, Forestdale MA 02644
Exec. Director: William B. Peirce
Members: 90-100 *Staff:* 2-5
Annual Budget: $50-100,000 *Tel:* (617) 477-2127
Hist. Note: Counselors who work directly with students and parents for a fee, and are not affiliated with any educational institution. Membership: $600/year.
Annual Meetings: With the Nat'l Ass'n of Independent Schools
1987-Boston, MA

Independent Electrical Contractors (1956)
1101 Connecticut Ave., N.W., Suite 700, Washington DC 20036
Exec. V. President: Mark Levin, CAE
Members: 2,500-3,000 companies *Staff:* 2-5
Annual Budget: $250-500,000 *Tel:* (202) 857-1141
Hist. Note: A federation of state and local groups promoting the common business interests of the electrical construction industry, particularly the independent electrical contractor. Until 1981 known as Associated Independent Electrical Contractors of America.
Publications:
News Circuit Newsletter. m. adv.
Directory. a.
Annual Meetings: Convention and Trade Show

Independent Free Papers of America (1980)
210 Washington St., Chardon OH 44024
Secy.-Treas.: Chalmers E. Bennett
Members: 240 *Staff:* 1
Annual Budget: $10-25,000 *Tel:* (216) 285-2218
Hist. Note: Publishers of locally distributed and independently owned free circulation shopping guides and community newspapers. Has no paid staff. Membership: $75/yr.
Publication:
The Independent Publisher. m. adv.
Annual Meetings: Semi-annual

Independent Gasoline Marketers Council (1969)
1133 15th St., N.W., Suite 1100, Washington DC 20005
President and Gen. Counsel: Jack A. Blum
Members: 15-20 *Staff:* 2-5
Annual Budget: $100-250,000 *Tel:* (202) 662-0618
Hist. Note: Supports the Independent Gasoline Marketers Council Political Action Committee. Represents the interests of independent gasoline marketers in Washington before such agencies as the Department of Energy.

Independent Insurance Agents of America (1896)
100 Church St., New York NY 10007
Exec. V. President and General Counsel: Jeffrey M. Yates
Members: 34,000 *Staff:* 40-45
Annual Budget: over $5,000,000 *Tel:* (212) 285-4250
Hist. Note: Formerly (1976) Nat'l Ass'n of Insurance Agents, Inc. Supports the Nat'l Agents Political Action Committee. Maintains Washington office. Has a budget of about $8,000,000.
Publications:
Independent Agent Magazine. m. adv.
IIAA Action News.
Annual Meetings: Fall/4,000
1987-Las Vegas, NV (Caesar's Palace)/Sept. 13-17
1988-Boston, MA(Marriott Copley & Westin)/Sept. 14-18
1989-Los Angeles, CA(Bonaventur)/Sept. 10-14
1990-Chicago, IL(Hyatt-Regency)/Sept.14-18
1991-Honolulu, HI(Sheraton Waikiki)/Sept. 29-Oct. 3

Independent Investors Protective League (1970)
8035-A West Oakland Park Blvd., Sunrise FL 33321
Exec. Officer: Merrill Sands
Members: 3,000 *Staff:* 2-5
Annual Budget: under $10,000 *Tel:* (305) 749-1551
Annual Meetings: December

Independent Jewelers Organization (1972)
64 Post Road West, Westport CT 06880
V. President, Marketing: Phyllis Trefz
Members: 1,000 companies *Staff:* 6-10
Annual Budget: $500-1,000,000 *Tel:* (203) 226-6941
Hist. Note: Restricted to one company per area, IJO is a buying and service organization for its members.
Semi-annual Meetings: Winter and Summer

Independent Liquid Terminals Ass'n (1974)
1133 15th St., N.W., Suite 204, Washington DC 20005
President: John Prokop
Members: 60 companies; 320 sustaining members *Staff:* 2-5
Annual Budget: $250-500,000 *Tel:* (202) 659-2301
Hist. Note: Owners and lessors of bulk storage tank space for oil, chemicals, edibles and other liquid commodities.
Publications:
Directory of Suppliers of Goods and Services. a.
Directory of Bulk Liquid Terminals and Storage Facilities. a.
Newsletter. m.

Independent Literary Agents Ass'n (1977)
55 Fifth Ave., New York NY 10003
President: Peter L. Skolnik
Members: 70 *Staff:* 1
Annual Budget: under $10,000 *Tel:* (212) 206-5600
Hist. Note: Nation-wide trade association of literary agents concerned with improving author/publisher relations and cooperating with other literary organizations on First Amendment matters and other issues of concern to the publishing industry. Membership: $75/yr.
Publication:
Newsletter. 7-8/yr.

Independent Livestock Marketing Ass'n (1945)
Route 3, Box 419, Elwood IN 46036
Exec. Director: S. Paul Juday
Members: 40 companies *Staff:* 2-5
Annual Budget: $25-50,000 *Tel:* (317) 552-3939
Publications:
Newsletter. m.
Market Journal. m.
Annual Meetings: Spring

Independent Local Newspaper Ass'n (1978)
Hist. Note: Ceased operations in 1985.

Independent Lubricant Manufacturers Ass'n (1948)
1055 Thomas Jefferson St., N.W., #302, Washington DC 20007
Exec. Director: Nancy DeMarco
Members: 250 companies *Staff:* 2-5
Annual Budget: $250-500,000 *Tel:* (202) 337-3470
Hist. Note: Independent blenders and compounders of lubricants and motor oils. Until 1980 known as the Independent Oil Compounders Association.
Publication:
ILMA Compoundings. m.
Annual Meetings: Fall
1987-Miami, FL/Oct. 10-13

Independent Media Producers Ass'n (1976)
Hist. Note: Founded to combat the federal government's approach in 1976 to limiting audio-video production. Became the Independent Media Producers Council within the Internat'l Communications Industries Ass'n in 1985.

Independent Medical Distributors Ass'n (1978)
5845 Horton St., Suite 201, Mission KS 66202
Exec. Director: Frank A. Bistrom
Members: 67 companies *Staff:* 2-5
Annual Budget: $50-100,000 *Tel:* (913) 262-4510
Hist. Note: Members are firms dealing in high-technology, sophisticated, medical equipment.
Publication:
Update. m.
Annual Meetings: December
1987-Southern Florida

Independent Motion Picture Producers Ass'n (1932)
Hist. Note: Inactive in 1984.

Independent Motorcycle Retailers of America (1983)
c/o Ass'ns Unlimited, 5116 North Cicero, Chicago IL 60618
Director: George Ericson
Members: 260 *Staff:* 3
Annual Budget: under $10,000 *Tel:* (312) 282-7106
Hist. Note: Trade association of independent retailers; over 40% of motorcycle retailers are indpendent and account for 45% of products sold. Membership: $50/yr.
Publication:
IMRA News. m.
Annual Meetings: February

Independent Petroleum Ass'n of America (1929)
1101 16th St., N.W., 2nd Fl., Washington DC 20036
President: H.B. Scoggins
Members: 8,600 *Staff:* 30-35
Annual Budget: $1-2,000,000 *Tel:* (202) 857-4722
Hist. Note: Members are small producers of oil and natural gas and their suppliers.
Publication:
Petroleum Independent. bi-m. adv.
Annual Meetings: Mid-Year (Spring) and Annual (Fall) Meetings

Independent Professional Painting Contractors Ass'n (1982)
Box 233, Huntington NY 11743
President: Heinz Hoffmann
Members: 16-20 companies *Staff:* 1
Annual Budget: under $10,000 *Tel:* (516) 423-3654
Hist. Note: Members consist only of open-shop painting contractors who formed the association to serve needs which they perceived as unsatisfied by the Painting and Decorators Contractors of America. Has no paid staff at present. Membership: $60/yr. (individual); $50/yr. (organization/company)

Independent Professional Typists Network (1980)
Hist. Note: Reported as defunct in 1984.

Independent Refiners Ass'n of America (1949)
Hist. Note: Merged April 1, 1983 with the American Petroleum Refiners Association to form the American Independent Refiners Association.

Independent Research Libraries Ass'n (1972)
c/o Massachusetts Historical Society, 1154 Boylston St., Boston MA 02215
Chairman: Louis L. Tucker
Members: 14 institutions *Staff:* 1
Annual Budget: under $10,000 *Tel:* (617) 536-1608
Hist. Note: Independently supported unaffiliated research libraries of which the American Antiquarian Soc. (Worcester) and the Huntington (San Marino) are examples.
Semi-annual Meetings:

Independent Sector (1980)
1828 L St., N.W., Washington DC 20036
President: Brian O'Connell
Members: 600 institutions *Staff:* 20-25
Annual Budget: $1-2,000,000 *Tel:* (202) 223-8100
Hist. Note: Formed from a merger of the Coalition of Nat'l Voluntary Organizations and the Nat'l Council on Philanthropy. Purpose is to encourage giving, volunteering and not-for-profit initiative.
Annual Meetings: Fall/600-800

00145 12 05 86 1233

1987-Washington, DC
1988-Houston, TX
1989-Open
1990-San Diego, CA

Independent Sewing Machine Dealers Ass'n (1952)
Box 338, Hilliard OH 43026
Exec. V. President: JoAnn Gram
Members: 1,200 *Staff:* 6-10
Annual Budget: $100-250,000 *Tel:* (614) 870-7211
Hist. Note: Formerly (until 1979) known as the Independent Sewing Machine Dealers of America, Inc. Regular membership is open to individual proprietorships, partnerships and corporations actively engaged in the retail sales and service of sewing machines. Membership: $100/yr. (individual); $150/yr. (organization/company)
Publication:
Round-Bobbin. m. adv.
Annual Meetings: June
1987-Anaheim, CA(Disneyland Hotel)/June 6-9/2,000

Independent Signcrafters of America (1976)
Box 605, Marietta OH 45750
Exec. Director: Regina Jeffers
Members: 400-450 *Staff:* 2-5
Annual Budget: $25-50,000 *Tel:* (614) 374-3276
Hist. Note: Members are signcrafters and sign suppliers. Formerly the Nat'l Independent Sign Ass'n, ISA assumed its present name in 1981.
Publications:
Newsletter. bi-m.
Sign Talk. bi-m.

Independent Terminal Operators Ass'n (1970)
1015 15th St., N.W., Suite 1100, Washington DC 20005
Secretary & Gen. Counsel: William H. Bode
Members: 11-15 companies *Staff:* 1
Annual Budget: $10-25,000 *Tel:* (202) 898-5800
Hist. Note: Has no office beyond the above, the law firm of Spriggs, Bode, & Hollingsworth.

Independent Watchmen's Union (1937)
Hist. Note: Became the International Security Officers, Police and Guards Union in 1981-82.

Independent Zinc Alloyers Ass'n (1959)
1000 16th St., N.W., Suite 603, Washington DC 20036
Exec. Director: Richard M. Cooperman
Members: 20-25 companies *Staff:* 2-5
Annual Budget: $50-100,000 *Tel:* (202) 785-0558
Hist. Note: Producers and suppliers of zinc alloy.

India Chamber of Commerce of America (1938)
445 Park Ave., 18th Floor, New York NY 10022
Director: M. Patricia Erdman
Members: 150
Tel: (212) 755-7181

Indiana Limestone Institute of America (1928)
Stone City Bank Bldg. , Ste. 400, Bedford IN 47421
Architectural Services Director: William H. McDonald
Members: 45-50 companies *Staff:* 2-5
Annual Budget: $100-250,000 *Tel:* (812) 275-4426
Hist. Note: Incorporated in 1928, ILI is the successor to the Quarryman's Club, an outgrowth of the Bedford Stone Club, which had been formed for promotional and political reasons. Absorbed the National Association for Indiana Limestone. As now constituted, ILI is the promotional arm of the Indiana Limestone Industry for limestone used as a building product and sets standards of quality and workmanship.

Industrial Ass'n of Juvenile Apparel Manufacturers (1933)
520 8th Ave., New York NY 10018
President: Alan D. Lubell
Members: 27 *Staff:* 1
Annual Budget: $100-250,000 *Tel:* (212) 244-2953
Hist. Note: A subsidiary of United Infants' and Children's Wear Ass'n. Membership: Based on sales volume.

Industrial Biotechnology Ass'n (1981)
2115 East Jefferson St., Suite 504, Rockville MD 20852
Exec. Director: Richard D. Godown
Members: 50-60 companies *Staff:* 6-10
Annual Budget: $500-1,000,000 *Tel:* (301) 984-9598
Hist. Note: Members are companies involved in genetic engineering and commercial biotechnology.
Publications:
What is Biotechnology? Primer.
Biotechnology at Work. Series.
Annual Meetings: October

Industrial Chemical Research Ass'n (1985)
1811 Monroe, Dearborn MI 48124
President: Harold Castor
Members: 50 companies; 2,200 individuals *Staff:* 3
Annual Budget: $1-2,000,000 *Tel:* (313) 563-0360
Hist. Note: Members are manufacturers, marketers, researchers, formulators, salesmen, executive officers, and suppliers of industrial chemicals united to promote research, safe practices, and increased selling efficiency in the industrial chemical industry. Membership: $50/yr.
Publications:
Newsletter. bi-m.
Bulletin Update. irreg.
Annual Meetings: Semi-Annual meetings

Industrial Communication Council (1955)
Hist. Note: Became the Council of Communication Management in 1985.

Industrial Designers Soc. of America (1965)
1142E Walker Road, Great Falls VA 22066
Exec. Director: Brian J. Wynne
Members: 2,000 *Staff:* 6
Annual Budget: $500-1,000,000 *Tel:* (703) 759-0100
Hist. Note: Merger of American Soc. of Industrial Designers (1944), Industrial Designers Institute (1938) and Industrial Design Education Ass'n. Membership: $204/yr.
Publications:
Innovation. q. adv.
Design Perspectives. m. adv.
Membership Directory. a. adv.
Annual Meetings: Summer
1987-Monterey, CA/Aug. 5-8

Industrial Development Research Council (1961)
40 Technology Park/Atlanta, Norcross GA 30092
Exec. Director: McKinley Conway
Members: 650 *Staff:* 8-10
Annual Budget: $1-2,000,000 *Tel:* (404) 446-6996
Hist. Note: Executives of industrial corporations engaged in site selection and facility planning.
Publications:
Industrial Development. bi-m.
Site Selection Handbook. a.
Semi-annual meetings: Spring and Fall
1987-Seattle, WA(Sheraton)/May 15-18
1987-San Antonio, TX(Hyatt Regency)/Oct. 25-28
1988-Chicago, IL (Marriott)/May 15-18
1988-Hilton Head, SC(Hyatt)/Oct. 30-Nov. 2
1989-St. Louis, MO(Adam's Mark)/May 14-17
1989-San Francisco, CA(Westin St. Francis)/Nov. 5-8

Industrial Diamond Ass'n of America (1946)
3008 Millwood Ave., Box 11187, Columbia SC 29205
Exec. Director: J. Edgar Eubanks
Members: 95 companies *Staff:* 8-10
Annual Budget: $50-100,000 *Tel:* (803) 252-5646
Hist. Note: Members are concerned with industrial diamonds, either as importers, dealers, or manufacturers of diamond tools.
Annual Meetings: Spring
1987-Bermuda(Princess)/April/130

Industrial Electronics and Control Instrumentation Soc.
Hist. Note: A subsidiary of the Institute of Electrical and Electronics Engineers. Membership in the Society, open only to IEEE members, includes subscription to a technical periodical in the field published by IEEE. All administrative support is provided by IEEE.

Industrial Fabrics Ass'n Internat'l (1912)
345 Cedar Bldg., Suite 450, St. Paul MN 55101
Exec. V. President: Robert C. Mead
Members: 2,200 companies *Staff:* 25-30
Annual Budget: $2-5,000,000 *Tel:* (612) 222-2508
Hist. Note: An association of the industrial fabrics industry. Founded as the Nat'l Canvas Goods Manufacturers Ass'n, it became the Canvas Products Ass'n Internat'l in 1956 and assumed its present name in 1980. Absorbed the Narrow Fabrics Institute in 1986.
Publications:
Buyers' Guide. a. adv.
Industrial Fabric Products Review. m. adv.
Who's Who in Canvas and Industrial Fabrics. a.
Geotechnical Fabrics Report. q. adv.
Annual Meetings: Fall
1987-Las Vegas, NV(MGM Grand)/Nov. 9-12

Industrial Fasteners Institute (1931)
1505 East Ohio Bldg., 1717 East 9th St., Cleveland OH 44114
Managing Director: C.G. (Dick) Scofield
Members: 75 companies *Staff:* 2-5
Annual Budget: $500-1,000,000 *Tel:* (216) 241-1482
Hist. Note: Formerly the American Institute of Bolt, Nut and Rivet Manufacturers, members are companies making industrial fasteners and formed parts.
Annual Meetings: Late Winter
1987-Litchfield Park, AZ(The Wigwam)/Feb. 16-20
1988-Laguna Beach, CA(Ritz Carlton)/Feb. 21-25
1989-Cypress Gardens, FL(Hyatt Cypress Gardens)/March 12-16
1990-Tuscon, AZ(Westin La Paloma)/Feb. 11-15

Industrial Gas Cleaning Institute (1960)
1707 L St., N.W., Suite 570, Washington DC 20036
Exec. Director: Jeffrey C. Smith
Members: 40 companies *Staff:* 2-5
Annual Budget: $250-500,000 *Tel:* (202) 457-0911
Hist. Note: Member of the Environmental Industry Council. Members are manufacturers of industrial air pollution control equipment for stationary sources. Membership: $3500/yr.
Publications:
Executive Update. bi-w.
Organization Directory. a.
Clean Air News. bi-m.
Annual Meetings: Spring
1987-Florida(Boca Raton Hotel)/April 8-12
1988-Bermuda(Southampton Princess)/April 13-17
1989-Alabama(The Grand Hotel)/April 19-23
1990-South Carolina(Kiawah Island Hotel)/April 18-22

Industrial Health Foundation (1935)
34 Penn Circle West, Pittsburgh PA 15206
President: Dr. Daniel C. Braun
Members: 120 companies *Staff:* 16-20
Annual Budget: $500-1,000,000 *Tel:* (412) 363-6600
Hist. Note: Organized as a multiple fellowship in the Mellon Institute of Industrial Research in 1935, it began operating as a non-profit independent research and service organization when the Institute merged with the Carnegie Institute of Technology in 1967. The Foundation serves as an independent consultant in the areas of occupational health, hygiene and safety for corporations which participate through membership. Annual dues are based on the number of employees in the corporation.
Publications:
Industrial Hygiene Digest. m.
Memos to Members. q.
Proceedings of Symposia. irreg.
Technical Bulletins. irreg.
Annual Meetings: December, at the University Club in Pittsburgh, PA

Industrial Heating Equipment Ass'n (1929)
1901 North Moore St., Suite 509, Arlington VA 22209
Exec. V. President: James J. Houston, CAE
Members: 50-55 *Staff:* 2-5
Annual Budget: $100-250,000 *Tel:* (703) 525-2513
Hist. Note: Manufacturers of industrial furnaces, ovens, combustion equipment, induction and dielectric heaters. Formerly (1954) Industrial Furnace Manufacturers Ass'n. Sponsors the IHEA Political Action Committee.
Publications:
Directory of Industrial Heat Processing and Combustion Equipment. bien.
IHEA Newsletter. q.
Legislative Reports. irreg.
Membership Directory. a.
News Compendium. irreg.
Heat Management. q.
Annual Meetings: Feb./March
1987-Palm Desert, CA(Marriott's Desert Springs)/March 1-5/200

Industrial Jacks Ass'n
Hist. Note: Reported defunct in 1986.

Industrial Management Soc. (1938)
Hist. Note: A professional society of executives interested in applying scientific principles to the measurement, evaluation and analysis of all phases of industrial activity. Merged with the American Institute of Industrial Engineers in 1982.

Industrial Marketing Associates (1946)
Hist. Note: Ceased operations in 1984.

Industrial Mathematics Soc. (1949)
Box 159, Roseville MI 48066
Secretary: Joseph Silvagi
Members: 100 *Staff:* 1
Annual Budget: under $10,000 *Tel:* (313) 771-0403
Hist. Note: Established in 1949 in Detroit. Members are individuals interested in extending the understanding and application of mathematics in industry. Has no paid staff. Membership: $15/yr.
Publication:
Industrial Mathematics. semi-a.
Annual Meetings: Semi-annual Meetings

Industrial Metal Containers Ass'n
8720 Red Oak Blvd., Suite 201, Charlotte NC 28210-3957
Management Exec.: William A. Dagar
Members: 9 *Staff:* 2-10
Tel: (704) 522-8644
Hist. Note: A product section of the Material Handling Institute. Membership: $1,350/yr.
Annual Meetings:
1987-Boca Raton, FL(Boca Raton Club)/Nov. 6-12
1988-Phoenix, AZ(Arizona Biltmore)/Oct. 7-13

Industrial Perforators Ass'n (1961)
710 North Plankinton, Suite 333, Milwaukee WI 53203
Secy.-Treas.: Delores Liebherr-Morris
Members: 15 companies *Staff:* 2-5
Annual Budget: $50-100,000 *Tel:* (414) 271-2263
Hist. Note: Members are companies making perforated metal products.

Industrial Relations Research Ass'n (1947)
7226 Soc. Sci. Bldg., Univ. of Wisconsin, Madison WI 53706
Secy.-Treas.: David R. Zimmerman
Members: 5,000 *Staff:* 2-5
Annual Budget: $50-100,000 *Tel:* (608) 262-2762
Hist. Note: Affiliated with Internat'l Industrial Relations Ass'n and member, Allied Social Science Ass'ns. Membership $36/year.
Publications:
IRRA Newsletter. q.
Proceedings. semi-a.

00146 12 05 86 1233

Volume of Research. a.
Membership Directory. trien.
Semi-annual Meetings: April and Dec. with Allied Social Science Ass'ns
1987-Boston, MA/April 29-May 1 and Chicago, IL/Dec. 28-30

Industrial Research Institute (1938)
100 Park Ave., Suite 3600, New York NY 10017
Exec. Director: Charles F. Larson
Members: 275-300 *Staff:* 6-10
Annual Budget: $1-2,000,000 *Tel:* (212) 683-7626
Hist. Note: Founded in 1938 under the auspices of the Nat'l Research Council and incorporated in New York in 1945. A company-membership ass'n to improve industrial research management and relations among industry, government and academics in science and technology.
Publication:
Research Management. bi-m.
Annual Meetings: Spring/7-800
1987-Phoenix, AZ(Biltmore)/May 3-6
1988-Palm Springs, CA(Desert Springs)May 1-4
1989-Williamsburg, VA/May 21-24
1990-Palm Beach, FL(The Breakers)/May 13-16
1991-Phoenix, AZ(Biltmore)/May 5-8

Industrial Safety Equipment Ass'n (1934)
1901 N. Moore St., Arlington VA 22209
President: Frank E. Wilcher, Jr.
Members: 80-85 *Staff:* 6
Annual Budget: $250-500,000 *Tel:* (703) 525-1695
Hist. Note: Members are makers of all types of apparel, supplies and equipment used for the protection of industrial workers.
Annual Meetings: May
1987-Litchfield Park, AZ(Wigwam)/May
1988-Bermuda(Castle Harbour)/May
1989-Asheville, SC(Grove Park Inn)/May

Industrial Truck Ass'n (1951)
1750 K St., N.W., Suite 210, Washington DC 20006
Exec. Director: William J. Montwieler
Members: 37 companies *Staff:* 3
Annual Budget: $250-500,000 *Tel:* (202) 296-9880
Hist. Note: Founded as the Electric Industrial Truck Ass'n, it assumed its present name in 1951. Members are manufacturers of powered lift trucks as well as their major components.
Annual Meetings: Fall
1987-Miami, FL(Doral Country Club)

Industrial Union of Marine and Shipbuilding Workers of America (1933)
5101 River Road, Suite 110, Bethesda MD 20816
President: Arthur Batson, Jr.
Members: 15,000 *Staff:* 11-15
Annual Budget: $1-2,000,000 *Tel:* (301) 951-4266
Hist. Note: Organized in Quincy, Massachusetts in September 1934. Affiliated with AFL-CIO.
Biennial meetings: Even years

Industry Applications Soc.
Hist. Note: A subsidiary of the Institute of Electrical and Electronics Engineers. Membership in the Society, open only to IEEE members, includes subscription to a technical periodical in the field published by IEEE. All administrative support is provided by IEEE.

Industry Council for Tangible Assets (1983)
1701 Pennsylvania Ave., N.W., Suite 560, Washington DC 20006
President: Howard Segermark
Annual Budget: $250-500,000 *Tel:* (202) 785-8600
Hist. Note: Promotes the interests of those individuals, partnerships, firms, associations and corporations who are engaged in the business of manufacturing, importing, distributing or selling at retail any tangible asset, including any precious metal, coin, antique or art object. Membership: from $250/yr.
Publications:
Washington Wire.
ICTA Membership Directory. a. adv.

Infant and Juvenile Manufacturers Ass'n (1912)
100 East 42nd St., New York NY 10017
Exec. Director: Aaron L. Solomon
Members: 23 *Staff:* 1
Annual Budget: $10-25,000 *Tel:* (212) 867-5720
Annual Meetings: New York, NY/1st Tuesday in December

Infant Formula Council (1970)
5775 Peachtree-Dunwoody Rd., Suite 500D, Atlanta GA 30342
President: Robert H. Kellen
Members: 5 companies *Staff:* 9
Tel: (404) 252-3663
Annual Meetings:
1987-Naples, Fl/Feb. 12-13

Infants' and Children's Wear Salesmen's Guild (1939)
160 West 34th St., New York NY 10001
Exec. Officer: William Rosenberg
Members: 500-700 *Staff:* 1
Annual Budget: under $10,000 *Tel:* (212) 279-3498

Infants', Children's and Girls' Sportswear and Coat Ass'n (1934)
450 Seventh Ave., New York NY 10123
Exec. Director: Stanley D. Halperin
Members: 50 companies *Staff:* 2-5
Tel: (212) 563-1118
Hist. Note: Formerly (until 1978) the Infants' and Children's Coat Ass'n. A member of the Federation of Apparel Manufacturers.
Annual Meetings: December

Infectious Diseases Soc. of America (1963)
6431 Fannin, 1728 Freeman Bldg., Houston TX 77030
Secretary: Herbert L. DuPont, M.D.
Members: 2,000-2,100 *Staff:* 2-5
Annual Budget: $50-100,000 *Tel:* (713) 792-4929
Publications:
Journal of Infectious Disease. m. adv.
Reviews of Infectious Diseases. bi-m.
Annual Meetings: Fall/2,000
1987-New York, NY/Oct. 8-8
1988-Los Angeles, CA/Oct. 27-28
1989-Houston, TX/Sept. 28-29
1990-Atlanta, GA

Inflatable Boat Ass'n
Hist. Note: A division of the Industrial Fabrics Association International. Members are makers and distributors of inflatable boats and rafts.
Annual Meetings: With the Industrial Fabrics Association International.

Inflight Food Services Ass'n (1965)
304 West Liberty St., Suite 301, Louisville KY 40202
President: Phillip Cook
Annual Budget: $250-500,000 *Tel:* (502) 583-3783
Hist. Note: Members are international airlines and caterers. Membership: $125/yr.
Annual Meetings:
1987-San Diego, CA(Intercontinental)/May/750
1988-Orlando, FL/May/750

Information Film Producers of America (1957)
Hist. Note: Became Ass'n of Visual Communicators (1985).

Information Industry Ass'n (1969)
555 New Jersey Ave., N.W., Suite 800, Washington DC 20001
President: Paul G. Zurkowski
Members: 460 companies *Staff:* 25-30
Annual Budget: $1-2,000,000 *Tel:* (202) 639-8262
Hist. Note: Trade association representing companies interested and involved in the business opportunities associated with the generation, distribution, and use of information. These firms participate in three IIA divisions which develop programs to meet their needs in Database and Publishing, Electrocin Services, and Financial Information Services. Information Services.
Publications:
Information Sources. a.
Information Times. q.
Friday Memo. w.
Tri-annual Meetings: Spring, Fall and Winter
1987-Boca Raton, FL(Boca Raton Hotel & Club)/Feb. 12-14
1987-Washington, DC(Omni Shoreham Hotel)/May 18-20
1988-Chicago, IL(Palmer House)/Nov. 15-18

Information Theory Soc.
Hist. Note: A subsidiary of the Institute of Electrical and Electronics Engineers. Membership in the Society, open only to IEEE members, includes subscription to a technical periodical in the field published by IEEE. All administrative support is provided by IEEE.

Inland Marine Underwriters Ass'n (1930)
14 Wall St., Room 2100, New York NY 10005
V. President: John C. Herman
Members: 350 companies *Staff:* 2-5
Annual Budget: $250-500,000 *Tel:* (212) 233-7958
Hist. Note: Addresses problems of common concern to companies doing Inland Marine insurance business. Membership: $500/yr.
Publications:
Impact. q.
Inland Marine Insurance Fact Book. quinquen.
Annual Meetings: May/125
1987-San Antonio, TX(Sheraton San Antonio Resort)/May 17-20

Inland River Ports and Terminals (1974)
Central Station, Box 863, St. Louis MO 63188
Secy.-Treas.: Wayne E. Weidemann
Members: 150
Annual Budget: $10-25,000 *Tel:* (314) 721-0900
Hist. Note: Incorporated in the State of Missouri to represent the interests of inland waterway ports, terminals and associated activities, throughout the U.S. Membership: $150-200/yr.
Publication:
Newsletter. m.
Annual Meetings: March/April

Input/Output Systems Ass'n (1959)
Hist. Note: Founded as the Tabulating Card Manufacturers Association, it became the Data Processing Cards and Forms Association and (in 1968) the Data Processing Supplies Association and assumed its present name in 1974. No longer in existence in 1983.

Insect Screening Weavers Ass'n (1940)
2000 Maple Hill St., Yorktown Heights NY 10598
Secretary: Peter M. Miranda
Members: 11-15 companies *Staff:* 2-5
Annual Budget: $10-25,000 *Tel:* (914) 962-9052
Hist. Note: Formerly (1968) Insect Wire Screening Bureau and (1977) Wire Weavers Ass'n.

Institute for Alternative Agriculture (1983)
9200 Edmonston Road, Suite 117, Greenbelt MD 20770
Exec. Director: Dr. I. Garth Youngberg
Members: 1,000 individuals *Staff:* 4
Annual Budget: $100-250,000 *Tel:* (301) 441-8777
Hist. Note: Formed to promote, through research and education programs, a more cost-effective, resource-conserving, and environmentally sound farming system. Membership: $15/yr.
Publications:
Alternative Agriculture News. m.
American Journal of Alternative Agriculture. q. adv.
Annual Meetings: March

Institute for Briquetting and Agglomeration (1949)
Box 794, Erie PA 16512
Exec. Director: Walter W. Eichenberger
Members: 225 individuals, 150 companies *Staff:* 1
Annual Budget: $50-100,000 *Tel:* (814) 838-1133
Hist. Note: Organized in 1949 as Internat'l Briquetting Ass'n, the present name was assumed in 1967. Members shape and form materials such as charcoal, lime, ores, chemicals, metal swarf and powders, coal fines, coke breeze, wood waste etc. which require size enlargement for efficient use. Membership: $30/yr. (individual); $60/yr. (organization/company)
Publications:
Newsletter. q.
Proceedings. bi-a. adv.
Biennial meetings: Uneven years
1987-Orlando, FL(Sheraton World)/Sept. 27-30/250-300

Institute for Certification of Computer Professionals (1973)
2200 E. Devon Ave., Suite 268, Des Plaines IL 60018
Exec. Director: George R. Eggert
Members: 13 associations *Staff:* 3-11
Annual Budget: $500-1,000,000 *Tel:* (312) 299-4227
Hist. Note: ICCP is supported by 13 major international computer societies. It exams and certifies professionals within the computer information processing industry, operating certification programs which lead to the designations: Certified Computer Programmer (CCP), Certified Data Processor (CDP), Certified Systems Professional (CSP), and Associate Computer Professional (ACP).
Publication:
Project ICCP. m. adv.
Annual Meetings: January
1987-San Antonio, TX(Radisson Gunther)/Jan. 22-25/45-60

Institute for Fermentation and Brewing Studies (1983)
P.O. Box 287, Boulder CO 80306
President: Charles N. Papazian
Members: 600 *Staff:* 8-12
Annual Budget: $100-250,000 *Tel:* (303) 447-0816
Hist. Note: Subsidiary of Ass'n of Brewers (same address). Members are professional brewers at micro, small, large and pub breweries. Publishes information on brewing techniques and brewery operations. Membership: $48/yr.
Publications:
New Brewer. bi-m. adv.
Microbrewers Resource Handbook & Directory.
Annual Meetings:
1987-New England/Sept./250-350

Institute for Interconnecting and Packaging Electronic Circuits (1957)
Hist. Note: See IPC.

Institute for Medical Record Economics (1979)
121 Mount Vernon St., Boston MA 02108
Exec. Director: C. Peter Waegemann
Members: 800 affiliates *Staff:* 3
Annual Budget: $250-500,000 *Tel:* (617) 720-2229
Hist. Note: Members are medical record, computer professionals and others concerned with research and education in medical documentation.
Publication:
Medical Documentation Update. 10/yr.
Annual Meetings: Spring
1987-Chicago, IL(Palmer House)/March 24-27/800
1988-New York, NY

Institute for Municipal Engineering (1966)
1313 East 60th St., Chicago IL 60637
Secretary: Rodney R. Fleming
Members: 3,600 *Staff:* 2-5
Annual Budget: $25-50,000 *Tel:* (312) 667-2200
Hist. Note: Established 1966 as one of the first two APWA institutes for professional development, of which there are now seven. The institute promotes the development, adoption and use of sound engineering policies and efficient management

00147 12 05 86 1233

principles by those people employed by public agencies who have responsibility for engineering and construction.
Publication:
APWA Reporter. m. adv.
Annual Meetings: Fall, with the American Public Works Asso'n
1987-Chicago, IL/Sept. 19-24
1988-Toronto, Ontario/Sept. 24-29
1989-Orlando, FL/Sept. 23-28
1990-St. Louis, MO/Sept. 8-13

Institute for Polyacrylate Absorbents (1985)
1330 Connecticut Ave., N.W., Suite 300, Washington DC 20036
Exec. Director: William H. Smock
Annual Budget: $100-250,000 *Tel:* (202) 659-0060
Hist. Note: IPA represents U.S. manufacturers and users of absorbent polymers made of cross-linked polyacrylates and manufacturers and users of acrylic acid or its salts. It addresses the scientific, regulatory and related issues which are likely to impact health, safety and environmental aspects of the manufacture, use and disposal of fluid-absorbing polyacrylates.

Institute for Safety in Transportation (1977)
Hist. Note: Became the International Institute for Safety in Transportation in 1984.

Institute for the Advancement of Engineering (1967)
Box 1305, Woodland Hills CA 91365
Exec. Manager: Lloyd Higginbotham
Members: 1,500 *Staff:* 2-5
Annual Budget: $25-50,000 *Tel:* (818) 992-8292
Annual Meetings: Four meetings during Engineering Week (February) and membership meetings every two months

Institute of Ass'n Management Companies (1963)
5820 Wilshire Blvd., Suite 500, Los Angeles CA 90036
Exec. V. President: Jean Replogle
Members: 135 companies *Staff:* 2-5
Annual Budget: $250-500,000 *Tel:* (213) 937-5514
Hist. Note: Membership consists of companies engaged in the management of 2 or more organizations on a professional client basis. Founded as the Multiple Ass'n Management Institute in 1963, it assumed its present name in 1977.
Publications:
Elected Leader. q adv.
IAMC Referral Directory. bi-a.
Annual Meetings: July
1987-Reno, NV(MGM Grand)/July 28-31/250

Institute of Business Appraisers (1978)
P.O. Box 1447, Boynton Beach FL 33435
Exec. Director: Raymond C. Miles
Members: 1,000 *Staff:* 2-5
Annual Budget: $100-250,000 *Tel:* (305) 433-0908
Hist. Note: Members are actively involved in the valuation and appraisal of businesses and major business assets. Membership: $125/yr.
Publication:
IBA Newsletter. m.

Institute of Business Designers (1963)
1155 Merchandise Mart, Chicago IL 60654
Exec. Director: Rena F. Berke, CAE
Members: 3,000, 30 chapters
Annual Budget: $500-1,000,000 *Tel:* (312) 467-1950
Hist. Note: Contract (commercial) interior designers.
Publication:
News Bulletin.
Annual Meetings: June, in Chicago, IL/300

Institute of Certified Financial Planners (1973)
Two Denver Highlands, 10065 E. Harvard Ave., Suite 320, Denver CO 80231
Exec. Director: Dianna Rampy
Members: 11,000 *Staff:* 27
Annual Budget: $2-5,000,000 *Tel:* (303) 751-7600
Hist. Note: Established in Denver with 42 charter members. Accepts members who have qualified for the CFP (Certified Financial Planner) designation. Membership: $150/year.
Publications:
Journal of the Institute of Certified Financial Planners. q.
Newsworthy. m. adv.
Membership Directory. a.
Annual Meetings:
1987-San Diego, CA(Intercontinental Hotel)/Feb. 12-15/500
1988-New Orleans, LA

Institute of Certified Professional Business Consultants (1975)
600 South Federal St., #400, Chicago IL 60605
Exec. Director: Durward Humes
Members: 225-250 *Staff:* 2-5
Tel: (312) 922-6222
Hist. Note: Members provide business management consulting services to doctors and other professionals. Awards the CPBC ("Certified Professional Business Consultant") designation.
Annual Meetings: With the Soc. of Professional Business Consultants and the Soc. of Medical-Dental Consultants

Institute of Certified Records Managers (1975)
Box 8188, Prairie Village KS 66208
Secretary: Dr. Helene L. Zimmerman, CRM
Members: 514 *Staff:* 1
Annual Budget: $10-25,000 *Tel:* (517) 774-3969
Hist. Note: Developed by the American Records Management Ass'n in 1966, the ICRM was incorporated in 1975. It is a separate and independent organization from its sponsoring associations which include: Ass'n of Records Managers and Administrators, Nat'l Ass'n of State Archivists and Records Administrators, the Soc. of American Archivists, and the Ass'n for Information and Image Management. ICRM is a certifying organization of professional records managers and administrative officers who specialize in the field of Records and Information Management Programs. All members have received the Certified Records Manager (CRM) designation. Membership: $25/yr.
Publications:
ICRM Newsletters. 3/yr.
Membership Directory. a.
Preparing for the CRM Examination: A Handbook.
Annual Meetings: Fall
1987-Anaheim, CA(Convention Ctr.)/Oct. 19-22/250-300
1988-Baltimore, MD
1989-New Orleans, LA
1990-San Francisco, CA

Institute of Certified Travel Agents (1964)
Hist. Note: A non-profit, educational institution chartered in Washington in 1964 to promote professionalism in the travel industry. Now based in Wellesley, Massachusetts, it conducts a training program leading to certification and the CTC ("Certified Travel Counselor") designation.

Institute of Chartered Financial Analysts (1961)
Box 3668, Charlottesville VA 22903
President and C.E.O.: Alfred C. Morley
Members: 9,000 *Staff:* 27
Annual Budget: $2-5,000,000 *Tel:* (804) 977-6600
Hist. Note: Members are individuals who have passed three examinations and received the professional designation, Chartered Financial Analyst (CFA). Incorporated in Virginia in 1962. Membership: $75/year.
Publications:
CFA Digest. q.
Newsletter. q.
Membership Directory. a.
Proceedings of ICFA-Sponsored Seminars. 2-3/yr.
Annual Meetings: With the Financial Analysts Federation
1987-Philadelphia, PA/June

Institute of Cost Analysis (1980)
7111 Marlan Drive, Alexandria VA 22307
Exec. Director: Leroy T. Baseman
Members: 2,000-3,000 *Staff:* 2
Annual Budget: $250-500,000 *Tel:* (703) 768-6405
Hist. Note: A professional organization of cost analysts in Government and industry incorporated in the State of Virginia. Awards the CCA ("Certified Cost Analyst") designation. Membership: $35/year.
Publications:
Journal of Cost Analysis. semi-a.
Newsletter of the Institute. q.

Institute of Diving (1977)
17314 Hutchinson Road, Panama City Beach FL 32407
Exec. Secretary: Bonnie Ingram
Members: 1,200 individuals and companies *Staff:* 2-5
Annual Budget: $50-100,000 *Tel:* (904) 325-4101
Hist. Note: Members are sports, commercial and military divers, individuals, organizations and corporations interested in diving and diving-related activities. Membership: $25/yr.
Publication:
IOD Newsletter. q. adv.
Annual Meetings: Spring

Institute of Electrical and Electronics Engineers (1884)
345 East 47th St., New York NY 10017
Exec. Director and Gen. Manager: Eric Herz
Members: 250,000 *Staff:* 375-400
Annual Budget: over $5,000,000 *Tel:* (212) 705-7900
Hist. Note: Merger (1963) of the American Institute of Electrical Engineers (1884) and Institute of Radio Engineers (1912). Includes chapters in Canada and throughout the rest of the world, with members in 130 countries. Maintains and provides administrative support for the following subsidiaries: Acoustics, Speech and Signal Processing; Aerospace and Electronic Systems; Antennas and Propagation; Broadcast, Cable and Consumer Electronics; Circuits and Systems; Communications; Components Hybrids and Manufacturing Technology; Computer (see separate listing); Control Systems; Education; Electrical Insulation; Electromagnetic Compatibility; Electron Devices; Engineering Management; Engineering in Medicine and Biology; Geoscience and Remote Sensing; Industry Applications; Information Theory; Instrumentation and Measurement; Magnetics; Microwave Theory and Techniques; Nuclear and Plasma Science Oceanic Engineering; Power Engineering; Professional Communications; Quantum Electronics and Applications; Reliability; Social Implications of Technology; Solid-State Circuits; Sonics and Ultrasonics; Systems, Man and Cybernetics; and Vehicular Technology. Has annual budget of over $45 million. Maintains library, Center for the History of Electrical Engineering and a Washington office.
Publications:
Proceedings. m.
Spectrum. m. adv.
Institute. m.
IEEE Potentials. q.
51 monthly Transactions and Journals.

Institute of Electrical and Electronics Engineers Computer Soc.
Hist. Note: See the Computer Society of the Institute of Electrical and Electronics Engineers.

Institute of Environmental Sciences (1954)
940 East Northwest Hwy., Mount Prospect IL 60056
Exec. Director: Janet A. Ehmann
Members: 3,800 individuals *Staff:* 6-10
Annual Budget: $500-1,000,000 *Tel:* (312) 255-1561
Hist. Note: Formed by a merger of the Institute of Environmental Engineers (founded in 1955) and the Soc. of Environmental Engineers. Absorbed the American Ass'n for Contamination Control in 1973. Members are individuals concerned with the effect on men, materials and equipment brought on by the operation of such advanced equipment as rockets, jet planes, reactors, submarines, etc. Membership: $40/yr. (individual); $800/yr. (organization).
Publications:
Journal of Environemntal Sciences. bi-m. adv.
Proceedings. a.
Annual Meetings: Spring
1987-San Jose, CA(Convention Ctr.)/May 4-8
1988-Valley Forge, PA(Convention Ctr.)/May 2-6
1989-Anaheim, CA(Disneyland Hotel)/May 1-5
1990-New Orleans, LA(Hyatt Regency)/April 30-May 4
1991-San Diego, CA(Town & Country)/May 6-10

Institute of Financial Education (1922)
111 East Wacker Drive, Chicago IL 60601
President: Dale C. Bottom
Members: 55,000 *Staff:* 70
Annual Budget: $2-5,000,000 *Tel:* (312) 644-3100
Hist. Note: Established as the American Savings and Loan Institute, it assumed its present name in 1975. It is the educational arm of the savings and loan industry, and is affiliated with the United States League of Savings Institutions. Membership: $8/yr.
Annual Meetings: March
1987-Kansas City, MO(Hyatt)/March 15-18
1988-Cleveland, OH(Stouffer Inn)/March 20-23

Institute of Food Technologists (1939)
221 North LaSalle St., Suite 300, Chicago IL 60601
Exec. Director: Calvert L. Willey
Members: 22,000 *Staff:* 30-35
Annual Budget: $2-5,000,000 *Tel:* (312) 782-8424
Hist. Note: Founded in 1939 and incorporated in Illinois. Promotes the application of science and engineering to the production, processing, packaging, distribution, preparation, evaluation and utilization of food. About 60% of IFT members work for food processors or ingredient manufacturers, principally in R&D, quality control, technical sales, or corporate management. Membership: $45/yr.
Publications:
Food Technology. m. adv.
Journal of Food Science. bi-m.
Annual Meetings: Summer/10,000
1987-Las Vegas, NV(Convention Ctr.)/June 16-19
1988-New Orleans, LA(Convention Ctr.)/June 19-22
1989-Chicago, IL(McCormick Place)/June 25-29
1990-New Orleans, LA(Convention Ctr.)/June 19-22

Institute of Home Office Underwriters (1937)
c/o The Independent Life & Accident, Insurance Co., One Independent Drive, Jacksonville FL 32276
V. President and Editor: Jack Rice
Members: 563 companies: 1,200-1,300 individuals
Annual Budget: $50-100,000 *Tel:* (904) 358-5036
Hist. Note: Sponsors an educational program leading to the FALU designation ("Fellow, Academy of Life Underwriting").
Publications:
On the Risk. q.
Proceedings. a.
Annual Meetings: Fall
1987-Seattle, WA(Westin)/Nov. 2-4
1988-Boston, MA(Marriott)/Oct. 17-18
1989-St. Louis, MO(Adam's Mark)/Oct. 23-25
1990-Washington, DC(Sheraton)/Oct. 22-24
1991-Chicago, IL(Hyatt Regency)/Oct. 21-23

Institute of Industrial Engineers (1948)
25 Technology Park/Atlanta, Norcross GA 30092
Exec. Director: David L. Belden, PE
Members: 43,000 *Staff:* 80
Annual Budget: over $5,000,000 *Tel:* (404) 449-0460
Hist. Note: Founded and chartered in Columbus, Ohio as the American Institute of Industrial Engineers; assumed its present name in 1981. Member of the American Ass'n of Engineering Societies, the Accreditation Board for Engineering and Technology and the Nat'l Council of Engineering Examiners. Absorbed the Industrial Management Soc. in 1982. Has an annual budget of $7.3 million. Membership: $65/yr.
Publications:
IIE Transactions. q.
The Engineering Economist. q.
Industrial Engineering. m. adv.
Industrial Management. bi-m.
Annual Meetings: May
1987-Washington, DC(Sheraton Washington)/May 17-21/3,000
1988-Orlando, FL(Marriott's World Center)/May 22-25/3,000

00148 12 05 86 1233

Institute of Industrial Launderers (1932)
1730 M St., N.W., Suite 610, Washington DC 20036
Manager: Bernard H. Ehrlich
Members: 900-1,000 companies *Staff:* 11-15
Annual Budget: $1-2,000,000 *Tel:* (202) 296-6744
Hist. Note: Members are companies renting and cleaning work uniforms, gloves, mats, towels, etc.
Publication:
Industrial Launderer. m. adv.
Annual Meetings: Fall
1987-Los Angeles, CA(Century Plaza)/Oct. 10-15
1988-Washington, DC

Institute of Intermodal Repairers (1983)
427 Grand Ave., Oakland CA 94610
Exec. Secy.: Mark C. North
Members: 70 companies *Staff:* 1
Annual Budget: $50-100,000 *Tel:* (415) 268-8410
Hist. Note: Begun in 1983 by approximately 40 repair companies from the U.S. and Canada to develop the industry in such areas as new repair techniques and to unify industry response to other trade associations and industry groups. Membership: $500/yr.
Publication:
IIR Newsletter. q. adv.
Annual Meetings: Winter
1987-New York, NY(Vista International)/Jan. 29-30/200

Institute of Internal Auditors (1941)
249 Maitland Ave., Box 1119, Altamonte Springs FL 32701
President: G. Peter Wilson
Members: 30,000 *Staff:* 75
Annual Budget: over $5,000,000 *Tel:* (305) 830-7600
Hist. Note: Membership composed of internal auditors, comptrollers and accountants in companies, government, and organizations. Grants the CIA (Certified Internal Auditor) designation. Has an annual budget of $6-7,000,000. Membership: $50-100/yr.
Publications:
Edpacs. m.
IIA Today. m.
The Internal Auditor. bi-m. adv.
Annual Meetings: Summer
1987-Dallas,TX(Anatole)/June 21-24/1,500
1988-London, England(Grovesnor)/July 3-6/1,000
1989-San Francisco, CA/June 25-28/1,800
1990-St. Louis, MO/June 17-20/1,500

Institute of Internat'l Container Lessors (1971)
Bedford Consultants Bldg., Box 605, Bedford NY 10506
Secretary & Counsel: Edward A. Woolley
Members: 12 companies *Staff:* 3
Annual Budget: $250-500,000 *Tel:* (914) 234-3696
Hist. Note: Membership is engaged in leasing marine cargo containers to ship operators and others on a broad international basis. Sponsors an inspectors' certification and examination testing program; distributes myriad technical bulletins; and is active in regulatory, tax and customs fields.
Publication:
Technical Publicatins.

Institute of Internat'l Finance (1983)
2000 Pennsylvania Ave., N.W., Suite 8500, Washington DC 20006
Managing Director: Andre' de Lattre
Members: 187 *Staff:* 37
Annual Budget: $2-5,000,000 *Tel:* (202) 857-3600
Hist. Note: Created as a center for the dissemination of information to member organizations and a forum in which lending institutions can communicate with borrowing countries, multilateral organizations and regulators, in order to improve the processs of international lending. Members include commercial banks from developed and developing countries. Associate members include development banks, central banks, export credit agencies and multinational corporations. Membership: $6,000/yr. (full), $15,000/yr. (associate).
Publications:
Brochure. a.
Newsletter. q.
Semi-Annual Meetings: Usually at Washington, DC headquarters

Institute of Judicial Administration (1952)
One Washington Square Village, New York NY 10012
Director: Margaret L. Shaw
Members: 900-1,000 *Staff:* 10-15
Annual Budget: $500-1,000,000 *Tel:* (212) 598-7721
Hist. Note: Founded by Arthur T. Vanderbilt in 1952 at the New York University Law Center. Members are judges, lawyers and others concerned with improving the operation of the court system.
Annual Meetings: October

Institute of Makers of Explosives (1913)
1120 19th St., N.W., Suite 310, Washington DC 20036
President: Frederick P. Smith, Jr.
Members: 22 companies *Staff:* 2-5
Annual Budget: $500-1,000,000 *Tel:* (202) 429-9280
Hist. Note: Members are U.S. and Canadian producers of commercial explosives. Sponsors the Explosive Manufacturers Political Action Committee.
Publication:
Publications List Available.
Annual Meetings: Spring
1987-Phoenix, AZ(Biltmore)/May 20-22/90

Institute of Management Consultants (1968)
19 West 44th St., New York NY 10036
Exec. Director: John F. Hartshorne, CAE
Members: 1,700 individuals *Staff:* 6-10
Annual Budget: $250-500,000 *Tel:* (212) 921-2885
Hist. Note: Awards the "CMC" (Certified Management Consultant) designation. Membership: $300/yr.
Publication:
Newsletter. irreg.
Annual Meetings: March

Institute of Management Sciences, The (1953)
290 Westminster St., Providence RI 02903
Exec. Director: Mary R. DeMelim
Members: 6,500-7,000 individuals *Staff:* 6-10
Annual Budget: $500-1,000,000 *Tel:* (401) 274-2525
Hist. Note: Founded in 1953 and incorporated in California. Affiliated with the American Ass'n for the Advancement of Science, Conference Board of the Mathematical Sciences, Internat'l Statistical Institute and the Nat'l Academy of Sciences. Promotes the understanding and practice of management. Membership: $36/yr. (individual); $90/yr. (corporate).
Publications:
Interfaces. bi-m. adv.
Management Science. m. adv.
Marketing Science. q. adv.
Mathematics of Operations Research. q. adv.
OR/MS Today. bi-m.
Semi-annual Meetings: Spring and Fall
1987-New Orleans, LA/Spring and St. Louis, MO/Fall
1988-Washington, DC/Spring and Denver, CO/Fall

Institute of Mathematical Statistics (1935)
Division of Statistics, University of California, Davis CA 95616
Exec. Secretary: Francisco Samaniego
Members: 3,000 *Staff:* 2-5
Annual Budget: $100-250,000 *Tel:* (916) 752-2361
Hist. Note: Established September 12, 1935 during the joint meeting of the American Mathematical Soc. and the Mathematical Ass'n of America in Ann Arbor. Member of the Conference Board of the Mathematical Sciences, and the Allied Social Science Ass'ns.
Publications:
Annals of Probability. q. adv.
Annals of Statistics. q. adv.
Institute of Mathematical Statistics Bulletin. bi-m. adv.
Statistical Science. q. adv.
Annual Meetings: Summer
1987-San Francisco, CA/Aug. 17-20
1988-Ft. Collins, CO/Aug. 8-11
1989-Washington, DC/Aug.

Institute of Medicine (1970)
2101 Constitution Ave., N.W., Washington DC 20418
President: Samuel O. Thier, M.D.
Members: 600-700 *Staff:* 50
Annual Budget: $2-5,000,000 *Tel:* (202) 334-3300
Hist. Note: Private membership organization established in 1970 under the charter of the National Academy of Sciences to address issues associated with public policies for the advancement of human health.
Publication:
IOM Newsletter.
Annual Meetings: October in Washington, D.C.

Institute of Nautical Archaeology (1973)
Drawer AU, College Station TX 77840
President: Dr. Don Frey
Members: 850-900 *Staff:* 6-10
Annual Budget: $1-2,000,000 *Tel:* (409) 845-6694
Hist. Note: Originally called the American Institute of Nautical Archaeology. Members are specialists in underwater archaeological excavation. Affiliated with Texas A. & M.
Publication:
Newsletter. q.

Institute of Navigation (1945)
815 15th St., N.W., Suite 832, Washington DC 20005
Exec. Director: Frank B. Brady
Members: 3,000 *Staff:* 2-5
Annual Budget: $100-250,000 *Tel:* (202) 783-4121
Hist. Note: Members are individuals interested in advancing the science of navigation on land, air and sea. Membership: $24/year (individual), $120-360/year (organization).
Publication:
Navigation. q. adv.
Semi-annual Meetings: Winter and Summer
1987-Anaheim, CA/Jan. 20-22/200
1987-Dayton, OH/June 23-25/150

Institute of Newspaper Controllers and Finance Officers (1947)
Hist. Note: Became Internat'l Newspaper Financial Executives in 1984.

Institute of Noise Control Engineering (1971)
Box 3206, Arlington Branch, Poughkeepsie NY 12603
Chairman, Administrative Committee: G.C. Maling, Jr.
Members: 7 companies, 1,300 individuals
Annual Budget: $100-250,000 *Tel:* (914) 462-4006
Hist. Note: Incorporated in Washington, DC, INCE is a non-profit professional organization concerned with the advancement of noise control technology with particular emphasis on engineering solutions to environmental noise problems. Membership: $50/year.
Publications:
Noise Control Engineering Journal. bi-m. adv.
Noise/News. bi-m.
Annual Meetings: June/July
1987-University Park, PA/June/300

Institute of Nuclear Materials Management (1958)
60 Revere Drive, Suite 500, Northbrook IL 60062
Exec. Director: John E. Messervey
Members: 800 *Staff:* 2-5
Annual Budget: $250-500,000 *Tel:* (312) 480-9080
Hist. Note: Individuals and companies concerned with the managing and safeguarding of nuclear materials. Membership: $45/yr.
Publications:
Journal. q. adv.
Proceedings. a.
Annual Meetings: Summer
1987-Newport Beach, CA(Marriott)/July 12-15/550

Institute of Nuclear Power Operations (1979)
1100 Circle 75 Parkway, Atlanta GA 30339
President: Zack T. Pate
Members: 100-125 companies *Staff:* 400
Annual Budget: over $5,000,000 *Tel:* (404) 953-3600
Hist. Note: Established in late 1979, incorporated in Delaware, to strengthen nuclear power plant construction quality and operational safety. Members are electric utilities owning a share in a nuclear power plant, operating one, or holding a license to construct one.
Publications:
Review. q.
Impact. m.

Institute of Paper Chemistry (1929)
1043 East South River St., Appleton WI 54912
President: Richard A. Matula
Members: 50 manufacturers of pulp, paper, or paperboard
Staff: 200-225
Annual Budget: over $5,000,000 *Tel:* (414) 734-9251
Hist. Note: Affiliated with Lawrence University, IPC is an educational research center for manufacturers of pulp paper. Has an annual budget of $11,000,000
Publication:
Abstract Bulletin. m.
Annual Meetings: Spring

Institute of Real Estate Management (1933)
430 North Michigan Ave., Chicago IL 60611
Exec. V. President: Ronald Vukas
Members: 7,000 *Staff:* 60-70
Annual Budget: over $5,000,000 *Tel:* (312) 661-1930
Hist. Note: A professional society of real estate managers affiliated with the Nat'l Ass'n of Realtors, it awards the Certified Property Manager (CPM), Accredited Resident Manager (ARM) and Accredited Management Organization (AMO) designations. Has an annual budget of approximately $6 million.
Publication:
Journal of Property Management. bi-m. adv.
Annual Meetings: Fall with the Nat'l Ass'n of Realtors

Institute of Scrap Iron and Steel (1928)
1627 K St., N.W., Suite 700, Washington DC 20006
Exec. Director: Dr. Herschel Cutler
Members: 1,300 companies *Staff:* 15
Annual Budget: $1-2,000,000 *Tel:* (202) 466-4050
Hist. Note: Established in New York City on March 17, 1928 as the Eastern Scrap Iron Association by 21 charter member scrap processors. Membership today comprises processors, brokers, suppliers and consumers. Assumed its present name the same year. Sponsors the Institute of Scrap Iron and Steel Political Action Committee.
Publications:
Facts. a.
ISIS Report. bi-w.
Phoenix Quarterly. q.
Annual Meetings:
1987-Las Vegas/Jan.

Institute of Shortening and Edible Oils (1932)
1750 New York Ave., N.W., Washington DC 20006
President: Robert M. Reeves
Members: 20 *Staff:* 2-5
Annual Budget: $100-250,000 *Tel:* (202) 783-7960
Hist. Note: Formerly the Institute of Shortening Manufacturers.
Publications:
Food Fats and Oils. quinquennial.
Treatment of Waste Water from Food Oil Plants. quinquennial.
Directory of Edible Oil Industry in the U.S. quinquennial.
Annual Meetings: Late Winter/Early Spring
1987-Phoenix, AZ/March
1988-Boca Raton, FL/March

Institute of Store Planners (1961)
211 West 43rd St., Suite 301, New York NY 10017
Internat'l President: Ronald Lubben
Members: 1,200
Annual Budget: $100-250,000 *Tel:* (212) 867-4876
Hist. Note: Members are store planners and designers, visual merchandisers, educators, as well as contractors and suppliers to the industry. Membership: $100/yr. (professional); $200/yr. (trade)
Publication:
ISP Newsletter. q.

00149 12 05 86 1233

Institute of Surplus Dealers (1947)
Hist. Note: Ceased operations in the summer of 1982.

Institute of Tax Consultants (1980)
Hist. Note: Incorporated in the state of Washington in 1980, the Institute is the certifying board for the National Association of Income Tax Practitioners.

Institute of the Ironworking Industry (1977)
1750 New York Ave., N.W., Washington DC 20006
Exec. Director: John J. McMahon
Members: 35 organizations *Staff:* 2-5
Annual Budget: $250-500,000 *Tel:* (202) 783-3998
Hist. Note: Began operations on April 4, 1977 as the joint creation of the Iron Workers Employers Ass'n of Washington, DC and the Internat'l Ass'n of Bridge, Structural and Ornamental Iron Workers (AFL-CIO). Co-partipants are 37 regional associations of steel fabricators and erectors. The Institute was formed to enhance the development of the Ironworking industry; its mission is, in part, "to assist workers and employers in the Ironworking Industry in solving problems of mutual concern not susceptible to resolution within the collective bargaining process; to study and explore ways of eliminating potential problems which reduce competitiveness and inhibit the economic development of the industry."
Semi-annual Meetings: June and November

Institute of Transportation Engineers (1930)
525 School St., S.W., Suite 410, Washington DC 20024
Exec. Director: Thomas W. Brahms
Members: 7,700 *Staff:* 11
Annual Budget: $1-2,000,000 *Tel:* (202) 554-8050
Hist. Note: Founded in Pittsburgh in 1930 and incorporated in 1954 in Connecticut as the Institute of Traffic Engineers; assumed its present name in 1976. Members are individual professionals responsible for planning, designing, and operating surface transportation facilities.
Publication:
ITE Journal. m. adv.
Annual Meetings: Aug./Sept.
1987-New York, NY/Aug. 16-20
1988-Vancouver, BC/Sept. 24-28
1989-San Diego, CA/Sept. 17-21
1990-Orlando, FL/Aug. 12-16
1991-Milwaukee, WI/Sept. 22-26

Institute on Religion in an Age of Science (1954)
Lutheran School of Theology at Chicago, 1100 E. 55th St., Chicago IL 60615
President: Philip Hefner
Members: 330
Annual Budget: $10-25,000 *Tel:* (312) 753-0764
Hist. Note: IRAS aims to understand, interpret, and advance in the light of the sciences and critical scholarship the continuing functions of evolving religion that guide humanity's relation to the ultimate conditions of its destiny. Member of the Council on the Study of Religion. Affiliate Society of the American Ass'n for the Advancement of Science.
Publications:
IRAS Newsletter. irreg.
Zygon, Journal of Religion and Science. q. adv.
Annual Meetings: Always Star Island, NH in July/200

Institutional and Municipal Parking Congress (1954)
904 Princess Anne St., #303, Fredericksburg VA 22401
Exec. Director: David L. Ivey
Members: 7-800 *Staff:* 2-5
Annual Budget: $250-500,000 *Tel:* (703) 371-7535
Hist. Note: Formerly known as the Internat'l Municipal Parking Congress; until 1956 IMPC was a branch of the National League of Cities. Members are cities, colleges, hospitals, airports, port authorities, civic centers, state/federal government agencies and others concerned with parking, as well as suppliers and consultants. Membership: $175-270/yr.
Publications:
Parking Professional. m. adv.
Who's Who in Parking Yearbook. a.
Parking Buyers Guide. a. adv.
Annual Meetings: Spring/500
1987-Miami, FL/April 27-May 2
1988-San Francisco, CA/June 4-9

Institutional and Service Textile Distributors Ass'n (1944)
93 Standish Road, Hillsdale NJ 07642-1110
Exec. Secretary: Bernard J. Ellis
Members: 20 companies *Staff:* 2-5
Annual Budget: $25-50,000 *Tel:* (201) 664-4600
Hist. Note: Members are wholesale distributors of textiles to hospitality and health care industries such as hospitals, hotels, railroads, nursing homes and restaurants. Membership: $500/yr. minimum, based on sales.
Semi-Annual Meetings: New York, NY(Sheraton Russell)/April & Oct./25
1987-New York, NY(Union League Club)/Jan. 13/150

Institutional Carpet Maintenance Council (1971)
Hist. Note: A division of the Ass'n of Specialists in Ccleaning and Restoration.

Instrument Contracting and Engineering Ass'n (1986)
P.O. Box 42558, Northwest Station, Washington DC 20015
Exec. Director: Walter M. Kardy
Members: 30 companies *Staff:* 1-2
Annual Budget: $25-50,000 *Tel:* (301) 933-7430
Hist. Note: A group of contractors which install automated controls and controls for robotics in power stations and other heavy industrial installations. Incorporated in Washington, DC. Membership: $1,500/yr.
Annual Meetings: Spring

Instrument Soc. of America (1945)
67 Alexander Dr., Box 12277, Research Triangle Pk NC 27709
Exec. Director: Glenn F. Harvey
Members: 40,000 *Staff:* 101
Annual Budget: over $5,000,000 *Tel:* (919) 549-8411
Hist. Note: Founded in Pittsburgh on April 28, 1945 by representatives of 18 local instrument societies from the U.S. and Canada. Incorporated the same year in Pennsylvania. A charter member of the American Automatic Control Council, an affiliate of the American Institute of Physics, member of the American Federation of Information Processing Societies, member of the American Nat'l Standards Institute and U.S. representative to the Internat'l Measurement Confederation. Has a budget of approximately $14 million. Membership: $35/yr.
Publications:
InTech. m. adv.
Programmable Controls. m. adv.
ISA Transactions. q.
ISA Directory of Instrumentation. a.
ISA Proceedings. a.
Annual Meetings: Fall/25,000
1987-Anaheim, CA(Convention Ctr.)/Oct. 5-8
1988-Houston, TX(Astrohall)/Oct. 17-20
1989-Philadelphia, PA(Civic Ctr.)/Oct. 23-26
1990-New Orleans, LA(Convention Ctr.)/Oct. 15-18
1991-Anaheim, CA(Convention Ctr.)/Oct. 28-31

Instrumentation and Measurement Soc.
Hist. Note: A subsidiary of the Institute of Electrical and Electronics Engineers. Membership in the Society, open only to IEEE members, includes subscription to a technical periodical in the field published by IEEE. All administrative support is provided by IEEE.

Insulated Cable Engineers Ass'n (1925)
Box P, South Yarmouth MA 02664
Secy.-Treas.: Edward McIlveen
Members: 105 *Staff:* 2
Annual Budget: $50-100,000 *Tel:* (617) 394-4424
Hist. Note: A professional society of individuals developing standards to promote the reliability of insulated wire and cable. Formerly (until 1979) known as the Insulated Power Cable Engineers Ass'n, Inc. Membership: $1,300/yr.
Publication:
Publications List Available.
Annual Meetings: September/50-60
1987-Niagara-on-the-Lake(Pillar & Post)/Sept. 22-25
1988-Williamsburg, VA(Hospitality House)/Sept. 15-18
1989-Atlanta, GA(Calloway Gardens)/Sept. 27-30

Insulated Steel Door Systems Institute (1975)
712 Lakewood Center North, 14600 Detroit Ave., Cleveland OH 44107
Mng. Director: Allen P. Wherry
Members: 6 companies *Staff:* 2-5
Tel: (216) 226-7700
Hist. Note: Members are producers of insulated steel door systems.

Insulation Contractors Ass'n of America (1977)
15819 Crabbs Branch Way, Rockville MD 20855
Exec. Director: R. Hartley Edes
Members: 300 companies *Staff:* 2-5
Annual Budget: $250-500,000 *Tel:* (301) 926-3083
Hist. Note: Incorporated in the District of Columbia in December 1977, with 32 charter members. Residential and commercial insulation contractors and suppliers.
Publications:
Member Bulletin. Bi-m.
ICAA News. m.
Annual Meetings: September/500
1987-Washington,DC(Marriott Crystal Gateway Hotel)/Oct. 7-9

Insurance Accounting and Systems Ass'n (1928)
Box 8857, Durham NC 27707
Secy.-Treas.: Elaine S. Powell
Members: 1,600-1,700 companies *Staff:* 2-5
Annual Budget: $500-1,000,000 *Tel:* (919) 683-2356
Hist. Note: Formed as the Insurance Accounting and Statistical Ass'n, Inc. at a meeting of representatives of 8 Illinois and Indiana life insurance companies at Peoria, IL on April 14, 1928. Adopted the name Insurance Accounting and Systems Ass'n, Inc. in 1983. The IASA serves life, property and liability, reinsurance and health care companies through the study, research, and development of modern insurance theory, practice, and procedures.
Publications:
Interpreter. m.
Proceedings. a.
Year Book. a.
Annual Meetings: May or June
1987-Chicago, IL(Hyatt)
1988-San Antonio, TX(Marriott)
1989-Toronto, Ontario(Sheraton Center)
1990-Anaheim, CA(Hilton)
1991-Nashville, TN(Opryland)
1992-Dallas, TX(Loews Anatole)
1994-Atlanta, GA(Marriott Marquis)

Insurance Advertising Conference
Hist. Note: Became the Insurance Marketing Communications Association in 1984.

Insurance Company Education Directors Soc. (1953)
Hist. Note: Became the Soc. of Insurance Trainers and Educators in 1985.

Insurance Conference Planners (1958)
Minnesota Mutual Life, 400 N. Robert St., St. Paul MN 55101
Exec. Officer: Robert D. Lewis, Jr.
Members: 300-400 individuals *Staff:* 1
Annual Budget: under $10,000 *Tel:* (612) 298-3882
Hist. Note: Established as the Insurance Convention Planners, it assumed its present name in 1976. Membership: $50/year.
Annual Meetings: November
1987-Palm Springs, CA(Marriott Desert Springs)/Nov. 3-6/150

Insurance Crime Prevention Institute (1971)
15 Franklin St., Westport CT 06880
Exec. Director: Wendall C. Harness
Members: 300-350 *Staff:* 125
Annual Budget: $2-5,000,000 *Tel:* (203) 226-6347
Hist. Note: Formerly the Casualty Insurance Fraud Ass'n. Members are insurance companies interested in the detection, prevention and prosecution of fraud.
Publication:
ICPI Report. bi-m.
Annual Meetings: June

Insurance Economics Soc. of America (1917)
1700 Pennsylvania Ave., N.W., Suite 590, Washington DC 20006
President-Mng. Director: John B. O'Day
Members: 100 insurance companies *Staff:* 2-5
Annual Budget: $100-250,000 *Tel:* (202) 393-2541
Hist. Note: Formed to oppose the proliferation of state and federal social insurance laws.
Publication:
Insurance Economics Surveys. m.

Insurance Industry Meetings Ass'n (1980)
2330 S. Brentwood Blvd., St. Louis MO 63144-2076
Vice President: Victor V. Viator
Members: 470 *Staff:* 2-5
Tel: (314) 961-2300
Hist. Note: Members are state and regional insurance companies and insurance company communications representatives. Conducts seminars on insurance practices and serves as an industry clearinghouse.
Publication:
Alert Bulletin. w.
Annual Meetings: Fall
1987-Las Vegas, NV/Nov. 3-6
1988-Victoria, BC/Nov. 1-5

Insurance Information Institute (1959)
110 William St., New York NY 10038
President: Mechlin D. Moore
Members: 300 companies *Staff:* 80
Annual Budget: over $5,000,000 *Tel:* (212) 669-9200
Hist. Note: An ass'n of property and casualty insurance companies whose primary activities include public education, information dissemination and bestowal of leadership awards. Maintains library and bibliographic data base, as well as a toll-free consumer hotline: (800) 221-4954.
Publications:
Journal of Insurance. bi-m.
Executive Letter. w.
Insurance Facts. a.
Insurance Review. m. adv.
Annual Meetings: Winter
1987-New York, NY(The Plaza)/Jan. 13-14

Insurance Institute for Highway Safety (1959)
Watergate 600, Washington DC 20037
President: Brian O'Neill
Members: 3 trade ass'ns and several companies *Staff:* 60
Annual Budget: over $5,000,000 *Tel:* (202) 333-0770
Hist. Note: An independent non-profit research and communications organization working to reduce property losses, deaths and injuries on the nation's highways. Supported by the American Insurance Highway Safety Ass'n, the American Insurers Highway Safety Alliance, the Nat'l Ass'n of Independent Insurers Safety Ass'n and several unaffiliated property and casualty insurance companies.
Publication:
Status Report. bi-w.

Insurance Institute of America (1909)
Hist. Note: Not a trade association. The educational arm of the American Institute for Property and Liability Underwriters.

00150 12 05 86 1233

Insurance Loss Control Ass'n (1932)
2425 E. Grand River Ave., Lansing MI 48912
Secretary: Jack Thomas
Members: 400 *Staff:* 1
Annual Budget: under $10,000 *Tel:* (517) 482-6211
Hist. Note: Established as the Ass'n of Mutual Fire Insurance Engineers, it became the Ass'n of Mutual Insurance Engineers in 1968 and assumed its present name in 1980.
Publication:
HELP Newsletter. q.

Insurance Marketing Communications Ass'n (1923)
175 West Jackson Blvd., Room A-1251, Chicago IL 60604
Exec. Director: C.F. Scheer
Members: 300-400 *Staff:* 1
Annual Budget: $100-250,000 *Tel:* (312) 427-6618
Hist. Note: Members represent mutual, stock and direct writer, property and casualty insurance companies. Formerly the Insurance Advertising Conference. Assumed its present name in 1984. Membership: $300/yr.
Publications:
Ad-Talk. bi-m.
Membership Roster. a.
Up-Date. bi-m.
Semi-annual meetings: January and June
1987-Coronado, CA(del Coronado)/Jan. 18-21
1987-Hyannis, MA(Dunfey's)/June 21-24
1988-Charleston, SC(Omni)/Jan. 24-27
1988-Vail, CO(Marriott's Mark Resort)/June 26-29

Insurance Workers Internat'l Union (1959)
Hist. Note: Merged with United Food and Commercial Workers Union as its Insurance Division in late 1983.

Intellectual Property Owners (1972)
1255 Twenty-Third St., N.W., Suite 850, Washington DC 20037
Exec. Director: Herbert C. Wamsley
Members: 125-150 *Staff:* 2
Annual Budget: $250-500,000 *Tel:* (202) 466-2396
Hist. Note: Holders of patents, trademarks and copyrights. Primary concern is to strengthen patent, trademark and copyright laws as an increased incentive for innovation and creativity. Membership: $150/yr. (individual); $250-7,500/yr. (institution).
Publication:
Newsletter. m.
Annual Meetings: January
1987-Ft. Lauderdale, FL/Jan. 19-20

Inter-American Bar Ass'n (1940)
1889 F St., N.W., Suite 450, Washington DC 20006-4499
Secy. General: John O. Dahlgren
Members: 3,000 *Staff:* 2-5
Annual Budget: $100-250,000 *Tel:* (202) 789-2747
Hist. Note: Founded in 1940 by a group of jurists and lawers representing 44 professional organizations throughout 17 nations of the Western hemisphere to fill the need for an unbiased and professional forum for the discussion of comparative law. Membership: $30/yr.(Junior); $50/yr.(Senior).
Publications:
Newsletter. q.
Proceedings. bi-a.
Annual Meetings:
1987-Buenos Aires/April 4-10/500

Inter-Financial Ass'n (1983)
21 Tamal Vista Blvd., Corte Madera CA 94925
Admin. Director: Nancy H. Norelli
Members: 350 individuals *Staff:* 2
Annual Budget: $50-100,000 *Tel:* (415) 924-1930
Hist. Note: Founded in 1983 to meet the professional needs of financial executives in a deregulated environment, the Inter-Financial Ass'n is a multi-industry national trade ass'n for the financial services industry. Members are from banks, savings and loans, the securities and investment field, insurance companies, credit unions, and suppliers to these companies. IFA sponsors about 30 educational conferences every year across the nation. Membership: $145/yr.
Publication:
IFA Newsletter. q.

Inter-Industry Conference on Auto Collision Repair (1979)
2600 River Road, Des Plaines IL 60018
Exec. V. President: Jeffrey N. Silver
Members: 75 *Staff:* 8
Annual Budget: $1-2,000,000 *Tel:* (312) 699-1670
Hist. Note: Founded in 1979 when the collision repair and insurance industries realized that the new generation of fuel efficient cars required new repair technology. Members are major auto manufacturers, insurance companies, auto collision repair shops, tool, equipment, and supply manufacturers and related industry and trade associations.
Annual Meetings: Summer

Inter-Society Color Council (1931)
U.S. Army Natick R&D Center, STRNC-ITC, Natick MA 01760-5019
Secretary: Therese R. Commerford
Members: 700 individuals, 28 organizations *Staff:* 2-5
Annual Budget: $10-25,000 *Tel:* (617) 651-5469
Hist. Note: Members are concerned with the standards, descriptions and specifications of color and their application to color problems. Established December 29, 1931 at the Museum of Science and Industry in New York City. Membership: $20/yr.(individual); $100/yr.(organization)
Publication:
ISCC News. bi-m.
Annual Meetings: Spring
1987-Philadelphia, PA(Barclay Hotel)/April 5-7/150-250
1988-Baltimore, MD
1989-Chicago, IL

Intercoiffure America (1915)
540 Robert E. Lee Blvd., New Orleans LA 70124
President: John Jay
Members: 180-190 companies *Staff:* 2-5
Annual Budget: $50-100,000 *Tel:* (504) 282-4907
Hist. Note: Formerly (1966) Internat'l des Coiffures de Dames Members are beauty salon owners. Has no permanent address or staff; the President serves two years.
Semi-annual Meetings: Spring and Fall in New York, NY

Intercollegiate Broadcasting System (1940)
3107 Westover Dr., S.E., Washington DC 20020
V. Chairman: Dr. George Abraham
Members: 7-800
Annual Budget: $100-250,000 *Tel:* (202) 582-7210
Hist. Note: College and university broadcasting stations.
Publications:
Journal of College Radio. irreg.
Newsletter. bi-m.
Annual Meetings: March
1987-New York, NY

Intercollegiate Musical Council, The Nat'l Ass'n of Male Choruses (1915)
Loyola Marymount Univ., West 80th and Loyola Blvd., Los Angeles CA 90045
Exec. Secretary: Fr. Richard H. Trame, S. J.
Members: 55 *Staff:* 1
Annual Budget: under $10,000 *Tel:* (213) 642-2780
Hist. Note: Promotes research, publication and production of quality music for male choruses. Moribund during and after World War II, the Council was revived in 1952; annual seminars have been held since 1954. Membership: $30/yr.(minimum)
Publication:
Quodlibet (Newsletter). 3/yr.
Annual Meetings: With the American Choral Directors Association
1987-San Antonio, TX(Hyatt Regency)/March 12-14

Intercollegiate Tennis Coaches Ass'n (1957)
Box 71, Princeton NJ 08544
Exec. Director: David A. Benjamin
Members: 1,200 *Staff:* 3
Annual Budget: $250-500,000 *Tel:* (609) 452-6332
Hist. Note: Formerly (1976) Nat'l Collegiate Tennis Coaches Ass'n. Sponsors a number of national championship; administers a complex and comprehensive ranking system for teams, singles and doubles; and awards honors to players and coaches. Membership: $75/year.
Publication:
Newsletter. m.

Interfaith Forum on Religion, Art and Architecture (1978)
1777 Church St., N.W., Washington DC 20036
Exec. Director: Tish Kendig
Members: 650 *Staff:* 1
Annual Budget: $50-100,000 *Tel:* (202) 387-8333
Hist. Note: Affiliated with the American Institute of Architects. Formed by a merger of the Guild for Religious Architecture, the American Soc. of Church Architects and the Nat'l Commission on Church Planning. The membership includes manufacturers, suppliers, architects and administrators of church buildings.
Publication:
Faith & Form. semi-a. adv.
Biennial Meetings: Even Years
1988-Houston, TX

Interior Design Educators Council (1962)
Design and Environmental Analysis, Cornell University, Ithaca NY 14853-4401
Corresp. Secretary: Paul Eschelman
Members: 400
Annual Budget: $10-25,000 *Tel:* (607) 255-3165
Hist. Note: Members are teachers of interior design in colleges and universities in the U.S. and Canada. Has no paid staff.
Publications:
The Journal of Interior Design Education and Research. semi-a.
IDEC Record. q.
Annual Meetings: April
1987-San Diego, CA

Interior Design Soc. (1973)
220 West Gerry Lane, Wood Dale IL 60191
Exec. Director: Faye Foley
Members: 2,500-3,000 individuals, 350-500 companies *Staff:* 2-5
Annual Budget: $100-250,000 *Tel:* (312) 595-0200
Hist. Note: Affiliated with the Nat'l Home Furnishings Ass'n.

Interior Plantscape Ass'n
Hist. Note: A division of the Associated Landscape Contractors of America.

Intermarket Ass'n of Advertising Agencies (1967)
1605 North Main St., Dayton OH 45405
President: Walter Ohlmann
Members: 22 companies
Annual Budget: under $10,000 *Tel:* (513) 278-0681
Hist. Note: Founded in 1967 as a network for small to medium agencies, the organization is comprised primarily of shops ranging from $2-15 million in billings.
Publication:
Newsletter. m.
Semi-annual meetings: Winter and Summer/25

Intermodal Transportation Ass'n (1981)
6410 Kenilworth Ave., Suite 108, Riverdale MD 20737
Exec. Director: Albert J. Mascaro
Members: 450-500 *Staff:* 6-10
Annual Budget: $250-500,000 *Tel:* (301) 864-2661
Hist. Note: Formed in 1981 by an ad-hoc committee of the Equipment Interchange Ass'n, ITA is an autonomous association. Members are air, motor, rail and water transportation companies and allied services united to establish standard practices for interchange of trailers and containers between companies doing business with one another. Membership: $150/yr.
Publication:
Newsletter. m.
Semi-annual Meetings: Spring and Fall

Internat'l Academy of Metabology (1971)
Hist. Note: Address unknown in 1985-86.

Internat'l Academy of Myodontics (1970)
Hist. Note: Address unknown in 1985-86; probably defunct.

Internat'l Academy of Pathology (U.S.-Canadian Div.) (1906)
Bldg. C, Suite B, 3515 Wheeler Road, Augusta GA 30909
Secy.-Treas.: Nathan Kaufman, M.D.
Members: 4,400-4,500 *Staff:* 2-5
Annual Budget: $500-1,000,000 *Tel:* (404) 733-7550
Hist. Note: Formerly Internat'l Ass'n of Medical Museums. Membership: $75/yr.
Publication:
Laboratory Investigation. m. adv.
Annual Meetings: February or March/2,000
1987-Chicago, IL(Palmer House)/March 7-13
1988-Washington, DC(Hilton)/Feb. 27-Mar. 4
1989-San Francisco, CA(Hilton)/March 4-10
1990-Boston, MA(Sheraton)/March 3-9
1991-Chicago, IL(Hyatt Regency)/March 16-22
1992-Orlando, FL(Marriott's World Ctr.)/March 14-20

Internat'l Academy of Preventive Medicine (1971)
P.O. Box 5832, Lincoln NE 68505
Exec. Director: Carroll Thompson
Members: 600 physicians, 1,300 lay people *Staff:* 2
Annual Budget: $100-250,000 *Tel:* (402) 467-2716
Hist. Note: Founded in 1971 and incorporated in the State of Texas. A main area of concern of the Academy is reducing the increasing incidence of chronic degenerative diseases through professional and public education.
Publications:
Journal of The Internat'l Academy of Preventive Medicine. q. adv.
Your Health. bi-m. adv.

Internat'l Academy of Proctology (1948)
1203 Hadley Road, Morresville IN 46158
Exec. Officer: Dr. George A. Donnally
Members: 900 *Staff:* 2-5
Annual Budget: $25-50,000 *Tel:* (317) 831-9300
Hist. Note: Members are specialists in diseases of the colon.
Publications:
American Journal of Proctology, Gastroenterology, Colon and Rectal
Surgery. m. adv.
Annual Meetings: Spring

Internat'l Academy of Trial Lawyers (1954)
210 South First St., San Jose CA 95113
Exec. Secretary: Barbara V. Laskin
Members: 475-500 *Staff:* 2
Annual Budget: $100-250,000 *Tel:* (408) 275-6767
Hist. Note: Members are defense and plaintiff attorneys who have had a minimum of 12 years of appellate practice. Membership: $500/yr.
Publications:
IATL Bulletin. semi-a.
Student Advocacy Report. a.
Annual Meetings: Spring/150
1987-Laguna Niguel, CA(Ritz Carlton)/Feb. 18-22
1988-Boca Raton, FL(Boca Raton Club)/March 2-6

Internat'l Agricultural Aviation Foundation (1978)
405 Main Street, Mount Vernon WA 98273
Exec. Secretary: Tom J. Wood
Members: 2,643 *Staff:* 5
Annual Budget: $100-250,000 *Tel:* (509) 522-4311
Hist. Note: Pilots and aircraft owners licensed by the FAA as agricultural aviators (crop dusters). Membership: $68/yr.
Publications:
IAAF Newsletter.
AG-Pilot Internat'l Magazine.
Annual Meetings: December
1987-Mobile, AL/Dec. 2-5/3,000

00151 12 05 86 1233

Internat'l Airforwarders and Agents Ass'n (1950)
310 Swann Ave., Alexandria VA 22301
Exec. Director: Robert Binder
Members: 100 *Staff:* 2-5
Annual Budget: $25-50,000 *Tel:* (202) 463-4800
Hist. Note: Formerly (1978) Internat'l Airfreight Agents Ass'n. Members are air cargo agents and air freight forwarders.
Publication:
Update. semi-m.
Annual Meetings: June

Internat'l Alliance of Theatrical Stage Employees and Moving Picture Machine Operators of the U.S. & Ca (1893)
1515 Broadway, Suite 601, New York NY 10036
President: Alfred W. DiTolla
Members: 65,000 *Staff:* 25-30
Annual Budget: $2-5,000,000 *Tel:* (212) 730-1770
Hist. Note: Established in New York City on July 20, 1893 as the Alliance of Theatrical Stage Employees of the United States and chartered by the American Federation of Labor in 1894. In 1899, with the acceptance of two Canadian locals, the words "and Canada" were added, and in 1902 "International" was subsituted for "National." When the union was granted jurisdiction over motion picture projectionists in 1914, the present name was adopted.
Publication:
Bulletin. q.
Biennial Meetings: Even years in Summer

Internat'l Allied Printing Trades Ass'n (1909)
6025 Chippewa, Room 302, St. Louis MO 63109
Secy.-Treas.: Leo L. Vohsen
Members: 2 labor unions
Annual Budget: over $5,000,000 *Tel:* (314) 353-2248
Hist. Note: Exercises jurisdiction throughout the United States and Canada in regard to the Allied Printing Trades Label. Member unions are the Graphic Communications Internat'l Union and the Internat'l Typographical Union. Adopted and owned by the Association, the label designates the products of the labor of its members.
Publications:
Typographical Journal. m. adv.
Review. m.

Internat'l Anesthesia Research Soc. (1922)
3645 Warrensville Center Rd., Cleveland OH 44122
Exec. Secretary: E. A. Moffitt, M.D.
Members: 14,500 individuals *Staff:* 6-10
Annual Budget: $500-1,000,000 *Tel:* (216) 295-1124
Publication:
Anesthesia and Analgesia. m. adv.
Annual Meetings: Spring
1987-Orlando, FL(Buena Vista Palace)/March 15-19
1988-San Diego, CA(Intercontinental)/March
1989-Orlando, FL(Buena Vista Palace)/March
1990-Honolulu, HI(Sheraton)/March

Internat'l Apple Institute (1970)
Suite 210, 6707 Old Dominion Dr., Box 1137, McLean VA 22101
Exec. V. President: Derl Derr
Members: 24 state organizations; 550 regular members *Staff:* 5
Annual Budget: $500-1,000,000 *Tel:* (703) 442-8850
Hist. Note: Merger of the Internat'l Apple Ass'n (1895) and the Nat'l Apple Institute (1935). Members are growers and handlers. Membership fee based on number of bushels handled.
Publication:
Apple News. bi-m.
Annual Meetings: June
1987-Grand Rapids, MI(Amway Grand Plaza)/June 28-July 1/400
1988-Williamsburg, VA(Fort Magrucer Inn & Conf. Ctr.)/June 24-29

Internat'l Arabian Horse Ass'n (1950)
Box 33696, Denver CO 80233
Exec. V. President: Wayne G. Hipsley
Members: 27,750 *Staff:* 60
Annual Budget: over $5,000,000 *Tel:* (303) 450-4774
Hist. Note: Promotes the Arabian breed. Maintains show records of Arabian horse placings, produces film, videotape and slide presentations, compiles statistics, holds Arabian horse fairs and Nat'l Show Finals annually. Membership: $30/yr.
Annual Meetings: November
1987-Denver, CO/Nov. 5-7
1988-Las Vegas, NV/Nov. 3-5

Internat'l Arthroscopy Ass'n (1974)
70 West Hubbard St., Suite 202, Chicago IL 60610
Exec. Director: Sanford J. Hill
Members: 700 *Staff:* 2-5
Annual Budget: $50-100,000 *Tel:* (312) 644-2623
Hist. Note: Membership, by invitation only, is about 70% American and costs $50/yr.
Publication:
IAA Newsletter. semi-a.
Annual Meetings: Triennial Meetings
1987-Sydney,Australia/April 4-6

Internat'l Ass'n for Aquatic Animal Medicine (1969)
33 Martin Drive, Novato CA 94947
President: Leslie Dierauf
Members: 300-350 *Staff:* 1
Annual Budget: $10-25,000 *Tel:* (415) 642-3785
Hist. Note: Members are veterinarians and marine biologists. Membership: $20/yr. (individuals); $50/yr. (organizations).
Publication:
Newsletter. q. adv.
Annual Meetings: Spring
1987- Monterey, CA(Monterey Bay Aquarium)/May 10-14/300-400

Internat'l Ass'n for Dental Research (1920)
1111 14th St.,N.W., Suite 1000, Washington DC 20005
Exec. Director: Dr. John A. Gray
Members: 7,000 individuals *Staff:* 8
Annual Budget: $100-250,000 *Tel:* (202) 898-1050
Hist. Note: About one half of the members are American. Membership: $82/yr. (U.S. citizen); $22/yr. (foreign without Journal) $49/yr. (foreign with Journal).
Publication:
Journal of Dental Research. m. adv.
Annual Meetings: March, with the American Ass'n of Dental Schools.
1987-Chicago, IL
1988-Montreal, Quebec
1989-Dublin
1989-San Francisco, CA

Internat'l Ass'n for Enterostomal Therapy (1968)
2081 Business Center Drive, Suite 290, Irvine CA 92715
Exec. Director: Fred S. Droz
Members: 40 agencies, 2,000 individuals *Staff:* 3
Annual Budget: $250-500,000 *Tel:* (714) 833-2445
Hist. Note: An ET nurse provides acute and rehabilitative care for people with select disorders of the gastrointestinal, genitourinary, and integumentary systems. Membership: $65/yr. (individual), $100/yr. (agency).
Publication:
Journal of Enterostomal Therapy. bi-m. adv.
Annual Meetings: June
1987-Las Vegas, NV(Caesar's Palace)/June 1-6

Internat'l Ass'n for Financial Planning (1969)
Two Concourse Parkway, Suite 800, Atlanta GA 30328
President: Hubert L. Harris
Members: 25,000 *Staff:* 80
Annual Budget: over $5,000,000 *Tel:* (404) 395-1605
Hist. Note: Established in Denver in 1969. Members work with clients in the areas of personal and business financial planning. Membership includes accountants, lawyers, bankers, stockbrokers, insurance agents, realtors, and others involved with securities, tax-sheltered investments and estate planning. Has an annual budget of approximately $12 million. Membership: $125/yr. (individual), $4,500/yr. (company).
Publications:
Financial Planning Magazine. m. adv.
Financial Planning Newspaper. m. adv.
IAFP Directory of Financial Planning Products & Services. a. adv.
Directory of the Registry of Financial Planning Practitioners. a.
Annual Meetings: Fall/6,000
1987-Atlanta, GA(World Congress Ctr.)/Oct. 5-8
1988-New York, NY
1989-San Francisco, CA

Internat'l Ass'n for Hospital Security (1968)
Box 637, Lombard IL 60148
President: Michael S. Stultz
Members: 1,500 individuals *Staff:* 2-5
Annual Budget: $100-250,000 *Tel:* (312) 953-0990
Hist. Note: An affiliate of the American Hospital Association. Membership: $60/yr.
Publications:
IAHS Newsletter. 5/yr.
Journal of Healthcare Protection Management. 3/yr.
Annual Meetings: June
1987-Washington, DC/June 28-July 2

Internat'l Ass'n for Hydrogen Energy (1975)
Box 248266, Coral Gables FL 33124
President: T. Nejat Veziroglu
Members: 2,500 *Staff:* 2-5
Annual Budget: $50-100,000 *Tel:* (305) 284-4666
Hist. Note: Established at the Hydrogen Economy Miami Energy Conference in Miami in March 1974 and incorporated in Florida in 1975. Members, hailing from 86 countries, are scientists and engineers professionally involved in the development of hydrogen energy. Membership: $45/yr.
Publication:
International Journal of Hydrogen Energy. m. adv.
Annual Meetings: Biennial Meetings; even years.
1988-Moscow, USSR/June 19-24/1,000

Internat'l Ass'n for Identification (1915)
2516 Otis Drive, Alameda CA 94501-6370
Secy.-Treas.: Ashley R. Crooker, Jr.
Members: 2,500 *Staff:* 3
Annual Budget: $50-100,000 *Tel:* (415) 865-2174
Hist. Note: Organized in 1915 in Oakland, CA as the Internat'l Ass'n for Criminal Identification, it assumed its present name in 1920. Absorbed the Internat'l Ass'n for Voice Identification in 1981. Membership consists of persons engaged in identification, investigation and scientific examination of physical evidence. IAI promotes research in forensic sciences and is responsible for two international certification programs for Latent Print Examiners and Voice Print Examiners. Membership: $40/yr.
Publications:
I.A.I. Roster. a. adv.
Identification News. m.
Annual Meetings: Summer
1987-Crystal City, VA(Radisson)/500
1988-California/July 4-11
1989-Pensacola, Fl
1990-Nashville, TN

Internat'l Ass'n for Impact Assessment (1980)
c/o F.A. Rossini, Office of, Interdisciplinary Programs, Georgia Tech, Atlanta GA 30332
Secretary: Alan Porter
Members: 35 companies, 500 individuals
Annual Budget: under $10,000 *Tel:* (404) 894-2330
Hist. Note: Founded and chartered in Atlanta, GA, IAIA is a professional society of those who assess environmental, social and technological impact for both the private and public sectors. Membership: $25/yr. (individual); $50/yr. (institution).
Publication:
Impact Assessment Bulletin. q. adv.
Annual Meetings:
1987-Barbados/May 30-June 4
1988-Nathan, Queensland, Australia/July 2-4/150

Internat'l Ass'n for Learning Laboratories (1965)
Dept. of Modern Languages, Ellis Hall, Ohio University, Athens OH 45701
Exec. Secretary: Charles Richardson
Members: 600
Annual Budget: under $10,000 *Tel:* (614) 594-5622
Hist. Note: Members are involved in the administration or operation of machine aided learning facilities and foreign language programs. Founded as the Nat'l Ass'n of Language Laboratory Directors, it became the Nat'l Ass'n Learning Lab Directors before assuming its present name in 1982. Affiliated with the American Council on the Teaching of Foreign Languages and the Ass'n for Educational Communications and Technology. Membership: $15/yr.
Publications:
NALLD Journal. q. adv.
Membership Directory. a.
Semi-annual:

Internat'l Ass'n for Mathematical Geology (1968)
c/o Kansas Geological Survey, 1930 Constant Ave., Lawrence KS 66046
President: Prof. J.C. Davis
Members: 800
Annual Budget: $25-50,000 *Tel:* (913) 864-4991
Hist. Note: Founded at the XXIII International Geological Congress, Prague, Czechoslovakia in 1968. Professional geologists, mathematicians and others interested in the application and use of mathematics in geological research and technology. Affiliated with the International Statistical Institute and the International Union of Geological Sciences.
Publications:
Computers & Geosciences. bi-m. adv.
Mathematical Geology. 8/yr.
Quadrennial Conventions: With Internat'l Geological Congresses

Internat'l Ass'n for Orthodontics (1961)
211 East Chicago Ave., Suite 915, Chicago IL 60611
Exec. Director: Joanna Carey
Members: 1,500 *Staff:* 2-5
Annual Budget: $250-500,000 *Tel:* (312) 642-2602
Hist. Note: Formerly Internat'l Academy of Orthodontics. A professional society of individuals interested in the treatment and prevention of malocclusion of the teeth. Membership: $95/year.
Publications:
Bandelette. q. adv.
Membership Directory. a.
The Journal.
Annual Meetings: Fall
1987-Orlando, FL(Hyatt)/Sept. 17-20/600
1988-Las Vegas, NV(Caesar's Palace)/Sept. 15-18/600
1989-Montreal, Quebec

Internat'l Ass'n for Personnel Women (1950)
5820 Wilshire Blvd., Suite 500, Los Angeles CA 90036
Exec. Director: Jean Replogle
Members: 2,500 *Staff:* 6-10
Annual Budget: $100-250,000 *Tel:* (213) 937-9000
Hist. Note: Membership: $60/yr.
Publications:
Human Resources: Journal of IAPW. q. adv.
Connections. q.
Annual Meetings: Spring
1987-Princeton, NJ/May 3-6
1988-Los Angeles, CA

Internat'l Ass'n for Shopping Center Security (1981)
2830 Clearview Place, N.E., Suite 300, Atlanta GA 30340
Exec. Director: Anthony N. Potter, Jr.
Members: 550 *Staff:* 2
Annual Budget: $50-100,000 *Tel:* (404) 457-3575
Hist. Note: Members are security directors, developers as well as operations personnel in shopping centers.
Publications:
Security Blanket. m. adv.
Training Bulletin. m.
Annual Meetings: April

00152 12 05 86 1233

Internat'l Ass'n for the Study of Organized Crime (1984)
Saint Xavier College, 3700 W. 103rd St., Chicago IL 60655
President: Howard Abadinsky
Members: 148 individuals *Staff:* 0
Annual Budget: under $10,000 *Tel:* (302) 779-3300
Hist. Note: Researchers, investigators, and educators interested in the study of organized crime. Membership: $15/yr.
Publication:
Update. q.
Annual Meetings: November
1987-Montreal, Canada(LeGrand Hotel)/Nov. 12-13
1988-Chicago, IL(Marriott)/Nov. 10-11

Internat'l Ass'n for the Study of Pain (1973)
909 NE 43rd St., Suite 306, Seattle WA 98105-6020
Exec. Officer: Louisa E. Jones
Members: 2,800 individuals, 6 companies *Staff:* 2
Annual Budget: $250-500,000 *Tel:* (206) 547-6409
Hist. Note: Founded in Seattle, Washington, IASP was incorporated in Washington, DC in 1974. Members are scientists, physicians and other health professionals actively engaged in pain research and those who have a special interest in diagnosis and treatment of pain syndromes. Membership: $50-85/year (individual) varies with income.
Publications:
Pain. m. adv.
IASP Newsletter. bi-m.
Directory. a.
Triennial Meetings:
1987-Hamburg, West Germany(Congress Centrum)/Aug. 2-7/2,500
1990-Adelaide, Australia(Convention Ctr.)

Internat'l Ass'n of Airport Duty Free Stores (1970)
1101 Connecticut Ave., N.W., Suite 700, Washington DC 20036
Exec. Director: Robert T. Chancler
Members: 300 *Staff:* 2-5
Annual Budget: $100-250,000 *Tel:* (202) 857-1184
Hist. Note: Membership: $350/yr.
Publication:
Trademarket Handbook and Membership Directory. a. adv.
Annual Meetings: March
1987-Bal Harbour, FL(Sheraton)/March 29-April 2

Internat'l Ass'n of Amusement Parks and Attractions (1920)
4230 King St., Alexandria VA 22302
Exec. Director and Counsel: John R. Graff
Members: 1,800 *Staff:* 9
Annual Budget: $1-2,000,000 *Tel:* (703) 671-5800
Hist. Note: Formed as Nat'l Ass'n of Amusement Parks, Pools and Beaches through a merger of the Nat'l Ass'n of Amusement Parks and the American Ass'n of Pools and Beaches, it became (1964) the Internat'l Ass'n of Amusement Parks and assumed its present name in 1972. Absorbed the Nat'l Water Slide Ass'n in 1982. Sponsors and supports the Internat'l Ass'n of Amusement Parks and Attractions Political Action Committee.
Publications:
Fun World. m. adv.
Directory and Guide. a. adv.
Annual Meetings: Fall
1987-New Orleans, LA(Exhibition Center)/Nov. 4-7
1988-Dallas, TX(Convention Center)/Nov. 16-19
1989-Atlanta, GA(GA World Congress Ctr.)/Nov. 14-18
1990-Washington, DC(Conv. Center)/Nov. 14-17
1991-Orlando, FL(Civic Center)/Nov. 13-16
1992-Dallas, TX(Conv. Center)/Nov. 18-21
1993-Washington, DC(Conv. Center)/Nov. 17-21
1994-Atlanta, GA(GA World Congress Center)/Nov. 16-19

Internat'l Ass'n of Approved Basketball Officials (1921)
Box 661, West Hartford CT 06107
Exec. Director: Paul Francis, Jr.
Members: 13,000 *Staff:* 2-3
Annual Budget: $250-500,000 *Tel:* (203) 232-7530
Hist. Note: A recruiting and training association for basketball officials. Membership: $15-20/yr.
Publications:
Sportorials. 8/yr.
Basketball Handbook. a.
Semi-annual meetings: Spring and Fall
1987-Baltimore, MD/April 10-12/350
1987-Atlanta, GA/Sept. 11-13/350

Internat'l Ass'n of Arson Investigators (1949)
25 Newton St., Box 600, Marlboro MA 01752
Exec. Secretary: Robert E. May
Members: 7,500 *Staff:* 16-20
Annual Budget: $100-250,000 *Tel:* (617) 481-5977
Hist. Note: Formed at Purdue University by U.S. and Canadian representatives of the insurance industry, fire services and law enforcement agencies. Membership: $25/yr.
Publications:
I.A.A.I. Directory. a.
The Fire and Arson Investigator. q. adv.
Book of Selected Articles for Arson Investigators.
Annual Meetings: Spring
1987-Las Vegas, NV/4-600

Internat'l Ass'n of Assessing Officers (1934)
1313 East 60th St., Chicago IL 60637
Exec. Director: Richard Almy
Members: 8,000 *Staff:* 15-20
Annual Budget: $1-2,000,000 *Tel:* (312) 947-2069
Hist. Note: Formerly (1959) the Nat'l Ass'n of Assessing Officers. Members are professionals involved in the administration of property taxes. Awards the CAE (Certified Evaluater) and RES (Residential Evaluation Specialist) designations. Sponsors numerous educational programs. Membership: $75/yr.
Publications:
Assessment and Valuation Legal Reporter. m.
Assessment Digest. bi-m. adv.
IAAO News Bulletin. m.
Property Tax Information Service. bi-m.
Property Tax Journal. q.
Annual Meetings: Fall/1,500
1987-New Orleans, LA(Marriott)/Sept. 13-16/1,500
1988-Nashville, TN(Opryland)/Sept. 7-10
1989-Fort Worth, TX(Americana & Hyatt)/Sept. 24-27
1990-Montreal, Quebec/Oct. 14-17/1,500

Internat'l Ass'n of Auditorium Managers (1924)
500 North Michigan Ave., Suite 1400, Chicago IL 60611
Exec. Director: Richard L. Bensen
Members: 1,200 *Staff:* 10-12
Annual Budget: $500-1,000,000 *Tel:* (312) 661-1700
Hist. Note: Managers of auditoriums, arenas, convention centers, stadiums and performing arts centers representing the most prominent sports, entertainment and convention facilities. Operates a placement service for managers; sponsors executive development courses in auditorium management. Membership: $225/yr.
Publications:
Facility Manager. q. adv.
IAAM News. m.
Program and Directory. a.
Annual Meetings: July/1,700
1987-Washington, DC(Sheraton Washington)
1988-Nashville, TN(Opryland)
1989-Reno, NV(Convention Center)

Internat'l Ass'n of Auto Theft Investigators (1935)
12416 Feldon St., Wheaton MD 20906
Secretary: Thomas J. Horrigan
Members: 1,500 individuals *Staff:* 1
Tel: (301) 946-1182
Hist. Note: Established and incorporated at the University of Oklahoma in Norman, OK. Active members include local and state police officers and national government agents. Affiliate members are from the insurance industry, car rental firms, and various automobile associations. Membership: $15-$20/yr.
Publications:
APB. q.
Training & Education Bulletin. q.
Seminar Proceedings. a.
Annual Meetings: Fall
1987-Salt Lake City, UT
1988-Galveston, TX

Internat'l Ass'n of Boards of Examiners of Optometry (1919)
5530 Wisconsin Ave., Suite 805, Bethesda MD 20815
Administrator: Jack Feldesman
Members: 300 *Staff:* 1
Annual Budget: under $10,000 *Tel:* (301) 951-6330
Hist. Note: Affiliated with the Federation of Ass'ns of Health Regulatory Boards.
Annual Meetings: With the American Optometric Ass'n

Internat'l Ass'n of Bomb Technicians and Investigators (1973)
Box 6609, Colorado Springs CO 80934
Exec. Administrator: Glenn E. Wilt
Members: 2,800 *Staff:* 2-5
Annual Budget: $100-250,000 *Tel:* (303) 636-2596
Hist. Note: Membership: $40/yr.
Publications:
Newsletter. bi-m.
Directory. a.
Annual Meetings: Spring

Internat'l Ass'n of Book Publishing Consultants
Hist. Note: Inactive since 1985.

Internat'l Ass'n of Bridge, Structural and Ornamental Iron Workers (1896)
1750 New York Ave., N.W., Suite 400, Washington DC 20006
President: Juel D. Drake
Members: 174,000-175,000 *Staff:* 11-15
Annual Budget: over $5,000,000 *Tel:* (202) 383-4800
Hist. Note: Organized in Pittsburgh, PA on February 4, 1896 as the Internat'l Ass'n of Bridge and Structural Iron Workers. Chartered by the American Federation of Labor in 1903. Became the Internat'l Ass'n of Bridge, Structural and Ornamental Iron Workers and Pile Drivers in 1915 and assumed its present name in 1917. Has a budget of about $18 million. Sponsors and supports the Ironworkers Political Action League.
Publication:
The Iron Worker. m.
Annual Meetings: Every 5 years in August (1991).

Internat'l Ass'n of Business Communicators (1970)
870 Market St., Suite 940, San Francisco CA 94102
President: Norman Leaper
Members: 12,200 *Staff:* 24
Annual Budget: $2-5,000,000 *Tel:* (415) 433-3400
Hist. Note: Merger (1970) of the International Council of Industrial Editors (1941), the American Association of Industrial Editors (1938), and Corporate Communicators Canada (1942). Members are communication and public relations professionals working as freelancers and consultants. Membership: $110/yr.
Publication:
Communication World. m. adv.
Annual Meetings: Summer/1,500
1987-London, England/July 13-16
1988-Anaheim, CA(Disneyland)/June 6-9
1989-New Orleans, LA/June 5-8
1990-Vancouver, BC
1991-Washington, DC
1992-San Francisco, CA

Internat'l Ass'n of Campus Law Enforcement Administrators (1958)
638 Prospect Ave., Hartford CT 06105
Exec. Director: Peter Berry
Members: 700-800 institutions *Staff:* 2-5
Annual Budget: $100-250,000 *Tel:* (203) 233-4531
Hist. Note: Formerly Nat'l Ass'n of College and University Security Directors, and (until 1980) Internat'l Ass'n of College and University Security Directors.
Publication:
Campus Law Enforcement Journal. bi-m. adv.
Annual Meetings: June
1987-Boston,MA(Hyatt)/750
1988-Arlington,TX/800

Internat'l Ass'n of Chain Stores - North American Headquarters (1953)
3800 Moore Place, Alexandria VA 22305
North American Representative: Sally Adamy-McMullen
Members: 500 companies *Staff:* 10
Tel: (703) 549-4525
Hist. Note: Provides management research on problems related to food distribution and serves as an international forum where food chain store executives can meet to exchange ideas and information. Membership: $400-2,500/yr. (organization).
Publication:
Quarterly Review
Annual Meetings: June
1987-Cannes

Internat'l Ass'n of Chiefs of Police (1893)
13 Firstfield Road, Gaithersburg MD 20878
Exec. Director: Jerald R. Vaughn
Members: 14,000 *Staff:* 50
Annual Budget: $2-5,000,000 *Tel:* (301) 948-0922
Hist. Note: Formerly (1895) Nat'l Chiefs of Police Union; (1898) Nat'l Ass'n of Chiefs of Police; (1902) Chiefs of Police of the United States and Canada. Sponsors the Institute for Police Management. Membership: $50-$100/year.
Publications:
Journal of Police Science and Administration. q.
The Police Chief. m. adv.
Annual Meetings: Fall/6,000
1987-Toronto, Canada/Oct. 24-29
1988-Portland, OR/Oct. 15-20
1989-Louisville,KY/Oct. 14-19
1990-Tulsa,OK/Oct. 6-11

Internat'l Ass'n of Clerks, Recorders, Election Officials and Treasurers (1971)
P.O. Box 1525, Houston TX 77001
President: Anita Rodeheaver
Members: 2,000 individuals and companies *Staff:* 1
Annual Budget: $50-100,000 *Tel:* (713) 221-6411
Hist. Note: Membership: $40/yr. (deputy and associate members).
Publication:
IACREOT News. q. adv.
Annual Meetings: Summer
1987-Nashville,TN(Opryland)
1988-Tucson,AZ
1989-San Diego,CA

Internat'l Ass'n of Clothing Designers (1911)
450 Seventh Ave., New York NY 10123
Exec. Director: Mike Kaplan
Members: 600 *Staff:* 2-3
Annual Budget: $100-250,000 *Tel:* (212) 239-6995
Hist. Note: Founded as the National Association of Clothing Designers it assumed its present name in 1919. Membership figure includes both designers and industrial members.
Publications:
International Designer. q.adv.
Bulletin. 10/yr.
Style Forecast. semi-a.
Industry Resources Book. semi-a.
Semi-annual Meetings: May and September

Internat'l Ass'n of Conference Centers (1981)
Box 989, Woodbury CT 06798
President: John Marenzana
Members: 100 facilities *Staff:* 2-5
Annual Budget: $100-250,000 *Tel:* (203) 266-4377
Publications:
Center Lines. q.
Directory. a.
Annual Meetings: April

00153 12 05 86 1233

Internat'l Ass'n of Convention and Visitor Bureaus (1914)
Box 758, Champaign IL 61820
Managing Director: Richard J. Newman
Members: 260 *Staff:* 2-5
Annual Budget: $250-500,000 *Tel:* (217) 359-8881
Hist. Note: Formerly (1975) Internat'l Ass'n of Convention Bureaus.
Publications:
Newsletter (Members only). m.
Membership Directory. a.
Annual Meetings: Summer
1987-Nashville, TN
1988-Undecided
1989-Reno, NV
1990-New Orleans, LA

Internat'l Ass'n of Cooking Professionals (1978)
1001 Connecticut Ave., N.W., Suite 800, Washington DC 20036
Exec. V. President: Marcie M. McNelis
Members: 200 schools, 935 individuals *Staff:* 4
Annual Budget: $250-500,000 *Tel:* (202) 293-7716
Hist. Note: Founded in 1978 as the Ass'n of Cooking Schools; known until 1985 as the Internat'l Ass'n of Cooking Schools. Members are cooking schools, cooking educators, cooking students, culinary specialists, caterers, and food writers. Membership: $100/yr. (individuals); $200/yr. (institution)
Publications:
Cooking Schools Commentary. m. adv.
Directory of Schools. a.
Research Reports. semi-a.
Annual Meetings: Spring
1987-Los Angeles, CA/March/600
1988-St. Louis, MO/March/600
1989-Boston, MA/March/600

Internat'l Ass'n of Cooking Schools (1978)
Hist. Note: Became the Internat'l Ass'n of Cooking Professionals in 1985.

Internat'l Ass'n of Coroners and Medical Examiners (1927)
6913 W. Plank Road, Peoria IL 61604
Exec. Secy.-Treas.: Herbert H. Buzbee
Members: 750 *Staff:* 1
Annual Budget: under $10,000 *Tel:* (309) 697-8100
Hist. Note: Established as the National Association of Coroners and Medical Examiners, it assumed its present name in 1968. Has no paid staff. Membership: $50/yr.
Publications:
Proceedings. bi-a.
Newsletter. q.
Annual Meetings: June
1987-New Orleans, LA(Fairmont Hotel)
1988-San Diego, CA

Internat'l Ass'n of Corporate Real Estate Executives (1969)
471 Spencer Drive South, Suite 8, West Palm Beach FL 33409
President: Joseph R. Bagby
Members: 3,000 *Staff:* 24
Annual Budget: $1-2,000,000 *Tel:* (305) 683-8111
Hist. Note: Formerly (1973) Nat'l Ass'n of Location Analysts and Negotiators and the Nat'l Ass'n of Corporate Real Estate Executives. Assumed its present name in 1983. Members are corporate executives responsible for any function related to the acquisition or management of real estate. Membership: $275/yr.
Publications:
Corporate Real Estate Executive. m. adv.
Meeting Program. 10/yr. adv.
NACORE Directory. a. adv.
Annual Meetings: Spring/1,000
1987-Toronto, Ontario(Sheraton Centre)/June 13-17
1988-San Francisco, CA(St. Francis)/March 19-22
1989-Baltimore, MD/June 17-21

Internat'l Ass'n of Correctional Officers (1977)
P.O. Box 7051, Marquette MI 49855
Exec. Director: Bob Barrington
Members: 7,000 *Staff:* 2-5
Annual Budget: $25-50,000 *Tel:* (906) 227-1689
Hist. Note: Officers in federal, state and local correctional facilities. Formerly (1978) the American Ass'n of Correctional Facility Officers and (until 1986), the American Ass'n of Correctional Officers. Membership: $15/yr. (individual), $20/yr. (organization).
Publication:
The Keeper's Voice. q.
Annual Meetings: Summer, prior to American Correctional Ass'n
1987-New Orleans, LA/August

Internat'l Ass'n of Counseling Services (1972)
5999 Stevenson Ave., Third Fl., Alexandria VA 22304
Admin. Officer: Nancy E. Roncketti
Members: 200 *Staff:* 2-5
Annual Budget: $50-100,000 *Tel:* (703) 823-9840
Hist. Note: Formerly the American Board on Professional Standards in Vocational Counseling; the American Board on Counseling Services. Established by and affiliated with the American Ass'n for Counseling and Development to evaluate college, community and private counseling services. Accredits private and public postsecondary educational institution counseling services. Accreditation fee: $375/yr. (company).
Publications:
IACS Newsletter. irreg.
Directory of Counseling Services. a.
Professional Series. irreg.
Annual Meetings: With American Ass'n for Counseling and Development
1987-Chicago, IL/March 15-18

Internat'l Ass'n of Credit Card Investigators (1968)
1620 Grant Ave., Novato CA 94947
Exec. Director: D.D. Drummond
Members: 3,021 individuals *Staff:* 3
Annual Budget: $50-100,000 *Tel:* (415) 897-8800
Hist. Note: Formerly the Ass'n of Credit Card Investigators. Membership: $30/yr. (regular); $15/yr. (law enforcement members).
Publication:
IACCI Newsletter. bi-m. adv.
Annual Meetings: Fall
1987-Toronto, Ontario(Inn on the Park)/Sept. 21-23
1988-Charlotte, NC(Adam's Mark)/Sept. 19-23

Internat'l Ass'n of Defense Counsel (1920)
20 N. Wacker Dr., Ste. 3100, Chicago IL 60606
Exec. Director: Richard J. Hayes
Members: 2,250 individuals *Staff:* 10
Annual Budget: $2-5,000,000 *Tel:* (312) 368-1494
Hist. Note: Formerly (1986) Internat'l Ass'n of Insurance Counsel. Members are defense attorneys and insurance and corporate counsel; membership is by invitation only. Membership: $400/yr.
Publication:
IADC News. q.
Semi-annual Meetings: Summer & Winter with Defense Research Institute

Internat'l Ass'n of Drilling Contractors (1940)
Box 4287, Houston TX 77210
Exec. V. President: Edwin McGhee
Staff: 16-20
Annual Budget: over $5,000,000 *Tel:* (713) 578-7171
Hist. Note: Formerly (1972) American Ass'n of Oilwell Drilling Contractors. Supports the Drilling Contractors Political Action Committee.
Publication:
The Drilling Contractor. m. adv.
Annual Meetings: Fall

Internat'l Ass'n of Electrical Inspectors (1928)
930 Busse Hwy., Park Ridge IL 60068
Exec. Director: W.I. Summers
Members: 17,500 *Staff:* 6-10
Annual Budget: $500-1,000,000 *Tel:* (312) 696-1455
Hist. Note: Members consist of inspectors, utilities, insurance groups, dealers, contractors, electricians, manufacturers and testing laboratories. IAEI cooperates in the formulation of standards for the safe installation and use of electrical materials, devices, and appliances. Membership: $25/yr.(individual); coporate rates vary.
Publications:
IAEI News. bi-m. adv.
Membership Directory. a. adv.
Annual Meetings: Fall (Regional Meetings)

Internat'l Ass'n of Energy Economists (1977)
1133 15th St., N.W., Suite 1000, Washington DC 20005
Exec. Director: Joan Walsh Cassedy
Members: 1,500 *Staff:* 2
Annual Budget: $100-250,000 *Tel:* (202) 293-5913
Hist. Note: Individuals from the energy industries, consulting and research organizations, goverment and universities who are professionally interested in energy economics. Membership: $55/yr.
Publications:
Directory. a.
IAEE Newsletter. q.
The Energy Journal. q. adv.
Proceedings. a.
Semi-annual Meetings: Summer and Winter
1987-Calgary, Alberta(Univ. of Calgary)/July

Internat'l Ass'n of Ethicists (1985)
323 S. Franklin Bldg., Suite I-104, Chicago IL 60606-7094
President: David A. Mrovka
Members: 20 individuals
Annual Budget: under $10,000 *Tel:* (800) 531-5314
Hist. Note: Headquartered in Colorado Springs, CO. IAE provides a repository and clearinghouse for information regarding scientific research in ethics and morals worldwide, a national system for information exchange between ethicist professionals and a public forum to enable ethicist professionals to address clients' needs. The Academy of Ethical Studies, a division of IAE, provides education and accreditation programs. Extension 3456 must be requested when using the toll-free number. Membership: $10/yr.
Publication:
Journal of Ethical Studies. q. adv.

Internat'l Ass'n of Fairs and Expositions (1920)
Box 985, Springfield MO 65801
Exec. V. President: Miller Lewis
Members: 1,600 *Staff:* 6-10
Annual Budget: $500-1,000,000 *Tel:* (417) 862-5771
Hist. Note: Membership consists of individual agricultural fairs and regional ass'ns of agricultural fairs.
Publication:
Fairs and Expositions. m. adv.
Annual Meetings: Fall/5,000

Internat'l Ass'n of Family Sociology (1972)
Dept. of Sociology, Northern Illinois University, DeKalb IL 60115-2854
Gen. Secretary: Man Singh Das
Members: 200 *Staff:* 1
Annual Budget: under $10,000 *Tel:* (815) 753-6423
Hist. Note: Sociologists interested in the field of family and marriage.
Publications:
Internatinal Journal of Sociology of the Family. semi-a.
IAFS Newsletter. q.
Annual Meetings: Every 5 years

Internat'l Ass'n of Fire Chiefs (1873)
1329 18th St., N.W., Washington DC 20036
Exec. Director: Garry L. Briese, CAE
Members: 7,500-8,000 *Staff:* 12
Annual Budget: $500-1,000,000 *Tel:* (202) 833-3420
Hist. Note: Formerly (1926) Nat'l Ass'n of Fire Engineers. Fire chiefs, equipment manufacturers and others concerned with fire prevention, protection and fighting.
Publications:
The International Fire Chief. m. adv.
Washington Scene. w.
Annual Meetings: September
1987-St. Louis, MO/Aug. 16-19

Internat'l Ass'n of Fire Fighters (1918)
1750 New York Ave., N. W., Washington DC 20006
President: John A. Gannon
Members: 164,000 *Staff:* 40-50
Annual Budget: over $5,000,000 *Tel:* (202) 737-8484
Hist. Note: Organized in Washington February 26, 1918 and chartered by the American Federation of Labor the same year. Sponsors and supports the Fire Fighters Interested in Registration and Election Political Action Committee. Has an annual budget of $7 million.
Publication:
The International Fire Fighter. m.
Biennial meetings: Even years in August
1988-Miami, FL(Hilton)
1990-St. Louis, MO

Internat'l Ass'n of Fish and Wildlife Agencies (1902)
1325 Massachusetts Ave., N.W., Washington DC 20005
Exec. V. President: Jack H. Berryman
Members: 425 *Staff:* 2-5
Annual Budget: $100-250,000 *Tel:* (202) 639-8200
Hist. Note: Established as the Nat'l Ass'n of Game Commissioners and Wardens, it became the Internat'l Ass'n of Game, Fish and Conservation Commissioners in 1917 and assumed its present name in 1976.
Publications:
Proceedings. a. adv.
Newsletter. bi-m.
Annual Meetings: September/250
1987-Winston-Salem, SC(Hyatt)/Sept. 13-17
1988-Toronto, Ontario(Convention Center)/Sept. 9-15
1989-Pierre, SD

Internat'l Ass'n of Geophysical Contractors (1971)
5335 West 48th Avenue, Suite 400, Denver CO 80212
President: Charles F. Darden
Members: 176 companies *Staff:* 3
Annual Budget: $100-250,000 *Tel:* (303) 458-8404
Hist. Note: Companies involved in oil exploration. Affilated with the Canadian Ass'n of Geophysical Contractors; operates chapters in Far East, Australia and Europe, Africa and Middle East (EAME) regions. Membership Fee: Based on gross geophysical expenditures or revenues.
Publication:
IAGC Newsletter. q.
Annual Meetings: May in Houston, TX

Internat'l Ass'n of Golf Administrators (1967)
125 Spencer Place, Mamaroneck NY 10543
President: Jay Mottola
Members: 60-70 *Staff:* 1
Annual Budget: under $10,000 *Tel:* (914) 698-0390
Hist. Note: Members are executives of local golf associations. Membership: $50/yr.
Annual Meetings: February

Internat'l Ass'n of Governmental Fair Agencies (1966)
Illinois Dept. of Agriculture, State Fairgrounds, Springfield IL 62706-1001
President: Thomas Doubet
Members: 35 *Staff:* 1
Annual Budget: under $10,000 *Tel:* (217) 782-7411
Hist. Note: U.S. and Canadian representatives of state/provincial agencies that are responsible for educational and agricultural fairs. Affiliated with the National Association of State Departments of Agriculture. Membership: $35/yr.
Annual Meetings: Spring

Internat'l Ass'n of Heat and Frost Insulators and Asbestos Workers (1904)
1300 Connecticut Ave., N.W., Suite 505, Washington DC 20036
President: Andrew T. Haas
Members: 20,000-21,000 *Staff:* 11-15
Annual Budget: $2-5,000,000 *Tel:* (202) 785-2388
Hist. Note: Chartered on September 22, 1904 by the American Federation of Labor as the Nat'l Ass'n of Heat, Frost, General Insulators and Asbestos Workers of America. The word "International" came into the title after the acceptance of

00154 12 05 86 1233

Canadian locals in 1910. Sponsors and supports the Internat'l Ass'n of Heat and Frost Insulators and Asbestos Workers Political Action Committee.
Publication:
The Asbestos Worker. q.
Annual Meetings: Every 5 years
1987-Philadelphia, PA

Internat'l Ass'n of Hospital Central Service Management (1958)
213 West Institute Place, Suite 412, Chicago IL 60610
Exec. Director: Betty Hanna
Members: 4,000 *Staff:* 4
Annual Budget: $50-100,000 *Tel:* (312) 440-0078
Hist. Note: Established in 1958 as the Nat'l Ass'n of Hospital Central Service Personnel. Became the Internat'l Ass'n of Hospital Central Service Management in 1969. Membership consists of persons serving in a technical, supervisory or management capacity in hospital departments responsible for the management and distribution of supplies. Affiliate members are technicians who have achieved a passing grade in national exam.
Publication:
Communique.
Semi-annual meetings:
1987-Las Vegas, NV

Internat'l Ass'n of Hospitality Accountants (1953)
Box 27649, Austin TX 78755
Exec. V. President: Barbara Byrd-Lawler
Members: 2,700 *Staff:* 5
Annual Budget: $250-500,000 *Tel:* (512) 346-5680
Hist. Note: A professional society of hotel, motel, and restaurant and club accountants. Founded as the Nat'l Ass'n of Hotel Accountants, it became the Nat'l Ass'n of Hotel-Motel Accountants and assumed its present name in 1975.
Publication:
The Bottom Line. bi-m.
Annual Meetings: Fall
1987-Toronto, Ontario/Oct.

Internat'l Ass'n of Ice Cream Manufacturers
Hist. Note: Became the Internat'l Ice Cream Ass'n in 1986.

Internat'l Ass'n of Independent Producers (1932)
Box 2801, Washington DC 20013
Exec. Director: Dr. Edward Von Rothkirch
Members: 2,800 domestic; 1,400 foreign *Staff:* 2-5
Annual Budget: $25-50,000 *Tel:* (202) 638-5595
Hist. Note: Formerly Internat'l Alliance of Independent Film Producers. Members are producers of records, films and tapes.
Publications:
Communication Arts Internat'l. q. adv.
Communication Arts Internat'l Newsletter. 8/yr.
Annual Meetings: Series of Regional Workshops; 8 in U.S., 3 in Canada, 8 abroad.

Internat'l Ass'n of Independent Scholars (1983)
1549 Armacost Ave., #2, Los Angeles CA 90025
President: Joan Leopold
Members: 20 individuals
Annual Budget: under $10,000 *Tel:* (213) 826-1186
Hist. Note: Membership is open to persons pursuing research while engaged in other professions or pursing research apart from traditional academic institutions. Encourages scholarly and collegial activity by: coordinating reading and study groups; supporting the dissemination of information regarding publications, lectures, grants, jobs, events of interest; conducting programs quarterly; assisting in low-cost grant administration and providing reference services. Membership: $10/yr.
Publication:
New and Notes (newsletter), q.
Annual Meetings: Los Angeles, CA/September

Internat'l Ass'n of Industrial Accident Boards and Commissions (1914)
Box 13449, Jackson MS 39236
Exec. Director: J.T. Noblin
Members: 400-450 *Staff:* 2-5
Annual Budget: $100-250,000 *Tel:* (601) 366-4582
Hist. Note: Members are governmental units, companies and others interested in improving workmen's compensation laws and their administration. Membership: $200/year.
Publications:
IAIABC Journal. q.
IAIABC Newsletter. m.
Annual Meetings:
1987-Hartford, CT
1988-Seattle, WA
1989-Baltimore, MD

Internat'l Ass'n of Insurance Counsel
Hist. Note: Became the Internat'l Ass'n of Defense Counsel in 1986.

Internat'l Ass'n of Law Enforcement Firearms Instructors (1981)
Box 47015, Forrestville MD 20747-0015
Exec. Director: Elizabeth A. Callahan
Members: 820 *Staff:* 1
Annual Budget: $25-50,000 *Tel:* (301) 736-1974
Hist. Note: Members are certified firearms instructors from police departments, security agencies, etc. Incorporated in the State of Massachusetts. Membership: $40/yr.

Internat'l Ass'n of Law Enforcement Intelligence Analysts (1980)
Box 876, Ben Franklin Station, Washington DC 20044
Exec. Director: Brian S. Boyd
Members: 900
Annual Budget: under $10,000 *Tel:* (919) 396-0270
Hist. Note: Members are presently or formerly employed in a specialized law enforcement intelligence capacity, sworn and civilian, by a government entity.
Publications:
Newsletter. q.
Criminal Intelligence Analysis Review. q.

Internat'l Ass'n of Lighting Designers (1969)
18 East 16th St., Suite 208, New York NY 10003
Exec. Director: Marion Greene
Members: 300-325 *Staff:* 1
Annual Budget: $100-250,000 *Tel:* (212) 206-1281
Hist. Note: Voting members are at the Corporate or Senior Associate grade, having respectively, four years' experience at the level of Chief Designer or above, or two years' experience at the level of Job Captain or above at a professional firm. Membership: $100 initiation fee plus $100/yr. (corporate); and $50 initiation fee plus $60/yr. (senior associate)
Publications:
Newsletter. m.
Membership Directory. a.
Annual Meetings: November, with the Lighting Awards Presentation

Internat'l Ass'n of Lighting Maintenance Contractors (1952)
2017 Walnut St., Philadelphia PA 19103
Exec. Director: Brent H. Farber, Jr.
Members: 200 companies *Staff:* 10
Annual Budget: $50-100,000 *Tel:* (215) 569-3650
Hist. Note: Companies that clean, repair and maintain commercial and industrial lighting fixtures. Formerly (until 1978) the Nat'l Ass'n of Lighting Maintenance Contractors.
Publication:
Main-Lighter. 9/yr. adv.
Semi-annual meetings: Spring and Fall

Internat'l Ass'n of Machinists and Aerospace Workers (1888)
1300 Connecticut Ave., N.W., Washington DC 20036
President: William W. Winpisinger
Members: 600,000 *Staff:* 225-250
Annual Budget: over $5,000,000 *Tel:* (202) 857-5200
Hist. Note: Founded May 5, 1888 in Atlanta, Georgia as the Order of United Machinists and Mechanical Engineers. Became the National Association of Machinists in 1889 and the International Association of Machinists in 1891. Assumed its present name in 1964. Has a budget of about $65 million. Sponsors and supports the International Association of Machinists and Aerospace Workers Political Action Committee.
Publication:
The Machinist. m.
Annual Meetings: Every 4 years
1988-Atlanta

Internat'l Ass'n of Merger and Acquisition Consultants (1973)
9575 West Higgins Road, Suite 903, Rosemont IL 60018
Administrator: Cheryl A. Cade
Members: 30 *Staff:* 1
Annual Budget: $50-100,000 *Tel:* (312) 696-4330
Hist. Note: Formerly (1982) Nat'l Ass'n of Merger and Acquisition Consultants. Members are specialists in selling, buying, and merging medium-sized businesses, both public and private firms.
Publication:
Newsletter. m. (for members only)
Semi-annual Meetings: Spring and Fall/30
1987-Los Angeles, CA/May

Internat'l Ass'n of Milk Control Agencies (1935)
Dept. of Agriculture, Div. of Dairy Industry Services, Albany NY 12235
Secy.-Treas.: Ronald Pearce
Members: 33 *Staff:* 1
Annual Budget: under $10,000 *Tel:* (518) 457-6773
Publication:
Proceedings. a.
Annual Meetings: Summer
1987 Alberta, Canada

Internat'l Ass'n of Milk, Food and Environmental Sanitarians (1911)
P.O. Box 701, Ames IA 50010
Exec. Manager: Kathy R. Hathaway
Members: 3,500-4,000 *Staff:* 8
Annual Budget: $250-500,000 *Tel:* (515) 232-6699
Hist. Note: Founded as the Internat'l Ass'n of Dairy and Milk Inspectors, it became the Internat'l Ass'n of Milk Sanitarians in 1937, the Internat'l Ass'n of Milk and Food Sanitarians in 1947 and assumed its present name in 1957. A professional society of individuals working in the field of sanitary handling of dairy and other food products. Membership: $28/yr.
Publications:
Dairy and Food Sanitation. m. adv.
Journal of Food Protection. m. adv.
Annual Meetings: August/350-400
1987-Anaheim, CA(Disneyland)

Internat'l Ass'n of Ocular Surgeons (1981)
233 E. Erie St., Suite 710, Chicago IL 60611
Director: Dr. John G. Bellows
Members: 2,000 *Staff:* 6
Annual Budget: $50-100,000 *Tel:* (312) 951-1400
Hist. Note: A division of the American Soc. of Contemporary Medicine, Surgery and Ophthalmology. Membership: $125/yr.
Publication:
Journal of Ocular Therapy and Surgery. bi-m. adv.
Annual Meetings: Fall

Internat'l Ass'n of Optometric Executives
P.O. Box 3312, Harrisburg PA 17101
Secy.-Treas.: Terry Stark
Members: 50-75 *Staff:* 0
Annual Budget: under $10,000
Hist. Note: Formerly called the Society of Association Optometric Executives.
Annual Meetings: June, with the American Optometric Association.

Internat'l Ass'n of Organ Teachers USA
Hist. Note: Became Keyboard Teachers Ass'n in 1986.

Internat'l Ass'n of Orofacial Myology (1972)
Hist. Note: Address unknown in 1985-86.

Internat'l Ass'n of Personnel in Employment Security (1913)
1801 Louisville Road, Frankfort KY 40601
Exec. Director: Michael R. Stone
Members: 27,000 *Staff:* 5
Annual Budget: $250-500,000 *Tel:* (502) 223-4459
Hist. Note: Members are involved in unemployment compensation and job placement in local, state and federal agencies. Formerly (1952) Internat'l Ass'n of Public Employment Services. Membership: $15/yr.
Publications:
IAPES News. 11/yr. adv.
Proceedings. a.
Perspectives: Review & Essays on Employment Security Issues. a.
Annual Meetings: June/July
1987-San Antonio,TX(Hyatt)/July 7-10/1,500
1988-Chicago,IL(Marriott)/July 11-15/2,000
1989-Louisville,KY(Galt House)/June 12-16/2,000
1990-Des Moines, IA(Marriott)/June 25-29/1,500

Internat'l Ass'n of Pet Cemeteries (1971)
P.O. Box 1346, South Bend IN 46624
Exec. Director: Wendell C. Morse, D.V.M.
Members: 230 *Staff:* 1
Annual Budget: $25-50,000 *Tel:* (219) 277-1115
Hist. Note: Founded in Chicago as the Nat'l Ass'n of Pet Cemeteries, it assumed its present name in 1978. Affiliated with the Nat'l Ass'n of the Pet Industry. Membership: $110/yr. (individual); $150/yr. (organization/company)
Publication:
News and Views. q. adv.
Annual Meetings: Fall
1987-Orlando, FL/Oct.
1988-Las Vegas, NV/Oct.
1989-New Orleans, LA/Oct.

Internat'l Ass'n of Piano Builders and Technicians (1979)
9140 Ward Parkway, Kansas City MO 64114
Communications Director: Larry Goldsmith
Members: 4 associations
Tel: (816) 444-3500
Hist. Note: Members consist of the Piano Technicians Guild, the Japanese Piano Technicians Ass'n, the Korea Ass'n of Piano Tuners, and the Taipei Piano Technicians Ass'n.
Publication:
IAPBT Bulletin. q.
Annual Meetings: Biennial Meetings (Odd Years)
1987-Toronto, Canada(Constellation)/July 24-26

Internat'l Ass'n of Plumbing and Mechanical Officials (1926)
5032 Alhambra Ave., Los Angeles CA 90032
Exec. Director: Tom Higham
Members: 2,000 *Staff:* 11-15
Annual Budget: $1-2,000,000 *Tel:* (213) 223-1471
Hist. Note: Formerly (1966) Western Plumbing Officials Ass'n. Administrative officials, government agencies, associations, manufacturers and suppliers in the plumbing industry.
Publication:
Official. bi-m. adv.
Annual Meetings: Fall
1987-Salt Lake City, UT(Marriott)/Oct. 11-15/450
1988-Seattle, WA(Marriott)/Sept. 25-29/400
1989-Reno, NV(Nuggett)/Sept. 24-28/400

Internat'l Ass'n of Printing House Craftsmen (1919)
7599 Kenwood Rd., Cincinnati OH 45236
Exec. V. President: Patricia A. Milligan
Members: 15-16,000 *Staff:* 2-5
Annual Budget: $100-250,000 *Tel:* (513) 891-0611
Hist. Note: The Internat'l Ass'n of Printing House Craftsmen, Inc. is open to printing plant executives. Membership: $15/yr.

00155 12 05 86 1233

Publication:
Review of the Graphic Arts. q. adv.
Annual Meetings: August/1,000
1987-Toronto, Ontario
1988-Cincinnati, OH
1989-Sparks, NV

Internat'l Ass'n of Professional Natural Hygienists (1978)
204 Stambaugh Building, Youngstown OH 44503
Secy.-Treas.: Mark A. Huberman
Members: 30 Individuals. *Staff:* 1
Annual Budget: under $10,000 *Tel:* (216) 746-5000
Hist. Note: The IAPNH promotes the clinical advancement of its profession, ethical responsibility, certification of other Professionals and the accredation of schools or training programs, and the health freedom of Ass'n members. Members are limited to Primary Care Doctors specializing in the supervision of fasting as an integral part of Natural Hygienic care. Members must be graduates of a university and have a legal practice. Membership: $50-200/yr.
Publication:
IAPNH Newsletter. q.
Annual Meetings: July/Aug.
1987-Ontario, Canada

Internat'l Ass'n of Professional Security Consultants (1984)
2 Sunrise Place, Armonk NY 10504
Exec. Director: Ernest J. Bolduc
Members: 35 individuals *Staff:* 1
Annual Budget: $10-25,000 *Tel:* (914) 273-8590
Hist. Note: Members are security management consultants. Membership: $150/yr.
Annual Meetings: Spring
1987-New York, NY

Internat'l Ass'n of Pupil Personnel Workers (1911)
Mt. View, P.O. Box 36, Barnesville MD 20838
Exec. Director: William E. Myer
Members: 600 individuals, 100 libraries *Staff:* 1
Annual Budget: under $10,000 *Tel:* (301) 972-8374
Hist. Note: Pupil personnel workers, social workers and others concerned with school attendance. Formerly (until) 1957) known as the Nat'l League to Promote School Attendance.
Publication:
IAPPW Journal. q. adv.
Annual Meetings: October
1987-Atlanta, GA

Internat'l Ass'n of Quality Circles (1977)
801-B W. 8th Street, Suite 301, Cincinnati OH 45203
Managing Director: Cathy E. Kramer, Ph.D.
Members: 6,000 *Staff:* 15
Annual Budget: $1-2,000,000 *Tel:* (513) 381-1959
Hist. Note: A quality circle is a group of employees, performing similar work, who meet regularly to analyze and solve work-related problems. The concept originated in Japan in 1962. Membership: $55/yr. (individual), $225/yr. (company), $32/yr. (quality circle).
Publications:
Quality Circles Journal. q. adv.
Circle Report. bi-m.
Annual Meetings: Spring
1987-New Orleans, LA/April 6-9/4,700
1988-Indianpolis, IN/April 11-15
1989-Kansas City, MO/April 30-May 4
1990-Cincinnati, OH

Internat'l Ass'n of Refrigerated Warehouses (1891)
7315 Wisconsin Ave., #1200 N, Bethesda MD 20814
President: J. William Hudson
Members: 255 companies *Staff:* 9
Annual Budget: $1-2,000,000 *Tel:* (301) 652-5674
Hist. Note: Formerly (1972) Nat'l Ass'n of Refrigerated Warehouses. Members are operators of public refrigerated warehouses. Membership: Varies by size of operation.
Publications:
Cold Facts. m. adv.
Annual Directory of Public Refrigerated Warehouses. a. adv.
Annual Meetings: Spring/650
1987-San Diego, CA(del Coronado)/May 3-6
1988-London(International)/April 25-28
1989-Denver, CO(Broadmoor)/May 3-6
1990-Orlando, FL(Hyatt)/April 22-25
1991-Desert Springs, CA(Marriott)/April 21-24

Internat'l Ass'n of Security Services (1973)
P.O. Box 8202, Northfield IL 60093
Exec. Director: Howard W. Ross
Members: 1,000 companies *Staff:* 2-5
Annual Budget: $100-250,000 *Tel:* (312) 973-7712

Internat'l Ass'n of Service Companies (1981)
Hist. Note: Merged into the North American Computer Service Ass'n in 1983.

Internat'l Ass'n of Siderographers (1899)
6090 Ansley Court, Manassas VA 22111
Internat'l President: Richard Warburton
Members: 13 *Staff:* 2-4
Annual Budget: under $10,000 *Tel:* (703) 590-2251
Hist. Note: Established in Washington, DC January 11, 1899 as the Steel Plate Transferrers' Ass'n and chartered by the American Federation of Labor in 1906, it assumed its present name in 1921. It is one of the smallest unions in the AFL-CIO, CLC. Siderographers are individuals who use engravers dies and, with a transfer press, pick up the die image on a roll which is used to make a currency die. The roll is then used to make a currency steel plate for printing of stock certificates, bonds, etc. Membership: $10 per month.
Biennial meetings: Uneven years, Labor Day weekend
1987-Ottawa, Canada/20

Internat'l Ass'n of Strategic Planning Consultants (1979)
Hist. Note: Ceased operations in 1984.

Internat'l Ass'n of Structural Movers (1983)
11811 S.E. Highway 212, Clackamas OR 97015
President: Terry Emmett
Members: 150-200 companies *Staff:* 1
Annual Budget: $50-100,000 *Tel:* (503) 655-7191
Hist. Note: Founded at the Marriott Hotel, Atlanta, Georgia January 15, 1983. Members are movers of heavy structural products, trusses, barns, houses and machinery. Has a small international membership.
Publication:
The Mover. q.

Internat'l Ass'n of Tool Craftsmen (1953)
1915 Arrowline Court, Bettendorf IA 52722
President: Arthur W. Dekoster
Members: 410 *Staff:* 1
Annual Budget: $10-25,000 *Tel:* (319) 332-6147
Hist. Note: Independent labor union.
Publication:
Tool and Die Journal. q.
Biennial meetings: Uneven years in Fall

Internat'l Ass'n of Tour Managers - North American Region (1961)
1646 Chapel St., New Haven CT 06511
Exec. Director: G. Dominic Passarelli
Members: 1,300 *Staff:* 2
Annual Budget: $100-250,000 *Tel:* (203) 777-5994
Hist. Note: Affiliated with American Soc. of Travel Agents and Universal Federation of Travel Agents Ass'n. Professional association of tour managers; tour operators are associate members. Membership: $75/yr.
Publication:
Tour Manager. q.

Internat'l Ass'n of Trade Exchanges
Hist. Note: Became the Internat'l Reciprocal Trade Ass'n in 1984.

Internat'l Ass'n of Trichologists (1973)
37320 22nd St., Kalamazoo MI 49009
Director: David Salinger
Members: 200-250 *Staff:* 2-5
Annual Budget: $25-50,000 *Tel:* (616) 375-4430
Hist. Note: Members are qualified to care for the hair and scalp. Awards the designations Certified Trichologist (IAT) and Master Certified Trichologist (MIAT). Membership: $70/year.
Publication:
Newsletter. bi-m.

Internat'l Ass'n of Wiping Cloth Manufacturers (1932)
Washington-Dulles Internat'l Airport, P.O. Box 17086, Washington DC 20041
Exec. V. President: Herbert L. Grossman
Members: 250 companies *Staff:* 2-5
Annual Budget: $100-250,000 *Tel:* (703) 661-6377
Hist. Note: Makers and distributors of industrial wiping materials and cloths. Founded as the Sanitary Institute of America, it became the Nat'l Ass'n of Wiping Cloth Manufacturers and, in 1977, the Internat'l Ass'n of Wiping Cloth Manufacturers.
Publication:
IAWCM Bulletin. m. adv.
Annual Meetings:
1987-San Diego, CA/March 8-13

Internat'l Ass'n of Women Police (1915)
Box 15207, Seattle WA 98115
Exec. Director: Beryl A. Thompson
Members: 1,000 individuals *Staff:* 1
Annual Budget: $10-25,000
Hist. Note: Originally founded as the Internat'l Policewoman's Ass'n in 1915 and disbanded in 1932; reorganized under its present name in 1956. Members are full-time law enforcement officers with powers of arrest. Men have been eligible for full membership since 1976. Membership: $25/yr.
Publication:
IAWP Bulletin. q. adv.
Annual Meetings: Fall
1987-New York, NY/Sept. 10-15
1988-Atlanta, GA

Internat'l Ass'n of Word Processing Specialists (1979)
Hist. Note: Reported defunct in 1985.

Internat'l Aviation Theft Bureau
Hist. Note: Superseded by Aviation Crime Prevention Institute, Inc.

Internat'l Banana Ass'n (1983)
1101 Vermont Ave., N.W., Suite 306, Washington DC 20005
President: Robert M. Moore
Members: 6-10 companies *Staff:* 2-5
Annual Budget: $1-2,000,000 *Tel:* (202) 371-1620
Hist. Note: Trade association of the banana industry.
Semi-Annual Meetings:

Internat'l Bankers Ass'n (1968)
Hist. Note: Address unknown in 1982. Perhaps defunct.

Internat'l Beefalo Breeders' Registry (1980)
Hist. Note: Merged with the American Beefalo Ass'n and the World Beefalo Ass'n to form the American Beefalo World Registry in 1983.

Internat'l Bio-Environmental Foundation (1977)
P.O. Box 794, Northridge CA 91328-0794
Administrative Secretary: Mark M. Viro
Members: 1500 individuals *Staff:* 2-5
Annual Budget: $25-50,000 *Tel:* (818) 882-7128
Hist. Note: Scientists concerned with the biological effects of atmospheric ions, electromagnetic fields, noise and artifical light. Formerly known as the American Bio-Enviromental Association.
Publication:
Bulletins. irreg.

Internat'l Black Writers Conference (1970)
P.O. Box 1030, Chicago IL 60690
Exec. Director: Mable Terrell
Members: 200 individuals *Staff:* 2
Annual Budget: under $10,000 *Tel:* (312) 995-5195
Hist. Note: IBWC is a writers organization formed to address the needs of Black and other minority-group writers. Membership: $15/yr.
Publications:
Black Writer Magazine. q. adv.
In-Touch (newsletter). m.
Annual Meetings: June

Internat'l Bottled Water Ass'n (1958)
113 N. Henry St., Alexandria VA 22314
Exec. V. President: William F. Deal, CAE
Members: 400-500 *Staff:* 6
Annual Budget: $500-1,000,000 *Tel:* (703) 683-5213
Hist. Note: Membership consists of owners and operators of bottled water plants, dealers, distributors and industry suppliers. Established as The American Bottled Water Association, it assumed its present name in 1982.
Publications:
Bottled Water Reporter. bi-m. adv.
Membership Roster. a. adv.
Newsletter. bi-m.
Technical Newsletter. bi-m.
Annual Meetings: Fall, usually October.
1987-Chicago, IL(Hyatt Regency)
1988-New Orleans, LA(Hyatt Regency)

Internat'l Boxing Writers Ass'n (1980)
P.O. Box 610, Millwood NY 10546
Secretary: Carol Capobianco
Members: 175 *Staff:* 4
Annual Budget: under $10,000 *Tel:* (914) 359-6334
Hist. Note: Writers and radio and TV broadcasters who cover amateur and professional boxing. Membership: $20/yr.
Publication:
Center Ring. q.
Annual Meetings:
1987-Philadelphia, PA/Nov.

Internat'l Brangus Breeders Ass'n (1949)
5750 Epsilon, San Antonio TX 78249
Exec. V. President: Jerry D. Morrow
Members: 2,400-2,500 *Staff:* 18
Annual Budget: $500-1,000,000 *Tel:* (512) 696-8231
Hist. Note: Breeders and merchandisers of Brangus beef cattle. Member of the National Society of Livestock Record Associations. Membership: $60/yr.
Publication:
Brangus Journal. m. adv.
Annual Meetings: February

Internat'l Bridge Press Ass'n
3601 Connecticut Ave., N.W., Washington DC 20008
Secretary: Eloene Griggs
Members: 400 *Staff:* 5
Annual Budget: $10-25,000 *Tel:* (202) 244-7353
Hist. Note: Persons who write on the game of contract bridge for newspapers, magazines, books and news letters. Affiliated with World Bridge Federation. Membership: $35/yr.
Publications:
Bulletin. m.
Directory of Members. a.
Annual Meetings: Fall
1987-Jamaica/Oct. 10-24
1987-Brighton, England/Aug. 1-15

00156 12 05 86 1233

Internat'l Bridge, Tunnel & Turnpike Ass'n (1932)
2120 L St. NW, Suite 305, Washington DC 20037
Exec. Director: John J. Hassett
Members: 200-225 *Staff:* 2-5
Annual Budget: $250-500,000 *Tel:* (202) 659-4620
Hist. Note: Founded as the American Toll Bridge Ass'n, it became the American Bridge, Tunnel and Turnpike Ass'n in 1948 and assumed its present name in 1964. Membership consists of public agencies and support organizations operating toll facilities.
Publication:
Tollways. m.
Annual Meetings: Fall/500
1987-Halifax, Canada(Sheraton)/Sept. 13-16
1988-San Francisco(Hyatt Regency Embarcadero)/Sept. 25-28
1989-Spain/Sept.
1990-Dallas, TX/Oct.

Internat'l Brotherhood of Boilermakers, Iron Shipbuilders, Blacksmiths, Forgers and Helpers (1881)
753 State Ave., 5th Floor, New Brotherhood Bldg., Kansas City KS 66101
President: Charles W. Jones
Members: 120,000 *Staff:* 125-150
Annual Budget: over $5,000,000 *Tel:* (913) 371-2640
Hist. Note: Organized in Chicago August 6, 1881 as the Nat'l Boilermaker and Helpers Protective and Benevolent Union. Renamed the Internat'l Brotherhood of Boilermakers and Iron Ship Builders Protective and Benevolent Union of the United States and Canada in 1883. Merged with the Nat'l Brotherhood of Boilermakers in 1893 to form the Internat'l Brotherhood of Boilermakers and Iron Ship Builders of America. Chartered by the American Federation of Labor in 1897, it became the Internat'l Brotherhood of Boilermakers, Iron Ship Builders and Helpers of America in 1912 and merged in 1951 with the Internat'l Brotherhood of Blacksmiths, Drop Forgers and Helpers and adopted its present name. Merged with the United Cement, Lime, Gypsum and Allied Workers Internat'l Union in 1984. Has a budget of about $27 million. Sponsors and supports the Legislative Education Action Program Campaign Assistance Fund.
Publication:
Boilermaker-Blacksmith Reporter. m.
Annual Meetings: Every 5 years (1991)

Internat'l Brotherhood of Electrical Workers (1891)
1125 15th St., N. W., Washington DC 20005
President: John J. Barry
Members: 1,100,000 *Staff:* 250
Annual Budget: over $5,000,000 *Tel:* (202) 833-7000
Hist. Note: Established in St. Louis November 21, 1891 as the National Brotherhood of Electrical Workers and chartered by the American Federation of Labor the same year. Assumed its present name in 1899 after the acceptance of the first Canadian local. Sponsors and supports the International Brotherhood of Electrical Workers Committee on Political Education.
Publication:
IBEW Journal. m.
Annual Meetings: Quadrennial Meetings (1990)

Internat'l Brotherhood of Firemen and Oilers (1898)
122 C St., N.W., Suite 280, Washington DC 20001
President: Jimmy L. Walker
Members: 43,000-44,000 *Staff:* 10
Annual Budget: $1-2,000,000 *Tel:* (202) 737-5300
Hist. Note: Organized in Kansas City December 18, 1898 as the Internat'l Brotherhood of Stationary Firemen and chartered by the American Federation of Labor the following year. In 1919 the charter was expanded to include oilers and boiler room helpers and the name was changed to its present form. Sponsors and supports the Internat'l Brotherhood of Firemen and Oilers Political League.
Publication:
Firemen and Oilers Journal. bi-m.
Annual Meetings: Every 5 years (1991)

Internat'l Brotherhood of Magicians (1925)
28 North Main St., Kenton OH 43326
Exec. Secretary: Theresa Zoeller
Members: 10,000-11,000 *Staff:* 2-5
Annual Budget: $100-250,000 *Tel:* (419) 675-7150
Hist. Note: Includes an international membership of professional and amateur magicians and their suppliers.
Publication:
The Linking Ring. m. adv.
Annual Meetings:
1987-Nashville, TN/July

Internat'l Brotherhood of Painters and Allied Trades (1887)
1750 New York Ave., N. W., Washington DC 20006
General President: William A. Duval
Members: 170,000-175,000 *Staff:* 100-125
Annual Budget: over $5,000,000 *Tel:* (202) 637-0700
Hist. Note: Organized in Baltimore March 15, 1887 as the Brotherhood of Painters and Decorators. Became the Brotherhood of Painters, Decorators and Paperhangers of America in 1890. Absorbed the United Scenic Artists, the Nat'l Paperhangers Ass'n and the Nat'l Union of Sign Painters. Merged with the Amalgamated Glass Workers Internat'l Ass'n in 1915. Assumed its present name in 1969. Has a budget of about $11 million. Sponsors and supports the IBPAT Political Action Together-Political Action Committee.
Publication:
The Painters and Allied Trades Journal. m.
Annual Meetings: Every 5 years (1989)

Internat'l Brotherhood of Pottery and Allied Workers (1890)
Hist. Note: Established in 1890 as the Brotherhood of Operative Potters, it assumed its present name in 1968. Merged in 1982 with the Glass Bottle Blowers of the United States and Canada to form the Glass, Pottery, Plastics and Allied Workers International Union.

Internat'l Brotherhood of Teamsters, Chauffeurs, Warehouseman and Helpers of America (1903)
25 Louisiana Ave., N.W., Washington DC 20001
General President: Jackie Presser
Members: 1,900,000 *Staff:* 300
Annual Budget: over $5,000,000 *Tel:* (202) 624-6800
Hist. Note: Established in Niagara Falls, New York in 1903 as the International Brotherhood of Teamsters through the merger of the Teamsters National Union (founded in 1902) and the Team Drivers International Union (founded in 1899). Assumed its present name in 1940 and merged in 1972 with the United Brewery, Flour, Cereal, Soft Drink and Distillery Workers. Formerly affiliated with the American Federation of Labor, from which it was expelled for corruption in 1957, it is now an independent union with a budget of about $73 million.
Publication:
International Teamster. m.
Annual Meetings: Every 5 years in Summer (1991)

Internat'l Buckskin Horse Ass'n (1971)
Box 357, St. John IN 46373
Exec. Secretary: Richard E. Kurzeja
Members: 2,000 *Staff:* 4
Annual Budget: $25-50,000 *Tel:* (219) 365-8326
Hist. Note: Maintains a registry of Buckskin, Dun, Red Dun and Grulla horses. Membership: $10/yr.
Publication:
Dun and Buckskin Journal. bi-m. adv.
Annual Meetings: Fall
1987-City of Industry, CA(Sheraton)/Aug. 10-14

Internat'l Builders Exchange Executives (1948)
1351 East Jefferson Ave., Detroit MI 48207
Managing Editor: Phyllis Brooks
Members: 65-70 individuals *Staff:* 3
Annual Budget: under $10,000 *Tel:* (313) 567-5500
Hist. Note: Members are executive heads of local building trade associations in the United States and Canada.
Publication:
President's Newsletter. m.
Annual Meetings: June or July

Internat'l Business Forms Industries (1953)
1730 North Lynn St., Suite 501, Arlington VA 22209-2096
President: Christopher R. Bevevino
Members: 620 companies *Staff:* 16
Annual Budget: $1-2,000,000 *Tel:* (703) 841-9191
Hist. Note: Members of IBFI are manufacturers are business forms and suppliers to the industry. Founded in 1953 as a section of Printing Industries of America, Inc. (PIA), IBFI is now a self-sustaining, wholly incorporated international association. Maintains a European Operations Office in England.
Publications:
IBFI Informs. m.
Tech Roundup. m.
Econoscope. q.
Annual Meetings: Spring
1987-Denver, CO(Fairmont Hotel)/May 10-13
1988-Washington, DC(Mayflower)/May 8-11

Internat'l Cargo Gear Bureau (1966)
17 Battery Place, New York NY 10004
President: Charles G. Visconti
Members: 30-35 *Staff:* 16-20
Annual Budget: $1-2,000,000 *Tel:* (212) 425-2750
Hist. Note: Members are makers and users of material handling equipment in ports.

Internat'l Carwash Ass'n (1953)
One Imperial Place, One East 22nd St., Suite 400, Lombard IL 60148
Exec. Director: Robert "Gus" Trantham
Members: 3,000 companies *Staff:* 15-18
Annual Budget: $1-2,000,000 *Tel:* (312) 495-0100
Hist. Note: Formerly American Auto Laundry Ass'n (1958) and Automatic Car Wash Ass'n Internat'l (1975); absorbed the Nat'l Car Wash Council in 1982 and included it in its name until 1985.
Publication:
ICA Directory. semi-a. adv.
Semi-Annual Meetings: January and June
1987-Las Vegas, NV/Jan. 26-28
1987-Atlanta, GA/June 29-July 1

Internat'l Castor Oil Ass'n (1957)
656 Linwood Ave., Ridgewood NJ 07450
Secy.-Treas.: David P. Dingley
Members: 50-60 *Staff:* 1
Annual Budget: under $10,000 *Tel:* (212) 563-3200
Hist. Note: Formed in New York City May 1, 1957 by members of the former Linseed-Castorseed Association of New York and incorporated in the State of New Jersey in 1963. Includes foreign members. Crushers of castor seed and exporters, importers, processors, consumers and distributors of castor oil.
Annual Meetings: Winter, in New York City.

Internat'l Cemetery Supply Ass'n (1955)
Box 07779, Columbus OH 43207
Secretary: Robert Loffer
Members: 75 companies *Staff:* 1
Annual Budget: under $10,000 *Tel:* (614) 443-4675
Hist. Note: Suppliers of equipment, materials and services to the cemtery industry. Formerly (until 1980) known as the Cemetery Supply Ass'n.
Annual Meetings: With American Cemetery Ass'n

Internat'l Ceramic Ass'n (1958)
Hist. Note: Inactive in 1984.
Publications:
Blue Book. a.
Trade Journal. bi-m. adv.
Annual Meetings: Summer

Internat'l Chain of Industrial and Technical Advertising Agencies (1962)
c/o U.S. Advertising, 2700 Route 22, Union NJ 07083
President: George Black
Members: 40-45 companies *Staff:* 2-5
Annual Budget: $10-25,000 *Tel:* (201) 688-2700
Hist. Note: Independent advertising agencies specializing in industrial and technical products united to market on the international level. Officers change every 2 years.
Publication:
Newsletter. q.

Internat'l Chain Salon Ass'n (1972)
8127 Powers Ferry Road, Suite 22, Marietta GA 30067
President: Raymond Belue
Members: 60-70 *Staff:* 1
Annual Budget: under $10,000 *Tel:* (404) 952-9530
Hist. Note: Formerly (1985) the Nat'l Beauty Salon Chain Ass'n.
Meetings: Every nine months

Internat'l Cheese and Deli Ass'n (1965)
Hist. Note: Became the Internat'l Dairy-Deli Ass'n on June 13, 1985.

Internat'l Chemical Workers Union (1944)
1655 West Market St., Akron OH 44313
President: Frank D. Martino
Members: 60,000 *Staff:* 40-50
Annual Budget: $2-5,000,000 *Tel:* (216) 867-2444
Hist. Note: The International Council of Chemical and Allied Industries Union was formed in Akron, Ohio September 7, 1940. Renamed the International Chemical Workers Union, this organization received a charter from the American Federation of Labor in September, 1944. Maintains a Washington office. Sponsors and supports the Labor Investment of Voter Ecucation Political Action Committee.
Publication:
International Chemical Worker. m.
Biennial meetings: Even years
1988-Hollywood,FL(Diplomat)/Oct./400
1990-Las Vegas, NV/Oct./400

Internat'l Childbirth Education Ass'n (1960)
Box 20048, Minneapolis MN 55420-0048
President: Jeanne Rose
Members: 12,000 *Staff:* 6-10
Annual Budget: $250-500,000 *Tel:* (612) 854-8660
Hist. Note: Association concerned with family-centered maternity care with minimal medical intervention. An international group functioning in 32 countries, ICEA membership is predominantly concentrated in the U.S. Membership: $20-35/yr. (individual)
Publications:
Internat'l Journal of Childbirth Education. q. adv.
ICEA Review. q.
ICEA Bookmarks. 3/yr.
Membership Directory. a. adv.
Annual Meetings:
1987-Los Angeles, CA(Los Angeles Airport Marriott)/July 3-5/750-1,000
1987-Washington, DC(Radisson Mark Plaza)/Aug. 14-16/750-1,000

Internat'l Chiropractors Ass'n (1926)
1901 L St., N.W., Suite 800, Washington DC 20036
Exec. V. President: B.E. Nordstrom, D.C.
Members: 9,000 *Staff:* 21
Annual Budget: $2-5,000,000 *Tel:* (202) 659-6476
Hist. Note: Established as the Chiropractic Health Bureau, it assumed its present name in 1941. A professional society of chiropractors which supports the International Chiropractors Political Action Committee.
Publications:
Internat'l Review of Chiropractic. q. adv.
ICA Today. bi-m.
Annual Meetings: Spring
1987-Las Vegas, NV/July 2-5

00157 12 05 86 1233

Internat'l Circulation Managers Ass'n (1898)
The Newspaper Center, 11600 Sunrise Valley Drive, Reston VA 22091
General Manager: Joseph B. Forsee
Members: 1,500-1,600 *Staff:* 2-5
Annual Budget: $500-1,000,000 *Tel:* (703) 620-9555
Hist. Note: Established in Detroit, MI as the Nat'l Ass'n of Newspaper Circulation Managers. Became international in 1910. Membership: $50-350/yr. (based on circulation).
Publications:
Buyers Guide and Convention Program. a. adv.
Conference Book of Proceedings. a.
Official ICMA Update. m. adv.
Annual Meetings: Spring/1,000
1987-Chicago, IL(Hyatt)/June 29-July 2
1988-Dallas, TX
1989-Nashville, TN
1990-San Francisco, CA
1991-Boston, MA

Internat'l City Management Ass'n (1914)
1120 G St., N.W., Suite 300, Washington DC 20005
Exec. Director: William H. Hansell, Jr.
Members: 7,000-7,200 *Staff:* 70-80
Annual Budget: $1-2,000,000 *Tel:* (202) 626-4600
Hist. Note: Founded as the Internat'l City Managers Ass'n, it assumed its present name in 1969. A professional society of city and county administrators.
Publications:
Management Information Service. m.
Municipal Year Book. a.
Public Management. m. adv.
Urban Data Service. m.
Annual Meetings: Fall
1987-Montreal, Quebec/Oct. 25-29

Internat'l Claim Ass'n (1909)
Mississippi River at 17th St., Rock Island IL 61201
Secretary: C. Ernest Beane
Members: 465 *Staff:* 1
Annual Budget: $250-500,000 *Tel:* (309) 786-6481
Hist. Note: Members are life and health insurance companies represented by claims employees and officers. Membership: $200/yr.
Publications:
ICA News. q.
Proceedings. a.
Annual Meetings: Fall
1987-New Orleans, LA(Fairmont)/Sept. 12-16/1,100
1988-Marco Island, FL(Marriott)/Oct. 16-19/1,100
1989-Palm Desert, CA(Marriott)/Sept. 17-20/1,100

Internat'l Cogeneration Soc. (1978)
1700 K St., N.W., Suite 1300, Washington DC 20006
President: Glenn Lovin
Members: 2,000 companies *Staff:* 2-5
Annual Budget: $100-250,000 *Tel:* (202) 659-1552
Hist. Note: Companies using "co-generation", a process in which the heat and steam produced in the generation of electricity are used for additional purposes. Incorporated in the District of Columbia in April 1978.
Publication:
Cogeneration World.
Annual Meetings: October

Internat'l Coil Winding Ass'n (1977)
Box 35395, Minneapolis MN 55435
Exec. Director: Frank McGuinn
Members: 80 companies, 300 individuals *Staff:* 2
Annual Budget: $250-500,000 *Tel:* (612) 935-7653
Hist. Note: Formerly the North American Council of the Internat'l Coil Winding Ass'n. Membership: $25/yr. (individual); $150/yr. (organization/company)
Publications:
ICWA Newsletter. q.
Directory of Members. a.
Technical Proceedings. a.
Annual Meetings: Fall
1987-Rosemont. IL(Rosemont Convention Center)/Oct.5-8/7,000
1988-Cincinnati, OH(Cincinnati Convention Center)/Oct. 3-6/6,000

Internat'l College of Applied Nutrition (1960)
Box 1050, Temple City CA 91780
Exec. Director: B. Stabell
Members: 1,200 *Staff:* 2-5
Annual Budget: $50-100,000 *Tel:* (818) 286-3123
Hist. Note: Formerly American Academy of Nutrition. Membership: $75/year.
Publications:
Journal of Applied Nutrition. semi-a.
Newsletter. bi-m.
Annual Meetings: Summer

Internat'l College of Dentists, U.S.A. Section (1928)
12651 South Dixie Highway, Miami FL 33156
Registrar: Franklin M. Kenward, D.D.S.
Members: 7,000 *Staff:* 2-5
Annual Budget: $50-100,000 *Tel:* (305) 255-7001
Hist. Note: Members are dentists who have made an outstanding contribution to the profession of dentistry.
Publications:
Letterette. a.
Newsletter. a.
Annual Meetings: Fall

Internat'l College of Real Estate Consulting Professionals (1972)
120 6th St. South, #808, Minneapolis MN 55402-1803
President: W.A. Russell
Members: 150 *Staff:* 2-5
Annual Budget: $10-25,000 *Tel:* (612) 665-6280
Hist. Note: Membership includes attorneys, appraisers, architects, brokers, engineers, planners, property managers and mortgage bankers. Established as the Amerciaan College of Real Estate Consultants, it absorbed the Nat'l Ass'n of Real Estate Counselors in 1979 and assumed its present name in 1981. Absorbed the Nat'l Ass'n of Real Estate Counselors in 1979. Awards the RECP ("Real Estate Consulting Professional") designation.
Publications:
Directory. a.
Newsletter. m.

Internat'l College of Surgeons (U.S. Section) (1935)
1516 Lake Shore Drive, Chicago IL 60610
Exec. Director (U.S. Section): Robert T. Shirley, CAE
Members: 7,000 *Staff:* 20-25
Annual Budget: $500-1,000,000 *Tel:* (312) 787-6274
Hist. Note: Founded in Geneva, Switzerland 1935 and incorporated in the District of Columbia in 1940, ICS is a federation of general surgeons and surgical specialists with a worldwide membership of 13,500. Admission to the U.S. section is contingent upon a candidate's board certification in his specialty or as deemed equivalent by the Qualifications Council. Membership: $170/yr.
Publications:
International Surgery. bi-m. adv.
U.S. News and Notes (newsletter). q.
Annual Meetings: Spring (U.S. Section) and Biennial International Meetings
1987-Washington, DC(Sheraton Washington)/April 3-5/300
1988-New Orleans, LA(Royal Orleans Hotel)/Feb. 12-14/300
1989-San Francisco, CA

Internat'l Communication Ass'n (1950)
Box 9589, Austin TX 78766
Exec. Director: Robert L. Cox
Members: 2,350 individuals *Staff:* 2-5
Annual Budget: $100-250,000 *Tel:* (512) 454-8299
Hist. Note: Founded December 1950 in Chicago as the Nat'l Soc. for the Study of Communication. Adopted its present name in 1969 when it was incorporated in Ohio. A founding member of the Council of Communication Socities and affiliate of the American Ass'n for the Advancement of Science. Encourages the systematic study of communication theories, processes and skills. Not to be confused with the Internat'l Communications Ass'n.
Publications:
Human Communication Research. q.
Journal of Communication. q.
ICA Newsletter. q. adv.
Membership Directory. bien. adv.
Annual Meetings: Spring
1987-Montreal, Quebec/May 21-25
1988-New Orleans, LA/May 29-June 2

Internat'l Communications Ass'n (1948)
12750 Merit, LB-89, Suite 710, Dallas TX 75251
Exec. Director: Stephen M. Christie
Members: 600 companies; 1,600 individuals *Staff:* 8
Annual Budget: $1-2,000,000 *Tel:* (214) 233-3889
Hist. Note: Founded as the Nat'l Committee of Communications Supervisors. Became the Industrial Communications Ass'n in 1953 and assumed its present name in 1966. Individuals responsible for telecommunications services within their companies. Membership: $500/yr.
Publications:
Communique. bi-m.
Membership Roster. a.
Annual Meetings: Spring
1987-New Orleans, LA(Hilton)/May 17-22
1988-Anaheim, CA(Hilton)/May 15-20
1989-Dallas, TX/May 21-26

Internat'l Communications Industries Ass'n (1939)
3150 Spring St., Fairfax VA 22031-2399
Exec. V. President: Harry R. McGee, CAE
Members: 900-1,000 *Staff:* 25
Annual Budget: $2-5,000,000 *Tel:* (703) 273-7200
Hist. Note: Members are audio-visual, video, computer dealers equipment manufacturers and material producers. Cooperates with other industry associations on projects such as legislation, copyright, international marketing, statistics, and technical standards. Awards the CTS (Certified Technology Specialist) designation. Sponsors and supports the Audio-Visual Communications Fund Political Action Committee. Absorbed the Ass'n of Media Producers in 1982. The Independent Media Producers Ass'n became a council within ICIA in 1985. Formerly (1983) the Nat'l Audio-Visual Ass'n.
Publications:
Equipment Directory of Audio-Visual, Computer and Video Products. a.
Communications Industries Report. bi-w.
Annual Meetings: Jan.-Feb./11,000
1987-Atlanta, GA/Feb. 24-28
1988-New Orleans, LA/Jan. 13-18
1989-Dallas, TX/Feb. 9-13
1990-Anaheim, CA/Jan. 18-22

Internat'l Communications Industries Ass'n Materials Division (1969)
3150 Spring St., Fairfax VA 22031
Chairman: Fay Paras
Members: 400 companies and individuals *Staff:* 2-5
Annual Budget: $25-50,000 *Tel:* (703) 273-7200
Hist. Note: Founded in 1969 as the Educational Materials Producers Council. Became the Educational Media Producers Council in 1973, the NAVA Materials Council in 1976, and the ICIA Materials Division in 1984. Is now a division of the International Communications Industries Association. Members include audio-visual and microcomputer software producers and dealers.
Annual Meetings: January/10-11,000
1987-Atlanta/Feb. 26-28
1988-New Orleans/Jan. 13-18
1989-Dallas, TX/Feb. 9-13

Internat'l Concatenated Order of Hoo-Hoo (1892)
Box 118, Gurdon AR 71743
Exec. Secretary: Billy W. Tarpley
Members: 7,000-7,500 *Staff:* 2-5
Annual Budget: $100-250,000 *Tel:* (501) 353-4997
Hist. Note: Does business under "Hoo-Hoo International" and "International Order of Hoo-Hoo". Members are represenatives of the forest products and lumber industry, lumber associations and lumber press. Originated in Gurdon, Arkansas when several lumber executives were stranded by a railroad washout. International in scope with chapters in Canada, Australia, New Zealand, New Guinea and Singapore, among others.
Publication:
Log & Talley. q. adv.
Annual Meetings: September
1987-Seattle, WA
1988-Orlando, FL
1989-Honolulu, HI
1990-San Francisco, CA

Internat'l Conference Industry Ass'n
Hist. Note: Ceased operations in 1986.

Internat'l Conference of Administrators of Residential Agencies (1923)
18 Prospect St., Stamford NY 12167
Secy.-Treas.: Frederick R. Allen
Members: 150-175 *Staff:* 1
Annual Budget: under $10,000 *Tel:* (607) 652-2576
Hist. Note: Formerly (until 1979) known as the Nat'l Conference of Superintendents of Training Schools and Reformatories.

Internat'l Conference of Building Officials (1922)
5360 South Workman Mill Rd., Whittier CA 90601
President: James E. Bihr
Members: 8,000 *Staff:* 80
Annual Budget: over $5,000,000 *Tel:* (213) 699-0541
Hist. Note: Membership in the Conference is open to all governmental units as well as all other segments of the building construction industry. Publishes the Uniform Building Code, related code documents and educational texts; maintains a products/systems evaluation service; and sponsors an educational program leading to inspector certification. Has an annual budget of $8 million.
Publications:
Building Standards Magazine. bi-m. adv.
Building Standards Newsletter. bi-m.
Annual Meetings: Fall/1,000-1,200
1987-Kansas City, MO(Vista)
1988-Seattle, WA
1989-Southern California
1990-Denver, CO
1991-Boise, ID(Red Lion)

Internat'l Conference of Police Chaplains (1973)
Rte. 5, Box 310, Livingston TX 77351
Exec. Secretary: David W. DeRevere
Members: 600-650 *Staff:* 1
Annual Budget: $50-100,000 *Tel:* (409) 327-2322
Hist. Note: Provides education and support for law enforcement chaplains. Assists law enforcement agencies start chaplaincy programs. Membership: $35/yr.
Publications:
Chaplains Handbook. irreg.
Directory of Police Chaplains. m.
Newsletter. 9/yr.
Annual Meetings: July
1987-Cincinnati, OH/July 13-17/125
1988-Baltimore, MD/July 4-9/150

Internat'l Conference of Symphony and Opera Musicians (1960)
Box 20013, Seattle WA 98102
Secretary: Nancy Griffin
Members: 4,500 *Staff:* 2-5
Annual Budget: $50-100,000 *Tel:* (206) 329-3118
Hist. Note: Professional symphony, opera and ballet musicians united to promote the welfare of and make more rewarding the livelihood of the orchestral performer and to disseminate inter-orchestra information through correspondence and a newsletter. Affiliated with the American Federation of Musicians.
Publications:
Senza Sordino. bi-m.
Directory. bien.

00158 12 05 86 1233

Internat'l Congress of Oral Implantologists (1976)
Box 2277, Grand Central Station, New York NY 10163
Exec. Director: Margaret M. Jackson
Members: 1,000 *Staff:* 3
Annual Budget: $250-500,000 *Tel:* (201) 783-6300
Hist. Note: Dentist, oral surgeons, research personnel and others involved in oral implant procedures. Membership: $200/yr.
Publication:
IMPLANTOLOGIST. semi-a. adv.
Annual Meetings:
1987-Leawood, KS/March 20-21/150

Internat'l Consumer Credit Ass'n (1912)
Hist. Note: Became the Internat'l Credit Ass'n. (1985)

Internat'l Coordinating Committee on Solid State Sensors and Actuators Research (1981)
c/o Electronics Design Center, Case Western Reserve University, Cleveland OH 44106
Chairman: Wen H. Ko
Members: 35
Annual Budget: $50-100,000 *Tel:* (216) 368-2071
Publication:
Digest of Internat'l Conference on Sensors & Actuators. Bien.
Annual Meetings: Biennial
1987-Tokyo, Japan/June
1989-Europe/June

Internat'l Copper Research Ass'n (1960)
708 Third Ave., New York NY 10017
President: William H. Dresher
Members: 21 *Staff:* 9
Annual Budget: $2-5,000,000 *Tel:* (212) 697-9355
Hist. Note: Formerly Copper Products Development Ass'n, INCRA is the technical research arm of the world copper industry. Without laboratories of its own, INCRA, through contracts with other organizations, carries out research designed to increase the world's use and knowledge of copper. Membership fee based on member's copper production.
Annual Meetings: June

Internat'l Council for Computer Communication (1972)
Box 9745, Washington DC 20016-9745
Exec. Secretary: Dr. Pramode Verma
Members: 60-70 individuals *Staff:* 1
Annual Budget: $10-25,000 *Tel:* (301) 530-7628
Hist. Note: An honorary society of computer communication professionals affiliated with the Internat'l Soc. for Information Processing.
Publication:
Computer Networks. bi-m. adv.
Biennial Meetings: even years.
1988-Tel Aviv

Internat'l Council for Computers in Education (1979)
1787 Agate St., Univ. of Oregon, Eugene OR 97403
C.E.O.: Dr. David Moursund
Members: 13,000 *Staff:* 11
Annual Budget: $250-500,000 *Tel:* (503) 686-4414
Hist. Note: Membership: $21.50/yr.
Publications:
The Computing Teacher. 9/yr. adv.
The SIG Bulletin. q.
Annual Meetings: Nat'l Educational Computing Conference
1987-Philadelphia, PA/3,000

Internat'l Council for Small Business (1956)
105 Harris Hall, University of Missouri-Rolla, Rolla MO 65401
President: Donald D. Myers
Members: 8-900 *Staff:* 2-5
Annual Budget: $25-50,000 *Tel:* (314) 341-4004
Hist. Note: Formerly (1977) Nat'l Council for Small Business Management Development. Membership: $60/yr.(individual with subscription) Questions concerning the Journal should be directed to: Editor, Stan Klock at the Bureau of Business Research, West Virginia University, P.O. Box 6025, Morgantown, WV 26506-6025.
Publications:
Journal of Small Business Management. q. adv.
ICSB Newsletter. q.
Annual Meetings: June

Internat'l Council of Airshows (1968)
Box 1105, Jackson MI 49204
Exec. Director: Rick Nadeau
Members: 360 *Staff:* 1
Annual Budget: $100-250,000 *Tel:* (517) 782-2424
Hist. Note: Members consist of sponsors, promoters, producers and air show performers. Membership: $150
Publications:
ICAS News Magazine. q. adv.
Newsletter. 8/yr.
Annual Meetings: Winter

Internat'l Council of Psychologists (1941)
4805 Regent St., Madison WI 53705
Secy.-Gen.: Mrs. Patricia W. Cautley, Ph.D.
Members: 1,700-1,800 *Staff:* 2-5
Annual Budget: $25-50,000 *Tel:* (608) 238-5373
Hist. Note: Established as Nat'l Council of Women Psychologists in the U.S.A. Became (1947) Internat'l Council of Women Psychologists, and (1960) Internat'l Council of Psychologists. Membership: $25/year.
Publications:
Directory of Members. bien. adv.
International Psychologist. q. adv.
Annual Meetings: July/August
1987-New York,NY/Aug. 23-26/200-300
1988-Singapore/Aug. 20-24/150-200

Internat'l Council of Shopping Centers (1957)
665 Fifth Ave., New York NY 10022
Exec. V. President: John Riordan
Members: 18,000 *Staff:* 60-65
Annual Budget: over $5,000,000 *Tel:* (212) 421-8181
Hist. Note: Owners, developers, managers, retailers and suppliers of shopping centers. Sponsors professional accreditation programs for Certified Shopping Center Manager (CSM) and certified Marketing Director (CMD). Has an annual budget of $12.5 million. Membership: $75/yr.(individual); $400/yr.(company).
Publications:
Public Affairs Report. m.
Shopping Centers Today. m. adv.
Research Quarterly.
Leasing Opportunities.
Annual Meetings: Spring in Las Vegas, NV(Hilton/Convention Ctr.)/10,000

Internat'l Craniopathic Soc. (1972)
Hist. Note: Merged in 1982 with the Sacro-Occipital Research Soc. Internat'l.

Internat'l Credit Ass'n (1912)
243 North Lindbergh Blvd., P.O. Box 27357, St. Louis MO 63141
President: William J. Henderson
Members: 18,000 individuals *Staff:* 15-20
Annual Budget: $500-1,000,000 *Tel:* (314) 991-3030
Hist. Note: Originally (1912) Nat'l Retail Credit Ass'n; most recently (1985) Internat'l Consumer Credit Ass'n. Awards the Certified Consumer Credit Executive, "CCCE", designation through its Soc. of Certified Credit Executives.
Publications:
Consumer Trends. m.
ICA Newsletter. m.
The Credit World. bi-m. adv.
Annual Meetings: June
1987-Seattle, WA(Westin)
1988-Maui, HI(Marriott)
1989-San Antonio, TX(Hyatt)

Internat'l Customer Service Ass'n (1981)
111 E. Wacker Drive, Suite 600, Chicago IL 60601
Exec. Director: Madalyn Duerr
Members: 1,400 *Staff:* 1
Annual Budget: $100-250,000 *Tel:* (312) 644-6610
Hist. Note: A professional association of customer service managers incorporated in the State of Illinois May 13, 1981.
Publication:
ICSA News. bi-m.
Annual Meetings: Fall

Internat'l Dairy-Deli Ass'n (1965)
Box 5528, Madison WI 53705
Exec. Director: Carol L. Christison
Members: 360 companies *Staff:* 7
Annual Budget: $500-1,000,000 *Tel:* (608) 238-7908
Hist. Note: Members are companies involved in the production, processing or selling of deli, dairy and bakery products. Formerly (1985) the Internat'l Cheese and Deli Ass'n.
Publication:
Dairy-Deli Wrap Up. q.
Annual Meetings: May
1987-Miami Beach, FL/May 17-19

Internat'l Dance-Exercise Ass'n (1982)
4501 Mission Bay Drive, Suite 2-F, San Diego CA 92109
Exec. Director: Kathie Davis
Members: 11,000 *Staff:* 22
Annual Budget: $1-2,000,000 *Tel:* (619) 274-2770
Hist. Note: The largest association for dance-exercise professionals, representing all 50 states and 32 foreign countries. Membership: $48/yr. (individual), $150/yr. (company).
Publications:
Dance Exercise Today. 9/yr. adv.
IDEA Annual Directory. a. adv.
Annual Meetings: June
1987-Anaheim, CA(Disneyland Hotel)/2,500

Internat'l Database Ass'n (1983)
Hist. Note: Reported defunct in 1985.

Internat'l Deli-Bakery Ass'n (1982)
P.O. Box 33235, Decatur GA 30033
Exec. V. President: Carl Baker
Members: 150 companies; 400 individuals *Staff:* 2
Annual Budget: $50-100,000 *Tel:* (404) 325-4322
Hist. Note: Membership open to any interested person or firm that supports Association efforts to achieve industry growth. Membership: $250-500/yr. (company).
Publications:
Newsletter. q.
Membership/Reference Book. a. adv.
The Advocate Newsletter. m.
Annual Meetings:
1987-Atlantic City, NJ(Convention Center)/March 29-31/800

Internat'l Desalination Ass'n (1973)
10 South Main St., Box 387, Topsfield MA 01983
Secretary General: Patricia A. Burke
Members: 450 individuals, companies and public agencies
Staff: 1
Annual Budget: $250-500,000 *Tel:* (617) 887-8101
Hist. Note: Established as the National Water Supply Improvement Association, became the Water Supply Improvement Ass'n in 1982, and assumed its present name in 1985 upon merging with the Internat'l Deslination and Environmental Ass'n. Members are producers and users of water desalinization equipment. In addition to the biennial meetings, the associaton holds regional affiliate meetings in even years and several seminars/workshops.
Publications:
Newsletter. bi-m.
Journal. semi-a.
Proceedings of Biennial Conference. bien.
Biennial Meetings: Odd years

Internat'l Die Sinkers' Conference (1940)
4807 Rockside Road, Independence OH 44131
President: James H. Anderson
Members: 3,000 *Staff:* 6-10
Annual Budget: $250-500,000 *Tel:* (216) 447-9797
Hist. Note: Independent labor union.
Publication:
News Flash. q.
Semi-annual meetings: Spring and Fall

Internat'l District Heating and Cooling Ass'n (1909)
1101 Connecticut Ave., N.W., Suite 700, Washington DC 20036
Exec. Director: Frederick R. Callowhill
Members: 300 *Staff:* 2-5
Annual Budget: $100-250,000 *Tel:* (202) 429-5111
Hist. Note: Formerly (1969) Nat'l District Healing Ass'n and the (1985) Internat'l District Heating Ass'n. Members are owners/operators of District (central) heating and cooling systems, suppliers of centralized piping systems and appurtenances that produce hot water, and architects/engineers associated with the design of such systems.
Publications:
District Heating. q. adv.
Proceedings. a.
Annual Meetings: June
1987-Baltimore, MD(Lord Baltimore)/June 21-25/350
1988-Chautauqua, NY/June 19-23

Internat'l District Heating Ass'n (1909)
Hist. Note: Became the Internat'l District Heating and Cooling Ass'n (1985).

Internat'l Documentary Ass'n (1982)
8480 Beverly Blvd., Los Angeles CA 90048
Administrative Director: Mark Bahny
Members: 25 companies, 450 individuals *Staff:* 2
Annual Budget: $50-100,000 *Tel:* (213) 655-7089
Hist. Note: Members are professionals in the fields of non-fiction and documentary film and video. Membership: $50/yr.
Publications:
International Documentary. q. adv.
IDA Membership Directory. a.

Internat'l Downtown Ass'n (1954)
915 15th St., N.W., Suite 900, Washington DC 20005
President: Richard H. Bradley
Members: 400 *Staff:* 6
Annual Budget: $250-500,000 *Tel:* (202) 783-4963
Hist. Note: Formerly (1986) Internat'l Downtown Executives Ass'n. Members are downtown development organizations represented by chief executive officer; city, county or state agencies involved with downtown economic development; and individuals and corporations with an interest in downtown development. Operates a subsidiary for program development, the Downtown Development Foundation.
Publication:
Center City Report. bi-m.
Annual Meetings: Fall
1987-Cleveland, OH/Sept. 20-24
1988-Denver, CO/Oct. 2-6

Internat'l Drapery Ass'n (1965)
11555 Monarch St., Garden Grove CA 92645
Exec. Director: James Hirashiki
Members: 150-200 companies *Staff:* 6-10
Annual Budget: $100-250,000 *Tel:* (714) 898-0583
Hist. Note: Established as the White Front Drapery Concessionaire, it assumed its present name in 1973. Members are retail drapery merchants with established stores.
Annual Meetings: July

Internat'l Drycleaners Congress (1959)
Box 8629, San Jose CA 95155
Exec. Director: George M. Shepherd
Members: 1,066 individuals *Staff:* 3
Annual Budget: $50-100,000 *Tel:* (408) 286-2969
Hist. Note: IDC is a world-wide organization of fabric care industry leaders in 45 countries who believe they can and should make a contribution to international understanding and goodwill. Membership: $38/yr.
Publication:
IDC News. bi-m.
Annual Meetings: Fall
1987-San Francisco, CA

00159 12 05 86 1233

1988-England
1989-Taiwan
1990-West Germany

Internat'l Dwarf Fruit Tree Ass'n (1958)
Plant & Oil Sciences Bldg., Michigan State University, East Lansing MI 48824-1112
Exec. Secretary: Ronald L. Perry
Members: 1,900-2,000 *Staff:* 2-5
Annual Budget: $25-50,000 *Tel:* (517) 355-5200
Hist. Note: Founded in a cold storage warehouse in Hartford, Michigan in 1958. Membership: $40/yr.
Publications:
Compact Fruit Tree, Proceedings of the Annual Conference.
Newsletter. q.
Annual Meetings: March
1987-Toronto, Ontario/March 1-4
1988-Hershey, PA
1989-Grand Rapids, MI

Internat'l Electrical Testing Ass'n
1718 Connecticut Ave., N.W., Suite 310, Washington DC 20009
Exec. Director: Dr. Mary R. Denton
Members: 61 companies *Staff:* 1
Annual Budget: $100-250,000 *Tel:* (704) 332-1682
Hist. Note: Formerly the Nat'l Electrical Testing Ass'n. Members are independent firms in testing, analysis and maintenance of electical power systems; associate members are firms supplying services for the power systems industry. Membership: $500/yr.
Publications:
NETA World. q. adv.
NETA Conference Program. a. adv.
Annual Meetings: March
1987-San Francisco, CA(Claremont)/March 17-20
1988-Orlando, FL(Contemporary)/March 15-18

Internat'l Electronic Facsimile Users Ass'n (1978)
Hist. Note: Commercial and inplant users of electronic facsimile equipment and their suppliers. Originally conceived as a division of the Nat'l Ass'n of Quick Printers, it became independent in 1979 and was inactive in 1982. Defunct.

Internat'l Electronic Packaging Soc. (1977)
114 N. Hale St., Wheaton IL 60187
Director: William D. Ashman
Members: 1,000 *Staff:* 1
Annual Budget: $100-250,000 *Tel:* (312) 260-1044
Hist. Note: Engineers responsible for the packaging design of electronic systems.
Publication:
Newsletter. q.
Annual Meetings: Fall/650
1987-Boston, MA(Marriott)/Nov.10-12
1988-Dallas, TX(Marriott)/Nov. 8-10

Internat'l Embryo Transfer Soc. (1974)
309 W. Clark St., Champaign IL 61820
Business Manager: Carl Johnson
Members: 870 individuals *Staff:* 2
Annual Budget: $100-250,000 *Tel:* (217) 356-3182
Hist. Note: Active members are persons interested in the technology of embryo transfer with a veterinary, master's or doctorate degree in a field related to embryo transfer. Membership: $60/yr.
Publication:
Embryo Transfer Newsletter. q.
Annual Meetings: January
1987-Dublin, Ireland(Burlington)/Jan. 25-27/350
1988-Ft. Collins, CO/Jan. 17-19/350

Internat'l Endodontic Soc.
Hist. Note: Defunct in 1984.

Internat'l Erosion Control Ass'n (1972)
Box 195, Pinole CA 94564
Exec. Director: Michael McMillan
Members: 300 individuals, 70 companies *Staff:* 1
Annual Budget: $25-50,000 *Tel:* (415) 223-2134
Hist. Note: Landscape contractors, architects, engineers, and suppliers, as well as government officials concerned about soil erosion. Membership: $50/yr.(individual), $200/yr.(organization).
Publications:
Newsletter. q.
Proceedings. a.
Annual Meetings: February/200
1987-Reno, NV/Feb. 26-27

Internat'l Exchangors Ass'n (1978)
Drawer L, Rancho Santa Fe CA 92067
Chairman: Dr. A.D. Kessler
Members: 3,200 *Staff:* 2
Annual Budget: $100-250,000 *Tel:* (619) 756-1441
Hist. Note: Professionals involved in exchanging real estate. Awards the C.E. (Certified Exchanger) designation.
Publications:
Creative Real Estate Magazine. m.
Listing Book. m.
Roster of Exchangors. q.
Annual Meetings: Spring

Internat'l Exhibitors Ass'n (1966)
5103-B Backlick Road, Annandale VA 22003
Exec. Director: Robert C. La Prad
Members: 1,200 companies *Staff:* 6-8
Annual Budget: $1-2,000,000 *Tel:* (703) 941-3725
Hist. Note: Members are companies using exhibits for marketing, advertising or public relations. Founded as the Natural Trade Show Exhibitors Association, it assumed its present name in 1983. Awards the CES ("Certified Exhibits Specialist") designation. Membership: $225/yr.
Publications:
"IDEAS" Newsletter. m. adv.
Exhibitor Industry Guide. a. adv.
Exhibitor Workbook. a.
Annual Budget Guide. a.
Salary Survey. bien.
Membership Directory.
Annual Meetings: Summer
1987-Louisville, KY
1988-Phoenix, AZ

Internat'l Fabricare Institute (1972)
12251 Tech Rd., Silver Spring MD 20904
Exec. V. President: Charles R. Riggott
Members: 11,000 companies *Staff:* 50
Annual Budget: $1-2,000,000 *Tel:* (301) 622-1900
Hist. Note: Merger (1972) of the American Institute of Laundering (1883) and the Nat'l Institute of Drycleaning (1907). The educational and research center for the drycleaning and laundry industries in the U.S.
Publications:
Fabricare News. m.
Focus. bi-m.
Special Reporter. bi-m.
Annual Meetings: Spring
1987-Atlanta, GA(April 27-30
1988-Open
1989-Dallas, TX/March 6-9

Internat'l Facility Management Ass'n (1980)
Summit Tower, Suite 1410, 11 Greenway Plaza, Houston TX 77046
Exec. Director: Mel Schlitt
Members: 3,500 individuals *Staff:* 6
Annual Budget: $500-1,000,000 *Tel:* (713) 623-4362
Hist. Note: Founded as the Nat'l Facility Management Ass'n, it assumed its present name in 1982. Regular membership is open to any individual who is an in-house member or manager of a department responsible for planning, designing or managing his organization's facilities. Membership: $125/yr. (individual); $300/yr. (organization/company)
Publications:
Facility Management News. bi-m.
Directory. a.
Conference Proceedings. a.
Conference Directory. a. adv.
Annual Meetings: Fall
1987-Dallas, TX(Fairmont)/Nov. 1-4/1,500
1988-Atlanta, GA(Westin Peachtree Plaza)/Oct. 23-26/2,000
1989-Baltimore, MD

Internat'l Federation for Choral Music (1982)
College of Music, CB 301, University of Colorado, Boulder CO 80309-0301
Sec. General: Walter S. Collins
Members: 50 organizations; 300 individuals
Annual Budget: $10-25,000 *Tel:* (303) 447-8537
Hist. Note: The Federation was formed to strengthen cooperation between national and international organizations interested in choral music, encourage formations of new choral organizations, promote international exchange programs and the inclusion of choral music in general education, and to inform the public of occurences in the choral field. Membership: $20/yr. (indidivual); variable for organizatins.
Publications:
International Choral Bulletin. q. adv.
World Census of Choral Music. irreg.
Triennial: August
1988-Pecs, Hungary

Internat'l Federation of Advertising Agencies (1950)
1605 Main St., Suite 1115, Sarasota FL 33577
Managing Director: Kenneth M. Hill
Members: 40-50 companies *Staff:* 2-5
Annual Budget: $50-100,000 *Tel:* (813) 366-2902
Hist. Note: Chartered in California as the National Federation of Advertising Agencies, it assumed its present name in 1979. Members are non-competing local advertising agencies, about 60% of which are American.
Publication:
Newsletter. m.
Annual Meetings: Spring
1987-Pebble Beach, CA(Pebble Beach Lodge)/April 12-16/75
1988-Copenhagen, Denmark/May 25-28/75

Internat'l Federation of Health Professionals (1970)
402 West 47th St., New York NY 10036
President: William Perry
Members: 8,573 individuals *Staff:* 22
Annual Budget: $2-5,000,000 *Tel:* (212) 489-9540
Hist. Note: Labor union. Members are medical personnel, blue and white collar workers and transport workers united to oppose the influence of "third party" health insurance organizations destructive of the classical doctor- patient realtionship.
Publication:
Local 6 Voice.
Annual Meetings: Every 3 years (August 1988)

Internat'l Federation of Professional and Technical Engineers (1918)
8701 Georgia Ave., Suite 701, Silver Spring MD 20910
President: Rodney A. Bower
Members: 26,000 *Staff:* 15
Annual Budget: $500-1,000,000 *Tel:* (301) 565-9016
Hist. Note: Founded in Washington, DC July 1, 1918 as the International Federation of Draftsmen's Unions and affiliated with the American Federation of Labor. Became the International Federation of Technical Engineers' Architects' and Draftsmen's Unions in 1919, the American Federation of Technical Engineers in 1953 and assumed its present name in 1973.
Publication:
Outlook. bi-m.
Biennial meetings: Even years in July

Internat'l Federation of Women's Travel Organizations
Hist. Note: No paid staff; address unknown in 1986.

Internat'l Fence Industry Ass'n (1962)
8609 Cross Park Drive, Austin TX 78754
Exec. V. President: Kay L. Knapp
Members: 750-800 companies *Staff:* 5
Annual Budget: $250-500,000 *Tel:* (512) 339-8376
Hist. Note: Membership: $265/yr.
Publication:
Fence Post. m. adv.
Annual Meetings: Jan.-Feb./2,000
1987-San Diego, CA(Town & Country)/Feb. 4-7
1988-Orlando, FL(Marriott World Resort)/Jan. 12-15
1989-New Orleans, LA(Marriott)/Jan. 11-14

Internat'l Festivals Ass'n (1956)
Box 1828, St. Petersburg FL 33731
Exec. V. President: Herbert C. Melleney
Members: 200-225 *Staff:* 2
Annual Budget: $100-250,000 *Tel:* (813) 898-1828
Hist. Note: Members are individuals employed by the administrations of community and civic festivals.
Publication:
Festivals International. q.
Annual Meetings: September
1987-El Paso, TX(Paso del Norte)/Aug. 25-30/350
1988-Ottawa, Ontario/400
1989-Seattle, WA(Westin)

Internat'l Fire Photographers Ass'n (1965)
Box 201, Elmhurst IL 60126-0201
President: William E. Reynolds
Members: 750-800 *Staff:* 3
Annual Budget: under $10,000 *Tel:* (312) 530-3097
Hist. Note: Photographers affiliated with a fire department. Dedicated to promoting the use of photography in arson investigations and in fire prevention education. Has no paid staff. Certification program awards designations of Journeyman, Craftsman and Master Fire Photographer. Membership: $18/yr.
Publication:
Fire Photography Journal. q. adv.
Annual Meetings: June
1987-Rolling Meadows, IL(Holiday Inn)/June 17-20/65

Internat'l Food Additives Council (1980)
5775 Peachtree-Dunwoody Rd., Suite 500D, Atlanta GA 30342
President: Robert H. Kellen
Members: 12 companies *Staff:* 6
Tel: (404) 252-3663
Hist. Note: Information clearing house concerning the use in food and safety of food additives. Serves as a regulatory and scientific liaison for industry concerning food additives.
Annual Meetings: Mid-December in Washington, DC

Internat'l Food Information Council (1985)
1250 Eye St., N.W., Suite 300, Washington DC 20005
Exec. Director: Thomas E. Stenzel
Members: 10 companies *Staff:* 2
Annual Budget: $250-500,000 *Tel:* (202) 289-2005
Hist. Note: Established in December, 1985, IFIC is primarily concerned with providing information on the health and safety aspects of food ingredients to a wide variety of concerned groups.
Annual Meetings: Fall

Internat'l Food Service Executives' Ass'n (1901)
111 East Wacker Dr., Chicago IL 60601
Exec. V. President: Barbara Chalik
Members: 3,000 *Staff:* 2-5
Annual Budget: $100-250,000 *Tel:* (312) 644-6610
Hist. Note: Formerly (1957) Internat'l Stewards' and Caterers' Ass'n and (1977) Food Service Executives' Ass'n, Inc. Administers the Certified Food Executive (CFE) program.
Annual Meetings: Summer
1987-Miami Beach, FL(Fountainebleu)

Internat'l Food, Wine and Travel Writers Ass'n (1956)
206 North Hermosa Drive, Palm Springs CA 92262

00160 12 05 86 1233

Exec. Director: Don Jackson
Members: over 100 individuals *Staff:* 1
Annual Budget: under $10,000 *Tel:* (619) 320-4271
Hist. Note: Established in Paris. Headquarters moved to California in 1981. Members are freelance and/or staff writers specializing in food, wine and/or travel writing. Membership: $50/yr.
Publication:
Hospitality World. q.
Annual Meetings: None held

Internat'l Foodservice Distributors Ass'n (1956)
201 Park Washington Court, Falls Church VA 22046
Exec. Director: Gilbert L. Kretzer
Members: 250 companies *Staff:* 2-5
Annual Budget: $100-250,000 *Tel:* (703) 532-9400
Hist. Note: Formerly Food Service Distributors Institute. Merged (1969) with Institutional Food Distributors of America. A semi-autonomous division of the National-American Wholesale Grocers' Association. Members supply the "eat-away-from-home" industry with food and supplies.
Publications:
IFDA Buyers' Bulletin. m.
IFDA Fiscal Controls Bulletin. m.
IFDA Foodservice Report. m.
IFDA Operations Bulletin. m.
IFDA Sales Manager's Bulletin. m.
IFDA Washington Report.
Annual Meetings: With Nat'l American Wholesale Grocers' Ass'n
1987-Chicago, IL(Hyatt)/March 22-25

Internat'l Foodservice Manufacturers Ass'n (1952)
875 North Michigan Ave., Chicago IL 60611
President: Michael J. Licata
Members: 400-450 companies *Staff:* 15-20
Annual Budget: $2-5,000,000 *Tel:* (312) 944-3838
Hist. Note: Founded as the Institutional Food Manufacturers of America, it became the Institutional Food-Service Manufacturers Association in 1964 and assumed its present name in 1970. Members are makers and processors of food and equipment for the away-from-home market, as well as their suppliers.
Publications:
Government Report.
IFMA World.

Internat'l Footwear Ass'n (1985)
47 West 34th St., New York NY 10001
Exec. Director: Ted Rowland
Members: 43 companies *Staff:* 3
Annual Budget: $250-500,000 *Tel:* (212) 714-2399
Hist. Note: Represents importers of footwear.
Publication:
IFA Newsletter. m.
Annual Meetings: January

Internat'l Foundation of Employee Benefit Plans (1954)
Box 69, 18700 West Blue Mound Road, Brookfield WI 53008-0069
Exec. V. President: Lee R. Polacheck, CAE
Members: 26,000 *Staff:* 105
Annual Budget: over $5,000,000 *Tel:* (414) 786-6700
Hist. Note: Formerly (1973) Nat'l Foundation of Health, Welfare and Pension Plans. Membership consists of individuals working in the field of employee benefits. Has an annual budget of $11 million. Membership: $350/yr.
Publications:
Digest. m.
Employee Benefits Journal. a.
Legal-Legislative Reporter News Bulletin. m.
Annual Meetings: Fall/5,000
1987-San Francisco, CA/Dec. 4-9
1988-New Orleans, LA/Nov. 11-16
1989-Orlando, FL/Nov. 10-15
1990-Honolulu, HI/Nov. 9-14

Internat'l Franchise Ass'n (1960)
1350 New York Ave., N.W., Suite 900, Washington DC 20005
President: William B. Cherkasky
Members: 700 companies *Staff:* 28
Annual Budget: $2-5,000,000 *Tel:* (202) 628-8000
Hist. Note: Membership consists of companies franchising the distribution of their goods or services. Supports the Franchising Political Action Committee, Inc. (FRAN-PAC).
Publications:
Franchising World Magazine. bi-m.
Franchise Legal Digest. bi-m.
Business Franchise Guide. m.
Franchise Insider. bi-m.
Franchise Law Report. q.
Journal of International Franchising and Distribution Law. q.
Annual Meetings: January
1987-Acapulco, Mexico
1988-San Francisco, CA(Fairmont)

Internat'l Frozen Food Ass'n (1974)
1764 Old Meadow Lane, Suite 350, McLean VA 22102
Director General: Thomas B. House, CAE
Members: 60 *Staff:* 2-5
Annual Budget: $10-25,000 *Tel:* (703) 821-0770
Hist. Note: Federation of ass'ns and companies involved in distribution, production, or marketing of frozen food for the internat'l market. Affiliated with the American Frozen Food Institute.
Publications:
Internat'l Frozen Food Report. m.
"Stag" Newsletter. 3/yr.

Annual Meetings: 4
Semi-annual meetings
1987-Honolulu, HI/May 14-17
1987-Toronto, Canada

Internat'l Fund-Raising Ass'n (1958)
Hist. Note: Became the Nat'l Ass'n of Professional Fund Raisers in 1983.

Internat'l Garden Horticultural Industry Ass'n (1977)
26 Pine St., Dover DA 19901
Chairman of the Board: Le Roy Rench
Members: 2,225 *Staff:* 5
Annual Budget: $250-500,000 *Tel:* (302) 736-6781
Hist. Note: Membership is open to all people in the industry. IGHIA works to help trade with all nations to improve and acknowledge new plants and products; coordinates the International Trade Show and Publication; keeps members informed on changes in export/import rules and regulations. Membership: $100/year.
Publication:
Green World. m.
Annual Meetings: September

Internat'l Glaucoma Congress (1977)
233 East Erie St., Suite 710, Chicago IL 60611
Director: Dr. John G. Bellows
Members: 6,000-6,500 *Staff:* 6-10
Annual Budget: $250-500,000 *Tel:* (312) 951-1400
Hist. Note: A division of the American Society of Contemporary Medicine, Surgery and Ophthalmology. Members are physcians interested in the latest developments in the knowledge and information of glaucomatous diseases. Membership: $125/yr.
Publications:
Glaucoma. bi-m. adv.
Annals of Opthalmology. m. adv.
Journal of Ocular Therapy and Surgery. bi-m.
Annual Meetings: March, with the ASCMSO.
1987-Las Vegas, NV(Caesar's Palace)/March 14-20/over 1,000
1988-Hollywood, FL(Diplomat Hotel)/March 12-16/over 1,000

Internat'l Glutamate Technical Committee (1973)
Box 76181, Atlanta GA 30358
Chairman: Andrew G. Ebert, Ph.D.
Members: 20 individuals; 20 companies
Tel: (404) 843-3177
Hist. Note: Composed of phyicians and/or scientists employed by producers or users of glutamic acid and its salts or doing research on it in University laboratories. Membership: $3,000/yr.
Annual Meetings: Fall

Internat'l Gold and Silver Plate Soc. (1974)
Hist. Note: Started by its parent organization, the International Foodservice Manufacturers Association, as a method of recognizing those individuals who have made outstanding contributions. One gold and seven silver plates are annually awarded.

Internat'l Graphic Arts Education Ass'n (1923)
4615 Forbes Ave., Pittsburgh PA 15213
Secretary: Kenneth B. Kulakowsky
Members: 500-600 *Staff:* 1
Annual Budget: $10-25,000 *Tel:* (412) 682-5170
Hist. Note: Founded in 1936 as the Nat'l Graphic Arts Education Ass'n. Adopted the present name in 1950 and was incorporated in 1969. Members are teachers of printing, photography and the graphic arts.
Publications:
The Communicator. 8/yr.
Visual Communications Journal. a.
Annual Meetings: Summer
1987-Springfield, MO(Southwest Missouri State Univ.)/Aug. 2-7

Internat'l Graphics
Hist. Note: Disbanded in 1986.

Internat'l Graphoanalysis Soc. (1929)
111 North Canal St., Chicago IL 60606
President: V. Peter Ferrara
Members: 15,000 *Staff:* 60
Annual Budget: $2-5,000,000 *Tel:* (312) 930-9446
Hist. Note: Graphoanalysis is the analysis of handwriting for personality assessment. Used in such areas as testing for employment and education counseling. Absorbed the American Institute of Grapho Analysis in 1949.
Publication:
Journal of Graphoanalysis. m.
Semi-annual meetings: Attendance 1,000
1987-Chicago, IL(Drake)/July 19-24/600

Internat'l Grooving and Grinding Ass'n (1972)
P.O. Box 1750, Briarcliff Manor NY 10510
Exec. Manager: Peter Silveri
Members: 35 companies *Staff:* 1
Annual Budget: $10-25,000 *Tel:* (914) 941-8444
Hist. Note: Members are businesses engaged in the grooving process to improve traction on wet pavement and the grinding process to rehabilitate and restore road surfaces.

Publication:
International Groover. q.
Annual Meetings: Winter
1987-Palm Springs, CA/Feb. 26-March 1

Internat'l Group of Agents and Bureaus (1986)
18825 Hicrest Rd., Glendora CA 91740
Exec. Director: Dottie Walters
Members: 75 speakers bureaus and agents *Staff:* 2-5
Annual Budget: $50-100,000 *Tel:* (818) 335-5127
Hist. Note: Members are bureaus, agents or management companies who actively book speakers and have been in business at least two years. Membership: $250/yr.
Publication:
G.A.B. (newsletter). m.
Annual Meetings: June

Internat'l Guards Union of America (1947)
Route 2, Box 54, Avery TX 75554
President: Marvin Burkett
Members: 2,600 *Staff:* 2-5
Annual Budget: $25-50,000 *Tel:* (214) 684-3687
Hist. Note: Independent labor union. Guards, watchmen and others hired to protect personnel and property.
Annual Meetings: Every 4 years (1989)

Internat'l Guild of Craft Journalists, Authors and Photographers (1976)
Hist. Note: Defunct as of 1985.

Internat'l Guild of Professional Electrologists (1979)
1018 North Davis, Arlington TX 76012
Corresp. Secretary: Sarah Walker
Members: 1,500-2,000 *Staff:* 1
Annual Budget: $50-100,000 *Tel:* (817) 274-7969
Hist. Note: A public relations organization whose members are professional electrologists and manufacturers of hair-removing equipment as well as owners and teachers of schools of electrolysis. Membership: $50/yr. (individual); $250/yr. (company).
Publication:
IGPE Newsletter. q. adv.
Biennial Meetings: Odd Years
1987-St. Louis, MO(Adam's Mark)/July 30-Aug. 1

Internat'l Halfway House Ass'n (1964)
P.O. Box 81826, Lincoln NE 68501
President: James Hemm
Members: 900-1,000 individuals and agencies
Annual Budget: $25-50,000 *Tel:* (402) 464-0602
Hist. Note: An affiliate of the American Correctional Ass'n. Public and private agencies involved in providing community based residential treatment alternatives for those with social disabilities. Membership: $25/yr. (individual); $100-600/yr. (organization).
Publications:
Newsletter. bi-m. adv.
Directory of Residential Programs. Every 3 yrs.
Semi-annual Meetings: Aug. with American Correctiona Ass'n & Spring
1987-Boston, MA(Boston Park Plaza)/March 28-31/350-500
1987-New Orleans, LA/August/25-50
1988-San Francisco, CA/Spring/350-500
1988-Cincinnati, OH/August/25-50

Internat'l Hardwood Products Ass'n (1956)
Box 1308, Alexandria VA 22313
Exec. V. President: Wendy J. Baer
Members: 225-250 companies *Staff:* 2-5
Annual Budget: $100-250,000 *Tel:* (703) 836-6696
Hist. Note: Formerly Imported Hardwood Plywood Ass'n and Imported Hardwood Products Ass'n (1982). Sponsors and supports the International Hardwood Products Ass'n Political Action Committee.
Publications:
Directory. a.
IHPA Flash Bulletins. irreg.
IHPA Newsletter. m.
Import/Export Hardwood Statistics. q.
Annual Meetings: Winter
1987-Tucson, AZ(Loew's Ventana Canyon)/March 3-7/250
1988-Naples, FL(The Registry Resort)/March 1-5/250

Internat'l Health Soc. (1944)
1001 East Oxford Lane, Englewood CO 80110
Secy.-Treas.: Franklin L. Bowling, M.D.
Members: 500 *Staff:* 1
Annual Budget: under $10,000 *Tel:* (303) 789-3003
Hist. Note: An agency member of the American Public Health Ass'n founded as the Civil Affairs/Military Government Public Health Ass'n. It then became the Civil Affairs/Internat'l Health Society and (in 1964) the Internat'l Health Soc. of the U.S. It assumed its present name in 1973. Members are medical and other personnel with an interest in international health. Membership: $20/yr.
Publication:
Bulletin. q.
Annual Meetings: With the American Public Health Ass'n.
1987-New Orleans, LA/Oct. 18-22
1988-Boston, MA/Nov. 13-17
1989-Chicago, IL/Oct. 22-26

00161 12 05 86 1233

Internat'l Hockey League (1945)
Hist. Note: Address unkown in 1984.

Internat'l Home Furnishings Representatives Ass'n (1934)
518 Davis St., Suite 210, Evanston IL 60201
Exec. Director: John D. Condit
Members: 6,000 individuals, 350-400 organizations *Staff:* 2-5
Annual Budget: $100-250,000 *Tel:* (312) 328-7733
Hist. Note: Formerly (1967) Nat'l Wholesale Furniture Salesmens' Ass'n and (1972) Nat'l Home Furnishings Representatives Ass'n. A federation of local home furnishings representatives associations.
Publications:
Homefurnishings Contact. 10/yr. adv.
Opportunity Center. 10/yr. adv.
Annual Meetings: Spring

Internat'l Ice Cream Ass'n (1906)
888 16th St., N.W., Washington DC 20006
President: John F. Speer, Jr.
Members: 210 *Staff:* 26
Annual Budget: $1-2,000,000 *Tel:* (202) 296-4250
Hist. Note: Established as the Nat'l Ass'n of Ice Cream Manufacturers, it became the Internat'l Ass'n of Ice Cream Manufacturers in 1933 and assumed its present name in 1986. Affiliated with the Marketing and Training Institute. Shares offices, staff and, to some extent, membership, with the Milk Industry Foundation. Supports the Milk Industry Foundation and International Association of Ice Cream Manufacturers Political Action Committee. Membership fee based on volume.
Publications:
Up-to-Date. m.
The Latest Scoop. a.

Internat'l Illawarra Ass'n (1975)
Hist. Note: Reported as defunct in 1984.

Internat'l Information Management Congress (1962)
P.O. Box 34404, Bethesda MD 20817
Exec. Director: Don M. Avedon
Members: 90 companies; 600 individuals *Staff:* 3
Annual Budget: $500-1,000,000 *Tel:* (301) 983-0604
Hist. Note: Members are involved in the document systems field. Membership: $75/yr.
Publications:
IMC Journal. bi-m. adv.
IMC Newsletter. m.
Annual Meetings: Fall
1987-Vienna(Austria Center)/Oct. 12-15/5,000
1988-Hong Kong(Ocean Terminal)/Sept. 12-15/5,000
1989-London(Barbican Centre)/Oct. 23-26/6,000

Internat'l Information/Word Processing Ass'n (1972)
Hist. Note: Became the Association of Information Systems Professionals June 1, 1983.

Internat'l Institute for Bio-Energetic Analysis (1956)
144 East 36th St., New York NY 10016
Exec. Director: Alexander Lowen, M.D.
Members: 1,050 *Staff:* 1
Annual Budget: $50-100,000 *Tel:* (212) 532-7742
Hist. Note: A professional society of individuals concerned with the energy processes of the human body and their effect on physical and mental health. Formerly (until 1979) known as the Institute for Bio-Energetic Analysis. Membership: $60/yr.
Publication:
Bioenergetic Analysis. a.

Internat'l Institute for Lath and Plaster (1976)
25332 Narbonne Ave., #170, Lomita CA 90717
Exec. Director: Clay M. Johnston
Members: 20 organizations *Staff:* 2
Annual Budget: $10-25,000 *Tel:* (213) 539-6080
Hist. Note: Formed by merger of the Associated Institute for Lath and Plaster and the Internat'l Council for Lathing and Plastering (founded 1952 and formerly the Nat'l Bureau for Lathing and Plastering). A federation of organizations representing contractors, unions and makers of lathing and plastering supplies.

Internat'l Institute for Safety in Transportation (1977)
Box 63, Franklin Square, New York NY 11010
Exec. Director: Dr. Edmund J. Cantilli
Members: 100-110 individuals; 10 firms *Staff:* 2
Annual Budget: $10-25,000 *Tel:* (516) 485-0050
Hist. Note: The Institute for Safety in Transportation was formed in October of 1977 for the express purpose of uncovering hazards in all modes of transportation and pressing agencies for their removal by providing technical and educational services. Formerly (1984) the Institute for Safety in Transportation. Membership: $50/yr. (individual), $500/yr. (company).
Publications:
The Safety Activist. q.
Transportation Safety Newsletter. m. adv.
Annual Meetings:
1987-Rio de Janiero, Brazil

Internat'l Institute of Ammonia Refrigeration (1971)
111 East Wacker Dr., Chicago IL 60601
Exec. Director: James E. Elsener
Members: 280 companies *Staff:* 2-5
Annual Budget: $50-100,000 *Tel:* (312) 644-6610
Hist. Note: Orginally formed to oppose the classification of ammonia as a hazardous substance in the 1971 National Electrical Code, IIAR has broadened its purpose to include public education, promotional and standards development programs in addition to legislative/regulatory concerns.
Publications:
IIAR Newsletter. q.
Membership Directory. a.
Proceedings. a.
Annual Meetings: Spring/260
1987-San Diego, CA(Hyatt Islandia)/March 29-April 1
1988-Savannah, GA(Hyatt)

Internat'l Institute of Foods and Family Living (1976)
225 W. Ohio St., Chicago IL 60610
President: Lucille J. Lampman
Members: 4 *Staff:* 6
Tel: (312) 670-0200
Hist. Note: Marketing and public relations arm of the Internat'l Natural Sausage Casing Ass'n and the Self-Rising Flour and Corn Meal Program.

Internat'l Institute of Municipal Clerks (1947)
160 N. Altadena Dr., Pasadena CA 91107
Exec. Director: John J. Hunnewell, CAE
Members: 8,000 *Staff:* 6-10
Annual Budget: $250-500,000 *Tel:* (818) 795-6153
Hist. Note: Founded in 1947 at French Lick, Indiana as the Nat'l Institute of City and Town Clerks. Became the Nat'l Institute of Municipal Clerks in 1949 and the Internat'l Institute of Municipal Clerks in 1960. Membership consists of persons serving as Clerks, Secretaries or Recorders at the state, provincial, county or local level of government. Awards the CMC (Certified Municipal Clerk) designation.
Publications:
Directory. a.
IIMC News Digest. m.
News for Officers of State Clerks' Ass'ns. q.
Technical Bulletins. irreg.
Annual Meetings: May
1987-Fort Worth, TX/May 17-21

Internat'l Institute of Synthetic Rubber Producers (1960)
2077 South Gessner, Suite 133, Houston TX 77063
Managing Director: W.E. Tessmer
Members: 45-50 companies *Staff:* 4-6
Annual Budget: $500-1,000,000 *Tel:* (713) 783-7511
Hist. Note: Has an international membership. Membership: $10,500/year (organization/company).
Publications:
Worldwide Rubber Statistics. a.
Synthetic Rubber Manual. trien.
Proceedings. a.
Directory of Members. a.
Annual Meetings: Spring/250-300
1987-Edinburgh, Scotland(Sheraton)/June
1988-Quebec City, Canada(Chateau Frontenac)/May
1989-Asia
1990-Europe

Internat'l Institute of Valuers (1975)
Hist. Note: Became the Internat'l Institute in 1984.

Internat'l Insurance Advisory Council (1966)
1615 H St., N.W., Washington DC 20062
Director: Gordon J. Cloney
Members: 30 companies and trade ass'ns *Staff:* 3
Annual Budget: $100-250,000 *Tel:* (202) 463-5480
Hist. Note: The IIAC, operating under the aegis of the Chamber of Commerce of the U.S., is composed of U.S. insurance and reinsurance companies that conduct business in international markets.
Publication:
Report. bi-a.
Annual Meetings: New York, NY(Pierre)/May/300

Internat'l Intelligent Buildings Ass'n (1985)
1815 H St., N.W., Suite 700, Washington DC 20006
Secretary: Joseph E. Hadley, Jr.
Members: 141 companies, 18 individuals *Staff:* 3
Annual Budget: $100-250,000 *Tel:* (202) 296-6320
Hist. Note: Established and incorporated in Washington, DC, IIBA is a worldwide federation of architects, engineers, building developers and other organizations and individuals in the industry. Membership: $250-500/yr.
Publication:
Newsletter. m.
Annual Meetings: Summer
1987-Washington, DC(Convention Center)/June 21-26)

Internat'l Jelly and Preserve Ass'n (1918)
5775 Peachtree-Dunwoody Rd., Suite 500D, Atlanta GA 30342
President: Robert H. Kellen
Members: 100-125 companies *Staff:* 8
Tel: (404) 252-3663
Hist. Note: Formerly (1978) the National Preservers Ass'n.
Annual Meetings: March
1987-Palm Beach, FL/March 22-25

Internat'l Juvenile Officers Ass'n (1957)
Box 2229, Florissant MO 63032
Exec. Director: Charles Fumagalli
Members: 1,300 *Staff:* 1
Annual Budget: $10-25,000 *Tel:* (314) 298-7788
Hist. Note: Police officers assigned to juvenile division.
Publications:
I.J.O.A. Magazine. a. adv.
I.J.O.A. Reporter. bi-m.
Annual Meetings: Last week in June

Internat'l Labor Communications Ass'n (1955)
815 16th St., N.W., Room 509, Washington DC 20006
Secy.-Treas.: James M. Cesnik
Members: 750 *Staff:* 1
Annual Budget: $100-250,000 *Tel:* (202) 637-5068
Hist. Note: Formed by a merger of the Internat'l Labor Press of America (1911) and the CIO Editors and Public Relations Conference (1940). Members are editors of union papers.
Biennial Meetings: Odd years

Internat'l Labor Press Ass'n
Hist. Note: Became the International Labor Communications Association in January of 1984.

Internat'l Ladies Garment Workers' Union (1900)
1710 Broadway, New York NY 10019
President: Jay Mazur
Members: 219,000 *Staff:* 1,250
Annual Budget: over $5,000,000 *Tel:* (212) 265-7000
Hist. Note: Organized in New York City June 3, 1900 and chartered by the American Federation of Labor on June 23rd.
Publication:
Justice. m.
Triennial Meetings: 1989

Internat'l League of Electrical Ass'ns (1936)
2101 L St., N.W., Suite 300, Washington DC 20037
Exec. Secretary: Richard H. Geissler
Members: 50 organizations *Staff:* 1
Annual Budget: under $10,000 *Tel:* (202) 457-8477
Hist. Note: A federation of state and local organizations affiliated with and given administrative support by the Nat'l Electrical Manufacturers Ass'n, in whose office it is based. Until 1979 known as the Internat'l Ass'n of Electrical Leagues.
Publication:
Electrical Industry Hotline. q.
Annual Meetings: Fall
1987-Indianapolis, IN/Oct.

Internat'l League of Professional Baseball Clubs (1884)
Box 608, Grove City OH 43123
President: Harold Cooper, Jr.
Members: 8 clubs *Staff:* 3-15
Annual Budget: $250-500,000 *Tel:* (614) 871-1300
Hist. Note: The oldest minor league in baseball.
Publication:
Record Book. a.

Internat'l Leather Goods, Plastics and Novelty Workers' Union (1937)
14th Floor, 265 West 14th St., New York NY 10011
President: Domenic DiPaola
Members: 18,000 *Staff:* 30-35
Annual Budget: $1-2,000,000 *Tel:* (212) 675-9240
Hist. Note: Chartered March 5, 1937 by the American Federation of Labor as the International Ladies' Handbag, Pocketbook and Novelty Workers Union. Adopted its present name in 1955.
Quinquennial Conventions: 1987

Internat'l Livestock Brand and Theft Conference (1946)
Box 94631, Lincoln NE 68509
Secy.-Treas.: Cynthia Monroe
Members: 20-30 states
Annual Budget: under $10,000 *Tel:* (402) 471-2237
Hist. Note: State employees and livestock associations' executives (in the U.S. and Canada) concerned with the use of livestock brands. Formerly (1969) the Nat'l Livestock Brand Conference and (1982) Internat'l Livestock Brand Conference.
Annual Meetings: July/50

Internat'l Longshoremen's and Warehousemen's Union (1937)
1188 Franklin St., San Francisco CA 94109
President: James R. Herman
Members: 55,000 *Staff:* 20-25
Annual Budget: $1-2,000,000 *Tel:* (415) 775-0533
Hist. Note: Formed in Aug., 1937 by dissidents from the Internat'l Longshoremen's Ass'n led by Harry Bridges; chartered by the Congress of Industrial Organizations. Certified by the NLRB in 1938 as the collective bargaining agent for all longshoremen on the Pacific Coast. Expelled in 1950 by the CIO for alleged Communist domination. Now an independent labor union.
Publication:
The Dispatcher. m.
Annual Meetings: Triennial Meetings
1988-Vancouver, B.C./Spring

00162 12 05 86 1233

Internat'l Longshoremen's Ass'n (1892)
17 Battery Place, Room 1530, New York NY 10004
President: Thomas W. Gleason
Members: 116,000 *Staff:* 25-30
Annual Budget: over $5,000,000 *Tel:* (212) 425-1200
Hist. Note: Established in Detroit in 1892 as the Nat'l Longshoremen's Ass'n of the United States. Became the Internat'l Longshoremen's Ass'n in 1895 and was chartered by the American Federation of Labor in 1896. Expelled for corruption and racketeering by the AFL in 1953, the ILA merged in 1959 with the International Brotherhood of Longshoremen (which had been set up in opposition by the AFL) and re-affiliated with AFL-CIO.
Publication:
ILA Newsletter. 4-5/yr.
Annual Meetings: Triennial Meetings
1987-Florida/July

Internat'l Magic Dealers Ass'n (1945)
Box 1359, Boston MA 02111
Corresp. Secretary: Hank Lee
Members: 150-175 companies *Staff:* 1
Annual Budget: under $10,000 *Tel:* (617) 482-8749
Hist. Note: Founded as the Magic Dealers Ass'n, it assumed its present name in 1974. Members are makers of magicians' equipment, dealers and publishers.
Publication:
M.D.A. Monthly Bulletin.
Annual Meetings: With Internat'l Brotherhood of Magicians or Soc. of American Magicians

Internat'l Magnesium Ass'n (1943)
7927 Jones Branch Drive, Lancaster Bldg., Suite 400, McLean VA 22102
Exec. Director: Byron B. Clow
Members: 90 companies *Staff:* 2-5
Annual Budget: $250-500,000 *Tel:* (703) 442-8888
Hist. Note: Formerly (1973) Magnesium Ass'n. The purpose of the association is to develop and increase the international use and acceptance of magnesium metal and its alloys in all product forms. Regular membership is open to organizations or individuals directly engaged in the production, manufacture or marketing of metallic magnesium in some product form. The Internat'l Magnesium Development Corporation is a wholly owned subsidiary of IMA which contracts cooperative research for its members. Membership: $1,250/yr.
Publications:
Magnesium Newsletter. m.
Magnesium Buyer's Guide. a.
Proceedings. a.
Annual Meetings: May-June/350
1987-Tokyo, Japan(Takanawa Prince)/Mary 17-20/300
1988-Washington, DC(JW Marriott)/May 1-3/300

Internat'l Maintenance Institute (1961)
Box 266695, Houston TX 77207
Exec. Secretary: Joyce Rhoden
Members: 1,800 individuals *Staff:* 1
Annual Budget: $50-100,000 *Tel:* (713) 481-0869
Publication:
The Maintenance Journal. bi-m. adv.
Annual Meetings: Semi-Annual Meetings
1987-Milwaukee, WI/March
1988-Houston, TX(Pasadena Convention Center)/October

Internat'l Management Council (1935)
2250 E. Devon, Suite 318, Des Plaines IL 60018
Exec. Director: J. Bruce Knox
Members: 13-14,000 *Staff:* 2
Annual Budget: $100-250,000 *Tel:* (312) 298-3930
Hist. Note: Sponsored by the Young Men's Christian Association as the National Council of Foremen's Clubs, it became the National Council of Industrial Management Clubs in 1948 and assumed its present name in 1971. Membership: $12/yr.
Publication:
IMC News and Views. q.
Annual Meetings: Spring
1987-Grand Rapids, MI(Amway Grand)/May 19-22/450-500
1988-Boston, MA(Boston Park Plaza)/May 25-27

Internat'l Map Dealers' Ass'n (1981)
P.O. Box 1789, Kankakee IL 60901
Exec. Secretary: Norman Strasma
Members: 125 companies *Staff:* 2
Annual Budget: $25-50,000 *Tel:* (815) 939-3509
Hist. Note: Membership comprised of retail stores featuring maps; distributors; and manufacturers. Incorporated in Florida. Membership: $100/yr.
Publication:
Newsletter. q.
Annual Meetings: Fall
1987-Reno, NV/Oct./200

Internat'l Marine Transit Ass'n (1977)
34 Otis Hill Road, Hingham MA 02043
Secy.-Treas.: Martha Reardon
Members: 200 companies, 300 individuals
Annual Budget: $25-50,000 *Tel:* (617) 749-0078
Hist. Note: Promotes and supports waterborne transit operations, ferries, hovercraft and the like. Members are marine transit operators, shipyard operators and suppliers, regulatory authorities and others interested in the waterborne transit industry. Formerly (until 1980) known as the Maritime Transit Association.
Annual Meetings:
1987-Sicily, Italy/Oct.

Internat'l Marketing Audit Ass'n (1977)
Hist. Note: An international organization, 25% of whose membership is from the United States.

Internat'l Masonry Institute (1970)
823 15th St., N.W., Suite 1001, Washington DC 20005
Exec. Vice President: Ray Lackey
Staff: 10-15
Annual Budget: $1-2,000,000 *Tel:* (202) 783-3908
Hist. Note: A Labor/Management Trust established by the Mason Contractors Ass'n of America and the Internat'l Union of Bricklayers & Allied Craftsmen which conducts market development, research and development, training and labor/management relations programs. Not a membership organization.

Internat'l Material Management Soc. (1945)
650 East Higgins Road, Schaumberg IL 60195
Exec. Director: James J. Prunty
Members: 6,500 *Staff:* 5-9
Annual Budget: $500-1,000,000 *Tel:* (312) 310-9570
Hist. Note: Founded as the American Material Handling Society, it assumed its present name in 1966. A professional society of individuals interested in advancing the theory and practice of the management and handling of all types of material. Membership: $65/yr. (individual), $1,000/yr. (company).
Publications:
Material Handling Outlook. q.
Membership Directory. a.
Who's Who in Material Handling. a. adv.
Annual Meetings: September
1987-Atlanta, GA
1988-New Orleans, LA
1989-Toronto, Canada

Internat'l Meat Processors Ass'n (1981)
Box 35880, Tucson AZ 85740
President: Raymond F. Thill
Members: 40-50 companies *Staff:* 1
Annual Budget: under $10,000
Publication:
Newsletter. irreg.

Internat'l Metallographic Soc. (1967)
Box 2489, Columbus OH 43216
Secretary: Japnell Braun
Members: 6-700 *Staff:* 2-5
Annual Budget: $50-100,000
Hist. Note: Members are individuals interested in the microscopic study of metals and other materials; interest is to benefit the art and science of, and to raise the professional standards of: optical and electron metallography, ceramography, petrography, micrography, and their allied sciences. Formerly known as the Internat'l Microstructural Analysis Soc. Membership: $35/yr.(individual); $100/yr.(organization).
Publications:
Metallography. q. adv.
Slip Lines. q.
Annual Meetings: Summer/200-300
1987-Monterey, CA(Sheraton)/July 26-30
1988-Toronto, Ontario(Hilton Harbour Castle)/July 23-27
1989-Charlotte, NC

Internat'l Microwave Power Institute (1966)
13542 Union Village Circle, Clifton VA 22024
Exec. Director: Robert C. LaGasse, CAE
Members: 700 *Staff:* 2-5
Annual Budget: $100-250,000 *Tel:* (703) 830-5588
Hist. Note: Members are engineers, educators, home economists and scientists interested in non-communication aspects of micro-wave power. Membership: $95/yr.(individual); $500/yr.(organization).
Publications:
Journal of Microwave Power. q.
Microwave World. bi-m. adv.
Annual Meetings: Summer/300
1987-Cincinnati, OH(Hyatt)/Aug. 31-Sept. 2

Internat'l Military Club Executives Ass'n (1971)
1438 Duke St., Alexandria VA 22314
Exec. Director: Larry Kelly
Members: 1,200 *Staff:* 6
Annual Budget: $250-500,000 *Tel:* (703) 548-0093
Hist. Note: Membership: $245/yr. (regular); $295/yr. (company).
Publication:
Military Clubs and Recreation. m. adv.
Annual Meetings: Regional Meetings throughout U.S., Europe, and the Far East

Internat'l Miniature Horse Registry
Hist. Note: Absorbed by the American Miniature Horse Ass'n in 1985.

Internat'l Minilab Ass'n (1985)
222 South Elm St., Greensboro NC 27401
V. President, Marketing: Carolyn Welty
Members: 500 *Staff:* 2-5
Annual Budget: $500-1,000,000 *Tel:* (919) 273-5897
Hist. Note: Members are individuals and firms whose business is providing on-premise retail photofinishing services to consumer/professional customers and producers/distributors of services/products to minilabs. Membership: $37/yr. (lab), $250/yr. (supplier).
Publications:
Minilab Developments. q. adv.
Newsletter. m.
Product & Services Directory. a. adv.
Minilab Buyers Guide. a.
Annual Meetings: Two Education Seminars/Expositions per year.

Internat'l Mobile Air Conditioning Ass'n (1958)
3303 LBJ Freeway, Suite 219, Dallas TX 75234
Exec. Director: Paul M. Allen
Members: 300 companies *Staff:* 6-10
Annual Budget: $100-250,000 *Tel:* (214) 484-5750
Hist. Note: Formerly (1970) Automotive Air Conditioning Ass'n, Inc. Members are makers of air conditioning units and other installed accessories (cellular phones, stereo, security systems, etc.) for vehicles, boats, and aircraft, as well as their distributors and suppliers. Membership: $125/yr. (individual); $500/yr. (company)
Publication:
Shop Talk. m.
Annual Meetings: February
1987-Dallas, TX(Fairmont)/Feb. 12-14/1,500

Internat'l Molders' and Allied Workers' Union (1859)
1225 East McMillan St., Cincinnati OH 45206
President: Bernard Butsavage
Members: 42,000 *Staff:* 38
Annual Budget: over $5,000,000 *Tel:* (513) 221-1525
Hist. Note: America's oldest internat'l union, IMAWU was established in Philadelphia on July 5, 1859 as the Nat'l Union of Iron Molders and renamed the Iron Molders' Union of American in 1861. Became the Internat'l Molders' Union in 1863 and charter member of the American Federation of Labor in 1886. Became the International Molders and Foundry Workers Union of North America in 1934 and assumed its present name in 1961. Sponsors and supports the International Molders' and Allied Workers' Union Political Action Committee. Membership: 2 hours' pay/yr.
Publications:
International Molders' and Allied Workers' Union Journal. m.
Molder's Journal. bi-m.
Annual Meetings: Every 4 years (1988)
1988-Cincinnati, OH(Convention Center)/Aug./2,000

Internat'l Motion Picture and Lecturers Ass'n (1970)
P.O. Box 494, Dowagiac MI 49047
President: Fran Reidleberger
Members: 60 individuals *Staff:* 1
Annual Budget: under $10,000 *Tel:* (616) 782-7451
Hist. Note: Sponsored by the Internat'l Travel Adventure Film Guild. Members produce personally narrated travel films.

Internat'l Motor Press Ass'n (1962)
c/o Kermish-Geylin, 211 West 56th St., Suite 265, New York NY 10019
President: Don Chaikin
Members: 450-500 *Staff:* 1
Annual Budget: $10-25,000 *Tel:* (212) 419-3500
Hist. Note: A professional group of writers and editors producing auto articles for the press, radio or TV. Concentrated in the New York area. US Chapter of the International Federation of Automotive Journalists. Membership: $50/yr.
Publication:
IMPAct. m.

Internat'l Municipal Signal Ass'n (1896)
Box 539, Newark NJ 14513
Exec. Director: Harold Glerum
Members: 2,500-3,000 *Staff:* 2-5
Annual Budget: $100-250,000 *Tel:* (315) 331-2182
Hist. Note: Members are government employees involved in public safety service operations: traffic signals installation and maintenance, police and fire alarm systems, street lights, radio communications, civil defense, etc. Associate membership is available to persons in private corporations responsible for promoting public safety. Membership: $40/yr. (individual); $300/yr. (company).
Publications:
IMSA Journal. bi-m. adv.
IMSA Official Wire and Cable Specifications.
IMSA Official Fire Alarm Manual.
IMSA Traffic Signal Manual of Installation & Maintenance Procedures.
Annual Meetings: Summer
1987-Providence, RI
1988-Colorado Springs, CO

Internat'l Museum Photographers Ass'n (1970)
Box 30051, Bethesda Station, Bethesda MD 20814
Exec. Director: Lowell Anson Kenyon
Members: 175-200 individuals *Staff:* 1
Annual Budget: under $10,000 *Tel:* (301) 897-0083
Hist. Note: A division of the Council on Fine Arts Photography, which handles its publications.
Annual Meetings: Monthly meetings

Internat'l Narcotic Enforcement Officers Ass'n (1958)
112 State St., Suite 1310, Albany NY 12207
Exec. Director:: John J. Bellizzi
Members: 7,500 *Staff:* 6-10

00163 12 05 86 1233

Annual Budget: $100-250,000 *Tel:* (518) 463-6232
Hist. Note: Membership: $25/year. Established in Albany, NY in October, 1960, and incorporated in the state of New York in the same year. In recognition of its growing international membership, the present name was adopted in 1963. Membership: $25/year.
Publications:
International Drug Report. m.
Narc Officer. bi-m. adv.
Annual Meetings:
1987-Orlando, FL/August
1988-New Orleans, LA/October

Internat'l Natural Sausage Casing Ass'n (1927)
225 W. Ohio St., Chicago IL 60610
Exec. Secretary: Lucille Lampman
Members: 200-250 companies *Staff:* 2-5
Annual Budget: $50-100,000 *Tel:* (312) 670-0200
Hist. Note: Formerly (1965) Natural Casing Institute.
Publication:
INSCA Annual. a. adv.
Semi-Annual Meetings: Spring in Europe, Fall in North America

Internat'l Newspaper Advertising and Marketing Executives, Inc. (1911)
Box 17210, Dulles Internat'l Airport, Washington DC 20041
Gen. Manager and Secy-Treas.: Reggie R. Hall
Members: 3,500 *Staff:* 12
Annual Budget: $500-1,000,000 *Tel:* (703) 620-0090
Hist. Note: Formerly Newspaper Advertising Executives Association. Until 1981 known as International Newspaper Advertising Executives, Inc. Offices are located in the Newspaper Center, 11600 Sunrise Valley Drive, Reston, VA. Membership fee based on size of circulation.
Semi-annual Meetings: Winter and Summer
1987-Miami Beach, FL(Fontainebleau)/Jan 25-28/1,500
1987-San Diego, CA(Del Coronado)/July 12-15/800
1988-New Orleans, LA(Hilton)/Jan./1,600
1988-Toronto, Canada(Sheraton)/July/800
1989-San Francisco, CA(Hilton)/Jan./1,600
1989-Boston, MA(Copley)/July/800

Internat'l Newspaper Financial Executives (1947)
P.O. Box 17573, Washington Dulles Internat'l Airport, Washington DC 20041
Exec. Director: Robert J. Kasabian
Members: 1,100 *Staff:* 2-5
Annual Budget: $250-500,000 *Tel:* (703) 620-9500
Hist. Note: The international press association for financial accounting and business management. The above address is the mailing address; executive offices are located at The Newspaper Center, 11600 Sunrise Valley Drive, Reston,VA, 22091.
Publication:
The Newspaper Financial Executive Journal. m.
Semi-annual Meetings: May and October
1987-Marco Island, FL(Marriott)/May 10-13
1987-Seattle, WA

Internat'l Newspaper Promotion Ass'n (1930)
P.O. Box 17422, Washington Dulles Internat'l Airport, Washington DC 20041
Exec. Director: Paula Markiewicz
Members: 1,400-1,500 *Staff:* 6
Annual Budget: $500-1,000,000 *Tel:* (703) 620-9560
Hist. Note: Founded in 1931 as the Nat'l Newspaper Promotion Ass'n. The name was changed in 1967 to the Internat'l Newspaper Promotion Ass'n to reflect the makeup of the membership from more than 40 countries including the United States and Canada. The INPA exists to be of service to newspapers and to work for the advancement and promotion of newspapers through marketing, public relations and research. Membership fee based on newspaper circulation size. The above address is the mailing address; executive offices are located at The Newspaper Center, 11600 Sunrise Valley Drive, Reston, VA, 22091.
Publications:
Idea Newsletter. m.
Idea Newspaper. a.
Promoting the Total Newspaper - a Handbook.
Annual Meetings: May
1987-Toronto, Ontario(Hilton Harbour Castle)/May 17-20
1988-Colorado Springs, CO(Broadmoor Hotel)/May 22-25
1989-Washington, DC
1990-New Orleans, LA(Fairmont Hotel)

Internat'l Nubian Breeders Ass'n (1956)
Box 130, Creswell OR 97426
Secretary: Shirley Gardner
Members: 600 *Staff:* 1
Annual Budget: under $10,000 *Tel:* (503) 895-2742
Hist. Note: Membership: $8/year.
Publication:
Internat'l Nubian Breeder. semi-m. adv.
Annual Meetings: October/November

Internat'l Oil Mill Superintendents Ass'n (1894)
3414 54th St., Lubbock TX 79413
Secy.-Treas.: Bentley H. Page
Members: 400-450 individuals *Staff:* 1
Annual Budget: $25-50,000 *Tel:* (806) 799-6571
Hist. Note: Founded in Waco, Texas May 2, 1894 as the Oil Mill Superintendents Ass'n of Texas. Several years later the name was changed to the Nat'l Oil Mill Superintendents Ass'n to reflect the fact that the membership included individuals from other cotton-growing states. In the 1950s the present name was assumed because the membership had come to include individuals from other countries growing edible oil seeds. Membership: $35/yr.
Publication:
Oil Mill Gazetteer. m. adv.
Annual Meetings: June
1987-Ventura, CA(Harbortown Marine)/June 14-16
1988-Corpus Christi, TX

Internat'l Oil Scouts Ass'n (1924)
Box 272949, Houston TX 77277
Secy.-Treas.: Charlsie Ramsey
Members: 500 *Staff:* 6
Annual Budget: $25-50,000 *Tel:* (713) 840-4294
Hist. Note: Formerly (1960) Nat'l Oil Scouts and Landmen's Ass'n. Federation of regional ass'ns of oil scouts and landmen. Records production in oil and gas fields and compiles exploratory well listings, in the U.S., Canada, and abroad. Membership: $65/year. Requests for the IOSA Yearbook should be directed to: Mason Map Service, Yearbook Editor, P.O. Box 338, Austin, TX 78767.
Publications:
Newsletter. q.
Directory. a. adv.
Magazine. a. adv.
Yearbook. semi-a.
Annual Meetings: Summer
1987-New Orleans, LA(June)/200

Internat'l Organization for the Education of the Hearing Impaired (1967)
3417 Volta Place, Washington DC 20007
Chairwoman: Sandy North
Members: 300-350 *Staff:* 2-5
Annual Budget: under $10,000 *Tel:* (202) 337-5220
Hist. Note: Affiliated with the Alexander Graham Bell Association for the Deaf, which provides staff support. Formerly (1982) American Organization for the Education of the Hearing Impaired.
Biennial meetings: even years

Internat'l Organization of Citrus Virologists (1969)
Plant Pathology Department, University of California, Riverside CA 92521
Secy.-Treas.: Dr. Howard Ohr
Members: 210 individuals
Annual Budget: under $10,000 *Tel:* (714) 787-4140
Hist. Note: Members are individuals engaged in research of citrus virus diseases and related disorders that are potential health hazards. Membership: $10/yr.
Publication:
Proceedings of Conference. Tri-a.
Triennial Meetings: (1989)

Internat'l Organization of Women Executives (1977)
Hist. Note: Defunct in 1982.

Internat'l Organization of Women in Telecommunications (1981)
2308 Oakwood Lane, Arlington TX 76012
Chairperson: Anne Bailey
Members: 1,600 *Staff:* 1
Annual Budget: $10-25,000 *Tel:* (817) 275-0683
Hist. Note: Incorporated in the State of California to enhance the image of women in the telecommunications industry. Membership: $75/year.
Publication:
IOWT Newsletter. q.

Internat'l Oxygen Manufacturers Ass'n (1943)
Box 16248, Cleveland OH 44116
Exec. Director: Richard S. Croy
Members: 180-190 *Staff:* 2-5
Annual Budget: $250-500,000 *Tel:* (216) 228-2166
Hist. Note: IOMA members are the manufacturers of all of the industrial and medical gases (oxygen, nitrogen, argon, acetylene, carbon dioxide, hydrogen, etc.) or of equipment and supplies (plants, cylinders, valves, tanks, etc.) used by the industrial gas companies.
Publication:
IOMA Broadcaster. bi-m.
Annual Meetings: Fall/350
1987-Hilton Head Island, SC(Marriott)/Oct. 17-22
1988-London(Inter-Continental)/Oct. 16-20
1989-Scottsdale, AZ(Camelback)/Oct. 26-Nov. 2
1990-Trinidad(Marriott's Sam Lordis Castle)/Oct. 27-Nov. 1
1991-Kiawah Island, SC(Kiawah Island Resort)/Oct. 26-31

Internat'l Ozone Ass'n-Pan American Committee Branch (1973)
83 Oakwood Avenue, Norwalk CT 06850
Exec. Director: Margit H. Istok
Members: 300-400 individuals, 60-70 companies *Staff:* 2
Annual Budget: $25-50,000 *Tel:* (203) 847-8169
Hist. Note: Represents the interests of environmental and other scientific communities, application engineers, users, manufacturers of ozone generation and contacting equipment, ozone analyzers, monitors and control equipment, as well as the interests of various supporting industries and professions. International headquarters in Zurich, Switzerland. Formerly (until 1978) the Internat'l Ozone Institute, Inc. Membership: $65/yr. (individual), $150-500/yr. (organization).
Publications:
Ozone Science and Engineering: The Journal of IOA. q. adv.
OZONews. bi-m. adv.
Biennial meetings: odd years
1987-Zurich, Switzerland/Sept./300
1989-New York, NY/Sept./300

Internat'l Passenger Ship Ass'n (1972)
Hist. Note: Became the Cruise Lines Internat'l Ass'n in July, 1984.

Internat'l Periodical Distributors Ass'n (1972)
341 Madison Ave., New York NY 10017
President: Robert B. Alleger
Members: 11-15 *Staff:* 2-5
Annual Budget: $250-500,000 *Tel:* (212) 986-8150
Hist. Note: Members are consumer magazine and paperback book distributors.
Annual Meetings: Not held

Internat'l Personnel Management Ass'n (1906)
1617 Duke St., Alexandria VA 22314
Exec. Director: Donald K. Tichenor, CAE
Members: 5,000-6,000 *Staff:* 17
Annual Budget: $1-2,000,000 *Tel:* (703) 549-7100
Hist. Note: Formerly (1906) Civil Service Assembly of the United States and Canada; (1957) Public Personnel Ass'n; and (1973) consolidated with Soc. for Personnel Administration. Membership: $60/yr. (individual); $100-1,255/yr. (company)
Publications:
Agency Issues. bi-w.
IPMA News. m.
Public Personnel management. q. adv.
Annual Meetings: Fall/700
1987-Ottowa, Ontario(Westin)/Oct. 4-8
1988-New Orleans, LA(Fairmont)/Oct. 2-6
1989-Phoenix, AZ(Hyatt)/Oct. 15-19
1990-Atlanta, GA(Marriott Downtown)/Sept. 23-27
1991-Philadelphia, PA(Wyndham Franklin Plaza Hotel)/Oct. 6-10

Internat'l Pesticide Applicators Ass'n (1963)
Box 1377, Milton WA 98354-1377
Editor: Dianna M. Tovoli
Members: 60-80 companies *Staff:* 1
Annual Budget: $10-25,000 *Tel:* (206) 848-3407
Hist. Note: Members are companies involved in all aspects of pesticide application and control. At present concentrated in the Pacific Northwest, Colorado, Ohio, and Canada. Membership: $150/yr.
Publication:
Pesticide Progress. q. adv.
Annual Meetings: Fall

Internat'l Philatelic Press Club (1963)
Box 127, New Britain CT 06050-0127
Exec. Chairman: David A. Kent
Members: 250 *Staff:* 5
Annual Budget: under $10,000 *Tel:* (203) 725-2544
Hist. Note: Members are professionals who write or edit news about stamps and stamp collecting. Associate members are persons or organizations who edit or publish catalogs or other materials intended to publicize profit-making philatelic enterprises. Formerly (1978) Philatelic Press Club. Membership: $12.50/yr. (individual), $50/yr. (organization).
Publications:
Membership List. a.
Report to Members. m.

Internat'l Photo Optical Show Ass'n
Hist. Note: Operations suspended as of January, 1986.

Internat'l Phycological Soc. (1961)
Dept. of Botany, Duke University, Durham NC 27706
Secretary: Richard B. Searles
Members: 850 individuals *Staff:* 1
Annual Budget: $10-25,000 *Tel:* (919) 684-3375
Hist. Note: Founded to develop phycology, distribute phycological information and promote internat'l cooperation among phycologists.
Publication:
Phycologia. q.

Internat'l Physical Fitness Ass'n (1960)
415 West Court St., Flint MI 48503
Secretary: Shelly Rhoades
Members: 1,700-1,800 physical fitness centers *Staff:* 1
Annual Budget: $10-25,000 *Tel:* (313) 239-2166
Hist. Note: Formerly (1975) Universal Gym Affiliates. Principal purpose at present is to facilitate the transfer of memberships from one center to another.

Internat'l Piano Guild (1929)
808 Rio Grande St., Box 1807, Austin TX 78767
President: Walter Merchant
Members: 11-12,000 *Staff:* 11-15
Annual Budget: $100-250,000 *Tel:* (512) 478-5575
Hist. Note: A division of the American College of Musicians. Professional society of piano teachers and music faculty members. Sponsors national examinations. Formerly (1981) the National Guild of Piano Teachers.
Publication:
Piano Guild Notes. bi-m. adv.

00164 12 05 86 1233

Internat'l Planetarium Soc. (1970)
c/o Hansen Planetarium, 15 S. State St., Salt Lake City UT 84111
Secretary: Jack Dunn
Members: 610-620 *Staff:* 0
Annual Budget: under $10,000 *Tel:* (801) 358-2104
Hist. Note: Planetarium personnel and suppliers. Until 1976 known as the International Society of Planetarium Educators. Has no paid staff. Membership: $34/year.
Publications:
Newsletter. q.
Planetarian. q.
Biennial meetings: even years

Internat'l Plant Propagators' Soc. (Eastern Region) (1951)
Box 910, Arlington VA 22216-2900
Secy.-Treas.: Dr. David F. Hamilton
Members: 700 *Staff:* 2-5
Annual Budget: $25-50,000 *Tel:* (202) 789-2900
Hist. Note: Established originally as the Plant Propagation Society, it has Eastern and Southern regional branches, as well as branches in England, Australia and New Zealand. Members are nurserymen and academicians engaged in the study and systematic cultivation of plants. Membership: $30/yr.
Publications:
The Plant Propagator. q.
Proceedings. a.
Annual Meetings: December/500
1987-Chicago, IL(O'Hare Sheraton)
1988-Norfolk, VA

Internat'l Plate Printers', Die Stampers' and Engravers' Union of North America (1892)
4910 Oxford Court, Bensalem PA 19020
Secy.-Treas: James Kopernick
Members: 400-450 *Staff:* 2-5
Annual Budget: $10-25,000 *Tel:* (215) 757-1621
Hist. Note: Members are employed in the printing of U.S. and Canadian currency as well as stocks, bonds and foreign currency. Organized in Boston in 1892 as the Nat'l Steel and Cooper Plate Printers of the United States of America and affiliated with the American Federation of Labor in 1898. Changed "National" to "International" in 1901 when a local was formed in Ontario, and became the Internat'l Plate Printers and Die Stampers Union of North America in 1921. A merger with the Internat'l Steel and Copper Plate Engravers League in 1925 resulted in adoption of the present title.
Biennial meetings: Uneven years in Spring

Internat'l Platform Ass'n (1831)
Box 250, Winnetka IL 60093
Exec. Director: Luvie Owens
Members: 5,000 *Staff:* 6-10
Annual Budget: $250-500,000 *Tel:* (312) 446-4321
Hist. Note: An outgrowth of the American Lyceum Association founded by Daniel Webster and Josiah Holbrook. Professional association of those interested in oratory and the power of the spoken word - including lecturers, musicians, actors, program chairman and booking agents, bringing together all facets of the American lecture platform.
Publication:
Newsletter.
Annual Meetings: First week of August.
1987-Washington, DC

Internat'l Porcelain Artist Teachers (1956)
706 East Third Flint MI 48503
Exec. Director: Steven Hoffman
Members: 2,900-3,000 *Staff:* 2-5
Annual Budget: $10-25,000 *Tel:* (313) 233 3627
Hist. Note: Founded as the Nat'l China Painting Teachers Organization. It became the Internat'l China Painting Teachers Organization in 1962 and assumed its present name in 1976.
Publications:
News. m.
Membership Rosters. bien.
Biennial Meetings: Even years

Internat'l Pot and Kettle Club (1924)
3700 Cambridge Road, Cameron Park CA 95682
Exec. Secretary: Dave Crockett
Members: 5-600 *Staff:* 1
Annual Budget: $25-50,000 *Tel:* (916) 677-9111
Hist. Note: Established in Los Angeles in January, 1924 as the Associated Pot and Kettle Clubs of America and incorporated in the State of California in 1926. The present name was assumed in 1979. The club is an association of individuals engaged in buying and selling non-food hard goods and kindred lines. It was originally organized to abate the animosity then existing between buyers for retail and wholesale establishments. Most charters are in the West. Membership: $20/year.
Publications:
Hints. 6/yr.
Membership Directory. a.
Annual Meetings: June/300

Internat'l Precious Metals Institute (1976)
Government Bldg., ABE Airport, Allentown PA 18103
Exec. Director: David E. Lundy
Members: 950 individuals, 185 companies *Staff:* 6-10
Annual Budget: $250-500,000 *Tel:* (215) 266-1570
Hist. Note: Members are miners, refiners, producers and users of precious metals, as well as research scientists and mercantilists. The Institute was formed Nov. 18, 1976, to encourage the exchange of information and technology in the precious metals industry. Cooperates with the American Soc. for Metals, the American Electroplaters' Soc., the American Institute of Mining Engineers, the American Soc. for Testing and Materials and the Manufacturing Jewelers and Silversmith Ass'n.
Publications:
IPMI Membership Directory. a.
IPMI News and Reviews. m.
Annual Meetings: June
1987-Brussels, Belgium
1988-Boston, MA(Copley Plaza)/June 5-9/400

Internat'l Prepress Ass'n (1892)
552 W. 167th St., South Holland IL 60473
Exec. Director: Henry L. Hatch
Members: 250 companies *Staff:* 6-10
Annual Budget: $250-500,000 *Tel:* (612) 920-0723
Hist. Note: Producers of pre-press materials for the graphics industry. Formerly (1968) the American Photoengravers Association and (1980) the American Photoplatemakers Association and (until 1984) Internat'l Ass'n of Photoplatemakers. Merged with the Photoengravers Ass'n (1967) and Peri, Inc. (1980).
Publication:
The Prepress Bulletin. bi-m. adv.
Annual Meetings:
1987-Dallas, TX(Wyndham)/April 7-8
1988-White Sulohur Springs, WV(Greenbrier)

Internat'l Printers Supply Salesmen's Guild (1913)
Printing Industries of Illinois, 70 E. Lake St., Chicago IL 60601
Nat'l Secretary: James R. Niesen
Members: 3-400 *Staff:* 1
Annual Budget: under $10,000 *Tel:* (312) 372-8501
Hist. Note: An associate organization of Printing Industries of America. Has chapters in eight major metropolitan areas of the U.S.
Publication:
International Guilder. semi-a.

Internat'l Printing and Graphic Communications Union (1973)
Hist. Note: A merger, October 2, 1973 of the Internat'l Pressmen and Assistants Union of North America founded in 1889 and the Internat'l Stereotypers', Electrotypers' and Platemakers' Union of North America (founded in 1902). Merged, July 1, 1983, with the Graphic Arts International Union to form the Graphic Communications International Union.

Internat'l Professional Rodeo Ass'n (1957)
106 East McClure, Box 615, Pauls Valley OK 73075
Secy.-Treas.: J.O. Cravens
Members: 19,000 *Staff:* 8
Annual Budget: $2-5,000,000 *Tel:* (405) 238-6488
Hist. Note: Formerly Interstate Rodeo Ass'n (1963) and the Internat'l Rodeo Ass'n (1983). Governing body for professional rodeo. Membership: $145/year.
Publications:
Rodeo News. m. adv.
Newsletter. m.
Annual Meetings: January

Internat'l Psychohistorical Ass'n (1976)
Box 314, Planetarium Station, New York NY 10024
President: Jerrold Atlas, Ph.D.
Members: 250-260 *Staff:* 1
Annual Budget: under $10,000 *Tel:* (201) 891-4980
Hist. Note: Membership is open to scholars from all disciplines who are interested in advancing the study of psychohistory.
Publications:
IPA Bulletin. irreg. adv.
Psychohistory News. 1-2/yr. adv.
Annual Meetings: June
1987-New York, NY(Hunter College)/June 10-12/125-150

Internat'l Quorum of Film and Video Producers (1966)
Box 395, Oakton VA 22124
Exec. Director: Barbara Blair
Members: 150 companies *Staff:* 1
Annual Budget: $25-50,000 *Tel:* (703) 648-0818
Hist. Note: Membership composed of non-theatrical motion picture producers making films and video for industry and government. Founded as the Internat'l Quorum of Motion Picture Producers, it assumed its present name in 1983.
Publication:
Quorum Quotes. q.

Internat'l Racquet Sports Ass'n (1981)
132 Brookline Ave., Boston MA 02215
Exec. Director: John McCarthy
Members: 1,100 clubs, 250 companies *Staff:* 24
Annual Budget: $2-5,000,000 *Tel:* (617) 236-1500
Hist. Note: The result of a merger between the National Court Clubs Association and the National Tennis Association. Members are commercial, for-profit racquet sports clubs as well as manufacturers and suppliers.
Publication:
Club Business. 11/yr.
Annual Meetings: Summer

Internat'l Radio and Television Soc. (1939)
420 Lexington Ave., New York NY 10170
Exec. Director: Stephen B. Labunski
Members: 1,800-1,900 *Staff:* 6-10
Annual Budget: $500-1,000,000 *Tel:* (212) 867-6650
Hist. Note: Formerly (1962) Radio and Television Executives Soc. Orginally formed by a merger in 1952 of the Radio Executives Club (1939) and the American Television Soc. (1940). Members are managers, salesmen, and executive producers in radio, television and cable. Membership: $60/year.
Publications:
Gold Medal Annual. a. adv.
Yearbook and Directory. a. adv.

Internat'l Reading Ass'n (1956)
800 Barksdale Rd. Box 8139, Newark DE 19714
Exec. Director: Ronald Mitchell
Members: 70,000 *Staff:* 75
Annual Budget: over $5,000,000 *Tel:* (302) 731-1600
Hist. Note: Founded January 1, 1956 through a merger of the Internat'l Council for the Improvement of Reading Instruction (established 1947) and the Nat'l Ass'n for Remedial Teaching (established 1946). Members are classroom teachers, reading specialists, consultants, administrators, supervisors, college teachers, researchers, psychologists, librarians - persons who promote the study of reading techniques and teaching methods. Membership: $18/yr.
Publications:
Journal of Reading. 8/yr. adv.
Lectura y Vida. q.
Reading Research Quarterly. q.
Reading Teacher. 8/yr. adv.
Reading Today. bi-m. adv.
Annual Meetings: April/May
1987-Anaheim, CA/May 3-7
1988-Toronto, Ontario
1989-New Orleans, LA
1990-Atlanta, GA

Internat'l Real Estate Institute (1975)
8715 Via De Commercio, Scottsdale AZ 85258
Exec. Director: Robert G. Johnson
Members: 5,000 *Staff:* 6-10
Annual Budget: $1-2,000,000 *Tel:* (602) 998-8267
Hist. Note: Formerly (1984) the Internat'l Institute of Valuers. Members represent the area of real estate valuation, finance investment, development and management on an international level. Membership: $150/year (individual), $250/year (organization/company).
Publications:
International Real Estate Journal. q. adv.
Newsletter - IREI. bi-m. adv.
International Property Report. 3/yr. adv.
Annual Meetings: May

Internat'l Reception Operators (1975)
Hist. Note: Reported inactive in 1985. Address unknown in 1986. Probably defunct.

Internat'l Reciprocal Trade Ass'n (1979)
4012 Moss Place, Alexandria VA 22304
Exec. Director: Paul E. Suplizio
Members: 110 *Staff:* 2-5
Annual Budget: $100-250,000 *Tel:* (703) 823-8707
Hist. Note: Members are organizations serving as intermediary in the barter exchange of goods and services among business firms and professionals. Formed to foster the common interest of the Commercial Barter Industry in the U.S. and worldwide. Supports the Barter Political Action Committee. Formerly the Internat'l Ass'n of Trade Exchanges. Assumed its present name in 1984.
Publications:
Fact Sheets. irreg.
IRTA Newsletter. irreg.
Annual Meetings: May

Internat'l Reprographic Ass'n (1927)
Box 879, Franklin Park IL 60131
Exec. V. President: Thomas F. Renk, CAE
Members: 1,000 companies *Staff:* 6-7
Annual Budget: $1-2,000,000 *Tel:* (312) 671-5356
Hist. Note: Membership consists of photocopy and blueprint service companies and engineering equipment manufacturers and suppliers. Formerly (until 1973) known as the International Association of Blue Print and Allied Industries and (1973-1980) as the International Reprographic Blueprint Association. Membership: $100-400/yr. (based on employee count).
Publications:
Plan and Print. m. adv.
Repro Report. m.
Annual Meetings: 6
May/900-1,000
1987-Las Vegas, NV(Caesra's Palace)/April 29-May 3
1988-Boston, MA(Marriott)/May 4-8
1989-San Antonio, TX/May 8-13
1990-Monterrey, CA/May 1-6
1991-Colorado Springs, CO(Broadmoor)/April 30-May 5

Internat'l Rescue and Emergency Care Ass'n (1948)
8107 Ensign Curve, Bloomington MN 55438
Exec. Director: Carol Moss
Members: 700-800 rescue squads, 25,000 individuals *Staff:* 1
Annual Budget: $50-100,000 *Tel:* (612) 941-2926
Hist. Note: Organized in 1948 in Atlantic City, New Jersey and incorporated in Ohio; known as Internat'l Rescue and First Aid Ass'n until 1980.

00165 12 05 86 1233

Publication:
International Rescuer. q.
Annual Meetings: Late August
1987-Virginia Beach, VA

Internat'l Right of Way Ass'n (1934)
9920 La Cienega Blvd., Suite 515, Inglewood CA 90301
Exec. V. President: Betsy Fan
Members: 10,000-11,000 *Staff:* 6-10
Annual Budget: $1-2,000,000 *Tel:* (213) 649-5323
Hist. Note: Members are individuals responsible for acquiring land over which to run power and telephone lines, pipelines, roads, etc. Founded as the Southern California Right of Way Association. Formerly (1946-1980) known as the American Right of Way Ass'n. Membership: $65/yr.
Publication:
Right of Way. bi-m. adv.
Annual Meetings: June/1,000
1987-Portland, OR
1988-Baltimore, MD
1989-Dearborn, MI
1990-Denver,CO

Internat'l Rodeo Ass'n (1962)
Hist. Note: Became the Internat'l Professional Rodeo Ass'n in 1983.

Internat'l Sanitary Supply Ass'n (1923)
5330 N. Elston Ave., Chicago IL 60630
Exec. V. President: Jack D. Ramaley
Members: 3,000 companies *Staff:* 11-15
Annual Budget: $2-5,000,000 *Tel:* (312) 286-2575
Hist. Note: Formerly the National Sanitary Supply Association. Manufacturers, distributors, manufacturer representatives, publisher and associate members engaged in the manufacture and distribution of cleaning and maintenance products.
Publications:
ISSA Today. m.
ISSAlert. m.
Annual Meetings: Fall
1987-Las Vegas, NV(Convention Center)/Oct. 21-24/10,500
1988-New York City, NY(Convention Center)/Nov. 2-5/10,500
1989-Chicago, IL(McCormick Place)/Oct. 18-21/10,500

Internat'l Saw and Knife Ass'n (1965)
Hector and Jones Streets, Conshohocken PA 19428
Secy.-Treas.: John V. Capozzi
Members: 110 companies *Staff:* 1
Annual Budget: $10-25,000 *Tel:* (215) 825-2055
Hist. Note: Members are companies repairing or servicing large band, circular saws and paper knives. Formerly the Nat'l Ass'n of Saw Shops, assumed its present name in 1983. Has no paid staff or permanent address.

Internat'l Security Officers, Police and Guards Union (1937)
8519 Fourth Ave., Brooklyn NY 11209
President: John J. Fanning
Members: 4,000 *Staff:* 2-5
Annual Budget: under $10,000 *Tel:* (718) 836-3508
Hist. Note: An independent labor union which was founded under the name, Independent Watchmen's Association. The present name was assumed around 1981-82.
Quinquennial Meetings: 1990

Internat'l Silk Ass'n (1950)
111 West 40th St., 18th Floor, New York NY 10018
President: Robert Kobelt
Members: 20-25 silk converters and importers *Staff:* 1
Annual Budget: $10-25,000 *Tel:* (212) 398-1133
Annual Meetings: Fall

Internat'l Silo Ass'n (1907)
1163 E. Ogden Ave., Suite 705-359, Naperville IL 60540
President: Tom Knight
Members: 125 *Staff:* 2
Annual Budget: $100-250,000 *Tel:* (312) 369-4120
Hist. Note: From 1912-1956 went under the name of the National Association of Silo Manufacturers. Members manufacture crop storage facilities.
Annual Meetings: Third week in January.

Internat'l Sleep Products Ass'n (1915)
1235 Jefferson Davis Highway, Suite 601, Arlington VA 22202
Exec. V. President: Russell L. Abolt
Members: 450-500 companies *Staff:* 10
Annual Budget: $500-1,000,000 *Tel:* (703) 979-3550
Hist. Note: Formerly (1986) Nat'l Ass'n of Bedding Manufacturers.
Publication:
Bedding. m. adv.
Biennial Trade Shows: Spring
1987-New Orleans, LA/March 19-21
1989-San Antonio, TX/March 16-18

Internat'l Slurry Seal Ass'n (1962)
1101 Connecticut Ave., N.W., Suite 700, Washington DC 20036
Exec. Director: Mark Levin
Annual Budget: $100-250,000 *Tel:* (202) 857-1160
Hist. Note: Contractors and suppliers of asphalt slurry seal.
Annual Meetings: Winter/200
1987-Paris, France(Intercontinental)/Mar. 29-Apr. 12/500
1988-San Diego(Sheraton Harbor Island)
1989-Kona, Hawaii(Kona Surf)

Internat'l Snowmobile Industry Ass'n (1965)
3975 University Drive, Suite 310, Fairfax VA 22030
President: Roy W. Muth
Members: 4 manufacturers, 11-15 suppliers and distributors
Staff: 2-5
Annual Budget: $250-500,000 *Tel:* (703) 273-9606
Hist. Note: Organized and incorporated in the District of Columbia. Acts as Secretariat for the International Snowmobile Council and the Internat'l Snowmobile Tourism Council. ISIA serves the interests of the snowmobile manufacturing industry as well as recreational snowmobiling.
Publication:
ISIA Newsline. irreg.
Annual Meetings: Late Spring in Canada or the U.S.

Internat'l Soc. for Artificial Organs (1977)
Editorial Office, 8937 Euclid Ave., Cleveland OH 44106
Editor-in-Chief: Yukihiko Nose, MD, PhD
Members: 1,000 *Staff:* 6
Annual Budget: $100-250,000 *Tel:* (216) 421-0757
Hist. Note: Members are involved in the research, development or application of artificial organs. Membership: $85/yr.
Publications:
Artificial Organs. bi-m. adv.
Progress in Artificial Organs. bi-a.
Annual Meetings: 987-
Biennial Meetings: Odd years
1987-Munich, West Germany

Internat'l Soc. for Cardiovascular Surgery - North American Chapter
13 Elm St., Box 1565, Manchester MA 01944
Exec. Director: William T. Maloney, CAE
Members: 1,200 *Staff:* 12
Annual Budget: $25-50,000 *Tel:* (617) 927-8330
Publication:
Journal of Vascular Surgery.
Annual Meetings: June
1987-Toronto, Ontario(Sheraton Centre)/June 7-10
1988-Chicago, IL(Hyatt Regency)/June 12-15
1989-New York, NY(Hilton)/June 18-21
1990-Los Angeles, CA(Century Plaza)/June 3-6
1991-Boston, MA(Sheraton/Hynes Aud.)/June 2-5

Internat'l Soc. for Chronobiology (1937)
Room 120, Building 307, BARC-E, Beltsville MD 20705
Secy.-Treas.: Dora K. Hayes
Members: 600
Annual Budget: $10-25,000 *Tel:* (301) 344-2474
Hist. Note: Founded at Ronneby, Sweden as Societas pro Studio Rhythmi Biologici, it assumed its present name in 1971. Seeks to further the development of studies on temporal parameters of biological variables (chronobiologic variation) and to pursue related scientific and educational purposes; to encourage the development of centers of chronobiological research; and to work toward the establishment of chronobiology as an academic discipline in its own right. Its principal activity is sponsorship of international conferences. Scientific Members: $45/yr.
Publications:
Chronobiologia. q.
Chronobiology International. q. adv.

Internat'l Soc. for Clinical Laboratory Technology (1962)
818 Olive, Suite 918, St. Louis MO 63101
Administrator: David Birenbaum
Members: 8,000 *Staff:* 11-15
Annual Budget: $100-250,000 *Tel:* (314) 241-1445
Hist. Note: Founded as the Registry of Medical Technologists International, it subsequently became the International Society of Clinical Laboratory Technology and assumed its present name in 1974. Members are registered medical technologists and laboratory technicians.
Publication:
Newsletter. bi-m. adv.
Annual Meetings: Summer
1987-St. Louis, MO(Omni at Union Station)/Aug.

Internat'l Soc. for Developmental Psychobiology (1967)
Department of Anatomy, University of British Columbia, Vancouver British Columbia V6T 1W5
Secretary: Dr. Joanne Weinberg
Members: 308 individuals *Staff:* 0
Annual Budget: $10-25,000 *Tel:* (604) 228-6214
Hist. Note: Formed to promote research into the relationship between behavioral and biological aspects of the developing organism at all levels of organization; membership open to any person engaged in the scientific study of human or animal development and holding a doctorate degree. Membership: $55/yr.
Publications:
Developmental Psychobiology. bi-m. adv.
Newsletter. 3/yr. adv.
Membership Directory. a. adv.
Annual Meetings: October/November
1987-New Orleans, LA/Nov. 13-16/200
1988-Toronto, Canada/Nov. 10-13/220
1989-San Francisco, CA/Oct. 25-28/220

Internat'l Soc. for Ecological Modelling-North AmericanChapter
School of Natural Resources, Ohio Sate University, Columbus OH 43210
Secretary General: Dr. William J. Mitsch
Members: 150 *Staff:* 1
Annual Budget: under $10,000 *Tel:* (614) 292-2265
Hist. Note: Individuals interested in constructing mathematical models of air, water and environmental pollution problems. Membership: $85/yr.
Publication:
Ecological Modelling.

Internat'l Soc. for General Semantics (1943)
P.O. Box 2469, San Francisco CA 94126
Exec. Director: Russell Joyner
Members: 2,500 *Staff:* 2-5
Annual Budget: $100-250,000 *Tel:* (415) 543-1747
Hist. Note: Members are educators, trainers, writers, scientists and others interested in how language shapes thought, behavior and communication with others. Membership: $25/yr.
Publications:
ETC: A Review of General Semantics. q. adv.
Glimpse. q.

Internat'l Soc. for Heart Transplantation (1981)
425 East River Road, Minnesota Hospital, Minneapolis MN 55455
Editor: Michael P. Kaye
Members: 50 companies, 800 individuals *Staff:* 1
Annual Budget: $100-250,000 *Tel:* (612) 625-5611
Hist. Note: Encouraes and stimulates discussion of all problems of interest and concern in the field of heart transplantation. Membership: $100/yr.
Publication:
Heart Transplantation. q. adv.
Annual Meetings: Spring

Internat'l Soc. for Hybrid Microelectronics (1967)
Box 2698, Reston VA 22090
Executive Director: Walter H. Biddle
Members: 6,000 *Staff:* 9
Annual Budget: $1-2,000,000 *Tel:* (703) 471-0066
Hist. Note: Promotes close interaction between the complementary technologies of ceramics, thin and thick films, semiconductor packaging, discrete semiconductor devices, and monolithic circuits. Formed in the fall of 1967 by a small group of engineers in the San Francisco Bay area. Membership: $30/year.
Publications:
Newsletter. bi-m.
Technical Journal. q.
Technical Proceedings. a.
Annual Meetings: Fall
1987-Minneapolis, MN(Hyatt)/Sept. 28-30
1988-Seattle, WA(Washington Plaza)/Oct. 17-19
1989-Baltimore, MD/Oct. 24-26
1990-Chicago, IL(Hyatt O'Hare)/Oct. 8-10
1991-Orlando, FL(Civic Ctr.)
1992-San Francisco, CA(Hilton)/Nov. 2-4

Internat'l Soc. for Intercultural Eductation, Training and Research (1985)
1505 22nd St., N.W., Washington DC 20037
Exec. Director: Diane L. Zeller, Ph.D.
Members: 1,400 individuals; 40 institutions *Staff:* 2-7
Annual Budget: $250-500,000 *Tel:* (202) 296-4710
Hist. Note: Founded as the Soc. for Intercultural Education, Training and Research in 1974, it added "International" to its name in 1985. An international professional association of individuals concerned with understanding the interaction between peoples of different national, cultural, racial and ethnic backgrounds.
Publications:
Communique. bi-m. adv.
Intercultural Resources Directories. 1-2/yr.
International Journal of Intercultural Relations. q.
Training Manuals. irreg.
Annual Meetings:
1987-Montreal, Canada
1988-Denver, CO
1989-Boston, MA

Internat'l Soc. for Medical and Psychological Hypnosis (1981)
45 West 67th St., New York NY 10023
President: Dr. Milton V. Kline
Staff: 15
Annual Budget: $100-250,000 *Tel:* (212) 799-2727
Hist. Note: Composed of professional societies in medicine and mental health and individuals involved in the health care profession. Membership: $100/yr. (individual); $300/yr. (organization/company)
Publications:
Morton Price Digest of Hypnotherapy and Hypnoanalysis. q.
Internat'l Journal of Psychological Hypnosis. q. adv.
Annual Meetings: Fall

Internat'l Soc. for Peritoneal Dialysis (1984)
3800 Reservoir Rd., N.W., Washington DC 20007
Secy.-Treas.: James F. Winchester, M.D.
Staff: 0
Annual Budget: $10-25,000 *Tel:* (202) 625-2092
Hist. Note: Stimulated by the growth of continuous ambulatory peritoneal dialysis, which is now used for renal failure management of 30,000 patients worldwide. Members are MD's, RN's, scientists, and dieticians interested in or having experience in peritoneal dialysis for the treatment of renal

00166 12 05 86 1233

failure. Membership: $50/yr.
Publications:
Frontiers in Peritoneal Dialysis. trienn.
Peritoneal Dialysis Bulletin. bi-m.
Annual Meetings: Triennial
1987-Venice, Italy/June 9-12

Internat'l Soc. for Prosthetics and Orthotics, United States Nat'l Member Soc. (1970)
317 East 34th St., New York NY 10016
Secretary-Treasurer: Joan E. Edelstein
Members: 325
Annual Budget: $10-25,000 *Tel:* (212) 340-6683
Hist. Note: Established and incorporated in Dover, Delaware. Membership: $50/yr.
Publication:
Prosthetics and Orthotics International. 3/yr. adv.
Annual Meetings: January, plus triennial international congress.

Internat'l Soc. for Range Management (1948)
Hist. Note: Became the Society for Range Management in 1982.

Internat'l Soc. of Air Safety Investigators (1964)
West Building, Room 259, Washington, National Airport, Washington DC 20001
President: Charles R. Mercer
Members: 900-1,000 individuals and companies *Staff:* 2-5
Annual Budget: $50-100,000 *Tel:* (703) 521-5195
Hist. Note: Established August 31, 1964 in Washington, DC to promote development of improved aircraft accident procedures. Has an international membership from 35 countries. Formerly (1977) the Soc. of Air Safety Investigators.
Publications:
The Forum. q.
ISASI News. q.
Annual Meetings: Fall
1987-Atlanta, GA

Internat'l Soc. of Appraisers (1979)
Box 726, Hoffman Estates IL 60195
President: Maurice E. Fry
Members: 2,000 *Staff:* 2-5
Annual Budget: $100-250,000 *Tel:* (312) 882-0706
Hist. Note: Members are appraisers specializing in property other than land or buildings. Membership: $150 initial fee; $115/yr. thereafter.
Publications:
Appraisers' Information Exchange. bi-m. adv.
Internat'l Journal of Personal Property Appraising. q.
Annual Meetings: Spring
1987-Baltimore, MD(Hyatt)/May
1988-Dallas, Houston or San Antonio, TX/May
1989-Honolulu, HI or Vancouver, BC/May

Internat'l Soc. of Arboriculture (1924)
5 Lincoln Square, P.O. Box 71, Urbana IL 61801
Exec. Director: Ervin C. Bundy
Members: 4,500 *Staff:* 4
Annual Budget: $250-500,000 *Tel:* (217) 328-2032
Hist. Note: Formerly (1976) Internat'l Shade Tree Conference.
Publications:
Journal of Arboriculture. m. adv.
Shade Tree Evaluation. a.
Yearbook and Convention Program. a. adv.
Tree and Shrub Transplanting Manual. a.
Annual Meetings: August/8-900
1987-Keystone, CO/Aug. 16-19
1988-Vancouver, BC(Univ. of British Columbia)/Aug. 14-17
1989-St. Charles, IL(Pheasant Run)/Aug. 13-16
1990-Toronto, Ontario(Sheraton Centre)/Aug. 12-15
1991-Philadelphia, PA(Adam's Mark Hotel)/Aug. 11-14

Internat'l Soc. of Barristers (1965)
3586 East Huron River Drive, Ann Arbor MI 48104
Admin. Secretary: John W. Reed
Members: 550-600 *Staff:* 1
Annual Budget: $100-250,000 *Tel:* (313) 764-0540
Hist. Note: Members are lawyers interested in encouraging advocacy under the adversary system and preserving the right to a jury trial. Membership: $300/yr.
Publication:
ISOB Quarterly. q.
Annual Meetings: Late Winter
1987-Kamuela, HI(Mauna Kea Beach Hotel)/Jan. 18-24/125

Internat'l Soc. of Certified Electronics Technicians (1970)
2708 West Berry, Fort Worth TX 76109
Exec. Director: Clyde Nabors
Members: 1,400-1,500 *Staff:* 5-7
Annual Budget: $100-250,000 *Tel:* (817) 921-9101
Hist. Note: Affiliated with the National Electronic Service Dealers Ass'n which provides administrative support. Awards the CET("Certified Electronics Technician") designation. Membership: $25/year.
Publications:
ISCET Newsletter. m.
Professional Electronics. bi-m. adv.
Annual Meetings: With the National Electronic Service Dealers Association in August.
1987-Memphis, TN(Peabody)Aug. 10-15
1988-Chicago, IL

Internat'l Soc. of Chemical Ecology (1983)
University of California, Department of Ecology, Irvine CA 92715
Secretary: Prof. Eloy Rodriguez
Members: 750 individuals *Staff:* 0
Annual Budget: under $10,000 *Tel:* (714) 856-6006
Hist. Note: Formed to promote the understanding of the origin, function, and significance of natural chemicals that mediate interactions with and among organisms. Membership: $15/yr.
Publication:
Journal of Chemical Ecology. (Published by Plenum Press, NY)
Annual Meetings: June
1987-Hull, England(Univ. of Hull)/June
1988-Montreal, Quebec(Laval Universite')
1989-Goteborg, Sweden(Univ. of Goteborg)

Internat'l Soc. of Communications Specialists (1984)
Hist. Note: Address unknown in 1985.

Internat'l Soc. of Copier Artists (1982)
800 West End Ave., New York NY 10025
Director: Louise Neaderland
Members: 125 individuals; 10 museums and libraries *Staff:* 0
Annual Budget: under $10,000 *Tel:* (212) 662-5533
Hist. Note: Founded to provide exposure to electrographic printmakers and book artists, the ISCA is a group of artists who use the copier as a creative tool. Membership: $25/yr. (individual); $90/yr. (institution)
Publications:
ISCA Quarterly. q.
ISCA Newsletter. 3/yr.
ISCA Bookworks Catalogue. a.

Internat'l Soc. of Developmental and Comparative Immunology (1978)
c/o 2080 Century Park East, Suite 1201, Los Angeles CA 90067
Secy.-Treas.: Dr. Richard K. Wright
Members: 500
Annual Budget: under $10,000 *Tel:* (213) 284-8003
Hist. Note: The ISDCI was founded to bring together research workers world-wide by fostering and maintaining international scientific cooperation and communication between individual scientists, regional groups and/ or national societies, interested in the study of developmental and comparative immunology. Affiliated with the Internat'l Union of Biological Sciences. Membership is open to all scientists and their graduate students. Membership: $35/yr.
Publication:
Developmental and Comparative Immunology, q.
Triennial meetings: next meeting in 1988

Internat'l Soc. of Financiers (1979)
31 Wildwood Ave., Suite 3, Asheville NC 28804-3555
Chairman: Ronald I. Gershen
Members: 500 *Staff:* 1
Annual Budget: $25-50,000 *Tel:* (704) 252-5907
Hist. Note: A professional society of brokers, consultants, investors and corporate lenders. 85% of the membership resides in the United States. Membership: $125/yr.
Publication:
International Financier. m.
Annual Meetings: None held

Internat'l Soc. of Fire Service Instructors (1960)
20 Main St., Ashland MA 01721
Exec. Director: Edward H. McCormack, Jr.
Members: 6,000 *Staff:* 13
Annual Budget: $1-2,000,000 *Tel:* (617) 881-5800
Hist. Note: Individuals responsible for the training of fire, police, ambulance and rescue personnel, and the public. Membership: $50/year.
Publication:
Rekindle. m.
Annual Meetings: March in Cincinnati, OH

Internat'l Soc. of Hotel Ass'n Executives (1974)
40 W. 38th St., New York NY 10018
President: James Marquart
Members: 75 *Staff:* 1
Annual Budget: under $10,000 *Tel:* (212) 921-8888
Hist. Note: Executive directors of hotel and motel ass'ns in the U.S. and Canada. Formerly (1974) American Hotel Trade Ass'n Executives. Affiliated with the American Hotel and Motel Ass'n. No permanent address. Officers change annually. Membership: $100/yr.
Annual Meetings:
1987-San Francisco, CA
1988-Dallas, TX
1989-Boston, MA

Internat'l Soc. of Industrial Fabric Manufacturers (1974)
1337 Garden Circle Drive, Newberry SC 29108
Secy.-Treas.: Sandy Saye
Members: 175-200 individuals *Staff:* 1
Annual Budget: $100-250,000 *Tel:* (803) 635-4651
Hist. Note: Engineers, executives, technicians and salespersons in the yarn industry. Formerly (1980) Internat'l Soc. of Industrial Yarn Manufacturers.
Publication:
American Textile Reporter. m. adv.
Semi-annual meetings: Spring and Fall

Internat'l Soc. of Interior Designers (1979)
433 S. Spring St., Suite 6-D, Los Angeles CA 90013
President: Patti Richards, FISID
Members: 2,500 *Staff:* 1
Annual Budget: $100-250,000 *Tel:* (213) 680-4240
Hist. Note: Professional membership in ISID is granted to those individuals who are regularly engaged in the practice of interior design and have completed coursework in interior design; other memberships are open to students, press and communications professionals and those working in affiliate professions. Membership: $135/yr. (professional); $125/yr. (trade)
Publication:
International Bulletin. bi-m.
Biennial Conferences: Odd Years
1987-Phoenix, AZ(Biltmore)/June 10-15
1989-Tokyo, Japan

Internat'l Soc. of Parametric Analysts (1979)
6803 Whittier Ave., McLean VA 22101
Business Manager: Dr. Armand B. Weiss
Members: 7-800 *Staff:* 2-5
Annual Budget: $100-250,000 *Tel:* (703) 442-8780
Hist. Note: Members are cost analysts working principally in the field of defense and weapons systems. Membership: $24/yr.
Publications:
Parametric World. m. adv.
Journal of Parametrics. q. adv.
Annual Meetings: Spring

Internat'l Soc. of Performing Arts Administrators (1948)
Box 200238, Austin TX 78720
Exec. Director: Clinton E. Norton
Members: 300 individuals and organizations *Staff:* 2
Annual Budget: $50-100,000 *Tel:* (512) 346-1328
Hist. Note: Formerly Nat'l Ass'n of Concert Managers and (1974) Internat'l Ass'n of Concert and Festival Managers. Incorporated in 1949 in the State of New York. A professional society whose membership is directly responsible for the presentation of cultural events on a world-wide scale. Membership: $150-250/yr. (individual), organizational fee based on budget.
Publications:
Forum. m.
Membership Directory. a.
Annual Meetings: New York City, in December.
1987-Dec. 13-17/150

Internat'l Soc. of Pharmaceutical Engineers (1980)
8910 North Dale Mabry Highway, Suite 27, Tampa FL 33614
Exec. Director: Robert Best
Members: 940 *Staff:* 5
Annual Budget: $250-500,000 *Tel:* (813) 932-6069
Hist. Note: Members are individuals concerned with the construction of pharmaceutical plants, particularly such matters as pure water, sterile environments, anti-pollution measures, etc. Membership: $95/yr.(individual); $600/yr.(company). U.S. members comprise 90% of membership.
Publications:
Pharmaceutical Engineering. bi-m. adv.
ISPE Newsletter. m. adv.
ISPE Membership Directory and By-Laws. a. adv.
Annual Meetings: November
1987-Lake Buena Vista, FL(Buena Vista Palace)/Nov. 8-11/175

Internat'l Soc. of Preretirement Planners (1975)
11312 Old Club Road, Rockville MD 20852
Exec. V. President: L. Malcolm Rodman, CAE
Members: 700 *Staff:* 1
Annual Budget: $50-100,000 *Tel:* (301) 881-4113
Hist. Note: Established in August, 1975 in Des Moines, Iowa as a professional society of individuals in business, industry, institutions, labor unions and academia concerned with the field of preparing mature individuals for retirement living. Membership: $75/year (individual).
Publications:
Retirement Planning. q. adv.
Perspective. m.
Annual Meetings: Fall
1987-San Francisco, CA(Ramada Renaissance)/Oct. 28-31
1988-Boston, MA

Internat'l Soc. of Statistical Science in Economics (1982)
333 Enterprise Drive #68, Rohnert Park CA 94928
Chairman: V.V. Shvyrkov
Members: 100 individuals
Annual Budget: under $10,000 *Tel:* (415) 585-0615
Hist. Note: Professional society of persons interested in the development of statistical science in economics on the basis of epistemological foundations. Membership: $15/yr.
Publications:
Newsletter. q. adv.
Proceedings. a. adv.
Annual Meetings: June

Internat'l Soc. of the Knee (1977)
70 West Hubbard St., Suite 202, Chicago IL 60610
Exec. Director: Sanford J. Hill
Members: 450 *Staff:* 2-5
Annual Budget: $100-250,000 *Tel:* (312) 644-2623
Hist. Note: Membership, by invitation only, costs $50/yr.
Publication:
ISK Newsletter. semi-a.
Annual Meetings: Biennially in uneven years.
1987-Sydney,Australia/April 6-10

00167 12 05 86 1233

Internat'l Soc. of Transport Aircraft Traders (1983)
1133 15th St., Suite 1000, Washington DC 20005
Exec. Director: Brian R. Cassedy
Members: 113 companies, 150 individuals *Staff:* 2
Annual Budget: $50-100,000 *Tel:* (202) 293-5910
Hist. Note: The Society was formed to provide a communications medium for those engaged in the purchase, sale, financing, appraisal or insuring of used airline aircraft. Membership: $300/yr.
Publication:
JeTrader. m. adv.
Annual Meetings: November

Internat'l Soc. of Weekly Newspaper Editors (1954)
Dept. of Journalism, Northern Illinois University, DeKalb IL 60115
Secy.-Treas.: Dr. Donald F. Brod
Members: 300 *Staff:* 2-5
Annual Budget: $10-25,000 *Tel:* (815) 753-1925
Hist. Note: Sponsors the Golden Quill Award for excellence in writing of editorials in weekly newspapers and the Eugene Cervi Award for that weekly newspaper person who has served as the conscience of the community. Membership: $25/yr.
Publications:
Grassroots Editor. q.
Newsletter. m.
Annual Meetings: July
1987-Santa Fe, NM

Internat'l Soc. of Weighing and Measurement (1916)
2506 Gross Point Road, Evanston IL 60201
Exec. Director: Arthur W. Engle, CAM
Members: 1,500 *Staff:* 3
Annual Budget: $100-250,000 *Tel:* (312) 475-1008
Hist. Note: Formerly titled the Nat'l Men's Scale Ass'n (1985). Members are engaged in the scale industry or weights and measurement enforcement.
Publication:
ISWM News. q. adv.
Annual Meetings: June/2,000
1987-Reno, NV(Bally Grand)
1988-New Orleans, LA(Hilton)

Internat'l Solar Energy Soc., American Section (1970)
Hist. Note: Became the American Solar Energy Society in 1982.

Internat'l Spa and Tub Institute (1978)
Hist. Note: Merged with the Nat'l Spa and Pool Institute in 1983.

Internat'l Staple, Nail and Tool Ass'n (1966)
435 North Michigan Ave., Chicago IL 60611
President: Bernie J. Mezger
Members: 7 *Staff:* 2-5
Annual Budget: $250-500,000 *Tel:* (312) 644-0828
Hist. Note: Founded as the Industrial Stapling Manufacturer's Institute, it became the Industrial Stapling and Nailing Technical Association in 1972 and assumed its present name in 1982. Financed and directed by manufacturers of collated fasteners and power tools for driving them.
Annual Meetings: November

Internat'l Stress and Tension Control Ass'n (1973)
U.S. International Univ., 10455 Pomerado Road, San Diego CA 92131
Exec. Director: F.J. McGuigan, Ph.D.
Members: 750 *Staff:* 1
Annual Budget: $10-25,000 *Tel:* (502) 588-6571
Hist. Note: An organization of people interested in the systematic relaxation of tension in everyday life. Formerly (1980) American Ass'n for the Advancement of Tension Control. Membership: $15/yr.
Publication:
Newsletter. q.
Annual Meetings: Spring

Internat'l Studies Ass'n (1959)
Byrnes Internat'l Center, Columbia SC 29208
Exec. Director: William A. Welsh
Members: 2,200 *Staff:* 7
Annual Budget: $100-250,000 *Tel:* (803) 777-2933
Hist. Note: A professional society with multinational and multidisciplinary membership concerned with the communication of national, international, and transnational issues, concerns, and ideas. Special areas of interest are directed within sectional subunits. Membership: Based upon annual income.
Publications:
International Studies Newsletter. 10/yr. adv.
International Studies Notes. 3/yr. adv.
International Studies Quarterly. q. adv.
New Dimensions in International Studies. a.
Membership Directory. a.
Annual Meetings: Spring
1987-Washington, DC(Omni Shoreham)/April 15-18/1,500
1988-St. Louis, MO
1989-London, England

Internat'l Tanning Manufacturers Ass'n (1979)
5100 Poplar, Suite 1219, Memphis TN 38137
President: William Richey
Members: 8 companies
Annual Budget: under $10,000 *Tel:* (901) 388-3050
Hist. Note: Members are manufacturers of suntanning equipment.
Annual Meetings: December

Internat'l Tape/Disc Ass'n (1970)
10 Columbus Circle, New York NY 10019
Exec. V. President: Henry Brief
Members: 450 companies *Staff:* 6-10
Annual Budget: $250-500,000 *Tel:* (212) 956-7110
Hist. Note: Manufacturers of audio and video tape and equipment, home computers, software and optical/laser media. Founded as the Internat'l Tape Ass'n, it assumed its present name in 1981.
Publications:
ITA Newsdigest. bi-m.
ITA Source Directory. a. adv.
Annual Meetings:
1987-Hilton Head Island, SC(Hyatt Regency)

Internat'l Tax Institute (1961)
101 Park Ave., 35th Floor, New York NY 10178-0061
President: Robert D. Whoriskey
Members: 300 *Staff:* 1
Annual Budget: $50-100,000 *Tel:* (212) 696-6031
Hist. Note: Formerly (1971) Institute on U. S. Taxation of Foreign Income, Inc. It is a professional organization of tax executives, lawyers and accountants concerned with taxation of international business income. Membership: $125/yr.(individual); $350/yr.(organization)
Publications:
Year Book. a.
Report to Members. m.
Annual Meetings: June

Internat'l Taxicab Ass'n (1917)
3849 Farragut Ave., Kensington MD 20895
Exec. V. President: Alfred B. LaGasse
Members: 600 *Staff:* 2-5
Annual Budget: $250-500,000 *Tel:* (301) 946-5701
Hist. Note: Formed in 1966 by a merger of the American Taxicabs Ass'n (1942), the Nat'l Ass'n of Taxicab Owners (1917), and the Cab Research Bureau (1938). Members are owners of taxi fleets. Sponsors the International Taxicab Association Political Action Committee.
Publication:
Taxicab Management. m. adv.
Annual Meetings: October or November/5-600
1987-Las Vegas, NV

Internat'l Technical Caramel Ass'n (1975)
1575 Eye St., N.W., Washington DC 20005
Secretary: Roger D. Middlekauff
Members: 12 companies
Annual Budget: $100-250,000 *Tel:* (202) 789-7589
Hist. Note: Ass'n sponsors research on caramel color and provides liaison with government offices throughout the world directly and through affiliated organizations.

Internat'l Technology Education Ass'n (1939)
1914 Association Drive, Reston VA 22091
Exec. Director: Kendall N. Starkweather
Members: 7-8,000 *Staff:* 2-5
Annual Budget: $250-500,000 *Tel:* (703) 860-2100
Hist. Note: Established as the American Industrial Arts Ass'n, ITEA assumed its present name in 1985. Membership consists of technology education teachers and supervisors. Affiliates of the ITEA are: Technology Education for Children Council, Council on Technology Teacher Education, American Council of Industrial Arts State Ass'n Officers, and American Council of Industrial Arts Supervisors. Membership: $40/yr.(individual); $120/yr.(institution)
Publications:
The Technology Teacher. 8/yr.
Technology Education News. q.
Annual Meetings: Spring
1987-Tulsa, OK/March 23-27
1988-Norfolk, VA/March 28-April 1

Internat'l Teleconferencing Ass'n (1982)
1299 Woodside Drive, #101, McLean VA 22102
Exec. Director: Robert Brouse
Members: 450 *Staff:* 3
Annual Budget: $100-250,000 *Tel:* (703) 556-6115
Hist. Note: Non-profit corporation founded to provide a clearinghouse for the exchange of information between users, researchers, and providers in the field of teleconferencing. Membership: $100/yr. (individual); $500/yr. (organization)
Publication:
ITCA Insiders Newsletter. m.
Annual Meetings: May

Internat'l Teleproduction Soc. (1969)
565 5th Ave., Suite 416, New York NY 10017
Exec. Director: Janet Luhrs
Members: 200 companies *Staff:* 2-5
Annual Budget: $100-250,000 *Tel:* (212) 986-1414
Hist. Note: Formerly (1986) the Videotape Production Ass'n. Videotape production firms and their suppliers, united to promote videotape as a communications medium.
Publication:
ITS News. q.
Annual Meetings: In conjunction with the Nat'l Ass'n of Broadcasters

Internat'l Television Ass'n (1971)
6311 N. O'Connor Road, LB, Irving TX 75039
Exec. Director: Frederick M. Wehrli, CAE, CEM
Members: 8,000 individuals *Staff:* 7
Annual Budget: $500-1,000,000 *Tel:* (214) 869-1112
Hist. Note: National organization of professional video communicators: individuals in non-broadcast video who use videotape and equipment in organizational settings producing, writing and editing video programs. Founded in 1971 as the Nat'l Industrial Television Ass'n. Merged in 1974 with the Industrial Television Society to become the Internat'l Industrial Television Ass'n. Assumed current name in 1978.
Publications:
International Television News. m. adv.
Corporate Television. bi-m. adv.
Membership Directory. a.
Salary Survey. a.
Annual Meetings: Spring, even years with the Nat'l Ass'n of Broadcasters and odd years on own.
1987-Washington, DC/May 27-31

Internat'l Test and Evaluation Ass'n (1980)
4400 Fair Lakes Court, Fairfax VA 22033
Administrator: Sherry A. Sieg
Members: 1,300 *Staff:* 1
Annual Budget: $50-100,000 *Tel:* (703) 631-6220
Hist. Note: A professional society of engineers concerned with the technology, process and management of test and evaluation. Members are concerned primarily with industrial and defense products (autos, tanks, aircraft, spacecraft, comand and control, simulation, weapon systems, etc). Membership: $40/year (individual), $500/year (corporate).
Publications:
Journal of Test and Evaluation. q. adv.
Symposium Proceedings. a. adv.
Annual Meetings: Fall
1987-Boston, MA(Park Plaza)/Nov. 10-12

Internat'l Theatrical Agencies Ass'n (1975)
Box 25505, Dallas TX 75225
President: C. W. Kendall
Members: 130-140 *Staff:* 1
Annual Budget: $25-50,000 *Tel:* (214) 349-3025
Hist. Note: Members are agencies booking entertainers into hotels, motels and lounges. Membership: $200/yr.
Publication:
The Bull Sheet. bi-m.
Semi-annual Meetings: First week in March, third week in September.

Internat'l Thermographers Ass'n (1973)
1730 N. Lynn St., Arlington VA 22209
Exec. Director: Nancy M. Yancey
Members: 100 companies *Staff:* 2-5
Annual Budget: $25-50,000 *Tel:* (703) 841-8100
Hist. Note: A section of the Printing Industries of America comprised of members who specialize in thermographic printing, or raised lettering.
Publication:
Newsletter. q.
Annual Meetings: Fall/250
1987-Marco Island, FL(Marriott)/Oct. 24-29

Internat'l Trade Commission Trial Lawyers Ass'n (1984)
1019 19th St., N.W., Washington DC 20036
President: Robert Swecker
Members: 340 individuals
Annual Budget: $10-25,000 *Tel:* (202) 785-4200
Hist. Note: Composed of attorneys who practice or are otherwise interested in Section 337 cases before the Internat'l Trade Commission. Membership: $15/yr. (government attorneys); $30/yr. (non-government attorneys).
Publication:
Section 337 Newsletter. m.
Annual Meetings: Fall

Internat'l Transactional Analysis Ass'n (1958)
1772 Vallejo St., San Francisco CA 94123
Exec. Director: Susan Sevilla
Members: 5,000 *Staff:* 6-10
Annual Budget: $500-1,000,000 *Tel:* (415) 885-5992
Hist. Note: Founded in 1954 by Dr. Eric Berne as the San Francisco Social Psychiatry Seminars, Inc. Became Internat'l Transactional Analysis Ass'n, Inc. in 1964. Members are interested in the analysis and social dynamics of interactions ("transactions") between individual and individual as well as individual and group. Membership: $45/yr.(individual); $25/yr.(institution)
Publications:
Transactional Analysis Journal. q. adv.
Script. 9/yr.
Semi-annual meetings: January and August

Internat'l Transfer Printing Institute
Hist. Note: Inactive in 1986.

00168 12 05 86 1233

Internat'l Trombone Ass'n (1971)
School of Music, North Texas State Univ., Denton TX 76203
Secy.-Treas.: Vern Kagarice
Members: 2,500 *Staff:* 1
Annual Budget: $25-50,000 *Tel:* (817) 565-3720
Hist. Note: Members are instrument makers, music publishers, professional performers, students, teachers and amateurs of the trombone.
Publication:
Journal. q.
Annual Meetings:
1987-Nashville, TN/May 25-29

Internat'l Truck Parts Ass'n (1974)
7127 Braeburn Place, Bethesda MD 20817
Exec. Director: Venlo J. Wolfsohn
Members: 115-120 companies *Staff:* 1
Annual Budget: $10-25,000 *Tel:* (202) 544-3090
Hist. Note: Members are dealers in used and rebuilt parts for heavy duty trucks. Membership: $200/yr.
Publications:
Membership Directory. a.
Newsletter. m.
Annual Meetings: Fall/200-250
1987-Scottsdale,AZ(Camelback)/Oct. 8-11
1988-Longboat Key,FL(Club)/Oct. 23-26/200

Internat'l Typographical Union (1852)
Box 157, Colorado Springs CO 80901
President: Robert S. McMichen
Members: 70,000 *Staff:* 90-100
Annual Budget: over $5,000,000 *Tel:* (303) 636-2341
Hist. Note: Established in Cincinnati on May 3, 1852 as the Nat'l Typographical Union, its present name was adopted in 1869 after the accession of Canadian locals. Merged in 1894 with the German-American Typographia (founded in 1873) and absorbed the Internat'l Mailers Union January 1, 1979. Affiliated with AFL-CIO, ITU is the oldest of the national unions and today has a budget of about $13 million.
Publications:
ITU Review. bi-w.
Typographical Bulletin. m.
Typographical Journal. m. adv.

Internat'l Union, Allied Industrial Workers of America (1935)
3520 West Oklahoma Ave., Milwaukee WI 53215
President: Dominick D'Ambrosio
Members: 65,000 *Staff:* 60
Annual Budget: over $5,000,000 *Tel:* (414) 645-9500
Hist. Note: Originally called the United Automobile Workers of America and chartered by the American Federation of Labor, this union received its present name in 1956 after the merger of the AFL-CIO. It draws its membership from a variety of trades, largely in the Midwest.
Publication:
Allied Industrial Worker. m.
Biennial Meetings: Uneven years

Internat'l Union of Allied Novelty and Production Workers (1965)
147-149 East 26th St., New York NY 10010
President: Julius Isaacson
Members: 34,000 *Staff:* 2-5
Annual Budget: $250-500,000 *Tel:* (212) 889-1212
Hist. Note: Labor union affiliated with AFL-CIO. Formerly (1978) Internat'l Union of Dolls, Toys, Playthings, Novelties and Allied Products of the United States and Canada.
Quinquennial Conventions: 1991

Internat'l Union of Bricklayers and Allied Craftsmen (1865)
815 15th St., N. W., Washington DC 20005
President: John T. Joyce
Members: 145-150,000 *Staff:* 40-50
Annual Budget: over $5,000,000 *Tel:* (202) 783-3788
Hist. Note: Organized October 16, 1865 in Painters Hall, Philadelphia as the Bricklayers International Union of the United States of North America. Around 1870 it was renamed the National Union of Bricklayers of the United States of America. About 1880 it became the Bricklayers and Masons International Union of America and, after plasterers were included in 1910, the Bricklayers, Masons and Plasterers' International Union of America. It affiliated with the American Federation of Labor in 1916 and assumed its present name in 1975. Sponsors and supports the International Union of Bricklayers and Allied Craftsmen Political Action Committee.
Publications:
Chalkline. m.
Journal. m. adv.
Quinquennial Meetings: 1990

Internat'l Union of Electronic, Electrical, Technical, Salaried and Machine Workers (1949)
1126 16th St., N. W., Suite 612, Washington DC 20036
President: William H. Bywater
Members: 200,000 *Staff:* 200
Annual Budget: over $5,000,000 *Tel:* (202) 296-1200
Hist. Note: Chartered November 2, 1949 by the Congress of Industrial Organizations after the expulsion, on grounds of being a Communist front, of the United Electrical, Radio and Machine Workers of America. Has a budget of about $17 million. Founded as the International Union of Electrical, Radio and Machine Workers, it assumed its present name in June 1983.
Publication:
IUE News. m.
Biennial meetings: Even years

Internat'l Union of Elevator Constructors (1901)
Suite 530, Clarke Bldg., 5565 Sterrett Place, Columbia MD 21044
President: Everett A. Treadway
Members: 25,000 *Staff:* 11-15
Annual Budget: $2-5,000,000 *Tel:* (301) 997-9000
Hist. Note: Established in Pittsburgh July 18, 1901 as the National Union of Elevator Constructors. Became the International Union of Elevator Constructors in 1903 and received a charter from the American Federation of Labor.
Publication:
The Elevator Constructor. m.
Quinquennial Conventions: 1991

Internat'l Union of Life Insurance Agents (1937)
161 West Wisconsin Ave., Milwaukee WI 53203
President: Robert C. Schuetz
Members: 1,500 *Staff:* 1
Annual Budget: $100-250,000 *Tel:* (414) 273-7849
Hist. Note: Independent labor union. Membership: $14/month.
Publication:
Our Voice. m.
Annual Meetings: Every 3 years
1988-Appleton, WI

Internat'l Union of Operating Engineers (1896)
1125 17th St., N.W., Washington DC 20036
President: Larry Dugan, Jr.
Members: 370,000 *Staff:* 160
Annual Budget: over $5,000,000 *Tel:* (202) 429-9100
Hist. Note: Established in Cincinnati on May 7, 1896 as the Nat'l Union of Steam Engineers and received a charter from the American Federation of Labor the following year. Became the Internat'l Union of Steam Engineers in 1898 following the acceptance of Canadian locals. Responding to changes in technology, it was renamed the Internat'l Union of Steam and Operating Engineers, which in 1927 merged with the Internat'l Brotherhood of Steam Shovel and Dredgemen, assuming its present name the same year. Absorbed the United Welders Internat'l Union in 1969. Has a budget of about $20,000,000. Sponsors and supports the Engineers Political Education Committee.
Publication:
International Operating Engineer. m.
Annual Meetings: Every 4 years in April (1988)

Internat'l Union of Petroleum and Industrial Workers (1945)
8131 E. Rosecrans Ave., Paramount CA 90723
President: George R. Beltz
Members: 3,800 *Staff:* 11-15
Annual Budget: $250-500,000 *Tel:* (213) 630-6232
Hist. Note: Founded and incorporated in 1945 as the Independent Petroleum Workers Union; affiliated with the Seafarer's Internat'l Union of North America (AFL-CIO) in 1962; adopted its present name in 1971.
Publication:
IUPIW Views. bi-m.
Annual Meetings: Every 5 years (1987)

Internat'l Union of Police Ass'ns (1978)
815 16th Street, N.W., Suite 507, Washington DC 20006
President: Robert B. Kliesmet
Members: 16,000 *Staff:* 3
Annual Budget: $500-1,000,000 *Tel:* (202) 628-2740
Hist. Note: Members are individual police local unions in the U.S. and Canada. Established December, 1978 in Washington, DC, when those members who wanted to affiliate with the AFL-CIO split away from the Internat'l Conference of Police Ass'ns. Affiliated with the AFL-CIO in February, 1979. Membership: $21/yr.
Publication:
The Law Officer. q. adv.
Annual Meetings:
1987-Shreveport, LA

Internat'l Union of Security Officers (1945)
2404 Merced St., San Leandro CA 94577
President: Charles Newport
Members: 10,000 *Staff:* 16-20
Annual Budget: $250-500,000 *Tel:* (415) 895-9905
Hist. Note: An independent labor union. Until 1980 known as the International Union of Guards and Watchmen.
Publication:
News Letter. bi-m.
Quadrennial Meetings: 1990

Internat'l Union of Tool, Die and Mold Makers (1972)
71 East Cherry St., Rahway NJ 07065
President: Henry F. Schickling
Members: 500 *Staff:* 2-5
Annual Budget: $50-100,000 *Tel:* (201) 388-3323
Hist. Note: An independent labor union.
Publication:
The Indicator. q.

Internat'l Union, United Plant Guard Workers of America (1948)
25510 Kelly Road, Roseville MI 48066
President: James C. McGahey
Members: 25,000 *Staff:* 16-20
Annual Budget: $1-2,000,000 *Tel:* (313) 772-7250
Hist. Note: Independent labor union.
Publication:
The Guard News. m.
Annual Meetings: Every 5 years (1990)

Internat'l Veterinary Acupuncture Soc. (1974)
RD #1, Chester Springs PA 19425
Exec. Director: Dr. Meredith L. Snader
Members: 200 individuals
Annual Budget: under $10,000 *Tel:* (215) 827-7742
Hist. Note: Incorporated in the State of Georgia, IVAS has about an 80% U.S. membership. Membership: $60/year.
Publication:
IVAS Newsletter. q.

Internat'l Visual Literacy Ass'n (1968)
701 Broce Drive, N.W., Blacksburg VA 24060
Treasurer: Alice D. Walker
Members: 200 *Staff:* 1
Annual Budget: under $10,000 *Tel:* (703) 961-5879
Hist. Note: Professionals involved in visual communication and visual literacy in relation to education. Affiliated with the Ass'n for Educational Communications and Technology.
Publications:
IVLA Newsletter. bi-m.
Journal of Visual Verbal Languaging. semi-a.
Proceedings. a.
Semi-annual Meetings: Late Winter and Fall
1987-Atlanta, GA(Commtex)/Feb. 28
1987-Tulsa, OK/Oct. 28-Nov. 1

Internat'l Wheat Gluten Ass'n (1979)
Hist. Note: An international association, the Wheat Gluten Industry Council is its national affiliate.

Internat'l Wild Rice Ass'n (1969)
2201/2 NW 1st Ave., Grand Rapids MN 55744
Exec. V. President: Ronald N. Nelson
Members: 100 *Staff:* 2
Annual Budget: $10-25,000 *Tel:* (218) 327-2229
Hist. Note: Membership concentrated in Minnesota, where most wild rice is grown. Formerly (until 1982) the Wild Rice Growers Ass'n. Membership: $100/yr.
Publication:
Newsletter. bi-m.
Annual Meetings: January

Internat'l Women's Writing Guild (1976)
Box 810, Gracie Station, New York NY 10028
Exec. Director: Hannelore Hahn
Members: 2,500 *Staff:* 3
Annual Budget: $100-250,000 *Tel:* (212) 737-7536
Hist. Note: A broad-based, grass roots alliance open to all women connected with the written word, regardless of previous professional accomplishments. Membership: $25/yr.
Publication:
Network. bi-m.

Internat'l Woodworkers of America (1936)
1622 North Lombard St., Portland OR 97217
President: Keith W. Johnson
Members: 107-108,000 *Staff:* 11-15
Annual Budget: $2-5,000,000 *Tel:* (503) 285-5281
Hist. Note: In September 1936 representatives of the Sawmill and Timber Workers Union met in Portland, Oregon and created the Federation of Woodworkers. On July 19, 1937 in Tacoma, Washington, this became the International Woodworkers of America and affiliated with the Congress of Industrial Organizations. Membership concentrated in the Northwest.
Publication:
International Woodworker. m.
Biennial Meetings:
1987-Portland, OR/Jan. 23-24

Internat'l Zebu Breeders Ass'n (1946)
783 Loop 337, New Braunfels TX 78130
Exec. V. President: Jimmy Hale
Members: 950 individuals *Staff:* 3
Annual Budget: $250-500,000 *Tel:* (512) 620-1744
Hist. Note: Formerly (1984) Pan American Zebu Breeders Ass'n. Formed to register, promote, and market all types of Zebu cattle on an international basis. Presently keeps six herd registry books: Indu-Brazil, Gyr, Guzerat, Nellore, Red Brahman, and Gray Brahman. Membership: $25/yr.
Publication:
American Zebu Journal. bi-m. adv.
Annual Meetings: June
1987-Austin, TX/June 10-14

Interprofessional Council on Environmental Design (1963)
Hist. Note: Established as the Interprofessional Commission on Environmental Design, it assumed its present name in 1969. A joint committee of the executives and elected heads of the American Consulting Engineers Council, the American Institute of Architects, the American Institute of Certified Planners, the American Society of Consulting Planners, the American Society of Landscape Architects, the American Society of Civil Engineers and the National Society of

00169 12 05 86 1233

Professional Engineers. Monitors federal legislation affecting the quality of human life.

Interstate Carriers Conference (1983)
2200 Mill Road, Alexandria VA 22314
Exec. Director: J. Terry Turner
Members: 700 carriers, 150 affiliates *Staff:* 4-6
Annual Budget: $500-1,000,000 *Tel:* (703) 838-1950
Hist. Note: The product of a merger on July 1, 1983 between the Common Carrier Conference-Irregular Route (founded in 1941) and the Contract Carrier Conference (founded in 1939). Affiliated with American Trucking Associations.
Publications:
Newsletter. semi-w.
Convention Newspaper. semi-a. adv.
Annual Meetings: March
1987-Miami Beach FL(Diplomat)/March 8-12

Interstate Conference of Employment Security Agencies (1937)
444 North Capitol St., N.W., Suite 126, Washington DC 20001-1571
Exec. V. President: William L. Heartwell, Jr.
Members: 53 state agencies *Staff:* 8-10
Annual Budget: $500-1,000,000 *Tel:* (202) 628-5588
Hist. Note: Representatives from state agencies that administer public service employment and unemployment insurance programs. Formerly (1939) the Interstate Conference of Unemployment Compensation Agencies. Membership: $10,000/yr.
Publications:
Update. m.
Labor Market Inform-the-Nation. q.
Semi-Annual Meetings: Spring and Fall
1987-Arlington, VA(Crystal Gateway Marriott)/Feb./150
1987-Reno, NV(Nugget)/Oct./250

Interstate Conference on Water Policy (1959)
955 L'Enfant Plaza, S.W., Suite 600, Washington DC 20024
Exec. Director: Joan M. Kovalic
Members: 70 *Staff:* 3
Annual Budget: $50-100,000 *Tel:* (202) 466-7287
Hist. Note: Established in 1959 and incorporated in Washington, DC in 1977. Members are state and regional agencies concerned with conservation, development and administration of water and land-related resources. Multi-state, interstate and intrastate agencies, as well as non-profit organizations and educational institutions, are eligible for associate membership; business and trade associations may apply for affiliate membership.
Publications:
Washington Report.
ICWP Policy Statement & Bylaws. a.
Membership Directory. a.
Proceedings. a.
Semi-annual Meetings: Spring and Fall
1987-Washington, DC/Spring
1987-San Antonio, TX/Spring

Interstate Natural Gas Ass'n of America (1944)
1660 L St., N.W., Washington DC 20036
President: Jerome J. McGrath
Members: 30 companies *Staff:* 30-35
Annual Budget: $2-5,000,000 *Tel:* (202) 293-5770
Hist. Note: Established in Kansas City, Missouri on January 11, 1944 as the Independent Natural Gas Ass'n of America by representatives of fourteen natural gas companies. In 1974 it assumed its present name and limited its voting membership to gas transmission companies, producers and distributors becoming associate members. Sponsors the Interstate Natural Gas Ass'n of America Political Action Committee.
Publication:
Washington Report. w.
Annual Meetings: Fall/400
1987-Hot Springs, VA(Homestead)/Sept. 27-30
1988-Laguna Niguel, CA(Ritz Carlton)/Oct. 2-5
1989-Naples, FL(Ritz Carlton)/Oct. 1-4

Interstate Oil Compact Commission (1935)
Box 53127, Oklahoma City OK 73152
Exec. Director: W. Timothy Dowd
Members: 6-700 *Staff:* 6-10
Annual Budget: $250-500,000 *Tel:* (405) 525-3556
Hist. Note: IOCC members are states that produce oil or gas; associate states support the conservation of America's energy resources. Establishes rules and guidelines for the proper maintenance of wells.
Publications:
Interstate Oil Compact Commission Committee Bulletin. semi-a.
Oil and Gas Compact Bulletin. semi-a.
Annual Report of IOCC.
National Stripper Well Survey. a.
Directory of Interstate Oil Commission and State Gas Agencies.
Semi-annual Meetings: June and December
1987-Coeur d'Alene, ID(Coeur d'Alene Resort)/June 21-24/400

Interstate Producers Livestock Ass'n (1962)
1705 W. Luthy Drive, Peoria IL 61615
Secretary: Eugene Kunkle
Members: 30,000 *Staff:* 300-350
Annual Budget: $2-5,000,000 *Tel:* (309) 691-5360
Hist. Note: Absorbed the Producers Livestock Marketing Association in 1968. A cooperative marketing organization.
Annual Meetings: December, in Chicago, IL

Interstate Towing Ass'n
Hist. Note: Address unknown in 1986.

Intersure, Ltd. (1966)
725 Teaneck Road, Teaneck NJ 07666
Exec. Secretary: Al Singer
Members: 30-35 insurance agencies *Staff:* 2-5
Annual Budget: $10-25,000 *Tel:* (201) 692-1700
Hist. Note: Formerly (1980) the Ass'n of Internat'l Insurance Agents; became Intersure: The Internat'l Insurance Agents Ass'n; assumed its present title in 1985.
Semi-annual meetings: Spring and Fall

Interuniversity Communications Council (1964)
Hist. Note: Became EDUCOM in 1984.

Intimate Apparel Manufacturers Ass'n (1931)
7 Hanover Square, New York NY 10004
Exec. Director: Jack Gross
Members: 15 companies *Staff:* 1
Annual Budget: $10-25,000 *Tel:* (212) 806-5400
Hist. Note: Membership concentrated in the New York area. Major purpose is labor negotiations with the International Ladies Garment Workers Union. The above address is the law firm of Stroock and Stroock and Lavan. Formed by the merger of the Lingerie Manufacturers Ass'n and the Negligee Manufacturers Ass'n in 1984.

Intraocular Lens Manufacturers Ass'n (1975)
Hist. Note: Dissolved in 1985.

Investigative Reporters and Editors (1975)
Box 838, Columbia MO 65205
Exec. Director: Steve Weinberg
Members: 3,000 *Staff:* 1-2
Annual Budget: $50-100,000 *Tel:* (314) 882-3364
Hist. Note: Membership: $25/yr.
Publication:
IRE Journal. q.
Annual Meetings: June
1987-Phoenix, AZ(Biltmore)/June 18-21/5-600

Investment Casting Institute (1953)
8521 Clover Meadow Dr., Dallas TX 75243
Exec. Director: Henry T. Bidwell
Members: 130 companies *Staff:* 1
Annual Budget: $100-250,000 *Tel:* (214) 341-0488
Hist. Note: Members are makers of precision castings by the lost-wax process.
Publication:
Newsletter. irreg.
Semi-annual Meetings: Spring and Fall

Investment Company Institute (1940)
1600 M St., N.W., Washington DC 20036
President: David Silver
Members: 1,600 companies *Staff:* 73
Annual Budget: over $5,000,000 *Tel:* (202) 293-7700
Hist. Note: Open-end and closed-end investment companies registered under the Investment Company Act of 1940, and their advisers and principal underwriters, as well as unit investment trust sponsors. Formerly (1961) Nat'l Ass'n of Investment Companies. Absorbed the Ass'n of Mutual Fund Plan Sponsors in 1973 and the Unit Investment Trust Ass'n in 1985. Sponsors the Investment Management Political Action Committee of the Investment Company Institute.
Publications:
Portfolio. bi-m.
Mutual Fund News. 5/yr.
Mutual Fund Fact Book. a.
Annual Meetings: Washington, DC in the Spring
1987-Washington, DC(Hilton)/May 19-21/1,200

Investment Counsel Ass'n of America (1937)
20 Exchange Place, New York NY 10005
Exec. Director: Gail F. Edwards
Members: 120 companies *Staff:* 1
Annual Budget: $50-100,000 *Tel:* (212) 344-0999
Hist. Note: A professional organization of experienced investment counseling firms.
Publication:
List of Member Firms. a.
Annual Meetings: May

Investment Recovery Ass'n (1981)
712 Lakewood Center North, 14600 Detroit Ave., Cleveland OH 44107
Exec. Director: Robert H. Ecker
Members: 180 companies
Annual Budget: $50-100,000 *Tel:* (216) 226-7700
Hist. Note: Members are firms that have an established investment recovery program providing for the disposition of recyclable products, capital assets, or surplus materials. Membership: $200/yr.
Publications:
Newsletter. q. adv.
Member Directory. a. adv.
Semi-annual Meetings: April and October
1987-Atlanta, GA/April and Toronto, Ontario/Oct.
1988-Denver, CO/April and Philadelphia, PA/Oct.
1989-San Francisco, CA/April and Minneapolis, MN/Oct.

Iota Tau Tau (1925)
641 Benfield Road, Severna Park MD 21146
Exec. Officer: Dr. Catherine M. Osborne
Members: 4-500 attorneys *Staff:* 1
Annual Budget: $10-25,000 *Tel:* (301) 647-6781
Hist. Note: Founded November 11, 1925 at Southwestern University, Los Angeles. Originally an honorary legal sorority, now also open to men. Has no permanent address or paid staff. The officers, except for the Treasurer, change every two years. Membership: $10.50/year.
Publication:
The Double Tau. a.
Biennial Meetings: Odd years
1987-Baltimore, MD/August/125-150

IPC (1957)
7380 N. Lincoln Ave., Lincolnwood IL 60646
Exec. Director: Raymond E. Pritchard
Members: 1,400 companies *Staff:* 27
Annual Budget: $1-2,000,000 *Tel:* (312) 677-2850
Hist. Note: Established as the Institute of Printed Circuits, it became the Institute for Interconnecting and Packaging Electronic Circuits in 1978, more commonly known as IPC. Members are makers of printed circuits, hybrid circuits and various types of discrete wiring techniques for electronic equipment. Membership: $800/yr.
Semi-annual Meetings: April and September
1987-Atlanta, GA(Westin Peachtree)/April 26-30

IPMA-A Graphic Communications Management Ass'n
Hist. Note: Became the In-Plant Management Ass'n in 1986.

Iron and Steel Soc. (1974)
410 Commonwealth Drive, Warrendale PA 15086
Exec. Director: Lawrence G. Kuhn
Members: 6,500 *Staff:* 14-18
Annual Budget: $1-2,000,000 *Tel:* (412) 776-1535
Hist. Note: One of the four member societies of the American Institute of Mining, Metallurgical, and Petroleum Engineers. Concerned with steel, castings, and ferroalloy production from raw material handling to the finished products. Membership: $45/yr.
Publication:
Iron and Steelmaker. m. adv.
Semi-annual meetings: Spring and Winter
1987-Pittsburgh, PA(Convention Ctr.)/March 29-April 1/1,500
1987-Chicago, IL(Hyatt Regency)/Dec. 8-11/1,500
1988-Toronto, Ontario(Sheraton Ctr.)/April 17-20/1,500
1988-Pittsburgh, PA(Convention Ctr.)/Dec. 6-9/1,800

Iron Castings Soc. (1982)
Hist. Note: Became the Metal Castings Soc. in 1986.

Irrigation Ass'n (1949)
1911 N. Fort Myer Drive, Suite 1009, Arlington VA 22209
Exec. V. President: Robert C. Sears
Members: 1,200 companies *Staff:* 11-12
Annual Budget: $500-1,000,000 *Tel:* (703) 524-1200
Hist. Note: Formerly the Sprinkler Irrigation Association, it adopted its present name in 1976 and absorbed the Drip Irrigation Association in 1979. Members are manufacturers, designers, suppliers, consultants, and contractors of all irrigation systems. Membership: $100/yr.(individual); $250-4,000/yr.(company).
Publications:
Newsletter. bi-m.
Newspaper. bi-m. adv.
Conference Proceedings. a.
Membership Directory and Buyers Guide. a. adv.
Annual Meetings: Fall
1987-Orlando, FL(Peabody Hotel)/Oct. 25-28
1988-Las Vegas, NV(MGM Grand)/Nov. 13-16
1989-Anaheim, CA(Marriott)/Nov. 12-15
1990-Phoenix, AZ/Oct. 28-31
1991-Dallas, TX(Anatole)/Nov. 16-20

Issues Management Ass'n (1982)
1615 L St., N.W., Suite 925, Washington DC 20036
Exec. Director: Joseph A. Cook
Members: 525 *Staff:* 1
Annual Budget: $50-100,000 *Tel:* (202) 296-9200
Hist. Note: Members are corporate/government executives and academics concerned with the foresight, analysis and effect of public issues on corporate, government and organization, policy. Membership: $75/yr.
Publication:
Issues Managers' Newsletter. m.
Semi-annual Meetings: June and October
1987-Atlanta, GA/May 27-29
1987-Philadelphia, PA(Sheraton Society Hill)/Sep. 30-Oct. 2
1988-Minneapolis, MN/June
1988-Los Angeles, CA/October

Italian Actors Union (1938)
184 5th Ave., New York NY 10010
President: Mimi Cecchini
Members: 75 *Staff:* 1
Annual Budget: under $10,000 *Tel:* (212) 675-1003
Hist. Note: An autonomous component of Associated Actors and Artistes of America, which chartered it in 1938. Founded in 1936 as the Lega di Miglioramento fra gli Artisti della Scena in New York City. Membership: $50/yr.

00170 12 05 86 1233

Italy-America Chamber of Commerce (1887)
350 Fifth Ave., New York NY 10118
Exec. Secretary: Roy A. Rossetti
Members: 1,200-1,300 *Staff:* 6-10
Annual Budget: $250-500,000 *Tel:* (212) 279-5520
Hist. Note: Formerly American Chamber of Commerce for Trade with Italy, it is the oldest foreign trade chamber in the U.S. Membership: $400/yr.
Publications:
News Letter. m.
Trade with Italy. bi-m. adv.
US-Italy Trade Directory. a. adv.
Annual Meetings: Spring

Jack Institute
Hist. Note: Ceased operations December 31, 1983.

Jean Piaget Soc. (1970)
Univ. of Delaware, Room 113, Willard Hall, Newark DE 19716
Editor: Frank B. Murray
Members: 500 educators and psychologists *Staff:* 1
Annual Budget: $10-25,000 *Tel:* (302) 451-2311
Hist. Note: The Society has no permanent office. The officers change annually. Mail may, however, be sent to the above address. Membership includes researchers and practitioners in the fields of psychology, education, philosophy and psychiatry who are interested in the nature of human knowledge. Membership: $15/yr.
Publication:
Genetic Epistemologist. q. adv.
Annual Meetings: June

Jesuit Philosophical Ass'n of the United States and Canada (1935)
Loyola University of Chicago, Chicago IL 60626
Secy.-Treas.: Rev. Harry Gensler, S.J.
Members: 120 *Staff:* 1
Annual Budget: under $10,000 *Tel:* (312) 274-3000
Hist. Note: Jesuits engaged in the teaching of philosophy.
Publication:
Proceedings. a.
Annual Meetings: Always Friday after Easter/50

Jesuit Secondary Education Ass'n (1970)
1424 16th St., N.W., Washington DC 20036
President: Charles P. Costello, S.J.
Members: 45-50 schools *Staff:* 2-5
Annual Budget: $50-100,000 *Tel:* (202) 667-3888
Hist. Note: Formerly, with the Ass'n of Jesuit College and Universities, a part of the Jesuit Education Ass'n.

Jewelers Board of Trade (1884)
70 Catamore Blvd., East Providence RI 02914
Exec. V. President: Robert W. Paul
Members: 3,000 *Staff:* 90
Annual Budget: $2-5,000,000 *Tel:* (401) 438-0750
Hist. Note: A credit reporting agency.
Publications:
J.B.T. Confidential Reference Book. semi-a.
Service Bulletin. w.
New Name Bulletin. w.

Jewelers of America (1957)
1271 Ave. of the Americas, New York NY 10020
Chairman of the Board: Michael Roman
Members: 12,500 *Staff:* 16-20
Annual Budget: $500-1,000,000 *Tel:* (212) 489-0023
Hist. Note: Formed by a merger of the American Nat'l Retail Jewelers Ass'n (1906) and the Nat'l Jewelers Ass'n (1942). Until July 1980, known as the Retail Jewelers of America, Inc.
Publication:
J Report. 10/yr.
Annual Meetings: July in New York, NY

Jewelers Security Alliance of the U. S. (1883)
6 East 45th St., New York NY 10017
President and Counsel: James B. White
Members: 4,000-5,000 *Staff:* 6-10
Annual Budget: $250-500,000 *Tel:* (212) 687-0328
Publication:
Crime Prevention Flash Bulletin. q.

Jewelers Shipping Ass'n (1962)
125 Carlsbad St., Cranston RI 02920
Gen. Manager: Richard M. Daley
Members: 2,300 companies *Staff:* 75
Annual Budget: $1-2,000,000 *Tel:* (401) 943-6020
Hist. Note: Membership: $10/yr.
Annual Meetings: Providence, RI/Fall

Jewelers Vigilance Committee (1912)
1180 Ave. of the Americas, New York NY 10036
Exec. V. President & General Counsel: Joel A. Windman
Members: 2,500-3,000 companies *Staff:* 6-10
Annual Budget: $100-250,000 *Tel:* (212) 869-9505

Jewelry Industry Council (1946)
130 West 42nd St., New York NY 10036
President: Gerry Hansen
Members: 1,000-1,500 *Staff:* 2-5
Annual Budget: $100-250,000 *Tel:* (212) 302-1770
Hist. Note: The promotional and education arm of the jewelry industry. Membership: $200-1,500/yr. (based on number of employees).

Jewelry Industry Distributors Ass'n (1946)
113 W. Franklin St., Baltimore MD 21201
Exec. Director: Thomas C. Shaner, CAE
Members: 125-150 companies *Staff:* 2-5
Annual Budget: $50-100,000 *Tel:* (301) 752-3318
Hist. Note: Formerly (1984) the Watch Material and Jewelry Distributors Ass'n of America.
Publication:
News and Views. q.
Annual Meetings: Spring, with American Jewelry Marketing Ass'n
1987-Hilton Head, SC(Intercontinental)/March 22-29
1988-Arizona or Las Vegas, NV

Jewelry Manufacturers Ass'n (1919)
475 Fifth Ave., New York NY 10017
General Counsel: Alex J. Glauberman
Members: 50 *Staff:* 2
Annual Budget: $25-50,000 *Tel:* (212) 725-5599
Hist. Note: Established as Jewelry Crafts Ass'n, it assumed its present name in 1961. Major activity is to conduct collective bargaining with the Jewelry Workers Union.
Annual Meetings: January, in New York City

Jewish Education Service of North America (1939)
730 Broadway, New York NY 10003
Exec. V. President: Dr. Jonathan Woocher
Members: 900-1,000 members; 80-90 organizations *Staff:* 15
Annual Budget: $500-1,000,000 *Tel:* (212) 260-0006
Hist. Note: The Jewish education service agency for the organized Jewish community in North America. Helps local federations and central agencies for Jewish education deal with community-wide Jewish education issues. Membership: $50/yr. (individual); for institutions, fee varies by size.
Publications:
Pedagogic Reporter. q.
Trends. q.
NISE Newsletter. q.

Jewish Funeral Directors of America (1927)
122 East 42nd St., Suite 1120, New York NY 10168
Exec. Director: Judith Weiss
Members: 200-225 *Staff:* 1
Annual Budget: $100-250,000 *Tel:* (212) 370-0024
Publication:
The Jewish Funeral Director. q. adv.
Annual Meetings: Fall/125
1987-Naples, FL(Ritz Carlton)/Nov. 1-6

Jewish Ministers Cantors Ass'n of America (1895)
3 West 16th St., New York NY 10011
President: Rev. Chaskele Ritter
Members: 300 *Staff:* 1
Annual Budget: under $10,000 *Tel:* (212) 675-6601
Hist. Note: Known at its inception as the Jewish Ministers Cantors Association of the United States and Canada, Canada has been dropped from the name because of limited Canadian membership. 75% of the membership is in the New York area.
Publication:
JMCA Bulletin. a.
Annual Meetings: June in New York, NY

Jewish Teachers Ass'n-Morim (1924)
45 East 33rd. St., New York NY 10016
President: Phyllis Pullman
Members: 28,000
Annual Budget: $25-50,000 *Tel:* (212) 684-0556
Hist. Note: Jewish teachers in public and private schools.
Publication:
Morim Bulletin. q.
Annual Meetings:
1987-New York, NY(Sheraton Centre Hotel)/March 15

Jockey Club, The (1894)
380 Madison Ave., New York NY 10017
Exec. Director: Hans Stahl
Members: 95 individuals *Staff:* 150
Tel: (212) 599-1919
Hist. Note: A service organization to the racing industry which encourages the development of thoroughbred horses, establishes regulations governing them and sets the foundation for rules adopted by all racing states. Members are individual owners/breeders and others connected with the racing industry.
Publications:
Racing Calendar. m.
Newsletter. bi-m.
Semi-annual: March and August

Jockeys' Guild (1940)
20 East 46th St., New York NY 10017
Nat'l Mng. Director: Nick Jemas
Members: 1,800-2,000 *Staff:* 14
Annual Budget: $1-2,000,000 *Tel:* (212) 687-7746
Hist. Note: Established as the Jockey's Community Fund and Guild, it assumed its present name in 1946. Members are licensed flat riding jockeys. Major thrust is to offer financial aid to needy members.
Publication:
Jockey News. m.
Annual Meetings: First week in December

Joint Council of Allergy and Immunology (1975)
Box 520, Mount Prospect IL 60056
Admin. Director: Joseph J. Lotharius
Members: 3,000 *Staff:* 2-5
Annual Budget: $100-250,000 *Tel:* (312) 255-1024
Hist. Note: The political affairs arm of four major allergy organizations: the American Academy of Allergy, the American Ass'n for Clinical Allergy and Immunology, the American Ass'n of Certified Allergists and the American College of Allergists.

Joint Council on Educational Telecommunications (1950)
c/o CPB, 1111 16th St., N.W., Washington DC 20036
Secretary: Douglas F. Bodwell
Members: 25-30
Annual Budget: under $10,000 *Tel:* (202) 293-6160
Hist. Note: Established as the Joint Council on Educational Broadcasting, it assumed its present name in 1967. Members are organizations of various types concerned with the development of educational television and radio. Has no paid staff. Membership: $250/yr. (company).

Joint Electron Device Engineering Council (1941)
2001 Eye St., N.W., Washington DC 20006
Exec. Director: John M. Kinn
Members: 750 *Staff:* 6-10
Annual Budget: $100-250,000 *Tel:* (202) 457-4971
Hist. Note: Affiliated with the Electronic Industries Ass'n. Manufacturers of solid state products. Membership: $3,000/yr.
Publications:
JEDEC Engineering Publications. irreg.
JEDEC Standards. irreg.

Journalism Education Ass'n (1924)
Box 99, Blue Springs MO 64015
Headquarters Manager: Lois Lauer Wolfe
Members: 1,300 *Staff:* 1
Annual Budget: $25-50,000 *Tel:* (816) 229-1666
Hist. Note: Established as Nat'l Ass'n of Journalism Directors in 1924, it became a division of Nat'l Education Ass'n in 1937; it has since severed this tie, and in 1963 assumed its present name. Members are principally secondary school journalism teachers and advisors.
Publications:
C:JET. q.
Newswire. q.
Semi-annual Meetings: Spring and Fall
1987-Portland, OR and Kansas City, MO
1988-San Francisco, CA and Washington, DC
1989-Anaheim, CA and St. Louis, MO

Judge Advocates Ass'n (1943)
1400 K St., N.W., Suite 915, Washington DC 20005
Exec. Secretary: Capt. John E. Corcoran
Members: 1,000-1,100 *Staff:* 1
Annual Budget: under $10,000 *Tel:* (202) 842-0300
Hist. Note: Members are lawyers who serve or have served in the Armed Forces. Fosters the development of an efficient military legal and judicial system.

Justice System Training Ass'n (1974)
Box 356, Appleton WI 54912
Exec. Director: Kevin Parsons
Members: 700 individuals *Staff:* 6-10
Annual Budget: $100-250,000 *Tel:* (414) 731-8893
Hist. Note: Trainers of defense tactics and physical training instructors from law enforcement, correctional and security agencies. Formerly (until 1979) known as the Law Enforcement Liaison Division of the U.S. Karate Ass'n. Membership: $45 (initial fee); $35/yr. (renewal)
Publication:
National PSDI Memorandum. bi-m.
Annual Meetings: First Week in June
1987-Orlando, FL/June 11-15/300
1988-Washington, DC

Jute Carpet Backing Council (1959)
30 Rockefeller Plaza, New York NY 10112
Secretary: Malcolm E. Martin
Members: 10-15 companies *Staff:* 0
Annual Budget: $100-250,000 *Tel:* (212) 408-5100
Hist. Note: Has no paid staff; the above address is the law firm of Chadbourne & Parke. Members are importers of jute carpet backings; purpose is to promote their product for use by domestic carpet mills in the manufacturing of tufted carpeting. Membership Fee: Based on previous year's imports and monthly assessments on current imports.
Publication:
Back Talk. m.
Annual Meetings: November in New York, NY at 30 Rockefeller Plaza

Juvenile Products Manufacturers Ass'n (1962)
66 East Main St., Moorestown NJ 08057
Exec. Director: William L. MacMillan, III
Members: 150 *Staff:* 7
Annual Budget: $500-1,000,000 *Tel:* (609) 234-9155
Hist. Note: Members are makers of baby furniture, carriages and related products.

00171 12 05 86 1233

JWB (1917)
15 East 26th St., New York NY 10010-1579
Exec. V. President: Arthur Rotman
Members: 250-275 organizations *Staff:* 35-40
Annual Budget: $2-5,000,000 *Tel:* (212) 532-4949
Hist. Note: A federation of Jewish Community Centers, YM-YWHAs and Camps. Founded as the National Jewish Welfare Board, it absorbed the Council of Young Men's Hebrew and Kindred Associations in 1921 and assumed its present name in 1977.
Publications:
Zarkor-program Ideas.
JWB Circle. m.
Personnel Reporter. q.
Biennial Meetings: Even years/1,200
1988-St. Louis

JWB Jewish Music Council (1944)
15 East 26th St., New York NY 10010
Coordinator: Paula G. Gottlieb
Members: 80 *Staff:* 1
Annual Budget: $10-25,000 *Tel:* (212) 532-4949
Hist. Note: Members represent national Jewish organizations and local community music councils. Presents Nat'l Jewish Music Award and sponsors performance season. Formerly Nat'l Jewish Music Council.
Publication:
Jewish Music Notes. semi-a.

Kaolin Clay Export (1963)
Hist. Note: Disbanded in 1985.

Kappa Delta Epsilon (1935)
Hist. Note: A professional fraternity of educators, originally restricted to women, founded in Washington March 26, 1933. Address unknown in 1987.

Keramos Fraternity (1902)
Materials Science and Engineering Dept.,110 Engineering Annex, Iowa State Univ., Ames IA 50011
Gen. Secretary: Thomas E. McGee
Members: 5,300-5,400 *Staff:* 1
Annual Budget: under $10,000 *Tel:* (515) 294-9619
Hist. Note: A professional fraternity of ceramic engineers. Has no paid staff.
Publication:
Keragram. 5-6/yr.
Annual Meetings: Spring

Keyboard Teachers Ass'n (1963)
13711 Taylorcrest, Houston TX 77079
President: Thelma C. Fisher
Members: 200-250
Annual Budget: $10-25,000 *Tel:* (713) 461-9982
Hist. Note: Formerly (1979) Nat'l Ass'n of Organ Teachers, Inc. and (1986) Internat'l Ass'n of Organ Teachers USA. Sponsors the Nat'l Soc. of Student Keyboardists. Membership: $22.50/yr. (individual); variable fee for organizations.
Publication:
The Keyboard Teacher. 5/yr.
Annual Meetings: Summer

Knitted Textile Ass'n (1965)
386 Park Avenue South, 9th Floor, New York NY 10016
Exec. Director: Herbert Rabinowitz
Members: 140-165 companies *Staff:* 2-5
Annual Budget: $100-250,000 *Tel:* (212) 689-3807
Hist. Note: Established as the Knitted Fabric Group, it assumed its present name in 1971. Affiliated with the American Fiber, Textile & Apparel Coalition. Members are makers of knitted fabrics of all types, and their suppliers. Membership: $375-5,000/year (company).
Annual Meetings: March in Miami at the Doral Country Club/200
1987-March 12-15

Knitting Guild of America, The (1984)
Box 1606, Knoxville TN 37901
Manager: Carol Wigginton
Members: 3,000 *Staff:* 5
Tel: (615) 524-2401
Hist. Note: Provides a source for communication and education to those persons wishing to advance the quality of workmanship and creativity in their Knitting endeavors. Membership: $15/yr.
Publication:
Cast On. q. adv.
Semi-annual Meetings: Spring and Summer
1987-New Orleans, LA(Clarion Hotel)/March 5-8
1987-Tacoma, WA(Univ. of Puget Sound)/June 12-14

Knitwear Employers Ass'n (1959)
75 Livingston Street, Brooklyn NY 11201
General Counsel: Leonard Brodsky
Members: 40 *Staff:* 1
Annual Budget: under $10,000 *Tel:* (212) 875-2300
Hist. Note: Major purpose is labor negotiations. Membership: $600/yr.

Label Printing Industries of America (1976)
1730 North Lynn St., Arlington VA 22209
Exec. Director: Betty B. Horn
Members: 45 companies *Staff:* 2-5
Annual Budget: $50-100,000 *Tel:* (703) 841-8122
Hist. Note: A special industry section of Printing Industries of America. Members are companies printing labels to be attached to retail merchandise.
Publication:
Labelgram. m.
Semi-annual Meetings: Spring and Fall
1987-Tempe, AZ/April and Baltimore, MD/Oct.

Laborers' Internat'l Union of North America (1903)
905 16th St., N.W., Washington DC 20006
President: Angelo Fosco
Members: 510,000 *Staff:* 200
Annual Budget: over $5,000,000 *Tel:* (202) 737-8320
Hist. Note: Organized in Washington DC April 13, 1903 as the International Hod Carriers and Building Laborers' Union of America and chartered by the American Federation of Labor. Reflecting the expanding scope of its organizing it changed its name twice in 1912, first to the International Hod Carriers' and Common Laborers' Union of America and next to the International Hod Carriers', Building and Common Laborers' Union of America. Merged in 1918 with the Compressed Air and Foundation Workers' International Union (founded in 1904) and in 1929 with the Tunnel and Subway Constructors' International Union (founded in 1910). Adopted it present name September 20, 1965. Has a budget of about $23 million. Sponsors and supports the Laborers' Political League.
Publications:
The Laborer. m.
The Mailhandler. 8/yr.
The Mailhandler Bulletin. w.
Quinquennial Conventions: 1991

Ladies Apparel Contractors Ass'n (1933)
450 Seventh Ave., New York NY 10123
Exec. Director: Sidney Reiff
Members: 150 companies *Staff:* 6
Annual Budget: $100-250,000 *Tel:* (212) 564-6161
Hist. Note: Founded as the United Popular Dress Manufacturers Ass'n. Formerly (1977) the Popular Price Dress Contractors Ass'n, Inc.
Annual Meetings: Always in New York, NY

Ladies Professional Golf Ass'n (1950)
4675 Sweetwater Blvd., Sugarland TX 77479
Commissioner: John D. Laupheimer
Members: 500-600 *Staff:* 16-20
Annual Budget: $1-2,000,000 *Tel:* (703) 980-5742
Hist. Note: In its 37th season, the LPGA is expected to play an international schedule of approximately 40 golf tournaments for a combined purse of $11 million. Separated into two divisions: teaching and tournament professionals.
Publications:
Annual Player Guide. a. adv.
Fairway Magazine. a. adv.
Annual Meetings: Winter

Ladies Professional Golf Ass'n of America (1950)
Hist. Note: Became the Ladies Professional Golf Ass'n in 1985.

Lake Carriers' Ass'n (1892)
915 Rockefeller Building, Cleveland OH 44113-1306
President: George J. Ryan
Members: 11-15 companies *Staff:* 8
Annual Budget: $250-500,000 *Tel:* (216) 621-1107
Hist. Note: Established in 1892 as the successor organization to Cleveland Vessel Owners Ass'n (1880) and Lake Carriers' Ass'n of Buffalo (1885). Members are Great Lakes vessel operators engaged in transportation of iron ore, coal, grain, limestone, cement and petroleum products.
Publication:
Annual Report. a.
Annual Meetings: With Dominion Marine Ass'n, alternately U.S. and Canada.

Lambda Alpha Epsilon (1937)
Hist. Note: See American Criminal Justice Association.

Laminated Fiberglass Insulation Producers Ass'n (1974)
Hist. Note: Disbanded in 1985.

Laminating Materials Ass'n (1985)
767 Park Avenue, Oradell NJ 07649
George M. Carter
Members: 80 compamies *Staff:* 1
Annual Budget: $10-25,000 *Tel:* (201) 265-7766
Hist. Note: Represents manufacturers and importers who produce one or more of five decorative surfacing materials. Collects production and import statistics for the five materials in the United States and Canada. Membership: $300/yr.
Publication:
Annual Statistical Report

Laminators Safety Glass Ass'n (1977)
3310 Harrison, Topeka KS 66611
Exec. V. President: William J. Birch
Members: 11-33 companies *Staff:* 2-5
Annual Budget: $50-100,000 *Tel:* (913) 266-7014
Hist. Note: Makers or distribution of flat laminated safety glass.
Semi-annual Meetings: Spring and Fall

Lamp and Shade Institute of America (1944)
230 5th Ave., Suite 1611, New York NY 10001
Secretary: Phyllis Southard
Members: 175-200 *Staff:* 2-5
Annual Budget: $25-50,000 *Tel:* (212) 683-5363
Hist. Note: Established in 1944 through a joint effort of New York, Chicago and Philadelphia Lamp and Shade Manufacturers. Membership: $215-$465/year (company) based on annual revenues.
Publication:
Suppliers Guide to Lighting Industry. bien. adv.
Annual Meetings: Not held

Land Improvement Contractors of America (1952)
1300 Maybrook Dr., P.O. Box 9, Maywood IL 60153
Exec. Manager: Donna C. Ambrose
Members: 4,000-4,500 *Staff:* 5
Annual Budget: $250-500,000 *Tel:* (312) 344-0700
Hist. Note: Supports the Land and Water Political Action Committee-LAW/PAC. Membership: $50/year.
Publications:
Membership Directory. a.
Newsletter. m.
Annual Meetings: February
1987-Las Vegas, NV(Riviera Hotel)/Feb. 16-19/1,500
1988-Atlanta, GA(Marriott Marquis & Hyatt)/Feb. 17-20
1989-Tulsa, OK

Land Mobile Communications Council (1967)
1150 17th St., N.W., Suite 1000, Washington DC 20036
General Counsel: Charles M. Meehan
Members: 22 organizations *Staff:* 1
Annual Budget: $100-250,000 *Tel:* (202) 956-5600
Hist. Note: Members are organizations representing users of mobile radio communication apparatus such as railroads, business, trucking companies and public safety services. Wishes to insure the reservation of a sufficient part of the radio spectrum to meet their requirements. Has no paid staff or permanent headquarters. The above address is the law firm of Keller & Heckman.
Annual Meetings: March in Washington, DC

Land Trust Exchange (1982)
13 Albert Meadow, Box 364, Bar Harbor ME 04609
Exec. Director: Benjamin R. Emory
Members: 500 organizations *Staff:* 5
Annual Budget: $100-250,000 *Tel:* (207) 288-9751
Hist. Note: A national association of local and regional non-profit land conservation groups. Membership: $30/yr.
Publications:
Exchange. q.
Nat'l Directory of Local and Regional Land Conservation Organizations.
Annual Meetings:
1987-Monterey, CA(Asilomar Conference Center)/Feb. 8-11/300

Laser Institute of America (1967)
5151 Monroe St. #102W, Toledo OH 43623
Gen. Manager: Haynes A. Lee
Members: 1,452 individuals, 99 companies *Staff:* 5
Annual Budget: $500-1,000,000 *Tel:* (419) 882-8706
Hist. Note: Established on September 25, 1967 in Washington, DC as the Laser Industry Ass'n. Chartered in the State of California. The name was changed to Laser Institute of America in 1972. Membership: $35/yr. (individual); $200/yr. (company).
Publication:
Laser Topics. q. adv.
Annual Meetings: Fall
1987-San Diego, CA(Town&Country)/Nov. 8-12

Latin American Anthropology Group (1969)
Hist. Note: Became the Society for Latin American Anthropology in 1983.

Latin American Manufacturers Ass'n (1973)
419 New Jersey Avenue, S.E., Washington DC 20003
President: Stephen Denlinger
Members: 500 companies *Staff:* 10
Annual Budget: $500-1,000,000 *Tel:* (202) 546-3803
Hist. Note: Represents Hispanic businessmen throughout the U.S. and is affiliated with industrial and commercial associations in Latin America. Emphasizes identification of contract opportunities for Latino firms in government agencies and with major corporations.
Publications:
Bulletin on Procurement Opportunities. m.
LAMA Newsletter. q.

Latin American Studies Ass'n (1966)
William Pitt Union, 9th Floor, Univ. of Pittsburgh, Pittsburgh PA 15260
Exec. Director: Reid Reading
Members: 2,400 individuals, 100 institutions *Staff:* 2-5
Annual Budget: $100-250,000 *Tel:* (412) 648-7929
Hist. Note: Members are both teachers and scholars concerned with the promotion of Latin American Studies. Includes the Consortium of Latin American Studies Programs (CLASP) formed in 1966 to coordinate programs for institutional members. Membership: $28-44/yr. scaled to income
Publications:
Forum. q. adv.
The Latin American Research Review. 3/yr. adv.
Annual Meetings: Every 18 months

00172 12 05 86 1233

1988-New Orleans, LA
1989-San Juan, PR
1991-Madrid, Spain

Laundry and Cleaners Allied Trades Ass'n (1920)
Hist. Note: Became the Textile Care Allied Trades Association in 1982.

Laundry and Dry Cleaning Internat'l Union (1959)
307 Fourth Ave., Bank Tower, Suite 908, Pittsburgh PA 15222
President: Frank H. Ervolino
Members: 17-18,000 *Staff:* 11-15
Annual Budget: $250-500,000 *Tel:* (412) 471-4829
Hist. Note: Organized in Washington May 12, 1959 by locals formerly members of the Laundry, Dry Cleaning and Dye House Workers' International Union (which had been expelled from the AFL-CIO in December, 1957). Chartered by the AFL-CIO. Sponsors and supports the League of Voter Education Political Action Committee.
Quinquennial Conventions: 1988

Laundry, Dry Cleaning and Dye House Workers' Internat'l Union (1898)
Hist. Note: Became the Textile Processors, Service Trade, Health Care, Professional and Technical Employees International Union in 1983.

Law and Society Ass'n (1964)
1900 Olive St., Denver CO 80220
Exec. Officer: Joyce Sterling
Members: 2,400 *Staff:* 2-5
Annual Budget: $50-100,000 *Tel:* (303) 871-6306
Hist. Note: Lawyers, sociologists and others interested in exploring the relationships between law and society. Membership: $35/yr. (individual), $65/yr. (company).
Publications:
Law and Society Review. q. adv.
Law and Society Newsletter. q.
Annual Meetings:
1987-Washington, DC/June 10-14

Lawn Institute
Hist. Note: See Better Lawn and Turf Institute.

Lead Industries Ass'n (1928)
292 Madison Ave., New York NY 10017
President: Werner T. Meyer
Members: 70-75 companies *Staff:* 2-5
Annual Budget: $500-1,000,000 *Tel:* (212) 578-4750
Hist. Note: LIA serves as the research, marketing and promotional arm of the lead industry in North America.
Publications:
Lead. semi-a.
Lead Lines. 3/yr.
Annual Meetings: With the Zinc Institute
1987-San Francisco, CA(Fairmont)/March 30-April 1/400

Lead-Zinc Producers Committee (1957)
1320 19th Street, N.W., Suite 600, Washington DC 20036
Secretary: Stanley Nehmer
Members: 3 companies *Staff:* 2-5
Annual Budget: $25-50,000 *Tel:* (202) 466-7720
Hist. Note: Founded as the Emergency Lead-Zinc Committee, it assumed its present name in 1970. Major interests are tariffs, taxation and international trade.

Leading Jewelers Guild (1957)
2050 South Bundy Drive, Los Angeles CA 90025
Exec. Director: Bart L. Sutton
Members: 40-45 companies with 160 stores *Staff:* 9-10
Annual Budget: $250-500,000 *Tel:* (213) 879-9351
Semi-annual Meetings: Summer in Los Angeles and Winter

Leaf Tobacco Exporters Ass'n (1939)
3716 National Dr., Suite 114, Raleigh NC 27612
Exec. V. President: J.T. Bunn
Members: 40-50 *Staff:* 2-5
Annual Budget: $100-250,000 *Tel:* (919) 782-5151
Hist. Note: Affiliated with the Tobacco Ass'n of the U.S.
Annual Meetings: May, at the Greenbrier in White Sulphur Springs, WV

Leafy Greens Council (1976)
Box 76067, St. Paul MN 55175
Exec. Director: Ray L. Clark, Jr.
Members: 30-35 individuals; 20-25 companies *Staff:* 1
Annual Budget: under $10,000 *Tel:* (612) 222-3232
Hist. Note: Growers, shippers, packers and sellers of spinach, cabbage, lettuce and other fresh green vegetables. Founded in 1976 as the Nat'l Spinach Ass'n. Became the Leafy Greens Council in 1977.
Annual Meetings: Usually timed to coordinate with those of the United Fresh Fruit and Vegetable Ass'n in February.

League for Innovation in the Community College (1968)
23276 South Pointe Drive, Suite 101, Laguna Hills CA 92653
Exec. Director: Terry O'Banion
Members: 50-60 community colleges *Staff:* 2-5
Annual Budget: $100-250,000 *Tel:* (714) 855-0710
Hist. Note: A national consortium of 20 districts established to stimulate innovation in community college education. Assists its members in experimenting in teaching, learning, student services and other aspects of community college operation, and in sharing the results of these experiments.
Publications:
Innovator. q.
League Reports. 10/yr.

League of Advertising Agencies (1951)
10 West 33rd St., Suite PH-A, New York NY 10001
Exec. Director: Mary C. Boland
Members: 80-100 *Staff:* 2-5
Tel: (212) 967-8089
Hist. Note: An organization, composed of medium-to-small-sized agencies, whose purpose is to provide a forum for, and encourage, the exchange of management information and creative ideas among its members through seminars and published material.
Publications:
Feedback. 5/yr.
Meeting Journal. m.
Monthly Dinner Meetings:

League of Federal Recreation Ass'ns (1960)
Box 24144, Washington DC 20024
Exec. Director: Austin Gattis
Members: 90 organizations *Staff:* 3
Annual Budget: $100-250,000 *Tel:* (202) 554-6910
Hist. Note: Membership, concentrated in the Washington, DC area, is composed of state, county and federal employee associations which sponsor recreational and employee benefit activities. Membership: $8/yr.
Publication:
Recreation News. m.

Leak Detection Technology Ass'n (1985)
1801 K St., N.W., Suite 800, Washington DC 20036
Exec. Director: Marc L. Marks
Members: 8 companies *Staff:* 2
Annual Budget: $50-100,000 *Tel:* (202) 835-2355
Hist. Note: Composed of businesses involved in environmental protection and safeguarding human health through the development and use of leak detection technology. Membership: $2,500/yr.
Annual Meetings: February

Leather Industries of America (1917)
2501 M St., N.W., Suite 350, Washington DC 20037
President: Charles S. Myers
Members: 260 companies *Staff:* 10
Annual Budget: $1-2,000,000 *Tel:* (202) 785-9400
Hist. Note: Formed by a merger of the Nat'l Ass'n of Tanners, the Morocco Manufacturers Nat'l Ass'n and the Patent and Enamelled Leather Manufacturers Ass'n as the Tanners' Council of America; it absorbed the Leather Industries of America in 1975 and assumed this name in 1986. Affiliated with the Sole Leather Council and the Auto Leather Guild.
Publications:
Newsbreak. bi-w.
Industry Statistics. a.
Trade Shows: LeatherWorld/Spring, Accessory & Garment Leather/Fall

Leather Workers Internat'l Union (1954)
Box 32, Peabody MA 01960
Secy.-Treas.: Al Quadros
Members: 1,100 *Staff:* 2-5
Annual Budget: $50-100,000 *Tel:* (617) 531-5605
Hist. Note: In May 1939 the Nat'l Leather Workers Ass'n (formerly the United Leather Workers Internat'l Union of America) joined the Internat'l Fur Workers Union to form the Internat'l Fur and Leather Workers Union. After the CIO expelled this union in 1950 for alleged Communist domination, the leather workers split away to form the present organization which is now an affiliate of AFL-CIO.
Quinquennial Meetings: 1987

Legal Assistant Management Ass'n (1984)
Box 40129, Overland Park KS 66204
Sandra L. Sabanske
Members: 270 *Staff:* 1
Annual Budget: $25-50,000 *Tel:* (913) 381-4458
Hist. Note: Organized as an outgrowth of a Steering Committee of the Paralegal Manager's Conference, the LAMA is an association of persons responsible for managerial and administrative duties related to legal assistant personnel. Membership: $50/yr
Publications:
Newsletter. q.
Directory of Legal Assistant Managers.
Annual Meetings: Fall
1987-New Orleans, LA

Legal Industry Advisory Council (1984)
104 Wilmot Road, Suite 201, Deerfield IL 60015-5195
Exec. Director: Carl A. Wangman, CAE
Members: 76 *Staff:* 2
Annual Budget: $10-25,000 *Tel:* (312) 940-8800
Hist. Note: Members provide products and services to the legal community. Membership: $300/year.
Publication:
LIAC News. q.
Semi-annual Meetings:
1987-Orlando, FL/May 16-22

Legislative Council for Photogrammetry (1963)
Hist. Note: Defunct in 1983.

Lepidopterists' Soc. (1947)
50 Cleveland Road, #3, Pleasant Hill CA 94523
Secretary: Richard A. Arnold
Members: 1,500-1,600
Annual Budget: $50-100,000 *Tel:* (415) 825-3784
Hist. Note: Formed in May, 1947 and formally constituted in December, 1950. Membership consists of persons interested in the study of butterflies and moths. Has no paid staff; officers rotate annually. Membership: $25/year (individual), $40/year (institution).
Publications:
Journal of the Lepidopterists' Society. q.
News of the Lepidopterists' Society. bi-m.
Annual Meetings: Spring
1987-Berkeley, CA(Univ. of CA)/July/150
1988-Pittsburgh, PA
1989-Albuquerque, NM

Liaison Committee of Cooperating Oil and Gas Ass'ns (1957)
105 S. Broadway #500, Wichita KS 67202
Secy.-Treas.: Donald P. Schnacke
Members: 21 ass'ns *Staff:* 1
Annual Budget: under $10,000 *Tel:* (316) 263-7297

Library Administration and Management Ass'n (1957)
50 East Huron St., Chicago IL 60611
Exec. Director: John W. Berry
Members: 4,400 *Staff:* 3
Annual Budget: $100-250,000 *Tel:* (312) 944-6780
Hist. Note: Formerly titled the Library Administration Division of the American Library Ass'n; it remains a division of the ALA. Membership: $25/yr., membership restricted to ALA members.
Publications:
Newsletter. q.
Library Building Consultant List. a.

Library Binding Institute (1935)
150 Allens Creek Road, Rochester NY 14618
Exec. Director: Sally M. Grauer
Members: 90 *Staff:* 2-5
Annual Budget: $100-250,000 *Tel:* (716) 461-4380
Hist. Note: Members are firms binding books for libraries, their suppliers and certain libraries with an in-house binding capacity.
Publications:
The New Library Scene. bi-m. adv.
The Endpaper (in-house newsletter). m.
Semi-annual Meetings: Spring and Fall
1987-Charleston, SC(Kiawah Island Resort)/May 2-5/70-100

Licensed Beverage Information Council (1979)
1250 I St., N.W., Washington DC 20005
Secy.-Treas.: Paul F. Gavaghan
Members: 11 *Staff:* 6
Tel: (202) 628-3544
Hist. Note: Formerly (until 1982) the Beverage Alcohol Information Council. A consortium of alcohol beverage industry associations conducting public and professional education programs.

Licensed Merchandisers' Ass'n
Hist. Note: Responsibilities taken over by the Licensing Industry Merchandisers' Ass'n in 1985.

Licensing Executives Soc. (1965)
71 East Ave., Norwalk CT 06851
Exec. Director: Penny Dalziel
Members: 2,000-2,200 individuals *Staff:* 2-5
Annual Budget: $100-250,000 *Tel:* (203) 852-7168
Hist. Note: Membership consists of individuals concerned with licensing patents, trademarks, processes and the like.
Publication:
Newsletter. q.

Licensing Industry Ass'n (1979)
Hist. Note: Became the Licensing Industry Merchandisers' Ass'n in 1985.

Licensing Industry Merchandisers' Ass'n (1979)
350 Fifth Ave., Suite 6210, New York NY 10118
Exec. Director: Murray Altchuler
Members: 250 *Staff:* 2
Annual Budget: $250-500,000 *Tel:* (212) 244-1944
Hist. Note: Formerly (1985) the Licensing Industry Ass'n. Members are agencies, agents, manufacturers, retailers and support groups involved in the merchandising of licensed properties.
Annual Meetings: June
1987-New York, NY(Jacob Javits Convention Center)/June 3-5

Life Communicators Ass'n (1933)
900 Des Moines St., Suite 200, Des Moines IA 50309
Account Manager: Nancy Brimeyer
Members: 700-750 *Staff:* 1

00173 12 05 86 1233

Annual Budget: under $10,000 *Tel:* (515) 266-2189
Hist. Note: Formerly Life Advertisers Ass'n and Life Insurance Advertisers Ass'n. Assumed its present name in 1984. Members are salaried employees of life insurance companies responsible for advertising, public relations, sales promotion and communication with the public.
Publications:
Life Communications. q.
Membership Roster. a.
Annual Meetings: Fall
1987-Washington, DC/Sept. 20-23

Life Insurance Advertisers Ass'n
Hist. Note: Became the Life Communicators Ass'n in 1984.

Life Insurance Marketing and Research Ass'n (1916)
8 Farm Springs, Farmington CT 06032
President & CEO: Ernest E. Cragg
Members: 500-600 *Staff:* 225-250
Annual Budget: over $5,000,000 *Tel:* (203) 677-0033
Hist. Note: Formerly (1974) Life Insurance Agency Management Ass'n. Has a budget of $16,000,000.
Publications:
Marketfacts. m.
Managers Magazine. m.
Annual Meetings: October/1,500
1987-Nashville, TN(Opryland)
1988-Washington, DC(Sheraton)
1989-Toronto, Ontario(Sheraton)

Life Insurers Conference (1910)
1004 North Thompson St., Richmond VA 23230
President: G. Mason Connell, Jr.
Members: 80 *Staff:* 2-5
Annual Budget: $100-250,000 *Tel:* (804) 359-5006
Hist. Note: Established as the Southern Casualty and Surety Conference, it became Southern Industrial Insurers' Conference in 1917, the Industrial Insurers Conference in 1925 and assumed its present name in 1948. Members are life insurance companies writing accident and health insurance.
Annual Meetings: Spring/400
1987-Boca Raton, FL(Boca Raton Hotel & Club)/May 13-16
1988-Palm Beach, FL(Breakers)/May 8-11
1989-White Sulphur Springs, WV(Greenbrier)/May 3-6

Life Office Management Ass'n (1924)
5770 Powers Ferry Road, Atlanta GA 30327
President: Lynn G. Merritt
Members: 800 *Staff:* 130
Annual Budget: over $5,000,000 *Tel:* (404) 951-1770
Hist. Note: Administers the FLMI Insurance Education Program and awards the FLMI (Fellow, Life Management Institute) designation. Membership Fee: based on premium income
Publications:
Journal of Information Management. q.
Resource. m.
Annual Meetings: Fall
1987-Montreal, Quebec(Queen Elizabeth)/Sept. 27-29
1988-Orlando, FL(Marriott)/Sept. 25-27
1989-Boston, MA(Marriott)/Sept. 10-12

Lightning Protection Institute (1955)
48 North Ayer St., Harvard IL 60033
Mng. Director: Marvin M. Frydenlund
Members: 200 *Staff:* 2-5
Annual Budget: $100-250,000 *Tel:* (815) 943-7211
Hist. Note: Members are manufacturers and installers of lightning protection equipment. The LPI Professional Division has a membership of about 100 engineers and others.
Publications:
Lightning Protection Guide. a.
Zeus News.

Lightweight Aggregate Producers Ass'n (1954)
Hist. Note: Inactive and moribund in 1982.

Linen Trade Ass'n (1890)
11 West 42nd St., New York NY 10036
Secretary: Laura E. Jones
Members: 30-35 *Staff:* 1
Annual Budget: under $10,000 *Tel:* (212) 944-2230
Hist. Note: Members, concentrated in the New York area, are makers, importers and dealers in decorative table linens. Has no separate headquarters but operates from the offices of the American Association of Exporters and Importers.

Lingerie Manufacturers Ass'n
Hist. Note: Merged with the Negligee Manufacturers Ass'n to become the Intimate Apparel Manufacturers Ass'n in 1984.

Linguistic Ass'n of Canada and the United States (1974)
360 MacLaren Lane, Lake Bluff IL 60044
Exec. Director: Dr. Adam Makkai
Members: 15 institutions, 500 individuals
Annual Budget: under $10,000 *Tel:* (312) 234-3997
Hist. Note: Established and incorporated in Illinois. Membership: $20-30/yr.
Publications:
LACUS Forum. a.
Forum Linguisticum. 3/yr. adv.
Annual Meetings: Fall/100
1987-Toronto, Ontario(York University)/Aug. 4-8
1988-East Lansing, MI(Michigan State University)
1989-Kingston, Ontario(Queen's University)

Linguistic Soc. of America (1924)
1325 18th Street, N.W., Washington DC 20036-6501
Associate Secretary-Treasurer: Margaret W. Reynolds
Members: 7,000 *Staff:* 2-5
Annual Budget: $250-500,000 *Tel:* (202) 835-1714
Hist. Note: Founded December 28, 1924 at the American Museum of Natural History in New York City and incorporated in 1940 in the District of Columbia. A constituent member of the American Council of Learned Societies, affiliate of Permanent Internat'l Committee of Linguistics (CIPL), founding member of the Consortium of Social Science Associations (COSSA). Membership: $15-45/yr. (individual), $75/yr. (institution).
Publications:
Language. q. adv.
LSA Bulletin. q. adv.
Directory of Programs in Linguistics in the U.S. & Canada. trien. adv.
Guide to Grants and Fellowships in Linguistics (1985). trien. adv.
Annual Meeting Handbook. adv.
Annual Meetings: December
1987-San Francisco, CA(Hyatt Regency Embarcadero)/600-1,200

Lipizzan Ass'n of America (1968)
233 Broadway, New York NY 10279
President: John Nicholas Iannuzzi
Members: 175 *Staff:* 3
Annual Budget: $10-25,000 *Tel:* (212) 619-1313
Hist. Note: Members own and breed Lipizzan horses. Formerly (1980) the Royal Internat'l Lipizzan Club. Membership: $25/yr.
Publication:
Lipizzan. q.

Liquid Waste and Sludge Transporter Council (1982)
Hist. Note: Became the Chemical Waste Transportation Council in 1985.

Lithographic Preparatory Services Ass'n (1960)
Hist. Note: Merged in 1983 with the Printing Platemakers Association to form the Graphic Preparatory Association.

Livestock Conservation Institute (1951)
239 Livestock Exchange Bldg., South St. Paul MN 55075
President: Neal Black
Members: 220 *Staff:* 2-5
Annual Budget: $100-250,000 *Tel:* (612) 457-0132
Hist. Note: Formed by a merger of the Nat'l Livestock Sanitary Committee and the Nat'l Livestock Loss Prevention Board (founded in 1916). Formerly (1976) Livestock Conservation, Inc.
Publications:
Newsletter. m.
Proceedings. a.
Annual Meetings:
1987-Milwaukee, WI(Red Carpet Inn)/April 7-9
1988-Kansas City, KS(Adam's Mark)/April 12-14
1989-Des Moines, IA(Marriott)/April 11-13
1990-Louisville, KY(Galt House)/April 3-5
1991-St. Paul, MN

Livestock Industry Institute (1970)
Hist. Note: A division within the Livestock Marketing Ass'n.

Livestock Marketing Ass'n (1976)
301 East Armour Blvd., Room 500, Kansas City MO 64111
Gen. Manager: James Ed Frost
Members: 1,400 *Staff:* 60-70
Annual Budget: over $5,000,000 *Tel:* (816) 531-2235
Hist. Note: Formed by a merger (July 1, 1976) of the Competitive Livestock Marketing Ass'n and the Nat'l Livestock Dealers Ass'n. The Livestock Industry Institute and the Livestock Merchandising Institute are divisions of the LMA.
Publications:
Livestock Marketing Business Letter. w.
Livestock Marketing Guide. a.
Annual Meetings: June
1987-Toronto, Ontario/June 9-11

Livestock Merchandising Institute (1970)
Hist. Note: Became the Livestock Industry Institute in 1985.

Livestock Publications Council (1974)
927 Elmview Drive, Encinitas CA 92024
Exec. Director: Forrest Bassford
Members: 116 organizations, 39 individuals
Annual Budget: $25-50,000 *Tel:* (619) 753-1322
Hist. Note: Established in Texas and incorporated in Colorado. Members are magazines, newspapers and other periodicals devoting at least 50% of their average content to the livestock industry. Individuals and periodicals not qualifying for full membership may become associate members. Membership: $50/yr. (individual); $100/yr. (publication)
Publication:
Actiongram (newsletter). m.
Annual Meetings: July/August
1987-Denver, CO
1988-San Antonio, TX

Living Plant Growers Ass'n (1963)
Hist. Note: Members are growers and suppliers interested in the marketing of indoor foliage plants. Inactive in 1983.

Loading Dock Equipment Manufacturers
8720 Red Oak Blvd., Suite 201, Charlotte NC 28210
Management Executive: Thomas Meinert
Staff: 2-5
Annual Budget: under $10,000 *Tel:* (704) 522-8644
Hist. Note: A product section of The Material Handling Institute.
Annual Meetings: Fall
1987-Boca Raton, FL(Hotel & Club)/Nov. 7-11
1988-Phoenix, AZ(Biltmore)/Oct. 8-12

Local and Short Haul Carriers Nat'l Conference (1943)
Hist. Note: Became the Regional and Distribution Carriers Conference in 1982.

Locomotive Maintenance Officers' Ass'n (1905)
3144 Brereton Court, Huntington WV 25705
Secy.-Treas.: Lou Koerner
Members: 2,000 *Staff:* 1
Annual Budget: $50-100,000 *Tel:* (304) 523-7276
Hist. Note: Established as the Internat'l Railway General Foremen's Ass'n, it assumed its present name in 1938 and absorbed the Master Boilermaker's Ass'n in 1955. Today its membership consists of railway executives and others concerned with diesel engine maintenance.

Log Homes Council (1977)
Hist. Note: Became the North American Log Homes Council in 1985.

Logsplitter Manufacturers Ass'n (1981)
710 East Ogden, Suite 113, Naperville IL 60540
Exec. V. President: Arthur W. Seeds, CAE
Members: 32 companies *Staff:* 5
Annual Budget: $10-25,000 *Tel:* (312) 369-2406
Hist. Note: Formerly the Nat'l Hydraulic Woodsplitters Manufacturers Ass'n. Exists to promote, develop, and maintain professional integrity and growth of the logsplitter industry and the safety of its products. Membership: $600/yr.
Publications:
Industry Update. 2-3/yr.
Splitter News. a. adv.
Annual Meetings: July

Long Distance Running Directors Ass'n (1980)
Hist. Note: Directors of road races. Defunct, 1983.

Loss Executives Ass'n (1931)
c/o Maryland Casualty Co., Box 1228, Baltimore MD 21203
President: Charles Ward
Members: 250-300
Annual Budget: under $10,000 *Tel:* (301) 366-1000
Hist. Note: Formed for the discussion, study and consideration of loss and loss adjustment problems.

Luggage and Leather Goods Manufacturers of America (1938)
350 Fifth Ave., Suite 1317, New York NY 10118
Exec. V. President: Robert K. Ermatinger
Members: 250 *Staff:* 6
Annual Budget: $500-1,000,000 *Tel:* (212) 695-2340
Hist. Note: Sponsors and supports the Luggage and Leather Goods Manufacturers of America Political Action Committee (LUGPAC). Membership: $250-1,250/yr. (company).
Publications:
Insider. m.
Showcase. bi-m. adv.
Annual Meetings: January
1987-Waikoloa, HI(Sheraton Waikoloa)/Jan. 15-22/120
1988-Puerto Rico(Cerromar)/Jan. 13-20/120

Luggage and Leather Goods Salesmen's Ass'n of America (1933)
76 Woodbury Road, Hauppauge NY 11788
Exec. Secretary: John Gualtieri
Members: 150-200 *Staff:* 1
Annual Budget: under $10,000 *Tel:* (212) 689-5741
Annual Meetings:
1987-Anaheim, CA/Feb.

Lutheran Church Library Ass'n (1958)
122 W. Franklin Ave., Minneapolis MN 55404
Exec. Director: Wilma Jensen
Members: 1,800-1,900 *Staff:* 2-5
Annual Budget: $25-50,000 *Tel:* (612) 870-3623
Hist. Note: Founded in 1958 in Minneapolis. Membership: $15/yr. (individual); $25/yr. (churches).

00174 12 05 86 1233

Publication:
Lutheran Libraries. q. adv.
Annual Meetings: Fall
1987-Brainerd, MN(Cragun's Conference Ctr.)/Oct. 8-10

Lutheran Education Ass'n (1942)
7400 Augusta, Concordia College, River Forest IL 60305
Office Manager: Barbara Goodwin
Members: 4,000 *Staff:* 1
Annual Budget: $50-100,000 *Tel:* (312) 771-8300
Hist. Note: Teachers, administrators and board members of Lutheran day schools, as well as Lutheran pastors. LEA departments include: Theological Educators in Associated Ministries (TEAM), Department of Early Childhood Education (DECE), Lutheran Elementary Teachers (LET) and Department of Lutheran Elementary School Principals (DLESP). Membership: $18/yr.
Publications:
Lutheran Education. 5/yr.
LEA News. q.
Annual Meetings:
1987-St. Louis, MO/May 19-21

Lutheran Educational Conference of North America (1910)
122 C St., N.W., Suite 300, Washington DC 20001
Secy.-Treas.: Dr. Arthur E. Puotinen
Members: 40-50 *Staff:* 2-5
Annual Budget: $100-250,000 *Tel:* (202) 783-7501
Hist. Note: Members are Lutheran colleges and boards of higher education. Formerly (until 1967) known as the Nat'l Lutheran Educational Conference, it is the oldest inter-Lutheran organization in North America. Membership: $150-600/yr. varies with type of institution.
Publication:
Papers and Proceedings of LECNA. a.
Annual Meetings: January
1987-Tarpon Springs, FL(Innisbrook Resort Hotel)/Jan. 18-21/100

Lutheran Hospital Ass'n of America (1948)
Lutheran Hospital, 501 10th Ave., Moline IL 61265
Secy.-Treas.: Kenneth Moburg
Members: 65 hospitals *Staff:* 1
Annual Budget: $10-25,000 *Tel:* (309) 757-2611
Annual Meetings: March, with the Protestant Health and Welfare Assembly.

Machine Knife Manufacturers Ass'n (1933)
800 Custer St., Evanston IL 60202
Exec. Secretary: Thomas D. Dolan
Members: 8-10 companies *Staff:* 2-5
Annual Budget: under $10,000 *Tel:* (312) 864-8444

Machine Printers and Engravers Ass'n of the United States (1960)
690 Warren Ave., East Providence RI 02914
President: John J. Phillips
Members: 600-700 *Staff:* 6-10
Annual Budget: $250-500,000 *Tel:* (401) 438-5849
Hist. Note: Independent labor union formed by a merger of the Friendly Society of Engravers and Sketchmakers (founded in 1878) and the Machine Printers Beneficial Ass'n (founded in 1874).
Annual Meetings: Fall

Machine Vision Ass'n of SME (1984)
Box 930, One SME Drive, Dearborn MI 48121
Administrator: Toni Miller
Members: 3,500
Tel: (313) 271-1500
Hist. Note: MVA/SME is an individual member society of the Soc. of Manufacturing Engineers. Membership: $50/yr.(individual); $165/yr.(organization)
Publication:
Vision. q. adv.
Annual Meetings: With Soc. of Manufacturing Engineers

Machinery and Allied Products Institute (1933)
1200 18th St., N.W., Suite 400, Washington DC 20036
President: Charles W. Stewart
Members: 500 manufacturing companies, 20-25 associations
Staff: 40-50
Annual Budget: $2-5,000,000 *Tel:* (202) 331-8430
Hist. Note: Organized originally as a federation of product-line trade associations, MAPI now represents producers and users of capital goods and allied products. MAPI and its affiliate, the Council for Technological Advancement, act as national spokesman for these industries and conduct original research in economics and management. MAPI's constituency also includes leading companies in the electronics, precision instruments, telecommunications, computer, office systems, aerospace and similar high technology industries, and service organizations.
Annual Meetings: June in Washington, DC/50 (exec. committee & association reps)

Machinery Dealers Nat'l Ass'n (1941)
1110 Spring St., Silver Spring MD 20910
Exec. V. President: Darryl D. McEwen
Members: 450 companies *Staff:* 6
Annual Budget: $250-500,000 *Tel:* (301) 585-9494
Hist. Note: Represents used industrial machinery dealers. Connected with the Machinery Dealers Political Action Committee. Membership: $650/yr.

Publication:
MDNA News. m.
Annual Meetings: Spring/400
1987-Hollywood, FL(Diplomat)/May 7-10
1988-San Francisco, CA(Fairmont)/May 28-June 1
1989-Chicago, IL or Washington, DC
1990-Boston, MA
1991-Chicago, IL or Washington, DC

Magazine and Paperback Marketing Institute (1946)
2947 Felton Road, Norristown PA 19401
Director: Don DeVito
Members: 5-600 *Staff:* 2-5
Annual Budget: $100-250,000 *Tel:* (215) 279-4153
Hist. Note: Formerly known as the Bureau of Independent Publishers and Distributors. Marketing arm of the Atlantic Coast Independent Distributors Ass'n.

Magazine Printers Section/Printing Industries of America (1986)
1730 North Lynn St., Arlington VA 22209
Exec. Director: Lottie S. MacConnell
Members: 45 companies *Staff:* 2
Annual Budget: $25-50,000 *Tel:* (703) 841-8112
Hist. Note: A special industry group of Printing Industries of America, its goal is to find solutions to current problems unique to the magazine printing industry. Members are officers of magazine printing firms. Membership: $585/yr. (company)
Triannual Meetings: Feb., June and Oct.
1987-Scottsdale, AZ(Camelback Inn)/Feb. 4-6
1987-Erlanger, KY/June 17-19
1987-Washington, DC(Washington Hilton)/Oct. 5

Magazine Publishers Ass'n (1919)
575 Lexington Ave., New York NY 10022
President: William F. Gorog
Members: 212 companies; 800 magazines *Staff:* 35-40
Annual Budget: $2-5,000,000 *Tel:* (212) 752-0055
Hist. Note: Members are publishers of magazines appearing at least quarterly. Founded as the Nat'l Ass'n of Periodical Publishers, it became the Nat'l Publishers Ass'n in 1920, the Nat'l Ass'n of Magazine Publishers in 1947 and assumed its present name in 1952. Sponsors and supports the Magazine Publishers Association Political Action Committee. Promotes magazines as an advertising medium, provides information and education on circulation.
Annual Meetings: Fall/600-650
1987-Palm Desert, CA(Marriott's Palm Desert Hotel)/Oct. 10-14

Magnetic Materials Producers Ass'n (1959)
800 Custer St., Evanston IL 60202
Exec. Secretary: Thomas D. Dolan
Members: 15-20 companies *Staff:* 2-5
Annual Budget: $25-50,000 *Tel:* (312) 864-8444
Hist. Note: Established as the Permanent Magnet Producers Association, it assumed its present name in 1967.
Annual Meetings: Spring

Magnetics Soc.
Hist. Note: A subsidiary of the Institute of Electrical and Electronics Engineers. Membership in the Society, open only to IEEE members, includes subscription to a technical periodical in the field published by IEEE. All administrative support is provided by IEEE.

Mail Advertising Service Ass'n Internat'l (1920)
7315 Wisconsin Ave., Ste. 440 W, Bethesda MD 20814
President: Robert M. Huse
Members: 450-500 companies *Staff:* 7
Annual Budget: $500-1,000,000 *Tel:* (301) 654-6272
Hist. Note: Members are producers of direct commercial mail, letter shops, list brokers, etc.
Publications:
Membership Directory. a.
Postscripts Newsletter. bi-w.
Annual Meetings: Spring/250
1987-Nashville, TN(Opryland)/June 3-7
1988-Washington, DC(JW Marriott)/June 1-5

Mail Order Ass'n of America (1933)
2550 M St., N.W., 9th Floor, Washington DC 20037
General Counsel: David C. Todd
Members: 5 companies *Staff:* 1
Annual Budget: under $10,000 *Tel:* (202) 457-6000
Hist. Note: Activities of the Ass'n are limited to matters pertaining to regulations issued by the Postal Rate Commission, Interstate Commerce Commission, the Department of Commerce and similar regulatory agencies and governmental offices. Members are retail firms selling by mail order. The above address is the law firm of Patton, Boggs and Blow.

Mail Systems Management Ass'n (1982)
Box 2155, New York NY 10116
President: Walter Justice
Members: 500 individuals and companies *Staff:* 1
Annual Budget: $10-25,000
Hist. Note: Members are mail room managers and directors and owners of administrative service companies. Membership: $35/yr. (individual), $60/yr. (company).
Annual Meetings: Winter, at the time of the Postal Forum.

Mailing List Users and Suppliers Ass'n (1984)
4010 South 57th Avenue, Suite 202, Lake Worth FL 33463
Exec. Director: Michael R. Cloney
Members: 110 companies *Staff:* 5
Annual Budget: $100-250,000
Hist. Note: Full membership: $750/yr.
Publication:
Newsletter. m.
Semi-annual Meetings: with Direct Marketing Association.
1987-March and Oct.

Mailorder Ass'n of Nurserymen (1934)
Hist. Note: Dissolved in 1985.

Maintenance Council of American Trucking Ass'ns (1979)
2200 Mill Road, Alexandria VA 22314
Exec. Director: Paul T. Domer
Members: 1,000-1,100 companies *Staff:* 6-10
Annual Budget: $250-500,000 *Tel:* (703) 838-1763
Hist. Note: Trucking executives, maintenance specialists, manufacturers, and suppliers interested in the efficient maintenance of trucking fleets. Membership: $300/yr.(Trucking Indiv.); $350/yr.(Manuf. Indiv.).
Publications:
Maintenance Manager. bi-m. adv.
Membership Directory. a.
Recommended Practices Manual.
Radial Tire Wear Conditions Manual.
Wheel & Rim Out of Service Guide.
Newsletter. q.
Annual Meetings: Three each year in Spring, Summer and Fall

Major Indoor Soccer League (1978)
757 3rd Ave., New York NY 10017
Commissioner: Bill Kentling
Members: 12 teams *Staff:* 16-20
Annual Budget: $1-2,000,000 *Tel:* (212) 486-7070
Hist. Note: Professional indoor soccer clubs, each having administrative staffs, coaches, trainers and players. Indoor soccer is an Americanized version of the sport, combining elements of soccer and hockey. Affiliated with the United States Soccer Federation.
Publication:
Missile. bi-m. adv.
Annual Meetings: June

Major Indoor Soccer League Players Ass'n (1978)
1300 Connecticut Ave., N.W., Suite 407, Washington DC 20036
Director: John Kerr
Members: 240 individuals *Staff:* 2-5
Annual Budget: $250-500,000 *Tel:* (202) 463-2200
Hist. Note: A labor union of professional soccer players, affiliated with the AFL-CIO under the umbrella of the Federation of Professional Athletes.

Major League Baseball Players Ass'n (1953)
805 Third Ave., 11th Floor, New York NY 10022
Exec. Director: Donald Fehr
Members: 1,100-1,200 *Staff:* 6-10
Annual Budget: $1-2,000,000 *Tel:* (212) 826-0808
Hist. Note: Independent labor union
Annual Meetings: First week in December

Major League Umpires Ass'n (1969)
1 Logan Square, Suite 1004, Philadelphia PA 19103
General Counsel: Richard G. Phillips
Members: 56 *Staff:* 1
Annual Budget: $10-25,000 *Tel:* (215) 568-7368
Hist. Note: Merger of the Ass'n of National Baseball League Umpires (1963) and the Ass'n of American League Umpires.

Malting Barley Improvement Ass'n (1945)
Hist. Note: Became the American Malting Barley Improvement Association in 1982.

Man and Cybernetics Systems Soc.
Hist. Note: A subsidiary of the Institute of Electrical and Electronics Engineers. Membership in the Society, open only to IEEE members, includes subscription to a technical periodical in the field published by IEEE. All administrative support is provided by IEEE.

Man-Made Fiber Producers Ass'n (1933)
1150 17th St., N. W., Washington DC 20036
President: Paul T. O'Day
Members: 15 *Staff:* 6-10
Annual Budget: $1-2,000,000 *Tel:* (202) 296-6508
Hist. Note: Members are producers of chemically-based or cellulosic fibers such as polyester, nylon, rayon, etc.
Annual Meetings: October

Management Systems Group - Nat'l Ass'n of Quick Printers
111 E. Wacker Drive, Chicago IL 60601
Chairman: William P. Hanrahan
Members: 460 companies *Staff:* 1
Annual Budget: $25-50,000 *Tel:* (312) 644-6610
Hist. Note: A special interest group within the Nat'l Ass'n of Quick Printers which provides administrative support. Members are printers and printer suppliers interested in manual and computerized management systems. Membership: $45/yr. plus NAQP membership.

00175 12 05 86 1233

Publication:
NAQP Quick Bytes. m.
Semi-annual Meetings: Feb. and August
1987-New Orleans, LA/Feb. and Anaheim, CA(Hyatt)/Aug.

Manufactured Housing Institute (1936)
1745 Jefferson Davis Hwy., Arlington VA 22202
President: Jerry C. Connors
Members: 250-300 companies *Staff:* 16-20
Annual Budget: $1-2,000,000 *Tel:* (703) 979-6620
Hist. Note: Established as Trailer Coach Manufacturers Ass'n. Became Mobile Homes Manufacturers Ass'n in 1956 and the Manufactured Housing Institute in 1975. Primary functions are public and governmental relations, establishment of construction standards, financial and statistical services and stimulation of business through expositions. Sponsors the Manufactured Housing Political Action Committee.
Annual Meetings: October

Manufacturers' Agents Nat'l Ass'n (1947)
23016 Mill Creek Road, P.O. Box 3467 (Zip: 92654), Laguna Hills CA 92653
President: James J. Gibbons
Members: 9-10,000 *Staff:* 16-20
Annual Budget: $1-2,000,000 *Tel:* (714) 859-4040
Hist. Note: Promotes the agency method of selling. Members are individuals representing two or more principals. Membership: $50 initiation fee; $135/yr. (US & Canada) and $65 initiation fee; $165/yr. (foreign)
Publications:
Agency Sales Magazine. m. adv.
Directory of Manufacturers' Sales Agencies. a.
Financial Fax. m.
Quarterly Meetings:
1987-San Jose, CA(Red Lion Inn)/Feb. 26-27
1987-Baltimore, MD(Tremont Plaza Hotel)/May 14-15
1987-Madison, WI(Sheraton)/Sept. 10-11
1987-Dallas, TX(Sheraton Park Central)/Nov. 12-13
1988-Memphis, TN(Peabody)/Feb.
1988-Denver, CO(Stouffer's Concourse)/May
1988-Providence, RI(Omni)/Sept.
1988-Seattle, WA/Nov.

Manufacturers Council on Color and Appearance (1972)
340 Herndon Pkwy., Herndon VA 22070
Secretary: Charles G. Leete
Members: 10 companies
Annual Budget: $25-50,000 *Tel:* (703) 481-1125
Hist. Note: Members are companies making instruments to measure color and appearance.
Annual Meetings: Spring

Manufacturers of Aerial Devices and Digger-Derricks Council
Hist. Note: A division of the Farm and Industrial Equipment Institute.

Manufacturers of Emission Controls Ass'n (1976)
1707 L St., N.W., Suite 520, Washington DC 20036
Exec. Director: Bruce I. Bertelsen
Members: 16 companies *Staff:* 2-5
Tel: (202) 296-4797
Annual Meetings: March, in Wasington, DC

Manufacturers of Telescoping and Articulating Cranes Council
Hist. Note: A division of the Farm and Industrial Equipment Institute.

Manufacturers Representatives of America (1978)
117 Miramar Ave., Biloxi MS 39530
Exec. Director: William R. Bess
Members: 425 *Staff:* 2-5
Annual Budget: $100-250,000 *Tel:* (601) 374-6537
Hist. Note: Manufacturers' representatives in the paper, plastic and sanitary supply fields.
Publications:
Newsline.m.
Yearbook.a.adv.
Annual Meetings: April
1987-Houston, TX(Houstonian)/April 1-5
1988-Jacksonville, FL(Sawgrass Resort)/April 6-10

Manufacturers Standardization Soc. of the Valve and Fittings Industry (1924)
127 Park Street, N.E., Vienna VA 22180
Exec. Director: Olen Thornton
Members: 80 companies *Staff:* 3
Annual Budget: $100-250,000 *Tel:* (703) 281-6613
Hist. Note: An engineering society devoted to bringing about uniform codes, standards and specifications. Membership: $1,750/yr.
Annual Meetings: Spring/140
1987-Naples, FL(Naples Beach Hotel & Golf Club)/May 3-7
1988-Longboat Key, FL(Longboat Key Club)/April 24-28
1989-St. Petersburg, FL(Don Cesar)/April 30-May 4

Manufacturing Automation Protocol and Technical Office Protocol Users Group
Hist. Note: A special interest group within the Soc. of Manufacturing Engineers which recommends industrial standard in automated manufacturing and factory floor communications.

Manufacturing Jewelers and Silversmiths of America (1903)
Biltmore Plaza, Providence RI 02903
Exec. Director: Matthew A. Runci
Members: 2,000 *Staff:* 120
Annual Budget: $2-5,000,000 *Tel:* (401) 274-3840
Hist. Note: Established as the New England Manufacturing Jewelers' and Silversmiths' Ass'n, it assumed its present name in 1956.
Publications:
American Jewelry Manufacturer. m. adv.
Action Report to Members. q.
Annual Meetings: Providence,RI/Oct./400

Manufacturing Jewelers Sales Ass'n (1952)
Hist. Note: Became the Fashion Jewelry Ass'n of America, Inc. (1985).

Manuscript Soc. (1948)
350 N. Niagara St., Burbank CA 91505
Exec. Director: David R. Smith
Members: 1,200-1,300 *Staff:* 2-5
Annual Budget: $50-100,000
Hist. Note: Dealers, curators, collectors and others interested in original manuscripts, autographs, letters and documents. Formerly (1953) Nat'l Soc. of Autograph Collectors. Membership: $20/year.
Publications:
Manuscripts. q.
News. 3/yr.
Annual Meetings: Spring
1987-Washington, DC/150

Maple Flooring Manufacturers Ass'n (1897)
60 Revere Drive, Suite 500, Northbrook IL 60062
Exec. V. President: John E. Messervey
Members: 96 companies *Staff:* 2-5
Annual Budget: $100-250,000 *Tel:* (312) 480-9138

Maraschino Cherry and Glace Fruit Processors (1906)
Hist. Note: A section of the Ass'n of Food Industries.

Marble Institute of America (1944)
33505 State St., Farmington MI 48024
Mng. Director: Robert Hund
Members: 500-525 companies *Staff:* 2-5
Annual Budget: $250-500,000 *Tel:* (313) 476-5558
Hist. Note: Absorbed the National Association of Marble Dealers in 1962. Members include producers, exporters/importers, distributors, fabricators, finishers, installers and industry suppliers. Membership: $450/yr. (U.S. company), $650/yr. (foreign company).
Publications:
Through the Ages. q. adv.
Dimensional Stone Vol. III-Design Manual.
Annual Meetings: Fall/200
1987-San Diego, CA

Marine Corps Reserve Officers Ass'n (1926)
201 North Washington St., Suite 206, Alexandria VA 22314
Exec. Director: Col. Laurence Gaboury, USMCR(Ret)
Members: 5,500 *Staff:* 2-5
Annual Budget: $100-250,000 *Tel:* (703) 548-7607
Publication:
The Word. bi-m. adv.
Annual Meetings: Spring
1987-New York, NY
1988-Washington, DC

Marine Engine Manufacturers Ass'n (1945)
Hist. Note: Became the Ass'n of Marine Engine Manufacturers in 1985.

Marine Retailers Ass'n of America (1971)
155 N. Michigan Ave., Suite 523, Chicago IL 60601
Exec. Director: Mathew J. Kaufman
Members: 2,000-2,500 companies *Staff:* 2-5
Annual Budget: $100-250,000 *Tel:* (312) 938-0359
Hist. Note: Members are manufacturers, distributors and dealers in marine equipment. Sponsors and supports the Marine Retailers Political Action Committee. Membership: $50-1,000/yr.
Publication:
MRAA Newsletter. m.
Annual Meetings: Fall

Marine Technology Soc. (1963)
2000 Florida Avenue, N.W., Suite 500, Washington DC 20009
Exec. Director: Harold D. Palmer
Members: 3,000-3,500 *Staff:* 4
Annual Budget: $250-500,000 *Tel:* (202) 462-7557
Hist. Note: Founded and incorporated in New York in 1963; merged in 1971 with the American Soc. for Oceanography. Affiliated with the American Ass'n for the Advancement of Science. Concerned with such issues as coastal zone management, law of the sea, marine mineral and energy resources, marine environmental protection and the economic potential of the sea. Membership: $50/yr.(individual); $275-650/yr.(organization)
Publications:
Marine Technology Society Journal. q. adv.
MTS Newsletter. m.
Remotely Operated Vehicles Conference Proceedings. a.
Oceans Conference Proceedings. a.
Annual Meetings: Fall/1,500
1987-Halifax, Canada(Convention Ctr.)/Sept. 28-Oct. 1
1988-Baltimore, MD(Convention Ctr.)/Oct. 30-Nov. 1
1989-Seattle, WA(Convention Ctr.)/Sept. 18-21

Maritime Law Ass'n of the U.S. (1899)
Hill, Rivkins, Carey, Loesberg, etc., 21 West St., New York NY 10006
President: Francis J. O'Brien
Members: 3,200
Annual Budget: $100-250,000 *Tel:* (212) 825-1000
Hist. Note: Affiliated with the American Bar Ass'n.
Publications:
MLA Proceedings. semi-a.
MLA Reports. semi-a.
Semi-annual meetings: May and November

Maritime Transportation Research Board (1965)
Hist. Note: Operates under the Commission on Sociotechnical Systems of the Nat'l Research Council. Formed by a merger of the Maritime Cargo Transportation Conference and the Ship Hull Research Committee.

Marketing Agents for Food Service Industry (1949)
111 East Wacker Drive, Suite 600, Chicago IL 60601
Exec. Director: James M. Dickinson
Members: 400 companies *Staff:* 2-5
Annual Budget: $100-250,000 *Tel:* (312) 644-6610
Hist. Note: Independent manufacturers representatives. Formerly (1975) Manufacturers' Agents for Food Service Industry.
Publications:
Food Service Industry Marketing Agents LOCATOR. a. adv.
REP Report. q.
Headquarters Report. 8/yr.
Annual Meetings: Feb./March in a resort area/300

Marketing and Distributive Education Ass'n
Hist. Note: Became the Marketing Education Ass'n in 1985.

Marketing and Management Council
Hist. Note: Affiliate of the Farm & Industrial Equipment Institute

Marketing Communications Executives Internat'l (1954)
Hist. Note: Ceased operations in 1985.

Marketing Education Ass'n (1982)
1908 Association Drive, Reston VA 22091
Admin. Coordinator: Carol Keith
Members: 2,000 *Staff:* 1
Annual Budget: $25-50,000 *Tel:* (703) 476-4299
Hist. Note: Formerly (1985) Marketing and Distributive Education Ass'n. Formed by a merger of the Council of Distributive Teacher Educators (founded in 1960), the Nat'l Ass'n of Distributive Education Local Supervisors, the Nat'l Ass'n of Distributive Education Teachers (founded in 1957) and Nat'l Ass'n of State Supervisors of Distributive Education (founded in 1947). Affiliated with the American Vocational Association. Membership: $20/year.
Publications:
Marketing Educators Journal. semi-a. adv.
Marketing Educators News. 3/yr. adv.
Annual Meetings: With the American Vocational Association.

Marketing Research Ass'n (1954)
111 East Wacker Drive, Suite 600, Chicago IL 60601
Exec. Director: Martha A. DeGraaf
Members: 2,000 *Staff:* 2-5
Annual Budget: $500-1,000,000 *Tel:* (312) 644-6610
Hist. Note: Companies and individuals involved in the design, administration, or analysis of market research studies. Formerly (1971) Marketing Research Trade Ass'n.
Publications:
Alert. bi-m. adv.
Journal of Data Collection. semi-a.
Research Service Directory. a. adv.
Manager's Notebook Series. 10/yr.
Semi-annual meetings: May and October
1987-San Francisco, CA/May 13-16
1987-Atlanta, GA/Oct. 28-30
1988-Chicago, IL/May
1988-Houston, TX/Oct.

Marking Device Ass'n (1910)
708 Church St., Evanston IL 60201
Exec. Secretary: Thomas H. Brinkmann
Members: 5-600 companies *Staff:* 2-5
Annual Budget: $100-250,000 *Tel:* (312) 328-3540
Hist. Note: Formerly Internat'l Stamp Manufacturers Ass'n. Manufacturers of rubber and metal stamps, plates and signs.
Annual Meetings: Fall/500
1987-San Diego, CA/Nov.
1988-Southeast
1989-Chicago, IL/Sept.
1990-Hawaii
1991-East
1992-Canada
1993-Chicago, IL

00176 12 05 86 1233

Marky Cattle Ass'n
Hist. Note: See American International Marchigiana Society.

Mason Contractors Ass'n of America (1950)
17 West 601 14th St., Oakbrook Terrace IL 60181
Exec. V. President: George A. Miller
Members: 1,500 *Staff:* 2-5
Annual Budget: $250-500,000 *Tel:* (312) 620-6767
Publication:
Masonry. bi-m. adv.
Annual Meetings: Late Winter
1987-Dallas, TX(Loew's Anatole)/March 14-18

Masonry and Concrete Saw Manufacturers Institute (1981)
712 Lakewood Center North, 14600 Detroit Ave., Cleveland OH 44107
Manager/Secretary-Treasurer: Allen P. Wherry
Members: 12 companies *Staff:* 2-5
Annual Budget: $10-25,000 *Tel:* (216) 226-7700
Hist. Note: Formerly (1985) the Masonry and Concrete Saw Manufacturers Ass'n.
Semi-annual Meetings: February and August

Mass Finishing Job Shops Ass'n (1981)
3801 Winding Way, Kalamazoo MI 49007
Exec. Director: John B. Kittredge
Members: 27 companies *Staff:* 1
Annual Budget: under $10,000 *Tel:* (616) 382-4713
Hist. Note: Members are companies engaged in the surface finishing, deburring and cleaning of metals and other materials owned through such techniques as tumbling, vibratory finishing, sandblasting, etc.
Semi-Annual Meetings:
1987-Toronto, Canada/Oct.

Mass Marketing Insurance Institute (1969)
1900 Arch St., Philadelphia PA 19103
Exec. Director: John W. Kane
Members: 300 companies *Staff:* 2-5
Annual Budget: $50-100,000 *Tel:* (215) 564-3484
Hist. Note: An international organization of independent brokers and carriers currently active in mass marketing insurance.
Publication:
Information Exchange. bi-m.
Annual Meetings: April

Mass Merchandising Distributors' Ass'n (1973)
Hist. Note: Defunct in 1983.

Master Brewers Ass'n of the Americas (1887)
4513 Vernon Blvd., Suite 202, Madison WI 53705
Exec. Secretary: Daniel C. Sommers
Members: 3,500 *Staff:* 2-5
Annual Budget: $250-500,000 *Tel:* (608) 231-3446
Hist. Note: Founded as the Master Brewers Ass'n of America, it assumed its present name in 1979. Members are brewery executives, suppliers and technical personnel in related industries. Membership: $60/yr.
Publications:
MBAA Communications. bi-m.
MBAA Technical Quarterly. q. adv.
Annual Meetings: Fall
1987-Milwaukee, WI(Mecca)/Sept. 27-Oct. 1

Master Furriers Guild of America (1929)
101 West 30th St., New York NY 10001
Exec. Director: Konnie Karopoulos
Members: 820-830 *Staff:* 2-5
Annual Budget: $250-500,000 *Tel:* (212) 244-8570
Publication:
The Master Furrier. 8/yr.
Annual Meetings: June or July at a resort within 200 miles of New York City.

Master Gemology Ass'n (1985)
2000 E. Sunrise Blvd., Fort Lauderdale FL 33304
President: Cary Keno
Members: 241 individuals *Staff:* 2
Annual Budget: $10-25,000 *Tel:* (305) 462-1119
Hist. Note: Membership is restricted to certified gemologists. Membership: $75/yr.
Publication:
MGA Quarterly Journal. q. adv.
Annual Meetings: February in Tucson, AZ

Master Printers of America (1945)
1730 North Lynn St., Arlington VA 22209
President: Brian W. Gill
Members: 8,500 *Staff:* 6-10
Annual Budget: $500-1,000,000 *Tel:* (703) 841-8130
Hist. Note: A division of Printing Industries of America. Members are open shop printers.
Publication:
Views. m.
Annual Meetings: Spring

Master Weavers Institute (1933)
Grotta, Glassman and Hoffman, P.A., 75 Livingston Ave., Roseland NJ 07068
Counsel: Stephen A. Ploscowe
Members: 9 companies *Staff:* 1
Annual Budget: under $10,000 *Tel:* (201) 992-4800
Hist. Note: Members, mainly in Northern New Jersey, are jacquard novely textile weavers. Major activity is collective bargaining and labor activities.

Mastercard Internat'l (1966)
888 Seventh Ave., New York NY 10106
President and CEO: Russell E. Hogg
Members: 29,000 financial institutions *Staff:* 600
Annual Budget: over $5,000,000 *Tel:* (212) 974-5700
Hist. Note: Administers the MasterCard credit card and other MasterCard products for 29,000 member banks around the world. Formerly (1981) Interbank Card Ass'n. Has an annual budget of over $150 million.
Publication:
Insight. bi-m.
Annual Meetings: Late Winter
1987-San Francisco, CA(Fairmont Hotel)/March 25-26
1988-Ft. Lauderdale, FL(Marriott's Harbor Beach/March 24

Material Handling Equipment Distributors Ass'n (1955)
201 Route #45, Vernon Hills IL 60061
Exec. V. President: Daniel R. Reilly
Members: 850 companies *Staff:* 6-10
Annual Budget: $500-1,000,000 *Tel:* (312) 680-3500
Hist. Note: Membership: $325-550/yr. (company).
Publication:
Material Handling Distribution. q. adv.
Annual Meetings: Spring/750-1,000
1987-Maui, HI(Hyatt)/May 10-14
1988-Las Vegas, NV(MGM Grand)/April 24-28
1989-Boston, MA(Marriott Copley Plaza)/May 7-11
1990-San Diego, CA(Intercontinental)/May 6-10

Material Handling Institute (1945)
8720 Red Oak Blvd., Suite 201, Charlotte NC 28210
Exec. V. President: Albert L. Leffler
Members: 300 companies *Staff:* 20
Annual Budget: $2-5,000,000 *Tel:* (704) 522-8644
Hist. Note: Member, Machinery and Allied Products Institute. Makers of industrial material handling equipment such as conveyors, racks, hoists and cranes, lift trucks. Membership: $1,100/yr. (company).
Semi-annual meetings: Fall and Spring
1987-Charlotte, NC/May

Materials and Methods Standards Ass'n (1962)
315 South Hicks Road, Palatine IL 60067
President: A. Robert Moore
Members: 35-45 companies *Staff:* 1
Annual Budget: $10-25,000 *Tel:* (312) 358-9500
Hist. Note: Incorporated in 1962 in Texas as the Mortar Manufacturers Standards Ass'n, it assumed its present name in 1977. Membership is composed of manufacturers of ceramic tile and ceramic tile installation products. MMSA is represented on the Tile Council of America and the ANSI A108/118/136 committees. MMSA issues bulletins on ceramic tile industry materials and practices not covered in the TCA handbook or ANSI standards.
Publication:
Bulletins. irreg.
Semi-annual Meetings: With ATTMCA and CTDA

Materials Handling Council
Hist. Note: A division of the Farm and Industrial Equipment Institute.

Materials Marketing Associates (1963)
638 Prospect Ave., Hartford CT 06105
Exec. Director: Charles G. Peterman
Members: 14 companies *Staff:* 2-5
Annual Budget: $50-100,000 *Tel:* (203) 233-5617
Hist. Note: Manufacturers' representatives marketing chemical raw material specialties to makers of coatings, inks, pharmaceuticals, adhesives, cosmetics, plastics, soaps and detergents and the like.
Publication:
Newsletter. m.

Materials Properties Council, The (1966)
345 East 47th Street, New York NY 10017
Acting Exec. Director: Martin Prager
Members: 250 companies or organizations, 600 individuals
Staff: 4
Annual Budget: $2-5,000,000 *Tel:* (212) 705-7693
Hist. Note: Formerly (1986) The Metal Properties Council. MPC is an outgrowth of the ASTM-ASME Joint Committee on the Effect of Temperature on the Properties of Metals which was founded in 1925 to meet the apparent need for information on the subject in the construction of central power stations. After 40 years it was apparent that a permanently staffed organization was needed to ensure the availability of valid data on materials to meet advancing technology. MPC was founded in 1966 to meet this need. Sponsored by American Soc. of Mechanical Engineers, American Soc. for Testing and Materials, American Soc. for Metals, Engineering Foundation and American Welding Soc.
Publications:
Committee List. a.
Frontiers. q.
Yearbook. a.
Annual Meetings: Board of Directors meeting, 2nd Thursday in October/45

Materials Research Soc. (1973)
9800 McKnight Road, Suite 327, Pittsburgh PA 15237
Exec. Director: John B. Ballance
Members: 5,000 *Staff:* 12
Annual Budget: $1-2,000,000 *Tel:* (412) 367-3003
Hist. Note: Members are individuals adopting a multi-disciplinary approach towards the problems of research on organic and inorganic materials. Membership: $45/year.
Publications:
MRS Bulletin. bi-m.
Journal of Materials Research. bi-m.
Semi-annual Meetings: Spring on the West Coast and Fall in Boston
1987-Anaheim, CA
1987-Boston, MA/Nov. 30-Dec. 5
1988-Reno, NV
1988-Boston, MA

Mathematical Ass'n of America (1915)
1529 18th St., N.W., Washington DC 20036
Exec. Director: Alfred B. Willcox
Members: 25,000 *Staff:* 25
Annual Budget: $2-5,000,000 *Tel:* (202) 387-5200
Hist. Note: Founded in Columbus, Ohio in 1915 to promote the teaching of mathematics, especially on the collegiate level. A constituent member of the Conference Board of the Mathematical Sciences. Membership: $48/yr.
Publications:
American Mathematical Monthly. 10/yr. adv.
Mathematics Magazine. 5/yr. adv.
College Mathematics Journal. 5/yr. adv.
Focus Newsletter. 10/yr.
Annual Meetings: Winter, with the American Mathematical Soc./3,000
1987-San Antonio, TX/Jan. 21-25
1988-Atlanta, GA/Jan. 6-9
1989-Phoenix, AZ/Jan. 11-14

MDS Industry Ass'n
Hist. Note: Merged with Microwave Communication Ass'n in 1986.

Meat Importers' Council of America (1962)
1901 North Fort Myer Dr., Arlington VA 22209
Exec. Director: William Morrison
Members: 175-200 companies *Staff:* 2-5
Annual Budget: $250-500,000 *Tel:* (703) 522-1910
Annual Meetings: Always Chicago, IL(Conrad Hilton)/Fall

Meat Industry Suppliers Ass'n (1948)
7297 Lee Hwy., Suite N, Falls Church VA 22042
President: Harry Buzzerd
Members: 100-150 companies *Staff:* 5-10
Annual Budget: $100-250,000 *Tel:* (703) 533-1159
Hist. Note: Formerly (1981) Meat Industry Supply and Equipment Ass'n. Members are suppliers to the meat, poultry and seafood packing and processing industries. Absorbed the Meat Machinery Manufacturers Institute and the Food Machinery Service Institute in 1984; these are now autonomous divisions of MISA.
Semi-annual Meetings: March and September
1987-Naples, FL(Ritz Carlton)/March 29-April 1

Meat Machinery Manufacturers Institute (1938)
Hist. Note: Merged into the Meat Industry Supplier Ass'n in 1984.

Mechanical Contractors Ass'n of America (1889)
5410 Grosvenor Lane, Suite 120, Bethesda MD 20814
Exec. V. President: James R. Noble
Members: 1,400 *Staff:* 20-25
Annual Budget: $1-2,000,000 *Tel:* (301) 897-0770
Hist. Note: Established as the Master Steam and Hot Water Fitters Ass'n of the United States, it became the Heating and Piping Contractors Nat'l Ass'n in 1918, the Heating, Piping and Air Conditioning Contractors Nat'l Ass'n in 1933 and assumed its present name in 1956. Sponsors the Mechanical Contractors Association of America Political Action Committee.
Publications:
The Reporter. m.
Membership Directory. a. adv.
Annual Meetings: January/February
1987-San Francisco, CA(Hyatt Embarcadero and Fairmont)/Feb. 1-5/2,000
1988-Palm Springs, CA(Marriott Desert Springs)/Feb. 7-11/2,000

Mechanical Jack Manufacturers Ass'n
Hist. Note: Dissolved in 1985.

Mechanical Power Transmission Ass'n (1933)
800 Custer St., Evanston IL 60202
Exec. Secretary: Thomas D. Dolan
Members: 15-20 *Staff:* 2-5
Annual Budget: $25-50,000 *Tel:* (312) 864-8444
Hist. Note: Formerly Multiple V-Belt Drive & Mechanical Power Transmission Ass'n

Mechanics Educational Soc. of America (1933)
15300 East Seven Mile Rd., Detroit MI 48205
President: Alfred J. Smith
Staff: 6-10

00177 12 05 86 1233

Annual Budget: $500-1,000,000 *Tel:* (313) 372-5700
Hist. Note: Organized by a group of Detroit tool and die makers in 1933 and affiliated with AFL-CIO in 1955.
Publication:
MESA Educator. 11/yr.

Media Credit Ass'n (1903)
575 Lexington Ave., Rm. 540, New York NY 10022
V. President: James E. Van Meter
Members: 150 *Staff:* 2-5
Tel: (212) 752-0055
Hist. Note: Organized to provide Guideline credit services on advertising agencies to publisher members of association.

Medical and Laboratory Instrumentation Soc. (1982)
Hist. Note: Address unknown in 1985-86.

Medical-Dental-Hospital Bureaus of America (1939)
70 West Hubbard St., Suite 202, Chicago IL 60610
Exec. Director: Sanford J. Hill
Members: 220 *Staff:* 2-5
Annual Budget: $100-250,000 *Tel:* (312) 644-2623
Publication:
Newscope. m.
Annual Meetings: Fall
1987-Incline Village, NV/Oct.

Medical Group Management Ass'n (1926)
1355 S. Colorado Blvd., Suite 900, Denver CO 80222
Exec. Director: Richard V. Grant, Ph.D.
Members: 6,100 individuals and 2,900 medical groups *Staff:* 50
Annual Budget: $2-5,000,000 *Tel:* (303) 753-1111
Hist. Note: Founded as the Ass'n of Clinic Managers, it became the Nat'l Ass'n of Clinic Managers in 1946 and assumed its present name in 1963. Affiliated with the honorary organization, the American College of Medical Group Administrators, and parent organization of the Center for Research in Ambulatory Health Care Administration. Members are managers of medical group practices.
Publications:
MGMA Directory. a. adv.
Medical Group Management. bi-m. adv.
Management Update. m. adv.
Annual Meetings: Fall
1987-Washington, DC(Sheraton Washington)/Oct. 25-28
1988-Kansas City, MO(Convention Ctr.)/Oct. 9-12
1989-Las Vegas, NV(Hilton)/Oct. 29-Nov. 1

Medical Library Ass'n (1898)
919 North Michigan Ave., Ste. 3208, Chicago IL 60611
Exec. Director: Raymond A. Palmer
Members: 5,000 *Staff:* 11-15
Annual Budget: $1-2,000,000 *Tel:* (312) 266-2456
Hist. Note: Originated in 1898 as the Ass'n of Medical Librarians and became the Medical Library Ass'n in 1907. Incorporated in Maryland in 1934. Affiliated with the American Ass'n for the Advancement of Science, and the Council of Nat'l Library Ass'ns. Membership: $75/yr. (individual); $125-295/yr. (organization).
Publications:
Bulletin of the MLA. q. adv.
Current Catalog Proof Sheets. w.
MLA News. m.
Directory. a. adv.
Annual Meetings: Spring/1,500
1987-Portland, OR(Hilton)
1988-New Orleans, LA
1989-Boston, MA
1990-Detroit, MI(Westin Renaissance)
1991-San Francisco, CA

Medical Mycological Soc. of the Americas (1966)
Dept. of Microbiology, Methodist Central,Hosp., Dallas TX 75222
Secy.-Treas.: Geoffrey A. Land
Members: 500-525 individuals *Staff:* 1
Annual Budget: under $10,000 *Tel:* (214) 944-8247
Hist. Note: Founded in 1966 to promote the development of medical mycology, the study of human pathogenic fungi among scientists of the Americas. Membership: $5/year.
Annual Meetings: March, with the American Soc. for Microbiology.

Medieval Academy of America (1925)
1430 Massachusetts Ave., Cambridge MA 02138
Exec. Director: Luke Wenger
Members: 3,900 individuals *Staff:* 2-5
Annual Budget: $100-250,000 *Tel:* (617) 491-1622
Hist. Note: Member American Council of Learned Societies Members are scholars with an interest in the period 500-1500 AD.
Publication:
Speculum. q. adv.
Annual Meetings: Spring

Meeting Planners Internat'l (1972)
Infomart, 1950 Stemmons Freeway, Dallas TX 75207
Exec. V. President: Douglas A. Heath, CAE
Members: 7,800 individuals *Staff:* 25
Annual Budget: $1-2,000,000 *Tel:* (214) 746-5222
Hist. Note: Professional meeting managers self-employed or employed by corporations and associations throughout the world. Membership: $175/yr.
Publications:
Meeting Manager. m. adv.
Membership Directory. a.
Semi-Annual Meetings: Summer and Winter
1987-Winnipeg, Canada/June 7-9
1987-Miami, FL/Dec. 6-9
1988-Seattle, WA/June 19-20
1988-Nashville, TN/Dec. 4-7

Melamine Tableware Ass'n (1979)
Hist. Note: Defunct 1984.

Men's Fashion Ass'n of America (1955)
240 Madison Ave., New York NY 10016
Exec. Director: Norman Karr
Members: 400 *Staff:* 10
Annual Budget: $500-1,000,000 *Tel:* (212) 683-5665
Hist. Note: The public relations and educational arm of the men's and boy's apparel industry. Founded as the American Institute of Men's and Boy's Wear, it assumed its present name in 1970.
Annual Meetings: Spring/Summer and Fall/Winter press previews
1987-Atlanta, GA(Marriott Marquis)/Jan. 22-25/400
1987-Rye, NY(Rye Town Hilton)/June 3-7/500

Menswear Retailers of America (1914)
2011 Eye St., N.W., Suite 600, Washington DC 20006
Exec. Director: Douglas Wiegand
Members: 4,000 stores *Staff:* 15-20
Annual Budget: $1-2,000,000 *Tel:* (202) 347-1932
Hist. Note: Established as the Nat'l Ass'n of Retail Clothiers and Furnishers, it assumed its present name in 1965 and absorbed the Nat'l Clothier Service in 1973. Supports the Menswear Public Affairs Committee.
Annual Meetings: February
1987-Atlanta, GA/Feb. 7-10

Merion Bluegrass Ass'n (1954)
12341 25th St., N.E., Seattle WA 98125
Exec. Secretary: A. E. Bonnicksen
Members: 100-125 growers *Staff:* 2-5
Tel: (206) 365-7548
Annual Meetings: June

Metal Belt Institute (1964)
Hist. Note: Ceased operations in 1985.

Metal Building Components Manufacturers Ass'n (1976)
1133 15th St., N.W., Washington DC 20005
Exec. Director: David W. Barrack
Members: 40-45 companies *Staff:* 2-5
Annual Budget: $10-25,000 *Tel:* (202) 293-5910

Metal Building Manufacturers Ass'n (1956)
1230 Keith Bldg., Cleveland OH 44115-2180
General Manager: Charles M. Stockinger
Members: 25 companies *Staff:* 2-5
Annual Budget: $100-250,000 *Tel:* (216) 241-7333
Annual Meetings: Nov.-Dec./50

Metal Castings Soc. (1975)
Cast Metals Federation Bldg., 455 State St., Des Plaines IL 60016
Exec. Director: Peter Dudchenko
Members: 180 companies *Staff:* 6-10
Annual Budget: $500-1,000,000 *Tel:* (312) 299-9160
Hist. Note: Formerly (1986) Iron Castings Soc. Ferrous and non-ferrous foundries producing castings. Merger (1975) of the Gray and Ductile Iron Founders' Soc. (1928) and the Malleable Founders Soc. (1897).
Publications:
Buyers' Guide and Directory. bien.
Metalcaster. m.
Annual Meetings: Fall/300
1987-Rancho Mirage, CA(Marriott)/Oct. 11-14
1988-Pinehurst, NC(Pinehurst)/Sept. 18-21

Metal Construction Ass'n (1983)
1133 15th St., N.W., Suite 620, Washington DC 20005
Exec. Director: David W. Barrack
Members: 105 companies *Staff:* 2-5
Annual Budget: $50-100,000 *Tel:* (202) 293-5910
Hist. Note: MCA is dedicated to the promotion of the use of metal in all types of construction: residential, industrial, commercial, farm, institutional and retrofit.

Metal Cutting Knife Ass'n (1953)
Hist. Note: Dissolved December 31, 1983.

Metal Cutting Tool Institute (1932)
1230 Keith Bldg., Cleveland OH 44115-2180
Secy.-Treas.: Charles M. Stockinger
Members: 40-50 *Staff:* 2-5
Annual Budget: $100-250,000 *Tel:* (216) 241-7333
Semi-annual Meetings:

Metal Findings Manufacturers Ass'n (1930)
P.O. Box 6765, Providence RI 02940
President: Steve Guyot
Members: 55-60 companies
Annual Budget: under $10,000 *Tel:* (617) 222-2000
Hist. Note: Makers of metal parts and fittings used in the assembly of jewelry. Has no paid staff or permanent address. Officers change every two years.
Annual Meetings: May in the Providence region.

Metal Finishing Suppliers Ass'n (1951)
1025 East Maple Rd., Birmingham MI 48011
Exec. Director: King Ruhly
Members: 240 companies *Staff:* 2-5
Annual Budget: $100-250,000 *Tel:* (313) 646-2728
Annual Meetings: Held with American Electroplaters' Society

Metal Framing Manufacturers Ass'n (1981)
111 East Wacker Drive, Suite 600, Chicago IL 60601
Exec. Director: Jack M. Springer
Members: 9 companies *Staff:* 4
Tel: (312) 644-6610
Hist. Note: MFMA Standards Publication. a. Guidelines for the Use of Metal Framing. a.
Publications:
MFMA Standards Publication. a.
Guidelines for the Use of Metal Framing. a.
Annual Meetings: Fall

Metal Ladder Manufacturers Ass'n (1949)
P.O. Box 580, Greenville PA 16125
Secretary: Richard L. Werner
Members: 5-10 companies
Annual Budget: under $10,000 *Tel:* (412) 588-8600

Metal Lath/Steel Framing Ass'n (1910)
600 S. Federal St., #400, Chicago IL 60605
Mng. Director: Durward Humes, CAE
Members: 7 companies *Staff:* 2-5
Annual Budget: $50-100,000 *Tel:* (312) 346-1600
Hist. Note: Formerly Metal Lath Manufacturers Ass'n and (1974) Metal Lath Ass'n. Promotes the increased use of expanded metal lath and accessories, and 20-gage and heavier steel framing products.
Publication:
Specifications for Metal Lathing and Furring. a.

Metal Polishers, Buffers, Platers and Allied Workers Internat'l Union (1892)
5578 Montgomery Rd., Cincinnati OH 45212
President: Glenn L. Holt
Members: 6,000 *Staff:* 4
Annual Budget: $25-50,000 *Tel:* (513) 531-2500
Hist. Note: Established in Toledo, Ohio in 1892 as the Metal Polishers, Buffers and Platers' International Union and chartered by the American Federation of Labor the same year. Merged in 1896 with the United Brotherhood of Brass and Composition Metal Workers, Polishers and Buffers to form the Metal Polishers, Buffers, Platers and Brass Workers International Union of North America. Renamed the Metal Polishers International Union in 1917, it became the Metal Polishers, Buffers, Platers and Helpers International Union in 1936 and assumed its present name in 1970.
Triennial Meetings:
1987-Louisville, KY(Galt House)/May/100-150

Metal Powder Industries Federation (1958)
105 College Rd., East, Princeton NJ 08540
Exec. Director: Kempton H. Roll
Members: 260 companies *Staff:* 12
Annual Budget: $1-2,000,000 *Tel:* (609) 452-7700
Hist. Note: Represents the trade, commercial and technological interests of the metal powder producing and consuming industries. The Federation consists of the following constituent ass'ns: the Powder Metallurgy Parts Ass'n, Metal Powder Producers Asns, Powder Metallurgy Equipment Ass'n, Refractory Metals Ass'n, Metal Powder Technology Ass'n.
Publications:
International Journal of Powder Metallurgy. q. adv.
P/M Technology Newsletter. m.
Semi-annual meetings: Fall at a resort area and Spring in a major city.
1987-Dallas, TX(Loew's Anatole)/May 17-20
1987-Napa, CA/Oct. 4-7

Metal Powder Producers Ass'n
Hist. Note: A Constituent member of the Metal Powder Industries Federation.

Metal Properties Council, The
Hist. Note: Became The Materials Properties Council in 1986.

Metal Treating Institute (1933)
300 N. 2nd St., Jacksonville Beach FL 32250
Exec. Director: M. Lance Miller, CAE
Members: 325 heat treating companies *Staff:* 2-5
Annual Budget: $100-250,000 *Tel:* (904) 249-0448
Publication:
Open Hearth. m.
Semi-annual Meetings: Spring and Fall
1987-Cancun/April and Toronto, Ontario(Four Seasons)/Oct.

00178 12 05 86 1233

1988-San Diego, CA(Rancho Bernardo)/April and Tampa, FL(Saddlebrook)
1989-Maui, HI/April

Metal Tube Packaging Council of North America (1957)
Hist. Note: Became the Tube Council of North America in 1983.

Metallurgical Soc., The (1871)
420 Commonwealth Drive, Warrendale PA 15086
Exec. Director: Alexander Scott
Members: 12,000 *Staff:* 20-25
Annual Budget: $2-5,000,000 *Tel:* (412) 776-9000
Hist. Note: The Metals Branch of the American Institute of Mining, Metallurgical and Petroleum Engineers (AIME, founded in 1871) was established in 1947 and the name changed to its present form in 1957; it became a separately incorporated entity in 1985. Membership: $60/yr.
Publications:
Journal of Electronic Materials. m. adv.
Journal of Metals. m. adv.
Metallurgical Transactions. m.
Annual Meetings: Winter
1987-Denver, CO(Marriott)/Feb. 22-26/5,000
1988-Phoenix, AZ(Hilton)/Jan. 25-29/5,000
1989-Las Vegas, NV(Hilton)/Feb. 28-March 3/6,000

Metaphysical Soc. of America (1950)
Dept. of Philosophy, Loyola College, 4501 North Charles St., Baltimore MD 21210-2699
Secy.-Treas.: William J. Desmond
Members: 600 individuals *Staff:* 1
Annual Budget: under $10,000 *Tel:* (301) 323-1010
Hist. Note: Promotes philosophic metaphysics. Founded as an alternative to prevailing views in other philosophic societies. Member American Council of Learned Societies. Membership: $10/yr.
Publication:
Newsletter. 3/yr.
Annual Meetings: March
1987-New York, NY/March 12-14

Meteoritical Soc. (1933)
Dept. of Geological Sciences, University of Tennessee, Knoxville TN 37996-1410
Secretary: Harry Y. McSween
Members: 800 *Staff:* 1
Annual Budget: $10-25,000 *Tel:* (615) 974-2366
Hist. Note: Established in 1933 to promote the study of meteorites and other samples of extraterrestrial matter and their relation to the origin and history of the solar system. Formerly (1946) Soc. for Research on Meteorites. Membership: $15/yr.(individual); $40/yr.(organization).
Publication:
Meteoritics. q.
Annual Meetings: Late Summer or early Fall
1987-Newcastle, England(Univ. of Newcastle)/July 20-24

Methods and Materials Standards Ass'n (1962)
Hist. Note: Became the Materials and Methods Standards Ass'n in 1984.

Methods Time Measurement Ass'n for Standards and Research (1951)
16-01 Broadway, Fair Lawn NJ 07410
Exec. Director: James P. O'Brien
Members: 1,000 *Staff:* 17
Annual Budget: $500-1,000,000 *Tel:* (201) 791-7720
Hist. Note: Membership consists of industrial psychologists and industrial engineers and academicians. Conducts research and training on the efficiency of human motion. Also known as MTM Association for Standards and Research. Membership: $25/yr. (individual), $350/yr. (company).
Publication:
MTM Journal. q. $8/yr.
Annual Meetings:
1987-Nashville, TN(Opryland)/Oct. 14-16/150

Methyl Chloride Industry Ass'n (1981)
c/o Richard Friedman, Covington and, Burling, 1201 Pennsylvania Ave., N.W., Washington DC 20044
Chairman: Ed Hobbs
Annual Budget: $10-25,000 *Tel:* (202) 662-5260
Hist. Note: Formed to serve the industry needs with respect to government regulation of methyl chloride.

Metropolitan Pharmaceutical Secretaries Ass'n (1928)
Box 8194, St. Louis MO 63156
Secy.-Treas.: Jack Samuel
Members: 25-30
Annual Budget: under $10,000 *Tel:* (314) 531-6929
Hist. Note: A very small organization of less than 30 members, without headquarters or paid staff, consisting of individuals who are secretaries of pharmaceutical associations in large urban areas.

Metropolitan Symphony Managers Ass'n
Hist. Note: A sub-group of the American Symphony Orchestra League without dues structure or separate headquarters.

Mexican American Engineering Soc. (1974)
Box 3520, Fullerton CA 92634
Nat'l Secretary: Reynaldo Trevino
Members: 13 chapters *Staff:* 2
Annual Budget: $50-100,000 *Tel:* (805) 378-2619
Hist. Note: Formed to provide meetings, seminars and forums for the presentation of technical papers and to bring about improved methods between industry, government, and the academic communities for the assimilation of qualified persons of Mexican-American extraction within the engineering and scientific disciplines. Membership: $25/yr. (professional); $7/yr. (student).
Publications:
PACE Newsletter. q.
Annual MAES Symposium Proceedings. a. adv.
Directory. semi-a.

Mexican Chamber of Commerce of the United States (1921)
15 Park Row, Suite 1700, New York NY 10038
Exec. V. President: L. D. Balseiro
Members: 800 companies *Staff:* 6-10
Annual Budget: $50-100,000 *Tel:* (212) 227-9171
Hist. Note: Seeks to foster trade and commerce between the United States and Mexico.
Publication:
Monthly Digest
Annual Meetings: April, September and November in New York

Mica Industry Ass'n (1953)
Hist. Note: Dissolved at the end of 1986.

Microbeam Analysis Soc. (1968)
Department of Geology 170-25, Cal Tech, Pasadena CA 91125
Secretary: John Armstrong
Members: 1,300 individuals, 50 companies *Staff:* 2-5
Annual Budget: $10-25,000 *Tel:* (818) 356-6253
Hist. Note: Formerly (1973) Electron Probe Analysis Soc. of America. Members involved with all types of electron and ion probes.
Publication:
Micronews. q.
Annual Meetings: Summer

Microcirculatory Soc. of America (1955)
Dept. of Physiology, Temple Med. School,3420 North Broad Street, Philadelphia PA 19140
Secretary: Dr. Ronald F. Tuma
Members: 325-350
Annual Budget: under $10,000 *Tel:* (215) 221-3276
Hist. Note: Incorporated in Massachusetts as the Microcirculatory Conference, it assumed its present name in 1965.
Annual Meetings: Prior to Federation of American Socs. for Experimental Biology

Microneurography Soc. (1981)
Cardiovascular Physiology, Veterans Administration Med. Center, Richmond VA 23249
Secretary: Dr. Dwain L. Eckberg
Members: 50-60 *Staff:* 1
Annual Budget: under $10,000 *Tel:* (804) 230-0001
Hist. Note: Members are individuals interested in the technique of inserting needles into nerves to record neurological activity in humans. Membership: $5/year.
Annual Meetings: With the Soc. for Neuroscience

Microwave Communications Ass'n (1975)
2000 L St., N.W., Suite 200, Washington DC 20036
Secretary: Elena Selin
Members: 28 *Staff:* 1
Tel: (202) 659-4417
Hist. Note: Absorbed MDS Industry Ass'n in 1986.
Publication:
Newsletter.

Microwave, Theory and Techniques Soc.
Hist. Note: A subsidiary of the Institute of Electrical and Electronics Engineers. Membership in the Society, open only to IEEE members, includes subscription to a technical periodical in the field published by IEEE. All administrative support is provided by IEEE.

Mid-Continent Oil and Gas Ass'n (1917)
711 Adams Office Bldg., Tulsa OK 74103
President: Wayne Gibbens
Members: 7-8000 individuals *Staff:* 6-10
Annual Budget: $500-1,000,000 *Tel:* (918) 582-5166
Hist. Note: Maintains a Washington government liaison office wherein the President sits but is headquartered in Tulsa. Sponsors the Mid-Continent-Oil and Gas Association Political Action Committee.
Annual Meetings: March

Mid-Continent Wildcatters Ass'n (1977)
Hist. Note: Formerly (1981) Small Producers for Energy Independence. Defunct in 1985.

Middle East Librarians' Ass'n (1972)
308 Main Library, Ohio State University,1858 Neil Avenue Mall, Columbus OH 43210
Secy.-Treas.: Dona Straley
Members: 125 individuals, 50 institutions *Staff:* 1
Annual Budget: under $10,000 *Tel:* (614) 422-3362
Hist. Note: Members are librarians and others who support the study or dissemination of information about the Middle East. Membership: $10/year.
Publication:
MELA Notes. 3/yr.
Annual Meetings: November, with the Middle East Studies Ass'n
1987-Baltimore, MD
1988-Toronto, Ontario

Middle East Studies Ass'n of North America (1966)
Dept. of Oriental Studies, University of Arizona, Tucson AZ 85721
Exec. Secretary: Prof. Michael Bonine
Members: 1600-1700 *Staff:* 2-5
Annual Budget: $50-100,000 *Tel:* (602) 621-5850
Hist. Note: Organized by a group of U. S. and Canadian scholars concerned with the study of the Middle East, from Morocco to Pakistan, Turkey to the Sudan. Membership: $50/yr.
Publications:
International Journal of Middle East Studies. q. adv.
MESA Bulletin. semi-a. adv.
Newsletter. 3/yr.
Annual Meetings: November or December
1987-Baltimore, MD
1988-Beverly Hills, CA

Military Chaplains Ass'n of the U.S. (1925)
Box 645, Riverdale MD 20737-0645
Exec. Director: William F. Emery
Members: 1,875 *Staff:* 2
Annual Budget: $50-100,000 *Tel:* (301) 699-3505
Hist. Note: A professional association of military chaplains, including reserve and retired, of all religious faiths. Members include chaplains of the Veterans Administration and Civil Air Patrol as well as the Armed Forces. Membership: $25/yr.
Publication:
Military Chaplain. bi-m.
Annual Meetings: Spring/300
1987-Newport, RI(The Viking)/April 28-May 1
1988-Colorado Springs, CO

Military Educators and Counselors Ass'n (1984)
5999 Stevenson Ave., Alexandria VA 22304
Exec. Director: Dr. Patrick J. McDonough
Members: 700
Tel: (703) 823-9800
Hist. Note: An organizational affiliate of the American Ass'n for Counseling and Development. Membership: $12/year.
Publication:
MECA Newsletter.
Annual Meetings: With the American Ass'n for Counseling and Development

Military Operations Research Soc. (1966)
101 South Whiting St., Room 202, Alexandria VA 22304
Exec. Director: Richard I. Wiles
Members: 7,000 *Staff:* 2-5
Annual Budget: $100-250,000 *Tel:* (703) 751-7290
Hist. Note: A professional society incorporated in the State of Virginia for the purpose of enhancing the quality and effectiveness of military operations research. Conducts a classified symposium annually and workshops as needed. Has no dues structure or general membership in the usual sense.
Publication:
Phalanx. q.
Annual Meetings: Spring
1987-Montgomery, AL(Air War College)/May/800

Military Reform Institute (1986)
1255 Twenty-Third St., N.W., #850, Washington DC 20037
President: William Lind
Members: 6 *Staff:* 2-5
Tel: (202) 452-8100
Hist. Note: MRI is a national organization of supporters of the military reform initiative; its purpose is to propose changes in the strategy, structure, and operation of the U.S. defense forces to promote deterrence, improve military effectiveness and to obtain full value for defense expenditures.

Milk Industry Foundation (1908)
888 16th St., N.W., Washington DC 20006
President: John F. Speer, Jr.
Members: 225 *Staff:* 26
Annual Budget: $1-2,000,000 *Tel:* (202) 296-4250
Hist. Note: Members are processors and distributors of milk and milk by-products. Shares offices, staff and, to some extent, membership with the International Association of Ice Cream Manufacturers. Membership fee based on volume.
Publications:
Milk Facts. a.
Up-to-Date. m.
Annual Meetings: Fall
1987-Chicago, IL(Chicago Marriott)/Sept. 25-30
1988-Orlando, FL(Marriott Resort)/Oct. 16-19
1989-Anaheim, CA(Marriott)/Oct. 1-4

00179 12 05 86 1233

Milking Machine Manufacturers Council
Hist. Note: Affiliate of the Farm and Industrial Equipment Institute.

Mill Mutual Fire Prevention Bureau
Hist. Note: Dissolved in Dec., 1985.

Millers' Nat'l Federation (1902)
600 Maryland Ave., S.W., Suite 305W, Washington DC 20024
President: Roy M. Henwood
Members: 50 *Staff:* 6-10
Annual Budget: $500-1,000,000 *Tel:* (202) 484-2200
Hist. Note: Represents mills grinding 80% of U.S. wheat, rye and durum flour. Absorbed (April, 1976) the Nat'l Soft Wheat Ass'n. Membership fee based on hundredweights of production.
Publications:
Newsletter. w.
Directory. bi-a.
Annual Meetings: Spring/200
1987-Naples, FL(Ritz Carlton)/May 10-12
1988-Laguna Niguel, CA(Ritz Carlton)/May 1-4
1989-Washington, DC
1990-Colorado Springs, CO(Broadmoor)/May 6-9
1991-Sea Island, GA(The Cloister)/April 21-24

Millinery Institute of America (1955)
99 University Place, New York NY 10003
Exec. Director: Burt Champion
Members: 100 *Staff:* 2-5
Annual Budget: $50-100,000 *Tel:* (203) 259-3632
Hist. Note: Members are hat manufacturers, retailers and suppliers united to promote the wearing of hats by every woman. Organization functions are strictly limited to work with the general press and stores.
Annual Meetings: Not held

Million Dollar Round Table (1927)
2340 River Rd., Des Plaines IL 60018
Exec. V. President: Roderick L. Geer, CLU
Members: 28,000 individuals *Staff:* 50-55
Annual Budget: $2-5,000,000 *Tel:* (312) 298-1120
Hist. Note: Life Insurance salesmen who have sold more than $2,000,000 of life insurance in a given year. Members must qualify annually and be members of the Nat'l Ass'n of Life Underwriters.
Publications:
Membership Directory. a.
Proceedings. a.
Round The Table. q.
Annual Meetings: June/July
1987-Chicago, IL/July 12-16
1988-Atlanta, GA/June 19-23
1989-Toronto, Ontario/June 18-22

Mine Inspectors' Institute of America (1912)
1900 Grant Bldg., Pittsburgh PA 15219
Secretary: John D. Woods
Members: 500
Annual Budget: under $10,000 *Tel:* (412) 281-2620
Hist. Note: Members are state, provincial and federal mine inspectors in the United States and Canada.
Annual Meetings: Spring
1987-Greensboro, NC/June 21-24

Mineral Insulation Manufacturers Ass'n (1933)
1420 King St., Suite 410, Alexandria VA 22314
Exec. V. President: Kenneth D. Mentzer
Members: 10 companies *Staff:* 2-5
Annual Budget: $250-500,000 *Tel:* (703) 684-0084
Hist. Note: Formerly the National Rock and Slag Wool Association, the National Mineral Wool Association and (until 1980) the National Mineral Wool Insulation Association, Inc.
Annual Meetings: Fall

Mineralogical Soc. of America (1919)
1625 I St., N.W., Suite 414, Washington DC 20006
Exec. Secretary: Barbara B. Minich
Members: 3,000-3,100 *Staff:* 2-5
Annual Budget: $250-500,000 *Tel:* (202) 775-4344
Hist. Note: Established at Harvard University on December 30, 1920; incorporated in the District of Columbia in 1937. A professional society of mineralogists, petrologists, crystallographers and others interested in the study of minerals. A member society of the American Geological Institute. Membership: $35/yr.
Publications:
American Mineralogist. bi-m.
Mineralogical Abstracts. q.
Reviews in Mineralogy. a.
The Lattice. q.
Annual Meetings: With Geological Soc. of America
1987-Phoenix, AZ/Oct. 26-29
1988-Denver, CO/Oct. 31-Nov. 3
1989-St. Louis, MO/Nov. 6-9
1990-San Diego, CA.Oct. 22-25

Miniatures Industry Ass'n of America (1979)
319 East 54th St., Elmwood Park NJ 07407
Exec. Director: Fred Polk
Members: 125 companies *Staff:* 2-5
Annual Budget: $100-250,000 *Tel:* (201) 794-1133
Hist. Note: Makers of one-inch-to-one-foot furniture and household effects.
Publication:
MIAA News. q.
Annual Meetings: August

Mining and Metallurgical Soc. of America (1908)
275 Madison Ave., New York NY 10016
Secretary: Mark Emerson
Members: 350 *Staff:* 2-5
Annual Budget: $10-25,000 *Tel:* (212) 684-4150
Hist. Note: Members are individuals concerned with the conservation of the nation's mineral resources and the well-being of the mining and metallurgical industries. Membership: $75/yr.
Publication:
Bulletin. irreg.
Annual Meetings: In conjuction with the American Institute of Mining, Metallurgical and Petroleum Engineers
1987-Denver, CO/Feb.

Mining and Reclamation Council of America (1977)
1575 Eye St., N.W., Room 525, Washington DC 20005
President: Daniel R. Gerkin
Members: 250 companies *Staff:* 12
Annual Budget: $1-2,000,000 *Tel:* (202) 789-0220
Hist. Note: Members are coal producing companies, industry suppliers and state or regional associations involved in coal mining. Created in response to the Surface Mining Control and Reclamation Act of 1977, MARC is involved in organizing a "grassroots" voice for the coal industry, particularly the small to medium sized operator. Sponsors and supports MARC-PAC, a political action committee, and MARC-EX, the exporters section of MARC intended to increase participation by smaller operators in exporting U.S. coal.
Publications:
Coal Now. bi-w.
Landmarc. bi-m. adv.
Semi-Annual Meetings: Spring and Fall

Missouri Fox Trotting Horse Breed Ass'n (1948)
Box 1027, Ava MO 65608
Secretary: Roy Brown
Members: 2,700 *Staff:* 2-5
Annual Budget: $50-100,000 *Tel:* (417) 683-2468
Hist. Note: Members are owners and breeders of Missouri Fox Trotting horses. Member of the Nat'l Soc. of Livestock Records Ass'ns. Membership: $10/yr.
Publications:
MFTHBA Journal. m.
Show and Celebration Book. a.
Annual Meetings: Always 4th Saturday in October

Mobile Air Conditioning Soc. (1981)
Box 267, Harleysville PA 19438
President: Simon A. Oulouhojian
Members: 235 companies *Staff:* 6-10
Annual Budget: $25-50,000 *Tel:* (215) 256-4246
Publications:
R-12. m.
AC Action.
ACJ.

Mobile Industrial Caterers' Ass'n Internat'l (1964)
7300 Artesia Blvd., Buena Park CA 90621
Exec. Director: Kelly Ramirez
Members: 100-125 companies *Staff:* 2-5
Annual Budget: $50-100,000 *Tel:* (714) 521-6000
Hist. Note: Members are companies using mobile equipment for industrial feeding.
Publications:
MICA Newsletter. m.
MICA Handbook and Roster. a.
Semi-annual Meetings: Spring and Fall, and Biennial Trade Show

Mobile Modular Office Ass'n (1983)
Box 986, Irmo SC 29063
Exec. Director: Toni S. Sylvester
Members: 150 companies *Staff:* 1
Annual Budget: $25-50,000 *Tel:* (803) 781-1638
Hist. Note: Member are makers and distributors of mobile office trailers. Membership: $300/yr.
Publications:
MMOA Newsletter. q.
National Directory of Manufacturers. a.
Annual Meetings: Winter
1987-Las Vegas, NV(MGM Grand)/Feb. 4-7/150

Model Railroad Industry Ass'n (1967)
Box 72, Cedarburg WI 53012
Exec. Secretary: Hugh Stephens
Members: 150-160 *Staff:* 1
Annual Budget: $25-50,000 *Tel:* (414) 377-3078
Hist. Note: Members are makers and importers of model railroad equipment as well as their suppliers. Affiliated with the Hobby Industry Ass'n of America.
Publications:
Reporter. bi-m.
Membership Roster. a.
Annual Meetings: October

Modeling Ass'n of America Internat'l (1958)
210 Central Park South, #14-C, New York NY 10019
Exec. Director: John W. Johnson
Members: 100 companies *Staff:* 1
Annual Budget: $10-25,000 *Tel:* (212) 753-1555
Hist. Note: Members are finishing, modeling and fashion arts schools and talent agencies.
Annual Meetings: April in New York, NY

Modern Greek Studies Ass'n (1968)
Box 1826, New Haven CT 06508
Exec. Director: John Iatrides
Members: 4-500 *Staff:* 1
Annual Budget: $25-50,000 *Tel:* (203) 397-4189
Hist. Note: Membership: $30.00
Publications:
Bulletin. semi-a.
Journal of Modern Greek Studies. semi-a.
Business meeting: annual
Scholarly conference: biennial

Modern Humanities Research Ass'n (1918)
Department of English, George Washington University, Washington DC 20052
American Secretary: John P. Reesing, Jr.
Members: 450-500 individuals *Staff:* 1
Annual Budget: under $10,000 *Tel:* (202) 676-6634
Hist. Note: American section of an international organization of modern language scholars with headquarters in London, England.
Publications:
Modern Language Review. q.
Slavonic and East European Review. q.
Annual Meetings: December, with the Modern Language Ass'n
1987-San Francisco, CA
1988-New Orleans, LA

Modern Language Ass'n of America (1883)
10 Astor Place, New York NY 10003
Exec. Director: Phyllis Franklin
Members: 29-30,000 *Staff:* 65-75
Annual Budget: $2-5,000,000 *Tel:* (212) 475-9500
Hist. Note: Founded at Columbia University, December 27-28, 1883 and incorporated in 1900 to elevate the study and teaching of modern languages to the status then held by the classics. Members are college-level teachers of modern languages. A member of the American Council of Learned Societies.
Publications:
MLA International Bibliography. a.
MLA Newsletter. q.
Publications of the Modern Language Association (PMLA). bi-m. adv.
Annual Meetings: December
1987-San Francisco, CA/Dec. 27-30
1988-New Orleans, LA/Dec. 27-30

Mohair Council of America (1966)
516 CNB Bldg., San Angelo TX 76902
Exec. Director: Robert M. Paschal
Members: 10,000-11,000 *Staff:* 2-5
Tel: (915) 655-3161
Hist. Note: Angora goat breeders.
Semi-annual meetings:

Monorail Manufacturers Ass'n (1933)
8720 Red Oak Blvd., Suite 201, Charlotte NC 28210-3957
Exec. Director: Albert L. Leffler
Members: 6 companies *Staff:* 2-5
Tel: (704) 522-8644
Hist. Note: A product section of the Material Handling Institute, Inc. Membership: $2500/yr.
Semi-annual Meetings: With Material Handling Institue

Montadale Sheep Breeders Ass'n
Hist. Note: No paid staff; address unknown in 1986.

Monument Builders of North America (1906)
1612 Central St., Evanston IL 60201
Exec. V. President: John E. Dianis, CAE
Members: 1,300 companies *Staff:* 6-10
Annual Budget: $500-1,000,000 *Tel:* (312) 869-2031
Hist. Note: Formed by a merger of the Monument Builders of America (formerly Memorial Craftsmen of America, founded in 1906) and the American Historic Monument Society. Members are makers, retailers, wholesalers and suppliers of cemetary markers and monuments.
Publication:
Monument Builder News. m. adv.
Annual Meetings: First week of February/1,200
1987-Vancouver, BC
1988-Nashville, TN
1989-Reno, NV

Moped Ass'n of America (1975)
130 East Main St., Malone NY 12953
Chairman: James Coughlin
Members: 3 companies; 2 associates
Tel: (518) 483-0106
Hist. Note: Membership consists of manufacturers, importers and distributors of small "motor-assisted" bicycles, or "mopeds." Formerly (1978) Motorized Bicycle Ass'n.
Annual Meetings: Feb. in New York, NY with the Internat'l Cycle Show

00180 12 05 86 1233

Mortgage Bankers Ass'n of America (1914)
1125 15th Street, N. W., Washington DC 20005
Exec. V. President: Warren Lasko
Members: 2,333 organizations *Staff:* 160-170
Annual Budget: over $5,000,000 *Tel:* (202) 861-6500
Hist. Note: Formed to promote growth and excellence in the mortgage banking correspondent system and the secondary market for mortgages. Encourages sound business practices that serve the needs of investors and borrowers. Informs members of changes in law, regulations, and pending legislation that affect the real estate and mortgage business. Members include mortgage banking firms, banks, insurance companies and savings and loan associations. Supports the Mortgage Bankers Political Action Committee. Has an annual budget of approximately $7 million.
Publications:
Mortgage Banking. m. adv.
Mortgage Banking Financial Statements and Operating Ratios. a.
Mortgage Banking Loans Closed and Servicing Volume. a.
National Delinquency Survey. a.
State and Local Report. 10/yr.
Washington Report. m.
Real Estate Finance Today. m. adv.
Membership Directory. a.
Annual Meetings: Fall
1987-Boston, MA(Sheraton Boston Hotel)/Oct. 11-14
1988-San Francisco, CA(Hilton)/Oct. 23-26
1989-Washington, DC(Hilton)/Oct. 22-25
1990-Los Angeles, CA(Westin Bonaventure)/Oct. 21-24

Mortgage Insurance Companies of America (1973)
1615 L St., N.W., Suite 1230, Washington DC 20036
Exec. V. President: Steven P. Doehler
Members: 14 companies *Staff:* 2-5
Annual Budget: $500-1,000,000 *Tel:* (202) 785-0767
Hist. Note: Supports the Mortgage Insurance Political Action Committee.
Publications:
Fact Book and Directory. a.
Washington Report. irreg.
Semi-Annual Meetings: Spring in Washington, DC and Fall

Motion Picture and Television Credit Ass'n (1956)
1653 Beverly Blvd., Los Angeles CA 90026
Administrator: Fabian Berke
Members: 103 companies *Staff:* 2-5
Annual Budget: $25-50,000 *Tel:* (213) 250-8278
Hist. Note: Established as the Motion Picture and Television Credit Managers Ass'n, it assumed its present name in 1966.
Publication:
Industry Credit Interchange.

Motion Picture Ass'n of America (1922)
1133 Ave. of the Americas, New York NY 10036
President: Jack J. Valenti
Members: 9 companies *Staff:* 100-125
Tel: (212) 840-6161
Hist. Note: Formerly (1945) Motion Picture Producers and Distributors of America. Membership includes the principal producers and distributors of films in the United States. Affiliated with the Motion Picture Export Ass'n of America. Maintains offices in Washington, DC and Los Angeles. Sponsors the Motion Picture Association Political Action Committee.

Motion Picture Export Ass'n of America (1945)
1133 Ave. of the Americas, New York NY 10036
Chairman: Jack J. Valenti
Members: 6-10 *Staff:* 100-125
Tel: (212) 840-6161
Hist. Note: A Webb-Pomerene Act Association affiliated with the Motion Picture Association of America.

Motor and Equipment Manufacturers Ass'n (1904)
300 Sylvan Ave., Englewood Cliffs NJ 07632-0638
President: William A. Raftery, CAE
Members: 7-800 companies *Staff:* 73
Annual Budget: $2-5,000,000 *Tel:* (201) 836-9500
Hist. Note: Serves manufacturers of automotive products used on, in or for the servicing of cars, trucks and buses; conducts market research. MEMA's TRANSNET Division provides coputerized electronic data interchange services. Maintains a Washington office. Annual membership fee based upon sales volume.
Publications:
Automotive Insight. q.
Credit and Sales Reference Directory. 3/yr.
Distributors Analysis. a.
Buyer's Guide. a.
Market Research Studies.
Annual Meetings: Feb./March/April
1987-Atlanta, GA/March 9
1988-Las Vegas, NV/March 1
1989-Chicago, IL/Feb. 27
1990-Las Vegas, NV/April 3
1991-Chicago, IL/Feb. 25

Motor Carrier Lawyers Ass'n (1937)
Hist. Note: Became the Transportation Lawyers Ass'n in 1983.

Motor Vehicle Manufacturers Ass'n of the United States (1913)
300 New Center Bldg., Detroit MI 48202
President: Thomas H. Hanna
Members: 11 companies *Staff:* 108
Annual Budget: over $5,000,000 *Tel:* (313) 872-4311
Hist. Note: Founded as the Automobile Manufacturers Ass'n, it assumed its present name in 1972. Maintains a Washington office and eight regional offices. Has an annual budget of over $10,000,000.
Publications:
Motor Vehicle Facts & Figures. a.
World Motor Vehicle Data. a.
Annual Meetings: June

Motorcycle Industry Council (1914)
3151 Airway Ave. Bldg. P-1, Costa Mesa CA 92626
President: Alan R. Isley
Members: 110-120 *Staff:* 8-12
Annual Budget: $1-2,000,000 *Tel:* (714) 241-9251
Hist. Note: Formerly (1970) Motorcycle, Scooter and Allied Trades Ass'n. Represents motorcycle manufacturers, and members of allied trades.
Publication:
Motorcycle Statistical Annual. a.
Annual Meetings: Established by Board of Directors annually during Feb.-April period.

Motorcycle Safety Foundation (1973)
3151 Airway Ave., Building K-200, Costa Mesa CA 92626
President: Alan Isley
Members: 5 companies *Staff:* 30
Annual Budget: $1-2,000,000 *Tel:* (714) 241-9922
Hist. Note: Founded by the five leading manufacturers and distributors of motorcycles for the purpose of public motorcycle safety education, licensing improvement, public information and research.
Publication:
Safe Cycling. q.
Annual Meetings: Not held

Movers' and Warehousemen's Ass'n of America (1935)
1001 North Highland St., Suite 100, Arlington VA 22201
Exec. Director: Edward P. Bocko
Members: 550-600 companies *Staff:* 2-5
Annual Budget: $50-100,000 *Tel:* (703) 525-4311
Hist. Note: Formerly Independent Mover's and Warehousemen's Ass'n; became the Movers' & Warehousemen's Ass'n of America, Inc. in 1954. Members are interstate carriers of household goods. A rate bureau, sanctioned by the I.C.C. and exempt from anti-trust regulation, which publishes rate schedules for member carriers.
Publication:
The Pick-Up. m.
Annual Meetings: Spring

MTM Ass'n for Standards in Research (1951)
Hist. Note: Abbreviation for Methods Time Measurement Ass'n for Standards in Research.

Mu Phi Epsilon (1903)
833 Laurel Ave., Highland Park IL 60035
Exec. Secy.-Treas.: Mrs. Mimi Angster Altman
Members: 45,000 *Staff:* 2-5
Annual Budget: $100-250,000 *Tel:* (312) 940-1222
Hist. Note: An international professional music fraternity founded November 13, 1903 at the Metropolitan College of Music, Cincinnati, Ohio. Membership is open to music majors or minors enrolled in schools where chapters exist. Concert artists, teachers, composers and other music leaders are also included. Membership: $10-$12/yr.
Publications:
Metronome-Opus. semi-a.
The Triangle. q.
Annual Meetings: August

Multi-Housing Laundry Ass'n (1959)
Box 2598, 1100 Raleigh Building, Raleigh NC 27602
Exec. Director: Michael Olson
Members: 250-275 companies *Staff:* 2-5
Annual Budget: $100-250,000 *Tel:* (919) 821-1435
Hist. Note: Formerly (until 1982) Nat'l Ass'n of Coin Laundry Equipment Operators.
Publication:
MLA News. m
Annual Meetings: June
1987-Colorado Springs, CO(Broadmoor)/June 17-21

Municipal Finance Officers Ass'n of the United States and Canada (1906)
Hist. Note: Changed name to Government Finance Officers Ass'n in 1984.

Municipal Treasurers Ass'n of the United States and Canada (1965)
3655 Hightide Drive, Rancho Palos Verdes CA 90274
Exec. Director: Beth Walker Durocher
Members: 1,500 individuals *Staff:* 2-5
Annual Budget: $100-250,000 *Tel:* (213) 377-0555
Hist. Note: Awards the Certified Municipal Finance Adminstrator credential (CMFA).
Publication:
Treasury Notes. bi-m. adv.
Annual Meetings: August/450
1987-Seattle, WA
1988-Austin, TX

Munitions Carriers Conference (1952)
7021 Tilden Lane, Rockville MD 20852
Mng. Director: William Burns
Members: 22 companies *Staff:* 2
Annual Budget: $25-50,000 *Tel:* (301) 984-1114
Hist. Note: Affiliate of American Trucking Ass'ns. Members are transporters of munitions and explosive materials.
Annual Meetings: With American Trucking Ass'ns
1987-last week in July

Museum Store Ass'n (1955)
61 South Pine St., Doylestown PA 18901
Exec. Director: Beverly Barsook
Members: 1,000 museums, 600 associates *Staff:* 3
Annual Budget: $100-250,000 *Tel:* (215) 348-7144
Hist. Note: Affiliated with the American Association of Museums.
Publications:
MUST. q.
Museum Store. q. adv.
Directory. a. adv.
Annual Meetings:
1987-Minneapolis, MN/May/1,500

Music and Entertainment Industry Educators Ass'n (1978)
Division of Music, Univ. of Texas at San Antonio, San Antonio TX 78285
Vice President: Michael Fink
Members: 150
Annual Budget: under $10,000 *Tel:* (512) 691-5319
Hist. Note: Established in Nashville, TN by the Nat'l Academy of Recording Arts and Sciences Institute as the Music Industry Educators Ass'n, it assumed its present name in April, 1986. Members are individuals and companies concerned with establishing educational standards for the creative production and management aspects of the music/recording industry. Has no paid staff or permanent headquarters. Membership: $25/yr. (individual); $150-250/yr. (company)
Publication:
MEIEA Notes. 3/yr.
Annual Meetings: Spring
1987-Atlanta, GA(Holiday Inn)/April 3-4
1988-New York, NY
1989-Los Angeles, CA

Music Critics Ass'n (1957)
6201 Tuckerman Lane, Rockville MD 20852
Exec. Director: Richard D. Freed
Members: 225-250 individuals *Staff:* 1
Annual Budget: $50-100,000 *Tel:* (301) 530-9527
Hist. Note: Members are music critics from the various communications media. Seeks to improve the calibre of music criticism and to promote an interest in music in the U.S. and Canada.
Publication:
Newsletter of The MCA. 3/yr.
Annual Meetings: Usually late summer in conjunction with some significant musical event.

Music Distributors Ass'n (1939)
135 West 29th St., New York NY 10001
Exec. V. President: Jerome Hershman
Members: 90 *Staff:* 1
Annual Budget: $25-50,000 *Tel:* (212) 564-0251
Hist. Note: Formerly (1977) the Nat'l Ass'n of Musical Merchandise Wholesalers. Membership: $350/yr. (supplier), $600/yr. (distributor).
Publications:
Newsletter. 6-10/yr.
Dealer Ad Planner Manual a.
Semi-annual meetings: In connection with the National Association of Music Merchants, January and June.
1987-Anaheim, CA(Marriott)/Jan. 7-13/75-100
1987-Puerto Vallarta, Mexico(Holiday Inn)
1988-Anaheim, CA/Jan. 6-12/75-100
1988-Maui, HI

Music Educators Nat'l Conference (1907)
1902 Association Drive, Reston VA 22091
Exec. Director: John J. Mahlmann
Members: 55,000 *Staff:* 30-35
Annual Budget: $2-5,000,000 *Tel:* (703) 860-4000
Hist. Note: Established as the Music Supervisors National Conference, it assumed its present name in 1934. A professional organization of music teachers, administrators and students. Affiliated with numerous other musical organizations.
Publications:
Journal of Research in Music Education. q.
Music Educators Journal. 9/yr. adv.
Biennial Meetings: Even years/6-8,000
1988-Indianapolis, IN(Hyatt Regency)

Music Industry Council (1923)
Hist. Note: Formerly Music Education Exhibitors Ass'n. The auxiliary of The Music Educators Nat'l Conference. Coordinates the Commercial Exhibits at National and Regional Music Educator Conferences. Address unknown since 1984.

Music Industry Manufacturers Ass'n (1981)
Hist. Note: Dissolved June 30, 1984.

Music Library Ass'n (1931)
Box 487, Canton MA 02021
Exec. Secretary: Linda Solow Blotner
Members: 1,750-1,800 *Staff:* 1
Annual Budget: $50-100,000 *Tel:* (617) 828-8450
Hist. Note: Affiliated with the Council of National Library Ass'ns.
Publications:
Music Cataloging Bulletin. m.
Notes. q. adv.

Music Publishers' Ass'n of the United States (1895)
130 West 54th St., Room 3-C, New York NY 10019
General Counsel: Howard Wattenberg
Members: 60 publishers *Staff:* 1
Annual Budget: $10-25,000 *Tel:* (212) 582-1122
Publication:
MPA Newsletter. q.

Music Teachers Nat'l Ass'n (1876)
2113 Carew Tower, Cincinnati OH 45202
Exec. Director: Robert J. Elias
Members: 22,500-23,500 *Staff:* 6
Annual Budget: $500-1,000,000 *Tel:* (513) 421-1420
Hist. Note: Founded by Theodore Presser in Delaware, Ohio December 26, 1876 with 62 charter members, MTNA is a professional society of music teachers in schools, studios, conservatories and colleges. Membership: $25/yr.
Publication:
American Music Teacher. bi-m. adv.
Annual Meetings: Spring
1987-New York, NY/Mar. 22-27
1988-Salt Lake City, UT/Mar. 20-25
1989-Wichita, KS/April 2-7

Music Video Ass'n
Hist. Note: Address unknown in 1986; probably defunct.

Musical Theatres Ass'n (1955)
Hist. Note: Defunct 1984.

Musicians Nat'l Hotline Ass'n (1980)
277 East 6100 South, Salt Lake City UT 84107
Exec. Director: Marvin C. Zitting
Members: 1,500 individuals *Staff:* 2-5
Annual Budget: $10-25,000 *Tel:* (801) 268-2000
Hist. Note: A non-profit association with a goal to increase the employment of musicians and related occupations. Membership is open to musicians, musical groups, schools, instructors, students, businesses that hire musicians, suppliers of music related products and services, and music related occupations. Regular membership: $20/yr.
Publication:
Hotline News. bi-m. adv.
Annual Meetings: January

Mutual Advertising Agency Network (1946)
8335 Jefferson Ave., Detroit MI 48214
Exec. Secretary: Clarence J. McLeod
Members: 30-40 companies *Staff:* 1
Annual Budget: $10-25,000 *Tel:* (313) 821-0120
Hist. Note: Formerly (founded as) Midwestern Advertising Agency Network in Chicago, Illinois.
Triannual Meetings:

Mutual Atomic Energy Liability Underwriters (1957)
Hist. Note: An insurance underwriting syndicate, not a trade or professional ass'n.

Mycological Soc. of America (1931)
Dept. of Botany, Louisiana State University, Baton Rouge LA 70803
Secretary: Meredith Blackwell
Members: 1,400-1,500 *Staff:* 1
Tel: (504) 388-8485
Hist. Note: Founded in New Orleans in 1931 as an outgrowth of the Microbiological Section of the Botanical Society of America and incorporated in 1966 in the District of Columbia. Individuals interested in the study of fungi. Affiliated with the American Association for the Advancement of Science and the American Institute of Biological Sciences. Membership: $35/yr. (individual), $60/yr. (organization).
Publications:
MSA Newsletter. semi-a.
Mycologia. bi-m.
Mycologia Memoirs. irreg.
Annual Meetings: With the American Institute of Biological Sciences.
1987-Ottawa, Canada(Carlton University)/June 22-25
1988-Davis, CA(University of California)/Aug. 14-18

Mystery Writers of America (1945)
236 West 27th St., New York NY 10001
Exec. Secretary: Mary A. Frisque
Members: 1,500 *Staff:* 1
Annual Budget: $25-50,000 *Tel:* (212) 255-7005
Hist. Note: Professional writers of crime and mystery stories and novels. Unpublished writers are affiliate members. Publishers and agents are associate members. Membership: $50/yr.
Publications:
Third Degree. m.
MWA Annual. a.

Annual Meetings: February and May in New York, NY

NAMRI/SME (1981)
One SME Drive, Box 930, Dearborn MI 48121
Exec. Director: Catherine A. Bender
Members: 150 *Staff:* 2-5
Annual Budget: $10-25,000 *Tel:* (313) 271-1500
Hist. Note: Founded and supported by the Society of Manufacturing Engineers. Members are individuals engaged in manufacturing research and technology development. Full name: North American Manufacturing Research Institution. Membership: $40/year, plus $15 initial fee.
Annual Meetings: Spring
1987-Bethlehem, PA(Lehigh University)/May 27-30/300

Narrow Fabrics Institute
Hist. Note: Merged with Industrial Fabrics Ass'n Internat'l in 1986.

Nat'l Abortion Federation (1977)
900 Pennsylvania Ave., S.E., Washington DC 20003
Exec. Director: Barbara Radford
Members: 311 institutions; 150 individuals *Staff:* 7
Annual Budget: $250-500,000 *Tel:* (202) 546-9060
Hist. Note: A national, non-profit professional organization serving both institutional and individual providers of abortion services. Membership: $25-250/year (individual).
Publication:
Update. q.
Annual Meetings: May/June
1987-Salt Lake City, UT

Nat'l Academic Advising Ass'n (1979)
c/o Aquinas College, 1607 Robinson Road, Grand Rapids MI 45906
V. President, Membership: Michael Keller
Members: 1,400 individuals *Staff:* 0
Annual Budget: $50-100,000 *Tel:* (616) 459-8281
Hist. Note: Membership open to professionals, faculty, and students working through academic advising to ensure the educational development of students in educational institutions. Membership: $30/yr. (professional); $15/yr. (student).
Publications:
NACADA Journal. bi-a. adv.
Newsletter. bi-a. adv.
Annual Meetings: October
1987-Chicago, IL(Conrad Hilton)/Oct. 11-14

Nat'l Academic Athletic Advisors' Ass'n (1976)
8090 Engineer Road, San Diego CA 92111
President: Lee McElroy
Members: 250 *Staff:* 1
Annual Budget: $10-25,000 *Tel:* (619) 560-4057
Hist. Note: An affiliate of the Nat'l Collegiate Athletic Ass'n, NAAAA serves professional advisors giving guidance to student activities at the college level. Membership: $40/yr.
Publications:
Athletic Advisor Newsletter. m.
Academic Outlook Journal.
Annual Meetings: January with Nat'l Collegiate Athletic Ass'n

Nat'l Academy of Arbitrators (1947)
Univ. of Michigan School of Business, Ann Arbor MI 48109
Secy.-Treas.: Dallas L. Jones
Members: 600 individuals *Staff:* 2-5
Annual Budget: $100-250,000 *Tel:* (313) 763-9714
Hist. Note: Founded in Chicago, September 14, 1947 to upgrade the professionalism of those engaged in the arbitration of labor-management disputes.
Publication:
The Chronicle. irreg.
Annual Meetings: Spring

Nat'l Academy of Code Administration
Hist. Note: Address unknown in 1986; probably defunct.

Nat'l Academy of Conciliators (1979)
5530 Wisconsin Ave., Suite 1130, Chevy Chase MD 20815
President: Lester B. Wolff
Members: 1,000 *Staff:* 15
Annual Budget: $1-2,000,000 *Tel:* (301) 654-6515
Hist. Note: Professionals who mediate and arbitrate disputes in the areas of construction, labor-management, consumer, human rights, family and environment as well as train third party neutrals.
Publications:
Newsletter. semi-a.
NAC Information Bulletin. m.

Nat'l Academy of Design (1825)
1083 Fifth Ave., New York NY 10028
Director: John H. Dobkin
Members: 350-400 professional artists *Staff:* 16-20
Annual Budget: $250-500,000 *Tel:* (212) 369-4880
Hist. Note: Founded in November 1825 as the New York Drawing Ass'n in order to furnish young artists with a place to study. In January 1826 it became the Nat'l Academy of the Arts of Design and incorporated in New York under its present title in 1828. Members are painters, sculptors, architects and print makers interested in promoting the arts. Supports a School of Fine Arts and holds exhibitions of paintings, sculpture and graphic arts.
Annual Meetings: Annual Exhibition

Nat'l Academy of Education (1965)
Grad. School of Education, Harvard Univ., Longfellow Hall, Cambridge MA 02138
Exec. Director: Gail Keeley
Members: 63 *Staff:* 2-5
Annual Budget: $500-1,000,000 *Tel:* (617) 495-9701
Hist. Note: Membership, constitutionally limited to 75 (plus members emeriti and foreign associates), is extended by invitation to individuals who have made a distinguished contribution to educational scholarship. Administers the Spencer Fellowship Program for research on the improvement of education in all its forms. Membership: $50/yr.
Publications:
Academy Notes. semi-a.
Academy Proceedings. a.
Semi-Annual meetings: Spring and Fall

Nat'l Academy of Engineering of the United States of America (1964)
2101 Constitution Ave., N.W., Washington DC 20418
President: Robert M. White
Members: 1,279 *Staff:* 35
Annual Budget: $1-2,000,000 *Tel:* (202) 334-3200
Hist. Note: A private organization established in 1964 to share in the responsibility given the National Academy of Sciences under its Congressional charter of 1863 to examine questions of science and technology at the request of the federal government; to sponsor engineering programs aimed at meeting national needs; to encourage engineering research and to recognize distinguished engineers. Membership is by peer election only. Membership: $100/yr.
Publication:
The Bridge. q.
Annual Meetings: October in Washington, DC
1987-Oct. 13-14/500

Nat'l Academy of Opticianry
10111 Martin Luther King, Jr. Hwy., #112, Bowie MD 20715
Exec. Director: Floyd H. Holmgrain, Jr., Ed.D.
Members: 3,600 individuals *Staff:* 4
Annual Budget: $250-500,000 *Tel:* (301) 577-4828
Hist. Note: An association of individual opticians who are state licensed or nationally certified, NAO's purpose is to promote continuing education through home study courses and seminars. Membership: $47.50/yr.
Publication:
ARCHIVES (newsletter within The Dispensing Optician magazine). m.
Annual Meetings: June
1987-Reno, NV/June 25-28

Nat'l Academy of Public Administration
Hist. Note: Part of the American Society for Public Administration.

Nat'l Academy of Recording Arts and Sciences (1957)
303 North Glenoaks Blvd., Suite 140, Burbank CA 91502
Nat'l Exec. Director: Christine M. Farnon
Members: 6,000 *Staff:* 16
Tel: (213) 849-1313
Hist. Note: Singers, musicians, engineers, composers, arrangers and others engaged in producing commercial recordings. Presents the annual "Grammy" awards for outstanding recordings.
Publication:
Grammy Pulse. q.
Annual Meetings: Spring

Nat'l Academy of Sciences (1863)
2101 Constitution Ave., N.W., Washington DC 20418
President: Frank Press
Members: 1,300-1,400 *Staff:* 900-1,000
Annual Budget: over $5,000,000 *Tel:* (202) 334-2000
Hist. Note: Private honorary organization of scholars in scientific and engineering research, chartered by act of Congress March 3, 1863 to serve as an advisor to the federal government on questions of science and technology. Conducts studies in all disciplines of natural and social sciences and engineering, with special emphasis on science advisory role in public policy issues.
Publications:
Proceedings. m.
News Report. m.
Annual Meetings: April in Washington, D.C.

Nat'l Academy of Television Arts and Sciences (1947)
110 West 57th St., Suite 301, New York NY 10019
President: John Cannon
Members: 14,000 *Staff:* 6-10
Annual Budget: $500-1,000,000 *Tel:* (212) 586-8424
Hist. Note: Maintains an archival program library on the campus of UCLA. Members are writers, engineers, editors, musicians and others engaged in the creative aspects of the television industry. Presents the annual "Emmy" awards for excellence.
Publications:
Emmy Awards Directory. a.
Television Quarterly. q. adv.
Semi-annual Meetings: June and November.

00182 12 05 86 1233

Nat'l Account Marketing Ass'n (1964)
50 East 41st St., New York NY 10017
Exec. Director: Ernest C. Biglow, Jr.
Members: 325 individuals *Staff:* 2-5
Annual Budget: $100-250,000 *Tel:* (212) 685-6712
Hist. Note: Members are company executives concerned with sales or marketing to major national accounts and the special treatment they sometimes require. Incorporated in the State of New York. Membership: $375/yr.
Publication:
NAMA News. q.
Annual Meetings: Spring
1987-Point Clear, AL(Marriott Grand Hotel/May 3-6/225
1988-Hilton Head, SC(Marriott)/May 1-4

Nat'l Accounting and Finance Council (1954)
2200 Mill Road, Alexandria VA 22314
Exec. Director: Samuel H. Gill
Members: 1,300 *Staff:* 7
Annual Budget: $500-1,000,000 *Tel:* (703) 838-1915
Hist. Note: NAFC is a member organization of chief financial officers within the American Trucking Ass'n.
Publication:
Motor Freight Controller. 10/Yr.
Annual Meetings: June/500
1987-Atlantic City, NJ/June 21-24
1988-San Francisco, CA(St. Francis)/June 26-29
1989-Dallas, TX(Loew's Anatole)
1990-Montreal
1991-Seattle, WA

Nat'l Advertising Agency Network (1932)
14 East 48th St., 5th Floor, New York NY 10017
President: Robert M. Purcell
Members: 50 advertising companies *Staff:* 2-5
Annual Budget: $250-500,000 *Tel:* (212) 355-7230
Hist. Note: A cooperative network of independent, non-competitive advertising agencies organized to provide branch office services for their clients. Formerly (1937) Allied Service Agencies.
Publications:
NAAN Staff Report. m.
NAAN Headquarters Report. m.
Semi-annual meetings: Spring and Fall

Nat'l Aeronautic Ass'n (1905)
1400 I St., N.W., Suite 550, Washington DC 20005
President: Maj.Gen. Clifton F. Von Kann, USA(Ret.)
Members: 2,500-3,000 *Staff:* 6-10
Annual Budget: $250-500,000 *Tel:* (202) 898-1313
Hist. Note: In addition to members at large, NAA's membership includes aerospace corporations, aero clubs, affiliates and the major national sporting aviation organizations including the Academy of Model Aeronautics, the Experimental Aircraft Ass'n, the United States Parachute Ass'n, the Internat'l Aerobatic Club, the Soaring Soc. of America, the Balloon Federation of America, the Helicopter Club of America and the United States Hang Gliding Ass'n. Absorbed the Aero Club of America in 1922. Membership: $7.50/yr. (individual); $500-10,000/yr. (organization).
Publications:
NAA Newsletter. m.
Year in Review. a.
Annual Meetings: October

Nat'l Aerosol Ass'n (1986)
5100 Forbes Blvd., Lanham MD 20706
Exec. Director: George Brown
Members: 25 companies *Staff:* 2
Annual Budget: $50-100,000 *Tel:* (301) 459-5927
Hist. Note: Membership is open to individuals, firms, and agencies engaged in business related to the development, manufacture, packaging, sale or distribution of aerosol products.
Annual Meetings: Winter
1987-Naples, FL(Ritz-Carlton)/Jan. 21-23

Nat'l Aesthetician and Nail Artist Ass'n (1981)
457 Busse Road, Elk Grove Village IL 60007
Exec. Director: John J. Savas
Members: 2,000-3,000 *Staff:* 2-5
Annual Budget: $25-50,000 *Tel:* (312) 956-1040
Hist. Note: Members are manicurists, pedicurists and aestheticians as well as manufacturers and suppliers. Formerly (1984) the Nat'l Ass'n of Nail Artists.
Publication:
NANA Magazine. q. adv.

Nat'l Agri Marketing Ass'n (1956)
9500 Nall Ave., Shawnee Mission KS 66207
Exec. Director: Rex Parsons
Members: 2,500 *Staff:* 2-5
Annual Budget: $500-1,000,000 *Tel:* (913) 341-5445
Hist. Note: Originated as the Chicago Area Agricultural Advertising Association with 39 charter members. In 1963 the name was changed to the National Agricultural Advertising and Marketing Association and the present name was assumed in 1973. Membership: $85/year.
Publications:
National NAMA Directory. a. adv.
Newsletter. m.
Annual Meetings: Spring/1,500
1987-St. Louis, MO(Adams Mark)/April 26-29
1988-Reno, NV(MGM Grand)/April 17-20

Nat'l Agricultural Aviation Ass'n (1967)
115 D St., S.E., Suite 103, Washington DC 20003
Exec. Director: Harold Collins
Members: 1,300 crop sprayers and allied companies *Staff:* 3
Annual Budget: $500-1,000,000 *Tel:* (202) 546-5722
Hist. Note: Formerly (1971) Nat'l Aerial Applicators Ass'n.
Publication:
Agricultural Aviation. m. adv.
Annual Meetings: December
1987-Mobile, AL/Nov. 30-Dec. 3

Nat'l Agricultural Chemicals Ass'n (1933)
Madison Bldg., 1155 15th St., N.W., Suite 900, Washington DC 20005
President: Dr. Jack D. Early
Members: 100 companies *Staff:* 25
Annual Budget: $2-5,000,000 *Tel:* (202) 296-1585
Hist. Note: Established as the Agricultural Insecticides and Fungicides Manufacturers' Association, it became the Agricultural Insecticide and Fungicide Association in 1933 and assumed its present name in 1949. Members are companies producing chemical controls for fungi, rodents, pests and weeds.
Annual Meetings: White Sulphur Springs, WV in the Fall

Nat'l Agricultural Marketing Officials (1920)
1100 Bank St., Room 805, Richmond VA 23219
Secy.-Treas.: Thomas R. Yates
Members: 50-55 *Staff:* 1
Annual Budget: under $10,000 *Tel:* (804) 786-3530
Hist. Note: Formerly (1977) Nat'l Ass'n of Marketing Officials. Has no paid staff or permanent address. Officers, except Secretary-Treasurer, change annually. Members are state officials responsible for marketing programs for agricultural products. Membership: $150/yr. (individual).
Publications:
Directory and Report. a.
Newsletter. irreg.

Nat'l Agricultural Plastics Ass'n (1960)
P.O. Box 767, Manchester MO 63011
Exec. Secretary: H. Carl Hoefer, Jr.
Members: 400 individuals and companies *Staff:* 1
Annual Budget: $25-50,000 *Tel:* (314) 394-9292
Hist. Note: Provides a forum for the investigation and discussion of the applications of plastics in agricultural production and marketing systems. Membership: $25/yr. (individual); $100/yr. (individual-commercial); $350/yr. (company)
Publications:
Agri-Plastics News. 6/yr.
Conference Proceedings. every 14-20 mos.
Annual Meetings: Every 14-20 months
1987-Portland, OR/Aug. 20-25/300
1988-Florida

Nat'l Agricultural Transportation League (1954)
215 N. Second Street, Suite A, Leesburg FL 32748
Manager-Treasurer: James H. Tilly
Members: 5-6,000 truckers, truck brokers and truck stops
Staff: 2-5
Annual Budget: $50-100,000 *Tel:* (904) 326-2188
Hist. Note: Represents truckers and truck brokers in exempt hauling of fruits and vegetables. Members include truckers, truck brokers, trucking firms, associated fields (insurance agencies, parts suppliers, truck stops, fuel and oil suppliers, etc.). Membership: $35-$150/year.
Publications:
N.A.T.L. News. bi-m. adv.
Bulletin. m.
Semi-Annual Meetings: February and November

Nat'l Air Carrier Ass'n (1962)
1730 M St., N.W., Suite 710, Washington DC 20036
President and C.E.O.: Edward J. Driscoll
Members: 9 companies *Staff:* 7-8
Tel: (202) 833-8200
Hist. Note: Members are certificated scheduled and charter airlines and air freight forwarders.
Annual Meetings: January, usually in Washington

Nat'l Air Filtration Ass'n (1980)
Hist. Note: Address unknown in 1985.

Nat'l Air Tankers Ass'n (1970)
Hist. Note: Ceased operations in 1984.

Nat'l Air Transportation Ass'n (1940)
4226 King St., Alexandria VA 22302
President: Lawrence L. Burian
Members: 1,200 air carriers & airport service organizations
Staff: 11-15
Annual Budget: $1-2,000,000 *Tel:* (703) 845-9000
Hist. Note: Established December, 1940 as the Nat'l Air Training Ass'n and became the Nat'l Aviation Trades Ass'n in 1944. In 1968 the Ass'n of Commuter Airlines merged with the Nat'l Air Taxi Conference and changed its name to the Nat'l Air Transportation Conferences. In 1974 the Nat'l Aviation Trades Ass'n merged with NATC and assumed its present name in 1976. The Air Cargo and Mail Ass'n is a unit of NATA. The Air Taxi/Charter Ass'n is also a unit of NATA. Sponsors the Nat'l Air Transportation Ass'n Political Action Committee and the Nat'l Air Transportation Foundation.
Publications:
Air Tran News. m. adv.
Airport Business Review.
Annual Wage and Salary Handbook. a.
Annual Report. a.
Annual Meetings: March or April

Nat'l Alcoholic Beverage Control Ass'n (1938)
4216 King St., West, Alexandria VA 22302
Exec. V. President & Treasurer: Paul C. Dufek
Members: 18 state agencies *Staff:* 15-20
Annual Budget: $1-2,000,000 *Tel:* (703) 578-4200
Publication:
Contacts Membership Directory.
Annual Meetings: Spring

Nat'l Alliance for Hydroelectric Energy (1980)
Hist. Note: Superceded by the National Hydropower Association in 1983.

Nat'l Alliance of Black School Educators (1970)
2816 Georgia Ave., N.W., Washington DC 20001
Nat'l Office Manager: William J. Saunders
Members: 2,500-3,000 *Staff:* 2-5
Annual Budget: $100-250,000 *Tel:* (202) 483-1549
Hist. Note: Formerly (until 1973) the Nat'l Alliance of Black School Superintendents. Membership: $50/yr.
Publications:
NABSE News Briefs. q.
Newsletter. q.
Annual Meetings: Fall
1987-Detroit, MI(Westin)/Nov. 18-22
1988-New Orleans, LA/Nov. 16-20

Nat'l Alliance of Cardiovascular Technologists (1976)
5 W. Hargett St., Suite 1100, Raleigh NC 27602
Exec. Director: JoAnne Harvey-Roundy
Members: 1,400 *Staff:* 3
Annual Budget: $50-100,000 *Tel:* (919) 821-1435
Hist. Note: Members are technicians, technologists, supervisors, department directors and physicians who work in cardiology and peripheral vascular studies. Founded as the National Society of Cardiology Technologists and incorporated in Florida, it assumed its present name in 1980 when it merged with the American Association of Cardiographic Technologists and the Colorado and Michigan Cardiology Technologists Associations. Membership: $40/yr.
Publication:
NACT News. bi-m. adv.
Annual Meetings: Spring/200-300

Nat'l Alliance of Homebased Businesswomen (1980)
P.O. Box 306, Midland Park NJ 07432
Staff Administrator: Marie MacBride
Members: 1,400 *Staff:* 1
Annual Budget: $25-50,000 *Tel:* (201) 423-9131
Hist. Note: Founded by nine women in 1980; incorporated in New Jersey in 1981. Its purpose is to support the option of individuals to participate in free enterprise by means of a homebased business and to enjoy the same privileges and to fulfill the same obligations as other businesses. Membership: $30/yr.
Publications:
Alliance. bi-m. adv.
Membership Directory. bi-a.
Annual Meetings: October/100
1987-Boston, MA

Nat'l Alliance of Independent Crop Consultants (1978)
2180 Elder Road, Bishop GA 30621
Exec. V. President: Louise G. Henry, Ph.D.
Members: 150-175 *Staff:* 1
Annual Budget: $10-25,000 *Tel:* (404) 769-7860
Hist. Note: Founded in 1978, NAICC is an outgrowth of the Southern Alliance of Independent Crop Consultants. Membership: $100/yr. (individual), $200-500/yr. (company).
Publication:
Newsletter. 4/yr.
Annual Meetings: Third week in October

Nat'l Alliance of Postal and Federal Employees (1913)
1628 11th St., N.W., Washington DC 20001
President: Robert L. White
Members: 29-30,000 *Staff:* 20-25
Annual Budget: $2-5,000,000 *Tel:* (202) 939-6325
Hist. Note: Established as the Nat'l Alliance of Postal Employees in 1913 with the immediate purpose of preventing elimination of blacks from railway mail service; became the first industrial Union in the U.S. in 1923 when it opened its membership to any postal employee who desired to join; assumed its present name in 1965 when it expanded its membership eligibility requirements to include federal employees. Supports the Nat'l Alliance for Political Action.
Publications:
National Alliance. m. adv.
Newsletter. q.
Reporter. m.
Biennial meetings: Even years in Summer/1,500-2,000
1988-Jackson, MS/Aug.
1990-Mobile, AL/Aug.

00183 12 05 86 1233

Nat'l Aloe Science Council (1981)
940 E. 51st St., Austin TX 78751
Mng. Director: Pat Miller
Members: 40-50 *Staff:* 2-5
Annual Budget: $50-100,000 *Tel:* (512) 454-8626
Annual Meetings: June in the Dallas/Ft. Worth area.

Nat'l Ambucs (1922)
Box 5127, High Point NC 27262
Exec. Secretary: Paul E. Skoglund
Members: 6,500-7,000 individuals *Staff:* 6-10
Annual Budget: $250-500,000 *Tel:* (919) 869-2166
Hist. Note: Corporate title is Nat'l Ass'n of American Business Clubs. An organization of business and professional men joined together through local chapters to build better communities and to aid the functionally handicapped; primary assistance is in training of therapists in occupational, physical, music, and speech and hearing fields. Contribution: $42/yr.
Publications:
The AMBUC Leader. m.
The AMBUC Magazine. q. adv.
Annual Meetings: Summer
1987-Nashville, TN(Opryland)/July 1-4/1,000
1988-Kansas City, MO/June 29-July 2/800
1989-Grand Rapids, MI(Amway Grand Plaza)/June 28-July 1/750
1990-Lancaster, PA(Americana Host Farm Resort)/June 27-30

Nat'l American Indian Court Clerks Ass'n (1980)
1000 Connecticut Ave., N.W., Washington DC 20036
Secretary: E. Thomas Colosimo
Members: 257 individuals *Staff:* volunteer
Annual Budget: $10-25,000 *Tel:* (202) 296-0685
Hist. Note: A national professional association dedicated to improving the American Indian court system throughout the U.S. through research, professional advancement and continuing education.

Nat'l American Indian Court Judges Ass'n (1980)
Hist. Note: Became the Nat'l American Indian Court Clerks Ass'n in 1985.

Nat'l American Legion Press Ass'n (1923)
2975 Catalina Drive, Decatur GA 30032
Secy.-Treas.: George W. Hooten
Members: 1,800 *Staff:* 2-5
Annual Budget: under $10,000 *Tel:* (404) 284-2480
Hist. Note: Formerly (1973) American Legion Press Ass'n.
Publication:
NALPA News-Letter. bi-m.
Annual Meetings: With American Legion
1987-San Antonio, TX

Nat'l-American Wholesale Grocers' Ass'n (1906)
201 Park Washington Court, Falls Church VA 22046
President: John R. Block
Members: 300-325 *Staff:* 36
Annual Budget: $2-5,000,000 *Tel:* (703) 532-9400
Hist. Note: Absorbed the Institutional Food Distributors of America (founded in 1956) and United States Wholesale Grocers' Ass'n (founded in 1892) in 1969; contains the Internat'l Foodservice Distributors Ass'n as a semiautonomous division. NAWGA provides educational, research and governmental services to wholesale grocers servicing independent retail grocers and foodservice distributors.
Publications:
NAWGA Review. m.
Foodservice Report. m.
Capitol Report. m.
Annual Meetings: March in Chicago, IL at the Hyatt Regency

Nat'l Animal Damage Control Ass'n (1979)
3919 Alta Monte, N.E., Albuquerque NM 87110
Secretary: William D. Fitzwater
Members: 450-500 *Staff:* 1
Annual Budget: under $10,000 *Tel:* (505) 883-9249
Hist. Note: Membership includes vertebrate pest controllers and government officials involved with wildlife management. Membership: $10/yr.(individual); $30/yr.(organization).
Publication:
The Probe. 10/yr.

Nat'l Antique and Art Dealers Ass'n of America (1954)
15 East 57th St., New York NY 10022
Secretary: Donald Sack
Members: 41 companies *Staff:* 1
Annual Budget: $10-25,000 *Tel:* (212) 517-5760
Hist. Note: A member of the Confederation Internationale des Negociants en Oeuvres d'Art. Formerly New York Antique and Art Dealers Ass'n, Inc.

Nat'l Apartment Ass'n (1939)
1111 14th St., N.W., #900, Washington DC 20005
Exec. V. President: Scott L. Slesinger
Members: 150-175 organizations *Staff:* 16-20
Annual Budget: $1-2,000,000 *Tel:* (202) 842-4050
Hist. Note: Established as Nat'l Apartment Owners Ass'n, it assumed its present name in 1967. A federation of local and state associations of owners, builders, investors and managers of rental property. Awards the CAM ("Certified Apartment Manager"), CAMT ("Certified Apartment Maintenance Technician") and CAPS ("Certified Apartment Property Supervisor") designations. Sponsors the Apartment Political Action Committee.
Publications:
Multi-Housing Advocate. m.
Units. q. adv.
Annual Meetings: Fall
1987-Washington, DC/2,500
1988-Dallas, TX/2,800

Nat'l Appliance Parts Suppliers Ass'n (1966)
600 S. Federal St., Suite 400, Chicago IL 60605
Managing Director: Durward Humes, CAE
Members: 150 companies *Staff:* 2-5
Annual Budget: $100-250,000 *Tel:* (312) 346-1600
Hist. Note: Provides distributors of home appliance parts (both replacement and OEM) with information and services. Sponsors industry trade show. Emphasis on supplier relations/activities to promote mutual understanding.
Publications:
NAPSA Results. bi-m.
YES Newsletter. bi-m.
Annual Meetings: Spring
1987-Orlando, FL(Hilton at Walt Disney World)/April 28-May 2

Nat'l Appliance Service Ass'n (1949)
1308 Pennylvania, Kansas City MO 64105
Exec. V. President: John S. McDermott, CAE
Members: 100-125 *Staff:* 1
Annual Budget: $50-100,000 *Tel:* (816) 221-1808
Hist. Note: Members are owners of portable small appliance repair centers.
Annual Meetings: Spring
1987-San Antonio, TX/May 31-June 4

Nat'l Aquaculture Industry Ass'n (1980)
Hist. Note: Promotes the development of aquaculture technology in the United States. Address unknown in 1983.

Nat'l Arborist Ass'n (1938)
174 Route 101, Bedford Station, Box 238, Bedford NH 03102
Exec. V. President: Robert Felix
Members: 450-500 tree service companies *Staff:* 5
Annual Budget: $250-500,000 *Tel:* (603) 472-2255
Publications:
NAA Reporter. m.
Treeworker. m.
Annual Meetings: February
1987-Marco Island, FL

Nat'l Armored Car Ass'n
Hist. Note: Address unknown in 1986; probably defunct.

Nat'l Art Education Ass'n (1947)
1916 Association Dr., Reston VA 22091
Exec. Director: Dr. Thomas A. Hatfield
Members: 9-10,000 teachers *Staff:* 11-15
Annual Budget: $500-1,000,000 *Tel:* (703) 860-8000
Hist. Note: Originally an auxiliary of the National Education Ass'n, NAEA became fully autonomous in 1947. Membership: $50/yr.
Publications:
Art Education. 6/yr. adv.
Studies in Art Education. q. adv.
NAEA News. bi-m. adv.
Annual Meetings: Spring
1987-Boston, MA
1988-Los Angeles, CA

Nat'l Art Materials Trade Ass'n (1950)
178 Lakeview Ave., Clifton NJ 07011
Exec. Director: Howard Wolfe
Members: 2,100-2,200 *Staff:* 6-10
Annual Budget: $1-2,000,000 *Tel:* (201) 546-6400
Publications:
Art Material Trade News. m.
News and Views. m.
Annual Meetings: May
1987-Atlanta, GA
1988-New York, NY
1989-San Francisco, CA
1990-Chicago, IL

Nat'l Artists Equity Ass'n (1947)
Box 28068, Washington DC 20038
Exec. Director: Olive Mosier
Members: 5,000 individuals *Staff:* 2-5
Annual Budget: $100-250,000 *Tel:* (202) 628-9633
Hist. Note: A society of professional artists working in the visual arts. Formerly (1984) the Artists Equity Ass'n. Membership: $40/yr.
Publication:
Artists Equity News. q.

Nat'l Ash Ass'n (1968)
Hist. Note: Became the American Coal Ash Ass'n in 1985.

Nat'l Asphalt Pavement Ass'n (1955)
6811 Kenilworth Ave., Riverdale MD 20737
President: John Gray
Members: 900-1,000 companies *Staff:* 16-20
Annual Budget: $1-2,000,000 *Tel:* (301) 779-4880
Hist. Note: Founded as the National Bituminous Concrete Association, it assumed its present name in 1965. Members are producers of asphaltic concrete for paving roads, airfields and other surfaces.
Publications:
Action News. w.
HMAT. q.
QIP Publications. irreg.
Focus. q.
Annual Meetings: Winter
1987-Las Vegas, NV(Caesar's Palace)
1988-San Francisco, CA(St. Francis)
1989-Los Angeles, CA(Century Plaza)
1990-Honolulu, HI(Sheraton)

Nat'l Assembly of Local Arts Agencies (1978)
1785 Massachusetts Ave., N.W., Suite 413, Washington DC 20036
Exec. Director: Robert Lynch
Members: 505 organizations *Staff:* 9
Annual Budget: $500-1,000,000 *Tel:* (202) 483-8670
Hist. Note: Formed as the Nat'l Assembly of Community Arts Agencies as a standing committee of the American Council for the Arts, NALAA became independent in 1978 and assumed its present name in 1983. Membership: $75/yr. (individual); $60/yr. mimimum (company).
Publications:
Connections Monthly. m.
Connections Quarterly. q.
Annual Meetings: June
1987-Portland, OR(Hilton)/June 21-24
1988-Washington, DC/June

Nat'l Assembly of Nat'l Voluntary Health and Social Welfare Organizations (1923)
1319 F St., N.W., Suite 601, Washington DC 20004
Exec. Director: Leonard W. Stern
Members: 29 organizations *Staff:* 3
Annual Budget: $100-250,000 *Tel:* (202) 347-2080
Hist. Note: Established as the National Social Work Council, it became the National Social Welfare Assembly in 1945, the National Assembly for Social Policy and Development in 1967 and assumed its present name in 1974. Association of 29 health and social welfare organization formed to facilitate communication and cooperation among member agencies, advancing their work and the mission of human service sector as a whole.
Publication:
Assemblyline. irreg.
Annual Meetings: Spring

Nat'l Assembly of State Arts Agencies (1974)
1010 Vermont Ave., N.W., Suite 920, Washington DC 20005
Exec. Director: Jonathan Katz
Members: 56 *Staff:* 6-10
Annual Budget: $500-1,000,000 *Tel:* (202) 347-6352
Hist. Note: Founded June 1968 as the North American Assembly of State and Provincial Arts Agencies and affiliated with the Associated Councils of the Arts. The organization became independent and assumed its present name in 1976. Members are state agencies receiving appropriations from their states and designated by federal legislation to receive funding from the National Endowment for the Arts.
Publication:
NASAA News. m.
Annual Meetings: October

Nat'l Assistance Management Ass'n (1978)
Box 57051, Washington DC 20037
President: Thomas L. Hadd
Members: 400 *Staff:* 1
Annual Budget: $10-25,000 *Tel:* (202) 223-1448
Hist. Note: Membership: $35/yr.
Publication:
Assistance Management. a.
Annual Meetings: Spring
1987-Washington, DC (George Washington University)/March 19-20/300

Nat'l Ass'n For Ambulatory Care (1981)
5151 Belt Line Rd., Suite 1017, Dallas TX 75240
President: John Rupke, M.D.
Members: 750 ambulatory care centers *Staff:* 3
Annual Budget: $100-250,000 *Tel:* (214) 788-2456
Hist. Note: Formerly (1981) Nat'l Ass'n of Centers for Urgent Treatment, (1984) Nat'l Ass'n of Freestanding Emergency Centers and (1985) Nat'l Ass'n of Freestanding Medical Centers. NAFAC represents the business, economic, and legislative interests of ambulatory care centers (ACC's) and provides services and information to individuals and corporations planning to open clinics and vendors to the industry. Membership: $300/yr. (organization).
Publications:
Ambulatory Care. m. adv.
Convention Program. a. adv.
Membership Directory. a. adv.
Accreditation Guidebook. a.
Annual Meetings: Early Summer

Nat'l Ass'n for Applied Arts and Sciences (1955)
Hist. Note: Inactive 1984-85.

Nat'l Ass'n for Armenian Studies and Research (1955)
175 Mt. Auburn St., Cambridge MA 02138
Exec. Secretary: Sandra L. Jurigian
Members: 1,000 *Staff:* 3-5
Annual Budget: $50-100,000 *Tel:* (617) 876-7630
Hist. Note: Founded in 1955 by a group of Greater Boston Armenian-Americans and Harvard University professors in order to foster Armenian studies in America through

00184 12 05 86 1233

institutions of higher education and through a multi-faceted program in support of research, scholarship and publications. Membership is open to all who are interested in furthering Armenian studies, culture and heritage. Regular membership: $35/yr.
Publications:
Books on Armenia and the Armenians. semi-a.
Journal of Armenian Studies. semi-a. adv.
NAASR Newsletter. q. adv.
Annual Meetings: Spring or Fall, in the greater Boston area.

Nat'l Ass'n for Bank Cost Analysis & Management Accountint (1980)
Box 27448, San Francisco CA 94127
Admin. Coordinator: Linda A. Feldman
Members: 625 individuals *Staff:* 1
Annual Budget: $25-50,000
Hist. Note: Membership open to individuals employed by any commercial bank, trust company, Federal Reserve bank, bank holding company or thrift institution located in the United States (including U.S.-based offices of foreign banks). Membership: $75/yr.
Publications:
NABCA News. q.
Journal for Bank Cost & Management Accounting.
Triannual Meetings:
1987-Houston, TX(Westin Galleria)/Feb. 11-13
1987-New York, NY(Marriott Center)/May 27-29
1987-Washington, DC(Marriott)/July 29-31

Nat'l Ass'n for Bilingual Education (1975)
1201 16th St., N.W., Room 407, Washington DC 20036
Secretary: Carolyn L. Riddick
Members: 2,133 *Staff:* 3
Annual Budget: $50-100,000 *Tel:* (202) 822-7870
Hist. Note: Professional association which represents the interests of Limited English Proficient (LEP) children, its members come from the education field - teachers, professors, researchers - and parents as well as community leaders who wish to promote the provision of bilingual education services to children. Incorporated in Texas. Membership: $35/yr. (individual); $50/yr. (organization/company)
Publications:
NABE Journal. 3/yr. adv.
NABE Newsletter. 5/yr. adv.
Annual Meetings: Spring/3-4,000
1987-Denver, CO(Conrad Hilton)/March 29-April 3
1988-Houston, TX/April 24-30

Nat'l Ass'n for Biomedical Research (1979)
818 Connecticut Ave., N.W., Suite 303, Washington DC 20006
Exec. Director: Frankie L. Trull
Members: 300 organizations *Staff:* 2-5
Annual Budget: $250-500,000 *Tel:* (202) 857-0540
Hist. Note: Members are institutions, professional societies and companies that use animals in biomedical research and testing. The association's purpose is to keep members informed of legislative and regulatory activity in the field. Founded as the Research Animal Alliance, it became the Ass'n for Biomedical Research in 1981. Absorbed the Nat'l Soc. for Medical Research and assumed its present name in 1985.
Publications:
NABR Update. irreg.
NABR Alert. irreg.
Annual Meetings: Fall

Nat'l Ass'n for Business Teacher Education (1927)
Hist. Note: A division of the Nat'l Business Education Ass'n

Nat'l Ass'n for Campus Activities (1960)
3700 Forest Drive, Suite 200, Box 6828 (Zip 29260), Columbia SC 29204
Exec. Director: G. Stephen Slagle
Members: 1,000 schools, 600 entertainment agencies *Staff:* 20
Annual Budget: $1-2,000,000 *Tel:* (803) 782-7121
Hist. Note: A non-profit organization of schools, colleges, entertainers and booking agents whose purpose is to assist in marketing entertainment services to educational institutions. Does no booking itself but attempts to make needed information available to both parties.
Publications:
Membership Directory. semi-a. adv.
Programming. m. adv.
Annual Meetings: February/2,500
1987-Nashville, TN(Opryland)
1988-Washington, DC(Sheraton Washington)
1989-Nashville, TN(Opryland)
1990-Chicago, IL(Hyatt Regency)
1991-Nashville, TN(Opryland)

Nat'l Ass'n for Check Safekeeping (1981)
1120 Connecticut Ave., N.W., Washington DC 20036
Asst. Director: William Miller
Members: 47 banks, 25 associated suppliers *Staff:* 1
Annual Budget: $50-100,000 *Tel:* (202) 663-5292
Hist. Note: Incorporated in the District of Columbia, NACS is an affiliate of the American Bankers Ass'n, from which it receives staff support. Its members advocate less legislative restrictions surrounding the return of all customers' cancelled checks.
Annual Meetings: Spring, with ABA National Operations and Automation Conference

Nat'l Ass'n for Child Care Management (1972)
1255 Twenty-Third St., N.W., Washington DC 20037
Exec Director: Carole M. Rogin
Members: 200 child care companies *Staff:* 2-5
Annual Budget: $100-250,000 *Tel:* (202) 659-5955
Hist. Note: Until 1981 known as the Nat'l Ass'n for Child Development and Education.
Publications:
NACCM News. m. adv.
Membership Directory. a.
Annual Meetings: Winter/200
1987-New Orleans, LA(Hotel Meridian)
1988-Houston, TX(Hotel Intercontintental)
1989-San Diego, CA(Hotel Intercontinental)

Nat'l Ass'n for Core Curriculum (1953)
404 R.I. White Hall, Kent State University, Kent OH 44242
Secy.-Treas.: Dr. Gordon F. Vars
Members: 300 *Staff:* 1
Annual Budget: under $10,000 *Tel:* (216) 672-2792
Hist. Note: An outgrowth of the National Conference of Core Teachers, first held in Morgantown, West Virginia on the campus of West Virginia Univ. on October 30-31, 1953, the present name was adopted in 1966. Membership: $10/yr.
Publication:
The Core Teacher. q.
Annual Meetings: Fall
1987-Washington, DC

Nat'l Ass'n for Creative Children and Adults (1974)
8080 Springvalley Dr., Cincinnati OH 45236
Chief Executive Officer: Ann Fabe Isaacs
Members: 600 individuals and schools *Staff:* 1
Annual Budget: $25-50,000 *Tel:* (513) 631-1777
Hist. Note: Sponsors in-service teacher training, conferences, programs, projects, school evaluation, and serves as a contact for the commissioning of art works and musical compositions. Members are teachers, school officials, counselors, executives and gifted children and adults. Membership: $50/yr. (individual), $100/yr. (organization/company).
Publications:
It's Happening. irreg.
The Creative Child and Adult. q.
Annual Meetings:
1987-Tarrytown, NY

Nat'l Ass'n for Drama Therapy (1979)
19 Edwards St., New Haven CT 06511
Corresponding Secretary: Dave Read
Members: 300 *Staff:* 1
Annual Budget: $10-25,000 *Tel:* (203) 624-2146
Hist. Note: Established and incorporated in New York. Members are professionals trained in theatre arts, psychology and psychotherapy making use of drama/theatre processes to achieve therapeutic goals. Awards the designation R.D.T. (Registered Drama Therapist) to individuals meeting professional standards. Membership: $40/year.
Publications:
Monographs on Drama Therapy. a.
Dramascape Newsletter.
Annual Meetings:
1987-New York, NY(New York University)/Nov.

Nat'l Ass'n for Environmental Education (1971)
Hist. Note: Became the North American Ass'n for Environmental Education (1985).

Nat'l Ass'n for Equal Opportunity in Higher Education (1969)
2243 Wisconsin Avenue, N.W., Washington DC 20007
President: Dr. Samuel L. Myers
Members: 114 Institutions *Staff:* 16-20
Annual Budget: $250-500,000 *Tel:* (202) 333-3855
Hist. Note: Members are black colleges and educational institutions united in an attempt to sensitize public policy makers and funders to the importance of enhancing the education of blacks.
Annual Meetings: Spring in Washington, DC/2,000

Nat'l Ass'n for Ethnic Studies (1975)
1861 Rosemount Ave., Claremont CA 91711
Editor: Charles Irby
Members: 200-250 individuals; 100 institutions *Staff:* 1
Annual Budget: $10-25,000 *Tel:* (714) 625-8070
Hist. Note: Promotes activities and scholarship in the field of ethnic studies. Formerly (1984) the Nat'l Ass'n of Interdisciplinary Ethnic Studies. Membership: $25/year.
Publications:
Explorations in Ethnic Studies. bi-a.
Explorations in Sights and Sounds. a.
Ethnic Reporter. bi-a.
Annual Meetings: Late Winter
1987-San Diego, CA(Grosvenor Inn)/Feb. 25-28

Nat'l Ass'n for Foreign Student Affairs (1948)
1860 19th St., N.W., Washington DC 20009
Exec. V. President: John F. Reichard
Members: 5,400 *Staff:* 35
Annual Budget: $1-2,000,000 *Tel:* (202) 462-4811
Hist. Note: Founded (1948) as Nat'l Ass'n of Foreign Students Advisors, became (1964) Nat'l Ass'n for Foreign Student Affairs. Members are admissions officers, English teachers, service group representatives, counselors and others interested in and responsible for the welfare of foreign students in the United States as well as U.S. students abroad. The Ass'n of Teachers of English as a Second Language is a section of the NAFSA. Membership: $67.50-470/yr. (institution, based on number of foreign students).
Publications:
NAFSA Directory. bien. adv.
NAFSA Newsletter. 8.yr. adv.
NAFSA Government Affairs Bulletin. 8/yr.
Annual Meetings: May
1987-Long Beach, CA(Hyatt)/May 27-31/2,000
1988-Washington, DC(Sheraton)/May 31-June 3
1989-Minneapolis, MN(Hyatt)/May 30-June 2
1990-Portland, OR(Portland Marriott)/May 15-18

Nat'l Ass'n for Health Care Recruitment (1975)
Box 93851, Cleveland OH 44101-5851
President: Karen Hart
Members: 600 *Staff:* 0
Annual Budget: $100-250,000 *Tel:* (216) 771-8010
Hist. Note: Formerly the Nat'l Ass'n of Nurse Recruiters. Assumed its present name in 1984. Has no paid staff. Membership: $50-$100/yr.
Publication:
NANR Newsletter. m. adv.
Annual Meetings: Summer
1987-Cincinnati, OH(Omni)/July 21

Nat'l Ass'n for Hearing and Speech Action (1919)
Hist. Note: Established as American Ass'n for the Hard of Hearing. Became (1922) American Federation of Organizations for the Hard of Hearing; (1935) American Soc. for the Hard of Hearing; (1945) American Hearing Soc., and Nat'l Ass'n for Hearing and Speech Action in 1966. Not a professional group.

Nat'l Ass'n for Home Care (1970)
519 C Street, N.E., Washington DC 20002
President: Val J. Halamandaris
Members: 5,000 agencies *Staff:* 40
Annual Budget: over $5,000,000 *Tel:* (202) 547-7424
Hist. Note: Members are concerned with the provision of health care and related services in the home. Formerly (1982) Nat'l Ass'n of Home Health Agencies. Merged with Home Health Services and Staffing Ass'n in 1986.
Publications:
Caring Magazine.
NAHC Report.
Homecare '86.

Nat'l Ass'n for Hospital Development (1967)
112-B East Broad St., Falls Church VA 22046
President: William C. McGinly, CAE
Members: 1,680 development directors and consultants *Staff:* 7
Annual Budget: $500-1,000,000 *Tel:* (703) 532-6243
Hist. Note: A professional association of hospital and health care executives involved in hospital development and fund-raising programs. Established as Developartners, the present name was adopted in 1968. Membership: $250/year.
Publications:
NAHD Journal. semi-a. adv.
NAHD News. 10/yr. adv.
Annual Meetings: Fall
1987-Boston, MA(Marriott)
1988-Dallas, TX
1989-Toronto, Ontario(Sheraton)

Nat'l Ass'n for Humanities Education (1967)
Dept. of Philosophy & Humanities, College of Liberal Arts, U. of MN, Duluth MN 55812
President: Fred E.H. Schroeder
Members: 500 *Staff:* 1
Annual Budget: under $10,000 *Tel:* (218) 726-8237
Hist. Note: Growing out of a series of programs sponsored by the New York State Department of Education, NAHE is a multidisciplinary professional educational organization. Membership: $12/year.
Publication:
Humanities Education. q.
Biennial meetings: Odd years
1987-St. Paul, MN(St. Paul Hotel)/April 10-12

Nat'l Ass'n for Individually Guided Education (1972)
c/o Elliot Elementary School, 225 South 25th St., Lincoln NE 68510
President: Robert L. Bussmann
Members: 1,200 *Staff:* 3
Annual Budget: $100-250,000 *Tel:* (402) 474-4349
Hist. Note: Promotes a teaching method that matches learning programs to individual student's needs; allows each student to progress at his or her own pace.
Publications:
The Forum. a.
Scope Newsletter. q.
Annual Meetings: November

Nat'l Ass'n for Industry-Education Cooperation (1949)
235 Hendricks Blvd., Buffalo NY 14226
President and C.E.O.: Dr. Donald M. Clark
Members: 900-1,000 organizations *Staff:* 2-5
Annual Budget: $250-500,000 *Tel:* (716) 834-7047
Hist. Note: Established as the Business-Industry Section of the National Science Teachers Association, it assumed its present name in 1964 and absorbed the Community Resources Workshop Association in 1972. Advocates improved coordination between industry and schools in school improvement and economic development. Membership: $25/yr. (individual), $100/yr. (institution), $250-1,000/yr. (corporate) based on net earnings.

00185 12 05 86 1233

Publications:
Journal of Industry-Education Cooperation. semi-a. adv.
NAIEC Newsletter. bi-m. adv.
Annual Meetings: Fall

Nat'l Ass'n for Law Placement (1971)
440 First St., N.W., Suite 302, Washington DC 20001
Administrator: Melanie R. Kersey
Members: 810 law schools and employers of lawyers *Staff:* 2-5
Annual Budget: $250-500,000 *Tel:* (202) 783-5171
Hist. Note: An incorporated not-for-profit organization of hiring partners, legal administrators, law school placement officers and deans. Members are American Bar Association-approved law schools and employers of lawyers. Membership: $325/yr.; $75/yr. (govt. agencies & public interest grps)
Publications:
NALP Notes. m.
Employment Report/Salary Survey. a.
Employer's Guide to Law Schools. a.
Directory of Legal Employers. a.
Judicial Clerkship Directory. a.
Annual Meetings: Spring
1987-New Orleans, LA(Westin Canal Place)/April 26-29

Nat'l Ass'n for Milk Marketing Reform (1974)
Hist. Note: Merged with the National Independent Dairies Association to form the National Independent Dairy-Foods Association in 1982.

Nat'l Ass'n for Music Therapy (1950)
505 11th St., S.E., Washington DC 20003
Exec. Director: Edward L. Norwood
Members: 3,100 individuals *Staff:* 4
Annual Budget: $100-250,000 *Tel:* (202) 543-6864
Hist. Note: Seeks to develop the therapeutic use of music in hospital and educational settings. Membership: $70/yr.
Publications:
Journal of Music Therapy. q.
Music Therapy Index.
NAMT Notes Newsletter. bi-m.
Membership Directory. a. adv.
Music Therapy Perspectives. a.
Annual Meetings: Fall
1987-San Francisco, CA(Hotel Meridian)/Nov. 20-24
1988-Atlanta, GA
1989-Kansas City, MO

Nat'l Ass'n for Physical Education in Higher Education (1978)
Box 1843, Bensalem PA 19020
Exec. Secretary: Marjorie Owen
Members: 1,000 individuals *Staff:* 1
Annual Budget: $25-50,000 *Tel:* (215) 787-1947
Hist. Note: The result of a merger between the National Association for Physical Education of College Women and the National College Physical Education Association for Men (founded in 1907). A professional society of physical education instructors at the college level. Has no paid staff.
Publications:
Quest Journal.
NAPEHE Newsletter. q.
NAPEHE Proceedings. bien.
Biennial meetings: even years

Nat'l Ass'n for Poetry Therapy (1981)
1029 Henhawk Road, Baldwin NY 11510
Secretary: Beverly Bussolati, O.T.R.
Members: 200
Annual Budget: under $10,000
Hist. Note: Provides an information network to all those interested in poetry therapy at professional, paraprofessional, patient, and agency-interface levels. Membership: $25/yr.
Publications:
NAPT Newsletter. q.
Journal.
Annual Meetings: Spring
1987-May

Nat'l Ass'n for Practical Nurse Education and Service (1941)
10801 Pear Tree Lane, Suite 151, St. Ann MO 63074
Exec. Director: Helen M. Larsen, LPN
Members: 30-35,000 *Staff:* 5
Annual Budget: $500-1,000,000 *Tel:* (314) 426-2662
Hist. Note: Membership: $31/yr.
Publication:
The Journal of Practical Nursing. m. adv.
Annual Meetings: Spring/1,500-2,000

Nat'l Ass'n for Professional Saleswomen (1980)
Box 255708, Sacramento CA 95865
Exec. Director: Dr. Barbara A. Pletcher
Members: 5,000 *Staff:* 7
Annual Budget: $100-250,000 *Tel:* (916) 484-1234
Hist. Note: A non-profit organization founded to offer training and education for women in professional sales and marketing careers. Membership composed of women selling industrial products, insurance, securities, etc.
Publication:
Successful Saleswoman. m. adv.
Annual Meetings: Fall

Nat'l Ass'n for Public Continuing and Adult Education (1952)
Hist. Note: Merged with the Adult Education Association in 1982 to become the American Association for Adult and Continuing Education.

Nat'l Ass'n for Regional Ballet (1956)
1123 Broadway, New York NY 10010
Exec. Director: Doris Hering
Members: 150 companies *Staff:* 4
Annual Budget: $250-500,000 *Tel:* (212) 645-0042
Hist. Note: Formerly (until 1964) known as the Nat'l Regional Ballet Ass'n. Dance companies affiliated with five regional associations in the U.S. Membership: $35/yr. (individual); $100/yr. (organization/company)
Publications:
Company Handbook. q.
Dance/America. q.
Director's Bulletin. q.
Pro-Wing Bulletin. q.
Gleanings. a.
Choreo/Network. irreg.
Semi-annual meetings: Spring & 2nd Friday of October in New York City
1987-Ft. Wayne, IN

Nat'l Ass'n for Research in Science Teaching (1928)
Univ. of Cincinnati, Coll. of Education,401 Teachers College, ML 2, Cincinnati OH 45221
Exec. Secretary: Dr. Glenn Markle
Members: 700-800 *Staff:* 3
Annual Budget: $25-50,000 *Tel:* (513) 475-2335
Hist. Note: A professional association of science educators. Affiliated with the National Science Teachers Association, the American Association for the Advancement of Science and the International Council of Science Associations for Education.
Publications:
Investigations in Science Education. a.
Journal of Research in Science Teaching. bi-m.
Newsletter. q.
Review of Research in Science Education. a.
Annual Meetings: Alternately with the National Science Teachers Association and the American Education Research Association

Nat'l Ass'n for Rural Mental Health (1976)
Nat'l Council of Community Mental Health,101 Montrose Rd., Suite 360, Rockville MD 20852
Administrative Officer: Virginia London
Members: 300 *Staff:* 1
Tel: (301) 984-6200
Hist. Note: Social workers, psychiatrists, psychologists and others who work in rural community mental health settings. A cooperating organization of the Nat'l Council of Community Mental Health Centers. Membership: $25/yr. (individual), $75/yr. (organization).
Publication:
Rural Community Mental Health Newsletter. 4/yr.
Annual Meetings: June/125

Nat'l Ass'n for Search and Rescue (1970)
Box 50178, Washington DC 20004
Exec. Director: Gregory J. McDonald
Members: 2,300 *Staff:* 1
Annual Budget: $100-250,000 *Tel:* (703) 352-1349
Hist. Note: Established as the Nat'l Ass'n of Search and Rescue Coordinators, it assumed its present name in 1975. Members belong to various emergency medical, fire or survival rescue services. Membership: $35/yr. (individual); $50/yr. (organization); $125/yr. (agency).
Publication:
Response! The Magazine for Search, Rescue and Recovery.
Annual Meetings:
1987-Orlando, FL(Sheraton Twin Towers)/May 13-17/1,000
1988-Salt Lake City, UT

Nat'l Ass'n for Sport and Physical Education (1974)
1900 Association Drive, Reston VA 22091
Exec. Director: Dr. Roswell D. Merrick
Members: 30,000 *Staff:* 4-5
Annual Budget: $100-250,000 *Tel:* (703) 476-3410
Hist. Note: An amalgamation of the Division of Men's Athletics and the Physical Education Division of the American Association for Health, Physical Education, Recreation and Dance. An independent member of the American Alliance for Health, Physical Education, Recreation and Dance. Membership: $42/year.
Publications:
The Athletic Director. bi-m.
Physical & Sport Education Review.
NASPE News. semi-a.
Update. m.
Annual Meetings: With AAHPERD.
1987-Kansas City/7,000-9,000

Nat'l Ass'n for State Information Systems (1969)
Box 11910, Iron Works Pike, Lexington KY 40578
Exec. Director: Carl W. Vorlander
Members: 50 states *Staff:* 2-5
Annual Budget: $100-250,000 *Tel:* (606) 252-2291
Hist. Note: A cooperating agency of the Council of State Governments, its membership consists of three representatives from each state. Main purpose is to assist the states in making the best use of their information systems resources.
Publications:
Information Systems Technology in State Government. a.
NASIS Newsletter. q.
Annual Meetings: Summer/200
1987-Sparks, NV/Aug.

Nat'l Ass'n for Stock Car Auto Racing (1947)
Box K, Daytona Beach FL 32015
President: William C. France
Members: 18,000 *Staff:* 35-40
Annual Budget: $1-2,000,000 *Tel:* (904) 253-0611
Publication:
NASCAR Newsletter. bi-m. adv.
Annual Meetings: Daytona Beach, FL/mid-February

Nat'l Ass'n for the Cottage Industry (1982)
Box 14460, Chicago IL 60614
Exec. Director: CoraLee Smith Kern
Members: 11,000 individuals *Staff:* 2-5
Annual Budget: $100-250,000 *Tel:* (312) 472-8116
Hist. Note: Members are owners of home-based businesses or individuals who work at flexible or remote work sites. Incorporated in the State of Illinois. Membership: $45/yr.
Publications:
Mind Your Own Business at Home. q.
The Cottage Connection. q.

Nat'l Ass'n for the Education of Young Children (1926)
1834 Connecticut Ave., N. W., Washington DC 20009
Exec. Director: Dr. Marilyn M. Smith
Members: 54,000 *Staff:* 30
Annual Budget: $2-5,000,000 *Tel:* (800) 424-2460
Hist. Note: Established as the National Association for Nursery Education, it assumed its present name in 1964. Members are administrators and teachers in schools for the very young.
Publication:
Young Children. 6/yr. adv.
Annual Meetings: Fall
1987-Chicago, IL/Nov. 12-15

Nat'l Ass'n for the Self-Employed (1981)
Box 612067 DFW, Dallas-Ft. Worth TX 75261
President: William K. Witcher
Members: 80,000-100,000 *Staff:* 7
Annual Budget: $2-5,000,000 *Tel:* (800) 433-8004
Hist. Note: Formed in 1981 by a group of independent businessmen in the Dallas/Fort Worth area. Members are small businesses of 5 or less employees. Membership: $42/yr.
Publication:
Small Business America. bi-m.

Nat'l Ass'n for the Speciality Food Trade (1951)
215 Park Ave. South, #1606, New York NY 10003
Exec. Director: Jeanne M. Maraz
Members: 1,500 companies *Staff:* 8
Annual Budget: $500-1,000,000 *Tel:* (212) 505-1770
Hist. Note: Members are manufacturers, importers, distributors, and retailers of specialty gourmet and fancy foods.
Publications:
NASFT Showcase Magazine. bi-m.
RD Trends. bi-m.
Semi-annual: Winter and Summer
1987-Anaheim, CA(Convention Center)/Feb. 15-17
1987-New York, NY(Javits Convention Center)/July 12-15

Nat'l Ass'n for Trade and Industrial Education (1974)
Box 1665, Leesburg VA 22075
Acting Exec. Officer: Dr. Ethel M. Smith
Members: 1,400 *Staff:* 1
Annual Budget: under $10,000 *Tel:* (703) 777-1740
Hist. Note: Membership includes instructors, state supervisors, teacher educators, representatives from labor organizations, and companies concerned with vocational education and training. Affiliated with the Vocational Industrial Clubs of America, Inc., American Vocational Association, et al.
Publication:
NATIE News Notes. q. adv.
Annual Meetings: With the American Vocational Association and the Vocational Industrial Clubs of America.

Nat'l Ass'n for Uniformed Services (1968)
5535 Hempstead Way, Springfield VA 22151
Exec. V. President: Maj.Gen. James C. Pennington, USA(Ret.)
Members: 40,000 *Staff:* 6-10
Annual Budget: $250-500,000 *Tel:* (703) 750-1342
Hist. Note: Promotes development and support of legislation to benefit all career service personnel. Sponsors the Nat'l Ass'n for Uniformed Services Political Action Committee (NAUS-PAC). Membership: $15/year.
Publications:
Legislative Guide. a.
Uniformed Services Journal. bi-m.
Annual Meetings: In Washington, DC area, last Wednesday in October/200-300.

Nat'l Ass'n for Veterinary Acupuncture (1973)
1905 Sunnycrest, Fullerton CA 92635
President: Dr. Richard S. Glassberg, D.V.M.
Members: 350 *Staff:* 1
Annual Budget: under $10,000 *Tel:* (714) 871-3000
Hist. Note: Veterinarians and others, mainly in the West, interested in the study and use of acupuncture in veterinary practice.

00186 12 05 86 1233

Nat'l Ass'n for Women Deans, Administrators, and Counselors (1916)
1325 18th Street, N.W., Suite 210, Washington DC 20036
Exec. Director: Dr. Patricia A. Rueckel
Members: 2,000 *Staff:* 2-5
Annual Budget: $100-250,000 *Tel:* (202) 659-9330
Hist. Note: Formerly (1956) Nat'l Ass'n of Deans of Women, and (1973) Nat'l Ass'n of Women Deans and Counselors. Membership: $55/yr.
Publication:
Journal. q. adv.
Annual Meetings: Spring
1987-Baltimore, MD
1988-Pittsburgh, PA

Nat'l Ass'n General Merchandise Representatives (1949)
111 East Wacker Dr., Suite 600, Chicago IL 60601
Exec. Director: Jack M. Springer
Members: 175-200 *Staff:* 2-5
Annual Budget: $500-1,000,000 *Tel:* (312) 644-6610
Hist. Note: Formerly (1976) Nat'l Ass'n of Drug Manufacturer's Representatives, and (until 1978) the Nat'l Ass'n of Diversified Manufacturers' Representatives.
Publications:
Representative. m.
Roster. semi-a.
Annual Meetings: Fall
1987-Palm Beach, FL(Breakers)
1988-Palm Springs, CA(Desert Springs)

Nat'l Ass'n of Academies of Science (1926)
Dep't. of Biology, Lafayette College, Easton PA 18042
Secretary: Shyamal K. Majumdar
Members: 45 academies *Staff:* 1
Annual Budget: $10-25,000 *Tel:* (215) 250-5464
Hist. Note: Before 1919 various academies were informally associated with the American Ass'n for the Advancement of Science (AAAS). In 1920 they were given the right of representation on the AAAS Council and became known as the Affiliated Academies. In 1926 they became a more organized group known as the Academy Conference, and in 1969 became known as the Ass'n of Academies of Science. Sponsored in part by the AAAS. Until 1979 known as the Ass'n of Academies of Science.
Publications:
Proceedings. a.
Directory. a.
Handbook. a.
Annual Meetings: With American Ass'n for the Advancement of Science
1987-Chicago, IL/Feb.

Nat'l Ass'n of Accountants (1919)
10 Paragon Drive, Montvale NJ 07645-1760
Exec. Director: Robert L. Shultis
Members: 96,000 *Staff:* 105
Annual Budget: over $5,000,000 *Tel:* (201) 573-9000
Hist. Note: A professional society of accountants established as the National Association of Cost Accountants. It assumed its present name in 1957. Has an annual budget of $12 million.
Publications:
Management Accounting. m. adv.
Controller's Quarterly.
Business Planning.
Annual Meetings: June
1987-San Diego, CA(Town & Country)

Nat'l Ass'n of Accredited Cosmetology Schools (1956)
5201 Leesburg Pike, Suite 205, Falls Church VA 22041
Exec. Director: Dr. James P. Murphy
Members: 900-1,000 *Staff:* 6
Annual Budget: $250-500,000 *Tel:* (703) 845-1333
Publications:
Cosmetology Instructor. 4-6/yr.
Membership Directory. a.
Educational and Legislative Newsletter.

Nat'l Ass'n of Activity Professionals (1981)
P.O. Box 274, Park Ridge IL 60068
Exec. Director: Marilyn Lamken
Members: 800 individuals *Staff:* 1
Annual Budget: $25-50,000 *Tel:* (312) 692-2564
Hist. Note: Active members are activity directors, coordinators, or consultants in long-term care facilities, senior retirement housing, senior centers, or adult day-care programs. Membership: $20-25/yr.
Publication:
NAAP News. bi-m. adv.
Annual Meetings: April
1987-Chicago, IL(Americana Congress)/April 23-25

Nat'l Ass'n of Administrators of Federal Education Programs (1975)
Hist. Note: Became the Nat'l Ass'n of Federal Education Program Administrators in 1985.

Nat'l Ass'n of Administrators of State and Federal Education Programs (1975)
Hist. Note: Became the Nat'l Ass'n of Administrators of Federal Education Programs in 1984. Which in turn became the Nat'l Ass'n of Federal Education Program Administrators in 1985.

Nat'l Ass'n of Advertising Publishers (1950)
111 East Wacker Drive, Suite 600, Chicago IL 60601
Exec. Director: Henry S. Givray
Members: 300 *Staff:* 2-5
Annual Budget: $250-500,000 *Tel:* (312) 644-6610
Hist. Note: Members are publishers of free-circulation community papers. Membership: $350 base plus $6/1000 circulation.
Publications:
NAAP Membership Directory. a.
NAAP Journal. semi-a. adv.
Ink Newsletter. adv.
Annual Meetings: June
1987-Las Vegas, NV(Tropicana)/June 2-5

Nat'l Ass'n of Advisors for the Health Professions (1974)
Box 5017, Station A, Champaign IL 61820-9017
Exec. Director: Julian M. Frankenberg
Members: 1,156 *Staff:* 4-6
Annual Budget: $100-250,000 *Tel:* (217) 344-6013
Hist. Note: Members are college faculty who counsel students on careers in the health professions. Membership dues: Varies according to region from $50-65/yr. (individual), $100/yr. (institution).
Publications:
The Advisor. q.
Directory. a.
Special Advisory. irreg.
Annual Meetings:
1987-Charleston, SC(Charleston Place)/July 8-11/400-500
1988-Washington, DC(Loew's L'Enfant Plaza)/April 21-24

Nat'l Ass'n of Aeronautical Examiners (1959)
Box 352, Delzura CA 92017
Nat'l President: James Pendleton
Members: 500 *Staff:* 1
Annual Budget: under $10,000
Hist. Note: Has no permanent staff or headquarters. Address changes with the President, who is elected every two years. Members are civilians employed by the Navy at Naval Air Re-Work Facilities.

Nat'l Ass'n of Aeronautical Production Controllers
Hist. Note: Independent Labor Union. Formerly (1973) Aeronautical Production Controlmen Ass'n Local chapters remain active. National chapter inactive since 1982.
Annual Meetings: Summer

Nat'l Ass'n of Agricultural Stabilization and Conservation Service County Office Employees
Hist. Note: See the National Association of ASCS County Office Employees.

Nat'l Ass'n of Agriculture Employees (1954)
P.O. Box 82369, Hapeville GA 30354
Exec. Chairwoman: Rebecca Lee
Members: 450 *Staff:* 10
Annual Budget: $25-50,000 *Tel:* (404) 763-7716
Hist. Note: NAEE is an independent federal labor union which represents employees working for the Dept. of Agriculture, Plant Protection and Quarantines. Members are professional employees with college degrees in Biological Sciences. Bargaining unit consists of Federal officers enforcing Federal agricultural quarantines relating to foreign and domestic programs. Formerly (1981) the Federal Plant Quarantine Inspectors Nat'l Ass'n. Membership: $135/yr.
Publication:
Newsletter. bi-m. adv.
Biennial Meetings: Even years in April

Nat'l Ass'n of Air Traffic Specialists (1960)
415 Wheaton Plaza North, Wheaton MD 20902
President: Bruce B. Henry
Members: 2,000 *Staff:* 2-5
Annual Budget: $250-500,000 *Tel:* (301) 946-0882
Hist. Note: Supports the NAATS Political Action Fund. An independent labor union.
Publication:
NAATS Bulletin. bi-m.
Biennial Meetings: Fall (1988)

Nat'l Ass'n of Alcoholism and Drug Abuse Counselors (1972)
3717 Columbia Pike, Suite 300, Arlington VA 22204
Exec. Director: Stephen H. Kreimer
Members: 7,000 individuals; 12 companies *Staff:* 7
Annual Budget: $250-500,000 *Tel:* (703) 920-4644
Hist. Note: NAADAC represents alcoholism and drug abuse counselors working in hospitals, treatment centers, private practice, councils and agencies on alcoholism and drug abuse, and employee assistance programs. Incorporated in Arlington, VA. Membership: $45/yr.
Publication:
The Counselor Magazine. bi-m. adv.
Annual Meetings: Summer
1987-New Orleans, LA(Fairmont)/June 17-20

Nat'l Ass'n of Aluminum Distributors (1951)
1900 Arch St., Philadelphia PA 19103
Exec. V. President: R. Bruce Wall
Members: 110 *Staff:* 2-5
Annual Budget: $250-500,000 *Tel:* (215) 564-3484
Annual Meetings: November/400
1987-Boca Raton(Hotel and Club)/Nov. 18-21
1988-Phoenix(Biltmore)/Nov. 13-16
1989-Boca Raton(Boca Raton Hotel)/Nov. 15-18

Nat'l Ass'n of American Business Clubs
Hist. Note: See Nat'l Ambucs.

Nat'l Ass'n of Animal Breeders (1947)
Box 1033, Columbia MO 65205
Exec. V. President: William M. Durfey
Members: 35 organizations *Staff:* 6-10
Annual Budget: $500-1,000,000 *Tel:* (314) 445-4406
Hist. Note: Formerly the National Association of Artificial Breeders, members are farmer coops and others interested in livestock improvement.
Publication:
Proceedings. a. adv.
Annual Meetings: Summer/500-700
1987-Columbus, OH/Aug.
1988-Tyson's Corner, VA/Aug.

Nat'l Ass'n of Architectural Metal Manufacturers (1937)
600 S. Federal St., #400, Chicago IL 60605
Exec. V. President: August L. Sisco
Members: 130-150 *Staff:* 2-5
Annual Budget: $100-250,000 *Tel:* (312) 922-6222
Hist. Note: Formerly the National Association of Ornamental Metal Manufacturers. Absorbed the National Steel Door and Frame Association in 1962.
Annual Meetings:
1987-Lake Tahoe, CA(Hyatt)
1988-Puerto Rico
1989-Palm Springs, CA
1990-Orlando, FL

Nat'l Ass'n of Area Agencies on Aging (1976)
600 Maryland Ave., S.W., Suite 208-W, Washington DC 20024
Exec. Director: Raymond C. Mastalish
Members: 675 area agencies on aging *Staff:* 14
Annual Budget: $500-1,000,000 *Tel:* (202) 484-7520
Hist. Note: Members include Area Agencies on Aging, Title VI Grantees, Service Provider Organizations, Network on Aging Advisory Council Members and others with a commitment to meeting the needs of older Americans. Its mission is to promote a national policy that would allow older Americans to remain independent in their communities and homes for as long as possible.
Publication:
Network News. bi-m. adv.
Annual Meetings: Summer
1987-Washington, DC(Marriott)/Aug. 8-13/800
1988-New Orleans, LA/700
1989-Washington, DC(Marriott)/800

Nat'l Ass'n of Artists' Organizations (1982)
930 F St., N.W., Suite 607, Washington DC 20004
Exec. Director: Charlotte B. Murphy
Members: 197 organizations; 43 individuals *Staff:* 3
Annual Budget: $50-100,000 *Tel:* (202) 737-8493
Hist. Note: A service organization for non-profit organizations dedicated to the creation and presentation of contemporary visual and performing arts in all media. Membership: $50-250/yr.(Based on budget size)
Publications:
NAAO Bulletin. bi-m.
Directory of Artists' Organizations. a. adv.
Annual Meetings: Every 18 months
1987-Los Angeles, CA/March/200

Nat'l Ass'n of ASCS County Office Employees
134 Ivy Ave., Chesterfield SC 29709
President: Willard Page
Members: 9,750 *Staff:* 2-5
Annual Budget: $100-250,000 *Tel:* (803) 623-7778
Hist. Note: An independent labor association. Members are county office employees of the U.S. Department of Agriculture's Agricultural Stabilization and Conservation Service. Membership: $20/yr. (individual).
Publication:
NASCOE Newsletter. bi-m.
Annual Meetings: August
1987-Norfolk, VA(Holiday Inn)/Aug. 5-9

Nat'l Ass'n of Attorneys General (1907)
444 North Capitol St., Suite 403, Washington DC 20001
Exec. Director/General Counsel: Christine Milliken
Members: 55 individuals *Staff:* 20
Annual Budget: $500-1,000,000 *Tel:* (202) 628-0435
Hist. Note: Attorneys General of the various states and territories. Issues six monthly newsletters that deal with legal developments in various fields at the state level, and occasional reports.
Publication:
Membership Directory. a.
Triannual Meetings: March & June in Washington, DC and December

Nat'l Ass'n of Auto Trim Shops (1953)
1623 Grand Ave., Baldwin NY 11510
Exec. Director: Nat W. Danas
Members: 8,800 *Staff:* 2-5

00187 12 05 86 1233

Annual Budget: $100-250,000 *Tel:* (516) 223-4334
Hist. Note: Members specialize in enhancing the appearance of cars and other vehicles by installation of new upholstery, convertible tops, etc.
Publication:
Auto Trim News. 11/yr. adv.
Annual Meetings:
1987-West Coast
1988-East Coast

Nat'l Ass'n of Band Instrument Manufacturers (1920)
c/o G. Leblanc Corp., 30th Ave. at 71st St., Kenosha WI 53141
Secy.-Treas.: Richard Hammond
Members: 15-20 companies *Staff:* 1
Annual Budget: $10-25,000 *Tel:* (414) 658-1644
Hist. Note: Membership fee varies by sales.
Annual Meetings: August

Nat'l Ass'n of Bank Servicers (1972)
5008 Pine Creek Drive, Suite B, Westerville OH 43081
Exec. Director: James R. Bannister
Members: 120 *Staff:* 2
Annual Budget: $100-250,000 *Tel:* (614) 895-1208
Hist. Note: Established as the Multi-Bank Data Processing Organization, it assumed its present name in 1975. Members are centers providing central computer services to banks and other financial institutions.
Semi-annual Meetings: Spring and Fall
1987-Tampa, FL(Harbour Island Hotel)/March 17-20
1987-Seattle, WA(Four Seasons Olympic Hotel)/Sept. 15-18
1988-Tucson, AZ/March 15-18 and Salt Lake City, UT/Sept. 13-16

Nat'l Ass'n of Bank Women (1921)
500 North Michigan Ave., Suite 1400, Chicago IL 60611
Exec. V. President: Phyllis M. Haeger
Members: 30,000 *Staff:* 20
Annual Budget: $2-5,000,000 *Tel:* (312) 661-1700
Hist. Note: Membership: $65/yr.
Publications:
Executive Financial Woman. bi-m.
Exchange Newsletter. bi-m.
Annual Meetings: Fall
1987-Nashville, TN (Opryland Hotel)/September
1988-Boston, MA(Marriott)/Sept. 24-27/1,000

Nat'l Ass'n of Bankruptcy Trustees (1981)
3008 Millwood Ave., Box 11187, Columbia SC 29211
Exec. Secretary: Carol H. Davis
Members: 900 individuals *Staff:* 9
Annual Budget: $25-50,000 *Tel:* (803) 252-5646
Hist. Note: Membership: $75/yr.
Publication:
NABTalk. q. adv.
Semi-annual Meetings:

Nat'l Ass'n of Baptist Professors of Religion (1927)
Mercer University, Macon GA 31207
Exec. Secretary: Watson Mills
Members: 600-650 *Staff:* 1
Annual Budget: under $10,000 *Tel:* (912) 744-2880
Hist. Note: Formerly (1983) the Ass'n of Baptist Professors of Religion. Membership: $15/yr. (individual).
Publications:
Perspectives in Religious Studies. q. adv.
Newsletter. irreg.
Bibliographic Series. irreg.
Monograph Series. irreg.
Dissertation Series. irreg.
Annual Meetings: in conjunction with AAR/SBL

Nat'l Ass'n of Bar Executives (1953)
750 North Lake Shore Drive, Chicago IL 60611
Staff Assistant: Callie R. Lacy
Members: 375-400 *Staff:* 2-5
Annual Budget: $25-50,000 *Tel:* (312) 988-5354
Hist. Note: Formerly (1962) Nat'l Conference of Bar Secretaries, and (1965) Nat'l Conference of Bar Executives.
Publication:
NABE Roster and By-laws. a.
Semi-annual meetings: With American Bar Ass'n

Nat'l Ass'n of Bar-Related Title Insurers (1965)
6390 Greenwich Drive, Suite 150, San Diego CA 92122
Exec. V. President: Douglas E. Miles
Members: 9 companies *Staff:* 2-5
Annual Budget: $25-50,000 *Tel:* (619) 453-8663
Hist. Note: Formerly (until 1979) known as the Nat'l Conference of Bar-Related Title Insurers. Members are title insurance companies "bar-related" as registered as a service mark with the U.S. Patent Office.
Publications:
Newsletter. bi-m.
Membership Directory. bien.
Annual Meetings: With the American Bar Ass'n

Nat'l Ass'n of Barber Styling Schools (1927)
304 South 11th St., Lincoln NE 68508
Secy.-Treas.: Alyce M. Howard
Members: 65-70 *Staff:* 1
Annual Budget: under $10,000 *Tel:* (402) 474-4244
Hist. Note: Formerly (1984) the Nat'l Ass'n of Barber Schools. Membership: $175/yr.
Publications:
NABS Newsletter. q.
Your Career in Professional Barber Styling.
Annual Meetings: May
1987-San Antonio, TX

Nat'l Ass'n of Basketball Coaches of the United States (1927)
Box 307, Branford CT 06405
Exec. Director: Joseph R. Vancisin
Members: 3,200 *Staff:* 2-5
Annual Budget: $100-250,000 *Tel:* (203) 488-1232
Publication:
The Basketball Bulletin. q.
Annual Meetings: March/2,000-2,400
1987-New Orleans, LA(Sheraton)/March 26-30
1988-Kansas City, MO/March 31-April 4
1989-Seattle, WA/March 30-April 3
1990-Denver, CO/March 29-April 2
1991-Indianapolis, IN/March 28-April 1
1992-Minneapolis, MN/March 26-30

Nat'l Ass'n of Basketball Referees (1977)
475 Park Ave. South, 17th Floor, New York NY 10016
Treasurer: Richard Bavetta
Members: 28 *Staff:* 1
Annual Budget: $10-25,000 *Tel:* (212) 725-1800
Hist. Note: A independent union of professional basketball referees. Conducts basketball camps.

Nat'l Ass'n of Bedding Manufacturers
Hist. Note: Became the Internat'l Sleep Products Ass'n in March, 1987.

Nat'l Ass'n of Beverage Importers-Wine-Spirits-Beer (1934)
1025 Vermont Ave., N.W., Suite 1205, Washington DC 20005
President: Robert J. Maxwell
Members: 115-120 companies *Staff:* 2-5
Annual Budget: $500-1,000,000 *Tel:* (202) 638-1617
Hist. Note: Members are required to hold a Federal Basic Importer's Permit and must be sponsored by an officer or member of the ass'n. Founded in New York City January 12, 1934 by eighteen charter members for the purpose of electing an NRA code authority. After the NRA was declared unconstitutional in 1935 the present organization was formed. Formerly (until 1979) known as the Nat'l Ass'n of Alcoholic Beverage Importers, Inc.
Publications:
Import Report. m.
Statistics. m.
Statistical Report. a.
Annual Meetings: Spring
1987-New York, NY(Grand Hyatt)/March 26/300-350

Nat'l Ass'n of Biology Teachers (1938)
11250 Roger Bacon Dr., #19, Reston VA 22090
Exec. Director: Patricia J. McWethy
Members: 6,000 individuals *Staff:* 6
Annual Budget: $250-500,000 *Tel:* (703) 471-1134
Hist. Note: Founded in 1938 and incorporated in Illinois in 1956. Affiliated with the American Ass'n for the Advancement of Science. Membership: $30/yr.
Publications:
The American Biology Teacher. 8/yr.
News and Views. q.
Annual Meetings: Fall/1,500
1987-Cincinnati, OH(Netherlands Plaza)/Oct. 15-18
1988-Chicago, IL(Marriott)/Nov. 17-20

Nat'l Ass'n of Black Accountants (1970)
300 I St., N.E., Suite 107, Washington DC 20002
Exec. Director: Linda Saulsby Gaston
Members: 2,500 *Staff:* 2-5
Annual Budget: $250-500,000 *Tel:* (202) 543-6656
Hist. Note: Established and incorporated in New York. Membership: $80/yr.
Publications:
News Bulletin. m.
Spectrum. semi-a.
Student News. q.
Annual Meetings: May-June
1987-Cleveland, OH/600

Nat'l Ass'n of Black and Minority Chambers of Commerce (1983)
7700 Edgewater Drive, Suite 742, Oakland CA 94621
Exec. V. President: Dr. Malcolm R. LaPlace, II, Ph.D.
Staff: 8
Tel: (415) 639-7915
Hist. Note: The creation of the Nat'l Chamber is a national strategy for local chamber members to share in the collective buying power of Black and Minority communities. Membership: $150/yr. (minimum).
Publications:
Black Business News. q. adv.
Nat'l Minority Chamber Directory. a.
Nat'l Minority Meeting Directory. a.
Annual Meetings: August

Nat'l Ass'n of Black Consulting Engineers (1975)
6406 Georgia Ave., N.W., Washington DC 20012
Secy.-Treas.: Knox Tull, Jr.
Members: 100 companies
Annual Budget: under $10,000 *Tel:* (202) 291-3550
Hist. Note: Founded as the Nat'l Council of Minority Consulting Engineers, it represented the merging of the Western Ass'n of Minority Consulting Engineers, the American Indian Council, and the Eastern Ass'n of Black Consulting Engineers; assumed its present name in 1978. Member firms are composed of all the consulting engineering disciplines: civil, structural, environmental, transportation, electrical, mechanical engineering, planning, architecture, land surveying, and construction management. Membership: $200/yr.
Annual Meetings: September

Nat'l Ass'n of Black Hospitality Professionals (1985)
P.O. Box 5443, Plainfield NJ 07060
Director: Mikoel Turner
Members: 50 individuals
Annual Budget: under $10,000 *Tel:* (201) 753-7856
Hist. Note: Purpose is to provide a forum for black professionals in the hotel and restaurant industry. Membership: $85/yr.
Quarterly Meetings:

Nat'l Ass'n of Black Journalists (1975)
Hist. Note: Address unknown in 1985.

Nat'l Ass'n of Black Manufacturers (1971)
Hist. Note: Emphasis is on procuring government contracts for member minority firms. Address unknown in 1983, reported defunct.

Nat'l Ass'n of Black-Owned Broadcasters (1977)
1730 M Street, N.W., Suite 412, Washington DC 20036
Exec. Director: James Winston
Members: 70-80 individuals; 130 stations *Staff:* 2-5
Annual Budget: $50-100,000 *Tel:* (202) 463-8970
Hist. Note: Founded in September, 1976 and incorporated in the District of Columbia in 1977. Members are blacks who own radio and/or television stations, cable television systems and related businesses.
Publication:
NABOB Info. m.
Annual Meetings: Awards Dinner in Washington, DC
1987-Sheraton Washington/April 16/600

Nat'l Ass'n of Black Social Workers (1968)
271 West 125th St., New York NY 10027
Administration Consultant: William T. Merritt
Members: 4-5,000 *Staff:* 2-5
Annual Budget: $250-500,000 *Tel:* (212) 749-0470
Hist. Note: Membership: $50/yr. (individual); $300/yr. (organization/company)
Publications:
Black Caucus. semi-a.
Position Statements. a.
Annual Meetings: April/2,000
1987-Boston, MA(Sheraton)/April 18-26
1988-San Francisco, CA(Hilton)
1989-Richmond, VA or Miami, FL
1990-Los Angeles, CA(Airport Hilton)

Nat'l Ass'n of Black Women Attorneys (1972)
508 5th St., N.W., Washington DC 20001
President: Mabel D. Haden
Members: 500 *Staff:* 1
Annual Budget: $25-50,000 *Tel:* (202) 638-5715
Hist. Note: Formerly (until 1978) the Nat'l Ass'n of Black Women Lawyers. Maintains a scholarship fund begun in 1978. Membership: $50/yr. (individual), $100/yr. (organization).
Publications:
Souvenir Booklet. a. adv.
NABWA News. bi-m. adv.
Annual Meetings:
1987-Washington, DC(Hyatt Regency)/Feb. 12-14/400

Nat'l Ass'n of Black Women Entrepreneurs (1978)
Box 1375, Detroit MI 48231
Exec. Director: Marilyn French-Hubbard
Members: 4,500 *Staff:* 5
Annual Budget: $100-250,000 *Tel:* (313) 341-7400
Hist. Note: Formed in Detroit to help its members obtain information about business opportunities and generally support black businesswomen.
Publication:
NABWE Newsletter. bi-m.
Annual Meetings: Detroit, MI/October

Nat'l Ass'n of Blind Teachers (1971)
1010 Vermont Ave., N.W., Suite 1100, Washington DC 20005
President: Dana Walker
Members: 185
Annual Budget: $10-25,000 *Tel:* (202) 393-3666
Hist. Note: Members are teachers who are blind. Affiliated with the American Council of the Blind, which provides administrative support. Membership: $10/yr.
Publication:
The Blind Teacher. q.
Annual Meetings: July
1987-Los Angeles, CA

00188 12 05 86 1233

Nat'l Ass'n of Blouse Manufacturers (1933)
450 Seventh Ave., New York NY 10123
Exec. Director: Stephen Thomas
Members: 150-175 *Staff:* 2-5
Tel: (212) 563-6390
Hist. Note: Membership concentrated in the New York area. Major purpose is labor negotiations with the Internat'l Ladies Garment Workers Union. A member of the Federation of Apparel Manufacturers.

Nat'l Ass'n of Boards of Education (1972)
1077 30th St., N.W., Suite 100, Washington DC 20007
Exec. Director: Sr. Lourdes Sheehan, RSM
Staff: 2-5
Annual Budget: $25-50,000 *Tel:* (202) 337-6232
Hist. Note: A service department of the Nat'l Catholic Educational Ass'n. Memberhip: $48/yr.
Publication:
PolicyMaker. q.
Annual Meetings:
1987-New Orleans, LA(April 19-22
1988-Undetermined/April 4-7

Nat'l Ass'n of Boards of Examiners of Nursing Home Administrators (1970)
1511 K St., N.W., #716, Washington DC 20005
Exec. Director: J.A. Miller, CAE
Members: 45 State Licensing Boards; 25 individuals *Staff:* 7
Annual Budget: $100-250,000 *Tel:* (202) 393-7003
Hist. Note: Purpose is to consider questions of common interest (i.e. educational and professional standards, uniformity of laws and regulations) to the nursing home administrators' examination and licensing boards and authorities of the United States. Membership: $25/yr.
Publication:
NAB Newsletter. q.
Annual Meetings: June
1987-Minneapolis, MN(Hyatt Regency)/June 9-12

Nat'l Ass'n of Boards of Pharmacy (1904)
1300 Higgins Road, Suite 103, Park Ridge IL 60068
Exec. Director: Fred T. Mahaffey
Members: 57 states or jurisdictions *Staff:* 11-16
Annual Budget: $500-1,000,000 *Tel:* (312) 698-6227
Hist. Note: Serves all American boards of pharmacy in matters of interstate reciprocity of licensure, uniform examination and licensing as well as other matters of mutual concern.
Publications:
NABP Newsletter. m.
NABP Proceedings. a.
NABP Survey of Pharmacy Law. a.
Annual Meetings: Spring/300
1987-Seattle, WA(Madison)/May 16-20
1988-San Antonio, TX(La Mansion del Rio)/May 5-11/350

Nat'l Ass'n of Boat Manufacturers (1945)
401 North Michigan Ave., Chicago IL 60611
Exec. Director: Jeff W. Napier
Members: 350 *Staff:* 35
Annual Budget: $100-250,000 *Tel:* (312) 836-4747
Hist. Note: Members are makers of pleasure boats. A partner-affiliate of the Nat'l Marine Manufacturers Ass'n, which provides administrative support and with which it shares offices.
Annual Meetings: Chicago in conjunction with the Marine Trade Exhibition.

Nat'l Ass'n of Bond Lawyers (1979)
Box 397, Hinsdale IL 60522
Exec. Director: Rita J. Carlson
Members: 2,800 *Staff:* 3
Annual Budget: $500-1,000,000 *Tel:* (312) 920-0160
Hist. Note: Members are lawyers specializing in the legal problems of debt obligations of the various states and their political subdivisions. Membership: $125/year (over 7 years of practice), $60/year (less than 7 years of practice).
Publications:
Directory. a.
Newsletter. q.
Annual Meetings: Chicago, in October
1987-O'Hare Hyatt/Oct. 13-16
1988-Marriott/Oct. 5-7
1989-Marriott/Oct. 18-20

Nat'l Ass'n of Book Manufacturers (1977)
Hist. Note: A section of Printing Industries of America. Inactive in 1985.

Nat'l Ass'n of Brick Distributors (1956)
1000 Duke Street, Alexandria VA 22314
Exec. Director: Walter E. Galanty, Jr.
Members: 350-400 *Staff:* 2-5
Annual Budget: $250-500,000 *Tel:* (703) 549-2555
Hist. Note: Formerly (1972) Nat'l Ass'n of Distributors and Dealers of Structural Clay Products. Membership: $550/yr.
Publications:
NABD Newspaper. bi-m. adv.
NABD Membership Directory. a.
NABD Statistical Profile. a.
Annual Meetings: Spring
1987-Key Biscayne, FL(Sonesta Beach Hotel)/March 11-15/500
1988-Hilton Head, SC(Intercontinental Hotel)/March 23-27/500

Nat'l Ass'n of Broadcast Employees and Technicians (1934)
7101 Wisconsin Ave., Suite 800, Bethesda MD 20814
Internat'l President: James P. Nolan
Members: 10,000 *Staff:* 6-10
Annual Budget: over $5,000,000 *Tel:* (301) 657-8420
Hist. Note: Organized as a company union in 1934 by the National Broadcasting Company under the title, Association of Technical Employees. Broke away from NBC in 1940 and changed its name to the National Association of Broadcast Engineers and Technicians. Chartered as an industrial union in 1951 by the Congress of Industrial Organizations under the name, National Association of Broadcast Employees and Technicians. Affiliated with the AFL-CIO and the Canadian Labour Congress.
Publication:
NABET News. bi-m.
Quadrennial Meetings: 1990

Nat'l Ass'n of Broadcasters (1922)
1771 N St., N.W., Washington DC 20036
President & C.E.O.: Edward O. Fritts
Members: 5,400 *Staff:* 130-140
Annual Budget: over $5,000,000 *Tel:* (202) 429-5300
Hist. Note: In 1951 NAB merged with the Television Broadcasters Ass'n and changed its name to the Nat'l Ass'n of Radio and Television Broadcasters; in 1958 the present name was reassumed. Absorbed the Nat'l Radio Broadcasters Ass'n in 1986. It is connected with the Television and Radio Political Action Committee. NAB upholds the American system of broadcasting, free from government censorship; and combats discriminatory legislative proposals against broadcasting and advertising.
Publications:
NAB Today. w.
Radioactive. m.
Engineering Conference Proceedings. a.
Annual Meetings: Spring
1987-Dallas, TX/March 29-April 1
1988-Las Vegas, NV/April 10-13
1989-Las Vegas, NV/April 30-May 3
1990-Dallas, TX/March 25-28

Nat'l Ass'n of Business and Educational Radio (1965)
1501 Duke St., Suite 200, Alexandria VA 22314
President & Gen. Manager: Emmett B. Kitchen, Jr.
Members: 10,000 companies *Staff:* 20-30
Annual Budget: $1-2,000,000 *Tel:* (703) 739-0300
Hist. Note: Formed in March 1965 in Chicago by 15 business 2-way radio users in order to obtain a portion of the radio spectrum for business radio and for all land mobile radio servces in general. Membership is composed of those who use, make, service or sell 2-way land mobile radio.
Publications:
Business Radio. m. adv.
Shop Talk. m. adv.
Tech Talk. q. adv.
Annual Meetings: March

Nat'l Ass'n of Business and Industrial Saleswomen (1979)
2221 West Lake St., Fort Collins CO 80521
Exec. Director: Debra A. Benton
Members: 700-800 *Staff:* 2-5
Annual Budget: $25-50,000 *Tel:* (303) 484-4687
Hist. Note: Saleswomen selling a business or industrial product or service united to enhance their position in what is regarded as a man's environment.
Publication:
Interchange. bi-m.

Nat'l Ass'n of Business Economists (1959)
28349 Chagrin Blvd., Cleveland OH 44122
President: Jerry L. Jordan
Members: 4,200 *Staff:* 1
Annual Budget: $50-100,000 *Tel:* (216) 464-7986
Hist. Note: A professional society of full-time business economists.
Publications:
Business Economics. q. adv.
NABE News. bi-m. adv.
Annual Meetings: Fall
1987-New Orleans, LA/Sept.
1988-Pitssburgh, PA/Sept.
1989-San Francisco, CA/Sept.
1990-Washington, DC/Sept.
1991-Los Angeles, CA/Sept.

Nat'l Ass'n of Business Political Action Committees (1977)
218 North Lee St., Alexandria VA 22314
Exec. Director: Patti Jo Baber
Members: 150 companies *Staff:* 2-5
Annual Budget: $100-250,000 *Tel:* (703) 549-7681
Hist. Note: Members are companies sponsoring political action committees for their employees. Membership: $750/yr.
Publications:
NABPAC Employee Education Newsletter. q.
NABPAC Newsletter. bi-m.

Nat'l Ass'n of Buying Services (1973)
9730 South Western Ave., Suite 328, Evergreen Park IL 60642
Director: Arnold L. Watland
Members: 10 *Staff:* 1
Annual Budget: under $10,000 *Tel:* (312) 778-5000
Hist. Note: Members are credit unions, labor unions, employee clubs, insurance agencies, and companies. The association puts them in touch with dealers from whom their own members may purchase such items as new cars, furniture, carpeting and appliances at a discount.
Annual Meetings: Winter

Nat'l Ass'n of Canoe Liveries and Outfitters (1977)
1847 Peeler Rd., Suite A, Dunwoody GA 30338
Exec. Director: Joan Heflinger
Members: 350 companies *Staff:* 2-5
Annual Budget: $50-100,000 *Tel:* (404) 393-8625
Hist. Note: Incorporated in the state of Michigan. Seeks to preserve open access to the nation's rivers and waters by commercial canoe outfitters.
Publications:
NACLO News. m.
Let's Go Paddling. a. adv.
Annual Meetings: December

Nat'l Ass'n of Casual Furniture Retailers (1980)
1190 Merchandise Mart, Chicago IL 60654
Exec. Director: Mariann B. Gregory
Members: 300 *Staff:* 2-5
Annual Budget: $25-50,000 *Tel:* (312) 321-0563
Hist. Note: Incorporated in Illinois, members are retailers; manufacturers and sales representatives qualify as associate members.
Publications:
Newsletter. q.
Ad Book. a.
Directory. q.
Annual Meetings: Fall

Nat'l Ass'n of Casualty and Surety Agents (1913)
6931 Arlington Road, Suite 308, Bethesda MD 20814
Exec. V. President: Bruce T. Wallace
Members: 260 *Staff:* 12
Annual Budget: $500-1,000,000 *Tel:* (301) 986-4166
Hist. Note: Supports the Nat'l Ass'n of Casualty and Surety Agents (NACSA) Political Action Committee.
Annual Meetings: Always at White Sulphur Springs(Greenbrier)/Oct./1,500

Nat'l Ass'n of Casualty and Surety Executives (1911)
85 John St., 12th Floor, New York NY 10038
Exec. Secretary: Lawrence M. Zippin
Members: 80-85 *Staff:* 2-5
Annual Budget: $10-25,000 *Tel:* (212) 669-0444
Annual Meetings: White Sulphur Springs, WV(Greenbrier)/Fall/1,500

Nat'l Ass'n of Catalog Showroom Merchandisers (1972)
2 Sound View Drive, Suite 100, Greenwich CT 06830
President: Marion Baker
Members: 850-900 companies *Staff:* 3-6
Annual Budget: $250-500,000 *Tel:* (203) 629-9033
Hist. Note: Regular members are catalog showroom operators and catalog publishers and associate members are suppliers.
Publications:
Member Bulletin. m.
Year Census of Catalog Showrooms. a.
Meetings:
Chicago, March-April and October, in conjuction with the Housewares
Shows
New York City, July, at time of the J.A. Jewelry Show
New York City, November, at time of the Table Top Show

Nat'l Ass'n of Catering Executives (1958)
2500 Wilshire Blvd., Suite 603, Los Angeles CA 90057
Exec. Director: Raymond P. Delrich
Members: 1,300-1,500 *Staff:* 3
Annual Budget: $100-250,000 *Tel:* (213) 384-3179
Hist. Note: Founded as the Banquet Managers Guild in New York City on June 3, 1958; assumed its present name in 1977. Membership: $75/yr. (individual); $1,500/yr. (company)
Publication:
NACE Newsletter. m.
Annual Meetings: Summer
1987-Atlanta, GA(Westin Peachtree Plaza)/June 29-July 2/500

Nat'l Ass'n of Catholic Chaplains (1965)
3257 South Lake Drive, Milwaukee WI 53207
Acting Exec. Director: Sr. Helen Hayes, O.S.F.
Members: 3,300-3,400 *Staff:* 2-5
Annual Budget: $250-500,000 *Tel:* (414) 483-4898
Hist. Note: Members are Catholic priests, permanent deacons and laity engaged in professional health care and related institutional ministries. Membership: $75/yr.
Publication:
Camillian. m.
Annual Meetings: Late Summer

Nat'l Ass'n of Cemeteries (1929)
Hist. Note: Merged with the American Cemetery Association in October, 1980.

00189 12 05 86 1233

Nat'l Ass'n of Certified Mortgage Bankers (1978)
Hist. Note: Became the National Society for Real Estate Finance in 1983.

Nat'l Ass'n of Chain Drug Stores (1933)
413 N. Lee Street, P.O. Box 1417-D49, Alexandria VA 22313
President: Robert J. Bolger
Members: 180 chains with 18,000 outlets *Staff:* 25-30
Annual Budget: $2-5,000,000 *Tel:* (703) 549-3001
Hist. Note: Connected with the Chain Drugstores Political Action Committee.
Publications:
ENL. bi-w.
Membership Directory. a.
Annual Meetings: Always in Palm Beach, FL/April/2,000
1987-The Breakers/April 26-29
1988-The Breakers/April 16-21
1989-Marriott
1990-The Breakers
1991-The Breakers

Nat'l Ass'n of Chain Manufacturers (1932)
20 North Wacker Drive, Chicago IL 60606
Exec. V. President: Richard F. Friedeman, Jr.
Members: 11 companies *Staff:* 2-6
Annual Budget: $50-100,000 *Tel:* (312) 558-1849
Tri-annual Meetings: Winter, Late Spring and Early Fall
1987-Chicago, IL(Westin O'Hare)/Jan. 29

Nat'l Ass'n of Chemical Distributors (1972)
1615 L St., N.W., Suite 925, Washington DC 20036
Exec. V. President: Sandford Hill
Members: 300 companies *Staff:* 8-10
Annual Budget: $500-1,000,000 *Tel:* (202) 296-9200
Hist. Note: Purchasers of bulk raw chemicals. Supports the Chemical Distributors Political Action Committee.
Publication:
The Chemical Distributor. m.

Nat'l Ass'n of Chewing Gum Manufacturers (1918)
66 E. Main St., Moorestown NJ 08057
Secretary-Treasurer: William L. MacMillan, III, CAE
Members: 15 companies *Staff:* 2-5
Annual Budget: $100-250,000 *Tel:* (609) 234-9155

Nat'l Ass'n of Chiefs of Police (1962)
1100 N.E. 125th St., North Miami FL 33161
Exec. Secretary: Gerald S. Arenberg
Members: 8,000 *Staff:* 2-5
Annual Budget: $250-500,000 *Tel:* (305) 891-1700
Hist. Note: Formerly Nat'l Police Museum. Maintains a Washington Congressional liaison office and operates the American Police Academy in Washington as its educational arm. Also maintains the American Police Hall of Fame and Museum. Membership: $30/yr.
Publication:
Police Command. m.
Annual Meetings: With the American Federation of Police

Nat'l Ass'n of Children's Hospitals and Related Institutions (1968)
401 Wythe St., Alexandria VA 22314
President: Robert H. Sweeney
Members: 93 hospitals *Staff:* 15-20
Annual Budget: $250-500,000 *Tel:* (703) 684-1355
Publication:
Newsletter. semi-a.
Semi-annual Meetings:

Nat'l Ass'n of Christian Colleges and Universities (1969)
Hist. Note: Inactive in 1982.

Nat'l Ass'n of Christians in Social Work (1953)
Hist. Note: Became the North American Association of Christians in Social Work in 1983.

Nat'l Ass'n of Christians in the Arts (1983)
Box 2995, Boston MA 02101
Nat'l Director: Roberta J. Ramzy
Members: 1225 individuals *Staff:* 4
Tel: (617) 574-0668
Hist. Note: Membership: $25/yr.
Publications:
Creativity. q.
Art Speak. bi-m.
Annual Meetings:
1987-Washington, DC/Aug.-Sept.
1988-San Fransisco, CA/Aug.-Sept.

Nat'l Ass'n of Church and Institutional Financing Organizations (1967)
Hist. Note: Dissolved in 1983.

Nat'l Ass'n of Church Business Administrators (1957)
Hist. Note: Became (1985) the Nat'l Ass'n of Church Business Administration.

Nat'l Ass'n of Church Business Administration (1957)
7001 Grapevine Hwy., Suite 324, Fort Worth TX 76180
Exec. Director: F. Marvin Myers
Members: 1,200 *Staff:* 2-5
Annual Budget: $100-250,000 *Tel:* (817) 284-1732
Hist. Note: Managers of local congregations, military chapels or religious institutions. Formerly (1985) the Nat'l Ass'n of Church Business Administrators.
Publications:
NACBA Gram. m.
NACBA Ledger. q.
Annual Meetings: July
1987-Houston, TX/July 13-16/550
1988-Denver, CO/July 18-21/575
1989-Tulsa, OK/July 17-20/600
1990-Atlanta, GA/July 16-19/600
1991-Seattle, WA/July 14-19
1992-Washington, DC/July

Nat'l Ass'n of Church Personnel Administrators (1972)
100 East 8th St., Cincinnati OH 45202
Exec. Director: Sr. Christine Matthews, O.P.
Members: 760 *Staff:* 2-5
Annual Budget: $100-250,000 *Tel:* (513) 421-3134
Hist. Note: Formed by the National Federation of Priests' Councils at the University of Notre Dame in October, 1972. Members are personnel administrators of religious congregations and dioceses. Membership: $110/yr. (individual), $300/yr. (company).
Publication:
NACPA Newsletter. bi-m. adv.
Annual Meetings: Fall
1987-Chicago, IL/440
1988-Philadelphia, PA(Holiday Inn Center City)/480

Nat'l Ass'n of Classroom Educators in Business Education (1968)
Lincoln High School, Cambridge City IN 47327
Corresp. Secretary: Larry Shinn
Members: 650-675 individuals *Staff:* 1
Annual Budget: under $10,000 *Tel:* (317) 478-3261
Hist. Note: Affiliated with the American Vocational Ass'n. Members are teachers at the high school or junior college level. Not incorporated, the association has no paid staff or permanent address other than the above. Formerly the Nat'l Ass'n of Classroom Educators in Business and Office Education. Membership: $3/yr.
Publications:
Directory of Officers and Committee Members. a.
Newsletter. q.
Annual Meetings: With the American Vocational Ass'n

Nat'l Ass'n of Clergy Hypnotherapists (1984)
501 Maynard Ave., Florence SC 29501
President: Dr. William N. Curtis
Members: 68 individuals *Staff:* 1
Annual Budget: under $10,000 *Tel:* (803) 662-9248
Hist. Note: A non-sectarian organization for ministers, rabbis, and priests interested in hypnosis, NACH was organized to clarify the negative attitudes and misconceptions held by religious people concerning hypnosis. Membership: $35/yr.
Publication:
Newsletter. bi-m.
Annual Meetings: Fall

Nat'l Ass'n of Coin Laundry Equipment Operators (1959)
Hist. Note: Became the Multi-Housing Laundry Association in 1982.

Nat'l Ass'n of Cold Storage Contractors (1981)
1255 23rd St., N.W., Washington DC 20037
Exec. Director: Mark T. Engle
Members: 60 companies *Staff:* 2-5
Annual Budget: $50-100,000 *Tel:* (202) 452-8100
Hist. Note: Trade association for the low-temperature facility construction industry.
Publications:
Newsletter. m.
Directory. a.

Nat'l Ass'n of College Admission Counselors (1937)
9933 Lawler Ave., Ste. 500, Skokie IL 60077
Exec. Director: Frank E. Burtnett
Members: 2,146 organizations; 1,295 individuals *Staff:* 20-25
Annual Budget: $2-5,000,000 *Tel:* (312) 676-0500
Hist. Note: Formerly (1968) Ass'n of College Admissions Counselors, and (1939) Ass'n of College Representatives. Membership: $40/yr. (individual); $120/yr. (high school); $225/yr. (college).
Publications:
NACAC Journal. q.
NACAC Membership Directory. a.
NACAC Bulletin. 10/yr.
Annual Meetings: Fall
1987-Seattle, WA(Westin)/Sept. 29-Oct. 2
1988-Milwaukee, WI(Mecca)/Oct. 4-7
1989-New York, NY/Oct. 4-7
1990-Louisville, KY(Galt House)/Oct. 2-5
1991-Hartford, CT(Sheraton & Hartford Civic Ctr.)/Sept. 29-Oct. 2

Nat'l Ass'n of College and University Attorneys (1961)
One Dupont Circle, N.W., Suite 620, Washington DC 20036
Exec. Director: Phillip M. Grier
Members: 620 colleges, universities, and university systems
Staff: 9
Annual Budget: $500-1,000,000 *Tel:* (202) 833-8390
Hist. Note: Membership: $200/year (individual), $230-2415/year (institutional).
Publications:
Directory of College and University Attorneys. a.
The College Law Digest. bi-m.
Journal of College and University Law. q.
Annual Meetings: June/400
1987-Albuquerque, NM/June 23-26
1988-Kansas City, MO/June 26-29
1989-Boston, MA/June 28-July 1
1990-Hawaii

Nat'l Ass'n of College and University Business Officers (1951)
One Dupont Circle, Suite 500, Washington DC 20036
Exec. V. President, Interim: James A. Hyatt
Members: 14,700 individuals, 2,028 institutions *Staff:* 45-50
Annual Budget: $2-5,000,000 *Tel:* (202) 861-2500
Hist. Note: Formerly (1962) Nat'l Federation of College and University Business Officers Ass'ns. Represents accredited, non-profit institutions of higher learning approved for membership by a regional business officers ass'n.
Publication:
Business Officer. m.
Annual Meetings: Summer/700-800
1987-Houston, TX/July
1988-St. Louis. MO/July

Nat'l Ass'n of College and University Chaplains and Directors of Religious Life (1948)
c/o Kalamazoo College, Kalamazoo MI 49007
President: Robert Dewey
Members: 225-250 *Staff:* 1
Annual Budget: under $10,000 *Tel:* (616) 383-8609
Hist. Note: Interfaith professional society of those responsible for the religious life within academic communities. Membership: $40/year (individual), $90-100/year (institutional).
Publications:
Membership List. a.
NACUC News. q.
Annual Meetings: February/100
1987-Winter Park, FL(Rollins College)/Feb. 22-25

Nat'l Ass'n of College and University Food Services (1958)
Michigan State Univ., 7 Olds Hall, East Lansing MI 48824
Exec. Director: Clark DeHaven
Members: 550-600 *Staff:* 3
Annual Budget: $250-500,000 *Tel:* (517) 332-2494
Hist. Note: Membership: $100-275/yr.
Publications:
NACUFS Journal. a.
NACUFS Newsletter/Digest. q.
NACUFS Facts & Findings. m.
NACUFS Directory/Update a.
Annual Meetings: June-July/5-600
1987-Boston, MA(Marriott Copley Plaza)/June 29-July 3
1988-Honolulu, HI(Hilton Hawaiian Village)/June 21-28
1990-Minneapolis, MN(Radisson Hotel South)/July 19-22

Nat'l Ass'n of College Automotive Teachers (1973)
501 West Algonquin Road, Arlington Heights IL 60005-4411
Exec. Manager: James E. Bates, CAE
Members: 525 *Staff:* 1
Annual Budget: $50-100,000 *Tel:* (312) 593-8250
Hist. Note: Membership: $30/year.
Publication:
NACAT News. q. adv.
Annual Meetings:
1987-Oakland, CA/600
1988-Columbus, OH

Nat'l Ass'n of College Auxiliary Services (1969)
Box 870, Staunton VA 24401
Exec. Director: Stan Clark
Members: 1,300 *Staff:* 2-5
Annual Budget: $250-500,000 *Tel:* (703) 885-8826
Hist. Note: Members are directors of college auxiliary services such as book stores, laundries, food services, housing, vending, printing, etc. Founded as the Association of College Auxiliary Services, it assumed its present name in 1973.
Publication:
College Service Administration. bi-m. adv.
Annual Meetings: Fall/650
1987-Baltimore, MD(Hyatt Regency)/Nov. 1-5
1988-Las Vegas, NV(Riviera)/Oct 23-27
1989-New Orleans, LA(Hyatt Regency)/Nov. 8-11
1990-Nashville, TN(Opryland)/Oct. 25-28
1991-Seattle, WA(Sheraton)/Nov. 6-9

Nat'l Ass'n of College Deans, Registrars, and Admissions Officers (1925)
917 Dorsett Ave., Albany GA 31701
Exec. Secretary: Helen Mayes
Members: 300-325 *Staff:* 1
Annual Budget: under $10,000 *Tel:* (912) 435-4945

00190 12 05 86 1233

Hist. Note: Deans, registrars and admissions officers of colleges with predominately black enrollments. Formerly (until 1949) known as the Nat'l Ass'n of Collegiate Deans and Registrars in Negro Schools, and (until 1970) the Nat'l Ass'n of College Deans and Registrars. Membership: $60-75/yr. based on size of enrollment.
Publications:
NACDRAO Newsletter. semi-a.
Proceedings of Annual Meeting. a.
Membership Directory. a.
Annual Meetings: March/100
1987-Baltimore, MD/March 15-18
1988-Atlanta, GA/March 13-16
1989-Knoxville, TN/March 12-15

Nat'l Ass'n of College Stores (1923)
528 East Lorain St., Box 58, Oberlin OH 44074
Exec. Director: Garis F. Distelhorst, CAE
Members: 3,700 *Staff:* 100
Annual Budget: over $5,000,000 *Tel:* (216) 775-7777
Hist. Note: Organized in 1924 as an offshoot of the American Booksellers Ass'n. Originally known as the College Bookstore Ass'n. Has an annual budget of $16-17 million.
Publications:
NACS Weekly Bulletin. w. adv.
College Store Journal. 6/yr. adv.
Campus Market Report. m.
NACS College Store Buyers Guide. a. adv.
NACS Book Buyers Manual. a. adv.
NACS Directory of Colleges and College Stores. a.
Annual Meetings: April/4,000
1987-Anaheim, CA(Convention Center)
1988-Cincinnati, OH(Convention Center)
1989-Baltimore, MD(Convention Center)

Nat'l Ass'n of College Wind and Percussion Instructors (1952)
Division of Fine Arts, Northeast Missouri State Univ., Kirksville MO 63501
Exec. Secy.-Treas.: Richard Weerts
Members: 1,400 individuals *Staff:* 1
Annual Budget: $10-25,000 *Tel:* (816) 785-4442
Hist. Note: Associated with the Music Educators Nat'l Conference. Members are those responsible for teaching wind and percussion instruments in American colleges and universities. Membership: $20/yr.
Publications:
Bibliography of Papers Appearing in the NACWPI Journal. a.
Holdings of the NACWPI Research Library. a.
NACWPI Journal. q. adv.
Annual Meetings:
1988-Indianapolis, IN/April 20-24

Nat'l Ass'n of Colleges and Teachers of Agriculture (1955)
608 W. Vermont, Univ. of Illinois, Urbana IL 61801
Editor: Dr. Jack C. Everly
Members: 1,500-1,600 *Staff:* 2-5
Annual Budget: $10-25,000 *Tel:* (217) 344-5738
Hist. Note: Membership: $15/year.
Publication:
NACTA Journal. q. adv.
Annual Meetings: Summer
1987-Columbia, MD/June/380
1988-Corvallis, OR/June

Nat'l Ass'n of Collegiate Directors of Athletics (1965)
Box 16428, Cleveland OH 44116-0428
Exec. Director: Michael J. Cleary
Members: 1,200 institutions *Staff:* 2-5
Annual Budget: $100-250,000 *Tel:* (216) 892-4000
Publication:
Athletic Administration. bi-m. adv.
Annual Meetings: June
1987-San Diego, CA(Town & Country)/June 7-10
1988-Marco Island, FL(Marriott's Marco Beach)/June 5-11

Nat'l Ass'n of Collegiate Gymnastics Coaches (Men) (1950)
University of Pittsburgh Athletic Dep't,P.O. Box 7436, Pittsburgh PA 15213
Secretary-Treasurer: Frank D'Amico
Members: 250 *Staff:* 0
Annual Budget: under $10,000 *Tel:* (412) 648-8334
Hist. Note: Promotes men's gymnastics at all levels. Formerly (1977) the Nat'l Ass'n of College Gymnastic Coaches. Has no paid staff. Membership: $50/year (active), $10/year (associate)
Publications:
Statistical Service. bi-w.(Dec.-Apr.) adv.
Newsletter. bi-m.
Semi-annual Meetings: Spring with NCAA Championships, and Fall with US Gymnastics Federation.
1987-Los Angeles, CA(UCLA)/April/80

Nat'l Ass'n of Colored Women's Clubs (1896)
5808 16th St., N.W., Washington DC 20011
Secretary: Carole A. Early
Members: 1,000 organizations *Staff:* 2-5
Annual Budget: $25-50,000 *Tel:* (202) 726-2044
Hist. Note: Formed through a merger of the Nat'l Colored Women's League and the Nat'l Federation of Afro-American Women. Sponsors the National Association of Girls Clubs.
Publication:
National Notes. semi-a.
Biennial Meetings: Even years
1988-Orlando, FL

Nat'l Ass'n of Community Action Agencies (1968)
1411 K St., N.W., Suite 1010, Washington DC 20005
Exec. Director: Edward L. Block
Members: 600 *Staff:* 3
Annual Budget: $100-250,000 *Tel:* (202) 737-9895
Hist. Note: Formerly (1982) the Nat'l Community Action Agency Executive Directors Ass'n. Members are community action and limited purpose agencies. Membership: $200-750/yr.
Publication:
Network. m.
Annual Meetings: Fall
1987-San Francisco, CA

Nat'l Ass'n of Community Health Centers (1970)
1330 New Hampshire Ave., N.W., Washington DC 20036
Exec. Director: Thomas Van Coverden
Members: 950 *Staff:* 20
Tel: (202) 833-9280
Hist. Note: Formerly (1970) Nat'l Ass'n of Neighborhood Health Center Directors and Administrators and (1977) Nat'l Ass'n of Neighborhood Health Centers. NACHC is an advocacy organization which works to assure the continued growth and development of community-based health care programs by providing education, training, and technical assistance to health center staff and board members. Membership: $30/yr.(individual); organizational fee based on budget.
Publication:
Washington Update. bi-w.
Annual Meetings: September
1987-New Orleans, LA(Fairmont)
1988-San Diego, CA(Town & Country)

Nat'l Ass'n of Community Leadership Organizations
1454 Duke St., Alexandria VA 22314
Exec. V. President: Rosemary Harper
Tel: (703) 836-7904
Hist. Note: Affiliated with the American Chamber of Commerce Executives.
Annual Meetings: September

Nat'l Ass'n of Companion Sitter Agencies and Referral Services (1978)
801 Princeton Ave., S.W., Birmingham AL 35211
President: Nancy J. Ripp
Members: 60-65 organizations *Staff:* 1
Annual Budget: $10-25,000 *Tel:* (205) 786-4219
Hist. Note: Incorporated in Alabama. Members are independently owned, private referral services and agencies that specialize in home care services for the elderly, the long-term infirmed and children. Membership: $200/yr.
Publication:
Newsletter. q.
Annual Meetings: May
1987-Philadelphia, PA(Adams Mark)/May 19-24/60-100

Nat'l Ass'n of Computer Stores
Hist. Note: Reported defunct in 1986.

Nat'l Ass'n of Computerized Tax Processors (1973)
2670 Cunningham Hole Road, Annapolis MD 21401
Exec. Secretary: L.D. Caracciolo
Members: 65 companies *Staff:* 1
Annual Budget: under $10,000 *Tel:* (301) 266-8560
Hist. Note: Members are companies processing tax forms by computer. Membership: $200/yr.
Annual Meetings: August
1987-Arlington, VA(Crystal Gateway Marriott)/Aug. 13-15/80-100

Nat'l Ass'n of Concession Services (1978)
Hist. Note: Defunct in 1983.

Nat'l Ass'n of Concessionaires (1944)
35 East Wacker Drive, Suite 1849, Chicago IL 60601
Exec. Director: Charles A. Winans
Members: 450-500 companies *Staff:* 2-5
Annual Budget: $250-500,000 *Tel:* (312) 236-3858
Hist. Note: Founded as the National Association of Popcorn Manufacturers, it became the International Popcorn Association and then the Popcorn and and Concessions Association before assuming its present name. Members are popcorn processors, operators of food, vending and beverage concessions and their suppliers. Membership: $125-350/yr.
Publications:
The Concessionaire. m.
Insite. a. adv.
Annual Meetings: Fall/2,500
1987-Atlanta, GA(Marriott Marquis)/Nov. 17-22
1988-Los Angeles, CA(Century Plaza)/Oct.
1989-Nashville, TN(Opryland)/Oct.

Nat'l Ass'n of Conservation Districts (1946)
1025 Vermont Ave., N.W., Suite 730, Washington DC 20005
Exec. V. President: Ernest C. Shea
Members: 2,900-3,000 districts *Staff:* 35-40
Annual Budget: $500-1,000,000 *Tel:* (202) 347-5995
Hist. Note: Conservation districts are local subdivisions of state governments which work to conserve and develop land, water, forests, wildlife and related natural resources. Formerly (1970) Nat'l Ass'n of Soil and Water Conservation Districts.
Publication:
Tuesday Letter. w.
Annual Meetings: First week in February/1500
1987-Reno, NV/Feb. 1-5
1988-Little Rock, AR/Feb. 7-11
1989-Salt Lake City, UT/Feb. 5-9

Nat'l Ass'n of Consumer Agency Administrators (1976)
1010 Vermont Ave., N.W., Suite 514, Washington DC 20005
Exec. Director: Jill H. Pace
Members: 110 consumer agencies *Staff:* 2-5
Annual Budget: $50-100,000 *Tel:* (703) 347-7395
Hist. Note: Members are municipal, county or state supported consumer affairs agencies. Qualified individuals are eligible for associate membership. Membership: $70-450/yr. (vaires with agency budget).
Publications:
NACAA News. 10/yr.
Recall Clearinghouse Service. m.
Annual Meetings:
1987-Charleston, WV/June 3-6

Nat'l Ass'n of Consumer Credit Administrators (1935)
Bataan Memorial Bldg., Room 137, Santa Fe NM 87501
Secy.-Treas.: Marce Saykally
Members: 50-60 *Staff:* 1
Annual Budget: $25-50,000 *Tel:* (505) 827-7740
Hist. Note: Formerly Ass'n of Small Loan Administrators; Nat'l Ass'n of Small Loan Supervisors. Membership: $200/year.
Annual Meetings: May/60
1987-Honolulu, HI (Sheraton Waikiki)/May 16-22

Nat'l Ass'n of Container Distributors (1925)
1900 Arch St., Philadelphia PA 19103
Exec. Director: William L. Robinson
Members: 33 companies *Staff:* 1
Annual Budget: $25-50,000 *Tel:* (215) 564-3484
Hist. Note: Formerly (1964) Nat'l Ass'n of Glass Containers Distributors.
Publication:
Exchange Packet. 8/yr.

Nat'l Ass'n of Convenience Stores (1961)
1605 King St., Alexandria VA 22314
President: Kerley LeBoeuf
Members: 1,250 retail; 47,000 outlets; 800 associates *Staff:* 18
Annual Budget: $2-5,000,000 *Tel:* (703) 684-3600
Hist. Note: Retail food stores carrying a more limited selection than supermarkets and usually open longer hours. Sponsors the National Association of Convenience Stores Political Action Committee. Membership: $250/yr.
Publications:
NACS SCAN. m.
State of the Convenience Store Industry. a.
Compensation Survey. a.
Membership and Services Directory. a.
Annual Meetings: Fall
1987-Toronto, Canada(Hilton Harbour Castle)/Sept. 27-30/2,700
1988-Las Vegas, NV(Hilton)/Sept. 25-28/4,250
1989-Boston(Marriott/Westin)/Sept. 24-27/2,700
1990-Dallas, TX(Lowes Anatole)/Sept. 23-26/5,000
1991-Orlando, FL(Marriott)/Oct. 13-16/3,000

Nat'l Ass'n of Corporate and Professional Recruiters (1978)
146 Blackberry Drive, Stamford CT 06903
Exec. Director: Linda J. Meagher
Members: 370 individuals *Staff:* 2
Annual Budget: $100-250,000 *Tel:* (203) 329-2349
Hist. Note: Founded in New York and incorporated in Delaware, NACPR was established to address the common concerns of corporate staffing executives and executive search consultants. Members are professionals with at least five years experience in the recruiting of management personnel. Membership: $250/yr.
Publications:
Searchlight. q.
NACPR Today. m.
Annual Meetings: Fall
1987-Orlando, FL(Hyatt Regency Grand Cypress)/Nov. 4-6

Nat'l Ass'n of Corporate Directors (1977)
450 Fifth St., N.W., Suite 1140, Washington DC 20001
President & C.E.O.: John M. Nash
Members: 1,800 *Staff:* 6-10
Annual Budget: $500-1,000,000 *Tel:* (202) 347-3123
Hist. Note: A not-for-profit educational association dedicated to ongoing information and education for corporate directors in board practices and corporate governance; focuses on issues such as Director's and Officer's liability, shareholder concerns, and responsible board decision making. Provides publications, seminars and in-house training, as well as a Register for filling board vacancies with qualified candidacies. Membership: $300/yr.
Publications:
Directors Monthly. m.
Board Practices Monographs. q.

00191 12 05 86 1233

Annual Meetings: October
1987-New York, NY(The Plaza)/Oct. 18-20/225

Nat'l Ass'n of Corporate Real Estate Executives (NACORE) (1969)
Hist. Note: Became the Internat'l Ass'n for Corporate Real Estate Executives in 1983.

Nat'l Ass'n of Corporate Speaker Activities (1983)
P.O. Box 690454, Houston TX 77269-0454
Exec. Director: Fred Beck
Members: 215 individuals
Annual Budget: $25-50,000 *Tel:* (713) 329-2114
Hist. Note: NACSA was established to foster the highest standards of professional development and performance in speech related fields of the corporate world. Its members include professionals responsible for aspects of corporate oral communications programs, academicians specializing in oral communication and communications consultants. Incorporated in Tulsa, OK. Membership: $85/yr.
Publication:
NACSA News. q.
Annual Meetings: Sept./Oct.
1987-San Francisco, CA

Nat'l Ass'n of Corrosion Engineers (1943)
Box 218340, Houston TX 77218
Exec. Director: Chip Lee
Members: 15,500-16,500 *Staff:* 50-55
Annual Budget: $2-5,000,000 *Tel:* (713) 492-0535
Hist. Note: Established in October, 1943 and incorporated in Texas in 1944. Addresses degradation of all materials. Has accreditation program for individual members and has certification program for coating inspectors. Membership: $55/yr. (individual), $300/yr. (organization).
Publications:
Corrosion. m. adv.
Corrosion Abstracts. semi-m.
Materials Performance. m. adv.
Annual Meetings: Spring
1987-San Francisco, CA(Moscone Center)/March 9-13/4,500
1988-St. Louis, MO(Gateway Convention Center)/March 21-25/5,000

Nat'l Ass'n of Cosmetology Schools
Hist. Note: See Nat'l Ass'n of Accredited Cosmetology Schools.

Nat'l Ass'n of Counties (1935)
440 1st St., N.W., Washington DC 20001
Exec. Director: John Thomas
Members: 2,300-2,400 *Staff:* 50-60
Annual Budget: $2-5,000,000 *Tel:* (202) 393-6226
Hist. Note: Formerly Nat'l Ass'n of County Officials. Membership is by county and includes all officials within the county. Today, nearly 75% of the 3106 counties in the United States are represented. Nineteen associations of professionally-related county officials are affiliated with it.
Publications:
County Employment Reporter. bi-m.
County News. w.
Annual Meetings: Summer/5,000
1987-Indianapolis, IN(Conv. Center)/July 11-14
1988-Anaheim, CA(Conv. Center)/July 16-19
1989-Cincinnati, OH(Conv. Center)/July 15-18

Nat'l Ass'n of Counties Council of Intergovernmental Coordinators (1966)
440 First St., N.W., 8th Floor, Washington DC 20001
Exec. Secretary: Robert Fogel
Members: 300 *Staff:* 1
Annual Budget: under $10,000 *Tel:* (202) 393-6226
Hist. Note: Established in 1966 as the Nat'l Ass'n of County Development Coordinators to satisfy the need for a greater exchange of ideas in coordinating federal and state aid programs at the county level. The name was changed to Nat'l Ass'n of Counties Council of Intergovernmental Coordinators in 1975. An affiliate of the Nat'l Ass'n of Counties.
Annual Meetings: Fall, in Washington, DC

Nat'l Ass'n of County Administrators (1961)
440 First St., N.W., Washington DC 20001
Staff Liaison: Ed Ferguson
Members: 375-400 individuals *Staff:* 1
Annual Budget: under $10,000 *Tel:* (202) 393-6226
Hist. Note: An affiliate of the Nat'l Ass'n of Counties.
Annual Meetings: With NACO

Nat'l Ass'n of County Aging Programs (1978)
440 First St., N.W., Washington DC 20001
Staff Liaison: Thomas Joseph
Members: 350 *Staff:* 1
Tel: (202) 393-6226
Hist. Note: An affiliate of the Nat'l Ass'n of Counties, which provides administrative support. Members are heads of county aging offices.
Annual Meetings: With the Nat'l Ass'n of Counties

Nat'l Ass'n of County Agricultural Agents (1915)
Courthouse, Room 203, Laramie WY 82070
Secretary: Arlowe Hulett
Members: 7,000 *Staff:* 1
Annual Budget: $250-500,000 *Tel:* (307) 742-3749
Hist. Note: Organized in Chicago in the old Livestock Record Building by a small group of county agents from 10 states. An association of associations, NACAA members are employees of the U.S. Department of Agriculture's Cooperative Extension Service.
Publication:
The County Agent. q.
Annual Meetings: Summer
1987-Fargo, ND/Aug. 9-13
1988-Charlotte, NC/Aug. 14-18
1989-New Brunswick, NJ/July 30-Aug. 3
1990-Washington State

Nat'l Ass'n of County Civil Attorneys (1957)
440 First St., N.W., Washington DC 20001
Staff Liaison: Donald Murray
Members: 225-250 *Staff:* 1
Annual Budget: under $10,000 *Tel:* (202) 393-6226
Hist. Note: An affiliate of and supported by the Nat'l Ass'n of Counties. Has no dues structure.
Annual Meetings: With NACO

Nat'l Ass'n of County Community Development Directors (1977)
440 First St., N.W., Washington DC 20001
Director, Community Development Programs: Donald Pepe
Members: 100 *Staff:* 2
Annual Budget: $100-250,000 *Tel:* (202) 393-6226
Hist. Note: An affiliate of the National Association of Counties, which provides staff support.
Annual Meetings: Fall

Nat'l Ass'n of County Engineers (1956)
326 Pike Rd., Ottumwa IA 52501
Exec. Secretary: Milton L. Johnson, P.E.
Members: 1,200-1,300 *Staff:* 1
Annual Budget: $50-100,000 *Tel:* (515) 684-6928
Hist. Note: Members are county engineering professionals or road management authorities. NACE is an affiliate of the Nat'l Ass'n of Counties. Membership: $50/yr.
Publications:
NACE Action Guides. 3 volumes.
NACE Training Guide Series. 7 volumes.
Annual Meetings:
1987-Orlando, FL
1988-Mobile, AL
1989-Wichita, KS
1990-Ohio

Nat'l Ass'n of County Health Facility Administrators (1978)
440 First St., N.W., Washington DC 20001
Staff Liaison: Benjamin Latt
Members: 225-250 *Staff:* 1
Annual Budget: under $10,000 *Tel:* (202) 393-6226
Hist. Note: An affiliate of the National Association of Counties, which provides administrative support. Works to improve the quality of healthcare available from county nursing homes and other long-term care institutions. Membership: $10/yr. (individual), $100/yr. (organization).
Annual Meetings: With NACO in July
1987-Indianapolis, IN/July 11-14
1988-Anaheim, CA/July 16-19
1989-Cincinnati, OH/July 15-18

Nat'l Ass'n of County Health Officials (1966)
440 First St., N.W., Washington DC 20001
Exec. Director: Grace Starbird
Members: 1,500 *Staff:* 2
Annual Budget: $100-250,000 *Tel:* (202) 783-5550
Hist. Note: An affiliate of the Nat'l Ass'n of Counties. Incorporated in 1985. Membership: $50-400/yr. (organization).
Publications:
NACHO News. bi-m.
Annual Report. a.
Annual Meetings: With NACO in July and the American Public Health Ass'n.
1987-Indianapolis, IN/July
1988-Anaheim, CA/July
1989-Cincinnati, OH/July

Nat'l Ass'n of County Human Services Administrators (1935)
c/o Nat'l Ass'n of Counties, 440 First St., N.W., Washington DC 20001
Staff Liaison: Thomas Joseph, III
Staff: 1
Tel: (202) 393-6226
Hist. Note: An affiliate of the Nat'l Ass'n of Counties formerly (1981) called the Nat'l Association of County Welfare Directors.
Annual Meetings: With the Nat'l Ass'n of Counties

Nat'l Ass'n of County Information Officers (1965)
440 First St., N.W., Washington DC 20001
Staff Liaison: Ralph Rathburn
Members: 300-350 *Staff:* 1
Annual Budget: under $10,000 *Tel:* (202) 393-6226
Hist. Note: An affiliate of the Nat'l Ass'n of Counties, which provides administrative support. Members are county public information officers and staff.
Annual Meetings: With Nat'l Ass'n of Counties

Nat'l Ass'n of County Park and Recreation Officials (1964)
440 First St., N.W., Washington DC 20001
Staff Liaison: Barbara Paley
Members: 750-800 individuals *Staff:* 1
Annual Budget: under $10,000 *Tel:* (202) 393-6226
Hist. Note: An affiliate of the Nat'l Ass'n of Counties, which provides administrative support. Members are professionals in the field of parks, recreation and leisure-related services.
Annual Meetings: With NACO.

Nat'l Ass'n of County Planning Directors (1965)
440 First St., N.W., Washington DC 20001
Staff Liaison: Donald Pepe
Members: 642 *Staff:* 1
Annual Budget: under $10,000 *Tel:* (202) 393-6226
Hist. Note: An affiliate of and supported by the National Association of Counties. Membership: $25/yr.
Annual Meetings: With NACO

Nat'l Ass'n of County Recorders and Clerks (1948)
440 First St., N.W., Washington DC 20001
Staff Liaison: Edward Ferguson
Members: 1200 *Staff:* 1
Annual Budget: under $10,000 *Tel:* (202) 393-6226
Hist. Note: An affiliate of and supported by the National Association of Counties. Members include county officials who are responsible for adminstration of public records, courts and elections. Membership: $35/yr.
Publication:
County News.
Annual Meetings: With NACO/July
1987-Indianapolis, IN
1988-Anaheim, CA
1989-Cincinnati, OH

Nat'l Ass'n of County Training and Employment Professionals (1974)
440 First St., N.W., Washington DC 20001
Staff Liaison: Jerald McNeil
Members: 1,000 *Staff:* 1
Annual Budget: $10-25,000 *Tel:* (202) 393-6226
Hist. Note: An affiliate of the National Association of Counties, which provides administrative support. Formerly (1985) the Nat'l Ass'n of County Employment and Training Administrators.
Annual Meetings: Fall

Nat'l Ass'n of County Treasurers and Finance Officers (1950)
440 First St., N.W., Washington DC 20001
Staff Liaison: Susan White
Members: 1,100-1,200 *Staff:* 1
Annual Budget: under $10,000 *Tel:* (202) 393-6226
Hist. Note: Established as the County Treasurers Association of the United States, it assumed its present name about 1969. An affiliate of the Nat'l Ass'n of Counties, which provides administrative support.
Annual Meetings: With NACO

Nat'l Ass'n of County Welfare Directors (1935)
Hist. Note: An affiliate of the Nat'l Ass'n of Counties which became the Nat'l Ass'n of County Human Service Administrators in 1981.

Nat'l Ass'n of Credit Management (1896)
520 8th Ave., New York NY 10018-5070
President: Clyde E. Williams, ABCE
Members: 43,000 companies *Staff:* 30
Annual Budget: $2-5,000,000 *Tel:* (212) 947-5070
Hist. Note: Founded June 23, 1896 in Toledo, Ohio by 82 charter member credit executives. Provides credit reports on business customers, collection service, assistance to creditors and commercial fraud detection and prevention. The Nat'l Institute of Credit is its educational arm. Maintains a Washington office.
Publications:
Credit and Financial Management. m. adv.
Credit Manual of Commercial Laws. a.
Annual Meetings: Spring
1987-Anaheim, CA(Disneyland)/May 17-21
1988-New Orleans, LA(Marriott)/May 22-26/3,000
1989-Nashville, TN(Opryland)/May 21-25
1990-Las Vegas, NV
1991-Atlanta, GA(Marriott Marquis)/May 12-16
1992-Boston, MA(Marriott/Westin)/May 17-20

Nat'l Ass'n of Credit Union Presidents (1977)
1133 15th St., N.W., Suite 620, Washington DC 20005
Exec. Director: David W. Barrack
Members: 260 *Staff:* 10
Annual Budget: $25-50,000 *Tel:* (202) 293-5910
Hist. Note: Conceived at Williamsburg in July 1976 at a conference of presidents of Southeast credit unions, the association was formally established the following year at the Hilton Inn in Albuquerque by 47 charter members representing credit unions with more than 20 million dollars in assets. It was incorporated in Alabama in 1978. Today about half the membership represents smaller credit unions on an associate basis. Membership: $125/year.
Publication:
NACUP Newsletter. q.
Annual Meetings: Fall

00192 12 05 86 1233

Nat'l Ass'n of Criminal Defense Lawyers (1958)
1815 H St., N.W., Suite 550, Washington DC 20006
Exec. Director: David B. Dorsey
Members: 4,200 *Staff:* 6
Annual Budget: $500-1,000,000 *Tel:* (202) 872-8688
Hist. Note: Formerly (1972) Nat'l Ass'n of Defense Lawyers in Criminal Cases. Membership: $100/yr.
Publication:
The Champion. adv.
Annual Meetings: August
1987-Snowmass, CO

Nat'l Ass'n of Criminal Justice Planners (1971)
1500 Massachusetts Ave., N.W., Suite 129, Washington DC 20005
Exec. Director: Mark A. Cunniff
Members: 150-200 *Staff:* 2-5
Annual Budget: $50-100,000 *Tel:* (202) 223-3171
Hist. Note: Members include individuals in state and local agencies as well as in police and corrections departments. Formerly the National Association of Urban Criminal Justice Directors. Membership: $45/yr.
Publications:
News Update. bi-m.
Newsletter. bi-m.
Annual Meetings: Fall.

Nat'l Ass'n of Dealers in Antiques (1961)
5859 N. Main Road, Rockford IL 61103
Exec. Secretary: Shirley Oler Kowing
Members: 1,500 individuals, 850 shops *Staff:* 2-5
Annual Budget: $50-100,000 *Tel:* (815) 877-4282
Hist. Note: Promotes fairness and honesty in the antiques trade. Membership: $65/yr.
Publication:
Bulletin. m.
Annual Meetings: Last week in September
1987-Rockford, IL(Clock Tower)/Sept. 27-Oct. 3/60
1988-Macinac, WI(Grand Hotel)

Nat'l Ass'n of Decorative Architectural Finishes (1968)
112 N. Alfred St., Alexandria VA 22314
Exec. Secretary: Wilhelmina T. Loomis
Members: 20-30 *Staff:* 2-5
Annual Budget: $10-25,000 *Tel:* (703) 836-7670
Hist. Note: Members are contractors installing decorative plastic surfaces.

Nat'l Ass'n of Decorative Fabric Distributors (1969)
3008 Millwood Ave., Columbia SC 29205
Exec. Director: J. Edgar Eubanks
Members: 100-125 companies *Staff:* 8-10
Annual Budget: $100-250,000 *Tel:* (803) 252-5646
Hist. Note: Established in 1969 as the Nat'l Ass'n of Upholstery Fabric Distributors, it assumed its present name in 1975.
Publications:
Swatches. m.
Potomac Patterns. m.
Annual Meetings:
1987-San Diego, CA(Del Coronado)/Sept. 200

Nat'l Ass'n of Demolition Contractors (1972)
4415 W. Harrison St., Hillside IL 60162
Exec. Director: William L. Baker
Members: 280 *Staff:* 2-5
Annual Budget: $100-250,000 *Tel:* (312) 449-5959
Hist. Note: Demolition equipment manufacturers and contractors. Membership: $250-500/year (based on revenues).
Publication:
Demolition Age. m. adv.
Annual Meetings: March
1987-Phoenix, AZ(Pointe)/March 8-11/500-600

Nat'l Ass'n of Dental Assistants (1974)
3837 Plaza Drive, Fairfax VA 22030
Exec. Director: Joseph Salta
Members: 7,000 individuals *Staff:* 2-5
Annual Budget: $50-100,000 *Tel:* (703) 273-3906
Hist. Note: Membership open to anyone employed by a dentist, including office personnel. Membership: $24/yr.
Publication:
The Explorer. m. adv.
Annual Meetings: Fall

Nat'l Ass'n of Dental Laboratories (1950)
3801 Mt. Vernon Ave., Alexandria VA 22305
Exec. Director: Robert W. Stanley
Members: 3,000-3,100 *Staff:* 10-12
Annual Budget: $1-2,000,000 *Tel:* (703) 683-5263
Hist. Note: A federation of state laboratory ass'ns formed by a merger of the Dental Laboratory Institute of America and the American Dental Laboratory Ass'n. From 1968-71 it was known as the Nat'l Ass'n of Certified Dental Laboratories. Affiliated with the Nat'l Board for Certification in Dental Laboratory Technology, granting the Certified Dental Technician (CDT) designation and the Nat'l Board for Certification of Dental Laboratories, granting the Certified Dental Laboratory (CDL) designation. Membership: $150/yr.
Publications:
Who's Who in the Dental Laboratory Industry. 11/yr. adv.
Trends and Techniques. 10/yr. adv.
NADL Leadership and Newsletter.
Annual Meetings: June
1987-Boston, MA(Copley Place Marriott)
1988-Las Vegas, NV
1989-Nashville, TN

Nat'l Ass'n of Development Companies (1982)
1730 Rhode Island Ave., N.W., Suite 209, Washington DC 20036
Exec. Director: Jeanne Morin
Members: 200-225 *Staff:* 5
Annual Budget: $100-250,000 *Tel:* (202) 785-8484
Hist. Note: Organized to represent Certified Development Companies that participate in the Small Business Administration's "503" lending program. Through the program, CDCs provide long-term, fixed asset financing to eligible small businesses. Membership: $250/yr. or 0.1% of Sec. 503 debentures (up to $1,000)
Publication:
NADCO News. m.
Annual Meetings: Spring

Nat'l Ass'n of Development Organizations (1967)
400 North Capitol St., N.W., Suite 372, Washington DC 20001
Exec. Director: Aliceann Wohlbruck
Members: 200-300 organization *Staff:* 3
Annual Budget: $250-500,000 *Tel:* (202) 624-7806
Hist. Note: Multi-county planning and economic development districts, mainly in rural areas. Primary concern is to promote economic development in non-metropolitan regions.
Publication:
NADO News. w.
Annual Meetings: October
1987-Las Vegas, NV(Caesar's Palace)/Oct. 4-6

Nat'l Ass'n of Developmental Disabilities Councils (1975)
1234 Massachusetts Ave., N.W., Washington DC 20005
Exec. Director: Susan Ames-Zierman
Members: 54 councils *Staff:* 2-5
Annual Budget: $100-250,000
Hist. Note: State and territorial councils on the developmentally disabled. Known as the National Conference on Developmental Disabilities until 1978.
Publication:
Forum. q.
Annual Meetings: October

Nat'l Ass'n of Diaper Services (1946)
2017 Walnut St., Philadelphia PA 19103
Exec. Director: John A. Shiffert, CAE
Members: 350 companies *Staff:* 6-10
Tel: (215) 569-3650
Hist. Note: Established in 1946 as the Diaper Service Institute of America. Became the Diaper Service Industry Ass'n in 1960. Merged in 1970 with the Nat'l Institute of Diaper Services (1938), and became the Nat'l Institute of Infant Services in 1971. It assumed its present name in 1985. Members are diaper rental and laundry services, the major threat whose existence comes from the increasing use of disposable diapers.
Publication:
Newsletter. q.
Annual Meetings: May
1987-Williamsburg, VA/May 5-8

Nat'l Ass'n of Diemakers and Diecutters (1972)
Box 2, Mount Morris IL 61054
Exec. Director: Ronald S. Ballard
Members: 236 firms and 400 individuals *Staff:* 1
Annual Budget: $100-250,000 *Tel:* (815) 734-4178
Hist. Note: Founded as the Diemakers and Diecutters Ass'n, it assumed its present name on January 1, 1980. Members are firms involved in die making, diecutting and related equipment and supply areas. Membership: $215/yr.
Publication:
Cutting Edge. m. adv.
Annual Meetings: September

Nat'l Ass'n of Disability Examiners (1963)
Box 7229, Springfield IL 62791
President: P.E. Rusche
Members: 2,500-2,800 *Staff:* 0
Annual Budget: $50-100,000
Hist. Note: Established and incorporated in 1968 as a division of the National Rehabilitation Association, but became autonomous in late 1978. Members are doctors and examiners engaged in judging social security disability claims. Promotes disability evaluation as a science and a profession. Has no paid staff or permanent officers. Membership: $30/yr.
Publications:
NADE Advocate. bi-m.
Nationwide Report. semi-a.
Annual Meetings: October
1987-Portland, OR/Oct. 4-9/350

Nat'l Ass'n of Display Industries (1942)
419 Park Ave. South, 3rd Floor, New York NY 10016
Exec. Director: Marvin H. Dorfmann
Members: 250 *Staff:* 2-5
Annual Budget: $1-2,000,000 *Tel:* (212) 213-2662
Hist. Note: Members are makers and distributors of materials used in retail and service stores, fixtures and display.
Publication:
NADI Newsletter. q.
Semi-annual meetings: June and December in New York City

Nat'l Ass'n of Distributive Education Local Supervisors
Hist. Note: An affiliate of the American Vocational Association. Became a component of the Marketing and Distributive Education Association in 1982.

Nat'l Ass'n of Distributive Education Teachers (1957)
Hist. Note: An affiliate of the American Vocational Association. Staff support is provided by Distribution Education Services Center, of which it is a component. Became a component of the Marketing and Distributive Education Association in 1982.

Nat'l Ass'n of Division Order Analysts (1974)
Box 64980, Lockbox #213, Dallas TX 75206
Exec. Coordinator: Linda B. Hoffman
Members: 900-1,000 *Staff:* 1
Annual Budget: $25-50,000 *Tel:* (214) 373-1046
Hist. Note: Individuals in the energy field who handle royalty payments from the sale of energy products.
Publications:
Directory. a.
Newsletter. q.

Nat'l Ass'n of Doctors in the United States (1958)
Hist. Note: Defunct 1984.

Nat'l Ass'n of Doll and Stuffed Toy Manufacturers (1983)
605 Third Ave., 18th Floor, New York NY 10158
President: Ralph Katz
Members: 30-40
Annual Budget: $25-50,000 *Tel:* (212) 916-9200
Hist. Note: Membership concentrated in the New York area. Major purpose is labor negotiations. Formed by a merger of the Nat'l Ass'n of Doll Manufacturers and the Stuffed Toy Manufacturers Ass'n (1934) in 1983.

Nat'l Ass'n of Doll Manufacturers
Hist. Note: Merged with the Stuffed Toy Manufacturers Ass'n in 1983 to form the Nat'l Ass'n of Doll and Stuffed Toy Manufacturers.

Nat'l Ass'n of Dredging Contractors (1935)
1625 Eye St., N.W., Suite 321, Washington DC 20006
Wash. Representative: Worth Hager
Members: 20-25 companies *Staff:* 1
Annual Budget: $100-250,000 *Tel:* (202) 223-4820
Hist. Note: Formerly (1975) Nat'l Ass'n of River and Harbor Contractors.

Nat'l Ass'n of Ecumenical Staff (1940)
475 Riverside Drive, Rm. 870, New York NY 10115
Exec. Officer: Margaret Koehler
Members: 350-400 *Staff:* 1
Annual Budget: under $10,000 *Tel:* (212) 870-2158
Hist. Note: A merger of Employed Council Officers Ass'n and the Ass'n of Executive Secretaries. Formerly (1971) Ass'n of Council Secretaries.
Annual Meetings: Second week in July

Nat'l Ass'n of Educational Buyers (1920)
180 Froehlich Farm Blvd., Woodbury NY 11797
Exec. V. President: Neil D. Markee
Members: 2,200 *Staff:* 2-5
Annual Budget: $250-500,000 *Tel:* (516) 921-7100
Hist. Note: Founded as the Educational Buyers Association, it assumed its present name in 1947. Members are college and university purchasing directors.
Publications:
Annual Meeting Proceedings. a.
NAEB Bulletin. m.
Annual Meetings: May
1987-Las Vegas, NV(Hilton)/April 22-25
1988-New Orleans, LA(Hyatt)/April 27-30

Nat'l Ass'n of Educational Negotiators (1970)
Hist. Note: Individuals who negotiate on the behalf of college and school administrations, and school boards. Formerly known as the Ass'n of Educational Negotiators. Address unknown in 1985.

Nat'l Ass'n of Educational Office Personnel (1934)
1902 Association Dr., Reston VA 22091
Exec. Secretary: Rebecca Grim
Members: 6,500-7,000 *Staff:* 2
Annual Budget: $50-100,000 *Tel:* (703) 860-2888
Hist. Note: Formerly (until 1979) the Nat'l Ass'n of Educational Secretaries. Members are office personnel in educational institutions. Sponsors a professional standards program which awards the designation "Certified Educational Office Employee." Membership: $25/yr.
Publications:
The National Educational Secretary. q. adv.
Crossroads. q.
The Beam. q.
Annual Meetings: July
1987-Hot Springs, AR(Arlington Resort Hotel & Spa)
1988-San Francisco, CA
1989-Wichita, KS
1990-Denver, CO

00193 12 05 86 1233

Nat'l Ass'n of Electrical Distributors (1908)
28 Cross St., Norwalk CT 06851
President: Marvin V. Schylling
Members: 3,000 *Staff:* 35-40
Annual Budget: $2-5,000,000 *Tel:* (203) 846-6800
Hist. Note: Formerly (1928) Electrical Supply Jobbers Ass'n and (1949) Nat'l Electric Wholesalers Ass'n
Publication:
The Electrical Distributor. m. adv.
Annual Meetings: Spring
1987-San Francisco, CA/May 3-6

Nat'l Ass'n of Electronic Keyboard Manufacturers (1963)
c/o Kimball Piano and Organ Co., 1600 Royal St., Jasper IN 47546
President: Gary Moeller
Members: 8 companies *Staff:* 1
Annual Budget: under $10,000 *Tel:* (812) 482-1600
Hist. Note: Affiliated with the American Music Conference and founded as the Nat'l Ass'n of Electronic Organ Manufacturers, NAEKM assumed its present name in 1983. Membership: $1,500/yr.
Annual Meetings: Trade Shows with the Nat'l Ass'n of Music Merchants/Jan. and June

Nat'l Ass'n of Elementary School Principals (1921)
1615 Duke St., Alexandria VA 22314-3406
Exec. Director: Dr. Samuel G. Sava
Members: 22,000 individuals *Staff:* 20-25
Annual Budget: $2-5,000,000 *Tel:* (703) 684-3345
Hist. Note: Founded in 1921 as a division of the National Education Ass'n, it became autonomous in 1972. Represents the professional interests of 22,000 elementary and middle school principals in the U.S., Canada, and 41 foreign countries. Serves as advocate for high-quality educational and social programs to benefit children and youth. Membership: $110/yr.(individual); $140/yr.(institution).
Publications:
Communicator. m.
Principal. 5/yr. adv.
Streamlined Seminar. bi-m.
Report to Parents. bi-m.
Here's How. bi-m.
NAESP Research Roundup. semi-a.
Education Almanac. bi-a.
Annual Meetings: Spring
1987-Orlando, FL/March 28-April 1
1988-San Francisco, CA/April 16-20
1989-Atlanta, GA/April 15-19
1990-San Antonio, TX/April 7-11
1991-Anaheim, CA/April 6-10
1992-New Orleans, LA/March 28-April 1

Nat'l Ass'n of Elevator Contractors (1951)
2964 Peachtree Rd., N.W., Suite 665, Atlanta GA 30305
Exec. Director: Jack F. Faser, CAE
Members: 500 companies *Staff:* 2-5
Annual Budget: $100-250,000 *Tel:* (404) 261-0166
Hist. Note: Installers of elevators and suppliers of equipment.
Annual Meetings:
1987-Orlando, FL(Buena Vista Palace)/800

Nat'l Ass'n of Emergency Medical Technicians (1975)
Box 627, Boulder MT 59632
President: John Murray
Members: 2,5000 *Staff:* 2
Annual Budget: $100-250,000 *Tel:* (406) 225-4222
Hist. Note: Formed in 1975 by various state EMT associations. Members are state certified and/or nationally registered emergency medical technicians (EMTs). The association consists of three divisions: the Nat'l Soc. of EMT-Paramedics; the Nat'l Soc. of EMT Instructor/Coordinators and the Nat'l Soc. of EMS Administrators. Membership: $40/yr.
Publication:
The NAEMT Newsletter. q.
Annual Meetings:
1987-Biloxi, MS(Biloxi Coliseum & Conv. Center)/April 29-May 3/1,200

Nat'l Ass'n of Employers on Health Care Alternatives (1976)
Suite 304, Key Executive Bldg., 104 Crandon Blvd., Key Biscayne FL 33149
Exec. Director: Ruth H. Stack
Members: 150 companies *Staff:* 4
Annual Budget: $250-500,000 *Tel:* (305) 361-2810
Hist. Note: Developed from the regional ass'n Twin City Health Care Development Project (1972). Seeks to educate and assist employers in implementing health care alternatives. Membership consists of companies with 25 or more employees. Incorporated February 17, 1976. Operational July 1, 1976. Formerly (1981) National Association of Employers on Health Maintenance Organizations. Membership: $900/yr. (associate), $1,800/yr. (company).
Publications:
NAEHCA Health Directions Letter. q.
NAECHA Blue Book Digest of HMO's. a. adv.
NAECHA Blue Book Digest of PPO's. a. adv.
Annual Meetings: Spring
1987-San Diego, CA(del Coronado)/May 14-15/150
1988-Phoenix, AZ(Arizona Biltmore)/June 1-2/150

Nat'l Ass'n of Energy Service Companies (1983)
2300 M St., N.W., Washington DC 20037
Contact: Terry Singer
Members: 33 private sector mbrs.; 77 public sector mbrs. *Staff:* 2
Annual Budget: $50-100,000 *Tel:* (202) 955-9795
Hist. Note: A non-profit corporation formed by energy service companies to meet the needs of the growing energy service industry. Represents the interests of the industry before legislative and administrative bodies; informs the public of the benefits of third party financing of energy conservation and alternative energy programs; educates members about the growth, development, and status of the energy service industry.
Publication:
NAESCO News. bi-m.
Annual Meetings: Fall
1987-Washington, DC/Oct.

Nat'l Ass'n of Enrolled Agents (1972)
6000 Executive Blvd., Suite 205, Rockville MD 20852
Exec. V. President: Larry R. Fink
Members: 5,000 *Staff:* 4-5
Annual Budget: $250-500,000 *Tel:* (301) 984-6232
Hist. Note: Membership consists of individuals who have been certified, or "enrolled", to represent clients to the Internal Revenue Service. Formerly (until 1978) the Ass'n of Enrolled Agents. Membership: $90/yr.
Publications:
E.A. The Journal of the Nat'l Ass'n of Enrolled Agents. q. adv.
Enrolled Agent. q.
The EAlert. m.
Annual Meetings: Summer/3-400
1987-Phoenix, AZ/Aug. 24-29/300-400
1988-Washington, DC

Nat'l Ass'n of Enrolled Federal Tax Accountants (1960)
6108 North Harding Ave., Chicago IL 60659-3108
Exec. Director: Seymour A. Rish, EFTA
Members: 400-500 *Staff:* 1
Annual Budget: under $10,000 *Tel:* (312) 463-5577
Hist. Note: Membership restricted to persons who have been authorized to use the "Enrolled Federal Tax Accountant" (EFTA) Service Mark designation and who have a Federal license as an "enrolled agent", or are otherwise qualified, to practice before the Internal Revenue Service, of the U.S. Department of the Treasury, as taxpayer's representatives.
Publication:
The E.F.T.A. q.
Annual Meetings: Summer

Nat'l Ass'n of Entrepreneurs (1985)
2378 S. Broadway, Denver CO 80210
Exec. Director: Elsa C. Kaiser
Members: 2-5 *Staff:* 600
Tel: (303) 698-1820
Hist. Note: Members are those who operate their own businesses or plan to do so. At present, membership is concentrated in Colorado, but members are welcome from anywhere in the nation.
Publications:
Newsletter. bi-m.
Journal. q.
Monthly Meetings:

Nat'l Ass'n of Environmental Professionals (1975)
Box 9400, Washington DC 20016
Exec. Secretary: Jane M. Thurber
Members: 850-900 *Staff:* 2-5
Annual Budget: $50-100,000 *Tel:* (301) 229-7171
Hist. Note: Members are involved in environmental planning, assessment, management, review and research. Awards the CEP (Certified Environmental Professional) designation. Membership: $70/yr. (individual), $500/yr. (institution/corporation).
Publications:
The Environmental Professional. q. adv.
Newsletter. m.
Annual Meetings: Spring
1987-Chicago, IL

Nat'l Ass'n of Episcopal Schools (1954)
815 Second Ave., New York NY 10017
Exec. Director: Ann Gordon
Members: 350 *Staff:* 2
Annual Budget: $100-250,000 *Tel:* (212) 867-8400
Hist. Note: Formerly (1965) Episcopal School Ass'n . Membership includes pre-school through secondary level Episcopal schools. Membership Fee: Based on size of school and number of students.
Publications:
Network (newsletter). bi-m.
Journal. a. adv.
Directory of Episcopal Schools. bien.
Triennial Meetings:
1987-New Orleans, LA(Fairmont)/Nov. 4-8/1,000

Nat'l Ass'n of Estate Planning Councils (1963)
1010 Wisconsin Ave., Suite 630, Washington DC 20007
President: Charles D. Rumbarger, CAE
Members: 260-270 councils, 25,000 individuals *Staff:* 2-5
Annual Budget: $25-50,000 *Tel:* (202) 965-7510
Hist. Note: Members are life insurance agents, trust department officers and attorneys, trust officers, life insurance agents, CPA's and others engaged in financial estate planning.
Publication:
Newsletter. q.

Nat'l Ass'n of Evangelicals (1942)
P.O. Box 28, Wheaton IL 60189
Exec. Director: Billy A. Melvin
Members: 45,000 churches; 4 million individuals
Annual Budget: $1-2,000,000 *Tel:* (312) 665-0500
Hist. Note: A voluntary fellowship of evangelical denominations, churches, schools, organizations, and individuals providing cooperative witness and extended outreach for four million Christians. Currently represents 45 complete denominations and individual churches from 33 other groups. Has a service constituency of more than 15 million people through its 14 commissions, affiliates and service agencies. Membership: $20/yr. (individual); organizational fee based on size.
Publications:
United Evangelical Action. bi-m.
National Evangelical, Directory. bien.
Dateline. irreg.
NAE Washington Insight. m.
Annual Meetings: March
1987-Buffalo, NY(Hyatt Regency)/March 3-5/1,200

Nat'l Ass'n of Executive Secretaries (1975)
3837 Plaza Drive, Fairfax VA 22030
President: Joseph Salta
Members: 2,000 individuals *Staff:* 2-5
Annual Budget: $50-100,000 *Tel:* (703) 273-5118
Hist. Note: Membership: $24/yr.
Publications:
The Exec-U-Tary. m.
Executive Secretary Salary Survey Report. a.
Annual Meetings: Fall

Nat'l Ass'n of Export Companies (1965)
396 Broadway, Suite 603, New York NY 10013
Exec. Director: Peter F. Greene
Members: 200 *Staff:* 2-5
Annual Budget: $25-50,000 *Tel:* (212) 966-2271
Hist. Note: Members are export trading and export management companies having exclusive representation agreements with two or more U.S. manufacturers for one or more overseas markets. Until 1983 known as the National Association of Export Management Companies. Membership: $200-300/yr. (company) depending on location.
Publication:
NEXCO Newsletter. m.
Annual Meetings: New York City in Spring

Nat'l Ass'n of Export Management Companies (1965)
Hist. Note: Became the National Association of Export Companies in 1983.

Nat'l Ass'n of Exposition Managers (1928)
334 East Garfield Rd., Box 377, Aurora OH 44202
Exec. Director: Donald J. Walter, CEM
Members: 2,400 *Staff:* 8
Annual Budget: $250-500,000 *Tel:* (216) 562-8255
Hist. Note: Originated in Cleveland in June 1928 and incorporated in 1947 as the Nat'l Ass'n of Exhibit Managers; adopted the present name in 1969. Members are managers of shows, exhibits and expositions; associate members are industry suppliers. Awards the designation CEM (Certified Exposition Manager).
Publications:
NAEM Newsletter. bi-m. adv.
Who's Who in Exposition Management. a. adv.
Checklist for Hall Contracts.
Hotel/Client Agreement Guidelines and Information.
NAEM White Paper.
Salary Survey Report.
NAEM Labor Guide.
Semi-Annual Meetings: June and December
1987-Boston, MA/June 2-5 and Anaheim, CA/Dec. 1-4
1988-Philadelphia, PA/June 7-10 and Houston, TX/Nov. 29-Dec. 2
1989-Memphis, TN/June 6-9 and New York, NY/Nov. 28-Dec. 2
1990-Denver, CO/June 5-8 and Phoenix, AZ/Nov. 27-30
1991-Seattle, WA/June 4-7 and Dallas, TX/Dec. 3-6

Nat'l Ass'n of Extension Home Economists (1933)
Box 172, 300 Edward St., Henry IL 61537
President: Carryllyn L. Hunt
Members: 3,700
Annual Budget: $250-500,000 *Tel:* (309) 364-2356
Hist. Note: Formerly Nat'l Home Demonstration Agents' Ass'n. Extension Home Economists are employees fo the Cooperative Extension Service, a joint venture of the U.S. Department of Agriculture, county government and State Land Grand Universities. Has no paid staff. Membership: $20/year.
Publication:
The Reporter. q. adv.
Annual Meetings: Fall
1987-Louisville, KY(Commonwealth Conv. Center/Hyatt/Galt)/Oct. 4-8
1988-Pittsburgh, PA(Conv. Center/Vista Int'l/Wm Penn)/Oct. 2-6
1989-Honolulu, HI(Sheraton)/Sept. 17-21
1990-Chicago, IL(Palmer House)/Sept. 23-27
1991-Tulsa, OK(Radisson Excelsior Hotel)/Oct. 6-10

Nat'l Ass'n of Extension 4-H Agents (1946)
c/o Nat'l 4-H Council, 7100 Connecticut,Ave., Chevy Chase MD 20815
President: Carole Hansen

00194 12 05 86 1233

Members: 3,000 *Staff:* 1
Annual Budget: $100-250,000 *Tel:* (301) 961-2800
Hist. Note: Established as the National Association of County Club Agents, it became the National Association of County 4-H Club Agents and in 1969 asssumed its present name. Has no paid staff. Administrative support is provided by the 4-H Council. Membership: $25/year.
Publication:
News & Views. q. adv.
Annual Meetings: Fall
1987-San Diego/Nov. 8-12/1,500
1988-Minneapolis, MN/Nov. 6-10
1989-Mobile, AL/November

Nat'l Ass'n of Extradition Officials (1964)
506 Toluca Park Dr., Burbank CA 91505
Exec. Director: Elvyn Holt
Members: 50 states, Puerto Rico and Virgin Islands *Staff:* 1
Annual Budget: under $10,000 *Tel:* (818) 845-1912
Hist. Note: Extradition officials (two representatives from each state) who are concerned with carrying out the provisions of the Uniform Extradition Act.
Publications:
Law Report. a.
Association Directory. a.

Nat'l Ass'n of Farm and Ranch Trailer Manufacturers
Hist. Note: Members are small to medium size manufacturers. Address unknown in 1985.

Nat'l Ass'n of Farm Broadcasters (1944)
Box 119, Topeka KS 66601
Exec. Secretary: George Logan
Members: 700-750 *Staff:* 6-10
Tel: (913) 272-3456
Hist. Note: Established as the National Association of Radio Farm Directors, it became the National Association of Television-Radio Farm Directors in 1956 and assumed its present name in 1964. Membership: $75/year.
Publications:
Chats. m.
NAFB Directory. a.
Annual Meetings: November in Kansas City, MO(Crown Center)/700
1987-Nov. 12-15
1988-Nov. 10-13
1989-Nov. 9-12

Nat'l Ass'n of Farmworker Organizations (1973)
Hist. Note: Ceased operations in 1983.

Nat'l Ass'n of Fashion and Accessory Designers (1949)
Hist. Note: Address unknown in 1985.

Nat'l Ass'n of Federal Credit Unions (1967)
1111 North 19th St., Suite 700, Arlington VA 22209
Exec. V. President: Kenneth L. Robinson
Members: 625 credit unions *Staff:* 25-30
Annual Budget: $2-5,000,000 *Tel:* (703) 522-4770
Hist. Note: Originated in Los Angeles in 1966 at a meeting of 56 credit union leaders to consider ways to shape the laws and regulations under which federal credit unions operate and incorporated in the state of California the next year. Supports the Nat'l Ass'n of Federal Credit Unions Political Action Committee.
Publications:
Update. w.
The Federal Credit Union. bi-m.
Annual Meetings: July/1,500
1987-Hawaii/July 19-22
1988-Washington, DC(Sheraton)/July 24-27

Nat'l Ass'n of Federal Education Program Administrators (1975)
1801 N. Moore St., Arlington VA 22209
Exec. Director: Stanley J. McFarland
Members: 3,400 *Staff:* 1
Annual Budget: $50-100,000 *Tel:* (703) 528-0700
Hist. Note: Organized in 1975 to represent those professional educators employed by local school districts, by intermediate school districts, by state departments of education, by non-public schools, by colleges and universities, and by education-product suppliers, who have responsibility for supervising, coordinating or administering federally-funded education programs. Formerly (1984) the Nat'l Ass'n of Administrators of State and Federal Education Programs and (1985) the Nat'l Ass'n of Administrators of Federal Education Programs. Membership: $50/yr. (individual).
Publication:
Quarterly Newsletter. q.
Annual Meetings: Spring in Washington, DC/300-350
1987-(Loew's L'Enfant Plaza)/April 5-8/450

Nat'l Ass'n of Federal Veterinarians (1918)
1522 K St., N.W., Suite 836, Washington DC 20005
Exec. V. President: Dr. Edward L. Menning
Members: 1,600-1,700 *Staff:* 2-5
Annual Budget: $100-250,000 *Tel:* (202) 223-3590
Hist. Note: An association of professional veterinarians. Affiliated with the American Veterinary Medical Ass'n and Nat'l Federation of Professional Organizations. Supports the Nat'l Ass'n of Federal Veterinarians Political Action Committee. Sponsors American Academy of Veterinary Preventive Medicine. Sponsors the NAFV Memorial Scholarship Fund.
Publication:
The Federal Veterinarian. m.
Annual Meetings: With Amer. Vet. Medical Ass'n and U.S. Animal Health Ass'n

Nat'l Ass'n of Federally Impacted Schools
444 North Capitol St., Suite 612, Washington DC 20001
Exec. Director: Thomas R. Shipley, Ed.D.
Members: 600 school districts *Staff:* 3-5
Annual Budget: $100-250,000 *Tel:* (202) 624-5455
Hist. Note: Association of school districts receiving federal impact aid. Serves children in areas of military, Indian, handicapped and poverty. Provides direct reimbursement to districts in lew of real tax or federal property. Membership: $200-7,000/yr. (based on amount of aid received).
Publication:
Newsletter. irreg.
Semi-annual Meetings: Washington, DC(Capitol Hyatt)/March and October

Nat'l Ass'n of Financial Consultants (1976)
5300 Denver Tech Parkway, Suite 200, Englewood CO 80111
Exec. Director: Robert W. Fisher
Members: 275-280 *Staff:* 2-5
Annual Budget: $50-100,000 *Tel:* (303) 771-5511
Hist. Note: Members are professional financial cosultants working with companies and individuals to secure financing for commercial projects, real estate or venture captial.
Publication:
The Financial Consultant. q.

Nat'l Ass'n of Fire Equipment Distributors (1963)
111 East Wacker Drive, Chicago IL 60601
Exec. Director: Walter G. Purcell
Members: 1,100 companies *Staff:* 6-10
Annual Budget: $500-1,000,000 *Tel:* (312) 644-6610
Publications:
Firewatch. q. adv.
Firewire. q.
Firesystems. bi-m.
Input/Output. q.
Annual Meetings: In conjunction with the Nat'l Fire Protection Ass'n/May
1987-Cincinnati, OH
1988-Los Angeles, CA
1989-Alexandria, VA
1990-San Antonio, TX

Nat'l Ass'n of Fire Investigators (1961)
53 West Jackson Blvd., Chicago IL 60604
President: John Kennedy
Members: 2,000-2,500 *Staff:* 16-20
Annual Budget: $25-50,000 *Tel:* (312) 939-6050
Hist. Note: Primary purposes are to increase the knowledge and improve the skills of persons engaged in the investigation of fires, explosions, arson, subrogation, fire prevention, and related fields, or in the litigation which ensues from such investigation. Membership: $25/yr.
Publication:
NAFI Newsletter. q.
Annual Meetings: Annual Seminar on Determining the Cause & Origin of Fires, Arson, and
Explosion
1987-Chicago, IL(Bismarck Hotel)/Sept. 16-18

Nat'l Ass'n of Fleet Administrators (1957)
6th Floor; 120 Wood Ave. South, Iselin NJ 08830
Exec. Director: David P. Lefever
Members: 2,700 *Staff:* 6-10
Annual Budget: $1-2,000,000 *Tel:* (201) 494-8100
Hist. Note: Individuals responsible for administration of a fleet of 25 or more motor vehicles not for hire commercially. Organized at a luncheon meeting at the Congress Hotel in Chicago, March 12, 1957 and incorporated with 25 charter members in the State of Illinois, April 11, 1957. Membership: $260/yr.
Publications:
NAFA's Fleet Executive. m. adv.
NAFA Reference Book. a. adv.
NAFA Newsletter. m.
Annual Meetings: Spring/1,500
1987-Montreal, Quebec(Queen Elizabeth)/April 26-29
1988-San Francisco, CA(Hilton)/May 1-4
1989-New York, NY(Hilton)/April 16-19
1990-Houston, TX(Westin & Intercontinental)/April 22-25
1991-Atlanta, GA(Marriott Marquis)/April 7-10

Nat'l Ass'n of Flight Instructors (1966)
Box 793, Dublin OH 43017
President: Jack J. Eggspuehler
Members: 2,500 *Staff:* 2-5
Annual Budget: $10-25,000 *Tel:* (614) 889-6148
Hist. Note: Members are flight instructors certified by the Federal Aviation Administration. Seeks to raise the professional standards of the flight instructors through educationa and organization. Membership: $24/yr.
Publication:
NAFI Newsletter. q. adv.
Annual Meetings: Not held.

Nat'l Ass'n of Floor Covering Distributors (1970)
13-126 West Merchandise Mart Plaza, Chicago IL 60654
Exec. Director: Wade Newman
Members: 600 companies *Staff:* 2-5
Annual Budget: $250-500,000 *Tel:* (312) 467-0116
Hist. Note: Membership: $350/yr.
Publication:
News and Views. bi-m.
Annual Meetings: Spring
1987-Orlando, FL(Peabody Hotel)/May 9-13
1988-San Diego, CA(Hotel Intercontinental)/March 19-23
1989-Marco Island, FL(Marriott's Marco Beach Resort)/April 8-12
1990-Orlando, FL(Hyatt Regency Grand Cypress)/March 24-28
1991-Washington, DC(Sheraton Washington)/March 16-20

Nat'l Ass'n of Floor Covering Installers (1968)
Hist. Note: Became a division of the Carpet and Rug Institute in 1983.

Nat'l Ass'n of Flour Distributors (1919)
Box 249, Yonkers NY 10710
Chairman of the Board: Ernest Brehm, Jr.
Members: 175-200 companies *Staff:* 1
Annual Budget: $50-100,000 *Tel:* (914) 968-6100
Hist. Note: Members are brokers, distributors and salesmen allied with the distribution of bakery flour.
Publication:
The Flour Distributor. 3/yr.
Annual Meetings: Spring
1987-Hilton Head, SC(Marriott)/May 14-17
1988-Rancho Mirage, CA(Rancho Las Palmas)/May 12-15

Nat'l Ass'n of Food Equipment Manufacturers (1948)
111 East Wacker Drive, Chicago IL 60601
Exec. V. President: William W. Carpenter
Members: 450 *Staff:* 2-5
Annual Budget: $250-500,000 *Tel:* (312) 644-6610
Biennial meetings: Odd years/20,000
1987-Las Vegas, NV(Conv. Center)/Sept. 19-22

Nat'l Ass'n of Foreign-Trade Zones (1973)
1101 Connecticut Ave., N.W., Suite 700, Washington DC 20036
Exec. Director: Robert T. Chancler
Members: 200 companies *Staff:* 2-5
Annual Budget: $100-250,000 *Tel:* (202) 857-1132
Hist. Note: Foreign-Trade Zones are sites where foreign or U.S. goods may be stored, tested, repackaged, assembled, etc. and where neither customs duty nor government excise tax is levied on exported products. Membership is composed of companies who are operators, grantees and users of these sites.
Publications:
Zones Report. m.
Reference Guide. a.
Annual Meetings: October
1987-Phoenix, AZ

Nat'l Ass'n of Franchise Companies (1969)
Box 6996, Hollywood FL 33081
Exec. Director: Edward J. Foley
Members: 108 companies, 50 individuals *Staff:* 2-5
Annual Budget: $50-100,000 *Tel:* (305) 966-1530
Hist. Note: Membership: $200/year (individual).
Publication:
Franchising/Investments Around The World. m.

Nat'l Ass'n of Fraternal Insurance Counsellors (1950)
Box 642, Sheboygan WI 53081
Secy.-Treas.: Peter Schmitt, Jr.
Members: 2,500-3,000
Tel: (414) 458-1996
Hist. Note: Formerly (1966) Fraternal Insurance Counsellors Ass'n. Affiliate of the Fraternal Field Managers Ass'n.
Publication:
The Fraternal Monitor. m.

Nat'l Ass'n of Freestanding Medical Centers (1981)
Hist. Note: Became the Nat'l Ass'n for Ambulatory Care in 1985.

Nat'l Ass'n of Freight Payment Banks (1977)
c/o North Carolina Nat'l Bank, One NCNB Plaza, Charlotte NC 28255
Acting Chairperson: Deborah Maluchnik
Members: 25-30 *Staff:* 1
Annual Budget: $10-25,000 *Tel:* (919) 829-6861
Hist. Note: Incorporated in the State of Delaware, this organization has no paid staff or permanent address. Officers are elected annually. Members are banks offering shippers special arrangements for timely payment of freight charges. Membership: $425/yr.
Annual Meetings: April/50
1987-Florida

Nat'l Ass'n of Freight Transportation Consultants (1959)
Box 221, Brookville MD 20833
Exec. Director: Donna F. Behme
Members: 90-100 *Staff:* 1
Annual Budget: $10-25,000 *Tel:* (301) 924-3614

00195 12 05 86 1233

Publication:
The Supplement. m.
Annual Meetings: Third Monday and Tuesday of November
1987-Louisville, KY
1988-Phoenix, AZ

Nat'l Ass'n of Fruits, Flavors and Syrups (1917)
Box 776, Mattawan NJ 07747
Exec. Director: Richard J. Sullivan
Members: 130 companies *Staff:* 5
Annual Budget: $50-100,000 *Tel:* (201) 583-8272
Hist. Note: Formerly (1974) Nat'l Fruit & Syrup Manufacturers Ass'n, Inc.
Annual Meetings: Fall
1987-Danvers, MA(Sheraton Tara)/Oct. 14-16
1988-Longboat Key, FL(Longboat Key CLub)/Sept. 28-30

Nat'l Ass'n of Furniture Manufacturers
Hist. Note: Merged with the Southern Furniture Manufacturers Ass'n in 1984 to become the American Furniture Manufacturers Ass'n.

Nat'l Ass'n of Futures Trading Advisors (1980)
111 East Wacker Dr., Chicago IL 60601
Exec. Director: Robert F. Hartman
Members: 175-200 *Staff:* 2-5
Annual Budget: $100-250,000 *Tel:* (312) 644-6610
Hist. Note: Members are commodity trading advisors and pool operators as well as professionals in all aspects of commodity trading. Membership: $500-2,200/yr.
Publication:
NAFTA News. bi-m.
Annual Meetings: July
1987-Chicago, IL(Ritz-Carlton)/July 22-24

Nat'l Ass'n of Gambling Regulatory Agencies (1984)
c/o Louisiana Dedpartment of Justice, 234 Loyala St., Suite 700, New Orleans LA 70112
President: William B. Faust, III
Tel: (504) 568-5550
Hist. Note: Members are government entities involved in state regulation of gambling activities. Membership: $100/yr. (organization).
Semi-annual Meetings:

Nat'l Ass'n of Garage Door Manufacturers (1968)
655 Irving Park at Lake Shore Drive, Suite 201 Park Place, Chicago IL 60613-3198
Exec. V. President: Frank S. Fitzgerald, CAE
Members: 70 companies *Staff:* 6-10
Annual Budget: $100-250,000 *Tel:* (312) 525-2644
Hist. Note: Formerly (1972) Midwest Garage Door Manufacturers Ass'n. Membership: $1,210/yr.
Publication:
Garage Door Business. q.
Tri-annual Meetings: Jan., May and Sept.
1987-San Francisco, CA(Fairmont)/Jan. 7-10
1987-Chicago, IL(Hyatt Regency O'Hare)/May 6-7
1987-Naples, FL(Naples Beach Hotel & Club)/Sept. 14-16
1988-Ft. Lauderdale, FL/Jan. 6-9
1988-Chicago, IL/May 4-6
1988-West/Sept. 19-21

Nat'l Ass'n of Geology Teachers (1938)
Box 368, Lawrence KS 66044
Secy.-Treas.: Alan R. Geyer
Members: 1,800 *Staff:* 9
Annual Budget: $25-50,000 *Tel:* (913) 843-1234
Hist. Note: Founded in Rock Island, IL as the Ass'n of College Geology Teachers; dropped "College" from name in 1946; assumed present name in 1958. A member society of the American Geological Institute. Membership: $20/yr. (individual); $28/yr. (organization/company)
Publication:
Journal of Geological Education. 5/yr. adv.
Annual Meetings: Fall with Geological Soc. of America
1987-Phoenix, AZ/Oct. 26-29
1988-Denver, CO/Oct. 31-Nov. 3
1989-St. Louis, MO/Nov. 9-12
1990-Dallas, TX/Oct. 29-Nov. 1
1991-San Diego, CA/Oct. 21-24
1992-Cincinnati, OH/Oct. 26-29
1993-Boston, MA/Oct. 25-28

Nat'l Ass'n of Girls Clubs (1930)
5808 16th St., N.W., Washington DC 20011
Headquarters Secretary: Carole A. Early
Members: 250 clubs *Staff:* 2-5
Annual Budget: $10-25,000 *Tel:* (202) 726-2044
Hist. Note: Membership consists of black girls aged 6-18. Sponsored by the National Association of Colored Women's Clubs. Aims are to begin training toward moral, mental and material development of its members and to give girls the right conceptions of health, beauty, love, home and service. Formerly (1976) National Association of Colored Girls Clubs.
Biennial Meetings: Even years with the National Association of Colored
Women's Clubs.

Nat'l Ass'n of Glove Manufacturers (1917)
Hist. Note: Address unknown in 1985.

Nat'l Ass'n of Glue Manufacturers (1923)
Hist. Note: Defunct in 1982.

Nat'l Ass'n of Golf Club Manufacturers (1924)
Hist. Note: Reported as inactive in 1986.

Nat'l Ass'n of Government Archives and Records Administrators (1984)
Room 10A75, Cultural Education Center, New York State Archives, Albany NY 12230
Exec. Director: Bruce W. Dearstyne
Members: 204 individuals
Annual Budget: $25-50,000 *Tel:* (518) 474-8037
Hist. Note: Incorporated in New York State, NAGARA is a nationwide association of local, state and federal records administrators and others concerned with improving administration of government records. Membership: $100/program/year (records management & archival agencies) ; $20/year (all others).
Publication:
The Clearinghouse. q.
Annual Meetings:
1987-Atlanta, GA/July 22-25

Nat'l Ass'n of Government Communicators (1976)
80 South Early St., Alexandria VA 22304
Exec. Director: Debbie Trocchi
Members: 1,000 *Staff:* 1
Annual Budget: $50-100,000 *Tel:* (703) 823-4821
Hist. Note: A merger of the Federal Editors Ass'n, the Government Information Organization, and the Armed Forces Writers' League. Member of the Council of Communication Societies. Membership: $45/yr. (individual), $75/yr. (company).
Publications:
Journal of Public Communication. a.
NAGC Communicator. m.

Nat'l Ass'n of Government Employees (1961)
285 Dorchester Ave., Boston MA 02127
President: Kenneth T. Lyons
Members: 195,000 *Staff:* 35-40
Annual Budget: $2-5,000,000 *Tel:* (617) 268-5002
Hist. Note: An independent labor union of civilian government employees. Sponsors and supports the Government Employees' Political Research Institute and the Nat'l Ass'n of Government Employees Political Action Committee.
Publication:
Fednews. m.
Quadrennial Meetings: (1987)

Nat'l Ass'n of Government Inspectors and Quality Assurance Personnel (1954)
Naval Air Rework Facility, Jacksonville Naval Air Station, Jacksonville FL 32212
President: Gary Nickels
Members: 1,000 *Staff:* 1
Annual Budget: under $10,000 *Tel:* (904) 772-2323
Hist. Note: Independent labor union. Formerly (1972) Nat'l Ass'n of Government Inspectors. Has no paid staff.
Publication:
National News Letter.

Nat'l Ass'n of Governmental Labor Officials (1914)
Department of Labor, Box 11329, Columbia SC 29211
Secy.-Treas.: Edgar McGowan
Members: 55
Annual Budget: $25-50,000 *Tel:* (803) 758-2851
Hist. Note: Founded as the Internat'l Ass'n of Governmental Labor Officials, it assumed its present name in 1979. Members are directors and commissioners of state labor departments. Has no paid staff or permanent address. Membership: $200/yr.
Semi-annual Meetings: Summer and Winter

Nat'l Ass'n of Governors' Highway Safety Representatives (1969)
444 North Capitol St., Suite 524, Washington DC 20001
Exec. Director: Judith Stone
Members: 57 states and territories *Staff:* 2
Annual Budget: $100-250,000 *Tel:* (202) 624-5877
Hist. Note: Members are state officials who administer the Highway Safety Act.
Publication:
Newsletter. bi-m.
Annual Meetings: Fall
1987-Winston-Salem, NC/Nov. 8-12

Nat'l Ass'n of Greenhouse Vegetable Growers (1937)
Hist. Note: Merged with the Western Greenhouse Vegetable Growers Ass'n to form the American Greenhouse Vegetable Growers Ass'n in 1984.

Nat'l Ass'n of Greeting Card Publishers (1941)
Hist. Note: Became the Greeting Card Association in 1983.

Nat'l Ass'n of Health and Welfare Ministries, United Methodist Church (1940)
Hist. Note: Became the United Methodist Association of Health and Welfare Ministries in 1983.

Nat'l Ass'n of Health Career Schools (1968)
9570 West Pico Blvd., Suite 200, Los Angeles CA 90035
General Counsel: J.S. Olins
Members: 200 *Staff:* 2
Annual Budget: $50-100,000 *Tel:* (213) 553-8626
Hist. Note: Formerly (1975) Ass'n of Accredited Medical Laboratory Schools, Inc.
Publications:
Bulletin. bi-m.
Newsletter. 2-3/yr.
Annual Meetings: Winter
1987-San Diego, CA(del Coronado)/Feb.

Nat'l Ass'n of Health Underwriters (1930)
1000 Connecticut Ave., N.W., Suite 1111, Washington DC 20036
Exec. V. President: William F. Flood
Members: 8,000 *Staff:* 6-10
Annual Budget: $250-500,000 *Tel:* (202) 638-0455
Hist. Note: Formerly (1962) Nat'l Ass'n of Accident & Health Underwriters, and Internat'l Ass'n of Health Underwriters (1978). Awards the RHU (Registered Health Underwriter) designation. Membership: $50/yr. (individual), $500/yr. (organization).
Publication:
Health Insurance Underwriter. m. adv.
Annual Meetings: June
1987-San Diego, CA(Del Coronado)/June 21-25/400
1988-Orlando, FL(Hyatt Grand Cypress)/June 28-July 1/400-450
1989-Tulsa, OK/June/450-500
1990-San Antonio, TX/June/500-550

Nat'l Ass'n of Health Unit Clerks/Coordinators (1980)
Hist. Note: Address unknown in 1985-86.

Nat'l Ass'n of Hebrew Day School Administrators (1960)
1114 Ave. J, Brooklyn NY 11230
Exec. Coordinator: Dr. Alfred Schnell
Members: 400
Tel: (718) 258-7767
Publication:
NAHDSA Review. 8/yr.

Nat'l Ass'n of Hebrew Day School PTAs (1948)
Hist. Note: Inactive since 1983.

Nat'l Ass'n of Hispanic Journalists (1984)
Nat'l Press Bldg., Suite 634, Washington DC 20045
Exec. Director: Frank Newton, Ph.D.
Members: 25 companies; 450 individuals *Staff:* 4
Annual Budget: $250-500,000 *Tel:* (202) 783-6228
Hist. Note: Its purposes are to increase educational and career opportunities in journalism for Hispanic Americans, to organize and provide mutual support by Hispanic Journalists, and to promote fair treatment of Hispanics by the news media. Membership: $35.yr. Membership: $35/yr.
Publications:
NAHJ Membership Newsletter. m.
National Hispanic Media Directory.
Annual Meetings: April
1987-Los Angeles, CA(Hilton)/April 22-25

Nat'l Ass'n of Hispanic Publications (1982)
1436 S. Main, Los Angeles CA 90017
Administrative Coordinator: Magdalena Whisler
Members: 106 publications *Staff:* 2
Annual Budget: $25-50,000 *Tel:* (702) 883-0186
Hist. Note: Membership open to publications which serve or cover the Hispanic and/or Spanish speaking community in the U.S. Associate membership open to individuals, corporations, or new services who support the NAHP' goals. Membership: $100/yr.
Publications:
Marketing Hispanic Print. m. adv.
National Hispanic Media Directory. a.
Annual Meetings: April, in conjunction with the Nat'l Hispanic Media Conference.
1987-Los Angeles, CA(Hilton)/2,400
1988-Mexico

Nat'l Ass'n of Home and Workshop Writers (1973)
Palomar Mountain CA 92060
President: Richard Day
Members: 45 *Staff:* 0
Annual Budget: under $10,000
Hist. Note: Writers of articles, books and video material on such subjects as home maintenance, repair and improvement, and on workshop projects. Membership: $25/year.
Publication:
Newsletter. bi-m.

Nat'l Ass'n of Home Builders of the U.S. (1942)
15th and M Streets, N.W., Washington DC 20005
Exec. V. President and C.E.O.: Kent W. Colton
Members: 145,100 *Staff:* 275
Annual Budget: over $5,000,000 *Tel:* (202) 822-0200
Hist. Note: Connected with the Builders Political Campaign Committee. Also supports the Homeowners Warranty Corporation and the NAHB Research Foundation and the Home Builders Institute. Absorbed the National Association of Home Manufacturers in 1981.
Publications:
Builder. m. adv.
NAHB News. w.

00196 12 05 86 1233

Annual Meetings: Winter
1987-Dallas, TX(Convention Center)/Jan./50,000
1988-Dallas, TX(Convention Center)/Jan./50,000
1989-Atlanta, GA

Nat'l Ass'n of Home Health Agencies (1970)
Hist. Note: Became the National Association for Home Care in 1982.

Nat'l Ass'n of Homes for Children (1975)
Box 1459, Millbrook NY 12545
President: Dr. Neil Howard
Members: 500-525 facilities and agencies *Staff:* 2-5
Annual Budget: $250-500,000 *Tel:* (914) 677-3283
Publications:
Newsletter. q.
Public Affairs Bulletin. bi-m.
Caring.
Annual Meetings: September
1987-Chicago, IL
1988-Los Angeles, CA

Nat'l Ass'n of Hose and Accessories Distributors (1985)
1900 Arch St., Philadelphia PA 19103
Exec. V. President: John W. Kane
Members: 175 companies; 200 individuals *Staff:* 2
Annual Budget: $50-100,000 *Tel:* (215) 564-3484
Hist. Note: A member of the National Association of Wholesaler Distributors. Membership: $150-350/yr.
Publication:
Connections. m.
Annual Meetings: Spring

Nat'l Ass'n of Hosiery Manufacturers (1905)
447 South Sharon Amity Road, Charlotte NC 28211
President and CEO: Sid Smith
Members: 300 *Staff:* 6-10
Annual Budget: $500-1,000,000 *Tel:* (704) 365-0913
Hist. Note: Manufacturers of hosiery as well as suppliers of raw materials, machinery and packaging. Members make and distribute more than 85% of U.S. hosiery, including socks and pantyhose.
Publications:
Hosiery News. m. adv.
Hosiery Statistics. a.
Annual Meetings:
1987-Hilton Head, NC(Hyatt)/April 22-26/500
1988-Charlotte, NC(Adams Mark)/April 24-27/600

Nat'l Ass'n of Hospital Admitting Managers (1974)
1101 Connecticut Ave., N.W., Suite 700, Washington DC 20036
Exec. Director: Carol A. Lively
Members: 1,600 *Staff:* 2
Annual Budget: $100-250,000 *Tel:* (202) 857-1125
Hist. Note: Established and incorporated in New York. Membership: $100/year (individual), $1,000/year (corporate).
Publication:
Journal for Hospital Admitting Management. q. adv.
Annual Meetings: Late spring
1987-New Orleans, LA (Fairmont)/April 23-27/500
1988-Washington, DC (Crystal Gateway Marriott)/April 28-May 1/500

Nat'l Ass'n of Hospital Purchasing Materials Management (1957)
Box 1046, Lewistown PA 17044-1046
President: Tedd Heckathorn
Members: 200 *Staff:* 2-5
Annual Budget: $25-50,000 *Tel:* (717) 242-0106
Hist. Note: Established in 1957 as the Nat'l Ass'n of Hospital Purchasing Agents, it became the Nat'l Ass'n of Hospital Purchasing Management in 1968 and assumed its present name in 1979. Members are individuals in administrative positions in the purchasing departments of health care institutions and may advance to fellowship status through a certification program. Membership: $80/year.
Annual Meetings: Fall/100

Nat'l Ass'n of Housing and Redevelopment Officials (1933)
1320 18th St., N.W., Washington DC 20036
Exec. Director: Robert Maffin
Members: 8-9000 *Staff:* 20-25
Annual Budget: $2-5,000,000 *Tel:* (202) 333-2020
Hist. Note: Formerly (1953) Nat'l Ass'n of Housing Officials.
Publications:
Journal of Housing. bi-m. adv.
NAHRO Monitor. semi-m.
Annual Meetings: Fall
1987-New Orleans, LA(Hilton)/Oct. 18-20

Nat'l Ass'n of Housing Cooperatives (1950)
2501 M St., N.W., Washington DC 20037
Exec. Director: Herbert Levy
Members: 700 *Staff:* 2-5
Annual Budget: $100-250,000 *Tel:* (202) 887-0706
Hist. Note: Affiliated with Cooperative League of the U.S.A. The ass'n defines a housing cooperative as a residential community whose residents collectively own their property, vote to determine policy, and receive only a limited return on invested capital. Members are housing cooperatives, management firms, attorneys, accountants, neighborhood organizations, tenant associations government agencies and individuals interested in cooperative housing. Membership: $35/yr. (individual); $200/yr. (organization/company).
Publications:
Cooperative Housing Bulletin. m. adv.
Cooperative Housing Journal.
Annual Meetings: Fall/400-600
1987-Arlington, VA(Hyatt Regency Crystal City)/Oct. 21-25
1988-Atlanta, GA(Hyatt Regency)/Sept. 28-Oct. 2
1989-New York, NY or Boston, MA

Nat'l Ass'n of Human Rights Workers (1947)
315 Court St., Clearwater FL 33516
President: Leon Russell
Members: 500
Annual Budget: $10-25,000 *Tel:* (813) 462-4880
Hist. Note: Formerly (1971) Nat'l Ass'n of Intergroup Relations Officials. Has no paid staff or permanent address; officers are elected annually. Membership: $35/yr.
Publications:
Journal of Intergroup Relations.
NAHRW Newsletter. bi-m. adv.
Annual Meetings: October
1987-Charlotte, NC(Marriott Inn-City Center)/Oct. 16-21

Nat'l Ass'n of Human Services Technologies (1961)
Hist. Note: Address unknown in 1985.

Nat'l Ass'n of Ice Cream Vendors (1969)
5600 Brookwood Terrace, Nashville TN 37205
Exec. Officer: Joe E. Maxwell, CAE
Members: 100-125 companies *Staff:* 2-5
Annual Budget: $10-25,000 *Tel:* (615) 356-4240
Hist. Note: Truckers of wholesale ice cream.
Publication:
Newsletter. m.
Annual Meetings: November

Nat'l Ass'n of Income Tax Practitioners (1972)
Hist. Note: Became the Nat'l Ass'n of Income Tax Preparers in 1985.

Nat'l Ass'n of Income Tax Preparers (1972)
Box 1414, North Windham ME 04062
President: Richard Hunt
Members: 548
Annual Budget: $25-50,000 *Tel:* (207) 892-6642
Hist. Note: Awards the designations Certified Tax Practitioner, Certified Tax Practitioner Specialist, and Certified Master Tax Consultant. Formerly known as the Nat'l Ass'n of Income Tax Accountants and the Nat'l Ass'n of Income Tax Practitioners, NAITP assumed its present name in 1985. The Institute of Tax Consultants is its certification arm. Membership: $65/year.
Publication:
The Communicator. bi-m. adv.

Nat'l Ass'n of Independent Businessmen (1968)
Hist. Note: Incorporated in Minnesota in 1968, this organization became dormant in the mid-1970s, was reactivated in 1981, but reported as defunct in 1983.

Nat'l Ass'n of Independent Colleges and Universities (1969)
122 C St., N.W., Suite 750, Washington DC 20001
President: Dr. Richard F. Rosser
Members: 900 *Staff:* 17
Annual Budget: $1-2,000,000 *Tel:* (202) 383-5950
Hist. Note: Founded as Federation of State Ass'ns of Colleges and Universities, a lobbying group for the Ass'n of American Colleges, it became the Nat'l Council of Independent Colleges and Universities in 1971 and assumed independence under its present name in 1976. Promotes private and government support for the nation's 1200 private institutions of higher learning and underwrites the Nat'l Institute of Independent Colleges and Universities as its research arm. Membership: $450-4,500/year (institution).
Publications:
Week In Review. w.
Voice of Independents. q.
Annual Meetings: Winter in Washington, DC(Hyatt Regency)/400-600
1987-Feb. 4-6
1988-Feb. 3-5
1989-Feb. 1-3
1990-Jan. 31-Feb. 2

Nat'l Ass'n of Independent Fee Appraisers (1961)
7501 Murdoch St., St. Louis MO 63119
Exec. V. President: Robert G. Kaestner
Members: 4,300-4,500 *Staff:* 6-10
Annual Budget: $250-500,000 *Tel:* (314) 781-6688
Hist. Note: Founded in Phoenix, Arizona in 1961. Members in large part are self-employed appraisers specializing in the appraisal of real estate held in fee simple. Awards three designations: Independent Fee Appraiser (IFA), IFA Senior (IFAS) and IFA Counselor (IFAC). Membership: $175/yr.
Publications:
Appraisal Review. q.
Appraiser-Gram. q.

Nat'l Ass'n of Independent Insurance Adjusters (1937)
222 West Adams, Suite 845, Chicago IL 60606
Exec. Director: David F. Mehren
Members: 450-500 companies *Staff:* 4
Annual Budget: $100-250,000 *Tel:* (312) 853-0808
Hist. Note: Members are companies and individuals adjusting claims for insurance companies on a fee basis.
Publications:
The Independent Adjuster. q. adv.
Membership Directory. a.
Status Report Member Newsletter. q.
Annual Meetings: May
1987-Orlando, FL/May 5-8

Nat'l Ass'n of Independent Insurance Auditors and Engineers (1963)
c/o Brandanger & Associates, 11995 Singletree Lane, Eden Prairie MN 55344
President: Dennis Brandanger
Members: 24 organizations
Annual Budget: under $10,000 *Tel:* (612) 944-0400
Hist. Note: Has no paid staff or permanent address; officers change annually.
Publication:
Independent Thoughts. m.
Annual Meetings: Always October

Nat'l Ass'n of Independent Insurers (1945)
2600 North River Road, Des Plaines IL 60018
President: Lowell R. Beck
Members: 500 *Staff:* 150
Annual Budget: over $5,000,000 *Tel:* (312) 297-7800
Hist. Note: Membership consists of property-liability companies. Maintains a Washington office. Supports the Nat'l Ass'n of Independent Insurers Political Action Committee.
Annual Meetings: Fall

Nat'l Ass'n of Independent Life Brokerage Agencies (1982)
1010 Wisconsin Ave., N.W., Suite 630, Washington DC 20007
Exec. Director: Charles D. Rumbarger, CAE
Members: 167 agencies *Staff:* 2-5
Annual Budget: $50-100,000 *Tel:* (202) 965-8998
Publication:
NAILBA News. q.
Annual Meetings: November

Nat'l Ass'n of Independent Publishers (1985)
2299 Riverside Drive, Box 850, Moore Haven FL 33471-1069
Exec. Director: Betty Wright
Members: 80 companies, 400 individuals *Staff:* 4
Annual Budget: $10-25,000 *Tel:* (813) 946-0293
Hist. Note: Established and incorporated in Florida, NAIP members are small, independent publishers and self-publishing writers. Membership: $50/year (individual).
Publication:
Publisher's Report. bi-m. adv.
Annual Meetings:
1987-Ft. Lauderdale, FL/Feb.

Nat'l Ass'n of Independent Record Distributors and Manufacturers (1971)
6935 Airport Highway Lane, Pennsauken NJ 08109
Exec. Director: Holly Cass
Members: 200 companies *Staff:* 1
Annual Budget: $10-25,000 *Tel:* (609) 665-8085
Hist. Note: Members are makers and distributors or records, tapes, music videos, compact discs, etc., and suppliers and distributors in related fields. Membership: $75/yr.
Publication:
Newsletter. irreg.
Annual Meetings: Spring
1987-San Francisco, CA
1988-New Orleans, LA

Nat'l Ass'n of Independent Resurfacers (1973)
5806 West 127th St., Elsip IL 60658
Exec. Secretary: Nancy Surprenant
Members: 90-100 companies
Annual Budget: $10-25,000 *Tel:* (312) 371-6384
Hist. Note: Members are companies engaged in refinishing bowling lanes, and their suppliers. Membership: $250/yr.
Publication:
Newsletter. q.
Annual Meetings: Oct./Nov.
1987-Reno, NV/Oct. 21-25

Nat'l Ass'n of Independent Schools (1962)
18 Tremont St., Boston MA 02108
President: John C. Esty, Jr.
Members: 958 schools, 66 associations *Staff:* 37
Annual Budget: $2-5,000,000 *Tel:* (617) 723-6900
Hist. Note: The result of a merger in 1962 of the Nat'l Council of Independent Schools and the Independent Schools Education Board. Independent elementary and secondary schools.
Publication:
Independent School. q. adv.
Annual Meetings: February-March/4-5,000
1987-Boston, MA/Feb. 26-28
1988-New York, NY/Feb. 25-27
1989-Chicago, IL/March 9-11

Nat'l Ass'n of Individual Investors
Hist. Note: A division of the Nat'l Ass'n of Investors.

00197 12 05 86 1233

Nat'l Ass'n of Industrial and Office Parks (1967)
1215 Jefferson Davis Highway, Suite 100, Arlington VA 22202
Exec. V. President: Sid R. Peters
Members: 5,600 companies *Staff:* 21
Annual Budget: $2-5,000,000 *Tel:* (703) 979-3400
Hist. Note: Formerly (Sept., 1976) the Nat'l Ass'n of Industrial Parks.
Publications:
Protective Covenants.
NAIOP News. q. adv.
Marketing Office and Industrial Parks.
Office Park Development.
Annual Meetings: October/600

Nat'l Ass'n of Industrial and Technical Teacher Educators (1937)
Education 200, Ferris State College, Big Rapids MI 49307
Secretary: Edward D. Cory
Members: 750-800 *Staff:* 1
Annual Budget: $10-25,000 *Tel:* (616) 796-0461
Hist. Note: NAITTE represents trade and industrial teacher educators, business and industrial trainers as well as persons in college and university trade and technical teacher education. Membership: $20/yr.
Publications:
Directory. a.
Journal of Industrial Teacher Education. q.
NAITTE Mailings. 3/yr.
Annual Meetings: December with American Vocational Ass'n
1987-Las Vegas, NV/Dec. 4-8
1988-St. Louis, MO/Dec. 2-6
1989-Orlando, FL/Dec. 1-5
1990-Cincinnati, OH/Nov. 30-Dec. 4

Nat'l Ass'n of Industrial Technology (1967)
College of Technology, Eastern Michigan University, Ypsilanti MI 48197
Exec. Director: Dr. Alvin E. Rudisill
Members: 1,200 *Staff:* 2-5
Annual Budget: $50-100,000 *Tel:* (313) 487-0358
Hist. Note: Membership consists of individuals and companies active in the field of industrial technology. Major purpose is to improve baccalaureate degree-level curricula of industrial technology. Membership: $25/year (individual), $100/year (institution).
Publications:
Journal of Industrial Technology. q.
Program Directory - Industrial Technology. a. adv.
Annual Meetings: October
1987-Nashville, TN(Stouffer's Nashville)/Oct. 21-23/400

Nat'l Ass'n of Insect Electrocutor Manufacturers
Hist. Note: Ceased operations in 1986.

Nat'l Ass'n of Installation Developers (1978)
P.O. Box 2145, Northbrook IL 60065-2145
Exec. V. President: Donald J. Walker
Members: 55-60
Tel: (312) 272-3930
Hist. Note: Members are individuals interested in the industrial development of closed military bases. Membership: $150/yr.
Publication:
Newsletter. q.
Annual Meetings: Fall/75
1987-Lake Charles, LA/Sept. 13-16

Nat'l Ass'n of Installment Companies (1951)
Hist. Note: Formerly (1969) Nat'l Ass'n of House to House Installment Companies. Firms engaged in direct selling to final consumers on a credit basis. Address unknown in 1985.

Nat'l Ass'n of Institutional Laundry Managers (1939)
Hist. Note: Became the Nat'l Ass'n of Institutional Linen Management in 1985.

Nat'l Ass'n of Institutional Linen Management (1985)
2130 Lexington Road, Suite H, Richmond KY 40475
Exec. Director: James Hartman
Members: 1,250 *Staff:* 2-5
Annual Budget: $100-250,000 *Tel:* (606) 624-0177
Hist. Note: Founded as the Nat'l Ass'n of Institutional Laundry Managers in 1939; assumed its present name in 1985. Membership: $80/yr.
Publications:
NAILM News. m.
Roster. a.
Annual Meetings: Spring
1987-Atlanta, GA/April 26-29
1988-Dallas, TX/March 10-15

Nat'l Ass'n of Insurance Brokers (1934)
1401 New York Ave., N.W., Suite 720, Washington DC 20005
Exec. Director: David F. Lambert, III
Members: 100 *Staff:* 6-10
Tel: (202) 628-6700
Hist. Note: Represents commercial insurance brokers.
Publication:
The Friday Flash. bi-w.
Annual Meetings: Spring
1987-Sea Island, GA(The Cloister)/May 26-30/200
1988-Pebble Beach, CA(The Lodge at P.B.)/May 10-14/200
1989-Sea Island, GA(The Cloister)/May 30-June 2/200

Nat'l Ass'n of Insurance Commissioners (1871)
1125 Grand Avenue, Suite 1900, Kansas City MO 64106
Exec. V. President: Karl Koch
Members: 55-60 *Staff:* 60
Annual Budget: $1-2,000,000 *Tel:* (816) 842-3600
Hist. Note: Members are the chief insurance regulatory officials of the 50 states, the District of Columbia, Guam, Puerto Rico and the Virgin Islands. Formerly Nat'l Conference of Insurance Commissioners.
Publication:
Proceedings. semi-a.
Semi annual meetings: Summer and Winter
1987-Chicago, IL/June
1987-Phoenix, AZ/Dec.

Nat'l Ass'n of Insurance Women (Internat'l) (1940)
1847 East 15th St., Box 4410, Tulsa OK 74159
Exec. Vice President: Susan Mills Caldwell
Members: 19,000 *Staff:* 8
Annual Budget: $500-1,000,000 *Tel:* (918) 744-5195
Hist. Note: Promotes insurance education and supports the professional advancement of its members; offers education programs through 430 local chapters in the United States and Western Canada. Offers the Certified Professional Insurance Woman/Man (CPIW/CPIM) designation.
Publication:
Today's Insurance Woman. bi-m. adv.
Annual Meetings: June
1987-Boston, MA(Marriott Copley Plaza)/June 21-24
1988-Indianapolis, IN(Hyatt Regency)/ June 19-22
1989-Honolulu, HI(Sheraton Waikiki)June 18-21
1990-Denver, CO(Fairmont)/June 16-19
1991-Grand Rapids, MI(Amway Grand Plaza)/June 16-19
1992-Atlanta, GA/June 14-17
1993-Reno, NV

Nat'l Ass'n of Interdisciplinary Ethnic Studies (1975)
Hist. Note: Became the Nat'l Ass'n for Ethnic Studies in 1984.

Nat'l Ass'n of Investigative Specialists (1984)
P.O. Box 33244, Austin TX 78764-6104
Director: Ralph D. Thomas
Members: 400 individuals; 200 companies *Staff:* 1
Annual Budget: $25-50,000 *Tel:* (512) 834-8500
Hist. Note: NAIS promotes the private investigative profession; it provides members with case assignments from other members; provides training manuals for the investigative profession; trains new private investigators. Membership: $65/yr.(one year); $85/yr.(two year)
Publication:
Tracer Magazine. bi-m.
Annual Meetings: Fall

Nat'l Ass'n of Investment Clubs (1951)
Hist. Note: Became the Nat'l Ass'n of Investors in 1984.

Nat'l Ass'n of Investment Companies (1971)
7th Floor, 915 15th St., N.W., Washington DC 20005
President: JoAnn H. Price
Members: 100 *Staff:* 4
Annual Budget: $250-500,000 *Tel:* (202) 347-8600
Hist. Note: Formerly (1986) the American Ass'n of Minority Enterprise Small Business Investment Companies. Minority enterprise small business investment companies (also known as MESBICs) are privately owned companies, licensed by the Small Business Administration, to provide equity financing or long term loans to minority small businesses. Membership: $15/yr. per $10,000 of private capital.
Publications:
Journal of Minority Business Finance. semi-a. adv.
Perspective. m. adv.
Annual Meetings: October/250-300

Nat'l Ass'n of Investors (1951)
1515 East Eleven Mile Road, Royal Oak MI 48067
Exec. Director: Thomas E. O'Hara
Members: 6,400 clubs, 118,000 individuals *Staff:* 23
Annual Budget: $2-5,000,000 *Tel:* (313) 543-0612
Hist. Note: A federation of investment clubs and individual investors concerned with teaching investment principles and representing individual investors in Washington. Formerly (1984) the Nat'l Ass'n of Investment Clubs, which is now one of two divisions; the other being the Nat'l Ass'n of Individual Investors. Membership: $30/yr. (individual); $30/yr. plus $7/yr. per individual for an organization.
Publications:
Better Investing. m. adv.
Investment Club Manual. tri-a.
Investment Club Accounting Manual.
Annual Meetings: Fall
1987-Detroit, MI(Westin)/Oct. 14-18
1988-Philadelphia, PA(Adams Mark)/Oct. 26-30

Nat'l Ass'n of Jai Alai Frontons (1977)
Daytona Beach Jai Alai, P.O. Box 2630, Daytona Beach FL 32015
Exec. Officer: Milton Roth
Members: 11 frontons *Staff:* 2-5
Annual Budget: $25-50,000 *Tel:* (904) 255-7395
Hist. Note: Established January 1, 1977 and incorporated in Florida.
Publications:
NAJF Notes. q.
Tounament Programs. bi-m. adv.

Nat'l Ass'n of Jazz Educators (1968)
Box 724, Manhattan KS 66502
Exec. Director: Bill McFarlin
Members: 6,000 individuals *Staff:* 2-5
Annual Budget: $250-500,000 *Tel:* (913) 776-8744
Hist. Note: Music teachers at all educational levels, librarians, musicians, and representatives from the music industry. A member of the Music Educators National Conference. Membership: $22/yr. (individual), $85-700/yr. (company).
Publications:
Educator. q. adv.
Jazz Educators Journal. q. adv.
Annual Meetings: January/2,000
1987-Atlanta, GA(Hyatt Regency)/Jan. 8-11
1988-Detroit, MI(Westin)/Jan. 7-10

Nat'l Ass'n of JD/MBA Professionals (1982)
c/o AE Capital, 745 5th Ave., 19th Floor, New York NY 10151
President: Bruce C. Rivkin
Members: 250-300
Annual Budget: under $10,000 *Tel:* (212) 888-6800
Hist. Note: Members are lawyers who also hold an MBA degree. Has no paid staff at present.
Publication:
JD/MBA Quarterly Journal. q.

Nat'l Ass'n of Jewelry Appraisers (1981)
4210 N. Brown Ave., Scottsdale AZ 85251
Exec. Director: Richard E. Baron
Members: 850 *Staff:* 3
Annual Budget: $100-250,000 *Tel:* (602) 941-8088
Hist. Note: Purpose is to maintain professional standards and education in the field of jewelry appraisal. Members include jewelers, jewelry appraisers, importers, brokers and other professionally interested trade members. Membership: $125/yr. (individual); $100/yr. (company)
Publications:
The Jewelry Appraiser. bi-m. adv.
Membership Directory. a.
Annual Meetings: February
1987-Tucson, AZ(Park Hotel)

Nat'l Ass'n of Jewish Family, Children's and Health Professionals (1964)
c/o New York Ass'n for New Americans, 225 Park Ave. S, New York NY 10003
Exec. Director: Dr. Solomon Henry Green
Members: 300 individuals *Staff:* 1
Annual Budget: $10-25,000 *Tel:* (212) 674-7400
Hist. Note: Established in 1964 as the Nat'l Ass'n of Jewish Family, Children's and Health Services. Membership: $25-60/yr.
Publication:
Newsletter. semi-a.
Annual Meetings: May/June

Nat'l Ass'n of Jewish Vocational Services (1939)
225 Park Ave. South, 17th Floor, New York NY 10003
Exec. Director: Harvey P. Goldman
Members: 34 organizations *Staff:* 6-10
Annual Budget: $100-250,000 *Tel:* (212) 529-7474
Hist. Note: Formerly (1976) the Jewish Occupational Council. Voluntary Jewish vocational guidance, employment, training and rehabilitation organizations in the U.S., Canada and Israel.
Publication:
Newsletter. m.
Annual Meetings: Spring

Nat'l Ass'n of Juvenile Correctional Agencies (1903)
36 Locksley Lane, Springfield IL 62704
Exec. Secy.-Treas.: Donald G. Blackburn
Members: 250 *Staff:* 1
Annual Budget: under $10,000 *Tel:* (217) 787-0690
Hist. Note: An affiliate of the American Correctional Ass'n. Founded as the National Ass'n of Training Schools and Juvenile Agencies, it assumed its present name in 1981. Merged with the Ass'n of State Juvenile Justice Administrators in 1984.
Publication:
Proceedings. a.
Annual Meetings: With the American Correctional Ass'n

Nat'l Ass'n of Laboratory Suppliers (1977)
P.O. Box 1229, Metairie LA 70004
Exec. Director: Barry W. Zander
Members: 30 companies *Staff:* 2
Annual Budget: $10-25,000 *Tel:* (504) 838-7969
Hist. Note: Brings together distributors and manufacturers of laboratory supplies and equipment for educational and business purposes. Membership: $300/yr.
Publication:
NALS News. q. adv.
Annual Meetings: Semi-annual meetings

Nat'l Ass'n of Latino Elected and Appointed Officials (1975)
708 G St., S.E., Washington DC 20003
Exec. Director: Dr. Harry Pachon
Members: 1,700 *Staff:* 11
Annual Budget: $500-1,000,000 *Tel:* (202) 546-2536
Hist. Note: NALEO is a non-partisan advocacy group which works to initiate public policies responsive to the Hispanic community and to inform that community of issues affecting them. While membership includes state representatives, mayors, and members of Congress, it is open to all who support its objectives. Membership: $25/yr. (individual);

00198 12 05 86 1233

$1,500/yr. (organization/company)
Publications:
Citizenship Newsletter. q.
NALEO National Report. q.
National Directory of Citizenship Services. bi-a.
National Roster of Hispanic Elected Officials. a.
Audit of Federal Contracting with Hispanic Firms. a.
Annual Meetings: Spring

Nat'l Ass'n of Lawn and Garden Manufacturers
Hist. Note: Ceased operations in 1985.

Nat'l Ass'n of Leagues, Umpires and Scorers (1931)
Box 1420, Wichita KS 67201
President: Joe Ryan
Members: 9,000-10,000 *Staff:* 1
Annual Budget: under $10,000 *Tel:* (316) 267-7333
Hist. Note: Affiliated with Nat'l Baseball Congress.
Publication:
Official Playing And Scoring Rules For Baseball. a.
Annual Meetings: Wichita, KS/August

Nat'l Ass'n of Learning Lab Directors (1965)
Hist. Note: Became the Internat'l Ass'n for Learning Laboratories in 1982.

Nat'l Ass'n of Legal Assistants (1975)
1420 S. Utica, Tulsa OK 74104
Exec. Director: Marge Dover
Members: 2,000 *Staff:* 2-5
Annual Budget: $100-250,000 *Tel:* (918) 587-6828
Hist. Note: Members are professional legal assistants. Awards the Certified Legal Assistant (CLA) designation.
Publication:
Facts and Findings. bi.-m.
Annual Meetings: July

Nat'l Ass'n of Legal Investigators (1967)
5319 N. Dixie Highway, Fort Lauderdale FL 33334
Nat'l Director: Charles G. Michaels
Members: 500
Annual Budget: $50-100,000 *Tel:* (305) 771-6900
Hist. Note: Membership: $80/yr.
Publication:
The Legal Investigator. q. adv.
Annual Meetings: June

Nat'l Ass'n of Legal Secretaries (Int'l) (1929)
2250 East 73rd, Suite 550, Tulsa OK 74136
Exec. Administrator: Judi A. Kruse
Members: 17,000 *Staff:* 6-10
Annual Budget: $500-1,000,000 *Tel:* (918) 493-3540
Hist. Note: Has certification program leading to designation as a Professional Legal Secretary (PLS). Established as the California Association of Legal Secretaries, it became Legal Secretaries, Inc. in 1940 and assumed its present name in 1950.
Publication:
The NALS Docket. bi-m. adv.
Annual Meetings: Summer/1,000
1987-Washington, DC(J.W. Marriott)/July 25-30
1988-Salt Lake City, UT(Sheraton Hotel Tower)/July 23-28
1989-Birmingham, AL(Wynfrey Hotel)/July 15-20

Nat'l Ass'n of Letter Carriers of the United States of America (1889)
100 Indiana Ave., N. W., Washington DC 20001
President: Vincent R. Sombrotto
Members: 286,000 *Staff:* 160
Annual Budget: over $5,000,000 *Tel:* (202) 393-4695
Hist. Note: Organized in Milwaukee, Wisconsin August 30, 1889 and chartered by the American Federation of Labor in 1917. Has a budget of about $12 million. Sponsors and supports the Committee on Letter Carriers Political Education. Membership: $72/year.
Publications:
NALC Bulletin Bulletin. w.
The Postal Record. m. adv.
The Activist. q.
Postmark Washington. q.
The Retiree. q.
Biennial meetings: Even years
1988-Portland, OR
1990-New Orleans, LA

Nat'l Ass'n of Life Companies (1955)
1455 Pennsylvania Ave., N.W., Suite 1250, Washington DC 20004
Exec. V. President: S. Roy Woodall, Jr.
Members: 500 companies *Staff:* 5
Annual Budget: $250-500,000 *Tel:* (202) 783-6252
Hist. Note: Small life and health insurance companies. Formerly Nat'l Institute of Life Insurers. Sponsors and supports the National Association of Life Companies Political Action Committee.
Publication:
Newsletter. m.
Semi-annual Meetings: Summer and Fall/250-300

Nat'l Ass'n of Life Underwriters (1890)
1922 F St., N.W., Washington DC 20006
Exec. V. President: Jack E. Bobo
Members: 130-135,000 *Staff:* 80-100
Annual Budget: over $5,000,000 *Tel:* (202) 331-6000
Hist. Note: A federation of 950-1,000 state and local ass'ns of career life insurance underwriters, NALU is a professional organization of life insurance agents, general agents and managers. Has an annual budget of $10 million. Supports the Life Underwriters Political Action Committee (LUPAC). Membership: $40/per capita.
Publications:
Life Association News. m. adv.
Wheelhorse Newsletter. m.
Annual Meetings: September/3-4000
1987-Orlando, FL/Sept. 13-17
1988-Dallas, TX(Anatole)/Sept. 25-29
1989-Boston, MA/Sept. 17-21
1990-Nashville, TN/Sept. 9-13

Nat'l Ass'n of Lighting Representatives (1980)
Box 214, Sea Girt NJ 08750
Exec. Director: Paul E. Saunders
Members: 600 *Staff:* 2
Annual Budget: $25-50,000 *Tel:* (201) 974-1900
Hist. Note: Individuals who sell residential lighting fixtures and accessories, and their manufacturers and/or importers.
Publications:
Lantern. m.
NALR Profile Directory. a.
Semi-annual Meetings:
1987-Nassau, Bahamas (Business Meeting)
1987-Texas (National Lighting Fair)

Nat'l Ass'n of Limited Edition Dealers (1975)
26 S. La Grange Road, La Grange IL 60525
Exec. Director: Ray Kiefer
Members: 240 companies *Staff:* 1
Annual Budget: $25-50,000 *Tel:* (312) 482-3650
Hist. Note: Members are dealers in limited edition prints.
Publication:
Bulletin. q.
Annual Meetings: July
1987-South Bend, IN

Nat'l Ass'n of List Compilers (1975)
Hist. Note: Defunct in 1983.

Nat'l Ass'n of Litho Clubs (1946)
Box 1258, Clifton NJ 07012
Exec. V. President: Philip W. Battaglia, CAE
Members: 4-5000 *Staff:* 3
Annual Budget: $25-50,000 *Tel:* (201) 777-6727
Hist. Note: Members are supervisory personnel in lithographic plants.
Publication:
Litho Tips. q. adv.
Annual Meetings: June
1987-Houston, TX(Hyatt)/June 24-27/400
1988-Minnesota(Breezy Point Resort)/June 22-26/400
1989-Baltimore, MD/June 21-25/425

Nat'l Ass'n of Lithographic Plate Manufacturers (1966)
1730 N. Lynn St., Arlington VA 22209
Exec. Director: Nancy Bigger
Members: 16-20 companies *Staff:* 2-5
Annual Budget: under $10,000 *Tel:* (703) 841-8100
Hist. Note: A special industry group of Printing Industries of America. Formerly (1975) the Nat'l Ass'n of Grained Plate Manufacturers.
Annual Meetings:
1987-Hawaii/March

Nat'l Ass'n of Mail Service Pharmacies (1975)
One Prince St., Alexandria VA 22314
Exec. Director: Delbert D. Konnor
Members: 6 companies *Staff:* 2
Annual Budget: under $10,000 *Tel:* (703) 684-8242
Hist. Note: NAMSP's purpose is to assist in informing consumers on obtaining maximum health benefits and prescription services through the purchase of highest quality drugs. There is one class of members consisting of licensed pharmacies which for a period of two years must have dispensed a minimum of 100,000 prescriptions per year. Also, the pharmacy must have received and dispensed by mail a majority of these prescriptions serviced during that two-year period.
Annual Meetings: Late fall

Nat'l Ass'n of Management and Technical Assistance Centers (1980)
733 15th St., N.W. Suite 917, Washington DC 20005
Washington Representative: Harold Williams
Members: 75 Centers *Staff:* 1
Annual Budget: $25-50,000 *Tel:* (202) 347-6740
Hist. Note: NAMTAC is an association of leading universities across the country that share a mutual objective of economic growth through university- related assistance. This broad definition ranges from high technology transfer programs to small business assistance centers and entepreneurial institutes. The primary goal of NAMTAC is to strengthen these initiatives through organized mutual support. Membership: $250/yr.
Publication:
NAMTAC Newsletter. q.
Annual Meetings: Fall, usually in Washington, DC

Nat'l Ass'n of Management/Marketing Educators (1968)
Lima Technical Institute, 4240 Campus Drive, Lima OH 45805
President: Norman P. Spricker
Members: 70 individuals; 15 companies
Annual Budget: under $10,000 *Tel:* (419) 227-5131
Hist. Note: Formerly (1978) Nat'l Ass'n of Management Educators. Members are teachers at two-year community colleges, technical schools and four-year private colleges. Has no paid staff. Membership: $30/yr. (individual); $50/yr. (organization).
Publication:
Newsletter. semi-a.
Annual Meetings: November

Nat'l Ass'n of Manufacturers (1895)
1331 Pensylvania Ave., N.W., Suite 1500, Washington DC 20004
President: Alexander B. Trowbridge
Members: 13,000-13,500 *Staff:* 200-250
Annual Budget: over $5,000,000 *Tel:* (202) 637-3000
Hist. Note: Established in Cincinnati January 22, 1895 to promote foreign trade, rehabilitate the merchant marine, advocate higher tariffs, support a trans-Isthmian canal and foster the manufacturing industry. With four divisions and two regional field offices, NAM is a voice for industry at the national level, representing as it does over 13,000 companies, 150 state and local associations of manufacturers and 110 national manufacturing trade associations. Supports the National Industrial Council, and CUE, an organization for Positive Employee Relations. Has an annual budget of over $10,000,000.
Publications:
Enterprise. m.
PAC Manager. m.
Briefing. w.
Annual Meetings:
1987-Washington, DC(JW Marriott)/March

Nat'l Ass'n of Manufacturing Opticians (1975)
13140 Coit Road, LB 144, Dallas TX 75240
Exec. V. President: William J. Flannery, III
Members: 35 companies *Staff:* 2
Annual Budget: $50-100,000 *Tel:* (214) 231-6266
Hist. Note: Membership is comprised of individuals and businesses engaged in the manufacture and production of prescription eyewear or related opthalmic goods and services; members must possess the ability to "full service" fabricate eyewear.
Semi-annual meetings: Winter and Summer
1987-Dallas, TX/Feb.

Nat'l Ass'n of Margarine Manufacturers (1920)
1625 Eye St., N.W., Suite 1024A, Washington DC 20006
President: S. F. Riepma
Members: 15-20 companies *Staff:* 2-5
Tel: (202) 785-3232
Annual Meetings: March

Nat'l Ass'n of Marine Products and Services (1972)
401 North Michigan Ave., Chicago IL 60611
President: Jeff W. Napier
Members: 875 *Staff:* 35
Annual Budget: $100-250,000 *Tel:* (312) 836-4747
Hist. Note: Formerly (1979) the Marine Accessories and Services Ass'n, it absorbed the Trailer Manufacturers Ass'n in 1980. Members are manufacturers of marine recreational equipment and accessories. A partner-affiliate of the Nat'l Marine Manufacturers Ass'n, which provides administrative support and with which it shares offices.
Annual Meetings: Chicago, in conjunction with the Marine Trade Exhibition

Nat'l Ass'n of Marine Services (1951)
1900 Arch Street, Philadelphia PA 19103
Exec. Director: William L. Robinson
Members: 90-100 companies *Staff:* 2-5
Annual Budget: $25-50,000 *Tel:* (215) 564-3484
Hist. Note: Established as Associated Ship Chandlers, it became the National Associated Marine Suppliers in 1951 and assumed its present name in 1969. Members are purveyors of supplies and equipment to ocean-going commercial vessels.
Publication:
Directory of American Ship Services. a. adv.

Nat'l Ass'n of Marine Surveyors (1960)
3450 Baychester Ave., Bronx NY 10475
Nat'l Secretary: Robert E. Christoverson
Members: 400-425 *Staff:* 1
Annual Budget: $100-250,000 *Tel:* (212) 881-8354
Hist. Note: Incorporated in the State of New York, September, 1962. Originally Corresponding Surveyors to the Yacht Safety Bureau. Membership: $220/yr.
Publications:
Conference Proceedings. a.
Membership List. a.
NAMS News. q.
Surveyors Practices. a.
Annual Meetings: Holds four zone meetings per year with an attendance of 100-200

Nat'l Ass'n of Market Developers (1953)
JP Martin Associates, 100 Fifth Ave., New York NY 10011
President: Joel Martin
Members: 500-750 *Staff:* 2-5

00199 12 05 86 1233

Annual Budget: $25-50,000 *Tel:* (212) 741-5301
Hist. Note: Black men and women engaged in marketing, sales, public relations, and advertising concerned with goods and services on the minority market. Membership: $100/yr.
Publications:
Briefcase. bi-m.
Emphasis. a. adv.
Annual Meetings: May
1987-Atlanta, GA(Hyatt Regency)/May 17-20/500
1988-Kansas City, MO

Nat'l Ass'n of MDS Service Companies (1979)
Hist. Note: Became the MDS Industry Ass'n in 1983.

Nat'l Ass'n of Meat Purveyors (1942)
8365-B Greensboro Drive, McLean VA 22102
Exec. V. President: Stanley J. Emerling
Members: 325-350 *Staff:* 4-6
Annual Budget: $500-1,000,000 *Tel:* (703) 827-5754
Hist. Note: Formerly (1966) Nat'l Ass'n of Hotel & Restaurant Meat Purveyors
Publications:
Newsletter. semi-m.
Meat Buyers Guide, NAMP Guide to Quality Assurance.
Annual Meetings: Fall/350-375
1987-Palm Springs, CA(Rancho Las Palmas at Rancho Mirage)/Nov. 2-6

Nat'l Ass'n of Media Women (1965)
1185 Niskey Lake Road, S.W., Atlanta GA 30331
Nat'l President: Mrs. Xernona Clayton Brady
Members: 250-300 individuals
Annual Budget: $10-25,000 *Tel:* (404) 344-5862
Hist. Note: Women in the communications industry united to recognize achievement and solve common problems.
Publication:
Media Woman. a.
Annual Meetings:
1987-Los Angeles, CA/Oct.

Nat'l Ass'n of Medical Equipment Suppliers (1982)
625 States Lane, Suite 200, Alexandria VA 22314
Exec. V. President: Janet A. Bourne
Members: 1,200 companies
Annual Budget: $1-2,000,000 *Tel:* (703) 836-6263
Hist. Note: NAMES was formed in May, 1982 in Las Vegas, Nevada by the merger of the Nat'l Affiliation of Durable Medical Equipment Companies and the Associated Independent Medical Equipment Suppliers. Trade association of durable medical equipment dealers. Membership: $395/yr.
Publications:
Washington Report. m. adv.
NAMES News. bi-wk.
State Forum. bi-wk.
NAMES Resources. q.
Annual Meetings: Spring
1987-Dallas, TX

Nat'l Ass'n of Medical Examiners (1966)
1402 S. Grand Blvd., Room C-305, St. Louis MO 63104
Secy.-Treas.: George E. Gantner, M.D.
Members: 715
Annual Budget: under $10,000 *Tel:* (314) 577-8000
Publication:
Journal of Forensic Medicine and Pathology. q.
Annual Meetings: Fall
1987-San Francisco, CA/Sept. 18-22

Nat'l Ass'n of Membership Directors of Chambers of Commerce (1941)
1454 Duke St., Alexandria VA 22314
Exec. V. President: Rosemary M. Harper
Members: 650 *Staff:* 3
Annual Budget: $100-250,000 *Tel:* (703) 836-7904
Hist. Note: Affiliated with the American Chamber of Commerce Executives. Membership: $50/yr. minimum (individual).
Publications:
NAMD Newsletter. semi-m.
Statistical Summary. a.
Who's Who Directory. a.
Compendium of Membership Letters.
Compendium of Dues Formulas.
Annual Meetings: August
1987-Charlotte, NC/Aug. 9-12
1988-Schaumberg, IL

Nat'l Ass'n of Men's Sportswear Buyers (1954)
535 Fifth Ave., 27th Floor, New York NY 10017
Exec. Director: Jack Herschlag
Members: 1,000 *Staff:* 3
Tel: (212) 490-2090
Hist. Note: Formed in 1954 by men's wear retailers to provide industry services and to sponsor a trade show for men's wear. Membership: $10/yr. Granted a license to Schimel Co. (same address) in 1985 to handle the four trade shows per year in New York City.
Publications:
NAMSB Newsletter. m.
NAMSB New York, the Show Week Magazine. semi-a. adv.
Annual Meetings: Always in New York, NY at the Jacob Javits Convention Center.

Nat'l Ass'n of Merger and Acquisition Consultants (1973)
Hist. Note: Became INTERMAC/NAMAC, the International Association of Merger and Acquisition Consultants in 1982.

Nat'l Ass'n of Metal Finishers (1955)
111 East Wacker Drive, #600, Chicago IL 60601
Exec. Director: Jeff Tanchon
Members: 1,100 *Staff:* 6-10
Annual Budget: $100-250,000 *Tel:* (312) 644-6610
Hist. Note: Merger of the National Federation of Metal Finishers and the National Association of Plating. Members are executives of firms engaged in all methods of finishing metal surfaces.
Publication:
Finishers' Management. m. adv.
Annual Meetings: March/500
1987-Maui, HI(Hyatt)/March 1-5

Nat'l Ass'n of Milliners, Dressmakers and Tailors (1966)
157 W. 126th St., New York NY 10027
President: Alma Goss
Members: 200
Annual Budget: under $10,000 *Tel:* (212) 666-1320
Hist. Note: Black members of the fashion industry united to recognize achievement and solve common problems.
Publications:
Journal. semi-a. adv.
Newsletter. m.
Semi-annual meetings: April and Oct. in New York, NY

Nat'l Ass'n of Minority Contractors (1969)
806 15th St., N.W., Suite 340, Washington DC 20005
Exec. Director: Ralph C. Thomas, III
Members: 3,500 companies and individuals *Staff:* 10-15
Annual Budget: $500-1,000,000 *Tel:* (202) 347-8259
Hist. Note: Established in Washington, DC in 1969 and incorporated in 1984. Membership consists of, but is not limited to, general contractors, subcontractors, construction managers, manufacturers, suppliers, local minority contractor associations, funded technical assistance organizations, state and local government agencies, attorneys and accountants. Regular Membership: $250/yr.
Publications:
American Contractor Publication. m.
Building Concerns. m. adv.
Reflections of NAMC. a. adv.
Annual Meetings: June
1987-Atlanta, GA

Nat'l Ass'n of Minority CPA Firms (1971)
Hist. Note: Reported defunct in 1984.

Nat'l Ass'n of Mirror Manufacturers (1957)
9005 Congressional Court, Potomac MD 20854
Exec. Secretary & Gen'l Counsel: James E. Mack, CAE
Members: 25 companies *Staff:* 2-5
Annual Budget: $100-250,000 *Tel:* (301) 365-4080
Semi-annual meetings: Spring and Fall
1987-Ft. Lauderdale, FL(Bonaventure Hotel)/April 4-8

Nat'l Ass'n of Miscellaneous, Ornamental and Architectural Products Contractors (1969)
10382 Main St., Box 225, Suite 200, Fairfax VA 22030
Exec. V. President: Fred H. Codding
Members: 900-1,000 companies *Staff:* 2-5
Annual Budget: $50-100,000 *Tel:* (703) 591-1870
Hist. Note: Members are companies fabricating and installing decking systems, ornamental iron, steel and aluminum sheathing and architectural motifs on building exteriors.
Annual Meetings:
1987-Lake Tahoe, CA

Nat'l Ass'n of Mortgage Brokers (1973)
1001 Connecticut Ave., N.W., Suite 800, Washington DC 20036
Exec. V. President: Randy Dyer, CAE
Members: 1,700 individuals *Staff:* 5
Annual Budget: $100-250,000 *Tel:* (202) 293-8877
Hist. Note: Formed to provide a focal point for mortgage brokers and a communications link with mortgage bankers and underwriters. Membership: $130/yr.
Publication:
Mortgage Broker News. bi-m. adv.
Annual Meetings: Fall

Nat'l Ass'n of Music Executives in State Universities (1935)
Dept. of Music, Univ. of Hawaii, 2411 Dole St., Honolulu HI 96822
Exec. Officer: John Mount
Members: 50
Annual Budget: under $10,000 *Tel:* (808) 948-7756
Hist. Note: Members are chairmen of departments of music at state universities (one from each state). Holds an annual, informal, two-day meeting at a state university which is devoted to the discussion of mutual problems.
Annual Meetings: Fall
1987-Honolulu, HI

Nat'l Ass'n of Music Merchants (1901)
5140 Avenida Encinas, Carlsbad CA 92008
Exec. V. President: Larry R. Linkin
Members: 3,745 companies *Staff:* 15
Tel: (619) 438-8001
Hist. Note: Members are musical instrument stores and manufacturers and their suppliers. Membership: $150/yr. (retail); $100/yr. (commercial).
Publications:
Business Barometer. m.
Music Retailer News. bi-m.
Retail Music Products Industry Report. a.
Biannual Trade Shows: NAMM Internat'l Music & Sound Expo/June/25,000
and the NAMM Winter Market/Anaheim, CA/23,000
1987-Anaheim, CA(Convention Center)/Jan. 16-18
1987-Chicago, IL(McCormick Place)/June 13-16
1988-Anaheim, CA(Convention Center)/Jan. 15-17
1988-Atlanta, GA(World Congress Center)/June 25-28

Nat'l Ass'n of Mutual Insurance Companies (1895)
3707 Woodview Trace, Box 68700, Indianapolis IN 46268
President: Harold W. Walters, CAE
Members: 1,200-1,276 *Staff:* 40
Annual Budget: $2-5,000,000 *Tel:* (317) 875-5250
Hist. Note: Membership consists of fire and casualty insurance companies.
Publication:
Mutual Insurance Bulletin. m. adv.
Annual Meetings: Fall
1987-San Antonio, TX(Marriott,Hilton&Hyatt Regency)/Sept. 20-23/1,600
1988-Honolulu, HI(Sheraton Waikiki)/Sept. 25-28/1,400
1989-Nashville, TN(Opryland)/Oct. 1-4/1,600
1990-Orlando, FL/Sept. 23-26
1991-San Francisco, CA/Sept. 15-18

Nat'l Ass'n of Mutual Savings Banks (1920)
Hist. Note: Merged on November 1, 1983 with the National Savings and Loan League to form the National Council of Savings Institutions.

Nat'l Ass'n of Nail Artists (1981)
Hist. Note: Became the Nat'l Aesthetician and Nail Artist Ass'n in 1984.

Nat'l Ass'n of Name Plate Manufacturers (1951)
1700 East Dyer Road, Suite 165, Santa Ana CA 92705
Exec. V. President: James A. Kinder
Members: 100-125 companies *Staff:* 2
Annual Budget: $50-100,000 *Tel:* (714) 261-2591
Hist. Note: Incorporated July 24, 1951 in the State of Delaware as a result of meetings by manufacturers during World War II to discuss metal shortages. Established as the Metal Etching and Fabricating Ass'n, it became Nat'l Ass'n of Metal Name Plate Manufacturers in 1967 and the Nat'l Ass'n of Name Plate Manufacturers in 1979. Publishes the only book of standards for the name plate industry.
Publication:
Bulletin. m.
Annual Meetings: March

Nat'l Ass'n of Naturopathic Physicians
Hist. Note: Reported inactive in 1986; a new association, however, has been formed at this time - American Ass'n of Naturopathic Physicians.

Nat'l Ass'n of Negotiated Commission Brokers (1973)
202 East 39th St., New York NY 10016
Chairman: G. Maxwell Ule, Jr.
Members: 10-15 brokerage firms *Staff:* 1
Annual Budget: under $10,000 *Tel:* (212) 687-0706
Hist. Note: Members are brokerage houses charging lower commissions than those set by the New York Stock Exchange.

Nat'l Ass'n of Negro Business and Professional Women's Clubs (1935)
1806 New Hampshire Ave., N.W., Washington DC 20009
Admin. Assistant: Diane L. Harvey
Members: 375-400 clubs, 10,000 individuals *Staff:* 2-5
Annual Budget: $25-50,000 *Tel:* (202) 483-4206
Hist. Note: Membership: $35/yr.
Publication:
Responsibility. q.
Annual Meetings: Summer
1987-Reno, NV/Aug. 12-15

Nat'l Ass'n of Neighborhoods (1975)
1651 Fuller St., N.W., Washington DC 20009
Exec. Director: Stephen Glaude
Members: 600 organizations, 500 individuals *Staff:* 2-5
Annual Budget: $250-500,000 *Tel:* (202) 332-7766
Hist. Note: Urban and rural organizations and coalitions working to strengthen neighborhood rights and responsibilities. Membership: $10-$25/year.
Publication:
NAN Bulletin. m.
Annual Meetings: Fall
1987-New Orleans, LA

00200 12 05 86 1233

Nat'l Ass'n of Noise Control Officials (1978)
53 Cubberley Road, Trenton NJ 08690
Administrator: Edward J. Di Polvere
Members: 200
Annual Budget: under $10,000 *Tel:* (609) 984-4161
Hist. Note: Incorporated in the State of New Jersey. Members are employees of the federal or state governments, consultants, scientists and students concerned with acoustical control of the environment. Membership: $30/yr.
Publication:
Vibrations. m. adv.
Annual Meetings: Fall, with the Nat'l Environmental Health Ass'n

Nat'l Ass'n of Numismatic Professionals (1982)
Hist. Note: Ceased operations in 1984.

Nat'l Ass'n of Nurse Recruiters
Hist. Note: Became the Nat'l Ass'n for Health Care Recruitment in 1984.

Nat'l Ass'n of Optometrists and Opticians (1959)
18903 South Miles Road, Cleveland OH 44128
Vice President: Frank Rozak
Members: 15,500 *Staff:* 2-5
Annual Budget: $50-100,000 *Tel:* (216) 475-8925
Hist. Note: Formerly the National Optical Association.
Semi-annual Meetings: Spring and Fall
1987-Washington, DC/March

Nat'l Ass'n of Orthopaedic Nurses (1980)
North Woodbury Road, Box 56, Pitman NJ 08071
Director of Education: Terri Pellino
Members: 6,500 *Staff:* 2-5
Annual Budget: $250-500,000 *Tel:* (609) 582-0111
Hist. Note: Members are registered nurses, licensed practical or licensed vocational nurses associated with any facet of the orthopaedic patient's care. Membership: $40/year.
Publications:
Orthopaedic Nursing. bi-m.
NAON News. bi-m.
Annual Meetings: Spring/1,500
1987-Baltimore, MD(Civic Center)/May 31-June 2
1988-Phoenix, AZ(Hyatt)/May 22-26
1989-Orlando, FL/May 20-25
1990-Chicago, IL/June 10-14
1991-San Antonio, TX/May 19-23

Nat'l Ass'n of OTC Companies (1973)
1735 K St., N.W., Suite 200, Washington DC 20006
President: Alan T. Rains, Jr.
Members: 550 *Staff:* 3
Annual Budget: $250-500,000 *Tel:* (202) 728-8316
Hist. Note: Members are companies whose securities are traded in over-the-counter markets, rather than on the major exchanges. Membership: $200-650/yr.
Publications:
Newsletter. m.
Bulletin. q.
Membership Directory. a.
Annual Meetings: Spring
1987-Washington, DC(Willard)/April 29-May 1
1988-Dallas, TX
1989-Washington, DC

Nat'l Ass'n of Paralegal Personnel (1975)
Box 8202, Northfield IL 60093
Exec. Director: Howard W. Ross
Members: 1,200 individuals and institutions *Staff:* 2-5
Annual Budget: $50-100,000 *Tel:* (312) 973-7712

Nat'l Ass'n of Park Rangers (1981)
Hist. Note: Became the American Park Rangers Ass'n in 1982.

Nat'l Ass'n of Parliamentarians (1930)
6301 James A. Reed Rd., Suite 114, Kansas City MO 64133-4751
Exec. Secretary: Elaine Fulton
Members: 4,000 *Staff:* 2-5
Annual Budget: $250-500,000 *Tel:* (816) 356-5604
Hist. Note: Organized in 1930 for the purposes of studying, teaching and promoting the rules of deliberative assemblies. See also American Institute of Parliamentarians.
Publication:
National Parliamentarian. q.
Annual Meetings: Always in Fall. Even years in Kansas City, uneven years, elsewhere.
1987-Dallas, TX
1988-Kansas City, MO
1989-New Orleans, LA

Nat'l Ass'n of Pastoral Musicians (1976)
225 Sheridan St., N.W., Washington DC 20011
President: Rev. Virgil C. Funk
Members: 8,300 *Staff:* 6-10
Annual Budget: $500-1,000,000 *Tel:* (202) 723-5800
Hist. Note: Formerly (1976) Nat'l Catholic Music Educators Ass'n, NPM is a national membership organization for parish musicians and parish clergy. Membership: $30/yr.
Publication:
Pastoral Music. q. adv.

Nat'l Ass'n of Pattern Manufacturers (1962)
21010 Center Ridge Rd., Rocky River OH 44116
Exec. Secretary: Benjamin J. Imburgia
Members: 170-180 companies *Staff:* 2-5
Annual Budget: $100-250,000 *Tel:* (216) 333-7417
Hist. Note: Members make wood, metal and plastic models and patterns for foundries and other industries.
Publication:
Industrial Models & Patterns. bi-m.
Annual Meetings: Fall

Nat'l Ass'n of Pediatric Nurse Associates & Practitioners (1973)
1000 Maplewood Drive, Suite 104, Maple Shade NJ 08052
Exec. Director: Mavis McGuire
Members: 2,600 *Staff:* 4
Annual Budget: $250-500,000 *Tel:* (609) 667-1773
Hist. Note: The goals of NAPNAP are to provide continuing education for pediatric nurse practitioners, as well as standards and certification for practice; and to support legislation designed to improve the quality of infant, child and adolescent health. Membership: $60/yr.
Publications:
Pediatric Nursing. bi-m. adv.
The Practitioner. bi-m.
Annual Meetings: Spring
1987-St. Louis, MO(Adams Mark)/March 22-25
1988-Boston, MA(Copley Plaza)/March 20-23
1989-Orlando, FL(Hyatt Orlando)/March 15-18

Nat'l Ass'n of Pension Consultants and Administrators (1974)
359 East Paces Ferry Road, N.E., Atlanta GA 30305
Exec. Director: John W. Baker, C.L.U.
Members: 300 individuals; 200 companies *Staff:* 2-5
Annual Budget: $50-100,000 *Tel:* (404) 231-0100
Hist. Note: Pension planners, consultants and administrators for individuals and companies. Initially organized to help its members understand and comply with ERISA.
Publication:
Newsletter. m.
Annual Meetings: First Wednesday in March/Washington, DC

Nat'l Ass'n of Personnel Consultants (1917)
1432 Duke St., Alexandria VA 22314
Exec. V. President: John Lisack, Jr.
Members: 1,500 *Staff:* 6
Annual Budget: $500-1,000,000 *Tel:* (703) 684-0180
Hist. Note: Formerly (1917) the Nat'l Employment Board. Merged (1960) with Employment Agencies Ass'n (1923) and Nat'l Ass'n of Employment Agencies (1956), to become the Nat'l Employment Ass'n. Changed to present name in 1978. Awards the Certified Personnel Consultant (CPC) designation.
Publication:
Personnel Consultant. bi-m. adv.
Annual Meetings: Fall

Nat'l Ass'n of Personnel Workers (1954)
Hist. Note: Black counterpart of the Nat'l Ass'n of Student Personnel Administrators. Members are student affairs personnel in the fields of teaching, housing, financial aid and social services.
Annual Meetings: In February at a college or university setting.

Nat'l Ass'n of Pharmaceutical Manufacturers (1955)
747 Third Ave., New York NY 10017
Exec. Director: George Schwartz
Members: 125-150 *Staff:* 2-5
Annual Budget: $250-500,000 *Tel:* (212) 838-3720
Hist. Note: Formerly (1968) Drug & Allied Products Guild.
Publication:
Bulletin. m.
Semi-annual Meetings: Summer and Winter
1987-Dorado Beach, PR(Cerromar Beach Hotel)/Jan. 17-23/300

Nat'l Ass'n of Photo Equipment Technicians (1973)
3000 Picture Place, Jackson MI 49201
NAPET Liaison: Keith Anderson
Members: 165 *Staff:* 1
Annual Budget: under $10,000 *Tel:* (517) 788-8100
Hist. Note: A division (1976) of the Photo Marketing Ass'n Internat'l. Provides information on the photographic industry to those engaged in photographic repair.
Publication:
NAPET News. bi-m.
Annual Meetings: February
1987-Chicago, IL (McCormick Pl)/Feb. 22-25

Nat'l Ass'n of Photographic Manufacturers (1946)
600 Mamaroneck Ave., Harrison NY 10528
Exec. V. President: Thomas J. Dufficy
Members: 35-40 companies *Staff:* 6-10
Annual Budget: $250-500,000 *Tel:* (914) 698-7603
Annual Meetings: Fall

Nat'l Ass'n of Physical Therapists (1961)
Box 367, West Covina CA 91793
Secretary: Shela Iva Denton, CAE
Members: 22,000 *Staff:* 6-10
Annual Budget: $50-100,000 *Tel:* (818) 332-7755
Hist. Note: Founded Nov. 29, 1961 as the Nat'l Ass'n of Independent Physiotherapy. Incorporated in California in 1961 as the Nat'l Ass'n of Independent Physical Therapists. Became the Nat'l Ass'n of Physical Therapists in 1962. Membership: $65/yr. (individual), $250/yr. (organization).
Publications:
NAPT Journal. bi-m. adv.
NAPT Newsletter. q.
National Directory of Physical Therapists. a.

Nat'l Ass'n of Physician Nurses (1973)
3837 Plaza Drive, Fairfax VA 22030
Exec. Director: Joseph Salta
Members: 3,000 *Staff:* 2-5
Annual Budget: $100-250,000 *Tel:* (703) 273-6262
Hist. Note: Membership: $24/yr.
Publication:
The Nightingale. m.
Annual Meetings: Spring

Nat'l Ass'n of Pipe Coating Applicators (1965)
717 Commercial National Bank Bldg., Shreveport LA 71101
Mng. Director: Merritt B. Chastain, Jr.
Members: 90-100 *Staff:* 2-5
Annual Budget: $100-250,000 *Tel:* (318) 227-2769
Hist. Note: Members apply exterior and interior protective pipe coatings to steel pipes in permanently established facilities. Membership: $1,000/year (company).
Publications:
Newsletter. q.
Membership Roster. a. adv.
Annual Meetings: Spring/200
1987-Scottsdale, AZ(Sunburst)/April 5-9

Nat'l Ass'n of Pipe Nipple Manufacturers (1933)
800 Roosevelt Road, Suite C-20, Glen Ellyn IL 60137
Exec. Secretary: Richard W. Church
Members: 40-45 *Staff:* 1
Tel: (312) 858-7337
Semi-annual Meetings: Fall, with American Supply Ass'n & Spring

Nat'l Ass'n of Pizza Operators (1982)
Box 114, Santa Claus IN 47579
President: Gerry Durnell
Staff: 28
Annual Budget: $50-100,000 *Tel:* (812) 937-4464
Hist. Note: Pizza equipment manufacturers, ingredient and equipment suppliers, franchise and independent pizza operators and frozen pizza producers. Provides liaison between pizza industry and governmental agencies. Researches industry data and statistics.
Publication:
Pizza Today. m. adv.

Nat'l Ass'n of Planners, Estimators and Progressmen (1943)
428 Madison Avenue, Room 8A, Orange Park FL 32073
Nat'l Secy.-Treas.: Terry R.. Taylor
Members: 1,000-1,100 *Staff:* 7
Annual Budget: $10-25,000 *Tel:* (305) 272-0640
Hist. Note: Independent labor union.
Biennial meetings: Even years
1988-Bremerton, WA/June

Nat'l Ass'n of Plant Patent Owners (1939)
1250 Eye St., N.W., Suite 500, Washington DC 20005
Exec. V. President: Robert F. Lederer, CAE
Members: 50-60 *Staff:* 1
Annual Budget: under $10,000 *Tel:* (202) 789-2900
Hist. Note: Owners of patents on newly propagated flowers, trees and plants. Affiliated with American Ass'n of Nurserymen.
Annual Meetings: With American Ass'n of Nurserymen.

Nat'l Ass'n of Plastic Fabricators (1956)
Hist. Note: Became the Decorative Laminate Products Ass'n in 1984.

Nat'l Ass'n of Plastics Distributors (1956)
5001 College Blvd., Suite 214, Leawood KS 66211
Exec. Director: Carol K. Wagner
Members: 340 companies *Staff:* 3
Annual Budget: $250-500,000 *Tel:* (913) 491-4698
Hist. Note: Formerly United Plastics Distributors Ass'n and (1970) Nat'l Plastics Distributors Ass'n.
Publications:
Plasti-Gram Newsletter. m.
The NAPD Magazine.
Annual Meetings: Fall
1987-Nashville, TN(Opryland)/Sept. 17-20/800
1988-Palm Springs, CA(Desert Springs)/Oct. 12-16/900
1989-Boston, MA(Westin Copley)/Sept. 13-17/900
1990-Vancouver, Canada(Hyatt Regency)/Sept. 12-16/900

Nat'l Ass'n of Plumbing-Heating-Cooling Contractors (1883)
180 South Washington St., Box 6808, Falls Church VA 22046
Exec. V. President: Joe A. Childress
Members: 6,500 *Staff:* 18
Annual Budget: $2-5,000,000 *Tel:* (703) 237-8100
Hist. Note: Established as the Nat'l Ass'n of Master Plumbers, it became the Nat'l Ass'n of Plumbing Contractors in 1953 and assumed its present name in 1962. Sponsors and supports the NAPHCC Political Action Committee, Education and

00201 12 05 86 1233

Technical Foundation, Scholarship Trust, and Legal Action Trust. Membership: $150/yr.
Publications:
Execugram. m.
NAPHCC News. m. adv.
Annual Meetings: Fall
1987-New York, NY(Marriott Marquis)/Oct. 14-20/10,000
1988-New Orleans, LA(Hilton)/Oct. 27-Nov. 2/7,000
1989-Las Vegas, NV(MGM Grand)/Oct. 12-17/8,000
1990-Chicago, IL(Hilton)/Oct. 5-9/7,000

Nat'l Ass'n of Police-Community Relations Officers (1969)
Norwalk Police Department, 297 West Ave., Norwalk CT 06852
President: Dep.Chf. Malcolm Skeeter
Members: 200-225
Annual Budget: $10-25,000 *Tel:* (203) 854-3002
Hist. Note: Has no paid staff or permanent address. Officers change every two years.
Publication:
Newsletter. q.
Annual Meetings: Spring
1987-Milwaukee, WI/June 18-19

Nat'l Ass'n of Police Organizations (1979)
c/o Detroit Police Officers Ass'n, 6525 Lincoln, Detroit MI 48202
President: Robert Scully
Members: 200,000
Tel: (313) 871-0484
Hist. Note: Members are police officers not affiliated with a labor union. Has no permanent headquarters or paid staff.

Nat'l Ass'n of Postal Supervisors (1908)
490 L'Enfant Plaza, S.W., Suite 3200, Washington DC 20024-2120
President: Rubin Handelman
Members: 40,000 *Staff:* 13
Annual Budget: $2-5,000,000 *Tel:* (202) 484-6070
Hist. Note: An independent professional association founded in Louisville, Kentucky, September 7, 1908. Sponsors the Supervisors Political Action Committee.
Publications:
NAPS letter. bi-w.
The Postal Supervisor. m. adv.
Biennial meetings: Even years in August
1988-San Antonio, TX
1990-San Diego, CA

Nat'l Ass'n of Postmasters of the U.S. (1898)
4212 King St., Alexandria VA 22302-1595
Exec. Director: Emmett F. Good
Members: 41,000 *Staff:* 11-15
Annual Budget: $1-2,000,000 *Tel:* (703) 671-6800
Hist. Note: Sponsors and supports the Political Education for Postmasters Political Action Committee.
Publications:
Postmaster's Gazette. m. adv.
Update Newsletter. bi-w.
Annual Meetings: Fall/3,500
1987-Portland, OR
1988-Virginia Beach, VA
1989-San Francisco, CA
1990-Niagara Falls, NY

Nat'l Ass'n of Power Engineers (1882)
2350 East Devon Ave., Suite 115, Des Plaines IL 60018
Office Coordinator: C. Dalgard
Members: 6,500 *Staff:* 6
Annual Budget: $100-250,000 *Tel:* (312) 298-0600
Hist. Note: Members include those in power plant operation and maintenance responsible for suppling industry and service establishments with process power, heat, air conditioning, lighting, ventilation and related building and plant services.
Publication:
National Engineer. m. adv.
Annual Meetings: Summer
1987-Chicago, IL(Holiday Inn Hart Plaza)/July 6-11/250-300
1988-French Lick, IN/July/250-300

Nat'l Ass'n of Principals of Schools for Girls (1921)
Route 3, Box 149-D, Hendersonville NC 28739
Exec. Director: Nancy E. Kussrow
Members: 600 *Staff:* 1
Annual Budget: $25-50,000 *Tel:* (704) 693-8248
Hist. Note: NASPG addresses common concerns of administrators of American and Canadian independent schools and colleges which enroll women.
Annual Meetings: Late Winter
1987-Hot Springs, VA/Mar. 1-4
1988-Colorado Springs, CO(Broadmoor)/Feb. 28-March 2/315
1989-Clearwater, FL/Feb. 26-March 1
1990-Tucson, AZ/Feb. 25-28

Nat'l Ass'n of Printers and Lithographers (1933)
780 Palisade Ave., Teaneck NJ 07666
President: Charles A. Alessandrini
Members: 3,700 companies *Staff:* 33
Annual Budget: $2-5,000,000 *Tel:* (201) 342-0700
Hist. Note: Established as the National Association of Photo-Lithographers, it assumed its present name in 1972. Membership: $235-925/yr. (company) based on annual sales/annual payroll.
Publications:
Printing Manager. m.
Business Indicator. q.
Marketing Action Planner. m.
Printing's P.C. q.
Annual Meetings:
1987-Naples, FL(Registry)/Feb. 9-12/300
1988-Phoenix, AZ(Pointe at South Mountain)/Feb. 8-11/350

Nat'l Ass'n of Printing Ink Manufacturers (1914)
47 Halstead Ave., Harrison NY 10528
Exec. Director: James E. Renson
Members: 90-100 *Staff:* 2-5
Annual Budget: $250-500,000 *Tel:* (914) 835-5650
Hist. Note: Established as the National Association of Printing Ink Makers, it assumed its present name in 1967. Sponsors the Nat'l Printing Ink Research Institute.
Publication:
American Ink-Maker. m.
Annual Meetings: Spring/400-500
1987-Boca Raton, FL(Boca Raton Club)/March 29-April 2
1988-San Diego, CA(Rancho Las Playas Marriott)/March 13-17
1989-Bermuda(Southhampton Princess)/April 23-27
1990-Phoenix, AZ(Biltmore)/March 11-15

Nat'l Ass'n of Printing Purchasers (1980)
Hist. Note: Defunct, 1982.

Nat'l Ass'n of Private Industry Councils (1979)
1015 15th St., N.W., Suite 600, Washington DC 20005
Exec. Director: Robert F. Knight
Members: 200 councils *Staff:* 2-5
Annual Budget: $100-250,000 *Tel:* (202) 289-2950
Hist. Note: Private industry councils and private employers concerned with employment and training policies in the context of economic development and education. Membership: $100-300/yr.
Publication:
Directory of Private Industry Councils. a.
Annual Meetings: Spring
1987-Washington, DC(Washington Marriott)/Feb. 1-3/300

Nat'l Ass'n of Private, Nontraditional Schools and Colleges (1974)
182 Thompson Road, Grand Junction CO 81503
Exec. Director: Dr. H. Earl Heusser
Members: 15 institutions *Staff:* 2-5
Annual Budget: $50-100,000 *Tel:* (303) 243-5441
Hist. Note: Formerly (1977) Nat'l Ass'n of Schools and Colleges. NAPNSC is the only national, institutional accrediting body which has developed criteria, standards and guidelines expressly for private, nontraditional or alternative education at postsecondary, secondary, elementary and pre-school levels. Also serves as the clearinghouse information center for nontraditional schools at all levels.
Publications:
Accreditation Fact Sheet. q.
Handbook for Accreditation. a.
Index of Project Findings. a.
Annual Meetings: June or December

Nat'l Ass'n of Private Psychiatric Hospitals (1933)
1319 F St., N.W., Washington DC 20004
Exec. Director: Robert L. Thomas, CAE
Members: 240 hospitals *Staff:* 15
Annual Budget: $1-2,000,000 *Tel:* (202) 393-6700
Hist. Note: An association of freestanding psychiatric hospitals for the private treatment of mental illness, alcohol, and drug dependencies. Sponsors the National Association of Private Psychiatric Hospitals Political Action Committee.
Publications:
Journal. q. adv.
Newsletter. bi-m. adv.
Annual Meetings: January/850
1987-Bal Harbour, FL(Sheraton)/Jan. 25-29
1988-Phoenix, AZ(The Pointe)/Jan. 24-28
1989-Ft. Lauderdale, FL(Marriott Harbor Beach)/Jan 29-Feb. 2
1990-San Diego, CA(Sheraton Harbor Island)/Jan. 28-Feb. 1
1991-Marco Island, FL(Marriott Marco Beach Resort)/Jan. 27-31

Nat'l Ass'n of Private Residential Facilities for the Mentally Retarded (1970)
6400 H Seven Corners Pl #1, Falls Church VA 22044-2009
Exec. Director: Joni Fritz
Members: 620 *Staff:* 3
Annual Budget: $100-250,000 *Tel:* (703) 536-3311
Hist. Note: Represents and assists the providers of private residential facilities which serve people with developmental disabilities. Affiliated with the American Ass'n on Mental Deficiency; participates in the Commission on Accreditation of Rehabilitation Facilitates.
Publications:
Links. m. adv.
Directory of Members. a.
Executive's Notebook. m.
Semi-annual Meetings: Spring with AAMD and Fall (Govt. Activities)

Nat'l Ass'n of Private Schools for Exceptional Children (1971)
2021 K St., N.W., Suite 315, Washington DC 20006
Exec. Director: Dr. Susan B. Nelson
Members: 600 schools *Staff:* 2-5
Annual Budget: $100-250,000 *Tel:* (202) 296-1800
Publications:
Directory. bi-a.
The NAPSEC Voice. 3/yr. adv.
Annual Meetings: January

Nat'l Ass'n of Private Security Vaults (1981)
135 West Morehead St., Charlotte NC 28202
President: Rick Drummond
Members: 130-150 companies *Staff:* 2-5
Annual Budget: $10-25,000 *Tel:* (704) 372-7233
Hist. Note: Established in 1981 as the National Association of Independent Security Vaults, NAPSV assumed its present name six months later. Members are private facilities providing leased security and data storage space.
Publication:
Newsletter. bi-m.

Nat'l Ass'n of Produce Market Managers (1946)
Connecticut Marketing Authority, 101 Reserve Road, Hartford CT 06114
President: Thomas Moriarty
Members: 200 *Staff:* 1
Annual Budget: under $10,000 *Tel:* (203) 527-5047
Hist. Note: Members are managers of farmers' markets, produce dealers, county agents, etc. Has no paid staff or permanent address, other than the above. Officers are elected annually.
Publication:
The Green Sheet. bi-m.
Annual Meetings: Spring/100

Nat'l Ass'n of Professional Band Instrument Repair Technicians (1976)
Box 51, Normal IL 61761
Exec. Director: Chuck Hagler
Members: 800 *Staff:* 1
Annual Budget: $50-100,000 *Tel:* (309) 452-4257
Hist. Note: A non-profit organization dedicated to integrity and professionalism in the craft of repair, restoration, and maintenance of band instruments. Membership: $60/yr.
Publications:
Techni-Com. bi-m. adv.
Newsletter. q.
Directory. a.
Annual Meetings: April
1987-Kansas City, MO
1988-Delavan, WI(Lake Lawn Lodge)/April 8-13/300

Nat'l Ass'n of Professional Baseball Leagues (1901)
201 Bayshore Dr. S.E., Box A, St. Petersburg FL 33731
President: John H. Johnson
Members: 17 minor leagues *Staff:* 11-15
Annual Budget: $250-500,000 *Tel:* (813) 822-6937
Hist. Note: Oversees the activity of minor league baseball.
Publications:
Baseball. a.
Baseball News. 10/yr.
Annual Meetings: First week in December/2,000.

Nat'l Ass'n of Professional Engravers (1982)
21010 Center Ridge Road, Rocky River OH 44116
Exec. Director: Benjamin J. Imburgia
Members: 300 companies *Staff:* 2-5
Annual Budget: $50-100,000 *Tel:* (216) 333-7417
Hist. Note: Established as the Northern Ohio Engravers Association in 1979, it assumed its present name in 1982 when its membership became national and incorporated in the State of Ohio. Members are engravers and industry suppliers and manufacturers. Membership: $60-325/yr.
Publication:
The Professional Engraver. q.
Annual Meetings: Spring - Trade Show Exhibition and Annual Meeting
St. Louis, MO(Sheraton Downtown)/April 9-12/1,100

Nat'l Ass'n of Professional Fund Raisers (1984)
501 West Algonquin Road, Arlington Heights IL 60005-4411
Exec. Manager: James E. Bates, CAE
Members: 60 companies
Annual Budget: $50-100,000 *Tel:* (312) 593-8350
Hist. Note: Membership: $400/year.
Publication:
Member News. q. adv.

Nat'l Ass'n of Professional Insurance Agents (1931)
400 North Washington St., Alexandria VA 22314
Exec. V. President: Donald K. Gardiner
Members: 42,000 *Staff:* 103
Annual Budget: over $5,000,000 *Tel:* (703) 836-9340
Hist. Note: Members are independent insurance agents and employees of American Agency System. Supports the Professional Insurance Agents Political Action Committee. Formerly (1976) the Nat'l Ass'n of Mutual Insurance Agents.
Publications:
PIAction. bi-m.
Professional Agent. m. adv.
Annual Meetings: Fall/2,000
1987-Chicago, IL (Hyatt)/Oct. 25-28
1988-Orlando, FL (Marriott)/Nov. 13-16

Nat'l Ass'n of Professional Surplus Lines Offices (1975)
Box 1507, Roswell GA 30077
Exec. Director: J. Dale Bohm
Members: 650 firms *Staff:* 2-5
Annual Budget: $500-1,000,000 *Tel:* (404) 998-9075

00202 12 05 86 1233

Hist. Note: Members are brokerage firms writing excess and surplus insurance lines. Founded and incorporated in the State of New York, the office was moved to Georgia in 1978.
Publication:
NAPSLO Newsletter. q.
Annual Meetings: Fall/1,200
1988-San Francisco, CA
1989-New York, NY
1990-Dallas, TX

Nat'l Ass'n of Professional Upholsterers (1985)
200 S. Main St., P.O. Box 2754, High Point NC 27261
Exec. Director: Roscoe C. Smith, III
Members: 3,086 *Staff:* 6
Annual Budget: $500-1,000,000 *Tel:* (919) 889-0113
Hist. Note: Members are professional upholsterers united to increase productivity and profitability in the industry. Membership: $49/yr.
Publication:
The Professional Upholster Magazine. m. adv.

Nat'l Ass'n of Professional Word Processing Technicians (1980)
110 West Byberry Road, E2, Philadelphia PA 19116
Exec. Director: Khalil Abdul Muhammad
Members: 420 *Staff:* 4
Annual Budget: under $10,000 *Tel:* (215) 698-8525
Hist. Note: Purpose is to test, certify and document word processing hardware, software companies and competent word processors. Membership: $100 (individual), $500 (organization).

Nat'l Ass'n of Professors of Hebrew in American Institutions of Higher Learning (1950)
1356 Van Hise Hall, Univ. of Wisconsin, 1220 Linden Drive, Madison WI 53706
Secretary: Gilead Morahg
Members: 250-300 individuals
Annual Budget: under $10,000 *Tel:* (608) 262-2968
Hist. Note: A service and information organization comprised of professors in colleges, universities and seminaries who specialize in the area of Bible, Hebrew and related subjects and non-academic associate members whose occupations or interests are related to Hebrew studies. Membership: $20/yr.
Publications:
Iggeret. semi-a.
Hebrew Studies. a.
Bulletin of Higher Hebrew Education. a.
Annual Meetings: With the Soc. for Biblical Literature

Nat'l Ass'n of Property Owners (1974)
Hist. Note: Established to preserve and protect the rights of private property holders threatened by government takeovers for park or other purposes. Inactive in 1983.

Nat'l Ass'n of Public Child Welfare Administrators
1125 15th St., N.W., Suite 300, Washington DC 20005
Project Manager: Betsey Rosenbaum
Members: 500
Tel: (202) 293-7550
Hist. Note: A constituent unit of the American Public Welfare Ass'n. Members are state or local administrators responsible for public social services to children, youth and families.

Nat'l Ass'n of Public Hospitals (1980)
1426 21st St., N.W., Washington DC 20036
President and General Counsel: Larry S. Gage
Members: 70 hospitals and hospital systems *Staff:* 2-5
Annual Budget: $250-500,000 *Tel:* (202) 861-0434
Annual Meetings:
1987-Sarasota, FL/June

Nat'l Ass'n of Public Insurance Adjusters (1951)
1133 15th St., N.W., Suite 620, Washington DC 20005
Exec. Director: David W. Barrack
Members: 70-80 companies *Staff:* 10
Annual Budget: $50-100,000 *Tel:* (202) 293-5910
Publication:
NAPIA Bulletin. m.
Annual Meetings: June

Nat'l Ass'n of Public Television Stations (1980)
1818 N St., N.W., Suite 410, Washington DC 20036
President: Peter M. Fannon
Members: 175 *Staff:* 10
Annual Budget: $1-2,000,000 *Tel:* (202) 887-1700
Hist. Note: Established in January, 1980 as the Ass'n for Public Broadcasting, the present name was adopted in July, 1980. NAPTS represents public television before the federal government and provides research and planning support to the industry. Members are public television licensees.
Publication:
Washington Update. irreg. (for member stations only)
Annual Meetings: Spring
1987-St. Louis, MO/April/500

Nat'l Ass'n of Publishers' Representatives (1950)
114 East 32nd St., Suite 1406, New York NY 10016
Exec. Director: Thomas F. Kenny
Members: 300 *Staff:* 2
Annual Budget: $25-50,000 *Tel:* (212) 683-1836
Hist. Note: Members are independent advertising space salespeople who have their own firms. Formerly (1982) the Association of Publishers' Representatives.

Publications:
NAPR Bulletin. m.
Membership Directory. a.

Nat'l Ass'n of Punch Manufacturers (1963)
1173 West River Pkwy., Grand Island NY 14072
Exec. Secretary: Charles H. Till
Members: 20-25 companies *Staff:* 1
Annual Budget: $10-25,000 *Tel:* (716) 773-5720
Hist. Note: Membership: $725/yr.
Annual Meetings: March

Nat'l Ass'n of Pupil Personnel Administrators (1965)
660 Chaffin Ridge, Columbus OH 43214
Exec. Director: Dr. Charles M. Wilson
Members: 900-1,000 *Staff:* 1
Annual Budget: $10-25,000 *Tel:* (614) 457-0066
Hist. Note: Members are public and private school administrative personnel with district or state-wide responsibility for pupil services.
Publication:
NAPPA News. q.
Annual Meetings: October
1987-El Paso, TX/Oct. 25-28

Nat'l Ass'n of Purchasing Management (1915)
496 Kinderkamack Road, Oradell NJ 07649
Exec. V. President: R. Jerry Baker, C.P.M.
Members: 28,000 individuals *Staff:* 29
Annual Budget: $2-5,000,000 *Tel:* (201) 967-8585
Hist. Note: Established as the Nat'l Ass'n of Purchasing Agents, it assumed its present name in 1968. Sponsors the Certified Purchasing Manager ("C.P.M.") program of professional competency. Membership: $60/yr.
Publications:
Insight. m.
Report on Business. m.
Journal of Purchasing and Materials Management. q.
Annual Meetings: May/3,000
1987-New York, NY(Hilton)
1988-Nashville, TN(Opryland)
1989-Boston, MA(Westin)
1990-New Orleans, LA(Hilton)

Nat'l Ass'n of Quality Assurance Professionals (1976)
104 Wilmot Road, Suite 201, Deerfield IL 60015-5195
Exec. Director: David L. Stumph
Members: 2,400 individuals; 52 companies *Staff:* 2-5
Annual Budget: $250-500,000 *Tel:* (312) 944-8800
Hist. Note: Members are concerned with the quality of health care delivery. Membership: $60/year (individual), $210/year (organization).
Publication:
Journal of Quality Assurance. q. adv.
Annual Meetings: Fall/600
1987-Orlando, FL (Hyatt)/Sept. 27-30
1988-Baltimore, MD(Stouffer)/Sept. 25-28
1989-Minneapolis, MN(Marriott)/Sept. 23-27

Nat'l Ass'n of Quick Printers (1975)
111 East Wacker Drive, Chicago IL 60601
Exec. Director: Tracy Poyser
Members: 2,600 companies *Staff:* 8-10
Annual Budget: $500-1,000,000 *Tel:* (312) 644-6610
Hist. Note: Owners and managers of duplicating shops who employ the photo direct printing process.
Publications:
NAQP Newsletter. m.
QP Outlook. q.
Semi-Annual Meetings: February and August

Nat'l Ass'n of Radio and Telecommunications Engineers (1982)
Box 15029, Salem OR 97309
President: Ray D. Thrower
Members: 5,500 *Staff:* 5
Annual Budget: $100-250,000 *Tel:* (503) 581-3336
Hist. Note: Organized September 11, 1982 at the Jantzen Beach Red Lion, Portland, Oregon and incorporated in that state. Certifies corporate telecommunications centers; certifies engineers an the radio and telecommunications industry after successful completion of a formal examination. Membership: $30-60/yr. depending on certification level.
Publication:
NARTE Newsletter. m.
Annual Meetings: March

Nat'l Ass'n of Rail Shippers (1937)
50 F St., N.W., Washington DC 20001
Director, Shipper Relations: Martha McManus Kappel
Members: 3-4,000 *Staff:* 2-5
Tel: (202) 639-2378
Hist. Note: Industrial Traffic Executives using rail transportation. Has no dues. Administrative support provided by Ass'n of American Railroads. Formerly (1984) the Nat'l Ass'n of Shippers Advisory Boards and the Nat'l Ass'n of Rail Shippers Advisory Board (1985).
Annual Meetings: Transportation seminar in May.
1987-Denver, CO/May 5-7/200-250
1988-Minneapolis, MN/May 3-5/200-250

Nat'l Ass'n of Rail Shippers Advisory Boards (1937)
Hist. Note: Became the Nat'l Ass'n of Rail Shippers (1985).

Nat'l Ass'n of Railroad Trial Counsel (1954)
881 Alma Real Drive, Suite 103A, Pacific Palisades CA 90272
Exec. Director: Henry M. Moffat
Members: 1,100 *Staff:* 3
Annual Budget: $100-250,000 *Tel:* (213) 459-7659
Hist. Note: Membership: $100/yr.
Publications:
NARTC Newsletter. bi-m.
The Chronicle. bi-m.
Annual Meetings: Summer/7-800
1987-Coronado, CA(Hotel del Coronado)/July 19-22
1988-Vancouver, Canada(Vancouver)/July 21-23
1989-White Sulphur Springs, WV(Greenbrier)/July 30-Aug. 2

Nat'l Ass'n of Railway Business Women (1941)
210 Bonny Knoll Road, Roseville CA 95678
President: Rozan Prizmich
Members: 3,500-4,000 *Staff:* 1
Annual Budget: $50-100,000 *Tel:* (916) 783-4650
Hist. Note: Established as the Railway Business Women's Ass'n, it assumed its present name in 1954. Has no paid staff or permanent address. President changes every 2 years. Membership: $10/yr.
Publication:
Capsule. m.
Annual Meetings: Spring
1987-Houston, TX(Westin Oaks)/May 22-26/250
1988-Fort Worth, TX

Nat'l Ass'n of Railway Tax Commissioners (1963)
Norfolk Southern Corp., 8 North Jefferson St., Roanoke VA 24042
Secy.-Treas.: Nova Painter
Members: 125
Annual Budget: under $10,000 *Tel:* (703) 981-5793
Hist. Note: Formerly Western Ass'n of Railway Tax Commissioners. Has no paid staff or permanent address; officers change annually. Membership: $5/yr.

Nat'l Ass'n of Real Estate Brokers (1947)
1101 14th St., #1000, Washington DC 20005
President: Thom Holmes
Members: 7,500 *Staff:* 2-5
Annual Budget: $100-250,000 *Tel:* (202) 289-6655
Hist. Note: Membership consists principally of black real estate brokers. Certifies qualified members to use the title, "Realtists." Membership: $100/yr.
Publications:
Convention Journal. a. adv.
The Realtist. q. adv.
Communicator. q.
Annual Meetings: August
1987-Chicago, IL(Marriott)/Aug. 1-8

Nat'l Ass'n of Real Estate Developers (1982)
Hist. Note: Inactive in 1985.

Nat'l Ass'n of Real Estate Editors (1929)
4575 Martin Drive, North Olmsted OH 44070
Exec. Secretary: Robert F. Brennan
Members: 375 *Staff:* 1
Annual Budget: under $10,000 *Tel:* (216) 779-1624
Hist. Note: In Birmingham, Alabama, January, 1929 as the National Conference of Real Estate Editors. The present name was assumed in 1936. Membership: $50-75/yr.
Publication:
Naree News. m.
Semi-annual meetings: with Nat'l Ass'n of Realtors and Nat'l Ass'n of Home Builders.

Nat'l Ass'n of Real Estate Investment Trusts (1960)
1101 17th St., N.W., Suite 700, Washington DC 20036
Exec. V. President: Mark O. Decker
Members: 350-400 *Staff:* 10-15
Annual Budget: $500-1,000,000 *Tel:* (202) 785-8717
Hist. Note: Formerly Nat'l Ass'n of Real Estate Investment Funds, it assumed its present name in 1972. Membership is open to qualified REITs and other organizations and individuals in related fields such as law, accounting, financial advising, mortgage and investment banking and real estate services. REIT's primary purpose is to represent the industry before Congress and the Executive branch; it also provides education and information for the industry and holds three major conferences each year. Membership: $650/yr. (individual); company fee determined by assets.
Publications:
The REIT Line. m.
The REIT Report. q.
REIT Factbook. a.
Compendium. a.
Membership Directory. a.
Administrative Survey. a.
How to Form a REIT Kit. a.
State and Course of the Industry. bi-a.
Member Report. irreg.
Annual Meetings: October/200
1987-Dallas, TX/Oct. 21-23
1988-Los Angeles, CA/Oct. 19-21
1989-New York, NY

00203 12 05 86 1233

Nat'l Ass'n of Real Estate License Law Officials (1930)
50 South Main St., Suite 600, Salt Lake City UT 84144
Exec. V. President: Stephen J. Francis
Members: 59 jurisdictions *Staff:* 90
Annual Budget: $50-100,000 *Tel:* (801) 531-8202
Hist. Note: Formerly Nat'l Ass'n of License Law Officials. An association of all the Real Estate Commissions in the United States and territories. Purpose is to upgrade the states' regulation of the real estate industry.
Publications:
NARELLO News. q.
Digest of Real Estate License Laws.
Directory.

Nat'l Ass'n of REALTORS (1908)
430 North Michigan Ave., Chicago IL 60611
Exec. V. President: William D. North
Members: 700,000 *Staff:* 550
Annual Budget: over $5,000,000 *Tel:* (312) 329-8200
Hist. Note: Founded in Chicago as the National Association of Real Estate Exchanges by 120 representatives from 19 local boards and one state association. Became the National Association of Real Estate Boards in 1916 and assumed its present name in 1974. Today it is a federation of about 1800 local boards and 50 state associations. Maintains a Washington office. Supports the National Realtors Political Action Committee and a number of state political action groups. Has a budget of over $50 million.
Publications:
Realtor News. bi-w.
Real Estate Today. m.
Annual Meetings: Mid-November
1987-Honolulu, HI/Nov. 12-17

Nat'l Ass'n of Recording Merchandisers (1958)
3 Eves Drive, Suite 307, Marlton NJ 08053
Exec. V. President: Mickey Granberg
Members: 450 tape and record companies *Staff:* 15
Annual Budget: $500-1,000,000 *Tel:* (609) 424-7404
Hist. Note: Formerly Nat'l Ass'n of Record Merchandisers. Regular members include all categories of phonograph record and tape merchandisers: retailers, rack-jobbers, one-stops, independent distributors and wholesalers; associates are manufacturers and suppliers to the industry. Membership Fee: Based on annual sales volume.
Publication:
NARM Sounding Board. m.
Annual Meetings: Late Winter
1987-Miami Beach, FL(Fontainbleau Hilton)/Feb. 13-17

Nat'l Ass'n of Recycling Industries (1913)
330 Madison Ave., New York NY 10017
Exec. V. President: M. J. Mighdoll
Members: 1,000 *Staff:* 16-20
Annual Budget: $1-2,000,000 *Tel:* (212) 867-7330
Hist. Note: Dealers, processors and consumers of scrap metal, paper, textiles, and rubber. Formerly (1960) Nat'l Ass'n of Waste Material Dealers, and (1973) Nat'l Ass'n of Secondary Material Industries, Inc. Absorbed the Rubber Reclaimers Ass'n, Inc. in 1977. Sponsors the Recycling Industry Political Action Committee.
Annual Meetings:
1987-New York, NY(Waldorf Astoria)/April 22-26

Nat'l Ass'n of Regional Councils (1967)
1700 K Street, N.W., Room 1300, Washington DC 20006
Exec. Director: Richard C. Hartman
Members: 338 *Staff:* 11-15
Annual Budget: $500-1,000,000 *Tel:* (202) 457-0710
Hist. Note: Established in 1967 by the Nat'l League of Cities and the Nat'l Ass'n of Counties. Incorporated as a membership organization in 1968. Members are regional councils of local governments and governmental agencies.
Publications:
Directory of Regional Councils. a. adv.
Washington Report. bi-w.
News and Notes. w.
Special Report. irreg.
Annual Meetings: Spring
1987-Reno, NV(MGM)/May 7-9
1988-Hartford, CT(Hilton)/May 22-25

Nat'l Ass'n of Regional Media Centers (1979)
Montgomery Co. Instruct'l Material Srvcs,ontgomery Ave. & Paper Mill Road, Erdenheim PA 19118
President: Charles Forsythe
Members: 250-275
Annual Budget: $25-50,000 *Tel:* (215) 233-9550
Hist. Note: State or regional repositories of instructional materials or services on which individual school systems can draw. Membership: $25/yr.
Publications:
Directory. a.
ETIN. q.
Semi-annual Meetings: January, with the Ass'n for Educational Communications and Technology and the Internat'l Communications
Industries Ass'n and in late summer or early fall in conjunction with another educational organization.

Nat'l Ass'n of Regulatory Utility Commissioners (1889)
Box 684, 1102 I.C.C. Bldg., Washington DC 20044
Gen. Counsel & Administrative Director: Paul Rodgers
Members: 350-375 *Staff:* 16-20
Annual Budget: $1-2,000,000 *Tel:* (202) 898-2200
Hist. Note: State and Federal regulatory commissioners. Formerly (1918) Nat'l Ass'n of Railway Commissioners; (1923) Nat'l Ass'n of Railroad and Utilities Commissioners and (1967) Nat'l Ass'n of Regulatory Utility Commissioners.
Publications:
Blue Bulletin. w.
Proceedings. a.
Annual Report on Utility and Carrier Regulations a.
Annual Meetings: Fall
1987-New Orleans, LA(Hilton)/Nov. 16-19/1,700
1988-San Francisco, CA(Westin St. Francis)/Oct. 31-Nov. 3/1,700
1989-Boston, MA(Marriott)/Nov. 13-16
1990-Lake Buena Vista, FL(Marriott Orlando)/Nov. 12-15
1992-Los Angeles, CA(Westin Bonaventure)/Nov. 16-19
1993-New York, NY(Marriott Marquis)/Nov. 15-18
1994-Reno, NV(Bally's Grand)/Nov. 14-17

Nat'l Ass'n of Rehabilitation Facilities (1969)
PO Drawer 17675, Washington DC 20041
Exec. Director: John A. Doyle
Members: 800 *Staff:* 16-20
Annual Budget: $1-2,000,000 *Tel:* (703) 556-8848
Hist. Note: Canadian and U.S. rehabilitation centers. Formed in 1969 by a merger of the Ass'n of Rehabilitation Centers (founded in 1952 as the Conference of Rehabilitation Centers and Facilities) and the Nat'l Ass'n of Sheltered Workshops and Homebound Programs (founded in 1954). Formerly (1975) Internat'l Ass'n of Rehabilitation Facilities and (1979) Ass'n of Rehabilitation Facilities. Represents both medical and vocational rehabilitation facilities.
Publication:
Rehabilitation Review. m.
Annual Meetings: June
1987-Seattle, WA
1988-Puerto Rico

Nat'l Ass'n of Rehabilitation Professionals in the Private Sector (1978)
Box 218, Blue Jay CA 92317
Exec. Director: Richard H. LaFon
Members: 400 companies, 1,500 individuals *Staff:* 4
Annual Budget: $500-1,000,000 *Tel:* (714) 337-0746
Hist. Note: Incorporated in Pennsylvania, NARPPS is an organization of companies, non-profit organizations and individuals involved in providing rehabilitation services to the disabled. Membership: $125/yr. (individual), $200/yr. (company).
Publications:
NARPPS News. bi-m. adv.
Journal of Private Sector Rehabilitation. q. adv.
Annual Meetings:
1987-Dallas, TX(Fairmont)/April 2-5/500

Nat'l Ass'n of Rehabilitation Secretaries (1971)
633 South Washington St., Alexandria VA 22314
Exec. Director: David L. Mills
Members: 1,200 *Staff:* 1
Annual Budget: under $10,000 *Tel:* (202) 836-0850
Hist. Note: Division of the Nat'l Rehabilitation Ass'n. Secretaries, stenographers and clerical assistants who work in the field of rehabilitation, either for a government or private agency. Officers change annually.
Publication:
NARS Newsletter. q. adv.
Annual Meetings: Fall, with Nat'l Rehabilitation Ass'n
1987-New Orleans, LA(Hyatt Regency)/Nov. 5-9
1988-Reno, NV(MGM Grand)/Nov. 29-Dec. 2
1989-Orlando, FL
1990-Minneapolis, MN

Nat'l Ass'n of Reimbursement Officers (1954)
1001 Third St., S.W., Suite 114, Washington DC 20024
President: Ted Thatcher
Members: 250 *Staff:* 1
Annual Budget: under $10,000 *Tel:* (202) 554-7807
Hist. Note: An organization of state mental health and mental retardation officials who are concerned with securing reimbursement for the cost of services provided to patients in state and county hospitals. Affiliated with the National Association of State Mental Health Program Directors. Has no paid staff.
Publication:
Newsletter. q.

Nat'l Ass'n of Reinforcing Steel Contractors (1969)
10382 Main St., Box 225, Suite 200, Fairfax VA 22030
Exec. Director: Fred H. Codding
Members: 400-450 companies *Staff:* 2-5
Annual Budget: $50-100,000 *Tel:* (703) 591-1870
Annual Meetings:
1987-Manzanillo, Mexico(Las Hadas)/Feb. 20-26/120-125

Nat'l Ass'n of Relay Manufacturers (1947)
Box 1505, Elkhart IN 46515
Exec. Director: A. C. Johnson
Members: 45-50 *Staff:* 1
Annual Budget: $50-100,000 *Tel:* (219) 264-9421
Hist. Note: NARM is a trade association for the elector-mechanical relay and associated switching devices industry. Membership: $1,250/yr.
Publication:
Proceedings. a.
Annual Meetings: Winter, also holds annual Nat'l Relay Conference at OK State Univ.
(School of Computer & Elec. Eng.), Stillwater, OK each April.
1987-San Diego, CA(Rancho Bernardo)/March 4-8

Nat'l Ass'n of Reporter Training Schools (1974)
Hist. Note: Defunct in 1985.

Nat'l Ass'n of Retail Dealers of America (1944)
10 E. 22nd St., #310, Lombard IL 60148
Exec. Director: John Shields
Members: 4,500-5,000 dealers *Staff:* 34
Annual Budget: $2-5,000,000 *Tel:* (312) 454-0944
Hist. Note: Formerly (until 1979) the Nat'l Appliance and Radio TV Dealers Ass'n.
Publication:
NARDA News. m. adv.

Nat'l Ass'n of Retail Druggists (1898)
205 Daingerfield Road, Alexandria VA 22314
Exec. V. President: Charles M. West
Members: 25-30,000 *Staff:* 35-40
Annual Budget: $2-5,000,000 *Tel:* (703) 683-8200
Hist. Note: Promotes the needs of the independent pharmacist. Supports the Nat'l Ass'n of Pharmacists Political Action Committee.
Publications:
NARD Almanac. a. adv.
NARD Journal. m. adv.
Newsletter. semi-m.
Annual Meetings: Fall
1987-Las Vegas, NV/Oct. 18-22

Nat'l Ass'n of Retail Grocers of the United States (1893)
Hist. Note: Merged in 1982 with the Cooperative Food Distributors of America to become the National Grocers Association.

Nat'l Ass'n of Retired Federal Employees (1921)
1533 New Hampshire Ave., N.W., Washington DC 20036-1279
President: H.T. Morrissey
Members: 490,000 *Staff:* 75-80
Annual Budget: $2-5,000,000 *Tel:* (202) 234-0832
Hist. Note: Formerly (1971) Nat'l Ass'n of Retired Civil Employees Sponsors and supports the National Association of Retired Federal Employees Political Action Committee. Membership: $12/yr.
Publication:
Retirement Life. m. adv.
Biennial meetings: Even years/2,200
1988-Little Rock, AR(Excelsior)/Sept. 25-30
1990-Louisville, KY

Nat'l Ass'n of Review Appraisers and Mortgage Underwriters (1975)
8715 Via De Commerico, Scottsdale AZ 85258
Exec. Director: Robert G. Johnson
Members: 7,000 *Staff:* 12
Annual Budget: $1-2,000,000 *Tel:* (602) 998-3000
Hist. Note: Members, mainly from financial institutions, are responsible for overseeing, reviewing or supervising the work of appraisers. Awards the CRA ("Certified Review Appraisal") designation. Membership: $150/year.
Publications:
Appraisal Review and Mortgage Underwriting Journal. q. adv.
NARA Newsletter. 6/yr. adv.
Annual Meetings: Fall/350

Nat'l Ass'n of Royalty Owners (1980)
119 North Broadway, Ada OK 74820
Exec. Director: James L. Stafford
Members: 5,000 *Staff:* 2-5
Annual Budget: $100-250,000 *Tel:* (405) 436-0034
Hist. Note: Organized in Oklahoma City in June 1980 after the passage of the Windfall Profits Tax, members are mineral, surface and royalty (producing sub-surface interests) owners concerned with the tax aspects of federal and state legislation, and with the effective management of their mineral properties. Incorporated in the State of Oklahoma. Membership: $50/yr.
Publication:
Royalty Owners Action Report (ROAR). m.
Annual Meetings: October or November

Nat'l Ass'n of Sailing Instructors and Sailing Schools (1980)
15 Renier Court, Middletown NJ 07748
Exec. Director: Richard A. Herbst
Members: 100-125 schools and individuals *Staff:* 1
Annual Budget: under $10,000 *Tel:* (201) 671-6190
Hist. Note: Primary function to to accredit sailing school courses and instructors. Membership: $10-150/yr.
Publications:
NASISS Newsletter. q.
NASISS/School Administrators Manual.

Nat'l Ass'n of Sales and Marketing Professionals (1986)
1130 Berkshire Lane, Newport Beach CA 92660
Secretary: Rosemarie Barbatti
Members: Projected at 5000 individuals.
Annual Budget: under $10,000 *Tel:* (714) 650-0387
Hist. Note: Incorporated in Arizona January, 1986. Established to promote professional standards in the industry, professional sales training and education, political representation, and communication among the professionals. Membership: $75/

00204 12 05 86 1233

year individual.

Nat'l Ass'n of Salespeople (1976)
Hist. Note: Absorbed the American Soc. of Professional Salesmen in 1978. Address unknown in 1983.

Nat'l Ass'n of Saw Shops
Hist. Note: Became the Internat'l Saw and Knife Ass'n in 1983.

Nat'l Ass'n of School Music Dealers (1962)
317 E. Walnut, Springfield MO 65806
President: Daniel L. Palen
Members: 300 *Staff:* 1
Annual Budget: $25-50,000 *Tel:* (417) 866-1986
Hist. Note: Formed by a charter group of music dealers during the 1962 Trade Show in Chicago. Has no paid staff. Membership: $150/year.
Publication:
NASMD Newsletter. q.
Annual Meetings:
1987-San Diego, CA
1988-Orlando, FL

Nat'l Ass'n of School Nurses (1968)
Box 1300, Scarborough ME 04074
Exec. Director: Beverly Farquhar
Members: 4,100 *Staff:* 4
Annual Budget: $250-500,000 *Tel:* (207) 883-2117
Hist. Note: Originally established as a department of the National Education Ass'n, NASN set up its own office in 1978 and is now an affiliate of NEA. Membership: $40/yr.
Publications:
NASN Newsletter. q.
The School Nurse. q. adv.
Annual Meetings: Last week of June/800-1,000
1987-Chicago, IL/June 26-30
1988-Washington, DC(Crystal City Hyatt)/June 28-July 2
1989-Los Angeles, CA
1990-New Orleans, LA

Nat'l Ass'n of School Psychologists (1969)
P.O. Box 55, Southfield MI 48037
Exec. Manager: Sharon Petty
Members: 9-10,000 *Staff:* 2-5
Annual Budget: $500-1,000,000 *Tel:* (313) 851-3229
Hist. Note: Membership: $59/year.
Publications:
Convention Proceedings. a.
School Psychology Review. q. adv.
Communique. 10/yr.
Annual Meetings: March
1987-New Orleans, LA(Hilton)/March 4-8

Nat'l Ass'n of School Security Directors (1970)
Charlotte-Mecklenburg Schools, 3101 Wilkinson Blvd., Charlotte NC 28208
Secy.-Treas.: Roland M. Smith
Members: 150-200 *Staff:* 1
Annual Budget: under $10,000 *Tel:* (704) 394-8900
Hist. Note: Formerly (1973) Internat'l Ass'n of School Security Directors. Promotes the profession of educational and institutional security among school security representatives and their institutions. Has no paid staff or permanent headquarters. Membership: $30/yr.(individual); $50/yr.(institution)
Publication:
Newsletter. bi-m.
Annual Meetings: July
1987-Washington, DC
1988-Indianapolis, IN

Nat'l Ass'n of Schools and Colleges of the United Methodist Church (1940)
Box 871, Nashville TN 37202
Secy.-Treas.: Julius S. Scott, Jr.
Members: 120 *Staff:* 2
Annual Budget: $50-100,000 *Tel:* (615) 327-2700
Semi-annual Meetings: Winter and Summer.

Nat'l Ass'n of Schools of Art and Design (1944)
11250 Roger Bacon Drive #5, Reston VA 22090
Exec. Director: Samuel Hope
Members: 120 schools *Staff:* 7
Annual Budget: $100-250,000 *Tel:* (703) 437-0700
Hist. Note: Established as the Nat'l Conference of Schools of Design, it became the Nat'l Ass'n of Schools of Design in 1948, the Nat'l Ass'n of Schools of Art in 1961, and assumed its present name in 1981.
Publications:
Directory. a.
Handbook. bien.
Annual Meetings: October

Nat'l Ass'n of Schools of Dance (1980)
11250 Roger Bacon Drive, #5, Reston VA 22090
Exec. Director: Samuel Hope
Members: 47 schools *Staff:* 7
Annual Budget: $25-50,000 *Tel:* (703) 437-0700
Hist. Note: An outgrowth of the Joint Commission on Dance and Theatre Accreditation. NASD is the recognized accrediting agency for education programs in dance.
Publications:
Directory. a.
Handbook. a.

Nat'l Ass'n of Schools of Music (1924)
11250 Roger Bacon Drive, #5, Reston VA 22090
Exec. Director: Samuel Hope
Members: 530 schools *Staff:* 7
Annual Budget: $500-1,000,000 *Tel:* (703) 437-0700
Hist. Note: The accrediting agency for educational programs in music in the U.S.
Publications:
Directory. a.
Handbook. bien.
Proceedings of the Annual Meeting. a.
Annual Meetings: November
1987-Boston, MA(Westin)

Nat'l Ass'n of Schools of Public Affairs and Administration (1969)
1120 G St., N.W., Suite 520, Washington DC 20005
Exec. Director: Alfred M. Zuck
Members: 250 institutions *Staff:* 6-10
Annual Budget: $100-250,000 *Tel:* (202) 628-8965
Hist. Note: Concerned with public service education and research in public policy and administration Membership: $300-950/year (institution) based on FTE. Membership: $300-950/yr. (institution) based on FTE.
Publication:
Directory of Programs in Public Affairs&Administration Programs. bi-a.
Annual Meetings: Fall
1987-Seattle, WA(Madison)/Oct. 20-24/200

Nat'l Ass'n of Schools of Theatre (1969)
11250 Roger Bacon Drive, #5, Reston VA 22090
Exec. Secretary: Samuel Hope
Members: 38 schools *Staff:* 7
Annual Budget: $10-25,000 *Tel:* (703) 437-0700
Hist. Note: The outgrowth of a study committee set up by the American Theatre Association, NAST was established as a division of ATA but is now autonomous. Its primary purpose is accreditation. NAST is the recognized accrediting agency for educational programs in theatre.
Publications:
Directory of Member Institutions. a.
Handbook of Accreditation Standards. bien.
Annual Meetings: August

Nat'l Ass'n of Science Writers (1934)
Box 294, Greenlawn NY 11740
Admin. Secretary: Diane McGurgan
Members: 1,260 *Staff:* 1
Annual Budget: $50-100,000 *Tel:* (516) 757-5664
Hist. Note: Journalists and others who convey information about scientific developments to the public. Organized September 14, 1934, by twelve science reporters. Incorporated in the State of New York in 1955.
Publication:
NASW Newsletter. q.
Annual Meetings: With the American Ass'n for the Advancement of Science
1987-Chicago, IL/Feb.
1988-Boston, MA/Feb.

Nat'l Ass'n of Scientific Materials Managers (1974)
Chemistry Dept., Univ. of New Orleans, New Orleans LA 70148
Treasurer: Cecil M. Wells
Members: 250-300 *Staff:* 1
Annual Budget: under $10,000 *Tel:* (504) 286-6324
Hist. Note: Members are stockroom managers, mainly in university and commercial research laboratories, who purchase scientific equipment. Membership: $15/yr. (individual); $50/yr. (organization/company)
Publication:
Newsline. q. adv.
Annual Meetings: July or August
1987-Las Vegas, NV
1988-Atlanta, GA

Nat'l Ass'n of Scissors and Shears Manufacturers (1925)
425 Post Road, Fairfield CT 06430
President: J. F. Farrington
Members: 6-10 companies *Staff:* 2-5
Annual Budget: under $10,000 *Tel:* (203) 255-2744
Hist. Note: Formerly (1970) Shears, Scissors & Manicure Implement Mfrs. Ass'n
Annual Meetings: December

Nat'l Ass'n of Secondary School Principals (1916)
1904 Association Dr., Reston VA 22091
Exec. Director: Scott D. Thomson
Members: 35,000 *Staff:* 75
Annual Budget: over $5,000,000 *Tel:* (703) 860-0200
Hist. Note: Administers 4 non-profit organizations: Nat'l Ass'n of Student Councils, Nat'l Ass'n of Student Activity Advisers, Nat'l Honor Soc., and Nat'l Junior Honor Soc. Has an annual budget of $9 million. Membership: $95/yr.
Publications:
Bulletin. 9/yr.
Curriculum Report. 5/yr.
Legal Memorandum. 5/yr.
NewsLeader. 9/yr.
Practitioner. 5/yr.
Student Activities. 9/yr.
Schools in the Middle. 5/yr.
Tips for Principals. 5/yr.
Annual Meetings: Winter
1987-San Antonio, TX/Feb. 6-10
1988-Anaheim, CA/March 4-8
1989-New Orleans, LA/Feb. 24-28

Nat'l Ass'n of Secretarial Services (1980)
100 2nd Ave. South, Suite 604, St. Petersburg FL 33701
Director: Cindy Fox
Members: over 1,000 *Staff:* 2-5
Annual Budget: $100-250,000 *Tel:* (813) 823-3646
Hist. Note: Independent secretarial services, word processing service bureaus, telephone answering services, and related office support services. Membership: $96/yr.
Publications:
NASS Newsletter. m.
Nat'l Membership Directory. a.
Annual Meetings:
1987-St. Petersburg, FL(Trade Winds)/May 14-16/350-400

Nat'l Ass'n of Secretaries of State (1904)
c/o The Council of State Governments, Iron Works Pike, Box 11910, Lexington KY 40578
President: James H. Douglas
Members: 50-55 *Staff:* 2
Annual Budget: $25-50,000 *Tel:* (606) 252-2291
Hist. Note: Established at the St. Louis World's Fair in 1904 as the Ass'n of American Secretaries of State, it is the oldest organization of major public officials in the U.S.; assumed its present name in 1921. An affiliate organization of the Council of State Governments which provides administrative support. Membership: $350-500/yr.
Publications:
NASS News. q.
NASS Handbook. a.
Office and Duties of the Secretary of State.
Annual Meetings: July
1987-Boston, MA/July 11-16

Nat'l Ass'n of Securities Dealers (1938)
1735 K St., N.W., Washington DC 20006
President: Gordon S. Macklin
Members: 6,500 broker/dealers *Staff:* 1,300
Annual Budget: over $5,000,000 *Tel:* (202) 728-8000
Hist. Note: Established as the Investment Bankers Conference, it assumed its present name in 1939. Has an annual budget of $100 million.
Publications:
Annual Report. a.
NASD News. bi-m.

Nat'l Ass'n of Selective Distributors (1978)
3690 Jefferson, S.E., Grand Rapids MI 49508
Acting President: Phillip Miller
Members: 30 companies
Annual Budget: $10-25,000 *Tel:* (616) 247-4733
Hist. Note: Members are companies engaged in publishing or distributing subscription magazines, books, records or periodicals.
Annual Meetings: Spring

Nat'l Ass'n of Self-Instructional Language Programs (1971)
c/o Critical Language Center, Temple University 022-38, Philadelphia PA 19122
Exec. Director: Dr. John B. Means
Members: 135 institutions *Staff:* 3
Annual Budget: $10-25,000 *Tel:* (215) 787-1715
Hist. Note: High schools, colleges and universities which teach foreign languages in a self-study format.
Publication:
"NASILP Journal". semi-a.
Annual Meetings: Fall

Nat'l Ass'n of Senior Living Industries (1985)
125 Cathedral St., Annapolis MD 21401
Exec. V. President: Robert G. Kramer
Members: 450 companies; 800 individuals *Staff:* 7
Annual Budget: $1-2,000,000 *Tel:* (301) 263-0991
Hist. Note: NASLI is a non-profit resource network of organizations, professionals and private citizens devoting efforts and resources to meeting the shelter, health, services and consumer product needs of the older populations. Membership: $850/yr.
Publication:
NASLI Newsletter. m. adv.
Annual Meetings: Spring
1987-Orlando, FL(Marriott World Trade Ctr.)/April 26-29/6-800
1988-San Francisco, CA

Nat'l Ass'n of Service Managers (1955)
60 Revere Drive, Suite 500, Northbrook IL 60062
Exec. Director: Robert Kay
Members: 1,000 *Staff:* 6
Annual Budget: $100-250,000 *Tel:* (312) 480-9575
Hist. Note: Membership: $25 initial fee; $135/yr. thereafter.
Publications:
NASM Memberline. m.
Directory. a. adv.
Annual Meetings: Fall

Nat'l Ass'n of Service Merchandising (1979)
221 North LaSalle St., Suite 863, Chicago IL 60601
Exec. V. President: Jay Spaulding
Members: 700-800 *Staff:* 6-10
Annual Budget: $1-2,000,000 *Tel:* (312) 368-1278

00205 12 05 86 1233

Hist. Note: Service distributors and suppliers of general merchandise and health and beauty items merchandised through supermarkets, department, drug, discount and variety stores. Formerly the American Rack Merchandisers Institute and (until 1979) the American Research Merchandising Institute. Consolidated with the Service Merchandisers of America and the Toiletry Merchandisers Ass'n, Inc., July 1, 1979.
Annual Meetings: Fall
1987-Washinton, DC(Shoreham Hotel)/Oct. 17-23/1,000

Nat'l Ass'n of Seventh-Day Adventist Dentists (1944)
Box 101, Loma Linda CA 92354
Exec. Secretary: Karen Sutton
Members: 500-600 *Staff:* 1
Annual Budget: $25-50,000 *Tel:* (714) 824-4633
Hist. Note: Affiliated with the American Dental Ass'n.
Publications:
News. q.
SDA Dentist. a.

Nat'l Ass'n of Sewer Service Companies (1976)
101 Wymore Road, Room 501, Altamonte FL 32714
Exec. Director: James T. Conklin
Members: 100-125 *Staff:* 2-5
Annual Budget: $25-50,000 *Tel:* (305) 774-0304
Hist. Note: Members inspect and rehabilitate sewer lines.
Annual Meetings: February

Nat'l Ass'n of Shippers Advisory Boards (1937)
Hist. Note: Became the Nat'l Ass'n of Rail Shippers Advisory Boards in 1984.

Nat'l Ass'n of Shippers' Agents (1968)
1511 K St., N.W., Suite 531, Washington DC 20005
Exec. Director: John F. Murphy
Members: 150 companies *Staff:* 2-3
Annual Budget: $250-500,000 *Tel:* (202) 737-5656
Hist. Note: Agents who act on behalf of shippers to consolidate freight so as to take advantage of volume rates.
Publication:
NASA Newsletter. m. adv.
Semi-annual Meetings:
1987-Destin, FL/April and Chicago, IL/Oct.

Nat'l Ass'n of Shooting Range Owners (1985)
P.O. Box 469, Sterling VA 22170
President: James R. Fleckenstein, CAE
Staff: 2
Annual Budget: under $10,000 *Tel:* (703) 450-6046
Hist. Note: Formed to serve the owners and operators of commercial and other public target shooting facilities. Sponsors the Legal Action for Range Preservation (LARP) program. Membership: $100-175/yr.
Publications:
Downrange Magazine. q. adv.
Ready on the Firing Line Newsletter. m.
Annual Meetings: Winter

Nat'l Ass'n of Small Business Investment Companies (1958)
1156 15th St., N.W., Suite 1101, Washington DC 20005
President: Walter B. Stults
Members: 500 companies *Staff:* 6-10
Annual Budget: $1-2,000,000 *Tel:* (202) 833-8230
Hist. Note: Members are companies licenced under the Small Business Investment Act of 1958. Sponsors the National Association of Small Business Investment Companies Political Action Committee.
Publications:
Membership Directory. a.
NASBIC News. semi-m.
Annual Meetings: Fall
1987-San Francisco, CAFairmont)/Oct. 18-22
1988-Washington, DC(Marriott)/Oct. 16-20
1989-Coronado, CA(Del Coronado)/Nov. 9-14
1990-Boca Raton, FL(Hotel & Club)/Nov. 8-13

Nat'l Ass'n of Small Government Contractors (1981)
2045 N. 15th St., Suite 1000, Arlington VA 22201
Exec. V. President: Dr. John F. Magnotti
Members: 30-35 companies *Staff:* 2-5
Annual Budget: $10-25,000 *Tel:* (703) 528-0072

Nat'l Ass'n of Smaller Communities (1977)
Hist. Note: Formerly the Ad Hoc Committee for Adequate and Assured Community Development Funding. Members are towns, small cities, municipal employees and consulting firms. Ceased effective operations in 1979. Absorbed by the Nat'l Ass'n of Towns and Townships in 1983.

Nat'l Ass'n of Social Workers (1955)
7981 Eastern Ave., Silver Spring MD 20910
Exec. Director: Mark G. Battle
Members: 102,748 *Staff:* 116
Annual Budget: over $5,000,000 *Tel:* (301) 565-0333
Hist. Note: A professional association of social workers formed Oct. 1, 1955 through the merger of the American Ass'n of Group Workers, the American Ass'n of Medical Social Workers, the American Ass'n of Psychiatric Social Workers, the American Ass'n of Social Workers, Ass'n for the Study of Community Organization, the Nat'l Ass'n of School Social Workers and the Social Work Research Group. Administers the Academy of Certified Social Workers and awards the ACSW designation. Publication office in New York City; 55 chapters. Supports PACE (a political action committee). Membership: $120/yr.
Publications:
Health and Social Work. q. adv.
NASW News. m. adv.
NASW Register of Clinical Social Workers. a.
Social Work. bi-m.
Social Work in Education. q. adv.
Social Work Research and Abstracts. q.
Annual Meetings: Biennial symposia, becoming annual in 1987.

Nat'l Ass'n of Solar Contractors (1977)
Box 15240, Phoenix AZ 85060
President: Edward A. Schein
Members: 500 *Staff:* 1
Annual Budget: $50-100,000 *Tel:* (602) 957-2365
Hist. Note: Members are contractors, architects, engineers, manufacturers and others involved in the installation of solar equipment. Serves as a clearinghouse for technical information, and represents the industry before Congress and the Department of Energy. Absorbed the American Solar Energy Ass'n in 1978.
Publications:
NASC News. bi-m.
Tech Bulletin q. adv.

Nat'l Ass'n of Solvent Recyclers (1980)
1333 New Hampshire Ave., N.W., Suite 1100, Washington DC 20036
Exec. Director: Barbara L. Barchard
Members: 100 companies *Staff:* 4
Annual Budget: $100-250,000 *Tel:* (202) 463-6956
Hist. Note: Members are companies whose primary business is the reclamation of solvents from industrial waste streams and the recycling of those refined materials for industrial use.
Publication:
Flashpoint. bi-w.
Semi-annual Meetings: April and October.

Nat'l Ass'n of Spanish Broadcasters (1979)
Hist. Note: Ceased operations in 1984.

Nat'l Ass'n of Specialized Carriers
Hist. Note: Address unknown in 1986.

Nat'l Ass'n of Specialty Food and Confection Brokers (1966)
6501 Poco Court, Fort Worth TX 76133
Secretary: Larry Burgess
Members: 80-90 *Staff:* 1
Annual Budget: under $10,000 *Tel:* (817) 292-8495
Publication:
Newsletter. q.
Semi-annual meetings: February and July

Nat'l Ass'n of Sporting Goods Wholesalers (1953)
Box 11344, Chicago IL 60611
Exec. Director: Rebecca A. Maddy
Members: 90 wholesalers; 300 manufacturers *Staff:* 1
Annual Budget: $50-100,000 *Tel:* (312) 565-0233
Hist. Note: 4 Formerly the Sporting Goods Jobbers Ass'n. Membership includes 90 wholesalers of primarily fishing and shooting sports equipment and approximately 300 manufacturers of this equipment.
Publications:
Sporting Goods Wholesaler. bi-m.
Membership Directory. a.
Annual Meetings: November/December

Nat'l Ass'n of Sports Officials (1980)
2017 Lathrop Ave., Racine WI 53405
Admin. Director: Sally Norwick
Members: 9-10,000 *Staff:* 6-10
Annual Budget: $250-500,000 *Tel:* (414) 632-5448
Hist. Note: A non-profit organization providing services and benefits (mainly medical and insurance) to amateur sports officials and umpires. Membership: $40/yr.
Publications:
NASO Newsletter. m.
Referee. m.
Annual Meetings: Summer
1987-San Francisco, CA(Marriott-Burlingame)/July 22-25/500

Nat'l Ass'n of State Administrators and Supervisors of Private Schools (1971)
Box 6Q, Richmond VA 23216
President: Charles Finley
Members: 33
Tel: (804) 225-2081
Hist. Note: Members are state licensure staff for private, post-secondary vocational schools Has no paid staff or permanent office. Officers change annually.

Nat'l Ass'n of State Agencies for Surplus Property (1947)
c/o Council of State Governments, Iron Works Pike, Box 11910, Lexington KY 40578
Staff Director: Marysia Tobin
Members: 54 *Staff:* 2
Annual Budget: $25-50,000 *Tel:* (606) 252-2291
Hist. Note: Members are surplus property agencies in the states and territories. Affiliated with the Council of State Governments which provides administrative support. Officers change annually.
Publication:
Newsletter. semi-a.
Annual Meetings:
1987-Orlando, FL/July

Nat'l Ass'n of State Alcohol and Drug Abuse Directors (1972)
444 N. Capitol St., N.W., Suite 530, Washington DC 20001
Exec. Director: Dr. William Butynski
Members: 67 *Staff:* 7
Annual Budget: $250-500,000 *Tel:* (202) 783-6868
Hist. Note: Formerly (until 1978) known as the Nat'l Ass'n of State Drug Abuse Program Coordinators. Composed of directors of State and Territorial alcoholism authorities and single State agencies for drug abuse prevention and their programs. Basic purpose is to foster, support and share information on the development of effective alcohol and drug abuse prevention and treatment services; serves as a focal point for public and private agency contacts. Membership: varies by state agency.
Publications:
NASADAD Alcohol and Drug Abuse Monthly Report. m.
NASADAD Alcohol and Drug Abuse Special Report. m.
Resource Directory of Nat'l Alcohol-Related Ass'ns, Agencies, & Orgs.
State Alcohol and Drug Abuse Profile. a.
Annual Meetings:
1987-Burlington, VT(Burlington Radisson)/May 31-June 3/150

Nat'l Ass'n of State and Provincial Lotteries (1971)
401 Marina Blvd., #220, South San Francisco CA 94080
Exec. Administrator: Jere Gilmour
Members: 147 companies *Staff:* 3
Annual Budget: $100-250,000 *Tel:* (415) 742-9711
Hist. Note: Established as the Nat'l Ass'n of State Lotteries, it became the North American Ass'n of State Lotteries in 1984 and assumed its present name in 1986.
Publications:
Directory of Members. a.
Annual Report.
Semi-annual Meetings:
1987-San Francisco, CA(Hyatt)/Feb. 13-17/600

Nat'l Ass'n of State Approving Agencies (1944)
Bureau of School Management, State House Complex, Station 23, Augusta ME 04333
President: C. Donald Sweeney
Members: 72 agencies, 185 individuals
Annual Budget: under $10,000 *Tel:* (207) 289-5857
Hist. Note: Administrators of federal and state laws pertaining to the approval and supervision of education and training programs for military personnel, veterans and their dependents.
Publication:
Directory. a.
Annual Meetings: Summer/120

Nat'l Ass'n of State Archaeologists (1978)
Star Route 1, Hackensack MN 56452
Secy.-Treas.: Christy A.H. Caine
Members: 40
Annual Budget: under $10,000 *Tel:* (218) 682-2110
Hist. Note: Has no permanent office or paid staff.
Publications:
NASA Newsletter. q.
NASA Directory. a.
Annual Meetings: With the Society for American Archaeology.
1987-Toronto, Ontario/May 6-10

Nat'l Ass'n of State Auditors, Comptrollers and Treasurers (1916)
2401 Regency Road, Suite 202, Lexington KY 40503
Exec. Director: Relmond Van Daniker
Members: 235 *Staff:* 7
Annual Budget: $250-500,000 *Tel:* (606) 276-1147
Hist. Note: Membership consists of 3 individuals from each state who serve in the capacity of auditors, comptrollers and treasurers of state fiscal agencies.
Publications:
Newsletter. bi-m.
Directory. a.
Annual Meetings:
1987-Hershey, PA/Aug. 15-19

Nat'l Ass'n of State Aviation Officials (1931)
777 14th St., N.W., Suite 717, Washington DC 20005
Exec. V. President: Robert T. Warner
Members: 50 states, Puerto Rico & Guam *Staff:* 2-5
Annual Budget: $250-500,000 *Tel:* (202) 783-0588
Hist. Note: Incorporated an affiliated research arm in 1986, the NASAO Center for Aviation Research and Education.
Publications:
NASAO Newsletter. m.
Directory. a.
Annual Meetings: Fall/350
1987-Lexington, KY(Regency Hyatt)/Oct. 18-22
1988-Montgomery, AL(Governors House)

00206 12 05 86 1233

Nat'l Ass'n of State Boards of Accountancy (1908)
545 Fifth Avenue, New York NY 10017
Exec. Director: William H. Van Rensselaer
Members: 54 state boards *Staff:* 6-10
Annual Budget: $500-1,000,000 *Tel:* (212) 490-3868
Hist. Note: Formerly (1967) Ass'n of Certified Public Accountant Examiners.
Publication:
The State Board Report. m.
Annual Meetings: Sept./Oct.
1987-New York, NY

Nat'l Ass'n of State Boards of Education (1959)
701 North Fairfax St., Suite #340, Alexandria VA 22314
Exec. Director: Phyllis L. Blaunstein
Members: 600-700 *Staff:* 16-20
Annual Budget: $1-2,000,000 *Tel:* (703) 684-4000
Hist. Note: Comprised of state board of education members from 48 states and six territories.
Publications:
State Board Connection. 10/yr.
Boardsmanship Briefs. 10/yr.
Annual Meetings: Third week in October
1987-Lexington, KY
1988-Chicago, IL

Nat'l Ass'n of State Boating Law Administrators (1961)
c/o Council of State Governments, Iron Works Pike, P.O. Box 11910, Lexington KY 40578
Exec. Director: Ed Feigenbaum
Members: 60-70 individuals *Staff:* 1
Annual Budget: under $10,000 *Tel:* (606) 252-2291
Annual Meetings: Fall
1987-Salt Lake City, UT(Marriott)/Sept. 28-30

Nat'l Ass'n of State Budget Officers (1945)
Hall of The States, 400 N. Capitol St., Suite 295, Washington DC 20001
Exec. Director: Gerald H. Miller
Members: 100-150 individuals *Staff:* 2-7
Annual Budget: $250-500,000 *Tel:* (202) 624-5382
Hist. Note: Membership limited to three budget officers per state. Affiliated with the Nat'l Governors Ass'n.
Semi-Annual Meetings: Spring and Summer

Nat'l Ass'n of State Catholic Conference Directors (1967)
521 S. 14th St., Lincoln NE 68508
President: James Cunningham
Members: 31 *Staff:* 1
Annual Budget: under $10,000 *Tel:* (402) 477-7517
Hist. Note: Directors of state Catholic Conferences.
Semi-annual meetings: summer and winter

Nat'l Ass'n of State Charity Officials (1978)
Hist. Note: Dissolved in 1985.

Nat'l Ass'n of State Credit Union Supervisors (1966)
1600 Wilson Blvd., Suite 905, Arlington VA 22209
Exec. Director: William M. Drohan, CAE
Members: 500 *Staff:* 3
Annual Budget: $250-500,000 *Tel:* (703) 821-2243
Hist. Note: State chartered credit unions and state credit union supervisors. Membership: $50-$400/yr.
Publication:
Stateline. m.
Annual Meetings: Autumn
1987-Scottsdale, AZ(Camelback Inn)/Sept. 20-23/600
1988-Boca Raton, FL(Boca Raton Hotel)/Sept. 17-23/600
1989-Monterey, CA(Doubletree Inn)/Sept. 6-10/600
1990-Vail, CO(Marriott's Mark Resort)/Sept. 23-26
1991-Palm Springs, CA(Rancho Las Palmas)/Sept. 14-18
1992-Marco Island, FL(Marriott's Marco Beach)/Oct. 3-7

Nat'l Ass'n of State Departments of Agriculture (1918)
1616 H St., N. W., Suite 704, Washington DC 20006
Exec. Secretary: James B. Grant
Members: 54 *Staff:* 10-15
Annual Budget: $250-500,000 *Tel:* (202) 628-1566
Hist. Note: Purpose is to increase public awareness of the value and services of State Departments of Agriculture. Includes 50 states, Puerto Rico, Samoa, Virgin Islands and Guam.
Annual Meetings:
1987-Atlanta, GA(Waverly Hotel)/Oct. 4-7/400
1988-Reno, NV(MGM Grand)/Sept. 23-28/400

Nat'l Ass'n of State Development Agencies (1946)
444 North Capitol St., Suite 611, Washington DC 20001
Exec. Director: Miles Friedman
Members: 200 *Staff:* 6-10
Annual Budget: $250-500,000 *Tel:* (202) 624-5411
Hist. Note: Formerly (1970) Ass'n of State Planning & Development Agencies.
Publications:
The NASDA Newsletter. 10/yr.
Trade Monitor. semi-a.
Legislative Watch. m.
Expenditure & Salary Survey. bi-a.

Nat'l Ass'n of State Directors of Migrant Education (1968)
250 East 500 South, Salt Lake City UT 84111
President: I. Peter Moreno
Members: 51 *Staff:* 0
Annual Budget: under $10,000 *Tel:* (801) 533-6092
Hist. Note: The person at each state level who has responsibility for the Chapter One Migrant Education Program operation is the state director and automatically becomes a member. The Ass'n is designed to promote interstate coordination and cooperation and provide direction for the policy decision makers at the national level.
Annual Meetings:
1987-Minneapolis, MN(Hyatt Regency)/April 26-29/1,500

Nat'l Ass'n of State Directors of Special Education (1938)
2021 K St., N.W., Suite 315, Washington DC 20036
Exec. Director: William Schipper
Members: 425 *Staff:* 6-10
Annual Budget: $500-1,000,000 *Tel:* (202) 296-1800
Hist. Note: Primarily a training organization operating on grants and affiliated with the National Education Association.
Publication:
Liaison Bulletin. bi-w.
Annual Meetings: October
1987-Scottsdale, AZ

Nat'l Ass'n of State Directors of Teacher Education and Certification (1922)
Arkansas State Department of Education, Bldg. 4, Capital Mall, Room 107-B, Little Rock AR 72201
President: Austin Hanner
Members: 90-100
Annual Budget: $10-25,000 *Tel:* (501) 371-1475
Hist. Note: Primarily concerned with educational personnel certification (licensing) and development.

Nat'l Ass'n of State Directors of Veterans Affairs (1946)
941 North Capitol St., N.W., Room 1211 F, Washington DC 20421
Record Custodian: A. Leo Anderson
Members: 51 *Staff:* 1
Annual Budget: under $10,000 *Tel:* (202) 737-5050
Hist. Note: Membership: $125/yr.
Annual Meetings:
1987-Atlantic City, NJ/125

Nat'l Ass'n of State Directors of Vocational Education (1920)
200 Lamp Post Lane, Camp Hill PA 17011
Exec. Director: John W. Struck
Members: 204 individuals *Staff:* 1
Annual Budget: $25-50,000 *Tel:* (717) 763-1120
Hist. Note: Membership: $25/yr.
Tri-annual meetings: Spring, Sept. and Dec.
The December meeting is always held with the American Vocational
Ass'n.
1987-Washington, DC(Quality Inn Capitol Hill)/May 4-8
1987-Hilton Head, SC/Sept. 14-17
1987-Las Vegas, NV/Dec. 3-5

Nat'l Ass'n of State Education Department Information Officers (1963)
Wyoming Dept. of Education, Hathaway Building, Cheyenne WY 82002
President: Dennis Kane
Members: 65 *Staff:* 1
Annual Budget: under $10,000 *Tel:* (307) 777-6203
Hist. Note: Membership: $10/yr.(individual); $50/yr.(institution)
Publication:
Newsliner. 8/yr.
Annual Meetings: July, with the Nat'l School Public Relations Ass'n

Nat'l Ass'n of State Emergency Services Directors (1981)
c/o Dept. of Health and Rehabilitation, 1317 Winewood Blvd., PDHEMS, Tallahassee FL 32301
Administrator: Larry Jordan
Members: 52 *Staff:* 1
Tel: (904) 487-1911
Hist. Note: Members are directors of state emergency medical services.

Nat'l Ass'n of State Foresters (1920)
444 North Capitol St., N.W., Hall of the States, Washington DC 20001
Washington Representative: Melinda Cohen
Members: 50-60 *Staff:* 2
Annual Budget: $50-100,000 *Tel:* (202) 624-5415
Hist. Note: Founded as the Ass'n of State Foresters in 1920, nationwide successor to the Ass'n of Eastern Forester (1911), NASF assumed its present name in 1964. Has no staff or permanent office other than the above. Officers are elected annually. Membership: $2,000/yr. (individual).
Publication:
Directory. a.
Annual Meetings: Fall

Nat'l Ass'n of State Land Reclamationists (1973)
c/o Council of State Governments, Irons Works Pike, P.O. Box 11910, Lexington KY 40578
Exec. Secretary: R. Steven Brown
Members: 140
Annual Budget: under $10,000 *Tel:* (606) 252-2291
Hist. Note: Organized to bring together State reclamation officials for activities of mutual interest and to promote cooperation between the states, private mining groups and the federal government on matters affecting the reclamation of mined lands. Membership: $5/yr. (individual); $100/yr. (corporate); $200/yr. (state)
Publications:
NASLR Newsletter. q.
Proceedings and Technical Papers of Annual Meeting. a.
Annual Meetings: Sept./Oct.
1987-Little Rock, AR/Oct.

Nat'l Ass'n of State Mental Health Program Directors (1963)
1101 King St., Alexandria VA 22314
Exec. Director: Harry C. Schnibbe
Members: 55 state and territorial mental health agencies *Staff:* 12
Annual Budget: $250-500,000 *Tel:* (202) 554-7807
Hist. Note: State commissioners in charge of the state government programs for the mentally disabled. Promotes cooperation and exchange of ideas in the administration of public mental health programs. A cooperating agency of the Nat'l Governors' Ass'n and the Council of State Governments.
Publications:
State Report.
U.S. Congress Report.
Federal Agencies Report.
Children & Youth Update.
Legal Issues.
Semi-annual meetings: Washington DC, Winter & Summer/100

Nat'l Ass'n of State Mental Retardation Program Directors (1963)
113 Oronoco St., Alexandria VA 22314
Exec. Director: Robert M. Gettings
Members: 53 *Staff:* 2-5
Annual Budget: $250-500,000 *Tel:* (703) 683-4202
Hist. Note: Formerly the Nat'l Ass'n of Coordinators of State Programs for the Mentally Retarded. Changed to its current name on December 7, 1977.
Publications:
Capitol Capsule. m. adv.
New Directions. m. adv.
Federal Funding Inquiry. irreg.
Annual Meetings: December

Nat'l Ass'n of State Park Directors (1962)
414 West Century Ave., Suite 202, Bismarck ND 58502
Secy.-Treas.: Douglas K. Eiken
Members: 50 states
Annual Budget: $10-25,000 *Tel:* (701) 224-4887
Hist. Note: Members are chief administrative officer of each state park agency. Has no permanent office. Officers are elected biennially. Membership: $100/yr.
Publications:
Annual Information Exchange. a.
Directory of State Park Directors. a.
State Parks Newsletter. a.
Annual Meetings: September
1987-Sacramento, CA/Sept. 9-12/100
1988-Lake Barclay, KY(Lake Barclay Lodge)/Sept. 7-10/100

Nat'l Ass'n of State Public Health Veterinarians (1953)
Dept. of Public Health, 100 North 9th Ave., Nashville TN 37219-5405
Secretary: Gary Swinger, DVM, MPH
Members: 50
Tel: (615) 741-7247
Hist. Note: Founded as the Ass'n of State Public Health Veterinarians, the association was successively the Ass'n of State and Territorial Public Health Veterinarians (1968), the Nat'l Ass'n of State and Territorial Public Health Veterinarians (1979), before assuming its present name in 1984. Members are heads of state veterinary public health agencies.
Annual Meetings:
1987-Undecided/Sept.-Oct.
1988-Portland, OR/July
1988-Undecided/Sept.-Oct.

Nat'l Ass'n of State Purchasing Officials (1947)
Box 11910, Iron Works Pike, Lexington KY 40578
Exec. Secretary: Linda Carroll
Members: 100-125 *Staff:* 1
Annual Budget: $10-25,000 *Tel:* (606) 252-2291
Hist. Note: Membership: $600/yr. (individual).
Publication:
NASPO Newsletter. q.

Nat'l Ass'n of State Racing Commissioners (1934)
535 West 2nd St., Suite 300, Lexington KY 40508
Exec. V. President: Anthony Chamblin
Members: 225-250 *Staff:* 6-10
Annual Budget: $100-250,000 *Tel:* (606) 254-4060
Publications:
Weekly News Bulletins. w.
Proceedings. a.
Statistical Reports on Greyhound Racing. a.
Statistical Reports on Horse Racing. a.

00207 12 05 86 1233

Book of Racing Law. a.
Annual Meetings: March/April
1987-Los Angeles, CA(Airport Hilton)/March 22-26

Nat'l Ass'n of State Recreation Planners (1981)
800 West Washington St., Suite 415, Phoenix AZ 85007
President: Don Myers
Members: 48 individuals
Annual Budget: under $10,000 *Tel:* (602) 255-1996
Hist. Note: Membership: $15/yr.
Publication:
Newsletter. q.
Annual Meetings: Spring/50
1987-Phoenix, AZ/May 26-29

Nat'l Ass'n of State Retirement Administrators (1956)
State Retirement Office, 540 East 2nd South, Salt Lake City UT 84102
Admin. Officer: Bert Hunsaker
Members: 53 *Staff:* 1
Annual Budget: under $10,000 *Tel:* (801) 355-3884
Publication:
Survey of State Retirement Systems. bi-a.
Annual Meetings: With Nat'l Conference of State Social Security Administrators
1987-Myrtle Beach, SC/Oct.

Nat'l Ass'n of State Savings and Loan Supervisors (1939)
1600 Wilson Blvd., Suite 905, Rosslyn VA 22209
Exec. Director: William M. Drohan, CAE
Members: 800 *Staff:* 4
Annual Budget: $250-500,000 *Tel:* (703) 821-2243
Hist. Note: Regulators of state chartered savings and loan ass'ns. Educational arm is the Institute for Continuing Regulatory Education. Associate membership includes 600 state chartered savings and loan associations.
Publications:
Profile of State Savings and Loan Supervisory Departments and their
Chartered Associations. bi-a. adv.
The State Advisor. m. adv.
Annual Meetings: May/June
1987-Nashville, TN(Opryland)/May 31-June 2/220
1988-Lake Tahoe, NV(Hyatt)/May 22-25/220
1989-Hilton Head, SC(Hyatt)/May 13-17/220
1990-Monterey, CA(Hyatt Monterey)/June 3-6/220

Nat'l Ass'n of State Supervisors and Directors of Secondary Education
c/o Dept. of Public Instruction, Grimes,State Office Bldg., E 14th & Grand, Des Moines IA 50319
President: Donald Cox
Members: 75 *Staff:* 1
Annual Budget: under $10,000 *Tel:* (515) 281-5609
Hist. Note: Formerly (1965) the Nat'l Ass'n of State Directors and Supervisors of Secondary Education.
Annual Meetings: In conjunction with the Nat'l Ass'n of Secondary School Principals

Nat'l Ass'n of State Supervisors of Distributive Education (1947)
Hist. Note: Affiliate of the American Vocational Ass'n. Members are state officials responsible for distributive education-marketing, wholesaling and retailing. Became a component of the Marketing and Distribution Education Association in 1982.

Nat'l Ass'n of State Supervisors of Home Economics Education
Hist. Note: A division of the American Vocational Ass'n.

Nat'l Ass'n of State Supervisors of Music (1940)
Virginia Dept. of Education, P.O. Box 6-Q, Richmond VA 23216
Chairman: John Yeager
Staff: 1
Annual Budget: under $10,000 *Tel:* (804) 225-2059
Hist. Note: Established as the Nat'l Council of State Supervisors of Music, members are supervisors of music in state departments of education. Affiliated with the Music Educators Nat'l Conference.
Publication:
Directory of State Supervisors of Music. a.
Annual Meetings: With the Music Educators Nat'l Conference

Nat'l Ass'n of State Supervisors of Trade and Industrial Education (1925)
State Dept. of Education, P. O. Box 6 Q, Richmond VA 23216
President: Ben Baines
Members: 200 *Staff:* 1
Annual Budget: under $10,000 *Tel:* (804) 225-2090
Hist. Note: Has no paid staff or permanent officer beyond the Treasurer at the above address.
Semi-annual Business Meetings: December and June

Nat'l Ass'n of State Telecommunications Directors (1978)
Box 11910, Iron Work Pike, Lexington KY 40578
Research Assistant: Pam Yost
Members: 78 *Staff:* 1
Annual Budget: $10-25,000 *Tel:* (606) 252-2291
Hist. Note: With directors representing all fifty states, NASTD is concerned with providing a forum for the exchange of ideas and practices; the development of a unified position on matters of national telecommunications policy and regulatory issues; and the improvement of state telecommunications systems. Administrative support is provided by the Council of State Governments .
Publication:
Gateway to Integration. q.
Annual Meetings:
1987-Chicago,IL/November

Nat'l Ass'n of State Textbook Administrators
Ford Education Bldg., Room 104B, Little Rock AR 72201
President: Sue Owens
Members: 25-30 individuals *Staff:* 1
Annual Budget: under $10,000 *Tel:* (501) 371-1461
Hist. Note: A rather informal group with no dues structure, permanent office or staff. Officers are elected annually. Members are adminstrators of state agencies repsponsible for the selection and distribution of texts for state schools.

Nat'l Ass'n of State Treasurers (1976)
Box 7871, Madison WI 53707
Secy.-Treas.: Charles P. Smith
Members: 51
Annual Budget: $50-100,000 *Tel:* (608) 266-3711
Hist. Note: Membership consists of State Treasureres, their deputies and staffs. Has no paid staff or permanent address; officers change annually. Membership: $250/yr.(State); $500-2,000/yr.(corporate).
Publications:
NAST Notes.
NAST Handbook. bien.
Annual Meetings:
1987-Newport, RI(Sheraton Goat Islander)/July 12-17

Nat'l Ass'n of State Units on Aging (1964)
600 Maryland Ave., S.W., Suite 208, Washington DC 20024
Exec. Director: Daniel A. Quirk
Members: 57 state units on aging *Staff:* 13
Annual Budget: $500-1,000,000 *Tel:* (202) 484-7182
Hist. Note: Members are the state units on aging of the fifty states, the District of Columbia and U.S. territories. Serves as an information clearinghouse. Provides an agency through which state units may join efforts to promote social policy responsive to the needs of older Americans.
Annual Meetings: In July/August with the Nat'l Ass'n of Area Agencies on Aging
1987-Washington, DC
1988-New Orleans, LA
1989-Washington, DC

Nat'l Ass'n of State Universities and Land Grant Colleges (1962)
One Dupont Circle, N.W., Suite 710, Washington DC 20036
President: Dr. Robert L. Clodius
Members: 149 institutions *Staff:* 20-25
Annual Budget: $2-5,000,000 *Tel:* (202) 293-7120
Hist. Note: Established as the Ass'n of State Universities and Land-Grant Colleges by a merger of the Ass'n of Land-Grant Colleges and State Universities (1887), the Nat'l Ass'n of State Universities (1895) and the State Universities Ass'n (1917). Assumed its present name in 1963.
Publications:
Greensheet. bi-w.
The Internat'l Newsletter. m.
Annual Meetings: November

Nat'l Ass'n of State Utility Consumer Advocates (1979)
1424 16th St., N.W., Suite 105, Washington DC 20036
Washington Counsel: Frederick B. Goldberg
Members: 40-50 *Staff:* 2
Annual Budget: $25-50,000 *Tel:* (202) 328-8600
Hist. Note: Members are state-appointed advocates who represent consumers before state public service commissions. Officers change every two years. The above address is the law office of Frederick B. Goldberg, P.C.
Publication:
Washington Report. m.
Annual Meetings: May/June

Nat'l Ass'n of Steel Pipe Distributors (1975)
1726 Augusta, Suite 102, Houston TX 77057
Exec. Director: Ann Saunders Muffeny
Members: 250 companies *Staff:* 2-5
Annual Budget: $250-500,000 *Tel:* (713) 781-6405
Hist. Note: Distributors and manufacturers of steel pipes and tubing. Organized in San Antonio, Texas, in April 1975, and incorporated in the same state. Membership: $550/yr.
Publications:
Pipeline. m. adv.
Tubular Products Manual. a.
Membership Directory. a. adv.
Annual Meetings: Spring
1987-Houston, TX(Houstonian)/April 8-12/400
1988-Phoenix, AZ

Nat'l Ass'n of Stevedores (1933)
2011 Eye Street, N.W., Washington DC 20006
Exec. Director and General Counsel: Thomas D. Wilcox
Members: 44 companies *Staff:* 3-5
Annual Budget: $250-500,000 *Tel:* (202) 296-2810
Hist. Note: Privately owned stevedore contractors and marine terminal operators.
Publications:
NAS Newsletter. m.
NAS Legislative Report. m.
NAS Legal Report. q.
NAS Bulletins. as needed.
Annual Meetings: March/April

Nat'l Ass'n of Store Fixture Manufacturers (1956)
5975 West Sunrise Blvd., Sunrise FL 33313
Exec. Director: Robert L. Strauss
Members: 150-175 *Staff:* 2-5
Annual Budget: $100-250,000 *Tel:* (305) 587-9190
Hist. Note: Manufacturers of store, bank and office fixtures. Membership: $500-1,750/yr.
Publications:
NASFM News. m.
NASFM Directory. a.
Annual Meetings: March/150
1987-Montego Bay, Jamaica(Rose Hall)/March 18-20

Nat'l Ass'n of Student Activity Advisers (1971)
1904 Association Drive, Reston VA 22091
Exec. Director: Dale Hawley
Members: 7,000 *Staff:* 10
Tel: (703) 860-0200
Hist. Note: Administrative support is provided by the Division of Student Activities of the Nat'l Ass'n of Secondary School Principals. Members are education professionals involved with student activity programs.
Publications:
Student Activities. m.
Monographs. q.
Annual Meetings: June

Nat'l Ass'n of Student Councils (1932)
Hist. Note: An activity administered by the Office of Student Activities of the Nat'l Ass'n of Secondary School Principals. Now includes more than 7,000 student councils and their advisers.

Nat'l Ass'n of Student Financial Aid Administrators (1968)
1776 Massachusetts Ave., N.W., Suite 100, Washington DC 20036
Exec. Director: A. Dallas Martin
Members: 2,600 institutions *Staff:* 16
Annual Budget: $100-250,000 *Tel:* (202) 785-0453
Publications:
NASFAA Newsletter. bi-m.
Journal of Student Financial Aid. q.
Annual Meetings:
1987-Washington, DC
1988-Salt Lake City, UT
1989-Washington, DC
1990-Boston, MA

Nat'l Ass'n of Student Personnel Administrators (1919)
986 Goodale Blvd., #111, Columbus OH 43212
Exec. Director: John E. Perkins
Members: 1,100-1,200 institutions, 3,500 individuals *Staff:* 6
Annual Budget: $500-1,000,000 *Tel:* (614) 294-4600
Hist. Note: Established in 1919 as the Nat'l Ass'n of Deans and Advisers of Men by a group of midwestern deans. The name was changed to the Nat'l Ass'n of Student Personnel Administrators in 1951.
Publications:
NASPA Journal. q.
NASPA Monograph Series. bi-a.
NASPA Forum. m.
Annual Meetings: Spring
1987-Chicago, IL(Marriott)/March 15-18/1,800
1988-St. Louis, MO/March 27-30
1989-Denver, CO/March 16-19

Nat'l Ass'n of Suggestion Systems (1942)
230 North Michigan Ave., Suite 1200, Chicago IL 60601
Exec. Director: George M. Otto
Members: 900-1,000 companies *Staff:* 2-5
Annual Budget: $250-500,000 *Tel:* (312) 372-1770
Hist. Note: Members are local, state and federal governments, and Fortune 500 companies. NASS tests the feasibility of employees' suggestions of new methods for improving job performance.
Publications:
NASS Pak. q.
News/Views. bi-m.
Roster and Statistical Report. a. adv.
Annual Meetings:
1987-New Orleans, LA(Sheraton)/Sept. 14-18

Nat'l Ass'n of Supervisors of Agricultural Education (1962)
State Dept. of Vocational Education, 1500 West 7th Street, Stillwater OK 74074
Past President: Joseph Raunikar
Members: 275-300
Annual Budget: under $10,000 *Tel:* (405) 377-2000
Hist. Note: Affiliated with American Vocational Ass'n. Has no paid staff or permanent headquarters. Officers rotate annually.
Publication:
Newsleter. q.
Annual Meetings: With American Vocational Ass'n.

00208 12 05 86 1233

Nat'l Ass'n of Supervisors of Business Education (1955)
Pulaski County Special School District, 1500 Dixon Road, P.O. Box 6409, Little Rock AR 72216
Contact: Doris Robey
Members: 100 *Staff:* 1
Annual Budget: under $10,000 *Tel:* (501) 490-2000
Hist. Note: Affiliated with the American Vocational Ass'n. Formerly (until 1975) the Nat'l Ass'n of Supervisors of Business and Office Education. Has no paid staff or permanent address. Membership: $10/yr.
Publication:
Newsletter. irreg.
Annual Meetings: With American Vocational Ass'n/December With Nat'l Business Education Ass'n/Spring

Nat'l Ass'n of Surety Bond Producers (1942)
6931 Arlington Road, Suite 308, Bethesda MD 20814
Exec. V. President: Bruce T. Wallace
Members: 540 *Staff:* 6-10
Annual Budget: $250-500,000 *Tel:* (301) 986-4166
Publication:
Producers Pipeline. m.
Annual Meetings: Spring/800
1987-San Francisco, CA (St. Francis)/April 8-11
1988-Palm Beach, FL (Breakers)/May 4-7

Nat'l Ass'n of Swine Records (1954)
Box 1803 West Detweiler Drive, Peoria IL 61615
President: Dan Parrish
Members: 8 secretaries of swine ass'ns, 8 breeders *Staff:* 2-5
Annual Budget: $100-250,000 *Tel:* (309) 691-8094
Publication:
Purebred Picture. q. adv.

Nat'l Ass'n of Synagogue Administrators (1948)
P.O. Box 2056, 27375 Bell Road, Southfield MI 48086-2056
1st V. President: Thomas Jablonski
Members: 160
Annual Budget: $10-25,000 *Tel:* (313) 357-5544
Hist. Note: A professional organization for conservative synagogue administrators. Affiliated with the Conference of Jewish Communal Service and the United Synagogue of America. Has no paid staff.
Publications:
NASA Journal. bi-a. adv.
Newsletter. q.
Annual Meetings: First quarter

Nat'l Ass'n of Tax Administrators (1934)
444 North Capitol St., N.W., Washington DC 20001
Exec. Secretary: Leon Rothenberg
Staff: 6-10
Tel: (202) 624-5890
Hist. Note: A constituent organization of the Federation of Tax Administrators. Absorbed the North American Gasolene Tax Conference and the Nat'l Tobacco Tax Ass'n in 1984.
Publication:
Revenue Administration. a.
Annual Meetings: June
1987-Oklahoma
1988-Toronto, Ontario
1989-Portland, OR

Nat'l Ass'n of Tax Consultors (1970)
454 N. 13th St., San Jose CA 95112
President: Lester J. Berlemann
Members: 1,800 companies *Staff:* 2
Annual Budget: $100-250,000 *Tel:* (408) 298-1458
Hist. Note: NATC provides a forum created as a source of news, information, political action and other programs for tax practitioners. Membership: $60/yr.
Publication:
National Consultor. q. adv.

Nat'l Ass'n of Tax Practitioners (1979)
1015 W. Wisconsin Ave., Kaukauna WI 54130
Chief Exec. Officer: Douglas E. Bennett, Sr.
Members: 8,000 individuals *Staff:* 12
Annual Budget: $1-2,000,000 *Tel:* (414) 766-9491
Hist. Note: Membership is open to any individual, group or business interested in the betterment of those engaged in the practice of preparing federal or state tax returns. Provides a tax research center and over 130 tax workshops for its members each year. Membership: $12/yr.
Publications:
1040 Report Newsletter. m.
Tax Information Guide for Preparers. semi-a.
Conference News. a. adv.
Who's Who in Tax Preparation (membership directory). a. adv.
Annual Meetings: August
1987-San Francisco, CA/Aug. 12-15/500
1988-Orlando, FL/Aug. 17-20
1989-Green Bay, WI(Embassy Suites)/Aug. 16-19/650

Nat'l Ass'n of Teachers' Agencies (1915)
c/o GA Agency, 11 Firethorne Lane, Valley Stream NY 11581
President: Sandra Alexander
Members: 25-30
Annual Budget: under $10,000 *Tel:* (516) 791-1390
Hist. Note: Members are private employment agencies concentrating on the placement of teachers. Absorbed the Ass'n of Southern Teacher Agencies (1909).
Publication:
Membership List. a.
Annual Meetings: Fall

Nat'l Ass'n of Teachers of Singing (1944)
2800 University Blvd. North, J.U. Station, Jacksonville FL 32211
Exec. Secretary: Dr. Bob M. Downing
Members: 4,600 *Staff:* 2-5
Annual Budget: $250-500,000 *Tel:* (904) 744-9022
Hist. Note: Teachers of singing and vocal instruction in private studios, conservatories, schools, colleges and community life. Membership: $40/yr.
Publications:
Inter Nos Newsletter. 3/yr.
NATS Journal. 5/yr. adv.
Annual Meetings: Every 18 months
1987-San Antonio, TX(Palacio Hilton)/Dec. 27-30/800
1989-Los Angeles, CA/July 1-5/850

Nat'l Ass'n of Telemarketing Consultants (1986)
356 Stadium Ave., Provo UT 84604
President: R.K. Fudge, CTC
Members: under 100 *Staff:* 1
Annual Budget: under $10,000 *Tel:* (801) 375-0927
Hist. Note: Members are individuals and companies in the U.S. and Canada who provide coonsulting and training services in the area of professional business telephone usage, including telephone marketing, sales and related topics. Recognizes excellence among members by awarding the Certified Telemarketing Consultant (CTC) designation. Membership: $100/yr. (individual); $300/yr. (company).
Publications:
The Telemarketing Consultant. q.
NATC Membership Directory. a.
Annual Meetings: October
1987-Salt Lake City, UT(Marriott Hotel)/Oct. 21-23
1988-New York, NY(Plaza Hotel)/Oct. 19-21
1989-Bermuda(South Hampton Princess)/Oct. 25-27
1990-Maui, HI(Hyatt)/Oct. 27-29
1991-Palm Springs, CA(Marquis)/Oct. 28-30

Nat'l Ass'n of Television and Electronic Servicers of America
Hist. Note: Merged with the Nat'l Electronic Sales and Service Dealers Ass'n in 1986.

Nat'l Ass'n of Television Program Executives (1963)
342 Madison Ave., Suite 933, New York NY 10173
Exec. Director: A. Philip Corvo
Members: 1,700 *Staff:* 8
Annual Budget: $2-5,000,000 *Tel:* (212) 949-9890
Hist. Note: Membership: $300/year (organization/company).
Publications:
NATPE Programmer. m. adv.
Programmers Guide. a. adv.
Pocket Station Listing Guide. semi-a. adv.
NATPE Daily. a. adv.
Annual Meetings: Winter
1987-New Orleans, LA(Convention Center)/Jan. 23-27/6,000
1988-Houston, TX(George Brown Center)/Feb. 26029/8,000
1989-Houston, TX(George Brown Center)/Feb. 15-19/8,000

Nat'l Ass'n of Temple Administrators (1941)
838 Fifth Ave., New York NY 10021
Dir. of Administration: Myron E. Schoen
Members: 175
Annual Budget: $50-100,000 *Tel:* (212) 249-0100
Hist. Note: Members are synagogue executive directors in the Reform Jewish movement. Affiliated with the Union of American Hebrew Congregations. Established as the Nat'l Ass'n of Temple Secretaries, it assumed its present name in 1959.
Publication:
NATA Journal. q.
Annual Meetings: Fall

Nat'l Ass'n of Temple Educators (1955)
Congregation Beth Israel, 5600 North Braeswood Blvd., Houston TX 77096
President: Kenneth Midlo
Members: 600 *Staff:* 1
Annual Budget: $25-50,000 *Tel:* (713) 771-6221
Hist. Note: Affiliated with Union of American Hebrew Congregations
Publication:
NATE News. irreg.

Nat'l Ass'n of Temporary Services (1967)
119 South Saint Asaph St., Alexandria VA 22314
Exec. V. President: Samuel R. Sacco
Members: 490 companies *Staff:* 2-5
Annual Budget: $500-1,000,000 *Tel:* (703) 549-6287
Hist. Note: Formerly (1971) Institute of Temporary Services. Members are companies supplying labor to others on a temporary basis. Sponsors and supports the National Association of Temporary Services Political Action Committee.
Publications:
Contemporary Times Magazine. q.
P.R. Overview. q.
Legislative Lookout. q.
Souvenir Journal. a.
Annual Meetings: Fall/500
1987-Chicago, IL
1988-Phoenix, AZ
1989-Boston, MA

Nat'l Ass'n of Textile and Apparel Distributors (1904)
Box 1325, Melbourne FL 32902
Exec. Director: Frank Keifer
Members: 98 *Staff:* 2-5
Annual Budget: $50-100,000 *Tel:* (305) 725-3129
Hist. Note: Established as the Nat'l Wholesale Dry Goods Ass'n which merged in 1955 with the Southern Wholesale Dry Goods Ass'n to form the Wholesale Dry Goods Institute. Became the Nat'l Wholesale Dry Goods Ass'n in 1955, the Nat'l Ass'n of Textile and Apparel Wholesalers in 1960 and assumed its present name in 1981. Membership: $300-600/yr. (company, based on volume).
Publication:
NATAD Newsletter. q. adv.

Nat'l Ass'n of Textile Supervisors (1883)
22 West Street, Millbury MA 01527
Secretary: Jack Vaidya
Members: 500-600 *Staff:* 2-5
Annual Budget: under $10,000 *Tel:* (617) 865-4401
Hist. Note: Formerly (1976) the Nat'l Ass'n of Woolen and Worsted Overseers. Superintendents, designers, production personnel and allied trade personnel.
Semi-annual Meetings: May and November

Nat'l Ass'n of the Pet Industry (1954)
Hist. Note: Inactive since 1983.

Nat'l Ass'n of the Remodeling Industry (1982)
1901 North Moore Street, Suite 808, Arlington VA 22209
Exec. Director: James Tolliver
Members: 4,500 members, 60 chapters *Staff:* 7
Annual Budget: $500-1,000,000 *Tel:* (703) 276-7600
Hist. Note: Manufacturers of building products, remodeling contractors, lending institutions and other firms in the home improvement industry. The result of a merger (1982) between the Nat'l Remodelers Ass'n and the Nat'l Home Improvement Council.
Publication:
Newsletter. m.
Annual Meetings: Late Winter or Early Spring
1987-Washington, DC/Feb. 26-28

Nat'l Ass'n of Theatre Owners (1920)
1560 Broadway, Suite 714, New York NY 10036
Exec. Director & Vice President: Joseph G. Alterman
Members: 8,000 theatres *Staff:* 6-10
Annual Budget: $250-500,000 *Tel:* (212) 730-7420
Hist. Note: Formerly (1966) Theatre Owners of America
Publications:
Encyclopedia of Exhibition. a. adv.
NATO News & Views.
Annual Meetings: Fall/2,000
1987-Atlanta, GA(Marriott)/Nov.
1988-Los Angeles, CA(Century Plaza)/Oct.
1989-Nashville, TN(Opryland)/Nov.

Nat'l Ass'n of Tobacco Distributors (1933)
1199 N. Fairfax St., Suite 701, Alexandria VA 22314
Exec. Director: Terry J. Burns
Members: 670 corporations *Staff:* 11-15
Annual Budget: $1-2,000,000 *Tel:* (703) 683-8336
Publications:
Distributor. m.
NATD Directory. a. adv.
Annual Meeting Program Directory. a. adv.
Annual Review. a. adv.
Annual Meetings: Spring
1987-New Orleans, LA(Hilton Rivergate)/March 25-28/2,000
1988-Orlando, FL(Marriott)/April 20-23/2,000
1989-Nashville, TN(Opryland)/March 29-April 1/2,000
1990-Miami, FL(Fontainbleu)/April 25-28/2,000

Nat'l Ass'n of Towns and Townships (1963)
1522 K Street, N.W., Suite 730, Washington DC 20005
Exec. Director: Jeffrey H. Schiff
Members: 15-20 state organizations, 13,000 local govts. *Staff:* 11-15
Annual Budget: $500-1,000,000 *Tel:* (202) 737-5200
Hist. Note: Established as the Nat'l Ass'n of Town and Township Officials, NATTO assumed its present name and opened a Washington office in 1977. NATaT is a non-profit membership organization offering technical assistance, educational services and public policy support to local government officials from 13,000 small communities across the U.S. Absorbed the Nat'l Ass'n of Smaller Communities in 1983; created the Nat'l Center for Small Communities in 1984.
Publications:
Nat'l Community Reporter. m.
Town Crier. q.
Community Development Exchange. bi-m.
Annual Meetings: September

Nat'l Ass'n of Trade and Technical Schools (1965)
2251 Wisconsin Ave., N.W., Suite 200, Washington DC 20007
Exec. Director: Stephen Blair
Members: 966 schools *Staff:* 28
Annual Budget: $2-5,000,000 *Tel:* (202) 333-1021
Hist. Note: Trade association of private, postsecondary vocational schools.
Publications:
Bulletin. irreg.
Handbook of Trade and Technical Careers and Training. a.
NATTS News. m.

00209 12 05 86 1233

Career Digest.
Career Training Journal.
Annual Meetings:
1987-San Antonio, TX
1988-San Diego, CA
1989-Nashville, TN
1990-Washington, DC
1991-San Francisco, CA

Nat'l Ass'n of Treasurers of Religious Institutes (1981)
8824 Cameron St., Silver Spring MD 20910
Exec. Director: Kathleen Steinkamp, RSM
Members: 490 *Staff:* 3
Annual Budget: $100-250,000 *Tel:* (301) 587-7776
Hist. Note: NATRI's mission is to address the fiscal, legal and administrative responsibilities specific to religious institutes in the U.S. Membership: $215/yr.
Publication:
Newsletter. m.
Annual Meetings: October
1987-San Francisco, CA(Sheraton Palace)/Oct. 7-11/450
1988-St. Paul-Minneapolis, MN
1989-Nashville, TN

Nat'l Ass'n of Truck Stop Operators (1960)
Box 1285, Alexandria VA 22313
President: Ronald L. Ziegler
Members: 1,000 *Staff:* 11-15
Annual Budget: $1-2,000,000 *Tel:* (703) 549-2100
Hist. Note: Owners and operators of large fully-equipped truck stops. Allied members are oil companies and other suppliers. Sponsors the Nat'l Ass'n of Truck Stop Operators Political Action Committee (NATSO/PAC).
Publications:
NATSO Truckers News. m. adv.
Washington Memo. m.
Semi-annual Meetings: Winter and Summer.
1987-New Orleans, LA/January
1987-Boston, MA/Summer

Nat'l Ass'n of Unclaimed Property Administrators (1962)
P.O. Box 3-R, Richmond VA 23207
President: Vivian Herbert
Members: 48
Annual Budget: under $10,000 *Tel:* (804) 225-2393
Hist. Note: Has no paid staff or permanent address; officers rotate. State officials who administer unclaimed property laws; members are usually the State Treasurer and members of his staff. Formerly (1980) the Ass'n of Unclaimed Property Administrators.
Publication:
Newsletter.
Annual Meetings: August

Nat'l Ass'n of Underwater Instructors (1960)
Box 14650, Montclair CA 91763
Exec. Director: Sam Jackson
Members: 6,500 *Staff:* 24
Annual Budget: $500-1,000,000 *Tel:* (714) 621-5801
Hist. Note: Certified instructors of basic, advanced, and specialized courses in underwater diving. Offers instructor certification programs and training programs. Affiliated with the Council for Nat'l Cooperation in Aquatics and the Underwater Soc. of America.
Annual Meetings: November/800-900
1987-Santa Ana, CA

Nat'l Ass'n of Uniform Manufacturers and Distributors (1932)
1156 Ave. of the Americas, New York NY 10036
Exec. Director: Bernard J. Lepper
Members: 450-500 *Staff:* 5
Annual Budget: $250-500,000 *Tel:* (212) 869-0670
Hist. Note: Membership: $300-2,250/yr. (organization, depending on size).
Publication:
NAUMD News. m.
Annual Meetings: February
1987-Palm Springs, CA (Canyon Club)/600

Nat'l Ass'n of Urban Bankers (1975)
111 East Wacker Drive, Chicago IL 60601
Exec. Director: Melanie Jones
Members: 22 chapters, 23 corporations, 1,500 individuals *Staff:* 1
Annual Budget: $25-50,000 *Tel:* (312) 644-6610
Hist. Note: Members are black bank executives. Has no paid staff. Officers are elected annually.
Publication:
The Urban Banker. q.
Annual Meetings: June
1987-Detroit, MI(Westin)/June 8-13

Nat'l Ass'n of Urban Flood Management Agencies (1977)
1015 18th St., N.W., Suite 1002, Washington DC 20036
Exec. Director: Ron M. Linton
Members: 25-30 *Staff:* 2-5
Annual Budget: $50-100,000 *Tel:* (202) 293-4844
Hist. Note: Members are state, county and municipal organizations concerned with the management of water resources in metropolitan areas.

Nat'l Ass'n of VA Physicians (1975)
3400 Internat'l Drive N.W., Pod K-2, Washington DC 20008
Exec. Director: Dr. Paul W. Schafer
Members: 13,000 individuals *Staff:* 4
Annual Budget: $250-500,000 *Tel:* (202) 363-3838
Hist. Note: Membership: $75/yr. (part-time); $150/yr. (full time).
Publication:
NAVAP News. m.
Annual Meetings: May
1987-Washington, DC(Nat'l Headquarters)

Nat'l Ass'n of Van Pool Operators (1976)
Hist. Note: Became the Ass'n for Commuter Transportation in 1984.

Nat'l Ass'n of Variety Stores (1943)
7646 West Devon Ave., Chicago IL 60631
Exec. V. President: Marvin E. Smith, Sr.
Members: 375-400 store owners *Staff:* 2-5
Annual Budget: $50-100,000 *Tel:* (312) 775-2232
Hist. Note: Independent variety store operators in rural America, comprising approximately 1,000 retail outlets.
Annual Meetings: Chicago

Nat'l Ass'n of Veteran Program Administrators
c/o California State University, Chico, Veterans Affairs Office, Chico CA 95929-0711
President: Bertie Rowland
Members: 350 universities/colleges, 20 individuals
Annual Budget: $10-25,000 *Tel:* (916) 895-5911
Hist. Note: Members are coordinators of veterans programs on college campuses. Concerned with preserving the educational benefits promised by the the military to service persons upon their enlistment. Membership: $30/year (individual).
Publication:
NAVPA News. q.
Annual Meetings: Last week in October
1987-Washington, DC

Nat'l Ass'n of Video Distributors (1981)
1255 Twenty-Third St., N.W., Washington DC 20037
Exec. Director: Sheldon J. Hauck
Members: 25 *Staff:* 2-5
Annual Budget: $100-250,000 *Tel:* (202) 452-8100
Hist. Note: Members are wholesale distributors of home video software; associate members are manufacturers of such equipment.

Nat'l Ass'n of Vision Professionals (1976)
1775 Church St., N.W., Washington DC 20036
President: Dr. Arnold Simonse
Members: 100 *Staff:* 1
Annual Budget: $10-25,000 *Tel:* (202) 234-1010
Hist. Note: Formerly (1985) Nat'l Ass'n of Vision Program Consultants. Professionals in the field of eye health and safety. Has no paid staff. Membership: $25/yr.
Annual Meetings: August
1987-Washington, DC/250

Nat'l Ass'n of Vision Program Consultants (1976)
Hist. Note: Became the Nat'l Ass'n of Vision Professionals in 1985.

Nat'l Ass'n of Vocational Home Economics Teachers
Rural Route 1, Box 34, Bristow OK 74010
President: Caroline Cotton
Members: 2,500-3,000 *Staff:* 1
Annual Budget: under $10,000 *Tel:* (918) 367-2241
Hist. Note: Affiliated with the American Vocational Ass'n. Formerly known as the Nat'l Ass'n of Vocational Homemakers Teachers. Has no paid staff. Officers change annually. Membership: $3/yr.
Annual Meetings: With the American Vocational Ass'n

Nat'l Ass'n of Water Companies (1895)
1725 K St., N.W., Suite 1212, Washington DC 20006
Exec. Director: James B. Groff
Members: 275-300 *Staff:* 6-10
Annual Budget: $500-1,000,000 *Tel:* (202) 833-8383
Hist. Note: Established July 30, 1895 at a meeting in Cresson Springs, Pennsylvania, as the Pennsylvania Water Works Ass'n. Became the Eastern Water Company Conference in 1959, and in 1963 the Nat'l Water Company Conference. Adopted its present name in 1971. Sponsors the Nat'l Ass'n of Water Companies Political Action Committee (NAWC/PAC).
Publications:
Newsletter. m.
Water. q.
Annual Meetings: October
1987-Orlando, FL(Hyatt Regency)/Oct. 10-15
1988-Boston, MA(Westin)/Oct. 1-7
1989-Colorado Springs, CO(Broadmoor)/Oct. 8-12
1990-St. Louis, MO(Adams Mark)/Oct. 7-11

Nat'l Ass'n of Wheat Growers (1950)
415 Second Street, N.E., #300, Washington DC 20002
Exec. V. President: Carl Schwensen
Members: 60,000 wheat farmers *Staff:* 10-20
Annual Budget: $1-2,000,000 *Tel:* (202) 547-7800
Hist. Note: A non-profit federation of state wheat organizations. Sponsors and supports the Nat'l Ass'n of Wheat Growers Foundation and the Nat'l Ass'n of Wheat Growers political action committee. Membership: $50/yr. (individual), $2,000/yr. (company).
Publications:
The Wheat Grower. m. adv.
Report from Washington. w.
Wheat Technology. bi-m. adv.
Annual Meetings: January
1987-San Diego, CA(Town & Country)/Jan. 27-30
1988-New Orleans, LA/Jan. 20-23

Nat'l Ass'n of Wholesaler-Distributors (1946)
1725 K St., N.W., Suite 710, Washington DC 20006
President: Dirk Van Dongen
Members: 7,000 companies, 120-130 ass'ns *Staff:* 25-30
Annual Budget: $2-5,000,000 *Tel:* (202) 872-0885
Hist. Note: Established as the National Association of Wholesalers by a group of leading wholesaler-distributor commodity line associations-trade associations that specialized in a particular product such as auto parts, drugs, lumber, food or tobacco. Its present name was assumed in 1970. A federation of national, state and local wholesaler associations, together with individual wholesalers. Supports the National Association of Wholesaler-Distributor Political Action Committee. Maintains the Distribution Research and Education Foundation and the NAW Service Corporation.
Publication:
Channels. m.
Annual Meetings: Winter
1987-Boca Raton, FL
1988-Kuaui, HI

Nat'l Ass'n of Women Artists (1889)
41 Union Square, Room 906, New York NY 10003
Office Secretary: Ann Hermanson Chennault
Members: 600-650 *Staff:* 1
Annual Budget: $10-25,000 *Tel:* (212) 675-1616
Hist. Note: Established in 1889 as the Women's Art Club of the City of New York. Holds an annual exhibition of members' works in New York City in Spring. Sponsors group traveling art shows of works by members, shown both in the U.S. and abroad.
Publications:
Exhibition Catalog. a. adv.
Quarterly Newsletter. 3/yr.
Semi-annual Meetings: May and November in New York, NY/100

Nat'l Ass'n of Women Business Owners (1974)
600 South Federal St., #400, Chicago IL 60605
President: Mary Del Brady
Members: 2,500 *Staff:* 2
Annual Budget: $100-250,000 *Tel:* (312) 346-2330
Hist. Note: Established in Washington D.C. as the Ass'n of Women Business Owners, NAWBO assumed its present name in 1976 and exists to provide education and training to its members, promote business ownership by women and serve as a forum through which women can establish themselves in the business world. Membership: $60/yr. (national, plus chapter dues & initiation fee).
Publication:
Statement. m.
Annual Meetings: Spring/300
1987-Denver, CO
1988-New York, NY

Nat'l Ass'n of Women Federal Contractors (1980)
Hist. Note: Merged in March 1983 with the Association of Women Government Contractors to form the National Associaton of Women Government Contractors.

Nat'l Ass'n of Women Government Contractors (1983)
402 Maple Ave., West, Suite C, Vienna VA 22180
Exec. Director: Nancy L. Stephens
Members: 200 *Staff:* 1
Annual Budget: $10-25,000 *Tel:* (703) 281-1044
Hist. Note: Incorporated in the District of Columbia, NAWGC is the product of a merger in March, 1983 of the Ass'n of Women Government Contractors and the Nat'l Ass'n of Women Federal Contractors. Its major purpose is to provide its members with a Washington voice and supply information on Federal legislation and programs affecting their interests.

Nat'l Ass'n of Women Highway Safety Leaders (1967)
7206 Robin Hood Dr., Upper Marlboro MD 20772
Exec. Director: Agnes Beaton
Members: 100,000 individuals *Staff:* 2-5
Annual Budget: $100-250,000 *Tel:* (301) 868-7583
Hist. Note: Promotes safety belt usage, alcohol education, child passenger seats, car care, gasoline saving tips, motorcycle safety and police enforcement.
Publications:
President's Newsletter. m.
Tempest. q.
Semi-annual Meetings:
1987-Winston-Salem, NC

Nat'l Ass'n of Women in Construction (1954)
327 South Adams St., Fort Worth TX 76104
Exec. Director: Betty Kornegay
Members: 8,000-9,000 *Staff:* 2-5
Annual Budget: $250-500,000 *Tel:* (817) 877-5551
Publication:
NAWIC Image. m. adv.
Annual Meetings: September

00210 12 05 86 1233

Nat'l Ass'n of Women Judges (1979)
c/o National Center for State Courts, 300 Newport Ave., Williamsburg VA 23187-8798
Staff Director: Susan Keilitz
Members: 790 *Staff:* 12
Annual Budget: $50-100,000 *Tel:* (804) 253-2000
Hist. Note: Organized in Los Angeles, October 28, 1979. Membership: $75/year.
Publication:
NAWJ News & Announcements. 3/yr.
Annual Meetings: October/200
1987-Seattle, WA/Oct. 9-12

Nat'l Ass'n of Women Lawyers (1911)
750 North Lake Shore Drive, Chicago IL 60611
Director: Patricia O'Mahoney
Members: 1,200 *Staff:* 1
Annual Budget: $25-50,000 *Tel:* (312) 988-6186
Hist. Note: Founded in 1899 as the Women Lawyers Club. Re-organized in 1911 as the Nat'l Ass'n of Women Lawyers.
Publications:
President's Letter. q.
Women Lawyers Journal. q. adv.
Annual Meetings: With American Bar Ass'n.

Nat'l Ass'n of Women's and Children's Apparel Salesmen (1945)
Hist. Note: A member of the Bureau of Salesmen's National Associations. Merged (1980) with the National Association of Men's and Boys' Apparel Clubs to become the Bureau of Wholesale Sales Representatives.

Nat'l Ass'n of Writing Instrument Distributors (1961)
1740 E. Joppa Road, P.O. Box 28279, Baltimore MD 21234
Exec. Director: Calvin K. Clemons
Members: 86 companies *Staff:* 5
Annual Budget: $100-250,000 *Tel:* (301) 661-4400
Hist. Note: Chief executives of wholesale pen companies, and sales and general management of pen manufacturing companies.
Publication:
NAWID Bluebook. q. adv.
Annual Meetings: Late Winter
1987-Orlando, FL(Wyndham Sea World)/Feb. 21-26/150
1988-Phoenix, AZ(Camelback)

Nat'l Athletic Trainers' Ass'n (1950)
1001 East Fourth St., Greenville NC 27858
Exec. Director: Otho Davis
Members: 9,620 *Staff:* 12
Annual Budget: $250-500,000 *Tel:* (919) 752-1725
Hist. Note: Athletic trainers from high schools, universities, colleges and junior colleges, professional football, baseball, basketball and hockey teams as well as military organizations. Membership: $75/yr. (individual-nat'l) and $10/yr. (indiv.-district)
Publication:
Athletic Training. q. adv.
Annual Meetings: Second weekend in June
1987-Columbus, OH
1988-Baltimore, MD

Nat'l Auctioneers Ass'n (1949)
8880 Ballentine St., Overland Park KS 66214
Exec. V. President: Harvey L. McCray
Members: 5,500-6,000 *Staff:* 6-10
Annual Budget: $250-500,000 *Tel:* (913) 541-8084
Hist. Note: Formerly (1950) National Society of Auctioneers.
Publication:
The Auctioneer. m. adv.
Annual Meetings: July
1987-Hollywood, FL(Diplomat)
1988-Kansas City, MO(Hyatt Regency)
1989-Cincinnati, OH(Clarion)
1990-Baltimore, MD(Hyatt Regency)

Nat'l Audio-Visual Ass'n (1939)
Hist. Note: Became the International Communications Industries Association in 1983.

Nat'l Auto Auction Ass'n (1945)
5701 Russell Dr., Box 29100, Lincoln NE 68529
Exec. Secretary: Bernard Hart
Members: 150 auction owners *Staff:* 2
Annual Budget: $100-250,000 *Tel:* (402) 464-2170
Hist. Note: NAAA represents dealers wholesale auto auctions, held in a permanent location on a regular weekly schedule. Promotes exchange of ideas and works in public relations in the used car merchandising industry.
Publication:
Membership Directory.
Annual Meetings: September/October
1987-Columbus, OH(Hyatt Regency)/Oct. 8-11/700
1988-Atlanta, GA(Marriott Marquis)/Oct. 6-9/700
1989-San Diego, CA(Intercontinental)/Oct. 19-22/750

Nat'l Automated Clearing House Ass'n (1974)
1901 L St., N.W., Suite 640, Washington DC 20036
President and C.E.O.: William R. Moroney
Members: 31 ass'ns & 17,500 financial institutions *Staff:* 15
Annual Budget: $2-5,000,000 *Tel:* (202) 659-4343
Hist. Note: Industry self-regulatory organization for automated clearing house (ACH) payment system. Also engages in national marketing and product development in the ACH payment system.
Publications:
Automated Payments Update. m.
NACHA Operating Rules & Guidelines. a.
Annual Meetings: March
1987-San Diego, CA(Inter-Continental)/March 15-18/1,100
1988-Dallas, TX/1,400

Nat'l Automatic Laundry and Cleaning Council (1960)
Hist. Note: Became the Coin Laundry Association in 1983.

Nat'l Automatic Merchandising Ass'n (1936)
20 North Wacker Drive, Chicago IL 60606
President: G. Richard Schreiber
Members: 2,300-2,400 companies *Staff:* 25-30
Annual Budget: $1-2,000,000 *Tel:* (312) 346-0370
Hist. Note: Members are makers and operators of automatic vending equipment together with the providers of food and other merchandise dispensed. Founded to provide government affairs service to the vending industry. Programs in public health and safety, public relations, education and training, accounting, and statistics comprise NAMA's other services.
Publications:
Directory of Members. a.
Members Newsletters. m.
Quarterly Labor Relations Report. q.
Vending/Foodservice Management Review. a.
Semi-annual meetings: Spring and Fall
1987-Reno, NV(Convention Center)/March 6-8/3,300
1987-Philadelphia, PA(Convention Center)/Oct. 29-Nov. 1/7,000
1988-Anaheim, CA(Convention Center)/April 15-17/3,400
1988-New Orleans, LA(Convention Center)/Oct. 20-23/7,200

Nat'l Automatic Sprinkler and Fire Control Ass'n (1914)
Hist. Note: Became the National Fire Sprinkler Association in 1983.

Nat'l Automobile Dealers Ass'n (1917)
8400 Westpark Drive, McLean VA 22102
Exec. V. President: Frank E. McCarthy
Members: 19,000 *Staff:* 300
Annual Budget: over $5,000,000 *Tel:* (703) 821-7000
Hist. Note: Organized in Chicago, June 10-11, 1917 as the result of the U.S. entry into World War I and a proposed luxury tax of 5% on automobiles. Incorporated in Illinois the same year, it represents dealers franchised by manufactuers and importers to sell and service new cars and trucks. Affiliated with Nat'l Automobile Dealers Used Car Guide Company. Connected with the Dealers Election Action Committee and the Nat'l Dealers Charitable Foundation. The Nat'l Truck Dealers Ass'n is a division of the NADA.
Publication:
Automotive Executive. m. adv.
Annual Meetings: Winter
1987-Las Vegas, NV(Convention Ctr.)
1988-San Francisco, CA/Feb. 7-10
1989-New Orleans, LA/Feb. 11-14

Nat'l Automobile Theft Bureau (1912)
10330 South Roberts Rd., Palos Hills IL 60465
President: Paul W. Gilliland
Members: 600 insurance companies *Staff:* 252
Annual Budget: over $5,000,000 *Tel:* (312) 430-2430
Hist. Note: Established in 1912 as the Automobile Protective and Information Bureau. A non-profit association of insurance companies writing physical damage and theft insurance, NATB serves as an agency for the location and identification of stolen vehicles, the promotion of anti-vehicle theft activities, the deterence of vehicle crime and fraud. Has an annual budget of $10 million.
Publications:
NATB Journal. 3/yr.
Annual Report. a.
Annual Meetings:
1987-Boston, MA/March 17

Nat'l Automobile Transporters Ass'n (1934)
615 Griswold #815, Detroit MI 48226
Gen'l Manager and Exec. V. President: Robert P. Farrell
Members: 50-75 *Staff:* 2-5
Annual Budget: $250-500,000 *Tel:* (313) 965-6533
Hist. Note: Affiliate of American Trucking Ass'ns, Inc. Members transport motor vehicles from assembly plants, railheads and seaports to dealers in U.S.A. and Canada by both "truckaway" and "driveaway".
Publications:
Bulletin. irreg.
Membership Directory. a.
Annual Meetings: May, in Dearborn, MI at the Hyatt with an attendance of 350-400.

Nat'l Automotive Parts Ass'n (1925)
2999 Circle 75 Parkway, Atlanta GA 30339
President: Robert E. McKenna
Members: 5 companies *Staff:* 20
Annual Budget: $1-2,000,000 *Tel:* (404) 956-2200
Hist. Note: Members are wholesalers and warehouse owners dealing in auto parts, accessories and supplies.
Publications:
NAPA News. 3/yr.
NAPA Outlook. every 6 weeks. adv.
Annual Meetings: October
1987-Atlanta, GA
1988-Atlanta, GA

Nat'l Automotive Radiator Service Ass'n (1953)
P.O. Box 267, Harleysville PA 19438
Director of Operations: Joan M. Williamson
Members: 1,200 *Staff:* 7-10
Annual Budget: $500-1,000,000 *Tel:* (215) 256-4246
Hist. Note: Industry trade association.
Publications:
Automotive Cooling Journal. m.
Nat'l Newsletter.
Technical Newsletter.
Annual Meetings: Spring/2,000
1987-Nashville, TN(Opryland)/March 25-29
1988-Las Vegas, NV(MGM Grand)/March 9-13
1989-Atlanta, GA(Westin Peachtree Plaza)/March 29-April 2

Nat'l Avionics Soc. (1973)
P.O. Box 23055, Richfield MN 55423
Secy.-Treas.: John Gera
Members: 100-125 *Staff:* 1
Annual Budget: under $10,000 *Tel:* (612) 866-8800
Hist. Note: Began in Minnesota with 62 charter members and was incorporated in that state in 1973. Members are involved in the engineering, manufacturing and operating of navigational and electrical systems as well as of communication equipment in airplanes. Membership: $15/yr.
Publication:
Avionics Newsletter. m.

Nat'l Award and Trophy Manufacturing Ass'n (1975)
Hist. Note: Address unknown since 1984, reported defunct.

Nat'l Bakery Suppliers Ass'n (1917)
1625 K St., N. W., Washington DC 20006
Counsel: Wayne K. Hill
Members: 30-35 *Staff:* 1
Annual Budget: $10-25,000 *Tel:* (202) 628-5530
Hist. Note: Formerly the National Bakery Supply House Association. Members are wholesale suppliers to the baking industry. Has no headquarters or permanent staff. The above address is the law firm of Markel, Hill and Byerley.

Nat'l Ballroom and Entertainment Ass'n (1948)
Box 33057, Minneapolis MN 55433
Exec. Secretary: Doris Pease
Members: 65 *Staff:* 1
Annual Budget: under $10,000 *Tel:* (612) 478-6661
Hist. Note: Origins go back to the late 1930s when a state organization was formed to work out mutual problems of the ballroom industry. In 1941 this became the Midwestern Ballroom Operators Association and, in 1948, the National Ballroom Operators Association. In 1970 the name was changed to the Entertainment Operators of America and the present name was adopted in 1976. Membership is open to anyone operating a ballroom or club featuring live music for public dancing. Membership: $100/year.
Publication:
Newsletter. q.
Annual Meetings:
1987-McFarland, WI(Park Ponderosa Ballroom)/July 26-28/100

Nat'l Band Ass'n (1960)
Box 121292, Nashville TN 37212
Exec. Secretary: L. Howard Nicar, Jr.
Members: 3,000 *Staff:* 1
Annual Budget: $50-100,000 *Tel:* (615) 329-2620
Hist. Note: Members are band directors, music teachers, musical instrument makers and others interested in band development. Affiliated with the Music Educators Nat'l Conference. Membership: $25/yr. (individual); $30/yr. (institution); $40/yr. (industrial).
Publication:
Journal. q.
Biennial Meetings: Even years
1988-Knoxville, TN

Nat'l Bankers Ass'n (1927)
122 C St., N.W., Suite 240, Washington DC 20001
V. President: John P. Kelly, Jr.
Members: 60-70 banks *Staff:* 3-5
Annual Budget: $250-500,000 *Tel:* (202) 783-3200
Hist. Note: Formerly (1951) Nat'l Negro Bankers Ass'n. Members are minority banking instirutions, minority individuals employed by majority banks and majority institutions. Membership: Institutional (minority bank) based on assets, Associate (minority individual employed in a majority bank) $150/yr., Affiliate (majority institution) $1,000/yr.
Publications:
NBA News Report. m.
NBA Today.
Annual Meetings: Fall
1987-Norfolk, VA/Oct. 21-24/350-400

Nat'l Bar Ass'n (1925)
1225 11th St., N.W., Washington DC 20001
Exec. Director: John Crump
Members: 10,000 *Staff:* 11-15
Annual Budget: $500-1,000,000 *Tel:* (202) 842-3900
Hist. Note: Membership consists principally of black lawyers. Oldest ass'n of minority attorneys in the U.S. Membership: $110/yr.

00211 12 05 86 1233

Publication:
NBA Bulletin. bi-m. adv.
Annual Meetings: Summer
1987-New York, NY
1988-Washington, DC
1989-Oakland, CA
1990-Houston, TX

Nat'l Bark Producers Ass'n (1971)
13542 Union Village Circle, Clifton VA 22024
Exec. Director: Robert C. LaGasse, CAE
Members: 65-70 *Staff:* 2-5
Annual Budget: $10-25,000 *Tel:* (703) 830-5367
Hist. Note: Producers of bark products and suppliers of services and products to the industry.
Publications:
Bark Producers Report. q.
Special Regional Releases. irreg.
Annual Meetings: Fall

Nat'l Barrel and Drum Ass'n (1940)
1030 Fifteenth Street, N.W., Suite 1030, Washington DC 20005
Exec. Director: Pamela Joan Terry
Members: 175-200 *Staff:* 2-5
Annual Budget: $100-250,000 *Tel:* (202) 296-8028
Hist. Note: Reconditioners and dealers of steel containers. Supports the Drum Reconditioners Environmental Committee.
Publication:
Membership and Industrial Supply Directory. a. adv.
Semi-annual meetings: Spring and Fall
1987-Charleston, SC(Omni)/April 23-25
1987-Arlington, VA(Crystal Gateway Marriott)/Nov. 5-8

Nat'l Bartenders Ass'n (1986)
1377 K St., N.W., P.O. Box 67, Washington DC 20005
Exec. Director: David J. Craver
Members: 3,000 individuals *Staff:* 4
Annual Budget: $50-100,000 *Tel:* (800) 227-8637
Hist. Note: Formed to promote bartending as a profession, NBA is incorporated in Virginia. Membership: $75/yr.
Publication:
Bar Tab. q. adv.
Annual Meetings: Spring
1987-Washington, DC

Nat'l Basketball Ass'n (1946)
645 Fifth Avenue, 15th Floor, New York NY 10022
Commissioner: David Stern
Members: 23 clubs *Staff:* 55-60
Annual Budget: over $5,000,000 *Tel:* (212) 826-7000
Hist. Note: The association which administers professional basketball.
Publication:
Hoop. m.

Nat'l Basketball Players Ass'n
15 Columbus Circle, 6th Floor, New York NY 10023
General Counsel: Lawrence Fleisher
Members: 270 individuals, 23 clubs *Staff:* 1
Annual Budget: $25-50,000 *Tel:* (212) 541-7118
Hist. Note: Independent labor union
Publication:
Time out. m.
Semi-annual Meetings:

Nat'l Bath, Bed and Linen Ass'n (1967)
15 East 26th St., Suite 1602, New York NY 10010
Exec. Director: Donald H. Roberts
Members: 500 companies *Staff:* 7
Annual Budget: $500-1,000,000 *Tel:* (212) 689-5550
Hist. Note: Established as the National Association of Bath Products Manufacturers, it assumed its present name in 1974. Members are makers and distributors of consumer products for the bedroom, bath and table. Membership: $250/yr. (company).
Publications:
Show Talk Newsletter. a.
NBB&L Directory of Exhibitors. a. adv.
Annual Meetings: May in New York City
1987-(Conv. Center)/May 10-13/12,000
1988-(Conv. Center)
1989-(Conv. Center)

Nat'l Beauty and Barber Manufacturers Ass'n (1941)
Hist. Note: Merged with the UBA in March, 1985 to form the American Beauty Ass'n.

Nat'l Beauty Culturists' League (1919)
25 Logan Circle, N.W., Washington DC 20005
President: Cleolis Richardson
Members: 10,000 *Staff:* 2-5
Tel: (202) 332-2695
Hist. Note: Established as the National Hair System Culture League, it assumed its present name in 1920. Members are black beauticians and cosmetologists.
Annual Meetings: Summer
1987-Detroit, MI(Westin Renaissance)/July 25-Aug. 1

Nat'l Beauty Salon Chain Ass'n (1972)
Hist. Note: Became the Internat'l Chain Salon Ass'n in 1985.

Nat'l Bed and Breakfast Ass'n (1981)
P.O. Box 332, Norwalk CT 06852
President: Phyllis Featherston
Members: 12,000 indvidual B&B homes and inns *Staff:* 11
Annual Budget: $10-25,000 *Tel:* (203) 847-6196
Hist. Note: Membership: $25/y.
Publication:
Bed & Breakfast Guide for the U.S. & Canada. bi-a. adv.

Nat'l Beer Wholesalers' Ass'n (1938)
5205 Leesburg Pike, Suite 505, Falls Church VA 22041
President: Ronald R. Rumbaugh
Members: 2,200-2,400 *Staff:* 25
Annual Budget: $2-5,000,000 *Tel:* (703) 578-4300
Hist. Note: Represents the independent wholesaling segment of the U.S. malt beverage industry. Sponsors and supports the National Beer Wholesalers Association Political Action Committee. Established (1985) the NBWA Education Foundation to sponsor national research, development and placement of alcohol awareness programs. Membership: fees proportional to member company's annual sales.
Publications:
Beer Marketing Management. m. adv.
NBWA Washington Update. bi-m.
NBWA Handbook (members only). a.
Who's Who in Beer Wholesaling (members only). bien.
NBWA Legislative and Regulatory Issues Alert. a.
NBWA Associate Member Update. q.
Distributor Productivity Report. a.
Annual Meetings: Fall/4,500
1987-Baltimore, MD(Baltimore Convention Center)/Oct. 11-14
1988-Anaheim, CA(Anaheim Convention Center)/Sept. 25-28

Nat'l Beverage Dispensing Equipment Ass'n (1971)
2011 Eye St., N.W., Suite 500, Washington DC 20006
Exec. Director: Sonya Parris
Members: 176 Companies *Staff:* 2-5
Annual Budget: $100-250,000 *Tel:* (202) 775-4885
Hist. Note: Established as the Nat'l Soda Dispensing Equipment Ass'n, it assumed its present name in 1982. Members are companies which sell, rent or service beverage dispensing equipment.
Publication:
NBDEA Report. bi-m. adv.
Annual Meetings: Late Winter
1987-St. Petersburg, FL

Nat'l Bicycle Dealers Ass'n (1946)
129 Cabrillo St., Suite 201, Costa Mesa CA 92627
Exec. Director: Steve Ready
Members: 600 *Staff:* 2-5
Annual Budget: $50-100,000 *Tel:* (714) 722-6909
Hist. Note: Trade association of independent bicycle dealers. Manufacturers and distributors are elligible for associate membership. Membership: $60/yr. (dealer); $150/yr. (associate).
Publication:
NBDA Spokesman. bi-a. adv.
Annual Meetings:
1987-Reno, NV(Convention Center)/Oct. 31-Nov. 2

Nat'l Black Caucus of State Legislators (1977)
444 North Capitol St., N.W., Suite 206, Washington DC 20001
Administrative Director: Marian Collins
Members: 396 *Staff:* 6
Annual Budget: $100-250,000 *Tel:* (202) 624-5457
Hist. Note: Membership: $25/yr.
Annual Meetings: Nov/Dec

Nat'l Black Coalition of Federal Aviation Employees (1976)
P.O. Box 1782, Bethany OK 73008
Secretary: Alethia E. Futtrell
Members: 500
Annual Budget: $500-1,000,000 *Tel:* (405) 787-1239
Hist. Note: NBCFAE represents the concerns of minority FAA employees. Membership: 1% of base pay per annum (individual); $1,000/yr. (company/organization).
Publications:
Unity. bi-m. adv.
Update. a. adv.
Annual Meetings: Fall
1987-Atlanta, GA/Sept./300
1988-Texas/Sept./300

Nat'l Black Health Planners Ass'n (1981)
2635 41st St., N.W., Washington DC 20007
President: Iris Lee
Members: 85
Annual Budget: under $10,000 *Tel:* (202) 727-0744
Hist. Note: A voluntary, non-profit organization concerned with planning for the improvement of health care resources and services for Black Americans. Membership: $25/yr.
Publication:
NETWORK. bi-m.
Annual Meetings: June

Nat'l Black Nurses Ass'n (1971)
Box 18358, Boston MA 02118
Exec. Director: Sadako S. Holmes
Members: 5,000 *Staff:* 2-5
Annual Budget: $100-250,000 *Tel:* (617) 266-9703
Hist. Note: Functions as a professional support group and as an advocacy group for the Black community and their health care. Recruits and assists Blacks and minorities interested in pursuing a nursing career. Membership: $75/yr. (national), $100/yr. (chapters).
Publications:
NBNA Newsletter. q. adv.
Journal NBNA. semi-a. adv.
Annual Meetings: August
1987-Phoenix, AZ(Hyatt)/Aug. 6-9/800
1988-Washington, DC(Hyatt)/Aug. 5-12/1,000

Nat'l Black Police Ass'n (1972)
1624 V St., N.W., Washington DC 20009
National Chairman: Ron Hampton
Members: 100 ass'ns
Annual Budget: $10-25,000 *Tel:* (202) 673-6920
Hist. Note: Established in November 1972 by eleven charter police associations and incorporated in the District of Columbia. A federation of police associations with about 30,000 individuals.
Publication:
NBPA Newsletter. q.
Annual Meetings: Late summer-Early fall

Nat'l Blacksmiths and Weldors Ass'n (1875)
Box 327, Arnold NE 69120
Information Director: James Holman
Members: 250 *Staff:* 1
Annual Budget: under $10,000 *Tel:* (308) 848-2913
Hist. Note: Blacksmiths, weldors, manufacturing machine shops and general repair shops. Has no paid staff or permanent headquarters; officers change annually. Membership principally in the Midwest. Membership: $25/yr.
Publication:
The Modern Blacksmith. q. adv.
Annual Meetings: First week of December.

Nat'l Block and Bridle Club (1919)
Animal Science Dept., South Dakota State University, Brookings SD 57007
President: Dr. Dan Gee
Members: 64 Active Chapters *Staff:* 2-5
Annual Budget: under $10,000 *Tel:* (605) 688-5165
Hist. Note: Professional fraternity of men and women working in animal husbandry and affiliated with the American Soc. of Animal Science.

Nat'l Blue Crab Industry Ass'n (1977)
2000 M St., N.W., Suite 580, Washington DC 20036
Exec. Director: Roy E. Martin
Members: 60-70 individuals *Staff:* 1
Tel: (202) 296-5170
Hist. Note: Harvesters and processors of blue crabs. In 1983 became a division of the Nat'l Fisheries Institute.
Annual Meetings:
1987-Orlando, FL/Feb.

Nat'l Board of Boiler and Pressure Vessel Inspectors (1919)
1055 Crupper Ave., Columbus OH 43229
Exec. Director: D.J. McDonald
Members: 55 *Staff:* 44
Annual Budget: $1-2,000,000 *Tel:* (614) 888-8320
Hist. Note: Membership is comprised of Chief Inspectors of states and cities of the United States and of provinces of Canada.
Publications:
Bulletin. q.
Proceedings. a.
Annual Meetings:
1987-New Orleans, LA
1988-Las Vegas, NV
1989-Oklahoma, OK

Nat'l Board of Fur Farm Organizations (1944)
13965 Burleigh Road, Brookfield WI 53005
Admin. Officer: Bruce W. Smith
Members: 42 national, regional & state mink and fox breeder
Staff: 2-5
Annual Budget: $50-100,000 *Tel:* (414) 786-4242
Hist. Note: Membership: $10/year (organization).
Publications:
Research References on Mink and Foxes. a.
Proceedings of Technical Short Course. a.
Annual Meetings: August

Nat'l Book Critics Circle (1974)
756 S. 10th St., Philadelphia PA 19147
V. President & Secretary: Alida Becker
Members: 450
Annual Budget: $10-25,000
Hist. Note: Non-profit, professional organization to improve the quality of book reviewing and to extend book review coverage. Membership: $30/yr.
Publication:
NBCC Journal. q.
Annual Meetings: January in New York, NY.

Nat'l Border Patrol Council (1967)
2169 Watts Drive, Ransomville NY 14131
President: Richard L. Bevans
Members: 1,000-1,100 *Staff:* 1
Annual Budget: $100-250,000 *Tel:* (716) 791-3585
Hist. Note: A labor union of Immigration and Naturalization Service Employees, affiliated with the AFL-CIO and the American Federation of Government Employees.
Publication:
The Educator. bi-m.

00212 12 05 86 1233

Nat'l Bowling Council (1943)
1919 Pennsylvania Ave., N.W., Washington DC 20006
Exec. Director: R. Lance Elliott
Members: 16 *Staff:* 11-15
Annual Budget: $2-5,000,000 *Tel:* (202) 659-9070
Hist. Note: NBC represents all facets of the sport of bowling: equipment manufacturers, bowling centers, and players' associations. Its purpose is to promote the sport of bowling.
Quarterly Meetings:

Nat'l Broiler Council (1954)
1155 15th St., N.W., Suite 614, Washington DC 20005
President: George B. Watts
Members: 125-150 companies *Staff:* 6-10
Annual Budget: $1-2,000,000 *Tel:* (202) 296-2622
Hist. Note: Organized at a meeting in Atlanta, Georgia, sponsored by the Broiler Institute in May, 1954 and incorporated in 1955. Members are producers and processors of broiler chickens, and their suppliers. Absorbed the Nat'l Broiler Ass'n in 1956. Supports the National Broiler Council PAC.
Publication:
NBC Washington Report. w.
Annual Meetings: Washington in the Fall

Nat'l Broom and Mop Council (1906)
Hist. Note: Broom and mop manufacturers, broom corn dealers and suppliers. Formerly (1949) Nat'l Broom Manufacturers Ass'n, (1968) Nat'l Broom Manufacturers and Allied Industries Ass'n and (1976) Nat'l Broom Council. Became the Broom and Mop Division of the American Brush Manufacturers Association in 1982.

Nat'l Broom Corn and Supply Dealers Ass'n (1938)
Hist. Note: Reported as defunct in 1983.

Nat'l Brotherhood of Packinghouse and Industrial Workers (1939)
524 Brown Court, Hurst TX 76053
President: J.R. Markham
Members: 1,400-1,500 *Staff:* 2-5
Annual Budget: $50-100,000 *Tel:* (817) 282-0309
Hist. Note: Independent Labor Union. Affiliated with Nat'l Federation of Independent Unions. Formerly Nat'l Brotherhood of Packinghouse and Dairy Workers.

Nat'l Buffalo Ass'n (1966)
Box 565, Fort Pierre SD 57532
Exec. Director: Judi Hebbring
Members: 900-1,000 *Staff:* 2-5
Annual Budget: $100-250,000 *Tel:* (605) 223-2829
Hist. Note: Owners and breeders of buffalo herds. Emphasis on control of buffalo diseases and movement and promotion of the live animals as well as buffalo products such as hides and meat. Membership: $50/yr.
Publication:
Buffalo. bi-m. adv.
Semi-annual meetings: Spring and Fall
1987-Lawton, OK/March 5-7/150
1987-Missoula, MT(Sheraton)/Sept. 10-12/150

Nat'l Building Granite Quarries Ass'n (1917)
c/o John Swenson Granite Co., North State St., Concord NH 03301
Secretary: Kurt Swenson
Members: 10 companies *Staff:* 1
Annual Budget: $10-25,000 *Tel:* (603) 225-2783
Hist. Note: Annual dues based on sales volume.

Nat'l Building Material Distributors Ass'n (1952)
1417 Lake Cook Road, Suite 130, Deerfield IL 60015
Exec. V. President: Al Leitschuh, CAE
Members: 550 companies *Staff:* 5
Annual Budget: $500-1,000,000 *Tel:* (312) 945-6940
Hist. Note: Absorbed (1964) Nat'l Plywood Distributors Ass'n.
Annual Meetings:
1987-Boston, MA(Westin)/Nov. 8-11
1988-New Orleans, LA(Hyatt)/Oct. 31-Nov. 2
1989-Nashville, TN(Opryland)/Nov. 12-15

Nat'l Bulk Vendors Ass'n (1949)
200 N. LaSalle St., Suite 2100, Chicago IL 60601-1095
Counsel: Morrie Much
Members: Not divulged *Staff:* 2-5
Tel: (312) 346-3100
Hist. Note: Founded as the National Vendors Association, it assumed its present name in 1977. Members are makers and operators of bulk vending equipment and supplies.
Publication:
Bulletin. bi-m.
Annual Meetings:
1987-San Francisco, CA
1988-Cancun, Mexico
1989-Hawaii

Nat'l Burglar and Fire Alarm Ass'n (1948)
1120 19th St., N.W., Suite LL-20, Washington DC 20036
Exec. Director: Richard J. Lucas
Members: 1,000 *Staff:* 6
Annual Budget: $500-1,000,000 *Tel:* (202) 296-9595
Hist. Note: Shares office space with the Central Station Electrical Protection Ass'n and the Alarm Industry Research and Education Foundation. Membership: $150-5,200/year (company) based on number of employees.
Publications:
NBFAA Roster. a. adv.
SDM Magazine. m. adv.
Annual Meetings: Spring, in conjunction with the Internat'l Security Conference.
1987-Orlando, FL/Feb. 22-25

Nat'l Business Aircraft Ass'n (1947)
1200 18th St., N.W., Washington DC 20036
President: Jonathan Howe
Members: 2,750-3,000 companies *Staff:* 20-25
Annual Budget: $2-5,000,000 *Tel:* (202) 783-9000
Hist. Note: Formed at the Cleveland Air Show of 1946 by 13 charter members and incorporated as the Corporation Aircraft Owners' Association in New York in 1947. The present name was adopted in 1953. Members are companies and individuals who utilize aircraft in the conduct of their business.
Publications:
Business Aircraft Report. bi-m.
Business Flying. a.
Maintenance Bulletin. m.
Annual Meetings: Fall/10-12,000
1987-New Orleans, LA/Sept. 29-Oct. 1
1988-Dallas, TX/Sept. 20-22
1989-Atlanta, GA/Oct. 3-5
1990-New Orleans, LA/Oct. 2-4
1991-Houston, TX/Oct. 1-3

Nat'l Business Circulation Ass'n (1948)
c/o Institutional Investor, 488 Madison Avenue, New York NY 10022
President: Vern W. Weiher
Members: 200 *Staff:* 1
Annual Budget: $25-50,000 *Tel:* (212) 303-3542
Hist. Note: Provides an opportunity for circulation managers of business publications to keep abreast of recent publishing developments, discuss successful and unsuccessful experiences, and interchange with peers in the publishing industry. Membership: $50/year.
Publication:
Newsletter. m.

Nat'l Business Education Ass'n (1946)
1914 Association Drive, Reston VA 22091
Exec. Director: Dr. O.J. Byrnside, Jr.
Members: 18,000 *Staff:* 6-10
Annual Budget: $500-1,000,000 *Tel:* (703) 860-8300
Hist. Note: Formed in Buffalo, NY as the United Business Education Ass'n through a merger of the Dept. of Business Education of the Nat'l Education Ass'n (founded in 1892) and the Nat'l Council for Business Education. Absorbed the Nat'l Business Teachers Ass'n (formerly the Nat'l Commercial Teachers Federation) and assumed its present name in 1962. The Nat'l Ass'n for Business Teacher Education is a division. Membership: $35/yr.
Publications:
Business Education Forum. 8/yr. adv.
NBEA Yearbook. a.
Annual Meetings: Spring/2,000
1987-Boston, MA(Marriott)/April 15-18
1988-Denver, CO(Marriott City Ctr. and Fairmont)/March 30-April 2
1989-Chicago, IL(Marriott)/March 22-25

Nat'l Business Forms Ass'n (1945)
433 E. Monroe Ave., Alexandria VA 22301
Exec. V. President: Meredith R. Smith, Jr. CAE
Members: 1,750 *Staff:* 30
Annual Budget: $2-5,000,000 *Tel:* (703) 836-6225
Hist. Note: Formerly (1963) Nat'l Business Forms Associates
Publication:
FORM. m. adv.
Annual Meetings:
1987-Boston, MA(Marriott)
1988-Palm SPrings, CA(Marriott)

Nat'l Business Law Council (1975)
Hist. Note: Reported as defunct in 1984.

Nat'l Business League (1900)
4324 Georgia Ave., N.W., Washington DC 20011
President: Arthur E. Teele, Jr.
Members: 9,000-10,000 *Staff:* 11-15
Annual Budget: $250-500,000 *Tel:* (202) 829-5900
Hist. Note: Formerly Nat'l Negro Business League. Founded by Booker T. Washington, the NBL now has 100-125 affiliates in 37 states. NBL membership ranges from international trading concerns and high-tech manufacturers to small service establishments and single proprietorships. Serves as the primary advocate for business development and expansion in the black community.
Publications:
National Memo. q.
The President's Briefs. bi-m.
Annual Meetings: Fall

Nat'l Cable Television Ass'n (1952)
1724 Massachusetts Ave., N.W., Washington DC 20036
President: James P. Mooney
Members: 3,000 *Staff:* 70-75
Annual Budget: over $5,000,000 *Tel:* (202) 775-3550
Hist. Note: Formerly (1968) Nat'l Community Television Ass'n. Members are cable TV systems; associate members are manufacturers, distributors, suppliers of hardware, programmers and other services. Has an annual budget of $7.5 million.
Publication:
Tech Line. m.
Annual Meetings: Spring
1987-Las Vegas, NV/May 17-20
1988-Los Angeles, CA/April 30-May 2
1989-Dallas, TX/May 21-24

Nat'l Campground Institute (1974)
Hist. Note: Promotional arm of the National Campground Owners Association.

Nat'l Campground Owners Ass'n (1967)
804 D St., N.E., Washington DC 20002
Exec. Director: Peter Verhoven
Members: 3,200 *Staff:* 2-5
Annual Budget: $100-250,000 *Tel:* (202) 543-6260
Hist. Note: Commercial campground owners and operators, manufacturers and suppliers of campground products and services. Supports the Nat'l Campground Institute.
Publication:
NCOA News. m. adv.
Annual Meetings: Late Fall
1987-Milwaukee, WI

Nat'l Camping Ass'n (1947)
353 West 56th St., New York NY 10019
Exec. Secretary: Katherine Morus
Tel: (212) 246-0052
Hist. Note: Members are camp owners and directors.
Biennial Conventions:

Nat'l Candle Ass'n (1933)
2045 N. 15th St., Suite 1000, Arlington VA 22201
Exec. V. President: John F. Magnotti, Jr.
Members: 30-35 companies *Staff:* 3
Annual Budget: $25-50,000 *Tel:* (703) 528-7018
Hist. Note: Established as the Candle Manufacturers Ass'n, it assumed its present name in 1974.

Nat'l Candy Brokers Ass'n (1981)
1747 Pennsylvania Ave., N.W., Suite 1000, Washington DC 20006
Exec. V. President: Gerard Paul Panaro
Members: 450 companies *Staff:* 2-5
Annual Budget: $50-100,000 *Tel:* (202) 785-9500
Hist. Note: Established as the Candy Brokers Ass'n of America, it became the Nat'l Candy Brokers and Sales Ass'n in 1981 and assumed its present name in 1982. Membership: $100/yr.
Publication:
The Candy Dish. m.
Annual Meetings: Chicago, in December

Nat'l Candy Wholesalers Ass'n (1945)
1120 Vermont Ave., N.W., Washington DC 20005
Exec. V. President: Russell L. Shipley
Members: 2,400-2,500 companies *Staff:* 11-15
Annual Budget: $1-2,000,000 *Tel:* (202) 463-2124
Publications:
Candy Wholesaler. m.adv.
Quick Topics Newsletter. bi-w.
Semi-annual meetings: Winter and Summer

Nat'l Capon Council
Hist. Note: Reported inactive in 1986.

Nat'l Car Wash Council (1967)
Hist. Note: Established as the National Coin Carwash Council, it absorbed the National Coinamatic Auto Wash Asscoiation in 1967 and became the National Car Wash Council in 1969. In 1982 it became part of the International Car Wash Association.

Nat'l Career Development Ass'n (1913)
5999 Stevenson Ave., Alexandria VA 22304
Exec. Director: E. Niel Carey
Members: 5-6,000 *Staff:* 2-5
Annual Budget: $100-250,000 *Tel:* (703) 823-9800
Hist. Note: Founded as the Nat'l Vocational Guidance Ass'n, NCDA assumed its present name in 1985. Members are counselors and career development professionals who work in education, business/industry, community agencies, military installations and private practince. A division of the American Association for Counseling and Development. Membership: $6-12/yr.
Publications:
Career Development Newsletter. 5/yr. adv.
Career Development Quarterly. q. adv.
Annual Meetings: With the AACD
1987-New Orleans, LA(Sheraton)/April 21-24
1988-Chicago, IL
1989-Boston, MA

Nat'l Cargo Bureau (1952)
One World Trade Center, Suite 2757, New York NY 10048
President: Capt. S. Fraser Sammis
Members: 300-350 *Staff:* 130-140
Annual Budget: over $5,000,000 *Tel:* (212) 432-1280
Hist. Note: Formed by the merger of the Bureau of Inspection of the Board of Underwriters of New York (founded in 1820) and the Board of Marine Underwriters of San Francisco (founded in 1886). Promotes the safe loading, stowage, securing and unloading of cargo on all vessels.
Annual Meetings: New York, second Monday in April.

00213 12 05 86 1233

Nat'l Cartoonists Soc. (1946)
9 Ebony Court, Brooklyn NY 11229
Scribe: Marge Duffy Devine
Members: 450-500 *Staff:* 1
Annual Budget: under $10,000 *Tel:* (718) 743-6510
Hist. Note: A professional organization of cartoonists. Editors, writers and others interested in cartooning are accepted as associate members. Membership: $75/yr. (New York, New Jersey, Connecticut); $50/yr. (elsewhere) plus $35 initiation fee.
Publication:
The Cartoonist. a. adv.
Annual Meetings: April
1987-New York, NY(Plaza Hotel)/April 17-19

Nat'l Catalog Managers Ass'n (1974)
Kelsey Hayes Co., 38481 Huron River Drive, Romulus MI 48174
President: Linda Rudolfi
Members: 94
Annual Budget: $10-25,000 *Tel:* (313) 941-2000
Hist. Note: Members are producers of automotive products catalogues. Has no paid staff or function beyond standardizing the publications its members prepare. Affiliated with the Automotive Service Industry Ass'n.
Publication:
Newsletter. q.

Nat'l Caterers Ass'n (1981)
Box 4510, Akron OH 44310
President: Tony Rubino
Members: 1,300 companies *Staff:* 6
Annual Budget: $100-250,000 *Tel:* (216) 836-0803
Hist. Note: Formed in 1981 as a non-profit organization serving northeastern Ohio, NCA became national in scope in 1983. Membership: $150/yr.
Publication:
At Your Service. m.

Nat'l Catholic Bandmasters' Ass'n (1953)
Box 1023, Notre Dame IN 46556
Secy.-Treas.: Robert F. O'Brien
Members: 250-300 *Staff:* 1
Annual Budget: under $10,000 *Tel:* (219) 239-7136
Hist. Note: Active membership open to any qualified band director who teaches in a Catholic grammar school, high school or college, and to woodwind, brass or percussion instructors in a Catholic band program. Membership: $20/yr.(individual); $35/yr.(institution).
Publication:
The Newsletter. bi-m.
Annual Meetings: First week in August
1987-Quincy, IL(Quincy College)/Aug. 7-9

Nat'l Catholic Business Education Ass'n (1945)
Box 982, Emporia KS 66801
C.E.O.: Richard F. Reicherter
Members: 500-600 *Staff:* 1
Annual Budget: under $10,000
Hist. Note: Until 1978 known as the Catholic Business Education Association. Membership: $10/year.
Publications:
The Review. q.
Regional Bulletins. semi-a.

Nat'l Catholic Cemetery Conference (1949)
710 North River Rd., Des Plaines IL 60016
Exec. Secretary: Leo A. Droste
Members: 1,900 *Staff:* 5
Annual Budget: $250-500,000 *Tel:* (312) 824-8131
Publication:
The Catholic Cemetery. m. adv.
Annual Meetings: Fall
1987-Boston, MA(Marriott Copley Plaza)/August 24-27
1988-Chicago, IL
1989-San Francisco, CA
1990-Washington, DC
1991-Toronto, Canada
1992-Cleveland, OH

Nat'l Catholic Development Conference (1968)
86 Front St., Hempstead NY 11550
Exec. Director: George T. Holloway
Members: 450 *Staff:* 6-10
Annual Budget: $500-1,000,000 *Tel:* (516) 481-6000
Hist. Note: NCDC members include the development officers and key fund raisers of charitable institutions and agencies, religious orders, dioceses, hospitals and educational institutions. While active membership is restricted to Catholic organizations, non-Catholic groups may apply for affiliate or associate memberships. Membership dues based upon philanthropic income.
Publications:
Dimensions. m.
Fund Raising Forum. m.
Monitor. q.
Annual Meetings: Fall
1987-Baltimore, MD(Omni International)/Sept. 28-Nov. 1

Nat'l Catholic Educational Ass'n (1904)
Suite 100, 1077 30th St., N.W., Washington DC 20007
President: Catherine T. McNamee, C.S.J.
Members: 14,000 *Staff:* 35-40
Annual Budget: $2-5,000,000 *Tel:* (202) 337-6232
Hist. Note: Founded in St. Louis June 12-14, 1904 as the Catholic Education Association through the merger of the Association of Catholic Colleges (1899), the Parish School Conference (1902) and the Educational Conference of Seminary Faculties (1898).
Publication:
Momentum. q. adv.
Annual Meetings: Week after Easter
1987-New Orleans, LA(Superdome)/April 20-23
1988-New York, NY(Jacob Javits Convention Center)/April 4-7

Nat'l Catholic Educational Exhibitors (1950)
2451 East River Road, Dayton OH 45439
Exec. Director: Peter Li
Members: 300-350 *Staff:* 2
Annual Budget: under $10,000 *Tel:* (513) 294-5785
Hist. Note: Members are companies selling to Catholic schools. Associate members are 150 Catholic school superintendents and administrators.
Publications:
Membership Directory. a.
NCEE Bulletin. q.
Annual Meetings: Easter week with the Nat'l Catholic Educational Ass'n

Nat'l Catholic Pharmacists Guild of the United States (1962)
1012 Surrey Hills Dr., St. Louis MO 63117
Exec. Director: John Paul Winkelmann
Members: 375 *Staff:* 1
Annual Budget: under $10,000 *Tel:* (314) 645-0085
Hist. Note: Founded on September 19, 1962 in New York City through the auspices of the Nat'l Catholic Welfare Conference (currently known as the United States Catholic Conference.) Affiliated with the Nat'l Council of Catholic Laity and the Internat'l Federation of Catholic Pharmacists. Membership: $10/year.
Publication:
The Catholic Pharmacist. q. adv.
Biennial meetings: odd years
1987-Green Bay, WI(St. Norbert's Abbey)/July 18

Nat'l Cattlemen's Ass'n (1977)
Box 3469, 5420 South Quebec St., Englewood CO 80155
Exec. V. Pres.: John Meetz
Members: 35,000 individuals, 70 ass'ns *Staff:* 40-45
Annual Budget: $2-5,000,000 *Tel:* (303) 694-0305
Hist. Note: A merger of the American Nat'l Cattlemen's Ass'n (founded in 1898) and the Nat'l Livestock Feeders Ass'n (founded in 1943). Absorbed the Nat'l Livestock Tax Committee in 1978. Maintains a Washington office. Supports the Public Lands Council and sponsors the Cattle Political Action Committee.
Publications:
Beef Business Bulletin. w.
National Cattlemen. m. adv.
Annual Meetings: Winter/5,500-6,000
1987-Reno, NV/Jan. 26-28
1988-Orlando, FL/Feb. 15-17

Nat'l Caucus of Gay and Lesbian Counselors (1974)
Box 216, Jenkintown PA 19046
Contact: Brenda Hawkins
Members: 150
Annual Budget: under $10,000
Hist. Note: An unofficial caucus of members of the American Ass'n for Counseling and Development focusing on issues of gay and lesbian concern. Affiliated with the Nat'l Gay Task Force and the Nat'l Gay Health Coalition. Membership: $15/year.
Publication:
Caucus Comments. q.
Annual Meetings: During the American Ass'n of Couseling and Development
1987-New Orleans,LA

Nat'l Caves Ass'n (1965)
Rt. 9, Box 106, McMinnville TN 37110
Secy.-Treas.: Barbara Munson
Members: 68 *Staff:* 1
Annual Budget: $10-25,000 *Tel:* (615) 668-3925
Hist. Note: NCA is a non-profit organization which sets and maintains standards for show caves throughout the country. Membership: $200-400/yr.
Publications:
NCA Cave Talk. bi-m.
Caves and Caverns. a.

Nat'l Center for Homoeopathy (1974)
1500 Massachusetts Ave., N.W., Suite 41, Washington DC 20005
Exec. Director: Suzanne B. Roethel
Members: 2,000 *Staff:* 2-5
Annual Budget: $250-500,000 *Tel:* (202) 223-6182
Hist. Note: Formerly associated with the American Foundation for Homoeopathy, but now independent. Membership: $25/yr.
Publication:
Homoeopathy Today. m.
Annual Meetings: Spring

Nat'l Ceramic Dealers Ass'n
Hist. Note: Absorbed by the Ceramic Arts Federation Internat'l in 1983.

Nat'l Ceramic Manufacturers Ass'n (1962)
Hist. Note: Absorbed by the Ceramic Arts Federation Internat'l in 1983.

Nat'l Ceramic Teachers Ass'n
Hist. Note: Absorbed by the Ceramic Arts Federation Internat'l in 1983.

Nat'l Ceramics Ass'n (1958)
Hist. Note: Became the International Ceramic Association in 1982.

Nat'l Certified Pipe Welding Bureau (1944)
5410 Grosvenor Lane, Suite 120, Bethesda MD 20814
Exec. Secretary: James R. Noble
Members: 600 companies *Staff:* 2
Annual Budget: $100-250,000 *Tel:* (301) 897-0770
Hist. Note: A department of the Mechanical Contractors Association of America. Membership: $250/yr.
Publication:
NCPWB Newsletter. semi-a.
Annual Meetings: Spring/150
1987-Hamilton, Bermuda(Hamilton Princess)/April 27-30
1988-Phoenix, AZ(Arizona Biltmore)/April 11-15
1989-San Diego, CA(Del Coronado)/March 27-31
1990-Longboat Key, FL(Longboat Key Club)/April 15-20

Nat'l Cheese Institute (1927)
699 Prince Street, Box 20047, Alexandria VA 22320
Exec. Director: Robert F. Anderson
Members: 125-150 *Staff:* 2-5
Annual Budget: $25-50,000 *Tel:* (703) 549-2230
Hist. Note: Absorbed the American Blue Cheese Ass'n, Inc. (1954)
Publication:
Newsletter. bi-w.

Nat'l Chemical Credit Ass'n (1936)
142 Lexington Ave., New York NY 10016
Secretary: William N. Otte
Members: 160 companies *Staff:* 14
Annual Budget: $100-250,000 *Tel:* (212) 683-4370
Annual Meetings:
1987-Palm Springs, CA/March 8

Nat'l Child Support Enforcement Ass'n (1952)
444 North Capitol St., N.W., Suite 613, Washington DC 20001
Exec Director: Mary Nathan
Members: 1,000 *Staff:* 2-5
Annual Budget: $100-250,000 *Tel:* (202) 624-8180
Hist. Note: Formerly the Nat'l Conference on Uniform Reciprocal Enforcement of Support and the Nat'l Reciprocal and Family Support Enforcement Ass'n. Assumed its present name in August of 1984. Members are officials responsible for enforcing family support laws. Membership: $35/yr.
Publication:
NRFSEA News. bi-m. adv.

Nat'l Children's Eye Care Foundation (1970)
1101 Connecticut Ave., N.W., Suite 700, Washington DC 20036
Exec. Director: Judith Walker
Members: 200 individuals; 30 companies *Staff:* 1-2
Annual Budget: $50-100,000 *Tel:* (202) 857-1185
Hist. Note: Supports the training of pediatric ophthalmologists and research into the special problems of children's eye care.
Publication:
Newsletter. q.

Nat'l Chimney Sweep Guild (1976)
Box 1078, Merrimack NH 03054
General Manager: Elaine Edwards
Members: 1,000 sweeps *Staff:* 3
Annual Budget: $100-250,000 *Tel:* (603) 424-2394
Hist. Note: Members are professional chimney sweeps and their suppliers. Membership: $195/yr.
Publication:
Sweeping. m.
Annual Meetings:
1987-Louisville, KY
1988-New Orleans, LA

Nat'l Christmas Tree Ass'n (1956)
611 East Wells St., Milwaukee WI 53202
Exec. Director: Donald L. McNeil
Members: 2,500 *Staff:* 6-8
Annual Budget: $500-1,000,000 *Tel:* (414) 276-6410
Hist. Note: Formerly (1974) the National Christmas Tree Growers' Ass'n. Membership: $55/yr.
Publication:
American Christmas Tree Journal. q. adv.
Annual Meetings: Winter
1987-Atlantic City, NJ(Resorts Internat'l)/Feb. 4-6/700

Nat'l Church Goods Ass'n (1908)
1114 Greenfield Lane, Mount Prospect IL 60056
Exec. Secretary: Don Latendresse
Members: 300 companies *Staff:* 1
Annual Budget: $50-100,000 *Tel:* (312) 253-5513
Semi-annual Meetings: Winter and Spring
1987-Palm Springs, CA/January
1987-Chicago, IL/May

00214 12 05 86 1233

Nat'l Cigar Leaf Tobacco Ass'n (1954)
1100 17th St., N.W., Suite 902, Washington DC 20036
Exec. Director: Benjamin F. Reeves
Members: 60-70 *Staff:* 2-5
Annual Budget: under $10,000 *Tel:* (202) 296-6820
Annual Meetings: Washington, DC at the ass'n headquarters in Winter

Nat'l Classification Management Soc. (1964)
6116 Roseland Drive, Rockville MD 20852
Exec. Secretary: Eugene J. Suto
Members: 1,400 *Staff:* 1
Annual Budget: $100-250,000 *Tel:* (301) 231-9191
Hist. Note: Members consist of individuals concerned with identifying and assigning a security classification to information and materials needing protection in the national interest. Membership: $25 entrance fee plus $40/yr.
Publications:
Classification Management. a.
NCMS Bulletin. bi-m.
Annual Meetings: Summer
1987-Huntsville, AL(Marriott)/June/400
1988-Torrance, CA(Marriott)/June 400-500
1989-Tampa, FL/June/400-500

Nat'l Clay Pipe Institute (1942)
201 North Fairfax St., Suite 32, Alexandria VA 22314
President: E. Jack Newbould
Members: 6 companies *Staff:* 3
Annual Budget: $100-250,000 *Tel:* (703) 548-1463
Hist. Note: Formerly National Clay Pipe Manufacturers. Makers of vitrified clay sewer pipes and fittings.
Semi-annual meetings:

Nat'l Clay Pot Manufacturers Ass'n (1956)
Drawer 485, Jackson MO 63755
President: Stone Manes
Members: 8 companies *Staff:* 1
Annual Budget: under $10,000 *Tel:* (314) 243-3138
Hist. Note: Members are makers of flower pots. NCPMA is a small organization with no headquarters or paid staff; the present president, who runs the organization, has held this office for some years.
Annual Meetings: Winter
1987-Marco Island, FL(Marriott)/Jan. 22-24

Nat'l Clearinghouse on Licensure, Enforcement and Regulation (1980)
Iron Works Pike, Box 11910, Lexington KY 40578
Exec. Director: Frances S. Berry
Members: 50 state licensing boards, 150 individuals *Staff:* 5
Annual Budget: $100-250,000 *Tel:* (606) 252-2291
Hist. Note: Members are licensing board members and administrators across all professions, central agency administrators and others in the occupation regulation community. Membership: $75/yr. (individual); $750/yr. (state)
Publications:
CLEAR News. q.
NDIS Reports. q.
National Clearinghouse on Examination Information Newsletter.
Annual Meetings: Fall
1987-Kansas City, MO/Sept. 2-5/600

Nat'l Club Ass'n (1961)
1625 Eye St., N.W., Suite 609, Washington DC 20006
Exec. V. President: Gerard F. Hurley, CAE
Members: 1,000 private clubs *Staff:* 8-12
Annual Budget: $500-1,000,000 *Tel:* (202) 466-8424
Hist. Note: Members are private clubs. Membership: $500-2,500/yr.; varies with gross revenue.
Publications:
Newsletter. m.
Reference Series. m.
Perspective. 10/yr. adv.
Semi-Annual Meetings: May and November

Nat'l Coaches Council (1974)
1900 Association Drive, Reston VA 22091
Exec. Director: Sue G. Mottinger
Members: 250 *Staff:* 2-5
Annual Budget: under $10,000 *Tel:* (703) 476-3450
Hist. Note: A subsidiary of the Nat'l Ass'n for Girls and Women in Sport.

Nat'l Coal Ass'n (1917)
1130 17th St., N.W., Washington DC 20036
President: Carl E. Bagge
Members: 225 companies *Staff:* 52
Annual Budget: over $5,000,000 *Tel:* (202) 463-2625
Hist. Note: Originated with a letter from Newton D. Baker, Secretary of War in the Wilson Cabinet, to the President of the Peabody Coal Company proposing that the coal industry voluntarily organize for war. As a result, industry leaders met in Washington at the Powhatan Hotel on June 27, 1917 and organized the present association. In 1953 the Bituminous Coal Institute was absorbed and in 1960, the American Coal Sales Ass'n. Affiliated with Coal Exporters Ass'n of the United States. Represents the coal industry in all matters except labor relations. Sponsors and supports the Committee on American Leadership Political Action Committee.
Publications:
Coal Data. a.
Coal News. w.
Coal Traffic Annual. a.
Steam Electric Plant Factors. m.
International Coal. a.
Annual Meetings: June/600

Nat'l Coalition of Alternative Community Schools (1978)
P.O. Box 378, R.D. 1, Glenmoore PA 19343
Exec. Director: Jerry Mintz
Members: 200-400 *Staff:* 1
Annual Budget: $25-50,000 *Tel:* (215) 458-5138
Hist. Note: Founded in Ann Arbor, NCACS is a group of individuals and schools supporting alternatives to the traditional educational system including educating children at home and developing tools and skills to work for social change. Membership: $30/yr.
Publications:
There Ought to Be Free Choice - Directory of Alternative Schools.
Newsletter. 5/yr. adv.
Annual Meetings: Spring
1987-Escondido, CA/April 22-26/150

Nat'l Coalition of Hispanic Health and Human Services Organizations (1973)
1030 15th St., N.W., #1053, Washington DC 20005
President: Jane L. Delgado, Ph.D.
Members: 200 companies; 200 individuals *Staff:* 15
Annual Budget: $2-5,000,000 *Tel:* (202) 371-2100
Hist. Note: Formerly (1986) Nat'l Coalition of Hispanic Mental Health and Human Services Organizations. Formed to expand and improve services, research, and training opportunities for the advancement of health status and quality of life of Hispanic families, youth, aged, handicapped and special Membership: $40/yr.(individual); $50-250/yr.(organization)
Publications:
COSSMHO Reporter. bi-m. adv.
COSSMHO Roadrunner. m.
Biennial Meetings: Even Years

Nat'l Coalition of Hispanic Mental Health and Human Services Organization
Hist. Note: Became Nat'l Coalition of Hispanic Health and Human Services Organizations in 1986.

Nat'l Coffee Ass'n of the U.S.A. (1911)
120 Wall St., New York NY 10005
President: George E. Boecklin
Members: 200-225 *Staff:* 6-10
Annual Budget: $500-1,000,000 *Tel:* (212) 344-5596
Hist. Note: Formerly (1939) Associated Coffee Industries of America.
Publication:
Newsletter. w.
Annual Meetings: Winter

Nat'l Coffee Service Ass'n (1965)
301 Maple Ave., West, Sec 1, Unit 3, Vienna VA 22180
President: G. Dean Wood
Members: 6-700 companies *Staff:* 2-5
Annual Budget: $250-500,000 *Tel:* (703) 255-0455
Hist. Note: Firms engaged in furnishing coffee, refreshment, snack and vending services.
Publications:
What's Brewing. m.
Membership Directory. a. adv.
Annual Meetings: Summer/1,500

Nat'l Coil Coaters Ass'n (1962)
1900 Arch St., Philadelphia PA 19103
Exec. Director: Kenneth R. Dickson
Members: 205 companies *Staff:* 6-10
Annual Budget: $250-500,000 *Tel:* (215) 564-3484
Hist. Note: Manufacturers of continuously coated metal coil and suppliers of materials or services used in coil coating.
Publications:
Membership Directory. a.
Newsletter. m.
Annual Meetings: April/800
1987-Ft. Lauderdale, FL(Marriott Harbor Beach)/April 25-30
1988-Palm Springs, CA(Rancho Las Palmas)/April 9-13

Nat'l Coin Machine Institute
Hist. Note: Address unknown in 1986; probably defunct.

Nat'l Collegiate Baseball Writers Ass'n (1960)
Arizona State University, Tempe AZ 85287
Secy.-Treas.: Mark Brand
Members: 250 *Staff:* 1
Annual Budget: under $10,000 *Tel:* (602) 965-6592
Hist. Note: An association of writers, sportscasters and sports publicity people who cover collegiate baseball.
Publication:
Newsletter. 8/yr.
Annual Meetings: June

Nat'l Collegiate Honors Council (1966)
Academic Building, Room 302, Univ. of Georgia, Athens GA 30602
Exec. Secy.-Treas.: Lothar L. Tresp
Members: 315 institutions; 354 individuals *Staff:* 4
Annual Budget: $50-100,000 *Tel:* (404) 542-1050
Hist. Note: An outgrowth of the Inter-University Committee on the Superior Student (ICSS) which was funded by the Carnegie Foundation from 1958 to 1965. A professional organization composed of faculty, administrators, and students dedicated to the encouragement of undergraduate honors learning; includes both public and private universities and colleges. Membership: $25/yr. (individual), $100/yr. (institution).
Publications:
Forum for Honors. q.
Nat'l Honors Report. q.
Annual Meetings: Fall
1987-Dallas, TX(Westin)/Oct. 29-Nov. 2
1988-Las Vegas, NV

Nat'l Commercial Finance Ass'n (1943)
225 West 34th St., New York NY 10001
Exec. Director: Leonard Machlis
Members: 230 *Staff:* 11
Annual Budget: $1-2,000,000 *Tel:* (212) 594-3490
Hist. Note: Founded as the National Conference of Commercial Receivable Companies, it became the National Commercial Finance Conference in 1953 and assumed its present name in 1983. Members are banks and commercial finance and factoring companies.
Publications:
Secured Lender. bi-m. adv.
Compendium of Commercial Finance Law. a.
Annual Meetings: Fall/1000
1987-San Francisco, CA(Fairmont)/Nov. 4-6
1988-New York, NY(Marriott Marquis)/Oct. 19-21

Nat'l Commercial Refrigeration Sales Ass'n (1946)
1900 Arch St., Philadelphia PA 19103
Exec. Director: Kenneth R. Dickson
Members: 100-125 *Staff:* 2
Annual Budget: $25-50,000 *Tel:* (215) 564-3484
Hist. Note: Installing contractors, manufacturers and distributors of commercial refrigeration equipment. Membership: $300-550/yr.
Publications:
Refrigeration News (newsletter). m.
Membership Directory.
Annual Meetings: Fall
1987-Marco Beach, FL(Marriott)/Oct. 25-28/100

Nat'l Committee for Clinical Laboratory Standards (1968)
771 East Lancaster Ave., Villanova PA 19085
Exec. Director: John V. Bergen, Ph.D.
Members: 940 organizations *Staff:* 11
Annual Budget: $500-1,000,000 *Tel:* (215) 525-2435
Hist. Note: Develops voluntary consensus standards for clinical laboratories. Affiliated with the American National Standards Institute.
Publications:
Update. bi-m.
Standards. irreg.
Annual Meetings: Spring/250
1987-Philadelphia, PA(Sheraton Society Hill)/April 23-24
1988-March 24-25
1989-March 30-31
1990-March 29-30
1991-March 21-22

Nat'l Committee for Motor Fleet Supervisor Training (1945)
Highway Traffic Safety Program, Michigan State University, East Lansing MI 48824
Exec. Director: Dr. Donald Smith
Members: 1,000-1,100 individuals and organizations *Staff:* 2-5
Annual Budget: $100-250,000 *Tel:* (517) 353-1790
Hist. Note: Provides certification which designates competence in the fleet industry's universal standards. Members are those in the industry and related organizations concerned with training and standards. Membership: $25/yr. (individual); $100/yr. (organization).
Publication:
Newsletter. q.
Annual Meetings: Spring

Nat'l Communications Ass'n (1955)
404 Park Ave. South, 7th Floor, New York NY 10016-8412
President:
Members: 75 *Staff:* 2-5
Annual Budget: $25-50,000 *Tel:* (212) 682-2627
Hist. Note: Companies making and selling privately-marketed communications equipment such as telephone and data systems, intercoms, pages, security and fire alarms. Formerly (1977) Private Communications Ass'n, Inc.
Publication:
NCA News. q.

Nat'l Community Action Agency Directors Ass'n
Hist. Note: Became the Nat'l Ass'n of Community Action Agencies in 1986.

Nat'l Community Action Agency Executive Directors Ass'n (1968)
Hist. Note: Became the Nat'l Community Action Agency Directors in 1982.

Nat'l Community Education Ass'n (1966)
119 North Payne St., Alexandria VA 22314
Exec. Director: William S. DeJong
Members: 1,500 *Staff:* 2-5
Annual Budget: $250-500,000 *Tel:* (703) 683-6232

00215 12 05 86 1233

Hist. Note: Established as the National Community School Education Association, it assumed its present name in 1974. Membership: $75/yr. (individual), $175/yr. (organization).
Publications:
Community Education Journal. q. adv.
Community Education Today. m.
Annual Meetings:
1987-Minneapolis, MN(Hyatt Regency)/Dec. 3-6/1,300-1,500
1988-Orlando, FL

Nat'l Composition Ass'n (1961)
1730 North Lynn St., Arlington VA 22209
President: Tina H. Allman
Members: 700-750 companies *Staff:* 2-5
Annual Budget: $500-1,000,000 *Tel:* (703) 841-8165
Hist. Note: A national affiliate of the Printing Industries of America. Formerly (1971) Nat'l Cold Type Composition Section/PIA. Membership: $265/yr.
Publications:
Newsline. m.
Technical Publications. m.
Software.
Annual Meetings: Spring
1987-New York, NY(Marriott Marquis)/April 9-11
1988-Toronto, Ontario(Metro Convention Center)/Sept. 7-9
1989-Philadelphia, PA(Civic Center)/May 11-13
1990-Chicago, IL(Hyatt Regency)/Aug. 23-25

Nat'l Computer Graphics Ass'n (1979)
2722 Merrilee Drive, Suite 200, Fairfax VA 22031
General Manager: James S. Werking
Members: 7,000 *Staff:* 30-35
Annual Budget: over $5,000,000 *Tel:* (703) 698-9600
Hist. Note: Manufacturers, vendors and users of computer graphics equipment. Membership: $25/yr.
Publications:
Computer Graphics News. m.
Graphic Network News. bi-m.
Proceedings. a.
Annual Meetings: Spring/25,000-30,000

Nat'l Concrete Burial Vault Ass'n (1929)
Box 64, South Chelmsford MA 01824
Exec. Director: Gerald Hardy
Members: 300 *Staff:* 1
Annual Budget: $25-50,000 *Tel:* (612) 452-3588
Annual Meetings: June/200
1987-Washington, DC
1988-Lake of the Ozarks, MO
1989-Louisville, KY

Nat'l Concrete Masonry Ass'n (1920)
Box 781, Herndon VA 22070
President: John A. Heslip
Members: 750-800 companies *Staff:* 25-30
Annual Budget: $2-5,000,000 *Tel:* (703) 435-4900
Hist. Note: Membership consists of manufacturers of concrete blocks and suppliers. Sponsors the Concrete Masonry Political Action Committee.
Publication:
C/M News. m. adv.
Annual Meetings: Winter/2,800
1987-Tampa, FL(Hyatt)/Feb. 15-18
1988-Nashville, TN(G.O. Opry)/Feb. 7-10
1989-Cincinnati, OH(Stouffers)

Nat'l Confectioners Ass'n of the United States (1883)
7900 Westpark Drive, Suite 514, McLean VA 22102
President: Richard T. O'Connell, CAE
Members: 300 *Staff:* 8
Annual Budget: $500-1,000,000 *Tel:* (703) 790-5750
Hist. Note: Manufacturers of confectionery products and their suppliers. Maintains a Chicago office at 645 N. Michigan Ave., Suite 1006, Chicago, IL 60611. (312) 280-1460. Is connected with the Nat'l Confectioners Ass'n of the United States Political Action Committee.
Publication:
Confection NEWS. m.
Annual Meetings: June
1987-San Francisco, CA(St. Francis)/June 18-20
1988-Boca Raton, FL

Nat'l Confectionery Salesmen's Ass'n of America (1899)
5 Jupiter St., New Monmouth NJ 07748
Exec. Secretary: John T. Mullarkey
Members: 700-750 *Staff:* 1
Annual Budget: under $10,000 *Tel:* (201) 671-3435
Hist. Note: Founded in 1899 and incorporated in 1912. Sponsors the Candy Hall of Fame, established in 1971. Membership: $35/yr.
Publications:
NCSA Journal. a. adv.
Spotlight. q.
Annual Meetings: Spring
1987-Grand Island, NY(Holiday Inn)/May 1-3/400

Nat'l Conference of Appellate Court Clerks (1974)
Nat'l Center For State Courts, 300 Newport Ave., Williamsburg VA 23185
Secreratiat Liaison: Mary Hogan
Members: 145 *Staff:* 1
Annual Budget: under $10,000 *Tel:* (804) 253-2000
Hist. Note: To improve the appellate process. Officers are elected annually, administrative support provided by the Nat'l Center for State Courts.
Publications:
Appellate Court Administration Review
NCACC Newsletter. bi-m.

Nat'l Conference of Bankruptcy Judges (1926)
U.S. Courthouse, 500 Camp St., New Orleans LA 70130
President: T. Hartley Kingsmill, Jr.
Members: 200-225 *Staff:* 1
Annual Budget: $10-25,000 *Tel:* (504) 589-6001
Hist. Note: An organization of bankruptcy judges and former judges organized to further the administration of bankruptcy laws. Established as the Nat'l Ass'n of Referees in Bankruptcy, it became the Nat'l Conference of Referees in Bankruptcy in 1969 and assumed its present name in 1973. Has no permanent address or paid staff.
Publication:
American Bankruptcy Law Journal. q.
Annual Meetings: Fall

Nat'l Conference of Bar Examiners (1931)
333 North Michigan Ave., Suite. 1025, Chicago IL 60601
Director of Administration: Anthony Nigro
Members: 1,000-2,000 *Staff:* 16-20
Annual Budget: $500-1,000,000 *Tel:* (312) 641-0963
Hist. Note: Conducts character investigations pertinent to admission to the practice of law at the request of state bar examiners boards, principally in cases of lawyers moving across state lines. An affiliated organization of the American Bar Ass'n.
Publication:
The Bar Examiner. q.
Annual Meetings: With American Bar Ass'n in August
1987-San Francisco, CA
1988-Toronto, Ontario
1989-Honolulu, HI

Nat'l Conference of Bar Foundations (1977)
c/o American Bar Ass'n, Div of Bar Svcs,750 North Lake Shore Drive, Chicago IL 60611
Staff Liaison: Callie R. Lacy
Members: 162
Annual Budget: under $10,000 *Tel:* (312) 988-5354
Hist. Note: Bar foundations and other educational and charitable foundations affiliated with state or local bar associations.
Publication:
Proceedings. semi-a.
Semi-annual meetings: Winter, and August with the American Bar
Association
1987-New Orleans, LA/Feb. and San Francisco, CA/Aug.
1988-Philadelphia, PA/Feb. and Toronto, Quebec/Aug.

Nat'l Conference of Bar Presidents (1950)
750 North Lake Shore Drive, Chicago IL 60611
President: James R. Crouch
Members: 650-700 *Staff:* 1
Annual Budget: under $10,000 *Tel:* (312) 988-5354
Hist. Note: Officers change annually. Composed of presidents and past presidents of State bar associations. Affiliated with American Bar Ass'n.
Publications:
Prexy. q.
Proceedings. semi-a.
Annual Meetings: With American Bar Ass'n.

Nat'l Conference of Black Lawyers (1968)
126 West 119th St., New York NY 10026
Nat'l Director: Dr. Gerald C. Horne
Members: 2,000 lawyers, 1,200 law students *Staff:* 6-10
Annual Budget: $250-500,000 *Tel:* (212) 864-4000
Hist. Note: Membership in the U.S., Canada, and the Virgin Islands. A progressive organization of lawyers, law students, judges and lay people committed to utilizing legal remedies to eliminate institutional racism and aid in the development of the black community.
Publications:
NCBL Notes. q.
Community Organization Legal Assistance Project (COLA) Notes. q.
Various Section Newletters.
Biennial Meetings: Odd years in October

Nat'l Conference of Black Mayors (1974)
1430 West Peachtree St., N.W., Suite 318, Atlanta GA 30309
Exec. Director: Michelle D. Kourouma
Members: 290 *Staff:* 16-20
Annual Budget: $500-1,000,000 *Tel:* (404) 892-0127
Hist. Note: Organized in 1973 in Tuskegee, Alabama as the Southern Conference of Black Mayors. Changed to its present name in January, 1977. Membership fee based on sliding scale according to population.
Publications:
Newsletter. m.
Membership Roster. a.
Souvenir Calendar. a.
Convention Program and Journal. a.
Annual Meetings: April
1987-Miami, FL(Hyatt Regency)/April 22-25/500-1,000

Nat'l Conference of Catholic Bishops (1966)
1312 Massachusetts Ave., N. W., Washington DC 20005
Gen. Secretary: Msgr. Daniel F. Hoye
Members: 350 *Staff:* 250
Annual Budget: over $5,000,000 *Tel:* (202) 659-6600
Hist. Note: Affiliated with the United States Catholic Conference, with which it shares staff. Has an annual budget of approximately $26 million.
Publication:
NCCB/USCC Report. m.
Annual Meetings: November in Washington, DC

Nat'l Conference of Catholic Charities
Hist. Note: Became Catholic Charities USA in 1986.

Nat'l Conference of Commissioners on Uniform State Laws (1892)
645 N. Michigan Ave., Ste. 510, Chicago IL 60611
Exec. Secretary: Edith Davies
Members: 302 *Staff:* 6-10
Annual Budget: $250-500,000 *Tel:* (312) 321-9710
Hist. Note: The Conference, one of the oldest of state organizations designed to encourage interstate cooperation, was organized in 1892 to promote uniformity by voluntary action of each state government. Since its organization, the Conference has drafted over two hundred uniform laws on numerous subjects in various fields of law, many of which have been widely enacted.
Publication:
Handbook and Proceedings. a.

Nat'l Conference of Editorial Writers (1947)
6223 Executive Blvd., Rockville MD 20852
Exec. Secretary: Cora Everett
Members: 560 *Staff:* 2-5
Annual Budget: $50-100,000 *Tel:* (301) 984-3015
Hist. Note: Members are editorial writers and editorial page columnists on newspapers of general circulation in the United States and Canada and journalism teachers. Membership: $50-$100/year.
Publication:
The Masthead. q.
Annual Meetings: By invitation of a host member or newspaper.
1987-Vancouver, BC(Pan-Pacific)/Sept. 22-25
1988-Fort Worth, TX(Worthington)/Sept. 13-16/250-300
1989-St. Paul, MN/Sept./250-300
1990-Orlando, FL

Nat'l Conference of Lieutenant Governors (1962)
Iron Works Pike, Box 11910, Lexington KY 40578
Staff Director: Edward D. Feigenbaum
Members: 54 *Staff:* 2
Annual Budget: $50-100,000 *Tel:* (606) 252-2291
Hist. Note: Affiliated with the Council of State Governments, which serves as its secretariat. Promotes the exchange of information; fosters interstate cooperation; and seeks to improve the efficiency and the effectiveness of the office of the lieutenant governor.
Publications:
NCLG Newsletter. q.
NCLG Biographical Sketchbook. bien.
Office of Lieutenant Governor & Its Powers. quadrennial.
NCLG Staff Directory. a.
Annual Meetings:
1987-Basin Harbor, VT/Aug. 23-28

Nat'l Conference of Local Environmental Health Administrators (1938)
Allegheny County Health Department, 3333 Frbes Ave., Pittsburg PA 15213
Chairman: Albert H. Brunwasser
Members: 200-300 *Staff:* 1
Annual Budget: under $10,000 *Tel:* (412) 578-8026
Hist. Note: Formerly (1966) the Conference of Municipal Public Health Engineers and (1983) Conference of Local Environmental Health Administrators. An organization of environmental health administrators employed at the local level and at universities. Purpose is to promote efficient and effective local environmental health programs. Affiliated with the National Environmental Health Association. Membership: $10/year.
Publication:
Newsletter. q.
Annual Meetings: June, with the Nat'l Environmental Health Ass'n
1987-San Diego, CA
1988-Cleveland, OH
1989-Seattle, WA

Nat'l Conference of Regulatory Utility Commission Engineers (1923)
Georgia Public Service Commission, 244 Washington St., S.W., Atlanta GA 30334
Secretary: Robert C. Evans
Members: 100-150 *Staff:* 1
Annual Budget: under $10,000 *Tel:* (404) 656-4516
Hist. Note: Formerly (1972) Conference of State Utility Commission Engineers.
Publication:
Proceedings. a.
Annual Meetings: June

Nat'l Conference of Standards Laboratories (1961)
1800 30th St., Suite 305B, Boulder CO 82301
Business Manager: L. Kenneth Armstrong
Members: 800 laboratories *Staff:* 2
Annual Budget: $100-250,000 *Tel:* (303) 440-3339
Hist. Note: Originally sponsored by the National Bureau of Standards, NCSL is now an independent non-profit association of academic, scientific, industrial, commercial and governmental laboratories concerned with the measurement of

00216 12 05 86 1233

physical quantities, the callibration of standards and instruments, and the development of standards of practice. Membership: $125/yr.
Publications:
NCSL Newsletter. q.
NCSL Directory of Standards Laboratories. bien.
Conference Proceedings. a.
Annual Meetings: Summer
1987-Denver, CO(Regency Hotel)/July 12-16/500
1988-Gaithersburg, MD

Nat'l Conference of State Historic Preservation Officers (1969)
Suite 332, Hall of the States, 444 North Capitol St., N.W., Washington DC 20001
Exec. Director: Eric Hertfelder
Members: 51 *Staff:* 3
Annual Budget: $100-250,000 *Tel:* (202) 624-5465
Hist. Note: Members state officials appointed by the governors of the states and territories to develop and administer state and federal historic preservation programs and to work with private and public organizations and individuals interested in historic preservation.
Publication:
Newsletter. m.

Nat'l Conference of State Legislatures (1975)
1050 17th St., Suite 2100, Denver CO 80265
Exec. Director: Earl S. Mackey
Members: 50 states and 7,500-8,000 legislators and staffs *Staff:* 90-100
Annual Budget: over $5,000,000 *Tel:* (303) 623-7800
Hist. Note: Formed by a merger of the National Legislative Conference (founded in 1947), the National Conference of State Legislative Leaders (founded 1959) and the National Society of State Legislators (founded in 1965). An organization of state legislators and their legislative staffs. Maintains a Washington office. Supported by the Foundation for State Legislatures, a center for public/private sector interaction. Affiliated with the Council of State Governments and the National Governors' Association.
Publications:
State Legislatures Magazine. 10/yr.
Capital to Capital. 22/yr.
Annual Meetings: Summer
1987-Indianapolis, IN
1988-Reno, NV
1989-Tulsa, OK
1990-Orlando, FL
1991-Nashville, TN
1992-Cincinnati, OH

Nat'l Conference of State Liquor Administrators (1934)
Box 718, Clarkston GA 30021
Exec. Secy.-Treas.: Ed Vaughn
Members: 35 states and territories *Staff:* 1
Annual Budget: $25-50,000 *Tel:* (404) 656-4263
Hist. Note: Membership: $200/yr.
Publication:
Directory. a.
Annual Meetings: June
1987-Albuquerque, NM(Marriott)/June 7-11
1988-New Orleans, LA/June 5-9

Nat'l Conference of State Retail Ass'ns (1968)
Hist. Note: A federation of 50 state retail associations meeting annually in Washington in May under the auspices of the American Retail Federation.

Nat'l Conference of State Social Security Administrators (1952)
Two Northside 75, Suite 300, Atlanta GA 30318
Deputy Director: Jim Larche
Members: 100-125 *Staff:* 1
Annual Budget: under $10,000 *Tel:* (404) 352-6414
Hist. Note: Founded in January 1952 in Bloomington, Indiana. Formerly (1963) Conference of State Social Security Administrators.
Publication:
Proceedings. a.
Annual Meetings:
1987-Myrtle Beach, SC/Nov.
1988-Boston, MA/Aug.
1989-Coeur d'Alene, ID/Aug.

Nat'l Conference of States on Building Codes and Standards (1967)
481 Carlisle Dr., Herndon VA 22070
Exec. Director: Robert C. Wible
Members: 400 *Staff:* 30-35
Annual Budget: $250-500,000 *Tel:* (703) 437-0100
Hist. Note: Serves the building code and public safety interests of the 50 states and territories. Provides a forum for the discussion and solution of problems of state building codes and regulations and coordinates intergovernmental reforms in the area of building codes and standards. Executive branch organization of the Nat'l Governors' Ass'n. Works closely with the Center for Building Technology of the Nat'l Bureau of Standards.
Publications:
Legislative Bulletin. bi-m.
Newsletter. bi-m.
Directory of State Building Codes & Regulations. bien.
Annual Meetings: September/100-125
1987-St. Paul, MN/Sept. 13-17

Nat'l Conference of Yeshiva Principals (1947)
160 Broadway, New York NY 10038
Exec. V.President: Rabbi A. Moshe Possick
Members: 375-400
Annual Budget: $25-50,000 *Tel:* (212) 227-1000
Hist. Note: Affiliated with the Nat'l Soc. for Hebrew Day Schools.
Publication:
Hamenahel-The Principal. 8/yr.
Annual Meetings: May in New York, NY

Nat'l Conference on Public Employee Retirement Systems (1942)
275 East Broad St., Columbus OH 43215
Secretary: Victor A. Miller
Members: 1,000 *Staff:* 1
Annual Budget: $100-250,000 *Tel:* (614) 227-4040
Publication:
Word from Washington. m.
Annual Meetings:
1987-Hawaii
1988-Chicago, IL
1989-California

Nat'l Conference on Research in English (1937)
211 Education Bldg., Indiana University, Bloomington IN 47401
Secretary: Dr. Jerome C. Harste
Members: 300-400 *Staff:* 1
Annual Budget: under $10,000
Hist. Note: Teachers and researchers in English. Membership by invitation only; $10/yr.
Publication:
Newsletter. semi-a.
Annual Meetings: May/100

Nat'l Conference on Social Welfare (1873)
Hist. Note: Reported as inactive in 1986.

Nat'l Conference on Weights and Measures (1905)
Box 3137, Gaithersburg MD 20878
Exec. Secretary: Albert Tholen
Members: 1,500 *Staff:* 2-5
Annual Budget: $25-50,000 *Tel:* (301) 921-3677
Hist. Note: Members are weights and measures enforcement officials from state, county and local governments; associate members from industry. Sponsored by the National Bureau of Standards. Membership: $35/yr.
Publications:
Annual Report. a.
Handbooks. a.
Directory of Weights and Measures Officials.
Annual Meetings: July/450
1987-Little Rock, AK(Excelsior)/July 19-24

Nat'l Congress of Floor Covering Ass'ns (1973)
470 Merchandise Mart, Chicago IL 60654
Chairman: James W. Bidwill
Members: 30 ass'ns *Staff:* 2-5
Annual Budget: $25-50,000 *Tel:* (312) 527-7514
Hist. Note: The umbrella organization of ass'ns in the floorcovering industry.
Publication:
Newsletter. q.
Annual Meetings: Chicago, IL in January during the Nat'l Floorcovering Market

Nat'l Consortium for Child Mental Health Services (1971)
3615 Wisconsin Ave., N.W., Washington DC 20016
Chairman: Joseph Palombi, M.D.
Members: 19 organizations *Staff:* 1
Annual Budget: under $10,000 *Tel:* (202) 966-7300
Hist. Note: National psychiatric, psychological, educational, social welfare, medical and consumer organizations. Serves as a forum for exchange of information on child mental health services.

Nat'l Constables Ass'n (1977)
16 Stonybrook Drive, Levittown PA 19055
Exec. Director: Hal Lefcourt
Members: 8-900 *Staff:* 2-5
Annual Budget: $100-250,000 *Tel:* (215) 547-6400
Hist. Note: Founded originally in New Jersey in 1972 as the National Police Constables Association and incorporated in Pennsylvania in March 1977. The present name was assumed in 1976. A non-profit, professional fraternal organization of constables, geared to a rebirth of the constable system and dedicated to upgrading their quality of performance. Membership: $15/year.
Publications:
APB. q. adv.
Buyer's Guide. semi-a. adv.
Annual Meetings: Spring
1987-Las Vegas, NV(Tropicana)/March 5-8

Nat'l Construction Employers Council (1978)
1101 15th St., N.W., Suite 1040, Washington DC 20005
President: James R. Baxter
Members: 15 nat'l trade ass'ns *Staff:* 2-5
Annual Budget: under $10,000 *Tel:* (202) 223-1510
Hist. Note: Formed to provide a single voice for construction industry management in labor relations. Members are nat'l trade ass'ns whose members employ union building tradesmen.

Nat'l Construction Industry Council (1974)
2100 M St., N.W., Suite 600, Washington DC 20037
Exec. Secretary: Anthony M. Ponticelli
Members: 30 construction ass'ns *Staff:* 2-5
Annual Budget: $100-250,000 *Tel:* (202) 296-7019
Publication:
The Voice Newsletter. m.
Quarterly meetings:

Nat'l Construction Machinery Credit Group (1939)
315 South Northwest Hwy., Park Ridge IL 60068
Secretary: George Zander
Members: 55-60 companies
Annual Budget: $10-25,000 *Tel:* (312) 696-3000

Nat'l Constructors Ass'n (1947)
1101 15th St., N.W., Suite 1000, Washington DC 20005
President: William R. Jones, Jr.
Members: 26-30 companies *Staff:* 9
Annual Budget: $1-2,000,000 *Tel:* (202) 466-8880
Hist. Note: Large, unionized engineering and construction companies. Sponsors the Nat'l Constructors Ass'n Political Action Committee.
Publications:
Directory. a.
NCA Newsletter. bi-m.
Semi-annual Meetings: January and September

Nat'l Consumer Finance Ass'n (1916)
Hist. Note: Became the American Financial Services Association on February 1, 1983.

Nat'l Consumers League (1899)
815 15th St., N.W., Suite 516, Washington DC 20005
Exec. Director: Linda F. Golodner
Members: 3,000 plus affiliates *Staff:* 6-10
Annual Budget: $100-250,000 *Tel:* (202) 639-8140
Hist. Note: The pioneer consumer organization in the country, the League supports public policies promoting the production of quality goods and services which are made in fair, safe and healthy working conditions. Absorbed the National Consumers Congress in 1978. Membership: $20/yr.(individual); $25-250/yr.(organization).
Publications:
Bulletin. bi-m.
Consumer Report Card. a.
Consumer Guides.
Annual Meetings: December

Nat'l Contract Management Ass'n (1959)
6728 Old McLean Village Dr., McLean VA 22101
Exec. Director: Kathleen Linse
Members: 19,000 individuals *Staff:* 17
Annual Budget: $1-2,000,000 *Tel:* (703) 442-0137
Hist. Note: Members are concerned with various forms of contracting with federal, state and local governments and industry. Formerly (1965) Nat'l Ass'n of Professional Contracts Administrators. Absorbed Gov't Contract Management Ass'n of America in 1965. Membership: $45/yr.
Publications:
NCMA Contract Management. m. adv.
NCMA Journal. semi-a.
Semi-annual Meetings: Los Angeles in July, Washington, DC in November

Nat'l Contract Sweepers Institute (1980)
1730 Rhode Island Avenue, N.W., Suite 1000, Washington DC 20036
Director: Charles Johnson
Members: 225-250 *Staff:* 2-5
Annual Budget: $25-50,000 *Tel:* (202) 659-4613
Hist. Note: Members are street, parking lot and industrial area sweeping contractors and their suppliers. Formerly the Nat'l Contract Sweepers Ass'n. Became a division of the Nat'l Solid Wastes Management Ass'n in 1984. Membership: $250/yr.(company)
Publications:
Member Directory. a.
News Sweep. q. adv.
Member Memo. m.
Annual Meetings:
1987-Chicago, Il/Sept.

Nat'l Cooperative Business Ass'n (1916)
1401 New York Ave., N.W., Suite 1100, Washington DC 20005
Interim President and C.E.O.: Frank B. Sollars
Members: 300 organizations, plus 400 individuals *Staff:* 50
Annual Budget: over $5,000,000 *Tel:* (202) 638-6222
Hist. Note: Founded as the Cooperative League of the U.S.A., NCBA assumed its present name in 1985. Represents American cooperatives in Internat'l Cooperative Alliance. Serves as Chamber of Commerce for all types of cooperatives. Sponsors and supports the Nat'l Cooperative Business Political Action Committee. Has an annual budget of $7,500,000. Membership: $25/yr.(individual); $250/yr.(organization).
Publications:
Cooperative Business Journal. bi-m.
New Clips. semi-m.
Annual Meetings: Spring at the Washington Plaza Hotel, Washington, DC
1987-April 27-29
1988-April 25-27
1989-May 1-3
1990-April 23-25

00217 12 05 86 1233

Nat'l Coordinating Council on Emergency Management (1952)
7297 Lee Hwy., Suite N, Falls Church VA 22042
Exec. Director: David S. O'Bryon
Members: 1,700 *Staff:* 2-5
Annual Budget: $100-250,000 *Tel:* (703) 533-7672
Hist. Note: Representatives of city and county government departments responsible for civil defense. Formerly the United States Civil Defense Council. Assumed its present name in 1983. Membership: $15-$125/yr.
Publications:
Bulletin. m.
Emergency Management Review. q.
Annual Meetings: October

Nat'l Corn Growers Ass'n (1957)
1000 Executive Pkwy., Suite 224, St. Louis MO 63141
C.E.O.: Jeff Gain
Members: 14,000 *Staff:* 16
Annual Budget: $1-2,000,000 *Tel:* (314) 275-9915
Hist. Note: Membership: $20-50/yr. (varies by state).
Publication:
Corn Grower Newsletter. m.
Annual Meetings:
1987-Minneapolis, MN(Hyatt)/July 19-21

Nat'l Correctional Recreational Ass'n (1966)
P.O. Drawer C, Earleton FL 32631
President: Dr. Gail McCall
Members: 300 *Staff:* 1
Annual Budget: under $10,000 *Tel:* (904) 468-2801
Hist. Note: Known as the Nat'l Corrections Recreational Ass'n from 1966 to 1971. Affiliate of the American Correctional Ass'n. Membership: $25/yr.
Publication:
NCRA Grapevine. q.
Annual Meetings: October

Nat'l Corrugated Steel Pipe Ass'n (1955)
2011 Eye St., N.W., Suite 500, Washington DC 20006
Chief Engineer: Corwin L. Tracy, P. E.
Members: 175-200 *Staff:* 10-16
Annual Budget: $500-1,000,000 *Tel:* (202) 223-2217
Hist. Note: Formerly Nat'l Corrugated Metal Pipe Ass'n.
Publications:
Membership Directory. a. adv.
Corrugations. bi-m.
NCSPA News. bi-m. adv.
Pipeline. q. adv.
Annual Meetings: March
1987-Kauai, HI

Nat'l Cosmetology Ass'n (1921)
3510 Olive St., St. Louis MO 63103
Meetings Coordinator: JoAnn Johnson
Members: 58,000 *Staff:* 20-25
Annual Budget: $1-2,000,000 *Tel:* (314) 534-7980
Hist. Note: Owners and operators of beauty shops.
Publication:
American Hairdresser/Salon Owner Maggazine. m. adv.
Annual Meetings: July
1987-San Diego, CA(Town & Country Hotel)
1988-Atlanta, GA(Hilton)
1989-San Francisco, CA(Hilton)
1990-Washington, DC(Hilton)/July 14-17

Nat'l Costumers Ass'n (1923)
3038 Hayes Ave., Fremont OH 43420
Secy.-Treas.: La Mar C. Kerns
Members: 200-250 theatrical customers and suppliers. *Staff:* 1
Annual Budget: $50-100,000 *Tel:* (419) 334-3236
Hist. Note: Membership: $100/yr.
Publication:
The Costumers Magazine. m. adv.
Annual Meetings: July
1987-Los Angeles, CA(Airport Hilton)/July 18-23/400
1988-Omaha, NE(Holiday Inn Convention Ctr.)/July 15-20/400
1989-Indianapolis, IN(Hyatt Regency)/July 20-25

Nat'l Cotton Batting Institute (1954)
1918 North Parkway, Box 12287, Memphis TN 38112
Exec. Secretary: David Hull
Members: 62 companies *Staff:* 2-5
Annual Budget: $25-50,000 *Tel:* (901) 274-9030
Annual Meetings:
1987-New Orleans, LA(Sheraton)/March/55

Nat'l Cotton Council of America (1938)
P.O. Box 12285, 1918 North Pkwy., Memphis TN 38182
Exec. V. President: Earl W. Sears
Members: 275-300 delegates *Staff:* 70-75
Annual Budget: $2-5,000,000 *Tel:* (901) 274-9030
Hist. Note: Membership consists of approximately 300 delegates named by cotton interests in the cotton-producing states. Seeks to increase the consumption of cotton and cottonseed products. Maintains a Washington office. Supports the Committee for the Advancement of Cotton (political action).
Publications:
Cotton Review. m.
Cotton's Week. w.
Annual Meetings: Winter
1987-San Diego, CA

Nat'l Cotton Ginners' Ass'n (1937)
Box 12285, Memphis TN 38182
NCC Staff Coordinator for the NCGA: Fred Johnson
Members: 15-16 state socs.,7 state ass'ns, 2 regional ass'n
Annual Budget: under $10,000 *Tel:* (901) 274-9030
Hist. Note: Has no paid staff, administrative support provided by the Nat'l Cotton Council.
Annual Meetings: Winter with Nat'l Cotton Council
1987-San Diego, CA(Sheraton Harbor Island)/Jan. 25-27/75-100
1988-Memphis, TN(Peabody)/Feb. 7-9/75-100

Nat'l Cottonseed Products Ass'n (1897)
P.O. Box 12023, Memphis TN 38182
Exec. V. President: Kenneth O. Lewis
Members: 275-325 *Staff:* 6-10
Annual Budget: $250-500,000 *Tel:* (901) 324-4417
Hist. Note: Founded as the Interstate Cottonseed Crushers Ass'n, it assumed its present name in 1929.
Annual Meetings: May
1987-Savannah, GA(Hyatt Regency)/May 17-19/350
1988-Nashville, TN(Opryland)/May 12-14/350
1989-San Antonio, TX(Hyatt Regency)/May 14-16/300
1990-San Diego, CA(Del Coronado)/May 6-8/300

Nat'l Council for Community Relations (1974)
El Paso Community College, Box 20500, El Paso TX 79998
President: John Lencyk
Members: 635 individuals *Staff:* 0
Annual Budget: $25-50,000 *Tel:* (915) 775-6064
Hist. Note: Affiliated with the American Ass'n of Community and Junior Colleges. Organization created to focus on the responsibilities of officers of community colleges as communicators. Membership: $35/yr.(individual); $75/yr.(institution)
Publication:
Counsel. q.
Annual Meetings: Spring
1987-Las Vegas, NV

Nat'l Council for Critical Analysis (1968)
Box 137, Port Jefferson NY 11777
President: Pasqual S. Schievella
Members: 400
Annual Budget: under $10,000 *Tel:* (516) 928-6745
Hist. Note: Formerly (1970) Nat'l Council of Teachers for Critical Analysis. Members are educators and teachers of philosophy interested in bringing philosophy to the masses, introducing it, in particular, to earlier years of education. Has no paid staff. Membership: $10/yr. (individual); $12/yr. (organization).
Publication:
Journal of Critical Analysis. irreg.

Nat'l Council for Geographic Education (1915)
Western Illinois University, Macomb IL 61455
Exec. Director: James W. Vining
Members: 3,200 *Staff:* 2-5
Annual Budget: $50-100,000 *Tel:* (309) 298-2470
Hist. Note: Formerly Nat'l Council of Geography Teachers. Seeks to enhance the status, quality, and effectiveness of geography teaching in North America.
Publications:
Journal of Geography. m. adv.
Perspective. 5/yr.
Annual Meetings: Fall
1987-Springfield, MO/450
1988-Snowbird, UT/450
1989-Cincinnati, OH
1990-Williamsburg, VA
1991-St. Paul, MN

Nat'l Council for Textile Education (1933)
Box 391, Charlottesville VA 22902
President: Charles G. Tewksbury
Members: 30 *Staff:* 1
Annual Budget: under $10,000 *Tel:* (804) 296-5511
Hist. Note: Founded as The National Council of Textile School Deans, it assumed its present name in 1953. Members are college textile departments.
Annual Meetings: With the American Textile Manufacturers Institute

Nat'l Council for the Social Studies (1921)
3501 Newark St., N.W., Washington DC 20016
Exec. Director: Frances Haley
Members: 22,000 *Staff:* 11-15
Annual Budget: $500-1,000,000 *Tel:* (202) 966-7840
Hist. Note: Formed by a group of college and public school educators in 1921 in Atlantic City, NJ as the Nat'l Council of Teachers of the Social Studies, it was transformed into the Nat'l Council for the Social Studies a year later with a new constitution. This subsequently became a department of the Nat'l Education Ass'n in 1925 and completely independent in 1973. Membership: $43/yr.
Publications:
NCSS Bulletin. irreg.
Social Education. 7/yr. adv.
Annual Meetings: November
1987-Dallas, TX/Nov. 13-17
1988-Orlando, FL/Nov. 18-22
1989-St. Louis, MO(Adam's Mark & Clarion Hotels)/Nov. 10-14

Nat'l Council for U.S.-China Trade (1973)
1818 N St., N.W., Washington DC 20036
President: Roger W. Sullivan
Members: 450 companies *Staff:* 35-40
Annual Budget: $2-5,000,000 *Tel:* (202) 429-0340
Hist. Note: Companies that trade or hope to trade with the People's Republic of China.
Publication:
The China Business Review. bi-m. adv.
Annual Meetings: June in Washington, DC(Mayflower)/200-300

Nat'l Council for Urban Economic Development (1967)
1730 K St., N.W., Suite 1009, Washington DC 20006
Exec. Director: Jeff Finkle
Members: 1,000 *Staff:* 12
Annual Budget: $500-1,000,000 *Tel:* (202) 223-4735
Hist. Note: Established as the HUB Council, it became the Council for Urban Economic Development in 1971 and assumed its present name in 1974. Members are concerned with urban revitalization and economic development. Membership: $250/yr. (individual); $550/yr. (organization).
Publications:
Commentary. q.
Information Service Report. irreg.
Legislative Report. irreg.
Economic Developments. bi-w.
Annual Meetings: Washington, DC in Spring
1987-(Capitol Hilton)/March 29-April 1

Nat'l Council of Acoustical Consultants (1962)
Box 359, 66 Morris Ave., Springfield NJ 07081
Exec. Director: Steven Changaris
Members: 85 companies *Staff:* 2-5
Annual Budget: $25-50,000 *Tel:* (201) 379-1100
Hist. Note: Dedicated to management and related concerns of professional acoustical consulting firms and to safeguarding the interests of the clients and public which they serve.
Publications:
Directory. bi-a.
Newsletter. q. adv.
Annual Meetings: With Acoustical Soc. of America

Nat'l Council of Acupuncture Schools and Colleges (1982)
Box 954, Columbia MD 21044
Mary Ellen Zorbaugh
Members: 15 schools
Annual Budget: $10-25,000 *Tel:* (301) 997-4888
Hist. Note: Founded in Chicago and incorporated in the District of Columbia. Membership is open to all established 2-year acupuncture training programs.
Semi-Annual Meetings: May and October

Nat'l Council of Administrative Women in Education (1915)
17 Forsyth Road, Pittsburgh PA 15220
Exec. Officer:
Members: 3,000 *Staff:* 1
Annual Budget: $25-50,000 *Tel:* (412) 571-7400
Hist. Note: Founded in 1915 at the Nat'l Education Ass'n convention in Oakland, California. Became an accredited department of the NEA in 1932, and an autonomous organization in 1973. Main purpose is to encourage women to prepare for and accept administrative and executive positions in education.
Publication:
NCAWE News. 5/yr. adv.
Annual Meetings: Spring

Nat'l Council of Agricultural Employers (1964)
499 South Capitol St., S.W., Suite 411, Washington DC 20003
Exec. V. President: Elizabeth D. Whitley
Members: 500 *Staff:* 2
Annual Budget: $100-250,000 *Tel:* (202) 544-6400
Hist. Note: Members are growers and producers who employ agricultural laborers, as well as processors and organizations related to the agriculture business. Strictly an information center; does not negotiate contracts.
Publication:
NCAE News. m.
Annual Meetings: February
1987-Washington, DC/Feb. 25-27/100

Nat'l Council of Architectural Registration Boards (1920)
1735 New York Ave., N.W., Ste. 700, Washington DC 20006
Exec. Director: Samuel T. Balen
Members: 55 State Registration Boards *Staff:* 30
Annual Budget: $2-5,000,000 *Tel:* (202) 783-6500
Hist. Note: Assists state regulatory agencies in developing regulations for the practice of architecture and the licensing of persons wishing to practice.
Publications:
Annual Report. a.
Newsletter. q.
Annual Meetings: June/300
1987-Seattle, WA (Four Seasons)/June 24-27
1988-Chicago, IL (Westin Chicago)/June 27-30
1989-Boston, MA (Westin Copley Sq.)/June 27-30

00218 12 05 86 1233

Nat'l Council of Area and Regional Travel Organizations
Hist. Note: A nursling of the Travel Industry Association of America, which provides administrative support.

Nat'l Council of Career Women (1975)
1701 K St., N.W., Suite 1004, Washington DC 20006
President: Janice M. Covey
Members: 600
Annual Budget: under $10,000 *Tel:* (202) 659-6599
Hist. Note: A voluntary organization with members concentrated in the Washington, DC area. NCCW offers opportunities for members to enhance the professional skills and awareness of women to become better prepared to succeed in today's business world in traditional as well as non-traditional career fields.
Publication:
Newsletter. bi-m.
Bi-monthly meetings: Washington, DC

Nat'l Council of Catholic Women (1920)
1312 Massachusetts Ave., N.W., Washington DC 20005
Administrator: Annette Kane
Members: 10,000 organizations *Staff:* 6-10
Annual Budget: $250-500,000 *Tel:* (202) 638-6050
Hist. Note: A federation of nat'l, state, diocesan, inter-parochial, and parochial organizations of Catholic women. Membership fee based upon size of organization.
Publication:
Catholic Woman. bi-m.
Biennial meetings: odd years

Nat'l Council of Coal Lessors (1951)
1050 One Valley Square, Charleston WV 25301
Secretary: David Stemple
Members: 75-80 companies *Staff:* 2-5
Tel: (304) 346-0569
Hist. Note: Supports the National Council of Coal Lessors Political Action Committee. Members are owners of coal-bearing land concerned with taxes, depletion allowances, black lung payments, etc.

Nat'l Council of College Publication Advisers (1954)
Hist. Note: Became College Media Advisers in 1983.

Nat'l Council of Commercial Plant Breeders (1954)
1030 15th St., N.W., Suite 964, Washington DC 20005
Exec. V. President: William T. Schapaugh
Members: 60-65 companies *Staff:* 2-5
Annual Budget: $50-100,000 *Tel:* (202) 223-4080
Hist. Note: Founded in 1954 by representatives of thirteen commercial firms as a non-profit organization to promote the achievement and interest of American plant breeders both in the United States and abroad.
Annual Meetings: June
1987-Boston, MA(Westin)/July 1

Nat'l Council of Community Hospitals (1974)
1000 Thomas Jefferson St., N.W., Suite 500, Washington DC 20007
Exec. Director: Katie Bolt
Members: 100-125 institutions *Staff:* 6-10
Annual Budget: $500-1,000,000 *Tel:* (202) 342-7300
Hist. Note: Primary purpose is to insure that the point of view of its members is adequately represented to the Federal Government. Membership: $300/yr. (individual); $3,500-6,500/yr. (organization).
Publication:
Washington Update. irreg.
Semi-annual Meetings: Spring in the East, Fall in the West.
1987-Key Biscayne, FL(Spring) and Tucson, AZ(Fall)

Nat'l Council of Community Mental Health Centers (1970)
6101 Montrose Road, Suite 360, Rockville MD 20852
Exec. Director: Frank Bailey
Members: 600-700 agencies *Staff:* 9-12
Annual Budget: $1-2,000,000 *Tel:* (301) 984-6200
Hist. Note: Promotes a unified network of community mental health providers, organizations and indivduals on the national, state and local level. Memberhip: $156/yr. (individual); organizational membership based on budget.
Publication:
National Council News. m. adv.
Annual Meetings: Spring
1987-Miami Beach, FL(Fontainbleau)/June 3-6/1,500
1988-Boston, MA(Marriott Copley Place)/March 30-April 2/1,500
1989-New York, NY(Sheraton Center)/March 29-April 1/1,600
1990-Chicago, IL(Marriott Downtown)/May 30-June 2/1,500
1991-New Orleans, LA(Sheraton New Orleans)/May 29-June 1/1,700

Nat'l Council of County Ass'n Executives (1948)
440 First St., N.W., Washington DC 20001
Staff Liaison: Ed Ferguson
Members: 140-150 *Staff:* 2-5
Annual Budget: under $10,000 *Tel:* (202) 393-6226
Hist. Note: An affiliate of the National Association of Counties. Formerly (1973) Conference of Executives of State Associations of Counties.
Annual Meetings: With Nat'l Ass'n of Counties

Nat'l Council of Elected County Executives (1970)
440 First St., N.W., Washington DC 20001
Staff Liaison: Ed Ferguson
Members: 156 *Staff:* 1
Annual Budget: under $10,000 *Tel:* (202) 393-6226
Hist. Note: An affiliate of the National Association of Counties, which provides administrative support.
Annual Meetings: With NACO

Nat'l Council of Engineering Examiners (1920)
Box 1686, Clemson SC 29633
Exec. Director: Roger B. Stricklin, Jr.
Members: 55 state boards, 600 individuals *Staff:* 18
Annual Budget: $2-5,000,000 *Tel:* (803) 654-6824
Hist. Note: Formerly (1967) Nat'l Council of State Boards of Engineering Examiners. Coordinates evaluation and registration of professional engineers and land surveyors.
Publications:
Proceedings. a.
Registration Bulletin. q.
Annual Meetings: August/350
1987-Baltimore/Aug. 13-16
1988-Albuquerque, NM
1989-Birmingham, AL
1990-Wisconsin
1991-New Hampshire

Nat'l Council of Erectors, Fabricators and Riggers (1969)
2200 Mill Road, Suite 616, Alexandria VA 22314
V. President: Thomas Kollins
Members: 3 organizations *Staff:* 1
Annual Budget: $10-25,000 *Tel:* (703) 838-1980
Hist. Note: Members are the Specialized Carriers and Rigging Ass'n, the Nat'l Ass'n of Reinforcing Steel Contractors and the Nat'l Ass'n of Miscellaneous Ornamental and Architectural Products Contractors. Serves as interface with the labor union.

Nat'l Council of Farmer Cooperatives (1929)
50 F St., N.W., 9th Floor, Washington DC 20001
President: Wayne A. Boutwell
Members: 150-160 *Staff:* 20-25
Annual Budget: $2-5,000,000 *Tel:* (202) 628-6676
Hist. Note: Absorbed Nat'l Federation of Grain Cooperatives in 1973. Sponsors and supports the National Council of Farmer Cooperatives Political Action Committee. Affiliated with Farm Credit Council, Agricultural Cooperative Development Internat'l and American Institute of Cooperation. Sponsors Co-op PAC.
Publications:
Washington Councilor. w.
Co-op Monitor. q.
NCFC Highliter. m.
Washington Cooperator. bi-m.
Annual Meetings: Winter
1987-Washington, DC/Jan. 18-22
1988-Honolulu, HI/Jan. 22-27
1989-Washington, DC/Jan. 21-26
1990-Nashville, TN/Jan. 20-25

Nat'l Council of Forestry Ass'n Executives (1949)
1205 East Main St., Richmond VA 23219
President: Charles Finley, Jr.
Members: 30-40
Tel: (804) 644-8462
Hist. Note: National organization with no paid staff, headquarters or dues. Officers are elected annually. Members, who represent state and regional forest associations, meet 1-2 times annually to share experiences, workable ideas and to formulate policy on forestry issues.

Nat'l Council of Health Centers (1969)
Hist. Note: Founded and known as the Nat'l Council of Health Care Services until 1980. Merged with the American Health Care Ass'n in 1984.

Nat'l Council of Investigation and Security Services (1975)
Hist. Note: Address unknown in 1987.

Nat'l Council of Juvenile and Family Court Judges (1937)
Box 8970, Reno NV 89507
Exec. Director: Dean Louis W. McHardy
Members: 2,500 *Staff:* 55-60
Annual Budget: over $5,000,000 *Tel:* (702) 784-6012
Hist. Note: Located on the campus of Univ. of Nevada at Reno. Operates National College of Juvenile Justice at Reno and National Center for Juvenile Justice, a research center, at Pittsburgh, PA.
Publications:
Juvenile and Family Law Digest. m.
Juvenile and Family Court Journal. q.
Juvenile and Family Court Newsletter. 8/yr.
Annual Meetings: July

Nat'l Council of Local Administrators of Vocational Education and Practical Arts (1942)
NYC Board of Education, Trade and Tech.,Educ., 66 Rugby Rd., Brooklyn NY 11226
Exec. Secretary: Dr. Harry Lewis
Members: 900-1,000 *Staff:* 1
Annual Budget: under $10,000 *Tel:* (212) 282-3269
Hist. Note: Administrators and supervisors of vocational and practical arts education in public and technical schools. Formed by a merger of the Nat'l Ass'n of Trade School Principals and the Nat'l Council of City Administrators of Industrial Arts and Vocational Education. Affiliated with the American Vocational Ass'n. Membership: $25/year.
Publication:
Council-Gram. q.
Annual Meetings: With the American Vocational Ass'n

Nat'l Council of Local Public Welfare Administrators (1940)
1125 15th St., N.W., Suite 300, Washington DC 20005
Contact: David Racine
Members: 150 *Staff:* 1
Annual Budget: under $10,000 *Tel:* (202) 293-7550
Hist. Note: A constituent unit of the American Public Welfare Ass'n.

Nat'l Council of Music Importers and Exporters (1966)
135 West 29th St., New York NY 10001
Exec. V. President: Jerome Hershman
Members: 68 *Staff:* 1
Annual Budget: $10-25,000 *Tel:* (212) 564-0251
Hist. Note: Formerly Nat'l Ass'n of Music Importers Membership: $285/yr. (company).
Publication:
Newsletter. 10/yr.
Annual Meetings:
1987-Chicago, IL(Marriott)/June 15/60
1988-Atlanta, GA(Marriott)/June 27/60
1989-Chicago, IL(Marriott)/June/65
1990-Chicago, IL(Marriott)/June/65

Nat'l Council of Patent Law Ass'ns (1935)
277 Park Ave., New York NY 10172
Secretary: Charles P. Baker
Members: 52 state & local ass'ns
Tel: (212) 758-2400
Hist. Note: Began as a branch of the American Intellectual Property Law Ass'n; now an independent association. Has no paid staff.
Publications:
Chairman's Letter. m.
Legislative Letter. m.
Newsletter. q.
Semi-Annual Meetings: Feb. and Oct. in Washington, DC

Nat'l Council of Physical Distribution Management (1963)
Hist. Note: Became the Council of Logisitics Management in 1985.

Nat'l Council of Professional Services Firms (1972)
Hist. Note: Became the Professional Services Council in 1982.

Nat'l Council of Real Estate Investment Fiduciaries (1982)
276 Fifth Ave., New York NY 10001
Exec. Director: Judy Kalvin
Members: 40 companies; 70 individuals *Staff:* 2
Annual Budget: $100-250,000 *Tel:* (212) 475-4316
Hist. Note: Members are real estate investment managers, including insurance companies, banks and independent investment advisors, serving the pension fund industry. Membership: $200/yr. (subscription membership); $3,000/yr. (voting membership).
Publication:
NCREIF Report. q.
Semi-Annual Meetings: Spring and Fall
1987-Hawaii(with Urban Land Institute)/May
1987-Los Angeles, CA/Oct.

Nat'l Council of Salesmen's Organizations (1946)
225 Broadway, Suite 515, New York NY 10007
Exec. Director: Agnes Johnson
Members: 50,000 *Staff:* 2-5
Annual Budget: $50-100,000 *Tel:* (212) 349-1707
Publication:
The Voice. q. adv.

Nat'l Council of Savings Institutions (1983)
1101 15th Street, N.W., Washington DC 20005
President: John H. Rousselot
Members: 600 *Staff:* 75-80
Annual Budget: over $5,000,000 *Tel:* (202) 857-3100
Hist. Note: The product of a merger on November 1, 1983 between the National Association of Mutual Savings Banks (founded in 1920) and the National Savings and Loan League (founded in 1943). Members are savings and loan institutions and mutual savings banks. Supports the Thriftpac Political Action Committee. Has an annual budget of $8 million.
Publications:
Bottomline. m.
Washington Memo. w.
Membership Directory. a.
Annual Meetings: May/1,000
1987-San Francisco, CA(Fairmont)/May 10-13

00219 12 05 86 1233

Nat'l Council of Self-Insurers (1945)
10 S. Riverside Plaza, Chicago IL 60606
Exec. Director: Douglas F. Stevenson
Members: 300
Annual Budget: $25-50,000 *Tel:* (312) 454-5110
Hist. Note: Formerly (1973) Nat'l Council of State Self-insurers Ass'ns. Organizations and individuals concerned with self-insurance under the workmen's compensation laws. The above address is the law firm of Stevenson, Rusin & Friedman.

Nat'l Council of Social Security Management Ass'ns (1970)
P.O. Box 2067, Minot ND 58702
Contact: Steve Bauer
Members: 10 associations; 4,000 individuals
Annual Budget: $100-250,000 *Tel:* (701) 852-3651
Hist. Note: Members are managers and supervidors of Social Security field offices and teleservice centers in the U.S. and Puerto Rico.
Publication:
Mass Media. 8x/yr.
Annual Meetings: October
1987-Philadelphi, PA/Oct. 13-15
1988-San Juan, PR

Nat'l Council of State Boards of Nursing (1978)
625 North Michigan Ave., Suite 1544, Chicago IL 60611
Exec. Director: Eileen McQuaid Dvorak
Members: 61 *Staff:* 14
Annual Budget: $2-5,000,000 *Tel:* (312) 787-6555
Hist. Note: Members are state boards of nursing.
Publications:
Newsletter. bi-w.
Issues. q.
Annual Meetings: Summer
1987-Chicago, IL(Marriott)/Aug. 25-29
1988-Des Moines, IA/Aug.
1989-Chicago, IL/Aug.

Nat'l Council of State Consultants in Elementary Education (1940)
Hist. Note: Dissolved in 1984.

Nat'l Council of State Directors of Community Junior Colleges (1969)
102 Breckinridge Hall, University of Kentucky, Lexington KY 40506
Chairman: Charles T. Wethington, Jr.
Members: 35-40
Annual Budget: $10-25,000 *Tel:* (606) 257-8607
Hist. Note: Affiliated with American Ass'n of Community and Junior Colleges. Membership: $20/yr.
Annual Meetings: Workshop in July; meeting in October.

Nat'l Council of State Education Ass'ns (1966)
1201 16th St., N.W., Washington DC 20036
Exec. Director: Kai Erickson
Members: 52 associations, 182 individuals *Staff:* 2-5
Annual Budget: $250-500,000 *Tel:* (202) 822-7745
Hist. Note: Merger in 1966 of the Nat'l Ass'n of Secretaries of State Teachers Ass'ns (1924) and the Nat'l Council of State Ass'n Presidents (1961). Members are secretaries and presidents of state education ass'ns. Members are executive directors, presidents, vice presidents presidents-elect and treasurers of state education ass'ns.
Publications:
Information Service Reports. irreg.
NCSEA Newsletter. m.
Profiles of State Associations. a.
Annual Meetings: November
1987-Phoenix, AZ

Nat'l Council of State Emergency Medical Services Training Coordinators (1977)
Box 3824, Pojoaque NM 87501-0824
Chairperson: Randy Kuykendall
Members: 159
Annual Budget: $50-100,000 *Tel:* (505) 827-2523
Hist. Note: Members are supervisors or coordinators of state EMS training programs (limited to three members from each state). Affiliated with the American College of Emergency Physicians, Nat'l Ass'n of State Emergency Medical Service Directors, Nat'l Ass'n of Emergency Technicians, and the Nat'l Registry of Emergency Medical Technicians. Purpose is to improve EMS education and promote standardized training and licensure. Membership: $110/yr.
Publication:
Minutes of the Annual Meeting. a.
Annual Meetings: Fall
1987-Rapid City, SD/Oct.
1988-Santa Fe, NM/Oct.

Nat'l Council of State Garden Clubs (1929)
4401 Magnolia Ave., St. Louis MO 63110
Office Manager: Jane Schlereth
Members: 325-350,000 individuals, 11,000 clubs *Staff:* 11-15
Tel: (314) 776-7574
Hist. Note: A federation of garden clubs united to protect and conserve natural resources through teacher training and environmental workshops. Supported by dues of 25 cents per person from its member clubs.
Publication:
The National Gardener. bi-m. adv.
Annual Meetings: May/1,000
1987-Bal Harbour, FL(Sheraton)/May 11-13
1988-Houston, TX/May 2-4
1989-Rochester, NY/May 23-25
1990-Seattle, WA
1991-Des Moines, IA

Nat'l Council of State Human Service Administrators (1939)
1125 15th St., N.W., Suite 300, Washington DC 20005
Chairperson: Michael R. Petit
Members: 200
Tel: (202) 293-7550
Hist. Note: Formerly (1984) Nat'l Council of State Public Welfare Administrators. A constituent unit of the American Public Welfare Ass'n.
Quarterly Meetings:

Nat'l Council of State Pharmaceutical Ass'n Executives (1929)
156 E. Market St., #900, Indianapolis IN 46204
Secy.-Treas.: David A. Clark
Members: 50-60 *Staff:* 2-5
Annual Budget: under $10,000 *Tel:* (317) 634-4968
Annual Meetings: With American Pharmaceutical Ass'n and Nat'l Ass'n of Retail Druggists

Nat'l Council of State Public Welfare Administrators (1938)
Hist. Note: Became the Nat'l Council of State Human Service Administrators in 1984 .

Nat'l Council of State Supervisors of Foreign Languages (1960)
Div. of Curriculum Dev., Tx Ed. Agency, 1701 North Congress, Austin TX 78701
President: Carl H. Johnson
Members: 70-80 *Staff:* 1
Annual Budget: under $10,000 *Tel:* (512) 463-9556
Hist. Note: Provides support at the state level for foreign language programs and liaison with other agencies and federal and local government.
Annual Meetings: With the American Council on the Teaching of Foreign Languages

Nat'l Council of State Travel Directors (1972)
c/o Travel Industry Ass'n, 1899 L St., N.W., Suite 600, Washington DC 20036
TIA Staff Liaison: Patty Hubbard
Members: 56 *Staff:* 1
Annual Budget: under $10,000 *Tel:* (202) 293-1433
Hist. Note: A council of the Travel Industry Ass'n of America, which provides administrative support. Members are state and territorial government travel offices. Formerly (1978) the Council of Regional Travel Executives (CORTE). Membership: $910/yr.
Publication:
Stateside. q.
Annual Meetings: Educational Seminar for State Travel Officials (ESSTO)
1987-Grand Lake, OK/July 12-16

Nat'l Council of Teachers of English (1911)
1111 Kenyon Rd., Urbana IL 61801
Exec. Director: John C. Maxwell
Members: 53,000 individuals; 19,000 institutions *Staff:* 80
Annual Budget: $2-5,000,000 *Tel:* (217) 328-3870
Hist. Note: Membership: $35/year.
Publications:
CSSEDC Newsletter. q.
College Composition and Communication. q. adv.
College English. 8/yr. adv.
English Education. q. adv.
English Journal. 8/yr. adv.
Language Arts. 8/yr. adv.
Research in the Teaching of English. q. adv.
SLATE Newsletter. bi-m.
Livewire. 5/yr.
Teaching English in the Two-Year College. q. adv.
Annual Meetings: Fall/4,000
1987-Los Angeles, CA(Hilton)/Nov. 20-24
1988-St. Louis, MO(Adams Mark)/Nov. 18-23
1989-Baltimore, MD(Stouffer's)/Nov. 17-22

Nat'l Council of Teachers of Mathematics (1920)
1906 Association Dr., Reston VA 22091
Exec. Director: James D. Gates
Members: 62,000 *Staff:* 43
Annual Budget: $2-5,000,000 *Tel:* (703) 620-9840
Hist. Note: Affiliate of the American Association for the Advancement of Science. Membership: $35/yr. (individual), $40/yr. (organization).
Publications:
The Arithmetic Teacher. 9/yr. adv.
The Journal for Research in Mathematics Education. 5/yr. adv.
The Mathematics Teacher. 9/yr. adv.
NCTM News Bulletin. 5/yr.
Annual Meetings: Spring
1987-Anaheim, CA/April 8-11
1988-Chicago, IL/April 6-9
1989-Orlando, FL/April 12-15
1990-Salt Lake City, UT/April 18-20
1991-New Orleans, LA/April 17-20

Nat'l Council of the Churches of Christ in the U.S.A. (1950)
475 Riverside Dr., Room 880, New York NY 10115
Gen. Secretary: Arie Brouwer
Members: 31 communions *Staff:* 400
Annual Budget: over $5,000,000 *Tel:* (212) 870-2511
Hist. Note: Founded in 1950 by representatives of 29 major Protestant and Orthodox denominations who met to unite 12 nationwide interchurch agencies and form the Nat'l Council of Churches, NCC is now the primary expression of the ecumenical movement in the United States with 31 communions - Protestant, Orthodox and Anglican church bodies with a combined membership of 40 million Christians. Has an annual budget of over $40 million.
Publications:
Ecu-Link. 10/yr.
Yearbook of American and Canadian Churches. a.
Semi-annual Governing Board Meetings: Spring and Fall
1987-Kansas City, MO/May 13-15 and New York, NY/Nov. 4-6

Nat'l Council of the Paper Industry for Air and Stream Improvement (1943)
260 Madison Ave., New York NY 10016
Exec. V. President: Dr. Isaiah Gellman
Members: 125 companies *Staff:* 60
Annual Budget: $2-5,000,000 *Tel:* (212) 532-9000
Hist. Note: A technical organization devoted to finding solutions to environmental protection problems related to the manufacture of pulp, paper and wood products and industrial forestry. Formerly (1968) Nat'l Council for Stream Improvement.
Publications:
Bulletin Board. Bi-w.
Technical Bulletins. irreg.
Annual Meetings: New York(Waldorf Astoria)every March/150

Nat'l Council of Travel Attractions
Hist. Note: A nursling of the Travel Industry Association of America, which provides administrative support.

Nat'l Council of University Research Administrators (1959)
One Dupont Circle, N.W., Suite 618, Washington DC 20036
Director, National Office: Natalie A. Kirkman
Members: 1,800 *Staff:* 2-5
Annual Budget: $250-500,000 *Tel:* (202) 466-3894
Hist. Note: Individuals with professional interests in problems and policies relating to the administration of sponsored research, education and training activities at colleges and universities. Membership: $25/year.
Publications:
NCURA Directory. a.
NCURA Newsletter. 10/year.
Intellectual Property.

Nat'l Council of Urban Tourism Organizations
Hist. Note: A nursling of the Travel Industry Association of America, which provides administrative support.

Nat'l Council on Compensation Insurance (1922)
One Penn Plaza, 250 West 34th St., New York NY 10119
President: Kevin M. Ryan
Members: 740 insurance companies *Staff:* 1,200
Annual Budget: over $5,000,000 *Tel:* (212) 560-1000
Hist. Note: Formerly the Nat'l Council on Workmen's Compensation Insurance, NCCI is a voluntary, non-profit, statistical research and ratemaking organization. Supported by the insurance industry, NCCI's primary functions are the preparation and administration of rates, rating plans and systems for worker's compensation insurance in 32 states and providing similar assistance in about one-half of the remaining states. Members include stock companies, mutual companies, competitive state funds and reciprocals. Has an annual budget of $55,000,000.
Publications:
Annual Statistical Bulletin. a.
Legal Insight. 3/yr.
NCCI Digest. q.
Scopes. a.
Annual Meetings: April
1987-Boca Raton, FL(Park Place Suite)/April 2/250

Nat'l Council on Crime and Delinquency (1907)
77 Maiden Lane, 4th Floor, San Francisco CA 94108
President: Dr. Barry Krisberg
Members: 10,000 *Staff:* 30-40
Annual Budget: $2-5,000,000 *Tel:* (415) 956-5651
Hist. Note: Established in 1907 as the Nat'l Probation Ass'n. Is concerned with upgrading criminal justice practices. Membership: $25/yr.
Publications:
Crime and Delinquency. q. adv.
Journal of Research in Crime and Delinquency. semi-a. adv.
Annual Meetings: Spring

Nat'l Council on Education for the Ceramic Arts (1967)
P.O. Box 1677, Bandon OR 97411
Exec. Secretary: Regina Brown
Members: 1,400 *Staff:* 2
Tel: (503) 347-4394
Hist. Note: Members are teachers, professional studio artists, students and others concerned with the ceramic arts. NCECA became an independent organization in 1967 after several years of affiliation with the Ceramic Educational Council of the American Ceramic Society. Purpose is to promote and improve

00220 12 05 86 1233

education in the ceramic arts. Membership: $30/yr. (domestic), $35/yr. (foreign).
Publications:
NCECA Journals. semi-a.
Newsletter. q.
Annual Meetings:
1987-Syracuse, NY
1988-Portland, OR
1989-Kansas City, MO

Nat'l Council on Family Relations (1938)
1910 West County Road B, Suite 147, Roseville MN 55113
Exec. Officer: Mary Jo Czaplewski
Members: 5,000 *Staff:* 12
Annual Budget: $500-1,000,000 *Tel:* (612) 633-6933
Hist. Note: Professionals, academicians and others interested in education and research about the family, development of community services for and government policies concerning families, and related issues. Membership: $70/yr. (individual); $100/yr. (organization).
Publications:
Family Relations. q. adv.
Journal of Marriage and the Family. q. adv.
Newsletter q. adv.
Annual Meetings: Fall

Nat'l Council on Governmental Accounting (1933)
Hist. Note: Sponsored by Municipal Finance Officers Ass'n of the U.S. & Canada. Established as the National Committee on Municipal Accounting, it became the National Committee on Governmental Accounting in 1949 and assumed its present name in 1974. Ceased operations in 1984.

Nat'l Council on Harness Racing (1980)
Hist. Note: Moribund in 1982 and probably destined for oblivion.

Nat'l Council on Measurement in Education (1938)
1230 17th St., N.W., Washington DC 20036
Exec. Officer: William J. Russell
Members: 2,200-2,300 *Staff:* 2-5
Annual Budget: $100-250,000 *Tel:* (202) 223-9318
Hist. Note: Founded as the National Council on Measurements used in Education, it assumed its present name in 1960. Membership: $20/year.
Publications:
Educational Measurement: Issues and Practice. q.
Journal of Educational Measurement. q. adv.
Annual Meetings: With American Educational Research Association in Spring
1987-Washington, DC(Sheraton-Shoreham)/April 21-23
1988-New Orleans, LA(Marriott-Sheraton)/April 6-8
1989-San Francisco, CA(Hilton)/March 28-30
1990-Boston, MA(Sheraton-Marriott)/April 6-8
1991-Chicago, IL(Hyatt Marriott(/April

Nat'l Council on Public Polls (1969)
Box 183, Princeton NJ 08542
President: Harry W. O'Neill
Members: 20 companies
Annual Budget: under $10,000 *Tel:* (609) 924-6570
Hist. Note: Formerly Nat'l Committee on Public Polls. Members are public opinion polling companies. Has no paid staff. The modest dues barely cover operating expenses.
Annual Meetings: No set pattern.

Nat'l Council on Radiation Protection and Measurements (1964)
7910 Woodmont Ave., Ste. 1016, Bethesda MD 20814
Exec. Director: W. Roger Ney
Members: 300-325 *Staff:* 6-10
Annual Budget: $500-1,000,000 *Tel:* (301) 657-2652
Hist. Note: Formerly (1929) Advisory Committee on X-ray and Radium Protection; (1947) Nat'l Committee on Radiation Protection; (1957) Nat'l Committee on Radiation Protection and Measurements.
Publications:
NCRP Reports. irreg.
Proceedings. a.
Annual Meetings: Spring in Washington, DC

Nat'l Council on Synthetic Fuels Production (1980)
Hist. Note: Became the Council on Synthetic Fuels in 1985.

Nat'l Council on Teacher Retirement (1924)
P.O. Box 1882, Austin TX 78767-1882
Secy.-Treas.: Bruce Hineman
Members: 222 organizations *Staff:* 2-5
Annual Budget: $50-100,000 *Tel:* (512) 397-6401
Hist. Note: Members are 46 state and 15 local retirement systems, 23 educaation associations, 12 state pension and investment boards and 126 commercial firms.
Publications:
Proceedings and Membership Directory. a.
Newsletter. m.
Annual Meetings: Fall
1987-Nashville, TN(Opryland)/Sept. 27-Oct. 2
1988-Reno, NV(MGM Grand)/Sept. 25-30

Nat'l Council on the Aging (1950)
600 Maryland Ave., S.W., West Wing 100, Washington DC 20024
Exec. Director: Jack Ossofsky
Members: 6,000 *Staff:* 90
Annual Budget: over $5,000,000 *Tel:* (202) 479-1200
Hist. Note: A nonprofit voluntary organization in the field of aging; a central national resource for planning information, technical consultation and advocacy and materials for professionals in the field. Supports the Nat'l Institute on Age, Work and Retirement; the Nat'l Institute of Senior Centers; the Nat'l Center on Rural Aging; the Center of the Arts and Aging; the Nat'l Institute of Senior Housing, the Nat'l Institute on Adult Daycare; the Nat'l Ass'n of Older Worker Employment Services, the Nat'l Voluntary Organizations for Independent Living for the Aging and the Nat'l Institute on Community-Based Long-Term Care. Membership: $60/yr. (individual); $125/yr. (organization).
Publications:
Current Literature on Aging. q.
Perspective on Aging. bi-m.
Senior Center Report. q.
Annual Meetings: Spring/3,000
1987-Chicago, IL/March 29-April 1

Nat'l Counter Intelligence Corps Ass'n (1947)
3969 Applewood Lane, Kettering OH 45429
Chairman: Otto E. Fiedler
Members: 1,600 *Staff:* 1
Annual Budget: $10-25,000 *Tel:* (513) 293-0878
Hist. Note: Former counter intelligence agents of the U.S. Army, Marines and Air Force. Membership: $10/yr.
Publication:
Golden Sphinx. q.
Annual Meetings: Fall
1987-Philadelphia, PA

Nat'l CPA Group (1972)
233 Broadway, Suite 743, New York NY 10279
Director of Administration: Maureen S. Schwartz
Members: 35-40 companies *Staff:* 3
Annual Budget: $250-500,000 *Tel:* (212) 766-4260
Hist. Note: Formerly known as the Nat'l Group of CPA Firms. The Group is an international association of accounting firms formed to provide services to its member firms: professional development programs, exchange of management information, development of technical and promotional materials, interfirm peer reviews, and availability of specialized knowledge.
Publications:
Newsletter. bi-m.
Personal Financial Planning Quarterly. q.
Roster. bi-a.
Directory of Specialists.
Semi-annual Meetings: Spring and Fall/150
1987-Palm Springs, CA/May and Orlando, FL/Sept.

Nat'l Credit Union Management Ass'n (1949)
Box 140099, Dallas TX 75214-0099
Treasurer: L. Phil Davis
Members: 4,200 credit unions *Staff:* 1
Annual Budget: $250-500,000 *Tel:* (214) 328-0093
Hist. Note: Members are credit unions whose assets total more than $1,000,000.
Annual Meetings: September or October
1987-Orlando, FL/Oct. 4-7
1988-San Diego, CA(Town & Country)/Oct. 2-5
1989-Nashville, TN(Opryland)/Sept. 24-27
1990-Honolulu, HI(Hawaian Village)/Sept. 21-27

Nat'l Crime Prevention Institute (1971)
9001 Shelbyville Road, Burhans Hall, Room 134, Louisville KY 40292
Director: Timothy D. Crowe
Members: 350 individuals; 60 companies *Staff:* 8
Annual Budget: $250-500,000 *Tel:* (502) 588-6987
Hist. Note: Businesses, law enforcement and correction agencies, government officials, educators and community action groups interested in efficient, on-going crime prevention programs. Serves as a central exchange for technical, statistical and educational information on crime prevention.
Annual Meetings: NCPI Alumni Annual Conference

Nat'l Criminal Justice Ass'n (1971)
444 N. Capitol St., N.W., Suite 608, Washington DC 20001
Exec. V. President: Gwen A. Holden
Members: 500 *Staff:* 8
Annual Budget: $250-500,000 *Tel:* (202) 347-4900
Hist. Note: Membership open to all criminal justice system practitioners and others with interest in crime prevention and control, law enforcement, the courts, corrections or other aspects of the administration of justice. Incorporated in the District of Columbia in 1974. Formerly (until 1979) known as the Nat'l Conference of State Criminal Justice Planning Administrators. Membership: $55/yr.
Publications:
Justice Bulletin. m.
Juvenile Justice. irreg.
Justice Research. irreg.
Legislative Report. a.
Justice Alert. irreg.
Annual Meetings: Spring
1987-Wilmington, DE(Blockade Runner)/May 26-28/100-150

Nat'l Crop Insurance Ass'n (1915)
8400 West 164th St., #400, Overland Park KS 66210
Exec. V. President: George A. Bender
Members: 105-110 *Staff:* 8-9
Annual Budget: $500-1,000,000 *Tel:* (913) 451-3656
Hist. Note: Formerly (1975) Hail Insurance Adjustment and Research Ass'n. NCIA is an association of insurance companies limited to those writing insurance for damage by hail, fire and other weather perils to growing crops.
Annual Meetings: Late Winter/200-250
1987-Scottsdale, AZ(Granada Royale Homotel)/March 1-3
1988-Kansas City, MO

Nat'l Crop Insurance Council (1966)
Hist. Note: Inactive in 1984.

Nat'l Crushed Stone Ass'n (1918)
Hist. Note: Merged with the Nat'l Limestone Institute to become the Nat'l Stone Ass'n in 1985.

Nat'l Customs Brokers and Forwarders Ass'n of America (1897)
Five World Trade Center, Suite 9273, New York NY 10048
Exec. V. President: John Hammon, CAE
Members: 510 *Staff:* 2-5
Annual Budget: $250-500,000 *Tel:* (212) 432-0050
Hist. Note: Founded (1897) as the Customs-Clerks Ass'n of the Port of New York. Became the New York Customs Brokers Ass'n (1922) and was incorporated under the same name in 1933. Accepted nat'l membership in 1945, and was incorporated as the Customs Brokers and Forwarders Ass'n of America, Inc., in 1948. Name changed to Nat'l Customs Brokers and Forwarders Ass'n of America, Inc., in 1962.
Publications:
Membership Directory. a. adv.
Newsletter. m.
Annual Meetings:
1987-Palm Springs, CA(Desert Princess)/March 2-5

Nat'l Dairy Council (1915)
6300 North River Rd., Rosemont IL 60018
President: Elwood W. Speckmann
Members: 2,500-3,000 *Staff:* 30-35
Annual Budget: $2-5,000,000 *Tel:* (312) 696-1020
Hist. Note: Supported by all segments of the dairy industry in its promotion of nutrition research and nutrition education insofar as they apply to dairy products. Funds are channelled through the United Dairy Industry Ass'n to the Nat'l Dairy Council.
Publications:
Catalog of Nutrition Education Materials. a.
Dairy Council Digest. bi-m.
Nutrition News. q.
Annual Meetings: With United Dairy Industry Ass'n

Nat'l Dance Ass'n (1932)
1900 Association Dr., Reston VA 22091
Exec. Director: Dr. Margie R. Hanson
Members: 3,000 *Staff:* 2
Annual Budget: $25-50,000 *Tel:* (703) 476-3436
Hist. Note: Until 1974 a division of the American Ass'n for Health, Physical Education and Recreation. It is now an ass'n of the American Alliance for Health, Physical Education, Recreation and Dance (AAHPERD). Members are dance and physical education instructors mostly in public and private schools and universities. Membership: $42/yr.
Publications:
Focus. bien.
Journal of Physical Education, Recreation and Dance. 9/yr. adv.
Spotlight on Dance. q.
Annual Meetings: Spring, with AAHPERD
1987-Las Vegas, NV/April 13-17
1988-Kansas City, MO/April 6-10
1989-Boston, MA/April 19-23
1990-New Orleans, LA/March 28-April 1

Nat'l Decorating Products Ass'n (1947)
1050 North Lindbergh Blvd., St. Louis MO 63132
Exec. V. President: Robert E. Petit
Members: 6,000-7,000 *Staff:* 40-50
Annual Budget: over $5,000,000 *Tel:* (314) 991-3470
Hist. Note: Formerly Retail Paint & Wallpaper Distributors of America. Merged (1971) with Southern Paint & Wallpaper Dealers Ass'n. Formerly (1972) Paint and Wallpaper Ass'n of America, Inc. Annual budget is in excess of $12 million.
Publication:
Decorating Retailer. m. adv.
Annual Meetings: November/9-10,000
1987-Chicago, IL (McCormick Place)/Nov. 20-22
1988-Chicago, IL (McCormick Place)/Nov. 18-20

Nat'l Defense Transportation Ass'n (1944)
727 North Washington St., Suite 200, Alexandria VA 22314-1976
President: Norman C. Venyke
Members: 140-150 organizations; 8,000 individuals *Staff:* 6-10
Annual Budget: $250-500,000 *Tel:* (703) 836-3303
Hist. Note: Established October 11, 1944 as the Army Transport Association by seven officers from the Army Transportation Corps, it assumed its present name in 1949. Originally intended as a liaison between government and private transportation officials, it has evolved into a major spokesman for the U.S. transportation industry and private enterprise. Sustaining members are air, sea and land transportation companies of all types, together with their suppliers.
Publication:
Defense Transportation Journal. bi-m. adv.
Annual Meetings: Fall/500
1987-Little Rock, AR/Sept. 27-30
1988-Honolulu, HI/Sept. 25-28
1989-Seattle, WA/Sept. 24-27
1990-El Paso, TX

00221 12 05 86 1233

Nat'l Dental Ass'n (1913)
5506 Connecticut Ave., N.W., Suite 24-25, Washington DC 20015
Director: Leslie L. Atkinson
Members: 1,500-2,000 *Staff:* 2-5
Annual Budget: $100-250,000 *Tel:* (202) 244-7555
Hist. Note: Founded in Hampton, VA. Members are minority dentists dedicated to providing quality dental care to the unserved and underserved.
Publication:
National Dental Ass'n Journal. q. adv.
Annual Meetings: Summer/1,000
1987-Los Angeles(Hilton)/July 31-Aug. 6
1988-Open
1989-Open
1990-Houston, TX
1991-Atlanta, GA

Nat'l Dental Technicians Ass'n (1977)
Box 1236, Tulsa OK 74101
Exec. Secretary: Ray Mullins
Members: 2,500 *Staff:* 1
Annual Budget: $25-50,000 *Tel:* (918) 438-7697
Hist. Note: Membership: $50/year.
Annual Meetings: Tulsa, OK

Nat'l Dimension Manufacturers Ass'n (1929)
1000 Johnson Ferry Road, Suite A-130, Marietta GA 30067
Exec. Director: Steven V. Losser
Members: 80 companies *Staff:* 3-5
Annual Budget: $100-250,000 *Tel:* (404) 565-6660
Hist. Note: Founded in 1929 as Hardwood Dimension Manufacturers Ass'n; assumed its present name in 1985. Members are manufacturers of wood component products for the furniture and kitchen cabinet industries as well as other wood parts users.
Annual Meetings: Spring
1987-Reno, NV(Harrah's)/April 11-14
1988-Charleston, SC

Nat'l Disabled Law Officers Ass'n (1971)
c/o 75 New St., Nutley NJ 07110
Founder: Peter A. Frazza
Members: 5,000 individuals *Staff:* 1
Annual Budget: under $10,000 *Tel:* (201) 667-9569
Hist. Note: A service organization for disabled law enforcement officers; advocates retraining and placement of officers. No membership fee.
Publication:
Newsletter. irreg.

Nat'l District Attorneys Ass'n (1950)
1033 N. Fairfax St., Suite 200, Alexandria VA 22314
Exec. Director: Jack E. Yelverton
Members: 7,000 *Staff:* 15-20
Annual Budget: $500-1,000,000 *Tel:* (703) 549-9222
Hist. Note: Established as the Nat'l Ass'n of County and Prosecuting Attorneys, it assumed its present name in 1959.
Publications:
Capital Perspective. bi-m.
Case Commentaries & Briefs. m.
The Prosecutor. q. adv.
Annual Meetings: Summer
1987-Tuscon, AZ(Westin La Paloma)/July 26-29

Nat'l Dog Groomers Ass'n of America (1969)
Box 101, Clark PA 16113
Exec. Director: Jeffrey L. Reynolds
Members: 2,200 groomers and supply distributors *Staff:* 2-5
Annual Budget: $50-100,000 *Tel:* (412) 962-2711
Hist. Note: Membership: $40/year (individual), $25/year (organization/company).
Publication:
Groomers Voice. q. adv.

Nat'l Dome Ass'n (1976)
Hist. Note: Formerly (until 1980) known as the National Ass'n of Dome Home Manufacturers. Members are companies making prefabicated domes. Absorbed by the Home Manufacturers Council of the National Association of Home Builders in 1983.

Nat'l Drilling Contractors Ass'n (1977)
3008 Millwood Ave., Columbia SC 29205
Exec. Director: J. Edgar Eubanks
Members: 110 companies *Staff:* 8-10
Annual Budget: $50-100,000 *Tel:* (803) 252-5646
Hist. Note: Members are oil and water well drillers. Incorporated in the State of Pennsylvania.
Annual Meetings: February-March, with the National Drilling Federation.

Nat'l Drilling Federation (1980)
3008 Millwood Ave., Columbia SC 29205
Exec. Director: J. Edgar Eubanks
Members: 2 organizations, 40-50 associates *Staff:* 8-10
Annual Budget: $25-50,000 *Tel:* (803) 252-5646
Hist. Note: Members are the Diamond Core Drill Manufacturers Association and the National Drilling Contractors Association. Incorporated in the District of Columbia.
Annual Meetings: Trade Show

Nat'l Drug Trade Conference (1913)
Box 238, Alexandria VA 22313
President: Charles S. Trefrey
Members: 8
Annual Budget: under $10,000 *Tel:* (703) 684-6400
Hist. Note: A group of associations meeting periodically to discuss issues facing the industry. Members are: American Pharmaceutical Ass'n, American Ass'n of Colleges of Pharmacy, Nat'l Ass'n of Chain Drug Stores, Nat'l Ass'n of Retail Druggists, Nat'l Wholesale Druggists Ass'n, Pharmaceutical Manufacturers Ass'n, and The Proprietary Ass'n, and the Cosmetic, Toiletry, and Fragrance Ass'n. Has no paid staff or permanent address. Officers change annually.
Annual Meetings: Winter

Nat'l Dry Bean Council (1950)
c/o Agri Sales, Inc., 385 East Marley Drive., Box 2028, Saginaw MI 48605
President: Jim Stein
Members: 6 ass'ns *Staff:* 1
Annual Budget: under $10,000 *Tel:* (517) 753-5432
Hist. Note: Formerly Nat'l Dried Bean Council. Has no permanent headquarters.
Annual Meetings: Washington, DC in January.

Nat'l Duckling Council (1965)
Box 76067, St. Paul MN 55175
Exec. Director: Ray L. Clark, Jr.
Members: 15-20 companies *Staff:* 2-5
Annual Budget: $50-100,000 *Tel:* (612) 222-3232
Annual Meetings: Atlanta in January with The Southeastern Poultry Conference

Nat'l Economic Ass'n (1969)
Off. of Systems VP for Academic Affairs,Southern University, Baton Rouge LA 70813
Secretary-Treasurer: Dr. Gus T. Ridgel
Members: not divulged
Annual Budget: under $10,000
Hist. Note: Formerly (1975) Caucus of Black Economists. NEA promotes black representation in the economics profession, acts as a job clearing house and gives financial assistance to black students of economics. Membership: $36/year.
Publication:
Journal of Black Political Economy. q.
Annual Meetings: In conjunction with the American Economic Ass'n

Nat'l Education Ass'n of the U.S. (1857)
1201 16th St., N.W., Washington DC 20036
Exec. Director: Don Cameron
Members: 1,700,000 individuals *Staff:* 500-600
Annual Budget: $1-2,000,000 *Tel:* (202) 833-4000
Hist. Note: Formerly (1870) Nat'l Teachers Ass'n. Merged with American Teachers Ass'n in 1966. Supports the Nat'l Education Ass'n Political Action Committee. Strives to enhance and strengthen public education in America in order to futher equity and excellence for all Americans. Also works to advance human and civil rights. Engages in political action through its political action committee (NEA-PAC). Membership: $66/yr.
Publications:
NEA Addresses and Proceedings. a.
NEA Handbook. a.
NEA Today. 10/yr.
Today's Education. a.
Annual Meetings: June/July
1987-Los Angeles, CA

Nat'l Electric Sign Ass'n (1944)
801 North Fairfax St., Suite 205, Alexandria VA 22314
President: George M. Kopecky
Members: 900 *Staff:* 6-10
Annual Budget: $250-500,000 *Tel:* (703) 836-4012
Hist. Note: Manufacturers of all types of on-premise signs, the materials for them, and suppliers to the industry. Sponsors and supports the National Electric Sign Association Political Action Committee.
Publications:
NESA Directory a.
NESA News. m.
Annual Meetings: Spring
1987-Las Vegas, NV(Bally Grand)/April 3-7/5,000
1988-Orlando, FL(Peabody Hotel)/April 15-20/5,000
1989-Phoenix, AZ

Nat'l Electrical Contractors Ass'n (1901)
7315 Wisconsin Ave., Bethesda MD 20814
Exec. V. President: John M. Grau
Members: 5,500 companies *Staff:* 75-80
Annual Budget: over $5,000,000 *Tel:* (301) 657-3110
Hist. Note: Members are electrical contruction companies. Sponsors and supports the Electrical Construction Political Action Committee.
Publication:
Electrical Contractor. m. adv.
Annual Meetings:
1987-San Francisco, CA/Oct. 25-29
1988-New Orleans, LA/Oct. 23-27
1989-Chicago, IL/Oct. 1-4

Nat'l Electrical Manufacturers Ass'n (1926)
2101 L St., N.W., Washington DC 20037
President: Bernard H. Falk
Members: 500-600 companies *Staff:* 85-100
Annual Budget: over $5,000,000 *Tel:* (202) 467-8400
Hist. Note: The largest trade organization for manufacturers of electrical products in the U.S. Organized in 1926 through the merger of several organizations, the oldest of which, The Electrical Manufacturers Club, was formed in 1905. Has an annual budget of $6 million.
Publication:
NEMA News Bulletin
Annual Meetings: Fall/400-500
1987-New Orleans, LA(Fairmont)/Nov. 15-18
1988-Undecided
1989-Washington, DC(Capital Hilton)/Nov. 12-15

Nat'l Electrical Manufacturers Representatives Ass'n (1970)
222 Westchester Ave., White Plains NY 10604
Exec. Director: Henry P. Bergson
Members: 1,000 companies *Staff:* 7
Annual Budget: $1-2,000,000 *Tel:* (914) 428-1307
Hist. Note: Members are independent electrical sales representatives. Membership: $600/yr.
Publications:
Headquarters Report. bi-m.
NEMRA Locator. a. adv.
Annual Meetings:
1987-Reno, NV(Bally Grand)/April 2-7
1988-Orlando, FL(Marriott Orlando World Center)/Feb. 15-22
1989-Nashville, TN(Opryland)/April 4-9
1990-Dallas, TX(Loew's Anatole)/March 21-26
1991-San Diego, CA or Chicago, IL/late March or early April
1992-Boston, MA(Marriott Copley Place)/April 8-15
1993-San Francisco, CA/late March or early April

Nat'l Electrolysis Organization (1975)
Hist. Note: Merged with the Electrolysis Soc. of America to form the Soc. of Clinical and Medical Electrologists in 1985.

Nat'l Electronic Distributors Ass'n (1937)
35 E. Wacker Drive, Suite 3202, Chicago IL 60601
Exec. V. President: Toby Mack
Members: 500-550 *Staff:* 7
Annual Budget: $500-1,000,000 *Tel:* (312) 558-9114
Hist. Note: Formerly National Radio Parts Distributors Association. Members are distributors of high technology components to industry.
Annual Meetings: Spring
1987-Las Vegas, NV(MGM Grand)/May 13-15

Nat'l Electronic Sales and Service Dealers Ass'n (1963)
2708 West Berry, Fort Worth TX 76109
Exec. Director: Clyde W. Nabors
Members: 2,500-2,700 *Staff:* 10-12
Annual Budget: $250-500,000 *Tel:* (817) 921-9061
Hist. Note: 5 Electronics sales and service shops. Sponsors the International Society of Certified Electronics Technicians. Formerly (1974) the Nat'l Electronic Ass'n and (1983) the Nat'l Electronic Service Dealers Ass'n. Absorbed the Nat'l Ass'n of Television and Electronic Servicers of America in 1986. Membership: $72/yr.
Publications:
Professional Electronics Yearbook. a. adv.
Newsletter.
Professional Electronics. m. adv.
Annual Meetings:
1987-Memphis, TN(Peabody)/Aug. 10-15/500
1988-Chicago, IL
1989-Tucson, AZ

Nat'l Elevator Industry (1934)
630 Third Ave., New York NY 10016
Exec. Director: Frank S. Aquilino
Members: 70-80 companies *Staff:* 6-10
Annual Budget: $500-1,000,000 *Tel:* (212) 986-1545
Hist. Note: Formerly (1969) Nat'l Elevator Manufacturing Industry, Inc.
Publication:
Newsletter. bi-m.

Nat'l Emergency Management Ass'n (1950)
1410 Riverside Dr., Jackson MS 39202
President: James E. Wahler
Members: 75
Annual Budget: $10-25,000 *Tel:* (601) 352-9100
Hist. Note: Founded as the National Association of State Civil Defense Directors, it became the National Association of State Directors for Disaster Preparedness in 1974 and assumed its present name in 1980. Members include State Directors of Emergency Management, local emergency management representatives and interested individuals and corporations. Has no paid staff or permanent address. Officers change annually. Membership: $10/yr. (individual), $500/yr. (state/company).
Semi-annual meetings: Spring and Fall

Nat'l Employee Benefits Institute (1977)
2550 M St., N.W., Suite 785, Washington DC 20037
Associate Director: Thomas G. Schendt
Members: 100 plus *Staff:* 4-6
Tel: (800) 558-7258
Hist. Note: Corporations concerned about employee benefits and related legislation.
Publication:
Legislative Update. q.
Annual Meetings: Quarterly, with at least one meeting in Washington, DC.

00222 12 05 86 1233

Nat'l Employee Services and Recreation Ass'n (1941)
2400 South Downing, Westchester IL 60153
Exec. Director: Patrick B. Stinson
Members: 4,000 companies *Staff:* 6
Annual Budget: $250-500,000 *Tel:* (312) 562-8130
Hist. Note: A professional association for employee services and recreation management. Founded as the National Industrial Recreation Association, it assumed its present name in 1982. Members include managers of such programs as employee assistance, pre- retirement planning, fitness, child care, sports, travel and educational and cultural programs in business, the government and military. Membership: $75/yr. (company).
Publications:
Employee Services Management. adv.
Keynotes. m.
Annual Meetings: May
1987-Minneapolis, MN(Hyatt Regency)/May 13-17

Nat'l Employment and Training Ass'n (1966)
IJC Tupelo, 653 Eason Blvd., Tupelo MS 38801
President: Nancy White
Members: 1,300-1,500 *Staff:* 1
Annual Budget: $10-25,000 *Tel:* (601) 842-5621
Hist. Note: An affiliate of the Employment and Training Division of the American Vocational Association. Formerly (1967) Manpower Training Ass'n and (1978) the Nat'l Manpower Training Ass'n.
Publication:
Manpower Newsletter. m.
Annual Meetings: With American Vocational Ass'n

Nat'l Employment Counselors Ass'n (1964)
5999 Stevenson Ave., Alexandria VA 22304
Exec. Director: Dr. Patrick J. McDonough
Members: 1,400-1,500
Annual Budget: $10-25,000 *Tel:* (703) 823-9800
Hist. Note: Division of the American Ass'n for Counseling and Development. Membership: $9/yr.
Publications:
Journal of Employment Counseling. q. adv.
NECA Newletter.
Annual Meetings: With American Ass'n for Counseling and Development
1987-New Orleans, LA/April 22-25

Nat'l Energy Specialist Ass'n (1984)
2035 Western, Suite 201, Topeka KS 66604
Exec. Director: Michael C. Cooper
Members: 300 companies; 500 individuals *Staff:* 3
Annual Budget: $500-1,000,000 *Tel:* (913) 232-1702
Hist. Note: Incorporated in 1984 as a non-profit organization dedicated to enhancing consumer investment in energy conservation products and services through those professional companies and individuals that promote safe, cost efficient solutions to the energy crisis. Membership open to all energy-involved manufacturers, distributors, dealers and individuals. Awards the designation CERS (Certified Energy Reduction Specialist) to qualified individuals.
Publication:
The Energy Specialist. q. adv.
Annual Meetings: Spring

Nat'l Engine Parts Manufacturers Ass'n (1944)
20 North Wacker Drive, Chicago IL 60606
Exec. V. President: Richard F. Friedeman
Members: 16-20 companies *Staff:* 2-5
Annual Budget: $25-50,000 *Tel:* (312) 236-6169
Hist. Note: Absorbed (1972) Piston and Pin Standardization Group and Automotive Engine Bearings Group. Formerly (1972) Piston Ring Manufacturers Group.

Nat'l Engineering Consortium (1944)
505 North Lake Shore Drive, Suite 4808, Chicago IL 60611
Exec. Director: Robert Janowiak
Members: 17 institutions *Staff:* 15
Tel: (312) 828-9134
Hist. Note: Formerly (1974) Nat'l Electronics Conference. A non-profit engineering education organization sponsored by major technological universities.
Publication:
Proceedings. a.
Annual Meetings: Annual Nat'l Communications Forum
1987-Chicago, IL(Ramada)/Sept. 28-30/4,000
1988-Stamford, CT/May 4-6/2,000

Nat'l Environmental Balancing Bureau (1971)
8224 Old Courthouse Road, Vienna VA 22180
Administrator: William C. Abernathy
Members: 380 companies *Staff:* 4
Annual Budget: $100-250,000 *Tel:* (703) 734-3840
Hist. Note: Co-sponsored by the Mechanical Contractors Ass'n of America and the Sheet Metal and Air Conditioning Contractors Nat'l Ass'n. Function is to establish and direct a management oriented industry program to upgrade and maintain uniform standards for the testing, adjusting, and balancing of environmental systems, and measurement for sound and vibration levels. Membership: $300/yr.
Publication:
The Balance Sheet Newsletter. q.
Annual Meetings: Fall
1987-Nashville,TN(Vanderbilt Plaza)/Nov. 4-7

Nat'l Environmental Development Ass'n (1972)
1440 New York Ave., N.W., Suite 300, Washington DC 20005
Exec. V. President: Steven B. Hellem
Members: 300-310 companies, labor unions and organizations
Annual Budget: $50-100,000 *Tel:* (202) 638-1230
Hist. Note: Companies and others concerned with the impact of environmental legislation on business and industrial profits.
Publication:
Balance. m.
Annual Meetings: Always March, in Washington, DC

Nat'l Environmental Health Ass'n (1937)
720 S. Colorado Blvd., South Tower, Suite 970, Denver CO 80222
Exec. Director: Nelson E. Fabian
Members: 4,200 *Staff:* 6
Annual Budget: $500-1,000,000 *Tel:* (303) 756-9090
Hist. Note: Incorporated in California in 1937 as the Nat'l Ass'n of Sanitarians. Became the Nat'l Environmental Health Ass'n in 1970. NEHA members represent virtually all environmental health and protection professions. NEHA administers a certification program, as well as offering continuing education programs and special seminars. Membership: $40/year (individual), $300/year (organization/company).
Publications:
Journal of Environmental Health. bi-m. adv.
NEHA Newsletter. q.
NEHA Environmental Health Trends Report. q.
Annual Meetings: June/1,000-1,500
1987-San Diego, CA(Sheraton Harbor Island)/June 13-17
1988-Cleveland, OH(Stouffers Inn on the Park)
1989-Seattle, WA(Westin Hotel)
1990-Charlotte, NC

Nat'l Environmental Training Ass'n (1977)
8687 Via de Ventura, #214, Scottsdale AZ 85258
Exec. Director: George A. Kinias
Members: 700-750 *Staff:* 5
Annual Budget: $250-500,000 *Tel:* (602) 951-1440
Hist. Note: Trainers of personnel in the field of air and noise pollution and hazardous waste control, water supply and waste-water treatment. Membership: $30/yr. (individual), $125/yr. (organization/company).
Publications:
NETA News. q. adv.
Who's Who in Environmental Training a.
Conference Proceedings. a.
Annual Meetings: August
1987-Portland, ME/100-150
1988-Reno, NV

Nat'l Equipment Distributors Ass'n (1985)
4300-L Lincoln Ave., Rolling Meadows IL 60008
Exec. Director: Donn W. Sanford
Staff: 3
Annual Budget: $10-25,000 *Tel:* (312) 359-8160
Hist. Note: Incorporated in Illinois.
Annual Meetings:
1987-Phoenix, AZ(Hyatt)/Feb.

Nat'l Equipment-Servicing Dealers Ass'n (1981)
Box 121, East Main St., Jefferson Valley NY 10535
Exec. Director: Norman Beck
Staff: 1
Annual Budget: $10-25,000 *Tel:* (914) 245-5678
Hist. Note: Organized in Pittsburgh September 11, 1981, members are dealers servicing lawn and garden power equipment. Membership: $20/year.
Publication:
Newsletter. q.
Annual Meetings: Fall

Nat'l Erectors Ass'n (1969)
1501 Lee Highway, Suite 202, Arlington VA 22209
Exec. V. President: Noel C. Borck
Members: 150-175 companies *Staff:* 2-7
Annual Budget: $500-1,000,000 *Tel:* (703) 524-3336
Hist. Note: A construction employers trade ass'n consisting of steel erectors, iron workers and industrial maintenance firms. Primary function is labor relations. Formerly Nat'l Steel Erectors Ass'n.
Publications:
I-Beam Newsletter. m.
NEA Notes. m.
Safety Spotlight. bi-m.
Labor Update. q.
Semi-annual Meetings: Spring, and Fall in Washington, DC
1987-Tampa, FL
1988-Palm Springs, CA

Nat'l Estimating Soc. (1966)
1001 Connecticut Ave., N.W., Suite 800, Washington DC 20036
Exec. V. President: Jeffrey A. Bell
Members: 1,340-1,400 *Staff:* 2
Annual Budget: $100-250,000 *Tel:* (202) 466-5499
Hist. Note: Individuals who deal primarily in the field of government contract estimating and pricing. Founded in San Diego in 1966 by aerospace cost estimators and incorporated in California. Membership: $45/yr.
Publications:
Dollars and Sense. m.
The National Estimator. q. adv.
Annual Meetings:
1987-Atlanta, GA/late April or early May

Nat'l Executive Housekeepers Ass'n (1930)
1001 Eastwind Drive, Suite 301, Westerville OH 43081
Exec. Director: James H. Powell
Members: 5,135 individuals *Staff:* 2-5
Annual Budget: $250-500,000 *Tel:* (614) 895-7166
Hist. Note: A professional organization for administrators of housekeeping programs in commercial, institutional and industrial facilities. Membership: $65/yr.
Publication:
Executive Housekeeping Today. m. adv.
Biennial Meetings: Even years, in Summer
1988-Boston, MA(Marriott)

Nat'l Exhaust Distributors Ass'n (1984)
300 John Q. Hammons Pkwy., Suite 112, Springfield MO 65806
Exec. Director: Larry Dixon
Members: 47 companies
Annual Budget: $50-100,000 *Tel:* (417) 864-4756
Hist. Note: Members include the manufacturers and warehouse distributors of products specific to the exhaust industry. Membership: $100-1,200/yr.
Publication:
Newsletter. q.

Nat'l Export Traffic League (1946)
234 Fifth Ave., New York NY 10001
President: Helga A. Jalkio
Members: 125-150 individuals
Annual Budget: under $10,000 *Tel:* (212) 697-5895
Hist. Note: Formed in New York City in May 1946 by a group of export-import traffic executives to promote higher standards in internat'l distribution. Has no permanent staff. Officers rotate. Membership: $56/yr.
Publications:
Network. m. adv.
Journal/Membership Directory. a. adv.

Nat'l Eye Research Foundation (1956)
899 Skokie Blvd., Suite 300, Northbrook IL 60062
President: Dr. Roy K. A. Wesley
Members: 500 *Staff:* 3
Annual Budget: $250-500,000 *Tel:* (800) 621-2258
Hist. Note: Membership: $125/year.
Publication:
Contacto. bi-m. adv.
Semi-Annual Meetings:
1987-Chicago, IL(Hyatt Regency)/June 10-11(Centennial of Contact Lens)
1987-Las Vegas, NV/Fall

Nat'l Family Business Council (1971)
60 Revere Drive, Suite 500, Northbrook IL 60062
Director: John E. Messervey
Members: 1,000 *Staff:* 5
Annual Budget: $100-250,000 *Tel:* (312) 480-9574
Publication:
Family Business Resource Guide.
Annual Meetings: Fall

Nat'l Family Planning and Reproductive Health Ass'n (1971)
122 C St., N.W., Suite 380, Washington DC 20001-2109
Exec. Director: Scott R. Swirling
Members: 1,000 *Staff:* 5
Annual Budget: $250-500,000 *Tel:* (202) 628-3535
Hist. Note: A professional membership group concerned with the delivery and availability of family planning services in the United States. Its members are primarily government-funded agencies involved in the provision of family planning and related health services. NFPRHA follows legislative and administrative developments affecting reproductive health issues, conducts policy research analysis and provides technical assistance. Funding sources include private donations, membership dues and foundation grants. Until 1979 known as the National Family Planning Forum. Membership: $125/yr.(individual); $500/yr.(organization).
Publications:
NFPRHA News. m. adv.
NFPRHA Alert. irreg.
NRPRHA Action. irreg.
Annual Meetings: Early Spring in Washington, DC at the Sheraton Washington
1987-March 9-11
1988-Feb. 29-March 2

Nat'l Farm and Power Equipment Dealers Ass'n (1900)
10877 Watson Rd., St. Louis MO 63127
Exec. V. President: William E. Galbraith
Members: 9,000 retail dealers *Staff:* 60-65
Annual Budget: $250-500,000 *Tel:* (314) 821-7220
Hist. Note: Founded as the Nat'l Retail Farm Equipment Ass'n, it assumed its present name in 1962.
Publications:
Farm and Power Equipment. m. adv.
Official Guide - Tractors and Farm Equipment. semi-a.
Official Industrial Equipment Guide. semi-a.
Outdoor Power Equipment Official Guide. a.
Cost of Doing Business Study. a.
Annual Meetings: August
1987-Milwaukee, WI/Aug. 2-6
1988-Vancouver, BC/Aug. 7-11
1989-Boston, MA/Aug. 6-10
1990-Salt Lake City, UT/Aug. 5-9

00223 12 05 86 1233

Nat'l Farmers Organization (1955)
720 Davis Ave., Corning IA 50841
President: DeVon R. Woodland
Members: 30,000-40,000 *Staff:* 250-300
Annual Budget: $1-2,000,000 *Tel:* (515) 322-3131
Hist. Note: Advocates collective bargaining through contract marketing by farmers. Formerly Collective Bargaining for Agriculture. Maintains a Washington office. Sponsors and supports the Nat'l Farmers Organization-Grass Roots in Politics Political Action Committee. Membership: $75/yr.
Publication:
NFO Reporter. m.
Annual Meetings: December
1987-Las Vegas, NV

Nat'l Farmers Union
Hist. Note: Official name is the Farmers Educational and Co-operative Union of America.

Nat'l Fastener Distributors Ass'n (1968)
3094 Cressing Place, Columbus OH 43227
Exec. Director: Mary Ann Langholz
Members: 164 companies *Staff:* 1-2
Annual Budget: $100-250,000 *Tel:* (614) 237-0252
Hist. Note: Absorbed the Southern Ass'n of Industrial Fastener Distributors in 1972. Membership: $600/yr.
Publications:
NFDA Now. q.
NFDA Stock Guide. a. adv.
Semi-annual meetings: Spring and Fall/250
1987-Nashville, TN(Opryland)/April 8
1987-Grand Traverse Village, MI(Grand Traverse Resort)/Oct. 7-11
1988-Hilton Head, SC(Intercontinental)/April 20-24

Nat'l Federation of Abstracting and Information Services (1958)
112 South 16th St., Philadelphia PA 19102
Exec. Director: Betty Unruh
Members: 50 *Staff:* 2-5
Annual Budget: $250-500,000 *Tel:* (215) 563-2406
Hist. Note: Formerly (1972) Nat'l Federation of Science Abstracting and Indexing Services and (1982) Nat'l Federation of Abstracting and Indexing Services. Cooperates with the American Soc. for Information Science, the American Library Ass'n and other national and international organizations concerned with information science. Members are private organizations (25) and government offices here and abroad (14) which abstract and index scientific and technical data in print and machine-readable form. Membership fee varies with revenues.
Publications:
Directory. bien.
NFAIS Newsletter. bi-m.
Trainers' Circuit Newsletter. q.
Annual Meetings:
1987-Arlington, VA(Gateway Marriott)/March 1-4
1988-Philadelphia, PA(Four Seasons)/Feb. 28-March 2

Nat'l Federation of Business and Professional Womens Clubs (1919)
2012 Massachusetts Ave., N.W., Washington DC 20036
Nat'l President: MaRy Ray Oaken
Members: 155,000 individuals *Staff:* 25-30
Annual Budget: $1-2,000,000 *Tel:* (202) 293-1100
Hist. Note: The membership is divided among about 3,800 clubs and 53 state and territorial organizations. Sponsors the Business and Professional Women's Foundation and the Business and Professional Women's Political Action Committee. Membership: $11/yr.
Publication:
National Business Woman. bi-m. adv.
Annual Meetings: Summer

Nat'l Federation of Catholic Physicians' Guilds (1932)
850 Elm Grove Rd., Elm Grove WI 53122
Exec. Secretary: Robert H. Herzog
Members: 6,800 *Staff:* 4
Annual Budget: $50-100,000 *Tel:* (414) 784-3435
Publication:
The Linacre. q.
Annual Meetings:
1987-New York, NY/late September

Nat'l Federation of Community Broadcasters (1975)
3rd Floor, 1314 14th St., N.W., Washington DC 20005
President: Carol Schatz
Members: 175 *Staff:* 6-10
Annual Budget: $250-500,000 *Tel:* (202) 797-8911
Hist. Note: Members are non-commercial public radio stations licensed to community organizations, as well as university and other licensees, independent producers and production groups. NFCB's purpose is to advance community-oriented non-commercial broadcasting; provide programming, services, and resources to community licensees; foster cooperation among local broadcasting organizations; and participate at the national level in the development of public broadcasting policy. Membership: $75/yr. (individual); $2,000/yr. (organization/company)
Publications:
NFCB Newsletter. m. adv.
Producer's Classifieds. q. adv.
Annual Meetings: Summer/2-300
1987-Boulder, CO(Hilton)/July 2-6
1988-Washington, DC

Nat'l Federation of Federal Employees (1917)
1016 16th St., N.W., Washington DC 20036
President: James M. Peirce
Members: 52,000 *Staff:* 85
Annual Budget: $2-5,000,000 *Tel:* (202) 862-4400
Hist. Note: Chartered by the American Federation of Labor in 1917, NFFE withdrew from the AFL in 1931 objecting to the AFL's position that civil service classification should not be extended to skilled crafts. It is now an independent labor union in competition with the American Federation of Government Employees (AFL-CIO). Sponsors the Public Affairs Council (NFFE), a political action committee.
Publications:
The Federal Employee. m.
Action. bi-m.
Biennial meetings: Even years
1988-St. Louis, MO/350
1990-Little Rock, AR/350

Nat'l Federation of Federal Land Bank Ass'ns (1947)
Hist. Note: Inactive in 1984.

Nat'l Federation of Fishermen (1969)
2424 Pennsylvania Ave., N.W., Suite 516, Washington DC 20037
Exec. Director: Lucy Sloan
Members: 20 ass'ns
Hist. Note: Formed by merger of Nat'l Fishermen and Wives and Congress of American Fishermen. Represents the majority of organized commerical fisherman in the United States.
Annual Meetings: With Fish Expo, alternately in Seattle (uneven years) and Boston (even years).

Nat'l Federation of Grange Mutual Insurance Companies (1934)
769 Hebron Ave., Box 71, Glastonbury CT 06033
Secretary: Alden A. Ives
Members: 11-15 *Staff:* 1
Annual Budget: under $10,000 *Tel:* (203) 633-4678
Annual Meetings: With Nat'l Ass'n of Mutual Insurance Companies

Nat'l Federation of Independent Business (1943)
600 Maryland Ave., S.W., Washington DC 20024
President: John Sloan
Members: 500,000 *Staff:* 780
Annual Budget: over $5,000,000 *Tel:* (202) 554-9000
Hist. Note: Established as the National Federation of Small Business, it assumed its present name about 1950. In addition to the Washington office, it maintains offices in San Mateo, CA and all 50 state capitals. Its principal focus is legislative relations and research. Sponsors the National Federation of Independent Business Political Action Committee. Membership: $1,000/yr. (maximum).
Publications:
The Mandate. bi-m.
Economic Report. q.
State Reports.
Action Report. a.
How Congress Voted. a.
NFIB Business Edge. bi-m.
Annual Meetings: Quadrennial Meetings
1987-Washington, DC

Nat'l Federation of Independent Unions (1963)
1166 South 11th St., Philadelphia PA 19147
President: F. J. Chiappardi
Members: 55,000-60,000 *Staff:* 2-5
Annual Budget: $25-50,000 *Tel:* (215) 336-3300
Hist. Note: Independent labor federation. Merger of Nat'l Independent Union Council and Confederated Unions of America.
Publication:
News for Independent Unions. q.
Semi-annual Meetings: March and September
1987-Washington, DC/March
1987-Oklahoma/September

Nat'l Federation of Licensed Practical Nurses (1949)
Box 11038, 214 S. Driver St., Durham NC 27703
Exec. Director: Sammy K. Griffin
Members: 10,000 *Staff:* 5
Annual Budget: $250-500,000 *Tel:* (919) 596-8202
Hist. Note: Independent professional association. Sponsors the Political Education for Nurses Political Action Committee. Membership: $51/yr.
Publication:
Licensed Practical Nurse. m. adv.
Annual Meetings: Fall
1987-Virgin Islands and Bahamas(S.S. Norway)/Oct. 3-10

Nat'l Federation of Local Cable Programmers (1976)
906 Pennsylvania Ave., S.E., Washington DC 20003
Exec. Director: Sue Miller Buske
Members: 1,500 *Staff:* 5
Annual Budget: $250-500,000 *Tel:* (202) 544-7272
Hist. Note: Organized to foster citizen participation in community television programming. Membership: $50/year (individual).
Publications:
Community Television Review. q. adv.
NFLCP Newsletter. q. adv.
Annual Meetings: Summer
1987-Chicago, IL
1988-Tampa, FL

Nat'l Federation of Modern Language Teachers Ass'ns (1916)
Gannon University, Erie PA 16541
Secy.-Treas.: Paul W. Peterson
Members: 7,000 *Staff:* 2-5
Annual Budget: $100-250,000 *Tel:* (815) 871-7330
Hist. Note: Provides a forum for the exchange of information of interest to teachers of modern languages. Membership: $13/yr. (individual); $30/yr. (company).
Publication:
The Modern Language Journal. q. adv.
Annual Meetings: With the American Council on the Teaching of Foreign Languages
1988-New York, NY/Dec. 29

Nat'l Federation of Music Clubs (1898)
1336 North Delaware St., Indianapolis IN 46202
Exec. Secetary: Patricia M. Midgley
Members: 5-600,000 *Staff:* 2-5
Annual Budget: $100-250,000 *Tel:* (317) 638-4003
Hist. Note: Dedicated to finding and fostering young musical talent.
Publications:
Junior Keynotes. q. adv.
Music Clubs Magazine. q. adv.

Nat'l Federation of Paralegal Ass'ns (1974)
104 Wilmot Road, Suite 201, Deerfield IL 60015-5195
Exec. Director: Sheila L. Wertz
Members: 40 state and local ass'ns *Staff:* 1
Annual Budget: $100-250,000 *Tel:* (312) 940-8800
Hist. Note: Founded in Chicago, Illinois by eight charter member paralegal associations. Members of the Federation now represent over 8,500 individual paralegals. Offers a forum for paralegals practicing in all sectors, including private and public law firms, legal services, financial institutions, the courts, trade associations and federal, state and local government .
Publication:
National Paralegal Reporter. bi-m.
Annual Meetings: June
1987-Boston, MA
1988-Dallas, TX
1989-San Diego, CA

Nat'l Federation of Press Women (1937)
Box 99, Blue Springs MO 64015
Exec. Administrator: Lois Lauer Wolfe
Members: 5,000 *Staff:* 1
Annual Budget: $100-250,000 *Tel:* (816) 229-1666
Hist. Note: Writers, editors and other communications professionals for newspapers, magazines, radio-TV, institutions, wire services, and agencies. Organized at the Chicago Women's Club, May 6, 1937 under the leadership of Helen Miller Malloch as a federation of state affiliates of working press women. Membership: $20/yr.
Publication:
Press Woman. m. adv.
Annual Meetings: Summer
1987-Williamsburg, VA/June 25-27
1988-Little Rock, AR/June 8-12
1989-Coeur d'Alene, ID

Nat'l Federation of Priests' Councils (1968)
1307 South Wabash Ave., Chicago IL 60605
President: Rev. Richard P. Hynes
Members: 100-125 councils *Staff:* 2-5
Annual Budget: $100-250,000 *Tel:* (312) 427-0115
Hist. Note: Members are priest's councils, no individual membership.
Publications:
Touchstone - Newsletter. q.
Council Exchange - Newsletter. q.
Annual Meetings: April-May/300
1987-Minneapolis/St.Paul, MN(Undetermined)/May 10-14
1988-Louisville, KY/April 24-28
1989-New Orleans, LA/April

Nat'l Federation of Professional Organizations (1966)
P.O. Box 19684, Alexandria VA 22320-0684
President: Wayne A. Nagel
Members: 8 federal professional societies *Staff:* 1
Annual Budget: under $10,000 *Tel:* (703) 765-7906
Hist. Note: The member societies represent civil service professionals.

Nat'l Federation of State High School Ass'ns (1920)
11724 Plaza Circle, Box 20626, Kansas City MO 64195
Exec. Director: Brice B. Durbin
Members: 50-60 state association; 20,000 high schools *Staff:* 43
Annual Budget: $2-5,000,000 *Tel:* (816) 464-5400
Hist. Note: Established as the National Federation of State High School Athletic Associations, it assumed its present name in 1970. The governing body for the interscholastic athletic activity of more than 20,000 high schools in the United States, Canada, the Phillipines, Guam and the Virgin Islands.
Publications:
National Federation News.
Interscholastic Athletic Administration Magazine. q.

00224 12 05 86 1233

Nat'l Athletic Director Conference Proceedings. a.
Semi-annual Meetings: Summer and Winter
1987-Point Clear(Marriott Grand)/Jan. 5-8/180
1987-Denver, CO(Marriott City Center)/June 29-July 3/1,000
1988-Colorado Springs, CO(Broadmoor)/Jan. 4-7/180
1989-Kansas City, MO(Hyatt Regency)/July 5-9/1,200
1989-Tampa, FL(Saddlebrook Resort)/July 3-7/1,200

Nat'l Feed Ingredients Ass'n (1920)
One Corporate Place, 1501 42nd St., West Des Moines IA 50265
President: Marvin L. Vinsand, CAE
Members: 250-300 *Staff:* 6-10
Annual Budget: $500-1,000,000 *Tel:* (515) 225-9611
Hist. Note: Established as the National Mineral Feed Association, it assumed its present name in 1958. Members are makers and suppliers of trace minerals and feed additives.
Annual Meetings: Fall/750
1987-Boston, MA
1988-New Orleans, LA

Nat'l Fellowship of Child Care Executives (1954)
P.O. Box 2549, Billings MT 59103
Exec. Secretary: Wes Robbie
Members: 80 homes for boys
Annual Budget: under $10,000 *Tel:* (406) 252-9301
Hist. Note: Administrators of homes maintaining group residential care for children who are in need of supervision away from their homes. Formerly (1981) Nat'l Ass'n of Homes for Boys. Membership: $100/yr.
Publication:
Book of Proceedings. a.
Annual Meetings: Last full week of June

Nat'l Fencing Coaches Ass'n of America (1941)
118 Fayette St., Ithaca NY 14850
President: Jean-Jacques Gillet
Members: 250-275
Annual Budget: $10-25,000 *Tel:* (607) 255-2368
Hist. Note: Members are coaches, teachers and others interested in fencing. Affiliated with the U. S. Olympic Committee.
Publication:
Swordmaster. q. adv.

Nat'l Fenestration Council (1979)
3310 Harrison, Topeka KS 66611
Exec. V. President: William J. Birch
Members: 100 companies *Staff:* 2-5
Annual Budget: $100-250,000 *Tel:* (913) 266-7014
Hist. Note: Members are makers of residential windows, both wood and glass and their suppliers.
Publication:
News from NFC. q.
Semi-annual Meetings:

Nat'l Fertilizer Solutions Ass'n (1955)
10777 Sunset Office Drive, Suite 10, St. Louis MO 63127
Exec. V. President, C.E.O.: Jay J. Vroom
Members: 1,400-1,500 *Staff:* 20-23
Annual Budget: $1-2,000,000 *Tel:* (314) 821-0340
Hist. Note: Formerly Nat'l Nitrogen Solutions Ass'n. Members are fluid fertilizer dealers; manufacturers and suppliers of related products and services, nutrient materials, pesticides; and fertilizer organizations. The Fluid Fertilizer Foundation is its research and education division.
Publication:
Solutions. 7/yr.
Annual Meetings: December
1987-Kansas City, MO(Convention Ctr.)/Dec. 11-14/3,000
1988-Cincinnati, OH(Convention Ctr.)/Dec. 2-5/3,000
1989-Las Vegas, NV(Convention Ctr.)/Dec. 8-11/3,000
1990-St. Louis, MO(Convention Ctr.)/Dec. 7-10/3,000

Nat'l Film Carriers (1932)
2200 Mill Road, Alexandria VA 22314
Exec. Director: George H. Mundell
Members: 38 companies *Staff:* 3
Annual Budget: $50-100,000 *Tel:* (703) 838-1887
Hist. Note: Founded as Nat'l Film Carriers Corporation, it became affiliated with American Truckings Ass'ns as the Film Carriers Conference in 1935. Merged in 1969 with the Air Freight Motor Carriers Conference (established in 1964) and assumed its present name as part of the Film, Air and Package Carriers Conference, which provides administrative support. Members are deliverers of film from warehouse to theatre and back, as well as (given the present state of the film industry) truckers of magazines and newspapers.
Annual Meetings:
1987-Newport Beach, CA(Marriott)/April 26-29

Nat'l Fire Protection Ass'n (1896)
Batterymarch Park, Quincy MA 02269
President: Robert Grant
Members: 35,000 individuals and organizations *Staff:* 225-250
Annual Budget: over $5,000,000 *Tel:* (617) 770-3000
Hist. Note: Founded in 1896 and incorporated in Massachusetts in 1930. Promotes the science and improves the methods of fire protection and prevention, promulgates standards and gives advice on safety. The Nat'l Ass'n of Chief Electrical Inspectors is one of its sections. Has an annual budget of $20,000,000. Maintains a Washington office. Membership: $60/year.
Publications:
Fire Command. m. adv.
Fire Journal. bi-m. adv.
Fire News.
Fire Technology. a.
Semi-Annual Meetings: Spring and Fall
1987-Cincinnati, OH/May 18-21
1987-Portland, OR/Nov. 9-12
1988-Los Angeles, CA/May 16-20
1988-Nashville, TN/Nov. 14-17

Nat'l Fire Sprinkler Ass'n (1914)
Route 22 and Robin Hill Park, Box 1000, Patterson NY 12563
President: John A. Viniello
Members: 500-600 *Staff:* 16-20
Annual Budget: $2-5,000,000 *Tel:* (914) 878-4200
Hist. Note: Founded as the Nat'l Automatic Sprinkler Ass'n, it became the Nat'l Automatic Sprinkler and Fire Control Ass'n and assumed its present name in 1983. Members are makers and installers of automatic fire sprinklers and related equipment.
Publications:
Sprinkler Quarterly. q.
Sprinkler Technotes. bi-m.
NFSA Grassroots. m.
Annual Meetings: Spring
1987-Tucson, AZ/May 4-8

Nat'l Fish Meal and Oil Ass'n (1950)
2000 M Street, N.W., Suite 580, Washington DC 20036
Exec. Director: Lee J. Weddig
Members: 25-30 *Staff:* 2-5
Annual Budget: $25-50,000 *Tel:* (202) 296-5090
Hist. Note: Merger (1966) of the Industrial Products Division of the Nat'l Fisheries Institute and the Virginia Fisherman's Ass'n to form a division of the Nat'l Fisheries Institute. Became (Sept., 1975) an autonomous division of the Nat'l Ocean Industries Ass'n and (Feb. 1980) an autonomous division of the National Fisheries Institute.

Nat'l Fisheries Institute (1945)
2000 M St., N.W., Suite 580, Washington DC 20036
Exec. V. President: Lee J. Weddig
Members: 1,100 *Staff:* 18
Annual Budget: $2-5,000,000 *Tel:* (202) 296-5090
Hist. Note: Absorbed (1970) American Seafood Distributors Ass'n, (1983) the Shellfish Institute of North American and (1983) the National Blue Crab Industry Association. Sponsors the Fisheries Political Action Committee.
Publication:
Fisheries Blue Book. a. adv.
Annual Meetings: Spring/1,800-2,000
1987-Dallas, TX(Anatole)/April 8-11

Nat'l Flaxseed Processors Ass'n (1977)
Hist. Note: Ass'n exists solely to provide a vehicle for collection and dissemination of monthly statistical reports. It is an unincorporated entity. Inactive in 1986.

Nat'l Fluid Power Ass'n (1953)
3333 North Mayfair Rd., Milwaukee WI 53222
President and Secretary: James I. Morgan, CAE
Members: 175-200 companies *Staff:* 11-15
Annual Budget: $1-2,000,000 *Tel:* (414) 778-3344
Hist. Note: Companies which have designed, manufactured and nationally marketed a fluid power component for at least two years in the United States.
Publications:
NFPA Membership Directory. a.
NFPA Reporter. m.
Semi-annual Meetings: Spring and Fall

Nat'l Food and Conservation Through Swine (1970)
Fox Run Rd., R.D. 4, Box 397, Sewell NJ 08080
Secretary: Mrs. Ronnie Polen
Members: 500 *Staff:* 1
Annual Budget: under $10,000 *Tel:* (609) 468-5447
Hist. Note: Members are farmers feeding edible food waste to swine.
Annual Meetings: Spring

Nat'l Food and Energy Council (1957)
409 Vandiver West, Suite 202, Columbia MO 65202
Exec. Manager: Kenneth L. McFate
Members: 250 energy suppliers *Staff:* 2-5
Annual Budget: $100-250,000 *Tel:* (314) 875-7155
Hist. Note: Formerly (1957) Inter-Industry Farm Electric Utilization Council, (1962) Farm Electrification Council and (1977) the Food and Energy Council, it assumed its present name in 1982. Electric utilities, agricultural cooperatives and related organizations concerned with assuring sufficient inexpensive electrical energy for food production.
Publication:
FEC News and Notes. bi-m.
Annual Meetings: Nat'l Agri-Lectic Conference

Nat'l Food Brokers Ass'n (1904)
1010 Massachusetts Ave., N.W., Washington DC 20001
President: Charles F. Haywood
Members: 2,500 companies *Staff:* 29
Annual Budget: $2-5,000,000 *Tel:* (202) 789-2844
Publications:
Newsline. bi-w.
FBQ (Food Broker Quarterly). q. adv.
NFBA Directory. a.
Convention Times. a. adv.
Annual Meetings: First week in December/18,000
1987-New Orleans, LA/Dec. 4-9
1988-San Francisco, CA/Dec. 2-7
1989-New Orleans, LA(Tentative)/Dec. 1-6

Nat'l Food Distributors Ass'n (1927)
111 East Wacker Dr., Chicago IL 60601
Managing Director: Arthur H Klawans,
Members: 550-600 *Staff:* 2-5
Annual Budget: $250-500,000 *Tel:* (312) 644-6610
Hist. Note: Independent truck distributors delivering to chains or retail outlets.
Publication:
NFDA Newsletter.
Annual Meetings: Summer/1,500
1987-Nashville, TN(Opryland)/July 25-28
1988-Las Vegas, NV(MGM)/July 26-28

Nat'l Food Processors Ass'n (1907)
1401 New York Ave., N.W., Washington DC 20005
President: Charles J. Carey
Members: 500-600 companies *Staff:* 200
Annual Budget: over $5,000,000 *Tel:* (202) 639-5900
Hist. Note: Founded in 1907 through a merger of the Atlantic State Canners Ass'n and the Western Packers Ass'n. Commercial packers of canned, frozen and dehydrated foods. Established scientific research facilities in 1913, currently located in Dublin, California, Seattle, Washington and at its headquarters in Washington, DC. Acts as liaison for the food industry to regulatory and legislative bodies on scientific and technical issues. The Nat'l Food Laboratory is its wholly owned subsidiary to conduct contract research on a proprietary basis. The Food Processors Institute is its educational and training arm. Formerly (1977) the Nat'l Canners Ass'n. Sponsors the National Food Processors Association Political Action Committee.
Publication:
Information Letter. w.
Annual Meetings: Winter/3,000

Nat'l Food Processors Institute (1973)
Hist. Note: An educational organization established and managed by the National Food Processors Association. Also known as the Food Processors Institute.

Nat'l Football League (1920)
410 Park Ave., New York NY 10022
Commissioner: Alvin Rozelle
Members: 28 teams *Staff:* 40-45
Annual Budget: over $5,000,000 *Tel:* (212) 758-1500
Hist. Note: Founded as the American Professional Football Association on September 17, 1920 in the showroom of the Huppmobile agency in Canton, Ohio with Jim Thorpe as President. Assumed its present name in 1922 and merged with the American Football League on February 1, 1970.

Nat'l Football League Players Ass'n (1970)
2021 L St., N.W., Washington DC 20036
Exec. Director: Gene Upshaw
Members: 1,500 active; 1,500 retired *Staff:* 26-30
Annual Budget: $1-2,000,000 *Tel:* (202) 463-2200
Hist. Note: The result of a merger on January 8, 1970 of the Nat'l Football League Players Ass'n (formed in 1956) and the American Football League Players Ass'n (formed about 1959). Labor union affiliated with AFL/CIO under the umbrella of the Federation of Professional Athletes. Membership: $1,500/yr.
Publications:
The Checkoff. w.
Touchback. m.
The Laudible. m.
Annual Meetings:
1987-Los Angeles, CA/March 25-29

Nat'l Foreign Trade Council (1914)
100 East 42nd St., #910, New York NY 10017
President: Richard W. Roberts
Members: 600-650 *Staff:* 30-35
Annual Budget: $1-2,000,000 *Tel:* (212) 867-5630
Hist. Note: Established in New York City pursuant to a resolution of the First National Foreign Trade Convention in 1914 as a private non-profit organization for the promotion and protection of U.S. international trade and investments.
Publications:
Noticias. w.
Report to Members. q.
Annual Meetings: Fall, in New York, NY

Nat'l Forensic Ass'n (1972)
Dept. of Communication & Theatre Arts, Univ. of Wisconsin, Eau Claire WI 54702
Exec. Secretary: Chirstina Reynolds
Members: 225 colleges *Staff:* 1
Annual Budget: $10-25,000 *Tel:* (715) 836-3305
Hist. Note: Promotes individual speaking. Membersip: $25/yr. (institution).
Publications:
Newsletter. 3/yr.
NFA Journal. semi-a.
Semi-annual Meetings: Spring and Fall
1987-Mankato, MN/April

Nat'l Forest Products Ass'n (1902)
1250 Connecticut Ave., N.W., Washington DC 20036
President: David E. Stahl
Members: 45-50 forest industry ass'ns and companies *Staff:* 70-75

00225 12 05 86 1233

Annual Budget: $2-5,000,000 *Tel:* (202) 463-2700
Hist. Note: A federation of forest products ass'ns and companies. Formerly (1965) Nat'l Lumber Manufacturers Ass'n. Member of the Forest Industries Council. Connected with the Forest Industry Political Action Committee. Concerned with such issues as federal and private land management, wood markets and international trade.
Publications:
In Focus.
Washington Letter.
Congressional Update.
Economics Monthly.
Semi-annual Meetings: May, in Washington, DC, and Fall
1987-San Francisco, CA(Fairmont)/Nov. 8-11

Nat'l Forest Recreation Ass'n (1948)
Rt. 3, Box 210, Flagstaff AZ 86004
President: Gaylord Staveley
Members: 4,500-5,000 *Staff:* 2-5
Annual Budget: $50-100,000 *Tel:* (602) 526-4330
Hist. Note: Owners and operators of recreational and commercial facilities on National Forest, National Park Service and Bureau of Land Management lands, principally in the West.
Publication:
NFRA News. q. adv.
Annual Meetings:
1987-Sacramento, CA/April 1-3

Nat'l Forum for Executive Women
Hist. Note: Ceased operations in 1986.

Nat'l Foundation for Consumer Credit (1942)
8701 Georgia Ave., Suite 507, Silver Spring MD 20910
President: Donald L. Badders
Members: 2-300 credit-counseling services *Staff:* 2-5
Annual Budget: $250-500,000 *Tel:* (301) 589-5600
Hist. Note: Members are non-profit community consumer credit counseling services. Absorbed the Retail Credit Institute of America in 1951.
Publication:
Newsletter. m.
Annual Meetings: Fall

Nat'l Foundry Ass'n
Hist. Note: Merged with Cast Metals Federation to form the Cast Metals Ass'n in April, 1986.

Nat'l Frame Builders Ass'n (1970)
1163 E. Ogden Ave., Suite 705-359, Naperville IL 60540
President: Tom Knight
Members: 300 companies *Staff:* 2
Annual Budget: $100-250,000 *Tel:* (312) 369-4114
Hist. Note: Members are building contractors specializing in post frame construction of agricultural and commercial buildings. Membership: $275/yr. minimum (company).
Publications:
Newsletter. m. adv.
Membership Directory. a. adv.
Annual Meetings: November
1987-Pittsburg, PA

Nat'l Franchise Ass'n Coalition (1975)
Hist. Note: Coalition members are associations of franchise holders liscensed by various fast-food chains, Burger Chef, McDonalds, etc., united to prevent the franchiser from terminating their lease against their will. Defunct, 1983.

Nat'l Fraternal Congress of America (1913)
1300 Iroquois Drive, Suite 260, Naperville IL 60540
Exec. V. President: Raymond A. Klee
Members: 100 societies *Staff:* 6-10
Annual Budget: $500-1,000,000 *Tel:* (312) 355-6633
Hist. Note: Membership open to any fraternal organization which is without capital stock, is carried on solely for the mutual benefit of its members and their beneficiaries, having a lodge system and a representative form of government which provides for the payment of death, sickness or disability benefits. Formed by a merger of the National Fraternal Congress (founded in 1886) and the Associated Fraternities of America (founded in 1901).
Publications:
Statistics of Fraternal Benefit Societies. a.
Manual and Directory. a.
Report of Annual Meeting. a.
Annual Meetings: September/600
1987-Chicago, IL(Hilton & Towers)/Sept. 30-Oct.3
1988-New Orleans, LA(Sheraton)/Sept. 21-24

Nat'l Fraternity of Student Musicians (1927)
808 Rio Grande St., Box 1807, Austin TX 78767
President: Walter Merchant
Members: 115,000 *Staff:* 11-15
Tel: (512) 478-5775
Hist. Note: A division of the American College of Musicians. Affiliated with the Internat'l Piano Guild. Piano students whose teachers are members of the Nat'l Guild of Piano Teachers and who enter sponsored auditions.

Nat'l Free Lance Photographers Ass'n (1962)
Hist. Note: Inactive in 1984.

Nat'l Freight Claim and Security Council of the American Trucking Ass'ns (1936)
2200 Mill Rd., Alexandria VA 22314
Exec. Director: Fred Favor
Members: 500 *Staff:* 2-5
Annual Budget: $100-250,000 *Tel:* (703) 838-1864
Hist. Note: Formerly (1985) the Nat'l Freight Claim Council, an autonomous part of the American Trucking Association. Works to establish uniform standards of loss and damage claims, as well as ajudication of claims.
Publication:
Newsletter. m.
Annual Meetings: Early Summer/200
1987-San Diego, CA(Hyatt)
1988-Miami Beach, FL(Sheraton)
1989-Toronto, Canada(Westin)/July 12-15

Nat'l Freight Claim Council of the American Trucking Ass'n (1936)
Hist. Note: Became the Nat'l Freight Claim and Security Council of the American Trucking Ass'ns in 1985.

Nat'l Freight Transportation Ass'n (1905)
Box 16219, Rocky River OH 44116
Exec. Secy.-Treas.: Walter C. Mayo
Members: 500-550 *Staff:* 2-5
Annual Budget: $100-250,000 *Tel:* (216) 331-6064
Hist. Note: Formerly (1977) Nat'l Freight Traffic Ass'n. A professional organization of executives in the transportation industry.
Semi-annual Meetings: Spring and Fall

Nat'l Frozen Food Ass'n (1945)
Box 398, Hershey PA 17033
President: Nevin B. Montgomery
Members: 1,050 companies *Staff:* 11-15
Annual Budget: $500-1,000,000 *Tel:* (717) 534-1601
Hist. Note: Maintains a Washington Office. Supports the National Frozen Food Association Political Action Committee. Sponsors Nat'l Frozen Food Month.
Publications:
Frozen Food Executive. m. adv.
National Frozen Food Association Directory. a. adv.
Annual Meetings: Fall/3,000
1987-Dallas, TX(Loew's Anatole)/Oct. 11-14
1988-Chicago, IL/Oct. 29-Nov. 2
1989-Atlanta, GA/Oct. 22-25
1990-San Francisco, CA/Nov. 11-14

Nat'l Frozen Pizza Institute (1975)
1764 Old Meadow Lane, Suite 350, McLean VA 22102
Exec. Director: Francis G. Williams
Members: 43 Companies *Staff:* 2-5
Annual Budget: $25-50,000 *Tel:* (703) 821-0770
Hist. Note: Managed by American Frozen Food Institute.

Nat'l Funeral Directors and Morticians Ass'n (1938)
5723 S. Indiana Ave., Chicago IL 60637
Exec. Secretary: Gertrude L. Roberts
Members: 1,900-2,000 *Staff:* 2-5
Annual Budget: $100-250,000 *Tel:* (312) 752-7419
Hist. Note: Membership in respective state association required.
Publications:
Scope Newsletter. q. adv.
Directory. bien. adv.
Annual Meetings: August
1987-Milwaukee, WI(Hyatt Regency)/Aug. 8-13/600

Nat'l Funeral Directors Ass'n (1882)
11121 W. Oklahoma Ave., Milwaukee WI 53227
President: Roy Pfeffer
Members: 15,000 *Staff:* 15-17
Annual Budget: $2-5,000,000 *Tel:* (414) 541-2500
Publications:
The Director. m.
NFDA Report. m.
Annual Meetings:
1987-Salt Lake City, UT(Convention Ctr.)/Oct. 18-22
1988-New Orleans, LA
1989-Baltimore, MD

Nat'l Furniture Traffic Conference (1927)
32 Pleasant St., Gardner MA 01440
Mng. Director and President: Raynard F. Bohman, Jr.
Members: 300 *Staff:* 2-5
Annual Budget: $50-100,000 *Tel:* (617) 632-1913
Hist. Note: Members are furniture manufacturers, wholesalers, warehouses, retailers and makers of allied products. Represents furniture interests before the Interstate Commerce Commission and other rate and classification bodies.
Publications:
The Furniture Transporter. semi-m.
Traffic Newsletter. m.
National Directory of Specialized Furniture Carriers. bi-a.
Annual Meetings: Fall

Nat'l Futures Ass'n (1982)
200 West Madison St., Suite 1600, Chicago IL 60606
President and CEO: Robert K. Wilmouth
Members: 2,800 firms *Staff:* 315
Annual Budget: over $5,000,000 *Tel:* (312) 781-1300
Hist. Note: Registered as a futures association under the Commodity Exchange Act in the fall of 1981 and began operations October 1, 1982 as an industry-wide self-regulatory organization for the futures industry. Members are futures commission merchants, commodity trading advisors, pool operators, introducing brokers, exchanges and associated personnel.
Publications:
Newsletter. q.
Annual Review. a.
Annual Meetings: Fourth Thursday in February
1987-New York, NY/Feb. 26

Nat'l Garden Bureau (1976)
1311 Butterfield Road, Suite 310, Downers Grove IL 60515
Exec. Director: Nona Wolfram-Koivula
Members: 50-60 companies *Staff:* 2-4
Annual Budget: $50-100,000 *Tel:* (312) 963-6999
Hist. Note: Non-profit educational service of the North American vegetable and flower seed industry. Regular membership is limited to members of American Seed Trade Ass'n. Incorporated in 1976 in the District of Columbia. Assists garden writers, broadcasters and teachers in promoting the value of growing vegetables and flowers from seeds.
Publication:
Press Service Sheets. q.
Semi-annual Meetings: In conjunction with the American Seed Trade
Ass'n, midwinter and midsummer.

Nat'l Gas Measurement Ass'n (1965)
Box 35819, Houston TX 77035
Secretary: Ken Kridner
Members: 225-250 *Staff:* 1
Annual Budget: under $10,000 *Tel:* (713) 723-7456
Hist. Note: Members are technical personnel of the gas industry interested in measuring the quantity and quality of natural gas, either as it comes from the ground or is delivered to the consumer.

Nat'l Gasohol Commission (1978)
Hist. Note: Purpose is to gather and disseminate information about fuels made from alcohol extracted from natural matter. Reported in 1983 as defunct.

Nat'l Genealogical Soc. (1903)
4527 17th St. N., Arlington VA 22207
Exec. Director: Margaret M. Redmond
Members: 7,500 *Staff:* 3-6
Annual Budget: $250-500,000 *Tel:* (703) 525-0050
Hist. Note: Established April 24, 1903 at 920 S St., N.W. Washington, DC by Newton L. Collamer and other genealogists. Incorporated as a nonprofit organization under the laws of the District of Columbia in 1904 to collect and preserve genealogical, historical and heraldic data, to inculcate and promote interest in research, to foster careful documentation and promote scholarly writing, to issue publications relating to the field of genealogy. Membership: $30/yr.
Publications:
National Genealogical Society Quarterly. q. adv.
Newsletter. bi-m.
Annual Meetings: Spring
1987-Raleigh, NC(Radisson)/May 13-16

Nat'l Geriatrics Soc. (1953)
212 West Wisconsin Ave., Milwaukee WI 53203
Exec. Director: Thomas J. Bergen
Members: 200 individuals; 70-80 institutions *Staff:* 2-5
Annual Budget: $10-25,000 *Tel:* (414) 272-4130
Hist. Note: Membership includes public, voluntary and proprietary nursing homes and hospitals, homes for the aged, sanitariums, extended care facilities, physicians, nurses, health care administrators and para-medical professionals. The Society is concerned with the advancement of techniques of care for the aged, infirm, chronically ill, handicapped and convalescent. Membership: $35-85/yr. (individual); $50-100/yr. (organization)
Publications:
Newsletter. m.
Nursing Care Requirements in Nursing Homes in States of the Union.
trien.
Annual Meetings: At a University location throughout the U.S., Mexico and Canada

Nat'l Gift and Art Ass'n (1925)
Hist. Note: Dissolved in 1983.

Nat'l Glass Ass'n (1948)
8200 Greensboro Drive, McLean VA 22102
President & CEO: Philip J. James
Members: 2,500 companies *Staff:* 31
Annual Budget: $2-5,000,000 *Tel:* (703) 442-4890
Hist. Note: Formerly the Nat'l Auto & Flat Glass Dealers Ass'n and the Nat'l Glass Dealers Ass'n (until 1984). Incorporated in the State of Michigan in 1948. Reincorporated in the District of Columbia in 1978. Members are architectural and automobile glass manufacturers, wholesalers, fabricators, distributors, installers and related industries such as mirrors, sealants, tools, and material handling equipment.
Publications:
Glass Magazine. m. adv.
The Update. m.
Glass Market Quarterly. q.
Membership Directory. a.
Member Services Catalogue. a.
Annual Meetings: March
1987-Las Vegas, NV

00226 12 05 86 1233

1988-Houston, TX
1989-San Francisco, CA
1990-New Orleans, LA
1991-Orlando, FL

Nat'l Golf Foundation (1936)
1150 South U.S. Hwy. 1, Jupiter FL 33477
Members: 3,000 golf facilities; 1,000 companies *Staff:* 35
Annual Budget: $1-2,000,000 *Tel:* (305) 744-6006
Hist. Note: Members are organizations involved in the game of golf.
Annual Meetings:
1987-October

Nat'l Goose Council (1971)
P.O. Box 267, Sisseton SD 57262-0267
President: Marlin Schiltz
Members: 40-50 individuals, 6-10 companies *Staff:* 2-5
Annual Budget: $10-25,000 *Tel:* (605) 698-7651
Hist. Note: Members are breeders of market geese and their suppliers.
Annual Meetings: Winter, in the Minneapolis/St. Paul area.

Nat'l Governors' Ass'n (1908)
Hall of the States, Suite 250, 444 N. Capitol St., N.W., Washington DC 20001
Exec. Director: Dr. Raymond C. Scheppach
Members: 55 Governors *Staff:* 100
Annual Budget: $2-5,000,000 *Tel:* (202) 624-5300
Hist. Note: Members are Governors of the 50 states and 5 territories--Guam, the Virgin Islands, Puerto Rico, American Samoa, and Northern Marianas. Funded by individual states. Informs members of federal legislation that will have an impact on their constituencies. Attempts collective influence through development of national policy voted on by members. Includes an Office of State Services which offers technical and consultant services, as well as an Office of Research and Development which handles demonstration projects. Formerly (1977) Nat'l Governors' Conference.
Publications:
Governors' Bulletin. w.
Capital Ideas. bi-m.
Governors of the American States. a.
Directory of Staff Assistants to the Governors. a.
Policy Positions. a.
Semi-Annual Meetings: Winter and Summer
1987-Traverse City, MI(Grand Traverse Resort)/July 26-28
1987-Washington, DC(Hyatt Regency)/Feb. 22-24

Nat'l Grain and Feed Ass'n (1896)
500 Folger Bldg., 725 15th St., N.W., Washington DC 20005
Exec. V. President: Rich L. Pennell
Members: 1,300 *Staff:* 11-15
Annual Budget: $500-1,000,000 *Tel:* (202) 783-2024
Hist. Note: Formerly (1970) Grain and Feed Dealers Nat'l Ass'n.
Publications:
Feed and Feeding Digest. m.
National Grain and Feed Association Directory Yearbook. a. adv.
National Newsletter. w.
Annual Meetings: March
1987-Washington, DC

Nat'l Grain Sorghum Producers Ass'n (1985)
Box 350, Abernathy TX 79311-0530
Exec. Director: Elbert Harp
Members: 2,500-3,000 *Staff:* 2-5
Annual Budget: $250-500,000 *Tel:* (806) 298-2543
Hist. Note: Founded as the Grain Sorghum Producers Ass'n in 1955; assumed its present name in 1985. Affiliated with the Texas Grain Sorghum Producers Board and the U.S. Feed Grains Council. Membership: $25/yr. (individual), $100/yr. (company).
Publications:
Grain Sorghum News. m. adv.
Feedfacts.
Annual Meetings: Lubbock, TX(Holiday Inn - Civic Center)/ Feb. 16-18/200

Nat'l Grain Trade Council (1936)
1030 15th St., N.W., Suite 476, Washington DC 20005
President: Robert R. Petersen
Members: 50-60 *Staff:* 2-5
Annual Budget: $50-100,000 *Tel:* (202) 842-0400
Hist. Note: Federated membership of grain exchanges, as well as distributors, exporters and warehousemen.

Nat'l Graphic Arts Dealers Ass'n (1982)
Box 1302, Boca Raton FL 33429
Exec V. President: Robert L. Fitzpatrick
Members: 140 companies *Staff:* 2
Annual Budget: $50-100,000 *Tel:* (305) 391-4934
Hist. Note: Members are independent (not owned by a manufacturer or distributor) local dealers of supplies and equipment to the printing industry. Membership: $450/yr.
Publications:
Dealer Update. m.
The Eagle. bi-m.
Membership Directory. a.
Semi-annual Meetings: Summer and Mid-Winter

Nat'l Greenhouse Manufacturers Ass'n (1958)
Box 567, Pana IL 62557
Exec. Director: Dr. Harold Gray
Members: 70 companies *Staff:* 2
Annual Budget: $25-50,000 *Tel:* (217) 562-2644
Hist. Note: Membership: $400-650/yr.
Semi-annual meetings: Spring and Fall.
1987-Sedona, AZ(Los Abragados)/April 5-8
1987-Kiawah Island, SC/Oct. 17-21

Nat'l Grocers Ass'n (1982)
1825 Samuel Morse Drive, Reston VA 22090
President and C.E.O.: Thomas K. Zaucha
Members: 2,000 *Staff:* 25-30
Annual Budget: $2-5,000,000 *Tel:* (703) 437-5300
Hist. Note: The result of a merger between the National Association of Retail Grocers of the United States (founded in 1893) and the Cooperative Food Distributors of America (founded in 1937). Members are independent retailers and regional wholesalers. Supports the Grocers Political Action Committee.
Publications:
National Grocer.
Bit by Bit.
The N.G.A. Technology Newsletter
Annual Meetings: Winter/6,000

Nat'l Guard Ass'n of the U.S. (1878)
One Massachusetts Ave., N.W., Washington DC 20001
Exec. Director: Ltg. LaVern E. Weber
Members: 40,000-50,000 *Staff:* 35
Annual Budget: $1-2,000,000 *Tel:* (202) 789-0031
Hist. Note: Founded at Richmond, Virginia in 1878. Membership is open to any officer or warrant-officer who serves or has served in the Army or Air Nat'l Guard. Membership Fee: Scaled according to rank.
Publication:
The National Guard. m. adv.
Annual Meetings: September
1987-Portland, OR(Red Lion)
1988-San Antonio, TX(Convention Center)
1989-Detroit, MI
1990-Reno, NV
1991-Honolulu, HI

Nat'l Guild of Catholic Psychiatrists (1950)
1211 Boulevard, Seaside Park NJ 08752
Exec. Secretary: Sr. Anna Polcino, M.D.
Members: 66
Annual Budget: under $10,000 *Tel:* (201) 830-4078
Hist. Note: Regular membership in the Guild is open to Catholic physicians; associate membership open to non-Catholic physicians and other mental health professionals. Regular membership: $40/yr.
Publication:
Bulletin. a. adv.
Annual Meetings: With American Psychiatric Ass'n, usually first Sunday in May
1987-Chicago, IL/May 10/30-40

Nat'l Guild of Community Schools of the Arts (1937)
P.O. Box 8018, Englewood NJ 07631
Exec. Director: Lolita Mayadas
Members: 160 institutions *Staff:* 2-5
Annual Budget: $100-250,000 *Tel:* (201) 871-3337
Hist. Note: Non-profit, non-degree granting schools teaching music, dance, drama and the visual arts incorporated 1954. Membership: $30/year (individual), $75-$400/year (insitution).
Publications:
Employment Opportunities. m.
Guildnotes. m.
Membership Directory. a.
Annual Report.
Annual Meetings:
1987-New York, NY/250

Nat'l Guild of Piano Teachers (1929)
808 Rio Grande St., Box 1807, Austin TX 78767
President: Walter Merchant
Members: 10-11,000 *Staff:* 11-15
Annual Budget: $500-1,000,000 *Tel:* (512) 478-5775
Hist. Note: A division of the American College of Musicians. Professional society of piano teachers and music faculty members. Sponsors national examinations.
Publication:
Piano Guild Notes. bi-m. adv.

Nat'l Guild of Professional Paperhangers (1974)
Box 574, Farmingdale NY 11735
President: Edwin Watzel, Sr.
Members: 475 individuals *Staff:* 1
Annual Budget: $25-50,000 *Tel:* (516) 798-4339
Hist. Note: Founded at Hicksville, NY in 1974, incorporated in Pennsylvania in 1982. Membership: $75/yr. (individual or company).
Publication:
NGPP National News. bi-m. adv.
Annual Meetings: June/150
1987-Williamsburg, VA(Hospitality House)/June 26-20
1988-Boston, MA

Nat'l Gymnastic Judges Ass'n (1969)
1150 Morehead, Ann Arbor MI 48103
Exec. Director: Mike Milidonis
Members: 570
Annual Budget: under $10,000 *Tel:* (313) 662-4472
Hist. Note: Founded in 1969 and incorporated in 1980, the NGJA acts as a service organization, providing technical and educational knowledge, training and certification for gymnastic officials. Affiliated with the U.S. Gymnastics Federation. Membership: $25/yr.
Publications:
Men's Rules Interpretations Book. quadren. adv.
Men's Rules Interpretations Book pdate. a.
NGJA News. q.
Annual Meetings: Fall, with the United States Gynmastics Federation
1987-St. Louis, MO(Adams Mark)/Sept. 25-29/1,200
1988-Chicago, IL/Sept. 23-26
1989-Chicago, IL/Oct. 19-22

Nat'l Hairdressers and Cosmetologists Ass'n
Hist. Note: Became the Nat'l Cosmetology Ass'n in 1986.

Nat'l Hand Embroidery and Novelty Manufacturers Ass'n (1930)
225 West 34th St., New York NY 10122
Exec. Director: Sheldon M. Edelman
Members: 25-30 companies *Staff:* 1
Annual Budget: $10-25,000 *Tel:* (212) 564-2500
Hist. Note: Membership concentrated in New York City. Major activity is labor negotiations with the International Ladies Garment Workers Union.

Nat'l Handbag Ass'n/Nat'l Fashion Accessories Ass'n (1916)
330 Fifth Ave., Suite 205, New York NY 10001
Exec. Director: Harold Sachs
Members: 175-200 *Staff:* 6
Annual Budget: $100-250,000 *Tel:* (212) 947-3424
Hist. Note: Formerly (1966) Nat'l Authority for the Ladies Handbag Industry, NHA constitutes the unification of the handbag and accessories industry. Added the title, Nat'l Fashion Accesories Ass'n, in 1986.

Nat'l Hardwood Lumber Ass'n (1898)
Box 34518, Memphis TN 38184-0518
Exec. Manager: S. Carroll White
Members: 1,225 companies *Staff:* 40
Annual Budget: $2-5,000,000 *Tel:* (901) 377-1818
Hist. Note: Trade association of the hardwood lumber industry. Establishes offical grading rules for hardwood lumber, provides lumber inspection service in the U.S. and Canada and conducts the Hardwood Institute promotion program. Operates school for teaching hardwood lumber grading rules.
Publications:
Newsletter. m.
Year Book. a. adv.
Annual Meetings: Fall/1,500
1987-Washington, DC(Hilton)/Oct. 18-21
1988-New Orleans, LA(Fairmont)/Oct. 15-18
1989-St. Louis, MO(Clarion)/Oct. 16-18
1990-Toronto, Ontario(Royal York)/Oct. 22-24
1991-San Francisco, CA(Fairmont)/Sept. 30-Oct. 2

Nat'l Hay Ass'n (1895)
P.O. Box 1059, Jackson MI 49204
Exec. Secretary: Carol L. Gates
Members: 300-350 *Staff:* 2-5
Annual Budget: $50-100,000 *Tel:* (517) 782-2688
Hist. Note: Represents the interests of both companies and individuals which make up the "hay industry" as it moves hay and straw from surplus to deficit areas. Membership: $200/yr.
Publications:
Hay There. m. adv.
Yearbook and Membership Directory. a. adv.
Annual Meetings: Fall
1987-Fontana, WI(The Abbey on Lake Geneva)/Oct. 8-10/350

Nat'l Health Council (1920)
622 3rd Ave., 34th Fl., New York NY 10017-6765
Exec. V. President: Edward H. Van Ness
Members: 65 nat'l organizations *Staff:* 8
Annual Budget: $500-1,000,000 *Tel:* (212) 972-2700
Hist. Note: A federation of voluntary health agencies, professional societies, business groups, government bodies and other organizations concerned with the nation's health.
Annual Meetings: March

Nat'l Health Lawyers Ass'n (1972)
522 21st St., N.W., Suite 120, Washington DC 20006
Exec. Director: David J. Greenburg
Members: 4,000 *Staff:* 12
Annual Budget: $500-1,000,000 *Tel:* (202) 833-1100
Hist. Note: Private, corporate and institutional lawyers involved with or practicing law in the health care field. Associate Membership available to non-lawyers. Conducts non-partisan educational programs and sponsors research in the interest of both consumers and providers of health care. Membership: $110/yr.
Publications:
Health Law Digest. m.
News Report. m.
Annual Meetings: Spring
1987-New Orleans, LA/May 13-15

00227 12 05 86 1233

Nat'l Hearing Aid Soc. (1951)
20361 Middlebelt Rd., Livonia MI 48152
Exec. V.President: Anthony DiRocco
Members: 4,000 individuals *Staff:* 7
Annual Budget: $500-1,000,000 *Tel:* (313) 478-2610
Hist. Note: Formerly (1966) Soc. of Hearing Aid Audiologists. Professional association of hearing aid specialists. Membership: $150/year.
Publications:
Audecibel. q. adv.
Directory. a.
Annual Meetings: Fall/2,000
1987-New Orleans, LA(Hyatt Regency)/Oct. 7-11

Nat'l Hearing Conservation Ass'n (1976)
900 Des Moines St., Des Moines IA 50309
Exec. Director: Karen Loihl
Members: 285 companies and individuals *Staff:* 3
Tel: (515) 266-2189
Hist. Note: Established and incorporated in Florida. Members are individuals holding advanced academic degrees in disciplines dealing with hearing and hearing loss or a related discipline. Membership: $50/yr. (individual); $195/yr. (company).
Publication:
Newsletter. q. adv.
Annual Meetings: February
1987-Washington, DC/Feb. 26-28

Nat'l Hemophilia Foundation (1948)
110 Greene St., Suite 406, New York NY 10012
Exec. Director: Alan P. Brownstein
Members: 19,000 *Staff:* 15-20
Annual Budget: $500-1,000,000 *Tel:* (212) 219-8180
Hist. Note: Chartered in New York as the Hemophilia Foundation, it assumed is present name in 1956. Member of the Nat'l Health Council and charter member of the World Federation of Hemophilia Organizations.
Publication:
News Notes. q.
Annual Meetings: Fall
1987-Omaha, NE

Nat'l Hereford Hog Record Ass'n (1933)
Route 1, Box 37, Flandreau SD 57028
Secy.-Treas.: Ruby Schrecengost
Members: 150 *Staff:* 1
Annual Budget: under $10,000 *Tel:* (605) 997-2116
Hist. Note: Established and incorporated in Iowa. Maintains registry of pedigrees. Member of the Nat'l Soc. of Livestock Record Ass'ns.
Publications:
Newsletter. a.
Advertiser. q. adv.
Annual Meetings: September
1987-Iola, KS/Sept. 11-12

Nat'l High School Athletic Coaches Ass'n (1965)
P.O. Box 1808, Ocala FL 32678
Exec. Director: Carey E. McDonald
Members: 50,000 *Staff:* 2-6
Annual Budget: $250-500,000 *Tel:* (904) 622-3660
Publication:
National Coach. q. adv.
Annual Meetings: June/1,000
1987-New Orleans, LA(Hyatt Regency)/June 20-26
1988-Cromwell, CT/June 25-July 1
1989-Phoenix, AZ(Hyatt Regency)/June 24-30

Nat'l Hispanic Ass'n of Construction Enterprises (1980)
1625 Eye St., N.W., Washington DC 20006
Nat'l Exec. Director: David J. Morales
Members: 1,500 individuals *Staff:* 7
Annual Budget: $250-500,000 *Tel:* (202) 293-0001
Hist. Note: Formed to promote the utilization of Hispanic construction firms in both the private and public sectors of the construction industry and to provide said firms technical assistance in improving their financial and management capabilities. Membership: $250-1,000/yr.
Publications:
NHACE Newsletter. m. adv.
NHACE Summary. m. adv.
NHACE Industry Bulletin. m. adv.
NHACE Annual Convention Program. a. adv.
Annual Meetings: October

Nat'l Hispanic Psychological Ass'n (1980)
5077 Lankershim Blvd., #400, North Hollywood CA 91601
President: Dr. Floyd H. Martinez
Members: 250
Annual Budget: under $10,000 *Tel:* (818) 508-7800
Hist. Note: Incorporated in Colorado. Professional society organized to foster the development of Hispanic psychology as a science, to lend visibility to Hispanic issues in psychology and to promote the training of Hispanic psychologists.
Annual Meetings: Late summer

Nat'l Hockey League (1917)
1155 Metcalfe St., Montreal Quebec H3B 2W2
President: John A. Ziegler, Jr.
Members: 21 teams *Staff:* 100-110
Annual Budget: over $5,000,000 *Tel:* (514) 871-9220

Nat'l Hockey League Player's Ass'n (1967)
65 Queen St. West, Suite 210, Toronto Ontario M5H 2M5
Exec. Director: R. Alan Eagleson
Members: 500 *Staff:* 2-5
Annual Budget: $2-5,000,000 *Tel:* (416) 868-6574
Hist. Note: Independent labor union established in Montreal in June, 1967. Membership: $1,000/yr.
Annual Meetings: Summer

Nat'l Home Fashions League (1947)
107 World Trade Center, Box 58045, Dallas TX 75258
Exec. Director: Marilyn J. Miller, CAE
Members: 1,800-1,900 *Staff:* 2-5
Annual Budget: $250-500,000 *Tel:* (214) 747-2406
Hist. Note: Executives in the interior furnishings industry.
Publications:
NHFL Who's Who in Interior Furnishings. a. adv.
NHFL Newsbriefs. q.
Annual Meetings: Spring/300
1987-Phoenix, AZ(Arizona Biltmore)/May 21-24

Nat'l Home Furnishings Ass'n (1920)
405 Merchandise Mart Plaza, Chicago IL 60654
Exec. V. President: David K. Murray
Members: 12,000 *Staff:* 40
Annual Budget: $2-5,000,000 *Tel:* (312) 836-0777
Hist. Note: Formerly (1970) Nat'l Retail Furniture Ass'n. Membership consists of retail stores. Supports the Retail Furnishings Task Force as well as the National Home Furnishings Association Political Action Committee.
Publication:
Competitivedge. m. adv.
Biennial Meetings: even years/800.
1988-Las Vegas, NV(Riviera)/Sept. 14-18

Nat'l Home Improvement Council (1956)
Hist. Note: Founded as the Home Improvement Council, Inc., NHIC merged with the National Remodelers Association in 1982 to become the National Association of the Remodeling Industry.

Nat'l Home Study Council (1926)
1601 18th St., N.W., Washington DC 20009
Exec. Director: William A. Fowler
Members: 70-90 home study schools *Staff:* 6-10
Annual Budget: $500-1,000,000 *Tel:* (202) 234-5100
Hist. Note: A federally-recognized accrediting agency and trade association whose members cover 80-90% of all correspondence students.
Publications:
Directory of Accredited Home Study Schools. a.
NHSC News.
NHSC Report.
Annual Meetings: March/200
1987-Ottawa, Canada(Chateau Laurier)/May 10-13
1988-San Diego, CA(del Coronado)

Nat'l HomeCaring Council (1962)
519 C St., N.E., Washington DC 20002
Exec. Director: Bill Halamandaris
Staff: 18
Tel: (202) 547-6586
Hist. Note: A division of the Foundation for Hospice and HomeCare (same address). Agencies, other organizations and individuals concerned with ensuring quality in-home services for children, the aged and others. Conducts programs in the areas of consumer education/protection; the development of basic standards and accreditation for home care services and training programs; technical assistance and legislative

Nat'l Honey Packers and Dealers Ass'n (1952)
Box 8, Edgewater FL 32032
Exec. Secretary: Douglas McGinnis
Members: 30-40 *Staff:* 1
Annual Budget: under $10,000 *Tel:* (904) 428-9027
Annual Meetings: Winter
1987-New Orleans, LA(Hyatt Regency)/Jan. 12-13

Nat'l Hospice Organization (1977)
1901 N. Fort Myer Drive, Suite 307, Arlington VA 22209
President: John J. Mahoney
Members: 3,300 hospice programs and individuals *Staff:* 6-10
Annual Budget: $1-2,000,000 *Tel:* (703) 243-5900
Hist. Note: The hospice concept cares for the terminally ill by centering the caring process in the home and family backed up by in-patient facilities when needed and appropriate.
Publication:
NHO Hospice News. m.
Annual Meetings: Fall

Nat'l Housewares Manufacturers Ass'n (1938)
1324 Merchandise Mart, Chicago IL 60654-1273
Secretary:
Members: 1,200 *Staff:* 6-10
Annual Budget: $2-5,000,000 *Tel:* (312) 644-3333
Hist. Note: Manufacturers served include: kitchen tools and gadgets, cooking and bakeware items, serving and buffet products, glassware and china, bath and closet accessories, small electrical appliances, outdoor products and accessories, decorative accessories. Membership: $100/yr.
Publications:
NHMA Internat'l Housewares Expo Directory. semi-a.
NHMA Manufacturers Market Research Study. a.
NHMA Newsletter. q.
Export Newsletter. 3-4/yr.
Show Directory. a.
Consumer Buying and Purchasing Habits. quadrenn.
Annual Meetings: Chicago, IL(McCormick Place)/January (beginning 1988)
1987-April 5-9
1988-Jan. 10-13
1989-Jan. 8-11
1990-Jan. 7-10
1991-Jan. 6-9
1992-Jan. 12-15

Nat'l Housing Conference (1931)
1126 16th St., N.W., Suite 211, Washington DC 20036
Exec. Dir.: Juliette B. Madison
Members: 1,000 *Staff:* 2-5
Annual Budget: $250-500,000 *Tel:* (202) 223-4844
Hist. Note: Formerly the National Public Housing Conference, members are individuals and organizations pressing for a more effective public housing program.
Publication:
NHC Report from Washington. m.
Annual Meetings: March, in Washington, DC
1987-Loews L'Enfant Plaza
1988-Loews L'Enfant Plaza

Nat'l Humanities Alliance (1981)
1527 New Hampshire Ave., N.W., Washington DC 20036
Exec. Director: Dr. Marsha Nye Adler
Members: 60 ass'ns *Staff:* 1
Annual Budget: $50-100,000 *Tel:* (202) 328-2121
Hist. Note: NAA, made up of associations, organizations and institutes in the humanities, is a representation of the interests in the humanities - scholarly, higher education, museums, libraries, state and local organizations.
Publication:
The Alliance. m.
Annual Meetings: April
1987-Washington, DC(Park Terrace)/April 22/100

Nat'l Hydropower Ass'n (1983)
1133 21st St., N.W., Suite 500, Washington DC 20036
Exec. Director: Elaine Evans
Members: 80-100 companies *Staff:* 1
Annual Budget: $50-100,000 *Tel:* (202) 887-5200
Hist. Note: Members are developers of hydro sites and makers of hydropower equipment. Incorporated in the District of Columbia. Membership: $400/yr. (individual); $3,000/yr. (organization/company)
Publication:
Hydro Update. bi-m.

Nat'l Ice Cream Mix Ass'n (1945)
5610 Crawfordsville Rd., Suite 1104, Indianapolis IN 46224
Exec. Director: Peter Holm
Members: 100-125 companies *Staff:* 1
Annual Budget: $10-25,000 *Tel:* (317) 243-9342
Hist. Note: Suppliers of ice cream mix to fast food service operations.
Semi-Annual meetings: January in Florida, and Fall.

Nat'l Ice Cream Retailers Ass'n (1933)
1429 King Ave., Suite 210, Columbus OH 43212
Exec. Director: Don Buckley
Members: 387 companies *Staff:* 2-5
Annual Budget: $100-250,000 *Tel:* (614) 486-1444
Hist. Note: Established as the Nat'l Ass'n of Retail Ice Cream Manufacturers, it assumed its present name in the mid-1960s. Membership: $95-410/yr. (company, based on number of retail locations the company operates).
Publications:
Bulletin. m.
NICRA Yearbook. a. adv.
Annual Meetings: Fall
1987-Chicago, IL/Sept. 24-26

Nat'l Independent Automobile Dealers Ass'n (1946)
600 E. Las Colinas Blvd., Suite 314, Irving TX 75039
Exec. V. President: Charles F. Tupper, Jr.
Members: 12,000 *Staff:* 4-6
Annual Budget: $500-1,000,000 *Tel:* (214) 556-0044
Hist. Note: Founded as the Nat'l Used Car Dealers Ass'n, it assumed its present name in 1955. Regular membership is open to any person, company or corporation licensed to buy, sell or auction motor vehicles. Regular membership: $40/yr.
Publication:
Used Car Dealer. m. adv.
Semi-Annual Meetings: February and August
1987-Orlando, FL(Peabody)/March 4-7/750
1987-Minneapolis, MN/Aug. 12-15/200
1988-San Diego, CA/Feb./800
1988-Portland, OR/Aug./250

Nat'l Independent Bank Equipment and Systems Ass'n (1973)
1411 Peterson, Park Ridge IL 60068
Exec. Director: Ann M. Walk
Members: 250 dealers and manufacturers *Staff:* 2
Annual Budget: $100-250,000 *Tel:* (312) 825-8419
Hist. Note: Established as the Nat'l Independent Bank Equipment and Suppliers Ass'n, it assumed its present name in 1977. Membership: $325/yr.

00228 12 05 86 1233

Publication:
Newsletter. m.
Annual Meetings: Spring/400
1987-Orlando, FL(Orlando Hyatt)/April 25-28
1988-Colorado Springs, CO(Broadmoor)/April 24-28
1989-New Orleans, LA/April 28-May 2

Nat'l Independent Coal Operators Ass'n (1960)
Box 354, Richlands VA 24641
Exec. V. President: Louis Hunter
Members: 4,500-5,000 small bituminous operators *Staff:* 2-5
Annual Budget: $25-50,000 *Tel:* (703) 963-9011
Hist. Note: Operators of small bituminous, union and non-union coal mines, not owned by other large companies, principally in Appalachia and often engaged in stripping. Membership fee based on tonnage.
Publication:
The National Independent Coal Leader. m. adv.
Annual Meetings: April/4-500
1987-Lexington, KY(Holiday Inn North)/April 23-25

Nat'l Independent Dairy-Foods Ass'n (1982)
321 D St., N.E., Washington DC 20002
Washington Representative: Donald Randall
Members: 200 companies *Staff:* 2-5
Annual Budget: $100-250,000 *Tel:* (202) 543-3838
Hist. Note: The result of a merger on January 1, 1982 between the National Association for Milk Marketing Reform (established in 1974) and the National Independent Dairies Association (established in 1957). Members are private dairy processors. Works for legislative changes to eliminate major "anti-competitive" elements in milk marketing, the major target being cooperatives. Works also for revision of the Federal milk marketing regulations. Has no office other than the above.

Nat'l Independent Nursery Furniture Retailers Ass'n (1975)
Hist. Note: Address unknown in 1985.

Nat'l Independent Poultry and Food Distributors Ass'n (1967)
3000 Old Canton Road, #265, Jackson MS 39216-4213
Exec. Secretary: Thomas Charles Stratton
Members: 225 companies *Staff:* 2-5
Annual Budget: $50-100,000 *Tel:* (601) 981-0513
Publication:
NIPFDA News. m.
Annual Meetings: Spring

Nat'l Independent Truckers Unity Council (1974)
Hist. Note: Address unknown in 1982. Reported defunct.

Nat'l Indian Education Ass'n (1970)
1115 Second Ave. South, Minneapolis MN 55403
President: Karen C. Fenton
Members: 1,700 *Staff:* 2
Annual Budget: $50-100,000 *Tel:* (612) 333-5341
Hist. Note: American Indian teachers. Membership: $35/year (individual).
Publication:
Indian Education. irreg.
Annual Meetings:
1987-Bismarck, ND

Nat'l Indoor Track Meet Directors Ass'n (1955)
Box 342, Cardiff NJ 08232
Secy.-Treas.: Jack Milne
Members: 26 organizations *Staff:* 1
Annual Budget: under $10,000 *Tel:* (609) 645-3310
Hist. Note: Membership: $50/year.
Publication:
Indoor Track Meet Directors Schedule. a.

Nat'l Industrial Belting Ass'n (1887)
1900 Arch St., Philadelphia PA 19103
Exec. V. President: Robert G. Clifton
Members: 160 companies *Staff:* 2-5
Annual Budget: $50-100,000 *Tel:* (215) 564-3484
Hist. Note: Founded as the American Leather Belting Association, it became the National Industrial Leather Association in 1926 and assumed its present name in 1977. Composed of distributors and manufacturers of flat industrial belting used for conveying, elevating and power transmission.
Annual Meetings: Fall
1987-Toronto, Ontario(Westin)/Sept. 27-30

Nat'l Industrial Council - Industrial Relations Group (1907)
1331 Pennsylvania Ave., Suite 1500, North Lobby, Washington DC 20004-1703
Exec. Director: Argyll Campbell
Members: 88 organizations *Staff:* 2-5
Annual Budget: $250-500,000 *Tel:* (202) 637-3052
Hist. Note: A federation of national, state and local manufacturers' associations. Affiliated with Nat'l Ass'n of Manufacturers. Founded as the National Council for Industrial Defense by the National Association of Manufacturers in 1907; became the National Industrial Council in 1918. Composed of two groups of industrial employer associations, each with its own executive director: the Industrial Relations Group and the State Associations Group (see separate entry). Primarily interested in labor relations. Membership: $250-1,200/year (association).
Publications:
Industrial Relations Report. m.
Washington Week. w. to bi-w.
Semi-annual Meetings: Spring and Fall
1987-Captiva Island, FL(South Seas Plantation)/March

Nat'l Industrial Council - State Ass'ns Group (1907)
1331 Pennsylvania Ave., N.W., Suite 1500,orth Lobby, Washington DC 20004-1703
Exec. Director: Barry Buzby
Members: 47 state ass'ns *Staff:* 2-5
Annual Budget: $250-500,000 *Tel:* (202) 637-3054
Hist. Note: The NIC is composed of two groups of industrial employer associations: the State Ass'ns Group and the Industrial Relations Group. For more information the preceding entry, Nat'l Relations Council - Industrial Relations Group.
Annual Meetings: May

Nat'l Industrial Distributors Ass'n (1905)
1900 Arch St., Philadelphia PA 19103
Exec. V. President: Robert G. Clifton
Members: 710 comapnies *Staff:* 6-10
Annual Budget: $250-500,000 *Tel:* (215) 564-3484
Hist. Note: Formerly the National Supply and Machinery Distributors Association, members are wholesalers of industrial equipment and supplies.
Annual Meetings:
1987-Los Angeles, CA/May 10-13
1988-Boston, MA
1989-Chicago, IL

Nat'l Industrial Glove Distributors Ass'n (1959)
310 Riva Road & Holiday Court, Annapolis MD 21401
Exec. Director: E.H. Steinberg
Members: 130 companies *Staff:* 2
Annual Budget: $50-100,000 *Tel:* (301) 266-6032
Publication:
NIGDA Newsletter. m.
Annual Meetings: March
1987-Orlando, FL(Mission Inn)/March 15-18/135

Nat'l Industrial Recreation Ass'n (1941)
Hist. Note: Became the National Employee Services and Recreation Association in 1982.

Nat'l Industrial Sand Ass'n (1936)
900 Spring St., Silver Spring MD 20910
Mng. Director: Vincent P. Ahearn, Jr.
Members: 50 *Staff:* 11-15
Tel: (301) 587-1400
Semi-annual Meetings: Spring in varying locations and Fall, always in
White Sulphur Springs, WV
1987-Napa, CA/May 5-8
1987-Oct. 13-16
1988-Kauai, HI/May 10-13
1988-Oct. 11-14

Nat'l Industrial Transportation League (1907)
1090 Vermont Ave., N.W., Suite 410, Washington DC 20005
Exec. V. President: James E. Bartley
Members: 1,400 *Staff:* 6-10
Annual Budget: $500-1,000,000 *Tel:* (202) 842-3870
Hist. Note: Founded as the National Industrial Traffic League, it assumed its present name in 1982. Presents the viewpoint of the transportation industry to the government. Represents industrial and commercial shippers, boards of trade, chambers of commerce, and similar groups. Its members use all modes of transportation, and directly or indirectly represent an estimated 80 per cent of the commercial traffic that moves in the United States.
Publications:
The Notice. w.
Transportation Policies. a.
Proceedings of Annual Meeting. a.
Annual Meetings: November/1,000
1987-Louisville, KY(Galt House)/Nov. 19-20
1988-Dallas, TX(Loews Anatole)/Nov. 17-18
1989-Open/Nov. 16-17
1990-Boston, MA(Marriott Copley Place)/Nov. 15-16

Nat'l Industrial Workers Union (1955)
768 North Main St., Lima OH 45801
President: Duard Bellamy
Members: 580 *Staff:* 2-5
Annual Budget: $25-50,000 *Tel:* (419) 224-1031
Hist. Note: Independent labor union. Affiliated with the National Federation of Independent Unions.

Nat'l Industrial Zoning Committee (1948)
Box 21398, Columbus OH 43221
Secretary: James M. Jennings
Members: 8 national organizations
Annual Budget: under $10,000 *Tel:* (614) 488-2643
Hist. Note: Concerned with improving the techniques and practices for zoning land for industry as a part of comprehensive community planning.
Annual Meetings: Infrequent

Nat'l Industries for the Blind (1938)
524 Hamburg Turnpike, Wayne NJ 07470
President: George J. Mertz
Members: 106 agencies *Staff:* 90
Annual Budget: $2-5,000,000 *Tel:* (201) 595-9200
Hist. Note: Congress passed the Wagner-O'Day Act in 1938 directing the Federal Government to purchase, under certain conditions, products from agencies employing blind people. To carry out the provisions of the Act, the Committee for Purchase from the Blind was established; it designated Nat'l Industries for the Blind as a central non-profit agency to facilitate equitable distribution of Federal Government contracts to its associated agencies for the blind throughout the country. In 1971, the Act was amended to include the purchase of both products and services from workshops from the blind and provided that workshops for the other severely handicapped participate in the Act, which became known as the Javits-Wagner-O'Day Act.
Publication:
Opportunity. q.
Semi-annual Meetings: Spring and Fall

Nat'l Inholders Ass'n (1978)
Box 588, Sonoma CA 95476
Exec. Director: Charles S. Cushman
Members: 15,000 *Staff:* 10
Annual Budget: $250-500,000 *Tel:* (707) 935-1279
Hist. Note: Formerly (1980) Nat'l Park Inholders Ass'n. Individuals holding property, equity interest, grazing permits, leases cabins, mining claims or real estate in or adjacent to federally managed areas such as national parks, forests, refuges and other reserves. Maintains a Washington representative. Membership: $35/yr.
Publications:
National Inholder News. q.
Congressional Directory. bien.
Inholder Action Guide. bien.
Annual Meetings: Not held

Nat'l Institute for Architectural Education (1894)
30 West 22nd St., New York NY 10010
Exec. Secretary: Lillian Marus
Members: 250-300 *Staff:* 1-2
Annual Budget: $25-50,000 *Tel:* (212) 924-7000
Hist. Note: Established as the Society of Beaux-Arts Architects, it became the Beaux-Arts Institute of Design in 1941 and assumed its present name in 1956.
Annual Meetings: New York City, in December

Nat'l Institute of American Doll Artists (1963)
RR 1, Box 9640, Loomis Hill, Waterbury Center VT 05677
President: Mirren Barrie
Members: 200
Annual Budget: under $10,000 *Tel:* (802) 244-6995
Hist. Note: Professional doll artists creating original dolls. Membership by election: $25/year.
Publications:
Newsletter. q.
Directory.
Yearbook. a. adv.
Annual Meetings:
1987-Boston, MA(Sheraton Boston Hotel & Towers)/Aug. 14-17/200

Nat'l Institute of Building Sciences (1976)
1015 15th St., N.W., Suite 700, Washington DC 20005
President: Gene C. Brewer
Members: 700 *Staff:* 16-20
Annual Budget: $2-5,000,000 *Tel:* (202) 347-5710
Hist. Note: A non-governmental, non-profit organization created by Congress to encourage a more rational building regulatory environment and to facilitate the introduction of new and existing technology into the building process. Membership includes individuals, companies, associations, government bodies and unions.
Publication:
Building Sciences. m.
Annual Meetings: November/200

Nat'l Institute of Ceramic Engineers (1938)
65 Ceramic Dr., Columbus OH 43214
Exec. Director: W. Paul Holbrook
Members: 2,000 *Staff:* 2-5
Annual Budget: $50-100,000 *Tel:* (614) 268-8645
Hist. Note: Professional society of ceramic engineers, dedicated to the development, promotion and advancement of ceramic engineering interests. Founded by the American Ceramic Soc. of which it remains a class. Also affiliated with the American Ass'n of Engineering Socs., the Accreditation Board for Engineering and Technology, the Nat'l Soc. of Professional Engineers and the Nat'l Council of Engineering Examiners. Membership: $8/year. (Applicants must be members of the ACerS and approved for admission.)
Annual Meetings: Spring, with the ACerS
1987-Pittsburgh, PA/April 26-30
1988-Cincinnati, OH/May 1-5

Nat'l Institute of Certified Moving Consultants (1974)
124 South Royal St., Alexandria VA 22314
President: Dr. T. Peter Ruane
Members: 1,000 individuals, 100 companies *Staff:* 2-5
Annual Budget: $100-250,000 *Tel:* (703) 549-6003
Hist. Note: Established by the National Moving and Storage Association as a separate educational membership organization. Awards the CMC (Certified Moving Consultant) designation to those who have passed an exam testing their ability "to give sound moving advice, accurate estimates and coordinate moving services." Membership: $85/yr. (individual), $150/yr.

00229 12 05 86 1233

(company).
Publications:
CMC Membership Directory. a.
Moving Consultants Certification Manual.
Selling and Servicing Office and Industrial Moves.

Nat'l Institute of Credit (1918)
Hist. Note: A non-profit credit educational organization sponsored by the National Association of Credit Management.

Nat'l Institute of Fire Restoration (1968)
Hist. Note: A division of the Ass'n of Specialists in Cleaning and Restoration.

Nat'l Institute of Governmental Purchasing (1944)
115 Hillwood Ave., Falls Church VA 22046
Exec. V. President: Lewis E. Spangler, CPPO
Members: 1,500 *Staff:* 6-10
Annual Budget: $250-500,000 *Tel:* (703) 533-7300
Hist. Note: Members are government buying agencies at local, state and federal level in the U.S. and Canada. Promotes professional development, uniform purchasing laws and procedures. Affiliated with the United States Conference of Mayors and the Institute of Purchasing & Supply of Great Britain. Conducts a two-tier certification program awarding CPPO (Certified Public Purchasing Officer) and PPB (Professional Public Buyer) designations. Conducts seminars in public purchasing. Membership: $150-300/yr. (agency)
Publications:
NIGP Letter Service Bulletin. semi-m.
NIGP Technical Bulletin. semi-m.
NIGP Dictionary of Purchasing Terms. irreg.
NIGP Journal. a. adv.
Annual Meetings: Summer
1987-Kansas City, MO(Hyatt Regency/Conv. Ctr.)/July 25-29
1988-Atlanta, GA
1989-Portland, OR

Nat'l Institute of Independent Colleges and Universities (1976)
Hist. Note: The research arm of the National Association of Independent Colleges and Universities.

Nat'l Institute of Management Counsellors (1954)
Box 193, 45 North Station Plaza, Great Neck NY 11022
Exec. Director: Willard Warren
Members: 200-300 *Staff:* 2-5
Tel: (516) 482-5683

Nat'l Institute of Municipal Law Officers (1935)
1000 Connecticut Ave., N.W., Suite 800, Washington DC 20036
Gen'l Counsel: Charles S. Rhyne
Members: 1,800 cities *Staff:* 11-15
Annual Budget: $1-2,000,000 *Tel:* (202) 466-5424
Hist. Note: Founded by municipal attorneys attending an annual conference of the United States Conference of Mayors in 1935 as an organization of municipalities acting through their chief legal officer. Participates in federal and state cases of nation-wide importance and serves as a source of municipal legal information. Membership Fee: Varies by population.
Publications:
The Municipal Attorney. bi-m.
Municipal Law Docket. bi-m.
Newsletter for Municipal Attorneys.
Municipal Law Journal. m.
Municipal Ordinance Review. bi-m.
Municipal Law Court Decisions. bi-m.
NIMLO Congressional News.
Annual Meetings: Fall/700
1987-Salt Lake City, UT

Nat'l Institute of Oilseed Products (1934)
111 Sutter St., San Francisco CA 94104
Exec. Secretary: Robert L. Moon
Members: 250-275 companies *Staff:* 2-5
Annual Budget: $50-100,000 *Tel:* (415) 392-5718
Hist. Note: Members are importers, dealers and brokers in copra, palm and coconut and other edible oils. The above address is the law firm of Hoffman, Davis and Moon.
Publications:
Trading Rules. a.
Washington Correspondence. w.

Nat'l Institute of Packaging, Handling and Logistic Engineers (1956)
Box 2765, Arlington VA 22202
Chairman, Advisory Board: James A. Russell
Members: 250
Annual Budget: under $10,000 *Tel:* (703) 557-0947
Hist. Note: Originally the DC chapter of the Society of Packaging and Handling Engineers, the Institute became independent in an effort to give more emphasis to the government liaison responsibilities of its members. The majority of its membership still is to be found in the greater metropolitan Washington area. Has no headquarters or paid staff. Membership: $30/yr.
Publication:
Newsletter. m.
Monthly Meetings: 10/year

Nat'l Institute of Pension Administrators (1983)
1700 East Dyer Road, Suite 165, Santa Ana CA 92705
Exec. Director: James A. Kinder
Members: 200 individuals *Staff:* 8
Annual Budget: $100-250,000 *Tel:* (714) 250-8749
Hist. Note: The Institute is responsible for the formation of professional standards and awards the APA (Accredited Pension Administrator) designation by examination and experience.
Publication:
Newsletter. bi-m.

Nat'l Institute of Rug Cleaning (1945)
Hist. Note: A division of the Ass'n of Specialists in Cleaning and Restoration.

Nat'l Institute of Senior Centers (1970)
600 Maryland Ave., S.W., West Wing 100, Washington DC 20024
Coordinator: Robert Cosby
Members: 2,000 *Staff:* 2-5
Annual Budget: $50-100,000 *Tel:* (202) 479-1200
Hist. Note: Originally (1962) the Nat'l Advisory Committee on Senior Centers of the Nat'l Council on the Aging.
Publications:
Senior Center Report. bi-m.
Proceedings. a.
Annual Meetings: With Nat'l Council on the Aging

Nat'l Institute of Steel Detailing (1969)
2506 Gross Point Rd., Evanston IL 60201
Exec. Director: Arthur W. Engle, C.A.M.
Members: 141 *Staff:* 2-5
Annual Budget: $50-100,000 *Tel:* (312) 475-7300
Hist. Note: Steel detailing is the production, from architectural and engineering drawings, of fabrication drawings that can be read by workers in a fabrication shop, where designs for steel skeletons of buildings are created. Founded May 10, 1969 in Houston by thirty-eight detailing firms.
Publication:
The Connection. q.
Annual Meetings: Late Spring
1987-Hawaii/May

Nat'l Institute on Age, Work and Retirement (1967)
Hist. Note: Formerly (1978) Nat'l Institute of Industrial Gerontology. The research arm of the Nat'l Council on the Aging. Not a membership organization.

Nat'l Institute on Park and Grounds Management (1975)
Box 1936, Appleton WI 54913
Exec. Secretary: Erik L. Madisen, Jr.
Members: 1,050 *Staff:* 2-5
Annual Budget: $50-100,000 *Tel:* (414) 733-2301
Hist. Note: Managers of parks, campuses and other large outdoor areas. Seeks to improve grounds management through education and exchange of information. Membership: $50/yr. (individual), $100/yr. (company).
Publications:
Clearing House Newsletter. 10/yr. adv.
Roster (members only). a. adv.
Annual Meetings: Fall or Winter
1987-Tulsa, OK(Excelsior)/Nov. 8-12/550

Nat'l Institutional Food Distributor Associates (1958)
Hist. Note: Became NIFDA, Inc. in 1985.

Nat'l Insulation Certification Institute (1977)
Hist. Note: Defunct July 1, 1982.

Nat'l Insulation Contractors Ass'n (1954)
1025 Vermont Ave., N.W., Suite 410, Washington DC 20005
Exec. V. President: William W. Pitkin
Members: 500 companies *Staff:* 6-10
Annual Budget: $250-500,000 *Tel:* (202) 783-6277
Hist. Note: Formerly (1970) Insulation Distributor-Contractors Nat'l Ass'n. Members are industrial and commercial insulation contractors, manufacturers and distributors.
Publication:
Insulation Outlook. m. adv.
Annual Meetings: April
1987-Marco Island, FL/April 5-8

Nat'l Insurance Ass'n (1921)
2400 South Michigan Ave., Chicago IL 60616
Exec. Director: Clarice M. Hal
Members: 28-30 black-owned companies *Staff:* 2-5
Annual Budget: $250-500,000 *Tel:* (312) 842-5125
Hist. Note: Formerly (1954) Nat'l Negro Insurance Ass'n.

Nat'l Intercollegiate Soccer Officials Ass'n (1964)
131 Moffitt Blvd., Islip NY 11751
President: Richard Jamison
Members: 3,200 *Staff:* 1
Annual Budget: $100-250,000 *Tel:* (516) 277-3878
Hist. Note: Membership: $35/year.
Publication:
Newsletter. 6-8/yr. adv.
Annual Meetings: Winter

1987-Boston, MA(Marriott)
1988-Washington, DC(Hyatt)
1989-Cincinnati, OH(Hyatt)
1990-Philadelphia, PA

Nat'l Interfraternity Conference (1909)
3901 West 86th St., Suite 280, Indianapolis IN 46268
Exec. Director: Jonathan J. Brant
Members: 59 fraternities *Staff:* 2-5
Annual Budget: $100-250,000 *Tel:* (317) 872-1112
Hist. Note: An association of men's national social fraternities whose members convened originally November 27, 1909 at the University Club in New York City.
Publications:
Campus Commentary.
Directory of Deans and Greek Advisors. a.
Foundation Forum. q.
Annual Meetings: Always week after Thanksgiving.

Nat'l Interstate Council of State Boards of Cosmetology (1936)
Box 11390, Capitol Station, Columbia SC 29211
General Counsel: O. Wayne Corley
Members: 50-55 boards, 200-250 individuals
Annual Budget: $50-100,000 *Tel:* (803) 799-9800
Hist. Note: Merger (1956) of Nat'l Council of State Boards of Cosmetology and Interstate Council of State Boards of Cosmetology. Persons commissioned by state governments to administer cosmetology laws and examine applicants for cosmetology licenses.
Publications:
NIC Bulletin. bi-m.
NIC Directory. a.
Annual Meetings:
1987-Rapid City, SD/Aug. 22-26

Nat'l Intravenous Therapy Ass'n (1973)
87 Blanchard Road, Cambridge MA 02138
Exec. Director: Mary Larkin, CRNI
Members: 4,000 *Staff:* 10
Annual Budget: $500-1,000,000 *Tel:* (617) 576-1282
Hist. Note: Membership consists primarily of Registered Nurses involved in the clinical practice of intravenous therapies. Membership: $55/yr.
Publications:
NITA Journal. bi-m. adv.
NITA Update. bi-m.
Health Care Decisions. semi-a.
CRNI News. semi-a.
Annual Meetings: Spring
1987-Nashville, TN(Opryland)/May 9-14/1,800
1988-San Diego, CA(Town & Country)/May 7-12/2,000
1989-Miami, FL(Fountainbleau Hilton)/May 4-11/2,200
1990-Undecided/2,400
1991-Miami, FL(Fontainbleau Hilton)/May 2-9/2,600

Nat'l Investor Relations Institute (1969)
1730 M St., N.W., Suite 806, Washington DC 20036
President: Louis M. Thompson, Jr.
Members: 1,850 *Staff:* 6
Annual Budget: $500-1,000,000 *Tel:* (202) 861-0630
Hist. Note: A professional association of corporate officers and investor relations consultants. Membership: $275/yr.
Publications:
Directory of Analyst Societies, Splinter Groups, Stockholders Clubs.
a.
NIRI Membership Directory. a.
Legislative Bulletin. irreg.
Investor Relations Resource Guide. a.
Newsletter. m.
Semi-annual Meetings: Spring and Fall
1987-Orlando, FL(Hyatt Grand Cypress)/June/400
1987-New York, NY/Nov./400
1988-San Diego, CA/May/425
1988-New York, NY/Nov./425

Nat'l Juice Products Ass'n (1957)
Box 1531, 215 Madison St., Tampa FL 33601
Secy. & General Counsel: David C.G. Kerr
Members: 84 companies; 45 associates *Staff:* 2
Annual Budget: $100-250,000 *Tel:* (813) 229-1089
Hist. Note: Established by a group of citrus juice processors in Dallas, TX in Jan., 1957 as the Nat'l Ass'n of Citrus Juice Processors and incorporated in Florida in June of that year; became the Nat'l Orange Juice Ass'n in 1960; and assumed its present name in 1966. Its objectives are the promulgation of uniform standards and uniform advertising and labeling practices; the promotion of high standards of quality; liaison between Federal and state regulatory agencies; and promotion of research, technology and distribution of chilled fruit juices. Membership: $2,000/yr.
Annual Meetings: Spring/350-450
1987-Napa Valley, CA(Silverado)/June 3-7
1988-White Sulphur Springs, WV(Greenbrier)/May 25-29
1989-West Coast
1990-Hilton Head, SC(Intercontinental)/April 18-22

Nat'l Juvenile Detention Ass'n (1971)
P.O. Box 70243, Louisville KY 40270
Exec. Director: Earl Dunlap
Members: 5-600 *Staff:* 3
Annual Budget: $25-50,000 *Tel:* (502) 425-6176
Hist. Note: An affiliate of the Amercian Correctional Ass'n. Membership: $25/yr. (Administrator); $12/yr. (Supervisor); $6/yr. (Line Staff).

00230 12 05 86 1233

Publications:
NJDA News. q. adv.
Rader Papers. semi-a. adv.
Directory.
Semi-annual Meetings: March and October
1987-Pittsburgh, PA/March and Orlando, FL/Oct.
1988-Atlantic City, NJ/March and Illinois/Oct.

Nat'l Kerosene Heater Ass'n (1981)
First American Center, Suite 15, Nashville TN 37238
Exec. V. President: J. Thomas Smith
Members: 65 companies *Staff:* 2-5
Annual Budget: $250-500,000 *Tel:* (615) 254-1961
Hist. Note: Members are individuals, partnerships and corporations involved in the manufacturing and marketing of kerosene heaters.
Publication:
Bulletins. irreg.
Annual Meetings: August

Nat'l Kidney Foundation (1950)
2 Park Ave., New York NY 10016
Exec. Director: John Davis
Staff: 27
Annual Budget: over $5,000,000 *Tel:* (212) 889-2210
Hist. Note: An organization supporting research and public information on the diagnosis and treatment of diseases of the kidney. Formerly (1958) Nat'l Nephrosis Foundation and (1964) Nat'l Kidney Disease Foundation.
Publications:
The Kidney. m.
Kidney '87. q.
Council of Nephrology Social Workers Newsletter. q.
Council on Renal Nutrition Newsletter. q.
Council on Renal Nutrition Quarterly. q.
Council of Nephrology Nurses and Technicians Action Update. q.
American Journal of Kidney Diseases. q.
Perspectives: Journal of the Council of Nephrology Social Workers. a.
Annual Meetings: Late Fall

Nat'l Kitchen and Bath Ass'n (1963)
124 Main St., Hackettstown NJ 07840
Exec. Director: Francis J. Jones
Members: 2,500 companies *Staff:* 15-20
Annual Budget: $1-2,000,000 *Tel:* (201) 852-0033
Hist. Note: Kitchen equipment manufacturers, suppliers, wholesalers, retail dealers, distributors and designers. Awards the designation Certified Kitchen Designer (CKD). Formerly (until 1982) the American Institute of Kitchen Dealers.
Publications:
Directory. a.
Newsletter. m.
Annual Meetings:
1987-Atlanta, GA/May 3-6/22,000

Nat'l Kitchen Cabinet Ass'n (1955)
P.O. Box 6830, Falls Church VA 22046
V. President: C. Richard Titus
Members: 277 *Staff:* 5
Annual Budget: $250-500,000 *Tel:* (703) 237-7580
Hist. Note: Formerly (1962) Nat'l Institute of Wood Kitchen Cabinets. Members are manufacturers of assembled prefinished kitchen cabinets.
Annual Meetings: Spring

Nat'l Knitwear and Sportswear Ass'n (1918)
386 Park Ave. South, New York NY 10016
Exec. Director: Seth M. Bodner
Members: 900 *Staff:* 25-30
Annual Budget: $100-250,000 *Tel:* (212) 683-7520
Hist. Note: Until 1980 known as the National Knitted Outerwear Association.
Publications:
Knitting Times. w. adv.
Apparel World. w. adv.
Knitting Times Yearbook. a. adv.
Apparel World Buyers Guide.
Annual Meetings: November

Nat'l Knitwear Manufacturers Ass'n (1866)
365 South St., Morristown NJ 07960
President: Robert E. Blanchard
Members: 100-125 *Staff:* 2-5
Annual Budget: $100-250,000 *Tel:* (201) 326-1650
Hist. Note: Manufacturers of underwear, nightwear, knit shirts, fleecewear and allied products. Established in 1866 "to secure (in questions where our interests are concerned) the advantages which will always accrue to united action over individual effort." Formerly (1934) Nat'l Ass'n of Knit Goods Manufacturers and (1968) the Underwear Institute.
Annual Meetings: Spring, with Industry Leaders Meeting in Fall
1987-Hilton Head Island, SC(Mariner's Inn)/April 9-12/225-250
1987-Carefree, AZ(The Boulders)/Nov. 5-8
1988-White Sulphur Springs, WV(Greenbrier)/May 5-8/225-250
1988-Ponte Vedra, FL(Ponte Vedra Inn & Club)/Oct. 13-16

Nat'l Kraut Packers Ass'n (1907)
Hist. Note: Reported inactive in 1984.

Nat'l Labor Relations Board Professional Ass'n (1962)
1717 Pennsylvania Ave., N.W., Washington DC 20006
Secy.-Treas.: Dennis Walsh
Members: 200
Annual Budget: $10-25,000 *Tel:* (202) 254-9084
Hist. Note: Independent union of lawyers working for the N.L.R.B. in Washington. In additon to representing attorneys, the association also represents law clerks and law students employed by the Board's Division of Administrative Law Judges. Has no headquarters or paid staff. Officers are elected annually. Membership: $52/year.
Annual Meetings: January

Nat'l Labor Relations Board Union (1963)
c/o NLRB Region 30, H.S. Reuss Fed.Plaza,10 W. Wisconsin Ave., Suite 1240, Milwaukee WI 53203
President: Irving E. Gottschalk
Members: 1,300-1,400
Annual Budget: $50-100,000 *Tel:* (414) 291-3871
Hist. Note: Independent labor union of N.L.R.B. employees. Has no paid staff.
Publication:
NLRBU Remedy. bi-m.
Biennial meetings: Uneven years in Fall

Nat'l Lamb Feeders Ass'n (1950)
Box 238, Bristol IL 60512
President: Howard E. Wyman
Members: 800 *Staff:* 1
Annual Budget: $25-50,000 *Tel:* (312) 553-5512
Publication:
Newsletter. m.
Semi-annual meetings: Winter and Late Summer
1987-Chicago, IL(Marriott), Feb. 1-3/125

Nat'l Landscape Ass'n (1939)
1250 Eye St., N.W., Suite 500, Washington DC 20005
Exec. V. President: Robert F. Lederer, CAE
Members: 5-600 landscaping companies. *Staff:* 2-5
Annual Budget: $25-50,000 *Tel:* (202) 789-2900
Hist. Note: Formerly (1972) Nat'l Landscape Nurserymen's Ass'n, Inc. Affiliated with American Ass'n of Nurserymen.
Publication:
News Letter. m.
Annual Meetings: February, in Louisville.

Nat'l Lawn and Garden Distributors Ass'n (1969)
1900 Arch St., Philadelphia PA 19103
Exec. Director: William L. Robinson
Members: 150-200 *Staff:* 2-5
Annual Budget: $25-50,000 *Tel:* (215) 564-3484
Hist. Note: Members are wholesale distributors of lawn and garden supplies; associate members are makers of such and affiliates are sales representatives. Until 1979 known as the Lawn and Garden Distributors Association.
Publication:
Membership Directory. a.
Annual Meetings: September

Nat'l Lawyers Guild (1937)
853 Broadway, Suite 1705, New York NY 10003
Exec. Director: Barbara Dudley
Members: 8,000 *Staff:* 2-5
Annual Budget: $100-250,000 *Tel:* (212) 260-1360
Hist. Note: Funded as a progressive, anti-racist alternative to the American Bar Association. The Guild is open to lawyers, law students, legal workers and jailhouse lawyers, supporting the movement for social change in the U.S. Progressive membership fee schedule.
Publications:
Guild Notes. q.
Guild Practitioner. q.
Annual Meetings: June
1987-Washington, DC

Nat'l Lead Burning Ass'n (1945)
Box 200, Pratt Station, Brooklyn NY 11205
Secy.-Treas.: Francis L. Kiernan
Members: 6 companies *Staff:* 1
Annual Budget: under $10,000 *Tel:* (718) 855-1964
Hist. Note: Fabricators of lead-lined equipment for handling corrosive chemicals and radiation shielding.
Annual Meetings: New York, NY in Spring

Nat'l League for Nursing (1952)
10 Columbus Circle, New York NY 10019
Exec. Director: Pamela Maraldo, RN, Ph.D.
Members: 17,000 individuals, 1,900 organizations *Staff:* 160
Annual Budget: over $5,000,000 *Tel:* (212) 582-1022
Hist. Note: Founded and incorporated in Washington, DC in 1952 as a merger of the Nat'l League of Nursing Education, Nat'l Organization for Public Health Nursing, Ass'n of Collegiate Schools of Nursing, Joint Committee on Practical Nurses and Auxiliary Workers in Nursing, Services, Joint Committee on Careers in Nursing, Nat'l Committee for the Improvement of Nursing Services, and the Nat'l Nursing Accrediting Service.
Publication:
Nursing and Health Care. m. adv.
Biennial Meetings: Odd years/4,000
1987-Washington, DC/June 14-18

Nat'l League of American Pen Women (1897)
1300 17th St., N.W., Washington DC 20036
Secretary: Laura Crowe
Members: 6,000 *Staff:* 2-5
Annual Budget: $100-250,000 *Tel:* (202) 785-1997
Hist. Note: Organized April 26, 1897 in Washington, DC as the League of American Pen Women; assumed its present name and was incorporated in 1926. Promotes the development of the creative talents of professional women artists, writers, dramatists, lecturers and composers. Membership: $25/yr.
Publication:
The Pen Women. 9/yr. adv.
Biennial Meetings: Even years

Nat'l League of Cities (1924)
1301 Pennsylvania Ave., N.W., 6th Floor, Washington DC 20004
Exec. Director: Alan Beals
Members: 1,300 municipalities & 49 state municipal leagues
Staff: 60-65
Annual Budget: over $5,000,000 *Tel:* (202) 626-3000
Hist. Note: Known until 1964 as the American Municipal Association, the National League of Cities was founded in 1924 by reform-minded state municipal leagues to represent the interests of its members to the federal and state governments. Has an annual budget of $6.4 million. Membership: $556-46,275/year (city).
Publications:
Nation's Cities Weekly. w. adv.
Urban Affairs Abstracts. w.
Annual Meetings: Fall-Annual Congress,Business Meeting,and Exhibition
Winter-Annual Congressional Conference
1987-Philadelphia, PA/Dec. 5-9
1988-Las Vegas, NV/Nov. 26-30

Nat'l League of Postmasters of the U.S. (1904)
1023 North Royal St., Alexandria VA 22314-1569
President: Ron Swisher
Members: 22,000 *Staff:* 140
Annual Budget: $2-5,000,000 *Tel:* (703) 548-5922
Hist. Note: Organized in Wasington, DC December 13-15, 1887 by about 200 Third and Fourth Class Postmasters to represent the interests of professional postmasters. Membership: Amount varies according to grade of Postmaster.
Publications:
Postmasters Advocate. bi-w.
Postmasters Advocate. m. adv.
Semi-Annual Meetings: Summer/1,400-2,000 and Winter/400
1987-Houston, TX(Hyatt Regency)/Aug. 9-14
1988-St. Louis, MO(Adams Mark)/Aug. 7-13
1989-Atlanta, GA(Marriott Marquis)
1990-Anaheim, CA(Hilton)

Nat'l League of Professional Baseball Clubs (1876)
350 Park Ave., 18th Floor, New York NY 10022
President: A. Bartlett Giamatti
Members: 12 clubs *Staff:* 6-10
Annual Budget: $2-5,000,000 *Tel:* (212) 371-7300
Hist. Note: Established February 2, 1876 at the Grand Central Hotel in New York City.

Nat'l Leased Housing Ass'n (1972)
2300 M St., N.W., Suite 260, Washington DC 20037
Exec. Director: Janet S. Charlton
Members: 750-800 companies and individuals
Annual Budget: $250-500,000 *Tel:* (202) 785-8888
Hist. Note: Founded by developers and financers of federally funded housing under the government's Section 8 rent subsidy program for the poor. With the demise of Section 8 new construction/substantial rehabilita- tion program, NLHA has broadened its purview to all government related rental housing programs.
Publication:
NLHA Bulletin. m.
Semi-Annual Meetings: January and June

Nat'l Legal Aid and Defender Ass'n (1911)
8th Floor, 1625 K St., N.W., Washington DC 20006
Exec. Director: Clinton Lyons
Members: 5,000 *Staff:* 20
Annual Budget: $500-1,000,000 *Tel:* (202) 452-0620
Hist. Note: Organized in 1911 by fifteen legal assistance programs as the Nat'l Alliance of Legal Aid Socs., it became the Nat'l Ass'n of Legal Aid Organizations in 1949 and assumed its present name in 1958. The only private, non-profit organization devoting all its resources to the support and development of quality legal assistance to the poor. Membership: $50/yr. (individual); organizational fee based on a percentage of budget.
Publications:
Cornerstone. 5/yr. adv.
Directory of Legal Aid and Defender Services. bi-a.
Annual Meetings: Fall/800
1987-Miami, FL(Fontainebleau Hilton)/Dec. 1-4/700
1988-San Diego, CA

Nat'l Librarians Ass'n (1975)
Box 586, Alma MI 48801
Director: P. Dollard
Members: 300 *Staff:* 1
Annual Budget: under $10,000 *Tel:* (517) 463-7227
Hist. Note: Formed by 5 librarians who felt the need for a professional librarians ass'n separate from those organizations already established. Has no paid staff.

00231 12 05 86 1233

Publication:
Newsletter. q. adv.
Annual Meetings: Held with American Library Ass'n in June.

Nat'l Licensed Beverage Ass'n (1950)
309 North Washington St., Alexandria VA 22314
Exec. Director: Gerald E. Murphy
Members: 30-31,000 *Staff:* 2-5
Annual Budget: $250-500,000 *Tel:* (703) 683-6633
Publication:
NLBA News. bi-m. adv.
Annual Meetings: Fall
1987-Las Vegas, NV

Nat'l Lime Ass'n (1902)
3601 N. Fairfax Drive, Arlington VA 22201
Exec. Director: Thomas L. Potter
Members: 35-45 *Staff:* 6-10
Annual Budget: $500-1,000,000 *Tel:* (703) 243-5463
Hist. Note: Members are manfacturers of quicklime and hydrated lime for environmental, industrial, construction, and other purposes.
Publication:
Lime-Lites. m.
Semi-annual Meetings: Spring and Fall

Nat'l Limestone Institute (1960)
Hist. Note: Merged with the Nat'l Crushed Stone Ass'n to become the Nat'l Stone Ass'n in 1985.
Publication:
Limestone. q. adv.
Annual Meetings: Washington, in January at the Capital Hilton

Nat'l Lincoln Sheep Breeders Ass'n (1889)
R.R. #6, Box 24, Decatur IL 62521
Secretary: Teresa M. Kruse
Members: 75 breeders *Staff:* 1
Annual Budget: under $10,000 *Tel:* (217) 864-3601
Hist. Note: Breeders and fanciers of Lincoln sheep. Membership: $4/yr. plus $10 initiation fee.
Biennial Meetings:

Nat'l Liquor Stores Ass'n (1934)
5101 River Road, Suite 108, Bethesda MD 20816
Exec. Director: John B. Burcham, Jr.
Members: 11,000-12,000 *Staff:* 2-5
Annual Budget: $100-250,000 *Tel:* (301) 656-1494
Hist. Note: Formerly National Retail Liquor Package Stores Association.
Publication:
News and Views. q.
Annual Meetings: Spring

Nat'l Live Stock and Meat Board (1922)
444 North Michigan Ave., Chicago IL 60611
President: John L. Huston
Members: 28 organizations *Staff:* 55-60
Annual Budget: over $5,000,000 *Tel:* (312) 467-5520
Hist. Note: Meat Board was formed to protect and increase demand for beef, pork, lamb, veal and processed meat products through consumer marketing programs on behalf of the livestock and meat industry. Financed through a check-off system - a fixed amount is deducted from the livestock producers' receipts when they sell their cattle, hogs and lambs. Members are national and regional livestock and meat industry organizations and state beef, pork and lamb councils. Has an annual budget of $13.3 million.
Publications:
Food and Nutrition News. 5/yr.
Meat Board Reports. m.
Annual Meetings: August
1987-Portland, OR(Red Lion Inn Lloyd Center)/Aug. 23-25/400

Nat'l Live Stock Producers Ass'n (1922)
307 Livestock Exchange Bldg., Denver CO 80216
Exec. V. President: Darrell D. Hipes
Members: 200-250,000 *Staff:* 2-5
Annual Budget: $250-500,000 *Tel:* (303) 296-1077
Hist. Note: Formerly (1943) Nat'l Live Stock Marketing Ass'n. A Federation of cooperative live stock marketing agencies and regional credit corporations.
Annual Meetings: Fourth Tuesday in March.

Nat'l Livestock Exchange (1888)
c/o Burnett-Carter Co., Box 552, Memphis TN 38101
President: Jim Carter
Members: 5 stockyards *Staff:* 1
Annual Budget: under $10,000 *Tel:* (901) 948-4322
Hist. Note: Stockyards at terminal livestock markets throughout the country.
Publication:
NLE Report. bi-m.
Semi-annual Meetings: Spring and Fall

Nat'l Locksmith Suppliers Ass'n (1950)
1900 Arch St., Philadelphia PA 19103
Exec. Director: Patricia A. Lilly
Members: 160 *Staff:* 3
Annual Budget: $100-250,000 *Tel:* (215) 564-3484
Annual Meetings: April/May
1987-Orlando, FL(Hotel Royal Plaza)/May 2-6/300

Nat'l LP-Gas Ass'n (1931)
1301 W. 22nd St., Oak Brook IL 60521
Exec. V. President: J. D. Capps
Members: 4-5,000 *Staff:* 35-40
Annual Budget: $1-2,000,000 *Tel:* (312) 573-4800
Hist. Note: Producers and distributors of liquefied petroleum gas and manufacturers of equipment for its use. Formed by a merger of the Nat'l Liquified Petroleum Gas Ass'n and the Nat'l LP Gas Council. Supports the Propane Industry Political Action Committee as well as the National LP-Gas Association Political Action Committee. Maintains a Washington, DC area office.
Publication:
Newsletter. w.
Annual Meetings: Spring/3,000
1987-New Orleans, LA(Marriott-Sheraton Hotels)/May 31-June 3
1988-Baltimore, MD(Convention Center)/May 22-25
1989-Las Vegas, NV(Bally's Las Vegas Hotel)/May 14-17
1990-Nashville, TN(Opryland Hotel)/May 6-9

Nat'l Lubricating Grease Institute (1933)
4635 Wyandotte St., Kansas City MO 64112
General Manager: Edward J. Palecki
Members: 200-225 companies *Staff:* 2-5
Annual Budget: $100-250,000 *Tel:* (816) 931-9480
Hist. Note: Incorporated as the Nat'l Ass'n of Lubricating Grease Manufacturers. Assumed its present name in 1937. Members are companies who manufacture and market all types of lubricating greases and research and educational groups whose interests are primarily technical.
Publication:
NLGI Spokesman. m. adv.
Annual Meetings: Fall
1987-Toronto, Ontario/Oct. 25-28

Nat'l Luggage Dealers Ass'n (1925)
350 Fifth Ave., Suite 814, New York NY 10118
Exec. Director: M. Howard Kaplan
Members: 125-150 *Staff:* 7
Annual Budget: $1-2,000,000 *Tel:* (212) 947-8080
Hist. Note: Members are retailers of luggage, leather goods, gifts and handbags. Membership fee based on retail volume.
Semi-annual Meetings: March and July
1987-Newport Beach, CA/March/400
1987-New York, NY(Sheraton Centre)/July/600

Nat'l Luggage Dealers Ass'n
Hist. Note: See NLDA Associates.

Nat'l Lumber and Building Material Dealers Ass'n (1916)
40 Ivy St., S.E., Washington DC 20003
Exec. V. President: Harlan Hummel
Members: 15,000 dealers and manufacturers *Staff:* 6-10
Annual Budget: $250-500,000 *Tel:* (202) 547-2230
Hist. Note: Formerly the National Retail Lumber Dealers Association, it absorbed the Lumber Dealers Research Council (founded in 1966). Supports the Lumber Dealers Political Action Committee - LUDPAC.
Publications:
Capitol Comments. m.
Building Material Retailer. m. adv.
Annual Meetings: Fall
1987-Boston, MA(Marriott Copley Place)/Oct. 14-18
1988-Palm Springs, CA(The Spa & Marquis)/Oct. 15-19
1989-Orlando, FL(Marriott World Center)/Sept. 12-17
1990-Colorado Springs, CO(Broadmoor)/Nov. 4-8

Nat'l Lumber Exporters Ass'n (1900)
c/o Nat'l Forest Products Ass'n, 1250 Connecticut Ave., Suite 200, Washington DC 20036
Exec. Director: John V. Ward
Members: 30-40 *Staff:* 2-5
Annual Budget: $25-50,000 *Tel:* (202) 463-2700
Hist. Note: Managed by staff of Southern Hardwood Lumber Manufacturers Ass'n. NLEA's sole purpose is to help American companies export more hardwood lumber, logs, dimension and other products. Membership: $500-2,500/yr. (based on export volume).

Nat'l Machine Tool Builders' Ass'n (1902)
7901 Westpark Dr., McLean VA 22102-4269
President: James A. Gray
Members: 300 companies *Staff:* 65
Annual Budget: over $5,000,000 *Tel:* (703) 893-2900
Hist. Note: Supports the Machine-Tool Political Action Committee. Has an annual budget of 10.1 million.
Publications:
Production. m. adv.
Directories of Machine Tools. a.
Economic Handbook of Machine Tool Industry. a.
Semi-Annual Meetings: Spring and Fall
1987-Palm Beach, FL(Breakers)/April 8-11
1987-Rancho Mirage, CA(Rancho Las Palmas)/Oct. 21-25
1988-Naples, FL(Ritz-Carlton)/April 6-9
1988-Chicago, IL(McCormick Place)/Sept. 7-15
1988-Monterey, CA(Hyatt Regency)/Nov. 9-12

Nat'l Mail Order Ass'n (1972)
5818 Venice Blvd., Los Angeles CA 90019
Chairman: Paul Muchnick
Tel: (213) 934-7986
Hist. Note: Mail order marketers. Membership: $42/yr.
Publications:
Mail Order Digest. m.
Washington Newsletter. m.

Nat'l Male Nurse Ass'n (1971)
Hist. Note: Became the American Assembly for Men in Nursing in 1982.

Nat'l Management Ass'n (1925)
2210 Arbor Boulevard, Dayton OH 45439
President, C.E.O.: Ronald E. Leigh
Members: 74,000 *Staff:* 25-30
Annual Budget: $1-2,000,000 *Tel:* (513) 294-0421
Hist. Note: Formerly (1956) Nat'l Ass'n of Foremen. Members are middle level and supervisory management personnel united to professionalize management and promote American competitive enterprise.
Publication:
Manage. q.
Annual Meetings:
1988-Denver, CO
Fall
1987-San Diego, CA
1988-Demver, CO

Nat'l Manufactured Housing Federation (1977)
1015 15th St., N.W., Suite 1240, Washington DC 20005
President: Daniel Gilligan
Members: 45 state ass'ns *Staff:* 2-5
Annual Budget: $100-250,000 *Tel:* (202) 789-8690
Hist. Note: A federation of state associations of mobile home manufacturers, retailers and park owners. Sponsors and supports the National Manufactured Housing Federation Federal Political Action Committee.
Publication:
Focus Newsletter. bi-w.
Annual Meetings:
1987-Washington, DC/March 23-24

Nat'l Manufactured Housing Finance Ass'n (1979)
1350 New York Ave., N.W., Suite 800, Washington DC 20005
Secretary: James A. Brodsky
Members: 25-30 companies *Staff:* 2-5
Annual Budget: $50-100,000 *Tel:* (202) 628-2009
Hist. Note: Members are primarily lenders who finance the purchase of manufactired homes, mainly through federal programs.
Publication:
Newsletter. irreg.
Semi-annual Meetings: April and October

Nat'l Marina Manufacturers Consortium (1986)
Box 6040, Macomb IL 61455
Exec. Director: Dr. Douglass G. Norvell
Members: 5 companies; 11 individuals *Staff:* 2
Annual Budget: under $10,000 *Tel:* (309) 833-1117
Hist. Note: The purpose of the Consortium is to provide information to the public on marinas. Membership: $25/yr. (individual), $100/yr. (company).
Publication:
Newsletter. m.
Annual Meetings: Miami, FL/TBA

Nat'l Marine Bankers Ass'n (1979)
401 N. Michigan Ave., Suite 2950, Chicago IL 60611
Exec. Director: Gregory Proteau
Members: 150 companies *Staff:* 0
Annual Budget: $25-50,000 *Tel:* (312) 836-4747
Hist. Note: Any bank, savings institution or credit union which holds marine loans directly in its portfolio is eligible for membership. Membership: $200/yr.
Publication:
The Business of Pleasure Boats. q.
Annual Meetings: Fall

Nat'l Marine Distributors Ass'n (1965)
1810 South Rittenhouse Square, Suite 411, Philadelphia PA 19103
Exec. Director: Elizabeth A. Kelly
Members: 100 *Staff:* 2-5
Annual Budget: $100-250,000 *Tel:* (215) 735-3303
Hist. Note: Wholesalers of marine accessories and hardware.
Publication:
The Journal. q.

Nat'l Marine Education Ass'n (1976)
Box 666, Narragansett RI 02882
Exec. Director: Prentice K. Stout
Members: 1,700 individuals; 8 institutions *Staff:* 1
Annual Budget: $25-50,000 *Tel:* (401) 792-6211
Hist. Note: Members are interested in all types of marine education at the high school and college levels as well as continuing education and informal instruction in the marine environment. The association's primary goal is to promote a "marine literate" society. Membership: $18/yr.
Publication:
Current. q. adv.
Annual Meetings: Second week in August

Nat'l Marine Engineers' Beneficial Ass'n (1875)
444 North Capitol St., Suite 800, Washington DC 20001
President: C.E. DeFries
Members: 12,000 *Staff:* 25-30
Annual Budget: $500-1,000,000 *Tel:* (202) 347-8585
Hist. Note: Established in Cleveland in February 1875 as the Nat'l Marine Engineers Ass'n and assumed its present name in 1883. Affiliated with AFL-CIO.

00232 12 05 86 1233

Publication:
The American Marine Engineer. m.
Biennial meetings: Even years

Nat'l Marine Manufacturers Ass'n (1979)
401 North Michigan Ave., Chicago IL 60611
President: Jeff W. Napier
Members: 1,200 companies *Staff:* 35-40
Annual Budget: $500-1,000,000 *Tel:* (312) 836-4747
Hist. Note: Manufacturers of pleasure boats, boating supplies and marine engines. Formed by the merger of Boating Industry Ass'ns and the Nat'l Ass'n of Engine and Boat Manufacturers, Inc., NMMA is now an umbrella support organization for three affiliates - the Nat'l Ass'n of Marine Products and Services, the Ass'n of Marine Engine Manufacturers and the Nat'l Ass'n of Boat Manufacturers. Sponsors the National Marine Manufacturers Association Political Action Committee. Maintains New York, Miami, and Washington, DC offices.
Publications:
Boating News. w. adv.
Inter/port. w.
Annual Meetings: Fall
1987-Naples, FL(Ritz Carlton)/Nov. 15-19/400-500
1988-Coronado, CA(Hotel del Coronado/Oct. 23-27/400-500

Nat'l Marine Representatives Ass'n (1960)
16-2 St. Thomas Colony, Fox Lake IL 60020
Exec. Director: Teddee Grace
Members: 352 *Staff:* 1
Annual Budget: $50-100,000 *Tel:* (312) 587-1253
Hist. Note: Members are independent boat and marine accessory salesmen. Membership: $160/year.
Publications:
NMRA Newsletter. m.
Membership Directory. a.
Annual Meetings: With International Marine Trades Exhibit & Conference in Chicago.

Nat'l Maritime Union of America (1937)
346 West 17th St., New York NY 10011
President: Shannon J. Wall
Members: 35,000 *Staff:* 35-40
Annual Budget: over $5,000,000 *Tel:* (212) 620-5700
Hist. Note: Founded May 3, 1937 in New York City and affiliated with AFL-CIO. Has a budget of about $7 million.
Publications:
ITPE News. m.
NMU Government Operations News. q.
The NMU Pilot. m.
Quadrennial Meetings: October (1988)

Nat'l Mass Retailing Institute (1965)
570 Seventh Ave., New York NY 10018
President: Richard I. Hersh
Members: 150 mass retail chains *Staff:* 14
Annual Budget: $1-2,000,000 *Tel:* (212) 354-6600
Hist. Note: Formerly (1969) Mass Merchandising Research Foundation and (1976) Mass Retailing Institute. Sponsors the National Mass Retailing Institute Political Action Committee.
Publication:
Discount Data. m.
Annual Meetings: May/2,200
1987-Miami, FL(Fountainbleau)/May 9-13
1988-Nashville, TN(Opryland)/May 21-25
1989-Orlando, FL(Marriott World Ctr.)/May 13-17

Nat'l Mastitis Council (1961)
1840 Wilson Blvd., Arlington VA 22201
Secy.-Treas.: John B. Adams
Members: 500-600 bovine mastitis professionals *Staff:* 2-5
Annual Budget: $50-100,000 *Tel:* (703) 243-8268
Hist. Note: Shares office space with the Nat'l Milk Producers Federation. Membership: $20/yr.
Publication:
Udder Topics Newsletter.
Annual Meetings: February
1987-Orlando, Fl(Marriott Int'l Drive)/Feb. 20-23

Nat'l Meat Ass'n
Hist. Note: Merged into the American Meat Insitute in 1984.

Nat'l Meat Canners Ass'n (1923)
P.O. Box 3556, Washington DC 20007
Exec. Secretary: A. Dewey Bond
Members: 35 companies *Staff:* 1
Annual Budget: $25-50,000 *Tel:* (703) 841-2424
Hist. Note: Promotes the interests of packers of commercially sterile canned meats, and encourages scientific and practial research. Affiliated with the American Meat Institute. Membership: $400/year.
Annual Meetings: Spring
1987-White Sulphur Springs, WV(Greenbrier)/May 17-20/100

Nat'l Medical Ass'n (1895)
1012 10th St., N.W., Washington DC 20001
Exec. V. President: William C. Garrett
Members: 14,500 *Staff:* 6-10
Annual Budget: $500-1,000,000 *Tel:* (202) 347-1895
Hist. Note: Professional society of black physicians. Membership: $300/yr.
Publications:
Journal of the National Medical Association. q. adv.
NMA Newsletter. q.
Annual Meetings: Summer
1987-New Orleans, LA
1988-Los Angeles, CA
1989-Orlando, FL
1990-Houston, TX

Nat'l Mental Health Ass'n (1909)
1021 Prince St., Alexandria VA 22314-2971
Exec. Director: Preston J. Garrison
Members: 650 *Staff:* 20-25
Annual Budget: $1-2,000,000 *Tel:* (703) 684-7722
Hist. Note: Formed by a merger of the Nat'l Committee for Mental Hygiene, the Nat'l Mental Health Foundation and the Psychiatric Foundation. Absorbed the Nat'l Organization for Mentally Ill Children. Formerly (until 1978) the National Association for Mental Health and (until 1980) the Mental Health Association.
Publication:
FOCUS. m.
Annual Meetings: November
1987-Washington, DC
1988-Hartford, CT
1989-Washington, DC
1990-Indianapolis, IN

Nat'l Metal Decorators Ass'n (1936)
435 N. Michigan Ave., Chicago IL 60611
Exec. Director: Alfred Van Horn, III
Members: 350 individuals *Staff:* 1
Annual Budget: $50-100,000 *Tel:* (312) 644-0828
Hist. Note: Members are individuals in firms that apply decoration to metal surfaces through lithography or rollercoating. Membership: $35/year.
Annual Meetings: Fall/700
1987-San Antonio(Hyatt Regency)/Nov. 8-11

Nat'l Micrographics Ass'n (1943)
Hist. Note: Became the Association for Information and Image Management in 1983.

Nat'l Middle School Ass'n (1973)
Box 14882, Columbus OH 43214
Exec. Director: Robert M. Malinka
Members: 2,500
Annual Budget: $250-500,000 *Tel:* (614) 263-5407
Hist. Note: Educators and parents interested in middle school education. Formerly (until 1973) known as the Midwest Middle School Ass'n. Membership: $35/year (individual), $80/year (organization).
Publication:
Middle School Journal. q. adv.
Annual Meetings: Fall
1987-St. Louis, MO(Clarion)/Nov. 12-15

Nat'l Midwives Ass'n (1977)
Hist. Note: Merged with the Midwives Alliance of North America.

Nat'l Military Intelligence Ass'n (1974)
c/o GTE, Gov't. Systems Corp., Stategic Sys. Div., 6608 Electronic Dr., Springfield VA 22151-4381
President: Roy Yonkers
Members: 1,700 *Staff:* 1
Annual Budget: $10-25,000 *Tel:* (703) 354-1565
Hist. Note: Members are either engaged in the military intelligence profession in the Armed Forces of the United States or are U.S. citizens who have an interest in military intelligence and support the role of MI in the safeguarding of our nation's security. Membership: $10-25/yr.
Publications:
The American Intelligence Journal. q. adv.
NMIA Newsletter. q.
Annual Meetings: Winter

Nat'l Milk Producers Federation (1916)
4th Floor, 1840 Wilson Blvd., Arlington VA 22201
Chief Exec. Officer: James C. Barr
Members: 60-70 dairy cooperatives *Staff:* 20-25
Annual Budget: $2-5,000,000 *Tel:* (703) 243-6111
Hist. Note: Established as the National Cooperative Milk Producers Federation, it assumed its present name in 1966 and absorbed the National Creameries Association in 1966.
Publications:
News for Dairy Co-ops. w.
Economics Report. m.
Legislature Report. m.
Annual Meetings: November/1,500

Nat'l Minority Supplier Development Council (1972)
1412 Broadway, 11th Floor, New York NY 10018
President: Alfonso Whitfield
Members: 165 companies *Staff:* 10
Annual Budget: $100-250,000 *Tel:* (212) 944-2430
Hist. Note: Established to assist minorities in obtaining a larger slice of the economic pie. Formerly (until 1980) known as the Nat'l Minority Purchasing Council.
Publication:
Minority Supplier News. q.
Annual Meetings:
1987-Pittsburgh, PA/Oct. 19-22

Nat'l Mobile Radio Ass'n (1955)
Hist. Note: Established as the California Mobile Maintainers Association, it assumed its present name in 1980. Members are companies or individuals selling or servicing mobile communications equipment. Washington office closed in late 1984. Address unkown.

Nat'l Motor Freight Traffic Ass'n (1956)
2200 Mill Road, Alexandria VA 22314
Exec. Director: Martin Foley
Members: 2,000 *Staff:* 30-35
Annual Budget: $2-5,000,000 *Tel:* (703) 838-1810
Hist. Note: Members are regulated motor common carriers of general freight. Membership: $75-7,000/yr.
Publications:
National Motor Freight Classification Tariff. a.
ATA Hazardous Materials Tariff. a.
Directory of Standard Carrier Agent Codes. a.
Continental Directory of Standard Point Location Codes. a.
Annual Meetings: Winter/200
1987-Palm Springs, CA(Spa Hotel)/Jan. 31-Feb. 5
1988-Longboat Key, FL(Longboat Key CLub)/Feb. 2-10

Nat'l Motorcycle Dealers Ass'n (1974)
Hist. Note: Retail motorcycle dealers, primarily franchise owners. Dissolved in 1978. Re-established in 1984, it then merged with Motorcyle Retailers of America to form the National Motorcycle Retailers Ass'n.

Nat'l Motorcycle Retailers Ass'n (1984)
1441 Q St., N.W., Washington DC 20009
Exec. Director: Wayne H. Dickson
Tel: (202) 682-1558
Hist. Note: Members are retailers, manufactureres and aftermarket suppliers. Formed by a merger of the Motorcycle Retailers of America and the Nat'l Motorcycle Dealers Ass'n. Membership: $250/yr. (individual).
Publication:
Dealer Trends. m.
Annual Meetings: Fall

Nat'l Motorsports Press Ass'n (1959)
Box 500, Darlington SC 29532
Exec. Secretary: William Kiser
Members: 350 *Staff:* 1
Tel: (803) 393-7251
Hist. Note: Formerly Southern Motorsports Press Ass'n. Membership: $75/yr.
Publication:
Bulletin. m.
Annual Meetings:
1987-Charlotte, NC/January
1987-Florence, SC/August 31

Nat'l Moving and Storage Ass'n (1920)
124 South Royal St., Alexandria VA 22314
President: Dr. T. Peter Ruane
Members: 1,400 *Staff:* 10-15
Annual Budget: $500-1,000,000 *Tel:* (703) 549-9263
Hist. Note: Represents moving companies with storage facilities throughout the world. Until 1981 known as the Nat'l Furniture Warehousemen's Ass'n. Sponsors and supports the Nat'l Moving and Storage Ass'n Political Action Committee, the Nat'l Moving and Storage Technical Foundation and the Nat'l Institute of Certified Moving Consultants. Membership: $350/yr. and up (company, fee varies with size).
Publications:
Direction. m. adv.
National Moving and Storage Times. w.
Annual Meetings: Spring/350
1987-Las Vegas, NV(Bally's Grand)/ March 31- April 5
1988-San Juan, PR(Caribe Hilton)/April 12-17

Nat'l Multi Housing Council (1978)
1250 Connecticut Ave., N.W., #620, Washington DC 20036
Exec. V. President: Stephen D. Driesler
Members: 6,000 individuals and companies *Staff:* 6
Annual Budget: $500-1,000,000 *Tel:* (202) 659-3381
Hist. Note: Land developers, realtors, apartment owners, builders and developers, and others concerned with issues relating to rent, rent control, multifamily housing, condominium conversions, and tax legislation. Formerly (until 1980) known as the National Rental Housing Council. Sponsors and supports the National Multi Housing Council Political Action Committee.
Publication:
NMHC Newsletter. m.

Nat'l Multiple Sclerosis Soc. (1946)
205 East 42nd St., New York NY 10017
President and CEO: Adm. Thor Hanson
Members: 550-600,000 individuals *Staff:* 130
Annual Budget: over $5,000,000 *Tel:* (212) 986-3240
Hist. Note: Until 1947 known as the Ass'n for the Advancement of Research on Multiple Sclerosis. Promotes research into the cause, prevention, treatment and cure of multiple sclerosis, a neurological disorder and provides services to persons with MS and their families. Has an annual budget of $13.3 million. Membership: $10/yr.
Publication:
Inside Ms. q. adv.
Biennial Meetings: Even years
1988-Seattle, WA/June

00233 12 05 86 1233

Nat'l Music Council (1940)
45 W. 34th St., Suite 1010, New York NY 10001
Exec. V. President: Benjamin S. Dunham
Members: 50 organizations *Staff:* 2
Annual Budget: $25-50,000 *Tel:* (212) 563-3734
Hist. Note: Federation of music organizations chartered by the U.S. Congress as a forum for discussion of national music problems.
Publication:
Nat'l Music Council News. q.
Annual Meetings: June

Nat'l Music Publishers' Ass'n (1917)
205 East 42nd St., New York NY 10017
President and C.E.O.: Edward P. Murphy
Members: 300 companies *Staff:* 6-10
Annual Budget: $1-2,000,000 *Tel:* (212) 751-1930
Hist. Note: Established as the Music Publishers Protective Ass'n; assumed its present name in 1966. Members are publishers of popular music concentrated principally around New York, Los Angeles and Nashville. A separate staff presides over subsidiary, the Harry Fox Agency, a licensing group for the members' product.
Annual Meetings: New York, NY/June

Nat'l Neckwear Ass'n (1943)
75 Livingston St., Brooklyn NY 11201
Counsel: Leonard Brodsky
Members: 20-30 companies *Staff:* 1
Annual Budget: under $10,000 *Tel:* (718) 875-2300
Hist. Note: Major purpose of the association is to represent its members in labor negotiations. Closely associated with the Bow Tie Manufacturers Ass'n. Membership: $600/yr. (company)

Nat'l Needlework Ass'n (1974)
230 Fifth Ave., New York NY 10001
Exec. Director: Mary Colucci
Members: 400-450 *Staff:* 2-5
Annual Budget: $100-250,000 *Tel:* (212) 685-1646
Hist. Note: In the spring of 1974, 34 companies met to form the Nat'l Needlework Ass'n for the purposes of advancing needlework quality, understanding and marketing in the United States. Members are needlework manufacturers, retailers, and distributors. Holds both a national and regional shows.
Annual Meetings: National Show
1987-Anaheim, CA(Convention Center)/Jan. 25-28

Nat'l Newspaper Ass'n (1885)
1627 K St., N.W., Suite 400, Washington DC 20006
Exec. V. President: David C. Simonson
Members: 5,000 *Staff:* 11-15
Annual Budget: $1-2,000,000 *Tel:* (202) 466-7200
Hist. Note: Founded as the Nat'l Editorial Ass'n and assumed its present name in 1960. Members are the editors and publishers of about 70% of the country's weeklies and half its dailies--many quite small with circulations of under 5,000. Membership: $25/year (individual), institutional dues varies with circulation.
Publications:
News Media Update.
Publishers' Auxiliary. w. adv.
Annual Meetings: Fall
1987-Portland, OR(Portland Marriott)/Sep.30-Oct.3/800
1988-San Antonio(Marriott)/Oct. 26-29/800

Nat'l Newspaper Publishers Ass'n (1940)
948 National Press Bldg., Washington DC 20045
Exec. Director: Steve G. Davis
Members: 160-170 *Staff:* 2-5
Annual Budget: $50-100,000 *Tel:* (202) 662-7324
Hist. Note: Formerly Nat'l Negro Publishers Ass'n. Membership: $150/yr.
Annual Meetings: June
1987-Detroit, MI/250
1988-St. Louis, MO(Hyatt)/250

Nat'l Notary Ass'n (1957)
23012 Ventura Blvd., Box 4625, Woodland Hills CA 91365-4625
Exec. Director: Deborah M. Thaw
Members: 61,000 notaries public *Staff:* 40
Annual Budget: $1-2,000,000 *Tel:* (818) 347-2035
Hist. Note: Established in 1957 by Raymond C. Rothman as the California Notary Ass'n; assumed its present name in 1965. Membership: $18/yr.
Publications:
Notary Viewpoint. bi-m. adv.
The National Notary. bi-m. adv.
Annual Meetings: Spring
1987-New York, NY(Halloran House)/June 25-28

Nat'l Notion Ass'n (1976)
Hist. Note: Inactive in 1986.

Nat'l Nurses Soc. on Addictions (1974)
2506 Gross Point Road, Evanston IL 60201
Exec. Director: Dagny N. Engle, RN, CAE
Members: 560 individuals *Staff:* 2-5
Annual Budget: $25-50,000 *Tel:* (312) 475-1000
Hist. Note: A national specialty nursing organization for addictions nurses. Membership: $50/yr.
Publication:
Newsletter. q. adv.
Annual Meetings: Fall
1987-Chicago, IL

Nat'l Nutrition Consortium (1974)
Hist. Note: Ceased operations in early 1986.

Nat'l Nutritional Foods Ass'n (1936)
125 E. Baker Ave., Suite 230, Costa Mesa CA 92626
Exec. Director: Patricia Heydlauff
Members: 3,300 *Staff:* 10
Annual Budget: $1-2,000,000 *Tel:* (714) 966-6632
Hist. Note: Formerly (1970) Nat'l Dietary Foods Ass'n. Absorbed the American Dietary Retailers Ass'n in 1969. Natural, nutritional and dietary food retailers, distributors, and producers. Supports the Nat'l Nutritional Foods Political Action Committee. Membership: $55/year (individual), $100-500/year (company).
Annual Meetings:
1987-Las Vegas, NV
1988-Las Vegas, NV
1989-Las Vegas, NV
1990-Boston, MA

Nat'l Oak Flooring Manufacturers Ass'n (1909)
8 North Third, Suite 804 Sterick Bldg., Memphis TN 38103
Managing Director: James H. Lee
Members: 20-30 *Staff:* 2-5
Annual Budget: $50-100,000 *Tel:* (901) 526-5016
Hist. Note: Main purpose is to establish manufacturing and grading standards for the industry and to see that these standards are observed by a continuous inspection service. Open to manufacturers in the U.S. who make solid hardwood flooring. Formerly the Oak Flooring Manufacturers of the United States and Southern Oak Flooring Industries. NOFMA sponsors the Hardwood Flooring Installation School (since 1979) with the American Parquet Ass'n and the Maple Flooring Manufacturers Ass'n. The Oak Flooring Institute is the promotional arm of NOFMA.
Semi-Annual Meetings: Summer and Winter
1987-Nashville, TN/July and Memphis, TN/Dec.

Nat'l Ocean Industries Ass'n (1966)
1050 17th St., N.W. #700, Washington DC 20036
President: Charles D. Matthews
Members: 325-350 companies *Staff:* 6-10
Annual Budget: $500-1,000,000 *Tel:* (202) 785-5116
Hist. Note: Oil and gas companies, their suppliers, and support companies drilling and exploring on the outer continental shelf; also deep seabed mining, and fishing. Established as the Nat'l Oceanographic Ass'n, it became the Nat'l Oceanography Ass'n in 1970 and assumed its present name in 1972. Sponsors the Nat'l Ocean Industries Ass'n Political Action Committee.
Publications:
NOIA Membership Directory. a.
NOIA Leaders. a.
Washington Report. bi-w.
Annual Meetings:
1987-Washington, DC(Vista International)/April 5-7/250-325

Nat'l Office Machine Dealers Ass'n (1924)
12411 Wornall, Kansas City MO 64145
Exec. Director: Kenneth E. Shrier
Members: 6,000 *Staff:* 25-30
Annual Budget: $2-5,000,000 *Tel:* (816) 941-3100
Hist. Note: Founded in 1926 as the Nat'l Ass'n of Typewriter Dealers. Became the Nat'l Typewriter and Office Machine Dealers Ass'n and later assumed its present name. Sponsors and supports the Nat'l Office Machine Dealers Ass'n Political Action Committee.
Publications:
Hotline. 24/yr.
Spokesman. m. adv.
Annual Meetings: Summer/15,000
1987-Atlanta, GA/July

Nat'l Office Products Ass'n (1904)
301 North Fairfax St., Alexandria VA 22314
Exec. V. President: Donald P. Haspel
Members: 8,500 *Staff:* 50
Annual Budget: over $5,000,000 *Tel:* (703) 549-9040
Hist. Note: Established in 1904 as the Nat'l Stationers Ass'n, it became the Nat'l Stationery and Office Equipment Ass'n in 1950 and assumed its present name in 1968. Absorbed the Nat'l Office Furniture Ass'n in 1965. Members are manufacturers, wholesalers and retailers of office equipment, supplies and furniture. Sponsors the National Office Products Association Political Action Committee.
Publications:
Office Products Industry Report. bi-w.
Office Products Special Report. bi-m. adv.
Annual Meetings: Chicago in the Fall

Nat'l Oil Jobbers Council (1941)
Hist. Note: Became the Petroleum Marketers Ass'n of America in 1984.

Nat'l Onion Ass'n (1913)
One Greeley National Plaza, Suite 510, Greeley CO 80631
Exec. V. President: Wayne Mininger
Members: 550 *Staff:* 3
Annual Budget: $100-250,000 *Tel:* (303) 353-5895
Hist. Note: Formerly Nat'l Statistical Onion Ass'n.
Publications:
News Letter. m.
Statistical Report. m.
Annual Meetings: December/300

Nat'l Opera Ass'n (1955)
Route 2, Box 93, Commerce TX 75428
Exec. Secretary: Mary Elaine Wallace
Members: 800-850 *Staff:* 1
Annual Budget: $25-50,000 *Tel:* (214) 886-3830
Hist. Note: Members are opera companies, schools of music, opera directors, composers, conductors, librettists, teachers, and other professionals whose work is opera-related. Membership: $30/yr.
Publications:
Membership Directory. a.
NOA Newsletter. q.
Opera Journal. q.
Annual Meetings: November
1987-Orlando, FL
1988-Columbus, OH
1989-Banff, Alberta

Nat'l Options and Futures Soc. (1979)
322 Eighth Ave., 12th Fl., New York NY 10001
Exec. Director: Carol Bensky
Members: 500 individuals *Staff:* 1
Annual Budget: $50-100,000 *Tel:* (212) 206-8301
Hist. Note: NOFS includes a broad representation of institutional investors and securities industry professionals involved in research, brokerage, and trading. Membership: $10/yr.
Publication:
Options and Futures News. p.
Annual Meetings: Fall

Nat'l Optometric Ass'n (1969)
1489 Livingston Ave., Columbus OH 43205
Exec. Director: Dr. Edwin Marshall
Members: 400 *Staff:* 1
Annual Budget: $10-25,000 *Tel:* (614) 253-5593
Hist. Note: Established and incorporated in Atlanta, NOA is a professional society of predominantly minority optometrists especially concerned with the delivery of vision/eye health care to the minority community. Affiliated with the American Optometric Ass'n, American Public Health Ass'n, Ass'n of Schools and Colleges of Optometry and Nat'l Health Council. Membership: $100/yr.
Publication:
NOA Newsletter. q. adv.
Annual Meetings: June-July
1987-Las Vegas, NV
1988-Washington, DC

Nat'l Order of Women Legislators (1938)
1377 K St., N.W., Suite 169, Washington DC 20005
Exec. Director: Joy Stone
Members: 500-525 *Staff:* 1
Annual Budget: under $10,000 *Tel:* (202) 737-3999
Hist. Note: Founded in Washington, DC in 1938. Members must have served in a State legislature. Plans to move in December, 1986; mail to the above address will be forwarded.
Publication:
Owletter. q.
Annual Meetings: Fall
1987-Tulsa, OK
1988-Hartford, CT

Nat'l Organization of Bar Counsel (1964)
555 Franklin St., San Francisco CA 94102
President: Ronald W. Stovitz
Members: 290
Annual Budget: under $10,000 *Tel:* (415) 561-8359
Hist. Note: Attorneys representing bar associations and disciplinary agencies on the state, local and national levels. Holds semi-annual meetings with the American Bar Ass'n, with which it is informally affiliated. Has no permanent office or staff. Officers are elected annually.
Semi-annual Meetings: In conjunction with the annual and mid-year
meetings of the American Bar Ass'n

Nat'l Organization of Industrial Trade Unions (1954)
148-06 Hillside Ave., Jamaica NY 11435
President: Daniel Lasky
Members: 7,500 *Staff:* 6-10
Annual Budget: $250-500,000 *Tel:* (718) 291-3434
Hist. Note: Independent labor union.
Publication:
Unioncraft. a.
Annual Meetings: December

Nat'l Organization of Social Security Claimants' Representatives (1979)
19 East Central Ave., Pearl River NY 10965
Exec. Director: Nancy G. Shor
Members: 2,300 *Staff:* 2-5
Annual Budget: $50-100,000 *Tel:* (914) 735-8812
Hist. Note: Composed mostly of lawyers.
Publication:
NOSSCR Forum. m.
Semi-annual Meetings: Summer and Fall
1987-Washington, DC/June
1987-San Francisco, CA

Nat'l Organization of Test, Research and Training Reactors (1982)
c/o Research Reactor Facility, Univ. of,Missouri, Columbia MO 65211

00234 12 05 86 1233

Chairman: Don M. Alger
Members: 50 companies; 80 individuals
Annual Budget: under $10,000 *Tel:* (314) 882-4211
Hist. Note: Members must be on operations staff of reactor.
Annual Meetings: October
1987-Washington, DC (Nat'l Bureau of Standards)

Nat'l Organization on Legal Problems of Education (1954)
3601 SW 29th St., Suite 223, Southwest Plaza, Topeka KS 66614
Exec. Director: Thomas N. Jones, J.D.
Members: 2,700 *Staff:* 6-10
Annual Budget: $250-500,000 *Tel:* (913) 273-3550
Hist. Note: Membership consists of law professors, school administrators, school attorneys, etc. Purpose is to promote research and publication in the field of school law.
Publications:
School Law Update. a.
NOLPE Case Citation Series. 5/yr.
Yearbook of School Law. a.
Annual Meetings:
1987-New Orleans, LA(Fairmont Hotel)/Nov. 18-21/400
1988-Washington, DC(Omni Shoreham)/Nov. 16-19

Nat'l Ornament and Electric Lights Christmas Ass'n (1975)
230 Fifth Ave., Suite 1611, New York NY 10001
President: Ronald Schoenfeld
Members: 40-45 companies *Staff:* 2
Annual Budget: $10-25,000 *Tel:* (212) 889-8343
Hist. Note: Formed by a merger of the Christmas Decorations Ass'n and the Decorative Lighting Guild of America. The bulk of the members are in the New York area. Membership: $500/yr. (sales under $1 mil.), $1,000/yr. (sales over $1 mil.).
Publication:
Membership Directory. irreg.
Annual Meetings: February, in New York City.

Nat'l Ornamental and Miscellaneous Metals Ass'n (1958)
2996 Grandview Ave., N.E., Suite 109, Atlanta GA 30305
Exec. Director: Blanche Blackwell
Members: 525 companies *Staff:* 3
Annual Budget: $100-250,000 *Tel:* (404) 237-5334
Hist. Note: Organized at the Claridge Hotel, Memphis, Tennessee in January, 1958 as the National Ornamental Iron Manufacturers Association. In 1961 the name was changed to National Ornamental Metal Manufacturers Association and the present name adopted in 1977. Membership: $200/yr. (company).
Publication:
NOMMA Ornamental/Miscellaneous Metal Fabricator. bi-m. adv.
Annual Meetings: Winter/1,000
1987-San Diego, CA(Town & Country)/Feb. 10-14
1988-Open
1989-Las Vegas, NV(Sahara)

Nat'l Outerwear and Sportswear Ass'n (1942)
Hist. Note: Became a division of the American Apparel Manufacturers Ass'n in 1983.

Nat'l Paint and Coatings Ass'n (1933)
1500 Rhode Island Ave., N.W., Washington DC 20005
Exec. Director: Larry L. Thomas
Members: 900-1,000 *Staff:* 50
Annual Budget: $2-5,000,000 *Tel:* (202) 462-6272
Hist. Note: Manufacturers of paints and industrial coatings, and suppliers to the industry. Formed in 1933 as the Nat'l Paint, Varnish and Lacquer Ass'n through a merger of the American Paint Manufacturers Ass'n and the Nat'l Paint, Oil and Varnish Ass'n, the name was changed to the Nat'l Paint and Coatings Ass'n in 1972.
Publications:
Abstract Review. m.
Coatings. m.
Member/Services Directory. a. adv.
Trade Mark Directory. tri-a.
Annual Meetings: Fall
1987-Washington, DC(Washington Hilton)
1988-Chicago, IL(Palmer House)
1989-New Orleans, LA(New Orleans Hilton)
1990-Washington, DC(Washington Hilton)
1991-San Francisco, CA(San Francisco Hilton)

Nat'l Paint Distributors (1960)
2 Talcott Road, Park Ridge IL 60068
Exec. Director: John F. Roberts
Members: 32 companies *Staff:* 6-10
Annual Budget: $100-250,000 *Tel:* (312) 696-1590
Hist. Note: Membership: $4,800/yr.
Publication:
News. w.
Annual Meetings: Just prior to Nat'l Decorating Products Show/November
1987-Chicago, IL
1988-Chicago, IL

Nat'l Pan Hellenic Council (1929)
1316 Underwood St., N.W., Washington DC 20012
Corresponding Secretary: Grace W. Phillips
Members: 8 national fraternities/sororities
Hist. Note: Black fraternities and sororities.
Annual Meetings: Fall

Nat'l Panhellenic Conference (1902)
3901 West 86th Street, Suite 285, Indianapolis IN 46268
Chairman: Sidney G. Allen
Members: 26 national sororities *Staff:* 1
Tel: (317) 872-3185
Hist. Note: Organized in Chicago, May 24, 1902.
Biennial Meetings: Odd years

Nat'l Panhellenic Conference of Central Office Executives
Hist. Note: Became the Ass'n of the Nat'l Panhellenic Conference of Central Office Executives in 1984.

Nat'l Paper Trade Ass'n (1903)
111 Great Neck Road, Great Neck NY 11021
President: John J. Buckley, Jr.
Members: 1,700-1,800 companies *Staff:* 13
Annual Budget: $1-2,000,000 *Tel:* (516) 829-3070
Hist. Note: Wholesalers of printing and industrial paper.
Publication:
Management News. m.
Annual Meetings: Fall
1987-Atlanta, GA/Sept. 19-22

Nat'l Paperbox and Packaging Ass'n (1918)
231 Kings Highway East, Haddonfield NJ 08033
Exec. Director: Lawrence Lynch
Members: 350 companies *Staff:* 8
Annual Budget: $500-1,000,000 *Tel:* (609) 429-7377
Hist. Note: Formed in 1918 as the Nat'l Federation of Paper Box Manufacturers; developed into the Nat'l Paper Box Manufacturers Ass'n in 1919; changed name to the Nat'l Paper Box Ass'n in 1972; and adopted its present name in 1981. In 1982 NPPA opened membership to all independent manufacturers of packaging including rigid paper boxes, folding cartons and thermoform materials. Annual membership fee based upon sales volume.
Publications:
Newsletter (2). bi-m.
Key Ratios of the Folding Carton Industry.
Key Ratios of the Rigid Box Industry.
Wage Rates of the Rigid Box and Folding Carton Industries.
Monthly Billing Reports for Rigid Box and Folding Carton Industries.
Annual Meetings: Spring/300
1987-Oahu, HI(Turtle Bay Hilton)/May 13-17
1988-Charleston, SC(Omni Charleston Place)/May 11-15
1989-Puerto Rico(Caribe Hilton)/May 17-21
1990-London, England(The Grovsner House)/May
1991-San Francisco, CA

Nat'l Paralegal Ass'n (1982)
10 South Pine St., Doylestown PA 18901
Exec. Director: H. Jeffrey Valentine
Members: 3,500-4,000 *Staff:* 6-10
Annual Budget: $250-500,000 *Tel:* (215) 348-5575
Hist. Note: Members are paralegals, paralegal educators, law libraries, law firms, schools and others with an interest in the advancement of the profession. Membership: $70 (first year); $45/year (thereafter).
Publications:
The Paralegal. bi-m.
Annual Nat'l Salary & Employment Survey. a. adv.
Nat'l School & Institute Directory. a.
Paralegal Career Booklet. a.
Directory of Local Paralegal Clubs. a.

Nat'l Park and Recreation Soc. (1932)
Hist. Note: Formerly the American Park and Recreation Association, it is now a branch of the Nat'l Recreation and Park Association. Has no paid staff. Administrative support provided by the National Recreation and Park Association. Members are professional recreation directors in towns and cities throughout the country.

Nat'l Parking Ass'n (1951)
1112 16th St., N.W., Suite 2000, Washington DC 20036
Exec. V. President: Thomas G. Kobus
Members: 800 off-street parking companies, 250 organization
Staff: 6
Annual Budget: $1-2,000,000 *Tel:* (202) 296-4336
Hist. Note: Sponsors the National Parking Association Political Action Committee. Membership: $200-$7,500/yr. (organizations and companies).
Publications:
NPA Government Reports. 10/yr.
Parking Angle. m.
Parking Magazine. semi-m. adv.
Parking World. 10/yr. adv.
Annual Meetings: June
1987-San Francisco, CA(Fairmont)/May 17-20
1988-New York, NY(Marriott Marquis)/May 22-25
1989-Vancouver, BC(Pan Pacific)/May 21-24/800
1990-Chicago, IL(Fairmont)/May 13-16/800

Nat'l Parks and Conservation Ass'n (1919)
1015 31st. St., N.W., Washington DC 20007
President: Paul C. Pritchard
Members: 55,000 *Staff:* 34
Annual Budget: $2-5,000,000 *Tel:* (202) 265-2717
Hist. Note: Established as the National Parks Association, it assumed its present name in 1970. Members are individuals interested in conservation, protection of National Parks, wildlife and the wilderness. Varying membership fees available.
Publication:
National Parks Magazine. bi-m. adv.
Annual Meetings: Annual Dinner, third Thursday in November in Washington, DC/250-300.

Nat'l Particleboard Ass'n (1960)
18928 Premiere Court, Gaithersburg MD 20879
Exec. V. President: William H. McCredie
Members: 15-20 companies *Staff:* 11-16
Annual Budget: $500-1,000,000 *Tel:* (301) 670-0604
Publications:
U.S. Particleboard/MDF Plant Capacity. a.
U.S. Particle Board/MDF Shipments. a.
Semi-annual Meetings:
1987-Ponte Vedra Beach, FL(Ponte Vedra Inn)/April 26-29/100
1987-Portland, OR(Red Lion Inn)/Oct. 18-21

Nat'l Passenger Traffic Ass'n (1969)
516 Fifth Ave., Suite 406, New York NY 10036
President: Richard Rudkin
Members: 750 *Staff:* 4
Annual Budget: $250-500,000 *Tel:* (212) 221-6782
Hist. Note: The voice of the business traveler in communication to government and the travel industry. Membership: $175/yr.
Publications:
Business Travel Review. m. adv.
Conference Journal. a. adv.
Annual Meetings: Fall
1987-Atlanta, GA/Sept. 19-23
1988-Boston, MA/Sept. 25-28
1989-Dallas, TX

Nat'l Pasta Ass'n (1904)
1901 North Ft. Myer Dr., Suite 1000, Arlington VA 22209
President: Joseph M. Lichtenberg
Members: 100 *Staff:* 2-5
Annual Budget: $500-1,000,000 *Tel:* (703) 841-0818
Hist. Note: Established as the National Macaroni Manufacturers Association, it absorbed the National Macaroni Institute in 1979 and assumed its present name in 1981.
Publications:
PASTA Journal. m. adv.
NPA Newsletter. w.
Pastahh. q.
Annual Meetings:
1987-Laguna Niguel, CA(Ritz-Carlton)/March 22-26/20
1988-Naples, FL(Ritz Carlton)/March
1989-Palm Desert, CA(Marriott Desert Springs)/Feb. 10-16/200

Nat'l Patent Council (1945)
Hist. Note: No longer a membership organization (since 1986).

Nat'l Peach Council (1942)
P.O. Box 1085, Martinsburg WV 25401
Exec. Director: Lillie E. Hoover Largent
Members: 2,000 individuals *Staff:* 2
Annual Budget: $100-250,000 *Tel:* (304) 267-6024
Hist. Note: Formed in 1942 and incorporated in 1945 in West Virginia. A federation of state associations of peach growers and allied industry members.
Publications:
Convention Proceedings. a.
Peach-Times. m. adv.
Annual Meetings: February/4-500

Nat'l Peanut Council (1940)
101 South Peyton St., Suite 301, Alexandria VA 22314
President: Perry A. Russ
Members: 250-300 *Staff:* 8
Annual Budget: $500-1,000,000 *Tel:* (703) 838-9500
Hist. Note: Founded in June, 1940 and incorporated in Georgia in 1941, the Council counts among its members peanut farmers, shellers, brokers, special processors, the manufacturers of peanut products and peanut butter, as well as the allied support trades. As the umbrella for the entire peanut industry, the Council promotes increased peanut consumption, research and the dissemination of knowledge of new technology, as well as improved processing, storage, handling and packaging techniques. The Council also acts as a clearinghouse for information pertaining to actions by the federal government and is the industry forum for the exchange of ideas and information by the industry's leaders.
Publication:
Peanut News. m.
Annual Meetings: Spring/500
1987-Tuscon, AZ(Westin La Paloma)/April 1-4
1988-Tampa, FL(Hyatt)/April 6-9

Nat'l Pecan Marketing Council (1979)
219 North Main, Suite 513, Bryan TX 77803
Exec. Director: Norman Winter
Members: 600 *Staff:* 2-5
Annual Budget: $500-1,000,000 *Tel:* (409) 775-4009
Hist. Note: Promotes the pecan industry through cooperative programs with American companies, contact with press representatives, trade show representation and a European marketing program. Membership: $100/yr.
Publication:
Newsletter. q.

00235 12 05 86 1233

Nat'l Pecan Shellers and Processors Ass'n (1943)
Hist. Note: Became the Nat'l Pecan Shellers Ass'n in 1985.

Nat'l Pecan Shellers Ass'n (1943)
5775 Peachtree-Dunwoody Road, Suite 500D, Atlanta GA 30342
President: Robert H. Kellen
Members: 60 *Staff:* 4
Tel: (404) 252-3663
Hist. Note: Formerly (1985) the Nat'l Pecan Shellers and Processors Ass'n.
Semi-annual Meetings:
1987-Nashville, TN/Feb. 11-13
1987-San Diego, CA/Sept. 16-18

Nat'l Pedigreed Livestock Council (1911)
4700 East 63rd St., Kansas City MO 64130
Secy.-Treas.: Dr. T.D. "Dusty" Rich
Members: 50-55 registry ass'ns *Staff:* 1
Annual Budget: under $10,000 *Tel:* (816) 333-7731
Hist. Note: A federation of cattle, horse, swine, goat and sheep breeders having a common interest in purebred stock as a means of livestock improvement. Formerly (1985) the Nat'l Soc. of Livestock Record Ass'ns.
Annual Meetings: May, usually in Kansas City, MO

Nat'l Pegboard Systems Ass'n (1983)
Box 964, Alexandria VA 22313-0964
President: Larry Burch
Members: 80 companies *Staff:* 3
Annual Budget: $50-100,000 *Tel:* (703) 683-5656
Hist. Note: Trade association of pegboard accounting systems (one write or single write systems) manufacturers.
Publication:
NPSA News. bi-m.
Annual Meetings: Spring

Nat'l Perinatal Ass'n (1974)
101 1/2 S. Union St., Alexandria VA 22314
Exec. Director: Sandra Butler Whyte
Members: 10,000 *Staff:* 3
Annual Budget: $250-500,000 *Tel:* (703) 549-5523
Hist. Note: Members are individuals promoting the belief that health care is affected by all factors in the human life cycle from prior to conception through the next generation. Particular emphasis on care for the pregnant women, fetus and newborn. Membership: $10-40/yr. (individual), $100/yr. (organization)
Publications:
NPA Bulletin. bi-m. adv.
Annual Report. a. adv.
Directory. adv.
State Reports. adv.
Annual Meetings: Fall
1987-St. Louis, MO(Adams Mark)/Nov. 7-11/850-1,000
1988-San Diego, CA(Sheraton Harbor Island)/Oct. 8-11/850-1,000
1989-Washington, DC(Washington Hilton)/Nov. 11-14/1,200-1,500
1990-Dallas, TX

Nat'l Perishable Transportation Ass'n (1975)
400 Lathrop, River Forest IL 60305
Attorney: William Towle
Members: 225
Annual Budget: $10-25,000 *Tel:* (312) 771-6330
Hist. Note: Founded as the Nat'l Perishable Traffic Ass'n, it assumed its present name in 1979. Members are executives of motor carriers, shippers and receivers of perishable commodities interested in the transportation thereof. Has no paid staff or permanent address at present. Officers change annually.
Annual Meetings: First week after Labor Day
1987-Geneva, WI(Americana)/Sept.
1988-Colorado Springs, CO(Broadmoor)

Nat'l Personal Robot Ass'n
Hist. Note: Became the Nat'l Service Robot Ass'n in 1986.

Nat'l Pest Control Ass'n (1933)
8100 Oak St., Dunn Loring VA 22027
Exec. V. President: Harvey S. Gold
Members: 2,100 *Staff:* 20-25
Annual Budget: $2-5,000,000 *Tel:* (703) 573-8330
Hist. Note: Formerly (1937) Nat'l Ass'n of Exterminators and Fumigators. Members are companies engaged in the integrated management of insects, rodents, birds and other pests which inhabit buildings or structures of any kind. Supports the Nat'l Pest Control Ass'n Political Action Committee.
Annual Meetings: Late October
1987-Honolulu, HI
1988-Nashville, TN

Nat'l Pet Dealers and Breeders Ass'n (1972)
Box 35, Lancaster KS 66041
President: Virginia D. Billings
Members: 150-160 *Staff:* 1
Annual Budget: $10-25,000 *Tel:* (913) 874-2343
Hist. Note: Has no paid staff or permanent headquarters.
Publication:
Newsletter. bi-m.
Annual Meetings: First Sunday in May

Nat'l Petroleum Council (1946)
1625 K St., N.W., Washington DC 20006
Exec. Director: Marshall Nichols
Members: 120 *Staff:* 15-20
Annual Budget: $1-2,000,000 *Tel:* (202) 393-6100
Hist. Note: Self-supporting advisory body to the Secretary of Energy established in 1946 at the request of President Truman.
Semi-annual Meetings: Spring and Fall in Washington, DC

Nat'l Petroleum Refiners Ass'n (1902)
1899 L St., N.W., Suite 1000, Washington DC 20036
President: Urvan R. Sternfels
Members: 250-300 *Staff:* 25-30
Annual Budget: $2-5,000,000 *Tel:* (202) 457-0480
Hist. Note: Merger in 1961 of the Nat'l Petroleum Ass'n (1902) and the Western Petroleum Refiners Ass'n (1912). Members are petroleum, petrochemical, and refining companies.
Annual Meetings: Spring/4,000
1987-San Antonio, TX(Conv. Center)/March 29-31
1988-San Antonio, TX(Conv. Center)/March 20-22
1989-San Francisco, CA(Hilton)/March 19-21
1990-San Antonio, TX(Conv. Center)/March 25-27
1991-San Antonio, TX(Conv. Center)/March 17-19
1992-New Orleans, LA(Sheraton/Marriott-Conv.Center)/March 29-31

Nat'l Pharmaceutical Ass'n (1947)
Box 934, Howard University, Washington DC 20059
Exec. Director: James N. Tyson
Members: 350-400 individuals *Staff:* 1
Annual Budget: under $10,000 *Tel:* (202) 636-6544
Hist. Note: Members are black pharmacists and pharmacy students.
Publication:
Journal of the NPhA. q. adv.
Annual Meetings: First week of August/350
1987-Kansas City, MO(Westin Crown Center)/Aug. 2-6
1988-Washington, DC

Nat'l Pharmaceutical Council (1953)
1894 Preston White Drive, Reston VA 22091
President: Mark R. Knowles
Members: 25-30 companies *Staff:* 11-15
Annual Budget: $1-2,000,000 *Tel:* (703) 620-6390
Hist. Note: Members are research-intensive companies producing brand name prescription medicines.

Nat'l Phlebotomy Ass'n (1978)
2623 Bladensburg Road, N.E., Washington, DC 20018
Exec. Director: Diane C. Crawford
Members: Over 4,200 individuals *Staff:* 14
Annual Budget: $250-500,000 *Tel:* (202) 636-4515
Hist. Note: NPA's primary focus is on education and research in phlebotomy; it provides an accreditation mechanism for phlebotomy training programs. Registry Fee: $25
Publication:
The Tourniquet. 3/yr. adv.
Annual Meetings: August
1987-Denver, CO/Aug. 8-10/60
1988-Washington, DC(Shoreham)/Aug. 8-10/100

Nat'l Piano Manufacturers Ass'n
Hist. Note: Became the Piano Manufacturers Ass'n Internat'l in 1986.

Nat'l Piano Travelers Ass'n
Hist. Note: Defunct in 1986.

Nat'l Planning Ass'n (1934)
1616 P St., N.W., Suite 400, Washington DC 20036
President: Edward E. Masters
Members: 3,000 *Staff:* 20
Annual Budget: $1-2,000,000 *Tel:* (202) 265-7685
Hist. Note: Founded during the Great Depression of the 1930's as the Nat'l Economic and Social Planning Ass'n, NPA assumed its present name in 1941. NPA is a private, non-profit, non-political organization that brings together leaders from business, agriculture, and the applied and academic professions to identify emerging problems confronting the nation and agree upon policies and programs to cope with them. Membership: $45/yr. (individual); $1,000/yr. (institution)
Publications:
Looking Ahead. q.
Policy Reports. 6-8/yr.
Annual Meetings: Not held.

Nat'l Plant Board (1925)
Box CN 330, New Jersey Dept. of Agriculture, Trenton NJ 08625
Chairman: William Metterhouse
Members: 51 *Staff:* 1
Annual Budget: under $10,000 *Tel:* (609) 292-5440
Hist. Note: Representatives from each state and Puerto Rico interested in protecting agriculture, forestry and horticulture throughout the U.S. by pest control and plant quarantine. Affiliated with the Nat'l Ass'n of State Departments of Agriculture. Has no paid staff.
Publication:
Minutes of Annual Meeting. a.
Annual Meetings: Second week of August/75
1987-Far Western U.S.
1988-Eastern U.S.
1989-Southern U.S.

Nat'l Plastercraft Ass'n (1972)
3910 Kamer-Miller Road, New Albany IN 47150
Exec. V. President: William L. Ferguson
Members: 300 companies *Staff:* 2-5
Annual Budget: $25-50,000 *Tel:* (812) 944-7960
Hist. Note: Makers and dealers in plaster and plaster products and molds for the hobby industry. Affiliated with the Hobby Industry Association of America. Formerly (until 1980) known as the Plastercraft Association.
Publication:
The Plastercrafter. bi-m.
Annual Meetings: June/3-400
1987-Dallas, TX/June 18-21

Nat'l Police Officers Ass'n of America (1955)
1316 Gardiner Lane, Suite 204, Louisville KY 40213
Nat'l Exec. Director and Editor: John W. Lewis
Members: 4,000-4,500 *Staff:* 6-10
Annual Budget: $100-250,000 *Tel:* (502) 451-7550
Hist. Note: NPOA consists of full-time law enforcement officers; the Nat'l Police Reserve Officers Ass'n consists of members other than full-time law enforcement officers (civilians, guards, etc.). Offers an Awards program for law enforcement officers on and off duty as well as civilians, media and others supportive of law enforcement.
Publication:
Enforcement Journal. q. adv.
Biennial Meetings: uneven years
1987-Sanibel Island, FL/Oct. 21-23

Nat'l Pork Producers Council (1954)
Box 10383, 1776 N.W. 14th St., Des Moines IA 50306
Exec. V. President: Orville K. Sweet
Members: 110,000 *Staff:* 40-45
Annual Budget: over $5,000,000 *Tel:* (515) 223-2600
Hist. Note: Established as the National Swine Growers Council, NPPC assumed its present name in 1967 and is now a federation of 35-40 state associations. Has an annual budget over $10 million.
Publication:
Newsletter. m.
Annual Meetings: March, during the American Pork Congress/15,000

Nat'l Postsecondary Agriculture Student Organization (1979)
Box 34, Cobleskill NY 12043
Exec. Director: Kenneth W. Olcott
Members: 80 institutions; 8,500 individuals *Staff:* 1
Annual Budget: $50-100,000 *Tel:* (518) 234-7309
Hist. Note: Members are institutions educating vocational agricultural students on the junior college level. Membership: $3/yr.(individual), $30/yr.(institution).
Publication:
Newsletter. 3/yr.
Annual Meetings: March
1987-Spokane, WA/March 16-18
1988-Green Bay, WI/March 14-16

Nat'l Potato Council (1948)
9085 East Mineral Circle, Suite 155, Englewood CO 80112
Exec. Director: Ron Walker
Members: 13,500 commercial growers *Staff:* 2-5
Annual Budget: $250-500,000 *Tel:* (303) 790-1141
Hist. Note: Represents all U.S. potato growers on federal legislative and regulatory issues. Membership: $25/yr. (individual); $0.50/1,000 cwt production/yr. (states)
Publications:
Spudletter. 6/yr. adv.
Statistical Report. a. adv.
North American Seed Potato Seminar Proceedings Book. a. adv.
Annual Meetings: Early January/400
1987-San Diego, CA/Jan. 8-10
1988-Tamppa Bay, FL/Jan. 8-10

Nat'l Potato Promotion Board (1972)
1385 S. Colorado Blvd., Denver CO 80222
President: Robert L. Mercer
Members: 15,000 potato growers *Staff:* 20-25
Annual Budget: over $5,000,000 *Tel:* (303) 758-7783
Hist. Note: Also known as The Potato Board. Operates a national promotion plan for potatoes. Has an annual budget of $5-6 million.
Publication:
Spotlight. m.
Annual Meetings: Last week of March in Denver(Marriott)

Nat'l Precast Concrete Ass'n (1965)
825 East 64th St., Indianapolis IN 46220
Exec. V. President: Robert W. Walton
Members: 6-700 companies *Staff:* 6-10
Annual Budget: $100-250,000 *Tel:* (317) 253-0486
Publication:
The North American Precaster. m.
Annual Meetings: February/1,200
1987-San Diego, CA(Sheraton Harbor Island)/Feb. 20-25

Nat'l Premium Sales Executives (1956)
1600 Rt. 22, Union NJ 07083
Exec. Director: Howard C. Henry
Members: Limited to 400 individuals *Staff:* 6-10
Annual Budget: $250-500,000 *Tel:* (201) 687-3090
Hist. Note: Members are professional premium/incentive marketing executives. Membership: $495/yr.

00236 12 05 86 1233

Publications:
Directory of Members. a. adv.
NPSE Newsletter. m.
Incentive Report. semi-a.
Annual Meetings: Chicago, IL(Hyatt Regency)/Sept./400
1987-Sept. 13-17
1988-Sept. 18-22

Nat'l Prepared Frozen Food Ass'n
Hist. Note: Address unknown in 1986.

Nat'l Press Photographers Ass'n (1946)
3200 Croasdaile Drive, Suite 306, Durham NC 27705
Exec. Director: Charles H. Cooper
Members: 8,000-9,000 *Staff:* 6-10
Annual Budget: $500-1,000,000 *Tel:* (919) 383-7246
Publications:
News Photographer. m. adv.
NPPA Membership Directory. a. adv.
Annual Meetings: June-July
1987-Toronto, Ontario/June 30-July 5
1988-Seattle, WA

Nat'l Pretzel Bakers Institute (1940)
P.O. Box 1433, Lancaster PA 17603
Exec. Director: Wendy S. Phillips
Members: 40 companies *Staff:* 2
Annual Budget: $10-25,000 *Tel:* (717) 394-3108
Annual Meetings: September
1987-Phoenix, AZ(The Pointe)/Sept. 23-27

Nat'l Printing Equipment and Supply Ass'n (1933)
6849 Old Dominion Drive, Suite 200, McLean VA 22101
President: Regis J. Delmontagne
Members: 250 *Staff:* 21
Annual Budget: $1-2,000,000 *Tel:* (703) 734-8285
Hist. Note: Established as the Nat'l Printing Equipment Ass'n, it assumed its present name in 1979. Members are makers of graphic arts equipment and supplies.
Annual Meetings: Fall

Nat'l Printing Ink Research Institute
Hist. Note: Sponsored by the Nat'l Ass'n of Printing Ink Manufacturers. Not a trade ass'n.

Nat'l Psychological Ass'n (1947)
Hist. Note: Founded in 1947 and chartered in Maryland. Membership open to all behavioral scientists. Inactive and moribund in 1983.

Nat'l Psychological Ass'n for Psychoanalysis (1950)
150 West 13th St., New York NY 10011
Exec. Administrator: Annabella B. Nelken
Members: 295 *Staff:* 2-5
Tel: (212) 924-7440
Hist. Note: Founded in 1950 by the late Dr. Theodor Reik.
Publications:
News and Reviews. bi-m.
The Psychoanalytic Review. q. adv.

Nat'l Publishers Ass'n (1985)
Hist. Note: Reported as inactive in 1986.

Nat'l Purchasing Institute (1968)
201 W. Belt Line Road, Cedar Hill TX 75104
Exec. Director: J. Nelson Slater
Members: 550 *Staff:* 2-5
Annual Budget: $50-100,000 *Tel:* (214) 333-3278
Hist. Note: Established in 1968 in Galveston, Texas as The Southern Purchasing Institute; assumed its present name in 1973. Educational, government and institutional purchasing administrators. Membership: $75/year.
Publications:
Purchasing News. m.
Membership Directory. a. adv.
Conference Program. a. adv.
Annual Meetings:
1987-Fort Worth, TX(Hyatt Regency)

Nat'l Quartz Producers Council (1967)
Box 1719, Wheat Ridge CO 80034
Secy.-Treas.: Mel Busley
Members: 6 *Staff:* 1
Annual Budget: under $10,000 *Tel:* (303) 424-6777
Hist. Note: Members are producers of crushed quartz for use in decorative architectural concrete.

Nat'l Radio Broadcasters Ass'n
Hist. Note: Merged in 1986 with Nat'l Ass'n of Broadcasters.

Nat'l Railroad Construction and Maintenance Ass'n (1967)
6989 Washington Ave. South, Suite 200, Edina MN 55435
Exec. Director: Daniel Foth
Members: 150-175 companies *Staff:* 3
Annual Budget: $100-250,000 *Tel:* (612) 941-8693
Hist. Note: Originated in 1967 with labor negotiations with the Laborers' Internat'l Union of North America and the Internat'l Union of Operating Engineers for a national agreement on railroad construction and maintenance. Incorporated in Illinois in 1972. Members are railroad construction and maintenance contractors, manufacturing, supply and service firms. Formerly (until 1978), Railroad Construction and Maintenance Ass'n. Membership: $450/yr. (contractors); $300/yr. (suppliers)
Publications:
Directory. a. adv.
Safety Manual. a.
Manual of Supplemental Specification for RR Rehabilitation Projects. a
Manual of Recommended Practice for RR Track Construction. a.
Annual Meetings: Winter
1987-Orlando, FL(Walt Disney World Village Hotel)/Jan. 25-29
1988-Scottsdale, AZ
1989-Bahamas

Nat'l Railroad Intermodal Ass'n
Box 337, Palos Park IL 60464
Exec. Secretary: Pat Crowe
Members: 250 companies and individuals *Staff:* 1
Annual Budget: under $10,000 *Tel:* (312) 974-4363
Hist. Note: Formerly (until 1978) the Nat'l Railroad Piggyback Ass'n.

Nat'l Reading Conference (1953)
1070 Sibley Tower, Rochester NY 14604
Exec. Director: Peter O. Allen
Members: 500 *Staff:* 2-5
Annual Budget: $50-100,000 *Tel:* (716) 546-7241
Hist. Note: Teachers involved in college and adult education literacy programs and research. Membership: $35/yr.
Publication:
Journal of Reading Behavior. q.
Annual Meetings: December
1987-Florida/Dec. 1-5/500
1988-Arizona/Nov. 29-Dec. 3/550
1989-San Antonio, TX/Nov. 28-Dec. 2/550

Nat'l Ready Mixed Concrete Ass'n (1930)
900 Spring St., Silver Spring MD 20910
President: Vincent P. Ahearn, Jr.
Members: 900-1,000 *Staff:* 25-30
Annual Budget: $250-500,000 *Tel:* (301) 587-1400
Hist. Note: Sponsors the National Ready Mixed Concrete Association Political Action Committee.
Annual Meetings: January

Nat'l Realty Committee (1971)
1250 Connecticut Ave., N.W., Suite 630, Washington DC 20036
President: E. Wayne Thevenot
Members: 300 firms *Staff:* 6-10
Annual Budget: $1-2,000,000 *Tel:* (202) 785-0808
Hist. Note: NRC's membership is comprised of those individuals and companies concerned with the development, ownership and financing of large scale income producing real estate in the U.S. Supports the Nat'l Realty Political Action Committee.
Publications:
Newsletter. m.
Periodic Economic Analyses.
Annual Meetings: Quarterly Executive Committee Meetings in Washington or New York

Nat'l Reciprocal and Family Support Enforcement Ass'n
Hist. Note: Became the Nat'l Child Support Enforcement Ass'n in August of 1984.

Nat'l Reciprocal Ass'n (1932)
1350 New York Ave., N.W., Suite 207, Washington DC 20005
Exec. Secretary: C. Aliquo
Members: 250-300 *Staff:* 2-5
Annual Budget: $10-25,000
Publication:
NRA Review. m.
Semi-Annual meetings: Spring and Fall

Nat'l Recreation and Park Ass'n (1965)
3101 Park Center Drive, Alexandria VA 22302
Exec. Director: R. Dean Tice
Members: 18,000 *Staff:* 40-50
Annual Budget: $2-5,000,000 *Tel:* (703) 820-4940
Hist. Note: Formed by a merger of the American Ass'n of Zoological Parks and Aquariums (founded in 1924), the American Institute of Park Executives (formed in 1898), the American Recreation Soc. (formed in 1938), the Nat'l of State Parks (founded in 1921) and the Nat'l Recreation Ass'n(founded in 1906).
Publications:
Journal of Leisure Research, q.
Parks and Recreation. m. adv.
Therapeutic Research Journal. q.
Annual Meetings: Fall

Nat'l Red Cherry Institute (1947)
Box 30285, Lansing MI 48909-7785
Exec. Director: Harry A. Foster
Members: 3 state ass'ns *Staff:* 2-5
Annual Budget: $500-1,000,000 *Tel:* (517) 321-1231
Hist. Note: Established June 2, 1947, and incorporated March 30, 1949. Members are the Michigan Cherry Commission, the Pennsylvania Red Cherry Growers Ass'n and the Wisconsin Red Cherry Growers Ass'n.

Nat'l Rehabilitation Ass'n (1925)
633 South Washington St., Alexandria VA 22314
Exec. Director: David L. Mills
Members: 24-25,000 *Staff:* 6-10
Annual Budget: $500-1,000,000 *Tel:* (703) 836-0850
Hist. Note: Founded in 1925 and incorporated in the District of Columbia in 1963. Membership consists of those concerned with the rehabilitation of the physically and mentally impaired. Membership: $55/yr. (individual); $100-1,000/yr. (company).
Publications:
Journal of Rehabilitation. q. adv.
NRA Newsletter. 8/yr. adv.
Mary Switzer Monograph. a. adv.
Annual Meetings: November/1,500
1987-New Orleans, LA(Hyatt Regency)/Nov. 5-9
1988-Reno, NV(MGM Grand)/Nov. 28-Dec. 2
1989-Orlando, FL
1990-Minneapolis, MN

Nat'l Rehabilitation Counseling Ass'n (1958)
633 S. Washington St., Alexandria VA 22314
President: Susan Magruder
Members: 4,000 individuals *Staff:* 2-5
Annual Budget: $100-250,000 *Tel:* (703) 836-7677
Hist. Note: Affiliated with The Nat'l Rehabilitation Ass'n.
Publications:
Journal of Applied Rehabilitation Counselling. q.adv.
Professional Report. bi-m.
Annual Meetings: With Nat'l Rehabilitation Ass'n.

Nat'l Religious Broadcasters (1943)
CN 1926, Morristown NJ 07960
Exec. Director: Dr. Benjamin L. Armstrong
Members: 450 stations, 550 program producers, 150 associate
Staff: 25-30
Annual Budget: $1-2,000,000 *Tel:* (201) 428-5400
Hist. Note: The oldest and most comprehensive ass'n in the field of religious broadcasting, representing about 75% of those in the field. Strives to maintain free access to the U.S. airwaves by religious broadcasters and to improve quality of religious media. Membership Fee: Based on income.
Publications:
Directory of Religious Broadcasting. a. adv.
Religious Broadcasting. m. adv.
Religious Broadcasting Sourcebook. irreg.
Annual Meetings: February in Washington, DC at the Sheraton

Nat'l Reloading Manufacturers Ass'n (1958)
4905 S.W. Griffith Drive, Suite 101, Beaverton OR 97005
Exec. Secretary: William J. Chevalier
Members: 15-20 companies, 20-30 individuals *Staff:* 2-5
Annual Budget: $10-25,000 *Tel:* (503) 646-1384
Hist. Note: Manufacturers of tools and components for reloading ammunition.

Nat'l Remodelers Ass'n (1933)
Hist. Note: Founded as the National Established Repair Service and Improvement Contractors Association. Merged with the National Home Improvement Council in 1982 to become the National Association of the Remodeling Industry.

Nat'l Renal Administrators Ass'n (1978)
P.O. Box 129, Port Huron MI 48061-0129
Communications Director: Gloria Smith Justice
Members: 250 *Staff:* 5
Annual Budget: $25-50,000 *Tel:* (313) 987-3625
Hist. Note: NRAA was formed to provide a vehicle for the development of educational and informational services for administative personnel involved in the ESRD program. Membership: $100/yr. (professional).
Publications:
NRAA Newsletter. q. adv.
NRAA Membership Directory. a. adv.
Annual Meetings: Fall

Nat'l Renderers Ass'n (1933)
2250 East Devon Ave., Des Plaines IL 60018
President: Dean A. Specht
Members: 400 *Staff:* 20
Annual Budget: $2-5,000,000 *Tel:* (312) 827-8151
Hist. Note: Re-cyclers of animal by-products who produce tallow and grease as a by-product of meat packing.
Publications:
Render. bi-m.
Renditions. semi-m.
Annual Meetings: October/600
1987-Dallas, TX
1988-Palm Springs, CA
1989-Toronto, Canada

Nat'l Rental Service Ass'n
Hist. Note: Formerly the Folding Chair Rental Ass'n. Merged with the American Rental Ass'n in 1986.

Nat'l Rep/Wholesaler Ass'n (1979)
2179 South Shiloh, Suite 1, Garland TX 75041-1331
Exec. Officer: Don B. Akerman
Members: 40
Annual Budget: $25-50,000 *Tel:* (214) 864-0025
Hist. Note: Office furniture representatives that have wholesale outlets. Affiliated with the National Office Products Association.
Semi-annual meetings: June and October

00237 12 05 86 1233

Nat'l Research Council (1916)
Hist. Note: Established by the National Academy of Sciences in 1916 and perpetuated at the request of the President of the United States to serve as the operating arm of the National Academy of Sciences and the National Academy of Engineering for providing scientific and technical advice to the government, the public and the scientific and engineering communities. Administered by the National Academy of Sciences, the National Academy of Engineering and the Institue of Medicine. Not a membership organization.
Publication:
News Report. 10/yr.

Nat'l Resource Recovery Ass'n (1982)
1620 Eye St., N.W., Washington DC 20006
Exec. Secretary: Ronald Musselwhite
Members: 250 *Staff:* 2-5
Annual Budget: $50-100,000 *Tel:* (202) 293-7330
Hist. Note: Affiliated with U. S. Conference of Mayors, members are concerned with the recycling of municipal solid waste for the production of heat, energy, and other purposes. Active members are local government organizations; associate members are from the private sector. Active Membership fee varies according to population.
Publication:
City Currents. bi-m.
Annual Meetings: Always in Washington, DC/March
1987-Hyatt Regency/March 25-27/250-300

Nat'l Restaurant Ass'n (1919)
311 First St., N.W., Washington DC 20001
Exec. V. President: William Fisher
Members: 11,000 *Staff:* 100
Annual Budget: over $5,000,000 *Tel:* (202) 638-6100
Hist. Note: NRA is the foodservice industry's leading trade group with a membership representing more than 100,000 establishments. Maintains a Chicago office. Sponsors the National Restaurant Association Political Action Committee. Has an annual budget of $14.1 million. Membership: $90-8,000/yr. (company, based on sales volume).
Publications:
Restaurants U.S.A. m.
Washington Report. w.
Annual Meetings: Chicago, IL/3rd week in May/100,000
1987-Chicago Hilton

Nat'l Retail Hardware Ass'n (1900)
770 North High School Rd., Indianapolis IN 46224
Mng. Director: Richard H. Lambert
Members: 17-18,000 *Staff:* 90-100
Annual Budget: over $5,000,000 *Tel:* (317) 248-1261
Hist. Note: A federation of 20 affiliated U.S. and Canadian associations. Has an annual budget of $14,000,000.
Publications:
DIY Retailing. m. adv.
Worldwide Hardware. semi-a. adv.
Annual Meetings: Summer/1,400-1,500
1987-Washington, DC(Hilton)/July

Nat'l Retail Merchants Ass'n (1911)
100 West 31st St., New York NY 10001
President: James R. Williams
Members: 45,000 stores *Staff:* 90-100
Annual Budget: over $5,000,000 *Tel:* (212) 244-8780
Hist. Note: Established as Nat'l Retail Dry Good Ass'n, it assumed its present name in 1958. Membership includes larger chains and smaller stores from the United States and 50 countries abroad. NRMA counsels and assists in every aspect of store keeping; conducts seminars and workshops; and engages in research. Maintains a Washington, DC office and sponsors the Nat'l Retail Merchants Ass'n Political Action Committee.
Publications:
Creditalk. bi-m.
Employee Relations Bulletin. m.
Retail Control.
Stores. m. adv.
Traffic Topics. q.
Ad Pro. m.
Annual Meetings: New York, NY(Hilton & Sheraton)/Jan.
1987-Jan. 11-14
1988-Jan. 10-13

Nat'l Retail Pet Store and Groomers Ass'n (1951)
Box 1337, South Pasadena CA 91030
Secretary: Thomas H. McLaughlin
Members: 100 *Staff:* 1
Annual Budget: $10-25,000 *Tel:* (818) 799-7182
Hist. Note: Founded as the National Pet Supply and Groomers Association, it assumed its present name in 1978. Members are pet stores, animal groomers and their suppliers.
Annual Meetings: Spring/150

Nat'l Rice Growers Ass'n (1965)
Hist. Note: A federation of five county rice growers associations. Inactive in 1984.

Nat'l Rifle Ass'n of America (1871)
1600 Rhode Island Ave., N.W., Washington DC 20036
Acting Exec. V. President: J. Warren Cassidy
Members: 3,000,000 *Staff:* 375-400
Annual Budget: over $5,000,000 *Tel:* (202) 828-6000
Hist. Note: Formed August 19, 1871 in New York City "to promote and encourage rifle shooting on a scientific basis" and incorporated in the State of New York November 20, 1871 with General Ambrose Burnside as first President. It is the oldest sportsmen's organization in the U.S. Maintains the NRA Political Victory Fund and supports the Institute for Legislative Action (founded in 1975), its political action arm. Acts as the U. S. national governing body in shooting for the International Shooting Union and the U. S. Olympic Committee. Has an annual budget of $52,000,000 Membership: $20/yr.
Publications:
The American Hunter. m. adv.
The American Marksman. m. adv.
American Rifleman. m. adv.
Monitor. bi-w.
Annual Meetings: Spring/18,000
1987-Reno, NV/April 24-28
1988-Orlando, FL/April 22-26
1989-St. Louis, MO/April 28-May 2
1990-Anaheim, CA/June 8-12

Nat'l Roof Deck Contractors Ass'n (1959)
600 S. Federal St., #400, Chicago IL 60605
Exec. Director: Mary Meyers
Members: 35-40 companies *Staff:* 2-5
Annual Budget: $10-25,000 *Tel:* (312) 346-1600
Hist. Note: Members are contractors installing poured gypsum, lightweight insulating concrete and cementitious wood fibre structural roof deck systems. Formerly (until 1980) known as the Gypsum Roof Deck Foundation.

Nat'l Roofing Contractors Ass'n (1886)
One O'Hare Centre, 6250 River Road, Des Plaines IL 60018
Exec. V. President: Fred C. Good, CAE
Members: 3,000 *Staff:* 35
Annual Budget: over $5,000,000 *Tel:* (312) 318-6722
Hist. Note: Installers of all types of roofs and roofing materials. Sponsors the National Roofing Contractors Political Action Committee.
Publications:
The Roofing Spec. m. adv.
Roofing 86. a.
Annual Meetings: Late Winter
1987-San Francisco, CA(100th Anniversary)/Feb./March/10,000
1988-Dallas, TX/Feb. 22-26

Nat'l Rural Electric Cooperative Ass'n (1942)
1800 Massachusetts Ave., N.W., Washington DC 20036
Exec. V. President: Bob Bergland
Members: 1,000-1,100 *Staff:* 300-400
Annual Budget: over $5,000,000 *Tel:* (202) 857-9500
Hist. Note: Membership consists of cooperative systems, public power and public utility districts. Has an annual budget of over $40 million. Supports the Action Committee for Rural Electrification.
Publications:
Management Quarterly. q.
Rural Electric Newsletter. w.
Rural Electrification. m. adv.
Annual Meetings: Late Winter, 10-12,000
1987-Dallas, TX/Feb. 1-4
1988-New Orleans, LA/Feb. 7-10
1989-Washington, DC/Feb. 12-15

Nat'l Rural Health Care Ass'n (1978)
301 East Armour Blvd., Suite 420, Kansas City MO 64111
Exec. Director: Robert Van Hook
Members: 1,125 *Staff:* 6-10
Annual Budget: $500-1,000,000 *Tel:* (816) 756-3140
Hist. Note: Formerly the Nat'l Rural Primary Care Ass'n, it assumed its present name in 1984. Absorbed the American Rural Health Ass'n and the American Small and Rural Hospital Ass'n in 1986. Members are health professionals involved in rural health care. Membership: $75/yr. (individual); $250/yr. (organization)
Publications:
Rural Health Care Newsletter. bi-m. adv.
Journal of Rural Health. semi-a. adv.
Annual Meetings:
1987-Nashville, TN
1988-Washington, DC

Nat'l Rural Letter Carriers' Ass'n (1903)
1448 Duke St., Alexandria VA 22314
President: Olin F. Armentrout
Members: 66,000 *Staff:* 16-20
Annual Budget: $2-5,000,000 *Tel:* (703) 684-5545
Hist. Note: Independent labor union organized in Chicago in 1903 and composed of 47 state associations. Sponsors and supports the National Rural Letter Carriers Association Political Action Committee. Membership: $60/yr.
Publication:
The National Rural Letter Carrier. w. adv.
Annual Meetings: First full week in August/2,500
1987-Des Moines, IA
1988-Reno, NV
1989-Buffalo, NY

Nat'l Rural Primary Care Ass'n
Hist. Note: Became the Nat'l Rural Health Care Ass'n in 1984.

Nat'l Safe Transit Ass'n (1948)
43 East Ohio St., Suite 914, Chicago IL 60610
Exec. Director: Ellis Murphy
Members: 350 companies *Staff:* 2-5
Annual Budget: $100-250,000 *Tel:* (312) 645-0083
Hist. Note: Formerly (1974) Nat'l Safe Transit Committee, Inc. Members are shippers, carriers, manufacturers, packagers and testing laboratories interested in reducing damage to goods in transit. Membership: $350/yr. (company).
Publication:
Preshipment Testing. m. adv.
Annual Meetings: First week in May
1987-Toronto, Canada

Nat'l Safety Council (1913)
444 North Michigan Ave., Chicago IL 60611
President: T. C. Gilchrest
Members: 11-12,000 *Staff:* 325
Annual Budget: over $5,000,000 *Tel:* (312) 527-4800
Hist. Note: Founded September 24, 1913 in Chicago as the Nat'l Council for Industrial Safety. Became the Nat'l Safety Council in 1914 and was granted a charter by Congress August 13, 1953 to arouse and maintain the interest in safety and accident prevention, and to encourage the adoption and institution of safety methods by all persons, corporations and other organizations. Has an annual budget of $24 million.
Publications:
Family Safety. q.
Farm Safety Review. bi-m.
The Industrial Supervisor. m.
Journal of Safety Research. q.
National Safety and Health News. m. adv.
Safe Driver. m.
Safe Worker. m.
Traffic Safety. m. adv.
Nat'l Safety Congress & Exposition: Chicago, IL(Hyatt)/Fall/13,000

Nat'l Safety Management Soc. (1966)
3871 Piedmont Ave., Oakland CA 94611
President: Phil Wirtz
Members: 2,000
Annual Budget: $50-100,000 *Tel:* (415) 653-4148
Hist. Note: A professional society dedicated to the advancement of new concepts of accident prevention and loss control, promoting the role of safety management as an indispensable tool for management improvement, and providing the individual member an opportunity for professional growth. Membership is open to anyone with management responsibilities. Membership: $40-55/year.
Publications:
Insights - Journal of Safety Management. semi-a.
Update - Safety Management Newsletter. m.
Annual Meetings: May/200

Nat'l Sand and Gravel Ass'n (1916)
900 Spring St., Silver Spring MD 20910
President: Vincent P. Ahearn, Jr.
Members: 300-350 *Staff:* 31
Annual Budget: $500-1,000,000 *Tel:* (301) 587-1400
Hist. Note: Sponsors the National Sand and Gravel Association Political Action Committee.
Publication:
Sand Gravel Board Letter. m.
Annual Meetings: With Nat'l Ready-Mixed Concrete Ass'n

Nat'l Sash and Door Jobbers Ass'n (1935)
2300 E. Devon Ave., #358, Des Plaines IL 60018
Exec. V. President: Robert T. O'Keefe
Members: 750 companies *Staff:* 6-10
Annual Budget: $1-2,000,000 *Tel:* (312) 299-3400
Hist. Note: Formed by a merger of the Northern and Southern Sash and Door Jobbers Associations (both founded in 1935).
Publications:
Membership Directory and Products Guide. a.
NSDJA News. m.
Millwork Product Guide. a.
Millwork Home Study. a.
Business Math Home Study.
Annual Meetings: Fall
1987-Las Vegas, NV
1988-Nashville, TN
1989-Anaheim, CA
1990-Orlando, FL
1991-San Francisco, CA

Nat'l Satellite Cable Ass'n (1982)
888 16th St. NW, Washington DC 20006
Chairman: Robert Swander
Members: 225 *Staff:* 2-5
Annual Budget: $100-250,000 *Tel:* (202) 659-2928
Hist. Note: Members are operators of satellite master antenna systems(SMATV), owners and developers of multi-unit housing complexes, manufacturers, suppliers and distributors of equipment, program providers, consultants and attorneys.
Publication:
Downlink.

Nat'l Savings and Loan League (1943)
Hist. Note: Established as the Nat'l Savings and Loan League. Became the Nat'l League of Insured Savings Ass'ns in 1957 and changed its name back to the Nat'l Savings and Loan League in 1974. Merged on November 1, 1983 with the National Association of Mutual Savings Banks to form the National Council of Savings Institutions.

Nat'l Scale Men's Ass'n
Hist. Note: Name changed to the Internat'l Soc. of Weighing and Measurement (1985).

Nat'l Scholastic Press Ass'n
Hist. Note: See Associated Collegiate Press, Nat'l Scholastic Press Ass'n.

00238 12 05 86 1233

Nat'l School Boards Ass'n (1940)
1680 Duke St., Alexandria VA 22314
Exec. Director: Thomas A. Shannon
Members: 52 State Ass'ns *Staff:* 100
Annual Budget: over $5,000,000 *Tel:* (703) 838-6722
Hist. Note: Formerly (1948) Nat'l Council of State School Boards Assn's. Has an annual budget over $10,000,000.
Publications:
American School Board Journal. m. adv.
The Executive Educator. m. adv.
Annual Meetings: March/April/20,000
1987-San Francisco, CA/Apr. 4-7
1988-New Orleans, LA/March 25-29
1989-Anaheim, CA/March 31-April 3
1990-Las Vegas, NV
1991-San Francisco, CA

Nat'l School Orchestra Ass'n (1958)
345 Maxwell Drive, Pittsburgh PA 15236
Exec. Secretary, NSOA Service Office: Norman Mellin
Members: 1,500 individuals *Staff:* 1
Annual Budget: $25-50,000 *Tel:* (412) 882-6696
Hist. Note: Unified Associate of the Music Educators Nat'l Conference. Formed to promote and improve orchestras in the elementary and secondary schools, colleges, universities, and their surrounding communities. Membership: $20/yr.(individual); $25/yr.(institution)
Publications:
NSOA Bulletin. 5/yr. adv.
The Instrumentalist.

Nat'l School Public Relations Ass'n (1935)
1501 Lee Highway, Arlington VA 22209
Exec. Director: John H. Wherry
Members: 1,600 individuals *Staff:* 20-25
Annual Budget: $1-2,000,000 *Tel:* (703) 528-5840
Hist. Note: Formerly (1950) School Public Relations Ass'n. Individuals from school districts, nat'l, state and local ass'ns, state education agencies, school-community relations programs, and information agencies.
Publications:
Education U.S.A. w.
Education U.S.A. Ed-Line. twice daily.
It Starts in the Classroom. m.
NSPRA Network.
Annual Meetings: July/600
1987-San Antonio, TX/July 13-16

Nat'l School Supply and Equipment Ass'n (1916)
P.O. Box 17005, Arlington VA 22216
Exec. V. President: John L. Spalding
Members: 700 companies *Staff:* 7
Annual Budget: $500-1,000,000 *Tel:* (703) 524-8819
Hist. Note: Formerly (1958) Nat'l School Service Institute. Members are manufacturers, distributors, retailers and independent manufacturers representatives of school supplies, instructional materials and equipment. Absorbed the Education Industries Ass'n in 1978.
Publication:
Tidings. m.
Annual Meetings: Fall/1,500
1987-Las Vegas, NV(Tropicana Hotel)/April 10-12
1987-Nashville, TN(Opryland)/Nov. 20-23
1988-Las Vegas, NV(Hilton Conv. Center)/Nov. 4-7

Nat'l School Transportation Ass'n (1964)
6213 Old Keene Mill Court, Box 2639, Springfield VA 22152
Exec. Director: Karen E. Finkel
Members: 1,500 companies and individuals *Staff:* 2-5
Annual Budget: $100-250,000 *Tel:* (703) 644-0700
Hist. Note: Formerly (1975) Nat'l Ass'n of School Bus Contract-Operators. Supports the Non-Partisan Transportation Action Committee (political action). Membership: $40-5,200/year ($9/vehicle).
Publication:
National School Bus Report. q. adv.
Annual Meetings: July
1987-Denver, CO/July 26-29/550
1988-Baltimore, MD/July/550

Nat'l Science Supervisors Ass'n (1960)
P.O. Box AL, Amagansett NY 11930
Exec. Secretary: Robert Fariel
Members: 700-750 *Staff:* 1
Annual Budget: under $10,000 *Tel:* (516) 267-3692
Hist. Note: An affiliate of the Nat'l Science Teachers Ass'n, with which it annually meets. Has no permanent address or paid staff; its affairs are directed by an annually-elected President and Executive Board. Membership: $15/yr.
Publication:
NSSA Newsletter. q.
Annual Meetings: March with the Nat'l Science Teachers Ass'n
1987-Washington, DC/March 26-29

Nat'l Science Teachers Ass'n (1895)
1742 Connecticut Ave., N.W., Washington DC 20009
Exec. Director: Bill G. Aldridge
Members: 42,000, including 30,000 individuals *Staff:* 50
Annual Budget: $1-2,000,000 *Tel:* (202) 328-5800
Hist. Note: Established in 1895 as the Department of Science Instruction of the Nat'l Education Ass'n. Merged with the American Science Teachers Ass'n in 1944 and reorganized to form the Nat'l Science Teachers Ass'n. Incorporated in the District of Columbia in 1960. Affiliated with the American Ass'n for the Advancement of Science. Membership: $25/year.
Publications:
Journal of College Science Teaching. bi-m. adv.
Science and Children. m. adv.
Science Scope. q. adv.
The Science Teacher. 7/yr. adv.
Annual Meetings: Spring
1987-Washington, DC/March 26-29

Nat'l Screw Machine Products Ass'n (1933)
6700 West Snowville Rd., Brecksville OH 44141
Exec. V. President: Frank T. McGinnis, CAE
Members: 500 companies *Staff:* 11-15
Annual Budget: $500-1,000,000 *Tel:* (216) 526-0300
Hist. Note: Sponsors the National Screw Machine Products Association Political Action Committee.
Annual Meetings: Fall/500
1987-San Diego, CA(Inter-Continental)/OZct. 25-30
1988-Bay Point, FL(Marriott)/Oct. 30-Nov. 3
1989-Maui, HI(Marriott Kaanapali Beach)/Oct. 21-27

Nat'l Sculpture Soc. (1893)
15 East 26th St., New York NY 10010
Exec. Director: Mrs. Claire A. Stein
Members: 350 *Staff:* 2-5
Annual Budget: $100-250,000 *Tel:* (212) 889-6960
Hist. Note: Members are professional sculptors united to promote the development and appreciation of sculpture.
Publications:
Exhibit Catalogue. a.
National Sculpture Review. a. adv.
Annual Meetings: New York City second Tuesday in January/65-90

Nat'l Seasoning Manufacturers Ass'n (1972)
701 S. County Line Road, Hinsdale IL 60521
Exec. Secretary: Andrew E. Maren
Members: 25-30 companies *Staff:* 1
Annual Budget: under $10,000 *Tel:* (312) 323-6693
Hist. Note: Established as the Industrial Meat Seasoning Manufacturers Ass'n, it became the Nat'l Ass'n of Meat Seasoning Manufacturers. In 1981 it became the Nat'l Ass'n of Meat and Food Seasoning Manufacturers and assumed its present name in 1984. Membership: $150-200/yr.
Annual Meetings: With the American Meat Institute in the Fall of odd years.
With the Institute of Food Technologists in the summer of even years.
1987-Chicago, IL(McCormick Inn)/Oct.

Nat'l Second Mortgage Ass'n (1974)
1166 DeKalb Pike, Center Square PA 19422
Exec. Director: Perk Lodge
Members: 130 *Staff:* 2-5
Annual Budget: $100-250,000 *Tel:* (800) 342-1121
Hist. Note: Active members include banks, second mortgage companies, savings and loan and other financial institutions. Organized and incorporated in 1974 in Atlanta by 26 charter members. Active Membership: $350 intitiation fee, $650/yr.
Publications:
Equity Magazine. q.
Legislative Report. 3/yr.
NSMA Statistical Report. a.
Annual Meetings: Spring/300
1987-Laguna Beach, CA(Ritz Carlton)
1988-White Sulphur Springs, WV(The Homestead)
1989-Colorado Springs, CO(Broadmoor)
1990-Cerromar Beach, Puerto Rico

Nat'l Security Industrial Ass'n (1944)
1015 15th St., N.W., Suite 901, Washington DC 20005
President: Lt. Gen. Wallace H. Robinson, Jr. USMC
Members: 400 companies *Staff:* 27
Annual Budget: $2-5,000,000 *Tel:* (202) 393-3620
Hist. Note: Members are industrial, research, legal and educational organizations of all sizes and drawn from all segments of the industrial community interested in and related to the national security. Founded in 1944 at the instance of James Forrestal, then Secretary of the Navy and later the first Secretary of Defense. Fosters an effective working relationship between government and industry in the interest of national security.
Publications:
NSIA Annual Report. a.
NSIA Newsletter. q.
Annual Meetings: Washington, DC(Sheraton Washington)/3rd week in Sept./500

Nat'l Security Traders Ass'n (1934)
One World Trade Center, Suite 4511, New York NY 10048
President: John L. Watson
Members: 5,000 *Staff:* 2-5
Annual Budget: $250-500,000 *Tel:* (212) 524-0484
Hist. Note: Members are Over-the-Counter stock traders. Sponsors the Over-the-Counter Information Bureau.
Annual Meetings: October

Nat'l Selected Morticians (1917)
1616 Central St., Evanston IL 60201
Director: Fred L. Bates
Members: 950 funeral directors *Staff:* 6-10
Annual Budget: $500-1,000,000 *Tel:* (312) 475-3414
Publication:
NSM Bulletin. m.
Annual Meetings: Fall/900
1987-Orlando, FL (Disneyworld Contemporary)/Sep. 15-18
1988-Denver, CO (Marriott Center City)/Oct. 4-7

Nat'l Service Robot Ass'n (1984)
900 Victors Way, Box 3724, Ann Arbor MI 48106
Exec. V. President: Donald A. Vincent
Members: 20 companies; 300 individuals *Staff:* 10
Annual Budget: $50-100,000 *Tel:* (313) 994-6088
Hist. Note: Established and managed by the Robotic Industries Ass'n. Membership: $30/yr. (individual); $300/yr. (organization/company)
Publications:
Robot Times Newsletter. bi-m.
NSRA News. q.
Annual Meetings:
1987-Chicago, IL(McCormick Place)/April 28-29

Nat'l Shellfisheries Ass'n (1909)
Marine Sciences Research Center, SUNY, Stony Brook NY 11794
Secy.-Treas.: Scott Siddall
Members: 600-700
Annual Budget: $10-25,000 *Tel:* (516) 632-8668
Hist. Note: Organized as Nat'l Ass'n of Shellfish Commissioners, it assumed its present name in 1930 and was incorporated in Maryland in 1968. Members are individuals interested in research on that group of mollusks and crustaceans of economic importance known as shellfish. Has no paid staff or permanent address. Membership: $18/yr.
Publication:
Journal of Shellfish Research. semi-a.
Annual Meetings: Summer

Nat'l Sheriffs' Ass'n (1940)
1450 Duke St., Alexandria VA 22314
Exec. Director: L. Cary Bittick
Members: 45,000 *Staff:* 29-32
Annual Budget: $2-5,000,000 *Tel:* (703) 836-7827
Publications:
The National Sheriff. bi-m. adv.
The Roll Call. bi-m.
Annual Meetings: June/1,200
1987-Grand Rapids, MI(Amway Grand Plaza)/June 21-24
1988-Louisville, KY
1989-Hawaii
1990-Denver, CO
1991-Minneapolis, MN

Nat'l Shoe Retailers Ass'n (1912)
1414 Avenue of the Americas, 7th Floor, New York NY 10019
President: William Boettge
Members: 4,000 *Staff:* 8-10
Annual Budget: $500-1,000,000 *Tel:* (212) 752-2555
Publications:
Footwear Focus. q. adv.
NSRA Newsletter. m. adv.
Annual Meetings:
1987-Hilton Head, SC(Hyatt)/May 13-16/100

Nat'l Shoe Travelers Ass'n (1910)
230 South Bemiston Ave., St. Louis MO 63105
President: Arthur W. Jacob
Members: 6,500 *Staff:* 2-5
Annual Budget: $250-500,000 *Tel:* (314) 862-6264
Hist. Note: Membership: $60/year.
Publication:
Foot-Print. bi-m.

Nat'l Shooting Sports Foundation (1961)
Box 1075, Riverside CT 06878
Exec. Director: Robert T. Delfayng
Members: 400-450 *Staff:* 11
Annual Budget: $1-2,000,000 *Tel:* (203) 637-3618
Hist. Note: Absorbed (1963) Sportmen's Service Bureau. Manufacturers of hunting and shooting equipment and accessories. Supported by about 100 firms involved in all aspects of the shooting industry, as well as dealers, distributors and sales reps. The Sporting Arms and Ammunition Manufacturers' Institute became an autonomous subsidiary of NSSF in 1985.
Publication:
NSSF Reports
Annual Meetings: January/20,000
1987-New Orleans, LA(Conv. Center)
1988-Las Vegas, NV
1989-Dallas, TX

Nat'l Shorthand Reporters Ass'n (1899)
118 Park St., S.E., Vienna VA 22180
Exec. Director: Charles G. Hagee, CAE
Members: 20,000 *Staff:* 25-30
Annual Budget: $2-5,000,000 *Tel:* (703) 281-4677
Hist. Note: Merged (1970) with Associated Stenotypists of America. Sponsors and supports the National Shorthand Reporters Association Political Action Committee. Members are individuals "skilled in the art of verbatim reporting of proceedings by the use of shorthand symbols, manually or by machine". Membership: $90/yr.
Publications:
The National Shorthand Reporter. 10/year. adv.
Registry of Professional Reporters. a. adv.
Annual Meetings: August/1,200
1987-Seattle, WA(Westin)/Aug. 5-8
1988-Minneapolis, MN(Hyatt Regency)/July 27-30
1989-Orlando, FL(Marriott)/Aug. 2-5

00239 12 05 86 1233

Nat'l Showmen's Ass'n (1938)
Box 662, East Northport NY 11731
Secretary: Millie Sparks
Members: 150-200 individuals *Staff:* 1
Annual Budget: $10-25,000 *Tel:* (516) 261-2417
Hist. Note: Members are owners or operators of rides, concessions and other carnival attractions. Has no paid staff.
Semi-annual Meetings: March and October

Nat'l Shrimp Breaders and Processors Ass'n (1957)
Hist. Note: Became the Nat'l Shrimp Processors Ass'n in 1984.

Nat'l Shrimp Congress (1957)
Hist. Note: Defunct in 1983.

Nat'l Shrimp Processors Ass'n (1957)
55 Park Place, Suite 400, Atlanta GA 30335
General Counsel: William H. Kitchens
Members: 27 *Staff:* 1
Annual Budget: $10-25,000 *Tel:* (404) 577-5100
Hist. Note: Formerly (1984) the Nat'l Shrimp Breaders and Processors Ass'n. Membership: $500/yr.
Publication:
Newsletter. q.
Annual Meetings: February
1987-Longboat Key, FL(Colony Beach Resort)/Feb. 19-21

Nat'l Single Service Food Ass'n (1977)
5775 Peachtree-Dunwoody Road, Suite 500D, Atlanta GA 30342
President: Robert H. Kellen
Members: 55 *Staff:* 5
Tel: (404) 252-3663
Hist. Note: Manufacturers and packagers of individual packets of condiments and other portion control foods for the food service industry.
Annual Meetings:
1987-New Orleans, LA/Oct. 14-16

Nat'l Ski Areas Ass'n (1961)
20 Maple St., Box 2883, Springfield MA 01101
President: Cal Conniff
Members: 425 areas, 250 associates *Staff:* 10
Annual Budget: $1-2,000,000 *Tel:* (413) 781-4732
Hist. Note: Members are Ski area operators. Seeks to foster, stimulate and promote skiing and safety in skiing. Membership: .01% of gross lift receipts up to $5 million and .005% over $5 million, minimum dues $200/year.
Publication:
NSAA News. m.
Annual Meetings: May
1987-Reno, NV(Bally)/May 25-29/1,300
1988-Ft. Lauderdale, FL(Diplomat)/May 22-26/1,300
1989-Anaheim, CA(Anaheim Marriott)/May 10-14
1990-Boston, MA(Sheraton)/May 13-17

Nat'l Ski Credit Ass'n (1954)
83 Eastern Ave., St. Johnsbury VT 05819
Exec. Secretary: James J. Weinstein
Members: 425 companies *Staff:* 2-5
Annual Budget: $50-100,000 *Tel:* (802) 748-8080
Hist. Note: Formerly Nat'l Ski Clothing and Equipment Ass'n. Membership: $425/yr.
Annual Meetings: March

Nat'l Ski Patrol System (1938)
2901 Sheridan Blvd., Denver CO 80214
Exec. Director: Stephen Over
Members: 23-24,000 *Staff:* 8-10
Annual Budget: $500-1,000,000 *Tel:* (303) 237-2737
Hist. Note: Started in 1938 by Minot Dole. Chartered in 1980 by Act of Congress to promote ski safety and the sport of skiing, and assist ski area management by rendering immediate first aid to injured skiers and evacuating them from slopes for further attention. Members are trained in all phases of ski patrolling, including first aid, ski mountaineering, avalanche patrol and lift evacuation.
Publication:
Ski Patrol Magazine. q.
Annual Meetings: June
1987-Colorado Springs, CO

Nat'l Ski Touring Operations Ass'n (1976)
Hist. Note: Became Cross Country Ski Areas of America in 1983.

Nat'l Slag Ass'n (1918)
300 South Washington St., Alexandria VA 22314
President: Howard K. Eggleston
Members: 30-40 *Staff:* 2-5
Annual Budget: $100-250,000 *Tel:* (703) 549-3111
Hist. Note: Members are processors of steel industry slags for use as a mineral aggregate in construction and manufacturing applications.

Nat'l Small Business Ass'n (1937)
1155 15th St., N.W., Suite 710, Washington DC 20005
Exec. V. President: George A. Abbott
Members: 45,000-50,000 companies and individuals *Staff:* 12
Annual Budget: $2-5,000,000 *Tel:* (202) 293-8830
Hist. Note: Founded and incorporated in Ohio in 1937 as the Nat'l Small Business Men's Ass'n. Became the Nat'l Small Business Ass'n in 1962, the same year in which the American Ass'n of Small Business was absorbed. "To foster the birth and vigorous development of independent small business." Absorbed The Conference of American Small Business Organizations in 1982. Managed the Small Business Legislative Council until 1985 when it became an independent entity. Merged with Small Business United in 1986 and changed its name to the Nat'l Small Business United.
Publication:
Voice of Small Business. m.
Semi-annual Meetings: April and September

Nat'l Small Business Government Contractors Ass'n (1982)
405 Northfield Ave., Suite 113, West Orange NJ 07052
Exec. Director: Lydia Barbara Bashwiner
Members: 50-60 companies *Staff:* 2-5
Annual Budget: $25-50,000 *Tel:* (201) 736-1055
Hist. Note: A group of companies interested in liberalizing government procurement procedures and enabling smaller businesses to participate. Membership: $250/yr.

Nat'l Small Shipments Traffic Conference (1952)
1750 Pennsylvania Ave., N.W., Suite 1105, Washington DC 20006
Exec. Director: Joseph F. H. Cutrona
Members: 250-300 *Staff:* 2-5
Annual Budget: $250-500,000 *Tel:* (202) 393-5505
Hist. Note: Founded in 1952 by former members of The National Industrial Traffic League, making LTL ("less than truckload") shipments. Members are truck, air, rail and sea shippers of freight weighing less than 10,000 pounds. Membership fee based on gross annual sales.
Publication:
The Small Shipment. bi-w.
Semi-annual meetings: Spring and Fall/175
1987-Tampa, FL/April 22-24
1987-Arlington, VA(Marriott Crystal Gateway)/Sept. 16-18

Nat'l Soccer Coaches Ass'n of America (1940)
R.D. #5, Box 5074, Stroudsburg PA 18360
Exec. Director: John McKeon
Members: 4,500 *Staff:* 2-5
Annual Budget: $250-500,000 *Tel:* (717) 421-8720
Hist. Note: Membership: $25/year.
Publication:
Soccer Journal. q. adv.
Annual Meetings: January/1,500-1,700
1987-Boston, MA(Marriott Copley Square)
1988-Crystal City, VA(Hyatt Regency)
1989-Philadelphia, PA(Franklin Plaza)

Nat'l Soc. for Cardiopulmonary Technology (1967)
Hist. Note: Became the Nat'l Soc. for Cadiovascular and Pulmonary Technology in 1986.

Nat'l Soc. for Cardiovascular and Pulmonary Technology (1967)
1133 15th St., N.W., Suite 620, Washington DC 20005
Exec. Director: Jerry Lugmayer
Members: 2,500 individuals *Staff:* 2
Annual Budget: $100-250,000 *Tel:* (202) 293-5910
Hist. Note: Formerly the Nat'l Soc. of Cardiopulmonary Technologists, NSCPT became the Nat'l Soc. for Cardiopulmonary Technology in 1979 and assumed its present name in 1986. Membership: $52/year (individual), $250/year (organization/company).
Publications:
NSCPT Analyzer. q. adv.
CP Digest. m. adv.
Annual Meetings: May-June
1987-Boston, MA

Nat'l Soc. for Hebrew Day Schools (1944)
160 Broadway, New York NY 10038
Exec. V. President: Joshua Fishman
Members: 13,000-14,000 individuals *Staff:* 11-15
Annual Budget: $500-1,000,000 *Tel:* (212) 227-1000
Hist. Note: Torah Umesorah was organized by Rabbinical leaders of Eastern Europe who found haven in America and who wished to re-establish Jewish centers of learning on this continent. They therefore began together with the spiritual leaders in North America to found Hebrew Day Schools on all levels, combining religious and secular learning. It has now developed a gamut of services to these schools.
Publications:
Our World. m.
Torah Umesorah Report. q.

Nat'l Soc. for Histotechnology (1973)
5900 Princess Garden Pkwy., Suite 805, Lanham MD 20706
Exec. Secretary: Roberta Mosedale
Members: 2,000-2,100 *Staff:* 2-5
Annual Budget: $50-100,000 *Tel:* (301) 577-4907
Hist. Note: Members are laboratory personnel who study tissues and prepare slides for diagnosis by a pathologist.
Publications:
Journal of Histotechnology. q. adv.
NSH in Action. q.
Annual Meetings: Fall/800
1987-Seattle, WA(Sheraton)/Oct. 10-17
1988-Louisville, KY(Galt House)/Oct. 9-15

Nat'l Soc. for Medical Research (1946)
Hist. Note: Merged with the Ass'n for Biomedical Research to form the Nat'l Ass'n for Biomedical Research in 1985.

Nat'l Soc. for Performance and Instruction (1962)
1126 16th St., N.W., Suite 214, Washington DC 20036
Exec. Director: Paul W. Tremper
Members: 2,500 *Staff:* 2-5
Annual Budget: $250-500,000 *Tel:* (202) 861-0777
Hist. Note: Formerly (1973) Nat'l Soc. for Programmed Instruction. Concerned with improved performance in jobs. Membership: $80/yr.
Publication:
Performance & Instruction Journal. 10/yr. adv.
Annual Meetings: Spring
1987-San Antonio, TX/March 15-20
1988-Washington, DC
1989-Denver, CO

Nat'l Soc. for Real Estate Finance (1978)
2300 M St., N.W., Suite 800, Washington DC 20037
Exec. V. President: Lewis O. Kerwood
Members: 200 individuals *Staff:* 2-5
Tel: (202) 466-6015
Hist. Note: Incorporated in Delaware in 1978 as the National Association of Certified Mortgage Bankers, it began functioning in the spring of 1979 and was rechartered under its present name in 1982. Membership consists of individuals who have achieved distinction in some aspect of real estate/real estate finance.

Nat'l Soc. for the Study of Education (1895)
5835 South Kimbark Ave., Chicago IL 60637
Secy.-Treas.: Kenneth J. Rehage
Members: 2,500-3,000 *Staff:* 2
Annual Budget: $100-250,000 *Tel:* (312) 962-1582
Hist. Note: A professional society of teachers established as the National Herbart Society for the Scientific Study of Education, it assumed its present name in 1899. Membership: $20-40/yr.
Publications:
Contemporary Educational Issues. irreg.
Yearbooks of The N.S.S.E. a.
Annual Meetings: With one or more of the nat'l educational ass'ns.

Nat'l Soc. of Accountants for Cooperatives (1935)
6320 Augusta Drive, #802C, Springfield VA 22150
Exec. Director: Kimberly Smith
Members: 2,200-2,300 *Staff:* 2-5
Annual Budget: $250-500,000 *Tel:* (703) 569-3088
Hist. Note: Membership: $55/yr.
Publication:
Cooperative Accountant. q.
Annual Meetings: August/800
1987-Boston, MA(Copley Plaza)/Aug. 3-6
1988-Colorado Springs, CO(Broadmoor)/Aug. 8-11
1989-San Diego, CA(Intercontinental)/Aug. 7-10
1990-New Orleans, LA/Aug. 6-9
1991-Washington, DC(J.W. Marriott)/Aug. 4-8

Nat'l Soc. of Architectural Engineering (1984)
P.O. Box 395, Lawrence KS 66044
Exec. Director: Ronald N. Helms, P.E., Ph.D
Members: 350
Annual Budget: under $10,000 *Tel:* (913) 864-3434
Hist. Note: Members are architectural engineers, persons who are involved in the design and/or construction of the Engineered systems for buildings. Membership: $150/3 years.
Publication:
Membership Directory. a.
Semi-annual Meetings: Winter and Summer
1987-Nashville, TN/Jan. and Reno, NV/June

Nat'l Soc. of Cartographers (1977)
Hist. Note: Formed by a splinter group of the American Society of Cartographers. Members initially have been concentrated in the Washington area. Has no permanent staff. Officers are elected for one or two-year terms. Address unknown in 1983.

Nat'l Soc. of EMS Administrators
Hist. Note: A division of the National Association of Emergency Medical Technicians.

Nat'l Soc. of EMT Instructor-Coordinators
Hist. Note: A division of the National Association of Emergency Medical Technicians.

Nat'l Soc. of EMT Paramedics
Hist. Note: A division of the National Association of Emergency Medical Technicians.

Nat'l Soc. of Fund Raising Executives (1960)
1101 King St., Suite 3000, Alexandria VA 22314
President: J. Richard Wilson
Members: 6,000 *Staff:* 18
Annual Budget: $1-2,000,000 *Tel:* (703) 684-0410
Hist. Note: Individual fund raisers with experience in directing, managing or counseling fund raising programs. Formerly the Ass'n of Fund-Raising Directors, and (1978) the Nat'l Soc. of Fund Raisers, Inc.
Publications:
NSFRE News. 10/yr.
NSFRE Journal. bien. adv.

00240 12 05 86 1233

Directory. a.
Annual Meetings:
1987-Washington, DC(Sheraton)/March
1988-Nashville, TN(Opryland)

Nat'l Soc. of Genetic Counselors (1978)
431 W. Oakdale Ave., Chicago IL 60657
President: Beth Fine, MS
Members: 750
Annual Budget: $50-100,000 *Tel:* (312) 528-1019
Hist. Note: Incorporated in New York, NSGC was formed to further the professional interests of those with advanced education and experience in the areas of medical genetics and counseling. Membership: $35/yr.
Publication:
Perspectives in Genetic Counseling. q. adv.

Nat'l Soc. of Insurance Premium Auditors (1975)
Box 68401, Indianapolis IN 46268
Exec. Director: Richard A. Knarr
Members: 1,500 individuals *Staff:* 2
Annual Budget: $25-50,000 *Tel:* (317) 253-0943
Hist. Note: A professional society of auditors from insurance or fee service insurance auditing companies. Membership: $25/yr.
Publications:
National Auditor. m.
Premium Audit Ledger. semi-a.
Annual Meetings: May
1987-Indianapolis, IN
1988-Charlotte, NC
1989-New Orleans, LA
1990-Honolulu, HI

Nat'l Soc. of Livestock Record Ass'ns (1911)
Hist. Note: Became the Nat'l Pedigree Livestock Council in 1985.

Nat'l Soc. of Mural Painters (1893)
c/o Am. Fed. of Arts, 41 East 65th St., New York NY 10021
Secretary: Nan Tandy
Members: 150-160
Annual Budget: under $10,000 *Tel:* (212) 532-8233
Hist. Note: The oldest arts organization in the U.S., its members are muralists all over the nation chosen by a majority vote of the organization after a review of slides and biographical material. Membership: $25/yr.
Publication:
Newsletter. irreg.
Quarterly Meetings:

Nat'l Soc. of Painters in Casein and Acrylic (1952)
117 East 35th St., New York NY 10016
President: Mark Freeman
Members: 130
Annual Budget: $10-25,000 *Tel:* (212) 477-8295
Hist. Note: Membership limited to 130 professional artists. Sponsors exhibitions and demonstrations of painting in casein, acrylic and polymer watercolor.
Annual Meetings: May

Nat'l Soc. of Patient Representatives (1972)
840 N. Lake Shore Dr., Chicago IL 60611
Director: Alexandra Gekas
Members: 1,000 *Staff:* 1
Annual Budget: $250-500,000 *Tel:* (312) 280-6000
Hist. Note: Affiliated with the American Hospital Association. Formerly (1981) the Society of Patient Representatives. Membership: $60/yr.
Publication:
Patient Representation. q.
Annual Meetings: Fall
1987-Anaheim, CA(Disneyland)/Oct. 5-9/400
1988-Atlanta, GA(Omni)/Nov. 7-11

Nat'l Soc. of Professional Engineers (1934)
1420 King St., Alexandria VA 22314
Exec. Director: Donald G. Weinert
Members: 75,000 *Staff:* 80
Annual Budget: over $5,000,000 *Tel:* (703) 684-2800
Hist. Note: Founded in New York City in 1934 and incorporated the same year in South Carolina. Consists of 54 state societies and more than 500 chapters. Affiliated with the Accreditation Board for Engineering and Technology and the National Institute for Certification in Engineering Technologies. Supports the Nat'l Soc. of Professional Engineers Political Action Committee and the NSPE Education Foundation. Has an annual budget of $6.9 million.
Publication:
Engineering Times. m. adv.
Semi-annual Meetings: Winter & Summer
1987-Orlando, FL(Orlando Marriott)/Jan. 18-24
1987-Denver, CO(Denver Marriott)/July 12-18
1988-Mobile, AL(Riverview Plaza)/Jan. 24-30
1988-Seattle, WA(Sheraton)/July 17-23

Nat'l Soc. of Professional Resident Managers (1964)
1133 15th St., N.W., Suite 620, Washington DC 20005
Exec. Director: Frank A. Connors
Members: 600 *Staff:* 2-5
Annual Budget: $25-50,000 *Tel:* (202) 293-5910
Hist. Note: Members must be employed in some capacity in the housing management field. The society's main purpose is to upgrade the professional capabilities of its members. 60% of membership is at present in the greater Washington area.
Publications:
NSPRM Directory. a. adv.
NSPRM Newsletter. m. adv.
Annual Meetings: June

Nat'l Soc. of Professional Sanitarians (1956)
Department of Health, Box 570, Jefferson City MO 65102
Exec. Director: John Norris
Members: 500-600 *Staff:* 1
Annual Budget: under $10,000 *Tel:* (314) 751-6095
Hist. Note: Members are individuals involved in all aspects of environmental and public health.
Publication:
Professional Sanitarian. semi-a.
Annual Meetings: Fall

Nat'l Soc. of Professional Surveyors (1981)
Hist. Note: A member organization of the American Congress on Surveying and Mapping.

Nat'l Soc. of Public Accountants (1945)
1010 North Fairfax St., Alexandria VA 22314
Exec. V. President: Stanley H. Stearman, CAE
Members: 21,000 *Staff:* 20-25
Annual Budget: $2-5,000,000 *Tel:* (703) 549-6400
Hist. Note: Professional society of public accountants. Sponsors the Accreditation Council for Accountancy. Supports the National Society of Public Accountants Political Action Committee.
Publications:
The National Public Accountant. m. adv.
NSPA Washington Reporter. m.
Annual Meetings: August/800
1987-Boston, MA/800
1988-Las Vegas, NV
1989-Toronto, Canada
1990-Denver, CO

Nat'l Soc. of Sales Training Executives (1940)
1040 Woodcock Rd., Orlando FL 32803
Administrative Manager: Charles T. Harper, Jr.
Members: 150 *Staff:* 2-5
Annual Budget: $250-500,000 *Tel:* (305) 894-8312

Nat'l Soc. to Prevent Blindness (1908)
79 Madison Ave., New York NY 10016
Exec. Director: Michael L. Weamer
Members: 350 *Staff:* 200
Annual Budget: over $5,000,000 *Tel:* (212) 684-3505
Hist. Note: Formerly (1927) Nat'l Committee for the Prevention of Blindness and (1979) Nat'l Soc. for the Prevention of Blindness. Absorbed (1961) Ophthalmological Foundation.
Publications:
Prevent Blindness News. q.
SIGHTSAVING Magazine. q.

Nat'l Soda Dispensing Equipment Ass'n (1971)
Hist. Note: Became the National Beverage Dispensing Equipment Association in 1982.

Nat'l Soft Drink Ass'n (1919)
1101 16th St., N.W., Washington DC 20036
President: Frederick L. Webber
Members: 2,000 companies *Staff:* 50
Annual Budget: over $5,000,000 *Tel:* (202) 463-6732
Hist. Note: Established as the American Bottlers of Carbonated Beverages, it assumed its present name in 1967. Absorbed the National Bottlers Association and the National Bottlers Protective Association. Members are soft drink makers and their suppliers.
Publications:
NSDA Dateline. bi-w.
NSDA Quarterly. q.
Annual Meetings: Fall/25,000
1987-Chicago, IL/Nov. 2-5
1988-Atlanta, GA/Oct. 31-Nov. 4
1989-New York, NY/Oct. 2-5

Nat'l Solid Wastes Management Ass'n (1964)
1730 Rhode Island Ave., N.W., Suite 1000, Washington DC 20036
Exec. Director: Eugene J. Wingerter
Members: 2,800 companies *Staff:* 40-45
Annual Budget: $2-5,000,000 *Tel:* (202) 659-4613
Hist. Note: Absorbed the Incinerator Institute of America in 1974 and the Nat'l Contract Sweepers Ass'n in 1984.
Publication:
Waste Age. m.
Annual Meetings: Spring/4,000
1987-Dallas, TX(Convention Center)/May 3-8
1988-Washington, DC(Conv. Center)/May 3-6

Nat'l Sound and Communications Ass'n (1980)
501 W. Algonquin Road, Arlington Heights IL 60005-4411
Exec. Secretary: Francis C. Rebedeau
Members: 350 *Staff:* 3
Annual Budget: $100-250,000 *Tel:* (312) 593-8360
Hist. Note: Installers and servicers of audio-visual and electronic communications equipment.

Nat'l Soybean Processors Ass'n (1930)
1255 Twenty-Third St., N.W., Washington DC 20037
President: Sheldon J. Hauck
Members: 14 companies *Staff:* 4-6
Annual Budget: $500-1,000,000 *Tel:* (202) 452-8040
Hist. Note: Supports the Soybean News Service, its public information arm.
Publication:
NSPA Yearbook and Trading Rules. a.
Annual Meetings: June

Nat'l Spa and Pool Institute (1956)
2111 Eisenhower Ave., Alexandria VA 22314
Exec. V. President: William Sadd
Members: 3,600 companies *Staff:* 20-25
Annual Budget: $2-5,000,000 *Tel:* (703) 838-0083
Hist. Note: Founded in Chicago in 1956. Formerly (until 1980) known as the National Swimming Pool Institute. Absorbed the Internat'l Spa and Tub Institute in 1983.
Annual Meetings:
1987-Reno, NV(MGM Grand)/Feb. 15-17/3,000
1988-Houston, TX/Nov. 16-18/12,000
1989-Phoenix, AZ/Nov. 18-21/10,000

Nat'l Speakers Ass'n (1973)
4747 North 7th St., Suite 310, Phoenix AZ 85014
Exec. V. President: P. Douglas Kerr
Members: 2,600 individuals *Staff:* 9
Annual Budget: $500-1,000,000 *Tel:* (602) 265-1001
Hist. Note: Provides a common platform for those interested in increasing the quality, integrity and visibility of the speaking profession. Membership: $110/yr.
Publications:
Speakout. m.
Who's Who in Professional Speaking. a. adv. (members only)
Annual Meetings: Summer
1987-Nashville, TN(Opryland)/July 11-14/1,100
1988-Phoenix, AZ(Pointe at South Mountain)
1989-Dallas, TX
1990-Toronto, Ontario (tentative)

Nat'l Speleological Soc. (1941)
Cave Ave., Huntsville AL 35810
Secretary: Jeanne Pridmore
Members: 6,400 *Staff:* 2
Annual Budget: $50-100,000 *Tel:* (205) 852-1300
Hist. Note: Founded and incorporated in the District of Columbia in January 1941. Affiliated with the American Ass'n for the Advancement of Science, the Nat'l Parks and Conservation Ass'n and the Internat'l Union of Speleology. Dedicated to the exploration, study and conservation of caves and caverns. Membership: $22.50/year.
Publications:
NSS Bulletin. semi-a. adv.
NSS News. m. adv.

Nat'l Sporting Goods Ass'n (1929)
1699 Wall St., Mount Prospect IL 60056-9968
President: Dr. James L. Faltinek, CAE
Members: 18,000 retail outlets, 2,300 suppliers *Staff:* 40-50
Annual Budget: over $5,000,000 *Tel:* (312) 439-4000
Hist. Note: NSGA membership consists of suppliers, retailers, wholesalers and sales agents in the sporting goods industry. It is the largest sporting goods trade association in the U.S. The Athletic Goods Team Distributors is a division of NSGA comprised of members who specialize in supplying equipment to high schools, colleges and organized teams. NSGA also sponsors the Sports Foundation, Inc. to promote interest in active sports and Ass'n and Show Management, Inc., a trade show and association management subsidiary.
Publications:
Team Lineup. q.
Market Watch. m.
NSGA Sports Retailer. m. adv.
Sporting Goods Market. a.
NSGA Cost of Doing Business Survey. a.
NSGA Buying Guide. a.
Tri-annual Meetings:
1987-Dallas, TX(Convention Ctr.)/Sept. 20-22
1987-Anaheim, CA(Convention Ctr.)/Sept. 18-20
1987-Chicago, IL(McCormick Place)/Oct. 8-11
1988-Houston, TX(Brown Convention Ctr.)/Feb. 5-7
1988-Anaheim, CA(Convention Ctr.)/Sept. 16-18
1988-Chicago, IL(McCormick Place)/Oct. 14-17
1989-Dallas, TX(Convention Ctr.)/Feb. 3-5
1989-Chicago, IL(McCormick Place)/Sept. 15-18
1989-Anaheim, CA(Convention Ctr.)/Oct. 20-22
1990-Houston, TX(Brown Convention Ctr.)/Feb. 2-4
1990-Anaheim, CA(Convention Ctr.)/Sept. 14-16
1990-Chicago, IL(McCormick Place)/Oct. 10-13

Nat'l Sportscasters and Sportswriters Ass'n (1962)
Box 559, Salisbury NC 28144
Program Coordinator: Barbara Lockert
Members: 1,000 *Staff:* 1
Annual Budget: $10-25,000 *Tel:* (704) 633-4275
Hist. Note: Membership: $20/yr.
Publication:
NSSA News. semi-a.

Nat'l Spotted Saddle Horse Ass'n (1980)
Box 898, 108 N. Spring, Murfreesboro TN 37133
Secretary: Donna D. West
Members: 1,250 *Staff:* 1
Annual Budget: $25-50,000 *Tel:* (615) 890-2864

00241 12 05 86 1233

Hist. Note: Members own or breed Spotted Saddle horses.
Publication:
Nat'l Spotted Saddle Horse Journal. q. adv.
Semi-annual Meetings: Spring and Fall

Nat'l Spotted Swine Record (1914)
P.O. Box 2807, West Lafayette IN 47906
Secretary: Larry R. Williams
Members: 634 *Staff:* 6-10
Annual Budget: $100-250,000 *Tel:* (317) 497-3918
Hist. Note: Breeders and fanciers of spotted swine. Member of the National Society of Livestock Record Associations. Affiliated with the National Association of Swine Records.
Publication:
Spotted News. m. adv.
Annual Meetings: December

Nat'l Spray Equipment Manufacturers Ass'n (1922)
550 Randall Rd., Elyria OH 44035
Exec. Secretary: Don R. Scarbrough
Members: 11-15 companies *Staff:* 1
Annual Budget: under $10,000 *Tel:* (216) 988-9411
Hist. Note: Established as the National Spray Painting and Finishing Equipment Association, it assumed its present name in 1974. Serves as a technical forum for safety and environmental matters pertaining to the spray finishing industry. Membership: $500/yr. (company).
Annual Meetings: June

Nat'l Sprayer and Duster Ass'n (1946)
Hist. Note: Defunct in 1985.

Nat'l Staff Leasing Ass'n (1984)
1516 S. Pontius Ave., Los Angeles CA 90025
Exec. Director: Randy Bauler, CAE
Members: 60 companies *Staff:* 12
Annual Budget: $25-50,000 *Tel:* (213) 478-0215
Hist. Note: Established in Arizona and incorporated in Virginia, NSLA members are firms providing employee (or staff) leasing services. Membership: $500-1,000/yr. (based on number of employees).
Publication:
NSLA Staff Report. m.
Semi-annual Meetings: May and October

Nat'l Star Route Mail Carriers Ass'n (1933)
Hist. Note: Became the National Star Route Mail Contractors Association in 1982.

Nat'l Star Route Mail Contractors Ass'n (1933)
324 East Capitol St., N.E., Washington DC 20003
Exec. Director: John V. 'Skip' Maraney
Members: 5,500-6,000 *Staff:* 2-5
Annual Budget: $250-500,000 *Tel:* (202) 543-1661
Hist. Note: Members have mail delivery contracts with the U.S. Post Office to transport mail over the highways on authorized schedules. Until 1982 known as the National Star Route Mail Carriers Association.
Annual Meetings: August
1987-Mobile, AL(Riverview Plaza)/Aug. 3-7
1988-Louisville, KY(Sheraton Lakeview Hotel)/Aug. 1-5

Nat'l State Printing Ass'n
Box 11910, Iron Works Pike, Lexington KY 40578
Staff Director: Pam Yost
Members: 50 *Staff:* 1
Annual Budget: $10-25,000 *Tel:* (606) 252-2291
Hist. Note: An association of various states and other related political jurisdictions, NSPA is concerned with improving the management of printing programs, exchanging information, cooperating for more effective production and procurement of printing products. Administrative support is provided by The Council of State Governments .
Publication:
NSPA Newsletter. q.
Annual Meetings:
1987-Carson City, NV/October

Nat'l Steel Carriers Ass'n (1966)
4000 Town Center, Suite 1730, Southfield MI 48075
General Counsel: Robert L. Coopes
Members: 75 companies *Staff:* 2-5
Annual Budget: $100-250,000 *Tel:* (313) 354-0620
Hist. Note: Formed to assist trucking companies with reference to labor matters and grievance hearings.

Nat'l Stone Ass'n (1985)
1415 Elliot Place, N.W., Washington DC 20007
President: Robert G. Bartlett
Members: 375-400 companies *Staff:* 20-25
Annual Budget: $1-2,000,000 *Tel:* (202) 342-1100
Hist. Note: The result of a merger in 1984 between the Nat'l Crushed Stone Ass'n (1918) and the Nat'l Limestone Institute (1945). Quarry owners and operators, equipment manufacturers and service organizations connected with the crushed stone industry. Supports the Nat'l Stone Ass'n Political Action Committee.
Publication:
Magazine. bi-m.
Annual Meetings: Winter
1987-Orlando, FL(Hilton)/Jan. 25-28
1988-Houston, TX(Hyatt)/Jan. 24-28
1989-Washington, DC(Hyatt)/Jan. 21-25

Nat'l Strength and Conditioning Ass'n (1978)
Box 81410, Lincoln NE 68501
Exec. Director: Ken Kontor
Members: 10,500 *Staff:* 15
Annual Budget: $500-1,000,000 *Tel:* (402) 472-3000
Hist. Note: Members are primarily coaches involved in athletic conditioning. Formerly (1981) the Nat'l Strength Coaches Ass'n. Membership: $39/yr.
Publication:
NSCA Journal. bi-m. adv.
Annual Meetings: Summer
1987-Las Vegas, NV(Tropicana)/June 26-28/600
1988-Orlando, FL(Peabody)/June 24-26/800

Nat'l Stripper Well Ass'n (1934)
Box 3373, Abilene TX 79604
Exec. V. President: Glen Michel
Members: 27 associations *Staff:* 2
Annual Budget: $25-50,000 *Tel:* (915) 672-5225
Hist. Note: A stripper oil well produces a daily average of 10 barrels or less of crude petroleum. Membership: $100/year.
Publications:
National Stripper Well Survey. q.
Newsletter. q.
Semi-annual Meetings: With the Independent Petroleum Ass'n of America

Nat'l Student Nurses Ass'n (1953)
North Woodbury Road/Box 56, Pitman NJ 08071
Exec. Director: Robert Piemonte
Members: 30,000 *Staff:* 11
Annual Budget: $1-2,000,000 *Tel:* (609) 589-2319
Hist. Note: Membership: $30-$40/yr. (depending on state chapter). Membership: $30-$40/year (depending on state chapter).
Publications:
Imprint. 5/yr.
NSNA News. 7/yr.
Annual Meetings: Spring
1987-Chicago, IL(Hyatt)/April 1-5/3,000

Nat'l Student Osteopathic Medical Ass'n (1976)
Philadelphia College of Osteopathic, Medicine, 4190 City Ave., Philadelphia PA 19131
Nat'l President: Paul Zeitz
Members: 4,500 *Staff:* 2
Annual Budget: $10-25,000 *Tel:* (215) 581-6000
Hist. Note: Affiliated with the American Osteopathic Ass'n. Membership: $30/yr.
Publication:
Student DOctor.
Semi-annual Meetings: Fall and Spring

Nat'l Student Recreation and Park Soc.
Hist. Note: A branch of the Nat'l Recreation and Park Ass'n.

Nat'l Student Speech Language Hearing Ass'n (1972)
10801 Rockville Pike, Rockville MD 20852
Administrative Consultant: Sr. Charleen Bloom, Ph.D.
Members: 9,000 *Staff:* 1
Annual Budget: $100-250,000 *Tel:* (301) 897-5700
Hist. Note: Formed as Nat'l Student Speech and Hearing Ass'n through a merger of Sigma Alpha Eta and the Student Journal Group of American Speech and Hearing Ass'n; assumed its present name in 1980. Members are undergraduates and master's degree candidates working in the field of speech-language pathology and audiology. Recognized by the American Speech-Language-Hearing Ass'n as the only official national student association in speech and hearing. Membership: $30/yr.
Publications:
NSSLHA Journal. a.
Clinical Series. bien.
Annual Meetings: With the American Speech-Language-Hearing Association.
1987-New Orleans, LA
1988-Boston, MA

Nat'l Suffolk Sheep Ass'n (1935)
Box 324, 3316 Ponderosa, Columbia MO 65205
Secy.-Treas.: Betty J. Biellier
Members: 9,700 *Staff:* 9-12
Annual Budget: $100-250,000 *Tel:* (314) 442-4103
Hist. Note: Breeders and fanciers of Suffolk sheep. Maintains pedigree registry and promotes breed. Member of the National Society of Livestock Record Associations.
Publications:
Sheep Breeder and Sheepman. m. adv.
The Shepherd. m. adv.
Suffolk Banner. adv.
Semi-annual Meetings: Louisville at the North American Livestock
Exhibition and Sedalia in June at the Midwest Ram Sale.

Nat'l Sugar Brokers Ass'n (1903)
One World Trade Center, Suite 1531, New York NY 10048
Exec. Secretary: Gwen Cody
Members: 100-150 *Staff:* 1
Annual Budget: under $10,000 *Tel:* (212) 432-0813
Hist. Note: Members are brokers of refined sugar.
Annual Meetings: Jan. in New York, NY

Nat'l Sunflower Ass'n (1975)
4023 N. State St., Bismarck ND 58501
Exec. Director: Larry Kleingartner
Members: 100 organizations, 15,000 growers *Staff:* 6-10
Annual Budget: $250-500,000 *Tel:* (701) 224-3019
Hist. Note: Companies associated with sunflower products, including growers' councils, seed companies, processors, exporters, researchers, chemical firms, shippers, commission firms and merchandisers. Established as the Sunflower Association of America, it assumed its present name in 1981.
Publication:
The Sunflower. m. adv.
Annual Meetings: December, alternately North and South Dakota
1987-Bismarck, ND(Kirkwood Motor Inn)

Nat'l Supply Distributors Ass'n (1933)
5152 Bower Ave., Dayton OH 45431
President: Earl Bohachek
Members: 190-200 stores *Staff:* 2-5
Annual Budget: $100-250,000 *Tel:* (513) 258-2424
Hist. Note: Founded as Nat'l Plumbing and Heating Ass'n, it became Nat'l Supply Ass'n of America and assumed its present name in 1967. Members are home improvement centers.
Publication:
NSDA Bulletin. w.
Annual Meetings: Spring
1987-Tucson, AZ/March 28-April 1

Nat'l Surplus Dealers Ass'n (1947)
Hist. Note: Dissolved in 1985.

Nat'l Swim and Recreation Ass'n (1970)
Hist. Note: Ceased operations in 1985.

Nat'l Swine Improvement Federation (1975)
101 Peters Hall, Univ. of Minnesota, St. Paul MN 55112
Secy.-Treas.: Dr. Charles J. Christians
Members: 50
Annual Budget: under $10,000 *Tel:* (612) 624-0766
Hist. Note: Established in Kansas City, MO and incorporated in Nebraska. Members are central testing stations, field performance testing programs, purebred breed associations and the Nat'l Pork Producers Council. Membership: $50/yr.
Publications:
Proceedings. a.
Newsletter. q.
Annual Meetings: December

Nat'l Tank Truck Carriers (1945)
2200 Mill Rd., Alexandria VA 22314
President: Clifford J. Harvison
Members: 200-225 *Staff:* 6-10
Annual Budget: $250-500,000 *Tel:* (202) 838-1960
Hist. Note: Conference of American Trucking Ass'ns, Inc. Membership: $250-6,000/yr.
Publications:
Directory. a. adv.
Cargo Tank Truck Regulation. a. adv.
Mutual Aid Handbook. a.
Annual Meetings: May
1987-Toronto, Ontario(Harbor Castle)/May 17-20

Nat'l Tax Ass'n-Tax Institute of America (1973)
21 East State St., Columbus OH 43215
Exec. Director: Stanley J. Bowers
Members: 2,000 *Staff:* 3
Annual Budget: $250-500,000 *Tel:* (614) 224-8352
Hist. Note: Formed by merger of National Tax Association (1907) and Tax Institute of America (1932). Provides the taxpayer, tax administrator, practitioner, educator, and student with a vehicle for national research, discussion, and dissemination of related information. Membership: $50-100/yr.(individual); $250/yr.(organization).
Publications:
National Tax Journal. q.
Proceedings. a.
Annual Meetings: Fall/400
1987-Pittsburgh, PA(Sheraton-Hilton)/Nov. 9-12
1988-Des Moines, IA(Marriott)/Sept. 25-28
1989-Atlanta, GA(Marriott Downtown)/Oct. 8-11
1990-Dearborn, MI(Hyatt Regency)/Oct. 7-10

Nat'l Taxidermists Ass'n (1970)
18626 St. Clair Ave., Cleveland OH 44110
Exec. Director: William Lee Birch
Members: 2,500 individuals; 35 companies *Staff:* 2-5
Annual Budget: $50-100,000 *Tel:* (216) 531-1971
Hist. Note: Membership: $30/year.
Publication:
NTA Newsletter. bi-m.
Annual Meetings:
1987-Las Vegas, NV/July 16-18
1988-Washington, DC/July 5-7

Nat'l Tay-Sachs and Allied Diseases Ass'n (1957)
385 Elliot St., Newton MA 02164
Exec. Director: Dale Carre
Members: 4,500-5,000 *Staff:* 2
Annual Budget: $100-250,000 *Tel:* (617) 964-5508
Hist. Note: Tay-Sachs disease is an inherited genetic disorder, caused by the absence of a vital enzyme and resulting in the destruction of the nervous system; about 85% of reported cases are Jewish, most are of Eastern-Central European ancestry. NTSAD's purpose is public and professional education, prevention, services to families, detection and research of Tay-

00242 12 05 86 1233

Sachs and related allied diseases.
Publication:
Breakthrough. semi-a.
Annual Meetings: Late Spring
1987-Newton, MA(Newton Marriott)/May 29-31/150

Nat'l Technical Services Ass'n (1966)
1255 Twenty-Third St., N.W., Washington DC 20037
Exec. Director: Sheldon J. Hauck
Members: 75-100 firms *Staff:* 2-5
Annual Budget: $100-250,000 *Tel:* (202) 452-8100
Hist. Note: Formerly the Technical Services Industry Ass'n. Trade association of contract tecnical services firms (engineering, designing and drafting companies).
Publication:
NTSA Reporter. q.
Annual Meetings: Fall
1987-Hilton Head, SC(Hotel Intercontinental)/Sept. 20-23
1988-Monterey, CA(Hyatt Regency)/Sept. 28-30

Nat'l Telephone Cooperative Ass'n (1954)
2626 Pennsylvania Ave., N.W., Washington DC 20037
Exec. V. President: Michael E. Brunner
Members: 450 *Staff:* 100
Annual Budget: $2-5,000,000 *Tel:* (202) 298-2300
Hist. Note: Represents both cooperative and commercial, independent rural phone companies, which receive financing from the Rural Electrification Administration under the Department of Agriculture.
Publications:
Rural Telecommunications. q.
NTCA Exchange. 10/yr.
Washington Report. w.
Annual Meetings: First quarter/2,000
1987-Orlando, FL(Marriott)/Feb. 7-13
1988-Las Vegas, NV(Caesar's Palace)/March 6-11
1989-New Orleans, LA(Hilton-Marriott-Sheraton)/Feb. 17-25
1990-San Antonio, TX/Feb.18-23

Nat'l Terrazzo and Mosaic Ass'n (1924)
3166 Des Plaines Ave., Suite 132, Des Plaines IL 60018
Exec. Director: Edward A. Grazzini
Members: 700 *Staff:* 2-5
Annual Budget: $250-500,000 *Tel:* (312) 635-7744
Publications:
NTMA Newsletter. q.
Convention Program Journal. a. adv.
Annual Meetings: March/April
1987-New Orleans, LA(Sheraton)/March 15-20

Nat'l Textile Processors Guild (1933)
75 Livingston St., Brooklyn NY 11201
Secy-Counsel: Leonard Brodsky
Members: 30-35 *Staff:* 1
Annual Budget: under $10,000 *Tel:* (718) 875-2300
Hist. Note: Dyers and finishers of knitted fabrics, yarns and sweaters. Major purpose is labor negotiations. The above address is the law firm of Rothstein and Korzenik. Membership: $600/year (company).

Nat'l Therapeutic Recreation Soc. (1966)
3101 Park Center Drive, Alexandria VA 22302
Branch Liaison: Yvonne A. Washington
Members: 3,200 *Staff:* 2
Tel: (703) 820-4940
Hist. Note: Formed by a merger of the Nat'l Ass'n of Recreation Therapists (founded in 1953) and the Hospital Section of the American Recreation Soc. A branch of the Nat'l Recreation and Park Ass'n. Members are interested in applying recreation towards therapy of the handicapped and ill.
Publication:
Journal. q.
Annual Meetings: With Nat'l Recreation and Park Ass'n

Nat'l Tile Roofing Manufacturers Ass'n (1976)
3127 Los Feliz Blvd., Los Angeles CA 90039
Exec. V. President: Walter F. Pruter
Members: 40 companies, 91 individuals *Staff:* 2
Annual Budget: $50-100,000 *Tel:* (213) 660-4411
Hist. Note: Manufacturers of clay and concrete roof tiles. Membership: $1,000-8,000/yr.
Semi-annual Meetings:
1987-San Francisco, CA/Feb.
1987-Williamsburg, VA/June

Nat'l Tire Dealers and Retreaders Ass'n (1921)
1250 Eye St., N.W., Suite 400, Washington DC 20005
Exec. V. President: Philip P. Friedlander, Jr.
Members: 5,000 *Staff:* 25-35
Annual Budget: $2-5,000,000 *Tel:* (202) 789-2300
Hist. Note: Formerly Nat'l Ass'n of Independent Tire Dealers. Absorbed the Tire Retreading Institute in 1978. Sponsors TIDE-PAC, a political action committee.
Publications:
Dealer News. m. adv.
NTDRA Who's Who. a. adv.
MEMBERGRAM. m. adv.
Annual Meetings: September/10,000
1987-Dallas, TX/Sept. 18-21
1988-New Orleans, LA/Sept. 16-19
1989-Anaheim, CA(Convention Ctr.)/Sept. 14-17
1990-Atlanta, GA(World Congress Ctr.)/Sept. 20-23

Nat'l Tobacco Tax Ass'n (1927)
Hist. Note: Absorbed into the Nat'l Ass'n of Tax Administrators in 1984, formerly a constituent organization of the Federation of Tax Administrators.

Nat'l Tooling and Machining Ass'n (1943)
9300 Livingston Road, Fort Washington MD 20744
President: Matthew B. Coffey
Members: 3,600 *Staff:* 55-60
Annual Budget: $2-5,000,000 *Tel:* (301) 248-6200
Hist. Note: Established as the Nat'l Tool and Die Manufacturers Ass'n, it became the Nat'l Tool, Die and Precision Machining Ass'n in 1960 and assumed its present name in 1980. Members are makers of jigs, molds, tools, gauges, dies and fixtures for companies doing precision machining. Supports the Tooling and Machining Industry Political Action Committee.
Publications:
Buyers Guide. a. adv.
The Record. m. adv.
Annual Meetings: January/1,400

Nat'l Tour Ass'n (1951)
546 East Main, Lexington KY 40508
Exec. V. President: W. James Host
Members: 3,000 *Staff:* 20-25
Annual Budget: $2-5,000,000 *Tel:* (606) 253-1036
Hist. Note: Founded as Nat'l Tour Brokers Ass'n, it assumed its present name in 1983. A non-profit organization of group tour operators and allied suppliers, it sponsors the Nat'l Tour Ass'n Political Action Committee.
Publications:
Tuesday. bi-w.
NTA Courier. m. adv.
Annual Meetings: November
1987-Baltimore, MD/Nov. 8-13
1988-Kansas City, MO/Nov. 13-18
1989-Salt Lake City, UT/Oct. 29-Nov. 3

Nat'l Trade Show Exhibitors Ass'n (1967)
Hist. Note: Became the International Exhibitors Association in 1983.

Nat'l Translator Ass'n (1962)
Box 628, Riverton WY 82501
President: Darwin Hillberry
Members: 250
Annual Budget: $100-250,000 *Tel:* (307) 856-3322
Hist. Note: Translator FM and TV stations boost normal signals over mountains into rural areas.
Annual Meetings: Spring
1987-Albuquerque, NM

Nat'l Trappers Ass'n (1959)
P.O. Box 3667, Bloomington IL 61702
Exec. Director: John Thorson
Members: 20,000 *Staff:* 2-5
Annual Budget: $250-500,000 *Tel:* (309) 829-2422
Hist. Note: Formerly (1969) Nat'l Trappers Ass'n of America. Membership: $10/yr.
Publication:
Voice of the Trapper. q. adv.
Annual Meetings: Third Weekend of August
1987-Mansfield, OH(Fairgrounds)
1988-Dayton, OH

Nat'l Treasury Employees Union (1938)
1730 K St., N.W., Suite 1100, Washington DC 20006
Nat'l President: Robert M. Tobias
Members: 65-70,000 *Staff:* 100
Annual Budget: over $5,000,000 *Tel:* (202) 785-4411
Hist. Note: Formerly (1957) Nat'l Ass'n of Collectors of Internal Revenue and (1973) Nat'l Ass'n of Internal Revenue Service Employees. Absorbed (1970) Nat'l Ass'n of Alcohol and Tobacco Tax Officers (1935). An independent labor union. Absorbed the National Custom Service Ass'n in 1975. Sponsors and supports the National Treasury Employees Union Political Action Committee. Has an annual budget of $7 million.
Publication:
NTEU Bulletin. every 3 wks.
Biennial meetings: Uneven years in August
1987-Chicago, IL
1989-Las Vegas, NV

Nat'l Truck Equipment Ass'n (1964)
25900 Greenfield Rd., Suite 410, Oak Park MI 48237
Exec. Director: James D. Carney
Members: 1,350 companies *Staff:* 15
Annual Budget: $1-2,000,000 *Tel:* (313) 968-3680
Hist. Note: Formerly (until 1979) known as the Truck Equipment and Body Distributors Ass'n, Inc. Membership comprised of companies engaged in the manufacture, distribution and repair of truck bodies and accessories; companies involved in the manufacture, purchase and sales of truck equipment. NTEA includes the Fire Apparatus Manufacturers Ass'n, the Towing Equipment Manufacturers Ass'n, the Ambulance Manufacturers Ass'n and the American Institute of Service Body Manufacturers. Membership: $350/yr. (distributor); $700/yr. (manufacturer)
Publications:
TENews. m.
Excise Tax Quarterly. q.
Regulations Report. m.
Annual Meetings: Winter
1987-Orlando, FL/Jan. 27-31
1988-Houston, TX/April 20-22

Nat'l Truck Leasing System (1944)
2625 Butterfield Road, #110E, Oak Brook IL 60521-1211
President: William J. Ford
Members: 125-150 *Staff:* 6-10
Annual Budget: $1-2,000,000 *Tel:* (312) 782-2991
Hist. Note: Members are independent truck leasing companies.
Publication:
Nationalease Newsletter. w.
Annual Meetings: Fall, in Chicago, IL

Nat'l Tumor Registrar's Ass'n (1974)
104 Wilmot Rd., Suite 201, Deerfield IL 60015-5195
Administrator: Carol Godiksen
Members: 1,200 *Staff:* 3
Annual Budget: $50-100,000 *Tel:* (312) 724-7700
Hist. Note: Members are persons involved with hospital, state or regional data banks that maintain statistics on cancer. Membership: $40/yr.
Publication:
The Abstract. q. adv.
Annual Meetings: May/June
1987-Minneapolis, MN(Marriott City Ctr.)/May 27-30/400
1988-Seattle, WA(Westin)/May 23-28/500

Nat'l Tunis Sheep Registry (1929)
Wayland NY 14572
Secy.-Treas.: Leona Fitzpatrick
Members: 150 *Staff:* 2-5
Annual Budget: under $10,000 *Tel:* (716) 669-2664
Hist. Note: Breeders and fanciers of Tunis sheep, which were first imported into the U.S. in 1799 from Tunis, North Africa. Membership: $5/year.
Publication:
Newsletter. q. adv.
Annual Meetings: Syracuse, NY(State Fair)/Summer

Nat'l Turf Writers Ass'n (1960)
2362 Winston, Louisville KY 40205
Secretary-Treasurer: Mike Barry
Members: 300 *Staff:* 1
Annual Budget: $10-25,000 *Tel:* (502) 452-6965
Annual Meetings: Louisville before the Kentucky Derby.

Nat'l Turkey Federation (1939)
11319 Sunset Hills Road, Reston VA 22090
Exec. V. President: G. L. 'Lew' Walts
Members: 2,000-2,500 *Staff:* 6-10
Annual Budget: $500-1,000,000 *Tel:* (703) 435-7206
Hist. Note: Supports the Turkey Industry Political Action Committee.
Publication:
NTF Newsletter. m.
Annual Meetings: January
1987-Lake Buena Vista, FL(Walt Disney World Hilton)/Jan. 14-16

Nat'l Unfinished Furniture Institute (1980)
1850 Oak St., Northfield IL 60093
Exec. Director: Ray Passis
Members: 6-7,000 *Staff:* 2-5
Annual Budget: $250-500,000 *Tel:* (312) 446-8434
Hist. Note: Membership composed of manufacturers and retailers in the unfinished furniture industry.
Publications:
Newsletter. bi-m.
Unfinished Furniture Industry. bi-m. adv.
Semi-annual Meetings: March and August
1987-Anaheim, CA(Disneyland)/March 29-31
1987-Rosemont, IL(O'Hare Expo Center)/Aug. 2-4

Nat'l United Licensees Beverage Ass'n (1964)
7141 Frankstown Ave., Pittsburgh PA 15208
Exec. Secretary: Vivian Lane
Members: 2,000-2,200 *Staff:* 1
Annual Budget: under $10,000 *Tel:* (412) 241-8773
Hist. Note: Minority holders of liquor licenses.
Annual Meetings: Fall
1987-Chicago, IL

Nat'l University Continuing Education Ass'n (1915)
One Dupont Circle, N.W., Suite 420, Washington DC 20036-1168
Exec. Director: Dr. Kay Kohl
Members: 300-350 institutions *Staff:* 6-10
Annual Budget: $250-500,000 *Tel:* (202) 659-3130
Hist. Note: Formerly (until 1980) known as the Nat'l University Extension Ass'n. Colleges and universities with continuing education programs and professional staff.
Publications:
Continuing Education Recruiter. m. adv.
Continuum. 3/yr.
NUCEA Newsletter. 10/yr.
Annual Meetings: April
1987-Kansas City, MO(Hyatt Regency)/April 5-8
1988-Philadelphia, PA(Adams Mark)/April 16-20
1989-Salt Lake City, UT(Westin, Marriott, Sheraton Triad)/April 12-19

00243 12 05 86 1233

Nat'l Utility Contractors Ass'n (1964)
1235 Jefferson Davis Highway, Suite 606, Arlington VA 22202
Exec. Director: William G. Harley
Members: 2,000 companies *Staff:* 6-10
Annual Budget: $1-2,000,000 *Tel:* (703) 486-2100
Hist. Note: Members are sewer, water and underground utility contractors. Absorbed the Horizontal Earth Borers Ass'n in 1980. Supports the Nat'l Utility Contractors Ass'n Legislative Information and Action Committee.
Publications:
Directory of Members. a. adv.
The National Utility Contractor. m. adv.
NUCA News.
Annual Meetings: Late Winter
1987-Orlando, FL(Marriott World Center)/Feb. 4-7/1,200
1988-San Antonio, TX(Hilton)/Feb. 20-24/1,500

Nat'l Vehicle Leasing Ass'n (1976)
3710 South Robertson Blvd., Suite 225, Culver City CA 90232
Exec. Director: Bill Nerenberg
Members: 850 companies *Staff:* 7
Annual Budget: $500-1,000,000 *Tel:* (213) 838-3170
Hist. Note: Founded as an amalgamation of two separate groups of pioneer lessors in 1968 in San Francisco as the Automotive Leasing Ass'n; merged with the Southern California Leasing Ass'n to become the California Vehicle Leasing Ass'n; expanded its membership in 1981 to become the Western Vehicle Leasing Ass'n; and in 1984 voted to act as a national body under the name Nat'l Vehicle Leasing Ass'n. As the central representative body for all members of the vehicle leasing industry in the U.S., NVLA's activities include: governmental affairs, education, publishing, conferences, legal and other member services, industry relations and certification. Membership: $500/yr.
Publications:
Vehicle Leasing Today. bi-m. adv.
Lifeline. bi-m.
National Guide to Leasing Suppliers & Services. a. adv.
Action Bulletin. q.
Annual Meetings: May
1987-Colorado Springs, CO(Broadmoor)/May 6-10/750
1988-Nashville, TN(Opryland Hotel)/May 17-22/800
1989-San Diego, CA(Hotel Intercontinental)/May 3-7/850

Nat'l Venture Capital Ass'n (1973)
1655 North Fort Myer Drive, Suite 700, Arlington VA 22209
Exec. Director: Daniel T. Kingsley
Members: 200 companies *Staff:* 2
Tel: (703) 528-4370
Hist. Note: Membership by invitation. Members consist of corporations, corporate financiers and private individuals who are responsible for investing private capital in young companies on a professional basis.
Annual Meetings: Spring in Washington, DC

Nat'l Vocational Agricultural Teachers Ass'n (1948)
5600 Mount Vernon Memorial Hwy., Box 15051, Alexandria VA 22309
Exec. Director: Sam Stenzel
Members: 9,000 *Staff:* 2-5
Annual Budget: $100-250,000 *Tel:* (703) 780-1862
Hist. Note: A federation of fifty affiliated state voactional agricaultural teacher associations, NVATA was organized in 1948 in Milwaukee, WI. A member of the Agricultural Education Division of the American Vocational Ass'n. Membership: $35/yr. (individual), $175/yr. (company).
Publication:
News and Views of NVATA. m.
Annual Meetings: With the American Vocational Ass'n.
1987-Las Vegas, NV/Dec. 4-8
1988-St. Louis, MO/Dec. 2-6
1989-Orlando, FL/Dec. 1-5
1990-Cincinnati, OH/Nov. 30-Dec. 1
1991-Los Angeles, CA/Dec. 6-10

Nat'l Vocational Guidance Ass'n (1952)
Hist. Note: Became (1985) the Nat'l Career Development Ass'n.

Nat'l Water Resources Ass'n (1932)
955 L'Enfant Plaza North, S.W., Suite 1202, Washington DC 20024
Exec. V. President: Thomas F. Donnelly
Members: 5,000 *Staff:* 3
Annual Budget: $100-250,000 *Tel:* (202) 488-0610
Hist. Note: Formerly (1970) Nat'l Reclamation Ass'n. Operates in 16 western states. Members are directors of water resource development projects such as irrigation districts, canal companies, conservancy districts and water users in general. Memberships available through state ass'ns.
Publication:
Water Line. m.
Annual Meetings: Fall/1,200
1987-Reno, NV(MGM Grand)
1988-Spokane, WA

Nat'l Water Slide Ass'n (1980)
Hist. Note: Merged with the International Association of Amusement Parks and Attractions in 1982.

Nat'l Water Supply Improvement Ass'n (1973)
Hist. Note: Became the Water Supply Improvement Association in 1982.

Nat'l Water Well Ass'n (1948)
6375 Riverside Drive, Dublin OH 43107
Exec. Director: Dr. Jay H. Lehr
Members: 11,500 *Staff:* 60
Annual Budget: $2-5,000,000 *Tel:* (614) 761-1711
Hist. Note: Members are water well contractors, makers and suppliers of well drilling equipment, and scientists/engineers interested in the problems of locating and using underground water. The Ass'n of Ground Water Scientists and Engineers is a division of NWWA. Membership: $44-120/yr. (individual); $83-220/yr. (org./company)
Publications:
Ground Water Monitoring Review. q. adv.
Water Well Journal. m. adv.
Ground Water. bi-m.
Membership Directory. trien.
Newsletters.
Annual Meetings: September/4,000
1987-Minneapolis, MN/Sept. 14-16
1988-Las Vegas, NV/Sept. 26-28
1989-Houston, TX/Sept. 11-13
1990-Anaheim, CA/Sept.

Nat'l Waterbed Retailers Ass'n (1972)
36 S. State St., #1506, Chicago IL 60603
Exec. Director: Ralph J. Bloch
Members: 360 *Staff:* 5
Annual Budget: $250-500,000 *Tel:* (312) 236-6662
Hist. Note: Founded as the Waterbed Retailers Ass'n, it assumed its present name in 1978. Membership: $100-$150/year.
Publication:
Flotation News. q.
Annual Meetings: September

Nat'l Watercolor Soc. (1920)
5441 Alcove St., N. Hollywood CA 91607
President: Arthur L. Kaye
Members: 1,070
Annual Budget: $10-25,000
Hist. Note: A non-profit, nationwide 1,000 member organization dedicated to the exhibition and promotion of excellence in water media painting.
Publication:
NWS Catalogue. a.
Annual Meetings: February
1987-Brea, CA

Nat'l Waterfowl Council (1952)
Department of Game, 600 North Capitol Way, Olymphia WA 98504
Chairman: Jack S. Wayland
Members: 50 *Staff:* 1
Annual Budget: under $10,000
Hist. Note: Membership consists of state and provincial government fish and game departments. Coordinates waterfowl research, management, and planning. Has no paid staff or permanent address. Officers change annually.
Semi-annual Meetings: March and August, held in conjunction with North American Wildlife Conference and the Fish and Wildlife Service.

Nat'l Waterways Conference (1960)
1130 17th St., N.W., Washington DC 20036
President: Harry N. Cook
Members: 500-550 *Staff:* 2-5
Annual Budget: $100-250,000 *Tel:* (202) 296-4415
Hist. Note: An umbrella group of shippers, barge lines and local waterways authorities working to promote a better understanding of the public value of the American waterways system.
Publications:
Washington Watch (Members Only)
Newsletter. q.
Annual Meetings: September/450
1987-Little Rock, AR
1988-Nashville, TN

Nat'l Weather Ass'n (1976)
4400 Stamp Road, Room 404, Temple Hills MD 20748
Exec. Director: Sol Hirsch
Members: 1,600-1,700 *Staff:* 1
Annual Budget: $50-100,000 *Tel:* (301) 899-3784
Hist. Note: Individuals and groups interested in practical meteorology on a professional basis. Membership: $20/yr. (individual); $25/yr. (organization/company)
Publications:
National Weather Digest. q. adv.
Newsletter. 8/yr.
Meeting Program. a. adv.
Annual Meetings: Fall
1987-New Orleans, LA or Houston, TX/Oct. 20-23/100

Nat'l Weather Service Employees Organization (1976)
400 North Capitol St., Suite 326, Washington DC 20001
President: John Quadros
Members: 1,400 *Staff:* 2-5
Tel: (202) 783-3131
Publications:
Four Winds Flyer. m.
Four Winds Newsletter. bi-m.
Annual Meetings: Fall
1987-Honolulu, HI/Sept.

Nat'l Welding Supply Ass'n (1945)
1900 Arch St., Philadelphia PA 19103
Exec. Secretary: G. A. Taylor Fernley
Members: 1,400-1,500 *Staff:* 6-10
Annual Budget: $250-500,000 *Tel:* (215) 564-3484
Publications:
Spatter.
Welding Supply Index.
Annual Meetings: Fall

Nat'l Wellness Ass'n (1985)
Univ. of Wisconsin Stevens Point, South Hall, Stevens Point WI 54481
Exec. Director: David A. Emmerling, Ed.D.
Staff: 1
Annual Budget: $250-500,000 *Tel:* (715) 346-2172
Hist. Note: Organized under the Nat'l Wellness Institute at the Univ. of Wisconsin at Stevens Point, NWA is composed of professionals working in all areas of health and wellness promotion. Its mission is to meet the growing need of these professionals for information, services and networking. Membership: $45/yr. (individual); $95/yr. (organization)
Publication:
Wellness Management (newsletter). q.
Annual Meetings: With Nat'l Wellness Conference in July at Univ. of WI - Stevens Pt.
1987-July 19-24
1988-July 17-22
1989-July 16-21
1990-July 15-20

Nat'l Wheel and Rim Ass'n (1924)
4836 Victor St., Jacksonville FL 32207
Exec. V. President: Bryan W. Lewis
Members: 45-50 *Staff:* 2-5
Annual Budget: $100-250,000 *Tel:* (904) 737-2900
Hist. Note: Organized in Chicago in 1924 at the Metropole Hotel. Warehouse distributors of wheels, rims and related parts. Affiliated with the Nat'l Ass'n of Wholesaler-Distributors.
Annual Meetings: Fall/200
1987-Orlando, FL(Contemporary)/Sept. 27-Oct. 2
1988-Long Beach, CA(Hyatt)/Sept. 25-30
1989-Boston, MA(Copley)/Sept. 17-22
1990-Vancouver, BC(Bayshore Inn)/Sept. 23-28
1991-Colorado Springs, CO(Broadmoor)/Sept. 15-20

Nat'l Wholesale Druggists' Ass'n (1876)
105 Oronoco St., Alexandria VA 22314
President: Charles S. Trefrey
Members: 700-750 companies *Staff:* 27
Annual Budget: $2-5,000,000 *Tel:* (703) 684-6400
Hist. Note: Established as Western Wholesale Druggists, it assumed its present name in 1881. Absorbed the Druggists Service Council in 1972 and the Drug Wholesalers Ass'n in 1984. Merged with the Drug Wholesalers Ass'n in August 1984.
Publications:
Executive Newsletter. semi-m.
Government Affairs Newsletter. semi-m.
Annual Meetings: Fall
1987-Toronto, Ontario(Sheraton Centre)/Sept. 12-17/1,700
1988-Maui, HI(Hyatt & Marriott)/Oct. 22-26/1,700

Nat'l Wholesale Furniture Ass'n (1933)
Box 2482, High Point NC 27261-2482
Exec. Director: Bobbie C. Shaw
Members: 90-100 companies *Staff:* 2-5
Annual Budget: $50-100,000 *Tel:* (919) 884-1566
Hist. Note: Organized under the auspices of the Nat'l Ass'n of Furniture Manufacturers, members are wholesale furniture distributors.
Publications:
Newsletter. m.
Who's Who in Furniture Distribution. a.
Annual Meetings: Spring
1987-Scottsdale, AZ(Camelback)/Feb. 28-March 4/125

Nat'l Wholesale Hardware Ass'n (1894)
1900 Arch St., Philadelphia PA 19103
Managing Director: Thomas A. Fernley, III
Members: 130 Full-line distributors, 150 manufacturers *Staff:* 6-10
Tel: (215) 564-3484
Annual Meetings: October/1,500
1987-Toronto, Ontario(Sheraton Centre)/Oct. 18-21
1988-Seattle, WA(Sheraton/Westin)/Oct. 9-12
1989-Boston, MA(Marriott/Westin-Copley)/Oct. 15-18

Nat'l Wholesale Lumber Distributing Yard Ass'n (1966)
1015 15th St., N.W., Suite 700, Washington DC 20005
Corporate Agent: John M. Dickerman
Members: 55-60 companies *Staff:* 1
Annual Budget: under $10,000 *Tel:* (202) 289-7797
Annual Meetings: With Nat'l Hardwood Lumber Ass'n

Nat'l Wine Ass'n (1958)
Kasser Liquor Company, 220 West Luzerne St., Philadelphia PA 19140
President: Raymond H. Kasser
Members: 75-100
Annual Budget: under $10,000 *Tel:* (215) 223-3100
Hist. Note: Formerly (1973) Nat'l Ass'n of Wine Bottlers and (1976) Nat'l Ass'n of Wine Producers and Bottlers.
Publication:
NWA Bulletin. m.

00244 12 05 86 1233

Nat'l Wine Distributors Ass'n (1978)
501 W. Algonquin Road, Arlington Heights IL 60005-4411
Exec. Director: Francis C. Rebedeau
Members: 200-225 companies *Staff:* 2-5
Annual Budget: $100-250,000 *Tel:* (312) 593-8360
Publication:
Wine Marketing Perspectives. m.

Nat'l Women's Ass'n of Allied Beverage Industries (1944)
1250 Eye St., N.W., Suite 900, Washington DC 20005
Headquarters Administrator: Norene M. Yoch
Members: 26 chapters *Staff:* 2
Annual Budget: $25-50,000 *Tel:* (202) 628-3544
Hist. Note: Membership: $7/yr.
Publication:
Industry Woman. q.
Annual Meetings: Between June 1st and September 15th/200.
1987-Portland, OR

Nat'l Women's Neckwear and Scarf Ass'n (1933)
1350 Avenue of the Americas, New York NY 10019
General Counsel: Jacob M. Weinstein
Members: 10 companies *Staff:* 1
Annual Budget: under $10,000 *Tel:* (212) 708-0316
Hist. Note: Major purpose is labor negotiations with the International Ladies Garment Workers Union. Membership is concentrated in the New York area. Has no headquarters; the above address is a private law office.

Nat'l Wood Energy Ass'n (1979)
The Hill-Jeremiah Hart House, Box 4548, Portsmouth NH 03801
Chairman: Robert Kennel
Members: 300 companies *Staff:* 3
Annual Budget: $100-250,000 *Tel:* (603) 436-1921
Hist. Note: Trade association for the wood energy industry. Originated in Bloomfield Hills, Michigan in October 1979 and incorporated in Washington, DC. Became moribund in 1980. Reactivated in 1983. Membership: $500/yr.
Publications:
Biologue. bi-m. adv.
BioEnergy Update. bi-m. adv.
Insiders Report. bi-m.

Nat'l Wood Flooring Ass'n (1986)
2714 Breckenridge Industrial Court, St. Louis MO 63144
Exec. Secretary: Bonnie J. Holmes
Members: 150 companies *Staff:* 1
Annual Budget: $50-100,000 *Tel:* (800) 422-4556
Hist. Note: Membership includes all segments of the flooring industry: distributors, manufacturers, retailers/contractors, etc. NWFA's purposes include advertising and promotion, education and training, the development of standards and grade levels and intra-industry communications. Membership: $375/yr.
Publication:
Newsletter. q.
Annual Meetings: Spring
1987-St. Louis, MO(Marriott Pavilion)/April 29 - May 2
1988-Kansas City, MO
1989-Chicago, IL
1990-Minneapolis, MN
1991-Dallas, TX

Nat'l Wood Window and Door Ass'n (1926)
1400 East Touhy Ave., Des Plaines IL 60018
Exec. V. President: John W. Shoemaker
Members: 100-140 *Staff:* 6-10
Annual Budget: $250-500,000 *Tel:* (312) 299-5200
Hist. Note: Founded as the Nat'l Door Manufacturers Ass'n and became the Nat'l Woodwork Manufacturers Ass'n, Inc. in 1950; assumed its present title in 1985. Absorbed the Ponderosa Pine Woodwork Ass'n in 1975. Members are makers of standard building products such as doors, windows, and frames.
Semi-annual Meetings:

Nat'l Wooden Box Ass'n (1897)
Hist. Note: Dissolved in December, 1984.

Nat'l Wooden Pallet and Container Ass'n (1947)
1625 Massachusetts Ave., N.W., Washington DC 20036
Exec. V. President: William C. Baldwin
Members: 270 companies *Staff:* 7
Annual Budget: $250-500,000 *Tel:* (202) 667-3670
Hist. Note: A pallet is a portable platform for moving and storing freight.

Nat'l Woodland Owners Ass'n (1983)
374 Maple Ave. E., Suite 210, Vienna VA 22180
President: Keith A. Argow
Members: 10,500 individuals *Staff:* 2
Annual Budget: under $10,000 *Tel:* (703) 255-2700
Hist. Note: Founded with the purpose of uniting non-industrial private woodland owners in America; membership includes landowners in 48 states. Although independent of the forest products industry and public agencies, NWOA works with all organizations to promote non-industrial forestry and the interests of woodland owners. Membership: $10/yr. (individual); $50/yr. (organization/company)
Publication:
Woodland Report. m.
Annual Meetings: Not held

Nat'l Woodwork Manufacturers Ass'n (1926)
Hist. Note: Became the Nat'l Wood Window and Door Ass'n in 1985.

Nat'l Wool Growers Ass'n (1865)
8 East 300 South, Suite 415, Salt Lake City UT 84111
Exec. V. President: Jay Wilson
Members: 31 associations *Staff:* 6
Annual Budget: $250-500,000 *Tel:* (801) 363-4484
Hist. Note: Organized in Syracuse, NY in 1865 for protection and promotion of the U.S. sheep industry. Membership composed of 31 state and area sheep organizations where 90% of the nation's lambs and wool are produced. Supports Responsible Action to Maintain Sheep (RAMS), a Political Action Committee. Maintains a Washington office.
Publication:
National Wool Grower. m. adv.
Annual Meetings:
1987-Sparks, NV

Nat'l Wool Marketing Corporation (1929)
P.O. Box 32445, Columbus OH 43232-0445
General Manager: V. Arnold MacDonald
Members: 6 state associations *Staff:* 5-10
Annual Budget: $250-500,000 *Tel:* (614) 863-3716
Hist. Note: A marketing agency for a number of state associations of sheep growers.
Semi-annual meetings: February and September

Nat'l Wrestling Coaches Ass'n (1946)
Univ. of Utah, Salt Lake City UT 84112
Exec. V. President: Marvin G. Hess
Members: 1,070 *Staff:* 1
Annual Budget: $50-100,000 *Tel:* (801) 581-3836
Hist. Note: Formerly (1962) American Wrestling Coaches and Officials Ass'n, and (1969) Nat'l Collegiate Athletic Ass'n of Wrestling Coaches and Officials. Affiliated with the Nat'l Collegiate Athletic Ass'n. Membership: $25/yr. (high school), $35/yr. (college).
Publication:
Amateur Wresting News. 14/yr. adv.
Annual Meetings: Fall

Nat'l Writers Club (1937)
1450 S. Havana, Suite 620, Aurora CO 80012
Director: James Lee Young
Members: 5,000 *Staff:* 4-6
Annual Budget: $250-500,000 *Tel:* (303) 751-7844
Hist. Note: Founded in 1937 by David Raffelock to serve freelance writers. Membership: $50/yr.
Publications:
Flash Market News. m.
NWC Newsletter. 10/yr.
Authorship. bi-m. adv.
Professional Freelance Writers Directory. a.

Nat'l Writers Union (1983)
13 Astor Place, New York NY 10003
Director: Kim Fellner
Members: 2,000 *Staff:* 3
Annual Budget: $50-100,000 *Tel:* (212) 254-0279
Hist. Note: An independent union originated in New York City at the Roosevelt Hotel in October 1981 in connection with the American Writers Congress and formally established in May, 1983. Membership: $25-$100/yr. (based on income).
Publication:
The American Writer. bi-m.
Annual Meetings: May

Nat'l Yellow Pages Agency Ass'n (1975)
801 North Shepherd Hills Drive, Tucson AZ 85710
Exec. Director: Kenneth Hudnall
Members: 70 companies
Annual Budget: $50-100,000 *Tel:* (602) 722-3177
Hist. Note: Established at Columbus, Ohio and incorporated in Minnesota, NYPAA members are advertising agencies and suppliers. Membership: $750/yr.
Publication:
NYPAA Newsletter. m.
Annual Meetings: Fall

Natural Gas Supply Ass'n (1965)
1730 Rhode Island Ave., N.W., Suite 200, Washington DC 20036
President: Nicholas J. Bush
Members: 90 companies *Staff:* 11-15
Annual Budget: $2-5,000,000 *Tel:* (202) 331-8900
Hist. Note: Members are gas and oil producers who favor new exploration for natural gas. Formerly (until 1979) known as the Natural Gas Supply Committee.
Publication:
FYI. m.
Annual Meetings: Fourth Quarter of the Year

Natural Product Broker Ass'n (1982)
P.O. Box 1177, St. Augustine FL 32084
Secretary: Wayne Ellison
Members: 22 companies
Annual Budget: under $10,000 *Tel:* (904) 824-5884
Hist. Note: Purpose is to open channels between manufacturers/distributors and brokers of natural food and nonfood products. Membership: $100/yr.
Annual Meetings: Semi-annual
1987-Anaheim, CA/March
1987-Las Vegas,NV/July

Natural Rubber Shippers Ass'n (1971)
1400 K St., N.W., 9th Floor, Washington DC 20005
Vice President: T.I. Lemon
Members: 57 companies *Staff:* 5
Annual Budget: $250-500,000 *Tel:* (202) 682-1325
Hist. Note: Membership: $250/year.
Annual Meetings: New York City in Spring

Natural-Source Vitamin E Ass'n (1984)
1050 Connecticut Ave., N.W., Washington DC 20036-5339
Exec. Director: William R. Pendergast
Members: 3 companies *Staff:* 3
Annual Budget: $500-1,000,000 *Tel:* (202) 857-6029
Hist. Note: Purpose is to promote the sale of natural source vitamin E by use of a certification mark to identify retail products that have been tested and found to contain 100% natural source vitamin E.
Annual Meetings: Semi-Annual Meetings

NAUI
Hist. Note: See Nat'l Ass'n of Underwater Instructors.

Naval Civilian Administrators Ass'n (1947)
Hist. Note: Has no office or permanent staff. Officers change annually. Address unknown in 1987.

Navy Field Safety Ass'n (1957)
Hist. Note: Address unknown in 1985.

Neckwear Ass'n of America (1946)
151 Lexington Ave., #2F, New York NY 10016
Exec. Director: Gerald Andersen
Members: 110 companies *Staff:* 2-5
Annual Budget: $100-250,000 *Tel:* (212) 683-8454
Hist. Note: Formerly (1979) known as the Men's Tie Foundation, Inc.
Semi-annual Meetings: May and October in New York, NY

Negligee Manufacturers Ass'n (1933)
Hist. Note: Merged in 1984 with the Lingerie Manufacturers Ass'n to become the Intimate Apparel Manufacturers Ass'n.

Netherlands Chamber of Commerce in the United States (1903)
1 Rockefeller Plaza, New York NY 10020
Managing Director: Kersen J. DeJong
Members: 900-1,000 *Staff:* 10-12
Annual Budget: $500-1,000,000 *Tel:* (212) 265-6460
Hist. Note: Membership: $100/yr. (individual); $250/yr. (corporate)
Publication:
Holland-USA. q.
Annual Meetings: New York City

Network Users Ass'n (1981)
National Trade Productions, 2111 Eisenhower Ave., Suite 400, Alexandria VA 22314
President: Al Zacharias
Members: 125-135 companies *Staff:* 1
Annual Budget: $25-50,000 *Tel:* (703) 683-8500
Hist. Note: NUA is a non-profit organization of private and public sector companies, institutions and agencies whose mission is to promote development and availability of effective information systems networks through its collective power to influence industry and standards development. Membership: $300/yr. (users); $500/yr. (vendors)
Publication:
NUA Interconnection. bi-m.
Semi-annual Meetings: Spring and Fall
1987-Atlanta, GA/April and San Diego, CA/Oct.

Neuroelectric Soc. (1967)
8700 West Wisconsin Ave., Milwaukee WI 53226
President: Anthony Sances, Ph.D.
Members: 150-200
Annual Budget: $10-25,000 *Tel:* (414) 257-5307
Hist. Note: Members are interested in the effect of electricity on biological systems as well as on head and spine injuries. Affiliated with the Alliance for Engineering in Medicine and Biology. Membership: $25/yr.
Publication:
Neuroelectric News. 3/yr. adv.
Annual Meetings: Fall

Neurosurgical Soc. of America (1948)
c/o Neurosurgical Associates, 152 Zandale, Lexington KY 40503
Secretary: Russell Travis, M.D.
Members: 175-200
Annual Budget: under $10,000 *Tel:* (606) 277-6143

New York Academy of Sciences (1817)
2 East 63rd St., New York NY 10021
Exec. Director: Dr. Heinz R. Pagels
Members: 52,783 *Staff:* 85
Annual Budget: over $5,000,000 *Tel:* (212) 838-0230
Hist. Note: Originally known as the Lyceum of Natural History, the New York Academy of Sciences is an independent international organization representing all scientific disciplines from the 50 states and more than 85 nations worldwide. It is dedicated to disseminating scientific information, to educating scientists and the general public on scientific issues, and to promoting the role of science in human welfare. Membership is

00245 12 05 86 1233

open to anyone with an interest in science and current research and is subject to approval by the board of Governors. Composed of 25 sections which meet monthly Sept.-June, the Academy sponsors 18-20 Scientific Conferences every year, primarily in New York City. Membership: $55/yr.
Publications:
Annals of the New York Academy of Sciences. 25/yr.
The Sciences. bi-m. adv.
Annual Meetings: December

New York Cotton Exchange (1870)
4 World Trade Center, New York NY 10048
President: Joseph J. O'Neill
Members: 450 *Staff:* 55-60
Annual Budget: over $5,000,000 *Tel:* (212) 938-2650
Hist. Note: Oldest of the New York commodity futures exchanges. Formed Citrus Associates in 1966 and Petroleum Division in 1971.

New York Mercantile Exchange (1872)
4 World Trade Center, New York NY 10048
President: Rosemary T. McFadden
Members: 800-850 individuals *Staff:* 140
Annual Budget: over $5,000,000 *Tel:* (212) 938-2214
Hist. Note: Formerly (1880) Butter, Cheese, and Egg Exchange of the City of New York. Concerned with the trading of commodity futures. Has a budget of over $10,000,000.
Publications:
Exchange News. q.
Membership Directory. a.
Newsletter. q.
Annual Meetings: Second Tuesday in March

New York State Safe Deposit Ass'n (1906)
c/o Morgan Guaranty Trust Co., 522 Fifth Ave., New York NY 10036
President: Lawrence Owens
Members: 2,000
Annual Budget: $25-50,000 *Tel:* (212) 997-8286
Hist. Note: Banks and other institutions with safe deposit facilities from all over the nation are members.
Publication:
The Safe Deposit Bulletin. m.

New York Stock Exchange (1792)
11 Wall St., New York NY 10005
Chairman: John J. Phelan, Jr.
Members: 1,366 *Staff:* 1,800
Annual Budget: over $5,000,000 *Tel:* (212) 656-3000
Hist. Note: The Exchange member organizations number 628 with a total of 5,800 sales offices in the U.S. and foreign countries. The NYSE is the premier marketplace for the securities of some 1,500 major U.S. and foreign corporations and also provides a marketplace to trade options on the NYSE index and stock options. The New York Futures Exchange, an NYSE subsidiary, provides the world's most modern marketplace for index futures.

Newsletter Ass'n (1964)
1401 Wilson Blvd., Suite 403, Arlington VA 22209
Exec. Director: Frederick D. Goss
Members: 900 publishing companies *Staff:* 2-5
Annual Budget: $500-1,000,000 *Tel:* (703) 527-2333
Hist. Note: Founded as the Independent Newsletter Ass'n, it became the Newsletter Ass'n of America in 1977 and was incorporated in the District of Columbia. Merged with the Nat'l Ass'n of Investment Advisory Publishers in 1979 and assumed its present name in 1983. Membership: $265/yr.
Publications:
NA Hotline. bi-w.
Guidebook to Newsletter Publishing.
Success in Newsletter Publishing.
Annual Meetings: Spring, in Washington, DC
1987-Mayflower Hotel/May 31-June 2

Newspaper Advertising Bureau (1913)
1180 Sixth Ave., New York NY 10036
President: Craig C. Standen
Members: 970-980 *Staff:* 135-145
Annual Budget: over $5,000,000 *Tel:* (212) 921-5080
Hist. Note: Formerly (1973) Bureau of Advertising of the ANPA, Inc. Members are daily newspapers united to promote their use as an advertising medium. Has an annual budget of $14 million.
Publication:
Newspaper Advertising Planbook. a.
Annual Meetings: Spring
1987-New York, NY/April

Newspaper Advertising Co-op Network (1970)
501 W. Algonquin Road, Arlington Heights IL 60005-4411
Exec. Director: Francis C. Rebedeau
Members: 150-160 papers *Staff:* 2
Annual Budget: $25-50,000 *Tel:* (312) 593-8360
Hist. Note: The association of co-op advertising managers from the U.S. and Canada.
Publication:
The Coordinator. m.
Semi-annual Meetings: Winter and Summer

Newspaper Advertising Sales Ass'n (1907)
c/o Sawyer-Ferguson-Walker, 245 Park Ave., New York NY 10167
President: Roy Blackfield
Members: 15 companies *Staff:* 2
Annual Budget: $10-25,000 *Tel:* (212) 661-6262
Hist. Note: Formerly (1974) American Ass'n of Newspaper Representatives. Members are national sales agents for about 1,500 daily papers in the U.S. and Canada. Membership: $1,000/yr.
Annual Meetings:
1987-New York, NY/June 11/55

Newspaper Ass'n Managers (1923)
Box 17407, Dulles Airport, Washington DC 20041
Exec. Secretary: Stephen E. Palmedo
Members: 68 *Staff:* 1
Annual Budget: $10-25,000 *Tel:* (703) 648-1123
Hist. Note: An association of managers of state, regional, national and international press associations. Offices are located in The Newspaper Center, 11600 Sunrise Valley Drive, Reston, VA 22091.
Annual Meetings: August

Newspaper Comics Council
Hist. Note: Became the Newspaper Features Council in 1984.

Newspaper Farm Editors of America (1953)
312 Valley View Drive, Huron OH 44839
Exec. Secy.-Treas.: Audrey Mackiewicz
Members: 160-170
Annual Budget: under $10,000 *Tel:* (419) 433-5412
Hist. Note: A professional organization of farm editors and farm writers. Formerly Newspaper Farm Editors Association.
Publication:
Newsletter. m.
Semi-annual Meetings: April, in Washington and November

Newspaper Features Council (1955)
Ward Castle, Comly Ave., Rye Brook NY 10573
Exec. Director: Catherine Walker
Members: 125-150 *Staff:* 1
Tel: (914) 939-3919
Hist. Note: Formerly (1984) Newspaper Comics Council. NFC is a forum for newspapers, editors, writers, columnists, cartoonists and syndicates to exchange views and improve the content of newspapers for the betterment of the general public and the industry.
Annual Meetings: Fall

Newspaper Guild, The (1933)
1125 15th St. N.W., Washington DC 20005
President: Charles A. Perlik, Jr.
Members: 32,000 *Staff:* 32
Annual Budget: $2-5,000,000 *Tel:* (202) 296-2990
Hist. Note: A labor union representing editorial and commercial department employees of newspapers, wire and news services, magazines and related enterprises in the U.S., Canada and Puerto Rico. Established as the American Newspaper Guild in Washington, DC, December 15, 1933. Assumed its present name in 1971. Affiliatd with AFL-CIO, the Canadian Labour Congress, and the Internat'l Federation of Journalists.
Publication:
Guild Reporter. semi-m.
Annual Meetings: Summer/350

Newspaper Personnel Relations Ass'n (1949)
Dulles Internat'l Airport, Box 17407, Washington DC 20041
Exec. Director: Patricia P. Renfroe
Members: 500 *Staff:* 1
Annual Budget: $50-100,000 *Tel:* (703) 648-1000
Hist. Note: Members are personnel and labor relations officers of newspapers. Membership: $150/yr. (1st member); $50/yr. (2nd member) NPRA is headquartered at The Newspaper Center, 11600 Sunrise Valley Drive, Reston, VA 22091.
Publication:
NPRA News. m.
Annual Meetings: June/2-300
1987-Chicago, IL(Marriott Downtown)/June 28-July 1
1988-Coronado, CA(del Coronado)/June 26-29
1989-Ottawa, Ontario(Westin)/June 25-28
1990-New York, NY(Omni Park Central)/June 22-26

Newspaper Purchasing Management Ass'n (1957)
c/o Purchasing Director, News and Sun-Sentinel, Ft. Lauderdale FL 33302
President: Stephen S. Grant
Members: 140-150 individuals
Annual Budget: $10-25,000 *Tel:* (305) 761-4323
Hist. Note: Formerly (1969) Nat'l Ass'n of Newspaper Purchasing Executives. Officers change annually. Has no permanent headquarters or staff.
Annual Meetings: Spring

Newspaper Systems Group (1967)
Newsday, Inc., 235 Pinelawn Road, Melville NY 11747
President: Dennis O'Leary
Members: 40
Hist. Note: Members are concerned with computer systems applications in newspapers and related organizations.

NIFDA (1958)
P.O. Box 724945, Atlanta GA 30339
President: Shannon D. Talley
Members: 115 *Staff:* 80
Tel: (404) 952-0871
Hist. Note: Formerly Nat'l Institutional Food Distributors Associates; adopted the acronym NIFDA, Inc. in 1985. NIFDA is a national buying and marketing association of wholesale foodservice distributors.
Semi-Annual Meetings: Spring and Fall
1987-Orlando, FL and Nashville, TN
1988-Dallas, TX and Las Vegas, NV
1989-Phoenix, AZ and Washington, DC

Nine to Five Nat'l Ass'n of Working Women (1973)
614 Superior Ave., N.W., #852, Cleveland OH 44113-1306
Exec. Director: Karen Nussbaum
Members: 12,000 *Staff:* 4
Annual Budget: $500-1,000,000 *Tel:* (216) 566-9308
Hist. Note: Established in Boston. Membership: $20/yr.
Publication:
Nine to Five Newsletter. bi-m.
Annual Meetings:
1987-Evanston, IL(Northwestern Univ.)

Nitrobenzene Ass'n (1981)
Hist. Note: Inactive in 1985.

Nitrogen Tree Fixing Ass'n (1981)
P.O. Box 680, Waimanalo HI 96795
Exec. Secretary: Dale Withington
Members: 1,000 individuals *Staff:* 7
Annual Budget: $100-250,000 *Tel:* (808) 259-8685
Hist. Note: Encourages research and development efforts concerning the use of nitrogen fixing trees to provide firewood, forage, green manure, and other products that benefit people and relieve pressure on dwindling natural forests. Membership: $5-10/yr.
Publications:
Leucaena Research Reports. a.
Nitrogen Fixing Tree Research Reports. a.
NFTA Highlights. irreg.
NFTA Newsletter. semi-a.

No-Load Mutual Fund Ass'n (1971)
11 Penn Plaza, Suite 2204, New York NY 10001
Exec. Director: Laura J. Berger
Members: 375 funds *Staff:* 6
Annual Budget: $250-500,000 *Tel:* (212) 563-4540
Hist. Note: Investment companies who market their shares at net asset value.
Publications:
No-Load Newsletter. m.
Investor Directory. a.
Annual Meetings: Fall, in New York City.

Noah Worcester Dermatological Soc. (1958)
9500 Kenwood Road, Cincinnati OH 45242
Secy.-Treas.: K. William Kitzmiller, M.D.
Members: 170-180 *Staff:* 1
Annual Budget: $50-100,000 *Tel:* (513) 891-8045
Hist. Note: Named for Noah Worcester, author of the first American text on dermatology, published in 1845. Officers remain for five-year terms.
Annual Meetings:
1987-Rancho Mirage/Feb. 15-21
1988-Monte Carlo/April 19-24

Noise Control Products and Materials Ass'n (1976)
2506 Gross Point Road, Evanston IL 60201
Exec. V. President: Arthur W. Engle
Members: 10-15 companies *Staff:* 1-2
Annual Budget: $25-50,000 *Tel:* (312) 475-7300
Publication:
Noise Control Feedback. q.
Semi-Annual Meetings:

Non-Commissioned Officers Ass'n of the U.S.A. (1960)
Box 33610, San Antonio TX 78233
President: Walter Kruger
Members: 200,000 individuals *Staff:* 30
Annual Budget: $2-5,000,000 *Tel:* (512) 653-6161
Hist. Note: Individuals who serve or have served in U.S. Military forces in grades E4 through E9. Membership: $15/yr.
Publications:
NCOA Newsbrief. bi-w.
NCOA Journal. m. adv.
NCOA in Action. bien.
Annual Meetings: July/600
1987-Las Vegas, NV(Bally's Grand)
1988-San Antonio, TX(Hyatt Regency)
1989-Orlando, FL
1990-San Antonio, TX(Hyatt Regency)

Non-Ferrous Founders' Soc. (1943)
455 State St., Suite 100, Des Plaines IL 60016
Exec. Director: James L. Mallory, CAE
Members: 150-200 companies *Staff:* 2-5
Annual Budget: $100-250,000 *Tel:* (312) 299-0950
Hist. Note: Members are manufacturers of bronze, brass and aluminum castings.
Publications:
Crucible. bi-m. adv.
North American Directory of Non-Ferrous Foundries. a. adv.
Annual Meetings: Fall
1987-Tucson, AZ(Sheraton El Conquistador)/Sept. 27-30/125
1988-Kohala, HI(Sheraton Waikoloa)/Oct. 1-5/150

00246 12 05 86 1233

Non-Heatset Web Unit
1730 North Lynn St., Suite 200, Arlington VA 22209
Exec. Director: Edward W. Hill, Jr.
Members: 650 *Staff:* 2-5
Annual Budget: $100-250,000 *Tel:* (703) 841-8140
Hist. Note: A special industry group of Printing Industries of America.
Annual Meetings: November
1987-Hilton Head, SC(Intercontinental)/Nov. 8-11/500
1988-Palm Springs, CA(Americana Canyon)/Nov. 13-16/500

Non-Powder Gun Products Ass'n (1975)
200 Castlewood Drive, North Palm Beach FL 33480
Executive Director: Anthony L. Kucera
Members: 18 companies *Staff:* 1
Annual Budget: $10-25,000 *Tel:* (305) 842-4100
Hist. Note: Members are manufacturers and distributors of air guns and ammunition. Affiliated with the Sporting Goods Manufacturers Association which provides administrative support.
Annual Meetings: January with The "SHOT" Show (Shooting, Hunting, Outdoors show).

Nonprofit Mailers Federation (1982)
3050 K St., N.W., Suite 310, Washington DC 20007
President: George Miller
Members: 600 organizations *Staff:* 2-5
Annual Budget: $100-250,000 *Tel:* (202) 944-4188
Hist. Note: Members are nonprofit groups using direct mail to fund their activities or disseminate information.
Publication:
Bulletin. irreg.

North American Academy of Ecumenists (1967)
Bellarmine College, 2001 Newburg Road, Louisville KY 40205
Membership Secretary: Eugene Zoeller
Members: 160 *Staff:* 1
Annual Budget: under $10,000 *Tel:* (502) 452-8178
Hist. Note: Formerly Ass'n of Professors of Ecumenics. Membership includes ecumenically active clergy and laity as well as professors and students. Affiliated with the Journal of Ecumenical Studies. Membership: $20/yr.
Annual Meetings: September

North American Academy of Manipulative Medicine (1965)
5021 Seminary Road, Suite 125, Alexandria VA 22311
Exec. Secretary: Tisha R. Levin
Members: 300 individuals *Staff:* 1
Annual Budget: $25-50,000 *Tel:* (703) 931-0099
Hist. Note: Founded in 1965 by a group of United States and Canadian physicians to promote and conduct scientific studies in manipulation and to facilitate the utilization of this modality in clinical practice. (Manipulative medicine is the use of mechanical forces applied though the hands to diagnose and treat functional disorders of the musculo-skeletal system.) NAAMM is the North American affiliate of the Internat'l Federation of Manual Medicine.
Publication:
The Touchstone. q. adv.
Annual Meetings: Fall
1987-Las Vegas, NV/Oct./100-150
1988-Quebec, Canada(Loews Le Concorde)/Aug./100-150

North American Ass'n for Environmental Education (1971)
Box 400, Troy OH 45373
Exec. V. President: Joan C. Heidelberg
Members: 700 *Staff:* 2-5
Annual Budget: $10-25,000 *Tel:* (513) 698-6493
Hist. Note: Formerly (1985) the Nat'l Ass'n for Environmental Education. Purpose is to assist and support the work of individuals and groups engaged in environmental education, research and service. NAEE is organized into three interactive sections: Elementary and Secondary Education Section; Environmental Studies Section; and the Non-Formal Section. Membership: $25/yr. (individual); $100/yr. (institution).
Publications:
Environmental Communicator. bi-m.
Current Issues in Environmental Education. a.
Recent Graduate Works. a.
Monographs. a.
Conference Proceedings. a
Annual Meetings: Fall
1987-Quebec(Le Chateau Frontenac)/Oct. 17-22/300

North American Ass'n of Christians in Social Work (1953)
Box 90, St. David's PA 19087
Exec. Director: Edward G. Kuhlmann
Members: 1,000 *Staff:* 2-5
Annual Budget: $25-50,000 *Tel:* (215) 687-5777
Hist. Note: Growing out of a series of annual conferences held at Wheaton College beginning in 1950, the Evangelical Social Work Conference was incorporated in 1953 as the National Association of Christians in Social Work. Became the present organization in 1983. Membership: $50/yr.
Publications:
Catalyst. bi-m. adv.
Social Work and Christianity. semi-a. adv.
Practice Monograph Series. a.
Annual Meetings: Fall
1987-Nashville, TN(Maxwell House)/Oct. 8-11
1988-San Antonio, TX

North American Ass'n of State Lotteries
Hist. Note: Became the Nat'l Ass'n of State and Provincial Lotteries in 1986.

North American Ass'n of Summer Sessions (1964)
11728 Summerhaven Drive, Creve Coeur MO 63146
Exec. Secretary: Michael U. Nelson
Members: 414 schools *Staff:* 2-5
Annual Budget: $25-50,000 *Tel:* (314) 872-8406
Hist. Note: Established as the National Association of College and University Summer Sessions, it became the National Association of Summer Sessions in 1968 and assumed its present name in 1975. Membership: $10/year (individual), $45/year (institution).
Publications:
Newsletter. q.
Proceedings.
Membership Directory.
Annual Meetings: Fall
1987-Toronto, Canada

North American Ass'n of Wardens and Superintendents (1870)
Box 607, Carson City NV 89710
President: George Sumner
Members: 250 *Staff:* 1
Annual Budget: under $10,000
Hist. Note: Formerly (1971) Wardens' Ass'n of America and (1980) American Ass'n of Wardens and Superintendants. Has no permanent headquarters. An affiliate of the American Correctional Ass'n.
Annual Meetings: With American Correctional Ass'n

North American Blueberry Council (1965)
Box 166, Marmora NJ 08223
Secretary/Manager: Myrtle L. Ruch
Members: 40-50 growers/organizations *Staff:* 2-5
Annual Budget: $250-500,000 *Tel:* (609) 399-1559
Hist. Note: Blueberry growers and marketers from the U.S. and Canada. Membership: Assessed on annual production (minimum 250,000 lbs.).
Publications:
Calyx. bi-m.
Proceedings. a.
Annual Meetings: Winter
1987-Vancouver, BC(Pan Pacific Hotel)
1988-New Orleans, LA(Marriott)
1989-Orlando, FL

North American Boxing Federation (1967)
Hist. Note: Address unknown in 1985.

North American Cartographic Information Soc. (1980)
Nat'l Ocean Service, Room 100, 6010 Executive Blvd., Rockville MD 20852
Exec. Secretary: Ron Bolton
Members: 200-250
Annual Budget: under $10,000 *Tel:* (301) 443-8075
Hist. Note: Members are cartographers and others interested in the creation of accurate maps. Incorporated in the State of Wisconsin. Membership: $15/year.
Publications:
Map Gap. q.
Journal. semi-a.
Annual Meetings: October/100

North American Catalysis Soc. (1955)
Univ. of Illinois, Dept. of Chemical, Engineering, Box 4348, Chicago IL 60680
Secretary: Richard D. Gonzalez
Members: 2,000 *Staff:* 1
Annual Budget: $10-25,000 *Tel:* (312) 996-9430
Hist. Note: Fosters an interest in heterogeneous and homogeneous catalysis in the US and Canada. Organizes national meetings for the purpose of discussing the latest developments in the field. Membership: $1/yr.
Publication:
Catalysis Soc. Newsletter. bi-a.
Annual Meetings: Biennial meetings in Spring, uneven years.
1987-San Diego, CA
1989-Detroit, MI

North American Clinical Dermatological Soc. (1959)
Hist. Note: NACDS has requested that its address and telephone number not be liste d.

North American Clun Forest Ass'n (1973)
55 North Main St., East Longmeadow MA 01028
Exec. Secretary: Richard Bean
Members: 50 *Staff:* 1
Annual Budget: under $10,000 *Tel:* (413) 525-4171
Hist. Note: Breeders and fanciers of Clun Forest sheep. Maintains registry of pedigrees and promotes standards of the breed. Membership: $15/yr.
Publication:
Clun Forest Sheep. tri-a. adv.
Annual Meetings: Fall

North American Computer Service Ass'n (1982)
Hist. Note: Address unknown in 1986.

North American Corriente Ass'n (1982)
4400 East 12th St., Casper WY 82609
Asst. Secretary: Roberta M. Nelson
Members: 70 *Staff:* 1
Tel: (307) 237-4491
Hist. Note: The NACA promotes the use of the Corriente Bull and has instituted and proceeds to monitor a registered breeding program to preserve the true breed and make it available for the fast growing rodeo circuit. Membership: $250/life; $25/yr. (active member); $10/yr. (associate).
Publication:
The Corresponder. q. adv.
Annual Meetings: April

North American District Heating and Cooling Institute (1982)
Box 19428, Washington DC 20036
Exec. Director: Richard Eckfield
Members: 120 companies
Annual Budget: $100-250,000 *Tel:* (202) 223-4922
Hist. Note: An association of district heating and cooling utilities (centralized suppliers of heating and cooling through piping systems), DHC product manufacturers and professional service providers organized to promote the use of DHC technology. NADHCI conducts research, sponsors training programs and public education programs promoting DHC, and develops national product performance standards through ANSI. Membership: $75/yr. (individual); $800-14,000/yr. (company).
Publications:
Washington Letter.
DHC/CHP in America. adv.

North American Electric Reliability Council (1968)
101 College Road East, Princeton NJ 08540-6601
President: Michehl R. Gent
Members: 9 regional councils *Staff:* 16-20
Annual Budget: $1-2,000,000 *Tel:* (609) 452-8060
Hist. Note: Founded as the National Electric Reliability Council, it assumed its present name September 2, 1981. Formed by the electric utility industry in 1968, NERC promotes the reliability of bulk power supply in the electric utility systems in North America.
Publications:
Annual Report. a.
Annual Review of Overall Reliability and Adequacy of North American
Bulk Power Systems. a.
Annual Summary of Projected Peak Demand, Generating Capability and
Fossil Fuel Requirement. a.
Annual Meetings: Not held.

North American Export Grain Ass'n (1920)
1747 Pennsylvania Ave., N.W., Suite 1175, Washington DC 20006
Exec. Director: Joseph Halow
Members: 38 companies *Staff:* 2-5
Annual Budget: $250-500,000 *Tel:* (202) 223-8285
Hist. Note: Canadian and U.S. grain exporters.
Publication:
Bulletins. irreg.
Annual Meetings: Washington, D.C.

North American Farm Show Council (1972)
560 Morning St., Worthington OH 43085
Exec. Coordinator: Dale T. Friday
Members: 32 organizations
Annual Budget: $10-25,000 *Tel:* (614) 885-7206
Hist. Note: Established in Chicago and incorporated in Ohio, NAFSC members are agricultural trade shows. Membership: $650/yr.
Semi-annual Meetings: May and November
1987-Chicago, IL(O'Hare Hilton)/May 4-5
1987-Atlanta, GA(Hyatt Regency)/Nov. 16-17

North American Flowerbulb Wholesalers Ass'n (1984)
Hist. Note: Address unknown in 1985.

North American Gamebird Ass'n (1931)
Box 2105, Cayce-West Columbia SC 29171
Exec. Secretary: Walter S. Walker
Members: 1,550 *Staff:* 2-5
Annual Budget: $25-50,000 *Tel:* (803) 796-8163
Hist. Note: Formerly (1981) North American Game Breeders and Shooting Preserve Operators Association. Membership: $35/yr. The phone number listed above is good Aug. 15-June 1; from June 1 to Aug. 15, it is (803) 364-3659.
Publication:
Wildlife Harvest. q. adv.
Annual Meetings: Winter
1987-New Orleans, LA/Jan. 8-11

North American Gasoline Tax Conference (1926)
Hist. Note: Aborbed into the Nat'l Ass'n of Tax Administrators as the NATA Motor Fuel Tax Section in 1984. Formerly a constituent organization of the Federation of Tax Administrators.

00247 12 05 86 1233

North American Indian Museums Ass'n (1979)
c/o Seneca-Iroquois Nat'l Museum, Box 442, Salamanca NY 14779
Chairman: George Abrams
Members: 50
Annual Budget: under $10,000 *Tel:* (716) 945-1790
Hist. Note: Native American cultural centers and museums and employees of such institutions.
Publications:
Directory of Indian Museums. a.
Newsletter. irreg.
Annual Meetings: Fall

North American Jewish Youth Council (1964)
515 Park Ave., New York NY 10022
Chairman: Jonathan Goldstein
Members: 20-25 organizations & 60 local councils *Staff:* 2-5
Annual Budget: under $10,000 *Tel:* (212) 751-6070
Hist. Note: Founded to provide a forum for all Jewish youth organizations. Funded largely by a grant from the American Zionist Youth Foundation.

North American Limousin Foundation (1968)
100 Livestock Exchange Bldg., Denver CO 80216
Exec. V. President: Gregory L. Martin
Members: 50,000 *Staff:* 15-20
Annual Budget: $1-2,000,000 *Tel:* (303) 296-8835
Hist. Note: Registers, promotes and develops limousin beef cattle, a French breed introduced into the U.S.A. in 1968. Lifetime Membership: $200
Annual Meetings: January, in Denver at the Fairmont with an attendance of 500.

North American Log Builders Ass'n (1981)
Hist. Note: Merged with the Log Homes Council to become the North American Log Homes Council in 1985.

North American Log Homes Council (1985)
15th and M Sts., N.W., Washington DC 20005
Exec. Director: James Birdsong
Members: 55 companies *Staff:* 2-5
Annual Budget: $50-100,000 *Tel:* (202) 822-0576
Hist. Note: Founded in 1977 as the Log Homes Council; assumed its present name in 1985. A division of the Nat'l Ass'n of Home Builders.
Annual Meetings: With the Nat'l Ass'n of Home Builders

North American Manufacturing Research Institution (1981)
Hist. Note: See NAMRI/SME.

North American Morab Horse Ass'n (1984)
W3174 Faro Springs Road, Hilbert WI 54129
Exec. Director: Patricia Fochs
Members: 150 *Staff:* 1
Annual Budget: under $10,000 *Tel:* (414) 853-3086
Hist. Note: Members are owners and breeders of Morab horses, a crossbreed of Arabian and Morgan horses. Absorbed the Hearst Memorial Morab Horse Registry in 1985. Membership: $15 first year, $10/year thereafter (individual).
Publication:
Morab News. q.
Annual Meetings: October

North American Mycological Ass'n (1959)
4245 Redinger Rd., Portsmouth OH 45662
Exec. Director: Harry S. Knighton
Members: 1,500 *Staff:* 2-5
Annual Budget: under $10,000 *Tel:* (614) 354-2018
Hist. Note: Originated at Ohio State University in November 1959 as the Committee on Fungi and was incorporated in Ohio as the North American Mycological Ass'n in 1967. Membership: $15/year.
Publications:
McIlvainea. a.
Mycophile. bi-m.
Annual Meetings:
1987-Gulfport, MS(Univ. of Southern MS)/July 16-19

North American Normande Ass'n (1982)
RR 1, Box 63, McCallsburg IA 50154-9728
V. President: Dennis Book
Tel: (515) 434-2391
Hist. Note: Breeders of Normande Cattle. Absorbed the American Normande Soc. in 1985.

North American Photonics Ass'n (1980)
Hist. Note: Dissolved in 1985.

North American Professional Driver Education Ass'n (1958)
4935 West Foster Ave., Chicago IL 60630
Exec. Secretary: W.E. Rumsfield
Members: 275-300 schools *Staff:* 2-5
Annual Budget: $50-100,000 *Tel:* (312) 777-9605
Hist. Note: Formerly (1970) Nat'l Professional Driver Education Ass'n, Inc., and (1960) Nat'l Ass'n of Driving Schools. Members are individuals and companies involved in driver education. Awards the "Qualified Driving School" designation. Membership: $200/year.
Regional Meetings: January, July and November.

North American Securities Administrators Ass'n (1917)
2930 S.W. Wanamaker Drive, Suite 5, Topeka KS 66614
Exec. Director: Bruce Burditt
Members: 65 *Staff:* 5
Tel: (913) 273-2600
Hist. Note: Formerly (1945) Nat'l Ass'n of Securities Administrators. Members consist of state officials administering "blue sky" laws controlling securities sales. Includes officers of every U. S. state securities authority, The District of Columbia, Puerto Rico, the provincial securities commissions of Canada and national equivalents in Mexico.
Publications:
NASAA. m.
Proceedings. a.
Semi-Annual Meetings: Spring and Fall

North American Simulation and Gaming Ass'n (1961)
c/o Department of Political Science, University of N. Carolina-Asheville, Asheville NC 28804-3299
Exec. Director: Dr. Bob Farzanegan
Members: 250-300 *Staff:* 1
Annual Budget: under $10,000 *Tel:* (704) 258-6434
Hist. Note: Established as Nat'l Gaming Council, it assumed its present name in 1974. Members are teachers, trainers and others interested in the concept of using simulated situations and games as educational and planning tools. Membership: $35/yr.
Publication:
Simulation & Games Magazine. q.
Annual Meetings: Fall, in an academic environment.

North American Soccer League (1966)
Hist. Note: Merger (1968) of the National Professional Soccer League (1966) and the United Soccer Association (1966). With only one team remaining in late 1985, NASL was inactive.

North American Soccer League Players Ass'n (1977)
Hist. Note: A labor union of professional soccer players, formerly (1980) the North American Soccer Players Association. With only one NASL team remaining in 1985, the union may be presumed inactive.

North American Soc. for Corporate Planning (1966)
Hist. Note: Merged with the Planning Executives Institute to form Planning Forum in 1985.

North American Soc. for Pediatric Gastroenterology (1971)
4540 Sand Point Way, N.E., Seattle WA 98105
Secretary-Treasurer: Jane Todaro, MD
Members: 270 *Staff:* 1
Annual Budget: under $10,000 *Tel:* (206) 522-8841
Hist. Note: Membership: $50/year (individual).
Publication:
Newsletter. irreg.
Semi-annual Meetings: in conjunction with American Pediatric Soc. and
American Soc. for the Study of Liver Disease

North American Soc. for the Psychology of Sport and Physical Activity (1966)
University of Oregon, 131 Esslinger Hall, Eugene OR 97403
Secy.-Treas.: Dr. Maureen Weiss
Members: 650 individuals *Staff:* 1
Annual Budget: under $10,000 *Tel:* (503) 686-4108
Hist. Note: Scholars whose research interests focus on aspects of motor behavior. Membership: $20/yr. (professional); $5/yr. (student).
Publication:
NASPSPA Newsletter. 3/yr.
Annual Meetings:
1987-Vancouver, BC/June 4-7

North American Soc. of Adlerian Psychology (1952)
159 North Dearborn St., Suite 419, Chicago IL 60601
Exec. Director: Neva L. Hefner
Members: 1,050-1,200 *Staff:* 2-5
Annual Budget: $50-100,000 *Tel:* (312) 977-1944
Hist. Note: Formerly (1976) American Soc. of Adlerian Psychology. Members are individuals interested in the teachings of the Austrian psychiatrist, Alfred Adler (1870-1937). His system emphasizes the uniqueness of each individual and that individual's relationships with society. Membership: $65/yr.
Publications:
Individual Psychology: Journal of Adlerian Theory, Research and Practice. q.
NASAP Newsletter. bi-m.
Annual Meetings: Memorial Day weekend/400-500
1987-Fort Wayne, IN(Hilton)/May 22-25

North American Soc. of Pacing and Electrophysiology (1979)
13 Eaton Court, Wellesley Hills MA 02181
Administrator: Carol J. McGlinchey
Members: 825 *Staff:* 5
Annual Budget: $500-1,000,000 *Tel:* (617) 237-1866
Hist. Note: Members are physicians and others involved in the development and implantation of heart pacemakers. Membership: $175/yr.
Publications:
NASPE News. q.
Journal A. bi-m. adv.
Journal B. bi-m. adv.
Annual Meetings: Spring/700
1987-Boston, MA(Marriott Copley Place)/April 30-May 2
1988-Los Angeles, CA/May 12-14

North American Students of Cooperation (1968)
Box 7715, Ann Arbor MI 48107
Director of Publications & Info.: Sharon Pedersen
Members: 35 organizations, 10,000 individuals *Staff:* 3-5
Annual Budget: $100-250,000 *Tel:* (313) 663-0889
Hist. Note: Formerly (until 1978) the North American Student Cooperative Organization. Formed to provide technical assistance and information to cooperative enterprises in the U.S. and Canada, in particular campus co-operatives. Membership: $35/yr. (individual), $150/yr. (organization).
Publications:
Directory of Campus Co-ops. a.
Leadership Directions.
NASCO Newsbriefs.
Annual Meetings: Fall in Ann Arbor, MI at the Michigan Union

North American Telecommunications Ass'n (1970)
2000 M St., N.W., Suite 550, Washington DC 20036
President: Edwin B. Spievack
Members: 745 companies *Staff:* 27
Annual Budget: $1-2,000,000 *Tel:* (202) 296-9800
Hist. Note: Manufacturers and installers of telephone equipment and related technologies. The so-called "interconnect" industry. Known as the North American Telephone Association, 1970-1982.
Publications:
Market Update (newsletter). bi-w. adv.
Washington Update (newsletter). bi-w.
Telecommunications Sourcebook. a. adv.
Telecommunications Equipment Industry Statistical Review. a.
Compensation & Benefits Survey of Telecommunications Equipment
Personnel. a.
Annual Meetings:
1987-Dallas, TX(Dallas Infomart)/Dec. 1-4

North American Telephone Ass'n (1970)
Hist. Note: Became The North American Telecommunications Association in 1984.

North American Thermal Analysis Soc. (1968)
c/o AT&T Bell Labs 600 Mountain Ave., 2D-225, Murray Hill NJ 07974
Secretary: Bonnie Bachman
Members: 750 *Staff:* 1
Annual Budget: $25-50,000 *Tel:* (201) 582-6085
Hist. Note: Incorporated in Delaware. Affiliated with the Internat'l Conference on Thermal Analysis. Membership: $10/year.
Publication:
NATAS Notes. q. adv.
Annual Meetings:
1987-Washington, DC(Capitol Hilton)/Sept. 27-30/400
1988-Orlando, FL/Oct. 9-12
1989-San Diego, CA

North American Transplant Coordinators Organization (1980)
5000 Van Nuys Blvd., Suite 400, Sherman Oaks CA 91403
Administrative Director: Michael Sciacca
Members: 550 individuals
Annual Budget: $250-500,000 *Tel:* (818) 995-7338
Hist. Note: Health professionals, involved in obtaining and distributing human organs and tissues for transplant, or working with recipients.
Publication:
NATCO Newsletter. q. adv.

North American Travel Ass'n (1981)
Hist. Note: Disbanded in 1984.

North American Wholesale Lumber Ass'n (1893)
2340 S. Arlington Heights Rd., Suite 680, Arlington Heights IL 60005
Exec. V. President: H. M. Pete Niebling
Members: 575 *Staff:* 7
Annual Budget: $500-1,000,000 *Tel:* (312) 981-8630
Hist. Note: Formerly (1972) Nat'l American Wholesale Lumber Ass'n. Membership: $450-850/year (organization/company), depending on membership category and size.
Publications:
NAWLA Forum. bi-m.
NAWLA Observation and Expectation Report. bi-m.
Annual Directory of Membership. a.
NAWLA Bulletin. bi-w.
Annual Meetings: Spring
1987-Scottsdale, AZ(Camelback Inn)/April 25-29/600-750
1988-Tarpon Springs, FL(Innsbrook)/April 17-21/600-700
1989-Tuscon, AZ(El Conquistador)/April 16-19/600-800
1990-Jasper, Canada(Jasper Lodge)/June 11-15/650-800
1991-Boca Raton, FL(Boca Raton Hotel)/April 11-15/750
1992-Colorado Springs, CO(Broadmoor)/May 16-20/750
1993-White Sulphur Springs, WV(Greenbrier)/May 12-16/600

00248 12 05 86 1233

North American Wildlife Foundation (1911)
1266 W. Northwest Highway, Suite 806, Palatine IL 60067
Senior Vice President: Matthew B. Connolly, Jr.
Members: 500 companies and individuals
Annual Budget: $500-1,000,000 *Tel:* (312) 991-1208
Hist. Note: Formerly (1935) American Game Protective Ass'n, (1946) American Wildlife Institute, and (1951) American Wildlife Foundation. Aims to help maintain, restore and advance sound natural resource and wildlife management programs. Supported by both individual and corporate members interested in its aims.

North Coast Export Company (1980)
1339 Fay Ave., Fairhaven CA 95564
Manager: William Gross
Members: 4 members *Staff:* 1
Tel: (707) 443-9348
Hist. Note: A Webb-Pomerene Act association. Members are exporters of wood fiber in chip form.

North Coast Export Cooperative (1971)
Hist. Note: Dissolved in 1985.

Northamerican Heating and Airconditioning Wholesalers Ass'n (1947)
P.O. Box 16790, Columbus OH 43216
Exec. V. President: James D. Wilder
Members: 500 *Staff:* 6-10
Annual Budget: $500-1,000,000 *Tel:* (614) 488-1835
Hist. Note: Affiliated with the Nat'l Ass'n of Wholesaler-Distributors. Formerly Nat'l Heat Wholesalers Ass'n; Nat'l Heating and Air Conditioning Wholesalers Absorbed (1969) the Northamerican Ass'n of Sheet Metal Distributors.
Publication:
NHAW Scene. m.

Northeastern Lumber Manufacturers Ass'n (1933)
272 Tuttle Road, P.O. Box 87A, Cumberland Center ME 04021
Exec. V. President: Stephen S. Clark
Members: 200 *Staff:* 7
Annual Budget: $100-250,000 *Tel:* (207) 829-6901
Hist. Note: Affiliated with the Nat'l Forest Products Ass'n, members are manufacturers of wood products principally in New England, New York, and Pennsylvania. Membership: $15/yr. (individual); fee for manufacturers based on shipments and/or minimum.
Publications:
Information Log (newsletter). m.
Purchasers' Guide. a.
Standard Grading Rules for Northeastern Lumber. irreg.
Semi-annual meetings: Spring and Fall
1987-Boston, MA(Marriott Longwharf)/March 26-29/250
1987-Sturbridge, MA(Sheraton)/Sept. 17-20/200
1988-Boston, MA(Copley Plaza)/March 23-27/250
1988-Hyannis, MA(Dunphey's Hyannis)/Sept. 14-18/200

Northeastern Retail Lumberman's Ass'n (1894)
339 East Ave., Rochester NY 14604
Exec. V. President: John J. Brill
Members: 1,365 *Staff:* 20-25
Annual Budget: $2-5,000,000 *Tel:* (716) 325-1626
Hist. Note: Membership: $500-1,200/year.
Publication:
The Lumber Co-Operator. m. adv.
Annual Meetings: January in Boston, MA/10,000
1987-Marriott
1988-Westin

Northeastern Weed Science Soc. (1947)
Plant Sci. Dept., Univ. of Connecticut, Storrs CT 06268
Secy.-Treas.: Richard A. Ashley
Members: 400-450 *Staff:* 1
Annual Budget: $10-25,000 *Tel:* (203) 486-3435
Hist. Note: Membership: $10/year.
Publication:
NEWSS Proceedings and Supplement. a.
Annual Meetings: January
1987-Williamsburg, VA(Williamsburg Inn)/Jan. 5-8
1988-Hartford, CT

Northern Hardwood and Pine Manufacturers Ass'n (1892)
Hist. Note: Dissolved in 1985.

Northern Nut Growers Ass'n (1910)
Box 340, Niagara College, St. Catharines Ontario L2R 6V6
Secretary: R. Douglas Campbell
Members: 2,000-2,100 growers *Staff:* 1
Annual Budget: $25-50,000 *Tel:* (416) 735-2211
Hist. Note: Promotes interest in nut-bearing trees, their culture and products. Mainly concerned with 14 different species of nut trees grown in the Northern U.S. and southern Canada. Has no paid staff.
Publications:
Nutshell. q. adv.
Proceedings. a. adv.
Annual Meetings: Summer/250
1987-Kentucky/Aug.
1988-Nebraska

Northern Textile Ass'n (1854)
230 Congress St., Boston MA 02110
President: Karl Spilhaus
Members: 275-300 mills *Staff:* 6-10
Annual Budget: $250-500,000 *Tel:* (617) 542-8220
Hist. Note: Originally established as the New England Cotton Manufacturers Association, it changed its name to the Nat'l Ass'n of Cotton Manufacturers about 1890 and assumed its present name in 1956. Its core membership today consists of makers of cotton and synthetic yarns, but it also provides staff support for and includes three semi-autonomous Councils- Wool Manufacturers (absorbed in 1956), Felt Manufacturers (absorbed in 1961) and Elastic Fabric Manufacturers (formerly the Elastic Fabric Manufacturers Institute, established in 1953 and absorbed in 1970). Sponsors the Northern Textile Ass'n Political Action Committee.
Annual Meetings: September

Northwest Dried Fruit Export Ass'n (1927)
Hist. Note: Defunct in 1982.

Northwest Fruit Exporters (1980)
1005 Tieton Dr., Yakima WA 98902
Manager: Arthur Mattig
Members: 19 companies
Annual Budget: $250-500,000 *Tel:* (509) 453-4837
Hist. Note: A Webb-Pomerene Act association.

Norwegian-American Chamber of Commerce (1915)
825 Third Ave., New York NY 10022
Ass't. General Manager: Mrs. Inger M. Tallaksen
Members: 1,000 companies *Staff:* 2-5
Annual Budget: $50-100,000 *Tel:* (212) 421-9210
Hist. Note: Membership: $175/year (individual), $800/year (company).
Publications:
Norwegian American Commerce. q. adv.
Norwegian Trade Bulletin. 8/yr.
Annual Meetings: New York City, in March/150-200

Norwegian Fjord Ass'n of North America (1977)
24750 W. Chardon Road, Grayslake IL 60030
Secy.-Treas.: Wandalyn Rice
Members: 40-50 *Staff:* 1
Annual Budget: under $10,000 *Tel:* (312) 546-7881
Hist. Note: Members own and breed Norwegian Fjord horses. Membership: $25/yr.
Publication:
Newsletter. a.

Nuclear and Plasma Sciences Soc.
Hist. Note: A subsidiary of the Institute of Electrical and Electronics Engineers. Membership in the Society, open only to IEEE members, includes subscription to a technical periodical in the field published by IEEE. All administrative support is provided by IEEE.

Nuclear Information and Records Management Ass'n (1978)
210 Fifth Ave., New York NY 10010
Admin. Assistant: Jane Hannum
Members: 415 *Staff:* 1
Annual Budget: $25-50,000 *Tel:* (212) 683-9221
Hist. Note: Purpose is to improve the management of corporate records relating to nuclear facilities. Membership includes utility company employees, architectural engineers and industrial consultants. Formerly (1985) the Nuclear Records Management Ass'n. Membership: $40/yr.
Publication:
Newsletter. q.
Annual Meetings: September
1987-Southern California
1988-Chicago, IL

Nuclear Records Management Ass'n (1978)
Hist. Note: Became (1985) the Nuclear Information and Records Management Ass'n.

Numerical Control Soc. (1962)
Hist. Note: Became the Ass'n for Integrated Manufacturing Technology in 1984.

Nursery Ass'n Executives (1947)
Box 1871, Bozeman MT 59771-1871
Secretary-Treasurer: Jane R. Barry
Members: 40-50 *Staff:* 1
Annual Budget: under $10,000 *Tel:* (406) 586-6042
Hist. Note: Chief executives of nursery ass'ns of the U.S. and Canada. Formerly (1972) Nursery Ass'n Secretaries. The association was formed primarily for educational purposes.
Semi-annual Meetings: summer with Amer. Ass'n of Nurserymen and winter
1987-Grand Rapids, MI(Amway Grand Plaza)/July 17-20/40
1987-Washington, DC/Feb. 19-21
1988-Vancouver, Canada/Feb. 25-27/40

Nursery Marketing Council (1977)
1250 Eye St., N.W., Suite 500, Washington DC 20005
Exec. V. President: Robert F. Lederer, CAE
Members: 500 companies *Staff:* 11-15
Annual Budget: $500-1,000,000 *Tel:* (202) 789-2900
Hist. Note: Established to promote the purchase of nursery stock by consumers. Affiliated with the American Ass'n of Nurserymen.
Annual Meetings: With American Ass'n of Nurserymen.

Nurses Ass'n of the American College of Obstetricians and Gynecologists (1969)
600 Maryland Ave., S.W., Ste. 200 East, Washington DC 20024
Exec. Director: Sallye B. Shaw
Members: 20,000 *Staff:* 24
Annual Budget: $1-2,000,000 *Tel:* (202) 638-0026
Hist. Note: Members specialize in obstetric, gynecologic, or neonatal nursing. Membership: $70/yr.
Publications:
Journal of Obstetric, Gynecologic and Neonatal Nursing. bi-m. adv.
Newsletter. m.
Biennial Meetings: Odd Yrs. & Biennial Research Conferences: Even Yrs.

Nurses Organization of the Veterans Administration (1980)
505 East Hawley Street, Mundelein IL 60060
Exec. Director: Edward J. Stygar, Jr.
Members: 3,000 *Staff:* 2-5
Annual Budget: $50-100,000 *Tel:* (312) 949-6057
Hist. Note: Membership: $48/yr.
Publication:
News from NOVA. q.
Annual Meetings: Fall/250
1987-Washington, DC

Nutrition Today Soc. (1974)
Hist. Note: Discontinued operations in 1985.

Occupational Medical Administrators' Ass'n (1959)
Advisor, Medical & Environmental Health,,xxon Co. Internat'l, 200 Park Ave., Florham Park NJ 07932-1002
Secy.-Treas.: Paul P. Dauzickas, Jr.
Members: 40-50 *Staff:* 1
Annual Budget: under $10,000 *Tel:* (201) 765-5897
Hist. Note: Established as the Industrial Medical Administrator's Ass'n, it assumed its present name in 1978. A professional association of medical administrators in government, business and industry, OMAA has no paid staff or permanent headquarters; officers change biennially.
Annual Meetings: Spring
1987-Montreal, Quebec/May/30-40

Oceanic Engineering Council
Hist. Note: A subsidiary of the Institute of Electrical and Electronics Engineers. Membership in the Council open to only to IEEE members, includes subscription to a technical periodical in the field published by IEEE. All administrative support is provided by IEEE.

Oceanic Soc. (1969)
1536 16th St., N.W., Washington DC 20036
President: Clifton Curtis
Members: 40-50,000 *Staff:* 14
Annual Budget: $1-2,000,000 *Tel:* (202) 328-0098
Hist. Note: Concerned with education and research about, and conservation of, the marine environment. Supports Oceanic Soc. Expeditions, based in San Francisco. Membership: $18/yr.
Publications:
Chapter Newsletters. bi-m. adv.
Oceans. bi-m. adv.
Symposia Proceedings. irreg.
Semi-Annual Meetings: Board of Trustees and Membership
1987-West Coast/Spring and Washington, DC/Fall

OCR Users Ass'n (1970)
Hist. Note: See Recognition Technology Users Association.

Office and Professional Employees Internat'l Union (1945)
265 West 14th St., Suite 610, New York NY 10011
President: John Kelly
Members: 150,000 *Staff:* 50-55
Annual Budget: $2-5,000,000 *Tel:* (212) 675-3210
Hist. Note: Organized in Cincinnati, Ohio January 8, 1945 as the Office Employees International Union and chartered by the American Federation of Labor at the same time. Absorbed the Associated Unions of America in 1972. Sponsors and supports the Voice of the Electorate Political Action Committee. Membership Fee varies by local union.
Publications:
White Collar. q.
Research News. q.
Annual Meetings: Every three years in June (1989)

Office Automation Soc. Internat'l (1982)
15269 Mimosa, Suite B, Dumfries VA 22026
Exec. Director: Paul D. Oyer
Members: 3,500 *Staff:* 6
Annual Budget: $100-250,000 *Tel:* (703) 690-3880
Hist. Note: Incorporated in the District of Columbia July 1, 1982. Provides information exchange between office professionals, vendors, and consultants. Maintains a program for certification of office professionals. Membership: $30/yr.(individual); $500/yr.(company).

00249 12 05 86 1233

Publications:
Office Automation News. bi-m. adv.
Proceedings. a. adv.
Office Automation Glossary.
Semi-Annual Meetings: May and September
1987-Atlantic City, NJ(Resorts Internat'l)/May 19-22/500
1987-Chicago, IL(Ramada O'Hare)/Sept. 8-11/500

Office Education Ass'n (1966)
5454 Cleveland Ave., Columbus OH 43229
Exec. Director: Mrs. Dorothy M. Goodman
Members: 70,000 *Staff:* 6-10
Annual Budget: $500-1,000,000 *Tel:* (614) 895-7277
Hist. Note: A non-profit vocational student organization for students enrolled in high school and post secondary office occupations education programs. Membership: $5/yr.
Publications:
Advisors Newsletter. 5/yr. adv.
Student Magazine. q. adv.
Annual Meetings: Spring/3,500
1987-Des Moines/May 2-10
1988-Louisville, KY(Golt House)/April 23-May 1
1989-Dallas, TX(Loew's Anatole)/April 21-30
1990-Minneapolis, MN/April 28-May 6

Office Systems Research Ass'n (1981)
University Center, Room 574, Cleveland State University, Cleveland OH 44115
Exec. Director: Edward G. Thomas
Members: 300 *Staff:* 1
Annual Budget: $10-25,000 *Tel:* (216) 687-4740
Hist. Note: Organized in Washington, DC in the fall of 1980 and officially chartered in the State of Ohio in June 1981. Members are individuals from business, government or education interested in a professional approach to the planning of office systems. Membership: $55/yr.
Publications:
Newsletter. m.
Office Systems Research Journal. semi-a.
Annual Meetings: Feb./March
1987-New York, NY(Hotel Inter-Continental)/March 21-22/100

Office Technology Management Ass'n (1972)
9401 West Beloit Road, Suite 211, Milwaukee WI 53227
President: Marsha Radaj
Members: 500 *Staff:* 2-5
Tel: (414) 321-0880
Hist. Note: Formerly the Word Processing Society of Wisconsin, founded in Milwaukee in March, 1972. Assumed its present name in 1983. Membership: $30-$50/year.
Publication:
The Word. bi-m. adv.
Annual Meetings: Spring/8,000

Offshore Marine Service Ass'n (1957)
2 Canal St., Suite 2312, New Orleans LA 70130
Exec. Director: Capt. William Mayberry
Members: 140 *Staff:* 2-5
Annual Budget: $100-250,000 *Tel:* (504) 523-7363
Hist. Note: Members are owners and operators of vessels servicing offshore installations, and their suppliers.
Publication:
OMSA Newsletter. m.
Quarterly Meetings: New Orleans, LA

Offshore Valve Ass'n
1620 Eye St., N.W., Suite 603, Washington DC 20006
Exec. V. President: George G. Pagonis
Members: 40 companies; 10 individuals *Staff:* 2
Annual Budget: $50-100,000 *Tel:* (202) 452-8811
Hist. Note: Membership fee varies from $300-$3,000/yr.

Oil, Chemical and Atomic Workers Internat'l Union (1955)
Box 2812, Denver CO 80201
President: Joseph M. Misbrener
Members: 120-130,000 *Staff:* 75-100
Annual Budget: over $5,000,000 *Tel:* (303) 987-2229
Hist. Note: The product of a merger in 1955 of the Oil Workers International Union (founded in 1918) and the United Gas, Coke and Chemical Workers International Union (founded in 1942). Has a budget of about $14 million. Sponsors and supports the Oil, Chemical and Atomic Workers Committee on Political Education Fund.
Publication:
OCAW Reporter.
Triennial meetings: Summer

Oil Field Haulers Ass'n (1936)
Box 488, 700 East 11th St., Austin TX 78767
President: Scott Pospisil
Members: 450-500 companies *Staff:* 11-15
Annual Budget: $250-500,000 *Tel:* (512) 476-5326
Hist. Note: Affiliate of American Trucking Ass'ns.
Publication:
Newsletter. bi-m.
Annual Meetings: April

Oil Investment Institute (1969)
1750 K St., N.W., Suite 1200, Washington DC 20006
Gen. Counsel: Richard A. Cantor
Members: 85 companies *Staff:* 2-5
Annual Budget: $100-250,000 *Tel:* (202) 775-0770
Hist. Note: Public drilling programs registered with the Securities and Exchange Commission, as well as law and accounting firms connected with such projects.

Olive Oil Ass'n of America (1917)
Hist. Note: A section of the Association of Food Industries.

Omega Tau Sigma (1907)
1003 Ellis Drive, Charles City IA 50616
President: Dr. John P. Donohue
Members: 5-6,000 *Staff:* 1
Annual Budget: under $10,000 *Tel:* (515) 257-3408
Hist. Note: Professional veterinary medical fraternity, established at the University of Pennsylvania School of Veterinary Medicine. Member of the Professional Fraternity Ass'n.

Omicron Kappa Upsilon (1914)
College of Dentistry, Room 105, Lincoln NE 68583-0740
Secy.-Treas.: Stephen H. Leeper, D.D.S.
Members: 16,000-18,000 dentists *Staff:* 2-5
Annual Budget: $10-25,000 *Tel:* (402) 472-1339
Hist. Note: Honorary dental society. Organized May 21, 1914 by the faculty of Northwestern University Dental School.
Annual Meetings: Spring

Oncology Nursing Soc. (1975)
3111 Banksville Road, Pittsburgh PA 15216
Exec. Director: Pearl Moore, R.N.
Members: 10,000 *Staff:* 11
Annual Budget: $1-2,000,000 *Tel:* (412) 344-3899
Hist. Note: Members are nurses involved in the treatment and care of cancer patients. Membership: $53/yr.(individual); $1,000/yr.(organization).
Publication:
Oncology Nursing Forum. q. adv.
Annual Meetings: Spring/2,400
1987-Denver, CO(Hilton)/May 6-9
1988-Pittsburgh, PA(Convention Ctr.)/May 4-7
1989-San Francisco, CA(Convention Ctr.)/May 17-20
1990-Washington, DC(Hilton)/May 16-19
1991-San Antonio, TX(Convention Ctr.)/May 8-11

Onion Export Associates of New York (1981)
50 Chestnut Drive, Hastings-on-Hudson NY 10706
President: Louis H. Vorzimer
Members: 65-70 *Staff:* 1
Annual Budget: under $10,000
Hist. Note: A Webb-Pomerene Act Association.

Open Pit Mining Ass'n (1944)
c/o Consolidation Coal Co., Consol Plaza, Pittsburgh PA 15241
Secy.-Treas.: Henry E. Gilham
Members: 30-35 companies, 650 individuals
Annual Budget: $10-25,000 *Tel:* (412) 831-4440
Hist. Note: Open pit and strip mining companies for coal and minerals, suppliers and electric utilities. Has no paid staff.
Annual Meetings: June

OPERA America (1970)
633 E St., N.W., Washington DC 20004
Exec. Director: Martin I. Kagan
Members: 105 opera companies *Staff:* 10
Annual Budget: $500-1,000,000 *Tel:* (202) 347-9262
Hist. Note: Established to facilitate communication and cooperation among professional opera producing companies in the U.S., Canada, Central and South America. Purpose is to: promote the growth and expansion of opera; assist in development of resident professional opera companies through cooperative artistic management services to its members; assist improvement of operatic presentations; encourage the appreciation and enjoyment of opera by all segments of American society; and to foster the education, training and development of operatic composers, singers and allied talents. Membership: Sliding scale based on budget.
Publications:
Intercompany Announcements. 10/yr.
Profile. a.
Season Performance Schedule. a.
Membership List.
Scenery, Costumes and Musical Materials Directory. bien.
List of Educational Resource Materials.
Survey of Professional Training/Apprentice Programs.
Repertoire Survey.
Annual Meetings: Winter
1987-Dallas, TX(Sheraton)/Jan. 9-11
1988-Houston, TX/Feb.

Operations Research Soc. of America (1952)
Mount Royal & Guilford Avenues, Baltimore MD 21202
Exec. Director: Patricia H. Morris
Members: 7,000 *Staff:* 2-5
Annual Budget: $500-1,000,000 *Tel:* (301) 528-4146
Hist. Note: Founded May 26, 1952 and incorporated in the District of Columbia the same year. A member society of the Internat'l Federation of Operational Research Societies. Members are investigators, students, teachers and managers that deal with the application of scientific methods to decision making, especially to the allocation of resources. Membership: $15-65/yr. (individual), $96/yr. (organization/company).
Publications:
OR/MS Today. bi-m. adv.
Interfaces. bi-m. adv.
Marketing Science. q. adv.
Mathematics of Operations Research. q.
Operations Research. bi-m. adv.
Operations Research Letters, bi-m.
ORSA/TIMS Bulletin. semi-a. adv.
Transportation Science. q.
Semi-annual Meetings: Spring and Fall
1987-New Orleans, LA(Marriott)/May 4-6
1987-St. Louis, MO(Adams Mark)/Oct. 26-28
1988-Washington, DC(Washington Hilton)/April 25-27
1988-Denver, CO(Marriott & Fairmont)/Oct. 24-26

Operative Plasterers' and Cement Masons' Internat'l Ass'n of the United States and Canada (1864)
1125 17th St., N. W., Washington DC 20036
President: Melvin H. Roots
Members: 54,000 *Staff:* 43
Annual Budget: $2-5,000,000 *Tel:* (202) 393-6569
Hist. Note: Founded in 1864 as the National Plasterers' Organization of the United States, it was renamed the Operative Plasterers International Association of the United States and Canada in 1889. Affiliated with the American Federation of Labor in 1908, it absorbed the cement finishers of the United Brotherhood of Cement Workers in 1915 and changed its name to the Operative Plasterers' and Cement Finishers' International Association of the United States and Canada. The present name was adopted in 1950. Sponsors and supports the Plasterers' and Cement Masons' Political Action Committee.
Publication:
The Plasterer and Cement Mason. m. adv.
Quinquennial Conventions: 1989

Optical Character Recognition Users Ass'n (1970)
Hist. Note: Became the Recognition Technologies Users Association in 1982.

Optical Laboratories Ass'n (1939)
P.O. Box 2000, Merrifield VA 22116-2000
Exec. Director: Irby N. Hollans, CAE
Members: 338 companies *Staff:* 2-5
Annual Budget: $500-1,000,000 *Tel:* (703) 849-8550
Hist. Note: Formerly the Optical Wholesalers Ass'n, it adopted its present name in 1977. Independent ophthalmic laboratories and supply houses making prescription glasses to requirements of ophthalmologists, optometrists and opticians.
Annual Meetings: November/1,800-2,100
1987-San Antonio, TX
1988-Las Vegas, NV
1989-Nashville, TN
1990-Orlando, FL
1991-New Orleans, LA

Optical Manufacturers Ass'n (1916)
6055A Arlington Blvd., Falls Church VA 22044
Exec. V. President: Eugene Adams Keeney
Members: 80 companies *Staff:* 4
Annual Budget: $500-1,000,000 *Tel:* (703) 237-8433
Hist. Note: Members are makers of spectacle frames, lenses, cases and machinery.
Semi-Annual Meetings: Spring in Washington, DC and Fall

Optical Soc. of America (1916)
1816 Jefferson Place, N.W., Washington DC 20036
Exec. Director: Dr. Jarus W. Quinn
Members: 9,000 *Staff:* 25-30
Annual Budget: $2-5,000,000 *Tel:* (202) 223-8130
Hist. Note: Composed of individuals interested in any aspect of the subject of optics-teaching, research, manufacturing or physiology. Membership: $40/yr.
Publications:
Applied Optics. semi-m. adv.
Journal of the Optical Soc. of America A. m.
Journal of the Optical Soc. of America B. m.
Optics and Spectroscopy. m.
Optics Letters. m.
Optics News. m. adv.
Soviet Journal of Optical Technology. m.
Journal of Lightwave Technology. bi-m.
Chinese Physics-Lasers. q.
Annual Meetings: October
1987-Rochester, NY/Oct. 19-23

Opticians Ass'n of America (1926)
10341 Democracy Lane, Box 10110, Fairfax VA 22030
Exec. Director: James D. Hawkins, CAE
Members: 900-1,000 retail optical companies *Staff:* 11-15
Annual Budget: $1-2,000,000 *Tel:* (703) 691-8355
Hist. Note: Formerly (1972) Guild of Prescription Opticians of America, Inc.
Publication:
Dispensing Optician. m. adv.
Annual Meetings: Spring/1,000

Oral History Ass'n (1966)
Hist. Note: Address unknown in 1987. Probably defunct.

Organization Development Institute (1968)
11234 Walnut Ridge Road, Chesterland OH 44026
President: Dr. Donald W. Cole, RODC
Members: 455 individuals *Staff:* 1
Annual Budget: $25-50,000 *Tel:* (216) 461-4333
Hist. Note: Regular members believe they are professionally qualified in organization development by training and experience and support the O.D. code of ethics. They may use the initials "RODP" after their name (Registered O.D.

00250 12 05 86 1233

Professional). Membership: $70-110/yr. (individual), $500/yr. (corporate).
Publications:
Internat'l Registry of O.D. Professionals & O.D. Handbook. a.
The Organization Development Journal. q. adv.
Organizations and Change. m. adv.
Semi-Annual: Spring and Fall
1987-Warsaw, Poland & Moscow/Sept. 22-25 & Sept. 27-Oct. 3
1988-Singapore/Nov. 15-18/88

Organization for the Protection and Advancement of Small Telephone Companies (1963)
2301 M St., N.W., Suite 530, Washington DC 20037
Exec. V. President: Andrew G. Mulitz
Members: 350 companies *Staff:* 6-10
Annual Budget: $500-1,000,000 *Tel:* (202) 659-5990
Hist. Note: Is concerned with protecting the interests of small, mainly rural, telephone companies.
Publication:
Newsletter. q.
Semi-annual Meetings: July and January

Organization for Tropical Studies (1963)
P.O. Box DM, Duke Station, Durham NC 27706
Exec. Director: Donald E. Stone
Members: 40 institutions *Staff:* 16-20
Annual Budget: $1-2,000,000 *Tel:* (919) 684-5774
Hist. Note: Universities and research institutions with graduate programs in tropical studies. Maintains an office and research stations in Costa Rica.
Publication:
OTS Newsletter. q.
Annual Meetings: March-April in San Jose, Costa Rica/100

Organization of American Historians (1907)
112 N. Bryan St., Bloomington IN 47401-3841
Exec. Secretary: Joan Hoff-Wilson
Members: 8,500 individuals, 3,500 institutions *Staff:* 6-10
Annual Budget: $250-500,000 *Tel:* (812) 335-7311
Hist. Note: Formerly (1964) Mississippi Valley Historical Ass'n. Membership Fee: $80/yr. (organization/company); graduated scale based on income for individual.
Publications:
Journal of American History. q. adv.
OAH Magazine of History. q. adv.
OAH Annual Program. a. adv.
OAH Newsletter. a. adv.
Annual Meetings: April/1,800-2,000
1987-Philadelphia, PA(Wyndham Franklin Plaza)/April 2-5
1988-Reno, NV(Bally's Grand)/March 30-April 2
1989-St. Louis, MO
1990-Washington, DC

Organization of Athletic Administrators (1974)
Hist. Note: Inactive in 1982.

Organization of Biological Field Stations (1966)
Box 351, Eureka MO 63025
Secretary/Treasurer: Dr. Richard W. Coles
Members: 64 stations, 43 individuals
Annual Budget: under $10,000 *Tel:* (314) 938-5271
Hist. Note: Founded in 1966 as the Organization of Inland Biological Field Stations at Lake Texoma, OK. Members are Biological Field Stations and individuals concerned with biological field facilities in the U.S. and Canada. Has no paid staff. Membership: $10/year (individual), $50/year (institution).
Publication:
OBFS Newsletter. semi-a.
Annual Meetings: September
1987-Ogallala, NE(Cedar Point Biological Station)/Sept. 25-28
1988-Bodega Bay, CA(Bodega Marine Station)
1989-Maine(Audubon Science Camp)

Organization of Black Airline Pilots (1976)
Box 86 LaGuardia Airport, New York NY 11371
General Manager: Eddie R. Hadden
Members: 500 individuals; 4 companies *Staff:* 1
Annual Budget: $10-25,000 *Tel:* (201) 568-8145
Hist. Note: Seeks to enhance the participation of minorities in the aerospace industry. Provides a communication network and job search assistance. Regular membership is open to cockpit crewmembers of commercial air carriers including corporate pilots. Sponsors a summer flight academy for youth at Tuskegee, Alabama. Membership: $100/year(individual), $200/year (organization).
Publications:
OBAP Monthly Newsletter.
OBAP Quarterly Newsletter. adv.
Semi-annual Meetings: Spring and August

Organization of Manufacturers Representatives (1986)
1377 K St., N.W., Suite 831, Washington DC 20005
Exec. Director: George Brown
Members: 20 companies *Staff:* 2
Annual Budget: $100-250,000 *Tel:* (202) 362-3009
Hist. Note: Organized to further the profession of manufacturers' representatives and independent manufacturers' agents.

Organization of Plastics Processors (1974)
Hist. Note: Reported as dissolved in 1984.

Organization of Professional Employees of the U.S. Department of Agriculture (1929)
Box 381, Rm. 1414 So. Bldg. U.S.D.A., Washington DC 20044
Exec. Director: John H. Miner
Members: 8-9,000 *Staff:* 2-5
Annual Budget: $100-250,000 *Tel:* (202) 447-4898
Hist. Note: Membership: $26/yr.
Publications:
OPEDA News. m.
OPEDA Journal. 3/yr.
Annual Meetings: October
1987-Washington, DC(Quality Inn-Arlington Hotel)/Oct. 5-8/50
1988-Washington, DC/Oct. 2-5/50
1989-Washington, DC/Oct. 1-4/50

Organization of Teachers of Oral Diagnosis (1963)
Univ. of Michigan School of Dentistry, Ann Arbor MI 48109-1078
Secy.-Treas.: Sharon L. Brooks, DDS
Members: 200
Annual Budget: under $10,000 *Tel:* (313) 764-1565
Hist. Note: Conceived at a workshop for oral diagnosis teachers in 1963 at Iowa State University. Membership: $50/year.
Publication:
OTOD Newsletter. q.
Annual Meetings: With American Ass'n of Dental Schools

Organized Flying Adjusters (1958)
Box 3476, Corpus Christi TX 78404
Central Records Office: William G. Holmes
Members: 75-100 companies and individuals *Staff:* 1
Annual Budget: under $10,000 *Tel:* (512) 852-2735
Hist. Note: Aircraft insurance adjusters who process aviation insurance claims and investigate causes of aircraft accidents. Membership: $150/yr.(individual); $50/yr.(company).
Publication:
OFA Newsletter. q.
Annual Meetings: October-By invitation only
1987-Fort Worth, TX
1988-Atlantic City, NJ

Oriental Rug Importers Ass'n of America (1928)
267 Fifth Ave., New York NY 10016
Secretary: Trudy Klein
Members: 60-65 companies *Staff:* 1
Annual Budget: $10-25,000 *Tel:* (212) 685-1761
Hist. Note: Membership is concentrated in the New York area.
Publication:
Oriental Rug Magazine. 4-5/yr. adv.
Annual Meetings: New York, NY

Oriental Rug Retailers of America (1970)
P.O. Box 4728, Medford OR 97501
Exec. Director: Otto A. Ewaldsen
Members: 236 *Staff:* 4
Annual Budget: $250-500,000 *Tel:* (503) 779-8409
Hist. Note: Membership of 236 represents over 460 store locations. Membership: $250/yr.
Publication:
Newletter. 10/yr.
Annual Meetings: Summer
1987-Chicago, IL(Chicago Hilton)/Aug. 2-7/1,200
1988-Washington, DC(Washington Hilton)/July 17-22/1,400

Orthodox Theological Soc. in America (1968)
Hellenic College, 50 Goddard Ave., Brookline MA 02146
Editor: Dr. George Papademetriou
Members: 100 individuals *Staff:* 1
Annual Budget: under $10,000 *Tel:* (617) 731-3500
Hist. Note: Members are Orthodox theologians of various ethnic backgrounds. Has no paid staff. The above phone number should be used with extension #243. Membership: $10/yr.
Publications:
Bulletin. q.
Directory. every 5 years.
Annual Meetings: Spring
1987-Brookline, MA

Orthopaedic Research Soc. (1954)
222 South Prospect St., Suite 127, Park Ridge IL 60068
Exec. Secretary: Karen J. Jared
Members: 984 *Staff:* 2
Annual Budget: $100-250,000 *Tel:* (312) 698-1625
Hist. Note: Orthopedic surgeons in the U.S. and Canada. Membership: $115/yr.
Publications:
Journal of Orthopaedic Research. q. adv.
Transaction Book of the Annual Meeting. a.
Annual Meetings: Winter
1987-San Francisco, CA(Convention Center)/Jan. 19-22/1,600
1988-Atlanta, GA/Feb. 1-4
1989-Las Vegas, NV/Feb. 6-9

Orthopedic Surgical Manufacturers Ass'n (1955)
1450 Brooks Road, Memphis TN 38116
Secy.-Treas.: Frank M. Lewis
Members: 20-30 companies
Annual Budget: under $10,000 *Tel:* (901) 396-2121
Hist. Note: Members are manufacturers of orthopedic surgical items.
Triannual Meetings: Winter, Spring and Summer

Orton Dyslexia Soc. (1949)
724 York Road, Baltimore MD 21204
Exec. Director: Anne L. O'Flanagan
Members: 8,300 individuals *Staff:* 6
Annual Budget: $250-500,000 *Tel:* (301) 296-0232
Hist. Note: An international organization with branches in Canada, Bermuda and the United States named after Dr. Samuel T. Orton (1879-1948) to disseminate information on specific language disabilities-dyslexia. Membership: $45/yr.
Publications:
Perspectives on Dyslexia. q.
Annals of Dyslexia. a.
Annual Meetings: Fall
1987-San Francisco, CA/Nov.

Osborne Ass'n (1932)
135 East 15th St., New York NY 10003
Exec. Director: Robert Gangi
Members: 300-500 *Staff:* 6-10
Annual Budget: $250-500,000 *Tel:* (212) 673-6633
Hist. Note: Formed by merger of the National Society of Penal Information and the Welfare League Association of New York. Named after Thomas Mott Osborne (1859-1926), pioneer prison reformer and founder of the Mutual Welfare League. Members are professional correctional personnel and others interested in assisting prisoner rehabilitation.

Osteopathic College of Ophthalmology and Otorhinolaryngology (1916)
405 Grand Ave., Dayton OH 45405
Exec. Director: G. Joseph Strickler, CAE
Members: 345 physicians *Staff:* 5
Annual Budget: $50-100,000 *Tel:* (513) 222-4213
Publication:
Newsletter. q.
Annual Meetings: Spring/225-250
1987-Colorado Springs, CO(Broadmoor)/May 3-7
1988-Hilton Head, SC(Marriott Hilton Head Resort)/April 17-21
1989-San Diego, CA(Hotel Del Coronado)/April 9-13
1990-Boca Raton, FL(Hotel & Club)/April 22-26
1991-Monterey, CA(Hyatt Regency)/April 14-18

Otosclerosis Study Group (1947)
27555 Middlebelt, Farmington Hills MI 48018
President: T. Manford McGee, M.D.
Members: 125-150
Annual Budget: under $10,000 *Tel:* (313) 476-4622
Hist. Note: Physicians specializing in diseases of the ear. Affiliated with the American Academy of Otolaryngology.

Outdoor Advertising Ass'n of America (1891)
1899 L St., N.W., Suite 403, Washington DC 20036
President: Vernon A. Clark
Members: 200 *Staff:* 6-10
Annual Budget: $500-1,000,000 *Tel:* (202) 223-5566
Hist. Note: Recommends standards for outdoor display structures and disseminates information on the outdoor medium. Supports the Outdoor Advertising Political Action Committee located in Washington, DC. Maintains a Washington office.
Publication:
Buyers Guide to Outdoor Advertising. a.
Biennial meetings: odd years

Outdoor Amusement Business Ass'n (1965)
4600 West 77th St., Minneapolis MN 55435
Exec. Director: Roland K. Larson
Members: 4000 *Staff:* 2-5
Annual Budget: $100-250,000 *Tel:* (612) 831-4643
Hist. Note: Membership consists of road shows, carnivals and equipment suppliers.
Publications:
Newsletter. m. adv.
OABA Annual. a. adv.
Semi-annual Meetings: Feb. in Tampa, FL and Nov. in Chicago, IL

Outdoor Education Ass'n (1940)
143 Fox Hill Road, Denville NJ 07834
President: Dr. Edward J. Ambry
Members: 200
Annual Budget: under $10,000 *Tel:* (201) 627-7214
Hist. Note: Advocates of outdoor learning as part of school and organization programs.

Outdoor Power Equipment Aftermarket Ass'n (1986)
1001 Connecticut Ave., N.W., Suite 800, Washington DC 20036
Exec. V. President: William S. Bergman
Members: 75 companies *Staff:* 3
Annual Budget: $100-250,000 *Tel:* (202) 775-8605
Hist. Note: OPEAA is a group of small to medium-sized businessmen dedicated to promoting the use of aftermarket (spare) parts in outdoor power equipment (lawnmowers, chain saws, etc.), as well as to ensuring an atmosphere of free and unrestrained trade in the industry.
Publication:
Aftermarket Advocate. bi-m. adv.
Annual Meetings: February
1987-Orlando, FL(Sonesta Village Hotel)/Feb. 1-4/150

00251 12 05 86 1233

Outdoor Power Equipment Distributors Ass'n (1980)
1900 Arch St., Philadelphia PA 19103
Exec. Director: John W. Kane
Members: 150 companies *Staff:* 2-5
Annual Budget: $50-100,000 *Tel:* (215) 564-3484
Annual Meetings: February

Outdoor Power Equipment Institute (1952)
1901 L St., N.W., Suite 700, Washington DC 20036
Exec. Director and C.O.O.: Dennis C. Dix, CAE
Members: 72 companies *Staff:* 6-10
Annual Budget: $1-2,000,000 *Tel:* (202) 296-3484
Hist. Note: Established as the Lawn Mower Institute, OPEI assumed its present name in 1960. Members are manufacturers of all types of mechanized lawn and garden equipment and industry suppliers of major components.
Publication:
Executive Update. irreg.
Annual Meetings: June
1987-Monterey, CA/June 21-24/250
1988-Napa, CA(Silverado Country Club)/June 19-22/200-225
1989-Charleston, SC(Kiawah Inn)/June 18-21/200-225

Outdoor Writers Ass'n of America (1927)
2017 Cato Avenue, Suite 101, State College PA 16801
Exec. Director: Sylvia G. Bashline
Members: 1,600-1,700 *Staff:* 2-5
Annual Budget: $100-250,000 *Tel:* (814) 234-1011
Hist. Note: OWAA was formed at a meeting April 9, 1927 in Chicago by a group of writers attending an Izaak Walton League of America convention. Members are broadcasters, writers and editors, authors, photographers and artists who pledge to support conservation of natural resources. Membership: $50/yr. (individual), $250/yr. (organization).
Publication:
Outdoors Unlimited. m.
Annual Meetings: May/June
1987-Kalispell, MT(Westin)/June 21-26
1988-Marco Island, FL(Marriott)/May 22-26
1989-Des Moines, IA/June 11-15

Overseas Automotive Club (1923)
300 Sylvan Ave., Englewood Cliffs NJ 07632
Secretary: Stephen Bomer
Members: 1,000-1,100 individuals *Staff:* 2-5
Annual Budget: $250-500,000 *Tel:* (201) 836-6999
Hist. Note: An international organization whose membership comes about 50% from the United States, of individuals engaged in the export and import of U.S. parts, tools and products used in automotive maintenance.
Publications:
OAC News. q.
OAC Roster. a.
Annual Meetings: Late Winter/Early Spring
1987-Atlanta, GA/March 10-12
1988-Las Vegas, NV/March 2-4

Overseas Education Ass'n (1956)
1201 16th St., N.W., Washington DC 20036
Exec. Director: Ronald R. Austin
Members: 5,100 *Staff:* 12
Annual Budget: $500-1,000,000 *Tel:* (202) 822-7850
Hist. Note: A labor union affiliated with the National Education Association and representing about 5,100 teachers on overseas military bases. Membership: $274/yr.
Publication:
Journal. 9/yr.

Overseas Press Club of America (1939)
52 East 41st St., New York NY 10017
President: Herbert Kupferberg
Members: 1,500 professional journalists *Staff:* 2
Annual Budget: under $10,000 *Tel:* (212) 679-9650
Hist. Note: Membership: $275/yr.
Publications:
Dateline. a. adv.
Overseas Press Bulletin. w. adv.
Semi-annual meetings: Awards Dinner in April (NYC) and October

Owner-Operator Independent Drivers Ass'n of America (1973)
P.O. Box 88, Oak Grove MO 64075
President: James J. Johnston
Members: 6,000 individuals *Staff:* 22
Annual Budget: $2-5,000,000 *Tel:* (816) 229-5791
Hist. Note: Membership: $50/yr. (driver), $90/yr. plus $10/truck (owner/operator).
Publications:
Land Line Magazine. bi-m. adv.
OOIDA News Update. q.
Annual Meetings: June & November (Open Board of Directors Meeting)

Owner Operators of America (1982)
Hist. Note: Provides business and legislative information to self-employed truckers; represents self-employed truckers on Capitol Hill; Discounts on services and supplies for self-employed members. Address unknown in 1986.

Oxygenated Fuels Ass'n (1983)
1330 Connecticut Ave., N.W., Washington DC 20036
Exec. Director: George S. Dominguez
Staff: 1
Annual Budget: $100-250,000 *Tel:* (202) 659-0060
Hist. Note: An affiliate of the Synthetic Organic Chemical Manufaturers Ass'n which provides administrative support.
Publication:
Newsletter. m.
Annual Meetings:
1987-Washington, DC/December

P/M Industries Ass'n (1958)
Hist. Note: A constituent part of the Metal Powder Industries Federation. Formerly (1970) Magnetic Powder Core Ass'n, merged with the In-Plant Powder Metallurgy Ass'n to form the Metal Powder Technology Ass'n in 1985.

Pacific Agricultural Cooperative for Export (1972)
21 Tamal Vista Blvd., #106, Corte Madera CA 94925
Exec. Secretary: J. Murray Fox
Members: 18 companies *Staff:* 1
Annual Budget: $25-50,000 *Tel:* (415) 924-2442
Hist. Note: A Webb-Pomerene Act Ass'n.

Package Designers Council (1952)
Box 3753, Grand Central Station, New York NY 10017
Secretary: William O'Connor
Members: 180 *Staff:* 1
Annual Budget: under $10,000 *Tel:* (212) 682-1980
Hist. Note: The sole organization representing package designers and practitioners in marketing communications throughout the USA and abroad. Membership: $275/yr.
Publications:
Newswrap. semi-a.
PDC Update. bi-m.
Annual Meetings: October in New York City.

Packaged Ice Ass'n (1917)
111 East Wacker Dr., Suite 600, Chicago IL 60601
Exec. Director: Robert F. Hartman
Members: 400 *Staff:* 2-5
Annual Budget: $250-500,000 *Tel:* (312) 644-6610
Hist. Note: Manufacturers and distributors of ice and their suppliers. Develops new uses for ice. Founded as the National Association of Ice Industries, it became the National Ice Association in 1958 and assumed its present name in December, 1980.
Publications:
Ice News. bi-m. adv.
Membership Directory. a. adv.
Annual Meetings: Fall

Packaging Institute Internat'l (1939)
20 Summer St., Stamford CT 06901
Exec. Director: Carol M. Newman
Members: 2,900-3,000 *Staff:* 6-10
Annual Budget: $250-500,000 *Tel:* (203) 325-9010
Hist. Note: Incorporated in 1939 as Packaging Institute U.S.A., the association adopted the title Packaging Institute Internat'l in 1986. It is a society of both individuals and companies whose objectives include educating the packaging professional, advancing packaging technology, and increasing the value of packaging and packaged products in the marketplace. Membership: $80/yr. (individual); $1,000/yr. (organization)
Publications:
PACK-INFO. q.
Who's Who in Packaging. a. adv.
Glossary of Packaging Terms. triennial. adv.
Directory of Contract Packagers. triennial. adv.
Annual Meetings: Fall
1987-Tampa Bay, FL/Oct. 7-9

Packaging Machinery Manufacturers Institute (1932)
1343 L St., N.W., Washington DC 20005
Exec. Director: Claude S. Breeden, Jr.
Members: 250 *Staff:* 11-15
Annual Budget: $1-2,000,000 *Tel:* (202) 347-3838
Hist. Note: Owns and manages PACK EXPO, an exposition of packaging machinery and materials. Sponsors the Packaging Machinery Manufacturers Institute Political Action Committee.
Publications:
Pack-age. q.
Packaging Machinery Directory. bi-a.

Paint, Body and Equipment Ass'n (1975)
9140 Ward Parkway, Kansas City MO 64114
Exec. Director: Barbara Parks
Members: 100 companies *Staff:* 7-8
Annual Budget: $50-100,000 *Tel:* (816) 444-3500
Hist. Note: Warehouse distributors of automotive paint and other repair products and affiliate manufacturer suppliers.
Publication:
Membership Directory. a. adv.
Annual Meetings: Fall

Painting and Decorating Contractors of America (1884)
7223 Lee Hwy., Falls Church VA 22046
Exec. Director: Charles H. Holes
Members: 3,500 *Staff:* 6-10
Annual Budget: $500-1,000,000 *Tel:* (703) 534-1201
Hist. Note: Membership: $170/yr. plus council and chapter dues.
Publication:
Painting and Wallcovering Contractor. bi-m. adv.
Annual Meetings: March
1987-Phoenix(Hyatt)/March 3-6
1988-Minneapolis(Hyatt)/March 1-4
1989-New Orleans, LA(Sheraton)/March 14-17
1990-San Diego, CA
1991-Atlanta, GA
1992-San Antonio, TX

Paleontological Research Institution (1932)
1259 Trumansburg Rd., Ithaca NY 14850
Director: Dr. Peter R. Hoover
Members: 725-750 *Staff:* 2-5
Annual Budget: $100-250,000 *Tel:* (607) 273-6623
Hist. Note: Founded in Ithaca in 1932 and incorporated in New York in 1936. Affiliated with the American Ass'n for the Advancement of Science and the Association of Systematics Collections.
Publications:
Bulletins of American Paleontology. a.
Paleontographica Americana. irreg.
Annual Meetings: Second Saturday in May

Paleontological Soc. (1908)
United States Geological Survey, E-501 U.S. Nat'l Museum, Washington DC 20560
Secretary: Dr. John Pojeta, Jr.
Members: 2,000 *Staff:* 1
Annual Budget: $50-100,000 *Tel:* (202) 343-5097
Hist. Note: Affiliated with the Geological Society of America. Membership: $43/yr.
Publications:
Journal of Paleontology. bi-m.
Memoirs of The Paleontological Society. irreg.
News and Notes. semi-a.
Paleobiology. q.
Short Course Notes. a.
Annual Meetings: Fall, with the Geological Soc. of America.
1987-Phoenix, AZ

Palomino Horse Ass'n (1936)
Box 324, Jefferson City MO 65102
Exec. Secretary: Robert E. Dallmeyer
Members: 375-400 *Staff:* 2-5
Annual Budget: $10-25,000 *Tel:* (314) 635-5511
Hist. Note: Members are owners and breeders of Palomino horses. Provides a registry for Palominos.
Publication:
Palomino Parade. m. adv.

Palomino Horse Breeders of America (1941)
15253 E. Skelly Dr., Tulsa OK 74116-2620
General Manager: Cindy Chilton
Members: 6,000 *Staff:* 6-10
Annual Budget: $250-500,000 *Tel:* (918) 438-1234
Hist. Note: Members are owners and breeders of Palomino horses. Maintains a registry as well as show records. Membership: $30/yr.
Publication:
Palomino Horses. m. adv.
Annual Meetings: Summer
1987-Orlando, FL/June 11-13
1987-Tulsa, OK/July 11-18

Pan-American Biodeterioration Soc. (1985)
Dept. of Forensic Sciences, George Washington University, Washington DC 20052
Corres. Secy.: Dr. Charles O'Rear
Members: 75
Annual Budget: under $10,000 *Tel:* (202) 676-7319
Hist. Note: Membership open to those involved in the study of the deterioration of materials of economic importance by organisms. Membership: $15/yr.
Publication:
Newsletter. q.
Annual Meetings: Summer

Paper Bag Institute (1935)
2 Overhill Rd., Scarsdale NY 10583
Exec. V. President: Brent C. Dixon
Members: 11-15 *Staff:* 2-5
Annual Budget: $100-250,000 *Tel:* (914) 723-7610
Annual Meetings: Fall

Paper Distribution Council (1958)
111 Great Neck Road, Great Neck NY 11021
Secretary: John J. Buckley, Jr.
Members: 20-25 companies *Staff:* 1
Annual Budget: under $10,000 *Tel:* (516) 829-3070
Hist. Note: Members are manufacturers and distributors concerned with the problems of wholesale paper distribution. Affiliated with the American Paper Institute and the Nat'l Paper Trade Ass'n, which provides administrative support.

Paper Industry Management Ass'n (1919)
2400 East Oakton St., Arlington Heights IL 60005
Exec.Director: George J. Calimafde
Members: 3,500-4,000 *Staff:* 12-14
Annual Budget: $1-2,000,000 *Tel:* (312) 956-0250
Hist. Note: Founded as the American Pulp and Paper Mill Superintendents Association, it assumed its present name in 1959. Members are executives in paper and pulp mills.
Publications:
PIMA-Magazine. m. adv.
PIMA Membership Directory. a. adv.

00252 12 05 86 1233

PIMA-Catalog a. adv.
Annual Meetings: June
1987-Minneapolis, MN(Radisson)/June 16-19/1,000
1988-Atlanta, GA(Marriott Marquis)/June 15-18/1,000

Paper Makers Advertising Ass'n (1911)
Hist. Note: Defunct in 1982.

Paper Shipping Sack Manufacturers Ass'n (1933)
2 Overhill Rd., Scarsdale NY 10583
Exec. V. President: Brent C. Dixon
Members: 20-30 *Staff:* 2-5
Annual Budget: $250-500,000 *Tel:* (914) 723-6440
Hist. Note: Formerly the Rope Paper Sack Manufacturers Ass'n.
Annual Meetings: October

Paperboard Packaging Council (1967)
1101 Vermont Ave., N.W., Suite 411, Washington DC 20005
President: S. Edward Iciek
Members: 100 *Staff:* 12
Annual Budget: $500-1,000,000 *Tel:* (202) 289-4100
Hist. Note: Formed by a merger of the Folding Paper Box Association of America (founded in 1929) and the Institute for Better Packaging (founded in 1929). Members are companies making folding cartons.
Annual Meetings: Chicago, in March(Drake)

Parapsychological Ass'n (1957)
Box 12236, Research Triangle Pk NC 27709-2236
President: Dr. Richard Broughton
Members: 300 *Staff:* 1
Annual Budget: $10-25,000 *Tel:* (919) 688-8241
Hist. Note: Membership restricted to persons doing research or scholarly work in the field which is of publishable quality. Affiliated with the American Ass'n for the Advancement of Science. Membership: $30/yr.
Publication:
Research in Parapsychology. a.
Annual Meetings: August/200

Parcel Shippers Ass'n (1953)
1211 Connecticut Ave., N.W., Suite 406, Washington DC 20036
Exec. V. President: David A. Bunn
Members: 175-200 companies *Staff:* 2-5
Annual Budget: $50-100,000 *Tel:* (202) 296-3690
Hist. Note: Formerly (1977) the Parcel Post Ass'n. Sponsors and supports the Parcel Shippers Association Political Action Committee.
Annual Meetings: Chicago, in the Spring, at an airport site.

Parenteral Drug Ass'n (1946)
1407 Avenue of the Arts Bldg., Philadelphia PA 19107
Exec. Director: Solomon C. Pflag
Members: 1,800 *Staff:* 6-10
Annual Budget: $500-1,000,000 *Tel:* (215) 735-9752
Hist. Note: Members are makers of parenteral (injectable) drugs, and their suppliers. Membership: $60/yr.(individual); $375/yr.(company).
Publications:
Journal of Parenteral Science and Technology. bi-m.
PDA Letter. m.
Annual Meetings: Fall/1,500
1987-Philadelphia, PA(Wyndham Franklin Place)/Nov. 18-20/1,700

Paso Fino Horse Ass'n
P.O. Box 600, Bowling Green FL 33834
Exec. Director: Jerold Knight
Members: 2,500 *Staff:* 6-7
Annual Budget: $250-500,000 *Tel:* (813) 375-4331
Hist. Note: Formerly (1986) Paso Fino Owners and Breeders Ass'n. Members are owners and breeders of Paso Fino horses. Incorporated in Tennessee. Membership: $35/yr.
Publication:
Paso Fino Horse World. m.

Passive Solar Industries Council (1980)
1414 Prince St., Alexandria VA 22314
Exec. Director: Elena Marcheso-Moreno
Members: 60 companies; 14 individuals *Staff:* 2-5
Annual Budget: $100-250,000 *Tel:* (703) 683-5003
Hist. Note: Founded in 1980, PSIC grew out of an informal group of trade associations representing the building industry. Membership is comprised mainly of trade associations, manufacturers and suppliers interested in the construction of buildings that, by their design, use and store solar energy.
Publications:
Passive Solar News. m.
Passive Solar Trends.
Annual Meetings: Fall

Passive Solar Products Ass'n (1979)
Hist. Note: A division of the Industrial Fabrics Association International. Members are makers of screens, awnings, movable insulation, window glazings and thermal storage units.

Patent and Trademark Office Soc. (1917)
Box 2089, Eads Station, Arlington VA 22202
Secretary: Judy Hartman
Members: 1,000 *Staff:* 7
Annual Budget: $50-100,000
Hist. Note: Formerly (1986) Patent Office Soc. Members are past and present examiners in the U.S. Patent and Trademark Office, together with registered patent attorneys and agents, trademark practitioners, patient practitioners for federal agencies, judges and other patent professionals. Membership: $18/yr.
Publications:
Journal of Patent and Trademark Office Society. m. adv.
Newsletter. m.
Annual Meetings: February in Arlington, VA
1987-Crystal City, VA(Crystal City Theater)/Feb./5-700

Patent Office Professional Ass'n (1962)
Box 2745, Arlington VA 22202
President: Ronald J. Stern
Members: 1,400 *Staff:* 7
Annual Budget: $50-100,000 *Tel:* (703) 557-2975
Hist. Note: Independent labor union representing all non-managerial professionals (other than trademark professionals) in the U.S. Patent and Trademark Office. Affiliated with the National Federation of Professional Organizations. Membership: $104/yr.
Publication:
POPA Newsletter. m.
Annual Meetings: First Thursday in December near Washington.

Patent Office Soc.
Hist. Note: Became the Patent and Trademark Office Soc. in 1986.

Pathology Practice Ass'n (1980)
1225 Connecticut Ave., N.W., Suite 303, Washington DC 20036
Washington Representative: Paul Johnson
Members: 500 individuals *Staff:* 2-5
Annual Budget: $100-250,000 *Tel:* (202) 659-0330
Hist. Note: Founded to provide government relations and professional services to pathologists.
Publication:
PPA Newsletter. bi-m.
Annual Meetings: December

Pattern Makers' League of North America (1887)
501 15th St., Suite 204, Moline IL 61265
President: Jack L. Gabelhausen, Sr.
Members: 9,600 *Staff:* 2-5
Annual Budget: $500-1,000,000 *Tel:* (309) 764-2013
Hist. Note: Established in Philadelphia May 18, 1887 and chartered by the American Federation of Labor in 1894.
Publication:
Pattern Markers' Journal. q.
Quinquennial Meetings: 1991

Pattern Recognition Soc. (1966)
Georgetown Univ. Medical Center, 3900 Reservoir Road, N. W., Washington DC 20007
Exec. Director: Dr. Robert S. Ledley
Members: 450-550 *Staff:* 2-5
Annual Budget: $10-25,000 *Tel:* (202) 625-2121
Hist. Note: Members are scientists and engineers interested and working in the field of pattern recognition in the broad sense.
Publication:
Pattern Recognition. bi-m.
Annual Meetings: Not held

Peanut Butter and Nut Processors Ass'n (1969)
9005 Congressional Court, Potomac MD 20854
Mng. Director & General Counsel: James E. Mack, CAE
Members: 190-225 companies *Staff:* 2-5
Annual Budget: $100-250,000 *Tel:* (301) 365-4080
Hist. Note: A merger of The Peanut Butter Manufacturers Ass'n (1939) and The Peanut and Nut Salters Ass'n (1941). Absorbed The Peanut Butter Sandwich and Cookie Manufacturers Ass'n. Formerly (until 1978) known as the Peanut Butter Manufacturers and Nut Salters Ass'n. Sponsors and supports the Peanut Butter and Nut Processors Association Political Action Committee.
Annual Meetings: November

Pediatric Orthopaedic Soc. of North America
Hist. Note: Became a division of American Academy of Orthopaedic Surgeons in 1986.

Pencil Makers Ass'n (1918)
66 East Main St., Moorestown NJ 08057
Exec. V. President: William L. MacMillan, III
Members: 20-25 companies *Staff:* 2-5
Annual Budget: $100-250,000 *Tel:* (609) 234-9155
Hist. Note: Formerly (1970) Lead Pencil Manufacturers Ass'n, Inc.

Pennsylvania Grade Crude Oil Ass'n (1923)
Pringle Power Company, P.O. Box 201, Bradford PA 16701
President: John W. Bryner
Members: 200-225 *Staff:* 2-5
Annual Budget: $50-100,000 *Tel:* (814) 368-8172

Pension Real Estate Ass'n (1982)
1101 17th St., N.W., Suite 700, Washington DC 20036
Exec. Director: Mark O. Decker
Members: 350-400 *Staff:* 10-15
Annual Budget: $500-1,000,000 *Tel:* (202) 296-4141
Hist. Note: Membership open to qualified pension funds, plan sponsors, asset managers and other supportive firms. Represents the industry before Congress and the Executive branch; holds three conferences per year. Membership: $1,000/yr.
Publications:
PREA Newsletter. q.
Membership Directory. semi-a.
Tri-Annual Meetings: Jan., May and October
1987-San Francisco, CA/Jan.
1987-Dallas, TX/May
1987-New York, NY/Oct.

Percheron Horse Ass'n of America (1876)
138 Columbus Road, Fredericktown OH 43019
Secy.-Treas.: Alex T. Christian
Members: 2,000 *Staff:* 3
Annual Budget: $50-100,000 *Tel:* (614) 694-3602
Hist. Note: Formerly Percheron Soc. of America, it assumed its present name in 1934. Members are owners and breeders of Percheron horses. Membership: $10/yr.
Publication:
Percheron News. q. adv.
Annual Meetings: First Saturday in November

Percussive Arts Soc. (1961)
214 West Main St., Urbana IL 61801
Admin. Manager: David Via
Members: 5,500 *Staff:* 1
Annual Budget: $100-250,000 *Tel:* (217) 367-4098
Hist. Note: Members are teachers and performers on drums and other percussion instruments. Membership: $25/yr.
Publications:
Percussive Notes. q.
Percussion Notes Research Edition. semi-a.
Percussion News. m.
Annual Meetings: Fall/2,500
1987-St. Louis, MO(Adam's Mark Hotel)/Oct. 29-Nov. 1
1988-San Antonio, TX(Hilton Palacio Del Rio)/Nov. 17-20

Perennial Plant Ass'n (1983)
2001 Fyffe Road, Columbus OH 43210
Exec. Secretary: Dr. Steven M. Still
Members: 1,000 firms and individuals *Staff:* 1
Annual Budget: $100-250,000 *Tel:* (614) 422-6027
Hist. Note: Voting membership in PPA is open to firms or individuals who are actively engaged in the growing, landscape planting, landscape designing or merchandising of perennials. Membership: Based upon gross volume of business in perennials.
Publications:
Newsletter. q. adv.
Proceedings of Herbaceous Perennial Plant Symposium. a. adv.
Annual Meetings: August
1987-Baltimore, MD(Omni Internat'l)/Aug. 3-8
1988-Portland, OR(Hilton)/Aug. 1-5
1989-St. Louis, MO(Omni Internat'l)/July 31-Aug. 4

Performance Registry Internat'l (1955)
Hist. Note: Became Production Records Inc. (1985).

Periodical and Book Ass'n of America (1965)
Hist. Note: Address unknown in 1985.

Perlite Institute (1949)
6268 Jericho Turnpike, Commack NY 11725
Mng. Director: Robert S. Milanese
Members: 60-70 companies *Staff:* 2-5
Annual Budget: $250-500,000 *Tel:* (516) 499-6384
Hist. Note: Mining firms, processors of expanded perlite, roof deck applicators, furnace manufacturers and other processors of perlite, a volcanic rock used for building and industrial insulation, plaster and concrete aggregate and in fillers applications.
Annual Meetings: May
1987-Switzerland
1988-San Francisco, CA

Personal Protective Armor Ass'n (1977)
2800 Belcaro Circle, Nashville TN 37215
Exec. Director: Larry Gates
Members: 21 companies
Annual Budget: $25-50,000 *Tel:* (615) 244-2400
Hist. Note: Members are manufacturers of personal body armor primarily used by law enforcement agencies. Membership: $1,000-3,000/yr. (company).
Semi-annual Meetings: Spring and Fall

Personnel/Burden Carrier Manufacturers Ass'n (1974)
8770 Red Oak Blvd., Suite 201, Charlotte NC 28210-3957
Management Exec.: William A. Dagar
Members: 4 *Staff:* 2
Annual Budget: under $10,000 *Tel:* (704) 522-8644
Hist. Note: A product section of the Material Handling Institute. Membership: $1,300/yr.
Annual Meetings:
1987-Boca Raton, FL(Boca Raton Hotel)/Nov. 6-12
1988-Phoenix, AZ(Arizona Biltmore)/Oct. 7-13

Peruvian Paso Horse Registry of North America (1970)
Box 325, Guerneville CA 95446
Registrar: Ann Miles
Members: 450 *Staff:* 1
Annual Budget: $50-100,000 *Tel:* (707) 869-2818
Hist. Note: Members breed and own Peruvian Paso horses. Maintains the stud book for purebred Peruvian Pasos, formulates rules and regulations for showing, promotes shows and exhibitions. Membership: $35/year (individual).

00253 12 05 86 1233

Publications:
Nuestro Caballo (newsletter). irreg.
Membership Directory.

Pesticide Producers Ass'n (1975)
1200 17th Street, N.W., Washington DC 20036
Exec. Secretary: Denise M. Larr
Members: 60 *Staff:* 2-5
Annual Budget: $25-50,000 *Tel:* (202) 857-9800
Hist. Note: Incorporated in the District of Columbia in 1975. Smaller pesticide formulators and manufacturers. Until 1979, Pesticide Formulators Association. The above address is the law firm of Bishop, Liberman, Cook, Purcell & Reynolds.
Semi-annual Meetings: February and Fall.

Pet Food Institute (1958)
1101 Connecticut Ave., N.W., Suite 700, Washington DC 20036
Exec. Director: Duane H. Ekedahl
Members: 100-125 *Staff:* 2-5
Annual Budget: $250-500,000 *Tel:* (202) 857-1120
Hist. Note: Makers of dry, semi-moist and canned pet food.
Publication:
PFI Monitor.
Annual Meetings: September

Pet Industry Distributors Ass'n (1969)
1740 E. Joppa Road, P.O. Box 28279, Baltimore MD 21234
Exec. Director: Calvin K. Clemons
Members: 267 companies *Staff:* 2-5
Annual Budget: $50-100,000 *Tel:* (301) 661-4400
Hist. Note: Affiliated with the Nat'l Ass'n of Wholesaler-Distributors and the Pet Industry Joint Advisory Council. Membership: $300/yr.
Publication:
PIDA News Bulletin. q.
Annual Meetings: Winter
1987-Scottsdale, AZ/Feb./200
1988-Hawaii/Feb./200
1989-Palm Springs, CA/Feb./200

Pet Industry Joint Advisory Council (1970)
1710 Rhode Island Ave., N.W., 2nd Fl., Washington DC 20036
General Counsel: N. Marshall Meyers
Members: 1,500 firms and individuals *Staff:* 3-6
Annual Budget: $500-1,000,000 *Tel:* (202) 452-1525
Hist. Note: Members are pet shop retailers, livestock breeders and importers, product manufacturers and distributors. Monitors federal and state legislation affecting the industry; sponsors research on human/companion animal bond; publishes managment and training manuals for pet shops; and disseminates information on pet ownership responsibility.
Publications:
Pet Abstracts. semi-a.
Pet Letter. m.
Pet Alert. irreg.
Annual Meetings: March

Petroleum Electric Power Ass'n
Hist. Note: Dissolved in 1986.

Petroleum Equipment Institute (1951)
Box 2380, Tulsa OK 74101
Exec. V. President: Howard B. Upton, Jr. CAE
Members: 1,100 *Staff:* 6-10
Annual Budget: $500-1,000,000 *Tel:* (918) 743-9941
Hist. Note: Established as the Nat'l Ass'n of Oil Equipment Jobbers, it assumed its present name in 1966. Members are makers and distributors of equipment used in service stations, bulk plants and other marketing facilities.
Publications:
Petro Equipment Directory. a.
Tulsa Letter w.
Annual Meetings: Fall/2,500
1987-Toronto, Ontario(Convention Ctr.)/Oct. 14-16
1988-San Francisco, CA(Moscone Convention Ctr.)/Oct. 13-15
1989-Nashville, TN(Opryland)/Sept. 26-28
1990-Las Vegas, NV(Hilton)/Oct. 2-4
1991-Cincinnati, OH(Convention Ctr.)/Oct. 1-3

Petroleum Equipment Suppliers Ass'n (1933)
9225 Katy Freeway, Suite 401, Houston TX 77024
Exec. V. President: J. Stephen Larkin
Members: 302 *Staff:* 11-15
Annual Budget: $500-1,000,000 *Tel:* (713) 932-0168
Hist. Note: Makers of oil field production and drilling equipment, well site services and supplies. Formerly American Petroleum Equipment Suppliers.
Annual Meetings: Spring
1987-Scottsdale, AZ(Marriott)/March 24-29/400

Petroleum Industry Security Council (1982)
6448 Hwy. 290 East, Suite C100, Austin TX 78723
Exec. Director: Boyd Burdett
Members: 300-400 companies *Staff:* 2-5
Annual Budget: $250-500,000 *Tel:* (512) 454-3562
Hist. Note: Founded in April 1982 by a group of Texans to combat the growing problem of oil theft of all types. Membership open nationally.
Publication:
Newsletter.

Petroleum Marketers Ass'n of America (1941)
1120 Vermont Ave., N.W., Suite 1130, Washington DC 20005
Exec V. President: Phillip R. Chisholm
Members: 41 associations *Staff:* 16-20
Annual Budget: $1-2,000,000 *Tel:* (202) 331-1198
Hist. Note: A federation of state and regional petroleum marketing ass'ns comprising about 14-15,000 individuals. Formerly (1942) Council of Independent Petroleum Marketers; (1948) Nat'l Council of Independent Petroleum Ass'ns; and Nat'l Oil Jobbers Council (until 1984). Absorbed the Nat'l Oil Fuel Institute in 1974. Maintains the Petroleum Marketers Small Businessmen's Committee.
Publication:
Petroleum Marketing Management. m.
Semi-Annual Meetings:

Petroleum Marketing Education Foundation (1968)
101 North Alfred St., Alexandria VA 22314
Exec. V. President: Michael T. Scanlon, Jr.
Members: 1,500 companies *Staff:* 4-5
Annual Budget: $500-1,000,000 *Tel:* (703) 684-0000
Hist. Note: Founded in 1968 as a 501(c)(3) tax-exempt educational institution designed to educate petroleum marketing executives. Publishes 8-10 new book each year as well as educational video tapes. Corporate Sponsorship: $500/yr.
Publications:
Foundation Flag Newsletter. q. adv.
Annual Petroleum Marketing Databook. a. adv.
Annual Meetings:
1987-Winter Management Institute in Vail, CO/Jan. 11-14
1987-Annual Board Meeting in Palm Springs, CA/Feb. 20-21
1987-Annual Leadership Course in Charlottesville, VA/June 21-26

Pharmaceutical Advertising Council (1934)
342 Madison Ave., Suite 457, New York NY 10173
Exec. Secretary: Kathryn M. Cronin
Members: 1,500 *Staff:* 2
Annual Budget: $250-500,000 *Tel:* (212) 370-1701
Hist. Note: Formerly the Pharmaceutical Advertising Club. Organization of communications and marketing specialists serving the pharmaceutical industry. Membership: $75/year.

Pharmaceutical Manufacturers Ass'n (1958)
1100 15th St., N.W., Suite 900, Washington DC 20005
President: Gerald J. Mossinghoff
Members: 109 *Staff:* 90-100
Annual Budget: over $5,000,000 *Tel:* (202) 835-3400
Hist. Note: Formed by merger of the American Drug Manufacturers Ass'n and the American Pharmaceutical Manufacturers Ass'n. Makers of ethical pharmaceutical and biological products sold under their own labels. Supports the Pharmaceutical Manufacturers Ass'n Foundation and the Pharmaceutical Manufacturers Ass'n Better Government Committee. Has an annual budget of $9-10 million.
Publications:
PMA Newsletter. w.
State Capitol Reports. w.
Science and Technology Notes. m.
Trademark Bulletin. m.
Annual Meetings: April/650
1987-White Sulphur Springs, WV(Greenbrier)/May 17-20
1988-Phoenix, AZ(Biltmore)/April 24-26

Phi Alpha Delta (1902)
10722 White Oak Ave., Box 3217, Granada Hills CA 91344
Exec. Director: Frederick J. Weitkamp
Members: 110,000 *Staff:* 6-10
Annual Budget: $500-1,000,000 *Tel:* (213) 360-1941
Hist. Note: Professional law fraternity formed in Chicago, Nov. 8, 1902. Absorbed Phi Delta Delta, a women's professional law sorority, in 1972.
Publication:
The Reporter. q.
Biennial Meetings: August, even years

Phi Beta Lambda
Hist. Note: See Future Business Leaders of America

Phi Beta Pi - Theta Kappa Psi (1891)
111 East Wacker Drive, Suite 600, Chicago IL 60601
Exec. Secretary: Christine Norris
Members: 18,500 *Staff:* 1
Annual Budget: $25-50,000 *Tel:* (312) 644-6610
Hist. Note: A professional medical fraternity, Phi Beta Pi was founded on March 10, 1891 at Western Pennsylvania Medical College; Theta Kappa Psi was founded on November 30, 1879 in New Haven, CT; and the two fraternities were officially merged on February 8, 1961. Major purpose is to provide a better environment for medical student members and to help with student loans and alumni relations.
Publication:
PBPTKP Newsletter. 3/yr.
Annual Meetings: Spring
1987-Detroit, MI

Phi Delta Phi (1869)
1750 N St., N.W., Washington DC 20036
Exec. Director: Sam S. Crutchfield
Members: 80,000 *Staff:* 2-5
Annual Budget: $250-500,000 *Tel:* (202) 628-0148
Hist. Note: Professional international legal fraternity. Founded at Ann Arbor Michigan, December 13, 1869. Membership: $40 initiation fee; voluntary alumni dues.

Publication:
The Headnoter. q.
Annual Meetings: Biennial Meetings (uneven years) in August

Philippine-American Chamber of Commerce (1920)
565 Fifth Ave., Suite 809, New York NY 10017
Exec. Secretary: Nenita O. Santiago
Members: 150-160 *Staff:* 2-5
Annual Budget: $25-50,000 *Tel:* (212) 972-9326
Annual Meetings: New York City, at the India House

Philosophy of Education Soc. (1941)
Dept. of Educational Fdns, University of Alberta, Edmonton Alberta T5K 2E5
Secy.-Treas.: Allen Pearson
Members: 500
Annual Budget: $25-50,000 *Tel:* (403) 432-3726
Hist. Note: Has no paid staff.
Publications:
Educational Theory. q.
Proceedings. a.
Newsletter. irreg.

Philosophy of Science Ass'n (1934)
Philosophy Dept., Michigan State Univ., East Lansing MI 48824
Exec. Secretary: Dr. Peter D. Asquith
Members: 900-1,000 individuals *Staff:* 1
Annual Budget: $50-100,000 *Tel:* (517) 353-9392
Hist. Note: Member of the Internat'l Union of History and Philosophy of Science and affiliate of the American Ass'n for the Advancement of Science. Membership: $35/yr.
Publications:
Newsletter. q.
Philosophy of Science. q. adv.
Proceedings of Biennial Meetings. bi-a.
Biennial Meetings: even years in Fall

Phlebology Soc. of America (1962)
5530 Wisconsin Ave., N.W., Suite 917, Washington DC 20815
Exec. Director: Ken Biegeleisen, M.D., Ph.D
Members: 100-150 *Staff:* 4
Annual Budget: $50-100,000 *Tel:* (301) 656-2214
Hist. Note: Established and incorporated in New York in 1962 as a professional membership society for the purpose of exchanging scientific information, nationally, in the field of peripheral vascular disease. Members are designated as Fellows, Associate Fellows, and Clinical Fellows, depending upon the extent of their involvement in the research or clinical practice in phlebology. Membership: $150/yr.
Publication:
Phlebology. q.

Phobia Soc. of America (1981)
133 Rollins Ave., Suite 4-B, Rockville MD 20852
Exec. Director: Susan B. Kanaan
Members: 5,000 *Staff:* 2-4
Annual Budget: $100-250,000 *Tel:* (301) 231-9350
Hist. Note: PSA includes people who suffer from panic and phobic disorders and professionals who study and treat them. Its purpose is to provide information and support. Membership: $25/yr. (general); $40/yr. (professional)
Publications:
Newsletter. q. adv.
National Phobia Treatment Directory.
Annual Meetings: Fall
1987-San Francisco, CA(Hyatt Regency)/Oct./4-500

Phosphate Chemicals Export Ass'n (1975)
8410 West Bryn Mawr Ave., Suite 1000, Chicago IL 60631
Sr. V.P.-Finance & Administration: Robert L. Schmidt
Members: 14 companies *Staff:* 25
Annual Budget: $2-5,000,000 *Tel:* (312) 399-1010
Hist. Note: A Webb-Pomerene Act association.

Phosphate Rock Export Ass'n (1970)
1311 N. West Shore Blvd., Suite 301, Tampa FL 33607
Chairman and CEO: James J. Gavin
Members: 8 companies *Staff:* 20-25
Annual Budget: $2-5,000,000 *Tel:* (813) 879-7310
Hist. Note: A Webb-Pomerene Act Ass'n, incorporated in the State of Delaware in 1970.
Monthly Meetings: Tampa, FL

Photo Chemical Machining Institute (1968)
4113 Barberry Drive, Lafayette Hill PA 19444
Exec. Director: Judith Ginsberg
Members: 85 companies *Staff:* 2-5
Annual Budget: $50-100,000 *Tel:* (215) 825-2506
Hist. Note: Members are companies producing metal products through photo etching. In addition, the Institute includes member companies that service the pcm industry and supply its needs. Membership: $250-500/yr.
Publications:
The Journal. q. adv.
Membership Directory. a.
Semi-annual Meetings: Feb. and Sept.
1987-Anaheim, CA(Emerald Hotel)/Feb. 22-27/100
1987-Amsterdam, Holland(Hilton)/Sept. 13-16/100
1988-Anaheim, CA/Feb. and Bedford, MA/Sept.

00254 12 05 86 1233

Photo Marketing Ass'n-Internat'l (1924)
3000 Picture Place, Jackson MI 49201
Exec. Director: Roy S. Pung
Members: 11,000 *Staff:* 50-55
Annual Budget: over $5,000,000 *Tel:* (517) 788-8100
Hist. Note: Merger of Nat'l Photo Dealers Ass'n (1946) and Master Photo Finishers of America. Formerly (1974) Master Photo Dealers and Finishers' Ass'n. Maintains branches in Canada, Mexico, Australia and New Zealand. Manages The Ass'n of Professional Color Laboratories.
Publication:
Photo Marketing Magazine. m. adv.
Annual Meetings: March
1987-Chicago, IL(McCormick Place)/March 15-18
1988-Chicago, IL(McCormick Place)/Feb. 28-March 2

Photographic Industry Council (1969)
Eastman Kodak, 343 State St., Rochester NY 14650
Secy.-Treas.: Kenneth T. Lassiter
Members: 16-20 organizations *Staff:* 2-5
Annual Budget: under $10,000 *Tel:* (716) 724-2284
Hist. Note: Established by the Nat'l Ass'n of Photographic Manufacturers, the Professional Photographers of America, the Photo Marketing Ass'n, the Photographic Soc. of America and the Studio Suppliers Ass'n to handle matters of common concern to the photographic industry.

Photographic Manufacturers and Distributors Ass'n (1939)
866 United Nations Plaza, Suite 436, New York NY 10017
Exec. Manager: Norman C. Lipton
Members: 75-80 companies *Staff:* 1
Annual Budget: $25-50,000 *Tel:* (212) 688-3520
Hist. Note: Formerly Photographic Merchandising and Distributing Association.

Photovoltaic Institute of America
Hist. Note: A sub-division of the Solar Energy Institute of America.

Phycological Soc. of America (1946)
Department of Botany, Louisiana State University, Baton Rouge LA 70803
Secretary: Dr. Russell L. Chapman
Members: 1,800
Annual Budget: $100-250,000 *Tel:* (504) 388-8558
Hist. Note: Established in 1946 to promote basic and applied research in the algae. Affiliated with the American Ass'n for the Advancement of Science and the American Institute of Biological Sciences. Membership: $35/yr.(individual); $95/yr.(institution).
Publications:
Journal of Phycology (volume 1 appeared in 1965)
Journal of Phycology. q.
Phycological Newsletter. 3/yr.
Applied Phycology Forum. 3/yr.
Annual Meetings: Summer, at a university environment.
1987-Columbus, OH(Ohio State Univ.)/August
1988-Davis, CA(Univ. of California)/August
1989-Toronto,Ontario(Univ. of Toronto)/August
1990-Raleigh, NC(North Carolina State Univ.)/August

Physicians Forum (1939)
220 South State St., Suite 1926, Chicago IL 60604
Secretary: Daniel Blumenthal, M.D.
Staff: 1
Tel: (312) 922-1968
Hist. Note: Physicians and allied health care workers who support a comprehensive national health insurance system. Membership: $75/yr.
Publication:
The Physicians Forum Bulletin. q.
Annual Meetings: November

Phytochemical Soc. of North America (1967)
Dept. of Botany, University of Iowa, Iowa City IA 52242
Treasurer: Dr. Jonathan E. Poulton
Members: 400
Annual Budget: $10-25,000 *Tel:* (319) 353-6834
Hist. Note: Formerly Plant Phenolics Group of North America. Members are individuals interested in all aspects of the chemistry of plants. Full membership: $15/yr.
Publications:
Phytochemical Newsletter. q.
Recent Advances in Phytochemistry. a.
Annual Meetings: June/July
1987-Tampa, FL(Univ. of So. Florida)/June 22-26

Pi Beta Alpha (1947)
215 Eisenhower Drive, Bloomington IL 61701
Exec. Secretary: Larry Efaw
Members: 950 *Staff:* 1
Annual Budget: $10-25,000 *Tel:* (309) 828-8140
Hist. Note: Established in Columbus, Ohio August 8, 1947 as the Professional Bookmen of America, Inc. The present name was adopted in 1976. A professional and honorary association whose members are concerned with the marketing of school textbooks and other educational materials. Membership: $20/yr.
Publication:
PBA News/Infoline. q.
Annual Meetings: Summer
1987-Hershey, PA(Hershey Lodge & Convention Ctr.)/July 12-15

Pi Lambda Theta (1910)
4101 East Third St., Bloomington IN 47401
Exec. Director: Anabel Demetrius, MPA
Members: 16,000 *Staff:* 6-10
Annual Budget: $250-500,000 *Tel:* (812) 339-3411
Hist. Note: A professional and honor organization in the field of education. Established November 1910 at the University of Missiouri. Founded as a women's organization, but permitted men to join in 1974. Incorporated in the State of Indiana in 1976. Membership: $30/yr.
Publications:
Educational Horizons. q.
Pi Lambda Theta Newsletter. bi-m.
Biennial meetings: uneven years in summer.

Pi Sigma Epsilon
Hist. Note: Professional fraternity affiliated with Sales and Marketing Executives, International, Inc.

Piano Manufacturers Ass'n Internat'l (1897)
15080 Beltwood Parkway East, Suite 108, Dallas TX 75244-2715
Exec. Director: Donald W. Dillon
Members: 16 *Staff:* 2-5
Annual Budget: $100-250,000 *Tel:* (214) 241-8957
Hist. Note: Formerly (1986) the Nat'l Piano Manufacturers Ass'n. Supports the Nat'l Piano Foundation (same address) as its educational arm.
Semi-annual Meetings: Winter and Summer
1987-Anaheim, CA(Conv. Center)/Jan 16-18
1987-Chicago, IL(McCormick Place)/June 27-30

Piano Technicians Guild (1958)
9140 Ward Parkway, Kansas City MO 64114
Exec. Director: Barbara Parks
Members: 3,500 *Staff:* 6-10
Annual Budget: $250-500,000 *Tel:* (816) 444-3500
Hist. Note: Formed in 1958 by consolidation of the American Soc. of Piano Technicians and the Nat'l Ass'n of Piano Tuners. Membership as Registered Technician acquired by examination.
Publications:
Membership Update.
The Piano Technician's Journal. m. adv.
Annual Meetings:
1987-Toronto, Canada(Constellation Hotel)

Pickle Packers Internat'l (1893)
Box 606, St. Charles IL 60174
Exec. V. President: William R. Moore
Members: 150-175 *Staff:* 2-5
Annual Budget: $100-250,000 *Tel:* (312) 584-8950
Hist. Note: Formerly (1963) Nat'l Pickle Packers Ass'n. Members are manufacturers of pickles, suppliers of salt, salt stock brokers, and other suppliers to the industry.
Publication:
Pickle Pak Science. a.
Annual Meetings: Fall
1987-Colorado Springs, CO(Broadmoor Hotel)/Oct. 29-31
1988-Toronto, Ontario(Inn on the Park)/Sept. 28-30

Piece Goods Salesman's Ass'n (1933)
Hist. Note: Became the Fabric Salesmen's Ass'n in 1982.

Pilots Internat'l Ass'n (1965)
4000 Olson Memorial Highway, Minneapolis MN 55422
President: Richard J. Wildberger
Members: 10,000-11,000 *Staff:* 2-5
Annual Budget: $50-100,000 *Tel:* (612) 588-5175
Hist. Note: Members are military, commercial, airline, private and student pilots. Provides travel, chart, career placement and airplane title search services.
Publications:
Plane and Pilot. m. adv.
PIA/Flight Line. q.

Pin, Clip and Fastener Services (1933)
179 Allyn St., #304, Hartford CT 06103
Secretary: Edward Isenberg
Members: 10-15 *Staff:* 2-5
Tel: (203) 246-6566
Hist. Note: Formerly (1980) Pin, Clip and Fastener Association. Includes Safety Pin Research Council. Manufacturers of straight and safety pins, paper clips, etc.

Pinto Horse Ass'n of America (1956)
7525 Mission Gorge Road, Suite C, San Diego CA 92120
Exec. V. Pres.: Garry Freeman
Members: 5,500 *Staff:* 10
Annual Budget: $250-500,000 *Tel:* (619) 286-1570
Hist. Note: Members are breeders and owners of Pinto horses. Membership: $60/yr.
Publication:
Pinto Horse.

Pipe Fabrication Institute (1913)
P.O. Box 173, Springdale PA 15144
Exec. Director: Lois A. Moore
Members: 10 *Staff:* 1
Annual Budget: $50-100,000 *Tel:* (412) 274-4722
Hist. Note: Members are producers and designers of high-temperature, high-pressure piping systems.
Annual Meetings: Semi-annual
1987-New Orleans, LA(Royal Sonestal)/Feb. 8-11
1987-Ponte Vedra Beach, FL(Sawgrass Resort)/Sept. 13-15
1988-Palm Springs, CA(Americana Canyon Hotel & Resort)/Feb. 7-10
1988-Kansas City, MO(Hyatt Regency at Crown Center)/June 12-15

Pipe Line Contractors Ass'n (1947)
4100 First City Center, 1700 Pacific Ave., Dallas TX 75201
Managing Director: Hailey A. Roberts
Members: 136 companies *Staff:* 2-5
Annual Budget: $500-1,000,000 *Tel:* (214) 969-2700
Hist. Note: Members are builders of cross-country pipeline, and their suppliers.
Annual Meetings: Boca Raton, FL(Hotel & Club)/Feb.

Pitless Adapter Division (Water Systems Council) (1966)
600 S. Federal St., Suite 400, Chicago IL 60605
Exec. Directory: Charles Stolberg
Members: 10 *Staff:* 2-3
Tel: (312) 346-1600

Planning Executives Institute (1951)
Hist. Note: Merged with the North American Society for Corporate Planners to form Planning Forum in 1985.

Planning Forum: The Internat'l Society for Planning andStrategic Management (1985)
5500 College Corner Pike, Box 70, Oxford OH 45056
President: Ronald L. Lerman
Members: 8,000 *Staff:* 12
Annual Budget: $1-2,000,000 *Tel:* (513) 523-4185
Hist. Note: A merger of the North American Soc. for Corporate Planning (1966) and the Planning Executives Institute (1951). Members are both professionals and executives with planning responsibilities in the private or public sectors. Focuses on planning and strategic management as tools of corporate performance. Membership: $70/yr.
Publication:
Planning Review. bi-m. adv.
Annual Meetings: Spring
1987-Chicago,IL(Hyatt)/April/800

Plant Growth Regulator Soc. of America (1971)
700 Experiment Station Road, Lake Alfred FL 33850
Business Manager: Dr. William C. Wilson
Members: 100 companies; 750 individuals *Staff:* 0
Annual Budget: $25-50,000 *Tel:* (813) 956-1151
Hist. Note: Established as the Plant Growth Regulator Working Group; functions as a non-profit educational and scientific organization. Membership: $15/yr.
Publications:
PRGSA Bulletin. q.
Proceedings. a.
Annual Meetings: August
1987-Honolulu, HI(Sheraton)/Aug. 2-6/over 150
1988-San Antonio, TX
1989-Washington, D.C. area

Plastic and Metal Products Manufacturers Ass'n (1937)
225 West 34th St., New York NY 10122
Exec. Director: Sheldon M. Edelman
Members: 150-200 *Staff:* 6-10
Annual Budget: $100-250,000 *Tel:* (212) 564-2500
Hist. Note: Formerly (1970) Plastic Products Manufacturers Ass'n, Inc.

Plastic Bag Ass'n (1986)
2 Overhill Road, Scarsdale NY 10583
Exec. V. President: Brent C. Dixon
Members: 21 companies *Staff:* 2
Annual Budget: $50-100,000 *Tel:* (914) 723-7610
Hist. Note: Members are U.S. and Canadian manufacturers of plastic retail bags.

Plastic Container Manufacturers Institute (1962)
Hist. Note: Dissolved in 1985.

Plastic Pipe and Fittings Ass'n (1978)
800 Roosevelt Road, Bldg. C, Suite 20, Glen Ellyn IL 60137
Exec. Director: Richard W. Church
Members: 60-70 companies *Staff:* 2-5
Annual Budget: $250-500,000 *Tel:* (312) 858-6540
Hist. Note: PPFA is the national trade association of manufacturers of plastic piping products used for plumbing applications. Members include pipe and fitting processors, prime resin suppliers, equipment suppliers, solvent cement manufacturers and suppliers of compounding indredients.
Publication:
Pipelines. m.
Semi-annual meetings: March and October/150

Plastic Shipping Container Institute (1976)
1411 Opus Place, Suite 111, Downers Grove IL 60515
Attorney and Secretary: Robert C. Hultquist
Members: 35-40 companies *Staff:* 1
Annual Budget: $25-50,000 *Tel:* (312) 969-4500
Hist. Note: Members are manufacturers of open head plastic shipping containers. Associate members are companies producing virgin high density polyethylene and component parts for shipping containers.

00255 12 05 86 1233

Semi-annual Meetings: Winter and Fall
1987-Longboat Key, FL/Feb.
1987-Vail, CO/Sept.

Plastic Soft Materials Manufacturers Ass'n (1937)
225 West 34th St., New York NY 10001
Exec. Director: Sheldon M. Edelman
Members: 80-90 *Staff:* 2-5
Annual Budget: $50-100,000 *Tel:* (212) 564-2500

Plastic Surgery Research Council (1955)
SIU School of Medicine, 800 North Rutledge, Springfield IL 62702
Secretary-Treasurer: Dr. Robert Russell
Members: 243 individuals *Staff:* 1
Annual Budget: under $10,000 *Tel:* (217) 782-8872
Hist. Note: To promote basic research in plastic and reconstructive surgery. Membership: $100/yr.
Annual Meetings: Spring/200

Plastics Pipe Institute (1949)
355 Lexington Ave., New York NY 10017
Exec. Director: Stanley A. Mruk
Members: 36 companies *Staff:* 2-5
Annual Budget: $100-250,000 *Tel:* (212) 503-0600
Hist. Note: A division of Soc. of the Plastics Industry, PPI promotes the effective use of plastics piping systems, contributes to the development of standards, publishes technical reports and statistics, educates designers, installers, users and officials and maintains liaison with other groups.
Semi-annual Meetings: Spring and Fall
1987-Toronto, Ontario(Four Seasons Inn on the Park)/April 21-24/85
1987-Denver, CO(Marriott City Ctr.)/Nov. 16-18

Pleaters, Stitchers and Embroiderers Ass'n (1920)
225 West 34th St., New York NY 10001
Exec. Director: Sheldon M. Edelman
Members: 90 *Staff:* 6-10
Tel: (212) 564-2500

Plumbing and Drainage Institute (1928)
5342 Boulevard Place, Indianapolis IN 46208
Exec. Secretary-Treasurer: Austin O. Roche, Jr.
Members: 3 companies *Staff:* 1
Annual Budget: $50-100,000 *Tel:* (317) 251-5298
Hist. Note: Formerly (1949) Plumbing and Drainage Manufacturers Ass'n. Incorporated in 1954 in the State of Illinois.
Annual Meetings: April in Indianapolis

Plumbing-Heating-Cooling Information Bureau (1917)
Three Illinois Center, Chicago IL 60601
Exec. Director: David L. Weiner
Members: 1,300-1,400 *Staff:* 3
Tel: (312) 372-7331
Hist. Note: Formed by a merger of the Plumbing and Heating Modernization Committee (founded in 1955) and the Plumbing and Heating Industries Bureau (founded in 1919).

Plumbing Manufacturers Institute (1956)
800 Roosevelt Road, Suite C-20, Glen Ellyn IL 60137
President: Richard W. Church
Members: 64 companies *Staff:* 2-5
Annual Budget: $100-250,000 *Tel:* (312) 858-9172
Hist. Note: The national trade association of plumbing products manufacturers. It has been, successively, the Sanitary Brass Institute, the Brass Gas Stop Institute, the Tubular Brass Institute and, most recently, in 1975, the Plumbing Brass Institute.
Publications:
Plumbenomics. q.
Waterlines. m.
Semi-annual Meetings: February and September

Poetry Soc. of America (1910)
15 Gramercy Park, New York NY 10003
Admin. Director: Judith Baumel
Members: 1,600 professional poets *Staff:* 2-5
Annual Budget: $100-250,000 *Tel:* (212) 254-9628
Hist. Note: Membership: $30/yr.
Publication:
Newsletter. 3-4/yr.
Annual Meetings: April in New York City

Point-of-Purchase Advertising Institute (1938)
2 Executive Drive, Fort Lee NJ 07024
President and C.O.O.: John Kawula
Members: 500-600 *Staff:* 11
Annual Budget: $1-2,000,000 *Tel:* (201) 585-8400
Hist. Note: Members are producers, buyers and users of signs and displays at retail.
Publications:
POPAI News. 5/yr. adv.
Quarterly Reports.
Research Bulletins. 6/yr.
Annual Meetings: April
1987-Boca Raton(Hotel & Club)/April 5-9
1988-Phoenix(Biltmore)/April 10-14
1989-Palm Beach, FL(The Breaker's)

Poland China Record Ass'n (1876)
Box 2537, W. Lafayette IN 47906-0537
Exec. Secretary:
Members: 300-400 *Staff:* 2-5
Annual Budget: $100-250,000 *Tel:* (317) 497-3718
Hist. Note: Breeders and fanciers of Poland China swine. Member of the Nat'l Soc. of Livestock Record Ass'ns. Membership: $10 first year; $25/yr. thereafter.
Publication:
Purebred Picture. 10/yr. adv.
Semi-Annual Meetings:

Police Executive Research Forum (1975)
2300 M Street, N.W., Suite 910, Washington DC 20037
Exec. Director: Darrel W. Stephens
Members: 90 police chiefs *Staff:* 11-15
Annual Budget: $1-2,000,000 *Tel:* (202) 466-7820
Hist. Note: A national organization of chief executives of city, county, and state police agencies. Membership is limited to the leaders of large police departments - those with more than two hundred members or which are the principal police agency for a iurisdiction of at least 100,000 people. Originated in January, 1975; officially established in July, 1976; and incorporated in the District of Columbia in May, 1977. Membership: $100/yr.

Police Management Ass'n (1980)
1001 22nd St., N.W., Suite 200, Washington DC 20037
Exec. Director: E. Roberta Lesh
Members: 1,080 *Staff:* 2
Annual Budget: $250-500,000 *Tel:* (202) 833-1460
Hist. Note: Created from a national constitutional convention in 1980, PMA's principles include integrating results of research into police management decisions and exchanging ideas and experiences through scholarly discussion and debate. Internat'l membership includes police managers ranking from sergeants with management responsibility through chiefs of police. Membership: $25/yr.(individual); $150/yr.(organization)
Publication:
The Police Manager. q.
Annual Meetings: Fall

Political Products Manufacturers Ass'n (1972)
Hist. Note: Address unknown in 1985-86.

Pollution Liability Insurance Ass'n (1982)
1333 Butterfield Road, Suite 100, Downers Grove IL 60515
President: Thomas E. Knowlton
Members: 20-30 companies *Staff:* 10-20
Annual Budget: over $5,000,000 *Tel:* (312) 969-5300
Hist. Note: PLIA is a reciprocal pool reinsuring pollution liability policies written by member insurance companies. Membership is limited to licensed insurance or reinsurance companies with ratings of B+ or better in BEST's. Has a written premium of $20 million.
Annual Meetings: Spring

Polyurethane Division-Soc. of the Plastics Industry (1985)
355 Lexington Ave., New York NY 10017
Manager: Fran Walker Lichtenberg
Members: 45-50 companies *Staff:* 2-5
Annual Budget: $1-2,000,000 *Tel:* (212) 503-0600
Hist. Note: Founded as the Urethane Institute in 1959; assumed its present name in 1985. Members are suppliers and fabricators of foam, elastomers, and molded products for the insulation, cushioning, and automotive industries. Membership: $900/yr. plus SPI dues.
Publication:
Polyurethane News. q.
Annual Meetings: Fall
1987-Aachen, West Germany/Sept. 28-Oct. 2/1,500
1988-Philadelphia, PA(Wyndham Franklin Plaza)/Oct. 18-21/900
1989-San Francisco, CA(Westin St. Francis)/Oct. 1-3/900
1990-Orlando, FL

Polyurethane Manufacturers Ass'n (1971)
800 Roosevelt Road, Suite C-20, Glen Ellyn IL 60137
Exec. Director: Richard W. Church
Members: 110 *Staff:* 2-5
Tel: (312) 858-2670
Hist. Note: Membership includes processors of solid cast, microcellular, RIM and thermoplastic urethane elastomers; manufacturers, suppliers, distributors and sales agents of raw materials, additives or processing equipment; and individuals or companies providing publishing, education, research, or consulting services to the industry.
Publication:
Polytopics. m.
Semi-annual meetings: Spring and Fall/200
1987-Dallas, TX(Fairmont)/April 26-29
1987-Quebec City, Quebec(Hilton International Quebec)/Oct. 18-21
1988-San Diego, CA/April 23-27
1988-Buffalo, NY/Oct. 22-26

Popcorn Institute (1943)
111 East Wacker Drive, Chicago IL 60601
Exec. Director: William E. Smith
Members: 40 *Staff:* 2-5
Annual Budget: $100-250,000 *Tel:* (312) 644-6610
Hist. Note: Official trade ass'n of the popcorn industry representing 85% of the world's sales. Members are popcorn processors. Absorbed the Popcorn Processors Ass'n in 1960.

Popular Culture Ass'n (1967)
Bowling Green University, Bowling Green OH 43403
Secy.-Treas.: Ray B. Browne
Members: 3,000 individuals *Staff:* 2-5
Annual Budget: $10-25,000 *Tel:* (419) 372-7861
Hist. Note: Educators interested in various aspects of popular culture, i.e., cartoons, folklore, protest music, soap operas, black culture, motion pictures, etc.
Publications:
Journal of American Cultures. q.
Journal of Popular Culture. q.
Journal of Regional Cultures. q.
Popular Culture Methods. q.
Journal of Popular Literature.
Annual Meetings:
1987-Montreal, Canada(Queen Elizabeth)/Late March/2,700
1988-New Orleans, LA(Clarion)/Late March/3,000

Population Ass'n of America (1931)
806 15th St., N.W., Suite 640, Washington DC 20005
Exec. Associate: Jean Smith
Members: 2,700 *Staff:* 2-5
Annual Budget: $100-250,000 *Tel:* (202) 393-3253
Hist. Note: Established in 1931 and incorporated in New York in 1937. Promotes research in human population. Membership: $40/yr.
Publications:
Demography. q. adv.
PAA Affairs. q.
Population Index. q.
Annual Meetings: 5
Spring/1,000
1987-Chicago, IL(Marriott)/April 30-May 2
1988-New Orleans, LA(Hyatt)/April 21-23
1989-Baltimore, MD(Omni)/March 30-April 2
1990-Toronto, Ontario(Royal York)
1991-Washington, DC

Porcelain Enamel Institute (1930)
1111 North 19th St., Suite 200, Arlington VA 22209
Exec. V. President: John C. Oliver
Members: 70-80 companies *Staff:* 6-10
Annual Budget: $250-500,000 *Tel:* (703) 527-5257
Hist. Note: Suppliers and makers of porcelain enamel products and raw materials.
Annual Meetings: November

Portable Drilling Rig Manufacturers Ass'n (1976)
600 S. Federal St., Suite 400, Chicago IL 60605
Exec. Director: Charles Stolberg
Members: 9 companies *Staff:* 2-3
Annual Budget: $10-25,000 *Tel:* (312) 346-1600
Hist. Note: Members are producers of portable drilling rigs for water wells, blastholes, shallow oil and gas wells, mineral exploration and construction uses.
Publications:
Glossary of Terms.
Safety Manual.

Portable Power Equipment Manufacturers Ass'n (1959)
4720 Montgomery Lane, Bethesda MD 20814
President: Donald E. Purcell
Members: 21 companies *Staff:* 4
Annual Budget: $250-500,000 *Tel:* (301) 652-0774
Hist. Note: Formerly (1977) Power Saw Manufacturers Ass'n and until 1984, the Chain Saw Manufacturers Ass'n.
Annual Meetings: May

Portable Sanitation Ass'n Internat'l (1971)
7800 Metro Pkwy., Suite 104, Bloomington MN 55420
Exec. Director: T.C. Anderson
Members: 350-425 *Staff:* 2-5
Annual Budget: $100-250,000 *Tel:* (612) 854-8300
Hist. Note: Makers of chemical toilets and companies that rent and service them.
Publications:
PSA In Action. m.
Who's Who in Portable Sanitation. a.
Annual Meetings: Fall
1987-Nashville, TN/Oct.

Portland Cement Ass'n (1916)
5420 Old Orchard Rd., Skokie IL 60077
President: John P. Gleason, Jr.
Members: 35-40 companies *Staff:* 315
Annual Budget: over $5,000,000 *Tel:* (312) 966-6200
Hist. Note: Maintains a Washington office. Has an annual budget of $20,000,000.
Semi-annual Meetings: Chicago in May and other cities in November.

Portugal-U.S. States Chamber of Commerce (1979)
5 West 45th St., New York NY 10036
Exec. Director: Paulo Almeida d'Eca
Members: 250 *Staff:* 5
Annual Budget: $100-250,000 *Tel:* (212) 354-4627
Hist. Note: A bilateral Chamber of Commerce. Founded in 1979. Exists to promote trade and investment between the two countries. Membership: $150/yr. (individual); $300/yr. (organization).
Publication:
Newsletter. m.
Annual Meetings: Winter

00256 12 05 86 1233

Post Card Manufacturers Ass'n (1964)
1819 H Street, N.W., Suite 630, Washington DC 20006
Exec. Secretary: Harry J. Lambeth
Members: 8 *Staff:* 1
Annual Budget: $10-25,000 *Tel:* (202) 775-1150
Hist. Note: Primary concern is with postal rates for post cards. Has no headquarters beyond the above, the law firm of Barton and Lambeth.

Post-Tensioning Institute (1976)
301 West Osborn, Suite 3500, Phoenix AZ 85013
Exec. Director: Clifford L. Freyermuth
Members: 830 individuals *Staff:* 2-5
Annual Budget: $250-500,000 *Tel:* (602) 265-9158
Hist. Note: Members are concerned with the advancement of post-tensioned prestressed concrete design and construction. Formerly the Post-Tensioning division of The Prestressed Concrete Institute.
Publication:
PTI Newsletter. bi-m.
Annual Meetings: Fall
1987-New Orleans, LA

Potash and Phosphate Institute (1935)
2801 Buford Hwy., N.E., Suite 401, Atlanta GA 30329
President: Robert E. Wagner
Members: 18 companies *Staff:* 35-40
Annual Budget: $2-5,000,000 *Tel:* (404) 634-4274
Hist. Note: Formerly (1971) American Potash Institute, Inc., (1975) Potash Institute of North America and (1977) Potash and Phosphate Institute.
Publication:
Better Crops with Plant Food. q.
Annual Meetings: October

Potato Ass'n of America (1913)
University of Wisconsin, Hancock WI 54943
Secretary: Dr. David Curwen
Members: 1,500-1,600 *Staff:* 2-5
Annual Budget: $50-100,000 *Tel:* (715) 249-5712
Hist. Note: Founded in New York, NY in 1912 as the Nat'l Potato Ass'n of America and incorporated in New Jersey in 1913; became the Potato Ass'n of America, Inc. in 1917. PAA is a professional society for potato research, extension, utilization and technical workers in all aspects of the American potato industry. Membership: $25/yr.
Publication:
American Potato Journal. m. adv.
Annual Meetings: Summer
1987-Minneapolis, MN/Aug. 2-6
1988-Fort Collins, CO
1989-Oregon
1990-Quebec City, Quebec
1991-Pasco, WA

Potato Board (1972)
Hist. Note: Common name for the Nat'l Potato Promotion Board.

Potato Chip/Snack Food Ass'n
Hist. Note: Became the Snack Food Ass'n in 1986.

Poultry and Egg Institute of America (1971)
Hist. Note: Ceased operations in 1984.

Poultry Science Ass'n (1908)
309 West Clark St., Champaign IL 61820
Business Manager: Carl D. Johnson
Members: 1,700 *Staff:* 1
Annual Budget: $100-250,000 *Tel:* (217) 356-3182
Hist. Note: Originated in 1908 as the Internat'l Ass'n of Instructors and Investigators in Poultry Husbandry. Became the American Ass'n of Instructors and Investigators in Poultry Husbandry in 1912 and the Poultry Science Ass'n, Inc. 1926. Affiliated with the American Ass'n for the Advancement of Science and the World's Poultry Science Ass'n.
Publication:
Poultry Science. bi-m. adv.
Annual Meetings: Summer
1987-Corvallis, OR(Oregon State Univ.)/Aug. 10-14
1988-Baton Rouge, LA(Louisiana State Univ.)/July 24-28
1989-Madison, WI(Univ. of Wisconsin)/July 24-28

Poured Concrete Wall Contractors Ass'n of America (1975)
825 East 64th Street, Indianapolis IN 46220
Exec. Director: James E. Tilford
Members: 200 companies *Staff:* 7
Annual Budget: $25-50,000 *Tel:* (317) 253-5655
Publication:
Newsletter. bi-m.
Semi-annual Meetings: Winter (with World of Concrete) and Summer
1987-Houston, TX(Lincoln Park Hotel)/Jan. 25
1987-Williamsburg, VA/Aug.

Powder Actuated Tool Manufacturers Institute (1952)
100 S. Third St., St. Charles MO 63301
Exec. Director: James Borchers
Members: 8 companies *Staff:* 1
Annual Budget: $50-100,000 *Tel:* (314) 947-6610
Hist. Note: Powder Actuated Tool Manufacturers Institute, Inc. represents manufacturers of construction tools used to fasten to and into steel and concrete. PATMI is a member of the Nat'l Safety Council and the American Nat'l Standards Institute, Inc.
Publication:
PATMI Basic Training Manual.
Annual Meetings:
1987-Jan., May and Sept.

Powder Coating Institute (1981)
1800 Diagonal Road, #600, Alexandria VA 22314
Exec. Director: Gregory J. Bocchi
Members: 57 companies *Staff:* 2
Annual Budget: $100-250,000 *Tel:* (703) 684-4409
Hist. Note: Members are companies producing powder coatings and related application equipment used to coat and protect metals.
Publication:
PCI Newsletter. bi-m.
Annual Meetings: Spring

Powder Metallurgy Equipment Ass'n (1958)
Hist. Note: A constituent part of the Metal Powder Industries Federation. Equipment suppliers for powder metallurgy parts and products.

Powder Metallurgy Parts Ass'n (1957)
Hist. Note: A constituent part of the Metal Powder Industries Federation. Manufacturers of powder metallurgy parts and products. Formerly (1967) Powder Metallurgy Parts Manufacturers Ass'n.

Power and Communication Contractors Ass'n (1945)
6301 Stevenson Ave., Suite One, Alexandria VA 22304
Exec. V. President: Michael E. Strother
Members: 250 companies *Staff:* 2-5
Annual Budget: $100-250,000 *Tel:* (703) 823-1555
Hist. Note: Contractors and suppliers specializing in electric power line, telephone and cable television construction and their suppliers. Formerly (1950) Rural Electrical Contractors Ass'n.
Publication:
Reporter. m. adv.
Annual Meetings:
1987-Maui, HI(Hyatt Regency)/Feb.

Power Conversion Products Council, Internat'l (1974)
Box 637, Libertyville IL 60048
Exec. Director: Elizabeth B. Bevington
Members: 67 companies *Staff:* 2-5
Annual Budget: $25-50,000 *Tel:* (312) 362-3201
Hist. Note: Members are manufacturers and suppliers to the wall plug-in transformer/transformer charger/converter industry. Major purpose is to work for industry standards.
Publications:
Newsletter.
Directory.
Tri-annual Meetings: Winter, Spring and Fall/75
1987-Clearwater Beach, FL(Sheraton Sand Key)/Feb. 18-20
1987-Baltimore, MD(Omni International)/May 13-15

Power Crane and Shovel Ass'n (1945)
Hist. Note: A bureau of the Construction Industry Manufacturers Association.

Power Engineering Soc.
Hist. Note: A subsidiary of the Institute of Electrical and Electronics Engineers. Membership in the Society, open only to IEEE members, includes subscription to a technical periodical in the field published by IEEE. All administrative support is provided by IEEE.

Power Industry Biologists Task Force (1973)
Hist. Note: Biologists doing environmental work for electric power companies. Has no permanent headquarters or paid staff. Officers change annually. Formerly (1983) the Soc. of Power Industry Biologists. Became a division of the Energy and Environment Committee of the Edison Electric Institute in 1983.

Power Industry Laboratory Ass'n (1984)
Dept. of Energy, Bonneville Power Adminstration, Box 491, Vancouver WA 98666
Secretary: A.S. "Stan" Capon
Members: 53 companies, 80 individuals
Annual Budget: under $10,000 *Tel:* (206) 690-2601
Hist. Note: Established June, 1984 at Chattanooga, Tennesee. Members are managers of laboratory and testing facilities of electric and gas utilities.
Publication:
Membership Directory. a.
Annual Meetings: April

Power Sources Manufacturers Ass'n (1985)
8833 Sunset Blvd., Suite 311, Los Angeles CA 90069
President: Tim A. Parrot
Members: 42 companies *Staff:* 2
Annual Budget: $50-100,000 *Tel:* (213) 652-9107
Hist. Note: Regular members are U.S. based or owned manufacturers of power sources and conversion equipment. Regular membership: $500-2,500/yr. (based on number of employees)
Annual Meetings: Sept.-Oct./2-300
1987-New York, NY
1988-Los Angeles, CA
1989-Boston, MA
1990-San Francisco, CA
1991-New York, NY

Power Sprayer and Duster Council
Hist. Note: Affiliate of the Farm and Industrial Equipment Institute

Power Tool Institute (1937)
501 West Algonquin Road, Arlington Heights IL 60005-4411
Exec. Manager: James E. Bates, CAE
Members: 14 *Staff:* 2-5
Annual Budget: $100-250,000 *Tel:* (312) 593-8350
Hist. Note: Formerly (1969) Electric Tool Institute.

Power Transmission Distributors Ass'n (1960)
100 Higgins Rd., Park Ridge IL 60068
Exec V. President: Beate Halligan
Members: 450 companies *Staff:* 3
Annual Budget: $500-1,000,000 *Tel:* (312) 825-2000
Hist. Note: Established as Mechanical Power Transmission Equipment Distributors Ass'n, it assumed its present name in 1966. Members are distributors and manufacturers of power transmission/motion control equipment.
Publication:
Transmissions. q.
Annual Meetings: October/800
1987-Las Vegas, NV(Caesar's Palace)/Oct. 18-21
1988-Toronto, Ontario(Sheraton Centre)/Oct. 18-23

Power Transmission Representatives Ass'n (1972)
5845 Horton, Suite 201, Shawnee Mission KS 66202
Exec. Director: Frank A. Bistrom
Members: 170 *Staff:* 2-5
Annual Budget: $50-100,000 *Tel:* (913) 262-4512
Annual Meetings: Spring
1987-Maui, HI(Inter-Continental)/March 7-11/250
1988-Charleston, SC(Undecided)/April/260

Powered Ultralight Manufacturers Ass'n
Hist. Note: Reported defunct in 1986.

Pre-Arrangement Interment Ass'n of America (1956)
1133 15th St., N.W., Suite 620, Washington DC 20005
Exec. Director: John H. Ganoe
Members: 5-600 *Staff:* 2-5
Annual Budget: $50-100,000 *Tel:* (202) 293-5910
Hist. Note: Cemeteries, funeral homes and sales companies promoting, pre-arranging and pre-paying for burial and funeral arrangements. Formerly (1956) Interment Ass'n of America. Absorbed the Pre-Arrangement Interment Exchange of America in 1971. Membership: $250/year.
Publications:
Ideas. q. adv.
PIAA Notes. bi-m. adv.
Semi-Annual Meetings: Winter and Summer

Precious Metals Industry Ass'n (1984)
Hist. Note: Reported as inactive in 1986.

Precision Chiropractic Research Soc. (1976)
1412 Alta Mesa Way, Brea CA 92621
President: A.C. Fulkerson
Members: 200 *Staff:* 1
Annual Budget: under $10,000 *Tel:* (213) 694-4181
Hist. Note: Also known as Spinal Stress Research Society. Members are chiropractors specializing in spinal stress.
Annual Meetings: November

Precision Measurements Ass'n (1958)
9681 Business Center Drive, Rancho Cucamonga CA 91730
Exec. Director: Phillip A. Painchaud
Members: 600 *Staff:* 1
Annual Budget: $25-50,000 *Tel:* (714) 980-6166
Hist. Note: Members are professionals in the measurement science field. Membership: $35/yr.
Publication:
Newsnotes. bi-m.
Annual Meetings: With the Nat'l Scale Men's Ass'n
1987-Gaithersburg, MD(Nat'l Bureau of Standards)

Preferred Funeral Directors Internat'l (1937)
6009 Wayzata Blvd., Suite 104, Minneapolis MN 55416
Exec. Director: Dayne Sieling
Members: 90-100 Companies *Staff:* 2-5
Annual Budget: $50-100,000 *Tel:* (612) 541-0551
Hist. Note: Established as the Advertising Funeral Directors of America, it assumed its present name in the mid-50s. Members are larger-volume funeral homes.
Publication:
P.F.D.I. Bulletin. bi-m.
Semi-Annual Meetings: Spring and Fall.

00257 12 05 86 1233

Preferred Hotels Ass'n (1968)
1901 Soutn Meyers Road, Suite 220, Oakbrook Terrace IL 60148
Exec. V. President: Ronald R. Beaumont
Members: 72 hotels *Staff:* 25
Annual Budget: $2-5,000,000 *Tel:* (312) 953-0404
Hist. Note: An exclusive group of independently operated and marketed luxury hotels and resorts in the U.S. and abroad. Founded to give independent hotels a way to compete with the central reservations systems and marketing impact of hotel chains. Membership dues computed on a per-room basis.
Publication:
The Presidents Newsletter.
Annual Meetings: Spring
1987-Dallas, TX(Mansion on Turtle Creek)/June 17-19

Prescription Footwear Ass'n (1956)
1414 Avenue of the Americas, New York NY 10019
Exec. Director: William Boettge
Members: 600-650 individuals and companies *Staff:* 6-10
Annual Budget: $50-100,000 *Tel:* (212) 752-2555
Hist. Note: Affiliated with the National Shoe Retailers Association. Members are manufacturers and retailers of footwear orthopedic devices.
Publications:
Ped Oscope. bi-m.
Directory. a.
Annual Meetings: November

Pressure Sensitive Tape Council (1953)
104 Wilmot Road, Suite 201, Deerfield IL 60015-5195
Exec. V. President: Glen R. Anderson
Members: 21 companies *Staff:* 2-5
Annual Budget: $100-250,000 *Tel:* (312) 724-7700
Annual Meetings: November/60
1987-Florida
1988-San Diego, CA

Pressure Vessel Manufacturers Ass'n (1975)
600 S. Federal St., Suite 400, Chicago IL 60605
Exec. Director: August L. Sisco
Members: 20-30 companies *Staff:* 2-5
Annual Budget: $50-100,000 *Tel:* (312) 922-6222
Hist. Note: Members are manufacturers and suppliers for the pressure vessel fabricating industry. Membership: $850-3,600/yr. (based on sales).
Triannual meetings: Spring, Summer and Fall

Prestressed Concrete Institute (1954)
201 N. Wells St., Chicago IL 60606
Exec. Director: Fromy Rosenberg
Members: 2,500-2,600 *Staff:* 16-20
Annual Budget: $2-5,000,000 *Tel:* (312) 346-4071
Publications:
Ideas. m.
PCI Journal. bi-m. adv.
Annual Meetings: Fall

Print Council of America (1956)
Houghton Library, Harvard University, Cambridge MA 02138
President: Eleanor Garvey
Members: 125
Annual Budget: under $10,000 *Tel:* (617) 495-2444
Hist. Note: Professional organization of museum curators of prints. Has no paid staff.
Annual Meetings: Spring

Print Information Center
Hist. Note: A special industry group of Printing Industries of America.

Printing Brokerage Ass'n (1985)
1700 N. Moore St., Suite 714, Arlington VA 22209
V. President & Exec. Director: Glenna T. McWilliams
Members: 25 companies; 75 individuals *Staff:* 3
Annual Budget: $100-250,000 *Tel:* (703) 243-3666
Hist. Note: PBA promotes business relationships between brokers, manufacturers and related companies in the printing industry; sets standards and codes of ethical conduct and acts as a source of information and referral. Membership: $300/yr.
Annual Meetings: Spring

Printing Industries of America (1887)
1730 North Lynn St., Arlington VA 22209
Acting President: G. William Teare, Jr.
Members: 12,200 *Staff:* 90
Annual Budget: over $5,000,000 *Tel:* (703) 841-8100
Hist. Note: The umbrella organization of the graphic arts industry. PIA is a federation of national, regional, state, and city associations incorporated under the laws of the District of Columbia. Established as United Typothetae of America, it became Printing Industry of America in 1945 and assumed its present name in 1965. Absorbed the Lithographers and Printers National Association in 1964. Supports the Printing Industries of America Political Action Committee, PrintPac. Has an annual budget of over $11,000,000.
Publications:
Printlines. m.
The Capital Letter. w.
Annual Meetings: Fall
1987-Washington, DC(Hilton)/Oct./150
1988-Washington, DC/Oct./100

Printing Industry Financial Executives
Hist. Note: A special industry group of Printing Industries of America.

Printing Platemakers Ass'n (1897)
Hist. Note: Established as the National Association of Electrotypers, it became the International Association of Electrotypers in 1921, the International Association of Electrotypers and Sterotypers in 1935 and the Printing Platemakers Association in 1969. Merged in January 1983 with the Lithographic Preparatory Services Association to form the Graphic Preparatory Association.

Private Carrier Conference (1945)
2200 Mill Road, Alexandria VA 22314
Exec. Director: Thomas L. Moore
Members: 2,200 *Staff:* 6
Annual Budget: $500-1,000,000 *Tel:* (703) 838-1995
Hist. Note: Manufacturers, processors and distributors who operate trucks within the scope and in furtherance of another non-transportation enterprise. Formed to defend such concerns from persistent attacks on their rights to operate. Affiliated with American Trucking Ass'ns, Inc.
Publications:
Private Carrier. m. adv.
Private Carrier Bulletin. m.
Semi-Annual Meetings:
1987-St. Louis, MO(Adam's Mark)/May 26-29/1,700

Private Doctors of America (1968)
3422 Bienville St., New Orleans LA 70119
Chairman: Dr. Jose L. Garcia-Oller
Members: 44,000 *Staff:* 11-15
Annual Budget: $250-500,000 *Tel:* (504) 486-5891
Hist. Note: Founded in New Orleans to represent exclusively private practicing doctors nationwide. Formerly (1977) the American Ass'n of Councils of Medical Staffs of Private Hospitals. Membership: $220/year.
Publication:
Private Doctor. 10/yr.
Annual Meetings: Spring, in New Orleans, LA

Private Label Manufacturers Ass'n (1979)
41 East 42nd Street, New York NY 10017
President: Brian Sharoff
Members: 500 companies
Annual Budget: $1-2,000,000 *Tel:* (212) 972-3131
Hist. Note: Promotes the purchase of private label or store brand products by consumers.
Publication:
Newsletter. q.
Annual Meetings: Fall in Chicago, IL at the O'Hare Expo Center.

Private Security Liaison Council (1981)
Box 24967, Nashville TN 37202
Chairman: Joe Duncan, Sr.
Members: 6 associations
Tel: (615) 259-2084
Hist. Note: A group of associations representing guard services, makers of burglar and fire alarms and the like united to confront legislative issues (for example, a proposal that the Government not be allowed to hire private security services) that threaten the industry.

Private Truck Council of America (1939)
2022 P Street, N.W., Washington DC 20036
Exec. V. President: Richard D. Henderson
Members: 1,600 *Staff:* 5
Annual Budget: $250-500,000 *Tel:* (202) 785-4900
Hist. Note: Founded as the Nat'l Council of Private Motor Truck Owners, it assumed its present name about 1954. Represents the interests of non-transportation companies which operate trucks in furtherance of a primary commercial enterprise other than for-hire transportation.
Publications:
News Line. m.
Private Line. bi-m.
Annual Meetings: Spring
1987-New Orleans, LA(Hyatt Regency)/April 8-10

Process Equipment Manufacturers' Ass'n (1960)
7297 Lee Highway, Suite N, Falls Church VA 22042
Exec. Director: Harry W. Buzzerd, Jr.
Members: 60 companies *Staff:* 2-5
Annual Budget: $100-250,000 *Tel:* (703) 533-0286
Hist. Note: Companies engaged in the manufacture and supply of equipment for food, chemical, pulp & paper, water and wastewater processing, air pollution control, liquids-solids separation, etc.
Publication:
PEMA Press. bi-m.
Annual Meetings: February
1987-Naples, FL(Ritz Carlton)/Feb. 18-20

Processed Apples Institute (1951)
5775 Peachtree-Dunwoody Road, Suite 500D, Atlanta GA 30342
President: Robert H. Kellen
Members: 90 *Staff:* 4
Tel: (404) 252-3663
Hist. Note: Members are producers of processed apple products and their suppliers.
Annual Meetings:
1987-Tucson, AZ/March 8-11

Procurement Round Table (1984)
2045 North 15th St., Suite 1000, Arlington VA 22201
Secy.-Treas.: Dr. John F. Magnotti, Jr.
Members: 25 individuals *Staff:* 2
Annual Budget: under $10,000 *Tel:* (703) 528-0072
Hist. Note: Members provide advice on federal procurement policy matters.

Produce Marketing Ass'n (1949)
1500 Casho Mill Rd., P.O. Box 6036, Newark DE 19714
Exec. V. President: Robert L. Carey, CAE
Members: 1,800 companies, 600 individuals *Staff:* 20-25
Annual Budget: $2-5,000,000 *Tel:* (302) 738-7100
Hist. Note: A national trade association whose members are companies, corporations, organizations or individuals engaged in any facet of marketing fresh produce and floral products, or providing equipment, supplies, transportation, or other services to the fresh produce and floral industry. Founded as the Produce Prepackaging Ass'n, it became the Produce Packaging Ass'n in 1956, the Produce Packaging and Marketing Ass'n in 1967 and assumed its present name in 1971.
Publications:
PMA Almanac. a. adv.
PMA Floral Marketing Directory and Buyer's Guide. a. adv.
PMA Food Service Guide to Fresh Produce. a. adv.
PMA Newsletter. bi-w.
PMA Directory of International Trade. a. adv.
Annual Meetings: Fall/4,500-5,000
1987-Anaheim, CA(Convention Center)/Oct. 24-28
1988-Nashville, TN(Opryland)/Oct. 22-26
1989-Reno, NV(Convention Center/MGM Grand)/Oct. 14-18

Producer's Guild of America (1950)
292 S. LaCienega Blvd., Beverly Hills CA 90211
Exec. Director: Charles B. Fitz Simons
Members: 575-600 *Staff:* 2-5
Tel: (213) 659-6898
Hist. Note: Formerly (1967) Screen Producers Guild. Members are producers of motion pictures and television shows mainly in the Los Angeles area.
Publication:
The Journal of the Producers Guild of America. q.

Product Development and Management Ass'n (1976)
Graduate Sch. of Business, Indiana Univ.,01 West Michigan St., Indianapolis IN 46202
Secy.-Treas.: Thomas P. Hustad
Members: 375 *Staff:* 0
Annual Budget: $25-50,000 *Tel:* (317) 274-4984
Hist. Note: International association designed to serve people with a professional interest in improving the management of product innovation. Membership: $85/yr.
Publications:
Journal of Product Innovation Management. q.
Newsletter. q.
Directory. a.
Annual Meetings: Fall
1987-New York, NY/Oct.
1988-Chicago, IL/Oct.

Production Engine Remanufacturers Ass'n (1946)
512 East Wilson Ave., Suite 311, Glendale CA 91206
Exec. V. President: Alvin P. Bean
Members: 240 companies *Staff:* 2-5
Annual Budget: $250-500,000 *Tel:* (818) 240-8666
Hist. Note: Formerly (1970) Western Engine Rebuilders Ass'n and (1973) Production Engine Rebuilders Ass'n. Members are manufacturers, remanufacturers and parts suppliers to the production line combustion engine industry. Membership: $450/yr.
Annual Meetings: Fall/500
1987-Los Angeles, CA(Sheraton Premier)/Sept. 16-20
1988-Boston, MA(Copley Plaza)/Sept. 21-25
1989-Kauai, HI/Sept. 27-Oct. 1
1990-Orlando, FL/Sept. 26-30

Production Music Library Ass'n (1982)
40 East 49th St., Suite 605, New York NY 10017
President: Michael Nurko
Annual Budget: under $10,000 *Tel:* (212) 832-1098
Hist. Note: Members are music libraries supplying producers with music under license; thus clearing the producer from any possibility of copyright infringement.
Semi-annual Meetings:

Production Records (1985)
Route 1, Box 126, Fairland OK 74343
Manager: Glenn E. Butts
Members: 1,000-1,500 *Staff:* 2-5
Annual Budget: $10-25,000 *Tel:* (918) 676-3266
Hist. Note: Founded in 1955 as the Performance Registry Internat'l; assumed the title Production Records Inc. in 1985. Members are cattle ranchers, farmers, and related companies which promote better breeding practices in beef cattle, research, programming, and franched software. Membership: $100/yr.
Publication:
News Releases. irreg.

Production Service and Sales District Council
100 Livingston St., Brooklyn NY 11201
President: Robert J. Rao
Members: 21,000 *Staff:* 16-20
Annual Budget: $500-1,000,000 *Tel:* (718) 858-4900

00258 12 05 86 1233

Hist. Note: An independent labor union for hotel workers. Formerly known as the Internat'l Production, Service and Sales Union.
Annual Meetings: Every 5 years (1990)

Professional Aeromedical Transport Ass'n (1986)
P.O. Box 579, Moorestown NJ 08057
Exec. Director: Dennis C. Neff
Members: 25 companies; 10 individuals *Staff:* 3
Annual Budget: $10-25,000 *Tel:* (609) 234-0330
Hist. Note: PATA's primary purpose is to standardize and upgrade services of aeromedical transport operations. Membership is open to companies which provide such services or are suppliers to the industry and to individuals with an interest in the industry. Membership: $100/yr. (individual); $500/yr. (company)
Semi-annual Meetings:

Professional Air Traffic Controllers Organization (1968)
Hist. Note: A labor union affiliated (1971) with Nat'l Marine Engineers Beneficial Ass'n (AFL-CIO). Seriously damaged by the strike of the summer of 1981 and the consequent dismissal of most of its members by President Reagan. Bankrupt in 1982.

Professional Airways Systems Specialists (1977)
444 North Capitol St., N.W., Suite 840, Washington DC 20001
President: Howard E. Johannssen
Members: 2,000 *Staff:* 6-10
Annual Budget: $500-1,000,000 *Tel:* (202) 347-6065
Hist. Note: A labor union of flight safety specialists established in Chicago February 15-18, 1977 and certified by the Federal Labor Relations Authority December 31, 1981.
Publication:
PASS Dateline. q.
Biennial Meetings: Memorial Day weekend even years.

Professional Archers Ass'n (1961)
7315 North Fan Anna Drive, Tucson AZ 85704
Secy.-Treas.: R. Arlyne Rhode
Members: 350-400 *Staff:* 2-5
Annual Budget: $100-250,000 *Tel:* (602) 742-5846
Hist. Note: Members are professional archery competitors and instructors. Sponsors professional tournaments. Membership: $200/yr. plus $20 initiation fee.
Publications:
Newsletter. m.
U.S. Archer Magazine. bi-m.
Annual Meetings: Summer

Professional Ass'n of Diving Instructors (1966)
1243 East Warner Ave., Santa Ana CA 92705
V.P.-Education & Public Affairs: Al Hornsby
Members: 12,000 *Staff:* 100
Annual Budget: over $5,000,000 *Tel:* (714) 540-7234
Hist. Note: PADI is a professional diving organization that certifies scuba diving instructors. Over 10,000 PADI instructor members and 1,100 Dive Store members (PADI Training Facilities) conduct training in over 90 countries. PADI provides educational/training materials and retail support to its members.
Publications:
Dive Industry News. q.
Diving Ventures. q.
Undersea Journal. q.
Annual Meetings: DEMA Trade Show - Jan./Feb.
1987-Las Vegas, NV
1988-New Orleans, LA
1989-Las Vegas, NV
1990-Orlando, FL
1991-Houston, TX

Professional Ass'n of Secretarial Services (1980)
Hist. Note: Dissolved in December, 1984.

Professional Audio-Video Retailers Ass'n (1979)
9140 Ward Parkway, Kansas City MO 64114
Exec. V. President: Jerry Fogel
Members: 128 companies *Staff:* 2-5
Annual Budget: $100-250,000 *Tel:* (816) 444-3500
Hist. Note: Membership: $350-1,200/yr.
Publication:
Parascope. bi-m.
Annual Meetings: March/April
1987-Wesley Chapel, FL(Saddlebrook)/March 22-27/250
1988-San Diego, CA(Intercontinental)/April 17-22/250

Professional Aviation Maintenance Ass'n (1972)
500 Northwest Plaza, Suite 912, St. Ann MO 63074
Exec. Administrator: Patti J. Campbell
Members: 1,800 individuals, 230 companies *Staff:* 3
Annual Budget: $100-250,000 *Tel:* (314) 739-2580
Hist. Note: Members are technicians holding an A&P (Air Frame and Power Plant) license and aviation maintenance companies. Membership: $25/yr. (individual); $300/yr. (company)
Publication:
The PAMA News. bi-m. adv.
Annual Meetings: March
1987-Houston, TX(Albert Thomas Convention Ctr.)/Feb. 11-13
1988-Houston, TX(Hyatt Regency)/March

Professional Basketball Writers' Ass'n of America (1972)
26 Woodside Park, Pleasant Ridge MI 48069
Secy.-Treas.: William Halls
Members: 175 *Staff:* 1
Annual Budget: under $10,000 *Tel:* (313) 222-2260
Hist. Note: Members are sports editors and reporters who cover professional basketball. Membership: $15/yr.
Publication:
Newsletter. 8/yr.
Annual Meetings: During the NBA All-Star Game.
1987-Seattle, WA/Feb. 6-8/100

Professional Bowlers Ass'n of America (1958)
1720 Merriman Rd., Akron OH 44313
Commissioner: Joseph R. Antenora
Members: 3,000 *Staff:* 16-20
Tel: (216) 836-5568
Hist. Note: Members must have a minimum average of 190 established for 66 or more games per season for the 2 most recent seasons prior to applying for membership. Hosts regional and national tournaments throughout the year. Membership: $125/yr. (regional membership).
Publication:
Tournament Annual. a. adv.

Professional Comedians Ass'n (1984)
Box 222, New York NY 10185
Secretary: Bill Miller
Members: 140
Annual Budget: under $10,000 *Tel:* (212) 614-1123
Hist. Note: The PCA is an organization of comedians that was formed to support the interests and well-being of its members and to enhance their professional and economic standing. Membership: $120 intitiation(one year);$48/year dues.
Publication:
Stand Up, m.
Annual Meetings: February

Professional Communication Soc.
Hist. Note: A subsidiary of the Institute of Electrical and Electronic Engineers. Membership in the Society, open only to IEEE members, includes subscription to a technical periodical in the field published by IEEE. All administrative support is provided by IEEE.

Professional Convention Management Ass'n (1958)
100 Vestavia Office Park, Suite 220, Birmingham AL 35216
Exec. V. President: Roy B. Evans, Jr. CAE
Members: 1,300 individuals *Staff:* 2-5
Annual Budget: $500-1,000,000 *Tel:* (205) 251-1717
Hist. Note: Incorporated in Illinois February 28, 1958. Membership consists of convention managers, CEO's, meeting planners, and suppliers representing 1,000 organizations in the medical, dental, hospital, and allied professions. Membership: $150-300/yr.
Publication:
News and views. q.
Annual Meetings: Winter
1987-Orlando, FL(Marriott)/Jan. 6-9/1,400
1988-Nashville, TN(Opryland)/Jan. 4-7/1,500
1989-Anaheim, CA(Marriott & Hilton)/Jan. 4-7
1990-New Orleans, LA(Marriott & Sheraton)/Jan. 3-6

Professional Dance Teachers Ass'n
Box 38, Waldwick NJ 07463
Secretary: Danny Hoctor
Members: 1,000 *Staff:* 2-5
Annual Budget: $50-100,000 *Tel:* (201) 652-7767
Hist. Note: Members are professional teachers of jazz, ballet and modern dance. The association helps its members to improve their teaching techniques and provides them with ideas for new dance routines to use in their studios. Membership: $60/yr.
Publication:
Newsletter and Dance Routines. a.
Annual Meetings: July

Professional Engineers in Private Practice (1955)
1420 King St., Alexandria VA 22314
Staff Director: Frank Musica
Members: 11,000 *Staff:* 4
Annual Budget: $500-1,000,000 *Tel:* (703) 684-2862
Hist. Note: Formed in 1955 as an autonomous division of the Nat'l Soc. of Professional Engineers to address concerns of individual consulting professional engineers; reorganized in 1965 with independent dues structure. Provides information and lobbying efforts on practice management, professional liability, and career development interests of members. Membership: $50/yr.
Publications:
Private Practice News. m.
Directory of Engineers in Private Practice. bien.
Semi-annual Meetings: With Nat'l Soc. of Professional Engineers.
1987-Orlando, FL(Marriott)/Jan. 18-24/500
1987-Denver, CO(Marriott City Center)/July 12-18/500
1988-Mobile, AL(Riverview Plaza)/Jan. 17-23/500
1988-Seattle, WA(Sheraton)/July 17-23/500
1989-Atlanta, GA(Marriott)/Jan. 8-14/500
1989-Minneapolis, MN(Amfac)/July 23-30/500

Professional Football Trainers
1001 East 4th St., Greenville NC 27858
Admin. Assistant: Mary Edgerley
Members: 80-100 *Staff:* 1
Annual Budget: under $10,000 *Tel:* (919) 752-1725
Annual Meetings: June
1987-Las Vegas, NV
1988-Washington, DC

Professional Football Writers of America (1962)
12042 Mereview Drive, St. Louis MO 63146
Secretary-Treasurer: Howard Balzer
Members: 250
Annual Budget: under $10,000 *Tel:* (314) 997-7111
Hist. Note: Members are sportswriters and columnists who cover professional football regularly. Promotes good working relationships between writers and leagues, clubs and players' associations.
Publication:
Newsletter. bi-m.
Annual Meetings: Friday preceeding Super Bowl.

Professional Fraternity Ass'n (1977)
1226 West Michigan, #134, Indianapolis IN 46202
Exec. Secretary: Harriet Rodenberg
Members: 35-40 professional fraternities and sororities *Staff:* 1
Annual Budget: under $10,000 *Tel:* (317) 639-6165
Hist. Note: Established October 22, 1977, through merger of the Professional Panhellenic Ass'n (established 1925) and the Professional Interfraternity Conference (established 1928). Membership: $200/yr. (organization).
Publications:
PFA Newsletter. 4-6/yr.
Membership Directory. a.
Annual Meetings: Late September
1987-Tucson, AZ(Sheraton El Conquistador)/Sept. 17-19

Professional Golf Club Repairmen's Ass'n (1977)
2053 Harvard Ave., Dunedin FL 33528
Exec. Director: Thelma Schloss
Members: 1,000-2,000 *Staff:* 2-5
Annual Budget: $10-25,000 *Tel:* (813) 733-4348
Hist. Note: Persons engaged in golf club repair and/or custom golf club making and golf professionals whose jobs include repair work. Membership: $15/yr.
Publication:
Golf Club Maker. q.
Annual Meetings: None held

Professional Golfers Ass'n of America (1916)
100 Ave. of the Champions, Palm Beach Gardens FL 33418
Exec. Director: Lou King
Members: 9,620, plus 5,280 apprentices *Staff:* 60
Annual Budget: $2-5,000,000 *Tel:* (305) 626-3600
Hist. Note: Founded in New York City in 1916. Runs local, national and international tournaments. Most members are club professionals managing golf courses.
Publication:
PGA Magazine. m. adv.

Professional Grounds Management Soc. (1911)
3701 Old Court Road, Suite 15, Pikesville MD 21208
Exec. Director: Allan Shulder
Members: 1,236 *Staff:* 3
Annual Budget: $100-250,000 *Tel:* (301) 653-2742
Hist. Note: Formerly (1971) Nat'l Ass'n of Professional Gardeners. Members are managers of parks, golf courses, botanical gradens, arboretums and similar recreational areas accessible to the public. Awards the CGM (Certified Grounds Manager) designation. Membership: $60/yr.
Publications:
PGMS Membership Directory. a. adv.
Grounds Management Forum. m. adv.
Grounds Maintenance Estimating Guidelines. bi-a.
Grounds Maintenance Management Guidelines. bi-a.
Grounds Management Forms and Job Descriptions Guide. bi-a.
Annual Meetings: Fall
1987-Washington, DC(Hyatt Crystal City)/Nov. 8-11

Professional Handlers Ass'n
Hist. Note: No paid staff; address unknown in 1986.

Professional Independent Mass Marketing Administrators (1975)
Hist. Note: Became the Professional Insurance Mass-Marketing Association in 1982.

Professional Insurance Communicators of America (1955)
P.O. Box 68700, Indianapolis IN 46268
Secy.-Treas.: E. H. Wright
Members: 100-120 *Staff:* 1
Annual Budget: under $10,000 *Tel:* (317) 875-5250
Hist. Note: Founded as the Mutual Insurance Council of Editors, it became the Mutual Insurance Communicators in 1969 and assumed its present name in 1981. An affiliate of the Nat'l Ass'n of Mutual Insurance Companies. Members are editors of insurance company newsletters.
Publication:
The Mutual Piper. irreg.
Annual Meetings: Spring
1987-Philadelphia, PA

00259 12 05 86 1233

Professional Insurance Mass-Marketing Ass'n (1975)
4733 Bethesda Ave., Suite 330, Bethesda MD 20814
Exec. V. President: John J. McManus
Staff: 2-5
Annual Budget: $250-500,000 *Tel:* (301) 951-1260
Hist. Note: Formerly (1982) the Professional and Independent Mass-Marketing Administrators. Members are leading third-party administrators and companies active in mass-marketing all lines of insurance.
Publications:
PIMA News. m.
PIMA Membership Directory. a.
Annual Meetings: February/250
1987-Laguna Niguel, CA(Ritz-Carlton)/Feb. 8-11
1988-Phoenix, AZ(Biltmore)

Professional Lawn Care Ass'n of America (1979)
1225 Johnson Ferry Rd. N.E., Suite B-220, Marietta GA 30067
Exec. V. President: James R. Brooks
Members: 900 companies *Staff:* 2-5
Annual Budget: $250-500,000 *Tel:* (404) 977-5222
Hist. Note: Lawn care operators and manufacturers/suppliers of associated products. Membership Fee: Based on gross sales volume.
Publication:
Turf Talks Newsletter. bi-m.
Annual Meetings: Fall
1987-San Antonio, TX(Convention Center)/Nov. 13-16
1988-New Orleans, LA(Superdome)/Nov. 7-10

Professional Managers Ass'n (1981)
Box 7762 Ben Franklin Station, Washington DC 20044
President: Helene Benson
Members: 1,000 *Staff:* 1-3
Annual Budget: $25-50,000 *Tel:* (202) 535-4322
Hist. Note: Members are federal employees in mid-level management positions. In process of establishing chapters throughout the country. Membership: $52/year.
Publication:
Update. bi-m.

Professional Mariners Alliance (1983)
55 John St., New York NY 10038
Exec. Director: Randy O'Neill
Members: 5,000 individuals *Staff:* 4
Annual Budget: $25-50,000 *Tel:* (212) 608-3081
Hist. Note: Members include deck and engineering officers, marine insurers, admiralty attorneys, corporate managers, naval architects, surveyors, agents, and brokers. Membership: $50/yr.
Publications:
The Professional Mariner. q. adv.
PMA Soundings. bi-w. adv.

Professional Numismatists Guild (1947)
Box 430, Van Nuys CA 91408
Exec. Director: Paul L. Koppenhaver
Members: 200-210 *Staff:* 2-5
Annual Budget: $100-250,000 *Tel:* (818) 781-1764
Hist. Note: Members are individuals who have been full-time coin dealers for at least five years. Promotes high standards of ethics in the hobby of numismatics. Affiliated with the American Numismatic Association and the American Numismatic Society. Until 1969 known as the Professional Numismatic Guild.
Semi-Annual Meetings: April and August
1987-St. Louis, MO/April
1987-Atlanta, GA/August

Professional Photographers of America (1880)
1090 Executive Way, Des Plaines IL 60018
Exec. Director: Robert E. Becker, CAE
Members: 14,000 *Staff:* 50
Annual Budget: over $5,000,000 *Tel:* (312) 299-8161
Hist. Note: Professional society of portrait, commercial, wedding, industrial and specialized photographers. Grants the Master of Photography, Photographic Craftsman and Photographic Specialist degrees in recognition of exceptional ability and service. Sponsors the Winona School of Professional Photography. Formerly (1958) the Photographers' Ass'n of America.
Publications:
PP of A Today Newsletter. m.
The Professional Photographer. m. adv.
Directory of Professional Photography. a. adv.
Annual Meetings: Summer
1987-Rosemont, IL(O'Hare Expo Ctr.)/Aug. 1-5/6,000
1988-Orlando, FL(Orange County Civic Ctr.)/July 8-13/6,000

Professional Picture Framers Ass'n (1971)
4305 Sarellen Road, Richmond VA 23231
Exec. Director: Michael C. Kromer, CAE
Members: 6,200 *Staff:* 16-20
Annual Budget: $1-2,000,000 *Tel:* (804) 226-0430
Hist. Note: A trade ass'n of manufacturers, wholesalers, print publishers, importers and retailers selling and making art and framing supplies.
Publication:
The Framer. m.
Semi-annual meetings: Winter and Summer/5,000
1987-Atlanta, GA(Congress Center/Marriott Marquis)/Jan. 14-20
1987-Chicago, IL(O'Hare Exp. Center/Hyatt/Holiday Inn)/July 23-28
1988-Las Vegas, NV(Cashman Center/MGM Grand)/Feb. 18-22
1988-New York, NY(Convention Center/Marriott Marquis)/July 20-27
1989-New Orleans, LA(Superdome/Hyatt Regency)Jan. 12-17
1989-San Francisco, CA(Moscone Center/Hilton/Towers)/July 13-18
1990-Atlanta, GA(Congress Center/Hyatt Regency)/Feb. 22-27
1990-Chicago, IL(O'Hare Expo Center/Hyatt Regency)/Jyly 19-25

Professional Pool Players Ass'n (1975)
422 North Broad St., Elizabeth NJ 07206
Secretary: Arno Bollhardt
Members: 1,500 *Staff:* 1
Annual Budget: $25-50,000 *Tel:* (201) 355-1302
Hist. Note: Formed by a group of players who broke away from the Billiard Congress of America.
Publication:
PPPA Newsletter. m.
Annual Meetings: August

Professional Publishers Marketing Group (1980)
c/o Columbia University Press, 562 West 113th St., New York NY 10025
Contact: Ann Zeller
Members: 30 companies
Annual Budget: under $10,000 *Tel:* (212) 316-7125
Hist. Note: Publishers of books and magazines who exchange marketing data.
Publication:
Newsletter. q.

Professional Putters Ass'n (1959)
Box 35237, Fayetteville NC 28303
Commissioner: David Lloyd
Members: 1,117 *Staff:* 32
Annual Budget: $500-1,000,000 *Tel:* (919) 485-7131
Hist. Note: Members are individuals over the age of 16 who compete in national putting tournaments as well as golf course owners, managers and suppliers. Membership: $20/yr.
Publications:
Facts and Membership. a.
Putt-Putt World. q.
Official Rules and Regulations of the PPA.

Professional Race Pilots Ass'n (1939)
Box 60084, Reno NV 89506
Exec. Director: Jane Skliar
Members: 150 *Staff:* 1
Annual Budget: under $10,000 *Tel:* (702) 322-1421
Hist. Note: Affiliate of Nat'l Aeronautic Ass'n. Founded as the Professional Race Pilots Ass'n in 1934 and incorporated in 1939. Became the United States Air Racing Ass'n in 1977. In 1984, PRPA returned to its original name, and incorporated in Nevada. Eastern regional affiliate has adopted the USARA title. Membership: $25/yr. (technical), $35/yr. (pilots and owners).
Publication:
News Letter. m.
Annual Meetings: Mid-September in Reno, NV at Karl's Silver Cub Hotel & Casino

Professional Reactor Operator Soc. (1981)
Box 181, Mishicot WI 54288-0181
President: James Peterson
Members: 465 *Staff:* 2-5
Annual Budget: $10-25,000 *Tel:* (414) 863-6996
Hist. Note: Members are operators of nuclear power facilities. Membership: $25/yr.(individual); $500/yr.(organization)
Publication:
The Communicator. q. adv.
Annual Meetings: Spring
1987-Washington, DC/June

Professional Rodeo Cowboys Ass'n (1936)
101 Prorodeo Dr., Colorado Springs CO 80919
Exec. V. President: Bob Eidson
Members: 9-10,000 *Staff:* 25-30
Annual Budget: $2-5,000,000 *Tel:* (303) 593-8840
Hist. Note: Founded as Cowboys Turtle Ass'n. Became Rodeo Cowboys Ass'n in 1945 and Professional Rodeo Cowboys Ass'n in 1975.
Publication:
Prorodeo Sports News. bi-w. adv.
Annual Meetings: Held the week before the National Finals
1987-Las Vegas, NV

Professional School Photographers of America (1951)
Hist. Note: Dissolved in 1985, it now functions as a section of Photo Marketing Ass'n with headquarters in Jackson, MI.

Professional Secretaries Internat'l (1942)
301 East Armour Blvd., Kansas City MO 64111-1299
Exec. Director: Jerome A. Heitman
Members: 42,000 *Staff:* 31
Annual Budget: $1-2,000,000 *Tel:* (816) 531-7010
Hist. Note: Formerly (1981) Nat'l Secretaries Ass'n (Internat'l). Incorporated in the State of Missouri, PSI is a non-profit professional association sponsoring the Institute for Certifying Secretaries which awards the designation "Certified Professional Secretary" (CPS). PSI services include the PSI Research and Educational Foundation, a nonprofit trust which coordinates and authorizes research, distributes findings and provides public instruction related to the secretarial profession. Membership: $15 initial fee; $27/yr. renewal
Publication:
The Secretary Magazine. 9/yr. adv.
Annual Meetings: Summer/1,700
1987-Los Angeles, CA(Biltmore)/July 27-30/1,800
1988-Kansas City, MO(Hyatt)/July 24-26
1989-San Antonio, TX(Marriott)/July 16-21
1990-Seattle, WA/July 22-27
1991-Dallas, TX/July

Professional Services Council (1972)
World Center Building, Suite 406, 918 16th St., N.W., Washington DC 20006
Exec. Director: Virginia Littlejohn
Members: 100 companies, 6 ass'ns *Staff:* 2-5
Annual Budget: $250-500,000 *Tel:* (202) 296-2030
Hist. Note: Companies providing professional and technical services to the government and private industry. Sponsors and supports the Professional Services Council Political Action Committee Formerly (until 1982) the National Council of Professional Services Firms. Membership: $100/yr. (trade ass'ns), $300-15,000/yr. (company).
Publication:
News Update. m.
Annual Meetings: Semi-annual meetings

Professional Services Management Ass'n (1975)
1213 Prince Street, Alexandria VA 22314
Exec. Director: Kerry Harding
Members: 1,000 *Staff:* 2-5
Annual Budget: $250-500,000 *Tel:* (703) 684-3993
Hist. Note: Members are business managers of professional service firms (i.e. engineering, architecture, landscape architecture, interior design, managemenat consultants, etc.) seeking to promote the exchange of ideas and information and to establish guidelines in the field of professional and service firm management. Membership: $150/yr.
Publications:
Ascent. bi-m. adv.
Management Reports. 3-4/yr.
Focus on Marketing. semi-a.
Focus on Operations. sem-a.
Focus on Human Resources. semi-a.
Focus on Management. semi-a.
Focus on Finance. semi-a.
PSMA Member Services Manual. a. adv.
Hot Line Directory.
Annual Meetings: October

Professional Ski Instructors of America (1961)
5541 Central Ave., Boulder CO 80301
Exec. Director: David A. Hamilton
Members: 16,000 individuals, 350 ski schools, 35 companies
Staff: 5
Annual Budget: $500-1,000,000 *Tel:* (303) 447-0842
Hist. Note: Provides on-going education for certified ski instructors and international educational training.
Publication:
The Ski Pro Journal of Professional Ski Instruction. q. adv.
Semi-annual Meetings: Spring and Fall

Professional Soccer Reporters Ass'n (1975)
c/o Chicago Tribune, 435 N. Michigan Ave., Chicago IL 60611
President: John Leptich
Members: 300 individuals
Annual Budget: under $10,000 *Tel:* (312) 222-3475
Hist. Note: Formed to further and foster better working conditions for those covering soccer in North America. Membership: $15/yr.
Annual Meetings: Winter
1987-Los Angeles, CA/Feb.

Professional Stringers Ass'n (1973)
2209 South 32nd Ave., Omaha NE 68105
Exec. Director: Frank Fochek
Members: 800 individuals *Staff:* 1
Annual Budget: under $10,000 *Tel:* (402) 345-9996
Hist. Note: Tennis racquet stringers at stores and clubs. Membership: $18/yr. (U.S., Canada and Mexico), $21/yr. (elsewhere).
Publication:
Newsletter. bi-m. adv.

Professional Tennis Registry, USA (1976)
Box 4739, Hilton Head SC 29938
President: Dennis Van der Meer
Members: 3,600 *Staff:* 2-5
Annual Budget: $100-250,000 *Tel:* (803) 785-9602
Hist. Note: An international association of officially recognized, certified and registered tennis teaching professionals. Developed the "Official Standard Method" of instruction to certify tennis professionals through an internationally standardized test. Membership: $95 application fee; $75/yr.
Publication:
The TENNISPRO. q. adv.
Annual Meetings: Hilton Head, SC in October
1987-Oct. 4-11/600

Professional Travel Film Directors Ass'n (1967)
7 South Dearborn St., Chicago IL 60603
1st V. President: William S. Fisher
Members: 50-60 *Staff:* 1
Annual Budget: under $10,000 *Tel:* (312) 726-5293
Hist. Note: Formerly (1971) Professional Travel Film Managers Ass'n. Promotes communication between sponsors, speakers and managers. Membership: $25-$50/year.
Annual Meetings: Winter

00260 12 05 86 1233

Professional Ultralight Manufacturers Ass'n (1980)
Hist. Note: Became the Powered Ultralight Manufacturers Association in 1982.

Professional Women Photographers (1975)
c/o Photgraphics Unlimited, 17 West 17th St., #14, New York NY 10011-5510
Chairwoman: Mariette Pathy Allen
Members: 500
Annual Budget: under $10,000 *Tel:* (212) 255-9676
Hist. Note: Began in 1975 with the exhibition, "Breadth of Vision: Portfolios of Women Photographers" at the Fashion Institute of Technology in New York City. PWP proceeded with monthly meetings, newsletters and exhibitions. Incorporated in New York City. Membership: $15/yr., $20/yr. (New York City)
Publication:
PWP Newsletter. bi-m. adv.
Monthly Meetings: New York City(Nikon House) 2nd Wednesday Sept.-May

Professional Women's Appraisal Ass'n (1986)
8715 Via De Commercio, Scottsdale AZ 85258
Exec. Director: Lori A. Laughlin
Members: 2,200 individuals *Staff:* 3
Annual Budget: $250-500,000 *Tel:* (602) 998-4422
Hist. Note: PWAA provides professional recognition to women involved in real estate valuation. Membership: $150/yr.
Publications:
Newsletter. 6/yr. adv.
Professional Women's Appraisal Journal. q. adv.
Annual Meetings: September

Profit Sharing Council of America (1947)
20 North Wacker Dr., Chicago IL 60606
President: Walter Holan
Members: 1,200 companies *Staff:* 6-10
Annual Budget: $250-500,000 *Tel:* (312) 372-3411
Hist. Note: Formerly (1973) Council of Profit Sharing Industries. Members are companies with profit-sharing plans. Membership fee based on size of company.
Publication:
Profit Sharing. m.
Annual Meetings: October
1987-Washington, DC
1988-Chicago, IL

Project Management Institute (1969)
Box 43, Drexel Hill PA 19026
Exec. Director: Bonnie J. McGarr
Members: 5,000 individuals *Staff:* 2-5
Annual Budget: $500-1,000,000 *Tel:* (215) 622-1796
Hist. Note: Dedicated to advancing the state-of-the-art in the profession of project management. Membership: $60/yr.
Publications:
Proceedings. a.
Project Management Journal. 5/yr. adv.
Annual Meetings: Fall
1987-Milwaukee, WI
1988-San Francisco, CA
1989-Atlanta, GA

Prolotherapy Ass'n (1962)
Hist. Note: Doctors specializing in the rehabilitation of ligaments and tendons by the induced proliferation of new cells. Absorbed by the American Association of Orthopaedic Medicine in February 1984.

Promotion Marketing Ass'n of America (1911)
322 8th Ave., Suite 1201, New York NY 10001
President: Parker C. Lindberg
Members: 500-600 *Staff:* 6
Annual Budget: $250-500,000 *Tel:* (212) 867-3990
Hist. Note: Founded as American Manufacturers Premiums Ass'n, it became Premium Advertising Ass'n of America in 1934 and Promotion Marketing Ass'n of America, Inc. in 1977. This last name change reflects an expansion of PMAA's interest into promotional fields other than those concerned primarily with premiums and incentives. Members are premium users, premium manufacturers, consultants and advertising agencies. Sponsors the New York Premium Show and the Nat'l Premium Show in Chicago.

Propeller Club of the U.S. (1927)
1030 15th St., N.W., Suite 430, Washington DC 20005
Exec. V. President: J. Daniel Smith
Members: 17,000 individuals, 106 local clubs *Staff:* 4
Annual Budget: $250-500,000 *Tel:* (202) 898-0680
Hist. Note: Promotes and supports American water-borne commerce and the development of river, Great Lakes and harbor improvements. Founded in 1923 as The Propeller Club of New York, it became a multi-club national organization and assumed its present name in 1927.
Publications:
Proceedings of American Merchant Conference. a.
The Propeller Club Quarterly. q.
Annual Meetings: Fall
1987-San Francisco, CA/550
1988-Galveston, TX
1989-Honolulu, HI
1990-Tacoma, WA
1992-Brownsville-Port Isabel, TX

Property Loss Research Bureau (1947)
Suite 400 West, 1501 Woodfield Road, Schaumburg IL 60173
President: Franklin W. Nutter
Members: 215 insurance companies *Staff:* 11-15
Annual Budget: $1-2,000,000 *Tel:* (312) 490-8650
Hist. Note: Founded as the Mutual Loss Research Bureau, it assumed its present name in 1972. Members are mutual and stock insurance companies.
Annual Meetings: April/1,200
1987-San Diego, CA(Sheraton Harbor Island)/April 6-8

Property Management Ass'n of America (1979)
8811 Colesville Road, Suite G106, Silver Spring MD 20910
Exec. V. President: John P. Bachner
Members: 450 individuals, 300 companies *Staff:* 6-10
Annual Budget: under $10,000 *Tel:* (301) 587-6543
Hist. Note: Managers of residential and commercial properties.
Publications:
Bulletin. m.
Directory. a.

Proprietary Ass'n, The (1881)
1150 Connecticut Ave., N.W., Washington DC 20036
President: James D. Cope
Members: 80 active, 135 associates *Staff:* 35-40
Annual Budget: $2-5,000,000 *Tel:* (202) 429-9260
Hist. Note: Organized in New York City on November 26, 1881 as the Proprietary Medicine Manufacturers and Dealers Ass'n. Members are makers and distributors of medicines for self-care sold over the counter without a prescription. Supports The Proprietary Industry Political Action Committee-PIPAC. Membership fee based on sales volume.
Publications:
Executive Newsletter. w.
Legislative News Bulletins. irreg.
Scientific Bulletin. irreg.
Membership Directory. a.
Annual Meetings: Spring
1987-White Sulphur Springs, WV(Greenbrier)/May 9-13/700
1988-Palm Beach, FL(Breakers)/March 26-30/700
1989-White Sulphur Springs, WV(Greenbrier)/May 13-17/700
1990-White Sulphur Springs, WV(Greenbrier)/May 12-16/700
1991-Palm Beach, FL(Breakers)/March 23-27/700

Protestant Church-Owned Publishers Ass'n (1951)
P.O. Box 801, Nashville TN 37202
Exec. Secretary: Harold L. Fair
Members: 33 publishing houses *Staff:* 2-5
Annual Budget: $25-50,000 *Tel:* (615) 749-6405
Hist. Note: Trade association of church-owned publishing houses, incorporated in Pennsylvania.
Publication:
The Round Table. m.
Biennial Meetings: February or March

Psi Omega (1892)
1030 Lincoln Ave., Prospect Park PA 19076
Exec. Director: Edward M. Grosse
Members: 24-25,000 individuals *Staff:* 2-5
Annual Budget: $100-250,000 *Tel:* (215) 532-2330
Hist. Note: Professional dental fraternity. Organized at the Baltimore College of Dental Surgery in 1892. Affiliated with the Professional Fraternity Association.
Publication:
The Frater of Psi Omega. q.
Annual Meetings: With American Dental Ass'n

Psychometric Soc. (1935)
ACT Box 168, 2201 North Dodge Street, Iowa City IO 52243
Secretary: Mark Reckase
Members: 1,100-1,200 *Staff:* 2
Annual Budget: $10-25,000 *Tel:* (319) 337-1105
Hist. Note: Founded in Chicago in 1935 and incorporated in New Jersey in 1962. Affiliated with the American Psychological Ass'n and the American Ass'n for the Advancement of Science. Promotes the use of mathematical concepts in testing the theoretical and experimental data of psychology. Membership: $30/year.
Publication:
Psychometrika. q.
Annual Meetings: Spring
1987-Montreal, Quebec/June 17-19/300

Psychonomic Soc. (1959)
Dept. of Psychology, Florida State University, Tallahassee FL 32306
Secy.-Treas.: Michael Rashotte
Members: 2,000 *Staff:* 6-10
Annual Budget: $100-250,000 *Tel:* (904) 644-3511
Hist. Note: Members are psychologists conducting or supervising research.
Publications:
Animal Learning and Behavior. q.
Behavior Research Methods, Instruments and Computers. bi-m.
Bulletin of The Psychonomic Society. bi-m.
Memory and Cognition. bi-m.
Perception and Psychophysics. m.
Physiological Psychology. q.
Annual Meetings: November/1,000
1987-Seattle, WA
1988-Chicago, IL

Public Affairs Council (1954)
1255 23rd St., N.W., Suite 750, Washington DC 20037
President: Richard A. Armstrong
Members: 455 corporate members, 30 individuals *Staff:* 11-15
Annual Budget: $500-1,000,000 *Tel:* (202) 872-1790
Hist. Note: Formed as the Effective Citizens Organization, it assumed its present name in 1965. The Council is a bi-partisan organization of corporate public affairs officers. It serves its members through a clearinghouse of information on programs and problems, counseling, workshops and conferences, publications and job referral. Membership is largely by company. Affiliated with the Foundation for Public Affairs. Membership: $1,000-1,200/yr.
Publications:
IMPACT. m.
Directory of Public Affairs Officers. bi-a. (For & of members only)
Annual Meetings: Periodically

Public Agency Risk Managers Ass'n (1974)
5750 Almaden Expressway, San Jose CA 95118
Secy.-Treas.: Ben C. Francis
Members: 300 public and private agencies *Staff:* 1
Annual Budget: $10-25,000 *Tel:* (408) 265-2600
Hist. Note: A forum for public agencies (cities, counties, universities, school districts, special districts) and associate members to discuss and exchange ideas for the improvement and functioning of risk management within governmental agencies.
Publication:
Parmafacts. m.
Annual Meetings: January

Public Employees Roundtable (1982)
Interstate Commerce Commission, 1201 Connecticut Ave., N.W., Rm. 1220-NW, Washington DC 20423
Chairman: G. Jerry Shaw
Members: 25 associations *Staff:* 1
Annual Budget: $25-50,000 *Tel:* (202) 535-4324
Hist. Note: The Roundtable is composed of 25 association representing 750,000 public employees. Its purposes are to: inform the American citizenry of the quality of people in government and the value of the services they perform; develop a stronger espirit de corps among public service employees; and encourage interest in civil service careers.
Publication:
Unsung Heroes. q.

Public Housing Authorities Directors Ass'n (1979)
444 N. Capitol St., N.W., Suite 614, Washington DC 20001
Exec. Director: Wallace Johnson
Members: 800 *Staff:* 2-5
Annual Budget: $100-250,000 *Tel:* (202) 624-5445
Hist. Note: Association of public housing agency executive directors. Membership: $60-500/yr. (based on agency size).
Publication:
News Notes. semi-m.
Annual Meetings: May/June

Public Interest Computer Ass'n (1984)
2001 O St., N.W., Washington DC 20036
Exec. Director: Denise Jesuvio
Members: 200 organizations *Staff:* 3
Annual Budget: $100-250,000 *Tel:* (202) 775-1588
Hist. Note: A non-profit, tax-exempt educational organization dedicated to helping the nonprofit community make effective use of microcomputer-based information technology. PICA members are concentrated in the Washington, DC area. Membership: $100-150/yr.
Publications:
PICA Newsletter. 11/yr.
Resource Notebook. q.

Public Library Ass'n (1944)
50 East Huron St., Chicago IL 60611
Exec. Director: Eleanor Jo Rodger
Members: 5,600 *Staff:* 5
Annual Budget: $250-500,000 *Tel:* (312) 944-6780
Hist. Note: A division of the American Library Association, membership in which is a prerequisite. Membership: $25/year.
Publication:
Public Libraries. q. adv.
Annual Meetings: PLA National Conference
1988-April

Public Offender Counselors Ass'n (1975)
5999 Stevenson Ave., Alexandria VA 22304
Exec. Director (AACD): Dr. Patrick J. McDonough
Members: 900-1,000 *Staff:* 1
Annual Budget: under $10,000 *Tel:* (703) 823-9800
Hist. Note: An organizational affiliate of the American Ass'n for Counseling and Development. Membership: $10/yr.
Publications:
Journal of Offender Counseling. bi-a.
POCA Report. bi-m.
Annual Meetings: With the American Ass'n for Counseling and Development.
1987-New Orleans, LA/April 22-25

Public Relations Soc. of America (1947)
845 Third Ave., New York NY 10022
Exec. V. President: Elizabeth Ann Kovacs, CAE
Members: 13,216 *Staff:* 35-40
Annual Budget: $2-5,000,000 *Tel:* (212) 826-1750
Hist. Note: The major professional association of public relations practitioners in the U.S. Absorbed the American Public Relations Ass'n in 1961, the Nat'l Communication Council for Human Services in 1976, and the Academy of Hospital Public Relations in 1986. Membership: $150/yr.

00261 12 05 86 1233

Publications:
Public Relations Journal. m. adv.
Public Relations Journal/Register Issue. a. adv.
Annual Meetings: November/1,500
1987-Los Angeles, CA(Bonaventure)
1988-Cincinnati, OH(Clarion Hotel and Convention Ctr.)
1989-Dallas, TX(Loew's Anatole)
1990-New York, NY(Marriott Marquis)

Public Risk and Insurance Management Ass'n (1978)
1120 G St., N.W., Suite 400, Washington DC 20005
Exec. Director: Natalie Wasserman
Members: 1,350 *Staff:* 2-5
Annual Budget: $500-1,000,000 *Tel:* (202) 626-4650
Hist. Note: Members are risk managers in municipal and state governments.
Publications:
Public Risk Magazine.
RiskWatch Newsletter.
Annual Meetings: May/June

Public Securities Ass'n (1977)
40 Broad St., New York NY 10004
Exec. Director: Heather L. Ruth
Members: 300 *Staff:* 30
Annual Budget: over $5,000,000 *Tel:* (212) 809-7000
Hist. Note: Members are dealers and dealer banks who underwrite and trade federal, state and local government securities and mortgage-backed securities. Absorbed the Government Guaranteed Loan Dealers Ass'n in 1980 and the Ass'n of Primary Dealers in U.S. Government Securities in 1983. Maintains a Washington, DC office. Has an annual budget of approximately $7 million.
Publications:
Government Securities Newsletter. irreg.
Mortgage-Backed Securities Newsletter. irreg.
Municipal Market Developments. m.
Municipal Securities Newsletter. m.
Washington Newsletter. semi-m.
Annual Meetings: October/700
1987-Phoenix, AZ(Biltmore)
1988-Grand Cypress, FL(Hyatt Regency)
1989-Phoenix, AZ(Biltmore)
1990-Boca Raton, FL(Hotel & Club)
1991-Phoenix, AZ(Biltmore)

Public Service Satellite Consortium (1975)
600 Maryland Ave., S.W., Suite 220, Washington DC 20024
President: Louis A. Bransford
Members: 100 *Staff:* 15
Annual Budget: $1-2,000,000 *Tel:* (202) 863-0890
Hist. Note: Public service organizations interested in seeing low-cost audio and data telecommunications services developed through efficient use of satellite systems. Membership includes hospitals, universities, associations and state telecommunications authorities. Maintains offices in Denver and Washington, DC. Membership: $500/yr.
Publication:
Report to Members. bi-m.
Annual Meetings: October

Public Utilities Communicators Ass'n (1922)
122 Decker Drive, New Castle PA 16105
Exec. Director: Walter K. Conover
Members: 375-400 individuals *Staff:* 1
Annual Budget: $25-50,000 *Tel:* (412) 654-1350
Hist. Note: Advertising, public relations and communications directors of public utilities, their agencies and trade allies. Formerly (1977) Public Utilities Advertising Ass'n. Membership: $125/yr.
Publications:
PUCA Communicator/Showcase. q.
Newsletter. 8/yr.
Annual Meetings: 44
June
1987-Miami Beach, FL(Fontainebleau)/June 10-12/200-250
1988-Dallas, TX
1989-Edmonton, Canada
1990-Kansas City, MO

Public Works Historical Soc. (1975)
1313 East 60th St., Chicago IL 60637
Exec. Secretary: Howard Rosen
Members: 1,300 *Staff:* 2-5
Annual Budget: $50-100,000 *Tel:* (312) 667-2200
Hist. Note: Scholars, public agencies, and academic institutions collecting and preserving public works history. Affiliated with the American Public Works Ass'n. Membership: $20/yr. (individual); $35/yr. (public agencies)
Publications:
Newsletter. q.
Essays in Public Works History. a.
Oral Histories. a.
Annual Meetings: In conjunction with Internat'l Public Works Congress & Equipment Show

Publishers' Alliance (1978)
Hist. Note: Reported as defunct in 1984.

Publishers' Publicity Ass'n (1957)
c/o Peter Bedrick Books, 125 E. 23rd St., New York NY 10010
President: Jill Danzig
Members: 250 *Staff:* 1
Annual Budget: $10-25,000 *Tel:* (212) 777-1187
Hist. Note: Founded as the Publishers' Adclub, it assumed its present name in 1963. Membership: $70-110/yr.

Pulp and Paper Machinery Manufacturers' Ass'n (1933)
5313 38th St., N.W., Washington DC 20015
Exec. Director: Frank M. McManus, Jr.
Members: 35 companies *Staff:* 1-2
Annual Budget: $50-100,000 *Tel:* (202) 362-6034
Hist. Note: Formerly (1971) Pulp and Paper Machinery Ass'n. Membership: $750-1,500/yr.
Publication:
Newsletter (for members only). m.
Annual Meetings: Spring
1987-New York, NY/March/50
1988-Atlanta, GA/March/50

Pulp Chemicals Ass'n (1947)
60 East 42nd St., Room 824, New York NY 10165
Exec. Director: Douglas E. Campbell
Members: 25-30 *Staff:* 2-5
Annual Budget: $100-250,000 *Tel:* (212) 697-4816
Hist. Note: Membership consists of international manufacturers of chemical products (other than pulp and paper) produced by or from products of the wood pulp industry.
Annual Meetings: Fall/200-250
1987-San Francisco, CA(Hyatt Regency)/Sept. 21-23/300
1988-Lisbon, Portugal/Oct.

Pulp, Paper and Paperboard Export Ass'n of the U.S. (1952)
528 N. New Street, Suite 200, Bethlehem PA 18018
Manager-Secy-Treas: Robert L. Kerridge
Members: 9 companies *Staff:* 1
Tel: (215) 694-0832
Hist. Note: A Webb-Pomerene Act Ass'n

Pulverized Limestone Ass'n (1954)
Colorado Lien Co., Box 1961, Fort Collins CO 80522
Secy.-Treas.: Paul V. Haerr
Members: 16 companies *Staff:* 1
Annual Budget: $10-25,000 *Tel:* (303) 493-6294
Hist. Note: Membership: $500/yr.
Annual Meetings: Always in Sea Island, GA(The Cloisters)/ October/over50
1987-Oct. 18-21
1988-Oct. 16-19
1989-Oct. 15-18
1990-Oct. 21-24

Purebred Dairy Cattle Ass'n (1940)
P.O. BOx 160, Cabool MO 65689920
Secretary: Bradford E. Ellsworth
Members: 6 cattle breeders ass'ns *Staff:* 1
Annual Budget: under $10,000 *Tel:* (417) 962-3141
Hist. Note: Members are breeders of Ayrshire, Brown-Swiss, Guernsey, Holstein, Milking Shorthorn, and Jersey cattle and dairy cattle breed registry ass'ns.
Annual Meetings: February
1987-Columbus, OH/Feb. 19-20

PVC Belting Manufacturers Ass'n (1973)
1819 H Street, N.W., Suite 630, Washington DC 20006
Exec. Director: Harry J. Lambeth
Members: 8 companies *Staff:* 1
Annual Budget: $10-25,000 *Tel:* (202) 775-1150
Hist. Note: Manufacturers of Poly Vinyl Chloride industrial belts. Above address is that of the law firm of Barton & Lambeth.
Annual Meetings: Semi-annual Meetings

Pyrotechnic Signal Manufacturers Ass'n (1973)
c/o Olin Corp., 1730 K St., N.W., Washington DC 20006
Asst. Secy.-Treas.: Phyllis S. Black
Members: 6-10 companies *Staff:* 2-5
Annual Budget: $10-25,000 *Tel:* (202) 331-7400

Quality Bakers of America Cooperative (1922)
70 Riverdale Ave., Greenwich CT 06830
Interim General Manager: Ernie Stolzer
Members: 80 bakeries *Staff:* 100
Annual Budget: $1-2,000,000 *Tel:* (203) 531-7100
Hist. Note: Members are independent wholesale bakeries and their suppliers.
Annual Meetings: New York, NY in October

Quality Chekd Dairy Products Ass'n (1945)
201 E. Ogden Ave., Hinsdale IL 60521
Mng. Director: Mel W. Rapp
Members: 40-50 *Staff:* 11-15
Annual Budget: $2-5,000,000 *Tel:* (312) 325-0660
Hist. Note: Dairy foods processors who use the Quality Chekd trademark on their products, and engage in group purchasing of ingredients and supplies.
Publication:
Scope. bi-m.

Quality Control Council of America (1986)
P.O. Box 42558, Northwest Station, Washington DC 20015
Exec. Director: Walter M. Kardy
Members: 8 companies *Staff:* 1-2
Annual Budget: $10-25,000 *Tel:* (301) 933-7430
Hist. Note: A group of contractors concerned with non-destructive testing of weldments in piping in power stations and other heavy industrial installations, they engage in quality assurance testing in such installations. Incorporated in Washington, DC. Membership: $2,000-4,000/yr.
Annual Meetings: Spring

Quantum Electronics and Applications Soc.
Hist. Note: A subsidiary of the Institute of Electrical and Electronics Engineers. Membership in the Society, open only to IEEE members, includes subscription to a technical periodical in the field published by IEEE. All administrative support is provided by IEEE.

Race Directors Ass'n (1980)
Hist. Note: Ceased operations in 1983.

Rack Manufacturers Institute (1958)
8720 Red Oak Blvd., Charlotte NC 28210
Management Executive: John B. Nofsinger
Members: 35-40 companies *Staff:* 3
Annual Budget: $25-50,000 *Tel:* (704) 522-8644
Hist. Note: Makers of steel industrial storage racks.
Annual Meetings: Semi-Annual Meetings with Material Handling Institute
1987-Charlotte, NC
1987-Boca Raton, FL(Hotel and Club)/Nov. 6-11
1988-Phoenix, AZ(Biltmore)/Oct. 7-12
1989-Undetermined
1990-Palm Springs, CA(Marriott's Ranchos Las Palmas Resort)/Oct. 19-24

Racking Horse Breeders Ass'n of America (1971)
Route 2, Box 72-A, Decatur AL 35603
President: Joe D. Bright
Members: 3,000 *Staff:* 2-5
Annual Budget: $10-25,000 *Tel:* (205) 353-7225
Hist. Note: Members are persons directly connected with Racking horses and the Racking horse industry.
Publications:
Racking Review. m.
Racking Horse Times.
Annual Meetings: January

Radiation Research Soc. (1952)
925 Chestnut St., Philadelphia PA 19107
Admin. Director: Meg Keiser
Members: 1,700 *Staff:* 2
Tel: (215) 574-3153
Hist. Note: Founded in 1952 and incorporated in the District of Columbia. A professional society of individuals studying radiation and its effects. Affiliated with the Internat'l Ass'n for Radiation Research. Membership: $20/year.
Publications:
Newsletter. q.
Radiation Research. m. adv.
Annual Meetings: Spring
1987-Atanta, GA(Peachtree Plaza)/Feb. 21-26
1988-Philadelphia, PA(Franklin Plaza)/April 15-21/1,000

Radio Advertising Bureau (1951)
304 Park Ave. South, New York NY 10010
President & C.E.O.: William Stakelin
Members: 3,500 *Staff:* 50-60
Annual Budget: over $5,000,000 *Tel:* (212) 599-6666
Hist. Note: Established originally as the Department of Radio Advertising of the National Association of Broadcasters, it became independent in 1951 as the Broadcast Advertising Bureau and assumed its present name in 1955. Members are radio stations, networks and station sales representatives united to promote radio time as a sales medium. Awards the CRMC (Certified Radio Marketing Consultant) designation.
Publication:
Sound Management. m. adv.
Annual Meetings:
1987-Atlanta, GA(Hyatt Regency)/Feb. 7-10/1,300

Radio and Television Correspondents Ass'n (1939)
U.S. Capitol, Room H-320, Washington DC 20515
Chairman: Charles Gibson
Members: 2,000
Annual Budget: $10-25,000 *Tel:* (202) 225-5214
Hist. Note: Formerly (1946) Radio Correspondents Ass'n. Members are correspondents covering Congress. Its sole purpose is to oversee the work of the Senate and House press galleries. Has no paid staff; officers change annually.

Radio-Television News Directors Ass'n (1946)
1717 K St., N.W., Suite 615, Washington DC 20006
Exec. V. President: Ernie Schultz
Members: 3,000 *Staff:* 7
Annual Budget: $1-2,000,000 *Tel:* (202) 659-6510
Hist. Note: Member of the Council of Communication Societies.
Publication:
RTNDA Communicator. m. adv.
Annual Meetings: Fall
1987-Orlando, FL/Sept. 1-4

00262 12 05 86 1233

Radiological Soc. of North America (1915)
Oak Brook Regency Towers, 1415 West 22nd St., Tower B, Oak Brook IL 60521
Exec. Director: Mary Ann Tuft, CAE
Members: 19,000 *Staff:* 36
Annual Budget: over $5,000,000 *Tel:* (312) 576-2670
Hist. Note: Founded as the Western Roentgen Society and assumed its present name in 1915. Members are individuals interested in the application of radiology to medicine.
Publications:
Radiology. m. adv.
RadioGraphics. q.
Annual Meetings: Always in Chicago at McCormick Place in November/29,000
1987-Nov. 29-Dec. 4
1988-Nov. 27-Dec. 2
1989-Nov. 12-17

Radiologists' Business Managers Ass'n (1968)
8047 Parallel Parkway #7, Kansas City KS 66112
Exec. Director: Nancy L. Story
Members: 1,100 *Staff:* 2
Annual Budget: $100-250,000 *Tel:* (913) 299-2805
Hist. Note: Strives for improvement of radiology practice management through management education and study of practice ecomonics, legislative issues and consumer trends. Membership: $155/yr.
Publications:
The RBMA Bulletin. m.
Radiology Business Journal. q. adv.
Annual Meetings: May/300-400
1987-San Antonio, TX(Hilton Palacio Del Rio)/May 3-6
1988-New York, NY(Waldorf Astoria)/April 20-24
1989-Colorado Springs, CO(Broadmoor)/May 17-21

Railroad Public Relations Ass'n (1952)
50 F St., N.W., Washington DC 20001
Secy.-Treas.: Diane S. Liebman
Members: 150-175 individuals
Annual Budget: $10-25,000 *Tel:* (202) 639-2545
Hist. Note: Organized to strengthen effectiveness of public relations activities of the railroads at a time when the industry was being challenged by alternative means of transportation. Includes railroad public relations officers, public relations officers from allied industries and editors of railroad industry publications. Membership: $50/yr.
Publication:
Interline. bi-m.
Annual Meetings: June
1987-White Sulphur Springs, WV(Greenbrier)/June 21-24

Railroad Yardmasters of America
Hist. Note: Merged with United Transportation Union in 1985 and became the Yardmasters Dept./UTU.

Railway Automotive Management Ass'n (1966)
1160 Raymond Blvd., Newark NJ 07102
Coordinator: Lima Perreira
Members: 50 fleet managers
Annual Budget: $25-50,000 *Tel:* (201) 648-7750
Hist. Note: Dedicated to the safe, efficient, and economic operation of railroad fleets. Membership available to fleet representatives from all railroads in the U.S. and Canada.
Annual Meetings: May

Railway Engineering-Maintenance Suppliers Ass'n (1965)
6120 West North Ave., Suite 202A, Chicago IL 60639
Exec. Secretary: J.J. Stallmann
Members: 290 *Staff:* 2
Annual Budget: $100-250,000 *Tel:* (312) 622-6653
Hist. Note: Merger (1965) of Nat'l Railway Appliance Ass'n (Est. 1894) and Ass'n of Track and Structures Suppliers (Est. 1914). Members are distributors and manufacturers of railway track machinery and supplies.
Publication:
Newsletter. q.
Semi-Annual Meetings: Spring and Fall
1987-Chicago, IL(Palmer House)/March/900
1987-Kansas City, MO(Westin Crowne Center)/Sept./600
1988-Chicago, IL(Palmer House)/March/900
1988-Chicago, IL(Palmer House)/Sept./600
1989-Chicago, IL(Palmer House)/March/900
1989-Toronto,Ontario(Metro Convention Center)/Aug./3,000

Railway Fuel and Operating Officers Ass'n (1892)
Box 1189, Champaign IL 61820
Secy.-Treas.: W. N. Hull
Members: 1,200-1,300 *Staff:* 1
Annual Budget: $10-25,000 *Tel:* (217) 586-3705
Hist. Note: The oldest of the railroad professional associations, RFOOA was founded as the Traveling Engineers Association. It merged in 1936 with the Railway Fuel Association to become the Railway Fuel and Traveling Engineers Association and assumed the present name in 1956. Incorporated in the State of Connecticut in 1981. Membership: $20/yr.
Publications:
The Manifest. bi-m.
Annual Book of Proceedings. a. adv.
Annual Meetings:
1987-Chicago, IL(Hilton)/Sept. 13-16
1988-Chicago, IL(Hilton)/Sept. 17-22
1989-Atlanta, GA(Hilton)

Railway Labor Executives Ass'n (1926)
400 First St., N.W., Washington DC 20001
Exec. Secy.-Treas.: Andrew M. Ripp
Members: 18 *Staff:* 2-5
Annual Budget: $50-100,000 *Tel:* (202) 737-1541
Hist. Note: Composed of the chief executive officers of railway labor organizations. Affiliated with AFL-CIO Sponsors and supports the Railway Labor Executives Association Political League.

Railway Progress Institute (1908)
700 North Fairfax St., Alexandria VA 22314
President: Robert A. Matthews
Members: 150 companies *Staff:* 6-10
Annual Budget: $500-1,000,000 *Tel:* (703) 836-2332
Hist. Note: The trade association of the railway equipment and supply industry. Formerly (1956) Railway Business Ass'n. Membership: $500-13,350/yr. (company).
Publications:
Railway Progress News. m.
Annual Report. a.
Washington Report. m.
Annual Meetings: Fall/900
1987-Washington, DC(Hilton)/Nov. 5
1988-Chicago, IL(Hilton)/Sept. 21-22
1989-Washington, DC(Hilton)/Nov. 9

Railway Supply Ass'n (1962)
1150 Wilmette Ave., Office #3, Wilmette IL 60091
Exec. Director: William J. Burrows
Members: 350-370 *Staff:* 1
Annual Budget: $50-100,000 *Tel:* (312) 251-5476
Hist. Note: Merger of Allied Railway Supply Ass'n (1931) and Railway Electrical and Mechanical Supply Ass'n (1909). Principally coordinators of railway supply exhibitions.
Annual Meetings: Chicago, in Fall
1987-(Conrad Hilton)/Sept. 13-16/2,000
1988-(Conrad Hilton)/Sept. 18-21/5,000
1989-(Conrad Hilton)/Sept. 17-20/2,500

Railway Systems Suppliers (1906)
561 Middlesex Ave., Suite 5, Metuchen NJ 08840
Exec. Director: W. Edward Rowland
Members: 162 companies *Staff:* 2
Annual Budget: $100-250,000 *Tel:* (201) 494-2910
Hist. Note: Merger (1961) of the Railway Communications Suppliers Ass'n and Signal Appliance Ass'n. Formerly (1971) Railway Signal and Communications Suppliers Ass'n, and (1977) Railway Systems Suppliers Ass'n, Inc.
Publications:
Modern Railroads. adv.
Progressive Railroading. adv.
Railway Age. m. adv.
International Railway Journal.
Annual Meetings: Fall
1987-Pittsburgh, PA(Hilton)/Oct. 11-14/1,500

Railway Tie Ass'n (1919)
314 North Broadway, Rm. 1040, St. Louis MO 63102
Exec. Secretary: D.B. Mabry
Members: 575 companies *Staff:* 2-5
Annual Budget: $50-100,000 *Tel:* (314) 231-8099
Hist. Note: Formerly the Nat'l Ass'n of Railroad Tie Producers. Membership is comprised of crosstie producers, sawmill owners, wood preservation companies railroad maintenance engineers, purchasing officials and others interested in the manufacture and procurement of wood railroad ties.
Publication:
Crossties Magazine. m. adv.
Annual Meetings: Fall
1987-New Orleans, LA(Royal Orleans)/Sept. 23-25/300

Real Estate Aviation Chapter (1948)
5440 St. Charles Road, Berkeley IL 60163-1287
Director: Warren J. Haeger
Members: 125 *Staff:* 1
Annual Budget: under $10,000 *Tel:* (312) 547-7100
Hist. Note: Formerly (1976) the Nat'l Real Estate Fliers Ass'n and (until 1978) the Real Estate Aviation Council. Main objective is to educate members and the public on the economic and social impact of aviation on cities, land values and uses and real estate ownership. A chapter of the Farm and Land Institute of the National Association of Realtors. Membership. $25/yr. (individual).
Publication:
Flight Lines. q.
Annual Meetings: With the Nat'l Ass'n of Realtors

Real Estate Educators Ass'n (1979)
230 North Michigan Ave., Suite 1200, Chicago IL 60601
Exec. Director: George Otto
Members: 1,000 *Staff:* 2-5
Annual Budget: $50-100,000 *Tel:* (312) 372-9800
Hist. Note: Members are individuals involved in all types of real estate training and education. Membership: $45/yr. (individual); $100/yr. (organization/company)
Publications:
REEAction. q. adv.
Proceedings. a.
Conference Journal. a. adv.
Annual Meetings: May
1987-Chicago, IL/May 20-22
1988-Houston, TX
1989-Chicago, IL

Real Estate Securities and Syndication Institute (1971)
430 North Michigan Ave., Chicago IL 60611-4091
Exec. V. President: Mary Walker Fleischmann
Members: 4,000 individuals *Staff:* 15-20
Annual Budget: $1-2,000,000 *Tel:* (312) 670-6760
Hist. Note: Established in 1972 as an affiliate of the Nat'l Ass'n of Realtors, RESSI represents a membership of over 4,000 individuals and/or firms who are specialists in the creation, issuance, analysis, promotion, marketing, and management of real estate securities. Membership: $320/yr. (individual); company fee based on revenues.
Publications:
RESSI Review. m.
Real Estate Securities Journal. 3/yr. adv.
RESSI Membership Directory. a. adv.
Annual Meetings: November
1987-Honolulu, HI(Hawaiian Regency)/Nov. 10-15
1988-Dallas, TX(Holiday Inn Union Square)/Nov. 10-15
1989-Dallas, TX(Plaza of the Americas)/Nov. 9-14
1990-New Orleans, LA(Monteleone)/Nov. 8-13

Real Estate Trainers Ass'n Internat'l (1979)
Hist. Note: Ceased to operate in 1982.

REALTORS Land Institute (1944)
430 North Michigan Ave., Chicago IL 60611
Exec V. President: Linda J. Thompson
Members: 4,000 individuals *Staff:* 6-10
Annual Budget: $500-1,000,000 *Tel:* (312) 329-8440
Hist. Note: Formerly (1975) Nat'l Institute of Farm and Land Brokers and (1986) Farm and Land Institute, RLI is an affiliate of the Nat'l Ass'n of REALTORS. Members are those interested in the development and sale of all types of land. Offers the Accredited Farm and Land Member (AFLM) designation.
Publications:
Land Realtor. m.
Membership Roster. a.
Annual Meetings: With Nat'l Ass'n of REALTORS
1987-Honolulu, HI
1988-San Francisco, CA

Realtors Nat'l Marketing Institute (1923)
430 N. Michigan Ave., Suite 500, Chicago IL 60611
V. President, Administration: Nanci Gentile
Members: 24,500 *Staff:* 65
Annual Budget: over $5,000,000 *Tel:* (312) 670-3780
Hist. Note: Formerly (1975) Nat'l Institute of Real Estate Brokers. Affiliated with the Nat'l Ass'n of Realtors.
Publications:
Real Estate Business. q.
Commercial-Investment Journal. q.
Annual Meetings: With Nat'l Ass'n of REALTORS
1987-Honolulu, HI/Nov. 12-17

Reclaim Managers Ass'n (1981)
478 W. Hamilton Ave., Suite 223, Campbell CA 95008
President: Jill Hayashida
Members: 35-40 companies *Staff:* 5
Annual Budget: under $10,000 *Tel:* (408) 982-6755
Hist. Note: Promotes the recovery of reusable resources generated by electronic and other companies. Membership: $100/yr.
Annual Meetings: June

Recognition Technologies Users Ass'n (1970)
Box 2016, Manchester Center VT 05255
Exec. Director: Franklin Cooper
Members: 500 companies *Staff:* 2-5
Annual Budget: $100-250,000 *Tel:* (802) 362-4151
Hist. Note: Users and marketers of data processing equipment for optical character, mark read, optical bar code, magnetic ink character, image and voice recognition technologies. Formerly (1982) the Optical Character Recognition Users Association.
Publications:
Recognition Technology Today. bi-m.
Recognition Technology Today Buyer's Guide. a. adv.
Semi-annual meetings: Winter and Summer
1987-Ft. Lauderdale, FL(Harbor Beach)/Jan. 11-14
1987-San Francisco, CA(Hyatt Regency)/Aug. 2-5
1988-Scottsdale, AZ(Camelback)/Jan. 10-13
1988-Philadelphia, PA(Adams Mark)/July 24-27
1989-Ft. Lauderdale, FL(Marriott Marina)/Jan. 15-18

Recording Industry Ass'n of America (1952)
888 Seventh Ave., 9th Floor, New York NY 10106
President: Jason S. Berman
Members: 40 companies *Staff:* 22
Annual Budget: $2-5,000,000 *Tel:* (212) 765-4330
Hist. Note: Makers of phonograph and video discs as well as pre-recorded tapes. Formerly (1970) Record Industry Ass'n of America. Major thrust is combating unauthorized copying ("piracy") of recorded material. RIAA will be moving to Washington, DC in early 1987.

Recreation Vehicle Dealers Ass'n of North America (1968)
3251 Old Lee Hwy., Suite 500, Fairfax VA 22030
Exec. V. President: Robert Strawn
Members: 940-950 *Staff:* 7
Annual Budget: $500-1,000,000 *Tel:* (703) 591-7130
Hist. Note: Absorbed (1969) Recreational Dealer Ass'n; formerly (1970) Recreation Vehicle Dealers Institute, and (1976) the Recreational Vehicle Dealers of America, Inc.

00263 12 05 86 1233

Publications:
Legislative Bulletin. m.
RV Rental Directory. semi-a.
RVDA News. m. adv.
Annual Meetings: Fall
1987-New Orleans, LA
1988-Houston, TX

Recreation Vehicle Industry Ass'n (1963)
1896 Preston White Drive, Reston VA 22090
President: David J. Humphreys
Members: 615 companies *Staff:* 30-35
Annual Budget: $2-5,000,000 *Tel:* (703) 620-6003
Hist. Note: Established in 1963 as the Recreational Vehicle Institute, Inc. Merged in 1968 with Camping Trailer Manufacturers Ass'n and American Institute of Travel Trailer and Camper Manufacturers, Inc. The name was changed in 1975 to Recreation Vehicle Industry Ass'n. Members are manufacturers of motor homes, travel trailers, truck campers, fold-down camping trailers, pick-up covers and van converters as well as suppliers of RV component parts.
Publications:
RVIA Marketing Report. m.
RV Road Signs. q.
Directory. a.
Year End Report. a.
Annual Meetings: February

Recreation Vehicle Rental Ass'n (1982)
3251 Old Lee Hwy., Suite 500, Fairfax VA 22030
Exec. Director: Robert J. Strawn
Members: 200 companies *Staff:* 1
Annual Budget: $10-25,000 *Tel:* (703) 591-7130
Hist. Note: Established in Washington, DC on March 10, 1982 by 18 founding members as a division of the Recreation Vehicle Dealers Ass'n of North America. Staff support is provided by RVDA to which all members of RVRA belong.
Publication:
Who's Who in RV Rentals. semi-a.
Annual Meetings: With The Recreation Vehicle Dealers Ass'n

Recreational Vehicle Club Directors Ass'n (1973)
Hist. Note: Inactive as of 1983.

Red Angus Ass'n of America (1954)
4201 I-35 North, Denton TX 76201
Exec. Director: Lyle V. Springer
Members: 1,000 *Staff:* 6-10
Annual Budget: $250-500,000 *Tel:* (817) 387-3502
Hist. Note: Members are breeders and improvers of Red Angus Beef Cattle. Member of: Nat'l Pedigree Livestock Council; Nat'l Cattlemen's Ass'n; U.S. Beef Breeds Council; and Beef Improvement Federation. Membership: $40 to join, then $50 plus $1 per animal/yr.
Publication:
American Red Angus. m. adv.
Annual Meetings: Fall
1987-Reno, NV/Sept./100

Red Cedar Shingle and Handsplit Shake Bureau (1915)
515 116th Ave., N.E., Suite 275, Bellevue WA 98004
President and C.E.O.: Michael M. Westfall
Members: 300-350 *Staff:* 25-30
Annual Budget: $1-2,000,000 *Tel:* (206) 453-1323
Hist. Note: Founded in 1915 as Shingle Branch of West Coast Lumber Manufacturers Ass'n. Incorporated as the Red Cedar Shingle Bureau in 1926. Absorbed (1963) the Hand Split Red Cedar Shake Ass'n.
Annual Meetings: 3rd Friday of Sept. in Seattle

Refractories Institute (1951)
301 Fifth Avenue, Suite 1517, Pittsburgh PA 15222
President: Mark S. Gleeson
Members: 100 companies *Staff:* 5
Annual Budget: $500-1,000,000 *Tel:* (412) 281-6787
Hist. Note: Incorporated in 1951 as the national trade association for refractory manufacturers, suppliers of equipment and raw material. Refractories are heat-resistant materials that are used for lining high-temperature furnaces and reactors. Membership: $1,200/yr.
Annual Meetings: June
1987-Ponte Vedra, CA(Ponte Vedra Country Club)
1988-Kiawha Island, SC
1989-White Sulphur Springs, WV(Greenbrier)
1990-Ponte Vedra, CA(Ponte Vedra Country Club)

Refractory Metals Ass'n (1970)
Hist. Note: Producers of powders and products made from tungsten, molybdenum, tatalum and niobium. Formerly (1975) Refractory and Reactive Metals Ass'n. A constituent member of the Metal Powder Industries Federation.

Refrigerating Engineers and Technicians Ass'n (1910)
230 North Michigan Ave., Room 1200, Chicago IL 60601
Managing Director: Kenneth B. Andersen, CAE
Members: 1,900-2,000 *Staff:* 2-5
Annual Budget: $50-100,000 *Tel:* (312) 853-0432
Hist. Note: Formerly Nat'l Ass'n of Practical Refrigerating Engineers. Designers, installers, operators and maintainers of central refrigeration and air conditioning equipment. Membership: $25/yr. (individual); $75/yr. (company).
Publication:
RETA Breeze. q.
Annual Meetings: November
1987-Baltimore, MD(Sheraton)/Nov. 4-7/175

Refrigeration Service Engineers Soc. (1933)
1666 Rand Rd., Des Plaines IL 60016
Exec. V. President: Nari Sethna
Members: 29,000 *Staff:* 16-20
Annual Budget: $1-2,000,000 *Tel:* (312) 297-6464
Hist. Note: Membership: $25/yr.
Publication:
Refrigeration Service and Contracting. m.
Annual Meetings: Fall
1987-Norfolk, VA/Nov. 12-15
1988-New Orleans, LA/Nov. 3-5
1989-Omaha, NE(Holiday Inn)/Oct. 19-21
1990-Honolulu, HI

Regional Airline Ass'n (1968)
1101 Connecticut Ave., N.W., Suite 700, Washington DC 20036
President: Duane H. Ekedahl
Members: 150-200 companies and organizations *Staff:* 6-10
Annual Budget: $500-1,000,000 *Tel:* (202) 857-1170
Hist. Note: In 1968 the Ass'n of Commuter Airlines merged with the Nat'l Air Taxi Conference to form what became the Nat'l Air Transportation Conferences and, later, the Nat'l Air Transportation Ass'ns. In 1975 this group again became independent under the name Commuter Airline Ass'n of America until 1981 when it assumed its present name. A regional, or commuter, airline is one whose planes carry 60 or fewer passengers. Members consists of more than 100 carriers, plus associates and affiliates.
Publication:
Times Magazine.
Semi-annual meetings: Spring and Fall/2-300

Regional and Distribution Carriers Conference (1943)
2200 Mill Road, Alexandria VA 22314
Exec. Director: Warren H. Wiedhahn
Members: 370 *Staff:* 6
Annual Budget: $250-500,000 *Tel:* (703) 838-1990
Hist. Note: Affiliate of American Trucking Ass'ns. Formerly (1982) the Local and Short Haul Carriers National Conference. Members are "for-hire motor common carriers of general (mixed) freight in packaged lots."
Publication:
The Grapevine. m. adv.
Annual Meetings: Spring/250
1988-San Antonio, TX(Hyatt Regency)/April 20-24

Regional Orchestra Managers Ass'n
Hist. Note: A sub-group of the American Symphony Orchestra League without dues structure or separate headquarters.

Regional Science Ass'n (1954)
Dept. of Geography, University of Illinois, Champaign-Urbana IL 61801
Secretary: Dr. G. Hewings
Members: 2,500
Tel: (217) 333-1880
Hist. Note: Members are professionals concerned with urban and regional planning.
Publications:
Int'l Regional Science Review. 2-3/yr.
Papers, RSA. semi-a.
Annual Meetings: November

Registered Mail Insurance Ass'n (1921)
127 John St., New York NY 10038
Manager: Jane B. Hotchkiss
Members: 12 *Staff:* 8
Annual Budget: $250-500,000 *Tel:* (212) 363-2950
Hist. Note: A joint operation of insurance companies to provide insurance for shipments of currency, securities and other valuables. Formerly the Registered Mail Central Bureau.

Regular Common Carrier Conference (1939)
2200 Mill Road, Suite 350, Alexandria VA 22314
Exec. Director: James C. Harkins
Members: 375 *Staff:* 11-15
Annual Budget: $1-2,000,000 *Tel:* (703) 838-1967
Hist. Note: RCCC is the only national organization created solely to serve the needs of highway common carriers of general commodity freight. Affiliated with the American Trucking Ass'ns, Inc., yet is still an autonomous organization.
Publications:
Highway Common Carrier Newsletter. semi-m.
Motor Carrier Computer News. m.
Semi-annual meetings: Fall and Winter/400
1987-San Diego, CA/Feb. 8-12 and New York, NY/Oct. 23-27

Regulatory Affairs Professionals Soc. (1976)
1100 Connecticut Ave., N.W., Suite 700, Washington DC 20036
Director of Meetings: Lori Engle
Members: 1,350 *Staff:* 2-5
Annual Budget: $250-500,000 *Tel:* (202) 857-1148
Hist. Note: Members are management personnel, lawyers and consultants from drug, medical supply, cosmetic and health care related industries who work with the Food and Drug Administration and other regulatory agencies. Incorporated in the District of Columbia. Membership: $70/year.
Publications:
RAPS Internat'l News. bi-m.
Membership Directory. a.
Annual Meetings: September in Washington, DC

Rehabilitation Nursing Institute
Hist. Note: The educational and research arm of the Association of Rehabilitation Nurses.

Reinforced Concrete Research Council (1948)
5420 Old Orchard Rd., Skokie IL 60077
Secretary: Anthony E. Fiorato
Members: 35-40 individuals *Staff:* 0
Annual Budget: $10-25,000 *Tel:* (312) 966-6200
Hist. Note: Affiliated with American Society of Civil Engineers. Has no paid staff.
Publication:
RCRC Bulletins. irreg.
Annual Meetings: Late August in Skokie, IL/25-30.

Reinsurance Ass'n of America (1968)
1025 Connecticut Ave., N.W., Suite 512, Washington DC 20036
President: Andre Maisonpierre
Members: 27 companies *Staff:* 9
Annual Budget: $1-2,000,000 *Tel:* (202) 293-3335
Hist. Note: Incorporated in the District of Columbia as the Nat'l Ass'n of Property and Casualty Reinsurers. Became the Reinsurance Ass'n of America in 1970.
Annual Meetings: May

Reliability Soc.
Hist. Note: A subsidiary of the Institute of Electrical and Electronics Engineers. Membership in the Society, open only to IEEE members, includes subscription to a technical periodical in the field published by IEEE. All administrative support is provided by IEEE.

Religion Newswriters Ass'n of U.S. and Canada (1949)
Dallas Morning News, Communications Center, Dallas TX 75265
President: Helen Parmley
Members: 250 individuals
Annual Budget: $10-25,000 *Tel:* (214) 977-8222
Hist. Note: A professional association of journalists covering religion for the secular press. Has no permanent address. Officers change every two years. Membership: $25/yr.
Publication:
News Letter. bi-m.

Religious Conference Management Ass'n (1972)
One Hoosier Dome, Suite 120, Indianapolis IN 46225
Exec. Director: Dr. DeWayne S. Woodring
Members: 650 *Staff:* 3
Annual Budget: $100-250,000 *Tel:* (317) 632-1888
Hist. Note: Non-profit international organization of men and women who have responsibility for planning and/or managing meetings, seminars, conferences, conventions, assemblies, or other gatherings for religious organizations. Formerly (1982) the Religious Convention Managers Ass'n. Membership: $50/yr.
Publications:
"RCMA Highlights" published in Convention World. bi-m. adv.
Who's Who in Religious Conference Management. a.
Annual Meetings: January
1987-Long Beach, CA(Hyatt)/Jan. 27-30/650
1988-Rochester, NY(Hyatt)/Jan. 26-29/675
1989-Milwaukee, WI(Hyatt)/Jan. 24-27

Religious Education Ass'n (1903)
409 Prospect St., New Haven CT 06511-2177
Exec. Secretary: Dorothy Savage
Members: 3,000 individuals, 1,400 libraries *Staff:* 2-5
Annual Budget: $100-250,000 *Tel:* (203) 865-6141
Hist. Note: Founded in Chicago by William Rainey Harper to promote religious and moral education. Membership: $35/year.
Publications:
REACH. q.
Religious Education. q. adv.

Religious Public Relations Council (1929)
357 Righters Mill Road, P.O. Box 315, Gladwyne PA 19035
Exec. Secretary: Anne M. Reimel
Members: 750 *Staff:* 52
Annual Budget: $50-100,000 *Tel:* (215) 642-8895
Hist. Note: Founded in Washington, DC, RPRC membership is open to individuals devoting a major portion of their service in professional public relations to any religious communion, organization or related agency. Formerly the Religious Publicity Council. Membership: $75/yr.
Publications:
The Counselor. q.
The MediaKit.
Annual Meetings: April
1987-Philaelphia, PA(Sheraton University)/April 7-10
1988-Dallas, TX
1989-Washington, DC
1990-Nashville, TN

Religious Speech Communication Ass'n (1973)
Manhattan Christian College, Manhattan KS 66502
Exec. Secretary: Franklin Karns
Members: 200-250 individuals and institutions *Staff:* 1

00264 12 05 86 1233

Annual Budget: under $10,000 *Tel:* (913) 539-3571
Hist. Note: Promotes oral religious communication. Until 1973 was the Religious Speech Division of the Speech Communication Association. Membership: $15/yr.(individual); $50/yr.(institution).
Publications:
Religious Communication Today. a. adv.
Homiletic. semi-a. adv.
RSCA Newsletter. 3/yr.
Annual Meetings: With the Speech Communication Association
1987-Boston, MA/Nov. 5-8
1988-New Orleans, LA/Nov. 3-6
1989-San Francisco, CA/Nov. 18-21

Relocation Assistance Ass'n of America
Hist. Note: Became American on the Move in 1986.

Renaissance Soc. of America (1954)
1161 Amsterdam Ave., New York NY 10027
Exec. Director: Eugence F. Rice, Jr.
Members: 2,800 *Staff:* 2-5
Annual Budget: $50-100,000 *Tel:* (212) 280-2318
Hist. Note: A professional society of scholars of the Renaissance. Member of the American Council of Learned Societies. Membership: $35/yr. (individual); $45/yr. (organization/company)
Publication:
Renaissance Quarterly. q. adv.
Annual Meetings: March
1987-Tempe, AZ(Arizona State Univ.)/March 12-14
1988-New York, NY(Columbia Univ.)/March 17-19
1989-Cambridge, MA(Harvard Univ.)

Renewable Fuels Ass'n (1981)
225 Pennsylvania Ave., S.E., Third Floor, Washington DC 20003
President: Eric Vaughn
Members: 50-60 *Staff:* 2-5
Annual Budget: $100-250,000 *Tel:* (202) 543-3802
Hist. Note: Members are companies and individuals interested in the development of renewable fuels such as ethanol and methane. Membership Fee: Based on capacity for producers.
Publications:
RFA Newsletter. m.
Conference Proceedings. a.
Annual Meetings: Fall

Renewable Natural Resources Foundation (1972)
5410 Grosvenor Lane, Bethesda MD 20814
Exec. Director: Robert D. Day
Members: 10 professional societies *Staff:* 2-5
Annual Budget: $500-1,000,000 *Tel:* (301) 493-9101
Hist. Note: A federation of 10 professional societies whose members are directly concerned with the advancement of research, education, scientific practice and policy formulation for the conservation, replenishment and use of the earth's renewable natural resources. The member societies are: Ass'n for Conservation Information; American Fisheries Soc.; American Geophysical Union; American Water Resources Ass'n; Ecological Soc. of America; Soc. for Range Management; The Wildlife Soc.; American Soc. for Photogrammetry and Remote Sensing; The Coastal Soc.; and Resources for the Future. Incorporated in the District of Columbia in January, 1972. Membership: $50/yr. (individual); $100/yr. (organization/company)
Publication:
Renewable Resources Journal. q.
Annual Meetings: Nov./Dec.

Renown Shippers (1980)
303 Brookside Ave., Redlands CA 92373
Members: 13 companies
Hist. Note: A Webb-Pomerene Act association.

Research and Development Associates for Military Food and Packaging Systems (1946)
103 Biltmore Drive, Suite 106, San Antonio TX 78213
Exec. Director: Col. Merton Singer, USA (Ret.)
Members: 350-400 *Staff:* 3-5
Annual Budget: $100-250,000 *Tel:* (512) 344-5773
Hist. Note: Founded as a forum for the interchange of technical data on food products, feeding systems, food and feeding equipment and food packaging between industry and professors of Food Science and Technology on one hand and the U.S. Armed Forces and Government on the other. Membership: $250/yr.
Publications:
Newsletter - "The Link". q.
Activities Report. semi-a.
Annual Meetings: April/400
1987-Norfolk, VA(Omni International)
1988-San Antonio, TX(Marriott on the River)

Research and Engineering Council of the Graphic Arts Industry (1950)
Marshallton Bldg., Rte. 1, Chadds Ford West, Chadds Ford PA 19317
Mng. Director: Fred M. Rogers
Members: 300 companies *Staff:* 2-5
Annual Budget: $250-500,000 *Tel:* (215) 388-7394
Hist. Note: Members are companies, organizations and individuals interested in developing better methods of printing and composition. Membership: $425/yr.
Publication:
Coordinator. m.
Annual Meetings: Spring
1987-Atlanta, GA(Colony Square)/March 5-6/150

Research Council on Structural Connections (1946)
Civil Engineering Structural Dept., Univ. of Texas, Austin TX 78712
Secretary: Karl H. Frank
Members: 40-50
Tel: (512) 471-7259
Hist. Note: Researches the effects of stress on bolted and riveted joints for its member companies and institutions. Formerly (until 1980) known as the Research Council on Riveted and Bolted Structural Joints.

Reserve Officers Ass'n of the U.S. (1922)
One Constitution Ave., N. E., Washington DC 20002
Exec. Director: Maj.Gen. Evan L. Hultman, AUS(Ret.)
Members: 121,000 individuals, 700 groups *Staff:* 30-35
Annual Budget: $2-5,000,000 *Tel:* (202) 479-2200
Hist. Note: Membership is open to any regular, reserve or former officer of the Army, Navy, Air Force, Marine Corps, Coast Guard, Public Health Service, or National Oceanic and Atmospheric Administration. Membership: $25/yr.
Publications:
The Officer. m. adv.
National Security Report. m.
Annual Meetings: Late June/1,200
1987-Orlando, FL
1988-Las Vegas, NV(Riviera)
1989-Houston, TX
1990-Atlanta, GA
1991-Phoenix, AZ

Resilient Floor Covering Institute (1929)
966 Hungerford Drive, Suite 12-B, Rockville MD 20850
Mng. Director: Robert D. Maurer
Members: 25-30 companies *Staff:* 2-5
Annual Budget: $100-250,000 *Tel:* (301) 340-8580
Hist. Note: Formerly (1973) Asphalt and Vinyl Asbestos Tile Institute and (Jan. 1, 1976) the Resilient Tile Institute.

Resistance Welder Manufacturers Ass'n (1936)
1900 Arch St., Philadelphia PA 19103
Exec. Director: R. Bruce Wall
Members: 34 *Staff:* 2-5
Annual Budget: $100-250,000 *Tel:* (215) 564-3484
Annual Meetings:
1987-Longboat Key, FL(Colony Beach and Tennis Resort)/ Nov. 4-8/80

RESNA, Ass'n for the Advancement of Rehabilitation Technology (1979)
1101 Connecticut Ave., N.W., Suite 700, Washington DC 20036
Exec. Director: Patricia I. Horner
Members: 800 *Staff:* 3
Annual Budget: $100-250,000 *Tel:* (202) 857-1199
Hist. Note: Formerly Rehabilitation Engineering Soc. of North America, it assumed its present in 1986. A professional organization of the rehabilitation engineering community, the society brings together a diverse group of individuals whose credentials, activities and interests vary widely but who are all committed to designing, developing, evaluating and providing external and internal devices that will put the benefits of technology to work for disabled persons. Membership: $50/yr.
Publications:
Rehabilitation Technology Review. q. adv.
Proceedings of the RESNA Annual Conference. a.
Annual Meetings: Summer/500
1987-San Jose, CA/June 19-23
1988-Montreal, Quebec/June

Resources Council (1958)
979 Third Ave., New York NY 10022
Exec. Director: Pauline Delli-Carpini
Members: 450 *Staff:* 2-5
Annual Budget: $50-100,000 *Tel:* (212) 752-9040
Hist. Note: Membership consists of manufacturers and suppliers in the interior furnishings industry who sell strictly to interior designers, architects, and specifiers. Main objective is to promote members products and act as liaison between the trade and people who buy from them.
Publication:
Resources Council News. a. adv.
Semi-annual meetings:

Retail Advertising Conference (1952)
67 Oak St., Chicago IL 60611
Exec. Director: Douglas E. Raymond
Members: 1,150 individuals *Staff:* 2-5
Annual Budget: $500-1,000,000 *Tel:* (312) 280-9344
Hist. Note: International association of marketing and advertising executives. Membership: $45/year.
Publications:
RAC Digest. bi-m.
RAC Membership Directory. a.
Washington Report.
Annual Meetings: Late Jan. in Chicago, IL at the Marriott Downtown
1987-Jan. 29-Feb. 1/1,400

Retail Bakers of America (1918)
6525 Belcrest Rd., Suite 250, Hyattsville MD 20782
Exec. V. Pres. and Secy.: Richard C. Gohla
Members: 2,660 *Staff:* 14
Annual Budget: $500-1,000,000 *Tel:* (301) 277-0990
Hist. Note: Established in Chicago July 16, 1918 as The Retail Merchant Bakers of America, it became the Associated Bakers of America in 1925, the Associated Retail Bakers of America in 1938 and assumed its present name in 1978. Sponsors and supports the Political Action Committee of the Retail Bakers of America. Membership fee based on annual sales volume.
Publications:
Donut Ideas Exchange. irreg.
Fresh Baked. m.
MUR Inter-Com. q.
Washington Bulletins. irreg.
Annual Meetings: RBA Supermarket Bakery Conference and RBA Convention-Exhibition run sequentially at same site.
1987-Baltimore, MD(Convention Ctr.)/March 20-24/7,500
1988-Dallas, TX(Convention Ctr.)/April 15-19/7,500
1989-Cincinnati, OH/April 14-18/7,500
1990-Boston, MA/March 16-20/7,500

Retail Confectioners Internat'l (1918)
1807 Glenview Road, Suite 204, Glenview IL 60025
Exec. Director: Evans N. Billington
Members: 600 companies *Staff:* 2-5
Annual Budget: $250-500,000 *Tel:* (312) 724-6120
Hist. Note: Founded in 1918 as Associated Retail Confectioners of the United States. In 1960 name was changed to Associated Retail Confectioners of North America to recognize members in Canada and Mexico. In 1969 changed to Retail Confectioners International to recognize membership in Europe, Australia and Japan.
Publications:
Kettletalk. m. adv.
RCI Magazine. q.
RCI Annual Convention Program. a. adv.
Annual Meetings: Summer/1,500
1987-San Francisco, CA(St. Francis)/June 14-17
1988-Salt Lake City, UT
1989-Chicago, IL

Retail Floorcovering Institute (1973)
13-154 Merchandise Mart, Chicago IL 60654
Exec. Director: Edward S. Korczak
Members: 1,800 companies *Staff:* 2-5
Annual Budget: $1-2,000,000 *Tel:* (312) 644-1243
Publications:
Retail Cost of Doing Business. a.
Contract Cost of Doing Business. a.
The Square Yard. m. adv.
Annual Meetings: March/April
1987-Las Vegas, NV
1988-Hollywood, FL

Retail, Wholesale and Department Store Union (1937)
30 East 29th St., New York NY 10016
President: Lenore Miller
Members: 250,000 *Staff:* 40-50
Annual Budget: over $5,000,000 *Tel:* (212) 684-5300
Hist. Note: Established in 1937 by dissidents from the Retail Clerks International Union and chartered by the Congress of Industrial Organizations as the United Retail Employees of America. Became the United Retail, Wholesale and Department Store Employees of America in 1940, a title that was later shortened to its present form. Absorbed the Distributive, Processing and Office Workers of America as well as the Playthings, Jewelry and Novelty Workers International Union in 1954 and the Cigar Makers International Union of America in 1974.
Publication:
RWDSU Record. m.
Annual Meetings: Every 4 years in Spring (1990)

Reticuloendothelial Soc. (1954)
Medical College of Georgia, Augusta GA 30912
Exec. Director: Dr. Sherwood M. Reichard
Members: 1,100 *Staff:* 2-5
Annual Budget: $100-250,000 *Tel:* (404) 828-2601
Hist. Note: Founded in 1954 and incorporated in 1965. Membership consists of those interested in phagocytic cells of the body, especially when concerned with host defense, immunity and cancer.
Publication:
The Journal of Leucocyte Biology. m. adv.
Annual Meetings: October
1987-Kona, Hawaii/Oct. 17-22

Retired Officers Ass'n (1929)
201 North Washington St., Alexandria VA 22314
President: V. Adm. Thomas J. Kilcline, USN(Ret.)
Members: 349,000 individuals, 375 chapters *Staff:* 60-65
Annual Budget: over $5,000,000 *Tel:* (703) 549-2311
Hist. Note: Comprised of veteran and active members of the Army, Navy, Air Force, Marine Corps, Coast Guard, National Oceanic and Atmospheric Administration, and the Public Health Service, and widow(er)s of the above. Represents over two-thirds of the total retired officer community. Established in Los Angeles February 23, 1929 with 63 members to counsel and render assistance to its members in connection with their retired status. Moved to Washington in 1944 and expanded its purpose to include representing its members' rights and interests when service matters are considered by the Government. Now takes positions on a variety of defense matters. Has an annual budget of $5,500,000. Membership: $15/yr.
Publications:
The Retired Officer Magazine. m. adv.
TROA-Gram. m.
Annual Meetings: Biennial, even years, in Fall
1988-Hawaii(Sheraton Waikiki)/Nov. 10-13
1990-Marriott's Desert Springs Resort/Sept. 9-12

00265 12 05 86 1233

Rhetoric Soc. of America (1968)
Dep't. of English, Ohio State Univ., Columbus OH 43210
Exec. Secretary: Edward P. J. Corbett
Members: 5-600 *Staff:* 1
Annual Budget: under $10,000 *Tel:* (614) 422-6866
Hist. Note: Teachers and students interested in promoting the development and dissemination of research and theory about the production and analysis of rhetorical discourse.
Publication:
Rhetoric Society Quarterly. q.
Annual Meetings: Held in conjunction with meetings of large organizations concerned
with speech, English, philosophy, etc.

Rice Council of America (1957)
Box 740123, Houston TX 77274
Exec. V. President: Bill Goldsmith
Members: 35,000 *Staff:* 15-20
Annual Budget: $2-5,000,000 *Tel:* (713) 270-6699
Hist. Note: Absorbed U.S. Rice Export Development Ass'n in 1964. Formerly (1960) The Rice Industry. Represents the rice industry in Texas, Arkansas, Louisiana, Mississippi, California and Missouri.

Rice Millers' Ass'n (1899)
1235 Jefferson Davis Hwy., Arlington VA 22202
Exec. V. President: J. Stephen Gabbert
Members: 30-40 mills and cooperatives *Staff:* 5
Annual Budget: $500-1,000,000 *Tel:* (703) 920-1281
Publications:
Export Date. m.
Statistical Statement. m.
Annual Meetings: May/June
1987-San Diego, CA(Sheraton Harbor Island)/June 17-20/600
1988-Colorado Springs, CO(Broadmoor)/June 15-18/600
1989-Hawaii/June/600

Risk and Insurance Management Soc. (1950)
205 East 42 St., New York NY 10017
Exec. Director: Ron Judd
Members: 3,800-3,900 organizations *Staff:* 40-50
Annual Budget: $2-5,000,000 *Tel:* (212) 286-9292
Hist. Note: Founded as the National Insurance Buyers Association, it became the American Society of Insurance Management in 1954 and assumed its present name in 1975. Membership consists of corporations, municipalities, universities and other entities who plan and purchase insurance or insurance services. No insurance brokers or consultants.
Publications:
Rimscope. bi-w.
Risk Management. m. adv.
Annual Meetings: April
1987-Las Vegas, NV/March 29-April 3

Roadmasters and Maintenance of Way Ass'n of America (1883)
18154 Harwood Ave., Homewood IL 60430
Secretary: Patricia Weissmann
Members: 2,000-2,100 individuals *Staff:* 1
Annual Budget: under $10,000 *Tel:* (312) 799-4650
Hist. Note: Founded to raise the standards and improve the methods of track and roadway maintenance of American railways.
Publication:
Proceedings. a. adv.
Annual Meetings: Fall
1987-Kansas City, MO
1988-Chicago, IL
1989-Toronto, Ontario

Roadside Business Ass'n (1936)
Hist. Note: Became the American Council of Highway Advertisers in 1985.

Robert Morris Associates, the Nat'l Ass'n of Bank Loan and Credit Officers (1914)
Philadelphia Nat'l Bank Bldg., #1616, Philadelphia PA 19107
Exec. V. President: Clarence R. Reed
Members: 3,000 financial institutions; 13,500 individuals *Staff:* 65
Annual Budget: over $5,000,000 *Tel:* (215) 665-2850
Hist. Note: Seeks to improve the principles and practice of commercial lending and credit functions, loan administration and asset management in commercial banks. Has an annual budget of $7.8 million.
Publications:
Annual Statement Studies. a.
Commercial Lending Newsletter. m.
Commercial Loan Charge-off Report. a.
The Journal of Commercial Bank Lending. m.
Legislative & Regulatory Report. bi-m.
Annual Meetings: Fall
1987-Hawaii/Nov. 8-11
1988-Chicago, IL/Oct. 16-19

Robotic Industries Ass'n (1974)
900 Victors Way, Box 3724, Ann Arbor MI 48106
Exec. V. President: Donald A. Vincent
Members: 350 companies *Staff:* 12
Annual Budget: $1-2,000,000 *Tel:* (313) 994-6088
Hist. Note: Trade association of the robotics industry concerned with developing industry guidelines and collecting and dispensing accurate information on developments and applications. Formerly (1980) known as the Robot Institute of America. Established in Dearborn, Michigan, incorporated in Washington, DC. Established as Nat'l Service Robot Ass'n and Automated Vision Ass'n in 1984. Membership: $200-1,000/yr. (depending on class).
Publications:
Robot Times. q.
RIA Worldwide Robotics Survey and Directory. a.
Robotics Glossary. a.
AVA Machine Vision Glossary. a.
Machine Vision: A Delphi Study to 1990. a.
Annual Meetings: Spring

Robotics Internat'l of SME (1980)
1 SME Drive, Box 930, Dearborn MI 48121
Exec. Director: Catherine A. Bender
Members: 11,500 *Staff:* 2-5
Tel: (313) 271-1500
Hist. Note: A member association of the Soc. of Manufacturing Engineers. Members are scientists, engineers and managers concerned with robotS. Membership: $52/year (initiation fee $15).
Publications:
RI Newsletter. q.
Robotics Today. bi-m.
SME News. 9/yr.
Annual Meetings: Spring
1987-Chicago, IL(Hilton & Towers)/April 26-30/2,000
1988-Detroit, MI(Westin)/June/2,000

Rodeo Media Ass'n (1969)
Hist. Note: Inactive in 1985.

Rolf Institute (1972)
302 Pearl St., Boulder CO 80302
Managing Director: Richard A. Stenstadvold
Members: 500 *Staff:* 10
Annual Budget: $1-2,000,000 *Tel:* (303) 449-5903
Hist. Note: Established and incorporated California, members are practioners of the technique of connective tissue manipulation developed by Dr. Ida P. Rolf. Membership: $450/yr.
Publication:
Rolf Lines. m.
Annual Meetings: August
1987-Boulder, CO

Roll Manufacturers Institute (1948)
Hist. Note: Manufacturers of cast steel and cast iron rolls used in mills rolling and shaping steel and non-ferrous metals. Dissolved October 29, 1982.

Roller Skating Foundation of America (1956)
Kilmer Professional Park, 23 Kilmer Dr., Bldg. 2, Suite F-2, Morganville NJ 07751
Exec. Secretary: Irwin N. Rosee
Members: 5,400
Tel: (201) 536-1311
Hist. Note: Roller skaters and skating rink owners and operators and skate manufacturers. Conducts public relations programs for the industry.
Publication:
Rinksider. bi-m.
Annual Meetings: Not held

Roller Skating Rink Operators Ass'n of America (1937)
7700 A St., Lincoln NE 68510
Exec. Director: George H. Pickard
Members: 1,600 *Staff:* 25
Annual Budget: $1-2,000,000 *Tel:* (402) 489-8811
Hist. Note: Independent, for-profit, recreational roller skating facilities. Sponsors the Soc. of Roller Skating Teachers of America.
Publications:
Roller Skating Business. m.
Skate. q. adv.
Annual Meetings: Spring/1,500
1987-Las Vegas, NV(Caesar's Palace)/May 10-15
1988-Orlando, FL(Sheraton Twin Towers)/May 8-13
1989-Las Vegas, NV
1990-San Francisco, CA(Hilton)/May 27-31

Romance Writers of America (1981)
5206 F.M. 1960 West, Suite 207, Houston TX 77069
Exec. Secretary: Patricia Higgins
Members: 3,000 *Staff:* 1
Annual Budget: $50-100,000 *Tel:* (713) 440-6885
Hist. Note: Supports beginning, intermediate and advanced romance writers. Promotes recognition of the genre of romance writing as a serious book form. Conducts workshops, sponsors national qnd regional conferences and awards accomplishments. Membership: $35/yr.
Publications:
Romance Writers Report. bi-m. adv.
Chapter Advisory Letter. m.
Annual Meetings: Summer
1987-Dallas, TX/July 16-19

Romanian Studies Ass'n of America (1973)
90 Laslo Terrace, Fairfield CT 06430
Secretary: Aurelio Ciufecu
Staff: 1
Annual Budget: under $10,000 *Tel:* (203) 789-6994
Hist. Note: An "allied" organization of the Modern Language Association. Has no paid staff. Membership: $9/year.
Publication:
Yearbook of Romanian Studies. a.
Annual Meetings: December, with the Modern Language Ass'n
1987-San Francisco, CA
1988-New Orleans, LA

Roof Coatings Manufacturers Ass'n (1982)
60 Revere Drive, Suite 500, Northbrook IL 60062
Exec. Director: Carla M. Helm
Members: 100 companies *Staff:* 2-5
Annual Budget: $50-100,000 *Tel:* (312) 480-9080
Publications:
RCMA Report. m.
Directory. a.
Annual Meetings: January
1987-Naples, FL

Roses Incorporated (1936)
Box 99, Haslett MI 48840
Exec. V. President: James C. Krone
Members: 411 commercial growers *Staff:* 2-6
Tel: (517) 339-9544
Hist. Note: Members produce about 80% of the greenhouse roses grown in the United States and Canada.
Publication:
Bulletin. m.

Roundalab (1977)
3 Churchill Road, Cresskill NJ 07626-1698
Exec. Secretary: Peg Tirrell
Members: 1,000 *Staff:* 1
Annual Budget: $25-50,000 *Tel:* (201) 568-5857
Hist. Note: A professional society of individuals who teach round dancing at any phase. Fee: $45/Teaching Unit Renewal
Publications:
Journal. q.
Roundalab Manual. a.
Annual Meetings: June/150
1987-Houston, TX(Stouffers Greenway Plaza)/June 21-23
1988-Anaheim, CA(The Grand Hotel)/June 19-21
1989-Oklahoma City, OK/June 18-20
1990-Memphis, TN/June 24-26

Roundtable for Women in Foodservice (1983)
325 E. 57th St., Suite 2A, New York NY 10022
Exec. V. President: Beverly Barbour
Members: 1,600 individuals *Staff:* 3
Annual Budget: $50-100,000 *Tel:* (212) 593-2791
Hist. Note: Established and incorporated in New York, the Roundtable serves as a central source of education and information and a catalyst for career advancement for women in food service. Open to all members of the industry. Membership: $90/yr., including chapter dues.
Publications:
RWF Directory. a.
RWF News. q.
Annual Meetings: Fall
1987-Chicago, IL/May 17/125

Rubber Manufacturers Ass'n (1900)
1400 K St., N.W., Washington DC 20005
President: Donald G. Brotzman
Members: 200-215 *Staff:* 50-55
Annual Budget: $2-5,000,000 *Tel:* (202) 682-4800
Hist. Note: Founded in 1900 as the New England Rubber Club. Incorporated in 1915 as the Rubber Club of America and became the Rubber Ass'n of America in 1917. Name changed to Rubber Manufacturers Ass'n in 1929. Members are manufacturers of rubber products of all types. Supports the Rubber Manufacturers Ass'n Political Action Committee.
Annual Meetings: 3rd Thursday in November

Rural Education Ass'n (1907)
300 Education Building, Colorado State University, Fort Collins CO 80523
Exec. Director: Joseph T. Newlin
Members: 700-800 *Staff:* 2-5
Annual Budget: $50-100,000 *Tel:* (303) 491-7022
Hist. Note: Established as the Department of Rural and Agricultural Education of the National Education Association, it became the Rural Education Association in 1959, the Rural Regional Education Association in 1975 and reassumed its present name in October 1980 when it became fully independent of NEA. Purpose is to improve and expand public education in rural areas. Membership: $40/yr. (individual), $140/yr. (company).
Publications:
Rural Education News. q.
Rural Educator Journal. 3/yr.
Annual Meetings: Fall
1987-Lake Placid, NY(Hilton)/400
1988-Bismark, ND

Rural Sociological Soc. (1937)
Dept. of Sociology, Wilson Hall, Montana State University, Bozeman MT 59717
Business Office Mgr.: Bonita Spoerl
Members: 900-1,000 individuals *Staff:* 1
Annual Budget: $100-250,000 *Tel:* (406) 994-5248
Hist. Note: Originally a section of the American Sociological Soc., the Rural Sociological Soc. became independent in 1937. Membership: $30/yr.
Publications:
The Rural Sociologist. bi-m.
Rural Sociology. q. adv.

00266 12 05 86 1233

Annual Meetings: August at a University environment/350
1987-Madison, WI
1988-Athens, GA

Ruth Jackson Soc. (1983)
1217 St. Paul St., Baltimore MD 21202
Secretary: Mary L. Morden, M.D.
Members: 110
Annual Budget: under $10,000 *Tel:* (301) 484-3234
Hist. Note: Women engaged in the practice of orthopaedic surgery. All members are certified by the American Board of Orthopaedic Surgery, belong to the American Academy of Orthopaedic Surgeons, or are in training programs leading to these two qualifications. Women in allied fields are also candidates for membership. Membership: $50/yr.
Annual Meetings: With the American Academy of Orthopaedic Surgeons.

Sacro-Occipital Research Soc. Internat'l (1925)
Box 358, Sedan KS 67361
Treasurer: Dr. M.L. Rees
Members: 1,500 chiropractors *Staff:* 2
Annual Budget: $100-250,000 *Tel:* (316) 725-5110
Hist. Note: Formerly (until 1979) known as the Sacro-Occipital Research Soc. Merged in 1982 with the Internat'l Craniopathic Soc.
Publication:
The Source. q.
Annual Meetings: Omaha, NE/September or October

SAF (1884)
1601 Duke St., Alexandria VA 22314
Exec. V. President: Betty O. Sapp
Members: 10,000 *Staff:* 25-30
Annual Budget: $2-5,000,000 *Tel:* (703) 836-8700
Hist. Note: SAF stands for the Society of American Florists and Ornamental Horticulturists. Sponsors the American Floral Marketing Council and the Society of American Florists Political Action Committee.
Publication:
SAF-Business News for the Floral Industry.
Annual Meetings: July
1987-St. Louis, MO/July 22-25

SAFE Ass'n (1957)
15723 Vanowen St., Suite 246, Van Nuys CA 91406
Business Administrator: Jeani Benton
Members: 900-1,000 *Staff:* 1
Annual Budget: $100-250,000 *Tel:* (818) 994-6495
Hist. Note: Established as the Space and Flight Equipment Ass'n at Edwards Air Force Base in 1957 and moved to Los Angeles in 1960. Incorporated in California in 1964 as the Survival and Flight Equipment Ass'n and became the SAFE Ass'n in 1977. Promotes the science of survival and the development of air safety in all forms of transportation.
Publications:
SAFE Journal. bi-m. adv.
Symposium Proceedings. a.
Annual Meetings: December/600
1987-Las Vegas, NV(Riviera)/Dec. 6-10
1988-Las Vegas, NV(Riviera)/Dec. 4-8

Safety Equipment Distributors Ass'n (1968)
111 East Wacker Drive, Suite 600, Chicago IL 60601
Exec. Director: James E. Elsener
Members: 270-280 companies *Staff:* 2-5
Annual Budget: $100-250,000 *Tel:* (312) 644-6610
Hist. Note: Incorporated July 1, 1968 from a nucleus group of distributors who were formerly associate members of the Industrial Safety Equipment Association. Financial independence from ISEA was gained the following year. Membership: $300-700/yr.
Publications:
The SEDA Scene. bi-m.
AV Library. irreg.
SEDA Catalog Program. irreg.
Industry Profile Summary (IPS). a.
Annual Meetings: Summer
1987-Banff, Canada(Banff Springs Hotel)/June 12-18/250
1988-White Sulphur Springs, WV(Greenbrier)/July 16-20

Safety Helmet Council of America (1967)
2228 Cotner Ave., Los Angeles CA 90064
Exec. Director: Jodi DeLucca
Members: 16-25 *Staff:* 2-5
Annual Budget: $25-50,000
Hist. Note: Non-profit corporation designed to serve the interests of those persons and firms engaged in the manufacture and distribution of high performance safety helmets.

Safety Soc., The (1959)
1900 Association Dr., Reston VA 22091
Exec. Director: Raymond A. Ciszek
Members: 2,000 *Staff:* 2-5
Annual Budget: $10-25,000 *Tel:* (703) 476-3430
Hist. Note: Formerly (1985) the American School and Community Safety Ass'n. Until 1974 a division of the American Ass'n for Health, Physical Education and Recreation. An independent member of the American Alliance for Health, Physical Education, Recreation and Dance until 1985, it is now an autonomous society within the Ass'n for Research, Administration, Professional Councils and Societies. Members are school and community personnel with an interest in and responsiblity for safety.
Publication:
Safety Forum. 3/year.
Annual Meetings: With AAHPER.

Sailmakers' Institute (1969)
Hist. Note: A division of The Industrial Fabrics Association International.
Annual Meetings: With The Industrial Fabrics Association International (IFAI)

Salad Manufacturers Ass'n (1980)
2971 Flowers Road South, Suite 204, Atlanta GA 30341
Exec. Director: Judy Stokes
Members: 150-160 *Staff:* 2-5
Tel: (404) 452-0660
Hist. Note: Concerned with the manufacture and sale of prepared (wet) salads.
Publications:
Directory a.
The Salad Special. q.
Annual Meetings: First quarter of each year
1987-Nashville, TN(Opryland)/Feb. 19-21

Sales and Marketing Executives, Internat'l (1935)
Statler Office Tower, #446, Cleveland OH 44115
Exec. Director-Programs: Jack Criswell
Members: 12,000 *Staff:* 5
Annual Budget: $1-2,000,000 *Tel:* (216) 771-6650
Hist. Note: Established as Nat'l Federation of Sales Executives, it became Nat'l Sales Executives Internat'l in 1949 and assumed its present name in 1961. Members are most commonly professionals in the fields of sales and marketing management, market research management, sales training, distribution management and other senior executives in small and medium businesses. Offers many career development services including: Sales Management Institute, Graduate School of Sales Management and Marketing (with Syracuse Univ.) and professional certification. Pi Sigma Epsilon, a professional fraternity, is an affiliate. Membership: $95/yr.
Publications:
Marketing Times. bi-m. adv.
SME-I Digest. bi-m.
Leadership Directory. a.
Annual Meetings: Spring
1987-Little Rock, AR(Excelsior)/June 6-9/5-700
1988-Buffalo, NY
1989-Oklahoma City, OK

Sales Ass'n of the Chemical Industry (1921)
50 East 41st St., New York NY 10017
Admin. Assistant: Paul B. Slawter, Jr.
Members: 850 individuals *Staff:* 1
Annual Budget: $50-100,000 *Tel:* (212) 686-1952
Hist. Note: Founded as the Salesmen's Association of the American Chemical Industry by 96 charter members September 7, 1921 at the Chemist's Club, New York City. Incorporated 1944 in the State of New York.
Publications:
The Chemical Paddler. a. adv.
SACI Slants. semi-a
Annual Meetings: Semi-annual meetings

Sales Ass'n of the Paper Industry (1919)
260 Madison Ave., New York NY 10016
Exec. V. President: Anne G. Toomey
Members: 300 *Staff:* 1
Annual Budget: $25-50,000 *Tel:* (212) 340-0648
Hist. Note: Formed in 1919, it opened its own office in New York in 1950. Formerly (1972) Salesmen's Ass'n of the Paper Industry. Membership: $40/yr.
Publication:
Bulletin. m.
Annual Meetings: With American Paper Institute.

Salmon Institute (1957)
Hist. Note: Defunct in 1982.

Salt Institute (1914)
206 North Washington St., Alexandria VA 22314
President: William E. Dickinson
Members: 20-30 *Staff:* 6-10
Annual Budget: $500-1,000,000 *Tel:* (703) 549-4648
Hist. Note: Founded in 1914 as the Salt Producers Ass'n. Became the Salt Institute in 1963. Supported by major salt producers in the Western hemisphere, Europe, and Australia.
Publications:
Agricultural Digest. bien.
Highway Digest. bien.
Annual Meetings: February/60
1987-Boca Raton, FL(Hotel & Club)/Feb. 16-21

Sanitation Suppliers and Contractors Institute (1957)
Hist. Note: A component of the Environmental Management Association.

Santa Gertrudis Breeders Internat'l (1951)
Box 1257, Kingsville TX 78364
Exec. Director: Dr. W.M. Warren
Members: 5,200 *Staff:* 16-20
Annual Budget: $500-1,000,000 *Tel:* (512) 592-9357
Hist. Note: Incorporated April 9, 1951 with 169 charter members to standardize and certify those animals designated as "purebred" and to establish rigorous controls for grading-up to purebred herds. Member of the Nat'l Soc. of Livestock Record Ass'n. Membership: $25/year.
Publications:
Membership Book. a.
Santa Gertrudis Journal. m. adv.
Annual Meetings: Spring
1987-Nashville, TN(Marriott)/April 8-11/500

Satellite Broadcasting and Communications Ass'n (1980)
300 N. Washington St., Suite 208, Alexandria VA 22314
Exec. V. President: Charles C. Hewitt
Members: 4,000-5,000 companies *Staff:* 6
Annual Budget: $1-2,000,000 *Tel:* (703) 549-6990
Hist. Note: Formerly (1985) the Soc. for Private and Commercial Earth Stations and (1986) Satellite Television Industry Ass'n. Represents manufacturers, distributors, dealers, and owners of earth stations and provides data and representation on legislative and regulatory actions affecting them. Membership: $100/yr. (individual); corporate rate varies.
Semi-annual Meetings: Spring and Fall
1987-Las Vegas, NV/March 2-4
1987-Nashville, TN/Sept.

Satellite Television Industry Ass'n
Hist. Note: Name changed in 1986 to Satellite Broadcasting and Communications Ass'n.

Sauna Soc. of America (1965)
1001 Connecticut Ave., N.W., Washington DC 20036
Exec. Director: V.S. Choslowsky
Members: 30-35 companies *Staff:* 2-5
Tel: (202) 331-1365
Hist. Note: Established by importers, manufacturers, builders and suppliers of saunas and sauna equipment and accessories to provide information to the general public on the construction and use of authentic Finnish sauna and to conduct a program of medical, historical, architectural and other research of the sauna, in cooperation with the Internat'l Sauna Soc. in Helsinki, Finland.
Publication:
Newsletter. m.
Semi-annual Meetings: Washington, DC

Savings and Loan Foundation (1951)
Hist. Note: Became the Foundation for Savings Institutions in 1985.

Savings Institutions Marketing Soc. of America (1965)
Hist. Note: Became the Financial Institutions Marketing Society of America in 1983.

Scaffold Industry Ass'n (1972)
14039 Sherman Way, Van Nuys CA 91405
Exec. V. President: D. Victor Saleeby
Members: 700-800 *Staff:* 2-5
Annual Budget: $250-500,000 *Tel:* (818) 782-2012
Hist. Note: Formerly (1975) the Scaffold Contractors Ass'n. Membership: $450/yr.
Publications:
Directory/Handbook. a. adv.
SIA Newsletter. m. adv.
Annual Meetings: June
1987-Reno, NV(Bally)/July 7-11/600
1988-Minneapolis, MN
1989-Seattle, WA
1990-Boston, MA

Scaffolding, Shoring and Forming Institute (1960)
1230 Keith Bldg., Cleveland OH 44115-2180
Mng. Director: John H. Addington
Members: 15-20 companies *Staff:* 2-5
Annual Budget: $25-50,000 *Tel:* (216) 241-7333
Hist. Note: Formerly Steel Scaffolding and Shoring Institute and (1980) Scaffolding and Shoring Institute.

Scale Manufacturers Ass'n (1945)
152 Rollins Avenue, Suite 208, Rockville MD 20852
Exec. Director: Raymond J. Lloyd
Members: 25-30 *Staff:* 4
Annual Budget: $100-250,000 *Tel:* (301) 984-9080
Hist. Note: Manufacturers of general industrial scales, load cell weighing devices, retail scales, and vehicle and livestock scales. Purpose is to advance the science of weighing and force measuring, and the engineering and manufacture of instruments, apparatus, equipment and facilities.
Publications:
Directory. a.
Weighlog. q.
Annual Meetings: April/100
1987-Napa Valley, CA(Silverado)/April 26-29
1988-Tarpon Springs, FL(Innisbrook)April 24-27

Schiffli Lace and Embroidery Manufacturers Ass'n (1940)
512 23rd St., Union City NJ 07087
Exec. Director: I. Leonard Seiler
Members: 275-300 companies *Staff:* 2-5
Annual Budget: $100-250,000 *Tel:* (201) 863-7300
Hist. Note: Formerly Embroidery Manufacturers Bureau. Membership concentrated principally in Northern New Jersey and New York City. Membership: $125/yr./machine.

00267 12 05 86 1233

Publications:
Embroidery Directory. a. adv.
Embroidery News. 8-10/yr.
Annual Meetings: November

School Management Study Group (1969)
860 18th Ave., Salt Lake City UT 84103
Exec. Secretary: M. Donald Thomas
Members: 3-400
Annual Budget: under $10,000 *Tel:* (801) 532-5340
Hist. Note: School and college administrators interested in improving educational institutions. Membership: $20/yr.
Publication:
Newsletter. 10/yr.
Annual Meetings: In conjunction with the American Ass'n of School Administrators

School Science and Mathematics Ass'n (1902)
126 Life Science Bldg., Bowling Green University, Bowling Green OH 43403
Exec. Secretary: Dr. Darrel W. Fyffe
Members: 4,300 *Staff:* 2-5
Annual Budget: $100-250,000 *Tel:* (419) 372-7393
Hist. Note: Incorporated in Illinois in 1902 as the Central Ass'n of Science and Mathematics Teachers, Inc. Affiliated with the American Ass'n for the Advancement of Science.
Publication:
School Science and Mathematics. 8/yr. adv.
Annual Meetings: Fall
1987-Billings, MT(Holiday Inn)/Oct. 15-17/1,000

Science Fiction Writers of America (1965)
Box H, Wharton NJ 07885
Exec. Secretary: Peter D. Pautz
Members: 800 *Staff:* 1
Annual Budget: $25-50,000
Hist. Note: SFWA is an organization of professional writers in the science fiction and fantasy field. The minimum requirement for active membership is professional publication of three short stories or one full-length single-author fiction book. Institutional membership is open to organizations with a legitimate interest in science fiction. Membership: $50/yr.
Publications:
Bulletin. q.
Directory of the Science Fiction Writers of America. a.
SFWA Forum. bi-m.
Nebula Awards Report. 6-8/yr.
Annual Meetings: April; odd years in New York City, even years on the West Coast.

Scientific Apparatus Makers Ass'n (1918)
1101 16th St., N.W., Suite 300, Washington DC 20036
President: Graydon R. Powers, Jr.
Members: 225-250 companies *Staff:* 15-20
Annual Budget: $1-2,000,000 *Tel:* (202) 223-1360
Hist. Note: Serves the manufacturers and distributors of high-technology instrumentation, apparatus, equipment and supplies marketed worldwide in the industrial, medical-clinical, and scientific research communities. Established as the Scientific Apparatus Makers Association of America, it assumed its present name in 1948 and absorbed the Association of Nuclear Instrument Manufacturers in 1972.
Publications:
Government Bulletin. m.
International Bulletin. m.

Scientific Manpower Commission
Hist. Note: Became the Commission on Professionals in Science and Technology in 1986.

Screen Actors Guild (1933)
7065 Hollywood Blvd., Hollywood CA 90028-7594
Exec. Secretary: Kendall Orsatti
Members: 64,000 *Staff:* 200
Annual Budget: over $5,000,000 *Tel:* (213) 465-4600
Hist. Note: Labor union affiliated with AFL-CIO with a budget of about $12 million. An autonomous branch union of Associated Actors and Artistes America, representing actors in film, television, and commercials.
Publications:
Screen Actor Magazine. q.
Screen Actor Newsletter. q.
Annual Meetings: December in Hollywood, CA.

Screen Extras Guild (1945)
3629 Cahuenga Blvd. West, Los Angeles CA 90068
Nat'l Exec. Secretary: H. O'Neil Shanks
Members: 5,300 *Staff:* 11-15
Annual Budget: $500-1,000,000 *Tel:* (213) 851-4301
Hist. Note: Collective bargaining agent for screen and TV extras. Affiliated with AFL-CIO. An autonomous branch of Associated Actors and Artistes of America. Membership: $110/year.
Annual Meetings: Los Angeles

Screen Manufacturers Ass'n (1955)
655 Irving Park at Lake Shore Drive, Suite 201 Park Place, Chicago IL 60613-3198
Exec. Secretary: June G. Fitzgerald, CAE
Members: 25-30 companies *Staff:* 2-5
Annual Budget: $50-100,000 *Tel:* (312) 525-2644
Hist. Note: Formerly (1957) Frame Screen Manufacturers Ass'n.
Publication:
Screening Industry News. q.
Semi-annual Meetings: April in Birmingham, AL and Fall
1987-Birmingham, AL/April 15-16
1987-Pine Mountain, GA(Callaway Gardens)/Sept. 30-Oct. 3

Screen Printing Ass'n Internat'l (1948)
10015 Main St., Fairfax VA 22031
President: John M. Crawford, Jr. CAE
Members: 2,800 *Staff:* 16-20
Annual Budget: $1-2,000,000 *Tel:* (703) 385-1335
Hist. Note: Formerly (1967) Screen Process Printing Association. Contains eight industry sections: Decal Division; Outdoor Advertising Division; Point-of-Purchase Division; Associate Members Council; Textile Graphics Division; Industrial/Electronic/Container Division; Small Shops Group; and Radiation Curing Group. Supports the Screen Printing Technical Foundation to conduct research, tests, studies and scientific examinations designed to provide information on screen printing and related processes. Membership Fee: Sliding scale based on sales volume.
Publications:
Tabloid. m.
Who's Who in Screen Printing. a.
Annual Meetings: Fall/7,000-8,000
1987-St. Louis, MO(Convention Center)/Oct. 7-10
1988-Houston, TX(Brown Convention Center)/Oct. 5-8
1989-Los Angeles, CA(Convention Center)/Nov. 1-4
1990-Atlanta, GA(World Congress Center)/Oct. 10-13
1991-Cleveland, OH(Cleveland Convention Center)/Oct. 9-12
1992-Indianapolis, IN(Indiana Convention Center)/Oct. 28-31

Seafarers' Internat'l Union of North America (1938)
5201 Auth Way, Camp Springs MD 20746
President: Frank Drozak
Members: 80,000 *Staff:* 100-125
Annual Budget: $2-5,000,000 *Tel:* (301) 899-0675
Hist. Note: Composed of 27 autonomous affiliated unions of seamen, fishermen, fish cannery workers, inland boatmen, transportation workers and industrial workers in the U.S., Canada, and Puerto Rico. Product of labor in-fighting in the maritime industry, SIU was chartered by the American Federation of Labor October 14, 1938 as an outgrowth of the Sailor's Union of the Pacific, oldest affiliate of the former International Seaman's Union of America. Sponsors and supports the Marine Fireman's Union Political Action Fund as well as the Sailors Political Fund.
Publication:
Seafarers Log. m.
Triennial Meetings:

Sealant and Waterproofers Institute (1976)
3101 Broadway, Suite 300, Kansas City MO 64111
Exec. Director: Ken Bowman
Members: 110-125 companies *Staff:* 2-5
Annual Budget: $100-250,000 *Tel:* (816) 561-8230
Hist. Note: Regular members are sealant and waterproofing contractors; associate members are suppliers to the industry.
Publication:
The Applicator. q. adv.
Semi-annual Meetings:
1987-St. Petersburg, FL/Feb. 22-25

Sealant Engineering and Associated Lines (1964)
7867 Convoy Court, Suite 301, San Diego CA 92111
Exec. Director: Edward W. Johnson, CAE
Members: 38 companies *Staff:* 3
Annual Budget: $50-100,000 *Tel:* (619) 569-7906
Hist. Note: Membership open to distributors and manufacturers of sealant and waterproofing products. Membership: $1,000-1,500/yr.
Semi-annual meetings: Spring and Winter
1987-Boston, MA(Parker House)/April 21-24
1987-Virgin Islands(Frenchmans Reef)/Dec. 1-5

Sealed Insulating Glass Manufacturers Ass'n (1963)
111 East Wacker Drive, Suite 600, Chicago IL 60601
Exec. V. President: James Dickinson
Members: 153 *Staff:* 2-5
Annual Budget: $100-250,000 *Tel:* (312) 644-6610
Publications:
SIGMA Newsletter. m.
Directory. a.
Annual Meetings: Semi-annual meetings
1987-Scottsdale, AZ(Registry)/March 8-11/260
1987-Bloomington, IN(Indian Lake Resort)/Aug. 16-19/225

Seaplane Pilots Ass'n (1972)
421 Aviation Way, Frederick MD 21701
Exec. Director: Mary F. Silitch
Members: 4,000 *Staff:* 2
Annual Budget: $100-250,000 *Tel:* (301) 695-2083
Hist. Note: Established in Little Ferry, NJ as the U.S. Seaplane Pilots Ass'n. Seeks to protect right of access for seaplanes to waterways in the U.S. and Canada, to promote seaplane flying and to disseminate information to seaplane pilots. Membership: $28/yr.
Publications:
Water Flying Annual a. adv.
Water Flying. q. adv.
SPA Seaplance Landing Directory. a. adv.
Annual Meetings: September (1st weekend after Labor Day), Greenville, ME/1,500

Secondary Lead Smelters Ass'n (1976)
6000 Lake Forest Drive, Suite 350, Atlanta GA 30328
Exec. Secretary: Michael L. Sappington
Members: 40 companies *Staff:* 2
Annual Budget: $50-100,000 *Tel:* (404) 257-9634
Hist. Note: Investigates means/methods to achieve compliance with OSHA and EPA regulations impacting the secondary lead smelting industry. Membership: $4,000/yr.
Publication:
Minutes of Technical Sessions, 3x a.
Triannual Meetings:

Secondary School Theatre Ass'n (1959)
Hist. Note: A division of the American Theatre Association. Formerly the Secondary School Theatre Conference.

Securities Industry Ass'n (1912)
120 Broadway, 35th Floor, New York NY 10271
President: Edward I. O'Brien
Members: 500 firms *Staff:* 60
Annual Budget: over $5,000,000 *Tel:* (212) 608-1500
Hist. Note: Merger in 1972 of the Ass'n of Stock Exchange Firms (1913) and the Investment Bankers Ass'n of America (1912). Investment bankers, brokers, dealers, mutual funds and others accounting for about 95% of the securities business in North America. Maintains a Washington office. Sponsors the Securities Industry Political Action Committee, the Municipal Securities Industry Political Action Committee and the Securities Industry Foundation for Economic Education.

Security Container Institute (1978)
Hist. Note: Formed in 1978 after the dissolution of the Safe Manufacturers' Nat'l Ass'n to keep communication open between members if and when necessary. Inactive in 1985.

Security Equipment Industry Ass'n (1971)
2800 28th St., Suite 124, Santa Monica CA 90405
Exec. Director: Donna J. Gentry
Members: 130 companies *Staff:* 2-5
Annual Budget: $250-500,000 *Tel:* (213) 450-4141
Hist. Note: A merger of the Security Equipment Manufacturers Ass'n and the Security Equipment Distributors Ass'n, both founded in 1969. Incorporated in Illinois in 1971; 1977 in California. Membership: based on a three-tier sliding scale.
Publications:
News Brief. m.
Market Research Reports. 3/yr.
Quarterly meetings: February, April, June and August.

Security Lithographers Section
Hist. Note: A special industry group of Printing Industries of America.

SEDESCO-USA (1956)
Hist. Note: More commonly known as the American Association of Esthetics.

Seismological Soc. of America (1906)
6431 Fairmount Ave., Suite 7, El Cerrito CA 94530
Association Director: Susan B. Newman
Members: 1,600-1,700 *Staff:* 2-5
Annual Budget: $100-250,000 *Tel:* (415) 525-5474
Hist. Note: Originated in San Francisco in August 1906 shortly after the earthquake and incorporated in California the same year. A member society of the American Geological Institute.
Publications:
Bulletin. bi-m.
Seismological Research Letters. q. adv.
Annual Meetings: Spring
1987-Santa Barbara, CA
1988-Honolulu, HI

Selenium-Tellurium Development Ass'n (1938)
Box 3096, Darien CT 06820
Secretary: Prescott C. Fuller
Members: 11 companies *Staff:* 2-5
Annual Budget: $50-100,000 *Tel:* (203) 655-0470
Hist. Note: Originally the Selenium Development Committee, the STDA was incorporated in New York in 1963 and now includes US, Canadian, Swedish, Japanese and Peruvian producers of selenium and tellurium. Members are companies producing copper, from whose ores selenium and tellurium are derived.
Publications:
Selenium and Tellurium Selects. m.
Bulletin-STDA.
Annual Meetings: May

Self Insurance Institute of America (1981)
1700 East Dyer Road, Suite 165, Santa Ana CA 92705
Exec. V. President: James A. Kinder
Members: 600 companies *Staff:* 9
Annual Budget: $500-1,000,000 *Tel:* (714) 261-2553
Hist. Note: Established in Santa Ana, CA in 1981 in order to bring the three principal entities of the self-insurance industry - consumer employers, third party administrators and reinsurance companies - and other interested parties together for dialogue; incorporated in California. Members are companies involved or interested in self-funding risk for workers compensation insurance programs, employee benefit plans or property and casualty protection. Membership: $500/yr.
Publications:
The Self Insurer Magazine.
Hotline Legislative Report.

00268 12 05 86 1233

Annual Meetings: Fall
1987-Orlando, FL(Wyndham)/Oct. 18-24/800

Self-Rising Flour and Corn Meal Program (1933)
225 W. Ohio, 6th Fl., Chicago IL 60610
Asst. Secy.-Treas.: J.R. Yurkus
Members: 30-35 *Staff:* 5-7
Annual Budget: $50-100,000 *Tel:* (312) 670-0200
Hist. Note: An association of the millers of self-rising wheat and corn consumer products and their allied trades formed for the purpose of conducting an educational program on behalf of those products. Formerly Self Rising Flour Institute.

Self-Service Storage Ass'n (1975)
P.O. Box 110, Eureka Springs AR 72632
Exec. Director: Gail P. Pohl
Members: 1,500 *Staff:* 16
Annual Budget: $1-2,000,000 *Tel:* (501) 253-7701
Hist. Note: Self-service storage facilities. Membership: $300/yr.(minimum)
Publication:
Self-Service Storage. m. adv.
Annual Meetings: October
1987-Phoenix, AZ(Hyatt Regency)

Semiconductor Equipment and Materials Institute (1970)
805 East Middlefield Road, Mountain View CA 94043
Exec. Director: William H. Reed
Members: 500 individuals; 1,100 corporations *Staff:* 46
Annual Budget: over $5,000,000 *Tel:* (415) 964-5111
Hist. Note: SEMI is an international trade association representing firms supplying equipment, materials and services to the semiconductor industry. Membership: $50/yr. (individual); $1-5,000/yr. (corporate)
Publications:
Membership Directory. a.
SEMI Outlook. q.
SEMI News. bi-m.
SEMI Standards. q.
Forecast. a.
SEMI Standards Information Alert. q.
SEMI Japan News. bi-m. (in Japanese)
Annual Meetings: Holds several regional trade shows

Semiconductor Industry Ass'n (1977)
10201 Torre Ave., Suite 275, Cupertino CA 95014
President: A.A. (Andy) Procassini
Members: 45-50 companies *Staff:* 10
Annual Budget: $500-1,000,000 *Tel:* (408) 973-9973
Hist. Note: Represents producers of all semiconductor products, such as discrete components, integrated circuits and microprocessors.
Publications:
SIA Circuit Newsletter. q.
Yearbook/Directory. bien.
Annual Meetings: November/50

Senior Executives Ass'n (1980)
Box 7610, Washington DC 20044
President: Carol A. Bonosaro
Members: 2,100 *Staff:* 6-10
Annual Budget: $250-500,000 *Tel:* (202) 535-4328
Hist. Note: Founded in 1980 as a tax-exempt, non-profit corporation representing Federal executives. SEA is committed to effective and productive leadership in government; seeks to obtain fair pay, benefits, training and recognition for the almost 7,000 Federal executives who manage the government's departments and agencies. Membership: $156/yr.
Publication:
Action. 10/yr. adv.
Annual Meetings: Summer in Washington, DC/400

Service Employees Internat'l Union (1921)
1313 L St., N.W., Washington DC 20005
Internat'l President: John J. Sweeney
Members: 850,000 *Staff:* 200
Annual Budget: over $5,000,000 *Tel:* (202) 898-3200
Hist. Note: Chartered by the American Federation of Labor on April 23, 1921 as a union of custodial and building service employees. Originally, the Building Service Employees Internat'l Union, it assumed its present name in 1968. Affiliated with AFL-CIO-CLC. Merged with the Internat'l Jewelry Workers Union on July 1, 1980 and the Nat'l Ass'n of Government Employees on December 1, 1982. Sponsors and supports the PET COPE Political Action Committee. Has an annual budget of over $25 million.
Publications:
SEIU Leadership News Update. m.
Service Employee. m.
Annual Meetings: Every 4 years (1988)

Service Station Dealers of America (1947)
304 Pennsylvania Ave., S.E., Washington DC 20003
Exec. Director: Victor Rasheed
Members: 60,000 *Staff:* 2-5
Annual Budget: $500-1,000,000 *Tel:* (202) 546-6868
Hist. Note: Members are independent gasoline dealers who sell gasoline under the brand name of their supplier. Sponsors the SSDA Political Action Committee. Known as National Congress of Petroleum Retailers, Inc. until 1980.
Publications:
American Dealer Magazine. 3/yr.
ActionGram. irreg.
Annual Meetings: Summer
1987-Niagara Falls, NY/Aug. 9-12

Sewing Machine Trade Ass'n (1933)
Hist. Note: Became the American Apparel Machinery Trade Ass'n in 1984.

Shade Tobacco Growers Agricultural Ass'n (1942)
Box 389, East Haddam CT 06423
Exec. Director: Anthony F. Amenta
Members: 5 *Staff:* 1
Annual Budget: $25-50,000 *Tel:* (203) 873-8257
Hist. Note: Growers and processors of shade-grown leaf tobacco for cigar wrappers.
Annual Meetings: March in Glastonbury, CT

Sheet Metal and Air Conditioning Contractors' Nat'l Ass'n (1943)
8224 Old Courthouse Road, Vienna VA 22180
Exec. V. President: Donald D. Clark
Members: 2,700-2,800 *Staff:* 25-30
Annual Budget: $1-2,000,000 *Tel:* (703) 790-9890
Hist. Note: Formerly (1956) Sheet Metal Contractors Nat'l Ass'n. Supports the Sheet Metal and Air Conditioning Political Action Committee.
Publication:
SMACNA Update. bi-w.
Annual Meetings: Fall

Sheet Metal Workers' Internat'l Ass'n (1888)
1750 New York Ave., N.W., 6th Floor, Washington DC 20006
President: Edward J. Carlough
Members: 148,000-149,000 *Staff:* 100-125
Annual Budget: over $5,000,000 *Tel:* (202) 783-5880
Hist. Note: Established in Toledo, Ohio on January 25, 1888 as the Tin, Sheet Iron and Cornice Workers' Internat'l Ass'n and chartered by the American Federation of Labor the following year. Became the Amalgamated Sheet Metal Workers' Internat'l Ass'n in 1899 and merged with the Sheet Metal Workers' Nat'l Alliance in 1903 to become the Amalgamated Sheet Metal Workers' Internat'l Alliance. Merged in 1907 with the Coppersmiths' Internat'l Union and assumed Has a budget of about $20 million. Sponsors and supports the Sheet Metal Workers Internat'l Ass'n Political Action Committee. Membership: $130/yr.
Publications:
The Scene Today. bi-w.
Sheet Metal Workers' Journal. m.
Focus on Funds. m.
Annual Meetings: September/600
1988-Toledo, OH

Shellfish Institute of North America (1908)
2000 M St., N.W., Suite 580, Washington DC 20036
Exec. Director: Roy E. Martin
Members: 100 *Staff:* 1
Annual Budget: $50-100,000 *Tel:* (202) 296-5170
Hist. Note: Formerly (1970) Oyster Institute of North America. Became a division of the Nat'l Fisheries Institute in 1983.
Annual Meetings: With Nat'l Shellfisheries Ass'n

Shelving Manufacturers Ass'n (1972)
8720 Red Oak Blvd., Charlotte NC 28210
Management Executive: John B. Nofsinger
Members: 15 *Staff:* 2-5
Annual Budget: $10-25,000 *Tel:* (704) 522-8644
Annual Meetings: Semi-Annual Meetings with Material Handling Institute
1987-Charlotte, NC
1987-Boca Raton, FL(Hotel & Club)/Nov. 6-11
1988-Phoenix, AZ(Biltmore)/Oct. 7-12
1989-Undecided
1990-Palm Springs, CA(Marriott's Ranchos Las Palmas Resort)/Oct. 19-24

Shipbuilders Council of America (1921)
1110 Vermont Ave., N.W., Washington DC 20005
President: John J. Stocker
Members: 50-60 companies *Staff:* 6-10
Annual Budget: $1-2,000,000 *Tel:* (202) 775-9060
Hist. Note: Formerly Nat'l Council of American Shipbuilders. Absorbed Atlantic and Gulf Coasts Drydock Ass'n. Private shipbuilding and repair companies and related firms such as manufacturers of marine equipment and supplies, many of which do work for the federal government.
Publications:
Report. a.
Shipyard Weekly. w.
Annual Meetings: Washington, in March

Shipowners Claims Bureau
5 Hanover Sq., New York NY 10004
President: Thomas J. McGowan
Members: 31 *Staff:* 35
Tel: (212) 269-2350
Hist. Note: Members are claim managers and adjusters for shipping lines and protection and indemnity clubs.
Annual Meetings: November

Shippers Nat'l Freight Claim Council (1974)
Box Z, Huntington NY 11743
Exec. Director/Gen. Counsel: William J. Augello
Members: 850 companies *Staff:* 6-10
Annual Budget: $250-500,000 *Tel:* (516) 549-8984
Hist. Note: Founded as a non-profit membership association of U.S. and Canadian shippers, receivers, and carriers, SNFCC is dedicated to the reduction of transit losses and the improvement of freight claim procedures in domestic and international commerce. Membership: $295/yr.
Publications:
Directory of Freight Claim Officers. a.
Claim Digest. m. adv.
Freight Claims in Plain English. (text)
Transportation Insurance in Plain English. (text)
Annual Meetings: March
1987-New Orleans, LA(Hilton)/March 4-6/300
1988-Las Vegas, NV

Shippers Oil Field Traffic Ass'n (1951)
105 East Vilbig Road, Irving TX 75060
Exec. Secretary: Wm. 'Mac' Sprucew
Members: 23 companies *Staff:* 1
Annual Budget: under $10,000 *Tel:* (214) 253-4988
Annual Meetings: March

Shock Soc. (1978)
Medical College of Georgia, Augusta GA 30912
Exec. Director: Dr. Sherwood M. Reichard
Members: 450 *Staff:* 3
Annual Budget: $50-100,000 *Tel:* (404) 828-2601
Hist. Note: Membership composed of individuals interested in extending basic clinical knowledge of the nature and treatment of shock and trauma.
Publications:
Circulatory Shock. m. adv.
Directory. a.
Annual Meetings: June
1987-Montreal, Quebec/June 7-11

Shoe Pattern Manufacturers Ass'n (1947)
715 Boylston St., Boston MA 02116
Mng. Director: Richard S. Guild, CAE
Members: 6 companies *Staff:* 1
Annual Budget: under $10,000 *Tel:* (617) 266-6800
Hist. Note: Makers of patterns for women's shoes. Formed by a merger of the Nat'l Shoe Pattern Manufacturers Ass'n and the Shoe Pattern Manufacturers Ass'n of New England.
Annual Meetings: February

Shoe Service Institute of America (1904)
112 Calendar Court Mall, Lagrange IL 60525
Exec. V. President: Robert L. Landwerlen
Members: 175-200 companies *Staff:* 2-5
Annual Budget: $250-500,000 *Tel:* (312) 482-8010
Hist. Note: Formerly Nat'l Leather and Shoe Finders Ass'n, it assumed its present name in 1949. Members are wholesalers and suppliers of shoe repair, shoe care and related items to the shoe service industry. Membership Fee: $250-500/yr. (Based on sales volume)
Publications:
Shoe Service Magazine. m. adv.
Findings Newsletter. m. adv.
Annual Meetings: July
1987-Chicago, IL/1,000

Shoe Suppliers Ass'n of America (1968)
Box 366, East Bridgewater MA 02333
Exec. V. President: Frank Underhill
Members: 51-55 companies *Staff:* 1
Annual Budget: under $10,000 *Tel:* (617) 378-2035
Hist. Note: Incorporated in Massachusetts. Membership principally from New England. Members are suppliers of some component going into the making of shoes, either raw materials or machinery. Has no paid staff. Membership: $125/yr. (company).
Annual Meetings: May, in New England.

Showmen's League of America (1913)
300 West Randolph St., Chicago IL 60606
Secretary: Noble Case
Members: 1,400-1,500 *Staff:* 2-5
Annual Budget: $25-50,000 *Tel:* (312) 332-6236
Hist. Note: A fraternal and benevolent organization of outdoor amusement operators and showmen.
Publication:
Directory. a. adv.

Sigma Delta Chi
Hist. Note: See The Soc. of Professional Journalists.

Sigma Tau Kappa
Hist. Note: An honorary society for members of the American Society of TV Cameramen.

Silicones Health Council (1982)
1330 Connecticut Ave., N.W., Washington DC 20036
Exec. Director: William H. Smock
Annual Budget: $50-100,000 *Tel:* (202) 659-0060
Hist. Note: An affiliate of the Synthetic Organic Chemical Manufacturers Ass'n which provides administrative support, SHC is an organization of organosilicones manufacturers. The group was formed to coordinate programs dealing with health, environmental and safety issues of interest to the industry and to disseminate scientifically sound information regarding silicones.

Silk and Rayon Printers and Dyers Ass'n of America (1942)
401 Hamburg Pike, Suite 103, Wayne NJ 07470
Exec. Secretary: Kenneth G. Monaghan

00269 12 05 86 1233

Members: 100-125 companies *Staff:* 6-10
Annual Budget: $50-100,000 *Tel:* (201) 942-7000
Hist. Note: Affiliated with the Textile Printers and Dyers Labor Relations Institute. Absorbed the Skein Dyers Association of America in 1977.

Silk Commission Manufacturers Ass'n (1920)
Hist. Note: Defunct in 1983.

Silver Institute (1971)
1026 16th St., N.W., Suite 101, Washington DC 20036
Exec. Director: John H. Lutley
Members: 100 companies *Staff:* 6-10
Annual Budget: $250-500,000 *Tel:* (202) 783-0500
Hist. Note: Members, drawn from 24 foreign countries as well as the U.S., are companies which mine and refine silver, fabricators and manufacturers of products containing silver.
Publications:
Silver Institute Letter. bi-m.
Modern Silver Coinage. a.
Silver Mine Production - Worldwide. a.
New Silver Technology. q.

Silver Users Ass'n (1947)
1717 K St., N.W., Suite 404, Washington DC 20006
Exec. V. Pres. and Secy.: Walter L. Frankland, Jr.
Members: 25-30 companies *Staff:* 2-5
Annual Budget: $100-250,000 *Tel:* (202) 785-3050
Hist. Note: Founded in 1947 and incorporated in Washington, DC in April, 1971, the Silver Users Ass'n represents manufacturers and distributors of products in which silver is an essential material, such as photographic materials, medical and dental supplies, batteries and electrical equipment, silverware, mirrors, commemorative art and jewelry. SUA works for the recognition of silver as a commodity and the removal of governmental regulations which retard its free exchange in commerce both foreign and domestic.
Publications:
Analysis of Bureau of Mines Silver Statistics. q.
U. S. Silver Summmary. a.
Annual Meetings: New York(Waldorf-Astoria)/Jan./85
1987-Jan. 9

Single Ply Roofing Institute (1982)
104 Wilmot Road, Suite 201, Deefield IL 60015-5195
Exec. V. President: Carl A. Wangman, CAE
Members: 95-100 companies *Staff:* 2-5
Annual Budget: $100-250,000 *Tel:* (312) 940-8800
Hist. Note: Established in Los Angeles, SPRI is comprised of manufacturers and marketers of sheet-applied Membrane roofing materials. Membership: $1,650/yr.
Publication:
Sprinfo. bi-m.
Annual Meetings: January
1987-Coronado, CA(del Coronado)
1988-Ft. Lauderdale, FL(Bonaventure)

Single Service Institute (1933)
1025 Connecticut Ave., N.W., Suite 513, Washington DC 20036
Exec. V. President: Joseph W. Bow, CMP, CAE
Members: 35-40 companies *Staff:* 2-5
Annual Budget: $250-500,000 *Tel:* (202) 347-0020
Hist. Note: Manufacturers of one-time use cups and plates for food service, nestable containers, placemats, prepackaging trays, egg cartons, etc. Formed by the merger in 1966 of the Paper Cup and Container Institute (1933), the Paper Plate Ass'n (1948) and the Linen and Lace Paper Institute (1954). Absorbed the Food Tray and Board Ass'n in 1971 (formerly Pulp and Paper Prepackaging Ass'n.) Absorbed the Egg Packaging Ass'n in 1975.
Publication:
Environment News Digest. 6/yr.
Annual Meetings: October/Washington, DC/50-75
1987-(Westin)/Oct. 14-16

Ski Industries America (1954)
8377 B Greensboro Drive, McLean VA 22102
President: David J. Ingemie
Members: 500 companies *Staff:* 16
Annual Budget: $2-5,000,000 *Tel:* (703) 556-9020
Hist. Note: Incorporated in New York December 10, 1954 as the National Ski Equipment and Clothing Association-primarily a credit reporting agency. The first organizational meeting was held May 22, 1955 at Shine's Restaurant, New York City and the present name was adopted in 1960.
Publications:
SIA Trade Show Directory. a.
Ski Retailer Advisor. m.
SIA Ski Rep Newsletter. 3/yr.
SIA Marketing Matters. bi-m.
SIA Membership Newsletter. m.
Annual Meetings: Las Vegas(Convention Center)/March/17,000
1987-March 13-18

Ski Retailers Council (1971)
600 Madison Ave., New York NY 10022
Director: Doris Taplinger
Members: 350-400 companies *Staff:* 2-5
Annual Budget: $50-100,000 *Tel:* (212) 874-3030
Publication:
SRC Newsletter. irreg.
Semi-annual meetings: Las Vegas and New York

Ski Retailers Internat'l (1968)
Hist. Note: Reported defunct in 1984.

Sleep Research Soc. (1961)
Univ. of Texas Health Science Center at,Dallas, 5323 Harry Hines, Dallas TX 75235-9070
President: Dr. Howard Roffwarg
Members: 425 *Staff:* 1
Annual Budget: $25-50,000 *Tel:* (214) 688-3040
Hist. Note: Founded as Ass'n for the Psychophysiological Study of Sleep, it assumed its present name in 1983. Membership: $125/yr. (individual); $1,000/yr. (organization/company)
Publication:
Sleep. bi-m. adv.
Annual Meetings:
1987-Copenhagen, Denmark (with European Sleep Soc.)

Slide Fastener Ass'n
Hist. Note: Became American Fastener Enclosure Ass'n in 1986.

Slovak Studies Ass'n (1977)
700 Penfield Ave, Havertown PA 19083
Editor: M. Mark Stolarik
Members: 120 individuals
Annual Budget: under $10,000 *Tel:* (215) 853-1363
Hist. Note: The SSA promotes inter-disciplinary scholarly research, publication, and teaching related to the Slovak experience the world over. Any person seriously engaged in Slovak studies is eligible. Membership: $5.
Publication:
Newsletter of the Slovak Studies Ass'n. ba.

Slurry Technology Ass'n (1975)
1800 Connecticut Ave., N.W., Suite 300, Washington DC 20009
Exec. Director: George H. Eatman
Members: 55-60 companies, 10-15 individuals *Staff:* 4
Annual Budget: $250-500,000 *Tel:* (202) 332-5751
Hist. Note: Organized in Houston, August, 1975. Pipeline and energy companies and manufacturers interested in pipeline delivery of solid liquid mixtures and direct firing of coal. Formerly the Slurry Transport Ass'n. Assumed present name in 1984.
Publication:
Proceedings, International Technical Conference. a.
Annual Meetings:
1987-New Orleans, LA(Hyatt Regency)/March 31-April 3/400

Slurry Transport Ass'n
Hist. Note: Became the Slurry Technology Ass'n in 1984.

Small Business Development Center Directors Ass'n
Hist. Note: Became the Ass'n of Small Business Development Centers in 1984.

Small Business Legislative Council (1977)
1025 Vermont Ave., N.W., Suite 1201, Washington DC 20005
President: John Satagaj
Members: 87 small businesses *Staff:* 2
Annual Budget: $100-250,000 *Tel:* (202) 639-8500
Hist. Note: Formerly affiliated with the Nat'l Small Business Ass'n, the SBLC became independent in 1985.
Publication:
SBLC Journal. m.
Annual Meetings: Late Winter in Washington, DC

Small Engine Servicing Dealers Ass'n (1975)
Box 6312, St. Petersburg FL 33736
Exec. Director: Raymond D. Jordan
Members: 3-400 *Staff:* 2-5
Annual Budget: $10-25,000 *Tel:* (813) 397-3925
Hist. Note: Members are dealers in equipment powered by small engines - lawn mowers, power saws, tractors, etc.

Small Hydro Soc. (1979)
Hist. Note: Inactive in 1986.

Small Independent Record Manufacturers Ass'n (1980)
c/o Starvision Internat'l Records, 2001 West Main St., Suite 205E, Stamford CT 06902
Chairman: Jimmy Dockett
Members: 27 companies
Annual Budget: under $10,000 *Tel:* (203) 358-9948
Hist. Note: Members are black-owned record companies grossing less than $250,000 per year. Membership: $25-200/yr.
Publication:
SIRMA Newsletter. q.
Annual Meetings: Semi-annual

Small Motor Manufacturers Ass'n (1975)
Box 637, Libertyville IL 60048
Exec. Director: Betsy Bevington
Members: 97 companies *Staff:* 2-5
Annual Budget: $50-100,000 *Tel:* (312) 362-3201
Hist. Note: Users, suppliers, and original equipment manufacturers of fractional and sub-fractional horsepower motors.
Publications:
Newsletter.
Membership Directory.
Meter Market Statistics.
Semi-annual Meetings: Spring and Fall
1987-Wesley Chapel, FL(Saddlebrook)/March 18-20/150

Small Press Writers and Artists Organization (1978)
411 Main Trail, Ormond Beach FL 32074
President: Audrey Parente
Members: 400 *Staff:* 4
Annual Budget: under $10,000 *Tel:* (904) 672-9461
Hist. Note: Writers of science fiction and fantasy who publish in small press journals. Membership: $10/year.
Publications:
Newsletter. bi-m.
Showcase. a.
Annual Meetings: Not held

Smaller Manufacturers Council (1945)
339 Blvd. of Allies, Pittsburgh PA 15222
President: Leo R. McDonough
Members: 2,500 companies *Staff:* 7
Annual Budget: $500-1,000,000 *Tel:* (412) 391-1622
Hist. Note: Membership open to all business except legal, medical, and financial employing less than 500 people.
Publications:
Dynamic Business. m. adv.
Product and Services Directory. bi-a. adv.
Council News. bi-m.
Annual Meetings: September

Smelter Control Research Ass'n
Hist. Note: Six copper, lead and zinc producers. Has no paid staff or permanent office. Administrative support, when needed, is provided by the American Bureau of Metal Statistics.

Smelter Environment Research Ass'n
Hist. Note: Ten to fifteen copper, lead and zinc producers. Has no paid staff or permanent office. Intermittently becomes inactive. Administrative support, when needed, is provided by the American Bureau of Metal Statistics.

Smokeless Tobacco Council (1968)
1925 K St., N.W., Suite 504, Washington DC 20006
President: Michael J. Kerrigan
Members: 5 companies *Staff:* 5
Annual Budget: $2-5,000,000 *Tel:* (202) 452-1252
Hist. Note: Formerly (1971) Snuff Producers Council. Media source and information bureau for producers of snuff and chewing (smokeless) tobacco.

Snack Food Ass'n (1937)
1711 King St., Suite 1, Alexandria VA 22314
President: John R. Cady
Members: 600 companies *Staff:* 14
Annual Budget: $2-5,000,000 *Tel:* (703) 836-4500
Hist. Note: Formerly (1976) the Potato Chip Institute Internat'l and (1985) the Potato Chip/Snack Food Ass'n. Represents manufacturers of snacks made from vegetables, grains, fruits, meats and nuts. Supports the Snack Political Action Committee.
Publication:
Chipper/Snacker. m. adv.
Annual Meetings: Winter
1987-Nashville, TN(Opryland)/March 8-11/1,500-1,900
1988-Dallas, TX(Loew's Anatole)/March 20-24/1,500-1,900
1989-New Orleans, LA(Rivergate)/Feb. 19-23/1,500-1,900

Soap and Detergent Ass'n (1926)
475 Park Avenue South, New York NY 10016
President: Theodore E. Brenner
Members: 145 companies *Staff:* 22
Annual Budget: $2-5,000,000 *Tel:* (212) 725-1262
Hist. Note: Formerly Ass'n of American Soap & Glycerine Producers. Four divisions: Household; Industrial & Institutional; Technical & Materials; Glycerine & Oleochemical.
Publication:
Newsletter. m.
Annual Meetings: Boca Raton in January

Social Implications of Technology Soc.
Hist. Note: A subsidiary of the Institute of Electrical and Electronics Engineers. Membership in the Society, open only to IEEE members, includes subscription to a technical periodical in the field published by IEEE. All administrative support is provided by IEEE.

Social Science Research Council (1923)
605 Third Ave., New York NY 10158
President: Frederic Wakeman
Members: 7 societies, 9 elected individuals *Staff:* 25-30
Annual Budget: over $5,000,000 *Tel:* (212) 661-0280
Hist. Note: A not-for-profit corporation governed by a board of directors to advance research in the social sciences. Some members of the board are elected from seven national scientific societies; the American Anthropological Ass'n, the American Economic Ass'n, the American Historical Ass'n, the American Political Science Ass'n, the American Psychological Ass'n, the American Sociological Ass'n, and the American Statistical Ass'n. Has an annual budget of $6-8 million.
Publications:
Social Science Research Council Items. q.
Annual report. a.

00270 12 05 86 1233

Soc. for Adolescent Medicine (1968)
Box 3462, Granada Hills CA 91344
Exec. Secretary: Richard C. Brown
Members: 900 *Staff:* 4
Annual Budget: $100-250,000 *Tel:* (818) 368-5996
Hist. Note: Doctors, nurses, social workers, and psychologists involved with health care for adolescents.
Publication:
Journal of Adolescent Health Care. bi-m.
Annual Meetings: Spring
1987-Boston, MA
1988-Seattle, WA
1989-San Francisco, CA
1990-Atlanta, GA

Soc. for Advancement of Management (1912)
2331 Victory Parkway, Cincinnati OH 45206
Exec. Director: Joseph L. Bush, Jr.
Members: 3-4,000 *Staff:* 2-5
Annual Budget: $100-250,000 *Tel:* (513) 751-4566
Hist. Note: A professional organization of management executives, it was formed by a merger of the Taylor Soc. and the Soc. of Industrial Engineers; Absorbed the Industrial Methods Soc. in 1946. Merged in 1973 with the American Management Ass'n, Inc. (1923), the American Foundation for Management Research, Inc. (1960), the Internat'l Management Ass'n, Inc., and the Presidents Ass'n, Inc. (1961), to form the American Management Ass'ns, of which it was a semi-autonomous division. SAM returned to independent status on July 1, 1983 and is no longer affiliated with American Management Associations. Membership: $65/year (individual).
Publication:
Advanced Management Journal. q.
Annual Meetings: Spring
1987-Lancaster, PA/May 3-5

Soc. for American Archaeology (1934)
1511 K St., N.W., Suite 716, Washington DC 20005
Exec. Director: Jerome A. Miller
Members: 4,500 *Staff:* 1
Annual Budget: $250-500,000 *Tel:* (202) 638-6079
Hist. Note: Organized in Pittsburgh December 28, 1934 to speak for the entire American archaeological discipline. Membership: $50/year.
Publication:
American Antiquity. q. adv.
Annual Meetings: Spring/1,500
1987-Toronto,Ontario(Royal York)/May 6-10
1988-Phoenix, AZ(Hilton)/April 27-May 1

Soc. for American Cuisine (1986)
304 West Liberty St., Louisville KY 40202
Exec. V. President: Phillip S. Cooke
Members: 300 *Staff:* 2-5
Tel: (502) 583-3783
Hist. Note: A professional association for the advancement of American food and wine.
Annual Meetings: Fall
1987-Charleston, SC/Sept. 13-16

Soc. for Applied Anthropology (1941)
P.O. Box 24083, Oklahoma City OK 73124-0083
President: Theodore Downing
Members: 2,500 individuals *Staff:* 2-5
Annual Budget: $100-250,000 *Tel:* (602) 326-3338
Hist. Note: Promotes the interdisciplinary scientific study of the principles controlling the relations of human beings to one another, and the wide application of those principles to practical problems. Membership: $42/yr.
Publications:
Human Organization. q.
Practicing Anthropology. q.
Annual Meetings: Spring
1987-Oaxaca, Mexico/April 8-12
1988-Tampa, FL

Soc. for Applied Learning Technology (1972)
50 Culpeper St., Warrenton VA 22186
President: Raymond G. Fox
Members: 550-600 individuals *Staff:* 2-5
Annual Budget: $250-500,000 *Tel:* (703) 347-0055
Hist. Note: Founded in Washington, DC in 1972. Members include industrial, military and academic managers involved in the design production or use of technology-based educational systems. Membership: $30/yr.
Publication:
Journal of Educational Technology Systems. q.
Annual Meetings: February
1987-Orlando, FL/Feb. 18-20

Soc. for Applied Spectroscopy (1956)
Box 1438, Frederick MD 21701
Exec. Administrator: Donna L. Welch
Members: 4,000-4,200 *Staff:* 3
Annual Budget: $500-1,000,000 *Tel:* (301) 694-8122
Hist. Note: The Federation of Spectroscopic Societies was founded in Pittsburgh in March 1956. From this grew the Society for Applied Spectroscopy established in New York in November 1958 and incorporated in Pennsylvania in 1960. Affiliated with the Iron and Steel Chemists Association, the Fourier Transform Spectroscopy Group and the Coblentz Soc. Membership: $30/yr. (individual), $200/yr. (company).
Publications:
Applied Spectroscopy. 8/yr. adv.
Newsletter. 3/yr.
Annual Meetings: Fall/2,000
1987-Detroit, MI
1988-Boston, MA

Soc. for Biomaterials (1985)
University of Alabama, Department of Biomaterials, Birmingham AL 35294
Exec. Secy.: L. Rachel Sellers
Members: 600-700 *Staff:* 1
Annual Budget: $50-100,000 *Tel:* (205) 254-0377
Hist. Note: Members are scientists, surgeons, dentists and others interested in the problems of developing replacements for living tissue. Seeks to encourage research and development and education in the biomaterials sciences. Membership: $90/yr.
Publications:
Journal of Biomedical Materials Research. 9/yr.
The Torch. semi-a.
Annual Meetings: Spring
1987-New York, NY/June 2-6
1988-Kyoto, Japan/Late April
1989-Orlando, FL/April 28-May 2

Soc. for Clinical and Experimental Hypnosis (1949)
128-A Kings Park Dr., Liverpool NY 13090
Admin. Director: Marion Kenn
Members: 1,100-1,200 *Staff:* 2-5
Annual Budget: $100-250,000 *Tel:* (315) 652-7299
Hist. Note: Founded June 12, 1949 and incorporated in New York in 1963. Affiliated with the American Ass'n for the Advancement of Science, the World Federation for Mental Health and the Internat'l Soc. of hypnosis. Membership: $70/yr.
Publications:
International Journal of Clinical and Experimental Hypnosis. q. adv.
SCEH Newsletter. q.
Annual Meetings: Fall
1987-Los Angeles, CA(Ambassador)/Oct. 26-31/350-400
1988-Ashville, NC(Grove Park Inn)/Oct. 31-Nov. 5/350-400

Soc. for Clinical Ecology (1965)
Hist. Note: Changed name to American Academy of Environmental Medicine in 1984.

Soc. for Clinical Trials (1978)
600 Wyndhurst Ave., Baltimore MD 21210
Vice President: Paul Meier
Members: 1,500 individuals *Staff:* 2
Annual Budget: $25-50,000 *Tel:* (301) 435-4200
Hist. Note: Incorporated in the State of Maryland, members of the Society are individuals involved in the controlled medical testing of procedures, drugs and other therapeutic agents. Membership: $58/yr.
Publication:
Controlled Clinical Trials. q. adv.
Annual Meetings: Spring
1987-Atlanta, GA(Westin Peachtree Plaza Hotel)/May 17-20/800
1988-San Diego, CA(Town & Country Hotel)/May 21-26/850

Soc. for Clinical Vascular Surgery (1970)
Box 1565, 13 Elm St., Manchester MA 01944
Conference Administrator: Charlene Terranova
Members: 500 individuals *Staff:* 1
Annual Budget: $100-250,000 *Tel:* (617) 927-8330
Hist. Note: Membership: $100/yr.
Annual Meetings: March
1987-Scottsdale, AZ(Hyatt Regency at Gainey Ranch)

Soc. for College and University Planning (1966)
2026 M School of Education Bldg., University of Michigan, Ann Arbor MI 48109-1259
Exec. Secretary: Joanne E. MacRae
Members: 1,800 *Staff:* 2-5
Annual Budget: $100-250,000 *Tel:* (313) 763-4776
Hist. Note: Represents university and college presidents and other officers involved in long-range planning, government agencies and private consulting firms. Membership: $65/yr.
Publications:
News. q.
Planning for Higher Education. q.
Annual Meetings: Summer
1987-Washington, DC(J.W. Marriott)/July 19-22
1988-Toronto, Canada
1989-Denver, CO

Soc. for Computer Applications in Engineering, Planning and Architecture (1965)
15713 Crabbs Branch Way, Rockville MD 20855
Exec. Director: Patricia C. Johnson
Members: 400 *Staff:* 2-5
Annual Budget: $100-250,000 *Tel:* (301) 926-7070
Hist. Note: Known as CEPA, Inc., CEPA originally stood for "Civil Engineering Program Applications." Formed in 1965 by a small group of civil engineers concerned with the effective use of computers in the engineering field. Principal objective is to further the effective application of computers in engineering, architecture, and related fields. Provides a means for the exchange of information and for the exchange and cooperative development of computer programs and systems pertaining to engineering, planning, and architecture. CEPA has an international membership. Membership: $225/yr. (organization)
Publications:
CEPA Newsletter. q. adv.
Computer Software Directory. bien.
Proceedings. semi-a.
Semi-annual meetings: Spring and Fall
1987-Washington, DC/June 22-24 and Chicago, IL/Fall

Soc. for Computer Simulation (1952)
Box 17900, San Diego CA 92117
Exec. Director: Charles A. Pratt
Members: 2,300 engineers, scientists, educators *Staff:* 10-14
Annual Budget: $500-1,000,000 *Tel:* (619) 277-3888
Hist. Note: Founded in Oxnard, CA in 1952 as the Simulation Council and incorporated in California in 1957 as Simulation Councils, Inc. Became Soc. for Computer Simulation in 1973. A founding member of the American Federation of Information Processing Societies and the Nat'l Computer Conference Board. A sponsoring society of the American Automatic Control Council. Membership: $35/yr.
Publications:
Simulation. m. adv.
Simulation Series. q.
Transactions. q.
Annual Meetings: In conjunction with the Summer Computer Simulation Conference
1987-Montreal, Quebec/July 27-29
1988-Seattle, WA
1989-Austin, TX

Soc. for Conceptual and Content Analysis by Computer (1983)
Department of German and Russian, Bowling Green State University, Bowling Green OH 43403
Secretary: Prof. Klaus M. Schmidt
Members: 200
Annual Budget: under $10,000 *Tel:* (419) 372-2260
Hist. Note: Established in Raleigh, NC, SCCAC is a loosely organized group, composed of scholars from various disciplines interested and active in the field of conceptual and content analysis of texts by computer.
Publications:
Newsletter. a.
Membership List. a.
Annual Meetings: Meets semi-annually, usually with a group with related interests.
1987-Columbia, SC(Univ. of SC)/April
1987-West Germany(Univ. of Trier)/Sept.

Soc. for Cryobiology (1964)
9650 Rockville Pike, Bethesda MD 20814
Secretariat:
Members: 450
Annual Budget: $25-50,000 *Tel:* (301) 530-7120
Hist. Note: Organized March 20, 1964 and incorporated the same year in Maryland. Promotes research and disseminates knowledge in low temperature biology and medicine. Membership: $15/yr.
Publication:
Cryobiology. bi-m. adv.
Annual Meetings: Summer, at a University.

Soc. for Developmental Biology (1939)
Hist. Note: Address unknown in 1987.

Soc. for Economic Botany (1959)
Medicinal Chemistry and Pharmacognosy, College of Pharmacy, Univ. of Illinois, Chicago IL 60612
Secretary: A. Douglas Kinghorn
Members: 700 individuals *Staff:* 0
Annual Budget: under $10,000 *Tel:* (312) 996-0914
Hist. Note: Promotes research on the past, present and future uses of plants. Has no paid staff. Membership: $20/yr.
Publication:
Economic Botany. q.
Annual Meetings: Summer
1987-Chicago, IL(University of Illinois at Chicago)/June/120

Soc. for Environmental Geochemistry and Health (1971)
Life Science Dept., Univ. of Missouri, Rolla MO 65401
Secy.-Treas.: Dr. Nord L. Gale
Members: 300-350 *Staff:* 1
Annual Budget: under $10,000 *Tel:* (314) 341-4831
Hist. Note: Members are individuals interested in the relationship between geochemistry and health and the study of such questions as the role of iodine in goiter, fluorine in tooth decay, the effect of trace metals on the environment and occupational diseases such as silicosis and beryliosis. Affiliated with the American Ass'n for the Advancement of Science. Membership: $25/yr.
Publications:
Interface. q. adv.
Environmental Geochemistry and Health. q.
Annual Meetings: June at the Conference on Trace Substances in Environmental Health
1987-St. Louis, MO(Clarion Hotel)/May 25-28

Soc. for Epidemiologic Research (1967)
c/o American Journal of Epidemiology, 624 N. Broadway, Room 225, Baltimore MD 21205
Secretary-Treasurer: Susan T. Sacks, Ph.D.
Members: 2,100 *Staff:* 1
Annual Budget: $50-100,000 *Tel:* (301) 955-3441
Hist. Note: Established in 1967 in Washington, DC.
Publication:
American Journal of Epidemiology. m. adv.
Annual Meetings: June

00271 12 05 86 1233

Soc. for Ethnomusicology (1956)
P.O. Box 2984, Ann Arbor MI 48106
Secretary: Joseph Hickerson
Members: 2,200 *Staff:* 1
Annual Budget: $50-100,000 *Tel:* (313) 665-9400
Hist. Note: Member American Council of Learned Societies. Has an internat'l membership.
Publications:
Ethnomusicology. q. adv.
Newsletter. 3/yr.
Annual Meetings: Fall
1987-Ann Arbor, MI
1988-Open
1989-Madison, WI

Soc. for Experimental Biology and Medicine (1903)
630 West 168th St., New York NY 10032
Exec. Secretary: Dr. Mero Nocenti
Members: 2,450 *Staff:* 3
Tel: (212) 927-6485
Hist. Note: Established February 25, 1903 to cultivate the experimental method of investigation in biology and medicine.
Publication:
Proceedings. 11/yr. adv.

Soc. for Experimental Mechanics (1943)
7 School St., Bethel CT 06801
Mng. Director: Kenneth A. Galione
Members: 2,700-3,300 *Staff:* 10-12
Annual Budget: $250-500,000 *Tel:* (203) 790-6373
Hist. Note: Founded in 1943 and incorporated in Delaware in 1961. Formerly (1984) the Soc. for Experimental Stress Analysis. Promotes research in experimental mechanics. Membership: $45/yr.
Publications:
Experimental Mechanics. q.
Experimental Techniques. m. adv.
Semi-annual Meetings: Spring and Fall/500

Soc. for Experimental Stress Analysis (1943)
Hist. Note: Became the Soc. for Experimental Mechanics in 1984.

Soc. for Foodservice Management (1979)
304 West Liberty St., Suite 301, Louisville KY 40202
Exec. V. President: Phillip Cooke
Members: 850 individuals *Staff:* 5
Annual Budget: $100-250,000 *Tel:* (502) 583-3783
Hist. Note: Executives and managers of employee food service operations and contract companies providing food at places of employment. Formed as the result of a merger between the Ass'n for Food Service Management (established 1970) and the Nat'l Industrial Cafeteria Managers' Ass'n (established 1949) on July 1, 1979. Membership $150/yr.
Publications:
Newsletter. m.
Management Report. irreg.
Membership Roster. a.
Annual Meetings: Fall
1987-Las Vegas, NV(Desert Inn)/Sept. 21-25/250

Soc. for Foodservice Systems (1980)
HITM, 830 Transfer Road, St. Paul MN 55114
President: O. Peter Snyder
Members: 95-115 *Staff:* 1
Annual Budget: $10-25,000 *Tel:* (612) 646-7077
Hist. Note: Members are professionals involved in all aspects of commercial and non-commercial foodservice. Membership: $50/yr. (individual); $500/yr. (organization/company)
Publication:
Journal of Foodservice Systems. q. adv.
Annual Meetings: Spring
1987-Dallas, TX

Soc. for French Historical Studies (1955)
Dept. of History, Mills College, 5000 Mac Arthur Blvd., Oakland CA 94613
Exec. Officer: Bertram M. Gordon
Members: 1,400-1,500 *Staff:* 1
Annual Budget: under $10,000 *Tel:* (804) 924-3478
Publication:
French Historical Studies. semi-a.

Soc. for General Systems Research (1954)
Univ. of Louisville, Louisville KY 40292
President: Peter B. Checkland
Members: 900-1,000 *Staff:* 2-5
Annual Budget: $50-100,000 *Tel:* (502) 588-6996
Hist. Note: Originated in 1954 as the Soc. for the Advancement of General Systems Theory and incorporated in Michigan in 1955. Became the Soc. for General Systems Research in 1957. Affiliated with American Ass'n for the Advancement of Science, United Nations Educational, Scientific and Cultural Organization, and Internat'l Federation for Systems Research. Promotes the development of theoretical systems applicable to more than one of the traditional fields of knowledge. Membership: $54/yr. (individual); $150/yr. (organization/company)
Publications:
Behavioral Science. bi-m.
General Systems Bulletin. 3/yr.
General Systems Yearbook. a.
Systems Research Journal. q.
Annual Meetings: With American Ass'n for the Advancement of Science

Soc. for Gynecologic Investigation (1952)
600 Maryland Ave., S.W., Suite 300E, Washington DC 20024-2588
Administrator: Ava Tayman
Members: 455 *Staff:* 1
Annual Budget: $50-100,000 *Tel:* (202) 863-2544
Hist. Note: Membership: $50/year.
Annual Meetings: March
1987-Atlanta, GA/March 18-21
1988-Baltimore, MD/March 17-20
1989-San Diego, CA/March 15-18

Soc. for Health and Human Values (1969)
1311-A Dolley Madison Blvd., 3A, McLean VA 22101
Exec. Director: George K. Degnon, CAE
Members: 900-1,000 *Staff:* 2-5
Annual Budget: $25-50,000 *Tel:* (703) 556-9222
Hist. Note: Membership: $40/year.
Annual Meetings: Fall
1987-Rosslyn, VA(Rosslyn Hyatt)/Nov. 5-7/300
1988-Chicago, IL/300

Soc. for Historians of American Foreign Relations (1967)
Dept. of History, North Texas State U., P.O. Box 13735, North Texas Station, Denton TX 76203
Exec. Secy.-Treas.: William Kamman
Members: 975 *Staff:* 1
Annual Budget: $10-25,000 *Tel:* (817) 565-2288
Hist. Note: Affiliated with the American Historical Ass'n and the Organization of American Historians. Promotes the study of diplomatic history in cooperation with the National Archives and other government agencies. Membership: $16.50/yr.
Publications:
Diplomatic History. q. adv.
Newsletter. q. adv.
Roster and Research List. a.
Annual Meetings: Summer
1987-Annapolis, MD(U.S. Naval Academy)/June 24-27

Soc. for Historical Archaeology (1967)
P.O. Box 231033, Pleasant Hill CA 94523
Secy.-Treas.: Stephanie H. Rodeffer
Members: 1,700-1,800
Annual Budget: $25-50,000 *Tel:* (415) 686-4660
Hist. Note: Is concerned with the identification, excavation, interpretation and conservation of sites and materials and applies archaeological methods to the study of history. Membership: $20/yr.(individual); $40/yr.(organization). Business office for membership and back issues of publications: P.O. Box 241, Glassboro, NJ, 08028.
Publications:
Historical Archaeology. semi-a. adv.
SHA Newsletter. q.
Special Publications. a.
Annual Meetings: Winter
1987-Savannah, GA
1988-Reno, NV(MGM Grand)/Jan.
1989-Baltimore, MD(Convention Center)/Jan.

Soc. for History Education (1972)
Cal. State Univ., 1250 Bellflower Blvd., Long Beach CA 90840
Secretary: Eugene L. Asher
Members: 3,000 *Staff:* 2-5
Annual Budget: $50-100,000 *Tel:* (213) 498-4503
Hist. Note: Formerly (1972) History Teachers Ass'n. Concerned with the way history is taught at the secondary and post-secondary levels. Membership: $22/yr.(individual); $28/yr.(institution)
Publications:
The History Teacher. q. adv.
Network News Exchange. semi-a. adv.

Soc. for History in the Federal Government (1979)
Box 14139, Benjamin Franklin Station, Washington DC 20044
Secretary: JoAnne McCormick
Members: 500
Annual Budget: $10-25,000
Hist. Note: Professional society of historians, archivists, curators and others with an interest in the historical and archival activities of the U.S. government. Affiliated with the American Historical Ass'n. Membership: $12/yr.
Publications:
The Federalist. q.
Roster. a.
Annual Meetings: Spring
1987-Washington, DC(Hyatt)/April 24-26/300

Soc. for Hospital Social Work Directors (1966)
840 North Lake Shore Dr., Chicago IL 60611
Director: Carolyn Hatzis
Members: 2,000-2,500 *Staff:* 2-5
Annual Budget: $250-500,000 *Tel:* (312) 280-6414
Hist. Note: Full membership is open to social work administrators or consultants in the administration of social work programs in a hospital or related health care institution who hold a masters degree from a graduate school of social work accredited by the Council on Social Work Education. The Society is affiliated with the American Hospital Ass'n. Membership: $79/yr.
Publications:
Social Work Administration (newsletter). bi-m.
Discharge Planning Update. q.
Annual Meetings:
1987-Orlando, FL/800
1988-Seattle, WA/700

Soc. for Humanistic Anthropology
1703 New Hampshire Ave., N.W., Washington DC 20009
Secretary: Marea Teski
Members: 201
Tel: (202) 232-8800
Hist. Note: An affiliate of the American Anthropological Association, which provides administrative support. Members are interested in the human meaning of anthropological inquiry and the anthropologist's commitment to experience and evaluation. Membership: $20/yr.
Publication:
Anthropology and Humanism. q.
Annual Meetings: With the American Anthropological Association.

Soc. for Humanistic Judaism (1969)
28611 West Twelve Mile Road, Farmington Hills MI 48018
Exec. Director: Miriam Jerris
Members: 1,500 *Staff:* 1
Annual Budget: $100-250,000 *Tel:* (313) 478-7610
Hist. Note: Creates, publishes and shares holiday and life cycle materials for secular humanistic Jews. Membership: $25/yr. (individual); $35/yr. (household).
Publications:
Humanistic Judaism. q.
Halmanorah. q.
Annual Meetings: May
1987-Deerfield, IL(Congregation Beth Or)/May 1-3
1988-Farmington Hills, MI(Birmingham Temple)/May 6-8

Soc. for Industrial and Applied Mathematics (1952)
1405 Architects Building, 117 South 17th Street, Philadelphia PA 19103
Mng. Director: I. Edward Block
Members: 6,500 individuals, 245 organizations *Staff:* 30-35
Annual Budget: $2-5,000,000 *Tel:* (215) 564-2929
Hist. Note: Organized in Philadelphia in Nov., 1951 and incorporated in Delaware in April, 1952. Affiliated with the American Federation of Information Processing Societies and the American Ass'n for the Advancement of Science. Member of the Conference Board of the Mathematical Sciences and the Division of Mathematics of Nat'l Research Council. Furthers the application of mathematics to problems of industry and science. Membership: $52/yr.
Publications:
SIAM Journal on Algebraic and Discrete Methods. q. adv.
SIAM Journal on Applied Mathematics. bi-m. adv.
SIAM Journal on Computing. bi-m. adv.
SIAM Journal on Control and Optimization. bi-m. adv.
SIAM Journal on Mathematical Analysis. bi-m. adv.
SIAM Journal on Numerical Analysis. bi-m. adv.
SIAM Journal on Scientific and Statistical Computing. bi-m.
SIAM News. bi-m. adv.
SIAM Review. q. adv.
Theory of Probability and its Applications. q. adv.
Annual Meetings:
1987-Denver, CO/Oct./600

Soc. for Industrial Archeology (1971)
National Museum of American History, Room 5020, Washington DC 20560
President: Thorwald Torgersen
Members: 1,200 *Staff:* 1
Annual Budget: $10-25,000 *Tel:* (202) 357-2228
Hist. Note: Founded in Washington at the National Museum of American History to promote the study of the physical survivals of our technical and industrial past. Membership: $25/yr.(individual), $30/yr. (organizaiton). Has no paid staff. Officers change bi-annually.
Publications:
IA. a. adv.
SIA Newsletter. q.
Semi-annual meetings: Spring and Fall

Soc. for Industrial Microbiology (1949)
P.O. Box 12534, Arlington VA 22209-8534
Business Secy.: Ann Kulback
Members: 1,700-1,800 *Staff:* 2
Annual Budget: $50-100,000 *Tel:* (703) 941-5373
Hist. Note: Founded in 1949 and incorporated in 1960. Promotes the advancement of the microbiological sciences especially as applied to industry. The Society is an Adherent Society member of the American Institute of Biological Sciences, Inc. Membership: $35-50/yr.(individual); $200/yr.(corporation).
Publications:
Journal Industrial Microbiology. bi-m. adv.
Newsletter. bi-m. adv.
Proceedings of Annual Meeting. a.
Annual Meetings: August
1987-Baltimore, MD(Hyatt Regency)/Aug. 9-14/550-750

Soc. for Information Display (1962)
8055 West Manchester, Suite 615, Playa Del Rey CA 90293
Office Manager: Bettye Burdett
Members: 2,000-2,500 *Staff:* 2-5
Annual Budget: $50-100,000 *Tel:* (213) 305-1502
Hist. Note: Membership: $35/yr.
Publications:
Digest of Technical Papers. a.
Information Display Journal. adv.
Proceedings of SID. a.
Seminar Lecture Notes. a.
Conference Record. a.
Semi-annual Meetings: Spring and Fall
1987-New Orleans, LA(Hyatt Regency)/May 11-15
1987-London, England(Savoy Place)

00272 12 05 86 1233

Soc. for Information Management (1969)
111 East Wacker Drive, Suite 600, Chicago IL 60601
Exec. Director: Henry Givray
Members: 1,400 individuals, 80 companies *Staff:* 2-5
Annual Budget: $100-250,000 *Tel:* (312) 644-6610
Hist. Note: SOI was formed to enhance international recognition of information as a basic organizational resource and to promote the effective utilization and management of this resource towards the improvement of management performance. It attempts to enhance communications between MIS directors and the senior executives responsible for management of the business enterprise. Formerly (until 1982) the Soc. for Management Information Systems.
Publications:
Conference Proceedings. a.
MIS Quarterly. q.
Newsletter. bi-m.
Annual Meetings: September

Soc. for Intercultural Education, Training and Research (1974)
Hist. Note: Became the Internat'l Soc. for Intercultural Education, Training and Research in 1985.

Soc. for Invertebrate Pathology (1967)
Dept. of Zoology, Arizona State University, Tempe AZ 85287
Secretary: Elizabeth W. Davidson
Members: 723 *Staff:* 1
Annual Budget: $10-25,000
Hist. Note: Has no paid staff or permanent headquarters. Membership: $11/yr.
Publications:
Directory. irreg.
Newsletter. q.
Annual Meetings: Fall

Soc. for Investigative Dermatology (1937)
San Francisco General Hospital, Room 269, Bldg. 100, San Francisco CA 94110
Secy.-Treas.: Ervin H. Epstein, Jr.
Members: 2,600 *Staff:* 2-5
Annual Budget: $100-250,000 *Tel:* (415) 647-3992
Hist. Note: Founded and incorporated in New York, April 24, 1937.
Publication:
Journal of Investigative Dermatology. m. adv.
Annual Meetings: Spring

Soc. for Italian Historical Studies (1955)
Boston College, Chestnut Hill MA 02167
Exec. Secretary: Alan J. Reinerman
Members: 350 *Staff:* 1
Annual Budget: under $10,000 *Tel:* (617) 969-0100
Hist. Note: Members are professors and students of Italian history. Encourages the study and teaching of Italian history; promotes research; and awards prizes. Membership: $3/yr.
Publication:
Newsletter. a.
Annual Meetings: With the American Historical Ass'n
1987-Washington, DC/Dec. 28-30/150

Soc. for Latin American Anthropology (1969)
1703 New Hampshire Ave., N.W., Washington DC 20009
Treasurer: Jane H. Hill
Members: 528
Annual Budget: under $10,000 *Tel:* (202) 232-8800
Hist. Note: Professional anthropologists interested in Latin America. Affiliated with the American Anthropological Association, which provides administrative support. Founded as the Ad Hoc Group on Latin American Anthropology, it became the Latin American Anthropology Group in 1971 and assumed its present name in 1982.
Publication:
LAAG Contributions. a.
Annual Meetings: With the American Anthropological Association

Soc. for Magnetic Resonance Imaging (1982)
1340 Old Chain Bridge Road, Suite 300, McLean VA 22101
President: Richard J. Burk, Jr.
Members: 1,000 *Staff:* 6-10
Annual Budget: $25-50,000 *Tel:* (703) 790-1745
Hist. Note: Physicians and basic scientists promoting the applications of magnetic resonance techniques to medicine and biology, with special emphasis on imaging. Membership: $65/yr.
Publication:
Magnetic Resonance Imaging. q. adv.

Soc. for Management Information Systems (1969)
Hist. Note: Became the Society for Information Management in 1982.

Soc. for Marketing Professional Services (1973)
801 North Fairfax St., Suite 215, Alexandria VA 22314
Exec. Director: Jeanne M. Murphy
Members: 3,800 *Staff:* 2-5
Annual Budget: $500-1,000,000 *Tel:* (703) 549-6117
Hist. Note: Employees of architectural, engineering, planning, landscape architectural, interior design and construction management firms who are responsible for marketing their organizations' services. Membership: $175/yr.
Publication:
SMPS news. m.
Annual Meetings: September
1987-Chicago, IL(Hilton)/Sept. 29-Oct. 2

Soc. for Medical Anthropology (1968)
1703 New Hampshire Ave., N.W., Washington DC 20009
Secy.-Treas.: Joan Anderson
Members: 1,400-1,500
Tel: (202) 232-8800
Hist. Note: An affiliate of the American Anthropological Association, which provides administrative support. Members are interested in the anthropological aspects of health, illness, health care and related topics. Membership: $12/year.
Publication:
Medical Anthropology Quarterly. q.
Annual Meetings: With the American Anthropological Association.

Soc. for Music Teacher Education (1983)
c/o Music Educators Nat'l Conference, 1902 Association Drive, Reston VA 22091
Staff Liaison: Harriet M. Mogge
Members: 750 individuals
Tel: (703) 860-4000
Hist. Note: Formed in response to a need felt by college instructors within the Music Educators Nat'l Conference for more specific meetings and programs aimed at their instruction and curriculum.
Annual Meetings: Meets biennially with the Music Educators Nat'l Conference.

Soc. for Natural Philosophy (1963)
Dept. of Mathematics, Southern Illinois Univ. at Carbondale, Carbondale IL 62901
Secretary: Scott Spector
Members: 300
Annual Budget: under $10,000 *Tel:* (618) 453-5302
Hist. Note: Mathematicians, physicists, chemists, engineers and other scientists interested in the foundations of mathematical sciences in nature. Areas of concern to the Society's members include rational continuum mechanics, electromagnetism, and statistical mechanics.
Annual Meetings: Usually at a University Environment
1987-New Haven, CT(Yale University)/Fall
1988-Baltimore, MD(Johns Hopkins University)/Spring

Soc. for Neuroscience (1969)
11 Dupont Circle, N.W., Washington DC 20036
Exec. Director: Nancy Beang
Members: 10,000 *Staff:* 10
Annual Budget: $1-2,000,000 *Tel:* (202) 462-6688
Hist. Note: Affiliated with the Nat'l Soc. for Medical Research. Membership: $45/yr. (individual).
Publications:
Neuroscience Abstracts. a.
Journal of Neuroscience. m. adv.
Neuroscience Newsletter. bi-m.
Neuroscience Training Programs in North America. bien.
Annual Meetings: Fall/8-10,000
1987-New Orleans, LA(Conv. Center)/Nov. 16-21
1988-Toronto, Ontario(Conv. Center)/Nov. 13-18
1989-Phoenix, AZ(Conv. Center)/Oct. 29-Nov. 3
1990-St. Louis, MO/Oct. 28-Nov. 2

Soc. for New Language Study (1972)
Box 10596, Denver CO 80210
Treasurer: R. P. Tripp, Jr.
Members: 15 *Staff:* 1
Annual Budget: under $10,000 *Tel:* (803) 777-6115
Hist. Note: To stimulate consideration, evaluation and cultivation of the study of language, literature and philosophy from new perspectives.
Publication:
In Gear Dargum. a.
Annual Meetings: With Rocky Mountain Modern Language Association in the fall.

Soc. for Nursing History (1979)
Teachers College, Columbia Univ., 525 W. 120th St., New York NY 10027
Secretary: Althea Davis
Members: 130
Annual Budget: under $10,000 *Tel:* (212) 678-3421
Hist. Note: Members are researchers, teachers and individuals interested in the history of nursing. Works to stimulate interest in the history of nursing and to incorporate nursing history into the curriculum of appropriate institutions.
Publication:
Gazette. semi-a.
Annual Meetings: Not held.

Soc. for Nutrition Education (1969)
1700 Broadway, Suite 300, Oakland CA 94612
Exec. Director: Michael McKechnie
Members: 4,000 nutrition educators *Staff:* 9
Annual Budget: $500-1,000,000 *Tel:* (415) 444-7133
Hist. Note: Membership: $55/yr.
Publications:
Journal of Nutrition Education. q. adv.
SNE Exchange.
Annual Meetings:
1987-San Francisco, CA

Soc. for Obstetric Anesthesia and Perinatology (1969)
c/o Grace Maternity Hospital, 5821 University Ave, Halifax Nova Scotia B3H 1W3
Editor: Dr. W. D. R. Writer
Annual Budget: under $10,000 *Tel:* (902) 422-6501
Hist. Note: Has no paid staff.
Publication:
SOAP Newsletter. 3-4/yr.
Annual Meetings: Spring
1987-Halifax, Canada(Halifax Sheraton)/May 20-23/350
1988-San Francisco, CA

Soc. for Occlusal Studies (1964)
4920 Loughboro Road, N.W., Washington DC 20016
Exec. Secretary: Mrs. Peter A. Neff
Members: 400 *Staff:* 1
Annual Budget: $25-50,000 *Tel:* (202) 244-2701
Hist. Note: Occlusion is the bringing of the opposing surfaces of the teeth of the upper and lower jaws into contact. Members are dentists and dental technicians. Membership: $50/yr.
Publication:
Newsletter. q.
Biennial meetings: even year

Soc. for Occupational and Environmental Heatlh (1972)
2021 K St., N.W., Suite 305, Washington DC 20006
President: James Merchant, MD, PhD
Members: 500 *Staff:* 1
Annual Budget: $25-50,000 *Tel:* (202) 737-5045
Hist. Note: Founded at the New York Academy of Sciences on November 12, 1972. Incorporated in the District of Columbia. Members include physicians, hygienists, economists, laboratory scientists, academicians, labor and industry representatives. Officers are elected biennially; governing councillors triennially. Membership: $50/yr.
Publications:
SOEH Letter. q.
Archives of Environmental Health. bi-m.
Annual Meetings: Spring
1987-Bethesda, MD(Holiday Inn)/April 6-8

Soc. for Office Based Surgery
Hist. Note: Became the American Soc. of Outpatient Surgeons in 1986.

Soc. for Pediatric Radiology, The (1958)
Children's Hospital Med. Ctr., Elland & Bethesda Aves., Cincinnati OH 45229-2899
Secretary: Donald R. Kirks, M.D.
Members: 550
Annual Budget: $25-50,000 *Tel:* (513) 559-8058
Hist. Note: Members are health professionals interested in pediatric imaging.
Publication:
Membership Directory. a.
Annual Meetings: Spring/225
1987-Toronto, Ontario(Westin)/June 7-12
1988-San Diego, CA(del Coronado)/April 28-May 1

Soc. for Pediatric Research (1930)
Dept. of Pediatrics, Univ. of NM School,of Medicine, Albuquerque NM 87131
Exec. Secretary: Debbie Wogenrich
Members: 800-900 *Staff:* 1
Annual Budget: $100-250,000 *Tel:* (505) 277-4361
Hist. Note: Purpose is to provide a forum for pediatric researchers to present and receive information currently available in all fields of pediatric research. Membership: $50/yr.
Publication:
Pediatric Research Program Issue. a. adv.
Annual Meetings: Spring
1987-Anaheim, CA(Disneyland Hotel)April 27-May 1
1988-Washington, DC(Sheraton Washington)/May 2-6
1989-Washington, DC(Sheraton Washington)/May 1-5
1990-Anaheim, CA(Anaheim Hilton)/May 7-11
1991-New Orleans, LA(Rivergate Hilton)April 29-May 3

Soc. for Pediatric Urology
J. Hillis Miller Health Center, Box J-247, Gainesville FL 32610
Secretary: Dr. R. Dixon Walker
Members: 275-300 *Staff:* 1
Annual Budget: under $10,000 *Tel:* (904) 392-2501
Hist. Note: An invitational professional society whose secretary changes every three years
Annual Meetings: Immediately preceeding those of the American Urological Ass'n

Soc. for Peripheral Vascular Nursing (1982)
1070 Sibley Tower, Rochester NY 14604
Exec. Director: Margaret M. Crevey
Members: 300 individuals *Staff:* 8
Annual Budget: $10-25,000 *Tel:* (716) 546-7241

Soc. for Personality Assessment (1938)
866 Amelia Court Northeast, St. Petersburg FL 33702
Admin. Officer: Ann M. O'Roark
Members: 1,000 *Staff:* 1
Annual Budget: $25-50,000 *Tel:* (813) 527-9863
Hist. Note: Founded and incorporated in Newark, New Jersey in 1939 as the Rorschach Research Exchange. The name was later changed to the Soc. for Projective Techniques, then to the Soc. for Projective Techniques and Personality Assessment and, finally, in 1971 to the Soc. for Personality Assessment. Membership: $30/yr.

00273 12 05 86 1233

Publication:
Journal of Personality Assessment. bi-m. adv.
Annual Scientific Meetings: March
1987-San Francisco, CA(Sir Francis Drake)/March 14-16

Soc. for Philosophy of Religion (1940)
Dept. of Philosophy, Univ. of Georgia, Athens GA 30602
Secy.-Treas.: Frank R. Harrison, III
Members: 90-125 *Staff:* 1
Annual Budget: under $10,000 *Tel:* (404) 542-2821
Hist. Note: Members are leading scholars in the philosophy of religion who must be nominated and voted upon. Membership is limited to 125. Sponsors the Southern Humanities Conference. Membership: $10/yr.
Annual Meetings: February-March

Soc. for Photographic Education (1963)
Box 1651, FDR Station, New York NY 10150
Chairman: Helmmo Kindermann
Members: 1,500 *Staff:* 4
Annual Budget: $50-100,000
Hist. Note: College and university teachers of photography, photographers, museum curators and students of photography. Membership: $50/yr.
Publications:
Exposure. q. adv.
Newsletter. q.
Annual Meetings: Spring
1987-San Diego, CA(Hotel del Coronado)/April 12-15

Soc. for Private and Commercial Earth Stations (1980)
Hist. Note: Became the Satellite Television Industry Ass'n, Inc. in 1985.

Soc. for Psychological Anthropology
1703 New Hampshire Ave., N.W., Washington DC 20009
Secretary: Kathryn M. Anderson-Levitt
Members: 699 *Staff:* 1
Annual Budget: $10-25,000 *Tel:* (202) 232-8800
Hist. Note: An affiliate of the American Anthropological Association, which provides administrative support. Membership: $20/yr.
Publication:
Ethnos: Journal of the Society for Psychological Anthropology. q.
Annual Meetings: With the American Anthropological Association.

Soc. for Psychophysiological Research (1960)
401 Parnassus Ave., San Francisco CA 94143
Secy.-Treas.: Robert W. Levenson
Members: 800-900 *Staff:* 1
Annual Budget: $25-50,000 *Tel:* (415) 476-7622
Hist. Note: A multidisciplinary society of physicians, psychologists and engineers. Membership: $37/yr.
Publication:
Psychophysiology. bi-m. adv.
Annual Meetings: Early Fall
1987-Amsterdam, Holland(Okura)/3rd wk. Sept./300

Soc. for Public Health Education (1950)
703 Market St., Suite 535, San Francisco CA 94103
Exec. Director: James P. Lovegren
Members: 1,000 *Staff:* 1
Annual Budget: $50-100,000 *Tel:* (415) 546-7601
Hist. Note: Formerly (1970) Soc. of Public Health Educators, Inc.
Publication:
Health Education Quarterly. q.
Annual Meetings: With American Public Health Association.

Soc. for Radiation Oncology Administrators (1984)
925 Chestnut St., 7th Fl., Philadelphia PA 19107
Exec. Secretary: Suzanne Bohn
Members: 125 individuals *Staff:* 2
Annual Budget: $10-25,000 *Tel:* (215) 574-3181
Hist. Note: Established in Philadelphia, SROA is concerned with the administration of the business and non-medical management aspects of radiation oncology. Membership: $50/yr.
Annual Meetings: Fall/75
1987-Boston, MA(Sheraton)/Oct. 23-29
1988-New Orleans, LA(Hilton)/Oct. 9-14
1989-Los Angeles, CA(Bonaventure)/Oct. 16-21

Soc. for Range Management (1948)
2760 West Fifth Ave., Denver CO 80204
Exec. V. President: Peter V. Jackson
Members: 5,500-6,000 *Staff:* 6-10
Annual Budget: $250-500,000 *Tel:* (303) 571-0174
Hist. Note: Founded in Salt Lake City in January 1948 as the American Soc. of Range Management and incorporated in Wyoming in 1949. Became the Soc. for Range Management in 1971. Studies rangeland ecosystems and the principles of managing range resources. Member Society of the Renewable Natural Resources Foundation.
Publications:
Journal of Range Management. bi-m. adv.
Rangelands.
Abstracts. a.
Annual Meetings: Feb./1,500
1987-Boise, ID
1988-Corpus Christi, TX
1989-Billings, MT
1990-Reno, NV

Soc. for Reformation Research (1947)
Department of History, Carthage College, Kenosha WI 53141
Secretary: Jonathan W. Zophy
Members: 400
Annual Budget: under $10,000
Hist. Note: Affiliated with the American Historical Ass'n and the American Society of Church History. Formerly (1985) the American Soc. for Reformation Research. Member of the Council on the Study of Religion. Membership: $7/year.
Publications:
Archive for Reformation History. a.
Newsletter. a.
Annual Meetings: With the American Historical Ass'n

Soc. for Research in Child Development (1933)
Tolman Hall, Univ. of California, Institute of Human Development, Berkeley CA 94720
Exec. Officer: Dr. Dorothy H. Eichorn
Members: 4,000 *Staff:* 15
Annual Budget: $1-2,000,000 *Tel:* (415) 642-6401
Hist. Note: Founded in 1933 in the District of Columbia as an outgrowth of the Committee on Child Development of the Nat'l Research Council. The Committee, formed in 1925, was the successor to a subcommittee on Child Development under the Division of Anthropology and Psychology of the Nat'l Research Council which began in 1922. Incorporated in Illinois in 1950, in Indiana in 1956 and in Wisconsin in 1970. Affiliated with the American Ass'n for the Advancement of Science. Membership: $90/yr.
Publications:
Child Development. bi-m. adv.
Child Development Abstracts and Bibliography. 3/yr.
Monographs of the SRCD. 4-5/yr.
Biennial meetings: uneven years in Spring
1987-Baltimore, MD(Hyatt Regency)/April 23-26

Soc. for Risk Analysis (1982)
1340 Old Chain Bridge Road, Suite 300, McLean VA 22101
President: Richard J. Burk, Jr.
Members: 1,500 *Staff:* 10
Annual Budget: $10-25,000 *Tel:* (703) 790-1745
Hist. Note: Founded to study and understand on a scientific basis the risks posed by technological development. Membership: $38/yr.
Publications:
Risk Analysis Journal. q. adv.
Risk Newsletter. q. adv.

Soc. for Scholarly Publishing (1978)
2000 Florida Ave., N.W., Washington DC 20009
Administrator: Alice O'Leary
Members: 1,200 individuals, 85 organizations *Staff:* 1
Annual Budget: $100-250,000 *Tel:* (202) 328-3555
Hist. Note: Established on June 16, 1978, in Washington, DC. Members are individuals, publishing companies and professional societies involved in the production of scholarly books and periodicals. Membership: $36/yr.
Publications:
SSP Newsletter. bi-m.
Directory of Members. a.
Annual Meetings: Late Spring/350
1987-New Orleans, LA

Soc. for Slovene Studies (1973)
Institute on East Central Europe, Columbia Univ., 420 W. 118th St., New York NY 10027
President: Carole Rogel
Members: 160-175 *Staff:* 1
Annual Budget: under $10,000 *Tel:* (212) 280-4008
Hist. Note: Affiliated since 1977 with the American Ass'n for the Advancement of Slavic Studies. Has no paid staff.
Publication:
Slovene Studies. semi-a. adv.
Annual Meetings: With the American Ass'n for the Advancement of Slavic Studies.

Soc. for Social Studies of Science (1975)
Dept. of Sociology, Indiana University, Bloomington IN 47405
Secretary: Thomas F. Gieryn
Members: 450-500 *Staff:* 1
Annual Budget: under $10,000 *Tel:* (812) 335-4127
Hist. Note: Affiliated with American Ass'n for the Advancement of Science. Membership: $15/yr. (individual); $30/yr. (organization/company)
Publication:
Science and Technology Studies. q.
Annual Meetings: Fall
1987-Worcester, MA/Oct.

Soc. for Spanish and Portuguese Historical Studies (1969)
Dept. of History, Univ. of Minnesota, 614 Soc.Sci. Bldg., 267 19th Ave. S., Minneapolis MN 55455
Gen. Secretary: Carla Phillips
Members: 400-450 *Staff:* 1
Annual Budget: $10-25,000 *Tel:* (619) 226-2573
Hist. Note: Founded to promote research in all aspects and epochs of Iberian historical studies. Membership: $15/yr.
Publication:
Bulletin of the Soc. for Spanish & Portuguese Historical Studies. 3/yr
Annual Meetings: April/60
1987-Austin, TX/April 24-26
1988-Nashville, TN
1989-St. Louis, MO

Soc. for Surgery of the Alimentary Tract (1960)
Northwestern Memorial Hospital, 250 E. Superior St., Suite 201, Chicago IL 60611
Secretary: Dr. David Nahrwold
Members: 950-1000 *Staff:* 1
Annual Budget: $10-25,000 *Tel:* (312) 908-8060
Hist. Note: Formerly Association of Colon Surgery.
Annual Meetings: Spring

Soc. for Technical Communication (1953)
815 15th St., N.W., Suite 400, Washington DC 20005
Exec. Director & Counsel: William C. Stolgitis
Members: 10-11,000 *Staff:* 2-5
Annual Budget: $500-1,000,000 *Tel:* (202) 737-0035
Hist. Note: In 1953, two organizations interested in improving the practice of technical communication, the Soc. of Technical Writers and the Ass'n of Technical Writers and Editors, were founded simultaneously on the East Coast. These organizations merged in 1957 to form the Soc. of Technical Writers and Editors. This grew rapidly and, in 1960, merged with a Pacific Coast group, the Technical Publishing Soc., founded in 1954. This merger resulted in the Soc. of Technical Writers and Publishers. In 1971, the name was changed to Soc. for Technical Communication. Today, STC is the largest professional society in the world concerned primarily witn all phases of technical communication. Incorporated in New York in 1958. Member of the International Council of Communication Societies. Membership: $50/yr.
Publications:
Conference Proceedings. a.
INTERCOM. m.
Technical Communication. q. adv.
Annual Meetings: Spring, International Technical Communication Conference/1,400
1987-Denver, CO(Radisson)/May 10-13
1988-Philadelphia, PA(Franklin Plaza)/May 10-13
1989-Chicago, IL(Marriott)/May 14-17
1990-San Jose, CA(Convention Ctr.)/May 20-23
1991-New York, NY(Hilton)/May 12-15

Soc. for Textual Scholarship (1979)
Ph.D. Program in English, CUNY Graduate Center, 33 W. 42nd St., New York NY 10036
Exec. Director: D.C. Greetham
Members: 40 institutions; 600 individuals *Staff:* 1
Annual Budget: $10-25,000 *Tel:* (212) 790-4598
Hist. Note: STS was founded to overcome the disciplinary isolation of textual scholarship in various fields. It aims to discover common theories and procedures which could be of value to researchers in all areas of textual study. Membership: $10/yr.
Publications:
TEXT. a.
Newsletter. irreg.
Bulletin. irreg.
Annual Meetings: Biennial Meetings in April
1987-New York, NY(CUNY Graduate Center)/April 8-11/200
1989-New York, NY(CUNY Graduate Center)/250

Soc. for the Advancement of Behavior Analysis (1980)
Dep't of Psychology, Western Michigan Univ., Kalamazoo MI 49008
Managing Editor: Shery Chamberlain
Members: 400 *Staff:* 2
Annual Budget: $25-50,000 *Tel:* (616) 383-0452
Hist. Note: Purpose is to provide instruction and training in behavior analysis and to disseminate information concerning it. Varying membership categories.
Publication:
The Behavior Analyst. semi-a.
Annual Meetings: With the Ass'n for Behavior Analysis.

Soc. for the Advancement of Education (1939)
99 W. Hawthorne Ave., Suite 518, Valley Stream NY 11580-6101
President: Stanley Lehrer
Members: 1,800-2,000 *Staff:* 2-5
Annual Budget: $100-250,000 *Tel:* (516) 568-9191
Hist. Note: Membership: $19.95/year.
Publication:
USA Today Magazine. m. adv.

Soc. for the Advancement of Fission Energy (1976)
Hist. Note: Inactive in 1983, the Society has no dues or paid staff. It is not a professional society and operates through volunteers.

Soc. for the Advancement of Food Service Research (1958)
304 West Liberty St., Suite 301, Louisville KY 40202
Exec. V. President: Phillip S. Cooke
Members: 200 *Staff:* 4
Tel: (502) 583-3783
Hist. Note: SAFSR is the only national professional association devoted to the advancement of foodservice research and development.
Publications:
Newsletter. q. adv.
Proceedings. a. adv.

00274 12 05 86 1233

Abstracts. a.
Annual Meetings: Spring
1987-Dallas, TX/March 11-14

Soc. for the Advancement of Material and Process Engineering (1944)
Box 2459, 843 West Glentana St., Covina CA 91722
Manager: Marge Smith
Members: 8,000 individuals *Staff:* 11
Annual Budget: $1-2,000,000 *Tel:* (818) 331-0616
Hist. Note: Originated March 17, 1944 in Hawthorne, CA as the Soc. of Aircraft Material and Process Engineers. Incorporated in California in 1960 as the Soc. of Aerospace Material and Process Engineers and became the Soc. for the Advancement of Material and Process Engineering in 1973. Membership: $26/yr.
Publications:
SAMPE Journal. bi-m. adv.
SAMPE Quarterly. q.
Semi-Annual Meetings: Spring and Fall
1987-Anaheim, CA(Convention Ctr.)/April 6-9/7,000
1987-Arlington, VA(Hyatt at Crystal City)/Oct. 13-15/700

Soc. for the Advancement of Scandinavian Study (1911)
Germanic Languages, Univ. of Illinois, Urbana IL 61801
Secy.-Treas.: Marianne E. Kalinke
Members: 800 members and subscribers *Staff:* 1
Annual Budget: $10-25,000 *Tel:* (217) 333-4852
Hist. Note: Scholars, teachers, and researchers in Scandinavian language, literature and culture. Regular membership: $25/yr.
Publications:
Scandinavian Studies. q.
SS News and Notes.
Annual Meetings: May
1987-Columbus, OH(Ohio State University)/May 1-3/200

Soc. for the Anthropology of Visual Communication (1968)
Hist. Note: Became the Soc. for Visual Anthropology in 1984.

Soc. for the Comparative Study of Society and History (1959)
Dept. of History, Univ. of Michigan, Ann Arbor MI 48109
Secretary: Jacob M. Price
Staff: 1
Annual Budget: $50-100,000 *Tel:* (313) 764-6362
Hist. Note: Members are historians, anthropologists, sociologists and other social scientists. Membership: $30/yr.
Publication:
Comparative Studies in Society and History. q.

Soc. for the History of Discoveries (1960)
45 Mill Rock Rd., Hamden CT 06511
Secy.-Treas.: Barbara B. McCorkle
Members: 275 *Staff:* 1
Annual Budget: under $10,000 *Tel:* (203) 436-8638
Hist. Note: Affiliated with the American Historical Ass'n. Established as a result of the International Congress for the History of Discoveries, held in Lisbon in 1960. Membership: $15/yr.
Publications:
Newsletter. a.
Terrae Incognitae. a. adv.
Annual Report. a.
Annual Meetings: Fall
1987-London, England(British Library & Royal Geographical Soc.)/Sept.

Soc. for the History of Technology (1958)
Dept. of History, Duke Univ., Durham NC 27706
Secretary: Alex Roland
Members: 1,400 *Staff:* 2-5
Annual Budget: $25-50,000 *Tel:* (919) 684-2758
Hist. Note: Formed in Cleveland in 1958 and incorporated in Ohio in 1959. Affiliated with the American Ass'n for the Advancement of Science and the American Historical Ass'n. Membership: $26/yr.
Publications:
Newsletter. m.
Technology and Culture. q. adv.
Annual Meetings:
1987-Raleigh,NC

Soc. for the Preservation of Oral Health (1960)
Hist. Note: Address unknown in 1984.

Soc. for the Psychological Study of Social Issues (1936)
Box 1248, Ann Arbor MI 48106-1248
Admin. Associate: Lynda J. Fuerstnau
Members: 2,900-3,000 *Staff:* 3
Annual Budget: $100-250,000 *Tel:* (313) 662-9130
Hist. Note: Seeks to bring behavioral and social science theory, empirical evidence and practice into focus on human problems. Members must be graduate students or professionals. A division (#9) of the American Psychological Ass'n. Membership: $12/yr.
Publication:
Journal of Social Issues. q.
Annual Meetings: Annual meeting with American Psychological Ass'n; Mid-year Meeting in Feb.-March

Soc. for the Scientific Study of Religion (1949)
Catholic University of America, Marist Hall, Room 108, Washington DC 20064
Exec. Secretary: Hart Nelsen
Members: 1,400 individuals, 1,300 libraries *Staff:* 1
Annual Budget: $50-100,000 *Tel:* (202) 635-5447
Hist. Note: Founded at Harvard University in 1949 and incorporated the same year in Connecticut. Membership: $24/yr.
Publication:
Journal for the Scientific Study of Religion. q. adv.
Annual Meetings: October/500

Soc. for the Scientific Study of Sex (1957)
Box 29795, Philadelphia PA 19117
Exec. Director: Deborah Weinstein, M.S.W.
Members: 1,000 *Staff:* 2
Annual Budget: $100-250,000 *Tel:* (215) 782-1430
Hist. Note: An international professional association of researchers, clinicians educators, who share an interest and competency in the scientific pursuit of knowledge concerning sexuality. Membership: $70/yr.
Publications:
Journal of Sex Research. q. adv.
SSSS Newsletter. bi-m.
Membership Handbook. a.
Annual Meetings: November

Soc. for the Study of Amphibians and Reptiles (1958)
Glendale Community College, Glendale AZ 85302-3090
Secretary: James S. Jacob
Members: 1,800 individuals, 400 institutions *Staff:* 12
Annual Budget: $50-100,000 *Tel:* (602) 934-2211
Hist. Note: Formerly (1967) Ohio Herpetological Soc. Membership: $27/yr.
Publications:
Herpetological Review. q. adv.
Journal of Herpetology. q.
Annual Meetings: August
1987-Vera Cruz, Mexico
1988-Ann Arbor, MI(Univ. of Michigan)

Soc. for the Study of Evolution (1946)
Dep't. of EPO Biology, Univ. of Colorado, Campus Box 334, Boulder CO 80309
Exec. V. Pres.: Dr. Jeffrey B. Mitton
Members: 2,400 *Staff:* 1
Annual Budget: $250-500,000 *Tel:* (303) 492-8956
Hist. Note: Founded in St. Louis on March 30, 1946 as an outgrowth of the Committee on Common Problems of Genetics, Paleontology and Systematics established in 1943 by the Nat'l Research Council. Absorbed the Society for the Study of Speciation. Promotes the study of organic evolution and the integration of the various fields of science concerned with evolution.
Publication:
Evolution. bi-m. adv.
Annual Meetings: June
1987-Bozeman,MN(Montana State Univ.)/June 21-24/400

Soc. for the Study of Reproduction (1967)
309 West Clark St., Champaign IL 61820
Exec. Secy.: Carl D. Johnson
Members: 2,400-2,500 *Staff:* 1
Annual Budget: $250-500,000 *Tel:* (217) 356-3182
Hist. Note: Evolved from the Biennial Symposium and Animal Reproduction in 1949 at Iowa State University. Formed in 1967 at the University of Illinois. Adherent society of the American Institute of Biological Sciences.
Publication:
Biology of Reproduction. 10/yr. adv.
Annual Meetings: Summer
1987-Urbana, IL(Univ. of Illinois)/July 20-23

Soc. for the Study of Social Biology (1926)
c/o Social Science Research Council, 605 3rd Ave., New York NY 10158
Secy.-Treas.: Lonnie R. Sherrod
Members: 350 *Staff:* 1
Annual Budget: under $10,000 *Tel:* (212) 661-0280
Hist. Note: Founded, organized and incorporated in New York in January 1926 as the American Eugenics Soc., Inc.; assumed its present name in 1973. Promotes the study of the biologial and sociocultural forces affecting the structure and composition of human populations. Membership: $20/yr.
Publication:
Social Biology. q.
Annual Meetings: Fall

Soc. for the Study of Social Problems (1951)
N531, School of Nursing, Univ. of California - San Francisco, San Francisco CA 94143-0646
Exec. Officer: Elinore E. Luire, Ph.D.
Members: 1,200 individuals *Staff:* 2-3
Annual Budget: $100-250,000 *Tel:* (415) 476-8022
Hist. Note: The primary objective of the Society is to promote social science research and teaching in order to bring scholarly and practical attention to the social world and its problems. Incorporated in Indiana.
Publications:
Social Problems. 5/yr. adv.
SSSP Newsletter. 3/yr. adv.
Annual Meetings: August
1987-Chicago, IL(Bismark)/Aug. 14-16/800
1988-Atlanta, GA/Aug. 21-23
1989-San Francisco, CA/Aug. 6-8
1990-Washington, DC

Soc. for the Study of Symbolic Interaction (1975)
Dept. of Sociology, Univ. of Arkansas, Fayetteville AR 72701
Corresponding Secy.-Treas.: Donna Darden
Members: 375 individuals
Annual Budget: under $10,000 *Tel:* (501) 575-3205
Hist. Note: Members are interested in symbolic interaction, the concept that people react to things because of the meanings they attach to them. Has no paid staff. Membership: According to employment status.
Publications:
SSSI Notes. q.
Symbolic Interaction. semi-a.
Annual Meetings:
1987-Chicago, IL(Palmer House)/mid-Aug./75-100

Soc. for Theriogenology (1973)
Association Building, Ninth & Minnesota, Hastings NE 68901
Exec. Director: Don Ellerbee
Members: 1,950 *Staff:* 2-5
Annual Budget: $25-50,000 *Tel:* (402) 463-0392
Hist. Note: Formerly (1975) American Veterinary Soc. for the Study of Breeding Soundness. Members are veterinarians interested in animal reproduction. Membership: $50/yr.
Publications:
Newsletter. bi-m.
Proceedings. a.
Annual Meetings: September with the American College of Theriogenologists
1987-Austin, TX
1988-Orlando, FL

Soc. for Values in Higher Education (1923)
409 Prospect Street, New Haven CT 06510
Exec. Director: David C. Smith
Members: 1,500-1,600 *Staff:* 2-5
Annual Budget: $100-250,000 *Tel:* (203) 865-8839
Hist. Note: A network of persons in the academic world and the professions who have a special concern for the ethical and religious dimensions of their work. Formerly (1962) Nat'l Council on Religion in Higher Education and (1976) Soc. for Religion in Higher Education.
Publication:
SOUNDINGS. q. adv.
Annual Meetings: August
1987-Olympia, WA(Evergreen State College)/Aug. 8-13

Soc. for Vascular Surgery (1945)
13 Elm St., Box 1565, Manchester MA 01944
Exec. Secretary: Gardner V. McCormick
Members: 350-400 *Staff:* 1
Annual Budget: $10-25,000 *Tel:* (617) 927-8330
Hist. Note: Organized in Hot Springs, VA on December 5, 1945 at a meeting of the Southern Surgical Ass'n.
Publication:
Journal of Vascular Surgery.
Annual Meetings: Spring/1,500
1987-Toronto, Ontario(Sheraton Centre)/June 7-10
1988-Chicago, IL(Hyatt Regency)/June 12-15
1989-New York, NY(Hilton)/June 18-21
1990-Los Angeles, CA(Century Plaza)/June 3-6
1991-Boston, MA(Sheraton/Hynes Aud.)/June 2-5

Soc. for Visual Anthropology (1968)
Dept. of Anthropology, Brigham Young University, Provo UT 84602
President: Thomas Blakely
Members: 800-900 individuals
Annual Budget: under $10,000 *Tel:* (801) 378-2565
Hist. Note: Formerly (1972) Program in Ethnographic Film and (1984) Soc. for the Anthropology of Visual Communication. Membership: $10/yr.
Publication:
Visual Anthropology Newsletter. q.
Annual Meetings: November, with the American Anthropological Ass'n

Soc. of Actuaries (1949)
500 Park Blvd., Itasca IL 60143
Exec. Director: John E. O'Connor, Jr.
Members: 10,300 *Staff:* 40
Annual Budget: $2-5,000,000 *Tel:* (312) 773-3010
Hist. Note: Merger of the American Institute of Actuaries (1909) and the Actuaries Soc. of America (1889). Membership: $185/yr.(fellow); $140/yr. (associate for 5-9 yrs.); $95/yr.(associate for under 5 yrs.)
Publications:
Committee Reports. irreg.
Transactions. a.
Record. 4/yr.
The Actuary. 10/yr.
Annual Meetings: October/1,300
1987-Montreal, Quebec(Queen Elizabeth)/Oct. 19-21
1988-Boston, MA(Marriott)/Oct. 24-26
1989-New York, NY(Marriott Marquis)/Oct. 23-25

Soc. of Air Force Physicians (1958)
USAF/SGPC, HQ Bolling Air Force Base, Washington DC 20332
Secretary: Col. J. William Myers
Members: 175-200 *Staff:* 1
Annual Budget: under $10,000 *Tel:* (202) 767-1872
Annual Meetings: With American College of Physicians.

00275 12 05 86 1233

1987-New Orleans, LA(Fairmont)
1988-Washington, DC

Soc. of Allied Weight Engineers (1939)
344 E. 'J' St., Chula Vista CA 92010
Exec. Secretary: Fred H. Wetmore
Members: 1,300-1,400 individuals; 45 companies *Staff:* 1
Annual Budget: $25-50,000 *Tel:* (619) 427-8262
Hist. Note: Organized in Los Angeles in 1939 as the Society of Aeronautical Weight Engineers and incorporated as a nonprofit organization on April 2, 1941, the Society now includes international memberships. Assumed its present name on January 1, 1973. The membership consists predominantly of engineers in the aerospace industry concerned with mass properties or weight engineering. Membership: $20/yr. (individual); $200/yr. (company)
Publications:
SAWE Newsletter. bi-m.
Weight Engineering. 3/yr. adv.
Annual Meetings: Middle of May/200
1987-Seattle, WA(Four Seasons Olympic Hotel)/May 18-20
1988-Detroit, MI
1989-Baltimore, MD-Washington, DC area

Soc. of American Archivists (1936)
600 South Federal St., Suite 504, Chicago IL 60605
Exec. Director: Donn C. Neal
Members: 4,000 *Staff:* 6-10
Annual Budget: $500-1,000,000 *Tel:* (312) 922-0140
Hist. Note: A professional society of individuals and institutions interested in preservation and use of archives, manuscripts and current records as well as machine-readable records, sound recordings, pictures, films and maps.
Publications:
American Archivist. q. adv.
SAA Newsletter. bi-m.
Annual Meetings: Fall
1987-New York City(Grand Hyatt)/September2-6/1,200
1988-Atlanta, GA(Peachtree Plaza)

Soc. of American Business and Economic Writers (1963)
Hist. Note: Became the Soc. of American Business Editors and Writers in May, 1986.

Soc. of American Business Editors and Writers (1963)
Univ. of Missouri School of Journalism, 76 Gannett Hall, Columbia MO 65211
Exec. Director: James Gentry
Members: 300 *Staff:* 3
Annual Budget: $10-25,000 *Tel:* (314) 882-7862
Hist. Note: Founded in 1963 as an offspring of the professional journalist society, Sigma Delta Chi, seminar program on business news. The name was originally the Soc. of American Business Writers and was changed to the Soc. of American Business and Economic Writers in April, 1976. The present name became effective in May, 1986. Members are financial, business and economic news writers and editors for newspapers and magazines. Membership: $25/year.
Publication:
Business Journalist.
Annual Meetings:
1987-Washington, DC
1988-St. Paul, MN
1989-New York, NY

Soc. of American Florists (1884)
Hist. Note: Became SAF: The Center for Commercial Floriculture in 1983.

Soc. of American Foresters (1900)
5400 Grosvenor Lane, Bethesda MD 20814
Exec. V. President: Ronald R. Christensen
Members: 20-21,000 *Staff:* 30-35
Annual Budget: $2-5,000,000 *Tel:* (301) 897-8720
Hist. Note: Founded by Gifford Pinchot and six other pioneer foresters. Scientific and educational association representing all segments of the forestry profession; including private and public practitioners, educators, researchers, technicians and students. It serves as the accreditation agency for professional forestry education in the U.S.
Publications:
Forest Science. q.
Journal of Forestry. m. adv.
Northern Journal of Applied Forestry. q. adv.
Southern Journal of Applied Forestry. q. adv.
Western Journal of Applied Forestry. q. adv.
Annual Meetings: Fall
1987-Minneapolis, MN(Hyatt)/Oct. 18-21/1,800
1988-Syracuse, NY/Sept.-Oct./1,800
1989-Pacific Northwest/Sept.-Oct/2,000
1990-Washington, DC

Soc. of American Graphic Artists (1915)
32 Union Square, Room 1214, New York NY 10003
President: Steven Yamin
Members: 250
Tel: (212) 260-5706
Hist. Note: Founded (1915) as the Brooklyn Soc. of Etchers, it became the Soc. of American Graphic Artists in 1952 to include woodcut, lithography and other media. Any artist who has been selected twice for a SAGA exhibition in the last five years is eligible for invitation to membership. Membership enables artists to show their work in New York City through important exhibitions with substantial awards. Membership: $20/yr.
Publications:
Newsletter. q. (for members only)
SAGA National Print Exhibition Catalogue.

Soc. of American Historians (1939)
Columbia Univ., 610 Fayerweather Hall, New York NY 10027
Secy.-Treas.: Kenneth T. Jackson
Members: 250-275 *Staff:* 2-5
Annual Budget: $10-25,000 *Tel:* (212) 280-2555
Hist. Note: Membership, by invitation, is composed of individuals who have written a scholarly historical work of literary distinction.

Soc. of American Historical Artists (1980)
Hist. Note: A small group of Eastern U.S. artists interested in promoting historical accuracy of dress, architecture, equipment, etc. in the scenes depicted. Membership by invitation only. Has no permanent headquarters or paid staff and a modest budget.

Soc. of American Magicians (1902)
P.O. Box 368, Mango FL 34262-0368
Nat'l Secretary: Joyce Zachary
Members: 5,500-6,000 *Staff:* 2-5
Annual Budget: $100-250,000 *Tel:* (813) 684-9787
Hist. Note: Membership is open to professional and amateur magicians, manufacturers of magical apparatus, collectors, writers, and hobbyists. Membership: $25/year.
Publication:
MUM. m. adv.
Annual Meetings: July
1987-Las Vegas, NV(Riviera Hotel)/July 8-11/1,000
1988-Florida

Soc. of American Military Engineers (1920)
607 Prince St., P.O. Box 21289, Alexandria VA 22320-2289
Exec. Director: Brg.Gen. Walter Bachus, USA(Ret.)
Members: 28,000 individuals; 2,100 corporations *Staff:* 11-15
Annual Budget: $1-2,000,000 *Tel:* (703) 549-3800
Hist. Note: Founded January 1, 1920 and incorporated in the District of Columbia in 1924. SAME's primary mission is to encourage the free exchange of ideas between military and civilian engineers. Members are military officers, civilian professionals (most of whom have had military service and hold Nat'l Guard or reserve commissions), major construction businesses and engineering students. An associate member of the Engineers Joint Council. Membership: $24/yr. (individual); $240-500/yr. (corporate).
Publication:
The Military Engineer. bi-m. adv.
Annual Meetings: Spring
1987-San Francisco, CA
1988-Atlanta, GA
1989-Kansas City, MO

Soc. of American Registered Architects (1956)
320 N. Michigan Ave., Chicago IL 60601
President: Alex Gravesen
Members: 900-1,000 *Staff:* 1
Annual Budget: $100-250,000 *Tel:* (312) 726-5880
Hist. Note: Established in Kansas City by Wilfred Gregson of Atlanta. Has no permanent, paid staff. Membership: $150/yr.
Publications:
Arascope. q.
Practicing Architect. q. adv.
Annual Meetings: Fall/150-200

Soc. of American Travel Writers (1956)
1120 Connecticut Ave., N.W., Suite 940, Washington DC 20036
Admin. Coordinator: Ken Fischer
Members: 750 *Staff:* 1
Annual Budget: $100-250,000 *Tel:* (202) 785-5567
Hist. Note: Organized as the American Ass'n of Travel Writers in Ellinor Village, FL during a convention of the Nat'l Ass'n of Travel Organizations. Assumed its present name in 1957 and was incorporated in the District of Columbia in 1958. Membership: $90/year.
Publications:
Directory. a.
The Travel Writer. 10/yr.
Travel Photo Source Book. bien.
Annual Meetings: Fall

Soc. of American Value Engineers (1959)
600 S. Federal St., #400, Chicago IL 60605
Exec. Director: August L. Sisco
Members: 1,500-2,000 *Staff:* 2-5
Annual Budget: $100-250,000 *Tel:* (312) 346-3265
Hist. Note: Awards the Certified Value Specialist (CVS) designation.
Publications:
Interactions. m.
Value World. q. adv.

Soc. of American Wood Preservers (1958)
7297 Lee Highway, Unit P, Falls Church VA 22042
President and C.E.O.: George K. Eliades, CAE
Members: 105 companies *Staff:* 2-5
Annual Budget: $250-500,000 *Tel:* (703) 237-0900
Hist. Note: Chartered in Georgia in 1958 and opened national office in 1969. Membership consists of pressure-treated wood preserving plants and their chemical suppliers. Sponsors the Soc. of American Wood Preservers Political Action Committee.
Publication:
Action Update. m.
Annual Meetings: With American Wood Preservers Ass'n in Spring
1987-Toronto, Ontario(Hilton)/May 9-14/650

Soc. of Applied Experimental and Engineering Psychology (1953)
Hist. Note: Became the Div. of Applied Experimental and Engineering Psychology in 1985.

Soc. of Architectural Administrators (1965)
1735 New York Ave., N.W., Washington DC 20006
Acting AIA/SAA Liaison: James Franklin
Members: 600 *Staff:* 1
Annual Budget: $25-50,000 *Tel:* (202) 626-7566
Hist. Note: Formerly (1974) The Architectural Secretaries Association. Operates a certification program for its members. Membership: $45/yr.
Publications:
News Journal. m.
Handbook for Architectural Administrators. Revised.
Annual Meetings: With American Institute of Architects

Soc. of Architectural Historians (1940)
1700 Walnut St., Suite 716, Philadelphia PA 19103-6085
Exec. Secretary: David Bahlman
Members: 4,000 *Staff:* 2-5
Annual Budget: $100-250,000 *Tel:* (215) 735-0246
Hist. Note: Provides an international forum for those interested in architecture, encourages scholarly research in the field and promotes the preservation of significant architectural monuments. A member of the American Council of Learned Societies. Membership: $48/year.
Publications:
Journal. q. adv.
Newsletter. bi-m. adv.
Annual Meetings: April
1987-San Francisco(Palace)/April 22-26/500
1988-Chicago, IL/April 13-17
1989-Montreal, Canada/April 12-16

Soc. of Authors' Representatives (1928)
39 1/2 Washington Sq., Apt. 10, New York NY 10012
Exec. Secretary: Georgie Lee
Members: 50-55 *Staff:* 1
Annual Budget: $10-25,000 *Tel:* (212) 228-9740
Hist. Note: Membership, concentrated in the New York area, consists of literary and dramatic agents. Membership: $175/yr.
Publication:
The Literary Agent. a.
Annual Meetings: Winter
1987-New York, NY(Harvard Club)/Dec./55

Soc. of Automotive Engineers (1905)
400 Commonwealth Dr., Warrendale PA 15096-0001
Exec. V. President: Max E. Rumbaugh, Jr.
Members: 43,000 *Staff:* 180
Annual Budget: over $5,000,000 *Tel:* (412) 776-4841
Hist. Note: Originated in 1905 as the Soc. of Automobile Engineers and became the Soc. of Automotive Engineers in 1916. Incorporated in New York the same year. Advances all aspects of the design, construction and use of self-propelled mechanisms, prime movers, their components and related equipment. Has an annual budget of $12 million. Membership: $50/year or less.
Publications:
Automotive Engineering. m. adv.
Aerospace Engineering. m. adv.
SAE Transactions. a.
SAE Update. m. adv.
Annual Meetings: Feb. in Detroit, MI(Cobo Hall)/30,000

Soc. of Behavioral Medicine (1978)
Box 8530, Univ. Station, Knoxville TN 37996
Exec. Director: Judith C. Woodward
Members: 2,000 *Staff:* 2-5
Annual Budget: $100-250,000 *Tel:* (615) 974-5164
Hist. Note: Members are primarily physicians, psychologists and nurses concerned with the effect of behavior on health. Membership: $60/yr.
Publications:
Behavioral Medicine Abstracts. q. adv.
Annals of Behavioral Medicine. q. adv.
Directory. bien.
Proceedings. a.
Annual Meetings: Spring
1987-Washington, DC(J.W. Marriott)/March 19-22/800-1,000
1988-Boston, MA/April

Soc. of Biblical Literature (1880)
2201 S. University Blvd., Denver CO 80210
Exec. Secretary: Prof. Kent H. Richards
Members: 5,000 *Staff:* 2-5
Annual Budget: $250-500,000 *Tel:* (303) 744-1287
Hist. Note: Formerly Soc. of Biblical Literature and Exegesis. A member of the American Council of Learned Societies. Membership: $15-50/yr.
Publications:
Journal of Biblical Literature. q. adv.
Semeia. q. adv.
Annual Meetings: November

00276 12 05 86 1233

Soc. of Biological Psychiatry (1945)
Dept. of Psychology & Behavioral Science,tanford University, Stanford CA 94305
Secy.-Treas.: Philip A. Berger, M.D.
Members: 800 *Staff:* 1
Annual Budget: $25-50,000 *Tel:* (415) 497-0852
Hist. Note: Founded in San Francisco in 1945 and incorporated in California in 1949. Promotes the study of the biological basis of human behavior.
Publication:
Biological Psychiatry. m. adv.
Annual Meetings: Spring
1987-Chicago, IL(Hyatt Regency)/May 6-10
1988-Montreal, Quebec(Hyatt Regency)/May 3-7
1989-San Francisco, CA(Hilton & Tower)/May 3-7

Soc. of Biomedical Equipment Technicians (1976)
1901 North Fort Myer Drive, Suite 602, Arlington VA 22209
Exec. Director: Michael J. Miller
Members: 900-1,000 *Staff:* 1
Annual Budget: $25-50,000 *Tel:* (703) 525-4890
Hist. Note: Sponsored by the Ass'n of Advancement of Medical Instrumentation to recognize biomedial equipment technicians as a specialty group. Sponsors a certification program (administered by the AAMI) in which the designation "CBET" (Certified Biomedical Equipment Technician) is awarded. Membership: $50/yr.
Publication:
Biomedical Technology Today. bi-m.
Annual Meetings: Spring
1987-Los Angeles, CA(Westin Bonaventure)/May 16-20/2,000
1988-Washington, DC(Sheraton Washington)/May 14-18/2,000

Soc. of Broadcast Engineers (1963)
Box 50844, Indianapolis IN 46250
Exec. Secretary: Helen Pfeifer
Members: 4-5,000 individuals; 60-70 companies *Staff:* 2-3
Annual Budget: $50-100,000 *Tel:* (317) 842-0836
Hist. Note: Membership includes studio and transmitter operators, announcer technicians, chief engineers of large and small stations and others involved in broadcast engineering. Founded in 1963 as the Institute of Broadcast Engineers. Membership: $20/yr. (individual), $300/yr. (organization/company).
Publication:
SBE Signal. bi-m.
Annual Meetings: With the Nat'l Ass'n of Broadcasters

Soc. of Cable Television Engineers (1969)
Box 2389, West Chester PA 19380
Exec. V. President: William Riker
Members: 3,200 individuals, 110 companies *Staff:* 2-5
Annual Budget: $250-500,000 *Tel:* (215) 363-6888
Hist. Note: Membership: $40/year.
Publications:
The Interval. m. adv.
Membership Directory. a. adv.
Annual Meetings: Spring
1987-Orlando, FL(Hyatt)/April 2-5

Soc. of Carbide and Tool Engineers (1947)
c/o ASM International, Metals Park OH 44073
President: J.A. Swartley-Loush
Members: 1,700
Annual Budget: $50-100,000 *Tel:* (216) 338-5151
Hist. Note: Formerly (1976) the Soc. of Carbide Engineers. Membership: $45/yr.
Publication:
The Carbide and Tool Journal. bi-m. adv.
Annual Meetings:
1987-Scottsdale, AZ(Doubletree Hotel)/Feb. 25-27/1,000

Soc. of Cardiovascular Anesthesiologists (1978)
Box 11083, 2315 Westwood Ave., Richmond VA 23230
Exec. Secretary: John A. Hinckley
Members: 1,600 *Staff:* 5
Annual Budget: $250-500,000 *Tel:* (804) 257-7154
Publication:
Newsletter. q.
Annual Meetings: Spring
1987-Palm Desert(Marriott Palm Desert Hotel)/April 10-13
1988-New Orleans, LA(Sheraton)/April 10-13

Soc. of Certified Consumer Credit Executives (1961)
Hist. Note: Merged with the International Consumer Credit Association in 1983.

Soc. of Certified Data Processors (1942)
Hist. Note: Became the Association of the Institute for Certification of Computer Professionals in 1983.

Soc. of Certified Insurance Counselors (1969)
3630 North Hills Drive, Austin TX 78731
President: William T. Hold, Ph.D.
Members: 8,250 individuals *Staff:* 28
Tel: (512) 345-7932
Hist. Note: The Society is the largest professional association for insurance agents with a mandatory continuing education requirement. Membership: $60/yr.
Publications:
The Counselor. bi-m.
Ruble Seminar News. bi-m.

Soc. of Certified Kitchen Designers (1967)
124 Main St., Hackettstown NJ 07840
Exec. Director: Francis Jones
Members: 1,000 individuals *Staff:* 2-5
Annual Budget: $50-100,000 *Tel:* (201) 852-0033
Hist. Note: The certifying arm of the National Kitchen and Bath Association, which provides administrative support. Awards the "CKD" (Certified Kitchen Designer) designation. Membership: $40/yr.
Publication:
The Professional to Consult. a.
Annual Meetings: In conjunction with the National Kitchen and Bath Conference.

Soc. of Chartered Property and Casualty Underwriters (1944)
Kahler Hall, 720 Providence Rd. (CB#9), Malvern PA 19355
Exec. V. President: James W. Hamilton, CPCU,CLU
Members: 16,000-17,000 *Staff:* 25-30
Annual Budget: $2-5,000,000 *Tel:* (215) 251-2728
Hist. Note: Insurance professionals who have passed the exam of the American Institute for Property and Liability Underwriters and have become a Chartered Property Casualty Underwriter (CPCU). Membership: $80/yr.
Publications:
CPCU Journal. q.
CPCU News. 9/yr.
Directory. bien.
Annual Meetings: Fall/2,500
1987-San Antonio, TX/Oct. 11-14
1988-Cincinnati, OH/Oct. 9-12
1989-Anaheim, CA/Oct. 15-18/3,000
1990-Washington, DC/Oct. 7-10

Soc. of Children's Book Writers (1968)
Box 296, Mar Vista Station, Los Angeles CA 90066
Exec. Director: Lin Oliver
Members: 3,000
Annual Budget: $10-25,000 *Tel:* (818) 347-2849
Hist. Note: SCBW acts as a network for the exchange of knowledge between children's writers, illustrators, editors, publishers and agents. Members include writers and illustrators of children's books, magazine stories and articles; writers and producers of children's television; children's book and magazine editors and publishers; agents; children's librarians, teachers and educators; bookstore owners and personnel. Membership: $30/yr.
Publication:
SCBW Bulletin. bi-m.
Annual Meetings: August at the Ambassador Hotel in Los Angeles, CA/250-300

Soc. of Christian Ethics (1959)
Vancouver School of Theology, 6000 Iona Drive, Vancouver British Columbia V6T 1L4
Exec. Secretary: Terence R. Anderson
Members: 675 individuals *Staff:* 1
Annual Budget: $10-25,000 *Tel:* (604) 228-9031
Hist. Note: The purpose of the Society is to promote scholarly work in the field of Christian ethics and in the relation of Christian ethics to other traditions of ethics and to social, economic, political and cultural problems. The Society also seeks to encourage and improve the teaching of these fields in colleges, universities, and theological schools and to provide a fellowship of discourse and debate for those engaged professionally within these general fields. Member of the Council of Societies for the Study of Religion. Formerly (until 1980) known as the American Society of Christian Ethics.
Publication:
Annual of the Society of Christian Ethics. a.
Annual Meetings: Third weekend in January/275
1987-Boston, MA(Copley Plaza)/Jan. 16-18

Soc. of Collision Repair Specialists (1982)
Box 1326, Blue Springs MO 64015
V. President: Sharon Dye
Members: 600 companies *Staff:* 2-5
Annual Budget: $100-250,000 *Tel:* (816) 228-6699
Hist. Note: Organized in Schaumburg, Illinois September 24, 1982. Members are owners of auto repair shops, insurance companies, educational associates and suppliers.
Publications:
SCRS News. m.
Collision Repair Specialist. m.
Annual Meetings: Summer
1987-Toronto, Canada/June 18-21

Soc. of Commercial Seed Technologists (1922)
P.O. Box 1712, Brandon Manitoba R7A 6C4
Secy-Treas: Marie Greeniaus
Members: 100-125 *Staff:* 1
Annual Budget: $10-25,000 *Tel:* (503) 998-8243
Hist. Note: Formerly (1946) Ass'n of Commercial Seed Analysts of North America. Professional involved in the testing and analysis of seeds, research on seed physiology, and seed production and handling based on the modern botanical and agricultural sciences. Membership: $45/yr.
Publications:
Seed Technologist News. 3/yr.
Proceedings, SCST. a.
Annual Meetings: With the Ass'n of Official Seed Analysts.
1987-Sacramento, CA(Red Lion)/June/65-75

Soc. of Company Meeting Planners (1971)
2600 Garden Road, #208, Monterey CA 93940
Exec. Director: Randy Lindner
Members: 200 *Staff:* 5
Annual Budget: $25-50,000 *Tel:* (408) 649-6544
Hist. Note: Corporate meeting planners and convention service managers. Founded in Chicago in 1971, incorporated in California. Membership: $200/yr.
Publication:
Newsletter. q.
Semi-Annual Meetings: Summer and Fall
1987-St. Louis, MO(Adam's Mark)/June 23-26
1987-Anaheim, CA(Disneyland)/Nov. 9-11

Soc. of Construction Superintendents (1935)
Hist. Note: A professional society of construction superintendents, supervisors and engineers. Address unknown in 1983.

Soc. of Consumer Affairs Professionals in Business (1973)
4900 Leesburg Pike, Suite 400, Alexandria VA 22302
Exec. Director: Louis Garcia, CAE
Members: 1,400 *Staff:* 2-5
Annual Budget: $500-1,000,000 *Tel:* (703) 998-7371
Hist. Note: Individuals responsible for the management of consumer affairs in all types of businesses. Operates the SOCAP Foundation as a conduit for corporate contributions in the field of consumer affairs. Membership: $150/yr.
Publications:
Mobius. bi-a.
Update. m.
Annual Meetings: Fall/400
1987-Los Angeles, CA

Soc. of Cosmetic Chemists (1945)
1995 Broadway, Suite 1701, New York NY 10023
Executive Administrator: William Hanley
Members: 3,298 *Staff:* 2-5
Annual Budget: $500-1,000,000 *Tel:* (212) 874-0600
Hist. Note: Founded in May 1945 and incorporated in Delaware in 1947. A member of the Internat'l Federation of Societies of Cosmetic Chemists. Membership: $50/yr.
Publication:
Journal of the Society of Cosmetic Chemists. bi-m. adv.
Semi-annual Meetings: May and December
1988-Minneapolis, MN/May
1987-Parsippany, NJ/December

Soc. of Craft Designers (1975)
6175 Barfield Road, Suite 220, Atlanta GA 30328
Exec. Director: Nancy Horne
Members: 399 *Staff:* 1
Annual Budget: $25-50,000 *Tel:* (404) 252-2454
Hist. Note: Affiliated with the Hobby Industry Ass'n of America. Members are designers of craft items and writers for the craft industry. Membership: $60/yr.(individual); $100/yr.(company).
Publication:
Newsletter. bi-m.
Annual Meetings: January
1987-Anaheim, CA
1988-St. Louis, MO

Soc. of Critical Care Medicine (1970)
251 East Imperial, Suite 480, Fullerton CA 92635
Exec. Director: Norma Shoemaker
Members: 2,800 individuals *Staff:* 14
Annual Budget: $1-2,000,000 *Tel:* (714) 870-5243
Hist. Note: Physicians, scientists, engineers, nurses and allied health personnel with involvement in critical care medicine, patient care, teaching and research. Established the Foundation for Critical Care Medicine in 1983 to provide funding for research and education in critical care medicine. It is located in Washington, DC. Membership: $160/yr.
Publications:
Journal of Critical Care Medicine. m. adv.
Concern Newsletter. q. adv.
State of the Art. a.
New Horizons. a.
Annual Meetings: May/June
1987-Anaheim, CA(Disneyland Hotel)/May 26-30/1,500
1988-Orlando, FL(Marriott's Orlando World Center)/May 16-20/1,500
1989-New Orleans, LA
1990-San Francisco, CA

Soc. of Diagnostic Medical Sonographers (1969)
10300 N. Central Expwy , Bldg.1, Ste.276, Dallas TX 75231
Exec. Director: Gwen Grim
Members: 4,000 *Staff:* 2-5
Annual Budget: $250-500,000 *Tel:* (214) 369-4332
Hist. Note: Individuals employing high frequency sound for medical diagnosis. Designed to provide members with continuing education, current information on standards, trends and opportunities in the field of ultrasound. Membership: $56/year.
Publications:
Journal of Dignostic Medical Sonography. bi-m.
SDMS Newsletter. q.
Annual Meetings: April
1987-Chicago, IL(Marriott Downtown)/April 24-26/3-500
1988-Anaheim, CA
1989-Atlanta, GA

Soc. of Die Casting Engineers (1954)
2000 N. 5th Ave., River Grove IL 60171
Exec. V. President: Larry G. Hayes

00277 12 05 86 1233

Members: 3,500 *Staff:* 11
Annual Budget: $1-2,000,000 *Tel:* (312) 452-0700
Hist. Note: Founded in Detroit on Oct. 4, 1954; incorporated in Michigan in 1955 and Illinois in 1980. Membership: $55/yr. (individual), $250-1,350/yr. (corporate).
Publication:
Die Casting Engineer. bi-m. adv.
Biennial meetings: odd years.
1987-Toronto,Ontario/May 11-14

Soc. of Economic Geologists (1920)
Box 571, Golden CO 80402
Secretary: Jack Murphy
Members: 2,700 *Staff:* 2-5
Annual Budget: $50-100,000 *Tel:* (303) 236-5538
Hist. Note: Founded in Chicago December 28, 1920 and incorporated in New York in 1930. Affiliated with the Geological Soc. of America and the American Geological Institute. Advances the science of geology in relation to mining and related industries. Membership: $43/year.
Publication:
Economic Geology. 8/yr.
Semi-Annual meetings: February (with AIME) and November (with
Geological Soc. of America)

Soc. of Economic Paleontologists and Mineralogists (1926)
Box 4756, Tulsa OK 74159-0756
Exec. Director: Joseph R. Huffstetler
Members: 8,000 *Staff:* 10
Annual Budget: $500-1,000,000 *Tel:* (918) 743-9765
Hist. Note: Originated in Fort Worth in 1926 and became an affiliated society of the American Ass'n of Petroleum Geologists in 1927, later a section, and in 1930 a technical division. A member society of the American Geological Institute.
Publications:
Journal of Sedimentary Petrology. bi-m.
PALAIOS. bi-m.
Semi-Annual Meetings: Annual with AAPG and Mid-Year

Soc. of Electronic Endodontology (1972)
Hist. Note: Dissolved in 1983.

Soc. of Engineering Psychologists (1953)
Hist. Note: Became the Soc. of Applied Experimental and Engineering Psychology in 1984.

Soc. of Engineering Science (1963)
ESM Department, 118 Norris Hall, Virginia Tech, Blacksburg VA 24061
Secretary: Prof. Carl T. Herakovich
Members: 400-500 *Staff:* 2-5
Annual Budget: $10-25,000 *Tel:* (703) 961-5372
Hist. Note: Multidisciplinary society of scientists and engineers concerned with research and communication between the fields of engineering and science. Membership: $15/year (individual).
Publications:
The Engineering Science Perspective. q.
Abstracts of the Annual Meeting. a.
Annual Meetings: November at a university and biennial int'l conferences (even years)

Soc. of Experimental Psychologists (1904)
Dept. of Psychology, UCLA, Los Angeles CA 90024
Secretary: Dr. Edward Carterette
Members: 153 *Staff:* 1
Annual Budget: under $10,000 *Tel:* (213) 825-2961
Hist. Note: An honorary society founded in 1904 and incorporated in 1939. Confers the annual Howard Crosby Warren Medal.
Annual Meetings: At University locations

Soc. of Experimental Social Psychology (1964)
Department of Psychology, Williams College, Williamstown MA 01267
Secy.-Treas.: Dr. George R. Goethals
Members: 470-500 social psychologists
Annual Budget: under $10,000 *Tel:* (413) 597-2443
Hist. Note: Has no paid staff. Membership: $6/yr.
Annual Meetings: 3rd week in October
1987-Charlottesville, VA
1988-Madison, WI

Soc. of Experimental Test Pilots (1955)
P.O. Box 986, Lancaster CA 93534
Exec. Director: Thomas H. Smith
Members: 1,600-1,700 *Staff:* 6
Annual Budget: $100-250,000 *Tel:* (805) 942-9574
Hist. Note: Founded September 14, 1955 and incorporated in California in 1956. Sponsors the Society of Experimental Test Pilots Scholarship Foundation. Has an international membership. Membership: $50/year.
Publication:
S.E.T.P. Technical Review. 5/yr.
Annual Meetings: Spring in Europe and Fall in Los Angeles.

Soc. of Exploration Geophysicists (1930)
Box 702740, Tulsa OK 74170
Exec. Director: John H. Hyden, CAE
Members: 18,000 *Staff:* 37
Annual Budget: over $5,000,000 *Tel:* (918) 493-3516
Hist. Note: Founded in Houston in 1930 and incorporated in Oklahoma.
Publications:
Geophysics. m. adv.
The Leading Edge of Exploration. m. adv.
Yearbook. a. adv.
Annual Meetings: Fall
1987-New Orleans, LA
1988-Anaheim, CA
1989-Dallas, TX
1990-San Francisco, CA

Soc. of Explosives Engineers (1974)
6990 Summers Rd., Box 185, Montville OH 44064
Exec. Director: Dr. Calvin J. Konya
Members: 1,760 *Staff:* 2
Annual Budget: $50-100,000 *Tel:* (216) 474-8436
Hist. Note: Members are individuals and organizations concerned with the use, supply or safeguarding of explosive substances. Membership is international. Absorbed the American Blasting Association in 1979. Membership: $25/yr.(individual); $175/yr.(organization).
Publications:
SEE Journal. bi-m.
Membership Directory. a.
General Proceedings. a.
Annual Meetings: February
1987-Florida/Jan. 31-Feb. 7
1988-Anaheim, CA/Feb. 1-6

Soc. of Eye Surgeons (1969)
7801 Norfolk Ave., Bethesda MD 20814
Exec. Secretary: Lawrence M. King, Jr.
Members: 1,000 *Staff:* 2-5
Annual Budget: $50-100,000 *Tel:* (301) 986-1830
Hist. Note: Sponsored by The Internat'l Eye Foundation. Membership: $100/yr.
Publication:
Eye To Eye Newsletter. semi-a.
Biennial Meetings: Even years (1988)

Soc. of Federal Labor Relations Professionals (1973)
2025 I St. N.W., Suite 216, Washington DC 20006
Exec. Secretary: Betty L. Ziska
Members: 800-825 *Staff:* 1
Annual Budget: $25-50,000 *Tel:* (202) 466-4048
Hist. Note: Membership is open to representatives of unions and management and neutrals. Membership: $35/yr.
Publication:
Newsletter. bi-m.
Annual Meetings: Late Winter

Soc. of Federal Linguists (1930)
Box 7765, Washington DC 20044
President: Richard S. Relac
Members: 125-150 *Staff:* 1
Annual Budget: under $10,000
Hist. Note: Formerly (1960) the Soc. of Federal Translators. Membership includes non-government linguists. Membership: $15/yr.
Publications:
Membership Directory. a.
Newsletter. 9/yr.
Annual Meetings: January, in Washington, DC

Soc. of Financial Examiners (1973)
Box 2598, 1100 Raleigh Building, Raleigh NC 27602
Exec. Director: Sharon Perry
Members: 1,400 *Staff:* 2-5
Annual Budget: $100-250,000 *Tel:* (919) 821-1435
Hist. Note: Membership: $35/yr.
Publications:
The Examiner. m.
The INSIGHT.
Annual Meetings: July

Soc. of Fire Protection Engineers (1950)
60 Batterymarch St., Boston MA 02110
Exec. Director: D. Peter Lund, CAE
Members: 3,200 *Staff:* 2-5
Annual Budget: $250-500,000 *Tel:* (617) 482-0686
Hist. Note: Founded October 31, 1950 as the professional section of the Nat'l Fire Protection Ass'n. Became independent of the NFPA on Feb. 10, 1971. Membership: $85/yr.
Publications:
Directory. bien.
SFPE Bulletin. 5/yr.
Technology Reports. m.
Proceedings. a.
Annual Meetings: With Nat'l Fire Protection Ass'n in Spring.
1987-Cincinnati, OH
1988-Los Angeles, CA
1989-San Antonio, TX

Soc. of Fire Protection Technicians (1973)
Hist. Note: Address unknown in 1985.

Soc. of Flight Test Engineers (1968)
Box 4047, Lancaster CA 93539
Exec. Director: Dianne Van Norman
Members: 1,000-1,100 individuals; 26-30 companies *Staff:* 1
Annual Budget: $10-25,000 *Tel:* (805) 948-3067
Hist. Note: Members are engineers whose principal professional interest is the flight testing of aircraft. Purpose of the Society is to improve communications in the fields of flight test operations, analysis, instrumentation and data systems.
Publications:
National Symposium Proceedings. a.
Flight Test news. m.
Annual Meetings: September
1987-Europe
1988-North Texas
1989-Lancaster, CA

Soc. of Former Special Agents of the Federal Bureau of Investigation (1937)
2416 Queens Plaza South, Room 312, Long Island City NY 11101
Exec. Secretary: Fran Keogh
Members: 8,000 *Staff:* 2-5
Annual Budget: $100-250,000 *Tel:* (718) 361-0051
Hist. Note: Founded and incorporated in New York in 1937. Created the Former Agents of the F.B.I. Foundation which assists needy members, deceased members' families, rehabilitation of the ill and education. Membership: $40/yr.
Publications:
The Grapevine. m.
Directory. a.
Annual Meetings:
1987-Dallas, TX(Loew's Anatole)
1988-Nashville, TN(Opryland)
1989-Orlando, FL(Peabody)

Soc. of Gastrointestinal Assistants (1973)
1070 Sibley Tower, Rochester NY 14604
Exec. Director: Margaret Crevey
Members: 2,300 *Staff:* 6-10
Annual Budget: $250-500,000 *Tel:* (716) 546-7241
Hist. Note: Nurses and other allied health care individuals working in the fields of gastroenterology/endoscopy. Membership: $50/yr.
Publication:
SGA Journal. q. adv.
Annual Meetings: Spring/1,000
1987-Chicago, IL(Westin)/May 9-13
1988-New Orleans, LA(Hyatt)/May

Soc. of General Physiologists (1946)
P.O. Box 257, Woods Hole MA 02543
Secretary: Dr. Luis Reuss
Members: 1,000 *Staff:* 1
Annual Budget: $10-25,000 *Tel:* (409) 761-1986
Hist. Note: Founded in 1946 at the Marine Biological Laboratory, Woods Hole, and incorporated in Massachusetts in 1966. Affiliate of the American Ass'n for the Advancement of Science, Internat'l Union of Physiological Sciences, the Nat'l Research Council, Internat'l Union of Pure and Applied Biophysics, and the American Physiological Soc.. Membership: $20/yr.
Publications:
Journal of General Physiology. m.
Symposium. a.
Annual Meetings: Woods Hole, MA(Marine Biological Lab.)/ Sept./200
1987-Sept. 9-13
1988-Sept. 7-11

Soc. of Geriatric Ophthalmology (1975)
3003 Woodward, Berkley MI 48072
Secy.-Treas.: Henry J. Sprio, M.D.
Annual Budget: $10-25,000 *Tel:* (313) 546-2133
Hist. Note: Professional society of ophthalmologists concerned about the problems of the elderly patient, including the special aspects of geriatric ophthalmologic examination. A satellite organization of the American Academy of Ophthalmology. Membership: $100/yr.
Annual Meetings:
1987-Canton, OH/March 21-22

Soc. of Glass and Ceramic Decorators (1963)
207 Grant St., Port Jefferson NY 11777
Exec. Secretary: Frank S. Child
Members: 500 *Staff:* 2-5
Annual Budget: $100-250,000 *Tel:* (516) 473-0232
Hist. Note: Formerly (1984) the Soc. of Glass Decorators. Membership: $165/yr. (individual); $250/yr. (company).
Publications:
Newsletter. adv. 10-12/yr.
Proceedings. a.
SGCD Directory.
SGCD Seminar Program.
Annual Meetings: Winter
1987-Atlanta, GA(Hyatt Regency Peachtree Center)/Nov. 23-25

Soc. of Glass Decorators (1963)
Hist. Note: Became the Soc. of Glass and Ceramic Decorators in 1984.

Soc. of Government Economists (1970)
Box 9622, Friendship Station, Washington DC 20016
Hist. Note: Members are economists interested in the economic aspects of government policy. Membership concentrated in the Washington area.
Publications:
Directory. a.
Newsletter. m.
Annual Meetings: Washington, DC in March

00278 12 05 86 1233

Soc. of Government Meeting Planners (1980)
1606 17th St., N.W., Washington DC 20009
Exec. Director: Alan M. Weil
Members: 300 companies; 300 individuals *Staff:* 2
Annual Budget: $50-100,000 *Tel:* (202) 232-6883
Hist. Note: Members are persons involved in planning government meetings and individuals who supply services to government planners. Membership: $35-175/yr.
Publication:
Newsletter. m. adv.
Annual Meetings: Feb.-March
1987-Washington, DC(J.W. Marriott)/Feb. 17-20/600

Soc. of Gynecological Oncologists (1969)
111 East Wacker Drive, Suite 600, Chicago IL 60601
Exec. Director: Rosemary Zuern
Members: 500 *Staff:* 3
Tel: (312) 644-6610
Hist. Note: Founded in 1969 by a small group of doctors interested in advancing knowledge and raising standards of practice in gynecologic oncology within the disciplines of obstetrics and gynecology. Membership: $175/yr.
Annual Meetings: February/500
1987-Miami, FL(Doral Hotel & Country Club)/Feb. 1-4
1988-Miami, FL(Doral Hotel & Country Club)/Feb. 7-10
1989-Maui, HI(Hyatt Regency)/Feb. 5-9

Soc. of Head and Neck Surgeons (1954)
13 Elm Street, Box 1565, Manchester MA 01944
Exec. Director: Gardner V. McCormick
Members: 5-600 *Staff:* 1
Annual Budget: $25-50,000 *Tel:* (617) 927-8330
Publication:
Head and Neck Surgery.
Annual Meetings: Spring with American Soc. of Clinical Oncology
1987-England/April 26-May 1
1988-New Orleans, LA/May 22-25
1989-San Francisco, CA/May 21-24
1990-Washington, DC/May 13-16

Soc. of Hydrogen Sulphide Safety Contractors (1982)
Hist. Note: Members are companies from the oil and gas industries working with hydrogen sulphide. Address unknown in 1984.

Soc. of Illustrators (1901)
128 East 63rd St., New York NY 10021
Director: Terrence Brown
Members: 950 *Staff:* 6-11
Annual Budget: $250-500,000 *Tel:* (212) 838-2560
Hist. Note: A professional society of illustrators and art directors founded in New York in 1901 by ten of America's leading illustrators. Established a Hall of Fame in 1958 to recognize distinguished achievement in the field of illustration and a Museum of American Illustration in 1981. Most members come from the New York Area. Membership: $275-325/yr.
Publication:
Annual of American Illustration. a. adv.

Soc. of Incentive Travel Executives (1974)
271 Madison Ave., Suite 904, New York NY 10016
Vice President: Andre G. Abbate, Jr.
Members: 1,300 *Staff:* 5
Annual Budget: $250-500,000 *Tel:* (212) 889-9340
Hist. Note: SITE is an individual membership society covering 43 countries. Members are: corporate users, airlines, Tourist Boards, cruise lines, destination management companies, consultants, hotels/resorts, travel agents, incentive travel houses and publications. Membership: $200/yr.
Publication:
SITE Newsletter. q.
Semi-Annual Meetings:
University of Incentive Travel/June
International Conference/Nov.

Soc. of Independent Financial Advisors (1975)
Hist. Note: Address unknown in 1985.

Soc. of Independent Gasoline Marketers of America (1958)
1730 K St., N.W., Suite 907, Washington DC 20006
Exec. Director: Kenneth A. Doyle
Members: 300 companies *Staff:* 5-10
Annual Budget: $1-2,000,000 *Tel:* (202) 429-9333
Hist. Note: Private brand gasoline marketers. Sponsors and supports the Society of Independent Gasoline Marketers of America Political Action Committee.
Publications:
Roster. a.
SIGMA Update. m.
Semi-annual Meetings: Spring and Fall(with American Petroleum Institute).
1987-San Diego, CA(Intercontinental)/April 11-13/475

Soc. of Independent Professional Earth Scientists (1962)
4925 Greenville Ave., Suite 170, Dallas TX 75206
Exec. Secretary: Diane Finstrom
Members: 1,300 *Staff:* 1
Annual Budget: $25-50,000 *Tel:* (214) 363-1780
Hist. Note: Founded in Houston, TX and chartered as a professional and scientific scoiety in 1963, SIPES is a member society of the American Geological Institute. Members are geologists, geophysicists, engineers and other earth scientists with at least twelve years professional experience who are independent or self-employed. Sponsors and supports the SIPES Foundation, a charitable and educational foundation, chartered in Texas in 1981. Membership: $60/yr.
Publications:
Newsletter. q. adv.
Membership Directory. bien. adv.
Annual Meetings: Feb./March
1987-Shreveport, LA

Soc. of Industrial Realtors (1941)
777 14th St., N.W., Suite 400, Washington DC 20005
Exec. V. President: Robert E. Boley
Members: 1,670 individuals *Staff:* 11-15
Annual Budget: $1-2,000,000 *Tel:* (202) 383-1150
Hist. Note: A professional affiliate of the Nat'l Ass'n of Realtors, SIR was founded in Washington just prior to World War II at the instigation of the then War Department to help locate specialized facilities suitable for the production of military equipment. Incorporated in the State of Illinois, active members are brokers, consultants and appraisers, all of whom must first be members of the Nat'l Ass'n of Realtors. Membership: $650/yr. (active members).
Publications:
Industrial Market Survey. semi-a.
SIR Reports. 6/yr.
Office Market Survey. semi-a.
Semi-annual meetings:
1987-Boca Raton,FL(Boca Raton Hotel)/May 8-13
1987-Hawaii(Hyatt Regency)/Nov. 3-7
1988-Colorado Springs, CO(Broadmoor)/April 30 - May 5
1988-San Francisco, CA(St. Francis Hotel)/Nov. 3-7
1989-Boston, MA(Copley Place)/May 10-14
1989-Dallas, TX(Sheraton Plaza of America)/Nov. 2-7
1990-Palm Desert, CA(Marriott Desert Springs)/April 18-22
1990-New Orleans, LA(Sheraton)/Nov. 1-6

Soc. of Insurance Accountants (1960)
Route 3, Box 166, Crozet VA 22932
Admin. Services: George Sumsion
Members: 8-900 *Staff:* 1
Annual Budget: $10-25,000 *Tel:* (804) 823-4839
Hist. Note: Formed by a merger of the Insurance Accountants Ass'n and the Ass'n of Casualty Accountants and Statisticians.
Publication:
Proceedings. a.
Annual Meetings: October

Soc. of Insurance Research (1970)
Box 933, Appleton WI 54912
Admin. Secretary: Debra Krueger
Members: 600 individuals *Staff:* 1
Annual Budget: $25-50,000 *Tel:* (414) 731-2405
Hist. Note: Founded under the sponsorship of the Griffith Foundation for Insurance Education, Ohio State University to provide a communication channel and a forum for the exchange of research ideas. Members are individuals actively engaged in some form of insurance research. Membership: $100/yr.
Publications:
Research Review. bi-m.
Membership Directory. a.
Member Skills Matrix. a.
Annual Meetings: November
1987-New Orleans, LA
1988-Detroit, MI
1989-Denver, CO
1990-Columbus, OH

Soc. of Insurance Trainers and Educators (1953)
200 Hembree Park Drive, Roswell GA 30076
President: William C. Priegnitz
Members: 500
Annual Budget: $25-50,000 *Tel:* (404) 442-8633
Hist. Note: Formerly (1985) the Insurance Company Education Directors Soc. Membership composed of education and training personnel, personnel directors, and those responsible for the training function in insurance. Voting Membership: $60/yr.
Publications:
In-Site. bi-m.
Training Journal. bi-a.
Annual Meetings: June
1987-Keystone, CO(Keystone Lodge)/June 16-19
1988-Hyannisport, MA(Dunfey's)
1989-Lake Lanier, GA(Stouffer's Pineisle)

Soc. of Logistics Engineers (1966)
125 West Park Loop, Suite 201, Huntsville AL 35806-1745
Exec. Director: Robert R. Leonard
Members: 9,500 *Staff:* 10
Annual Budget: $500-1,000,000 *Tel:* (205) 837-1092
Hist. Note: Founded in 1966 as a non-profit international professional society of individuals to promote logistics education and technical activities. Membership: $40/yr.
Publications:
Annals. a.
Directory. a.
Logistics Spectrum. q. adv.
SOLEtter. m.
Annual Meetings: Summer/750
1987-St. Louis(Clarion)/Aug. 18-20
1988-San Francisco, CA/Aug.

Soc. of Manufacturing Engineers (1932)
One SME Drive, Box 930, Dearborn MI 48121
Exec. V. President and General Manager: Kenneth L. Thorpe
Members: 80,000 *Staff:* 280
Annual Budget: over $5,000,000 *Tel:* (313) 271-1500
Hist. Note: Founded as the American Soc. of Tool Engineers, it became the American Soc. of Tool and Manufacturing Engineers in 1960 and the Soc. of Manufacturing Engineers in 1969. SME is a technical society dedicated to advancing scientific knowledge in the field of manufacturing and to applying its resources to research, writing, publishing and disseminating information. Supports a number of associations and technical groups, including: Ass'n for Finishing Processes, Computer and Automated Systems Ass'n, Electronics Manufacturing Group, Composites Group, Machine Vision Ass'n, North American Manufacturing Research Institute, Robotics Internat'l and Manufacturing Automation Protocol and Technical Office Protocol (MAP/TOP) Users Group. Sponsors the Manufacturing Engineerging Education Foundation and the Manufacturing Engineering Certification Insitute, which grants the "CMFgE" (Certified Manufacturing Engineer) and "CMFgT" (Certified Manufacturing Technologist) designations. Membership: $40/yr. (individual); $155/yr. (organization/company)
Publications:
Manufacturing Engineering. m. adv.
Robotics Today. bi-m. adv.
CIM Technology. q. adv.
Newsletters: Machine Vision, Composites, Finishing & MAP/TOP. q. adv.
Journal of Manufacturing Systems. semi-a.
Manufacturing Insights.
Annual Meetings: May
1987-Detroit, MI(Cobo Hall)/May 4-7/25,000
1988-Cleveland, OH(Convention Ctr.)/May 2-5/20,000
1989-Detroit, MI(Cobo Hall)/May 1-4/25,000
1990-Philadelphia, PA(Civic Ctr.)/May 7-10/20,000
1991-Detroit, MI(Cobo Hall)/May 6-9/25,000

Soc. of Marine Port Engineers (1946)
21 West St., Suite 3102, New York NY 10006
Secy.-Treas.: James H. Dickey
Members: 400-450 engineers *Staff:* 1
Annual Budget: under $10,000 *Tel:* (212) 269-4840
Hist. Note: Membership: $45/yr.
Publication:
The De-Air-Eator. q.
Annual Meetings: May, in New York, NY

Soc. of Maritime Arbitrators (1963)
26 Broadway, Suite 1200, New York NY 10004
President: Alexis Nichols
Members: 120-130 *Staff:* 2-5
Annual Budget: $50-100,000 *Tel:* (212) 483-0616
Hist. Note: Members are drawn from such fields as surveying, engineering, finance, brokerage, stevedoring, construction, repairs, sales, insurance, and terminal and vessel operations; the bulk of the membership is in the New York area. SMA's purpose is to help settle disputes arising from contracts for and all movements by water or involving shipbuilding and repair, and to maintain uniformity in U.S. maritime arbitration proceedings.
Publication:
The Arbitrator. q.
Annual Meetings:
1987-Madrid, Spain(Hotel Palace)/Oct. 12-16

Soc. of Medical Administrators (1914)
1901 Pennsylvania Ave., N.W., Suite 207, Washington DC 20006
Treasurer: Marvin H. Goldberg
Members: 50 *Staff:* 1
Annual Budget: under $10,000 *Tel:* (202) 659-5939
Hist. Note: Membership limited to 50 physicians active in administrative medicine.
Annual Meetings: Winter/65-70
1987-Palm Beach(The Breakers)

Soc. of Medical Consultants to the Armed Forces (1946)
4301 Jones Bridge Road, Bethesda MD 20814-4799
Staff Asst. to the President: Dr. John W. Bullard
Members: 900-1,000 *Staff:* 1
Annual Budget: $10-25,000 *Tel:* (301) 295-3107
Hist. Note: Organized by specialists who were consultants to the Armed Forces during World War II, SMCAF now includes individuals who have been consultants at any time to the Armed Services. Formerly Soc. of U.S. Medical Consultants in W.W. II.
Annual Meetings: Washington, DC/Fall

Soc. of Medical-Dental Management Consultants (1968)
7318 Raytown Road, Raytown MO 64133
Exec. Secretary: William Kidd
Members: 75-100 individuals *Staff:* 1
Annual Budget: $25-50,000 *Tel:* (800) 826-2264
Hist. Note: A professional society established in Kansas City, Missouri by 20 charter members in the spring of 1968. Membership: $295/yr.
Publication:
Consultant's Newsletter. bi-m.
Semi-annual Meetings: Winter and Summer
1987-Las Vegas, NV or Chicago, IL/Feb.
1987-Philadelphia, PA/June

00279 12 05 86 1233

Soc. of Mining Engineers (1957)
Caller #D, Littleton CO 80127
Exec. Director: Claude L. Crowley
Members: 25,000 *Staff:* 24
Annual Budget: $2-5,000,000 *Tel:* (303) 973-9550
Hist. Note: Member of the American Institute of Mining, Metallurgical, and Petroleum Engineers (1871). Membership: $60/yr.
Publications:
Mining Engineering. m. adv.
Mining Transactions, AIME. a.
Minerals and Metallurgical Processing Journal. q. adv.
Semi-annual Meetings: 2,500
1987-Denver, CO(Convention Complex)/Feb. 24-27
1987-New Orleans, LA(Sheraton)/June 14-18
1988-Phoenix/Jan. 26-29
1989-Las Vegas/Feb. 28-March 3

Soc. of Motion Picture and Television Art Directors (1960)
14724 Ventura Blvd., P.H., Sherman Oaks CA 91403
Exec. Director: Gene Allen
Members: 3-400 *Staff:* 2-5
Tel: (818) 905-0599
Hist. Note: A labor union formerly (until 1960) known as the Soc. of Motion Picture Art Directors. Affiliated with the Internat'l Alliance of Theatrical Stage Employees and Moving Picture Machine Operators of the U.S. and Canada, Local 876.

Soc. of Motion Picture and Television Engineers (1916)
585 W. Hartsdale Ave., White Plains NY 10607
Exec. Director: Lynette A. Robinson
Members: 9,000 *Staff:* 25-30
Annual Budget: $1-2,000,000 *Tel:* (914) 761-1100
Hist. Note: Founded in 1916 as the Soc. of Motion Picture Engineers. Incorporated in the District of Columbia. Became the Soc. of Motion Picture and Television Engineers in 1950. Membership: $50/year.
Publication:
SMPTE Journal. m. adv.
Annual Meetings: Fall
1987-Los Angeles, CA/Oct.

Soc. of Multivariate Experimental Psychology (1960)
Department of Psychology, University of Virginia, Charlottesville VA 22901
Secy.-Treas.: Dr. J. Jack McArdle
Members: 65 *Staff:* 1
Annual Budget: under $10,000 *Tel:* (804) 924-3374
Hist. Note: A small professional group of active behavioral scientists who use mathematical approaches to complex problems. Membership: $40/yr.
Publication:
Multivariate Behavioral Research. q. adv.
Annual Meetings:
1987-Vancouver, BC/Nov./35

Soc. of Municipal Arborists (1964)
R.R. 3, Box 614, Williston ND 58801
Exec. Secretary: Dale L. Gaasland
Members: 90-100 individuals; 5-10 companies *Staff:* 1
Annual Budget: $10-25,000 *Tel:* (701) 774-0485
Hist. Note: Full-time municipal arborists and companies representing products in the field. Membership: $30/yr.
Publication:
City Trees. m. adv.

Soc. of Nat'l Ass'n Publications (1963)
1010 Wisconsin Ave., N.W., Suite 630, Washington DC 20007
Exec. Director: Anita S. Bollt
Members: 250 *Staff:* 2-5
Annual Budget: $100-250,000 *Tel:* (202) 965-7510
Hist. Note: Members are publications of voluntary ass'ns and professional societies.
Publications:
Directory of Members. a.
Snapshot. m.
Editorial and Graphic Awards Competition Booklet.
Annual Meetings: June in Washington, DC
1987-(Washington Marriott)/June 14-17

Soc. of Naval Architects and Marine Engineers (1893)
One World Trade Center, Suite 1369, New York NY 10048
Secy. and Exec. Director: Robert G. Mende
Members: 13,000 *Staff:* 20-25
Annual Budget: $1-2,000,000 *Tel:* (212) 432-0310
Hist. Note: Incorporated in New York April 28, 1893.
Publications:
Journal of Ship Research. q.
Marine Technology. q.
STAR Proceedings. a.
Transactions. a.
Journal of Ship Production. q.
Annual Meetings: New York City in Fall(New York Hilton)/2,000

Soc. of Nematologists (1961)
Dept. of Plant Pathology and Physiology,Clemson University, Clemson SC 29634-0377
Secretary: S.A. Lewis
Members: 800-900 *Staff:* 1
Annual Budget: $50-100,000 *Tel:* (803) 656-5471
Hist. Note: Members are individuals interested in nematodes, such as roundworms or threadworms. Member of the American Institute of Biological Sciences. Has no paid staff. Membership: $15/yr.
Publications:
Journal of Nematology. q.
Nematology Newsletter. q.
Membership Directory. bien.
Annual Meetings: Summer/400-600
1987-Hawaii(Ala Moana Americana)/July 19-22
1988-Raleigh, NC(Radisson Plaza)/June 12-16
1989-Davis, CA

Soc. of Neurological Surgeons (1920)
Medical Univ. of South Carolina, 171 Ashley Ave., Charleston SC 29425
Secretary: Phanor L. Perot, Jr.
Members: 300 *Staff:* 1
Annual Budget: $10-25,000 *Tel:* (803) 792-2421
Hist. Note: The honorary society of neurological surgery. Membership restricted.
Annual Meetings: Spring

Soc. of Neurosurgical Anesthesia and Neurological Supportive Care (1973)
2315 Westwood Avenue; Box 11083, Richmond VA 23230
Exec. Secretary: John A. Hinckley
Members: 600 individuals *Staff:* 2-5
Annual Budget: $10-25,000 *Tel:* (804) 353-9529
Hist. Note: Members are board-certified anesthesiologists or surgeons. Membership: $45/yr.
Publication:
Newsletter. 3-4/yr.
Annual Meetings: With the American Soc. of Anesthesiologists in the Fall

Soc. of Newspaper Design (1979)
Box 17290, Dulles Airport, Washington DC 20041
Exec. Secretary: Pat Kelly
Members: 1,600 *Staff:* 1
Annual Budget: $25-50,000 *Tel:* (703) 620-1083
Hist. Note: Originally the Society of Newspaper Designers (the name was changed in 1981), membership is open to anyone interested in newspapers or newspaper design. Membership: $45/yr.
Publication:
Design. q.
Annual Meetings: Fall
1987-Texas

Soc. of Noninvasive Vascular Technology (1977)
1101 Connecticut Ave., N.W., Suite 700, Washington DC 20036
Exec. Director: Patricia Horner
Members: 2,800 *Staff:* 2-5
Annual Budget: $250-500,000 *Tel:* (202) 857-1149
Hist. Note: Founded and incorated in Ohio. Members perform diagnostic tests to determine the location of blockages in the body's circulatory system. Approximately 60% of SNIVT members are practicing noninvasive technologists or are involved in supervision and/or education in a clinical setting. Other members include physicians, researchers, manufacturers and other health care providers. Serves as an education and information resource in matters pertaining to noninvasive vascular technology. Membership: $40/yr.
Publications:
BRUIT. 5/yr. adv.
Spectrum. 5/yr. adv.
Annual Meetings: June
1987-Toronto, Canada(Royal York)/June 3-7/500
1988-Chicago, IL(Marriott)/June 8-11/600
1989-New York, NY
1990-Los Angeles, CA
1991-Boston, MA

Soc. of North American Goldsmiths (1970)
9421 Hunting Ct., Charlotte NC 28105
President: Michael Croft
Members: 4,000 individuals *Staff:* 3
Annual Budget: $100-250,000
Hist. Note: Concerned with the educational, scientific and aesthetic aspects of goldsmithing and metalsmithing. Membership: $45/yr.
Publication:
Metalsmith. q. adv.
Annual Meetings:
1987-Bloomfield, MI(Cranbrook Academy)

Soc. of Nuclear Medicine (1954)
136 Madison Ave., New York NY 10016
Exec. Director: Henry L. Ernstthal, CAE
Members: 10,000 *Staff:* 31-35
Annual Budget: $2-5,000,000 *Tel:* (212) 889-0717
Hist. Note: A multidisciplinary organization of physicians, physicists, chemists, radiopharmacists, technologists, etc. interested in diagnostic and therapeutic uses of radioactive and stable isotopes. Membership: $90/yr.
Publications:
Journal of Nuclear Medicine m. adv.
Journal of Nuclear Medicine Technology. q. adv.
Annual Meetings: Spring/5,000
1987-Toronto, Ontario/June 2-5
1988-San Francisco, CA
1989-St. Louis, MO
1990-Washington, DC

Soc. of Office Automation Professionals (1981)
AMS Building, 2360 Maryland Road, Willow Grove PA 19090
Administrator: Elizabeth Hand
Members: 150 *Staff:* 1
Annual Budget: $10-25,000 *Tel:* (215) 659-4300
Hist. Note: Membership is composed of professionals involved in data processing, word processing, voice and data telecommunications as well as library, behavioral and management science. Affiliated with the Administrative Management Soc. Membership: $50/yr.(individual); $250/yr.(organization)
Publications:
SOAPBox. q.
OA Newsletter. q.
Directory of Members. a.
Annual Meetings: Not Held

Soc. of Oral Physiology and Occlusion (1954)
3 Linden Place, Middletown NY 10940
Secy.-Treas.: Dr. Irving Anderman
Members: 150-175 *Staff:* 1
Annual Budget: under $10,000 *Tel:* (914) 343-2133
Hist. Note: Founded by Dr. Nathan Allen Shore for the study of the pain syndromes associated with tempero-mandibular joint dysfunction and occlusion.
Annual Meetings: New York City, in November, at the New York Athletic Club.

Soc. of Packaging and Handling Engineers (1945)
11800 Sunrise Valley Dr., Reston VA 22091
Exec. Director: William C. Pflaum
Members: 3,000 *Staff:* 2-5
Annual Budget: $250-500,000 *Tel:* (703) 620-9380
Hist. Note: Founded in 1945 as the Industrial Packaging Engineers Ass'n and incorporated in Illinois the same year. Became the Soc. of Industrial Packaging and Materials Handling Engineers in 1948 and the Soc. of Packaging and Handling Engineers in 1958. Member of the Council of Engineering and Scientific Soc. Executives. Membership: $60/yr. (individual), $600/yr. (company).
Publications:
Newsletter. bi-m.
SPHE Technical Journal. bi-a.
Directory. a.
Semi-Annual Meetings: Spring and Fall

Soc. of Park and Recreation Educators (1966)
3101 Park Center Drive, Alexandria VA 22302
Exec. Secretary: Donald Henkel
Members: 400-500 individuals *Staff:* 1
Annual Budget: $25-50,000 *Tel:* (703) 820-4940
Hist. Note: A branch of the Nat'l Recreation and Park Ass'n.
Publication:
Newsletter. q.
Annual Meetings: With Nat'l Recreation and Park Ass'n

Soc. of Pediatric Orthopedics (1982)
Hist. Note: Became the Pediatric Orthopaedic Soc. of North America in 1985 and a division of the American Academy of Orthopaedic Surgeons in 1986.

Soc. of Pelvic Surgeons (1952)
1600 North State St., Suite 304, Jackson MS 39202
Secy.-Treas.: Dr. Richard Boronow
Members: 125-150 *Staff:* 1
Annual Budget: under $10,000 *Tel:* (601) 944-0220

Soc. of Petroleum Engineers (1913)
222 Palisades Creek Drive, Richardson TX 75080
Exec. Director: Dan Adamson
Members: 56,500 *Staff:* 75
Annual Budget: over $5,000,000 *Tel:* (214) 669-3377
Hist. Note: Technical engineers, scientists and managers engaged in the recovery of oil and gas related energy sources through wellbores. In 1913 a Standing Committee on Oil and Gas was established as part of the American Institute of Mining and Metallurgical Engineers. This became the Petroleum Division of the Institute in 1922, and the Petroleum Branch in 1949. Petroleum was added to the Institute name in 1955, and in 1957 the Soc. of Petroleum Engineers was formed as one of three largely autonomous societies within the AIME. In 1985, SPE incorporated separately from AIME. Membership: $30/yr.
Publications:
Journal of Petroleum Technology. m. adv.
SPE Drilling Engineering. q. adv.
SPE Production Engineering. q. adv.
SPE Formation Evaluation. q. adv.
SPE Reservoir Engineering. q. adv.
Annual Meetings: Fall
1987-Dallas, TX/Sept. 27-30
1988-Houston, TX/Oct. 2-5
1989-San Francisco, CA/Sept. 24-27
1990-New Orleans, LA/Sept. 23-26

Soc. of Philatelic Americans (1894)
Hist. Note: Address unkown in 1984; reported defunct.

Soc. of Philaticians (1972)
154 Laguna Court, St. Augustine Shores FL 32086-7031
Secretary: Gustav Detjen, Jr.
Members: 185 *Staff:* 1
Annual Budget: under $10,000 *Tel:* (904) 797-3513
Hist. Note: Professional philatelic journalists and publicists. Founded in November, 1972, in New York City during the Nat'l Postage Stamp Show. Membership: $15/yr.

00280 12 05 86 1233

Publications:
Philatelic Directory. a. adv.
The Philatelic Journalist. q. adv.
Membership List. a.
Annual Meetings: Spring and Fall in New York City

Soc. of Photo-Optical Instrumentation Engineers (1956)
Hist. Note: Became SPIE- International Society for Optical Engineering in 1983.

Soc. of Photo-Technologists (1959)
P.O. Box 9634, Denver CO 80209
Exec. Director: Elsa C. Kaiser
Members: 1,200 *Staff:* 2-5
Annual Budget: $50-100,000 *Tel:* (303) 698-1820
Hist. Note: A professional society of camera repair technicians. Holds seminars and workshops throughout the year. Membership: $100-200/yr. (based on sales volume).
Publications:
SPT Newsletter. m.
SPT Journal and Service Notes. bi-m. adv.

Soc. of Photographer and Artist Representatives (1965)
1123 Broadway, Suite 914, New York NY 10010
Exec. Officer: Anita Green
Members: 250 *Staff:* 1
Annual Budget: $50-100,000 *Tel:* (212) 924-6023
Hist. Note: Agents representing commercial artists and photographers. Membership: $175/yr.

Soc. of Photographic Scientists and Engineers
Hist. Note: Became SPSE: Soc. for Imaging Science and Technology in 1986.

Soc. of Physics Students (1968)
335 East 45th St., New York NY 10017
Exec. Director: Dr. Dion W. J. Shea
Members: 7,200 individuals *Staff:* 6-10
Annual Budget: $250-500,000 *Tel:* (516) 349-7800
Hist. Note: Formed through a merger of the Student Sections of the American Institute of Physics and the physics honor society, Sigma Pi Sigma. Affiliated with the American Institute of Physics, Inc. Membership: $10/year.
Publications:
Journal of Undergraduate Research in Physics. semi-a.
SPS Information Book. a.
SPS Newsletter. 5/yr.
Speakers, Tours & Films Book. a.
Annual Meetings: April
1987-Crystal City, VA(Hyatt Regency)/April 22-23

Soc. of Plastics Engineers (1942)
14 Fairfield Dr., Brookfield Center CT 06805
Exec. Director: Robert D. Forger
Members: 25,000 *Staff:* 35
Annual Budget: $2-5,000,000 *Tel:* (203) 775-0471
Hist. Note: Founded December 2, 1941 in Detroit as the Soc. of Plastics Sales Engineers and incorporated in Michigan in 1942. Membership: $55/yr.
Publications:
Journal of Vinyl Technology. q.
Plastics Engineering. m. adv.
Polymer Composites. bi-m.
Polymer Engineering and Science. 22/yr.
Annual Meetings: Spring/4-5,000
1987-Los Angeles, CA(Bonaventure/Biltmore)/May 4-7
1988-Atlanta, GA(Westin/Hyatt Regency/Merchandise Mart)/April 18-21
1989-New York, NY(Hilton)/May 1-4
1990-Dallas, TX(Loew's Anatole)/May 7-10
1991-Montreal,Quebec(Convention Center)/May 6-9
1992-Detroit, MI(Westin)/May 4-7

Soc. of Professional Archaeologists (1976)
Museum, Michigan State University, East Lansing MI 48824-1045
Secy.-Treas.: Dr. William Lovis
Staff: 1
Annual Budget: $25-50,000 *Tel:* (309) 788-5263
Hist. Note: Established to forward and speak for professional archaeologists and develop professional standards in training, conduct and research. Promulgates a Code of Ethics and certifies the qualifications of its members. Membership: $45/yr.

Soc. of Professional Audio Recording Studios (1978)
Box 11333, Beverly Hills CA 90213
Exec. Director: Gary Helmers
Members: 200-300 *Staff:* 5-10
Annual Budget: $250-500,000 *Tel:* (213) 466-1244
Hist. Note: Members are individuals, companies and studios connected with the professional recording industry.
Publication:
Data Track Newsletter. q.
Annual Meetings: October

Soc. of Professional Benefit Administrators (1975)
2033 M St., N.W., Suite 605, Washington DC 20036
President: Frederick D. Hunt, Jr.
Members: 370 companies *Staff:* 2-5
Annual Budget: $500-1,000,000 *Tel:* (202) 223-6413
Hist. Note: Independent third-party contract administration firms, which administer employee benefit plans for client emloyers and unions. One third of all U.S. workers, retirees and dependents are covered by SPBA plans. Membership: $475-2,500/yr. (Based on size)
Publications:
SPBA Update. w.
SPBA Roster. a.
SPBA Stop-Loss Directory. irreg.
Semi-annual meetings: Spring and Fall/244
1987-Washington, DC(L'Enfant Plaza)/Spring
1987-San Diego, CA(del Coronado)/Fall
1988-Washington, DC(L'Enfant Plaza)/Spring
1988-Kansas City, MO(Westin Crown Center)/Fall

Soc. of Professional Business Consultants (1956)
600 S. Federal St., Suite 400, Chicago IL 60605
Exec. Director: Durward Humes
Members: 200-250 *Staff:* 2-5
Tel: (312) 346-1600
Hist. Note: Consultants to the medical and dental professions.
Annual Meetings: June
1987-San Antonio, TX(Intercontinental)
1988-Denver, CO(Fairmont)

Soc. of Professional Investigators (1956)
Hist. Note: Address unknown in 1986. Probably defunct.

Soc. of Professional Journalists, Sigma Delta Chi (1909)
53 W. Jackson Blvd., Suite 731, Chicago IL 60604
Exec. Officer: Russell C. Tornabene
Members: 24,000 *Staff:* 12
Annual Budget: $1-2,000,000 *Tel:* (312) 922-7424
Hist. Note: Founded at DePauw University in Greencastle, IN in 1909 as Sigma Delta Chi; assumed its present name in 1973. Membership, by invitation only, is comprised of men and women in every field of journalism. Maintains over 325 local professional and campus chapters. Membership: $40/yr.
Publications:
The Quill. m. adv.
Freedom of Information Report. a.
Ethics Report. a.
Annual Meetings: November/900-1,000
1987-Chicago, IL
1988-Cincinnati, OH
1989-Houston, TX
1990-Louisville, KY
1991-Cleveland, OH

Soc. of Professional Management Consultants (1959)
163 Engle St., Englewood NJ 07631
Exec. Director: Marjorie Zelner
Members: 170 *Staff:* 2-5
Annual Budget: $10-25,000 *Tel:* (201) 569-6668
Hist. Note: Membership: $150/yr. (individual).
Publications:
Profile Directory. a.
Newsletter. bi-m.
Technical Articles. bi-m.
Annual Meetings: New York, NY/June

Soc. of Professional Well Log Analysts (1959)
6001 Gulf Freeway, Suite C-129, Houston TX 77023
Administrator: Vicki J. King
Members: 4,400 *Staff:* 2-5
Annual Budget: $250-500,000 *Tel:* (713) 928-8925
Hist. Note: Founded in Tulsa in January 1959 and incorporated in Oklahoma the same year. Promotes the evaluation of formations through well logging techniques, to locate gas, oil and other minerals. Membership: $20-25/yr.
Publications:
The Log Analyst. bi-m. adv.
Transactions. a.
Annual Meetings: June
1987-London, England(Grosevnor)/June 29-July 3/800
1988-San Antonio, TX(Marriott)/June 5-8/1,600

Soc. of Professionals in Dispute Resolution (1973)
1730 Rhode Island Ave., N.W., Suite 909, Washington DC 20036
Exec. Director: Laurene Hughes Church
Members: 1,800 *Staff:* 2-5
Annual Budget: $100-250,000 *Tel:* (202) 833-2188
Hist. Note: Members are specialists in labor, environment, family, community and other types of dispute resolution. Incorporated in the State of New York. Administrative support provided by the American Arbitration Ass'n. Membership: $65/yr.
Publications:
Occasional papers. 1-3/yr.
SPIDR News. q.
Proceedings. a.
Annual Meetings: Mid-October/400
1987-New York, NY(Grand Hyatt)/Oct. 22-25

Soc. of Professors of Education (1902)
School of Education, #135, Pan American University, Edinburg TX 78539
Secy.-Treas.: Martha Tevis
Members: 200-250 *Staff:* 1
Annual Budget: under $10,000 *Tel:* (512) 381-3436
Hist. Note: Established as the Nat'l Soc. of College Teachers of Education, it assumed its present name in 1969. Membership: $15/yr.

Publications:
DeGarmo Lectures. a.
SPE Monograph Series. a.
Annual Meetings: February/100

Soc. of Prospective Medicine (1972)
Box 20548, Indianapolis IN 46220-0548
Office Manager: Cindi L. Weber
Members: 450-500 *Staff:* 2
Annual Budget: $50-100,000 *Tel:* (317) 924-4878
Hist. Note: Individuals interested in health care programs to extend life expectancy. Membership: $55/yr.
Publications:
An Ounce of Prevention. q.
Proceedings. a.
Directory. a.
Annual Meetings: Fall/200
1987-Atlanta, GA/Sept. 17-20
1988-Indianapolis, IN

Soc. of Protozoologists (1947)
12301 Parklawn Drive, Rockville MD 20852
Secretary: Pierre-Marc Daggett
Members: 1,000-1,100 *Staff:* 1
Annual Budget: $50-100,000 *Tel:* (301) 881-2600
Hist. Note: Founded in 1947 as an international scientific society. An affiliate of the American Ass'n for the Advancement of Science and member of the World Federation of Parasitologists. Members are concerned with all aspects of the study of protozoa.
Publication:
Journal of Protozoology. q. adv.
Annual Meetings: Summer

Soc. of Publication Designers (1964)
25 West 43rd St., Suite 711, New York NY 10036
Exec. Director: Bride M. Whelan
Members: 500 *Staff:* 2-5
Annual Budget: $100-250,000 *Tel:* (212) 354-8585
Hist. Note: A professional organization which includes art directors, designers, illustrators, photographers, printers and publishers. Serves the needs of the editorial designer and art director by sponsoring annual competitions, speakers evenings, exhibitions and other activities. Membership: $150/yr. (individual); $350/yr. (corporate)
Publications:
Grids. 5/yr.
Publication Design Annual. a. adv.

Soc. of Radiological Engineering (1968)
Georgetown Univ. Hosp., Radiology Dept.,3800 Reservoir Road, N.W., Washington DC 20007
Exec. Director: Dave Whitbeck
Members: 375-400 *Staff:* 1
Annual Budget: $25-50,000 *Tel:* (202) 625-2573
Hist. Note: Originated in Chicago at the annual meeting of the Radiological Soc. of North America. Membership: $30/yr.
Publication:
Journal of Radiological Engineering. q. adv.
Annual Meetings: Concurrently with the Radiological Soc. of North America

Soc. of Real Estate Appraisers (1935)
645 North Michigan Ave., Chicago IL 60611
Exec. V. President: Robert E. Palmer
Members: 17,000 *Staff:* 60
Annual Budget: over $5,000,000 *Tel:* (312) 346-7422
Hist. Note: Formerly the Soc. of Residential Appraisers. Awards the designations SRA (Senior Residential Appraiser), SRPA (Senior Real Property Appraiser), and SREA (Senior Real Estate Analyst). Sponsors and supports the Society of Real Estate Appraisers Political Action Committee. Has an annual budget of $7 million.
Publications:
Briefs. bi-w.
The Real Estate Appraiser and Analyst. q.
Annual Meetings: August
1987-Montreal, Quebec(Queen Elizabeth)/Aug. 2-5/1,000
1988-Reno, NV(MGM Grand)/Aug. 7-10/1,000
1989-Atlanta, GA/Aug. 6-9

Soc. of Research Administrators (1967)
1505 4th St., Suite 203, Santa Monica CA 90401
Exec. Director: Julie M. Carthane
Members: 1,800 *Staff:* 3
Annual Budget: $100-250,000 *Tel:* (213) 393-3137
Hist. Note: A professional association of individuals in industry, academia and government to improve the efficiency of research administration and the interface between the investigators and their administrative overseers. Membership: $60/year.
Publications:
Membership Directory. a. adv.
Newsletter. bi-m.
SRA Journal. q. adv.
Annual Meetings: Fall
1987-New Orleans, LA(Fairmont)/Sept. 20-23/5-600
1988-Boston, MA(Park Plaza Hotel)/Oct. 9-12/5-600

Soc. of Rheology (1929)
335 East 45th St., New York NY 10017
Secretary: Don Baird
Members: 1,250
Annual Budget: $10-25,000 *Tel:* (212) 661-9404
Hist. Note: Chemists, physicists, biologists, chemical engineers, and others concerned with the theory and precise measurement of the flow of matter, and the response of materials to mechanical force. Has a permanent address at the American Institute of Physics, and is one of the 5 founding members of

00281 12 05 86 1233

that organization. Membership: $20/yr.
Publications:
Journal of Rheology. bi-m.
Rheology Bulletin. 1-2/yr.
Annual Meetings: Late Fall

Soc. of Risk Management Consultants (1984)
3255 Fritchie Drive, Baton Rouge LA 70809
Secretary: Robert S. Felton
Members: 110 *Staff:* 1
Annual Budget: $10-25,000 *Tel:* (504) 925-2833
Hist. Note: Formed in 1984 by the consolidation of the Insurance Consultants Soc. and the Institute of Risk Management Consultants. Membership: $100/yr.
Publication:
SRMC Journal. irreg.
Annual Meetings: October/100-150

Soc. of Roller Skating Teachers of America (1945)
7700 A St., Lincoln NE 68510
Exec. Director: George H. Pickard
Members: 1,300-1,400 *Staff:* 2-5
Annual Budget: $25-50,000 *Tel:* (402) 489-8811
Hist. Note: Sponsored by Roller Skating Rink Operators of America.
Publication:
SRSTA Newsletter. m.
Annual Meetings: Winter

Soc. of Satellite Professionals (1983)
P.O. Box 7154, McLean VA 22106
Administrator: Elizabeth Harrington
Members: 675 *Staff:* 1
Annual Budget: $10-25,000 *Tel:* (703) 356-3787
Hist. Note: Members are individuals in the field of satellite communications. There are twenty-one corporate sponsors. Membership: $45/yr.
Publications:
Update. m.
ORBITER. q.
Membership Directory. a.
Annual Meetings: In conjunction with the Satellite Communications Users Conference.

Soc. of Small Craft Designers (1949)
V195 Fontenoy East, Boyne City MI 49712
President: William R. Mehaffey
Members: 250 *Staff:* 1
Annual Budget: under $10,000 *Tel:* (616) 582-2924
Hist. Note: Members are small craft designers concerned with the scientific design of yachts and small commercial vessels (up to 200 feet). Members are primarily naval architects.
Publications:
Planimeter. semi-a.
Roster. bien.

Soc. of Soft Drink Technologists (1953)
P.O. Box 259, Brentwood MD 20722
Secy.-Treas.: Harry E. Korab
Members: 975 *Staff:* 2-5
Annual Budget: $10-25,000 *Tel:* (301) 277-0018
Hist. Note: A professional society of individuals engaged in the soft drink industry. Membership: $40/yr.
Publication:
Annual Meeting Proceedings. a.
Annual Meetings: April/400
1987-Las Vegas, NV(Las Vegas Hilton)/April 6-8

Soc. of State Directors of Health, Physical Education and Recreation (1926)
9805 Hillridge Dr., Kensington MD 20895
Secy.-Treas.: Simon A. McNeely
Members: 180 *Staff:* 1
Annual Budget: under $10,000 *Tel:* (301) 949-2226
Hist. Note: Seeks to promote and improve programs of health, physical education, recreation, athletics, dance and related subjects in elementary schools, secondary schools, colleges and universities, and teacher education programs in these disciplines. Membership: $25/yr.
Annual Meetings: With American Alliance for Health, Physical Education, Recreation and Dance.
1987-Las Vegas, NV(MGM Grand)/April 11-14/150
1988-Kansas City, MO/April 4-7/150

Soc. of Surgical Oncology (1940)
13 Elm St., Box 1565, Manchester MA 01944
Exec. Director: William T. Maloney, CAE
Members: 800 cancer specialists *Staff:* 12
Annual Budget: $50-100,000 *Tel:* (617) 927-8330
Hist. Note: Founded in 1940 as the James Ewing Soc. Became the Soc. of Surgical Oncology in 1975.
Annual Meetings: Spring
1987-England/April 26-May
1988-Los Angeles, CA(Century Plaza)/April 17-21

Soc. of Systematic Zoology (1948)
Nat'l Marine Fisheries, Systematics Lab,U.S. National Museum, Washington DC 20560
Secretary: Austin B. Williams
Members: 900-1,000 *Staff:* 1
Annual Budget: under $10,000 *Tel:* (202) 357-2639
Hist. Note: Founded in the District of Columbia in 1948. Affiliated with the American Ass'n for the Advancement of Science, the American Institute of Biological Sciences, the National Research Council and the American Soc. of Zoologists. Promotes zoological classification. Membership: $20/yr.
Publication:
Systematic Zoology. q.
Annual Meetings: With the American Soc. of Zoologists
1987-Nashville, TN
1988-New Orleans, LA
1989-San Francisco, CA
1990-Boston, MA

Soc. of Teachers of Emergency Medicine (1975)
Box 619911, Dallas TX 75261-9911
Staff Executive: Ellen Stewart
Members: 615 *Staff:* 2
Annual Budget: $50-100,000 *Tel:* (214) 550-0921
Hist. Note: Physicians who teach emergency medicine, emergency medicine residents, non-physicians teaching emergency care, medical suppliers and others interested in emergency medicine. Affiliated with the American College of Emergency Physicians and the Ass'n of American Medical Colleges. Active Membership: $90/yr.
Publications:
Stemletter. bi-m. adv.
Educational Resources Compendium. a.
Membership Directory. a.
Annual Meetings: Spring
1987-Philadelphia, PA(Franklin Plaza)/May 17-19/150
1988-Cincinnati, OH(Netherland Plaza)/May 22-24/150
1989-San Diego, CA/May/175

Soc. of Teachers of Family Medicine (1968)
1740 West 92nd St., Kansas City MO 64114
Exec. Director: Roger A. Sherwood, CAE
Members: 2,300 *Staff:* 6-10
Annual Budget: $500-1,000,000 *Tel:* (816) 333-9700
Hist. Note: Multidisciplinary society of health professionals concerned with family medicine education. Affiliated with the American Board of Family Practice, the American Academy of Family Physicians, and the Family Health Foundation of America. Represents family medicine as an academic discipline on the Council of Academic Societies of the Ass'n of American Medical Colleges.
Publication:
Family Medicine. bi-m. adv.
Annual Meetings: Spring/750
1987-New Orleans, LA(Marriott)/April 25-29
1988-Montreal, Quebec(Queen Elizabeth)/April 26-30
1989-Denver, CO(Marriott)/April 25-29

Soc. of the Plastics Industry (1937)
1025 Connecticut Avenue, N.W., #409, Washington DC 20036
President: Charles E. O'Connell
Members: 1,600 companies *Staff:* 90
Annual Budget: over $5,000,000 *Tel:* (202) 822-6700
Hist. Note: Promotes the application and use of plastics and is the principal representative of the plastics industry.
Publications:
SPI Membership Directory and Buyers Guide. a.
Facts and Figures of the U.S. Plastics Industry. a.
Annual Meetings: Regional show also triennial National Plastics Exposition (NPE)

Soc. of Thoracic Surgeons (1964)
111 East Wacker Dr., Chicago IL 60601
Business Manager: Walter G. Purcell
Members: 2,500 *Staff:* 6-10
Tel: (312) 644-6610
Publication:
Annals of Thoracic Surgery. a. adv.
Annual Meetings: September
1987-Toronto, Ontario/Sept. 20-23
1988-New Orleans, LA/Sept. 25-28
1989-Baltimore, MD/Sept. 10-13

Soc. of Toxicology (1961)
1133 15th St., N.W., Suite 1000, Washington DC 20005
Exec. Secretary: Joan Walsh Cassedy
Members: 2,200 *Staff:* 2
Annual Budget: $250-500,000 *Tel:* (202) 293-5935
Hist. Note: Founded and incorporated in the District of Columbia in 1961. Members are individuals concerned with the effects of chemicals on living organisms. Membership: $85/yr. (individual); $1,000/yr. (organization).
Publications:
Fundamental and Applied Toxicology. bi-m. adv.
Toxicology and Applied Pharmacology. m. adv.
Annual Meetings: Late Winter/3,000
1987-Washington, DC(Hilton)/Feb. 23-27
1988-Dallas, TX(Loews Anatole)/Feb. 14-19
1989-Atlanta, GA(Hilton)/Feb. 26-March 3
1990-St. Louis, MO(Adam's Mark)/March 11-16

Soc. of United States Air Force Flight Surgeons (1960)
Box 35387, Brooks AFB TX 78235
Exec. Officer: Sharon A. Falkenheimer
Members: 7-800 *Staff:* 1
Annual Budget: under $10,000 *Tel:* (512) 536-3475
Hist. Note: Affiliated with Aerospace Medical Ass'n. Membership: $10/yr.
Publication:
Soc. of USAF Flight Surgeons' Newsletter. q.
Annual Meetings: With Aerospace Medical Ass'n.

Soc. of University Otolaryngologists (1964)
Eye and Ear Infirmary, 1855 West Taylor St., Chicago IL 60612
Exec. Secretary: Edward L. Applebaum, M.D.
Members: 380 *Staff:* 1
Annual Budget: under $10,000 *Tel:* (312) 996-6582
Hist. Note: Otolaryngology is a medical specialty concerned with the ear, nose and throat and their disorders.

Soc. of University Patent Administrators (1975)
Harvard Medical School, 221 Longwood Avenue, Room 202, Boston MA 02115
President: Stephen Atkinson
Members: 525 individuals *Staff:* 1
Annual Budget: $25-50,000 *Tel:* (617) 732-0920
Hist. Note: Incorporated as a non-profit group in the state of Illinois. Members are individuals overseeng the marketing and sale of the results of government-financed research at educational institutions. Membership: $30/yr.
Publications:
SMPA Newsletter. q.
SMPA Journal. semi-a.
SMPA Membership Directory. a.
Annual Meetings: Semi-annual
1987-Arlington, VA(Stouffer)/Feb. 22-24/250-300
1987-Boulder, CO/June/125-150

Soc. of University Surgeons (1939)
Dept. of Surgery, UCLA Medical Center, Los Angeles CA 90024
Secretary: Ronald W. Busuttil
Members: 950-1,000 *Staff:* 1
Annual Budget: $25-50,000 *Tel:* (213) 825-5318
Annual Meetings: February
1987-Columbus, OH/Feb. 12-14
1988-San Antonio, TX/Feb. 11-13
1989-Baltimore, MD/Feb. 9-11

Soc. of University Urologists (1967)
Milton S. Hershey Medical Center, Div. of Urology, P.O. Box 850, Hershey PA 17033
Secy.-Treas.: Thomas J. Rohner, Jr., M.D.
Members: 425 *Staff:* 1
Annual Budget: under $10,000 *Tel:* (717) 534-8849
Hist. Note: Promotes high standards of urologic education and research. Membership: $30/yr.
Annual Meetings: In conjunction with the American College of Surgeons/125

Soc. of Vacuum Coaters (1957)
1133 15th St., N.W., Suite 620, Washington DC 20005
Exec. Director: John H. Ganoe
Members: 400-500 *Staff:* 2-5
Annual Budget: $50-100,000 *Tel:* (202) 293-5910
Hist. Note: Individuals concerned with the capabilities of vacuum coating for decorative and thin film applications.
Publication:
Proceedings. a.

Soc. of Vector Ecologists (1968)
Box 87, Santa Ana CA 92702
Secy.-Treas.: Frank W. Pelsue
Members: 450-500 *Staff:* 1
Annual Budget: under $10,000 *Tel:* (714) 971-2421
Hist. Note: A vector ecologist studies the environmental interrelationships of arthropods and other animals of public health importance (eg mosquitoes) as a basis for developing improved prevention and control measures. Members work in Mosquito Abatement Districts, Health, Agricultural and Fish and Game Departments, universities, private industry, and the Armed Forces. Has no paid staff. Membership: $25/yr.
Publication:
Bulletin of the Society of Vector Ecologists. irreg.
Annual Meetings: November
1987-Monterey, CA(Asilimar)/Nov. 18-20
1988-Arrowhead, CA(Convention Ctr.)

Soc. of Vertebrate Paleontology (1940)
Natural History Museum, 900 Exposition Boulevard, Los Angeles CA 90007
Secy.-Treas.: David P. Whistler
Members: 1,100-1,200 *Staff:* 1
Annual Budget: $25-50,000 *Tel:* (213) 744-3310
Hist. Note: Established in December 1940. Formerly a section of the Paleontological Soc. Affiliated with the American Geological Institute.
Publications:
News Bulletin. 3/yr.
Journal of Vertebrate Palentology. q.
Annual Meetings:
1987-Tuscon, AZ/Nov./300-400
1988-Drumheller, Canada/Nov./300-400

Soc. of Wine Educators (1977)
132 Shaker Road, Suite 14, East Longmeadow MA 01028
Exec. Director: James J. Holsing
Members: 1,400 individuals; 350 companies *Staff:* 2
Annual Budget: $100-250,000 *Tel:* (413) 567-8272
Hist. Note: The purpose of the society is to provide education on wine to consumers, retailers and restaurateurs, and those with a genuine interest in wine. Members include those who teach wine education classes; those who write about wine; and those associated with wine in the production, restaurant, retail and wholesale areas. Membership: $35/yr. (individual); $100/yr. (industry)

00282 12 05 86 1233

Publication:
SWE Chronicle. q.
Annual Meetings: Summer, near a wine producing area/4-500
1987-Vancouver, BC(Univ. of British Columbia)/Aug. 4-7

Soc. of Woman Geographers (1925)
1619 New Hampshire Ave., N.W., Washington DC 20009
Exec. Secretary: Mrs. Ellen F. Schou
Members: 400-500
Annual Budget: under $10,000 *Tel:* (202) 265-2669
Hist. Note: Founded in New York City in 1925 and incorporated in the District of Columbia in 1937. Membership by invitation only.
Annual Meetings: Held every 3 years (1987)

Soc. of Women Engineers (1950)
345 East 47th St., Room 305, New York NY 10017
Acting Exec. Director: B.J. Harrod
Members: 14,000 *Staff:* 8
Annual Budget: $250-500,000 *Tel:* (212) 705-7855
Hist. Note: An educational service organization of graduate engineers. SWE was founded in 1949-50 when small groups of women engineers started meeting in New York, Boston, Philadelphia and Washington, D.C. The Society was incorporated in 1952. In 1976 membership was opened to men. Membership: $50/yr.(individual); $700-1,000/yr.(company).
Publication:
U.S. Woman Engineer. bi-m. adv.
Annual Meetings: June
1987-Kansas City, MO/1,200
1988-San Juan, Puerto Rico/1,200
1989-Oakland, CA/1,500

Soc. of Wood Science and Technology (1958)
Box 5062, Madison WI 53705
Exec. Secretary: Vicki Claas
Members: 4-500 *Staff:* 2
Annual Budget: $25-50,000 *Tel:* (608) 264-5747
Hist. Note: Founded in June 1958 as the American Soc. of Wood Engineering. Became the Soc. of Wood Science and Technology in 1961 and incorporated in Wisconsin in 1961.
Publication:
Wood and Fiber Science. q.
Annual Meetings: Summer/100
1987-Louisville, KY/June 21
1988-Quebec City, Quebec
1989-Reno, NV

Sod Growers Ass'n of Mid-America (1958)
101 West Lincoln St., Peotone IL 60468
Exec. Secretary: Beverly A. Haase
Members: 30-35 companies *Staff:* 1
Annual Budget: under $10,000 *Tel:* (312) 258-6636
Hist. Note: Trade association for the sod industry; disseminates practical and scientific information and financially encourages turf research at universities.
Publication:
Newsletter. 3/yr.
Annual Meetings: First Thursday in December

Software Publishers Ass'n (1984)
1111 19th St., N.W., Suite 1200, Washington DC 20036
Exec. Director: Kenneth A. Wasch
Members: 175 companies *Staff:* 2
Annual Budget: $250-500,000 *Tel:* (202) 452-1600
Hist. Note: Members are microcomputer software firms. Services include: data collection program, software protection, contracts reference disk, conferences, and lobbying. Membership Fee: Based on total organizational revenues.
Publication:
SPA News. m.
Annual Meetings:
1987-Berkeley, CA(Claremont)/Mrch 25-28/350

Soil Conservation Soc. of America (1945)
7515 Northeast Ankeny Road, Ankeny IA 50021
Exec. V. President: Walter N. Peechatka
Members: 13,000 *Staff:* 11-15
Annual Budget: $500-1,000,000 *Tel:* (515) 289-2331
Hist. Note: Founded in the District of Columbia in 1945 and incorporated there in 1949. Promotes better land use and management. Membership $37/year.
Publications:
Journal of Soil and Water Conservation. bi-m. adv.
SCSA Conservogram.
Annual Meetings: Summer/1,500
1987-Billings, MT(Sheraton and Northern)/Aug. 2-5
1988-Columbus, OH(Hyatt Regency)/July 31 - August 3
1989-Edmonton, Canada(Convention Centre)/July 30-Aug. 2

Soil Science Soc. of America (1936)
677 South Segoe Rd., Madison WI 53711
Exec. V. President: Robert F. Barnes
Members: 6,500 *Staff:* 2-5
Annual Budget: $250-500,000 *Tel:* (608) 273-8080
Hist. Note: Founded November 18, 1936 and incorporated in Wisconsin in 1952. Shares headquarters with the American Soc. of Agronomy and the Crop Science Soc. of America.
Publications:
Journal of Environmental Quality. q.
Soil Science Society of America Journal. bi-m.
Agronomy News. m.
Annual Meetings: With American Soc. of Agronomy and the Crop Science Soc. of America
1987-Atlanta, GA(Hilton, Hyatt Regency & Westin)/Nov. 20-Dec. 4/4,000

Solar Energy Industries Ass'n (1974)
1730 North Lynn St., Suite 610, Arlington VA 22209-2009
Exec. V. President: David Gorin
Members: 150-200 companies, 22 state chapters *Staff:* 3-9
Annual Budget: $250-500,000 *Tel:* (703) 524-6100
Hist. Note: Membership consists of companies and individuals concerned with the development of the sun as a source of energy. Supports the Solar Energy Research and Education Foundation as well as the Solar Energy Industries Association Political Action Committee.
Publications:
SEIA News.
SEIA Directory and Buyers Guide. a.
Annual Meetings: Winter
1987-Orlando, FL

Solar Energy Institute of North America (1976)
Hist. Note: Inactive in 1985.

Solar Rating and Certification Corp. (1980)
1001 Connecticut Ave., N.W., Suite 800, Washington DC 20036
Exec. V. President: Arlen G. Reimnitz
Members: 150 companies *Staff:* 3
Annual Budget: $250-500,000 *Tel:* (202) 452-0078
Hist. Note: The SRCC is a non-profit third party certification organization whose primary purpose is the development and implementation of certification programs and national rating standards for solar energy equipment including solar collectors, solar water heating systems and wind energy conversion systems. In addition to its certification programs, the corporation also administers a laboratory accreditation program for independent test facilities evaluating solar components, subsystems and systems. Program fee: $500/yr.
Publications:
Directory of SRCC Certified Solar Collector Ratings. semi-a.
Directory of SRCC Certified Solar Water Heating Systems Ratings.
semi-a.
Newsletter. 3/yr.

Solid-State Circuits Council
Hist. Note: A subsidiary of the Institute of Electrical and Electronics Engineers. Membership in the Society, open only to IEEE members, includes subscription to a technical periodical in the field published by IEEE. All administrative support is provided by IEEE.

Sommelier Soc. of America (1954)
35 West 36th St., New York NY 10018
Exec. Director: Richard J. Gaffney
Members: 500-600 *Staff:* 2-5
Annual Budget: $50-100,000 *Tel:* (212) 686-7435
Hist. Note: "Sommelier": French name for a wine steward. Members are wine importers and merchants, restaurant owners, caterers and others. Seeks to expand the knowledge and appreciation of fine wines and liquors. Membership: $50-$85/year.
Publication:
Newsletter. 11/yr.
Annual Meetings: New York City, in Spring.

Songwriters Guild of America (1931)
276 5th Ave., New York NY 10001
Exec. Director: Lewis M. Bachman
Members: 4,000-4,500 *Staff:* 11-15
Annual Budget: $250-500,000 *Tel:* (212) 686-6820
Hist. Note: Formerly (1958) Songwriters Protective Ass'n and (1984) American Guild of Authors and Composers. Negotiates agreements between songwriters, composers and publishers. Maintains a Copyright Renewal Service, and a Royalty Collection Service.
Publications:
Bulletin. q.
SGA News. 2/yr. adv.
Semi-annual meetings: New York in February and Los Angeles in April

Sonics and Ultrasonics Soc.
Hist. Note: A subsidiary of the Institute of Electrical and Electronics Engineers. Membership in the Society, open only to IEEE members, includes subscription to a technical periodical in the field published by IEEE. All administrative support is provided by IEEE.

Sorptive Minerals Institute (1970)
1440 New York Ave., N.W., Suite 300, Washington DC 20005
Exec. Director: Steven B. Hellem
Members: 6-10 companies *Staff:* 2-5
Annual Budget: $50-100,000 *Tel:* (202) 638-1200
Hist. Note: Members are companies mining and processing sorptive minerals (clays and diatomaceous earths that can absorb 75-125% of their weight in water).
Publication:
Memo. m.
Annual Meetings: May
1987-Colorado Springs, CO

Southern Cypress Manufacturers Ass'n (1905)
805 Sterick Bldg., Memphis TN 38103
Exec. Secretary: James H. Lee
Members: 10-15 companies *Staff:* 2-5
Tel: (901) 525-8221
Hist. Note: Managed by the staff of the Harwood Manufacturers Ass'n.

Southern Forest Institute
Hist. Note: A Division of the American Forest Institute.

Southern Forest Products Ass'n (1914)
Box 52468, New Orleans LA 70152
President: W. R. Ganser, Jr. CAE
Members: 175-200 companies *Staff:* 25-30
Annual Budget: $2-5,000,000 *Tel:* (504) 443-4464
Hist. Note: Formerly (1970) Southern Pine Ass'n. Lumber manufacturers of Southern pine. Member of the Forest Industries Council. Membership: $1,750-350,000/yr. (company, based on shipment size).
Publications:
Newsletter. w.
Marketing News. m.
Semi-annual meetings:
1987-New Orleans, LA(Hilton)/June 16-17/250
1987-Memphis, TN(Peabody)/Oct./250
1988-Washington, DC(J.W. Marriott)/May/200
1988-Charleston, SC(Omni)/Oct. 9-12/250
1989-Atlanta, GA(Marriott Marquis)/Oct. 15-17/300

Southern Furniture Manufacturers Ass'n (1905)
Hist. Note: Merged with the Nat'l Furniture Manufacturers Ass'n in 1984 to become the American Furniture Manufacturers Ass'n.

Southern Hardwood Lumber Manufacturers Ass'n
Hist. Note: Became the Hardwood Manufacturers Ass'n in 1984.

Southern Labor Union (1955)
Box Q, Cumberland KY 40823
Internat'l President: Rileith Adams
Members: 1,500 *Staff:* 1
Annual Budget: $100-250,000 *Tel:* (606) 589-2379
Hist. Note: Independent labor union.
Biennial Meetings: Even years

Southern Traffic League (1918)
Hist. Note: Became the Southern Transportation League in 1985.

Southern Transportation League (1985)
3426 North Washington Blvd., Box 1240, Arlington VA 22210
Exec. Director: William P. Jackson, Jr.
Members: 100-125 *Staff:* 2-5
Annual Budget: $10-25,000 *Tel:* (703) 525-4050
Hist. Note: Founded as the Southern Traffic League in 1918, it assumed its present name in 1985.
Publication:
The Southern Transportation Light. w.

Southwestern Craft and Hobby Ass'n (1974)
1100-H Brandywine Blvd., P.O. Box 2188, Zanesville OH 43702
Exhibit Manager: Walter E. Offinger
Members: 755 individuals *Staff:* 11
Tel: (614) 452-4541
Hist. Note: SWCHA has a national membership of professionals engaged in the manufacturing, buying and selling of craft industry supplies and merchandise. Membership: $15-25/yr.
Publication:
Southwestern Craft & Hobby Ass'n Newsletter. q.
Annual Meetings: Summer in Dallas, TX at the Dallas Market Center
1987-Aug. 1-3
1988-July 30-Aug. 1
1989-July 29-31

Souvenirs and Novelties Trade Ass'n (1962)
401 North Broad St., Philadelphia PA 19108
President: Scott C. Borowsky
Members: 20,000 *Staff:* 14
Annual Budget: $500-1,000,000 *Tel:* (215) 925-9744
Publications:
Souvenirs and Novelties Magazine. 7/yr. adv.
Tourist Attractions and Parks. 6/yr. adv.

Soy Protein Council (1971)
1255 Twenty-Third St., N.W., Washington DC 20037
Exec. V. President: Sheldon J. Hauck
Members: 6 companies *Staff:* 2-5
Annual Budget: $100-250,000 *Tel:* (202) 467-6610
Hist. Note: Members are processors and distributors of vegetable proteins and their products, for use and consumption in human food. Formerly (1982) the Food Protein Council.

Soycrafters Ass'n of North America
Hist. Note: Became the Soyfoods Ass'n of America in 1984.

Soyfoods Ass'n of America (1979)
1101 Connecticut Ave., N.W., Suite 700, Washington DC 20036
Exec. Director: Judith A. Walker
Members: 75 companies *Staff:* 2
Annual Budget: $25-50,000 *Tel:* (202) 857-1133
Hist. Note: Formerly Soyfoods Ass'n of North America. Membership: $125-$3,000/yr. (based on sales volume)

00283 12 05 86 1233

Publication:
Soyfoods Report. q. adv.
Annual Meetings: Winter
1987-Anaheim, CA

Space Commerce Roundtable Foundation (1985)
419 Park Ave. South, 3rd Floor, New York NY 10016
Exec. Director: Harry A. Hansen
Members: 40 individuals *Staff:* 1
Annual Budget: under $10,000 *Tel:* (212) 213-2539
Hist. Note: The Foundation's purposes are to: promulgate information to the general public concerning the financial requirements of space commerce; establish and operate periodic gatherings of financial and technical experts and groups for the exchange and dissemination of information concerning space commerce.

Spain-U.S. Chamber of Commerce (1959)
350 Fifth Ave., Suite 3514, New York NY 10118
Exec. Director: Miguel Sabastia
Members: 550-600 *Staff:* 2-5
Annual Budget: $100-250,000 *Tel:* (212) 967-2170
Hist. Note: Originated at a luncheon at the Biltmore Hotel February 9, 1959 and incorporated in New York April 2, 1959.
Publication:
Spain-U. S. Trade Magazine. bi-m. adv.

Special Industrial Radio Service Ass'n (1953)
1700 North Moore St., Suite 910, Rosslyn VA 22209
President and Managing Director: Mark E. Crosby
Members: 13,300 *Staff:* 16-20
Annual Budget: $1-2,000,000 *Tel:* (703) 528-5115
Hist. Note: Designated by the FCC in 1953 as the official Frequency Advisory Committee for the Special Industrial Radio Service. Formed to represent the interests of its members concerning 2-way radio communications.
Publication:
Mini-Signals. m.
Annual Meetings: Fall
1987-Denver, CO
1988-Phoenix, AZ
1989-Boston, MA

Special Interest Group for Architecture of Computer Systems
c/o Quintus Computer Systems, 1310 Villa St., Mountain View CA 94041
Chairman: Doug DeGroot
Members: 3,000
Tel: (212) 869-7440
Hist. Note: SIGARCH is concerned with the constituents and arrangement of the physical resources of the computer system. A semi-autonomous subsidiary of the Association for Computing Machinery. Membership: $20/year, $42/year (non-ACM).
Publications:
Computer Architecture News. q.
Proceedings of Annual Symposium on Computer Architecture. a.
Annual Meetings: With the Association for Computing Machinery

Special Interest Group for Automata and Computability Theory
Dept. of Computer Science, Columbia University, New York NY 10027
Chairman: Zvi Galil
Members: 1,600-1,700
Tel: (212) 869-7440
Hist. Note: SIGACT is concerned with theoretical computer science, including analysis of algorithms. A semi-autonomous subsidiary of the Association for Computing Machinery. Membership: $11/year, $33/year (non-ACM).
Publication:
SIGACT News. q.
Annual Meetings: With the Association for Computing Machinery

Special Interest Group for Biomedical Computing
15 Parsons Way, Los Altos CA 94022
Chairman: Karen A. Duncan
Members: 1,100
Annual Budget: $10-25,000 *Tel:* (212) 869-7440
Hist. Note: SIGBIO is a semi-autonomous subsidiary of the Ass'n for Computing Machinery. Membership: $14/yr., $21/yr. (non-ACM).
Publication:
SIGBIO Newsletter. q.
Annual Meetings: With the Association for Computing Machinery

Special Interest Group for Computer Graphics (1968)
11 West 42nd St., New York NY 10036
Chairman: Dr. Kellogg S. Booth
Members: 12,000 *Staff:* 10
Tel: (212) 869-7440
Hist. Note: A forum for the promotion and dissemination of current computer graphics research, technologies and applications. A semi-autonomous subsidiary of the Association for Computing Machinery. Membership: $18/year, $45/year (non-ACM).
Publication:
Computer Graphics. q. adv.
Annual Meetings: August
1987-Anaheim, CA(Convention Center)
1988-Atlanta, GA(Convention Center)
1989-Boston, MA(Hynes Center)
1990-Dallas, TX(Convention Center)

Special Interest Group for Computer Personnel Research (1962)
McIntire School of Commerce, University of Virginia, Charlottesville VA 22903
Chairman: Elias M. Awad
Members: 350-400
Tel: (212) 869-7440
Hist. Note: SIGCPR is concerned with the investigation of the nature of computer personnel and their jobs. A semi-autonomous subsidiary of the Association for Computing Machinery. Membership: $10/year, $12/year (non-ACM).
Publication:
SIGCPR Newsletter. q.
Annual Meetings: With the Ass'n for Computing Machinery

Special Interest Group for Computer Science Education (1970)
Univ. of South West Louisiana, Box 41690, Lafayeete LA 70501
Chairman: Della T. Bonnette
Members: 2,000-2,100
Annual Budget: $25-50,000 *Tel:* (212) 869-7440
Hist. Note: SIGCSE provides a forum for the problems common among college educators involved in computer science programs. A semi-autonomous subsidiary of the Association for Computing Machinery Membership: $11/yr.; $25/yr. (non-ACM).
Publication:
SIGCSE Bulletin. q.
Annual Meetings: With the Ass'n for Computing Machinery

Special Interest Group for Computer Uses in Education
Columbia University Teachers College, New York NY 10027
Chairman: Robert P. Taylor
Members: 1,500
Tel: (212) 869-7440
Hist. Note: SIGCUE is a semi-autonomous subsidiary of the Ass'n for Computing Machinery. Formerly Special Interest Group for Computer-assisted Instruction. Membership: $10/year, $24/year (non-ACM).
Publication:
SIGCUE Bulletin. q.
Annual Meetings: With the Ass'n for Computing Machinery

Special Interest Group for Computers and Human Interaction (1972)
1865 Tanglewood Drive, Glenview IL 60025
Chairman: Lorraine Borman
Members: 2,300
Tel: (212) 869-7440
Hist. Note: SIGCHI is a semi-autonomous subsidiary of the Ass'n for Computing Machinery. Formerly (1982) the Special Interest Group for Social and Behavioral Science Computing. Membership: $15/year, $37/year (non-ACM).
Publication:
SIGCHI Bulletin. q.

Special Interest Group for Computers and Society (1972)
Dept. of Computer Science, The City College (CUNY), New York NY 10031
Chairman: Abbe Mowshowitz
Members: 1,300 *Staff:* 1
Annual Budget: $10-25,000 *Tel:* (212) 690-6632
Hist. Note: SIGCAS was created by the Ass'n for Computing Machinery in 1969 and given permanent status in 1972. Concerned with the impact on society of computer enhancements to informational technology. Membership: $12/yr., $28/yr. (non-ACM).
Publication:
Computers and Society. q.
Annual Meetings: With the Association for Computing Machinery and the AFIPS Nat'l Computer Conference and Exposition.

Special Interest Group for Computers and the Physically Handicapped (1970)
USVA Rehab'n Research & Development Ctr., Box 20, Hines IL 60141
Chairman: Ross W. Lambert, Jr.
Members: 500
Annual Budget: $10-25,000 *Tel:* (212) 869-7440
Hist. Note: SIGCAPH is concerned with the professional interests of computing personnel with physical disabitlities and the application of computing technology to solutions of disability problems. A semi-autonomous subsidiary of the Association for Computing Machinery. Formerly (until 1978) the Special Interest Committee for Computers and the Physically Handicapped. Membership: $10/year, $24/year (non-ACM).
Publication:
SIGCAPH Newsletter. q.
Annual Meetings: With the Association for Computing Machinery

Special Interest Group for Data Communication
INRS Telecommunications, 3 Place du Commerce, Verdun Quebec H3E 1H6
Chairman: Michael J. Ferguson
Members: 4,900-5,000
Tel: (212) 869-7440
Hist. Note: SIGCOMM provides a forum on problems in data communication as applicable to the computer field. A semi-autonomous subsidiary of the Association for Computing Machinery. Membership: $15/year, $32/year (non-ACM)
Publication:
Computer Communications Review. q.
Annual Meetings: With the Association for Computing Machinery

Special Interest Group for Information Retrieval (1966)
Univ. of IL, Electrical Engineering &, Computer Science Dept., Box 4348, Chicago IL 60680
Chairman: Clement Yu
Members: 2,100
Tel: (312) 996-2318
Hist. Note: SIGIR is concerned with the application of machines to the storage, retrieval and dissemination of information. A semi-autonomous subsidiary of the Association for Computing Machinery. Membership: $6/year, $20/year (non-ACM).
Publications:
SIGIR Forum. q.
SIGIR Conference Proceedings. a.
Annual Meetings: With the Ass'n for Computing Machinery
1987-New Orleans, LA
1988-France
1989-Boston, MA

Special Interest Group for Management of Data
Univ. of WI, Computer Science Dept., 1210 West Dayton St., Madison WI 53706
Chairman: David J. DeWitt
Members: 4,200
Tel: (212) 869-7440
Hist. Note: SIGMOD is concerned with the development, management and evaluation of database technology. Formerly (1973) Special Interest Group for File Description and Translation. A semi-autonomous subsidiary of the Association for Computing Machinery. Membership: $15/year, $17/year (non-ACM).
Publication:
SIGMOD Record. q.
Annual Meetings: With the Association for Computing Machinery

Special Interest Group for Measurement and Evaluation (1971)
Ass'n for Computing Machinery, 11 West 42nd St., New York NY 10036
Chairman: Edward D. Lazowska
Members: 1,900
Annual Budget: $25-50,000 *Tel:* (212) 869-7440
Hist. Note: SIGMETRICS provides a forum for those interested in the measurement and evaluation of computer system performance. A semi-autonomous subsidiary of the Ass'n for Computing Machinery (ACM). Membership: $12/yr., $25/yr. (non-ACM).
Publication:
Performance Evaluation Review. q.
Semi-annual meetings: in May and with Ass'n for Computing Machinery.
1987-Banff, Alberta/May/200
1988-Santa Fe, NM/May/200
1989-Berkeley, CA/May/200

Special Interest Group for Microprogramming
c/o Ass'n for Computing Machinery, 11 West 42nd St., New York NY 10036
Chairman: Gearold R. Johnson
Members: 2,300
Tel: (212) 869-7440
Hist. Note: SIGMICRO is a semi-autonomous subsidiary of the Ass'n for Computing Machinery. Membership: $12/year, $34/year (non-ACM).
Publication:
SIGMICRO Newsletter. q.
Annual Meetings: With the Association for Computing Machinery

Special Interest Group for Simulation and Modeling (1968)
VPI, Department of Computer Science, 2990 Telstar Court, FaLls Church VA 22042
Chairman: Paul Roth
Members: 2,000-2,500
Tel: (212) 869-7440
Hist. Note: SIGSIM is a semi-autonomous subsidiary of the Ass'n for Computing Machinery. Members are interested in all aspects of modeling and simulation as performed in digital computers, including discrete, continuous and combined simulations. Membership: $12/yr.; $30/yr. (non-ACM).
Publications:
Proceeding. a.
Simuletter. q.
Annual Meetings: With the Association for Computing Machinery
1987-Washington, DC(Radisson)/Dec.
1988-Atlanta, GA

00284 12 05 86 1233

Special Interest Group for Social and Behavioral Science Computing
Hist. Note: Became the Special Interest Group for Computers and Human Interaction in 1982.

Special Interest Group for Symbolic and Algebraic Manipulation
Southern Methodist University, Dept. of Computer Science & Engineering, Dallas TX 75275
Chairman: David Y. Yun
Members: 700-800
Tel: (212) 869-7440
Hist. Note: SIGSAM is a semi-autonomous subsidiary of the Ass'n for Computing Machinery. Membership: $7.50/year, $15/year (non-ACM).
Publication:
SIGSAM Bulletin. q.
Annual Meetings: With the Association for Computing Machinery

Special Interest Group for University and College Computing Services (1962)
University of Delaware, Academic Computing Srvcs, 15 Smith Hall, Newark DE 19716
Chairperson: Jane S. Caviness
Members: 1,600 *Staff:* 1
Annual Budget: $50-100,000 *Tel:* (302) 451-8447
Hist. Note: SIGUCCS is a semi-autonomous subsidiary of the Ass'n for Computing Machinery. Formerly (1984) the Special Interest Group for University Computing Centers. Membership: $10/yr.; $32/yr. (non-ACM).
Publication:
SIGUCCS Newsletter. q.
Annual Meetings: With the Association for Computing Machinery

Special Interest Group for University Computing Centers (1962)
Hist. Note: Became the Special Interest Group for University and College Computing Services in 1984.

Special Interest Group on Ada Programming Language
c/o Computer Science Corp., 304 West Route 38, Moorestown NJ 08057
Chairman: Anthony Gargaro
Annual Budget: $100-250,000 *Tel:* (609) 234-8510
Hist. Note: SIGAda is a semi-autonomous subsidiary of the Ass'n for Computing Machinery. Membership: $32/yr. (individual); $500/yr. (organization/company)
Publication:
Ada Letters. bi-m.
Annual Meetings: Winter
1987-Boston, MA/Dec./1,000

Special Interest Group on APL Programming Language
VM Systems Group, 901 S. Highland St., Arlington VA 22204
Chairman: John W. Myrna
Tel: (212) 869-7440
Hist. Note: SIGAPL is a semi-autonomous subsidiary of the Ass'n for Computing Machinery. Membership: $15/year, $40/year (non-ACM).
Publication:
APL Quote Quad. q.

Special Interest Group on Artificial Intelligence
USC Information Science Institute, 4676 Admiralty Way, Marina del Rey CA 90292
Chairman: Bill Swartout
Members: 11,000
Annual Budget: $100-250,000 *Tel:* (213) 822-1511
Hist. Note: A scientific organization established in the mid-1960s, of individuals interested in the application of computers to tasks normally requiring intelligence and the enhancement of the computer's capacity in this field. SIGART is a semi-autonomous subsidiary of the Ass'n for Computing Machinery. Membership: $10/yr., $25/yr. (non-ACM).
Publication:
SIGART Newsletter. q.
Annual Meetings: With the Association for Computing Machinery or the American Association for Artificial Intelligence.

Special Interest Group on Business Data Processing and Management (1960)
General Mills Inc., 2EW, 9200 Wayzata Blvd., Minneapolis MN 55440
Chairman: Roger A. Rydberg
Members: 6,000
Annual Budget: $100-250,000 *Tel:* (212) 869-7440
Hist. Note: SIGBDP is a subsidiary of the Ass'n for Computing Machinery. Absorbed the Special Interest Group for Computer Systems Installation Management in 1980. Members are primarily interested in the use of computers in the business environment; emphasis is placed on pragmatic business information systems which utilize advanced technolgoy where beneficial. Membership: $10/yr. (ACM member); $25/yr. (non-ACM member)
Publication:
Database. q.
Annual Meetings: With the National Computer Conference, and ACM Conference.
1987-Coral Gables, FL(Coconut Grove)/March 5-6/300

Special Interest Group on Design Automation (1968)
c/o Ass'n for Computing Machinery, 11 W. 42nd St., New York NY 10036
Chairman: Charles A. Shaw
Members: 2,000
Annual Budget: $100-250,000 *Tel:* (212) 869-7440
Hist. Note: SIGDA is a semi-autonomous subsidiary of the Ass'n for Computing Machinery whose members are interested in theoretic, analytic and heuristic methods for performing and assisting design tasks and optimizing designs through the use of computer techniques, algorithms and programs. Awards travel grants and scholarships; provides University library support; and co-sponsors, with IEEE/CS's Design Automation Technical Council, the Design Automation Conference. All correspondence regarding the Conference should be sent to: MPA Assoc., 7366 Old Mill Tr., Boulder, CO 80301.
Publication:
SIGDA Newsletter. q.
Annual Meetings: Co-Sponsor of Design Automation Conference
1987-Miami Beach, FL(Convention Ctr.)/June 28-July 1/4,000
1988-Anaheim, CA(Convention Ctr.)/June 12-15/4,000
1989-Las Vegas, NV(Convention Ctr.)/June 25-28
1990-Orlando, FL(Convention Ctr.)/June 24-27

Special Interest Group on Documentation (1975)
Sysdoc International, 41 Britain St., Suite 300, Toronto Ontario M5A 1R7
Chairman: Diana Patterson
Members: 2,000
Tel: (212) 869-7440
Hist. Note: SIGDOC is a semi-autonomous subsidiary of the Ass'n for Computing Machinery. Membership: $12/year, $34/year (non-ACM).
Publication:
Asterisk. q.

Special Interest Group on Numerical Mathematics (1966)
University of Maryland, Computer Science Department, College Park MD 20742
Chairman: G.W. Stewart
Members: 1,300
Tel: (212) 869-7440
Hist. Note: SIGNUM is concerned with computational Mathematics. A semi-autonomous subsidiary of the Association for Computing Machinery. Membership: $11/year, $19/year (non-ACM).
Publication:
SIGNUM Newsletter. q.
Annual Meetings: With Ass'n for Computing Machinery

Special Interest Group on Office Automation
Hist. Note: Became Special Interest Group on Office Information Systems in 1986.

Special Interest Group on Office Information Systems (1980)
Computer Science Dept., 324 Alumni Hall,University of Pittsburgh, Pittsburgh PA 15260
Chairman: Siegfried Treu
Members: 3,000
Tel: (412) 624-6456
Hist. Note: Formerly (1986) Special Interest Group on Office Automation. SIGOIS is a semi-autonomous subsidiary of the Ass'n for Computing Machinery. Membership: $10/yr.; $25/yr. (non-ACM)
Publication:
SIGOIS Bulletin. q.

Special Interest Group on Operating Systems
Computer Science Div., Dept. EECS, University of California, Berkeley CA 94720
Chairman: Alan J. Smith
Members: 8,000
Annual Budget: $50-100,000 *Tel:* (212) 869-7440
Hist. Note: SIGOPS is a semi-autonomous subsidiary of the Ass'n for Computing Machinery. Membership: $8/yr., $30/yr. (non-ACM)
Publication:
Operating Systems Review. q.
Semi-annual Meetings: one with ACM, one symposium on operating prin.

Special Interest Group on Personal Computing
Hist. Note: Merged with the Special Interest Group on Small Computing Systems, a semi-autonomous subsidiary of the Association for Computing Machinery, in 1983.

Special Interest Group on Programming Languages (1966)
Sun Microsystems, Inc., 2550 Garcia Ave., Mountain View CA 94043
Chairman: Steven S. Muchnick
Members: 10,500
Annual Budget: $250-500,000 *Tel:* (212) 869-7440
Hist. Note: SIGPLAN is concerned with all aspects of programming languages and programming language processors. A semi-autonomous subsidiary of the Ass'n for Computing Machinery. Membership: $22/year, $36/year (non-ACM).
Publications:
SIGPLAN Notices. m. adv.
Fortran Forum. q.
Annual Meetings: June
1987-Minneapolis, MN(Radisson)

Special Interest Group on Security, Audit, and Control (1981)
IBM (E22/921-2) Box 390, Poughkeepsie NY 12602
Chairman: Stanley A. Kurzban
Members: 1,200
Annual Budget: $10-25,000 *Tel:* (914) 296-6344
Hist. Note: SIGSAC is a semi-autonomous subsidiary of the Ass'n for Computing Machinery. Membership: $12/year, $26/year (non-ACM).
Publication:
SIGSAC Review. q.
Annual Meetings: not held

Special Interest Group on Small and Personal Computing Systems and Applications (1975)
Prime Computer, Inc., 500 Old Connecticut Path, Framingham MA 01701
Chairman: Anne-Marie Claybrook
Members: 4,000
Tel: (212) 869-7440
Hist. Note: SIGSMALL/PC are primarily concerned with microprocessors and microcomputers. Formerly (1984) the Special Interest Group on Small Computing Systems and Applications. A semi-autonomous subsidiary of the Ass'n for Computing Machinery. Membership: $8/year, $24/year (non-ACM).
Publication:
SIGSMALL/PC Notes. q.

Special Interest Group on Software Engineering
COINS, University of Massachusetts, Amherst MA 01003
Chairman: W. Richards Adrion
Tel: (413) 545-2742
Hist. Note: SIGSOFT is a semi-autonomous subsidiary of the Ass'n for Computing Machinery. Membership: $10/year, $20/year (non-ACM).
Publication:
Software Engineering Notes. q.

Special Libraries Ass'n (1909)
1700 18th St., N.W., Washington DC 20009
Exec. Director: David R. Bender
Members: 11,500-12,000 *Staff:* 26-30
Annual Budget: $1-2,000,000 *Tel:* (202) 234-4700
Hist. Note: A member of the Council of Nat'l Library and Information Ass'ns, the Internat'l Federation of Library Ass'ns and the American Nat'l Standards Institute. Incorporated in Rhode Island in 1928 and later in New York in 1959. Members are professional librarians and information managers, serving industry, business, research and educational and technical institutions. Membership: $75/yr.
Publications:
Special Librairies. q. adv.
SpeciaList. m.
Annual Meetings: June/6,000
1987-Anaheim, CA(Convention Ctr.)June 6-11
1988-Denver, CO(Currigan Exhibition Ctr.)/June 11-16
1989-New York, NY/June 10-15
1990-Cleveland, OH/June 9-14
1991-San Antonio, TX/June 8-13
1992-San Francisco, CA/June 6-11
1993-Cincinnati, OH/June 5-10

Specialized Carriers and Rigging Ass'n (1948)
2200 Mill Road, Suite 616, Alexandria VA 22314
Exec. V. President: N. Eugene Brymer, CAE
Members: 600 companies *Staff:* 6-10
Annual Budget: $500-1,000,000 *Tel:* (703) 838-1980
Hist. Note: Established as the Heavy Specialized Carriers Section-Local Cartage National Conference, it became the Heavy Specialized Carriers Conference in 1959 and assumed its present name in 1981. Affiliated with American Trucking Associations, members are carriers, crane, rigging operators and millwrights engaged in the transport of heavy goods. The Crane and Rigging Ass'n is a subsidiary.
Publication:
Transportation Engineer. 6/yr. adv.
Annual Meetings: Spring
1987-Palm Springs, CA(Desert Princess)April 24-29/550

Specialty Advertising Ass'n, Internat'l (1964)
1404 Walnut Hill Lane, Irving TX 75038
President: H. Ted Olson
Members: 3,600 *Staff:* 30
Annual Budget: $2-5,000,000 *Tel:* (214) 580-0404
Hist. Note: Formerly Specialty Advertising Nat'l Ass'n (1903) and Specialty Membership: $214/yr. minimum.
Publications:
Specialty Advertising Business. m. adv.
Ideasworth. q.
Tri-Annual Meetings: Winter in Dallas, Spring and Summer/5-6,000
1987-Convention Center/Winter/10,000
1987-Los Angeles, CA/Spring
1987-Washington, DC/Summer
1988-Chicago, IL/Summer
1989-Cincinnati, OH/Summer
1989-Atlanta, GA/Spring

00285 12 05 86 1233

Specialty Automotive Manufacturers Ass'n (1978)
4667 MacArthur Blvd., Suite 314, Newport Beach CA 92660
Exec. Director: Dick Wells
Members: 40-50 companies *Staff:* 1
Annual Budget: $50-100,000 *Tel:* (714) 756-9053
Hist. Note: Members are makers and distributors of kits and materials to transform early chassis into classic and exotic cars.
Annual Meetings:
1987-Columbus, OH(Fairgrounds)/June

Specialty Coffee Ass'n of America (1982)
Box 200, 496 LaGuardia Place, New York NY 10012
Correspondent: Donald N. Schoenholt
Members: 150 companies *Staff:* 1
Annual Budget: $10-25,000
Hist. Note: Membership: $150/yr.
Publication:
In Good Taste. m.
Semi-annual Meetings: Summer and Winter

Specialty Equipment Market Ass'n (1963)
11540 East Slauson Ave., Whittier CA 90606
President: Charles R. Blum
Members: 1,800 companies *Staff:* 18-20
Annual Budget: $2-5,000,000 *Tel:* (213) 692-9402
Hist. Note: Formerly (1966) Speed Equipment Manufacturers Ass'n, and (1979) Specialty Equipment Manufacturers Ass'n. Composed of companies supplying performance motor vehicle parts and accessories.
Publication:
SEMA News. m.
Annual Meetings: Fall in Las Vegas, NV(Convention Ctr.)/ 16,000

Specialty Steel Industry of the United States (1962)
1055 Thomas Jefferson St., N.W., Suite 308, Washington DC 20007
Secretary: David Hartquist
Members: 15-20 companies *Staff:* 1
Annual Budget: $250-500,000 *Tel:* (202) 342-8400
Hist. Note: Has no headquarters other than the above, the law firm of Collier, Shannon, Rill and Scott. Known as the Tool and Stainless Steel Industry Committee, 1962-1983.

Specialty Tool and Fastener Distributors Ass'n (1976)
P.O. Box 44, Elm Grove WI 53122
Exec. Director: Morrie E. Halvorsen
Members: 1,250 companies *Staff:* 3
Annual Budget: $500-1,000,000 *Tel:* (414) 784-4774
Hist. Note: Members specialize in the sale of power tools, power-actuated tools, anchors, diamond drilling equipment, fastening systems and related construction supplies.
Publication:
Trade News. m.
Annual Meetings: November

Specialty Vehicle Institute of America (1983)
3151 Airway Ave., Bldg. K107, Costa Mesa CA 92626
Managing Director: Debby Pickett
Members: 4 companies *Staff:* 20
Tel: (714) 241-9256
Hist. Note: A national, non-profit trade association representing manufacturers and distributors of all-terrain vehicles, SVIA's purpose is to foster and promote the safe and responsible use of specialty vehicles manufactured and/or distributed in the U.S.
Publications:
Tips for the ATV Rider.
Parents, Youngsters and ATVs.
ATV Off Road Practice Guide.

Speech and Signal Processing Acoustics Soc.
Hist. Note: A subsidiary of the Institute of Electrical and Electronics Engineers. Membership in the Society, open only to IEEE members, includes subscription to a technical periodical in the field published by IEEE. All administrative support is provided by IEEE.

Speech Communication Ass'n (1914)
5105 Backlick Rd., Annandale VA 22003
Exec. Secretary: Dr. William Work, CAE
Members: 5,000-5,500 *Staff:* 10-15
Annual Budget: $500-1,000,000 *Tel:* (703) 750-0533
Hist. Note: Founded in 1914 as the Nat'l Ass'n of Academic Teachers of Public Speaking. Became the Nat'l Ass'n of Teachers of Speech in 1923, the Speech Ass'n of America in 1946 and the Speech Communication Ass'n in 1970. Incorporated in Missouri in 1950. A constituent of the American Council on Education. Members are teachers at all levels, media and communication consultants, students, libraries and persons in theatre production. Member of the Council of Communication Societies. Membership: $40/yr.
Publications:
Communication Education. q. adv.
Communication Monographs. q.
Critical Studies in Mass Communication. q.
Quarterly Journal of Speech. q.
Annual Meetings: November
1987-Boston, MA(Sheraton)/Nov. 5-8/2,500

Speed Coaches Ass'n (1979)
P.O. Box 81846, Lincoln NE 68501
Staff Liaison: Nance Kirk
Members: 400 *Staff:* 1
Annual Budget: under $10,000 *Tel:* (402) 489-8811
Hist. Note: A division of the Roller Skating Rink Operators Association which provides administrative support. Members are professional roller speed skating coaches, trainers and managers. Membership: $40/yr.
Publications:
Directory. a.
Newsletter. m.
Annual Meetings: With the National Roller Skating Championships

SPIE-Internat'l Soc. for Optical Engineering (1956)
Box 10, 1022 19th St., Bellingham WA 98227
Exec. Director: Joseph Yaver
Members: 7,119 *Staff:* 65-70
Annual Budget: $2-5,000,000 *Tel:* (206) 676-3290
Hist. Note: Scientists, engineers and companies interested in applications of optical, electro-optical, fiber-optic, laser, and photographic instrumentation systems and technology. Founded and incorporated in 1956 in California as the Soc. of Photographic Instrumentation Engineers, it later became the Soc. of Photo-Optical Instrumentation Engineers and assumed its present name in 1983. Membership: $60/yr.(individual); Institutional dues based on annual sales volume.
Publications:
Optical Engineering. m. adv.
Optical Engineering Reports. m. adv.
Tri-Annual Meetings: January in Los Angeles, CA; Spring on the East
Coast; August in San Diego, CA; Fall on East Coast.

Spill Control Ass'n of America (1973)
17117 West Nine Mile Road, Suite 1040, Southfield MI 48075
Exec. Director and Gen. Counsel: Marc K. Shaye
Members: 100-125 *Staff:* 2-5
Annual Budget: $100-250,000 *Tel:* (313) 552-0500
Hist. Note: Established as the Oil Spill Control Ass'n of America, it assumed its present name in 1978. Members are companies and individuals concerned with cleaning up spills of hazardous products and manufacturers of specialized products for spill control/clean-up and personnel protection. The above address is that of the law firm of Bornstein, Wishnow, Shaye and Schneiderman.
Publication:
News Brief. q.

Spinal Stress Research Soc. (1976)
Hist. Note: Also known as Precision Chiropractors Research Society.

Sponge and Chamois Institute (1933)
60 East 42nd St., New York NY 10165
Exec. Secretary: Jules Schwimmer
Members: 15-20 companies *Staff:* 2-5
Annual Budget: $10-25,000 *Tel:* (212) 867-2290
Hist. Note: Members are dealers and suppliers of natural sponges and chamois leather.
Annual Meetings: November

Sporting Arms and Ammunition Manufacturers' Institute (1926)
Box 1075, Riverside CT 06878
Exec. Director: Robert Pelfay
Members: 15 companies *Staff:* 2-5
Annual Budget: $100-250,000 *Tel:* (203) 637-3618
Hist. Note: The trade association of most of the leading U.S. producers of sporting firearms, ammunition and smokeless propellants, active primarily in technical matters relating to voluntary industry standards and product safety. SAAMI became an autonomous subsidiary of the Nat'l Shooting Sports Foundation in 1985, with NSSF providing administrative functions.

Sporting Goods Agents Ass'n (1934)
Box 998, Morton Grove IL 60053
Exec. Director: Lois Halinton
Members: 1,000 *Staff:* 2-5
Annual Budget: $50-100,000 *Tel:* (312) 296-3670
Hist. Note: Members consist of independent manufacturers' agents in the Sporting Goods Industry. Formerly (1977) Sporting Goods Representatives Ass'n. Membership: $150/yr.
Publication:
Membership Roster.
Annual Meetings: Always the day before the Nat'l Sporting Goods Ass'n Chicago Show
1987-Chicago, IL/Oct.

Sporting Goods Manufacturers Ass'n (1906)
200 Castlewood Drive, North Palm Beach FL 33408
President: Howard J. Bruns
Members: 180 regular, 700 associate companies *Staff:* 11-15
Annual Budget: $1-2,000,000 *Tel:* (305) 842-4100
Hist. Note: Established as the Athletic Goods Manufacturers Association, it assumed its present name in 1972. Supports the American Sports Education Institute, the Athletic Institute, the National Golf Foundation and the Tennis Foundation of North America-all headquartered at the same address. Maintains a Washington office.
Publications:
Internat'l Marketing Newsletter. q.
Census Report. a.
Annual Meetings: Spring
1987-Palm Beach Gardens, FL(PGA Sheraton Resort)/May 10-13
1988-Phoenix, AZ(Pointe at South Mountain)/May 8-11

Sports Turf Managers Ass'n (1981)
Hist. Note: Ceased operations in 1985.

Sportswear Apparel Ass'n (1933)
450 Seventh Ave., New York NY 10123
Exec. Director: Sidney Reiff
Members: 150 companies *Staff:* 6
Annual Budget: $100-250,000 *Tel:* (212) 564-6161
Hist. Note: Established as Infants and Children's Novelties Ass'n. Known as Infants, Children's and Sportswear Ass'n before assuming its present name.
Annual Meetings: Always in New York, NY

Sportswear Salesmen's Ass'n (1942)
147 West 33rd St., New York NY 10001
Exec. Secretary: Benjamin Honig
Members: 400-425 *Staff:* 1
Tel: (212) 594-0094

Spring Manufacturers Institute (1933)
380 West Palatine Road, Wheeling IL 60090
Exec. V. President: Charles G. Whitchurch
Members: 325-350 companies *Staff:* 2-5
Annual Budget: $250-500,000 *Tel:* (312) 520-3290
Hist. Note: Founded as the Spring Manufacturers Ass'n, it assumed its present name in 1961.
Publication:
Springs Magazine. semi-a. adv.
Semi-annual Meetings: Spring and Fall/350
1987-Palm Beach Gardens, FL(PGA Sheraton)/April 5-7
1987-Hawaii(Mauna Lani Bay)/Nov. 8-10
1988-San Francisco, CA(Fairmont)/March 27-29
1988-Hilton Head, SC(Inter-continental)/Sept. 25-27
1989-Laguna Niguel, CA(Ritz-Carlton)/May 14-16
1989-Hot Springs, VA(Homestead)/Sept. 17-19

Spring Service Ass'n (1981)
4015 Marks Road, Suite 2B, Medina OH 44256
Exec. V. President: Cara R. Giebner
Members: 140 companies *Staff:* 1
Annual Budget: $100-250,000 *Tel:* (216) 725-7160
Hist. Note: Members are persons, firms, or corporations who have operated a full line spring service shop for at least two years with sufficient inventory to service market area, have rebuilding department capable of making all necessary spring repairs, and have the following shop equipment: hydraulic press or heat treating furnace, U-bolt bender capable of bending up to one inch rod cold, punch and shear capable of cutting spring steel to certain specs, and two mechanics providing drive-in service. Membership: $500/yr.
Publication:
"The Leaf" newsletter. bi-m.
Annual Meetings: October
1987-Montreal,Quebec(Le Centre Sheraton)/Oct. 8-11
1988-Phoenix, AZ (The Pointe at Tapatio)/Oct. 13-15
1989-St. Louis, MO(Omni)/Oct. 26-29

SPSE: Soc. for Imaging Science and Technology (1947)
7003 Kilworth Lane, Springfield VA 22151
Exec. Director: Calva Lotridge
Members: 3,500-3,600 *Staff:* 7
Annual Budget: $250-500,000 *Tel:* (703) 642-9090
Hist. Note: Originated in 1947 as the Soc. of Photographic Engineers. In 1957 merged with the Technical Division of the Photographic Soc. of America to form the Soc. of Photographic Scientists and Engineers. Known as the Soc. of Photographic Scientists and Engineers until 1986 (hence the acronym, SPSE). Incorporated in the District of Columbia in 1966. Membership: $60/yr. (individual); $350/yr. (organization)
Publications:
Journal of Imaging Technology. bi-m. adv.
Journal of Imaging Science.
Semi-Annual Meetings: Spring and Fall

Stained Glass Ass'n of America (1903)
1125 Wilmington Ave., St. Louis MO 63111
Exec. Secretary: Naomi M. Mundy
Members: 700-750 *Staff:* 2
Annual Budget: $250-500,000 *Tel:* (314) 353-5128
Hist. Note: Membership is composed of stained glass studios, artists, designers, craft suppliers and others actively engaged in the craft of stained glass.
Publication:
Stained Glass. q. adv.
Annual Meetings: June
1987-Corning, NY
1988-Indianapolis, IN

Standards Engineering Soc. (1947)
6700 Penn Ave. South, Minneapolis MN 55423
Exec. Director: Ray Monahan
Members: 900-1,000 *Staff:* 1
Annual Budget: $25-50,000
Publications:
Proceedings. a.
SES Directory. a. adv.
Standards Engineering. m. adv.
Annual Meetings:
1987-Boston, MA

00286 12 05 86 1233

1988-Open
1989-Open
1990-Minnesota

State and Territorial Air Pollution Program Administrators (1968)
444 North Capitol St., N.W., Suite 306, Washington DC 20001
Exec. Director: S. William Becker
Members: 50-55 individuals *Staff:* 3
Annual Budget: $100-250,000 *Tel:* (202) 624-7864
Hist. Note: Members are representatives from each state and territory. Shares headquarters and staff with the Association of Local Air Pollution Control Officials. The association's semi-annual meetings are open to members only; the annual Air Toxics Conference, held in the Fall in Washington, DC, is open to the public.
Publication:
Washington Update. m. (for members only)
Annual Meetings: Semi-annual Membership Meetings & Annual Air Toxics Conference

State Environmental Education Coordinators Ass'n (1977)
Dept. of Education, Grimes Office Bldg., Des Moines IA 50319
Treasurer: Duane Toomsen
Members: 30
Tel: (515) 281-3146
Hist. Note: A small organization with nominal dues. Has no paid staff or permanent address. Members are individuals representing about 30 state Departments of Education.

State Governmental Affairs Council (1975)
1001 Connecticut Ave., N.W., Suite 800, Washington DC 20036
Exec. Director: Martha M. McNelis, CAE
Members: 106 companies *Staff:* 2-4
Annual Budget: $250-500,000 *Tel:* (202) 659-7605
Hist. Note: Formed in October 1975 as an outgrowth of the National Society of State Legislators. Members are representatives of major U.S. companies and associations engaged in interstate commerce. Works with the Nat'l Conference of State Legislatures, the Council of State Governments, and various other regional associations to improve state government and enhance cooperation between the business community and state government. Membership: $2,500/yr.
Publication:
SGAC News. 8/yr.
Annual Meetings: In conjunction with Nat'l Conference of State Legislatures
1987-Indianapolis, IN/July 26-31
1988-Reno, NV/July 25-29
1989-Oklahoma City, OK
1990-Orlando, FL
1991-Nashville, TN
1992-Cincinnati, OH

State Higher Education Executive Officers (1954)
1860 Lincoln St., Suite 310, Denver CO 80295
Exec. Director: James R. Mingle
Members: 50 states *Staff:* 12
Annual Budget: $250-500,000 *Tel:* (303) 830-3686
Hist. Note: Established in Colorado, SHEEO members are the full-time chief executive officers serving statewide coordinating boards and governing boards of postsecondary education. Membership: $1,000-3,250/yr.
Publications:
SHEEO Newsletter. q.
Directory of Professional Personnel. a.
Annual Meetings: Summer
1987-Vail, CO/July 12-15

State Medicaid Directors Ass'n
1125 15th St., N.W., Suite 300, Washington DC 20005
Coordinator: Richard Jensen
Members: 54 *Staff:* 1
Annual Budget: under $10,000 *Tel:* (202) 293-7550
Hist. Note: Members are directors of state and territorial medical assistance programs. An affiliate of the American Public Welfare Ass'n.
Semi-annual Meetings: May and December

Station Representatives Ass'n (1948)
230 Park Ave., New York NY 10169
Mng. Director: Jerome Feniger
Members: 25 organizations *Staff:* 2-5
Annual Budget: $250-500,000 *Tel:* (212) 687-2484
Hist. Note: Founded (1948) as the Nat'l Ass'n of Radio Station Representatives, Inc. Became Station Representatives Ass'n Inc., in 1952. Broadcast sales organizations, not affiliated with a nat'l network, who sell non-network broadcast advertising.
Publication:
The Must Carry Rules.
Annual Meetings: New York City, in July

Stationery and Office Equipment Board of Trade (1875)
P.O. Box 977, Great Neck NY 11022
Exec. V. President: Dominic A. Fitzpatrick
Members: 280 companies *Staff:* 6-10
Annual Budget: $250-500,000 *Tel:* (516) 466-6150
Hist. Note: Credit and financial reporting bureau servicing the stationery, office equipment and school supply industry. Organized 1875, incorporated 1879. Formerly The Stationers & Publishers Board of Trade.

Statistical Paper Group (1949)
24th Floor, 30 Rockefeller Plaza, New York NY 10112
Counsel: Michael B. Weir
Members: 25-30 companies *Staff:* 1
Annual Budget: $100-250,000 *Tel:* (212) 541-5800
Hist. Note: Has no headquarters other than the above, the law firm of Chadbourne, Parke, Whiteside and Wolfe.

Steel Bar Mills Ass'n (1911)
1221 Locust St., #405, St. Louis MO 63103
Exec. V. President: Oliver A. Dulle, Jr.
Members: 30 companies *Staff:* 2-5
Annual Budget: $50-100,000 *Tel:* (314) 231-2011
Hist. Note: Small electric furnace steel makers and steel rollers. Formerly (1966) Rail Steel Bar Ass'n.
Annual Meetings: Spring/30
1987-Palm Springs, CA(Marquis)

Steel Carriers Conference-ATA (1965)
Hist. Note: Affiliate of American Trucking Ass'ns, Inc. Absorbed by the Specialized Carriers and Rigging Ass'n in 1983.

Steel Carriers Tariff Ass'n (1957)
Box 724, Riverdale MD 20737
Managing Director: Daniel W. Wendel
Members: 50 companies *Staff:* 1
Annual Budget: $50-100,000 *Tel:* (301) 779-7822

Steel Deck Institute (1936)
P.O. Box 9506, Canton OH 44711
Mng. Director: Bernard E. Cromi
Members: 11 companies *Staff:* 2-5
Annual Budget: $50-100,000 *Tel:* (216) 493-7886
Hist. Note: Established as the Metal Roof Deck Technical Institute, it assumed its present name in 1939. A non-profit association of National Steel Deck Producers and associate Members furnishing products allied to steel deck use in construction. SDI is a regulatory agency disseminating design standards to the industry.
Publications:
SDI Design Manual. a. adv.
Diaphragm Design Manual. a. adv.
Comprehensive Steel Deck Institute Binder. a. adv.
Annual Meetings: May
1987-Naples, FL(La Playa)/May 4-5/40

Steel Door Institute (1954)
712 Lakewood Center North, 14600 Detroit Ave., Cleveland OH 44107
Managing Director: Allen P. Wherry
Members: 11 companies *Staff:* 2-5
Annual Budget: $50-100,000 *Tel:* (216) 226-7700
Hist. Note: Producers of all-metal frames and doors for commercial, industrial and residential construction.

Steel Founders' Soc. of America (1902)
Cast Metals Federation Bldg., 455 State St., Des Plaines IL 60016
Exec. V. President: Jack D. McNaughton, CAE
Members: 95 foundries *Staff:* 6-10
Annual Budget: $500-1,000,000 *Tel:* (312) 299-9160
Hist. Note: A technically oriented trade ass'n serving the steel casting industry. Absorbed the Alloy Casting Institute in 1970.
Annual Meetings: Fall
1987-Hershey, PA(Hotel Hershey)/Sept. 13-15/275
1988-Tucson, AZ(Sheraton El Conquistador)/Sept. 18-20

Steel Joist Institute (1928)
1205 48th Ave. North, Suite A, Myrtle Beach SC 29577
Mng. Director: E.T.E. Sprague
Members: 15-20 companies *Staff:* 2-5
Annual Budget: $250-500,000 *Tel:* (803) 449-0487
Hist. Note: Composed of active manufacturers, the SJI cooperates with government and business agencies to establish steel joist standards.
Publications:
Catalogue of Specifications and Lead Tables.
Technical Digests.
Annual Meetings: May
1987-Charleston, SC(Kiawah Island)/May 16-20

Steel Plate Fabricators Ass'n (1933)
1250 Executive Place, Suite 401, Geneva IL 60134
Exec. Director: Earl A. Bratton, CAE
Members: 100-125 *Staff:* 2-5
Annual Budget: $100-250,000 *Tel:* (312) 232-8750
Annual Meetings: Early Spring/200
1987-Litchfield Park, AZ(Wigwam)/May 3-6
1988-West Palm Beach, FL(Sheraton)/March 19-23
1989-Tucson, AZ(Westin La Paloma)/Feb. 25-March 1
1990-Naples, FL(Ritz Carlton)/March 3-7

Steel Service Center Institute (1907)
1600 Terminal Tower, Cleveland OH 44113
President: Andrew G. Sharkey, III
Members: 350-400 *Staff:* 11-15
Annual Budget: $2-5,000,000 *Tel:* (216) 694-3630
Hist. Note: Formerly (1926) American Iron and Steel and Heavy Hardware Ass'n; (1932) American Steel and Heavy Hardware Ass'n; (1959) American Steel Warehouse Ass'n, Inc.
Publications:
Center Lines. m.
Prologue. a.
Annual Meetings: May/1,000
1987-Nashville, TN(Opryland)/May 17-20
1988-Toronto, Ontario(Harbour Castle Hilton)/May 15-18
1989-Undecided
1990-Washington, DC(Hilton)/May 13-16
1991-San Francisco, CA(Fairmont)/May 5-8

Steel Shipping Container Institute (1944)
2204 Morris Ave., Union NJ 07083
President: Arthur J. Schultz, Jr.
Members: 55 companies *Staff:* 5
Annual Budget: $250-500,000 *Tel:* (201) 688-8750
Hist. Note: Makers of drums, barrels and pails.
Publication:
SSCI Reporter. semi-a.

Steel Structures Painting Council (1950)
4400 Fifth Ave., Pittsburgh PA 15213-2683
Director: Bernard R. Appleman
Members: 1,500 individuals; 225 organizations *Staff:* 6-10
Annual Budget: $25-50,000 *Tel:* (412) 268-3327
Hist. Note: Conducts research, develops standards, and disseminates information about surface preparation, application techniques, coatings, and related technology for protecting structural steel. Members include paint manufacturers, raw material suppliers, specifiers, applicators, government agencies, and a wide variety of end-users. Membership: $40/yr.(individual); $300-1,000/yr.(organization).
Publications:
Journal of Protective Coatings and Linings. m. adv.
Publications List. irreg.
Annual Meetings:
1987-New Orleans, LA(Fairmont Hotel)/Jan. 19-22/800-1,000
1987-Orlando, FL(Sheraton World)/Nov. 4-7/800-1,000

Steel Tank Institute (1916)
P.O. Box 4020, Northbrook IL 60065
Exec. V. President: Brian Donovan
Members: 85 companies *Staff:* 10-15
Annual Budget: $2-5,000,000 *Tel:* (312) 498-1980
Hist. Note: Conducts research, develops new technologies and standards for the industry; and represents interests of its members to Congress and the Executive branch. Membership: $2,500/yr.
Publications:
Tank Talk. bi-m.
Membership Roster. a.
Annual Report.
Semi-annual Meetings: Feb. and August/125
1987-Orlando, FL(Disneyworld)/Feb. and Colorado Springs, CO/Aug.
1988-Hawaii/Feb. and Williamsburg, VA(Williamsburg Inn)/Aug.

Steel Window Institute (1920)
1230 Keith Bldg., Cleveland OH 44115-2180
Exec. Director: John H. Addington
Members: 6-10 companies *Staff:* 2-5
Annual Budget: $10-25,000 *Tel:* (216) 241-7333
Hist. Note: Formerly the Metal Window Institute.
Publication:
Recommended standards for Steel windows. a.

Sterling Silversmiths Guild of America (1917)
312A Wyndhurst Ave., Baltimore MD 21210
Exec. V. President: Robert M. Johnston
Members: 6 Companies *Staff:* 2-5
Annual Budget: $500-1,000,000 *Tel:* (301) 532-7062
Hist. Note: Members are silver manufacturing companies.

Stock Transfer Ass'n (1911)
The Bank of New York, 90 Washington St., New York NY 10015
President: William J. Skinner
Members: 450-500 companies *Staff:* 2-5
Annual Budget: $100-250,000 *Tel:* (212) 530-8071
Hist. Note: An association of representatives from banks and corporations in the U.S. and Canada who are involved in the issuance, transfer and registration of corporate securities or related duties. Membership: $400/yr.
Publications:
Commerce Clearing House. m.
STA Rule Booklet.
Annual Meetings: Fall/500

Stove, Furnace and Allied Appliance Workers' Internat'l Union of North America (1882)
2929 South Jefferson Ave., St. Louis MO 63118
Internat'l Secy.-Treas.: Gary Louis Meyer
Members: 6,500 *Staff:* 2-5
Annual Budget: $500-1,000,000 *Tel:* (314) 664-3736
Hist. Note: Originated in Quincy, Illinois on April 24, 1882 and chartered by the American Federation of Labor on January 6, 1894 as the Stove Mounters International Union. Assumed its present name in 1962. Membership: $120/yr.
Publication:
S.F.& A.A.W. Journal. semi-a.
Annual Meetings: Every 3 years
1989-Chicago, IL

Street Rod Equipment Ass'n (1982)
Box 4967, Whittier CA 90607
Exec. Director: Richard Van Cleve
Members: 250 companies *Staff:* 2-5

00287 12 05 86 1233

Annual Budget: $25-50,000 *Tel:* (213) 692-9402
Hist. Note: Manufacturers, builders, distributors and jobbers making or servicing equipment for installation in cars made in the United States before 1948 which have been modified through installation of modern components.
Publication:
SREA Newsletter. m.
Annual Meetings: Summer

Structural Cement-Fiber Products Ass'n (1960)
Hist. Note: Inactive in 1984.

Structural Stability Research Council (1944)
Fritz Engineering Lab. #13, Lehigh Univ., Bethlehem PA 18015
Director: Dr. Lynn S. Beedle
Members: 200-225 individuals, 23 organizations, 70 companie
Staff: 2-5
Annual Budget: $50-100,000 *Tel:* (215) 758-3522
Hist. Note: An outgrowth of the American Society of Civil Engineers Committee on Design of Structural Members, The Column Research Council was established by the Engineering Foundation in 1944. In 1976, broadened scope of its interests led to the adoption of the present name. Members are individuals, organizations or firms concerned with the investigation and design of metal and composite structures. Membership: $45/3yrs. (individual), $125-1,000/yr. (organization).
Publication:
Proceedings, Annual Technical Session. a.
Annual Meetings: Spring
1987-Houston, TX(Adams Mark)/March 23-25/200
1988-Minneapolis, MN(Radisson University Hotel)/April 25-27/125
1989-New York, NY

Stucco Manufacturers Ass'n (1957)
14006 Ventura Blvd., Suite 207, Sherman Oaks CA 91423
Exec. Secretary: Robert F. Welch
Members: 20-25 companies *Staff:* 1
Annual Budget: under $10,000 *Tel:* (213) 789-8733

Student American Pharmaceutical Ass'n (1969)
2215 Constitution Ave., N.W., Washington DC 20037
Exec. Secretary: Anna T. Charuk
Members: 12,000 *Staff:* 2-5
Annual Budget: $50-100,000 *Tel:* (202) 628-4410
Hist. Note: A subdivision of the American Pharmaceutical Ass'n.
Publication:
The Pharmacy Student. m.
Annual Meetings: Early Spring
1987-Chicago, IL/March 28-April 1

Studio Suppliers Ass'n
Hist. Note: Defunct in 1986.

Stuffed Toy Manufacturers Ass'n (1934)
Hist. Note: Merged with the Nat'l Ass'n of Doll Manufacturers in 1983 to form the Nat'l Ass'n of Doll and Stuffed Toy Manufacturers.

Stunt Women of America
Hist. Note: Assumed the name Stuntwomen's Ass'n of Motion Pictures, Inc. in 1986.

Stuntwomen's Ass'n of Motion Pictures (1968)
202 Vance, Pacific Palisades CA 90272
President: Diane Peterson
Members: 15 individuals
Annual Budget: under $10,000 *Tel:* (213) 454-8228
Hist. Note: Formerly known as Stunt Women of America (until 1986). SWAMP is an organization with a miniscule budget and less than 20 members residing in California and belonging to the Screen Actors Guild or the American Federation of Television and Radio Artists.
Semi-Annual Meetings: May and November

Submersible Wastewater Pump Ass'n (1976)
600 S. Federal St., #400, Chicago IL 60605
Assoc. Director: Christine Payton
Members: 25 companies *Staff:* 2-5
Annual Budget: $25-50,000 *Tel:* (312) 346-1600
Hist. Note: Manufacturers of submersible wastewater pumps and their component suppliers.
Semi-annual Meetings:

Subscription Television Ass'n (1980)
Hist. Note: Ceased operations in 1984.

Substituted Anilines Task Force (1983)
Hist. Note: An affiliate of the Synthetic Organic Chemical Manufacturers Ass'n which provides administrative support.

Suburban Newspapers of America (1971)
111 East Wacker Dr., Chicago IL 60601
Exec. Director: James E. Elsener
Members: 1,200 papers *Staff:* 2-5
Annual Budget: $100-250,000 *Tel:* (312) 644-6610
Hist. Note: Merger of Accredited Home Newspapers of America (1942), the Suburban Press Foundation and the Suburban Section of the Nat'l Newspaper Ass'n.
Publications:
SNA Membership Directory. a.
Suburban Publisher. m. adv.
Four Conferences each year:
1987-Acapulco, Mexico(Acapulco Princess)/Jan. 25-31 (Publishers)
1987-New Orleans, LA(Royal Orleans)/Feb. 15-17 (Circulation)
1987-Los Angeles, CA(Century Plaza)/April 21-24 (Advertising)
1987-San Francisco, CA(Fairmont)/June 23-26 (Management)

Sugar Ass'n (1949)
1511 K Street, N.W., Suite 235, Washington DC 20005
President: J.R. O'Connell, Jr.
Members: 22 companies *Staff:* 10
Annual Budget: $2-5,000,000 *Tel:* (202) 628-0189
Hist. Note: Members are processors and refiners of beet and cane sugar. Administers funds to promote research on sucrose and for public relations. Maintains library.
Publication:
Sugar and Health. bi-m.

Sugar Industry Technologists (1941)
Box 2067, Martinez CA 94553
Exec. Director: R. Stuart Patterson
Members: 700 *Staff:* 2
Annual Budget: $50-100,000 *Tel:* (415) 372-8383
Hist. Note: Technical and administrative personnel in the cane sugar refining industry. Membership: $15/yr.(individual); $375/yr.(company).
Publication:
Proceedings. a.
Annual Meetings: May
1987-Sydney, Australia/May 11-14
1988-Savannah, GA/May 8-11
1989-New Orleans, LA
1990-Vancouver,B.C.
1991-New York, NY

Sulfate of Potash Magnesia Export Ass'n (1982)
421 E. Hawley St., Mundelein IL 60060
Secretary: Nicolaus Bruns, Jr.
Members: 2 companies
Annual Budget: under $10,000 *Tel:* (312) 565-8600
Hist. Note: A Webb-Pomerene Act Association.

Sulphur Export Corporation (1958)
Hist. Note: A Webb-Pomerene Act Association which dissolved January 1, 1982.

Sulphur Institute (1960)
1725 K St., N.W., Suite 508, Washington DC 20006
President: Harold L. Fike
Members: 35-30 *Staff:* 11-15
Annual Budget: $1-2,000,000 *Tel:* (202) 331-9660
Hist. Note: Membership: $7,500/yr.
Publication:
Sulphur in Agriculture. semi-a.
Annual Meetings: May/75-100
1987-San Diego, CA(Del Coronado)
1988-Strasbourg, France(Hilton)

Summer and Casual Furniture Manufacturers Ass'n (1959)
P.O. Box HP-7, High Point NC 27407
Exec. Director: Joseph Ziolkowski
Members: 50-60 companies *Staff:* 2-4
Annual Budget: $50-100,000 *Tel:* (919) 884-5000
Hist. Note: Division of American Furniture Manufacturers Ass'n. Membership fee based on sales volume.
Publication:
National Casual Market Review. semi-a. adv.
Annual Meetings: September in Chicago, IL at the Holiday Inn Mart

Sump and Sewage Pump Manufacturers Ass'n (1956)
560 W. Washington St., #301, Chicago IL 60606
Managing Director: Pamela Franzen
Members: 30-35 *Staff:* 2-3
Tel: (312) 332-4146
Hist. Note: Formerly (1981) Sump Pump Manufacturers Association.

Sunflowers Processors Ass'n (1981)
Hist. Note: Ass'n exists solely to provide a vehicle for collection and dissemination of monthly statistical reports. It is an unincorporated entity. Inactive in 1986.

Sunglass Ass'n of America (1970)
71 East Ave., Norwalk CT 06851
Exec. Director: Swea Nightingale
Members: 70-80 *Staff:* 2-5
Tel: (203) 852-7168
Hist. Note: Members of the Association consist of firms actively engaged in the manufacture and/or importation of sunglasses, sunglass parts, components or materials.
Publication:
Newsletter. q.
Annual Meetings: October

Supima Ass'n of America (1955)
4141 East Broadway Rd., Phoenix AZ 85040
President: Jesse W. Curlee
Members: 2,000 *Staff:* 4-5
Annual Budget: $500-1,000,000 *Tel:* (602) 437-1364
Hist. Note: Producers of Supima (extra-long staple) cotton. Most members are located in the Southwest. Supports SUPAC, a political action committee. Membership: $5/bale assessment.
Publication:
SAA Newsletter. m.
Annual Meetings:
1987-El Paso, TX/Feb./250

Suppliers of Advanced Composite Materials Ass'n (1984)
1600 Wilson Blvd., Suite 1008, Arlington VA 22209
Exec. Director: Joseph C. Jackson
Members: 61 companies *Staff:* 3
Annual Budget: $250-500,000 *Tel:* (703) 841-1556
Hist. Note: Formerly (1986) Suppliers of Advanced Composite Materials. An international non-profit trade association of "Free World" manufacturers which produce materials used in construction of fiber- reinforced advanced composite finished products. Membership fee varies with sales volume.
Annual Meetings: May
1987-West Coast/May 5-8/100

Surety Ass'n of America (1908)
100 Wood Ave. South, Iselin NJ 08830
President: Lloyd Provost
Members: 560-585 companies *Staff:* 25
Annual Budget: $1-2,000,000 *Tel:* (201) 494-7600
Hist. Note: Insurance companies underwriting fidelity, surety and forgery bonds. Absorbed the Towner Rating Bureau in 1947.
Annual Meetings: New York, NY, second Thursday in May
1987-New York, NY(Vista International)/May 7/200

Surface Design Ass'n (1976)
311 E. Washington St., Fayetteville TN 37334
Editor: Stephen Blumrich
Members: 1,500 *Staff:* 2
Annual Budget: $10-25,000 *Tel:* (615) 433-6804
Hist. Note: Membership consists of individuals involved in printing, designing and dyeing art fabrics. Incorporated in the State of Minnesota. Membership: $25/year.
Publication:
Surface Design Journal. q. adv.
Biennial Meetings: Odd years

Surface Mount Technology Ass'n (1985)
59 N. Santa Cruz Ave., Suite Q, Los Gatos CA 95030
President: Linda J. West
Members: 366 companies; 350 individuals
Annual Budget: $25-50,000 *Tel:* (408) 354-0700
Hist. Note: Membership: $50/yr.
Publications:
Newsletters. m.
Referral Directory. a. adv.
Membership Directory. a. adv.
Standard Guidelines. adv.
Annual Meetings: October 1st

Surplus Bearing Dealers Institute (1955)
Hist. Note: Inactive in 1982.

Survival and Flight Equipment Ass'n (1957)
Hist. Note: See the SAFE Ass'n.

Sussex Cattle Ass'n of America (1967)
P.O. Drawer AA, Regugio TX 78377
Director: Fred Eastwood
Members: 15 *Staff:* 0
Annual Budget: under $10,000 *Tel:* (512) 526-2380
Hist. Note: Members are either individuals, partnerships, corporations or firms actively engaged in the breeding of Sussex cattle. Membership: $10/yr.
Semi-annual Meetings: May and November

Swedish-American Chamber of Commerce (1906)
825 Third Ave., New York NY 10022
President & General Manager: Olle Wijkstrom
Members: 1,000 *Staff:* 10-12
Annual Budget: $250-500,000 *Tel:* (212) 838-5530
Publications:
Membership Directory. a.
Newsletter. bi-w.
Subsidiary Listing. a.
Annual Meetings: March, in New York

Sweet Potato Council of the United States (1961)
P.O. Box 14, McHenry MD 21541
Exec. Secretary: Harold H. Hoecker
Members: 2,500 farmers *Staff:* 2-5
Annual Budget: $25-50,000 *Tel:* (301) 387-9537
Annual Meetings: January
1987-Jackson, MS/Jan. 25-27

Synagogue Council of America (1926)
327 Lexington Ave., New York NY 10016
Exec. V. President: Rabbi Henry D. Michelman

00288 12 05 86 1233

Members: 6 organizations *Staff:* 6-10
Annual Budget: $250-500,000 *Tel:* (212) 686-8670
Hist. Note: A coordinating agency for Orthodox, Reform and Conservative Jewish congregations.

Synthetic Amorphous Silica and Silicates Industry Ass'n (1982)
c/o J.M. HJuber Co., Box 310, Havre de Grace MD 21078
Chairman: Rick Walker
Members: 11 companies *Staff:* 1
Annual Budget: under $10,000 *Tel:* (301) 939-3500
Hist. Note: A group of chemical manufacturers making synthetic amorphous silica, a substance used in paints, varnishes, toothpaste and scouring agents and capable of high toxicity under certain circumstances. Has no dues structure, offices or permanent staff, and a very limited budget at present. Officers are elected annually.

Synthetic Organic Chemical Manufacturers Ass'n (1921)
1330 Connecticut Ave., N.W., Washington DC 20036
President: Ronald A. Lang
Members: 130 companies *Staff:* 50
Annual Budget: over $5,000,000 *Tel:* (202) 659-0060
Hist. Note: Represents membership on legislative, regulatory and international trade issues; implements commercial programs to provide members with new opportunities to increase their sales. SOCMA provides administrative, technical, scientific and regulatory support for its affiliates including: Acrylamide Producers Ass'n; Acrylonitrile Group; Aklyl Amines Council; American Industrial Health Council; Aniline Ass'n; Aspirin Foundation of America; Biphenyl Work Group; Cationic Flocculants Producers Ass'n; Chlorinated Paraffins Industry Ass'n; Chlorobenzene Producers Ass'n; Diethylenetriamine Producers/Importers Alliance; Ethylbenzene Producers' Ass'n; Formadehyde Institute; Institute for Polyacrylate Absorbents; Oxygenated Fuels Ass'n; Silicones Health Council; Substituted Anilines Task Force; U.S. Operating Committee of the Ecological and Toxicological Ass'n of the Dyestuffs Manufacturing Industry. Has an annual budget of $7.5 million.
Publication:
SOCMA Newsletter. semi-m.
Semi-annual Meeting: December, in New York City, and Spring.

System Safety Soc. (1964)
7345 S. Pierce St., Suite 201-G, Littleton CO 80123
Mgr., Membership Services: James Gibble
Members: 1,100 individuals, 12 companies *Staff:* 1
Annual Budget: $50-100,000 *Tel:* (303) 973-8233
Hist. Note: Emphasis is on hazard identification and design of safety features of complex aerospace and transportation systems, as well as product liability prevention methodology. Formerly (1966) the Aerospace System Safety Society. Membership: $40/yr. (individual); $60/yr. (corporate)
Publication:
Hazard Prevention Journal. bi-m. adv.
Biennial Technical Conference: Odd Years
1987-New Orleans, LA(Marriott)/July 27-31/400

Systems Builders Ass'n (1968)
P.O. Box 117, W. Milton OH 45383-0117
Exec. V. President: Christopher Long
Members: 1,200 companies *Staff:* 2-5
Annual Budget: $500-1,000,000 *Tel:* (513) 698-4127
Hist. Note: Formerly (1984) the Metal Building Dealers Ass'n.
Annual Meetings: Winter

Systems, Man and Cybernetics Soc.
Hist. Note: A subsidiary of the Institute of Electrical and Electronics Engineers. Membership in the Society, open only to IEEE members, includes subscription to a technical periodical in the field published by IEEE. All administrative support is provided by IEEE.

Tackle and Shooting Sports Agents Ass'n (1953)
2625 Clearbrook Dr., Arlington Heights IL 60005
Managing Director: Thomas P. Conley
Members: 250 *Staff:* 2-5
Annual Budget: $10-25,000 *Tel:* (312) 364-4460
Hist. Note: Formerly (1976) Sporting Industries Representatives, (1977) Tackle Representatives Ass'n and (1985) Tackle Representatives Ass'n Internat'l. Assumed its present name in December 1986.
Publication:
Tackle Report. q.
Annual Meetings: Summer, in conjunction with trade show.
1987-Atlanta, GA(World Congress Center)/Aug. 6-9
1988-Las Vegas, NV(Convention Center)/July 28-31
1989-Las Vegas, NV(Convention Center)/July 27-30

Tackle Representatives Ass'n Internat'l (1953)
Hist. Note: Became the Tackle and Shooting Sports Agents Ass'n in December 1986.

Tag and Label Manufacturers Institute (1933)
104 Wilmot Road, Suite 201, Deerfield IL 60015-5195
Exec. Director: Glen Anderson
Members: 130 companies *Staff:* 2
Annual Budget: $100-250,000 *Tel:* (312) 940-8800
Hist. Note: Formally organized in Cleveland on June 15, 1933 as the Tag Manufacturers Institute. In 1962 the Bylaws were revised to include converters of pressure sensitive labels, and the present name was adopted. The supplier (Associates) division was formed in 1966 and now consists of suppliers of label base stocks, presses and auxiliary equipment, plates, dies, inks, adhesvies, tag & label papers.
Publications:
Illuminator. bi-m.
Buyers Guide. a.
Annual Meetings: Fall/300
1987-Homestead, WV/Sept. 13-16
1988-Tarpon Springs, FL(Innisbrook)

Talmex Export Corporation (1969)
World Trade Center, Suite 211, San Francisco CA 94111
Secy.-Treas.: Charles T. Caito
Members: 6 rendering companies *Staff:* 1
Tel: (415) 392-6304
Hist. Note: A Webb-Pomerene Act Ass'n

Tamworth Swine Ass'n (1923)
Hist. Note: Breeders and fanciers of Tamworth swine. Address unknown in 1987.

Tantalum Producers Ass'n (1968)
1230 Keith Bldg., Cleveland OH 44115-2180
Exec. Director: Charles M. Stockinger
Members: 7 companies *Staff:* 1
Annual Budget: under $10,000 *Tel:* (216) 241-7333
Hist. Note: Members are companies producing tantalum and columbium, additives used in producing steel with electronic applications.

Tapered Steel Transmission Pole Institute (1979)
111 East Wacker Drive, Suite 600, Chicago IL 60601
Information Director: Jack M. Springer
Members: 5-10 companies *Staff:* 2-5
Annual Budget: $25-50,000 *Tel:* (312) 644-6610
Hist. Note: Manufacturers of steel transmission poles for power lines. Affiliated with the Nat'l Electrical Manufacturers Ass'n.
Annual Meetings: Not held

Tax Executives Institute (1944)
1300 North 17th St., Suite 1300, Arlington VA 22209
Exec. Director: Thomas P. Kerester
Members: 3,900 individuals *Staff:* 6-10
Annual Budget: $1-2,000,000 *Tel:* (703) 522-3535
Hist. Note: A professional organization of corporate tax executives. Membership is open to corporate officers and employees charged with administering their company's tax affairs. Membership: $160/yr. Initiation fee: $160/yr.
Publications:
The Tax Executive. q. adv.
TEI News. bi-m.
Annual Meetings: Fall/1,250

Tea Ass'n of the United States of America (1899)
230 Park Ave., New York NY 10169
Exec. Secretary: Theresa K. Kulka
Members: 150-175 *Staff:* 1
Annual Budget: $25-50,000 *Tel:* (212) 986-9415
Publication:
Tea World. q.
Annual Meetings: November

Tea Council of the U.S.A. (1950)
230 Park Ave., New York NY 10169
Exec. Director: Donald A. Wiederecht
Members: 7 governments and 45-50 companies *Staff:* 6-10
Annual Budget: $500-1,000,000 *Tel:* (212) 986-6998
Hist. Note: Seeks to increase the consumption of hot and iced tea in competition with all else drunk in the U.S.

Teachers of English to Speakers of Other Languages (1966)
Georgetown University, 1118 22nd St., N.W., Washington DC 20037
Exec. Director: Dr. James E. Alatis
Members: 9,150 individuals; 1,850 institutions *Staff:* 8
Annual Budget: $500-1,000,000 *Tel:* (202) 625-4569
Hist. Note: Promotes instruction and research in the teaching of standard English to speakers of other languages or dialects. Membership: $40/yr.
Publications:
TESOL Membership Directory. bi-a. adv.
TESOL Newsletter. bi-m.
TESOL Quarterly. q. adv.
Annual Meetings: March-April
1987-Miami, FL(Diplomat)/April 21-25
1988-Chicago, IL(Conrad Hilton)/March 8-13/4,500
1989-San Antonio, TX(Conv. Center)/March 6-11/3,800
1990-San Francisco, CA(Hilton)/March 5-10/5,000

Technical Ass'n of the Graphic Arts (1948)
R.I.T., T&E Center, 1 Lomb Memorial Drive, Box 9887, Rochester NY 14623-0887
Exec. Director: Michael H. Bruno
Members: 900-1,000 individuals *Staff:* 1
Annual Budget: $50-100,000 *Tel:* (716) 272-0557
Hist. Note: Organized to advance the science and technology of the graphic arts. Membership: $45/yr.(individual). Other membership categories available for organizations.
Publications:
TAGA Newsletter. 3/yr.
TAGA Proceedings. a.
Annual Meetings: Spring
1987-San Diego, CA(U.S. Grant)/March 29-April 1/200-300
1988-Chicago, IL
1989-Savannah, GA
1990-Kansas City, MO

Technical Ass'n of the Pulp and Paper Industry (1915)
Box 105113, Technology Park, Atlanta GA 30348
Exec. Director: William L. Cullison, CAE
Members: 27,000 *Staff:* 80
Annual Budget: over $5,000,000 *Tel:* (404) 446-1400
Hist. Note: Organized in 1915 as a section of the American Paper and Pulp Ass'n. The articles of organization were revised at the first annual meeting in 1916 and the name was changed to the Technical Ass'n of the Pulp and Paper Industry. Today, members include those professionals who work in the pulp, paper, packaging, converting, and nonwovens industries. Has an annual budget of $8.3 million. Membership: $50/yr. (individual); $500/yr. (organization/company)
Publication:
Journal. m. adv.
Annual Meetings: Feb./March
1987-San Francisco, CA/Feb. 8-11
1988-Atlanta, GA(Congress Center)/Feb. 28-March 2
1989-New Orleans, LA
1990-Atlanta, GA/March 4-7

Technical Marketing Soc. of America (1975)
KB Bldg., #609, 3711 Long Beach Blvd., Long Beach CA 90807
Exec. Director: Mark R. Johnson
Members: 4,000 *Staff:* 7
Annual Budget: $100-250,000 *Tel:* (213) 595-0254
Hist. Note: Engineers interested in the marketing of aerospace technical products and data. Membership: $25/yr.
Publications:
Aerospace Market Outlook. bi-m.
TMSA Report. bi-m.
Seminar Proceedings. a.

Technology Education for Children Council (1965)
Dept. of Industry and Technology, California University of Pennsylvania, California PA 15419
President: John Lucy
Members: 250
Annual Budget: under $10,000 *Tel:* (412) 938-4381
Hist. Note: Formerly (1986) American Council for Elementary School Industrial Arts, TECC is a constituent member of the Internat'l Technology Education Ass'n. Membership: $8/yr. (individual); $38/yr. (organization/company)
Publications:
Newsletter. semi-a.
Membership Directory. a.
Monograph Series.
Annual Meetings: With Internat'l Technology Education Ass'n
1987-Tulsa, OK/March 23-27
1988-Norfolk, VA/March 28-April 1
1989-Dallas, TX/March 20-24
1990-Indianapolis, IN/April 6-9

Technology Transfer Soc. (1975)
279 S. Beverly Drive, #1078, Beverly Hills CA 90212-3807
Exec. Secretary: Norman Goldstone
Members: 600 *Staff:* 2-5
Annual Budget: $50-100,000 *Tel:* (213) 874-2535
Hist. Note: Concerned with the transfer of technology between such disciplines as science, engineering, management, education and information science. Membership: $45/yr.(individual); $150-500/yr.(organization).
Publications:
Journal of Technology Transfer. semi-a.
Newsletter. bi-m.
Proceedings. a.
Annual Meetings: June
1987-Washington, DC(Omni Shoreham)/June 23-25/200

Tele-Communications Ass'n (1961)
1515 West Cameron, Suite B-140, West Covina CA 91790
Manager: Charles Dobruck
Members: 1,000-1,100 companies; 2,300-2,500 individuals
Staff: 3-10
Annual Budget: $500-1,000,000 *Tel:* (818) 960-2849
Hist. Note: Members are organizations utilizing point-to-point telecommunication circuits for internal purposes. Membership at present concentrated in 13 Western states.
Publication:
Technical Bulletin. q. adv.
Annual Meetings: September, in San Diego.

Telecommunications Internat'l Union (1949)
Hist. Note: Address unknown in 1985.

Television Bureau of Advertising (1954)
477 Madison Ave., New York NY 10022
President: Roger D. Rice
Members: 600-700 *Staff:* 60-70
Annual Budget: over $5,000,000 *Tel:* (212) 486-1111
Hist. Note: Founded with the help and sponsorship of the National Association of Broadcasters, TVB has become the marketing organization of the television industry. Members are networks, stations, sales reps, program producers and syndicators. Has an international membership. Has an annual budget of $7-8 million.
Publications:
Co-op Plans Book. a.
Spot-Planning Guide. a.
TV Basics. a.

00289 12 05 86 1233

Annual Meetings: November
1987-Atlanta, GA(Marriott)/Nov. 11-13/1,200
1988-New Orleans, LA(Hilton)/Nov. 16-18/1,300
1989-Orlando, FL(Orlando Marriott)/Nov. 15-17/1,400
1990-Dallas, TX(Anatole)/Nov. 14-16/1,500
1991-Las Vegas, NV(Hilton)/Nov. 18-20/1,600
1992-Atlanta, GA(Marriott)/Nov. 11-13/1,700

Television Critics Ass'n (1978)
c/o Phoenix Gazette, Box 1950, Phoenix AZ 85004
Treasurer: Barbara Holsopple
Members: 100-110
Annual Budget: under $10,000 *Tel:* (602) 271-8000
Hist. Note: Members are professional journalists in the print media who specialize in or whose responsibilities include the regular coverage of television. Has no paid staff or permanent address. Membership: $25/yr.
Publication:
TCA Newsletter. m.
Semi-annual Meetings: June and January in Los Angeles(Century Plaza)

Television Information Office (1959)
Hist. Note: The PR area of the television industry. Based in New York City. Affiliated with the Nat'l Ass'n of Broadcasters.

Telocator Network of America (1949)
2000 M St., N.W., Suite 230, Washington DC 20036
President: Thomas H. Lamoureux
Members: 600 *Staff:* 20
Annual Budget: $1-2,000,000 *Tel:* (202) 467-4770
Hist. Note: Established as the National Mobile Radio System, it became the National Association of Radiotelephone Systems and assumed its present name in 1977. Members are radio common carriers and telephone companies who operate two-way mobile telephone and cellular telephone systems. Also encompasses manufacturers of mobile radio equipment. Assigns the (RCC) Radio Common Carrier identification numbers.
Publications:
Telocator Magazine. m. adv.
Bulletin. w.
Semi-annual Meetings: Spring and Fall
1987-Phoenix, AZ(Phoenix Civic Center)/April 29-May 1/1,800
1987-San Francisco, CA(Moscone Center)/Oct. 20-23/3,500

Tennessee Walking Horse Breeders and Exhibitors Ass'n (1935)
Box 286, Lewisburg TN 37091
Secretary: Sharon Brandon
Members: 5,200 *Staff:* 11-15
Annual Budget: $500-1,000,000 *Tel:* (615) 359-1574
Hist. Note: Members are owners and breeders of the Tennessee Walking horse. Formerly the Tennessee Walking Horse Breeders Ass'n of America (1974).
Publication:
Breedjournal, Voice of the Tennessee Walking Horse. m. adv.

Tennis Manufacturers Ass'n (1981)
200 Castlewood Drive, North Palm Beach FL 33408
Exec. Secretary: Brad Patterson
Members: 90-100 companies *Staff:* 2-5
Annual Budget: $50-100,000 *Tel:* (305) 848-1026
Hist. Note: Affiliated with the Tennis Foundation of America. Membership: $300-3,200/yr.
Publication:
Net Friends News. bi-m.
Semi-Annual Meetings: Atlanta, GA/Spring and New York, NY/Fall
1987-Atlanta, GA(Marriott Marquis)/Feb. 7-10/50,000
1987-New York, NY(Marriott Marquis)/Sept. 19-22/25,000

Terminal Elevator Grain Merchants Ass'n (1918)
1030 15th St., N.W., Suite 476, Washington DC 20005
Secy.-Treas.: Robert R. Petersen
Members: 40 companies *Staff:* 4
Annual Budget: $50-100,000 *Tel:* (202) 842-0400

Test Boring Ass'n (1941)
P.O. Box 5126, Old Bridge NJ 08857
Exec. Officer: Bette Katz
Members: 6-10 *Staff:* 1
Annual Budget: under $10,000
Hist. Note: Formerly (1969) Test Boring Contractors Ass'n.
Annual Meetings: Late Winter in New York, NY

Texas Longhorn Breeders Ass'n of America (1964)
2315 North Main St., Suite 402, Fort Worth TX 76106
Exec. Director: Roy D. Gregg
Members: 3,000 *Staff:* 10
Annual Budget: $500-1,000,000 *Tel:* (817) 625-6241
Hist. Note: Founded in Lawton, OK to serve as the breed registry and to preserve the Texas Longhorn through promotion, education and research, its members are breeders and fanciers of Texas Longhorn beef cattle. Member of the Nat'l Pedigree Livestock Council, Nat'l Cattlemen's Ass'n, and U.S. Beef Breeds Council. Membership: $35/yr.
Publication:
TLBAA Trails. m.
Annual Meetings: August/500
1987-Lake of the Ozarks, MO(Lodge of Four Seasons)/Aug. 9-12
1988-Ft. Worth, TX
1989-Colorado
1990-San Antonio, TX

Texas Produce Export Ass'n (1980)
6912 W. Exp. 83, Harlingen TX 78552
Secretary: William E. Weeks
Members: 24 companies *Staff:* 2
Annual Budget: $10-25,000
Hist. Note: A Webb-Pomerene Act association.

Textile Bag and Packaging Ass'n (1934)
1024 West Kinzie Ave., Chicago IL 60622
Secy.-Treas.: Sheldon Simon
Members: 175-200 companies *Staff:* 1
Annual Budget: $50-100,000 *Tel:* (312) 733-3660
Hist. Note: Formerly (1968) Nat'l Burlap Bag Dealers Ass'n and (1984) Textile Bag Processors Ass'n; assumed its present name in 1985. Members are recyclers and reclaimers of textile bags. Membership: $200/year.
Publication:
Roster. a.
Annual Meetings: Winter
1987-Ft. Lauderdale, FL(Marriott's Harbor Beach)/Feb. 15-22
1988-San Diego, CA

Textile Bag Manufacturers Ass'n (1925)
Box 2145, Northbrook IL 60065-2145
Exec. V. President: Donald J. Walker
Members: 40-45 companies *Staff:* 2-5
Tel: (312) 272-3930
Hist. Note: Makers of cloth bags principally for agricultural products.
Annual Meetings:
1987-Scottsdale, AZ(Camelback Inn)/March

Textile Bag Processors Ass'n
Hist. Note: Became the Textile Bag and Packaging Ass'n in 1985.

Textile Care Allied Trades Ass'n (1920)
543 Valley Rd., Upper Montclair NJ 07043
Exec. Director: Robert C. Knipe
Members: 350 *Staff:* 2-5
Annual Budget: $100-250,000 *Tel:* (201) 744-0090
Hist. Note: Absorbed the Nat'l Laundry Allied Trades Ass'n and the Laundry and Dry Cleaners Machinery Manufacturers Ass'n. Formerly (until 1982) the Laundry and Cleaners Allied Trades Ass'n. Members are makers and distributors of commercial laundry and dry cleaning machinery, equipment and supplies.
Annual Meetings: Spring

Textile Converters Ass'n (1958)
16th Floor, 100 East 42nd St., New York NY 10017
Exec. Director: Jacob P. Rosenbaum
Members: 90 *Staff:* 1
Annual Budget: $25-50,000 *Tel:* (212) 867-5720

Textile Distributors Ass'n (1938)
45 West 36th St., 3rd floor, New York NY 10018
Exec. Director: J. Wallace Kaine
Members: 200 *Staff:* 5
Tel: (212) 563-0400
Hist. Note: Converters and distributors of fabrics selling primarily to apparel manufacturers and over-the-counter trade. Formerly Textile Distributors Institute and (1965) Textile Fabric Distributors Ass'n. Provides administrative support to the American Printed Fabrics Council, formed to promote printed fabrics.
Annual Meetings: Spring, in the Poconos

Textile Fibers and By-Products Ass'n (1931)
Box 11065, Charlotte NC 28220
Acting Exec. Secretary: John Coleman
Members: 69 companies *Staff:* 1
Annual Budget: $25-50,000 *Tel:* (704) 527-5593
Hist. Note: Formerly (1966) Textile Waste Ass'n.
Publication:
General Communique. w.
Annual Meetings: Spring/105

Textile Foremen's Guild (1937)
300 Lafayette Ave., Hawthorne NJ 07506
President: Eugene S. Motyka
Members: 55 *Staff:* 2-5
Annual Budget: under $10,000 *Tel:* (201) 423-3079
Hist. Note: Independent labor union of the textile industry.

Textile Information Users Council (1969)
Box 20288, Greensboro NC 27420
Committee Member: Georgia Rodeffer
Members: 35-40 individuals
Hist. Note: Established March 21, 1969 at Myrtle Beach, SC. Promotes the development of comprehensive services for information handling in the areas of current awareness and retrospective searching of the textile and related industries.
Publications:
Textile Pathfinders.
Directory of Translators.
Semi-Annual Meetings: Spring and Fall

Textile Laundry Council
316 Chestnut St., Moorestown NJ 08057
Exec. V. President: Susan R. Heath
Members: 14 companies *Staff:* 1-2
Annual Budget: $10-25,000 *Tel:* (609) 722-1182
Hist. Note: Formerly Product Promotion Programs, Inc., TLC consists of a loosely organized group of individual diaper services which meet together periodically to exchange information on common problems. Membership: $1,200/year (company).
Annual Meetings: Not held

Textile Printers and Dyers Labor Relations Institute
401 Hamburg Turnpike, Suite 103, Wayne NJ 07470
Secy.-Treas.: Walter J. Stryker
Members: 35-40 plants *Staff:* 1
Annual Budget: $10-25,000 *Tel:* (201) 942-7000
Hist. Note: Major purpose is labor negotiating on behalf of its members.

Textile Processors, Service Trades, Health Care, Professional and Technical Employees Internat'l Union (1898)
360 North Michigan Ave., Suite 905, Chicago IL 60601
General President: Frank A. Scalish
Members: 28-29,000 *Staff:* 6-10
Annual Budget: $250-500,000 *Tel:* (312) 726-9416
Hist. Note: Organized in Troy, New York and chartered by the American Federation of Labor in 1900 as the Shirt, Waist and Laundry Workers Internat'l Union. Renamed the Laundry Workers Internat'l Union in 1909, it merged in 1956 with the Internat'l Ass'n of Cleaning and Dye House Workers to form the Laundry, Dry Cleaning and Dye House Workers' Internat'l Union; assumed its present name in 1980. Expelled for corruption from the AFL-CIO in Dec., 1957, it became a division of the Internat'l Brotherhood of Teamsters in 1962.
Publication:
Newsletter. q.
Annual Meetings: Every 5 years in Spring
1990-Chicago, IL/May

Textile Quality Control Ass'n (1951)
Box 76501, Atlanta GA 30328
Secy.-Treas.: L. Howard Olson
Members: 175-200 individuals *Staff:* 2-5
Annual Budget: $10-25,000 *Tel:* (404) 252-9037
Hist. Note: Membership: $25/yr.
Publication:
Proceedings. semi-a.
Semi-Annual Meetings: April and September
1987-Charlotte, NC(Holiday Inn-Woodlawn)/April/150
1987-Myrtle Beach, SC(Hilton)/Sept./150
1988-Charlotte, NC(Holiday Inn-Woodlawn)/April/150
1988-Charleston, SC/Sept./150

Textile Rental Services Ass'n of America (1913)
1250 East Hallandale Beach Blvd., Suite 703, Hallandale FL 33009
Exec. Director: John J. Contney, CAE
Members: 1,800-1,900 companies *Staff:* 20-25
Annual Budget: $1-2,000,000 *Tel:* (305) 457-7555
Hist. Note: Members are renters of uniforms, linen and towels to business and industry. Associate members are manufacturers, distributors and suppliers. Formerly (until 1979) known as the Linen Supply Ass'n of America. Supports TRSAPAC (a political action committee).
Publications:
Roster and Buyers' Guide. a. adv.
Textile Rental. m. adv.
Clean Scene. bi-m. adv.
Annual Meetings: Spring
1987-Atlanta, GA(Marriott Marquis)/April 24-26/600
1988-Palm Desert, CA(Marriott Desert Springs)/June 5-9/600

Textured Yarn Ass'n of America (1971)
Hist. Note: Address unknown in 1985.

Theatre Equipment Ass'n (1971)
244 West 49th St., New York NY 10019
Exec. Director: Robert Sunshine
Members: 110 companies *Staff:* 2
Annual Budget: $50-100,000 *Tel:* (212) 246-6460
Hist. Note: Merger of Theatre Equipment Dealers Ass'n and the Supply Manufacturers Ass'n founded in 1933.
Annual Meetings:
1987-Long Boat Key, FL
1988-Monterey, CA

Theatre Library Ass'n (1937)
111 Amsterdam Ave., New York NY 10023
Secy.-Treas.: Richard M. Buck
Members: 475-500 *Staff:* 1
Annual Budget: $10-25,000 *Tel:* (212) 870-1670
Hist. Note: An Affiliate of the American Library Association and the International Federation for Theatre Research. Membership: $20/yr. (individual), $25/yr. (institutional).
Publications:
Broadside. q.
Performing Arts Resources. a.
Semi-annual meetings: Summer with the American Library Association
and Fall in New York City.
1987-San Francisco, CA/Summer
1988-New Orleans, LA/Summer

00290 12 05 86 1233

Thermal Insulation Manufacturers Ass'n (1941)
7 Kirby Plaza, Box 686, Mount Kisco NY 10549
Exec. Director: John M. Barnhart
Members: 16-20 companies *Staff:* 2-5
Tel: (914) 241-2284
Hist. Note: The Industrial Mineral Fiber Institute merged in 1941 with the Industrial Mineral Wool Institute to form the Industrial Mineral Insulation Manufacturers Institute. This, in turn, merged in 1958 with the Magnesia-Silica Insulation Manufacturers Ass'n to form the Nat'l Insulation Manufacturers Ass'n. The present name was adopted in 1973.

Third Class Mail Ass'n (1947)
1333 F St., N.W., Suite 710, Washington DC 20004-1108
Exec. Director: Gene A. Del Polito
Members: 500 *Staff:* 2-5
Annual Budget: $250-500,000 *Tel:* (202) 347-0055
Hist. Note: Established as Associated Third Class Mail Users, it assumed its present name in October 1981.
Publications:
Membership Directory. a.
TCMA Bulletin. 50/yr. w.
Annual Meetings: Fall

Third Fertilizer Foundation (1982)
Hist. Note: The research and educational arm of the National Fertilizer Solutions Association.

Thoroughbred Club of America (1932)
Box 8098, Lexington KY 40533
Exec. Director: Maud Hann Thornton
Members: 1,300 *Staff:* 2-5
Annual Budget: $50-100,000 *Tel:* (606) 254-4282
Hist. Note: Founded as the Thoroughbred Club in 1932; name was changed to its present form the following year. Although most members live in Kentucky, the membership represents all branches of the Thoroughbred industry and comes from all parts of the U.S., Europe and Canada.

Thoroughbred Racing Ass'ns of North America (1942)
3000 Marcus Ave., Suite 2W4, Lake Success NY 11042
Exec. V. President: J. B. Faulconer
Members: 50 tracks *Staff:* 6-10
Annual Budget: $500-1,000,000 *Tel:* (516) 328-2660
Hist. Note: Supports the Thoroughbred Racing Protective Bureau. Formerly (1977) the Thoroughbred Racing Ass'ns of the U.S., Inc.
Publications:
TRA Directory & Record Book. a.
Newsletter. m.
Annual Meetings: February
1987-San Francisco, CA(Fairmont)/Feb. 4-6/400

Thread Institute (1933)
1101 Connecticut Ave., N.W., Suite 300, Washington DC 20036
Exec. Director: O'Jay Niles
Members: 35-40 *Staff:* 2-5
Annual Budget: $50-100,000 *Tel:* (202) 862-0518
Hist. Note: Members are makers, converters and distributors of thread and thread products. Administrative support provided by American Textile Manufacturers Institute.
Annual Meetings: May/June
1987-Wesley CHapel, FL(Saddlebrook Resort)/April 29-May 3

Tile Contractors' Ass'n of America (1904)
112 North Alfred St., Alexandria VA 22314
Exec. Director: Wilhelmina T. Loomis
Members: 200 *Staff:* 2-5
Annual Budget: $100-250,000 *Tel:* (703) 836-5995
Hist. Note: Sub-contractors engaged in installing ceramic tile. Formerly (1936) Tile and Mantle Contractors Ass'n of America.
Publication:
TCAA Products & Materials Guide. a. adv.
Annual Meetings: Fall
1987-Chicago, IL(Drake)/Sept. 26-Oct. 1

Tile Council of America (1945)
Box 326, Princeton NJ 08542
Exec. Director: Jeffrey H. Schott, PhD.
Members: 15-20 companies *Staff:* 11-15
Annual Budget: $1-2,000,000 *Tel:* (609) 921-7050
Hist. Note: Manufacturers and suppliers of ceramic wall and floor tiles.
Publication:
Handbook for Ceramic Tile. a.
Semi-annual Meetings: Spring and Fall

Tile, Marble, Terrazzo, Finishers, Shopworkers and Granite Cutters Internat'l Union (1901)
801 North Pitt St., Suite 116, Alexandria VA 22314
President: Gerald D. Bombassaro
Members: 9,000 *Staff:* 4
Annual Budget: $25-50,000 *Tel:* (703) 549-3050
Hist. Note: Organized in New York in 1901 and chartered by the American Federation of Labor in 1902 as the Internat'l Union of Marble Workers. This became the Internat'l Ass'n of Marble, Stone and Slate Polishers, Rubbers and Sawyers in 1917 and, after name changes resulting from changing jurisdictions too numerous to itemize, assumed its present name in 1980.
Biennial meetings: Even years/August

Tillage Council
Hist. Note: A division of the Farm and Industrial Equipment Institute.

Timber Operators Council (1960)
6825 S.W. Sandburg St., Tigard OR 97223
Exec. V. Pres. and CEO: John B. Stentz
Members: 460 companies *Staff:* 30
Annual Budget: $2-5,000,000 *Tel:* (503) 620-1710
Hist. Note: Formed by merger of Lumberman's Industrial Relations Council, Oregon Coast Operators, Plywood and Door Manufacturers Industrial Committee and Willamette Valley Lumber Operators Ass'n. Membership comprised of wood products manufacturing companies primarily in Washington, Oregon and Northern California. Concerned primarily with industrial/labor relations issues. Membership Fee: Based on size of production payroll.
Publications:
Newsletter. bi-w.
Labor Relations Report. irreg.
Safety Alert. irreg.
EEO-AAP Report. irreg.
Targeting In. irreg.
Annual Meetings: Portland, in the Spring, 350
1987-Jantzen Beach Thunderbird/May 20-21/250

Timber Products Manufacturers (1916)
951 East Third Ave., Spokane WA 99202
Manager & Gen. Counsel: Greg R. Tichy
Members: 300-325 *Staff:* 8
Annual Budget: $250-500,000 *Tel:* (509) 535-4646
Hist. Note: Established as the Timber Products Manufacturers Ass'n, it assumed its present name in 1969. It was established to improve, promote and advance the Timber Industry; serves 300 members throughout the Northwest and Intermountain area.
Publication:
T.P.M. Bulletin. w.
Annual Meetings: Spring
1987-Sun Valley, ID/June/150

Tin Research Institute (1949)
1353 Perry St., Columbus OH 43201
Manager: Daniel J. Maykuth
Staff: 6-10
Annual Budget: $250-500,000 *Tel:* (614) 424-6200
Hist. Note: Maintains an office in Palo Alto, CA. The U.S. representative of the International Tin Research Institute based in England.
Publications:
Annual Report. a.
Tin and Its Uses. q.

Tire and Rim Ass'n (1903)
3200 West Market St., Akron OH 44313
Exec. V. President: J. F. Pacuit
Members: 100-125 companies *Staff:* 2-5
Annual Budget: $100-250,000 *Tel:* (216) 836-5553
Hist. Note: The technical standardizing body for tire, rim and valve manufacturers.
Quarterly meetings: Akron, OH

Tire Industry Safety Council (1969)
National Press Building, Suite 844, Washington DC 20045
Director: Frank Holeman
Members: 14 companies *Staff:* 2-5
Tel: (202) 783-1022
Hist. Note: Affiliated with the Rubber Manufacturers Association, whose President is Chairman of the Council. Members are tire manufacturers.
Annual Meetings: Not held

Tire Retread Information Bureau (1974)
621 Forest Ave., Suite 4, Pacific Grove CA 93950
Managing Director: Harvey Brodsky
Members: 250 companies *Staff:* 2
Annual Budget: $100-250,000 *Tel:* (408) 649-0944
Hist. Note: Public relations arm of the retread industry. Receives logistical support from industry associations, suppliers and remanufacturers.

Tissue Culture Ass'n (1946)
19110 Montgomery Village Ave., Suite 300, Gaithersburg MD 20879
Exec. Director: William G. Momberger, CAE
Members: 2,500 *Staff:* 6
Annual Budget: $250-500,000 *Tel:* (301) 869-2900
Hist. Note: Founded in 1946 as the Tissue Culture Commission and became the Tissue Culture Ass'n in 1950. Incorporated in 1964 in the District of Columbia. Membership: $60/yr.
Publications:
In Vitro Cellular and Developmental Biology. 13/yr. adv.
Program. a. adv.
TCA Report. bi-m.
Tissue Culture Methods. q. adv.
Membeship Roster. bien.
Annual Meetings: June
1987-Washington, DC/May/1,200
1988-Las Vegas, NV/June/1,000

Titanium Development Ass'n (1984)
11 West Monument Ave., Box 2307, Dayton OH 45401
Exec. Director: Francine W. Rickenbach
Members: 60 companies, 200 individuals *Staff:* 4
Annual Budget: $250-500,000 *Tel:* (513) 223-8432
Hist. Note: Formed to promote titanium metal; seeks to expand existing markets and develop new markets for titanium.
Publications:
TiDBITS. m.
Buyers Guide. a.
Statistics. a.
Annual Meetings: Fall
1987-Annapolis, MD/Oct. 4-7/150
1987-Chicago, IL/Sept. 12-16/100

Tobacco Associates (1947)
1101 17th St., N.W., Washington DC 20036
President: Kirk Wayne
Members: 175-200,000 *Staff:* 6-10
Annual Budget: $250-500,000 *Tel:* (202) 659-1160
Hist. Note: Promotes flue-cured tobacco.
Annual Meetings: Raleigh, NC, in early Spring.

Tobacco Ass'n of the U.S. (1900)
3716 National Drive, Suite 114, Raleigh NC 27612
Exec. V. President: J.T. Bunn
Members: 50-60 *Staff:* 2-5
Annual Budget: $100-250,000 *Tel:* (919) 782-5151
Hist. Note: Affiliated with Leaf Tobacco Exporters Ass'n.
Annual Meetings: May, at the Greenbrier in White Sulphur Springs, WV/500.

Tobacco Export Ass'n of El Paso (1980)
Hist. Note: A Webb-Pomerene Act association. Address unknown in 1984. Probably defunct.

Tobacco Growers' Information Committee (1958)
P.O. Box 18089, Raleigh NC 27619
Mng. Director: Reginald L. Lester
Members: 46 *Staff:* 2-5
Annual Budget: $100-250,000 *Tel:* (919) 848-4920
Hist. Note: Membership consists of tobacco growers' organizations and other leaf groups and not individual farmers. Represents the nation's tobacco growers on public policy issues, including creating better public understanding of economic contribution of tobacco, the smoking and health controversy, punitive legislation and taxation of tobacco.
Publication:
Newsletter. q.
Annual Meetings: Usually in Raleigh, NC in Oct.

Tobacco Institute (1958)
1875 Eye St., N.W., Suite 800, Washington DC 20006
President: Samuel D. Chilcote, Jr.
Members: 11-15 companies *Staff:* 100
Annual Budget: over $5,000,000 *Tel:* (202) 457-4800
Hist. Note: Created in 1958 by a group of cigarette manufacturers to foster public understanding of the smoking and health controversy and to increase awareness of the historic role of tobacco and its place in the national economy.
Annual Meetings: New York City, in December

Tobacco Merchants Ass'n of the U.S. (1915)
231 Clarksville Road, Princeton NJ 08540
Exec. Director: Farrell Delman
Members: Not divulged *Staff:* 12
Annual Budget: $500-1,000,000 *Tel:* (609) 275-4900
Hist. Note: Non-lobbying think-tank supported by all sectors of the tobacco industry, financial companies, suppliers, and foreign-based companies. Organized to provide one-stop shopping on all tobacco industry information. Membership: $450/yr.
Publications:
Bits. bi-w.
International Executive Summary. w.
Issues Monitor. m.
Leaf Bulletin. w.
Legislative Bulletin. w.
Tobacco Barometers(2 parts). m & q.
Tobacco Trade Barometers(Import/Export)(6 parts). m.
Tobacco Update. q.
Executive Summary. w.
Special Reports. bi-m.
Annual Meetings: New York City, in Spring.

Tobacconists' Ass'n of America
Hist. Note: Dissolved in 1986.

Tool and Stainless Steel Industry Committee (1962)
Hist. Note: Became the Specialty Steel Industry of the United States in 1983.

Tooling Component Manufacturers Ass'n (1958)
5772 Garden Grove Blvd., Suite 236, Westminster CA 92683
Exec. Secretary: Ray Fuhrer
Members: 10 companies
Annual Budget: under $10,000 *Tel:* (714) 897-9590
Hist. Note: Founded as the National Institute of Jig and Fixture Component Manufacturers and incorporated in Michigan, it assumed its present name in 1981. Its members, most of whom are in the Midwest, are united primarily for the purpose of coordinating and standardizing sizes.
Publication:
TCMA Newsletter. m.
Semi-Annual Meetings: February and October

00291 12 05 86 1233

Tourist House Ass'n of America (1975)
Box 355-A, R.D. 2, Greentown PA 18426
Director: Betty R. Rundback
Members: 850 homeowners & 125 B&B Reservation Services
Staff: 2-5
Annual Budget: under $10,000 *Tel:* (717) 857-0856
Hist. Note: Membership: $15/yr.
Publications:
Bed and Breakfast, U.S.A.-A Guide to Guest Houses and Tourist Homes. a.

Towing and Recovery Ass'n of America (1979)
Box 2517, Winter Park FL 32790
Exec. Director: Michael P. McGovern
Members: 1,500 companies *Staff:* 5-7
Annual Budget: $500-1,000,000 *Tel:* (305) 788-6909
Hist. Note: Members are companies operating tow-trucks and automotive recovery equipment. Membership: $75/1st year; $150/year thereafter.
Publications:
National Towing News. m.
TRAA Annual Membership Directory. a.
TRAA REgulatory Report. bi-m.
Annual Meetings: June
1987-Chicago, IL(Hyatt O'Hare)/June 21-28/2,500
1988-Anaheim, CA
1989-Nashville, Louisville or Charlotte
1990-Las Vegas, NV

Toy Manufacturers of America (1916)
200 Fifth Ave., New York NY 10010
President: Douglas Thomson
Members: 250 *Staff:* 15
Annual Budget: $1-2,000,000 *Tel:* (212) 675-1141
Hist. Note: Formerly (1966) Toy Manufacturers of the U.S., Inc. Commonly referred to as the Toy Association.

Toy Wholesalers' Ass'n of America (1958)
66 East Main St., Moorestown NJ 08057
Exec. Director: William L. MacMillan, III
Members: 125 companies *Staff:* 2-5
Annual Budget: $50-100,000 *Tel:* (609) 234-9155
Hist. Note: Formerly National Toy Wholesalers Association.

Track and Field Ass'n/United States of America (1979)
Hist. Note: The result of merger between the United States Track and Field Federation (founded in 1962) and the United States Track Coaches Association (founded in 1933). Reported as defunct in 1983.

Trade Relations Council of the U.S. (1885)
1001 Connecticut Ave., N.W., Washington DC 20036
Exec. Secretary: Eugene L. Stewart
Members: 35-40 companies & associations *Staff:* 2-5
Annual Budget: $25-50,000 *Tel:* (202) 785-4185
Hist. Note: A non-profit research organization established as the American Tariff League. Assumed its present name in 1959. Concentrates on collecting statistics on trade and industry as they affect foreign economic policy. The above address is the law firm of Eugene L. Stewart.

Trade Show Bureau (1977)
8 Beach Road, Box 797, East Orleans MA 02643
President: William W. Mee
Members: 14 associations *Staff:* 2-5
Annual Budget: $100-250,000 *Tel:* (617) 240-0177
Hist. Note: Member ass'ns are the American Hotel and Motel Ass'n, American Soc. of Ass'n Executives, Exhibit Designers and Producers Ass'n, Exposition Service Contractors Ass'n, Internat'l Ass'n of Auditorium Managers, Internat'l Ass'n of Convention and Visitors Bureaus, Internat'l Ass'n of Fairs and Expositions, Nat'l Ass'n of Exposition Managers, Health Care Exhibitors Ass'n, Hotel Sales and Marketing Management, Internat'l Exhibitor's Ass'n, Professional Convention Management Ass'n, Canadian Ass'n of Exposition Managers, Meeting Planners Internat'l, and Nat'l Ass'n of Exposition Managers. The Exhibition Validatin Concil is a subsidiary of the TSB. Formed to act as a unified voice for the trade show industry in the areas of public relations and government affairs.

Trade Show Services Ass'n (1984)
17100 Norwalk Blvd. #116, Cerritos CA 90701-2750
Exec. Director: Anne H. Weber
Members: 40 companies *Staff:* 1
Annual Budget: $10-25,000 *Tel:* (213) 402-0531
Hist. Note: Members are companies which are actively involved in the erection, dismantling, and transportation of trade show exhibits. Membership: $500/yr.
Publication:
Newsletter. q.
Annual Meetings: August

Trademark Soc. (1963)
Box 2631, Eads Station, Arlington VA 22202
President: Craig Taylor
Members: 85
Annual Budget: under $10,000 *Tel:* (703) 557-2937
Hist. Note: Independent labor union of Patent Office Trademark examiners. All members are attorneys. Has no headquarters or paid staff; officers change annually.

Trading Stamp Institute of America (1957)
Hist. Note: Became TSIA Inc., the Association of Retail Marketing Services in 1982.

Traffic Audit Bureau (1933)
114 East 32nd St., New York NY 10016
President: Ken Sammon
Members: 400-450 *Staff:* 6-10
Annual Budget: $250-500,000 *Tel:* (212) 213-9640
Hist. Note: Audits the circulation of the outdoor advertising media--the organized poster medium and the standard rotating painted bulletin medium and establishes the standards for the measurement of the circulation of the outdoor advertising media.
Publications:
Circulation Values of Outdoor Advertising. q.
TAB Newsletter. m.
Research & Data Bulletins. irreg.
Annual Meetings: Late Winter

Trailer Hitch Manufacturers Ass'n (1967)
1050 Connecticut Ave., N.W., Washington DC 20036
Exec. Secretary and Counsel: Lawrence F. Henneberger
Members: 6 companies *Staff:* 1
Annual Budget: $10-25,000 *Tel:* (202) 857-6087
Hist. Note: A trade group of makers of trailer hitchers, couplers and tow bars united to monitor federal and state legislative and regulatory activity affecting their products. The above address is the law firm of Arent, Fox, Kintner, Plotkin and Kahn.

Training Media Distributors Ass'n (1978)
25605 Cielo Court, Valencia CA 91355
Exec. Director: Paul Kledzik
Members: 55-65 companies *Staff:* 1
Annual Budget: $50-100,000 *Tel:* (805) 254-7224
Hist. Note: Members are concerned with preventing unauthorized copying of training media, especially films, videotapes and printed media.
Publication:
The Monthly. m.
Annual Meetings: Spring
1987-Atlanta, GA/June

Trans-Atlantic American Flag Liner Operations (1985)
90 West St., Suite 1307, New York NY 10006
Chairman: David B. Letteney
Members: 4 steamship companies *Staff:* 2-5
Annual Budget: $50-100,000 *Tel:* (212) 513-0600
Hist. Note: Major purpose is publication of ocean freight rates on movements of military goods.

Transit Advertising Ass'n (1942)
1025 Thomas Jefferson St., N.W., Suite 502, Washington DC 20007
President: Jon L. Boisclair
Members: 12 *Staff:* 4
Annual Budget: $100-250,000 *Tel:* (202) 333-8540
Hist. Note: Formed as Transit Advertising Ass'n ; became (1942-61) Nat'l Ass'n of Transportation Advertising; and (1961-63) Nat'l Ass'n of Transit Advertising. Members sell advertising in the facilities of public transit companies.

Transmission Products Ass'n (1983)
25 North Broadway, Tarrytown NY 10591
Secretary: Richard C. Byrne
Members: 25 companies *Staff:* 2-4
Annual Budget: $10-25,000 *Tel:* (914) 332-0040
Hist. Note: Formerly (1984) the Institute of Transmission Parts Repackagers. Purpose is to promote use of industry products and to encourage expansion in general automotive usage of the industry's products.
Annual Meetings: Spring

Transplantation Soc. (U.S. Section) (1966)
New England Deaconess Hospital, 185 Pilgrim Road, Boston MA 02215
Secretary: Mary L. Wood
Members: 1,400-1,500 *Staff:* 2-5
Annual Budget: $250-500,000 *Tel:* (617) 732-8547
Hist. Note: An international society of scientists dealing with all aspects of transplantation of organs and tissues.
Publications:
Transplantation. m. adv.
Transplantation Proceedings. q. adv.
Biennial meetings: Even years
1988-Sydney, Australia/1,200

Transport Workers Union of America (1934)
80 West End Ave., New York NY 10023
Internat'l President: John E. Lawe
Members: 130,000 *Staff:* 50-60
Annual Budget: over $5,000,000 *Tel:* (212) 873-6000
Hist. Note: Organized in April, 1934 in New York City as the Transport Workers Union. Chartered by the Congress of Industrial Organizations under its present title in 1937. Sponsors and supports the Transport Workers Union Political Contribution Committee.
Publication:
T. W. U. Express. m.
International Convention: Every 4 years in Fall (1989).

Transportation Ass'n of America (1935)
Hist. Note: Representatives of all segments of the transportation industry united to oppose government ownership in any form. Dissolved in 1983.

Transportation Brokers Conference of America (1979)
14508 John Humphrey Dr., Orland Park IL 60462
Exec. Director: Charles M. Naylor
Members: 1,225 *Staff:* 7
Annual Budget: $500-1,000,000 *Tel:* (312) 460-0010
Hist. Note: Established as the Property Brokers Association of America, it assumed its present name in 1981. Members are individuals working with truckers, carriers and shippers to arrange the transport of general freight. Membership: $250/yr.
Publication:
The Professional Broker. m. adv.
Annual Meetings: Spring
1987-Chicago, IL(Hilton Hotel & Towers)/April 8-10/700

Transportation Institute (1968)
5201 Auth Way, Camp Springs MD 20746
Exec. Director: Peter J. Luciano
Members: 170 companies *Staff:* 25-30
Annual Budget: $1-2,000,000 *Tel:* (301) 423-3335
Hist. Note: Members are U.S.-flag shipping, towing and dredging companies. Is concerned with maintaining the strength of U.S. water-borne commerce.
Publication:
Currents. m.

Transportation Lawyers Ass'n (1937)
3310 Harrison, Topeka KS 66611
Exec. Director: William J. Birch
Members: 450-500 individuals
Annual Budget: $100-250,000 *Tel:* (913) 266-7013
Hist. Note: Founded in Louisville, KY as the Motor Carrier Lawyers Ass'n (MCLA), assumed its present name in 1983. Originally an international bar association for lawyers representing motor carriers before the Interstate Commerce Commission and Canadian regulatory agencies, membership is now open to attorneys representing any interstate, foreign or intrastate "transportation interest."
Publications:
Transportation Law Journal. semi-a.
Your Letter of The Law. 5/yr.
Annual Meetings: Spring

Transportation Research Forum (1961)
1133 15th St., N.W., Suite 1000, Washington DC 20005
Exec. Director: Joan Walsh Cassedy
Members: 700 individuals *Staff:* 1
Annual Budget: $50-100,000 *Tel:* (202) 293-5910
Hist. Note: An independent organization of transportation professionals, TRF's purpose is to provide an impartial meeting ground for carriers, shippers, government officials, consultants, university researchers, suppliers, and others seeking an exchange of information related to both passenger and freight transportation. Membership: $50/yr.
Publications:
Proceedings of Annual Meeting. a.
Newsletter. q.
Directory of Members.
Annual Meetings: Fall
1987-San Antonio, TX(Four Seasons)/Nov. 16-18/250

Transportation Safety Equipment Institute (1962)
300 Sylvan Ave., Box 1638, Englewood Cliffs NJ 07632-0638
Exec. Secretary: Howard L. Cook
Members: 28 companies *Staff:* 2-5
Annual Budget: $50-100,000 *Tel:* (201) -
Hist. Note: Formerly (1986) the Truck Safety Equipment Institute. Manufacturers of lighting, mirrors and emergency-vehicle products, reflectors and other devices related to motor vehicle safety.
Publication:
TSEI Reports. irreg.
Annual Meetings: October
1987-Tucson, AZ(Sheraton)/Oct. 21-25
1988-Captiva Island, FL(South Seas Plantation)/Oct. 19-23
1989-Napa, CA(Silverado)/Oct. 18-22

Transworld Advertising Agency Network (1936)
5200 DTC Parkway, Suite 400, Englewood CO 80111
President: Jay Tallant
Members: 25-30 *Staff:* 2-5
Annual Budget: $100-250,000 *Tel:* (303) 771-0960
Hist. Note: A group of medium-sized, cooperating, non-competitive advertising agen Established as the Transamerica Advertising Agency Network, it assumed its present name in 1975. The association is a group of medium-sized, cooperating, and non-competitive advertising agencies.
Publication:
TAAN-A-GRAM. m.
Semi-annual Meetings:
1987-Palm Springs, CA(Rancho Las Palmas)/Feb. 11-15
1987-Hong Kong(Regency)/June 27-July 2
1988-Las Vegas, NV(Desert Inn)/Feb.
1988-White Sulpher Springs, WV(Greenbrier)/June

Travel Agents Computer Soc. (1980)
238 Main St., Suite 302, Cambridge MA 02142
Exec. Director: Joan V. Halter
Members: 321 agencies *Staff:* 5
Annual Budget: $100-250,000 *Tel:* (617) 491-6001

00292 12 05 86 1233

Hist. Note: Industry association specifically dedicated to the advancment and betterment of automation within the travel industry. Membership: $250/yr.
Publication:
TACOS Update. bi-m.
Annual Meetings: Annual Trade Show
1987-New Orleans,LA(Hyatt)/Dec. 2-5/500
1988-San Francisco, CA(Hyatt)/Dec. 2-5

Travel and Tourism Research Ass'n (1970)
Box 8066, Foothill Sta., Salt Lake City UT 84108
Exec. Director: Mari Lou Wood
Members: 750 companies, universities, gov't agencies *Staff:* 1
Annual Budget: $100-250,000 *Tel:* (801) 581-3351
Hist. Note: Established as the Travel Research Association as the result of a merger of the Eastern and Western Councils for Travel Research on January 1, 1970. The present name was adopted in 1980. Membership: $130-225/yr.
Publications:
Journal of Travel Research. q. adv.
Proceedings of Annual Conference. a.
Travel Trends in the U.S. and Canada. tri. a.
Directory of Travel Research Suppliers. bi-a.
Directory of Members. a.
TTRA Members Newsletter. 5/yr.
Annual Meetings: June/350-400
1987-Seattle, WA(Westin)/June 9-12
1988-Montreal,Quebec(Sheraton)/June
1989-Oahu, HI/June
1990-New Orleans, LA(Fairmont)/June 10-14

Travel Industry Ass'n of America (1969)
1899 L St., N.W., Suite 600, Washington DC 20036
President: William D. Toohey
Members: 1,700 *Staff:* 20-25
Annual Budget: $2-5,000,000 *Tel:* (202) 293-1433
Hist. Note: The result of a merger of Discover America (founded in 1965) and the National Association of Travel Organizations (founded in 1941). Members are organizations such as hotels, airlines, travel agencies, etc. interested in promoting increased travel to and within the United States. Formerly (until 1980) known as Discover America Travel Organizations. National Councils: Area and Regional Travel Organizations, State Travel Directors, Travel Attractions, and Urban Tourism Organizations.
Publication:
News Line. m.
Annual Meetings: Fall

Travel Journalists Guild (1980)
Box 2498, Grand Central Station, New York NY 10163
Exec. Secretary: Olga Barbi
Members: 75
Tel: (212) 255-0893
Hist. Note: Established in Antigua, Guatemala in 1980, TJG members are freelance authors, photographers, artists, lecturers, feil makers, etc. specializing in travel with a minimum of three years experience. Membership: $100/year (individual) plus $25 initial fee.
Publication:
Travelwriter Marketletter. m.

Tree-Ring Soc. (1934)
University of Arizona, Laboratory of Tree-Ring Research, Tucson AZ 85721
Secretary: Dr. Jeffrey S. Dean
Members: 300-325 individuals and institutions *Staff:* 1
Annual Budget: under $10,000 *Tel:* (602) 621-2320
Hist. Note: Membership consists of those interested in dendrochronology, the science of determining dates by matching tree-rings for archaeological, hydrological or climatological purposes. Has no paid staff. Membership: $15/yr.
Publication:
Tree-Ring Bulletin. a.

Triological Soc.
Hist. Note: Abbreviated name for the American Laryngological, Rhinological and Otological Society.

Trophy Dealers and Manufacturers Ass'n (1980)
4644 West Jennifer St., Suite 101, Fresno CA 93722
Exec. Director: Don L. Neer
Members: 3,100 companies *Staff:* 12
Annual Budget: $1-2,000,000 *Tel:* (209) 275-5100
Hist. Note: Began in San Francisco, CA in 1966 as Bay Area Trophy Dealers; incorporated in California in 1967 as Trophy Dealers of Northern California; eventually expanded its membership to become the Trophy Dealers of America, Inc. This group merged in 1980 with the American Awards Manufacturers Ass'n (founded in 1976) and assumed its present name, Trophy Dealers and Manufacturers Ass'n, Inc. Membership: $75/yr. (Retail Dealer); $325/yr. (manufacturing supplier)
Publication:
The Trophy Dealer. m. adv.
Trade Exhibits: Seven Regional Exhibits each year

Truck and Heavy Equipment Claims Council (1961)
10054 Willdan, St. Louis MO 63123
Nat'l Corresp. Secretary: June Crawford
Members: 40-50 *Staff:* 1
Annual Budget: under $10,000 *Tel:* (314) 638-8424
Hist. Note: Established Oct. 3, 1961, in Chicago, to consider common problems of the members in the handling of insurance claims in trucks and heavy equipment.
Semi-annual meetings: October and May/250
1987-Oklahoma City, OK/May
1987-Pittsburg, PA(Hilton)/Oct. 3-5
1988-Fresno, CA/May
1988-Shreveport, LA/Oct. 1-3

Truck Body and Equipment Ass'n (1947)
Hist. Note: Address unknown in 1987.

Truck-frame and Axle Repair Ass'n (1966)
915 East 99th St., Brooklyn NY 11236-4011
Exec. Administrator: Silvie Licitra
Members: 74 chassis frame and axle shops *Staff:* 1
Annual Budget: $25-50,000 *Tel:* (718) 257-6133
Hist. Note: Founded in Louisville, Kentucky on May 16, 1966 by 13 frame and axle repair shops. Membership is open to all companies which have been in business for two years repairing heavy-duty trucks, tractors and trailers and straightening their frames, axles and housings, as well as aligning and balancing their wheels.
Publications:
TARA Newsletter. m.
TYE News. bi-m.
Annual Meetings: Tri-Annual
1987-San Diego, CA/Feb. 15-17
1987-Williamsport, PA/May 10-12
1987-Lake Tahoe, CA/Sept. 24-28

Truck Mixer Manufacturers Bureau (1944)
900 Spring St., Silver Spring MD 20910
Secretary: Terrence J. Keenan
Members: 9 companies *Staff:* 2-5
Annual Budget: $50-100,000 *Tel:* (301) 587-1400
Publication:
Truck Mixer & Agitator Standards. irreg.
Annual Meetings: Always in Litchfield Park, AZ at The Wigwam.

Truck Renting and Leasing Ass'n (1978)
2011 Eye St., N.W., 5th Floor, Washington DC 20006
Exec. Director: Beverley F. Walker
Members: 200 *Staff:* 6-10
Annual Budget: $250-500,000 *Tel:* (202) 775-4859
Hist. Note: Became separate organization on the dissolution in 1978 of the Car and Truck Renting and Leasing Ass'n.
Publications:
TRALA Legislative Report.
TRALA News Digest.
Membership Directory. a. adv.
Survey and Analysis of Truck Renting and Leasing Industry. bien.
Annual Meetings: Winter/400
1987-Las Vegas, NV(Caesar's Palace)/Feb.

Truck Safety Equipment Institute
Hist. Note: Became the Transportation Safety Equipment Institute in 1986.

Truck Trailer Manufacturers Ass'n (1941)
1020 Princess St., Alexandria VA 22314
President: Charles J. Calvin
Members: 200 *Staff:* 6-10
Annual Budget: $500-1,000,000 *Tel:* (703) 549-3010
Hist. Note: Represents the manufacturers of truck trailers and intermodal containers; members are responsible for the manufacture of over 90% of the commercial trailers produced in the U.S.
Publication:
TTMA Bulletin. w.
Annual Meetings: Spring/500
1987-Tucson, AZ(Westin La Paloma)/April 10-15/500

Trucking Management (1963)
2233 Wisconsin Ave., N.W., Suite 412, Washington DC 20007
President: Arthur H. Bunte, Jr.
Members: 47 motor common carriers of general freight *Staff:* 3
Annual Budget: $250-500,000 *Tel:* (202) 965-7660
Hist. Note: The main collective bargaining arm of the trucking industry. Represents about 47 firms with about 100,000 employees. Formerly (until 1978) Trucking Employers, Inc.
Annual Meetings: Chicago

Truss Plate Institute (1961)
583 D'Onofrio Drive, Suite 200, Madison WI 53719
Managing Director: Charles B. Goehring
Members: 250 companies *Staff:* 2
Annual Budget: $250-500,000 *Tel:* (608) 833-5900
Hist. Note: Trade association of truss plate manufacturers, allied suppliers and truss manufacturers. Incorporated in Florida.
Annual Meetings: Fall/800

TSIA, Inc., The Ass'n of Retail Marketing Services
Hist. Note: Became the Ass'n of Retail Marketing Services in 1983.

Tube Council of North America (1957)
740 Broadway, Suite 903, New York NY 10003
Exec. Secretary: Ted Klein
Members: 11-15 companies *Staff:* 2-5
Annual Budget: $25-50,000 *Tel:* (212) 477-9007
Hist. Note: Established as the Collapsible Metal Tube Association, it became the Metal Tube Packaging Council of North America in 1966 and assumed its present name in 1983.
Publication:
Tube Topics. q.
Annual Meetings: Spring

Tubular Exchanger Manufacturers Ass'n (1939)
25 North Broadway, Tarrytown NY 10591
Secretary: Richard C. Byrne
Members: 28 companies *Staff:* 5-7
Annual Budget: $25-50,000 *Tel:* (914) 332-0040
Hist. Note: Sets standards for the industry, known as TEMA Standards, which are sold to the chemical processing and petroleum refining industries.

Tubular Finishers and Processors Ass'n (1983)
1429 Murray Bay, Houston TX 77080
Exec. Director: R.S. Bennett
Members: 100 companies *Staff:* 2
Annual Budget: $25-50,000 *Tel:* (713) 467-7974
Hist. Note: Established and incorporated in Texas in 1983. Membership: company $300/year, additional company employees $100/year.
Annual Meetings: October

Tubular Rivet and Machine Institute (1937)
25 North Broadway, Tarrytown NY 10591
Secretary: Richard C. Byrne
Members: 11 companies *Staff:* 2-5
Annual Budget: $50-100,000 *Tel:* (914) 332-0040
Hist. Note: Formerly Tubular and Split Rivet Council. The Institute's Technical Council has developed metric and inch engineering standards as well as safety standards for the use of rivet setting machines.

Tuna Research Foundation (1916)
1101 17th St., N.W., Suite 910, Washington DC 20036
V. President: Randi P. Thomas
Members: 5 companies *Staff:* 2-5
Annual Budget: $100-250,000 *Tel:* (202) 296-4630
Hist. Note: The trade association of U.S. tuna canners. Organized in 1916 as the Southern California Fish Canners Ass'n. Reorganized in 1932 as the California Fish Canners Ass'n-Division, Tuna Research Foundation. Became (1964) the Tuna Research Foundation, Inc.
Annual Meetings:
1987-Chicago, IL

Tune-up Manufacturers Institute (1954)
222 Cedar Lane, Teaneck NJ 07666
Exec. Manager: Ralph W. Van Demark
Members: 17 companies *Staff:* 2
Annual Budget: $25-50,000 *Tel:* (201) 836-9500
Hist. Note: Founded as the Ignition Manufacturers Institute, it assumed its present name in 1981.

Typographers Internat'l Ass'n (1920)
2262 Hall Pl., N.W., Suite 101, Washington DC 20007
Exec. Director: Charles W. Mulliken
Members: 500-600 *Staff:* 2-5
Annual Budget: $500-1,000,000 *Tel:* (202) 965-3400
Hist. Note: Formerly (1980) the Internat'l Typographic Composition Ass'n. Members are management level executives of commercial typesetters.
Publications:
The Typographer. m. adv.
Typographic "i" (external). q.
Annual Meetings: Fall/2-250
1987-San Francisco, CA(Fairmont)/Oct. 5-12
1988-San Destin, FL/Oct.
1989-Vancouver, BC/Oct.
1990-Boston, MA

Ultrasonic Industry Ass'n (1956)
P.O. Box 5126, Old Bridge NJ 08857
Exec. Director: Bette Katz
Members: 20 companies *Staff:* 2-5
Annual Budget: under $10,000
Hist. Note: Formed by a merger of the Ultrasonic Manufacturers Association (formed in 1956) and the Ultrasonic Industry Council (formed in 1970). Membership: $75/yr.(individual); $400/yr.(organization)

UNDA-USA (1972)
850 Sligo Ave., Suite 602, Silver Spring MD 20910
President: Maury R. Sheridan
Members: 450 *Staff:* 2-5
Annual Budget: $500-1,000,000 *Tel:* (301) 588-0655
Hist. Note: Also known as the Nat'l Catholic Ass'n of Communications, it is the U.S. arm of UNDA, the international association of Catholic broadcasters. Absorbed the Catholic Broadcasters Ass'n (1948). Membership: $120/yr.
Publication:
UNDA-USA Newsletter.

Undergarment Accessories Ass'n
Hist. Note: Dissolved in 1986.

00293 12 05 86 1233

Underground Contractors Association (1957)
8550 West Bryn Mawr Ave., Chicago IL 60631
Exec. V. President: Gary L. Dowty
Members: 100 companies *Staff:* 2-5
Annual Budget: $100-250,000 *Tel:* (312) 693-6930
Hist. Note: Membership principally in the Midwest at present.
Publication:
Underground Contractors Newsletter. m.
Annual Meetings: Spring

Underground Equipment Council
Hist. Note: A division of the Farm and Industrial Equipment Institute.

Undersea and Hyperbaric Medical Soc. (1967)
9650 Rockville Pike, Bethesda MD 20814
Exec. Director: Dr. Leon J. Greenbaum, Jr.
Members: 2,500 *Staff:* 10-14
Annual Budget: $250-500,000 *Tel:* (301) 530-9225
Hist. Note: Formerly (1986) Undersea Medical Soc. Membership: $75/yr. (individual); $500/yr. (organization).
Publications:
Undersea Biomedical Research. bi-m.
Pressure. bi-m.
Journal of Hyperbaric Medicine. q.
Underwater Medicine· Abstracts from the Literature. bi-m.
Annual Meetings: Summer
1987-Baltimore, MD(Hyatt Regency)/May 26-30/350
1988-New Orleans, LA(Fairmont)/June 7-10/450

Undersea Medical Soc. (1967)
Hist. Note: Became the Undersea and Hyperbaric Medical Soc. in 1986.

Underwear-Negligee Associates (1935)
16th Floor, 100 East 42nd St., New York NY 10017
Exec. Director and Counsel: Jeffrey A. Russ
Members: 120 individuals *Staff:* 1
Tel: (212) 867-5720
Hist. Note: Formed by a merger of the Lingerie Salesmen Association and the Underwear Salesmen Association. Has no headquarters or staff. The above address is the law firm of Solomon & Rosenbaum, Drechsler & Leff. Most of the active members are concentrated in the New York area.

Uniform Boiler and Pressure Vessel Laws Soc. (1915)
2838 Long Beach Rd., Box 512, Oceanside NY 11572
Chairman: William J. Stuber
Members: 200-250 *Staff:* 2-5
Annual Budget: $50-100,000 *Tel:* (516) 536-5485
Hist. Note: Formerly American Uniform Boiler Law Society. Established to promote uniformity in rules, laws and regulations for boiler and pressure vessel safety based on the requirements of the American Society of Mechanical Engineers Boiler and Pressure Vessel Code and other related American and Canadian national standards.
Publications:
Bulletin. m.
Data Sheet. a.
'Synopsis of Boiler & Pressure Vessel Laws, Rules and Regulations by
States, Cities, Counties and Canadian Provinces' with Revisions. q.

Uniformed Services Academy of Family Physicians (1973)
P.O. Box 11083, 2315 Westwood Ave., Richmond VA 23230
Exec. Director: John A. Hinckley
Members: 1,652 *Staff:* 2-5
Annual Budget: $50-100,000 *Tel:* (804) 358-3950
Hist. Note: Family physicians in the armed services. Affiliated with the American Academy of Family Physicians.
Publication:
Newsletter. q.
Annual Meetings: Spring/400
1987-Orlando, FL(Hyatt)/May 3-7
1988-Salt Lake City, UT(Westin Hotel Utah)/March 27-April 1

Union for Radical Political Economics (1968)
155 West 23rd St., 12th Fl., New York NY 10011
Administrator: Michael P. Jacobs
Members: 2,000 *Staff:* 2
Annual Budget: $100-250,000 *Tel:* (212) 691-5722
Hist. Note: An interdisciplinary association devoted to the study, development, and application of political economic analysis to social problems. A member of the Allied Social Science Ass'ns. Membership: $20/yr. ($40/yr. with subscription).
Publications:
Review of Radical Political Economics. q.
URPE Newsletter. q.
Semi-annual Meetings: Summer Conference in August and with Allied
Social Science Ass'ns in December

Union of American Hebrew Congregations (1873)
838 Fifth Ave., New York NY 10021
President: Rabbi Alexander M. Schindler
Members: 800 congregations *Staff:* 240
Annual Budget: over $5,000,000 *Tel:* (212) 249-0100
Hist. Note: Has a budget of approximately $13 million.
Publications:
Reform Judaism. q. adv.
Keeping Posted. bi-m.
Reform Judaism. q.
Biennial Meetings: uneven years
1987-Chicago, IL(Hyatt)/Oct. 29-Nov. 3/2,500
1989-New Orleans, LA/Nov. 2-7/2,500

Union of American Physicians and Dentists (1972)
1730 Franklin St., Suite 200, Oakland CA 94612
Exec. Administrator: Gary Robinson
Members: 25,000 *Staff:* 20
Annual Budget: $1-2,000,000 *Tel:* (415) 839-0193
Hist. Note: A labor union representing physicians and dentists in fourteen states who bargain with government entities, hospitals and employers. Membership: $360/yr.
Publication:
UAPD Leadership News. m.
Triennial meetings: 1988

Union of Independent Colleges of Art (1966)
Hist. Note: Became the Alliance of Independent Colleges of Art in 1982.

Union of Journeymen Horseshoers of the United States
Hist. Note: No paid staff; address unknown in 1986.
Publication:
UJH Newsletter. a.
Annual Meetings: Every three years (1983)

United Allied Workers Internat'l Union (1957)
Box 723, Hammond IN 46320
President: Norma J. Baggett
Members: 320 *Staff:* 1
Annual Budget: under $10,000 *Tel:* (219) 932-9400
Hist. Note: Independent labor union
Publication:
News and Views. semi-a.
Quadrennial Meetings: 1990

United Ass'n of Journeymen and Apprentices of the Plumbing and Pipe Fitting Industry of the U.S. and Canada (1889)
901 Massachusetts Ave., N. W., Washington DC 20001
President: Marvin J. Boede
Members: 325,000-350,000 *Staff:* 125-150
Annual Budget: over $5,000,000 *Tel:* (202) 628-5823
Hist. Note: Organized in Washington, DC October 7, 1889 as the United Association of Journeymen, Plumbers, Gas Fitters, Steam Fitters and Steam Fitters Helpers of the United States and Canada. Affiliated with the American Federation of Labor in 1897 and adopted its present name in 1947. Has a budget of about $23 million. Sponsors and supports the U. A. Political Education Committee.
Publications:
General Officers Report. w.
U. A. Journal. m.
Annual Meetings: Every 5 years in Summer (1991)

United Automobile, Aerospace and Agricultural Implement Workers of America (1935)
8000 East Jefferson Ave., Detroit MI 48214
President: Owen F. Bieber
Members: 1,200,000 *Staff:* 800
Annual Budget: over $5,000,000 *Tel:* (313) 926-5000
Hist. Note: Chartered by the American Federation of Labor August 26, 1935 in Detroit under the name, United Automobile Workers of America. Joined the Congress of Industrial Organizations in 1938 and became independent (after the formation of AFL-CIO) in 1968 and affiliated with the AFL-CIO in 1981. Has a budget of about $217 million.
Publications:
Ammo. m.
Skill. q.
Solidarity. m.
Triennial Meeting: 1989

United Better Dress Manufacturers Ass'n (1939)
110 West 40th St., New York NY 10018
Members: 150 *Staff:* 2-5
Tel: (212) 354-7042
Hist. Note: Smaller manufacturers of quality dresses, mainly in the New York area. Major purpose is labor negotiating with the International Ladies Garment Workers Union.

United Brotherhood of Carpenters and Joiners of America (1881)
101 Constitution Ave., N. W., Washington DC 20001
President: Patrick Campbell
Members: 750-775,000 *Staff:* 125-150
Annual Budget: over $5,000,000 *Tel:* (202) 546-6206
Hist. Note: Established August 8, 1881 in Chicago as the Brotherhood of Carpenters and Joiners. Merged in 1888 with the United Order of Carpenters to form the present organization. Absorbed the Wood, Wire and Metal Lathers International Union in 1979. A charter member of the American Federation of Labor, the Brotherhood today has a budget of about $40 million.
Publication:
The Carpenter. m. adv.
Annual Meetings: Every 5 years (1991)

United Bus Owners of America (1971)
1275 K Street, N.W., Suite 800, Washington DC 20005
Exec. Director: Wayne J. Smith
Members: 2200 companies *Staff:* 4
Annual Budget: $250-500,000 *Tel:* (202) 484-5623
Hist. Note: UBOA serves the intercity bus industry, with particular emphasis on group travel and tourism.
Publication:
The Docket. m.
Annual Meetings: Spring

United Cancer Council (1963)
650 E. Carmel Drive, Suite 340, Carmel IN 46032
Exec. Director: Randall Grove
Members: 36 agencies *Staff:* 6
Annual Budget: $500-1,000,000 *Tel:* (317) 844-6627
Hist. Note: A federation of independent local cancer agencies across the country that receive financial support from United Way, the Council's mission is to promote, encourage and assist in programs of: service to cancer patients; public and professional education with regard to cancer; and research. Membership: $250/yr.
Publication:
Coordinator. q.
Annual Meetings: Spring
1987-Atlanta, GA(Omni)/June 10-14/150

United Cement, Lime, Gypsum And Allied Workers Internat'l Union (1939)
Hist. Note: An outgrowth of the National Council of United Cement Workers which had been formed in 1936, the present organization received a charter as an industrial union from the American Federation of Labor in St. Louis on September 12, 1939. Became a division of the Internat'l Brotherhood of Boilermakers, Iron Ship Builders, Blacksmiths, Forgers and Helpers on March 15,1984.
Publication:
Voice of the Cement, Lime Gypsum and Allied Workers. m.
Biennial meetings: Even years

United Choral Conductors Club of America
Hist. Note: Recorded in 1978 as being inactive or defunct.

United Dairy Industry Ass'n (1971)
6300 North River Rd., Rosemont IL 60018
C.E.O.: Edward A. Peterson
Members: 20 regional and state units *Staff:* 107
Annual Budget: over $5,000,000 *Tel:* (312) 696-1860
Hist. Note: The promotional arm of the dairy industry. Develops and coordinates programs of the American Dairy Ass'n, Dairy Research Inc, and the Dairy Council. Manages the Dairy Industry Foundation.
Publications:
Dairy Promotion Review. semi-a.
Pipeline. m.
Media Memo. semi-a.
Annual Meetings: March
1987-Chicago, IL(O'Hare Marriott)/600

United Dance Merchants of America (1958)
701 Beta Drive, Cleveland OH 44143
Secy.-Treas.: Taffy Epstein
Members: 60 *Staff:* 1
Annual Budget: under $10,000 *Tel:* (216) 461-3360
Hist. Note: Members are makers and distributors of dance costumes, dancing shoes, dance music and literature, etc.
Publication:
Update. 3/yr.
Semi-annual meetings: Summer and Winter

United Duroc Swine Registry (1936)
1803 West Detweiller Dr., Peoria IL 61615
Exec. Secretary: Gary E. Huffington
Members: 2,000
Annual Budget: $500-1,000,000 *Tel:* (309) 691-8094
Hist. Note: Breeders and fanciers of Duroc swine. Member of the National Pedigree Livestock Council. Membership: $10/yr.
Publication:
Duroc News. m. adv.
Annual Meetings: Always Peoria, IL, first Saturday in December

United Egg Internat'l
2296 Henderson Mill Road, Suite 401, Atlanta GA 30345
Hist. Note: A Webb-Pomerene Act association.

United Egg Producers (1968)
3951 Snapfinger Parkway, Suite 580, Decatur GA 30035
President: Albert E. Pope
Members: 5 regional co-ops *Staff:* 6-10
Annual Budget: $500-1,000,000 *Tel:* (404) 288-6700
Hist. Note: The largest trade group in the egg industry. Maintains a Washington government liaison office. Sponsors the Egg Political Action Committee.
Publication:
United Voices. bi-w.

United Electrical, Radio and Machine Workers of America (1936)
11 East 51st St., New York NY 10022
President: James M. Kane
Members: 160-170,000 *Staff:* 90-100

00294 12 05 86 1233

Annual Budget: $2-5,000,000 *Tel:* (212) 753-1960
Hist. Note: Established in Buffalo in March, 1936, and chartered by the Congress of Industrial Organizations the same year. Expelled from the CIO in 1949 on the grounds of being Communist dominated, it is now an independent union.
Publication:
UE News. every 3 weeks.
Annual Meetings: September
1987-Boston, MA

United Engineering Trustees (1904)
345 East 47th St., New York NY 10017
Secretary & General Manager (C.E.O.): Alexander D. Korwek
Members: 12 engineering organizations *Staff:* 60-70
Annual Budget: over $5,000,000 *Tel:* (212) 705-7828
Hist. Note: Formerly the United Engineering Society. Founded in New York City in 1904 as the United Engineering Society for the "advancement of the engineering arts and sciences in all their branches and to maintain a free public engineering library." Name changed in 1930 to Engineering Foundation, Inc., and again in 1931 to its present form. Constituent members include Founder (ASCE; AIME; ASME; IEEE; and AIChE) and Associate (IES; EI; WRC; MPC; ABET and SWE) Societies representing a collective membership of 750,000. In addition to ownership and operation of the United Engineering Center, the UET has two departments, the Engineering Foundation which supports engineering research projects and conducts interdisciplinary conferences; and the Engineering Societies Library which is one of the foremost public engineering libraries in existence. In addition, the UET manages the Daniel Guggenheim Medal Board of Award and the John Fritz Medal Board of Award and it also acts as fiscal agent for the Welding Research Council and the Metal Properties Council. Has an annual budget of $7 million.
Annual Meetings: Fourth Thursday in January in New York City (by invitation only).

United Farm Workers of America (1962)
La Paz, Keene CA 93531
President: Cesar E. Chavez
Members: 40,000 *Staff:* 6-200
Annual Budget: $2-5,000,000 *Tel:* (805) 822-5571
Hist. Note: Organized in 1962 by Cesar Chavez as the Nat'l Farm Workers Ass'n. In 1965 the Nat'l Farm Workers Ass'n and the Agricultural Workers Organizing Committee merged to become the United Farm Workers of America affiliated with the AFL-CIO. Sponsors and supports the National United Farm Workers Volunteer Political Action Committee.
Publications:
El Malcriado. m.
Food and Justice. m.
Biennial meetings: even years

United Food and Commercial Workers Internat'l Union (1979)
1775 K St., N. W., Washington DC 20006
Internat'l President: William H. Wynn
Members: 1,300,000 *Staff:* 500-550
Annual Budget: over $5,000,000 *Tel:* (202) 223-3111
Hist. Note: Labor union affiliated with AFL/CIO and the Canadian Labour Congress. Formed by a merger of the Retail Clerks Internat'l Union (founded in 1888), the Amalgamated Meat Cutters and Butcher Workmen of North America (founded in 1897) in 1979. Affiliated Barbers, Beauticians, and Allied Industries Internat'l Ass'n in 1980; United Retail Workers in 1981; Insurance Workers Internat'l Union in 1983; and Canadian Brewery and Distillery Workers in 1986. Has an annual budget of about $60 million. Membership: $70/yr.
Publication:
UFCW Action. bi-m.
Annual Meetings: Every 5 years (1988) in July or August
1988-San Francisco, CA(Fairmont)/July 25-29/4,000

United Food Animal Ass'n
Hist. Note: Reported inactive in 1986.

United Fresh Fruit and Vegetable Ass'n (1938)
727 North Washington St., Alexandria VA 22314
President: Roger J. Stroh
Members: 2,700-2,800 *Staff:* 25-30
Annual Budget: $2-5,000,000 *Tel:* (703) 836-3410
Hist. Note: Merger of Western Fruit Jobbers Ass'n (1904) and American Fruit and Vegetable Shippers Ass'n (1911). Absorbed (1952) Nat'l League of Wholesale Fresh Fruit and Vegetable Distributors. Membership consists of growers, shippers, distributors, dealers and retailers of fresh fruit, vegetables, nuts, plants, flowers and related products. Supports the United Political Action Committee.
Publications:
Outlook. 6/yr. bi-m.
Produce Merchandiser. m.
Spudlight. w.
Supply Letter. m.
United Newswire. w.
Foodservice Newsletter. m.
Annual Meetings: February
1987-Orlando, FL/Feb. 15-18
1988-Houston, TX/Feb. 21-24
1989-San Diego, CA/Feb. 12-15
1990-San Antonio, TX/Feb. 11-14

United Fur Manufacturers Ass'n (1925)
101 West 30th St., New York NY 10001
Manager: Ted Dardaganis
Members: 90-100 companies *Staff:* 2-5
Annual Budget: $50-100,000 *Tel:* (212) 736-5215
Hist. Note: Major purpose is to furnish credit information and conduct labor negotiations. Membership concentrated in a 2-3 block area of New York City.

United Furniture Workers of America
Hist. Note: Merged with IUE on Jan. 1, 1987 and became the Furniture Divison - Internat'l Union of Electronic, Electrical, Technical, Salaried, and Machine Workers.

United Garment Workers of America (1891)
4207 Lebanon Road, Hermitage TN 37076
President: William O'Donnell
Members: 25,000 *Staff:* 30
Annual Budget: $1-2,000,000 *Tel:* (615) 889-9221
Hist. Note: Organized in New York City in April 1891 and chartered by the American Federation of Labor the following month.
Publication:
The Garment Workers. m.
Annual Meetings: Every 5 years (1987)

United Glass and Ceramic Workers of North America
Hist. Note: Organized in 1934 as the Federation of Flat Glass Workers of America and chartered by the American Federation of Labor. Became the Federation of Glass, Ceramic and Silica Sand Workers of America in 1940 and assumed its present name in 1954. Merged on September 1, 1982 with the Aluminum, Brick and Clay Workers International Union to form the Aluminum, Brick and Glass Workers International Union.

United Golfers' Ass'n (1926)
663 E. 105th St., Chicago IL 60628
Nat'l Secretary: Mrs. Louise Simpson
Members: 50-60 clubs, with predominantly black memberships
Staff: 1
Annual Budget: under $10,000 *Tel:* (312) 785-5813
Annual Meetings: March
1987-Chicago, IL

United Hatters, Cap and Millinery Workers Internat'l Union (1901)
Hist. Note: Became the headware division of the Amalgamated Clothing and Textile Workers Union in December, 1983.

United Infants and Childrens Wear Ass'n (1933)
520 Eighth Avenue, New York NY 10018
President: Alan Oubell
Members: 26 *Staff:* 2-5
Annual Budget: $100-250,000 *Tel:* (212) 244-2953
Hist. Note: A member of the Federation of Apparel Manufacturers.
Publication:
Member News Bulletin. m.
Annual Meetings: Not held

United Inventors and Scientists of America (1942)
Hist. Note: Defunct in 1982.

United Knitwear Manufacturers League (1938)
225 West 39th St., New York NY 10018
Gen. Counsel: Arnold R. Harris
Members: 140-150 *Staff:* 2-5
Annual Budget: $25-50,000 *Tel:* (212) 819-1011
Hist. Note: Makers of knitted outergarments such as sweaters and swimming suits. Major purpose is the conduct of labor negotiations. Membership concentrated in the New York area.
Publication:
Bulletin. irreg.
Biennial Meetings:

United Methodist Ass'n of Health and Welfare Ministries (1940)
601 West Riverview Ave., Dayton OH 45406-5543
President: Robert F. Willner
Members: 355 *Staff:* 4
Annual Budget: $250-500,000 *Tel:* (513) 227-9494
Hist. Note: Organized in 1940 as the National Association of Methodist Hospitals a nd Homes. Became the National Association of Health and Welfare Ministries, United Methodist Church in 1969 and assumed its present name in 1983. Membership: $35/yr. (individual), $400-2,000/yr. (institutions, based on budget).
Publications:
Messenger Newsletter. q. adv.
Search. m.
CrossArms. q.
Caring. q.
Annual Meetings: March
1987-New Orleans, LA(Hyatt Regency)/March 14-18/360
1988-San Francisco, CA/Feb. 27-March 2

United Mine Workers of America (1890)
900 15th St., N. W., Washington DC 20005
President: Richard L. Trumka
Members: 240,000 *Staff:* 250
Annual Budget: over $5,000,000 *Tel:* (202) 842-7200
Hist. Note: Formed January 25, 1890, in Columbus, Ohio, by the merger of the Knights of Labor and the National Progressive Union of Miners and Mine Laborers. Chartered as an industrial union by the American Federation of Labor, it remained an AFL affiliate until 1947 when it became independent. Has a budget of about $18 million. Sponsors and supports the Coal Miners Political Committee.
Publication:
UMW Journal. m.
Annual Meetings: Every 4 years (1990)/2,000

United Mortgage Bankers of America
Hist. Note: No paid staff; address unknown in 1986.

United Nations Staff Union (1946)
United Nations, Room 525, New York NY 10017
President: Anna Frangipani Campino
Members: 12,000 individuals *Staff:* 3
Annual Budget: $500-1,000,000 *Tel:* (212) 754-7076
Hist. Note: Open to all staff of the United Nations Secretariat.
Publication:
UN Report. bi-m.

United Neighborhood Centers of America (1911)
1319 F St., N.W., Suite 603, Washington DC 20004
Exec. Director: Jerome C. Stevenson
Members: 150 agencies *Staff:* 10-15
Annual Budget: $250-500,000 *Tel:* (212) 393-3929
Hist. Note: Formerly (1959) Nat'l Federation of Settlement and (1979) Nat'l Federation of Settlements and Neighborhood Centers. United Neighborhood Centers of America was organized in 1911 by Jane Addams and other pioneer leaders of the settlement movement in the United States. The aim of the organization is to improve the quality of life at the neighborhood level.
Publication:
News & Round Table. bi-m.
Annual Meetings: May

United Ostomy Ass'n (1962)
2001 W. Beverly Blvd., Los Angeles CA 90057
Exec. Director: Sharon Underwood
Members: 50,000 individuals; 200 companies *Staff:* 8
Annual Budget: $1-2,000,000 *Tel:* (213) 413-5510
Hist. Note: Incorporated in New York, UOA is a not-for-profit mutual aid organization of individuals who have undergone ostomy surgery, their families, and members of the medical, enterostomal therapy and nursing professions.
Publications:
Ostomy Quarterly. q. adv.
The Phoenix.
Annual Meetings: August
1987-Cleveland, OH(Stouffer's Inn)/Aug. 20-22/1,500
1988-New Orleans, LA
1989-Miami, FL
1990-Las Vegas, NV

United Paperworkers Internat'l Union (1972)
815 16th St., N.W., Washington DC 20006
President: Wayne E. Glenn
Members: 275-300,000 *Staff:* 250
Annual Budget: over $5,000,000 *Tel:* (202) 783-5238
Hist. Note: The United Paperworkers of America (founded in 1944) and the International Brotherhood of Papermakers (founded in 1893) merged March 6, 1957 to form the United Papermakers and Paperworkers. This organization, in turn, merged on August 2, 1972 with the International Brotherhood of Pulp, Sulphite and Paper Mill Workers of the United States and Canada (founded in 1909) to form the present organization-the United Paperworkers International Union, the Canadian members of which formed a separate union in 1974. Has a budget of about $17 million. Sponsors and supports the United Paperworkers International Union Political Action Committee.
Publication:
The Paperworker. m.
Triennial Meetings: (1987)

United Pesticide Formulators and Distributors Ass'n (1968)
P.O. Box 398, Buford GA 30518
Exec. Director: Nancy Chandler
Members: 90-100 *Staff:* 1
Annual Budget: $25-50,000 *Tel:* (404) 945-8261
Hist. Note: Seeks to upgrade the pest control industry by promoting cooperation between customer and supplier and cooperating with government authorities for proper liaison and communication. Membership: $250/yr.
Publication:
Update. bi-m.
Annual Meetings:
1987-San Diego, CA/April 8-10

United Presbyterian Health, Education and Welfare Ass'n (1956)
475 Riverside Drive, Room 1268, New York NY 10155
Exec. Director: Rodney T. Martin
Members: 1,200 *Staff:* 2-5
Annual Budget: $50-100,000 *Tel:* (212) 870-2436
Hist. Note: Formerly (1969) Nat'l Presbyterian Health and Welfare Ass'n. Membership is composed of individuals, governing bodies, churches and organizations.
Publications:
Newsletter. q.
UPHEWA Directory. a.
Biennial Meetings: Uneven years
1987-San Antonio, TX/Jan. 27-Feb. 1

00295 12 05 86 1233

United Professional Horsemen's Ass'n (1968)
181 North Mill St., Lexington KY 40507
Exec. Director: Elizabeth B. Culley
Members: 1,200 *Staff:* 2
Annual Budget: $100-250,000 *Tel:* (606) 252-6888
Hist. Note: Professional horse trainers, owners and breeders. Membership: $35/yr.
Publications:
The UPHA Herald. q. adv.
UPHA Directory. a. adv.
UPHA Marketplace. m. adv.
Annual Meetings: January
1987-Nashville, TN(Opryland)/Jan. 8-10/400

United Professional Softball League (1976)
Hist. Note: Ceased operations in 1983.

United Rubber, Cork, Linoleum and Plastic Workers of America (1935)
87 South High St., URWA Bldg., Akron OH 44308
President: Milan Stone
Members: 115,000 *Staff:* 125-150
Annual Budget: over $5,000,000 *Tel:* (216) 376-6181
Hist. Note: Organized in Akron, Ohio September 12, 1935 as the United Rubber Workers of America and chartered as an industrial union the following year by the Congress of Industrial Organization. Assumed its present name in 1945.
Publication:
United Rubber Worker. bi-m.
Triennial meetings: 1987
1987-Las Vegas, NV(Riviera)/Sept. 27-Oct. 3

United Saw Service Ass'n (1932)
Hist. Note: Became the Food Machinery Service Institute in 1983 and merged into the Meat Industry Supplier Association in 1984.

United Scenic Artists (1918)
575 8th Ave., New York NY 10018
Business Representative: James J. Ryan
Members: 1,800 *Staff:* 12
Annual Budget: $500-1,000,000 *Tel:* (212) 736-4498
Hist. Note: Entertainment industry union. Members are highly skilled scenic artists, set designers, art directors, costume designers, lighting designers, mural artists for broadway, T.V. films, commercial and regional theatre.
Publication:
Newsletter. m.
Monthly Membership Meetings:

United Societies of Physiotherapists (1973)
1036 Olean Road, East Aurora NY 14052
President: Beverly Stewart
Members: 800-1,000
Annual Budget: $10-25,000 *Tel:* (716) 655-0165
Hist. Note: Established by a member of the American Physical Therapy Association who wished to give more emphasis to the interests of the individual practictioner. An umbrella organization for independent state organizations of licensed physiotherapists. Has no paid staff.
Publications:
Bulletin. irreg.
Newsletter. q.
Annual Meetings:
1987-Atlantic City, NJ/March

United Soft Serve and Fast Food Ass'n (1978)
Hist. Note: Address unknown in 1985.

United States Academy of Arms (1947)
Hist. Note: Became the United States Fencing Coaches Ass'n in 1985.

United States Air Racing Ass'n (1939)
Hist. Note: Became the Professional Race Pilots Ass'n in 1984. USARA is now the designation of PRPA's eastern regional affiliate.

United States Air Traffic Controllers Organization (1982)
Hist. Note: Ceased operations in 1984.

United States Animal Health Ass'n (1896)
Box 28176, Richmond VA 23228-0176
Admin. Secretary: Ella R. Blanton
Members: 1,000-1,200 individuals, 15-20 organizations *Staff:* 2-5
Annual Budget: $50-100,000 *Tel:* (804) 266-3275
Hist. Note: Formed in 1896 as the Nat'l Ass'n of State Livestock Sanitary Boards to combat one disease affecting cattle, it became the United States Livestock Sanitary Ass'n in 1911 and assumed its present name in 1968. Absorbed the Nat'l Assembly of Chief Livestock Health Officials in 1973. Seeks to prevent, control and eliminate livestock diseases. Membership: $30/yr. (individual); $200/yr. (organization/company)
Publications:
Newsletter. q.
Proceedings. a.
Foreign Animal Diseases. every 5 yrs.
Annual Meetings: October/900
1987-Salt Lake City, UT(Hotel Utah)/Oct. 28-30
1988-Little Rock, AR(Excelsior)/Oct. 16-21
1989-Las Vegas, NV(Riviera)/Oct. 22-27
1990-Omaha, NE(Howard Johnson's)/Oct. 7-12

United States Aquaculture Council (1977)
Hist. Note: Closely affiliated with the U.S. Aquaculture Federation, its lobbying arm. Inactive in 1984; the chairman has resigned and no successor has been designated.

United States-Arab Chamber of Commerce (1967)
One World Trade Center, Suite 4657, New York NY 10048
Exec. Director: Mhd. Thabet Al-Mahayni
Members: 600 companies *Staff:* 19
Annual Budget: $2-5,000,000 *Tel:* (212) 432-0655
Hist. Note: A service organization chartered in the State of New York. Membership consists of corporations, partnerships, financial institutions, and individuals in those professions whose commercial interests parallel the objectives of the organization. Membership dues vary according to annual sales and assets.
Publications:
U.S.-Arab Chamber Briefs. 26/yr. adv.
Annual Report. a.
Annual Directory. a.
Annual Meetings: April in New York City

United States Armor Ass'n (1885)
Box 607, Fort Knox KY 40121
Nat'l Secy.-Treas.: Major Charles E. Griffiths, USA (Ret.)
Members: 6,000-6,500 *Staff:* 2-5
Annual Budget: $50-100,000 *Tel:* (502) 942-8624
Hist. Note: Formerly U.S. Cavalry Ass'n and U.S. Armored Cavalry Ass'n. Membership composed of former military personnel. Membership: $16/yr.
Publication:
Armor. bi-m.
Annual Meetings: May

United States Army Warrant Officers Ass'n (1974)
Box 2040, Reston VA 22090
Exec. V. President: Don Hess
Members: 4,500 *Staff:* 3
Annual Budget: $50-100,000 *Tel:* (703) 620-3986
Hist. Note: Membership: $36/yr.
Publication:
Newsliner. m. adv.
Annual Meetings: Always in Washington, DC area/October

United States Ass'n of Independent Gymnastic Clubs (1972)
235 Pinehurst Road, Wilmington DE 19803
Exec. Director: Edgar M. Knepper
Members: 640 clubs *Staff:* 2-5
Annual Budget: $50-100,000 *Tel:* (302) 656-3706
Hist. Note: Members are not-for-profit clubs.
Publication:
Journal. q.
Triannual Meetings:
1987-Las Vegas, NV and Cherry Hill, NJ/August
1987-Chicago, IL/Nov.

United States-Austrian Chamber of Commerce (1949)
165 W. 46th St., New York NY 10036
Administrative Secy.: Erika Borozan
Members: 350 companies, 100 individuals *Staff:* 2
Annual Budget: $25-50,000 *Tel:* (212) 819-0117
Publication:
Austrian Business. q. adv.
Annual Meetings: New York, NY, last week in May

United States Basketball Writers Ass'n (1956)
200 N. Broadway, Suite 1905, St. Louis MO 63102
Exec. Officer: Joe Mitch
Members: 1,000 *Staff:* 1
Annual Budget: under $10,000 *Tel:* (314) 421-0339
Publication:
The Tip-Off. 7/yr.
Annual Meetings: In conjunction with finals of NCAA tournament

United States Beet Sugar Ass'n (1911)
1156 15th St., N.W., Washington DC 20005
President: David C. Carter
Members: 11 companies *Staff:* 6-10
Annual Budget: $250-500,000 *Tel:* (202) 296-4820
Hist. Note: Established as the United States Beet Sugar Industry, it became the United States Sugar Manufacturers Ass'n in 1914 and assumed its present name in 1926. Sponsors the Beet Sugar Political Action Committee.
Publication:
American Beet Sugar Companies. a.
Annual Meetings: First week in February

United States Brewers Ass'n (1862)
Hist. Note: Dissolved in 1986, to be succeeded by the Beer Institute.

United States Business and Industrial Council (1933)
220 National Press Bldg., Washington DC 20045
President: Anthony Harrigan
Members: 2,500 companies *Staff:* 10-15
Annual Budget: $500-1,000,000 *Tel:* (202) 662-8744
Hist. Note: Established as the Southern States Industrial Council, it became the United States Industrial Council in 1975 and assumed its present name in 1983. Expresses the "voice of free enterprise from the conservative viewpoint".
Publications:
Bulletin. bi-m.
Washington Business Wire. m.
Syndicated Newspaper Column. w.
Annual Meetings: Fall

United States Cane Sugar Refiners' Ass'n (1936)
1001 Connnecticut Ave., N.W., Washington DC 20036
President: Nicholas Kominus
Members: 6 companies *Staff:* 2-5
Annual Budget: $250-500,000 *Tel:* (202) 331-1458
Annual Meetings: Fall

United States Cigarette Export Ass'n (1982)
120 Park Ave., New York NY 10017
Members: 3 companies
Hist. Note: A Webb-Pomerene Act association.

United States Civil Defense Council
Hist. Note: Became the Nat'l Coordinating Council on Emergency Management in October 1983.

United States Conference of City Health Officers (1961)
Hist. Note: Became the United States Conference of Local Health Officers in 1984.

United States Conference of Local Health Officers (1961)
1620 Eye St., N.W., Washington DC 20006
Exec. Director: John J. Gunther
Members: 300 *Staff:* 2-5
Annual Budget: $10-25,000 *Tel:* (202) 293-7330
Hist. Note: Created by and affiliated with the U.S. Conference of Mayors. Members are commissioners, directors, chief health officers, and other heads of city, county or city-county health agencies. Formerly (1983) the United States Conference of City Health Officers.
Publication:
City Health Officers News. m.
Annual Meetings: In conjunction with the American Public Health Ass'n

United States Conference of Mayors (1932)
1620 Eye St., N.W., Washington DC 20006
Exec. Director: John J. Gunther
Members: 600 *Staff:* 50
Annual Budget: $2-5,000,000 *Tel:* (202) 293-7330
Hist. Note: An organization of city governments. Membership limited to the 880 U.S. cities with more than 30,000 population. Affiliated with the United States Conference of Local Health Officers and the U.S. Conference of Human Service Officers.
Annual Meetings: June/950
1987-Nashville, TN(Hermitage-Hyatt Regency)/June 13-17
1988-Salt Lake City, UT(Marriott-Westin)/June 11-15
1989-Charleston, SC

United States Council for Internat'l Business (1945)
1212 Ave. of the Americas, New York NY 10036
President: Abraham Katz
Members: 300 *Staff:* 35
Annual Budget: $2-5,000,000 *Tel:* (212) 354-4480
Hist. Note: Formerly (1982) United States Council-International Chamber of Commerce. U.S. affiliate of the following international organizations: the Internat'l Chamber of Commerce (ICC), the Internat'l Organization of Employers (IOE) and the Business and Industry Advisory Committee (BIAC) to the Organization for Economic Cooperation and Development (OECD). As the the U.S. representative of each of these associations, the Council assures that their views are those endorsed by the American business community and endeavors to similarly influence U.S. government policy. Also serves as the official issuing and guaranteeing authority for ATA Carnets (customs documents allowing temporary, duty-free import and export of goods destined for eventual export). Maintains a Washington, DC office.
Publications:
ICC Business World, the Magazine of Int'l Trade, Finance, Industry.
Council Newsletter.
IGO Report.
Focus on Issues.
Annual Meetings: Annual Dinner/Fall

United States Council-Internat'l Chamber of Commerce (1919)
Hist. Note: Became the United States Council for International Business in 1982.

00296 12 05 86 1233

ited States Cross Country Coaches Ass'n
)7 State Gyn, Iowa State University, Ames IA 50011
cretary: Bill Bergan
embers: 100-120 *Staff:* 1
nnual Budget: under $10,000 *Tel:* (515) 294-3723
ist. Note: Formerly Nat'l Collegiate Cross Country Coaches Ass'n
iblication:
Quarterly Review. q.
nnual Meetings: With Nat'l College Athletic Ass'n

ted States Durum Growers Ass'n (1957)
RT-T, Box 10, Goodrich ND 58444
cretary: Du Wayne Tessmann
embers: 3,000 wheat growers *Staff:* 2-5
nnual Budget: $10-25,000 *Tel:* (701) 884-2703
ist. Note: Until 1981 known as the Durum Growers Association of the United States.
iblication:
Durum Kernels. m.
nnual Meetings: Always March, at Devil's Lake, ND

ted States Electronic Mail Ass'n (1972)
ist. Note: Formerly (1977) the Facsimile Users Ass'n. Reported defunct in 1983.

ted States Environment and Resources uncil (1970)
st. Note: Inactive in 1984.

ted States Federation for Culture Collections
0)
ept. 47P, Bldg. AP9A, Abbott Laboratories, North Chicago IL 064
cy.-Treas.: Marianna Jackson
embers: 225-250 *Staff:* 1
nnual Budget: under $10,000 *Tel:* (312) 937-8764
st. Note: Members are individuals and organizations concerned with maintaining culture collections and running taxonomic studies on micro-organisms. Membership: $6/yr. (individual); $100/yr. (company).
blication:
Newsletter. q.
mi-annual Meetings: one with the American Soc. for Microbiology
1987-Atlanta, GA/March 3 or 4/50
1987-Baltimore, MD(Hyatt Regency Inner Harbor)/Aug. 14/100

ted States Feed Grains Council (1960)
00 K St., N.W., Suite 1200, Washington DC 20005
esident: Darwin E. Stolte
embers: 100 companies and organizations *Staff:* 90
nnual Budget: $2-5,000,000 *Tel:* (202) 789-0789
st. Note: Motivated by the grain sorghum and corn producer associations, representatives of the agricultural community formed the U.S. Feed Grains Council in 1960 as a non-profit organization which would work under contract with the Foreign Agricultural Service of the U.S. Department of Agriculture to increase dollar sales abroad of U.S. feed grains (corn, sorghum and barley).
blications:
Annual Report. a.
Directory. a.
Feed Grains Focus.
Meeting Program. semi-a.
mi-annual Meetings: March and August
1987-San Antonio, TX(La Mansion del Rio)/March 1-4/350
1987-Asheville, NC(Grove Park Inn)/Aug. 2-5/400

ted States Fencing Coaches Ass'n (1985)
x 274, New York NY 10159
cretary: Richard Gradkowski
embers: 250 individuals *Staff:* 1
nual Budget: $10-25,000 *Tel:* (212) 532-2557
st. Note: Established in 1947 as the United States Academy of Arms, it assumed its present name in 1985. Affiliated with the U.S. Olympic Committee and the Nat'l Collegiate Athletic Ass'n. Members are fencing masters who teach fencing, train instructors, develop fencing camps, conduct clinics, and administer accreditation exams to coaches. Membership: $25/yr.
blications:
Directory. a.
Swordmaster. q.

ed States Football League (1982)
Vanderbilt Ave., New York NY 10017
mmissioner: Harry Usher
ff: 25-30
: (212) 682-6363
st. Note: Originally organized to present football to the public during the spring and early summer. The USFL planned to change to a fall-winter schedule in 1986, however play was suspended after the league's anti- trust suit against the Nat'l Football League produced a damage award of one dollar. It is probable that the USFL will disolve if its damage award is not substantially increased on appeal.

ed States Football League Players Ass'n
)
21 L St., N.W., Washington DC 20036
ec. Director: Doug Allen
mbers: 709
Tel: (202) 463-2200
Hist. Note: Labor union affiliated with the AFL-CIO under the umbrella of the Federation of Professional Athletes.

United States Golf Ass'n (1894)
Golf House, Far Hills NJ 07931
Sr. Exec. Director: Frank Hannigan
Members: 5,400 clubs and courses *Staff:* 100-110
Annual Budget: over $5,000,000 *Tel:* (201) 234-2300
Hist. Note: An association of member clubs and courses formed on December 22, 1894. Sponsors the U.S. Open, Senior Open and Women's Open Championships, the Walker and Curtis Cup matches and nine national amateur championships. The governing body of U.S. Golf. Membership: $15-$1,000/yr. (individual), $30-1,300/yr. (couple).
Publications:
The Golf Journal. 8/yr.
Green Section Record. 6/yr.
Annual Meetings: January or February
1987-Seattle, WA(Westin Hotel)/Jan. 31

United States Harness Writers' Ass'n (1947)
Box Ten, Batavia NY 14020
Secretary: William F. Brown, Jr.
Members: 400-425 *Staff:* 1
Annual Budget: $25-50,000 *Tel:* (716) 343-5900
Hist. Note: Members are members of the media who cover harness racing. Has no paid staff or permanent headquarters. Membership: $40/yr.
Publication:
Newsletter. q.
Annual Meetings: April
1987-Freehold, NJ

United States Hide, Skin and Leather Ass'n (1980)
1707 N St., N.W., 3rd Fl., Washington DC 20036
President: Jerome J. Breiter
Members: 125 *Staff:* 2-5
Annual Budget: $100-250,000 *Tel:* (202) 833-2405
Hist. Note: Formed Nov. 4, 1980 in Chicago by a merger of the American Association of Hides, Skins and Leather Merchants (established 1918) and the National Hide Association (established 1945).
Publications:
Membership Directory. a.
Bulletin. m.
Trade Practices for Proper Packer Cattlehide Delivery. irreg.

United States Immigration and Naturalization Officers Ass'n (1923)
15 Park Row, Suite 439, New York NY 10038
Nat'l President: Sal Vassallo
Members: 1,100-1,200 *Staff:* 1
Annual Budget: $25-50,000 *Tel:* (212) 962-2057
Publication:
Guardian of the Gate. q.

United States Independent Telephone Ass'n (1897)
Hist. Note: Became the United States Telephone Association in 1983.

United States Institute for Theatre Technology (1960)
330 West 42nd St., Suite 1702, New York NY 10036-6978
Manager: Carol Lewis
Members: 300 organizations; 2,100 individuals *Staff:* 4
Annual Budget: $100-250,000 *Tel:* (212) 563-5551
Hist. Note: All factors that influence performance space planning, visual and auditory design, construction and operation, administration, and equipment are the objects of USITT's research and information exchange. Membership: $50/yr.
Publications:
USITT Newsletter. m. adv.
Theatre Design and Technology. q. adv.
USITT Membership Directory. a. adv.
Annual Meetings: Spring
1987-Minneapolis, MN(Hyatt Regency)/April 22-25
1988-Anaheim, CA(Disneyland Hotel)/March 23-26
1989-Calgary, Alberta(Convention Ctr.)/April 12-15
1990-Milwaukee, WI(Hyatt & MECCA)/March 28-31
1991-Hartford, CT(Sheraton Hartford Hotel)/March 20-23

United States Jaycees (1920)
Box 7, Tulsa OK 74121
Exec. V. President: Kevin Krepinevich
Members: 245,700 *Staff:* 80
Annual Budget: $2-5,000,000 *Tel:* (918) 584-2481
Hist. Note: Service training organization of individuals between 18 and 36 providing leadership training through participation in community programs. Formerly (1965) United States Junior Chamber of Commerce.
Publication:
Jaycees Magazine. m. adv.
Annual Meetings: June
1987-Reno, NV/June 15-18

United States Lacrosse Coaches' Ass'n (1935)
3 Roman Lane, West Islip NY 11795
Secretary: Francis McCall
Members: 600
Annual Budget: under $10,000 *Tel:* (516) 587-1748
Hist. Note: Promotes the sport of lacrosse on all levels through coaching clinics, clinic notes, award presentation and grants.
Publication:
Lacrosse Magazine. 9/yr.
Annual Meetings: First weekend in December.

United States Lanolin and Derivatives Manufacturers Ass'n (1973)
Hist. Note: Inactive in 1984.

United States League of Savings Institutions (1892)
111 East Wacker Dr., Chicago IL 60601
President: William O'Connell
Members: 3,500 *Staff:* 400-450
Tel: (312) 644-3100
Hist. Note: Established as the United States Savings and Loan League, it became the United States League of Savings Ass'ns in 1975 and assumed its present name in 1983. Maintains a Washington office. Supports the Savings Ass'n Political Elections Committee.
Publication:
Savings Institutions. m. adv.
Annual Meetings: Fall

United States Lifesaving Ass'n (1964)
425 East McFetridge Drive, Chicago IL 60605
President: Joe Pecoraro
Members: 6,000 *Staff:* 2-5
Annual Budget: $50-100,000 *Tel:* (312) 294-2332
Hist. Note: Founded as the Nat'l Surf Life Saving Ass'n of America, it assumed its present name in 1979. A professional and educational organization of open water lifeguards and rescue personnel, it supports the annual National Lifeguard Championhips. Membership: $15/yr.
Publication:
American Lifeguard. q. adv.
Annual Meetings: Summer
1987-Honolulu, HI
1988-Cape May, NJ

United States Marine Products Manufacturers' Ass'n (1985)
1230 Keith Building, Cleveland OH 44115
Exec. Director: John H. Addington
Members: 53 companies *Staff:* 3
Annual Budget: $50-100,000 *Tel:* (216) 241-7333
Hist. Note: Composed of companies that produce products for the marine industry, MPMA's primary goals are to provide a form through which executives in the industry can discuss common concerns and to explore news ways to enhance the domestic marine market and increase international trade of U.S. marine products.
Annual Meetings: Fall

United States Meat Export Federation (1976)
3333 Quebec St., Suite 7200, Denver CO 80207
President: Alan R. Middaugh
Members: 85-90 organizations *Staff:* 24
Annual Budget: $1-2,000,000 *Tel:* (303) 399-7151
Hist. Note: Trade ass'n of livestock producers and feeders, packers, purveyors and exporters, agribusiness, agriservice interests, farm organizations, and other promotional groups united in their interest in developing international markets for U.S. beef, pork, and lamb. Membership: $2,000-5,000/yr.
Publications:
MEF Action. m.
Annual Report. a.
Export Reports. irreg.
Exporter Directory. irreg.
Semi-annual Meetings: Spring and Fall
1987-Washington, DC/June
1987-Denver, CO/Nov.

United States-Mexico Chamber of Commerce (1973)
1000 Potomac St., N.W., Suite 102, Washington DC 20007
Exec. V. President: Gerard J. Van Heuven
Members: U.S. and Mexican companies *Staff:* 3-5
Annual Budget: $500-1,000,000 *Tel:* (202) 296-5198
Hist. Note: Maintains offices in Los Angeles and Mexico City. Membership: $300/yr. (individual), $1,200/yr. (company).
Publications:
Washington Letter. m.
Special Reports. m.
Binational Financial Reprot. semi-a.
Call to Action. q.
Annual Meetings: Semi-annual meetings

United States Nat'l Committee for Byzantine Studies (1962)
Hist. Note: Address unknown in 1985.

United States Nat'l Fruit Export Council (1954)
Hist. Note: Organizations interested in furthering the export of fruit products. Inactive in 1983.

United States of America National Committee of the Internat'l Dairy Federation (1980)
464 Central Ave., Northfield IL 60093
Secretary: Harold Wainess
Members: 35 companies, 13 individuals *Staff:* 3
Annual Budget: $25-50,000 *Tel:* (312) 446-2402
Hist. Note: Members consist of milk producers, dairy product maufacturers and suppliers, dairy scientists and educators, and other representatives of the U.S. dairy industry. IDF

headquarters are in Brussels, Belgium. Membership: $150/yr. (individual), $550-1,500/yr. (company).
Publications:
Technical Bulletins. 15-20/yr.
Technical Standards. 10-15/yr.
Prodeedings of IDF Seminars and Meetings. 5/yr.
Semi-annual meetings: February and August with IDF

United States Operating Committee of ETAD (1982)
1330 Connecticut Ave., N.W., Suite 300, Washington DC 20036
Exec. Secretary: Eric A. Clarke
Members: 10 companies *Staff:* 2-5
Annual Budget: $250-500,000 *Tel:* (202) 659-0060
Hist. Note: The international association, ETAD (Ecological and Toxicological Ass'n of the Dyestuffs Manufacturing Industry) was formed in 1974 to combine scientific and technical resources within companies in the dyestuffs industry to address ecotoxicological problems. In 1977 American companies formed the Dyes Environmental and Toxicology Organization (DETO); in 1982 most DETO members decided to join ETAD, and the two organizations were merged. The U.S. Committee of ETAD represents the interests of manufacturers of dyes with regard to environmental and health hazards in the manufacture, processing, shipment, use and disposal of their products. Affiliated with the Synthetic Organic Chemical Manufacturers Association, which provides administrative support.

United States Ordnance Producers Ass'n (1979)
Hist. Note: A Webb-Pomerene Act Association, inactive in 1983.

United States-Pakistan Economic Council (1977)
500 Fifth Ave., Suite 935, New York NY 10110
Administrator: Marian Baldwin
Staff: 2-5
Annual Budget: $25-50,000 *Tel:* (212) 221-7070
Hist. Note: Promotes U.S. trade with Pakistan.
Publication:
U.S.-Pakistan Bulletin. m.
Annual Meetings: January

United States Paper Exporters Council (1941)
Hist. Note: Ceased operations in 1982.

United States Pharmacopeial Convention (1820)
12601 Twinbrook Parkway, Rockville MD 20852
Exec. Director: William M. Heller, Ph.D.
Members: 330 *Staff:* 125
Annual Budget: over $5,000,000 *Tel:* (301) 881-0666
Hist. Note: Established January 1, 1820 as the result of a call by Dr. Lyman Spalding of New York for a convention to adopt a uniform national drug list. Composed of representatives of medical and pharaceutical organizations colleges and the Federal Government. Establishes standards for drug quality and publishes information about the proper dispensing and use of drugs. Has a budget of $8.5 million.
Publications:
About Your Medicines. a.
Abstract of Proceedings. quinquennial
United States Adopted Names and USP Dictionary of Drug Names. a.
United States Pharmacopeia-National Formulary. continuously revised.
Pharmacopeial Forum. bi-m.
Drug Information for the Health Care Provider. continuously revised.
Advice for the Patient. continuously revised.
USPDI Review. bi-m.
Annual Meetings: Quinquennial Meetings
1990-Washington, DC

United States Police K-9 Ass'n (1971)
4 Coed Lane, Farmingville NY 11738
Nat'l Secretary: Kevin J. Conroy
Members: 1,800 individuals, 250 companies *Staff:* 1
Annual Budget: $25-50,000 *Tel:* (516) 732-4565
Hist. Note: Merger (1971) of the Police K-9 Ass'n and the United States K-9 Ass'n. Membership is open to full time paid law enforcement officers, employees of a law enforcement agency, or members of the Military Police who are canine handlers, trainers, or administrators. Aim is to establish minimum standards for police dogs through uniform methods of training. Membership: $16/year.
Publication:
Canine Courier. bi-m. adv.
Semi-annual Meetings: May and October
1987-Mansfield, OH(Quality Court)/May/200

United States Potters' Ass'n (1875)
518 Market St., East Liverpool OH 43920
Secretary: Rose Chamberlin
Members: 2 companies *Staff:* 1
Annual Budget: under $10,000 *Tel:* (216) 386-4225
Hist. Note: Manufacturers of earthen and china table and kitchenware.

United States Poultry Export (1980)
771 Spring St., N.W., Atlanta GA 30308
Contact: G. Bland Byrne
Members: 5 companies
Hist. Note: A Webb-Pomerene Act association.

United States Professional Cycling Federation (1968)
R.D. #1, Box 130, New Tripoli PA 18066
Exec. Director: Jack W. Simes, III
Members: 125 individuals *Staff:* 5
Annual Budget: $10-25,000 *Tel:* (215) 298-3262
Hist. Note: Formerly (1985) United States Professional Racing Organization. Members are professional bicyclists united to further the sport in the U.S. The Federation serves as the exclusive governing body for professional cycling in the U.S. Membership: $70/yr.
Five Meetings per Year: Jan., March, June, Aug. and Oct.

United States Professional Tennis Ass'n (1927)
Saddlebrook, P.O. Box 7077, Wesley Chapel(Tampa) FL 34249
Exec. Director: Tim Heckler
Members: 5,200 *Staff:* 8-10
Annual Budget: $1-2,000,000 *Tel:* (813) 973-3777
Hist. Note: USPTA is the only non-profit trade association for professional tennis teachers. Membership: $110/yr.
Publications:
Advantage Magazine. bi-m. adv.
Convention Commemorative Program. a. adv.
Directory. a. adv.
USPTA Newsletter. bi-m. adv.
Annual Meetings: September
1987-Tampa, FL/Sept. 20-27

United States Racquet Club Ass'n (1973)
Hist. Note: Address unknown in 1982.

United States Shellac Importers Ass'n (1910)
Box 85, Islip NY 11751
Exec. Director: H. William Galland
Members: 10 companies *Staff:* 1
Annual Budget: under $10,000 *Tel:* (516) 581-3818
Hist. Note: Has no paid staff.
Annual Meetings: April in New York, NY

United States Ski Coaches Ass'n (1977)
P.O. Box 100, Park City UT 84060
Administrative Assistant: Gail Whitney
Members: 2,000 *Staff:* 2-5
Annual Budget: $25-50,000 *Tel:* (801) 649-9090
Publications:
Bulletin. bi-m.
Journal. q.

United States Ski Writers Ass'n (1963)
7 Kensington Road, Glens Falls NY 12801
President: Don A. Metivier
Members: 300 *Staff:* 1
Annual Budget: under $10,000 *Tel:* (518) 793-1201
Hist. Note: Members are photographers and writers of skiing. Membership: $20/yr.
Publication:
Ski Writers Bulletin. q.
Annual Meetings: Spring
1987-Calgary, Alberta/March

United States Soccer Federation (1913)
Nat'l Headquarters, 1750 East Boulder St., Colorado Springs CO 80909
Nat'l Administrator: Keith E. Walker
Members: 110 affiliated ass'ns;over 3.5 million individuals
Staff: 14-18
Annual Budget: $2-5,000,000 *Tel:* (303) 578-4678
Hist. Note: A federation of state senior and youth soccer ass'ns, formerly United States Football Ass'n.
Publication:
Soccer Monthly. m.

United States Targhee Sheep Ass'n (1951)
Box 34, Jordan MT 59337
Secy.-Treas.: Jack McRae
Members: 220-230 *Staff:* 1
Annual Budget: $25-50,000 *Tel:* (406) 557-6266
Hist. Note: Membership: $25/life (individual).
Publication:
Directory. a. adv.
Annual Meetings: Summer
1987-Douglas, WY/Aug.

United States Telecommunications Suppliers Ass'n (1979)
150 North Michigan Ave., Suite 600, Chicago IL 60601
Mng. Director: Donald R. Pollock
Members: 600 companies *Staff:* 12
Annual Budget: $1-2,000,000 *Tel:* (312) 782-8597
Hist. Note: Originally a part of the United States Independent Telephone Association with which it is affiliated, USTSA is a trade group of manufacturers, suppliers and support service organizations of the telecommunications industry.
Publication:
USTSA Newsletter. m.
Semi-annual Meetings:
1987-Indianapolis, IN/Feb. 17-19
1987-Las Vegas, NV/April 14-16
1987-Geneva,Switzerland/Oct. 20-27
1988-Atlanta, GA/May 24-26
1989-Anaheim, CA/May 23-25

United States Telephone Ass'n (1897)
900 19th St., N.W., Suite 800, Washington DC 20006-2102
President: John Sodolski
Members: 1,000 telephone companies; 500 non-telephone cos.
Staff: 30-35
Annual Budget: $2-5,000,000 *Tel:* (202) 835-3100
Hist. Note: Formerly Independent Telephone Ass'n of America and Nat'l Independent Telephone, it took its persent name in 1983. Originally represented 96% of the U.S. non-Bell system telephone industry, USTA now accepts membership from companies affiliated with AT&T previously. Supports the Communications Political Action Committee.
Publication:
Member Letter. bi-w.
Annual Meetings: Fall
1987-Lake Buena Vista, FL/Oct. 13-15

United States Tennis Ass'n (1881)
1212 Avenue of the Americas, New York NY 10036
Exec. Director and C.O.O.: John T. Fogarty
Members: 250,000 *Staff:* 100
Annual Budget: over $5,000,000 *Tel:* (212) 302-3322
Hist. Note: An association of organizations and individuals interested in the promotion of tennis. Formerly (1975) United States Lawn Tennis Ass'n. Sponsors the U.S. teams for the Wightman, Federation and Davis Cup competitions. Runs the U.S. Open Tennis Championships, held annually at Flushing, NY. Also runs the national championships for juniors, seniors and amateurs, as well as thousands of tournaments at the local level. Membership: $8-$16/yr.
Publications:
Tennis U.S.A. m. adv.
Yearbook and Tennis Guide. a. adv.
Annual Meetings:
1987-Tuscon, AZ(Sheraton El Conquistador)/Feb. 28-March 7

United States Tennis Court and Track Builders Ass'n (1965)
1004 East Jefferson St., Charlottesville VA 22901
Exec. Secretary: Sharon U. Black
Members: 150-160 *Staff:* 3
Annual Budget: $100-250,000 *Tel:* (804) 971-2860
Hist. Note: The only organization that represents tennis courts and track builders in the United States and Canada. Membership: $450/yr.
Publications:
Newsletter. q.
Membership Directory. a.
Annual Meetings: Technical Meeting/Trade Show
1987-Denver, CO/180

United States Tennis Writers' Ass'n (1928)
c/o H.O. Zimman, Inc., 156 Broad St., Lynn MA 01901
President: Bob Greene
Members: 180-190 *Staff:* 1
Annual Budget: under $10,000 *Tel:* (617) 598-9230
Hist. Note: Formerly (1976) the Lawn Tennis Writers Ass'n of America.
Publication:
Membership Directory. a.
Quarterly Meetings:

United States Tour Operators Ass'n (1972)
211 East 51st St., Suite 12B, New York NY 10022
Exec. V. President: Robert E. Whitley
Members: 40-50 companies *Staff:* 2-5
Annual Budget: $250-500,000 *Tel:* (212) 944-5727
Hist. Note: Organized in California but expanded to national membership in 1975. Members are wholesale tour operators.

United States Trademark Ass'n (1878)
6 East 45th St., New York NY 10017
Exec. Director: Robin A. Rolfe
Members: 1,700-1,800 *Staff:* 15
Annual Budget: $1-2,000,000 *Tel:* (212) 986-5880
Hist. Note: Established in New York City November 21, 1878 by twelve manufacturers responding to the need to protect their trademarks. Incorporated in the State of New York January 8, 1887.
Publications:
Trademark Reporter. bi-m.
Bulletin. w.
Executive Newsletter. q.
Trademark Stylesheets. a.
Annual Meetings: Spring/1,500
1987-Boston, MA(The Westin)/April
1988-Phoenix, AZ(Hyatt/Hilton)/May

United States Trout Farmers Ass'n (1952)
515 Rock St., Little Rock AR 72202
Exec. Director: Ray Cooper
Members: 350-400 farmers *Staff:* 2-5
Annual Budget: $50-100,000 *Tel:* (501) 372-3595
Hist. Note: The oldest commercial aquaculture organization in the United States. Active Membership: $60/yr.
Publication:
Salmonid. q. adv.
Annual Meetings: Fall

United States Tuna Foundation (1977)
2033 M St., N.W., Washington DC 20036
Exec. Director: David G. Burney
Members: 15-20 companies and organizations *Staff:* 3
Annual Budget: $250-500,000 *Tel:* (202) 857-0610
Hist. Note: Trade association representing the tuna industry. Maintains a Washington office.
Annual Meetings: San Diego, CA

00298 12 05 86 1233

United States Venetian Blind Ass'n (1942)
Hist. Note: Became the American Window Coverings Manufacturers Ass'n in 1985.

United States-Yugoslav Economic Council (1974)
1511 K St., N.W., Suite 431, Washington DC 20005
President: Richard E. Johnson
Members: 5-10 individuals, 150-200 companies *Staff:* 2-5
Annual Budget: $100-250,000 *Tel:* (202) 737-9652
Hist. Note: Purpose is to promote trade and investment with Yugoslavia on behalf of member companies.
Publication:
Business News. m.
Annual Meetings: Spring

United Steelworkers of America (1942)
Five Gateway Center, Pittsburgh PA 15222
President: Lynn Williams
Members: 750,000 *Staff:* 1,000
Annual Budget: over $5,000,000 *Tel:* (412) 562-2400
Hist. Note: The United Steelworkers of America had its origin in the creation, in 1936, of the Steel Workers Organizing Committee created to unionize steelworkers for the CIO. The Amalgamated Association of Iron, Steel and Tin Workers (founded in 1876) was incorporated in the effort. In 1942 the latter was dissolved and SWOC was transformed into the present organization. Merged in 1944 with Aluminum Workers of America (founded 1932); in 1967 with Internat'l Union of Mine, Mill and Smelter Workers (founded 1892); in 1970 with United Stone and Allied Products Workers of America (founded 1903); in 1972 with Internat'l Union of District 50, Allied and Technical Workers of the U.S. and Canada (founded 1936); and in 1985 with Upholsters' Internat'l Union of North America (founded 1882). Has a general, strike and defense fund of about $220 million. Affiliated with AFL-CIO and the Canadian Labour Congress. Sponsors and supports the United Steelworkers of America Political Action Fund.
Publication:
Steelabor. m.
Biennial meetings: Even years in Fall

United Synagogue of America (1913)
155 Fifth Ave., New York NY 10010
Exec. V. President: Rabbi Benjamin Z. Kreitman
Members: 850-900 *Staff:* 150
Annual Budget: $2-5,000,000 *Tel:* (212) 533-7800
Hist. Note: Conservative U.S. and Canadian congregations. Affiliated with the National Federation of Jewish Men's Clubs, the National Women's League, the United Synagogue Youth and the Jewish Theological Seminary of America.
Publications:
Achshav. bi-m.
Adult Jewish Education. q.
Advisors Newsletter. q.
Conservative Judaism. q.
Kol Atid. m.
Our Age-Dorenu. bi-w.
Outlook. q.
Synagogue School. q.
Torch. q.
United Synagogue Review. q.
Your Child. q.
Biennial Meetings: uneven years

United Telegraph Workers (1902)
701 Gude Drive, Rockville MD 20850
President: Richard C. Brockert
Members: 9,500 *Staff:* 2-5
Annual Budget: $500-1,000,000 *Tel:* (301) 762-4444
Hist. Note: Established as the Commercial Telegraph Union of America on July 19, 1902 as the result of a merger of the Commercial Telegraphers Union and the Order of Commercial Telegraphers. Affiliated with the AFL-CIO. Assumed its present name in 1968.
Publication:
Telegraph Workers Journal. m.
Biennial Meetings: odd years

United Textile Workers of America (1901)
420 Common St., Box 325, Lawrence MA 01842
President: Vernon Mustard
Members: 30,000 *Staff:* 30-35
Annual Budget: $2-5,000,000 *Tel:* (617) 686-2901
Hist. Note: Founded in Washington, DC on November 19, 1901 as the result of an AFL-sponsored merger of the International Union of Textile Workers (founded in 1890) and the American Federation of Textile Operatives (founded in 1900). Affiliated with the AFL-CIO and the Canadian Labour Congress.
Publication:
Textile Challenger. bi-m.
Annual Meetings: Every 4 years.
1988-Bal Harbour, FL(Sheraton)/April

United Thoroughbred Trainers of America (1958)
19363 James Couzens Highway, Detroit MI 48235
Exec. Secretary: Ruth A. Le Grove
Members: 1,850 *Staff:* 2-5
Annual Budget: $25-50,000 *Tel:* (313) 342-6144
Hist. Note: Established as the Nat'l Thoroughbred Trainers Guild, it assumed its present name in 1960. Members are licensed thoroughbred horse trainers united to elevate the standards of the professional trainer's vocation and to promote interest in the sport of thoroughbred racing. Membership: $50/yr.
Publication:
The Backstretch. q. adv.
Annual Meetings: Fall

United Transportation Union (1969)
14600 Detroit Ave., Lakewood OH 44107
President: Fred A. Hardin
Members: 210,000 *Staff:* 150-200
Annual Budget: $2-5,000,000 *Tel:* (216) 228-9400
Hist. Note: Merger of Brotherhood of Locomotive Firemen and Enginemen (1873) Brotherhood of Railroad Trainmen (1883); Order of Railway Conductors and Brakemen (1868); Switchmen's Union of North America (1894). Absorbed (1972) Federated Council of the Internat'l Ass'n of Railway Employees and merged with Railroad Yardmasters of America in 1985. Sponsors and supports the Transportation Political Education League.
Publication:
UTU News. m.
Annual Meetings: Every 4 years (1987)

United Union of Roofers, Waterproofers and Allied Workers (1919)
1125 17th St., N. W., Washington DC 20036
President: Earl Kruse
Members: 27,000 *Staff:* 30-40
Annual Budget: $2-5,000,000 *Tel:* (202) 638-3228
Hist. Note: The result of a merger in Pittsburgh, Pennsylvania, September 8, 1919 of the International Slate and Tile Roofers Union of America (founded in 1902) and the International Brotherhood of Composition Roofers, Damp and Waterproof Workers of the United States and Canada (founded in 1905). Chartered by the American Federation of Labor in 1919. Until 1978 known as the United Slate, Tile and Composition Roofers, Damp and Waterproof Workers Association.
Publications:
United Union of Roofers, Waterproofers and Allied Workers Journal. q.
adv.
Quinquennial Meetings in the Fall: 1988

Unites States Women's Track Coaches Ass'n (1967)
Athletic Department, University of Oregon, Eugene OR 97403
Contact: Tom Heinenon
Annual Budget: under $10,000 *Tel:* (503) 686-3395

Universities Council on Water Resources (1962)
113 Nebraska Hall, University of Nebraska, Lincoln NE 68588-0517
Exec. Secretary: Dr. William L. Powers
Members: 93 academic institutions *Staff:* 2-5
Annual Budget: under $10,000 *Tel:* (402) 472-3305
Hist. Note: Founded as the Universities Council on Hydrology in 1962; assumed its present name in 1964. A voluntary organization of universities engaged in education, research, public service, international activities, and legislative pursuits relevant to all aspects of water resources. Membership: $200/yr.
Publications:
Update. q.
Proceedings of Annual Meetings. a.
Careers in Water Resources. irreg.
Course Listings in Water Resources. irreg.
Graduate Studies in Water Resources. irreg.
Annual Meetings:
1987-Hilton Head, SC/July 29-Aug. 1/150-200

Universities Research Ass'n (1965)
1111 19th St., N.W.,, Suite 400, Washington DC 20036
President: Edward Knapp
Members: 50-60 *Staff:* 2-5
Annual Budget: $500-1,000,000 *Tel:* (202) 293-1382
Hist. Note: Members are chief executives of universities. Purpose is to cooperate in research in the physical and biological sciences. Among other things, URA runs the Fermi National Laboratory in Chicago. President is elected annually.
Annual Meetings: March

Universities Space Research Ass'n (1969)
American City Bldg., Suite 212, Columbia MD 21044
Exec. Director: Dr. W. D. Cummings
Members: 58 *Staff:* 6-10
Annual Budget: $250-500,000 *Tel:* (301) 730-2656
Hist. Note: A consortium of universities that manage research institutes and programs, primarily for NASA.
Publications:
Lunar and Planetary Information Bulletin. q.
NSRA Newsletter. q.
Annual Meetings: Washington, DC/March

University and College Designers Ass'n (1971)
2811 Mishawaka Avenue, South Bend IN 46615
Treasurer: Karen Reimer
Members: 750 *Staff:* 1
Annual Budget: $25-50,000 *Tel:* (219) 288-8232
Hist. Note: Individuals involved in visual communication design for colleges and universities. Membership: $45/yr.
Publication:
Designer. q.
Annual Meetings: September
1987-San Antonio, TX

University and College Theatre Ass'n
Hist. Note: A division of the American Theatre Association.

University Ass'n for Emergency Medicine (1970)
900 West Ottawa, Lansing MI 48915
Exec. Director: Mary Ann Schropp
Members: 1,100 *Staff:* 2-5
Annual Budget: $100-250,000 *Tel:* (517) 485-5484
Hist. Note: Formerly (1977) the University Association for Emergency Medical Services. Dedicated to promoting research and education in Emergency Medicine. Membership open to physicians, nurses, allied health professionals, and those interested in academic Emergency Medicine. Membership: $35-150/yr.
Publications:
Annals of Emergency Medicine. m. adv.
Status Report. q. adv.
Annual Meetings: May
1987-Philadelphia, PA(Franklin Plaza Hotel)/May 19-21
1988-Cincinnati, OH(Netherland Plaza)/May 25-28
1989-San Diego, CA
1990-Chicago, IL

University Council for Educational Administration (1957)
116 Farmer Building, Tempe AZ 85287
Exec. Director: Patrick B. Forsyth
Members: 45-50 universities *Staff:* 4
Annual Budget: $100-250,000 *Tel:* (602) 965-6690
Hist. Note: A private, non-profit corporation consisting of major universities of the United States and Canada. Established to improve the professional preparation of educational administrators. Proposed in 1954 and established at Columbia Univ. in 1957, the central office was moved to Ohio State and UCEA began operations with a full-time staff and 34 charter members in 1959.
Publications:
Educational Administration Abstracts. q.
Educational Administration Quarterly. q.
Journal of Educational Equity and Leadership. q.
UCEA Review. q.
Annual Meetings: Semi-annual meetings

University Film and Video Ass'n (1947)
C/O Dept. of Cinema and Photography, Southern Illinois University, Carbondale IL 62901
Membership Chairperson: Loren Cocking
Members: 800
Tel: (618) 453-2365
Hist. Note: Members are instructors and film makers concerned with the production and study of film. Originally the University Film Producers Ass'n, it became the University Film Ass'n in 1968 and assumed its present name in 1982. Member of the Council of Communication Societies. Membership: $35/yr.(individual); $75/yr.(institution)
Publications:
Digest. bi-m.
Journal. q.
Membership Directory. bien.
Annual Meetings: Late July or August

University Film Ass'n (1947)
Hist. Note: Formerly (1968) University Film Producers Ass'n. Became the University Film and Video Ass'n in 1982.

University Photographers Ass'n of America (1961)
News Bureau, N. Michigan Univ., Marquette MI 49855
President: Don Pavloski
Members: 250-275
Annual Budget: under $10,000 *Tel:* (906) 227-2720
Hist. Note: Members are college personnel who professionally practice photography. Has no paid staff or permanent address; officers change annually. Membership: $25/yr.
Publication:
UPAA Newsletter. q.
Annual Meetings: June
1987-Provo, UT(Brigham Young Univ.)
1988-Indianapolis, IN

University Resident Theatre Ass'n (1969)
1560 Broadway, Suite 801, New York NY 10036
Exec. Director: Berenice Weiler
Members: 40-45 *Staff:* 2-5
Annual Budget: $100-250,000 *Tel:* (212) 221-1130
Hist. Note: Operates The National Unified Auditions, the Artist Escrow Program, and a showcase of MFA graduates. Membership: $1,100/yr. (organization).
Annual Meetings: Semi-annual meetings

Upholsterers' Internat'l Union of North America (1882)
Hist. Note: Absorbed by the United Steelworkers of America in November, 1985.

Urban Affairs Ass'n (1969)
Univ. of Delaware, Newark DE 19716
Exec. Director: Mary Helen Callahan
Members: 225 *Staff:* 2-5
Annual Budget: $25-50,000 *Tel:* (302) 451-2394
Hist. Note: Urban specialists from private or public universities who are involved in teaching, research or public service. Promotes more effective policies and procedures relating to the study of urban affairs and urbanization. Formerly (1981) Council of University Institutes for Urban Affairs. Membership: $30/yr.(individual); $225/yr.(institution).

00299 12 05 86 1233

Publications:
Journal of Urban Affairs. q.
UAA Communication. bi-m.
University Urban Programs. trian.
Annual Meetings: Spring
1987-Akron, OH(Quaker Square Hilton)/April 22-26/200
1988-St. Louis, MO

Urban and Regional Information Systems Ass'n (1963)
319 C Stret, S.E., Washington DC 20003
Exec. Director: Thomas M. Palmerlee
Members: 1,300 *Staff:* 2
Annual Budget: $250-500,000 *Tel:* (202) 543-7141
Hist. Note: Users and providers of information systems in the public sector. Membership: $50/yr.
Publications:
Newsletter. bi-m. adv.
Conference Proceedings. a.
Exemplary Systems in Government. a.
Annual Meetings: Summer
1987-Ft. Lauderdale, FL/Aug. 1-6/850
1988-Los Angeles, CA/Aug. 6-11/850
1989-Boston, MA/July 29-Aug. 3

Urban Land Institute (1936)
1090 Vermont Ave., N.W., Suite 300, Washington DC 20005
Exec. V. President: James A. Cloar
Members: 10,500 *Staff:* 70-75
Annual Budget: over $5,000,000 *Tel:* (202) 289-8500
Hist. Note: Conducts practical research in various fields of real estate knowledge including indentifying and interpreting land use trends in relation to the changing needs of its users. Consists of developers, architects, public officials and others concerned with land planning and development. Official name is ULI-The Urban Land Institute. Membership: $200/yr.
Publications:
Land Use Digest. m.
Project Reference File. q.
Urban Land. m.
Semi-Annual Meetings: Spring and Fall

Urethane Foam Contractors Ass'n
Hist. Note: Reported defunct in 1986.

Urethane Institute (1959)
Hist. Note: Changed title to Polyurethane Division-Soc. of the Plastics Industry. (1985)

USA Rugby Football Union (1975)
600 S. Federal St., #400, Chicago IL 60605
Exec. Secretary: John S. Swinburn
Members: 700 clubs *Staff:* 2
Annual Budget: $250-500,000 *Tel:* (312) 346-1600
Hist. Note: Composed of four territorial unions whose membership includes approximately 700 rugby clubs.
Annual Meetings: Spring

USA Toy Library Ass'n (1984)
104 Wilmot Road, Suite 201, Deerfield IL 60015
Exec. Director: Judith Iacuzzi
Members: 30 companies, 350 individuals *Staff:* 1
Annual Budget: $50-100,000 *Tel:* (312) 940-8800
Hist. Note: Built on the idea that play and toys are an important part of a child's healthy growth and development; receives about eight inquiries week from individuals interested in establishing a toy library or bettering an existing one. Basic Memberhip: $35/yr.
Publications:
Child's Play Newsletter. m.
Toy Library Operators Manual. a.
Toys for Growing. a.
Toy Library Directory. a.
Annual Meetings: Fall
1987-Chicago, IL

Utilities Telecommunications Council (1948)
1150 17th St., N.W., Suite 1000, Washington DC 20036
Gen. Counsel: Charles M. Meehan
Members: 2,000-2,500 *Staff:* 2-5
Annual Budget: $500-1,000,000 *Tel:* (202) 956-5651
Hist. Note: Represents energy utilities in telecommunications matters before various federal and state agencies, particularly the FCC. The above address is that of the law firm Keller and Heckman.
Publication:
Newsletter. m.
Annual Meetings: June
1987-Portland, OR(Red Lion Inn)/June 15-18/1,000
1988-Boston, MA(Marriott Copley)/June 27-30

Utility Workers Union of America (1945)
815 16th St., N.W., Washington DC 20006
President: James Joy, Jr.
Members: 60,000 *Staff:* 25-30
Annual Budget: $2-5,000,000 *Tel:* (202) 347-8105
Hist. Note: Founded in 1945 through the merger of the Utility Workers Organizing Committee (which had been set up by the CIO in 1938) and the Brotherhood of Consolidated Edison Employees and chartered by the Congress of Industrial Organizations the same year. Affiliated with AFL-CIO. Sponsors and supports the Committee on Political Action as well as the Utility Workers Union of America Political Contributions Committee.

Publication:
Light. m.
Quadrennial Meetings:
1987-Hollywood, FL(Diplomat)/600-800

Vacuum Bag Manufacturers Ass'n (1974)
Hist. Note: Became inactive in 1984.

Vacuum Cleaner Manufacturers Ass'n (1913)
45 Pleasant Drive, Chagrin Falls OH 44022
Exec. Secretary: Joseph C. Frantz, Sr.
Members: 14 companies
Tel: (216) 247-2202
Annual Meetings: Fall in Hot Springs, VA

Vacuum Dealers Trade Ass'n (1981)
1200 Locust St., Des Moines IA 50309
Exec. Director: J.R. Beall
Members: 1,200 *Staff:* 7
Annual Budget: $250-500,000 *Tel:* (515) 282-9101
Hist. Note: Vacuum cleaner retailers, manufacturers and distributors.
Publication:
News. m.

Valve Manufacturers Ass'n of America (1938)
1050 17th St., N.W., Suite 701, Washington DC 20036
President: Malcolm E. O'Hagan
Members: 75-85 companies *Staff:* 6-10
Annual Budget: $500-1,000,000 *Tel:* (202) 331-8105
Hist. Note: Founded as the Valve Manufacturers Ass'n in 1938; added "of America" in 1985.
Publications:
Currents. m.
Valve Magazine. q.
Annual Meetings: Fall

Vanilla Bean Ass'n of America (1930)
c/o Fritzsche Dodge & Olcott, 76 9th Ave., New York NY 10011
President: Barry Coyle
Members: 11-15 companies
Annual Budget: under $10,000 *Tel:* (212) 929-4100

Variable Resistive Components Institute (1960)
7380 North Lincoln Ave., Lincolnwood IL 60646
Exec. Director: Raymond E. Pritchard
Members: 25-30 companies *Staff:* 2-5
Annual Budget: $25-50,000 *Tel:* (312) 677-2853
Hist. Note: Formerly Precision Potentiometer Manufacturers Ass'n.

Vatel Club (1913)
250 West 57th St., Room 2231, New York NY 10019
Manager: Christine Thongs
Members: 800 *Staff:* 1
Annual Budget: $25-50,000 *Tel:* (212) 246-9397
Hist. Note: The oldest association of chefs and members of the culinary profession in the United States. Membership: $50/yr.
Publication:
Toques Blanches. bi-m. adv.
Monthly Meetings: New York, NY

Veal Industry Council (1985)
435 N. Michigan Ave., Suite 1717, Chicago IL 60611-4067
Exec. Director: Sandy H. Sadler
Staff: 2
Annual Budget: under $10,000 *Tel:* (312) 644-0828
Hist. Note: Founded in Chicago, IL in 1985 and incorporated in West Virginia, the Council's primary purpose is to increase the consumption of veal. It was also designed to provide support for existing organizations lending support to the veal industry and to provide a forum for communication among all facets of the veal industry: growers, packers, feed companies, and suppliers. Membership: $25/yr.
Publication:
The Vealer. m. adv.
Annual Meetings: December

Vehicle Security Ass'n (1984)
5100 Forbes Road, Lanham MD 20706
Exec. Director: Aaron M. Lowe
Members: 64
Annual Budget: $10-25,000 *Tel:* (301) 459-5927
Hist. Note: VSA represents manufacturers, dealers, distributors and manufacturers representatives of vehicle security devices. Membership: $100/yr. (dealer), $250/yr. (distributor), $1,000/yr. (manufacturer).
Publication:
VSA News. q.
Annual Meetings: January
1987-Las Vegas, NV/Jan. 11

Vehicular Technology Soc.
Hist. Note: A subsidiary of the Institute of Electrical and Electronics Engineers. Membership in the Society, open only to IEEE members, includes subscription to a technical periodical in the field published by IEEE. All administrative support is provided by IEEE.

Venezuelan American Ass'n of the U.S. (1936)
111 Broadway, New York NY 10006
Secy.-Treas.: Paul E. Calvet
Members: 90 companies, 60 individuals *Staff:* 2
Annual Budget: $10-25,000 *Tel:* (212) 233-7776
Hist. Note: Promotes the expnasion of trade relations between the U.S. and Venezuela. Membership: $100/yr. (individual); $300/yr. (corporate).
Publication:
Venezuela News Bulletin. m.

Vermiculite Ass'n (1950)
600 South Federal St., Suite 400, Chicago IL 60605
Contact: Augie Sisco
Members: 23 companies *Staff:* 2-5
Annual Budget: $25-50,000 *Tel:* (312) 346-1600
Hist. Note: Membership: $400/yr.
Annual Meetings: Fall

Veterinary Cancer Soc. (1974)
Box 999, Battelle Pacific N.W. Labs, Richland WA 99352
Corresponding Secretary: Dr. Richard E. Weller
Members: 500 individuals
Annual Budget: under $10,000 *Tel:* (509) 376-3193
Hist. Note: Membership: $20/yr, $5/yr. (interns and students).
Publication:
Veterinary Cancer Society Newsletter. q.

Vibrating Screen Manufacturers Ass'n (1959)
30 Oak St., Stamford CT 06905
Secretary & Counsel: Herbert S. Blake, III
Members: 10 companies *Staff:* 2-5
Annual Budget: $10-25,000 *Tel:* (203) 324-0700
Hist. Note: Formerly Mechanical Vibrating Screen Mfrs. Ass'n. Manufacturers of mechanical vibrating screens and feeders for sizing materials in the aggregate, mining, chemical and food industries.
Annual Meetings: With the Crusher and Portable Plant Ass'n

Vibration Institute (1972)
115 West 55th St., Suite 401, Clarendon Hills IL 60514
Director: Dr. Ronald L. Eshleman
Members: 1,000 *Staff:* 6-10
Annual Budget: $250-500,000 *Tel:* (312) 654-2254
Hist. Note: Founded as the Vibration Foundation, it reorganized in 1973 under its present name. Members are companies and individuals concerned with machinery vibration. Membership: $25/year (individual).
Publications:
Vibrations Magazine. q. adv.
The Shock and Vibration Digest. m.
Annual Meetings: Spring/Summer
1987-St. Louis, MO(Omni Hotel)/June 9-11/200

Video Software Dealers Ass'n (1981)
3 Eves Drive, Suite 307, Marlton NJ 08053
Exec. V. President: Mickey Granberg
Members: 3,000 companies *Staff:* 15
Annual Budget: $2-5,000,000 *Tel:* (609) 424-7117
Hist. Note: Regular members are retailers and distributors of pre-recorded video products; associate members are manufacturers and suppliers of products to the industry. Membership fee varies with number of retail stores and volume.
Publication:
VSDA Reports. m. adv.
Annual Meetings: August at the Convention Center in Las Vegas, NV
1987-Aug. 16-19

Videotape Production Ass'n (1969)
Hist. Note: Became the Internat'l Teleproduction Soc. in 1986.

Videotex Industry Ass'n (1981)
1901 N. Fort Myer Drive, Suite 200, Rosslyn VA 22209
Exec. Director: Robert L. Smith, Jr.
Members: 180 companies *Staff:* 3
Annual Budget: $250-500,000 *Tel:* (703) 522-0883
Hist. Note: Membership consists of companies developing mass market electronic information and transaction services. Promotes the use of videotex and teletext, communications services for the transmission of news, business transactions or electronic messages over telephone or cable lines to television sets or home and office personal computers. Membership: $50/yr. (individual); $3,000/yr. (company)
Publications:
VIA Update. m.
Videotex and Teletext Resource: VIA Membership Directory. semi-a.
Videotex/Teletext Bibliography. a.
Annual Meetings: Spring
1987-New York, NY(Sheraton Centre)/June 15-17

Videtape Facilities Ass'n (1982)
6520 Selma Ave., Suite 352, Hollywood CA 90028
President and C.E.O.: Sam Holtz
Members: 45 companies
Tel: (213) 466-8511
Hist. Note: VFA members are companies supplying video production and post production services to the motion picture industry. Members are concentrated in the Los Angeles area. Membership: $350/yr.
Publications:
Newsletter.
Monitor Awards Magazine.

00300 12 05 86 1233

Monthly Breakfast Meetings: last Tuesday, plus three evening meetings
throughtout the year.

Vinegar Institute, The (1967)
5775 Peachtree-Dunwoody Rd., Suite 500D, Atlanta GA 30342
President: Robert H. Kellen
Members: 50 companies *Staff:* 4
Tel: (404) 252-3663
Hist. Note: Membership composed of makers and bottlers of vinegar, as well as suppliers to the industry.
Annual Meetings:
1987-San Diego, CA/Feb. 22-24

Vinifera Wine Growers Ass'n (1973)
Box P, The Plains VA 22171
President: R. de Treville Lawrence
Annual Budget: $10-25,000 *Tel:* (703) 754-8564
Hist. Note: Growers of the Vinifera grape, a European variety which produces a high-quality table wine, and makers of this wine. Disseminates information on new developments in wine-growing and wine-making techniques. Provides technical assistance for home and commercial vineyards. Membership: $17/yr.
Publication:
Vinifera Wine Growers Journal. q.
Annual Meetings: August

Vision Service Plan (1964)
1795 Clarkson Road, Suite 350, St. Louis MO 63017
Exec. Director: Larry Leiber
Members: 41 companies *Staff:* 2-5
Annual Budget: $100-250,000 *Tel:* (314) 532-0938
Hist. Note: Formerly (1977) Vision Institute of America. Eye care specialists involved in group vision care through vision service corporations.
Publications:
The Provider.
VSP Communicator. m.
Annual Meetings: Late Winter
1987-Charleston, SC(Mills House Hotel)/March 25-April 1/200

Visiting Nurse Ass'ns of America (1983)
518 17th St., Suite 388, Denver CO 80202
President: Robert Leduc
Members: 89 organizations *Staff:* 3
Annual Budget: $250-500,000 *Tel:* (303) 629-8622
Hist. Note: Superseded the American Affiliation of Visiting Nurse Ass'ns and Services in 1986. Members are non-profit, community-based home health care agencies.
Annual Meetings:
1987-La Jolla, CA(Marriott)/March 11-13

Vocational Evaluation and Work Adjustment Ass'n (1967)
633 S. Washington St., Alexandria VA 22314
President: Douglas Seiler
Members: 2,000
Annual Budget: $10-25,000 *Tel:* (703) 836-0850
Hist. Note: Has no permanent office or staff. It is a division of the Nat'l Rehabilitation Ass'n, which provides the secretariat.
Publications:
VEWAA Newsletter. q.
Vocational Evaluation and Work Adjustment Bulletin. q. adv.
Annual Meetings: With Nat'l Rehabilitation Ass'n

Vocational Industrial Clubs of America (1965)
Box 3000, Leesburg VA 22075
C.E.O.: Larry W. Johnson, CAE
Members: 275,000 *Staff:* 20-25
Annual Budget: $1-2,000,000 *Tel:* (703) 777-8810
Hist. Note: Founded in 1965 as the national organization for students in trade, industrial, technical and health occupations programs. Members are students in high schools, area vocational schools and in junior and community college training. Sponsors an annual National Leadership Conference and the United States Skills Olympics.
Publications:
The VICA, g. adv.
VICA, Professional Edition. q. adv.
VICA Professional News. 5/yr.
Annual Meetings: June
1987-Wichita, KS(Century II)/June 21-27

Volume Footwear Retailers of America (1944)
Hist. Note: Became the Footwear Retailers of America in 1985.

Walking Horse Owners Ass'n of America (1975)
Box 2397, Murfreesboro TN 37133-2397
Office Manager: Tommy Hall
Members: 800 *Staff:* 4
Annual Budget: $100-250,000 *Tel:* (615) 890-9120
Hist. Note: Members own and exhibit Tennessee Walking horses. Sponsors the Internat'l Grand Championship Walking Horse Show held in Murfreesboro, TN. Membership: $30/yr.
Publications:
Voice of TWH. m.
Walking Horse Report. w.
Annual Meetings: February

Walking Horse Trainers Ass'n (1968)
Box 61, Shelbyville TN 37160
Secretary: Frances C. Gentry
Members: 265 *Staff:* 1
Annual Budget: $25-50,000 *Tel:* (615) 684-5866
Hist. Note: Trainers of Tennessee Walking Horses. Works for unity in the horse industry and sponsors continuing research. Formerly Tennessee Walking Horse Trainers Association. Membership: $25/yr.
Annual Meetings: December

Wallcovering Distributors Ass'n (1920)
111 East Wacker Dr., Chicago IL 60601
Exec. Director: Edward Craft
Members: 120 companies *Staff:* 2-5
Annual Budget: $250-500,000 *Tel:* (312) 644-6610
Hist. Note: Formerly (until 1979) known as the Wallcovering Wholesalers Ass'n.
Annual Meetings: Jan./Feb.
1987-Honolulu, HI(Sheraton Waikiki)/Jan. 25-29

Wallcovering Manufacturers Ass'n (1973)
Box 359, 66 Morris Ave., Springfield NJ 07081
Exec. Director: Mauro A. Checchio
Members: 65-70 companies *Staff:* 2-5
Annual Budget: $250-500,000 *Tel:* (201) 379-1100
Hist. Note: Established as the first organization uniting manufacturers of wallpaper and vinyl wallcovering.
Publication:
Directory of Members. a.
Annual Meetings: Spring/150
1987-Rancho Mirage, CA(Marriott Rancho Las Palmas)/April 5-8
1988-Hilton Head, SC(Hyatt)/April 17-20/175

Warehouse Distributors Ass'n for Leisure and Mobile Products (1967)
P.O. Box 1908, Bradenton FL 33506-1908
Exec. Director: George L. Davison
Members: 225-275 companies *Staff:* 2-5
Annual Budget: $100-250,000 *Tel:* (813) 756-4298
Hist. Note: Formerly (1971) Warehouse Distributors Ass'n. Membership consists of wholesale distributors in parts for mobile homes and recreational vehicles.
Publication:
Tel-a-facts. m.
Annual Meetings: Fall
1987-Denver, CO/Oct.

Warehousing Education and Research Council (1977)
1100 Jorie Blvd., Suite 118, Oak Brook IL 60521
Exec. Director: Thomas E. Sharpe
Members: 1,400 individuals *Staff:* 2
Annual Budget: $250-500,000 *Tel:* (312) 990-0001
Hist. Note: A professional society for warehousing executives and managers designed to improve warehousing through education and research. Membership: $150/yr.
Publication:
WERCSHEET. m.
Annual Meetings: Spring
1987-Kansas City, MO(Hyatt/Westin)/May 31-June 3/750
1988-San Francisco, CA(Hyatt Regency)/May 22-25/800
1989-New Orleans, LA(Hyatt Regency)/May 7-10/800

Waste Oil Heating Manufactuers Ass'n (1981)
Hist. Note: Address unknown in 1986.

Watch Material and Jewelry Distributors Ass'n of America (1946)
Hist. Note: Became the Jewelry Industry Distributors Ass'n in 1984.

Water and Sewer Distributors of America (1979)
1600 Wilson Blvd., Suite 1008, Arlington VA 22209
Director of Member Services: Glenn L. Northrup
Members: 55 companies *Staff:* 2-5
Annual Budget: $25-50,000 *Tel:* (703) 841-1556
Hist. Note: Members are distributors of products to the municipal water and sewer markets. Membership: $300-900/yr. (company).
Publication:
Connections (newsletter). m.
Semi-annual Meetings: Winter and Fall
1987-Tucson, AZ(Loews)/March 8-12

Water and Wastewater Equipment Manufacturers Ass'n (1908)
Box 17402, Dulles Internat'l Airport, Washington DC 20041
President: Dawn C. Kristof
Members: 82 companies *Staff:* 2-5
Annual Budget: $100-250,000 *Tel:* (703) 661-8011
Hist. Note: Formerly Water and Sewage Works Manufacturers Ass'n.
Publications:
News from WWEMA
Washington Analysis. m.

Water Equipment Wholesalers and Suppliers Ass'n (1960)
Hist. Note: Division of Nat'l Water Well Ass'n

Water Lily Soc. (1984)
6800 Lilypons Road, Box 104, Buckeystown MD 21717-0104
Secretary: Charles B. Thomas
Members: 425 *Staff:* 1
Annual Budget: $10-25,000 *Tel:* (301) 662-2230
Hist. Note: Established and incorporated at Lilypons, MD, the Society is concerned with all aspects of water gardening. Membership: $15/yr. (individual), $45/yr. (organization).
Publication:
Water Garden Journal. q. adv.
Annual Meetings: August
1987-Denver, CO(Regency)/Aug. 19-23/150
1988-York, England

Water Pollution Control Federation (1928)
601 Wythe St., Alexandria VA 22314-1994
Exec. Director: Quincalee Brown
Members: 35,000 individuals, 700 companies *Staff:* 50
Annual Budget: over $5,000,000 *Tel:* (703) 684-2400
Hist. Note: Founded October 1928 as the Federation of Sewage and Industrial Wastes Ass'ns and incorporated in Illinois in 1941. Became the Water Pollution Control Federation January 1, 1960. Membership consists of autonomous regional ass'ns which are concerned with the treatment and disposal of domestic and industrial watewaters; groundwater; toxic and hazardous wastes. Has an annual budget of $6,500,000.
Publications:
Operations Forum. m. adv.
Highlights. m.
Journal. m. adv.
Annual Meetings: Fall/11,000
1987-Philadelphia, PA(Civic Center)/Oct. 4-8
1988-Dallas, TX(Convention Center)/Oct. 2-6
1989-San Francisco, CA(Moscone Center)/Oct. 15-19
1990-Washington, DC(Convention Center)/Oct. 7-11
1991-Toronto, Ontario(Convention Center)/Oct. 6-11
1992-New Orleans, LA(Convention & Exposition Center)/Sept. 20-24
1993-Salt Lake City, UT(Salt Palace)/Sept. 26-30

Water Quality Ass'n (1974)
4151 Naperville Road, Lisle IL 60532
Exec. Director: Douglas R. Oberhamer, CAE
Members: 1,700 *Staff:* 22
Annual Budget: $2-5,000,000 *Tel:* (312) 369-1600
Hist. Note: Merger of the Water Conditioning Ass'n Internat'l (1945) and the Water Conditioning Foundation (1948). A not-for-profit international trade association representing firms and individuals engaged in the design, manufacture, production, distribution, and sale of equipment, products, supplies and services for providing quality water for specific uses in residential, commercial, industrial and institutional establishments. Membership is voluntary. The Water Quality Research Council, formerly (1971) the Water Conditioning Research Council, is its research and educational arm.
Publication:
WQA Newsletter. m.
Annual Meetings: March
1987-Dallas, TX(Loew's Anatole)
1988-Reno, NV(MGM Grand)
1989-Orlando, FL

Water Quality Research Council (1950)
Hist. Note: Educational and research arm of the Water Quality Ass'n. Formerly (1971) the Water Conditioning Research Council.

Water Resources Congress (1971)
3800 N. Fairfax Drive, Suite 7, Arlington VA 22203
President: Ray Leonard
Members: 300 *Staff:* 2
Annual Budget: $50-100,000 *Tel:* (703) 525-4881
Hist. Note: Merger of the Nat'l Rivers and Harbors Congress (1901) and Water Resources Ass'n (1919); formerly (1970) Missipi Valley Ass'n. A federation of associations, governmental agencies and private firms concerned with land and water use, conservation, and control. Membership: $150/yr. (individual); $300/yr. (organization/company)
Publication:
Washington Report. semi-a.
Annual Meetings: May
1987-Washington, DC(Hyatt Capitol Hill)/May 10-12
1988-New Orleans, LA

Water Ski Industry Ass'n (1977)
200 Castlewood Drive, North Palm Beach FL 33408
Exec. Director: James Hotchkiss
Members: 46 companies *Staff:* 2-5
Annual Budget: $50-100,000 *Tel:* (305) 842-3600
Hist. Note: An affiliate of the Sporting Goods Manufacturers Ass'n, which provides administrative support. Incorporated in the State of Florida.
Annual Meetings: Fall, at the Marine Trade Show in Chicago, IL

Water Supply Improvement Ass'n (1973)
Hist. Note: Merged with the Internat'l Desalination and Environmental Ass'n to form the Internat'l Desalination Ass'n in 1985.

Water Systems Council (1932)
600 S. Federal St., #400, Chicago IL 60605
Exec. Director: Charles Stolberg
Members: 50 *Staff:* 2-3
Annual Budget: $100-250,000 *Tel:* (312) 346-1600

00301 12 05 86 1233

Hist. Note: Formerly the National Association of Domestic and Farm Pump Manufacturers, members make pumps and well drilling equipment and are prepared to install individual sources of water as opposed to central sources of supply. Affiliated with the Ground Water Council.
Semi-annual meetings: Spring and Fall in Chicago, IL

Water Transport Ass'n (1962)
Box 1460, Cincinnati OH 45201
Chairman of the Executive Committee: John Geary
Members: 25-30 *Staff:* 5-10
Annual Budget: $100-250,000 *Tel:* (513) 721-4000
Hist. Note: Established as the Common Carrier Conference of Domestic Water Carriers, it assumed its present name in 1965. Members are barge lines and steamship companies serving on inland waterways, the Great Lakes and coastal waters.

Waterbed Manufacturers Ass'n (1973)
2500 Wilshire Blvd., Suite 603, Los Angeles CA 90057
Exec. Director: Raymond P. Delrich, CAE
Members: 225 companies *Staff:* 5
Annual Budget: $1-2,000,000 *Tel:* (213) 384-3179
Publication:
Nightletter. m.
Annual Meetings: March/April
1987-Las Vegas, NV(Convention Center)/April 6-10/5,000
1988-San Francisco, CA(Moscone Center)/March 18-25/6,000
1989-Las Vegas, NV(Convention Center)/April 6-10/6,500

Waterbed Retailers Ass'n (1972)
Hist. Note: Also known as the Nat'l Waterbed Retailers Ass'n.

Weather Modification Ass'n (1951)
P.O. Box 8116, Fresno CA 93747
Exec. Secretary: Hilda Duckering
Members: 200 individuals, 10-15 companies *Staff:* 1
Annual Budget: under $10,000 *Tel:* (209) 291-8466
Hist. Note: Formerly (1967) Weather Control Research Ass'n.
Publications:
Newsletter. q.
Journal of Weather Modification. a.
Semi-annual meetings: Spring and Fall

Weaving and Spinning Council
Hist. Note: Ceased operations in 1986.

Web Offset Section
Hist. Note: A special industry group of Printing Industries of America.

Web Sling Ass'n (1973)
4010 S. 57th Ave., Suite 202, Lake Worth FL 33463
Exec. Director: Michael R. Cloney
Members: 30-40 *Staff:* 2-5
Annual Budget: $25-50,000
Hist. Note: Manufacturers of web slings which are used as hoists in various industrial operations.

Wedding Photographers Internat'l (1974)
Box 2003, 1312 Lincoln Blvd., Santa Monica CA 90406
President: Steve Sheanin
Members: 3,500-3,600 *Staff:* 2-5
Annual Budget: $250-500,000 *Tel:* (213) 451-0090
Hist. Note: Established as Wedding Photographers of America, WPI assumed its present name in 1977. Promotes high artistic and technical standards; serves as a forum for the exchange of knowledge and experience; and offers instruction in techniques, advertising, sales, promotion, marketing, public relations, accounting, management and tax planning. Membership: $42/yr.
Publication:
The Wedding Photographer. m.
Annual Meetings: Spring
1987-Las Vegas, NV(Tropicana)/Feb. 8-12/1,000

Weed Science Soc. of America (1953)
309 West Clark St., Champaign IL 61820
Exec. Secy.: Carl D. Johnson
Members: 3,200-3,300 *Staff:* 1
Annual Budget: $100-250,000 *Tel:* (217) 356-3182
Hist. Note: Founded as the Weed Society of America, it absorbed the Association of Regional Weed Control Conferences in 1956 and assumed its present name in 1963. Has members from Mexico and Canada.
Publication:
Weed Science. bi-m.
Annual Meetings: February

Welded Steel Tube Institute (1930)
522 Westgate Tower, Cleveland OH 44116
Exec. Director: Robert Boeddener
Members: 25 companies *Staff:* 2-5
Annual Budget: $100-250,000 *Tel:* (216) 333-4550
Hist. Note: Formerly (until 1960) the Formed Steel Tube Institute. Incorporated in 1955 in the State of Ohio. Members are producers of steel tubing produced from carbon, stainless, or alloy steel, for applications ranging from large structural tubing to small redrawn tubing. The Institute has four product councils - the Structural Tubing Producer Council, the Cold Drawn Tubing Producer Council, the Mechanical/Pressure Tubing Producer Council and the West Coast Tubing Producer Council.
Annual Meetings: Spring

Welding Research Council (1935)
345 East 47th St., Suite 1301, New York NY 10017
President & Exec. Director: Dr. Glenn W. Oyler
Members: 400 organizations *Staff:* 6-10
Annual Budget: $2-5,000,000 *Tel:* (212) 705-7956
Hist. Note: Established by the Engineering Foundation to conduct and coordinate welding research. Membership: $1,000/yr.
Publications:
Reports of Progress. bi-m.
WRC Bulletin. 10/yr.
Welding Research Abroad. 10/yr.
Welding Research News. q.
Welding Research Supplement. m.
Annual Meetings: Not held

Welsh Black Cattle Ass'n (1975)
Box 76B, Route 1, Shelburn IN 47879
Secretary: Susan Case
Members: 150 owners and breeders *Staff:* 1
Annual Budget: under $10,000 *Tel:* (812) 383-9233
Hist. Note: Breeders and fanciers of Welsh black cattle. Membership: $25/yr.
Publication:
Welsh World. a.
Annual Meetings:
1987-Douglas, AZ/Sept.

Welsh Pony and Cob Soc. of America (1906)
Box 2977, Winchester VA 22601
Secy.-Treas.: Victoria S. Headley
Members: 800 *Staff:* 3
Annual Budget: $50-100,000 *Tel:* (703) 667-6195
Hist. Note: Founded as the Welsh Pony and Cob Soc. of America in Illinois in 1906; reinstituted after a period of inactivity in Indiana in 1946 as Welsh Pony Soc. of America; reassumed its original name in 1986. Membership: $25/yr.
Publications:
Nat'l Welsh Pony Yearbook. a. adv.
Welsh Pony Soc. Newsletter. q.
Welsh Pony Studbook. a.
Annual Meetings:
1987-Lexington, KY/50-100

Welsh Pony Soc. of America
Hist. Note: Became the Welsh Pony and Cob Soc. of America in 1986.

West Coast Perishable Export Ass'n
Hist. Note: A Webb-Pomerene Act ass'n. Ceased operations in 1984.

Western and English Manufacturers Ass'n (1963)
789 Sherman St., Suite 360, Denver CO 80203
Exec. Director: Carl O. Norberg, CAE
Members: 100 companies *Staff:* 2-5
Annual Budget: $250-500,000 *Tel:* (303) 837-1280
Hist. Note: Manufacturers of Western and English style riding equipment and clothes. Until 1976 known as the Western and English Apparel and Equipment Manufacturers Association. Maintains a commercial credit program for membership and Salesman Representatives Registry.
Publications:
WAEMA Bulletin. bi-m.
Market Calendar Directory.
Annual Meetings: July/August
1987-Albuquerque, NM(Marriott)/Aug. 2-5/80

Western Ass'n of Equipment Lessors (1975)
1516 South Pontius Ave., Los Angeles CA 90025
Exec. V. President: Randy Bauler, CAE
Members: 500 companies *Staff:* 3
Annual Budget: $250-500,000 *Tel:* (213) 478-0215
Hist. Note: Represents bank-related leasing companies in 24 Western states. Membership: $400-700/yr.
Publications:
Newsline. bi-m. adv.
For Members Only. bi-m.
Funding Source Profile Directory. a.
Membership Directory. a.
Semi-annual Meetings: Spring and Fall
1987-San Diego, CA/May/300
1987-Hawaii/Sept./300

Western Awning Ass'n (1952)
25332 Narbonne Ave., Suite 170, Lomita CA 90717
Exec. Director: Clay M. Johnston
Members: 65 companies *Staff:* 2
Annual Budget: $10-25,000 *Tel:* (213) 539-6080
Hist. Note: Sellers and manufacturers of patio structures, screen enclosures and window awnings. Member of The Internat'l Conference of Building Officials. The only recognized awning ass'n in the U.S.
Publication:
News Bulletin. q.

Western/English Retailers of America (1976)
2011 Eye St., N.W., Suite 600, Washington DC 20006
Director: Ralph Beatty
Members: 200 *Staff:* 2-5
Annual Budget: $25-50,000 *Tel:* (202) 347-1932
Hist. Note: Established as the National Western/English Retailers Association, the word "National" was soon dropped and the present name assumed. A division of Menswear Retailers of America which provides administrative support, members are mostly smaller retail outlets.
Publication:
Business Newsletter. m.
Annual Meetings: Always in Denver, CO in Winter

Western Forest Industries Ass'n (1947)
1500 South West Taylor St., Portland OR 97205
President: Joseph W. McCracken
Members: 125 *Staff:* 10
Annual Budget: $500-1,000,000 *Tel:* (503) 224-5455
Hist. Note: Formed by a merger of the Pacific Lumber Remanufacturing Ass'n and the Portland Western Ass'n of Lumbermen and Loggers. Sponsors the Rosario Fund, a political action committee.
Publication:
Out-of-the Woods. w.
Annual Meetings: February

Western Railroad Ass'n (1970)
222 South Riverside Plaza, Suite 1100, Chicago IL 60606
President: James N. Baker
Members: 37 railroads *Staff:* 133
Annual Budget: over $5,000,000 *Tel:* (312) 648-7800
Hist. Note: Antecedent organizations were established as early as the 1880's for ratemaking and conducting matters related to Western regional interests. Since the Staggers Act, the association has confined its activities to railroad tariff publishing. The present organization resulted from a merger of the Ass'n of Western Railways and Western Railroad Traffic Ass'n. Has an annual budget of approximately $9 million.
Quarterly Meetings: in Chicago, IL

Western Range Ass'n (1950)
7844 Madison Ave., Suite 105, Fair Oaks CA 95628
Exec. Director: Larry Garro
Members: 290 *Staff:* 2-5
Annual Budget: $50-100,000 *Tel:* (916) 962-1500
Hist. Note: A group of western sheep producers united to expand the pool of shepherds from foreign and domestic labor sources.
Annual Meetings: Always June in Reno, NV

Western Red Cedar Ass'n (1898)
P.O. Box 2786, New Brighton MN 55112
Secy-Treas.: Arthur R. Zemske
Members: 6-10 companies *Staff:* 1
Annual Budget: under $10,000 *Tel:* (612) 633-4334
Hist. Note: Formerly the Western Red and Northern White Cedar Association. Affiliated with the Western Wood Products Ass'n. Membership: $300/yr.
Publication:
Cedar Notes. 3/yr.
Annual Meetings: March

Western Red Cedar Lumber Ass'n (1954)
Yeon Bldg., Portland OR 97204
Secy.-Manager: Robert H. Hunt
Members: 20 companies *Staff:* 2-5
Annual Budget: $100-250,000 *Tel:* (503) 224-3930
Hist. Note: Affiliated with the Western Wood Products Association.

Western States Meat Ass'n (1982)
1615 Broadway, Suite 900, Oakland CA 94612
Exec. Director: Rosemary Mucklow
Members: 700-750 *Staff:* 6-10
Annual Budget: $250-500,000 *Tel:* (415) 763-1533
Hist. Note: Has a national membership. Formed in 1982 by a merger of the Western States Meat Packers Ass'n and the Pacific Coast Meat Ass'n.
Publication:
Bulletin. w.
Annual Meetings: February
1987-Reno, NV/Feb. 26-March 1

Western Timber Ass'n (1952)
1251 Beacon Blvd., 1st Fl., West Sacramento CA 95691
Exec. V. President: William N. Dennison
Members: 27 companies *Staff:* 6
Annual Budget: $250-500,000 *Tel:* (916) 372-4786
Hist. Note: Formerly (1972) Western Lumber Manufacturers Ass'n. Members are sawmills dependent on government timber sources.
Semi-annual Meetings in California: Feb. and August
1987-West Sacramento, CA(Hotel El Rancho)/Feb. 26-27/100-110

Western Wood Products Ass'n (1964)
1500 Yeon Bldg., Portland OR 97204
President: Howard A. Roberts
Members: 300 companies *Staff:* 100
Annual Budget: over $5,000,000 *Tel:* (503) 224-3930
Hist. Note: A consolidation in 1964 of the Western Pine Association and the West Coast Lumbermen's Association. Operates a lumber grade inspection bureau to ensure uniform grading standards.
Publication:
Plumb Line. w.
Semi-Annual Meetings: Spring and Fall

Western World Pet Supply Ass'n (1951)
P.O. Box 1337, South Pasadena CA 91030
Exec. V. President: Thomas H. McLaughlin
Members: 287 companies *Staff:* 1

00302 12 05 86 1233

Annual Budget: $100-250,000 *Tel:* (818) 799-7182
Hist. Note: Represents the interests of pet industry manufacturers, importers, product distributors, breeder/livestock distributors and manufactuers' representatives.
Publication:
PET NEWS. q.
Semi-annual Meetings: July and October
1987-Long Beach, CA(Convention Center)/July 25-27
1987-Phoenix, AZ(Phoenix Civic Center)/Oct. 24-25

Western Writers of America (1953)
1753 Victoria, Sheridan WY 82801
Secy.-Treas.: Barbara Ketcham
Members: 550 *Staff:* 1
Annual Budget: $25-50,000 *Tel:* (307) 672-2079
Hist. Note: Professional writers and others interested in Western literature, biography, history and cinema. Sponsors the annual Spur Award in various fields of Western writing. Membership: $40/year.
Publication:
The Roundup. m.
Annual Meetings: Always third full week in June.
1987-Sheridan, WY
1988-San Diego, CA

Wet Ground Mica Ass'n (1933)
715 Boylston St., Boston MA 02116
Secretary: Richard Guild
Members: 3 companies *Staff:* 1
Annual Budget: under $10,000 *Tel:* (617) 266-6800
Hist. Note: Processors of wet ground mica, a component of paint, rubber, plastics, etc.
Annual Meetings: June

Wheat and Wheat Foods Foundation (1969)
Hist. Note: Defunct in 1982.

Wheat Gluten Industry Council (1979)
4510 W. 89th St., Prairie Village KS 66207
Exec. Director: J.M. Hesser
Members: 4 companies *Staff:* 2
Annual Budget: $10-25,000 *Tel:* (913) 341-1155
Hist. Note: WGIC members are domestic producers of wheat gluten and wheat starch on a commercial basis. Primary purpose is to expand and develop markets for these products and to coordinate regulatory matters pertaining to wheat gluten. Affiliated with the Internat'l Wheat Gluten Ass'n, an international trade association of 18 producers, located at the same address. Membership: $500/yr.
Publications:
Product Applications Bulletin. a.
Standard Test Method Bulletin. a.
Wheat Gluten - A Natural Protein for the Future. a.
Wheat Gluten World. q.
Membership Directory. bi-a.
Annual Meetings: June
1987-Vail, CO(Westin Hotel)/June 21-25/10-15
1988-Federal Republic of Germany/June 26-29/10-15
1989-Canada/June 18-21/10-15
1990-Argentina/June 24-27/10-15
1991-Bordeaux, France/June 23-26/10-15

Wheat Industry Council
Hist. Note: Dissolved in 1986.

Wheat Quality Council (1938)
404 Humboldt St., Suite G, Manhattan KS 66502
Exec. V. President: Thomas C. Roberts
Members: 185-200 *Staff:* 2-5
Annual Budget: $50-100,000 *Tel:* (913) 776-6348
Hist. Note: Established as the Kansas Wheat Improvemnt Association, it assumed its present name in 1980. A not-for-profit organization of Agri-Business groups that invest in continuing hard winter wheat quality improvement.
Publication:
Wheat Quality Notes. 9/yr.
Annual Meetings: January

Wheel Tractor and Attachments Council
Hist. Note: A division of the Farm and Industrial Equipment Institute.

Whey Products Institute (1971)
Hist. Note: Merged with the American Dry Milk Institute to form the American Dairy Products Institute in 1986.

White House Correspondents Ass'n (1914)
1067 Nat'l Press Bldg., Washington DC 20045
Office Manager:
Members: 500 *Staff:* 1
Annual Budget: under $10,000 *Tel:* (202) 737-2934
Hist. Note: Established in February, 1914. Newspaper, magazine, television and radio reporters of White House news.
Annual Meetings: Washington, DC in April

White House News Photographers Ass'n (1921)
Box 7119, Ben Franklin Station, Washington DC 20044-7119
President: Kenneth Lee Blaylock
Members: 450-500 *Staff:* 1
Annual Budget: $250-500,000 *Tel:* (703) 683-2557
Hist. Note: Founded in June 1921 with 24 charter members, membership is limited to professional photographers covering the White House or Capitol Hill on a regular basis. Major function is an annual dinner in honor of the President. Membership: $45/yr.
Publication:
The White House News Photographer. a.
Quarterly Meetings: in Washington, DC.

White Park Cattle Ass'n of America (1975)
419 North Water St., Madrid IA 50156
Office Secretary: Joyce Fisher
Members: 277 cattle owners and breeders *Staff:* 1
Annual Budget: $10-25,000 *Tel:* (515) 795-2013
Hist. Note: Breeders and fanciers of Park cattle.
Publication:
The Park Post. q.

Wholesale Florists and Florist Suppliers of America (1926)
5313 Lee Highway, Box 7308, Arlington VA 22207
Exec. V. President: Archie J. Clapp
Members: 1,100 *Staff:* 6-10
Annual Budget: $1-2,000,000 *Tel:* (703) 241-1100
Hist. Note: Until 1961 known as the Wholesale Commission Florists of America.
Publications:
Buyer's Guide. a.
Membership Directory. a. adv.
The Link. m. adv.
Annual Meetings: March/5-550
1987-Maui, HI/March 11-14
1988-Disney World, FL/March 2-5

Wholesale Nursery Growers of America (1965)
1250 Eye St., N.W., Suite 500, Washington DC 20005
Exec. V. President: Robert F. Lederer, CAE
Members: 700 companies *Staff:* 2-5
Annual Budget: $25-50,000 *Tel:* (202) 789-2900
Hist. Note: Affiliated with American Ass'n of Nurserymen.
Publication:
The Grower. q.
Semi-annual meetings: January in Chicago and July with the American Ass'n of Nurserymen

Wholesale Stationer's Ass'n (1916)
3166 Des Plaines Ave., Des Plaines IL 60018
Exec. V. President: John P. Danglade, CAE
Members: 300-325 companies *Staff:* 6
Annual Budget: $500-1,000,000 *Tel:* (312) 297-6882
Hist. Note: Established in 1916 as the Wholesale Stationers' Association of the U.S.A. and Canada. Formerly (1964) Wholesale Stationery and Office Equipment Association. Absorbed the Wholesale School, Art and Stationery Supplies Association (1962) in 1965. Membership includes both wholesalers and manufacturers. Membership dues based on dollar sales volume.
Publications:
Wholesaler Digest. bi-m.
Membership Roster. semi-a.
Wholesaler Catalog Guide. a.
Manufacturers Guide to Promotions and Advertising. a.
Annual Meetings: Spring/800
1987-Maui, HI(Marriott Resort)/April 5-9
1988-Miami, FL(Doral)/April 17-21
1989-Palm Desert, CA(Marriott Desert Springs)/April 9-13
1990-Orlando, FL(Hyatt Regency Grand Cypress)/April 1-5

Wild Bird Feeding Institute (1984)
1441 Shermer Road, Northbrook IL 60062
Exec. Secretary: Sue Wells
Members: 45 companies *Staff:* 3
Annual Budget: $10-25,000 *Tel:* (312) 272-0135
Hist. Note: Members are feed manufacturing, seed packing and processing companies. Organized primarily to promote the sales of bird feeding products.
Semi-Annual Meetings:

Wild Blueberry Ass'n of North America (1981)
18 Floral Ave., Fredericton New Brunswick E3A IK7
Exec. Director: Dr. G.W. Wood
Members: 15 companies, 37 individuals *Staff:* 2
Annual Budget: $250-500,000 *Tel:* (506) 472-2517
Hist. Note: An association of producers and processors of wild blueberries; open to anyone interested in the crop. Membership Fee: Based on production.
Annual Meetings: April
1987-Bangor, ME/April 10

Wild Rice Growers Ass'n (1969)
Hist. Note: Became the International Wild Rice Association in 1982.

Wildlife Disease Ass'n (1951)
Box 886, Ames IA 50010
Business Manager: Richard Dale
Members: 2,000 *Staff:* 1
Annual Budget: $25-50,000 *Tel:* (515) 233-1931
Hist. Note: Formed in March 1951 in Milwaukee at the North American Wildlife Conference. Originally the Committee on Wildlife Diseases, the name was changed to the Wildlife Disease Ass'n in 1952 and the ass'n was incorporated in Illinois in 1964. Membership: $30/yr. (individual), $48.50/yr. (organization).
Publications:
Journal of Wildlife Diseases. q.
Newsletter. q.
Annual Meetings: August

Wildlife Management Institute (1911)
1101 14th St., N.W., Suite 725, Washington DC 20005
President: Daniel A. Poole
Members: 700 *Staff:* 20
Annual Budget: $500-1,000,000 *Tel:* (202) 371-1808
Hist. Note: The programs of the Institute have been in existence under various names since 1911. Incorporated in New York in 1946. Sponsors the North American Wildlife and Natural Resources Conference.
Publications:
Outdoor News Bulletin. bi-w.
Transactions. a.
Annual Meetings: Spring/1,500
1987-Quebec City, Canada(Le Chateau Frontenac)/March 20-25

Wildlife Soc., The (1937)
5410 Grosvenor Lane, Bethesda MD 20814
Exec. Director: Harry E. Hodgdon
Members: 8,000 *Staff:* 6-10
Annual Budget: $500-1,000,000 *Tel:* (301) 897-9770
Hist. Note: Originated in the District of Columbia in 1936 during the North American Wildlife Conference. Originally the Soc. of Wildlife Specialists, it became The Wildlife Soc. in 1937 and was incorporated in the District of Columbia in 1948. Member society of the Renewable Natural Resources Foundation. Membership: $18/yr.
Publications:
Journal of Wildlife Management. q.
The Wildlifer. bi-m.
Wildlife Society Bulletin. q.
Annual Meetings: March/200-250
1987-Quebec City, Quebec(Le Chateau Frontenac)/March 20-25
1988-Louisville, KY(Galt House Hotel)/March 18-22

Window Shade Manufacturers Ass'n (1949)
Hist. Note: Voluntarily dissolved in 1982.

Wine and Spirits Guild of America (1947)
1766 Dupont Ave., South, Minneapolis MN 55403
Exec. Secretary: Max B. Green
Members: 40-50 (200-300 stores) *Staff:* 1
Annual Budget: $25-50,000 *Tel:* (612) 377-6459
Hist. Note: Membership: $600/yr.
Publication:
Newsletter. m.
Semi-annual Meetings: Spring and Fall
1987-New York, NY(Intercontinental)/May 3-6
1987-Colorado Springs, CO(Broadmoor)/Sept. 11-17
1988-Boston, MA(Copley Place)/Spring
1988-San Diego, CA/Fall

Wine and Spirits Shippers Ass'n (1976)
11800 Sunrise Valley Dr., Reston VA 22091
Mng. Director: Geoffrey Giovanetti
Members: 320 companies *Staff:* 6-10
Annual Budget: $500-1,000,000 *Tel:* (703) 860-2300
Hist. Note: Members are importers and distributors of alcoholic beverages. Primarily concerned with negotiating and arranging ocean freight for imports by members.
Annual Meetings:
1987-Los Angeles, CA(Biltmore/Bonaventure)/April 26-May 1

Wine and Spirits Wholesalers of America (1943)
2033 M St., N.W., Suite 400, Washington DC 20036
Exec. V. President and Gen. Counsel: Douglas W. Metz
Members: 800-850 establishments *Staff:* 12
Annual Budget: $1-2,000,000 *Tel:* (202) 293-9220
Hist. Note: Sponsors and supports the Wine and Spirits Wholesalers of America Political Action Committee.
Publications:
Bulletin. irreg.
Blue Book-Industry Directory. a.
Directions. bi-m.
Annual Meetings: Spring/3,500
1987-Los Angeles, CA(Bonaventure)/April 26-May 1
1988-Boston, MA(Marriott)/April 17-21
1989-Honolulu, HI(Sheraton)/April 30-May 5
1990-San Francisco, CA(Marriott)/May

Wine Institute (1934)
165 Post St., San Francisco CA 94108
Pres. and Gen. Manager: John A. De Luca
Members: 520 *Staff:* 40-50
Annual Budget: $2-5,000,000 *Tel:* (415) 986-0878
Hist. Note: Trade association of the California wine industry. Supports the Wine Institute Political Action Committee.
Publication:
Wine Institute Bulletin. m.
Annual Meetings: Summer

Wire Ass'n Internat'l (1930)
Box H, 1570 Boston Post Rd., Guilford CT 06437
Exec. Director: G.R."Monk" Munger
Members: 4,700 *Staff:* 25-30
Annual Budget: $1-2,000,000 *Tel:* (203) 453-2777
Hist. Note: Formerly (1977) the Wire Association Inc. Members are individuals involved in wire manufacturing, wire forming and fabricating and supplying the wire industry. Membership: $50/yr.
Publications:
Wire Journal International. m. adv.
Wire Journal International Directory/Catalog. a. adv.
WA Newsletter. q.

00303 12 05 86 1233

Annual Meetings: Fall
1987-Atlanta, GA(World Congress Center)/Oct. 27-30/8,000
1988-Toronto, Ontario(Sheraton)/Oct. 16-20/3,000
1989-Atlanta, GA(World Congress Center)/Nov. 7-10/8,000
1990-Boston, MA(Marriott and Westin)/Oct. 28-Nov. 1/3,000

Wire Fabricators Ass'n (1976)
710 East Ogden Ave., Suite 113, Naperville IL 60540
Exec. V. President: Arthur W. Seeds, CAE
Members: 32 companies *Staff:* 5
Annual Budget: $10-25,000 *Tel:* (312) 369-2406
Hist. Note: Members are manufacturers of items composed principally of low carbon steel wire. Membership: $250-350/yr. (company), based on number of employees.

Wire Machinery Builders Ass'n (1918)
7297 Lee Hwy., Suite N, Falls Church VA 22042
Exec. Director: Harry W. Buzzerd, Jr.
Members: 35
Annual Budget: $10-25,000 *Tel:* (703) 533-9530
Annual Meetings: Spring
1987-Williamsburg, VA(Williamsburg Hospitality House)/May 7-8

Wire Reinforcement Institute (1930)
8361 A Greensboro Drive, McLean VA 22102
President: William V. Wagner, Jr.
Members: 20 companies *Staff:* 2-5
Annual Budget: $100-250,000 *Tel:* (703) 790-9790
Hist. Note: Members are manufacturers of steel welded wire fabric produced according to the standards of the American Soc. for Testing & Materials.
Semi-annual meetings: May and November.

Wire Rope Technical Board (1959)
Box 849, Stevensville MD 21666
Exec. Secretary: John D. Ferry
Members: under 50 *Staff:* 2-5
Tel: (301) 643-4161

Wire Service Guild
133 West 44th St., New York NY 10036
Administrator: Kevin Keane
Members: 1,200-1,400 *Staff:* 2-5
Tel: (212) 869-9290
Hist. Note: Labor union representing editorial and commercial department employees of wire services. An affiliate of the Newspaper Guild.

Wirebound Box Manufacturers Ass'n (1934)
380 West Palatine Road, Wheeling IL 60090
Exec. V. President: Charles G. Whitchurch
Members: 20-25 *Staff:* 2-5
Annual Budget: $250-500,000 *Tel:* (312) 520-3280
Hist. Note: Manufacturers of wirebound boxes and crates designed to ship and store heavy industrial products, but also used for meat, poultry, fruit and vegetables.
Semi-annual Meetings: Spring and Fall/75-100
1987-Maui, HI(Inter-Continental)/March 8-10
1987-Chicago, IL/Sept.
1988-Hilton Head, SC(Inter-Continental)/Spring
1988-New Orleans, LA/Sept.
1989-Colorado Springs, CO(Broadmoor)/Spring
1989-Atlanta, GA(Terrace Garden Inn)/Sept.

Women in Communications (1909)
Box 9561, Austin TX 78766
Exec. V. President: Valerie Thurman
Members: 10,500-11,000 individuals *Staff:* 11-15
Annual Budget: $500-1,000,000 *Tel:* (512) 346-9875
Hist. Note: With 180 chapters across the U.S., seeks to improve women's opportunities in the communications professions. Founded as Theta Sigma Phi at the University of Washington, WICI. Assumed its present name in 1972. Membership: $55/yr.(plus local dues).
Publication:
The Professional Communicator. bi-m. adv.
Annual Meetings: Fall
1987-Minneapolis, MN/Oct.
1988-Washington, DC(Hyatt)/Sept. 28-Oct. 2
1989-San Antonio, TX/Oct.
1990-Boston, MA/Oct.

Women in Employee Benefits (1982)
1133 15th St., N.W., Suite 620, Washington DC 20005
Exec. Director: Maggie Greene
Members: 300 individuals *Staff:* 5
Annual Budget: $25-50,000 *Tel:* (202) 293-5910
Hist. Note: Headquartered in Washington, DC, WEB is a national network of professionals whose job responsibilities relate to employee benefits issues. Membership: $75/yr.
Publication:
Membership Directory. a.
Annual Meetings: March

Women in Energy (1981)
c/o Volt Energy Systems, 2500 McCain Place, #211, North Little Rock AR 72116
Nat'l Secretary: Terry Kessinger
Members: 250-300 individuals and companies
Annual Budget: under $10,000 *Tel:* (501) 753-7448
Hist. Note: Members are persons employed in energy and related energy businesses working in areas such as science, engineering, finance, consumer education, communications, home economics, etc. Membership: $35/yr.
Publication:
Women in Energy Newsletter. q.
Annual Meetings: September
1987-Tulsa, OK(Sheraton Kensington)/Sept. 13-15

Women in Government Relations (1975)
1311-A Dolley Madison Blvd. #3A, McLean VA 22101
Exec. Director: George K. Degnon, CAE
Members: 750 *Staff:* 1
Annual Budget: $100-250,000 *Tel:* (703) 556-9222
Hist. Note: An association of women professionals in government relations formed in Washington in December, 1975 by twelve charter members.
Publication:
Newsletter. m.
Annual Meetings: March
1987-Washington, DC(Four Seasons)/March 27/300

Women in Telecommunications (1981)
Hist. Note: Address unknown in 1985.

Women Library Workers (1975)
2027 Parker, Berkeley CA 94704
Nat'l Coordinator: Carol Starr
Members: 500 *Staff:* 1
Annual Budget: under $10,000 *Tel:* (415) 540-6820
Hist. Note: Members are professional librarians, clerks and library technicians interested in ending the discrimination against women in libraries. Has no paid staff. Membership: $15/year.
Publication:
Women Library Workers Journal. q. adv.

Women Life Underwriters Conference (1979)
1922 F St., N.W., Washington DC 20006
Exec. Director: Linda A. Turner, FLMI
Members: 2,000 *Staff:* 2-5
Annual Budget: $100-250,000 *Tel:* (202) 331-6008
Hist. Note: A Conference of the National Association of Life Underwriters. Membership: $50/year.
Publication:
Newsletter. m.
Annual Meetings: September/5,000
1987-Orlando, FL(Marriott World Center)/Sept. 13-17

Women of the Motion Picture Industry, Internat'l (1953)
MGM/UA, 2600 Century Parkway #450, Atlanta GA 30345
Internat'l President: Lynda Norris
Members: 610
Annual Budget: under $10,000 *Tel:* (404) 325-3470
Hist. Note: A federation of 13 clubs throughout the United States and Canada. Has no paid staff or permanent address. Officers change annually. Membership: $10/yr.
Annual Meetings: September
1987-Las Vegas, NV(Hilton)/Sept. 17-20/200

Women's Apparel Chains Ass'n (1945)
75 9th Ave., New York NY 10011
President: John Colletti
Members: 20 chains of stores *Staff:* 1
Annual Budget: $10-25,000 *Tel:* (212) 924-6585
Hist. Note: Principal activity is collective bargaining with labor unions. Has no paid staff.

Women's Caucus for Art (1972)
Moore College of Art, 20th and the Parkway, Philadelphia PA 19103
President: Annie Shaver-Crandell
Members: 3,500 *Staff:* 2
Annual Budget: $25-50,000 *Tel:* (215) 854-0922
Hist. Note: Women artists and educators, art historians and critics, and gallery and museum professionals. Membership: $30-35/yr.
Publications:
Newsletter. q. adv.
Hue Points. 11/yr.
Annual Meetings: February
1987-Boston, MA
1988-Houston, TX

Women's Caucus for the Modern Languages (1970)
Dept. of English, University of Arkansas,impel Hall 333, Fayetteville AR 72701
President: Dr. Margaret Jones Bolsterli
Members: 600-700
Annual Budget: under $10,000
Hist. Note: Women with a professional interest in the teaching and study of modern languages. Has no paid staff. Membership: $4.50-15/yr. (individual, varies with salary).
Publication:
Concerns. 3/yr.
Annual Meetings: With the Modern Language Ass'n
1987-San Francisco, CA
1988-New Orleans, LA

Women's College Coalition (1972)
1101 17th St., N.W., Washington DC 20036
Exec. Director: Marcia Sharp
Members: 65 institutions *Staff:* 3-4
Annual Budget: $50-100,000 *Tel:* (202) 466-5430
Hist. Note: Founded to serve as an advocate and resource for women's colleges, in cooperation with the Ass'n of American Colleges. Members are from 18 states and the District of Columbia, and include private and public, independent and church-related, and two and four year colleges.
Publication:
Publications List Available.

Women's Council of Realtors (1939)
430 North Michigan Ave, Chicago IL 60611
Exec. V. President: Catherine Collins
Members: 14,000 *Staff:* 6-10
Annual Budget: $500-1,000,000 *Tel:* (312) 329-8483
Hist. Note: A support group for women in real estate dedicated to preparing women for leadership roles in business and community service through its network of active state and local chapters. Membership: $34/yr.
Publications:
Communique. m.
Referral Roster. a. adv.
Annual Meetings: With the Nat'l Ass'n of Realtors.

Women's Internat'l Tennis Ass'n (1973)
Grand Bay Plaza, 2665 S. Bayshore Dr., Suite 1002, Miami FL 33133
Exec. Director: Merrett R. Stierheim
Members: 300 *Staff:* 32
Annual Budget: $1-2,000,000 *Tel:* (305) 856-4030
Hist. Note: Formerly (1986) Women's Tennis Ass'n. Members are professional women tennis players. Full membership: $500/yr.
Publications:
Inside Women's Tennis. m.
Media Guide. a.
Glamour Calendar Women of Tennis. a.
Annual Meetings: September at the U.S. Open

Women's Nat'l Book Ass'n (1917)
160 5th Ave., Room 604, New York NY 10010
President: Cathy Rentschler
Members: 1,000 *Staff:* 0
Annual Budget: $10-25,000 *Tel:* (212) 675-7805
Hist. Note: Founded in 1917 as an organization of women and men in all occupations allied to the book publishing industry. Members include publishers, authors, librarians, literary agents, editors, illustrators and booksellers. Has no paid staff.
Publication:
The Bookwoman. 3/yr.
Annual Meetings: Even-numbered years in conjunction with the Women's National Book Association Award; other years, at the discretion of the Board. Always in the Spring or Summer; 70th anniversary celebration: New York, NY/Oct. 29,1987.
1987-Washington, DC/May 21-22/25-30

Women's Professional Basketball League (1976)
Hist. Note: Defunct, 1982.

Women's Professional Rodeo Ass'n (1948)
Route 5, Box 698, Blanchard OK 73010
Secy.-Treas.: Lydia Moore
Members: 2,100 *Staff:* 1
Annual Budget: under $10,000 *Tel:* (405) 485-2277
Hist. Note: Competitors in professional girl rodeos and in barrel races in rodeos sanctioned by the Rodeo Cowboys Ass'n. Formerly (1980) the Girls' Rodeo Ass'n and (1981) the Professional Women's Rodeo Ass'n.
Publications:
News. m
Reference Book. a.
Rule Book. a.
Annual Meetings: December, in conjunction with the Nat'l Finals

Women's Tennis Ass'n
Hist. Note: Became the Women's Internat'l Tennis Ass'n in 1986.

Women's Transportation Seminar (1977)
Box 7753, Ben Franklin Station, Washington DC 20044
Exec. Secretary: Louise B. Morris
Members: 2,000 *Staff:* 1
Annual Budget: $50-100,000 *Tel:* (703) 256-5258
Hist. Note: A national organization of male and female transoportation professionals. Founded in Washington, DC as a mechanism to enhance personal advancement and professional recognition for members. Membership: $20-35/yr. (varies with chapter).
Publications:
WTS National Newsletter. bi-m.
WTS Nat'l Membership Directory. bi-a.
Local Chapter Newsletters. m.
Annual Meetings: May
1987-New York, NY(Vista International)/May 13-14
1988-Minneapolis, MN/May 11-13

Wood and Synthetic Flooring Institute (1954)
4415 West Harrison St., Suite 242C, Hillside IL 60162
Exec. V. President: Patricia Keating
Members: 50 companies *Staff:* 2
Annual Budget: $10-25,000 *Tel:* (312) 449-2933
Hist. Note: Formerly (1970) Wood Flooring Institute of America. Contractors and manufacturers of quality floors and sports surface. Publishes specifications for the design community.
Semi-annual Meetings: March and Nov.

00304 12 05 86 1233

Wood Fibre Exports
Hist. Note: Dissolved in 1984.

Wood Foundation Institute (1980)
P.O. Box 214, Hwy. 30 West, Toledo IA 52342
Exec. V. President: Ed J. Springer
Members: 30 *Staff:* 2
Annual Budget: under $10,000 *Tel:* (515) 484-4424
Hist. Note: Members are fabricators, suppliers, and others interested in wooden foundations. Membership: $500/yr. (individual); $100/yr. (company).
Annual Meetings: November

Wood Heating Alliance (1985)
1101 Connecticut Ave., N.W., Suite 700, Washington DC 20036
Exec. Director: Carter E. Keithley
Members: 820 companies *Staff:* 2-8
Annual Budget: $500-1,000,000 *Tel:* (202) 857-1181
Hist. Note: Members are makers of stoves, fireplaces, residential heating equipment and accesories; their suppliers and others (25% of membership) interested in promoting wood as a source of energy. The present organization is the product of a merger of the Wood Energy Institute, founded in 1974, and the Fireplace Institute, founded in 1973. Sponsors the Wood Heating Alliance Political Action Committee and the the Wood Heating Education-Research Foundation (WHERF), a public education and research foundation.
Publication:
WHA Reporter.
Annual Meetings: March

Wood Machinery Manufacturers of America (1899)
1900 Arch St., Philadelphia PA 19103
Exec. V. President: J. Gordon White, Jr.
Members: 115 companies *Staff:* 6-10
Annual Budget: $250-500,000 *Tel:* (215) 564-3484
Hist. Note: Formerly (1983) the Woodworking Machinery Manfacturers of America.
Publication:
Buyer's Guide and Directory. a.
Annual Meetings: Spring/280
1987-Marco Island, FL(Marriott's Marco Island Resort)/April 30-May 2
1988-Rancho Mirage, CA(Rancho Las Palmas)/April 20-23

Wood Moulding and Millwork Producers Ass'n (1963)
Box 25278, Portland OR 97225
Exec. V. President: Bernard J. Tomasko
Members: 60 companies *Staff:* 2-5
Annual Budget: $250-500,000 *Tel:* (503) 292-9288
Hist. Note: Established as the Western Wood Moulding Producers, it became the Western Wood Moulding and Millwork Producers in 1968 and assumed its present name in 1978.
Publication:
Case 'n Base News. m.
Semi-annual Meetings: February and August.
1987-San Diego, CA(Rancho Bernardo)/Aug. 20-23
1987-Phoenix, AZ/Feb. 18-21
1988-San Diego, CA(Del Coronado)/Feb. 10-13
1988-Coeur D'Alene, ID(North Shore Resort Hotel)/Aug. 10-13

Wood Products Manufacturers Ass'n (1929)
52 Racette Ave., Gardner MA 01440
Exec. Director: Albert J. Bibeau
Members: 225 *Staff:* 2-5
Annual Budget: $100-250,000 *Tel:* (617) 632-3923
Hist. Note: Formerly Wood Turners Service Bureau and Wood Turners and Shapers Ass'n (1978). Incorporated in Massachusetts in 1967, WPMA members represent all facets of the wood industry. Membership fee based on company size.
Publications:
Newsletter. m. adv.
Membership Directory. semi-a. adv.
Annual Meetings:
1987-Columbus, OH(Marriott North)/May 13-16/150
1988-Memphis, TN(Peabody)/March 23-26/200
1989-Lancaster, PA(Historic Strass Inn)/May 3-6/200
1990-Undecided
1991-Orlando, FL(Hyatt Regency)/March 17-19/150

Wood Tank Manufacturers Ass'n (1982)
Rt. 5, Renick WV 24966
President: Barry Glick
Members: 10 companies, 460 individuals *Staff:* 4
Annual Budget: $25-50,000 *Tel:* (304) 497-3163
Hist. Note: Formed to promote the manufacture and use of wooden hot tubs.

Wood Truss Council of America (1983)
111 East Wacker Drive, #600, Chicago IL 60601
Exec. Director: Henry Givray
Members: 400 companies *Staff:* 3
Annual Budget: $100-250,000 *Tel:* (312) 644-6610
Hist. Note: Members formerly constituted the component manufacturers division of the Truss Plate Institute. Membership: $300/yr.
Publication:
Wood Words Newsletter. m. adv.
Annual Meetings: October
1987-Las Vegas, NV

Woodworking Machinery Distributors' Ass'n (1959)
251 West DeKalb Pike, Adams Bldg., Suite 109, King of Prussia PA 19406
Exec. V. President: R. Franklin Brown, Jr.
Members: 110-120 companies *Staff:* 2-5
Annual Budget: $50-100,000 *Tel:* (215) 265-6658
Hist. Note: Dealers and distributors of new and used industrial woodworking machinery and sawmill equipment in the U.S. and Canada. Membership: $500/yr.
Publication:
Membership Directory/Buyers' Guide. a.
Semi-annual meetings: Spring and Fall
1987-Marco Island, FL(Marco Beach)/April 30-May 3/350
1987-New Orleans, LA(Royal Sonesta)/Oct. 27-30/130
1988-Rancho Mirage, CA(Rancho Las Palmas)/April 20-23/350

Woodworking Machinery Importers Ass'n of America (1978)
1740 E. Joppa Road, Box 28279, Baltimore MD 21234
Exec. Vice President: Calvin K. Clemons
Members: 46 members *Staff:* 5
Annual Budget: $100-250,000 *Tel:* (301) 661-4400
Hist. Note: Chief executives of woodworking machinery distributing companies primarily concerned with the import of woodworking machinery. Membership: $300/yr.
Publication:
Newsletter. q.
Biennial meetings: even years

Woodworking Machinery Manufacturers of America (1899)
Hist. Note: Became the Wood Machinery Manufacturers of America in 1983.

Wool Associates of the New York Cotton Exchange (1930)
Hist. Note: Defunct in 1982.

Woolknit Associates (1939)
267 Fifth Ave., Suite 806, New York NY 10016
Exec. Director: Eleanor Kairalla
Members: 100-125 *Staff:* 6-10
Annual Budget: $100-250,000 *Tel:* (212) 683-7785
Hist. Note: Research and promotional association for quality knitwear in natural animal fibers, its members consist of spinners, dyers, growers, knitters and designers.
Publications:
Knitvations. semi-a. adv.
Woolknit Industry Magazine. (fashion documentary for selected list of
retailers and designers).
Annual Meetings: All meetings held at New York headquarters

Word Processing Soc. (1972)
Hist. Note: Became the Office Technology Management Association May 1, 1983.

Work Glove Manufacturers Ass'n (1902)
1615 L St., N.W., Suite 925, Washington DC 20036
Exec. Director: Joseph Cook
Members: 75-100 companies *Staff:* 2-5
Annual Budget: $100-250,000 *Tel:* (202) 296-9200
Hist. Note: Formerly (1967) the Work Glove Institute.
Annual Meetings:
1987-Colorado Springs, CO(Broadmoor)/July 7-11/185

World Aquaculture Soc. (1970)
341 Pleasant Hall, LSU, Baton Rouge LA 70803
Manager, Home Office: Sheree Hohn Ellison
Members: 2,400 *Staff:* 5
Annual Budget: $50-100,000 *Tel:* (504) 388-3137
Hist. Note: Formerly (1986) the World Mariculture Soc. Members are individuals and companies interested in the cultivation of aquatic plants and animals for food purposes. Membership: $30/yr.(individual); $150/yr.(organization).
Publications:
Journal of the World Mariculture Soc. q.
Newsletter. q.
Annual Meetings: Late Winter
1987-Guayaquil, Ecuador/Jan. 18-23
1988-Hawaii

World Ass'n of Detectives (1925)
Box 5068, San Mateo CA 94402
Travel Director: Vance I. Morris
Members: 675-700 individuals
Tel: (415) 341-7277
Hist. Note: Formerly (1967) World Secret Service Ass'n.
Publication:
W.A.D. News. m. adv.
Annual Meetings:
1987-Jerusalem
1988-Denver, CO
1989-Australia or Stockholm

World Ass'n of Document Examiners (1973)
111 N. Canal St., Chicago IL 60606
Exec. Secretary: Lucille Range
Members: 500 *Staff:* 6
Annual Budget: $100-250,000 *Tel:* (312) 930-9446
Hist. Note: Document examiners organized to uphold high standards in the profession and to assist individual practitioners.
Publications:
WADE Journal. q.
WADE Newsletter. m.
Annual Meetings: Always Chicago in July

World Computer Graphics Ass'n (1981)
2033 M St., N.W., Suite 399, Washington DC 20036
President and CEO: Caby C. Smith
Members: 13 companies *Staff:* 7
Annual Budget: $500-1,000,000 *Tel:* (202) 775-9556
Hist. Note: Founded with the goal of promoting the growth and serving the needs of the global computer graphics community, through sponsoring exhibitions, conferences and seminars internationally.
Publications:
Conference Proceedings. q.
Association Update. semi-a.

World Court Clubs Ass'n (1978)
Hist. Note: Court clubs, individuals, and manufacturers of products for racquetball/fitness centers. Absorbed by Court Club Enterprises of Scottsdale, Arizona in 1984, no longer a non-profit association.

World Electroless Nickel Soc. (1980)
Hist. Note: Inactive in 1984.

World Future Soc. (1966)
4916 St. Elmo Ave., Bethesda MD 20814
President: Edward S. Cornish
Members: 30,000 individuals *Staff:* 15-20
Annual Budget: $1-2,000,000 *Tel:* (301) 656-8274
Hist. Note: An association of scientists, educators, government officials and others interested in social and technological developments of the future.
Publications:
Future Survey.
The Futurist. bi-m. adv.
Futures Research Quarterly. q.
Biennial Meetings:

World Population Soc. (1973)
1346 Connecticut Ave., N.W., Suite 906, Washington DC 20036
President: Philander P. Claxton, Jr.
Members: 1000 *Staff:* 2-5
Annual Budget: $50-100,000 *Tel:* (202) 463-6606
Hist. Note: A multidisciplinary group supporting research on and communicating information about population and its impact on the quality of life, and promoting fulfillment of the World Population Plan of Action agreed to by 136 nations in Bucharest in 1974.
Annual Meetings: Fall

World Pro Skiing-Racers Ass'n (1970)
Hist. Note: Professional ski racers who compete on the World Pro Skiing Tour. Reported defunct in 1982.

World Professional Squash Ass'n (1938)
12 Sheppard Street, Suite 401, Toronto Nova Scotia M5H-3-A1
President, marketing: Robert T. French
Members: 300 individuals *Staff:* 5-10
Annual Budget: $100-250,000 *Tel:* (416) 869-3499
Hist. Note: Conducts a squash tour consisting of 30 tournaments and provides a network of teaching programs. Formerly (1977) North American Professional Squash Racquets Association. Membership: $50/yr.(general); $100/yr.(touring pro)
Publication:
World Professional Squash Newsmagazine. 6-12/yr.
Annual Meetings:
1987-Toronto, Ontario(Sheraton Center)/Jan. 3/150

World's Poultry Science Ass'n, U.S.A. Branch (1965)
NPIP, VS, APHIS, USDA, Federal Center Building, Hyattsville MD 20782
Secy.-Treas.: Irvin L. Peterson
Members: 6-700 individuals and companies *Staff:* 1
Annual Budget: under $10,000 *Tel:* (301) 436-5140
Hist. Note: U.S. members of the World's Poultry Science Association. Promotes U.S. participation in World's Poultry Congresses held every 4 years. Membership: $15/yr.
Publication:
World's Poultry Science Journal. 3/yr.
Annual Meetings: With Poultry Science Ass'n.
1988-Nagoya, Japan(Fukiage Hall)/Sept. 5-9/4,000

World Waterpark Ass'n (1981)
7474 Village Drive, Prairie Village KS 66208
Exec. Director: Al Turner
Members: 130 suppliers; 300 parks *Staff:* 3
Annual Budget: $250-500,000 *Tel:* (913) 362-9440
Hist. Note: Membership: $150/yr.
Publications:
Splash. 9/yr. adv.
Buyer's Guide. a. adv.
Annual Meetings: Fall
1987-Orlando, FL(Buena Vista Palace)/Sept. 22-25/900

00305 12 05 86 1233

World Wide White and Creme Horse Registry (1936)
Naber NE 68755
Recording Secretary: Violet Stalhecker
Members: 100-125 *Staff:* 1
Annual Budget: under $10,000
Hist. Note: Founded as the American Albino Horse Club, it became the American Albino Ass'n and assumed its present name in 1980. Memberhip: $10/yr.
Publication:
Roundup News. q.
Annual Meetings: June

Woven Wire Products Ass'n (1942)
2515 N. Nordica Ave., Chicago IL 60635
Secretary: Margaret Tuchscher
Members: 40-50 companies *Staff:* 1
Annual Budget: under $10,000 *Tel:* (312) 637-1359
Hist. Note: Promotes the use of wire mesh products.
Publication:
Newsletter. m.
Semi-annual meetings: Spring and Fall

Writers Guild of America, East (1954)
555 West 57th St., New York NY 10019
Exec. Director: Mona Mangan
Members: 3,000 *Staff:* 20
Annual Budget: $1-2,000,000 *Tel:* (212) 245-6180
Hist. Note: Founded in New York City in 1954 as an independent labor union representing writers in motion pictures, television and radio. Affiliated with the Writers Guild of American, West.
Publication:
Newsletter. m.
Annual Meetings: New York, NY/3rd Thursday in September

Writers Guild of America, West (1954)
8955 Beverly Blvd., Los Angeles CA 90048
Exec. Director: Brian Walton
Members: 6,200 *Staff:* 70
Annual Budget: $1-2,000,000 *Tel:* (213) 550-1000
Hist. Note: Founded in Los Angeles, CA in 1954 as an independent labor union representing writers in motion pictures, television and radio. One of the two branches of the Writers Guild of America. Membership: $100/yr.
Publications:
Newsletter. 10/yr. adv.
Directory. a. adv.
Annual Meetings: September in Los Angeles.

Writing Instrument Manufacturers Ass'n (1943)
1625 Eye St., N. W., Washington DC 20006
Exec. V. President: Frank L. King
Members: 75-100 *Staff:* 2-5
Annual Budget: $100-250,000 *Tel:* (202) 331-1429
Hist. Note: Founded as the Fountain Pen and Mechanical Pencil Manufacturers Association, it assumed its present name in 1963.
Publications:
Manufacturers Directory. a. adv.
Trademark Directory. a.
Semi-annual Meetings: Spring and Fall/75-100

Xi Psi Phi (1889)
1005 East Main St., Ste. 7, Medford OR 97504
Supreme Secy-Treas.: William L. Barnum, D.M.D.
Members: 20,000 *Staff:* 2
Annual Budget: $100-250,000 *Tel:* (503) 772-6011
Hist. Note: A professional dental fraternity. Organized February 8, 1889 at the Unversity of Michigan. Affiliated with the Professional Fraternity Association and the American Dental Interfraternity Council.
Publication:
Xi Psi Phi Quarterly. q.
Annual Meetings: Board Meeting/Summer
1987-Medford, OR(Nendels)/June 4-6/25

Yearbook Printers Ass'n (1976)
Hist. Note: Defunct in 1984.

Young Presidents' Organization (1950)
52 Vanderbilt Ave., New York NY 10017
Exec. Director: Robert P. Paganelli
Members: 4,900 *Staff:* 50-60
Annual Budget: over $5,000,000 *Tel:* (212) 867-1900
Hist. Note: Members are elected corporate presidents between the ages of 40 and 50 whose companies must employ at least 50 individuals and have either $80 million total assets or $4 million annual sales. Has annual budget of over $12 million. Membership: $650/yr.
Publication:
Briefing. 10/yr.

Youth Symphony Orchestras
Hist. Note: A division of the American Symphony Orchestra League.

Zinc Institute (1918)
292 Madison Ave., New York NY 10017
President: Werner T. Meyer
Members: 50 companies *Staff:* 2-5
Annual Budget: $500-1,000,000 *Tel:* (212) 578-4750
Hist. Note: Formerly (1967) American Zinc Institute. Serving as the research, marketing, and promotional arm of the Zinc industry, the Zinc Institute shares administrative services with the Lead Industries Ass'n and the Cadmium Council.
Publications:
Zinc! semi-a.
ZincLines. 3/yr.
Annual Report.
Annual Meetings: With Lead Industries Ass'n
1987-San Francisco, CA(Fairmont)/March 30-April 1/400

Zonta Internat'l (1919)
35 E. Wacker Drive, Chicago IL 60601
Exec. Director: Valerie F. Levitan
Members: 35,000 *Staff:* 15
Annual Budget: $250-500,000 *Tel:* (312) 346-1445
Hist. Note: Classified service organization of executive women in business and professions. Membership: $20.50/year.
Publication:
The Zontian. q.
Biennial Meetings: June-July in even years
1988-Helsinki, Finland(Dipoli)/June
1990-Dallas, TX/June

00306 12 05 86 1233

1987

SUBJECT INDEX

Every active organization in this book has been indexed here under one or more subject headings. In some cases the subject headings used are the products or professions the organization represents. In other cases the subject heading may be the most significant word (the key word) in the title. For example, The American Ass'n of Nurserymen, Inc. will be found under the subject headings HORTICULTURE, LANDSCAPING, NURSERIES, and WHOLESALERS.

00001

SUBJECT INDEX

AGRONOMY

AIR CONDITIONING

AIR POLLUTION see also POLLUTION

AIRPLANES

AIRPORTS

ALLERGY

ALUMINUM

AMBULANCES

ANATOMY

ANESTHESIOLOGY

ANTHROPOLOGY

ANTIQUES

APPAREL

APPLIANCES

SUBJECT INDEX

00004

00005

SUBJECT INDEX

Tobacco Institute
United Cancer Council
Veterinary Cancer Soc.

CANS
Can Manufacturers Institute
Composite Can and Tube Institute

CARDIOLOGY
Academy of Veterinary Cardiology
American Cardiology Technologists Ass'n
American College of Angiology
American College of Cardiology
American Heart Ass'n
American Soc. of Echocardiography
Nat'l Alliance of Cardiovascular Technologists
Nat'l Soc. for Cardiovascular and Pulmonary Technology
North American Soc. of Pacing and Electrophysiology
Soc. of Cardiovascular Anesthesiologists

CAR WASH
Internat'l Carwash Ass'n
Texas Longhorn Breeders Ass'n of America

CARPETS see also RUGS
Ass'n of Specialists in Cleaning and Restoration
Carpet and Rug Institute
Carpet Cushion Council
Carpet Manufacturers Marketing Ass'n
Jute Carpet Backing Council
Nat'l Congress of Floor Covering Ass'ns
Oriental Rug Importers Ass'n of America
Oriental Rug Retailers of America
Retail Floorcovering Institute

CASTING see METAL WORKING

CATHOLIC
American Catholic Correctional Chaplains Ass'n
American Catholic Historical Ass'n
American Catholic Philosophical Ass'n
Ass'n for Religious and Value Issues in Counseling
Ass'n for Social Economics
Ass'n for the Sociology of Religion
Ass'n of Catholic Colleges and Universities
Ass'n of Catholic TV and Radio Syndicators
Ass'n of Jesuit Colleges and Universities
Catholic Actors Guild of America
Catholic Audio-Visual Educators
Catholic Biblical Ass'n of America
Catholic Campus Ministry Ass'n
Catholic Charities USA
Catholic Fine Arts Soc.
Catholic Health Ass'n of the United States
Catholic Library Ass'n
Catholic Press Ass'n
Catholic Theological Soc. of America
Conference of Major Superiors of Men, U.S.A.
Jesuit Philosophical Ass'n of the United States and Canada
Jesuit Secondary Education Ass'n
Nat'l Ass'n of Boards of Education
Nat'l Ass'n of Catholic Chaplains
Nat'l Ass'n of Pastoral Musicians
Nat'l Ass'n of State Catholic Conference Directors
Nat'l Catholic Bandmasters' Ass'n
Nat'l Catholic Business Education Ass'n
Nat'l Catholic Cemetery Conference
Nat'l Catholic Development Conference
Nat'l Catholic Educational Ass'n
Nat'l Catholic Educational Exhibitors
Nat'l Catholic Pharmacists Guild of the United States
Nat'l Conference of Catholic Bishops
Nat'l Council of Catholic Women
Nat'l Federation of Catholic Physicians' Guilds
Nat'l Federation of Priests' Councils
Nat'l Guild of Catholic Psychiatrists
North American Academy of Ecumenists
UNDA-USA

CATS
American Boarding Kennels Ass'n

CATTLE
American Angus Ass'n
American Ass'n of Bovine Practicioners
American Beefalo World Registry
American Blonde D'Aquitaine Ass'n
American Brahman Breeders Ass'n
American Breed Ass'n
American Buffalo Ass'n
American Chianina Ass'n
American Dexter Cattle Ass'n
American Galloway Breeders Ass'n
American Gelbvieh Ass'n
American Genetic Ass'n
American Guernsey Cattle Club
American Hereford Ass'n
American Internat'l Charolais Ass'n
American Internat'l Marchigiana Soc.
American Jersey Cattle Club
American Maine-Anjou Ass'n
American Milking Shorthorn Soc.
American Murray Grey Ass'n
American Pinzgauer Ass'n
American Polled Hereford Ass'n
American Polled Shorthorn Soc.
American Red Brangus Ass'n
American Red Poll Ass'n
American Scotch Highland Breeder's Ass'n
American Shorthorn Ass'n
American Simmental Ass'n
American Tarentaise Ass'n
Amerifax Cattle Ass'n
Ankina Breeders
Ayrshire Breeders Ass'n
Barzona Breeders Ass'n of America
Beef Improvement Federation
Beefmaster Breeders Universal
Brown Swiss Cattle Breeders Ass'n of the U.S.A.
Char-Swiss Breeders Ass'n
Holstein-Friesian Ass'n of America
Internat'l Brangus Breeders Ass'n
Internat'l Zebu Breeders Ass'n
Nat'l Ass'n of Animal Breeders
Nat'l Buffalo Ass'n
Nat'l Cattlemen's Ass'n
Nat'l Mastitis Council
Nat'l Pedigreed Livestock Council
North American Limousin Foundation
North American Normande Ass'n
Production Records
Purebred Dairy Cattle Ass'n
Red Angus Ass'n of America
Santa Gertrudis Breeders Internat'l
Sussex Cattle Ass'n of America
Welsh Black Cattle Ass'n
White Park Cattle Ass'n of America

CEDAR see WOOD & WOOD PRODUCTS

CEMENT see CONCRETE

CEMETERIES see also FUNERALS
American Cemetery Ass'n
American Institute of Commemorative Art
American Monument Ass'n
Continental Ass'n of Funeral and Memorial Socs.
Internat'l Ass'n of Pet Cemeteries
Internat'l Cemetery Supply Ass'n
Monument Builders of North America
Nat'l Catholic Cemetery Conference
Nat'l Concrete Burial Vault Ass'n
Pre-Arrangement Interment Ass'n of America

CERAMICS see also CHINA
American Ass'n of Ceramic Industries
American Ceramic Soc.
Associated Glass and Pottery Manufacturers
Ceramic Arts Federation Internat'l
Ceramic Tile Distributors Ass'n
Ceramic Tile Marketing Federation
Collector Platemakers Guild
Dry Process Ceramic and Steatite Manufacturers Ass'n
Internat'l Porcelain Artist Teachers
Keramos Fraternity
Materials and Methods Standards Ass'n
Nat'l Council on Education for the Ceramic Arts
Nat'l Institute of Ceramic Engineers
Tile Contractors' Ass'n of America

CHAINS
American Chain Ass'n
Chain Link Fence Manufacturers Institute
Nat'l Ass'n of Chain Manufacturers

CHAMBER OF COMMERCE
American-Arab Ass'n for Commerce and Industry
American Chamber of Commerce Executives
American Chamber of Commerce Researchers Ass'n
American Economic Development Council
American-Israel Chamber of Commerce and Industry
Argentina-American Chamber of Commerce
Belgian American Chamber of Commerce in the United States
Brazilian American Chamber of Commerce
British-American Chamber of Commerce
Chamber of Commerce of Latin America
Chamber of Commerce of the United States of America
Colombian American Ass'n
Council of Better Business Bureaus
Council of State Chambers of Commerce
Danish-American Chamber of Commerce (USA)
Ecuadorean American Ass'n
Egyptian-American Chamber of Commerce
Finnish American Chamber of Commerce
French-American Chamber of Commerce in the United States
German American Chamber of Commerce
Hong Kong Trade Development Council
India Chamber of Commerce of America
Internat'l Downtown Ass'n
Italy-America Chamber of Commerce
Mexican Chamber of Commerce of the United States
Nat'l Ass'n of Black and Minority Chambers of Commerce
Nat'l Ass'n of Membership Directors of Chambers of Commerce
Netherlands Chamber of Commerce in the United States
Norwegian-American Chamber of Commerce
Philippine-American Chamber of Commerce
Portugal-U.S. States Chamber of Commerce
Spain-U.S. Chamber of Commerce
Swedish-American Chamber of Commerce
United States-Arab Chamber of Commerce
United States-Austrian Chamber of Commerce
United States Council for Internat'l Business
United States Jaycees
United States-Mexico Chamber of Commerce
United States-Pakistan Economic Council
United States-Yugoslav Economic Council
Venezuelan American Ass'n of the U.S.

CHAPLAINS
American Catholic Correctional Chaplains Ass'n
American Protestant Correctional Chaplains' Ass'n
Ass'n of Jewish Chaplains of the Armed Forces
Ass'n of Mental Health Clergy
Catholic Campus Ministry Ass'n
Military Chaplains Ass'n of the U.S.
Nat'l Ass'n of Catholic Chaplains
Nat'l Ass'n of College and University Chaplains and Directors of Religious Life

CHEMICALS & CHEMICAL INDUSTRY
Acrylamide Producers Ass'n
Acrylonitrile Group
Alliance for Responsible CFC Policy
Alpha Chi Sigma
American Ass'n for Clinical Chemistry
American Ass'n of Cereal Chemists
American Ass'n of Textile Chemists and Colorists
American Carbon Soc.
American Chemical Soc.
American Coke and Coal Chemicals Institute
American College of Toxicology
American Industrial Health Council
American Institute of Chemical Engineers
American Institute of Chemists
American Leather Chemists Ass'n
American Microchemical Soc.
American Oil Chemists' Soc.
American Soc. for Mass Spectrometry
American Soc. for Neurochemistry
American Soc. of Biological Chemists
American Soc. of Brewing Chemists
Aniline Ass'n
Aspirin Foundation of America
Ass'n of Consulting Chemists and Chemical Engineers
Ass'n of Official Analytical Chemists
Ass'n of Official Racing Chemists
Catalysis Soc. of North America
Chemical Coaters Ass'n
Chemical Communications Ass'n
Chemical Fabrics and Film Ass'n
Chemical Manufacturers Ass'n
Chemical Marketing Research Ass'n
Chemical Specialties Manufacturers Ass'n
Chlorine Institute, The
Chlorobenzene Producers Ass'n
Combustion Institute
Commercial Development Ass'n
Compressed Gas Ass'n
Council on Soil Testing and Plant Analysis
Drug, Chemical and Allied Trades Ass'n
Dry Color Manufacturers Ass'n
Electrochemical Soc.
Ethylene Oxide Industry Council
Federation of Analytical Chemistry and Spectroscopy Societies
Federation of Societies for Coatings Technology
Fertilizer Institute
Fire Retardant Chemicals Ass'n
Formaldehyde Institute
Genetic Toxicology Ass'n
Geochemical Soc.
Halogenated Solvents Industry Alliance
Histochemical Soc.
Independent Liquid Terminals Ass'n
Industrial Chemical Research Ass'n
Institute for Polyacrylate Absorbents
Internat'l Chemical Workers Union
Internat'l Glutamate Technical Committee
Internat'l Ozone Ass'n-Pan American Committee Branch
Internat'l Pesticide Applicators Ass'n
Man-Made Fiber Producers Ass'n
Materials Marketing Associates
Methyl Chloride Industry Ass'n
Nat'l Aerosol Ass'n
Nat'l Agricultural Chemicals Ass'n
Nat'l Ass'n of Chemical Distributors
Nat'l Ass'n of Solvent Recyclers
Nat'l Chemical Credit Ass'n
Nat'l Fertilizer Solutions Ass'n
Nat'l Pest Control Ass'n
North American Catalysis Soc.
Northeastern Weed Science Soc.
Oil, Chemical and Atomic Workers Internat'l Union
Pesticide Producers Ass'n
Phytochemical Soc. of North America
Powder Coating Institute
Process Equipment Manufacturers' Ass'n
Professional Lawn Care Ass'n of America
Pulp Chemicals Ass'n
Sales Ass'n of the Chemical Industry
Silicones Health Council
Soc. for Environmental Geochemistry and Health
Soc. of American Wood Preservers
Soc. of Cosmetic Chemists
Soc. of Toxicology
Spill Control Ass'n of America

SUBJECT INDEX

Suppliers of Advanced Composite Materials Ass'n
Synthetic Amorphous Silica and Silicates Industry Ass'n
Synthetic Organic Chemical Manufacturers Ass'n
Tubular Exchanger Manufacturers Ass'n
United States Operating Committee of ETAD
United States Shellac Importers Ass'n

CHILDREN

American Academy of Pediatric Dentistry
American Ass'n of Children's Residential Centers
American Ass'n of Psychiatric Services for Children
American Ass'n of Youth Museums
Ass'n for Child Psychoanalysis
Ass'n for Childhood Education Internat'l
Ass'n for Library Service to Children
Ass'n for Maternal and Child Health and Crippled Children's Programs
Ass'n for the Care of Children's Health
Ass'n of Administrators of the Interstate Compact on the Placement of Children
Ass'n of Jewish Family and Children's Agencies
Children's Book Council
Children's Literature Ass'n
Childrenswear Manufacturers Ass'n
Choristers Guild
Council for Exceptional Children
Infant and Juvenile Manufacturers Ass'n
Infants' and Children's Wear Salesmen's Guild
Infants', Children's and Girls' Sportswear and Coat Ass'n
Nat'l Ass'n for Child Care Management
Nat'l Ass'n for Creative Children and Adults
Nat'l Ass'n for the Education of Young Children
Nat'l Ass'n of Children's Hospitals and Related Institutions
Nat'l Ass'n of Companion Sitter Agencies and Referral Services
Nat'l Ass'n of Homes for Children
Nat'l Ass'n of Jewish Family, Children's and Health Professionals
Nat'l Ass'n of Private Schools for Exceptional Children
Nat'l Ass'n of Public Child Welfare Administrators
Nat'l Children's Eye Care Foundation
Nat'l Consortium for Child Mental Health Services
Nat'l Fellowship of Child Care Executives
Soc. for Adolescent Medicine
Soc. for Research in Child Development
Soc. of Children's Book Writers
USA Toy Library Ass'n

CHINA see also CERAMICS

American Fine China Guild
China, Glass and Giftware Ass'n
Internat'l Porcelain Artist Teachers

CHINESE

American Ass'n for Chinese Studies
Ass'n for Asian Studies
Chinese Language Computer Soc.
Chinese Language Teachers Ass'n
Hong Kong Trade Development Council
Nat'l Council for U.S.-China Trade

CHIROPODY see PODIATRY

CHIROPRACTORS

American Chiropractic Ass'n
Council on Diagnostic Imaging to the A.C.A.
Internat'l Chiropractors Ass'n
Precision Chiropractic Research Soc.
Sacro-Occipital Research Soc. Internat'l

CHOCOLATE

American Cocoa Research Institute
Chocolate Manufacturers Ass'n of the U.S.A.
Cocoa Merchants' Ass'n of America
Nat'l Candy Brokers Ass'n

CIRCULATION

Internat'l Circulation Managers Ass'n
Internat'l Newspaper Promotion Ass'n

CLAY

American Ceramic Soc.
Brick Institute of America
Clay Minerals Soc.
Expanded Shale, Clay and Slate Institute
Nat'l Ass'n of Brick Distributors
Nat'l Clay Pipe Institute
Nat'l Clay Pot Manufacturers Ass'n
Nat'l Plastercraft Ass'n
Refractories Institute
Sorptive Minerals Institute
Stucco Manufacturers Ass'n
Tile Council of America
United States Potters' Ass'n

CLEANERS

Appliance Parts Distributors Ass'n
Ass'n of Specialists in Cleaning and Restoration
Building Service Contractors Ass'n Internat'l
Built-in Cleaning Systems Institute
Cleaning Equipment Manufacturers Ass'n
Cleaning Management Institute
Coin Laundry Ass'n
Institute of Industrial Launderers
Internat'l Ass'n of Wiping Cloth Manufacturers
Internat'l Drycleaners Congress
Internat'l Fabricare Institute
Internat'l Maintenance Institute
Laundry and Dry Cleaning Internat'l Union
Multi-Housing Laundry Ass'n
Nat'l Ass'n of Diaper Services
Nat'l Ass'n of Institutional Linen Management
Nat'l Chimney Sweep Guild
Nat'l Contract Sweepers Institute
Soap and Detergent Ass'n
Textile Care Allied Trades Ass'n
Textile Laundry Council
Textile Processors, Service Trades, Health Care, Professional and Technical Employees Internat'l Union
Textile Rental Services Ass'n of America
Vacuum Cleaner Manufacturers Ass'n

CLOTHING see APPAREL

CLUBS see also FRATERNAL ORGANIZATIONS

Alpha Alpha Gamma
Alpha Beta Alpha
Alpha Chi Sigma
Alpha Kappa Psi
Alpha Omega
Alpha Tau Delta
Alpha Zeta Omega
American Dental Interfraternity Council
American Yorkshire Club
Ass'n of American Air Travel Clubs
Ass'n of College Honor Societies
Ass'n of Community Travel Clubs
Automotive Booster Clubs Internat'l
Beta Alpha Psi
Boys Clubs of America
Boys Clubs Professional Ass'n
Cajal Club
Central Office Executives Ass'n of the Nat'l Panhellenic Conference
Club Managers Ass'n of America
College Fraternity Editors Ass'n
Continental Dorset Club
Delta Omicron
Delta Pi Epsilon
Delta Sigma Delta
Delta Sigma Pi
Delta Theta Phi
Distributive Education Clubs of America
Fraternity Executives Ass'n
Gamma Iota Sigma
General Federation of Women's Clubs
Girls Clubs of America
Gyro Internat'l
Internat'l Council for Computer Communication
Internat'l League of Professional Baseball Clubs
Internat'l Military Club Executives Ass'n
Internat'l Philatelic Press Club
Internat'l Pot and Kettle Club
Internat'l Racquet Sports Ass'n
Iota Tau Tau
Keramos Fraternity
Mu Phi Epsilon
Nat'l Ambucs
Nat'l Ass'n of Colored Women's Clubs
Nat'l Ass'n of Girls Clubs
Nat'l Ass'n of Investors
Nat'l Ass'n of Litho Clubs
Nat'l Ass'n of Negro Business and Professional Women's Clubs
Nat'l Block and Bridle Club
Nat'l Club Ass'n
Nat'l Council of State Garden Clubs
Nat'l Federation of Business and Professional Womens Clubs
Nat'l Federation of Music Clubs
Nat'l Interfraternity Conference
Nat'l League of Professional Baseball Clubs
Nat'l Pan Hellenic Council
Nat'l Panhellenic Conference
Nat'l Writers Club
Omega Tau Sigma
Omicron Kappa Upsilon
Overseas Automotive Club
Overseas Press Club of America
Phi Alpha Delta
Phi Beta Pi - Theta Kappa Psi
Phi Delta Phi
Pi Beta Alpha
Pi Lambda Theta
Professional Fraternity Ass'n
Psi Omega
United States Ass'n of Independent Gymnastic Clubs
Vocational Industrial Clubs of America
Xi Psi Phi

COACHES

American Baseball Coaches Ass'n
American Football Coaches Ass'n
American Hockey Coaches Ass'n
American Swimming Coaches Ass'n
College Swimming Coaches Ass'n of America
Golf Coaches Ass'n of America
ICAAAA Coaches Ass'n
Intercollegiate Tennis Coaches Ass'n
Nat'l Academic Athletic Advisors' Ass'n
Nat'l Ass'n of Basketball Coaches of the United States
Nat'l Ass'n of Collegiate Gymnastics Coaches (Men)
Nat'l Athletic Trainers' Ass'n
Nat'l Coaches Council
Nat'l Fencing Coaches Ass'n of America
Nat'l High School Athletic Coaches Ass'n
Nat'l Soccer Coaches Ass'n of America
Nat'l Strength and Conditioning Ass'n
Nat'l Wrestling Coaches Ass'n
Professional Ski Instructors of America
Speed Coaches Ass'n
United States Cross Country Coaches Ass'n
United States Lacrosse Coaches' Ass'n
United States Ski Coaches Ass'n
Unites States Women's Track Coaches Ass'n

COAL

American Coal Ash Ass'n
American Coke and Coal Chemicals Institute
American Mining Congress
Anthracite Industry Ass'n
Ass'n of Bituminous Contractors
Bituminous Coal Operators Ass'n
Coal Exporters Ass'n of the United States
Institute for Briquetting and Agglomeration
Mining and Reclamation Council of America
Nat'l Coal Ass'n
Nat'l Council of Coal Lessors
Nat'l Independent Coal Operators Ass'n
Open Pit Mining Ass'n
Slurry Technology Ass'n

COCOA see CHOCOLATE

COINS see NUMISMATICS

COLOR

Ass'n of Professional Color Laboratories
Certified Color Manufacturers Ass'n
Color Ass'n of the United States
Color Marketing Group
Dry Color Manufacturers Ass'n
Inter-Society Color Council
Manufacturers Council on Color and Appearance

COMMODITIES

American Soybean Ass'n
American Sugarbeet Growers Ass'n
Board of Trade of the Wholesale Seafood Merchants
Coffee, Sugar and Cocoa Exchange
Futures Industry Ass'n
Hop Growers of America
Nat'l Ass'n of Futures Trading Advisors
Nat'l Ass'n of Wheat Growers
Nat'l Futures Ass'n
Nat'l Grain Sorghum Producers Ass'n
Nat'l Grain Trade Council
Nat'l Live Stock and Meat Board
New York Cotton Exchange
Supima Ass'n of America

COMMUNICATIONS

American Academy of Advertising
American Ass'n of Disability Communicators
American SMR Network Ass'n
American Telemarketing Ass'n
Armed Forces Broadcasters Ass'n
Armed Forces Communications and Electronics Ass'n
Associated Public-Safety Communications Officers
Ass'n for Business Communication
Ass'n for Communication Administration
Ass'n for Conservation Information, The
Ass'n for Educational Communications and Technology
Ass'n for Multi-Image International
Ass'n of Federal Communications Consulting Engineers
Ass'n of Regional Religious Communicators
Ass'n of Schools of Journalism and Mass Communication
Ass'n of Visual Communicators
Cellular Telecommunications Industry Ass'n
Chemical Communications Ass'n
Communications Marketing Ass'n
Communications Security Ass'n
Communications Workers of America
Community Antenna Television Ass'n
Computer and Communications Industry Ass'n
Consolidated Tape Ass'n
Council of Biology Editors
Council of Communication Management
Drug Information Ass'n
EDUCOM
Energy Telecommunications and Electrical Ass'n
Exchange Carriers Standards Ass'n
Forest Industries Telecommunications
Forestry Conservation Communications Ass'n
Graphic Communications Ass'n
Health Sciences Communications Ass'n
Independent Data Communications Manufacturers Ass'n
Internat'l Ass'n of Business Communicators
Internat'l Communication Ass'n
Internat'l Communications Ass'n
Internat'l Documentary Ass'n
Internat'l Teleconferencing Ass'n
Joint Council on Educational Telecommunications
Land Mobile Communications Council
Microwave Communications Ass'n
Nat'l Ass'n of Hispanic Publications
Nat'l Ass'n of Media Women
Nat'l Ass'n of State Telecommunications Directors
Nat'l Avionics Soc.

CONSULTANTS
ACME, Inc.-The Association of Management Consulting Firms
America on the Move
American Ass'n of Dental Consultants
American Ass'n of Healthcare Consultants
American Ass'n of Medico-Legal Consultants
American Ass'n of Political Consultants
American Consultants League
American Consulting Engineers Council
American Soc. of Agricultural Consultants
American Soc. of Consultant Pharmacists
American Soc. of Consulting Arborists
American Soc. of Consulting Planners
American Soc. of Trial Consultants
APEC
Ass'n of Bridal Consultants
Ass'n of Consulting Chemists and Chemical Engineers
Ass'n of Consulting Foresters
Ass'n of Executive Search Consultants
Ass'n of Federal Communications Consulting Engineers
Ass'n of Graphic Arts Consultants
Ass'n of Internal Management Consultants
Ass'n of Management Consultants
Ass'n of Outplacement Consulting Firms
Ass'n of Productivity Specialists
Ass'n of Professional Material Handling Consultants
Ass'n of Professional Writing Consultants
ECRI
Foodservice Consultants Soc. Internat'l
Independent Computer Consultants Ass'n
Institute of Certified Professional Business Consultants
Institute of Management Consultants
Internat'l Ass'n of Ethicists
Internat'l Ass'n of Merger and Acquisition Consultants
Internat'l Ass'n of Professional Security Consultants
Internat'l College of Real Estate Consulting Professionals
Nat'l Alliance of Independent Crop Consultants
Nat'l Ass'n of Financial Consultants
Nat'l Ass'n of Freight Transportation Consultants
Nat'l Ass'n of Management and Technical Assistance Centers
Nat'l Ass'n of Pension Consultants and Administrators
Nat'l Ass'n of Telemarketing Consultants
Nat'l Ass'n of Vision Professionals
Nat'l Council of Acoustical Consultants
Nat'l Hispanic Ass'n of Construction Enterprises
Nat'l Institute of Certified Moving Consultants
Professional Services Council
Project Management Institute
Public Relations Soc. of America
Soc. of Medical Consultants to the Armed Forces
Soc. of Medical-Dental Management Consultants
Soc. of Professional Business Consultants
Soc. of Professional Management Consultants
Soc. of Risk Management Consultants

CONSUMERS
American Council on Consumer Interests
American Financial Services Ass'n
Ass'n for Consumer Research
Consumer Credit Insurance Ass'n
Consumer Federation of America
Electricity Consumers Resource Council
Nat'l Academy of Conciliators
Nat'l Ass'n of Consumer Agency Administrators
Nat'l Ass'n of State Utility Consumer Advocates
Nat'l Consumers League
Nat'l Cooperative Business Ass'n
Soc. of Consumer Affairs Professionals in Business

CONTAINERS see also BAGS, BOXES, CANS
Aluminum Foil Container Manufacturers Ass'n
Ass'n of Independent Corrugated Converters
Closure Manufacturers Ass'n
Compressed Gas Ass'n
Containerization and Intermodal Institute
Cylinder Manufacturers Ass'n
Detachable Container Ass'n
Fibre Box Ass'n
Fibre Drum Technical Council
Glass Packaging Institute
Nat'l Ass'n of Container Distributors
Nat'l Barrel and Drum Ass'n
Nat'l Food Processors Ass'n
Nat'l Wooden Pallet and Container Ass'n
Paper Shipping Sack Manufacturers Ass'n
Paperboard Packaging Council
Plastic Shipping Container Institute
Pressure Vessel Manufacturers Ass'n
Research and Development Associates for Military Food and Packaging Systems
Single Service Institute
Steel Shipping Container Institute

CONTRACTORS
Air Conditioning Contractors of America
American Subcontractors Ass'n
American Surety Ass'n
Associated Builders and Contractors
Associated General Contractors of America
Associated Landscape Contractors of America
Associated Specialty Contractors
Ass'n of Bituminous Contractors
Ass'n of Drilled Shaft Contractors
Ass'n of the Wall and Ceiling Industries-Internat'l
Ass'n of Tile, Terrazzo, Marble Contractors and Affiliates
Building Service Contractors Ass'n Internat'l
Ceilings and Interior Systems Construction Ass'n
Concrete Sawing and Drilling Ass'n
Construction Industry Management Board
Coordinating Council for Computers in Construction
Exposition Service Contractors Ass'n
Floor Covering Installation Contractors Ass'n
Greater Clothing Contractors Ass'n
Independent Electrical Contractors
Independent Professional Painting Contractors Ass'n
Instrument Contracting and Engineering Ass'n
Insulation Contractors Ass'n of America
Internat'l Ass'n of Geophysical Contractors
Internat'l Ass'n of Lighting Maintenance Contractors
Internat'l Institute for Lath and Plaster
Ladies Apparel Contractors Ass'n
Land Improvement Contractors of America
Mason Contractors Ass'n of America
Mechanical Contractors Ass'n of America
Nat'l Ass'n of Cold Storage Contractors
Nat'l Ass'n of Demolition Contractors
Nat'l Ass'n of Minority Contractors
Nat'l Ass'n of Miscellaneous, Ornamental and Architectural Products Contractors
Nat'l Ass'n of Plumbing-Heating-Cooling Contractors
Nat'l Ass'n of Reinforcing Steel Contractors
Nat'l Ass'n of Small Government Contractors
Nat'l Ass'n of Solar Contractors
Nat'l Ass'n of Women Government Contractors
Nat'l Certified Pipe Welding Bureau
Nat'l Constructors Ass'n
Nat'l Contract Management Ass'n
Nat'l Council of Erectors, Fabricators and Riggers
Nat'l Drilling Contractors Ass'n
Nat'l Drilling Federation
Nat'l Electrical Contractors Ass'n
Nat'l Environmental Balancing Bureau
Nat'l Insulation Contractors Ass'n
Nat'l Roof Deck Contractors Ass'n
Nat'l Roofing Contractors Ass'n
Nat'l School Transportation Ass'n
Nat'l Small Business Government Contractors Ass'n
Painting and Decorating Contractors of America
Pipe Line Contractors Ass'n
Poured Concrete Wall Contractors Ass'n of America
Procurement Round Table
Quality Control Council of America
Scaffold Industry Ass'n
Sealant and Waterproofers Institute
Sheet Metal and Air Conditioning Contractors' Nat'l Ass'n
Tile Contractors' Ass'n of America
Underground Contractors Association

CONVENTIONS see also EXHIBITS
Ass'n of Group Travel Executives
Convention Liaison Council
Electronic Industry Show Corporation
Exposition Service Contractors Ass'n
Foundation for Internat'l Meetings
Insurance Conference Planners
Internat'l Ass'n of Auditorium Managers
Internat'l Ass'n of Conference Centers
Internat'l Ass'n of Convention and Visitor Bureaus
Meeting Planners Internat'l
North American Farm Show Council
Professional Convention Management Ass'n
Religious Conference Management Ass'n
Soc. of Company Meeting Planners
Trade Show Bureau

COOKING
American Culinary Federation
Chefs de Cuisine Ass'n of America
Internat'l Ass'n of Cooking Professionals
Internat'l Food Service Executives' Ass'n
Nat'l Ass'n of Catering Executives
Vatel Club

COOPERATIVES
American Institute of Cooperation
American Turpentine Farmers Ass'n Co-op
Ass'n of Artist-Run Galleries
Ass'n of Co-operative Educators
Burley Tobacco Growers Cooperative Ass'n
Continental Ass'n of Funeral and Memorial Socs.
Cooperative Education Ass'n
Council for Interinstitutional Leadership
Council of 1890 College Presidents
Credit Union Nat'l Ass'n
Farm Credit Council
Farmers Educational and Co-operative Union of America
Flue-Cured Tobacco Cooperative Stabilization Corporation
Interstate Producers Livestock Ass'n
Nat'l Ass'n of Buying Services
Nat'l Ass'n of Housing Cooperatives
Nat'l Cooperative Business Ass'n
Nat'l Council of Farmer Cooperatives
Nat'l Farmers Organization
Nat'l Rural Electric Cooperative Ass'n
Nat'l Soc. of Accountants for Cooperatives
Nat'l Telephone Cooperative Ass'n
Newspaper Advertising Co-op Network
North American Students of Cooperation
Profit Sharing Council of America
Quality Bakers of America Cooperative
United Egg Producers

COPPER
American Bureau of Metal Statistics
American Copper Council
Ass'n of Brass and Bronze Ingot Manufacturers
Copper and Brass Fabricators Council
Copper and Brass Servicenter Ass'n
Copper Development Ass'n
Internat'l Copper Research Ass'n
Selenium-Tellurium Development Ass'n

CORN
American Corn Millers Federation
Corn Refiners Ass'n
Nat'l Corn Growers Ass'n
Nat'l Futures Ass'n
Self-Rising Flour and Corn Meal Program

CORRECTION see also LAW, POLICE, SECURITY
American Ass'n for Correctional Psychology
American Ass'n of Mental Health Professionals in Corrections
American Catholic Correctional Chaplains Ass'n
American Correctional Ass'n
American Correctional Chaplains Ass'n
American Correctional Food Service Ass'n
American Correctional Health Services Ass'n
American Criminal Justice Ass'n
American Jail Ass'n
American Jewish Correctional Chaplains Ass'n
American Protestant Correctional Chaplains' Ass'n
American Soc. of Criminology
Ass'n for Correctional Research and Information Management
Ass'n of State Correctional Administrators
Ass'n on Programs for Female Offenders
Correctional Education Ass'n
Correctional Industries Ass'n
Correctional Service Federation-U.S.A.
Federal Probation Officers Ass'n
Internat'l Ass'n of Correctional Officers
Internat'l Conference of Administrators of Residential Agencies
Internat'l Conference of Police Chaplains
Internat'l Halfway House Ass'n
Internat'l Juvenile Officers Ass'n
Nat'l Ass'n of Criminal Justice Planners
Nat'l Ass'n of Juvenile Correctional Agencies
Nat'l Correctional Recreational Ass'n
Nat'l Council on Crime and Delinquency
Nat'l Juvenile Detention Ass'n
North American Ass'n of Wardens and Superintendents
Osborne Ass'n
Public Offender Counselors Ass'n

COSMETICS & COSMETOLOGY
Aestheticians Internat'l Ass'n
American Ass'n of Esthetics
American Electrology Ass'n
American Health and Beauty Aids Institute
Ass'n of Cosmetologists and Hairdressers
Beauty and Barber Supply Institute
Certified Color Manufacturers Ass'n
Cosmetic Executive Women
Cosmetic Industry Buyers and Suppliers
Cosmetic, Toiletry and Fragrance Ass'n
Council on Electrolysis Education
Drug, Chemical and Allied Trades Ass'n
Foragers of America
Fragrance Foundation
Independent Cosmetic Manufacturers and Distributors
Intercoiffure America
Internat'l Ass'n of Trichologists
Internat'l Chain Salon Ass'n
Internat'l Guild of Professional Electrologists
Internat'l Tanning Manufacturers Ass'n
Modeling Ass'n of America Internat'l
Nat'l Aesthetician and Nail Artist Ass'n
Nat'l Ass'n of Accredited Cosmetology Schools
Nat'l Ass'n of Barber Styling Schools
Nat'l Beauty Culturists' League
Nat'l Cosmetology Ass'n
Nat'l Interstate Council of State Boards of Cosmetology
Regulatory Affairs Professionals Soc.
Soc. of Cosmetic Chemists

COTTON
American Cotton Shippers Ass'n
American Textile Manufacturers Institute
Cotton Council Internat'l
Cotton Warehouse Ass'n of America
Industrial Fabrics Ass'n Internat'l
Nat'l Cotton Batting Institute
Nat'l Cotton Council of America
Nat'l Cotton Ginners' Ass'n
New York Cotton Exchange
Supima Ass'n of America

COTTONSEED
American Oil Chemists' Soc.
Nat'l Cottonseed Products Ass'n

00009

SUBJECT INDEX

SUBJECT INDEX

ELECTRICITY & ELECTRONICS

00013

SUBJECT INDEX

SUBJECT INDEX

00017

SUBJECT INDEX

GRAIN see also FEED & GRAIN

GRAPHIC ARTS

GROCERS

GUNS see FIREARMS

GYNECOLOGY

HAIRDRESSERS see COSMETICS

HANDICAPPED see also BLIND, DEAF

SUBJECT INDEX

SUBJECT INDEX

INVESTMENTS see also FINANCE, SECURITIES INDUSTRY

IRON & STEEL INDUSTRY

ITALIAN

JEWELRY & GEMS

JEWISH

JOURNALISM

JUDGES

LABOR UNIONS

00022

LABORATORIES

LACE

LADDERS

LANDSCAPING

LANGUAGE

LARYNGOLOGY

LAUNDERERS see CLEANERS

LAW

00023

SUBJECT INDEX

LAW ENFORCEMENT see POLICE

LEAD

LEATHER GOODS see also SHOES

LECTURES

LIBRARIES

LIGHTING

LINGERIE & UNDERWEAR

LINGUISTICS

LIQUOR

LIVESTOCK

00025

SUBJECT INDEX

00027

SUBJECT INDEX

Soc. of Manufacturing Engineers
Soc. of the Plastics Industry
Solar Energy Industries Ass'n
Southern Cypress Manufacturers Ass'n
Specialty Automotive Manufacturers Ass'n
Specialty Equipment Market Ass'n
Sporting Arms and Ammunition Manufacturers' Institute
Sporting Goods Manufacturers Ass'n
Spring Manufacturers Institute
Steel Bar Mills Ass'n
Steel Deck Institute
Steel Door Institute
Steel Founders' Soc. of America
Steel Joist Institute
Steel Plate Fabricators Ass'n
Steel Shipping Container Institute
Steel Tank Institute
Steel Window Institute
Sterling Silversmiths Guild of America
Stucco Manufacturers Ass'n
Submersible Wastewater Pump Ass'n
Summer and Casual Furniture Manufacturers Ass'n
Sump and Sewage Pump Manufacturers Ass'n
Sunglass Ass'n of America
Suppliers of Advanced Composite Materials Ass'n
Synthetic Amorphous Silica and Silicates Industry Ass'n
Synthetic Organic Chemical Manufacturers Ass'n
Tag and Label Manufacturers Institute
Tantalum Producers Ass'n
Tapered Steel Transmission Pole Institute
Tennis Manufacturers Ass'n
Textile Bag Manufacturers Ass'n
Textile Care Allied Trades Ass'n
Textile Fibers and By-Products Ass'n
Theatre Equipment Ass'n
Thermal Insulation Manufacturers Ass'n
Thread Institute
Tile Council of America
Timber Operators Council
Timber Products Manufacturers
Tooling Component Manufacturers Ass'n
Toy Manufacturers of America
Trailer Hitch Manufacturers Ass'n
Transportation Safety Equipment Institute
Trophy Dealers and Manufacturers Ass'n
Truck Mixer Manufacturers Bureau
Truck Trailer Manufacturers Ass'n
Tube Council of North America
Tubular Exchanger Manufacturers Ass'n
Tune-up Manufacturers Institute
Ultrasonic Industry Ass'n
United Better Dress Manufacturers Ass'n
United Fur Manufacturers Ass'n
United Infants and Childrens Wear Ass'n
United Knitwear Manufacturers League
United Pesticide Formulators and Distributors Ass'n
United States Beet Sugar Ass'n
Vacuum Cleaner Manufacturers Ass'n
Valve Manufacturers Ass'n of America
Variable Resistive Components Institute
Vermiculite Ass'n
Vibrating Screen Manufacturers Ass'n
Vinegar Institute, The
Wallcovering Manufacturers Ass'n
Water Quality Ass'n
Water Systems Council
Waterbed Manufacturers Ass'n
Web Sling Ass'n
Welded Steel Tube Institute
Western and English Manufacturers Ass'n
Western Awning Ass'n
Wire Machinery Builders Ass'n
Wire Reinforcement Institute
Wire Rope Technical Board
Wirebound Box Manufacturers Ass'n
Wood and Synthetic Flooring Institute
Wood Machinery Manufacturers of America
Wood Moulding and Millwork Producers Ass'n
Wood Products Manufacturers Ass'n
Wood Tank Manufacturers Ass'n
Work Glove Manufacturers Ass'n
Woven Wire Products Ass'n
Writing Instrument Manufacturers Ass'n
Zinc Institute

MAPS

American Congress on Surveying and Mapping
Internat'l Map Dealers' Ass'n
North American Cartographic Information Soc.

MARKET RESEARCH

American Ass'n for Public Opinion Research
Chemical Marketing Research Ass'n
Council of American Survey Research Organizations
Marketing Research Ass'n
Nat'l Golf Foundation

MARKETING

Academy of Marketing Science
Advertising and Marketing Internat'l Network
Advertising Research Foundation
American Catfish Marketing Ass'n
American College of Healthcare Marketing
American Economic Development Council
American Film Marketing Ass'n
American Marketing Ass'n
American Railway Development Ass'n
American Soc. of Petroleum Operations Engineers
Armed Forces Marketing Council
Ass'n of Direct Marketing Agencies
Ass'n of Railroad Advertising and Marketing
Ass'n of Retail Marketing Services
Ass'n of Travel Marketing Executives
Automotive Cooling System Institute
Bank Marketing Ass'n
Biomedical Marketing Ass'n
Carpet Manufacturers Marketing Ass'n
Ceramic Tile Marketing Federation
Color Marketing Group
Communications Marketing Ass'n
Copper Development Ass'n
Council of Sales Promotion Agencies
Diamond and Gemstone Remarketing Ass'n
Direct Marketing Ass'n
Direct Marketing Computer Ass'n
Direct Marketing Creative Guild
Direct Marketing Credit Ass'n
Direct Selling Ass'n
Distributive Education Clubs of America
Electrical Generating Systems Ass'n
Financial Institutions Marketing Ass'n
Flat Glass Marketing Ass'n
Fulfillment Management Ass'n
Graphic Arts Marketing Information Service
Independent Gasoline Marketers Council
Independent Livestock Marketing Ass'n
Insurance Marketing Communications Ass'n
Internat'l Chain of Industrial and Technical Advertising Agencies
Internat'l Exhibitors Ass'n
Internat'l Institute of Foods and Family Living
Internat'l Newspaper Advertising and Marketing Executives, Inc.
Interstate Producers Livestock Ass'n
Life Insurance Marketing and Research Ass'n
Livestock Marketing Ass'n
Magazine and Paperback Marketing Institute
Mailing List Users and Suppliers Ass'n
Manufacturers' Agents Nat'l Ass'n
Marketing Education Ass'n
Marketing Research Ass'n
Mass Marketing Insurance Institute
Materials Marketing Associates
Nat'l Account Marketing Ass'n
Nat'l Agri-Marketing Ass'n
Nat'l Agricultural Marketing Officials
Nat'l Ass'n for Campus Activities
Nat'l Ass'n for Professional Saleswomen
Nat'l Ass'n of Display Industries
Nat'l Ass'n of Management/Marketing Educators
Nat'l Ass'n of Market Developers
Nat'l Ass'n of Produce Market Managers
Nat'l Ass'n of Sales and Marketing Professionals
Nat'l Energy Specialist Ass'n
Nat'l Exhaust Distributors Ass'n
Nat'l Mail Order Ass'n
Nat'l Pecan Marketing Council
Nat'l Potato Promotion Board
Nat'l Premium Sales Executives
Nat'l Wool Marketing Corporation
Nursery Marketing Council
Package Designers Council
Petroleum Marketers Ass'n of America
Petroleum Marketing Education Foundation
Photo Marketing Ass'n-Internat'l
Private Label Manufacturers Ass'n
Produce Marketing Ass'n
Product Development and Management Ass'n
Professional Insurance Mass-Marketing Ass'n
Professional Publishers Marketing Group
Promotion Marketing Ass'n of America
Realtors Nat'l Marketing Institute
Sales and Marketing Executives, Internat'l
Soc. for Marketing Professional Services
Soc. of Independent Gasoline Marketers of America
Specialty Equipment Market Ass'n
Technical Marketing Soc. of America

MATERIAL HANDLING

Ass'n of Professional Material Handling Consultants
Automatic Guided Vehicle Systems
Automatic Identification Manufacturers
Below/Hook Lifters Ass'n
Caster and Floor Truck Manufacturers Ass'n
Conveyor Equipment Manufacturers Ass'n
Crane Manufacturers Ass'n of America
Hoist Manufacturers Institute
Industrial Metal Containers Ass'n
Industrial Truck Ass'n
Institutional and Service Textile Distributors Ass'n
Internat'l Material Management Soc.
Loading Dock Equipment Manufacturers
Material Handling Equipment Distributors Ass'n
Material Handling Institute
Monorail Manufacturers Ass'n
Nat'l Industrial Belting Ass'n
Nat'l Institute of Packaging, Handling and Logistic Engineers
Nat'l Wooden Pallet and Container Ass'n
Personnel/Burden Carrier Manufacturers Ass'n
Rack Manufacturers Institute
Scale Manufacturers Ass'n
Shelving Manufacturers Ass'n
Soc. of Packaging and Handling Engineers
Web Sling Ass'n

MATHEMATICS

American Academy of Actuaries
American Mathematical Soc.
American Statistical Ass'n
Ass'n for Computing Machinery
Ass'n for Integrated Manufacturing Technology
Ass'n for Symbolic Logic
Ass'n for Women in Mathematics
Biometric Soc. (ENAR)
Casualty Actuarial Soc.
Conference Board of the Mathematical Sciences
Econometric Soc.
Industrial Mathematics Soc.
Institute of Management Sciences, The
Institute of Mathematical Statistics
Internat'l Ass'n for Mathematical Geology
Internat'l Soc. for Ecological Modelling-North AmericanChapter
Mathematical Ass'n of America
Nat'l Council of Teachers of Mathematics
North American Simulation and Gaming Ass'n
Operations Research Soc. of America
Psychometric Soc.
School Science and Mathematics Ass'n
Soc. for Industrial and Applied Mathematics
Soc. for Natural Philosophy
Soc. of Actuaries
Soc. of Multivariate Experimental Psychology
Special Interest Group for Symbolic and Algebraic Manipulation
Special Interest Group on Numerical Mathematics

MEASUREMENT

American Nat'l Metric Council
American Nat'l Standards Institute
Ass'n for Measurement and Evaluation in Counseling and Development
Mathematical Ass'n of America
Nat'l Conference on Weights and Measures
Nat'l Council of Teachers of Mathematics
Precision Measurements Ass'n
Tubular Rivet and Machine Institute

MEAT

American Ass'n of Meat Processors
American Meat Institute
American Meat Science Ass'n
Beef Improvement Federation
Canned and Cooked Meat Importers Ass'n
Internat'l Meat Processors Ass'n
Meat Importers' Council of America
Meat Industry Suppliers Ass'n
Nat'l Ass'n of Meat Purveyors
Nat'l Brotherhood of Packinghouse and Industrial Workers
Nat'l Buffalo Ass'n
Nat'l Food Processors Ass'n
Nat'l Live Stock and Meat Board
Nat'l Meat Canners Ass'n
Nat'l Pork Producers Council
Nat'l Renderers Ass'n
Nat'l Seasoning Manufacturers Ass'n
New York Mercantile Exchange
United States Meat Export Federation
Western States Meat Ass'n

MEDICINE

Academy of Ambulatory Foot Surgery
Academy of Aphasia
Academy of Osteopathic Directors of Medical Education
Academy of Psychosomatic Medicine
Acupuncture Internat'l Ass'n
Aerospace Medical Ass'n
AirLifeLine
Airline Medical Directors Ass'n
Alliance for Engineering in Medicine and Biology
Ambulatory Pediatric Ass'n
American Academy and Board of Neurological and Orthopaedic Surgery
American Academy for Cerebral Palsy and Developmental Medicine
American Academy of Allergy and Immunology
American Academy of Behavioral Medicine
American Academy of Cosmetic Surgery
American Academy of Craniomandibular Disorders
American Academy of Dental Electrosurgery
American Academy of Dental Radiology
American Academy of Dermatology
American Academy of Environmental Medicine
American Academy of Facial Plastic and Reconstructive Surgery
American Academy of Family Physicians
American Academy of Gnathologic Orthopedics
American Academy of Implant Dentistry
American Academy of Legal and Industrial Medicine
American Academy of Medical Administrators
American Academy of Medical Directors
American Academy of Medical Preventics
American Academy of Natural Family Planning
American Academy of Neurological Surgery
American Academy of Neurology
American Academy of Occupational Medicine

SUBJECT INDEX

MENTAL HEALTH

MERCHANDISING

METAL WORKING

METALS

METEOROLOGY

MICA

SUBJECT INDEX

MICROBIOLOGY
American College of Veterinary Microbiologists
American Soc. for Microbiology
Ass'n of Microbiological Diagnostic Manufacturers
Internat'l Phycological Soc.
Internat'l Soc. for Clinical Laboratory Technology
Microcirculatory Soc. of America
Soc. for Industrial Microbiology
United States Federation for Culture Collections

MICROFILMS
Ass'n for Information and Image Management

MICROSCOPES
American Ass'n of Feed Microscopists
American Microscopical Soc.
Electron Microscopy Soc. of America
Internat'l Metallographic Soc.
Scientific Apparatus Makers Ass'n

MILITARY
Adjutants General Ass'n of the United States
Air Force Ass'n
Air Force Sergeants Ass'n
American Defense Preparedness Ass'n
American Logistics Ass'n
American Soc. of Military Comptrollers
American Soc. of Naval Engineers
Armed Forces Broadcasters Ass'n
Armed Forces Communications and Electronics Ass'n
Ass'n for Unmanned Vehicle Systems
Ass'n of Military Colleges and Schools of the U.S.
Ass'n of Military Surgeons of the U.S.
Ass'n of Naval R.O.T.C. Colleges and Universities
Ass'n of Old Crows
Ass'n of Scientists and Engineers of the Naval Sea Systems Command
Ass'n of the United States Army
Chief Petty Officers Ass'n
Internat'l Military Club Executives Ass'n
Marine Corps Reserve Officers Ass'n
Military Chaplains Ass'n of the U.S.
Military Educators and Counselors Ass'n
Military Operations Research Soc.
Military Reform Institute
Nat'l Ass'n for Uniformed Services
Nat'l Ass'n of Planners, Estimators and Progressmen
Nat'l Ass'n of State Directors of Veterans Affairs
Nat'l Classification Management Soc.
Nat'l Counter Intelligence Corps Ass'n
Nat'l Guard Ass'n of the U.S.
Nat'l Military Intelligence Ass'n
Nat'l Security Industrial Ass'n
Non-Commissioned Officers Ass'n of the U.S.A.
Reserve Officers Ass'n of the U.S.
Retired Officers Ass'n
Soc. of Air Force Physicians
Soc. of American Military Engineers
Soc. of Medical Consultants to the Armed Forces
Soc. of United States Air Force Flight Surgeons
Uniformed Services Academy of Family Physicians
United States Armor Ass'n
United States Army Warrant Officers Ass'n
United States Marine Products Manufacturers' Ass'n

MILK
American Ass'n of Medical Milk Commissions
American Cultured Dairy Products Institute
American Dairy Products Institute
Certified Milk Producers Ass'n of America
Evaporated Milk Ass'n
Internat'l Ass'n of Milk Control Agencies
Internat'l Ass'n of Milk, Food and Environmental Sanitarians
Internat'l Dairy-Deli Ass'n
Milk Industry Foundation
Nat'l Frozen Pizza Institute
Nat'l Independent Dairy-Foods Ass'n
Nat'l Mastitis Council
Nat'l Milk Producers Federation
United Dairy Industry Ass'n

MILLERS see also FEED & GRAIN, GRAIN, WHEAT
American Ass'n of Cereal Chemists
American Corn Millers Federation
American Federation of Grain Millers Internat'l Union
Ass'n of Operative Millers
Millers' Nat'l Federation
Rice Millers' Ass'n

MILLINERY
Millinery Institute of America
Nat'l Ass'n of Milliners, Dressmakers and Tailors

MINERALOGY
American Crystallographic Ass'n
Geochemical Soc.
Mineralogical Soc. of America
Soc. of Economic Paleontologists and Mineralogists

MINERALS
American Gem and Mineral Suppliers Ass'n
American Iron Ore Ass'n
American Mining Congress
Asbestos Information Ass'n/North America
Ass'n of the Wall and Ceiling Industries-Internat'l
Clay Minerals Soc.
Gypsum Ass'n
Lead-Zinc Producers Committee
Mineral Insulation Manufacturers Ass'n
Nat'l Ass'n of Royalty Owners
Nat'l Slag Ass'n
Open Pit Mining Ass'n
Salt Institute
Slurry Technology Ass'n
Sulphur Institute

MINING INDUSTRY
American Institute of Mining, Metallurgical, and Petroleum Engineers
American Mining Congress
American Nuclear Energy Council
Anthracite Industry Ass'n
Asbestos Information Ass'n/North America
Ass'n of Bituminous Contractors
China Clay Producers Group
Crusher and Portable Plant Ass'n
Gold Institute
Mine Inspectors' Institute of America
Mining and Metallurgical Soc. of America
Mining and Reclamation Council of America
Nat'l Ass'n of State Land Reclamationists
Nat'l Ready Mixed Concrete Ass'n
Nat'l Sand and Gravel Ass'n
Nat'l Stone Ass'n
Open Pit Mining Ass'n
Perlite Institute
Phosphate Rock Export Ass'n
Selenium-Tellurium Development Ass'n
Silver Institute
Soc. of Economic Geologists
Soc. of Exploration Geophysicists
Soc. of Mining Engineers
Sorptive Minerals Institute
United Mine Workers of America
Vermiculite Ass'n

MINORITIES see also BLACKS
American Ass'n for Affirmative Action
American Indian Health Care Ass'n
American League of Financial Institutions
American Surety Ass'n
Ass'n for Multicultural Counseling and Development
Hispanic Nat'l Bar Ass'n
Latin American Manufacturers Ass'n
Mexican American Engineering Soc.
Nat'l Ass'n for Bilingual Education
Nat'l Ass'n for Ethnic Studies
Nat'l Ass'n of Black and Minority Chambers of Commerce
Nat'l Ass'n of Black Consulting Engineers
Nat'l Ass'n of Black Hospitality Professionals
Nat'l Ass'n of Community Action Agencies
Nat'l Ass'n of Investment Companies
Nat'l Ass'n of Latino Elected and Appointed Officials
Nat'l Ass'n of Minority Contractors
Nat'l Black Coalition of Federal Aviation Employees
Nat'l Black Health Planners Ass'n
Nat'l Business League
Nat'l Coalition of Hispanic Health and Human Services Organizations
Nat'l Hispanic Psychological Ass'n
Nat'l Indian Education Ass'n
Nat'l Minority Supplier Development Council
Nat'l Optometric Ass'n
Organization of Black Airline Pilots

MOTELS see HOTELS

MOTION PICTURES see FILMS

MOTOR VEHICLES see also AUTOMOBILES
Aftermarket Body Parts Ass'n
American Ass'n for Automotive Medicine
American Ass'n of Motor Vehicle Administrators
American Automotive Leasing Ass'n
American Bus Ass'n
American Car Rental Ass'n
American Internat'l Automobile Dealers Ass'n
American Retreaders' Ass'n
American Seat Belt Council
American Soc. of Body Engineers
American Trucking Ass'ns
Ass'n for Commuter Transportation
Auto Internacional Ass'n
Autoleather Guild
Automatic Transmission Rebuilders Ass'n
Automobile Importers of America
Automotive Advertisers Council
Automotive Affiliated Representatives
Automotive Battery Charger Manufacturers Council
Automotive Booster Clubs Internat'l
Automotive Cooling System Institute
Automotive Dismantlers and Recyclers Ass'n
Automotive Engine Rebuilders Ass'n
Automotive Exhaust Systems Manufacturers Council
Automotive Filter Manufacturers Council
Automotive Fleet and Leasing Ass'n
Automotive Industry Action Group
Automotive Information Council
Automotive Lift Institute
Automotive Market Research Council
Automotive Occupant Protection Ass'n
Automotive Parts and Accessories Ass'n
Automotive Parts Rebuilders Ass'n
Automotive Products Export Council
Automotive Refrigeration Products Institute
Automotive Service Ass'n
Automotive Service Industry Ass'n
Automotive Trade Ass'n Executives
Automotive Warehouse Distributors Ass'n
Bearing Specialist Ass'n
Brake System Parts Manufacturers Council
Bumper Recycling Ass'n of North America
Buses Internat'l Ass'n
Car Audio Specialists Ass'n
Car Care Council
Conference of American Renting and Leasing Assn's
Coordinating Research Council
Equipment and Tool Institute
Equipment Interchange Ass'n
Friction Materials Standards Institute
Heavy Duty Representatives Ass'n
Highway Users Federation for Safety and Mobility
Independent Armored Car Operators Ass'n
Independent Automotive Damage Appraisers Ass'n
Inter-Industry Conference on Auto Collision Repair
Intermodal Transportation Ass'n
Internat'l Mobile Air Conditioning Ass'n
Internat'l Motor Press Ass'n
Internat'l Taxicab Ass'n
Manufactured Housing Institute
Manufacturers of Emission Controls Ass'n
Mobile Air Conditioning Soc.
Moped Ass'n of America
Motor and Equipment Manufacturers Ass'n
Motor Vehicle Manufacturers Ass'n of the United States
Motorcycle Industry Council
Motorcycle Safety Foundation
Nat'l Ass'n for Stock Car Auto Racing
Nat'l Ass'n of Auto Trim Shops
Nat'l Ass'n of College Automotive Teachers
Nat'l Ass'n of Fleet Administrators
Nat'l Auto Auction Ass'n
Nat'l Automobile Dealers Ass'n
Nat'l Automobile Theft Bureau
Nat'l Automobile Transporters Ass'n
Nat'l Automotive Parts Ass'n
Nat'l Automotive Radiator Service Ass'n
Nat'l Independent Automobile Dealers Ass'n
Nat'l Tire Dealers and Retreaders Ass'n
Nat'l Truck Equipment Ass'n
Nat'l Truck Leasing System
Nat'l Wheel and Rim Ass'n
North American Professional Driver Education Ass'n
Overseas Automotive Club
Paint, Body and Equipment Ass'n
Pattern Makers' League of North America
Polyurethane Division-Soc. of the Plastics Industry
Power Transmission Representatives Ass'n
Production Engine Remanufacturers Ass'n
Recreation Vehicle Dealers Ass'n of North America
Recreation Vehicle Rental Ass'n
Soc. of Automotive Engineers
Soc. of Collision Repair Specialists
Specialty Automotive Manufacturers Ass'n
Specialty Equipment Market Ass'n
Street Rod Equipment Ass'n
Tire and Rim Ass'n
Tire Industry Safety Council
Tire Retread Information Bureau
Towing and Recovery Ass'n of America
Trailer Hitch Manufacturers Ass'n
Transmission Products Ass'n
Transportation Safety Equipment Institute
Truck-frame and Axle Repair Ass'n
Truck Mixer Manufacturers Bureau
Tune-up Manufacturers Institute
United Automobile, Aerospace and Agricultural Implement Workers of America
United Bus Owners of America
Vehicle Security Ass'n
Warehouse Distributors Ass'n for Leisure and Mobile Products

MOTORCYCLES
Independent Motorcycle Retailers of America
Moped Ass'n of America
Motorcycle Industry Council
Motorcycle Safety Foundation
Nat'l Motorcycle Retailers Ass'n

MUSEUMS
African American Museums Ass'n
American Ass'n of Museums
American Ass'n of Youth Museums
Ass'n for Living Historical Farms and Agricultural Museums
Ass'n of Art Museum Directors
Ass'n of Railway Museums
Ass'n of Science Museum Directors
Ass'n of Science-Technology Centers
Ass'n of Sports Museums and Halls of Fame
Ass'n of Systematics Collections
Council of American Maritime Museums
Internat'l Museum Photographers Ass'n
Museum Store Ass'n
North American Indian Museums Ass'n

SUBJECT INDEX

SUBJECT INDEX

American Ass'n of Public Health Dentistry
American Ass'n of Public Health Physicians
American Corrective Therapy Ass'n
American Epidemiological Soc.
American Mosquito Control Ass'n
American Public Health Ass'n
American School Health Ass'n
American Soc. of Allied Health Professions
American Soc. of Tropical Medicine and Hygiene
American Venereal Disease Ass'n
Ass'n for Practitioners in Infection Control
Ass'n for Vital Records and Health Statistics
Ass'n of Federal Safety and Health Professionals
Ass'n of Reserve Officers of the U.S. Public Health Service
Ass'n of Schools of Public Health
Ass'n of State and Territorial Health Officials
Ass'n of Teachers of Preventive Medicine
Cadmium Council
Commissioned Officers Ass'n of the United States Public Health Service
Conference of Public Health Laboratorians
Conference of Public Health Laboratorians
Conference of Public Health Veterinarians
Infectious Diseases Soc. of America
Internat'l Ass'n of Milk Control Agencies
Internat'l Health Soc.
Nat'l Assembly of Nat'l Voluntary Health and Social Welfare Organizations
Nat'l Ass'n of Advisors for the Health Professions
Nat'l Ass'n of County Health Officials
Nat'l Ass'n of Disability Examiners
Nat'l Ass'n of Public Hospitals
Nat'l Ass'n of Rehabilitation Secretaries
Nat'l Ass'n of State Alcohol and Drug Abuse Directors
Nat'l Conference of Local Environmental Health Administrators
Nat'l Council on Radiation Protection and Measurements
Nat'l Family Planning and Reproductive Health Ass'n
Nat'l Health Council
Nat'l Rehabilitation Ass'n
Nat'l Rehabilitation Counseling Ass'n
Nat'l Rural Health Care Ass'n
Nat'l Soc. of Professional Sanitarians
Physicians Forum
Soc. for Environmental Geochemistry and Health
Soc. for Epidemiologic Research
Soc. for Nutrition Education
Soc. for Public Health Education
Soc. of Vector Ecologists
Synthetic Amorphous Silica and Silicates Industry Ass'n
United Ostomy Ass'n
Vocational Evaluation and Work Adjustment Ass'n

PUBLIC RELATIONS
Agricultural Relations Council
Agriculture Council of America
American League of Lobbyists
American Soc. for Hospital Marketing and Public Relations
Ass'n for Conservation Information, The
Automotive Information Council
Baptist Public Relations Ass'n
Broadcast Promotion and Marketing Executives
Council for Advancement and Support of Education
Council of Communication Management
Electromagnetic Energy Policy Alliance
Internat'l Ass'n of Business Communicators
Internat'l Institute of Foods and Family Living
Issues Management Ass'n
Life Communicators Ass'n
Nat'l Ass'n of County Information Officers
Nat'l Council for Community Relations
Nat'l Council on Public Polls
Nat'l Golf Foundation
Nat'l Investor Relations Institute
Nat'l Reciprocal Ass'n
Nat'l School Public Relations Ass'n
Public Affairs Council
Public Relations Soc. of America
Railroad Public Relations Ass'n
Religious Public Relations Council
Tobacco Growers' Information Committee
Women in Government Relations

PUBLIC WORKS
American Public Works Ass'n
Oil Investment Institute
Public Works Historical Soc.

PUBLISHING
Agricultural Publishers Ass'n
American Ass'n of Academic Editors
American Ass'n of Yellow Pages Publishers
American Book Producers Ass'n
American Horse Publications
American Medical Publishers' Ass'n
American Newspaper Publishers Ass'n
American Soc. of Composers, Authors and Publishers
American Soc. of Indexers
Associated Construction Publications
Ass'n of American Publishers
Ass'n of American University Presses
Ass'n of Editorial Businesses
Ass'n of Jewish Book Publishers
Ass'n of North American Directory Publishers
Audit Bureau of Circulations
Book Industry Study Group
Business Publications Audit of Circulation
Christian Booksellers Ass'n
Church Music Publishers Ass'n
City and Regional Magazine Ass'n
Classroom Publishers Ass'n
Comics Magazine Ass'n of America
Coordinating Council of Literary Magazines
Copyright Soc. of the U.S.A.
COSMEP, Internat'l Ass'n of Independent Publishers
Council for Periodical Distributors Ass'ns
Educational Dealers and Suppliers Ass'n Internat'l
Engineering College Magazines Associated
Evangelical Christian Publishers Ass'n
Graphic Communications Ass'n
Independent Free Papers of America
Independent Literary Agents Ass'n
Information Industry Ass'n
Internat'l Periodical Distributors Ass'n
Livestock Publications Council
Magazine and Paperback Marketing Institute
Magazine Publishers Ass'n
Media Credit Ass'n
Music Publishers' Ass'n of the United States
Nat'l Ass'n of Advertising Publishers
Nat'l Ass'n of Hispanic Publications
Nat'l Ass'n of Independent Publishers
Nat'l Ass'n of Publishers' Representatives
Nat'l Business Circulation Ass'n
Nat'l Music Publishers' Ass'n
Nat'l Newspaper Publishers Ass'n
Newsletter Ass'n
Newspaper Advertising Bureau
Professional Publishers Marketing Group
Protestant Church-Owned Publishers Ass'n
Publishers' Publicity Ass'n
Soc. for Scholarly Publishing
Soc. for Technical Communication
Soc. of Nat'l Ass'n Publications
Soc. of Publication Designers
Software Publishers Ass'n

PULP see also PAPER INDUSTRY
American Pulpwood Ass'n
Ass'n of American Woodpulp Importers
Nat'l Forest Products Ass'n
Pulp and Paper Machinery Manufacturers' Ass'n
Pulp Chemicals Ass'n
Technical Ass'n of the Pulp and Paper Industry

PUMPS
American Concrete Pumping Ass'n
Contractors Pump Bureau
Gasoline Pump Manufacturers Ass'n
Hydraulic Institute
Submersible Wastewater Pump Ass'n
Sump and Sewage Pump Manufacturers Ass'n
Water Systems Council

PURCHASING
American Purchasing Soc.
American Soc. for Hospital Materials Management
Coalition for Common Sense in Government Procurement
Nat'l Ass'n of Educational Buyers
Nat'l Ass'n of Purchasing Management
Nat'l Ass'n of State Purchasing Officials
Nat'l Institute of Governmental Purchasing
Nat'l Purchasing Institute

RABBITS
American Rabbit Breeders Ass'n

RACING
American Greyhound Track Operators Ass'n
Ass'n for Internat'l Marathons (AIMS)
Ass'n of Official Racing Chemists
Harness Tracks of America
Jockeys' Guild
Nat'l Ass'n for Stock Car Auto Racing
Nat'l Ass'n of State Racing Commissioners
Professional Race Pilots Ass'n
Thoroughbred Racing Ass'ns of North America
United States Harness Writers' Ass'n

RADIOLOGY
American Academy of Dental Radiology
American Academy of Thermography
American College of Nuclear Physicians
American College of Podiatric Radiologists
American College of Radiology
American College of Veterinary Radiology
American Healthcare Radiology Administrators
American Institute of Ultrasound in Medicine
American Osteopathic College of Radiology
American Radium Soc.
American Registry of Clinical Radiography Technologists
American Roentgen Ray Soc.
American Soc. for Therapeutic Radiology and Oncology
American Soc. of Neuroimaging
American Soc. of Neuroradiology
American Soc. of Radiologic Technologists
Ass'n of University Radiologists
Cell Kinetics Soc.
Clinical Ligand Assay Soc.
Computerized Radiology Soc.
Conference of Radiation Control Program Directors
Council on Diagnostic Imaging to the A.C.A.
Fleischner Soc.
Microbeam Analysis Soc.
Nat'l Council on Radiation Protection and Measurements
Radiation Research Soc.
Radiological Soc. of North America
Radiologists' Business Managers Ass'n
Soc. for Pediatric Radiology, The
Soc. for Radiation Oncology Administrators
Soc. of Radiological Engineering

RADIO-TV
Alliance of Motion Picture and Television Producers
American Auto Racing Writers and Broadcasters Ass'n
American Federation of Musicians of the United States and Canada
American Federation of Television and Radio Artists
American Loudspeaker Manufacturers Ass'n
American Sportcasters Ass'n
American Women in Radio and Television
Associated Press Broadcasters
Associated Public-Safety Communications Officers
Ass'n for Broadcast Engineering Standards
Ass'n for Educational Communications and Technology
Ass'n of Catholic TV and Radio Syndicators
Ass'n of College and University Telecommunications Administrators
Ass'n of Federal Communications Consulting Engineers
Ass'n of Hospital Television Networks
Ass'n of Independent Commercial Producers
Ass'n of Independent Television Stations
Ass'n of Maximum Service Telecasters
Ass'n of Radio Reading Services
Ass'n of Regional Religious Communicators
Broadcast Credit Ass'n
Broadcast Education Ass'n
Broadcast Financial Management Ass'n
Broadcast Promotion and Marketing Executives
Cable Televison Administration and Marketing Soc.
Car Audio Specialists Ass'n
Clear Channel Broadcasting Service
Communications Marketing Ass'n
Community Antenna Television Ass'n
Concert Music Broadcasters Ass'n
Directors Guild of America
Electronic Industries Ass'n
Electronic Media Rating Council
Health Sciences Communications Ass'n
Intercollegiate Broadcasting System
Internat'l Documentary Ass'n
Internat'l Organization of Women in Telecommunications
Internat'l Radio and Television Soc.
Internat'l Teleproduction Soc.
Internat'l Television Ass'n
Internat'l Union of Electronic, Electrical, Technical, Salaried and Machine Workers
Joint Council on Educational Telecommunications
Land Mobile Communications Council
Motion Picture and Television Credit Ass'n
Music and Entertainment Industry Educators Ass'n
Nat'l Academy of Television Arts and Sciences
Nat'l Ass'n of Black-Owned Broadcasters
Nat'l Ass'n of Broadcast Employees and Technicians
Nat'l Ass'n of Broadcasters
Nat'l Ass'n of Business and Educational Radio
Nat'l Ass'n of Farm Broadcasters
Nat'l Ass'n of Public Television Stations
Nat'l Ass'n of Radio and Telecommunications Engineers
Nat'l Ass'n of Retail Dealers of America
Nat'l Ass'n of Television Program Executives
Nat'l Cable Television Ass'n
Nat'l Federation of Community Broadcasters
Nat'l Federation of Local Cable Programmers
Nat'l Religious Broadcasters
Nat'l Satellite Cable Ass'n
Nat'l Sportscasters and Sportswriters Ass'n
Nat'l Translator Ass'n
Public Service Satellite Consortium
Radio Advertising Bureau
Radio and Television Correspondents Ass'n
Radio-Television News Directors Ass'n
Satellite Broadcasting and Communications Ass'n
Screen Actors Guild
Soc. of Broadcast Engineers
Soc. of Cable Television Engineers
Soc. of Motion Picture and Television Art Directors
Soc. of Motion Picture and Television Engineers
Special Industrial Radio Service Ass'n
Station Representatives Ass'n
Tele-Communications Ass'n
Television Bureau of Advertising
Television Critics Ass'n
Telocator Network of America
UNDA-USA
United Electrical, Radio and Machine Workers of America
Video Software Dealers Ass'n
Videotex Industry Ass'n
Videtape Facilities Ass'n
Writers Guild of America, East
Writers Guild of America, West

RAILROADS
Air Brake Ass'n
American Ass'n of Railroad Superintendents
American Ass'n of Railway Surgeons
American Council of Railroad Women
American Institute for Shippers Ass'ns

00037

SUBJECT INDEX

READING

REAL ESTATE

RECORDS see PHONOGRAPHS

RECORDS MANAGEMENT

RECREATION

REFRACTORIES

REFRIGERATION

REHABILITATION

RELIGION see also CATHOLIC, JEWISH

RENTALS

SUBJECT INDEX

00041

SUBJECT INDEX

SUBJECT INDEX

00045

SUBJECT INDEX

WINDOWS

WINE

WIRE

WOMEN

WOOD & WOOD PRODUCTS

00047

1987

GEOGRAPHIC INDEX

All organizations in this book will be found here arranged

- Alphabetically by state.
- Alphabetically by city within state.
- Alphabetically by association within city within state.

ALABAMA

Birmingham
American Fertility Soc.
American Veterinary Exhibitors Ass'n
Ductile Iron Pipe Research Ass'n
Nat'l Ass'n of Companion Sitter Agencies and Referral Services
Professional Convention Management Ass'n
Soc. for Biomaterials

Decatur
Racking Horse Breeders Ass'n of America

Huntsville
Nat'l Speleological Soc.
Soc. of Logistics Engineers

Mobile
Ass'n of Internat'l Health Researchers

Montgomery
Ass'n of Conservation Engineers

Tuscaloosa
American Ass'n of University Administrators
Ass'n for University Business and Economic Research

ARIZONA

Flagstaff
Nat'l Forest Recreation Ass'n

Glendale
Soc. for the Study of Amphibians and Reptiles

Green Valley
American Automatic Control Council

Phoenix
Alpha Tau Delta
American Ass'n of Orthopaedic Medicine
American Burn Ass'n
Conference of Nat'l Park Concessioners
Nat'l Ass'n of Solar Contractors
Nat'l Ass'n of State Recreation Planners
Nat'l Speakers Ass'n
Post-Tensioning Institute
Supima Ass'n of America
Television Critics Ass'n

Prescott
Barzona Breeders Ass'n of America

Scottsdale
American Compensation Ass'n
American Professional Racquetball Organization
Internat'l Real Estate Institute
Nat'l Ass'n of Jewelry Appraisers
Nat'l Ass'n of Review Appraisers and Mortgage Underwriters
Nat'l Environmental Training Ass'n
Professional Women's Appraisal Ass'n

Sun City West
Engineering College Magazines Associated

Tempe
American Ass'n of Teachers of Slavic and East European Languages
Asphalt Rubber Producers Group
Nat'l Collegiate Baseball Writers Ass'n
Soc. for Invertebrate Pathology
University Council for Educational Administration

Tucson
American Ass'n of Correctional Training Personnel
American Ass'n of Poison Control Centers
American Ass'n of Veterinary Laboratory Diagnosticians
Art Libraries Soc./North America
Internat'l Meat Processors Ass'n
Middle East Studies Ass'n of North America
Nat'l Yellow Pages Agency Ass'n
Professional Archers Ass'n
Tree-Ring Soc.

ARKANSAS

Eureka Springs
Self-Service Storage Ass'n

Fayetteville
American Ass'n of Bible Colleges
Soc. for the Study of Symbolic Interaction
Women's Caucus for the Modern Languages

Gurdon
Internat'l Concatenated Order of Hoo-Hoo

Little Rock
American Parquet Ass'n
Nat'l Ass'n of State Directors of Teacher Education and Certification
Nat'l Ass'n of State Textbook Administrators
Nat'l Ass'n of Supervisors of Business Education
United States Trout Farmers Ass'n

North Little Rock
Women in Energy

Pine Bluff
American Ass'n for Correctional Psychology

CALIFORNIA

Agoura
American Academy of Sports Physicians

Alameda
Internat'l Ass'n for Identification

Alpine
American Osteopathic Academy of Sclerotherapy

Anaheim
Ceramic Arts Federation Internat'l

Arcadia
American Athletic Trainers Ass'n and Certification Board

Bakersfield
Academy of Dentistry Internat'l
Ass'n of Applied Insect Ecologists

Berkeley
Ass'n of Professional Bridge Players
Soc. for Research in Child Development
Special Interest Group on Operating Systems
Women Library Workers

Beverly Hills
Academy of Motion Picture Arts and Sciences
American Longevity Ass'n
Producer's Guild of America
Soc. of Professional Audio Recording Studios
Technology Transfer Soc.

Blue Jay
Nat'l Ass'n of Rehabilitation Professionals in the Private Sector

Brea
Precision Chiropractic Research Soc.

Buena Park
Mobile Industrial Caterers' Ass'n Internat'l

Burbank
American Auto Racing Writers and Broadcasters Ass'n
Manuscript Soc.
Nat'l Academy of Recording Arts and Sciences
Nat'l Ass'n of Extradition Officials

Cameron Park
Internat'l Pot and Kettle Club

Campbell
Reclaim Managers Ass'n

Capitola
American Hanoverian Soc.

Carlsbad
Nat'l Ass'n of Music Merchants

Carson
American Ass'n of Clinical Urologists

Century City
Ass'n of Representatives of Professional Athletes

Cerritos
Trade Show Services Ass'n

Chico
American Ass'n of Owners and Breeders of Peruvian Paso Horses
Nat'l Ass'n of Veteran Program Administrators

Chula Vista
College of Optometrists in Vision Development
Soc. of Allied Weight Engineers

City of Industry
Ass'n of Railway Museums
Certified Milk Producers Ass'n of America

Claremont
College Swimming Coaches Ass'n of America
Nat'l Ass'n for Ethnic Studies

Concord
Hydroponics Soc. of America

Corte Madera
Inter-Financial Ass'n
Pacific Agricultural Cooperative for Export

Costa Mesa
Motorcycle Industry Council
Motorcycle Safety Foundation
Nat'l Bicycle Dealers Ass'n
Nat'l Nutritional Foods Ass'n
Specialty Vehicle Institute of America

Covina
Educational Dealers and Suppliers Ass'n Internat'l
Soc. for the Advancement of Material and Process Engineering

Culver City
American Film Marketing Ass'n
Biomedical Engineering Soc.
Nat'l Vehicle Leasing Ass'n

Cupertino
Semiconductor Industry Ass'n

Cypress
American Soc. for Cytotechnology

Davis
American College of Veterinary Radiology
American Soc. for Enology and Viticulture
Geothermal Resources Council
Institute of Mathematical Statistics

Delzura
Nat'l Ass'n of Aeronautical Examiners

Diamond Bar
Christian Ministries Management Ass'n

El Cerrito
Seismological Soc. of America

El Dorado Hills
AirLifeLine

Encinitas
Livestock Publications Council

Encino
Federation of Trainers and Training Programs in Psychodrama

Fair Oaks
Western Range Ass'n

Fairhaven
North Coast Export Company

Fallbrook
Avocado Growers Bargaining Council

Foster City
American Ass'n of School Personnel Administrators

Fountain Valley
American College of Veterinary Ophthalmologists

Fresno
Trophy Dealers and Manufacturers Ass'n
Weather Modification Ass'n

Fullerton
American Endodontic Soc.
Mexican American Engineering Soc.
Nat'l Ass'n for Veterinary Acupuncture
Soc. of Critical Care Medicine

Garden Grove
Antique Appraisal Ass'n of America
Internat'l Drapery Ass'n

Gilroy
Fresh Garlic Ass'n

Glendale
Production Engine Remanufacturers Ass'n

Glendora
Internat'l Group of Agents and Bureaus

00001

GEOGRAPHIC INDEX

Granada Hills
Phi Alpha Delta
Soc. for Adolescent Medicine
Guerneville
Peruvian Paso Horse Registry of North America
Hollywood
American Soc. of Cinematographers
Ass'n of Independent Music Publishers
Directors Guild of America
Screen Actors Guild
Videtape Facilities Ass'n
Inglewood
Internat'l Right of Way Ass'n
Irvine
Ass'n of Pediatric Oncology Nurses
Avocado Export
Cleaning Management Institute
Internat'l Ass'n for Enterostomal Therapy
Internat'l Soc. of Chemical Ecology
Keene
United Farm Workers of America
La Habra
Ass'n of Christian Schools Internat'l
La Jolla
American Institute of Fishery Research Biologists
Ass'n of Firearm and Toolmark Examiners
Laguna Hills
League for Innovation in the Community College
Manufacturers' Agents Nat'l Ass'n
Lancaster
Soc. of Experimental Test Pilots
Soc. of Flight Test Engineers
Lindsay
Central Shippers
Loma Linda
Nat'l Ass'n of Seventh-Day Adventist Dentists
Lomita
Internat'l Institute for Lath and Plaster
Western Awning Ass'n
Long Beach
American Soc. for Aesthetic Plastic Surgery
Soc. for History Education
Technical Marketing Soc. of America
Los Altos
Special Interest Group for Biomedical Computing
Los Angeles
African Studies Ass'n
American Academy of Health Administration
American Academy of Medical Preventics
American Ass'n of Medical Milk Commissions
American Ass'n of Political Consultants
American Cinema Editors
American College of Internat'l Physicians
American College of Trial Lawyers
American Gem Soc.
Associated Surplus Dealers
Ceramic Tile Institute of America
College Theology Soc.
Congress of Neurological Surgeons
Exposition Service Contractors Ass'n
Institute of Ass'n Management Companies
Intercollegiate Musical Council, The Nat'l Ass'n of Male Choruses
Internat'l Ass'n for Personnel Women
Internat'l Ass'n of Independent Scholars
Internat'l Ass'n of Plumbing and Mechanical Officials
Internat'l Documentary Ass'n
Internat'l Soc. of Developmental and Comparative Immunology
Internat'l Soc. of Interior Designers
Leading Jewelers Guild
Motion Picture and Television Credit Ass'n
Nat'l Ass'n of Catering Executives
Nat'l Ass'n of Health Career Schools
Nat'l Ass'n of Hispanic Publications
Nat'l Mail Order Ass'n
Nat'l Staff Leasing Ass'n
Nat'l Tile Roofing Manufacturers Ass'n
Power Sources Manufacturers Ass'n
Safety Helmet Council of America
Screen Extras Guild
Soc. of Children's Book Writers
Soc. of Experimental Psychologists
Soc. of University Surgeons
Soc. of Vertebrate Paleontology
United Ostomy Ass'n
Waterbed Manufacturers Ass'n
Western Ass'n of Equipment Lessors
Writers Guild of America, West
Los Angelos
American Guides Ass'n
American Tour Managers Ass'n
Los Gatos
Surface Mount Technology Ass'n
Marina del Rey
Special Interest Group on Artificial Intelligence
Martinez
Sugar Industry Technologists
Menlo Park
American Ass'n for Artificial Intelligence
Ass'n for Women Geoscientists
Mill Valley
California Redwood Ass'n
Mission Vie o
American Ass'n of Attorney-Certified Public Accountants
Modesto
American Ass'n for Medical Transcription
Montclair
Nat'l Ass'n of Underwater Instructors
Monterey
Soc. of Company Meeting Planners
Monterey Park
Driving School Ass'n of America
Mountain View
Semiconductor Equipment and Materials Institute
Special Interest Group for Architecture of Computer Systems
Special Interest Group on Programming Languages
N. Hollywood
Nat'l Watercolor Soc.
Newport Beach
American Ass'n of Critical-Care Nurses
Nat'l Ass'n of Sales and Marketing Professionals
Specialty Automotive Manufacturers Ass'n
North Hollywood
Nat'l Hispanic Psychological Ass'n
Northridge
Internat'l Bio-Environmental Foundation
Novato
Internat'l Ass'n for Aquatic Animal Medicine
Internat'l Ass'n of Credit Card Investigators
Oakland
Institute of Intermodal Repairers
Nat'l Ass'n of Black and Minority Chambers of Commerce
Nat'l Safety Management Soc.
Soc. for French Historical Studies
Soc. for Nutrition Education
Union of American Physicians and Dentists
Western States Meat Ass'n
Orange
Ass'n of Medical School Pediatric Department Chairmen
Pacific Grove
Tire Retread Information Bureau
Pacific Palisades
Nat'l Ass'n of Railroad Trial Counsel
Stuntwomen's Ass'n of Motion Pictures
Palm Springs
Internat'l Food, Wine and Travel Writers Ass'n
Palo Alto
American Electronics Ass'n
Ass'n of Engineering Geologists
Electric Power Research Institute
Paramount
Internat'l Union of Petroleum and Industrial Workers
Pasadena
Internat'l Institute of Municipal Clerks
Microbeam Analysis Soc.
Pinole
Internat'l Erosion Control Ass'n
Playa Del Rey
Soc. for Information Display
Pleasant Hill
Lepidopterists' Soc.
Soc. for Historical Archaeology
Rancho Cucamonga
Precision Measurements Ass'n
Rancho Palos Verdes
Municipal Treasurers Ass'n of the United States and Canada
Rancho Santa Fe
Internat'l Exchangors Ass'n
Redding
American Buckskin Registry Ass'n
Redlands
Renown Shippers
Redondo Beach
Automotive Fleet and Leasing Ass'n
Riverside
Internat'l Organization of Citrus Virologists
Rohnert Park
Internat'l Soc. of Statistical Science in Economics
Roseville
Nat'l Ass'n of Railway Business Women
Sacramento
American Ambulance Ass'n
American Ass'n of Mental Health Professionals in Corrections
American Criminal Justice Ass'n
American Down Ass'n
American Institute of Building Design
Ass'n for Correctional Research and Information Management
Chief Officers of State Library Agencies
Nat'l Ass'n for Professional Saleswomen
San Diego
American Academy of Clinical Psychiatrists
American Soc. of Outpatient Surgeons
American Tunaboat Ass'n
American Venereal Disease Ass'n
ASHBEAMS
Ass'n of Science Museum Directors
Epigraphic Soc.
Internat'l Dance-Exercise Ass'n
Internat'l Stress and Tension Control Ass'n
Nat'l Academic Athletic Advisors' Ass'n
Nat'l Ass'n of Bar-Related Title Insurers
Pinto Horse Ass'n of America
Sealant Engineering and Associated Lines
Soc. for Computer Simulation
San Francisco
American Academy of Ophthalmology
American College of Foot Surgeons
American Council of Railroad Women
American Hypnotists' Ass'n
American Soc. of Ophthalmic Registered Nurses
American Soc. on Aging
Ass'n for Humanistic Psychology
Ass'n of Footwear Distributors
COSMEP, Internat'l Ass'n of Independent Publishers
Federation of Computer Users in the Medical Sciences
Internat'l Ass'n of Business Communicators
Internat'l Longshoremen's and Warehousemen's Union
Internat'l Soc. for General Semantics
Internat'l Transactional Analysis Ass'n
Nat'l Ass'n for Bank Cost Analysis & Management Accountint
Nat'l Council on Crime and Delinquency
Nat'l Institute of Oilseed Products
Nat'l Organization of Bar Counsel
Soc. for Investigative Dermatology
Soc. for Psychophysiological Research
Soc. for Public Health Education
Soc. for the Study of Social Problems
Talmex Export Corporation
Wine Institute
San Jose
Ass'n of Film Commissioners
California Export Ass'n
Internat'l Academy of Trial Lawyers
Internat'l Drycleaners Congress
Nat'l Ass'n of Tax Consultors
Public Agency Risk Managers Ass'n
San Leandro
Internat'l Union of Security Officers
San Mateo
World Ass'n of Detectives
Santa Ana
Nat'l Ass'n of Name Plate Manufacturers
Nat'l Institute of Pension Administrators
Professional Ass'n of Diving Instructors
Self Insurance Institute of America
Soc. of Vector Ecologists
Santa Clara
California Dried Fruit Export Ass'n
Santa Fe Springs
American Ass'n of Gynecological Laparoscopists
Santa Monica
American College of Probate Counsel
American Franchise Ass'n
Human Factors Soc.
Security Equipment Industry Ass'n
Soc. of Research Administrators
Wedding Photographers Internat'l
Sherman Oaks
Aerobics and Fitness Ass'n of America
Alliance of Motion Picture and Television Producers
North American Transplant Coordinators Organization
Soc. of Motion Picture and Television Art Directors
Stucco Manufacturers Ass'n
Sonoma
Nat'l Inholders Ass'n
South Laguna
American Institute of Oral Biology
South Pasadena
Ass'n of Visual Communicators
Nat'l Retail Pet Store and Groomers Ass'n
Western World Pet Supply Ass'n
South San Francisco
Nat'l Ass'n of State and Provincial Lotteries
Stanford
American Ass'n for the Advancement of Slavic Studies
American Soc. for Head and Neck Surgery
Soc. of Biological Psychiatry
Temple City
Internat'l College of Applied Nutrition
Thousand Oaks
American Soc. of Zoologists
Tustin
Diving Equipment Manufacturers Ass'n
Universal City
Gay and Lesbian Press Ass'n
Upland
American Gem and Mineral Suppliers Ass'n
Valencia
Training Media Distributors Ass'n
Valle o
American Concrete Pumping Ass'n
Van Nuys
Professional Numismatists Guild
SAFE Ass'n
Scaffold Industry Ass'n

Ventura
Automatic Transmission Rebuilders Ass'n
Vista
Evangelical Christian Publishers Ass'n
Walnut Creek
Ass'n of Human Resource Systems Professionals
West Covina
Nat'l Ass'n of Physical Therapists
Tele-Communications Ass'n
West Sacramento
Western Timber Ass'n
Westlake
American Soc. of Plumbing Engineers
Westminster
Tooling Component Manufacturers Ass'n
Whittier
Auto Internacional Ass'n
Internat'l Conference of Building Officials
Specialty Equipment Market Ass'n
Street Rod Equipment Ass'n
Woodland Hills
Institute for the Advancement of Engineering
Nat'l Notary Ass'n
Yucaipa
American Mustang Ass'n

COLORADO

Arvada
American Institute of Professional Geologists
Aurora
Affiliated Advertising Agencies Internat'l
American Academy of Cosmetic Surgery
American Soc. for Surgery of the Hand
Associated Business Writers of America
Nat'l Writers Club
Boulder
American Soc. of Plant Taxonomists
American Solar Energy Soc.
Ass'n for Experiential Education
Ass'n for Volunteer Administration
Behavior Genetics Ass'n
Caucus for Women in Statistics
CAUSE
College Football Ass'n
College Music Soc.
Geological Soc. of America
Institute for Fermentation and Brewing Studies
Internat'l Federation for Choral Music
Nat'l Conference of Standards Laboratories
Professional Ski Instructors of America
Rolf Institute
Soc. for the Study of Evolution
Colorado Springs
American Academy of Forensic Sciences
American Boarding Kennels Ass'n
Christian Booksellers Ass'n
General Merchandise Distributors Council
Internat'l Ass'n of Bomb Technicians and Investigators
Internat'l Typographical Union
Professional Rodeo Cowboys Ass'n
United States Soccer Federation
Denver
American Academy of Environmental Medicine
American Animal Hospital Ass'n
American Ass'n of Chairmen of Departments of Psychiatry
American Ass'n of Suicidology
American Buffalo Ass'n
American College of Medical Group Administrators
American Gelbvieh Ass'n
American Sheep Producers Council
American Soc. of Dermatopathology
American Soc. of Farm Managers and Rural Appraisers
American Water Works Ass'n
Ass'n of American Editorial Cartoonists
Ass'n of Audio-Visual Technicians
Ass'n of Operating Room Nurses
Boys Clubs Professional Ass'n
Ca al Club
Continental Basketball Ass'n
Farmers Educational and Co-operative Union of America
Government Management Information Sciences
Institute of Certified Financial Planners
Internat'l Arabian Horse Ass'n
Internat'l Ass'n of Geophysical Contractors
Law and Society Ass'n
Medical Group Management Ass'n
Nat'l Ass'n of Entrepreneurs
Nat'l Conference of State Legislatures
Nat'l Environmental Health Ass'n
Nat'l Live Stock Producers Ass'n
Nat'l Potato Promotion Board
Nat'l Ski Patrol System
North American Limousin Foundation
Oil, Chemical and Atomic Workers Internat'l Union
Soc. for New Language Study
Soc. for Range Management
Soc. of Biblical Literature
Soc. of Photo-Technologists
State Higher Education Executive Officers
United States Meat Export Federation
Visiting Nurse Ass'ns of America
Western and English Manufacturers Ass'n
Durango
American Aerobics Ass'n
Englewood
American Institute of Timber Construction
American School Food Service Ass'n
American Soc. of Bariatric Physicians
Internat'l Health Soc.
Nat'l Ass'n of Financial Consultants
Nat'l Cattlemen's Ass'n
Nat'l Potato Council
Transworld Advertising Agency Network
Fort Collins
American Soc. of Sugar Beet Technologists
Beet Sugar Development Foundation
Nat'l Ass'n of Business and Industrial Saleswomen
Pulverized Limestone Ass'n
Rural Education Ass'n
Ft. Collins
Ass'n of College and University Auditors
Golden
American Ass'n for Crystal Growth
American Ass'n of Equine Practitioners
Soc. of Economic Geologists
Grand Junction
Nat'l Ass'n of Private, Nontraditional Schools and Colleges
Greeley
American Soc. of Parasitologists
Nat'l Onion Ass'n
Lakewood
America on the Move
LaPorte
Dude Ranchers' Ass'n
Littleton
Ass'n for Women Veterinarians
Ass'n of Surgical Technologists
Soc. of Mining Engineers
System Safety Soc.
Westminster
Arabian Horse Registry of America
Wheat Ridge
Nat'l Quartz Producers Council
Wheatridge
Biofeedback Soc. of America

CONNECTICUT

Bethel
Soc. for Experimental Mechanics
Bloomfield
American Academy of Craniomandibular Disorders
Branford
Nat'l Ass'n of Basketball Coaches of the United States
Brookfield Center
Soc. of Plastics Engineers
Cos Cob
American Seafood Retailers Ass'n
Darien
Burlap and Jute Ass'n
Selenium-Tellurium Development Ass'n
East Haddam
Shade Tobacco Growers Agricultural Ass'n
East Haven
Ass'n of Master of Business Administration Executives
Enfield
Copier Dealers Ass'n
Fairfield
Nat'l Ass'n of Scissors and Shears Manufacturers
Romanian Studies Ass'n of America
Farmington
American Nuclear Insurers
Ass'n of Clinical Scientists
Life Insurance Marketing and Research Ass'n
Glastonbury
Nat'l Federation of Grange Mutual Insurance Companies
Goshen
American Connemara Pony Soc.
Greenwich
Academy of Family Mediators
Ass'n of Executive Search Consultants
Copper Development Ass'n
Nat'l Ass'n of Catalog Showroom Merchandisers
Quality Bakers of America Cooperative
Guilford
Wire Ass'n Internat'l
Hamden
Soc. for the History of Discoveries
Hartford
Accredited Gemologists Ass'n
American Epilepsy Soc.
Ass'n of Life Insurance Medical Directors of America
Internat'l Ass'n of Campus Law Enforcement Administrators
Materials Marketing Associates
Nat'l Ass'n of Produce Market Managers
Pin, Clip and Fastener Services
Kent
Ass'n of Business Officers of Preparatory Schools
Milford
American Soc. of Marine Artists
New Britain
Internat'l Philatelic Press Club
New Haven
American Oriental Soc.
Clowns of America, Internat'l
ICAAAA Coaches Ass'n
Internat'l Ass'n of Tour Managers - North American Region
Modern Greek Studies Ass'n
Nat'l Ass'n for Drama Therapy
Religious Education Ass'n
Soc. for Values in Higher Education
New Milford
Ass'n of Bridal Consultants
Norwalk
Carded Packaging Institute
Coblentz Soc.
Internat'l Ozone Ass'n-Pan American Committee Branch
Licensing Executives Soc.
Nat'l Ass'n of Electrical Distributors
Nat'l Ass'n of Police-Community Relations Officers
Nat'l Bed and Breakfast Ass'n
Sunglass Ass'n of America
Riverside
Nat'l Shooting Sports Foundation
Sporting Arms and Ammunition Manufacturers' Institute
Rocky Hill
Harness Horsemen Internat'l
Simsbury
Headmasters Ass'n
Stamford
Advertising and Marketing Internat'l Network
American Apparel Machinery Trade Ass'n
Ass'n for Employee Health and Fitness
Book Manufacturers Institute
Crusher and Portable Plant Ass'n
Data Entry Management Ass'n
Direct Marketing Credit Ass'n
Graphic Arts Advertisers and Exhibitors Council
Nat'l Ass'n of Corporate and Professional Recruiters
Packaging Institute Internat'l
Small Independent Record Manufacturers Ass'n
Vibrating Screen Manufacturers Ass'n
Storrs
American Ass'n of State Climatologists
Northeastern Weed Science Soc.
Watertown
Apartment Owners and Managers Ass'n of America
West Hartford
Handweavers Guild of America
Internat'l Ass'n of Approved Basketball Officials
West Haven
American Ass'n of Pathologists' Assistants
Westport
American Natural Soda Ash Corporation
Independent Jewelers Organization
Insurance Crime Prevention Institute
Wilton
Ass'n of Industrial Metallizers, Coaters and Laminators
Boating Writers Internat'l
Woodbury
Internat'l Ass'n of Conference Centers

DELAWARE

Greenville
Economic History Ass'n
Montchanin
Analytical Laboratory Managers Ass'n
Newark
American Philosophical Ass'n
Internat'l Reading Ass'n
Jean Piaget Soc.
Produce Marketing Ass'n
Special Interest Group for University and College Computing Services
Urban Affairs Ass'n
Wilmington
Ass'n of Sports Museums and Halls of Fame
Catalysis Soc. of North America
United States Ass'n of Independent Gymnastic Clubs

DISTRICT OF COLUMBIA

Washingon
American Ass'n of Acupuncture and Oriental Medicine
Washington
Academy of Pharmaceutical Sciences
Accountants for the Public Interest
Acrylamide Producers Ass'n
Acrylonitrile Group
Ad utants General Ass'n of the United States
Aeronautical Repair Station Ass'n
Aerospace Department Chairmen's Ass'n
Aerospace Industries Ass'n of America
Aerospace Medical Ass'n
African American Museums Ass'n
Agricultural Communicators in Education
Agricultural History Soc.
Agricultural Relations Council
Agriculture Council of America
Air Conditioning Contractors of America

GEOGRAPHIC INDEX

00004

Can Manufacturers Institute
Canadian-American Motor Carriers Ass'n
Canon Law Soc. of America
Car Audio Specialists Ass'n
Carbonated Beverage Institute
Catholic Biblical Ass'n of America
Catholic Charities USA
Cellular Telecommunications Industry Ass'n
Central Station Electrical Protection Ass'n
Ceramic Tile Marketing Federation
Certified Color Manufacturers Ass'n
Chain Link Fence Manufacturers Institute
Chamber of Commerce of the United States of America
Chemical Manufacturers Ass'n
Chemical Specialties Manufacturers Ass'n
Chemical Waste Transportation Council
China Clay Producers Group
Chlorine Institute, The
Chlorobenzene Producers Ass'n
Christian College Coalition
Cigar Ass'n of America
Classroom Publishers Ass'n
Clear Channel Broadcasting Service
Closure Manufacturers Ass'n
Coal Exporters Ass'n of the United States
Coalition for Common Sense in Government Procurement
Cold Finished Steel Bar Institute
College and University Personnel Ass'n
Color Marketing Group
Commercial Development Ass'n
Commercial Refrigerator Manufacturers Ass'n
Commission on Professionals in Science and Technology
Commissioned Officers Ass'n of the United States Public Health Service
Communications Security Ass'n
Communications Workers of America
Community Design Center Directors Ass'n
Competitive Telecommunications Ass'n
Composite Can and Tube Institute
Computer and Business Equipment Manufacturers Ass'n
Computer and Communications Industry Ass'n
Computer Dealers and Lessors Ass'n
Computer Soc. of the Institute of Electrical and Electronics Engineers
Computerized Radiology Soc.
Conference Board of the Mathematical Sciences
Conference of American Renting and Leasing Assn's
Conference of State Bank Supervisors
Construction Industry Management Board
Construction Management Ass'n of America
Consumer Federation of America
Continental Ass'n of Funeral and Memorial Socs.
Contract Services Ass'n of America
Convention Liaison Council
Cooperative Education Ass'n
Copper and Brass Fabricators Council
Corn Refiners Ass'n
Cosmetic, Toiletry and Fragrance Ass'n
Cotton Council Internat'l
Cotton Warehouse Ass'n of America
Council for Advancement and Support of Education
Council for American Private Education
Council for Basic Education
Council for Educational Development and Research
Council for Export Trading Companies
Council for Interinstitutional Leadership
Council for Responsible Nutrition
Council of American-Flag Ship Operators
Council of American Overseas Research Centers
Council of Chief State School Officers
Council of Defense and Space Industry Ass'ns
Council of Food Processors Ass'n Executives
Council of Graduate Schools in the U.S.
Council of Independent Colleges
Council of Pollution Control Financing Agencies
Council of Professional Ass'ns on Federal Statistics
Council of Scientific Soc. Presidents
Council of State Administrators of Vocational Rehabilitation
Council of State Chambers of Commerce
Council of State Community Affairs Agencies
Council of State Housing Agencies
Council of State Policy and Planning Agencies
Council of the Great City Schools
Council on Alternate Fuels
Council on Foundations
Council on Hotel, Restaurant and Institutional Education
Council on Postsecondary Accreditation
Council on Social Work Education
Criminal Justice Statistics Ass'n
Cylinder Manufacturers Ass'n
Dealer Bank Ass'n
Detachable Container Ass'n
Diplomatic and Consular Officers, Retired
Direct Selling Ass'n
Distilled Spirits Council of the United States
Edison Electric Institute
Education Writers Ass'n
Electricity Consumers Resource Council
Electromagnetic Energy Policy Alliance
Electronic Funds Transfer Ass'n
Electronic Industries Ass'n
Employee Benefit Research Institute
Employee Relocation Council
Employers Council on Flexible Compensation
Environmental Industry Council
ESOP Ass'n
Ethylene Oxide Industry Council
Exhibit Designers and Producers Ass'n
Exterior Insulation Manufacturers Ass'n
Eye Bank Ass'n of America
Farm Credit Council
Federal Administrative Law Judges Conference
Federal Bar Ass'n
Federal Communications Bar Ass'n
Federal Construction Council
Federal Energy Bar Ass'n
Federal Librarians Round Table
Federal Managers Ass'n
Federal Probation Officers Ass'n
Federal Water Quality Ass'n
Federally Employed Women
Federation of American Health Systems
Federation of American Scientists
Federation of Materials Societies
Federation of Nurses and Health Professionals
Federation of Organizations for Professional Women
Federation of Professional Athletes
Federation of Tax Administrators
Ferroalloys Ass'n
Ferrous Scrap Consumers Coalition
Fertilizer Institute
Fiberglass Fabrication Ass'n
Fibre Drum Technical Council
Financial Stationers Ass'n
Fire Marshals Ass'n of North America
Flavor and Extract Manufacturers Ass'n of the United States
Flexible Packaging Ass'n
Flight Engineers' Internat'l Ass'n
Food and Drug Law Institute
Food Industry Ass'n Executives
Food Marketing Institute
Food Processing Machinery and Supplies Ass'n
Foodservice and Lodging Institute
Footwear Retailers of America
Forestry Conservation Communications Ass'n
Formaldehyde Institute
Forum for Health Care Planning
Foundation for Internat'l Meetings
Foundation for Savings Institutions
Fragrance Materials Ass'n of the United States
Freight Forwarders Institute
Future Business Leaders of America-Phi Beta Lambda
Futures Industry Ass'n
Garden Centers of America
Gasoline Pump Manufacturers Ass'n
General Agents and Managers Conference of NALU
General Aviation Manufacturers Ass'n
General Federation of Women's Clubs
Gerontological Soc. of America
Gift Ass'n of America
Glass Packaging Institute
Gold Institute
Graphic Communications Internat'l Union
Greeting Card Ass'n
Grocery Manufacturers of America
Group Health Ass'n of America
Guild of Natural Science Illustrators
Halogenated Solvents Industry Alliance
Hazardous Waste Treatment Council
Health Industry Distributors Ass'n
Health Industry Manufacturers Ass'n
Health Insurance Ass'n of America
Hearing Industries Ass'n
High Speed Rail Ass'n
Highway Users Federation for Safety and Mobility
History of Earth Sciences Soc.
Home Economics Education Ass'n
Horticultural Research Institute
Hotel Employees and Restaurant Employees Internat'l Union
Hotel Sales and Marketing Ass'n Internat'l
Household Goods Forwarders Ass'n of America
Independent Bakers Ass'n
Independent Bankers Ass'n of America
Independent Data Communications Manufacturers Ass'n
Independent Electrical Contractors
Independent Gasoline Marketers Council
Independent Liquid Terminals Ass'n
Independent Lubricant Manufacturers Ass'n
Independent Petroleum Ass'n of America
Independent Sector
Independent Terminal Operators Ass'n
Independent Zinc Alloyers Ass'n
Industrial Gas Cleaning Institute
Industrial Truck Ass'n
Industry Council for Tangible Assets
Information Industry Ass'n
Institute for Polyacrylate Absorbents
Institute of Industrial Launderers
Institute of Internat'l Finance
Institute of Makers of Explosives
Institute of Medicine
Institute of Navigation
Institute of Scrap Iron and Steel
Institute of Shortening and Edible Oils
Institute of the Ironworking Industry
Institute of Transportation Engineers
Instrument Contracting and Engineering Ass'n
Insurance Economics Soc. of America
Insurance Institute for Highway Safety
Intellectual Property Owners
Inter-American Bar Ass'n
Intercollegiate Broadcasting System
Interfaith Forum on Religion, Art and Architecture
Internat'l Ass'n for Dental Research
Internat'l Ass'n of Airport Duty Free Stores
Internat'l Ass'n of Bridge, Structural and Ornamental Iron Workers
Internat'l Ass'n of Cooking Professionals
Internat'l Ass'n of Energy Economists
Internat'l Ass'n of Fire Chiefs
Internat'l Ass'n of Fire Fighters
Internat'l Ass'n of Fish and Wildlife Agencies
Internat'l Ass'n of Heat and Frost Insulators and Asbestos Workers
Internat'l Ass'n of Independent Producers
Internat'l Ass'n of Law Enforcement Intelligence Analysts
Internat'l Ass'n of Machinists and Aerospace Workers
Internat'l Ass'n of Wiping Cloth Manufacturers
Internat'l Banana Ass'n
Internat'l Bridge Press Ass'n
Internat'l Bridge, Tunnel & Turnpike Ass'n
Internat'l Brotherhood of Electrical Workers
Internat'l Brotherhood of Firemen and Oilers
Internat'l Brotherhood of Painters and Allied Trades
Internat'l Brotherhood of Teamsters, Chauffeurs, Warehouseman and Helpers of America
Internat'l Chiropractors Ass'n
Internat'l City Management Ass'n
Internat'l Cogeneration Soc.
Internat'l Council for Computer Communication
Internat'l District Heating and Cooling Ass'n
Internat'l Downtown Ass'n
Internat'l Electrical Testing Ass'n
Internat'l Food Information Council
Internat'l Franchise Ass'n
Internat'l Ice Cream Ass'n
Internat'l Insurance Advisory Council
Internat'l Intelligent Buildings Ass'n
Internat'l Labor Communications Ass'n
Internat'l League of Electrical Ass'ns
Internat'l Masonry Institute
Internat'l Newspaper Advertising and Marketing Executives, Inc.
Internat'l Newspaper Financial Executives
Internat'l Newspaper Promotion Ass'n
Internat'l Organization for the Education of the Hearing Impaired
Internat'l Slurry Seal Ass'n
Internat'l Soc. for Intercultural Eductation, Training and Research
Internat'l Soc. for Peritoneal Dialysis
Internat'l Soc. of Air Safety Investigators
Internat'l Soc. of Transport Aircraft Traders
Internat'l Technical Caramel Ass'n
Internat'l Trade Commission Trial Lawyers Ass'n
Internat'l Union of Bricklayers and Allied Craftsmen
Internat'l Union of Electronic, Electrical, Technical, Salaried and Machine Workers
Internat'l Union of Operating Engineers
Internat'l Union of Police Ass'ns
Interstate Conference of Employment Security Agencies
Interstate Conference on Water Policy
Interstate Natural Gas Ass'n of America
Investment Company Institute
Issues Management Ass'n
Jesuit Secondary Education Ass'n
Joint Council on Educational Telecommunications
Joint Electron Device Engineering Council
Judge Advocates Ass'n
Laborers' Internat'l Union of North America
Land Mobile Communications Council
Latin American Manufacturers Ass'n
Lead-Zinc Producers Committee
League of Federal Recreation Ass'ns
Leak Detection Technology Ass'n
Leather Industries of America
Licensed Beverage Information Council
Linguistic Soc. of America
Lutheran Educational Conference of North America
Ma or Indoor Soccer League Players Ass'n
Machinery and Allied Products Institute
Mail Order Ass'n of America
Man-Made Fiber Producers Ass'n
Manufacturers of Emission Controls Ass'n
Marine Technology Soc.
Mathematical Ass'n of America
Menswear Retailers of America
Metal Building Components Manufacturers Ass'n
Metal Construction Ass'n
Methyl Chloride Industry Ass'n
Microwave Communications Ass'n
Military Reform Institute
Milk Industry Foundation
Millers' Nat'l Federation
Mineralogical Soc. of America
Mining and Reclamation Council of America
Modern Humanities Research Ass'n
Mortgage Bankers Ass'n of America
Mortgage Insurance Companies of America
Nat'l Abortion Federation
Nat'l Academy of Engineering of the United States of America
Nat'l Academy of Sciences

00005

GEOGRAPHIC INDEX

FLORIDA

GEOGRAPHIC INDEX

GEORGIA

HAWAII

IDAHO

ILLINOIS

00009

GEOGRAPHIC INDEX

Underground Contractors Association
United Golfers' Ass'n
United States League of Savings Institutions
United States Lifesaving Ass'n
United States Telecommunications Suppliers Ass'n
USA Rugby Football Union
Veal Industry Council
Vermiculite Ass'n
Wallcovering Distributors Ass'n
Water Systems Council
Western Railroad Ass'n
Women's Council of Realtors
Wood Truss Council of America
World Ass'n of Document Examiners
Woven Wire Products Ass'n
Zonta Internat'l

Clarendon Hills
Vibration Institute

Country Club Hills
Building Officials and Code Administrators Internat'l

Crystal Lake
American Medical Publishers' Ass'n

Danville
Ass'n of Newspaper Classified Advertising Managers

Decatur
Nat'l Lincoln Sheep Breeders Ass'n

Deefield
Single Ply Roofing Institute

Deerfield
American Telemarketing Ass'n
Architectural Fabric Structures Institute
Ass'n for Corporate Growth
Ass'n of Legal Administrators
Ceilings and Interior Systems Construction Ass'n
Legal Industry Advisory Council
Nat'l Ass'n of Quality Assurance Professionals
Nat'l Building Material Distributors Ass'n
Nat'l Federation of Paralegal Ass'ns
Nat'l Tumor Registrar's Ass'n
Pressure Sensitive Tape Council
Tag and Label Manufacturers Institute
USA Toy Library Ass'n

DeKalb
Ass'n for Continuing Professional Education
Internat'l Ass'n of Family Sociology
Internat'l Soc. of Weekly Newspaper Editors

Des Plaines
American Architectural Manufacturers Ass'n
American Ass'n of Biofeedback Clinicians
American Die Casting Institute
American Foundrymen's Soc.
American Soc. of Clinical Hypnosis
American Soc. of Safety Engineers
Ass'n of the Institute for Certification of Computer Professionals
Broadcast Financial Management Ass'n
Cast Metals Ass'n
Die Casting Research Foundation
Institute for Certification of Computer Professionals
Inter-Industry Conference on Auto Collision Repair
Internat'l Management Council
Metal Castings Soc.
Million Dollar Round Table
Nat'l Ass'n of Independent Insurers
Nat'l Ass'n of Power Engineers
Nat'l Catholic Cemetery Conference
Nat'l Renderers Ass'n
Nat'l Roofing Contractors Ass'n
Nat'l Sash and Door Jobbers Ass'n
Nat'l Terrazzo and Mosaic Ass'n
Nat'l Wood Window and Door Ass'n
Non-Ferrous Founders' Soc.
Professional Photographers of America
Refrigeration Service Engineers Soc.
Steel Founders' Soc. of America
Wholesale Stationer's Ass'n

Downers Grove
American Guild of Music
Coin Laundry Ass'n
Nat'l Garden Bureau
Plastic Shipping Container Institute
Pollution Liability Insurance Ass'n

Elk Grove Village
American Academy of Pediatrics
Nat'l Aesthetician and Nail Artist Ass'n

Elmhurst
Herpetologists' League
Internat'l Fire Photographers Ass'n

Elsip
Nat'l Ass'n of Independent Resurfacers

Evanston
American Academy of Dermatology
American Board of Medical Specialties
American College of Chemosurgery
American Soc. for Dermatologic Surgery
Ass'n of Rehabilitation Nurses
Casket Manufacturers Ass'n of America
Caster and Floor Truck Manufacturers Ass'n
Econometric Soc.
Gypsum Ass'n
Healthcare Internal Audit Group
Internat'l Home Furnishings Representatives Ass'n
Internat'l Soc. of Weighing and Measurement
Machine Knife Manufacturers Ass'n
Magnetic Materials Producers Ass'n
Marking Device Ass'n
Mechanical Power Transmission Ass'n
Monument Builders of North America
Nat'l Institute of Steel Detailing
Nat'l Nurses Soc. on Addictions
Nat'l Selected Morticians
Noise Control Products and Materials Ass'n

Evergreen Park
Nat'l Ass'n of Buying Services

Fox Lake
Nat'l Marine Representatives Ass'n

Franklin Park
Internat'l Reprographic Ass'n

Geneva
Associated Church Press
Steel Plate Fabricators Ass'n

Glen Ellyn
Bearing Specialist Ass'n
Evangelical Church Library Ass'n
Nat'l Ass'n of Pipe Nipple Manufacturers
Plastic Pipe and Fittings Ass'n
Plumbing Manufacturers Institute
Polyurethane Manufacturers Ass'n

Glencoe
Chinese Language Computer Soc.

Glenview
Automotive Engine Rebuilders Ass'n
Computer Micrographics Technology
Equipment and Tool Institute
Retail Confectioners Internat'l
Special Interest Group for Computers and Human Interaction

Grayslake
American Ass'n of Credit Counselors
Norwegian F ord Ass'n of North America

Harvard
Lightning Protection Institute

Henry
Nat'l Ass'n of Extension Home Economists

Highland Park
Academy of Geriatric Dentistry
Guild of Temple Musicians
Mu Phi Epsilon

Hillside
Air Distributing Institute
American Sod Producers Ass'n
Dietary Managers Ass'n
Nat'l Ass'n of Demolition Contractors
Wood and Synthetic Flooring Institute

Hines
Special Interest Group for Computers and the Physically Handicapped

Hinsdale
American Ass'n of Handwriting Analysts
Ceramic Tile Distributors Ass'n
Nat'l Ass'n of Bond Lawyers
Nat'l Seasoning Manufacturers Ass'n
Quality Chekd Dairy Products Ass'n

Hoffman Estates
Internat'l Soc. of Appraisers

Homewood
American Ass'n of Railroad Superintendents
American Railway Bridge and Building Ass'n
Roadmasters and Maintenance of Way Ass'n of America

Itasca
Ass'n of Mill and Elevator Mutual Insurance Companies
Conference of Actuaries in Public Practice
Soc. of Actuaries

Jacksonville
American Dialect Soc.

Kankakee
Internat'l Map Dealers' Ass'n

La Grange
Nat'l Ass'n of Limited Edition Dealers

La Grange Park
American Nuclear Soc.

Lagrange
Shoe Service Institute of America

Lake Bluff
Linguistic Ass'n of Canada and the United States

Lake Forest
Civil Aviation Medical Ass'n
Council of Medical Specialty Societies

Libertyville
Power Conversion Products Council, Internat'l
Small Motor Manufacturers Ass'n

Lincolnshire
Controlled Release Soc.

Lincolnwood
IPC
Variable Resistive Components Institute

Lisle
American Purchasing Soc.
Water Quality Ass'n

Lombard
American Group of CPA Firms
Internat'l Ass'n for Hospital Security
Internat'l Carwash Ass'n
Nat'l Ass'n of Retail Dealers of America

Macomb
Nat'l Council for Geographic Education
Nat'l Marina Manufacturers Consortium

Maywood
Land Improvement Contractors of America

McHenry
American Horse Publications

Moline
American Rental Ass'n
Lutheran Hospital Ass'n of America
Pattern Makers' League of North America

Monticello
American Shropshire Registry Ass'n

Morton Grove
American Equilibration Soc.
Sporting Goods Agents Ass'n

Mount Morris
Graphic Preparatory Ass'n
Nat'l Ass'n of Diemakers and Diecutters

Mount Prospect
American Ass'n of Certified Allergists
American College of Allergists
Brotherhood of Railroad Signalmen
Institute of Environmental Sciences
Joint Council of Allergy and Immunology
Nat'l Church Goods Ass'n
Nat'l Sporting Goods Ass'n

Mundelein
American Art Therapy Ass'n
Ass'n for Practitioners in Infection Control
Biomedical Marketing Ass'n
Nurses Organization of the Veterans Administration
Sulfate of Potash Magnesia Export Ass'n

Naperville
Barbecue Industry Ass'n
Electronic Pest Control Ass'n
Incentive Manufacturers Representatives Ass'n
Internat'l Silo Ass'n
Logsplitter Manufacturers Ass'n
Nat'l Frame Builders Ass'n
Nat'l Fraternal Congress of America
Wire Fabricators Ass'n

Normal
American Vocational Education Research Ass'n
Nat'l Ass'n of Professional Band Instrument Repair Technicians

North Chicago
United States Federation for Culture Collections

Northbrook
American Soc. for Concrete Construction
Collector Platemakers Guild
Commercial Food Equipment Service Ass'n
Institute of Nuclear Materials Management
Maple Flooring Manufacturers Ass'n
Nat'l Ass'n of Installation Developers
Nat'l Ass'n of Service Managers
Nat'l Eye Research Foundation
Nat'l Family Business Council
Roof Coatings Manufacturers Ass'n
Steel Tank Institute
Textile Bag Manufacturers Ass'n
Wild Bird Feeding Institute

Northfield
Internat'l Ass'n of Security Services
Nat'l Ass'n of Paralegal Personnel
Nat'l Unfinished Furniture Institute
United States of America National Committee of the Internat'l Dairy Federation

Oak Brook
American Soc. of Neuroradiology
Associated Equipment Distributors
Council of Logistics Management
Healthcare Financial Management Ass'n
Nat'l LP-Gas Ass'n
Nat'l Truck Leasing System
Radiological Soc. of North America
Warehousing Education and Research Council

Oak Park
Cryogenic Soc. of America

Oakbrook Terrace
Mason Contractors Ass'n of America
Preferred Hotels Ass'n

Olympia Fields
American Railway Car Institute

Orland Park
Transportation Brokers Conference of America

Ottawa
American Oxford Sheep Ass'n

Palantine
Associated Laboratories

Palatine
American Hardboard Ass'n
American Soc. of Artists
Materials and Methods Standards Ass'n
North American Wildlife Foundation

Palos Hills
Nat'l Automobile Theft Bureau

INDIANA

IOWA

GEOGRAPHIC INDEX

Soc. of Eye Surgeons
Soc. of Medical Consultants to the Armed Forces
Undersea and Hyperbaric Medical Soc.
Wildlife Soc., The
World Future Soc.

Bowie
Nat'l Academy of Opticianry

Brentwood
Soc. of Soft Drink Technologists

Brookville
Nat'l Ass'n of Freight Transportation Consultants

Buckeystown
Water Lily Soc.

Camp Springs
Seafarers' Internat'l Union of North America
Transportation Institute

Chesapeake Beach
Academy of Security Educators and Trainers

Chestertown
American Pyrotechnics Ass'n

Chevy Chase
Nat'l Academy of Conciliators
Nat'l Ass'n of Extension 4-H Agents

College Park
American Ass'n of Physics Teachers
American Correctional Ass'n
American Educational Studies Ass'n
American Registry of Professional Entomologists
Asphalt Institute
Ass'n of College and University Printers
Correctional Education Ass'n
Entomological Soc. of America
Special Interest Group on Numerical Mathematics

Columbia
American Dance Therapy Ass'n
Council for Adult and Experiential Learning
Internat'l Union of Elevator Constructors
Nat'l Council of Acupuncture Schools and Colleges
Universities Space Research Ass'n

Derwood
American Soc. of Human Genetics
Ass'n of Interpretive Naturalists
Genetics Soc. of America

Forrestville
Internat'l Ass'n of Law Enforcement Firearms Instructors

Fort Washington
Nat'l Tooling and Machining Ass'n

Frederick
Aircraft Owners and Pilots Ass'n
Ass'n for Creative Change within Religious and other Social Systems
Aviation Crime Prevention Institute
Bioelectromagnetics Soc.
Diamond and Gemstone Remarketing Ass'n
Environmental Mutagen Soc.
Seaplane Pilots Ass'n
Soc. for Applied Spectroscopy

Gaithersburg
Air Taxi and Commercial Pilots Ass'n
American Ass'n for Laboratory Accreditation
Ass'n of Rehabilitation Programs in Data Processing
Fusion Power Associates
Internat'l Ass'n of Chiefs of Police
Nat'l Conference on Weights and Measures
Nat'l Particleboard Ass'n
Tissue Culture Ass'n

Greenbelt
American College of Psychiatrists
Institute for Alternative Agriculture

Hagerstown
American Correctional Chaplains Ass'n
American Jail Ass'n

Havre de Grace
Synthetic Amorphous Silica and Silicates Industry Ass'n

Hyattsville
Retail Bakers of America
World's Poultry Science Ass'n, U.S.A. Branch

Kensington
Ass'n of Military Surgeons of the U.S.
Bakery, Confectionery and Tobacco Workers' Internat'l Union
Internat'l Taxicab Ass'n
Soc. of State Directors of Health, Physical Education and Recreation

Lanham
Ass'n of Federal Safety and Health Professionals
Automotive Parts and Accessories Ass'n
Automotive Products Export Council
Automotive Refrigeration Products Institute
Nat'l Aerosol Ass'n
Nat'l Soc. for Histotechnology
Vehicle Security Ass'n

McHenry
Sweet Potato Council of the United States

Millersvillere
American Academy of Veterinary Nutrition

Pikesville
Professional Grounds Management Soc.

Poolesville
Construction Writers Ass'n

Potomac
American Academy of Podiatric Sports Medicine
Nat'l Ass'n of Mirror Manufacturers
Peanut Butter and Nut Processors Ass'n

Riverdale
Equipment Interchange Ass'n
Intermodal Transportation Ass'n
Military Chaplains Ass'n of the U.S.
Nat'l Asphalt Pavement Ass'n
Steel Carriers Tariff Ass'n

Rockville
Academy of Hazard Control Management
Academy of Product Safety Management
American Ass'n of Colleges of Osteopathic Medicine
American Ass'n of Colleges of Podiatric Medicine
American Chain Ass'n
American College Health Ass'n
American Institute for Design and Drafting
American Occupational Therapy Ass'n
American Soc. of Plant Physiologists
American Speech-Language-Hearing Ass'n
Asphalt Roofing Manufacturers Ass'n
Associated Information Managers
Ass'n of Civilian Technicians
Ass'n of Community Cancer Centers
Ass'n of Physical Fitness Centers
Ass'n of Schools and Colleges of Optometry
Brotherhood of Railway, Airline and Steamship Clerks, Freight Handlers, Express and Station Employees
Contractors Pump Bureau
Conveyor Equipment Manufacturers Ass'n
Dairy and Food Industries Supply Ass'n
Evaporated Milk Ass'n
Expanded Shale, Clay and Slate Institute
Federal Executive and Professional Ass'n
Industrial Biotechnology Ass'n
Insulation Contractors Ass'n of America
Internat'l Soc. of Preretirement Planners
Munitions Carriers Conference
Music Critics Ass'n
Nat'l Ass'n for Rural Mental Health
Nat'l Ass'n of Enrolled Agents
Nat'l Classification Management Soc.
Nat'l Conference of Editorial Writers
Nat'l Council of Community Mental Health Centers
Nat'l Student Speech Language Hearing Ass'n
North American Cartographic Information Soc.
Phobia Soc. of America
Resilient Floor Covering Institute
Scale Manufacturers Ass'n
Soc. for Computer Applications in Engineering, Planning and Architecture
Soc. of Protozoologists
United States Pharmacopeial Convention
United Telegraph Workers

St. Michaels
Council of American Maritime Museums

Severna Park
Iota Tau Tau

Silver Spring
American Ass'n of Black Women Entrepreneurs
American Ass'n of University Affiliated Programs
American Deafness and Rehabilitation Ass'n
American Federation of Home Health Agencies
American Hungarian Educators Ass'n
American Soc. for Parenteral and Enteral Nutrition
American Soc. of Psychoanalytic Physicians
Ass'n for Information and Image Management
Ass'n of Machinery and Equipment Appraisers
Ass'n of Soil and Foundation Engineers
Concrete Plant Manufacturers Bureau
Conference of Educational Administrators Serving the Deaf
Conference of Ma or Superiors of Men, U.S.A.
Convention of American Instructors of the Deaf
Governmental Refuse Collection and Disposal Ass'n
Internat'l Fabricare Institute
Internat'l Federation of Professional and Technical Engineers
Machinery Dealers Nat'l Ass'n
Nat'l Ass'n of Social Workers
Nat'l Ass'n of Treasurers of Religious Institutes
Nat'l Foundation for Consumer Credit
Nat'l Industrial Sand Ass'n
Nat'l Ready Mixed Concrete Ass'n
Nat'l Sand and Gravel Ass'n
Property Management Ass'n of America
Truck Mixer Manufacturers Bureau
UNDA-USA

Sparks
American Institute of Reciprocators

Stevensville
American Wood-Preservers' Ass'n
Fourdrinier Wire Council
Wire Rope Technical Board

Temple Hills
Air Force Sergeants Ass'n
Ass'n of Former Agents of the U.S. Secret Service
Nat'l Weather Ass'n

Towson
American Soc. of Trial Consultants

Upper Marlboro
Nat'l Ass'n of Women Highway Safety Leaders

Westminster
Conference of State Sanitary Engineers

Wheaton
Ass'n for Childhood Education Internat'l
Internat'l Ass'n of Auto Theft Investigators
Nat'l Ass'n of Air Traffic Specialists

MASSACHUSETTS

Abington
American Academy of Implant Dentistry

Amherst
Special Interest Group on Software Engineering

Ashland
Internat'l Soc. of Fire Service Instructors

Attleboro
Gold Filled Ass'n

Boston
American Boat Builders and Repairers Ass'n
American Meteorological Soc.
American Soc. of Law and Medicine
Archaeological Institute of America
Art and Craft Materials Institute
Ass'n for Field Archaeology
Ass'n of Professors of Missions
Boarding Schools
Dental Gold Institute
Governmental Research Ass'n
Independent Research Libraries Ass'n
Institute for Medical Record Economics
Internat'l Magic Dealers Ass'n
Internat'l Racquet Sports Ass'n
Nat'l Ass'n of Christians in the Arts
Nat'l Ass'n of Government Employees
Nat'l Ass'n of Independent Schools
Nat'l Black Nurses Ass'n
Northern Textile Ass'n
Shoe Pattern Manufacturers Ass'n
Soc. of Fire Protection Engineers
Soc. of University Patent Administrators
Transplantation Soc. (U.S. Section)
Wet Ground Mica Ass'n

Brookline
Orthodox Theological Soc. in America

Cambridge
American Academy of Arts and Sciences
American Ass'n of Variable Star Observers
Ass'n for Jewish Studies
Medieval Academy of America
Nat'l Academy of Education
Nat'l Ass'n for Armenian Studies and Research
Nat'l Intravenous Therapy Ass'n
Print Council of America
Travel Agents Computer Soc.

Canton
Music Library Ass'n

Chestnut Hill
Soc. for Italian Historical Studies

Chicopee
Ass'n of Brass and Bronze Ingot Manufacturers

Concord
Hospital Presidents Ass'n

East Bridgewater
Brotherhood of Shoe and Allied Craftsmen
Shoe Suppliers Ass'n of America

East Longmeadow
North American Clun Forest Ass'n
Soc. of Wine Educators

East Orleans
Trade Show Bureau

Forestdale
Independent Educational Counselors Ass'n

Framingham
Ass'n of Medical Rehabilitation Directors and Coordinators
CAMEO
Special Interest Group on Small and Personal Computing Systems and Applications

Gardner
Nat'l Furniture Traffic Conference
Wood Products Manufacturers Ass'n

Groton
Ass'n of North American Directory Publishers

Hingham
Cordage Institute
Internat'l Marine Transit Ass'n

Lawrence
United Textile Workers of America

Leeds
Amalgamated Printers' Ass'n

Lexington
Conference on Data Systems Languages

Lynn
United States Tennis Writers' Ass'n

Manchester
American Ass'n for Thoracic Surgery
American College of Gastroenterology
American Soc. for Gastrointestinal Endoscopy
Internat'l Soc. for Cardiovascular Surgery - North American Chapter

00013

GEOGRAPHIC INDEX

GEOGRAPHIC INDEX

NEW MEXICO

NEW YORK

00017

GEOGRAPHIC INDEX

NORTH CAROLINA

GEOGRAPHIC INDEX

Nat'l Wholesale Furniture Ass'n
Summer and Casual Furniture Manufacturers Ass'n

Raleigh
American Soc. of Echocardiography
Ass'n of Official Seed Certifying Agencies
Beef Improvement Federation
Bright Belt Warehouse Ass'n
Employment Management Ass'n
Flue-Cured Tobacco Cooperative Stabilization Corporation
History of Science Soc.
Leaf Tobacco Exporters Ass'n
Multi-Housing Laundry Ass'n
Nat'l Alliance of Cardiovascular Technologists
Soc. of Financial Examiners
Tobacco Ass'n of the U.S.
Tobacco Growers' Information Committee

Research Triangle Pk
American Ass'n for Aerosol Research
American Ass'n of Textile Chemists and Colorists
Instrument Soc. of America
Parapsychological Ass'n

Rural Hall
American Photographic Artisans Guild

Salisbury
Nat'l Sportscasters and Sportswriters Ass'n

Spindale
American Dairy Goat Ass'n

Wallace
Federation of Ass'ns of Regulatory Boards

NORTH DAKOTA

Bismarck
Nat'l Ass'n of State Park Directors
Nat'l Sunflower Ass'n

Goodrich
United States Durum Growers Ass'n

Minot
Nat'l Council of Social Security Management Ass'ns

Wahpeton
American Technical Education Ass'n

Williston
Soc. of Municipal Arborists

OHIO

Akron
American Industrial Hygiene Ass'n
Comparative and Internat'l Education Soc.
Council on Employee Benefits
Internat'l Chemical Workers Union
Nat'l Caterers Ass'n
Professional Bowlers Ass'n of America
Tire and Rim Ass'n
United Rubber, Cork, Linoleum and Plastic Workers of America

Ashtabula
American Soc. of Forensic Odontology
Council on Diagnostic Imaging to the A.C.A.

Athens
Internat'l Ass'n for Learning Laboratories

Aurora
Nat'l Ass'n of Exposition Managers

Bay Village
American Soc. of Sanitary Engineering

Bowling Green
Athletic Equipment Managers Ass'n
Popular Culture Ass'n
School Science and Mathematics Ass'n
Soc. for Conceptual and Content Analysis by Computer

Brecksville
Nat'l Screw Machine Products Ass'n

Canton
Steel Deck Institute

Cantongeles
American Ass'n for Pediatric Ophthalmology and Strabismus

Cedarville
Ass'n of Christian Librarians

Chagrin Falls
Vacuum Cleaner Manufacturers Ass'n

Chardon
Independent Free Papers of America

Chesterland
Organization Development Institute

Cincinnati
American Ass'n of Certified Appraisers
American Conference of Governmental Industrial Hygienists
American Institute of Plant Engineers
American Leather Chemists Ass'n
American Watchmakers Institute
Ass'n for Academic Surgery
Ass'n of Academic Physiatrists
Ass'n of Philosophy Journals Editors
Golf Writers Ass'n of America
Internat'l Ass'n of Printing House Craftsmen
Internat'l Ass'n of Quality Circles
Internat'l Molders' and Allied Workers' Union
Metal Polishers, Buffers, Platers and Allied Workers Internat'l Union
Music Teachers Nat'l Ass'n
Nat'l Ass'n for Creative Children and Adults
Nat'l Ass'n for Research in Science Teaching
Nat'l Ass'n of Church Personnel Administrators
Noah Worcester Dermatological Soc.
Soc. for Advancement of Management
Soc. for Pediatric Radiology, The
Water Transport Ass'n

Clayton
Ankina Breeders

Cleveland
Abrasive Grain Ass'n
Academy of Internat'l Business
Academy of Parish Clergy
American Ass'n for the Study of Neoplastic Diseases
American Ass'n of Industrial Social Workers
American Catholic Correctional Chaplains Ass'n
American College of Podopediatrics
American Iron Ore Ass'n
American Soc. of Business Press Editors
American Supply and Machinery Manufacturers Ass'n
Ass'n for Systems Management
Ass'n of Independent Conservatories of Music
Brotherhood of Locomotive Engineers
Building Systems Institute
Cemented Carbide Producers Ass'n
Certified Ballast Manufacturers Ass'n
Chemical Fabrics and Film Ass'n
Coated Abrasives Manufacturers' Institute
Compressed Air and Gas Institute
Concert Music Broadcasters Ass'n
Council on Library-Media Technical-Assistants
Custom Roll Forming Institute
Cutting Tool Manufacturers of America
Diamond Wheel Manufacturers Institute
Diesel Engine Manufacturers Ass'n
Fire Equipment Manufacturers' Ass'n
Forging Industry Ass'n
Grinding Wheel Institute
Hack and Band Saw Manufacturers Ass'n of America
Heat Exchange Institute
Hydraulic Institute
Industrial Fasteners Institute
Insulated Steel Door Systems Institute
Internat'l Anesthesia Research Soc.
Internat'l Coordinating Committee on Solid State Sensors and Actuators Research
Internat'l Oxygen Manufacturers Ass'n
Internat'l Soc. for Artificial Organs
Investment Recovery Ass'n
Lake Carriers' Ass'n
Masonry and Concrete Saw Manufacturers Institute
Metal Building Manufacturers Ass'n
Metal Cutting Tool Institute
Nat'l Ass'n for Health Care Recruitment
Nat'l Ass'n of Business Economists
Nat'l Ass'n of Collegiate Directors of Athletics
Nat'l Ass'n of Optometrists and Opticians
Nat'l Taxidermists Ass'n
Nine to Five Nat'l Ass'n of Working Women
Office Systems Research Ass'n
Sales and Marketing Executives, Internat'l
Scaffolding, Shoring and Forming Institute
Steel Door Institute
Steel Service Center Institute
Steel Window Institute
Tantalum Producers Ass'n
United Dance Merchants of America
United States Marine Products Manufacturers' Ass'n
Welded Steel Tube Institute

Columbus
American Ass'n for Chinese Studies
American Greenhouse Vegetable Growers Ass'n
American Guernsey Cattle Club
American Jersey Cattle Club
American Soc. for Nondestructive Testing
American Soc. of Criminology
Ass'n of College and University Housing Officers-Internat'l
Ass'n of Independent Mailing Equipment Dealers
Ass'n of Professional Directors of YMCAs in the United States
Ass'n on Handicapped Student Service Programs in Postsecondary Education
Aviation/Space Writers Ass'n
College Fraternity Editors Ass'n
Council of Educational Facility Planners, Internat'l
Delta Omicron
Electronic Music Consortium
Gamma Iota Sigma
Internat'l Cemetery Supply Ass'n
Internat'l Metallographic Soc.
Internat'l Soc. for Ecological Modelling-North AmericanChapter
Middle East Librarians' Ass'n
Nat'l Ass'n of Pupil Personnel Administrators
Nat'l Ass'n of Student Personnel Administrators
Nat'l Board of Boiler and Pressure Vessel Inspectors
Nat'l Conference on Public Employee Retirement Systems
Nat'l Fastener Distributors Ass'n
Nat'l Ice Cream Retailers Ass'n
Nat'l Industrial Zoning Committee
Nat'l Institute of Ceramic Engineers
Nat'l Middle School Ass'n
Nat'l Optometric Ass'n
Nat'l Tax Ass'n-Tax Institute of America
Nat'l Wool Marketing Corporation
Northamerican Heating and Airconditioning Wholesalers Ass'n
Office Education Ass'n
Perennial Plant Ass'n
Rhetoric Soc. of America
Tin Research Institute

Dayton
American Osteopathic Academy of Orthopedics
APEC
Bowling Writers Ass'n of America
Catholic Campus Ministry Ass'n
Flexicore Manufacturers Ass'n
Geochemical Soc.
Intermarket Ass'n of Advertising Agencies
Nat'l Catholic Educational Exhibitors
Nat'l Management Ass'n
Nat'l Supply Distributors Ass'n
Osteopathic College of Ophthalmology and Otorhinolaryngology
Titanium Development Ass'n
United Methodist Ass'n of Health and Welfare Ministries

Delaware
American Recreational Equipment Ass'n

Dublin
Nat'l Ass'n of Flight Instructors
Nat'l Water Well Ass'n

East Liverpool
United States Potters' Ass'n

Elyria
Nat'l Spray Equipment Manufacturers Ass'n

Fredericktown
Percheron Horse Ass'n of America

Fremont
Nat'l Costumers Ass'n

Grove City
Internat'l League of Professional Baseball Clubs

Hilliard
Independent Sewing Machine Dealers Ass'n

Huron
Newspaper Farm Editors of America

Independence
Internat'l Die Sinkers' Conference

Kent
American School Health Ass'n
Consortium of University Film Centers
Nat'l Ass'n for Core Curriculum

Kenton
Internat'l Brotherhood of Magicians

Kettering
Nat'l Counter Intelligence Corps Ass'n

Lakewood
United Transportation Union

Lima
Nat'l Ass'n of Management/Marketing Educators
Nat'l Industrial Workers Union

Louisville
Built-in Cleaning Systems Institute

Marietta
Independent Signcrafters of America

Medina
Heavy Duty Representatives Ass'n
Spring Service Ass'n

Metals Park
Soc. of Carbide and Tool Engineers

Montville
Soc. of Explosives Engineers

New Carlisle
Aeronautical Navigator Ass'n

Newark
American Academy of Osteopathy

North Olmsted
Nat'l Ass'n of Real Estate Editors

Nova
American and Delaine-Merino Record Ass'n

Oberlin
Nat'l Ass'n of College Stores

Oxford
American Classical League
Ass'n for Integrative Studies
Delta Sigma Pi
Planning Forum: The Internat'l Society for Planning andStrategic Management

Painesville
Gyro Internat'l

Portsmouth
North American Mycological Ass'n

Richmond Heights
American Metal Stamping Ass'n

Rocky River
Nat'l Ass'n of Pattern Manufacturers
Nat'l Ass'n of Professional Engravers
Nat'l Freight Transportation Ass'n

Rootstown
Ass'n of Academic Health Sciences Library Directors

Shaker Heights
Ass'n of Railroad Advertising and Marketing

Toledo
Advertising Media Credit Executives Ass'n, Internat'l
American Flint Glass Workers Union
American Scientific Glassblowers Soc.
Laser Institute of America
Troy
North American Ass'n for Environmental Education
Upper Sandusky
Columbia Sheep Breeders Ass'n of America
Vandalia
Ass'n of Theological Schools in the United States and Canada
W. Milton
Systems Builders Ass'n
West Milton
Door and Operator Dealers
Westerville
American Ceramic Soc.
American Trakehner Ass'n
Electrical Women's Round Table
Furniture Rental Ass'n of America
Home Economists in Business
Nat'l Ass'n of Bank Servicers
Nat'l Executive Housekeepers Ass'n
Wooster
Conference of Research Workers in Animal Diseases
Golf Coaches Ass'n of America
Worthington
American Monument Ass'n
Aviation Safety Institute
Delta Theta Phi
North American Farm Show Council
Yellow Springs
Fellowship of Religious Humanists
Youngstown
Internat'l Ass'n of Professional Natural Hygienists
Zanesville
American Ass'n of Ceramic Industries
Associated Glass and Pottery Manufacturers
Ass'n of Crafts and Creative Industries
Gift Retailers, Manufacturers and Representatives Ass'n
Southwestern Craft and Hobby Ass'n

OKLAHOMA

Ada
Nat'l Ass'n of Royalty Owners
Bethany
Nat'l Black Coalition of Federal Aviation Employees
Blanchard
Women's Professional Rodeo Ass'n
Bristow
Nat'l Ass'n of Vocational Home Economics Teachers
Edmond
American Registry of Clinical Radiography Technologists
Football Writers Ass'n of America
Fairland
Production Records
Langston
Council of 1890 College Presidents
Lawton
American Choral Directors Ass'n
Minco
American Honey Producers Ass'n
Muskogee
American Ass'n of Academic Editors
Colorado Ranger Horse Ass'n
Oklahoma City
Congress of County Medical Societies
Internat'l Porcelain Artist Teachers
Interstate Oil Compact Commission
Soc. for Applied Anthropology
Pauls Valley
Internat'l Professional Rodeo Ass'n
Seminole
Energy Consumers and Producers Ass'n
Stillwater
American Peanut Research and Education Soc.
American Soc. of Veterinary Ophthalmology
Nat'l Ass'n of Supervisors of Agricultural Education
Tulsa
American Ass'n of Petroleum Geologists
American Bridge Teachers' Ass'n
American Soc. of Photographers
Ass'n of Professional Writing Consultants
Distribution Contractors Ass'n
Gas Processors Ass'n
Gas Processors Suppliers Ass'n
Mid-Continent Oil and Gas Ass'n
Nat'l Ass'n of Insurance Women (Internat'l)
Nat'l Ass'n of Legal Assistants
Nat'l Ass'n of Legal Secretaries (Int'l)
Nat'l Dental Technicians Ass'n
Palomino Horse Breeders of America
Petroleum Equipment Institute
Soc. of Economic Paleontologists and Mineralogists
Soc. of Exploration Geophysicists
United States Jaycees

OREGON

Bandon
Nat'l Council on Education for the Ceramic Arts
Beaverton
Nat'l Reloading Manufacturers Ass'n
Clackamas
Internat'l Ass'n of Structural Movers
Corvallis
American Romney Breeders Ass'n
Creswell
Internat'l Nubian Breeders Ass'n
Estacada
American Poultry Ass'n
Eugene
Forest Industries Telecommunications
Internat'l Council for Computers in Education
North American Soc. for the Psychology of Sport and Physical Activity
Unites States Women's Track Coaches Ass'n
Forest Grove
Ass'n of Visual Science Librarians
Medford
Oriental Rug Retailers of America
Xi Psi Phi
Portland
American Tinnitus Ass'n
American Wood Chip Export Ass'n
Ass'n of Family and Conciliation Courts
Ass'n of Official Racing Chemists
Business Forms Management Ass'n
Internat'l Woodworkers of America
Western Forest Industries Ass'n
Western Red Cedar Lumber Ass'n
Western Wood Products Ass'n
Wood Moulding and Millwork Producers Ass'n
Roseburg
American Ass'n of Sheep and Goat Practitioners
Salem
Nat'l Ass'n of Radio and Telecommunications Engineers
Tigard
Timber Operators Council

PENNSYLVANIA

Allentown
Internat'l Precious Metals Institute
Bellefonte
American Southdown Breeders Ass'n
Bensalem
Internat'l Plate Printers', Die Stampers' and Engravers' Union of North America
Nat'l Ass'n for Physical Education in Higher Education
Bethlehem
College Placement Council
Pulp, Paper and Paperboard Export Ass'n of the U.S.
Structural Stability Research Council
Blue Bell
American Soc. of Internat'l Executives
Bradford
Pennsylvania Grade Crude Oil Ass'n
Bryn Mawr
American Council of Teachers of Russian
American Soc. of CLU & ChFC
Church and Synagogue Library Ass'n
California
Technology Education for Children Council
Camp Hill
American College of Utilization Review Physicians
Ass'n of Hospital Television Networks
Nat'l Ass'n of State Directors of Vocational Education
Center Square
Nat'l Second Mortgage Ass'n
Chadds Ford
Research and Engineering Council of the Graphic Arts Industry
Chambersburg
Academy of Oral Dynamics
Dairy Soc. Internat'l
Chester Springs
Internat'l Veterinary Acupuncture Soc.
Clark
Nat'l Dog Groomers Ass'n of America
Conshohocken
Internat'l Saw and Knife Ass'n
Coroapolis
Airline Operational Control Soc.
Doylestown
Museum Store Ass'n
Nat'l Paralegal Ass'n
Drexel Hill
Pro ect Management Institute
East Greenville
American Laryngological, Rhinological and Otological Soc.
Easton
Nat'l Ass'n of Academies of Science
Elizabethtown
American Ass'n of Meat Processors
Erdenheim
Nat'l Ass'n of Regional Media Centers
Erie
Institute for Briquetting and Agglomeration
Nat'l Federation of Modern Language Teachers Ass'ns
Gladwyne
Religious Public Relations Council
Glenmoore
Nat'l Coalition of Alternative Community Schools
Greentown
Tourist House Ass'n of America
Greenville
Metal Ladder Manufacturers Ass'n
Grove City
American Ass'n of Presidents of Independent Colleges and Universities
Harleysville
Mobile Air Conditioning Soc.
Nat'l Automotive Radiator Service Ass'n
Harrisburg
Anthracite Industry Ass'n
Automatic Damper Manufacturers Ass'n
Internat'l Ass'n of Optometric Executives
Haverford
Catholic Library Ass'n
Council of Nat'l Library and Information Ass'ns
Havertown
Slovak Studies Ass'n
Hershey
American College of Laboratory Animal Medicine
Nat'l Frozen Food Ass'n
Soc. of University Urologists
Honesdale
Evidence Photographers Internat'l Council
Indiana
Ass'n of Overseas Educators
Jenkintown
Nat'l Caucus of Gay and Lesbian Counselors
Kennett Square
American Ass'n of Avian Pathologists
American College of Veterinary Pathologists
American Mushroom Institute
King of Prussia
Copper and Brass Servicenter Ass'n
Woodworking Machinery Distributors' Ass'n
Lafayette Hill
Photo Chemical Machining Institute
Lancaster
Broadcast Promotion and Marketing Executives
Fire Retardant Chemicals Ass'n
Nat'l Pretzel Bakers Institute
Levittown
Nat'l Constables Ass'n
Lewistown
Nat'l Ass'n of Hospital Purchasing Materials Management
Malvern
American Institute for Property and Liability Underwriters
Soc. of Chartered Property and Casualty Underwriters
Maple Glen
American College of Legal Medicine
Drug Information Ass'n
Marshall Creek
American Ski Teachers Ass'n of Natur Teknik
McDonald
Black Top and Nat'l Delaine-Merino Sheep Breeders Ass'n
Mechanicsburg
American Ass'n of Feed Microscopists
Media
Glass, Pottery, Plastics and Allied Workers Internat'l Union
New Castle
Public Utilities Communicators Ass'n
New Tripoli
United States Professional Cycling Federation
Norristown
American Soc. for Clinical Pharmacology and Therapeutics
Magazine and Paperback Marketing Institute
Paoli
Clinical Laboratory Management Ass'n
Philadelphia
American Ass'n for Cancer Research
American Ass'n of Medico-Legal Consultants
American Ass'n of Scientific Workers
American Brush Manufacturers Ass'n
American Choral Foundation
American College of Clinical Pharmacology
American College of Physicians
American Entomological Soc.
American Institute of Medical Climatology
American Jewelry Marketing Ass'n
American Law Institute
American Musicological Soc.
American Philosophical Soc.
American Radium Soc.
American Railway Development Ass'n
American Schools of Oriental Research
American Soc. for Theatre Research
American Soc. of Cytology
American Soc. of Educators
American Soc. of Professional and Executive Women

GEOGRAPHIC INDEX

RHODE ISLAND

SOUTH CAROLINA

SOUTH DAKOTA

TENNESSEE

00023

GEOGRAPHIC INDEX

American School Counselor Ass'n
American Soc. for Horticultural Science
American Soc. for Personnel Administration
American Soc. for Training and Development
American Soc. of Naval Engineers
American Soc. of Professional Estimators
American Subcontractors Ass'n
American Trucking Ass'ns
American Vocational Ass'n
American Wind Energy Ass'n
Animal Health Institute
Associated Telephone Answering Exchanges
Ass'n for Counselor Education and Supervision
Ass'n for Education and Rehabilitation of the Blind andVisually Impaired
Ass'n for Humanistic Education and Development
Ass'n for Measurement and Evaluation in Counseling and Development
Ass'n for Multicultural Counseling and Development
Ass'n for Religious and Value Issues in Counseling
Ass'n for Specialists in Group Work
Ass'n for Supervision and Curriculum Development
Ass'n of American State Geologists
Ass'n of Earth Science Editors
Ass'n of Independent Corrugated Converters
Ass'n of Physical Plant Administrators of Universities and Colleges
Ass'n of Reproduction Materials Manufacturers
Community Ass'ns Institute
Computer Measurement Group
Construction Specifications Institute
Council for Therapeutic Recreation Certification
Dry Color Manufacturers Ass'n
Envelope Manufacturers Ass'n of America
Federated Ambulatory Surgery Ass'n
Film, Air and Package Carriers Conference
Future Farmers of America
Geoscience Information Soc.
Helicopter Airline Ass'n
Helicopter Ass'n Internat'l
Household Goods Carriers' Bureau
Institute of Cost Analysis
Internat'l Airforwarders and Agents Ass'n
Internat'l Ass'n of Amusement Parks and Attractions
Internat'l Ass'n of Chain Stores - North American Headquarters
Internat'l Ass'n of Counseling Services
Internat'l Bottled Water Ass'n
Internat'l Hardwood Products Ass'n
Internat'l Military Club Executives Ass'n
Internat'l Personnel Management Ass'n
Internat'l Reciprocal Trade Ass'n
Interstate Carriers Conference
Maintenance Council of American Trucking Ass'ns
Marine Corps Reserve Officers Ass'n
Military Educators and Counselors Ass'n
Military Operations Research Soc.
Mineral Insulation Manufacturers Ass'n
Nat'l Accounting and Finance Council
Nat'l Air Transportation Ass'n
Nat'l Alcoholic Beverage Control Ass'n
Nat'l Ass'n of Brick Distributors
Nat'l Ass'n of Business and Educational Radio
Nat'l Ass'n of Business Political Action Committees
Nat'l Ass'n of Chain Drug Stores
Nat'l Ass'n of Children's Hospitals and Related Institutions
Nat'l Ass'n of Community Leadership Organizations
Nat'l Ass'n of Convenience Stores
Nat'l Ass'n of Decorative Architectural Finishes
Nat'l Ass'n of Dental Laboratories
Nat'l Ass'n of Elementary School Principals
Nat'l Ass'n of Government Communicators
Nat'l Ass'n of Mail Service Pharmacies
Nat'l Ass'n of Medical Equipment Suppliers
Nat'l Ass'n of Membership Directors of Chambers of Commerce
Nat'l Ass'n of Personnel Consultants
Nat'l Ass'n of Postmasters of the U.S.
Nat'l Ass'n of Professional Insurance Agents
Nat'l Ass'n of Rehabilitation Secretaries
Nat'l Ass'n of Retail Druggists
Nat'l Ass'n of State Boards of Education
Nat'l Ass'n of State Mental Health Program Directors
Nat'l Ass'n of State Mental Retardation Program Directors
Nat'l Ass'n of Temporary Services
Nat'l Ass'n of Tobacco Distributors
Nat'l Ass'n of Truck Stop Operators
Nat'l Business Forms Ass'n
Nat'l Career Development Ass'n
Nat'l Cheese Institute
Nat'l Clay Pipe Institute
Nat'l Community Education Ass'n
Nat'l Council of Erectors, Fabricators and Riggers
Nat'l Defense Transportation Ass'n
Nat'l District Attorneys Ass'n
Nat'l Drug Trade Conference
Nat'l Electric Sign Ass'n
Nat'l Employment Counselors Ass'n
Nat'l Federation of Professional Organizations
Nat'l Film Carriers
Nat'l Freight Claim and Security Council of the American Trucking Ass'ns
Nat'l Institute of Certified Moving Consultants
Nat'l League of Postmasters of the U.S.
Nat'l Licensed Beverage Ass'n
Nat'l Mental Health Ass'n
Nat'l Motor Freight Traffic Ass'n
Nat'l Moving and Storage Ass'n
Nat'l Office Products Ass'n
Nat'l Peanut Council
Nat'l Pegboard Systems Ass'n
Nat'l Perinatal Ass'n
Nat'l Recreation and Park Ass'n
Nat'l Rehabilitation Ass'n
Nat'l Rehabilitation Counseling Ass'n
Nat'l Rural Letter Carriers' Ass'n
Nat'l School Boards Ass'n
Nat'l Sheriffs' Ass'n
Nat'l Slag Ass'n
Nat'l Soc. of Fund Raising Executives
Nat'l Soc. of Professional Engineers
Nat'l Soc. of Public Accountants
Nat'l Spa and Pool Institute
Nat'l Tank Truck Carriers
Nat'l Therapeutic Recreation Soc.
Nat'l Vocational Agricultural Teachers Ass'n
Nat'l Wholesale Druggists' Ass'n
Network Users Ass'n
North American Academy of Manipulative Medicine
Passive Solar Industries Council
Petroleum Marketing Education Foundation
Powder Coating Institute
Power and Communication Contractors Ass'n
Private Carrier Conference
Professional Engineers in Private Practice
Professional Services Management Ass'n
Public Offender Counselors Ass'n
Railway Progress Institute
Regional and Distribution Carriers Conference
Regular Common Carrier Conference
Retired Officers Ass'n
SAF
Salt Institute
Satellite Broadcasting and Communications Ass'n
Snack Food Ass'n
Soc. for Marketing Professional Services
Soc. of American Military Engineers
Soc. of Consumer Affairs Professionals in Business
Soc. of Park and Recreation Educators
Specialized Carriers and Rigging Ass'n
Tile Contractors' Ass'n of America
Tile, Marble, Terrazzo, Finishers, Shopworkers and Granite Cutters Internat'l Union
Truck Trailer Manufacturers Ass'n
United Fresh Fruit and Vegetable Ass'n
Vocational Evaluation and Work Ad ustment Ass'n
Water Pollution Control Federation

Annandale

Ass'n for Communication Administration
Ass'n of Community College Trustees
Internat'l Exhibitors Ass'n
Speech Communication Ass'n

Arlington

ADAPSO, the Computer Software and Services Industry Ass'n
Adhesive and Sealant Council
Air-Conditioning and Refrigeration Institute
Air Force Ass'n
Air Traffic Control Ass'n
Alliance for Responsible CFC Policy
American Academy of Physician Assistants
American Apparel Manufacturers Ass'n
American Ass'n of Blood Banks
American Ass'n of Equipment Lessors
American Ass'n of Healthcare Consultants
American Ass'n of School Administrators
American Ass'n of Tissue Banks
American Blood Commission
American Boiler Manufacturers Ass'n
American Chiropractic Ass'n
American Consultants League
American Defense Preparedness Ass'n
American Feed Industry Ass'n
American Gas Ass'n
American Intellectual Property Law Ass'n
American Meat Institute
American Soc. for Industrial Security
American Soc. for Psychoprophylaxis in Obstetrics
American Soc. of Consultant Pharmacists
American Surety Ass'n
American Waterways Operators
American Waterways Shipyard Conference
Architectural Woodwork Institute
Armed Forces Broadcasters Ass'n
Asbestos Information Ass'n/North America
Ass'n for the Advancement of Medical Instrumentation
Ass'n of Asbestos Cement Pipe Producers
Ass'n of Government Accountants
Ass'n of Graphic Arts Consultants
Ass'n of Labor-Management Administrators and Consultants on Alcoholism
Ass'n of Official Analytical Chemists
Ass'n of Old Crows
Ass'n of Physician Assistant Programs
Ass'n of Scientists and Engineers of the Naval Sea Systems Command
Ass'n of State Drinking Water Administrators
Ass'n of the United States Army
Ass'n of University Programs in Health Administration
Automobile Importers of America
Canned and Cooked Meat Importers Ass'n
Compressed Gas Ass'n
Conference Board of Ma or Printers
Construction Products Manufacturers Council
Consumer Bankers Ass'n
Convenient Automotive Services Institute
Council of Better Business Bureaus
Financial Printers Ass'n
Flight Safety Foundation
Gas Appliance Manufacturers Ass'n
Graphic Arts Employers of America
Graphic Arts Equipment and Supply Dealers Ass'n
Graphic Arts Marketing Information Service
Graphic Communications Ass'n
Industrial Heating Equipment Ass'n
Industrial Safety Equipment Ass'n
Internat'l Business Forms Industries
Internat'l Plant Propagators' Soc. (Eastern Region)
Internat'l Sleep Products Ass'n
Internat'l Thermographers Ass'n
Irrigation Ass'n
Label Printing Industries of America
Magazine Printers Section/Printing Industries of America
Manufactured Housing Institute
Master Printers of America
Meat Importers' Council of America
Movers' and Warehousemen's Ass'n of America
Nat'l Ass'n of Alcoholism and Drug Abuse Counselors
Nat'l Ass'n of Federal Credit Unions
Nat'l Ass'n of Federal Education Program Administrators
Nat'l Ass'n of Industrial and Office Parks
Nat'l Ass'n of Lithographic Plate Manufacturers
Nat'l Ass'n of Small Government Contractors
Nat'l Ass'n of State Credit Union Supervisors
Nat'l Ass'n of the Remodeling Industry
Nat'l Candle Ass'n
Nat'l Composition Ass'n
Nat'l Erectors Ass'n
Nat'l Genealogical Soc.
Nat'l Hospice Organization
Nat'l Institute of Packaging, Handling and Logistic Engineers
Nat'l Lime Ass'n
Nat'l Mastitis Council
Nat'l Milk Producers Federation
Nat'l Pasta Ass'n
Nat'l School Public Relations Ass'n
Nat'l School Supply and Equipment Ass'n
Nat'l Utility Contractors Ass'n
Nat'l Venture Capital Ass'n
Newsletter Ass'n
Non-Heatset Web Unit
Patent and Trademark Office Soc.
Patent Office Professional Ass'n
Porcelain Enamel Institute
Printing Brokerage Ass'n
Printing Industries of America
Procurement Round Table
Rice Millers' Ass'n
Soc. for Industrial Microbiology
Soc. of Biomedical Equipment Technicians
Solar Energy Industries Ass'n
Southern Transportation League
Special Interest Group on APL Programming Language
Suppliers of Advanced Composite Materials Ass'n
Tax Executives Institute
Trademark Soc.
Water and Sewer Distributors of America
Water Resources Congress
Wholesale Florists and Florist Suppliers of America

Blacksburg

American College of Veterinary Internal Medicine
Internat'l Visual Literacy Ass'n
Soc. of Engineering Science

Burke

Ass'n of American Physicians and Surgeons
Council of Industrial Boiler Owners

Charlottesville

Ass'n of University Anesthetists
Clinical Soc. of Genito-Urinary Surgeons
Institute of Chartered Financial Analysts
Nat'l Council for Textile Education
Soc. of Multivariate Experimental Psychology
Special Interest Group for Computer Personnel Research
United States Tennis Court and Track Builders Ass'n

Clifton

Internat'l Microwave Power Institute
Nat'l Bark Producers Ass'n

Crozet

Soc. of Insurance Accountants

Daleville

American Ass'n of Railway Surgeons

Dumfries

Office Automation Soc. Internat'l

Dunn Loring

Nat'l Pest Control Ass'n

Fairfax

Advanced Transit Ass'n
American Ass'n of Pastoral Counselors
American Soc. for Cybernetics
American Soc. of Cataract and Refractive Surgery
Animal Nutrition Research Council

WASHINGTON

GEOGRAPHIC INDEX

1981

BUDGET INDEX

All organizations in this book which have provided budget data will be found here listed alphabetically within ten budget categories, from under $10,000 to over $5,000,000.

OVER $5,000,000

Academy of Motion Picture Arts and Sciences
Advertising Council
Air Line Pilots Ass'n, Internat'l
Air Transport Ass'n of America
Alliance of American Insurers
Amalgamated Clothing and Textile Workers Union
Amalgamated Transit Union
American Academy of Ophthalmology
American Academy of Orthopaedic Surgeons
American Academy of Pediatrics
American Alliance for Health, Physical Education, Recreation and Dance
American Arbitration Ass'n
American Ass'n for Clinical Chemistry
American Ass'n for Respiratory Care
American Ass'n for the Advancement of Science
American Ass'n of Homes for the Aging
American Ass'n of Petroleum Geologists
American Ass'n of School Administrators
American Bankers Ass'n
American Bar Ass'n
American Bureau of Shipping
American Cancer Soc.
American Chemical Soc.
American College of Cardiology
American College of Emergency Physicians
American College of Healthcare Executives
American College of Obstetricians and Gynecologists
American College of Physicians
American College of Radiology
American College of Surgeons
American Concrete Institute
American Council of Life Insurance
American Council on Education
American Dairy Ass'n
American Dental Ass'n
American Diabetes Ass'n
American Dietetic Ass'n
American Egg Board
American Electronics Ass'n
American Farm Bureau Federation
American Federation of Government Employees
American Federation of Information Processing Societies
American Federation of Labor and Congress of Industrial Organizations
American Federation of Musicians of the United States and Canada
American Federation of State, County and Municipal Employees
American Federation of Teachers
American Gas Ass'n
American Geophysical Union
American Health Care Ass'n
American Heart Ass'n
American Hospital Ass'n
American Hotel and Motel Ass'n
American Institute for Property and Liability Underwriters
American Institute of Aeronautics and Astronautics
American Institute of Architects
American Institute of Certified Public Accountants
American Institute of Chemical Engineers
American Institute of Mining, Metallurgical, and Petroleum Engineers
American Institute of Physics
American Insurance Ass'n
American Iron and Steel Institute
American Library Ass'n
American Lung Ass'n
American Management Ass'n
American Marketing Ass'n
American Mathematical Soc.
American Medical Ass'n
American Mining Congress
American Nat'l Standards Institute
American Natural Soda Ash Corporation
American Newspaper Publishers Ass'n
American Nuclear Soc.
American Nurses' Ass'n
American Occupational Therapy Ass'n
American Optometric Ass'n
American Paper Institute
American Petroleum Institute
American Pharmaceutical Ass'n
American Physical Soc.
American Physical Therapy Ass'n
American Plywood Ass'n
American Postal Workers Union
American Production and Inventory Control Soc.
American Psychiatric Ass'n
American Psychological Ass'n
American Public Health Ass'n
American Public Transit Ass'n
American Quarter Horse Ass'n
American Soc. for Engineering Education
American Soc. for Microbiology
American Soc. for Personnel Administration
American Soc. for Training and Development
American Soc. of Anesthesiologists
American Soc. of Ass'n Executives
American Soc. of Civil Engineers
American Soc. of Clinical Pathologists
American Soc. of CLU & ChFC
American Soc. of Composers, Authors and Publishers
American Soc. of Heating, Refrigerating and Air-Conditioning Engineers
American Soc. of Hospital Pharmacists
American Soc. of Mechanical Engineers
American Soc. of Travel Agents
American Soybean Ass'n
American Speech-Language-Hearing Ass'n
American Stock Exchange
American Trucking Ass'ns
American Urological Ass'n
American Veterinary Medical Ass'n
American Water Works Ass'n
American Welding Soc.
Armed Forces Communications and Electronics Ass'n
Associated Builders and Contractors
Associated General Contractors of America
Ass'n for Computing Machinery
Ass'n for Supervision and Curriculum Development
Ass'n of American Medical Colleges
Ass'n of American Railroads
Ass'n of Flight Attendants
Ass'n of Mill and Elevator Mutual Insurance Companies
Ass'n of Old Crows
Ass'n of Operating Room Nurses
Ass'n of the United States Army
Ass'n of Trial Lawyers of America
ASTM
Atomic Industrial Forum
Audit Bureau of Circulations
Bank Administration Institute
Blue Cross and Blue Shield Ass'n
Boys Clubs of America
Brotherhood of Railway, Airline and Steamship Clerks, Freight Handlers, Express and Station Employees
Catholic Health Ass'n of the United States
Chamber of Commerce of the United States of America
Chemical Manufacturers Ass'n
Coffee, Sugar and Cocoa Exchange
College of American Pathologists
Communications Workers of America
Computer Soc. of the Institute of Electrical and Electronics Engineers
Construction Specifications Institute
Cosmetic, Toiletry and Fragrance Ass'n
Council for Tobacco Research-U.S.A.
Council of Better Business Bureaus
Credit Union Nat'l Ass'n
Cystic Fibrosis Foundation
Direct Marketing Ass'n
Directors Guild of America
Distilled Spirits Council of the United States
ECRI
Edison Electric Institute
Electric Power Research Institute
Electronic Industries Ass'n
Federation of American Societies for Experimental Biology
Federation of Apparel Manufacturers
Florists' Transworld Delivery Ass'n
Food Marketing Institute
Foreign Credit Insurance Ass'n
Graphic Arts Technical Foundation
Health Insurance Ass'n of America
Healthcare Financial Management Ass'n
Holstein-Friesian Ass'n of America
Hong Kong Trade Development Council
Hotel Employees and Restaurant Employees Internat'l Union
Independent Insurance Agents of America
Institute of Electrical and Electronics Engineers
Institute of Industrial Engineers
Institute of Internal Auditors
Institute of Nuclear Power Operations
Institute of Paper Chemistry
Institute of Real Estate Management
Instrument Soc. of America
Insurance Information Institute
Insurance Institute for Highway Safety
Internat'l Allied Printing Trades Ass'n
Internat'l Arabian Horse Ass'n
Internat'l Ass'n for Financial Planning
Internat'l Ass'n of Bridge, Structural and Ornamental Iron Workers
Internat'l Ass'n of Drilling Contractors
Internat'l Ass'n of Fire Fighters
Internat'l Ass'n of Machinists and Aerospace Workers
Internat'l Brotherhood of Boilermakers, Iron Shipbuilders, Blacksmiths, Forgers and Helpers
Internat'l Brotherhood of Electrical Workers
Internat'l Brotherhood of Painters and Allied Trades
Internat'l Brotherhood of Teamsters, Chauffeurs, Warehouseman and Helpers of America
Internat'l Conference of Building Officials
Internat'l Council of Shopping Centers
Internat'l Foundation of Employee Benefit Plans
Internat'l Ladies Garment Workers' Union
Internat'l Longshoremen's Ass'n
Internat'l Molders' and Allied Workers' Union
Internat'l Reading Ass'n
Internat'l Typographical Union
Internat'l Union, Allied Industrial Workers of America
Internat'l Union of Bricklayers and Allied Craftsmen
Internat'l Union of Electronic, Electrical, Technical, Salaried and Machine Workers
Internat'l Union of Operating Engineers
Investment Company Institute
Laborers' Internat'l Union of North America
Life Insurance Marketing and Research Ass'n
Life Office Management Ass'n
Livestock Marketing Ass'n
Mastercard Internat'l
Mortgage Bankers Ass'n of America
Motor Vehicle Manufacturers Ass'n of the United States
Nat'l Academy of Sciences
Nat'l Ass'n for Home Care
Nat'l Ass'n of Accountants
Nat'l Ass'n of Broadcast Employees and Technicians
Nat'l Ass'n of Broadcasters
Nat'l Ass'n of College Stores
Nat'l Ass'n of Home Builders of the U.S.
Nat'l Ass'n of Independent Insurers
Nat'l Ass'n of Letter Carriers of the United States of America
Nat'l Ass'n of Life Underwriters
Nat'l Ass'n of Manufacturers
Nat'l Ass'n of Professional Insurance Agents
Nat'l Ass'n of REALTORS
Nat'l Ass'n of Secondary School Principals
Nat'l Ass'n of Securities Dealers
Nat'l Ass'n of Social Workers
Nat'l Automobile Dealers Ass'n
Nat'l Automobile Theft Bureau.

Nat'l Basketball Ass'n
Nat'l Cable Television Ass'n
Nat'l Cargo Bureau
Nat'l Coal Ass'n
Nat'l Computer Graphics Ass'n
Nat'l Conference of Catholic Bishops
Nat'l Conference of State Legislatures
Nat'l Cooperative Business Ass'n
Nat'l Council of Juvenile and Family Court Judges
Nat'l Council of Savings Institutions
Nat'l Council of the Churches of Christ in the U.S.A
Nat'l Council on Compensation Insurance
Nat'l Council on the Aging
Nat'l Decorating Products Ass'n
Nat'l Electrical Contractors Ass'n
Nat'l Electrical Manufacturers Ass'n
Nat'l Federation of Independent Business
Nat'l Fire Protection Ass'n
Nat'l Food Processors Ass'n
Nat'l Football League
Nat'l Futures Ass'n
Nat'l Hockey League
Nat'l Kidney Foundation
Nat'l League for Nursing
Nat'l League of Cities
Nat'l Live Stock and Meat Board
Nat'l Machine Tool Builders' Ass'n
Nat'l Maritime Union of America
Nat'l Multiple Sclerosis Soc.
Nat'l Office Products Ass'n
Nat'l Pork Producers Council
Nat'l Potato Promotion Board
Nat'l Restaurant Ass'n
Nat'l Retail Hardware Ass'n
Nat'l Retail Merchants Ass'n
Nat'l Rifle Ass'n of America
Nat'l Roofing Contractors Ass'n
Nat'l Rural Electric Cooperative Ass'n
Nat'l Safety Council
Nat'l School Boards Ass'n
Nat'l Soc. of Professional Engineers
Nat'l Soc. to Prevent Blindness
Nat'l Soft Drink Ass'n
Nat'l Sporting Goods Ass'n
Nat'l Treasury Employees Union
New York Academy of Sciences
New York Cotton Exchange
New York Mercantile Exchange
New York Stock Exchange
Newspaper Advertising Bureau
Oil, Chemical and Atomic Workers Internat'l Union
Pharmaceutical Manufacturers Ass'n
Photo Marketing Ass'n-Internat'l
Pollution Liability Insurance Ass'n
Portland Cement Ass'n
Printing Industries of America
Professional Ass'n of Diving Instructors
Professional Photographers of America
Public Securities Ass'n
Radio Advertising Bureau
Radiological Soc. of North America
Realtors Nat'l Marketing Institute
Retail, Wholesale and Department Store Union
Retired Officers Ass'n
Robert Morris Associates, the Nat'l Ass'n of Bank Loan and Credit Officers
Screen Actors Guild
Securities Industry Ass'n
Semiconductor Equipment and Materials Institute
Service Employees Internat'l Union
Sheet Metal Workers' Internat'l Ass'n
Social Science Research Council
Soc. of Automotive Engineers
Soc. of Exploration Geophysicists
Soc. of Manufacturing Engineers
Soc. of Petroleum Engineers
Soc. of Real Estate Appraisers
Soc. of the Plastics Industry
Synthetic Organic Chemical Manufacturers Ass'n
Technical Ass'n of the Pulp and Paper Industry
Television Bureau of Advertising
Tobacco Institute
Transport Workers Union of America
Union of American Hebrew Congregations
United Ass'n of Journeymen and Apprentices of the Plumbing and Pipe Fitting Industry of the U.S. and Ca
United Automobile, Aerospace and Agricultural Implement Workers of America
United Brotherhood of Carpenters and Joiners of America
United Dairy Industry Ass'n
United Engineering Trustees
United Food and Commercial Workers Internat'l Union
United Mine Workers of America
United Paperworkers Internat'l Union
United Rubber, Cork, Linoleum and Plastic Workers of America
United States Golf Ass'n
United States Pharmacopeial Convention
United States Tennis Ass'n
United Steelworkers of America
Urban Land Institute
Water Pollution Control Federation
Western Railroad Ass'n
Western Wood Products Ass'n
Young Presidents' Organization

$2-5,000,000

Academy of General Dentistry
Actors' Equity Ass'n
ADAPSO, the Computer Software and Services Industry Ass'n
Aerospace Industries Ass'n of America
Air-Conditioning and Refrigeration Institute
Air Force Ass'n
Air Force Sergeants Ass'n
Air Line Employees Ass'n, International
Aluminum Ass'n
Aluminum, Brick and Glass Workers Internat'l Union
American Academy of Dermatology
American Academy of Facial Plastic and Reconstructive Surgery
American Academy of Family Physicians
American Academy of Neurology
American Academy of Otolaryngology-Head and Neck Surgery
American Academy of Physician Assistants
American Angus Ass'n
American Animal Hospital Ass'n
American Apparel Manufacturers Ass'n
American Ass'n for Counseling and Development
American Ass'n of Advertising Agencies
American Ass'n of Blood Banks
American Ass'n of Community and Junior Colleges
American Ass'n of Critical-Care Nurses
American Ass'n of Equipment Lessors
American Ass'n of Individual Investors
American Ass'n of Motor Vehicle Administrators
American Ass'n of Museums
American Ass'n of Nurse Anesthetists
American Ass'n of Oral and Maxillofacial Surgeons
American Ass'n of Orthodontists
American Ass'n of State Colleges and Universities
American Ass'n of State Highway and Transportation Officials
American Ass'n of University Professors
American Astronomical Soc.
American Booksellers Ass'n
American Bus Ass'n
American Business Women's Ass'n
American Camping Ass'n
American Ceramic Soc.
American Chamber of Commerce Executives
American Chiropractic Ass'n
American College of Chest Physicians
American College of Sports Medicine
American Compensation Ass'n
American Consulting Engineers Council
American Correctional Ass'n
American Craft Council
American Defense Preparedness Ass'n
American Dental Hygienists' Ass'n
American Federation of Grain Millers Internat'l Union
American Federation of Television and Radio Artists
American Financial Services Ass'n
American Flint Glass Workers Union
American Forest Council
American Foundrymen's Soc.
American Frozen Food Institute
American Geological Institute
American Hardware Manufacturers Ass'n
American Home Economics Ass'n
American Institute of Biological Sciences
American Institute of Real Estate Appraisers
American Institute of Steel Construction
American Jersey Cattle Club
American Land Title Ass'n
American Law Institute
American Meat Institute
American Medical Record Ass'n
American Metal Stamping Ass'n
American Meteorological Soc.
American Orthopaedic Ass'n
American Osteopathic Ass'n
American Paint Horse Ass'n
American Philosophical Soc.
American Physiological Soc.
American Planning Ass'n
American Podiatric Medical Ass'n
American Polled Hereford Ass'n
American Public Power Ass'n
American Rental Ass'n
American School Food Service Ass'n
American Sheep Producers Council
American Simmental Ass'n
American Soc. for Industrial Security
American Soc. for Medical Technology
American Soc. for Nondestructive Testing
American Soc. for Quality Control
American Soc. of Agricultural Engineers
American Soc. of Biological Chemists
American Soc. of Interior Designers
American Soc. of Internal Medicine
American Soc. of Landscape Architects
American Soc. of Plastic and Reconstructive Surgeons
American Soc. of Safety Engineers
American Soc. of Zoologists
American Symphony Orchestra League
American Textile Manufacturers Institute
American Vacuum Soc.
American Vocational Ass'n
Appaloosa Horse Club
Associated Construction Publications
Associated Credit Bureaus
Associated Equipment Distributors
Associated Surplus Dealers
Ass'n for Information and Image Management
Ass'n for Systems Management
Ass'n of American Publishers
Ass'n of Business Publishers
Ass'n of Christian Schools Internat'l
Ass'n of Independent Colleges and Schools
Ass'n of Iron and Steel Engineers
Ass'n of Legal Administrators
Ass'n of Nat'l Advertisers
Ass'n of Official Analytical Chemists
Ass'n of the Wall and Ceiling Industries-Internat'l
Audio Engineering Soc.
Automobile Importers of America
Automotive Parts and Accessories Ass'n
Automotive Service Ass'n
Automotive Service Industry Ass'n
Automotive Warehouse Distributors Ass'n
Bakery, Confectionery and Tobacco Workers' Internat'l Union
Bank Marketing Ass'n
Baseball - Office of Commissioner
Bowling Proprietors Ass'n of America
Brotherhood of Locomotive Engineers
Brotherhood of Maintenance of Way Employes
Brotherhood Railway Carmen of the United States and Canada
Building Officials and Code Administrators Internat'l
Building Owners and Managers Ass'n Internat'l
Business Forms Management Ass'n
Business Publications Audit of Circulation
Christian Booksellers Ass'n
Christian Medical Soc.
College Placement Council
Community Ass'ns Institute
Computer and Business Equipment Manufacturers Ass'n
Conference of State Bank Supervisors
Copper Development Ass'n
Council for Advancement and Support of Education
Council for Exceptional Children
Council of Chief State School Officers
Council of Logistics Management
Council of State Governments
Council on Foundations
Credit Union Executives Soc.
Crop-Hail Insurance Actuarial Ass'n
Data Processing Management Ass'n
Defense Research Institute
Direct Selling Ass'n
Door and Hardware Institute
EDUCOM
Employee Benefit Research Institute
Employee Relocation Council
Entomological Soc. of America
Exhibit Designers and Producers Ass'n
Factory Mutual System
Family Service America
Federation of State Medical Boards of the U. S.
Fertilizer Institute
Financial Analysts Federation
Financial Executives Institute
Footwear Industries of America
Foundation for Savings Institutions
Future Farmers of America
Geological Soc. of America
Girls Clubs of America
Glass Packaging Institute
Golf Course Superintendents Ass'n of America
Government Finance Officers Ass'n of the United States and Canada
Graphic Communications Internat'l Union
Grocery Manufacturers of America
Group Health Ass'n of America
Health Industry Manufacturers Ass'n
Highway Users Federation for Safety and Mobility
Independent Bankers Ass'n of America
Industrial Fabrics Ass'n Internat'l
Institute of Certified Financial Planners
Institute of Chartered Financial Analysts

BUDGET INDEX

Institute of Financial Education
Institute of Food Technologists
Institute of Internat'l Finance
Institute of Medicine
Insurance Crime Prevention Institute
Internat'l Alliance of Theatrical Stage Employees and Moving Picture Machine Operators of the U.S. & Ca
Internat'l Ass'n of Business Communicators
Internat'l Ass'n of Chiefs of Police
Internat'l Ass'n of Defense Counsel
Internat'l Ass'n of Heat and Frost Insulators and Asbestos Workers
Internat'l Chemical Workers Union
Internat'l Chiropractors Ass'n
Internat'l Communications Industries Ass'n
Internat'l Copper Research Ass'n
Internat'l Federation of Health Professionals
Internat'l Foodservice Manufacturers Ass'n
Internat'l Franchise Ass'n
Internat'l Graphoanalysis Soc.
Internat'l Professional Rodeo Ass'n
Internat'l Racquet Sports Ass'n
Internat'l Sanitary Supply Ass'n
Internat'l Union of Elevator Constructors
Internat'l Woodworkers of America
Interstate Natural Gas Ass'n of America
Interstate Producers Livestock Ass'n
Jewelers Board of Trade
JWB
Machinery and Allied Products Institute
Magazine Publishers Ass'n
Manufacturing Jewelers and Silversmiths of America
Material Handling Institute
Materials Properties Council, The
Mathematical Ass'n of America
Medical Group Management Ass'n
Metallurgical Soc., The
Million Dollar Round Table
Modern Language Ass'n of America
Motor and Equipment Manufacturers Ass'n
Music Educators Nat'l Conference
Nat'l Agricultural Chemicals Ass'n
Nat'l Alliance of Postal and Federal Employees
Nat'l-American Wholesale Grocers' Ass'n
Nat'l Ass'n for the Education of Young Children
Nat'l Ass'n for the Self-Employed
Nat'l Ass'n of Bank Women
Nat'l Ass'n of Chain Drug Stores
Nat'l Ass'n of College Admission Counselors
Nat'l Ass'n of College and University Business Officers
Nat'l Ass'n of Convenience Stores
Nat'l Ass'n of Corrosion Engineers
Nat'l Ass'n of Counties
Nat'l Ass'n of Credit Management
Nat'l Ass'n of Electrical Distributors
Nat'l Ass'n of Elementary School Principals
Nat'l Ass'n of Federal Credit Unions
Nat'l Ass'n of Government Employees
Nat'l Ass'n of Housing and Redevelopment Officials
Nat'l Ass'n of Independent Schools
Nat'l Ass'n of Industrial and Office Parks
Nat'l Ass'n of Investors
Nat'l Ass'n of Mutual Insurance Companies
Nat'l Ass'n of Plumbing-Heating-Cooling Contractors
Nat'l Ass'n of Postal Supervisors
Nat'l Ass'n of Printers and Lithographers
Nat'l Ass'n of Purchasing Management
Nat'l Ass'n of Retail Dealers of America
Nat'l Ass'n of Retail Druggists
Nat'l Ass'n of Retired Federal Employees
Nat'l Ass'n of State Universities and Land Grant Colleges
Nat'l Ass'n of Television Program Executives
Nat'l Ass'n of Trade and Technical Schools
Nat'l Ass'n of Wholesaler-Distributors
Nat'l Automated Clearing House Ass'n
Nat'l Beer Wholesalers' Ass'n
Nat'l Bowling Council
Nat'l Business Aircraft Ass'n
Nat'l Business Forms Ass'n
Nat'l Catholic Educational Ass'n
Nat'l Cattlemen's Ass'n
Nat'l Coalition of Hispanic Health and Human Services Organizations
Nat'l Concrete Masonry Ass'n
Nat'l Cotton Council of America
Nat'l Council for U.S.-China Trade
Nat'l Council of Architectural Registration Boards
Nat'l Council of Engineering Examiners
Nat'l Council of Farmer Cooperatives
Nat'l Council of State Boards of Nursing
Nat'l Council of Teachers of English
Nat'l Council of Teachers of Mathematics
Nat'l Council of the Paper Industry for Air and Stream Improvement
Nat'l Council on Crime and Delinquency
Nat'l Dairy Council
Nat'l Federation of Federal Employees
Nat'l Federation of State High School Ass'ns
Nat'l Fire Sprinkler Ass'n
Nat'l Fisheries Institute
Nat'l Food Brokers Ass'n
Nat'l Forest Products Ass'n
Nat'l Funeral Directors Ass'n
Nat'l Glass Ass'n
Nat'l Governors' Ass'n
Nat'l Grocers Ass'n
Nat'l Hardwood Lumber Ass'n
Nat'l Hockey League Player's Ass'n
Nat'l Home Furnishings Ass'n
Nat'l Housewares Manufacturers Ass'n
Nat'l Industries for the Blind
Nat'l Institute of Building Sciences
Nat'l League of Postmasters of the U.S.
Nat'l League of Professional Baseball Clubs
Nat'l Milk Producers Federation
Nat'l Motor Freight Traffic Ass'n
Nat'l Office Machine Dealers Ass'n
Nat'l Paint and Coatings Ass'n
Nat'l Parks and Conservation Ass'n
Nat'l Pest Control Ass'n
Nat'l Petroleum Refiners Ass'n
Nat'l Recreation and Park Ass'n
Nat'l Renderers Ass'n
Nat'l Rural Letter Carriers' Ass'n
Nat'l Security Industrial Ass'n
Nat'l Sheriffs' Ass'n
Nat'l Shorthand Reporters Ass'n
Nat'l Small Business Ass'n
Nat'l Soc. of Public Accountants
Nat'l Solid Wastes Management Ass'n
Nat'l Spa and Pool Institute
Nat'l Telephone Cooperative Ass'n
Nat'l Tire Dealers and Retreaders Ass'n
Nat'l Tooling and Machining Ass'n
Nat'l Tour Ass'n
Nat'l Water Well Ass'n
Nat'l Wholesale Druggists' Ass'n
Natural Gas Supply Ass'n
Newspaper Guild, The
Non-Commissioned Officers Ass'n of the U.S.A.
Northeastern Retail Lumberman's Ass'n
Office and Professional Employees Internat'l Union
Operative Plasterers' and Cement Masons' Internat'l Ass'n of the United States and Canada
Optical Soc. of America
Owner-Operator Independent Drivers Ass'n of America
Phosphate Chemicals Export Ass'n
Phosphate Rock Export Ass'n
Potash and Phosphate Institute
Preferred Hotels Ass'n
Prestressed Concrete Institute
Produce Marketing Ass'n
Professional Golfers Ass'n of America
Professional Rodeo Cowboys Ass'n
Proprietary Ass'n, The
Public Relations Soc. of America
Quality Chekd Dairy Products Ass'n
Recording Industry Ass'n of America
Recreation Vehicle Industry Ass'n
Reserve Officers Ass'n of the U.S.
Rice Council of America
Risk and Insurance Management Soc.
Rubber Manufacturers Ass'n
SAF
Seafarers' Internat'l Union of North America
Ski Industries America
Smokeless Tobacco Council
Snack Food Ass'n
Soap and Detergent Ass'n
Soc. for Industrial and Applied Mathematics
Soc. of Actuaries
Soc. of American Foresters
Soc. of Chartered Property and Casualty Underwriters
Soc. of Mining Engineers
Soc. of Nuclear Medicine
Soc. of Plastics Engineers
Southern Forest Products Ass'n
Specialty Advertising Ass'n, Internat'l
Specialty Equipment Market Ass'n
SPIE-Internat'l Soc. for Optical Engineering
Steel Service Center Institute
Steel Tank Institute
Sugar Ass'n
Timber Operators Council
Travel Industry Ass'n of America
United Electrical, Radio and Machine Workers of America
United Farm Workers of America
United Fresh Fruit and Vegetable Ass'n
United States-Arab Chamber of Commerce
United States Conference of Mayors
United States Council for Internat'l Business
United States Feed Grains Council
United States Jaycees
United States Soccer Federation
United States Telephone Ass'n
United Synagogue of America
United Textile Workers of America
United Transportation Union
United Union of Roofers, Waterproofers and Allied Workers
Utility Workers Union of America
Video Software Dealers Ass'n
Water Quality Ass'n
Welding Research Council
Wine Institute

$1-2,000,000

Acupuncture Internat'l Ass'n
Administrative Management Soc.
Advertising Research Foundation
Agriculture Council of America
Air Conditioning Contractors of America
Air Pollution Control Ass'n
Airport Operators Council Internat'l
American Academy and Institute of Arts and Letters
American Academy of Allergy and Immunology
American Academy of Arts and Sciences
American Academy of Cosmetic Surgery
American Academy of Medical Directors
American Academy of Periodontology
American Accounting Ass'n
American Advertising Federation
American Anthropological Ass'n
American Antiquarian Soc.
American Architectural Manufacturers Ass'n
American Assembly of Collegiate Schools of Business
American Ass'n for Artificial Intelligence
American Ass'n for Cancer Research
American Ass'n for Marriage and Family Therapy
American Ass'n for State and Local History
American Ass'n of Airport Executives
American Ass'n of Cereal Chemists
American Ass'n of Classified School Employees
American Ass'n of Colleges of Osteopathic Medicine
American Ass'n of Colleges of Pharmacy
American Ass'n of Collegiate Registrars and Admissions Officers
American Ass'n of Dental Schools
American Ass'n of Engineering Societies
American Ass'n of Medical Assistants
American Ass'n of Nurserymen
American Ass'n of Petroleum Landmen
American Ass'n of Physicists in Medicine
American Ass'n on Mental Deficiency
American Business Conference
American Cemetery Ass'n
American Collectors Ass'n
American College of Allergists
American College of General Practitioners in Osteopathic Medicine and Surgery
American College of Health Care Administrators
American Concrete Pipe Ass'n
American Conference of Governmental Industrial Hygienists
American Congress on Surveying and Mapping
American Council of Learned Societies
American Economic Ass'n
American Educational Research Ass'n
American Electroplaters and Surface Finishers Soc.
American Federation of Police
American Feed Industry Ass'n
American Film Marketing Ass'n
American Fisheries Soc.
American Fishing Tackle Manufacturers Ass'n
American Forestry Ass'n
American Gem Soc.
American Group Practice Ass'n
American Hereford Ass'n
American Home Sewing Ass'n
American Horticultural Soc.
American Industrial Health Council
American Industrial Hygiene Ass'n
American Institute of Nutrition
American Institute of Ultrasound in Medicine
American Internat'l Automobile Dealers Ass'n
American Internat'l Charolais Ass'n
American Judicature Soc.
American League of Professional Baseball Clubs
American Logistics Ass'n
American Machine Tool Distributors Ass'n
American Medical Care and Review Ass'n
American Medical Student Ass'n
American Medical Technologists
American Morgan Horse Ass'n
American Nuclear Energy Council
American Occupational Medical Ass'n
American Oil Chemists' Soc.
American Osteopathic Hospital Ass'n
American Phytopathological Soc.
American Political Science Ass'n
American Public Welfare Ass'n
American Public Works Ass'n
American Resort and Residential Development Ass'n
American Retail Federation
American Rheumatism Ass'n
American Road and Transportation Builders Ass'n
American Soc. for Horticultural Science

BUDGET INDEX

BUDGET INDEX

Special Industrial Radio Service Ass'n
Special Libraries Ass'n
Sporting Goods Manufacturers Ass'n
Sulphur Institute
Surety Ass'n of America
Tax Executives Institute
Telocator Network of America
Textile Rental Services Ass'n of America
Tile Council of America
Toy Manufacturers of America
Transportation Institute
Trophy Dealers and Manufacturers Ass'n
Union of American Physicians and Dentists
United Garment Workers of America
United Ostomy Ass'n
United States Meat Export Federation
United States Professional Tennis Ass'n
United States Telecommunications Suppliers Ass'n
United States Trademark Ass'n
Vocational Industrial Clubs of America
Waterbed Manufacturers Ass'n
Wholesale Florists and Florist Suppliers of America
Wine and Spirits Wholesalers of America
Wire Ass'n Internat'l
Women's Internat'l Tennis Ass'n
World Future Soc.
Writers Guild of America, East
Writers Guild of America, West

$500-1,000,000

Academy of Management
Accounting Firms Associated
ACME, Inc.-The Association of Management Consulting Firms
Adhesive and Sealant Council
Air-conditioning and Refrigeration Wholesalers Ass'n
Air Traffic Control Ass'n
Aircraft Electronics Ass'n
Airline Industrial Relations Conference
Alexander Graham Bell Ass'n for the Deaf
Alliance of Motion Picture and Television Producers
Aluminum Extruders Council
American Academy of Actuaries
American Academy of Forensic Sciences
American Academy of Hospital Attorneys
American Academy of Medical Preventics
American Academy of Orthotists and Prosthetists
American Academy of Physical Medicine and Rehabilitation
American Ass'n for Dental Research
American Ass'n for Higher Education
American Ass'n for Laboratory Animal Science
American Ass'n for Medical Transcription
American Ass'n for Vocational Instructional Materials
American Ass'n of Colleges for Teacher Education
American Ass'n of Colleges of Nursing
American Ass'n of Colleges of Podiatric Medicine
American Ass'n of Cost Engineers
American Ass'n of Crop Insurers
American Ass'n of Diabetes Educators
American Ass'n of Electromyography and Electrodiagnosis
American Ass'n of Endodontists
American Ass'n of Exporters and Importers
American Ass'n of Fund-Raising Counsel
American Ass'n of Gynecological Laparoscopists
American Ass'n of Law Libraries
American Ass'n of Physics Teachers
American Ass'n of Port Authorities
American Ass'n of Teachers of German
American Ass'n of Textile Chemists and Colorists
American Ass'n of University Affiliated Programs
American Bakers Ass'n
American Board of Medical Specialties
American Brahman Breeders Ass'n
American College Health Ass'n
American College of Musicians
American College of Nurse-Midwives
American College of Osteopathic Surgeons
American College of Probate Counsel
American College of Psychiatrists
American College of Trial Lawyers
American Concrete Pressure Pipe Ass'n
American Congress of Rehabilitation Medicine
American Corporate Counsel Ass'n
American Council for the Arts
American Council of Teachers of Russian
American Council on Science and Health
American Council on the Teaching of Foreign Languages
American Dairy Goat Ass'n
American Dairy Products Institute
American Dental Assistants Ass'n
American Dental Trade Ass'n
American Die Casting Institute
American Digestive Disease Soc.
American Economic Development Council
American Fertility Soc.
American Fire Sprinkler Ass'n
American Foreign Service Ass'n
American Fur Industry
American Furniture Manufacturers Ass'n
American Gear Manufacturers Ass'n
American Guernsey Cattle Club
American Guild of Musical Artists
American Guild of Organists
American Health Planning Ass'n
American Helicopter Soc. Internat'l
American Historical Ass'n
American Hockey League
American Home Lighting Institute
American Horse Council
American Hot Dip Galvanizers Ass'n
American Immigration Lawyers Ass'n
American Institute of Certified Planners
American Institute of Cooperation
American Institute of Food Distribution
American Institute of Graphic Arts
American Institute of Marine Underwriters
American Institute of Merchant Shipping
American Institute of Plant Engineers
American Institute of Technical Illustrators Ass'n
American Institute of Timber Construction
American Insurers Highway Safety Alliance
American Intellectual Property Law Ass'n
American Malting Barley Ass'n
American Medical Peer Review Ass'n
American Medical Women's Ass'n
American Montessori Soc.
American Movers Conference
American Nephrology Nurses' Ass'n
American Numismatic Soc.
American Organization of Nurse Executives
American Orthodontic Soc.
American Orthopsychiatric Ass'n
American Orthotic and Prosthetic Ass'n
American Pet Products Manufacturers Ass'n
American Psychoanalytic Ass'n
American Pulpwood Ass'n
American Rabbit Breeders Ass'n
American Recovery Ass'n
American Saddlebred Horse Ass'n
American Schools of Oriental Research
American Seed Trade Ass'n
American Short Line Railroad Ass'n
American Soc. for Aesthetic Plastic Surgery
American Soc. for Cell Biology
American Soc. for Information Science
American Soc. for Parenteral and Enteral Nutrition
American Soc. for Psychoprophylaxis in Obstetrics
American Soc. of Allied Health Professions
American Soc. of Clinical Hypnosis
American Soc. of Clinical Oncology
American Soc. of Consultant Pharmacists
American Soc. of Dentistry for Children
American Soc. of Farm Managers and Rural Appraisers
American Soc. of Hematology
American Soc. of Human Genetics
American Soc. of Internat'l Law
American Soc. of Law and Medicine
American Soc. of Lubrication Engineers
American Soc. of Magazine Photographers
American Soc. of Naval Engineers
American Soc. of Neuroradiology
American Soc. of Newspaper Editors
American Soc. of Plumbing Engineers
American Soc. of Real Estate Counselors
American Solar Energy Soc.
American Supply and Machinery Manufacturers Ass'n
American Telemarketing Ass'n
American Traffic Safety Services Ass'n
American Warehousemen's Ass'n
American Watchmakers Institute
American Wood Council
American Wood Preservers Bureau
American Wood Preservers Institute
American Yorkshire Club
Amusement and Music Operators Ass'n
Arabian Horse Registry of America
Asphalt Roofing Manufacturers Ass'n
Associated Landscape Contractors of America
Associated Public-Safety Communications Officers
Associated Telephone Answering Exchanges
Ass'n for Advanced Life Underwriting
Ass'n for Childhood Education Internat'l
Ass'n for Employee Health and Fitness
Ass'n for Multi-Image International
Ass'n for Research in Vision and Ophthalmology
Ass'n of Academic Health Centers
Ass'n of American Geographers
Ass'n of American Law Schools
Ass'n of American Universities
Ass'n of College Unions-Internat'l
Ass'n of College, University and Community Arts Administrators
Ass'n of Collegiate Schools of Architecture
Ass'n of Energy Engineers
Ass'n of Government Accountants
Ass'n of Labor-Management Administrators and Consultants on Alcoholism
Ass'n of Military Surgeons of the U.S.
Ass'n of Oil Pipe Lines
Ass'n of Oilwell Servicing Contractors
Ass'n of Private Pension and Welfare Plans
Ass'n of Progressive Rental Organizations
Ass'n of Research Libraries
Ass'n of Schools of Public Health
Ass'n of Science-Technology Centers
Ass'n of Specialists in Cleaning and Restoration
Ass'n of Surgical Technologists
Ass'n of Universities for Research in Astronomy
Automatic Transmission Rebuilders Ass'n
Automotive Dismantlers and Recyclers Ass'n
Automotive Industry Action Group
Bicycle Manufacturers Ass'n of America
BPI . . .A Growers' Organization
Broadcast Financial Management Ass'n
Brown Swiss Cattle Breeders Ass'n of the U.S.A.
Business/Professional Advertising Ass'n
Can Manufacturers Institute
Carpet and Rug Institute
Cast Iron Soil Pipe Institute
CAUSE
Ceilings and Interior Systems Construction Ass'n
Cellular Telecommunications Industry Ass'n
Chief Executives Organization
Children's Book Council
Christian College Coalition
Christian Ministries Management Ass'n
Cigar Ass'n of America
Clinical Laboratory Management Ass'n
Coin Laundry Ass'n
College and University Personnel Ass'n
College Art Ass'n of America
College Football Ass'n
Commercial Law League of America
Composites Institute
Compressed Gas Ass'n
Computer and Communications Industry Ass'n
Conference of Radiation Control Program Directors
Congress of Neurological Surgeons
Conservative Orthopedics Internat'l Ass'n
Construction Industry Manufacturers Ass'n
Consumer Credit Insurance Ass'n
Consumer Federation of America
Contract Services Ass'n of America
Corn Refiners Ass'n
Council for Periodical Distributors Ass'ns
Council for Responsible Nutrition
Council of American-Flag Ship Operators
Council of Independent Colleges
Council of Medical Specialty Societies
Council on Alternate Fuels
Country Music Ass'n
CPA Associates
Delta Sigma Pi
Dietary Managers Ass'n
Diving Equipment Manufacturers Ass'n
Dramatists Guild
Electronic Representatives Ass'n
Employers Council on Flexible Compensation
Employment Management Ass'n
Endocrine Soc.
Envelope Manufacturers Ass'n of America
ESOP Ass'n
Ethylene Oxide Industry Council
Farm Credit Council
Farm Equipment Manufacturers Ass'n
Fashion Group
FCIB-NACM Corp.
Federal Construction Council
Federal Managers Ass'n
Federation of American Controlled Shipping
Federation of American Health Systems
Federation of Computer Users in the Medical Sciences
Federation of Insurance and Corporate Counsel
Fibre Box Ass'n
Financial Institutions Marketing Ass'n
Flavor and Extract Manufacturers Ass'n of the United States
Flight Safety Foundation
Flue-Cured Tobacco Cooperative Stabilization Corporation
Footwear Retailers of America
Forest Products Research Soc.
Forging Industry Ass'n
Fourdrinier Kraft Board Group of the American Paper Institute
Fraternal Order of Police
French-American Chamber of Commerce in the United States
Future Business Leaders of America-Phi Beta Lambda
Gas Processors Ass'n
Genetics Soc. of America
Geothermal Resources Council
Governmental Refuse Collection and Disposal Ass'n
Grain Elevator and Processing Soc.
Graphic Arts Marketing Information Service
Gravure Research Institute
Gravure Technical Ass'n

00005

BUDGET INDEX

Gypsum Ass'n
Halogenated Solvents Industry Alliance
Handweavers Guild of America
Horsemen's Benevolent and Protective Ass'n
Hotel Sales and Marketing Ass'n Internat'l
Human Resource Planning Soc.
Independent Jewelers Organization
Industrial Biotechnology Ass'n
Industrial Designers Soc. of America
Industrial Fasteners Institute
Industrial Health Foundation
Institute for Certification of Computer Professionals
Institute of Business Designers
Institute of Environmental Sciences
Institute of Judicial Administration
Institute of Makers of Explosives
Institute of Management Sciences, The
Insurance Accounting and Systems Ass'n
Internat'l Academy of Pathology (U.S.-Canadian Div.)
Internat'l Anesthesia Research Soc.
Internat'l Apple Institute
Internat'l Ass'n of Auditorium Managers
Internat'l Ass'n of Electrical Inspectors
Internat'l Ass'n of Fairs and Expositions
Internat'l Ass'n of Fire Chiefs
Internat'l Bottled Water Ass'n
Internat'l Brangus Breeders Ass'n
Internat'l Circulation Managers Ass'n
Internat'l College of Surgeons (U.S. Section)
Internat'l Credit Ass'n
Internat'l Dairy-Deli Ass'n
Internat'l Facility Management Ass'n
Internat'l Federation of Professional and Technical Engineers
Internat'l Information Management Congress
Internat'l Institute of Synthetic Rubber Producers
Internat'l Material Management Soc.
Internat'l Minilab Ass'n
Internat'l Newspaper Advertising and Marketing Executives, Inc.
Internat'l Newspaper Promotion Ass'n
Internat'l Radio and Television Soc.
Internat'l Sleep Products Ass'n
Internat'l Television Ass'n
Internat'l Transactional Analysis Ass'n
Internat'l Union of Police Ass'ns
Interstate Carriers Conference
Interstate Conference of Employment Security Agencies
Irrigation Ass'n
Jewelers of America
Jewish Education Service of North America
Juvenile Products Manufacturers Ass'n
Laser Institute of America
Latin American Manufacturers Ass'n
Lead Industries Ass'n
Luggage and Leather Goods Manufacturers of America
Mail Advertising Service Ass'n Internat'l
Marketing Research Ass'n
Master Printers of America
Material Handling Equipment Distributors Ass'n
Mechanics Educational Soc. of America
Men's Fashion Ass'n of America
Metal Castings Soc.
Methods Time Measurement Ass'n for Standards and Research
Mid-Continent Oil and Gas Ass'n
Millers' Nat'l Federation
Monument Builders of North America
Mortgage Insurance Companies of America
Music Teachers Nat'l Ass'n
Nat'l Academy of Education
Nat'l Academy of Television Arts and Sciences
Nat'l Accounting and Finance Council
Nat'l Agri-Marketing Ass'n
Nat'l Agricultural Aviation Ass'n
Nat'l Art Education Ass'n
Nat'l Assembly of Local Arts Agencies
Nat'l Assembly of State Arts Agencies
Nat'l Ass'n for Hospital Development
Nat'l Ass'n for Practical Nurse Education and Service
Nat'l Ass'n for the Speciality Food Trade
Nat'l Ass'n General Merchandise Representatives
Nat'l Ass'n of Animal Breeders
Nat'l Ass'n of Area Agencies on Aging
Nat'l Ass'n of Attorneys General
Nat'l Ass'n of Beverage Importers-Wine-Spirits-Beer
Nat'l Ass'n of Boards of Pharmacy
Nat'l Ass'n of Bond Lawyers
Nat'l Ass'n of Casualty and Surety Agents
Nat'l Ass'n of Chemical Distributors
Nat'l Ass'n of College and University Attorneys
Nat'l Ass'n of Conservation Districts
Nat'l Ass'n of Corporate Directors
Nat'l Ass'n of Criminal Defense Lawyers
Nat'l Ass'n of Fire Equipment Distributors
Nat'l Ass'n of Hosiery Manufacturers
Nat'l Ass'n of Insurance Women (Internat'l)
Nat'l Ass'n of Latino Elected and Appointed Officials
Nat'l Ass'n of Legal Secretaries (Int'l)
Nat'l Ass'n of Meat Purveyors
Nat'l Ass'n of Minority Contractors
Nat'l Ass'n of Pastoral Musicians
Nat'l Ass'n of Personnel Consultants
Nat'l Ass'n of Professional Surplus Lines Offices
Nat'l Ass'n of Professional Upholsterers
Nat'l Ass'n of Quick Printers
Nat'l Ass'n of Real Estate Investment Trusts
Nat'l Ass'n of Recording Merchandisers
Nat'l Ass'n of Regional Councils
Nat'l Ass'n of Rehabilitation Professionals in the Private Sector
Nat'l Ass'n of School Psychologists
Nat'l Ass'n of Schools of Music
Nat'l Ass'n of State Boards of Accountancy
Nat'l Ass'n of State Directors of Special Education
Nat'l Ass'n of State Units on Aging
Nat'l Ass'n of Student Personnel Administrators
Nat'l Ass'n of Temporary Services
Nat'l Ass'n of the Remodeling Industry
Nat'l Ass'n of Towns and Townships
Nat'l Ass'n of Underwater Instructors
Nat'l Ass'n of Water Companies
Nat'l Automotive Radiator Service Ass'n
Nat'l Bar Ass'n
Nat'l Bath, Bed and Linen Ass'n
Nat'l Black Coalition of Federal Aviation Employees
Nat'l Building Material Distributors Ass'n
Nat'l Burglar and Fire Alarm Ass'n
Nat'l Business Education Ass'n
Nat'l Catholic Development Conference
Nat'l Christmas Tree Ass'n
Nat'l Club Ass'n
Nat'l Coffee Ass'n of the U.S.A.
Nat'l Committee for Clinical Laboratory Standards
Nat'l Composition Ass'n
Nat'l Confectioners Ass'n of the United States
Nat'l Conference of Bar Examiners
Nat'l Conference of Black Mayors
Nat'l Corrugated Steel Pipe Ass'n
Nat'l Council for the Social Studies
Nat'l Council for Urban Economic Development
Nat'l Council of Community Hospitals
Nat'l Council on Family Relations
Nat'l Council on Radiation Protection and Measurements
Nat'l Crop Insurance Ass'n
Nat'l District Attorneys Ass'n
Nat'l Electronic Distributors Ass'n
Nat'l Elevator Industry
Nat'l Energy Specialist Ass'n
Nat'l Environmental Health Ass'n
Nat'l Erectors Ass'n
Nat'l Feed Ingredients Ass'n
Nat'l Fraternal Congress of America
Nat'l Frozen Food Ass'n
Nat'l Grain and Feed Ass'n
Nat'l Guild of Piano Teachers
Nat'l Health Council
Nat'l Health Lawyers Ass'n
Nat'l Hearing Aid Soc.
Nat'l Hemophilia Foundation
Nat'l Home Study Council
Nat'l Independent Automobile Dealers Ass'n
Nat'l Industrial Transportation League
Nat'l Intravenous Therapy Ass'n
Nat'l Investor Relations Institute
Nat'l Legal Aid and Defender Ass'n
Nat'l Lime Ass'n
Nat'l Marine Engineers' Beneficial Ass'n
Nat'l Marine Manufacturers Ass'n
Nat'l Medical Ass'n
Nat'l Moving and Storage Ass'n
Nat'l Multi Housing Council
Nat'l Ocean Industries Ass'n
Nat'l Paperbox and Packaging Ass'n
Nat'l Particleboard Ass'n
Nat'l Pasta Ass'n
Nat'l Peanut Council
Nat'l Pecan Marketing Council
Nat'l Press Photographers Ass'n
Nat'l Red Cherry Institute
Nat'l Rehabilitation Ass'n
Nat'l Rural Health Care Ass'n
Nat'l Sand and Gravel Ass'n
Nat'l School Supply and Equipment Ass'n
Nat'l Screw Machine Products Ass'n
Nat'l Selected Morticians
Nat'l Shoe Retailers Ass'n
Nat'l Ski Patrol System
Nat'l Soc. for Hebrew Day Schools
Nat'l Soybean Processors Ass'n
Nat'l Speakers Ass'n
Nat'l Strength and Conditioning Ass'n
Nat'l Turkey Federation
Nat'l Vehicle Leasing Ass'n
Natural-Source Vitamin E Ass'n
Netherlands Chamber of Commerce in the United States
Newsletter Ass'n
Nine to Five Nat'l Ass'n of Working Women
North American Soc. of Pacing and Electrophysiology
North American Wholesale Lumber Ass'n
North American Wildlife Foundation
Northamerican Heating and Airconditioning Wholesalers Ass'n
Nursery Marketing Council
Office Education Ass'n
OPERA America
Operations Research Soc. of America
Optical Laboratories Ass'n
Optical Manufacturers Ass'n
Organization for the Protection and Advancement of Small Telephone Companies
Outdoor Advertising Ass'n of America
Overseas Education Ass'n
Painting and Decorating Contractors of America
Paperboard Packaging Council
Parenteral Drug Ass'n
Pattern Makers' League of North America
Pension Real Estate Ass'n
Pet Industry Joint Advisory Council
Petroleum Equipment Institute
Petroleum Equipment Suppliers Ass'n
Petroleum Marketing Education Foundation
Phi Alpha Delta
Pipe Line Contractors Ass'n
Power Transmission Distributors Ass'n
Private Carrier Conference
Pro ect Management Institute
Production Service and Sales District Council
Professional Airways Systems Specialists
Professional Convention Management Ass'n
Professional Engineers in Private Practice
Professional Putters Ass'n
Professional Ski Instructors of America
Public Affairs Council
Public Risk and Insurance Management Ass'n
Railway Progress Institute
REALTORS Land Institute
Recreation Vehicle Dealers Ass'n of North America
Refractories Institute
Regional Airline Ass'n
Renewable Natural Resources Foundation
Retail Advertising Conference
Retail Bakers of America
Rice Millers' Ass'n
Salt Institute
Santa Gertrudis Breeders Internat'l
Screen Extras Guild
Self Insurance Institute of America
Semiconductor Industry Ass'n
Service Station Dealers of America
Smaller Manufacturers Council
Soc. for Applied Spectroscopy
Soc. for Computer Simulation
Soc. for Marketing Professional Services
Soc. for Nutrition Education
Soc. for Technical Communication
Soc. of American Archivists
Soc. of Consumer Affairs Professionals in Business
Soc. of Cosmetic Chemists
Soc. of Economic Paleontologists and Mineralogists
Soc. of Logistics Engineers
Soc. of Professional Benefit Administrators
Soc. of Teachers of Family Medicine
Soil Conservation Soc. of America
Souvenirs and Novelties Trade Ass'n
Specialized Carriers and Rigging Ass'n
Specialty Tool and Fastener Distributors Ass'n
Speech Communication Ass'n
Steel Founders' Soc. of America
Sterling Silversmiths Guild of America
Stove, Furnace and Allied Appliance Workers' Internat'l Union of North America
Supima Ass'n of America
Systems Builders Ass'n
Tea Council of the U.S.A.
Teachers of English to Speakers of Other Languages
Tele-Communications Ass'n
Tennessee Walking Horse Breeders and Exhibitors Ass'n
Texas Longhorn Breeders Ass'n of America
Thoroughbred Racing Ass'ns of North America
Tobacco Merchants Ass'n of the U.S.
Towing and Recovery Ass'n of America
Transportation Brokers Conference of America
Truck Trailer Manufacturers Ass'n
Typographers Internat'l Ass'n
UNDA-USA
United Cancer Council
United Duroc Swine Registry
United Egg Producers
United Nations Staff Union
United Scenic Artists
United States Business and Industrial Council
United States-Mexico Chamber of Commerce
United Telegraph Workers
Universities Research Ass'n
Utilities Telecommunications Council
Valve Manufacturers Ass'n of America
Western Forest Industries Ass'n
Wholesale Stationer's Ass'n
Wildlife Management Institute
Wildlife Soc., The
Wine and Spirits Shippers Ass'n
Women in Communications
Women's Council of Realtors
Wood Heating Alliance
World Computer Graphics Ass'n
Zinc Institute

BUDGET INDEX

$250-500,000

ABCD: The Microcomputer Industry Ass'n
Academy of Ambulatory Foot Surgery
Academy of Political Science
Acoustical Soc. of America
Aerospace Medical Ass'n
Aestheticians Internat'l Ass'n
Affiliated Advertising Agencies Internat'l
Alcohol and Drug Problems Ass'n of North America
Alliance for Responsible CFC Policy
Alliance of Independent Colleges of Art
Alliance of Nonprofit Mailers
Alpha Kappa Psi
Alpha Omega
American Academy of Child and Adolescent Psychiatry
American Academy of Medical Administrators
American Academy of Optometry
American Academy of Otolaryngic Allergy
American Agricultural Economics Ass'n
American Ambulance Ass'n
American Amusement Machine Ass'n
American-Arab Ass'n for Commerce and Industry
American Arts Alliance
American Ass'n for Adult and Continuing Education
American Ass'n for Functional Orthodontics
American Ass'n for the Advancement of Slavic Studies
American Ass'n of Bioanalysts
American Ass'n of Bovine Practicioners
American Ass'n of Healthcare Consultants
American Ass'n of Immunologists
American Ass'n of Managing General Agents
American Ass'n of Meat Processors
American Ass'n of Neuroscience Nurses
American Ass'n of Pastoral Counselors
American Ass'n of Pathologists
American Ass'n of Sex Educators, Counselors and Therapists
American Ass'n of Teachers of French
American Ass'n of Teachers of Spanish and Portuguese
American Ass'n of Zoological Parks and Aquariums
American Astronautical Soc.
American Automotive Leasing Ass'n
American Blood Resources Ass'n
American Boarding Kennels Ass'n
American Boiler Manufacturers Ass'n
American Bureau of Metal Statistics
American Car Rental Ass'n
American Cement Trade Alliance
American Chianina Ass'n
American Choral Directors Ass'n
American Coal Ash Ass'n
American Cocoa Research Institute
American College of Angiology
American College of Dentists
American College of Foot Surgeons
American College of Gastroenterology
American College of Preventive Medicine
American College of Utilization Review Physicians
American College of Veterinary Internal Medicine
American Concrete Pavement Ass'n
American Council of Independent Laboratories
American Culinary Federation
American Dairy Science Ass'n
American Federation for Clinical Research
American Federation of School Administrators
American Gelbvieh Ass'n
American Gem Trade Ass'n
American Genetic Ass'n
American Geographical Soc.
American Geriatrics Soc.
American Greyhound Track Operators Ass'n
American Group Psychotherapy Ass'n
American Guild of Variety Artists
American Hardboard Ass'n
American Health and Beauty Aids Institute
American Healthcare Radiology Administrators
American Independent Refiners Ass'n
American Institute for Conservation of Historic and Artistic Works
American Institute of Chemists
American Institute of Professional Geologists
American Iron Ore Ass'n
American Jewish Historical Soc.
American League of Financial Institutions
American Legend Cooperative
American Licensed Practical Nurses Ass'n
American Medical Writers Ass'n
American Monument Ass'n
American Nat'l Metric Council
American Prepaid Legal Services Institute
American Productivity Management Ass'n
American Protestant Health Ass'n
American Public Gas Ass'n
American Railway Engineering Ass'n
American Recreation Coalition
American Red Brangus Ass'n
American Retreaders' Ass'n
American School Health Ass'n
American Shorthorn Ass'n
American Sightseeing Internat'l
American Ski Federation
American Soc. for Artificial Internal Organs
American Soc. for Clinical Nutrition
American Soc. for Clinical Pharmacology and Therapeutics
American Soc. for Enology and Viticulture
American Soc. for Environmental Education
American Soc. for Healthcare Education and Training
American Soc. for Histocompatability and Immunogenetics
American Soc. for Hospital Central Service Personnel
American Soc. for Hospital Food Service Administrators
American Soc. for Hospital Marketing and Public Relations
American Soc. for Hospital Risk Management
American Soc. of Abdominal Surgeons
American Soc. of Animal Science
American Soc. of Bakery Engineers
American Soc. of Bariatric Physicians
American Soc. of Cinematographers
American Soc. of Contemporary Medicine, Surgery and Ophthalmology
American Soc. of Directors of Volunteer Services
American Soc. of Educators
American Soc. of Extra-corporeal Technology
American Soc. of Limnology and Oceanography
American Soc. of Magazine Editors
American Soc. of Notaries
American Soc. of Pension Actuaries
American Soc. of Post-Anesthesia Nurses
American Soc. of Tropical Medicine and Hygiene
American Sod Producers Ass'n
American Spice Trade Ass'n
American Stamp Dealers' Ass'n
American Student Dental Ass'n
American Sugar Cane League of the U.S.A.
American Swimming Coaches Ass'n
American Textile Machinery Ass'n
American Theological Library Ass'n
American Truck Stop Operators Ass'n
American Tunaboat Ass'n
American Water Resources Ass'n
American Wind Energy Ass'n
American Women in Radio and Television
Anti-Friction Bearing Manufacturers Ass'n
APEC
Arthroscopy Ass'n of North America
Asbestos Information Ass'n/North America
Associated Accounting Firms Internat'l
Associated Master Barbers and Beauticians of America/Hair Internat'l
Ass'n for Advancement of Behavior Therapy
Ass'n for Asian Studies
Ass'n for Clinical Pastoral Education
Ass'n for Corporate Growth
Ass'n for Education and Rehabilitation of the Blind andVisually Impaired
Ass'n for Education in Journalism and Mass Communication
Ass'n for Humanistic Psychology
Ass'n for Integrated Manufacturing Technology
Ass'n for Manufacturing Excellence
Ass'n for Practitioners in Infection Control
Ass'n for Regulatory Reform
Ass'n for the Advancement of Psychology
Ass'n for the Care of Children's Health
Ass'n of Asbestos Cement Pipe Producers
Ass'n of Catholic Colleges and Universities
Ass'n of Civilian Technicians
Ass'n of Computer Retailers
Ass'n of Executive Search Consultants
Ass'n of Federal Investigators
Ass'n of Food Industries
Ass'n of Hispanic Arts
Ass'n of Human Resource Systems Professionals
Ass'n of Independent Corrugated Converters
Ass'n of Medical Illustrators
Ass'n of Metropolitan Sewerage Agencies
Ass'n of Physical Fitness Centers
Ass'n of Rehabilitation Nurses
Ass'n of Reserve City Bankers
Ass'n of Rotational Molders
Ass'n of State and Territorial Solid Waste Management Officials
Ass'n of Steel Distributors
Ass'n of Teachers of Preventive Medicine
Ass'n of Tile, Terrazzo, Marble Contractors and Affiliates
Ass'n of Transportation Practioners
Ass'n of Visual Communicators
Authors Guild
Aviation Maintenance Foundation
Aviation Safety Institute
Bankers' Ass'n for Foreign Trade
Barbecue Industry Ass'n
Beauty and Barber Supply Institute
Beet Sugar Development Foundation
Belgian American Chamber of Commerce in the United States
Beta Alpha Psi
Binding Industries of America
Biophysical Soc.
Biscuit and Cracker Manufacturers Ass'n
Box Office Management Internat'l
Broadcast Credit Ass'n
Builders Hardware Manufacturers Ass'n
Building Stone Institute
Bureau of Wholesale Sales Representatives
Burley Tobacco Growers Cooperative Ass'n
Business and Institutional Furniture Manufacturers Ass'n
Business Council
Catfish Farmers of America
Ceramic Tile Institute of America
Chamber Music America
Chester White Swine Record Ass'n
China Clay Producers Group
Choristers Guild
Christian Labor Ass'n of the United States of America
Christian Schools Internat'l
Cleaning Management Institute
Clinical Ligand Assay Soc.
Closure Manufacturers Ass'n
Cocoa Merchants' Ass'n of America
Color Marketing Group
Commissioned Officers Ass'n of the United States Public Health Service
Community Antenna Television Ass'n
Competitive Telecommunications Ass'n
Compressed Air and Gas Institute
Computer Dealers and Lessors Ass'n
Congress of Independent Unions
Construction Products Manufacturers Council
Cooling Tower Institute
Coordinating Council of Literary Magazines
Council for Agricultural Science and Technology
Council for Educational Development and Research
Council for Noncollegiate Continuing Education
Council for Therapeutic Recreation Certification
Council of American Building Officials
Council of Community Blood Centers
Council of Fleet Specialists
Council of Graduate Schools in the U.S.
Council of Industrial Boiler Owners
Council of Mutual Savings Institutions
Council of State Administrators of Vocational Rehabilitation
Council of State Chambers of Commerce
Council of State Community Affairs Agencies
Council of the Great City Schools
Council on Employee Benefits
Council on Postsecondary Accreditation
Criminal Justice Statistics Ass'n
Crop Science Soc. of America
Dance Educators of America
Dance Masters of America
Decision Sciences Institute
Delta Soc.
Delta Theta Phi
Direct Marketing Computer Ass'n
Do-It-Yourself Research Institute
Drug, Chemical and Allied Trades Ass'n
Dry Color Manufacturers Ass'n
Ecological Soc. of America
Educational Film Library Ass'n
Electrical Generating Systems Ass'n
Electronic Industry Show Corporation
Electronic Media Rating Council
Energy Telecommunications and Electrical Ass'n
Engine Manufacturers Ass'n
Environmental Management Ass'n
Evangelical Teacher Training Ass'n
Federated Ambulatory Surgery Ass'n
Federation of American Scientists
Federation of Tax Administrators
Fiberglass Fabrication Ass'n
Financial Management Ass'n
Food and Drug Law Institute
Foodservice Consultants Soc. Internat'l
Forest Farmers Ass'n
Forest History Soc.
Forest Industries Telecommunications
Fragrance Materials Ass'n of the United States
Fusion Power Associates
Gasoline and Automotive Service Dealers Ass'n
Gold Institute
Graphic Artists Guild Nat'l
Graphic Arts Employers of America
Greeting Card Ass'n
Hampshire Swine Registry
Hardwood Manufacturers Ass'n
Harness Horsemen Internat'l
Harness Tracks of America
Hazardous Waste Treatment Council
Hearing Industries Ass'n
History of Science Soc.
Hospital Management Systems Soc.
Hotel and Motel Brokers of America
Household Goods Forwarders Ass'n of America
Human Factors Soc.
Ice Skating Institute of America
In-Plant Management Ass'n
Independent Battery Manufacturers Ass'n
Independent College Funds of America
Independent Electrical Contractors
Independent Liquid Terminals Ass'n
Independent Lubricant Manufacturers Ass'n
Industrial Gas Cleaning Institute
Industrial Safety Equipment Ass'n
Industrial Truck Ass'n

BUDGET INDEX

BUDGET INDEX

Nat'l Kerosene Heater Ass'n
Nat'l Kitchen Cabinet Ass'n
Nat'l Leased Housing Ass'n
Nat'l Licensed Beverage Ass'n
Nat'l Live Stock Producers Ass'n
Nat'l Lumber and Building Material Dealers Ass'n
Nat'l Middle School Ass'n
Nat'l Organization of Industrial Trade Unions
Nat'l Organization on Legal Problems of Education
Nat'l Paralegal Ass'n
Nat'l Passenger Traffic Ass'n
Nat'l Perinatal Ass'n
Nat'l Phlebotomy Ass'n
Nat'l Potato Council
Nat'l Premium Sales Executives
Nat'l Ready Mixed Concrete Ass'n
Nat'l Security Traders Ass'n
Nat'l Shoe Travelers Ass'n
Nat'l Small Shipments Traffic Conference
Nat'l Soccer Coaches Ass'n of America
Nat'l Soc. for Performance and Instruction
Nat'l Soc. of Accountants for Cooperatives
Nat'l Soc. of Patient Representatives
Nat'l Soc. of Sales Training Executives
Nat'l Star Route Mail Contractors Ass'n
Nat'l Sunflower Ass'n
Nat'l Tank Truck Carriers
Nat'l Tax Ass'n-Tax Institute of America
Nat'l Terrazzo and Mosaic Ass'n
Nat'l Trappers Ass'n
Nat'l Unfinished Furniture Institute
Nat'l University Continuing Education Ass'n
Nat'l Waterbed Retailers Ass'n
Nat'l Welding Supply Ass'n
Nat'l Wellness Ass'n
Nat'l Wood Window and Door Ass'n
Nat'l Wooden Pallet and Container Ass'n
Nat'l Wool Growers Ass'n
Nat'l Wool Marketing Corporation
Nat'l Writers Club
Natural Rubber Shippers Ass'n
No-Load Mutual Fund Ass'n
North American Blueberry Council
North American Export Grain Ass'n
North American Transplant Coordinators Organization
Northern Textile Ass'n
Northwest Fruit Exporters
Oil Field Haulers Ass'n
Organization of American Historians
United Methodist Ass'n of Health and Welfare Ministries
United Neighborhood Centers of America
United States Beet Sugar Ass'n
United States Cane Sugar Refiners' Ass'n
United States Operating Committee of ETAD
United States Tour Operators Ass'n
United States Tuna Foundation
Universities Space Research Ass'n
Urban and Regional Information Systems Ass'n
USA Rugby Football Union
Vacuum Dealers Trade Ass'n
Vibration Institute
Videotex Industry Ass'n
Visiting Nurse Ass'ns of America
Wallcovering Distributors Ass'n
Wallcovering Manufacturers Ass'n
Warehousing Education and Research Council
Wedding Photographers Internat'l
Western and English Manufacturers Ass'n
Western Ass'n of Equipment Lessors
Western States Meat Ass'n
Western Timber Ass'n
White House News Photographers Ass'n
Wild Blueberry Ass'n of North America
Wirebound Box Manufacturers Ass'n
Wood Machinery Manufacturers of America
Wood Moulding and Millwork Producers Ass'n
World Waterpark Ass'n
Zonta Internat'l

$100-250,000

Abrasive Engineering Soc.
Academy of Criminal Justice Sciences
Academy of Dentistry Internat'l
Academy of Geriatric Dentistry
Academy of Pharmaceutical Sciences
Accountants for the Public Interest
Adhesives Manufacturers Ass'n
Advertising Typographers Ass'n of America
Aerobics and Fitness Ass'n of America
Affiliated Warehouse Companies
African American Museums Ass'n
African Studies Ass'n
Aftermarket Body Parts Ass'n
Air Freight Ass'n of America
Airport Security Council
Alliance for Engineering in Medicine and Biology
Allied Distribution
Alpha Chi Sigma
Aluminum Recycling Ass'n
Amatex Export Trade Ass'n
American Academy for Cerebral Palsy and Developmental Medicine
American Academy of Ambulatory Nursing Administration
American Academy of Crown and Bridge Prosthodontics
American Academy of Environmental Engineers
American Academy of Implant Dentistry
American Academy of Matrimonial Lawyers
American Academy of Osteopathy
American Academy of Psychoanalysis
American Academy of Religion
American Academy of Thermography
American Alfalfa Processors Ass'n
American Art Therapy Ass'n
American Ass'n for Clinical Immunology and Allergy
American Ass'n for Continuity of Care
American Ass'n for Laboratory Accreditation
American Ass'n for Medical Systems and Informatics
American Ass'n for the Study of Headache
American Ass'n for the Study of Liver Diseases
American Ass'n for Thoracic Surgery
American Ass'n of Attorney-Certified Public Accountants
American Ass'n of Avian Pathologists
American Ass'n of Bible Colleges
American Ass'n of Botanical Gardens and Arboreta
American Ass'n of Certified Appraisers
American Ass'n of Equine Practitioners
American Ass'n of Esthetics
American Ass'n of Hospital Dentists
American Ass'n of Industrial Management
American Ass'n of Medical Soc. Executives
American Ass'n of Medico-Legal Consultants
American Ass'n of Occupational Health Nurses
American Ass'n of Osteopathic Specialists
American Ass'n of Preferred Provider Organizations
American Ass'n of School Librarians
American Ass'n of Senior Physicians
American Ass'n of Swine Practitioners
American Ass'n of Tissue Banks
American Ass'n of Variable Star Observers
American Automatic Control Council
American Bankruptcy Institute
American Baseball Coaches Ass'n
American Berkshire Ass'n
American Blood Commission
American Boat Builders and Repairers Ass'n
American Brush Manufacturers Ass'n
American Buffalo Ass'n
American Cardiology Technologists Ass'n
American Chain Ass'n
American Cleft Palate Ass'n
American Clinical Laboratory Ass'n
American Coke and Coal Chemicals Institute
American College of Apothecaries
American College of Clinical Pharmacology
American College of Clinical Pharmacy
American College of Legal Medicine
American College of Neuropsychopharmacology
American College of Nuclear Physicians
American College of Nutrition
American College of Osteopathic Obstetricians and Gynecologists
American Composers Alliance
American Concrete Pumping Ass'n
American Consultants League
American Copper Council
American Council of Highway Advertisers
American Council on Consumer Interests
American Council on Internat'l Personnel
American Dance Therapy Ass'n
American Dental Soc. of Anesthesiology
American Down Ass'n
American Driver and Traffic Safety Education Ass'n
American Electrology Ass'n
American Endodontic Soc.
American Epilepsy Soc.
American Family Therapy Ass'n
American Fan Ass'n
American Fastener and Closure Ass'n
American Federation of Home Health Agencies
American Finance Ass'n
American Formalwear Ass'n
American Gastroenterological Ass'n
American Group of CPA Firms
American Hampshire Sheep Ass'n
American Holistic Medical Ass'n
American Indian Health Care Ass'n
American Industrial Arts Student Ass'n
American Institute for Design and Drafting
American Institute for Imported Steel
American Institute for Shippers Ass'ns
American-Israel Chamber of Commerce and Industry
American Ladder Institute
American Landrace Ass'n
American Littoral Soc.
American Longevity Ass'n
American Luggage Dealers Ass'n
American Maine-An ou Ass'n
American Maritime Ass'n
American Medical Electroencephalographic Ass'n
American Milking Shorthorn Soc.
American Mosquito Control Ass'n
American Mushroom Institute
American Music Conference
American Musicological Soc.
American Neurological Ass'n
American Ornithologists' Union
American Osteopathic Academy of Sports Medicine
American Osteopathic College of Radiology
American Peanut Research and Education Soc.
American Philological Ass'n
American Philosophical Ass'n
American Pilots' Ass'n
American Pipe Fittings Ass'n
American Powder Metallurgy Institute
American Prosthodontic Soc.
American Pyrotechnics Ass'n
American Rambouillet Sheep Breeders Ass'n
American Red Poll Ass'n
American Registry of Clinical Radiography Technologists
American Schizophrenia Ass'n
American School Counselor Ass'n
American Seafood Retailers Ass'n
American Soc. for Concrete Construction
American Soc. for Dermatologic Surgery
American Soc. for Gastrointestinal Endoscopy
American Soc. for Hospital Materials Management
American Soc. for Laser Medicine and Surgery
American Soc. for Performance Improvement
American Soc. for Photogrammetry and Remote Sensing
American Soc. of Agricultural Consultants
American Soc. of Brewing Chemists
American Soc. of Certified Engineering Technicians
American Soc. of Colon and Rectal Surgeons
American Soc. of Dermatopathology
American Soc. of Electro-Neurodiagnostic Technologists
American Soc. of Home Inspectors
American Soc. of Ichthyologists and Herpetologists
American Soc. of Journalists and Authors
American Soc. of Mammalogists
American Soc. of Military Comptrollers
American Soc. of Outpatient Surgeons
American Soc. of Pharmacognosy
American Soc. of Professional and Executive Women
American Soc. of Professional Estimators
American Soc. of Regional Anesthesia
American Soc. of Transportation and Logistics
American String Teachers Ass'n
American Studies Ass'n
American Sugarbeet Growers Ass'n
American Tinnitus Ass'n
American Train Dispatchers Ass'n
American Trakehner Ass'n
American Trauma Soc.
American Urological Ass'n Allied
American Watch Ass'n
American Woman's Soc. of Certified Public Accountants
American Yarn Spinners Ass'n
Apartment Owners and Managers Ass'n of America
Appalachian Hardwood Manufacturers
Appliance Parts Distributors Ass'n
Appraisers Ass'n of America
Argentina-American Chamber of Commerce
Armed Forces Marketing Council
Art and Craft Materials Institute
Art Dealers Ass'n of America
Art Libraries Soc./North America
ASHBEAMS
Asphalt Emulsion Manufacturers Ass'n
Asphalt Recycling and Reclaiming Ass'n
Asphalt Rubber Producers Group
Associated Air Balance Council
Associated Collegiate Press, Nat'l Scholastic Press Ass'n
Associated Independent Distributors
Associated Wire Rope Fabricators
Associated Writing Programs
Ass'n for Behavior Analysis
Ass'n for Business Communication
Ass'n for Canadian Studies in the United States
Ass'n for Commuter Transportation
Ass'n for Experiential Education
Ass'n for Finishing Processes
Ass'n for Gerontology in Higher Education
Ass'n for Hospital Medical Education
Ass'n for Institutional Research
Ass'n for Library Service to Children
Ass'n for Persons with Severe Handicaps
Ass'n for School, College and University Staffing
Ass'n for Symbolic Logic
Ass'n for the Advancement of International Education
Ass'n for the Advancement of Psychotherapy
Ass'n for the Development of Computer-Based Instructional Systems
Ass'n for the Study of Afro-American Life and History
Ass'n of Accounting Administrators
Ass'n of Advanced Rabbinical and Talmudic Schools
Ass'n of American Physicians and Surgeons
Ass'n of American University Presses
Ass'n of American Veterinary Medical Colleges

BUDGET INDEX

Ass'n of Area Business Publications
Ass'n of Biotechnology Companies
Ass'n of Bituminous Contractors
Ass'n of College and University Auditors
Ass'n of College and University Housing Officers-Internat'l
Ass'n of Commercial Mail Receiving Agencies
Ass'n of Community Cancer Centers
Ass'n of Credit Union League Executives
Ass'n of Diesel Specialists
Ass'n of Diving Contractors
Ass'n of Drilled Shaft Contractors
Ass'n of Edison Illuminating Companies
Ass'n of Engineering Geologists
Ass'n of Episcopal Colleges
Ass'n of Film Commissioners
Ass'n of Independent Video and Filmmakers
Ass'n of Industrial Metallizers, Coaters and Laminators
Ass'n of Information Managers Financial Institutions
Ass'n of Internat'l Photography Art Dealers
Ass'n of Jesuit Colleges and Universities
Ass'n of Jewish Family and Children's Agencies
Ass'n of Local Air Pollution Control Officials
Ass'n of Mental Health Administrators
Ass'n of Newspaper Classified Advertising Managers
Ass'n of North American Directory Publishers
Ass'n of Operative Millers
Ass'n of Professional Color Laboratories
Ass'n of Professional Design Firms
Ass'n of Professional Directors of YMCAs in the United States
Ass'n of Professional Vocal Ensembles
Ass'n of Professors of Gynecology and Obstetrics
Ass'n of Program Directors in Internal Medicine
Ass'n of Reproduction Materials Manufacturers
Ass'n of Retail Marketing Services
Ass'n of Retail Travel Agents
Ass'n of Schools and Colleges of Optometry
Ass'n of Ship Brokers and Agents (U.S.A.)
Ass'n of Sleep Disorders Centers
Ass'n of Small Business Development Centers
Ass'n of Soil and Foundation Engineers
Ass'n of State and Interstate Water Pollution Control Administrators
Ass'n of State Correctional Administrators
Ass'n of State Drinking Water Administrators
Ass'n of Systematics Collections
Ass'n of Teacher Educators
Ass'n of Tequila Producers
Ass'n of United States Night Vision Manufacturers
Ass'n on Handicapped Student Service Programs in Postsecondary Education
Auto Internacional Ass'n
Autoleather Guild
Automated Vision Ass'n
Automotive Affiliated Representatives
Automotive Engine Rebuilders Ass'n
Automotive Information Council
Aviation/Space Writers Ass'n
Ayrshire Breeders Ass'n
Barre Granite Ass'n
Battery Council Internat'l
Bearing Specialist Ass'n
Belgian Draft Horse Corp. of America
Better Vision Institute
Bibliographical Soc. of America
Billiard Congress of America
Biofeedback Soc. of America
Biological Photographic Ass'n
Boarding Schools
Book Industry Study Group
Book Manufacturers Institute
Botanical Soc. of America
Boxboard Research and Development Ass'n
Brazilian American Chamber of Commerce
Brewers Ass'n of America
British-American Chamber of Commerce
Burley and Dark Leaf Tobacco Export Ass'n
Business Planning Board
Cadmium Council
Callerlab-Internat'l Ass'n of Square Dance Callers
Car Audio Specialists Ass'n
Car Care Council
Career Apparel Institute
Carpet Cushion Council
Casket Manufacturers Ass'n of America
Cast Metals Ass'n
Catholic Biblical Ass'n of America
Catholic Campus Ministry Ass'n
Catholic Library Ass'n
Catholic Press Ass'n
Cement Employers Ass'n
Ceramic Tile Marketing Federation
Chain Link Fence Manufacturers Institute
Chemical Coaters Ass'n
Chief Petty Officers Ass'n
Chlorobenzene Producers Ass'n
Chocolate Manufacturers Ass'n of the U.S.A.
Christian College Consortium
City and Regional Magazine Ass'n
Clay Minerals Soc.
Clothing Manufacturers Ass'n of the U.S.A.
Coalition for Common Sense in Government Procurement
Cold Finished Steel Bar Institute
College Music Soc.
College of Optometrists in Vision Development
College of Osteopathic Healthcare Executives
Commercial Development Ass'n
Commission on Professionals in Science and Technology
Composite Can and Tube Institute
Conference Board of Ma or Printers
Conference of Actuaries in Public Practice
Conference of Casualty Insurance Companies
Conference of Ma or Superiors of Men, U.S.A.
Conference on College Composition and Communication
Congress of Lung Ass'n Staff
Construction Management Ass'n of America
Contact Lens Manufacturers Ass'n
Contact Lens Soc. of America
Controllers Council
Convention Liaison Council
Conveyor Equipment Manufacturers Ass'n
Copper and Brass Servicenter Ass'n
Cosmetic Executive Women
Cotton Warehouse Ass'n of America
Council for American Private Education
Council for European Studies
Council for Religion in Independent Schools
Council of American Survey Research Organizations
Council of Biology Editors
Council of Educational Facility Planners, Internat'l
Council of Landscape Architectural Registration Boards
Council of Planning Librarians
Council of Pollution Control Financing Agencies
Council of Sales Promotion Agencies
Council on Diagnostic Imaging to the A.C.A.
Council on Hotel, Restaurant and Institutional Education
Credit Women-Internat'l
Cremation Ass'n of North America
Crop Insurance Research Bureau
Cycle Parts and Accessories Ass'n
Decorative Laminate Products Ass'n
Delta Pi Epsilon
Delta Sigma Delta
Dental Gold Institute
Dental Laboratory Conference
Dental Manufacturers of America
Diamond Trade Ass'n of America
Die Casting Research Foundation
Diplomatic and Consular Officers, Retired
Distillers Feed Research Council
Distribution Contractors Ass'n
Door and Operator Dealers
Ductile Iron Soc.
Econometric Soc.
Egyptian-American Chamber of Commerce
Eight Sheet Outdoor Advertising Ass'n
Electromagnetic Energy Policy Alliance
Electron Microscopy Soc. of America
Energy Consumers and Producers Ass'n
Equipment and Tool Institute
Evangelical Christian Publishers Ass'n
Expanded Shale, Clay and Slate Institute
Exterior Insulation Manufacturers Ass'n
Eye Bank Ass'n of America
Farm Equipment Wholesalers Ass'n
Federal Energy Bar Ass'n
Federal Law Enforcement Officers Ass'n
Federally Employed Women
Federation of Analytical Chemistry and Spectroscopy Societies
Federation of Prosthodontic Organizations
Ferroalloys Ass'n
Film, Air and Package Carriers Conference
Fine Hardwoods-American Walnut Ass'n
Fire Equipment Manufacturers' Ass'n
Fire Suppression Systems Ass'n
Flat Glass Marketing Ass'n
Flexicore Manufacturers Ass'n
Flight Engineers' Internat'l Ass'n
Fluid Power Distributors Ass'n
Fluid Power Soc.
Foodservice and Lodging Institute
Foodservice Equipment Distributors Ass'n
Fragrance Foundation
Freight Forwarders Institute
Friction Materials Standards Institute
Furniture Rental Ass'n of America
Gas Processors Suppliers Ass'n
Gold Filled Ass'n
Golf Course Ass'n
Graphic Arts Equipment and Supply Dealers Ass'n
Greater Clothing Contractors Ass'n
Grinding Wheel Institute
Gummed Industries Ass'n
Gyro Internat'l
Hand Tools Institute
Health Industry Representatives Ass'n
Health Physics Soc.
Health Sciences Communications Ass'n
Healthcare Internal Audit Group
High Speed Rail Ass'n
Home Economists in Business
Hydraulic Institute
Incentive Manufacturers Representatives Ass'n
Independent Automotive Damage Appraisers Ass'n
Independent Bakers Ass'n
Independent Cash Register Dealers Ass'n
Independent Computer Consultants Ass'n
Independent Gasoline Marketers Council
Independent Sewing Machine Dealers Ass'n
Indiana Limestone Institute of America
Industrial Ass'n of Juvenile Apparel Manufacturers
Industrial Heating Equipment Ass'n
Institute for Alternative Agriculture
Institute for Fermentation and Brewing Studies
Institute for Polyacrylate Absorbents
Institute of Business Appraisers
Institute of Mathematical Statistics
Institute of Navigation
Institute of Noise Control Engineering
Institute of Shortening and Edible Oils
Institute of Store Planners
Insurance Economics Soc. of America
Insurance Marketing Communications Ass'n
Inter-American Bar Ass'n
Intercollegiate Broadcasting System
Interior Design Soc.
Internat'l Academy of Preventive Medicine
Internat'l Academy of Trial Lawyers
Internat'l Agricultural Aviation Foundation
Internat'l Ass'n for Dental Research
Internat'l Ass'n for Hospital Security
Internat'l Ass'n for Personnel Women
Internat'l Ass'n of Airport Duty Free Stores
Internat'l Ass'n of Arson Investigators
Internat'l Ass'n of Bomb Technicians and Investigators
Internat'l Ass'n of Campus Law Enforcement Administrators
Internat'l Ass'n of Clothing Designers
Internat'l Ass'n of Conference Centers
Internat'l Ass'n of Energy Economists
Internat'l Ass'n of Fish and Wildlife Agencies
Internat'l Ass'n of Geophysical Contractors
Internat'l Ass'n of Industrial Accident Boards and Commissions
Internat'l Ass'n of Lighting Designers
Internat'l Ass'n of Printing House Craftsmen
Internat'l Ass'n of Security Services
Internat'l Ass'n of Tour Managers - North American Region
Internat'l Ass'n of Wiping Cloth Manufacturers
Internat'l Brotherhood of Magicians
Internat'l Cogeneration Soc.
Internat'l Communication Ass'n
Internat'l Concatenated Order of Hoo-Hoo
Internat'l Council of Airshows
Internat'l Customer Service Ass'n
Internat'l District Heating and Cooling Ass'n
Internat'l Drapery Ass'n
Internat'l Electrical Testing Ass'n
Internat'l Electronic Packaging Soc.
Internat'l Embryo Transfer Soc.
Internat'l Exchangors Ass'n
Internat'l Festivals Ass'n
Internat'l Food Service Executives' Ass'n
Internat'l Foodservice Distributors Ass'n
Internat'l Hardwood Products Ass'n
Internat'l Home Furnishings Representatives Ass'n
Internat'l Insurance Advisory Council
Internat'l Intelligent Buildings Ass'n
Internat'l Labor Communications Ass'n
Internat'l Management Council
Internat'l Microwave Power Institute
Internat'l Mobile Air Conditioning Ass'n
Internat'l Municipal Signal Ass'n
Internat'l Narcotic Enforcement Officers Ass'n
Internat'l Piano Guild
Internat'l Reciprocal Trade Ass'n
Internat'l Silo Ass'n
Internat'l Slurry Seal Ass'n
Internat'l Soc. for Artificial Organs
Internat'l Soc. for Clinical Laboratory Technology
Internat'l Soc. for General Semantics
Internat'l Soc. for Heart Transplantation
Internat'l Soc. for Medical and Psychological Hypnosis
Internat'l Soc. of Appraisers
Internat'l Soc. of Barristers
Internat'l Soc. of Certified Electronics Technicians
Internat'l Soc. of Industrial Fabric Manufacturers
Internat'l Soc. of Interior Designers
Internat'l Soc. of Parametric Analysts
Internat'l Soc. of the Knee
Internat'l Soc. of Weighing and Measurement
Internat'l Studies Ass'n
Internat'l Technical Caramel Ass'n
Internat'l Teleconferencing Ass'n
Internat'l Teleproduction Soc.
Internat'l Union of Life Insurance Agents
Internat'l Women's Writing Guild
Investment Casting Institute
Jewelers Vigilance Committee
Jewelry Industry Council
Jewish Funeral Directors of America
Joint Council of Allergy and Immunology
Joint Electron Device Engineering Council
Justice System Training Ass'n
Jute Carpet Backing Council
Knitted Textile Ass'n
Ladies Apparel Contractors Ass'n
Land Mobile Communications Council
Land Trust Exchange
Latin American Studies Ass'n
Leaf Tobacco Exporters Ass'n
League for Innovation in the Community College
League of Federal Recreation Ass'ns
Library Administration and Management Ass'n
Library Binding Institute
Licensing Executives Soc.

The information in this directory is available in *Mailing List* form. See back insert.

00010

BUDGET INDEX

Life Insurers Conference
Lightning Protection Institute
Livestock Conservation Institute
Lutheran Educational Conference of North America
Magazine and Paperback Marketing Institute
Mailing List Users and Suppliers Ass'n
Manufacturers Representatives of America
Manufacturers Standardization Soc. of the Valve and Fittings Industry
Maple Flooring Manufacturers Ass'n
Marine Corps Reserve Officers Ass'n
Marine Retailers Ass'n of America
Maritime Law Ass'n of the U.S.
Marketing Agents for Food Service Industry
Marking Device Ass'n
Meat Industry Suppliers Ass'n
Medical-Dental-Hospital Bureaus of America
Medieval Academy of America
Metal Building Manufacturers Ass'n
Metal Cutting Tool Institute
Metal Finishing Suppliers Ass'n
Metal Treating Institute
Military Operations Research Soc.
Miniatures Industry Ass'n of America
Mu Phi Epsilon
Multi-Housing Laundry Ass'n
Municipal Treasurers Ass'n of the United States and Canada
Museum Store Ass'n
Nat'l Academy of Arbitrators
Nat'l Account Marketing Ass'n
Nat'l Alliance of Black School Educators
Nat'l Appliance Parts Suppliers Ass'n
Nat'l Artists Equity Ass'n
Nat'l Assembly of Nat'l Voluntary Health and Social Welfare Organizations
Nat'l Ass'n For Ambulatory Care
Nat'l Ass'n for Child Care Management
Nat'l Ass'n for Health Care Recruitment
Nat'l Ass'n for Individually Guided Education
Nat'l Ass'n for Music Therapy
Nat'l Ass'n for Professional Saleswomen
Nat'l Ass'n for Search and Rescue
Nat'l Ass'n for Sport and Physical Education
Nat'l Ass'n for State Information Systems
Nat'l Ass'n for the Cottage Industry
Nat'l Ass'n for Women Deans, Administrators, and Counselors
Nat'l Ass'n of Advisors for the Health Professions
Nat'l Ass'n of Architectural Metal Manufacturers
Nat'l Ass'n of ASCS County Office Employees
Nat'l Ass'n of Auto Trim Shops
Nat'l Ass'n of Bank Servicers
Nat'l Ass'n of Basketball Coaches of the United States
Nat'l Ass'n of Black Women Entrepreneurs
Nat'l Ass'n of Boards of Examiners of Nursing Home Administrators
Nat'l Ass'n of Boat Manufacturers
Nat'l Ass'n of Business Political Action Committees
Nat'l Ass'n of Catering Executives
Nat'l Ass'n of Chewing Gum Manufacturers
Nat'l Ass'n of Church Business Administration
Nat'l Ass'n of Church Personnel Administrators
Nat'l Ass'n of Collegiate Directors of Athletics
Nat'l Ass'n of Community Action Agencies
Nat'l Ass'n of Corporate and Professional Recruiters
Nat'l Ass'n of County Community Development Directors
Nat'l Ass'n of County Health Officials
Nat'l Ass'n of Decorative Fabric Distributors
Nat'l Ass'n of Demolition Contractors
Nat'l Ass'n of Development Companies
Nat'l Ass'n of Developmental Disabilities Councils
Nat'l Ass'n of Diemakers and Diecutters
Nat'l Ass'n of Dredging Contractors
Nat'l Ass'n of Elevator Contractors
Nat'l Ass'n of Emergency Medical Technicians
Nat'l Ass'n of Episcopal Schools
Nat'l Ass'n of Extension 4-H Agents
Nat'l Ass'n of Federal Veterinarians
Nat'l Ass'n of Federally Impacted Schools
Nat'l Ass'n of Foreign-Trade Zones
Nat'l Ass'n of Futures Trading Advisors
Nat'l Ass'n of Garage Door Manufacturers
Nat'l Ass'n of Governors' Highway Safety Representatives
Nat'l Ass'n of Hospital Admitting Managers
Nat'l Ass'n of Housing Cooperatives
Nat'l Ass'n of Independent Insurance Ad usters
Nat'l Ass'n of Institutional Linen Management
Nat'l Ass'n of Jewelry Appraisers
Nat'l Ass'n of Jewish Vocational Services
Nat'l Ass'n of Legal Assistants
Nat'l Ass'n of Marine Products and Services
Nat'l Ass'n of Marine Surveyors
Nat'l Ass'n of Membership Directors of Chambers of Commerce
Nat'l Ass'n of Metal Finishers
Nat'l Ass'n of Mirror Manufacturers
Nat'l Ass'n of Mortgage Brokers
Nat'l Ass'n of Pattern Manufacturers
Nat'l Ass'n of Physician Nurses
Nat'l Ass'n of Pipe Coating Applicators
Nat'l Ass'n of Power Engineers
Nat'l Ass'n of Private Industry Councils
Nat'l Ass'n of Private Residential Facilities for the Mentally Retarded
Nat'l Ass'n of Private Schools for Exceptional Children
Nat'l Ass'n of Radio and Telecommunications Engineers
Nat'l Ass'n of Railroad Trial Counsel
Nat'l Ass'n of Real Estate Brokers
Nat'l Ass'n of Royalty Owners
Nat'l Ass'n of Schools of Art and Design
Nat'l Ass'n of Schools of Public Affairs and Administration
Nat'l Ass'n of Secretarial Services
Nat'l Ass'n of Service Managers
Nat'l Ass'n of Solvent Recyclers
Nat'l Ass'n of State and Provincial Lotteries
Nat'l Ass'n of State Racing Commissioners
Nat'l Ass'n of Store Fixture Manufacturers
Nat'l Ass'n of Student Financial Aid Administrators
Nat'l Ass'n of Swine Records
Nat'l Ass'n of Tax Consultors
Nat'l Ass'n of Treasurers of Religious Institutes
Nat'l Ass'n of Video Distributors
Nat'l Ass'n of Women Business Owners
Nat'l Ass'n of Women Highway Safety Leaders
Nat'l Ass'n of Writing Instrument Distributors
Nat'l Auto Auction Ass'n
Nat'l Barrel and Drum Ass'n
Nat'l Beverage Dispensing Equipment Ass'n
Nat'l Black Caucus of State Legislators
Nat'l Black Nurses Ass'n
Nat'l Border Patrol Council
Nat'l Buffalo Ass'n
Nat'l Campground Owners Ass'n
Nat'l Career Development Ass'n
Nat'l Caterers Ass'n
Nat'l Certified Pipe Welding Bureau
Nat'l Chemical Credit Ass'n
Nat'l Child Support Enforcement Ass'n
Nat'l Chimney Sweep Guild
Nat'l Classification Management Soc.
Nat'l Clay Pipe Institute
Nat'l Clearinghouse on Licensure, Enforcement and Regulation
Nat'l Committee for Motor Fleet Supervisor Training
Nat'l Conference of Standards Laboratories
Nat'l Conference of State Historic Preservation Officers
Nat'l Conference on Public Employee Retirement Systems
Nat'l Constables Ass'n
Nat'l Construction Industry Council
Nat'l Consumers League
Nat'l Coordinating Council on Emergency Management
Nat'l Council of Agricultural Employers
Nat'l Council of Real Estate Investment Fiduciaries
Nat'l Council of Social Security Management Ass'ns
Nat'l Council on Measurement in Education
Nat'l Dental Ass'n
Nat'l Dimension Manufacturers Ass'n
Nat'l Environmental Balancing Bureau
Nat'l Estimating Soc.
Nat'l Family Business Council
Nat'l Fastener Distributors Ass'n
Nat'l Federation of Modern Language Teachers Ass'ns
Nat'l Federation of Music Clubs
Nat'l Federation of Paralegal Ass'ns
Nat'l Federation of Press Women
Nat'l Federation of Priests' Councils
Nat'l Fenestration Council
Nat'l Food and Energy Council
Nat'l Frame Builders Ass'n
Nat'l Freight Claim and Security Council of the American Trucking Ass'ns
Nat'l Freight Transportation Ass'n
Nat'l Funeral Directors and Morticians Ass'n
Nat'l Guild of Community Schools of the Arts
Nat'l Handbag Ass'n/Nat'l Fashion Accessories Ass'n
Nat'l Ice Cream Retailers Ass'n
Nat'l Independent Bank Equipment and Systems Ass'n
Nat'l Independent Dairy-Foods Ass'n
Nat'l Institute of Certified Moving Consultants
Nat'l Institute of Pension Administrators
Nat'l Intercollegiate Soccer Officials Ass'n
Nat'l Interfraternity Conference
Nat'l Juice Products Ass'n
Nat'l Knitwear and Sportswear Ass'n
Nat'l Knitwear Manufacturers Ass'n
Nat'l Lawyers Guild
Nat'l League of American Pen Women
Nat'l Liquor Stores Ass'n
Nat'l Locksmith Suppliers Ass'n
Nat'l Lubricating Grease Institute
Nat'l Manufactured Housing Federation
Nat'l Marine Distributors Ass'n
Nat'l Minority Supplier Development Council
Nat'l Needlework Ass'n
Nat'l Onion Ass'n
Nat'l Ornamental and Miscellaneous Metals Ass'n
Nat'l Paint Distributors
Nat'l Peach Council
Nat'l Police Officers Ass'n of America
Nat'l Precast Concrete Ass'n
Nat'l Railroad Construction and Maintenance Ass'n
Nat'l Rehabilitation Counseling Ass'n
Nat'l Safe Transit Ass'n
Nat'l Satellite Cable Ass'n
Nat'l School Transportation Ass'n
Nat'l Sculpture Soc.
Nat'l Second Mortgage Ass'n
Nat'l Slag Ass'n
Nat'l Soc. for Cardiovascular and Pulmonary Technology
Nat'l Soc. for the Study of Education
Nat'l Sound and Communications Ass'n
Nat'l Spotted Swine Record
Nat'l Steel Carriers Ass'n
Nat'l Student Speech Language Hearing Ass'n
Nat'l Suffolk Sheep Ass'n
Nat'l Supply Distributors Ass'n
Nat'l Tay-Sachs and Allied Diseases Ass'n
Nat'l Technical Services Ass'n
Nat'l Translator Ass'n
Nat'l Vocational Agricultural Teachers Ass'n
Nat'l Water Resources Ass'n
Nat'l Waterways Conference
Nat'l Wheel and Rim Ass'n
Nat'l Wine Distributors Ass'n
Nat'l Wood Energy Ass'n
Neckwear Ass'n of America
Nitrogen Tree Fixing Ass'n
Non-Ferrous Founders' Soc.
Non-Heatset Web Unit
Nonprofit Mailers Federation
North American District Heating and Cooling Institute
North American Students of Cooperation
Northeastern Lumber Manufacturers Ass'n
Office Automation Soc. Internat'l
Offshore Marine Service Ass'n
Oil Investment Institute
Organization of Manufacturers Representatives
Organization of Professional Employees of the U.S. Department of Agriculture
Orthopaedic Research Soc.
Outdoor Amusement Business Ass'n
Outdoor Power Equipment Aftermarket Ass'n
Outdoor Writers Ass'n of America
Oxygenated Fuels Ass'n
Paleontological Research Institution
Paper Bag Institute
Passive Solar Industries Council
Pathology Practice Ass'n
Peanut Butter and Nut Processors Ass'n
Pencil Makers Ass'n
Percussive Arts Soc.
Perennial Plant Ass'n
Phobia Soc. of America
Phycological Soc. of America
Piano Manufacturers Ass'n Internat'l
Pickle Packers Internat'l
Plastic and Metal Products Manufacturers Ass'n
Plastics Pipe Institute
Plumbing Manufacturers Institute
Poetry Soc. of America
Poland China Record Ass'n
Popcorn Institute
Population Ass'n of America
Portable Sanitation Ass'n Internat'l
Portugal-U.S. States Chamber of Commerce
Poultry Science Ass'n
Powder Coating Institute
Power and Communication Contractors Ass'n
Power Tool Institute
Pressure Sensitive Tape Council
Printing Brokerage Ass'n
Process Equipment Manufacturers' Ass'n
Professional Archers Ass'n
Professional Audio-Video Retailers Ass'n
Professional Aviation Maintenance Ass'n
Professional Grounds Management Soc.
Professional Numismatists Guild
Professional Tennis Registry, USA
Psi Omega
Psychonomic Soc.
Public Housing Authorities Directors Ass'n
Public Interest Computer Ass'n
Pulp Chemicals Ass'n
Radiologists' Business Managers Ass'n
Railway Engineering-Maintenance Suppliers Ass'n
Railway Systems Suppliers
Recognition Technologies Users Ass'n
Religious Conference Management Ass'n
Religious Education Ass'n
Renewable Fuels Ass'n
Research and Development Associates for Military Food and Packaging Systems
Resilient Floor Covering Institute
Resistance Welder Manufacturers Ass'n
RESNA, Ass'n for the Advancement of Rehabilitation Technology
Reticuloendothelial Soc.
Rural Sociological Soc.
Sacro-Occipital Research Soc. Internat'l
SAFE Ass'n
Safety Equipment Distributors Ass'n
Scale Manufacturers Ass'n
Schiffli Lace and Embroidery Manufacturers Ass'n
School Science and Mathematics Ass'n
Sealant and Waterproofers Institute
Sealed Insulating Glass Manufacturers Ass'n
Seaplane Pilots Ass'n
Seismological Soc. of America
Silver Users Ass'n
Single Ply Roofing Institute
Small Business Legislative Council
Soc. for Adolescent Medicine
Soc. for Advancement of Management
Soc. for Applied Anthropology
Soc. for Clinical and Experimental Hypnosis
Soc. for Clinical Vascular Surgery
Soc. for College and University Planning

BUDGET INDEX

Soc. for Computer Applications in Engineering, Planning and Architecture
Soc. for Foodservice Management
Soc. for Humanistic Judaism
Soc. for Information Management
Soc. for Investigative Dermatology
Soc. for Pediatric Research
Soc. for Scholarly Publishing
Soc. for the Advancement of Education
Soc. for the Psychological Study of Social Issues
Soc. for the Scientific Study of Sex
Soc. for the Study of Social Problems
Soc. for Values in Higher Education
Soc. of American Magicians
Soc. of American Registered Architects
Soc. of American Travel Writers
Soc. of American Value Engineers
Soc. of Architectural Historians
Soc. of Behavioral Medicine
Soc. of Collision Repair Specialists
Soc. of Experimental Test Pilots
Soc. of Financial Examiners
Soc. of Former Special Agents of the Federal Bureau of Investigation
Soc. of Glass and Ceramic Decorators
Soc. of Nat'l Ass'n Publications
Soc. of North American Goldsmiths
Soc. of Professionals in Dispute Resolution
Soc. of Publication Designers
Soc. of Research Administrators
Soc. of Wine Educators
Southern Labor Union
Soy Protein Council
Spain-U.S. Chamber of Commerce
Special Interest Group on Ada Programming Language
Special Interest Group on Artificial Intelligence
Special Interest Group on Business Data Processing and Management
Special Interest Group on Design Automation
Spill Control Ass'n of America
Sporting Arms and Ammunition Manufacturers' Institute
Sportswear Apparel Ass'n
Spring Service Ass'n
State and Territorial Air Pollution Program Administrators
Statistical Paper Group
Steel Plate Fabricators Ass'n
Stock Transfer Ass'n
Suburban Newspapers of America
Tag and Label Manufacturers Institute
Technical Marketing Soc. of America
Textile Care Allied Trades Ass'n
Tile Contractors' Ass'n of America
Tire and Rim Ass'n
Tire Retread Information Bureau
Tobacco Ass'n of the U.S.
Tobacco Growers' Information Committee
Trade Show Bureau
Transit Advertising Ass'n
Transportation Lawyers Ass'n
Transworld Advertising Agency Network
Travel Agents Computer Soc.
Travel and Tourism Research Ass'n
Tuna Research Foundation
Underground Contractors Association
Union for Radical Political Economics
United Infants and Childrens Wear Ass'n
United Professional Horsemen's Ass'n
United States Hide, Skin and Leather Ass'n
United States Institute for Theatre Technology
United States Tennis Court and Track Builders Ass'n
United States-Yugoslav Economic Council
University Ass'n for Emergency Medicine
University Council for Educational Administration
University Resident Theatre Ass'n
Vision Service Plan
Walking Horse Owners Ass'n of America
Warehouse Distributors Ass'n for Leisure and Mobile Products
Water and Wastewater Equipment Manufacturers Ass'n
Water Systems Council
Water Transport Ass'n
Weed Science Soc. of America
Welded Steel Tube Institute
Western Red Cedar Lumber Ass'n
Western World Pet Supply Ass'n
Wire Reinforcement Institute
Women in Government Relations
Women Life Underwriters Conference
Wood Products Manufacturers Ass'n
Wood Truss Council of America
Woodworking Machinery Importers Ass'n of America
Woolknit Associates
Work Glove Manufacturers Ass'n
World Ass'n of Document Examiners
World Professional Squash Ass'n
Writing Instrument Manufacturers Ass'n
Xi Psi Phi

$50-100,000

Academy of Dispensing Audiologists
Academy of Internat'l Business
Academy of Marketing Science
Academy of Operative Dentistry
Academy of Psychosomatic Medicine
Acrylonitrile Group
Adult Film Ass'n of America
Agricultural and Industrial Manufacturers' Representatives Ass'n
Agricultural Publishers Ass'n
Agricultural Research Institute
Air and Expedited Motor Carriers Conference
Airborne Law Enforcement Ass'n
Airport Ground Transportation Ass'n
Alliance of Metalworking Industries
Alternative Living Managers Ass'n
Ambulatory Pediatric Ass'n
American Academy of Craniomandibular Disorders
American Academy of Dental Practice Administration
American Academy of Esthetic Dentistry
American Academy of Gnathologic Orthopedics
American Academy of Oral Medicine
American Academy of Podiatric Sports Medicine
American Ass'n for Affirmative Action
American Ass'n for Partial Hospitalization
American Ass'n for Pediatric Ophthalmology and Strabismus
American Ass'n for Public Opinion Research
American Ass'n for Textile Technology
American Ass'n for the History of Medicine
American Ass'n of Anatomists
American Ass'n of Biofeedback Clinicians
American Ass'n of Black Women Entrepreneurs
American Ass'n of Children's Residential Centers
American Ass'n of Clinical Urologists
American Ass'n of Dental Examiners
American Ass'n of Orthopaedic Medicine
American Ass'n of Owners and Breeders of Peruvian Paso Horses
American Ass'n of Plastic Surgeons
American Ass'n of Poison Control Centers
American Ass'n of Political Consultants
American Ass'n of Professional Hypnotherapists
American Ass'n of Psychiatric Services for Children
American Ass'n of School Personnel Administrators
American Ass'n of Small Cities
American Ass'n of Small Research Companies
American Ass'n of Suicidology
American Ass'n of University Administrators
American Ass'n of Veterinary Laboratory Diagnosticians
American Beefalo World Registry
American Beekeeping Federation
American Catholic Philosophical Ass'n
American Choral Foundation
American College of Healthcare Marketing
American College of Internat'l Physicians
American College of Laboratory Animal Medicine
American College of Medical Group Administrators
American College of Osteopathic Pediatricians
American College of Physician Executives
American College of Prosthodontists
American College of Toxicology
American College of Veterinary Pathologists
American Commercial Collectors Ass'n
American Corn Millers Federation
American Correctional Health Services Ass'n
American Cultured Dairy Products Institute
American Cutlery Manufacturers Ass'n
American Deafness and Rehabilitation Ass'n
American Engineering Model Soc.
American Ethnological Soc.
American Farriers Ass'n
American Fur Merchant's Ass'n
American Gynecological and Obstetrical Soc.
American Hackney Horse Soc.
American Hanoverian Soc.
American Heartworm Soc.
American Holistic Nurses' Ass'n
American Innerspring Manufacturers
American Institute of Building Design
American Institute of Hydrology
American Institute of Parliamentarians
American Institute of Reciprocators
American Institute of the History of Pharmacy
American Jail Ass'n
American Judges Ass'n
American Laminators Ass'n
American League of Lobbyists
American Leather Chemists Ass'n
American Literary Translators Ass'n
American Massage Therapy Ass'n
American Naprapathic Ass'n
American Oriental Soc.
American Orthopaedic Soc. for Sports Medicine
American Package Express Carriers Ass'n
American Pain Soc.
American Pinzgauer Ass'n
American Polygraph Ass'n
American Radium Soc.
American Railway Car Institute
American Recreational Equipment Ass'n
American Registry of Certified Professionals in Agronomy, Crops and Soils
American Registry of Professional Entomologists
American Risk and Insurance Ass'n
American Roentgen Ray Soc.
American Safe Deposit Ass'n, The
American Scientific Glassblowers Soc.
American Seat Belt Council
American Shetland Pony Club
American Shrimp Processors Ass'n
American Soc. for Head and Neck Surgery
American Soc. for Mass Spectrometry
American Soc. for Photobiology
American Soc. for Therapeutic Radiology and Oncology
American Soc. of Artists
American Soc. of Church History
American Soc. of Criminology
American Soc. of Echocardiography
American Soc. of Electroplated Plastics
American Soc. of Hand Therapists
American Soc. of Nephrology
American Soc. of Ophthalmic Registered Nurses
American Soc. of Parasitologists
American Soc. of Sanitary Engineering
American Soc. of Women Accountants
American Spinal In ury Ass'n
American Sportscasters Ass'n
American Surety Ass'n
American Tarentaise Ass'n
American Turpentine Farmers Ass'n Co-op
American Underground-Space Ass'n
American Waterways Shipyard Conference
American Window Coverings Manufacturers Ass'n
American Wire Producers Ass'n
American Wood-Preservers' Ass'n
Animal Behavior Soc.
Archery Manufacturers Organization
Associated Actors and Artistes of America
Associated Church Press
Associated Corset and Brassiere Manufacturers Ass'n
Associated Funeral Directors Service
Associated Information Managers
Associated Specialty Contractors
Ass'n for Academic Surgery
Ass'n for Broadcast Engineering Standards
Ass'n for Computational Linguistics
Ass'n for Continuing Higher Education
Ass'n for Counselor Education and Supervision
Ass'n for Library and Information Science Education
Ass'n for Tropical Biology
Ass'n for Unmanned Vehicle Systems
Ass'n for Women Geoscientists
Ass'n for Women in Science
Ass'n of Academic Physiatrists
Ass'n of Art Museum Directors
Ass'n of Asphalt Paving Technologists
Ass'n of Black Psychologists
Ass'n of Collegiate Schools of Planning
Ass'n of Commercial Records Centers
Ass'n of Cosmetologists and Hairdressers
Ass'n of Crafts and Creative Industries
Ass'n of Family and Conciliation Courts
Ass'n of Food and Drug Officials
Ass'n of Former Intelligence Officers
Ass'n of Independent Camps
Ass'n of Independent Commercial Producers
Ass'n of Independent Mailing Equipment Dealers
Ass'n of Independent Microdealers
Ass'n of Industrial Manufacturers' Representatives
Ass'n of Internal Management Consultants
Ass'n of Interpretive Naturalists
Ass'n of Jewish Center Workers
Ass'n of Muslim Scientists and Engineers
Ass'n of North American Missions
Ass'n of Outplacement Consulting Firms
Ass'n of Part-Time Professionals
Ass'n of Pathology Chairmen
Ass'n of Petroleum Re-refiners
Ass'n of Physician Assistant Programs
Ass'n of Political Risk Analysts
Ass'n of Professors of Medicine
Ass'n of Racquetsports Manufacturers and Suppliers
Ass'n of Schools of Journalism and Mass Communication
Ass'n of Specialized and Cooperative Library Agencies
Ass'n of State and Territorial Health Officials
Ass'n of Teachers of Latin American Studies
Audio Visual Management Ass'n
Automotive Booster Clubs Internat'l
Automotive Fleet and Leasing Ass'n
Automotive Products Export Council
Automotive Trade Ass'n Executives
Aviation Crime Prevention Institute
Aviation Distributors and Manufacturers Ass'n Internat'l
Bakery Equipment Manufacturers Ass'n
Belt Ass'n
Better Lawn and Turf Institute
Bicycle Wholesale Distributors Ass'n

BUDGET INDEX

Billiard and Bowling Institute of America
Biological Stain Commission
Biometric Soc. (ENAR)
Biscuit and Cracker Distributors Ass'n
Black Music Ass'n
Bright Belt Warehouse Ass'n
Broadcast Education Ass'n
Brotherhood of Shoe and Allied Craftsmen
Bumper Recycling Ass'n of North America
Canon Law Soc. of America
Cantors Assembly
Captive Insurance Companies Ass'n
Carpet Manufacturers Marketing Ass'n
Casting Industry Suppliers Ass'n
Casualty Actuarial Soc.
Catholic Actors Guild of America
Cemented Carbide Producers Ass'n
Central Station Electrical Protection Ass'n
Certified Ballast Manufacturers Ass'n
Chefs de Cuisine Ass'n of America
Chemical Fabrics and Film Ass'n
Chemical Waste Transportation Council
Childrenswear Manufacturers Ass'n
Church and Synagogue Library Ass'n
Cleaning Equipment Manufacturers Ass'n
Clinical Orthopaedic Soc.
Clowns of America, Internat'l
Coalition of Labor Union Women
College Media Advisers
Collegiate Commissioners Ass'n
Columbia Sheep Breeders Ass'n of America
Comics Magazine Ass'n of America
Commercial Food Equipment Service Ass'n
Concrete Sawing and Drilling Ass'n
Conference of Educational Administrators Serving the Deaf
Conference of Nat'l Park Concessioners
Conference of State Court Adminstrators
Construction Financial Management Ass'n
Containerization and Intermodal Institute
Continental Ass'n of Funeral and Memorial Socs.
Convenient Automotive Services Institute
Convention of American Instructors of the Deaf
Cookware Manufacturers Ass'n
Cooperative Education Ass'n
Copper and Brass Fabricators Council
Cordage Institute
Correctional Education Ass'n
COSMEP, Internat'l Ass'n of Independent Publishers
Council of American Overseas Research Centers
Council of Professional Ass'ns on Federal Statistics
Cross Country Ski Areas of America
Cultured Pearl Ass'n of America
Custom Tailors and Designers Ass'n of America
Cutting Die Institute
Cutting Tool Manufacturers of America
Danish-American Chamber of Commerce (USA)
Diamond Council of America
Door Operator and Remote Controls Manufacturers Ass'n
Economic History Ass'n
Education Writers Ass'n
Electrical Equipment Representatives Ass'n
Electronic Motion Control Ass'n
Electronics Technicians Ass'n Internat'l
Engine Service Ass'n
Engraved Stationery Manufacturers Ass'n
Environmental Industry Council
Environmental Mutagen Soc.
Episcopal Conference of the Deaf
Epsilon Sigma Phi
Equipment Service Ass'n
Estuarine Research Federation
Evangelical Press Ass'n
Exposition Service Contractors Ass'n
Federal Communications Bar Ass'n
Federation of Materials Societies
Federation of Organizations for Professional Women
Ferrous Scrap Consumers Coalition
Financial Stationers Ass'n
Fire Retardant Chemicals Ass'n
Fleischner Soc.
Fluid Sealing Ass'n
Food Industry Ass'n Executives
Food Service Brokers of America, Inc.
Forum for Health Care Planning
Foundation for Internat'l Meetings
Fraternity Executives Ass'n
Garden Centers of America
Glass Tempering Ass'n
Graphic Preparatory Ass'n
Hardwood Research Council
Healthcare Information Systems Sharing Group
Heat Exchange Institute
Herpetologists' League
Hispanic Nat'l Bar Ass'n
History of Education Soc.
Home Economics Education Ass'n
Home Fashion Products Ass'n
Horticultural Research Institute
Independent Educational Counselors Ass'n
Independent Medical Distributors Ass'n
Independent Zinc Alloyers Ass'n
Industrial Diamond Ass'n of America
Industrial Perforators Ass'n
Industrial Relations Research Ass'n
Infectious Diseases Soc. of America
Institute for Briquetting and Agglomeration
Institute of Diving
Institute of Home Office Underwriters
Institute of Intermodal Repairers
Insulated Cable Engineers Ass'n
Inter-Financial Ass'n
Intercoiffure America
Interfaith Forum on Religion, Art and Architecture
Internat'l Arthroscopy Ass'n
Internat'l Ass'n for Hydrogen Energy
Internat'l Ass'n for Identification
Internat'l Ass'n for Shopping Center Security
Internat'l Ass'n of Clerks, Recorders, Election Officials and Treasurers
Internat'l Ass'n of Counseling Services
Internat'l Ass'n of Credit Card Investigators
Internat'l Ass'n of Hospital Central Service Management
Internat'l Ass'n of Lighting Maintenance Contractors
Internat'l Ass'n of Merger and Acquisition Consultants
Internat'l Ass'n of Ocular Surgeons
Internat'l Ass'n of Structural Movers
Internat'l College of Applied Nutrition
Internat'l College of Dentists, U.S.A. Section
Internat'l Conference of Police Chaplains
Internat'l Conference of Symphony and Opera Musicians
Internat'l Coordinating Committee on Solid State Sensors and Actuators Research
Internat'l Deli-Bakery Ass'n
Internat'l Documentary Ass'n
Internat'l Drycleaners Congress
Internat'l Federation of Advertising Agencies
Internat'l Group of Agents and Bureaus
Internat'l Guild of Professional Electrologists
Internat'l Institute for Bio-Energetic Analysis
Internat'l Institute of Ammonia Refrigeration
Internat'l Maintenance Institute
Internat'l Metallographic Soc.
Internat'l Natural Sausage Casing Ass'n
Internat'l Rescue and Emergency Care Ass'n
Internat'l Soc. of Air Safety Investigators
Internat'l Soc. of Performing Arts Administrators
Internat'l Soc. of Preretirement Planners
Internat'l Soc. of Transport Aircraft Traders
Internat'l Tax Institute
Internat'l Test and Evaluation Ass'n
Internat'l Union of Tool, Die and Mold Makers
Interstate Conference on Water Policy
Investigative Reporters and Editors
Investment Counsel Ass'n of America
Investment Recovery Ass'n
Issues Management Ass'n
Jesuit Secondary Education Ass'n
Jewelry Industry Distributors Ass'n
Label Printing Industries of America
Laminators Safety Glass Ass'n
Law and Society Ass'n
Leak Detection Technology Ass'n
Leather Workers Internat'l Union
Lepidopterists' Soc.
Locomotive Maintenance Officers' Ass'n
Lutheran Education Ass'n
Manuscript Soc.
Mass Marketing Insurance Institute
Materials Marketing Associates
Metal Construction Ass'n
Metal Lath/Steel Framing Ass'n
Mexican American Engineering Soc.
Mexican Chamber of Commerce of the United States
Middle East Studies Ass'n of North America
Military Chaplains Ass'n of the U.S.
Millinery Institute of America
Missouri Fox Trotting Horse Breed Ass'n
Mobile Industrial Caterers' Ass'n Internat'l
Movers' and Warehousemen's Ass'n of America
Music Critics Ass'n
Music Library Ass'n
Nat'l Academic Advising Ass'n
Nat'l Aerosol Ass'n
Nat'l Agricultural Transportation League
Nat'l Alliance of Cardiovascular Technologists
Nat'l Aloe Science Council
Nat'l Appliance Service Ass'n
Nat'l Ass'n for Armenian Studies and Research
Nat'l Ass'n for Bilingual Education
Nat'l Ass'n for Check Safekeeping
Nat'l Ass'n of Artists' Organizations
Nat'l Ass'n of Black-Owned Broadcasters
Nat'l Ass'n of Business Economists
Nat'l Ass'n of Canoe Liveries and Outfitters
Nat'l Ass'n of Chain Manufacturers
Nat'l Ass'n of Cold Storage Contractors
Nat'l Ass'n of College Automotive Teachers
Nat'l Ass'n of Consumer Agency Administrators
Nat'l Ass'n of County Engineers
Nat'l Ass'n of Criminal Justice Planners
Nat'l Ass'n of Dealers in Antiques
Nat'l Ass'n of Dental Assistants
Nat'l Ass'n of Disability Examiners
Nat'l Ass'n of Educational Office Personnel
Nat'l Ass'n of Energy Service Companies
Nat'l Ass'n of Environmental Professionals
Nat'l Ass'n of Executive Secretaries
Nat'l Ass'n of Federal Education Program Administrators
Nat'l Ass'n of Financial Consultants
Nat'l Ass'n of Flour Distributors
Nat'l Ass'n of Franchise Companies
Nat'l Ass'n of Fruits, Flavors and Syrups
Nat'l Ass'n of Government Communicators
Nat'l Ass'n of Health Career Schools
Nat'l Ass'n of Hose and Accessories Distributors
Nat'l Ass'n of Independent Life Brokerage Agencies
Nat'l Ass'n of Industrial Technology
Nat'l Ass'n of Legal Investigators
Nat'l Ass'n of Manufacturing Opticians
Nat'l Ass'n of Miscellaneous, Ornamental and Architectural Products Contractors
Nat'l Ass'n of Name Plate Manufacturers
Nat'l Ass'n of Optometrists and Opticians
Nat'l Ass'n of Paralegal Personnel
Nat'l Ass'n of Pension Consultants and Administrators
Nat'l Ass'n of Physical Therapists
Nat'l Ass'n of Pizza Operators
Nat'l Ass'n of Private, Nontraditional Schools and Colleges
Nat'l Ass'n of Professional Band Instrument Repair Technicians
Nat'l Ass'n of Professional Engravers
Nat'l Ass'n of Professional Fund Raisers
Nat'l Ass'n of Public Insurance Ad usters
Nat'l Ass'n of Railway Business Women
Nat'l Ass'n of Real Estate License Law Officials
Nat'l Ass'n of Reinforcing Steel Contractors
Nat'l Ass'n of Relay Manufacturers
Nat'l Ass'n of Schools and Colleges of the United Methodist Church
Nat'l Ass'n of Science Writers
Nat'l Ass'n of Solar Contractors
Nat'l Ass'n of Sporting Goods Wholesalers
Nat'l Ass'n of State Foresters
Nat'l Ass'n of State Treasurers
Nat'l Ass'n of Temple Administrators
Nat'l Ass'n of Textile and Apparel Distributors
Nat'l Ass'n of Urban Flood Management Agencies
Nat'l Ass'n of Variety Stores
Nat'l Ass'n of Women Judges
Nat'l Band Ass'n
Nat'l Bartenders Ass'n
Nat'l Bicycle Dealers Ass'n
Nat'l Board of Fur Farm Organizations
Nat'l Brotherhood of Packinghouse and Industrial Workers
Nat'l Candy Brokers Ass'n
Nat'l Children's Eye Care Foundation
Nat'l Church Goods Ass'n
Nat'l Collegiate Honors Council
Nat'l Conference of Editorial Writers
Nat'l Conference of Lieutenant Governors
Nat'l Costumers Ass'n
Nat'l Council for Geographic Education
Nat'l Council of Commercial Plant Breeders
Nat'l Council of Salesmen's Organizations
Nat'l Council of State Emergency Medical Services Training Coordinators
Nat'l Council on Teacher Retirement
Nat'l Dog Groomers Ass'n of America
Nat'l Drilling Contractors Ass'n
Nat'l Duckling Council
Nat'l Environmental Development Ass'n
Nat'l Exhaust Distributors Ass'n
Nat'l Federation of Catholic Physicians' Guilds
Nat'l Film Carriers
Nat'l Forest Recreation Ass'n
Nat'l Furniture Traffic Conference
Nat'l Garden Bureau
Nat'l Grain Trade Council
Nat'l Graphic Arts Dealers Ass'n
Nat'l Hay Ass'n
Nat'l Humanities Alliance
Nat'l Hydropower Ass'n
Nat'l Independent Poultry and Food Distributors Ass'n
Nat'l Indian Education Ass'n
Nat'l Industrial Belting Ass'n
Nat'l Industrial Glove Distributors Ass'n
Nat'l Institute of Ceramic Engineers
Nat'l Institute of Oilseed Products
Nat'l Institute of Senior Centers
Nat'l Institute of Steel Detailing
Nat'l Institute on Park and Grounds Management
Nat'l Interstate Council of State Boards of Cosmetology
Nat'l Labor Relations Board Union
Nat'l Manufactured Housing Finance Ass'n
Nat'l Marine Representatives Ass'n
Nat'l Mastitis Council
Nat'l Metal Decorators Ass'n
Nat'l Newspaper Publishers Ass'n
Nat'l Oak Flooring Manufacturers Ass'n
Nat'l Options and Futures Soc.
Nat'l Organization of Social Security Claimants' Representatives
Nat'l Pegboard Systems Ass'n
Nat'l Postsecondary Agriculture Student Organization
Nat'l Purchasing Institute
Nat'l Reading Conference
Nat'l Resource Recovery Ass'n
Nat'l Safety Management Soc.
Nat'l Service Robot Ass'n
Nat'l Ski Credit Ass'n
Nat'l Soc. for Histotechnology
Nat'l Soc. of Genetic Counselors
Nat'l Speleological Soc.
Nat'l Taxidermists Ass'n
Nat'l Tile Roofing Manufacturers Ass'n
Nat'l Tumor Registrar's Ass'n
Nat'l Weather Ass'n
Nat'l Wholesale Furniture Ass'n

BUDGET INDEX

$25-50,000

BUDGET INDEX

The information in this directory is available in *Mailing List* form. See back insert.

00015

BUDGET INDEX

Scaffolding, Shoring and Forming Institute
Science Fiction Writers of America
Shade Tobacco Growers Agricultural Ass'n
Showmen's League of America
Sleep Research Soc.
Soc. for Clinical Trials
Soc. for Cryobiology
Soc. for Health and Human Values
Soc. for Historical Archaeology
Soc. for Magnetic Resonance Imaging
Soc. for Occlusal Studies
Soc. for Occupational and Environmental Heatlh
Soc. for Pediatric Radiology, The
Soc. for Personality Assessment
Soc. for Psychophysiological Research
Soc. for the Advancement of Behavior Analysis
Soc. for the History of Technology
Soc. for Theriogenology
Soc. of Allied Weight Engineers
Soc. of Architectural Administrators
Soc. of Biological Psychiatry
Soc. of Biomedical Equipment Technicians
Soc. of Company Meeting Planners
Soc. of Craft Designers
Soc. of Federal Labor Relations Professionals
Soc. of Head and Neck Surgeons
Soc. of Independent Professional Earth Scientists
Soc. of Insurance Research
Soc. of Insurance Trainers and Educators
Soc. of Medical-Dental Management Consultants
Soc. of Newspaper Design
Soc. of Park and Recreation Educators
Soc. of Professional Archaeologists
Soc. of Radiological Engineering
Soc. of Roller Skating Teachers of America
Soc. of University Patent Administrators
Soc. of University Surgeons
Soc. of Vertebrate Paleontology
Soc. of Wood Science and Technology
Soyfoods Ass'n of America
Special Interest Group for Computer Science Education
Special Interest Group for Measurement and Evaluation
Standards Engineering Soc.
Steel Structures Painting Council
Street Rod Equipment Ass'n
Submersible Wastewater Pump Ass'n
Surface Mount Technology Ass'n
Sweet Potato Council of the United States
Tapered Steel Transmission Pole Institute
Tea Ass'n of the United States of America
Textile Converters Ass'n
Textile Fibers and By-Products Ass'n
Tile, Marble, Terrazzo, Finishers, Shopworkers and Granite Cutters Internat'l Union
Trade Relations Council of the U.S.
Truck-frame and Axle Repair Ass'n
Tube Council of North America
Tubular Exchanger Manufacturers Ass'n
Tubular Finishers and Processors Ass'n
Tune-up Manufacturers Institute
United Knitwear Manufacturers League
United Pesticide Formulators and Distributors Ass'n
United States-Austrian Chamber of Commerce
United States Harness Writers' Ass'n
United States Immigration and Naturalization Officers Ass'n
United States of America National Committee of the Internat'l Dairy Federation
United States-Pakistan Economic Council
United States Police K-9 Ass'n
United States Ski Coaches Ass'n
United States Targhee Sheep Ass'n
United Thoroughbred Trainers of America
University and College Designers Ass'n
Urban Affairs Ass'n
Variable Resistive Components Institute
Vatel Club
Vermiculite Ass'n
Walking Horse Trainers Ass'n
Water and Sewer Distributors of America
Web Sling Ass'n
Western/English Retailers of America
Western Writers of America
Wholesale Nursery Growers of America
Wildlife Disease Ass'n
Wine and Spirits Guild of America
Women in Employee Benefits
Women's Caucus for Art
Wood Tank Manufacturers Ass'n

$10-25,000

Academy for Implants and Transplants
Academy of Dental Materials
Academy of Dentistry for the Handicapped
Academy of Denture Prosthetics
Academy of Oral Dynamics
Academy of Orthomolecular Medicine
Advanced Transit Ass'n
Advertising and Marketing Internat'l Network
Affiliated Boards of Officials
Agricultural History Soc.
Agricultural Relations Council
Air Brake Ass'n
Air Cooled Heat Exchanger Manufacturers Ass'n
Allied Artists of America
Allied Stone Industries
Alpha Tau Delta
America on the Move
American Academy of Behavioral Medicine
American Academy of Clinical Psychiatrists
American Academy of Dental Group Practice
American Academy of Maxillofacial Prosthetics
American Academy of Restorative Dentistry
American Academy of Sports Physicians
American Academy of the History of Dentistry
American Academy of Veterinary and Comparative Toxicology
American Accordionists Ass'n
American Aerobics Ass'n
American Agricultural Editors Ass'n
American Agricultural Law Ass'n
American Analgesia Soc.
American Assembly for Men in Nursing
American Ass'n for Automotive Medicine
American Ass'n for Geriatric Psychiatry
American Ass'n for Leisure and Recreation
American Ass'n for Social Psychiatry
American Ass'n for the Study of Neoplastic Diseases
American Ass'n of Acupuncture and Oriental Medicine
American Ass'n of Certified Allergists
American Ass'n of Chairmen of Departments of Psychiatry
American Ass'n of Dental Editors
American Ass'n of Handwriting Analysts
American Ass'n of Housing Educators
American Ass'n of Medical Milk Commissions
American Ass'n of Neuropathologists
American Ass'n of Pathologists' Assistants
American Ass'n of Physical Anthropologists
American Ass'n of Police Polygraphists
American Ass'n of Psychiatric Administrators
American Ass'n of Public Welfare Information Systems Management
American Ass'n of Women Dentists
American Athletic Trainers Ass'n and Certification Board
American Bed & Breakfast Ass'n
American Beverage Alcohol Ass'n
American Book Producers Ass'n
American Breed Ass'n
American Bridge Teachers' Ass'n
American Butter Institute
American Carbon Soc.
American Catfish Marketing Ass'n
American Catholic Historical Ass'n
American Chamber of Commerce Researchers Ass'n
American Cinema Editors
American College of Cryosurgery
American College of Neuropsychiatrists
American College of Osteopathic Emergency Physicians
American College Personnel Ass'n
American Committee for Irish Studies
American Conference of Academic Deans
American Correctional Food Service Ass'n
American Corrective Therapy Ass'n
American Crystallographic Ass'n
American Dermatologic Soc. for Allergy and Immunology
American Dialect Soc.
American Diopter and Decibel Soc.
American Educational Studies Ass'n
American Fern Soc.
American Foreign Law Ass'n
American Fracture Ass'n
American Galloway Breeders Ass'n
American Greenhouse Vegetable Growers Ass'n
American Guild of Music
American Herbal Products Ass'n
American Hockey Coaches Ass'n
American Horse Publications
American Humor Studies Ass'n
American Institute of Nail and Tack Manufacturers
American Institutions Food Service Ass'n
American Jewish Press Ass'n
American Laryngological, Rhinological and Otological Soc.
American Loudspeaker Manufacturers Ass'n
American Malacological Union
American Meat Science Ass'n
American Microscopical Soc.
American Name Soc.
American Osteopathic Academy of Orthopedics
American Otological Soc.
American Poultry Ass'n
American Professional Racquetball Organization
American Protestant Correctional Chaplains' Ass'n
American Purchasing Soc.
American Real Estate and Urban Economics Ass'n
American Rose Council
American School Band Directors' Ass'n
American Shropshire Registry Ass'n
American Soc. for Clinical Investigation
American Soc. for Cybernetics
American Soc. for Dental Aesthetics
American Soc. for Geriatric Dentistry
American Soc. for the Study of Orthodontics
American Soc. for Theatre Research
American Soc. of Access Professionals
American Soc. of Aviation Writers
American Soc. of Business Press Editors
American Soc. of Gas Engineers
American Soc. of Genealogists
American Soc. of Group Psychotherapy and Psychodrama
American Soc. of Indexers
American Soc. of Internat'l Executives
American Soc. of Picture Professionals
American Soc. of Podiatric Dermatology
American Soc. of Podiatric Medical Assistants
American Soc. of Primatologists
American Soc. of Questioned Document Examiners
American Soc. of Sugar Beet Technologists
American Soc. of Test Engineers
American Soc. of Trial Consultants
American Southdown Breeders Ass'n
American Suffolk Sheep Soc.
American Veterinary Exhibitors Ass'n
American Warmblood Registry
American Wine Ass'n
American Women Composers
Aquatic Plant Management Soc.
Aromatic Red Cedar Closet Lining Manufacturers Ass'n
Art and Antique Dealers League of America
Ass'n for Applied Psychoanalysis
Ass'n for Business Simulation and Experiential Learning
Ass'n for Child Psychoanalysis
Ass'n for Comparative Economic Studies
Ass'n for Documentary Editing
Ass'n for Federal Information Resources Management
Ass'n for Maternal and Child Health and Crippled Children's Programs
Ass'n for Recorded Sound Collections
Ass'n for Religious and Value Issues in Counseling
Ass'n for Research, Administration, Professional Councils and Societies
Ass'n for Research in Nervous and Mental Disease
Ass'n for Social Economics
Ass'n for the Advancement of Health Education
Ass'n for the Advancement of Psychoanalysis
Ass'n for the Study of Man-Environment Relations
Ass'n for University Business and Economic Research
Ass'n of Agricultural Computer Companies
Ass'n of American Feed Control Officials
Ass'n of American Pesticide Control Officials
Ass'n of American Physicians
Ass'n of Applied Insect Ecologists
Ass'n of Artist-Run Galleries
Ass'n of Average Ad usters of the U.S.
Ass'n of Biomedical Communications Directors
Ass'n of Bridal Consultants
Ass'n of College Honor Societies
Ass'n of Environmental Engineering Professors
Ass'n of Graphic Arts Consultants
Ass'n of Information and Dissemination Centers
Ass'n of Jewish Book Publishers
Ass'n of Jewish Libraries
Ass'n of Management Analysts in State and Local Government
Ass'n of Medical Rehabilitation Directors and Coordinators
Ass'n of Medical School Pediatric Department Chairmen
Ass'n of Military Colleges and Schools of the U.S.
Ass'n of Naval R.O.T.C. Colleges and Universities
Ass'n of Official Racing Chemists
Ass'n of Osteopathic State Executive Directors
Ass'n of Otolaryngology Administrators
Ass'n of Paid Circulation Publications
Ass'n of Pediatric Oncology Nurses
Ass'n of Private Postal Systems
Ass'n of Productivity Specialists
Ass'n of Radio Reading Services
Ass'n of Scientists and Engineers of the Naval Sea Systems Command
Ass'n of Social and Behavioral Scientists
Ass'n of Teachers of Technical Writing
Ass'n of Travel Marketing Executives
Ass'n of Vacuum Equipment Manufacturers
Automatic Damper Manufacturers Ass'n
Automatic Guided Vehicle Systems
Automotive Advertisers Council
Automotive Battery Charger Manufacturers Council
Automotive Cooling System Institute
Automotive Market Research Council
Automotive Occupant Protection Ass'n
Automotive Refrigeration Products Institute
Baking Industry Sanitation Standards Committee
Baptist Public Relations Ass'n
Beef Improvement Federation
Behavior Genetics Ass'n
Bioelectromagnetics Soc.
Black Psychiatrists of America
Boating Writers Internat'l
Bowling Writers Ass'n of America
Brass and Bronze Ingot Institute

BUDGET INDEX

Building Systems Institute
Burley Leaf Tobacco Dealers Ass'n
Calorimetry Conference
CAMEO
Canadian-American Motor Carriers Ass'n
Carded Packaging Institute
Cartoonists Guild
Caster and Floor Truck Manufacturers Ass'n
Catalysis Soc. of North America
Cathodic Protection Industry Ass'n
Cell Kinetics Soc.
China, Glass and Giftware Ass'n
Chinese Language Teachers Ass'n
College Fraternity Editors Ass'n
College Language Ass'n
College Theology Soc.
Colorado Ranger Horse Ass'n
Communications Security Ass'n
Concert Music Broadcasters Ass'n
Conservation Education Ass'n
Consortium of University Film Centers
Coordinating Council for Computers in Construction
Correctional Industries Ass'n
Council for Intercultural Studies and Programs
Council of Colleges of Arts and Sciences
Council on Governmental Ethics Laws
Council on Soil Testing and Plant Analysis
Council on Technology Teacher Education
Crusher and Portable Plant Ass'n
Cylinder Manufacturers Ass'n
Dance Critics Ass'n
Dermatology Nurses Ass'n
Diamond Core Drill Manufacturers Ass'n
Die Set Manufacturers Service Bureau
Direct Marketing Creative Guild
Distribution Codes Institute
Electrical-Electronics Materials Distributors Ass'n
Electrical Women's Round Table
Engineering Reprographic Soc.
Epigraphic Soc.
Evangelical Church Library Ass'n
Executive Women Internat'l
Expansion Joint Manufacturers Ass'n
Fashion Jewelry Ass'n of America
Federal Court Clerks Ass'n
Federal Probation Officers Ass'n
Fiber Soc.
First Amendment Lawyers Ass'n
Floor Covering Installation Contractors Ass'n
Food Equipment Manufacturers Ass'n
Food Industries Suppliers' Ass'n
Fresh Garlic Ass'n
Fulfillment Management Ass'n
Game Manufacturers Ass'n
Gay and Lesbian Press Ass'n
Gelatin Manufacturers Institute of America
Geochemical Soc.
Gift Ass'n of America
Golf Course Builders of America
Golf Writers Ass'n of America
Governmental Research Ass'n
Graphic Arts Advertisers and Exhibitors Council
Guitar and Accessories Music Marketing Ass'n
Hebrew Actors Union
Home Office Life Underwriters Ass'n
Hydroponics Soc. of America
Independent Armored Car Operators Ass'n
Independent Free Papers of America
Independent Terminal Operators Ass'n
Infant and Juvenile Manufacturers Ass'n
Inland River Ports and Terminals
Insect Screening Weavers Ass'n
Institute of Certified Records Managers
Institute on Religion in an Age of Science
Inter-Society Color Council
Interior Design Educators Council
Internat'l Ass'n for Aquatic Animal Medicine
Internat'l Ass'n of Professional Security Consultants
Internat'l Ass'n of Tool Craftsmen
Internat'l Ass'n of Women Police
Internat'l Bridge Press Ass'n
Internat'l Chain of Industrial and Technical Advertising Agencies
Internat'l College of Real Estate Consulting Professionals
Internat'l Council for Computer Communication
Internat'l Federation for Choral Music
Internat'l Frozen Food Ass'n
Internat'l Graphic Arts Education Ass'n
Internat'l Grooving and Grinding Ass'n
Internat'l Institute for Lath and Plaster
Internat'l Institute for Safety in Transportation
Internat'l Juvenile Officers Ass'n
Internat'l Motor Press Ass'n
Internat'l Organization of Women in Telecommunications
Internat'l Pesticide Applicators Ass'n
Internat'l Phycological Soc.
Internat'l Physical Fitness Ass'n
Internat'l Plate Printers', Die Stampers' and Engravers' Union of North America
Internat'l Porcelain Artist Teachers
Internat'l Saw and Knife Ass'n
Internat'l Silk Ass'n
Internat'l Soc. for Chronobiology
Internat'l Soc. for Developmental Psychobiology
Internat'l Soc. for Peritoneal Dialysis
Internat'l Soc. for Prosthetics and Orthotics, United States Nat'l Member Soc.
Internat'l Soc. of Weekly Newspaper Editors
Internat'l Stress and Tension Control Ass'n
Internat'l Trade Commission Trial Lawyers Ass'n
Internat'l Truck Parts Ass'n
Internat'l Wild Rice Ass'n
Intersure, Ltd.
Intimate Apparel Manufacturers Ass'n
Iota Tau Tau
Jean Piaget Soc.
JWB Jewish Music Council
Keyboard Teachers Ass'n
Laminating Materials Ass'n
Legal Industry Advisory Council
Lipizzan Ass'n of America
Logsplitter Manufacturers Ass'n
Lutheran Hospital Ass'n of America
Ma or League Umpires Ass'n
Mail Systems Management Ass'n
Masonry and Concrete Saw Manufacturers Institute
Master Gemology Ass'n
Materials and Methods Standards Ass'n
Metal Building Components Manufacturers Ass'n
Meteoritical Soc.
Methyl Chloride Industry Ass'n
Microbeam Analysis Soc.
Mining and Metallurgical Soc. of America
Modeling Ass'n of America Internat'l
Music Publishers' Ass'n of the United States
Musicians Nat'l Hotline Ass'n
Mutual Advertising Agency Network
NAMRI/SME
Nat'l Academic Athletic Advisors' Ass'n
Nat'l Alliance of Independent Crop Consultants
Nat'l American Indian Court Clerks Ass'n
Nat'l Antique and Art Dealers Ass'n of America
Nat'l Assistance Management Ass'n
Nat'l Ass'n for Drama Therapy
Nat'l Ass'n for Ethnic Studies
Nat'l Ass'n of Academies of Science
Nat'l Ass'n of Band Instrument Manufacturers
Nat'l Ass'n of Basketball Referees
Nat'l Ass'n of Blind Teachers
Nat'l Ass'n of Casualty and Surety Executives
Nat'l Ass'n of College Wind and Percussion Instructors
Nat'l Ass'n of Colleges and Teachers of Agriculture
Nat'l Ass'n of Companion Sitter Agencies and Referral Services
Nat'l Ass'n of County Training and Employment Professionals
Nat'l Ass'n of Decorative Architectural Finishes
Nat'l Ass'n of Flight Instructors
Nat'l Ass'n of Freight Payment Banks
Nat'l Ass'n of Freight Transportation Consultants
Nat'l Ass'n of Girls Clubs
Nat'l Ass'n of Human Rights Workers
Nat'l Ass'n of Ice Cream Vendors
Nat'l Ass'n of Independent Publishers
Nat'l Ass'n of Independent Record Distributors and Manufacturers
Nat'l Ass'n of Independent Resurfacers
Nat'l Ass'n of Industrial and Technical Teacher Educators
Nat'l Ass'n of Jewish Family, Children's and Health Professionals
Nat'l Ass'n of Laboratory Suppliers
Nat'l Ass'n of Media Women
Nat'l Ass'n of Planners, Estimators and Progressmen
Nat'l Ass'n of Police-Community Relations Officers
Nat'l Ass'n of Private Security Vaults
Nat'l Ass'n of Punch Manufacturers
Nat'l Ass'n of Pupil Personnel Administrators
Nat'l Ass'n of Schools of Theatre
Nat'l Ass'n of Selective Distributors
Nat'l Ass'n of Self-Instructional Language Programs
Nat'l Ass'n of Small Government Contractors
Nat'l Ass'n of State Directors of Teacher Education and Certification
Nat'l Ass'n of State Park Directors
Nat'l Ass'n of State Purchasing Officials
Nat'l Ass'n of State Telecommunications Directors
Nat'l Ass'n of Synagogue Administrators
Nat'l Ass'n of Veteran Program Administrators
Nat'l Ass'n of Vision Professionals
Nat'l Ass'n of Women Artists
Nat'l Ass'n of Women Government Contractors
Nat'l Bakery Suppliers Ass'n
Nat'l Bark Producers Ass'n
Nat'l Bed and Breakfast Ass'n
Nat'l Black Police Ass'n
Nat'l Book Critics Circle
Nat'l Building Granite Quarries Ass'n
Nat'l Catalog Managers Ass'n
Nat'l Caves Ass'n
Nat'l Conference of Bankruptcy Judges
Nat'l Construction Machinery Credit Group
Nat'l Council of Acupuncture Schools and Colleges
Nat'l Council of Erectors, Fabricators and Riggers
Nat'l Council of Music Importers and Exporters
Nat'l Council of State Directors of Community Junior Colleges
Nat'l Counter Intelligence Corps Ass'n
Nat'l Emergency Management Ass'n
Nat'l Employment and Training Ass'n
Nat'l Employment Counselors Ass'n
Nat'l Equipment Distributors Ass'n
Nat'l Equipment-Servicing Dealers Ass'n
Nat'l Fencing Coaches Ass'n of America
Nat'l Forensic Ass'n
Nat'l Geriatrics Soc.
Nat'l Goose Council
Nat'l Hand Embroidery and Novelty Manufacturers Ass'n
Nat'l Ice Cream Mix Ass'n
Nat'l Labor Relations Board Professional Ass'n
Nat'l Military Intelligence Ass'n
Nat'l Optometric Ass'n
Nat'l Ornament and Electric Lights Christmas Ass'n
Nat'l Perishable Transportation Ass'n
Nat'l Pet Dealers and Breeders Ass'n
Nat'l Pretzel Bakers Institute
Nat'l Reciprocal Ass'n
Nat'l Reloading Manufacturers Ass'n
Nat'l Retail Pet Store and Groomers Ass'n
Nat'l Roof Deck Contractors Ass'n
Nat'l Shellfisheries Ass'n
Nat'l Showmen's Ass'n
Nat'l Shrimp Processors Ass'n
Nat'l Soc. of Painters in Casein and Acrylic
Nat'l Sportscasters and Sportswriters Ass'n
Nat'l State Printing Ass'n
Nat'l Student Osteopathic Medical Ass'n
Nat'l Turf Writers Ass'n
Nat'l Watercolor Soc.
Neuroelectric Soc.
Newspaper Advertising Sales Ass'n
Newspaper Ass'n Managers
Newspaper Purchasing Management Ass'n
Non-Powder Gun Products Ass'n
North American Ass'n for Environmental Education
North American Catalysis Soc.
North American Farm Show Council
Northeastern Weed Science Soc.
Office Systems Research Ass'n
Omicron Kappa Upsilon
Open Pit Mining Ass'n
Organization of Black Airline Pilots
Oriental Rug Importers Ass'n of America
Palomino Horse Ass'n
Parapsychological Ass'n
Pattern Recognition Soc.
Phytochemical Soc. of North America
Pi Beta Alpha
Popular Culture Ass'n
Portable Drilling Rig Manufacturers Ass'n
Post Card Manufacturers Ass'n
Production Records
Professional Aeromedical Transport Ass'n
Professional Golf Club Repairmen's Ass'n
Professional Reactor Operator Soc.
Psychometric Soc.
Public Agency Risk Managers Ass'n
Publishers' Publicity Ass'n
Pulverized Limestone Ass'n
PVC Belting Manufacturers Ass'n
Pyrotechnic Signal Manufacturers Ass'n
Quality Control Council of America
Racking Horse Breeders Ass'n of America
Radio and Television Correspondents Ass'n
Railroad Public Relations Ass'n
Railway Fuel and Operating Officers Ass'n
Recreation Vehicle Rental Ass'n
Reinforced Concrete Research Council
Religion Newswriters Ass'n of U.S. and Canada
Safety Soc., The
Shelving Manufacturers Ass'n
Small Engine Servicing Dealers Ass'n
Soc. for Foodservice Systems
Soc. for Historians of American Foreign Relations
Soc. for History in the Federal Government
Soc. for Industrial Archeology
Soc. for Invertebrate Pathology
Soc. for Psychological Anthropology
Soc. for Radiation Oncology Administrators
Soc. for Risk Analysis
Soc. for Spanish and Portuguese Historical Studies
Soc. for Surgery of the Alimentary Tract
Soc. for Textual Scholarship
Soc. for the Advancement of Scandinavian Study
Soc. for Vascular Surgery
Soc. of American Business Editors and Writers
Soc. of American Historians
Soc. of Authors' Representatives
Soc. of Children's Book Writers
Soc. of Christian Ethics
Soc. of Commercial Seed Technologists
Soc. of Engineering Science
Soc. of Flight Test Engineers
Soc. of General Physiologists
Soc. of Geriatric Ophthalmology
Soc. of Insurance Accountants
Soc. of Medical Consultants to the Armed Forces
Soc. of Municipal Arborists
Soc. of Neurological Surgeons
Soc. of Neurosurgical Anesthesia and Neurological Supportive Care
Soc. of Office Automation Professionals
Soc. of Professional Management Consultants
Soc. of Rheology
Soc. of Risk Management Consultants
Soc. of Satellite Professionals
Soc. of Soft Drink Technologists
Southern Transportation League
Special Interest Group for Biomedical Computing

BUDGET INDEX

Special Interest Group for Computers and Society
Special Interest Group for Computers and the Physically Handicapped
Special Interest Group on Security, Audit, and Control
Specialty Coffee Ass'n of America
Sponge and Chamois Institute
Steel Window Institute
Surface Design Ass'n
Tackle and Shooting Sports Agents Ass'n
Texas Produce Export Ass'n
Textile Laundry Council
Textile Printers and Dyers Labor Relations Institute
Textile Quality Control Ass'n
Theatre Library Ass'n
Trade Show Services Ass'n
Trailer Hitch Manufacturers Ass'n
Transmission Products Ass'n
United Societies of Physiotherapists
United States Conference of Local Health Officers
United States Durum Growers Ass'n
United States Fencing Coaches Ass'n
United States Professional Cycling Federation
Vehicle Security Ass'n
Venezuelan American Ass'n of the U.S.
Vibrating Screen Manufacturers Ass'n
Vinifera Wine Growers Ass'n
Vocational Evaluation and Work Ad ustment Ass'n
Water Lily Soc.
Western Awning Ass'n
Wheat Gluten Industry Council
White Park Cattle Ass'n of America
Wild Bird Feeding Institute
Wire Fabricators Ass'n
Wire Machinery Builders Ass'n
Women's Apparel Chains Ass'n
Women's Nat'l Book Ass'n
Wood and Synthetic Flooring Institute

UNDER $10,000

Academy for Sports Dentistry
Academy of Aphasia
Academy of Hazard Control Management
Academy of Product Safety Management
Academy of Veterinary Cardiology
Accordion Teachers' Guild
Accredited Gemologists Ass'n
Ad utants General Ass'n of the United States
Adhesion Soc.
Aeronautical Navigator Ass'n
Aerospace Department Chairmen's Ass'n
Afghanistan Studies Ass'n
African Heritage Studies Ass'n
Air Taxi and Commercial Pilots Ass'n
Airline Medical Directors Ass'n
Airline Operational Control Soc.
All-Breeds Rescue Conservancy
Allied Trades of the Baking Industry
Alpha Alpha Gamma
Alpha Beta Alpha
Amalgamated Lace Operatives of America
Amalgamated Printers' Ass'n
American Academy of Advertising
American Academy of Crisis Interveners
American Academy of Dental Electrosurgery
American Academy of Dental Radiology
American Academy of Equine Art
American Academy of Health Administration
American Academy of Neurological Surgery
American Academy of Physiologic Dentistry
American Academy of Teachers of Singing
American Academy of Veterinary Dermatology
American Academy of Veterinary Nutrition
American Academy on Mental Retardation
American and Delaine-Merino Record Ass'n
American Angora Goat Breeder's Ass'n
American Apparel Machinery Trade Ass'n
American Artists Professional League
American Ass'n for Aerosol Research
American Ass'n for Applied Linguistics
American Ass'n for Chinese Studies
American Ass'n for Correctional Psychology
American Ass'n for Rehabilitation Therapy
American Ass'n for Women Podiatrists
American Ass'n of Academic Editors
American Ass'n of Candy Technologists
American Ass'n of Ceramic Industries
American Ass'n of Computer Professionals
American Ass'n of Correctional Training Personnel
American Ass'n of Credit Counselors
American Ass'n of Dealers in Ancient, Oriental and Primitive Art
American Ass'n of Dental Consultants
American Ass'n of Disability Communicators
American Ass'n of Feed Microscopists
American Ass'n of Feline Practitioners
American Ass'n of Foot Specialists
American Ass'n of Genito-Urinary Surgeons
American Ass'n of Homeopathic Pharmacists
American Ass'n of Industrial Social Workers
American Ass'n of Industrial Veterinarians
American Ass'n of Language Specialists
American Ass'n of Osteopathic Examiners
American Ass'n of Phonetic Sciences
American Ass'n of Presidents of Independent Colleges and Universities
American Ass'n of Professional Hypnologists
American Ass'n of Professors of Yiddish
American Ass'n of Public Health Physicians
American Ass'n of Public Welfare Attorneys
American Ass'n of Railroad Superintendents
American Ass'n of Scientific Workers
American Ass'n of Sheep and Goat Practitioners
American Ass'n of State Climatologists
American Ass'n of Sunday and Feature Editors
American Ass'n of Teacher Educators in Agriculture
American Ass'n of Teachers of Arabic
American Ass'n of Veterinary Anatomists
American Ass'n of Veterinary Parasitologists
American Ass'n of Youth Museums
American Auto Racing Writers and Broadcasters Ass'n
American Bandmasters Ass'n
American Bashkir Curly Registry
American Bleached Shellac Manufacturers Ass'n
American Blind Lawyers Ass'n
American Blonde D'Aquitaine Ass'n
American Broncho-Esophagological Ass'n
American Buckskin Registry Ass'n
American Canoe Manufacturers Union
American Catholic Correctional Chaplains Ass'n
American Cheviot Sheep Soc.
American College of Osteopathic Internists
American College of Podiatric Radiologists
American College of Podopediatrics
American College of Veterinary Microbiologists
American College of Veterinary Ophthalmologists
American College of Veterinary Radiology
American Collegiate Retailing Ass'n
American Comparative Literature Ass'n
American Connemara Pony Soc.
American Correctional Chaplains Ass'n
American Cotton Exporter's Ass'n
American Council of Industrial Arts State Ass'n Officers
American Council of Industrial Arts Supervisors
American Council of Nanny Schools
American Council of Railroad Women
American Crossbred Pony Register
American Dental Interfraternity Council
American Dexter Cattle Ass'n
American Entomological Soc.
American Epidemiological Soc.
American Fine China Guild
American Gem and Mineral Suppliers Ass'n
American Goat Soc.
American Guides Ass'n
American Hungarian Educators Ass'n
American Hypnotists' Ass'n
American Institute for Archaeological Research
American Institute for Patristic and Byzantine Studies
American Institute of Fishery Research Biologists
American Institute of Indian Studies
American Institute of Medical Climatology
American Internat'l Marchigiana Soc.
American Jewish Correctional Chaplains Ass'n
American Karakul Sheep Registry
American Laryngological Ass'n
American Medallic Sculpture Ass'n
American Medical Publishers' Ass'n
American Mental Health Counselors Ass'n
American Metal Detector Manufacturers Ass'n
American Metal Importers Ass'n
American Microchemical Soc.
American Musicians Union
American Mustang Ass'n
American Nature Study Soc.
American Osteopathic Academy of Sclerotherapy
American Osteopathic College of Allergy and Immunology
American Osteopathic College of Dermatology
American Osteopathic College of Proctology
American Oxford Sheep Ass'n
American Park Rangers Ass'n
American Photographic Artisans Guild
American Polled Shorthorn Soc.
American Pomological Soc.
American Poultry Historical Soc.
American Producers of Italian Type Cheese Ass'n
American Psychopathological Ass'n
American Quaternary Ass'n
American Railway Bridge and Building Ass'n
American Railway Development Ass'n
American Retail Ass'n Executives
American Rhinologic Soc.
American Romney Breeders Ass'n
American Scotch Highland Breeder's Ass'n
American Shire Horse Ass'n
American Ski Teachers Ass'n of Natur Teknik
American Soc. for Conservation Archaeology
American Soc. for Legal History
American Soc. for Pediatric Neurosurgery
American Soc. for Stereotactic and Functional Neurosurgery
American Soc. for the Advancement of Anesthesia in Dentistry
American Soc. for the Study of Religion
American Soc. of Certified Business Counselors
American Soc. of Forensic Odontology
American Soc. of Interpreters
American Soc. of Knitting Technologists
American Soc. of Laboratory Animal Practitioners
American Soc. of Marine Artists
American Soc. of Master Dental Technologists
American Soc. of Petroleum Operations Engineers
American Soc. of Psychoanalytic Physicians
American Soc. of Psychopathology of Expression
American Soc. of Veterinary Ophthalmology
American Soc. of Veterinary Physiologists and Pharmacologists
American Sulphur Export Corporation
American Theatre Critics Ass'n
American Tin Trade Ass'n
American Tour Managers Ass'n
American Veterinary Soc. of Animal Behavior
American Vocational Education Research Ass'n
American Wholesale Booksellers Ass'n
American Wood Chip Export Ass'n
Analytical Laboratory Managers Ass'n
Animal Nutrition Research Council
Ankina Breeders
Antique Appraisal Ass'n of America
Apiary Inspectors of America
Apparel Guild
Armed Forces Broadcasters Ass'n
Asian/Pacific American Librarians Ass'n
Associated Antique Dealers of America
Associated Business Writers of America
Associated Glass and Pottery Manufacturers
Associated Laboratories
Associated Pipe Organ Builders of America
Associated Two-Year Schools in Construction
Ass'n for Biology Laboratory Education
Ass'n for Birth Psychology
Ass'n for Bridge Construction and Design
Ass'n for Computer Art and Design Education
Ass'n for Computers and the Humanities
Ass'n for Conservation Information, The
Ass'n for Consumer Research
Ass'n for Continuing Professional Education
Ass'n for Correctional Research and Information Management
Ass'n for Field Archaeology
Ass'n for Gnotobiotics
Ass'n for Integrative Studies
Ass'n for Jewish Studies
Ass'n for Living Historical Farms and Agricultural Museums
Ass'n for Population/Family Planning Libraries and Information Centers, Internat'l
Ass'n for Research in Growth Relationships
Ass'n for Social Anthropology in Oceania
Ass'n for the Anthropological Study of Play
Ass'n for the Bibliography of History
Ass'n for the Coordination of University Religious Affairs
Ass'n for the Education of Teachers in Science
Ass'n for Vital Records and Health Statistics
Ass'n for Women in Mathematics
Ass'n for Women Veterinarians
Ass'n of American Air Travel Clubs
Ass'n of American Editorial Cartoonists
Ass'n of American Plant Food Control Officials
Ass'n of American Seed Control Officials
Ass'n of American State Geologists
Ass'n of American Woodpulp Importers
Ass'n of Architectural Librarians
Ass'n of Bedding and Furniture Law Officials
Ass'n of Black Sociologists
Ass'n of Brass and Bronze Ingot Manufacturers
Ass'n of Business Officers of Preparatory Schools
Ass'n of Catholic TV and Radio Syndicators
Ass'n of Chairmen of Departments of Mechanics
Ass'n of Christian Librarians
Ass'n of Co-operative Educators
Ass'n of College and University Printers
Ass'n of Concert Bands
Ass'n of Conservation Engineers
Ass'n of Dark Leaf Tobacco Dealers and Exporters
Ass'n of Earth Science Editors
Ass'n of Editorial Businesses
Ass'n of Existential Psychology and Psychiatry
Ass'n of Federal Safety and Health Professionals
Ass'n of Firearm and Toolmark Examiners
Ass'n of Footwear Distributors
Ass'n of Former Agents of the U.S. Secret Service
Ass'n of Fundraising List Professionals
Ass'n of Graduate Liberal Studies Programs
Ass'n of Graduate Schools in Ass'n of American Universities
Ass'n of Independent Conservatories of Music
Ass'n of Independent Music Publishers

BUDGET INDEX

00019

BUDGET INDEX

Nat'l Ass'n of Scissors and Shears Manufacturers
Nat'l Ass'n of Shooting Range Owners
Nat'l Ass'n of Specialty Food and Confection Brokers
Nat'l Ass'n of State Approving Agencies
Nat'l Ass'n of State Archaeologists
Nat'l Ass'n of State Boating Law Administrators
Nat'l Ass'n of State Catholic Conference Directors
Nat'l Ass'n of State Directors of Migrant Education
Nat'l Ass'n of State Directors of Veterans Affairs
Nat'l Ass'n of State Education Department Information Officers
Nat'l Ass'n of State Land Reclamationists
Nat'l Ass'n of State Recreation Planners
Nat'l Ass'n of State Retirement Administrators
Nat'l Ass'n of State Supervisors and Directors of Secondary Education
Nat'l Ass'n of State Supervisors of Music
Nat'l Ass'n of State Supervisors of Trade and Industrial Education
Nat'l Ass'n of State Textbook Administrators
Nat'l Ass'n of Supervisors of Agricultural Education
Nat'l Ass'n of Supervisors of Business Education
Nat'l Ass'n of Teachers' Agencies
Nat'l Ass'n of Telemarketing Consultants
Nat'l Ass'n of Textile Supervisors
Nat'l Ass'n of Unclaimed Property Administrators
Nat'l Ass'n of Vocational Home Economics Teachers
Nat'l Avionics Soc.
Nat'l Ballroom and Entertainment Ass'n
Nat'l Black Health Planners Ass'n
Nat'l Blacksmiths and Weldors Ass'n
Nat'l Block and Bridle Club
Nat'l Cartoonists Soc.
Nat'l Catholic Bandmasters' Ass'n
Nat'l Catholic Business Education Ass'n
Nat'l Catholic Educational Exhibitors
Nat'l Catholic Pharmacists Guild of the United States
Nat'l Caucus of Gay and Lesbian Counselors
Nat'l Cigar Leaf Tobacco Ass'n
Nat'l Clay Pot Manufacturers Ass'n
Nat'l Coaches Council
Nat'l Collegiate Baseball Writers Ass'n
Nat'l Confectionery Salesmen's Ass'n of America
Nat'l Conference of Appellate Court Clerks
Nat'l Conference of Bar Foundations
Nat'l Conference of Bar Presidents
Nat'l Conference of Local Environmental Health Administrators
Nat'l Conference of Regulatory Utility Commission Engineers
Nat'l Conference of State Social Security Administrators
Nat'l Conference on Research in English
Nat'l Consortium for Child Mental Health Services
Nat'l Construction Employers Council
Nat'l Correctional Recreational Ass'n
Nat'l Cotton Ginners' Ass'n
Nat'l Council for Critical Analysis
Nat'l Council for Textile Education
Nat'l Council of Career Women
Nat'l Council of County Ass'n Executives
Nat'l Council of Elected County Executives
Nat'l Council of Local Administrators of Vocational Education and Practical Arts
Nat'l Council of Local Public Welfare Administrators
Nat'l Council of State Pharmaceutical Ass'n Executives
Nat'l Council of State Supervisors of Foreign Languages
Nat'l Council of State Travel Directors
Nat'l Council on Public Polls
Nat'l Disabled Law Officers Ass'n
Nat'l Drug Trade Conference
Nat'l Dry Bean Council
Nat'l Economic Ass'n
Nat'l Export Traffic League
Nat'l Federation of Grange Mutual Insurance Companies
Nat'l Federation of Professional Organizations
Nat'l Fellowship of Child Care Executives
Nat'l Food and Conservation Through Swine
Nat'l Gas Measurement Ass'n
Nat'l Guild of Catholic Psychiatrists
Nat'l Gymnastic Judges Ass'n
Nat'l Hereford Hog Record Ass'n
Nat'l Hispanic Psychological Ass'n
Nat'l Honey Packers and Dealers Ass'n
Nat'l Indoor Track Meet Directors Ass'n
Nat'l Industrial Zoning Committee
Nat'l Institute of American Doll Artists
Nat'l Institute of Packaging, Handling and Logistic Engineers
Nat'l Lead Burning Ass'n
Nat'l Librarians Ass'n
Nat'l Lincoln Sheep Breeders Ass'n
Nat'l Livestock Exchange
Nat'l Marina Manufacturers Consortium
Nat'l Neckwear Ass'n
Nat'l Order of Women Legislators
Nat'l Organization of Bar Counsel
Nat'l Organization of Test, Research and Training Reactors
Nat'l Pedigreed Livestock Council
Nat'l Pharmaceutical Ass'n
Nat'l Plant Board
Nat'l Quartz Producers Council
Soc. of Federal Linguists
Soc. of Marine Port Engineers
Soc. of Medical Administrators
Soc. of Multivariate Experimental Psychology
Soc. of Oral Physiology and Occlusion
Soc. of Pelvic Surgeons
Soc. of Philaticians
Soc. of Professors of Education
Soc. of Small Craft Designers
Soc. of State Directors of Health, Physical Education and Recreation
Soc. of Systematic Zoology
Soc. of United States Air Force Flight Surgeons
Soc. of University Otolaryngologists
Soc. of University Urologists
Soc. of Vector Ecologists
Soc. of Woman Geographers
Sod Growers Ass'n of Mid-America
Space Commerce Roundtable Foundation
Speed Coaches Ass'n
State Medicaid Directors Ass'n
Stucco Manufacturers Ass'n
Stuntwomen's Ass'n of Motion Pictures
Sulfate of Potash Magnesia Export Ass'n
Sussex Cattle Ass'n of America
Synthetic Amorphous Silica and Silicates Industry Ass'n
Tantalum Producers Ass'n
Technology Education for Children Council
Television Critics Ass'n
Test Boring Ass'n
Textile Foremen's Guild
Tooling Component Manufacturers Ass'n
Tourist House Ass'n of America
Trademark Soc.
Tree-Ring Soc.
Truck and Heavy Equipment Claims Council
Ultrasonic Industry Ass'n
United Allied Workers Internat'l Union
United Dance Merchants of America
United Golfers' Ass'n
United States Basketball Writers Ass'n
United States Cross Country Coaches Ass'n
United States Federation for Culture Collections
United States Lacrosse Coaches' Ass'n
United States Potters' Ass'n
United States Shellac Importers Ass'n
United States Ski Writers Ass'n
United States Tennis Writers' Ass'n
Unites States Women's Track Coaches Ass'n
Universities Council on Water Resources
University Photographers Ass'n of America
Vanilla Bean Ass'n of America
Veal Industry Council
Veterinary Cancer Soc.
Weather Modification Ass'n
Welsh Black Cattle Ass'n
Western Red Cedar Ass'n
Wet Ground Mica Ass'n
White House Correspondents Ass'n
Women in Energy
Women Library Workers
Women of the Motion Picture Industry, Internat'l
Women's Caucus for the Modern Languages
Women's Professional Rodeo Ass'n
Wood Foundation Institute
World's Poultry Science Ass'n, U.S.A. Branch
Woven Wire Products Ass'n
Nat'l Railroad Intermodal Ass'n
Nat'l Science Supervisors Ass'n
Nat'l Seasoning Manufacturers Ass'n
Nat'l Soc. of Architectural Engineering
Nat'l Soc. of Mural Painters
Nat'l Soc. of Professional Sanitarians
Nat'l Spray Equipment Manufacturers Ass'n
Nat'l Sugar Brokers Ass'n
Nat'l Swine Improvement Federation
Nat'l Textile Processors Guild
Nat'l United Licensees Beverage Ass'n
Nat'l Waterfowl Council
Nat'l Wholesale Lumber Distributing Yard Ass'n
Nat'l Wine Ass'n
Nat'l Women's Neckwear and Scarf Ass'n
Nat'l Woodland Owners Ass'n
Natural Product Broker Ass'n
Neurosurgical Soc. of America
Newspaper Farm Editors of America
North American Academy of Ecumenists
North American Ass'n of Wardens and Superintendents
North American Cartographic Information Soc.
North American Clun Forest Ass'n
North American Indian Museums Ass'n
North American Jewish Youth Council
North American Morab Horse Ass'n
North American Mycological Ass'n
North American Simulation and Gaming Ass'n
North American Soc. for Pediatric Gastroenterology
North American Soc. for the Psychology of Sport and Physical Activity
Norwegian F ord Ass'n of North America
Nursery Ass'n Executives
Occupational Medical Administrators' Ass'n
Omega Tau Sigma
Onion Export Associates of New York
Organization of Biological Field Stations
Organization of Teachers of Oral Diagnosis
Organized Flying Ad usters
Orthodox Theological Soc. in America
Orthopedic Surgical Manufacturers Ass'n
Otosclerosis Study Group
Outdoor Education Ass'n
Overseas Press Club of America
Package Designers Council
Pan-American Biodeterioration Soc.
Paper Distribution Council
Personnel/Burden Carrier Manufacturers Ass'n
Photographic Industry Council
Plastic Surgery Research Council
Power Industry Laboratory Ass'n
Precision Chiropractic Research Soc.
Print Council of America
Procurement Round Table
Production Music Library Ass'n
Professional Basketball Writers' Ass'n of America
Professional Comedians Ass'n
Professional Football Trainers
Professional Football Writers of America
Professional Fraternity Ass'n
Professional Insurance Communicators of America
Professional Publishers Marketing Group
Professional Race Pilots Ass'n
Professional Soccer Reporters Ass'n
Professional Stringers Ass'n
Professional Travel Film Directors Ass'n
Professional Women Photographers
Property Management Ass'n of America
Public Offender Counselors Ass'n
Purebred Dairy Cattle Ass'n
Real Estate Aviation Chapter
Reclaim Managers Ass'n
Religious Speech Communication Ass'n
Rhetoric Soc. of America
Roadmasters and Maintenance of Way Ass'n of America
Romanian Studies Ass'n of America
Ruth Jackson Soc.
School Management Study Group
Shippers Oil Field Traffic Ass'n
Shoe Pattern Manufacturers Ass'n
Shoe Suppliers Ass'n of America
Slovak Studies Ass'n
Small Independent Record Manufacturers Ass'n
Small Press Writers and Artists Organization
Soc. for Conceptual and Content Analysis by Computer
Soc. for Economic Botany
Soc. for Environmental Geochemistry and Health
Soc. for French Historical Studies
Soc. for Italian Historical Studies
Soc. for Latin American Anthropology
Soc. for Natural Philosophy
Soc. for New Language Study
Soc. for Nursing History
Soc. for Obstetric Anesthesia and Perinatology
Soc. for Pediatric Urology
Soc. for Philosophy of Religion
Soc. for Reformation Research
Soc. for Slovene Studies
Soc. for Social Studies of Science
Soc. for the History of Discoveries
Soc. for the Study of Social Biology
Soc. for the Study of Symbolic Interaction
Soc. for Visual Anthropology
Soc. of Air Force Physicians
Soc. of Experimental Psychologists
Soc. of Experimental Social Psychology

NO INFORMATION

Acrylamide Producers Ass'n
Afram Films
Air Diffusion Council
Aircraft Owners and Pilots Ass'n
All-America Rose Selections
American Academy and Board of Neurological and Orthopaedic Surgery
American Academy of Legal and Industrial Medicine
American Academy of Pediatric Dentistry
American Ass'n for the Surgery of Trauma
American Ass'n of Food Stamp Directors
American Ass'n of Yellow Pages Publishers
American Cargo War Risk Reinsurance Exchange
American Chain of Warehouses
American Cloak and Suit Manufacturers Ass'n
American College of Veterinary Surgeons
American Cotton Shippers Ass'n
American Court and Commercial Newspapers
American Electroencephalographic Soc.
American Equilibration Soc.
American Fastener Enclosure Ass'n

BUDGET INDEX

American Federation of Small Business
American Folklore Soc.
American Football Coaches Ass'n
American Franchise Ass'n
American Institute of Financial Brokers
American Nuclear Insurers
American Oceanic Organization
American Osteopathic College of Anesthesiologists
American Peanut Export Corporation
American Pediatric Soc.
American Psychosomatic Soc.
American Schools Ass'n
American Soc. of Cataract and Refractive Surgery
American Soc. of Cytology
American Surgical Ass'n
American Thyroid Ass'n
American Wire Cloth Institute
Antiquarian Booksellers Ass'n of America
ANV Export Corporation
Archery Range and Retailers Organization
Associated Gas Distributors
Associated Press Broadcasters
Ass'n for Dressings and Sauces
Ass'n for Multicultural Counseling and Development
Ass'n for Women in Psychology
Ass'n of Administrators of the Interstate Compact on the Placement of Children
Ass'n of Hospital Television Networks
Ass'n of Independent Television Stations
Ass'n of Local Housing Finance Agencies
Ass'n of Marine Engine Manufacturers
Ass'n of Master of Business Administration Executives
Ass'n of Maximum Service Telecasters
Ass'n of Southern Baptist Colleges and Schools
Ass'n of Tennis Professionals
Ass'n of Urban Universities
Authors League of America
Automatic Identification Manufacturers
Automotive Exhaust Systems Manufacturers Council
Automotive Lift Institute
Avocado Export
Avocado Growers Bargaining Council
Beer Institute
Biomedical Marketing Ass'n
Brake System Parts Manufacturers Council
Bureau of Salesmen's Nat'l Ass'ns
California Export Ass'n
Calorie Control Council
Carbonated Beverage Institute
Central Shippers
Cheese Importers Ass'n of America
Chemical Marketing Research Ass'n
Clear Channel Broadcasting Service
Color Ass'n of the United States
Combustion Institute
Computer and Automated Systems Ass'n of SME
Computer Measurement Group
Concord Grape Ass'n
Congress of County Medical Societies
Contact Lens Ass'n of Opthalmologists
Controlled Release Soc.
Copyright Soc. of the U.S.A.
Council for Jewish Education
Cultured Marble Institute
Dairy Research
Data Entry Management Ass'n
Deep Foundations Institute
Diamond Manufacturers and Importers Ass'n of America
Diamond Wheel Manufacturers Institute
Educational Dealers and Suppliers Ass'n Internat'l
Electricity Consumers Resource Council
Embroidery Council of America
Enteral Nutrition Council
Fabric Salesmen's Ass'n
Foragers of America
Fourdrinier Wire Council
Gasoline Pump Manufacturers Ass'n
Generic Pharmaceutical Industry Ass'n
German American Chamber of Commerce
Glass, Pottery, Plastics and Allied Workers Internat'l Union
Glutamate Ass'n, The (United States)
Greater Blouse, Skirt and Undergarment Ass'n
Health Care Exhibitors Ass'n
Heavy Duty Business Forum
Heavy Duty Manfacturers Ass'n
Hoist Manufacturers Institute
Honey Industry Council of America
In-Flight Food Service Ass'n
Independent Cosmetic Manufacturers and Distributors
Independent Data Communications Manufacturers Ass'n
India Chamber of Commerce of America
Industrial Metal Containers Ass'n
Infant Formula Council
Infants', Children's and Girls' Sportswear and Coat Ass'n
Institute of Certified Professional Business Consultants
Insulated Steel Door Systems Institute
Insurance Industry Meetings Ass'n
Internat'l Ass'n of Auto Theft Investigators
Internat'l Ass'n of Chain Stores - North American Headquarters
Internat'l Ass'n of Piano Builders and Technicians
Internat'l Food Additives Council
Internat'l Glutamate Technical Committee
Internat'l Institute of Foods and Family Living
Internat'l Jelly and Preserve Ass'n
Jockey Club, The
Knitting Guild of America, The
League of Advertising Agencies
Licensed Beverage Information Council
Machine Vision Ass'n of SME
Manufacturers of Emission Controls Ass'n
Media Credit Ass'n
Merion Bluegrass Ass'n
Metal Framing Manufacturers Ass'n
Microwave Communications Ass'n
Military Educators and Counselors Ass'n
Military Reform Institute
Mohair Council of America
Monorail Manufacturers Ass'n
Moped Ass'n of America
Motion Picture Ass'n of America
Motion Picture Export Ass'n of America
Mycological Soc. of America
Nat'l Academy of Recording Arts and Sciences
Nat'l Air Carrier Ass'n
Nat'l Ass'n for Rural Mental Health
Nat'l Ass'n of Black and Minority Chambers of Commerce
Nat'l Ass'n of Blouse Manufacturers
Nat'l Ass'n of Christians in the Arts
Nat'l Ass'n of Community Health Centers
Nat'l Ass'n of Community Leadership Organizations
Nat'l Ass'n of County Aging Programs
Nat'l Ass'n of County Human Services Administrators
Nat'l Ass'n of Diaper Services
Nat'l Ass'n of Entrepreneurs
Nat'l Ass'n of Farm Broadcasters
Nat'l Ass'n of Fraternal Insurance Counsellors
Nat'l Ass'n of Gambling Regulatory Agencies
Nat'l Ass'n of Hebrew Day School Administrators
Nat'l Ass'n of Installation Developers
Nat'l Ass'n of Insurance Brokers
Nat'l Ass'n of Margarine Manufacturers
Nat'l Ass'n of Men's Sportswear Buyers
Nat'l Ass'n of Music Merchants
Nat'l Ass'n of Pipe Nipple Manufacturers
Nat'l Ass'n of Police Organizations
Nat'l Ass'n of Public Child Welfare Administrators
Nat'l Ass'n of Rail Shippers
Nat'l Ass'n of State Administrators and Supervisors of Private Schools
Nat'l Ass'n of State Emergency Services Directors
Nat'l Ass'n of State Public Health Veterinarians
Nat'l Ass'n of Student Activity Advisers
Nat'l Ass'n of Tax Administrators
Nat'l Beauty Culturists' League
Nat'l Blue Crab Industry Ass'n
Nat'l Bulk Vendors Ass'n
Nat'l Camping Ass'n
Nat'l Council of Coal Lessors
Nat'l Council of Forestry Ass'n Executives
Nat'l Council of Patent Law Ass'ns
Nat'l Council of State Garden Clubs
Nat'l Council of State Human Service Administrators
Nat'l Council on Education for the Ceramic Arts
Nat'l Employee Benefits Institute
Nat'l Engineering Consortium
Nat'l Federation of Fishermen
Nat'l Fraternity of Student Musicians
Nat'l Hearing Conservation Ass'n
Nat'l HomeCaring Council
Nat'l Industrial Sand Ass'n
Nat'l Institute of Management Counsellors
Nat'l Mail Order Ass'n
Nat'l Motorcycle Retailers Ass'n
Nat'l Motorsports Press Ass'n
Nat'l Pan Hellenic Council
Nat'l Panhellenic Conference
Nat'l Pecan Shellers Ass'n
Nat'l Psychological Ass'n for Psychoanalysis
Nat'l Single Service Food Ass'n
Nat'l Soc. for Real Estate Finance
Nat'l Therapeutic Recreation Soc.
Nat'l Venture Capital Ass'n
Nat'l Weather Service Employees Organization
Nat'l Wholesale Hardware Ass'n
Newspaper Features Council
Newspaper Systems Group
NIFDA
North American Corriente Ass'n
North American Normande Ass'n
North American Securities Administrators Ass'n
North Coast Export Company
Office Technology Management Ass'n
Physicians Forum
Pin, Clip and Fastener Services
Pitless Adapter Division (Water Systems Council)
Pleaters, Stitchers and Embroiderers Ass'n
Plumbing-Heating-Cooling Information Bureau
Polyurethane Manufacturers Ass'n
Private Security Liaison Council
Processed Apples Institute
Producer's Guild of America
Professional Bowlers Ass'n of America
Pulp, Paper and Paperboard Export Ass'n of the U.S.
Radiation Research Soc.
Regional Science Ass'n
Renown Shippers
Research Council on Structural Connections
Robotics Internat'l of SME
Roller Skating Foundation of America
Roses Incorporated
Salad Manufacturers Ass'n
Sauna Soc. of America
Shipowners Claims Bureau
Soc. for American Cuisine
Soc. for Experimental Biology and Medicine
Soc. for Humanistic Anthropology
Soc. for Medical Anthropology
Soc. for Music Teacher Education
Soc. for the Advancement of Food Service Research
Soc. of American Graphic Artists
Soc. of Certified Insurance Counselors
Soc. of Government Economists
Soc. of Gynecological Oncologists
Soc. of Motion Picture and Television Art Directors
Soc. of Professional Business Consultants
Soc. of Thoracic Surgeons
Southern Cypress Manufacturers Ass'n
Southwestern Craft and Hobby Ass'n
Special Interest Group for Architecture of Computer Systems
Special Interest Group for Automata and Computability Theory
Special Interest Group for Computer Graphics
Special Interest Group for Computer Personnel Research
Special Interest Group for Computer Uses in Education
Special Interest Group for Computers and Human Interaction
Special Interest Group for Data Communication
Special Interest Group for Information Retrieval
Special Interest Group for Management of Data
Special Interest Group for Microprogramming
Special Interest Group for Simulation and Modeling
Special Interest Group for Symbolic and Algebraic Manipulation
Special Interest Group on APL Programming Language
Special Interest Group on Documentation
Special Interest Group on Numerical Mathematics
Special Interest Group on Office Information Systems
Special Interest Group on Small and Personal Computing Systems and Applications
Special Interest Group on Software Engineering
Specialty Vehicle Institute of America
Sportswear Salesmen's Ass'n
State Environmental Education Coordinators Ass'n
Sump and Sewage Pump Manufacturers Ass'n
Sunglass Ass'n of America
Talmex Export Corporation
Textile Bag Manufacturers Ass'n
Textile Distributors Ass'n
Textile Information Users Council
Thermal Insulation Manufacturers Ass'n
Tire Industry Safety Council
Travel Journalists Guild
Underwear-Negligee Associates
United Better Dress Manufacturers Ass'n
United Egg Internat'l
United States Cigarette Export Ass'n
United States Football League
United States Football League Players Ass'n
United States League of Savings Institutions
United States Poultry Export
University Film and Video Ass'n
Vacuum Cleaner Manufacturers Ass'n
Videtape Facilities Ass'n
Vinegar Institute, The
Wire Rope Technical Board
Wire Service Guild
World Ass'n of Detectives

00021

1987

ACRONYM INDEX

All organizations using an acronym will be found here listed by acronym. The order is alphabetical with lower case letters following upper case (i.e. a follows Z). The following signs precede A: &,-, and /.

AA	Academy of Aphasia
	Aniline Ass'n
AAA	Allied Artists of America
	American Academy of Actuaries
	American Academy of Advertising
	American Accordionists Ass'n
	American Accounting Ass'n
	American Aerobics Ass'n
	American Ambulance Ass'n
	American Angus Ass'n
	American Anthropological Ass'n
	American Arbitration Ass'n
	American Arts Alliance
	American Ass'n of Anatomists
	Appraisers Ass'n of America
	Ass'n of Accounting Administrators
AAA-CPA	American Ass'n of Attorney-Certified Public Accountants
AAAA	American Ass'n for Affirmative Action
	American Ass'n of Advertising Agencies
	Antique Appraisal Ass'n of America
	Associated Actors and Artistes of America
AAACE	American Ass'n for Adult and Continuing Education
AAACI	American-Arab Ass'n for Commerce and Industry
AAAE	American Ass'n of Academic Editors
	American Ass'n of Airport Executives
AAAI	Affiliated Advertising Agencies Internat'l
	American Academy of Allergy and Immunology
	American Ass'n for Artificial Intelligence
AAAL	American Ass'n for Applied Linguistics
AAAM	American Ass'n for Automotive Medicine
AAANA	American Academy of Ambulatory Nursing Administration
AAAOM	American Ass'n of Acupuncture and Oriental Medicine
AAAP	American Ass'n of Avian Pathologists
AAAR	American Ass'n for Aerosol Research
AAAS	American Academy of Arts and Sciences
	American Ass'n for the Advancement of Science
AAASS	American Ass'n for the Advancement of Slavic Studies
AAATC	Ass'n of American Air Travel Clubs
AAAUS	Ass'n of Average Adjusters of the U.S.
AAB	American Ass'n of Bioanalysts
AABB	American Ass'n of Blood Banks
AABC	American Ass'n of Bible Colleges
	American Ass'n of Biofeedback Clinicians
	Associated Air Balance Council
AABGA	American Ass'n of Botanical Gardens and Arboreta
AABM	American Academy of Behavioral Medicine
AABP	American Ass'n of Bovine Practicioners
	Ass'n of Area Business Publications
AABPA	American Ass'n for Budget and Program Analysis
AABT	Ass'n for Advancement of Behavior Therapy
AABWE	American Ass'n of Black Women Entrepreneurs
AAC	Ass'n of American Colleges
	Automotive Advertisers Council
AACA	American Ass'n of Certified Allergists
	American Ass'n of Certified Appraisers
AACAP	American Academy of Child and Adolescent Psychiatry
AACBP	American Academy of Crown and Bridge Prosthodontics
AACC	American Ass'n for Clinical Chemistry
	American Ass'n for Continuity of Care
	American Ass'n of Cereal Chemists
	American Ass'n of Credit Counselors
	American Automatic Control Council
	Argentina-American Chamber of Commerce
	Ass'n of Agricultural Computer Companies
AACD	American Academy of Craniomandibular Disorders
	American Ass'n for Counseling and Development
AACDP	American Ass'n of Chairmen of Departments of Psychiatry
AACE	American Ass'n for Cancer Education
	American Ass'n of Cost Engineers
AACG	American Ass'n for Crystal Growth
AACI	American Academy of Crisis Interveners
	American Ass'n of Ceramic Industries
	American Ass'n of Crop Insurers
AACIA	American Ass'n for Clinical Immunology and Allergy
AACJC	American Ass'n of Community and Junior Colleges
AACN	American Ass'n of Colleges of Nursing
	American Ass'n of Critical-Care Nurses
AACO	American Ass'n of Certified Orthoptists
AACOM	American Ass'n of Colleges of Osteopathic Medicine
AACP	American Academy of Clinical Psychiatrists
	American Ass'n for Correctional Psychology
	American Ass'n of Colleges of Pharmacy
	American Ass'n of Computer Professionals
AACPDM	American Academy for Cerebral Palsy and Developmental Medicine
AACPM	American Ass'n of Colleges of Podiatric Medicine
AACPP	Ass'n of Asbestos Cement Pipe Producers
AACR	American Ass'n for Cancer Research
AACRAO	American Ass'n of Collegiate Registrars and Admissions Officers
AACRC	American Ass'n of Children's Residential Centers
AACS	American Academy of Cosmetic Surgery
	American Ass'n for Chinese Studies
AACSB	American Assembly of Collegiate Schools of Business
AACSE	American Ass'n of Classified School Employees
AACSL	American Ass'n for the Comparative Study of Law
AACT	American Academy of Clinical Toxicology
	American Ass'n of Candy Technologists
AACTE	American Ass'n of Colleges for Teacher Education
AACTP	American Ass'n of Correctional Training Personnel
AACU	American Ass'n of Clinical Urologists
AAD	American Academy of Dermatology
AADA	Associated Antique Dealers of America
AADAOPA	American Ass'n of Dealers in Ancient, Oriental and Primitive Art
AADC	American Ass'n of Dental Consultants
	American Ass'n of Disability Communicators
AADE	American Academy of Dental Electrosurgery
	American Ass'n of Dental Editors
	American Ass'n of Dental Examiners
	American Ass'n of Diabetes Educators
AADGP	American Academy of Dental Group Practice
AADLA	Art and Antique Dealers League of America
AADPA	American Academy of Dental Practice Administration
AADR	American Academy of Dental Radiology
	American Ass'n for Dental Research
AADS	American Ass'n of Dental Schools
AAE	American Ass'n of Endodontists
	American Ass'n of Esthetics
AAEA	American Academy of Equine Art
	American Agricultural Economics Ass'n
	American Agricultural Editors Ass'n
AAEC	Ass'n of American Editorial Cartoonists
AAED	American Academy of Esthetic Dentistry
AAEE	American Academy of Environmental Engineers
	American Ass'n of Electromyography and Electrodiagnosis
AAEH	Ass'n to Advance Ethical Hypnosis
AAEI	American Ass'n of Exporters and Importers
AAEL	American Ass'n of Equipment Lessors
AAEM	American Academy of Environmental Medicine
AAEP	American Ass'n of Equine Practitioners
AAES	American Ass'n of Engineering Societies
AAF	American Advertising Federation
AAFCO	Ass'n of American Feed Control Officials
AAFI	Associated Accounting Firms Internat'l
AAFM	American Ass'n of Feed Microscopists
AAFO	American Ass'n for Functional Orthodontics
AAFP	American Academy of Family Physicians
	American Ass'n of Feline Practitioners
AAFPRS	American Academy of Facial Plastic and Reconstructive Surgery
AAFRC	American Ass'n of Fund-Raising Counsel
AAFS	Academy of Ambulatory Foot Surgery
	American Academy of Forensic Sciences
	American Ass'n of Foot Specialists
AAFSD	American Ass'n of Food Stamp Directors
AAG	Alpha Alpha Gamma
	Ass'n of American Geographers
AAGBA	American Angora Goat Breeder's Ass'n
AAGFO	American Academy of Gold Foil Operators
AAGL	American Ass'n of Gynecological Laparoscopists
AAGO	American Academy of Gnathologic Orthopedics
AAGP	American Ass'n for Geriatric Psychiatry
AAGUS	American Ass'n of Genito-Urinary Surgeons
AAHA	American Academy of Health Administration
	American Academy of Hospital Attorneys
	American Animal Hospital Ass'n
	American Ass'n of Handwriting Analysts
	American Ass'n of Homes for the Aging
AAHC	American Ass'n of Healthcare Consultants
	Ass'n of Academic Health Centers
AAHD	American Academy of the History of Dentistry
	American Ass'n of Hospital Dentists
AAHE	American Ass'n for Higher Education
	American Ass'n of Housing Educators
	Ass'n for the Advancement of Health Education
AAHM	American Ass'n for the History of Medicine
AAHP	American Ass'n of Homeopathic Pharmacists
AAHPERD	American Alliance for Health, Physical Education, Recreation and Dance
AAHSLD	Ass'n of Academic Health Sciences Library Directors
AAI	Alliance of American Insurers
	American Ass'n of Immunologists
AAIAL	American Academy and Institute of Arts and Letters
AAICPC	Ass'n of Administrators of the Interstate Compact on the Placement of Children
AAID	American Academy of Implant Dentistry
AAIE	Ass'n for the Advancement of International Education
	Ass'n of Applied Insect Ecologists
AAII	American Ass'n of Individual Investors
AAIM	American Ass'n of Industrial Management
AAISW	American Ass'n of Industrial Social Workers
AAIV	American Ass'n of Industrial Veterinarians
AAL	Ass'n of Architectural Librarians
AALA	American Agricultural Law Ass'n
	American Ass'n for Laboratory Accreditation
	American Automotive Leasing Ass'n
AALAS	American Ass'n for Laboratory Animal Science
AALIM	American Academy of Legal and Industrial Medicine
AALJ	Ass'n of Administrative Law Judges
AALL	American Ass'n of Law Libraries
AALR	American Ass'n for Leisure and Recreation
AALS	Ass'n of American Law Schools
AALU	Ass'n for Advanced Life Underwriting
AAM	American Ass'n of Museums
AAMA	African American Museums Ass'n
	American Academy of Medical Administrators
	American Amusement Machine Ass'n
	American Apparel Manufacturers Ass'n
	American Architectural Manufacturers Ass'n
	American Ass'n of Medical Assistants
AAMC	Ass'n of American Medical Colleges
AAMD	American Academy of Medical Directors
	American Ass'n on Mental Deficiency
	Ass'n of Art Museum Directors
AAMFT	American Ass'n for Marriage and Family Therapy
AAMGA	American Ass'n of Managing General Agents
AAMHPC	American Ass'n of Mental Health Professionals in Corrections
AAMI	Ass'n for the Advancement of Medical Instrumentation
AAML	American Academy of Matrimonial Lawyers
AAMLC	American Ass'n of Medico-Legal Consultants
AAMMC	American Ass'n of Medical Milk Commissions
AAMN	American Assembly for Men in Nursing
AAMP	American Academy of Maxillofacial Prosthetics
	American Academy of Medical Preventics
	American Ass'n of Meat Processors
AAMR	American Academy on Mental Retardation
AAMSE	American Ass'n of Medical Soc. Executives
AAMSI	American Ass'n for Medical Systems and Informatics
AAMT	American Ass'n for Medical Transcription
	American Ass'n for Music Therapy
AAMTA	American Apparel Machinery Trade Ass'n
AAMVA	American Ass'n of Motor Vehicle Administrators
AAN	American Academy of Neurology
	American Ass'n of Nurserymen
AANA	American Ass'n of Nurse Anesthetists
	Arthroscopy Ass'n of North America
AANFP	American Academy of Natural Family Planning
AANN	American Ass'n of Neuroscience Nurses
AANP	American Ass'n of Neuropathologists
AANS	American Academy of Neurological Surgery

ACRONYM INDEX

	American Ass'n of Neurological Surgeons
AAO	American Academy of Ophthalmology
	American Academy of Optometry
	American Academy of Osteopathy
	American Ass'n of Orthodontists
AAO-HNS	American Academy of Otolaryngology-Head and Neck Surgery
AAOA	American Academy of Otolaryngic Allergy
AAOBPPH	American Ass'n of Owners and Breeders of Peruvian Paso Horses
AAOE	American Ass'n of Osteopathic Examiners
AAOGP	American Academy of Orthodontics for the General Practitioner
AAOHN	American Ass'n of Occupational Health Nurses
AAOM	American Academy of Occupational Medicine
	American Academy of Oral Medicine
	American Ass'n of Orthopaedic Medicine
AAOMS	American Ass'n of Oral and Maxillofacial Surgeons
AAOS	American Academy of Orthopaedic Surgeons
	American Ass'n of Osteopathic Specialists
AAP	American Academy of Pediatrics
	American Academy of Periodontology
	American Academy of Psychoanalysis
	American Ass'n of Pathologists
	Ass'n for Applied Psychoanalysis
	Ass'n for the Advancement of Psychoanalysis
	Ass'n for the Advancement of Psychology
	Ass'n for the Advancement of Psychotherapy
	Ass'n of Academic Physiatrists
	Ass'n of American Physicians
	Ass'n of American Publishers
AAPA	American Academy of Physician Assistants
	American Alfalfa Processors Ass'n
	American Ass'n of Pathologists' Assistants
	American Ass'n of Physical Anthropologists
	American Ass'n of Port Authorities
	American Ass'n of Psychiatric Administrators
AAPC	American Ass'n of Pastoral Counselors
	American Ass'n of Political Consultants
AAPCC	American Ass'n of Poison Control Centers
AAPCO	Ass'n of American Pesticide Control Officials
AAPD	American Academy of Pediatric Dentistry
	American Academy of Physiologic Dentistry
AAPFCO	Ass'n of American Plant Food Control Officials
AAPG	American Ass'n of Petroleum Geologists
AAPH	American Ass'n for Partial Hospitalization
	American Ass'n of Professional Hypnologists
	American Ass'n of Professional Hypnotherapists
AAPHD	American Ass'n of Public Health Dentistry
AAPHP	American Ass'n of Public Health Physicians
AAPICU	American Ass'n of Presidents of Independent Colleges and Universities
AAPL	American Academy of Psychiatry and the Law
	American Artists Professional League
	American Ass'n of Petroleum Landmen
AAPM	American Ass'n of Physicists in Medicine
AAPMR	American Academy of Physical Medicine and Rehabilitation
AAPOR	American Ass'n for Public Opinion Research
AAPOS	American Ass'n for Pediatric Ophthalmology and Strabismus
AAPP	American Ass'n of Police Polygraphists
AAPPO	American Ass'n of Preferred Provider Organizations
AAPS	American Ass'n of Phonetic Sciences
	American Ass'n of Plastic Surgeons
	Ass'n of American Physicians and Surgeons
AAPSC	American Ass'n of Psychiatric Services for Children
AAPSM	American Academy of Podiatric Sports Medicine
AAPT	American Ass'n of Physics Teachers
	Ass'n of Asphalt Paving Technologists
AAPWA	American Ass'n of Public Welfare Attorneys
AAPWISM	American Ass'n of Public Welfare Information Systems Management
AAPY	American Ass'n of Professors of Yiddish
AAR	American Academy of Religion
	Ass'n of American Railroads
	Automotive Affiliated Representatives
AARC	American Ass'n for Respiratory Care
AARD	American Academy of Restorative Dentistry
AARG	Ass'n of Artist-Run Galleries
AARS	All-America Rose Selections
	American Ass'n of Railroad Superintendents
	American Ass'n of Railway Surgeons
AART	American Ass'n for Rehabilitation Therapy
AARTS	Ass'n of Advanced Rabbinical and Talmudic Schools
AARWBA	American Auto Racing Writers and Broadcasters Ass'n
AAS	American Analgesia Soc.
	American Antiquarian Soc.
	American Ass'n of Suicidology
	American Astronautical Soc.
	American Astronomical Soc.
	Ass'n for Academic Surgery
	Ass'n for Asian Studies
AASA	American Ass'n of School Administrators
	American Ass'n of Surgeon's Assistants
AASC	American Ass'n of Small Cities
	American Ass'n of State Climatologists
AASCO	Ass'n of American Seed Control Officials
AASCU	American Ass'n of State Colleges and Universities
AASE	American Ass'n of Special Educators
AASECT	American Ass'n of Sex Educators, Counselors and Therapists
AASFE	American Ass'n of Sunday and Feature Editors
AASG	Ass'n of American State Geologists
AASGP	American Ass'n of Sheep and Goat Practitioners
AASH	American Ass'n for the Study of Headache
AASHTO	American Ass'n of State Highway and Transportation Officials
AASL	American Ass'n of School Librarians
AASLD	American Ass'n for the Study of Liver Diseases
AASLH	American Ass'n for State and Local History
AASND	American Ass'n for the Study of Neoplastic Diseases
AASP	American Academy of Sports Physicians
	American Ass'n for Social Psychiatry
	American Ass'n of Senior Physicians
	American Ass'n of Stratigraphic Palynologists
	American Ass'n of Swine Practitioners
AASPA	American Ass'n of School Personnel Administrators
AASRC	American Ass'n of Small Research Companies
AAST	American Ass'n for the Surgery of Trauma
AASW	American Ass'n of Scientific Workers
AAT	American Academy of Thermography
AATA	American Art Therapy Ass'n
	American Ass'n of Teachers of Arabic
AATACB	American Athletic Trainers Ass'n and Certification Board
AATB	American Ass'n of Tissue Banks
AATCC	American Ass'n of Textile Chemists and Colorists
AATEA	American Ass'n of Teacher Educators in Agriculture
AATF	American Ass'n of Teachers of French
AATG	American Ass'n of Teachers of German
AATI	American Ass'n of Teachers of Italian
AATS	American Academy of Teachers of Singing
	American Ass'n for Thoracic Surgery
AATSEEL	American Ass'n of Teachers of Slavic and East European Languages
AATSP	American Ass'n of Teachers of Spanish and Portuguese
AATT	American Ass'n for Textile Technology
AAU	Ass'n of American Universities
AAUA	American Ass'n of University Administrators
AAUAP	American Ass'n of University Affiliated Programs
AAUP	American Ass'n of University Professors
	Ass'n of American University Presses
AAV	Ass'n of American Vintners
AAVA	American Ass'n of Veterinary Anatomists
AAVCT	American Academy of Veterinary and Comparative Toxicology
AAVD	American Academy of Veterinary Dermatology
AAVIM	American Ass'n for Vocational Instructional Materials
AAVLD	American Ass'n of Veterinary Laboratory Diagnosticians
AAVMC	Ass'n of American Veterinary Medical Colleges
AAVN	American Academy of Veterinary Nutrition
AAVP	American Ass'n of Veterinary Parasitologists
AAVSO	American Ass'n of Variable Star Observers
AAVT	Ass'n of Audio-Visual Technicians
AAWD	American Ass'n of Women Dentists
AAWI	Ass'n of American Woodpulp Importers
AAWP	American Ass'n for Women Podiatrists
AAYM	American Ass'n of Youth Museums
AAYPP	American Ass'n of Yellow Pages Publishers
AAZK	American Ass'n of Zoo Keepers
AAZPA	American Ass'n of Zoological Parks and Aquariums
AAZV	American Ass'n of Zoo Veterinarians
AAfPE	American Ass'n for Paralegal Education
AB	Ankina Breeders
ABA	Air Brake Ass'n
	Alpha Beta Alpha
	American Bakers Ass'n
	American Bandmasters Ass'n
	American Bankers Ass'n
	American Bar Ass'n
	American Beauty Ass'n
	American Berkshire Ass'n
	American Booksellers Ass'n
	American Breed Ass'n
	American Buffalo Ass'n
	American Burn Ass'n
	American Bus Ass'n
	Ass'n for Behavior Analysis
	Ayrshire Breeders Ass'n
ABAA	American Beverage Alcohol Ass'n
	American Blonde D'Aquitaine Ass'n
	Antiquarian Booksellers Ass'n of America
ABBA	American Bed & Breakfast Ass'n
	American Brahman Breeders Ass'n
ABBIM	Ass'n of Brass and Bronze Ingot Manufacturers
ABBRA	American Boat Builders and Repairers Ass'n
ABC	American Blood Commission
	American Business Conference
	Associated Builders and Contractors
	Ass'n for Business Communication
	Ass'n of Biotechnology Companies
	Ass'n of Bituminous Contractors
	Ass'n of Bridal Consultants
	Audit Bureau of Circulations
ABCA	American Baseball Coaches Ass'n
ABCD	ABCD: The Microcomputer Industry Ass'n
	Ass'n for Bridge Construction and Design
	Ass'n of Biomedical Communications Directors
ABCI	Automotive Booster Clubs Internat'l
ABCMC	Automotive Battery Charger Manufacturers Council
ABCR	American Bashkir Curly Registry
ABEA	American Broncho-Esophagological Ass'n
ABES	Ass'n for Broadcast Engineering Standards
ABF	American Beekeeping Federation
ABFLO	Ass'n of Bedding and Furniture Law Officials
ABGWIU	Aluminum, Brick and Glass Workers Internat'l Union
ABH	Ass'n for the Bibliography of History
ABHC	Ass'n of Bank Holding Companies
ABI	American Bankruptcy Institute
	American Butter Institute
ABJS	Ass'n of Bone and Joint Surgeons
ABKA	American Boarding Kennels Ass'n
ABLA	American Blind Lawyers Ass'n
	American Business Law Ass'n
ABLE	Ass'n for Biology Laboratory Education
ABLS	American Bryological and Lichenological Soc.
ABMA	American Boiler Manufacturers Ass'n
	American Brush Manufacturers Ass'n
ABMS	American Board of Medical Specialties
	American Bureau of Metal Statistics
ABO	Affiliated Boards of Officials
ABOPS	Ass'n of Business Officers of Preparatory Schools
ABP	Ass'n for Birth Psychology
	Ass'n of Business Publishers
ABPA	Aftermarket Body Parts Ass'n
	American Book Producers Ass'n
ABPsi	Ass'n of Black Psychologists
ABRA	American Blood Resources Ass'n
	American Buckskin Registry Ass'n
ABS	American Bureau of Shipping
	Animal Behavior Soc.
	Ass'n of Black Sociologists
ABSEL	Ass'n for Business Simulation and Experiential Learning
ABSMA	American Bleached Shellac Manufacturers Ass'n
ABTA	American Bridge Teachers' Ass'n
ABWA	American Business Women's Ass'n
	Associated Business Writers of America
ABWR	American Beefalo World Registry
ABYC	American Boat and Yacht Council
AC&CCI	American Coke and Coal Chemicals Institute
ACA	Agriculture Council of America
	American Camping Ass'n
	American Cemetery Ass'n
	American Chain Ass'n
	American Chianina Ass'n
	American Chiropractic Ass'n
	American Collectors Ass'n
	American College of Allergists
	American College of Angiology
	American College of Apothecaries
	American Compensation Ass'n
	American Composers Alliance
	American Correctional Ass'n
	American Council for the Arts
	American Crystallographic Ass'n
	Amerifax Cattle Ass'n
	Ass'n for Communication Administration
ACA+DE	Ass'n for Computer Art and Design Education
ACAA	American Coal Ash Ass'n
ACAD	American Conference of Academic Deans
ACB	Associated Credit Bureaus
	Ass'n of Concert Bands
ACBMA	Associated Corset and Brassiere Manufacturers Ass'n
ACC	American College of Cardiology
	American College of Chemosurgery
	American College of Cryosurgery
	American Copper Council
	American Craft Council
ACCA	Air Conditioning Contractors of America
	American Clinical and Climatological Ass'n
	American Commercial Collectors Ass'n
	American Corporate Counsel Ass'n
	American Correctional Chaplains Ass'n
ACCC	Ass'n of Community Cancer Centers
ACCCA	American Catholic Correctional Chaplains Ass'n
ACCCE	Ass'n of Consulting Chemists and Chemical Engineers
ACCE	American Chamber of Commerce Executives
ACCH	Ass'n for the Care of Children's Health
ACCI	American Council on Consumer Interests
	Ass'n of Crafts and Creative Industries
ACCN	American Court and Commercial Newspapers
ACCP	American College of Chest Physicians
	American College of Clinical Pharmacology
	American College of Clinical Pharmacy
ACCRA	American Chamber of Commerce Researchers Ass'n
ACCRSS	Ass'n for Creative Change within Religious and other Social Systems
ACCT	Ass'n of Community College Trustees
ACCU	Ass'n of Catholic Colleges and Universities
ACD	American College of Dentists
ACDA	American Choral Directors Ass'n
ACDM	Ass'n of Chairmen of Departments of Mechanics
ACDPI	American Cultured Dairy Products Institute
ACE	Agricultural Communicators in Education

ACRONYM INDEX

American Cinema Editors
American Council on Education
Ass'n of Co-operative Educators
Ass'n of Conservation Engineers
ACEA American Cotton Exporter's Ass'n
ACEC American Consulting Engineers Council
ACEI Ass'n for Childhood Education Internat'l
ACEP American College of Emergency Physicians
ACES Ass'n for Comparative Economic Studies
Ass'n for Counselor Education and Supervision
ACF American Choral Foundation
American Culinary Federation
Ass'n of Consulting Foresters
ACFO American College of Foot Orthopedists
ACFS American College of Foot Surgeons
ACFSA American Correctional Food Service Ass'n
ACG American College of Gastroenterology
Ass'n for Corporate Growth
ACGIH American Conference of Governmental Industrial Hygienists
ACGPOMS American College of General Practitioners in Osteopathic Medicine and Surgery
ACH Ass'n for Computers and the Humanities
Ass'n of Cosmetologists and Hairdressers
ACHA American Catholic Historical Ass'n
American College Health Ass'n
American Council of Highway Advertisers
ACHCA American College of Health Care Administrators
ACHE American College of Healthcare Executives
Ass'n for Continuing Higher Education
ACHEMA Air Cooled Heat Exchanger Manufacturers Ass'n
ACHM American College of Healthcare Marketing
ACHS Ass'n of College Honor Societies
ACHSA American Correctional Health Services Ass'n
ACI American Concrete Institute
Ass'n for Conservation Information, The
ACIA Associated Cooperage Industries of America
ACIAS American Council of Industrial Arts Supervisors
ACIASAO American Council of Industrial Arts State Ass'n Officers
ACIL American Council of Independent Laboratories
ACIP American College of Internat'l Physicians
American Council on Internat'l Personnel
ACIS American Committee for Irish Studies
ACJA American Criminal Justice Ass'n
ACJS Academy of Criminal Justice Sciences
ACL American Classical League
American Consultants League
Ass'n for Computational Linguistics
Ass'n of Christian Librarians
ACLA American Clinical Laboratory Ass'n
American Comparative Literature Ass'n
ACLAM American College of Laboratory Animal Medicine
ACLI American Council of Life Insurance
ACLM American College of Legal Medicine
ACLS American Council of Learned Societies
ACM American College of Musicians
Ass'n for Computing Machinery
ACMA American Catfish Marketing Ass'n
American Cutlery Manufacturers Ass'n
ACME ACME, Inc.-The Association of Management Consulting Firms
ACMF American Corn Millers Federation
ACMGA American College of Medical Group Administrators
ACMI Art and Craft Materials Institute
ACMRA Ass'n of Commercial Mail Receiving Agencies
ACMU American Canoe Manufacturers Union
ACN American College of Neuropsychiatrists
American College of Neuropsychopharmacology
American College of Nutrition
ACNM American College of Nuclear Medicine
American College of Nurse-Midwives
ACNP American College of Nuclear Physicians
ACNS American Council of Nanny Schools
ACOEP American College of Osteopathic Emergency Physicians
ACOG American College of Obstetricians and Gynecologists
ACOI American College of Osteopathic Internists
ACOMS American College of Oral and Maxillofacial Surgeons
ACOOG American College of Osteopathic Obstetricians and Gynecologists
ACOP American College of Osteopathic Pediatricians
ACOS American College of Osteopathic Surgeons
ACP American College of Physicians
American College of Podopediatrics
American College of Prosthodontists
American College of Psychiatrists
Associated Church Press
Associated Construction Publications
Ass'n for Child Psychoanalysis
ACPA American Catholic Philosophical Ass'n
American Cleft Palate Ass'n
American College Personnel Ass'n
American Concrete Pavement Ass'n
American Concrete Pipe Ass'n
American Concrete Pumping Ass'n
ACPC American College of Probate Counsel
ACPE American College of Physician Executives
Ass'n for Clinical Pastoral Education
Ass'n for Continuing Professional Education
ACPI Aviation Crime Prevention Institute
ACPM American College of Preventive Medicine
ACPNSPA Associated Collegiate Press, Nat'l Scholastic Press Ass'n
ACPPA American Concrete Pressure Pipe Ass'n
ACPR American College of Podiatric Radiologists
American Crossbred Pony Register
ACPS American Connemara Pony Soc.
ACR American College of Radiology
Ass'n for Consumer Research
Ass'n of Computer Retailers
ACRA American Car Rental Ass'n
American Collegiate Retailing Ass'n
ACRC Ass'n of Commercial Records Centers
ACRI American Cocoa Research Institute
ACRIM Ass'n for Correctional Research and Information Management
ACRL Ass'n of College and Research Libraries
ACRM American Congress of Rehabilitation Medicine
ACRW American Council of Railroad Women
ACS American Cancer Soc.
American Carbon Soc.
American Chemical Soc.
American College of Surgeons
Ass'n of Clinical Scientists
ACSA American Cotton Shippers Ass'n
Ass'n of Collegiate Schools of Architecture
ACSH American Council on Science and Health
ACSI Ass'n of Christian Schools Internat'l
Automotive Cooling System Institute
ACSM American College of Sports Medicine
American Congress on Surveying and Mapping
ACSMA American Cloak and Suit Manufacturers Ass'n
ACSP Ass'n of Collegiate Schools of Planning
ACSS American Cheviot Sheep Soc.
ACSUS Ass'n for Canadian Studies in the United States
ACT American College of Toxicology
Ass'n for Commuter Transportation
Ass'n of Civilian Technicians
ACTA American Cardiology Technologists Ass'n
American Cement Trade Alliance
American Corrective Therapy Ass'n
ACTC Ass'n of Community Travel Clubs
ACTFL American Council on the Teaching of Foreign Languages
ACTL American College of Trial Lawyers
ACTR American Council of Teachers of Russian
ACTRS Ass'n of Catholic TV and Radio Syndicators
ACTWU Amalgamated Clothing and Textile Workers Union
ACUA Ass'n of College and University Auditors
ACUCAA Ass'n of College, University and Community Arts Administrators
ACUHO-I Ass'n of College and University Housing Officers-Internat'l
ACUI Ass'n of College Unions-Internat'l
ACULE Ass'n of Credit Union League Executives
ACUP Ass'n of College and University Printers
ACURA Ass'n for the Coordination of University Religious Affairs
ACURP American College of Utilization Review Physicians
ACUTA Ass'n of College and University Telecommunications Administrators
ACVIM American College of Veterinary Internal Medicine
ACVL Ass'n of Cinema and Video Laboratories
ACVM American College of Veterinary Microbiologists
ACVO American College of Veterinary Ophthalmologists
ACVP American College of Veterinary Pathologists
ACVR American College of Veterinary Radiology
ACVS American College of Veterinary Surgeons
ACW American Chain of Warehouses
ACWRRE American Cargo War Risk Reinsurance Exchange
ACerS American Ceramic Soc.
AD Allied Distribution
AD-MRA American and Delaine-Merino Record Ass'n
ADA Academy of Dispensing Audiologists
American Dairy Ass'n
American Dental Ass'n
American Dermatological Ass'n
American Diabetes Ass'n
American Dietetic Ass'n
American Down Ass'n
ADAA American Dental Assistants Ass'n
Art Dealers Ass'n of America
ADAPSO ADAPSO, the Computer Software and Services Industry Ass'n
ADARA American Deafness and Rehabilitation Ass'n
ADC Advertising Council
Air Diffusion Council
Ass'n of Diving Contractors
ADCA Aerospace Department Chairmen's Ass'n
American Dexter Cattle Ass'n
ADCBIS Ass'n for the Development of Computer-Based Instructional Systems
ADCI American Die Casting Institute
ADDS American Digestive Disease Soc.
American Diopter and Decibel Soc.
ADE Ass'n for Documentary Editing
ADG American Dance Guild
ADGA American Dairy Goat Ass'n
ADH Academy of Dentistry for the Handicapped
ADHA American Dental Hygienists' Ass'n
ADI Academy of Dentistry Internat'l
Air Distributing Institute
ADIC American Dental Interfraternity Council
ADLTDE Ass'n of Dark Leaf Tobacco Dealers and Exporters
ADM Academy of Dental Materials
ADMA Ass'n of Direct Marketing Agencies
Automatic Damper Manufacturers Ass'n
Aviation Distributors and Manufacturers Ass'n Internat'l
ADMS American Donkey and Mule Soc.
ADP Academy of Denture Prosthetics
ADPA American Defense Preparedness Ass'n
ADPANA Alcohol and Drug Problems Ass'n of North America
ADPI American Dairy Products Institute
ADRA Automotive Dismantlers and Recyclers Ass'n
ADS American Dialect Soc.
Ass'n for Dressings and Sauces
Ass'n of Diesel Specialists
ADSA American Dairy Science Ass'n
American Dental Soc. of Anesthesiology
ADSAI American Dermatologic Soc. for Allergy and Immunology
ADSC Ass'n of Drilled Shaft Contractors
ADTA American Dance Therapy Ass'n
American Dental Trade Ass'n
ADTI American Dinner Theatre Institute
ADTSEA American Driver and Traffic Safety Education Ass'n
AE Avocado Export
AEA Actors' Equity Ass'n
Aircraft Electronics Ass'n
American Economic Ass'n
American Electrology Ass'n
American Electronics Ass'n
Nat'l Artists Equity Ass'n
AEB American Egg Board
Ass'n of Editorial Businesses
AEC Aluminum Extruders Council
Ass'n of Episcopal Colleges
AECT Ass'n for Educational Communications and Technology
AED Associated Equipment Distributors
AEDC American Economic Development Council
AEE Ass'n for Evolutionary Economics
Ass'n for Experiential Education
Ass'n of Energy Engineers
AEEGS American Electroencephalographic Soc.
AEEP Ass'n of Environmental Engineering Professors
AEG Ass'n of Engineering Geologists
AEHF Ass'n for Employee Health and Fitness
AEIC Ass'n of Edison Illuminating Companies
AEJMC Ass'n for Education in Journalism and Mass Communication
AEMA Asphalt Emulsion Manufacturers Ass'n
Athletic Equipment Managers Ass'n
AEMB Alliance for Engineering in Medicine and Biology
AEMCC Air and Expedited Motor Carriers Conference
AEMS American Engineering Model Soc.
AEPP Ass'n of Existential Psychology and Psychiatry
AER Ass'n for Education and Rehabilitation of the Blind andVisually Impaired
AERA American Educational Research Ass'n
Automotive Engine Rebuilders Ass'n
AES Abrasive Engineering Soc.
American Endodontic Soc.
American Entomological Soc.
American Epidemiological Soc.
American Epilepsy Soc.
American Equilibration Soc.
American Ethnological Soc.
Audio Engineering Soc.
AESA American Educational Studies Ass'n
AESC Ass'n of Executive Search Consultants
AESE Ass'n of Earth Science Editors
AESFS American Electroplaters and Surface Finishers Soc.
AESMC Automotive Exhaust Systems Manufacturers Council
AETA Amatex Export Trade Ass'n
American Embryo Transfer Ass'n
AETS Ass'n for the Education of Teachers in Science
AF Afram Films
AFA Air Force Ass'n
American Fan Ass'n
American Farriers Ass'n
American Finance Ass'n
American Forensic Ass'n
American Forestry Ass'n
American Formalwear Ass'n
American Fracture Ass'n
American Franchise Ass'n
Aspirin Foundation of America
Ass'n of Flight Attendants
AFAA Adult Film Ass'n of America
Aerobics and Fitness Ass'n of America
Air Freight Ass'n of America
AFAC Allied Finance Adjusters Conference
AFAUSSS Ass'n of Former Agents of the U.S. Secret Service
AFAi Accounting Firms Associated
AFBA Armed Forces Broadcasters Ass'n
AFBF American Farm Bureau Federation
AFBMA Anti-Friction Bearing Manufacturers Ass'n
AFC American Forest Council
Ass'n of Film Commissioners
AFCA American Fastener and Closure Ass'n
American Football Coaches Ass'n

The information in this directory is available in *Mailing List* form. See back insert.

ACRONYM INDEX

AFCC	Ass'n of Family and Conciliation Courts
AFCCE	Ass'n of Federal Communications Consulting Engineers
AFCEA	Armed Forces Communications and Electronics Ass'n
AFCG	American Fine China Guild
AFCMA	Aluminum Foil Container Manufacturers Ass'n
AFCR	American Federation for Clinical Research
AFD	Ass'n of Footwear Distributors
AFDO	Ass'n of Food and Drug Officials
AFDS	Associated Funeral Directors Service
AFEA	American Fastener Enclosure Ass'n
	Aviation Facilities Energy Ass'n
AFFA	Ass'n for Field Archaeology
AFFI	American Frozen Food Institute
AFFIRM	Ass'n for Federal Information Resources Management
AFGC	American Forage and Grassland Council
AFGE	American Federation of Government Employees
AFGM	American Federation of Grain Millers Internat'l Union
AFGWU	American Flint Glass Workers Union
AFHHA	American Federation of Home Health Agencies
AFI	American Fur Industry
	Ass'n of Federal Investigators
	Ass'n of Food Industries
AFIA	American Feed Industry Ass'n
AFIO	Ass'n of Former Intelligence Officers
AFIPS	American Federation of Information Processing Societies
AFL-CIO	American Federation of Labor and Congress of Industrial Organizations
AFLA	American Foreign Law Ass'n
	Automotive Fleet and Leasing Ass'n
AFLP	Ass'n of Fundraising List Professionals
AFM	Academy of Family Mediators
	American Federation of Musicians of the United States and Canada
AFMA	American Film Marketing Ass'n
	American Fur Merchant's Ass'n
	American Furniture Manufacturers Ass'n
AFMBT	Artificial Flower Manufacturers Board of Trade
AFMC	Armed Forces Marketing Council
	Automotive Filter Manufacturers Council
AFMCC	Air Freight Motor Carriers Conference
AFP	American Federation of Police
	Ass'n for Finishing Processes
AFS	American Fern Soc.
	American Fertility Soc.
	American Fisheries Soc.
	American Folklore Soc.
	American Foundrymen's Soc.
AFS&HP	Ass'n of Federal Safety and Health Professionals
AFSA	African Studies Ass'n
	Air Force Sergeants Ass'n
	American Federation of School Administrators
	American Financial Services Ass'n
	American Fire Sprinkler Ass'n
	American Foreign Service Ass'n
AFSB	American Federation of Small Business
AFSCME	American Federation of State, County and Municipal Employees
AFSI	Architectural Fabric Structures Institute
AFSMI	Ass'n of Field Service Managers, Internat'l
AFT	American Federation of Teachers
AFTA	American Family Therapy Ass'n
AFTE	Ass'n of Firearm and Toolmark Examiners
AFTHBA	American Fox Trotting Horse Breed Ass'n
AFTMA	American Fishing Tackle Manufacturers Ass'n
AFTRA	American Federation of Television and Radio Artists
AG	Acrylonitrile Group
	Apparel Guild
	Ass'n for Gnotobiotics
	Authors Guild
	Autoleather Guild
AGA	Abrasive Grain Ass'n
	Accredited Gemologists Ass'n
	American Gas Ass'n
	American Gastroenterological Ass'n
	American Gelbvieh Ass'n
	American Genetic Ass'n
	American Guides Ass'n
	Ass'n of Government Accountants
AGAC	Ass'n of Graphic Arts Consultants
AGAUS	Adjutants General Ass'n of the United States
AGBA	American Galloway Breeders Ass'n
AGBAD	Alexander Graham Bell Ass'n for the Deaf
AGBC	Avocado Growers Bargaining Council
AGBUC	Ass'n of Governing Boards of Universities and Colleges
AGCA	Associated General Contractors of America
AGCC	American Guernsey Cattle Club
AGCPAF	American Group of CPA Firms
AGD	Academy of General Dentistry
	Academy of Geriatric Dentistry
	Associated Gas Distributors
AGE	American Aging Ass'n
AGHE	Ass'n for Gerontology in Higher Education
AGI	American Geological Institute
AGLSP	Ass'n of Graduate Liberal Studies Programs
AGM	American Guild of Music
AGMA	American Gear Manufacturers Ass'n
	American Guild of Musical Artists
AGMC	Ass'n of General Merchandise Chains
AGMSA	American Gem and Mineral Suppliers Ass'n
AGO	American Guild of Organists
AGOS	American Gynecological and Obstetrical Soc.
AGPA	American Group Practice Ass'n
	American Group Psychotherapy Ass'n
AGPM	Associated Glass and Pottery Manufacturers
AGS	American Gem Soc.
	American Geographical Soc.
	American Geriatrics Soc.
	American Goat Soc.
AGSAAU	Ass'n of Graduate Schools in Ass'n of American Universities
AGTA	Airport Ground Transportation Ass'n
	American Gem Trade Ass'n
AGTE	Ass'n of Group Travel Executives
AGTOA	American Greyhound Track Operators Ass'n
AGU	American Geophysical Union
AGVA	American Guild of Variety Artists
AGVGA	American Greenhouse Vegetable Growers Ass'n
AGVS	Automatic Guided Vehicle Systems
AHA	American Hardboard Ass'n
	American Heart Ass'n
	American Hereford Ass'n
	American Historical Ass'n
	American Hospital Ass'n
	American Hypnotists' Ass'n
	Ass'n of Hispanic Arts
AHAM	Ass'n of Home Appliance Manufacturers
AHBAI	American Health and Beauty Aids Institute
AHC	American Horse Council
AHCA	American Health Care Ass'n
	American Hockey Coaches Ass'n
AHCM	Academy of Hazard Control Management
AHDGA	American Hot Dip Galvanizers Ass'n
AHEA	American Home Economics Ass'n
	American Hungarian Educators Ass'n
AHEAD	Ass'n for Humanistic Education and Development
AHHS	American Hackney Horse Soc.
AHI	Animal Health Institute
AHL	American Hockey League
AHLI	American Home Lighting Institute
AHMA	American Hardware Manufacturers Ass'n
	American Holistic Medical Ass'n
	American Hotel and Motel Ass'n
AHME	Ass'n for Hospital Medical Education
AHMI	Appalachian Hardwood Manufacturers
AHNA	American Holistic Nurses' Ass'n
AHP	American Horse Publications
	Ass'n for Humanistic Psychology
AHPA	American Health Planning Ass'n
	American Herbal Products Ass'n
	American Honey Producers Ass'n
AHRA	American Healthcare Radiology Administrators
	Arabian Horse Registry of America
AHS	Agricultural History Soc.
	American Hanoverian Soc.
	American Heartworm Soc.
	American Helicopter Soc. Internat'l
	American Horticultural Soc.
AHSA	African Heritage Studies Ass'n
	American Hampshire Sheep Ass'n
	American Home Sewing Ass'n
	American Humor Studies Ass'n
AHSSPPE	Ass'n on Handicapped Student Service Programs in Postsecondary Education
AHTN	Ass'n of Hospital Television Networks
AI	Asphalt Institute
AIA	Acupuncture Internat'l Ass'n
	Aerospace Industries Ass'n of America
	Aestheticians Internat'l Ass'n
	American Institute of Architects
	American Insurance Ass'n
	Anthracite Industry Ass'n
	Apiary Inspectors of America
	Archaeological Institute of America
	Ass'n of Insurance Attorneys
	Auto Internacional Ass'n
	Automobile Importers of America
AIA/NA	Asbestos Information Ass'n/North America
AIAA	American Institute of Aeronautics and Astronautics
AIADA	American Internat'l Automobile Dealers Ass'n
AIAG	Automotive Industry Action Group
AIAR	American Institute for Archaeological Research
AIASA	American Industrial Arts Student Ass'n
AIB	Academy of Internat'l Business
	Ass'n of Investment Brokers
AIBD	American Institute of Building Design
AIBS	American Institute of Biological Sciences
AIC	American Institute for Conservation of Historic and Artistic Works
	American Institute of Chemists
	American Institute of Cooperation
	Ass'n of Independent Camps
	Automotive Information Council
AICA	Alliance of Independent Colleges of Art
	American Institute of Commemorative Art
	American Internat'l Charolais Ass'n
AICC	Ass'n of Independent Corrugated Converters
AICCI	American-Israel Chamber of Commerce and Industry
AICCP	Ass'n of the Institute for Certification of Computer Professionals
AICM	Ass'n of Independent Conservatories of Music
AICP	American Institute of Certified Planners
	Ass'n of Independent Commercial Producers
AICPA	American Institute of Certified Public Accountants
AICS	Ass'n of Independent Colleges and Schools
AIChE	American Institute of Chemical Engineers
AIDD	American Institute for Design and Drafting
AIF	Atomic Industrial Forum
AIFB	American Institute of Financial Brokers
AIFD	American Institute of Food Distribution
AIFRB	American Institute of Fishery Research Biologists
AIFSA	American Institutions Food Service Ass'n
AIGA	American Institute of Graphic Arts
AIH	American Institute for Homeopathy
	American Institute of Hydrology
AIHA	American Industrial Hygiene Ass'n
AIHC	American Industrial Health Council
AIHCA	American Indian Health Care Ass'n
AIHP	American Institute of the History of Pharmacy
AIHR	Ass'n of Internat'l Health Researchers
AIHSA	American Insurers Highway Safety Alliance
AIIM	Ass'n for Information and Image Management
AIIS	American Institute for Imported Steel
	American Institute of Indian Studies
AILA	American Immigration Lawyers Ass'n
AIM	American Innerspring Manufacturers
	Associated Information Managers
	Ass'n of Independent Microdealers
	Automatic Identification Manufacturers
AIM/R	Ass'n of Industrial Manufacturers' Representatives
AIMC	American Institute of Medical Climatology
	Ass'n of Internal Management Consultants
AIMCAL	Ass'n of Industrial Metallizers, Coaters and Laminators
AIME	American Institute of Mining, Metallurgical, and Petroleum Engineers
AIMED	Ass'n of Independent Mailing Equipment Dealers
AIMFI	Ass'n of Information Managers Financial Institutions
AIMP	Ass'n of Independent Music Publishers
AIMRA	Agricultural and Industrial Manufacturers' Representatives Ass'n
AIMS	American Institute of Merchant Shipping
	American Internat'l Marchigiana Soc.
	Ass'n for Internat'l Marathons (AIMS)
AIMT	Ass'n for Integrated Manufacturing Technology
AIMU	American Institute of Marine Underwriters
AIN	American Institute of Nutrition
	Ass'n of Interpretive Naturalists
AINTM	American Institute of Nail and Tack Manufacturers
AIOA	American Iron Ore Ass'n
AIOB	American Institute of Oral Biology
AIP	American Institute of Parliamentarians
	American Institute of Physics
AIPAD	Ass'n of Internat'l Photography Art Dealers
AIPBS	American Institute for Patristic and Byzantine Studies
AIPE	American Institute of Plant Engineers
AIPG	American Institute of Professional Geologists
AIPLA	American Intellectual Property Law Ass'n
AIPLU	American Institute for Property and Liability Underwriters
AIR	American Institute of Reciprocators
	Ass'n for Institutional Research
AIRA	American Independent Refiners Ass'n
AIRC	Airline Industrial Relations Conference
AIREA	American Institute of Real Estate Appraisers
AIRS	Alliance of Information and Referral Systems
AIS	Ass'n for Integrative Studies
AISA	American Institute for Shippers Ass'ns
AISC	American Institute of Steel Construction
AISE	Ass'n of Iron and Steel Engineers
AISI	American Iron and Steel Institute
AISP	Ass'n of Information Systems Professionals
AIT	Academy for Implants and Transplants
AITC	American Institute of Timber Construction
AITIA	American Institute of Technical Illustrators Ass'n
AIUM	American Institute of Ultrasound in Medicine
AIVF	Ass'n of Independent Video and Filmmakers
AJA	American Jail Ass'n
	American Judges Ass'n
AJBP	Ass'n of Jewish Book Publishers
AJCAF	Ass'n of Jewish Chaplains of the Armed Forces
AJCC	American Jersey Cattle Club
AJCCA	American Jewish Correctional Chaplains Ass'n
AJCU	Ass'n of Jesuit Colleges and Universities
AJCW	Ass'n of Jewish Center Workers
AJFCA	Ass'n of Jewish Family and Children's Agencies
AJHS	American Jewish Historical Soc.
AJL	Ass'n of Jewish Libraries
	Ass'n of Junior Leagues
AJMA	American Jewelry Marketing Ass'n
AJPA	American Jewish Press Ass'n
AJS	American Judicature Soc.
	Ass'n for Jewish Studies
AKFM	Ass'n of Knitted Fabrics Manufacturers
AKFSR	American Karakul Sheep Registry
AKP	Alpha Kappa Psi
AL	American League of Professional Baseball Clubs
	Associated Laboratories
ALA	Aluminum Ass'n
	American Laminators Ass'n
	American Landrace Ass'n

ACRONYM INDEX

American Laryngological Ass'n
American Library Ass'n
American Logistics Ass'n
American Longevity Ass'n
American Lung Ass'n
Ass'n of Legal Administrators
Authors League of America
ALAPCO Ass'n of Local Air Pollution Control Officials
ALC American Legend Cooperative
ALCA American Leather Chemists Ass'n
Associated Landscape Contractors of America
ALCF Ass'n of Lutheran College Faculties
ALDA American Luggage Dealers Ass'n
ALEA Air Line Employees Ass'n, International
Airborne Law Enforcement Ass'n
ALFI American League of Financial Institutions
ALHFA Ass'n of Local Housing Finance Agencies
ALHFAM Ass'n for Living Historical Farms and Agricultural Museums
ALI American Ladder Institute
American Law Institute
Automotive Lift Institute
ALIC Ass'n of Life Insurance Counsel
ALIMDA Ass'n of Life Insurance Medical Directors of America
ALISE Ass'n for Library and Information Science Education
ALL AirLifeLine
American League of Lobbyists
ALMA Alternative Living Managers Ass'n
American Loudspeaker Manufacturers Ass'n
Analytical Laboratory Managers Ass'n
ALMACA Ass'n of Labor-Management Administrators and Consultants on Alcoholism
ALOA Amalgamated Lace Operatives of America
Associated Locksmiths of America
ALPA Air Line Pilots Ass'n, Internat'l
ALPNA American Licensed Practical Nurses Ass'n
ALROS American Laryngological, Rhinological and Otological Soc.
ALS American Littoral Soc.
ALSC Ass'n for Library Service to Children
ALTA American Land Title Ass'n
American Library Trustee Ass'n
American Literary Translators Ass'n
AM Academy of Management
AMA Adhesives Manufacturers Ass'n
American Management Ass'n
American Maritime Ass'n
American Marketing Ass'n
American Medical Ass'n
American Monument Ass'n
American Mustang Ass'n
AMAA American Maine-Anjou Ass'n
AMASLG Ass'n of Management Analysts in State and Local Government
AMBA American Malting Barley Ass'n
Ass'n of Master of Business Administration Executives
AMBBA/HI Associated Master Barbers and Beauticians of America/Hair Internat'l
AMBUCS Nat'l Ambucs
AMC American Mining Congress
American Movers Conference
American Music Conference
Ass'n of Management Consultants
AMCA Air Movement and Control Ass'n
American Mosquito Control Ass'n
AMCBO Ass'n of Major City Building Officials
AMCD Ass'n for Multicultural Counseling and Development
AMCEA Advertising Media Credit Executives Ass'n, Internat'l
AMCHCCP Ass'n for Maternal and Child Health and Crippled Children's Programs
AMCRA American Medical Care and Review Ass'n
AMCSUS Ass'n of Military Colleges and Schools of the U.S.
AMDA Airline Medical Directors Ass'n
Associated Minicomputer Dealers of America
AMDM Ass'n of Microbiological Diagnostic Manufacturers
AMDMA American Metal Detector Manufacturers Ass'n
AME Ass'n for Manufacturing Excellence
AMEA Ass'n of Machinery and Equipment Appraisers
AMECD Ass'n for Measurement and Evaluation in Counseling and Development
AMEEGA American Medical Electroencephalographic Ass'n
AMEM Ass'n of Marine Engine Manufacturers
AMFI Aviation Maintenance Foundation
AMGA American Murray Grey Ass'n
AMHA American Morgan Horse Ass'n
Ass'n of Mental Health Administrators
AMHC Ass'n of Mental Health Clergy
AMHCA American Mental Health Counselors Ass'n
AMHL Ass'n of Mental Health Librarians
AMI Alliance of Metalworking Industries
American Meat Institute
American Mushroom Institute
Ass'n for Multi-Image International
Ass'n of Medical Illustrators
AMIA American Metal Importers Ass'n
AMIN Advertising and Marketing Internat'l Network
AMO Archery Manufacturers Organization
AMOA Amusement and Music Operators Ass'n
AMPA American Medical Publishers' Ass'n
AMPAS Academy of Motion Picture Arts and Sciences
AMPRA American Medical Peer Review Ass'n
AMPTP Alliance of Motion Picture and Television Producers
AMQUA American Quaternary Ass'n
AMRA American Medical Record Ass'n
AMRC Automotive Market Research Council
AMRDC Ass'n of Medical Rehabilitation Directors and Coordinators
AMS Academy of Marketing Science
Administrative Management Soc.
American Mathematical Soc.
American Meteorological Soc.
American Microchemical Soc.
American Microscopical Soc.
American Montessori Soc.
American Musicological Soc.
AMSA American Meat Science Ass'n
American Medallic Sculpture Ass'n
American Medical Student Ass'n
American Metal Stamping Ass'n
Ass'n of Metropolitan Sewerage Agencies
AMSE Ass'n of Muslim Scientists and Engineers
AMSOV Ass'n of Major Symphony Orchestra Volunteers
AMSPDC Ass'n of Medical School Pediatric Department Chairmen
AMSS American Milking Shorthorn Soc.
AMST Ass'n of Maximum Service Telecasters
AMSUS Ass'n of Military Surgeons of the U.S.
AMT American Medical Technologists
AMTA American Massage Therapy Ass'n
AMTDA American Machine Tool Distributors Ass'n
AMU American Malacological Union
American Musicians Union
AMWA American Medical Women's Ass'n
American Medical Writers Ass'n
ANA Aeronautical Navigator Ass'n
American Naprapathic Ass'n
American Neurological Ass'n
American Nurses' Ass'n
Ass'n of Nat'l Advertisers
ANADP Ass'n of North American Directory Publishers
ANAM Ass'n of North American Missions
ANCAM Ass'n of Newspaper Classified Advertising Managers
ANEC American Nuclear Energy Council
ANI American Nuclear Insurers
ANM Alliance of Nonprofit Mailers
ANMC American Nat'l Metric Council
ANNA American Nephrology Nurses' Ass'n
ANPA American Newspaper Publishers Ass'n
ANRC Animal Nutrition Research Council
ANROTCCU Ass'n of Naval R.O.T.C. Colleges and Universities
ANS American Name Soc.
American Nuclear Soc.
American Numismatic Soc.
ANSAC American Natural Soda Ash Corporation
ANSI American Nat'l Standards Institute
ANSS American Nature Study Soc.
ANVEC ANV Export Corporation
AO Alpha Omega
AOA American Optometric Ass'n
American Orthopaedic Ass'n
American Orthopsychiatric Ass'n
American Osteopathic Ass'n
Ass'n of Otolaryngology Administrators
AOAC Ass'n of Official Analytical Chemists
AOAO American Osteopathic Academy of Orthopedics
AOAS American Osteopathic Academy of Sclerotherapy
AOASM American Osteopathic Academy of Sports Medicine
AOC Ass'n of Old Crows
AOCA American Osteopathic College of Anesthesiologists
AOCAI American Osteopathic College of Allergy and Immunology
AOCD American Osteopathic College of Dermatology
AOCF Ass'n of Outplacement Consulting Firms
AOCI Airport Operators Council Internat'l
AOCPr American Osteopathic College of Proctology
AOCR American Osteopathic College of Radiology
AOCS Airline Operational Control Soc.
American Oil Chemists' Soc.
AOD Academy of Operative Dentistry
Academy of Oral Dynamics
AODME Academy of Osteopathic Directors of Medical Education
AOE Ass'n of Overseas Educators
AOHA American Osteopathic Hospital Ass'n
AOM Academy of Orthomolecular Medicine
America on the Move
Ass'n of Operative Millers
AOMA American Occupational Medical Ass'n
Apartment Owners and Managers Ass'n of America
AONE American Organization of Nurse Executives
AOO American Oceanic Organization
AOPA Aircraft Owners and Pilots Ass'n
American Orthotic and Prosthetic Ass'n
Automotive Occupant Protection Ass'n
AOPL Ass'n of Oil Pipe Lines
AORC Ass'n of Official Racing Chemists
AORN Ass'n of Operating Room Nurses
AOS American Ophthalmological Soc.
American Oriental Soc.
American Orthodontic Soc.
American Otological Soc.
AOSA American Oxford Sheep Ass'n
Ass'n of Official Seed Analysts
AOSC Ass'n of Oilwell Servicing Contractors
AOSCA Ass'n of Official Seed Certifying Agencies
AOSED Ass'n of Osteopathic State Executive Directors
AOSSM American Orthopaedic Soc. for Sports Medicine
AOTA American Occupational Therapy Ass'n
AOU American Ornithologists' Union
AP/FPLIC Ass'n for Population/Family Planning Libraries and Information Centers, Internat'l
APA Acrylamide Producers Ass'n
Agricultural Publishers Ass'n
Amalgamated Printers' Ass'n
Ambulatory Pediatric Ass'n
American Parquet Ass'n
American Philological Ass'n
American Philosophical Ass'n
American Pilots' Ass'n
American Pinzgauer Ass'n
American Planning Ass'n
American Plywood Ass'n
American Polygraph Ass'n
American Poultry Ass'n
American Psychiatric Ass'n
American Psychological Ass'n
American Psychopathological Ass'n
American Pulpwood Ass'n
American Pyrotechnics Ass'n
Architectural Precast Ass'n
Ass'n of Paroling Authorities
APAA Automotive Parts and Accessories Ass'n
APAG American Photographic Artisans Guild
APALA Asian/Pacific American Librarians Ass'n
APAP Ass'n of Physician Assistant Programs
APB Associated Press Broadcasters
APBP Ass'n of Professional Bridge Players
APC Academy of Parish Clergy
Ass'n of Pathology Chairmen
APCA Air Pollution Control Ass'n
APCCA American Protestant Correctional Chaplains' Ass'n
APCL Ass'n of Professional Color Laboratories
APCO Associated Public-Safety Communications Officers
APCP Ass'n of Paid Circulation Publications
APDA Appliance Parts Distributors Ass'n
APDF Ass'n of Professional Design Firms
APDIM Ass'n of Program Directors in Internal Medicine
APDU Ass'n of Public Data Users
APDYMCA Ass'n of Professional Directors of YMCAs in the United States
APEC American Peanut Export Corporation
Automotive Products Export Council
APECA American Package Express Carriers Ass'n
APFA American Pipe Fittings Ass'n
APFC Ass'n of Physical Fitness Centers
APFO Ass'n on Programs for Female Offenders
APG American Pewter Guild, Ltd.
Ass'n of Professional Genealogists
APGA American Public Gas Ass'n
APGO Ass'n of Professors of Gynecology and Obstetrics
APHA American Paint Horse Ass'n
American Polled Hereford Ass'n
American Protestant Health Ass'n
American Public Health Ass'n
APHS American Poultry Historical Soc.
API Accountants for the Public Interest
American Paper Institute
American Petroleum Institute
APIC Ass'n for Practitioners in Infection Control
APICS American Production and Inventory Control Soc.
APITCA American Producers of Italian Type Cheese Ass'n
APJE Ass'n of Philosophy Journals Editors
APLSI American Prepaid Legal Services Institute
APM Academy of Psychosomatic Medicine
Ass'n for Psychoanalytic Medicine
Ass'n of Professors of Medicine
Ass'n of Professors of Missions
APMA American Podiatric Medical Ass'n
American Productivity Management Ass'n
APMHC Ass'n of Professional Material Handling Consultants
APMI American Powder Metallurgy Institute
APMS Aquatic Plant Management Soc.
APOBA Associated Pipe Organ Builders of America
APON Ass'n of Pediatric Oncology Nurses
APPA American Public Power Ass'n
Ass'n of Physical Plant Administrators of Universities and Colleges
APPMA American Pet Products Manufacturers Ass'n
APPP Ass'n of Planned Parenthood Professionals
APPS Ass'n of Private Postal Systems
APPWP Ass'n of Private Pension and Welfare Plans
APR Ass'n of Petroleum Re-refiners
APRA American Park Rangers Ass'n
Ass'n of Political Risk Analysts
Automotive Parts Rebuilders Ass'n
APRES American Peanut Research and Education Soc.
APRO American Professional Racquetball Organization
Ass'n of Progressive Rental Organizations

ACRONYM INDEX

APRRE	Ass'n of Professors and Researchers in Religious Education
APS	Academy of Pharmaceutical Sciences
	Academy of Political Science
	American Pain Soc.
	American Pediatric Soc.
	American Philosophical Soc.
	American Physical Soc.
	American Physiological Soc.
	American Phytopathological Soc.
	American Pomological Soc.
	American Prosthodontic Soc.
	American Psychosomatic Soc.
	American Purchasing Soc.
	Ass'n of Productivity Specialists
APSA	American Political Science Ass'n
APSM	Academy of Product Safety Management
APSS	American Polled Shorthorn Soc.
APTA	American Physical Therapy Ass'n
	American Public Transit Ass'n
APTIF	Ass'n of Publicly Traded Investment Funds
APTP	Ass'n of Part-Time Professionals
APVE	Ass'n of Professional Vocal Ensembles
APWA	American Public Welfare Ass'n
	American Public Works Ass'n
APWC	Ass'n of Professional Writing Consultants
APWU	American Postal Workers Union
APhA	American Pharmaceutical Ass'n
APsaA	American Psychoanalytic Ass'n
AQHA	American Quarter Horse Ass'n
ARA	Aluminum Recycling Ass'n
	American Recovery Ass'n
	American Rental Ass'n
	American Retreaders' Ass'n
	American Rheumatism Ass'n
ARAE	American Retail Ass'n Executives
ARAM	Ass'n of Railroad Advertising and Marketing
ARAPCS	Ass'n for Research, Administration, Professional Councils and Societies
ARBA	American Rabbit Breeders Ass'n
	American Red Brangus Ass'n
	American Romney Breeders Ass'n
ARBBA	American Railway Bridge and Building Ass'n
ARC	Agricultural Relations Council
	All-Breeds Rescue Conservancy
	American Recreation Coalition
	American Rose Council
	Ass'n of Railway Communicators
ARCA	American Rehabilitation Counseling Ass'n
ARCB	Ass'n of Reserve City Bankers
ARCCLMA	Aromatic Red Cedar Closet Lining Manufacturers Ass'n
ARCFCP	Alliance for Responsible CFC Policy
ARCI	American Railway Car Institute
ARCPACS	American Registry of Certified Professionals in Agronomy, Crops and Soils
ARCRT	American Registry of Clinical Radiography Technologists
ARD	Ass'n of Research Directors
ARDA	American Railway Development Ass'n
AREA	American Railway Engineering Ass'n
	American Recreational Equipment Ass'n
AREUEA	American Real Estate and Urban Economics Ass'n
ARF	Advertising Research Foundation
	American Retail Federation
ARGR	Ass'n for Research in Growth Relationships
ARI	Agricultural Research Institute
	Air-Conditioning and Refrigeration Institute
ARIA	American Risk and Insurance Ass'n
ARL	Ass'n of Research Libraries
ARLIS/NA	Art Libraries Soc./North America
ARM	Ass'n of Railway Museums
	Ass'n of Rotational Molders
ARMA	Asphalt Roofing Manufacturers Ass'n
	Ass'n of Records Managers and Administrators
ARMM	Ass'n of Reproduction Materials Manufacturers
ARMS	Ass'n of Racquetsports Manufacturers and Suppliers
	Ass'n of Retail Marketing Services
ARN	Ass'n of Rehabilitation Nurses
ARNMD	Ass'n for Research in Nervous and Mental Disease
AROUSPHS	Ass'n of Reserve Officers of the U.S. Public Health Service
ARPA	American Red Poll Ass'n
	Ass'n of Representatives of Professional Athletes
ARPDP	Ass'n of Rehabilitation Programs in Data Processing
ARPE	American Registry of Professional Entomologists
ARPG	Asphalt Rubber Producers Group
ARPI	Automotive Refrigeration Products Institute
ARR	Ass'n for Regulatory Reform
ARRA	Asphalt Recycling and Reclaiming Ass'n
ARRC	Ass'n of Regional Religious Communicators
ARRDA	American Resort and Residential Development Ass'n
ARRO	Archery Range and Retailers Organization
ARRS	American Roentgen Ray Soc.
	Ass'n of Radio Reading Services
ARS	American Radium Soc.
	American Rhinologic Soc.
ARSA	Aeronautical Repair Station Ass'n
ARSBA	American Rambouillet Sheep Breeders Ass'n
ARSC	Ass'n for Recorded Sound Collections
ARTA	Ass'n of Retail Travel Agents
ARTBA	American Road and Transportation Builders Ass'n
ARVIC	Ass'n for Religious and Value Issues in Counseling
ARVO	Ass'n for Research in Vision and Ophthalmology
ARW	Air-conditioning and Refrigeration Wholesalers Ass'n
AS	Adhesion Soc.
AS/RS	Automated Storage/Retrieval Systems
ASA	Acoustical Soc. of America
	Afghanistan Studies Ass'n
	American Schizophrenia Ass'n
	American Schools Ass'n
	American Shorthorn Ass'n
	American Simmental Ass'n
	American Soc. for Aesthetics
	American Soc. of Agronomy
	American Soc. of Anesthesiologists
	American Soc. of Appraisers
	American Soc. of Artists
	American Soc. on Aging
	American Sociological Ass'n
	American Soybean Ass'n
	American Sportcasters Ass'n
	American Statistical Ass'n
	American Studies Ass'n
	American Subcontractors Ass'n
	American Supply Ass'n
	American Surety Ass'n
	American Surgical Ass'n
	Automotive Service Ass'n
ASAAD	American Soc. for the Advancement of Anesthesia in Dentistry
ASAC	American Soc. of Agricultural Consultants
ASAE	American Soc. of Agricultural Engineers
	American Soc. of Ass'n Executives
ASAHP	American Soc. of Allied Health Professions
ASAIO	American Soc. for Artificial Internal Organs
ASALH	Ass'n for the Study of Afro-American Life and History
ASAM	Ass'n of Sales Administration Managers
ASAO	Ass'n for Social Anthropology in Oceania
ASAP	American Soc. for Adolescent Psychiatry
	American Soc. of Access Professionals
ASAPS	American Soc. for Aesthetic Plastic Surgery
ASAS	American Soc. of Abdominal Surgeons
	American Soc. of Animal Science
ASAW	American Soc. of Aviation Writers
ASBA	American Southdown Breeders Ass'n
	Ass'n of Ship Brokers and Agents (U.S.A.)
ASBC	American Seat Belt Council
	American Soc. of Biological Chemists
	American Soc. of Brewing Chemists
ASBCS	Ass'n of Southern Baptist Colleges and Schools
ASBDA	American School Band Directors' Ass'n
ASBDC	Ass'n of Small Business Development Centers
ASBE	American Soc. of Bakery Engineers
	American Soc. of Body Engineers
ASBO	Ass'n of School Business Officials Int'l
ASBP	American Soc. of Bariatric Physicians
ASBPE	American Soc. of Business Press Editors
ASBS	Ass'n of Social and Behavioral Scientists
ASC	Adhesive and Sealant Council
	Airport Security Council
	American Soc. for Cybernetics
	American Soc. of Cinematographers
	American Soc. of Criminology
	American Soc. of Cytology
	Associated Specialty Contractors
	Ass'n of Systematics Collections
	Automotive Service Councils
ASCA	American School Counselor Ass'n
	American Soc. for Conservation Archaeology
	American Soc. of Consulting Arborists
	American Swimming Coaches Ass'n
	Ass'n of State Correctional Administrators
ASCAP	American Soc. of Composers, Authors and Publishers
ASCB	American Soc. for Cell Biology
ASCBC	American Soc. of Certified Business Counselors
ASCC	American Soc. for Concrete Construction
ASCCP	American Soc. for Colposcopy and Cervical Pathology
ASCD	American Soc. of Computer Dealers
	Ass'n for Supervision and Curriculum Development
ASCE	American Soc. of Civil Engineers
ASCET	American Soc. of Certified Engineering Technicians
ASCH	American Soc. of Church History
	American Soc. of Clinical Hypnosis
ASCI	American Soc. for Clinical Investigation
ASCL	American Sugar Cane League of the U.S.A.
ASCLA	Ass'n of Specialized and Cooperative Library Agencies
ASCLU&ChFC	American Soc. of CLU & ChFC
ASCMSO	American Soc. of Contemporary Medicine, Surgery and Ophthalmology
ASCN	American Soc. for Clinical Nutrition
ASCO	American Soc. of Clinical Oncology
	Ass'n of Schools and Colleges of Optometry
ASCP	American Soc. of Clinical Pathologists
	American Soc. of Consultant Pharmacists
	American Soc. of Consulting Planners
ASCPT	American Soc. for Clinical Pharmacology and Therapeutics
ASCR	Ass'n of Specialists in Cleaning and Restoration
ASCRS	American Soc. of Cataract and Refractive Surgery
	American Soc. of Colon and Rectal Surgeons
ASCS	American Soc. of Corporate Secretaries
ASCT	American Soc. for Cytotechnology
ASCUS	Ass'n for School, College and University Staffing
ASD	Academy for Sports Dentistry
	American Soc. of Dermatopathology
	Associated Surplus Dealers
	Ass'n of Steel Distributors
ASDA	American Soc. for Dental Aesthetics
	American Stamp Dealers' Ass'n
	American Student Dental Ass'n
ASDAE	Ass'n of Seventh-day Adventist Educators
ASDC	American Soc. of Dentistry for Children
	Ass'n of Sleep Disorders Centers
ASDS	American Soc. for Dermatologic Surgery
ASDVS	American Soc. of Directors of Volunteer Services
ASDWA	Ass'n of State Drinking Water Administrators
ASE	American Soc. for Ethnohistory
	American Soc. of Echocardiography
	American Soc. of Educators
	American Stock Exchange
	Ass'n for Social Economics
ASEC	American Sulphur Export Corporation
ASEE	American Soc. for Engineering Education
	American Soc. for Environmental Education
ASEM	American Soc. for Engineering Management
ASENSSC	Ass'n of Scientists and Engineers of the Naval Sea Systems Command
ASEP	American Soc. of Electroplated Plastics
ASES	American Solar Energy Soc.
ASET	Academy of Security Educators and Trainers
	American Soc. of Electro-Neurodiagnostic Technologists
ASEV	American Soc. for Enology and Viticulture
ASF	American Ski Federation
ASFD	American Soc. of Furniture Designers
ASFE	Ass'n of Soil and Foundation Engineers
ASFMRA	American Soc. of Farm Managers and Rural Appraisers
ASFO	American Soc. of Forensic Odontology
ASFSA	American School Food Service Ass'n
ASG	American Soc. of Genealogists
ASGA	American Sugarbeet Growers Ass'n
ASGCA	American Soc. of Golf Course Architects
ASGD	American Soc. for Geriatric Dentistry
ASGE	American Soc. for Gastrointestinal Endoscopy
	American Soc. of Gas Engineers
ASGPP	American Soc. of Group Psychotherapy and Psychodrama
ASGS	American Scientific Glassblowers Soc.
ASGW	Ass'n for Specialists in Group Work
ASH	American Soc. of Hematology
ASHA	American Saddlebred Horse Ass'n
	American School Health Ass'n
	American Shire Horse Ass'n
	American Speech-Language-Hearing Ass'n
ASHBA	American Scotch Highland Breeder's Ass'n
ASHCSP	American Soc. for Hospital Central Service Personnel
ASHE	American Soc. for Hospital Engineering
ASHET	American Soc. for Healthcare Education and Training
ASHFSA	American Soc. for Hospital Food Service Administrators
ASHG	American Soc. of Human Genetics
ASHHRA	American Soc. for Healthcare Human Resources Administration
ASHI	American Soc. for Histocompatability and Immunogenetics
	American Soc. of Home Inspectors
ASHMM	American Soc. for Hospital Materials Management
ASHMPR	American Soc. for Hospital Marketing and Public Relations
ASHNS	American Soc. for Head and Neck Surgery
ASHP	American Soc. of Hospital Pharmacists
ASHRAE	American Soc. of Heating, Refrigerating and Air-Conditioning Engineers
ASHRM	American Soc. for Hospital Risk Management
ASHS	American Soc. for Horticultural Science
ASHT	American Soc. of Hand Therapists
ASI	Allied Stone Industries
	American Sightseeing Internat'l
	American Soc. of Indexers
	American Soc. of Interpreters
	Aviation Safety Institute
ASIA	American Spinal Injury Ass'n
	Automotive Service Industry Ass'n
ASID	American Soc. of Interior Designers
ASIDIC	Ass'n of Information and Dissemination Centers
ASIE	American Soc. of Internat'l Executives
ASIH	American Soc. of Ichthyologists and Herpetologists
ASIL	American Soc. of Internat'l Law
ASIM	American Soc. of Internal Medicine
ASIS	American Soc. for Industrial Security
	American Soc. for Information Science
ASIWPCA	Ass'n of State and Interstate Water Pollution Control Administrators
ASJA	American Soc. of Journalists and Authors

ACRONYM INDEX

ASJMC	Ass'n of Schools of Journalism and Mass Communication
ASKT	American Soc. of Knitting Technologists
ASL	Ass'n for Symbolic Logic
ASLA	American Soc. of Landscape Architects
ASLAP	American Soc. of Laboratory Animal Practitioners
ASLE	American Soc. of Lubrication Engineers
ASLH	American Soc. for Legal History
ASLM	American Soc. of Law and Medicine
ASLMS	American Soc. for Laser Medicine and Surgery
ASLO	American Soc. of Limnology and Oceanography
ASLRA	American Short Line Railroad Ass'n
ASM	American Soc. for Metals
	American Soc. for Microbiology
	American Soc. of Mammalogists
	American Soc. of Missiology
	Ass'n for Systems Management
ASMA	American Soc. of Marine Artists
ASMC	American Soc. of Military Comptrollers
ASMD	Ass'n of Science Museum Directors
ASMDT	American Soc. of Master Dental Technologists
ASME	American Soc. of Magazine Editors
	American Soc. of Mechanical Engineers
ASMER	Ass'n for the Study of Man-Environment Relations
ASMHF	Ass'n of Sports Museums and Halls of Fame
ASMMA	American Supply and Machinery Manufacturers Ass'n
ASMP	American Soc. of Magazine Photographers
ASMS	American Soc. for Mass Spectrometry
	American Soc. of Maxillofacial Surgeons
ASMT	American Soc. for Medical Technology
ASN	American Soc. for Neurochemistry
	American Soc. of Naturalists
	American Soc. of Nephrology
	American Soc. of Neuroimaging
	American Soc. of Neuroradiology
	American Soc. of Notaries
ASNA	American SMR Network Ass'n
ASNE	American Soc. of Naval Engineers
	American Soc. of Newspaper Editors
ASNT	American Soc. for Nondestructive Testing
ASOA	American Soc. of Ophthalmic Administrators
ASOR	American Schools of Oriental Research
ASORN	American Soc. of Ophthalmic Registered Nurses
ASOS	American Soc. of Outpatient Surgeons
ASP	American Soc. for Photobiology
	American Soc. of Papyrologists
	American Soc. of Parasitologists
	American Soc. of Pharmacognosy
	American Soc. of Photographers
	American Soc. of Primatologists
ASPA	American Shrimp Processors Ass'n
	American Soc. for Personnel Administration
	American Soc. for Public Administration
	American Soc. of Pension Actuaries
	American Soc. of Podiatric Medical Assistants
	American Sod Producers Ass'n
ASPAN	American Soc. of Post-Anesthesia Nurses
ASPC	American Sheep Producers Council
	American Shetland Pony Club
ASPD	American Soc. of Podiatric Dermatology
ASPE	American Soc. of Plumbing Engineers
	American Soc. of Professional Estimators
	American Soc. of Psychopathology of Expression
ASPEN	American Soc. for Parenteral and Enteral Nutrition
ASPET	American Soc. for Pharmacology and Experimental Therapeutics
ASPEW	American Soc. of Professional and Executive Women
ASPH	Ass'n of Schools of Public Health
ASPI	American Soc. for Performance Improvement
ASPN	American Soc. for Pediatric Neurosurgery
ASPO	American Soc. for Psychoprophylaxis in Obstetrics
ASPOE	American Soc. of Petroleum Operations Engineers
ASPP	American Soc. of Picture Professionals
	American Soc. of Plant Physiologists
	American Soc. of Psychoanalytic Physicians
ASPRS	American Soc. for Photogrammetry and Remote Sensing
	American Soc. of Plastic and Reconstructive Surgeons
ASPRSN	American Soc. of Plastic and Reconstructive Surgical Nurses
ASPT	American Soc. of Plant Taxonomists
ASQC	American Soc. for Quality Control
ASQDE	American Soc. of Questioned Document Examiners
ASR	Ass'n for the Sociology of Religion
ASRA	American Seafood Retailers Ass'n
	American Shropshire Registry Ass'n
	American Soc. of Regional Anesthesia
ASREC	American Soc. of Real Estate Counselors
ASRT	American Soc. of Radiologic Technologists
ASSBT	American Soc. of Sugar Beet Technologists
ASSE	American Soc. of Safety Engineers
	American Soc. of Sanitary Engineering
ASSFN	American Soc. for Stereotactic and Functional Neurosurgery
ASSH	American Soc. for Surgery of the Hand
ASSO	American Soc. for the Study of Orthodontics
ASSR	American Soc. for the Study of Religion
ASSS	American Suffolk Sheep Soc.
AST	Ass'n of Surgical Technologists
ASTA	American Seed Trade Ass'n
	American Soc. of Travel Agents
	American Spice Trade Ass'n
	American String Teachers Ass'n
ASTAN	American Ski Teachers Ass'n of Natur Teknik
ASTC	American Soc. of Trial Consultants
	Ass'n of Science-Technology Centers
ASTD	American Soc. for Training and Development
ASTDD	Ass'n of State and Territorial Dental Directors
ASTDN	Ass'n of State and Territorial Directors of Nursing
ASTE	American Soc. of Test Engineers
ASTHO	Ass'n of State and Territorial Health Officials
ASTL	American Soc. of Transportation and Logistics
ASTM	ASTM
ASTMH	American Soc. of Tropical Medicine and Hygiene
ASTR	American Soc. for Theatre Research
ASTRO	American Soc. for Therapeutic Radiology and Oncology
ASTSWMO	Ass'n of State and Territorial Solid Waste Management Officials
ASUC	American Soc. of University Composers
ASVO	American Soc. of Veterinary Ophthalmology
ASVPP	American Soc. of Veterinary Physiologists and Pharmacologists
ASWA	American Soc. of Women Accountants
ASYA	American Stock Yards Ass'n
ASYM	Ass'n of Synthetic Yarn Manufacturers
ASZ	American Soc. of Zoologists
ATA	Advertising Typographers Ass'n of America
	American Tarentaise Ass'n
	American Telemarketing Ass'n
	American Thyroid Ass'n
	American Tinnitus Ass'n
	American Trakehner Ass'n
	American Translators Ass'n
	American Trucking Ass'ns
	American Tube Ass'n
	American Tunaboat Ass'n
ATAA	Air Transport Ass'n of America
ATAE	Associated Telephone Answering Exchanges
	Automotive Trade Ass'n Executives
ATB	Ass'n for Tropical Biology
ATBI	Allied Trades of the Baking Industry
ATCA	Air Traffic Control Ass'n
	American Theatre Critics Ass'n
ATCPA	Air Taxi and Commercial Pilots Ass'n
ATD	Alpha Tau Delta
ATDA	American Train Dispatchers Ass'n
ATE	Ass'n of Teacher Educators
ATEA	American Technical Education Ass'n
ATFAC	American Turpentine Farmers Ass'n Co-op
ATG	Accordion Teachers' Guild
ATJ	Ass'n of Teachers of Japanese
ATLA	American Theological Library Ass'n
	Ass'n of Trial Lawyers of America
ATLAS	Ass'n of Teachers of Latin American Studies
ATMA	American Textile Machinery Ass'n
	American Tour Managers Ass'n
ATME	Ass'n of Travel Marketing Executives
ATMI	American Textile Manufacturers Institute
ATP	Ass'n of Tennis Professionals
	Ass'n of Tequila Producers
	Ass'n of Transportation Practioners
ATPM	Ass'n of Teachers of Preventive Medicine
ATRA	Advanced Transit Ass'n
	Automatic Transmission Rebuilders Ass'n
ATS	American Thoracic Soc.
	American Trauma Soc.
ATSOA	American Truck Stop Operators Ass'n
ATSSA	American Traffic Safety Services Ass'n
ATSUSC	Ass'n of Theological Schools in the United States and Canada
ATTA	American Tin Trade Ass'n
ATTMCA	Ass'n of Tile, Terrazzo, Marble Contractors and Affiliates
ATTW	Ass'n of Teachers of Technical Writing
ATU	Amalgamated Transit Union
ATYSC	Associated Two-Year Schools in Construction
AUA	American Underground-Space Ass'n
	American Urological Ass'n
	Ass'n of University Anesthetists
	Ass'n of University Architects
AUAA	American Urological Ass'n Allied
AUBER	Ass'n for University Business and Economic Research
AUPHA	Ass'n of University Programs in Health Administration
AUR	Ass'n of University Radiologists
AURA	Ass'n of Universities for Research in Astronomy
AUSA	Ass'n of the United States Army
AUSNVM	Ass'n of United States Night Vision Manufacturers
AUSS	Ass'n of University Summer Sessions
AUSUDIAP	Ass'n of United States University Directors of Interant'l Agricultural Programs
AUU	Ass'n of Urban Universities
AUVS	Ass'n for Unmanned Vehicle Systems
AVA	American Vocational Ass'n
	Ass'n for Volunteer Administration
	Automated Vision Ass'n
AVAS	Ass'n of Voluntary Action Scholars
AVC	Academy of Veterinary Cardiology
	Ass'n of Visual Communicators
AVDA	American Venereal Disease Ass'n
AVEA	American Veterinary Exhibitors Ass'n
AVEM	Ass'n of Vacuum Equipment Manufacturers
AVERA	American Vocational Education Research Ass'n
AVMA	American Veterinary Medical Ass'n
	Audio Visual Management Ass'n
AVRHS	Ass'n for Vital Records and Health Statistics
AVS	American Vacuum Soc.
AVSAB	American Veterinary Soc. of Animal Behavior
AVSL	Ass'n of Visual Science Librarians
AWA	American Warehousemen's Ass'n
	American Watch Ass'n
	American Wine Ass'n
	Ass'n of Women in Architecture
	Aviation/Space Writers Ass'n
AWBA	American Wholesale Booksellers Ass'n
AWC	Affiliated Warehouse Companies
	American Women Composers
	American Wood Council
	Ass'n for Women in Computing
AWCEA	American Wood Chip Export Ass'n
AWCI	American Wire Cloth Institute
	Ass'n of the Wall and Ceiling Industries-Internat'l
AWCMA	American Window Coverings Manufacturers Ass'n
AWDA	Automotive Warehouse Distributors Ass'n
AWEA	American Wind Energy Ass'n
AWG	Ass'n for Women Geoscientists
AWI	American Watchmakers Institute
	Architectural Woodwork Institute
AWIS	Ass'n for Women in Science
AWM	Ass'n for Women in Mathematics
AWO	American Waterways Operators
AWP	Associated Writing Programs
	Ass'n for Women in Psychology
AWPA	American Wire Producers Ass'n
	American Wood-Preservers' Ass'n
AWPB	American Wood Preservers Bureau
AWPI	American Wood Preservers Institute
AWR	American Warmblood Registry
AWRA	American Water Resources Ass'n
AWRF	Associated Wire Rope Fabricators
AWRT	American Women in Radio and Television
AWS	American Welding Soc.
AWSC	American Waterways Shipyard Conference
AWSCPA	American Woman's Soc. of Certified Public Accountants
AWTAO	Ass'n of Water Transportation Accounting Officers
AWV	Ass'n for Women Veterinarians
AWWA	American Water Works Ass'n
AYC	American Yorkshire Club
AYSA	American Yarn Spinners Ass'n
AZO	Alpha Zeta Omega
AmSect	American Soc. of Extra-corporeal Technology
ApHC	Appaloosa Horse Club
AsMA	Aerospace Medical Ass'n
B/H	Below/Hook Lifters Ass'n
B/PAA	Business/Professional Advertising Ass'n
BA	Belt Ass'n
BAA	Brewers Ass'n of America
BACC	Belgian American Chamber of Commerce in the United States
	Brazilian American Chamber of Commerce
	British-American Chamber of Commerce
BAEB	Bituminous and Aggregate Equipment Bureau
BAFT	Bankers' Ass'n for Foreign Trade
BAI	Bank Administration Institute
BAP	Beta Alpha Psi
BAWA	Burley Auction Warehouse Ass'n
BBAA	Barzona Breeders Ass'n of America
	Bridal and Bridesmaids Apparel Ass'n
BBIA	Billiard and Bowling Institute of America
BBII	Brass and Bronze Ingot Institute
BBSI	Beauty and Barber Supply Institute
BBU	Beefmaster Breeders Universal
BBWA	Bright Belt Warehouse Ass'n
BC	Business Council
BCA	Billiard Congress of America
	Boys Clubs of America
	Broadcast Credit Ass'n
BCBSA	Blue Cross and Blue Shield Ass'n
BCDA	Biscuit and Cracker Distributors Ass'n
BCI	Battery Council Internat'l
BCMA	Biscuit and Cracker Manufacturers Ass'n
BCOA	Bituminous Coal Operators Ass'n
BCPA	Boys Clubs Professional Ass'n
BCTWIU	Bakery, Confectionery and Tobacco Workers' Internat'l Union
BDHC	Belgian Draft Horse Corp. of America
BDLTEA	Burley and Dark Leaf Tobacco Export Ass'n
BEA	Broadcast Education Ass'n
BEMA	Bakery Equipment Manufacturers Ass'n
BEMS	Bioelectromagnetics Soc.
BFMA	Broadcast Financial Management Ass'n
	Business Forms Management Ass'n
BGA	Barre Granite Ass'n
	Behavior Genetics Ass'n
BHC	Business History Conference
BHMA	Builders Hardware Manufacturers Ass'n
BI	Beer Institute
BIA	Barbecue Industry Ass'n
	Binding Industries of America
	Brick Institute of America
	Buses Internat'l Ass'n

ACRONYM INDEX

BICSI	Built-in Cleaning Systems Institute
BIF	Beef Improvement Federation
BIFMA	Business and Institutional Furniture Manufacturers Ass'n
BISG	Book Industry Study Group
BISSC	Baking Industry Sanitation Standards Committee
BJA	Burlap and Jute Ass'n
BLE	Brotherhood of Locomotive Engineers
BLTDA	Burley Leaf Tobacco Dealers Ass'n
BLTI	Better Lawn and Turf Institute
BMA	Bank Marketing Ass'n
	Biomedical Marketing Ass'n
	Black Music Ass'n
BMAA	Bicycle Manufacturers Ass'n of America
BMC	Broker Management Council
BMES	Biomedical Engineering Soc.
BMI	Book Manufacturers Institute
BMMA	Beverage Machinery Manufacturers Ass'n
BMWE	Brotherhood of Maintenance of Way Employes
BOCAI	Building Officials and Code Administrators Internat'l
BOMA	Building Owners and Managers Ass'n Internat'l
BOMI	Box Office Management Internat'l
BPA	Biological Photographic Ass'n
	Black Psychiatrists of America
	Business Planning Board
	Business Publications Audit of Circulation
BPAA	Bowling Proprietors Ass'n of America
BPI	BPI . . .A Growers' Organization
BPME	Broadcast Promotion and Marketing Executives
BPRA	Baptist Public Relations Ass'n
BRAC	Brotherhood of Railway, Airline and Steamship Clerks, Freight Handlers, Express and Station Employees
BRANA	Bumper Recycling Ass'n of North America
BRCUSC	Brotherhood Railway Carmen of the United States and Canada
BRDA	Boxboard Research and Development Ass'n
BRMA	Business Records Manufacturers Ass'n
BRS	Brotherhood of Railroad Signalmen
BS	Biophysical Soc.
	Boarding Schools
BSA	Bearing Specialist Ass'n
	Bibliographical Soc. of America
	Biofeedback Soc. of America
	Botanical Soc. of America
BSAC	Brotherhood of Shoe and Allied Craftsmen
BSC	Biological Stain Commission
BSCAI	Building Service Contractors Ass'n Internat'l
BSCBA	Brown Swiss Cattle Breeders Ass'n of the U.S.A.
BSDF	Beet Sugar Development Foundation
BSI	Building Stone Institute
	Building Systems Institute
BSNA	Bureau of Salesmen's Nat'l Ass'ns
BSPMC	Brake System Parts Manufacturers Council
BTGCA	Burley Tobacco Growers Cooperative Ass'n
BTMA	Bow Tie Manufacturers Ass'n
BTNDMSA	Black Top and Nat'l Delaine-Merino Sheep Breeders Ass'n
BTRS	Behavior Therapy and Research Soc.
BTWSM	Board of Trade of the Wholesale Seafood Merchants
BVI	Better Vision Institute
BWAA	Baseball Writers Ass'n of America
	Bowling Writers Ass'n of America
BWDA	Bicycle Wholesale Distributors Ass'n
BWI	Boating Writers Internat'l
CA	Cantors Assembly
	Council of the Americas
	Cranial Academy
CAA	Cigar Ass'n of America
	College Art Ass'n of America
	Colombian American Ass'n
CABMA	College Athletic Business Managers Ass'n
CABO	Council of American Building Officials
CAEL	Council for Adult and Experiential Learning
CAF	Council on Alternate Fuels
CAFI	Ceramic Arts Federation Internat'l
CAFMS	Continental Ass'n of Funeral and Memorial Socs.
CAGA	Catholic Actors Guild of America
CAGI	Compressed Air and Gas Institute
CAI	Career Apparel Institute
	Clowns of America, Internat'l
	Community Ass'ns Institute
CAID	Convention of American Instructors of the Deaf
CAM-I	Computer Aided Manufacturing-Internat'l
CAMA	Civil Aviation Medical Ass'n
CAMCA	Canadian-American Motor Carriers Ass'n
CAMEO	CAMEO
CAMI	Coated Abrasives Manufacturers' Institute
CAMM	Council of American Maritime Museums
	Council of American Master Mariners
CANA	Cremation Ass'n of North America
CAORC	Council of American Overseas Research Centers
CAP	College of American Pathologists
CAPE	Council for American Private Education
CAPP	Conference of Actuaries in Public Practice
CARALA	Conference of American Renting and Leasing Assn's
CAS	Casualty Actuarial Soc.
CASA	Car Audio Specialists Ass'n
CASA/SME	Computer and Automated Systems Ass'n of SME
CASE	Council for Advancement and Support of Education
CASI	Convenient Automotive Services Institute
CASO	Council of American-Flag Ship Operators
CASRO	Council of American Survey Research Organizations
CAST	Council for Agricultural Science and Technology
CATA	Community Antenna Television Ass'n
CAUS	Color Ass'n of the United States
CAVE	Catholic Audio-Visual Educators
CBA	Catholic Biblical Ass'n of America
	Christian Booksellers Ass'n
	Consumer Bankers Ass'n
	Continental Basketball Ass'n
CBBB	Council of Better Business Bureaus
CBC	Children's Book Council
CBDNA	College Band Directors Nat'l Ass'n
CBE	Council for Basic Education
	Council of Biology Editors
CBEMA	Computer and Business Equipment Manufacturers Ass'n
CBFC	Copper and Brass Fabricators Council
CBI	Carbonated Beverage Institute
CBM	Certified Ballast Manufacturers Ass'n
CBMP	Conference Board of Major Printers
CBMS	Conference Board of the Mathematical Sciences
CBSA	Copper and Brass Servicenter Ass'n
CBUS	Clydesdale Breeders of the United States
CC	Cajal Club
	Calorimetry Conference
	Controllers Council
CCA	Chemical Coaters Ass'n
	Chemical Communications Ass'n
	Collegiate Commissioners Ass'n
CCAI	Collector Car Appraisers Internat'l
CCAR	Central Conference of American Rabbis
CCAS	Council of Colleges of Arts and Sciences
CCBC	Council of Community Blood Centers
CCBS	Clear Channel Broadcasting Service
CCC	Calorie Control Council
	Car Care Council
	Carpet Cushion Council
	Christian College Coalition
	Christian College Consortium
CCCC	Conference on College Composition and Communication
	Coordinating Council for Computers in Construction
CCFL	Conference on Consumer Finance Law
CCG	Custom Clothing Guild of America
CCI	Cadmium Council
	Cotton Council Internat'l
CCIA	Computer and Communications Industry Ass'n
	Consumer Credit Insurance Ass'n
CCIC	Conference of Casualty Insurance Companies
CCJ	Conference of Chief Justices
CCJA	Community College Journalism Ass'n
CCLA	Chamber of Commerce of Latin America
CCLM	Coordinating Council of Literary Magazines
CCM	Council of Communication Management
CCMA	Catholic Campus Ministry Ass'n
	Certified Color Manufacturers Ass'n
CCMIA	Canned and Cooked Meat Importers Ass'n
CCMS	Congress of County Medical Societies
CCPA	Cemented Carbide Producers Ass'n
CCPG	China Clay Producers Group
CCSAA	Cross Country Ski Areas of America
CCSGP	Coalition for Common Sense in Government Procurement
CCSSO	Council of Chief State School Officers
CCTI	Composite Can and Tube Institute
CDA	Commercial Development Ass'n
	Copier Dealers Ass'n
	Copper Development Ass'n
CDABO	College of Diplomates of the American Board of Orthodontics
CDC	Continental Dorset Club
CDCDA	Community Design Center Directors Ass'n
CDFEA	California Dried Fruit Export Ass'n
CDI	Council on Diagnostic Imaging to the A.C.A.
	Cutting Die Institute
CDLA	Computer Dealers and Lessors Ass'n
CDOA	Car Department Officers Ass'n
CDSHA-US	Country Day School Headmasters Ass'n of the U.S.
CEA	California Export Ass'n
	Cement Employers Ass'n
	College English Ass'n
	Conservation Education Ass'n
	Cooperative Education Ass'n
	Correctional Education Ass'n
CEAPRC	Construction Equipment Advertisers and Public Relations Council
CEASD	Conference of Educational Administrators Serving the Deaf
CEAUS	Coal Exporters Ass'n of the United States
CEB	Council on Employee Benefits
CEC	Council for Exceptional Children
CEDR	Council for Educational Development and Research
CEE	Conference on English Education
	Council on Electrolysis Education
CEFPI	Council of Educational Facility Planners, Internat'l
CEMA	Cleaning Equipment Manufacturers Ass'n
	Converting Equipment Manufacturers Ass'n
	Conveyor Equipment Manufacturers Ass'n
CEO	Chief Executives Organization
CEPA	Soc. for Computer Applications in Engineering, Planning and Architecture
CES	Council for European Studies
CESSE	Council of Engineering and Scientific Soc. Executives
CETC	Council for Export Trading Companies
CEW	Cosmetic Executive Women
CFA	Catfish Farmers of America
	College Football Ass'n
	Consumer Federation of America
CFAS	Catholic Fine Arts Soc.
CFC	Contract Furnishings Council
CFDA	Council of Fashion Designers of America
CFEA	College Fraternity Editors Ass'n
CFF	Cystic Fibrosis Foundation
CFFA	Chemical Fabrics and Film Ass'n
CFMA	Construction Financial Management Ass'n
CFPAE	Council of Food Processors Ass'n Executives
CFS	Council of Fleet Specialists
CFSBI	Cold Finished Steel Bar Institute
CFTMA	Caster and Floor Truck Manufacturers Ass'n
CG	Cartoonists Guild
	Choristers Guild
CGA	Compressed Gas Ass'n
	Concord Grape Ass'n
CGCS	Council of the Great City Schools
CGEL	Council on Governmental Ethics Laws
CGGA	China, Glass and Giftware Ass'n
CGGP	Conference Group on German Politics
CGS	Council of Graduate Schools in the U.S.
CHA	Camp Horsemanship Ass'n
CHA-US	Catholic Health Ass'n of the United States
CHIAA	Crop-Hail Insurance Actuarial Ass'n
CHRIE	Council on Hotel, Restaurant and Institutional Education
CI	Chlorine Institute, The
	Combustion Institute
	Composites Institute
	Cordage Institute
CIA	Correctional Industries Ass'n
CIAA	Cheese Importers Ass'n of America
CIASDC	Callerlab-Internat'l Ass'n of Square Dance Callers
CIBO	Council of Industrial Boiler Owners
CIBS	Cosmetic Industry Buyers and Suppliers
CIC	Council of Independent Colleges
CICA	Captive Insurance Companies Ass'n
CIES	Comparative and Internat'l Education Soc.
	Internat'l Ass'n of Chain Stores - North American Headquarters
CII	Containerization and Intermodal Institute
CIL	Council for Interinstitutional Leadership
CIMA	Construction Industry Manufacturers Ass'n
CIMB	Construction Industry Management Board
CIRB	Crop Insurance Research Bureau
CISCA	Ceilings and Interior Systems Construction Ass'n
CISP	Council for Intercultural Studies and Programs
CISPI	Cast Iron Soil Pipe Institute
CITBA	Customs and Internat'l Trade Bar Ass'n
CIU	Congress of Independent Unions
CIUNA	Coopers' Internat'l Union of North America
CJE	Council for Jewish Education
CJSA	Costume Jewelry Salesmen's Ass'n
	Criminal Justice Statistics Ass'n
CKS	Cell Kinetics Soc.
CLA	Catholic Library Ass'n
	Coin Laundry Ass'n
	College Language Ass'n
	Computer Law Ass'n
CLA-USA	Christian Labor Ass'n of the United States of America
CLAE	Council of Library Ass'n Executives
CLAO	Contact Lens Ass'n of Opthalmologists
CLARB	Council of Landscape Architectural Registration Boards
CLAS	Clinical Ligand Assay Soc.
	Congress of Lung Ass'n Staff
CLC	Convention Liaison Council
CLCS	Chinese Language Computer Soc.
CLEAR	Nat'l Clearinghouse on Licensure, Enforcement and Regulation
CLFMI	Chain Link Fence Manufacturers Institute
CLIA	Cruise Lines Internat'l Ass'n
CLLA	Commercial Law League of America
CLM	Council of Logistics Management
CLMA	Clinical Laboratory Management Ass'n
	Contact Lens Manufacturers Ass'n
CLMTA	Council on Library-Media Technical-Assistants
CLS	Christian Legal Soc.
	Consular Law Soc.
CLSA	Canon Law Soc. of America
	Contact Lens Soc. of America
CLTA	Chinese Language Teachers Ass'n
CLUW	Coalition of Labor Union Women
CMA	Cast Metals Ass'n
	Chamber Music America
	Chemical Manufacturers Ass'n
	Childrenswear Manufacturers Ass'n
	Chocolate Manufacturers Ass'n of the U.S.A.
	Closure Manufacturers Ass'n
	College Media Advisers
	Communications Marketing Ass'n
	Cookware Manufacturers Ass'n
	Country Music Ass'n
	Cylinder Manufacturers Ass'n

ACRONYM INDEX

CMA-USA	Clothing Manufacturers Ass'n of the U.S.A.
CMAA	Casket Manufacturers Ass'n of America
	Club Managers Ass'n of America
	Cocoa Merchants' Ass'n of America
	Comics Magazine Ass'n of America
	Construction Management Ass'n of America
	Crane Manufacturers Ass'n of America
CMBA	Concert Music Broadcasters Ass'n
CMG	Color Marketing Group
	Computer Measurement Group
CMI	Can Manufacturers Institute
	Cleaning Management Institute
	Cultured Marble Institute
CMMA	Carpet Manufacturers Marketing Ass'n
	Christian Ministries Management Ass'n
CMPA	Church Music Publishers Ass'n
CMPAA	Certified Milk Producers Ass'n of America
CMRA	Chemical Marketing Research Ass'n
CMS	Christian Medical Soc.
	Clay Minerals Soc.
	College Music Soc.
CMSI	Council of Mutual Savings Institutions
CMSM	Conference of Major Superiors of Men, U.S.A.
CMSS	Council of Medical Specialty Societies
CMT	Computer Micrographics Technology
CNCE	Council for Noncollegiate Continuing Education
CNLIA	Council of Nat'l Library and Information Ass'ns
CNPC	Conference of Nat'l Park Concessioners
CNS	Congress of Neurological Surgeons
COA	Commissioned Officers Ass'n of the United States Public Health Service
CODASYL	Conference on Data Systems Languages
CODSIA	Council of Defense and Space Industry Ass'ns
COEANPC	Central Office Executives Ass'n of the Nat'l Panhellenic Conference
COF	Council on Foundations
COHE	College of Osteopathic Healthcare Executives
COIA	Conservative Orthopedics Internat'l Ass'n
COMPTEL	Competitive Telecommunications Ass'n
COMSEC	Communications Security Ass'n
COPA	Council on Postsecondary Accreditation
COPAFS	Council of Professional Ass'ns on Federal Statistics
COPHL	Conference of Public Health Laboratorians
CORD	Congress on Research in Dance
COS	Clinical Orthopaedic Soc.
COSLA	Chief Officers of State Library Agencies
COSMEP	COSMEP, Internat'l Ass'n of Independent Publishers
COSSMHO	Nat'l Coalition of Hispanic Health and Human Services Organizations
COVD	College of Optometrists in Vision Development
CPA	Catholic Press Ass'n
	Chlorobenzene Producers Ass'n
	Classroom Publishers Ass'n
	Concrete Pipe Ass'n
CPAA	CPA Associates
	Cultured Pearl Ass'n of America
	Cycle Parts and Accessories Ass'n
CPB	Contractors Pump Bureau
CPC	College Placement Council
CPCFA	Council of Pollution Control Financing Agencies
CPCU	Soc. of Chartered Property and Casualty Underwriters
CPDA	Council for Periodical Distributors Ass'ns
CPG	Collector Platemakers Guild
CPHV	Conference of Public Health Veterinarians
CPI	Carded Packaging Institute
CPIA	Cathodic Protection Industry Ass'n
CPL	Council of Planning Librarians
CPMB	Concrete Plant Manufacturers Bureau
CPMC	Construction Products Manufacturers Council
CPOA	Chief Petty Officers Ass'n
CPPA	Crusher and Portable Plant Ass'n
CPST	Commission on Professionals in Science and Technology
CPTA	Corrugated Plastic Tubing Ass'n
CRA	California Redwood Ass'n
	Corn Refiners Ass'n
CRC	Coordinating Research Council
CRCPD	Conference of Radiation Control Program Directors
CRESA	Commercial Food Equipment Service Ass'n
CRFI	Custom Roll Forming Institute
CRHA	Colorado Ranger Horse Ass'n
CRI	Carpet and Rug Institute
CRIS	Council for Religion in Independent Schools
CRMA	City and Regional Magazine Ass'n
	Commercial Refrigerator Manufacturers Ass'n
CRN	Council for Responsible Nutrition
CRS	Computerized Radiology Soc.
	Controlled Release Soc.
CRSI	Concrete Reinforcing Steel Institute
CRWAD	Conference of Research Workers in Animal Diseases
CS	Central Shippers
	Classification Soc. of North America
	Coblentz Soc.
CSA	Caricaturist Soc. of America
	Cryogenic Soc. of America
CSAA	Contract Services Ass'n of America
CSAVR	Council of State Administrators of Vocational Rehabilitation
CSBA	Char-Swiss Breeders Ass'n
	Columbia Sheep Breeders Ass'n of America
CSCA	Conference of State Court Adminstrators
CSCAA	College Swimming Coaches Ass'n of America
	Council of State Community Affairs Agencies
CSCC	Council of State Chambers of Commerce
CSCE	Coffee, Sugar and Cocoa Exchange
CSDA	Concrete Sawing and Drilling Ass'n
CSEPA	Central Station Electrical Protection Ass'n
CSF-USA	Correctional Service Federation-U.S.A.
CSG	Council of State Governments
CSGUS	Clinical Soc. of Genito-Urinary Surgeons
CSHA	Council of State Housing Agencies
CSI	Christian Schools Internat'l
	Computer Security Institute
	Construction Specifications Institute
CSLA	Church and Synagogue Library Ass'n
CSMA	Chemical Specialties Manufacturers Ass'n
CSNA	Catalysis Soc. of North America
CSPA	Council of Sales Promotion Agencies
	Council of State Policy and Planning Agencies
CSS	Cognitive Science Soc.
CSSA	Crop Science Soc. of America
CSSE	Conference of State Sanitary Engineers
CSSEDC	Conference for Secondary School English Department Chairpersons
CSSP	Council of Scientific Soc. Presidents
CSSS	Conference of State Bank Supervisors
CSTDPHE	Conference of State and Territorial Directors of PublicHealth Education
CSTE	Council of State and Territorial Epidemiologists
CSTPA	Council on Soil Testing and Plant Analysis
CSUSA	Copyright Soc. of the U.S.A.
CSWE	Council on Social Work Education
CTA	Consolidated Tape Ass'n
CTAM	Cable Televison Administration and Marketing Soc.
CTDA	Ceramic Tile Distributors Ass'n
CTDAA	Custom Tailors and Designers Ass'n of America
CTFA	Cosmetic, Toiletry and Fragrance Ass'n
CTI	Cooling Tower Institute
CTIA	Cellular Telecommunications Industry Ass'n
CTIOA	Ceramic Tile Institute of America
CTMA	Cutting Tool Manufacturers of America
CTMF	Ceramic Tile Marketing Federation
CTR-USA	Council for Tobacco Research-U.S.A.
CTS	College Theology Soc.
CTSA	Catholic Theological Soc. of America
CTTE	Council on Technology Teacher Education
CUFC	Consortium of University Film Centers
CUNA	Credit Union Nat'l Ass'n
CUPA	College and University Personnel Ass'n
CUSS	Computer Use in Social Services Network
CWA	Comedy Writers Ass'n
	Communications Workers of America
	Construction Writers Ass'n
CWAA	Cotton Warehouse Ass'n of America
CWI	Credit Women-Internat'l
CWO	Council of Writers Organizations
CWS	Caucus for Women in Statistics
	Colonial Waterbird Society
CWSRA	Chester White Swine Record Ass'n
CWTC	Chemical Waste Transportation Council
CdCAA	Chefs de Cuisine Ass'n of America
ChLA	Children's Literature Ass'n
CoG/SME	Composites Group of SME
CoSIDA	College Sports Information Directors of America
DACC	Danish-American Chamber of Commerce (USA)
DACOR	Diplomatic and Consular Officers, Retired
DBA	Dealer Bank Ass'n
DBCAA	Dutch Belted Cattle Ass'n of America
DCA	Dance Critics Ass'n
	Detachable Container Ass'n
	Diamond Council of America
	Distribution Contractors Ass'n
DCAT	Drug, Chemical and Allied Trades Ass'n
DCDMA	Diamond Core Drill Manufacturers Ass'n
DCI	Distribution Codes Institute
DCMA	Dry Color Manufacturers Ass'n
DCRF	Die Casting Research Foundation
DDA	Dental Dealers of America
	Display Distributors Ass'n
DDPA	Delta Dental Plans Ass'n
DEA	Dance Educators of America
DECA	Distributive Education Clubs of America
DEMA	Data Entry Management Ass'n
	Diesel Engine Manufacturers Ass'n
	Diving Equipment Manufacturers Ass'n
DFI	Deep Foundations Institute
DFISA	Dairy and Food Industries Supply Ass'n
DFRC	Distillers Feed Research Council
DG	Dramatists Guild
DGA	Directors Guild of America
DGI	Dental Gold Institute
DGRA	Diamond and Gemstone Remarketing Ass'n
DHI	Door and Hardware Institute
DIA	Drug Information Ass'n
DIPRA	Ductile Iron Pipe Research Ass'n
DIS	Ductile Iron Soc.
DISCUS	Distilled Spirits Council of the United States
DLC	Dental Laboratory Conference
DLPA	Decorative Laminate Products Ass'n
DMA	Dance Masters of America
	Dental Manufacturers of America
	Dietary Managers Ass'n
	Direct Marketing Ass'n
DMCA	Direct Marketing Computer Ass'n
	Direct Marketing Credit Ass'n
DMCG	Direct Marketing Creative Guild
DMFA	Direct Mail Fundraisers Ass'n
DMIAA	Diamond Manufacturers and Importers Ass'n of America
DNA	Dermatology Nurses Ass'n
DO	Delta Omicron
DODA	Door and Operator Dealers
DORCMA	Door Operator and Remote Controls Manufacturers Ass'n
DPCSMA	Dry Process Ceramic and Steatite Manufacturers Ass'n
DPE	Delta Pi Epsilon
DPMA	Data Processing Management Ass'n
DRA	Dude Ranchers' Ass'n
DRI	Defense Research Institute
DRINC	Dairy Research
DSA	Direct Selling Ass'n
DSAA	Driving School Ass'n of America
DSD	Delta Sigma Delta
DSI	Dairy Soc. Internat'l
	Decision Sciences Institute
DSMSB	Die Set Manufacturers Service Bureau
DSP	Delta Sigma Pi
DTAA	Diamond Trade Ass'n of America
DTP	Delta Theta Phi
DWA	Domestic Wildcatters Ass'n
DWMI	Diamond Wheel Manufacturers Institute
DWU	Distillery, Wine and Allied Workers' Internat'l Union
DYIRI	Do-It-Yourself Research Institute
EAA	Ecuadorean American Ass'n
EACC	Egyptian-American Chamber of Commerce
EASA	Electrical Apparatus Service Ass'n
EBA	Experimental Ballistics Associates
EBAA	Eye Bank Ass'n of America
EBRI	Employee Benefit Research Institute
ECA	Embroidery Council of America
ECD	Episcopal Conference of the Deaf
ECFC	Employers Council on Flexible Compensation
ECLA	Evangelical Church Library Ass'n
ECMA	Engineering College Magazines Associated
ECPA	Energy Consumers and Producers Ass'n
	Evangelical Christian Publishers Ass'n
ECRI	ECRI
ECSA	Exchange Carriers Standards Ass'n
EDPA	Exhibit Designers and Producers Ass'n
EDPAA	EDP Auditors Ass'n, The
EDSA	Educational Dealers and Suppliers Ass'n Internat'l
EEI	Edison Electric Institute
EEMDA	Electrical-Electronics Materials Distributors Ass'n
EEPA	Electromagnetic Energy Policy Alliance
EERA	Electrical Equipment Representatives Ass'n
EFA	Editorial Freelancers Ass'n
EFLA	Educational Film Library Ass'n
EFTA	Electronic Funds Transfer Ass'n
EGSA	Electrical Generating Systems Ass'n
EHA	Economic History Ass'n
EHDA	Electric Housewares Distributors Ass'n
EIA	Electronic Industries Ass'n
	Equipment Interchange Ass'n
EIC	Environmental Industry Council
EIMA	Exterior Insulation Manufacturers Ass'n
EISC	Electronic Industry Show Corporation
EJMA	Expansion Joint Manufacturers Ass'n
ELCON	Electricity Consumers Resource Council
EM/SME	Electronics Manufacturing Group of SME
EMA	Employment Management Ass'n
	Engine Manufacturers Ass'n
	Environmental Management Ass'n
	Evaporated Milk Ass'n
EMAA	Envelope Manufacturers Ass'n of America
EMC	Electronic Music Consortium
EMCA	Electronic Motion Control Ass'n
EMMA	Emergency Medicine Management Ass'n
EMRA	Emergency Medicine Residents' Ass'n
EMRC	Electronic Media Rating Council
EMS	Environmental Mutagen Soc.
EMSA	Electron Microscopy Soc. of America
ENA	Emergency Nurses Ass'n
ENAR	Biometric Soc. (ENAR)
ENC	Enteral Nutrition Council
ENTELEC	Energy Telecommunications and Electrical Ass'n
EOIC	Ethylene Oxide Industry Council
EPA	Evangelical Press Ass'n
EPAA	Educational Press Ass'n of America
EPCA	Electronic Pest Control Ass'n
EPIC	Evidence Photographers Internat'l Council
EPRI	Electric Power Research Institute
ERA	Electronic Representatives Ass'n
ERC	Employee Relocation Council
ERF	Estuarine Research Federation
ERS	Engineering Reprographic Soc.
ES	Econometric Soc.
	Electrochemical Soc.
	Endocrine Soc.
	Epigraphic Soc.
ESA	Ecological Soc. of America
	Engine Service Ass'n
	Entomological Soc. of America
	Equipment Service Ass'n
ESCA	Exposition Service Contractors Ass'n
ESCSI	Expanded Shale, Clay and Slate Institute
ESMA	Engraved Stationery Manufacturers Ass'n
ESOAA	Eight Sheet Outdoor Advertising Ass'n

ACRONYM INDEX

ESP	Epsilon Sigma Phi
ESRS	Early Sites Research Soc.
ETA	Electronics Technicians Ass'n Internat'l
ETI	Equipment and Tool Institute
ETTA	Evangelical Teacher Training Ass'n
EWA	Education Writers Ass'n
EWI	Executive Women Internat'l
EWRT	Electrical Women's Round Table
FA	Ferroalloys Ass'n
	Foragers of America
FAANaOS	American Academy and Board of Neurological and Orthopaedic Surgery
FACC	Finnish American Chamber of Commerce
FACC-US	French-American Chamber of Commerce in the United States
FACS	Federation of American Controlled Shipping
FACSS	Federation of Analytical Chemistry and Spectroscopy Societies
FACTS	Nat'l Food and Conservation Through Swine
FAF	Financial Analysts Federation
FAHS	Federation of American Health Systems
FALA	First Amendment Lawyers Ass'n
FALJC	Federal Administrative Law Judges Conference
FAM	Federation of Apparel Manufacturers
FAPCC	Film, Air and Package Carriers Conference
FARB	Federation of Ass'ns of Regulatory Boards
FAS	Federation of American Scientists
FASA	Federated Ambulatory Surgery Ass'n
FASEB	Federation of American Societies for Experimental Biology
FBA	Federal Bar Ass'n
	Fibre Box Ass'n
FBLA-PBL	Future Business Leaders of America-Phi Beta Lambda
FCBA	Federal Communications Bar Ass'n
FCC	Farm Credit Council
	Federal Construction Council
FCCA	Federal Court Clerks Ass'n
	Forestry Conservation Communications Ass'n
FCI	Fluid Controls Institute
FCIA	Foreign Credit Insurance Ass'n
FCICA	Floor Covering Installation Contractors Ass'n
FCSI	Foodservice Consultants Soc. Internat'l
FCTCSC	Flue-Cured Tobacco Cooperative Stabilization Corporation
FDDS	Federation of Dental Diagnostic Sciences
FDLI	Food and Drug Law Institute
FDTC	Fibre Drum Technical Council
FEA	Farmstead Equipment Ass'n
	Fraternity Executives Ass'n
FEBA	Federal Energy Bar Ass'n
FEBMA	Forged Eye Bolt Manufacturers Ass'n
FECUA	Farmers Educational and Co-operative Union of America
FEDA	Foodservice Equipment Distributors Ass'n
FEI	Financial Executives Institute
FEIA	Flight Engineers' Internat'l Ass'n
FEMA	Casting Industry Suppliers Ass'n
	Farm Equipment Manufacturers Ass'n
	Fire Equipment Manufacturers' Ass'n
	Food Equipment Manufacturers Ass'n
FEMAUS	Flavor and Extract Manufacturers Ass'n of the United States
FEPA	Federal Executive and Professional Ass'n
FEW	Federally Employed Women
FEWA	Farm Equipment Wholesalers Ass'n
FF	Fragrance Foundation
FFA	Fiberglass Fabrication Ass'n
	Forest Farmers Ass'n
	Future Farmers of America
FFI	Freight Forwarders Institute
FFMA	Fraternal Field Managers Ass'n
FG	Fashion Group
FGA	Fresh Garlic Ass'n
FGMA	Flat Glass Marketing Ass'n
FH-AWA	Fine Hardwoods-American Walnut Ass'n
FHA	Future Homemakers of America
FHS	Forest History Soc.
FI	Fertilizer Institute
	Formaldehyde Institute
FIA	Footwear Industries of America
	Forging Industry Ass'n
	Futures Industry Ass'n
FIAE	Food Industry Ass'n Executives
FICC	Federation of Insurance and Corporate Counsel
FIEI	Farm and Industrial Equipment Institute
FIM	Foundation for Internat'l Meetings
FIMA	Financial Institutions Marketing Ass'n
FISA	Food Industries Suppliers' Ass'n
FIT	Forest Industries Telecommunications
FJAA	Fashion Jewelry Ass'n of America
FKBG-API	Fourdrinier Kraft Board Group of the American Paper Institute
FLEOA	Federal Law Enforcement Officers Ass'n
FLI	Foodservice and Lodging Institute
FLRT	Federal Librarians Round Table
FMA	Fabricators and Manufacturers Ass'n, Internat'l
	Federal Managers Ass'n
	Financial Management Ass'n
	Flexicore Manufacturers Ass'n
	Fragrance Materials Ass'n of the United States
	Fulfillment Management Ass'n
FMANA	Fire Marshals Ass'n of North America
FMI	Food Marketing Institute
FMPS	Federation of Modern Painters and Sculptors
FMS	Factory Mutual System
	Federation of Materials Societies
	Financial Managers Soc.
FMSI	Friction Materials Standards Institute
FNHP	Federation of Nurses and Health Professionals
FOA	Federation of Orthodontic Ass'ns
FOCUS	Federation of Computer Users in the Medical Sciences
FOP	Fraternal Order of Police
FOPW	Federation of Organizations for Professional Women
FPA	Federation of Professional Athletes
	Financial Printers Ass'n
	Flexible Packaging Ass'n
	Fusion Power Associates
FPDA	Fluid Power Distributors Ass'n
FPGAUS	Federated Pecan Growers' Ass'ns of the U.S.
FPMSA	Food Processing Machinery and Supplies Ass'n
FPO	Federation of Prosthodontic Organizations
FPOA	Federal Probation Officers Ass'n
FPPI	Frozen Potato Products Institute
FPRS	Forest Products Research Soc.
FPS	Fluid Power Soc.
FPSC	Forest Products Safety Conference
FRA	Footwear Retailers of America
FRAA	Furniture Rental Ass'n of America
FRCA	Fire Retardant Chemicals Ass'n
FRH	Fellowship of Religious Humanists
FS	Fiber Soc.
	Fleischner Soc.
FSA	Fabric Salesmen's Ass'n
	Family Service America
	Financial Stationers Ass'n
	Fluid Sealing Ass'n
FSBA	Food Service Brokers of America, Inc.
FSCC	Ferrous Scrap Consumers Coalition
FSCT	Federation of Societies for Coatings Technology
FSF	Flight Safety Foundation
FSI	Foundation for Savings Institutions
FSMBUS	Federation of State Medical Boards of the U. S.
FSSA	Fire Suppression Systems Ass'n
FTA	Federation of Tax Administrators
	Flexographic Technical Ass'n
FTDA	Florists' Transworld Delivery Ass'n
FTTPP	Federation of Trainers and Training Programs in Psychodrama
FUMWMOA	Fellowship of United Methodists in Worship, Music and Other Arts
FWAA	Football Writers Ass'n of America
FWC	Fourdrinier Wire Council
FWQA	Federal Water Quality Ass'n
GA	Gypsum Ass'n
GAA	Gift Ass'n of America
GAAEC	Graphic Arts Advertisers and Exhibitors Council
GACC	German American Chamber of Commerce
GAE	Graphic Arts Employers of America
GAESDA	Graphic Arts Equipment and Supply Dealers Ass'n
GAGN	Graphic Artists Guild Nat'l
GAMA	Game Manufacturers Ass'n
	Gas Appliance Manufacturers Ass'n
	General Aviation Manufacturers Ass'n
GAMC-NALU	General Agents and Managers Conference of NALU
GAMIS	Graphic Arts Marketing Information Service
GAMMA	Guitar and Accessories Music Marketing Ass'n
GAS	Glass Art Soc.
GASDA	Gasoline and Automotive Service Dealers Ass'n
GATF	Graphic Arts Technical Foundation
GBSUA	Greater Blouse, Skirt and Undergarment Ass'n
GBW	Guild of Book Workers
GCA	Garden Centers of America
	Girls Clubs of America
	Golf Course Ass'n
	Graphic Communications Ass'n
	Greeting Card Ass'n
GCAA	Golf Coaches Ass'n of America
GCBA	Golf Course Builders of America
GCCA	Greater Clothing Contractors Ass'n
GCIU	Graphic Communications Internat'l Union
GCSAA	Golf Course Superintendents Ass'n of America
GDC	Garage Door Council
GEAPS	Grain Elevator and Processing Soc.
GFA	Gasket Fabricators Ass'n
	Gold Filled Ass'n
GFOA	Government Finance Officers Ass'n of the United States and Canada
GFWC	General Federation of Women's Clubs
GHAA	Group Health Ass'n of America
GHBA	Galiceno Horse Breeders Ass'n
GI	Gold Institute
	Gyro Internat'l
GIA	Gummed Industries Ass'n
GIS	Gamma Iota Sigma
	Geoscience Information Soc.
GLPA	Gay and Lesbian Press Ass'n
GMA	Grocery Manufacturers of America
GMDA	Groundwater Management Districts Ass'n
GMDC	General Merchandise Distributors Council
GMIA	Gelatin Manufacturers Institute of America
GMIS	Government Management Information Sciences
GNSI	Guild of Natural Science Illustrators
GOTA	Green Olive Trade Ass'n
GPA	Gas Processors Ass'n
	Graphic Preparatory Ass'n
GPI	Glass Packaging Institute
GPIA	Generic Pharmaceutical Industry Ass'n
GPMA	Gasoline Pump Manufacturers Ass'n
GPPAW	Glass, Pottery, Plastics and Allied Workers Internat'l Union
GPSA	Gas Processors Suppliers Ass'n
GRA	Governmental Research Ass'n
GRC	Geothermal Resources Council
GRCDA	Governmental Refuse Collection and Disposal Ass'n
GRG	Gastroenterology Research Group
GRI	Gravure Research Institute
GRMRA	Gift Retailers, Manufacturers and Representatives Ass'n
GS	Geochemical Soc.
GSA	Genetics Soc. of America
	Geological Soc. of America
	Gerontological Soc. of America
GTA	Genetic Toxicology Ass'n
	Glass Tempering Ass'n
	Gravure Technical Ass'n
GTM	Guild of Temple Musicians
GWAA	Garden Writers Ass'n of America
	Golf Writers Ass'n of America
GWI	Grinding Wheel Institute
HA	Headmasters Ass'n
HAA	Helicopter Airline Ass'n
HAI	Helicopter Ass'n Internat'l
HAU	Hebrew Actors Union
HBPA	Horsemen's Benevolent and Protective Ass'n
HBSMAA	Hack and Band Saw Manufacturers Ass'n of America
HCEA	Health Care Exhibitors Ass'n
HDBF	Heavy Duty Business Forum
HDMA	Heavy Duty Manfacturers Ass'n
HDRA	Heavy Duty Representatives Ass'n
HEEA	Home Economics Education Ass'n
HEI	Heat Exchange Institute
HEIB	Home Economists in Business
HEREIU	Hotel Employees and Restaurant Employees Internat'l Union
HES	History of Economics Soc.
	History of Education Soc.
HESS	History of Earth Sciences Soc.
HFAA	Holstein-Friesian Ass'n of America
HFMA	Healthcare Financial Management Ass'n
HFPA	Home Fashion Products Ass'n
HFS	Human Factors Soc.
HGA	Handweavers Guild of America
	Hop Growers of America
HGCB	Household Goods Carriers' Bureau
HGFAA	Household Goods Forwarders Ass'n of America
HHA	Hickory Handle Ass'n
HHI	Harness Horsemen Internat'l
HI	Hydraulic Institute
	Hydronics Institute
HIA	Hearing Industries Ass'n
HIAA	Health Insurance Ass'n of America
	Hobby Industry Ass'n of America
HIAG	Healthcare Internal Audit Group
HICA	Honey Industry Council of America
HIDA	Health Industry Distributors Ass'n
HIMA	Health Industry Manufacturers Ass'n
HIRA	Health Industry Representatives Ass'n
HISSG	Healthcare Information Systems Sharing Group
HKTDC	Hong Kong Trade Development Council
HL	Herpetologists' League
HMA	Hardwood Manufacturers Ass'n
HMBA	Hotel and Motel Brokers of America
HMI	Hoist Manufacturers Institute
HMSS	Hospital Management Systems Soc.
HNBA	Hispanic Nat'l Bar Ass'n
HOLUA	Home Office Life Underwriters Ass'n
HPA	Hospital Presidents Ass'n
HPMA	Hardwood Plywood Manufacturers Ass'n
HPS	Health Physics Soc.
HRC	Hardwood Research Council
HRI	Horticultural Research Institute
HRPS	Human Resource Planning Soc.
HRSP	Ass'n of Human Resource Systems Professionals
HS	Harvey Soc.
	Histochemical Soc.
HSA	Hydroponics Soc. of America
HSIA	Halogenated Solvents Industry Alliance
HSMAI	Hotel Sales and Marketing Ass'n Internat'l
HSR	Hampshire Swine Registry
HSRA	High Speed Rail Ass'n
HSS	History of Science Soc.
HTA	Harness Tracks of America
HTI	Hand Tools Institute
HTMA	Hydraulic Tool Manufacturers Ass'n
HUFSM	Highway Users Federation for Safety and Mobility
HWTC	Hazardous Waste Treatment Council
HeSCA	Health Sciences Communications Ass'n
I-CAR	Inter-Industry Conference on Auto Collision Repair
IA	Intercoiffure America
	Irrigation Ass'n
IAA	Institute for Alternative Agriculture
	Internat'l Arthroscopy Ass'n
IAAA	Intermarket Ass'n of Advertising Agencies
	Internat'l Airforwarders and Agents Ass'n
IAAAM	Internat'l Ass'n for Aquatic Animal Medicine
IAABO	Internat'l Ass'n of Approved Basketball Officials
IAADFS	Internat'l Ass'n of Airport Duty Free Stores
IAAF	Internat'l Agricultural Aviation Foundation

ACRONYM INDEX

IAAI	Internat'l Ass'n of Arson Investigators
IAAM	Internat'l Ass'n of Auditorium Managers
IAAO	Internat'l Ass'n of Assessing Officers
IAAPA	Internat'l Ass'n of Amusement Parks and Attractions
IAATI	Internat'l Ass'n of Auto Theft Investigators
IABA	Inter-American Bar Ass'n
IABC	Internat'l Ass'n of Business Communicators
IABEO	Internat'l Ass'n of Boards of Examiners of Optometry
IABSOIW	Internat'l Ass'n of Bridge, Structural and Ornamental Iron Workers
IABTI	Internat'l Ass'n of Bomb Technicians and Investigators
IACC	Internat'l Ass'n of Conference Centers
	Italy-America Chamber of Commerce
IACCI	Internat'l Ass'n of Credit Card Investigators
IACD	Internat'l Ass'n of Clothing Designers
IACLEA	Internat'l Ass'n of Campus Law Enforcement Administrators
IACME	Internat'l Ass'n of Coroners and Medical Examiners
IACO	Internat'l Ass'n of Correctional Officers
IACOA	Independent Armored Car Operators Ass'n
IACP	Internat'l Ass'n of Chiefs of Police
	Internat'l Ass'n of Cooking Professionals
IACREOT	Internat'l Ass'n of Clerks, Recorders, Election Officials and Treasurers
IACS	Internat'l Ass'n of Counseling Services
IACVB	Internat'l Ass'n of Convention and Visitor Bureaus
IADC	Internat'l Ass'n of Defense Counsel
	Internat'l Ass'n of Drilling Contractors
IADR	Internat'l Ass'n for Dental Research
IAE	Institute for the Advancement of Engineering
	Internat'l Ass'n of Ethicists
IAEE	Internat'l Ass'n of Energy Economists
IAEI	Internat'l Ass'n of Electrical Inspectors
IAET	Internat'l Ass'n for Enterostomal Therapy
IAFC	Internat'l Ass'n of Fire Chiefs
IAFE	Internat'l Ass'n of Fairs and Expositions
IAFF	Internat'l Ass'n of Fire Fighters
IAFP	Internat'l Ass'n for Financial Planning
IAFS	Internat'l Ass'n of Family Sociology
IAFWA	Internat'l Ass'n of Fish and Wildlife Agencies
IAGA	Internat'l Ass'n of Golf Administrators
IAGC	Internat'l Ass'n of Geophysical Contractors
IAGFA	Internat'l Ass'n of Governmental Fair Agencies
IAHA	Internat'l Arabian Horse Ass'n
	Internat'l Ass'n of Hospitality Accountants
IAHCSM	Internat'l Ass'n of Hospital Central Service Management
IAHE	Internat'l Ass'n for Hydrogen Energy
IAHFIAW	Internat'l Ass'n of Heat and Frost Insulators and Asbestos Workers
IAHS	Internat'l Ass'n for Hospital Security
IAI	Internat'l Apple Institute
	Internat'l Ass'n for Identification
IAIA	Internat'l Ass'n for Impact Assessment
IAIABC	Internat'l Ass'n of Industrial Accident Boards and Commissions
IAIP	Internat'l Ass'n of Independent Producers
IAIS	Internat'l Ass'n of Independent Scholars
IAJAM	Industrial Ass'n of Juvenile Apparel Manufacturers
IALD	Internat'l Ass'n of Lighting Designers
IALEFI	Internat'l Ass'n of Law Enforcement Firearms Instructors
IALEIA	Internat'l Ass'n of Law Enforcement Intelligence Analysts
IALL	Internat'l Ass'n for Learning Laboratories
IAMA	Intimate Apparel Manufacturers Ass'n
IAMAW	Internat'l Ass'n of Machinists and Aerospace Workers
IAMC	Institute of Ass'n Management Companies
IAMCA	Internat'l Ass'n of Milk Control Agencies
IAMFES	Internat'l Ass'n of Milk, Food and Environmental Sanitarians
IAMG	Internat'l Ass'n for Mathematical Geology
IAO	Internat'l Ass'n for Orthodontics
IAOE	Internat'l Ass'n of Optometric Executives
IAOS	Internat'l Ass'n of Ocular Surgeons
IAP	Internat'l Academy of Pathology (U.S.-Canadian Div.)
	Internat'l Academy of Proctology
IAPBT	Internat'l Ass'n of Piano Builders and Technicians
IAPC	Internat'l Ass'n of Pet Cemeteries
IAPES	Internat'l Ass'n of Personnel in Employment Security
IAPHCI	Internat'l Ass'n of Printing House Craftsmen
IAPM	Internat'l Academy of Preventive Medicine
IAPMO	Internat'l Ass'n of Plumbing and Mechanical Officials
IAPNH	Internat'l Ass'n of Professional Natural Hygienists
IAPPW	Internat'l Ass'n of Pupil Personnel Workers
IAPSC	Internat'l Ass'n of Professional Security Consultants
IAPTA	Internat'l Allied Printing Trades Ass'n
IAPW	Internat'l Ass'n for Personnel Women
IAQC	Internat'l Ass'n of Quality Circles
IARS	Internat'l Anesthesia Research Soc.
IARW	Internat'l Ass'n of Refrigerated Warehouses
IAS	Internat'l Ass'n of Siderographers
IASA	Independent Automotive Service Ass'n
	Insurance Accounting and Systems Ass'n
IASCS	Internat'l Ass'n for Shopping Center Security
IASM	Internat'l Ass'n of Structural Movers
IASOC	Internat'l Ass'n for the Study of Organized Crime
IASP	Internat'l Ass'n for the Study of Pain
IASS	Internat'l Ass'n of Security Services
IAT	Internat'l Ass'n of Trichologists
IATC	Internat'l Ass'n of Tool Craftsmen
IATL	Internat'l Academy of Trial Lawyers
IATM	Internat'l Ass'n of Tour Managers - North American Region
IATSE	Internat'l Alliance of Theatrical Stage Employees and Moving Picture Machine Operators of the U.S. & Ca
IAU	Italian Actors Union
IAWCM	Internat'l Ass'n of Wiping Cloth Manufacturers
IAWP	Internat'l Ass'n of Women Police
IBA	Independent Bakers Ass'n
	Industrial Biotechnology Ass'n
	Institute for Briquetting and Agglomeration
	Institute of Business Appraisers
	Internat'l Banana Ass'n
IBAA	Independent Bankers Ass'n of America
IBBA	Internat'l Brangus Breeders Ass'n
IBBISBFGH	Internat'l Brotherhood of Boilermakers, Iron Shipbuilders, Blacksmiths, Forgers and Helpers
IBD	Institute of Business Designers
IBEE	Internat'l Builders Exchange Executives
IBEF	Internat'l Bio-Environmental Foundation
IBEW	Internat'l Brotherhood of Electrical Workers
IBFI	Internat'l Business Forms Industries
IBFO	Internat'l Brotherhood of Firemen and Oilers
IBHA	Internat'l Buckskin Horse Ass'n
IBM	Internat'l Brotherhood of Magicians
IBMA	Independent Battery Manufacturers Ass'n
IBPA	Internat'l Bridge Press Ass'n
IBPAT	Internat'l Brotherhood of Painters and Allied Trades
IBS	Intercollegiate Broadcasting System
IBTCWHA	Internat'l Brotherhood of Teamsters, Chauffeurs, Warehouseman and Helpers of America
IBTTA	Internat'l Bridge, Tunnel & Turnpike Ass'n
IBWA	Internat'l Bottled Water Ass'n
	Internat'l Boxing Writers Ass'n
IBWC	Internat'l Black Writers Conference
ICA	Institute of Cost Analysis
	Internat'l Carwash Ass'n
	Internat'l Chiropractors Ass'n
	Internat'l Claim Ass'n
	Internat'l Communication Ass'n
	Internat'l Communications Ass'n
	Internat'l Credit Ass'n
ICAA	Insulation Contractors Ass'n of America
	Investment Counsel Ass'n of America
ICAN	Internat'l College of Applied Nutrition
ICARA	Internat'l Conference of Administrators of Residential Agencies
ICAS	Internat'l Council of Airshows
ICBO	Internat'l Conference of Building Officials
ICC	Interstate Carriers Conference
ICCA	Independent Computer Consultants Ass'n
	India Chamber of Commerce of America
ICCC	Internat'l Council for Computer Communication
ICCE	Internat'l Council for Computers in Education
ICCP	Institute for Certification of Computer Professionals
ICCSSSAR	Internat'l Coordinating Committee on Solid State Sensors and Actuators Research
ICD-USA	Internat'l College of Dentists, U.S.A. Section
ICEA	Instrument Contracting and Engineering Ass'n
	Insulated Cable Engineers Ass'n
	Internat'l Childbirth Education Ass'n
ICESA	Interstate Conference of Employment Security Agencies
ICFA	Independent College Funds of America
	Institute of Chartered Financial Analysts
ICFP	Institute of Certified Financial Planners
ICGB	Internat'l Cargo Gear Bureau
ICGSCA	Infants', Children's and Girls' Sportswear and Coat Ass'n
ICI	Investment Casting Institute
	Investment Company Institute
ICIA	Internat'l Communications Industries Ass'n
ICITAA	Internat'l Chain of Industrial and Technical Advertising Agencies
ICMA	Internat'l Circulation Managers Ass'n
	Internat'l City Management Ass'n
ICMAD	Independent Cosmetic Manufacturers and Distributors
ICOA	Internat'l Castor Oil Ass'n
ICOHH	Internat'l Concatenated Order of Hoo-Hoo
ICOI	Internat'l Congress of Oral Implantologists
ICP	Insurance Conference Planners
	Internat'l Council of Psychologists
ICPBC	Institute of Certified Professional Business Consultants
ICPC	Internat'l Conference of Police Chaplains
ICPI	Insurance Crime Prevention Institute
ICRA	Industrial Chemical Research Ass'n
ICRDA	Independent Cash Register Dealers Ass'n
ICRECP	Internat'l College of Real Estate Consulting Professionals
ICRM	Institute of Certified Records Managers
ICS	Internat'l Cogeneration Soc.
	Internat'l College of Surgeons (U.S. Section)
	Metal Castings Soc.
ICSA	Internat'l Cemetery Supply Ass'n
	Internat'l Chain Salon Ass'n
	Internat'l Customer Service Ass'n
ICSB	Internat'l Council for Small Business
ICSC	Internat'l Council of Shopping Centers
ICSOM	Internat'l Conference of Symphony and Opera Musicians
ICTA	Industry Council for Tangible Assets
ICVS	Internat'l Soc. for Cardiovascular Surgery - North American Chapter
ICWA	Internat'l Coil Winding Ass'n
ICWP	Interstate Conference on Water Policy
ICWSG	Infants' and Children's Wear Salesmen's Guild
ICWU	Internat'l Chemical Workers Union
IDA	Industrial Diamond Ass'n of America
	Internat'l Desalination Ass'n
	Internat'l Documentary Ass'n
	Internat'l Downtown Ass'n
	Internat'l Drapery Ass'n
IDBA	Internat'l Deli-Bakery Ass'n
IDC	Internat'l Drycleaners Congress
IDCMA	Independent Data Communications Manufacturers Ass'n
IDDA	Internat'l Dairy-Deli Ass'n
IDEA	Internat'l Dance-Exercise Ass'n
IDEC	Interior Design Educators Council
IDFTA	Internat'l Dwarf Fruit Tree Ass'n
IDHCA	Internat'l District Heating and Cooling Ass'n
IDRC	Industrial Development Research Council
IDS	Interior Design Soc.
IDSA	Industrial Designers Soc. of America
	Infectious Diseases Soc. of America
IDSC	Internat'l Die Sinkers' Conference
IEA	Internat'l Exhibitors Ass'n
IEC	Independent Electrical Contractors
IECA	Independent Educational Counselors Ass'n
	Internat'l Erosion Control Ass'n
IEEE	Institute of Electrical and Electronics Engineers
IEEE-CS	Computer Soc. of the Institute of Electrical and Electronics Engineers
IEPS	Internat'l Electronic Packaging Soc.
IES	Institute of Environmental Sciences
IESA	Insurance Economics Soc. of America
IESNA	Illuminating Engineering Soc. of North America
IETS	Internat'l Embryo Transfer Soc.
IF	Internat'l Foundation of Employee Benefit Plans
IFA	Inter-Financial Ass'n
	Internat'l Festivals Ass'n
	Internat'l Footwear Ass'n
	Internat'l Franchise Ass'n
IFAA	Internat'l Federation of Advertising Agencies
IFAC	Internat'l Food Additives Council
IFAI	Industrial Fabrics Ass'n Internat'l
IFBS	Institute for Fermentation and Brewing Studies
IFC	Infant Formula Council
IFCM	Internat'l Federation for Choral Music
IFDA	Internat'l Foodservice Distributors Ass'n
IFE	Institute of Financial Education
IFFA	Internat'l Frozen Food Ass'n
IFHP	Internat'l Federation of Health Professionals
IFI	Industrial Fasteners Institute
	Internat'l Fabricare Institute
IFIA	Internat'l Fence Industry Ass'n
IFIC	Internat'l Food Information Council
IFMA	Internat'l Facility Management Ass'n
	Internat'l Foodservice Manufacturers Ass'n
IFPA	Independent Free Papers of America
	Internat'l Fire Photographers Ass'n
IFPTE	Internat'l Federation of Professional and Technical Engineers
IFRAA	Interfaith Forum on Religion, Art and Architecture
IFSA	In-Flight Food Service Ass'n
	Inflight Food Services Ass'n
IFSEA	Internat'l Food Service Executives' Ass'n
IFT	Institute of Food Technologists
IFWTWA	Internat'l Food, Wine and Travel Writers Ass'n
IGAB	Internat'l Group of Agents and Bureaus
IGAEA	Internat'l Graphic Arts Education Ass'n
IGAS	Internat'l Graphoanalysis Soc.
IGC	Internat'l Glaucoma Congress
IGCI	Industrial Gas Cleaning Institute
IGGA	Internat'l Grooving and Grinding Ass'n
IGHIA	Internat'l Garden Horticultural Industry Ass'n
IGMC	Independent Gasoline Marketers Council
IGPE	Internat'l Guild of Professional Electrologists
IGTC	Internat'l Glutamate Technical Committee
IGUA	Internat'l Guards Union of America
IHEA	Industrial Heating Equipment Ass'n
IHF	Industrial Health Foundation
IHFRA	Internat'l Home Furnishings Representatives Ass'n
IHHA	Internat'l Halfway House Ass'n
IHOU	Institute of Home Office Underwriters
IHPA	Internat'l Hardwood Products Ass'n
IHS	Immigration History Soc.
	Internat'l Health Soc.
IIA	Information Industry Ass'n
	Institute of Internal Auditors
IIAA	Independent Insurance Agents of America
IIAC	Internat'l Insurance Advisory Council
IIAR	Internat'l Institute of Ammonia Refrigeration
IIBA	Internat'l Institute for Bio-Energetic Analysis
	Internat'l Intelligent Buildings Ass'n
IICA	Internat'l Ice Cream Ass'n

ACRONYM INDEX

IICL	Institute of Internat'l Container Lessors
IIE	Institute of Industrial Engineers
IIF	Institute of Internat'l Finance
IIFFL	Internat'l Institute of Foods and Family Living
IIHS	Insurance Institute for Highway Safety
III	Institute of the Ironworking Industry
	Insurance Information Institute
IIL	Institute of Industrial Launderers
IILP	Internat'l Institute for Lath and Plaster
IIMA	Insurance Industry Meetings Ass'n
IIMC	Internat'l Institute of Municipal Clerks
IIPL	Independent Investors Protective League
IIR	Institute of Intermodal Repairers
IISRP	Internat'l Institute of Synthetic Rubber Producers
IIST	Internat'l Institute for Safety in Transportation
IJA	Institute of Judicial Administration
IJMA	Infant and Juvenile Manufacturers Ass'n
IJO	Independent Jewelers Organization
IJOA	Internat'l Juvenile Officers Ass'n
IJPA	Internat'l Jelly and Preserve Ass'n
ILA	Internat'l Longshoremen's Ass'n
ILAA	Independent Literary Agents Ass'n
ILBTC	Internat'l Livestock Brand and Theft Conference
ILCA	Insurance Loss Control Ass'n
	Internat'l Labor Communications Ass'n
ILEA	Internat'l League of Electrical Ass'ns
ILGPNWU	Internat'l Leather Goods, Plastics and Novelty Workers' Union
ILGWU	Internat'l Ladies Garment Workers' Union
ILI	Indiana Limestone Institute of America
ILMA	Independent Livestock Marketing Ass'n
	Independent Lubricant Manufacturers Ass'n
ILPBC	Internat'l League of Professional Baseball Clubs
ILTA	Independent Liquid Terminals Ass'n
ILWU	Internat'l Longshoremen's and Warehousemen's Union
IMA	Internat'l Magnesium Ass'n
	Internat'l Minilab Ass'n
	Issues Management Ass'n
IMACA	Internat'l Mobile Air Conditioning Ass'n
IMAWU	Internat'l Molders' and Allied Workers' Union
IMC	Industrial Metal Containers Ass'n
	Institute of Management Consultants
	Intercollegiate Musical Council, The Nat'l Ass'n of Male Choruses
	Internat'l Information Management Congress
	Internat'l Management Council
IMCA	Insurance Marketing Communications Ass'n
IMCEA	Internat'l Military Club Executives Ass'n
IMDA	Independent Medical Distributors Ass'n
	Internat'l Magic Dealers Ass'n
	Internat'l Map Dealers' Ass'n
IME	Institute for Municipal Engineering
	Institute of Makers of Explosives
IMI	Internat'l Maintenance Institute
	Internat'l Masonry Institute
IMMS	Internat'l Material Management Soc.
IMPA	Internat'l Meat Processors Ass'n
	Internat'l Motor Press Ass'n
	Internat'l Museum Photographers Ass'n
IMPALA	Internat'l Motion Picture and Lecturers Ass'n
IMPC	Institutional and Municipal Parking Congress
IMPI	Internat'l Microwave Power Institute
IMRA	Incentive Manufacturers Representatives Ass'n
	Independent Motorcycle Retailers of America
IMRE	Institute for Medical Record Economics
IMS	Industrial Mathematics Soc.
	Institute of Mathematical Statistics
	Internat'l Metallographic Soc.
IMSA	Internat'l Municipal Signal Ass'n
IMTA	Internat'l Marine Transit Ass'n
IMUA	Inland Marine Underwriters Ass'n
IN	Institute of Navigation
INA	Institute of Nautical Archaeology
INAME	Internat'l Newspaper Advertising and Marketing Executives, Inc.
INBA	Internat'l Nubian Breeders Ass'n
INCE	Institute of Noise Control Engineering
INCRA	Internat'l Copper Research Ass'n
INDA	INDA, Ass'n of the Nonwoven Fabrics Industry
INEOA	Internat'l Narcotic Enforcement Officers Ass'n
INFE	Internat'l Newspaper Financial Executives
INGAA	Interstate Natural Gas Ass'n of America
INMN	Institute of Nuclear Materials Management
INPA	Internat'l Newspaper Promotion Ass'n
INPO	Institute of Nuclear Power Operations
INRA	Investment Recovery Ass'n
INSCA	Internat'l Natural Sausage Casing Ass'n
INTEREX	Internat'l Exchangors Ass'n
INTERMAC	Internat'l Ass'n of Merger and Acquisition Consultants
INTV	Ass'n of Independent Television Stations
IOA-PACB	Internat'l Ozone Ass'n-Pan American Committee Branch
IOCC	Interstate Oil Compact Commission
IOCV	Internat'l Organization of Citrus Virologists
IOD	Institute of Diving
IOEHI	Internat'l Organization for the Education of the Hearing Impaired
IOM	Institute of Medicine
IOMA	Internat'l Oxygen Manufacturers Ass'n
IOMSA	Internat'l Oil Mill Superintendents Ass'n
IOSA	Internat'l Oil Scouts Ass'n
IOWT	Internat'l Organization of Women in Telecommunications
IPA	Industrial Perforators Ass'n
	Institute for Polyacrylate Absorbents
	Internat'l Platform Ass'n
	Internat'l Prepress Ass'n
	Internat'l Psychohistorical Ass'n
IPAA	Independent Petroleum Ass'n of America
	Internat'l Pesticide Applicators Ass'n
IPAT	Internat'l Porcelain Artist Teachers
IPC	Institute of Paper Chemistry
	IPC
IPDA	Internat'l Periodical Distributors Ass'n
IPFA	Internat'l Physical Fitness Ass'n
IPG	Internat'l Piano Guild
IPKC	Internat'l Pot and Kettle Club
IPLA	Interstate Producers Livestock Ass'n
IPMA	In-Plant Management Ass'n
	Internat'l Personnel Management Ass'n
IPMI	Internat'l Precious Metals Institute
IPO	Intellectual Property Owners
IPPA	Independent Professional Painting Contractors Ass'n
IPPC	Internat'l Philatelic Press Club
IPPDSEU-NA	Internat'l Plate Printers', Die Stampers' and Engravers' Union of North America
IPPS	Internat'l Plant Propagators' Soc. (Eastern Region)
IPRA	Internat'l Professional Rodeo Ass'n
IPS	Internat'l Phycological Soc.
	Internat'l Planetarium Soc.
IPSSG	Internat'l Printers Supply Salesmen's Guild
IQ	Internat'l Quorum of Film and Video Producers
IRA	Internat'l Reading Ass'n
	Internat'l Reprographic Ass'n
IRAS	Institute on Religion in an Age of Science
IRE	Investigative Reporters and Editors
IRECA	Internat'l Rescue and Emergency Care Ass'n
IREI	Internat'l Real Estate Institute
IREM	Institute of Real Estate Management
IRI	Industrial Research Institute
IRLA	Independent Research Libraries Ass'n
IRPT	Inland River Ports and Terminals
IRRA	Industrial Relations Research Ass'n
IRSA	Internat'l Racquet Sports Ass'n
IRTA	Internat'l Reciprocal Trade Ass'n
IRTS	Internat'l Radio and Television Soc.
IRWA	Internat'l Right of Way Ass'n
IS	Independent Sector
IS-SSE	Internat'l Soc. of Statistical Science in Economics
ISA	Independent Signcrafters of America
	Instrument Soc. of America
	Internat'l Silk Ass'n
	Internat'l Silo Ass'n
	Internat'l Soc. of Appraisers
	Internat'l Soc. of Arboriculture
	Internat'l Studies Ass'n
ISANTA	Internat'l Staple, Nail and Tool Ass'n
ISAO	Internat'l Soc. for Artificial Organs
ISASI	Internat'l Soc. of Air Safety Investigators
ISC	Internat'l Soc. for Chronobiology
ISCA	Internat'l Soc. of Copier Artists
ISCC	Inter-Society Color Council
ISCE	Internat'l Soc. of Chemical Ecology
ISCET	Internat'l Soc. of Certified Electronics Technicians
ISCLT	Internat'l Soc. for Clinical Laboratory Technology
ISDCI	Internat'l Soc. of Developmental and Comparative Immunology
ISDP	Internat'l Soc. for Developmental Psychobiology
ISDSI	Insulated Steel Door Systems Institute
ISEA	Industrial Safety Equipment Ass'n
ISEM	Internat'l Soc. for Ecological Modelling-North AmericanChapter
ISEO	Institute of Shortening and Edible Oils
ISF	Internat'l Soc. of Financiers
ISFSI	Internat'l Soc. of Fire Service Instructors
ISGS	Internat'l Soc. for General Semantics
ISHAE	Internat'l Soc. of Hotel Ass'n Executives
ISHBSS	Cheiron: The Internat'l Soc. of the History of Behavioral and Social Sciences
ISHM	Internat'l Soc. for Hybrid Microelectronics
ISHT	Internat'l Soc. for Heart Transplantation
ISIA	Ice Skating Institute of America
	Internat'l Snowmobile Industry Ass'n
ISID	Internat'l Soc. of Interior Designers
ISIFM	Internat'l Soc. of Industrial Fabric Manufacturers
ISIS	Institute of Scrap Iron and Steel
ISK	Internat'l Soc. of the Knee
ISKA	Internat'l Saw and Knife Ass'n
ISMDA	Independent Sewing Machine Dealers Ass'n
ISMPH	Internat'l Soc. for Medical and Psychological Hypnosis
ISOB	Internat'l Soc. of Barristers
ISOPGU	Internat'l Security Officers, Police and Guards Union
ISP	Institute of Store Planners
ISPA	Internat'l Soc. of Parametric Analysts
ISPAA	Internat'l Soc. of Performing Arts Administrators
ISPD	Internat'l Soc. for Peritoneal Dialysis
ISPE	Internat'l Soc. of Pharmaceutical Engineers
ISPO	Internat'l Soc. for Prosthetics and Orthotics, United States Nat'l Member Soc.
ISPP	Internat'l Soc. of Preretirement Planners
ISS	Iron and Steel Soc.
ISSA	Internat'l Sanitary Supply Ass'n
	Internat'l Slurry Seal Ass'n
ISTAT	Internat'l Soc. of Transport Aircraft Traders
ISTCA	Internat'l Stress and Tension Control Ass'n
ISTDA	Institutional and Service Textile Distributors Ass'n
ISWA	Insect Screening Weavers Ass'n
ISWM	Internat'l Soc. of Weighing and Measurement
ISWNE	Internat'l Soc. of Weekly Newspaper Editors
ITA	Industrial Truck Ass'n
	Intermodal Transportation Ass'n
	Internat'l Tape/Disc Ass'n
	Internat'l Taxicab Ass'n
	Internat'l Thermographers Ass'n
	Internat'l Trombone Ass'n
ITAA	Internat'l Theatrical Agencies Ass'n
	Internat'l Transactional Analysis Ass'n
ITCA	Intercollegiate Tennis Coaches Ass'n
	Internat'l Technical Caramel Ass'n
	Internat'l Teleconferencing Ass'n
ITCTLA	Internat'l Trade Commission Trial Lawyers Ass'n
ITE	Institute of Transportation Engineers
ITEA	Internat'l Technology Education Ass'n
	Internat'l Test and Evaluation Ass'n
ITI	Internat'l Tax Institute
ITMA	Internat'l Tanning Manufacturers Ass'n
ITOA	Independent Terminal Operators Ass'n
ITPA	Internat'l Truck Parts Ass'n
ITS	Internat'l Teleproduction Soc.
ITT	Iota Tau Tau
ITU	Internat'l Typographical Union
ITVA	Internat'l Television Ass'n
IU-UPGWA	Internat'l Union, United Plant Guard Workers of America
IUAIWA	Internat'l Union, Allied Industrial Workers of America
IUANPW	Internat'l Union of Allied Novelty and Production Workers
IUBAC	Internat'l Union of Bricklayers and Allied Craftsmen
IUE	Internat'l Union of Electronic, Electrical, Technical, Salaried and Machine Workers
IUEC	Internat'l Union of Elevator Constructors
IULIA	Internat'l Union of Life Insurance Agents
IUMSWA	Industrial Union of Marine and Shipbuilding Workers of America
IUOE	Internat'l Union of Operating Engineers
IUPA	Internat'l Union of Police Ass'ns
IUPIW	Internat'l Union of Petroleum and Industrial Workers
IUSO	Internat'l Union of Security Officers
IUTDMM	Internat'l Union of Tool, Die and Mold Makers
IVAS	Internat'l Veterinary Acupuncture Soc.
IVLA	Internat'l Visual Literacy Ass'n
IWA	Internat'l Woodworkers of America
IWRA	Internat'l Wild Rice Ass'n
IWWG	Internat'l Women's Writing Guild
IZAA	Independent Zinc Alloyers Ass'n
IZBA	Internat'l Zebu Breeders Ass'n
JA	Jewelers of America
JAA	Judge Advocates Ass'n
JBT	Jewelers Board of Trade
JCAI	Joint Council of Allergy and Immunology
JCBC	Jute Carpet Backing Council
JCET	Joint Council on Educational Telecommunications
JEA	Journalism Education Ass'n
JEDEC	Joint Electron Device Engineering Council
JESNA	Jewish Education Service of North America
JFDA	Jewish Funeral Directors of America
JG	Jockeys' Guild
JIC	Jewelry Industry Council
JIDA	Jewelry Industry Distributors Ass'n
JMA	Jewelry Manufacturers Ass'n
JMCA	Jewish Ministers Cantors Ass'n of America
JPA	Jesuit Philosophical Ass'n of the United States and Canada
JPMA	Juvenile Products Manufacturers Ass'n
JPS	Jean Piaget Soc.
JSA	Jewelers Shipping Ass'n
JSA-US	Jewelers Security Alliance of the U. S.
JSEA	Jesuit Secondary Education Ass'n
JSTA	Justice System Training Ass'n
JTA-M	Jewish Teachers Ass'n-Morim
JVC	Jewelers Vigilance Committee
KEA	Knitwear Employers Ass'n
KF	Keramos Fraternity
KTA	Keyboard Teachers Ass'n
	Knitted Textile Ass'n
LAA	League of Advertising Agencies
	Lipizzan Ass'n of America
LACA	Ladies Apparel Contractors Ass'n
LACUS	Linguistic Ass'n of Canada and the United States
LAMA	Latin American Manufacturers Ass'n
	Legal Assistant Management Ass'n
	Library Administration and Management Ass'n
LASA	Latin American Studies Ass'n
LBI	Library Binding Institute
LBIC	Licensed Beverage Information Council
LCA	Lake Carriers' Ass'n
LCCOGA	Liaison Committee of Cooperating Oil and Gas Ass'ns
LCI	Livestock Conservation Institute
LCLA	Lutheran Church Library Ass'n
LDCIU	Laundry and Dry Cleaning Internat'l Union

ACRONYM INDEX

LDTA	Leak Detection Technology Ass'n
LEA	Loss Executives Ass'n
	Lutheran Education Ass'n
LECNA	Lutheran Educational Conference of North America
LES	Licensing Executives Soc.
LFRA	League of Federal Recreation Ass'ns
LGC	Leafy Greens Council
LHAA	Lutheran Hospital Ass'n of America
LIA	Laser Institute of America
	Lead Industries Ass'n
	Leather Industries of America
LIAC	Legal Industry Advisory Council
LIC	Life Insurers Conference
LICA	Land Improvement Contractors of America
LIMA	Licensing Industry Merchandisers' Ass'n
LIMRA	Life Insurance Marketing and Research Ass'n
LIU	Laborers' Internat'l Union of North America
LJG	Leading Jewelers Guild
LLGMA	Luggage and Leather Goods Manufacturers of America
LLGSA	Luggage and Leather Goods Salesmen's Ass'n of America
LMA	Laminating Materials Ass'n
	Livestock Marketing Ass'n
	Logsplitter Manufacturers Ass'n
LMCC	Land Mobile Communications Council
LMOA	Locomotive Maintenance Officers' Ass'n
LODEM	Loading Dock Equipment Manufacturers
LOMA	Life Office Management Ass'n
LPC	Livestock Publications Council
LPGA	Ladies Professional Golf Ass'n
LPI	Lightning Protection Institute
LPIA	Label Printing Industries of America
LS	Lepidopterists' Soc.
LSA	Law and Society Ass'n
	Linguistic Soc. of America
LSGA	Laminators Safety Glass Ass'n
LSIA	Lamp and Shade Institute of America
LTA	Linen Trade Ass'n
LTE	Land Trust Exchange
LTEA	Leaf Tobacco Exporters Ass'n
LVA	Life Communicators Ass'n
LWIU	Leather Workers Internat'l Union
LZPC	Lead-Zinc Producers Committee
MAA	Mathematical Ass'n of America
	Medieval Academy of America
	Moped Ass'n of America
MAAI	Modeling Ass'n of America Internat'l
MAAN	Mutual Advertising Agency Network
MACS	Mobile Air Conditioning Soc.
MAES	Mexican American Engineering Soc.
MAFSI	Marketing Agents for Food Service Industry
MANA	Manufacturers' Agents Nat'l Ass'n
MAP/TOP	Manufacturing Automation Protocol and Technical Office Protocol Users Group
MAPI	Machinery and Allied Products Institute
MARC	Mining and Reclamation Council of America
MAS	Microbeam Analysis Soc.
MASAI	Mail Advertising Service Ass'n Internat'l
MBA	Merion Bluegrass Ass'n
MBAA	Master Brewers Ass'n of the Americas
	Mortgage Bankers Ass'n of America
MBCMA	Metal Building Components Manufacturers Ass'n
MBMA	Metal Building Manufacturers Ass'n
MBNA	Monument Builders of North America
MC	Mastercard Internat'l
MCA	Media Credit Ass'n
	Metal Construction Ass'n
	Microwave Communications Ass'n
	Military Chaplains Ass'n of the U.S.
	Mohair Council of America
	Music Critics Ass'n
MCAA	Mason Contractors Ass'n of America
	Mechanical Contractors Ass'n of America
MCATA	Maintenance Council of American Trucking Ass'ns
MCC	Munitions Carriers Conference
MCC-US	Mexican Chamber of Commerce of the United States
MCCA	Manufacturers Council on Color and Appearance
MCIA	Methyl Chloride Industry Ass'n
MCOGA	Mid-Continent Oil and Gas Ass'n
MCROA	Marine Corps Reserve Officers Ass'n
MCTI	Metal Cutting Tool Institute
MDA	Marking Device Ass'n
	Music Distributors Ass'n
MDHBA	Medical-Dental-Hospital Bureaus of America
MDNA	Machinery Dealers Nat'l Ass'n
MDRT	Million Dollar Round Table
MEA	Marketing Education Ass'n
MEAT BOARD	Nat'l Live Stock and Meat Board
MECA	Manufacturers of Emission Controls Ass'n
	Military Educators and Counselors Ass'n
MEIEA	Music and Entertainment Industry Educators Ass'n
MELA	Middle East Librarians' Ass'n
MEMA	Motor and Equipment Manufacturers Ass'n
MENC	Music Educators Nat'l Conference
MESA	Mechanics Educational Soc. of America
	Middle East Studies Ass'n of North America
MFAA	Men's Fashion Ass'n of America
MFGA	Master Furriers Guild of America
MFJSA	Mass Finishing Job Shops Ass'n
MFMA	Maple Flooring Manufacturers Ass'n
	Metal Findings Manufacturers Ass'n
	Metal Framing Manufacturers Ass'n
MFSA	Metal Finishing Suppliers Ass'n
MFTHBA	Missouri Fox Trotting Horse Breed Ass'n
MGA	Master Gemology Ass'n
MGMA	Medical Group Management Ass'n
MGSA	Modern Greek Studies Ass'n
MHEDA	Material Handling Equipment Distributors Ass'n
MHI	Manufactured Housing Institute
	Material Handling Institute
MHRA	Modern Humanities Research Ass'n
MIA	Marble Institute of America
	Millinery Institute of America
MIAA	Miniatures Industry Ass'n of America
MIC	Motorcycle Industry Council
MICA	Meat Importers' Council of America
	Mobile Industrial Caterers' Ass'n Internat'l
	Mortgage Insurance Companies of America
MIF	Milk Industry Foundation
MIIA	Mine Inspectors' Institute of America
MIMA	Mineral Insulation Manufacturers Ass'n
MISA	Meat Industry Suppliers Ass'n
MISL	Major Indoor Soccer League
MISLPA	Major Indoor Soccer League Players Ass'n
MJSA	Manufacturing Jewelers and Silversmiths of America
MKMA	Machine Knife Manufacturers Ass'n
ML/SFA	Metal Lath/Steel Framing Ass'n
MLA	Maritime Law Ass'n of the U.S.
	Medical Library Ass'n
	Multi-Housing Laundry Ass'n
	Music Library Ass'n
MLAA	Modern Language Ass'n of America
MLBPA	Major League Baseball Players Ass'n
MLMA	Metal Ladder Manufacturers Ass'n
MLUA	Major League Umpires Ass'n
MLUSA	Mailing List Users and Suppliers Ass'n
MMA	Materials Marketing Associates
	Monorail Manufacturers Ass'n
MMFPA	Man-Made Fiber Producers Ass'n
MMII	Mass Marketing Insurance Institute
MMOA	Mobile Modular Office Ass'n
MMPA	Magnetic Materials Producers Ass'n
MMSA	Materials and Methods Standards Ass'n
	Medical Mycological Soc. of the Americas
	Mining and Metallurgical Soc. of America
MNF	Millers' Nat'l Federation
MNHA	Musicians Nat'l Hotline Ass'n
MNS	Microneurography Soc.
MOA	Mail Order Ass'n of America
MOE	Mu Phi Epsilon
MORS	Military Operations Research Soc.
MPA	Magazine Publishers Ass'n
	Master Printers of America
	Music Publishers' Ass'n of the United States
MPAA	Motion Picture Ass'n of America
MPBP	Metal Polishers, Buffers, Platers and Allied Workers Internat'l Union
MPC	Materials Properties Council, The
MPEA	Machine Printers and Engravers Ass'n of the United States
MPEAA	Motion Picture Export Ass'n of America
MPI	Meeting Planners Internat'l
MPIF	Metal Powder Industries Federation
MPMA	United States Marine Products Manufacturers' Ass'n
MPMI	Magazine and Paperback Marketing Institute
MPS/PIA	Magazine Printers Section/Printing Industries of America
MPSA	Metropolitan Pharmaceutical Secretaries Ass'n
MPTA	Mechanical Power Transmission Ass'n
MPTCA	Motion Picture and Television Credit Ass'n
MRA	Manufacturers Representatives of America
	Marketing Research Ass'n
	Menswear Retailers of America
MRAA	Marine Retailers Ass'n of America
MRI	Military Reform Institute
MRIA	Model Railroad Industry Ass'n
MRS	Materials Research Soc.
MS	Manuscript Soc.
	Meteoritical Soc.
MSA	Metaphysical Soc. of America
	Microcirculatory Soc. of America
	Mineralogical Soc. of America
	Museum Store Ass'n
	Mycological Soc. of America
MSF	Motorcycle Safety Foundation
MSG-NAQP	Management Systems Group - Nat'l Ass'n of Quick Printers
MSMA	Mail Systems Management Ass'n
MSS	Manufacturers Standardization Soc. of the Valve and Fittings Industry
MTA US&C	Municipal Treasurers Ass'n of the United States and Canada
MTI	Metal Treating Institute
MTMASR	Methods Time Measurement Ass'n for Standards and Research
MTNA	Music Teachers Nat'l Ass'n
MTS	Marine Technology Soc.
MVA/SME	Machine Vision Ass'n of SME
MVMA	Motor Vehicle Manufacturers Ass'n of the United States
MWA	Mystery Writers of America
MWAA	Movers' and Warehousemen's Ass'n of America
MWI	Master Weavers Institute
NA	Newsletter Ass'n
NAA	Nat'l Academy of Arbitrators
	Nat'l Aeronautic Ass'n
	Nat'l Aerosol Ass'n
	Nat'l Apartment Ass'n
	Nat'l Arborist Ass'n
	Nat'l Ass'n of Accountants
	Nat'l Auctioneers Ass'n
	Neckwear Ass'n of America
NAAA	Nat'l Agricultural Aviation Ass'n
	Nat'l Auto Auction Ass'n
NAAAA	Nat'l Academic Athletic Advisors' Ass'n
	Nat'l Ass'n of Area Agencies on Aging
NAAB	Nat'l Ass'n of Animal Breeders
NAACOG	Nurses Ass'n of the American College of Obstetricians and Gynecologists
NAACS	Nat'l Ass'n of Accredited Cosmetology Schools
NAAD	Nat'l Ass'n of Aluminum Distributors
NAADAA	Nat'l Antique and Art Dealers Ass'n of America
NAADAC	Nat'l Ass'n of Alcoholism and Drug Abuse Counselors
NAAE	Nat'l Ass'n of Aeronautical Examiners
	Nat'l Ass'n of Agriculture Employees
	North American Academy of Ecumenists
NAAEE	North American Ass'n for Environmental Education
NAAG	Nat'l Ass'n of Attorneys General
NAAHP	Nat'l Ass'n of Advisors for the Health Professions
NAAMM	Nat'l Ass'n of Architectural Metal Manufacturers
	North American Academy of Manipulative Medicine
NAAN	Nat'l Advertising Agency Network
NAAO	Nat'l Ass'n of Artists' Organizations
NAAP	Nat'l Ass'n of Activity Professionals
	Nat'l Ass'n of Advertising Publishers
NAAS	Nat'l Ass'n of Academies of Science
NAASR	Nat'l Ass'n for Armenian Studies and Research
NAASS	North American Ass'n of Summer Sessions
NAATS	Nat'l Ass'n of Air Traffic Specialists
	Nat'l Ass'n of Auto Trim Shops
NAAWS	North American Ass'n of Wardens and Superintendents
NAB	Nat'l Ass'n of Boards of Examiners of Nursing Home Administrators
	Nat'l Ass'n of Broadcasters
	Newspaper Advertising Bureau
NABA	Nat'l Ass'n of Black Accountants
NABADA	Nat'l Barrel and Drum Ass'n
NABC	North American Blueberry Council
NABCA	Nat'l Alcoholic Beverage Control Ass'n
	Nat'l Ass'n for Bank Cost Analysis & Management Accountint
NABCE	Nat'l Ass'n of Black Consulting Engineers
NABCUS	Nat'l Ass'n of Basketball Coaches of the United States
NABD	Nat'l Ass'n of Brick Distributors
NABE	Nat'l Ass'n for Bilingual Education
	Nat'l Ass'n of Bar Executives
	Nat'l Ass'n of Boards of Education
	Nat'l Ass'n of Business Economists
NABER	Nat'l Ass'n of Business and Educational Radio
NABET	Nat'l Ass'n of Broadcast Employees and Technicians
NABHP	Nat'l Ass'n of Black Hospitality Professionals
NABI	Nat'l Ass'n of Beverage Importers-Wine-Spirits-Beer
NABIM	Nat'l Ass'n of Band Instrument Manufacturers
NABIS	Nat'l Ass'n of Business and Industrial Saleswomen
NABL	Nat'l Ass'n of Bond Lawyers
NABM	Internat'l Sleep Products Ass'n
	Nat'l Ass'n of Blouse Manufacturers
	Nat'l Ass'n of Boat Manufacturers
NABMCC	Nat'l Ass'n of Black and Minority Chambers of Commerce
NABOB	Nat'l Ass'n of Black-Owned Broadcasters
NABP	Nat'l Ass'n of Boards of Pharmacy
NABPAC	Nat'l Ass'n of Business Political Action Committees
NABPR	Nat'l Ass'n of Baptist Professors of Religion
NABR	Nat'l Ass'n for Biomedical Research
	Nat'l Ass'n of Basketball Referees
NABRTI	Nat'l Ass'n of Bar-Related Title Insurers
NABS	Nat'l Ass'n of Bank Servicers
	Nat'l Ass'n of Buying Services
NABSE	Nat'l Alliance of Black School Educators
NABSS	Nat'l Ass'n of Barber Styling Schools
NABSW	Nat'l Ass'n of Black Social Workers
NABT	Nat'l Ass'n of Bankruptcy Trustees
	Nat'l Ass'n of Biology Teachers
	Nat'l Ass'n of Blind Teachers
NABW	Nat'l Ass'n of Bank Women
NABWA	Nat'l Ass'n of Black Women Attorneys
NABWE	Nat'l Ass'n of Black Women Entrepreneurs
NAC	Nat'l Academy of Conciliators
	Nat'l Ass'n of Concessionaires
NACA	Nat'l Agricultural Chemicals Ass'n
	Nat'l Air Carrier Ass'n
	Nat'l Ass'n for Campus Activities
	Nat'l Ass'n of Christians in the Arts
	Nat'l Ass'n of County Administrators
	North American Corriente Ass'n
NACAA	Nat'l Ass'n of Community Action Agencies
	Nat'l Ass'n of Consumer Agency Administrators
	Nat'l Ass'n of County Agricultural Agents
NACAC	Nat'l Ass'n of College Admission Counselors

ACRONYM INDEX

NACADA	Nat'l Academic Advising Ass'n
NACAP	Nat'l Ass'n of County Aging Programs
NACAS	Nat'l Ass'n of College Auxiliary Services
NACAT	Nat'l Ass'n of College Automotive Teachers
NACBA	Nat'l Ass'n of Church Business Administration
NACC	Nat'l Ass'n for Core Curriculum
	Nat'l Ass'n of Catholic Chaplains
NACCA	Nat'l Ass'n for Creative Children and Adults
	Nat'l Ass'n of Consumer Credit Administrators
	Nat'l Ass'n of County Civil Attorneys
NACCDD	Nat'l Ass'n of County Community Development Directors
NACCIC	Nat'l Ass'n of Counties Council of Intergovernmental Coordinators
NACCM	Nat'l Ass'n for Child Care Management
NACD	Nat'l Ass'n of Chemical Distributors
	Nat'l Ass'n of Conservation Districts
	Nat'l Ass'n of Container Distributors
	Nat'l Ass'n of Corporate Directors
NACDA	Nat'l Ass'n of Collegiate Directors of Athletics
NACDL	Nat'l Ass'n of Criminal Defense Lawyers
NACDRAO	Nat'l Ass'n of College Deans, Registrars, and Admissions Officers
NACDS	Nat'l Ass'n of Chain Drug Stores
NACE	Nat'l Ass'n of Catering Executives
	Nat'l Ass'n of Corrosion Engineers
	Nat'l Ass'n of County Engineers
NACEBE	Nat'l Ass'n of Classroom Educators in Business Education
NACFA	North American Clun Forest Ass'n
NACFR	Nat'l Ass'n of Casual Furniture Retailers
NACGC(Men)	Nat'l Ass'n of Collegiate Gymnastics Coaches (Men)
NACGM	Nat'l Ass'n of Chewing Gum Manufacturers
NACH	Nat'l Ass'n of Clergy Hypnotherapists
NACHA	Nat'l Automated Clearing House Ass'n
NACHC	Nat'l Ass'n of Community Health Centers
NACHES	Nat'l Ass'n of Jewish Family, Children's and Health Professionals
NACHFA	Nat'l Ass'n of County Health Facility Administrators
NACHO	Nat'l Ass'n of County Health Officials
NACHRI	Nat'l Ass'n of Children's Hospitals and Related Institutions
NACHSA	Nat'l Ass'n of County Human Services Administrators
NACI	Nat'l Ass'n for the Cottage Industry
NACIO	Nat'l Ass'n of County Information Officers
NACIS	North American Cartographic Information Soc.
NACJP	Nat'l Ass'n of Criminal Justice Planners
NACLO	Nat'l Ass'n of Canoe Liveries and Outfitters
	Nat'l Ass'n of Community Leadership Organizations
NACM	Nat'l Ass'n of Chain Manufacturers
	Nat'l Ass'n of Credit Management
NACN	Newspaper Advertising Co-op Network
NACOP	Nat'l Ass'n of Chiefs of Police
NACORE	Internat'l Ass'n of Corporate Real Estate Executives
NACPA	Nat'l Ass'n of Church Personnel Administrators
NACPD	Nat'l Ass'n of County Planning Directors
NACPR	Nat'l Ass'n of Corporate and Professional Recruiters
NACPRO	Nat'l Ass'n of County Park and Recreation Officials
NACRC	Nat'l Ass'n of County Recorders and Clerks
NACS	Nat'l Ass'n for Check Safekeeping
	Nat'l Ass'n of College Stores
	Nat'l Ass'n of Convenience Stores
	North American Catalysis Soc.
NACSA	Nat'l Ass'n of Casualty and Surety Agents
	Nat'l Ass'n of Corporate Speaker Activities
NACSARS	Nat'l Ass'n of Companion Sitter Agencies and Referral Services
NACSC	Nat'l Ass'n of Cold Storage Contractors
NACSE	Nat'l Ass'n of Casualty and Surety Executives
NACSM	Nat'l Ass'n of Catalog Showroom Merchandisers
NACSW	North American Ass'n of Christians in Social Work
NACT	Nat'l Alliance of Cardiovascular Technologists
NACTA	Nat'l Ass'n of Colleges and Teachers of Agriculture
NACTEP	Nat'l Ass'n of County Training and Employment Professionals
NACTFO	Nat'l Ass'n of County Treasurers and Finance Officers
NACTP	Nat'l Ass'n of Computerized Tax Processors
NACUA	Nat'l Ass'n of College and University Attorneys
NACUBO	Nat'l Ass'n of College and University Business Officers
NACUCDRL	Nat'l Ass'n of College and University Chaplains and Directors of Religious Life
NACUFS	Nat'l Ass'n of College and University Food Services
NACUP	Nat'l Ass'n of Credit Union Presidents
NACWC	Nat'l Ass'n of Colored Women's Clubs
NACWPI	Nat'l Ass'n of College Wind and Percussion Instructors
NACo	Nat'l Ass'n of Counties
NAD	Nat'l Academy of Design
NADA	Nat'l Ass'n of Dealers in Antiques
	Nat'l Ass'n of Dental Assistants
	Nat'l Automobile Dealers Ass'n
NADAF	Nat'l Ass'n of Decorative Architectural Finishes
NADC	Nat'l Ass'n of Demolition Contractors
	Nat'l Ass'n of Dredging Contractors
NADCA	Nat'l Animal Damage Control Ass'n
NADCO	Nat'l Ass'n of Development Companies
NADD	Nat'l Ass'n of Diemakers and Diecutters
NADDC	Nat'l Ass'n of Developmental Disabilities Councils
NADE	Nat'l Ass'n of Disability Examiners
NADFD	Nat'l Ass'n of Decorative Fabric Distributors
NADHCI	North American District Heating and Cooling Institute
NADI	Nat'l Ass'n of Display Industries
NADL	Nat'l Ass'n of Dental Laboratories
NADO	Nat'l Ass'n of Development Organizations
NADOA	Nat'l Ass'n of Division Order Analysts
NADS	Nat'l Ass'n of Diaper Services
NADSTM	Nat'l Ass'n of Doll and Stuffed Toy Manufacturers
NADT	Nat'l Ass'n for Drama Therapy
NAE	Nat'l Academy of Education
	Nat'l Ass'n of Entrepreneurs
	Nat'l Ass'n of Evangelicals
	Nursery Ass'n Executives
NAEA	Nat'l Art Education Ass'n
	Nat'l Ass'n of Enrolled Agents
NAEB	Nat'l Ass'n of Educational Buyers
NAEC	Nat'l Ass'n of Elevator Contractors
NAED	Nat'l Ass'n of Electrical Distributors
NAEFTA	Nat'l Ass'n of Enrolled Federal Tax Accountants
NAEGA	North American Export Grain Ass'n
NAEHCA	Nat'l Ass'n of Employers on Health Care Alternatives
NAEHE	Nat'l Ass'n of Extension Home Economists
NAEKM	Nat'l Ass'n of Electronic Keyboard Manufacturers
NAEM	Nat'l Ass'n of Exposition Managers
NAEMT	Nat'l Ass'n of Emergency Medical Technicians
NAEO	Nat'l Ass'n of Extradition Officials
NAEOP	Nat'l Ass'n of Educational Office Personnel
NAEP	Nat'l Ass'n of Environmental Professionals
NAEPC	Nat'l Ass'n of Estate Planning Councils
NAES	Nat'l Ass'n for Ethnic Studies
	Nat'l Ass'n of Ecumenical Staff
	Nat'l Ass'n of Episcopal Schools
	Nat'l Ass'n of Executive Secretaries
NAESCO	Nat'l Ass'n of Energy Service Companies
NAESP	Nat'l Ass'n of Elementary School Principals
NAEUSA	Nat'l Academy of Engineering of the United States of America
NAEYC	Nat'l Ass'n for the Education of Young Children
NAE4-HA	Nat'l Ass'n of Extension 4-H Agents
NAF	Nat'l Abortion Federation
NAFA	Nat'l Ass'n of Fleet Administrators
NAFAC	Nat'l Ass'n For Ambulatory Care
NAFB	Nat'l Ass'n of Farm Broadcasters
NAFC	Nat'l Accounting and Finance Council
	Nat'l Ass'n of Financial Consultants
	Nat'l Ass'n of Franchise Companies
NAFCD	Nat'l Ass'n of Floor Covering Distributors
NAFCU	Nat'l Ass'n of Federal Credit Unions
NAFD	Nat'l Ass'n of Flour Distributors
NAFED	Nat'l Ass'n of Fire Equipment Distributors
NAFEM	Nat'l Ass'n of Food Equipment Manufacturers
NAFEO	Nat'l Ass'n for Equal Opportunity in Higher Education
NAFEPA	Nat'l Ass'n of Federal Education Program Administrators
NAFFS	Nat'l Ass'n of Fruits, Flavors and Syrups
NAFI	Nat'l Ass'n of Fire Investigators
	Nat'l Ass'n of Flight Instructors
NAFIC	Nat'l Ass'n of Fraternal Insurance Counsellors
NAFIS	Nat'l Ass'n of Federally Impacted Schools
NAFPB	Nat'l Ass'n of Freight Payment Banks
NAFSA	Nat'l Ass'n for Foreign Student Affairs
NAFSC	North American Farm Show Council
NAFTA	Nat'l Ass'n of Futures Trading Advisors
NAFTC	Nat'l Ass'n of Freight Transportation Consultants
NAFTZ	Nat'l Ass'n of Foreign-Trade Zones
NAFV	Nat'l Ass'n of Federal Veterinarians
NAGA	North American Gamebird Ass'n
NAGARA	Nat'l Ass'n of Government Archives and Records Administrators
NAGC	Nat'l Ass'n of Girls Clubs
	Nat'l Ass'n of Government Communicators
NAGDM	Nat'l Ass'n of Garage Door Manufacturers
NAGE	Nat'l Ass'n of Government Employees
NAGHSR	Nat'l Ass'n of Governors' Highway Safety Representatives
NAGIQAP	Nat'l Ass'n of Government Inspectors and Quality Assurance Personnel
NAGLO	Nat'l Ass'n of Governmental Labor Officials
NAGMR	Nat'l Ass'n General Merchandise Representatives
NAGRA	Nat'l Ass'n of Gambling Regulatory Agencies
NAGT	Nat'l Ass'n of Geology Teachers
NAHAD	Nat'l Ass'n of Hose and Accessories Distributors
NAHAM	Nat'l Ass'n of Hospital Admitting Managers
NAHB	Nat'l Alliance of Homebased Businesswomen
	Nat'l Ass'n of Home Builders of the U.S.
NAHC	Nat'l Ass'n for Home Care
	Nat'l Ass'n of Homes for Children
	Nat'l Ass'n of Housing Cooperatives
NAHCR	Nat'l Ass'n for Health Care Recruitment
NAHCS	Nat'l Ass'n of Health Career Schools
NAHD	Nat'l Ass'n for Hospital Development
NAHDSA	Nat'l Ass'n of Hebrew Day School Administrators
NAHE	Nat'l Ass'n for Humanities Education
NAHJ	Nat'l Ass'n of Hispanic Journalists
NAHM	Nat'l Ass'n of Hosiery Manufacturers
NAHP	Nat'l Ass'n of Hispanic Publications
NAHPMM	Nat'l Ass'n of Hospital Purchasing Materials Management
NAHRO	Nat'l Ass'n of Housing and Redevelopment Officials
NAHRW	Nat'l Ass'n of Human Rights Workers
NAHU	Nat'l Ass'n of Health Underwriters
NAHWW	Nat'l Ass'n of Home and Workshop Writers
NAIB	Nat'l Ass'n of Insurance Brokers
NAIC	Nat'l Ass'n of Insurance Commissioners
	Nat'l Ass'n of Investment Companies
	Nat'l Ass'n of Investors
NAICC	Nat'l Alliance of Independent Crop Consultants
NAICCA	Nat'l American Indian Court Clerks Ass'n
NAICU	Nat'l Ass'n of Independent Colleges and Universities
NAICV	Nat'l Ass'n of Ice Cream Vendors
NAID	Nat'l Ass'n of Installation Developers
NAIEC	Nat'l Ass'n for Industry-Education Cooperation
NAIFA	Nat'l Ass'n of Independent Fee Appraisers
NAIGE	Nat'l Ass'n for Individually Guided Education
NAII	Nat'l Ass'n of Independent Insurers
NAIIA	Nat'l Ass'n of Independent Insurance Adjusters
NAIIAE	Nat'l Ass'n of Independent Insurance Auditors and Engineers
NAILBA	Nat'l Ass'n of Independent Life Brokerage Agencies
NAILM	Nat'l Ass'n of Institutional Linen Management
NAIMA	North American Indian Museums Ass'n
NAIOP	Nat'l Ass'n of Industrial and Office Parks
NAIP	Nat'l Ass'n of Independent Publishers
NAIR	Nat'l Ass'n of Independent Resurfacers
NAIRD	Nat'l Ass'n of Independent Record Distributors and Manufacturers
NAIS	Nat'l Ass'n of Independent Schools
	Nat'l Ass'n of Investigative Specialists
NAIT	Nat'l Ass'n of Industrial Technology
NAITP	Nat'l Ass'n of Income Tax Preparers
NAITTE	Nat'l Ass'n of Industrial and Technical Teacher Educators
NAIW	Nat'l Ass'n of Insurance Women (Internat'l)
NAJA	Nat'l Ass'n of Jewelry Appraisers
NAJAF	Nat'l Ass'n of Jai Alai Frontons
NAJCA	Nat'l Ass'n of Juvenile Correctional Agencies
NAJD/MBAP	Nat'l Ass'n of JD/MBA Professionals
NAJE	Nat'l Ass'n of Jazz Educators
NAJVS	Nat'l Ass'n of Jewish Vocational Services
NAJYC	North American Jewish Youth Council
NALA	Nat'l Ass'n of Legal Assistants
NALAA	Nat'l Assembly of Local Arts Agencies
NALC	Nat'l Ass'n of Letter Carriers of the United States of America
	Nat'l Ass'n of Life Companies
	Nat'l Ass'n of Litho Clubs
NALED	Nat'l Ass'n of Limited Edition Dealers
NALEO	Nat'l Ass'n of Latino Elected and Appointed Officials
NALF	North American Limousin Foundation
NALHC	North American Log Homes Council
NALI	Nat'l Ass'n of Legal Investigators
NALMCO	Internat'l Ass'n of Lighting Maintenance Contractors
NALP	Nat'l Ass'n for Law Placement
NALPA	Nat'l American Legion Press Ass'n
NALPM	Nat'l Ass'n of Lithographic Plate Manufacturers
NALR	Nat'l Ass'n of Lighting Representatives
NALS	Nat'l Ass'n of Laboratory Suppliers
	Nat'l Ass'n of Legal Secretaries (Int'l)
NALU	Nat'l Ass'n of Life Underwriters
NALUS	Nat'l Ass'n of Leagues, Umpires and Scorers
NAM	Nat'l Ass'n of Manufacturers
	Newspaper Ass'n Managers
NAM/ME	Nat'l Ass'n of Management/Marketing Educators
NAMA	Nat'l Account Marketing Ass'n
	Nat'l Agri-Marketing Ass'n
	Nat'l Assistance Management Ass'n
	Nat'l Automatic Merchandising Ass'n
	North American Mycological Ass'n
NAMB	Nat'l Ass'n of Mortgage Brokers
NAMC	Nat'l Ass'n of Minority Contractors
NAMD	Nat'l Ass'n of Market Developers
NAMDCC	Nat'l Ass'n of Membership Directors of Chambers of Commerce
NAMDT	Nat'l Ass'n of Milliners, Dressmakers and Tailors
NAME	Nat'l Ass'n of Medical Examiners
	Nat'l Ass'n of Name Plate Manufacturers
NAMES	Nat'l Ass'n of Medical Equipment Suppliers
NAMESU	Nat'l Ass'n of Music Executives in State Universities
NAMF	Nat'l Ass'n of Metal Finishers
NAMHA	North American Morab Horse Ass'n
NAMIC	Nat'l Ass'n of Mutual Insurance Companies
NAMM	Nat'l Ass'n of Margarine Manufacturers
	Nat'l Ass'n of Mirror Manufacturers
	Nat'l Ass'n of Music Merchants
NAMO	Nat'l Agricultural Marketing Officials
	Nat'l Ass'n of Manufacturing Opticians

ACRONYM INDEX

NAMOA	Nat'l Ass'n of Miscellaneous, Ornamental and Architectural Products Contractors
NAMP	Nat'l Ass'n of Meat Purveyors
NAMPS	Nat'l Ass'n of Marine Products and Services
NAMS	Nat'l Ass'n of Marine Services
	Nat'l Ass'n of Marine Surveyors
NAMSB	Nat'l Ass'n of Men's Sportswear Buyers
NAMSP	Nat'l Ass'n of Mail Service Pharmacies
NAMT	Nat'l Ass'n for Music Therapy
NAMTA	Nat'l Art Materials Trade Ass'n
NAMTAC	Nat'l Ass'n of Management and Technical Assistance Centers
NAMW	Nat'l Ass'n of Media Women
NAN	Nat'l Ass'n of Neighborhoods
NANA	Nat'l Aesthetician and Nail Artist Ass'n
	North American Normande Ass'n
NANBPWC	Nat'l Ass'n of Negro Business and Professional Women's Clubs
NANCB	Nat'l Ass'n of Negotiated Commission Brokers
NANCO	Nat'l Ass'n of Noise Control Officials
NAO	Nat'l Academy of Opticianry
NAON	Nat'l Ass'n of Orthopaedic Nurses
NAOO	Nat'l Ass'n of Optometrists and Opticians
NAOSMM	Nat'l Ass'n of Scientific Materials Managers
NAOTC	Nat'l Ass'n of OTC Companies
NAP	Nat'l Ass'n of Parliamentarians
NAPA	Nat'l Agricultural Plastics Ass'n
	Nat'l Asphalt Pavement Ass'n
	Nat'l Automotive Parts Ass'n
NAPBIRT	Nat'l Ass'n of Professional Band Instrument Repair Technicians
NAPBL	Nat'l Ass'n of Professional Baseball Leagues
NAPC	Nat'l Ass'n of Personnel Consultants
NAPCA	Nat'l Ass'n of Pension Consultants and Administrators
	Nat'l Ass'n of Pipe Coating Applicators
NAPCRO	Nat'l Ass'n of Police-Community Relations Officers
NAPCWA	Nat'l Ass'n of Public Child Welfare Administrators
NAPD	Nat'l Ass'n of Plastics Distributors
NAPDEA	North American Professional Driver Education Ass'n
NAPE	Nat'l Ass'n of Power Engineers
	Nat'l Ass'n of Professional Engravers
NAPEHE	Nat'l Ass'n for Physical Education in Higher Education
NAPEP	Nat'l Ass'n of Planners, Estimators and Progressmen
NAPET	Nat'l Ass'n of Photo Equipment Technicians
NAPFE	Nat'l Alliance of Postal and Federal Employees
NAPFR	Nat'l Ass'n of Professional Fund Raisers
NAPH	Nat'l Ass'n of Public Hospitals
NAPHAIHL	Nat'l Ass'n of Professors of Hebrew in American Institutions of Higher Learning
NAPHCC	Nat'l Ass'n of Plumbing-Heating-Cooling Contractors
NAPIA	Nat'l Ass'n of Public Insurance Adjusters
NAPIC	Nat'l Ass'n of Private Industry Councils
NAPIM	Nat'l Ass'n of Printing Ink Manufacturers
NAPL	Nat'l Ass'n of Printers and Lithographers
NAPM	Nat'l Ass'n of Pattern Manufacturers
	Nat'l Ass'n of Pharmaceutical Manufacturers
	Nat'l Ass'n of Photographic Manufacturers
	Nat'l Ass'n of Punch Manufacturers
	Nat'l Ass'n of Purchasing Management
NAPMM	Nat'l Ass'n of Produce Market Managers
NAPN	Nat'l Ass'n of Physician Nurses
NAPNAP	Nat'l Ass'n of Pediatric Nurse Associates & Practitioners
NAPNES	Nat'l Ass'n for Practical Nurse Education and Service
NAPNM	Nat'l Ass'n of Pipe Nipple Manufacturers
NAPO	Nat'l Ass'n of Pizza Operators
	Nat'l Ass'n of Police Organizations
NAPP	Nat'l Ass'n of Paralegal Personnel
NAPPA	Nat'l Ass'n of Pupil Personnel Administrators
NAPPH	Nat'l Ass'n of Private Psychiatric Hospitals
NAPPO	Nat'l Ass'n of Plant Patent Owners
NAPR	Nat'l Ass'n of Publishers' Representatives
NAPRFMR	Nat'l Ass'n of Private Residential Facilities for the Mentally Retarded
NAPS	Nat'l Ass'n for Professional Saleswomen
	Nat'l Ass'n of Postal Supervisors
NAPSA	Nat'l Appliance Parts Suppliers Ass'n
NAPSEC	Nat'l Ass'n of Private Schools for Exceptional Children
NAPSG	Nat'l Ass'n of Principals of Schools for Girls
NAPSLO	Nat'l Ass'n of Professional Surplus Lines Offices
NAPSV	Nat'l Ass'n of Private Security Vaults
NAPT	Nat'l Ass'n for Poetry Therapy
	Nat'l Ass'n of Physical Therapists
NAPTS	Nat'l Ass'n of Public Television Stations
NAPU	Nat'l Ass'n of Professional Upholsterers
NAPUS	Nat'l Ass'n of Postmasters of the U.S.
NAPWPT	Nat'l Ass'n of Professional Word Processing Technicians
NAQAP	Nat'l Ass'n of Quality Assurance Professionals
NAQP	Nat'l Ass'n of Quick Printers
NAR	Nat'l Ass'n of REALTORS
NARAMU	Nat'l Ass'n of Review Appraisers and Mortgage Underwriters
NARAS	Nat'l Academy of Recording Arts and Sciences
NARB	Nat'l Ass'n for Regional Ballet
NARBW	Nat'l Ass'n of Railway Business Women
NARC	Nat'l Ass'n of Regional Councils
NARD	Nat'l Ass'n of Retail Druggists
NARDA	Nat'l Ass'n of Retail Dealers of America
NAREE	Nat'l Ass'n of Real Estate Editors
NAREIT	Nat'l Ass'n of Real Estate Investment Trusts
NARELLO	Nat'l Ass'n of Real Estate License Law Officials
NARF	Nat'l Ass'n of Rehabilitation Facilities
NARFE	Nat'l Ass'n of Retired Federal Employees
NARI	Nat'l Ass'n of Recycling Industries
	Nat'l Ass'n of the Remodeling Industry
NARM	Nat'l Ass'n of Recording Merchandisers
	Nat'l Ass'n of Relay Manufacturers
NARMC	Nat'l Ass'n of Regional Media Centers
NARMH	Nat'l Ass'n for Rural Mental Health
NARO	Nat'l Ass'n of Reimbursement Officers
	Nat'l Ass'n of Royalty Owners
NARPPS	Nat'l Ass'n of Rehabilitation Professionals in the Private Sector
NARS	Nat'l Ass'n of Rail Shippers
	Nat'l Ass'n of Rehabilitation Secretaries
NARSA	Nat'l Automotive Radiator Service Ass'n
NARSC	Nat'l Ass'n of Reinforcing Steel Contractors
NARST	Nat'l Ass'n for Research in Science Teaching
NARTC	Nat'l Ass'n of Railroad Trial Counsel
	Nat'l Ass'n of Railway Tax Commissioners
NARTE	Nat'l Ass'n of Radio and Telecommunications Engineers
NARUC	Nat'l Ass'n of Regulatory Utility Commissioners
NAS	Nat'l Academy of Sciences
	Nat'l Ass'n of Stevedores
	Nat'l Avionics Soc.
NASA	Nat'l Appliance Service Ass'n
	Nat'l Ass'n of Shippers' Agents
	Nat'l Ass'n of State Archaeologists
	Nat'l Ass'n of Synagogue Administrators
	Newspaper Advertising Sales Ass'n
NASAA	Nat'l Assembly of State Arts Agencies
	Nat'l Ass'n of State Approving Agencies
	Nat'l Ass'n of Student Activity Advisers
	North American Securities Administrators Ass'n
NASACT	Nat'l Ass'n of State Auditors, Comptrollers and Treasurers
NASAD	Nat'l Ass'n of Schools of Art and Design
NASADAD	Nat'l Ass'n of State Alcohol and Drug Abuse Directors
NASAE	Nat'l Ass'n of Supervisors of Agricultural Education
NASAO	Nat'l Ass'n of State Aviation Officials
NASAP	North American Soc. of Adlerian Psychology
NASAR	Nat'l Ass'n for Search and Rescue
NASASP	Nat'l Ass'n of State Agencies for Surplus Property
NASASPS	Nat'l Ass'n of State Administrators and Supervisors of Private Schools
NASBA	Nat'l Ass'n of State Boards of Accountancy
NASBE	Nat'l Ass'n of State Boards of Education
	Nat'l Ass'n of Supervisors of Business Education
NASBIC	Nat'l Ass'n of Small Business Investment Companies
NASBLA	Nat'l Ass'n of State Boating Law Administrators
NASBO	Nat'l Ass'n of State Budget Officers
NASBP	Nat'l Ass'n of Surety Bond Producers
NASC	Nat'l Aloe Science Council
	Nat'l Ass'n of Solar Contractors
NASC-NAPNSC	Nat'l Ass'n of Private, Nontraditional Schools and Colleges
NASCAR	Nat'l Ass'n for Stock Car Auto Racing
NASCCD	Nat'l Ass'n of State Catholic Conference Directors
NASCO	North American Students of Cooperation
NASCOE	Nat'l Ass'n of ASCS County Office Employees
NASCUMC	Nat'l Ass'n of Schools and Colleges of the United Methodist Church
NASCUS	Nat'l Ass'n of State Credit Union Supervisors
NASD	Nat'l Ass'n of Schools of Dance
	Nat'l Ass'n of Securities Dealers
	Nat'l Ass'n of Selective Distributors
NASDA	Nat'l Ass'n of State Departments of Agriculture
	Nat'l Ass'n of State Development Agencies
NASDAD	Nat'l Ass'n of Seventh-Day Adventist Dentists
NASDME	Nat'l Ass'n of State Directors of Migrant Education
NASDSE	Nat'l Ass'n of State Directors of Special Education
NASDTEC	Nat'l Ass'n of State Directors of Teacher Education and Certification
NASDVA	Nat'l Ass'n of State Directors of Veterans Affairs
NASDVE	Nat'l Ass'n of State Directors of Vocational Education
NASE	Nat'l Ass'n for the Self-Employed
NASEDIO	Nat'l Ass'n of State Education Department Information Officers
NASEMSD	Nat'l Ass'n of State Emergency Services Directors
NASF	Nat'l Ass'n of State Foresters
NASFAA	Nat'l Ass'n of Student Financial Aid Administrators
NASFCB	Nat'l Ass'n of Specialty Food and Confection Brokers
NASFM	Nat'l Ass'n of Store Fixture Manufacturers
NASFT	Nat'l Ass'n for the Speciality Food Trade
NASGA	North American Simulation and Gaming Ass'n
NASGC	Nat'l Ass'n of Small Government Contractors
NASGW	Nat'l Ass'n of Sporting Goods Wholesalers
NASILP	Nat'l Ass'n of Self-Instructional Language Programs
NASIS	Nat'l Ass'n for State Information Systems
NASISS	Nat'l Ass'n of Sailing Instructors and Sailing Schools
NASLI	Nat'l Ass'n of Senior Living Industries
NASLR	Nat'l Ass'n of State Land Reclamationists
NASM	Nat'l Ass'n of Schools of Music
	Nat'l Ass'n of Service Managers
	Nat'l Ass'n of Service Merchandising
NASMD	Nat'l Ass'n of School Music Dealers
NASMHPD	Nat'l Ass'n of State Mental Health Program Directors
NASMP	Nat'l Ass'n of Sales and Marketing Professionals
NASMRPD	Nat'l Ass'n of State Mental Retardation Program Directors
NASN	Nat'l Ass'n of School Nurses
NASO	Nat'l Ass'n of Sports Officials
NASP	Nat'l Ass'n of School Psychologists
NASPA	Nat'l Ass'n of Student Personnel Administrators
NASPAA	Nat'l Ass'n of Schools of Public Affairs and Administration
NASPD	Nat'l Ass'n of State Park Directors
	Nat'l Ass'n of Steel Pipe Distributors
NASPE	Nat'l Ass'n for Sport and Physical Education
	North American Soc. of Pacing and Electrophysiology
NASPG	North American Soc. for Pediatric Gastroenterology
NASPHV	Nat'l Ass'n of State Public Health Veterinarians
NASPL	Nat'l Ass'n of State and Provincial Lotteries
NASPO	Nat'l Ass'n of State Purchasing Officials
NASPSPA	North American Soc. for the Psychology of Sport and Physical Activity
NASR	Nat'l Ass'n of Solvent Recyclers
	Nat'l Ass'n of Swine Records
NASRA	Nat'l Ass'n of State Retirement Administrators
NASRC	Nat'l Ass'n of State Racing Commissioners
NASRO	Nat'l Ass'n of Shooting Range Owners
NASRP	Nat'l Ass'n of State Recreation Planners
NASS	Nat'l Ass'n of Secretarial Services
	Nat'l Ass'n of Secretaries of State
	Nat'l Ass'n of Suggestion Systems
NASSCO	Nat'l Ass'n of Sewer Service Companies
NASSD	Nat'l Ass'n of School Security Directors
NASSDSE	Nat'l Ass'n of State Supervisors and Directors of Secondary Education
NASSLS	Nat'l Ass'n of State Savings and Loan Supervisors
NASSM	Nat'l Ass'n of Scissors and Shears Manufacturers
	Nat'l Ass'n of State Supervisors of Music
NASSP	Nat'l Ass'n of Secondary School Principals
NASSTIE	Nat'l Ass'n of State Supervisors of Trade and Industrial Education
NASSTRAC	Nat'l Small Shipments Traffic Conference
NAST	Nat'l Ass'n of Schools of Theatre
	Nat'l Ass'n of State Treasurers
NASTA	Nat'l Ass'n of State Textbook Administrators
NASTD	Nat'l Ass'n of State Telecommunications Directors
NASUA	Nat'l Ass'n of State Units on Aging
NASUCA	Nat'l Ass'n of State Utility Consumer Advocates
NASULGC	Nat'l Ass'n of State Universities and Land Grant Colleges
NASW	Nat'l Ass'n of Science Writers
	Nat'l Ass'n of Social Workers
NATA	Nat'l Air Transportation Ass'n
	Nat'l Ass'n of Tax Administrators
	Nat'l Ass'n of Teachers' Agencies
	Nat'l Ass'n of Temple Administrators
	Nat'l Athletic Trainers' Ass'n
	Nat'l Automobile Transporters Ass'n
	North American Telecommunications Ass'n
NATAD	Nat'l Ass'n of Textile and Apparel Distributors
NATAS	Nat'l Academy of Television Arts and Sciences
	North American Thermal Analysis Soc.
NATB	Nat'l Automobile Theft Bureau
NATC	Nat'l Ass'n of Tax Consultors
	Nat'l Ass'n of Telemarketing Consultants
NATCO	North American Transplant Coordinators Organization
NATD	Nat'l Ass'n of Tobacco Distributors
NATE	Nat'l Ass'n of Temple Educators
NATIE	Nat'l Ass'n for Trade and Industrial Education
NATL	Nat'l Agricultural Transportation League
NATO	Nat'l Ass'n of Theatre Owners
NATP	Nat'l Ass'n of Tax Practitioners
NATPE	Nat'l Ass'n of Television Program Executives
NATRI	Nat'l Ass'n of Treasurers of Religious Institutes
NATS	Nat'l Ass'n of Teachers of Singing
	Nat'l Ass'n of Temporary Services
	Nat'l Ass'n of Textile Supervisors
NATSO	Nat'l Ass'n of Truck Stop Operators
NATTS	Nat'l Ass'n of Trade and Technical Schools
NATaT	Nat'l Ass'n of Towns and Townships
NAUB	Nat'l Ass'n of Urban Bankers
NAUFMA	Nat'l Ass'n of Urban Flood Management Agencies
NAUI	Nat'l Ass'n of Underwater Instructors
NAUMD	Nat'l Ass'n of Uniform Manufacturers and Distributors

ACRONYM INDEX

NAUPA	Nat'l Ass'n of Unclaimed Property Administrators
NAUS	Nat'l Ass'n for Uniformed Services
NAVA	Nat'l Ass'n for Veterinary Acupuncture
NAVAP	Nat'l Ass'n of VA Physicians
NAVD	Nat'l Ass'n of Video Distributors
NAVHET	Nat'l Ass'n of Vocational Home Economics Teachers
NAVP	Nat'l Ass'n of Vision Professionals
NAVPA	Nat'l Ass'n of Veteran Program Administrators
NAVS	Nat'l Ass'n of Variety Stores
NAW	Nat'l Ass'n of Wholesaler-Distributors
NAWA	Nat'l Ass'n of Women Artists
NAWBO	Nat'l Ass'n of Women Business Owners
NAWC	Nat'l Ass'n of Water Companies
	Nat'l Ass'n of Women in Construction
NAWDAC	Nat'l Ass'n for Women Deans, Administrators, and Counselors
NAWF	North American Wildlife Foundation
NAWG	Nat'l Ass'n of Wheat Growers
NAWGA	Nat'l-American Wholesale Grocers' Ass'n
NAWGC	Nat'l Ass'n of Women Government Contractors
NAWHSL	Nat'l Ass'n of Women Highway Safety Leaders
NAWID	Nat'l Ass'n of Writing Instrument Distributors
NAWJ	Nat'l Ass'n of Women Judges
NAWL	Nat'l Ass'n of Women Lawyers
NAWLA	North American Wholesale Lumber Ass'n
NBA	Nat'l Band Ass'n
	Nat'l Bankers Ass'n
	Nat'l Bar Ass'n
	Nat'l Bartenders Ass'n
	Nat'l Basketball Ass'n
	Nat'l Buffalo Ass'n
NBAA	Nat'l Business Aircraft Ass'n
NBBA	Nat'l Bed and Breakfast Ass'n
NBBC	Nat'l Block and Bridle Club
NBBLA	Nat'l Bath, Bed and Linen Ass'n
NBBPVI	Nat'l Board of Boiler and Pressure Vessel Inspectors
NBC	Nat'l Bowling Council
	Nat'l Broiler Council
NBCA	Nat'l Business Circulation Ass'n
NBCC	Nat'l Book Critics Circle
NBCFAE	Nat'l Black Coalition of Federal Aviation Employees
NBCIA	Nat'l Blue Crab Industry Ass'n
NBCL	Nat'l Beauty Culturists' League
NBCSL	Nat'l Black Caucus of State Legislators
NBDA	Nat'l Bicycle Dealers Ass'n
NBDEA	Nat'l Beverage Dispensing Equipment Ass'n
NBEA	Nat'l Ballroom and Entertainment Ass'n
	Nat'l Business Education Ass'n
NBFA	Nat'l Business Forms Ass'n
NBFAA	Nat'l Burglar and Fire Alarm Ass'n
NBFFO	Nat'l Board of Fur Farm Organizations
NBGQA	Nat'l Building Granite Quarries Ass'n
NBHPA	Nat'l Black Health Planners Ass'n
NBL	Nat'l Business League
NBMDA	Nat'l Building Material Distributors Ass'n
NBNA	Nat'l Black Nurses Ass'n
NBPA	Nat'l Bark Producers Ass'n
	Nat'l Basketball Players Ass'n
	Nat'l Black Police Ass'n
NBPC	Nat'l Border Patrol Council
NBPIW	Nat'l Brotherhood of Packinghouse and Industrial Workers
NBSA	Nat'l Bakery Suppliers Ass'n
NBVA	Nat'l Bulk Vendors Ass'n
NBWA	Nat'l Beer Wholesalers' Ass'n
	Nat'l Blacksmiths and Weldors Ass'n
NCA	Nat'l Camping Ass'n
	Nat'l Candle Ass'n
	Nat'l Caterers Ass'n
	Nat'l Cattlemen's Ass'n
	Nat'l Caves Ass'n
	Nat'l Club Ass'n
	Nat'l Coal Ass'n
	Nat'l Coffee Ass'n of the U.S.A.
	Nat'l Communications Ass'n
	Nat'l Composition Ass'n
	Nat'l Confectioners Ass'n of the United States
	Nat'l Constables Ass'n
	Nat'l Constructors Ass'n
	Nat'l Cosmetology Ass'n
	Nat'l Costumers Ass'n
	Nat'l Council on the Aging
NCAC	Nat'l Council of Acoustical Consultants
NCACC	Nat'l Conference of Appellate Court Clerks
NCACS	Nat'l Coalition of Alternative Community Schools
NCAE	Nat'l Council of Agricultural Employers
NCARB	Nat'l Council of Architectural Registration Boards
NCASC	Nat'l Council of Acupuncture Schools and Colleges
NCASI	Nat'l Council of the Paper Industry for Air and Stream Improvement
NCAWE	Nat'l Council of Administrative Women in Education
NCB	Nat'l Cargo Bureau
NCBA	Nat'l Candy Brokers Ass'n
	Nat'l Catholic Bandmasters' Ass'n
	Nat'l Cooperative Business Ass'n
NCBE	Nat'l Conference of Bar Examiners
NCBEA	Nat'l Catholic Business Education Ass'n
NCBF	Nat'l Conference of Bar Foundations
NCBFAA	Nat'l Customs Brokers and Forwarders Ass'n of America
NCBI	Nat'l Cotton Batting Institute
NCBJ	Nat'l Conference of Bankruptcy Judges
NCBL	Nat'l Conference of Black Lawyers
NCBM	Nat'l Conference of Black Mayors
NCBP	Nat'l Conference of Bar Presidents
NCBVA	Nat'l Concrete Burial Vault Ass'n
NCBWA	Nat'l Collegiate Baseball Writers Ass'n
NCC	Nat'l Coaches Council
	Nat'l Cotton Council of America
	Nat'l Council of the Churches of Christ in the U.S.A.
NCCA	Nat'l Chemical Credit Ass'n
	Nat'l Coil Coaters Ass'n
	Nat'l Council for Critical Analysis
NCCAE	Nat'l Council of County Ass'n Executives
NCCB	Nat'l Conference of Catholic Bishops
NCCC	Nat'l Catholic Cemetery Conference
NCCD	Nat'l Council on Crime and Delinquency
NCCEM	Nat'l Coordinating Council on Emergency Management
NCCH	Nat'l Council of Community Hospitals
NCCI	Nat'l Council on Compensation Insurance
NCCL	Nat'l Council of Coal Lessors
NCCLS	Nat'l Committee for Clinical Laboratory Standards
NCCMHC	Nat'l Council of Community Mental Health Centers
NCCMHS	Nat'l Consortium for Child Mental Health Services
NCCPB	Nat'l Council of Commercial Plant Breeders
NCCR	Nat'l Council for Community Relations
NCCUSL	Nat'l Conference of Commissioners on Uniform State Laws
NCCW	Nat'l Council of Career Women
	Nat'l Council of Catholic Women
NCDA	Nat'l Career Development Ass'n
NCDC	Nat'l Catholic Development Conference
NCEA	Nat'l Catholic Educational Ass'n
	Nat'l Community Education Ass'n
NCEC	Nat'l Construction Employers Council
	North Coast Export Company
NCECA	Nat'l Council on Education for the Ceramic Arts
NCECE	Nat'l Council of Elected County Executives
NCECF	Nat'l Children's Eye Care Foundation
NCEE	Nat'l Catholic Educational Exhibitors
	Nat'l Council of Engineering Examiners
NCEFR	Nat'l Council of Erectors, Fabricators and Riggers
NCEW	Nat'l Conference of Editorial Writers
NCFA	Nat'l Commercial Finance Ass'n
NCFAE	Nat'l Council of Forestry Ass'n Executives
NCFC	Nat'l Council of Farmer Cooperatives
NCFCA	Nat'l Congress of Floor Covering Ass'ns
NCFR	Nat'l Council on Family Relations
NCGA	Nat'l Church Goods Ass'n
	Nat'l Computer Graphics Ass'n
	Nat'l Corn Growers Ass'n
	Nat'l Cotton Ginners' Ass'n
NCGE	Nat'l Council for Geographic Education
NCGLC	Nat'l Caucus of Gay and Lesbian Counselors
NCH	Nat'l Center for Homoeopathy
NCHC	Nat'l Collegiate Honors Council
NCI	Nat'l Cheese Institute
NCIA	Nat'l Crop Insurance Ass'n
NCIC	Nat'l Construction Industry Council
NCICA	Nat'l Counter Intelligence Corps Ass'n
NCJA	Nat'l Criminal Justice Ass'n
NCJFCJ	Nat'l Council of Juvenile and Family Court Judges
NCL	Nat'l Consumers League
NCLAVEPA	Nat'l Council of Local Administrators of Vocational Education and Practical Arts
NCLEHA	Nat'l Conference of Local Environmental Health Administrators
NCLG	Nat'l Conference of Lieutenant Governors
NCLPWA	Nat'l Council of Local Public Welfare Administrators
NCLTA	Nat'l Cigar Leaf Tobacco Ass'n
NCMA	Nat'l Catalog Managers Ass'n
	Nat'l Concrete Masonry Ass'n
	Nat'l Contract Management Ass'n
NCMCG	Nat'l Construction Machinery Credit Group
NCME	Nat'l Council on Measurement in Education
NCMFST	Nat'l Committee for Motor Fleet Supervisor Training
NCMIE	Nat'l Council of Music Importers and Exporters
NCMS	Nat'l Classification Management Soc.
NCOA	Nat'l Campground Owners Ass'n
	Non-Commissioned Officers Ass'n of the U.S.A.
NCPA	Nat'l Cottonseed Products Ass'n
NCPAG	Nat'l CPA Group
NCPERS	Nat'l Conference on Public Employee Retirement Systems
NCPG	Nat'l Catholic Pharmacists Guild of the United States
NCPI	Nat'l Clay Pipe Institute
	Nat'l Crime Prevention Institute
NCPLA	Nat'l Council of Patent Law Ass'ns
NCPMA	Nat'l Clay Pot Manufacturers Ass'n
	Noise Control Products and Materials Ass'n
NCPP	Nat'l Council on Public Polls
NCPWB	Nat'l Certified Pipe Welding Bureau
NCRA	Nat'l Correctional Recreational Ass'n
NCRE	Nat'l Conference on Research in English
NCREIF	Nat'l Council of Real Estate Investment Fiduciaries
NCRPM	Nat'l Council on Radiation Protection and Measurements
NCRSA	Nat'l Commercial Refrigeration Sales Ass'n
NCRUCE	Nat'l Conference of Regulatory Utility Commission Engineers
NCS	Nat'l Cartoonists Soc.
NCSA	Nat'l Coffee Service Ass'n
	Nat'l Confectionery Salesmen's Ass'n of America
NCSBCS	Nat'l Conference of States on Building Codes and Standards
NCSBN	Nat'l Council of State Boards of Nursing
NCSEA	Nat'l Child Support Enforcement Ass'n
	Nat'l Council of State Education Ass'ns
NCSEMSTC	Nat'l Council of State Emergency Medical Services Training Coordinators
NCSG	Nat'l Chimney Sweep Guild
NCSGC	Nat'l Council of State Garden Clubs
NCSHPO	Nat'l Conference of State Historic Preservation Officers
NCSHSA	Nat'l Council of State Human Service Administrators
NCSI	Nat'l Contract Sweepers Institute
	Nat'l Council of Savings Institutions
	Nat'l Council of Self-Insurers
NCSL	Nat'l Conference of Standards Laboratories
	Nat'l Conference of State Legislatures
NCSLA	Nat'l Conference of State Liquor Administrators
NCSO	Nat'l Council of Salesmen's Organizations
NCSPA	Nat'l Corrugated Steel Pipe Ass'n
NCSPAE	Nat'l Council of State Pharmaceutical Ass'n Executives
NCSS	Nat'l Council for the Social Studies
NCSSFL	Nat'l Council of State Supervisors of Foreign Languages
NCSSMA	Nat'l Council of Social Security Management Ass'ns
NCSSSA	Nat'l Conference of State Social Security Administrators
NCSTD	Nat'l Council of State Travel Directors
NCTA	Nat'l Cable Television Ass'n
	Nat'l Christmas Tree Ass'n
NCTE	Nat'l Council for Textile Education
	Nat'l Council of Teachers of English
NCTM	Nat'l Council of Teachers of Mathematics
NCTR	Nat'l Council on Teacher Retirement
NCTRC	Council for Therapeutic Recreation Certification
NCUED	Nat'l Council for Urban Economic Development
NCUMA	Nat'l Credit Union Management Ass'n
NCURA	Nat'l Council of University Research Administrators
NCUSCT	Nat'l Council for U.S.-China Trade
NCWA	Nat'l Candy Wholesalers Ass'n
NCWM	Nat'l Conference on Weights and Measures
NCYP	Nat'l Conference of Yeshiva Principals
NDA	Nat'l Dance Ass'n
	Nat'l Dental Ass'n
NDAA	Nat'l District Attorneys Ass'n
NDBC	Nat'l Dry Bean Council
NDC	Nat'l Dairy Council
	Nat'l Duckling Council
NDCA	Nat'l Drilling Contractors Ass'n
NDF	Nat'l Drilling Federation
NDGAA	Nat'l Dog Groomers Ass'n of America
NDLOA	Nat'l Disabled Law Officers Ass'n
NDMA	Nat'l Dimension Manufacturers Ass'n
NDPA	Nat'l Decorating Products Ass'n
NDTA	Nat'l Defense Transportation Ass'n
	Nat'l Dental Technicians Ass'n
NDTC	Nat'l Drug Trade Conference
NEA	Nat'l Economic Ass'n
	Nat'l Education Ass'n of the U.S.
	Nat'l Erectors Ass'n
NEBB	Nat'l Environmental Balancing Bureau
NEBI	Nat'l Employee Benefits Institute
NEC	Nat'l Engineering Consortium
NECA	Nat'l Electrical Contractors Ass'n
	Nat'l Employment Counselors Ass'n
NEDA	Nat'l Electronic Distributors Ass'n
	Nat'l Environmental Development Ass'n
	Nat'l Equipment Distributors Ass'n
	Nat'l Exhaust Distributors Ass'n
NEHA	Nat'l Environmental Health Ass'n
	Nat'l Executive Housekeepers Ass'n
NEI	Nat'l Elevator Industry
NELMA	Northeastern Lumber Manufacturers Ass'n
NEMA	Nat'l Electrical Manufacturers Ass'n
	Nat'l Emergency Management Ass'n
NEMRA	Nat'l Electrical Manufacturers Representatives Ass'n
NEPMA	Nat'l Engine Parts Manufacturers Ass'n
NERC	North American Electric Reliability Council
NERF	Nat'l Eye Research Foundation
NES	Nat'l Estimating Soc.
NESA	Nat'l Electric Sign Ass'n
	Nat'l Energy Specialist Ass'n
NESDA	Nat'l Equipment-Servicing Dealers Ass'n
NESRA	Nat'l Employee Services and Recreation Ass'n
NESSDA	Nat'l Electronic Sales and Service Dealers Ass'n
NETA	Internat'l Electrical Testing Ass'n
	Nat'l Employment and Training Ass'n

ACRONYM INDEX

	Nat'l Environmental Training Ass'n
NETL	Nat'l Export Traffic League
NEXCO	Nat'l Ass'n of Export Companies
NFA	Nat'l Forensic Ass'n
	Nat'l Futures Ass'n
NFAIS	Nat'l Federation of Abstracting and Information Services
NFANA	Norwegian Fjord Ass'n of North America
NFBA	Nat'l Food Brokers Ass'n
	Nat'l Frame Builders Ass'n
NFBC	Nat'l Family Business Council
NFBPWC	Nat'l Federation of Business and Professional Womens Clubs
NFC	Nat'l Fenestration Council
	Nat'l Film Carriers
	Newspaper Features Council
NFCA	Nat'l Fencing Coaches Ass'n of America
	Nat'l Fraternal Congress of America
NFCB	Nat'l Federation of Community Broadcasters
NFCC	Nat'l Foundation for Consumer Credit
NFCCE	Nat'l Fellowship of Child Care Executives
NFCPG	Nat'l Federation of Catholic Physicians' Guilds
NFCSC	Nat'l Freight Claim and Security Council of the American Trucking Ass'ns
NFDA	Nat'l Fastener Distributors Ass'n
	Nat'l Food Distributors Ass'n
	Nat'l Funeral Directors Ass'n
NFDMA	Nat'l Funeral Directors and Morticians Ass'n
NFE	Northwest Fruit Exporters
NFEA	Newspaper Farm Editors of America
NFEC	Nat'l Food and Energy Council
NFF	Nat'l Federation of Fishermen
NFFA	Nat'l Frozen Food Ass'n
NFFE	Nat'l Federation of Federal Employees
NFFS	Non-Ferrous Founders' Soc.
NFGMIC	Nat'l Federation of Grange Mutual Insurance Companies
NFI	Nat'l Fisheries Institute
NFIA	Nat'l Feed Ingredients Ass'n
NFIB	Nat'l Federation of Independent Business
NFIU	Nat'l Federation of Independent Unions
NFL	Nat'l Football League
NFLCP	Nat'l Federation of Local Cable Programmers
NFLPA	Nat'l Football League Players Ass'n
NFLPN	Nat'l Federation of Licensed Practical Nurses
NFMC	Nat'l Federation of Music Clubs
NFMLTA	Nat'l Federation of Modern Language Teachers Ass'ns
NFMOA	Nat'l Fish Meal and Oil Ass'n
NFO	Nat'l Farmers Organization
NFPA	Nat'l Federation of Paralegal Ass'ns
	Nat'l Fire Protection Ass'n
	Nat'l Fluid Power Ass'n
	Nat'l Food Processors Ass'n
	Nat'l Forest Products Ass'n
NFPC	Nat'l Federation of Priests' Councils
NFPEDA	Nat'l Farm and Power Equipment Dealers Ass'n
NFPI	Nat'l Frozen Pizza Institute
NFPO	Nat'l Federation of Professional Organizations
NFPRHA	Nat'l Family Planning and Reproductive Health Ass'n
NFPW	Nat'l Federation of Press Women
NFRA	Nat'l Forest Recreation Ass'n
NFSA	Nat'l Fertilizer Solutions Ass'n
	Nat'l Fire Sprinkler Ass'n
NFSHSA	Nat'l Federation of State High School Ass'ns
NFSM	Nat'l Fraternity of Student Musicians
NFTA	Nat'l Freight Transportation Ass'n
	Nitrogen Tree Fixing Ass'n
NFTC	Nat'l Foreign Trade Council
	Nat'l Furniture Traffic Conference
NGA	Nat'l Glass Ass'n
	Nat'l Governors' Ass'n
	Nat'l Grocers Ass'n
	Nat'l Guard Ass'n of the U.S.
NGADA	Nat'l Graphic Arts Dealers Ass'n
NGB	Nat'l Garden Bureau
NGC	Nat'l Goose Council
NGCP	Nat'l Guild of Catholic Psychiatrists
NGCSA	Nat'l Guild of Community Schools of the Arts
NGF	Nat'l Golf Foundation
NGFA	Nat'l Grain and Feed Ass'n
NGJA	Nat'l Gymnastic Judges Ass'n
NGMA	Nat'l Gas Measurement Ass'n
	Nat'l Greenhouse Manufacturers Ass'n
NGPP	Nat'l Guild of Professional Paperhangers
NGPT	Nat'l Guild of Piano Teachers
NGS	Nat'l Genealogical Soc.
	Nat'l Geriatrics Soc.
NGSA	Natural Gas Supply Ass'n
NGSPA	Nat'l Grain Sorghum Producers Ass'n
NGTC	Nat'l Grain Trade Council
NHA	Nat'l Hay Ass'n
	Nat'l Humanities Alliance
	Nat'l Hydropower Ass'n
NHA/NFAA	Nat'l Handbag Ass'n/Nat'l Fashion Accessories Ass'n
NHACE	Nat'l Hispanic Ass'n of Construction Enterprises
NHAS	Nat'l Hearing Aid Soc.
NHAWA	Northamerican Heating and Airconditioning Wholesalers Ass'n
NHC	Nat'l Health Council
	Nat'l HomeCaring Council
	Nat'l Housing Conference
NHCA	Nat'l Hearing Conservation Ass'n
NHENMA	Nat'l Hand Embroidery and Novelty Manufacturers Ass'n
NHF	Nat'l Hemophilia Foundation
NHFA	Nat'l Home Furnishings Ass'n
NHFL	Nat'l Home Fashions League
NHHRA	Nat'l Hereford Hog Record Ass'n
NHL	Nat'l Hockey League
NHLA	Nat'l Hardwood Lumber Ass'n
	Nat'l Health Lawyers Ass'n
NHLPA	Nat'l Hockey League Player's Ass'n
NHMA	Nat'l Housewares Manufacturers Ass'n
NHO	Nat'l Hospice Organization
NHPA	Nat'l Hispanic Psychological Ass'n
NHPDA	Nat'l Honey Packers and Dealers Ass'n
NHSACA	Nat'l High School Athletic Coaches Ass'n
NHSC	Nat'l Home Study Council
NHWU	Non-Heatset Web Unit
NIA	Nat'l Inholders Ass'n
	Nat'l Insurance Ass'n
NIADA	Nat'l Independent Automobile Dealers Ass'n
	Nat'l Institute of American Doll Artists
NIAE	Nat'l Institute for Architectural Education
NIB	Nat'l Industries for the Blind
NIBA	Nat'l Industrial Belting Ass'n
NIBESA	Nat'l Independent Bank Equipment and Systems Ass'n
NIBS	Nat'l Institute of Building Sciences
NIC	Nat'l Industrial Council - Industrial Relations Group
	Nat'l Interfraternity Conference
NICA	Nat'l Insulation Contractors Ass'n
NICE	Nat'l Institute of Ceramic Engineers
NICMA	Nat'l Ice Cream Mix Ass'n
NICMC	Nat'l Institute of Certified Moving Consultants
NICOA	Nat'l Independent Coal Operators Ass'n
NICRA	Nat'l Ice Cream Retailers Ass'n
NICSBC	Nat'l Interstate Council of State Boards of Cosmetology
NIDA	Nat'l Independent Dairy-Foods Ass'n
	Nat'l Industrial Distributors Ass'n
NIEA	Nat'l Indian Education Ass'n
NIGDA	Nat'l Industrial Glove Distributors Ass'n
NIGP	Nat'l Institute of Governmental Purchasing
NIMC	Nat'l Institute of Management Counsellors
NIMLO	Nat'l Institute of Municipal Law Officers
NIOP	Nat'l Institute of Oilseed Products
NIPA	Nat'l Institute of Pension Administrators
NIPFDA	Nat'l Independent Poultry and Food Distributors Ass'n
NIPGM	Nat'l Institute on Park and Grounds Management
NIPHLE	Nat'l Institute of Packaging, Handling and Logistic Engineers
NIRI	Nat'l Investor Relations Institute
NIRMA	Nuclear Information and Records Management Ass'n
NISA	Nat'l Industrial Sand Ass'n
NISC	Nat'l Institute of Senior Centers
NISD	Nat'l Institute of Steel Detailing
NISOA	Nat'l Intercollegiate Soccer Officials Ass'n
NITA	Nat'l Intravenous Therapy Ass'n
NITL	Nat'l Industrial Transportation League
NITMDA	Nat'l Indoor Track Meet Directors Ass'n
NIWU	Nat'l Industrial Workers Union
NIZC	Nat'l Industrial Zoning Committee
NJDA	Nat'l Juvenile Detention Ass'n
NJPA	Nat'l Juice Products Ass'n
NKBA	Nat'l Kitchen and Bath Ass'n
NKCA	Nat'l Kitchen Cabinet Ass'n
NKF	Nat'l Kidney Foundation
NKHA	Nat'l Kerosene Heater Ass'n
NKMA	Nat'l Knitwear Manufacturers Ass'n
NKSA	Nat'l Knitwear and Sportswear Ass'n
NL	Nat'l League of Professional Baseball Clubs
NLA	Nat'l Landscape Ass'n
	Nat'l Librarians Ass'n
	Nat'l Lime Ass'n
NLADA	Nat'l Legal Aid and Defender Ass'n
NLAPW	Nat'l League of American Pen Women
NLBA	Nat'l Lead Burning Ass'n
	Nat'l Licensed Beverage Ass'n
NLBMDA	Nat'l Lumber and Building Material Dealers Ass'n
NLC	Nat'l League of Cities
NLDA	Nat'l Luggage Dealers Ass'n
NLE	Nat'l Livestock Exchange
NLEA	Nat'l Lumber Exporters Ass'n
NLFA	Nat'l Lamb Feeders Ass'n
NLG	Nat'l Lawyers Guild
NLGDA	Nat'l Lawn and Garden Distributors Ass'n
NLGI	Nat'l Lubricating Grease Institute
NLHA	Nat'l Leased Housing Ass'n
NLMFA	No-Load Mutual Fund Ass'n
NLN	Nat'l League for Nursing
NLPGA	Nat'l LP-Gas Ass'n
NLPM	Nat'l League of Postmasters of the U.S.
NLRBPA	Nat'l Labor Relations Board Professional Ass'n
NLRBU	Nat'l Labor Relations Board Union
NLSA	Nat'l Liquor Stores Ass'n
	Nat'l Locksmith Suppliers Ass'n
NLSBA	Nat'l Lincoln Sheep Breeders Ass'n
NLSPA	Nat'l Live Stock Producers Ass'n
NMA	Nat'l Management Ass'n
	Nat'l Medical Ass'n
NMBA	Nat'l Marine Bankers Ass'n
NMC	Nat'l Mastitis Council
	Nat'l Music Council
	Nursery Marketing Council
NMCA	Nat'l Meat Canners Ass'n
NMDA	Nat'l Marine Distributors Ass'n
	Nat'l Metal Decorators Ass'n
NMEA	Nat'l Marine Education Ass'n
NMEBA	Nat'l Marine Engineers' Beneficial Ass'n
NMF	Nonprofit Mailers Federation
NMFTA	Nat'l Motor Freight Traffic Ass'n
NMHA	Nat'l Mental Health Ass'n
NMHC	Nat'l Multi Housing Council
NMHF	Nat'l Manufactured Housing Federation
NMHFA	Nat'l Manufactured Housing Finance Ass'n
NMIA	Nat'l Military Intelligence Ass'n
NMMA	Nat'l Marine Manufacturers Ass'n
NMMC	Nat'l Marina Manufacturers Consortium
NMOA	Nat'l Mail Order Ass'n
NMPA	Nat'l Motorsports Press Ass'n
	Nat'l Music Publishers' Ass'n
NMPF	Nat'l Milk Producers Federation
NMRA	Nat'l Marine Representatives Ass'n
	Nat'l Motorcycle Retailers Ass'n
NMRI	Nat'l Mass Retailing Institute
NMSA	Nat'l Middle School Ass'n
	Nat'l Moving and Storage Ass'n
NMSDC	Nat'l Minority Supplier Development Council
NMSS	Nat'l Multiple Sclerosis Soc.
NMTBA	Nat'l Machine Tool Builders' Ass'n
NMU	Nat'l Maritime Union of America
NNA	Nat'l Neckwear Ass'n
	Nat'l Needlework Ass'n
	Nat'l Newspaper Ass'n
	Nat'l Notary Ass'n
NNFA	Nat'l Nutritional Foods Ass'n
NNGA	Northern Nut Growers Ass'n
NNPA	Nat'l Newspaper Publishers Ass'n
NNSA	Nat'l Nurses Soc. on Addictions
NOA	Nat'l Onion Ass'n
	Nat'l Opera Ass'n
	Nat'l Optometric Ass'n
NOBC	Nat'l Organization of Bar Counsel
NOEL	Nat'l Ornament and Electric Lights Christmas Ass'n
NOFMA	Nat'l Oak Flooring Manufacturers Ass'n
NOFS	Nat'l Options and Futures Soc.
NOIA	Nat'l Ocean Industries Ass'n
NOITU	Nat'l Organization of Industrial Trade Unions
NOLPE	Nat'l Organization on Legal Problems of Education
NOMDA	Nat'l Office Machine Dealers Ass'n
NOMMA	Nat'l Ornamental and Miscellaneous Metals Ass'n
NOPA	Nat'l Office Products Ass'n
NOSSCR	Nat'l Organization of Social Security Claimants' Representatives
NOVA	Nurses Organization of the Veterans Administration
NOWL	Nat'l Order of Women Legislators
NP&PA	Nat'l Paperbox and Packaging Ass'n
NPA	Nat'l Paralegal Ass'n
	Nat'l Parking Ass'n
	Nat'l Particleboard Ass'n
	Nat'l Pasta Ass'n
	Nat'l Perinatal Ass'n
	Nat'l Phlebotomy Ass'n
	Nat'l Planning Ass'n
	Nat'l Plastercraft Ass'n
NPAP	Nat'l Psychological Ass'n for Psychoanalysis
NPB	Nat'l Plant Board
NPBA	Natural Product Broker Ass'n
NPBI	Nat'l Pretzel Bakers Institute
NPC	Nat'l Panhellenic Conference
	Nat'l Peach Council
	Nat'l Peanut Council
	Nat'l Petroleum Council
	Nat'l Pharmaceutical Council
	Nat'l Potato Council
NPCA	Nat'l Paint and Coatings Ass'n
	Nat'l Parks and Conservation Ass'n
	Nat'l Pest Control Ass'n
	Nat'l Precast Concrete Ass'n
NPD	Nat'l Paint Distributors
NPDBA	Nat'l Pet Dealers and Breeders Ass'n
NPES	Nat'l Printing Equipment and Supply Ass'n
NPGPA	Non-Powder Gun Products Ass'n
NPHC	Nat'l Pan Hellenic Council
NPI	Nat'l Purchasing Institute
NPLC	Nat'l Pedigreed Livestock Council
NPM	Nat'l Ass'n of Pastoral Musicians
NPMA	Newspaper Purchasing Management Ass'n
NPMC	Nat'l Pecan Marketing Council
NPOA	Nat'l Police Officers Ass'n of America
NPPA	Nat'l Press Photographers Ass'n
NPPB	Nat'l Potato Promotion Board
NPPC	Nat'l Pork Producers Council
NPRA	Nat'l Petroleum Refiners Ass'n
	Newspaper Personnel Relations Ass'n
NPSA	Nat'l Pecan Shellers Ass'n
	Nat'l Pegboard Systems Ass'n
NPSE	Nat'l Premium Sales Executives
NPTA	Nat'l Paper Trade Ass'n
	Nat'l Passenger Traffic Ass'n
	Nat'l Perishable Transportation Ass'n
NPhA	Nat'l Pharmaceutical Ass'n
NQPC	Nat'l Quartz Producers Council
NR/WA	Nat'l Rep/Wholesaler Ass'n
NRA	Nat'l Reciprocal Ass'n
	Nat'l Rehabilitation Ass'n
	Nat'l Renderers Ass'n
	Nat'l Restaurant Ass'n

ACRONYM INDEX

	Nat'l Rifle Ass'n of America
NRAA	Nat'l Renal Administrators Ass'n
NRB	Nat'l Religious Broadcasters
NRC	Nat'l Railroad Construction and Maintenance Ass'n
	Nat'l Reading Conference
	Nat'l Realty Committee
NRCA	Nat'l Rehabilitation Counseling Ass'n
	Nat'l Roofing Contractors Ass'n
NRCI	Nat'l Red Cherry Institute
NRDCA	Nat'l Roof Deck Contractors Ass'n
NRECA	Nat'l Rural Electric Cooperative Ass'n
NRGA	Nat'l Rice Growers Ass'n
NRHA	Nat'l Retail Hardware Ass'n
NRHCA	Nat'l Rural Health Care Ass'n
NRIA	Nat'l Railroad Intermodal Ass'n
NRLA	Northeastern Retail Lumberman's Ass'n
NRLCA	Nat'l Rural Letter Carriers' Ass'n
NRMA	Nat'l Reloading Manufacturers Ass'n
	Nat'l Retail Merchants Ass'n
NRMCA	Nat'l Ready Mixed Concrete Ass'n
NRPA	Nat'l Recreation and Park Ass'n
NRPSGA	Nat'l Retail Pet Store and Groomers Ass'n
NRRA	Nat'l Resource Recovery Ass'n
NRSA	Natural Rubber Shippers Ass'n
NS	Neuroelectric Soc.
NSA	Nat'l Shellfisheries Ass'n
	Nat'l Sheriffs' Ass'n
	Nat'l Showmen's Ass'n
	Nat'l Slag Ass'n
	Nat'l Speakers Ass'n
	Nat'l Stone Ass'n
	Nat'l Sunflower Ass'n
	Neurosurgical Soc. of America
NSAA	Nat'l Ski Areas Ass'n
NSAC	Nat'l Soc. of Accountants for Cooperatives
NSAE	Nat'l Soc. of Architectural Engineering
NSBA	Nat'l School Boards Ass'n
	Nat'l Small Business Ass'n
	Nat'l Sugar Brokers Ass'n
NSBGCA	Nat'l Small Business Government Contractors Ass'n
NSC	Nat'l Safety Council
NSCA	Nat'l Satellite Cable Ass'n
	Nat'l Ski Credit Ass'n
	Nat'l Sound and Communications Ass'n
	Nat'l Steel Carriers Ass'n
	Nat'l Strength and Conditioning Ass'n
NSCAA	Nat'l Soccer Coaches Ass'n of America
NSCPT	Nat'l Soc. for Cardiovascular and Pulmonary Technology
NSDA	Nat'l Soft Drink Ass'n
	Nat'l Supply Distributors Ass'n
NSDJA	Nat'l Sash and Door Jobbers Ass'n
NSEMA	Nat'l Spray Equipment Manufacturers Ass'n
NSFRE	Nat'l Soc. of Fund Raising Executives
NSG	Newspaper Systems Group
NSGA	Nat'l Sand and Gravel Ass'n
	Nat'l Sporting Goods Ass'n
NSGC	Nat'l Soc. of Genetic Counselors
NSH	Nat'l Soc. for Histotechnology
NSHDS	Nat'l Soc. for Hebrew Day Schools
NSIA	Nat'l Security Industrial Ass'n
NSIF	Nat'l Swine Improvement Federation
NSIPA	Nat'l Soc. of Insurance Premium Auditors
NSLA	Nat'l Staff Leasing Ass'n
NSM	Nat'l Selected Morticians
NSMA	Nat'l Seasoning Manufacturers Ass'n
	Nat'l Second Mortgage Ass'n
NSMP	Nat'l Soc. of Mural Painters
NSMPA	Nat'l Screw Machine Products Ass'n
NSMS	Nat'l Safety Management Soc.
NSOA	Nat'l School Orchestra Ass'n
NSP	Nat'l Ski Patrol System
NSPA	Nat'l Shrimp Processors Ass'n
	Nat'l Soc. of Public Accountants
	Nat'l Soybean Processors Ass'n
	Nat'l State Printing Ass'n
NSPB	Nat'l Soc. to Prevent Blindness
NSPCA	Nat'l Soc. of Painters in Casein and Acrylic
NSPE	Nat'l Soc. of Professional Engineers
NSPI	Nat'l Soc. for Performance and Instruction
	Nat'l Spa and Pool Institute
NSPR	Nat'l Soc. of Patient Representatives
NSPRA	Nat'l School Public Relations Ass'n
NSPRM	Nat'l Soc. of Professional Resident Managers
NSPS	Nat'l Soc. of Professional Sanitarians
NSRA	Nat'l Service Robot Ass'n
	Nat'l Shoe Retailers Ass'n
	Nat'l Shorthand Reporters Ass'n
NSREF	Nat'l Soc. for Real Estate Finance
NSRMCA	Nat'l Star Route Mail Contractors Ass'n
NSS	Nat'l Sculpture Soc.
	Nat'l Speleological Soc.
NSSA	Nat'l Science Supervisors Ass'n
	Nat'l Sportscasters and Sportswriters Ass'n
	Nat'l Student Nurses Ass'n
	Nat'l Suffolk Sheep Ass'n
NSSE	Nat'l Soc. for the Study of Education
NSSEA	Nat'l School Supply and Equipment Ass'n
NSSF	Nat'l Shooting Sports Foundation
NSSFA	Nat'l Single Service Food Ass'n
NSSHA	Nat'l Spotted Saddle Horse Ass'n
NSSLHA	Nat'l Student Speech Language Hearing Ass'n
NSSR	Nat'l Spotted Swine Record
NSSTE	Nat'l Soc. of Sales Training Executives
NSTA	Nat'l Safe Transit Ass'n
	Nat'l School Transportation Ass'n
	Nat'l Science Teachers Ass'n
	Nat'l Security Traders Ass'n
	Nat'l Shoe Travelers Ass'n
NSVEA	Natural-Source Vitamin E Ass'n
NSWA	Nat'l Stripper Well Ass'n
NSWMA	Nat'l Solid Wastes Management Ass'n
NTA	Nat'l Taxidermists Ass'n
	Nat'l Tour Ass'n
	Nat'l Translator Ass'n
	Nat'l Trappers Ass'n
	Northern Textile Ass'n
NTA/TIA	Nat'l Tax Ass'n-Tax Institute of America
NTCA	Nat'l Telephone Cooperative Ass'n
NTDRA	Nat'l Tire Dealers and Retreaders Ass'n
NTEA	Nat'l Truck Equipment Ass'n
NTEU	Nat'l Treasury Employees Union
NTF	Nat'l Turkey Federation
NTLS	Nat'l Truck Leasing System
NTMA	Nat'l Terrazzo and Mosaic Ass'n
	Nat'l Tooling and Machining Ass'n
NTPG	Nat'l Textile Processors Guild
NTRA	Nat'l Tumor Registrar's Ass'n
NTRMA	Nat'l Tile Roofing Manufacturers Ass'n
NTRS	Nat'l Therapeutic Recreation Soc.
NTSA	Nat'l Technical Services Ass'n
NTSAD	Nat'l Tay-Sachs and Allied Diseases Ass'n
NTTC	Nat'l Tank Truck Carriers
NTWA	Nat'l Turf Writers Ass'n
NUA	Network Users Ass'n
NUCA	Nat'l Utility Contractors Ass'n
NUCEA	Nat'l University Continuing Education Ass'n
NUFI	Nat'l Unfinished Furniture Institute
NULBA	Nat'l United Licensees Beverage Ass'n
NVATA	Nat'l Vocational Agricultural Teachers Ass'n
NVCA	Nat'l Venture Capital Ass'n
NVLA	Nat'l Vehicle Leasing Ass'n
NWA	Nat'l Weather Ass'n
	Nat'l Wellness Ass'n
	Nat'l Wine Ass'n
NWAABI	Nat'l Women's Ass'n of Allied Beverage Industries
NWC	Nat'l Waterfowl Council
	Nat'l Waterways Conference
	Nat'l Writers Club
NWCA	Nat'l Wrestling Coaches Ass'n
NWDA	Nat'l Wholesale Druggists' Ass'n
	Nat'l Wine Distributors Ass'n
NWDS	Noah Worcester Dermatological Soc.
NWEA	Nat'l Wood Energy Ass'n
NWFA	Nat'l Wholesale Furniture Ass'n
	Nat'l Wood Flooring Ass'n
NWGA	Nat'l Wool Growers Ass'n
NWHA	Nat'l Wholesale Hardware Ass'n
NWLDYA	Nat'l Wholesale Lumber Distributing Yard Ass'n
NWMC	Nat'l Wool Marketing Corporation
NWNSA	Nat'l Women's Neckwear and Scarf Ass'n
NWOA	Nat'l Woodland Owners Ass'n
NWPCA	Nat'l Wooden Pallet and Container Ass'n
NWRA	Nat'l Water Resources Ass'n
	Nat'l Waterbed Retailers Ass'n
	Nat'l Wheel and Rim Ass'n
NWS	Nat'l Watercolor Soc.
NWSA	Nat'l Welding Supply Ass'n
NWSEO	Nat'l Weather Service Employees Organization
NWSS	Northeastern Weed Science Soc.
NWU	Nat'l Writers Union
NWWA	Nat'l Water Well Ass'n
NWWDA	Nat'l Wood Window and Door Ass'n
NYAS	New York Academy of Sciences
NYCE	New York Cotton Exchange
NYME	New York Mercantile Exchange
NYPAA	Nat'l Yellow Pages Agency Ass'n
NYSE	New York Stock Exchange
NYSSDA	New York State Safe Deposit Ass'n
OA	Osborne Ass'n
OAA	Opticians Ass'n of America
OAAA	Outdoor Advertising Ass'n of America
OABA	Outdoor Amusement Business Ass'n
OAC	Overseas Automotive Club
OAH	Organization of American Historians
OASI	Office Automation Soc. Internat'l
OBAP	Organization of Black Airline Pilots
OBFS	Organization of Biological Field Stations
OCAW	Oil, Chemical and Atomic Workers Internat'l Union
OCOO	Osteopathic College of Ophthalmology and Otorhinolaryngology
OD	Organization Development Institute
ODS	Orton Dyslexia Soc.
OEA	Office Education Ass'n
	Onion Export Associates of New York
	Outdoor Education Ass'n
	Overseas Education Ass'n
OFA	Organized Flying Adjusters
	Oxygenated Fuels Ass'n
OFHA	Oil Field Haulers Ass'n
OII	Oil Investment Institute
OKU	Omicron Kappa Upsilon
OLA	Optical Laboratories Ass'n
OMA	Optical Manufacturers Ass'n
OMAA	Occupational Medical Administrators' Ass'n
OMR	Organization of Manufacturers Representatives
OMSA	Offshore Marine Service Ass'n
ONS	Oncology Nursing Soc.
OOIDA	Owner-Operator Independent Drivers Ass'n of America
OPASTC	Organization for the Protection and Advancement of Small Telephone Companies
OPCA	Overseas Press Club of America
OPCMIA	Operative Plasterers' and Cement Masons' Internat'l Ass'n of the United States and Canada
OPEAA	Outdoor Power Equipment Aftermarket Ass'n
OPEDA	Organization of Professional Employees of the U.S. Department of Agriculture
	Outdoor Power Equipment Distributors Ass'n
OPEI	Outdoor Power Equipment Institute
OPEIU	Office and Professional Employees Internat'l Union
OPMA	Open Pit Mining Ass'n
ORIA	Oriental Rug Importers Ass'n of America
ORRA	Oriental Rug Retailers of America
ORS	Orthopaedic Research Soc.
ORSA	Operations Research Soc. of America
OS	Oceanic Soc.
OSA	Optical Soc. of America
OSG	Otosclerosis Study Group
OSMA	Orthopedic Surgical Manufacturers Ass'n
OSRA	Office Systems Research Ass'n
OTMA	Office Technology Management Ass'n
OTOD	Organization of Teachers of Oral Diagnosis
OTS	Omega Tau Sigma
	Organization for Tropical Studies
OTSA	Orthodox Theological Soc. in America
OVA	Offshore Valve Ass'n
OWAA	Outdoor Writers Ass'n of America
PA	Parapsychological Ass'n
	Proprietary Ass'n, The
PA-VRA	Professional Audio-Video Retailers Ass'n
PAA	Population Ass'n of America
	Potato Ass'n of America
	Professional Archers Ass'n
PABS	Pan-American Biodeterioration Soc.
PAC	Pharmaceutical Advertising Council
	Public Affairs Council
PACE	Pacific Agricultural Cooperative for Export
PAD	Phi Alpha Delta
	Pitless Adapter Division (Water Systems Council)
PADI	Professional Ass'n of Diving Instructors
PAI	Processed Apples Institute
PAMA	Professional Aviation Maintenance Ass'n
PARMA	Public Agency Risk Managers Ass'n
PAS	Nat'l Postsecondary Agriculture Student Organization
	Percussive Arts Soc.
PASS	Professional Airways Systems Specialists
PATA	Professional Aeromedical Transport Ass'n
PATMI	Powder Actuated Tool Manufacturers Institute
PBA	Pi Beta Alpha
	Plastic Bag Ass'n
	Printing Brokerage Ass'n
	Professional Bowlers Ass'n of America
PBC	Personnel/Burden Carrier Manufacturers Ass'n
PBEA	Paint, Body and Equipment Ass'n
PBI	Paper Bag Institute
PBNPA	Peanut Butter and Nut Processors Ass'n
PBP-TKP	Phi Beta Pi - Theta Kappa Psi
PBWAA	Professional Basketball Writers' Ass'n of America
PC/SNA	Potato Chip/Snack Food Ass'n
PCA	Popular Culture Ass'n
	Portland Cement Ass'n
	Print Council of America
	Professional Comedians Ass'n
	Pulp Chemicals Ass'n
PCC	Private Carrier Conference
PCCA	Power and Communication Contractors Ass'n
PCFS	Pin, Clip and Fastener Services
PCI	Powder Coating Institute
	Prestressed Concrete Institute
PCMA	Post Card Manufacturers Ass'n
	Professional Convention Management Ass'n
PCMI	Photo Chemical Machining Institute
PCPA	Protestant Church-Owned Publishers Ass'n
PCPCI	Power Conversion Products Council, Internat'l
PCRA	Poland China Record Ass'n
PCRS	Precision Chiropractic Research Soc.
PCUS	Propeller Club of the U.S.
PCWCA	Poured Concrete Wall Contractors Ass'n of America
PD-SPI	Polyurethane Division-Soc. of the Plastics Industry
PDA	Parenteral Drug Ass'n
	Private Doctors of America
PDC	Package Designers Council
	Paper Distribution Council
PDCA	Painting and Decorating Contractors of America
	Purebred Dairy Cattle Ass'n
PDI	Plumbing and Drainage Institute
PDMA	Product Development and Management Ass'n
PDRMA	Portable Drilling Rig Manufacturers Ass'n
PDTA	Professional Dance Teachers Ass'n
PEI	Petroleum Equipment Institute
	Porcelain Enamel Institute
PEMA	Process Equipment Manufacturers' Ass'n
PEPP	Professional Engineers in Private Practice
PER	Public Employees Roundtable
PERA	Production Engine Remanufacturers Ass'n
PERF	Police Executive Research Forum
PES	Philosophy of Education Soc.
PESA	Petroleum Equipment Suppliers Ass'n
PF	Physicians Forum

ACRONYM INDEX

	Planning Forum: The Internat'l Society for Planning andStrategic Management
PFA	Prescription Footwear Ass'n
	Professional Fraternity Ass'n
PFDI	Preferred Funeral Directors Internat'l
PFHA	Paso Fino Horse Ass'n
PFI	Pet Food Institute
	Pipe Fabrication Institute
PFT	Professional Football Trainers
PFWA	Professional Football Writers of America
PGA	Producer's Guild of America
	Professional Golfers Ass'n of America
PGCOA	Pennsylvania Grade Crude Oil Ass'n
PGCRA	Professional Golf Club Repairmen's Ass'n
PGMS	Professional Grounds Management Soc.
PGRSA	Plant Growth Regulator Soc. of America
PHA	Palomino Horse Ass'n
	Percheron Horse Ass'n of America
	Preferred Hotels Ass'n
PHADA	Public Housing Authorities Directors Ass'n
PHBA	Palomino Horse Breeders of America
PHCIB	Plumbing-Heating-Cooling Information Bureau
PHOSCHEM	Phosphate Chemicals Export Ass'n
PI	Perlite Institute
	Popcorn Institute
PI/Int'l	Packaging Institute Internat'l
PIA	Nat'l Ass'n of Professional Insurance Agents
	Packaged Ice Ass'n
	Pilots Internat'l Ass'n
	Printing Industries of America
PIAA	Pre-Arrangement Interment Ass'n of America
PIC	Photographic Industry Council
PICA	Professional Insurance Communicators of America
	Public Interest Computer Ass'n
PIDA	Pet Industry Distributors Ass'n
PIJAC	Pet Industry Joint Advisory Council
PILA	Power Industry Laboratory Ass'n
PIMA	Paper Industry Management Ass'n
	Professional Insurance Mass-Marketing Ass'n
PISC	Petroleum Industry Security Council
PLA	Public Library Ass'n
	Pulverized Limestone Ass'n
PLCA	Pipe Line Contractors Ass'n
PLCAA	Professional Lawn Care Ass'n of America
PLIA	Pollution Liability Insurance Ass'n
PLMA	Private Label Manufacturers Ass'n
PLRB	Property Loss Research Bureau
PLT	Pi Lambda Theta
PMA	Pencil Makers Ass'n
	Pharmaceutical Manufacturers Ass'n
	Photo Marketing Ass'n-Internat'l
	Police Management Ass'n
	Polyurethane Manufacturers Ass'n
	Precision Measurements Ass'n
	Produce Marketing Ass'n
	Professional Managers Ass'n
	Professional Mariners Alliance
	Property Management Ass'n of America
PMAA	Petroleum Marketers Ass'n of America
	Promotion Marketing Ass'n of America
PMDA	Photographic Manufacturers and Distributors Ass'n
PMEF	Petroleum Marketing Education Foundation
PMI	Plumbing Manufacturers Institute
	Project Management Institute
PMIA	Piano Manufacturers Ass'n Internat'l
PML	Pattern Makers' League of North America
PMLA	Production Music Library Ass'n
PMMI	Packaging Machinery Manufacturers Institute
PMPMA	Plastic and Metal Products Manufacturers Ass'n
PNG	Professional Numismatists Guild
POCA	Public Offender Counselors Ass'n
POPA	Patent Office Professional Ass'n
POPAI	Point-of-Purchase Advertising Institute
PPA	Pathology Practice Ass'n
	Perennial Plant Ass'n
	Pesticide Producers Ass'n
	Professional Photographers of America
	Professional Putters Ass'n
	Publishers' Publicity Ass'n
PPAA	Personal Protective Armor Ass'n
PPC	Paperboard Packaging Council
PPEMA	Portable Power Equipment Manufacturers Ass'n
PPFA	Plastic Pipe and Fittings Ass'n
	Professional Picture Framers Ass'n
PPHRNA	Peruvian Paso Horse Registry of North America
PPI	Pickle Packers Internat'l
	Plastics Pipe Institute
	Potash and Phosphate Institute
PPMG	Professional Publishers Marketing Group
PPMMA	Pulp and Paper Machinery Manufacturers' Ass'n
PPPA	Professional Pool Players Ass'n
PPPEA	Pulp, Paper and Paperboard Export Ass'n of the U.S.
PRCA	Professional Rodeo Cowboys Ass'n
PREA	Pension Real Estate Ass'n
	Phosphate Rock Export Ass'n
PRI	Paleontological Research Institution
	Production Records
PRIMA	Public Risk and Insurance Management Ass'n
PROS	Professional Reactor Operator Soc.
PRPA	Professional Race Pilots Ass'n
PRS	Pattern Recognition Soc.
PRSA	Public Relations Soc. of America
PRT	Procurement Round Table
PS	Paleontological Soc.
	Psychometric Soc.
	Psychonomic Soc.
PSA	Parcel Shippers Ass'n
	Philosophy of Science Ass'n
	Phlebology Soc. of America
	Phobia Soc. of America
	Phycological Soc. of America
	Poetry Soc. of America
	Poultry Science Ass'n
	Professional Stringers Ass'n
	Public Securities Ass'n
PSAI	Portable Sanitation Ass'n Internat'l
PSC	Professional Services Council
PSCA	Profit Sharing Council of America
PSCI	Plastic Shipping Container Institute
PSEA	Pleaters, Stitchers and Embroiderers Ass'n
PSI	Professional Secretaries Internat'l
PSIA	Professional Ski Instructors of America
PSIC	Passive Solar Industries Council
PSLC	Private Security Liaison Council
PSMA	Power Sources Manufacturers Ass'n
	Professional Services Management Ass'n
	Pyrotechnic Signal Manufacturers Ass'n
PSMMA	Plastic Soft Materials Manufacturers Ass'n
PSNA	Phytochemical Soc. of North America
PSRA	Professional Soccer Reporters Ass'n
PSRC	Plastic Surgery Research Council
PSSC	Public Service Satellite Consortium
PSSDC	Production Service and Sales District Council
PSSMA	Paper Shipping Sack Manufacturers Ass'n
PSTC	Pressure Sensitive Tape Council
PTCA	Private Truck Council of America
PTDA	Power Transmission Distributors Ass'n
PTFDA	Professional Travel Film Directors Ass'n
PTG	Piano Technicians Guild
PTI	Post-Tensioning Institute
	Power Tool Institute
PTOS	Patent and Trademark Office Soc.
PTRA	Power Transmission Representatives Ass'n
PUCA	Public Utilities Communicators Ass'n
PVCBMA	PVC Belting Manufacturers Ass'n
PVMA	Pressure Vessel Manufacturers Ass'n
PWAA	Professional Women's Appraisal Ass'n
PWHS	Public Works Historical Soc.
PWP	Professional Women Photographers
PtHA	Pinto Horse Ass'n of America
QBA	Quality Bakers of America Cooperative
QCCA	Quality Control Council of America
QCDPA	Quality Chekd Dairy Products Ass'n
R&DA	Research and Development Associates for Military Food and Packaging Systems
RAA	Regional Airline Ass'n
	Reinsurance Ass'n of America
RAAA	Red Angus Ass'n of America
RAB	Radio Advertising Bureau
RAC	Retail Advertising Conference
RAMA	Railway Automotive Management Ass'n
RAPS	Regulatory Affairs Professionals Soc.
RBA	Retail Bakers of America
RBMA	Radiologists' Business Managers Ass'n
RC	Resources Council
RCA	Rice Council of America
RCCC	Regular Common Carrier Conference
RCI	Retail Confectioners Internat'l
RCMA	Religious Conference Management Ass'n
	Roof Coatings Manufacturers Ass'n
RCRC	Reinforced Concrete Research Council
RCSC	Research Council on Structural Connections
RCSHSB	Red Cedar Shingle and Handsplit Shake Bureau
RDCC	Regional and Distribution Carriers Conference
REA	Religious Education Ass'n
	Rural Education Ass'n
REAC	Real Estate Aviation Chapter
REALTISTS	Nat'l Ass'n of Real Estate Brokers
RECGAI	Research and Engineering Council of the Graphic Arts Industry
REEA	Real Estate Educators Ass'n
REMSA	Railway Engineering-Maintenance Suppliers Ass'n
RES	Reticuloendothelial Soc.
RESNA	RESNA, Ass'n for the Advancement of Rehabilitation Technology
RESSI	Real Estate Securities and Syndication Institute
RETA	Refrigerating Engineers and Technicians Ass'n
RFA	Renewable Fuels Ass'n
RFCI	Resilient Floor Covering Institute
RFI	Retail Floorcovering Institute
RFOOA	Railway Fuel and Operating Officers Ass'n
RHBA	Racking Horse Breeders Ass'n of America
RI	Refractories Institute
	Rolf Institute
RI/SME	Robotics Internat'l of SME
RIA	Robotic Industries Ass'n
RIAA	Recording Industry Ass'n of America
RIMS	Risk and Insurance Management Soc.
RJS	Ruth Jackson Soc.
RLEA	Railway Labor Executives Ass'n
RLI	REALTORS Land Institute
RMA	Reclaim Managers Ass'n
	Rice Millers' Ass'n
	Robert Morris Associates, the Nat'l Ass'n of Bank Loan and Credit Officers
	Rubber Manufacturers Ass'n
RMI	Rack Manufacturers Institute
RMIA	Registered Mail Insurance Ass'n
RMWA	Roadmasters and Maintenance of Way Ass'n of America
RNA	Religion Newswriters Ass'n of U.S. and Canada
RNMI	Realtors Nat'l Marketing Institute
RNRF	Renewable Natural Resources Foundation
ROA	Reserve Officers Ass'n of the U.S.
RPI	Railway Progress Institute
RPRA	Railroad Public Relations Ass'n
RPRC	Religious Public Relations Council
RRS	Radiation Research Soc.
RS	Renown Shippers
RSA	Railway Supply Ass'n
	Regional Science Ass'n
	Renaissance Soc. of America
	Rhetoric Soc. of America
RSAA	Romanian Studies Ass'n of America
RSCA	Religious Speech Communication Ass'n
RSES	Refrigeration Service Engineers Soc.
RSFA	Roller Skating Foundation of America
RSNA	Radiological Soc. of North America
RSROA	Roller Skating Rink Operators Ass'n of America
RSS	Rural Sociological Soc.
RSSI	Railway Systems Suppliers
RTA	Railway Tie Ass'n
RTCA	Radio and Television Correspondents Ass'n
RTNDA	Radio-Television News Directors Ass'n
RTUA	Recognition Technologies Users Ass'n
RVDANA	Recreation Vehicle Dealers Ass'n of North America
RVIA	Recreation Vehicle Industry Ass'n
RVRA	Recreation Vehicle Rental Ass'n
RWA	Romance Writers of America
RWDSU	Retail, Wholesale and Department Store Union
RWF	Roundtable for Women in Foodservice
RWMA	Resistance Welder Manufacturers Ass'n
SA	Sugar Ass'n
SAA	Soc. for American Archaeology
	Soc. for Applied Anthropology
	Soc. of American Archivists
	Soc. of Architectural Administrators
	Soyfoods Ass'n of America
	Sportswear Apparel Ass'n
	Sunglass Ass'n of America
	Supima Ass'n of America
	Surety Ass'n of America
SAAI	Specialty Advertising Ass'n, Internat'l
SAAMI	Sporting Arms and Ammunition Manufacturers' Institute
SABA	Soc. for the Advancement of Behavior Analysis
SABEW	Soc. of American Business Editors and Writers
SAC	Soc. for American Cuisine
SACC	Swedish-American Chamber of Commerce
SACI	Sales Ass'n of the Chemical Industry
SACMA	Suppliers of Advanced Composite Materials Ass'n
SAE	Soc. for the Advancement of Education
	Soc. of Automotive Engineers
SAF	SAF
	Soc. of American Foresters
SAFP	Soc. of Air Force Physicians
SAFSR	Soc. for the Advancement of Food Service Research
SAG	Screen Actors Guild
SAGA	Soc. of American Graphic Artists
SAH	Soc. of American Historians
	Soc. of Architectural Historians
SALT	Soc. for Applied Learning Technology
SAM	Soc. for Adolescent Medicine
	Soc. for Advancement of Management
	Soc. of American Magicians
SAMA	Scientific Apparatus Makers Ass'n
	Specialty Automotive Manufacturers Ass'n
SAME	Soc. of American Military Engineers
SAMPE	Soc. for the Advancement of Material and Process Engineering
SANTA	Souvenirs and Novelties Trade Ass'n
SAPI	Sales Ass'n of the Paper Industry
SAR	Soc. of Authors' Representatives
SARA	Soc. of American Registered Architects
SAS	Soc. for Applied Spectroscopy
SASS	Soc. for the Advancement of Scandinavian Study
SASSIA	Synthetic Amorphous Silica and Silicates Industry Ass'n
SATW	Soc. of American Travel Writers
SAVE	Soc. of American Value Engineers
SAWE	Soc. of Allied Weight Engineers
SAWP	Soc. of American Wood Preservers
SB	Soc. for Biomaterials
SBA	Systems Builders Ass'n
SBCA	Satellite Broadcasting and Communications Ass'n
SBE	Soc. of Broadcast Engineers
SBET	Soc. of Biomedical Equipment Technicians
SBL	Soc. of Biblical Literature
SBLC	Small Business Legislative Council
SBM	Soc. of Behavioral Medicine
SBMA	Steel Bar Mills Ass'n
SBP	Soc. of Biological Psychiatry
SC	Soc. for Cryobiology
SCA	Shipbuilders Council of America
	Soc. of Cardiovascular Anesthesiologists
	Speech Communication Ass'n
	Speed Coaches Ass'n
	Sussex Cattle Ass'n of America
	Synagogue Council of America

ACRONYM INDEX

SCAA	Specialty Coffee Ass'n of America
	Spill Control Ass'n of America
SCB	Shipowners Claims Bureau
SCBW	Soc. of Children's Book Writers
SCC	Soc. of Cosmetic Chemists
SCCAC	Soc. for Conceptual and Content Analysis by Computer
SCCM	Soc. of Critical Care Medicine
SCD	Soc. of Craft Designers
SCE	Soc. of Christian Ethics
SCEH	Soc. for Clinical and Experimental Hypnosis
SCFMA	Summer and Casual Furniture Manufacturers Ass'n
SCI	Sponge and Chamois Institute
SCIC	Soc. of Certified Insurance Counselors
SCKD	Soc. of Certified Kitchen Designers
SCMA	Southern Cypress Manufacturers Ass'n
SCMP	Soc. of Company Meeting Planners
SCRA	Specialized Carriers and Rigging Ass'n
SCRF	Space Commerce Roundtable Foundation
SCRS	Soc. of Collision Repair Specialists
SCS	Soc. for Computer Simulation
SCSA	Soil Conservation Soc. of America
SCSSH	Soc. for the Comparative Study of Society and History
SCST	Soc. of Commercial Seed Technologists
SCT	Soc. for Clinical Trials
SCTA	Steel Carriers Tariff Ass'n
SCTE	Soc. of Cable Television Engineers
	Soc. of Carbide and Tool Engineers
SCUP	Soc. for College and University Planning
SCVS	Soc. for Clinical Vascular Surgery
SDA	Soap and Detergent Ass'n
	Surface Design Ass'n
SDCE	Soc. of Die Casting Engineers
SDI	Steel Deck Institute
	Steel Door Institute
SDMS	Soc. of Diagnostic Medical Sonographers
SEA	Senior Executives Ass'n
SEAL	Sealant Engineering and Associated Lines
SEB	Soc. for Economic Botany
SEBM	Soc. for Experimental Biology and Medicine
SEDA	Safety Equipment Distributors Ass'n
SEE	Soc. of Explosives Engineers
SEECA	State Environmental Education Coordinators Ass'n
SEG	Screen Extras Guild
	Soc. of Economic Geologists
	Soc. of Exploration Geophysicists
SEGH	Soc. for Environmental Geochemistry and Health
SEIA	Security Equipment Industry Ass'n
	Solar Energy Industries Ass'n
SEIU	Service Employees Internat'l Union
SEM	Soc. for Ethnomusicology
	Soc. for Experimental Mechanics
SEMA	Specialty Equipment Market Ass'n
SEMI	Semiconductor Equipment and Materials Institute
SEP	Soc. of Experimental Psychologists
SEPM	Soc. of Economic Paleontologists and Mineralogists
SER	Soc. for Epidemiologic Research
SES	Soc. of Engineering Science
	Soc. of Eye Surgeons
	Standards Engineering Soc.
SESDA	Small Engine Servicing Dealers Ass'n
SESP	Soc. of Experimental Social Psychology
SETP	Soc. of Experimental Test Pilots
SFA	Snack Food Ass'n
SFAAW	Stove, Furnace and Allied Appliance Workers' Internat'l Union of North America
SFCMP	Self-Rising Flour and Corn Meal Program
SFHS	Soc. for French Historical Studies
SFL	Soc. of Federal Linguists
SFLRP	Soc. of Federal Labor Relations Professionals
SFM	Soc. for Foodservice Management
SFPA	Southern Forest Products Ass'n
SFPE	Soc. of Fire Protection Engineers
SFS	Soc. for Foodservice Systems
	Steel Founders' Soc. of America
SFSAFBI	Soc. of Former Special Agents of the Federal Bureau of Investigation
SFTE	Soc. of Flight Test Engineers
SFWA	Science Fiction Writers of America
SGA	Soc. of Gastrointestinal Assistants
	Songwriters Guild of America
SGA of M-A	Sod Growers Ass'n of Mid-America
SGAA	Sporting Goods Agents Ass'n
	Stained Glass Ass'n of America
SGAC	State Governmental Affairs Council
SGBI	Santa Gertrudis Breeders Internat'l
SGCD	Soc. of Glass and Ceramic Decorators
SGE	Soc. of Government Economists
SGI	Soc. for Gynecologic Investigation
SGMA	Sporting Goods Manufacturers Ass'n
SGMP	Soc. of Government Meeting Planners
SGO	Soc. of Geriatric Ophthalmology
	Soc. of Gynecological Oncologists
SGP	Soc. of General Physiologists
SGSR	Soc. for General Systems Research
SHA	Soc. for Historical Archaeology
	Soc. for Humanistic Anthropology
SHAFR	Soc. for Historians of American Foreign Relations
SHC	Silicones Health Council
SHCA	Safety Helmet Council of America
SHD	Soc. for the History of Discoveries
SHE	Soc. for History Education
SHEEO	State Higher Education Executive Officers
SHFG	Soc. for History in the Federal Government
SHHV	Soc. for Health and Human Values
SHJ	Soc. for Humanistic Judaism
SHNS	Soc. of Head and Neck Surgeons
SHOT	Soc. for the History of Technology
SHSWD	Soc. for Hospital Social Work Directors
SI	Salt Institute
	Silver Institute
	Soc. of Illustrators
	Sulphur Institute
SIA	Scaffold Industry Ass'n
	Securities Industry Ass'n
	Semiconductor Industry Ass'n
	Ski Industries America
	Soc. for Industrial Archeology
	Soc. of Insurance Accountants
SIAM	Soc. for Industrial and Applied Mathematics
SID	Soc. for Information Display
	Soc. for Investigative Dermatology
SIETARI	Internat'l Soc. for Intercultural Eductation, Training and Research
SIGACT	Special Interest Group for Automata and Computability Theory
SIGAPL	Special Interest Group on APL Programming Language
SIGARCH	Special Interest Group for Architecture of Computer Systems
SIGART	Special Interest Group on Artificial Intelligence
SIGAda	Special Interest Group on Ada Programming Language
SIGBDP	Special Interest Group on Business Data Processing and Management
SIGBIO	Special Interest Group for Biomedical Computing
SIGCAPH	Special Interest Group for Computers and the Physically Handicapped
SIGCAS	Special Interest Group for Computers and Society
SIGCHI	Special Interest Group for Computers and Human Interaction
SIGCOMM	Special Interest Group for Data Communication
SIGCPR	Special Interest Group for Computer Personnel Research
SIGCSE	Special Interest Group for Computer Science Education
SIGCUE	Special Interest Group for Computer Uses in Education
SIGDA	Special Interest Group on Design Automation
SIGDOC	Special Interest Group on Documentation
SIGGRAPH	Special Interest Group for Computer Graphics
SIGIR	Special Interest Group for Information Retrieval
SIGMA	Sealed Insulating Glass Manufacturers Ass'n
	Soc. of Independent Gasoline Marketers of America
SIGMETRICS	Special Interest Group for Measurement and Evaluation
SIGMICRO	Special Interest Group for Microprogramming
SIGMOD	Special Interest Group for Management of Data
SIGNUM	Special Interest Group on Numerical Mathematics
SIGOIS	Special Interest Group on Office Information Systems
SIGOPS	Special Interest Group on Operating Systems
SIGPLAN	Special Interest Group on Programming Languages
SIGSAC	Special Interest Group on Security, Audit, and Control
SIGSAM	Special Interest Group for Symbolic and Algebraic Manipulation
SIGSIM	Special Interest Group for Simulation and Modeling
SIGSMALL/PC	Special Interest Group on Small and Personal Computing Systems and Applications
SIGSOFT	Special Interest Group on Software Engineering
SIGUCCS	Special Interest Group for University and College Computing Services
SIHS	Soc. for Italian Historical Studies
SIIA	Self Insurance Institute of America
SIM	Soc. for Industrial Microbiology
	Soc. for Information Management
SINA	Shellfish Institute of North America
SIP	Soc. for Invertebrate Pathology
SIPES	Soc. of Independent Professional Earth Scientists
SIR	Soc. of Industrial Realtors
	Soc. of Insurance Research
SIRMA	Small Independent Record Manufacturers Ass'n
SIRSA	Special Industrial Radio Service Ass'n
SIT	Sugar Industry Technologists
SITE	Soc. of Incentive Travel Executives
	Soc. of Insurance Trainers and Educators
SIU	Seafarers' Internat'l Union of North America
SJI	Steel Joist Institute
SLA	Showmen's League of America
	Special Libraries Ass'n
SLAA	Soc. for Latin American Anthropology
SLEMA	Schiffli Lace and Embroidery Manufacturers Ass'n
SLSA	Secondary Lead Smelters Ass'n
SLU	Southern Labor Union
SMA	Salad Manufacturers Ass'n
	Scale Manufacturers Ass'n
	Screen Manufacturers Ass'n
	Shelving Manufacturers Ass'n
	Soc. for Medical Anthropology
	Soc. of Maritime Arbitrators
	Soc. of Medical Administrators
	Soc. of Municipal Arborists
	Stucco Manufacturers Ass'n
SMACCNA	Sheet Metal and Air Conditioning Contractors' Nat'l Ass'n
SMC	Smaller Manufacturers Council
SMCAF	Soc. of Medical Consultants to the Armed Forces
SMD	Soc. of Medical-Dental Management Consultants
SMDA	State Medicaid Directors Ass'n
SME	Soc. of Manufacturing Engineers
	Soc. of Mining Engineers
SME-I	Sales and Marketing Executives, Internat'l
SMEP	Soc. of Multivariate Experimental Psychology
SMI	Masonry and Concrete Saw Manufacturers Institute
	Sorptive Minerals Institute
	Spring Manufacturers Institute
SMMA	Small Motor Manufacturers Ass'n
SMPE	Soc. of Marine Port Engineers
SMPS	Soc. for Marketing Professional Services
SMPTAD	Soc. of Motion Picture and Television Art Directors
SMPTE	Soc. of Motion Picture and Television Engineers
SMRI	Soc. for Magnetic Resonance Imaging
SMSG	School Management Study Group
SMTA	Surface Mount Technology Ass'n
SMTE	Soc. for Music Teacher Education
SMWIA	Sheet Metal Workers' Internat'l Ass'n
SN	Soc. for Neuroscience
SNA	Suburban Newspapers of America
SNAG	Soc. of North American Goldsmiths
SNAME	Soc. of Naval Architects and Marine Engineers
SNANSC	Soc. of Neurosurgical Anesthesia and Neurological Supportive Care
SNAP	Soc. of Nat'l Ass'n Publications
SND	Soc. of Newspaper Design
SNE	Soc. for Nutrition Education
SNFCC	Shippers Nat'l Freight Claim Council
SNH	Soc. for Nursing History
SNIVT	Soc. of Noninvasive Vascular Technology
SNLS	Soc. for New Language Study
SNM	Soc. of Nuclear Medicine
SNP	Soc. for Natural Philosophy
SNS	Soc. of Neurological Surgeons
SOA	Soc. of Actuaries
SOAP	Soc. for Obstetric Anesthesia and Perinatology
	Soc. of Office Automation Professionals
SOCAP	Soc. of Consumer Affairs Professionals in Business
SOCMA	Synthetic Organic Chemical Manufacturers Ass'n
SOEBT	Stationery and Office Equipment Board of Trade
SOEH	Soc. for Occupational and Environmental Heatlh
SOFE	Soc. of Financial Examiners
SOFTA	Shippers Oil Field Traffic Ass'n
SOLE	Soc. of Logistics Engineers
SOMA	Nat'l Student Osteopathic Medical Ass'n
SON	Soc. of Nematologists
SOPHE	Soc. for Public Health Education
SOPO	Soc. of Oral Physiology and Occlusion
SORSI	Sacro-Occipital Research Soc. Internat'l
SOS	Soc. for Occlusal Studies
SOT	Soc. of Toxicology
SP	Soc. of Philaticians
SPA	Seaplane Pilots Ass'n
	Soc. for Personality Assessment
	Soc. for Psychological Anthropology
	Soc. of Professional Archaeologists
	Software Publishers Ass'n
SPAI	Screen Printing Ass'n Internat'l
SPAR	Soc. of Photographer and Artist Representatives
SPARS	Soc. of Professional Audio Recording Studios
SPBA	Soc. of Professional Benefit Administrators
SPBC	Soc. of Professional Business Consultants
SPC	Soy Protein Council
	Sweet Potato Council of the United States
SPD	Soc. of Publication Designers
SPE	Soc. for Photographic Education
	Soc. of Petroleum Engineers
	Soc. of Plastics Engineers
	Soc. of Professors of Education
SPFA	Steel Plate Fabricators Ass'n
SPG	Statistical Paper Group
SPHE	Soc. of Packaging and Handling Engineers
SPI	Soc. of the Plastics Industry
SPIDR	Soc. of Professionals in Dispute Resolution
SPIE	SPIE-Internat'l Soc. for Optical Engineering
SPJ,SDX	Soc. of Professional Journalists, Sigma Delta Chi
SPM	Soc. of Prospective Medicine
SPMA	Shoe Pattern Manufacturers Ass'n
SPMC	Soc. of Professional Management Consultants
SPMEA	Sulfate of Potash Magnesia Export Ass'n
SPR	Soc. for Pediatric Radiology, The
	Soc. for Pediatric Research
	Soc. for Philosophy of Religion
	Soc. for Psychophysiological Research

ACRONYM INDEX

SPRE	Soc. of Park and Recreation Educators
SPRI	Single Ply Roofing Institute
SPS	Soc. of Pelvic Surgeons
	Soc. of Physics Students
SPSE	SPSE: Soc. for Imaging Science and Technology
SPSSI	Soc. for the Psychological Study of Social Issues
SPT	Soc. of Photo-Technologists
SPU	Soc. for Pediatric Urology
SPWAO	Small Press Writers and Artists Organization
SPWLA	Soc. of Professional Well Log Analysts
SR	Soc. of Rheology
SRA	Soc. for Risk Analysis
	Soc. of Research Administrators
	Station Representatives Ass'n
SRC	Ski Retailers Council
SRCC	Solar Rating and Certification Corp.
SRCD	Soc. for Research in Child Development
SRE	Soc. of Radiological Engineering
SREA	Soc. of Real Estate Appraisers
	Street Rod Equipment Ass'n
SRM	Soc. for Range Management
SRMC	Soc. of Risk Management Consultants
SROA	Soc. for Radiation Oncology Administrators
SRPDAA	Silk and Rayon Printers and Dyers Ass'n of America
SRR	Soc. for Reformation Research
SRS	Sleep Research Soc.
SRSTA	Soc. of Roller Skating Teachers of America
SS	Shock Soc.
SSA	Sauna Soc. of America
	Seismological Soc. of America
	Slovak Studies Ass'n
	Sommelier Soc. of America
	Sportswear Salesmen's Ass'n
	Spring Service Ass'n
SSAA	Shoe Suppliers Ass'n of America
SSAR	Soc. for the Study of Amphibians and Reptiles
SSAT	Soc. for Surgery of the Alimentary Tract
SSCD	Soc. of Small Craft Designers
SSCI	Steel Service Center Institute
	Steel Shipping Container Institute
SSDA	Service Station Dealers of America
SSDHPER	Soc. of State Directors of Health, Physical Education and Recreation
SSDT	Soc. of Soft Drink Technologists
SSE	Soc. for the Study of Evolution
SSFI	Scaffolding, Shoring and Forming Institute
SSGA	Sterling Silversmiths Guild of America
SSI	Single Service Institute
SSIA	Shoe Service Institute of America
SSIUS	Specialty Steel Industry of the United States
SSMA	School Science and Mathematics Ass'n
SSO	Soc. of Surgical Oncology
SSP	Soc. for Scholarly Publishing
	Soc. of Satellite Professionals
SSPC	Steel Structures Painting Council
SSPHS	Soc. for Spanish and Portuguese Historical Studies
SSPMA	Sump and Sewage Pump Manufacturers Ass'n
SSR	Soc. for the Study of Reproduction
SSRC	Social Science Research Council
	Structural Stability Research Council
SSS	Soc. for Slovene Studies
	System Safety Soc.
SSSA	Self-Service Storage Ass'n
	Soil Science Soc. of America
SSSB	Soc. for the Study of Social Biology
SSSI	Soc. for the Study of Symbolic Interaction
SSSP	Soc. for the Study of Social Problems
SSSR	Soc. for the Scientific Study of Religion
SSSS	Soc. for Social Studies of Science
	Soc. for the Scientific Study of Sex
SSZ	Soc. of Systematic Zoology
ST	Soc. for Theriogenology
STA	Slurry Technology Ass'n
	Stock Transfer Ass'n
STAPPA	State and Territorial Air Pollution Program Administrators
STC	Smokeless Tobacco Council
	Soc. for Technical Communication
STDA	Selenium-Tellurium Development Ass'n
STEM	Soc. of Teachers of Emergency Medicine
STFDA	Specialty Tool and Fastener Distributors Ass'n
STFM	Soc. of Teachers of Family Medicine
STGAA	Shade Tobacco Growers Agricultural Ass'n
STI	Steel Tank Institute
STL	Southern Transportation League
STS	Soc. for Textual Scholarship
	Soc. of Thoracic Surgeons
STUDENT APHA	Student American Pharmaceutical Ass'n
SUA	Silver Users Ass'n
SUO	Soc. of University Otolaryngologists
SUPA	Soc. of University Patent Administrators
SUS	Soc. of University Surgeons
SUU	Soc. of University Urologists
SVA	Soc. for Visual Anthropology
SVC	Soc. of Vacuum Coaters
SVE	Soc. of Vector Ecologists
SVHE	Soc. for Values in Higher Education
SVIA	Specialty Vehicle Institute of America
SVP	Soc. of Vertebrate Paleontology
SVS	Soc. for Vascular Surgery
SWAMP	Stuntwomen's Ass'n of Motion Pictures
SWCHA	Southwestern Craft and Hobby Ass'n
SWE	Soc. of Wine Educators
	Soc. of Women Engineers
SWG	Soc. of Woman Geographers
SWI	Sealant and Waterproofers Institute
	Steel Window Institute
SWPA	Submersible Wastewater Pump Ass'n
SWST	Soc. of Wood Science and Technology
TA	Tea Ass'n of the United States of America
	Tobacco Associates
TAA	Transit Advertising Ass'n
TAAFLO	Trans-Atlantic American Flag Liner Operations
TAALS	American Ass'n of Language Specialists
TAAN	Transworld Advertising Agency Network
TAASP	Ass'n for the Anthropological Study of Play
TAB	Traffic Audit Bureau
TACOS	Travel Agents Computer Soc.
TAGA	Technical Ass'n of the Graphic Arts
TAPPI	Technical Ass'n of the Pulp and Paper Industry
TARA	Truck-frame and Axle Repair Ass'n
TASDA	American Safe Deposit Ass'n, The
TASH	Ass'n for Persons with Severe Handicaps
TAUS	Tobacco Ass'n of the U.S.
TBA	Test Boring Ass'n
TBCA	Transportation Brokers Conference of America
TBMA	Textile Bag Manufacturers Ass'n
TBPA	Textile Bag and Packaging Ass'n
TC	Tea Council of the U.S.A.
TCA	Tele-Communications Ass'n
	Television Critics Ass'n
	Textile Converters Ass'n
	Thoroughbred Club of America
	Tile Council of America
	Tissue Culture Ass'n
TCAA	Tile Contractors' Ass'n of America
TCATA	Textile Care Allied Trades Ass'n
TCMA	Third Class Mail Ass'n
	Tooling Component Manufacturers Ass'n
TCNA	Tube Council of North America
TDA	Textile Distributors Ass'n
	Titanium Development Ass'n
TDMA	Trophy Dealers and Manufacturers Ass'n
TEA	Theatre Equipment Ass'n
TEC	Talmex Export Corporation
TECC	Technology Education for Children Council
TEGMA	Terminal Elevator Grain Merchants Ass'n
TEI	Tax Executives Institute
TEMA	Tubular Exchanger Manufacturers Ass'n
TESOL	Teachers of English to Speakers of Other Languages
TFBPA	Textile Fibers and By-Products Ass'n
TFG	Textile Foremen's Guild
TFPA	Tubular Finishers and Processors Ass'n
TGA-US	Glutamate Ass'n, The (United States)
TGIC	Tobacco Growers' Information Committee
THAA	Tourist House Ass'n of America
THECC	Truck and Heavy Equipment Claims Council
THMA	Trailer Hitch Manufacturers Ass'n
TI	Thread Institute
	Tobacco Institute
	Transportation Institute
TIA	Travel Industry Ass'n of America
	Typographers Internat'l Ass'n
TIMA	Thermal Insulation Manufacturers Ass'n
TIMS	Institute of Management Sciences, The
TISC	Tire Industry Safety Council
TIUC	Textile Information Users Council
TJC	Jockey Club, The
TJG	Travel Journalists Guild
TKGA	Knitting Guild of America, The
TLA	Theatre Library Ass'n
	Transportation Lawyers Ass'n
TLBAA	Texas Longhorn Breeders Ass'n of America
TLC	Textile Laundry Council
TLMI	Tag and Label Manufacturers Institute
TMA	Tennis Manufacturers Ass'n
	Tobacco Merchants Ass'n of the U.S.
	Toy Manufacturers of America
TMDA	Training Media Distributors Ass'n
TMI	Trucking Management
	Tune-up Manufacturers Institute
TMMB	Truck Mixer Manufacturers Bureau
TMS	Metallurgical Soc., The
TMSA	Technical Marketing Soc. of America
TMTFSGCIU	Tile, Marble, Terrazzo, Finishers, Shopworkers and Granite Cutters Internat'l Union
TNA	Telocator Network of America
TNG	Newspaper Guild, The
TOC	Timber Operators Council
TPA	Tantalum Producers Ass'n
	Transmission Products Ass'n
TPDLRI	Textile Printers and Dyers Labor Relations Institute
TPEA	Texas Produce Export Ass'n
TPI	Truss Plate Institute
TPM	Timber Products Manufacturers
TPSTHCPTEIU	Textile Processors, Service Trades, Health Care, Professional and Technical Employees Internat'l Union
TQCA	Textile Quality Control Ass'n
TRA	Thoroughbred Racing Ass'ns of North America
	Tire and Rim Ass'n
TRAA	Towing and Recovery Ass'n of America
TRALA	Truck Renting and Leasing Ass'n
TRC	Trade Relations Council of the U.S.
TRF	Transportation Research Forum
	Tuna Research Foundation
TRI	Tin Research Institute
TRIB	Tire Retread Information Bureau
TRMI	Tubular Rivet and Machine Institute
TROA	Retired Officers Ass'n
TRS	Tree-Ring Soc.
TRSA	Textile Rental Services Ass'n of America
TRTR	Nat'l Organization of Test, Research and Training Reactors
TS	Trademark Soc.
	Transplantation Soc. (U.S. Section)
TSB	Trade Show Bureau
TSEI	Transportation Safety Equipment Institute
TSS	Safety Soc., The
TSSA	Tackle and Shooting Sports Agents Ass'n
	Trade Show Services Ass'n
TSTPI	Tapered Steel Transmission Pole Institute
TTMA	Truck Trailer Manufacturers Ass'n
TTRA	Travel and Tourism Research Ass'n
TTS	Technology Transfer Soc.
TVB	Television Bureau of Advertising
TWAA	Toy Wholesalers' Ass'n of America
TWHBEA	Tennessee Walking Horse Breeders and Exhibitors Ass'n
TWS	Wildlife Soc., The
TWU	Transport Workers Union of America
UAA	Urban Affairs Ass'n
UAEM	University Ass'n for Emergency Medicine
UAHC	Union of American Hebrew Congregations
UAJAPPFIUSC	United Ass'n of Journeymen and Apprentices of the Plumbing and Pipe Fitting Industry of the U.S. and Ca
UAPD	Union of American Physicians and Dentists
UAW	United Automobile, Aerospace and Agricultural Implement Workers of America
UAWIU	United Allied Workers Internat'l Union
UBC	United Brotherhood of Carpenters and Joiners of America
UBDMA	United Better Dress Manufacturers Ass'n
UBOA	United Bus Owners of America
UBPVLS	Uniform Boiler and Pressure Vessel Laws Soc.
UCA	Underground Contractors Association
UCC	United Cancer Council
UCDA	University and College Designers Ass'n
UCEA	University Council for Educational Administration
UCOWR	Universities Council on Water Resources
UDIA	United Dairy Industry Ass'n
UDMA	United Dance Merchants of America
UDSR	United Duroc Swine Registry
UE	United Electrical, Radio and Machine Workers of America
UEI	United Egg Internat'l
UEP	United Egg Producers
UET	United Engineering Trustees
UFCW	United Food and Commercial Workers Internat'l Union
UFFVA	United Fresh Fruit and Vegetable Ass'n
UFMA	United Fur Manufacturers Ass'n
UFVA	University Film and Video Ass'n
UFW	United Farm Workers of America
UGA	United Golfers' Ass'n
UGWA	United Garment Workers of America
UHMS	Undersea and Hyperbaric Medical Soc.
UIA	Ultrasonic Industry Ass'n
UICWA	United Infants and Childrens Wear Ass'n
UKML	United Knitwear Manufacturers League
ULI	Urban Land Institute
UMA	United Methodist Ass'n of Health and Welfare Ministries
UMW	United Mine Workers of America
UNA	Underwear-Negligee Associates
UNCA	United Neighborhood Centers of America
UNSU	United Nations Staff Union
UOA	United Ostomy Ass'n
UPAA	University Photographers Ass'n of America
UPFD	United Pesticide Formulators and Distributors Ass'n
UPHA	United Professional Horsemen's Ass'n
UPHEWA	United Presbyterian Health, Education and Welfare Ass'n
UPIU	United Paperworkers Internat'l Union
URA	Universities Research Ass'n
URISA	Urban and Regional Information Systems Ass'n
URPE	Union for Radical Political Economics
URTA	University Resident Theatre Ass'n
URWA	United Rubber, Cork, Linoleum and Plastic Workers of America
USA	United Scenic Artists
	United Synagogue of America
USAA	United States Armor Ass'n
USACC	United States-Arab Chamber of Commerce
USAFP	Uniformed Services Academy of Family Physicians
USAHA	United States Animal Health Ass'n
USAIGC	United States Ass'n of Independent Gymnastic Clubs
USATLA	USA Toy Library Ass'n
USAWOA	United States Army Warrant Officers Ass'n
USBIC	United States Business and Industrial Council
USBSA	United States Beet Sugar Ass'n
USBWA	United States Basketball Writers Ass'n
USCCCA	United States Cross Country Coaches Ass'n
USCEA	United States Cigarette Export Ass'n
USCIB	United States Council for Internat'l Business
USCLHO	United States Conference of Local Health Officers
USCM	United States Conference of Mayors
USCSRA	United States Cane Sugar Refiners' Ass'n
USDGA	United States Durum Growers Ass'n
USFCA	United States Fencing Coaches Ass'n
USFCC	United States Federation for Culture Collections

ACRONYM INDEX

USFGC	United States Feed Grains Council
USFL	United States Football League
USFLPA	United States Football League Players Ass'n
USGA	United States Golf Ass'n
USHSLA	United States Hide, Skin and Leather Ass'n
USHWA	United States Harness Writers' Ass'n
USINOA	United States Immigration and Naturalization Officers Ass'n
USITT	United States Institute for Theatre Technology
USJ	United States Jaycees
USLA	United States Lifesaving Ass'n
USLCA	United States Lacrosse Coaches' Ass'n
USLSI	United States League of Savings Institutions
USMCOC	United States-Mexico Chamber of Commerce
USMEF	United States Meat Export Federation
USNAC	United States of America National Committee of the Internat'l Dairy Federation
USOC of ETAD	United States Operating Committee of ETAD
USP	United Societies of Physiotherapists
USPA	United States Potters' Ass'n
USPAK	United States-Pakistan Economic Council
USPC	United States Pharmacopeial Convention
USPCA	United States Police K-9 Ass'n
USPE	United States Poultry Export
USPRO	United States Professional Cycling Federation
USPTA	United States Professional Tennis Ass'n
USPTR	Professional Tennis Registry, USA
USRA	Universities Space Research Ass'n
USSCA	United States Ski Coaches Ass'n
USSF	United States Soccer Federation
USSIA	United States Shellac Importers Ass'n
USSWA	United States Ski Writers Ass'n
USTA	United States Telephone Ass'n
	United States Tennis Ass'n
	United States Trademark Ass'n
USTC&TBA	United States Tennis Court and Track Builders Ass'n
USTF	United States Tuna Foundation
USTFA	United States Trout Farmers Ass'n
USTOA	United States Tour Operators Ass'n
USTSA	United States Targhee Sheep Ass'n
	United States Telecommunications Suppliers Ass'n
USTWA	United States Tennis Writers' Ass'n
USWA	United Steelworkers of America
USWTCA	Unites States Women's Track Coaches Ass'n
USYEC	United States-Yugoslav Economic Council
UTC	Utilities Telecommunications Council
UTTA	United Thoroughbred Trainers of America
UTU	United Transportation Union
UTW	United Telegraph Workers
UTWA	United Textile Workers of America
UURWAW	United Union of Roofers, Waterproofers and Allied Workers
UWUA	Utility Workers Union of America
VA	Vermiculite Ass'n
VAAUS	Venezuelan American Ass'n of the U.S.
VBAA	Vanilla Bean Ass'n of America
VC	Vatel Club
VCMA	Vacuum Cleaner Manufacturers Ass'n
VCS	Veterinary Cancer Soc.
VDTA	Vacuum Dealers Trade Ass'n
VEWAA	Vocational Evaluation and Work Adjustment Ass'n
VFA	Videtape Facilities Ass'n
VI	Vibration Institute
	Vinegar Institute, The
VIA	Videotex Industry Ass'n
VIC	Veal Industry Council
VICA	Vocational Industrial Clubs of America
VMA	Valve Manufacturers Ass'n of America
VNAA	Visiting Nurse Ass'ns of America
VRCI	Variable Resistive Components Institute
VSA	Vehicle Security Ass'n
VSDA	Video Software Dealers Ass'n
VSMA	Vibrating Screen Manufacturers Ass'n
VSP	Vision Service Plan
VWGA	Vinifera Wine Growers Ass'n
WA	Woolknit Associates
WAA	Western Awning Ass'n
WACA	Women's Apparel Chains Ass'n
WAD	World Ass'n of Detectives
WADE	World Ass'n of Document Examiners
WAEL	Western Ass'n of Equipment Lessors
WAEMA	Western and English Manufacturers Ass'n
WAI	Wire Ass'n Internat'l
WAS	World Aquaculture Soc.
WASDA	Water and Sewer Distributors of America
WBANA	Wild Blueberry Ass'n of North America
WBCA	Welsh Black Cattle Ass'n
WBFI	Wild Bird Feeding Institute
WBMA	Wirebound Box Manufacturers Ass'n
WCA	Women's Caucus for Art
WCC	Women's College Coalition
WCGA	World Computer Graphics Ass'n
WCML	Women's Caucus for the Modern Languages
WCR	Women's Council of Realtors
WDA	Wallcovering Distributors Ass'n
	Wildlife Disease Ass'n
WDALMP	Warehouse Distributors Ass'n for Leisure and Mobile Products
WE	Women in Energy
WEB	Women in Employee Benefits
WERA	Western/English Retailers of America
WERC	Warehousing Education and Research Council
WFA	Wire Fabricators Ass'n
WFFSA	Wholesale Florists and Florist Suppliers of America
WFI	Wood Foundation Institute
WFIA	Western Forest Industries Ass'n
WFS	World Future Soc.
WGAE	Writers Guild of America, East
WGAW	Writers Guild of America, West
WGIC	Wheat Gluten Industry Council
WGMA	Wet Ground Mica Ass'n
	Work Glove Manufacturers Ass'n
WGR	Women in Government Relations
WHA	Wood Heating Alliance
WHCA	White House Correspondents Ass'n
WHNPA	White House News Photographers Ass'n
WHOA	Walking Horse Owners Ass'n of America
WHTA	Walking Horse Trainers Ass'n
WI	Wine Institute
WIC	Women in Communications
WIMA	Writing Instrument Manufacturers Ass'n
WITA	Women's Internat'l Tennis Ass'n
WLS	Water Lily Soc.
WLUC	Women Life Underwriters Conference
WLW	Women Library Workers
WMA	Wallcovering Manufacturers Ass'n
	Waterbed Manufacturers Ass'n
	Weather Modification Ass'n
WMBA	Wire Machinery Builders Ass'n
WMDA	Woodworking Machinery Distributors' Ass'n
WMI	Wildlife Management Institute
WMIAA	Woodworking Machinery Importers Ass'n of America
WMMA	Wood Machinery Manufacturers of America
WMMPA	Wood Moulding and Millwork Producers Ass'n
WNBA	Women's Nat'l Book Ass'n
WNGA	Wholesale Nursery Growers of America
WOMPI	Women of the Motion Picture Industry, Internat'l
WPCAA	White Park Cattle Ass'n of America
WPCF	Water Pollution Control Federation
WPCSA	Welsh Pony and Cob Soc. of America
WPI	Wedding Photographers Internat'l
WPMA	Wood Products Manufacturers Ass'n
WPRA	Women's Professional Rodeo Ass'n
WPS	World Population Soc.
WPSA	World Professional Squash Ass'n
	World's Poultry Science Ass'n, U.S.A. Branch
WQA	Water Quality Ass'n
WQC	Wheat Quality Council
WRA	Western Railroad Ass'n
	Western Range Ass'n
WRC	Water Resources Congress
	Welding Research Council
WRCA	Western Red Cedar Ass'n
WRCLA	Western Red Cedar Lumber Ass'n
WRI	Wire Reinforcement Institute
WRTB	Wire Rope Technical Board
WSA	Web Sling Ass'n
	Wholesale Stationer's Ass'n
WSC	Water Systems Council
WSFI	Wood and Synthetic Flooring Institute
WSG	Wire Service Guild
WSGA	Wine and Spirits Guild of America
WSIA	Water Ski Industry Ass'n
WSMA	Western States Meat Ass'n
WSSA	Weed Science Soc. of America
	Wine and Spirits Shippers Ass'n
WSTI	Welded Steel Tube Institute
WSWA	Wine and Spirits Wholesalers of America
WTA	Water Transport Ass'n
	Western Timber Ass'n
WTCA	Wood Truss Council of America
WTMA	Wood Tank Manufacturers Ass'n
WTS	Women's Transportation Seminar
WWA	Western Writers of America
	World Waterpark Ass'n
WWEMA	Water and Wastewater Equipment Manufacturers Ass'n
WWPA	Western Wood Products Ass'n
	Woven Wire Products Ass'n
WWPSA	Western World Pet Supply Ass'n
WWWCHR	World Wide White and Creme Horse Registry
YPO	Young Presidents' Organization
ZI	Zinc Institute
	Zonta Internat'l
9 to 5	Nine to Five Nat'l Ass'n of Working Women

U.S. Association Management Companies

1987

The association management firm is a comparatively recent phenomenon. The oldest company still in existence is the venerable firm of Fernley and Fernley of Philadelphia, founded in 1886. Today there are more than 200 association management firms in the United States, the vast majority formed since 1945. They serve over 500 national and perhaps 1,000 local or regional organizations.

Association management firms run a number of non-profit organizations (trade and professional associations, foundations, certifying organizations) on a contract basis. A full-service management firm provides a variety of services: legislative relations, financial management, conference and meeting planning and execution, publications, public relations, membership recruitment, fund-raising and training seminars. Associations may draw on them as needed for specific services, or they may surrender full management to the company, a relationship which assures greater continuity and appreciable tax advantages.

Contracts with the management company will usually provide for an account executive as Executive Director (who may handle several groups), a headquarters office and secretarial support. Direct costs such as telephone, postage, and travel are commonly billed to the client. A client can anticipate that the identity of his organization will be preserved and, if he wishes, will have his own stationery, convention program, newsletter, or magazine.

The advantage is obvious of being able to draw on a variety of skills as needed without the necessity of continuous high-overhead. This often makes sense to smaller groups. On the other hand, some feel that a management firm cannot be expected to provide more than housekeeping, and that the final responsibility for determining an association's problems and direction remains with its members. For this reason some associations outgrow their manager. They break away to set up their own headquarters, sometimes taking the account executive with them, a hazard of the business.

Some firms handle mostly national groups, some specializing in associations concerned with a specific industry of profession. Others concentrate on groups with regional, state or local memberships. We have chosen to list under the firm's name only the associations which fall within the scope of this book, i.e. national trade and professional associations. State and local clients, as well as educational and certifying arms and foundations, have not been included.

ACCENT ON MANAGEMENT
17 S. High St., Suite 1200, Columbus, OH 43215
(614) 221-1900
David W. Field, *President*
- Aviation/Space Writers Association
- National Institute for Real Estate Consultants

ADLER DROZ, INC.
2081 Business Center Drive, Suite 290, Irvine, CA 92715
(714) 833-2445
Fred Droz, *President*
- Association of Pediatric Oncology Nurses
- ET Foundation
- International Association for Enterostomal Therapy
- National ET Nursing Certification Board
- United Ostomy Association

THE ADMINISTRATORS, INC.
3602 E. Campbell St., Phoenix, AZ 85018
(602) 957-0773
Paulene Wampler, *President*

ADVANCEMENT PLANNING GROUPS
6320 Busch Blvd., Columbus, OH 43229
(614) 846-0771
Margaret H. Vild, *President*

AMERICAN FRATERNAL PROGRAMMERS
1100 Northeast 125th St., North Miami, FL 33161
(305) 891-9800
Gerald S. Arenberg, *President*
- American Federation of Police
- American Park Rangers Association
- American Police Academy
- National Association of Chiefs of Police

AMERICAN TRADE ASSOCIATION MANAGEMENT
9005 Congressional Court, Potomac, MD 20854
(301) 365-4080
James E. Mack, *President & General Counsel*
- National Association of Mirror Manufacturers
- Peanut Butter and Nut Processors Association

ASSOCIATION ALTERNATIVES, INC.
P.O. Box 36160, Raleigh, NC 27606
(919) 851-2901
Marcy Hege, CAE, *President*

ASSOCIATION DEVELOPMENT CENTER
1330 S. Bascom Ave., Suite D, San Jose, CA 95128
(408) 286-2969
Jan Shepherd, *President*
- International Drycleaners Congress
- Professional and Technical Consultants Association

ASSOCIATION EXCHANGE
P.O. Box 1519, Winter Haven, FL 33880
(813) 293-5710
David Boozer, President

ASSOCIATION HEADQUARTERS
277 East 6100 South, Salt Lake City, UT 84107
(801) 268-3000
Marvin C. Zitting, *President*
American Correctional Food Service Association
American Institutions Food Service Association
Musicians National Hotline Association

ASSOCIATION HEADQUARTERS, INC.
66 East Main St., Moorestown, NJ 08057
(609) 234-9155
William L. MacMillan, II, CAE, *President*
Childrenswear Manufacturers Association
Juvenile Products Manufacturers Association
National Association of Chewing Gum Manufacturers
Pencil Makers Association
Toy Wholesalers' Association of America

ASSOCIATION HEADQUARTERS, INC.
P.O. Box 2145, Northbrook, IL 60065-2145
(312) 272-3930
Donald J. Walker, *President*
National Association of Installation Developers
Textile Bag Manufacturers Association

ASSOCIATION LEADERSHIP
P.O. Box 469, Sterling, VA 22170
(703) 450-6046
James R. Fleckenstein, CAE, *President*
National Association of Shooting Range Owners

ASSOCIATION MANAGEMENT, INC.
P.O. Box 27187, Seattle, WA 98125
(206) 364-4250
Don L. Santy, *President*

ASSOCIATION MANAGEMENT, LTD.
900 Des Moines St., Des Moines, IA 50309
(515) 266-2189
Dennis Schneider, *President*
Academy of Dispensing Audiologists
Life Communicators Association
National Hearing Conservation Association

ASSOCIATION MANAGEMENT CENTER
2506 Gross Point Road, Evanston, IL 60201
(312) 475-7530
Arthur W. Engle, *President*
Association of Rehabilitation Nurses
Healthcare Internal Audit Group
International Society of Weighing and Measurement
National Institute of Steel Detailing
National Nurses Society on Addictions
Noise Control Products and Materials Association

ASSOCIATION MANAGEMENT CENTER, INC.
179 Allyn St., #304, Hartford, CT 06103
(203) 246-6566
Edward Isenberg, *President*
American Epilepsy Society
Pin, Clip and Fastener Service

ASSOCIATION MANAGEMENT CORP.
66 Morris Avenue, P.O. Box 359, Springfield, NJ 07081
(201) 379-1100
Mauro A. Checchio, *President*
American Association for Music Therapy
Converting Equipment Manufacturers Association
Council for Accreditation in Occupational Hearing Conservation
National Council of Acoustical Consultants
Wallcovering Manufacturers Association

ASSOCIATION MANAGEMENT GROUP
1010 Wisconsin Ave., N.W., Suite 630, Washington, DC 20007
(202) 965-7510
Charles D. Rumbarger, *President*
American Society of Home Inspectors
Fiberglass Fabrication Association
National Association of Estate Planning Councils
National Association of Independent Life Brokerage Agencies
Society of National Association Publications

ASSOCIATION MANAGEMENT PROFESSISONALS, INC.
P.O. Box 13066, St. Louis, MO 63119
(314) 534-4175
Robert James Cimasi, *President*

ASSOCIATION MANAGEMENT SERVICE
1070 Sibley Tower, Rochester, NY 14604
(716) 546-7241
Peter O. Allen, *President*
National Reading Conference
Society of Gastrointestinal Assistants

ASSOCIATION MANAGEMENT SERVICES, INC.
415 Parkway Drive, Box 545, Leeds, AL 35094
(205) 699-2272
George H. Jones, *President*

ASSOCIATION MANAGEMENT SERVICES OF THE U.S., INC.
10806 Trade Road, Richmond, VA 25236
(804) 379-2099
David Ottaway, *President*

ASSOCIATION MANAGEMENT SPECIALISTS
1156 - 15th St., N.W., Suite 525, Washington, DC 20005
(202) 659-1474
Elizabeth A. Dunleavy, *President*

ASSOCIATION MANAGEMENT SYSTEMS, INC.
710 East Ogden Ave., Suite 113, Naperville, IL 60540
(312) 369-2406
Arthur W. Seeds, *President*
Barbecue Industry Association
Electronic Pest Control Association
Incentive Manufacturers Representatives Association
Logsplitters Manufacturers Association
Wire Fabricators Association

ASSOCIATION MANAGEMENT & LEGISLATIVE SERVICES
4751 Lindle Road, Suites 126-128, Harrisburg, PA 17111
(717) 939-3333
John H. Burton, *President*

ASSOCIATION MANAGERS, INC.
3900 E. Timrod, Tucson, AZ 85711
(602) 881-1778
Phillip A. Gutt, *President*
American Association of Veterinary Diagnostic Laboratories

ASSOCIATION MEMBERS SERVICES, LTD.
P.O. Box 2104, Indianapolis, IN 46206
(317) 631-8124
N. Murray, *President & Board Chairman*

THE ASSOCIATION OFFICE
P.O. Box 441000-186, Aurora, CO 80044
(303) 750-2227
Dean Faulkner, *President*

ASSOCIATION OFFICES
1000 East 146th St., Suite 121, Burnsville, MN 55337
(612) 432-2228
Al Brodie, *Executive Vice President*

This list is available in Mailing Label form ($75.00)

ASSOCIATION REPRESENTATIVES, INC.
21010 Center Bridge Road, Rocky River, OH 44116
(216) 333-7417
Benjamin J. Imburgia, *President*
Forum of State Pest Control Associations
National Association of Pattern Manufacturers
National Association of Professional Engravers

ASSOCIATION SERVICES/ATLANTA, INC.
2786 N. Decatur Road, #220, Decatur, GA 30033
(404) 292-1113
Stewart M. Huey, *President*
National Asbestos Council

ASSOCIATION SERVICES CORP.
3310 Harrison St., Topeka, KS 66611
(913) 266-7014
William J. Birch, *President*
Flat Glass Marketing Association
Glass Tempering Association
Glazing Industry Code Committee
Laminators Safety Glass Association
National Fenestration Council
Transportation Lawyers Association

ASSOCIATION SERVICES INTERNATIONAL, LTD.
5845 Horton St., #201, Mission, KS 66202
(913) 262-4510
Frank A. Bistrom, *President*
Agricultural and Industrial Manufacturers Representatives Association
Asssociation of Industrial Manufacturers Representatives
Health Industry Representatives Association
Independent Medical Distributing Association
Petroleum Equipment Representatives Association
Power Transmission Representatives Association

ASSOCIATION SERVICES & MANAGEMENT
2021 Barberry Drive, Springfield, IL 62704
(217) 546-0532
Charles Miller, *President*

ASSOCIATION AND SOCIETY MANAGEMENT
210 Post St., Suite 1102, San Francisco, CA 94108
Robert M. Crum, CAE *President*
(415) 391-0545

ASSOCIATION AND SOCIETY MANAGEMENT, INC.
940 E. 51st St., Austin, TX 78751-2241
(512) 454-8626
Don R. McCullough, CAE, *President*
National Aloe Science Council
PIP Owners Association

ASSOCIATION AND SOCIETY MANAGEMENT INTERNATIONAL
7297 Lee Highway, Suite N, Falls Church, VA 22042
(703) 533-0251
Harry W. Buzzard, Jr., *President*
American Textile Machinery Association
American Tube Association
Meat Industry Suppliers Association
National Coordinating Council on Emergency Management
Process Equipment Manufacturers Association
Wire Machinery Builders Association

BANNISTER & ASSOCIATES, INC.
5008 Pine Creek, Suite B, Westerville, OH 43081
(614) 895-1355
James R. Bannister, *President*
American Trakehner Association
Electrical Women's Round Table
Furniture Rental Association of America
Hogan Users Group
Home Economists in Business
National Association of Bank Servicers
North American NCR Financial Users Group

BARBEE & ASSOCIATES
810 Merchants National Bank, Topeka, KS 66612
(913) 233-0555
George Barbee, *President*

BAXTER ASSOCIATES, INC.
P.O. Box 1333, Stamford, CT 06904
(203) 323-3143
Carroll A. Greathouse, *President*

BAYFIELD RESOURCES
71 East Ave., Norwalk, CT 06851
(203) 852-7168
Penny Dalziel, *President*
Carded Packaging Institute
Licensing Executives Society
Sunglass Association of America

BEAN & ASSOCIATES
512 East Wilson Ave., Suite 311, Glendale, CA 91206
(818) 240-8666
Alvin P. Bean, *President*
Production Engine Remanufacturers Association

WILLIAM S. BERGMAN ASSOCIATES
1001 Connecticut Ave., N.W., Suite 800, Washington, DC 20036
(202) 452-1520
William S. Bergman, *President*
American Association of Managing General Agents
Cooking Advancement and Research Education Foundation
Food Industry Association Executives
International Association of Cooking Professionals
National Association of Mortgage Brokers
National Estimating Society
Outdoor Power Equipment Aftermarket Association
Solar Rating and Certification Corp.
State Government Affairs Council
State Governmental Education and Research Foundation
Telemarking USA

BESS MANAGEMENT SERVICES
117 Miramar Ave., Biloxi, MS 39350
(601) 374-6537
William R. Bess, *President*
Broker Management Council
Manufacturers Representatives of America

DAVID BIRENBAUM AND ASSOCIATES
818 Olive St., Suite 918, St. Louis, MO 63101
(314) 241-1445
David Birenbaum, *Administrator*
American Association of Bioanalysts
International Society of Clinical Laboratory Technology

BLENHEIM MANAGEMENT ASSOCIATES
122 East 42nd St., Suite 1120, New York, NY 10168
(212) 867-4777
Randall S. Archibald, *President*
Jewish Funeral Directors of America

BOSTROM CORP.
435 N. Michigan Ave., Suite 1717, Chicago, IL 60611
(312) 644-0828
Glenn W. Bostrom, *President*
American Heartworm Society
American Home Lighting Institute
American Society of Clinical Oncology
Association of Rotational Molders
COMMON — An IBM Users Group
Cultured Marble Institute
Gift Association of America
International Association of Torch Clubs
International Society for Heart Transplantation
International Staple, Nail and Tool Association
Leukemia Society of America
National Association of Boards of Examiners of Nursing Home Administrators

National Association of School Psychologists
National Institute of Oilseed Products
National Metal Decorators Association
Nickel Producers Environmental Research Association
Society for American Archaeology
Society of Company Meeting Planners
Veal Industry Council

Other Offices:
1511 K St., N.W., Suite 716
Washington, DC 20005
(202) 638-6077

2600 Garden Road, Suite 208
Monterey, CA 93940
(408) 649-6544

DAN BOTKISS & ASSOCIATES
1001 Connecticut Ave., N.W., Suite 528, Washington, DC 20036
(202) 296-2207
Daniel A. Botkiss, *President*

G. DONALD BOYER & ASSOCIATES
3743 Arlington Ave., Riverside, CA 92506
(714) 684-7754
Don Boyer, *President*

THE BREEDEN COMPANY
1104 Wilmot Road, Suite 201, Deerfield, IL 60015-5196
(312) 940-8800
Carl A. Wangman, CAE, *Chairman*
American Telemarketing Association
Architectural Fabric Structures Institute
Association for Corporate Growth
Ceilings and Interior Systems Construction Association
Legal Industry Advisory Council
National Association of Quality Assurance Professionals
National Federation of Paralegal Associations
National Tumor Registrars Association
Pressure Sensitive Tape Council
Roof Insulation Council
Single Ply Roofing Institute
Tag and Label Manufacturers Institute
USA Toy Library Association

J. ROBERT BROUSE ASSOCIATES
1299 Woodside Drive, McLean, VA 22102
(703) 556-6114
Robin Critzer, *Executive Assistant*
International Teleconferencing Association

R. FRANKLIN BROWN, JR., INC.
251 W. DeKalb Pike, Adams Building, Suite 109
King of Prussia, PA 19406
(215) 265-6658
R. Franklin Brown, Jr., *President*
Copper and Brass Servicenter Association
Woodworking Machinery Distributors' Association

C. M. BROWNSTEIN AND ASSOCIATES
2001 S St., N.W., Suite 630, Washington, DC 20009
(202) 537-1220
Clifford M. Brownstein, *President*
Association of Accounting Administrators

BURNISON, MARTELLO AND ASSOCIATES
310 N. Alabama, Indianapolis, IN 46204
(317) 636-6059
Joyce M. Martello, *Principal*
Judith C. Burnison, *Principal*
American Association for Affirmative Action
Radiologist Business Managers
UNITEC Association

THE CATE CORP.
1980 Issac Newton Square South, Reston, VA 22090
(703) 435-6708
George M. Cate, *President*
American Association of Surgeon's Assistants
American Cardiology Technologists Association
American Society of Extra-corporeal Technology
Healthcare Information Systems Sharing Group
International Council of Perfusion Societies
Smocking Arts Guild of America

CLEMONS AND ASSOCIATES, INC.
P.O. Box 28279, 1740 E. Joppa Road, Baltimore, MD 21234
(301) 665-1276
Calvin K. Clemons, CAE, *President*
Fire Suppression Systems Association
National Association of Writing Instrument Distributors
Pet Industry Distributors Association
Woodworking Machinery Importers Association of America

RICHARD H. CLOUGH CO.
76 South State St., Box 1382, Concord, NH 03301
(603) 228-1231
Richard H. Clough, CAE, *President*

CM SERVICES, INC.
800 Roosevelt Road, #C-20, Glen Ellyn, IL 60137
(312) 858-7337
Richard W. Church, *President*
Bearing Specialist Association
National Association of Pipe Nipple Manufacturers
Plastic Pipe and Fittings Association
Plumbing Manufacturers Institute
Polyurethane Manufacturers Association
Whirlpool Bath Manufacturers Association

CONVENTION EVENTS, INC.
P.O. Box 3996, Littleton, CO 80161
(303) 797-7988
Richard Crandell, *President*

CRANSTON RESEARCH, INC.
6212-B Old Keene Hill Court, Springfield, VA 22152
(703) 866-0077
Carolyn F. Brown, *President*
American Astronautical Society

CREATIVE SYSTEMS, INC.
402 Maple Ave., W., Suite C, Vienna, VA 22180
(703) 281-1044
Nancy L. Stephens, *President*
National Association of Women Government Contractors

CROW-SEGAL MANAGEMENT COMPANY
1133 W. Morse Blvd., Suite 201, Winter Park, FL 32789
(305) 647-8839
Pat Crow-Segal, *President*

RICHARD S. CROY & COMPANY
14701 Detroit Ave., Cleveland, OH 44107
(216) 228-2166
Richard S. Crow, *President*
International Oxygen Manufacturers Association

BEN DAVIS ASSOCIATES
5420 Charter Oak Place, P.O. Box 12314, Jackson, MS 39236-2314
(601) 956-7787
Ben A. Davis, CAE, *President*

DAVIS/REPLOGLE & ASSOCIATES
5820 Wilshire Blvd., Suite 500, Los Angeles, CA 90036
(213) 937-5514
Jean Replogle, *President*
Association Management Education Foundation
Institute of Association Management Companies
International Association for Personnel Women

GEORGE K. DEGNON ASSOCIATES
1311-A Dolly Madison Blvd., #3-A, McLean, VA 22101
(703) 556-9222
George K. Degnon, *President*
- Ambulatory Pediatric Association
- American Psychosomatic Society
- Association of Behavioral Science and Medical Education
- Association of State and Territorial Health Officials
- Society for Health and Human Values
- Women in Government Relations

DEMPSEY MANAGEMENT SERVICES
3700 Market St., Suite 6-A, Clarkstown, GA 30021
(404) 297-9200
Frederick G. Dempsey, Jr., CAE, *President*

DICKSON-FELIX
1441 Que St., N.W., Washington, DC 20009
(202) 382-1540
Carol Felix, *Vice President*
- National Motorcycle Retailers Association

DIRECT CONNECTION INC.
1441 Shermer Road, #100, Northbrook, IL 60062
(312) 498-5550
Sue Wells, *President*
- Wild Bird Feeding Institute

H. P. DOLAN & ASSOCIATES
800 Custer Ave., Evanston, IL 60202
(312) 864-8444
Thomas D. Dolan, *President*
- Caster and Floor Truck Manufacturers Association
- Machine Knife Manufacturers Association
- Magnetic Materials Producers Association
- Mechanical Power Transmission Association

DOLCI MANAGEMENT SERVICES, INC.
322 Eighth Ave., 12th Floor, New York, NY 10001
(212) 206-8301
Joel A. Dolci, *President*
- National Options and Futures Society
- National Society of Fund Raising Executives

DOVE ASSOCIATES
531 Tobacco Quay, Alexandria, VA 22314
(703) 683-1260
Susan H. Dove, *President*
- Association of the Wall and Ceiling Industries - International
- Exterior Insulation Manufacturers Association
- Foundation of the Wall and Ceiling Industry

DROHAN MANAGEMENT GROUP
1600 Wilson Blvd., Suite 905, Arlington, VA 22209
(703) 821-2243
William M. Drohan, CAE, *President*
- Institute of Continuing Regulatory Education
- National Association of State Credit Union Supervisors
- National Association of State Savings and Loan Supervisors
- National Institute for State Credit Union Examination

ROGER L. DUERKSEN AND ASSOCIATES
P.O. Box 160587, Sacramento, CA 95816
(916) 626-7255
Roger L. Duerksen, *President*

DULLE AND COMPANY, INC.
1221 Locust St., #405, St. Louis, MO 63103
(314) 231-5582
Oliver A. Dulle, Jr., *President*
- Art Glass Suppliers Association
- Steel Bar Mills Association

EASTER ASSOCIATES
620 Stagecoach Road, Charlottesville, VA 22901
(804) 977-3716
Peter Easter, *President*

ELCOLE MANAGEMENT
2378 S. Broadway, Denver, CO 80210
(303) 698-1820
Elsa Kaiser, *President*
- Association of Audio-Visual Technicians
- National Association of Entrepreneurs
- Society of Photo-Technologists

B. J. ELLIS ASSOCIATES, INC.
93 Standish Road, Hillsdale, NJ 07642
(201) 664-4600
Bernard J. Ellis, *President*
- Association of International Photography Art Dealers
- Institutional and Service Textile Distributors Association

BARRY R. EPSTEIN ASSOCIATES, INC.
35 Eastmont Road, Hollywood, FL 33021
(305) 961-0000
Barry R. Epstein, APR, CCE, CID, *President*

J. EDGAR EUBANKS AND ASSOCIATES
3008 Millwood Ave., P.O. Box 11187, Columbia, SC 29205
(803) 252-5646
J. Edgar Eubanks, *President*
- American Fastener and Closure Association
- Automotive Lift Institute
- Diamond Core Drill Manufacturers Asksociation
- Flying Scot Sailing Association
- Industrial Diamond Association of America
- International Sunfish Class Association
- National Association of Bankruptcy Trustees
- National Association of Decorative Fabric Distributors
- National Drilling Contractors Association
- National Drilling Federation

EXECUTIVES CONSULTANTS INC.
13542 Union Village Circle, Clifton, VA 22204
(703) 830-5369
Robert C. LaGasse, *President*

EXECUTIVE DIRECTOR, INC.
611 East Wells St., Milwaukee, WI 53202
(414) 276-6445
Donald L. McNeil, *President*
- American Academy of Allergy and Immunology
- National Christmas Tree Association

EXECUTIVE MANAGEMENT ASSOCIATES
4454 Van Nuys Blvd., Suite 215, Box 5835
Sherman Oaks, CA 91403
(818) 986-8066
Jill McDonald, *President*

EXECUTIVE MANAGEMENT SERVICES, INC.
1940 Buford Blvd., Tallahassee, FL 32308
(904) 878-3134
Robert S. Rhinehart, *President*

EXECUTIVE SERVICES
800 St. Mary's St., Suite 203, Raleigh, NC 27605
(919) 821-2226
Annette S. Boutwell, *Owner*

DAVE FELLERS ASSOCIATES
5430 Neosho Lane, Shawnee Mission, KS 66205
(913) 362-5919
Dave Fellers, CAE, *President*

FERNLEY AND FERNLEY, INC.
1900 Arch St., Philadelphia, PA 19103
(215) 564-3484
Thomas A. Fernley, III, *President*
- American Brush Manufacturers Association
- American Jewelry Marketing Association
- Aviation Distributors and Manufacturers Association
- Bicycle Wholesale Distributors Association

Distribution Codes Institute
Fluid Power Distributors Association
Mass Marketing Insurance Institute
National Association of Aluminum Distributors
National Association of Container Distributors
National Association of Hose and Accessories Distributors
National Association of Marine Services
National Coil Coasters Association
National Commercial Refrigeration Sales Association
National Industrial Belting Association
National Industrial Distributors Association
National Lawn and Garden Distributors Association
National Locksmith Suppliers Association
National Welding Supply Association
National Wholesale Hardware Association
Outdoor Power Equipment and Distributors Association
Resistance Welders Manufacturers Association
Wood Machinery Manufacturers of America

J. D. FERRY ASSOCIATES
P.O. Box 849, Stevensville, MD 21666
(301) 643-4161
John D. Ferry, *Owner*
American Wood-Preservers' Association
Fourdrinier Wire Council
Wire Rope Technical Board

FITZGERALD MANAGEMENT CORP.
655 Irving Park Road, Suite 201, Park Place, Chicago, IL 60613
(312) 525-2644
June G. Fitzgerald, *President*
Door Operator and Remote Control Manufacturers Association
Garage Door Council
National Association of Garage Door Manufacturers
Screen Manufacturers Association

MARTIN FROMM & ASSOCIATES
9140 Ward Parkway, Kansas City, MO 64114
(816) 444-3500
Martin Fromm, *Chairman of the Board*
Association of Diesel Specialties
Automotive Warehouse Distributors Association
Diamond Council of America
International Association of Piano Builders and Technicians
Paint, Body and Equipment Association
Piano Technicians Guild
Professional Audio-Visual Retailers Association
State Defense Force Association of the U.S.

Washington Office:
1233 20th St., N.W., Suite 700
Washington, DC 20036
(202) 457-0393

P. R. GAGLE AND ASSOCIATES, INC.
420 West Roosevelt, Phoenix, AZ 85003
(602) 265-1699
Phillip R. Gagle, *President*

G GROUP MANAGEMENT FOR ASSOCIATIONS
16 California St., Suite 205, San Francisco, CA 94111
(415) 541-0244
George LaBar, *President*

GHORBANI ENTERPRISES, INC.
10506 Cavalcade St., Great Falls, VA 22066
(703) 759-2627
Danny Ghorbani, *President*

ED GLASSGOW & ASSOCIATES
P.O. Box 1580, 3927 West Omaha, Rapid City, SD 57709
(605) 343-6917
Ed Glassgow, CAE, *President*

G.M.O., INC.
Association Bldg., 9th & Minnesota, Hastings, NE 68901
(402) 463-5691
Don Ellerbee, *President*
American Embryo Transfer Association
Society for Theriogenology

GORMAN MANAGEMENT, INC.
1511 K St., N.W., Suite 508, Washington, DC 20005
R. Mickey Gorman, CAE, *President*
Beverage Machinery Manufacturers Association

GRAY & ASSOCIATES, INC.
692 Ritchie Highway, Suite F, Severna Park, MD 21146
(301) 647-7880
Carroll Gray, *President*

GROUP CONCEPTS, INC.
7300 Artesia Blvd., Buena Park, CA 90621
(714) 521-6000
Kelly Ramirez, *President*
Mobile Industrial Caterers Association International

G & T MANAGEMENT, INC.
211 E. 43rd St., Suite 301, New York, NY 10017
(212) 867-4480
Margaret Glos, CAE, *President*
American Society for Histocompatability and Immunogenetics
Institute of Store Planners
Joint Council of Mental Health Services
Women in Production

THE GUILD ASSOCIATES
715 Boylston St., Boston, MA 02116
(617) 266-6800
Richard S. Guild, *President*
American Boat Builders and Repairers Association
Art and Craft Materials Institute
Shoe Pattern Manufacturers Association
Wet Ground Mica Association

HAB ASSOCIATES, INC.
645 N. Michigan Ave., Chicago, IL 60611
(312) 951-0106
Betty Burns, *President*

P.M. HAEGER AND ASSOCIATES, INC.
500 N. Michigan Ave., Suite 1400, Chicago, IL 60611
(312) 661-1700
Phyllis M. Haeger, *President*
American Association of Diabetes Educators
American Woman's Society of Certified Public Accountants
Committee of 200
International Association of Auditorium Managers
National Association of Bank Women

HAGEN ASSOCIATION MANAGEMENT SERVICES
6845 Lake Shore Drive, P.O. Box 9379, Raytown, MO 64133
(816) 358-3317
Bruce R. Hagen, *President*
American Urological Association Allied

HARRY HANSEN MANAGEMENT, INC.
419 Park Ave., South, 3rd Floor, New York, NY 10016
(212) 213-2411
Harry A. Hansen, *President*
Space Commerce Roundtable Foundations

HARPER ADMINISTRATIVE SERVICES
1040 Woodcock Road, Orlando, FL 32802
(305) 894-8312
James Rapp, *President*
National Society of Sales Training Executives

HARRIS MANAGEMENT GROUP
1801 N. Meridian Road, Tallahassee, FL 32303
(904) 386-6000
Robert C. Harris, *President*

HAUCK AND ASSOCIATES, INC
1255 23rd St., N.W., Washington, DC 20037
(202) 452-1800
Sheldon J. Hauck, *President*
American Coke and Coal Chemicals Institute
American Family Therapy Association
Electromagnetic Energy Policy Alliance
Hearing Industries Association
Intellectual Property Owners
Military Reform Institute
National Association for Child Care Management
National Association of Cold Storage Contractors
National Association of Video Distributors
National Soybean Processors Association
National Technical Services Association
Soy Protein Council

HAWKINS & ASSOCIATES
804 D St., N.E., Washington, DC 20002
(202) 547-6696
Donald E. Hawkins, *President*
Association of Travel Marketing Executives
National Campground Owners Association

MARGARET HERBST
310 Madison Ave., New York, NY 10017
(212) 986-1160
Margaret Herbst, *President*

HESSER AND ASSOCIATES, INC.
4510 W. 89th St., Prairie Village, KS 66207
(913) 341-1155
J. M. Hesser, *President*
International Wheat Gluten Association
Wheat Gluten Industry Council

THE HILL GROUP
1615 L St., N.W., Suite 925, Washington, DC 20036
(202) 296-9200
Sanford J. Hill, *President*
Academy of Psychosomatic Medicine
American Orthopaedic Soc. for Sports Medicine
American Pain Society
Arthroscopy Association of North America
Ceramic Tile Marketing Federation
International Arthroscopy Association
International Society of the Knee
Issues Management Association
Medical-Dental-Hospital Services Bureaus of America
National Association of Chemical Distributors
National Association of NIDSPORT Users
Work Glove Manufacturers Association

Chicago Office:
70 West Hubbard St., Suite 202
Chicago, IL 60610
(312) 644-2623

THE HOFFMAN ORGANIZATION
706 East Third St., Flint, MI 48503
(313) 233-3627
Steven D. Hoffman, *President*
International Porcelain Art Teachers Association

HOST COMMUNICATIONS
546 East Main, Lexington, KY 40508
(606) 253-3230
W. James Host, *President*
National Tour Association

STANLEY G. HOUSE & ASSOCIATES
6001 Montrose Road, Rockville, MD 20852
(301) 984-7045
Stanley G. House, *Chairman*

HUMES & ASSOCIATES
600 S. Federal St., #400, Chicago, IL 60605
(312) 346-1600
August Sisco, *President*
Decorative Laminate Products Association
Institute of Certified Professional Business Consultants
Metal Lath/Steel Framing Association
National Appliance Parts Suppliers Association
National Association of Architectural Metal Manufacturers
National Association of Women Business Owners
National Roof Deck Contractors Association
National Trust Aid Systems Association
Portable Drilling Rig Manufacturers Association
Practice Management Information Center
Pressure Vessel Manufacturers Association
Society of American Value Engineers
Society of Professional Business Consultants
Submersible Wastewater Pump Association
USA Rugby Football Union
Water Systems Council

HUNT MANAGEMENT SYSTEMS
2033 M St., N.W., Suite 605, Washington, DC 20036
(202) 223-6413
Frederick D. Hunt, Jr., *President*
Society of Professional Benefit Administrators

THE HUNTE GROUP
436 Great Road, Acton, MA 01720
(617) 263-5144
Ronald B. Hunte, *President*

ALBERT E. HYDE & ASSOCIATES
P.O. Box 924555, Houston, TX 77292-4555
(713) 682-2877
Albert E. Hyde, *President*

INDUSTRY SERVICES CORPORATION
5100 Forbes Blvd., Lanham, MD 20706
(301) 459-5927
Lawrence S. Hecker
Automotive Products Export Council
Automotive Refrigeration Products Institute
500 Automotive Executives Club
Jesselson Benevolent Fund
National Aerosol Association
Organization of Manufacturers Representatives
Vehicle Security Association

INFORM, INC.
P.O. Box 1708, Hickory, NC 28603
(704) 322-7766
Paul F. Fogleman, *President*

INTEGRATED OPTIONS, INC.
P.O. Box 10140, Alexandria, VA 22310
(703) 971-3813
Linda S. Hartsock, CAE, *President*

INTERACTIVE MANAGEMENT
2150 W. 29th Ave., Suite 310, Denver, CO 80211
(303) 433-4446
Roberta Bourn, *President*

INTERFACE MANAGEMENT ASSOCIATES
8609 Cross Park Drive, Austin, TX 78754
(512) 339-8566
Kay L. Knapp, *President*
International Fence Industry Association

INTERNATIONAL MANAGEMENT GROUP, INC.
1133 15th St., N.W., Suite 1000, Washington, DC 20005
(202) 293-5910
Joan Walsh Cassedy, *Chairman*
Charles E. Perry, *Vice Chairman*
Brian R. Cassedy, *President*

American Association of Psychiatric Services for Children
American Cutlery Manufacturers Association
American Society of Electroplated Plastics
Asphalt Emulsion Manufacturers Association
Association for Unmanned Vehicle Systems
Association for Women in Computing
Association of Political Risk Analysts
Automotive Dismantlers Association of America
Bumper Recycling Association of North America
Commercial Development Association
International Association of Energy Economists
International Society of Transportation Aircraft Traders
Metal Construction Association
National Association of Credit Union Presidents
National Association of Public Insurance Adjusters
National Computer Services Network
National Society of Cardiopulmonary Technicians
National Society of Professional Resident Managers
Pre-Arrangement Interment Association of America
Society of Toxicology
Society of Vacuum Coaters
Transportation Research Forum
Women in Employee Benefits

JACKSON JACKSON & ASSOCIATES
10700 Richmond, Suite 201, Houston, TX 77042
(713) 780-9850
Robert M. Eaton, *Principal*

JAFIC ASSOCIATION MANAGEMENT, INC.
2469 Aloma Ave., Suite 214C, Winter Park, FL 32792
(305) 671-2612
Janice Ficarrotto, *President*

ANTHONY J. JANNETTI, INC.
North Woodbury Park, Box 56, Pitman, NJ 08071
(609) 589-2319
Anthony J. Jannetti, *President*
American Academy of Ambulatory Nursing Administration
American Nephrology Nurses' Association
American Society of Plastic and Reconstructive Surgical Nurses
Dermatology Nurses' Association
National Association of Orthopaedic Nurses
National Student Nurses' Association

JEBINC MANAGEMENT SERVICES
501 W. Algonquin Road, Arlington Heights, IL 60005-4411
(312) 577-8350
James E. Bates, *President*
Automotive Booster Clubs International
National Association of College Automotive Teachers
National Association of Professional Fund Raisers
Power Tool Institute

KAUTTER MANAGEMENT GROUP
P.O. Box 2156, Altamonte Springs, FL 32715-2156
(305) 774-7880
Willard S. Kautter, CAE, *President*
BLIS/COBOL Users Group
National Association of Physician Recruiters

THE ROBERT H. KELLEN COMPANY
5775 Peachtree-Dunwoody Road, Suite 500-D, Atlanta, GA 30342
(404) 252-3663
Robert H. Kellen, *President*
Association for Dressings and Sauces
Calorie Control Council
Concord Grape Association
Enteral Nutrition Council
Glutamate Association - United States
Health Care Exhibitors Association
Infant Formula Council
International Food and Additives Council
International Jelly and Preserve Association
National Pecan Shellers Association
National Single Service Food Association
Processed Apples Institute
Vinegar Institute

KIELTY REBEDEAU & ASSOCIATES
501 W. Algonquin Road, Arlington Heights, IL 60005-4411
(312) 593-8360
Francis C. Rebedeau, *President*
Communications Marketing Association
National Sound and Communications Association
National Wine Distributors Association
Newspaper Advertising Cooperative Network

KINDER AND ASSOCIATES, INC.
1700 East Dyer Road, Suite 165, Santa Ana, CA 92705
(714) 261-2591
James A. Kinder, *President*
National Association of Name Plate Manufacturers
National Institute of Pension Administrators
Self Insurance Institute of America

GENE P. KING & ASSOCIATES, INC.
1024 Dublin Road, Columbus, OH 43215
(614) 488-0617
Gene P. King, *President*

KLEIN & SAKS, INC.
1026 16th St., N.W., Suite 101, Washington, DC 20036
(202) 783-0500
John H. Lutley, *President*
Gold Institute
Silver Institute

KRISSOFF & ASSOCIATES, INC.
#3 Church Circle, Suite 250, Annapolis, MD 21401
(301) 267-0023
Michael R. Krissoff, *President*
Asphalt Recycling and Reclaiming Association

LINKS ASSOCIATION MANAGEMENT SERVICE
15 E. 40th St., Room 904-5, New York, NY 10016
(212) 532-5733
Mae E. Link, *President*

LLOYD & ASSOCIATES, INC.
152 Rollings Ave., Suite 208, Rockville, MD 20852
(301) 984-9080
Raymond J. Lloyd, *President*
American Chain Association
Conveyor Equipment Manufacturers Association
Scale Manufacturers Association

LOVELESS MANAGEMENT & LEGISLATIVE SERVICES, INC.
4161 Carmichael Ave., Suite 136, P.O. Box 43668
Jacksonville, FL 32202-3668
(904) 396-6941
Gary W. Loveless, CAE, *President*

MACO ASSOCIATED
2045 N. 15th St., Suite 1000, Arlington, VA 22201
(703) 528-0072
Dr. John F. Magnotti, *President*
American Surety Association
National Association of Small Government Contractors
National Candle Association
Procurement Round Table

MAMCO, INC.
21510 S. Main St., Carson, CA 90745
(213) 549-3470
Frank De Santis, *President*
American Association of Clinical Urologists

MANAGEMENT DIRECTIONS, INC.
766 Transfer Road, St. Paul, MN 55114
(612) 646-2121
Steven Pettersen, *Vice President*

MANAGEMENT EXCELLENCE, INC.
11 W. Monument Ave., Suite 510, Box 2307, Dayton, OH 45401
(513) 223-8008
F. W. Rickenbach, *President*
Titanium Development Association

MANAGEMENT SERVICES
P.O. Box 579, Moorestown, NJ 08057
(609) 234-0330
Dennis C. Neff, *President*
Professional Aeromedical Transport Association
Wise Foods Distributors Association

MANAGEMENT SERVICES FOR ASSOCIATIONS
106 "K" St., Suite 340, Sacramento, CA 95814
(916) 443-5090
Neil H. Ferstand, *President*

MANAGEMENT SPECIALTIES, INC.
1357 Washington St., No. 5, West Newton, MA 02165
(617) 964-4992
Cynthia Wilson, *President*
National Investment Company Service Association

MANAGEMENT SYSTEMS ASSOCIATES
729 Fischer Blvd., Toms River, NJ 08753
(201) 929-1667
Michael L. Redpath, *President*

MANAGEMENT 2
4720 Park Glen Road, Minneapolis, MN 55416
(612) 927-9220
Ed A. Harrington, CAE, *President*

MARKETING/ASSOCIATION SERVICES
1516 S. Pontius Ave., Los Angeles, CA 90025
(213) 478-0215
Randy Bauler, CAE, *Vice President - Association Operations*
Exposition Service Contractors Association
National Staff Leasing Association
Western Association of Equipment Lessors

THE MARTINEAU CORP.
4948 St. Elmo Ave., Suite 306, Bethesda, MDs 20814
(301) 652-8666
Jill M. Cornish, *President*

MAS MANAGEMENT
P.O. Box 2488, Pensacola, FL 32513
(904) 477-7843
JoAnne Krueger, *President*

MATTERSON ASSOCIATES, INC.
427 Kenwood Ave., Delmar, NY 12054
(518) 439-0981
Curtiss B. Matterson, CAE, *President*

MAXWELL MANAGEMENT ENTERPRISES
5600 Broodwood Terrace, Nashville, TN 37205
(615) 356-4240
Joe Maxwell, *President*

McCOLLUM MANAGEMENT & MEETINGS
P.O. Box 10523, Tallahassee, FL 32302
(904) 222-7924
Peggy K. McCollum, CAE, *President*

MEREDITH AND HENRY
1600 Route 2, Union, NJ 07083
(201) 687-3090
Howard C. Henry, *Partner*
George Meredith, *Partner*
Association of Retail Marketing Services
National Premium Sales Executives

Other Office:
3 Caro Court
Red Bank, NJ 07701
(201) 842-5070

THE MESSERSMITH GROUP
1730 "I" St., Suite 240, Sacramento, CA 95814
(916) 443-9023
Dr. Lloyd E. Messersmith, *President*

MILLER MANAGEMENT SERVICE
205 North 10th St., Suites 421-423, Boise, ID 83702
(208) 344-0781
Wendy Miller, *Owner*

MINETTA A. MILLER MULTIPLE MANAGEMENT
909 17th St., Suite 418, Denver, CO 80202
(303) 298-1700
Minetta A. Miller, *Owner*

MULTISERVICE MANAGEMENT
2017 Walnut St., Philadelphia, PA 19103
(215) 569-3650
John A. Shiffert, *President*
Aircraft Locknut Manufacturers Association
Fluid Sealing Association
Gasket Fabricators Association
International Association of Lighting Maintenance Contractors
National Association of Diaper Services
Professional Apparel Association

MURPHY AND MURPHY, INC.
43 East Ohio St., Chicago, IL 60611
(312) 645-0083
Ellis Murphy, *President*

RICHARD NEWMAN ASSOCIATES
P.O. Box 758, Champaign, IL 61820
(217) 352-1968
Richard J. Newman, *President*
International Association of Convention and Visitor Bureaus

NIKE ASSOCIATION MANAGEMENT, INC.
560 W. Washington St., Suite 301, Chicago, IL 60606
(312) 332-4146
Pamela W. Franzen, *President*
Sump and Sewage Pump Manufacturers Association

NORDIC MANAGEMENT, INC.
7867 Convoy Court, Suite 301, San Diego, CA 92111
(619) 569-7906
Edward W. Johnson, CAE, *President*
Sealant Engineering and Associated Lines

NPMC, INC.
3025 S. Parker Road, Suite 65, Aurora, CO 80014
(303) 755-4585
Gail M. Gorman, *President*
American Society for Surgery of the Hand

O'DONNELL ASSOCIATES
364 Parsippany Road, Parsippany, NJ 07054
(201) 887-s4889
Jeanne O'Donnell, *Executive Officer*
Association of Outplacement Consulting Firms

OFFICE ENTERPRISES
2353 North Rice St., Roseville, MN 55113
(612) 484-3315
Dave Locey, *President*

OFFINGER MANAGEMENT COMPANY
1100-H Brandywine Blvd., P.O. Box 2188, Zanesville, OH 43701
(614) 452-4541
Walter E. Offinger, *President*

American Association of Ceramic Industries
Association of Crafts and Creative Industries
Gift Retailers, Manufacturers and Representatives Association
Southwestern Craft and Hobby Association

OLSON MANAGEMENT GROUP
1100 Raleigh Bldg., Raleigh, NC 27601
(919) 821-1435
Michael S. Olson, CAE, *President*
American Society of Echocardiography
Employment Management Association
Multi-Housing Laundry Association
National Alliance of Cardiovascular Technologists
Society of Financial Examiners

ORECK ASSOCIATION MANAGEMENT
2410 Beverly Blvd., #1, Los Angeles, CA 90057
(213) 387-7432
Ruth Oreck, *President & C.E.O.*

ORGANIZATION MANAGEMENT, INC.
1121 L St., Suite 500, Sacrament, CA 95814
(916) 447-4113
Donald C. Burns, CAE, *President*

ORGANIZATION MANAGEMENT, INC.
660 Adams Ave., #254, Montgomery, AL 36104
(205) 263-3407
R. J. Cunningham, CAE, *President*

ORGANIZATION MANAGEMENT SERVICES OF WEST VIRGINIA
P.O. Box 1335, Charleston, WV 25325
(304) 342-4441
Floyd M. Sayre, Jr., CAE, *President*

ORGANIZATION MANAGEMENT SYSTEMS, INC.
60 Revere Drive, Suite 500, Northbrook, IL 60662
(312) 480-9080
John E. Messervey, *President*
Commercial Food Equipment Service Association
Institute of Nuclear Materials Management
Maple Flooring Manufacturers Association
National Association of Service Managers
National Family Business Council
Roof Coating Manufacturers Association

ORGANIZATION SERVICES, INC.
1405 Lilac Drive, Minneapolis, MN 55422
(612) 544-7256
William T. Harper, Sr., *President*

GEORGE M. OTTO ASSOCIATES, INC.
230 N. Michigan Ave., Suite 1200, Chicago, IL 60601
(312) 372-9800
George M. Otto, *President*

PACE, WEIL & ASSOCIATES INTERNATIONAL INC.
1606 17th St., N.W., Washington, DC 20009
(202) 232-0077
Alan M. Weil, *President*
Society of Government Meeting Planners

PAMI-PROFESSIONAL ASSOCIATION MANAGEMENT, INC.
Old National Bank Block, 247 Commercial St., N.E., Salem, OR 97301
(503) 399-8456
John V. Honey, Jr., *President*

PAYNE, MURCH AND ASSOCIATES
2011 Eye St., N.W., 5th Floor, Washington, DC 20006
(202) 223-3217
Roger A. Murch, *President*
American Car Rental Association
Conference of American Renting and Leasing Associations
National Beverage Dispensing Equipment Association
National Corrugated Steel Pipe Association
Truck Renting and Leasing Association

THE PEARSON GROUP
1317 King St., Alexandria, VA 22314
(703) 683-6334
Marion "Sandy" Pearson, *President*

PELICAN MANAGEMENT CORP.
10985 N. Harrell's Ferry, Road, Suite E, Baton Rouge, LA 70816
(504) 275-1791
Robert Mathews, *President*

PENN MICHAEL MANAGEMENT
4010 S. 57th Ave., Suite 202, Lake Worth, FL 33463
Michael R. Cloney, *President*
American Seat Belt Council
Home Fashion Products Association
Mailing List Users and Suppliers Association
Test Boring Association
Ultrasonic Industry Association
Web Sling Association

PRAGMA, INC.
P.O. Box 491, Jackson, CA 95642
(209) 223-1299
Ray B. Hunter, *President*

PRICE MANAGEMENT CORP.
815 Quarrier St., Suite 415, Charleston, WV 25301
(304) 345-4710
Roger K. Price, *President*

DANIEL B. PRIEST ASSOCIATES, INC.
1000 Connecticut Ave., N.W., Suite 707, Washington, DC 20036
(202) 463-3655
Daniel B. Priest, *President*

R. E. PRITCHARD & ASSOCIATES
7380 N. Lincoln Ave., Lincolnwood, IL 60646
(312) 677-2850
Raymond E. Pritchard, *President*
IPC (Institute for Interconnecting and Packaging Electronic Circuits)
Variable Resistive Components Institute

PROFESSIONAL ASSOCIATION MANAGEMENT
2786 N. Decatur Road, Suite 200, Decatur, GA 30033
(404) 292-6392
Sharon A. Hunt, *President*

PROFESSIONAL MANAGEMENT ASSOCIATES
P.O. Box 725, Belle Mead, NJ 08502
(201) 359-1184
Joanne Jeanguenin Cole, CAE, CMP, *President*

PROFESSIONAL RELATIONS AND RESEARCH INSTITUTE, INC.
P.O. Box 1565, 13 Elm St., Manchester, MA 01944
(617) 927-8330
William T. Maloney, *President*
American Association for Thoracic Surgery
American College of Gastroenterology
American Society for Gastrointestinal Endoscopy
International Society for Cardiovascular Surgery - North American Chapter
Society for Clinical Vascular Surgery
Society for Vascular Surgery
Society of Head and Neck Surgeons
Society of Surgical Oncology

P & S MANAGEMENT CO., INC.
P.O. Box 14350, Phoenix, AZ 85063
(602) 269-1406
Paul Hildebrand, *President*
Aspencade Motorcyclists Conventions
Gold Wing Road Riders Association
Women on Wheels Association

PUBLIC OFFICE SERVICES
204A East High St., Jefferson City, MO 65101
(314) 636-7521
Patricia S. Riner Amick, *President*

PUBLISHER SERVICES, INC.
80 South Early St., Alexandria, VA 22304
(703) 823-6966
Jack Cameron, *President*
National Association of Government Communicators

ROBERT W. REILLY, INC.
P.O. Box 3346, Annapolis, MD 21403
(301) 268-2011
Robert W. Reilly, *President*
American Blood Resources Association

ROGERS ENTERPRISES
13577 Grain Lane, San Diego, CA 92129
(619) 484-1681
Frederick J. Rogers, *President*

RUGGLES SERVICE CORP.
2315 Westwood Ave., P.O. Box 11083, Richmond, VA 23230
(804) 353-9259
John A. Hinckley, *President*
American Academy for Cerebral Palsy and Development Medicine
American Society of Post-Anesthesia Nurses
American Society of Regional Anesthesia
Society for Education in Anesthesia
Society of Cardiovascular Anesthesiologists
Society of Neurosurgical Anesthesia and Neurological Supportive Care
Uniformed Services Academy of Family Physicians

SALEEBY & ASSOCIATES, INC.
14039 Sherman Way, Van Nuys, CA 91405
(818) 782-2012
D. Victor Saleeby, *Executive Vice President*
Scaffold Industry Association

THE SANFORD ORGANIZATION, INC.
4300-L Lincoln Ave., Rolling Meadows, IL 60008
(312) 359-8160
Donn W. Sanford, *President*
Aluminum Extruders Council
National Equipment Distributors Association

PAUL SAUNDERS & ASSOCIATES
2175 Highway 35, Sea Girt, NJ 08750
(201) 974-1900
Paul Saunders, *President*
Electrical-Electronics Materials Distributors Association
National Association of Lighting Representatives

SDI MANAGEMENT COMPANY
2500 Wilshire Blvd., Suite 603, Los Angeles, CA 90057
(213) 384-3179
Raymond P. Delrich, *President*
National Association of Catering Executives
National Flotation Health Care Foundation
Waterbed Manufacturers Association

SERVICES FOR ORGANIZATION RENEWAL
P.O. Box 2502, San Rafael, CA 94912
Don L. Organ, CAE, *President*
Institute of Political Campaign Consultants

LARRY SHANE COMMUNICATIONS
1729 Glastonberry Road, Potomac, MD 20854
(301) 424-1000
Larry I. Shane, *President*
American Academy of Podiatric Sports Medicine

THE JOSEPH SHANER COMPANY
113 W. Franklin St., Baltimore, MD 21201
(301) 752-3320
Thomas C. Shaner, CAE, APR, *President*
American Institute of Floral Designers
Jewelry Industry Distributors Association
Kite Trade Association International
National Association of Nurse Attorneys
National Conference of Women's Bar Associations

SIEGEL-HOUSTON AND ASSOCIATES, INC.
1707 L St., N.W., Washington, DC 20036
(202) 296-9282
Martin Siegel, *President*
Betsy Houston, *Executive Vice President*
American Institute of Chemical Engineers
Federation of Materials Societies

SIMONELLI & ASSOCIATES
1011 St. Andrews Drive, Suite I, El Dorado Hills, CA 95630
(916) 933-3060
Frederick J. Simonelli, *President*
AirLifeLine

CHARLES B. SLACK, INC.
6900 Grove Road, Thorofare, NJ 08066
(609) 848-1000
Peter Slack, *President*
American Association for the Study of Liver Diseases
American Federation for Clinical Research
American Gastroenterological Association
American Society for Clinical Investigation
American Society for Colposcopy and Cervical Pathology
American Society of Hematology
American Society of Nephrology

SMITH, BUCKLIN & ASSOCIATES
111 E. Wacker Drive, Suite 600, Chicago, IL 60601
(312) 644-6610
William E. Smith, *Chairman*

1101 Connecticut Ave., N.W., Suite 700, Washington, DC 20036
(202) 857-1100

5000 Van Nuys Blvd., Suite 400, Sherman Oaks, CA 91403
(818) 995-7338

Adhesive Manufacturers Association
Agricultural Publishers Association
Alliance for Engineering in Medicine and Biology
American Association for Continuity of Care
American Association for Hospital Planning
American Association for Medical Systems and Informatics
American College of Nuclear Physicians
American Formalwear Association
American Hot Dip Galvanizers Association
American Ladder Institute
American Luggage Dealers Association
American Society of Allied Health Professions
American Wire Producers Association
American Women in Radio Television
Amusement and Music Operators Association
Association for Advancement of Rehabilitative Technology
Association for Hospital Medical Education
Association of Local Housing Finance Agencies
Association of Steel Distributors
Automotive Affiliated Representatives
Bakery Equipment Manufacturers Association
Baking Industry Sanitation Standards Committee
Battery Council International
Biscuit and Cracker Distributors Association
Casting Industry Suppliers Association

Chain Link Fence Manufacturers Institute
Cleaning Equipment Manufacturers Association
Commercial Refrigerator Manufacturers Association
Cremation Association of North America
Engine Manufacturers Association
Financial Stationers Association
Food Equipment Manufacturers Association
GUIDE International Corporation
Health Industry Bar Code Council
Ice Industry Research Foundation
IDMS User Association
Independent Electrical Contractors Association
International Association of Airport Duty Free Stores
International Customer Services Association
International District Heating and Cooling Association
International Food Service Executives Association
International Institute of Ammonia Refrigeration
International Quick Printing Foundation
International Slurry Seal Association
International Tandem Users' Group Association
Marketing Agents for the Food Service Industry
Marketing Representatives International
Marketing Research Association
Metal Framing Manufacturers Association
National Association General Merchandise Representatives
National Association of Advertising Publishers
National Association of Corporate Treasurers
National Association of Fire Equipment Distributors
National Association of Food Equipment Manufacturers
National Association of Foreign Trade Zones
National Association of Futures Trading Advisors
National Association of Hospital Admitting Managers
National Association of Metal Finishers
National Association of Quick Printers
National Children's Eye Care Foundation
National Food Distributors Association
North American Riding for the Handicapped Association
North American Transplant Coordinators Organization
Packaged Ice Association
Pet Food Institute
Phi Beta Pi - Theta Kappa Psi (Medical Fraternity)
Popcorn Institute
Regional Airline Association
Regulatory Affairs Professionals Society
Rehabilitation Engineering Society of North America
Safety Equipment Distributors Association
Sealed Insulating Glass Manufacturers Association
SHARE
Society for Information Management
Society of Gynecologic Oncologists
Society of Non-Invasive Vascular Technology
Society of Thoracic Surgeons
Soyfoods Association of America
Suburban Newspapers of America
Training Media Distributors Association
Wallcovering Distributors Association
Western Publications Association
Wood Heating Alliance
Wood Truss Council of America

SMITH, JONES & ASSOCIATES

111 East Wacker Drive, Suite 600, Chicago, IL 60601
(312) 644-6610
Lafayette Jones, *President*

1101 Connecticut Ave., N.W., Washington, DC 20036
(202) 857-1100

American Health and Beauty Aids Institute
Black Entertainment and Sports Lawyers Association
National Association of Urban Bankers
National Black MBA Association
National Society of Black Engineers

WAYNE SMITH COMPANY

1275 K St., N.W., Suite 800, Washington, DC 20005
(202) 484-5623
Wayne J. Smith, *President*

United Bus Owners of America

SOCIETY AND ASSOCIATION SERVICES CORP.

1340 Old Chain Bridge Road, Suite 300, McLean, VA 22101
(703) 790-1745
Richard J. Burk, Jr., *President*

American Society for Neurochemistry
American Society for Photobiology
Environmental Mutagen Society
Health Physics Society
Society for Magnetic Resonance Imaging
Society for Risk Analysis

SOUTHERN ASSOCIATION SERVICES

1239 Second St., Box 801, Macon, GA 31202
(912) 743-8612
Joe W. Andrews, Jr., *President*

SPANGLE & ASSOCIATES, INC.

2120 N. Meridian St., Indianapolis, IN 46202
(317) 924-5106
Warren Spangle, *President*

SPECIALTY CONTRACTORS MANAGEMENT, INC.

P.O. Box 42558, Northwest Station, Washington, DC 20015-0458
(301) 933-7430
Walter M. Kardy, *President*

Instrument Contracting and Engineering Association
Quality Control Council of America

THE SPENCE GROUP

1776 Massachusetts Ave., N.W., Suite 521
Washington, DC 20036
(202) 659-0600
Sandra Spence, *President*

Association for Commuter Transportation

S & S MANAGEMENT SERVICES

One Regency Drive, Box 30, Bloomfield, CT 06002
(203) 243-3977
Arthur N. Schuman, *President*

DUKE NORDLINGER STERN & ASSOCIATES

1336 54th Ave., N.E., St. Petersburg, FL 33703
(800) 237-8903
Dr. Duke Nordlinger Stern, CAE, CSP, CMC, *President*

STYGAR-WILLIS ASSOCIATES, INC.

505 E. Hawley St., Mundelein, IL 60060
(312) 949-6050
Edward J. Stygar, Jr., *Principal*
Robert B. Willis, *Principal*

American Art Therapy Asksociation
American Pathology Foundation
Association for Practitioners in Infection Control
Biomedical Marketing Association
Nurses Organization of the Veterans Administration

TAC, INC.

606 N. Larchmont Blvd., #4-A, Los Angeles, CA 90004
(213) 467-1158
Mrs. Rickey Gamore, *President*

THOMAS ASSOCIATES, INC.

1230 Keith Building, Cleveland, OH 44115-2180
(215) 241-7333
Charles M. Stockinger, *President*

American Supply and Machinery Manufacturers' Association
Building Systems Institute
Chemical Fabrics and Film Association
Coated Abrasives Manufacturers' Institute
Compressed Air and Gas Institute
Cutting Tool Manufacturers of America
Fire Equipment Manufacturers' Association
Hack and Band Saw Manufacturers Association of America
Heat Exchange Institute
Metal Building Manufacturers Association
Metal Cutting Tool Institute
Scaffolding, Shoring and Forming Institute
Steel Window Institute
Tantalum Producers Association
United States Marine Products Manufacturers' Association

TLC-THE LEGISLATIVE CENTER
Gold Bond Building, 677 Ala Moana Blvd., Suite 815
Honolulu, HI 96813-5416
(808) 537-4308

TRADE ASSOCIATION MANAGEMENT
3009 Rainbow Drive, #123, Decatur, GA 30034
(404) 241-4095
Ski Bashinski, *President*

TRADE ASSOCIATION MANAGEMENT, INC.
25 North Broadway, Tarrytown, NY 10591
(914) 332-0040
Richard C. Byrne, *President*
Air Cooled Heat Exchanger Manufacturers Association
American Institute of Nail and Tack Manufacturers
Die Set Manufacturers Service Bureau
Dry Process Ceramic and Steatite Manufacturers Association
Expansion Joint Manufacturers Association
Forged Eyebolt Manufacturers Association
Hand Tools Institute
Transmission Products Association
Tubular Exchanger Manufacturers Association
Tubular Rivet and Machine Institute

TRADE GROUP ASSOCIATES
60 East 42nd St., Suite 511, New York, NY 10165
(212) 682-8142
J. Dudley Waldner, *President*
Builders Hardware Manufacturers Association
Comics Magazine Association of America

VICKERMAN & COMPANY, INC.
1726 M St., N.W., Suite 1002, Washington, DC 20036
(202) 457-0909
John C. Vickerman, *President*
Business Records Manufacturers Association
Foundation for International Meetings

WALLACE & EDWARDS
1150 Connecticut Ave., N.W., Suite 507, Washington, DC 20036
(202) 331-4331
Donald L. Wallace, Jr., *President*
Cotton Warehouse Association of America

S. L. WALLACE & ASSOCIATES
8914 Rohan Court, Indianapolis, IN 46278
(317) 293-3833
Sonya L. Wallace, *President*

WALTON & ASSOCIATES
825 East 64th St., Indianapolis, IN 46220
(317) 251-1214
James E. Tilford, *President*
Architectural Precast Association
National Precast Concrete Association
Poured Concrete Wall Contractors Association

DANIEL M. WELDON ASSOCIATES
921 11th St., Suite 902, Sacramento, CA 95814
(916) 446-8110
Daniel M. Weldon, *President*

A. P. WHERRY & ASSOCIATES
712 Lakewood Center North, 14600 Detroit Ave.
Cleveland, OH 44107
(216) 226-7700
Allen P. Wherry, *President*
Abrasive Grain Association
Cemented Carbide Producers Association
Diamond Wheel Manufacturers Institute
Diesel Engine Manufacturers Association
Grinding Wheel Institute
Hydraulic Institute
Insulated Steel Door Systems Institute
Masonry and Concrete Saw Manufacturers Institute
Steel Door Institute

WHITCHURCH MANAGEMENT CORPORATION
380 West Palatine Road, Wheeling, IL 60090
(312) 520-3370
Charles G. Whitchurch, *President*
Association for Manufacturing Excellence
International Net Set
Spring Manufacturers Institute
Wirebound Box Manufacturers Association

WIDENER & ASSOCIATES
1847-C Peeler Road, Dunwoody, GA 30356
(404) 393-8625
Bruce Widener, *President*

W-L ASSOCIATES, LTD.
120 W. Church St., #4, Frederick, MD 81701
(301) 663-4252
William Wisecup, *President*
Bioelectromagnetics Society

WORLDWIDE MANAGEMENT COMPANY
P.O. Box 637, Libertyville, IL 60048
(312) 362-3201
Lincoln R. Samelson, *President*
Power Conversion Products Council International
Small Motor Manufacturers Association

BARRY W. ZANDER & ASSOCIATES
P.O. Box 1229, Metairie, LA 70004
(504) 838-7969
Barry W. Zander, *President*
National Association of Laboratory Suppliers

National Association

mailing list

Want to reach the Executives of 6250 National Trade and Professional Associations the easy way?

Here's how:

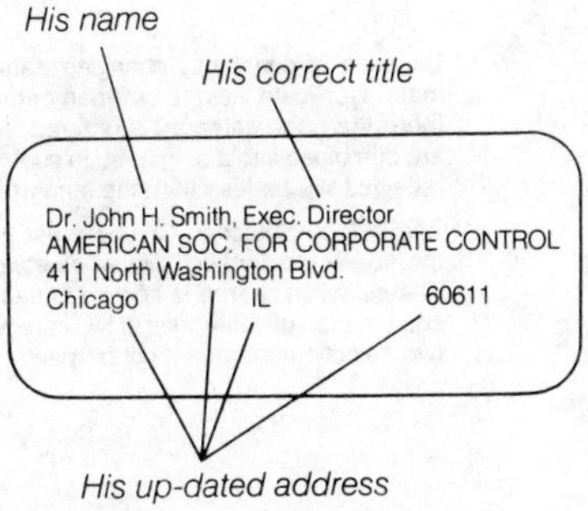

Our mailing list of national associations is warranted to be the most complete and accurate available. It is based on this directory and our staff is correcting it *every working day of the year.*

While some have found it useful to approach regional concentrations of associations (for example, Washington, D.C., Maryland and Virginia), others have mailed to associations in selected subjects — Medicine/Health, Consumer Affairs, etc. See the next page for a list of subject categories available.

Associations may also be isolated by the size of their budget. See the next page for the budget categories available.

For those marketing specialists who wish to contact the national associations systematically, in depth and over a long period, an alphabetical file of 3 x 5 cards, showing the Chief Executive, the address data and his telephone number, is a useful tool. All sorts of information can be entered on each card, and a completely updated file of cards can be obtained from Columbia Books when the current one grows outdated.

AN ANNUAL APPROACH to the 6000 national organizations in this book should be the basic marketing effort of any company wishing to expand its sales to the national association industry.

WHAT THEY SAY ABOUT IT!

"Without question the best and most accurate listing of (national) trade and professional organizations in the U.S."

FRANK MARTINEAU, Editor
Association Trends

"I buy it every year and always book conventions from it. These are the people I have to reach. A very effective tool."

HERB CURMUTT, Sales Manager
Safari Hotel
Scottsdale, Arizona

"Paid for itself many times over. We shall use it again."

WILLIAM TOLLEY, Engrosser
Washington, D.C.

"The mailing produced several continuing and a number of one-shot customers."

PAUL CUTLER, Court Reporter
Washington, D.C.

"Booked myself for a solid year."

CAVETT ROBERT, Convention Speaker
Phoenix, Arizona

ORDER FORM—ASSOCIATIONS MAILING LISTS

ASSOCIATION "ANNUAL BUDGET" MAILING LIST

The following selections by size of the association' annual budgets are available. Please check items desired. (There is NO selection charge for budget categories.)

BUDGET CATEGORY	APPROXIMATE NUMBER OF ASSOCIATIONS IN CATEGORY	PRESSURE SENSITIVE LABELS	3-UP CHESHIRE LABELS	3 x 5 CARDS w/tele. numbers	TOTAL
Over $1,000,000	1050	☐ $125	☐ $115	☐ $125	$
Over $500,000	1600	☐ $150	☐ $135	☐ $150	$
Over $250,000	2300	☐ $175	☐ $150	☐ $175	$
Over $100,000	3300	☐ $250	☐ $200	☐ $250	$
Over $50,000	3800	☐ $275	☐ $225	☐ $275	$
Over $25,000	4400	☐ $325	☐ $275	☐ $325	$
Over $10,000	5050	☐ $350	☐ $300	☐ $350	$
				6% tax (DC residents only)	$
				TOTAL	$

ASSOCIATION "SELECTED SUBJECT" MAILING LIST

Please check items ☑ desired. Enter total of each CATEGORY in column provided at right.

CATEGORY	APPROXIMATE NUMBER OF ASSOCIATIONS IN CATEGORY*	PRESSURE SENSITIVE LABELS	3-UP CHESHIRE LABELS	3 x 5 CARDS (w/tele. numbers)	TOTAL
Aerospace/Aviation	350	☐ $ 35.00	☐ $25.00	☐ $ 35.00	$
Agriculture/Forestry	500	☐ $ 40.00	☐ $35.00	☐ $ 40.00	$
Banking/Finance	400	☐ $ 35.00	☐ $25.00	☐ $ 35.00	$
Business	700	☐ $ 50.00	☐ $40.00	☐ $ 50.00	$
Chemicals/Plastics	450	☐ $ 40.00	☐ $35.00	☐ $ 40.00	$
Communications/Radio/TV	570	☐ $ 50.00	☐ $40.00	☐ $ 50.00	$
Construction	625	☐ $ 50.00	☐ $40.00	☐ $ 50.00	$
Consumer Affairs	1300	☐ $100.00	☐ $75.00	☐ $100.00	$
Drugs/Pharmaceuticals	175	☐ $ 30.00	☐ $25.00	☐ $ 30.00	$
Education	560	☐ $ 50.00	☐ $40.00	☐ $ 50.00	$
Electricity/Electronics	400	☐ $ 35.00	☐ $25.00	☐ $ 35.00	$
Engineering/Machinery	540	☐ $ 50.00	☐ $40.00	☐ $ 50.00	$
Environmental Affairs	630	☐ $ 50.00	☐ $40.00	☐ $ 50.00	$
Food/Beverages/Food Services	475	☐ $ 40.00	☐ $35.00	☐ $ 40.00	$
Foreign Trade	125	☐ $ 30.00	☐ $25.00	☐ $ 30.00	$
Insurance	165	☐ $ 30.00	☐ $25.00	☐ $ 30.00	$
Labor Unions	200	☐ $ 30.00	☐ $25.00	☐ $ 30.00	$
Manufacturing	830	☐ $ 75.00	☐ $65.00	☐ $ 75.00	$
Medicine/Health	1050	☐ $100.00	☐ $75.00	☐ $100.00	$
Metals/Mining/Minerals	280	☐ $ 35.00	☐ $25.00	☐ $ 35.00	$
Oil/Gas/Petroleum	250	☐ $ 35.00	☐ $25.00	☐ $ 35.00	$
Printing/Publishing	415	☐ $ 35.00	☐ $25.00	☐ $ 35.00	$
Recreation	540	☐ $ 50.00	☐ $40.00	☐ $ 50.00	$
Science	1100	☐ $100.00	☐ $75.00	☐ $100.00	$
Textiles/Apparel	170	☐ $ 30.00	☐ $25.00	☐ $ 30.00	$
Transportation	500	☐ $ 40.00	☐ $35.00	☐ $ 40.00	$
				Selection Charge**	$ 60.00
				6% tax (DC residents only)	$
				TOTAL	$

Name ______________________

Title ______________________

Organization ______________________

Street ______________________

City ______________________

State ______________ Zip ______________

______________ Date ______________________ Signature

* Because of constantly changing data, these totals are approximate. Duplicate listings between categories are eliminated when more than one category is ordered, and the selected categories are combined into a single list. In such cases, the number of labels received will be less than the sum of the category totals.

** The $60.00 Selection Charge must be added to any order from the "Selected Subject" list whether for one or more categories. The selection charge is applied to each order — for a category or combination of categories. If two categories are wanted separately, two selection charges must be paid.

National Association

mailing list

Want to reach the Executives of 6250 National Trade and Professional Associations the easy way?

Here's how:

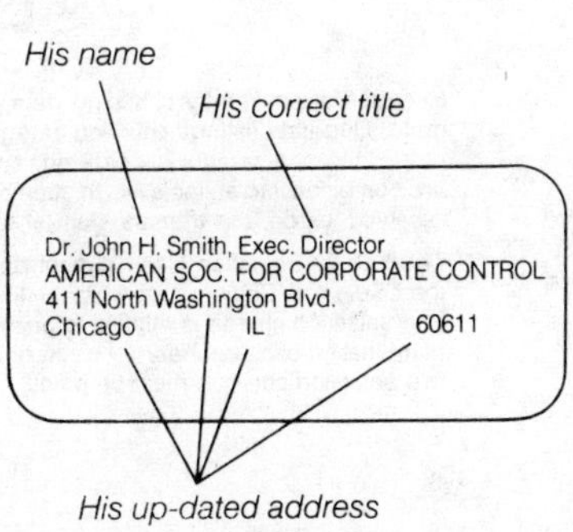

Our mailing list of national associations is warranted to be the most complete and accurate available. It is based on this directory and our staff is correcting it *every working day of the year.*

While some have found it useful to approach regional concentrations of associations (for example, Washington, D.C., Maryland and Virginia), others have mailed to associations in selected subjects — Medicine/Health, Consumer Affairs, etc. See the next page for a list of subject categories available.

Associations may also be isolated by the size of their budget. See the next page for the budget categories available.

For those marketing specialists who wish to contact the national associations systematically, in depth and over a long period, an alphabetical file of 3 x 5 cards, showing the Chief Executive, the address data and his telephone number, is a useful tool. All sorts of information can be entered on each card, and a completely updated file of cards can be obtained from Columbia Books when the current one grows outdated.

AN ANNUAL APPROACH to the 6000 national organizations in this book should be the basic marketing effort of any company wishing to expand its sales to the national association industry.

WHAT THEY SAY ABOUT IT!

"Without question the best and most accurate listing of (national) trade and professional organizations in the U.S."

FRANK MARTINEAU, Editor
Association Trends

"I buy it every year and always book conventions from it. These are the people I have to reach. A very effective tool."

HERB CURMUTT, Sales Manager
Safari Hotel
Scottsdale, Arizona

"Paid for itself many times over. We shall use it again."

WILLIAM TOLLEY, Engrosser
Washington, D.C.

"The mailing produced several continuing and a number of one-shot customers."

PAUL CUTLER, Court Reporter
Washington, D.C.

"Booked myself for a solid year."

CAVETT ROBERT, Convention Speaker
Phoenix, Arizona

ORDER FORM—ASSOCIATIONS MAILING LISTS

ASSOCIATION "ANNUAL BUDGET" MAILING LIST

The following selections by size of the association' annual budgets are available. Please check items desired. (There is NO selection charge for budget categories.)

BUDGET CATEGORY	APPROXIMATE NUMBER OF ASSOCIATIONS IN CATEGORY	PRESSURE SENSITIVE LABELS	3-UP CHESHIRE LABELS	3 x 5 CARDS w/tele. numbers	TOTAL
Over $1,000,000	1050	☐ $125	☐ $115	☐ $125	$
Over $500,000	1600	☐ $150	☐ $135	☐ $150	$
Over $250,000	2300	☐ $175	☐ $150	☐ $175	$
Over $100,000	3300	☐ $250	☐ $200	☐ $250	$
Over $50,000	3800	☐ $275	☐ $225	☐ $275	$
Over $25,000	4400	☐ $325	☐ $275	☐ $325	$
Over $10,000	5050	☐ $350	☐ $300	☐ $350	$
				6% tax (DC residents only)	$
				TOTAL	$

ASSOCIATION "SELECTED SUBJECT" MAILING LIST

Please check items ☑ desired. Enter total of each CATEGORY in column provided at right.

CATEGORY	APPROXIMATE NUMBER OF ASSOCIATIONS IN CATEGORY*	PRESSURE SENSITIVE LABELS	3-UP CHESHIRE LABELS	3 x 5 CARDS (w/tele. numbers)	TOTAL
Aerospace/Aviation	350	☐ $ 35.00	☐ $25.00	☐ $ 35.00	$
Agriculture/Forestry	500	☐ $ 40.00	☐ $35.00	☐ $ 40.00	$
Banking/Finance	400	☐ $ 35.00	☐ $25.00	☐ $ 35.00	$
Business	700	☐ $ 50.00	☐ $40.00	☐ $ 50.00	$
Chemicals/Plastics	450	☐ $ 40.00	☐ $35.00	☐ $ 40.00	$
Communications/Radio/TV	570	☐ $ 50.00	☐ $40.00	☐ $ 50.00	$
Construction	625	☐ $ 50.00	☐ $40.00	☐ $ 50.00	$
Consumer Affairs	1300	☐ $100.00	☐ $75.00	☐ $100.00	$
Drugs/Pharmaceuticals	175	☐ $ 30.00	☐ $25.00	☐ $ 30.00	$
Education	560	☐ $ 50.00	☐ $40.00	☐ $ 50.00	$
Electricity/Electronics	400	☐ $ 35.00	☐ $25.00	☐ $ 35.00	$
Engineering/Machinery	540	☐ $ 50.00	☐ $40.00	☐ $ 50.00	$
Environmental Affairs	630	☐ $ 50.00	☐ $40.00	☐ $ 50.00	$
Food/Beverages/Food Services	475	☐ $ 40.00	☐ $35.00	☐ $ 40.00	$
Foreign Trade	125	☐ $ 30.00	☐ $25.00	☐ $ 30.00	$
Insurance	165	☐ $ 30.00	☐ $25.00	☐ $ 30.00	$
Labor Unions	200	☐ $ 30.00	☐ $25.00	☐ $ 30.00	$
Manufacturing	830	☐ $ 75.00	☐ $65.00	☐ $ 75.00	$
Medicine/Health	1050	☐ $100.00	☐ $75.00	☐ $100.00	$
Metals/Mining/Minerals	280	☐ $ 35.00	☐ $25.00	☐ $ 35.00	$
Oil/Gas/Petroleum	250	☐ $ 35.00	☐ $25.00	☐ $ 35.00	$
Printing/Publishing	415	☐ $ 35.00	☐ $25.00	☐ $ 35.00	$
Recreation	540	☐ $ 50.00	☐ $40.00	☐ $ 50.00	$
Science	1100	☐ $100.00	☐ $75.00	☐ $100.00	$
Textiles/Apparel	170	☐ $ 30.00	☐ $25.00	☐ $ 30.00	$
Transportation	500	☐ $ 40.00	☐ $35.00	☐ $ 40.00	$
				Selection Charge**	$ 60.00
				6% tax (DC residents only)	$
				TOTAL	$

Name

Title

Organization

Street

City

State Zip

Date Signature

* Because of constantly changing data, these totals are approximate. Duplicate listings between categories are eliminated when more than one category is ordered, and the selected categories are combined into a single list. In such cases, the number of labels received will be less than the sum of the category totals.

** The $60.00 Selection Charge must be added to any order from the "Selected Subject" list whether for one or more categories. The selection charge is applied to each order — for a category or combination of categories. If two categories are wanted separately, two selection charges must be paid.

National Association

mailing list

Want to reach the Executives of 6250 National Trade and Professional Associations the easy way?

Here's how:

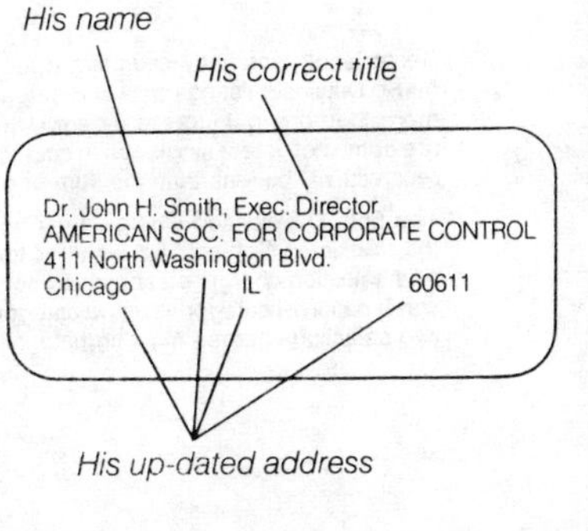

Our mailing list of national associations is warranted to be the most complete and accurate available. It is based on this directory and our staff is correcting it *every working day of the year.*

While some have found it useful to approach regional concentrations of associations (for example, Washington, D.C., Maryland and Virginia), others have mailed to associations in selected subjects — Medicine/Health, Consumer Affairs, etc. See the next page for a list of subject categories available.

Associations may also be isolated by the size of their budget. See the next page for the budget categories available.

For those marketing specialists who wish to contact the national associations systematically, in depth and over a long period, an alphabetical file of 3 x 5 cards, showing the Chief Executive, the address data and his telephone number, is a useful tool. All sorts of information can be entered on each card, and a completely updated file of cards can be obtained from Columbia Books when the current one grows outdated.

AN ANNUAL APPROACH to the 6000 national organizations in this book should be the basic marketing effort of any company wishing to expand its sales to the national association industry.

WHAT THEY SAY ABOUT IT!

"Without question the best and most accurate listing of (national) trade and professional organizations in the U.S."

FRANK MARTINEAU, Editor
Association Trends

"I buy it every year and always book conventions from it. These are the people I have to reach. A very effective tool."

HERB CURMUTT, Sales Manager
Safari Hotel
Scottsdale, Arizona

"Paid for itself many times over. We shall use it again."

WILLIAM TOLLEY, Engrosser
Washington, D.C.

"The mailing produced several continuing and a number of one-shot customers."

PAUL CUTLER, Court Reporter
Washington, D.C.

"Booked myself for a solid year."

CAVETT ROBERT, Convention Speaker
Phoenix, Arizona

ORDER FORM—ASSOCIATIONS MAILING LISTS

ASSOCIATION "ANNUAL BUDGET" MAILING LIST

The following selections by size of the association' annual budgets are available. Please check items desired. (There is NO selection charge for budget categories.)

BUDGET CATEGORY	APPROXIMATE NUMBER OF ASSOCIATIONS IN CATEGORY	PRESSURE SENSITIVE LABELS	3-UP CHESHIRE LABELS	3 x 5 CARDS w/tele. numbers	TOTAL
Over $1,000,000	1050	☐ $125	☐ $115	☐ $125	$
Over $500,000	1600	☐ $150	☐ $135	☐ $150	$
Over $250,000	2300	☐ $175	☐ $150	☐ $175	$
Over $100,000	3300	☐ $250	☐ $200	☐ $250	$
Over $50,000	3800	☐ $275	☐ $225	☐ $275	$
Over $25,000	4400	☐ $325	☐ $275	☐ $325	$
Over $10,000	5050	☐ $350	☐ $300	☐ $350	$
				6% tax (DC residents only)	$
				TOTAL	$

ASSOCIATION "SELECTED SUBJECT" MAILING LIST

Please check items ☑ desired. Enter total of each CATEGORY in column provided at right.

CATEGORY	APPROXIMATE NUMBER OF ASSOCIATIONS IN CATEGORY*	PRESSURE SENSITIVE LABELS	3-UP CHESHIRE LABELS	3 x 5 CARDS (w/tele. numbers)	TOTAL
Aerospace/Aviation	350	☐ $ 35.00	☐ $25.00	☐ $ 35.00	$
Agriculture/Forestry	500	☐ $ 40.00	☐ $35.00	☐ $ 40.00	$
Banking/Finance	400	☐ $ 35.00	☐ $25.00	☐ $ 35.00	$
Business	700	☐ $ 50.00	☐ $40.00	☐ $ 50.00	$
Chemicals/Plastics	450	☐ $ 40.00	☐ $35.00	☐ $ 40.00	$
Communications/Radio/TV	570	☐ $ 50.00	☐ $40.00	☐ $ 50.00	$
Construction	625	☐ $ 50.00	☐ $40.00	☐ $ 50.00	$
Consumer Affairs	1300	☐ $100.00	☐ $75.00	☐ $100.00	$
Drugs/Pharmaceuticals	175	☐ $ 30.00	☐ $25.00	☐ $ 30.00	$
Education	560	☐ $ 50.00	☐ $40.00	☐ $ 50.00	$
Electricity/Electronics	400	☐ $ 35.00	☐ $25.00	☐ $ 35.00	$
Engineering/Machinery	540	☐ $ 50.00	☐ $40.00	☐ $ 50.00	$
Environmental Affairs	630	☐ $ 50.00	☐ $40.00	☐ $ 50.00	$
Food/Beverages/Food Services	475	☐ $ 40.00	☐ $35.00	☐ $ 40.00	$
Foreign Trade	125	☐ $ 30.00	☐ $25.00	☐ $ 30.00	$
Insurance	165	☐ $ 30.00	☐ $25.00	☐ $ 30.00	$
Labor Unions	200	☐ $ 30.00	☐ $25.00	☐ $ 30.00	$
Manufacturing	830	☐ $ 75.00	☐ $65.00	☐ $ 75.00	$
Medicine/Health	1050	☐ $100.00	☐ $75.00	☐ $100.00	$
Metals/Mining/Minerals	280	☐ $ 35.00	☐ $25.00	☐ $ 35.00	$
Oil/Gas/Petroleum	250	☐ $ 35.00	☐ $25.00	☐ $ 35.00	$
Printing/Publishing	415	☐ $ 35.00	☐ $25.00	☐ $ 35.00	$
Recreation	540	☐ $ 50.00	☐ $40.00	☐ $ 50.00	$
Science	1100	☐ $100.00	☐ $75.00	☐ $100.00	$
Textiles/Apparel	170	☐ $ 30.00	☐ $25.00	☐ $ 30.00	$
Transportation	500	☐ $ 40.00	☐ $35.00	☐ $ 40.00	$
				Selection Charge**	$ 60.00
				6% tax (DC residents only)	$
				TOTAL	$

Name ______________________

Title ______________________

Organization ______________________

Street ______________________

City ______________________

State ______________ Zip ______________

______________ Date ______________________ Signature

* Because of constantly changing data, these totals are approximate. Duplicate listings between categories are eliminated when more than one category is ordered, and the selected categories are combined into a single list. In such cases, the number of labels received will be less than the sum of the category totals.

** The $60.00 Selection Charge must be added to any order from the "Selected Subject" list whether for one or more categories. The selection charge is applied to each order — for a category or combination of categories. If two categories are wanted separately, two selection charges must be paid.

National Association

mailing list

Want to reach the Executives of 6250 National Trade and Professional Associations the easy way?

Here's how:

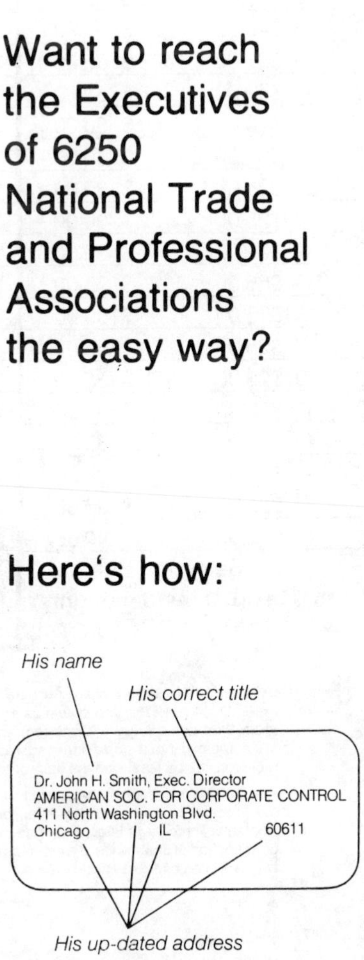

Our mailing list of national associations is warranted to be the most complete and accurate available. It is based on this directory and our staff is correcting it *every working day of the year.*

While some have found it useful to approach regional concentrations of associations (for example, Washington, D.C., Maryland and Virginia), others have mailed to associations in selected subjects — Medicine/Health, Consumer Affairs, etc. See the next page for a list of subject categories available.

Associations may also be isolated by the size of their budget. See the next page for the budget categories available.

For those marketing specialists who wish to contact the national associations systematically, in depth and over a long period, an alphabetical file of 3 x 5 cards, showing the Chief Executive, the address data and his telephone number, is a useful tool. All sorts of information can be entered on each card, and a completely updated file of cards can be obtained from Columbia Books when the current one grows outdated.

AN ANNUAL APPROACH to the 6000 national organizations in this book should be the basic marketing effort of any company wishing to expand its sales to the national association industry.

WHAT THEY SAY ABOUT IT!

"Without question the best and most accurate listing of (national) trade and professional organizations in the U.S."

FRANK MARTINEAU, Editor
Association Trends

"I buy it every year and always book conventions from it. These are the people I have to reach. A very effective tool."

HERB CURMUTT, Sales Manager
Safari Hotel
Scottsdale, Arizona

"Paid for itself many times over. We shall use it again."

WILLIAM TOLLEY, Engrosser
Washington, D.C.

"The mailing produced several continuing and a number of one-shot customers."

PAUL CUTLER, Court Reporter
Washington, D.C.

"Booked myself for a solid year."

CAVETT ROBERT, Convention Speaker
Phoenix, Arizona

ORDER FORM—ASSOCIATIONS MAILING LISTS

ASSOCIATION "ANNUAL BUDGET" MAILING LIST

The following selections by size of the association' annual budgets are available. Please check items desired. (There is NO selection charge for budget categories.)

BUDGET CATEGORY	APPROXIMATE NUMBER OF ASSOCIATIONS IN CATEGORY	PRESSURE SENSITIVE LABELS	3-UP CHESHIRE LABELS	3 x 5 CARDS w/tele. numbers	TOTAL
Over $1,000,000	1050	☐ $125	☐ $115	☐ $125	$
Over $500,000	1600	☐ $150	☐ $135	☐ $150	$
Over $250,000	2300	☐ $175	☐ $150	☐ $175	$
Over $100,000	3300	☐ $250	☐ $200	☐ $250	$
Over $50,000	3800	☐ $275	☐ $225	☐ $275	$
Over $25,000	4400	☐ $325	☐ $275	☐ $325	$
Over $10,000	5050	☐ $350	☐ $300	☐ $350	$
				6% tax (DC residents only)	$
				TOTAL	$

ASSOCIATION "SELECTED SUBJECT" MAILING LIST

Please check items ☑ desired. Enter total of each CATEGORY in column provided at right.

CATEGORY	APPROXIMATE NUMBER OF ASSOCIATIONS IN CATEGORY*	PRESSURE SENSITIVE LABELS	3-UP CHESHIRE LABELS	3 x 5 CARDS (w/tele. numbers)	TOTAL
Aerospace/Aviation	350	☐ $ 35.00	☐ $25.00	☐ $ 35.00	$
Agriculture/Forestry	500	☐ $ 40.00	☐ $35.00	☐ $ 40.00	$
Banking/Finance	400	☐ $ 35.00	☐ $25.00	☐ $ 35.00	$
Business	700	☐ $ 50.00	☐ $40.00	☐ $ 50.00	$
Chemicals/Plastics	450	☐ $ 40.00	☐ $35.00	☐ $ 40.00	$
Communications/Radio/TV	570	☐ $ 50.00	☐ $40.00	☐ $ 50.00	$
Construction	625	☐ $ 50.00	☐ $40.00	☐ $ 50.00	$
Consumer Affairs	1300	☐ $100.00	☐ $75.00	☐ $100.00	$
Drugs/Pharmaceuticals	175	☐ $ 30.00	☐ $25.00	☐ $ 30.00	$
Education	560	☐ $ 50.00	☐ $40.00	☐ $ 50.00	$
Electricity/Electronics	400	☐ $ 35.00	☐ $25.00	☐ $ 35.00	$
Engineering/Machinery	540	☐ $ 50.00	☐ $40.00	☐ $ 50.00	$
Environmental Affairs	630	☐ $ 50.00	☐ $40.00	☐ $ 50.00	$
Food/Beverages/Food Services	475	☐ $ 40.00	☐ $35.00	☐ $ 40.00	$
Foreign Trade	125	☐ $ 30.00	☐ $25.00	☐ $ 30.00	$
Insurance	165	☐ $ 30.00	☐ $25.00	☐ $ 30.00	$
Labor Unions	200	☐ $ 30.00	☐ $25.00	☐ $ 30.00	$
Manufacturing	830	☐ $ 75.00	☐ $65.00	☐ $ 75.00	$
Medicine/Health	1050	☐ $100.00	☐ $75.00	☐ $100.00	$
Metals/Mining/Minerals	280	☐ $ 35.00	☐ $25.00	☐ $ 35.00	$
Oil/Gas/Petroleum	250	☐ $ 35.00	☐ $25.00	☐ $ 35.00	$
Printing/Publishing	415	☐ $ 35.00	☐ $25.00	☐ $ 35.00	$
Recreation	540	☐ $ 50.00	☐ $40.00	☐ $ 50.00	$
Science	1100	☐ $100.00	☐ $75.00	☐ $100.00	$
Textiles/Apparel	170	☐ $ 30.00	☐ $25.00	☐ $ 30.00	$
Transportation	500	☐ $ 40.00	☐ $35.00	☐ $ 40.00	$
				Selection Charge**	$ 60.00
				6% tax (DC residents only)	$
				TOTAL	$

Name

Title

Organization

Street

City

State Zip

Date Signature

* Because of constantly changing data, these totals are approximate. Duplicate listings between categories are eliminated when more than one category is ordered, and the selected categories are combined into a single list. In such cases, the number of labels received will be less than the sum of the category totals.

** The $60.00 Selection Charge must be added to any order from the "Selected Subject" list whether for one or more categories. The selection charge is applied to each order — for a category or combination of categories. If two categories are wanted separately, two selection charges must be paid.

NATIONAL TRADE AND PROFESSIONAL ASSOCIATIONS
QUESTIONNAIRE

There is no charge to be listed in this Directory. If your organization qualifies as a trade or professional group with a national constituency, the publishers would be happy to consider listing it if you will return this completed form.

Organization name: ______________________________

Date and place established: ______________________________ Where incorporated. ______________________________

Street Address: ______________________________

City: ______________ State: ______________ Zip: ______________ Telephone: ______________

Chief **paid** executive (Title): ______________________________

(Name): ______________________________

(Note: We need the name of a **permanent** officer. If your organization does not support such a position, give us the Secretary or Corresponding Secretary.)

Size of membership: Companies? ______________ Individuals? ______________

Cost of annual **individual** membership: ______________ Size of paid staff ______________

Budget Category (All receipts, including convention receipts): Check one.

1.	under $10,000	☐	6.	$250-500,000	☐
2.	$10-25,000	☐	7.	$500-1,000,000	☐
3.	$25-50,000	☐	8.	$1-2,000,000	☐
4.	$50-100,000	☐	9.	$2-5,000,000	☐
5.	$100-250,000	☐	10.	over $5,000,000	☐

Serial Publications

Title	Frequency	Accepts ads	
		Yes	No
1.			
2.			
3.			
4.			

Membership meetings: Annual ☐ (What time of year? ______________) Semi-Annual ☐ Biennial ☐

Year	City	Hotel or Facility	Dates	Attendance
1987				
1988				
1989				
1990				
1991				

History: What is your purpose? What are your membership qualifications? Have you gone by another name, etc? Perhaps you can write something here, or send us your literature.

____

____

____

____

COLUMBIA BOOKS, Inc., *Publishers*
Suite 207, 1350 New York Avenue, NW
Washington, DC 20005
(202) 737-3777

SUBJECT AND KEY-WORD INDEX TO NTPA

How should your organization be coded?

0010 ABRASIVES
0030 ACCOUNTING
0040 ACOUSTICS
0045 ACTORS see also THEATRE
0047 ACTUARIES
0050 ADHESIVES
ADJUSTERS see CREDIT
0070 ADVERTISING INDUSTRY
0080 AEROSPACE
AGING see GERONTOLOGY
0090 AESTHETICS
0100 AGRICULTURE
0110 AGRONOMY
0120 AIR CONDITIONING
0130 AIR POLLUTION see also POLLUTION
0140 AIRPLANES
0150 AIRPORTS
0170 ALLERGY
0180 ALUMINUM
0185 AMBULANCES
0187 ANATOMY
0190 ANESTHESIOLOGY
0200 ANTHROPOLOGY
0210 ANTIQUES
0230 APPAREL
0240 APPLIANCES
0250 APPRAISERS
0255 ARABIC
0260 ARBITRATION
0270 ARCHAEOLOGY
0280 ARCHERY
0290 ARCHITECTURE
0300 ARCHIVISTS
0320 ARTS, THE
0330 ASBESTOS
0340 ASPHALT
0350 ASTROLOGY
ASTRONAUTICS see AEROSPACE
0370 ASTRONOMY
ATOMIC ENERGY see NUCLEAR ENERGY
0400 AUCTIONS
0410 AUDIO-VISUAL
0420 AUDITORIUM MANAGERS
0430 AUTHORS see also PRESS, WRITERS
AUTOMATIC VENDING see VENDING
0445 AUTOMOBILES see also MOTOR VEHICLES
AUTOMOTIVE INDUSTRY see GARAGES, MOTOR VEHICLES
0460 AVIATION
0480 BACTERIOLOGY
0490 BAGS see also BOXES, CONTAINERS
0510 BAKING
0525 BANDS see also MUSIC
0530 BANKING see also FINANCE, INVESTMENTS, SAVINGS & LOAN, SECURITIES INDUSTRY
0550 BARBERS
0560 BARRELS
0570 BASEBALL
0580 BASKETBALL
0590 BATTERIES
0600 BEARINGS
0610 BEER
0620 BEES
0630 BELTS
0640 BETTER BUSINESS BUREAUS
0650 BEVERAGE INDUSTRY
0660 BIBLE
0670 BICYCLES
0675 BILLIARDS
0680 BIOLOGY
0684 BIRDS
0685 BLACKS see also MINORITIES
0690 BLIND
0710 BLUEPRINTS
0720 BOATING
0730 BOILERS
BOOKKEEPING see ACCOUNTING
0750 BOOKS see also LIBRARIES
0755 BOTTLES see also BEVERAGE INDUSTRY
0760 BOTANY
0770 BOWLING
0780 BOXES see also BAGS, CONTAINERS
0785 BOXING
0790 BRASS
0800 BREWERS
0805 BRIDGE
0810 BRIQUETS
BROADCASTERS see RADIO-TV
0830 BRONZE
0840 BROOMS & BRUSHES
BUILDING see CONSTRUCTION
0880 BUSINESS
BUTTONS see FASTENERS
0885 BUTTERFLIES
0910 CAMPING
0920 CANCER
0923 CANS
0925 CARDIOLOGY
0930 CAR WASH
0940 CARPETS see also RUGS
CASTING see METAL WORKING
0975 CATHOLIC
0976 CATS
0980 CATTLE
CEDAR see WOOD & WOOD PRODUCTS
CEMENT see CONCRETE
1010 CEMETERIES see also FUNERALS
1020 CERAMICS see also CHINA
1030 CHAINS
1035 CHAMBER OF COMMERCE
1040 CHAPLAINS
1050 CHEMICALS & CHEMICAL INDUSTRY
1060 CHILDREN
1070 CHINA see also CERAMICS
1090 CHINESE
CHIROPODY see PODIATRY
1120 CHIROPRACTORS
1130 CHOCOLATE
1140 CIRCULATION
1150 CLAY
1160 CLEANERS
CLOTHING see APPAREL
1180 CLUBS see also FRATERNAL ORGANIZATIONS
1190 COACHES
1200 COAL
COCOA see CHOCOLATE
COINS see NUMISMATICS
1220 COLOR
1225 COMMODITIES
1230 COMMUNICATIONS
1240 COMPOSERS
1250 COMPTROLLERS
COMPUTERS see DATA PROCESSING
1270 CONCRETE
1280 CONFECTIONERS
1290 CONSERVATION
1300 CONSTRUCTION
1310 CONSULTANTS
1320 CONSUMERS
1330 CONTAINERS see also BAGS, BOXES,CANS
1350 CONTRACTORS
1360 CONVENTIONS see also EXHIBITS
1370 COOKING
1390 COOPERATIVES
1400 COPPER
1410 CORN
1420 CORRECTION see also LAW, POLICE, SECURITY
1430 COSMETICS & COSMETOLOGY
1450 COTTON
1460 COTTONSEED
1470 COUNSEL
COUNSELING see VOCATIONAL GUIDANCE
1475 COUNTY
1480 CREDIT see also FINANCE
1500 CRIMINOLOGY
1515 CRYOGENICS
1525 CUSTOMS
1530 CYBERNETICS
1540 CYTOLOGY
1550 DAIRY INDUSTRY
1556 DANCE
1560 DATA PROCESSING
1570 DEAF
1585 DECORATORS
1590 DEHYDRATORS
DEMOGRAPHY see POPULATION
1600 DENTISTS
1610 DERMATOLOGY
1620 DESIGNERS
1630 DIAMONDS
1640 DIETARY FOODS
DOCTORS see DENTISTS, MEDICINE, OSTEOPATHS, SURGEONS
1655 DOGS
1670 DOORS
1675 DRAFTING
DRESSES see APPAREL
1690 DRUGS see also PHARMACEUTICAL INDUSTRY
1700 DYERS
1710 ECONOMICS
1720 EDUCATION
1730 ELECTRICITY & ELECTRONICS
1740 ELEVATORS
EMBALMING see FUNERALS
1760 EMPLOYEES & EMPLOYMENT
1765 ENERGY
1770 ENGINEERS
1780 ENGINES
1790 ENGLISH
ENOLOGY see WINE
1810 ENTERTAINERS
1820 ENTOMOLOGY
1825 ENVIRONMENT
1850 EXAMINERS
1860 EXECUTIVES
1870 EXHIBITS see also CONVENTIONS
1880 EXPLOSIVES
1890 EXPORTERS
1900 FARMS
1910 FASTENERS
1920 FATS & OILS
1930 FEED & GRAIN
1940 FERTILIZERS
1950 FILMS
1970 FINANCE see also CREDIT
1980 FIRE
1985 FIREARMS see also RIFLERY
1990 FISH & FISHING
2010 FLOORING
FLOWERS see HORTICULTURE
2040 FOOD INDUSTRY
2050 FOOD PROCESSORS
2060 FOOD SERVICES
2070 FOOTBALL
2080 FOREIGN SERVICE
2090 FOREIGN TRADE see also EXPORTERS, IMPORTERS, WEBB—POMERENE ACT
2100 FORENSIC
2110 FORESTRY
FORGING see METAL WORKING INDUSTRY
2125 FOUNDATIONS
2130 FOUNDRIES
2140 FRANCHISES
2145 FRATERNAL ORGANIZATIONS see also CLUBS
2150 FREIGHT FORWARDERS
2160 FRENCH
2165 FRUIT
FUELS see COAL, GAS, OIL, PETROLEUM INDUSTRY
2180 FUND-RAISING
2190 FUNERALS see also CEMETERIES
2200 FURS
2210 FURNITURE
2230 GARAGES
2240 GARDENING
GARMENTS see APPAREL
2260 GAS
2270 GASOLINE
2280 GASTROENTEROLOGY
2290 GEARS
GEMS see JEWELRY & GEMS, MINERALS
2310 GENEALOGY
2320 GENETICS
2330 GEOGRAPHERS
2340 GEOLOGISTS
2350 GERONTOLOGY
2360 GERMAN
2370 GLASS see also BOTTLES
2380 GLOVES
2390 GOATS
2400 GOLD
2410 GOLF
2415 GOVERNMENT see also MILITARY
2420 GRAIN see also FEED & GRAIN
2440 GRAPHIC ARTS
2450 GROCERS
GUNS see FIREARMS
2460 GYNECOLOGY
HAIRDRESSERS see COSMETICS
2477 HANDICAPPED see also BLIND, DEAF
2480 HANDWRITING
2490 HARDWARE
HATS see MILLINERY
2510 HEALTH CARE
HEARING see DEAF
2530 HEATING
2540 HELICOPTERS
2550 HERPETOLOGY
2560 HISTORY
2570 HOCKEY
HOME BUILDERS see CONSTRUCTION
2590 HOME FURNISHINGS
2610 HONEY
2620 HORSES
2630 HORTICULTURE
2650 HOSPITALS
2660 HOTELS
2670 HOUSEWARES
2680 HYDRAULICS
2690 HYGIENE
2700 HYPNOSIS
2710 ICE
2730 IMMUNOLOGY
2740 IMPORTERS
2750 INDUSTRIAL PLANTS
2760 INDUSTRIAL RELATIONS
INFORMATION PROCESSING see DATA PROCESSING
2775 INSTRUMENTS
2780 INSULATION
2790 INSURANCE INDUSTRY
2800 INVENTORS
2810 INVESTMENTS see also FINANCE, SECURITIES INDUSTRY
2820 IRON & STEEL INDUSTRY
2830 ITALIAN
2840 JEWELRY & GEMS
2845 JEWISH
2850 JOURNALISM
2860 JUDGES
2875 LABOR UNIONS
2880 LABORATORIES
2890 LACE
2895 LACROSSE
2900 LADDERS
2910 LANDSCAPING
2920 LANGUAGE
2930 LARYNGOLOGY
LAUNDERERS see CLEANERS
2950 LAW
LAW ENFORCEMENT see POLICE
2960 LEAD
2970 LEATHER GOODS see also SHOES
2980 LECTURES
2990 LIBRARIES
3010 LIGHTING
3040 LINGERIE & UNDERWEAR
3050 LINGUISTICS
3080 LIQUOR
3090 LIVESTOCK
3100 LOCKS
3110 LUBRICANTS
LUMBER see WOOD & WOOD PRODUCTS
3130 MACHINE TOOL INDUSTRY
3140 MACHINERY
3150 MAGIC
3160 MAIL
3175 MAMMALOGY
3180 MANAGERS
3195 MANUFACTURERS
3200 MAPS
3210 MARKET RESEARCH
3220 MARKETING
3230 MATERIAL HANDLING
3240 MATHEMATICS
3250 MEASUREMENT
3260 MEAT
3270 MEDICINE
3280 MENTAL HEALTH
3290 MERCHANDISING
3310 METAL WORKING
3320 METALS
3340 METEOROLOGY
3350 MICA
3360 MICROBIOLOGY
3370 MICROFILMS
3380 MICROSCOPES
3385 MILITARY
3390 MILK
3400 MILLERS see also FEED & GRAIN, GRAIN, WHEAT
3405 MILLINERY
3410 MINERALOGY
3420 MINERALS
3430 MINING INDUSTRY
3435 MINORITIES see also BLACKS
MOTELS see HOTELS
MOTION PICTURES see FILMS
3480 MOTOR VEHICLES see also AUTOMOBILES
3483 MOTORCYCLES
3490 MUSEUMS
3500 MUSHROOMS
3510 MUSIC see also BANDS
NAILS see FASTENERS
3540 NATURALISTS
NAVAL see MILITARY
3550 NECKWEAR
NEGROES see BLACKS
3580 NEUROLOGY
3590 NEWSPAPERS
3600 NOTIONS
3610 NUCLEAR ENERGY
3620 NUMISMATICS
3630 NURSERYMEN
3640 NURSING
3650 NUTRITION
3660 NUTS
3670 OBSTETRICS
3680 OCEANOGRAPHY
3690 OFFICE EQUIPMENT
OFFICE PRODUCTS see STATIONERY
3710 OILS
3730 OPHTHALMOLOGY
3740 OPTICAL
3750 OPTOMETRY
3760 ORGANS
3770 ORIENTAL
ORNITHOLOGY see BIRDS
3790 ORTHODONTISTS
3795 ORTHOPEDICS
3800 OSTEOPATHS
3810 OXYGEN
3820 PACKAGING
3830 PAINT & PAINTING
3840 PALEONTOLOGY
3850 PAPER INDUSTRY see also PULP
3860 PARASITOLOGY
3870 PARKING
3880 PARKS
3890 PATENTS
3900 PATHOLOGY
3910 PATTFRNS
3930 PEDIATRICS
PENAL see CORRECTION, POLICE,SECURITY
3950 PENCILS & PENS
3960 PERSONNEL
3970 PEST CONTROL
3980 PETS see also specific animal
3990 PETROLEUM INDUSTRY
4010 PHARMACEUTICAL INDUSTRY see also DRUGS
4015 PHARMACOLOGY
4020 PHILATELY
4030 PHILOLOGY
4040 PHILOSOPHY
4050 PHONOGRAPHS
4070 PHOTOGRAPHY
4075 PHYSICAL EDUCATION
4080 PHYSICS
4090 PHYSIOLOGY
4100 PHYTOPATHOLOGY
4120 PILOTS
4130 PIPES
4140 PLANNING
PLANTS see HORTICULTURE
4150 PLASTICS INDUSTRY
4170 PLUMBING
4180 PLYWOOD
4185 PODIATRY
4190 POETS
4200 POLICE
4210 POLITICAL SCIENCE
4125 POLLUTION see also AIR POLLUTION
4225 POPULATION
4230 PORTUGUESE
4240 POST OFFICE
4250 POULTRY
4260 POWDER METALLURGY
4270 PREMIUMS
4280 PRESS see also AUTHORS,WRITERS
4290 PRINTING
PRISONS see CORRECTION
4295 PROCTOLOGY
4300 PSYCHOLOGISTS & PSYCHIATRISTS
4310 PUBLIC HEALTH
4320 PUBLIC RELATIONS
4330 PUBLIC WORKS
4340 PUBLISHERS
4350 PULP see also PAPER INDUSTRY
4360 PUMPS
4370 PURCHASERS
4390 RABBITS
4400 RACING
4410 RACK MERCHANDISERS
4420 RADIOLOGY
4430 RADIO-TV
4440 RAILWAYS
4450 READING
4460 REAL ESTATE
RECORDS see PHONOGRAPHS
4480 RECORDS MANAGEMENT
4490 RECREATION
4500 REFRACTORIES
4510 REFRIGERATION
4525 REHABILITATION
4530 RELIGION see also CATHOLIC, JEWISH
4550 RENTALS
4560 RESEARCH
4570 RESTAURANTS
4580 RETAILERS see also MERCHANDISING
4605 RICE
4608 RIFLERY see also FIREARMS
4610 ROADWAYS
4620 ROBOTICS
4627 ROLLER SKATING
4630 ROOFING
4640 RUBBER & RUBBER PRODUCTS
4650 RUGS see also CARPETS
4660 SAFETY
4670 SALESMEN
4675 SALVAGE
4680 SAND
4690 SANITATION
4700 SAVINGS & LOAN see also BANKING
4710 SAWS
4720 SCALES
SCHOOLS see EDUCATION
4750 SCIENCE
4760 SCIENTIFIC
4770 SCIENTISTS
SCREWS see FASTENERS
4785 SCULPTURE
4790 SECRETARIES
4800 SECURITIES INDUSTRY see also BANKING, FINANCE, INVESTMENTS
4810 SECURITY
4820 SEEDS
4840 SEWING MACHINES
4850 SEX
SHALE see CLAY
4870 SHEEP see also WOOL
4890 SHIPPING INDUSTRY
4900 SHOES see also LEATHER GOODS
4930 SIGNALS
4940 SIGNS
4950 SILK
4960 SILVER
4970 SINGING
4980 SKIING
5000 SLATE
5010 SLAVIC
5020 SMALL BUSINESS
5030 SOCCER
5040 SOCIAL WORKERS
5050 SOCIOLOGY
5070 SOYBEANS
5080 SPANISH
5090 SPEAKERS
5095 SPECTROSCOPY
5100 SPEECH
5110 SPELEOLOGY
5130 SPORTING GOODS
5140 SPORTS
STAMPS see PHILATELY
5160 STANDARDS
5170 STATIONERY
5180 STATISTICS
STEEL see IRON & STEEL INDUSTRY
5210 STONE
5220 STORAGE
5230 STORES
5250 SUGAR
5270 SURGEONS
5280 SURPLUS
5290 SURVEYORS
5300 SWIMMING
5310 SWINE
5320 TAXES
5330 TAXONOMY
TEACHERS see EDUCATION
5350 TELEPHONE
TELEVISION see RADIO-TV
5370 TENNIS
5380 TESTING
5390 TEXTILE INDUSTRY
5400 THEATRE
5410 THERAPEUTICS
TIES see NECKWEAR
5430 TILES
5440 TIMBER
5450 TIN
TIRES see RUBBER
5470 TOBACCO INDUSTRY
5480 TOOLS
5490 TOYS
5500 TRACK
5510 TRADEMARKS
5520 TRAFFIC
5530 TRAILERS
5540 TRAINING
5550 TRANSLATORS
5560 TRANSPORTATION
5570 TRAVEL INDUSTRY
5580 TREES
5600 TRUCKING INDUSTRY
5620 ULTRASONICS
5640 UNIFORMS
5650 UPHOLSTERY
5660 UROLOGY
5670 UTILITIES
5680 VACUUM
5690 VALVES
5700 VENDING
5720 VENTILATORS
5730 VETERINARY
5740 VITAMINS
5750 VOCATIONAL GUIDANCE
5770 WAREHOUSES
5780 WASTE
5790 WATCHES
5800 WATER
5810 WATERPROOFERS
5820 WATERWAYS
5830 WEBB-POMERENE ACT
WELDING see METAL WORKING INDUSTRY
5850 WELFARE
5860 WHEAT
5870 WHOLESALERS
5880 WINDOWS
5890 WINE
5910 WIRE
5920 WOMEN
5930 WOOD & WOOD PRODUCTS
5940 WOOL see also SHEEP
5950 WRITERS see also AUTHORS, PRESS
X-RAYS see RADIOLOGY
5990 YARN
6000 ZINC
6010 ZOOLOGY

ORDER FORM FOR THE ASSOCIATION MAILING LIST

Please send me the item(s) indicated ☐
☐CHECK ENCLOSED (Columbia Books pays postage)
Check or money order must accompany all initial orders.

	EXECUTIVES OF	PRESSURE-SENSITIVE LABELS	3-UP CHESHIRE LABELS*	3 x 5 CARDS (w/tele. nos.)	TOTAL COST
1.	THE NATIONAL LIST (All U.S. Associations) 6,250 associations	☐$350.00	☐$300.00	☐$350.00	$
2.	New York, New Jersey & Conn. 1,125 associations	☐$130.00	☐$110.00	☐$130.00	$
3.	D.C., Maryland & Virginia 1,900 associations	☐$175.00	☐$150.00	☐$175.00	$
4.	Illinois, Wisconsin & Indiana 1,100 associations	☐$125.00	☐$100.00	☐$125.00	$
				SUBTOTAL	$
				6% Tax (D.C. residents only)	$
				ORDER TOTAL	$

*Need Special equipment.

All lists are run in zip code sequence unless otherwise requested by the customer.

Name

Title

Organization

Street

City

State Zip

Date

Signature

ORDER FORM FOR THE ASSOCIATION MAILING LIST

Please send me the item(s) indicated ☐
☐CHECK ENCLOSED (Columbia Books pays postage)
Check or money order must accompany all initial orders.

	EXECUTIVES OF	PRESSURE-SENSITIVE LABELS	3-UP CHESHIRE LABELS*	3 x 5 CARDS (w/tele. nos.)	TOTAL COST
1.	THE NATIONAL LIST (All U.S. Associations) 6,250 associations	☐$350.00	☐$300.00	☐$350.00	$
2.	New York, New Jersey & Conn. 1,125 associations	☐$130.00	☐$110.00	☐$130.00	$
3.	D.C., Maryland & Virginia 1,900 associations	☐$175.00	☐$150.00	☐$175.00	$
4.	Illinois, Wisconsin & Indiana 1,100 associations	☐$125.00	☐$100.00	☐$125.00	$
				SUBTOTAL	$
				6% Tax (D.C. residents only)	$
				ORDER TOTAL	$

*Need Special equipment.

All lists are run in zip code sequence unless otherwise requested by the customer.

Name

Title

Organization

Street

City

State Zip

Date

Signature

ORDER FORM FOR THE ASSOCIATION MAILING LIST

Please send me the item(s) indicated ☐
☐CHECK ENCLOSED (Columbia Books pays postage)
Check or money order must accompany all initial orders.

	EXECUTIVES OF	PRESSURE-SENSITIVE LABELS	3-UP CHESHIRE LABELS*	3 x 5 CARDS (w/tele. nos.)	TOTAL COST
1.	THE NATIONAL LIST (All U.S. Associations) 6,250 associations	☐$350.00	☐$300.00	☐$350.00	$
2.	New York, New Jersey & Conn. 1,125 associations	☐$130.00	☐$110.00	☐$130.00	$
3.	D.C., Maryland & Virginia 1,900 associations	☐$175.00	☐$150.00	☐$175.00	$
4.	Illinois, Wisconsin & Indiana 1,100 associations	☐$125.00	☐$100.00	☐$125.00	$
				SUBTOTAL	$
				6% Tax (D.C. residents only)	$
				ORDER TOTAL	$

*Need Special equipment.

All lists are run in zip code sequence unless otherwise requested by the customer.

Name

Title

Organization

Street

City

State Zip

Date

Signature

AFFIX
STAMP
HERE

Association Mailing List

COLUMBIA BOOKS, INC.
1350 New York Avenue, N.W., Suite 207
Washington, DC 20005

AFFIX
STAMP
HERE

Association Mailing List

COLUMBIA BOOKS, INC.
1350 New York Avenue, N.W., Suite 207
Washington, DC 20005

AFFIX
STAMP
HERE

Association Mailing List

COLUMBIA BOOKS, INC.
1350 New York Avenue, N.W., Suite 207
Washington, DC 20005